W9-CVT-550

Reader's Digest

Complete Do-it-yourself Manual

Reader's Digest

Complete Do-it-yourself Manual

The Reader's Digest Association
Pleasantville, New York   Montreal, Canada   Sydney, Australia

The credits that appear on page 5 are hereby made a part of this copyright page.

 Library of Congress Catalog Card No. 72-87867.

Printed in the United States of America.

Seventh Printing

The editors are grateful for the assistance provided by the following manufacturers and organizations:

Adjustable Clamp Co.
Allegheny Natural Stone Co.
Allied Radio Corp.
American Brick & Stone Co.
American Gas Assn., Inc.
American Plywood Assn.
American Standard Inc.
American Vinyl Co.
Andersen Corp.
Armco Steel Corp.
Armstrong Cork Co.
Atlas Press Co.
Automatic Spray Co.
Bass, Rudolf
Bernzomatic Corp.
Black & Decker Mfg. Co.
Borden, Inc.
Bostitch Div. of Textron, Inc.
Brick and Clay Record Magazine
Bridgeport Brass Co.
Brinks & Cotton
Bruce Flooring Co.
Bryant Electric Co.
Building Stone Institute
Bulova Watch Co., Inc.
Carborundum Co.
Carrier Corp.
Cast Iron Pipe Research Assn., The
Champion International
Channellock, Inc.
Chicago Specialty Manufacturing Co.
Chrysler Corp.
Clarke Floor Machine Co.
Coastal Abrasive & Tool Co., Inc.
Columbus Coated Fabrics Co.
Consolidated Edison Co. of N.Y., Inc.
Constantine, Albert & Son, Inc.
Coplay Cement Manufacturing Company
Copper & Brass Research Assn.
Copper Development Assn., Inc.
Cory Corp.
Crane Co.
Crescent Niagara Corp.
Culligan, Inc.
Disston Co.
Dow Corning Corp.
Du Pont, E. I. de Nemours & Co.
Eaton, Yale and Towne
Edison Electric Institute
Edmund Scientific Co.
Emerson Electric of St. Louis
Fedders Corp.
Flintkote Co.
Fluidmaster, Inc.
Frigidaire Division, General Motors Corp.
General Electric Co.
Goldblatt Tool Co.
Goodyear Tire & Rubber Co.
Gothic Lumber & Millwork Inc.
Hanson, Henry L., Co., Inc.
Hexacon Elec. Co.
Holub Industries, Inc.
Honeywell
Hotpoint Division of General Electric Co.
Hyde Manufacturing Co.
Ideal Security Hardware Corp.
Irwin Auger Bit Co.
Jacobsen Mfg. Co.
Kedman Co.
Kemper Brothers
Kirsch Co.
Kwikset
Lafayette Radio Electronics Corp.
Lau Blower Co.
Lavelle Rubber Co.
Lennox Industries Inc.
Long Island Lighting Co.
Lufkin Div. of Cooper Industries, Inc.
Macklanburg-Duncan Co.
Majestic Company, Inc.
Masonite Corp.
Master Painting Co.
McCulloch Corp.
McGraw-Edison Co.
McPherson, Inc.
Meredith Separator Co.
Millers Falls Co.
Minnesota Mining & Mfg. Co.
Minwax Co., Inc.
Mobil Oil Corp.
Moen, Div. of Standard Screw Co.
Montgomery Ward & Co.
National Art Materials Trade Assn.
National Concrete Masonry Assn.
National Forest Products Assn.
National Gypsum Co.
Naval Jelly Co.
Nicholson File Co.
Norton Co.
Nutone Div., Scovill Mfg. Co.
Olin Corp.
Orangeburg Co.
Owens-Corning Fiberglas Corp.
Petersen Mfg. Co.
Pittsburgh Corning Corp.
Ponderosa Pine Wood Doors
Portable Electric Tools Div. of G.W. Murphy Industries
Porter, H. K., Co., Inc.
Portland Cement Assn.
PPG Industries, Inc.
Raaco Corp.
Ramset Olin Corp.
Rawlplug Company, Inc., The
Red Devil Inc.
Remington Arms Company, Inc.
Reynolds Metals Co.
Rheem Mfg. Co.
Rhodes, M.H., Inc.
Ridge Tool Co., The
Rockwell Mfg. Co.
Rohm and Haas Co.
Roto-Rooter Corp.
Rowe Manufacturing Co.
Rudd Mfg. Co.
Rudd, Nicholson
Russwin
St. Regis Paper Co.
Salton, Inc.
Schlage Lock Co.
Sears, Roebuck and Co.
Sherwin-Williams Co.
Shop-Vac Corp.
Simer Pump Co.
Sloan Valve Co.
Smith, H.B., Co., Inc., The
Spinning, Rolfe C., Inc.
Stanley Works, The:
  Stanley Door Systems Division
  Stanley Hardware Division
  Stanley Power Tools Division
  Stanley Tools Division
Structural Clay Products Institute
Tatko Brothers Slate Company, Inc.
Thomas Industries, Inc.
Thor Power Tool Co.
Tile Corp. of America
Toolkraft Corp.
Toro Manufacturing Corp.
Triumph Twist Drill Co.
Uniroyal, Inc.
United States Ceramic Tile Co.
U.S. Department of Agriculture
U.S. Department of Housing & Urban Development
United States Gypsum Co.
United States Steel Corp.
Universal-Rundle Corp.
Vulcan Basement Waterproofing Co.
Wallcoverings Council
Wallpaper Council
Watts Regulator Company, Inc.
Weil-McClain Co., Hydronic Div.
Weldwood Package Products
Weller Electric Corp.
Wendell Mfg. Co.
Wen Products, Inc.
Westinghouse Electric Corp.
Wetzler Clamp Co., Inc.

Contributing editors
Richard Day
George Daniels
Clarence Martin
Robert Scharff

Technical advisers
Dr. Ray R. Kriner
Joseph Luther
Larry Netti
Douglas Pribanie

Contributing artists
Ken Rice
Hisanori Morimoto
John Ballantine
George Kelvin
Rudie Hampel
Ted Lodigensky
Frank Schwartz
Peter Trojan

Black and white photography
Joseph Barnell
W.A. Sonntag
Ernest Coppolino
John & Roe Capotosto
Portland Cement Assn.
(pages 466 and 483)

Additional photo credits
Pages 526-29, 536-37, 540-41, 550-52, 554-57: The Stanley Book of Designs for Making Your Own Furniture and The Stanley Book of Designs for Home Storage. Sponsored by The Stanley Works, New Britain, Connecticut. Published by Spectator Publications Ltd., London. Photography by Ward Hart.

Contents

section 1: Hand tools: How to choose and use them

section 2: Power tools for the home workshop

section 3: Fasteners, hardware, and adhesives

section 4: Making your own interior repairs

section 5: Major and minor exterior repairs

section 6: Furniture: How to repair and restore it

section 7: Plumbing: How to keep it in working order

section 8: Electricity: Solving power problems safely

section 9: Climate control: Heating and air conditioning

section 10: Painting and decorating walls, ceilings, and floors

section 11: Working with wood

section 12: Metals: How to use them in home repair

section 13: Glass, ceramics, and plastics

section 14: Brickwork and stonework

section 15: Working with concrete

section 16: Guide to better planning

section 17: Fifty projects you can build

section 1:

Hand tools: How to choose and use them

Any job you do around the house is bound to involve hand tools at some stage. And not just any hand tool, but the right tool, correctly used. This means learning all that you can about hand tools and their purposes, and mastering the technique that each one requires. It is precisely this kind of instruction, applied to home repairs and improvements at every level, that you will find in this section.

contents

Your basic tool kit

Buying in stages

Apartment dwellers, as a rule, limit themselves to a few tools. Those shown below will take care of most of their needs—and a good many of the requirements of the homeowner as well. When purchasing any kind of tool, always buy the best. A good hammer, for example, is a lifetime investment. In the long run, it will cost you less than two or three cheap replacements. When you start adding to your tools, the first two items on your list should be an electric drill and a vise. The vise shown can be quickly attached to a kitchen table. For serious work, change to a vise with 3½-inch jaws and mount it on a sturdy workbench (p. 12). A toilet plunger will help save you many a ten-dollar bill when a drain gets stopped up; be sure that you get one with a long handle. Before buying any more tools, equip yourself with a tote box (not shown) that has a removable tray. You can use the box to store your tools and the tray to carry the necessary equipment to the job. Any other tool that you may add to the ones shown depends upon the particular type of work you are capable of doing. Last on our list of suggested purchases is the second power tool you should own—the electric saw. The first, of course, is the electric drill.

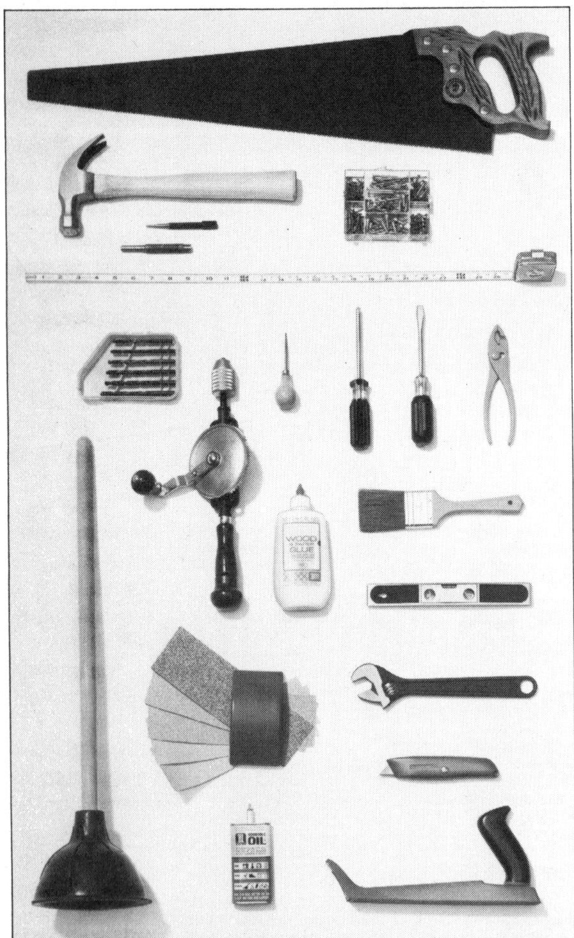

Basic tool kit: Crosscut saw, hammer, nail set, nail punch, assorted screws and nails, steel tape, bits and hand drill, awl, two screwdrivers (Phillips and regular), pliers, glue, brush, small level, sandpaper assortment and holder, adjustable wrench, knife, toilet plunger, oil, and surform plane.

Additions to consider: Hacksaw, plane, backsaw and miter box, set of three chisels, side-cutting pliers, large screwdriver, pipe wrench, combination plier-wrench, C-clamp, sharpening stone, file, level, combination square, propane torch, bits and brace, electric drill, vise, and small wrecking bar.

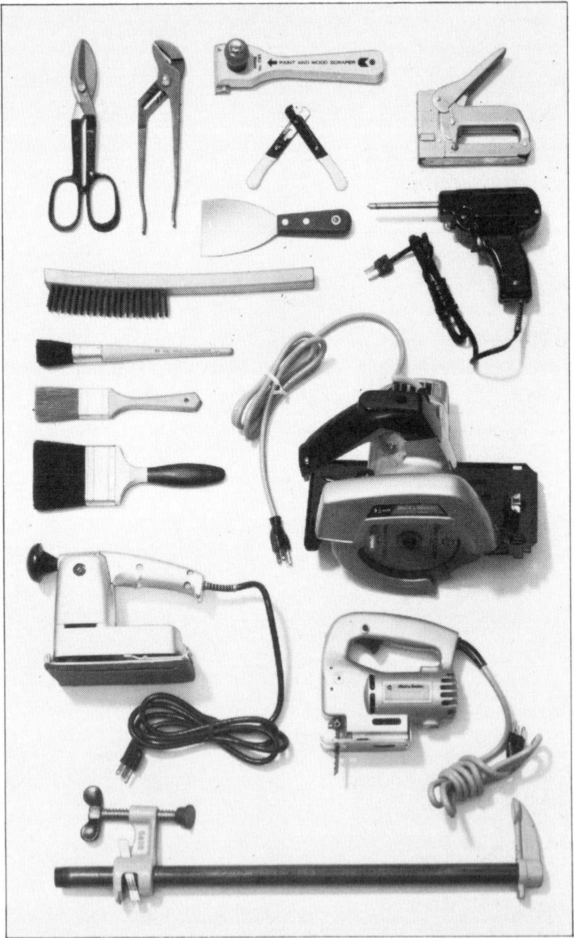

If your budget permits: Metal snips, channel-type pliers, scraper, wire stripper, stapler, putty knife, soldering gun, wire brush, paint brushes, portable power saw, finishing sander, jigsaw, and pipe clamp. For descriptions of other power tools you may want to add, see pages 44 to 66.

The right tools for the job

Job to be done	Appropriate hand tools	Useful power tools
Cutting round hole	hand drill brace keyhole saw file compass	jig saw drill and holesaw fly cutter
Cutting square opening	ruler keyhole saw hand drill	jig saw drill
Fastening to masonry	star drill hammer dowel masonry bolts	½″ drill carbide-tipped drills
Fastening to hollow wall	Molly bolts drill screwdriver	drill
Fastening to wood	drill awl hammer screwdriver	drill
Securing loose brick	cold chisel hammer mortar whiskbroom	
Repairing rotted clapboard	saw chisel hammer nail set pry bar paint and brush	circular or jig saw
Repairing popped nails in dry wall	pliers nails hammer nail set plaster mix	
Patching hole in plaster wall	saw knife plaster mix metal lath sandpaper primer	
Stopping pipe leak	pipe clamp wrench screwdriver	
Loosening binding door	screwdriver dowels shims plane	
Replacing broken windowpane	chisel hammer glazier's point paint sandpaper glass	
Replacing sash cord (with chain)	screwdriver chisel hammer chain knife string and weight	
Loosening stuck window	hammer putty knife wax	
Replacing socket or switch (after turning off current)	screwdriver socket or switch tape	

Job to be done	Appropriate hand tools	Useful power tools
Replacing defective lamp plug	new plug cutting pliers knife solder soldering gun flux tape	
Replacing frayed lamp wire	new wire screwdriver cutting pliers knife	
Correcting wobbly table or chair	lengthen leg with wood shim, glue and brad or cut down with fine saw	
Tightening loose chair rung	glue long clamp	
Removing cigaret burn on rug	wire brush	vacuum cleaner
Unclogging stopped drain	toilet plunger lye solution wrench pail	
Securing loose or missing ceramic wall tile or fixture	awl plaster mix tile rag	
Pasting down loose wallpaper	wallpaper paste scissors water rag	
Anchoring loose floor tile	putty knife chisel hammer sandpaper tile cement	
Removing floorboards	nail set saw hammer chisel pry bar	circular saw
Curing a squeaky floor	drill screw-type nails countersink hammer	drill
Sanding floor	scraper sandpaper nail set hammer pry bar	belt and disk sander vacuum cleaner
Installing door	chisel gauge hammer drill awl plane screwdriver	drill router
Installing door lock	brace drill chisel hammer screwdriver awl	drill router hole saw
Fixing loose handle	dowel glue drill awl screwdriver	drill

Back-of-door tool rack

This unit can be mounted on any closet door that has at least six inches of space between door and clothes—or shelves. Make it of ½-inch pine or plywood. Actual dimensions depend on the width of your closet door. Just be sure to leave plenty of clearance for the door to open and close. This particular unit is 32 inches high x 20 inches wide. The widest bottom dimension is eight inches. The back is of ⅛-inch pegboard. Tools can be hung from hooks inserted into pegboard or holes and slots cut into the cross supports. The holes should vary in size from ½ to ¼ inch and be elongated to hold such tools as chisels and files. The drawer can be sectioned for nails, screws, and other small hardware.

Center the rack on the door; mount it slightly above the knob with four long screws. Be sure to drive them into the solid part of the door. If necessary, span the hollow part with two battens screwed into the solid part and mount the rack on these.

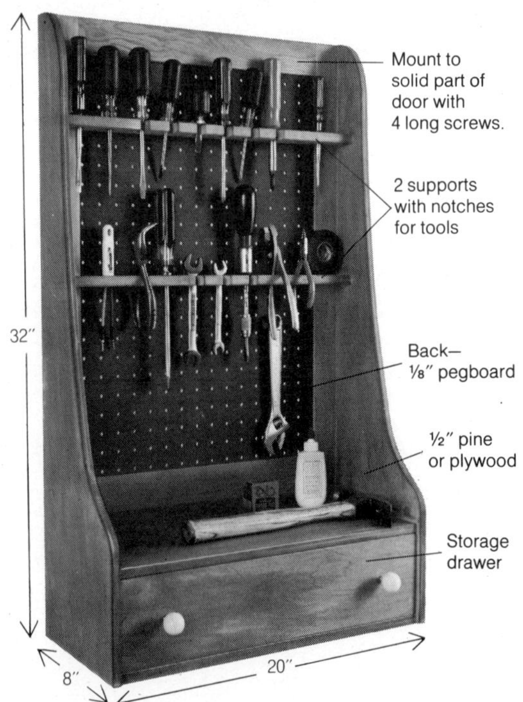

Simple workbench

This six-foot-long workbench can be easily built of 2 x 4s and ¾ inch plywood. First cut the 2 x 4s for the legs, using four pieces for each, cut to the size on the drawing. Next cut the two stretchers. Secure the leg sections with dowels and glue, then fasten them to the stretchers with four 6-x-⅜-inch bolts, passing them through holes drilled in the stretchers. Cut four pipe stubs from ¾-inch pipe and install into stretchers at points indicated in drawing. Each stub has a hole drilled in it for the bolts. This avoids the need to drive screws into end grain, which has very little holding strength.

The top is made of two pieces of ¾-inch fir plywood, covered with ¼-inch-thick hardboard. Back board and shelf complete the construction.

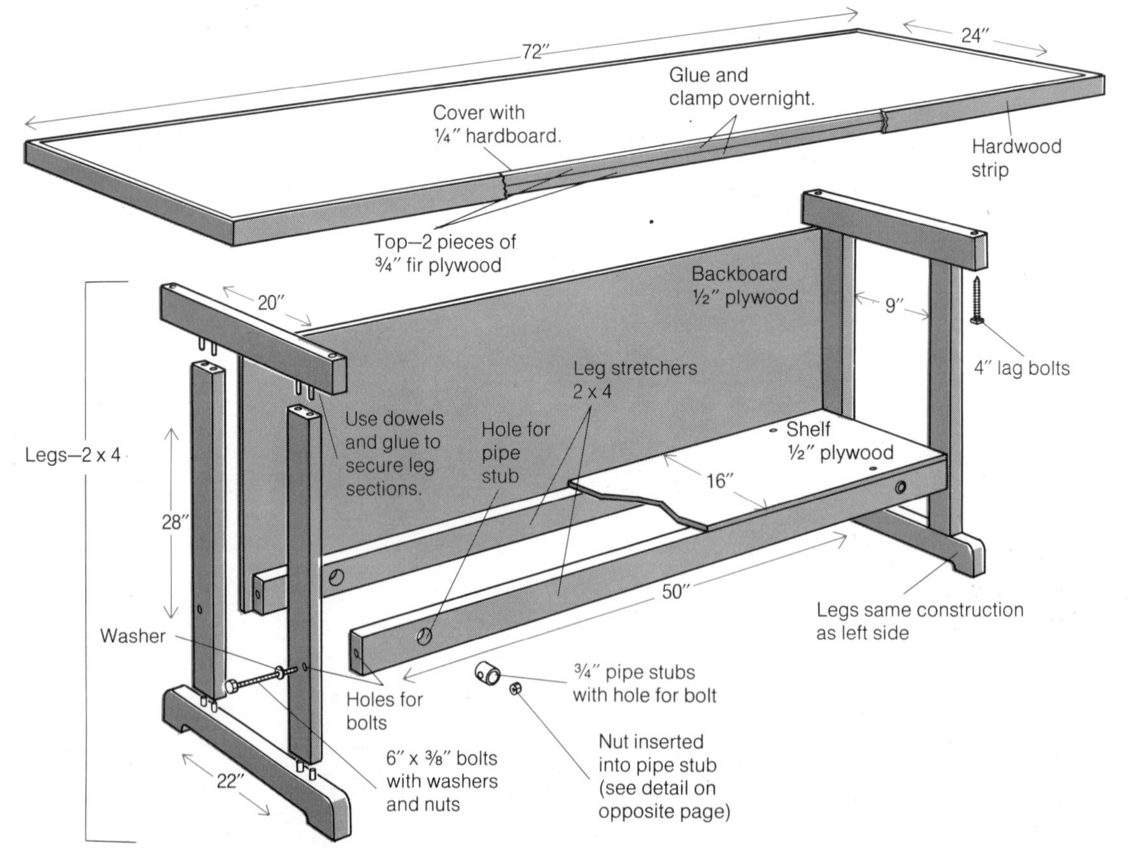

Advanced workbench

If you are a bit more ambitious, you can build this capacious workbench. Three drawers and a three-shelf cabinet give you ample storage space for tools, hardware, and paints. The first step: Making the end frames and bottom members. The end frames are attached to the bottom members with 6-inch bolts. Lag bolts, or long wood screws, could be used but this would mean forcing screws into end grain, which has little holding strength. Instead, four pipe stubs were cut from ¾-inch pipe and a hole drilled in each for a ⅜-inch bolt. The bolt passes through the leg of the end frame, into a predrilled hole in the bottom member, and through the hole in the pipe stub. A nut completes the assembly.

The top consists of two ¾-inch sheets of fir plywood topped with ¼-inch thick hardboard. Glue and clamp these together and let dry overnight. If you like, you can dress up the finished top by gluing a strip of oak or other hardwood around the sides to hide the end grain of the plywood.

Make the drawer compartments before you make the drawers; it is easier to fit a drawer to a compartment than the other way around. Each is fitted with a center guide and slides on two plastic-laminate runners.

A back panel covers the space between the drawer section and the cabinet section. You can vary the dimensions shown on the drawing to fit your own particular space requirements but, as a general guide, bear in mind that 36 inches is the ideal height for a workbench.

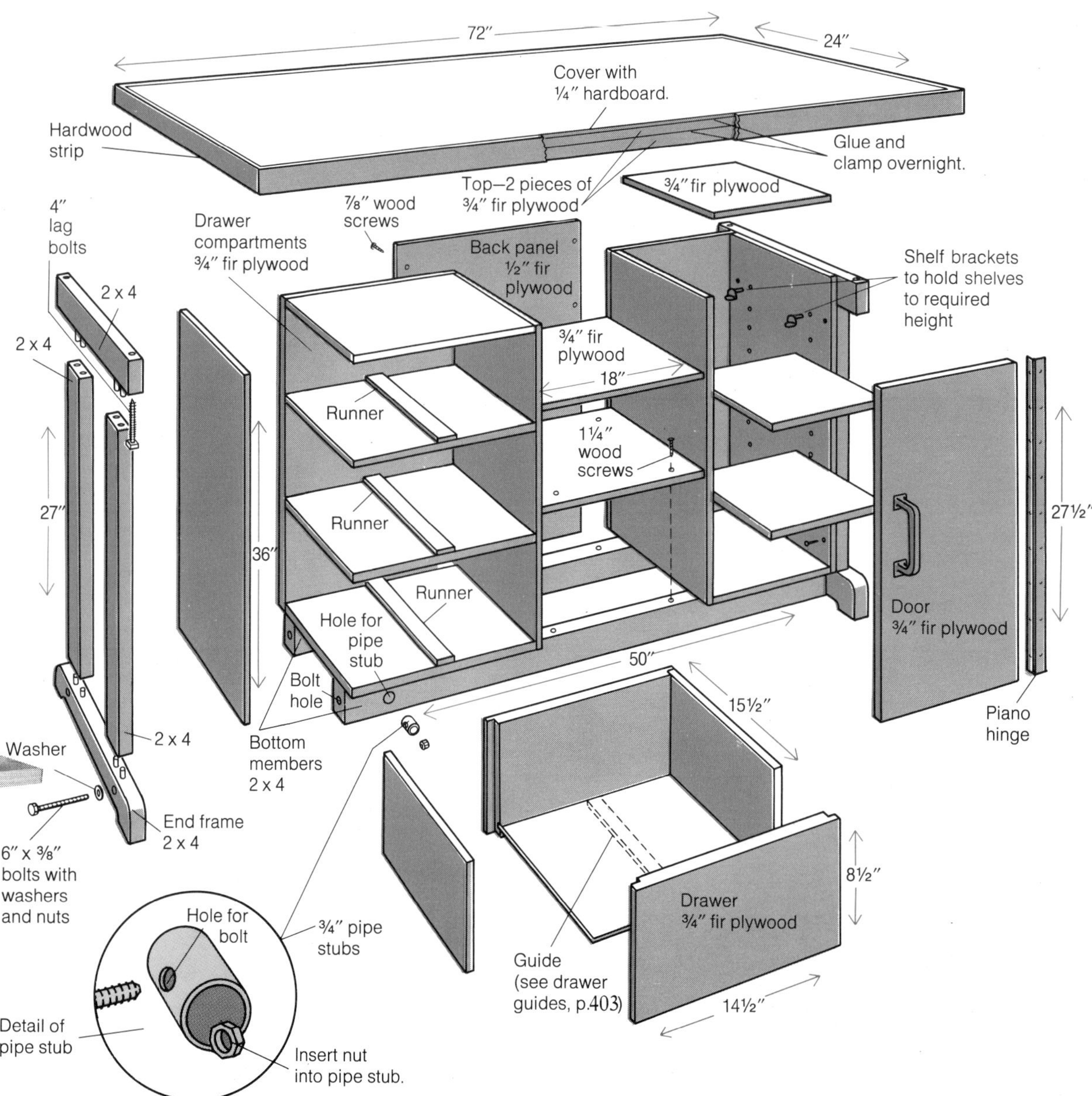

Hammers and hammering

Choosing the right hammer

The **curved claw nail hammer** is the tool to use for nailing and nail-pulling. Its usual bell-faced (slightly convex) striking surface minimizes marring when nails are driven flush, reduces nail deflection from off-angle blows. Hammer weights, based on head weight, are commonly 7 ounces for very light work, 13, 16, and 20 ounces for general carpentry. **Ripping hammers** (with straight claws) are designed for rough work and dismantling, as in opening crates, where the straight claws fit more readily between boards for prying. Their usual weight is 20 ounces, 28 or 32 ounces for heavy duty work. In either type, the head should be drop-forged steel rather than brittle cast iron. "Rim-tempering" of the striking face also greatly reduces the chance of breakage or chipping. Handle should be steel or fiber glass if the hammer must take excessive heat or humidity.

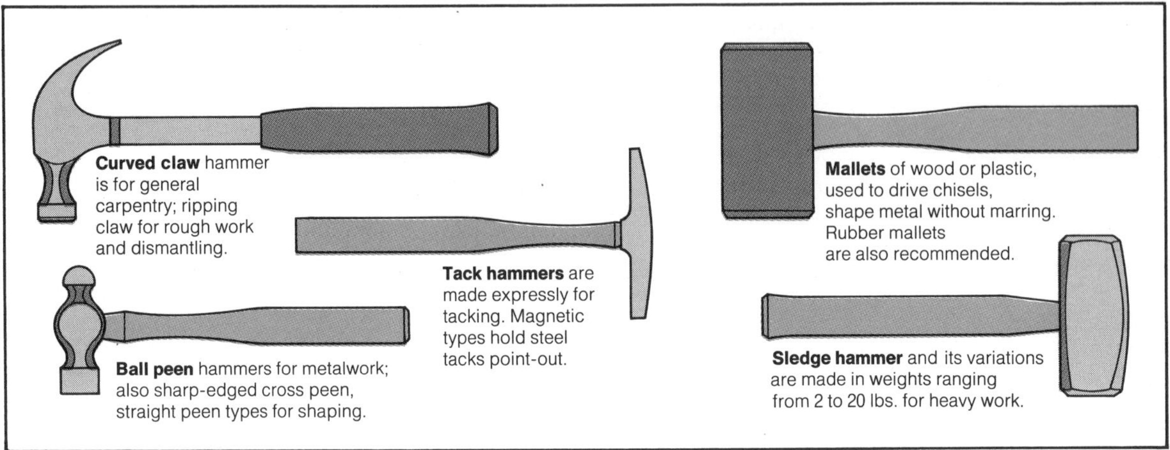

How to use hammers

In nailing, grasp the hammer near the end of the handle. Hold the nail between thumb and forefinger of your left hand and tap it lightly until it stands up in the wood. Then take your fingers away and drive the nail. To avoid marring a surface when pulling nails, place a thin piece of wood under the hammer head. (A thicker block gives you better leverage on long nails.) A ball peen hammer (not a claw hammer) is best for metal work. Using a nail hammer to strike metals harder than its face can damage it and cause dangerous chipping.

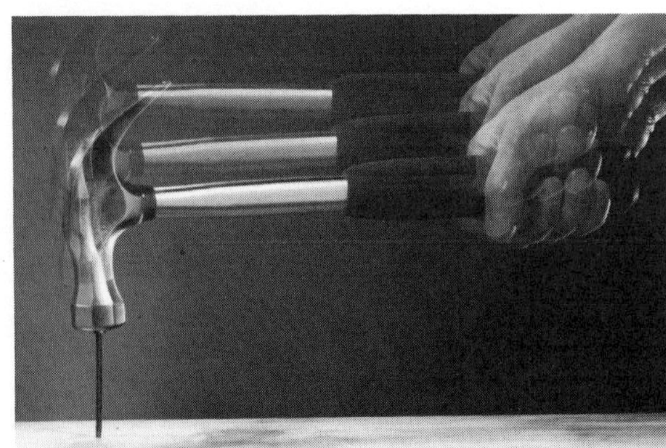
Hold nail hammer near handle end. Tap the nail so that it stands up, then release your hold and drive nail straight down.

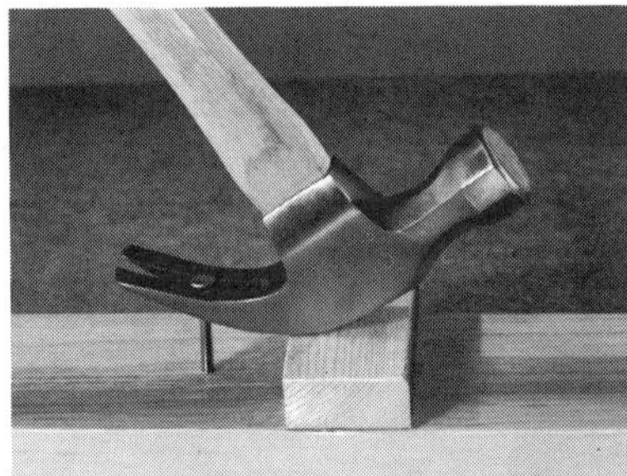
Wood block under hammer head prevents marring surface. A thicker block gives better leverage on long nails.

Straight claws of a ripping hammer fit between boards in dismantling work, such as removing floor boards, opening crates.

Wood or plastic mallet is needed to protect wood-handled chisels that are used in mortise and tenon work.

Start spreading a rivet head with the ball end of a ball peen hammer and finish the job with the face end.

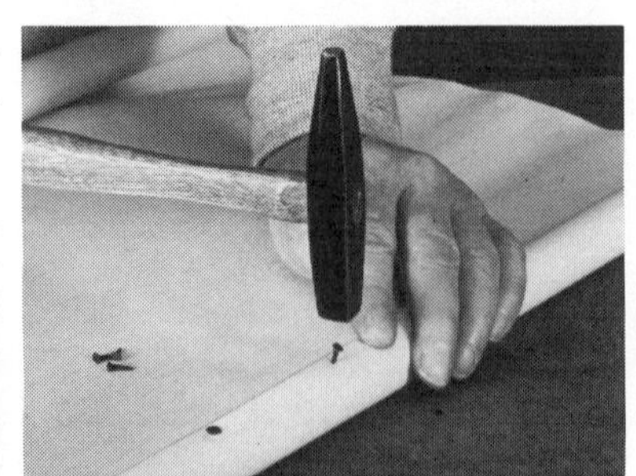
Magnetic tack-hammer helps two ways: It holds the tack point-out to start it in wood, then drives it home.

Rim-tempered sledge-type hammer is the right choice for heavy-duty jobs such as log splitting and masonry work.

Getting the most from your hammer

A quality hammer can last a lifetime if it is used properly and given reasonable care. Don't use a hammer for work it was not intended to do, like riveting with a nail hammer. Strike only with the striking face of a hammer (never with the side cheek) and don't use a hammer to hit anything that is harder than the hammer's striking face. The reason for this precaution: Impact power, often as high as 300 pounds, can damage the tool. Similarly, handle-leverage forces in nail-pulling may reach several thousand pounds, so use a nail-pulling wrecking bar instead of a claw hammer when you have to pull very large nails or spikes.

If you have a wood-handled hammer, keep it in a living area of the house, since high humidity, as for example in a damp basement, can swell the wood fibers inside the handle's head, crushing them, loosening the head, and making handle replacement necessary. Extreme dryness, as on a shelf above a radiator, can shrink the handle, which also causes looseness. The dry-shrunk handle can often be restored, however, by a brief water-soaking of the head end of the hammer. After this salvage operation, find a better storage spot for the hammer.

If a hammer (or other tool) is stored in an unheated area, such as an outbuilding or garage, condensation on the metal surfaces caused by temperature changes will produce rusting unless the metal is protected in storage by a film of oil. Light engine oil is suitable for the purpose.

Claw hammer can be used to straighten bent nails, working on a piece of scrap wood, as shown.

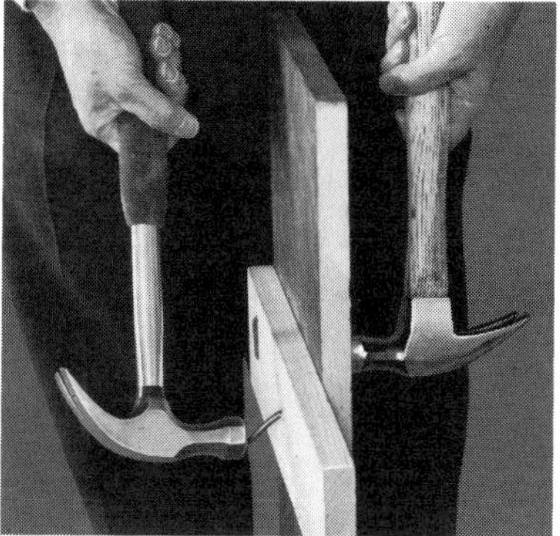

Use two hammers to clinch nails. Hold one hammer at the nail head and use the second one to bend and flatten nail.

Nail wedged into the V of the claw will hold it for starting when the other hand is needed to position the work.

Replacing a hammer handle

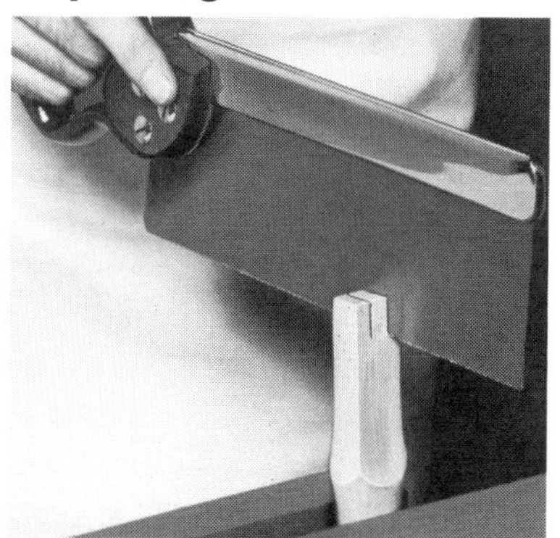

Saw off the old handle below the base of the head; drive remainder through the top. Shape new handle for a snug fit. Cut two slots in the handle top two-thirds of the head's depth.

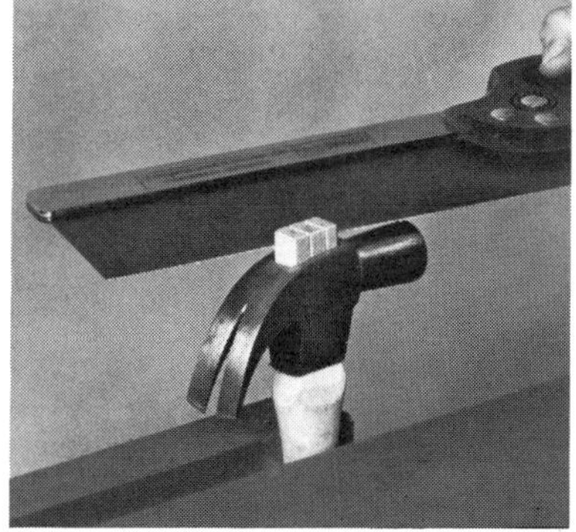

Drive the new handle into the head; cut off surplus wood flush with the head. To assure a well-seasoned, tight-fitting handle, place it in a 150° oven for an hour before final fitting.

Drive wedges into slots cut in the handle. Make wedges of hardwood or buy metal ones. File the handle top flush with the hammer head. Sand the handle and rub with linseed oil.

Nail sets

Nail sets, used to drive finishing nailheads below the surface of the work for concealment, are made to suit different nailhead diameters, ranging commonly from $\frac{1}{32}$ to $\frac{5}{32}$ in. by $\frac{1}{32}$ in. increments. (Heads should be sunk to a depth equal to their diameter). Self-centering nail sets are usually round. The square-headed forms offer the advantage of not rolling away when you work on sloping surfaces.

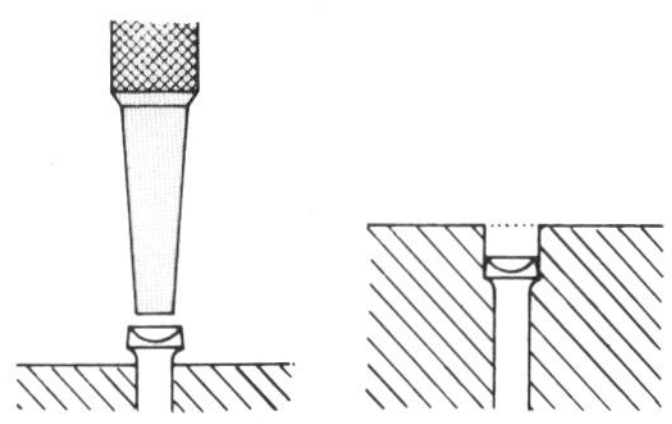

Where a nail set is to be used, the nail should not be driven flush with the surface, but should be left slightly above it to prevent possible hammer marring. The nail set, equipped with a tip slightly smaller than the nailhead, should then be set on the nailhead and hammer-driven to sink the head below the surface. Putty or wood filler may be used to fill in the recess that this leaves above the nailhead.

Saws and sawing

Types of saws

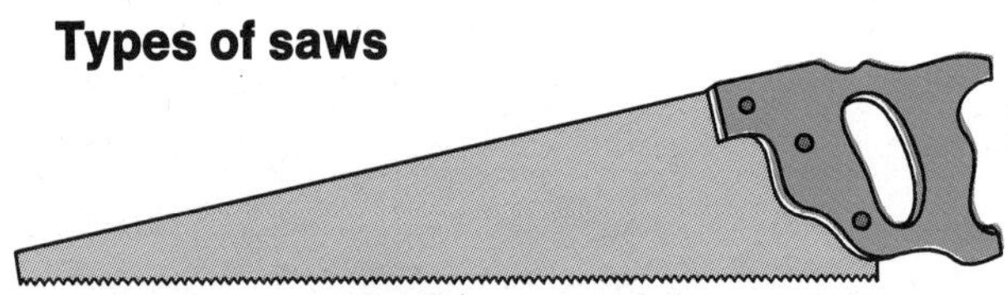

Hand saws for crosscutting or ripping come in two blade patterns. Upper edge of straight back pattern, above, can serve as line marker. Skew-backed type, not suited for marking, is preferred by some because saw seems more flexible.

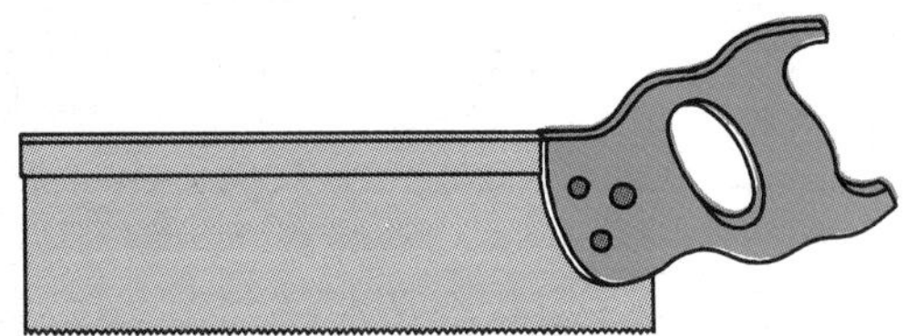

The backsaw, used for joint cutting, has reinforced back edge to keep blade rigid. Typical lengths are 10 to 16 in. A longer version called a miter box saw runs from 22 to 26 in. To cut smoothly, teeth are finer than on crosscut or rip saws.

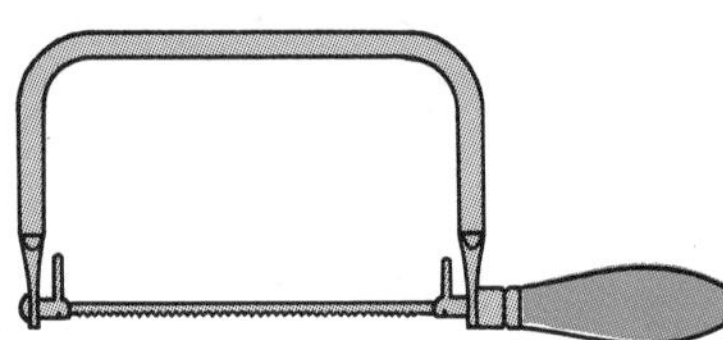

Coping saws, for cutting small-diameter curves, have spring steel frames with tension adjustment to hold blades taut. Blades are 1/16 to 1/8 in. wide, and from 6 to 6⅝ in. long. The blades mount to face in any direction.

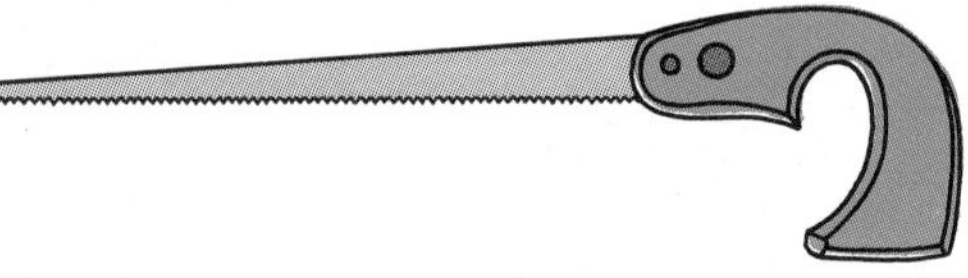

Compass saw has narrow, tapered blade for cutting curves or starting from bored hole. It is similar to the keyhole saw, which was once used to cut keyholes in wooden doors.

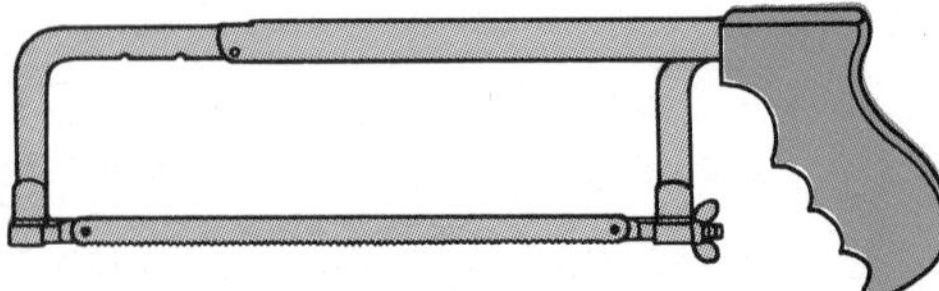

The hacksaw, for metal cutting, has a rigid frame that fits blades 8 to 12 in. long. High-speed steel blade mounts with teeth slanted away from handle and is drawn taut by wingnut.

Using the crosscut saw

A crosscut saw's performance depends on the quality of the saw and how you use it. In a high-quality crosscut saw, the teeth are usually precision-ground to tiny points that cut sharply across the wood fibers. The teeth of a low-priced saw, though the same shape, are rarely precision-ground. Quality saws cut faster with the same effort from you. The number of teeth per inch, referred to as points, commonly ranges from 7 to 12. (A saw that has 7 teeth to the

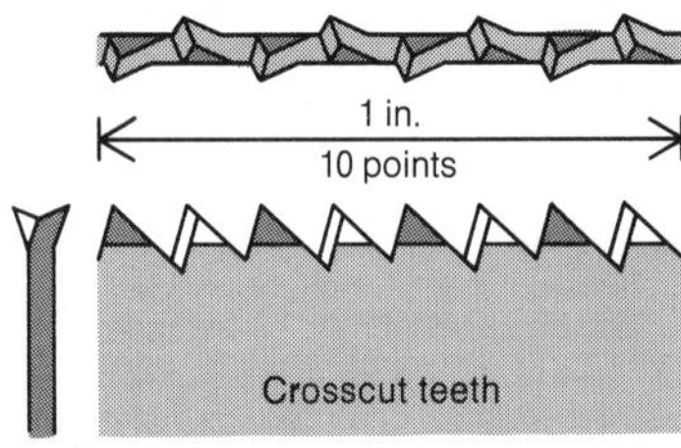

inch is called a 7-point saw.) When a saw has a low point number, it cuts fast but leaves a rough surface. High-number saws work more slowly but are smoother-cutting. For average work, 7 or 8 points is usual; for finer work, 10 points.

To reduce sawing friction and boost efficiency, alternate teeth are set (bent) outward about ¼ the blade thickness to opposite sides. This results in a cut slightly wider than blade thickness and lets the saw cut freely.

To begin a cut, use the butt portion of the blade near the handle. Use several pulling strokes to make a starting groove. Don't cut on the marked line, but on the waste (throwaway) side. This minimizes the chance of cutting short. Continue with full strokes

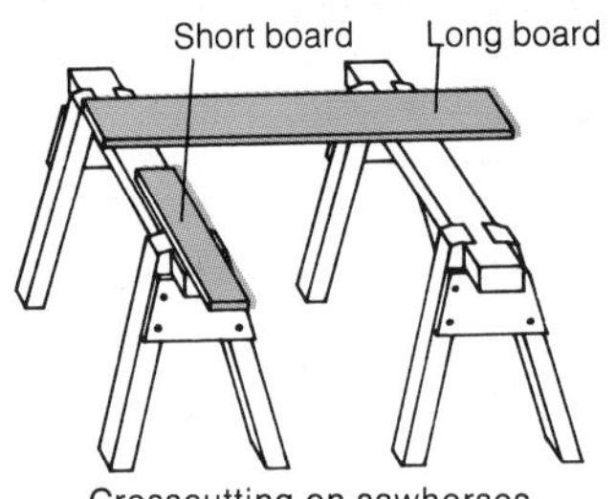

Crosscutting on sawhorses

for fast cutting and even distribution of tooth wear along the blade.

Because the crosscut saw cuts on both the forward and back strokes under its own weight, you only need to apply light pressure in using it. The most efficient cutting angle between the saw's edge and the surface of the work is 45 degrees.

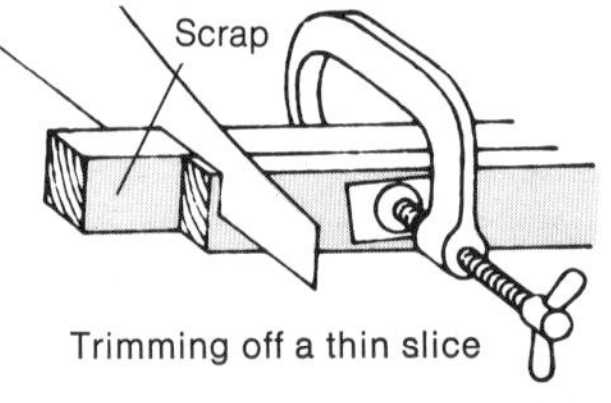

Trimming off a thin slice

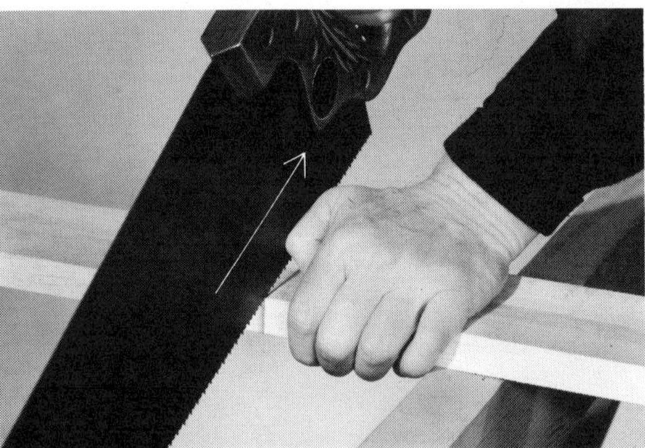

Plywood should be cut with a crosscut saw regardless of the direction of the surface grain. When sawing any wood, use your thumb to guide the draw strokes at the start.

At the finish of a crosscut, always support the waste piece while you are making the final cut-off strokes. Never break the piece off by twisting the saw blade.

Using a rip saw

The rip saw, designed to cut parallel to the grain, as in sawing a board lengthwise, usually has a 26-inch blade with 5½ teeth per inch. The teeth, shaped like miniature chisels with their cutting edges crosswise of the saw, literally chop their way through the wood. Alternate teeth are factory-set outward about ⅓ the blade thickness to opposite sides, to widen the cut and reduce friction.

To start a ripping cut, use the tip portion of the blade (not the butt, as with the crosscut saw), since quality rip-saw teeth are one point finer (6½) at the tip end. Use a few short pulling strokes to begin, then full strokes. Although the rip saw cuts only on the forward stroke, a sharp one can cut up to 10 feet a minute in nominal 1-inch white pine. A taper ground blade, thinner at the back edge than the toothed edge and thinner at the tip than the butt, reduces sawing effort considerably. (Available in high-quality rip and crosscut saws.) If the saw veers away from the line on long cuts, flex it slightly toward the line as you saw, to steer it back on course, but avoid sharp bending.

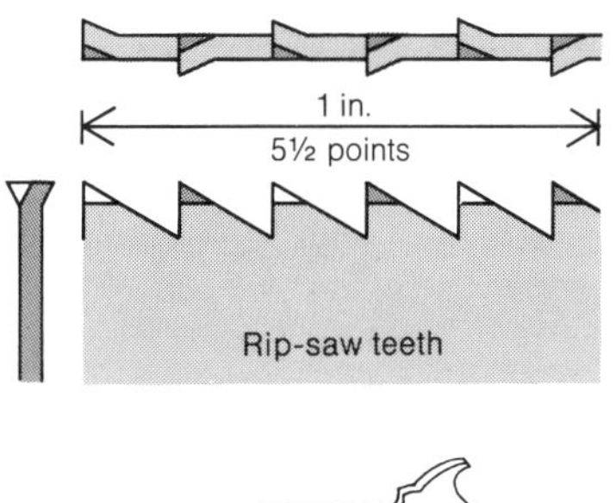

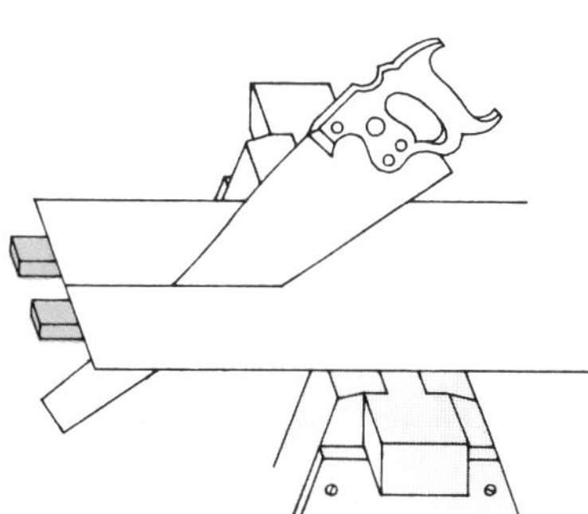
Support springy work on strips.

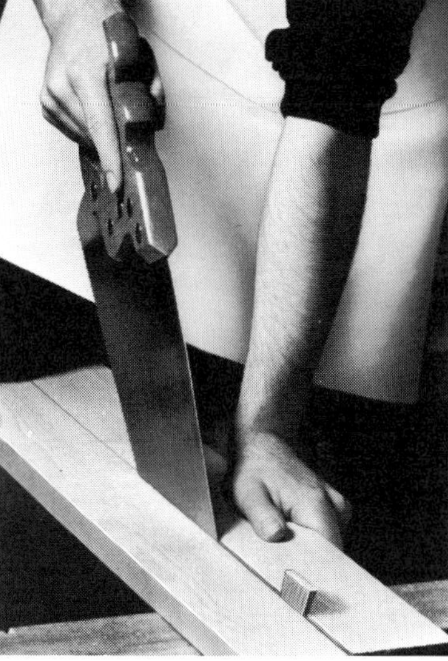
To prevent saw jamming in long cuts, drive wedge into starting end of cut.

For long ripping cuts, saw against a batten to assure a straight cut.

Using a backsaw

The backsaw, designed for joint-cutting work, is made in 10- to 16-inch lengths, usually with 12 or 13 teeth per inch, for smooth cuts with or across the grain. (The miter box saw is a longer version of the backsaw—up to 26 inches—and has 11 teeth per inch.)

To use a backsaw in a miter box, first mark the work for the cut, then line up the mark with the slots, to cut on the waste side of the line. Hold the work against the back of the box and start with a back stroke, holding the handle end tilted slightly upward. Level it as you proceed. To cut without a miter box, use a bench hook, as shown.

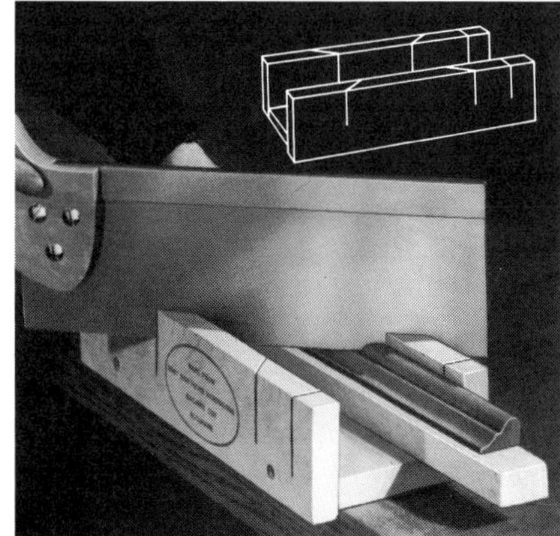
Miter box is used to cut moldings at 45° angles or for straight cuts. Lip seats against the front of the workbench.

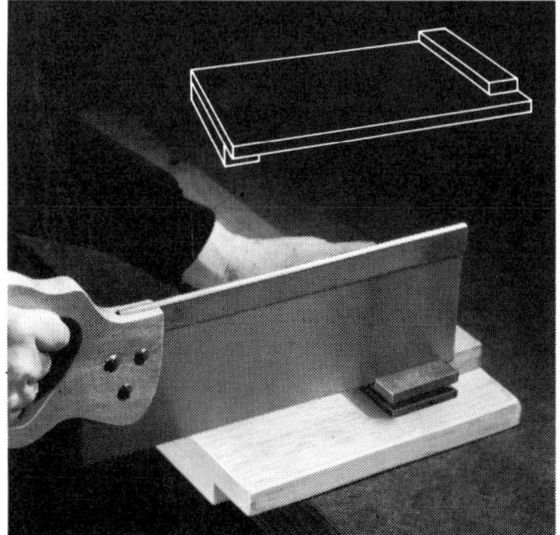
Bench hook holds the work but doesn't guide it. Used for making straight cuts, especially when work is too large to fit miter box.

Tenons are rip-cut in a vise, as pictured, on the waste side of the line. Start your cut with the saw tilted over the corner.

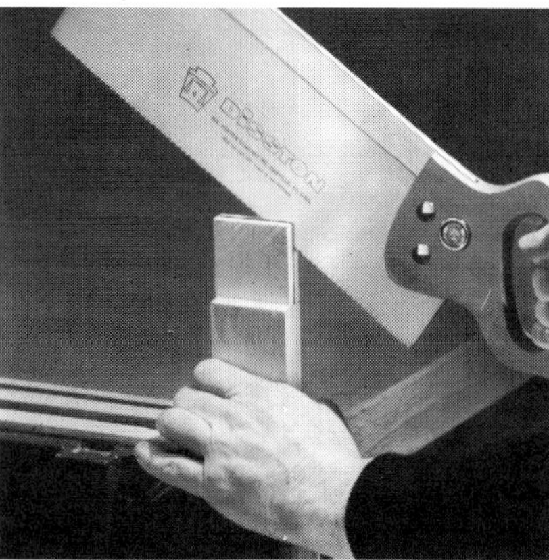
After making the first cut, turn work around in vise to make the second cut. Saw should be straight when it reaches bottom.

Special-purpose saws

Coping saw—for curve cutting and filigree work

The coping saw, used for delicate ornamental and filigree work, cuts curves smaller than pencil diameter, much smaller than can be cut with a compass or keyhole saw. Its replaceable blades, usually 6 to 6⅝ inches long, depending on the saw, may be as narrow as 7/100-inch, with 10 to 20 teeth per inch. (Spiral types are even slimmer.) Types are available for cutting wood, plastics, and thin metal. To change blades, turn the handle to loosen the threaded mounting grip, while springing the saw frame ends together between your body and the workbench. With frame ends sprung inward, the old blade can be removed and a new one inserted.

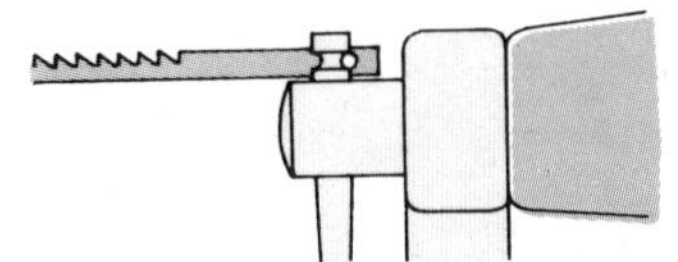

Mount blade so teeth slant to suit work

Slant of teeth depends on how the work is to be done. If it will be mounted vertically in a vise, the teeth should slant away from the handle, as you will be cutting on the push stroke. For exacting, delicate scroll work, the teeth should slant toward the handle, as you will be cutting on the pull stroke. The blade can be turned during the work, without removing it from the frame, to keep the frame clear of the edge of the material as the cut changes direction. Depth between blade and back of frame is usually from 4½ to 6½ inches.

Saws with frame depths of 8 to 12 inches are sometimes called **scroll saws, fret saws,** or **deep-throat coping saws.** Their blades are mounted with teeth slanting toward the handle to cut on the pull stroke, reducing the chance of blade spring-out.

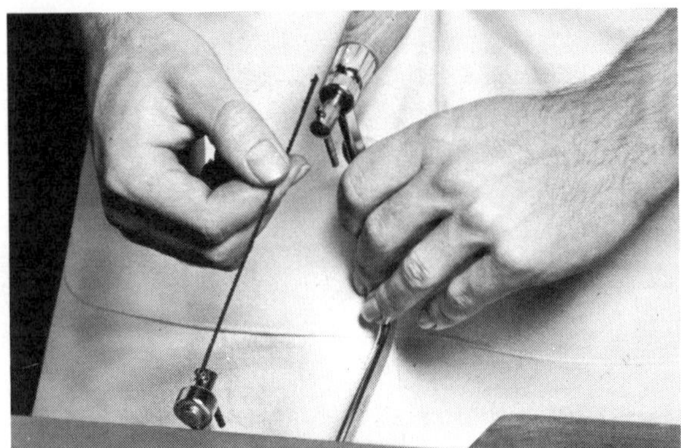

Spring ends of coping-saw frame towards each other to remove or replace blade. Blade holders permit turning of blade.

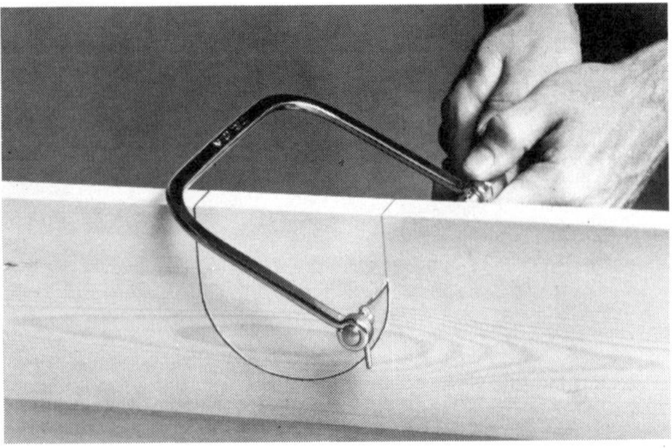

When work is mounted vertically in a vise for cutting, the saw teeth should be slanted away from the handle.

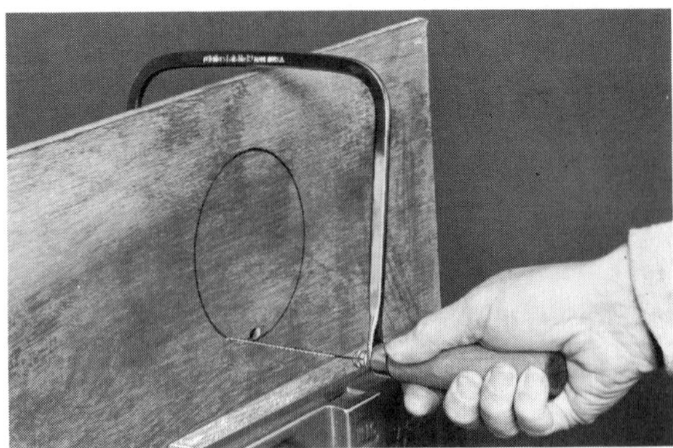

Special round cutting blade allows cut to be made in any direction without need for changing position of the blade.

Compass and keyhole saws—for hole cutting

Typical compass saws have 12- to 14-inch blades with 8 or 10 teeth per inch. Keyhole saws have narrower blades, usually 10 or 12 inches long, with 10 teeth per inch. Either can cut curves, though keyhole saws cut smaller diameters than compass saws. Both are also suited to making either curved or straight cuts starting from a bored hole. Since they are not frame types, they are not limited, as a coping saw is, to working near the edge of a panel. Hence, they can be used to cut openings in floors or walls for pipes or electrical outlets with the cut starting from a bored hole. When starting from a hole, use vertical strokes to begin. As the cut progresses, bring the saw to about a 45-degree angle. When you are starting a cut from the edge, the saw can be at that approximate angle from the beginning.

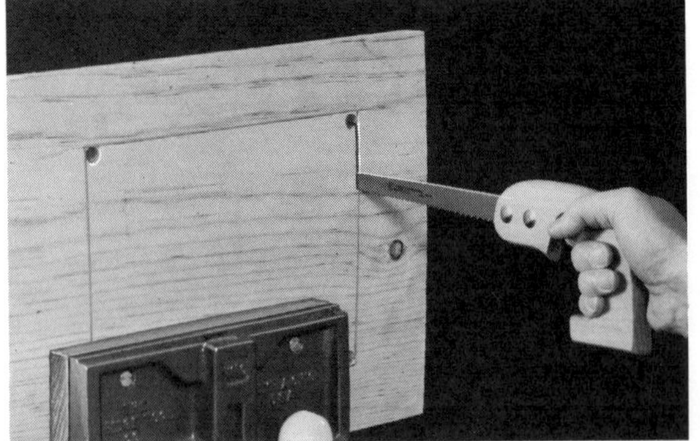

Start a cut like this with vertical strokes in hole; tip the saw to about 45° for cut; return to vertical at corner.

Pruning saw

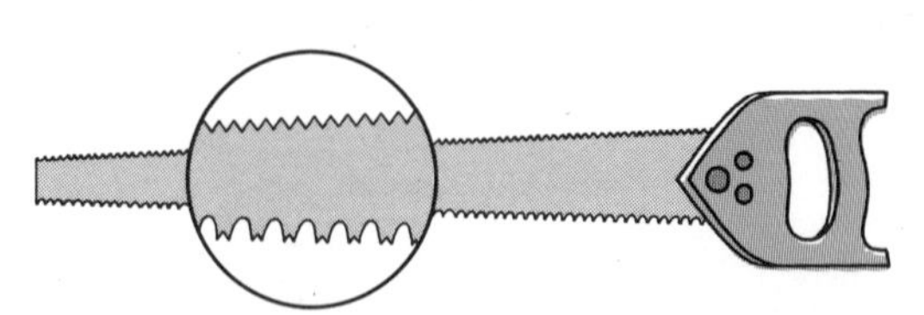

Pruning saws have deep-gullet teeth for cutting green wood. Straight blade types, like this, are also made with teeth on both edges—deep teeth for coarse cuts, plain 8-point crosscut teeth for trimming. Teeth slant toward tip, as on hand saws. Curved pattern pruning saws (down-curve on cutting edge) are designed for awkward places, also for use on a pole. Blade curve gives teeth back-slant for cutting on down stroke.

Hacksaws—for cutting metal

A hacksaw equipped with the correct blade can cut practically any metal you will encounter in shop work. To avoid breakage, draw the blade taut in the frame to prevent flexing. Blade choice depends on the material and its thickness. In general, use coarse teeth on thick metal, progressively finer teeth on thinner metal. At least two teeth should always be in contact with the material, so a thin section can't hook between teeth and break them. When you are cutting very thin stock, tip the saw so that the teeth

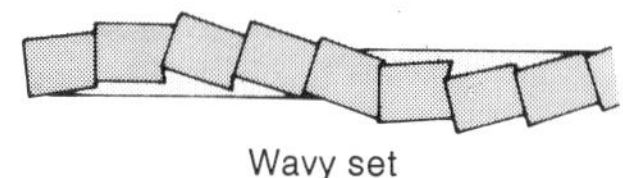

Wavy set

contact a part of the surface instead of the edge.

Standard high-speed steel blades can handle most of the cutting chores you are likely to be faced with. If you want blades that will perform well for a

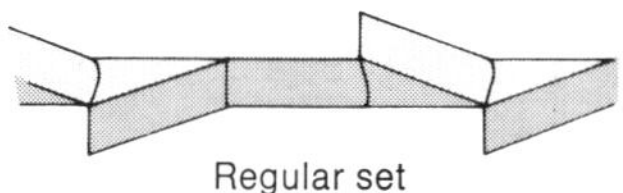

Regular set

longer time, use molybdenum alloy blades; they cost a little more than standard blades but can last up to 10 times as long. For the toughest cutting jobs, use a tungsten alloy blade.

Mount the work in a vise or jig so it cannot shift

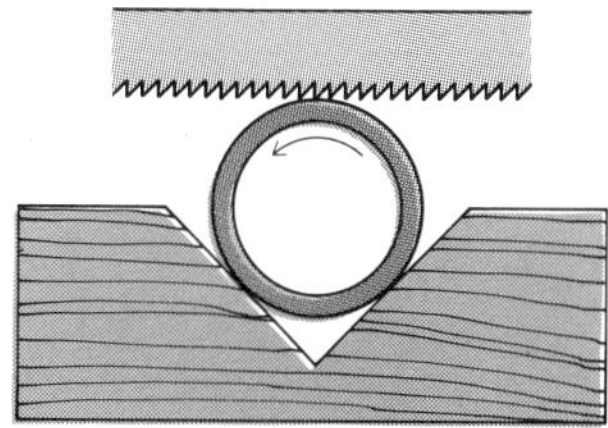

Tubing held in V-block is turned to complete cut.

and break the blade. Grip the handle of the saw in your right hand, hold the front of the frame with your left hand, and make slow strokes, using moderate down pressure on the forward cutting stroke and almost no pressure on the back stroke. Use as much of the blade length as you can for maximum cutting speed and minimum tooth wear.

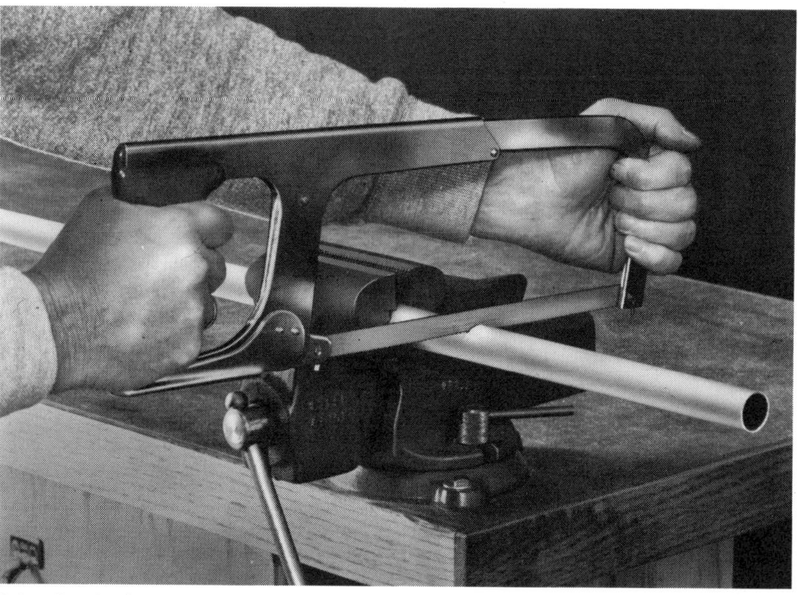

A two-hand grip is always used on a standard hacksaw to apply moderate down pressure on the forward cutting stroke, and to prevent the saw's tilting. Keep the saw in a vertical plane while cutting. For slanted cuts, mount the work in a vise so blade can operate in a vertical position. For fastest cut, use the coarsest blade recommended for the metal to be cut. For cuts deeper than the saw's frame, it is usually possible to turn the blade so its frame is swung over the end or the vertical edge of the work.

Mini-hacksaw takes standard blades, which are extended and held by screw clamp at the desired working length. The remainder is housed in the handle. Good for cutting jobs where other saws won't fit.

If available, use blades with wavy set teeth for thin stock, regular set for general work. Blades should have **14 teeth per inch** to cut bronze, aluminum, copper, brass, cast iron, or machine steel more

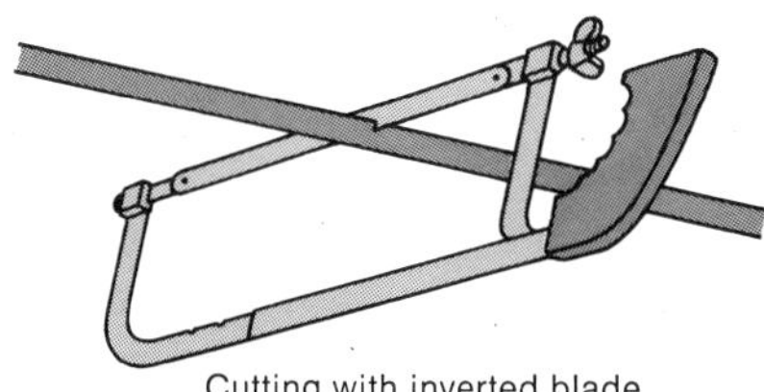

Cutting with inverted blade

than 1-inch thick; **18 teeth** for copper, aluminum, bronze, high-speed steel, tool steel, and annealed steel ¼- to 1-inch thick; **24 teeth** for ⅛- to ¼-inch iron, steel, wrought iron pipe, brass or copper tubing, drill rod, and items such as electrical conduit; and **32 teeth** for the same materials ⅛-inch thick or less.

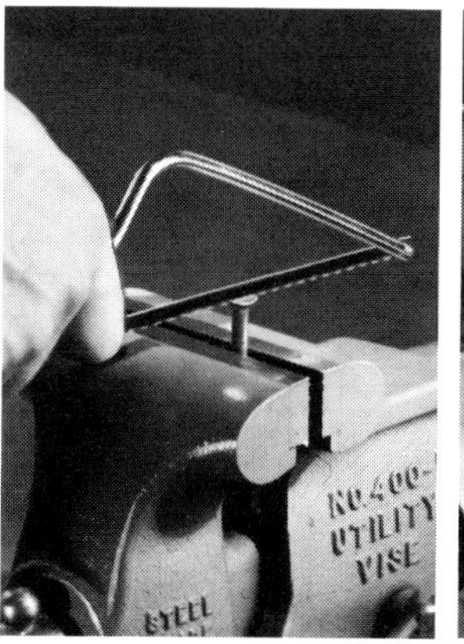

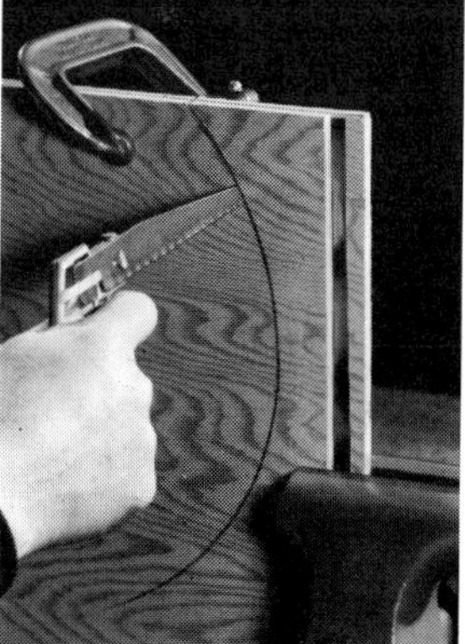

Special metal-cutting saws are made in many types for jobs that cannot be handled easily with an ordinary hacksaw. The tiny saw shown at the left is useful for cleaning out slots in screws and bolts. The saw at the right is used like a coping saw to cut thin metal. The metal is placed between a plywood sandwich so it will not buckle.

Sharpening and setting saws

Step-by-step procedure

Saw sharpening is necessary only when a saw's cutting rate slows down. This usually means a simple file touchup. Normally, you can restore full cutting speed this way four or five times before the teeth need to be reset.

As a preliminary step, slide a flat file (held absolutely level) along the top of the teeth to make very small flat areas on the tooth points. These will serve as guides in sharpening.

For sharpening, use a small triangular file. The same file is used for rip or crosscut teeth. To sharpen a crosscut saw, clamp it in a vise between two hardwood strips, as shown, with the gullet bottoms no more than ⅛ inch above the strips, to prevent file chatter.

Start at the blade tip (on your left), find the first tooth that is set toward you and rest the file in the gullet to the left of that tooth. Move the file handle to your left until the file seats against the bevel of the teeth. With the file held level at this angle, file down into the gullet until you cut away half of the adjacent flat tops made by the flat file. Skip the next gullet to the right and repeat procedure in the one after it. Continue the skip-and-file sequence, removing half of the tooth point flats, until you reach the handle end of the blade. Then reverse the saw in the vise, with the handle to the left.

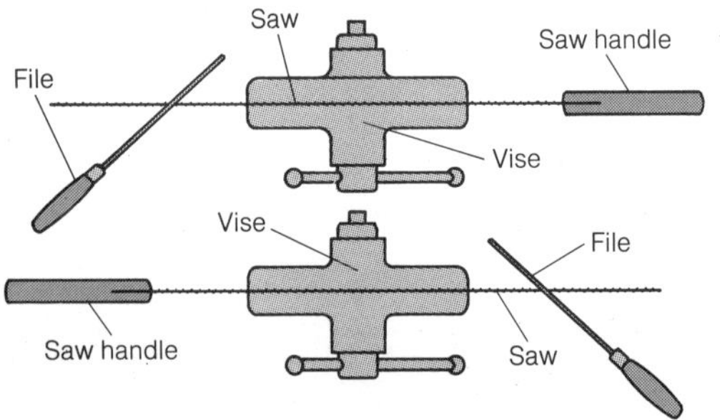

How crosscut saw is mounted in vise for first and second filing

Again starting at the blade tip (now on your right), place the file in the gullet to the right of the first tooth set toward you. (This is the first gullet you skipped when filing the other side of the blade.) Move the file handle to the right until the file seats on the tooth bevel and file until you have cut away the other half of the flats on adjacent tooth points. Skip the next gullet and file half the flats in the one after that. Continue this until you have sharpened all of the teeth.

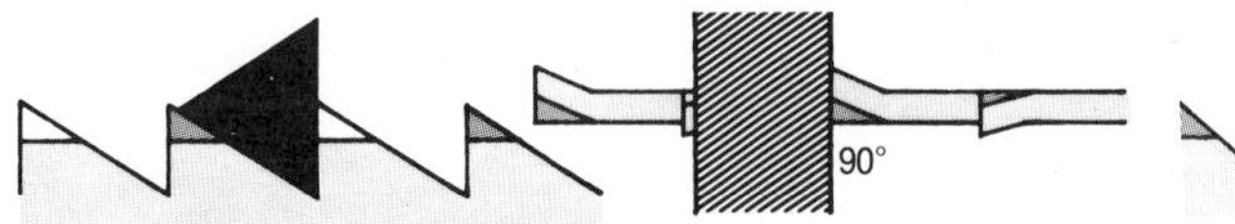

Filing a rip saw

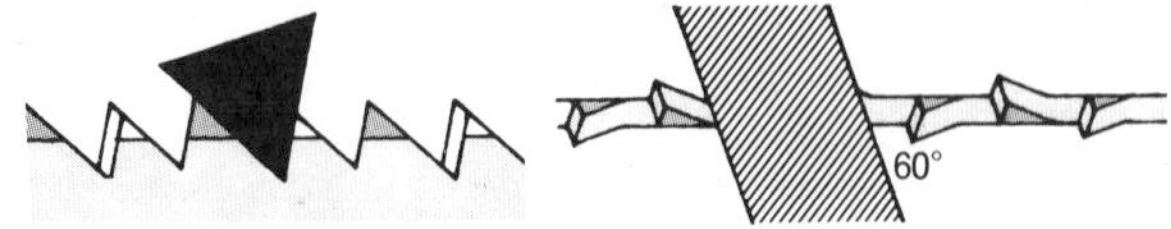

Filing a crosscut saw

Rip saws are sharpened in exactly the same way except that the file is used straight across the blade, at right angles to it. But do not try to do the entire job from one side of the saw. Reversing the saw in the vise is necessary to equalize filing variations that could otherwise cause a saw to veer to one side when cutting. After sharpening the teeth, check the bolts holding the handle and make sure they are tight.

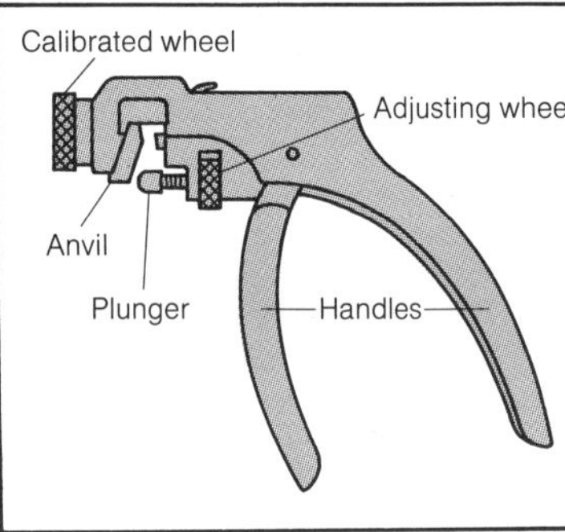

Saw set is used to bend each tooth in alternate direction. Necessary only after saw has had several sharpenings.

Saw clamped in a vise for sharpening should be held between two strips of hardwood extending the full length of the blade. The edges of the strips should not be more than ⅛ in. below the gullet bottoms of the saw teeth.

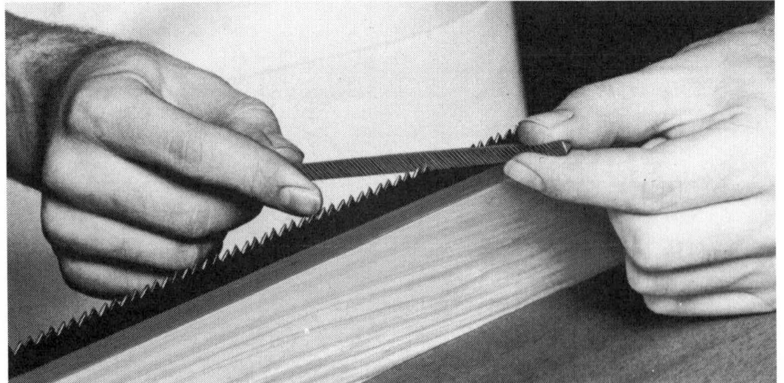

Triangular file sharpens both rip and crosscut saw teeth. In filing, keep the file perfectly level and at the correct angle. In crosscut types the angle should match the bevel. For a rip saw, file straight across, at right angles to the blade. Hold file by both ends and apply pressure on the forward stroke.

Saw set is used to bend teeth of saw to a predetermined angle. Can be used with saws having 4 to 16 teeth to the inch.

Using screwdrivers

Screwdrivers should be matched to screw size and type. Screws driven with an undersize screwdriver are likely to suffer slot and head damage. Oversize screwdrivers may fit the screw slot but may damage the work when used with flathead screws.

To take Phillips screws in an adequate range of sizes, you need at least two Phillips-type screw-

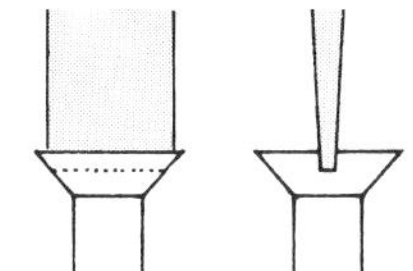

Blades must fit the screw slot.

drivers. To drive a number of screws rapidly by hand, a spiral ratchet screwdriver is best. Simply push down on the handle and the spiral ratchet spins the blade. It can be set in reverse to remove screws or locked for use as an ordinary screwdriver.

For hard-to-turn screws, you can use an offset screwdriver or one with a square blade (shank) equipped to take a wrench.

For hard-to-reach spaces, there are screw-holding screwdrivers that hold the screw to the tip. Starting holes for small screws are easily made with an awl. For larger screws, use a hand or electric drill.

Starting screws

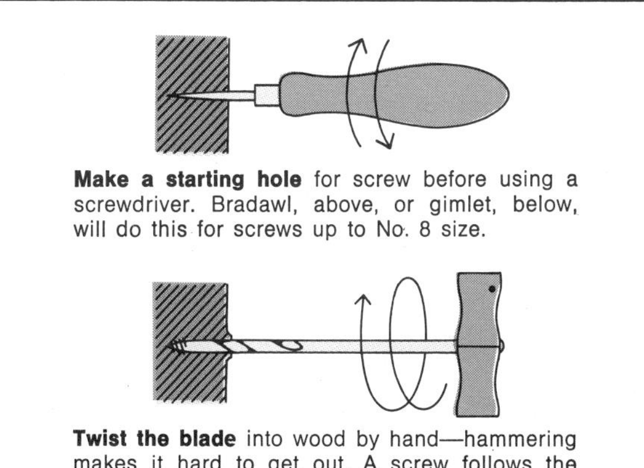

Make a starting hole for screw before using a screwdriver. Bradawl, above, or gimlet, below, will do this for screws up to No. 8 size.

Twist the blade into wood by hand—hammering makes it hard to get out. A screw follows the hole, so be sure that it is straight.

Screwdriver types

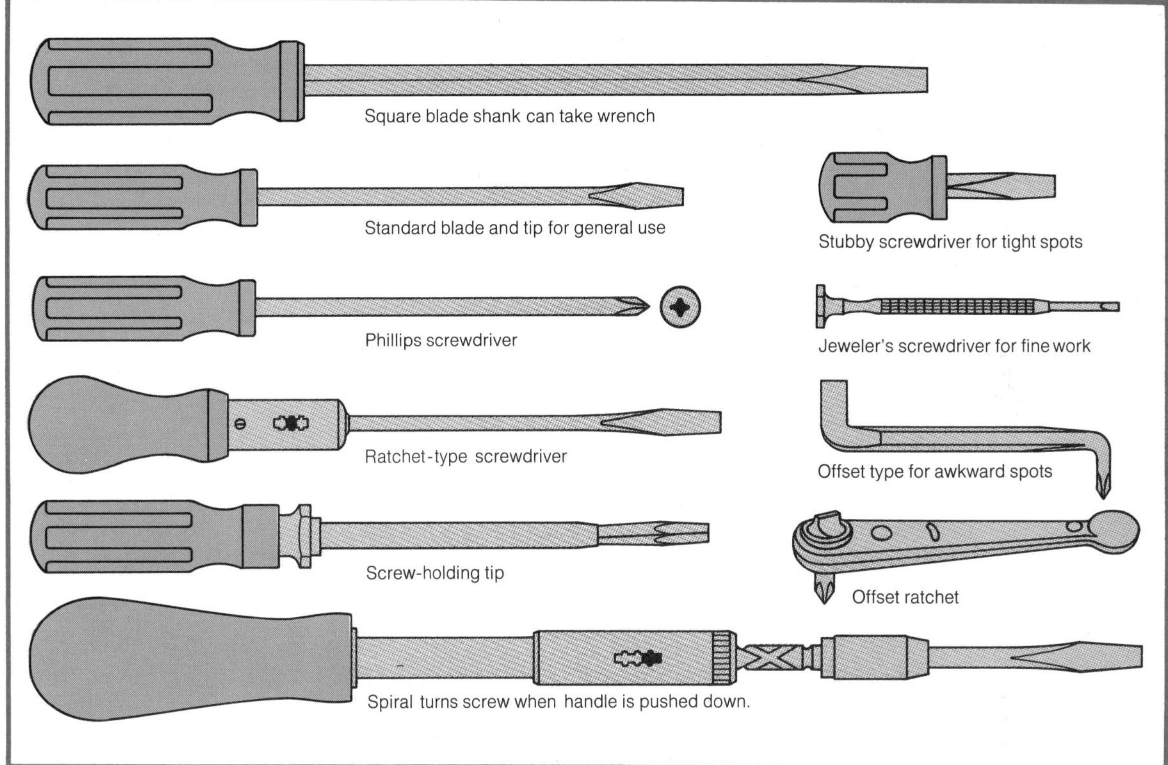

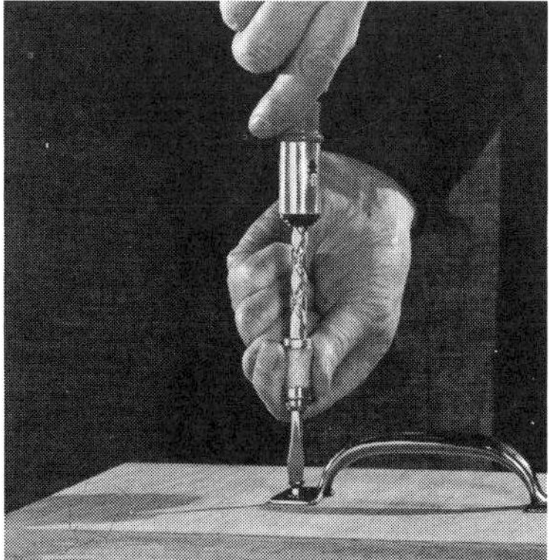

Spiral ratchet screwdriver has changeable blades for different screws. Depressing handle rotates blade; spring returns it. Useful to drive many screws.

Offset screwdriver gives more leverage than straight-handle type; drives or removes hard-to-turn screws. Works in tight places where others won't fit.

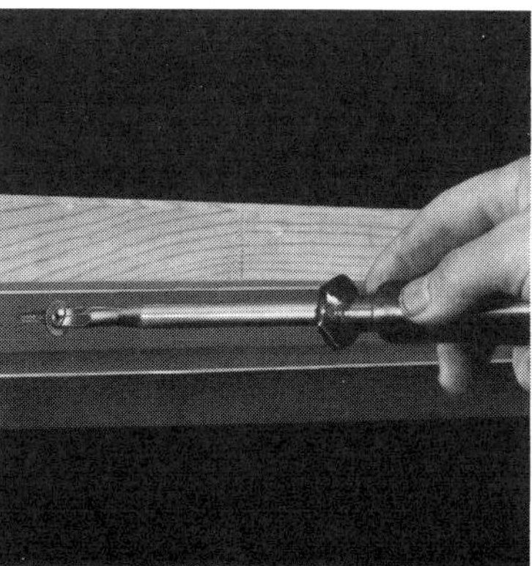

Screw-holding type holds screw on blade tip for starting in difficult spots. Made in several sizes; must be matched to size of screw to be driven.

Pliers

Types of pliers

The familiar **slip joint pliers** are named for the two-position pivot that provides both normal and wide jaw openings. Broad-jawed **lineman's pliers** have side cutters which equip them for heavy-duty wire cutting and splicing. **Channel-type pliers** with multi-position pivots adjust for jaw openings up to 2 inches and will grip any shape. **Long-nosed pliers** are used to shape wire and thin metal, and often for cutting as well. **Diagonal-cutting pliers** have no gripping jaws and are used for cutting only. Also for cutting only are **end-cutting nippers,** which can snip wire, small nails, and brads.

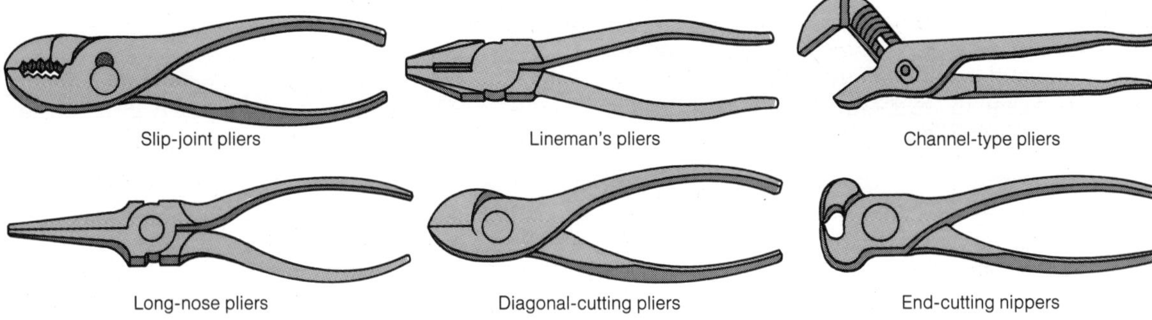

Using pliers

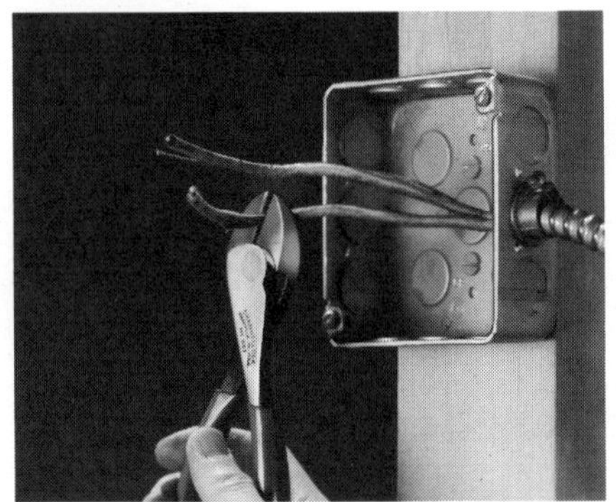

Diagonal-cutting pliers have hardened steel cutting edges for cutting wires, small brads.

End-cutting pliers also have hardened cutting edges, are used to pull nails and cut wire.

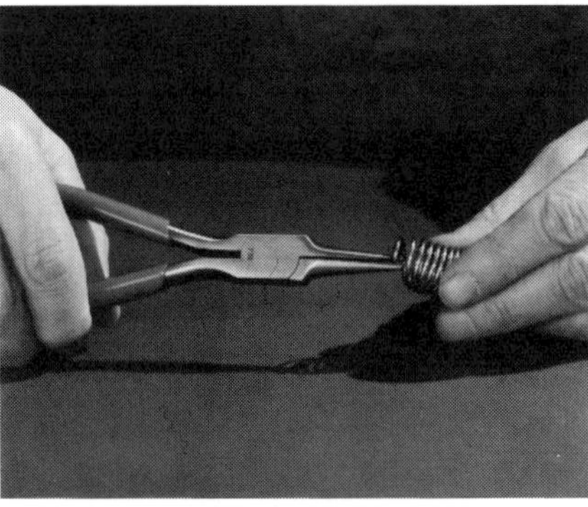

Long-nose pliers make terminal loops in wire, shape jewelry, insert small machine parts.

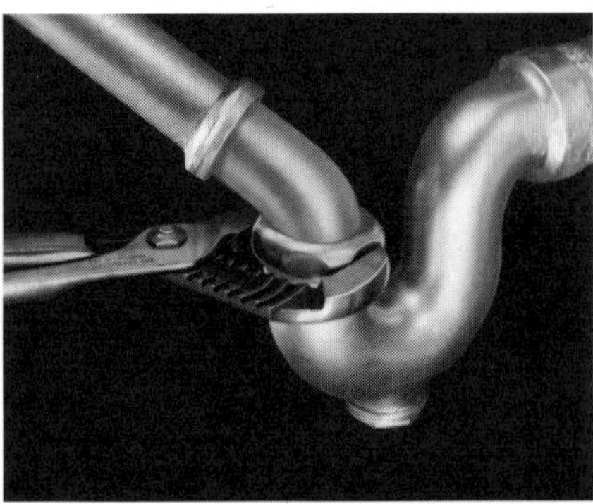

Channel-type pliers open wider than others, grip many shapes with long-handle leverage.

Combination plier-wrench

The **plier-wrench** functions as pliers, wrench, or vise. When it has been set to the desired gap, adjustable compound lever action locks it, auxiliary lever releases it. For work on round objects, such as pipe, use the curved-jaw type.

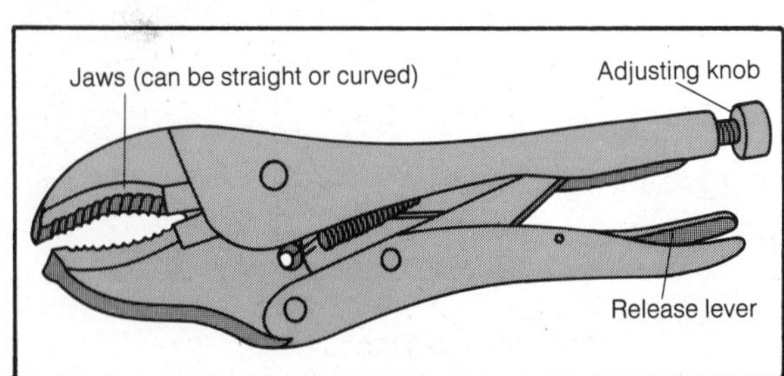

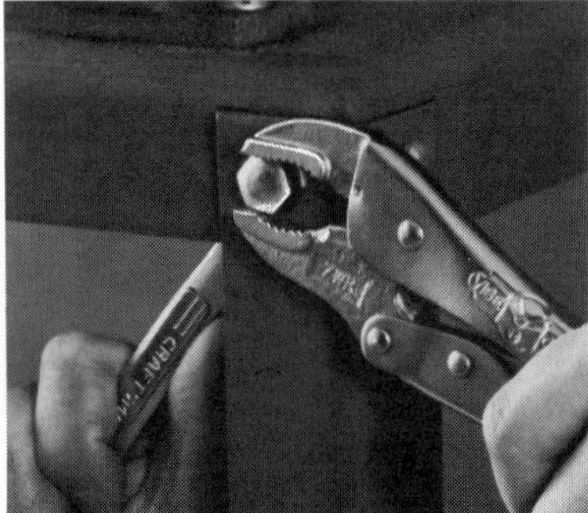

Combination plier-wrench is set to approximate grip gap with adjusting screw, then locked onto work with handles. Lever action releases its grip.

Plier-wrench, set to grip tightly, is handy for holding work against power grinding wheel. Point tool rest at wheel's center. Wear goggles.

This same tool will also protect your hands when you are using a star drill, by holding the drill in position. Keep plier-wrench close to drill point.

Wrench types and uses

Wrenches grip not only nuts and bolt heads but, in special forms, other objects from pipe to spark plugs. In general, where a wrench cannot be applied over the end of the work, as in tightening a fuel line connection, an **open-end wrench** is used. The adjustable open-end wrench fits many sizes. Where a wrench can be applied from the end of the work, as in removing a nut, a **box** or **socket wrench** is used; it can operate in tighter quarters than an open-end wrench. The **Allen wrench,** sometimes called a hex-key wrench, fits the hexagonal recesses in various Allen-type screws and setscrews. For round objects such as pipe, the **Stillson,** or **pipe wrench,** is used. Its movable upper jaw tightens automatically as pressure is applied to the handle.

Adjustable wrench

Double-end box wrench

Allen wrench

Ratchet box wrench speeds work

Double-end open-end wrench fits two sizes.

Combination open-end box wrench

Offset double-end box wrench

Nut driver

Deep-throat socket wrench

Ratchet handle and socket wrenches

Stillson (pipe) wrench

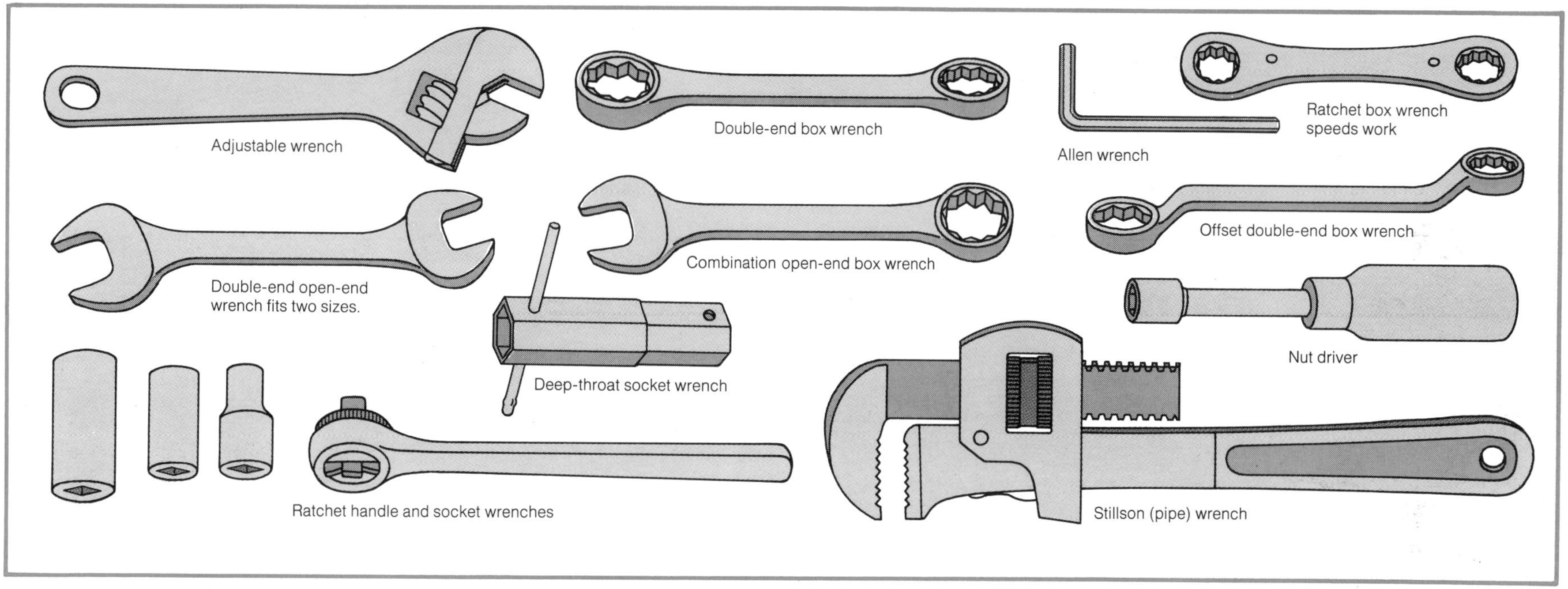

Nut driver is available in sizes to fit hex nuts from 3/16 to 1/2 in., some are self-adjusting from 1/4 to 7/16 in. Use the nut driver in the same way as you would a screwdriver.

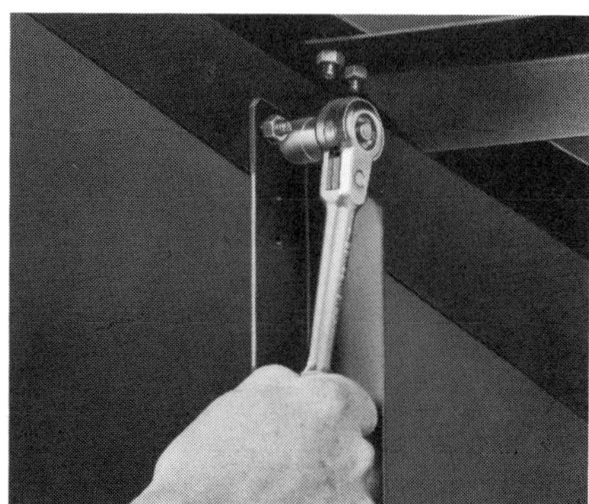

Socket wrenches are available in sets ranging from as few as six pieces to more than 200. Ratchet fittings and universal joints multiply its range of uses. Handy for auto work.

Box wrench has great strength, can be used where handle swing is limited to as little as 30° All box wrenches are available double-ended or in open-end combinations.

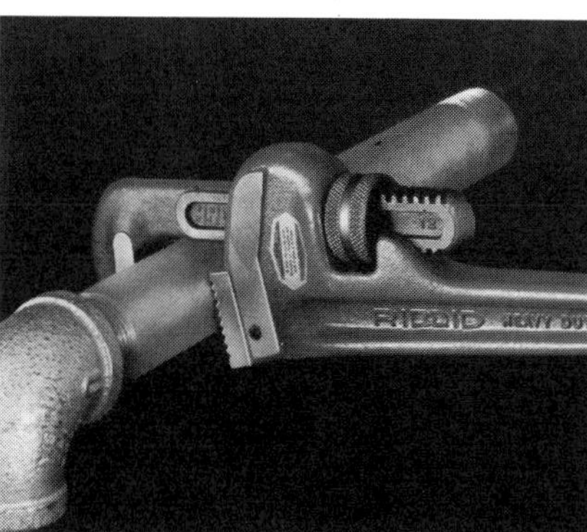

Pipe wrench jaws are adjusted so they contact pipe surface with a knurled nut in the upper handle. When pressure is applied to the handle, the jaws tighten automatically.

Measuring and marking

Using rules and tapes

The **folding wood rule** is used for general measuring, especially where its rigidity is needed, as in extending across wide openings like stairwells. The **steel tape rule**'s flexibility enables it to measure round as well as straight objects, and its compactness saves space in toolbox or pocket.

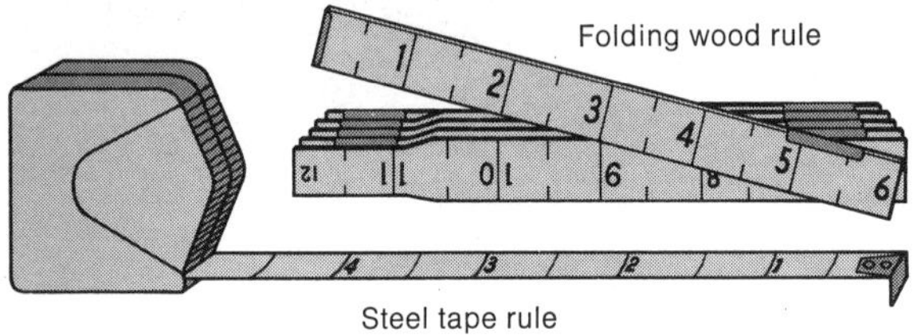

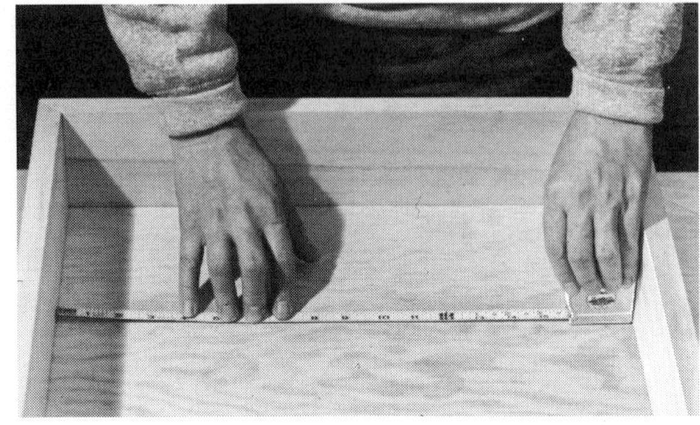

Inside measurements can be made with roll-type steel tape if 2 in. are added to compensate for width of tape case.

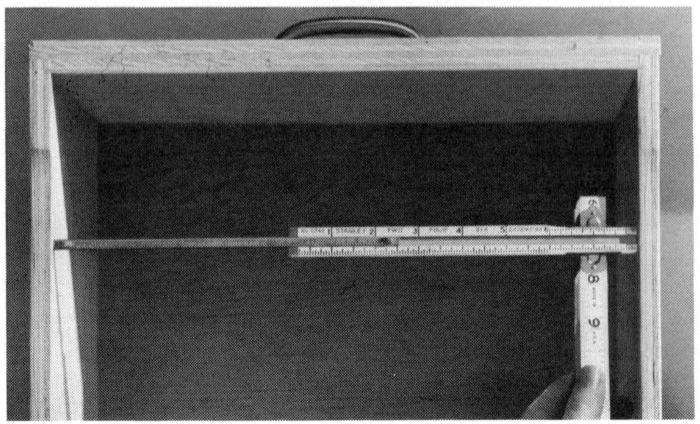

Open extension-type rule to nearest section; use slide-out extension for final measurement of inside dimensions.

Using squares

The **try square** is used to test adjoining surfaces for squareness, mark for right angle cuts. **Combination square** does these jobs and more, including miter marking. **Rafter** or **framing square** is both marking square and carpenter's calculator, scaled so you can mark for rafter cuts according to roof pitch. **T bevel** is used to measure an angle and then transfer it to another area.

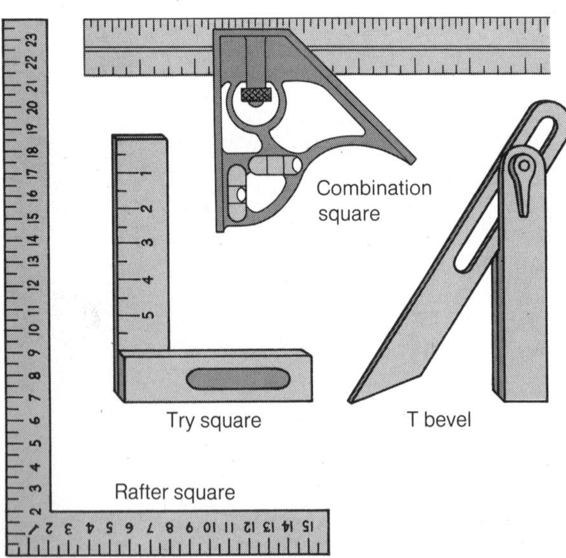

Using combination square for miter marking: Use other surface of square's body to mark right angles.

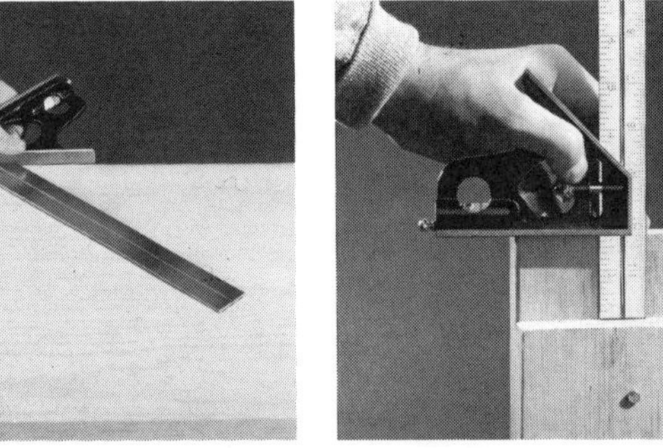

Measuring depth of holes or recesses using combination square: Slide rule-blade into hole; take reading at surface.

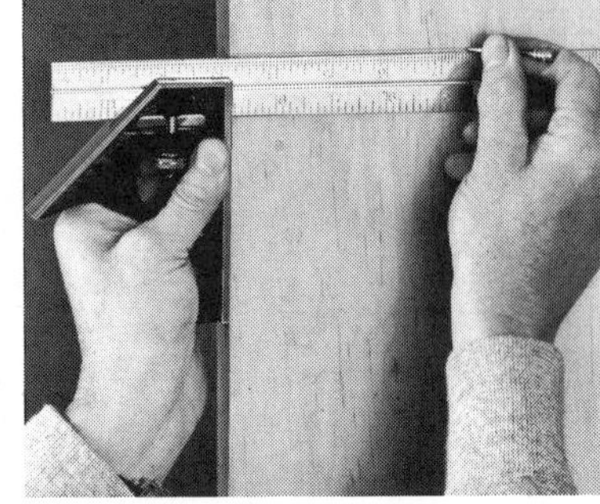

Combination square can also be used as a level, a marking gauge, a scribe, and a ruler for measuring and drawing.

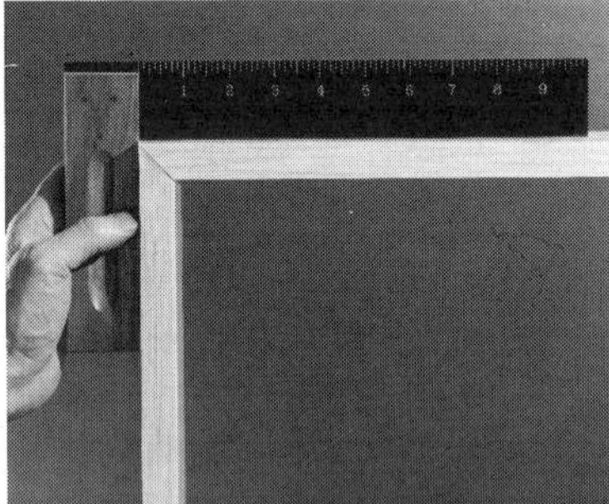

Use try square as shown here to test the adjoining surfaces for squareness. Use a plane to square work up, if necessary.

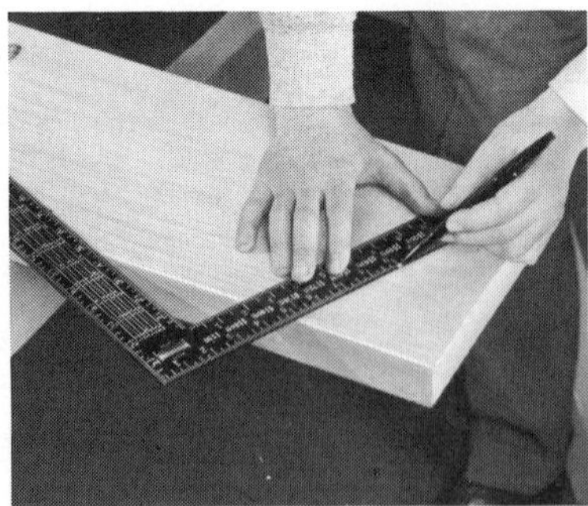

To mark rafter or stair stringer cuts along edges of square, set the special scale numbers along edge of lumber.

To duplicate angle cut, set T bevel on angle selected, tighten wing nut. Use setting to transfer angle to new work.

Using levels

Wood, aluminum, or magnesium levels come in lengths to suit their various purposes. Shortest is the **line level,** suspended on taut string for long-span leveling, as in grading or foundation work. Longest is the **mason's level,** usually four feet long. The **carpenter's level** is about two feet long. When the slightly curved bubble tubes, or **vials,** run length-

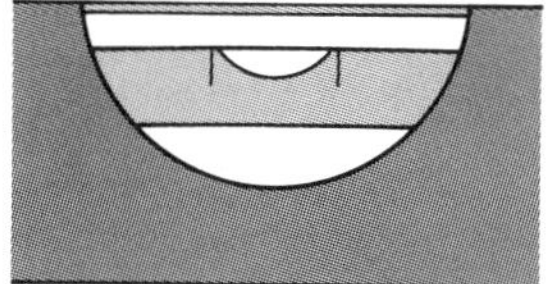

Bubble position, level

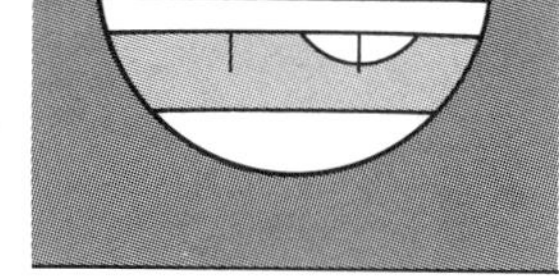

Bubble position, tilted

wise, they are **level** tubes used for checking horizontal surfaces. Vials that run crosswise are **plumb** for use in checking verticals. Some levels have adjustable vials calibrated from 0 to 90 degrees, for checking pitched surfaces. Others include a 45-degree tube. Select a level that can be read through the top for floor work, and one that can be read through the side for work at or above eye level.

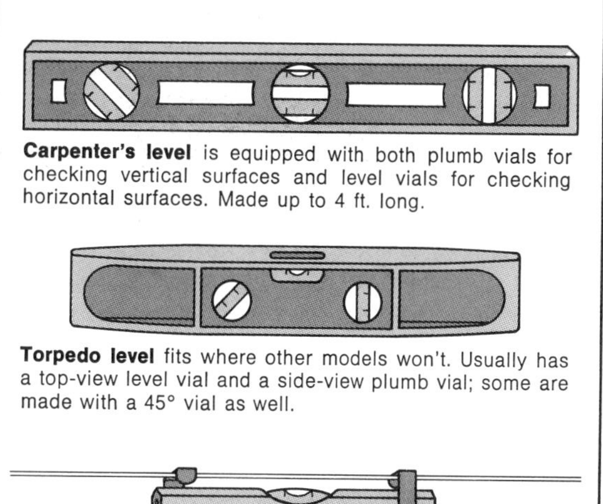

Carpenter's level is equipped with both plumb vials for checking vertical surfaces and level vials for checking horizontal surfaces. Made up to 4 ft. long.

Torpedo level fits where other models won't. Usually has a top-view level vial and a side-view plumb vial; some are made with a 45° vial as well.

Line level is usually about 3 in. long and very light in weight. Hooks at ends hang it on taut string for long-span leveling in grading and foundation work.

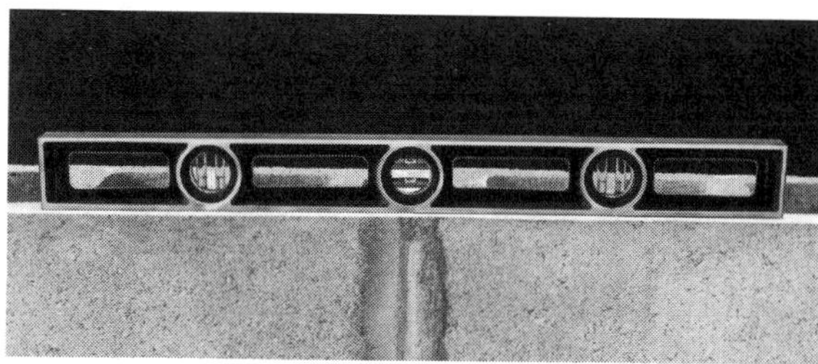

Mason's level covers broad span in concrete block work, shows which blocks need adjusting while mortar is still fresh.

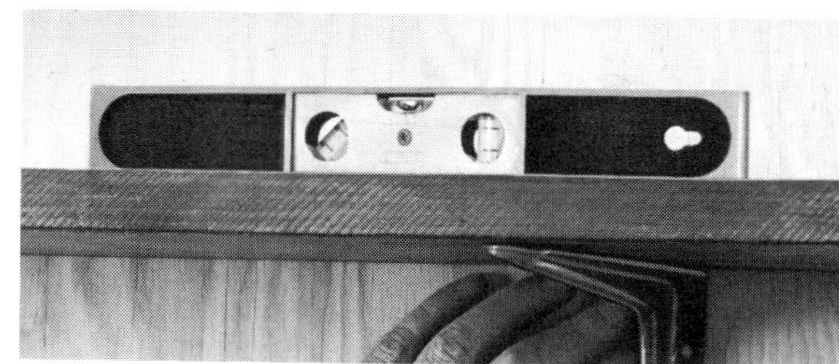

Torpedo level: Handy for checking sill level, angle of miter-positioned trim, level of stationary tools and appliances.

Tools for marking

The **marking gauge** is used to make a lengthwise scratch on a board for cutting to width. For a pencil mark, use a **combination square,** adjusted to width; slide it along the board edge with pencil held against the blade end. To mark for small circular cuts, use a **wing divider,** available with twin metal points for scratch marking or with point and pencil. For large circular marking, use a pair of **trammel points** mounted on a wood batten. Metal-pointed trammel must be used for center; marking trammel point may have pencil adapter. For very long straight marking, use a **chalk line.**

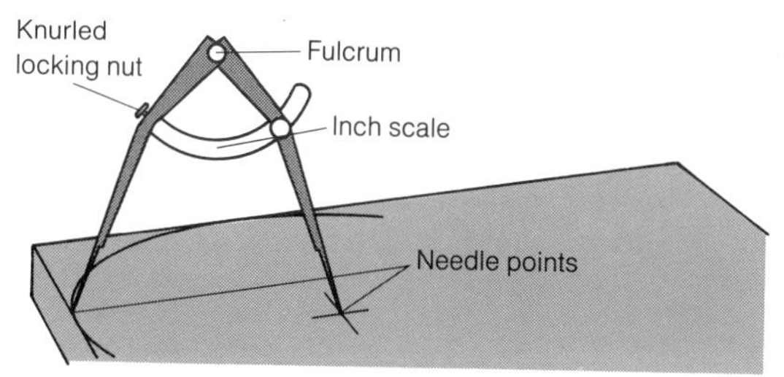

Marking gauge is used to draw a line parallel to the edge of a board at a predetermined distance. Gauge is marked in fractions of an inch. Marker is locked in place with thumbscrew. Some gauges have a brass liner that bears against wood to minimize friction. Hold the gauge at a slight angle as you move it along.

Trammel points clamped on a wood batten can be set at the spacing that is required for large circle marking. For scratch marking, use two metal-pointed trammels, one for center, the other for marking. For pencil mark, use one with a pencil holder. Make sure the pencil is sharp and does not wobble in the holder.

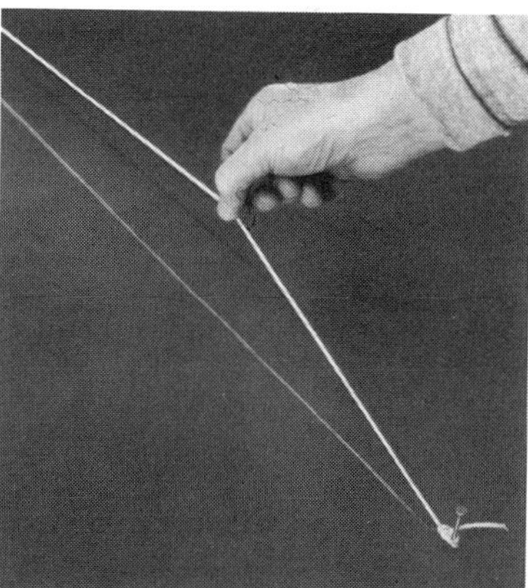

Use a taut chalk line for a very long straight-line mark, as in flooring-tile work. Available on reels that apply chalk automatically to line. You simply draw cord taut along the surface where you want the marked line to be, lift it up and snap it back. Chalk marks line. Use two nails as anchors for the chalk line.

Hand drills and braces

Using a brace and bit

The bit brace can bore a hole in any material a power drill can, but it takes longer. It does, however, have the advantage of being usable where no electric current is available, and it is practically noiseless. The chuck in which the bits are held requires taper shank bits in most models, though bit braces are also made with universal chucks that take round, square, or tapered shanks. For the uses encountered in the average shop, the regular tapered chuck is adequate.

An important feature of a quality bit brace is the ratchet, which can be set to transform a back-and-forth handle movement to a turning movement of the chuck in a clockwise or counterclockwise direction. This makes it possible to bore holes or to drive or remove screws in cramped spaces. The turning force (torque) of the tool depends on the "sweep." This is the diameter of the circle in which the handle turns, and ranges from 8 to 14 inches—the wider the sweep the greater the force. A 10-inch sweep is a good compromise that suits most purposes in the average shop.

To bore a hole perpendicular to the surface of the work, position a square or square block on it and align the bit with one corner. Bore from one side until just the tip of the bit emerges from the other side. Then remove the bit from the hole by backing it out, and continue the hole from the opposite side, carefully inserting the tip of the bit into the small exit hole. This will avoid splitting the wood when the full width of the bit emerges.

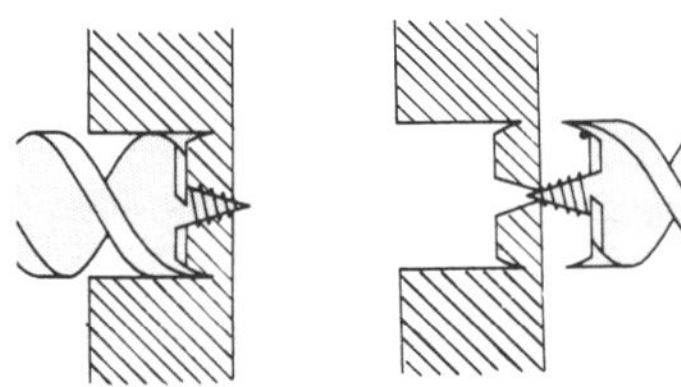

Drill from both sides to prevent splitting

If you want to drill partway through, stopping at a specified depth, wrap some tape around the shank of the bit at a point roughly equal to the depth of the required hole. Then make a pencil mark on the tape equal to the exact depth you want. With this marking to guide you, you won't be confused as to whether it is the top or the bottom of the tape that marks the required depth.

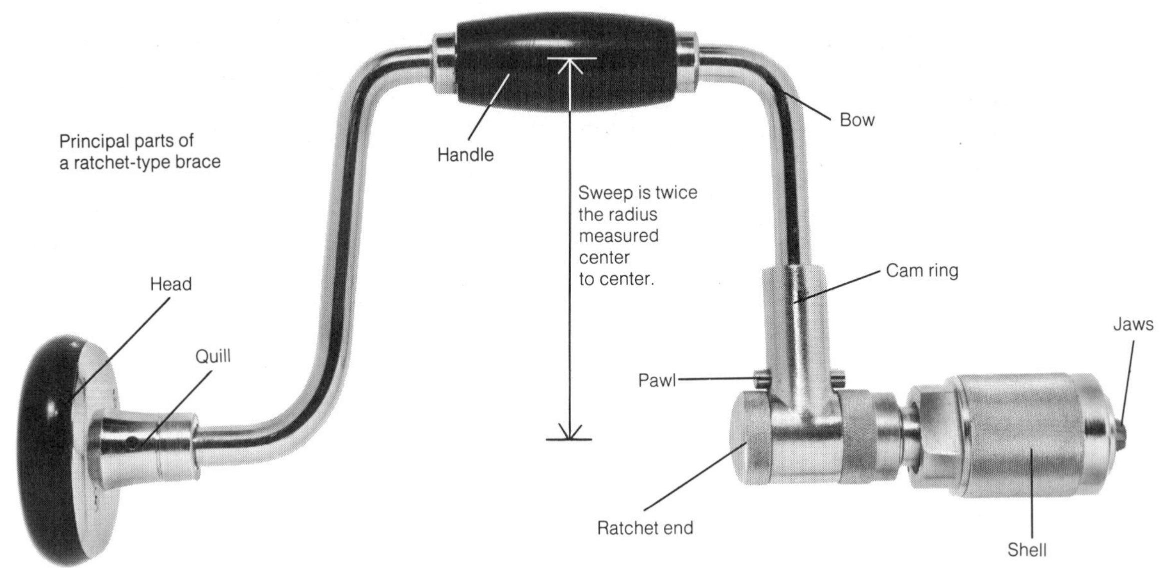

Principal parts of a ratchet-type brace

Bits

The corkscrew-shaped woodworking bits used in the bit brace are called **auger** bits. The most widely used forms are the **Jennings** type (also called double twist) and the **solid center** bit. The double twist leaves a cleaner hole; the solid center is stiffer, which is useful in deep holes or wavy grain. Both are readily available in diameters from ¼ to 1 inch and in lengths usually between 7 and 10 inches. For larger diameters, to 3 inches, use the adjustable **expansive** bit. For holes deeper than bit length, use a bit extension. **Spade** bits cost much less than auger-type bits, come in sizes from ¼ to 1 inch, in ¹⁄₁₆-inch increments. For shallow, flat-bottom holes, use a **Forstner** bit, which must be carefully located on the work, tapped lightly into the surface for starting. To drill metal, special twist drills, tempered for the purpose, are made in diameters from ¹⁄₁₆ inch up. **Countersink** bits recess holes for flathead screws. **Screwdriver** bits drive roundhead as well as flathead screws. They are handy for removing stubborn screws.

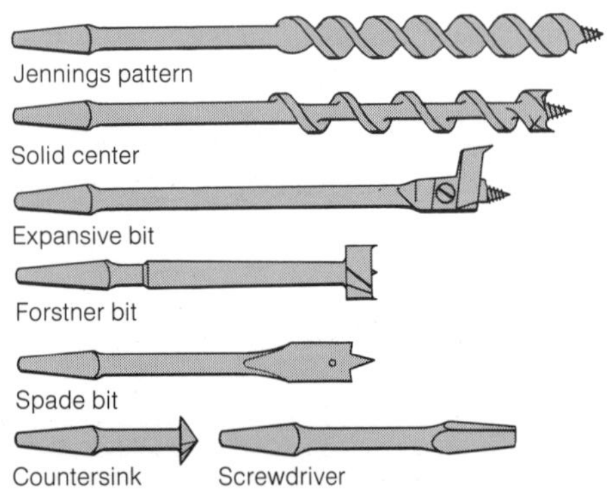

Drilling accurately: Sight bit against try square—or get someone else to do it—to assure straight drilling. For horizontal drilling, hold small round handle against body.

Using a hand drill

The hand drill is a crank-operated tool that utilizes a large wheel gear in mesh with a smaller pinion to turn the drill chuck approximately three revolutions for every turn of the crank. It provides adequate speed for drilling wood, metal, and plastic with straight-shank twist drills. The drills are sold singly or in sets. For use in the hand drill, diameters of drills generally range from 1/32 to 1/4 inch in increments of 1/64 inch. Although smaller sizes are made for doing certain types of work, they are seldom used with this particular tool.

To use the drill, hold the main handle in the left hand with thumb on top for vertical drilling, or in any manner that is comfortable and gives you firm control of the tool. Apply light to moderate pressure, the amount depending on the diameter of the drill. With very small drills, apply turning force to the crank handle on the up and down portions of the crank turn only, to avoid side thrust or wobble that might bend or break the twist drill. To make a hole

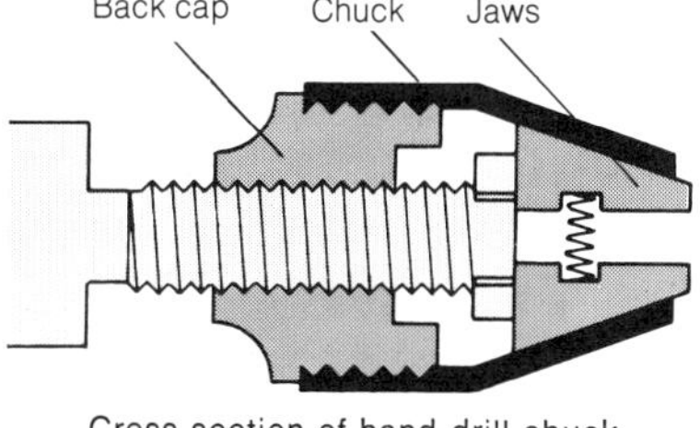

Cross section of hand drill chuck

in wood, use an awl to make a starting hole. In metal, use a centerpunch. This initial step is necessary to keep the drill from wandering. In metal drilling, lessen the pressure on the drill when it is about to break through the surface of the work, to prevent its catching on a burr and breaking. A few drops of oil applied occasionally to the moving parts is about all the maintenance that the tool requires.

Heavy-duty hand drills are called breast drills. Instead of a handle at the extreme end, they have a curved extension. Pressing against this extension enables the operator to apply considerable force for drilling into metal or hardwood. Some hand drills have a hollow detachable handle for storing extra drill bits. Hand drills accept bits up to 1/4 inch in diameter while breast drills take drill bits up to 3/8 inch in diameter.

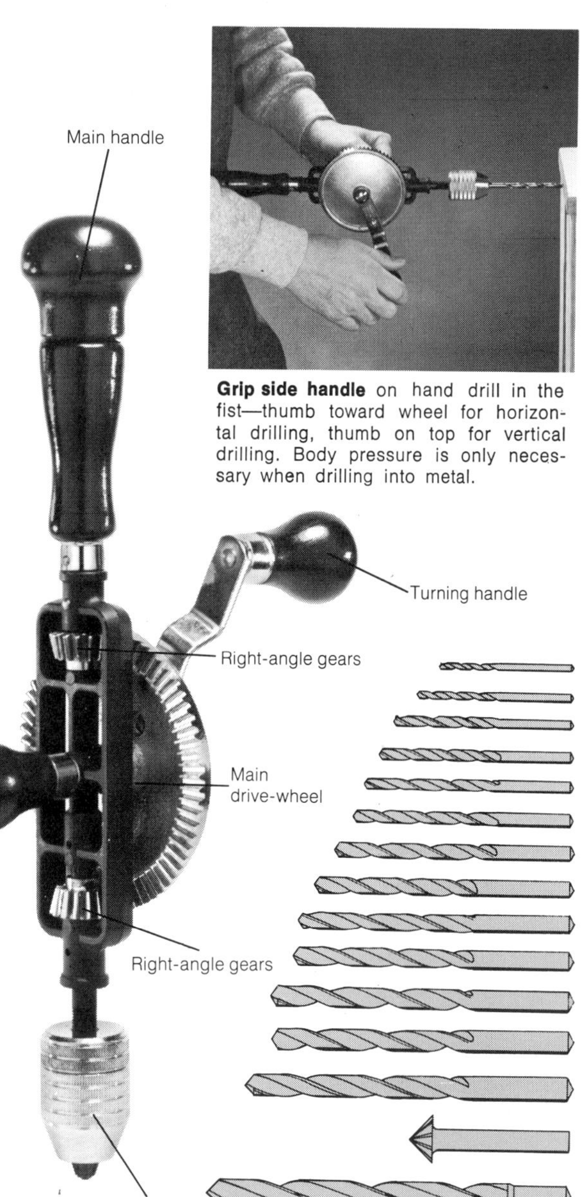

Grip side handle on hand drill in the fist—thumb toward wheel for horizontal drilling, thumb on top for vertical drilling. Body pressure is only necessary when drilling into metal.

Any twist drill or countersink that has a shank size up to 1/4 in. can be used with small hand drills.

Sharpening bits

The best tool for sharpening an auger bit is an **auger bit file,** shaped specially for the purpose and available at most hardware stores. The flat lateral cutters on the bit are beveled like a chisel on the surface toward the square shank of the bit, as shown in the left-hand drawing. File only on this bevel to restore a

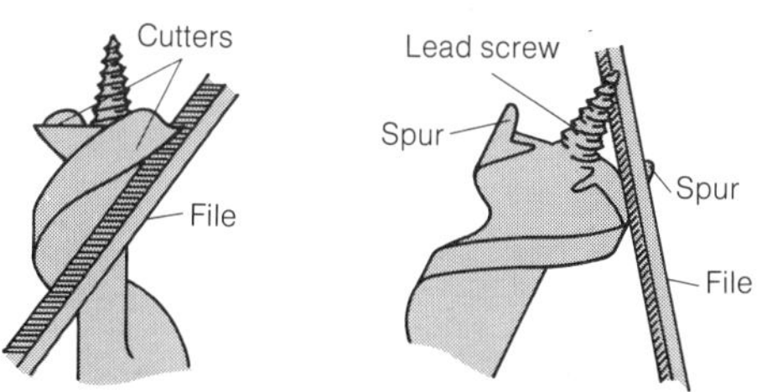

Sharpening an auger bit

sharp edge and remove as little metal as possible. In sharpening the rounded spurs at the perimeter of the bit tip, file only from the inside, as shown in the right-hand drawing, and do not attempt to sharpen any part of the pointed lead screw at the center of the bit tip.

The auger bit file may also be used to sharpen the expansive bit (see drawing below). File only the original bevel surfaces, as with the auger bit. If an auger bit file is not available, a flat needle file may be used for this sharpening job.

Twist drill bits, used for drilling metal, must be

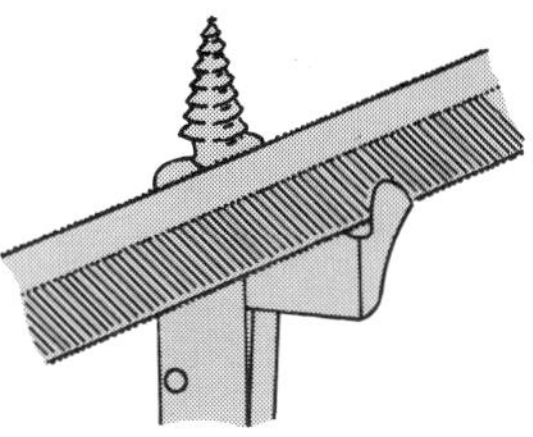

Sharpening an expansive bit

sharpened by grinding because of their hardness. This is best done in a drill-sharpening jig, which holds the drill at the proper angle to the grinding wheel. Jigs of this type are available with instructions at hardware stores. In bit brace use, however, twist drill bits seldom need sharpening if kept rust-free. Light oil, soap, or wax used as a lubricant in the hole being drilled eases the job and lessens bit wear. Apply it at intervals during the work.

Choosing and using planes

Planes are used to trim wood to size, to smooth it, to straighten irregular edges, to bevel and chamfer it, and, in special forms, to groove and shape wood into moldings. Types of planes vary according to use. The **block plane** is the smallest regular shop plane (about 6 inches long). The blade, or plane iron, is mounted bevel up at a low angle for planing along the grain or across ends. The best type for small smoothing and fitting jobs, the block plane can be operated with one hand. The **trimming plane,** usually 3½ inches long with an inch-wide blade, is for small and delicate work. A **model maker's plane,** unlike the preceding two, has a convex instead of a flat bottom, with curvatures sideways and lengthwise. It planes flat or mildly concave surfaces, is similar in size to trimming plane. The **smooth plane,** 7 to 10 inches long, has a blade about 1¾ inches wide, mounted bevel down. A cap on top of the blade bends and breaks shavings, minimizes surface roughening. Good for light to moderate general use. The **scrub plane** is sized comparably to the smooth plane but has a narrower blade (1¼ inches) with a rounded cutting edge. Choose it for fast rough cutting, also to produce a hand-hewn effect. The **jack plane** averages 12 to 15 inches in length, around 2 inches in blade width. A general-use plane much like the smooth plane, it is better for edge-straightening because of its greater length. **Fore** and **jointer planes,** like the jack plane but longer (from 18 to 24 inches), are the best choice for edge straightening.

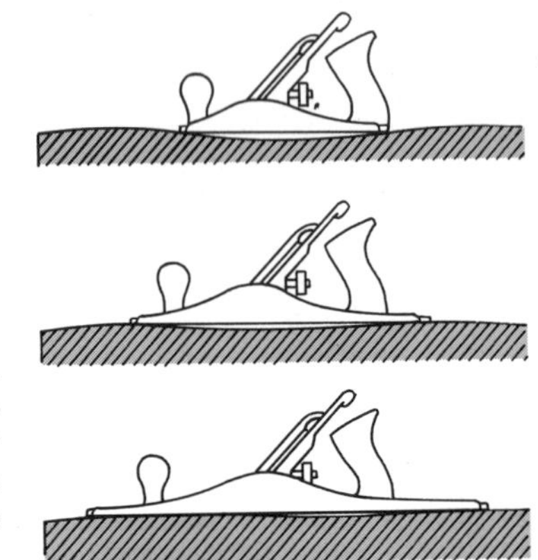

Small plane, such as block plane, rides up and down waves of irregular edge.

Longer jack plane spans several crests, has some straightening effect.

Very long jointer plane spans waves, cuts down high spots and straightens entire edge of work.

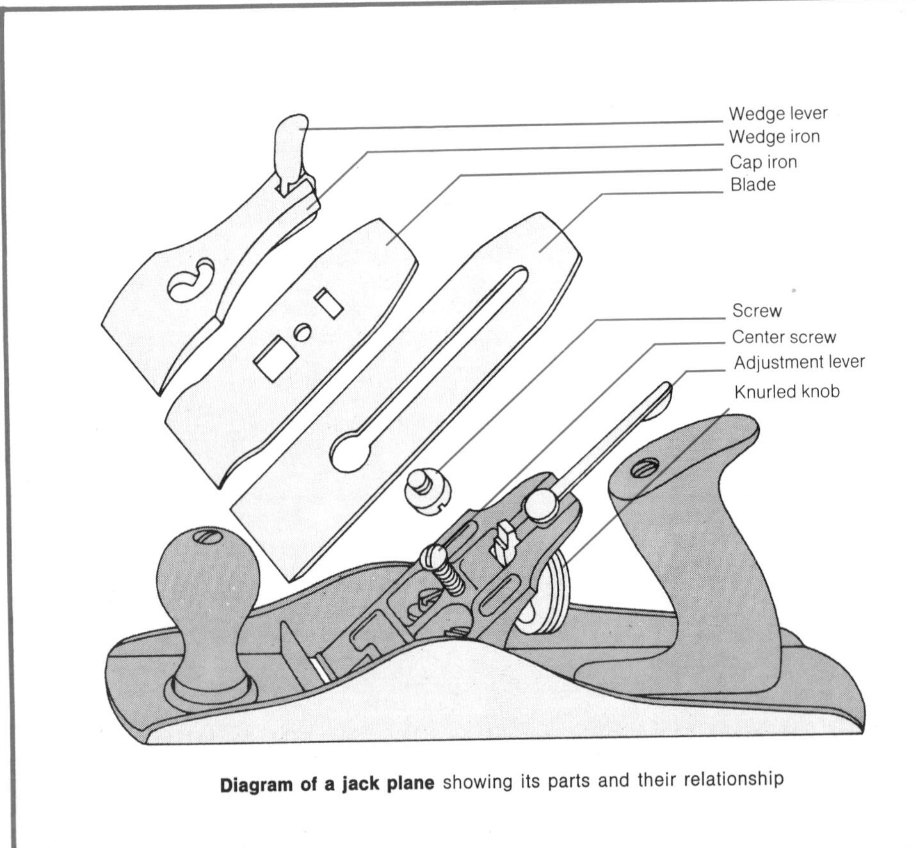

Diagram of a jack plane showing its parts and their relationship

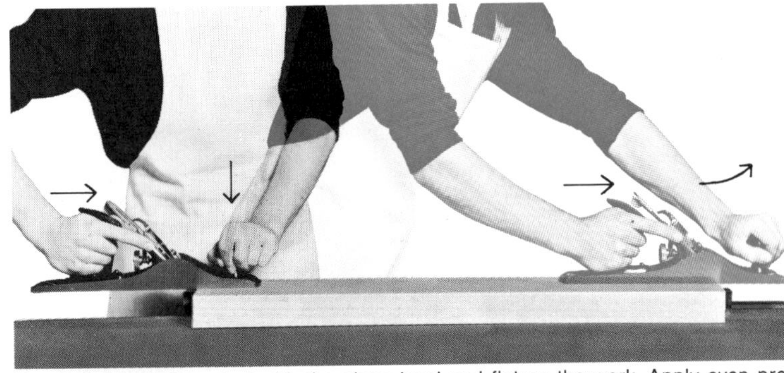

For straight planing, start with the plane level and flat on the work. Apply even pressure during the stroke to produce a continuous shaving. Hold the plane nose up at the end of the stroke to prevent a down curve. Always plane in direction of grain to minimize chipping. Planing against grain leaves rough surface.

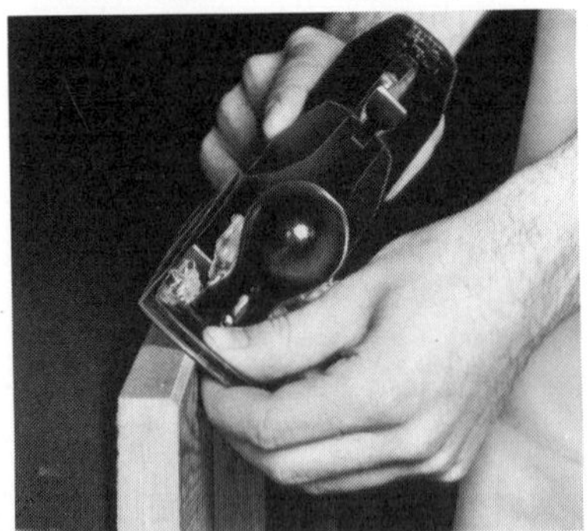

To chamfer or bevel using a plane, first mark the work, then tip the plane as shown. Plane with the grain.

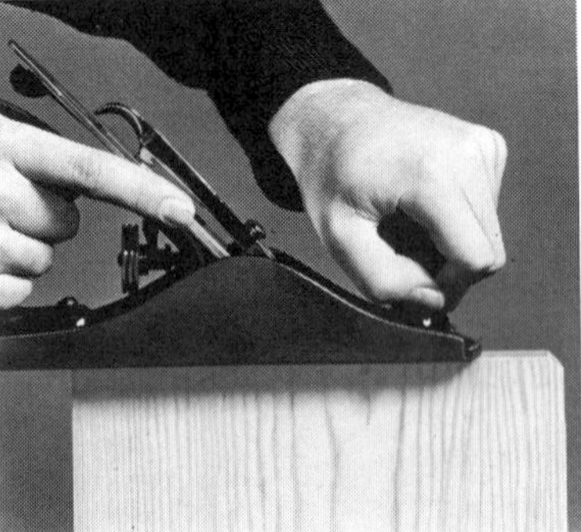

On end grain, plane from the edges toward the center. Then plane off the hump in the center to level edge.

Block planes

Although the basic block plane types are described as adjustable and nonadjustable, both of them can be adjusted. Cut depth is increased or decreased on the adjustable type by turning the adjusting wheel to loosen the blade, moving it in or out by hand and re-tightening the wheel. On either type, alignment of blade cutting edge with plane mouth must be done by hand with the blade loose. Block planes of the nonadjustable type are lower-priced, but the adjustable type is more convenient.

To plane across the end grain of a board, set the plane iron for a shallow cut, making sure the iron is sharp. Before starting the cut, be sure to bevel the ends slightly. This is important. If you don't, the plane will split the wood as it nears the end of the cut. Make the bevel cut with the plane at a 45-degree angle.

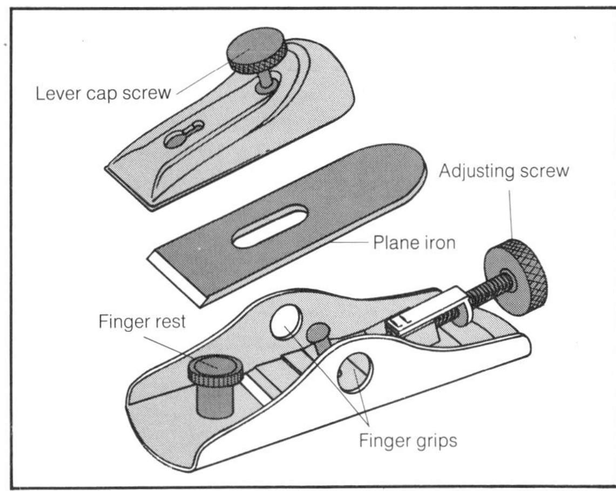

On end grain and wavy grain, hold block plane at 15° angle to direction of motion to cut with a minimum of wood roughening.

Blade adjustment

To remove a lot of material, set for deep cut at the start, shallow at the finish. If the grain isn't apparent, check the surface after the first stroke. If it is roughened noticeably, plane the opposite way. On wavy grain, set for a shallow cut, and plane at an angle. For general work, set the plane iron cap (on large planes) about 1/16 inch back from cutting edge; on curly wood, as close to edge as possible but not on it. To sharpen a large plane iron, grind only the original bevel, leaving top flat.

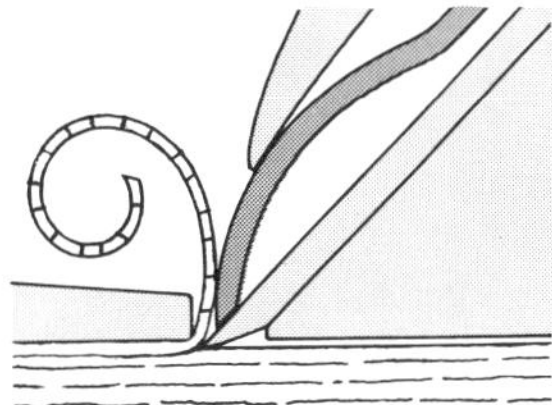
Plane iron cap breaks and curls shavings.

Screw cap tight to prevent wedged shavings.

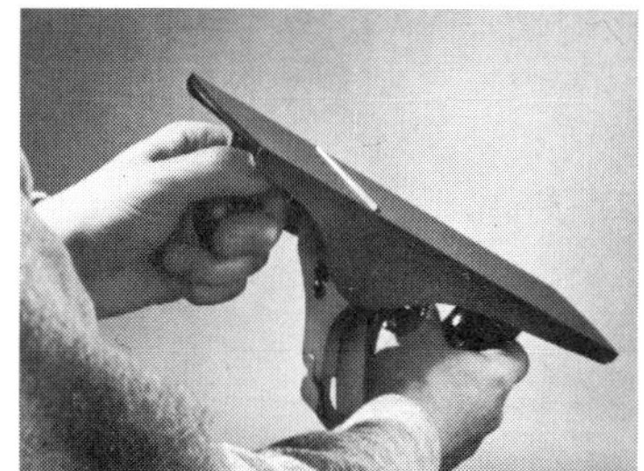
To align blade for even-width cut, sight along bottom and set cutting edge parallel to plane mouth. Move blade by hand on block plane, by lateral adjusting lever on larger plane types.

Using a shooting board

Shooting board is made by nailing one square-edged board higher than another on crosspieces, as shown in the drawing below, with a stop block at one end. With the work resting on the upper board, and end edge projecting, a plane can be tipped on its side and slid along the lower board to trim the work edge perfectly square.

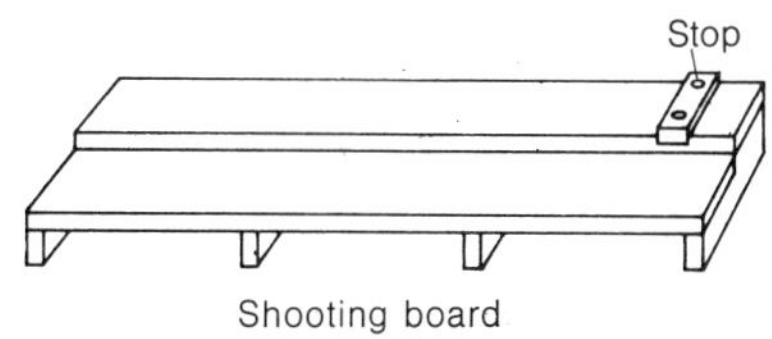

Shooting board

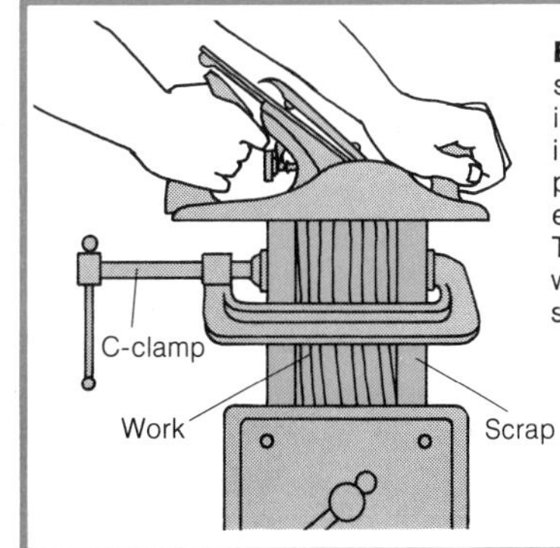

Easy way to prevent splitting of corners in end-grain planing is with scrap pieces clamped on each side of the work. The scrap, not the work, does the splitting.

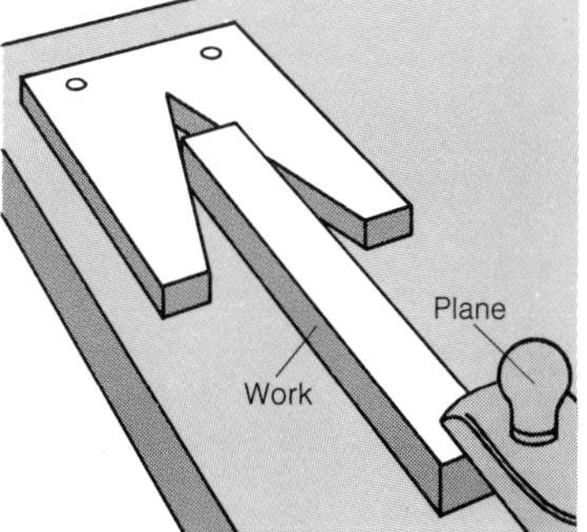

Jig to hold work for planing consists of piece of wood with a V cut out and screwed to bench top. Jig accepts work equal to width slightly less than V opening.

Special-purpose planes

How to use a rabbet plane

The rabbet plane makes a cut as wide as its bottom, descending into the cut as it deepens. Guided by a fence, or a batten on the work, it can cut a recessed step in the surface of a board adjoining the edge. Each stroke deepens the recess until the required depth is reached. For across-the-grain planing, a sharp spur attachment is used to score the edge of the cut and prevent tearing of fibers.

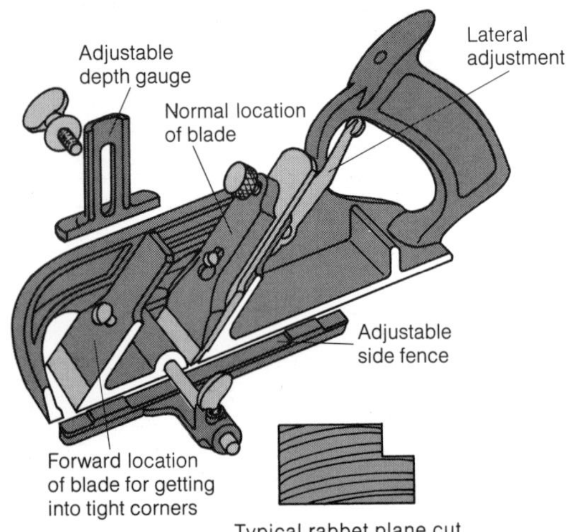

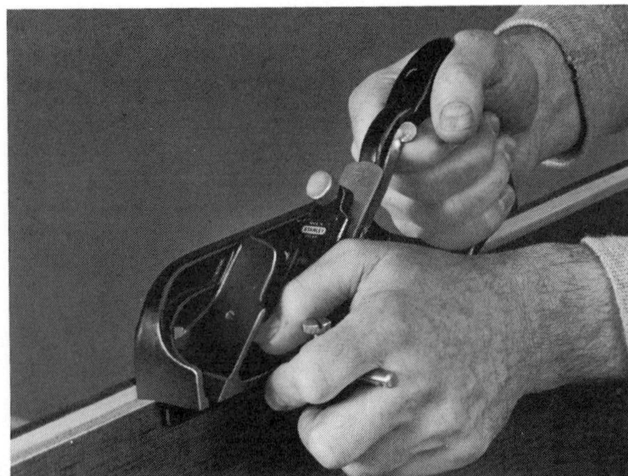

Rabbet plane is used to cut a recessed groove along the surface of a board along the edge. Cutter can be set to make a groove in a board even though board butts up against a wall.

How to use a hand router

The hand router is used chiefly to even and smooth the bottom of a squared groove, such as might receive the end of a shelf, after the material has been roughed out between saw cuts, usually with a chisel. The **open-throat router plane** shown below has an adjustable guide fence. The smaller **hand router** can be guided by a batten on the work. Cutting depth can be increased in steps to final level.

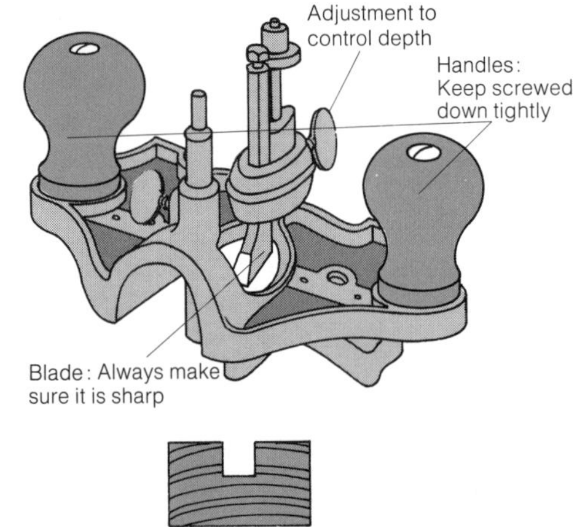

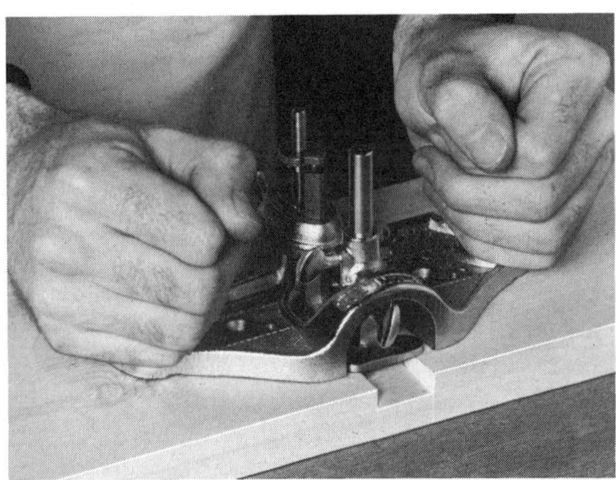

How the hand router is used to clean out a dado after most of the stock has been removed with a number of saw cuts. Cutting action consists of a series of short forward strokes.

How to use a spokeshave

The spokeshave is used to smooth or chamfer curved edges, convex or concave. Blade cutting depth is set by hand on some models, by screw adjustment on others. To use: With work in a vise, grasp both handles and push or pull along work. As a spokeshave must cut with the grain, it is often pushed along one section, then pulled along the other, to the center, to avoid having to shift work in the vise. Since the spokeshave is a kind of plane, the cutter must be kept sharp to do its job. Sharpen it as you would sharpen a plane iron (p. 31). Oil on the cutting edge, when tool is not in use, will prevent rusting.

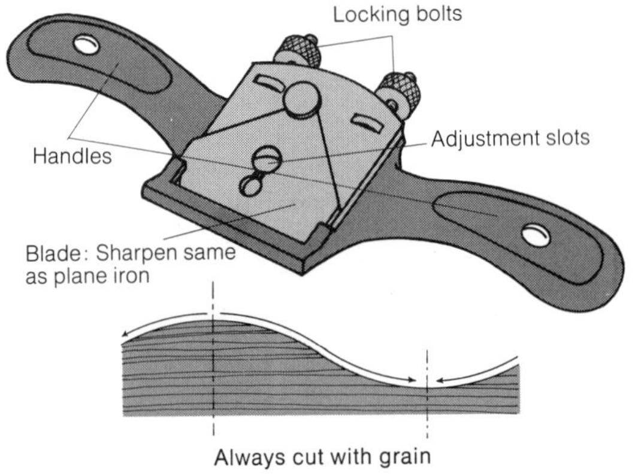

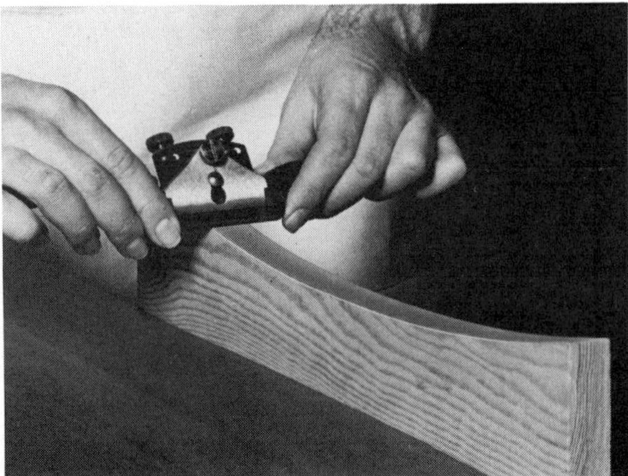

To use a spokeshave for cutting a concave curve, work from each end of the board toward the center. Always cut with grain and have blade at slight angle. Be sure blade is sharp.

Surform tools and their uses

Surform tools can be used plane- or file-fashion on wood, aluminum, copper, brass, plastic, laminates, and similar materials. (Shavings pass through the blade into the recess above, so the tool is used as a cheese grater by some.) Because of multiple cutting edges, the replaceable blades are well suited to end-grain cutting and smoothing of convex surfaces. Use with light to moderate pressure.

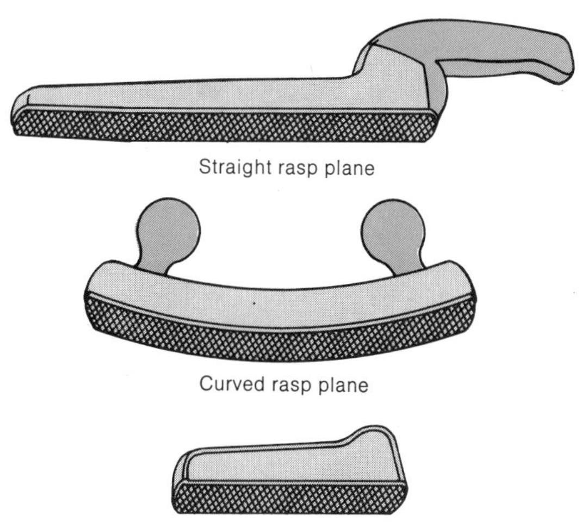

Surform, or rasp planes come in several styles and lengths. Handled in use like an ordinary plane; cannot, however, be adjusted for depth of cut. Less expensive than planes.

Using a drawknife

The drawknife removes material rapidly, operating somewhat like a spokeshave but taking much heavier cuts. It is held by the handles and drawn toward the user, with cutting depth controlled by the angle of the handles. It can be used to rough-cut large pieces prior to planing, as in removing large corner portions from square lumber at the start of rounding. Cutting edge widths run 10 to 12 inches.

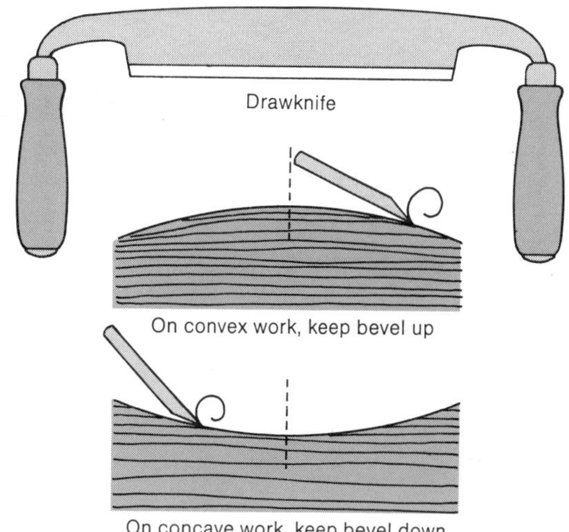

How the drawknife is used. Work should be securely held in a vise. Chief advantage of the drawknife is that it can cut right up to any obstruction on the work.

How to sharpen and hone a plane

Chisels and plane irons have two angles forming their cutting edge, a 25-degree ground angle and a 30-degree honed angle. Ground angle is formed on a grindstone and only needs occasional renewing. Honed angle is formed and maintained by rubbing on an oilstone. To hone a chisel or plane iron, oil the stone, then hold the blade at about a 30-degree angle to the stone, rubbing it to and fro along its length.

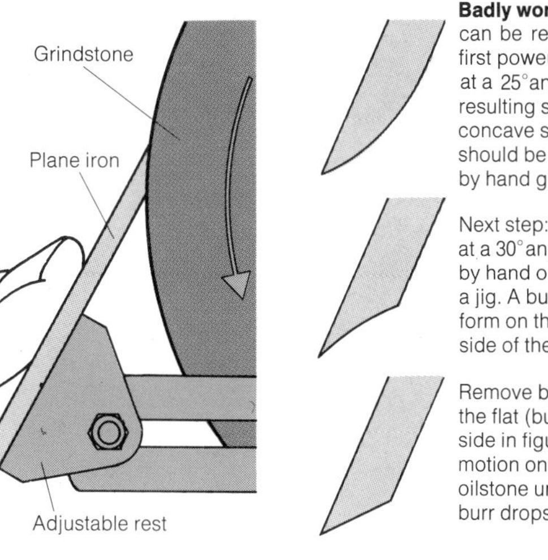

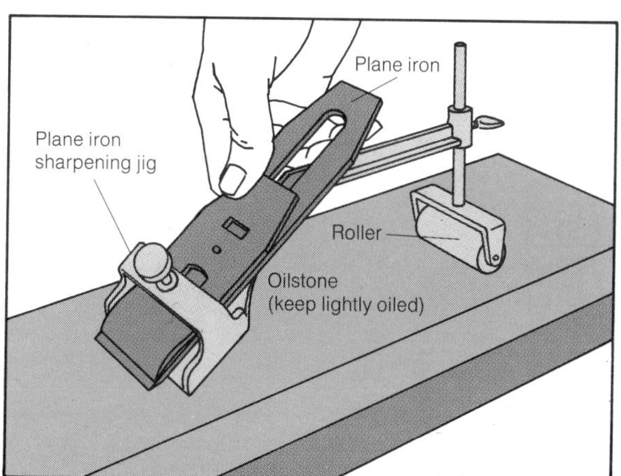

Jig for honing a plane iron keeps the iron at predetermined angle to the stone, generally 30°. The stone should be kept lubricated with light machine oil during honing process.

Chisels and gouges

Types of chisels

Most chisels today have plastic handles which can be struck with a hammer or with a mallet without danger of splitting. In fact, some chisels for use on wood are made of one-piece steel. Size is a factor in selection. The shortest is the **butt chisel,** about 7 to 9 inches long, for use in tight spaces. Next is the 9-to-10½-inch **pocket chisel,** preferred for general shop work. Largest is the **mill chisel,** 16 inches long, good for heavy work but seldom used in the home shop. Intended purpose is the other basic consideration. The **paring chisel** is thin-bladed, new-ground to a 25-degree edge, often re-ground to 15 degrees. Drive it by hand only for precise shave cuts in fitting work. The **firmer chisel** has a thick blade for heavy driving. The **gouge** is a hollow-blade type. **Firmer gouges** may be bevel-ground inside or outside, **paring gouges** are bevel-ground inside only.

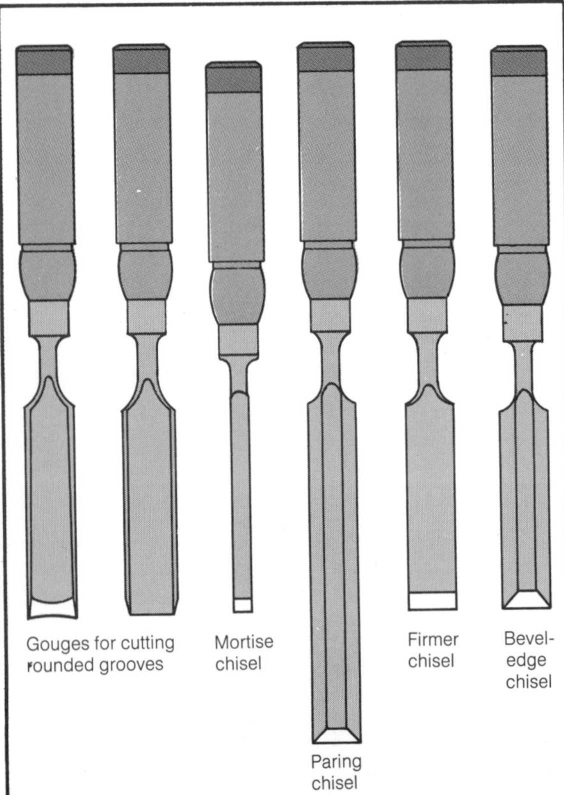

Using chisels

Work only with sharp chisels, and use them only for material removal that other tools cannot do. In lap-joint work, make close parallel saw cuts across the joint area, not quite to joint depth, and remove the material between the saw cuts. Then pare down to joint level with a chisel. In cutting a mortise, first score the outline with a knife so any surface splitting won't extend beyond it. Then bore out the bulk of the wood within the outline with an auger bit. Use the chisel to remove the rest and to finish the mortise to size and shape. Shallow recesses, such as for lock strike plates, can be made with a chisel by a series of close cross-grain cuts (within a knife outline), followed by paring cuts.

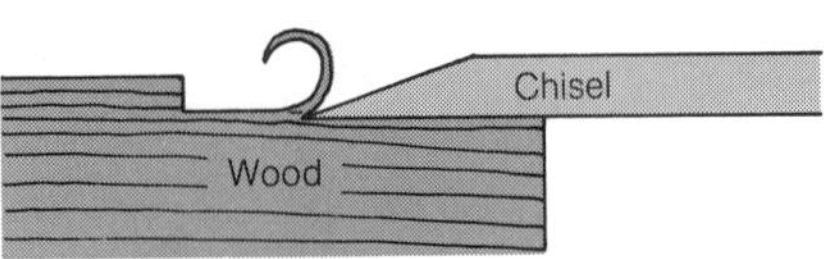

If the area to be cut extends to the end of the work chisel with bevel facing out, toward the waste

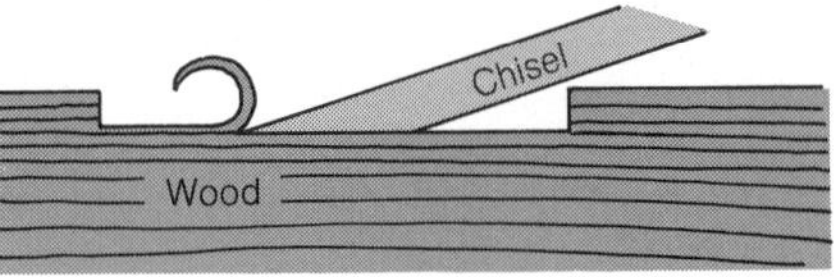

If the area is enclosed, it may be necessary to use the chisel with the bevel facing inward

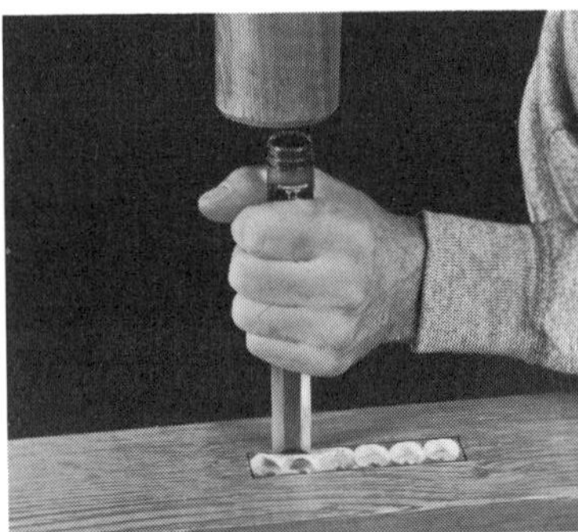

Using a chisel and a mallet to cut a mortise. First step is to drill a series of holes slightly narrower than required width. Then use chisel to clear out waste.

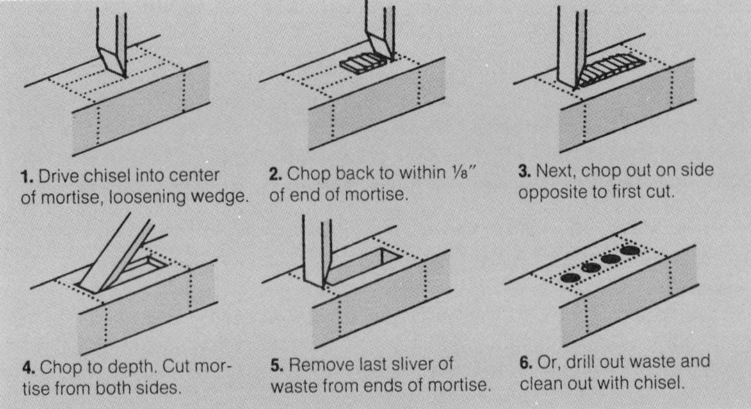

Hold a chisel so that the beveled edge faces the waste part of the wood. Start in at the extreme waste side of the wood and gradually work toward marking line.

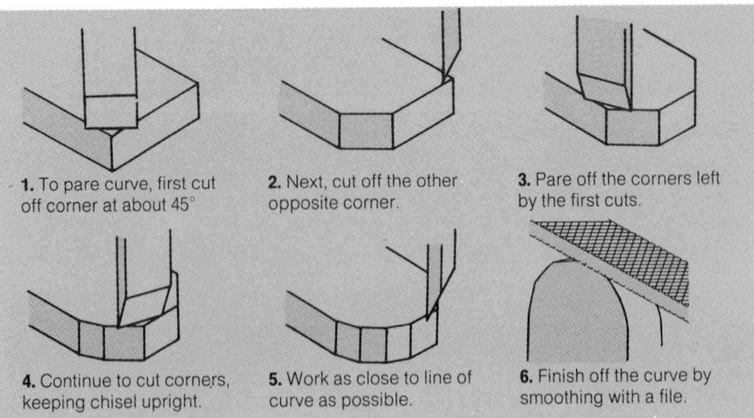

Cornering tools

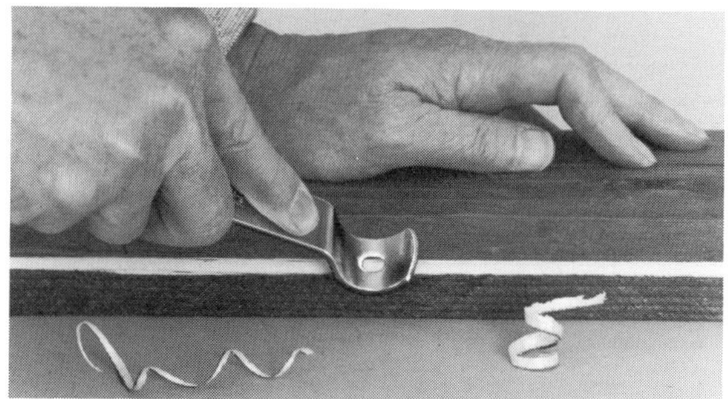

Cornering tools are used to round off sharp edges. Each end has different size opening. Made in 1/16- to 3/8-in. sizes.

Plug cutters

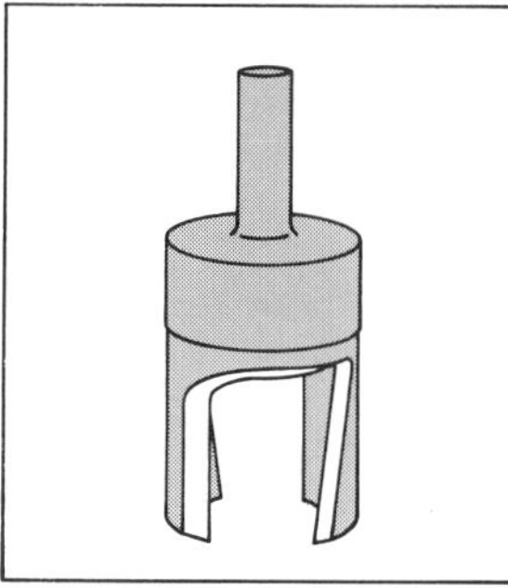

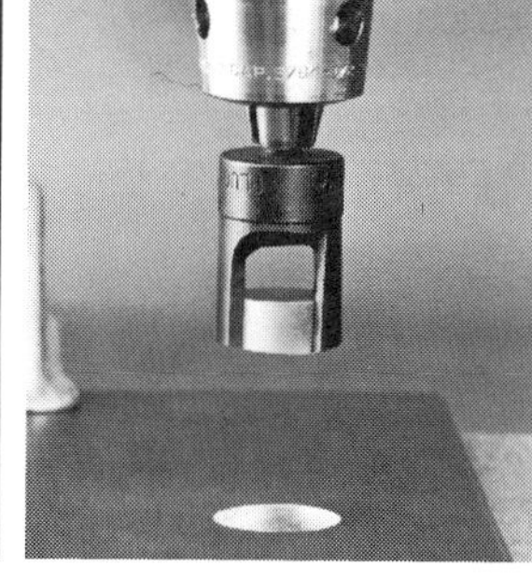

Plug cutters make plugs out of wood for covering recessed screws. Cutter is installed in a drill press to cut the plugs.

Cold chisels and their uses

The four general types of cold chisels are the flat chisel, cape chisel, round nose chisel, and diamond point chisel, as shown in the drawing, below left. Use a ball peen hammer to drive any of them, and always wear goggles when doing this kind of work.

Use the **flat chisel** to cut rods or small chain by driving a V cut into one or both sides, then bending the metal to break it off. You can use a flat chisel also to shear metal, starting from one end, at the top of the vise jaws.

Use a **cape chisel** to shear off rivet heads, by driving a groove through the center of the head and chipping off the rest. Use this chisel to deform threads so that nuts will not shake loose. The **round nose chisel** makes a round bottom cut, as in making oil grooves in bearing parts. In groove cutting, work from the ends toward the middle. Use the **diamond point** for sharp corners and V cuts.

Any cold chisel can be used to cut masonry block, tile, or brick by grooving deep enough for a breakoff. When the chisel head spreads from use, grind off the spread portion so chips won't fly off. If the cutting edge dulls, grind it to an angle of about 65 degrees between the surfaces of the cutting edge.

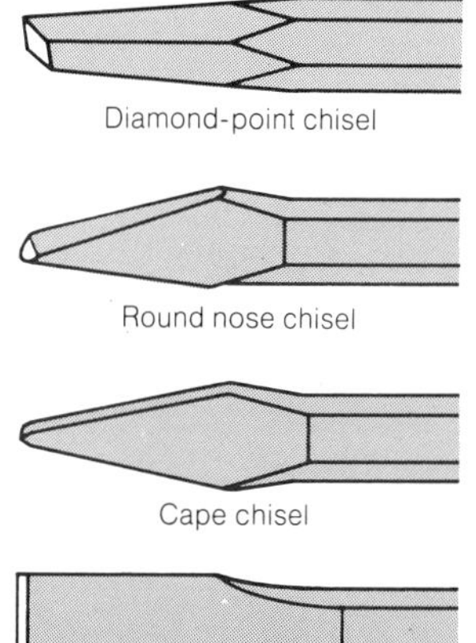

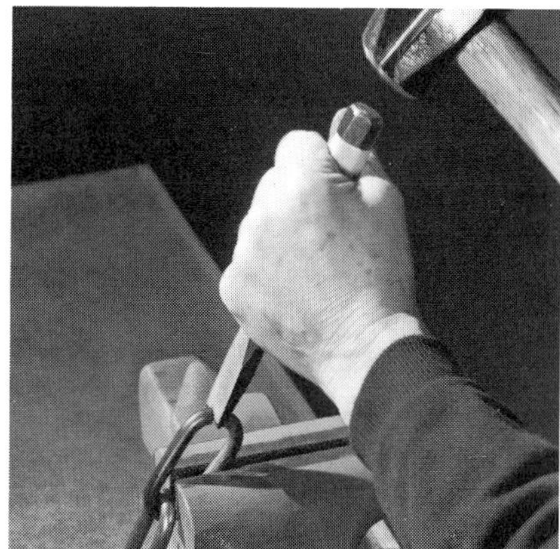

Using a flat cold chisel to make an opening in a concrete block for an electrical receptacle.

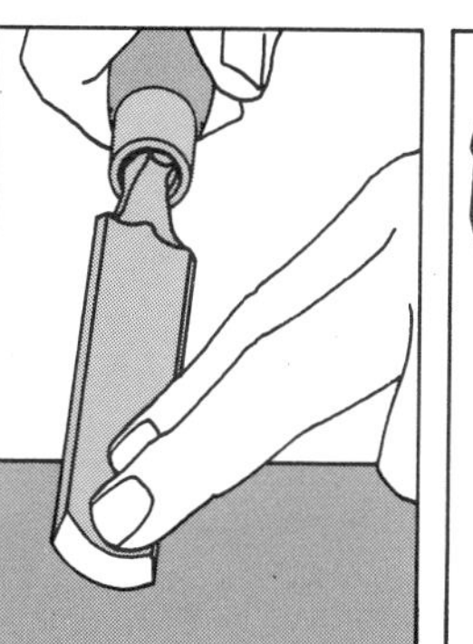

Use cold chisel and short-handled sledge to shorten a steel chain. Wear goggles.

Sharpening chisels and gouges

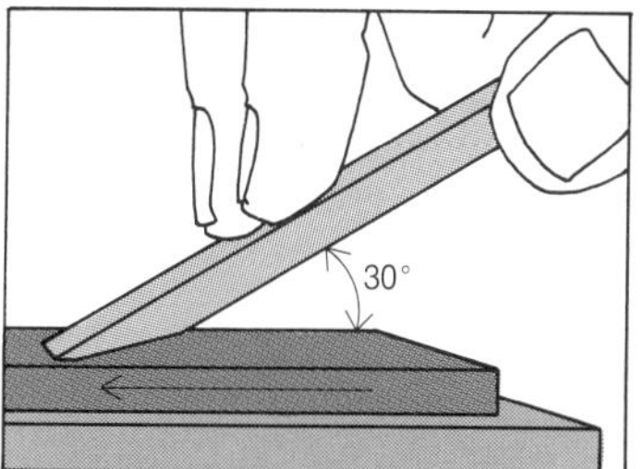

Chisels should be honed on a whetstone at a 30° angle. Use a figure 8 stroke. Lubricate the stone with a light machine oil and clean the stone after use with kerosene.

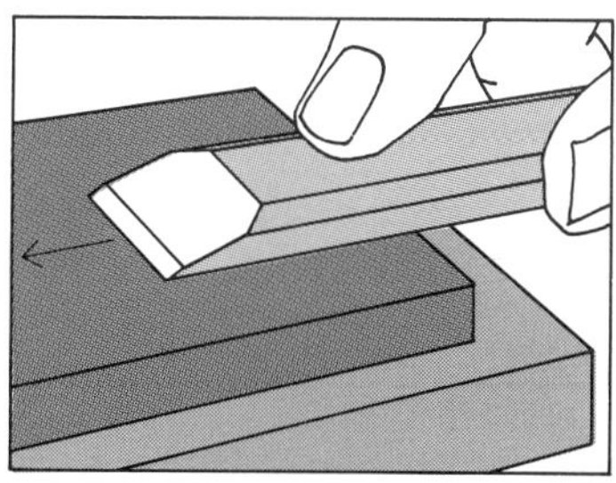

This operation will produce a burr on the flat side of the chisel which should be removed with light honing, with flat side down as shown. Use an elliptical stroke.

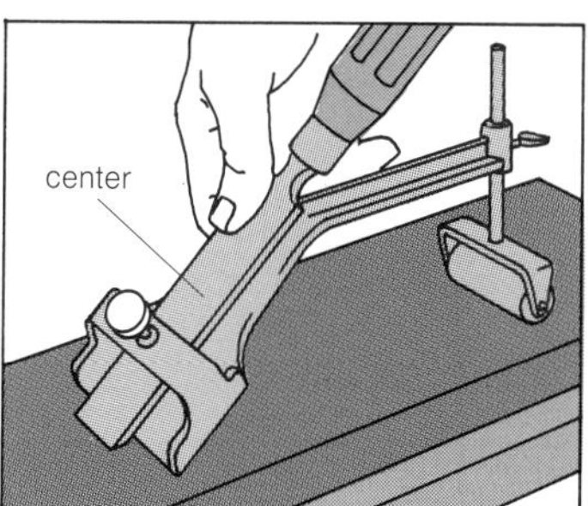

A store-bought sharpening jig will hold the chisel at exact angle for honing. Burr formed is then removed as shown in drawing.

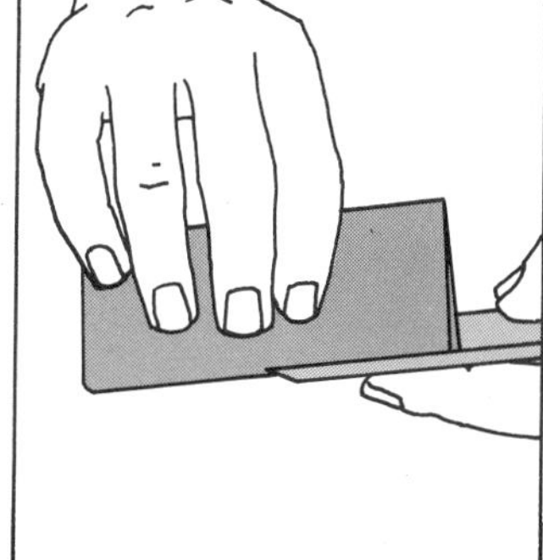

Gouges, because of their rounded surfaces, must be sharpened with specially made rounded and tapered stones as shown.

Files and filing

Types and uses of files

Files are classified by their cross-section shape, their length, and the "cut" and coarseness of the teeth. Typical file shapes are **flat, half-round, round, square,** and **triangular** (called 3-square when double-cut). Special-purpose shapes are usually named for their purpose, such as chain saw file, crosscut file, and so on. The common cuts of teeth are **single, double, rasp,** and **curved.**

In American files the coarseness of the teeth, starting with the coarsest, is rated as follows: Coarse (not available in all types), bastard, second cut, smooth cut, and in some types, dead smooth. The length of the file, which is measured from the "heel" where the tang begins to the "point" or opposite end (which may or may not actually be pointed), also affects the coarseness, as tooth size increases with the length of the file. Thus, a 12-inch bastard file has larger teeth than does a 6-inch bastard file, though both of them carry the same coarseness designation.

File selection calls for matching the file to the job. To produce a smooth surface, as for example on a rotary mower blade, use a single-cut file and apply light pressure. For rapid material removal, where a smooth finish isn't required, use a double-cut file with heavier pressure. For fast material removal in woodworking, use a rasp with the pressure that proves most efficient for the hardness of the particular wood. For surface filing of aluminum or steel, such as in auto body work, use a curved tooth file. For very delicate work, as on small machine parts such as clock mechanisms, use a "needle file" (a small slim form) of the most suitable shape. For unusual jobs, ask your supplier's advice, as special-purpose files are made in several dozen types. The proper filing motion on most jobs is straight filing, which calls for holding the file at both ends and moving it lengthwise or at a slight angle over the work.

Draw filing is done by holding the file at both ends, at a right angle to the surface to be filed, and moving it back and forth over the work to produce a somewhat finer finish than you would achieve with straight filing.

Work should be held, for any type of filing, by a vise or a clamp approximately at elbow height. Prevent vibration or chatter by mounting the surface to be filed close to the vise jaws or clamp. Store your files in a rack or at least in protective sleeves to prevent dulling from contact with tools.

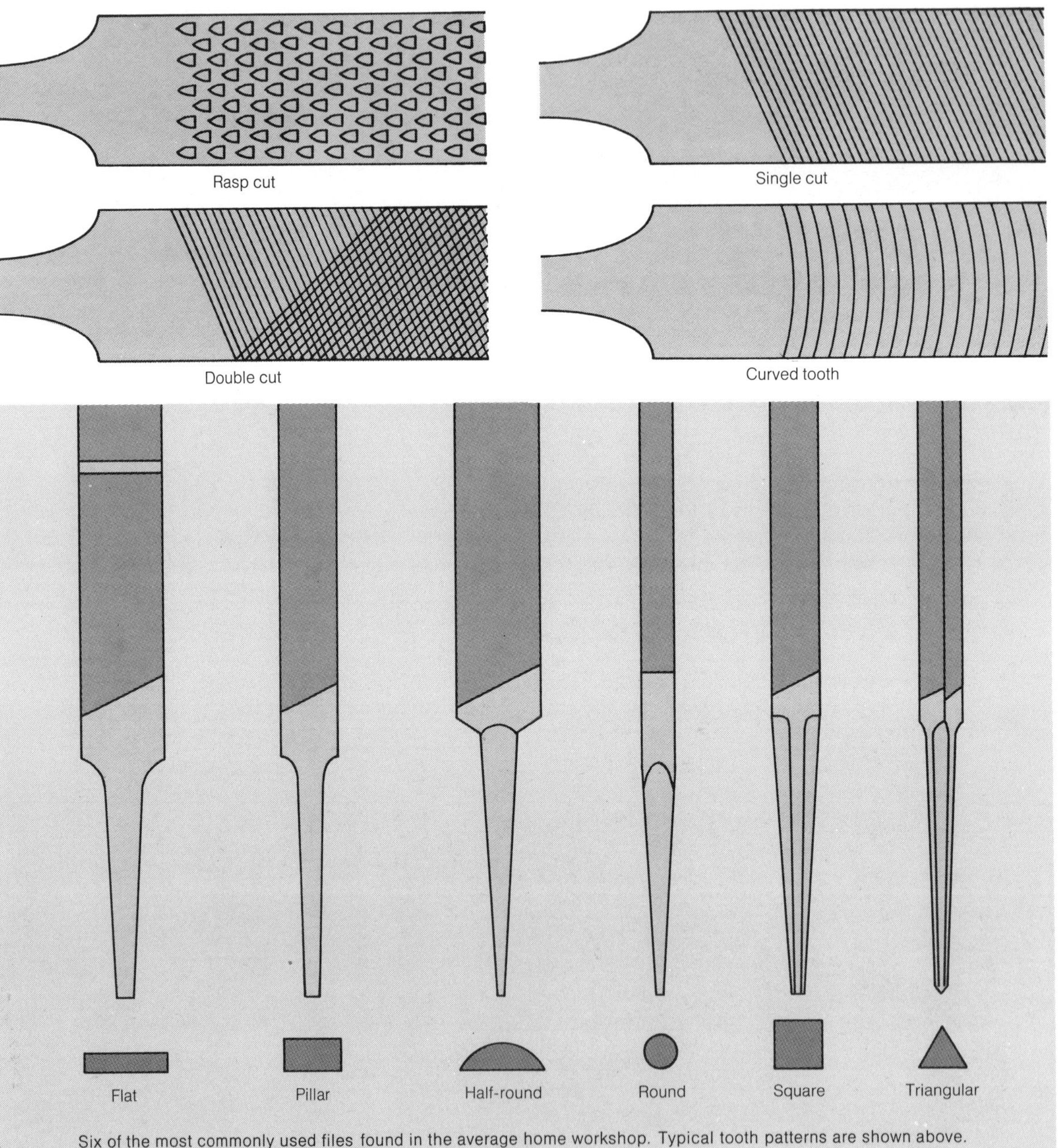

Six of the most commonly used files found in the average home workshop. Typical tooth patterns are shown above.

Special-purpose files

Cabinet rasp in half-round form is a versatile type of file for general woodworking. Fast cutting on soft materials but leaves a rough surface. Is also available in round form.

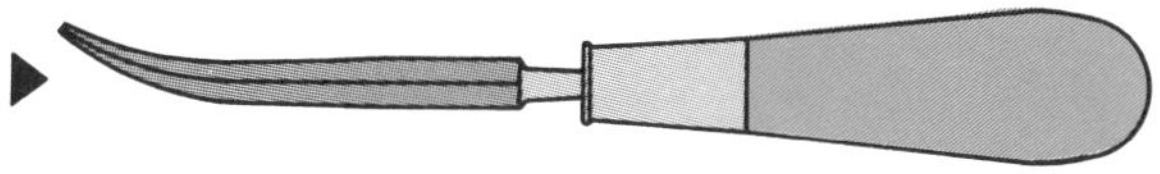

Bent riffler, triangular as shown here, is also available in flat, half-round, and round forms. A very useful type of file for finishing details in wood carving and metal work.

Cantsaw file is designed for sharpening saws that have less than 60° teeth, but it also handles filing jobs that require a file with a narrow triangular cross section.

Needle file, shown with knife cross section, is made in a wide variety of other shapes. Because it is very slender, it is the type to use for delicate machine and clock work.

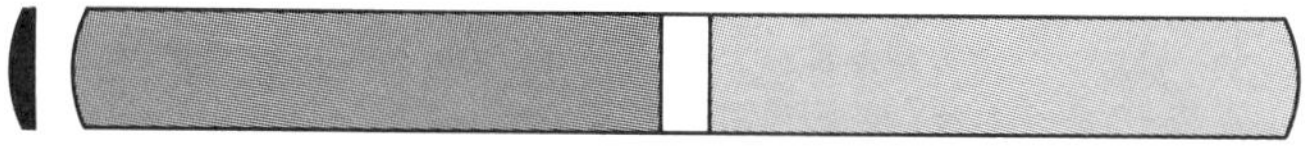

4-in-hand rasp file, originally called a shoe rasp, has half-round cross section. Half of each surface is file cut, the other half is rasp cut, for greater filing versatility.

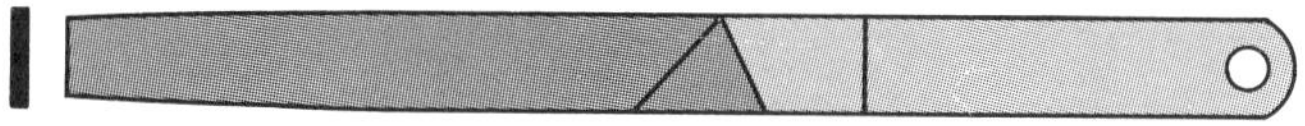

Mower blade file has an integral handle. Some types are double cut on both sides for fast cutting, others are single cut on one side to do smooth finishing after shaping cuts.

Rattail file, also called a tapered round file, is used to shape and smooth small round recesses, also to enlarge holes. The taper equips it for a wide range of shop work.

Auger bit file has toothed edges and smooth (toothless) surfaces on one pointed end and toothed surfaces and smooth edges on the other, which suits it for bit filing work.

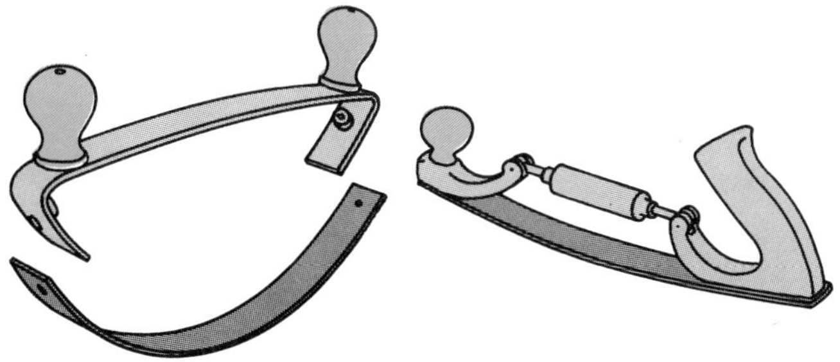

Curved tooth files are made in both rigid and flexible types. The flat types handle convex surfaces, convex types handle concave surfaces on large metal areas such as auto bodies.

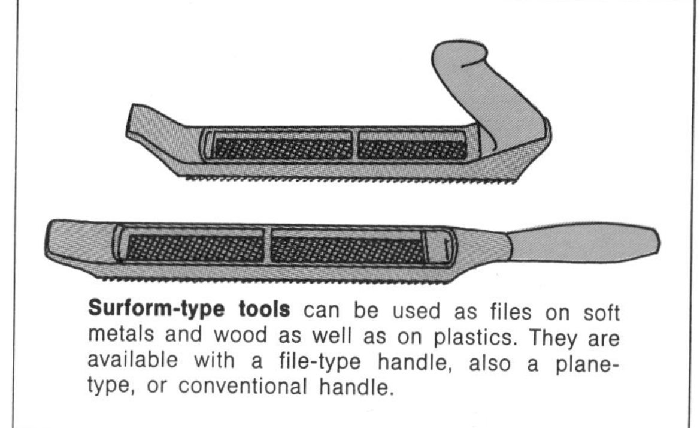

Surform-type tools can be used as files on soft metals and wood as well as on plastics. They are available with a file-type handle, also a plane-type, or conventional handle.

Care of files

Use a combination file card and brush to clean metal particles from spaces between teeth. A brush of soft iron wire removes hard-packed chips. Store files in a rack, never heaped on top of one another, as contact between files causes chipping.

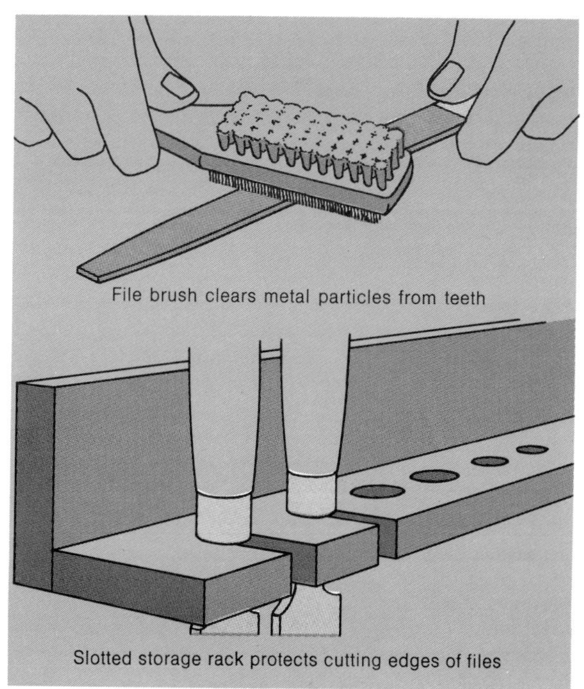

File brush clears metal particles from teeth

Slotted storage rack protects cutting edges of files

Vises and clamps

Types of bench vises

Bench vises are made in both **bolt-on** and **clamp-on** models. Bases may be either **rigid** or **swivel** types. For light duty, especially where a permanently installed vise might be an obstacle, it is best to select a clamp-on vise. For full-range use, buy a bolt-mounted vise, preferably one that has regular and pipe jaws, and a jaw width and opening of at least 3½ inches. Specialized vises include **vacuum-base** types that lock to any smooth surface and **multi-angle** vises which swivel horizontally and can be tilted vertically to any required position.

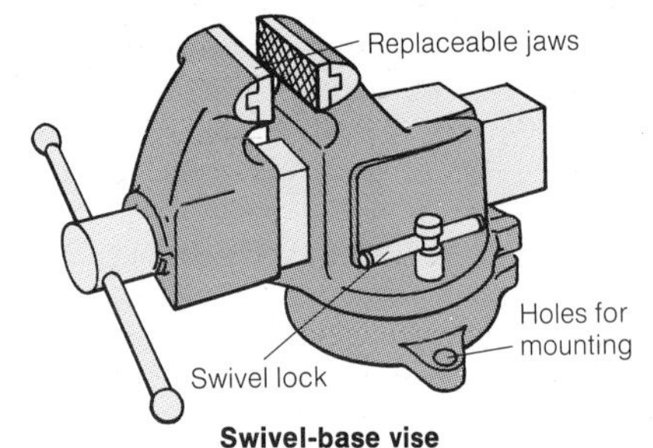

Swivel-base vise

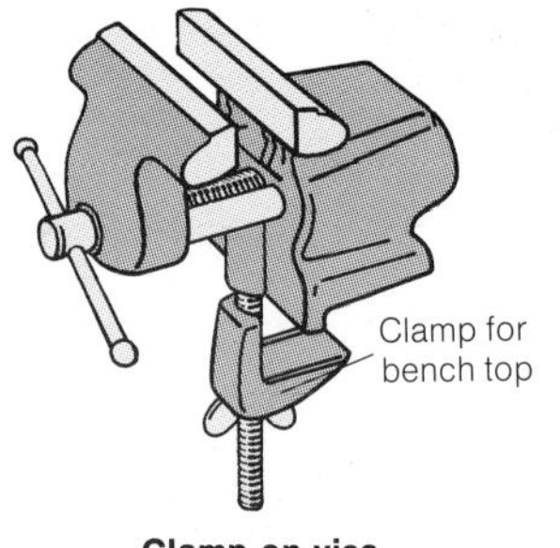

Clamp-on vise

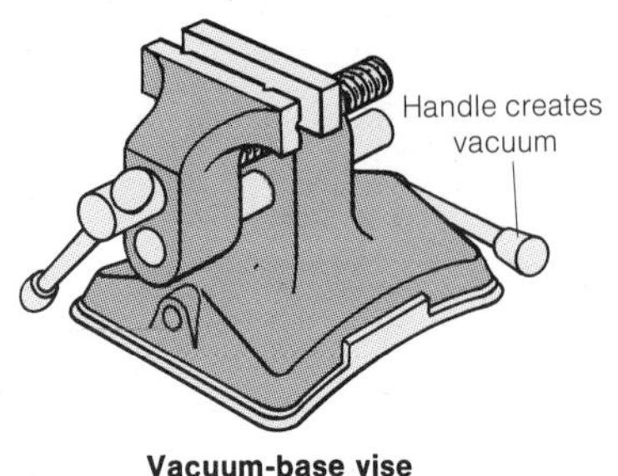

Vacuum-base vise

Woodworking vises

Woodworkers' vises do not mount on top of the workbench, as bench vises do, but at the edge of the bench, with their jaw tops flush with the bench top. Mounted in this way, they do not obstruct large work on the bench.

Jaws of woodworkers' vises are lined with wood or hardboard to protect the work clamped between them. A useful feature on some: A half thread that makes it possible to slide the jaw against the work without a lot of handle turning. The vise is then tightened with only a half turn.

When mounting a woodworking vise to a workbench, use heavy lag screws, which can be tightened with a wrench, instead of ordinary wood screws.

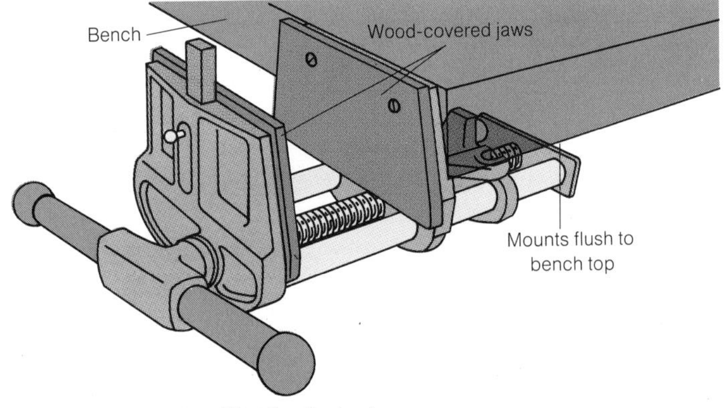

Woodworker's vise

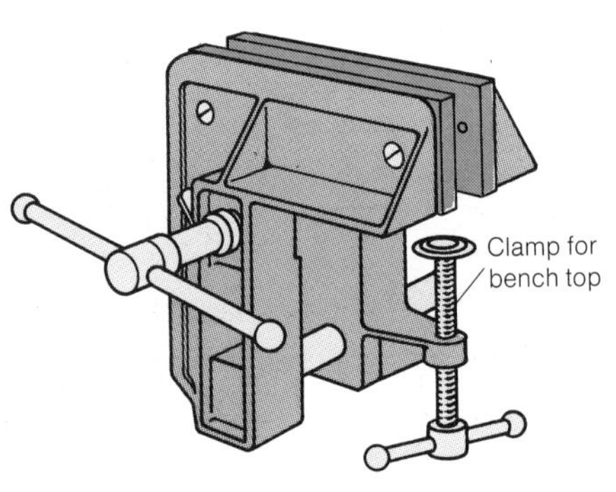

Clamp-on woodworker's vise

The versatile C-clamp

As a rule, C-clamps are made in sizes from 1 to 8 inches. (Sizes are based on the maximum opening.) The depth to the back of the clamp usually ranges from 1 inch to about 4 inches, depending on the size of the clamp. Deep-throated types are available, however, from some manufacturers.

Always insert pads of scrap wood between the clamp jaws and the work to protect the work's surface against marring. These protective pads also serve to distribute pressure uniformly. The ball joint at the foot of the clamp is designed to swivel so that work which is not absolutely flat can still be securely clamped. Buy C-clamps as required in sizes to suit each job as it comes up. After a few projects, you will have all the sizes you need.

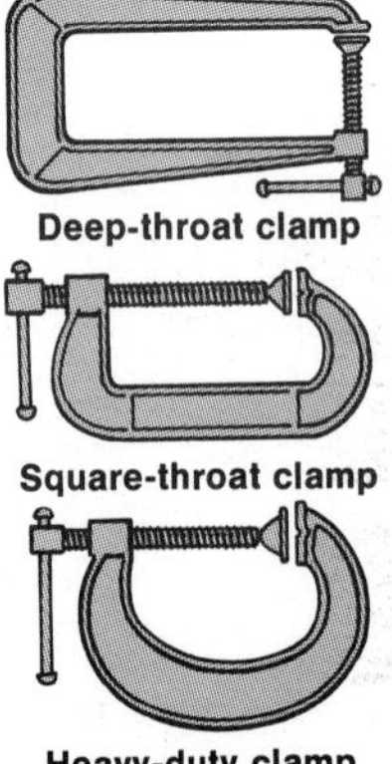
Deep-throat clamp

Square-throat clamp

Heavy-duty clamp

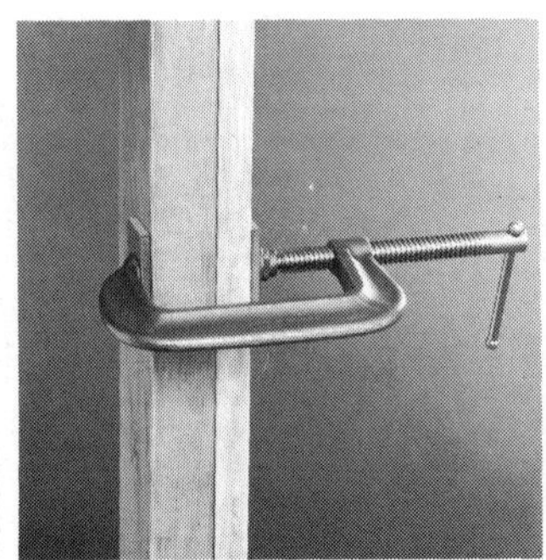
Wood between work and clamp jaws protects finish.

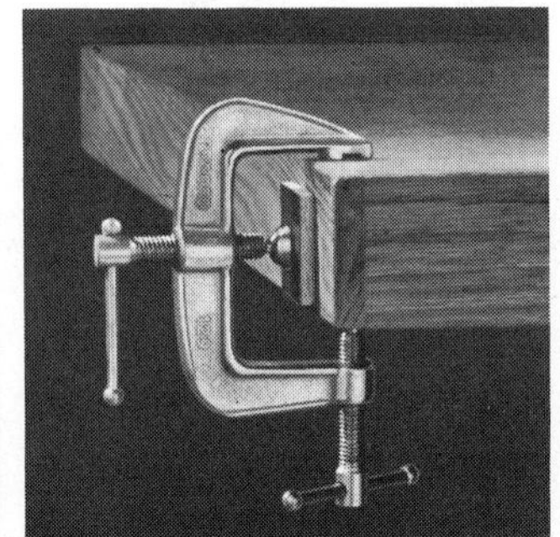
This clamp applies pressure in two directions for edge gluing.

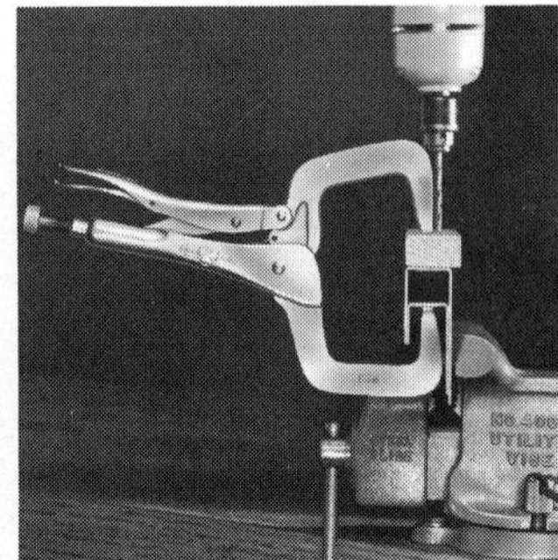
Vise-grip clamp, handy for holding any irregularly-shaped work.

Adjustable hand screws

Termed hand screws, these woodworking clamps have maple jaws that do not require pads of scrap wood to protect the work. Since the steel clamping screws operate through crosswise pivots in the wood jaws, they can be set at any required angle. Sizes, based on jaw length, range from 6 to 14 inches, openings from 3 to 10 inches, though the full size range is not stocked by all suppliers.

To open or close the hand screws, place the jaws' square ends toward you and grasp the right-hand spindle handle in your right hand, the left in your left hand. Rotate the entire clamp, "cranking" with your right hand, in the required direction to open or close the jaws evenly to the approximate gap. Then make final tightening adjustments.

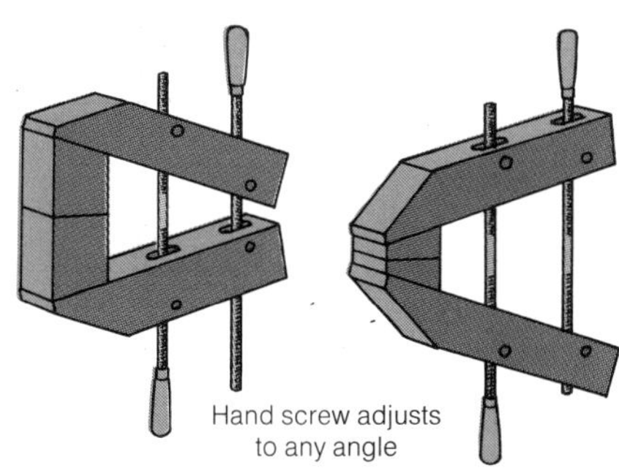

If new clamps have oil-finished jaws, clamp them tightly against blotting or other absorbent paper on a block before using them on actual work.

An adjustable hand screw is used to apply pressure to drawer guides while glue sets overnight. Avoid excessive pressure.

Spring clamps

Small spring clamps are the simplest type of gripping device to use on light-duty work where high clamping pressure is not required, as with modern gap-filler glues. The overall length of these clamps usually ranges from a little over 4 inches to about 8¼ inches, jaw openings from ⅞ inch to 3 inches. They are perfectly suited to fast-setting glue jobs where many clamps must be applied quickly. Some spring clamps have vinyl-covered jaws to protect the work from marring. Don't underrate the strength of these clamps. Some large ones have very heavy springs and actually require two hands to open.

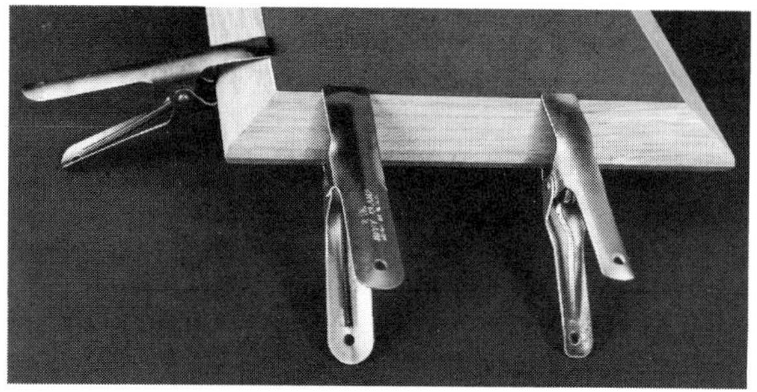

Use spring clamps where heavy pressure is not required.

Bar and pipe-bar clamps

Bar-type clamps (also called **cabinet** or **furniture clamps**) are made two ways: With jaws mounted on a flat steel bar, in 12- to 48-inch lengths; and with jaws designed to fit ½- and ¾-inch steel pipe. In the latter, the clamp assembly can be made to size by cutting pipe to length and threading one end. One jaw in both types has a clamping screw. To use the clamp, set the fixed jaw against one side of the work and slide the movable jaw against the other side, then tighten clamp with the hand screw.

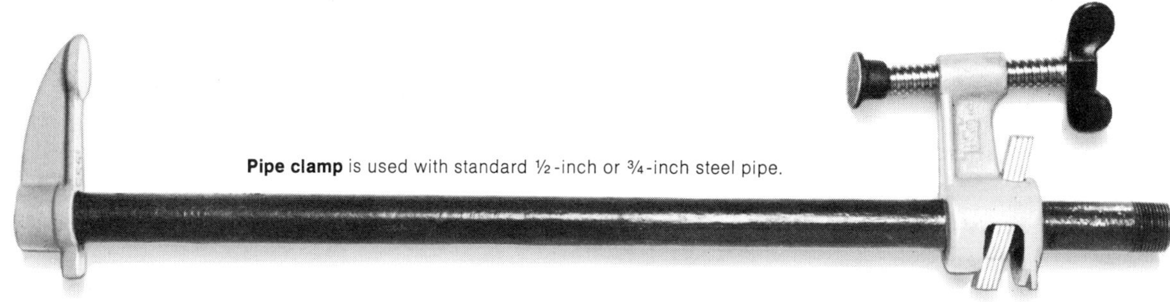

Pipe clamp is used with standard ½-inch or ¾-inch steel pipe.

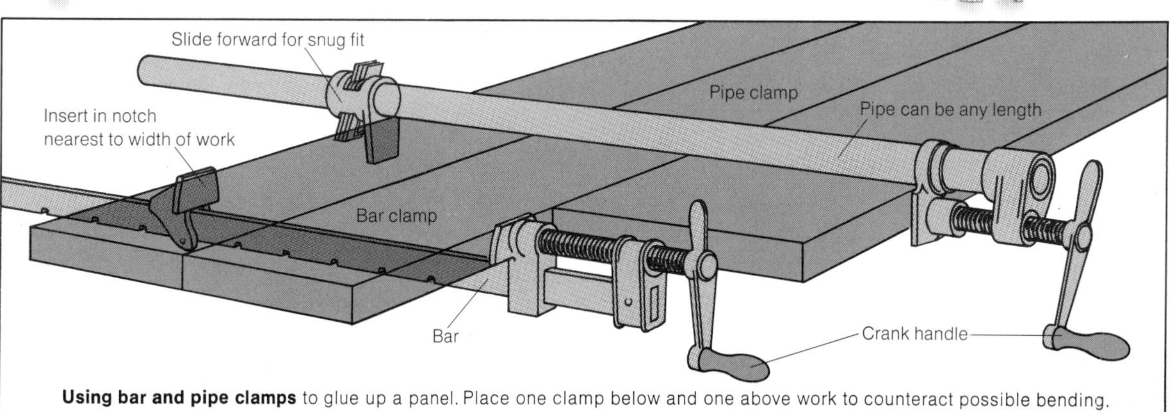

Using bar and pipe clamps to glue up a panel. Place one clamp below and one above work to counteract possible bending.

Vises and clamps

Band and web clamps

Clamps designed to tighten a fabric band (canvas or nylon) around the work are used to clamp irregular shapes and, simultaneously, to draw together several joints, as in gluing chair rungs. Band length commonly ranges from 12 to 15 feet. In clamping, the band is placed around the work and pulled snug at the clamp body, then tightened by a crank or ratchet mechanism, depending on the type and make.

Band clamp holds the chair parts in the correct position while the glue sets.

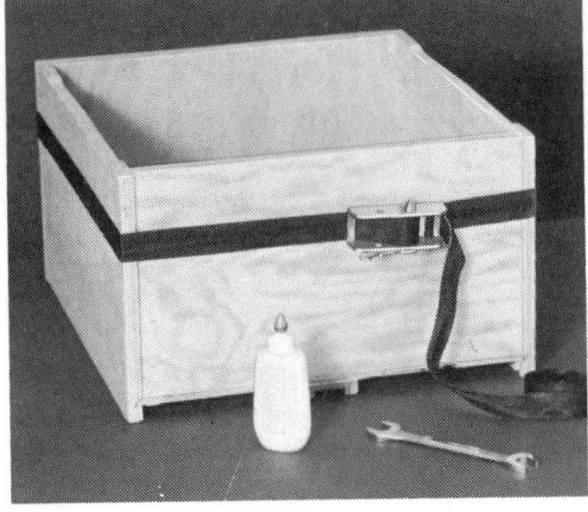

Assembling and gluing of a drawer is simplified by use of the band clamp.

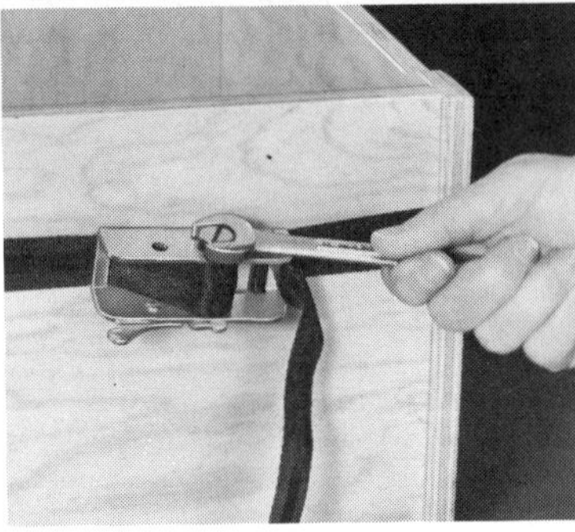

Nylon band clamp is tightened by means of a wrench, which is applied as shown.

Homemade clamping devices

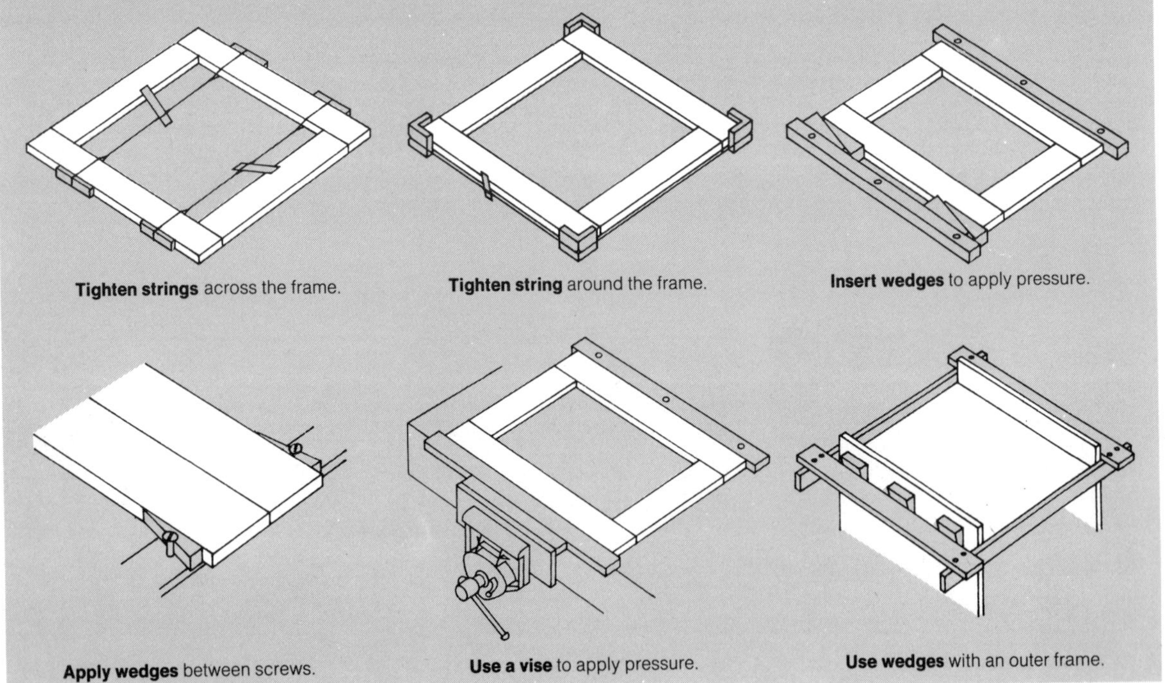

Tighten strings across the frame.

Tighten string around the frame.

Insert wedges to apply pressure.

Apply wedges between screws.

Use a vise to apply pressure.

Use wedges with an outer frame.

Special clamps

The **hold-down** is attached to a countersunk bolt on the workbench. When not needed, it is removed from the bolt, leaving the bench top clear. **Edge clamps** are useful where the work is too wide or long to use a C clamp or pipe clamp. After the bar clamp is attached, the edge clamp, shaped to fit it, is inserted. **Miter clamps** hold mitered joints while glue sets.

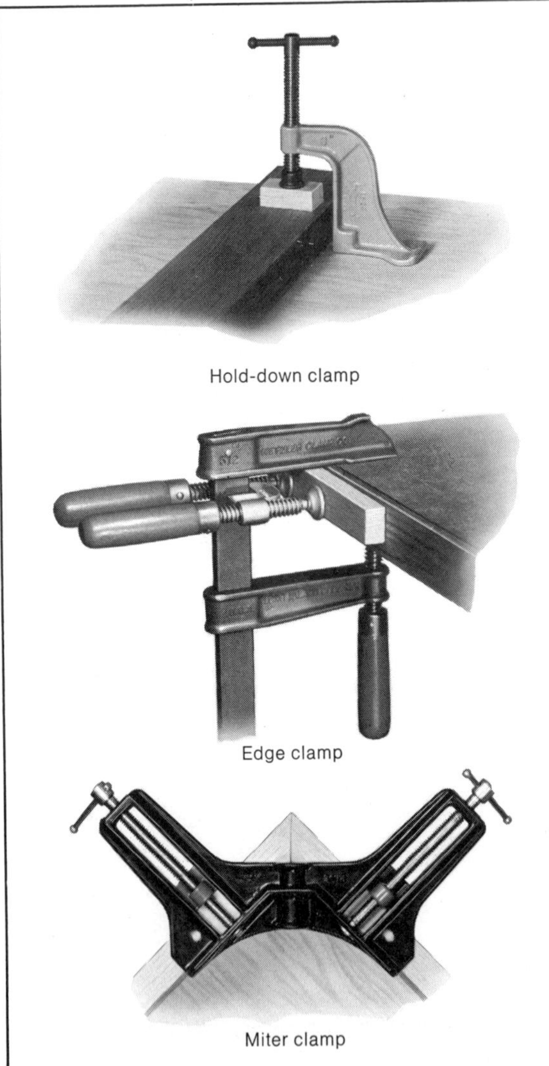

Hold-down clamp

Edge clamp

Miter clamp

Types and their uses

Choose **electric soldering irons** by size, using high-wattage irons for large areas, where heat loss is rapid. **Soldering guns** heat faster but have less heat-retaining mass, good for small jobs, wiring, shaping plastics. Use **propane torch** where massive heat is needed, as in plumbing connections. For outdoor soldering, soldering head can be fitted to torch.

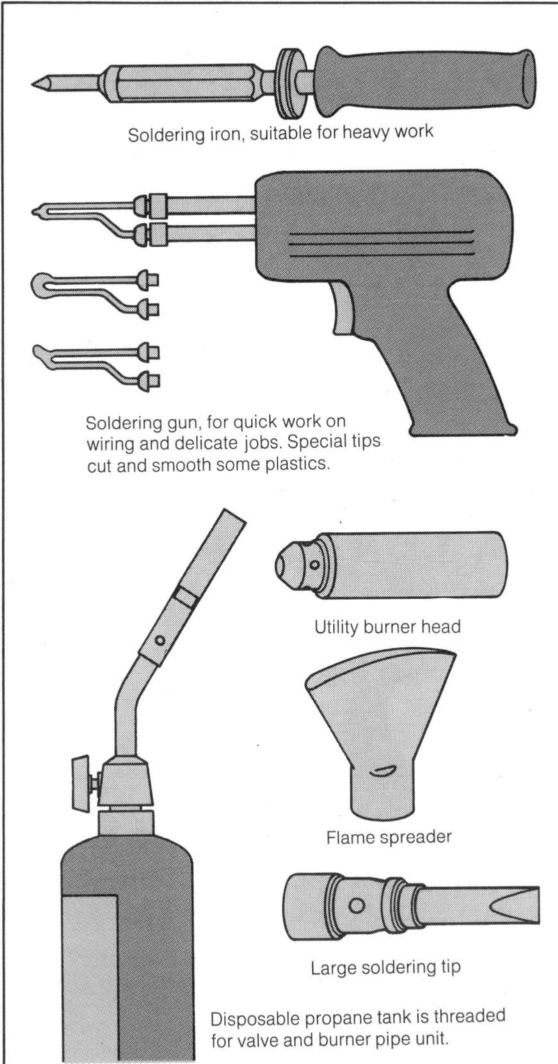

Using the soldering iron

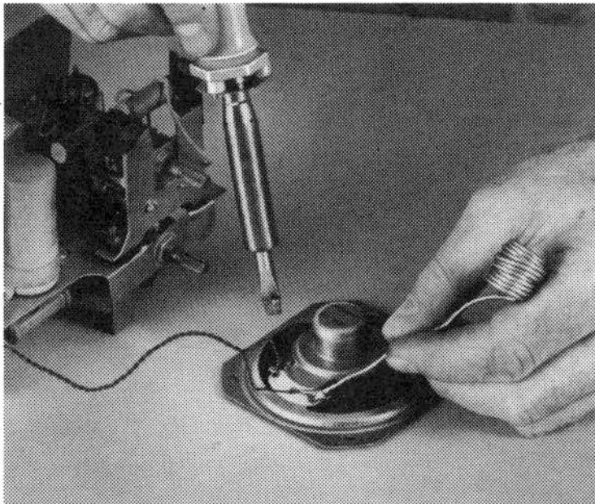

Small iron is used in radio work where excessive heat might damage components.

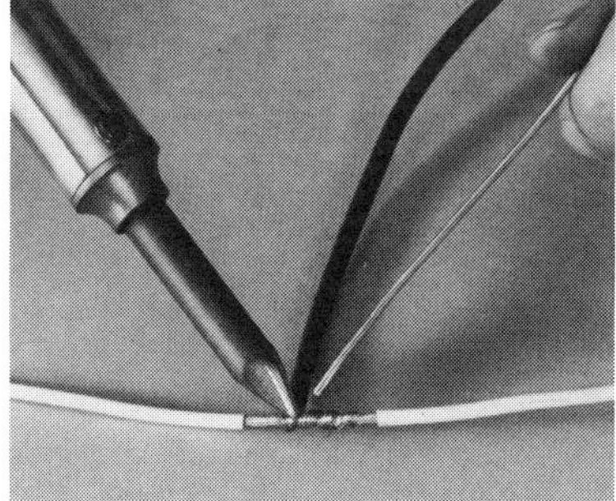

Medium-size soldering iron is used for soldering heavy wire connections.

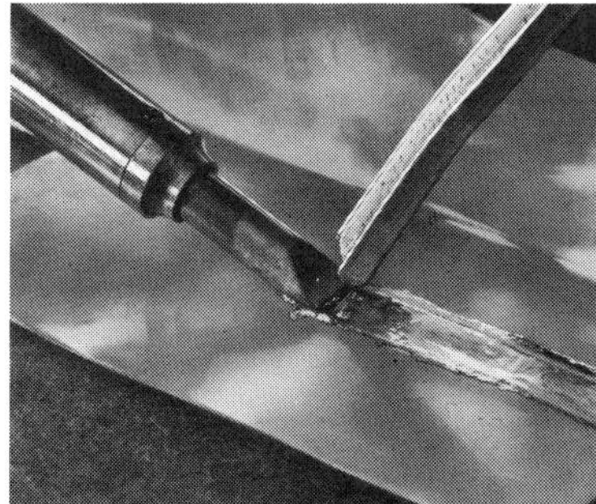

Work that conducts heat rapidly must always be soldered with a large iron.

Using the soldering gun

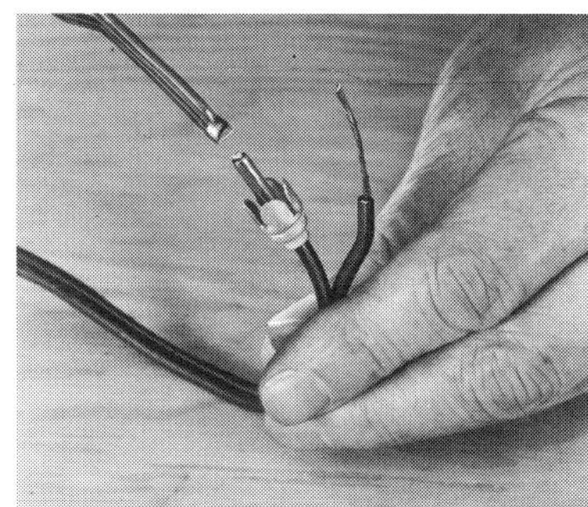

Chief advantage of soldering gun is that it reaches working heat in 5 seconds.

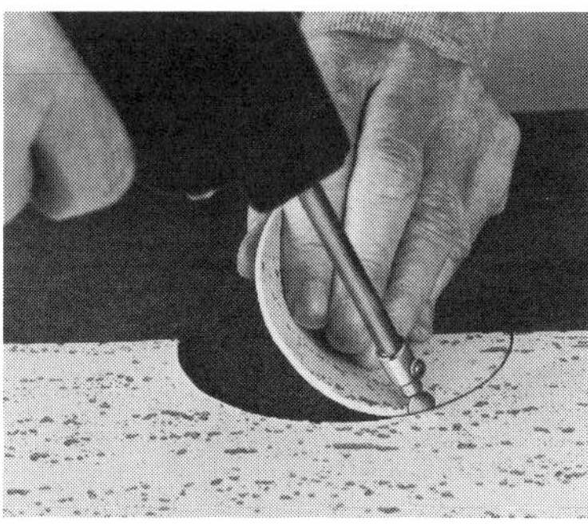

Special tip is available for soldering gun for cutting openings in floor tiles.

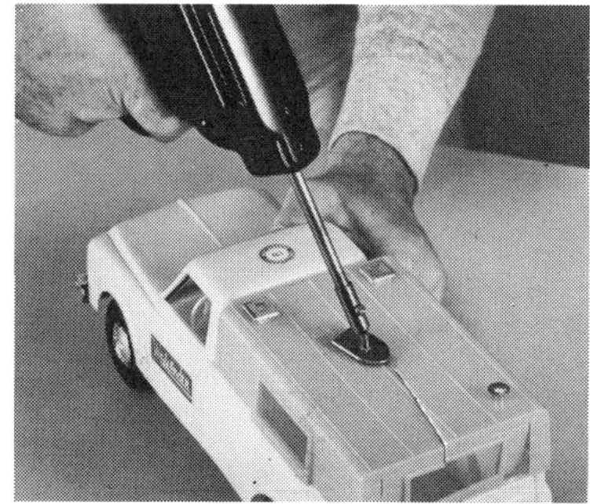

Flat tip is used to make repairs in plastic toys, for leather and wood burning.

Using the propane torch

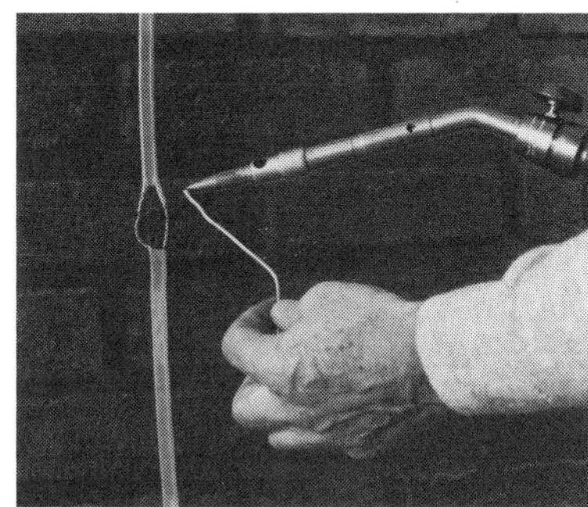

Torch with soldering tip used to solder wires where electricity isn't available.

Flame spreader mounted on propane torch is used to remove paint.

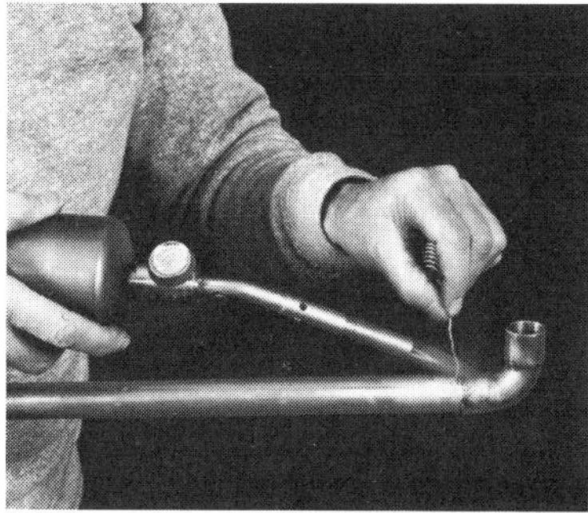

Sweating copper pipe and fittings is an easy job for the propane gas torch.

Sharpening

Knives and cutting tools

Knives and cutting tools may be sharpened by grinding, filing, or whetting, or by a combination of these methods, depending on the nature of the knife or tool. In general, if a cutting edge is very dull or nicked, it should first be power-ground to remove nicks and restore the bevel, then finished to a sharp edge on a whetstone.

Try to reproduce the original factory-made bevel and general blade section, since both are designed to suit the specific function of the tool or blade. Butcher knives usually have a flat-sided **V-grind** for strength as well as cutting ability. Because table carving knives require less strength, they are usually hollow ground for easier penetration. Fine slicing knives are **concave ground.** Similar to but thinner in section than the usual hollow-ground knife, they penetrate even more easily. Heavy-duty cutting implements such as meat cleavers and axes have convex sides (the reverse of a hollow grind) for greater strength. Also called **cleaver grind,** this grind tends to nick less than hollow, but also penetrates less easily.

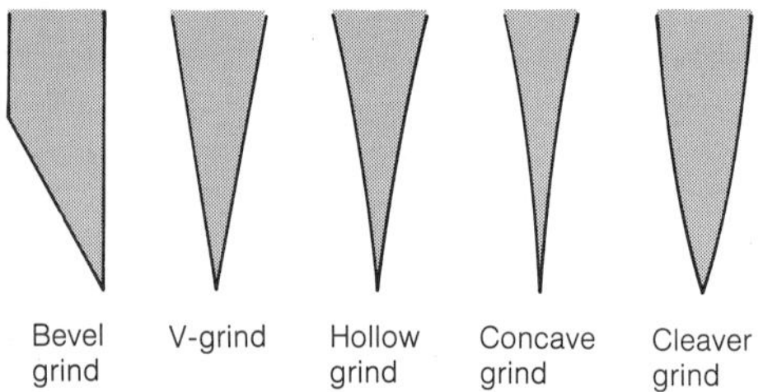

The visible cutting edge bevel for a flat or hollow-ground knife is about 30 degrees—15 on each side—which means the bevel width is about twice the blade thickness at the bevel's inner limit. On an ax, the visible cutting edge bevel is about 20 degrees, or nearly 3 times the blade thickness at the inner bevel limit, but is stronger because of the convex grind, not suitable for knives. The whetting angle that finishes the blade to a keen edge is about 5 degrees greater than that of the bevel. This results in a barely visible secondary bevel at the extreme edge of the blade. On a knife, this is produced by sliding the cutting edge backward over a whetstone, simultaneously moving it lengthwise to sharpen the full blade length. Sharpen the sides alternately, then (if you want an ultra-fine edge) do the same on a leather strop. On an ax or cleaver, do the job by sliding an ax stone along one side of the edge, then the other, in circular motion. The plane blade is ground on one side only to about a 25- or 30-degree bevel (a little longer than twice the blade thickness), then finished by sliding the edge back and forth on a whetstone at about 30 to 35 degrees. A variation of a few degrees doesn't matter so long as the whetting angle is about 5 degrees greater than the ground bevel angle.

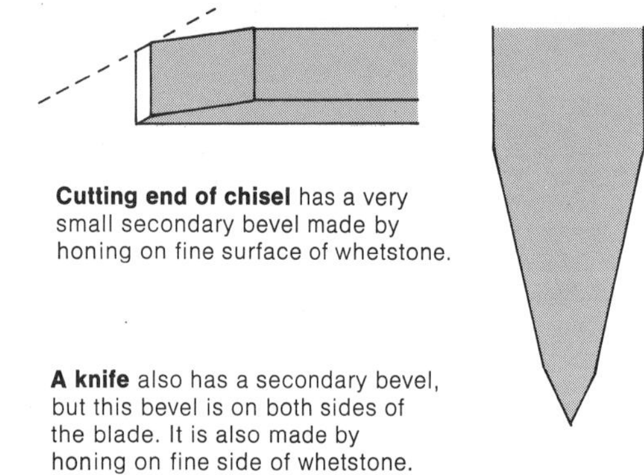

Cutting end of chisel has a very small secondary bevel made by honing on fine surface of whetstone.

A knife also has a secondary bevel, but this bevel is on both sides of the blade. It is also made by honing on fine side of whetstone.

Once sharpened, cutting edges can be kept keen for long intervals with just an occasional few strokes on the whetstone. A combination whetstone, which has both a coarse and a fine side, is best for average sharpening jobs. Sizes range from ⅝ x 1¾ x 4 inches to 1 x 2 x 8 inches (7 or 8 inch length is good for most edge tools and kitchen and carving knives). Use and store your stone in a wooden retainer (see sketch below); keep the stone's surface lubricated with light oil when using it. Remove loose grit and sludge from the surface with a solvent-soaked rag.

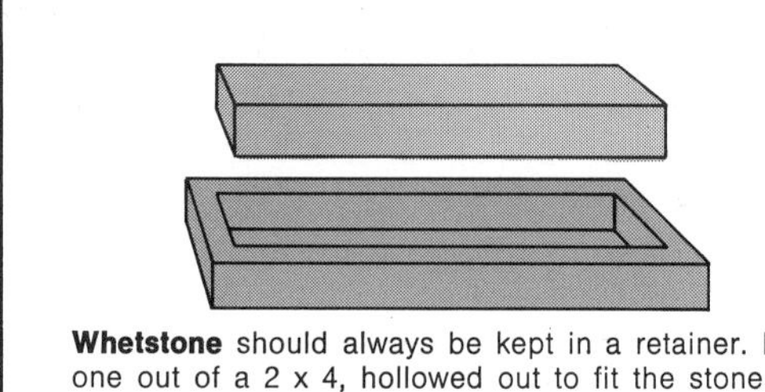

Whetstone should always be kept in a retainer. Make one out of a 2 x 4, hollowed out to fit the stone. Cement some rubber to the bottom so that it will not slip in use. Keep stone covered when not in use.

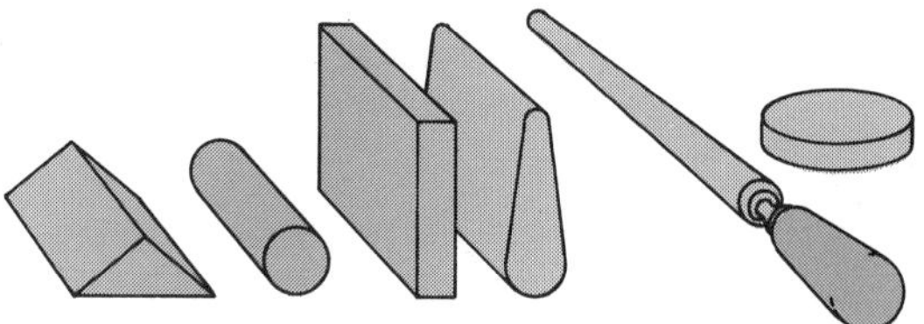

Slipstones are shaped for particular tools. They are rubbed along the edges to sharpen them—unlike whetstones, which remain stationary as the tool is moved over the whetstone's surface for sharpening.

Using a whetstone

Hold pocket knife against whetstone at a 30° angle; stroke the knife forward diagonally, turn over for return stroke.

Stroke scissors forward diagonally on the fine side of the stone. Always keep cutting bevel flat against stone.

You can sharpen an awl on a whetstone. Rotate the handle to get a needle-sharp point at the tip of the tool.

Using the slipstones

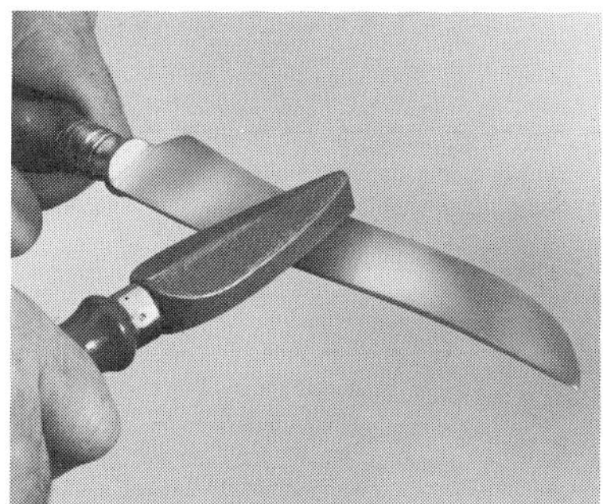

On carving knife blade, use stone this shape, circular motions on each side.

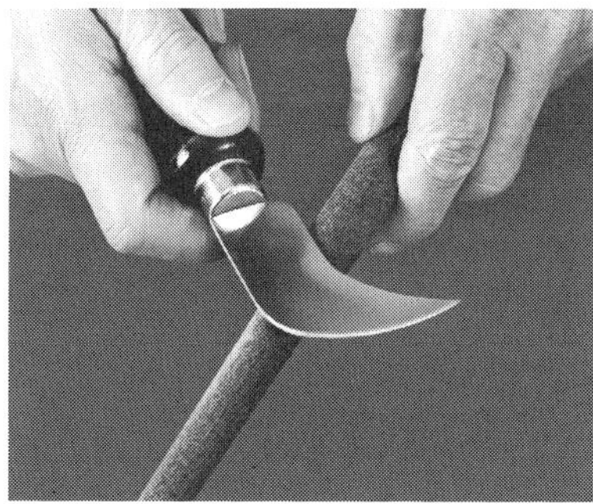

Linoleum knife's inside curves demand round-end stone, forward honing motion.

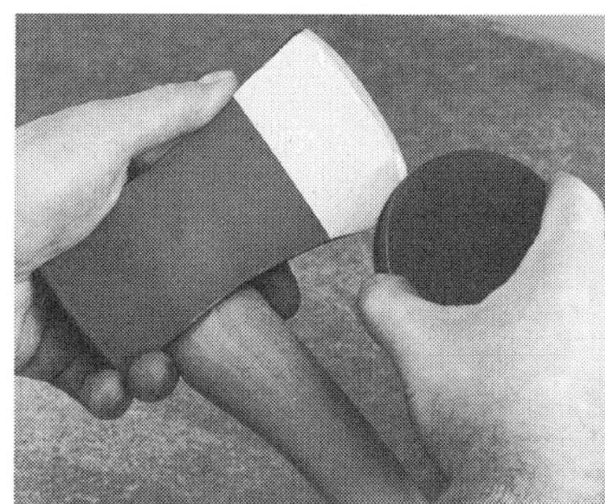

To sharpen an ax, slide stone along one side, then other, in a circular motion.

Using files

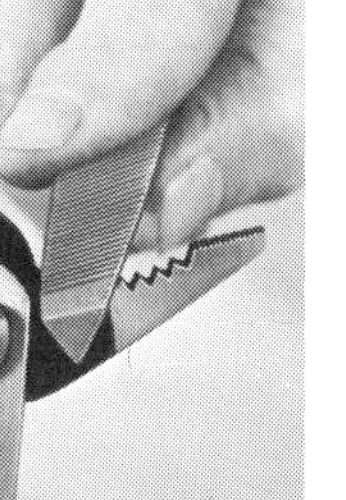

To improve pliers' grip, touch up teeth and wire cutters with triangular file.

Restore mower blade by filing (and removing nicks) to original bevel.

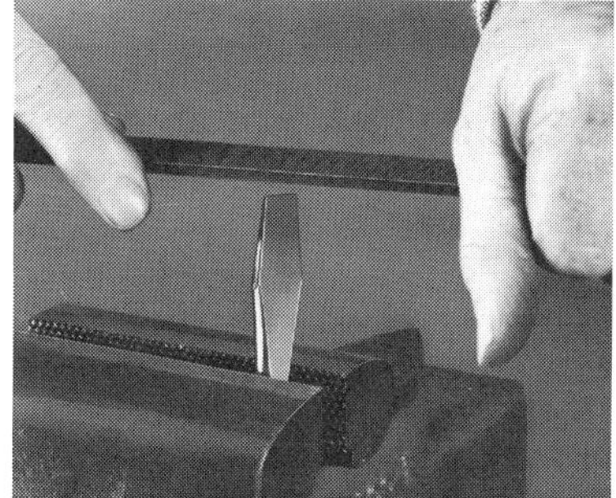

Screwdriver tip rounded? Square off by filing straight across, away from you.

Power grinders

Grind plane blade at 25° angle. Bevel should be twice thickness of blade.

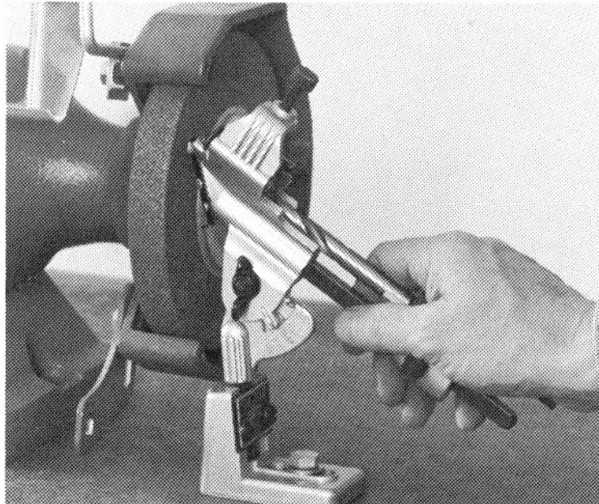

Drill sharpening jig adjusts to drill size, positions it for precise grinding.

Homemade drill grinding jig uses guide block to set drill to correct angle.

Grinding twist drills

Drill point gauge of flat steel (from hardware and power tool dealers) is held against drill body to check 59° angle at cutting lip of drill point. Angle at heel of cutting lip must be 12° less.

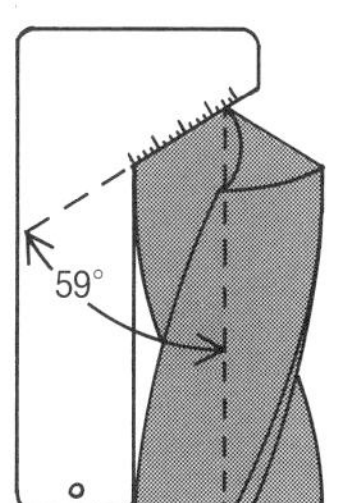

Correct angle at cutting edge of drill point lip

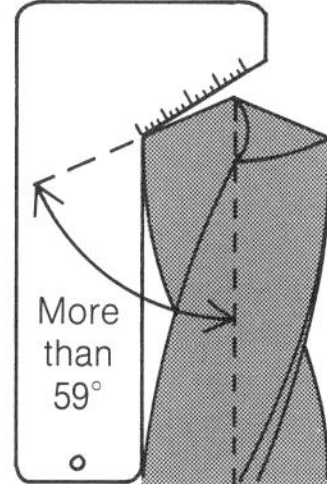

Point too flat, hard to center in punch mark

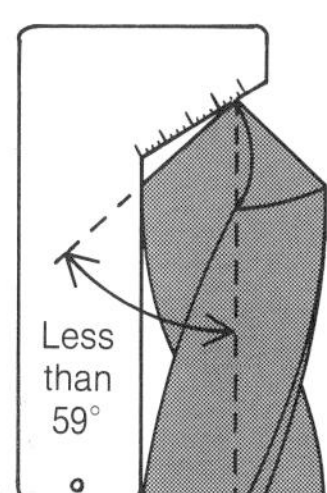

Point angle too acute, unsuitable for drilling metal

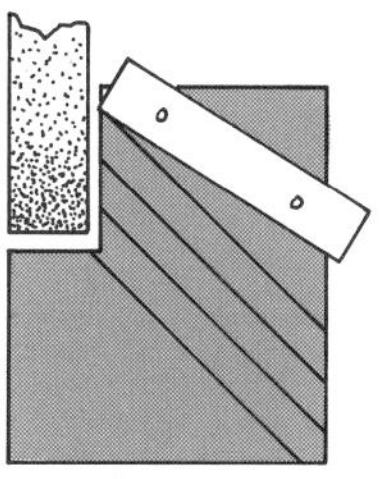

Drill grinding jig can be made with a guide fence at 59° to the flat face of grinding wheel for grinding cutting lips to correct angle. Lines on table are drawn at 12° in from fence to grind clearance at heel of lip after grinding cutting edge.

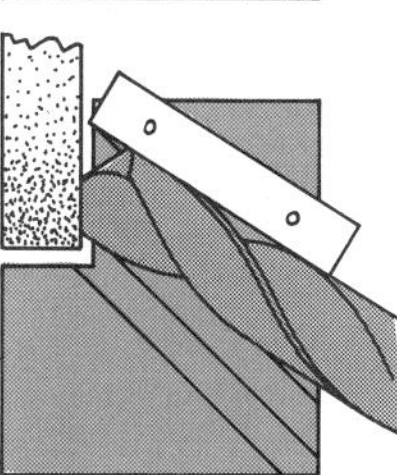

Hold drill cutting lip against side of wheel, with the drill body against the guide fence to grind the proper point angle at the cutting edge of lip. Be sure both lips have the same angle and are the same length. If not, drill will be off round and make oversize holes.

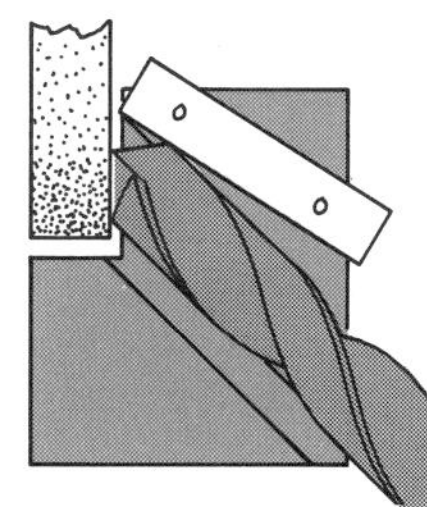

Rotate drill to grind heel (rear portion) of cutting lip, swinging drill at the same time to angles marked on jig table. This grinds away heel behind cutting lip to provide clearance so that only cutting edge contacts material being drilled.

Sanding and sandpaper

Coated abrasives

Modern coated abrasives include silicon carbide (hardest and sharpest, but brittle), aluminum oxide, garnet, flint, and emery. Abrasives come backed with cloth (stronger and more flexible) or paper, in standard and "wet" types (residue washes away). The abrasive particles may be close together (closed coat) for average work, or spaced widely apart (open coat) for materials that tend to clog. To hand sand heavily painted or pitchy surfaces, use inexpensive flint paper, discarding it as it clogs; hand sand clean wood with garnet paper, which is also low-priced. For power sanding of wood, aluminum oxide is fast and long-lasting. Silicon carbide cuts soft metals and plastics with light pressure, also rounds off the sharp edges of glass. For metal polishing, emery is customary. The work determines abrasiveness—very coarse for fast stock removal, fine for finishing.

Sandpaper grades range from very coarse to very fine. The oldest system uses grit symbols, from No. 4¼ (coarsest) to 10/0 (finest). Another system grades papers by numbers which represent the openings per inch in a screen through which abrasives can pass. Mesh numbers range from No. 12, very coarse, to No. 600, very fine.

Very fine:	Fine:	Medium:	Coarse:	Extra coarse:
For sanding between coats of varnish, paint, and lacquer; extra smooth final finish	For final sanding before primer or sealer; on metal, removing light rust and imperfections	For removing light stock and rust stains, and preparing walls prior to painting	For rough stock removal, smoothing deep scratches and imperfections	For removing heavy coats of paint, enamel, or varnish, and heavy rust deposits

Rubber sanding block grips the paper at both ends with recessed nails, thus relieving finger pressure. Useful for rounding ends, as pad is slightly resilient.

On wooden block, use enough sandpaper so that fingers can grip it securely. Tear the paper against a sharp edge rather than cutting it with scissors.

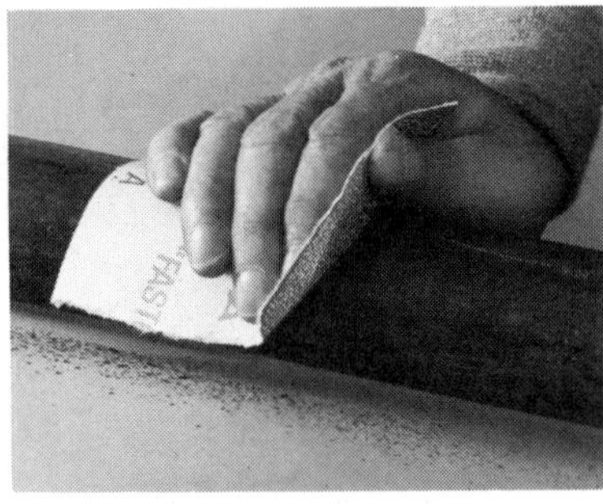
Wet-or-dry silicon-carbide paper has waterproof backing. Used wet, it cleans and smooths metal on car bodies prior to spraying; use it dry on wood.

A sanding shortcut for rungs and chair legs: Fold or tear the sandpaper into long strips. With one end in each hand, use as you would a shoe polishing rag.

Sanding pad made of nylon fibers is mildly abrasive; useful for sanding prior to final finishing or between coats. Pads are available palm-size.

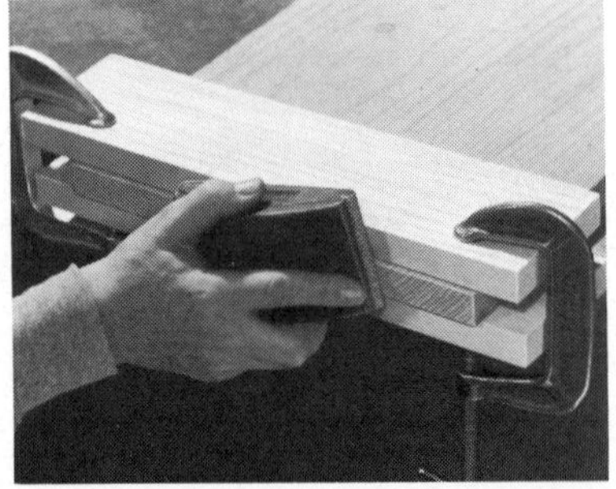
When sanding an end, protect other areas of wood by fastening a strip of wood at top and bottom of work. Hold strips firmly in position with C-clamps.

Choosing the right sandpaper

For wood, plastics, and fiber glass:
Use aluminum oxide paper. This man-made abrasive is tough and durable and well-suited for grinding and finishing extremely hard materials. It is capable of penetrating practically any surface, is a fast-cutting paper, and will continue to cut for an exceptionally long time.

Silicon carbide, an abrasive that is even harder than aluminum oxide, is also good for sanding hard plastics, glass, and ceramics.

For the sanding of metals:
Use an abrasive made of silicon carbide or aluminum oxide. Both of these are man-made materials and extremely hard.

Emery sandpaper was at one time generally regarded as the best abrasive to use on metal. However, because of its slow cutting action and tendency to wear out quickly, emery has been superseded by these powerful abrasives.

Aluminum oxide is used extensively for polishing stainless steel and for finishing high-carbon steel and bronze.

Silicon carbide is the sharpest and hardest substance known. It performs excellently for grinding and finishing brass, copper, and aluminum. Silicon carbide paper can be used wet or dry. When dry, it is used like garnet or flint paper; when wet, it is long-lasting and suitable for rubbing down paint work on metal, especially auto bodies.

section 2:

Power tools for the home workshop

Power tools can be great assets in the home workshop, equipping you for jobs you couldn't otherwise undertake. If they are to fulfill their potential, however, each purchase must be based on full knowledge of a tool's intended purposes and a careful judgment of its probable usefulness to you. This section gives you the facts that you will need to choose power tools wisely, confident that each acquisition will justify your investment.

contents

Choosing a drill

Because of its versatility, the electric drill is a wise choice for the homeowner's first portable power tool. It can drill metal, wood, plastic, and concrete, and perform many other operations as well.

The size of the drill is determined by the largest drill shank its chuck will accept, which may be ¼, ⅜, ½, or ¾ inch. The ¼-inch size is handiest for the average home workshop. A drill's power varies with size and make but typically ranges from about ⅕ hp in the ¼-inch size to as much as 1½ hp in ¾-inch models. Speed usually decreases with size (though turning power increases), ranging from about 2000 rpm for ¼-inch size to around 1200 rpm for ⅜ inch and 600 rpm for ½-inch drills. The ¾-inch size (largely for professional and industrial use) is commonly in the 250–475 rpm range. The slower speeds of the larger drills provide greater turning power (torque) necessary for driving large diameter bits and hole saws.

The high speed of the ¼-inch drills equips them not only to drill holes up to ¼-inch diameter in metal and ½ inch in wood, but also for sanding. Variable speed control is also available on many ¼- to ½-inch models; some ⅜- and ½-inch drills are also reversible. The speed control lets you select the best drilling speed. Reverse is useful in backing out wood bits from deep holes.

Heavy-duty drills of any given size vary more widely in price than do the light-duty models because of differences in bearings, wiring, and other features. For normal home use, heavy-duty features are not usually necessary.

Most drills are equipped with 3-wire grounding cords (with 3-prong plugs) to protect the user from shock in case of internal electrical damage. If you buy a drill with a 2-prong plug, be sure the tool is a type in which the outer shell and chuck are completely insulated from the wiring. Such drills are commonly termed double-insulated drills.

Many drills come with a polyethylene plastic carrying case which generally also contains an assortment of accessories. Whatever drill you buy, check the guarantee as well as the availability of parts. Your best guide to quality is a reputable manufacturer.

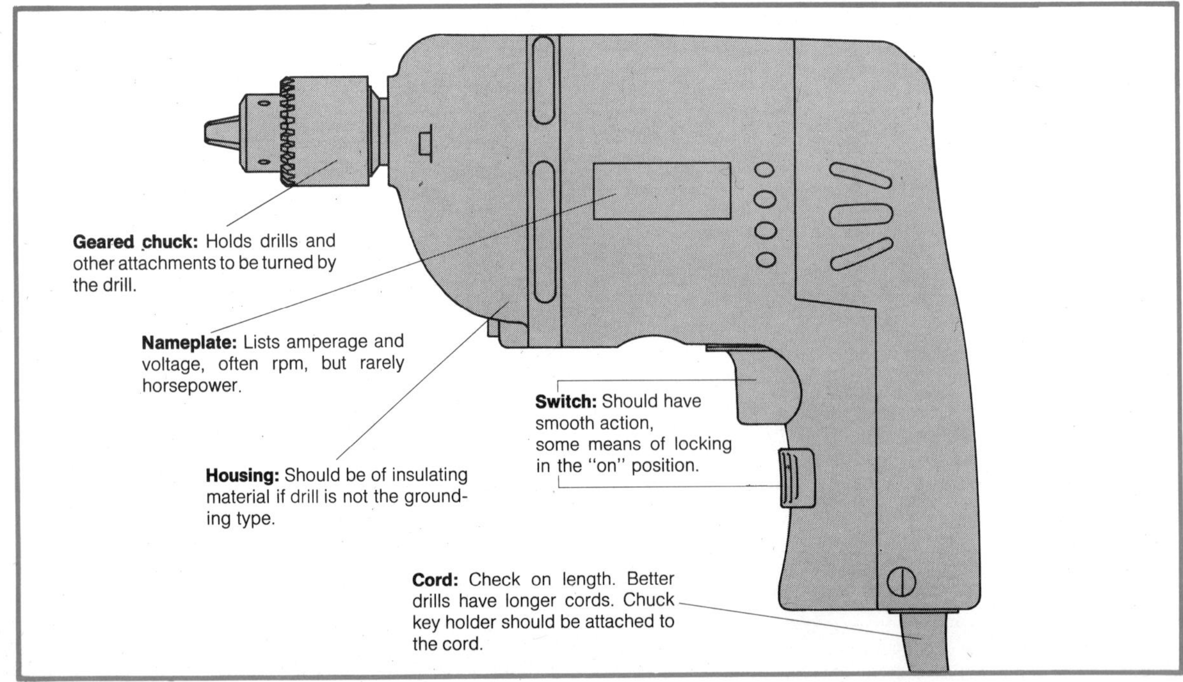

Bits

Shown below is a selection of the bits most often used in the average home workshop. Twist drills are among the most popular because they bore through both wood and metal. See the following pages for special-purpose attachments and how to use them.

Twist drills—for wood and metal

Oversize drill (cut-down shank)

Countersink

Countersink

Screw-mate

Auger-type bit

Spade bit

Carbide drill—for brick and masonry

Rotary rasp

Rotary file

Hole saw

Fly cutter

Drilling

Depth gauge locks to shaft of drill bit at any required distance to limit the depth of a hole. It is made of plastic.

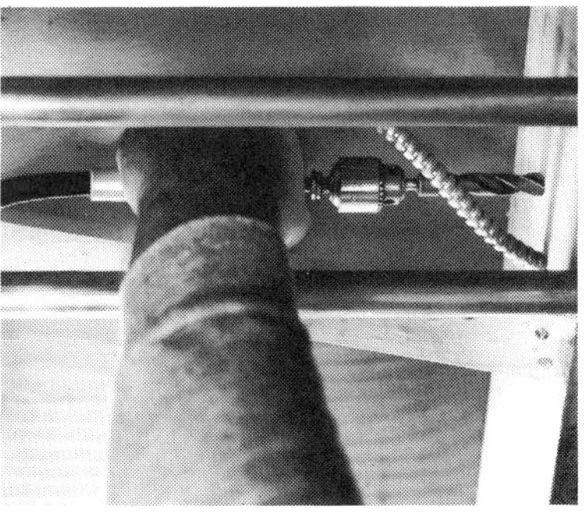

Flexible shaft attachment lets you get into tight places with any size drill. Accepts all accessories; is 40 in. long.

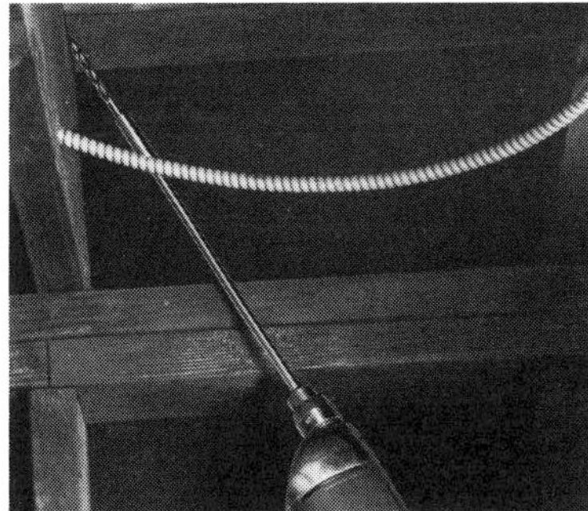

Extension is used for drilling holes beyond drill bit's length. Takes ¼-in. drills, which are locked to shaft.

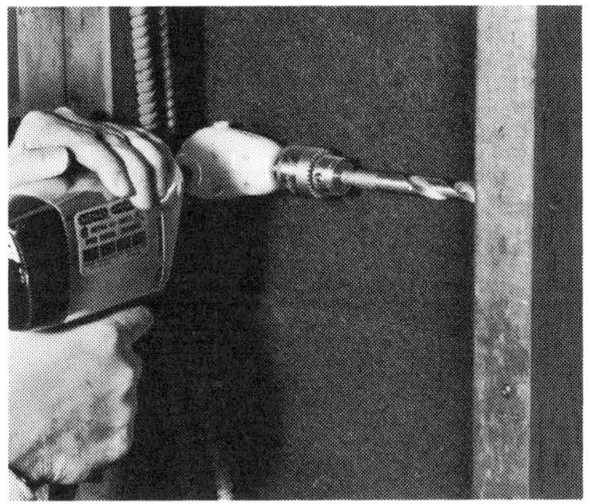

Right-angle attachment is used in areas where space is limited. Good for such jobs as running cable through beams.

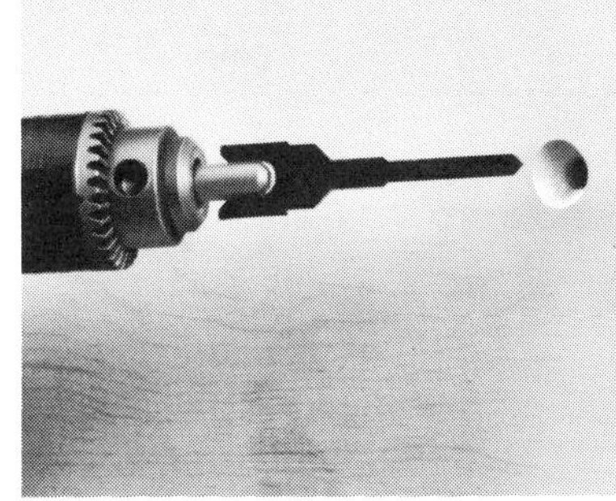

Screw-mate device enables you to drill pilot hole, shank clearance hole, and countersink all in one operation.

Auger for drilling holes into earth is a timesaver when planting bulbs or fertilizing shrubs and shade trees.

Grinding

Grinding wheel, which must be used with a stand, is handy for sharpening tools and drill bits. Wear goggles when using.

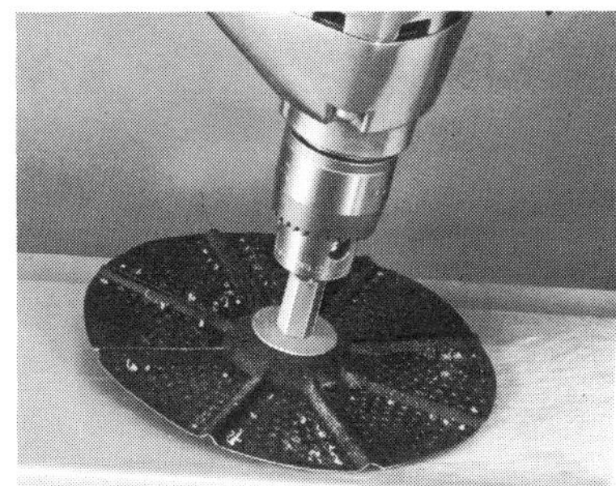

Grinding disk with sharp metal perforations that are hard to gum up, quickly removes paint from wood and metal.

Grinding stones come in many different sizes and shapes, all with a ¼-in. shank to fit chuck of electric drill.

The ½-inch drill

Because it has more power than smaller drills, the ½-inch drill can bore larger holes without overloading its motor and risking a burnout. It turns at a much lower rpm, however, and so is not as well suited for sanding, which requires high chuck speed.

Use the ½-inch drill for large-diameter drilling and boring in metal, masonry, or wood. Where deep holes are to be bored in large timbers, as in boat-building and heavy construction work, use a reversible drill. In reverse, the spiral-fluted bits can be quickly backed out of the holes they have made. Because of their greater power, all ½-inch drills have an extra handle mounted at the side, necessary for control. The handle is easily removed when it is necessary to get into a tight spot such as a corner.

The ½-in. drill is a must for drilling holes in masonry. If the going is tough, start with a small carbide drill and then finish the job with the desired size.

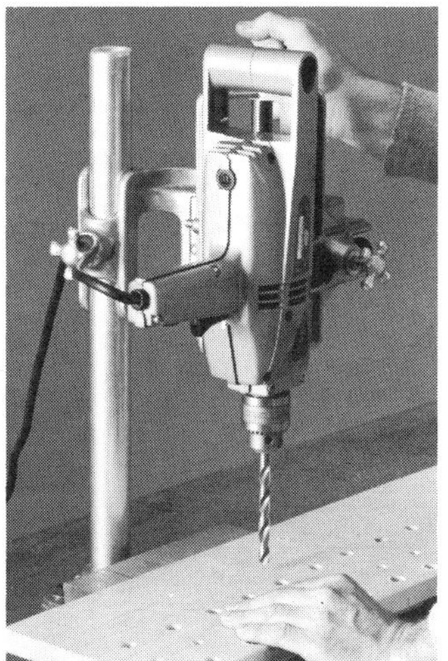

Special stands are made for most ½-in. drills to convert them into a small drill press. Removing the drill from the stand is just a matter of a few seconds.

Electric drills

Cutting

Circle cutter will make holes up to 12 in. in diameter. Bore hole for peg; start bit on any part of the circle's circumference.

Carbide-impregnated cutoff disk is used to cut metal. Drill should be mounted on a stand. Wear goggles; stand to one side.

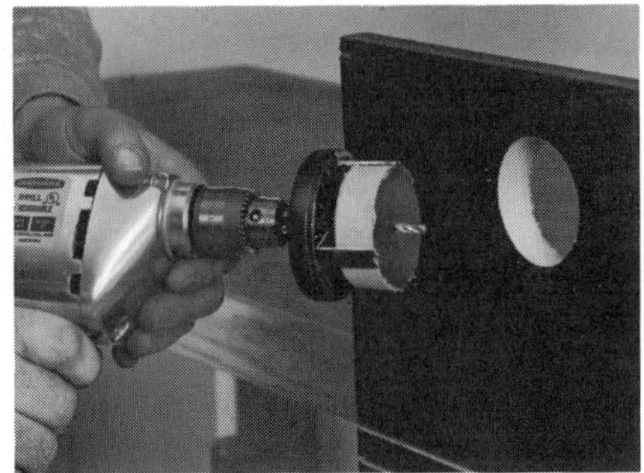

Hole cutter enables you to make perfectly circular cutouts in wood up to ¾ in. thick. Cutters range in size from ¾ to 2½ in.

Hacksaw attachment for cutting metal. Converts rotary motion of drill into reciprocating action. Uses broken-off hacksaw blades.

Sanding

Drum sander comes in various grit sizes for rough or fine work. Used mainly for smoothing edges, also sands curved and flat surfaces.

Ball-jointed rubber-backed disk sander can be used for rough sanding and paint removal. Can be fitted with bonnet for polishing.

Steel drum rasp, made in several sizes, has a ¼-in. shank to fit drill chuck. Used chiefly for rough sanding on curved surfaces.

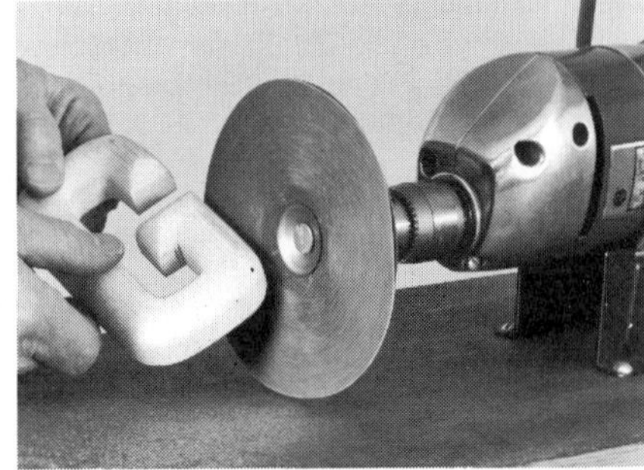

Disk sander can be used freehand or with the drill mounted on a stand. Stand to one side when using and wear protective goggles.

Miscellaneous

Chipping wheel for removing flaking paint from concrete floors and other surfaces. Rotating wheels have hardened steel points.

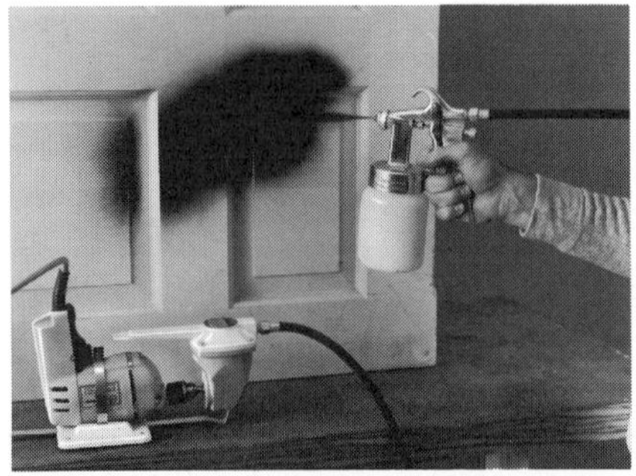

Paint sprayer attachment uses drill to power compressor. Comes with rubber hose, spray gun with pint cup, mounting hardware.

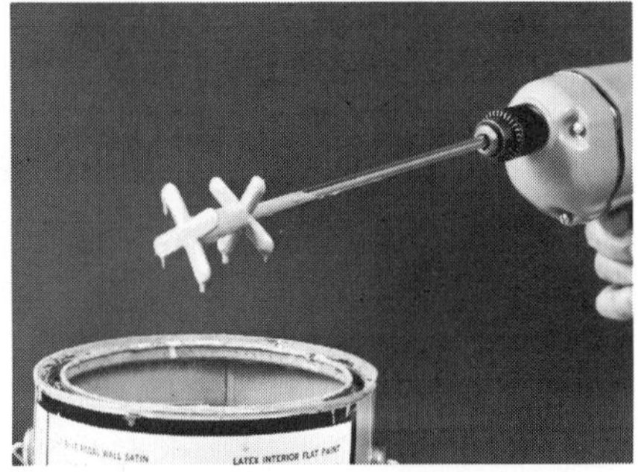

Paint stirrer mixes and thins. Put it in paint before turning on drill; leave it in 10 seconds after stopping drill.

Screwdriver attachment enables you to drive screws rapidly. Handy when many screws are to be driven, as in boat building.

Drill maintenance

In normal use, electric drills require little maintenance beyond periodic lubrication and, after considerable use, replacement of the motor brushes that make electrical contact with the rotating commutator. Since maintenance varies with make and model, your best guide is the instruction manual that comes with most new drills.

If no instruction manual is available for you to follow, make a rough pencil sketch of the visible parts at each stage of disassembly to guide you in reassembly. Some drill bodies are of the "clamshell" type—two halves held together with screws. You lift off the top half, leaving all internal parts in place in the bottom half.

Old grease should be removed from the gear case and replaced with grease made for drill and saber saw gears. This grease is available in tubes at hardware stores. Motor and gear shaft bearings (the bushing type) should be lubricated with light machine oil sold for general household use unless some other lubrication is specified by the manufacturer. Ball bearings are often permanently lubricated and sealed during manufacture and therefore require no subsequent oiling.

Your drill will let you know when it is in need of fresh grease and lubrication: It will start sounding unusually noisy. It is always better, however, to lubricate an electric drill well before it gets to this noisy condition.

With some drills, you will have to remove the front end to expose the gear case and the cover section of the handle to expose the brushes. Some drills have brush caps on opposite sides of the body at the rear. To replace the brushes, merely remove the caps, lift out the spring-loaded brushes, and insert the new brushes and the springs. Take care not to lose the springs. In the absence of instructions or a parts list, take the brushes to your dealer to be sure replacements are correct. Always replace both brushes, never one at a time.

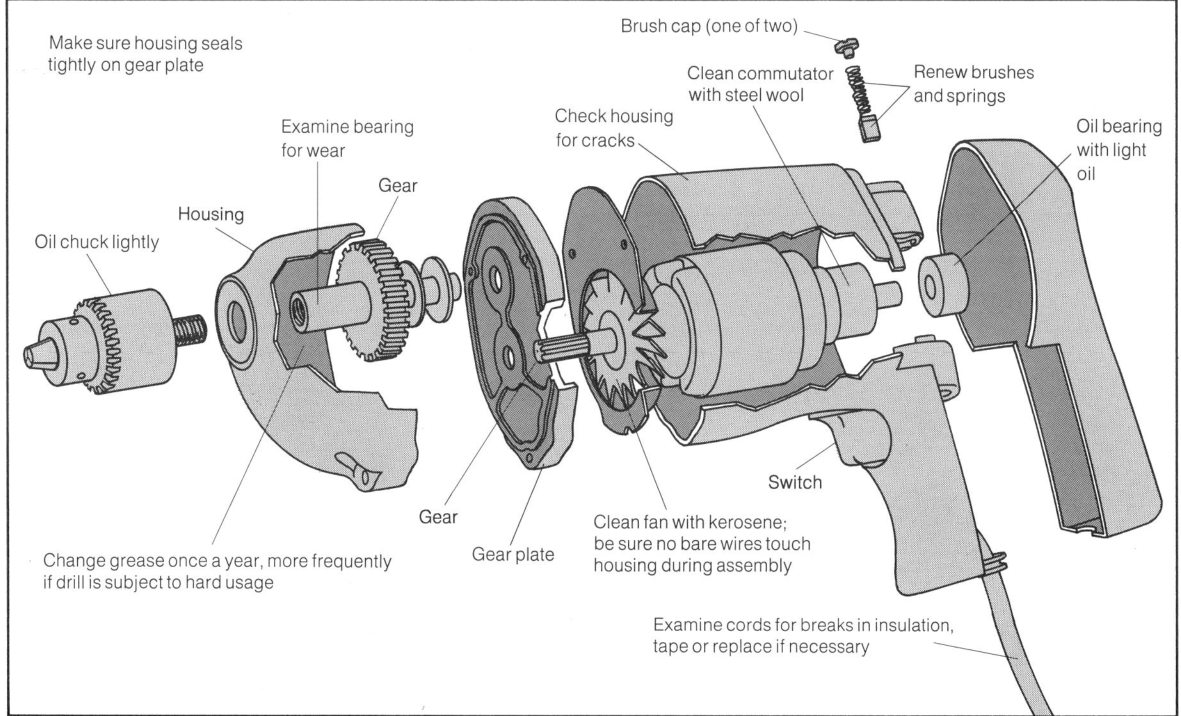

Electric screwdrivers

The electric screwdriver greatly reduces working time in large-scale screw fastening. With interchangeable tips, home workshop models can handle most slotted and Phillips-type screws. A reversing switch enables the tool to remove these same fastenings. To use an electric screwdriver, place the screw in the pilot hole, push the switch to "on," set the tool's driving tip on the screw and then push in gently. Because of a clutch, the tool will drive the screw only when you push on the handle.

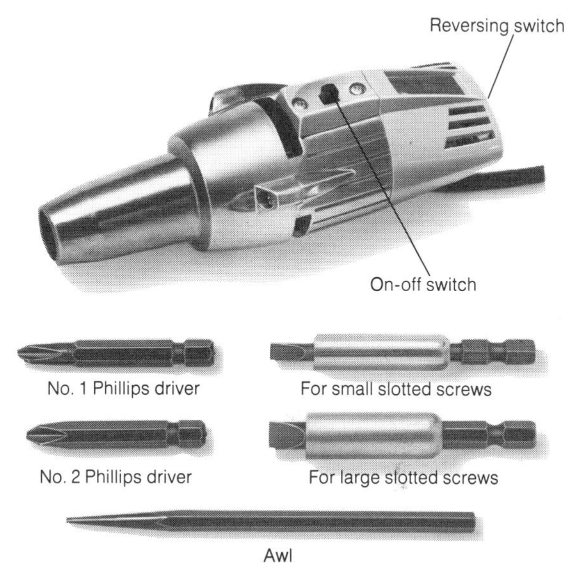

Driving garage-door hinge screws with an electric screwdriver

Circular power saws

How to select a circular saw

Any portable circular saw you buy for your shop should be capable of cutting a 2 x 4 at a 45-degree angle. In general, saws that have a blade diameter of 7 inches or more are good choices.

A number of other considerations have a bearing on your decision. The saw should have a depth adjustment, which enables you to make shallow cuts when required; an angle adjustment for cutting miters and bevels; and a ripping fence, which guides the saw when you want to rip a board to a specific width. It should also have an automatic spring-actuated blade guard that retracts as the blade enters the work, then covers the exposed part of the blade as soon as the cut has been completed.

Since most present-day saws have all of these features, your final choice often depends on how conveniently a saw operates and how easily the adjustments are made. Large-sized adjusting wing nuts are worthwhile details, as is an easy-to-grip handle on the blade guard. In addition to the saw handle, which contains the trigger starting switch, a knob on the end of the motor housing is convenient as an extra handle for awkward situations. This feature is not essential, however, with smaller saws.

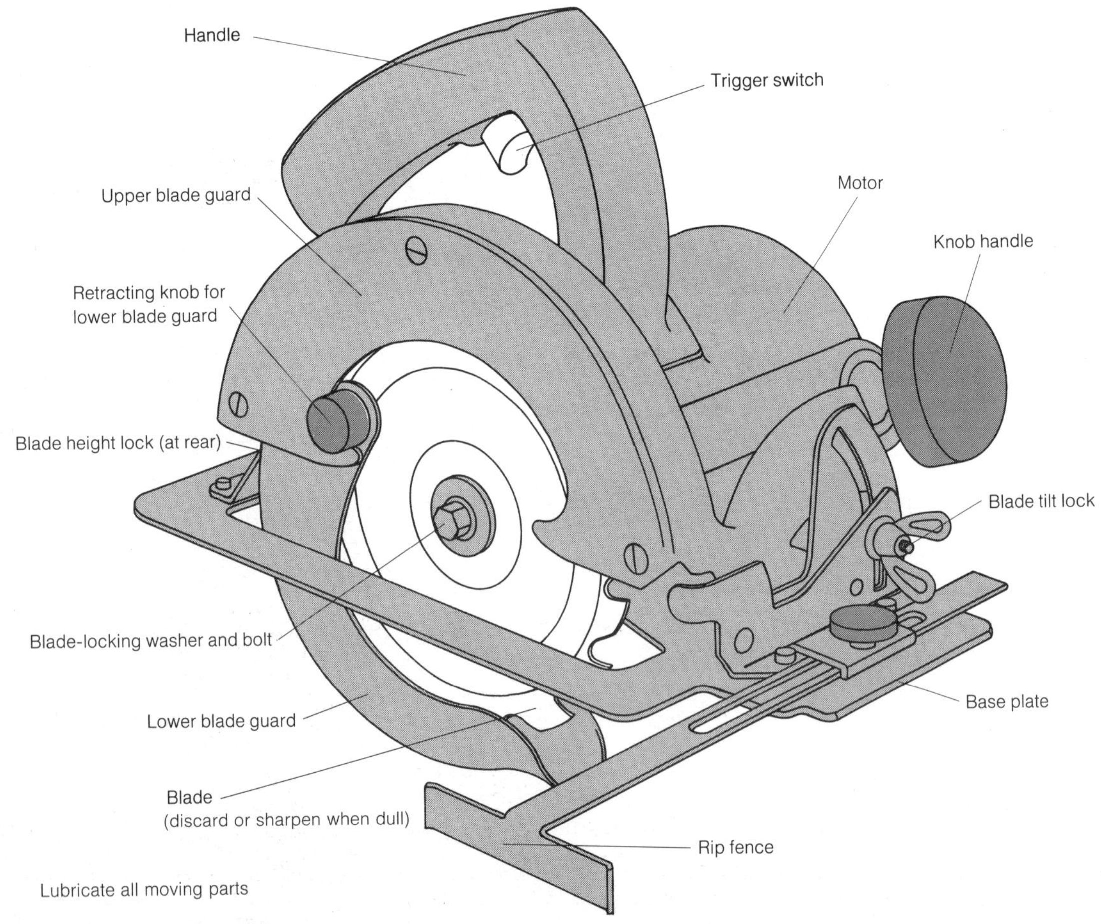

Safety practices

When using a portable circular saw, always be sure that the work to be cut is firmly supported, or held, so that it will not shift during the cut. Start the saw before the blade enters the work and guide it straight along the cutting line. Veering can cause jamming, stalling, even possible motor damage. (Be especially careful not to let the saw veer when you are using a masonry-cutting blade. In this case blade breakage could result.) If a long piece of wood is to be cut off, it should be supported by a helper. It must not be moved during the cut in such a way as to close the cut and bind the blade.

Keep a firm grip on the saw with your right hand, and keep your left hand well away from the saw. Make certain also that the cord is well out of the way so it will not be cut by the blade.

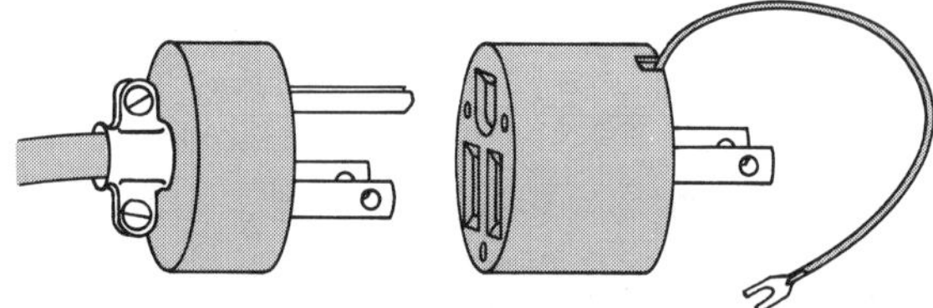
Always connect cord of three-pronged plug to properly grounded outlet or use adapter with ground wire.

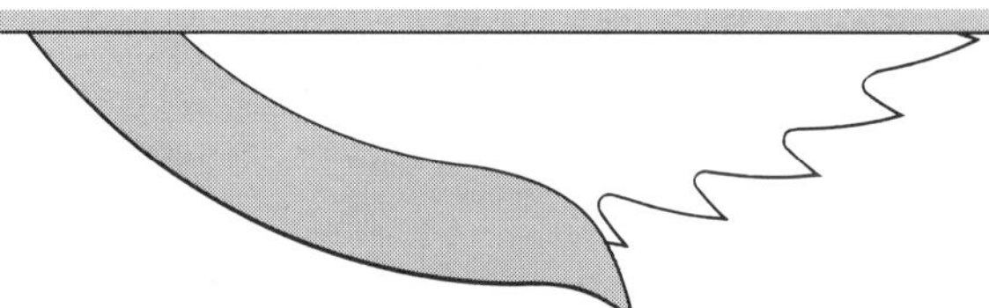
Lower blade guard covers the lower part of the blade; retracts as the blade enters the work.

Maintain a strong grip on the saw to keep it from tipping or dropping at the end of the cut. Keep your hands clear of the blade during the time required for it to come to a complete stop. Never adjust the saw without first disconnecting the power cord.

When replacing a blade, make sure that it will be turning in the right direction. This is generally indicated by an arrow on the blade. Also always be sure to use a sharp blade. A dull blade requires more power to cut through the work, tends to scorch the wood, and is a hazard to use because you tend to push the saw into the wood, instead of letting the saw do the work.

Adjusting and setting the saw

Although circular saws operate at maximum efficiency when they are adjusted to cut just through the bottom of the work, many users leave the blade at the full-depth adjustment for general work. The difference in performance is only noticeable when you are cutting thick stock.

If the tilt angle of the saw has been changed at a previous stage of the job, be sure that it is correctly readjusted. You can check for right-angle cuts by cutting a scrap piece and using a try square on the cut section. If you adjust the saw for a miter or bevel cut, test the angle by cutting a scrap piece before cutting the pieces to be actually used. A test is also advisable with shallow-depth adjustments and rip fence settings.

When trying out a new saw, familiarize yourself with all the adjustments by making several cuts on scrap wood. In this way you will learn how accurate the settings on the saw really are. The calibration on the saw, showing angles and distance, should only be used as a guide, never for actual measurements. Remember, too, that the width of the saw kerf (cut) and the types of blades used in construction work affect the precision of the final result. Use turps to remove gum, dirt, and pitch from the bottom of the saw. An occasional waxing of the bottom is a good idea. It will help the saw glide smoothly along the work. Also, make certain that the trigger switch is operating smoothly and that it does not lock inadvertently in the "on" position.

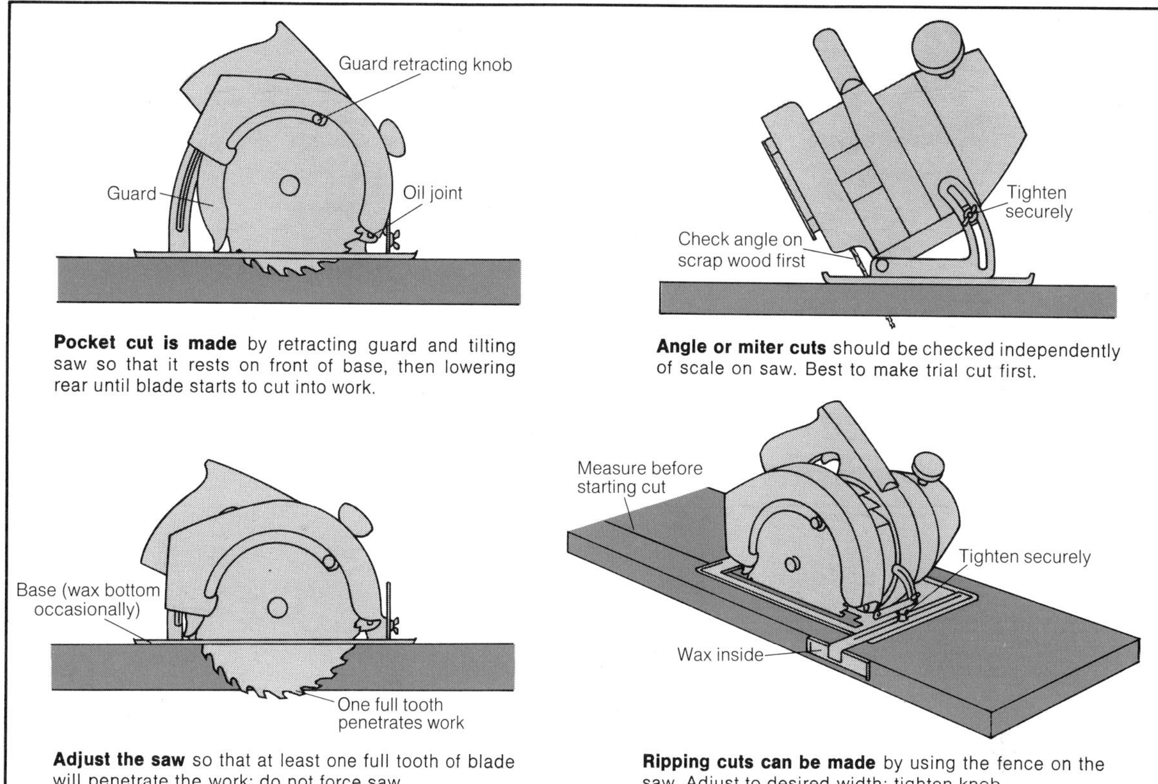

Pocket cut is made by retracting guard and tilting saw so that it rests on front of base, then lowering rear until blade starts to cut into work.

Angle or miter cuts should be checked independently of scale on saw. Best to make trial cut first.

Adjust the saw so that at least one full tooth of blade will penetrate the work; do not force saw.

Ripping cuts can be made by using the fence on the saw. Adjust to desired width; tighten knob.

How to choose blades

Combination crosscut and rip blade is suitable for most purposes. Does a good job of cutting thick or thin hardwoods and softwoods with or across the grain, as well as plywood and hardboard.

Crosscut blade's fine teeth cut smoothly across grain of hardwood and softwood. Suitable for cutting plywood, hardboard, veneers, also framing lumber such as 2 x 4s. Blade is not suitable for ripping.

Rip blade has larger teeth than combination blade. Recommended when you want to do a large amount of cutting with grain. Best used with rip fence or guide batten for easier, more accurate cutting.

Hollow ground blade makes smoothest cut, cuts thick or thin materials with little or no sanding required. Keep blades sharp to minimize the fiber fraying and wood scorching possible with dull blades.

Abrasive blades are made for masonry, metal, plastic, and other hard-to-cut materials. Excellent for scoring bricks or blocks for easy breaking. Buy the blade to suit the type of material to be cut.

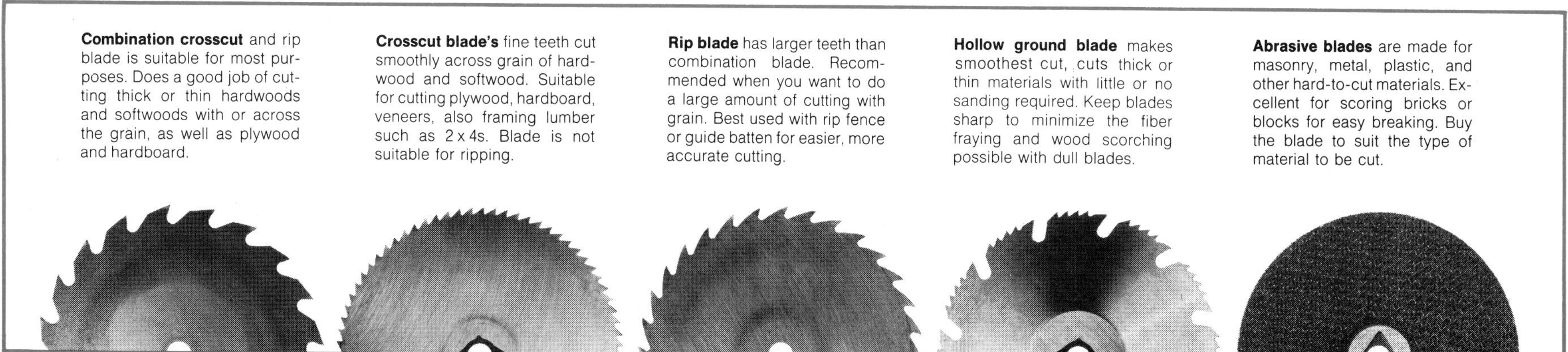

Circular power saws

Various uses

Crosscutting a 2 x 4 is a common operation for the portable saw. Support the work with your left hand as you guide saw with right.

A rip cut is a cut made with the grain of the wood. If the cut is not too wide, you can use the rip fence as a cutting guide.

A wide or long cut is best made with a batten clamped to the work as shown. Press against side of batten as you move saw forward.

Stringer cut for stairs should stop before the end of the line, be finished with a handsaw. Cutting beyond mark weakens wood.

To make a dado cut, first mark the area to be cut away on the board, allow for blade thickness and set blade for desired depth.

After making the first cut, make the second cut at the required width. Measure carefully and use a clamped batten as a guide.

Next, make a series of parallel passes between the two outside cuts. Reset the batten (or the rip fence) as required.

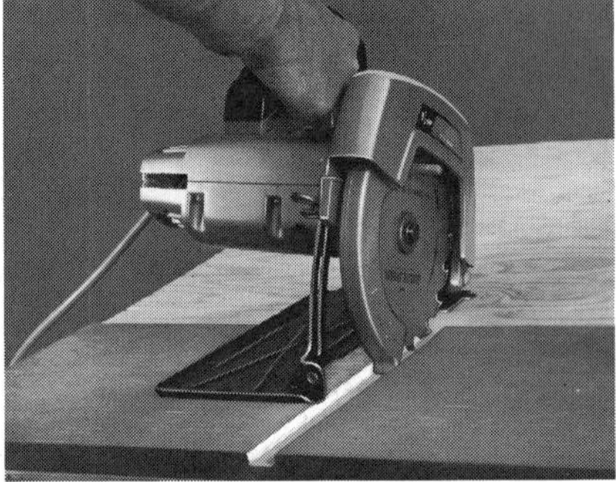

To remove the waste, you can use the saw or, if you prefer, a chisel and mallet. Cuts can be made with or across the grain.

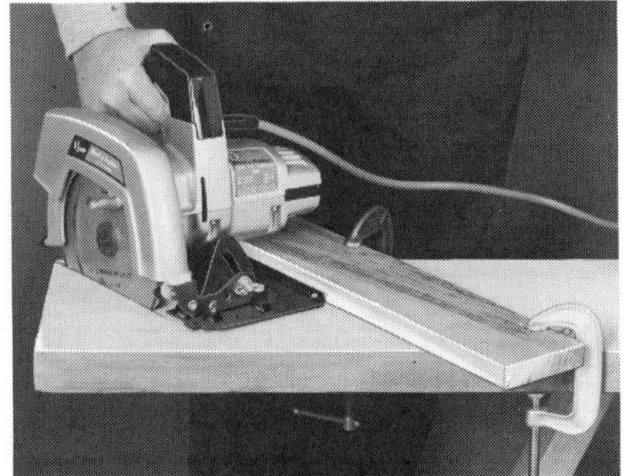

Miter: Clamp a straightedge over the wood to act as a miter guide fence. Make sure that the clamps will not foul the saw.

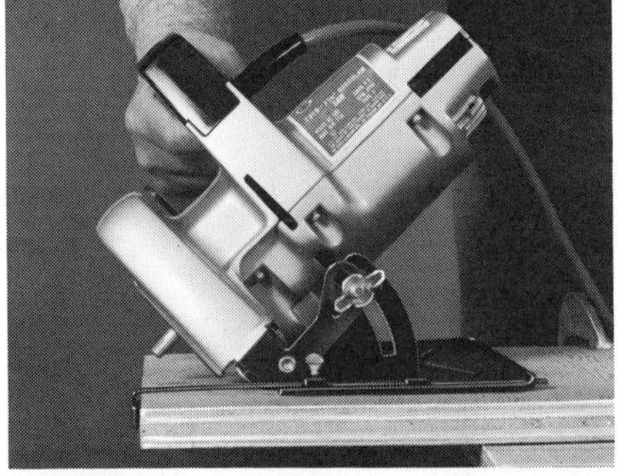

Bevel: Loosen the wing nut and set the saw at the desired angle; tighten the nut. Check on scrap wood before making a finish cut.

Compound bevel: This is a combination miter cut and a bevel cut, made at the same time. Always make trial cut first on scrap wood.

Grooving: Decorative cuts can be made on paneling by setting blade to make a shallow (⅛ in.-deep) cut. Use guide as shown.

Special applications

Cutting extra thick stock: Cut one side to maximum capacity of saw. Turn work over, align saw with cut, and finish.

To make a pocket cut, tilt the saw forward and lower the blade slowly. Cut almost to the end. Finish with handsaw.

Abrasive wheel cuts through brick and concrete. For marble, start shallow, increase depth slightly at each pass.

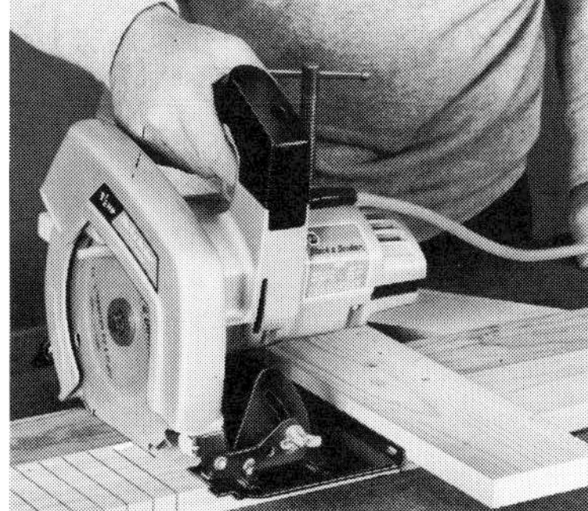
To bend wood around a corner, make many parallel cuts, ½ in. apart and equal to three-quarters of the wood's thickness.

Simple jig made of scrap wood and a C-clamp is used as a guide to make series of parallel cuts; or use saw freehand.

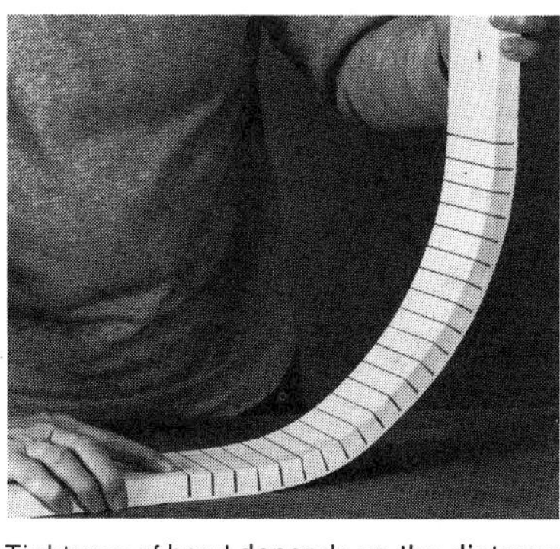
Tightness of bend depends on the distance between cuts, their depth, and the pliability of the lumber.

The 4½-inch trim saw

The trim saw with a 4½-inch blade does many jobs of larger saws but is lighter in weight and easier to handle. Because of its light weight (about 7 pounds), it can be used with one hand. A special base insert enables you to cut thin plywood and plastic laminates without danger of splintering. The saw's capability to cut at a 45-degree angle is limited to stock not more than 1 inch thick. For straight cutting, the saw will go through wood a little less than 2 inches thick. The saw is especially handy for freehand cutting of 4-x-8-foot plywood panels to approximate size and then trimming the pieces to exact size on a bench saw.

Maintenance

The instruction manual supplied with your saw is your best guide to maintenance, as procedures may vary with make and model. In some, bearings are permanently lubricated and sealed and gear housings require no further attention in normal use during the life of the saw. Others, by means of plainly marked oil holes in the housing, require regular applications of a few drops of light machine oil. The bearing of the retractable lower guard should be oiled from time to time to assure positive action. The blade should be kept sharp to maintain cutting speed and avoid motor-heating friction. You can eliminate the need for saw sharpening with throw-away blades. These are specially hardened to give relatively long life, but cannot be resharpened. Their low cost, however, makes disposal practical.

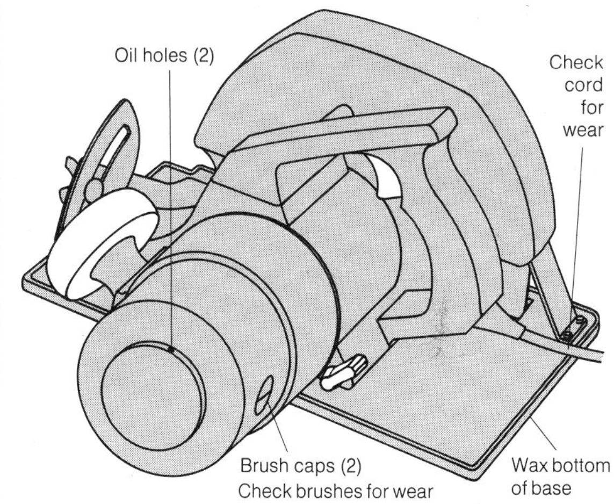

Oil all moving parts; use oil, grease, or gear lubricant as recommended by manufacturer

You can replace worn motor brushes in many models by removing the brush caps at the motor housing. In some saws, part of the housing must be removed for this purpose. Because of construction differences, if no instruction book is available, write to the saw manufacturer before tackling the job. If the saw comes with a case, store it there, and make sure the cord is not frayed or kinked.

Saber saw

Various uses

With various blades, the portable jigsaw, sometimes called a saber saw, can make straight or curved cuts in wood, plywood, hardboard, laminates, light metal, and even ceramics. It will rip a long piece of wood, crosscut, bevel, miter, and start a cut in the middle of a panel. With a special blade, it will cut flush to a perpendicular surface, permitting openings near a wall for heating ducts or plumbing. Most jigsaws cut through 2-inch stock.

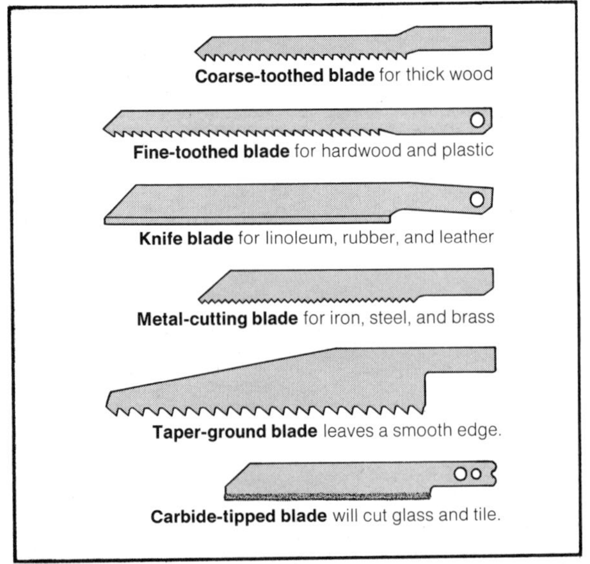

Coarse-toothed blade for thick wood

Fine-toothed blade for hardwood and plastic

Knife blade for linoleum, rubber, and leather

Metal-cutting blade for iron, steel, and brass

Taper-ground blade leaves a smooth edge.

Carbide-tipped blade will cut glass and tile.

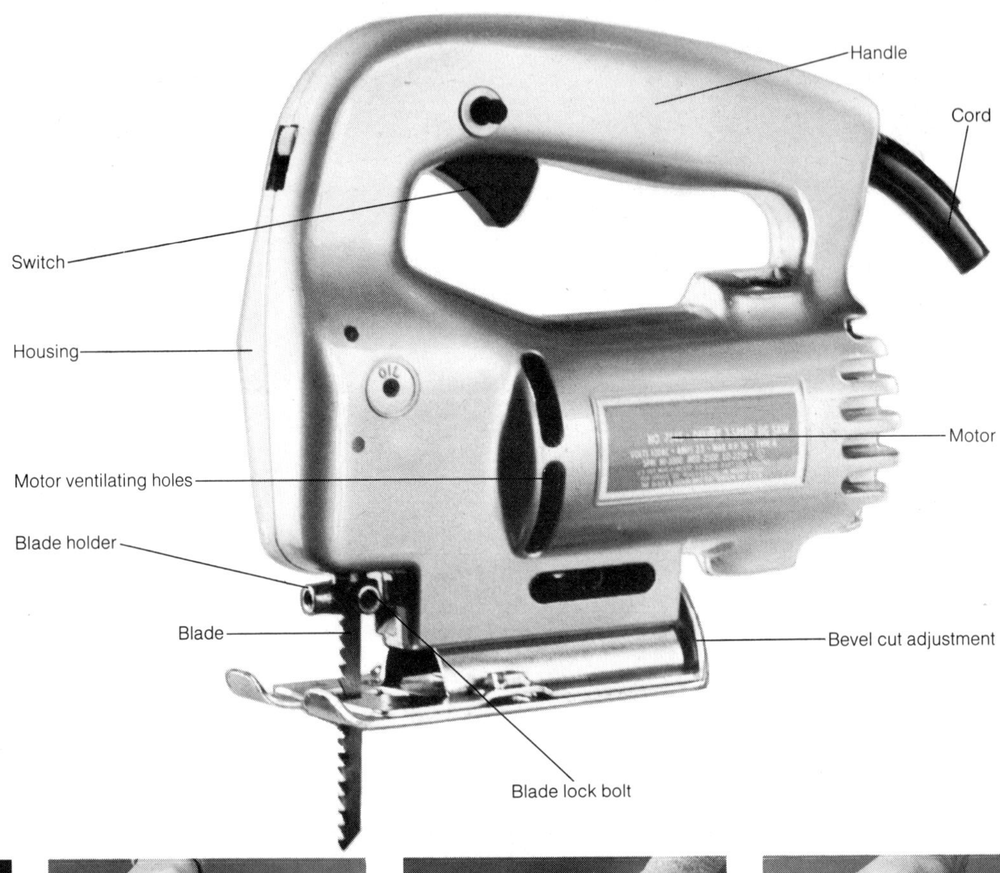

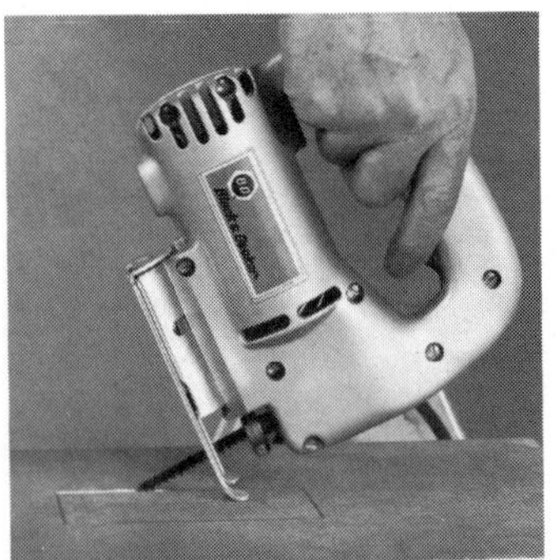

Pocket cut: Tilt the saw so that the base rests firmly on the work. Then tilt the base back slowly until the blade enters the wood.

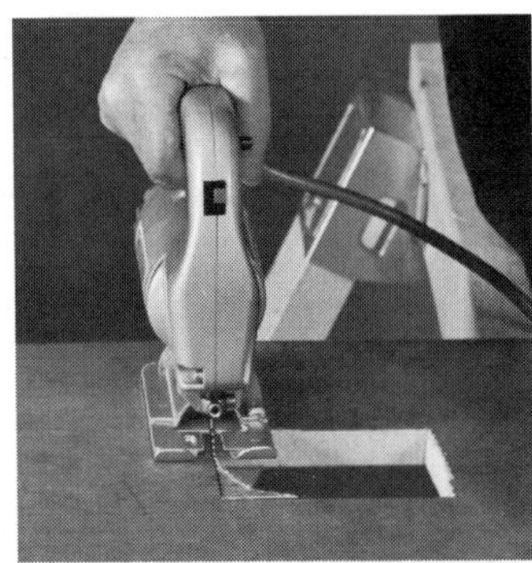

Near the end of the cut, turn the saw to make the next straight line cut and then finish off the leftover pieces in the corners.

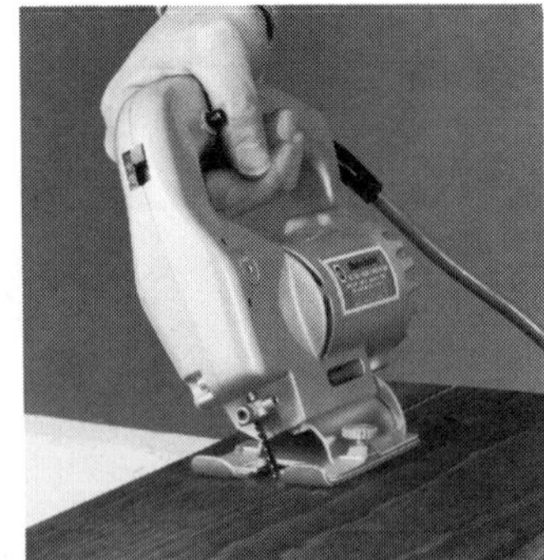

Bevel cut: Loosen the adjustment at the base plate and tilt the plate to the desired angle. Tighten and use the saw in the conventional way.

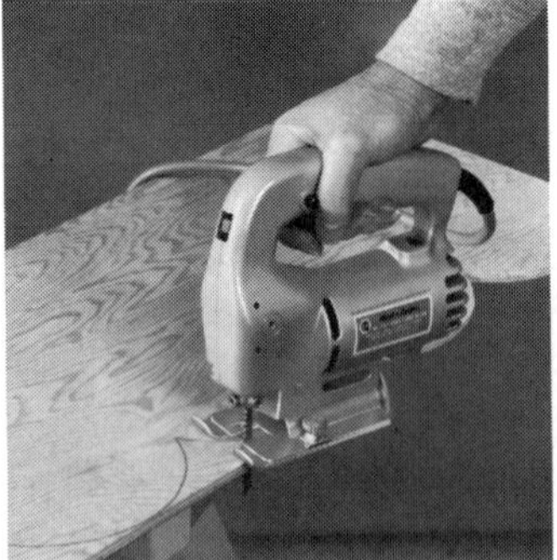

Curved cuts: Use narrowest blade to get sharpest curve. Start from edge, or make a pocket cut. Clamp work to prevent chattering.

Rip cut: Long straight cuts are termed ripping. This can be done with an accessory rip fence or with a board clamped to the work.

Reciprocating saw

The reciprocating saw is an adaptation of the saber saw, or jigsaw, for heavy duty such as in construction work. Blades, largely interchangeable among different makes, are available in lengths from 2½ to 12 inches. Generally heavier than saber saw blades, they range in purpose from cutting metal to cutting wood up to 6 inches thick.

In many models, blades may be mounted to cut up, down, or horizontally, and flush with an adjoining surface. In structural work and remodeling, long blades are sometimes used to cut right through a wall, after making sure wiring or plumbing won't be endangered. Blades for such use can cut through any nails they may encounter. Blades made specifically for cutting metal, such as pipe or bar stock, should be lubricated during use with light oil.

These saws are made in both single speed (about 2300 strokes per minute) and variable speed models. The lower speeds are more efficient for cutting steel and thermoplastics.

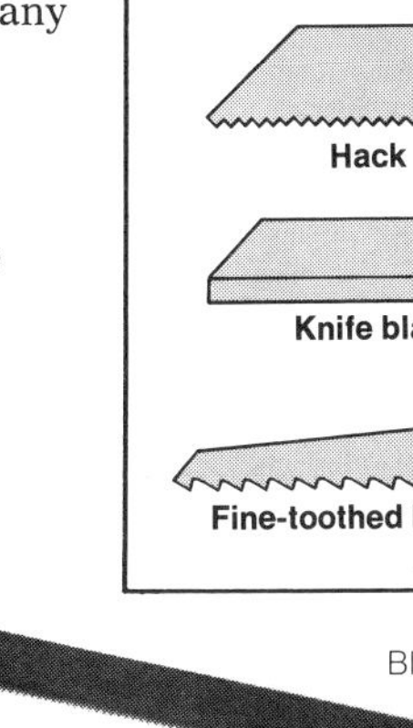

Coarse-toothed blade rough-cuts green wood.

Hack saw blade cuts metal to ⅛-in. thick.

Knife blade is for leather, rubber, cloth, linoleum.

Fine-toothed blade smooth-cuts wood, plastic, hardboard.

Reciprocating saw is ideal for rough-cutting lumber to size, for cutting firewood, and for general trimming where extreme accuracy is not important.

Cutting pipe hole: First drill a hole large enough to insert the blade, then proceed around marked area. Wear goggles if cutting directly overhead.

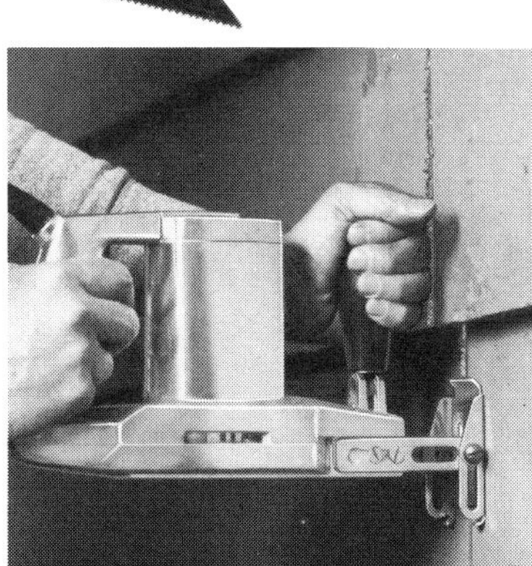

Removing clapboard (for air conditioner): Bore holes at corners to other side of wall as guide when finishing the cut from the inside of house. Cut all four sides.

Chain saw

For average use a gas- or electric-powered chain saw with a 12- to 16-inch bar (blade body) is a good choice. A typical model can cut through a 6-inch hardwood log in seconds. Gasoline-powered saws have a special clutch which prevents the chain from moving while the motor is idling. When the throttle is opened, the clutch engages and drives the chain.

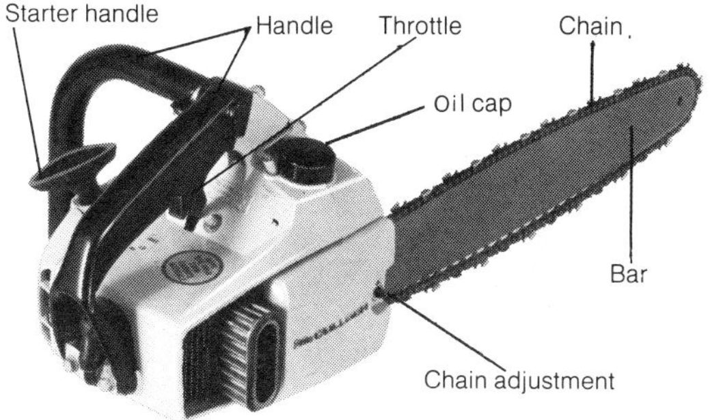

Felling a tree. This is the undercut, made on the side where you want the tree to fall. The actual felling, or main cut, is made on the opposite side, approximately 2 in. higher than the horizontal undercut.

A typical homeowner's gasoline-powered saw cutting logs into firewood. Cut the wood into 2-ft. lengths.

How to choose and use a router

The router is basically a simple portable tool, consisting of a high-speed electric motor (about 24,000 rpm) mounted vertically on a horizontal base plate. A chuck on the lower edge of its shaft holds keen-edged cutting bits that can be extended below the base to cut grooves, trim edges, form recesses, produce moldings, and otherwise shape wood on which the router is used.

The power of the router's motor (from ¼ to more than 1 hp in professional models) determines how deep and how fast the tool can cut through work, and what it costs. A low-powered router, however, can do many of the jobs a high-powered router can do, providing it does them in stages. It can make a deep cut, for example, by means of a number of shallow passes.

The router, with its cutter bit operating, may be lowered into the work from above, then moved along the path to be shaped or cut, or it may move into the work from the edge. The bits are set for depth of cut by an adjustment on the router body.

If the bit is to make a large recess, as in a meat platter, it may be mounted on a piece of plywood (large enough to span it from rim to rim) with the cutter projecting downward through a hole in the plywood support. Or you can buy accessories that enable the router to follow templates or guiding edges on the work. With some experience, you will be able to cut designs freehand and even write your name.

As motor shaft, chuck, and bit revolve clockwise (looking down), you should move the tool from left to right. **For safety:** Remember that the router shaft and bit turn at extremely high speed and cut very fast. Be sure the bit is locked tightly in the chuck, and always keep your fingers clear of it. Never change bits or cutters or make adjustments unless the cord is disconnected. Merely switching off the tool is not enough, as switches can be turned on accidentally. Hold the tool firmly on the work when using it, and "feed" from left to right.

To protect the tool, use sharp bits. (They retain their sharpness for a long time in normal use.) Try to get the feel of the most efficient cutting movement. The bit should cut easily with only slight reduction in motor speed. Moving it too slowly through the work may burn the wood and draw the temper of the bit. Moving it too fast slows the motor and causes overheating. Practice on scrap wood and watch performance carefully. The sound of the tool is an excellent guide, once you achieve efficient cutting. At the beginning, stop the tool frequently and check the cut for burned areas caused by too slow tool movement. Motor slowdown is a signal that you are forcing the cut. The knack usually takes only minutes to acquire. You will find the router especially handy when installing door locks and hinges. In fact, you can buy hinges with rounded corners to match the contour of the opening made by the router bit so that the need for chiseling by hand is eliminated.

When routing narrow work, the base of the router should be extended to gain extra support by fastening a block of wood to the base or to the work.

Motor: Oil bearings as shown in owner's manual

Switch: Hold router so that it is accessible

Handles: Keep clean and grasp firmly

Adjusting collar: Lock to desired depth and always make a trial cut first

Collet: Keep free of dirt and chips

Collet nut: Make sure it is always tight, use wrench supplied

Base: Wax occasionally for friction-free movement

Bit: Should be sharp and straight

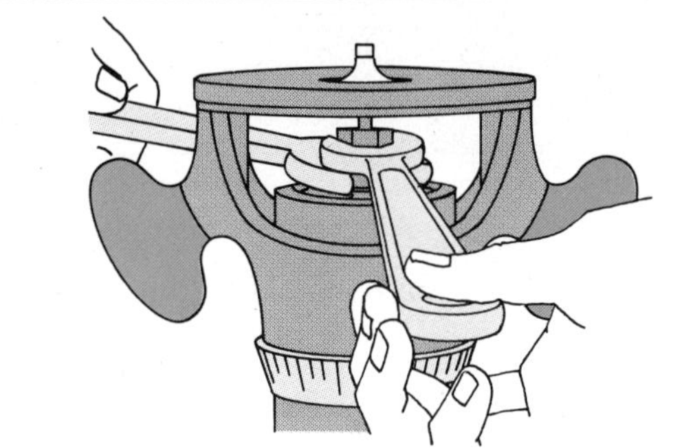

Inserting router bits: Disconnect router from power source. You will need two wrenches, unless your router has a locking device that prevents the motor shaft from turning. Hold one wrench on the lower nut and loosen (or tighten) collet nut with upper wrench.

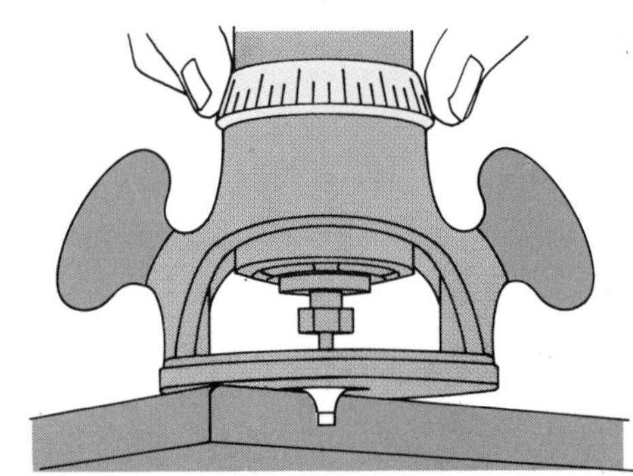

To adjust cutting depth: Place router on flat surface. Loosen wing nut and turn collar until bit just touches surface. Lift router and turn collar counterclockwise to lower bit to desired depth; tighten wing nut.

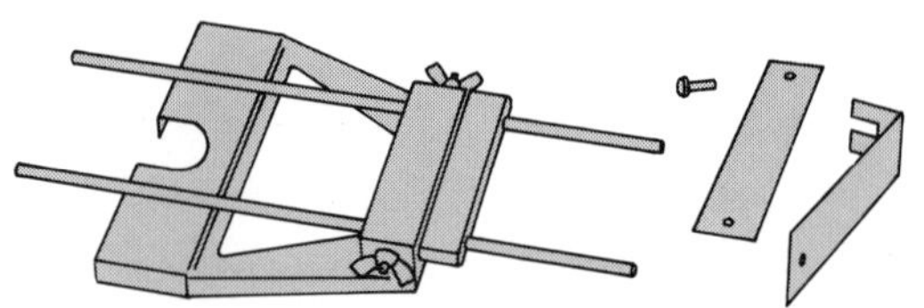

Router guide, available for most models, keeps the router bit at the exact desired distance from edge of work. Guide adjusts to and from router base and is held in place by locking screws. Can ride against rim of either straight or curved work as required.

Uses of the router

Grooving: Use straight bit. Set depth. Adjust router guide or straightedge at desired width. If work is narrow, clamp extra pieces on both sides to make wider base for router.

Dadoing: A cut across the width of a board is called a dado. It is used to make slots for shelves. If bit is narrower than desired dado width, make several passes.

Routing a circular groove: Mount guide bar to router base. Adjust width. Drill a hole in center of circle. Insert guide pin. Move the router in counterclockwise direction.

Rabbeting: Use straight bit. Set depth. If end and edge are to be cut, cut end first (across grain) to prevent edge chipping. Make large rabbets with several passes of bit.

Router bits and their purposes

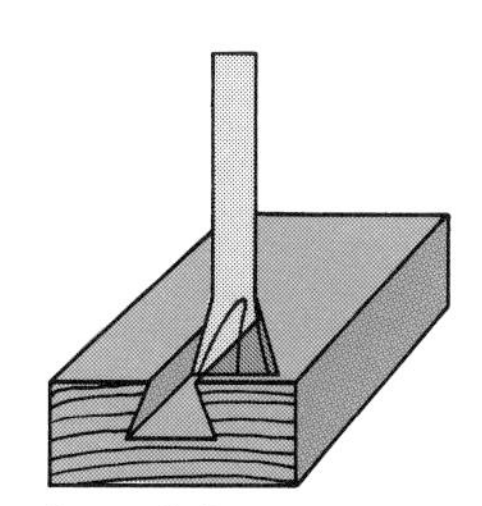

Dovetail: Creates strong joints for frames, shelves, bookcases, cabinets.

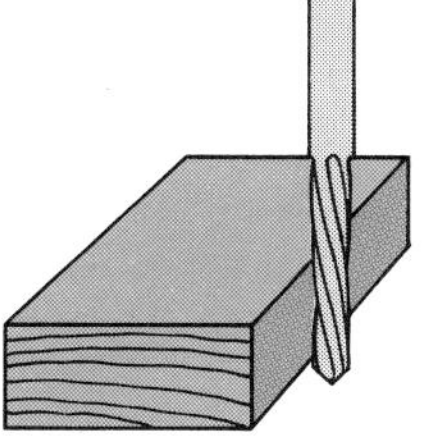

Spiral: Edge smoothing and trimming of plastic laminates, fiber glass.

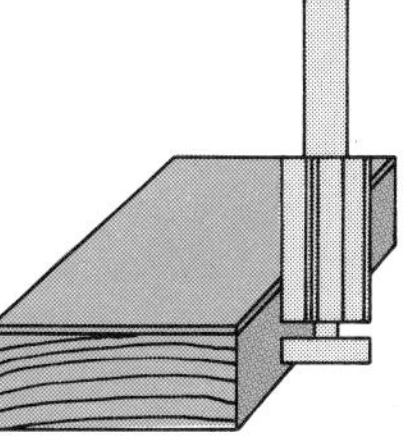

Combination panel: Veneer trimming, template panel routing.

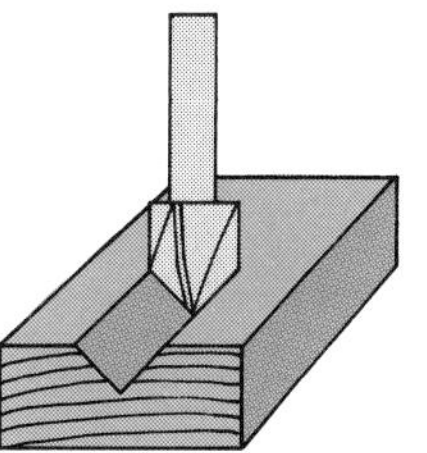

V-grooving: Lettering and sign work. Simulates planks on paneling.

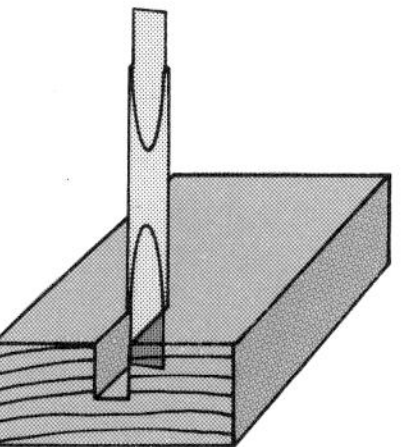

Straight, single flute: General stock removal. Grooves, dadoes, rabbets.

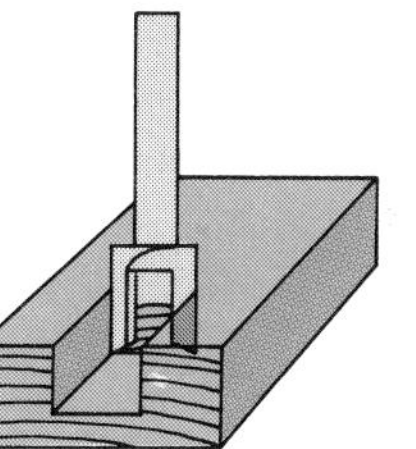

Stair routing: Stair tread bit for setting steps and riser grooves.

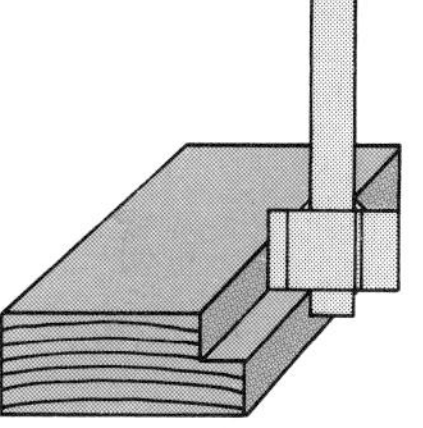

Rabbeting: Step-cutting edges for joints in cabinet doors and drawer fronts.

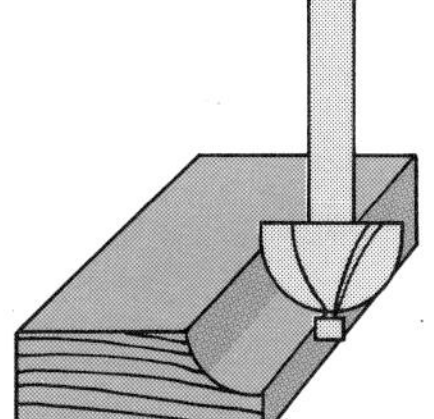

Cove: Decorative edges. With matching bit, makes drop-leaf joints.

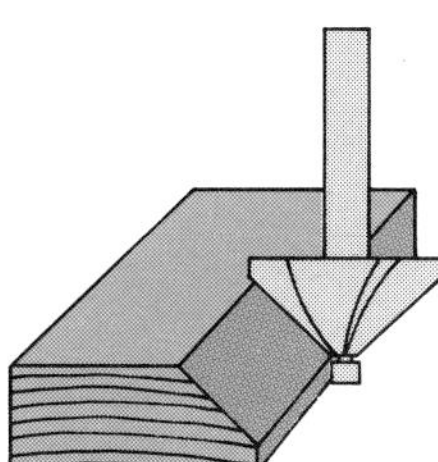

Chamfering: Angle cuts for concealed joints and decorative edges.

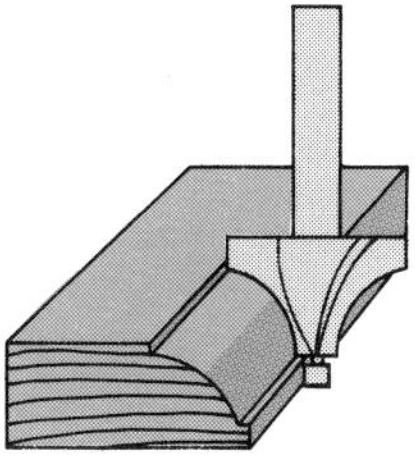

Beading: Decorative edges for veneered table tops, other furniture parts.

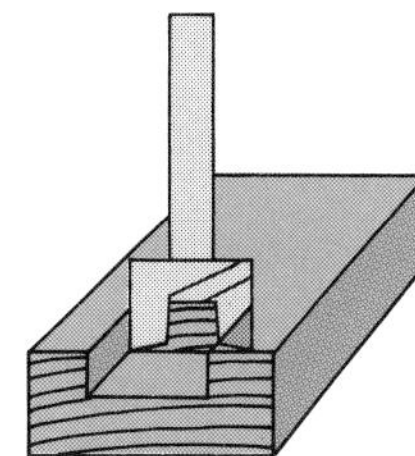

Straight: For wood and tile inlay in table tops and various game boards.

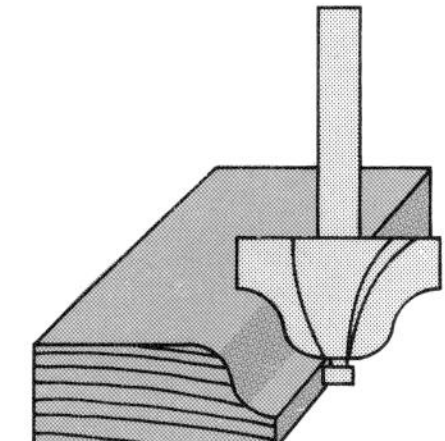

Roman ogee: Decorative edges for furniture of different periods.

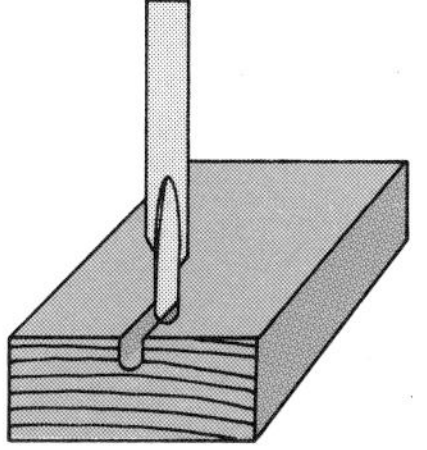

Veining: Decorative freehand, raised, or cut-in designs or letters.

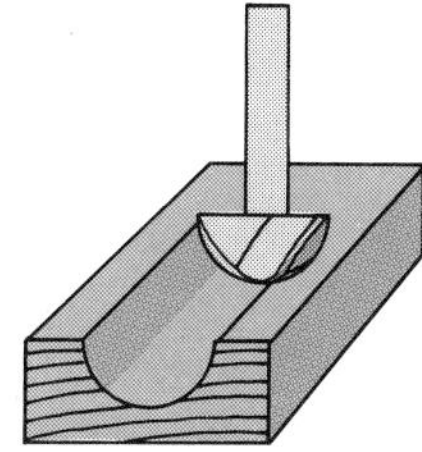

Core box: Fluting and reeding of flat surfaces. General ornamentation.

Electric planes

Block plane

The electric block plane is directly related to the electric jack plane. But because it is smaller, lighter, and easier to use, it is apt to be of far greater use to the average home handyman.

Like the conventional block plane, the electric unit is used with one hand, which is very convenient when the other hand must be used to support the work. The first time you use this tool, it will be with some trepidation, since it is held with the hand resting directly over the revolving cutters. This uneasiness will cease, however, once you get used to the fact that the cutters are nowhere near your fingers when the tool is held as shown. Hold the plane as indicated, with the index finger next to the switch.

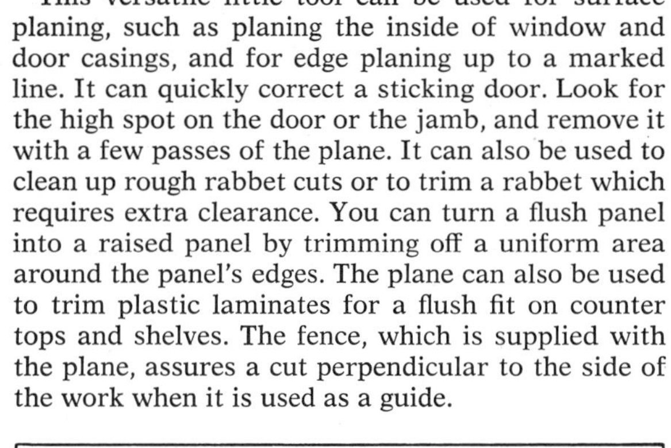

This versatile little tool can be used for surface planing, such as planing the inside of window and door casings, and for edge planing up to a marked line. It can quickly correct a sticking door. Look for the high spot on the door or the jamb, and remove it with a few passes of the plane. It can also be used to clean up rough rabbet cuts or to trim a rabbet which requires extra clearance. You can turn a flush panel into a raised panel by trimming off a uniform area around the panel's edges. The plane can also be used to trim plastic laminates for a flush fit on counter tops and shelves. The fence, which is supplied with the plane, assures a cut perpendicular to the side of the work when it is used as a guide.

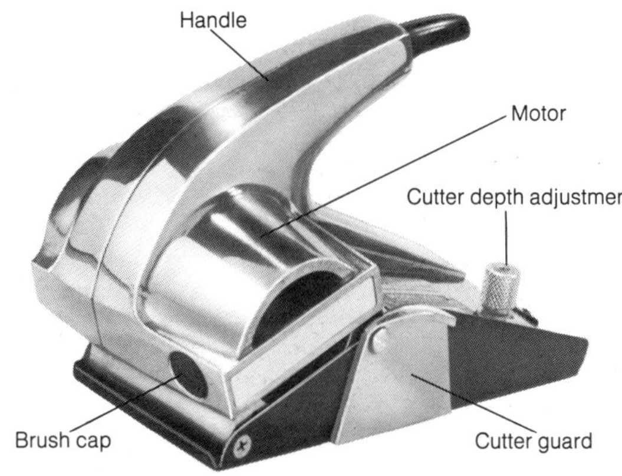

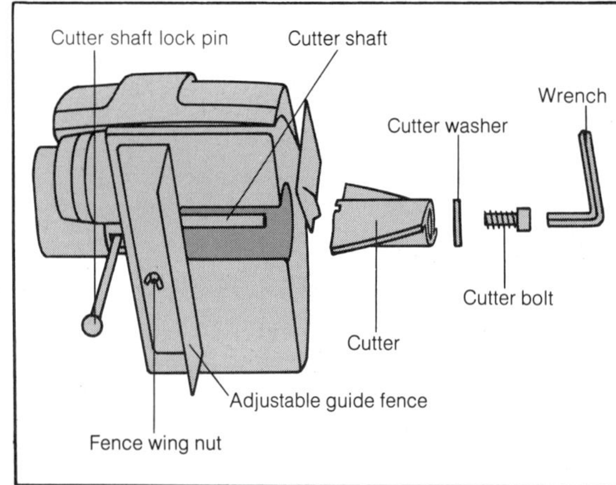

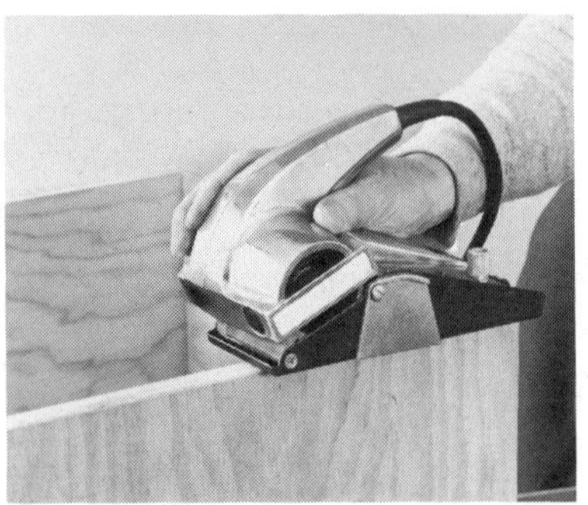

Electric block plane is held as shown, with index finger near switch (on far side, not visible). Plane can be used to make rabbet cuts with aid of fence.

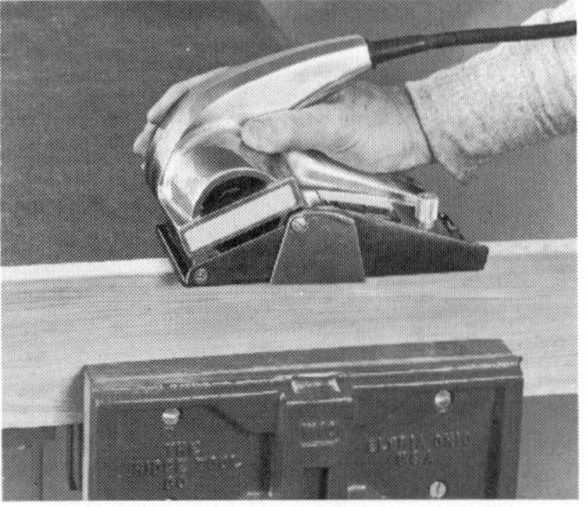

To ease a drawer, check the sides and edges for binding, usually indicated by dark, shiny spots. Plane only what is essential. Test often for fit.

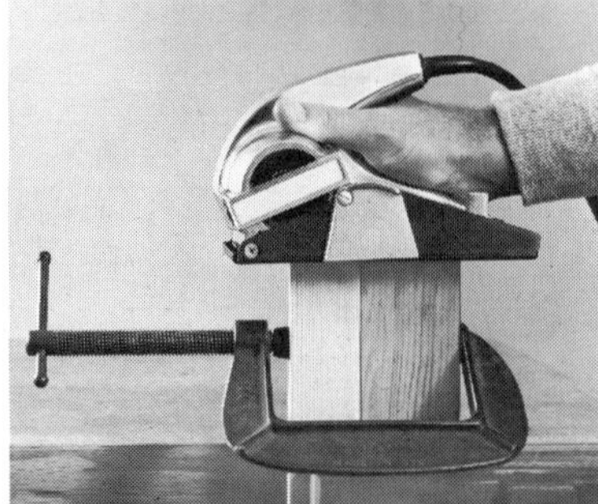

To cut across grain, work from the ends toward the center to avoid splitting. On a small piece, clamp scrap board at end and use very light strokes.

Jack plane

This plane does the work of a hand plane with less effort and produces a smoother job on knots and wavy grain. It planes by means of a revolving cutter that turns at about 22,000 rpm.

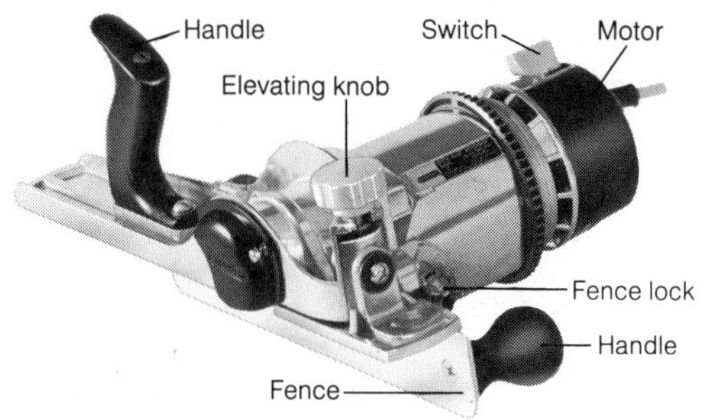

The plane has a fence which projects downward from one side perpendicular to the bottom. When you are planing the edge of a board or door, this fence is held against the side of the work to produce a perfectly square-edged cut. Fence can be removed for surface planing of broad areas and it can be tilted for bevel planing.

To plane a long board, clamp securely and grasp handles firmly. Use downward as well as side pressure to keep the guide snug against the work.

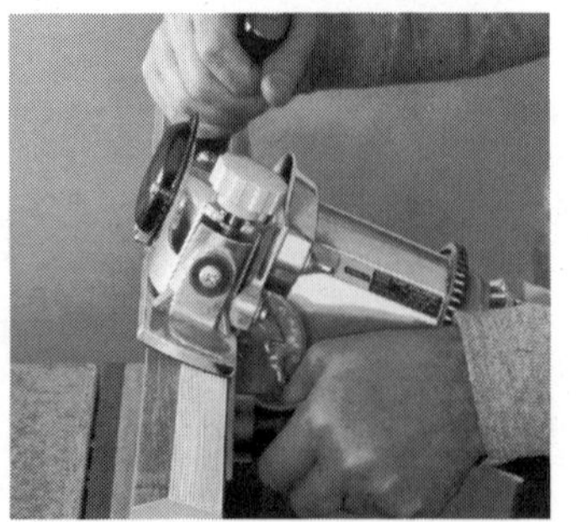

To make a bevel cut across the grain, set fence at desired angle. Follow instructions given above for planing a long board, but reduce downward pressure at front of plane to minimize chipping at the end of the cut. As an alternative, you can clamp some scrap at the end of the work.

The belt sander

Belt sanders are suited to fast material removal from flat surfaces and have a surface-flattening effect. For fast wood removal, operate the belt at about a 45-degree angle to the grain direction, using a fairly coarse belt. To produce a smooth final finish, use it parallel to the grain, first with a medium and then with a fine belt.

Cost of a belt sander depends on capacity, power, and refinements. Most of them use sandpaper 3 or 4 inches wide. For average use, one with a 3-inch belt is a good choice. One worthwhile feature is a high-low switch, low used chiefly for polishing metal and wood. Another is a dust pick-up system. The belt sander throws a lot of dust, and the pick-up system—a kind of miniature vacuum cleaner—sucks up most of it. When buying a sander, look for easy-to-use controls; a simple way to remove and install belts; a belt tightening system (belts tend to stretch after use); a means of adjusting one pulley so the belt tracks in a straight line; and a not-too-difficult means of installing new brushes.

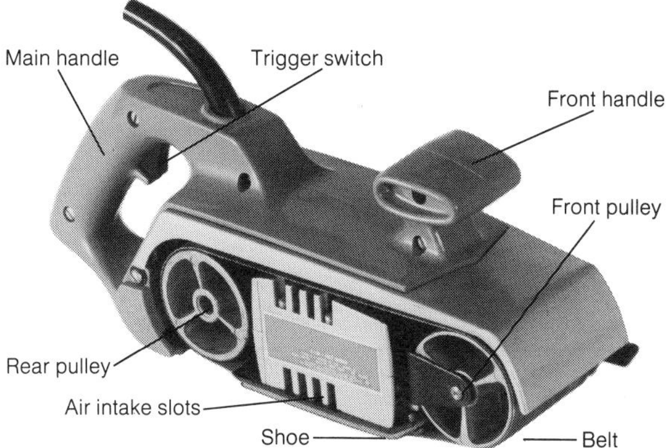

To change belt, pull lever to release tension and install new belt with arrow pointing in direction of travel.

Turn motor on and see if belt tracks properly. Rotate the tracking adjustment knob until belt tracks evenly.

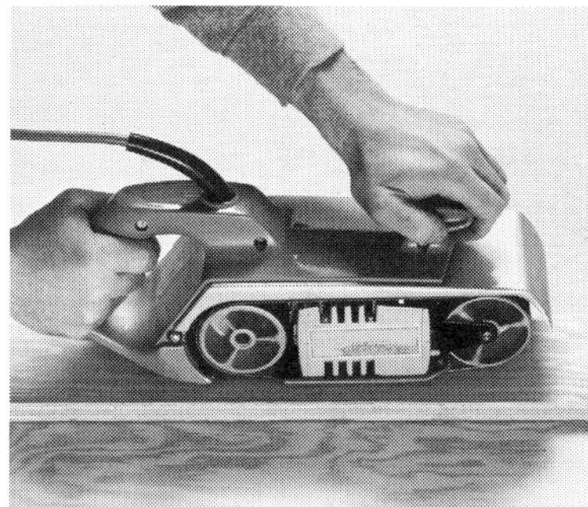

Use a coarse belt for fast stock removal. Always keep the sander moving and at a slight angle to the work.

The orbital sander

The orbital sander is not designed for removing material. It is strictly a finishing tool. Because its abrasive surface moves in a small-diameter circular motion, it is particularly effective where more than one grain direction is encountered, such as in miter joints or in checkerboard patterns. Many sanders now on the market can be switched from orbital sanding to straight-line sanding with merely the flip of a lever.

Sanding surfaces vary from about 3 x 7 to 4 x 9 inches. Most finishing sanders are motor-driven except for a few economy models which operate by means of a vibrator. The front knob on all sanders can be removed so that the sander can work right up to a vertical surface without interference. Practically every manufacturer has his own method of attaching the sandpaper to the operating end. Some use clamps, others use a knurled rod, or a sliding clip arrangement. A locking button, near the switch, will keep the motor running without the need of constant pressure on the spring-loaded switch. Check condition of sandpaper from time to time—worn paper won't cut.

Sandpaper is placed over the pad and stretched by means of a screwdriver applied to slots in knurled rollers.

Action of sander can be switched from straight-line to orbital sanding (and vice versa) by flipping a lever.

Orbital sanding cuts somewhat faster than straight-line sanding. Use it first, finish with straight-line sanding.

Uses and maintenance

Grinding wheels usually turn at about 3450 rpm, so always wear protective goggles when using a grinder, even if it comes with shatterproof, transparent eye shields. And never use one without the metal guards around wheels for protection against wheel failure.

Set the adjustable tool rest that supports the work about ⅛ inch from the wheel. Use the coarse wheel for soft materials (brass, copper, aluminum, etc.), the finer wheel for hard, brittle materials and smooth finishing. To avoid damage from overheating, let the work cool often between passes. If you replace a wheel, be sure the new one has the same rpm rating.

The grinder can also be used to clean and polish. Wire-brush wheels, available coarse and fine, are the choice to remove rust and corrosion from metal and to produce a scratch brush (medium luster) finish. You can get fiber-brush wheels for less abrasive scrubbing. For a high polish, use cloth buffing wheels with appropriate buffing compounds. For precious metals such as gold and silver, buff with red jeweler's rouge; for nickel, chrome, stainless steel, and aluminum, use white rouge; to polish brass, copper, and pewter, use brown tripoli.

Lubrication: Most grinders have ball bearings that need no lubrication. However, if yours has oil holes or grease cups, apply the recommended lubricant—sparingly—at least twice a year.

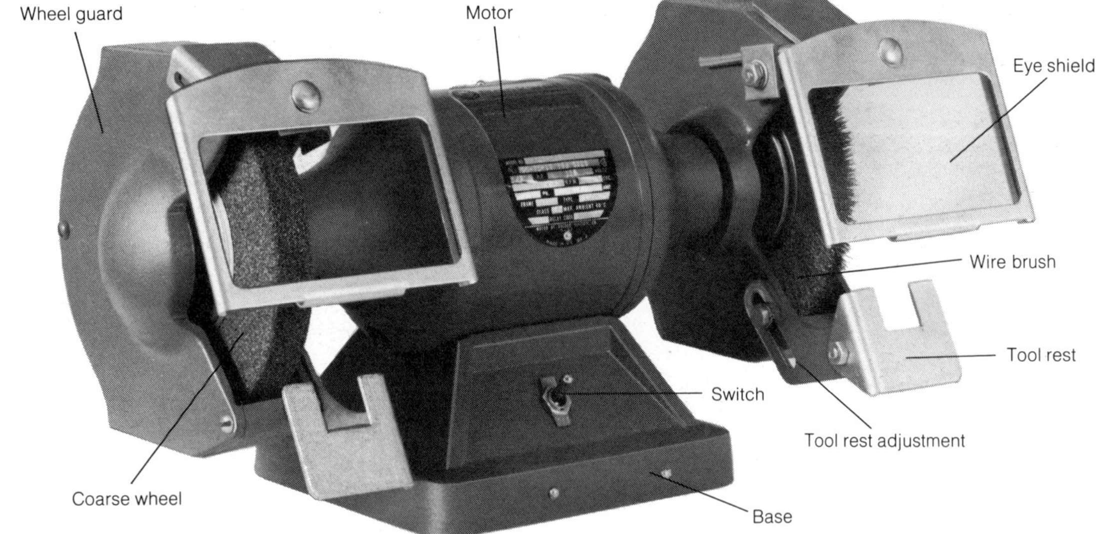

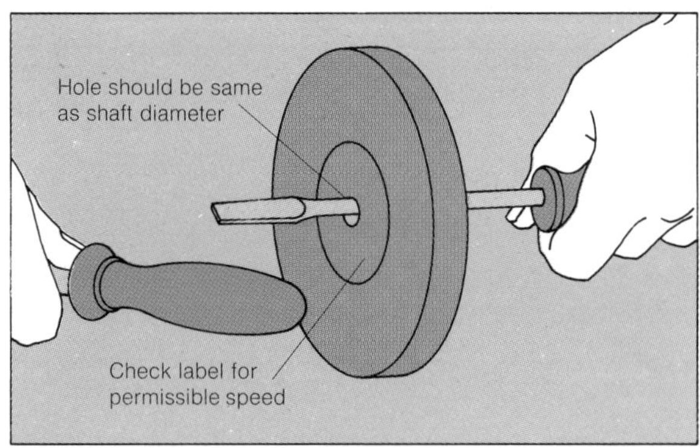

Testing a wheel: Supporting wheel as shown, tap with screwdriver handle 45° on each side of hole. Turn part way and repeat. If you don't get a ringing sound, discard the wheel.

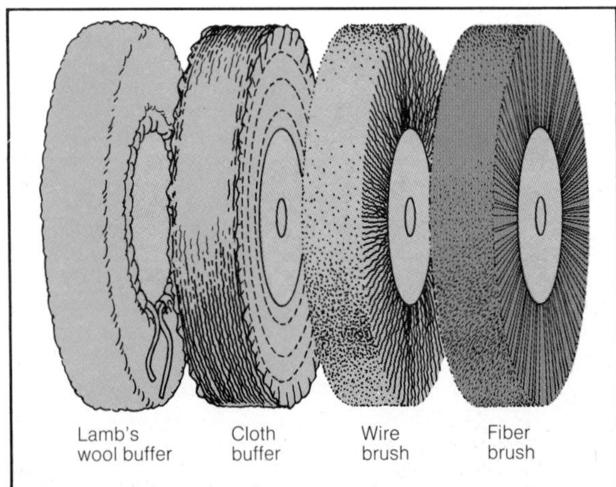

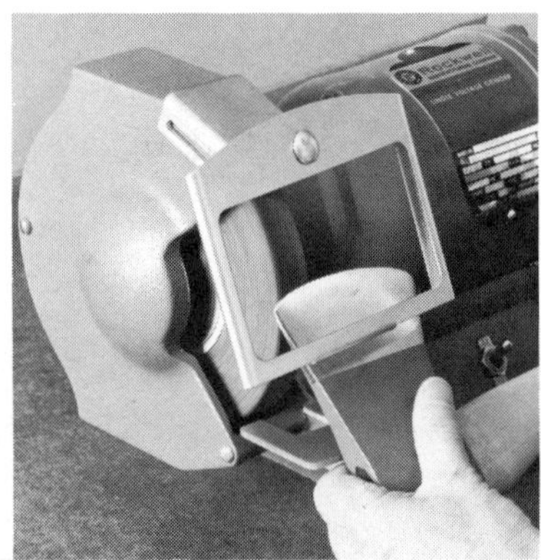

Use the fine stone for sharpening tools such as an ax. Support the ax head on the tool rest, hold firmly. Wear goggles.

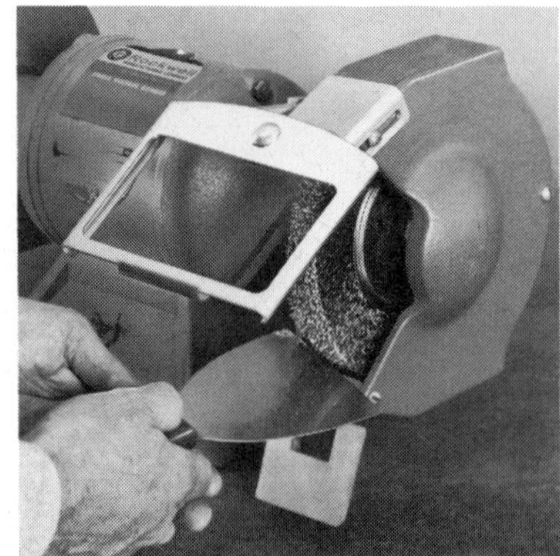

Coarse wire brush does quick job of removing rust from tools. Use fine wire brush to keep tools in mint condition.

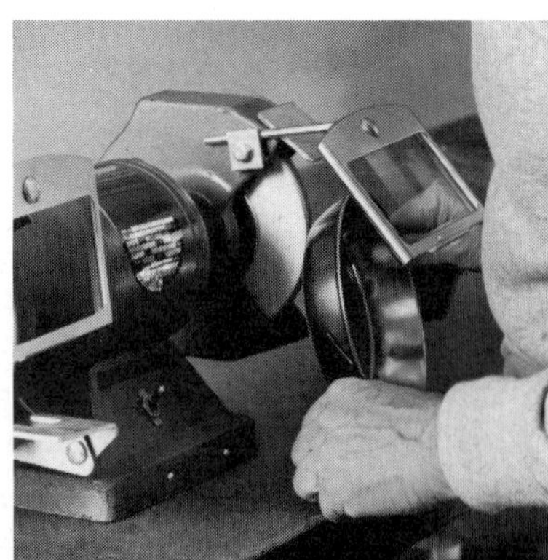

Polishing with the grinder is done with cloth buffing wheel. Charge wheel with polishing compound, then polish.

Combination belt and disk sander

This is a fast-cutting tool that smooths and also trims and shapes. The table at the sanding disk tilts from level to 45 degrees and is slotted for a miter gauge. For perfect fit in cabinetwork, saw parts slightly oversize, and then bring them to precise fit on the sander table, using a coarse belt for major trimming, fine for a final fit. Because the fast-cutting disk sander cuts across the grain, surfaces to be stained or left natural should get their final sanding parallel to the grain on the belt sander. The convex surface where the belt runs over the end rollers can do external curve sanding. The entire belt assembly tilts upward to a vertical position for convenience in using the sander on bulky work.

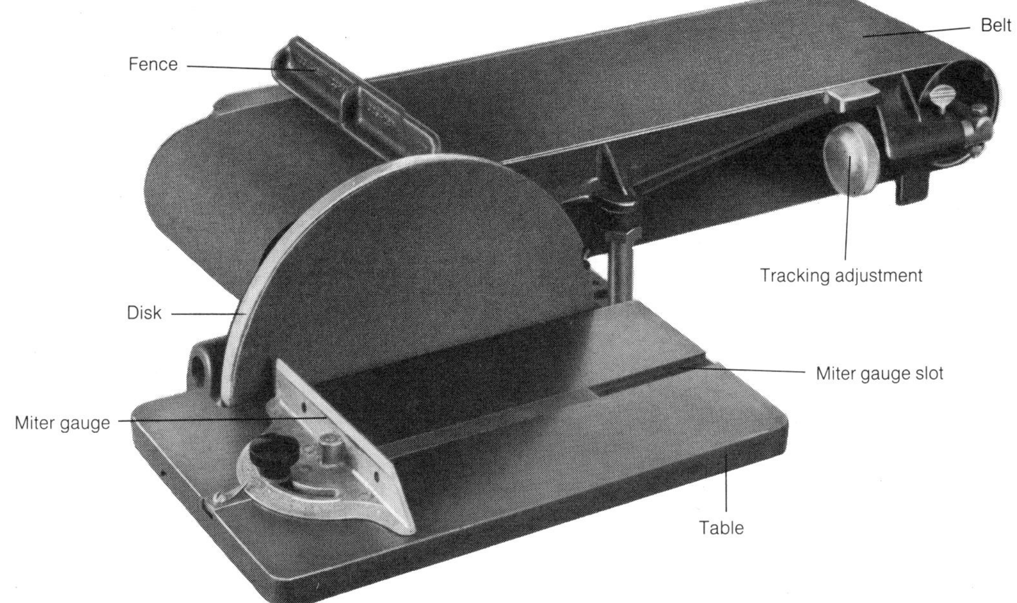

Sanding on the disk can be done freehand. Hold the work so that the rotating disk forces it down toward the table.

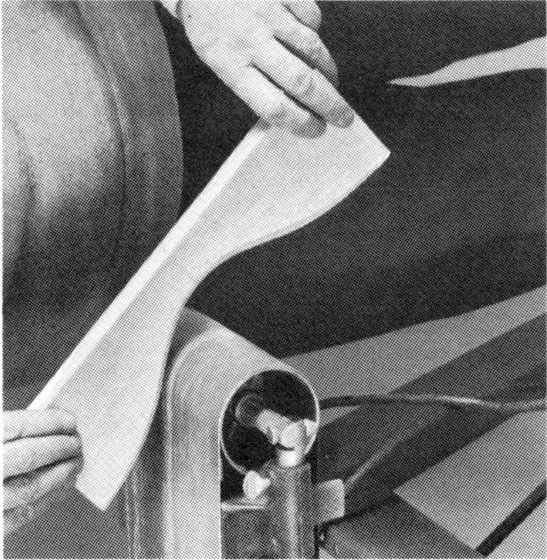

External curves can be sanded on the rounded area of the belt where it passes over the pulley. Keep the work moving.

When sanding flat areas on belt sander, keep work at slight angle to belt. Remove fence to sand work wider than belt.

Sander-grinder

With the proper belt, this tool can sand, grind, sharpen, and polish almost any material. Its belts cut faster and operate cooler than regular grinding wheels. To sand internal surfaces, remove belt from pulleys and pass it through inside of work.

Internal sanding can be done by passing the belt through the work. A system of movable pulleys and idlers permits this sanding operation.

Small pieces can be sanded comfortably on the sander-grinder as its belt is only 1 in. wide. Seven types of belts, from coarse to extra fine, are made for use on this machine.

How to use a bench saw

Today's workshop bench saws (also referred to as table saws or circular saws) range from 7½ to 10 inches in blade diameter, giving them a cutting depth of 1½ to 3⅜ inches. A popular size for average use is 8 inches.

Bench saws can cut long lengths at any width set by the fence, crosscut at any angle set on the miter gauge, and make bevel cuts when the blade is tilted. The blade can be raised or lowered to cut to any depth for grooving. A dado head, used in place of the saw blade, can cut grooves up to ¾-inch wide in a single pass.

The work is always fed to the saw from the front of the table. All settings, such as width, cutting depth, bevel, or miter gauge angle, should be made with the cord unplugged. To make the cut, start the saw and let it reach full speed before pushing in the work. Do not feed the work too fast as it will slow the blade noticeably. (The blade normally slows somewhat while cutting.)

Safety: Use the guard for all types of work that permit its use. The guard must be removed for such operations as grooving, coving, and dadoing, and for edge-cutting in wide stock. The photographs on this page have been taken with the guard removed so the operations they show could be seen more clearly. In addition to the guard, it is wise to use goggles when operating the saw. Always stand to one side of the blade, never directly in front of it. Remove your tie and make sure sleeves are snug around your wrists, or else roll them up.

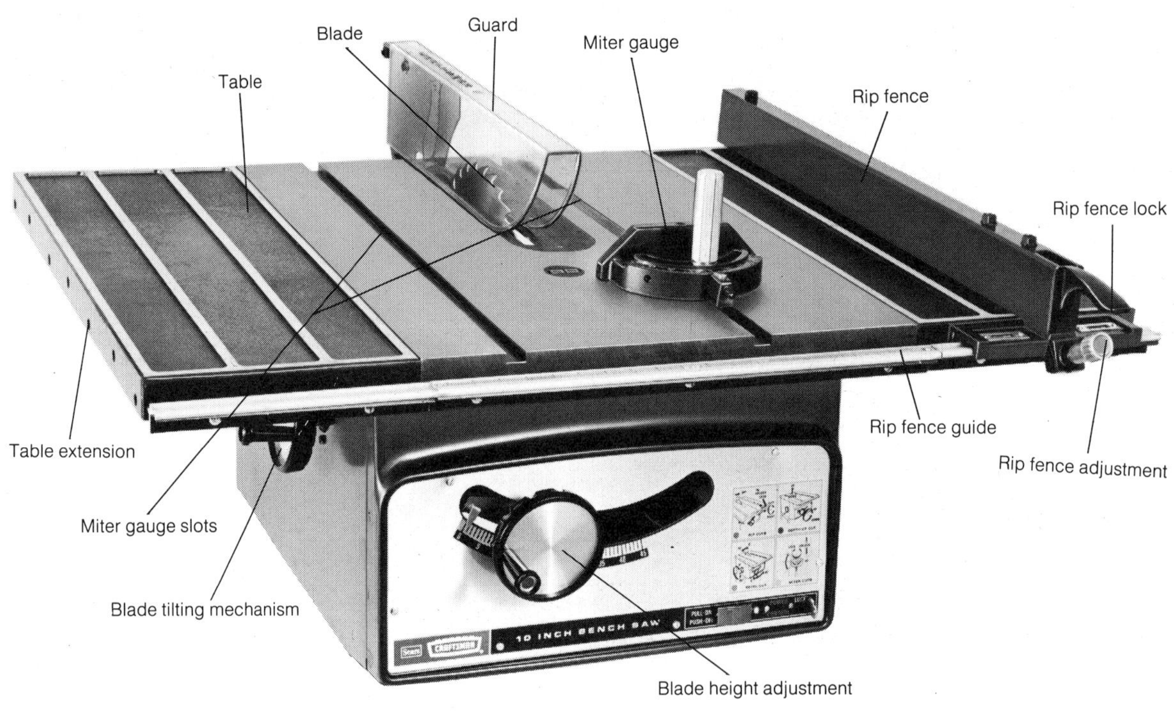

Bench saw is an ideal tool for the workshop with large floor area. Keep the table surface waxed so work will move smoothly into the blade.

Ripping: Set the fence for the desired width and hold the work against the fence as you push it through the saw. Do not force it.

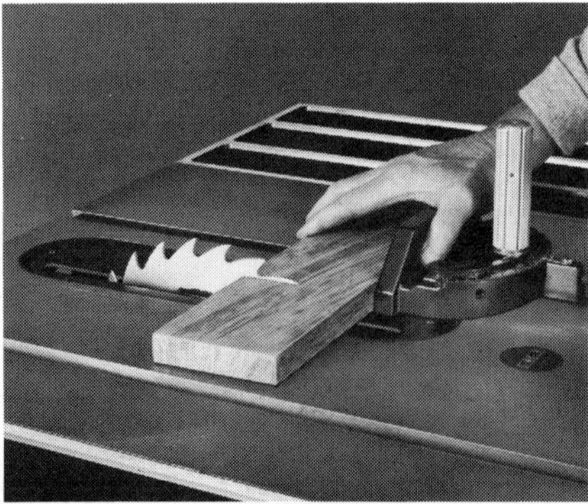

Crosscutting: Set the gauge at the desired angle (in this case 90°), hold the work firmly against the gauge, feed slowly.

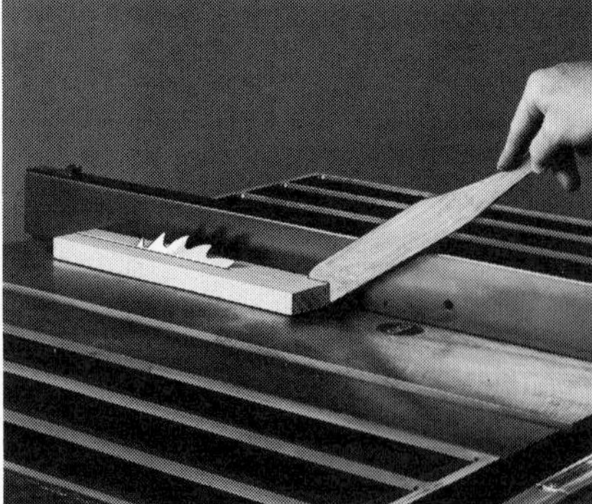

When ripping narrow work, always use a push stick, not your fingers, to feed the work into and through the saw blade.

Bevel cut is made by tilting the table to the desired angle. A scale at the tilting mechanism is marked off in degrees.

How to use a radial arm saw

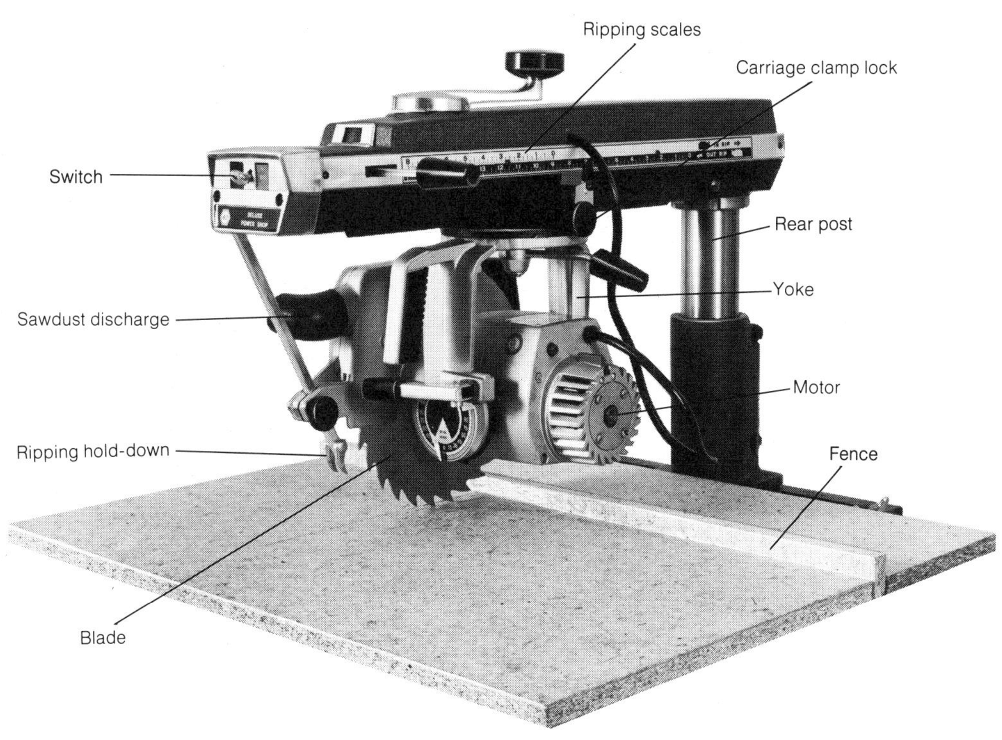

Radial arm saw is well suited for smaller workshops. Excellent for crosscutting; can also rip cut. Saw blade can be replaced by an abrasive wheel for grinding applications.

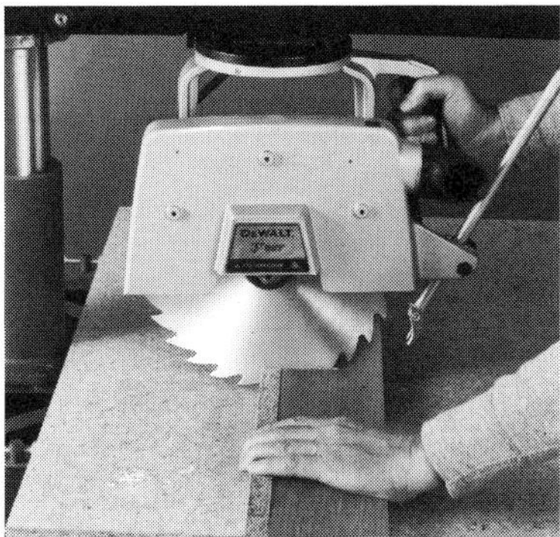

In crosscutting, the saw-motor unit is moved toward and across the work. Work is held against the fence.

To rip, the saw-motor is locked parallel to the fence at the desired distance and work is pushed through saw.

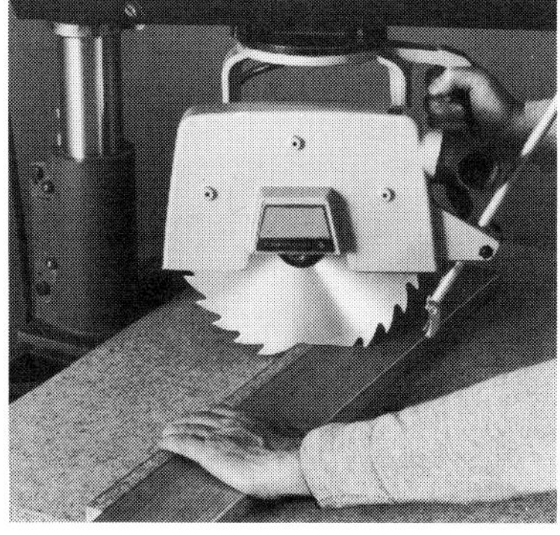

For an angle cut, the saw-motor is set at desired angle, work is held against fence, and saw is pulled across work.

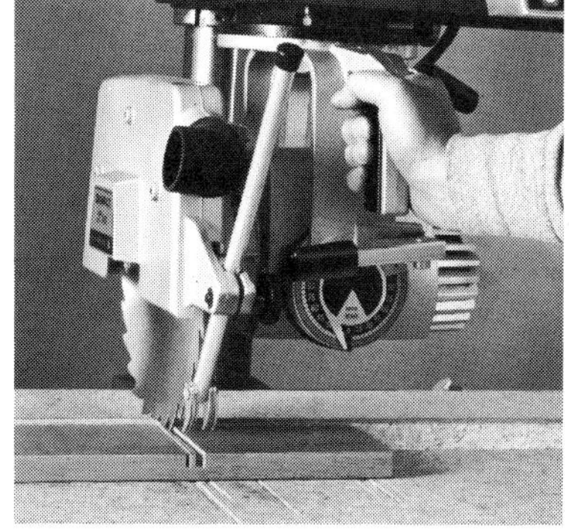

Decorative grooves are produced by raising blade to make a shallow cut. Dado cut is made with repeated passes.

The radial arm saw does much the same work as the bench saw but cuts from above the work instead of from below. In crosscutting, the radial arm saw has a great advantage over the bench saw. The work is stationary, in fact it can be clamped to the table, while the saw-motor unit moves across the work. This eliminates the awkward procedure of pushing long pieces of lumber across the saw table. The same is true of miter and angle cutting. In ripping, the saw-motor unit is locked parallel to the guide fence, and the work is pushed through the saw, the same as in bench-saw ripping.

Caution: When ripping on the radial arm saw, always push the work into the saw from the direction that is indicated on the saw guard, never from the rear.

In cutting completely through the work, the saw blade cuts slightly into the saw table surface (it is nonmetallic, so no harm is done to the blade). This table surface can be replaced when necessary.

The saw-motor unit can be moved in or out along the radial arm in relation to the upright column. The arm can be swung to any desired angle (for mitering or angle cutting), after which the entire assembly is locked in position. As the blade teeth travel away from the table front when crosscutting, the work is set firmly against the replaceable wood fence at the back of the table, and is held there by hand and saw action. In completing a cut, the blade passes through the fence. But as most crosscuts and 45-degree miter cuts follow the same paths, the blade passes through the fence at the original cuts, so that fence replacement is required only at long intervals. Replace the fence with wood the same thickness as the original.

Cutting depth is adjusted by raising the blade instead of lowering it, as on a bench saw. For dado work, remove the blade and install a dado head. For beveling, the saw-motor unit is tipped to the desired angle and locked. The radial arm saw gives the user a clear view of grooving and dado cuts that are concealed by the bench saw. However, because of its more complex design, the radial arm saw is usually higher in price.

Jigsaw and shaper

How to use the jigsaw

The jigsaw (also called the scroll saw) is a tool whose cutting blade moves in a reciprocating motion—up and down. With different blades, it can make straight and curved cuts in wood, light metal, and plastic. Capable of very small radius cuts, the tool is well suited for model and filigree work. The capacity of the saw is determined by the distance from the blade to the post at the rear.

Use only light pressure in moving the work into the blade, which normally faces forward. For long rip cuts, the blade can be mounted to face sideways. Set the rip fence for the required width. If the saw has no fence, you can make one by clamping a straight length of wood to the table. Use the slimmest blades (often called "jeweler's blades") for very small radius cuts. For fast cutting and gradual curves, use the heavier saber blades. Some saws can also use small machine files for rapid filing. To bevel, simply tilt the table to the desired angle and lock it in place.

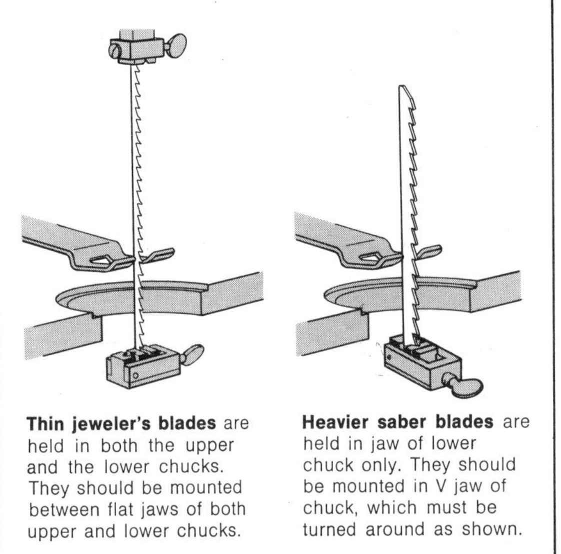

Thin jeweler's blades are held in both the upper and the lower chucks. They should be mounted between flat jaws of both upper and lower chucks.

Heavier saber blades are held in jaw of lower chuck only. They should be mounted in V jaw of chuck, which must be turned around as shown.

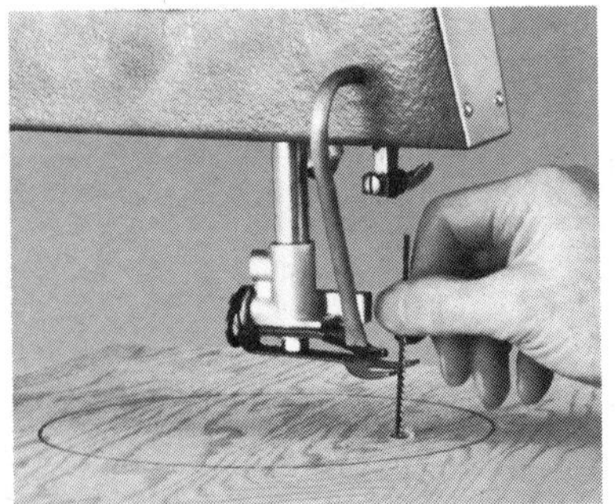

To cut an internal circle, drill a starting hole, remove the blade, pass it through the hole and replace blade.

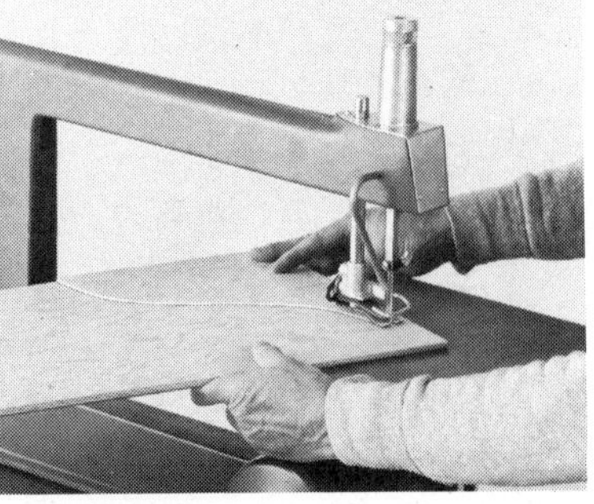

Cutting scrolls is an easy job for the jigsaw. Use a narrow blade for tight curves, wide blade for sweeping curves.

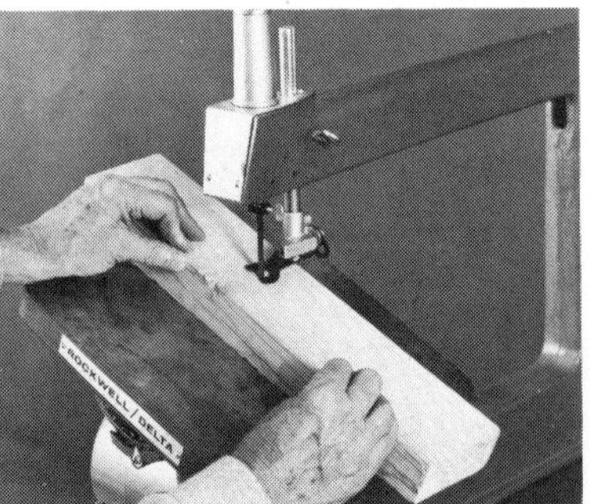

A 2 x 4 is about the maximum thickness the jigsaw can cut. The table can be tilted for cutting work at an angle.

Using the shaper

The shaper does work similar to that done by a router. Instead of the machine moving over the work, however, as with the router, the work is passed over the machine. Also, the shaper has greater capacity and power and is capable of many more intricate cuts. With a shaper, you can make your own molding, beading, and decorative cuts in wood, limited only by the number of cutters you have and your imagination. It is a high-speed machine—its spindle revolves at 10,000 rpm—so treat it with respect.

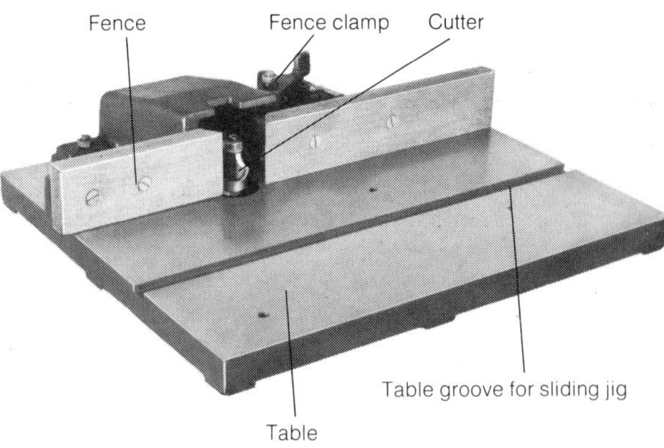

Making cove cut along side of board. Cutter is mounted on spindle and locked in place. Work is fed against the rotation of the cutter and at the same time pushed against fence.

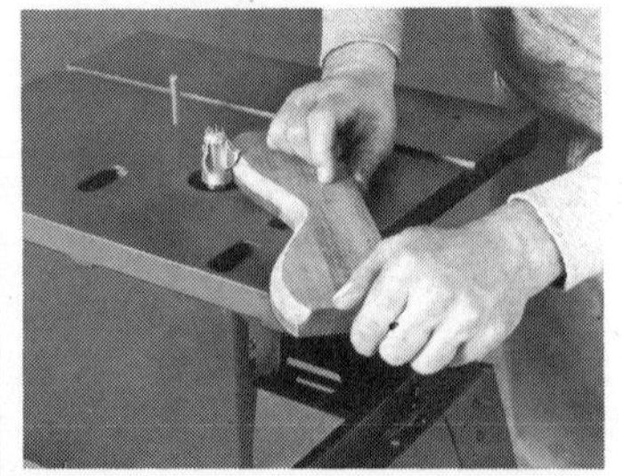

Work which cannot be shaped against the fence can usually be shaped by guiding it against a collar below the cutter. The only drawback is that the collar may slightly burn or score work if passed too slowly.

How to use a band saw

The fast-cutting band saw utilizes a flexible steel blade, in the form of a continuous loop, that runs over two rubber-tired wheels. Its size is determined by the diameter of the wheels.

To use the saw, feed the work into the blade at the point where it passes through the table. (A slot running to the table's edge permits blade removal and replacement.) For straight, fast cutting, use a wide, coarse-toothed blade. For curve cutting, use a narrower blade, the width depending on the radius you want to cut. A ⅜-inch wide blade can cut a 1-inch radius, though the slightly narrower ¼-inch blade provides a safety margin.

When operating the saw, set the upper blade guide about ¼ to ½ inch above the work. The sliding blade guide supports the blade as the work is pressed against it. It also tends to act as a guard against accidental hand contact with the blade. Only finger pressure is needed to feed the work through a sharp blade. Never use a dull blade. The extra pressure required makes accidental slips of the hand more likely. As band-saw blades are not expensive, and stay sharp a long time, it's practical to discard dull ones.

Most band saws are equipped with a tilting table for beveling and a fence for ripping. The fence should only be used with a wide blade; a narrow blade will tend to cut into the softer areas of the wood and thus cause wandering. The space between the blade and the upright arm often dictates the way work can be cut. Sometimes it is necessary to turn the work upside down to make certain parts of a cut. If you have a long cut in one direction, and a short one in another, it's best to make the short cut first. The work can then be easily backed out of the blade, and you will be in a position to start the long cut from the most practical point.

Upper wheel guard
Sliding blade guard
Ball bearing blade support
Blade guides
Blade
Arm
Blade slot
Table
Table insert
Miter gauge groove
Lower wheel guard

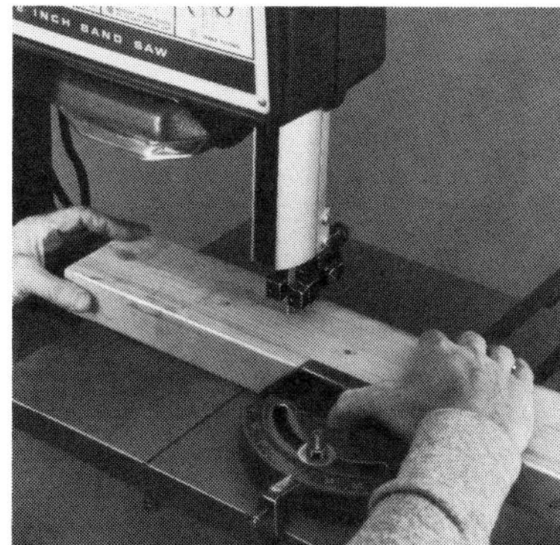

Crosscutting on the band saw with a miter gauge. Most cutting on the saw is done freehand, following a line.

Making a long rip cut: Work is guided into saw to follow a pencil line. Fence is recommended only with wide blade.

Cutting scallops: Cutting out short sections first will make it easier to back work out of the blade.

To cut a disk, start at the edge and cut into the guide line. Diameter is limited by distance to the post.

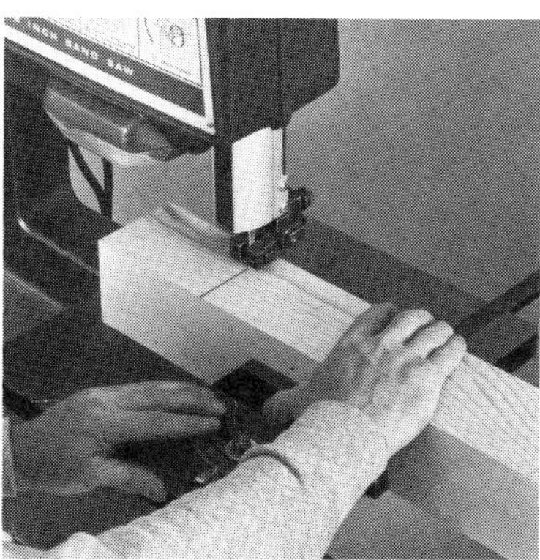

Band saw is capable of cutting wood up to 6 in. thick. Table can be tilted to make bevel cuts up to 45°.

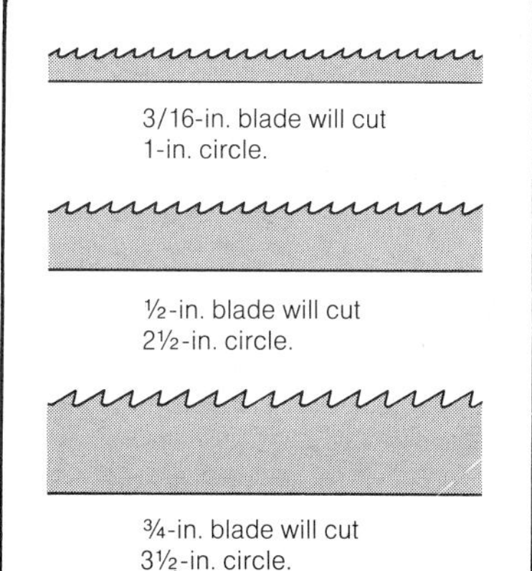

Adjusting and using a jointer

The jointer planes edges and surfaces of lumber by means of a 3-bladed cylindrical cutter that revolves at high speed between the tool's front and rear tables. Table heights are adjustable. The rear table (if adjustable) should be set and locked at the same height as the cutter blades and not be changed until required by cutter sharpening or for special work.

The depth of cut is established by lowering the front table to the required depth. To make a bevel cut, tilt the fence and lock it.

To plane an edge, hold the work firmly on the front table and against the fence with both hands, keeping hands over the table, not the cutter area. As soon as the first part of the work passes over the cutter, use your left hand to hold it down firmly on the rear table, while your right hand feeds the work into the cutter. Keep the work pressed against the fence as you move it along. **Note:** Guard has been removed in photos for the sake of clarity.

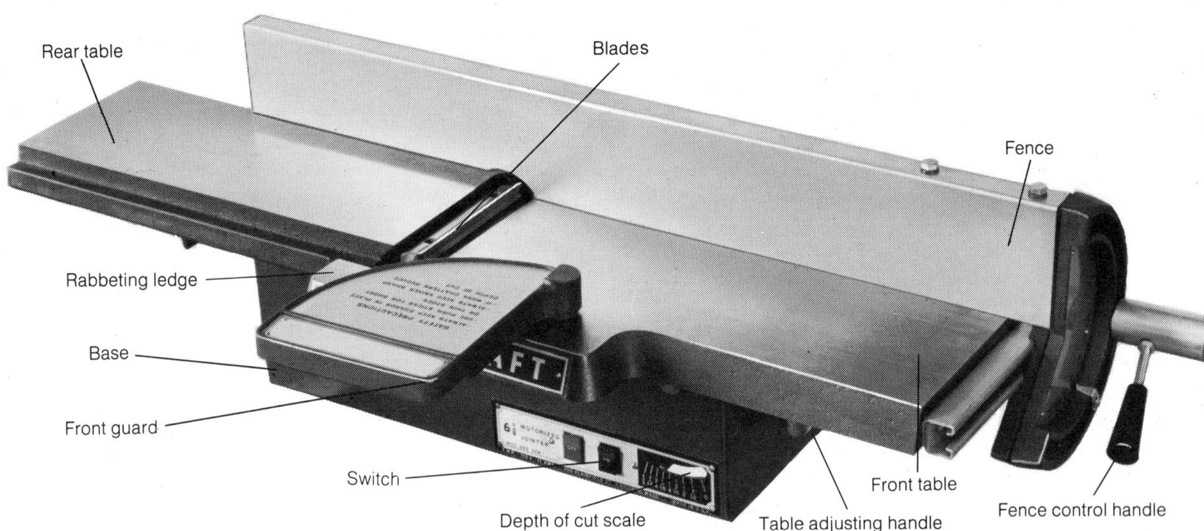

Adjusting rear table

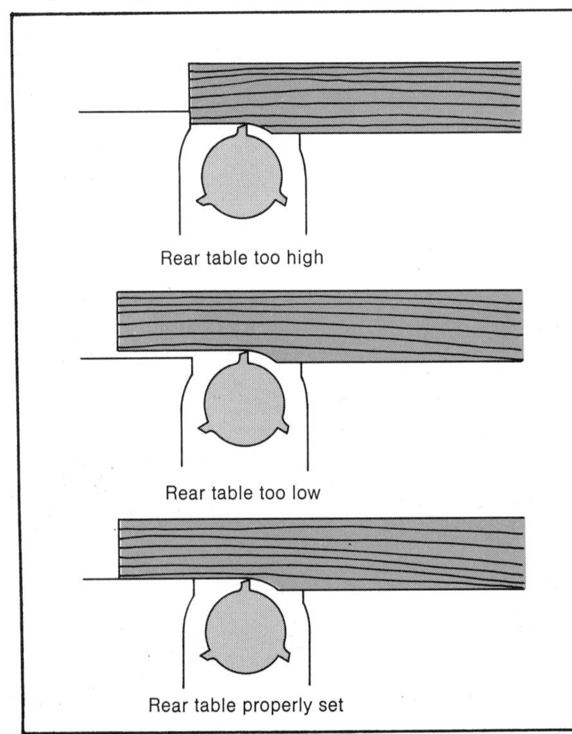

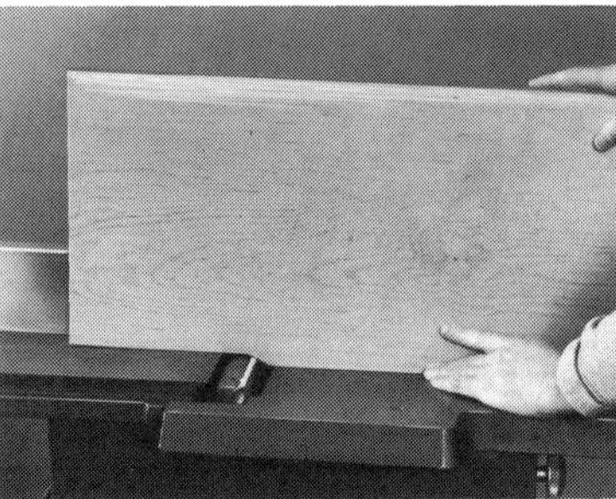

Planing the edge of a board: The drop of the front table is equal to the amount of wood to be removed.

Planing end grain: Short cut is made at end, work is reversed and finish cut made. This eliminates splintering.

To make a bevel cut, fence is tilted and locked at desired angle. Press work firmly against fence of jointer.

A deep rabbet cut may require several passes across the cutters to achieve the required depth of cut.

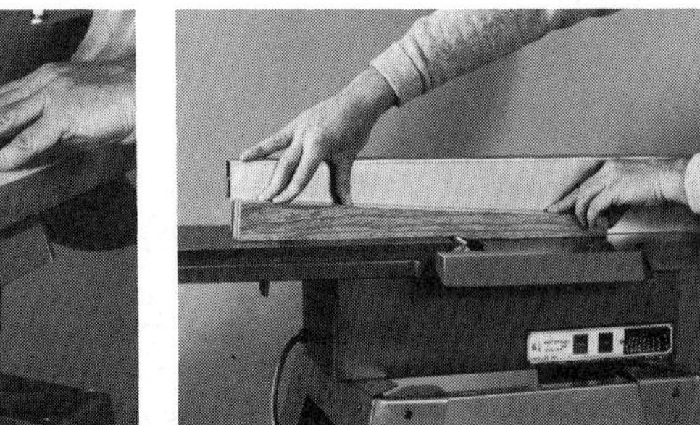

Planing to a taper is a useful jointer operation. The front table is lowered to the necessary depth of the cut.

Narrow or thin stock should always be pushed through the cutting area with a push stick, never with the fingers.

Adjusting and using a lathe

The lathe produces round forms by spinning the wood between its centers while the operator shapes it with various chisels and gouges pressed against the wood. Maximum turning diameter depends on the distance from spindle centers to bed of lathe. To turn a long object, find the approximate center at each end and mount it on the spur center supplied with the lathe. This center fits into and is turned by the motor-driven headstock spindle at the left end of the lathe. The other end of the work is supported by a cup center whose point is cranked into the wood by the tailstock feed handle. Center acts as support and bearing, must be oiled before turning begins.

Set the tool rest about ⅛ inch from the work. With the lathe at low speed, rough the wood to round form with a gouge. Start about 2 inches from the tailstock end. Repeat, working toward and finally off the headstock end. After roughing to shape, increase lathe speed to from 2400 to 2800 rpm (for diameters to 2 inches) and finish with tools to suit the shape. To shape a shallow form such as a bowl, screw the wood to a faceplate and mount this in turn to the headstock spindle. No cup center needed.
Safety: Always use goggles, remove your tie, wear snug-fitting sleeves or roll them up and stand to one side when turning on the motor.

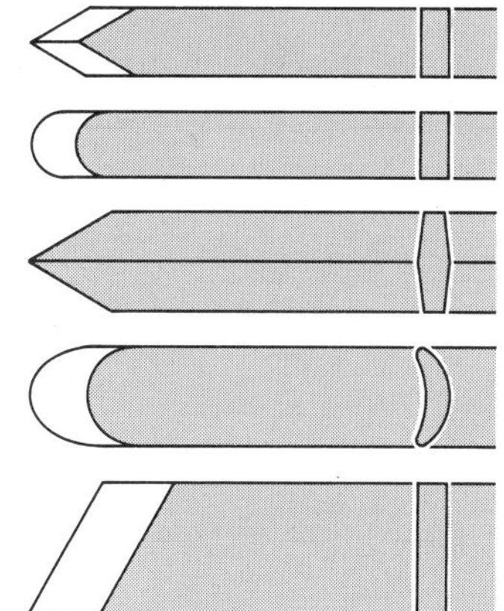

Spear chisel: Used where the shape fits the contour of the work.

Round nose chisel: Used for scraping cuts and where shape fits work.

Parting tool: For cutting off work and making straight cuts.

Gouge: For roughing work to shape and cove cutting.

Skew chisel: Used for smoothing cylinders and cutting shoulders.

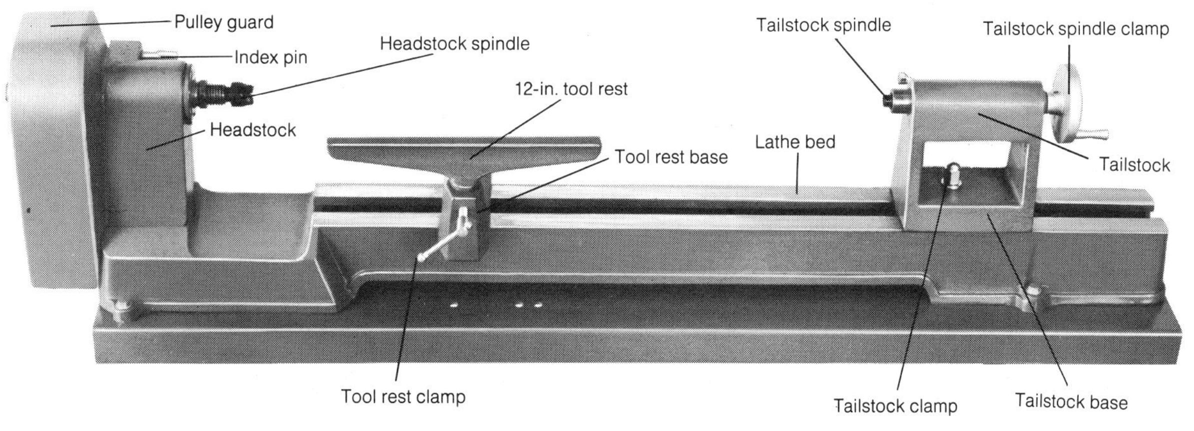

Lathe speed guide

Size of wood	First cut	Shaping cut	Finishing cut
Up to 2″	900	2500	4200
2–4″	800	2300	3300
4–6″	650	1800	2300
6–8″	600	1200	1800
8–10″	400	900	1000
10″+	300	600	600

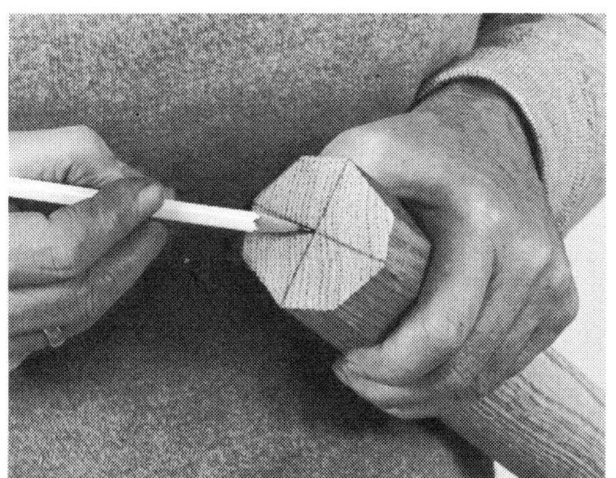

Locate the center of the work to be turned by drawing intersecting lines. Then mark the exact center with a punch or an awl.

Rough turning the central area of a cylinder. Tool rest should be ⅛ in. from work and ⅛ in. above the centerline.

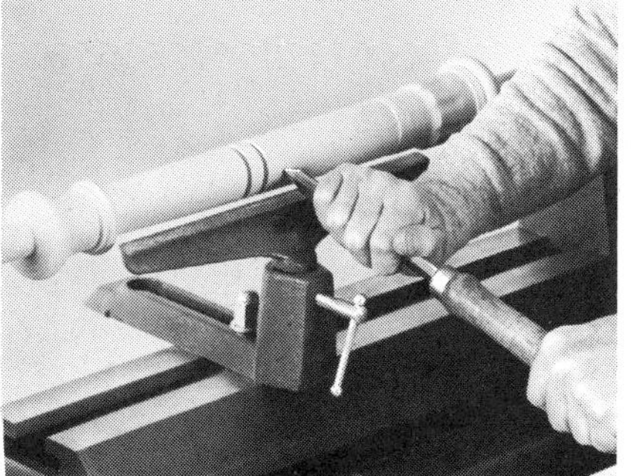

The parting tool is simply pushed into the work. Keep the handle low and raise it as the work diameter decreases.

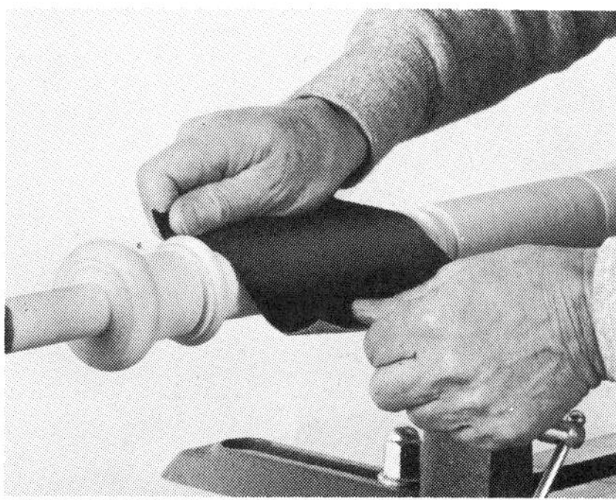

Sanding on the lathe is a pleasure. Just hold the sandpaper against the spinning work. Keep sandpaper moving back and forth.

Drill press

How to use a drill press

The drill press is the No. 2 stationary power tool in the home shop (the first is the bench or radial arm saw). It can drill round holes, or even square ones at any angle or to a pre-set depth in wood, metal, and plastic. The size of a drill press is based on the diameter of the circle through which the tool can drill a center hole.

To drill a hole at an angle, clamp the work to the drill press table and then tilt and lock the table to the desired angle. Always make sure that you have a supporting block of wood under the work to be drilled to avoid marring the drill press table and also to prevent splintering as the bit passes through the work. The drill press table should always be raised to bring the work as close as possible to the drill bit. In this way, it is possible to utilize fully the entire length of the drill.

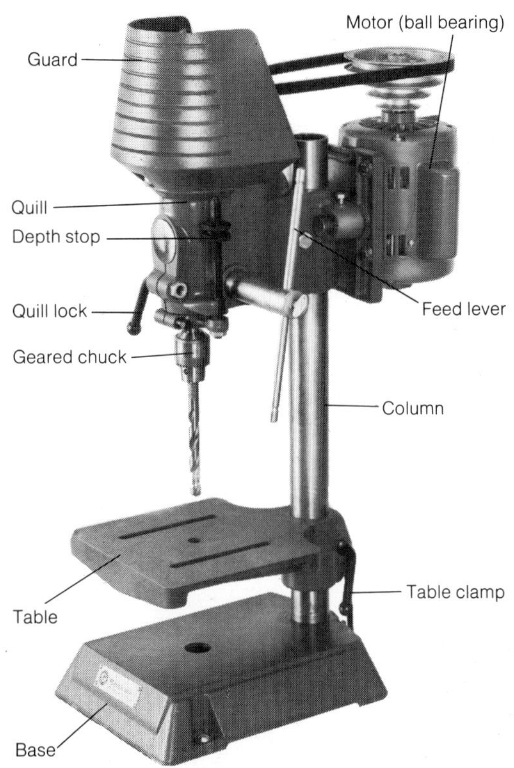

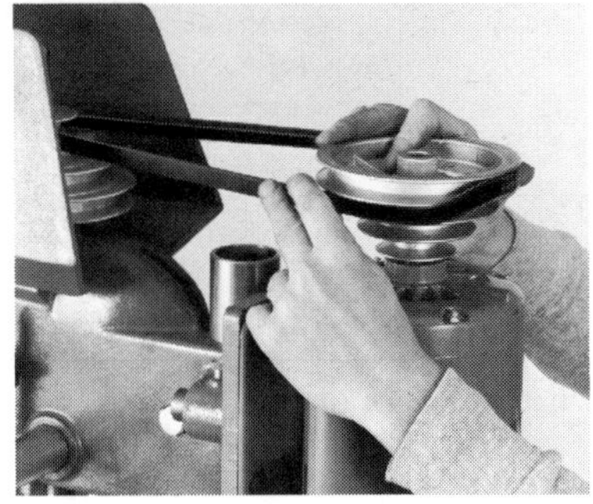

Adjust the belt for the proper drilling speed. Always use low speeds for drilling large holes in wood and metal.

When drilling a hole in metal, clamp the work to the drill press table and support it with a piece of scrap wood.

Use low speed when drilling holes larger than ½ in. in diameter. Clamp the work and use bit without a screw tip.

Attachments and jigs

Fly cutter is used to drill large diameter holes. Be sure cutter is locked in place before turning on power.

Drill press vise is a handy accessory for holding round or irregular work. Punch a starting mark in round work.

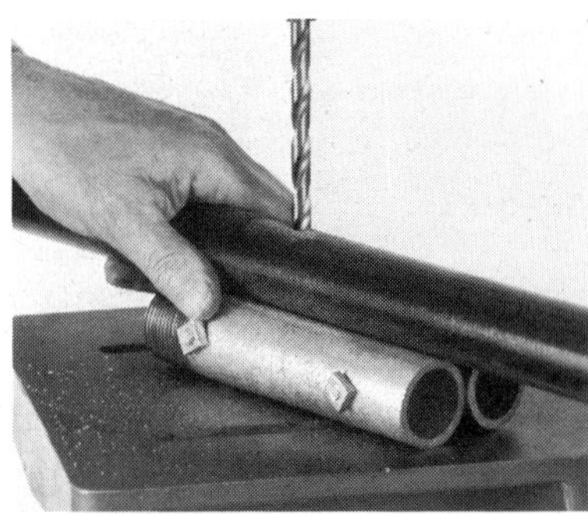

In an emergency you can make a pipe-holding jig by bolting together two short lengths of ¾-in. pipe.

Hole saw is used to cut holes from ¾ to 2½ in. wide in wood or metal; can cut through work ¾ in. thick.

Countersinking on the drill press is done with a special bit. Always adjust the stop to limit countersinking depth.

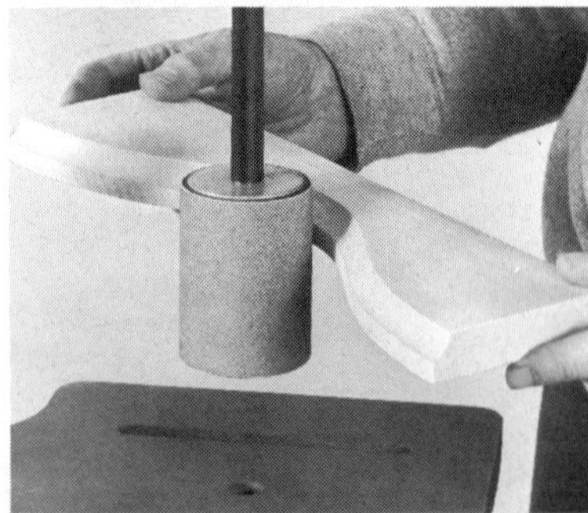

Drum sanding on the drill press. Make sure that shaft of sander is firmly locked before turning on power.

section 3:

Fasteners, hardware, and adhesives

In home repair and improvement, fasteners, hardware, and adhesives are critically important. The crucial question in judging any project is: How well does it work? And your choice of fasteners, hardware, and adhesives can make the difference between failure and success. This section explains these materials from every standpoint: The factors you must consider in making a selection; the alternatives you can choose; the procedures that you should follow to obtain a reliable result.

contents

Nail types and uses

General-purpose and woodworking nails

Common nail: General-purpose heavy-duty type used in construction and rough work. Large head won't pull through (see detail, right).

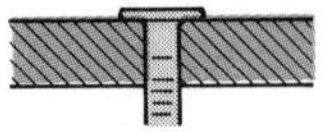

Finishing nail: Used on trim and cabinetwork where nailheads must be concealed. Head is sunk and then filled over.

Casing nail: Similar to finishing nail but heavier. Used for trim where strength and concealment (see detail) are required.

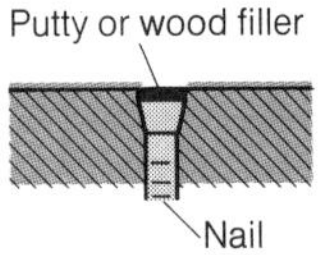

Putty or wood filler

Nail

Cut flooring nail: Has rectangular cross section and a blunt tip. Used to blind-nail flooring through edges without splitting.

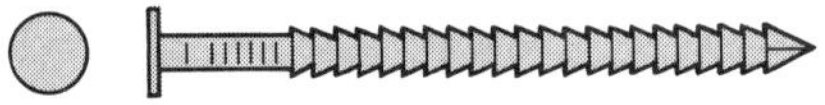

Annular ring nail: Has sharp-edged ridges that lock into wood fibers and greatly increase holding power.

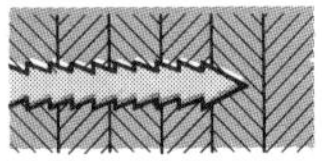

Spiral nails: Used in flooring to assure a tight and squeak-proof joining. Nail tends to turn into the wood like a screw as it is driven home.

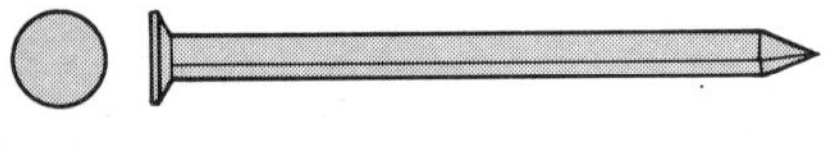

Square-shank concrete nail: Similar to round types used to fasten furring strips and brackets to concrete walls and floors.

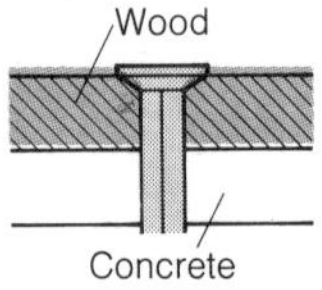

Wood

Concrete

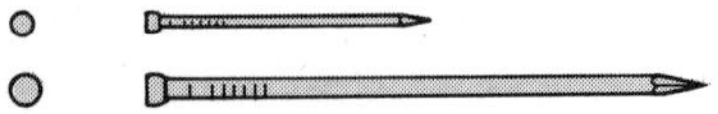

Common brads: Used for nailing parquet flooring to subfloor, attaching molding to walls and furniture. Brads are usually sunk and filled.

Tacks: Made in cut or round form; used to fasten carpet or fabric to wood, and for similar light fastening jobs.

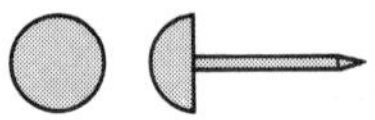

Upholstery nails: Made with both ornamental and colored heads; used to fasten upholstery where fastenings will show.

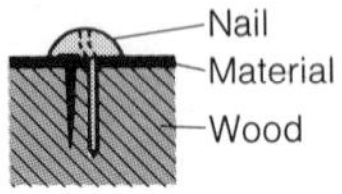

Nail

Material

Wood

Roofing nail: Has large head, is usually galvanized. Used to hold composition roofings; design resists pull-through.

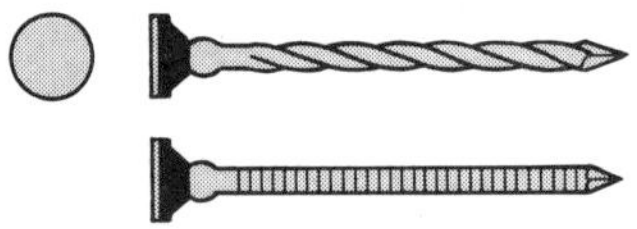

Sealing roofing nails: Have lead or plastic washer under head to provide watertight seal; used on metal roofing.

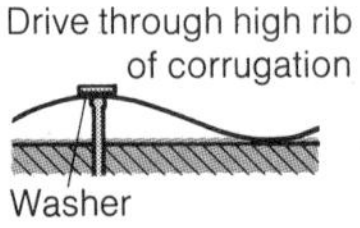

Drive through high rib of corrugation

Washer

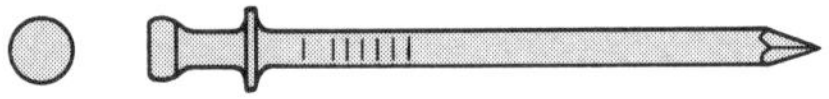

Duplex head nail: Can be driven tight against lower head, with upper head projecting for removal; for temporary work.

Barbed dowel pin: Has many purposes, such as aligning parts, serving as pivot, permitting disassembly or separation.

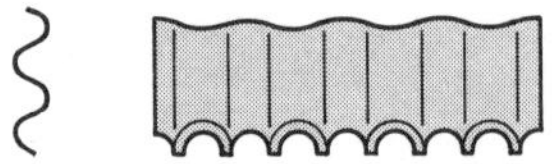

Corrugated fastener: Used in making light-duty miter joints, such as in screens and large picture frames. Drive it across joint.

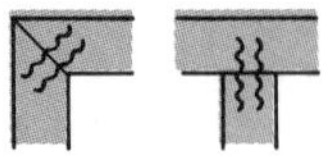

Staples: Made in many forms to hold wire fencing, bell wire, electric cable, screening; available with insulated shoulders.

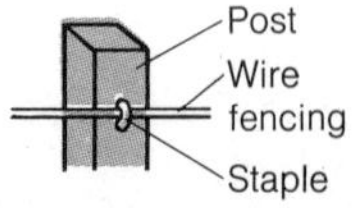

Post

Wire fencing

Staple

Nail sizes

Nail length is designated in inches and also by "penny" size, a term which originally related to the price per hundred, but now signifies only length. Nails are made in a wide range of lengths and types. Common nails, for example, are available in lengths from 1 inch, or 2 penny (abbreviated 2d), to 6 inches, or 60 penny.

Except in some special-purpose types, nail diameter increases with length; a 6-inch common nail is nearly four times the diameter of a 1-inch nail. Special-purpose nails, however, may come in only one size—as flooring brads do, for example—or in several lengths but only a single diameter, as some shingle nails do, depending on their purpose.

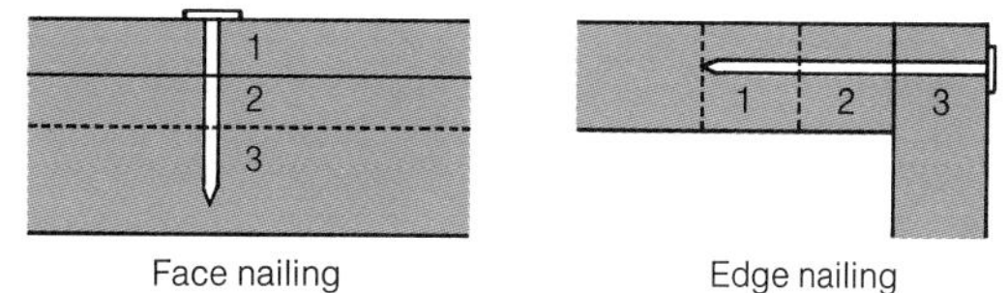

Face nailing Edge nailing

Driving nails: Nails should be driven, as a rule, through the thinner piece of wood into the thicker one, and the nail should be three times as long as the thickness of the thin piece through which it passes. Two-thirds of the nail will then be in the thicker piece for maximum holding power.

To get the best holding power from nails, drive them at angles, slanting toward or away from each other, so they cannot pull out without bending. In some cases, you can drive them through both pieces and bend (clinch) the protruding ends flat against the wood. You also get greater holding power from nails with spiral shafts or annular rings; in many, the holding power approximates the grip of screws.

Nailheads are another part of the selection story. Large heads hold best because they spread the load over a wider area, resisting pull-through. The heads of finishing nails, conversely, pull through wood quite readily. This is sometimes a welcome weakness, however, because it permits trim and cabinetwork to be disassembled by pulling through the nailheads, with a minimum of surface marring.

Penny nail gauge

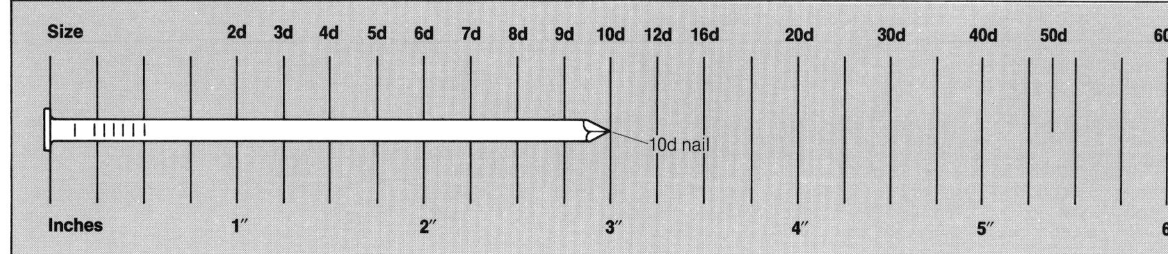

A nail's penny rating, originally its price per hundred, is now used as a measure of length. Since long nails were higher priced than short ones, they had a higher penny rating—as they still do. The penny abbreviation "d" (10d, for example, designates a 3-inch nail) derives from the denarius, an early Roman coin. Since the diameter of most widely used nail types increases with the length, the length designation, whether in inches or pennies, implies overall size and weight.

Quantity buying

Where nails will be regularly spaced, as in roofing and laying floors, you can avoid quantity errors in buying if you know the number per pound in the size required. The chart at the right provides the per-pound figures for some of the more widely used nail types. Your hardware dealer can usually give you the count on other types that he carries in stock. To avoid running short, allow about 10 percent more than you expect to need for the job, and add any surplus to your workshop assortment.

Metals and surfaces of special-purpose nails may vary with the application. Use copper and aluminum nails, for example, where there is a need to eliminate rust and corrosion. Nails for such applications as roofing and boat building are made in copper, brass, bronze, monel, stainless steel, and galvanized, the choice depending on the intended use. If desired types are not in stock, they can usually be ordered.

Approximate number of nails in a pound — *Nonstandard sizes—must be specially ordered

Length of nail in inches	⅞	1	1¼	1½	1¾	2	2¼	2½	2¾	3	3¼	3½	4	4½	5	5½	6
Common nail	—	847	543	294	254	167	150	101	92	66	61	47	30	23	17	14	11
Finishing nail	—	1,473*	880	630	535*	288	254*	196	178*	124	113*	93*	65*	—	—	—	—
Spiral flooring nail	—	—	—	—	—	177	158	142	—	—	—	—	—	—	—	—	—
Roofing nail	246	223	189	164	145	—	—	—	—	—	—	—	—	—	—	—	—
Square concrete nail	—	254	202	168	143	125	111	100	91	83	—	—	—	—	—	—	—
Fence staples (bright)	122	106	87	72	61	—	—	—	—	—	—	—	—	—	—	—	—

Nailing tips

Basic procedures

For extensive nailing, use a hammer that feels comfortable when you swing it. And keep it clean—a smudge on the face can be transferred almost indelibly to the work. If you should bend a nail in driving it, place a thin block of scrap wood under the hammer head to protect the work as you start pulling the nail; change to a thicker block to get extra leverage at the finish.

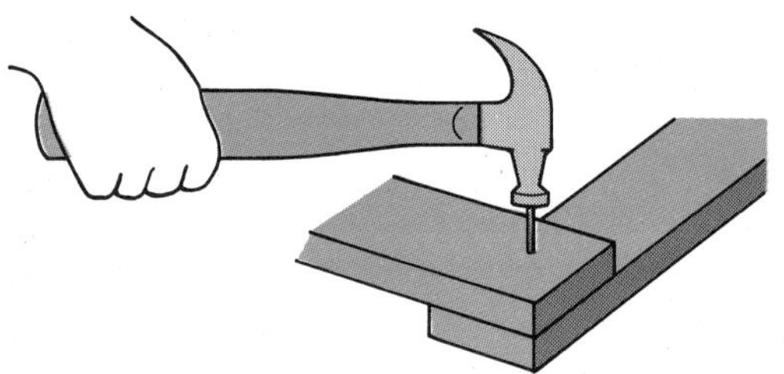

Right way to hold hammer

To drive a nail, hold it upright on the wood between the thumb and forefinger of your left hand. Hold the hammer near the end of the handle with your right hand and tap (don't bang) the nail a few times to drive it just far enough to stand up by itself. With the nail standing up, take your fingers away, and swing the hammer a little harder, but only a little. Don't use really heavy strokes until the nail is about an inch into the wood; a glancing blow can send it ricocheting, with possible injury to you.

If you're driving common nails in rough work, such as house framing, drive the heads in flush with the surface and don't bother to be careful about hammer marks. If you're driving finishing nails in work where appearance counts, stop when the head is just above the surface, and then sink it with a nail set (see illustration). When you work with hardened nails (many modern flooring and special-purpose types are hardened), always wear goggles. Such nails sometimes break instead of bending. The goggles will protect your eyes against flying pieces.

When nails must be driven close to the end of a piece, you can avoid splits any of several ways. You can drill pilot holes slightly smaller than the nails, if some loss of holding power is acceptable. Or you can blunt the nail point by tapping on it with the hammer while the head is on a solid surface. The blunt point shears the wood fibers instead of wedging them apart, reducing the chance of splitting.

Methods of nailing wood to wood

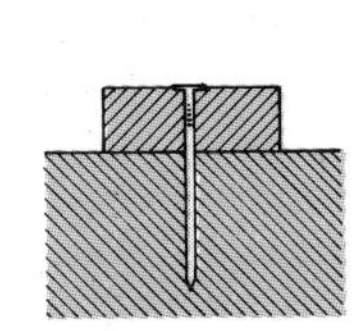

Use nails 2½ to 3 times longer than the thickness of the wood they must hold. Always nail light work to heavy.

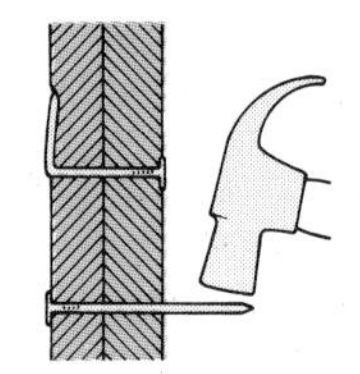

Clinch-nail for strong joints. Drive nails from opposite directions and bend the points into the wood.

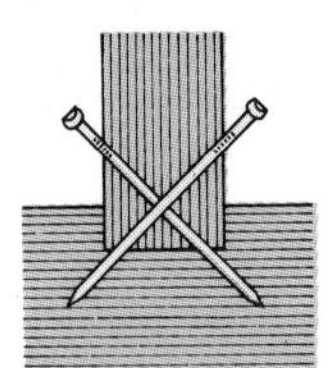

Toenail joints may be butted or recessed, as above. Opposing nails should be offset to pass each other.

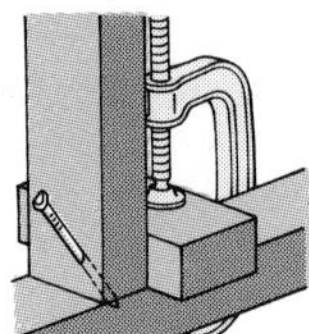

Use a clamp and a block of wood to steady a frame when toenailing. First nail will hold while the second is driven.

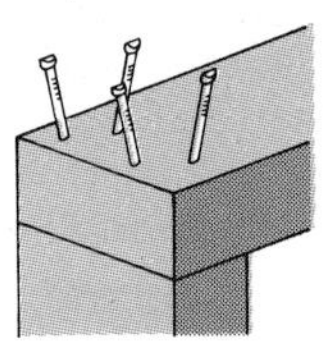

Dovetail nailing is done by driving nails at angles for better grip. Slant nails have hook effect.

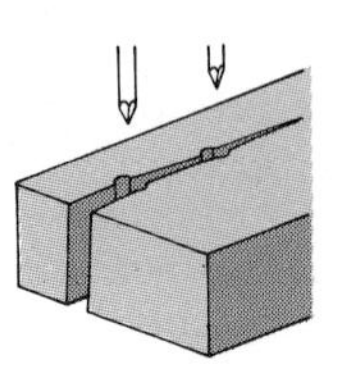

Avoid nailing into the same grain line—this will split the wood. Use blunt nails near the ends.

Split ends can be minimized by cutting wood overlength. Nail it in place before sawing off the excess.

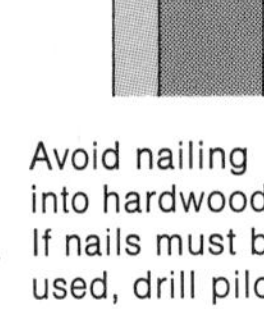

Avoid nailing into hardwood. If nails must be used, drill pilot holes slightly smaller than the nail shank.

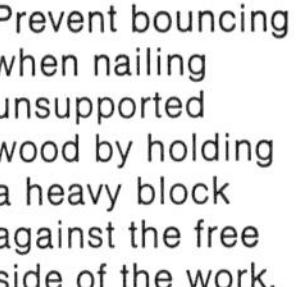

Prevent bouncing when nailing unsupported wood by holding a heavy block against the free side of the work.

Blind-nailing: Chisel up a wood sliver and drive a nail into the recess. Glue the sliver back in position.

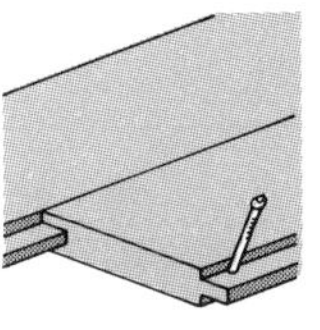

Blind-nail into floorboards by driving through tongue and shoulder. Drive at slight angle as shown.

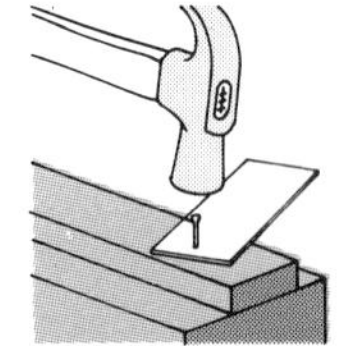

Push small nails and tacks through a thin cardboard holder so that fingers can be kept clear of the hammer.

How to use a nail set

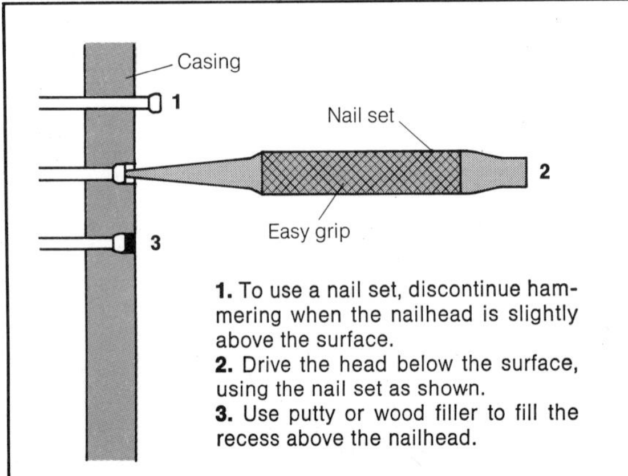

1. To use a nail set, discontinue hammering when the nailhead is slightly above the surface.
2. Drive the head below the surface, using the nail set as shown.
3. Use putty or wood filler to fill the recess above the nailhead.

New nail for wallboard

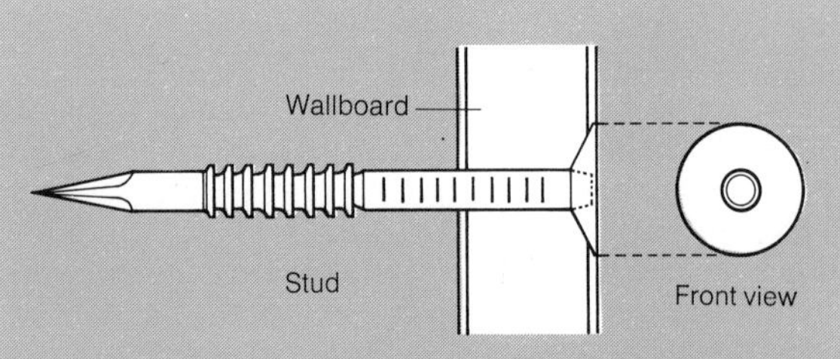

New drywall nail is especially designed to prevent popping. Shank of the nail has annular rings which bite into the wall stud. The head is dish-shaped and drives flush with the wallboard. The indentation in the middle takes the drywall finishing compound. Diameter is slightly smaller than conventional drywall nails.

Selecting the proper nail

Masonry nails are made round, square, and fluted, of hardened and tempered steel. They are often used to fasten framing parts, such as sills, furring, and window and door trim, to masonry and concrete.

The nails can usually be driven directly into concrete block walls and poured concrete floors. Driving into very hard concrete, however, may require a pilot hole. Drill through the part to be fastened and into the masonry to make sure the holes will line up. Most convenient tool for this: A carbide-tipped bit in a power drill. If drill diameter specifications are not available, always use a bit smaller than the nail diameter, so that the nail will be able to bite into the masonry and smooth-surfaced nails will develop maximum holding power.

Use heavy-duty nails for driving into masonry or concrete, without a pilot hole. Where many nails are to be driven this way, concrete stub nails are often used. Though these drive quickly, use a heavy-duty (2-or 3-pound) hammer. The hardened heads can dent a hammer's surface, risking breakage and impairing its usefulness.

In general, use masonry nails when a high load is not imposed on the fastening, and follow the chart below for length. Drive the heads flush with the surface of the part being fastened but do not continue pounding for a better grip. This will only loosen the nail in its hole.

Driving nails into brick is rather risky; brick is much harder than concrete and is apt to split. Your best bet is to drill a pilot hole with either a carbide-tipped drill or a star drill (p. 77).

Warning: Masonry nails are very hard, and tend to break rather than bend, so always wear goggles.

Nailing wood to masonry and concrete

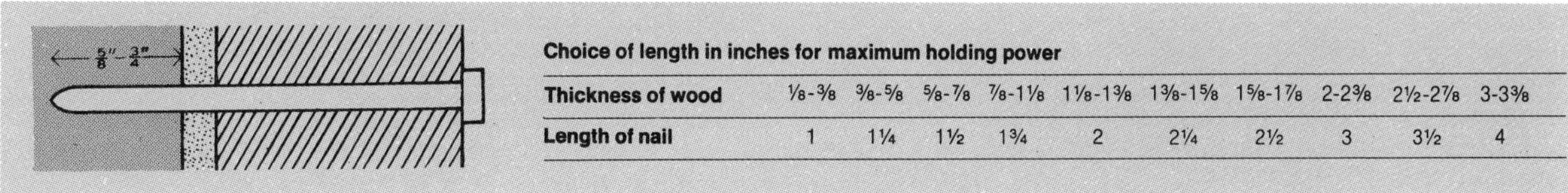

Choice of length in inches for maximum holding power

Thickness of wood	⅛-⅜	⅜-⅝	⅝-⅞	⅞-1⅛	1⅛-1⅜	1⅜-1⅝	1⅝-1⅞	2-2⅜	2½-2⅞	3-3⅜
Length of nail	1	1¼	1½	1¾	2	2¼	2½	3	3½	4

New fastening tool

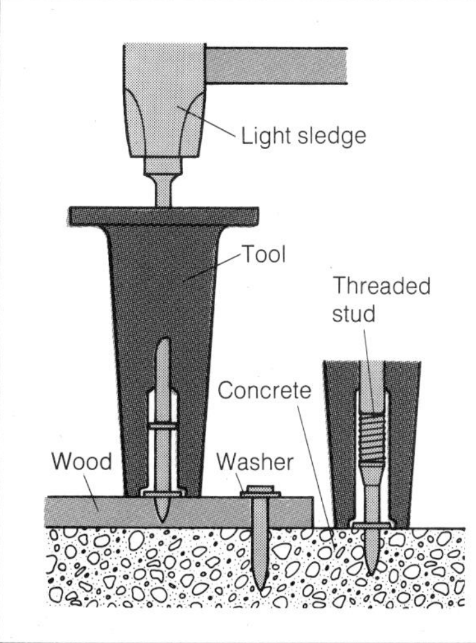

This new tool, especially designed for fastening to masonry and concrete, consists of a holding device and special nails. The holder keeps the nails from buckling and holds them upright until driven home. To select the right fastener, add the thickness of the material you are attaching to the penetration needed for best holding power. Fasteners should penetrate ½ to 1 in. in concrete and from ¾ to 1¼ in. in masonry block or mortar joints.

Fasteners are put through a special heat-treating process that produces high hardness and extra toughness. Because of this, they won't bend, buckle, or break. These extra-tough fasteners can hold loads up to 200 lbs. each. A special sliding washer, as shown in the detail at left, aids penetration and prevents pull-away.

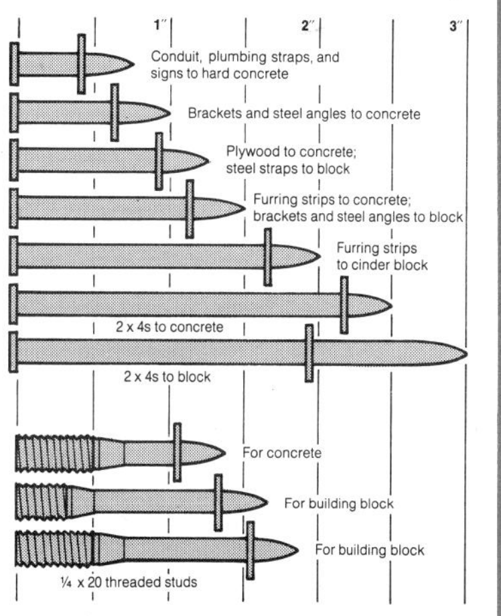

Available types

Concrete nails in three shank types for fastening sole plates to concrete; furring strips to concrete floors; furring strips to concrete, aggregate, or brick walls; and metal corner beading, door bucks, or carpet strips to concrete. They drive straight and set firmly; do the job without unnecessary drilling or filling. Their use can save time and money in building construction.

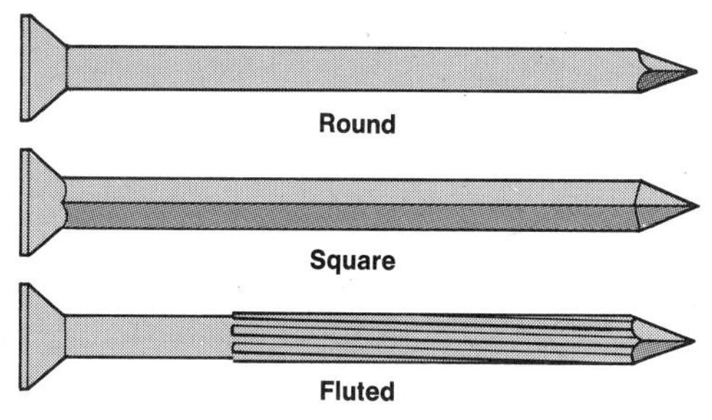

STANDARD SIZES

Approximate count per pound*

Length in inches (overall)	No. 5 gauge (½" head)	No. 6 gauge (7/16" head)	No. 7 gauge (⅜" head)	No. 8 gauge (11/32" head)	No. 9 gauge (21/64" head)	No. 10 gauge (5/16" head)
½	188	244	332	390	437	522
⅝	154	195	258	304	346	412
¾	130	163	211	249	285	342
⅞	113	139	178	211	243	292
1	99	121	154	186	211	254
1⅛	89	108	136	161	187	225
1¼	80	97	121	144	168	202
1½	67	81	100	119	139	168
1¾	58	70	85	102	119	143
2	51	61	74	88	104	125
2¼	46	54	66	78	92	111
2½	41	49	59	70	83	100
2¾	37	44	54	64	75	91
3	34	41	49	58	69	83
3¾	—	—	—	—	64	—

Fluted nail comes in No. 9 gauge only

*These counts are calculated for round shank nails. Variance in count may run 10%. Square nail count is between 20% and 30% less, due to extra steel in each nail. Changes in head styles also vary count. Standard-size nails are supplied with diamond points and flat countersunk heads. These nails can be furnished with nonstandard features such as cone head, or long diamond point, and in nonstandard lengths.

Screws

Where to use screws

Use screws where you need greater holding power than nails can provide, and when the fastened parts may later have to be taken apart.

The most common form of screw head is the **slotted** type, left. Crossed slots, such as the **Phillips,** right, and the **Reed & Prince,** reduce the chance of the screwdriver slipping and marring the work. Two screwdrivers will handle the usual range of Phillips screws; a single screwdriver size will drive all sizes of Reed & Prince screws.

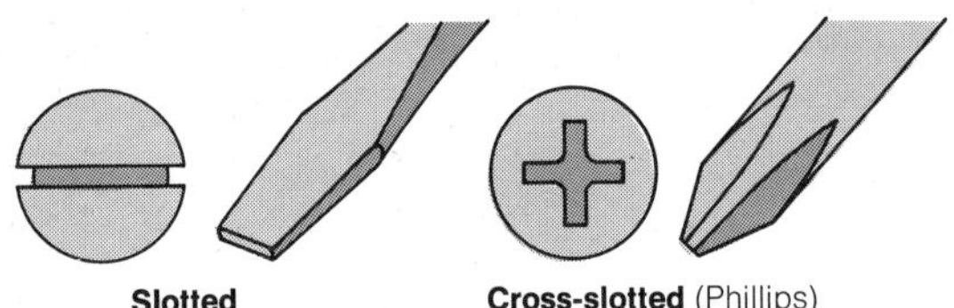

Slotted **Cross-slotted** (Phillips)

Thread forming and cutting screws

Screws that make their own threads are of two basic types: Thread **forming,** used for sheet metal, and thread **cutting,** used in heavier metal to cut a thread ahead of the main part of the screw—really a sort of bolt rather than a screw. Both are made in a variety of special forms. Among the most widely used, because of their versatility, are those shown below. Select screws according to the job to be done and the material in which they will be used.

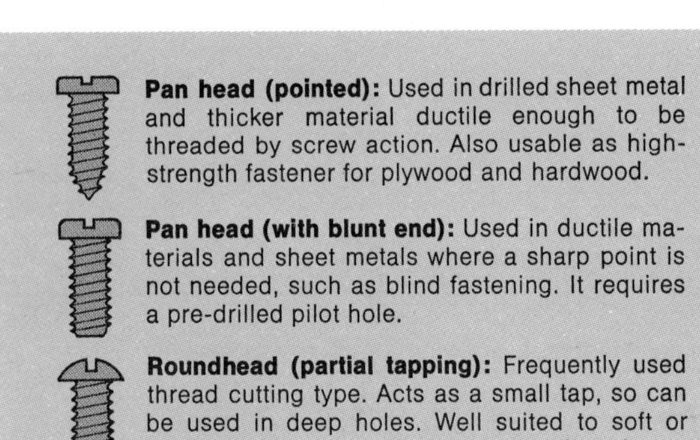

Pan head (pointed): Used in drilled sheet metal and thicker material ductile enough to be threaded by screw action. Also usable as high-strength fastener for plywood and hardwood.

Pan head (with blunt end): Used in ductile materials and sheet metals where a sharp point is not needed, such as blind fastening. It requires a pre-drilled pilot hole.

Roundhead (partial tapping): Frequently used thread cutting type. Acts as a small tap, so can be used in deep holes. Well suited to soft or hard materials; cuts machine-screw threads.

Roundhead (self-tapping): Used for similar applications but thicker materials. Also cuts machine-screw threads. Made in sizes to ¼ in. diameter; all require holes drilled to size.

Types of screws

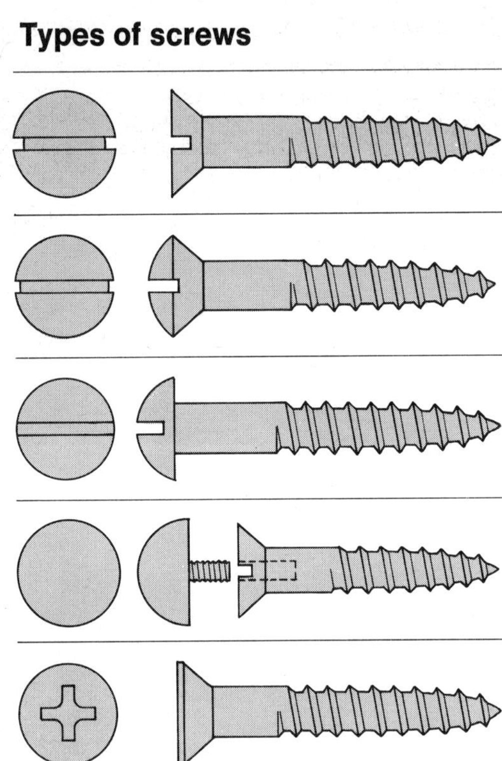

Flathead screws are used in applications where the head must be flush with the surface or slightly below it. Both slotted and cross-slot types are available.

In oval head screws, the lower portion of the head is countersunk and the top is rounded. They are easier to remove and better looking than flathead screws.

Roundhead screws are utility screws, used where the fastened piece is too thin to permit countersinking, and also on parts that may require a washer.

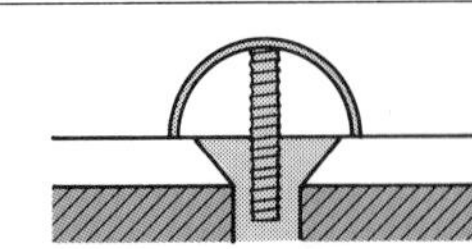

Dome head: This is a decorative form of flathead screw concealed by a dome cap. Dome heads are classed as ornamental and are available on special order only.

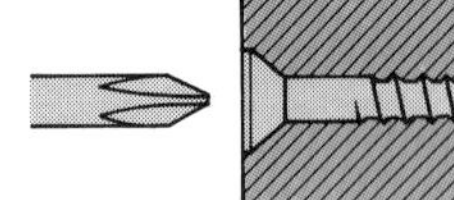

Phillips head screws have crossed slots to minimize screwdriver slip-out. Cross slots are available in most head types. A Phillips-type driver is required.

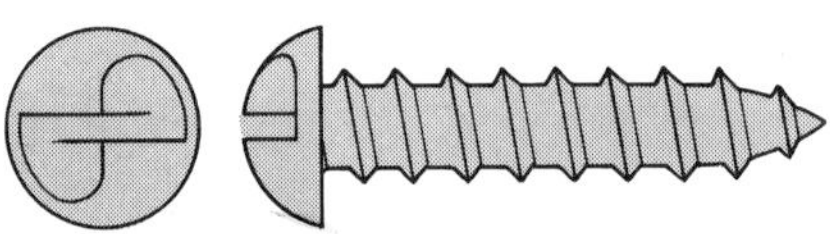

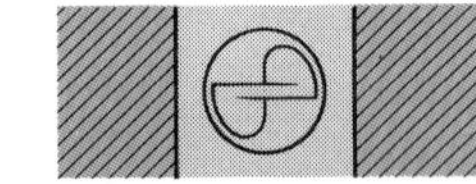

One-way screws are designed to prevent burglary and theft. If anyone should attempt to remove the screw, the screwdriver would slip out of the slot.

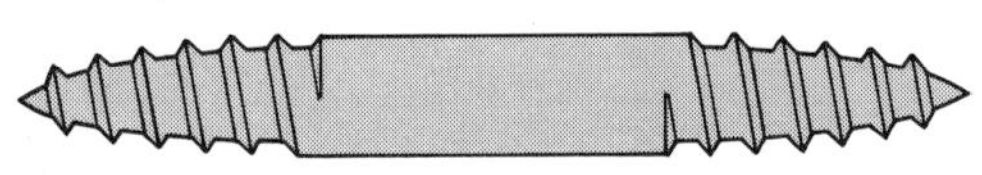

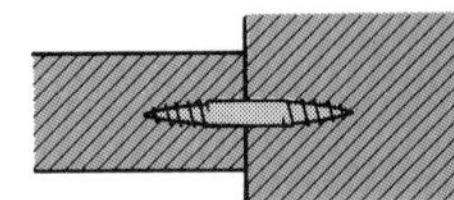

Dowel screw: This is the screw to use for end-to-end joints and similar applications unsuited to conventional screws. Usually available at large hardware outlets.

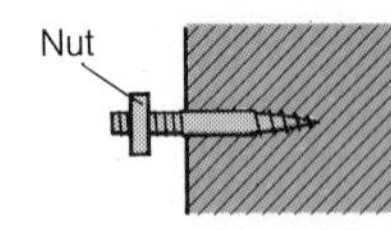

Hanger bolt (or screw) has one end that is threaded like a screw so it can be driven into wood; the other end is threaded to accept a square or a hex nut.

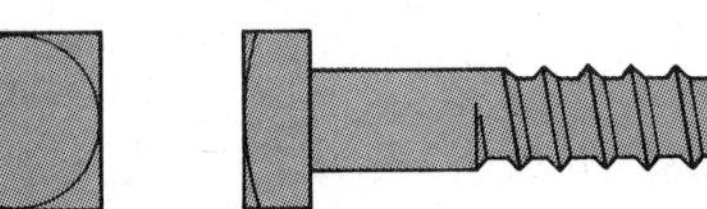

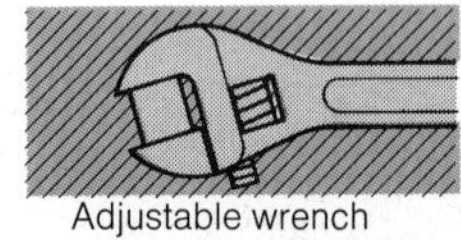

Adjustable wrench

Lag bolt (or screw) is actually a heavy-duty screw and is made in sizes up to 6 in. in length. The head end is square. Bolt is driven with a wrench, as shown.

Screw sizes

Screw sizes are measured by both length and diameter. Length is designated in inches; diameter, by gauge number. In general, screws are available in gauges 0 (about 1/16 inch) through 24 (approximately ⅜ inch). Lengths are from ¼ inch up to 6 inches.

The most commonly available screw sizes are numbers 2 through 16. If your job requires a larger gauge screw, you may have to place a special order.

Select screw lengths so that at least two-thirds of the screw length is in the base material to which you are fastening.

To enable screws to go into the work, you must first make a pilot hole. This can be done with an awl for screws up to No. 6 gauge. For larger screws, use a drill bit that is at least two sizes smaller than the thread diameter. When working in hardwood, or if working with large diameter screws in work that is subject to splitting, drill both a pilot hole and a clearance hole for the screw shank. Clearance holes should be the same diameter as the shank and drilled one-third the length of the screw.

When installing screws in new work, lubricate the threads with soap or wax.

Suiting the screws to the job

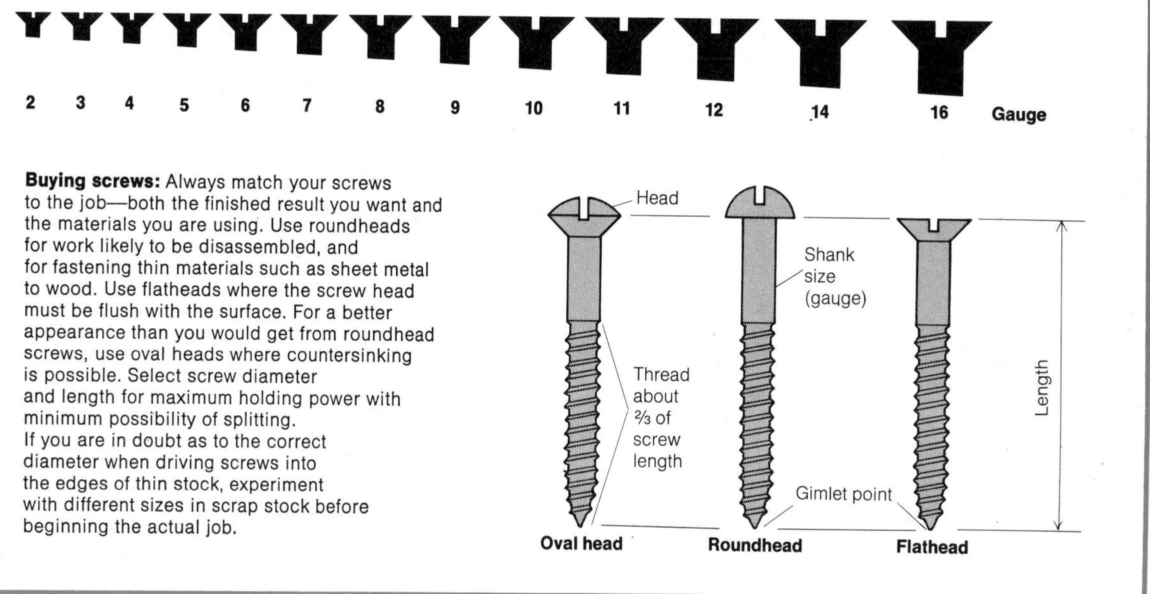

Buying screws: Always match your screws to the job—both the finished result you want and the materials you are using. Use roundheads for work likely to be disassembled, and for fastening thin materials such as sheet metal to wood. Use flatheads where the screw head must be flush with the surface. For a better appearance than you would get from roundhead screws, use oval heads where countersinking is possible. Select screw diameter and length for maximum holding power with minimum possibility of splitting. If you are in doubt as to the correct diameter when driving screws into the edges of thin stock, experiment with different sizes in scrap stock before beginning the actual job.

Screw washers

Washers are used under screw heads in some woodworking applications to provide added bearing surfaces and to avoid marring of the wood when removal is necessary, as in opening cabinet panels to gain access to inner parts. Stereo cabinets are a typical example. The washers should be matched to screw diameter and head type, as illustrated.

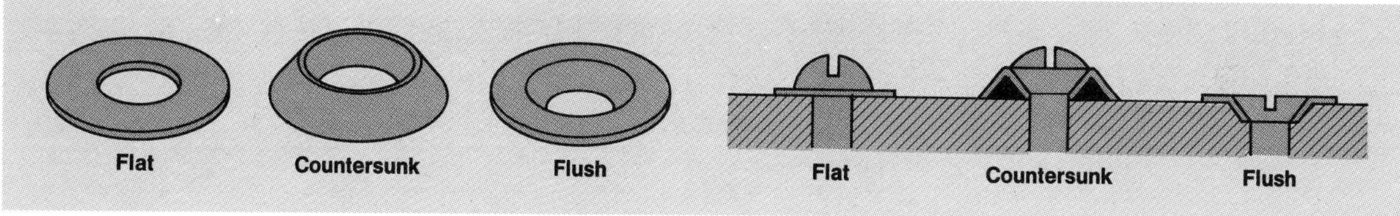

Screw hooks

Screw hooks are made to suit specific purposes. The **cup hook,** for example, is fitted with a stop cap to assure uniform extension when the hooks are used in rows. The ordinary **screw hook,** used to hang tools and utensils, has a sharp point to make insertion easy, and can be easily driven to the depth required. **Eye and ring** combinations take snap hooks, as on leashes. The common **screw eye** is formed from a single piece; for greater strength, cast and forged types are also available. The **square bend screw hook** is often used to support curtain rods and in the kitchen as a hanger for pots and utensils.

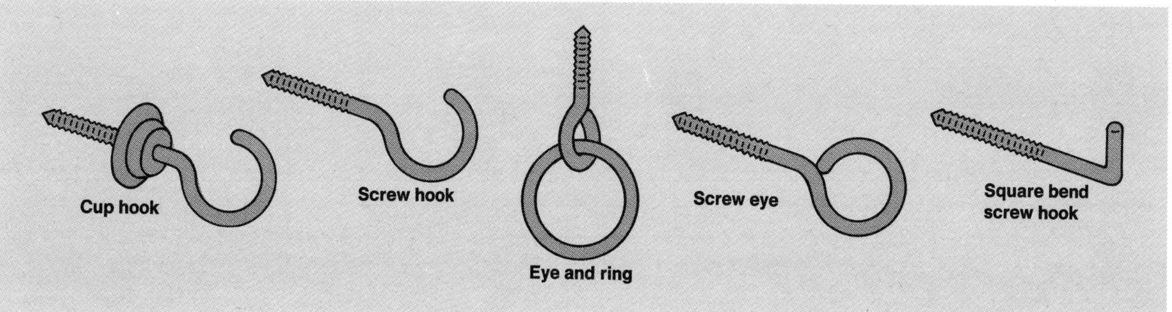

Screwing applications

General information

Screws are preferable to nails for fastening wood. They make a tighter joint; a joint that is screwed together can be taken apart without damage. With a pilot hole, a screw will never split the wood as a nail can. When two pieces of wood are being joined with a screw, the clearance hole in the wood through which the screw first passes should pass the shank without binding. The pilot hole in the second piece should be just that—a hole into which the screw thread can bite. Without a clearance hole, the screw will not be able to draw the two pieces of wood tightly together.

Fastening with screws

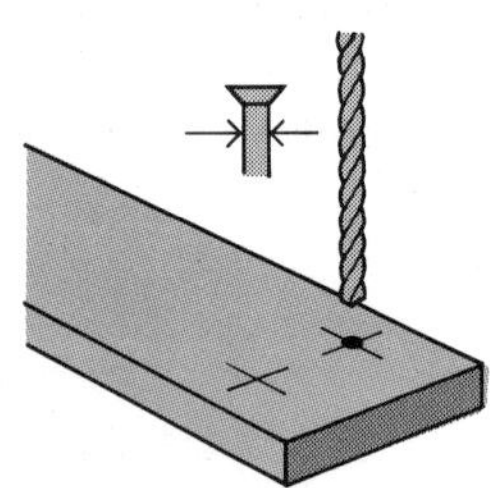

Locate and mark the screw position with intersecting lines. Hole drilled through the first piece of wood should pass shank of screw without binding.

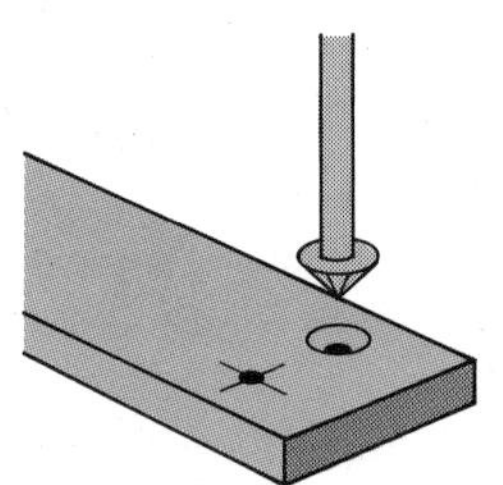

If you are using flathead screws, countersink the hole to match the diameter of the screw head. Check for right depth by dropping the screw through the hole. Fit should be flush.

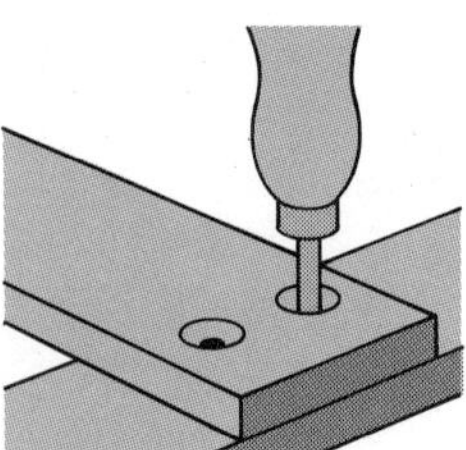

Next, lay the bottom piece in position and mark the position of the pilot holes by using an awl. Be careful that the work does not move as you do this.

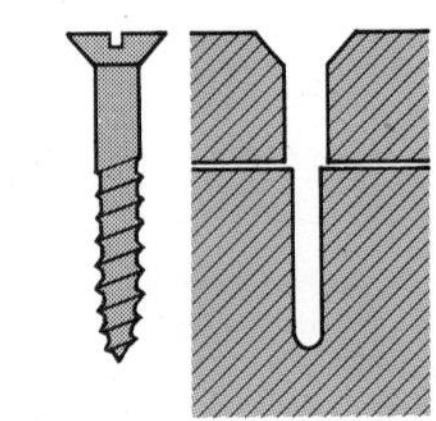

Now drill the pilot hole for the threaded part of the screw. This hole should be approximately half the depth of the length of the screw.

Screw-fixing tips

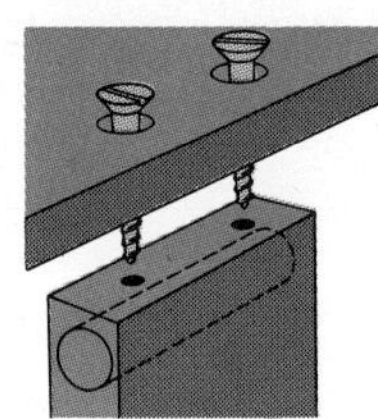

If you must drive screws into end grain, insert a hardwood dowel as shown. This will give the screws a better purchase than the weak end grain.

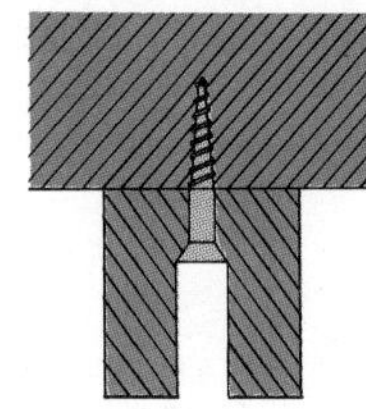

Counterboring the work will enable you to use a short screw when fastening extra-thick work. Countersink if using flathead screws.

Pockets, chiseled or bored in workpiece, provide seating for screws driven at an angle when fastening table or workbench tops in place.

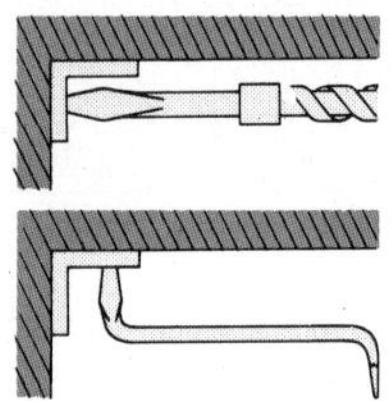

Awkward corner screws can be driven with spiral or ratchet screwdriver. An offset screwdriver is also useful for hard-to-get-at screws.

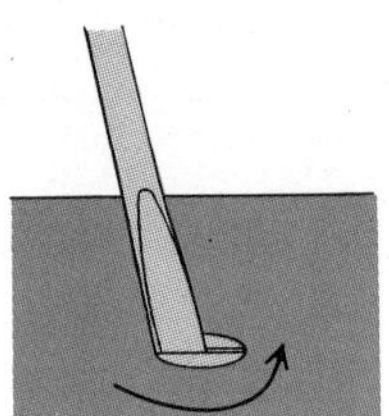

Loosen a stubborn screw by inserting screwdriver slightly past the slot and striking it with a mallet in direction the screw is to turn.

Special-purpose and special-order fittings

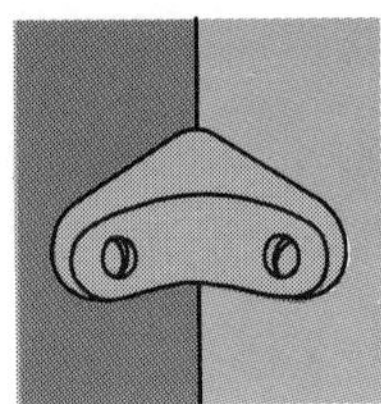

Corner brace is much more rigid than conventional angle iron. Holes are countersunk to accept flathead screws.

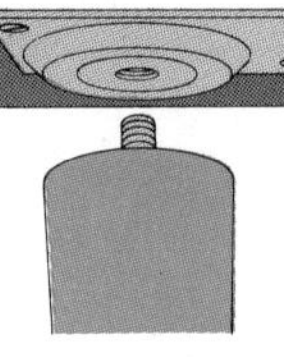

Leg plates are attached to bottom of table with screws, then the legs are screwed into the steel plates.

Self-locking fittings allow parts to slide together for friction-tight fit. Use for quick and easy disassembly of parts.

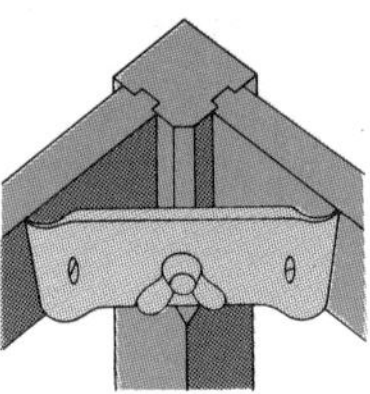

Corner table plates hold cross rails at an exact 90° angle. Plate is bolted to leg; screws go through plate and rails.

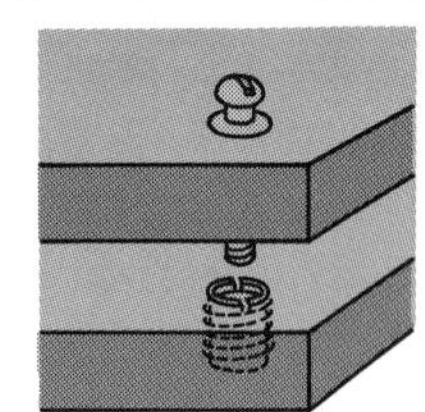

Insert has outside thread for installing into wood, machine thread to take a bolt in the inside. Made in many sizes.

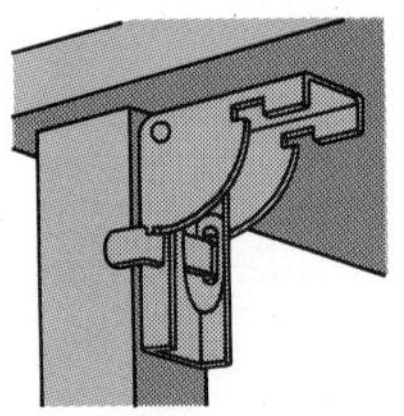

Folding bracket is used to hold cabinet lid in open position without danger of its falling down. Can be used at right or left.

Cam-action locking device draws two units together for extra-tight fit. Often used for connecting table halves.

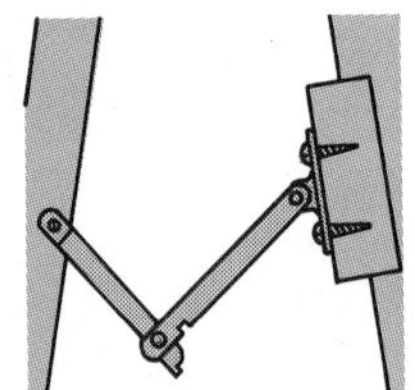

Folding leg bracket has spring action to lock automatically. Use for light tables. Also suitable for fold-down shelves.

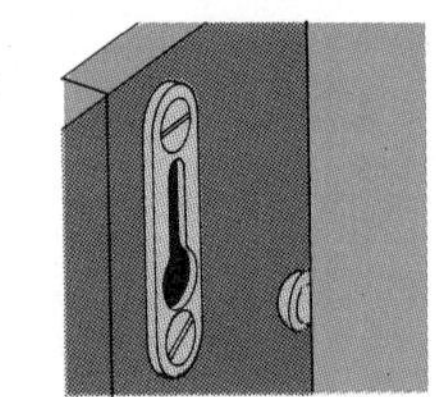

Keyhole plates are used for hanging cabinets on walls. Slot accepts roundhead screw projecting slightly from cabinet.

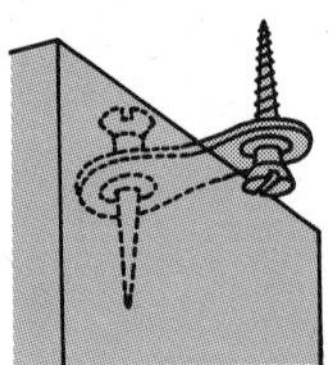

Clips are used to fasten desk tops to their supports. Useful when top should be detached for moving or storage.

Bolt sizes and threading

A bolt is generally defined as a fastener used with a nut and tightened by turning the nut. Machine bolts and threaded rods are available in a coarse or fine thread, coarse being the more common. The thread size of bolts is determined by the number of threads per inch. It is designated by a numeral following the bolt diameter; the diameter is given in fractions of an inch. Thus, a ¼ x 20 bolt would be ¼ inch in diameter and have 20 threads to the inch.

Bolt sizes ordinarily range from ⅛ x 40 to ½ x 13, and their lengths from ⅜ inch to 6 inches. Machine bolt diameters range from ¼ inch to as large as 2 inches; lengths, from ½ inch to 30 inches. The larger sizes are not generally stocked by most hardware dealers. Carriage bolts are made with coarse threads and are available in lengths from ½ inch to 10 inches and in diameters from 3/16 to ¾ inch. The average hardware store does not stock the very large sizes. The square section under the head of the carriage bolt sinks into the wood, preventing rotation of the bolt when the nut is tightened. This makes it possible to tighten the nut when the bolt head is not accessible. Use washer between nut and wood.

Washers and nuts

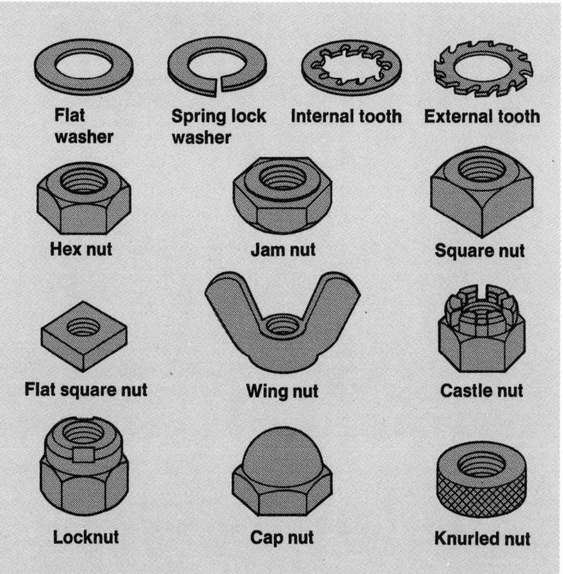

Types of bolts

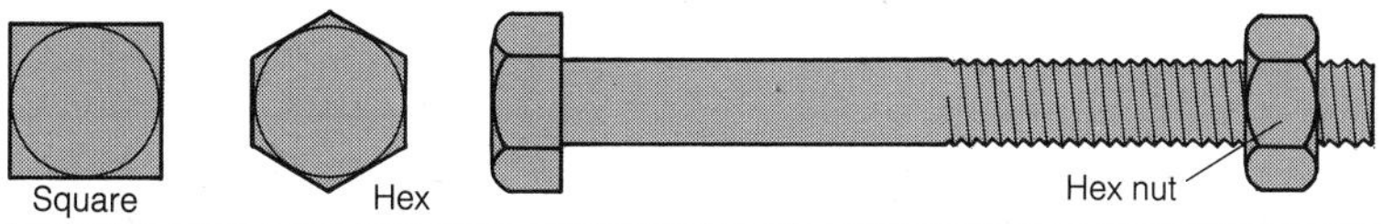

Machine bolts are made in both square and hex head forms and have either square or hex nuts. Bolts are available with coarse and with fine threads.

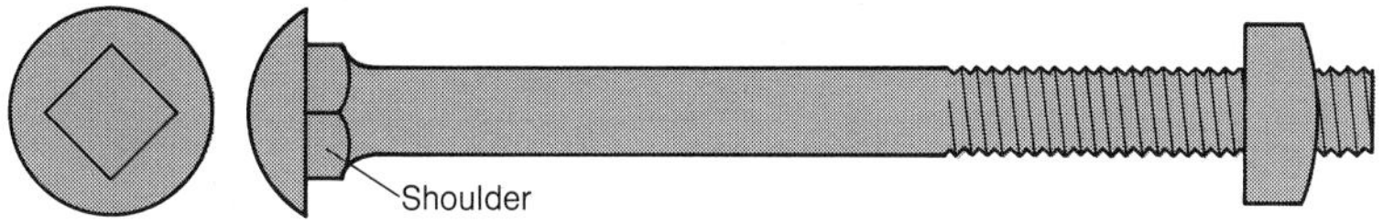

Carriage bolts have coarse threads. The head variations include a countersunk flat-topped head in addition to the roundhead. Shoulder keeps the bolt from turning when the nut is tightened.

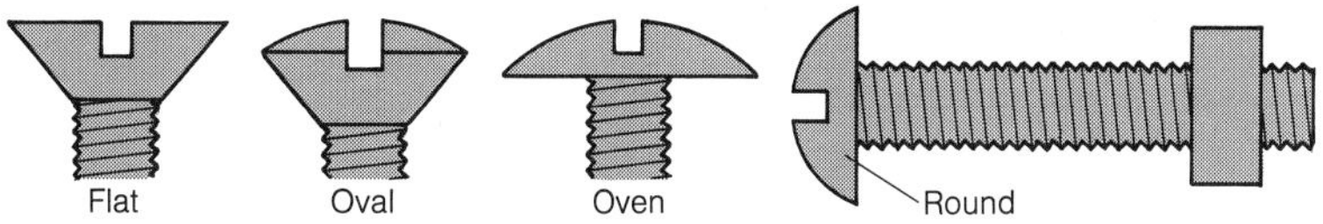

Stove bolts are made with slotted round, flat, or oval heads and they have coarse threads. Originally used in stove construction; now sold as general utility bolts.

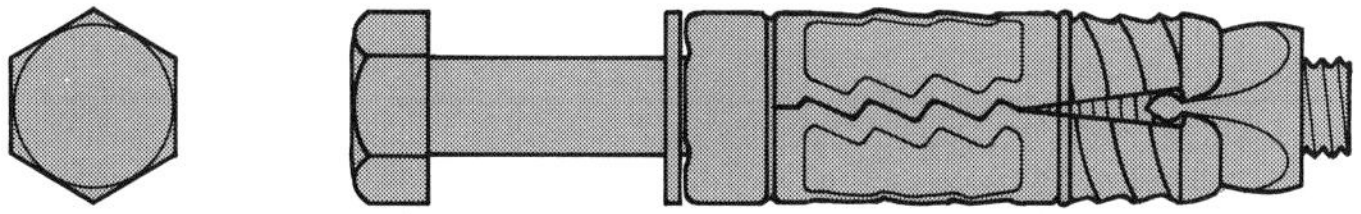

Masonry bolt and anchor is made in many forms. All of them work according to the same principle: As the bolt is tightened, the shell around it expands and grips the inside of the hole.

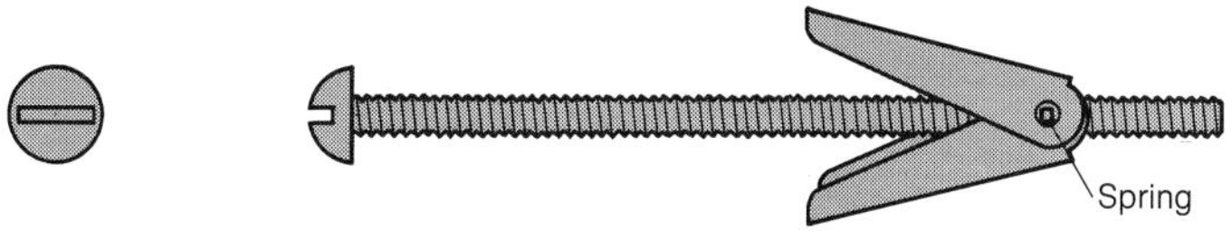

Toggle bolts are used for fastening to hollow walls. Hole large enough to pass the spring-loaded wings must be drilled in wall. Wings spread out and bear against the wall as the head is screwed home.

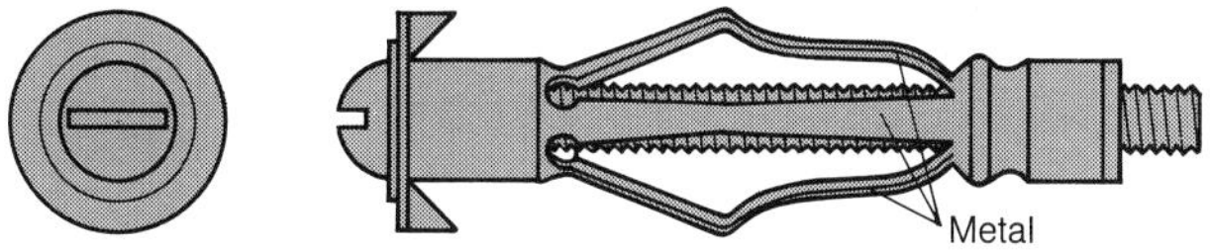

Molly bolt is similar to a toggle bolt and is also used for attaching to hollow surfaces. Bolt is passed through clearance hole and, as the head is turned, the legs are pushed outward to grip the wall.

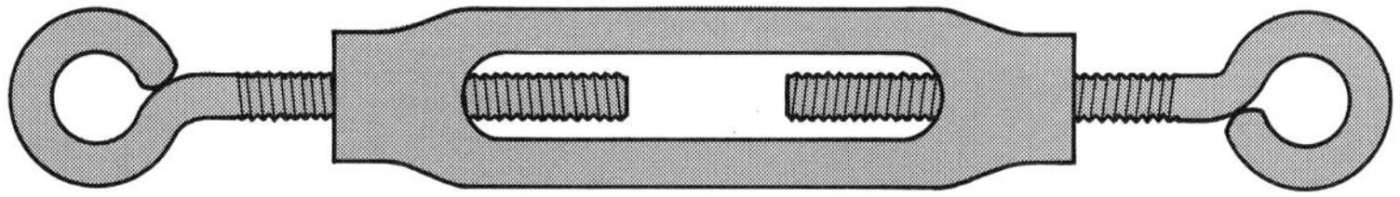

Turnbuckle consists of a steel sleeve and two screw eyes. Half of sleeve and one screw eye have right-hand thread, other half a left-hand thread. Turning sleeve left or right moves screw eyes in or out.

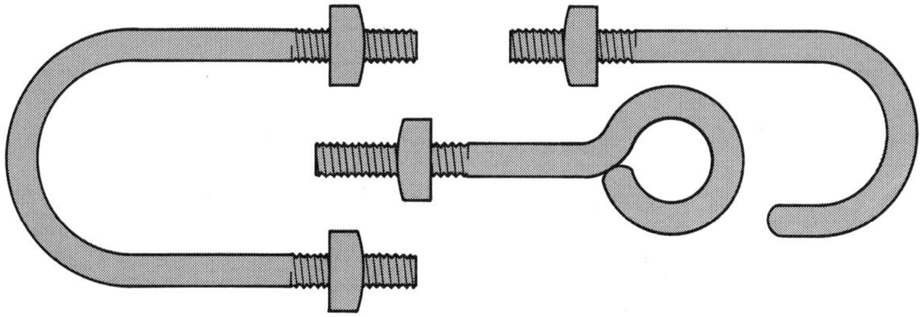

U bolts, J bolts, and eye bolts: These are all special-purpose fasteners and holders, produced in the shapes shown and used when that shape suits a particular application. They can also be made in the home workshop, to any diameter or size required by the job in hand, using threaded steel rods and bending them to the appropriate shape.

Attaching to hollow surfaces

Types of fasteners and how to use them

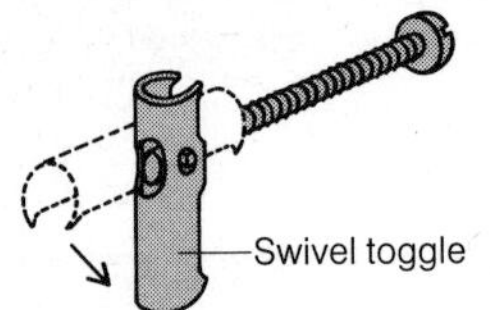

Gravity toggle bolts have a swivel toggle that drops vertically when pushed through a pre-drilled hole. Toggle is lost if bolt is removed. Sizes: ⅛, 3⁄16, ¼ in. diameter, and up to 3 in. length.

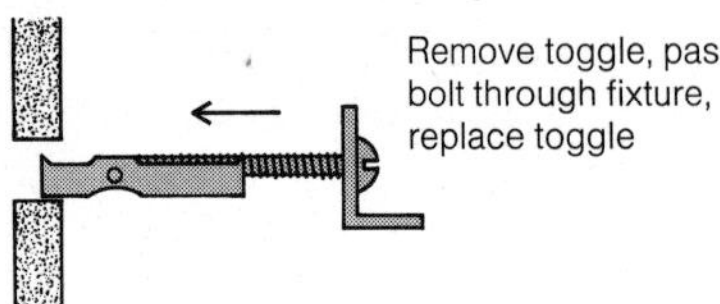
Remove toggle, pass bolt through fixture, replace toggle

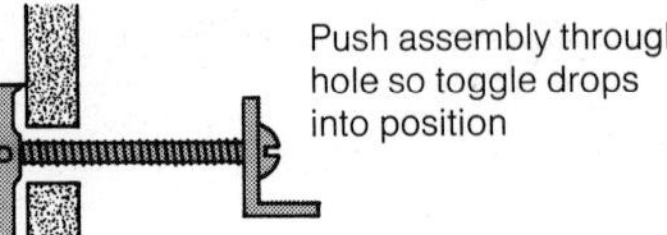
Push assembly through hole so toggle drops into position

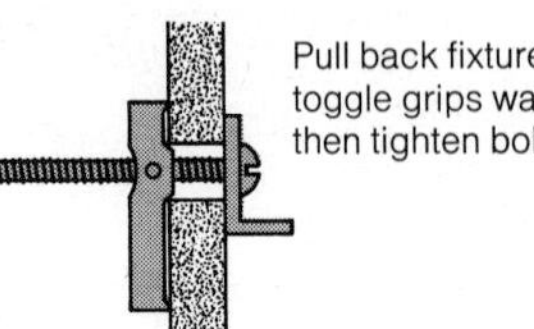
Pull back fixture so toggle grips wall and then tighten bolt

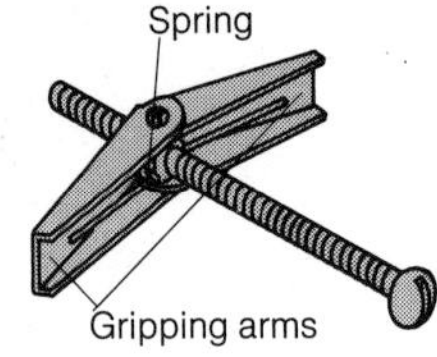

Split-wing toggles have two spring-loaded arms that expand after toggle is pushed through pre-drilled hole. Toggle is lost if bolt is removed. Sizes: ⅛, 3⁄16, ¼ in. diameter; lengths to 4 in.

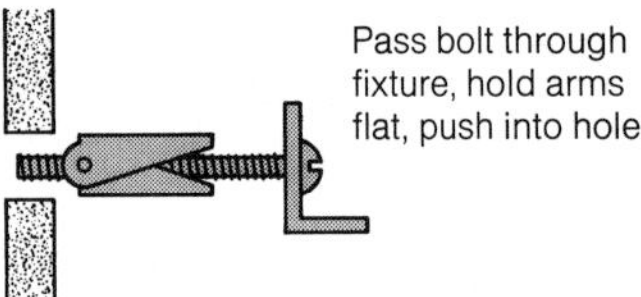
Pass bolt through fixture, hold arms flat, push into hole

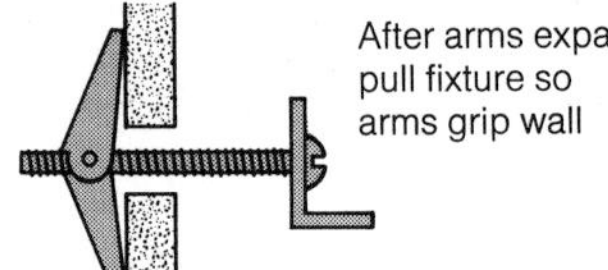
After arms expand, pull fixture so arms grip wall

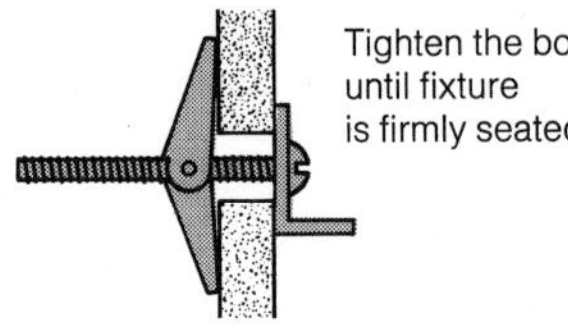
Tighten the bolt until fixture is firmly seated

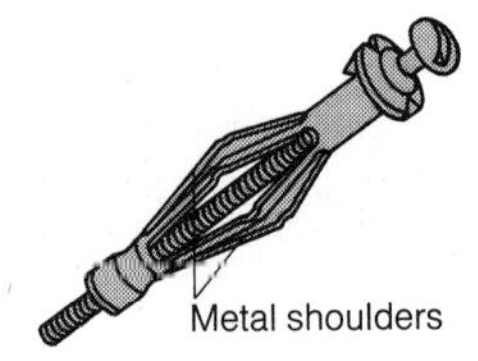

Collapsible anchors (Molly bolts) remain in place if bolt is removed. As bolt is turned, it draws metal-gripping shoulders against inner wall. Made in sizes for walls up to 1¾ in. thick.

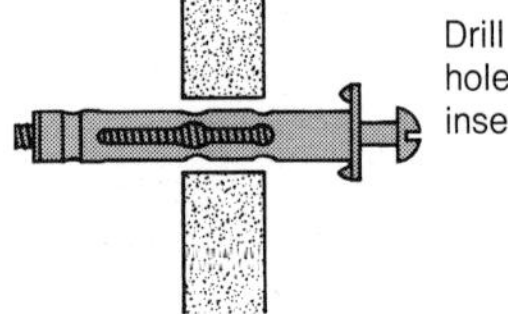
Drill passage hole for bolt, insert in hole

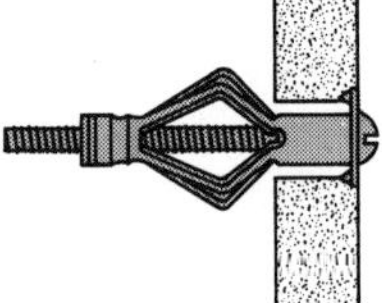
Tighten the bolt until pressure is felt

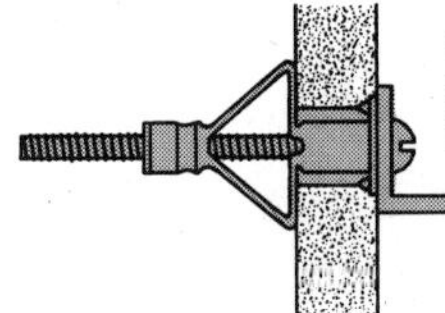
Remove bolt, pass through fixture, and tighten

Hollow door anchors (jack nuts): These are basically similar to Molly bolts but are used for very thin veneers such as are found on hollow-core closet and passageway doors.

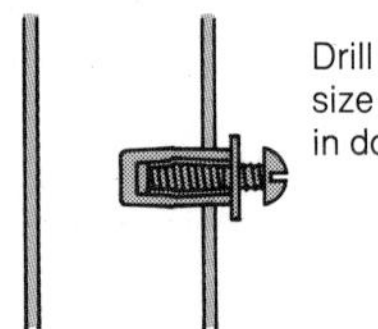
Drill recommended size passage hole in door

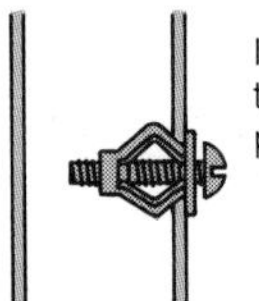
Insert anchor and tighten until pressure is felt

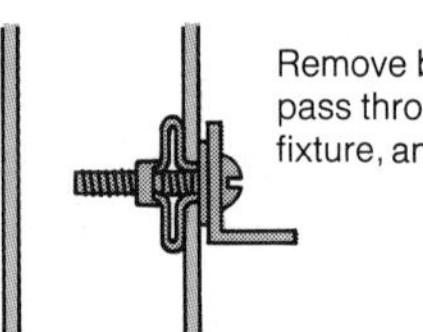
Remove bolt, pass through fixture, and tighten

Attaching heavy objects

Heavy picture frames and mirrors, and storage or bookcase shelves that will hold heavy books and magazines, should be supported by means of a cross member bridging the studs. Use No. 14 screws or lag bolts to secure the cross member to the studs. Locate the studs by tapping, or better still, probe for the studs with a ⅛-inch drill before drilling the pilot holes for the screws. Studs are generally 16 inches apart, measured from center to center.

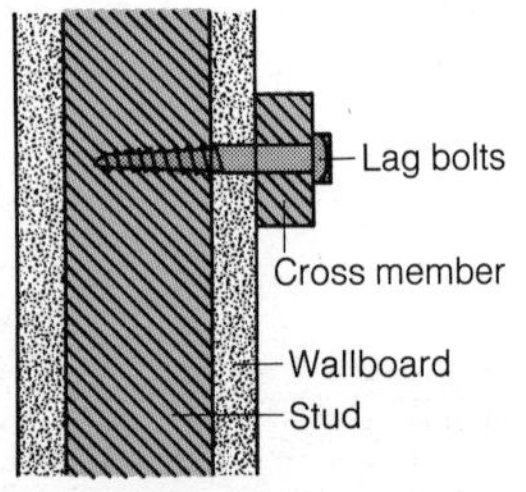

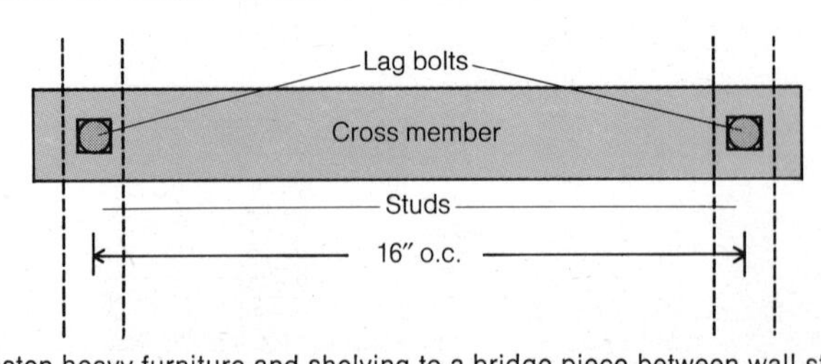

Fasten heavy furniture and shelving to a bridge piece between wall studs

How to use hole-drilling tools

The easiest way to drill holes for fastening into concrete or brick is with a carbide-tipped bit and ½-inch drill (p. 45). The average ¼-inch drill runs too fast for use with these bits. If you have to drill a large hole, it is best to start off with a small bit, $\frac{3}{16}$ or ¼ inch, then go to the larger size.

Hand drilling is also possible. For this you will need a heavy hammer and a drill. The star drill is the drill to use for making holes in masonry. (The Rawl drill shown at the top of the page is a sort of light-duty star drill.) The cutting end is fluted into a four-cornered star. Use gloves and grasp the drill near the center. (Wear goggles, too, when doing this work.) After each hammer blow, the drill should be rotated slightly. Every so often blow out the dust. Continue until the desired depth is reached.

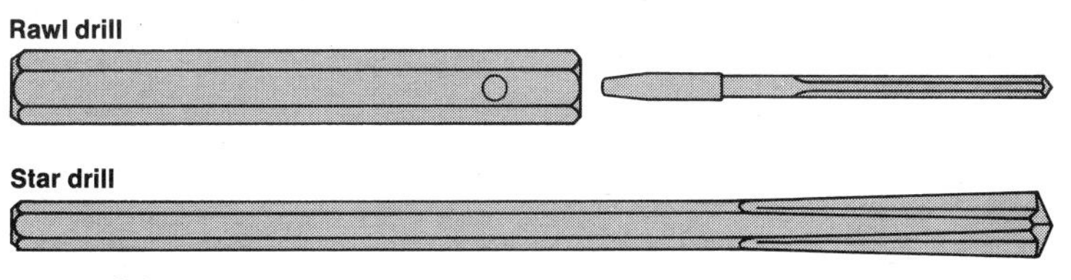

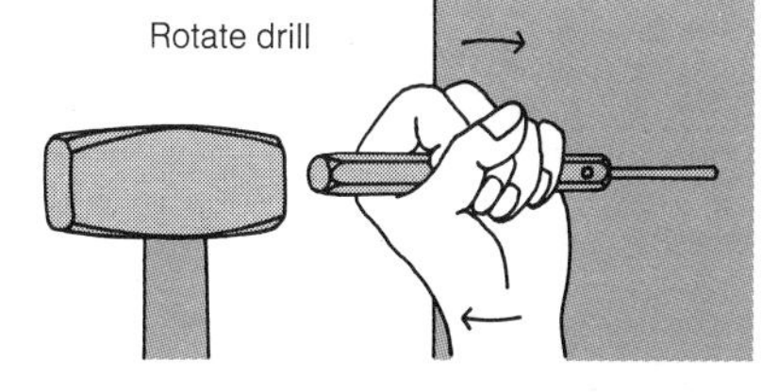

Hand drilling: Rawl drill is used for drilling holes smaller than ¼ in. in diameter in brick, stone, and concrete. Star drill is a heavy-duty hand-operated drill for making larger holes; available in sizes up to 1 in. in diameter.

Rotary carbide drill

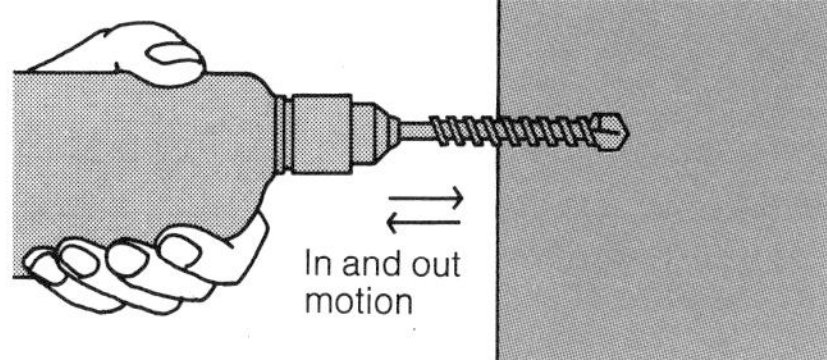

Power drilling: The carbide-tipped drill is the drill to use for making holes in masonry. Best results are obtained when used with a ½-inch drill. Made in sizes up to 1 in. in diameter.

Fasteners and how to use them

Wood dowel can be used for fastening to masonry. Make hole with carbide-tipped drill.

Use slightly oversize dowel. Grease it and drive it in flush with a hammer.

Wall plugs are fiber or plastic sheaths which are inserted into pre-drilled holes to provide a gripping base for screws. The screws cause the plug to expand and grip the sides of the hole.

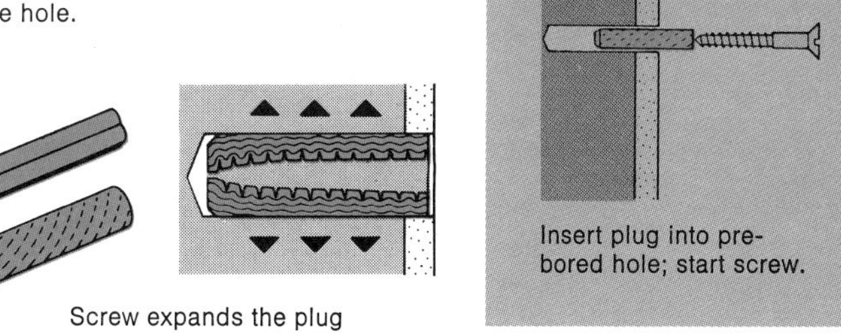

Screw expands the plug

Insert plug into pre-bored hole; start screw.

Slip the screw through object being fastened.

Drive the screw home, but do not overtighten.

Drill a pilot hole in the center of the dowel slightly smaller than the screw.

Use a roundhead screw and washer for fastening metal work to the masonry wall.

Masonry bolts are used for fixing heavy objects, such as furniture and construction framing, to solid walls. A plastic plug, inserted in a pre-drilled hole, expands as the bolt is threaded home. Bolts are available in a wide size range with a variety of head styles, including threaded ends which accept nuts.

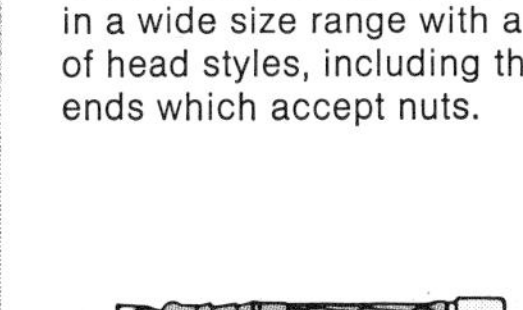

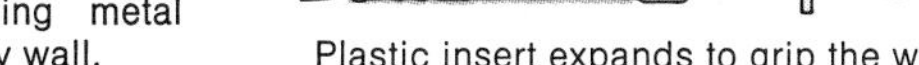

Plastic insert expands to grip the wall

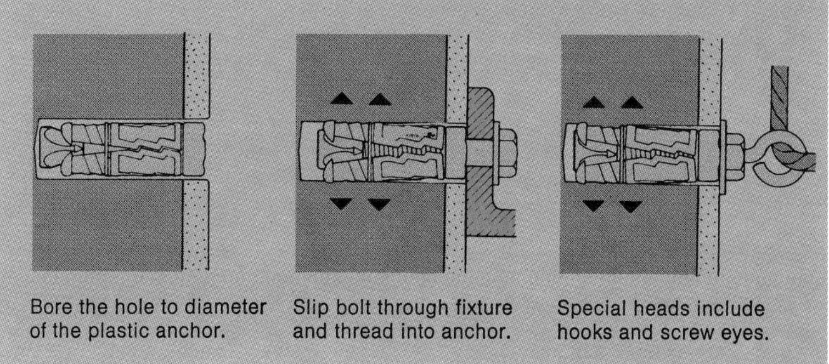

Bore the hole to diameter of the plastic anchor.

Slip bolt through fixture and thread into anchor.

Special heads include hooks and screw eyes.

Hinges

General information

Hinges for use on cabinets and chests are reversible—that is, they can be mounted right side up as well as upside down. Many door hinges, however, are not reversible; they must be of the correct "hand." If it is a loose-pin hinge, for example, the pin must be positioned so that it can be removed from the top. Also, some doors can be removed by lifting them from their hinges. Obviously, if the hinge were mounted upside down, the door would fall out of its hinges. Door hinges are specified, therefore, as "right hand" or "left hand." To determine the "hand" of a hinge, determine which is the "outside" of the door. This is the corridor side of an interior door. If, when you are standing on the outside of a door, the door opens **from** you to your **right,** it takes **right-hand hinges;** if it opens **from** you to your **left,** it takes **left-hand hinges.** But if the door opens **toward** you to your **left,** it is a **left-hand reverse** door and takes **right-hand** hinges; if the door opens **toward** you to your **right,** it is a **right-hand reverse** door and takes **left-hand hinges.**

Mounting hinges

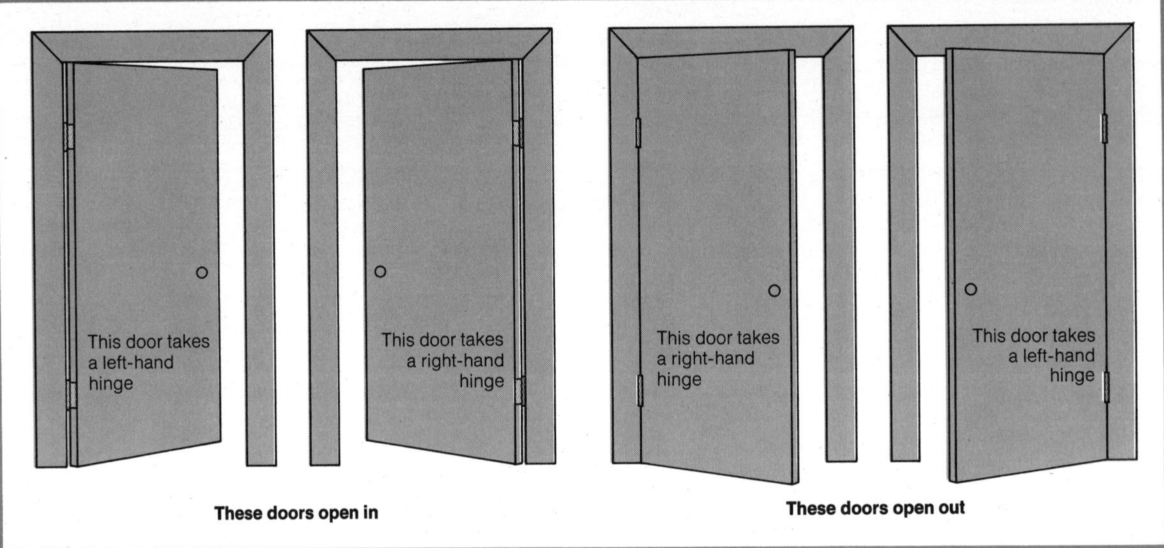

Types and uses

Simple butt hinges cannot be taken apart. They can be used for either right- or left-hand doors.
Loose-pin hinges should be used according to "hand" of door. Pin permits removal of door without unscrewing hinges.
Loose-joint hinge is used when it is desirable to remove door without disturbing hinges or pin. Door is merely raised enough to clear nonremovable pin, then detached.
Rising butt hinge is used when heavy carpeting interferes with opening of door. As door is swung open, the door rises slightly to clear the carpeting.

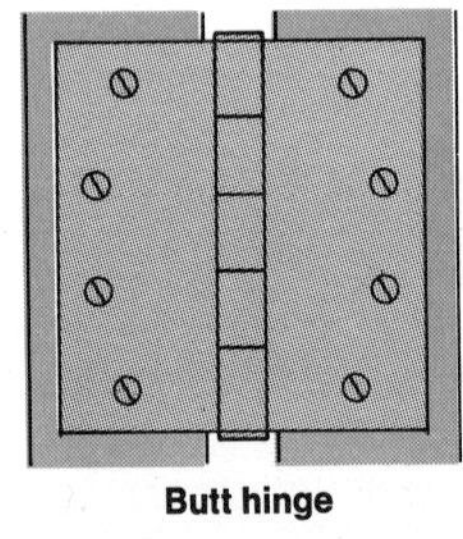
Butt hinge

Loose-pin hinge

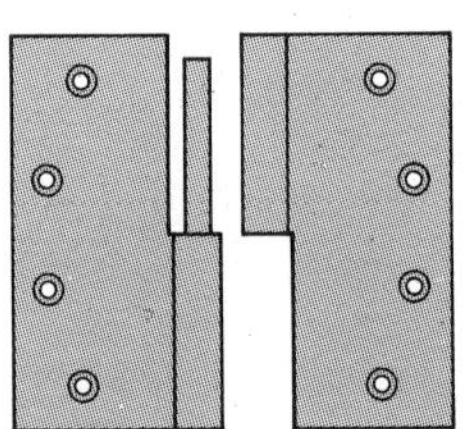
Loose-joint hinge

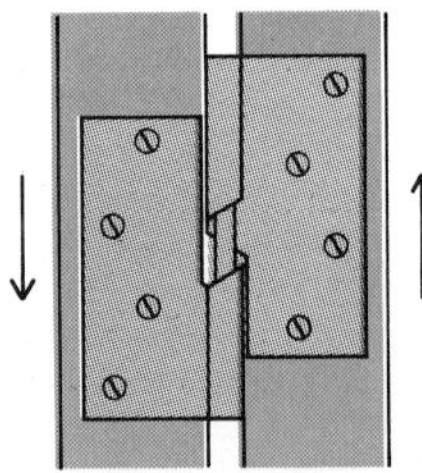
Rising butt hinge

Ball bearing hinges are permanently lubricated. They are especially recommended for heavy doors opening to the exterior.
Knuckle hinges are decorative—only the knuckle part of the hinge shows when the door is closed.
Flush door hinges are used on cabinets when it is desirable to have complete concealment of the hinge except for the barrel.
Pivot reinforced hinges are used for flush, recessed, or overlay doors. No door frame is required with this type of hinge.

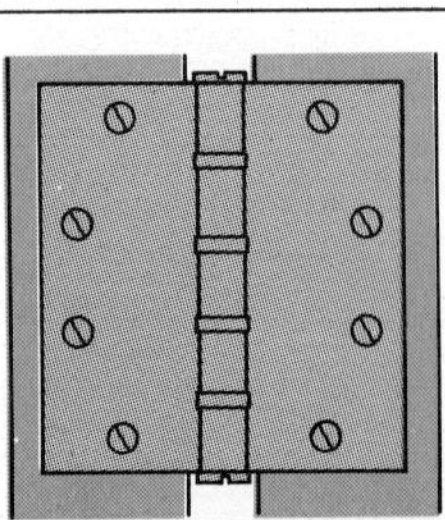
Ball bearing hinge

Knuckle hinge

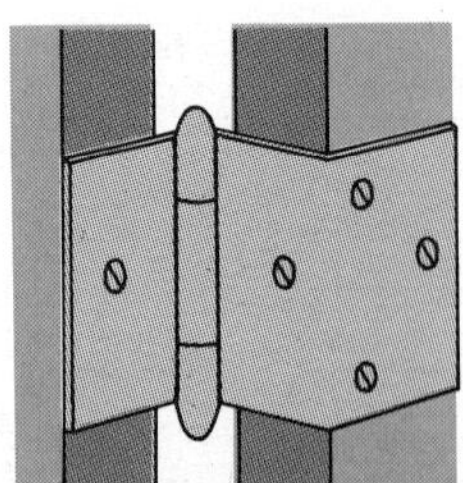
Flush door hinge

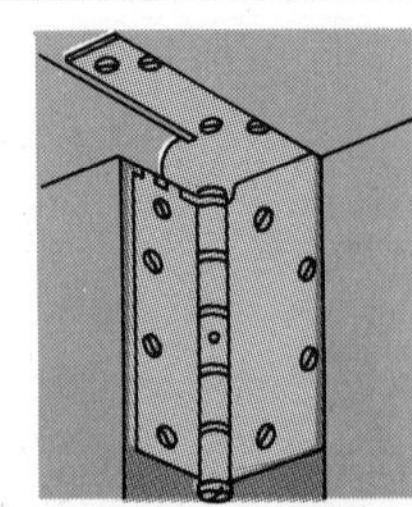
Pivot reinforced hinge

Types and uses

Gravity pivot hinges are used for light louvered or hall doors that must swing either way; some have a hold-open stop.
Double-acting hinges are used on folding doors. These hinges permit the door to swing either way.
Offset blind hinges are useful when a full opening screen or storm sash is required without interference from the hinges.
Spring-loaded hinges are used with heavy screen doors to automatically close the door after opening. On some models, spring tension is adjustable.

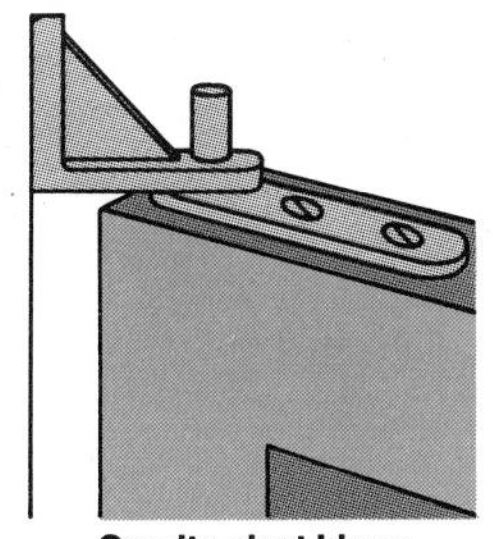
Gravity pivot hinge

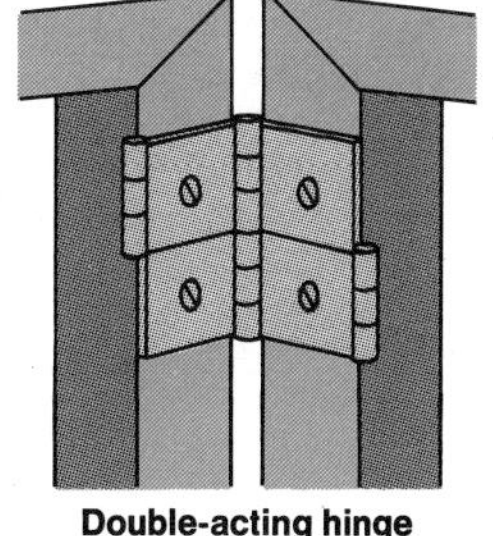
Double-acting hinge

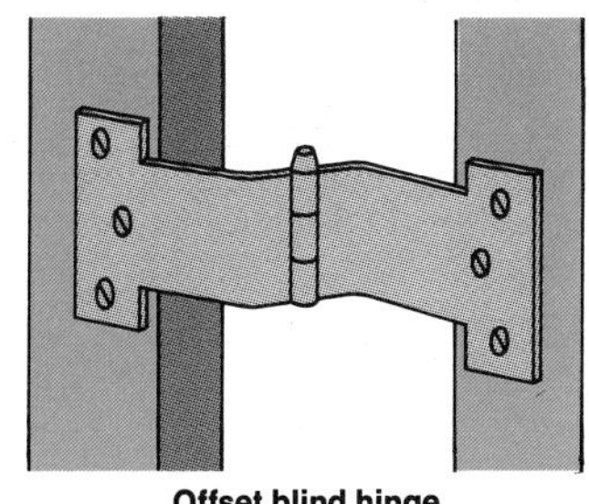
Offset blind hinge

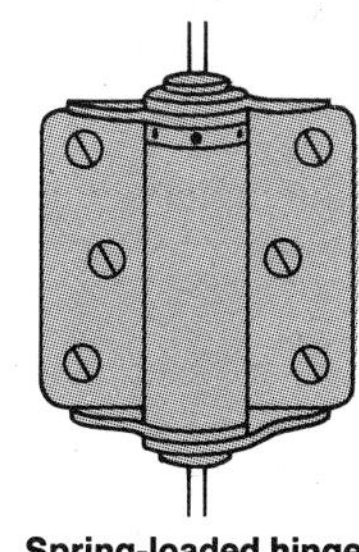
Spring-loaded hinge

Ornamental hinges are the choice when the hinges are to form part of the design of the cabinet or other item of furniture on which they are being used.
Rustic hinges come in H, H-L, and semi-concealed styles and are available in wrought iron, dead (flat) black, and copper finishes for a variety of decorative effects. They are generally supplied with pyramid head screws, which give the appearance of handmade nails when they are installed.

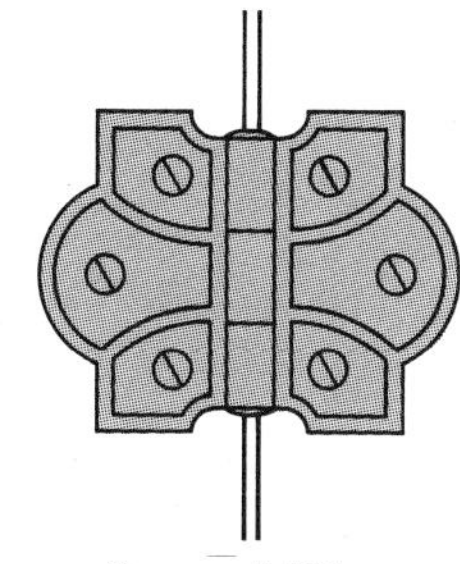
Ornamental hinge

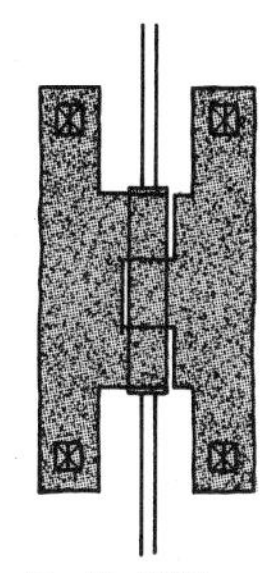
Rustic H hinge

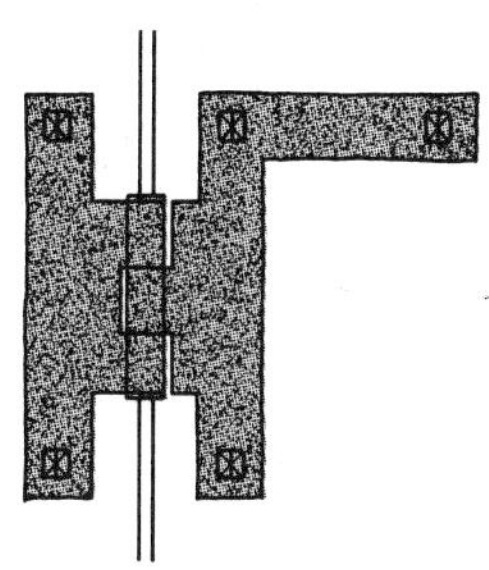
Rustic H-L hinge

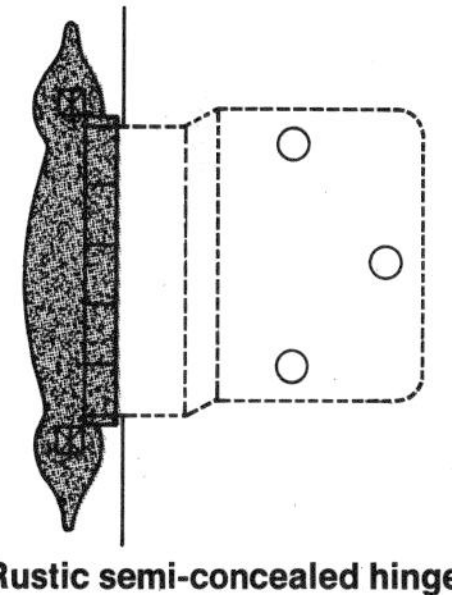
Rustic semi-concealed hinge

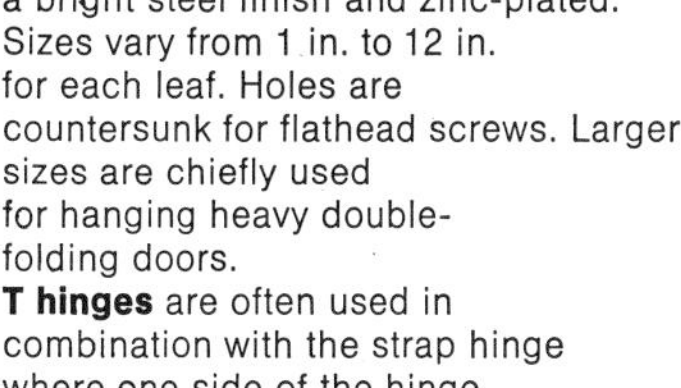

Strap hinges are made in both a bright steel finish and zinc-plated. Sizes vary from 1 in. to 12 in. for each leaf. Holes are countersunk for flathead screws. Larger sizes are chiefly used for hanging heavy double-folding doors.
T hinges are often used in combination with the strap hinge where one side of the hinge can be fastened to supports such as a post or door jamb. Sizes similar to strap hinges; also same finishes.

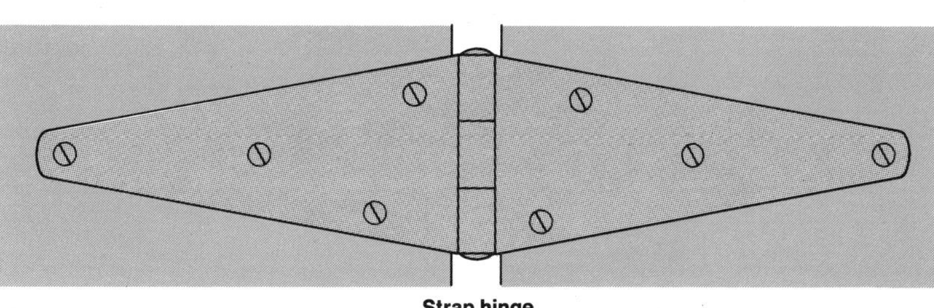
Strap hinge

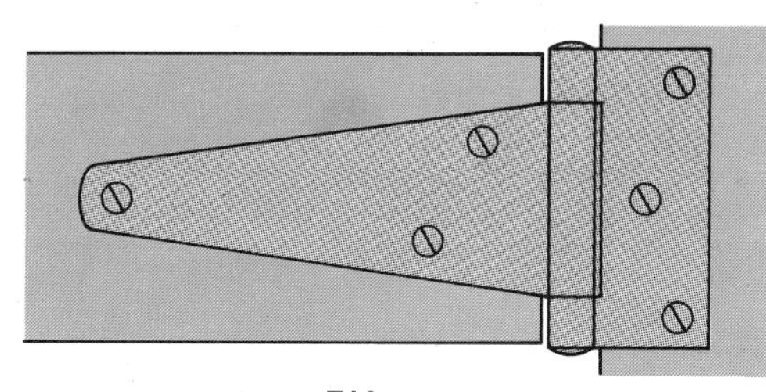
T hinge

The continuous hinge, which is also sometimes referred to as a piano hinge, is the type to use when full support of a door or lid is required. Typical examples, in addition to the piano application, are the lids of cedar chests, record players, and cabinets.
Continuous hinges are made of various metals—steel, brass, nickel, and aluminum—and in lengths up to 84 in. The holes in these hinges are usually 2 in. apart and countersunk for flathead screws.

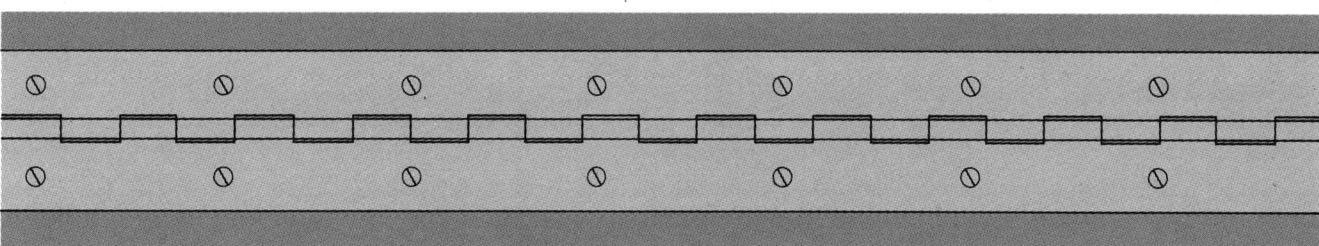
Continuous hinge

Door hardware

Types and uses

Door hardware includes hinges, locks, latches, stops, closers, holders, knobs, chains, peepholes, mail slots, and weatherstripping; see index for items not covered on this page.

Barrel bolts are used to lock doors from the inside; **chain fasteners** permit partial opening of a door. **Chain bolts** and **cane bolts** are used for locking garage doors.

Doorstops come in rigid types with rubber tips to prevent damage to the door and in a spring type that can be pushed aside while the floor is swept. **Latches** are used when key-locking is unnecessary.

Brass and bronze hardware is often coated with lacquer to prevent tarnishing. Do not polish it; polishing damages the lacquer seal and causes rapid tarnishing. Good serviceable hardware is also made of steel, but be wary of "hardware" made of plastic plated to resemble polished brass.

Latches

Latches are used for interior doors and are made in finishes that harmonize with period furniture: Rustic iron, dead black, copper, and brass.

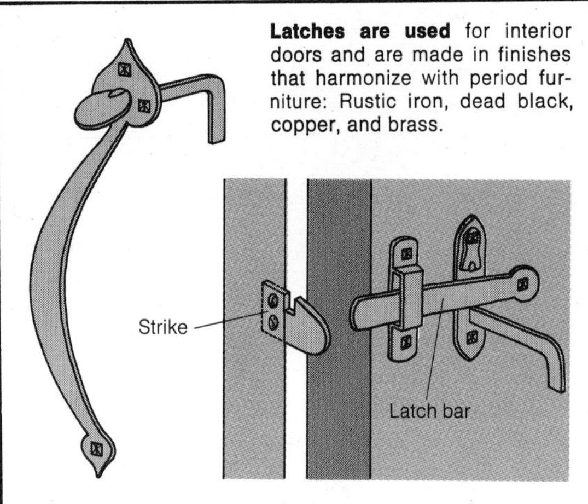

Bolts and fasteners

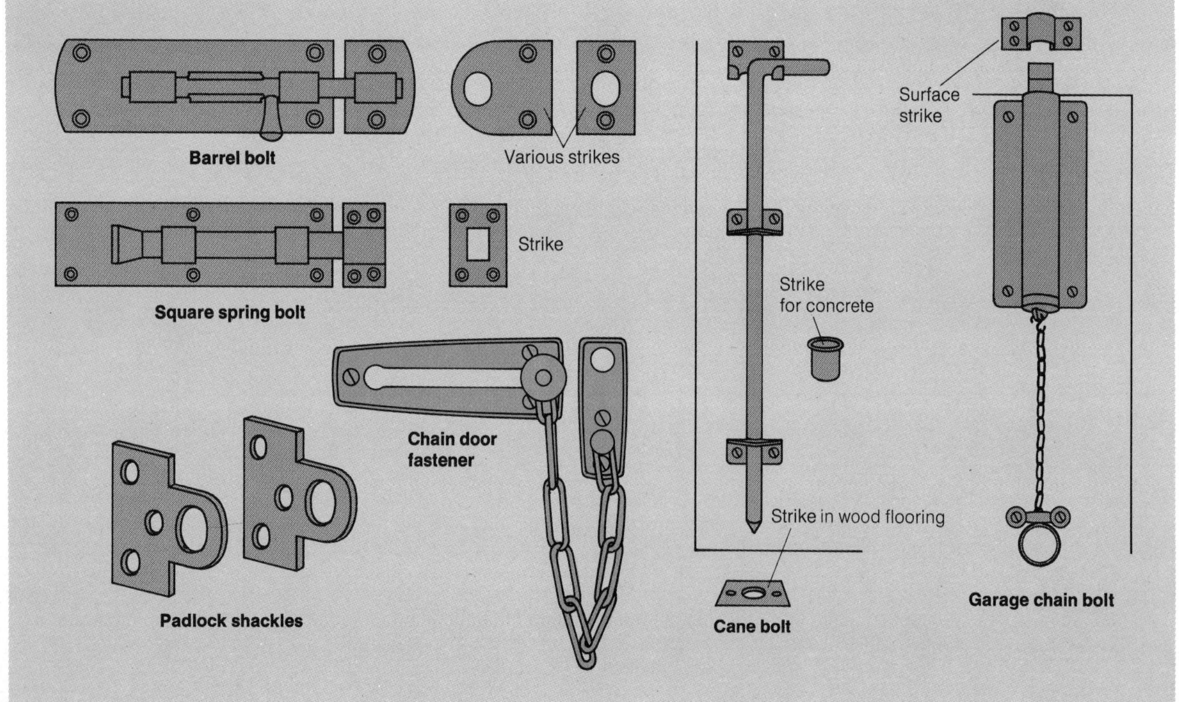

Stops and holders

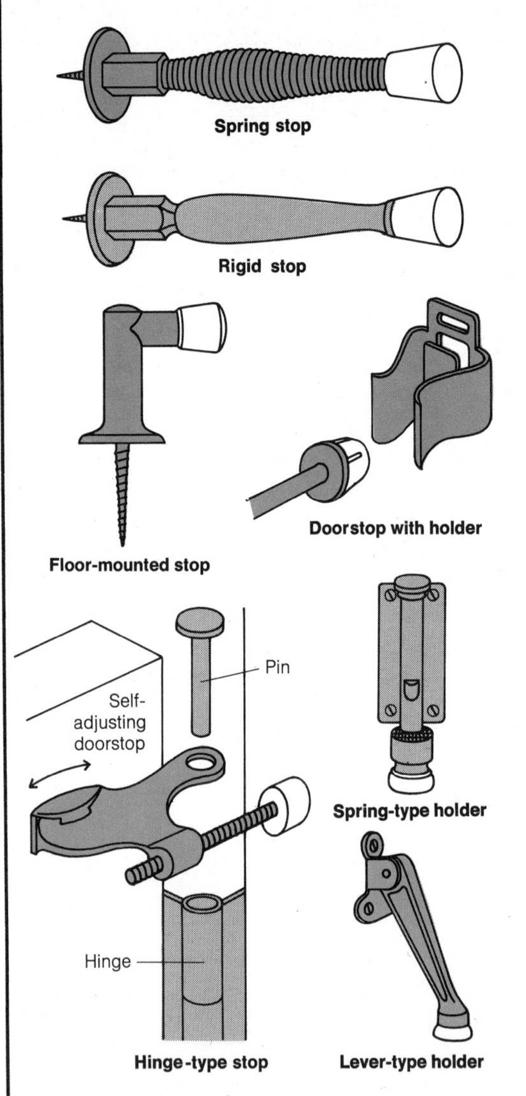

Stops and door holders are used to prevent doors from opening too wide, with possible damage to walls and hinges, and to hold doors in a fully opened or partially opened position. If a doorstop or a holder cannot be mounted on a wall, the stop can be mounted on the door, and of course vice versa. All doorstops have soft rubber tips to cushion the impact of the moving door.

Knobs and pulls

Knobs, drawer pulls, and handles come in a broad range of colors and materials: Bronze, steel, aluminum, porcelain, wood, plastic—even solid silver and gold-plated. There is no easier way to dress up an old piece of furniture than by replacing knobs and handles. They are simple to remove; all you need is a screwdriver. (Always remove them before doing any painting or refinishing.) Large hardware dealers feature panel displays of the knobs and handles they stock. Other sources are lumberyards that cater to the do-it-yourself trade, and mail-order houses.

Types of knobs

Screw type
Bolt type
Flush door type

Door
Screw

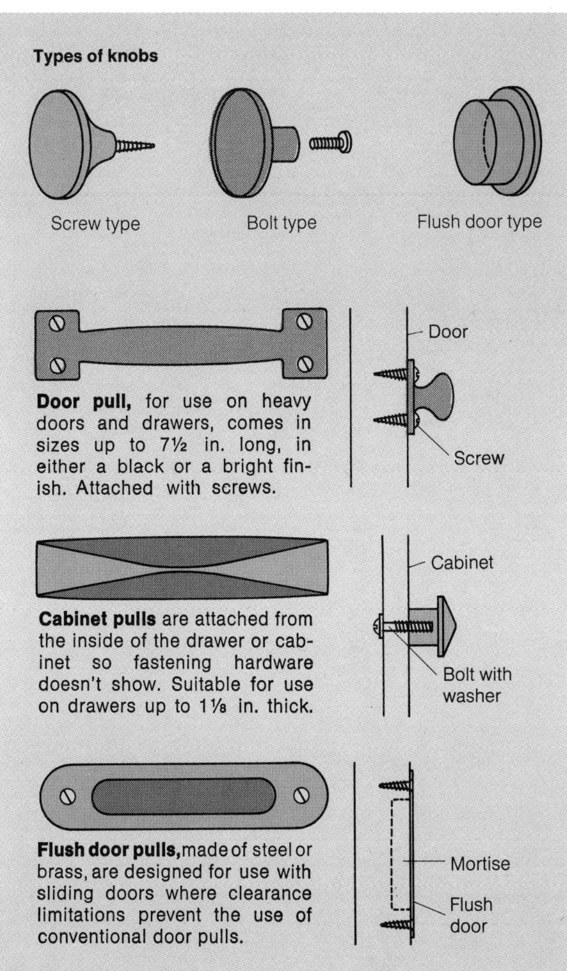

Door pull, for use on heavy doors and drawers, comes in sizes up to 7½ in. long, in either a black or a bright finish. Attached with screws.

Cabinet
Bolt with washer

Cabinet pulls are attached from the inside of the drawer or cabinet so fastening hardware doesn't show. Suitable for use on drawers up to 1⅛ in. thick.

Mortise
Flush door

Flush door pulls, made of steel or brass, are designed for use with sliding doors where clearance limitations prevent the use of conventional door pulls.

Types of catches and how they are used

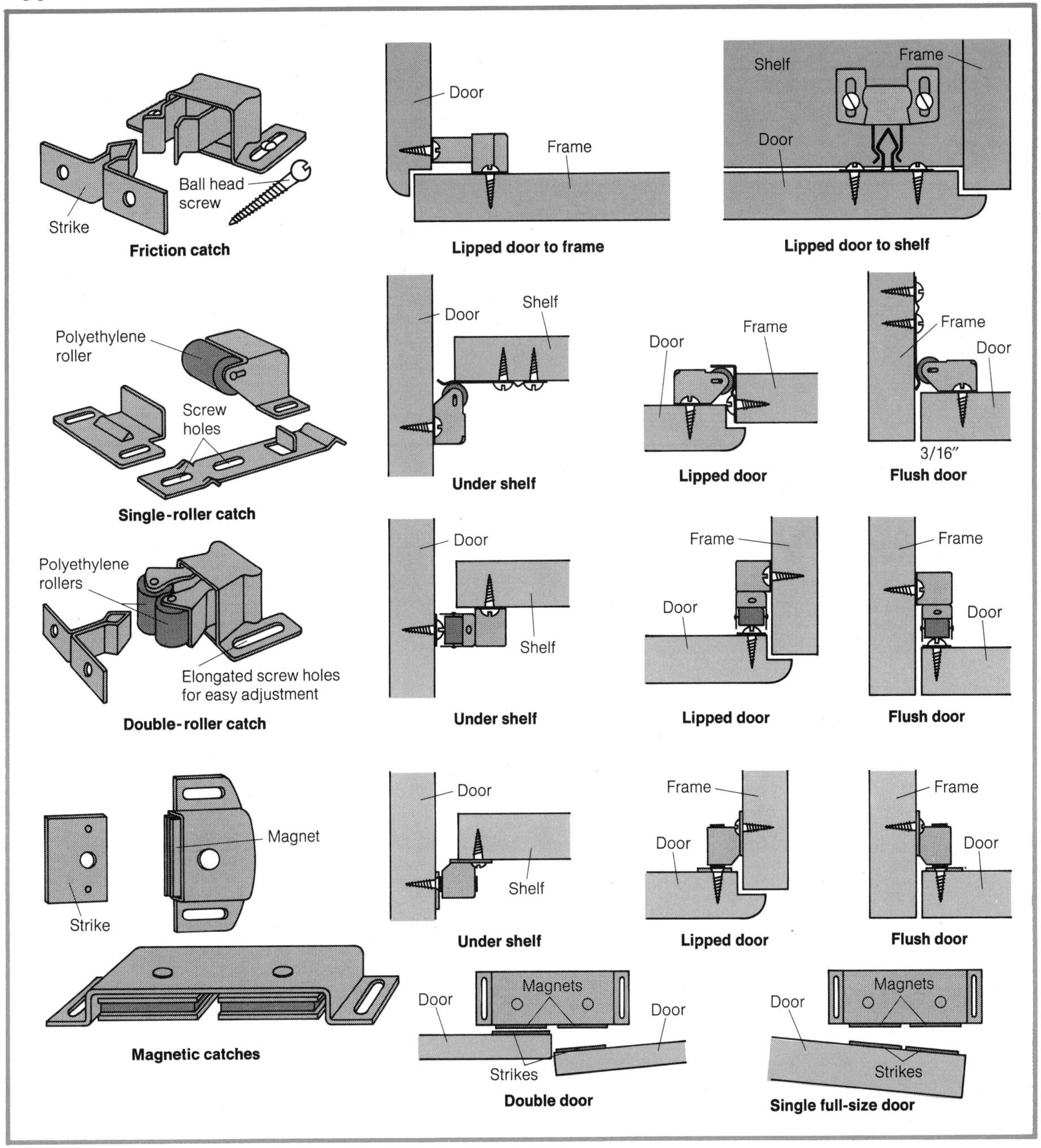

Strike
Ball head screw
Friction catch
Door
Frame
Lipped door to frame
Shelf
Frame
Door
Lipped door to shelf
Polyethylene roller
Screw holes
Single-roller catch
Door
Shelf
Under shelf
Door
Frame
Lipped door
Frame
Door
3/16″
Flush door
Polyethylene rollers
Elongated screw holes for easy adjustment
Double-roller catch
Door
Shelf
Under shelf
Frame
Door
Lipped door
Frame
Door
Flush door
Strike
Magnet
Door
Shelf
Under shelf
Frame
Door
Lipped door
Frame
Door
Flush door
Magnetic catches
Door
Magnets
Door
Strikes
Double door
Door
Magnets
Strikes
Single full-size door

Screen and storm door hardware

Simple screen door

Screen door hardware can be bought as a set containing hinges, door pull, and a hook and eye to keep the door closed. These, however, are just the bare essentials. In addition, the well-equipped screen door will have some sort of door closer (or a spring) and a snap catch if a door closer is not used. In place of a door closer, you can substitute spring-loaded hinges, which can be adjusted to increase or decrease spring tension. Don't forget a push bar to protect the screen. Without one, the screen will very soon bulge and ultimately tear.

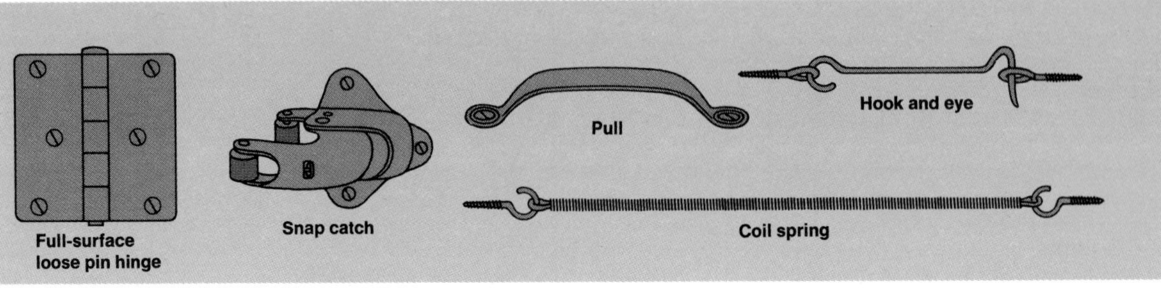

Storm door

Storm door hardware is very similar to hardware for screen doors. In fact, quite often the two doors are combined so that no extra hardware is required. At the start of winter, the screen panels are removed and glass panels substituted. At the start of summer, this is reversed. Combination screen and storm doors are usually sold complete with jambs which are inserted in front of the door serving the house. An added feature is a snubber—a chain-and-spring arrangement which keeps the door from opening too wide and also cushions it if it is opened too forcefully.

Screen and storm door hinges

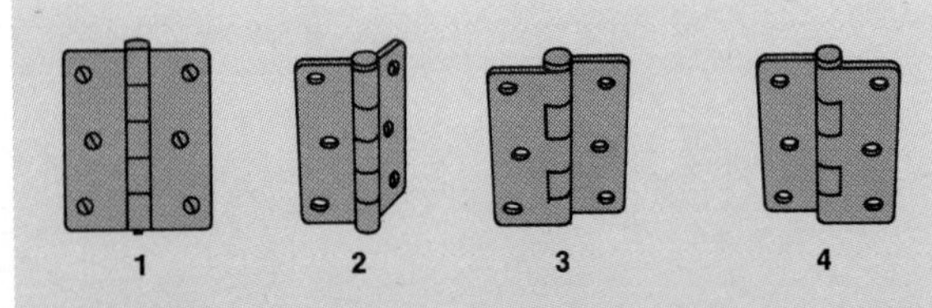

1. Full-surface hinge has two vertical bearings to sustain the door for right- or left-hand installation.
2. Half-surface hinge is used when the door jamb is too narrow to take a full-surface hinge. The inside leaf should be mortised.
3. Door thicker than the jamb can be neatly hung with this type of offset hinge.
4. Door thinner than the jamb takes a similar hinge but offset is in reverse direction, favoring the door.

Screen door hinges are often mounted without mortising into the door or the jamb, since the fit of a screen door is not as important as the fit of the exterior door. Nonmortising latches for screen doors are also available.

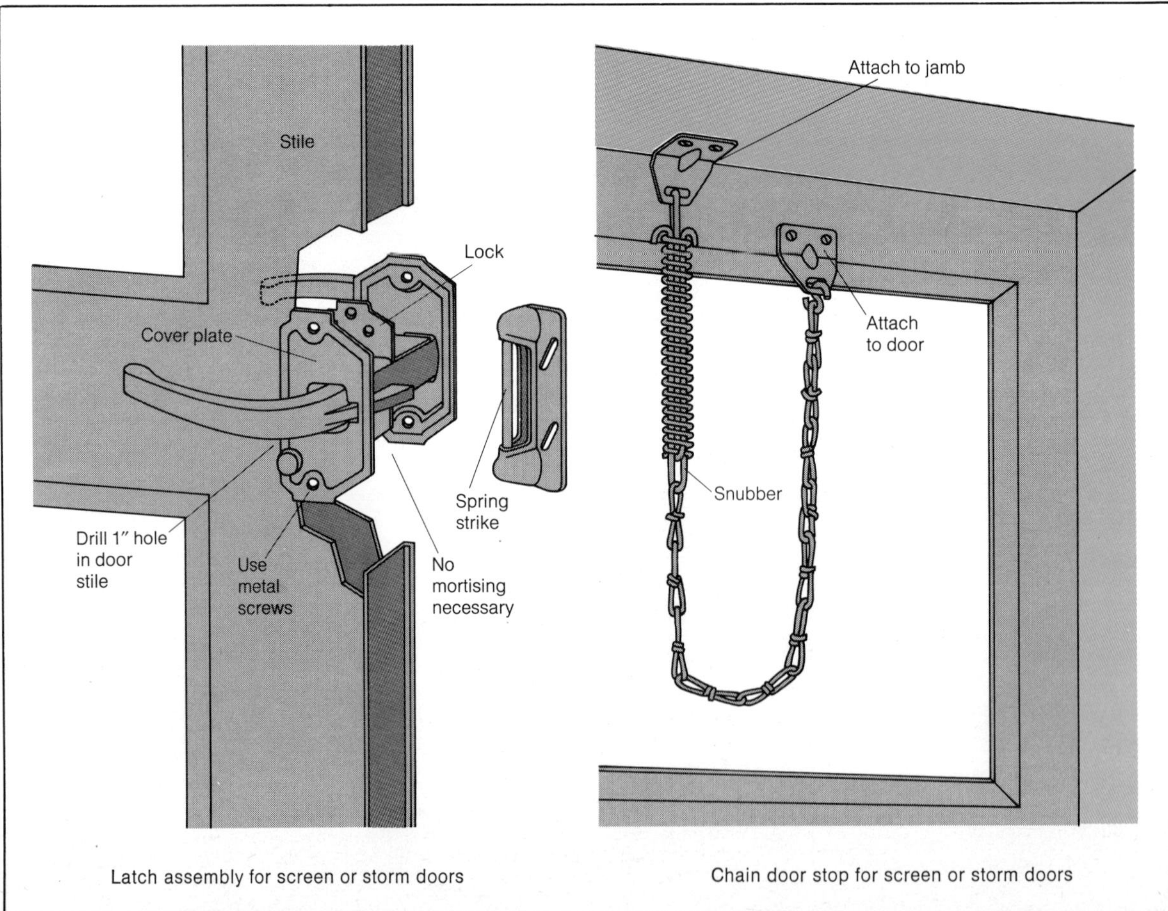

Latch assembly for screen or storm doors

Chain door stop for screen or storm doors

Door closers

Door closers serve several valuable purposes. They assure positive closing of a door, prevent the wind from opening it, stop a door from opening too wide and thus forcing the hinges, and cause doors to close smoothly without clatter. Closers are made in two types for residential use, the pneumatic and the hydraulic. As a general rule, all doors that face the outdoors should be fitted with a closer—even light screen doors, and of course storm doors. Because interior doors operate in such different circumstances, they do not require closers.

Before attempting to install any type of door closer, first make certain that the door does not bind, that it swings freely in any position, and that all accessory hardware (locks, hinges, and chains) are in place and securely fastened and will not interfere with the automatic closing of the door.

The pneumatic door closer, shown below, can be adjusted by turning the slotted screw in the center of the end cap. Turning it to the left (counterclockwise) will allow the door to close faster. Turning it to the right will make the door close more slowly. These closers also have a fast-latching feature – the last 3 inches of closing are accomplished rapidly to make certain the door will latch closed and not stay ajar. This fast-latching feature can be adjusted if necessary to keep the door from slamming. To adjust, open the door about 3 inches and hold it open with the hold-open washer. Then unscrew the door bracket and move it forward (away from the closer). This gives the closer less closing power. If more closing power is needed, the bracket should be moved back (toward the closer).

Installing a pneumatic door closer

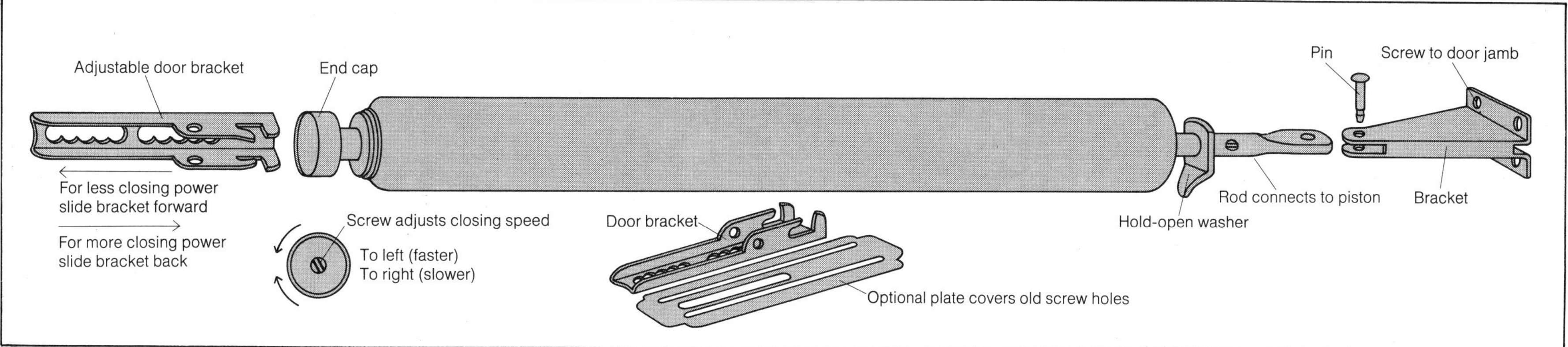

Installing a hydraulic door closer

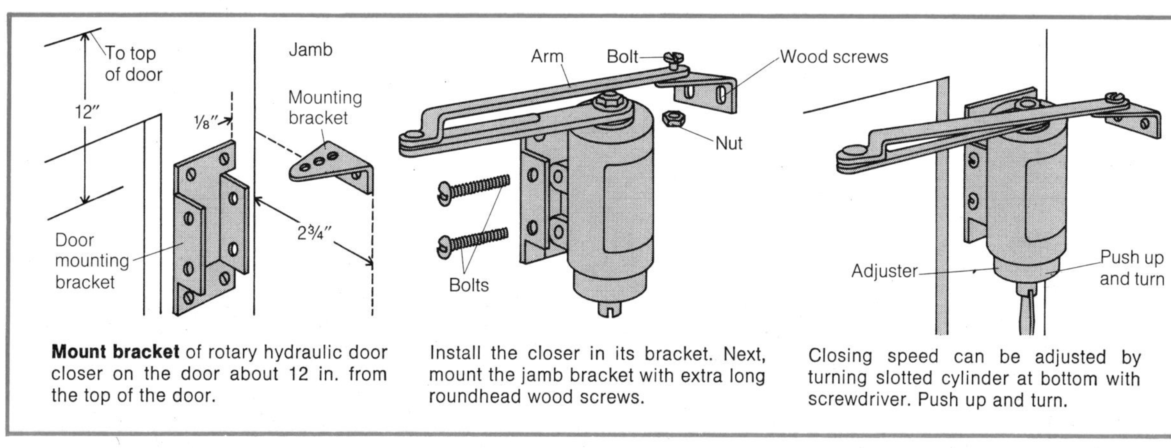

Mount bracket of rotary hydraulic door closer on the door about 12 in. from the top of the door.

Install the closer in its bracket. Next, mount the jamb bracket with extra long roundhead wood screws.

Closing speed can be adjusted by turning slotted cylinder at bottom with screwdriver. Push up and turn.

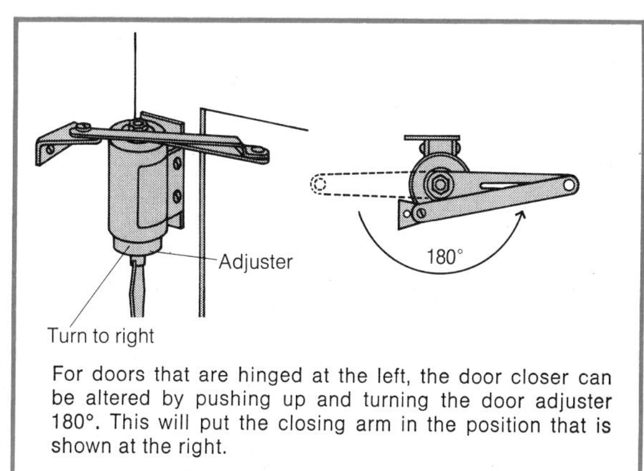

For doors that are hinged at the left, the door closer can be altered by pushing up and turning the door adjuster 180°. This will put the closing arm in the position that is shown at the right.

Miscellaneous hardware

Window hardware

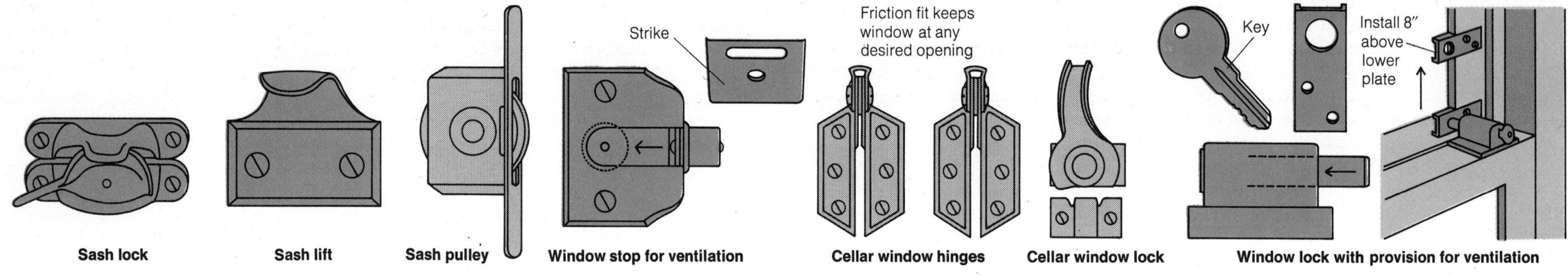

Sash lock **Sash lift** **Sash pulley** **Window stop for ventilation** **Cellar window hinges** **Cellar window lock** **Window lock with provision for ventilation**

Hasps and staples

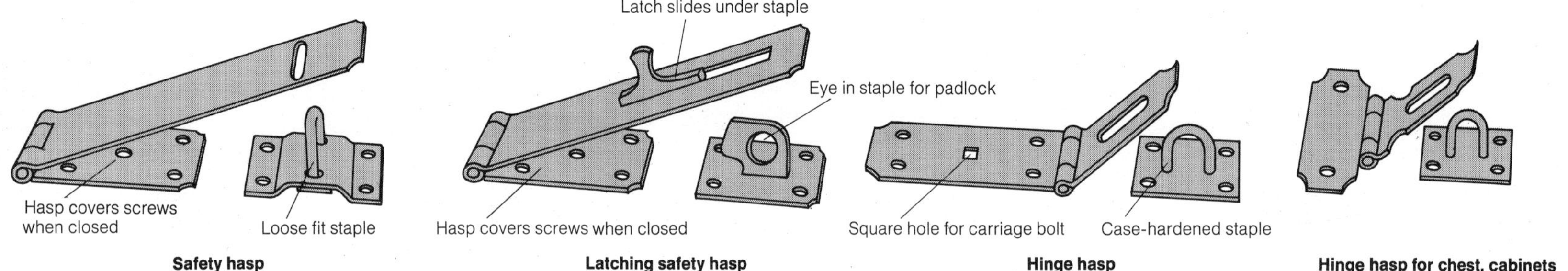

Safety hasp **Latching safety hasp** **Hinge hasp** **Hinge hasp for chest, cabinets**

Gate hardware

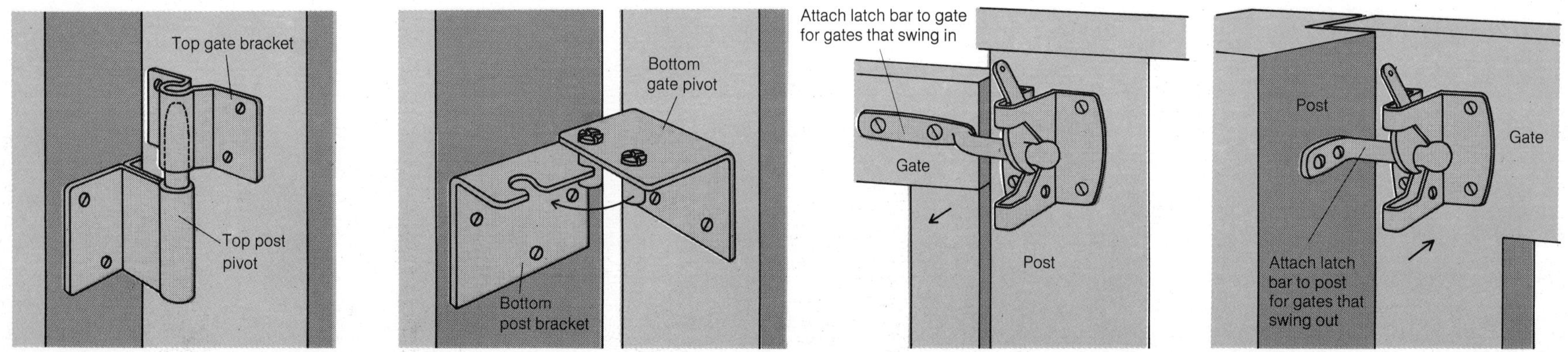

Hinge for gates that swing in or out

Gate latches for gates that swing one way only

Adjustable shelves

Adjustable shelving can be installed in closets or on walls. Shelves come in widths to 12 inches, and they are supported by movable brackets. A screwdriver and a hacksaw to cut uprights to length are the only tools required. Uprights should be spaced no more than 32 inches apart and screwed into wall studs. Be sure shelves extend at least 2 inches beyond brackets. Uprights can be joined to run from floor to ceiling.

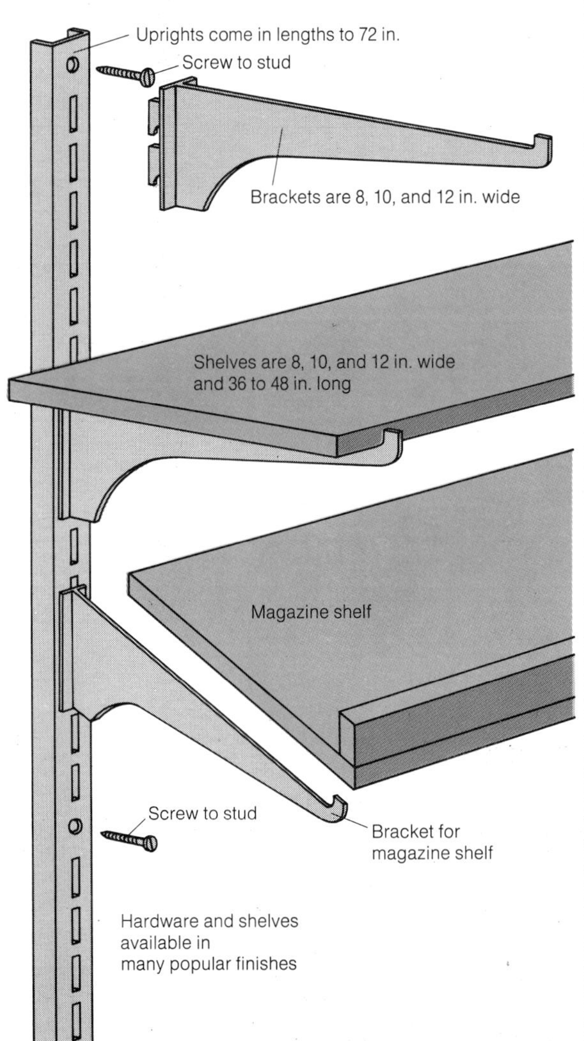

Clip-type supports

This type of shelving support is designed for use between narrow walls, such as are found in closets, and in bookcases and cabinets. The clip-in shelf supports fit into recesses 1 inch apart on the uprights and can be easily slipped out and repositioned to create any spacing desired. Two supports are required at each end of the shelf. Shelves should fit snugly against sides and back.

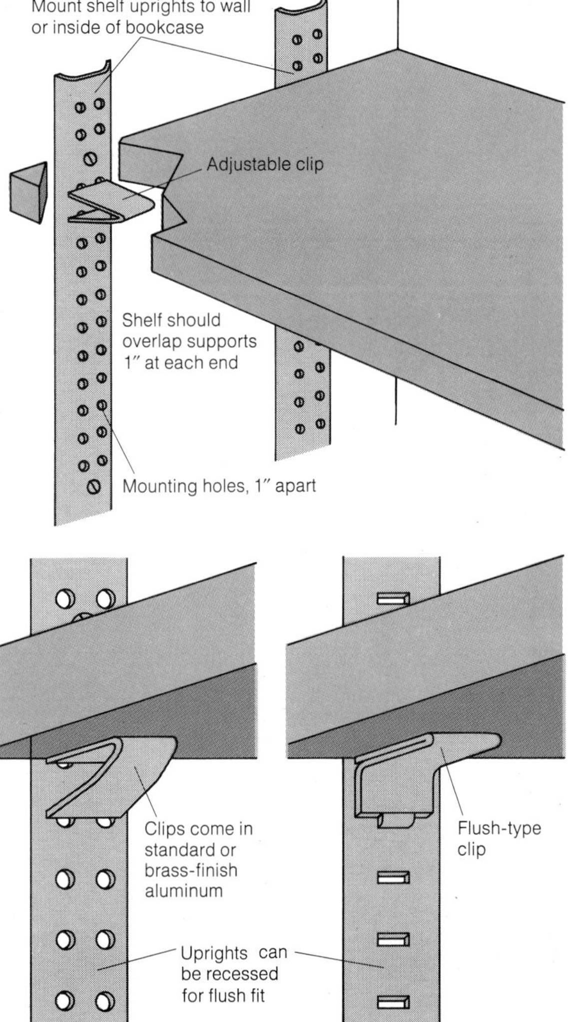

Tension-type uprights (freestanding)

This is a shelf support that can be installed independently of walls or other support and in any part of the house as a room divider. The posts extend from floor to ceiling and are held in place by spring-loaded ends which bear against the ceiling without marring it. They can be used with ceiling heights up to 8 feet 2 inches; supporting blocks can be added if your ceiling is a few inches higher.

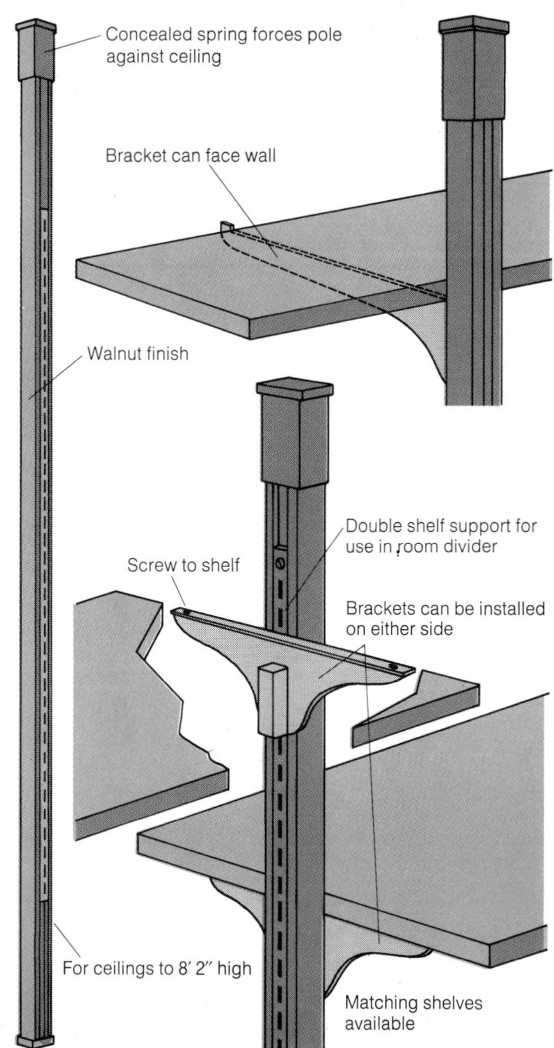

Choosing the right adhesive

Before choosing an adhesive, consider how the article you are gluing will be used when the job is finished. If making outdoor furniture, for example, select an adhesive which is waterproof; on kitchen and bathroom projects, use adhesives which resist moisture. When working in an unheated garage or basement, use glue that hardens at temperatures below 64°F. Consider, also, whether glued joints must be clamped, and the drying time involved.

To achieve satisfactory results from any adhesive, follow the manufacturer's instructions precisely, making sure joints are clean, dry and snug-fitting. The charts that follow describe the basic adhesive types available for household use.

TYPES AND USES

1. PVA adhesives: These are the familiar "white glues" that come ready-to-use in squeeze bottles. They are Polyvinyl resin adhesives suited to most interior woodworking jobs and household repairs. PVA dries clear; bonds are strong but will not resist high stress or dampness. Clean off excess glue with a damp cloth.

2. Contact cements: Use these adhesives to bond laminates (Formica, Micarta) to counter tops. Also good for gluing plastic foam, hardboard, and metal to wood. Apply adhesive to both work surfaces and allow to dry. Work pieces must be accurately positioned before glued surfaces touch since 50 to 75 percent of full bond strength is reached on contact. Bond strength is high, but not good for furniture building. Remove excess glue with special solvent or nail polish remover.

3. Rubber base cements: Rubber base cements have a wide range of non-structural bonding applications. Good to excellent bonds between wood to concrete, paper to wallboard, rubber to rubber and for pottery repairs. Use nail polish remover or special solvents to remove excess.

4. Epoxy adhesives: Almost any material can be glued with epoxies. They are particularly suitable for repairs to glass and china that will be immersed in warm water, and for strong metal to metal bonds. They are excellent for general repairs, but too expensive and awkward to manage for large projects. Epoxies are two part adhesives—a resin and a hardener—which must be mixed together in equal proportions. Some types are slow curing (up to 48 hours), although five minute curing epoxies are available.

5. Plastic cements: These adhesives are excellent for general household use. They are highly resistant to moisture and develop strong bonds. Plastic cements are most commonly used in model making, but can also be used to glue glass, wood, plastic and ornamental objects. Work must be clamped while cement hardens. These adhesives are moderately heat resistant. Clean excess with acetone.

6. Latex base adhesives: These are used for gluing fabrics, carpet, paper and cardboard. Available in tubes and tins, they dry quickly and form strong flexible bonds. They withstand washing in hot water, but not dry cleaning. Rub excess off with a damp rag before they set. Otherwise, soften them with lighter fluid.

7. Mastic adhesives: These are used to bond ceiling tiles, floor tiles, plywood wall panel or any similar building materials. There are two basic types; synthetic latex, which is a water-base adhesive; and rubber resin type which consists of synthetic rubbers in solvents. Both types bond well to concrete, cement screeds, hardboard, asphalt, ceramic tiles, leather and textiles. Rubber resin types are available in tubes that can be fitted into caulking guns for application. Surplus can be removed with a damp rag before setting; once hardened, use a petroleum solvent to remove.

8. Resorcinol and Formaldehyde adhesives: Both these glue types are excellent for bonding wood to wood where structural strength is needed in the adhesive. Resorcinol types are highly water resistant and are recommended for gluing outdoor furniture and in boat building. Formaldehydes are exceptionally strong, but limited to indoor furniture since weather resistance is poor. Both types require mixing: Resorcinols mix with resin: Formaldehyde with water. Both types require clamping times from 3 to 10 hours and neither should be used in work areas where temperatures are below 70 degrees.

9. Gums and pastes: This class of adhesives includes rubber cements, flour pastes, animal glues and vegetable derivatives such as starch and dextrine. These adhesives are only suitable for sticking paper, cardboard and leather. Many wallpaper adhesives fall into this category. Excess glues of this type can usually be cleaned off with water.

10. Silicone sealants: These cream-like adhesives are most commonly used as sealing compounds. The usual application is around sink and bathtub areas where the sink top or tub meets the wall.

VG=Very good; **G**=Good;
F=Fair; **P**=Poor;
INST=Instant; **FLX**=Flexible;
SR=Semirigid; **R**=Rigid

ADHESIVE TYPES	Stress Resistance	Weather Resistance	Setting Time (Hrs)	Curing Time (Hrs)	Open Time (Min)	Flexibility	Flammability	SAMPLE BRAND NAMES
1 **PVA adhesives**	G	P	4	24	10	SR	NO	Elmer's Glue-All; DuPont White glue; Sears white glue; Franklin Concrete Adhesive; Duralite; Evertite; Titebond.
2 **Contact cements**	F	VG	INST	24 TO 48	30 TO 60	FLX	YES	Devco rubber; Pliobond; Sears Miracle Pliobond; Craftsman; Weldwood; Duro; Woolworth's; Duralite.
3 **Rubber base cements**	P	G	INST TO 4	24 TO 48	1 TO 15	FLX	YES	Gripit; Ozite AP880; Scotch Grip; Miracle Adhesive; Black Magic; High Tak Super Adhesive No. 975; Poly-Chemical's Strip-Cure.
4 **Epoxy adhesives**	VG	VG	¼ TO 12	24	1 TO 180	R SR	NO	Helor Quik-Set; Kling Enterprises; 5-Minute epoxy; Epoxy 1177; Ruscoe epoxy; Elmer's epoxy; Devcon clear epoxy; Wilhold epoxy.
5 **Plastic cements**	P	F	6	48	1	SR	YES	Duco cement; Liquid Solder; Scotch Super-Strength adhesive; Wilhold china & glass cement; Devco Plastic Mender; Weldit cement.
6 **Latex base adhesives**	P	P	INST TO 1	8 TO 48	1 TO 120	FLX	NO	Devcon Patch; Sears Stitchless Mender; Duratite Formula 55; Franklin Indoor/Outdoor carpet adhesive.
7 **Mastic adhesives**	F	G TO VG	INST TO 1	48	10 TO 45	FLX *	YES *	Webtex 200 acoustical adhesive; Franklin Construction adhesive; Ruscoe Pan-L-Bond.
8 **Resorcinol and Formaldehyde**	VG	VG P	6 TO 10	24	15 TO 60	R	NO	Craftsman plastic resin glue; Weldwood plastic resin glue; Sears waterproof resorcinol glue; U.S. Plywood waterproof resorcinol glue.
9 **Gums and pastes**	P	P	¼	8	2	FLX	NO	Carters Liquid paste; Carters mucilage; Carters rubber cement; Higgins vegetable glue; LePage's paper cement.
10 **Silicone sealants**	P	VG	1	24	5	FLX	NO	Dow silicone adhesive; General Electric silicone seal; Sears silicone adhesive sealant; Duratite Formula 48 general purpose cement.

How to use this table

1. Determine which of the materials to be glued is movable and which is fixed. Look down the column on the left first and locate the movable material. Locate the fixed material in the column at the top of the page. If both objects to be glued are movable, it does not matter which column is referred to first.
2. Check the numbers in the boxes where the two columns intersect. The corresponding numbers in the chart (p. 86), indicate the adhesive(s) most suited to the job.
3. If more than one adhesive is recommended, study the properties of each adhesive to determine which will provide the most satisfactory bond in relation to conditions under which the glued object will be used. Select an adhesive from the list of brand names.

The numbers on this table correspond to the circled numbers in the chart on page 86. Find the recommended adhesive number on this table, then match with circled numbers on chart to find suggested brand names. Numbers in heavy type indicate the adhesive that is most suitable for work subject to extreme conditions.

	Acoustic tiles	Bricks and concrete	Carpets	Ceramic tiles	Cork (except tiles)	Cork tiles and sheeting	Fabrics and cloth	Glass, china, pottery	Hardboard	Leather	Vinyl	Metal	Paper and cardboard	Plaster	Drywall	Plastics, soft flexible	Plastics, hard rigid	Plastics, laminated (Formica, Micarta)	Plastics, floor tiles and sheeting	Plastic tiles	Polystyrene foam	Rubber	Rubber floor tiles and sheeting	Stone	Wood
Acoustic tiles	**7**,2	**7**	—	**7**	**2**,6,7	**2**,6,7	**6**	—	**7**,2	**7**	—	2	1,2	**7**,2	**7**,2	3	—	—	3	—	7	2	2	7,2	**7**,2
Bricks and concrete	—	—	—	7,2	—	—	—	—	—	—	—	**4**	—	—	—	—	—	—	—	—	—	—	—	**4**	**4**,7
Carpets	—	6,**2**	**6**	6,2	6	6	6	—	1,**2**	6	6,**2**	2	6	1,**2**	1,**2**	3	3,**2**	2	—	—	1	2	2	6,**2**	1,**2**
Ceramic tiles	7	7	—	2,**1**	2	2	7	2,5,**1**	7	2	2	2,**1**	7	7	7	3	2,**1**	2,**1**	3	—	7	2	2	7	7
Cork (except tiles)	6,**2**	3,**2**	6	2	3,**2**	3,**2**	6,**2**	3	1,**2**	2	3,**2**	2	1	1,**2**	1,**2**	3	3	2	7,**3**	—	7	2	2	3,**2**	1,**2**
Cork tiles and sheeting	2	7	—	2	3,**2**	2	6	3	7	3,5	—	2	3	7	7	3	2	2	7	—	—	2	2	7	7
Fabrics and cloth	6	6,**2**	6	7	6,**2**	6	6	1,3	1,**2**	6,**2**	6,**2**	3,**2**	6	1	1	3	2,**4**	2	3	—	6	2	2	6,**2**	1,8,**2**
Glass, china, pottery	—	3,**4**	—	2,**4**	3	3	3	3,5,**4**	—	3,5,**4**	3,5	3,5,**4**	3	3,**4**	3,**4**	3	3,5,**4**	2,**4**	3	—	—	2	3	3,**4**	—
Hardboard	2	1,**2**	—	2,**4**	1,**2**	2	1,**2**	—	1,**4**	2	1,**2**	2,**4**	1,**2**	2	2	3	2	2,**4**	3	—	1	2	2	2,**4**	1
Leather	2	3	6	2	2	3	6,**2**	3,5,**4**	2	2	3	2,5	3	2	2	3	3,**2**	2	3	—	6	2	2	2	2
Vinyl	—	3	**2**,6	2	3,**2**	—	6,**2**	3,5	1,**2**	3,5	3	3,5	3	3,**2**	3,**2**	3	3,**2**	2	—	—	—	2	—	3	1,**2**
Metal	2	2,**4**	—	2,**4**	2	2	3,**2**	3,5,**4**	2,**4**	2,5	3	2,5,**4**	3,**2**	2,**4**	2,**4**	3	2,5,**4**	2,5,**4**	3	—	—	2	2	2,**4**	2,**4**
Paper and cardboard	1,9,**2**	1,9,**2**	6	1,3,**2**	1,9	3	6	3,5	1,9,**2**	3,5	3	3,5,**2**	1,9	1,9	1,9	3	3	2	3	—	1,9	2	2	3	1,9,**2**
Plaster	—	—	—	—	1,**2**	2	1,**2**	3,5,**4**	2	2	3,**2**	2,**4**	1	1	1	3	2	2,**4**	3	—	—	2	2	—	1,**4**
Drywall	—	2	—	—	1,**2**	2	1,**2**	3,5,**4**	2	2	3,**2**	2,**4**	1	1	1	3	2	2,**4**	3	—	—	2	2	2	1
Plastics, soft flexible	3	3	3	3	3	3	3	3,5	3	3,5	3	3,5	3,5	3	3	3,5	3,5	3	3	—	—	3	3	3	3,5
Plastics, hard rigid	—	2,**4**	3,**2**	2,**4**	3	2	3,**2**	3,5,**4**	2,**4**	3,**2**	3,**2**	2,**4**	3,5	2,**4**	2,**4**	3,5	3,5,**4**	2,**4**	3	—	—	2	2	2,**4**	2,**4**
Plastics, laminated (Formica, Micarta)	2	2,**4**	—	2,**4**	2	2	2	2,**4**	2,**4**	2	2	2,**4**	2	2,**4**	2,**4**	3	2,**4**	2,**4**	3	—	1	2	2	2,**4**	2,**4**
Plastics, floor tiles and sheeting	3	7	—	3	7	7	3	3	7	3	—	3	3	7	7	3	3	3	3	—	—	3	3	7	7
Plastic tiles	—	7	—	—	—	—	—	—	7	—	—	3	—	7	7	—	—	—	—	7	7	—	—	7	7
Polystyrene foam	7	7	—	—	7	—	6	—	7	6	—	—	1	7	7	—	—	—	—	7	7	—	—	7	7
Rubber	2	2	—	2	2	2	2	2	2	2	2	2	2	2	2	3	2	2	3	—	—	2	2	2	2
Rubber floor tiles and sheeting	2	7	—	2	2	2	2	3	7	2	—	2	2	7	7	3	2	2	3	—	—	2	2	7	7
Stone	—	4	—	2	—	2	—	—	—	—	—	4	—	—	—	—	—	—	—	—	—	—	—	4	—
Wood	2,**7**	2,**4**	—	2,**4**,**8**	1,**2**	2	1,7,**6**	—	1,**8**	2,8	1,**2**	2,**4**	1,**2**	1,8	1,8	3	2,**4**	2,**4**	3	—	1	2	2	2,**4**	1,**8**

Adhesives for bonding plastics

How to use this table

Before selecting an adhesive for repairing a plastic, you must identify the type of plastic. The column dealing with identification and common uses will provide some basic clues. Generally, it is safe to assume that the cheaper the article, the more likely it is that the plastic is polyethylene or polystyrene. High-quality products are usually made of acrylics, nylon, acetal, or glass reinforced plastics.

Contact cements, plastic cements and epoxy are the three adhesive types that will take care of most repairs to plastic. Mastics, rubber base adhesives and resin-based resorcinol adhesives can also be used to bond many plastics. Test on scrap material first.

Use the tables below to help identify the type of plastic you want to bond. Find the material you are bonding to in the right-hand columns. Check the numbers with the corresponding adhesive type on page 86 and select a suitable brand name.

TYPE OF PLASTIC	IDENTIFICATION AND COMMON USES	ADHESIVE(S) FOR BONDING PLASTIC TO:			
		Itself	Ceramics	Metal	Wood
Thermo-setting plastics	Hard, brittle, heat resistant plastics that include epoxy, melamine, phenolic and others. Common uses: Non stick finish on pots and pans; washing machine agitators; plastic pipe; foam products.	2,4	4	4	4
Polystyrene, high impact	Rigid, brittle, makes metallic sound when dropped. Common uses: Toys; radio cases; water tumblers; plastic wall tiles; car parts such as instrument panel.	2,4,5,3	4,10	4	4,1
Polystyrene, clear	Transparent, glass-like, brittle. Tinny noise when dropped. Common users: Jugs; tumblers; model kits; food trays; canisters; cups and saucers.	2,4,5,3	4	4	4,1
ABS (Acrylonitrile-Butadiene-Styrene)	Tough, rigid, sinks in soapy water, metallic noise when dropped. Common uses: Refrigerator parts; luggage; cameras; picture frames; door and drawer handles.	2,4,3	4,10	4	4
Polyethylene and polypropylene	Tough and brightly colored. Both make dull noise when dropped and float in soapy water. Common uses: Cups; saucers; plates; trash bins; laundry baskets; squeeze bottles.	4,6	6	6	6
Acrylics	Usually transparent, makes dull noise when dropped. Common uses: Automobile tail and signal lights; plastic windows (Plexiglas, Acrylite); clear lampshades.	2,5,3	2	2	1,2
PVC, rigid (Polyvinylchloride)	Hard, glossy and weather resistant. Usually light colored. Common uses: Wall and floor tiles; picture frames; electric plugs; toys; shelving; bicycle mudguards.	2,5	5	2	5

TYPE OF PLASTIC	IDENTIFICATION AND COMMON USES	ADHESIVE(S) FOR BONDING PLASTIC TO:			
		Itself	Ceramics	Metal	Wood
Nylon and acetal	Tough, rigid moulding materials. Common uses: Door handles; gears; fishing reels and line; tennis racket strings; curtain tracks; drawer slides; auto dashboards.	2,4,8	2,4,10	4	4,8
PVC, flexible	Glossy; weather resistant. Common uses: Rainwear; flexible dolls; curtains; inflatable toys; shopping bags; garden hose; artificial leather; wire insulation.	2,5	5	2	5
Cellulose	Glossy, highly flammable. Common uses: Golf club heads; film; fountain pens; combs; eyeglasses frames; clock and watch frames; plastic pipe.	2,5	2	2	2
Decorative laminates	Hard, heat resistant and scratch resistant. Common uses: Counter tops; bathroom shower door panels; decorative panels.	2	2	2	1,2
Glass-reinforced plastics (GRP)	One side smooth, other rough. Fiber strands strengthen the plastic. Common uses: Boat hulls; car bodies; suitcases; furniture; corrugated panels.	2,4	2	2	2
Polyurethane foam, flexible	Brown, sponge-like honeycomb. Common uses: Foam cushions; insulation; mattresses; Christmas ornaments.	2,4	10	4	4
Polyurethane foam, rigid	Lightweight, firm, usually a brownish color. Common uses: Decorative imitation beams.	2,4	10	4	4
Polystyrene, expanded	White, rigid foam. It is easily crushed. Common uses: Packing material for appliances; insulation.	2,4,5,3	4,10	4	4,1

section 4:

Making your own interior repairs

A neglected house is a house on the way down—in livability, looks, and value. This is not news to any proud and penny-wise homeowner, nor is the cost of outside help. What is news is what this section will show you: The many repair jobs you can do yourself when you understand how. A ship-shape home yields hidden benefits too: Lower heating bills from improved insulation, less damage from such household pests as insects and rodents, and greater safety in such potentially dangerous areas as stairways.

contents

Interior maintenance

Inspection checklist

Make a thorough inspection of your home inside and out once or twice a year. Detecting and correcting repair problems before they become emergencies can save time, worry, and often money. Use the following list when you inspect the interior of the house. (For an exterior checklist, see p. 164.)

1. Attic: Look for evidence of roof leaks, also openings that permit entry of bats or other pests; inspect insulation, rafters, ventilation openings, chimney, and side walls.

2. Windows: Check for difficulty of operation, cracked or broken panes, sash cords or chains in need of replacement, faulty or hard-to-operate locks, worn weatherstripping.

3. Bathroom: Note dripping faucets, leaking shower heads, malfunctioning flush valves, inadequate hot-water supply.

4. Walls and ceilings: Examine condition of painted surfaces and wallpaper; look for cracks, holes, or bulges in plaster, signs of loose tape on wallboard.

5. Floors: Inspect for loose, creaking boards, worn areas, cracked and chipped baseboards and moldings, broken or missing floor tiles.

6. Staircase: Note loose, squeaking treads, shaky handrails and posts, cracked or broken balusters.

7. Radiators: Check leaking valves; bleed off air at start of heating season.

8. Air conditioners: Take out and clean filters before warm weather; cover exterior in winter.

9. Doors: Inspect for sticking or sagging; examine locks and chains; renew worn weatherstripping.

10. Fireplace: Check dampers, firebox, hearth, grate, andirons, screen, mantelpiece.

11. Kitchen: Examine appliance wiring; clean the ventilator fan and remove accumulations of dust and grease.

12. Doorbells: Test all sonic apparatus—chimes, buzzers, burglar alarms.

13. Furnace: Check for leaks in pipes, flue, firebox; examine damper; check blower belt and blades; replace filter; oil motor; test thermostat operation.

14. Electrical system: Look throughout the house for frayed cords, loose connections, malfunctioning switches and outlets.

15. Plumbing: Check drains, traps, waste pipes in basement, main water line and shutoff.

16. Basement in general: Look for signs of dampness, leaks, cracked or broken floors, cracked walls. Pay special attention to joint between floor and walls; this is where most basement leaks develop.

17. Basement pipes: Check all cold-water pipes in the basement. Wrap them with insulating material to prevent sweating and subsequent dripping during hot summer weather and possible freezing in winter.

18. Window sills: These take a beating, especially those that face the southern sun. Sand and paint them. You can make your window sills maintenance-free by covering them with a plastic laminate.

19. Basement windows: Those on grade, or slightly above grade, should be examined for termite damage, even if the foundation is concrete.

20. Beams: Make sure each beam is doing its share of the work with no visible space between a beam and the main house girder. Drive in shims if necessary.

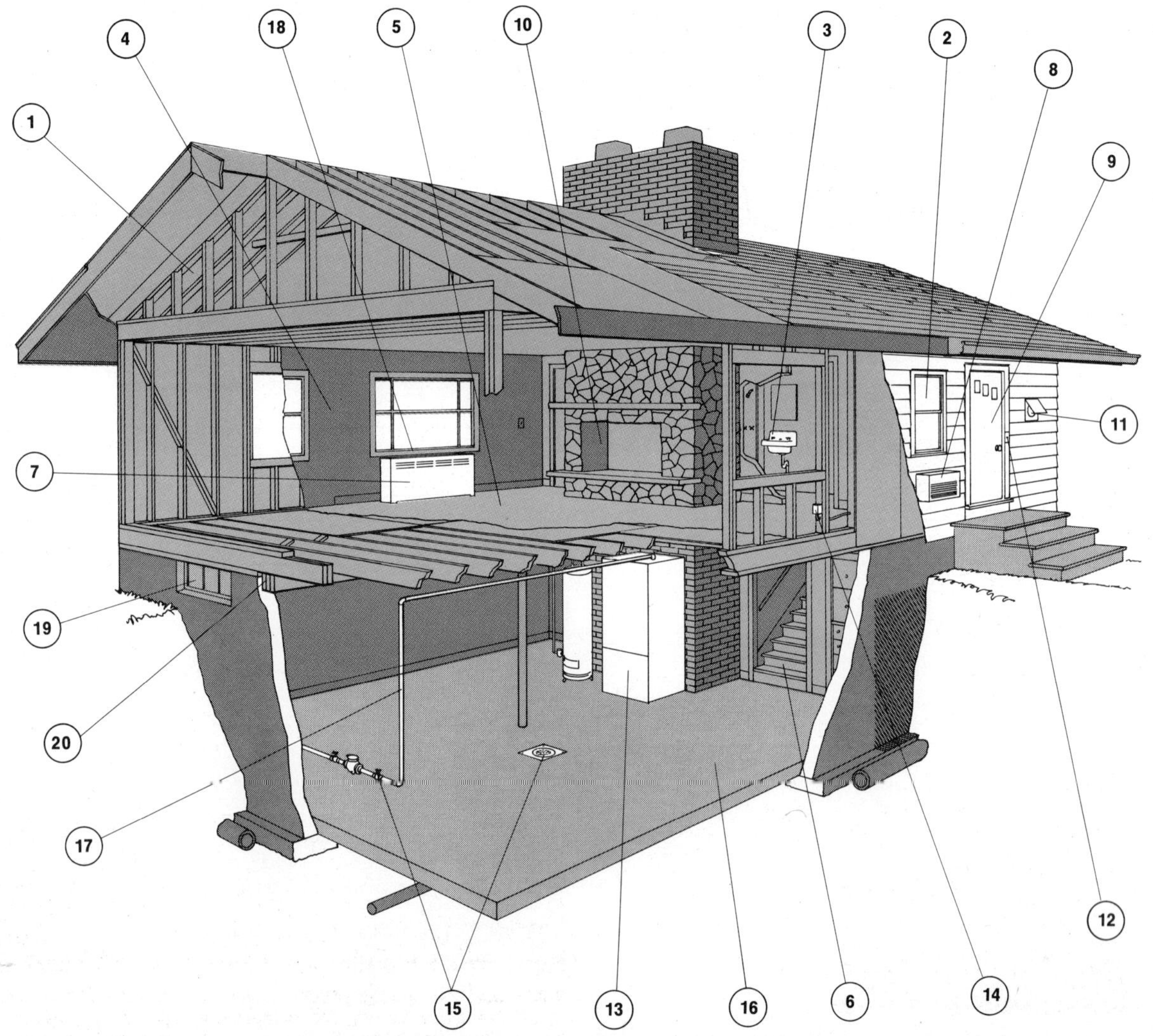

Patching cracks in plaster walls

Most cracks in plaster walls are caused by settlement, vibration, or atmospheric conditions, but some may be due to faulty construction. It takes careful inspection—particularly around doors, windows, moldings, and corners—to find hairline cracks that could become larger. Whatever their size, all cracks must be repaired before redecorating can begin.

Repair of cracks varies, not so much according to size as to origin. In most cases, repairs to settlement cracks will not need further attention. Vibration cracks are generally small and will probably require periodic repair. Cracks caused by atmospheric conditions may be prevented by controlling temperatures. Cracks due to faulty construction usually will not recur if the cause is eliminated.

Repairing hairline cracks

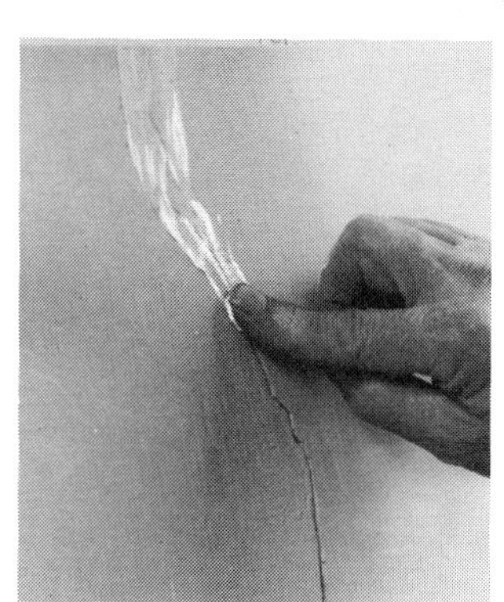

Remove loose particles by running a thin blade along crack. Brush out dust. Rub putty, spackle, or wood dough across crack with fingertip, forcing it in as deep as possible.

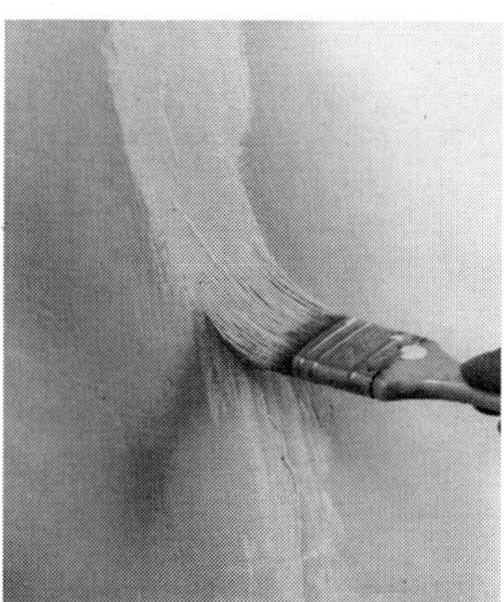

Make sure the repair is thoroughly dry and its surface sanded level before applying a finish. Then prime the repaired area with shellac or sealer to prevent absorption of paint.

Bend the tip of the tang end of a file into a hook; use to enlarge and undercut opening to provide grip for filler.

Prepare enough patching material to fill the crack; mix to a thick, buttery consistency for immediate use.

Apply water with brush or spray to thoroughly dampen the surface and the full depth of the opened crack.

Use flexible putty knife to fill opening completely with patching material. Remove excess from surface.

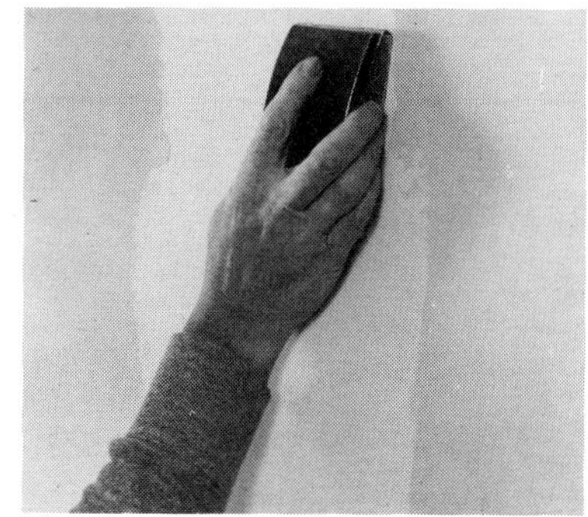

Use fine-grade sandpaper wrapped around a sanding block to smooth the patch and make it level.

When the patch has dried, apply a prime coat over the filled-in crack and the surrounding area.

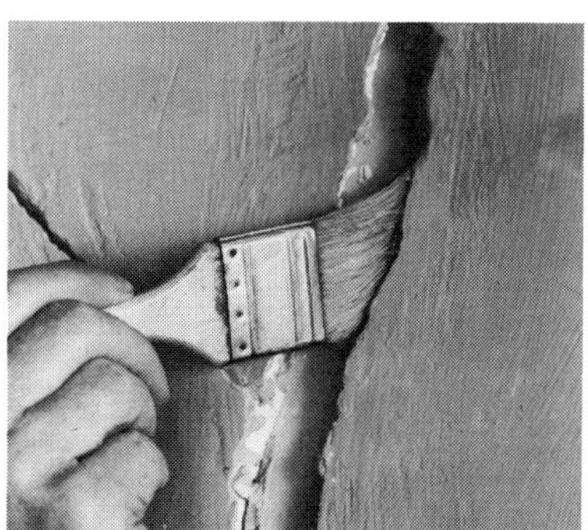

When patching a large crack, undercut it, remove loose plaster, and dampen as you would a small crack.

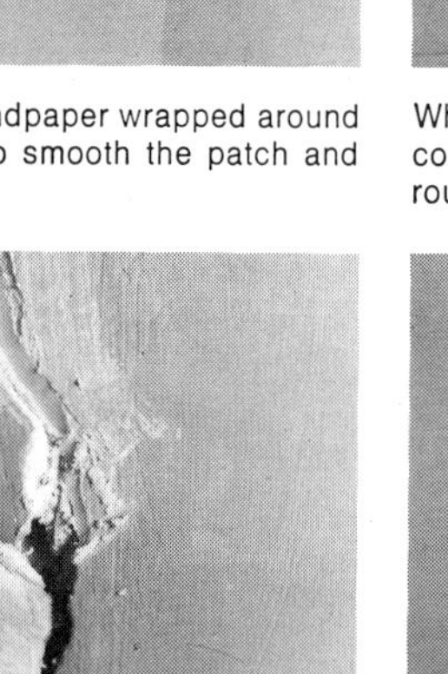

Mix a batch of plaster and fill the cavity. Allow a drying period of 24 hours. Shrinkage may occur during drying.

If shrinkage occurs, dampen patch area and fill cavity with fresh filler. Let dry. Sand smooth. Apply prime coat.

Patching holes in plaster walls

You can fill a small hole in a plaster wall, such as that made by a nail, or a dent caused by furniture, with spackle, wallboard compound, or other filling material suited to the purpose. To prepare the area for filling, first remove all loose plaster from around the perimeter of the hole. To be sure of getting a good bond, dampen the area around the edge of the cavity before applying the filler. After applying the patching material, let the area dry for several hours; then sand it smooth and flush, using a circular motion to blend in the edges of the patch. Prime the patched area before applying the first coat of paint.

A patch for a large hole is best made with plaster as the patching material, and requires some sort of backing support—wire mesh, expanded metal lath, or heavy hardware cloth. Put on at least two applications of plaster, forcing the first through the mesh of the backing to act as an anchor for the rest of the material, and filling the hole completely with the second. When the patching plaster is dry, sand the entire new area until it is smooth and level, then prime it for finishing.

Plaster is best for large holes or major areas, but patching materials such as spackle will serve if there are only a few relatively small holes to be filled. You can make spackle go further by combining it with plaster of Paris before adding water; use of this mixture also reduces the drying time.

When you are filling a large hole, it is a good idea to incorporate a small amount of heavy-duty nylon thread or horsehair in the patching material. This acts as a binder for the material, considerably strengthening the patch.

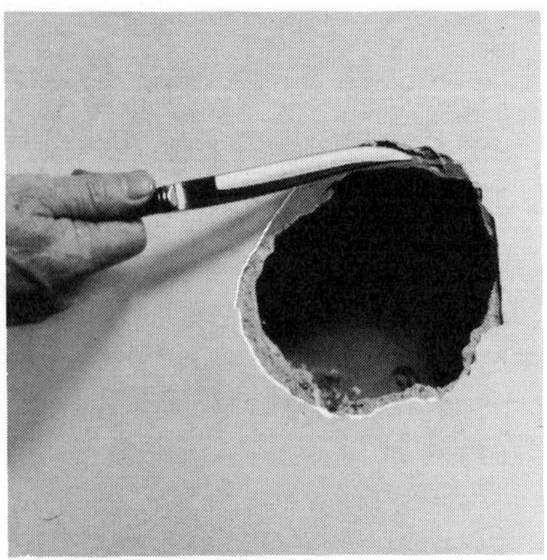

When preparing to fill a hole, first remove all loose plaster from around the perimeter.

Cut a piece of wire mesh larger than the hole. Thread a length of wire through it.

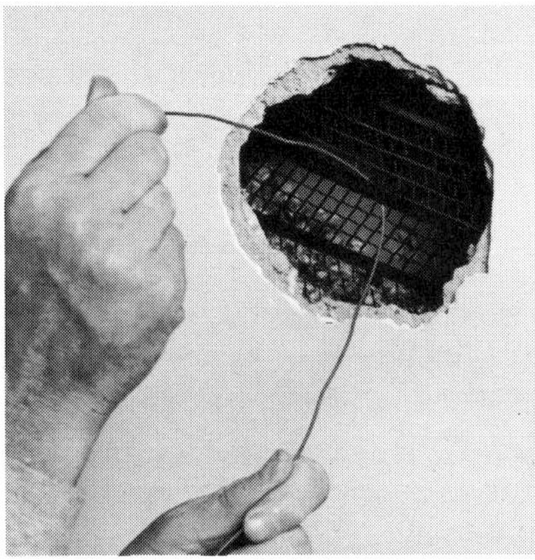

Insert the mesh in the hole. Pull on wire to keep mesh tight against inside of hole.

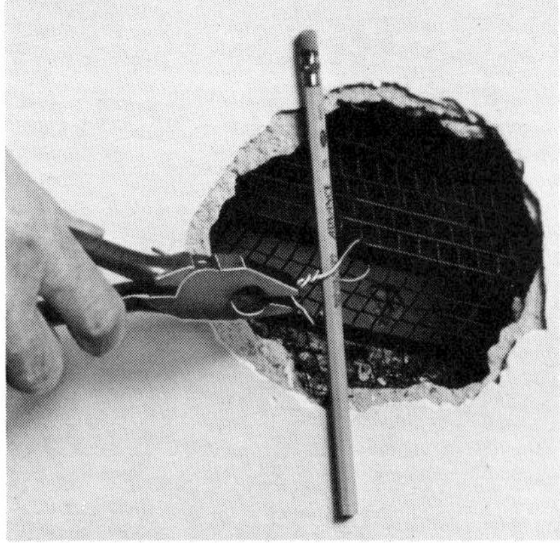

Twist the wire around a pencil or a piece of wood to hold the mesh in place.

Thoroughly dampen the interior and rim of the hole; use a spray or brush.

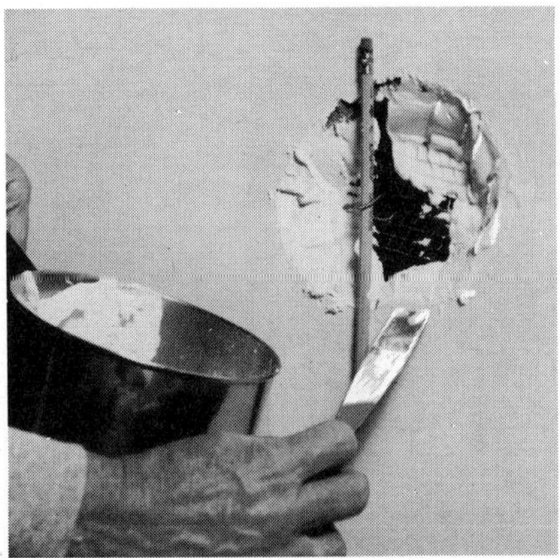

Apply first plaster coat, enough to penetrate the mesh and cover the edges of the hole.

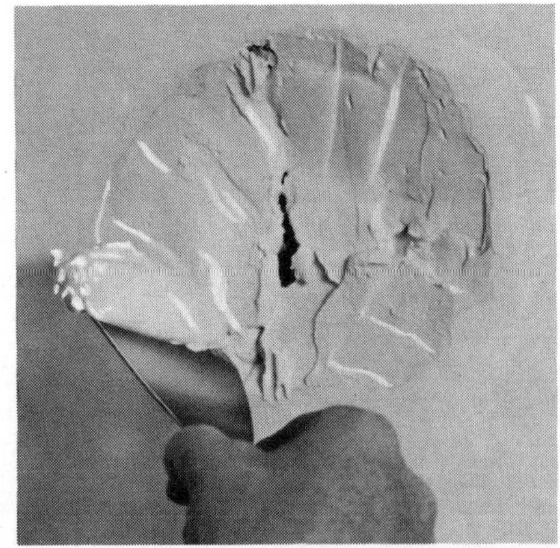

Let first coat dry. Untwist wire; remove pencil and wire. Apply second coat, filling hole.

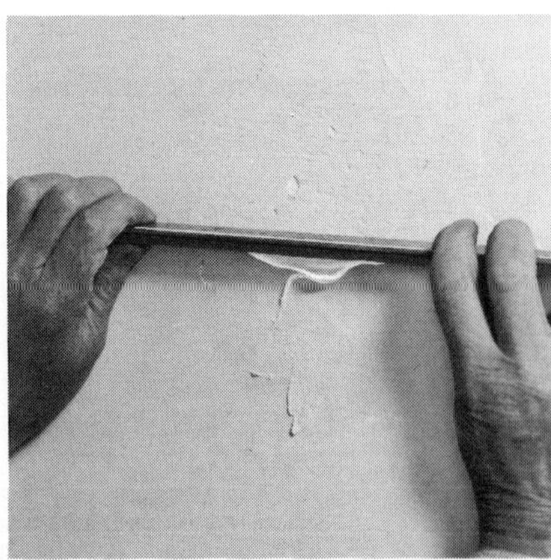

Scrape away excess plaster. Let patch dry thoroughly. Sand; prime before applying paint.

Working with wallboard

Wallboard consists of a fire-resistant gypsum core covered on both sides with a tough layer of paper. Standard wallboard is available in ⅜-, ½-, and ⅝-inch thicknesses; the panels are 4 feet wide and come in various lengths up to 16 feet, ready to finish or predecorated. Most wallboard panels are tapered on the face side to allow for the application of wallboard joint compound and the tape that spans adjoining panels to make a smooth, continuous wall surface. Other edges shown serve special, often decorative or architectural, purposes. Two coats of wallboard joint compound are usually used over wallboard tape; since the compound dries slowly, wait overnight between applications.

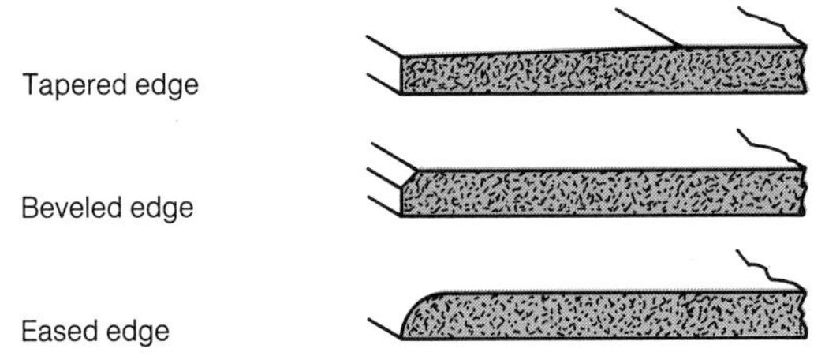

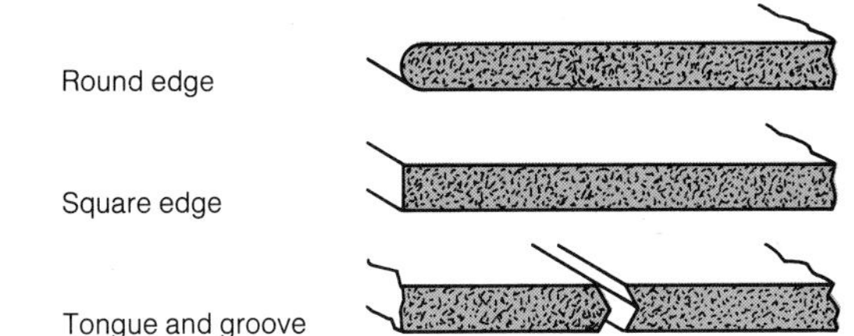

Tools and technique

The tools you need to work with wallboard include a **steel rule,** a **straightedge,** and a **trimming knife** equipped with a sharp, heavy, replaceable blade, used to score the surface of the board for breaking.

Among the necessary installation tools are a **crown-head hammer** to drive nails and to form a dimple (see photo, below right) in the wallboard; plastic pan to hold joint compound; 4-inch **finishing knife** and 10-inch **trowel;** medium-grade **sandpaper; keyhole saw** or **utility saw;** and **hacksaw** or **tinsnips.**

Also worth considering are tools that serve special purposes or make the work easier, such as a **circle cutter,** a **rubber mallet,** an **inside corner tool,** a **T-square,** and a **caulking gun.**

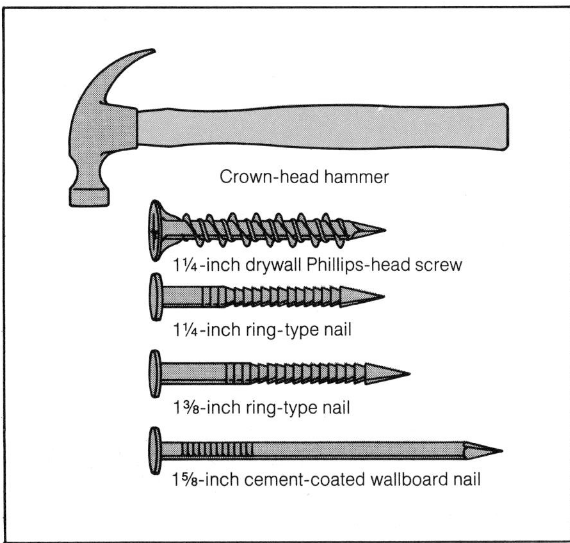

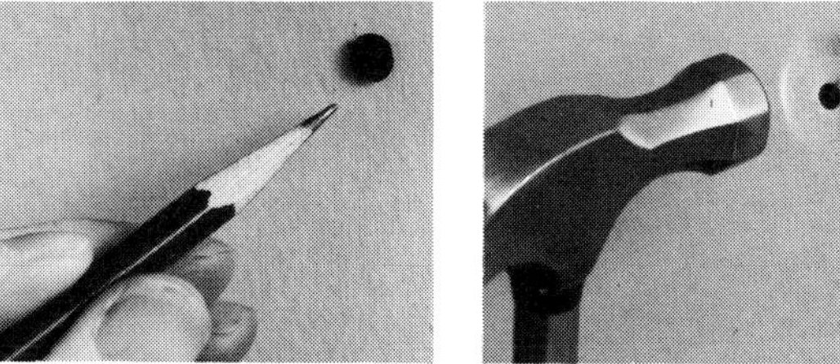

Use a crown-head hammer; set the nail flush (left). Do not puncture the wallboard surface by driving the nail too deep. Dimple the surface (right) with the last hammer blow.

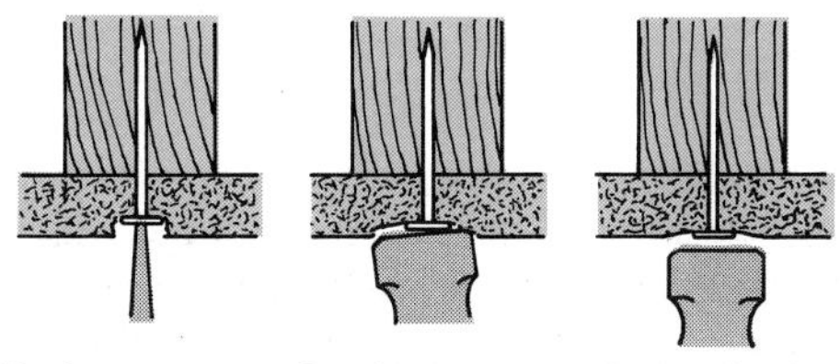

Estimating materials

Wallboard size	Nail size	Amount (per 1000 sq. ft.)
⅜ in., ½ in.	1⅝ in.	5¼ lbs.
⅝ in.	1⅞ in.	6¾ lbs.

COMPOUND AND TAPE

Wallboard area	Ready-mix compound	Compound required	Tape required
100—200 sq. ft.	1 gal.	12 lbs.	120 ft.
300—400	2	24	180
500—600	3	36	250
700—800	4	48	310
900—1000	5	60	500

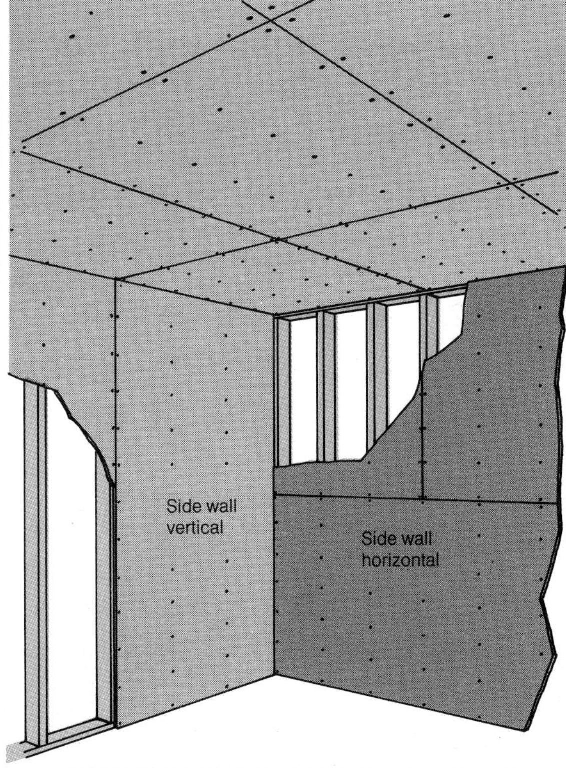

Apply wallboard first to ceilings, then to side walls. Install the side wallboards vertically, with edges parallel to the studs, or horizontally across the studs, whichever way will produce a minimum number of joints. Finish as described on p. 96.

Cutting wallboard

Before cutting the wallboard, check measurements carefully to be sure the panels will slip easily into place. Make straight cuts on the face side the full length or width of the board. Cuts can be made with a saw, if necessary, but a sharp trimming knife is recommended. Hold the blade at a right angle to the board and cut along a straightedge that is heavy enough not to move as you cut.

Score completely through the face paper and part way into the core. Break the core by snapping or bending away from the scored (paper) side. With the partially separated portion folded back, cut the exposed backing paper with the knife from either above or below. Smooth the edges with a rasp, coarse sandpaper, or metal lath wrapped around a wood block.

On the face of the board, carefully measure and mark with a pencil the location of holes for electrical outlets and other openings. Drill holes at corners of openings. Use a knife to score the outline of the piece to be removed. Score diagonal lines as well. Use light hammer blows to knock out the segments, or remove them with a fine-toothed keyhole saw. Be sure that the cutout is accurate so the cover plate will completely conceal the edges of the hole.

First score the wallboard through the face paper and into the core, using trimming knife and cutting along a heavy straightedge.

Next, break the core of the wallboard by bending or snapping the sides away from the scored (face paper) side.

With the partially broken portion folded back, cut the exposed backing paper from above or by an upward stroke from below.

Cut edges will be rough. Smooth them with a rasp or a piece of metal lath or coarse sandpaper wrapped around a wood block.

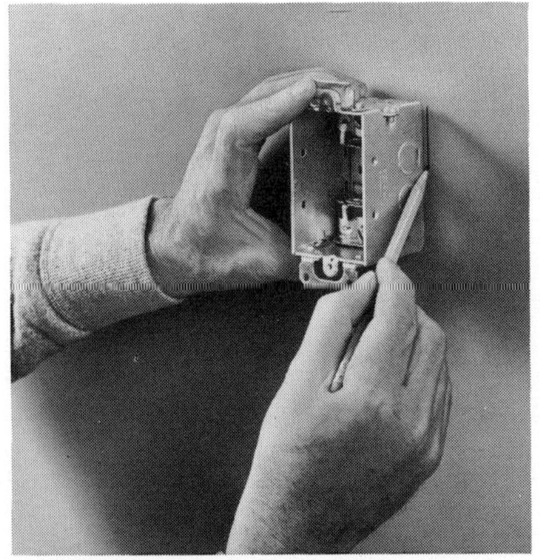

To make an opening for a switch box, place it at desired spot and trace its outline.

Drill a ¼-inch hole at each corner of the rectangular outline as shown.

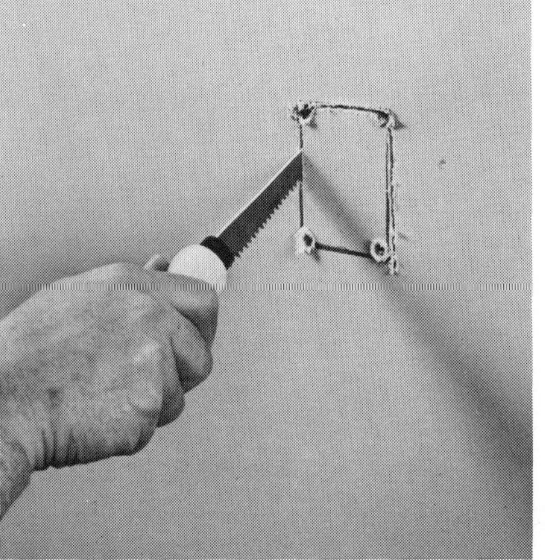

Using a keyhole or wallboard saw, cut the wallboard from hole to hole.

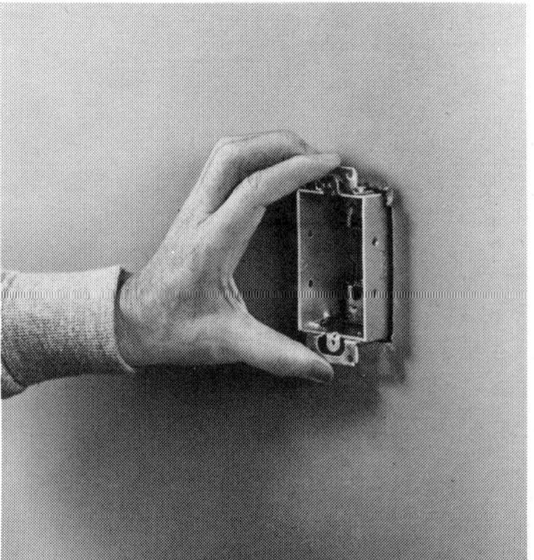

To allow for screw holes when outlining box, use the template shown on p. 265.

Replacing a wallboard panel

When damage to a wallboard panel is so severe that repairs are impractical, your only recourse is to replace the entire panel.

First make sure that the replacement wallboard is the same thickness as the one that is to be replaced. Then, using a sharp trimming knife, cut down the center of the tape and into the joint compound between the damaged board and the adjacent one. Take out all nails and remove the old panel. Pull away loose tape from the board to which it was joined, and sand the rough portions that remain.

After carefully measuring the opening to be filled, cut out the new panel, to size if necessary; use a sharp trimming knife. Sand the edges smooth.

A foot-powered wallboard lifter, improvised from two pieces of wood, will prove helpful in lifting the new section up and against the wall. When the board is in place and the fit is snug, nail the new panel securely, making sure that it butts against the length and width of adjoining panels. Use ring-type nails and, when hammering, exert firm hand pressure on the panel to hold the wallboard tight against the stud or framing member.

Drive all nails perpendicular to the wallboard, dimpling each nailhead. Cover the nails between joints with compound and fill the joints, then apply the tape (p. 96). When the compound has dried, add a second coat; let it dry and add a third, if necessary. Feather each coat out progressively farther from the center. When dry, sand and prime.

With trimming knife, cut down center of tape joining the panels, penetrating into joint compound.

Remove all nails from panel that is to be replaced. Be careful not to damage adjacent areas.

Tear off any loose tape and paper from edges of adjoining panel. Sand sections that remain attached.

Make foot lever of two pieces of wood; position one end under panel; raise panel into position for nailing.

Use one or two T braces (or shores) to force a ceiling board against joists for nailing.

Locate nails in about ⅜ to ½ in. from panel's edges. Drive nails perpendicular to the surface of the wallboard so heads are just flush.

Dimple each nail with the last blow of the hammer so that wallboard joint compound can be applied later to hide the nailheads.

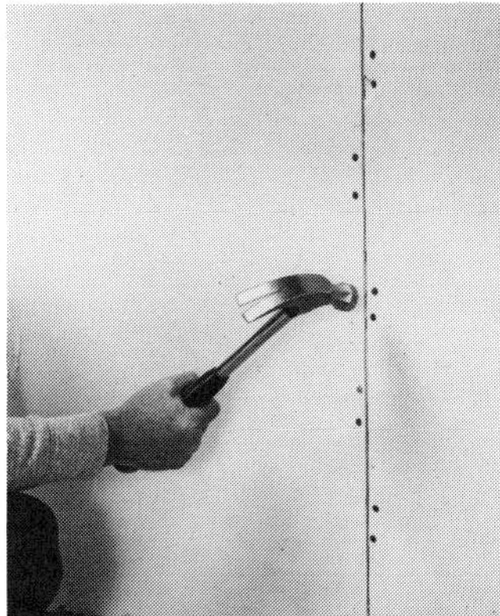

Staggered double nailing as shown is an effective way to secure wallboard to studs. The technique prevents nail popping later on.

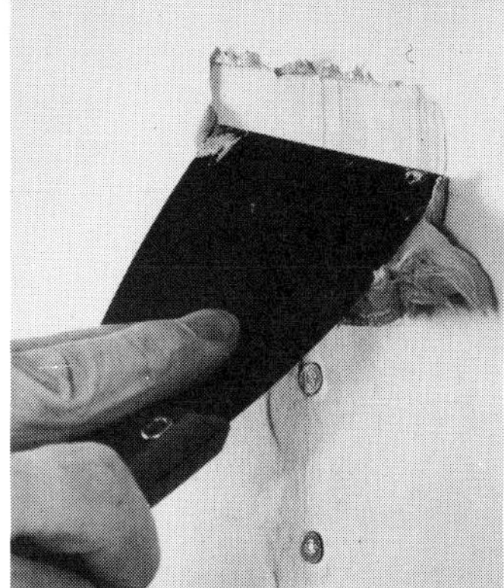

Use a putty knife to apply the wallboard joint compound to cover nailheads in the panel. Nailheads should be slightly below surface of panel.

Apply the tape before compound has a chance to set. Follow with another application of compound (p. 96). Feather out edges beyond tape area.

Taping a wallboard joint

If a wallboard joint is properly taped, it will blend in so well with the surrounding wall that it won't be noticeable. It takes time and careful application of both compound and tape, however, to obtain such a harmonious result.

Wallboard joint compound can be purchased ready-mixed or in a powder form that becomes a paste when it is mixed with water.

The standard wallboard tape is made of a tough 2-inch-wide perforated paper and comes in 75-, 250-, and 500-foot rolls. When the tape is embedded in the compound that fills the recess between the tapered edges of two adjoining wallboard panels, the compound oozes through the perforations to the surface, strengthening the bond.

After the embedded tape and the compound have dried, apply a second coat of compound directly over the first; make this coat from 6 to 8 inches wide and feather it out from the center. Allow the second coat to dry, then add the third coat. This third and final application should be feathered out 12 to 14 inches from the center. When the final coat is thoroughly dry, sand lightly with medium-grade sandpaper wrapped around a sanding block.

If it is necessary to make a butt joint in wallboard that is not tapered, follow the same procedure, but form a slight buildup at the center of the joint. It would be wise, in this case, to extend the feathering 2 to 4 inches beyond the distance that is suggested for a tapered-edge joint.

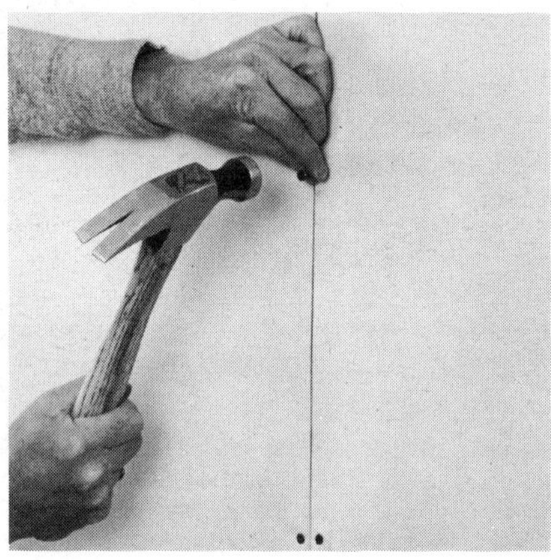

Space nails every 7 in. vertically, at least ⅜ in. in from edges of adjoining panels, and approximately opposite one another.

Apply a thick layer of joint compound to completely fill the channel formed by the tapered edges of the wallboard panels.

Center perforated tape over the length of the seam and press it firmly into the compound. Use a wallboard knife held at a 45° angle.

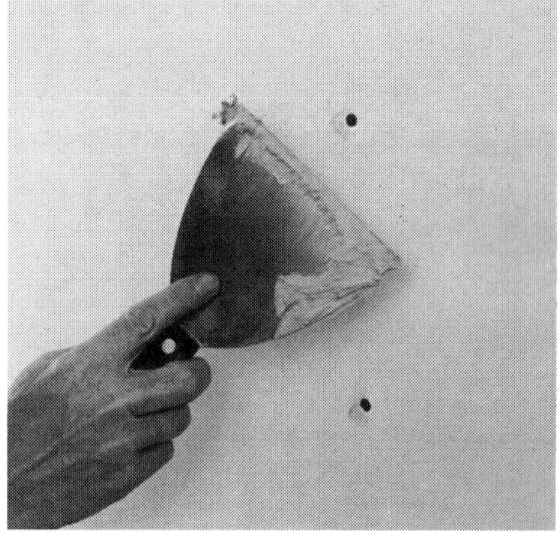

While the first coat of compound dries, use a putty knife to apply first coat of compound over any extra nails between joints.

When first coat is dry, apply a thin second coat, feathering it out 6 or 8 in. Apply second coat to nailheads between joints as well.

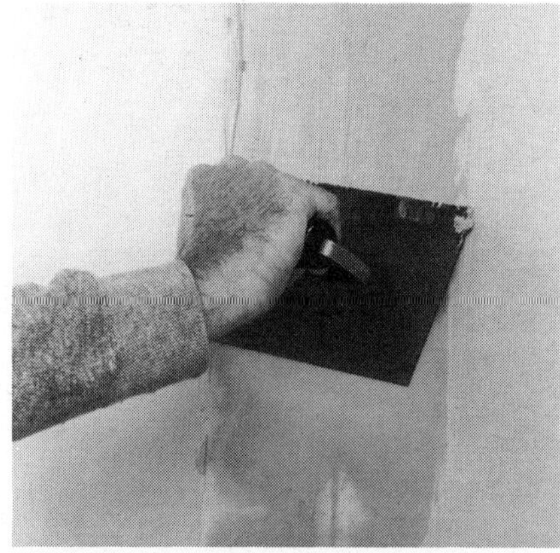

Add a third coat, making it thin and feathering it out 12 to 14 in. Apply third coat of compound to any extra nailheads between joints.

Wait until compound is thoroughly dry, then sand surface lightly with a medium sandpaper to make it smooth and even.

Apply primer coat to the section. If the wall is to be papered, use shellac; this will facilitate later removal of paper, if desired.

Taping an inside corner

Tape an inside corner as you would a flat seam (p. 96) but fold the tape into the corner angle. Use wallboard joint compound to fill the crack where the walls come together; then apply enough compound to the wall surfaces to embed the folded tape. Press compound firmly into corner with a finishing knife, feathering out the excess. Let dry; follow with second and third coats. When dry, sand and finish.

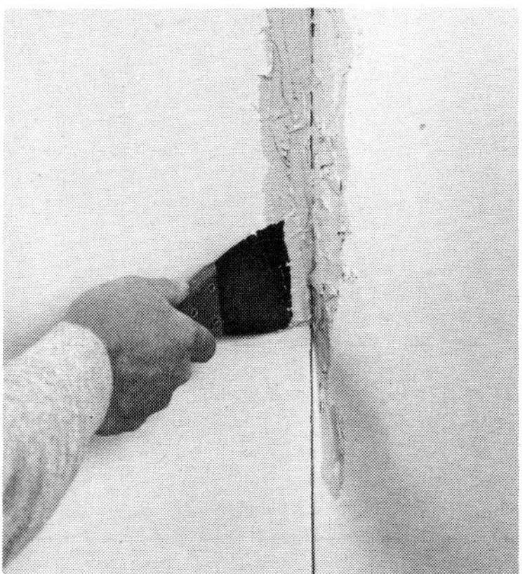

Fill crack with compound, allowing it to extend 1½ in. over adjoining surfaces.

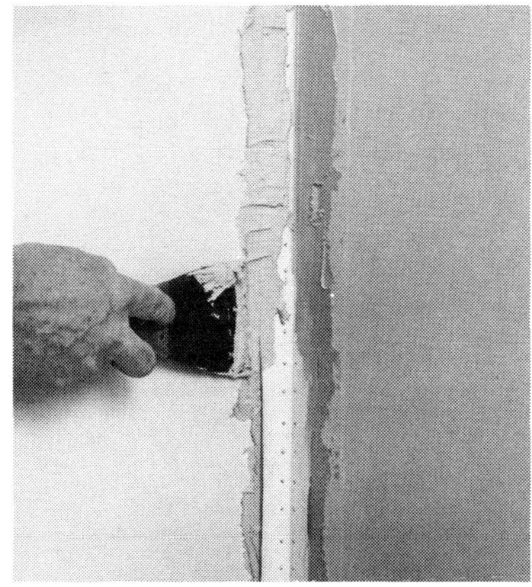

Fold perforated tape down center crease, then embed it in the compound.

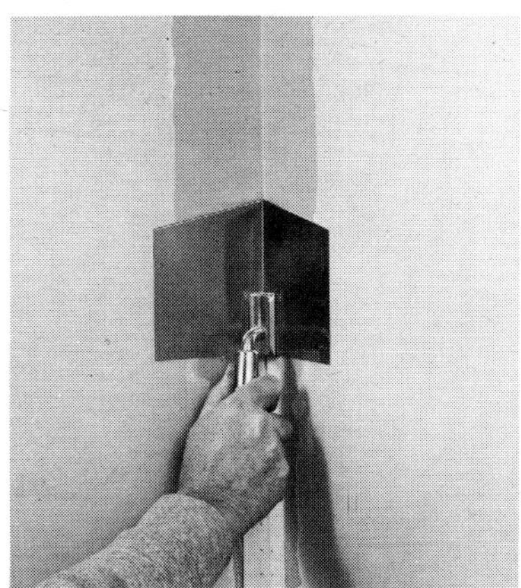

Apply second and third coats; use an inside corner tool to smooth the tape.

Repairing a small hole in wallboard

To fix a small hole in wallboard, insert a patch in the damaged area. Enlarge the opening to rectify its irregular shape, then cut a patch the same size and shape from scrap wallboard. Drive a screw part way into the center of the patch to act as a handle. Butter the edges of the patch with joint compound and fit into hole. When dry, remove screw, trowel compound on entire area, and finish as on p.98.

Enlarge opening around hole, cut patch to fit, and apply compound to edges.

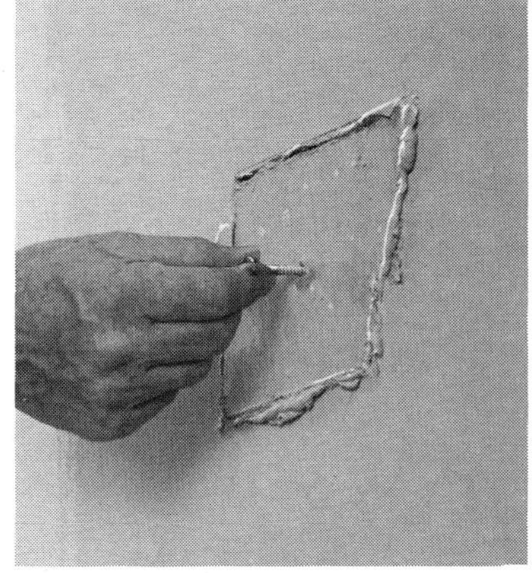

Use screw attached to patch to help handle it and to position it in hole.

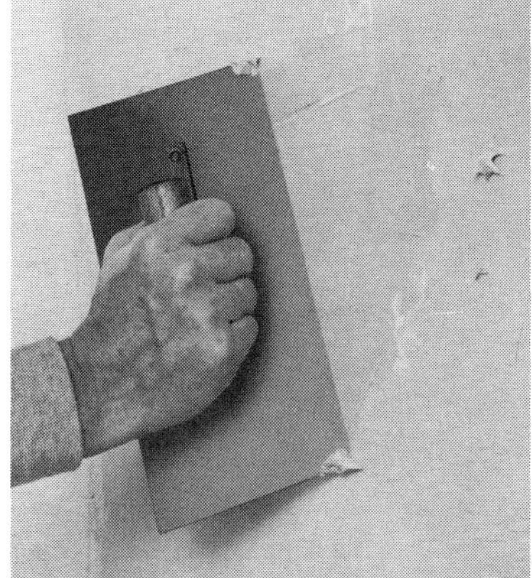

Remove screw, trowel compound onto the entire patch, finish as on p.98.

Taping an outside corner

Reinforce outside corners with metal edging, called a corner bead. One type, shown here, has paper flanges and is applied with joint compound; other types are nailed to framing through wallboard.

Lay bed of compound over outside corner before applying metal bead with paper flanges. If you use the all-metal type, make sure the nails are sufficiently countersunk.

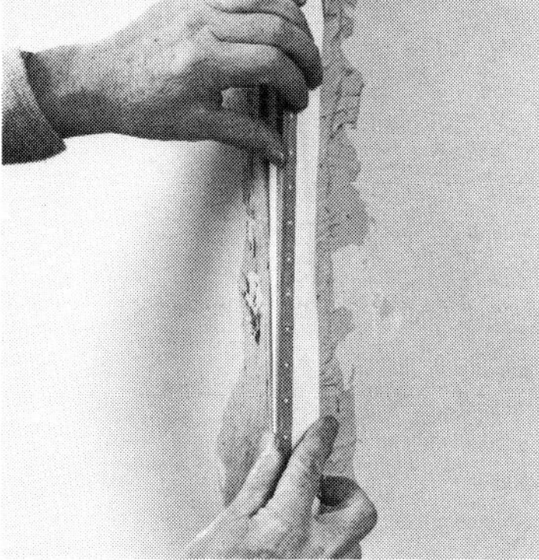

Attach metal bead; spread first coat of compound over and 3 to 4 in. beyond the tape. Feather the edges on both sides of the tape. Let it dry overnight.

Apply second coat. Feather edges wider than first coat; let it dry overnight and then sand it smooth the following day. Wipe thoroughly before applying prime coat.

Repairing a large hole in wallboard

You can effectively repair a large hole in a wallboard panel by cementing a patch, cut from scrap wallboard, in place against a backup plate. Use a keyhole saw to correct the hole's irregular shape and to enlarge it so the backup plate can be maneuvered into position. Use a piece of plywood or wallboard for the backup plate; make it 2 inches or more larger than the hole and cement it to the inner side of the damaged panel. Cut a patch from scrap wallboard about ⅛ inch smaller than the hole and cement it to the backup plate. Fill the crack around the patch, then cover the entire patch, with joint compound. When compound is dry, sand and finish patch area.

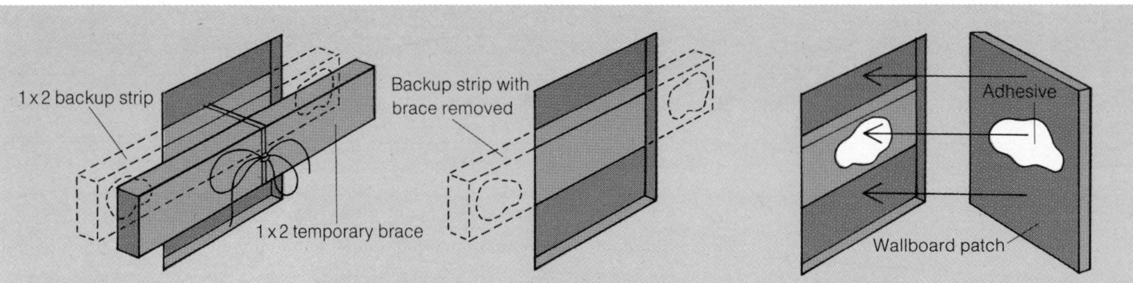

To brace a patch over a very large hole, cement a 1 x 2 to the inside of the wall, spanning the hole. Tie another 1 x 2 to this backup strip, spanning the hole on the wall's outside; remove it when adhesive dries. Apply patch as described below.

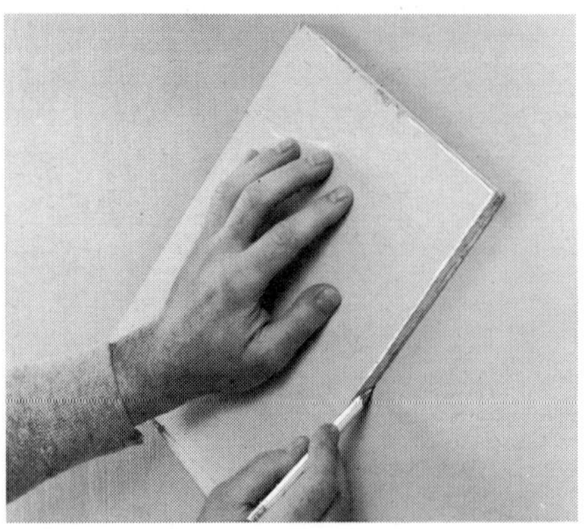

Saw a square of scrap wallboard to serve as a patch. Hold the patch over the area of the hole and outline with pencil.

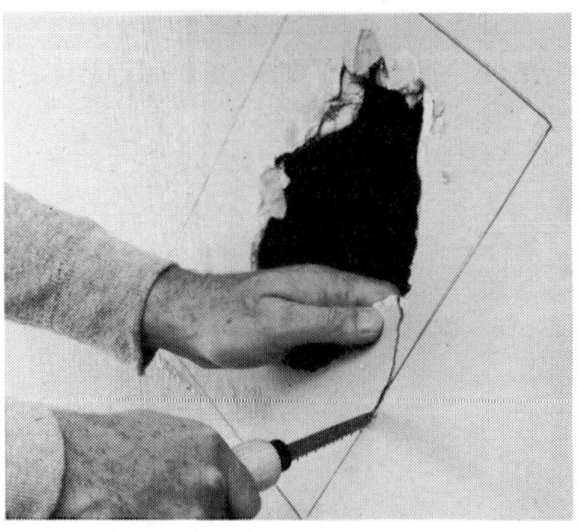

With the pencil line as a guide, use a keyhole saw to cut an opening in the wall around and slightly beyond the hole.

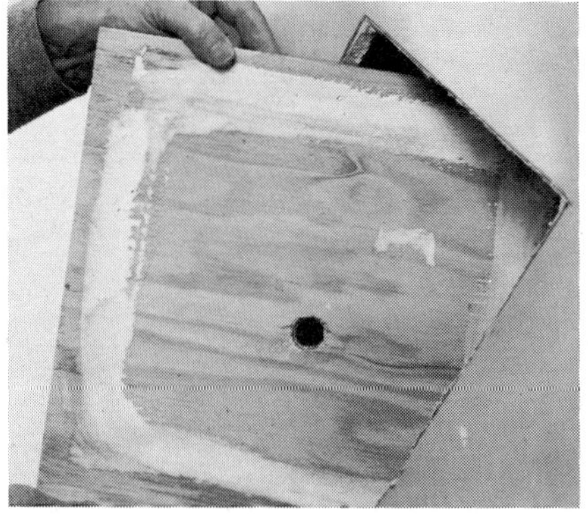

Cut backup plate larger than opening with finger hole in center. Coat border of backup with adhesive; tilt as shown and insert in opening.

Use finger hole to hold backup plate tight against the rear surface of the wall. Secure backup plate with screws.

With backup plate in place, apply joint compound to the sides and back of the patch and also to the face of the backup.

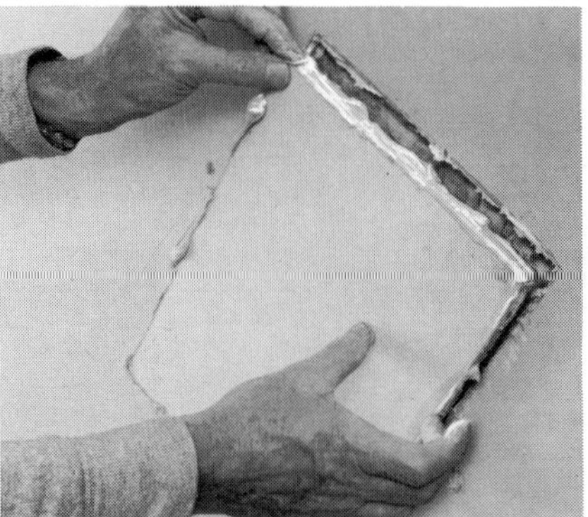

Fit patch in place, using steady gentle pressure against the backup area until the compound has begun to dry and take hold.

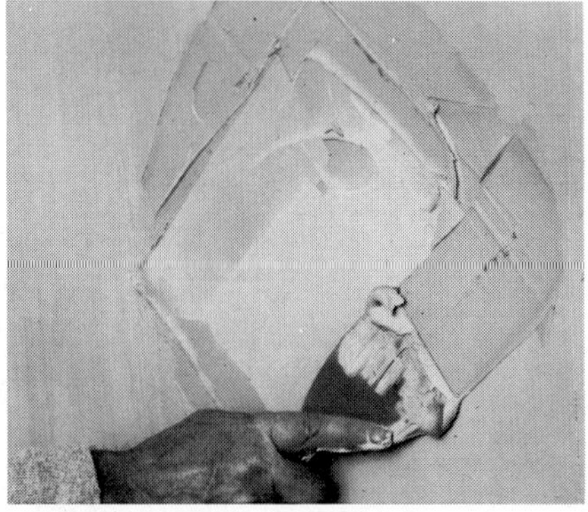

Apply joint compound liberally to fill in crack around patch and to cover entire surface. Allow compound to dry thoroughly.

Use medium sandpaper over a sanding block for final finishing after compound has dried. Feather edges for better concealment.

Repairing split wallboard tape

A split in wallboard tape that is not accompanied by a noticeable crack in the seam is generally caused by shrinkage of one or both panels.

To fix it, remove all loose segments of tape, large and small, so that they will not show up through the repair as bulges. Work carefully; try to avoid pulling away chunks of joint compound and wallboard core when you are removing the tape segments. Sand the section of split tape smooth. If there is a crack, fill it with joint compound; then apply new tape with compound over the damaged one.

Let the patch dry; then sand lightly with medium-grade sandpaper. A second coat of compound may be needed to conceal the damage completely.

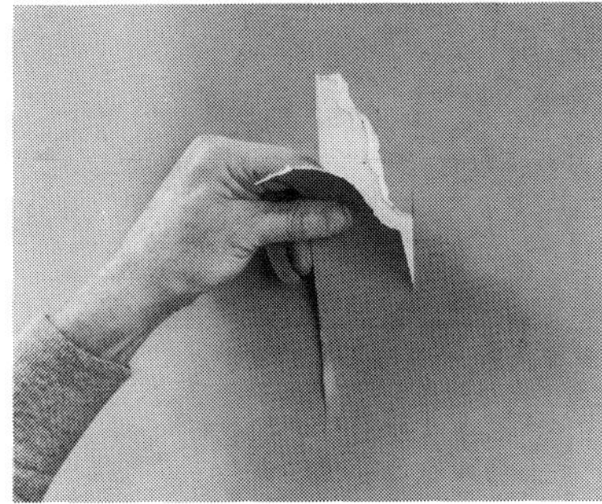

Pull off every bit of the damaged tape in the affected area.

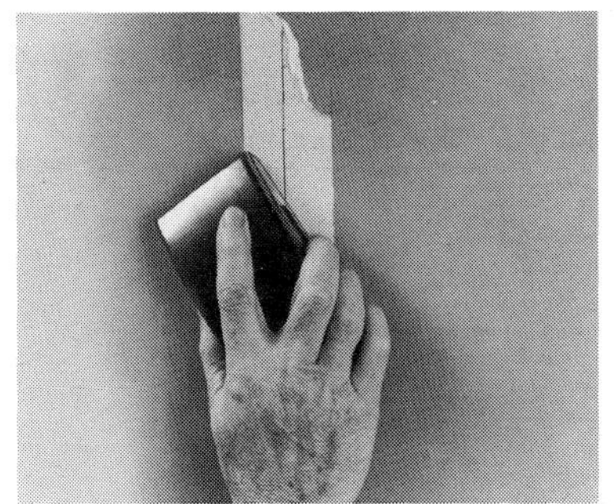

Sand the area the tape was removed from, to prevent appearance of bumps later.

Apply new tape over area with joint compound. Feather the edges.

Installing two layers of wallboard

Two layers of wallboard increase the sound-insulating qualities of a wall and eliminate popping nails. Attach the first layer of regular ⅜-inch wallboard in the usual way (p.95). Use a wide trowel to apply wallboard joint compound over the face of the base layer in dabs about 8 inches apart. Put the outer layer of wallboard in place. The joints of the two layers should be offset at least 10 inches.

To spread the adhesive and make a tight union, hold a 2x4 on the outer layer of wallboard and hammer-tap it, going over the entire panel this way. Nails may be driven part way into the studs to hold the two layers together until adhesive dries; then pull them out and fill the holes with compound.

After installing first layer of wallboard apply dabs of joint compound.

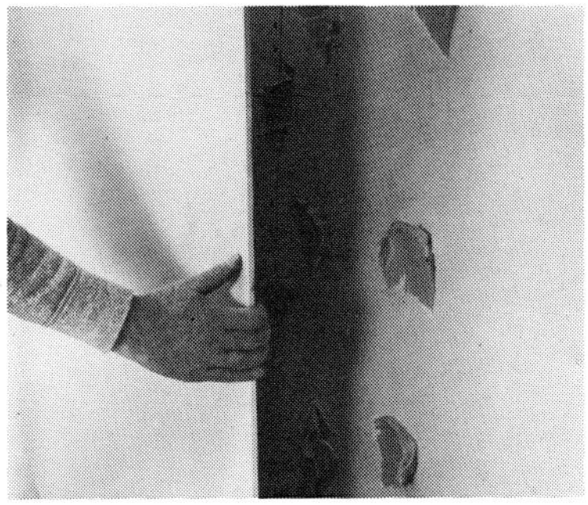

Put outer layer in place so that joints of the two boards do not coincide.

Hammer on block of wood to press outer layer firmly against inner board.

Repairing a dent in wallboard

Frequently damage to wallboard amounts to a dent rather than an actual break. Dent repair procedure is similar to that for repairing a large hole (p. 98), except that the dented wallboard itself becomes the backing material. Use coarse sandpaper to roughen the paper in the damaged area to provide a better grip for the joint compound filler. If the dent is large, apply a layer of wallboard joint compound and allow it to dry overnight. Then apply additional layers the same way until the large cavity is roughly filled with compound. When the patch is thoroughly dry, sand it and finish it. If the dent is small, you can fill it with a single application. Complete the job by sanding the patched area smooth and level.

Sand all surfaces of the dented section to provide a grip for the compound.

Fill in the cavity with one or more applications of the joint compound.

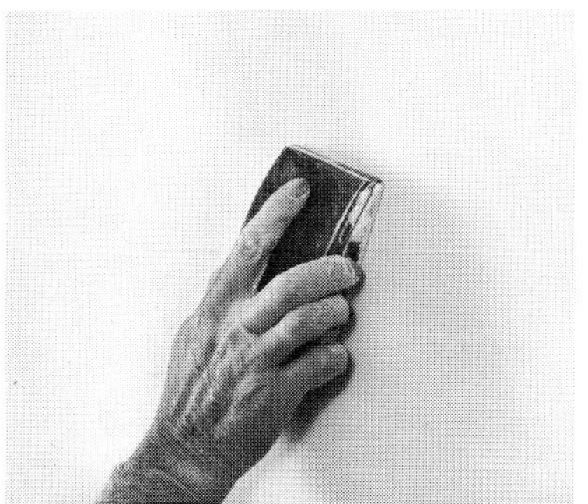

When dry, sand the patch and surrounding area smooth and even, then prime.

Fixing nail pops in wallboard

A nail pop occurs when a nail that has been sunk into wallboard begins to move outward, causing a protrusion, or bump, in the panel's otherwise smooth, paperlike surface.

There are several possible explanations for this nail movement. The nail may have been improperly set in the first place; the framing member may have shrunk or expanded under varying humidity conditions; or vibration or other building movement may be responsible for the gradual nail creep.

The usual repair procedure is to insert a new nail about 1½ inches away from the popped one. Drive the new nail home straight and true, and dimple (p. 93) the surrounding surface. While you are doing so, firmly press the wallboard back by hand against the framing so that there will be no movement of the panel on the nail shank.

If the popped nail cannot be removed easily, sink it below the surface, using a nail set if necessary. Remove all loose compound, dust, and other material, then repair both the damaged and dimpled areas with joint compound.

If a nail pop is minor and is not located in a prominent place, it can probably be ignored. Should it be in a glossy surface, however, or in a place that is brightly illuminated, repair is essential.

Sometimes the popped nail may have gotten so loose in its hole that sinking it again would do little good. If so, use a cement-coated nail of the next larger size in place of the popped one.

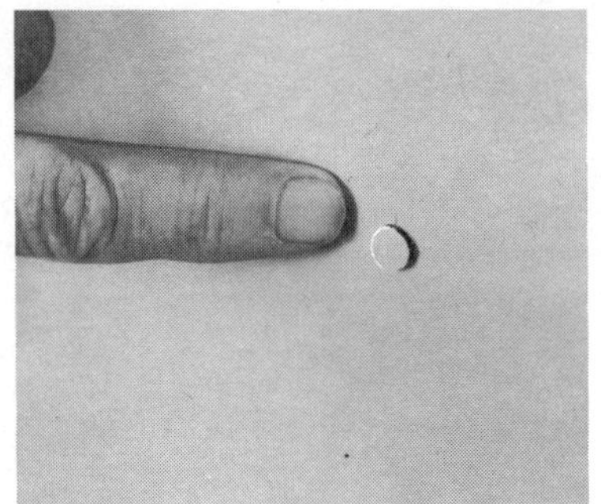

Nails that pop up from wallboard should be attended to at once so they won't cause further damage to the surface.

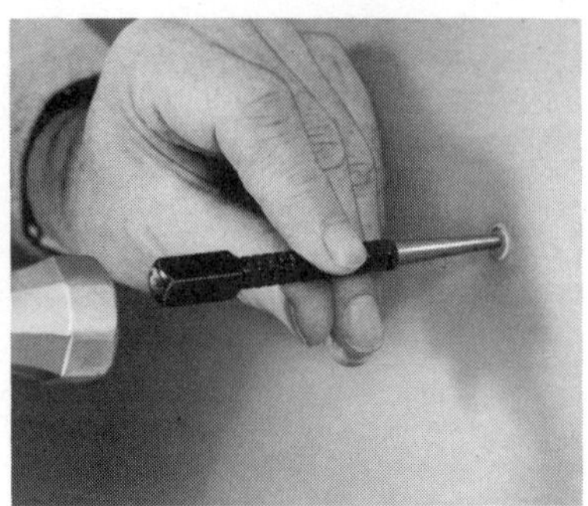

Either remove and replace the popped nail or drive it below the surface, using a nail set if necessary.

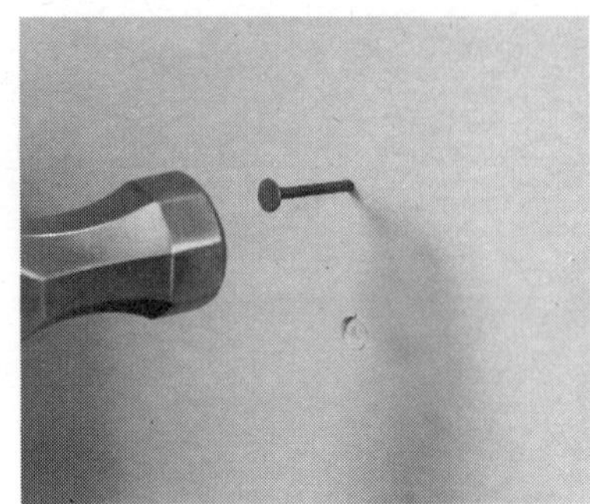

If nail still pops, remove it, push panel back in place, then hammer a new nail about 1½ in. from the popped nail.

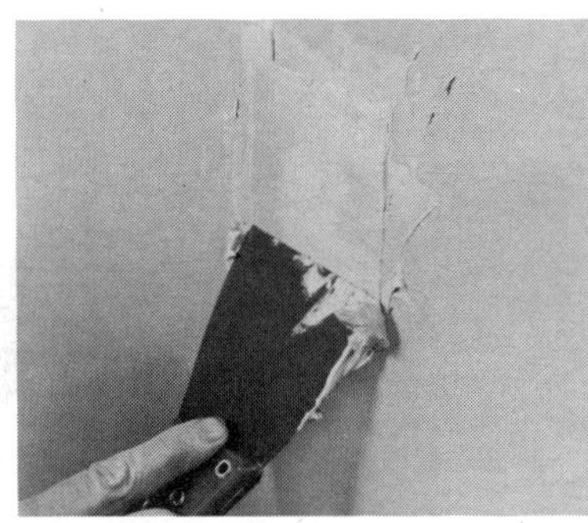

Use joint compound to fill in the new nail dimple and to repair the damaged area around the old nail.

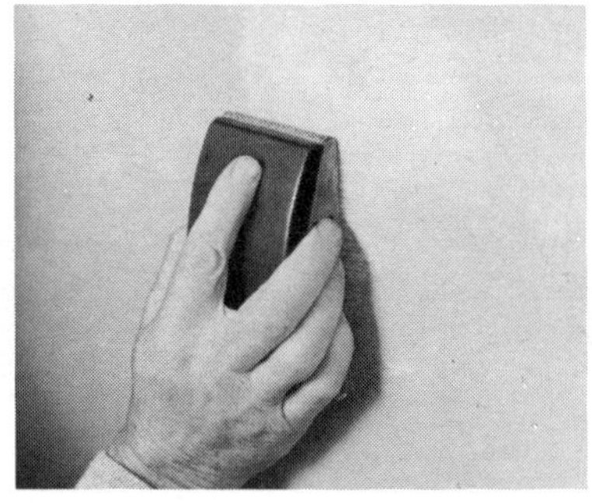

Sand the entire repaired area smooth and level, using a medium-grade sandpaper wrapped around a wood block.

Prime the area where new joint compound has been applied before doing any further painting or papering.

Replacing damaged ceiling tile

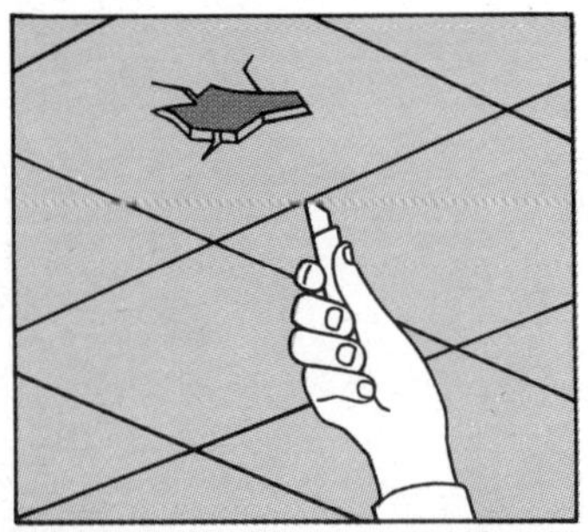

To remove a damaged ceiling tile, cut around the edges with a knife or a saw blade.

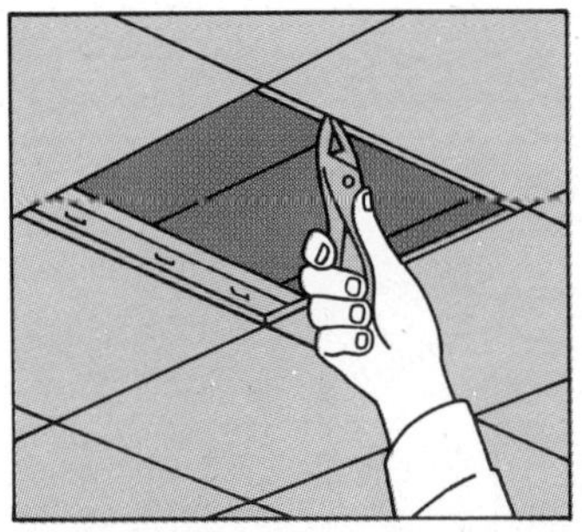

Pull out original nails or staples from the framing; then scrape off all remaining tile material.

Use a knife to cut the tongue edges from the new tile that is to replace the damaged one.

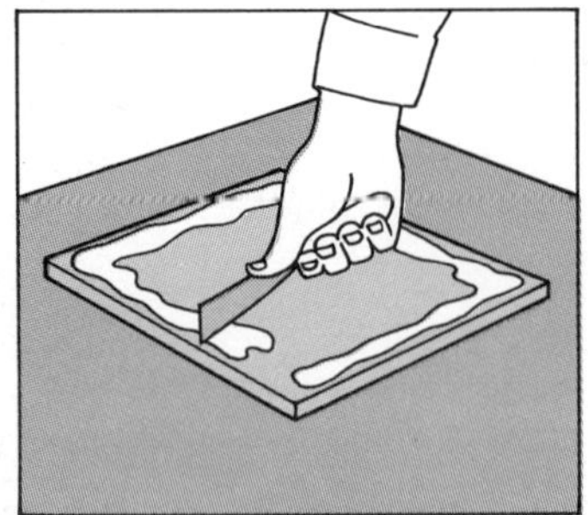

With a putty knife, apply a liberal amount of adhesive to the back of the replacement tile.

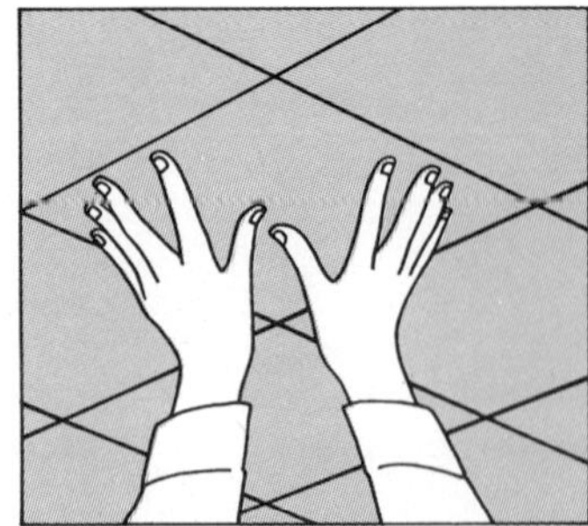

Insert the new tile in the opening in the ceiling. Use both hands to push it level with adjacent tiles.

Replacing a wood panel

In remodeling a room, it is often necessary to replace a wood panel either because one is damaged or for purposes of decoration. When you remove a panel, salvage as much as possible, particularly the crown molding and baseboard (p. 398); it may be difficult to match the original finish.

To pry off a wood panel, start with a putty knife and follow it with a wide flat chisel or a very thin pry bar. Work carefully to avoid damage to the pieces that are being removed or to the adjoining panels. In most cases, you will find that the panel is secured to the studs with glue at all points except under the molding and baseboard. You will probably have to scrape off the glue that remains on the studs, or the wall, before you can install a new panel.

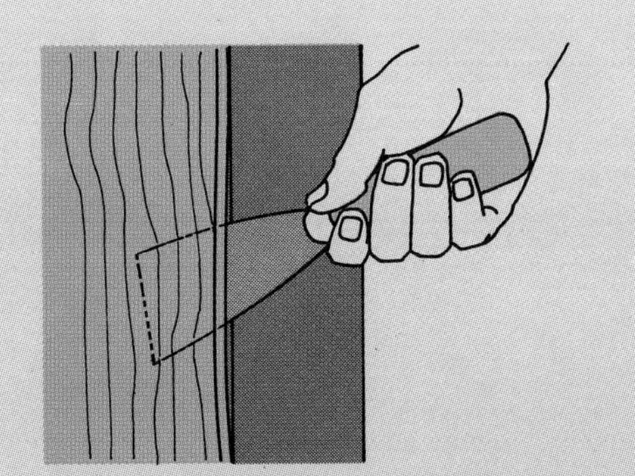

When removing a wood panel, first force putty knife between the panel and the stud.

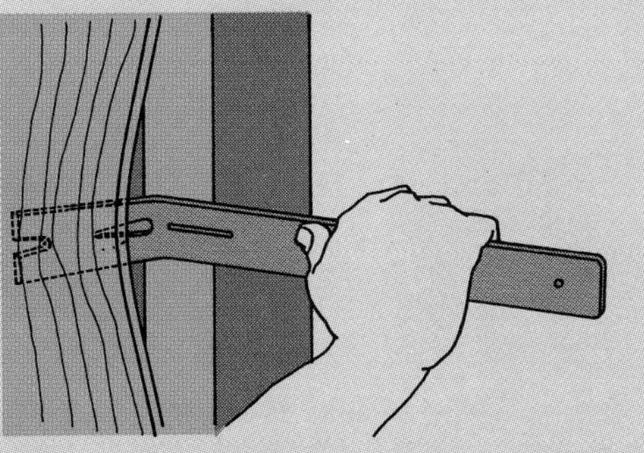

Then use a thin pry bar to get the added leverage needed to break the glue bond and remove any nails.

Try to salvage the entire baseboard and crown molding by taking pains to prevent damage when prying them off.

Remove brads still in panel with pincers, pry bar, or nail puller. Or sink brads, if necessary, with a nail set.

Split glued panel near one side with hammer and chisel to make room for prying remainder loose from the studs.

Pry with wrecking bar from split side and salvage as much of the panel as possible for use on other projects.

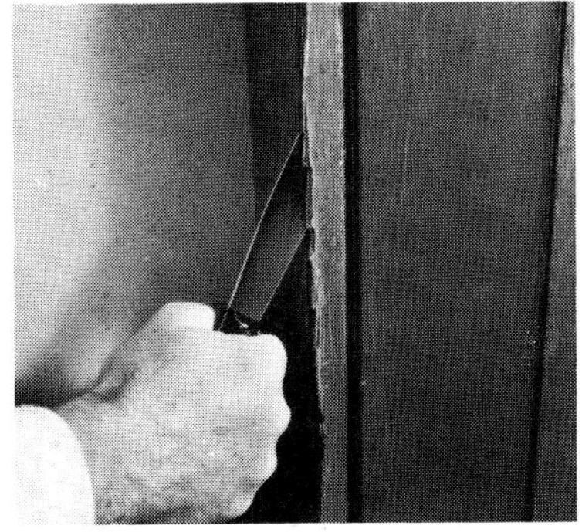

Use a putty knife to break the glue bond between the panel and the studs (or wall), then remove panel completely.

Scrape off old glue; put new panel in place to check fit, then remove it and apply bead of adhesive to studs or wall.

Install new panel. Pound glued areas with a padded block, then hammer in brads at evenly spaced intervals.

Use a nail set to sink brads level with or below surface of panel. Fill all of the holes with matching wood dough.

Replace salvaged crown molding and baseboard. Re-use of original holes requires longer and heavier-gauge brads.

Baseboards and moldings

Replacing damaged baseboard

Begin the removal of a section of damaged baseboard by inserting the end of a pry bar or chisel between wall and baseboard. Pry outward slowly and carefully so as to avoid splitting the wood. Place a wooden wedge into the gap created by the pry bar and continue the prying action, using a succession of wedges as you work along the baseboard.

When the baseboard is freed, place the new section alongside it and mark the length and required miter cuts. Use a miter box to make the cuts.

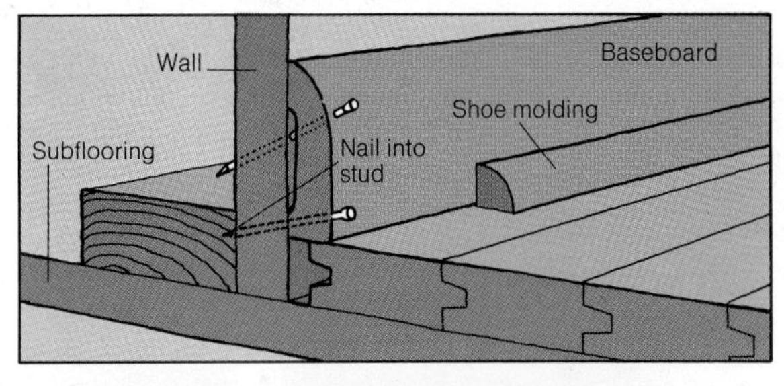

Insert the end of a thin pry bar or a chisel between baseboard and wall and pry carefully outward.

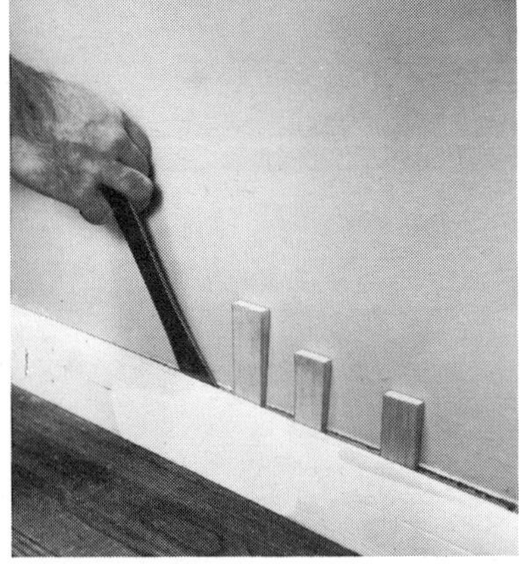

When the prying action has created a sufficient gap between baseboard and wall, insert a wooden wedge in the space.

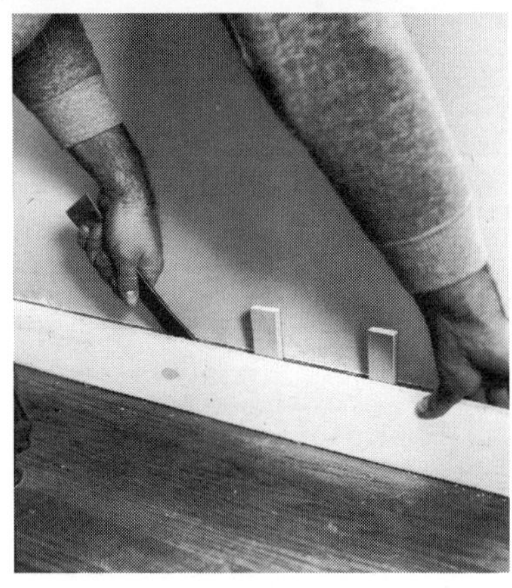

Continue prying, inserting more wedges as you are able to, until the baseboard is loose enough to pull away from wall.

Remove all nails remaining in the wall, using a wooden block as shown to prevent damage to the wall's surface.

Measure the replacement section of baseboard against the one you have removed, and mark off required corner angles.

Use a miter box for the cuts, then fit the new section into position and nail it in place. Sink nailheads; fill holes.

Fitting to an uneven floor

Measure widest gap between baseboard and floor. Cut wooden block a bit thicker than gap. Hold a pencil on block and slide it along floor to mark baseboard. Make sure pencil is sharp and keep it in firm contact with the baseboard.

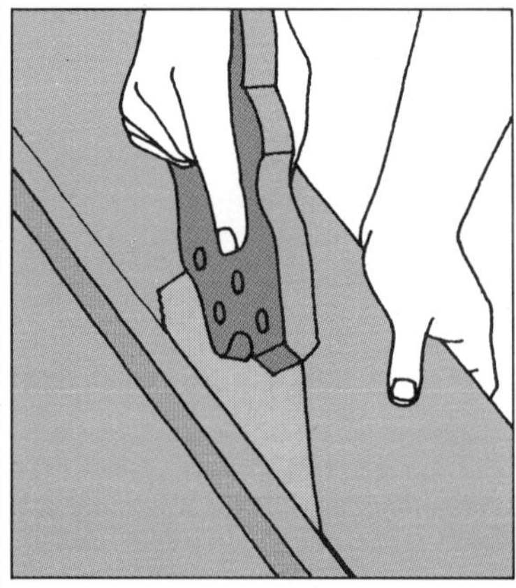

Cut along pencil line you have marked on baseboard. Angle the cut so that front of baseboard is slightly wider than back. If you have a band saw or a jigsaw, it will make the job less tedious and time-consuming.

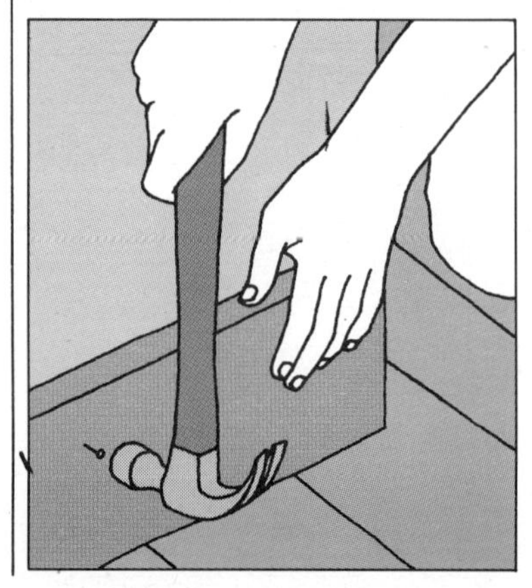

Position baseboard on floor and against wall. Press down on the baseboard, pushing it firmly against the floor, then nail it in place. Drive the upper nail at a slight downward angle. Toenailing does a better job of holding the board in place and at the same time forcing it against the floor.

Joining baseboard at corners

When the replacement of baseboard involves an inside corner, take special care in measuring and making the necessary cuts. The two sections that meet at an inside corner are brought together with a coped joint (p. 399). This joint is somewhat more difficult to make than a plain miter and takes more time. When it is well done, however, the result is trim and attractive. A miter joint (p. 393) is used when the two meeting sections of board must be cut and joined to fit an outside angle.

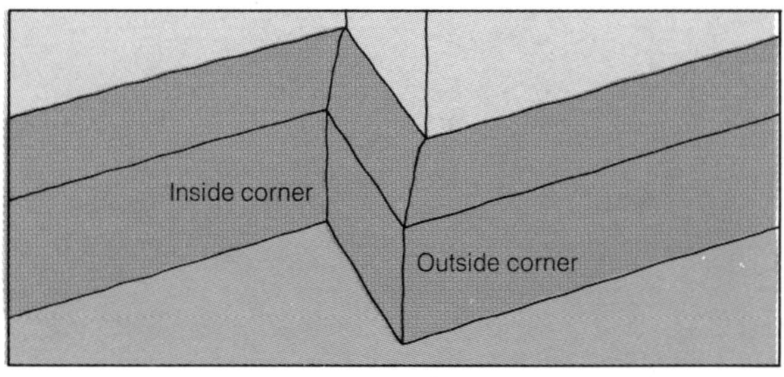

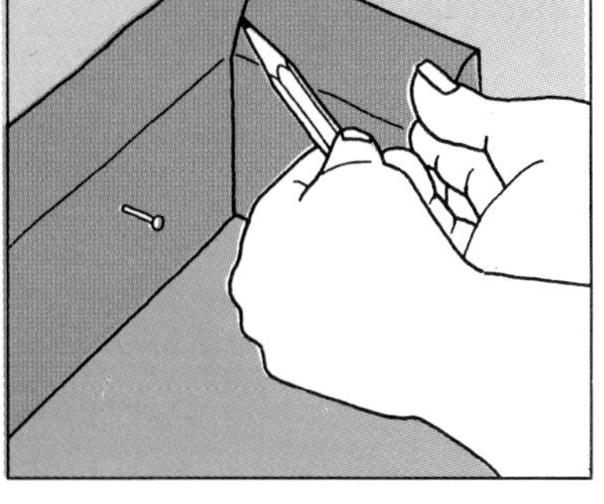

Inside corner: Temporarily nail piece of baseboard in corner. With pencil, trace on it the outline of a second piece.

Remove the temporarily nailed piece of baseboard. With a coping saw, cut carefully along the pencil line.

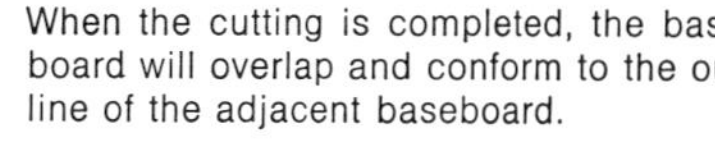

When the cutting is completed, the baseboard will overlap and conform to the outline of the adjacent baseboard.

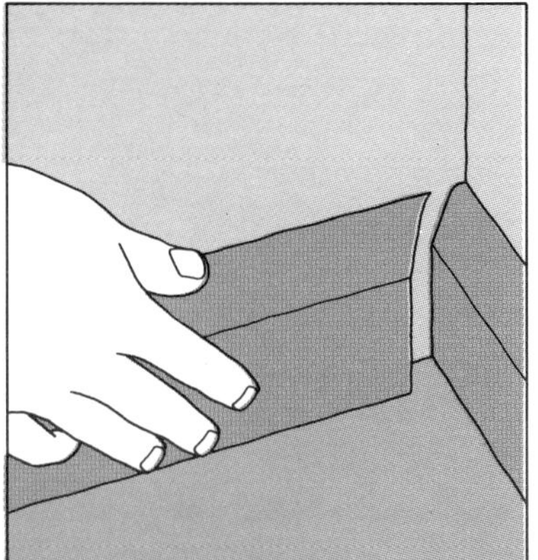

Butt the two baseboard pieces together to form a coped joint; nail to sole plate. Sink nailheads and fill holes.

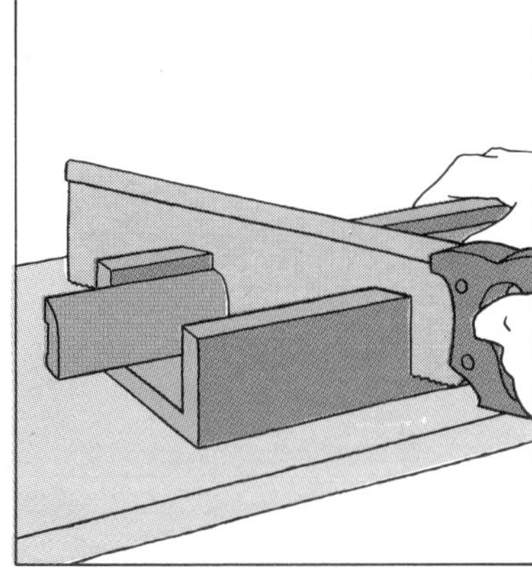

Fitting to an outside angle: Measure and cut the two pieces of baseboard at a 45° angle, using a miter box.

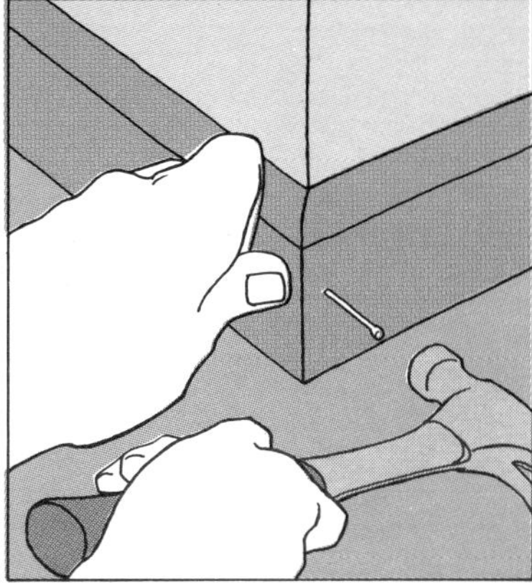

Bring cut ends together to form miter joint; nail to sole plate. Drive extra nails through joint into corner.

Installing shoe molding

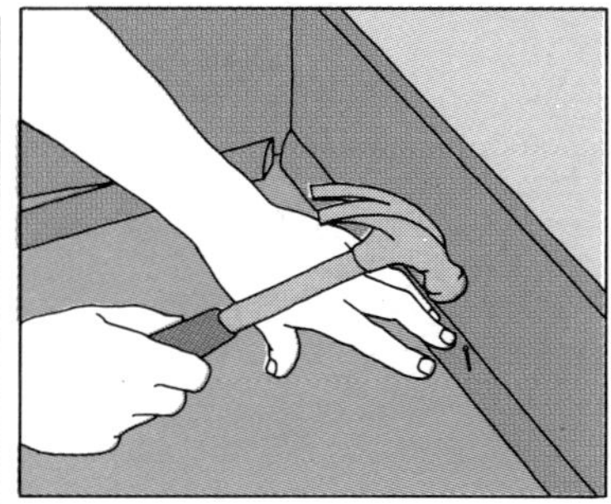

Cut molding to proper length to fill gap. Miter or cope all corners. Use brads long enough to penetrate the subfloor as well as the finish flooring.

At the points where the molding meets the door, mark it to make a curve to the door jamb. The job will look much better rounded off this way rather than leaving a straight end.

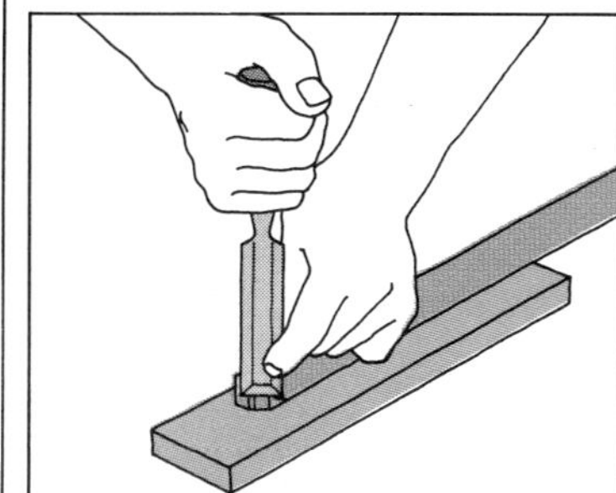

Place molding on scrap of wood and chisel off corner to match line of curve. Use coarse sandpaper, followed by fine, to make a smooth flowing curve on the molding.

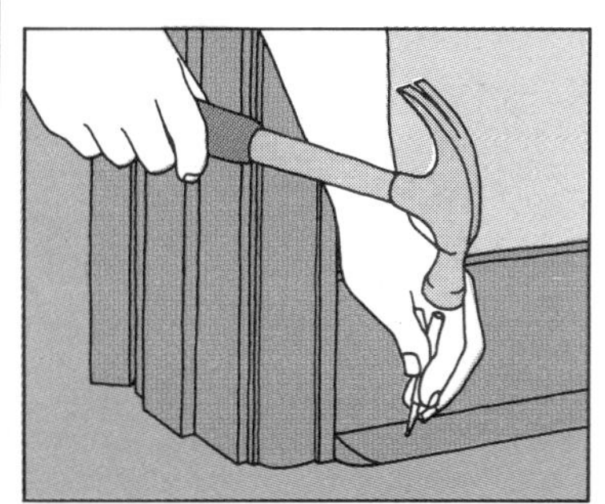

Finish by setting the brad heads below the surface of the molding with a nail set. Fill the holes with a matching putty, wipe off excess, then paint.

How a staircase is made

In its simplest form, a staircase consists of two pieces of wood (the stringers) sloping from one floor to another with steps fixed between them. There are, however, two basic types of staircase construction. In the **open-stringer** type, the top edges of the stringers are cut out sawtooth fashion, and the steps (horizontal treads and vertical risers) fitted to them. In **closed-stringer** construction, the edges of the stringers are straight, but grooves are cut into their inside faces to accommodate the steps.

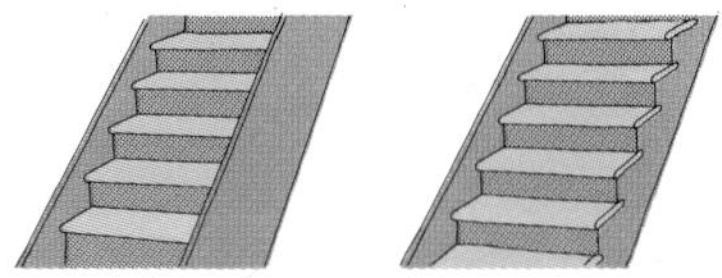

Closed-stringer stairs   Open stringer on right

Many staircases are made by a combination of methods. The steps are fixed to a closed stringer on one side—for example, against a wall; on the other side, they rest on the edges of an open stringer.

When one side of a staircase has an open stringer, repairs to the steps can be easily made from above. If both sides are closed, however, repairs must be done from under the stairs. This may involve stripping off lath and plaster or wallboard.

A complication arises when a staircase has additional supports running beneath the steps. This does not affect repairs to the open-stringer design, but it makes the replacement of steps in a closed staircase a major structural job.

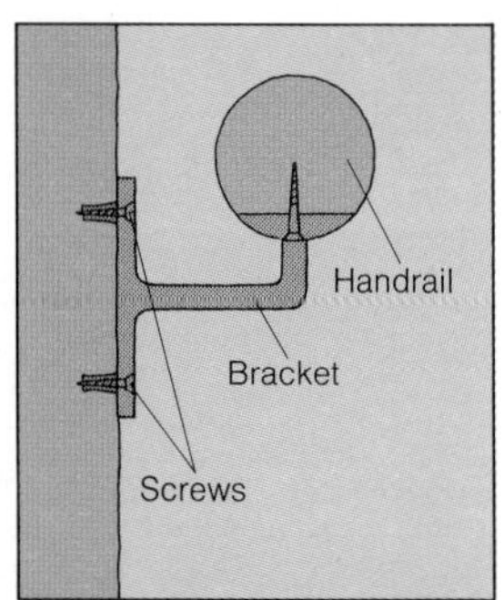

The handrail, usually made of wood but sometimes of plastic-covered metal, may be secured to wall by brackets.

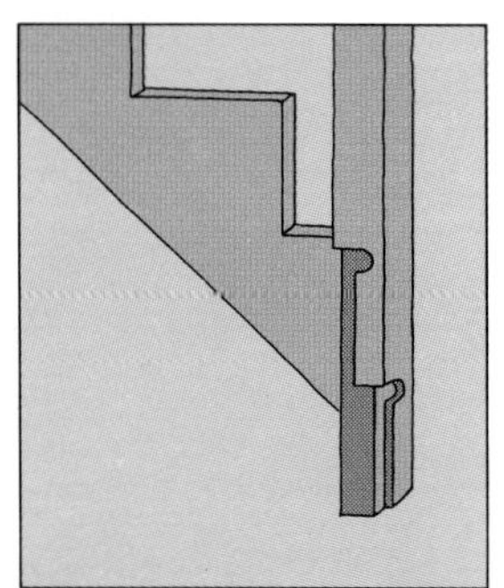

When no stringer support is available, the first steps are fixed in grooves in the starting newel.

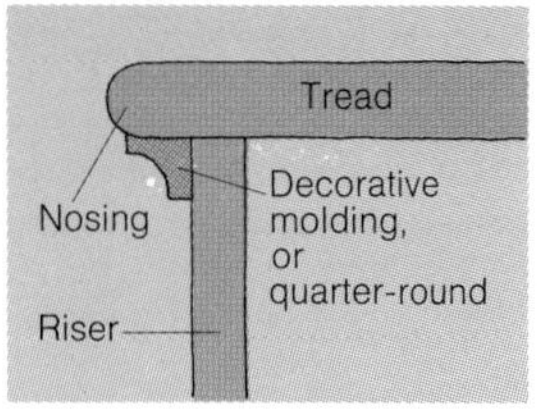

Tread

Nosing

Riser

Decorative molding, or quarter-round

Molding used to cover any gaps that may develop between tread and riser

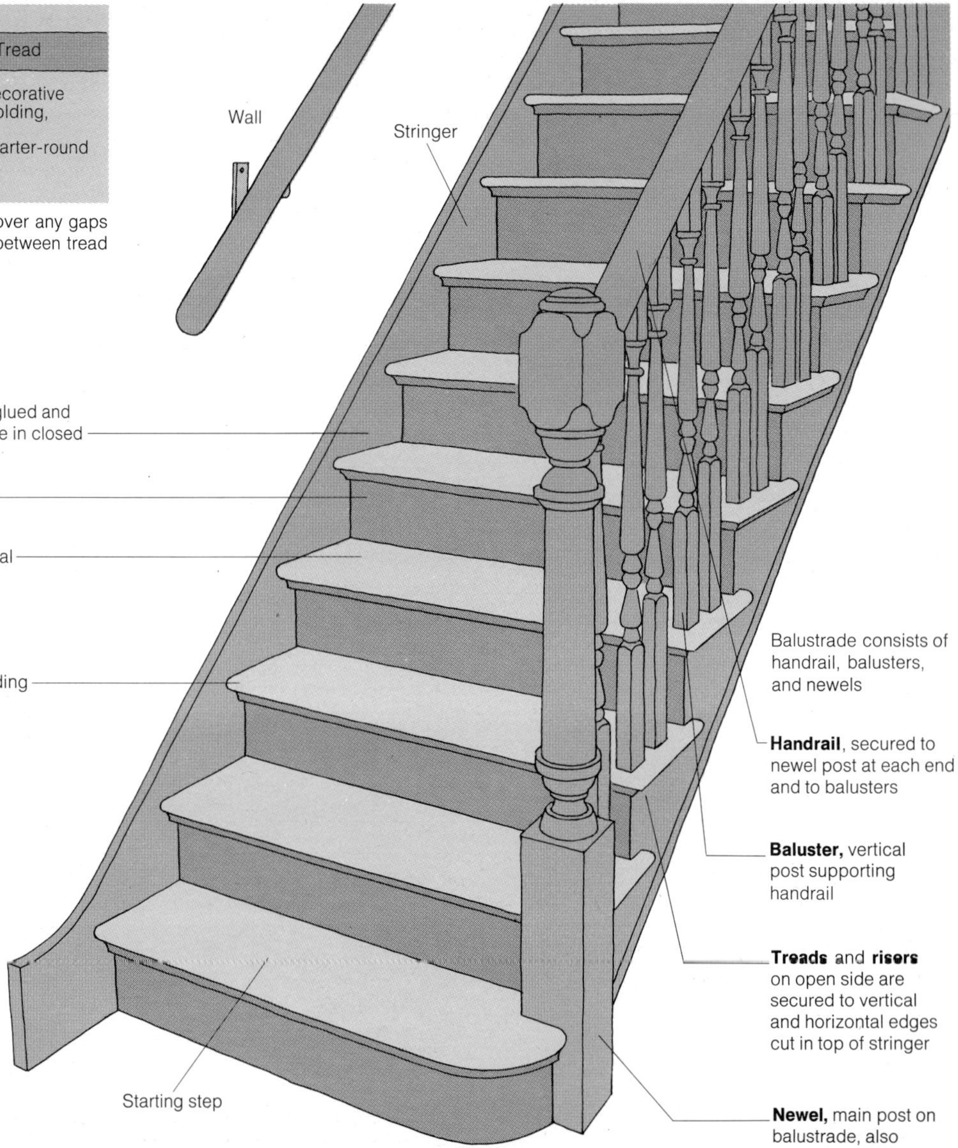

Wall

Stringer

Treads and risers glued and wedged into groove in closed side of staircase

Riser, the vertical part of step

Tread, the horizontal part of step

Nosing, the protruding front edge of tread, usually rounded.

Starting step

Balustrade consists of handrail, balusters, and newels

Handrail, secured to newel post at each end and to balusters

Baluster, vertical post supporting handrail

Treads and **risers** on open side are secured to vertical and horizontal edges cut in top of stringer

Newel, main post on balustrade, also supports bottom steps

Eliminating squeaks

Most squeaks in stairs are caused by a tread rubbing against the top or bottom of a riser or against a stringer at either end.

The visible parts of a stairway consist of treads, risers, stringers, and moldings. The important hidden parts include the nails and glue that hold the assembly together, the triangular-shaped glued-in blocks that strengthen the joint between the tread and the riser, and the wedges that are frequently glued into the closed-stringer dado joints to give the structure additional strength and stability.

Once you have determined the source of the squeak, a permanent cure is possible. If the underside of the stairway is open, and the repair can be made there, it will also be invisible.

Powdered graphite or other dry lubricants will silence or considerably muffle some squeaks, such as those that come from the area where the tread joins the riser. Dry lubricants do not, however, offer a permanent solution to the problem.

To stop a squeak that is coming from the front of a tread and the top of a riser, drive nails at opposing angles as shown, through the tread into the riser.

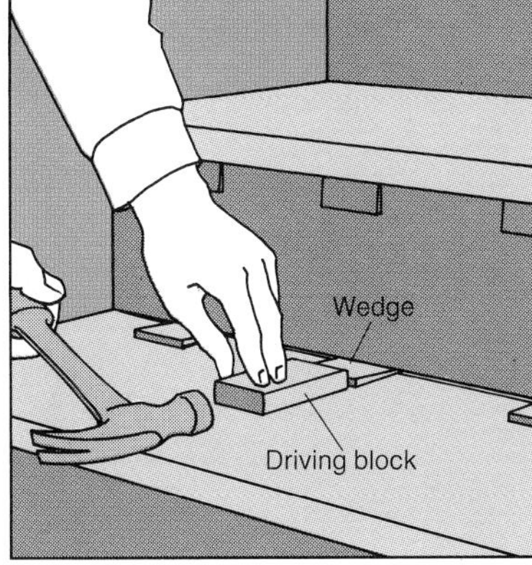

Correct squeaks that come from the top or bottom of a riser and the rear of a tread by inserting thin, glue-coated wood wedges at top or bottom.

Use a sharp knife to cut off the exposed ends of the wedges so that they are flush with riser. Then cover the repair with molding to conceal it.

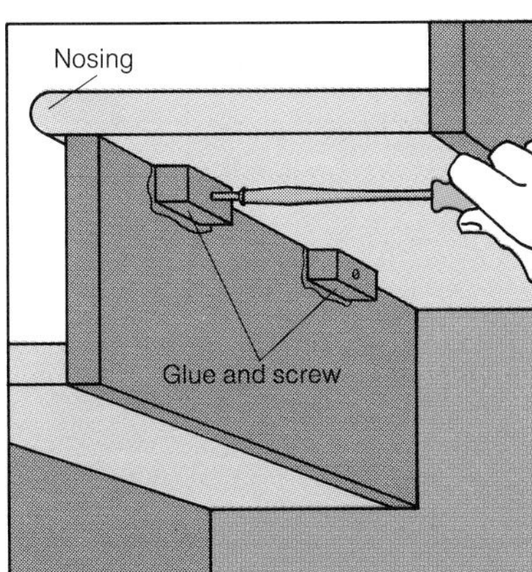

Another way to silence squeaks at bottom of tread and top of riser: Fasten wooden blocks underneath with glue and screws.

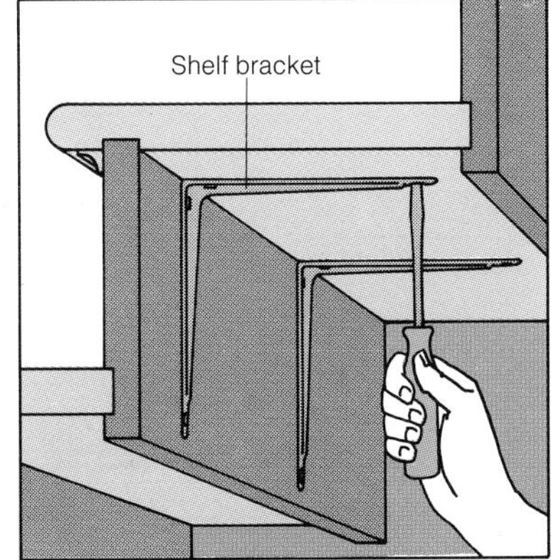

For general creaking of tread, install metal shelf brackets to underside of tread and back of riser.

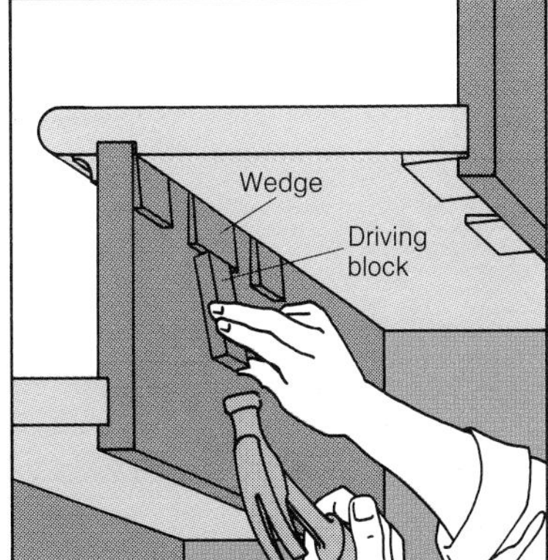

To secure and give extra support, tighten all existing wedges from below; install new ones where necessary.

Tightening loose balusters

Sometimes the settling of the house causes a flight of stairs to sag. This can bring about a loosening of the balusters, the vertical posts that support the handrail. Tighten the balusters by driving small hardwood wedges between the post and handrail.

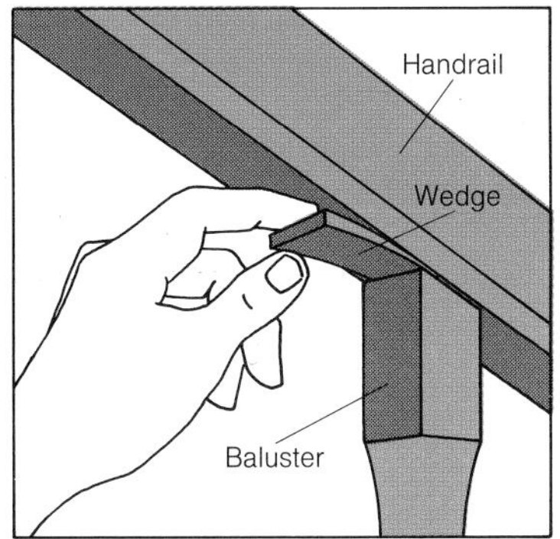

Tighten a loose baluster with a strip of wood slightly larger than the gap left by the sagging stairs. Sand it or plane it into a wedge shape with the grain running the length of the wedge.

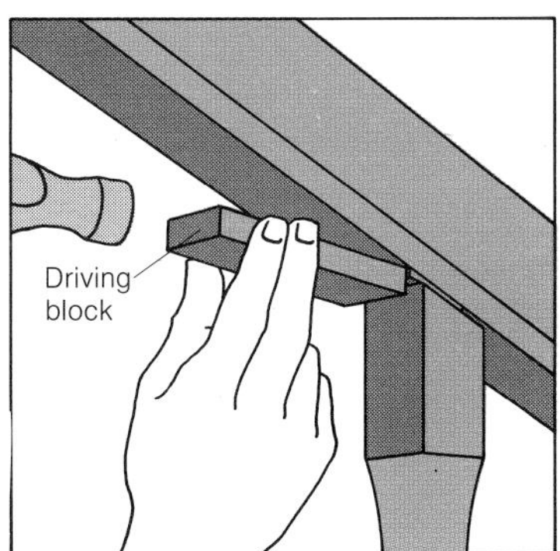

Insert the glue-coated wood strip at the top of the baluster. Tap it into position, then trim off any excess. Best to do this late at night when stairway will no longer be in use so that glue will set overnight.

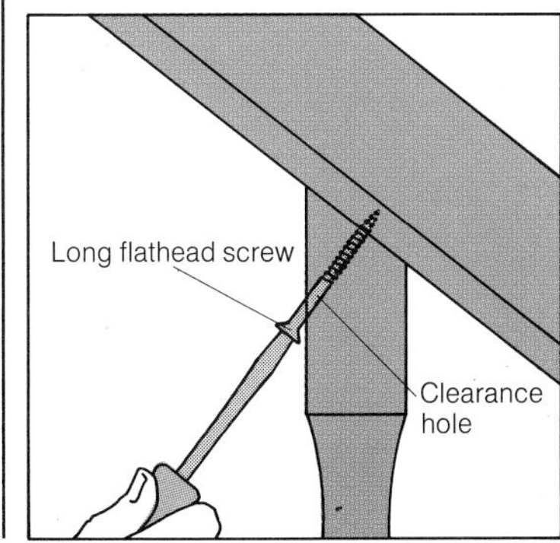

Alternatively, drill a hole at an angle and drive a screw through the baluster into the handrail. Hole through the baluster should be countersunk (p. 74) and large enough to pass the screw freely without binding.

Repairing treads and risers from above

Any homeowner is likely to run into a number of stairway repair problems, especially if his house is an old one. The entire stair structure could become shaky and need reinforcing, the handrails could require tightening, the balusters need to be reset.

If a wall of the house has settled, it may pull the stringer away from the steps. A simple way to correct this condition is to force the stringer back into position by driving wedges between the wall and the stringer. Do not use wedges, however, if the gap between the stringer and the steps is more than ½ inch; if you do, the stringer is liable to split. The only way to deal with such a wide separation is to replace all of the steps.

A repair problem that arises frequently with treads and risers is that of battered and worn treads. Instead of replacing the old treads with new, it is easier just to turn the treads over so the unsightly side is down and the undamaged side uppermost.

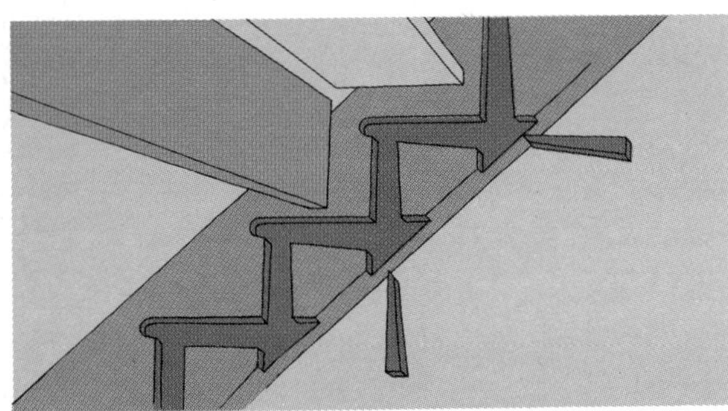

Stringer and wedge assembly showing positioning and securing of wedges between stringer and treads and risers.

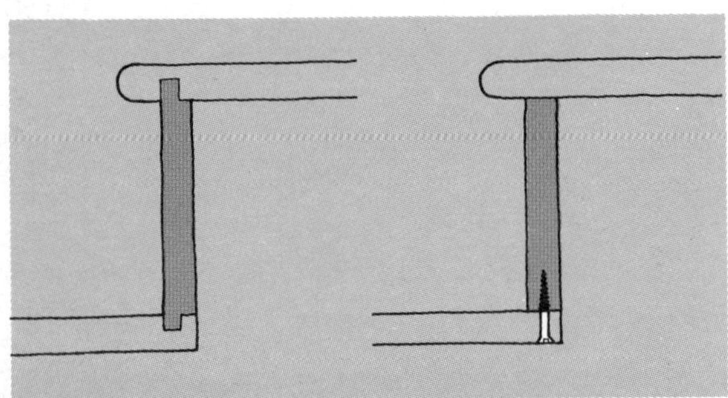

In well-made stairways, treads and risers are jointed (left); in others, they are secured by screws or nails (right).

When removing balusters that are fitted into slots at the bottom and holes at the top, first pry off end trim.

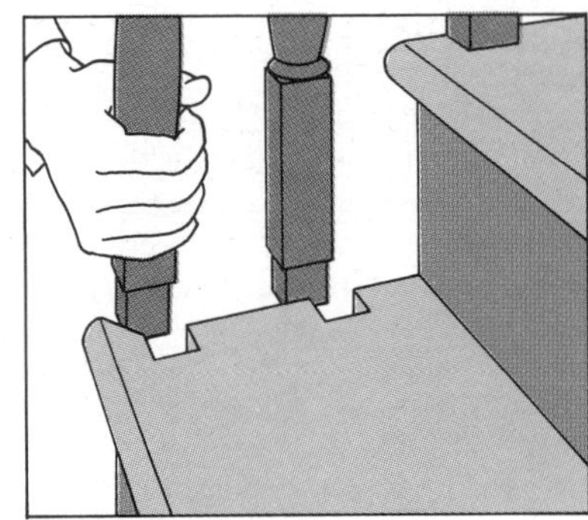

Slide the balusters out of their slots, then pull them down to free tips from holes bored in underside of handrail.

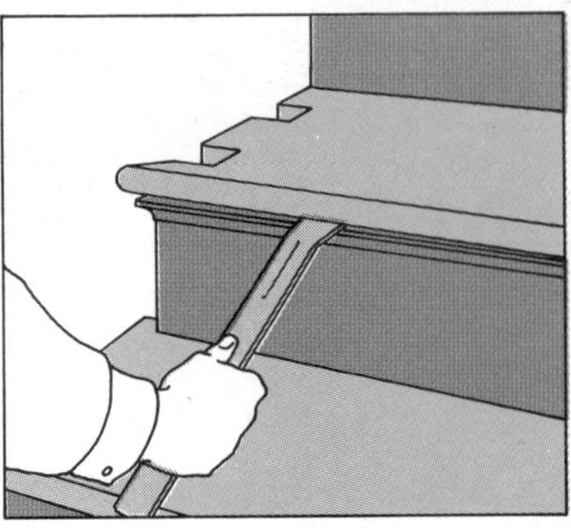

After balusters have been removed, carefully remove trim from under the front of the tread with a pry bar.

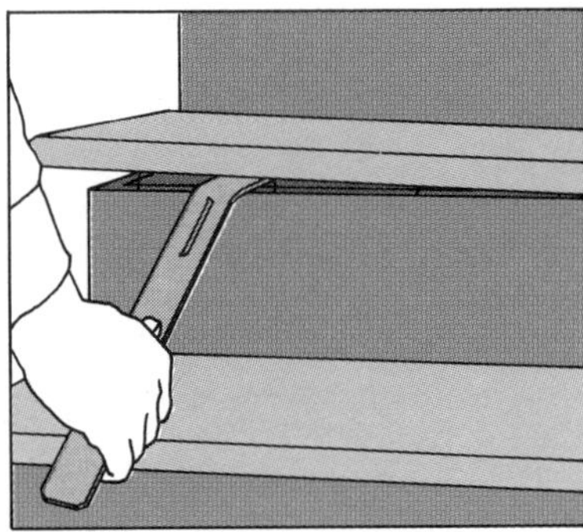

Next, pry up the tread from the riser just enough to allow the blade of a utility saw to be inserted.

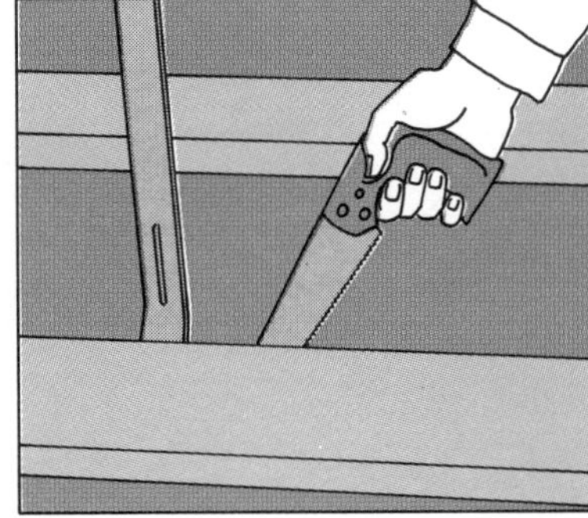

Do not try to pry the tread completely loose. Use utility saw to cut all nails hammered through riser into tread.

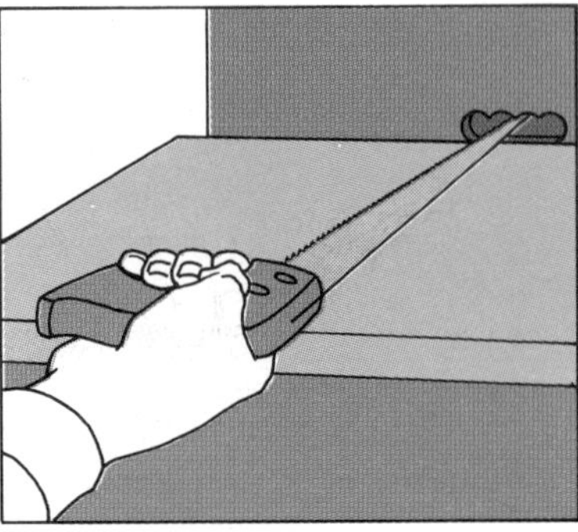

If tread and riser are dadoed, drill holes at base of riser and cut with saw blade along the joint.

Grasp the outside end of the tread and lift up. Twist and lift to free the other end from the stringer.

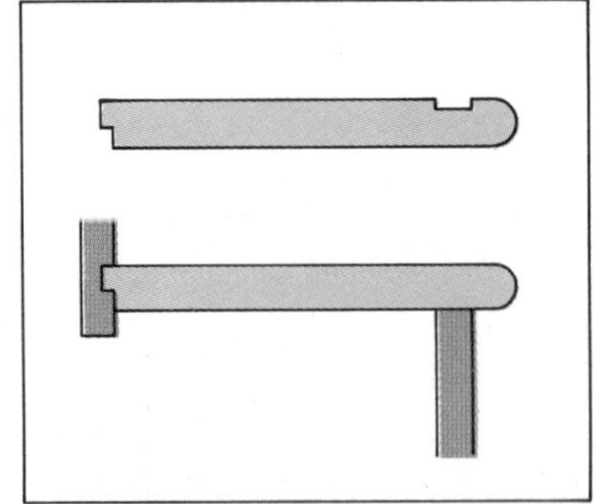

A worn tread can often be turned over and its underside used. Cut new slots; sand and finish new top surface.

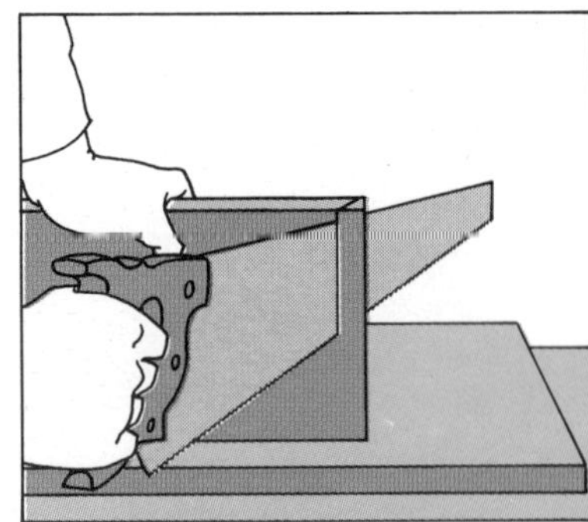

If a new riser is to be installed in open-stringer stairs, miter it to make an exact fit against the stringer.

Repairing treads and risers from above

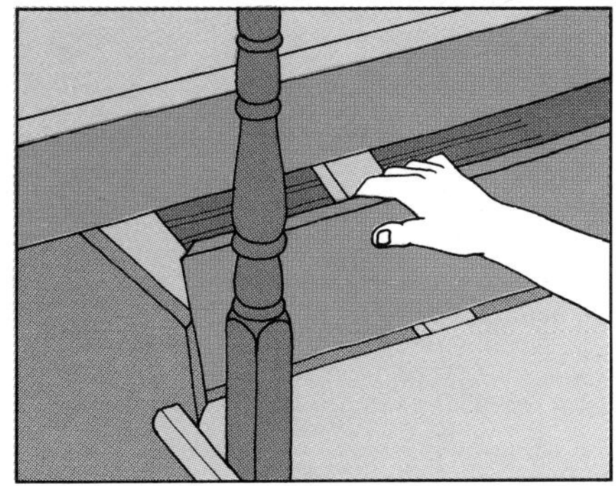

Position the riser with the miter joint against the outer stringer. If necessary, plane down the riser to make it fit properly.

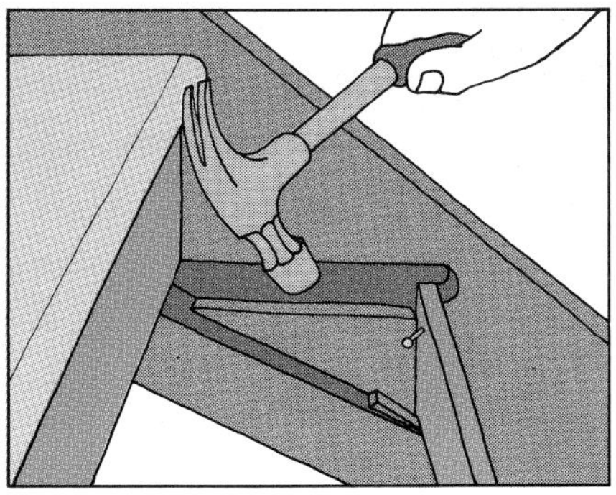

Glue in the wedge first, then the riser. Drive nails at an angle through the riser into the vertical stringer groove.

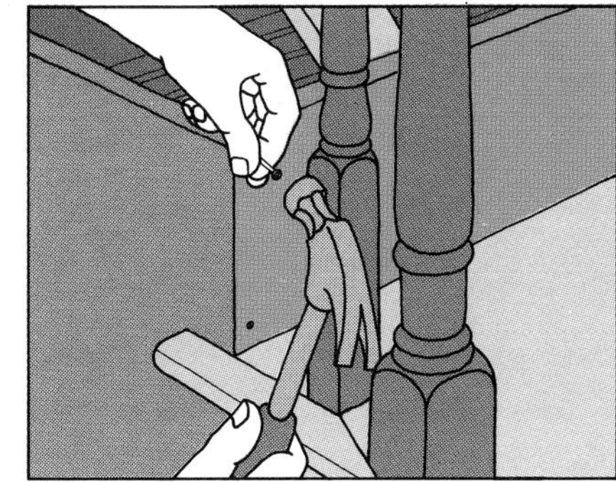

Glue and nail the miter joint on the outer corner. Wipe off surplus glue and sink nails below the surface with a nail set.

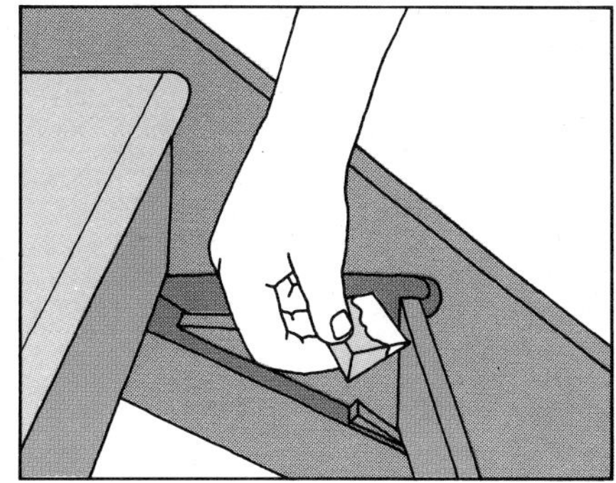

If a tighter fit is required, drive a glued wedge between the riser and the vertical groove of the inner stringer.

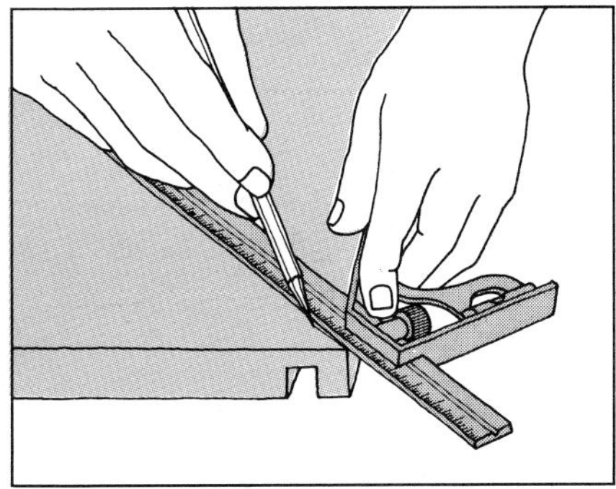

Turn the tread over and on its top mark a 45° miter at the outside corner where the side molding will fit.

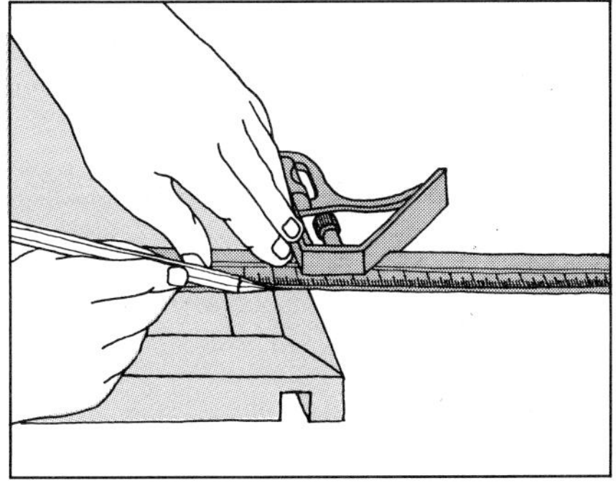

Measure the positions of the balusters on the old tread and mark them on the inside of the new miter line.

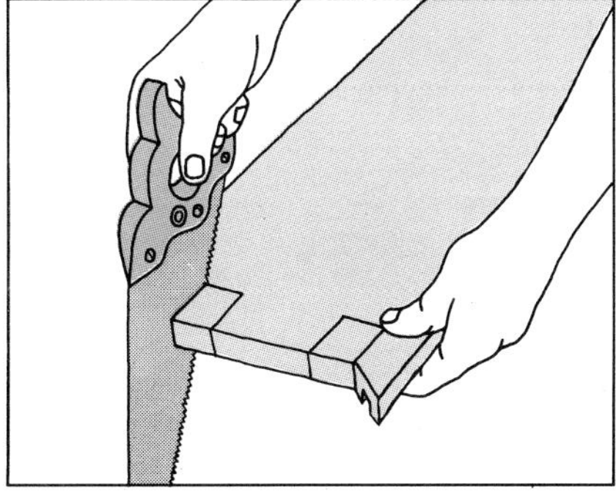

Cut out the miter joint to accommodate the side molding and saw along the lines of the baluster markings.

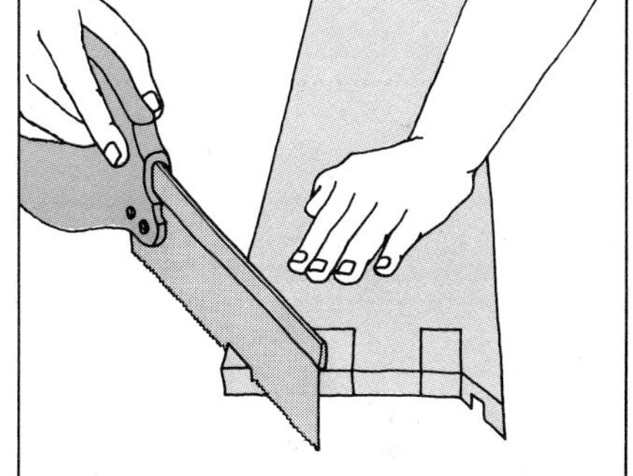

At the inner corner of the outside edge, cut off a piece to make a snug fit with the angled edge of the stringer.

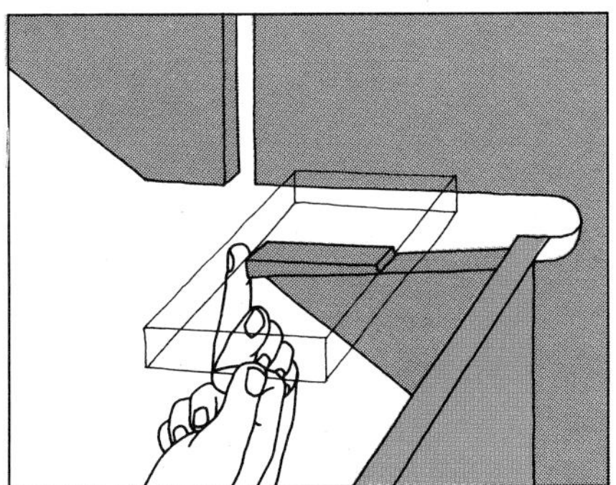

Fit a scrap as wide and thick as the tread into inner stringer groove. Fit a filler piece underneath. Remove the scrap.

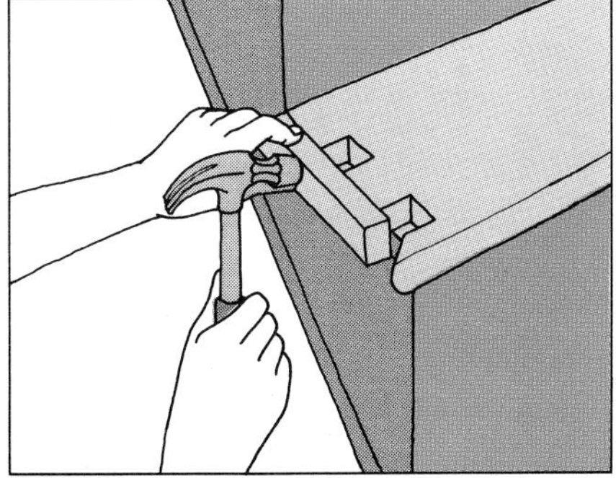

Glue the inner edge of tread and tap tread into position. Use a block of wood between hammer and tread to avoid scarring.

Nail the tread to the top of the outer stringer. To avoid splitting, do not nail too near the edges. Do not use glue.

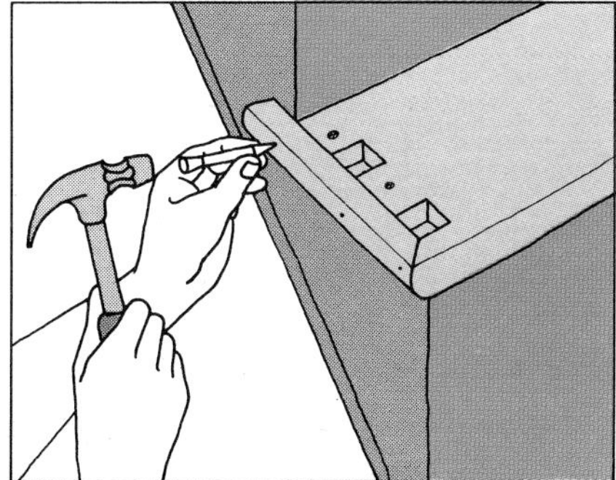

Replace old molding along the side. Sink nailheads below the surface and fill the holes with matching wood putty.

Repairing treads and risers from below

When a staircase is closed on both sides, damaged treads and risers must be removed from underneath. Such repairs can be done with relative ease if you can gain access to the rear of the stairs from the floor below. If this is impossible, it is best to get professional help.

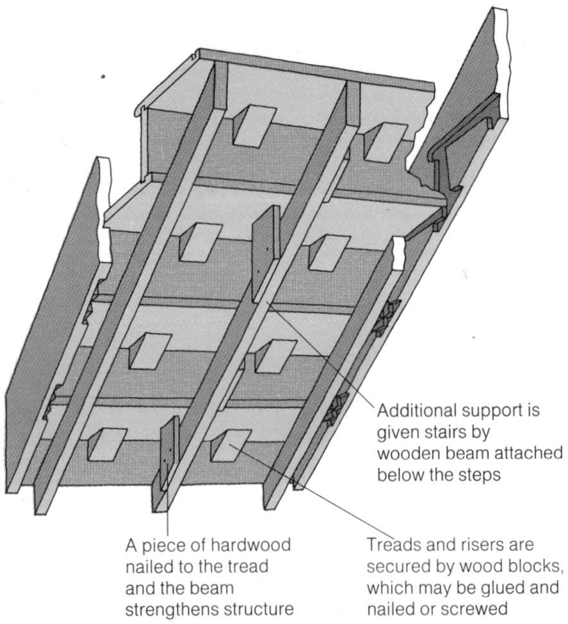

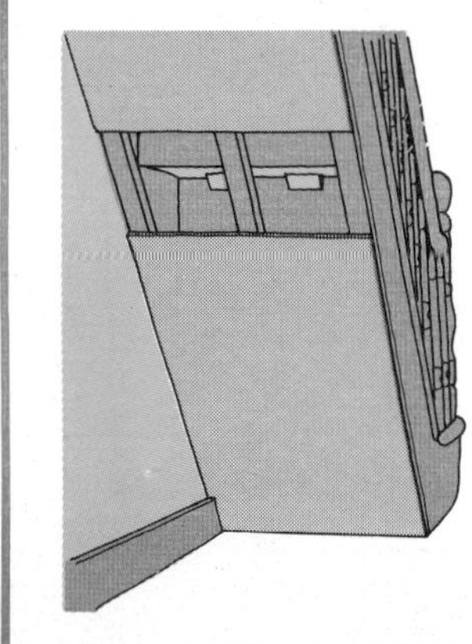

The undersides of some staircases are surfaced with lath and plaster, wallboard, or hardboard. To check whether there are supporting beams under stairs, remove a 6 in. strip the width of the staircase. This will permit you to look through to the underside. Use a chisel to remove plaster. If covering is wallboard or hardboard, drill a few small holes and cut out a 6-in. panel.

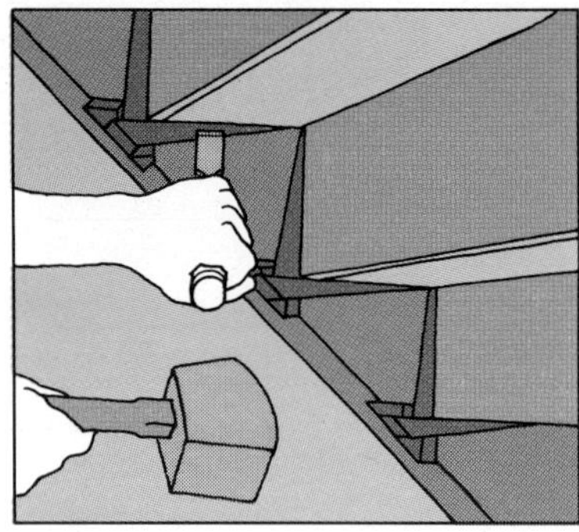

If treads and risers have been wedged into the stringer, remove the wedges with a chisel. Work carefully.

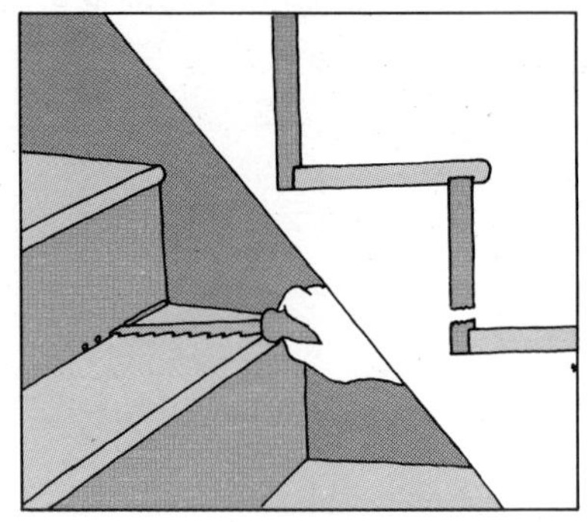

When the riser is jointed to the tread, drill a hole through the front, insert the blade of a keyhole saw, and cut.

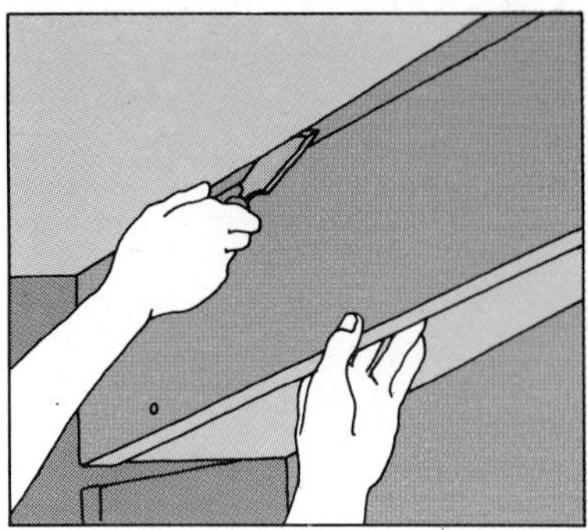

If tread and riser are not jointed, remove screws or nails. Then, using a chisel, force the riser down from the tread.

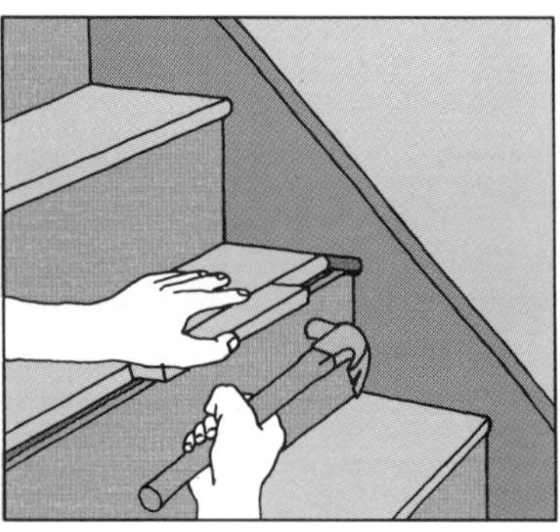

Use a hammer and wooden block at front to tap back the tread. Pull it free from underneath the stairs.

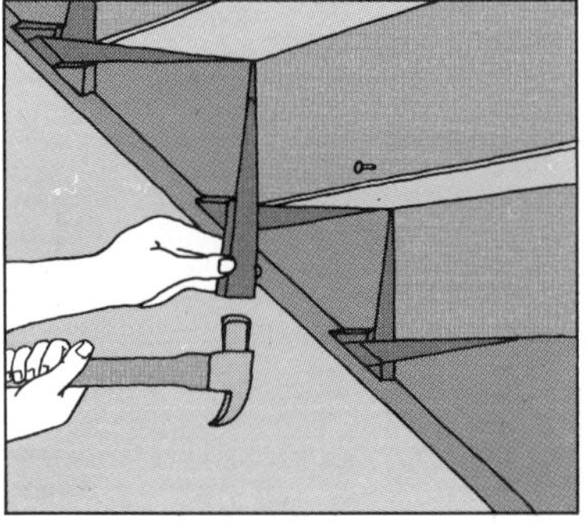

Cut and fit new tread and riser. Use nails at bottom to hold the riser temporarily, then drive in vertical wedges.

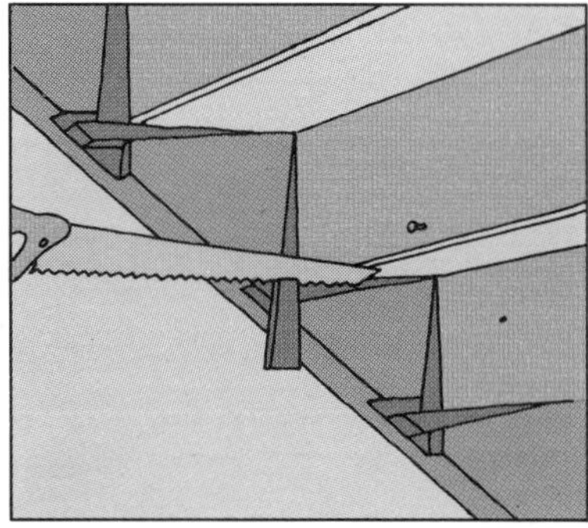

Remove the nails and saw off at an angle the part of the wedge that projects below the new riser.

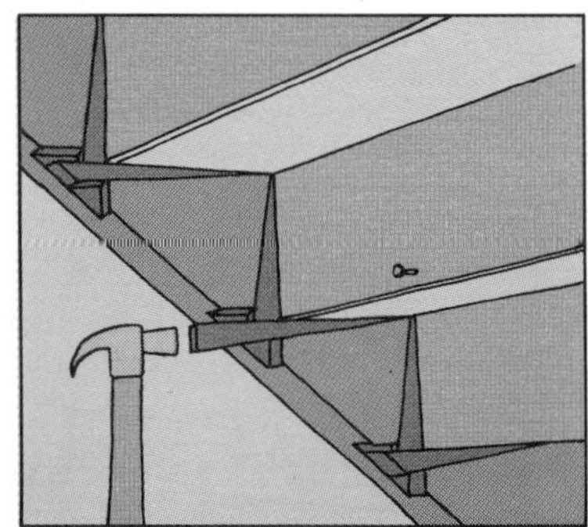

Coat the horizontal wedges with glue and then drive them tightly into the grooves below the tread.

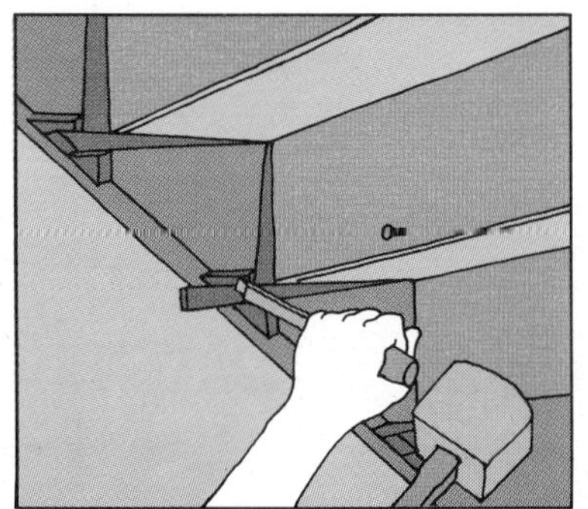

Chisel or saw off the part of the wedges still left projecting below the bottom edge of the stringer.

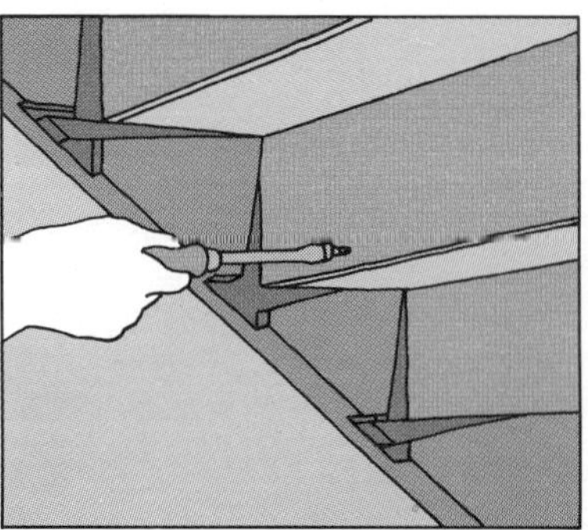

At a distance of about 6 in. from each end, drill pilot holes and drive screws through the riser above center of tread.

Eliminating squeaks

A squeak in a floor is often caused by a loose board rubbing against another board or against a nail. The looseness may be traceable to faulty original construction, use of improperly seasoned lumber, or just plain old age.

The first step in eliminating a squeaking or groaning sound is to pinpoint its location. Have someone walk on the floor to get it to squeak, while you trace the sound to its source.

If the squeaking occurs in the flooring of the main floor, and if the basement ceiling has exposed joists, you may be able to make repairs from below by installing additional bridging between joists. Toenail a solid piece of 2 x 8 in place or use two 2 x 4s staggered to permit nailing their ends from the opposite side of the joists. Or you can drive thin wooden wedges between the joist and the flooring at the point where the squeaking occurs.

If the basement ceiling is finished, or if the

Special flooring nail

squeak is in a floor above the main floor, the repair must be made at the surface of the floor itself. You can do this by driving special spiral-shaped flooring nails through the flooring into the joists or between joists into the flooring.

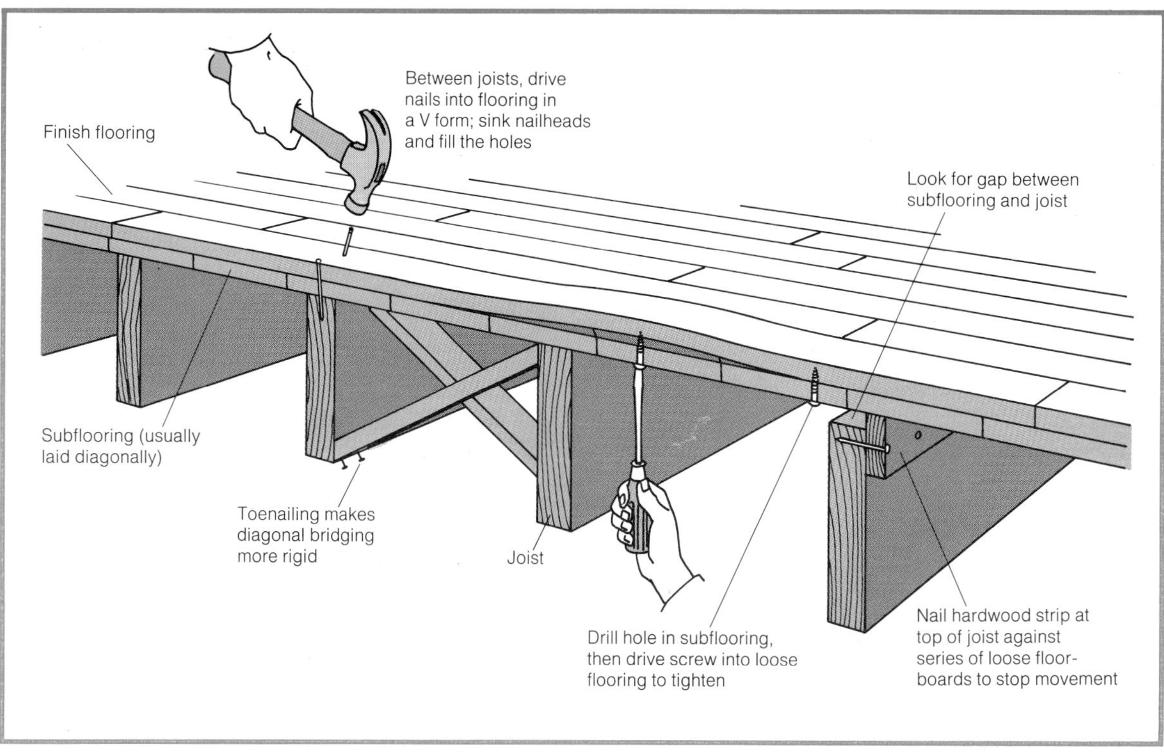

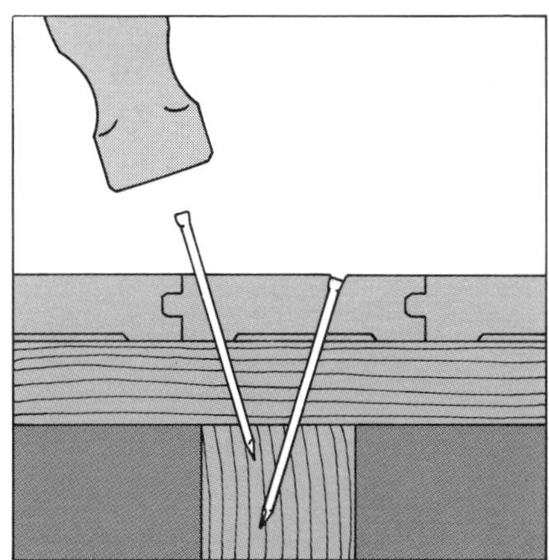

Locate squeak, then drill small pilot holes before driving annular-ring nails into the joists. Sink nailheads and fill holes.

When basement ceiling is open, you can tap shingle wedges under squeaking spots. Be sure the wedging does not raise entire flooring.

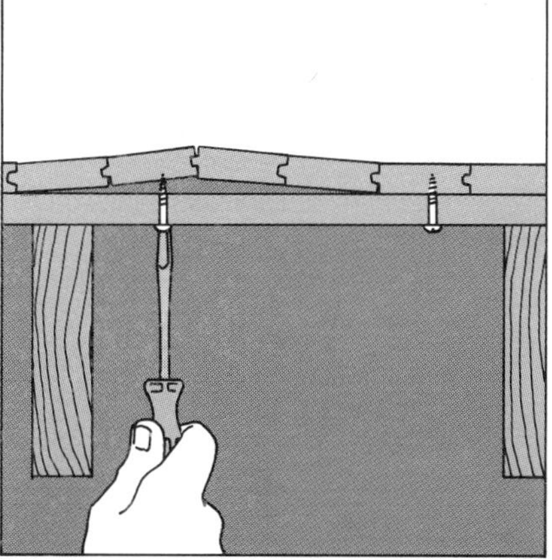

For loose finish flooring, drill clearance hole in subflooring, then use wood screws to draw flooring down, closing the space between.

For surface board movement, lubricate end joint crack with graphite, then secure and seal with wood putty or plastic wood.

Eliminating squeaks

Many squeaks in floors can be traced to changes that take place in the shape of the wood. A longitudinal warp in a joist will bring about a dip, causing insufficient support to be given to a section of the diagonally laid subflooring. When a portion of the floor is weakened in this way, a squeak can develop from any of several directions. You can repair this condition permanently by forcing a length of hardwood, longer than the gap, up against the subflooring. Use a wedge-pole set on the floor if necessary, then nail the patch securely in place against the joist.

Another change in shape takes the form of a warped floorboard, particularly one that curls up at an end. The remedy for this is to drill clearance holes, then drive spiral flooring nails through the high points of the warp and into the joist beneath.

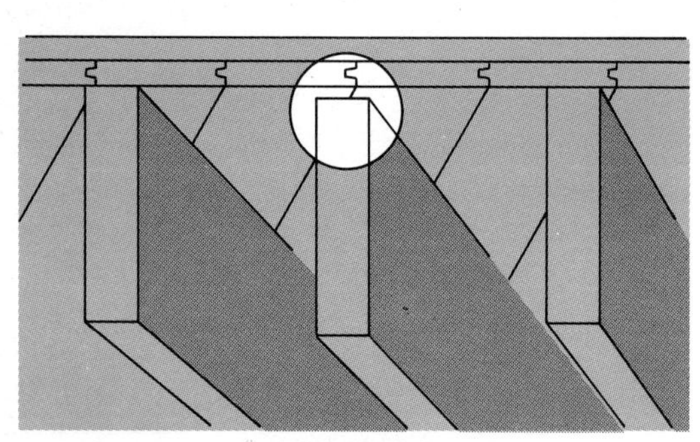

Sagging beam: A longitudinal warp or sag in a joist will leave a section of the flooring inadequately supported, causing a dip to develop.

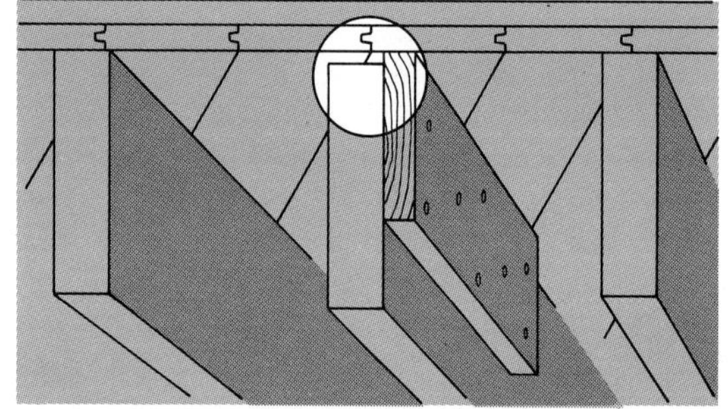

To correct this, force a piece of hardwood longer than the gap into place and nail it to the joist. This will permanently repair the fault.

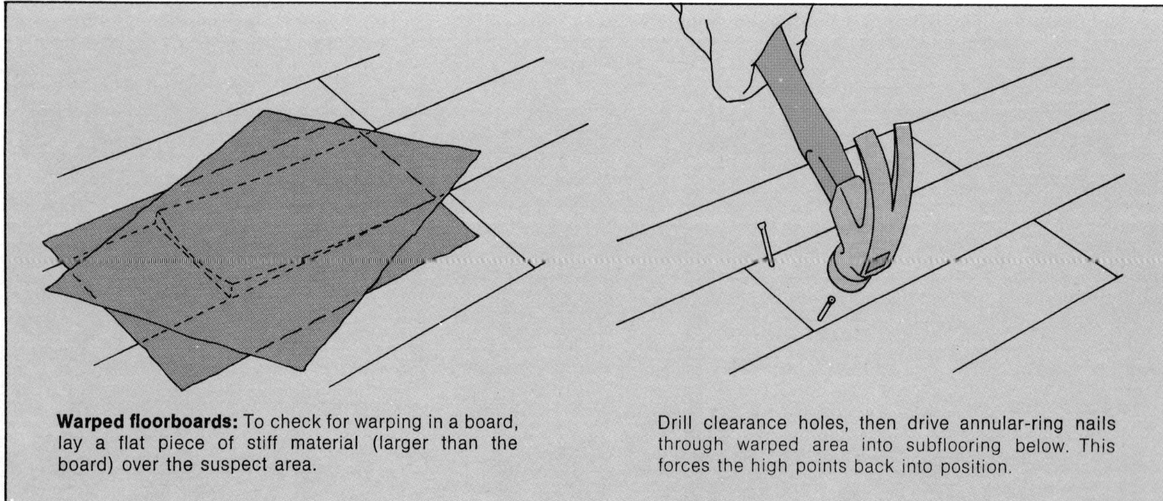

Warped floorboards: To check for warping in a board, lay a flat piece of stiff material (larger than the board) over the suspect area.

Drill clearance holes, then drive annular-ring nails through warped area into subflooring below. This forces the high points back into position.

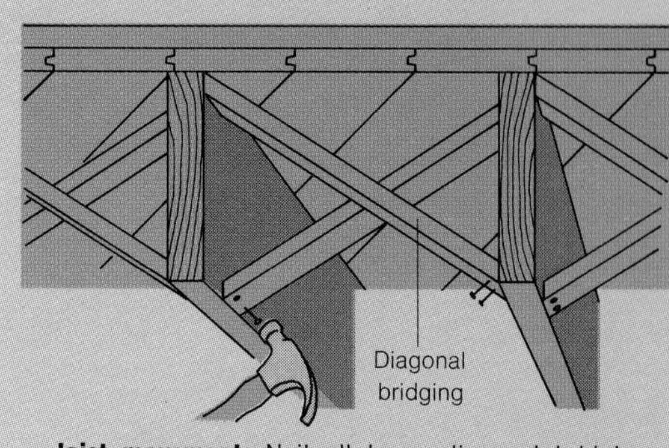

Joist movement: Nail all loose diagonal bridging. This gives rigidity to the joists.

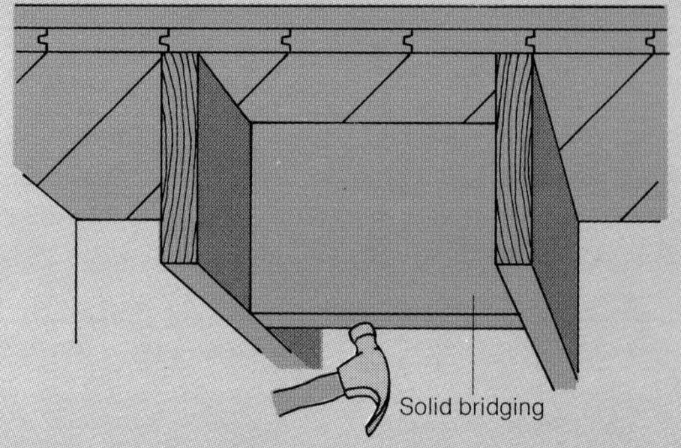

Cut additional bridging (needed for each 8 ft. of span) to exact size and force it into the opening.

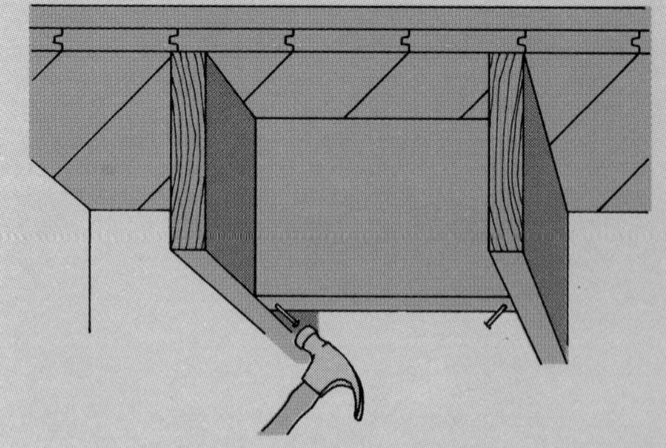

Toenail the top and bottom of both ends of the solid bridging into adjoining joists.

Correcting sags

A sagging floor can be the direct cause of such annoyances as sticking doors and windows, cracks in ceiling and wall plaster, even roof leaks. A sag must be corrected before any remodeling is attempted. A sag in the flooring of the first floor will affect all of the floors above and the roof as well. Its cause is insufficient support under the floor joists, and corrections that are made in the basement will take care of all sags.

One method is to use a short house jack equipped with a 4 x 4 vertical post extension to raise the sagging joists back up to their original position. Place a heavy beam on the concrete basement floor to act as a base for the jack. This will prevent the concrete from crumbling under the tremendous force that must be applied to raise the joists. Another beam is now put in position overhead under the sagging joists. It is held in place by the thrust against it of the jack's 4 x 4 post extension. The jack handle is turned, pushing the horizontal beam up against the sagging joists and gradually raising them. Caution must be exercised at this point, for as soon as resistance is felt on the jack handle, the operation must stop for at least 24 hours. Continued lifting could cause considerable damage to the house.

After 24 hours, it is safe to make a one-quarter turn of the handle, but no more. No matter how easy it is to lift with the jack, or how long it may take to remove the sag gradually, the quarter turn every 24 hours should not be exceeded.

You can make the repair permanent by installing a steel Lally column at each end of the supporting beam. Each column should be mounted on a concrete foundation at least 24 inches square and 12 inches thick. Adjustable steel jack posts are more convenient to install than Lally columns, but they are more expensive. Some building codes require that the jack post's screw mechanism be welded to prevent further turning; others require the mechanism to be buried in 6 inches of concrete.

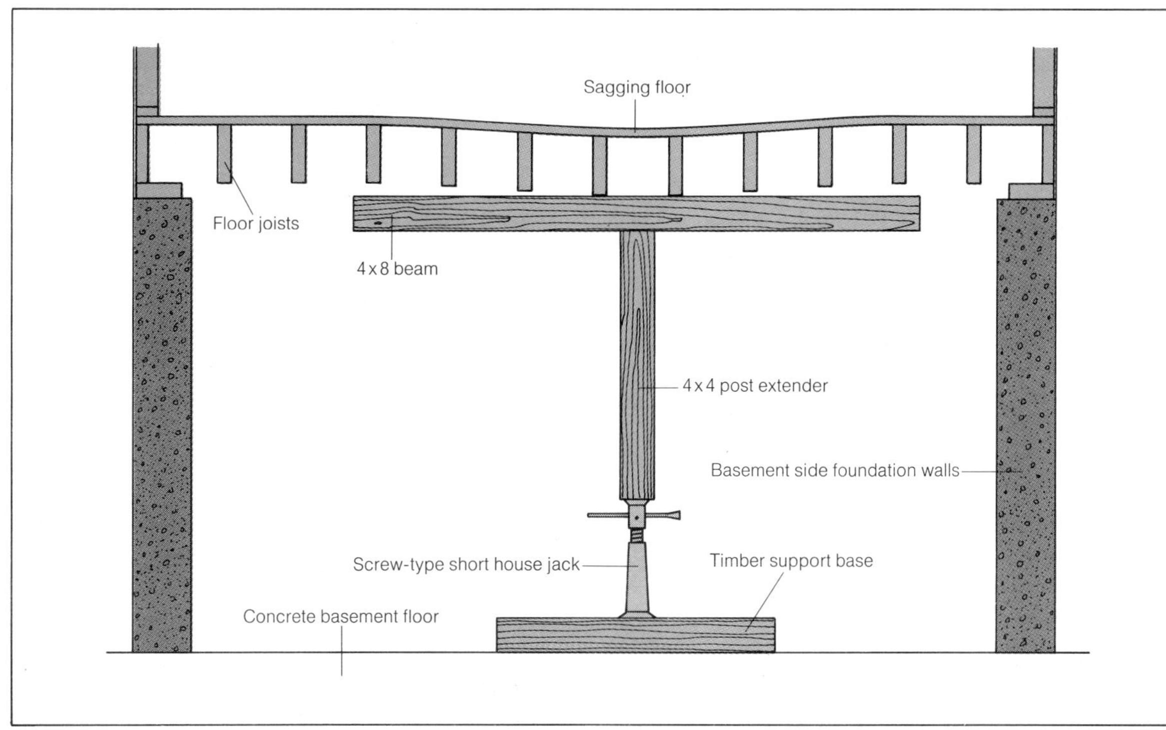

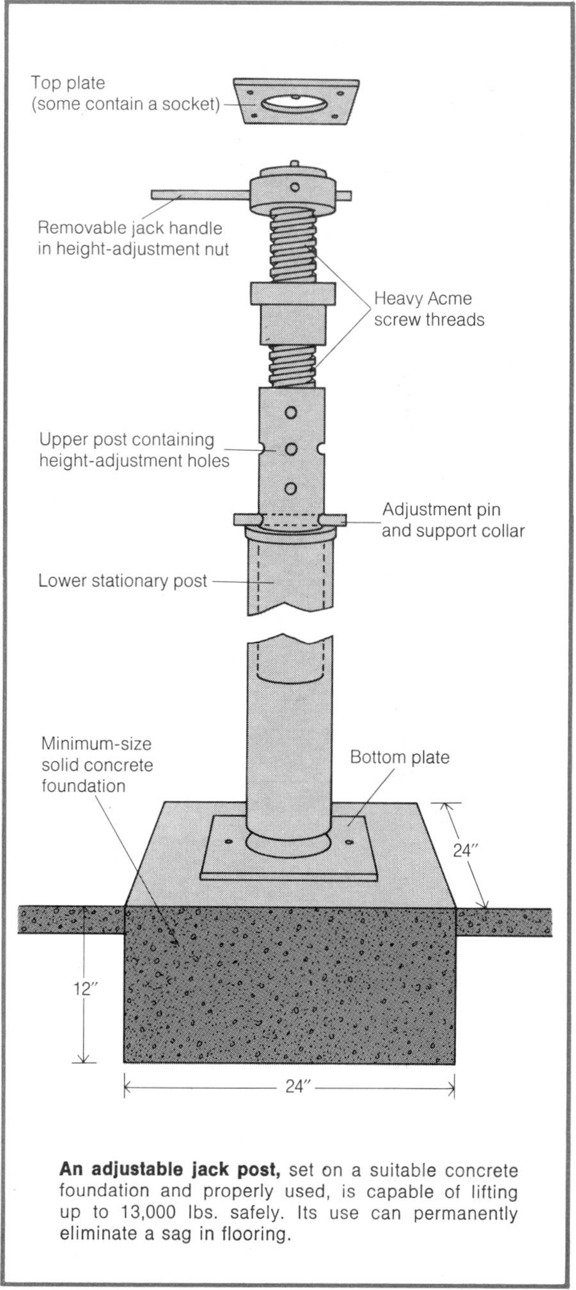

An adjustable jack post, set on a suitable concrete foundation and properly used, is capable of lifting up to 13,000 lbs. safely. Its use can permanently eliminate a sag in flooring.

Replacing damaged floorboards

There are many reasons for removing an old section of flooring and replacing it with new. A section may be damaged, or you may have to cut out a sound section to get at defective wiring or plumbing underneath. No matter what your reason may be, the method of replacement is always the same.

Bore a series of overlapping holes across the center of the damaged piece, taking care not to go too far into the subflooring. If there is no subflooring, center the holes over the joists to give support to the replacement. Either chisel off the tongue to get the section out or split it down the middle. Square off jagged edges of holes.

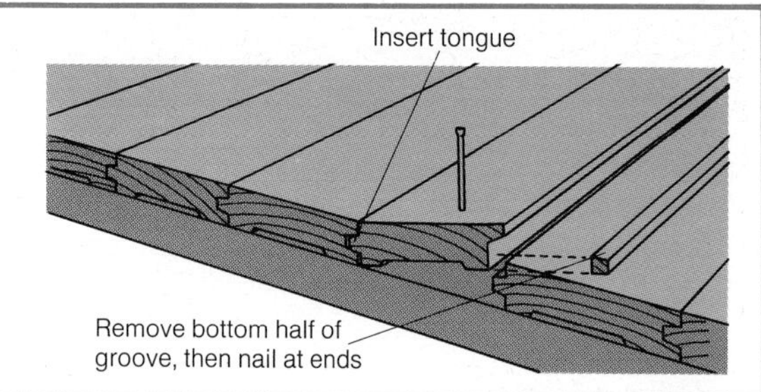

Cut the piece of new flooring to length for a snug fit. It will not go down into the opening, however, until the lower half of its groove is removed. Coat tongue and groove with glue. Insert the replacement tongue in the old flooring groove and drive the grooved side down into the opening. Drill pilot holes for nails at the ends of the board and along the grooved side of long boards. Drive in cement-coated nails and sink the nailheads.

Drill a series of large holes across center and against grain of board to be removed. Avoid drilling too far into the subflooring.

Use a sharp chisel to cut off the tongue of the board being replaced. Remove the board and trim the edges of the opening.

Alternate method of removing board: Split defective board down the center and along the grain with chisel. Pry out pieces.

Measure the opening and cut replacement board to size. Carefully test the new board against the opening for precise fit.

Turn replacement board over and chisel off lower half of its groove so that it will fit over the tongue of the adjoining board.

Coat tongue and groove with glue. Insert tongue, then drive it into place, using a wood block and mallet.

Drill pilot holes for nails at each end of board and along sides of long boards; make holes smaller than nail size. Sink nailheads.

After cement-coated nails have been sunk, fill holes and joints with color-matched putty and refinish to match the adjoining flooring.

Installing hardboard underlayment

Badly worn floorboards can be covered with tiles or linoleum. To get good results with either, an underlayment must first be put down over the damaged floorboards. Hardboard is excellent for this purpose.

You can buy hardboard made especially for underlayment in 4-x-4-foot squares (the easiest size to work with). This special hardboard is ¼ inch thick and smooth on both sides. Or you can buy 4-x-8-foot sheets of hardboard and cut them into 4-foot squares.

Stand hardboard on edge in the room where it is to be laid for 48 hours before installing. Prepare the floor by filling gaps and cracks and sanding and nailing down loose boards. Lay ordinary hardboard with its rough side down. Lightly bevel the edges of the hardboard before nailing.

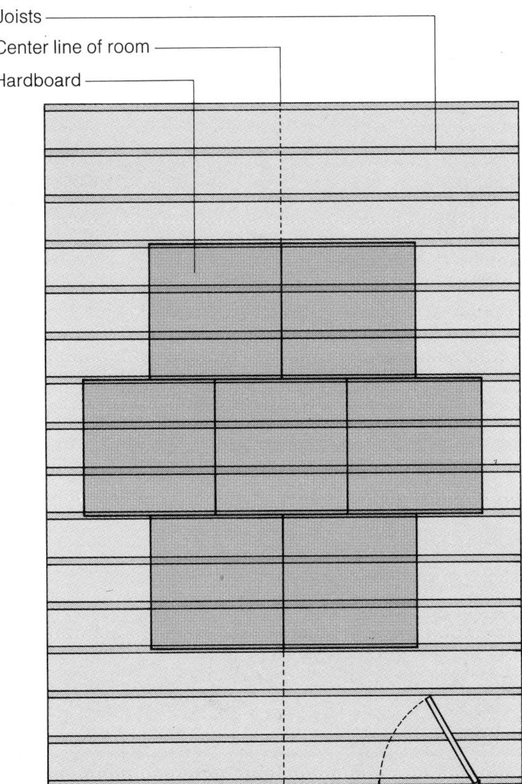

Laying hardboard squares: When putting down hardboard underlayment, try to position one edge of the first square over the center of a floor joist.

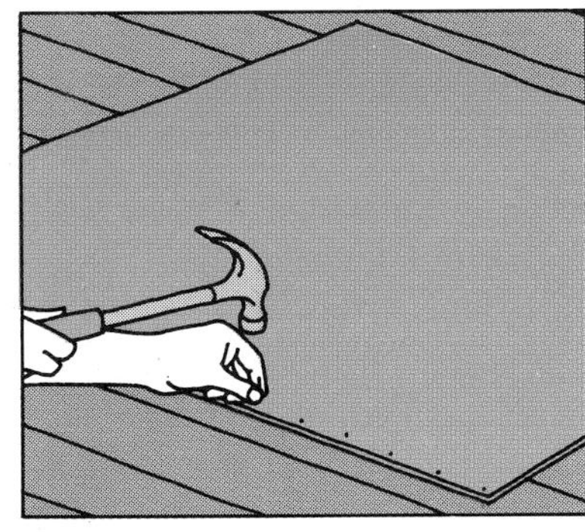

Start with a 4-ft. square in approximate center of room. Have one edge parallel to and centered on a joist.

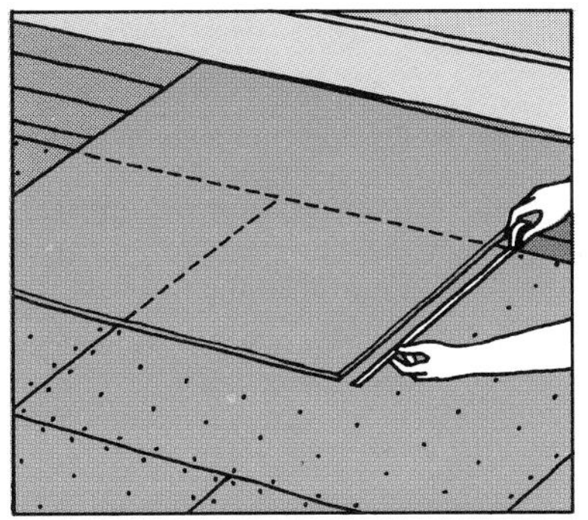

To cut border pieces flush with baseboard, place piece of hardboard flat on floor, then push it against baseboard.

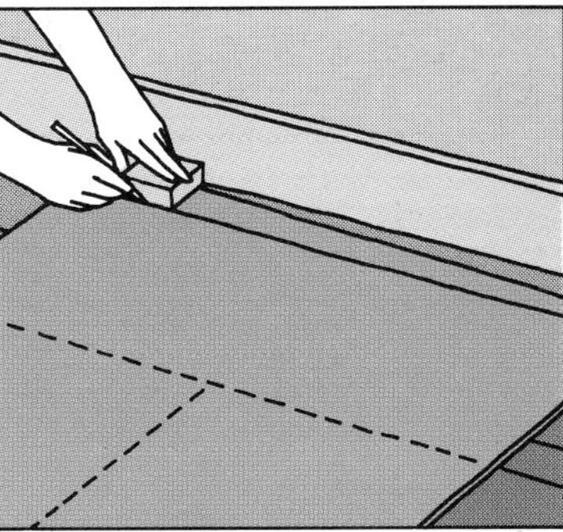

Hold a pencil against a small wood block and move block along baseboard so that pencil duplicates shape of baseboard.

Cut along this line, then fit the hardboard against the baseboard. Mark extent of overlap of hardboard underneath.

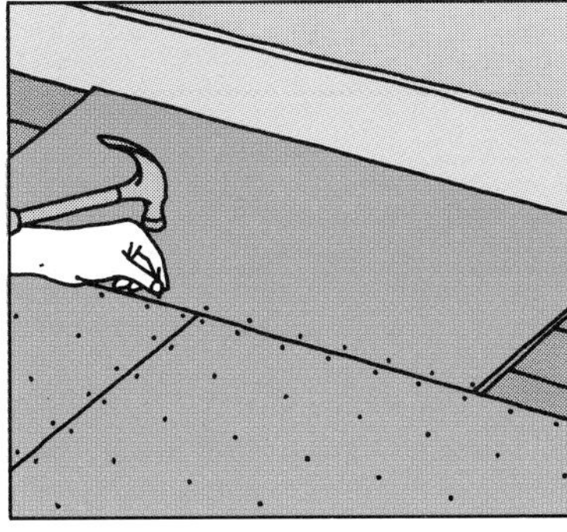

Cut off overlap; fit new section between baseboard and already laid hardboard. Do the same around entire border.

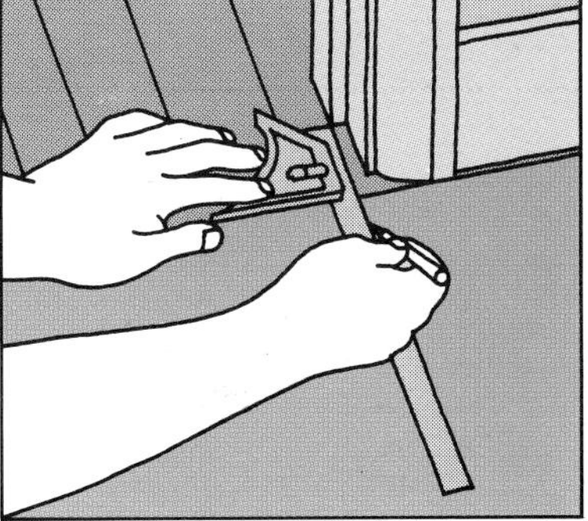

When you reach a doorway, use a combination square to mark distance from doorstop to edge of baseboard.

Use the block and pencil technique to mark the main points of the door frame on the hardboard.

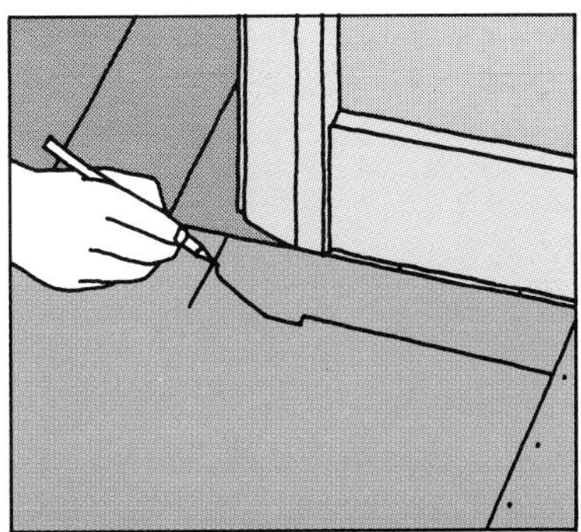

Join the marked points to duplicate shape of door frame. Draw curves freehand. Cut along pencil line with coping saw.

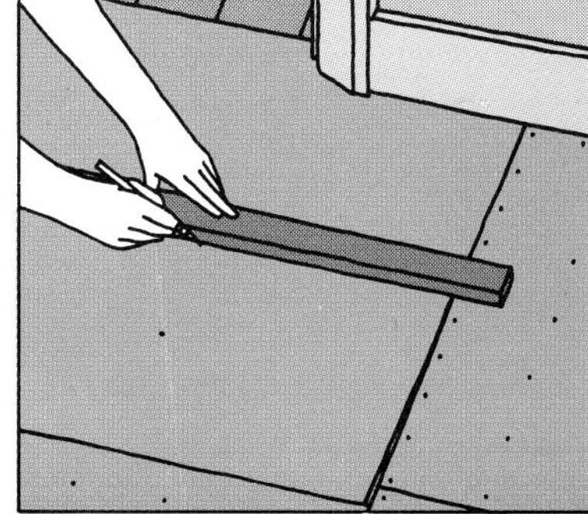

Place cutout board in position; mark extent of overlap of adjacent nailed board. Cut and nail every 4 in.

Using a drum sander

The drum sander, an inexpensive tool to rent, handles the major part of floor refinishing. The machine consists of a revolving rubber-covered drum mounted on a wheeled frame that tilts backward to lift the drum from the floor. A sheet of sandpaper is wrapped around the drum; a removable bag attached to a vacuum arrangement collects the dust.

A popular drum sander, excellent for home use, is powered by a 1½-hp motor that operates on 117 volts, 25 to 60 cycles AC or DC. It can be plugged into any wall outlet.

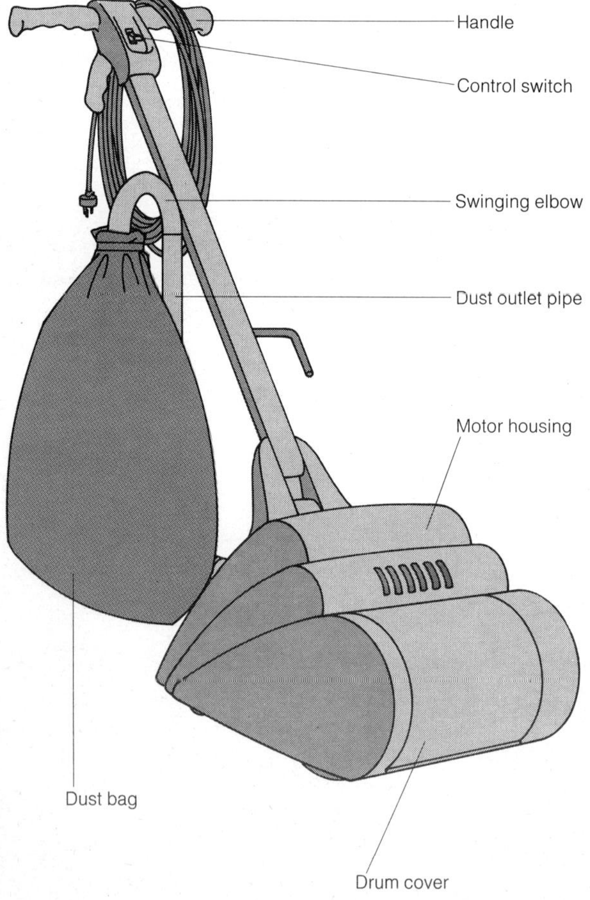

When you are ready to use the machine, first tilt it backward so that the drum clears the floor. Then switch on the power and gently lower the drum until it contacts the surface. If you lower the drum too quickly, the sandpaper will scar the floor.

The drum sander operates in both directions. Raise the drum at the beginning and end of each cut, or pass, across the floor. Sand with the grain whenever possible. This machine tends to pull away from the operator; hold it in check so that it moves at a slow and even pace throughout the operation.

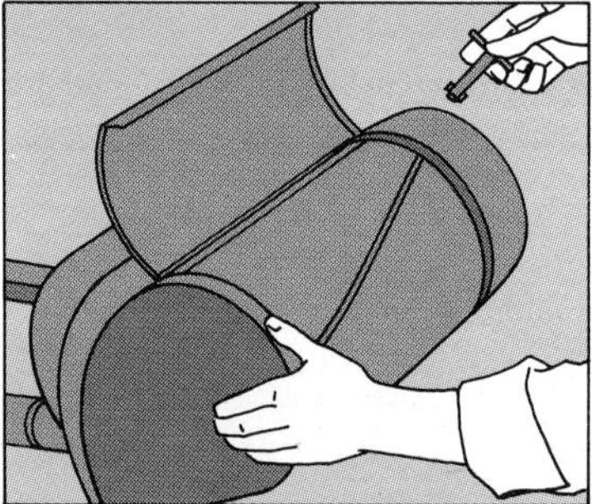

To insert paper, remove cord from outlet, tilt the machine, and lift the drum cover. Use the key supplied to loosen the drum that carries the sandpaper. Some models require an open-end wrench.

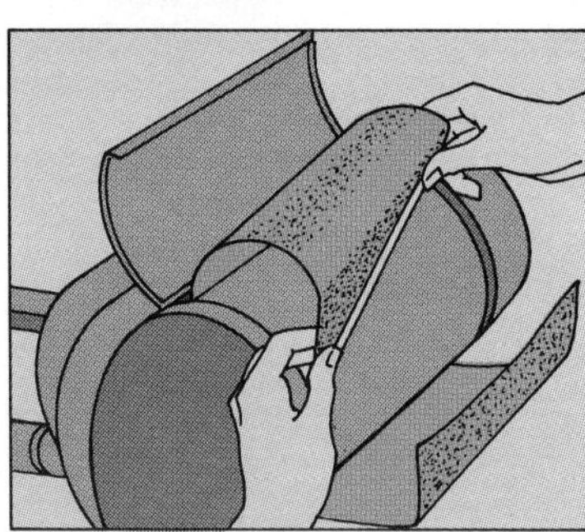

Wrap the new sheet of sandpaper around the drum and then tuck its ends into the slot. If you are using a small belt sander, make sure belt is traveling in direction of arrow printed on back of belt.

Pull the sandpaper tight on the drum. Use the key to tighten the paper around the drum. Plug in the cord and turn on the power. Stand clear and note whether belt is tracking evenly; adjust if necessary.

Using a disk sander

The disk sander, or floor edger, is used for sanding stair treads and along baseboards, in corners, inside closets, and in other places that are inaccessible to the large drum sander.

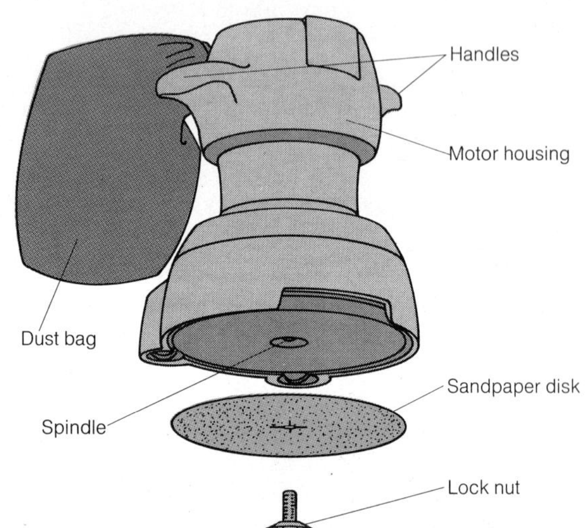

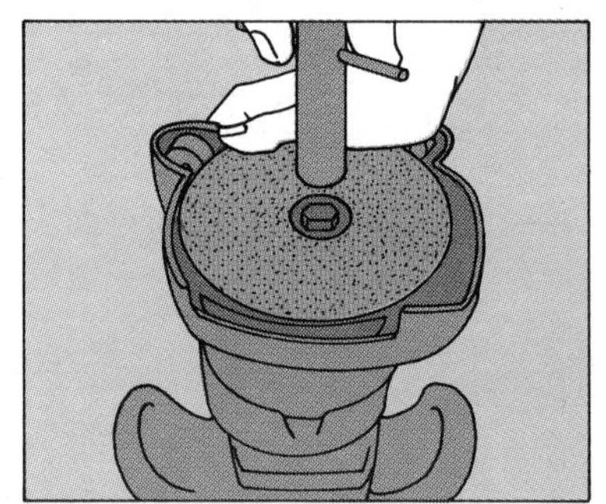

To remove old sandpaper disk, unplug the machine, turn it upside down, and use a wrench to loosen the lock nut. When renting the sander, ask for extra sandpaper in coarse, medium, and fine grades.

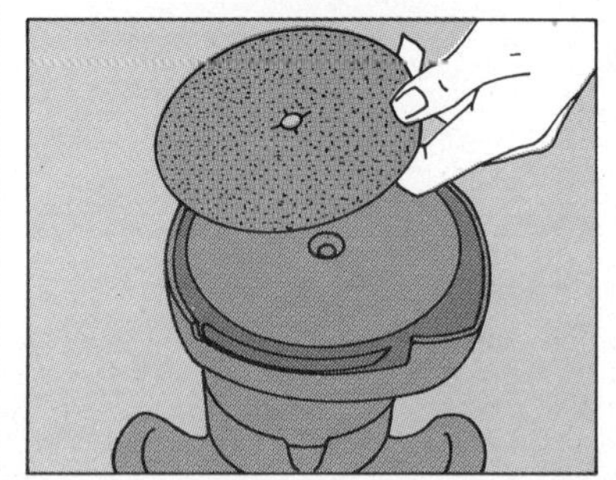

Make sure sandpaper disk is centered. Use coarse sandpaper first, follow with medium and fine. Start with an open-coat sandpaper to remove heavy coats of wax before switching to medium-grade paper.

Refinishing hardwood floors

Preparation is an important part of the job of refinishing floors. After taking all furnishings out of the room, remove the shoe molding (save it to put back later on). Removal of the molding will make edge sanding possible without damage to the baseboards. All projecting nails should be either pulled or set below the surface and loose boards nailed down.

Do the initial drum sanding with the grain in one continuous pass across the room. For the first sanding, use an open-coat (coarse) sandpaper belt on the drum. Make as many passes as are required to expose the bare wood. As you move to an unsanded section, overlap the area you have just sanded. Continue this way until you have done the entire floor.

Change the belt to a finer grade of sandpaper for the final drum sanding. Don't use a worn-out coarse belt instead of one with a finer grit.

The next part of the operation is done with the edger. For inaccessible sections, use a hand sander.

For the floor's finish, apply a penetrating sealer —varnish, shellac, lacquer, or one of the polyurethanes. The polyurethanes are more expensive but give you a durable surface that is moisture- and scratch-resistant. Use two coats of any finish.

Apply either a liquid or a paste polishing wax (never use a water wax) made specifically for hardwood floors. Use a soft cloth as an applicator and buff with an electric polisher. Apply a second coat over the dry initial coat and polish it. Complete the job by replacing the shoe molding.

Sink nails below surface or extract them; pull out all tacks to prevent tearing of sandpaper and possible damage to the sander.

Start drum sanding with coarse sandpaper; sand with grain whenever possible. Use this grade until entire floor has been sanded once.

Change to a medium-grade sandpaper for final sanding with drum sander. Start at one end of the room and work toward the other.

Disk sander, or floor edger, is designed to work near baseboards and door frames, on stair treads, and in other hard-to-reach spots.

Use sandpaper block or hand scraper in corners, under radiators, and in other out-of-the-way places where the disk sander cannot reach.

Clean floor thoroughly after sanding, using vacuum cleaner brush attachment to pick up the sawdust missed by the sander's collector.

Apply a polyurethane finish, then put on a second coat the following day. Use a brush or roller, or a combination of the two.

When finish has dried for three days, apply paste wax and buff with electric polisher; put on a second coat and buff the same way.

Replacing damaged tiles

The easiest way to remove a tile without damaging those around it is to apply heat from a torch or a warm iron. The warmth will soften the adhesive underneath, permitting the tile to be lifted off. Start lifting at one side or a corner and work toward the center. If this is impractical, you can chisel the tile away, starting from the center and progressing out to the edges. After you have removed the tile, scrape away the old adhesive. Try the new tile in the opening, matching the pattern if necessary. If it does not fit, trim or sand its edges. When the new tile fits exactly, warm it as you did the old one to make it flexible. Then apply adhesive to the area where the new tile will be laid. Install the tile and weight it down until the adhesive sets.

Warm the damaged tile with an iron or a torch; apply just enough heat to soften the adhesive underneath.

Using a putty knife, carefully pry up the damaged tile. Take care not to disturb the surrounding tiles.

An alternate method is to chisel out the damaged tile. Work carefully, from the center to the edges.

Remove all adhesive that remains from the setting of the old tile, scraping until you reach the bare foundation.

Try new tile in opening, matching pattern if design is involved. Tile sizes are standard so fit should be no problem.

New tile may require slight trimming. If so, use a knife or sandpaper with caution, testing frequently for fit.

Apply the amount and type of adhesive that is recommended for the kind of tile you are using as a replacement.

After first warming the new tile with an iron or torch sufficiently to make it flexible, lay it in place.

When replacement tile is in position, weight it down; leave weights in place for the entire drying period.

Flattening curled tiles

The tendency of tiles to curl up at the edges is probably their greatest fault. To cure this, first warm the tile, applying enough heat to soften its adhesive. Then lift the tile high enough to dab a small amount of adhesive under the curled area. Replace the tile and hold it down with weights until the adhesive is dry.

With an electric iron apply moderate heat to curled section of the tile long enough to soften the adhesive underneath.

Apply new adhesive as needed to the loose area; replace tile and keep weighted down until adhesive dries.

Repairing surface defects on tiles

To correct scratches or dents on tiles, scrape some of the surface from a scrap piece of the same material and grind it to a powder. Mix the powder with a colorless lacquer or quick-drying varnish to make a paste. Trowel the paste into the scratched or dented area. When the paste has dried, buff it smooth with fine steel wool and boiled linseed oil.

Take scrapings from a scrap of the same material as the floor covering, convert it to powder, and put in a container.

Add colorless lacquer and mix with the powder to a paste. Apply the paste to the section of the flooring that needs repair.

Removing stains from tiles

If food or grease spilled on resilient flooring is not removed fairly soon, the spill will become a stain. The substance that caused the stain determines the material that will remove it.

The most effective stain removers are everyday items in the average household: Household bleach, white vinegar and water, hydrogen peroxide, rubbing alcohol, household ammonia, lighter fluid, and nail polish remover.

If these are tried in the order given, one of them will eventually solve the problem. In most cases the first one, household bleach, will do the job.

If the stain covers the entire floor, and is somewhat gummy, the cause may be too much wax, or too many coats on top of one another. A strong ammonia solution or commercial cleaner should clear it up.

Patching sheet flooring

Worn sections of sheet flooring, such as linoleum or sheet vinyl, can be patched effectively and with relative ease. Get a piece of the same material as the floor covering to be patched; be sure it is larger than the damaged area. Place it over the worn section, being sure the pattern matches exactly, and tape it in position. Using a linoleum knife or other sharp knife, cut through both old and new thicknesses; extend the patch well beyond the damaged area. Remove both pieces, then thoroughly clean the area that was under the old floor covering. Trial-fit the patch, remove it, and apply adhesive to floor or back of patch. Put the patch in place and weight it down flat until the adhesive has dried.

Place a piece of the same material, larger than the worn area, over the spot to be patched; match the pattern exactly.

Tape patch material over worn area. Cut along steel straightedge through both thicknesses; make patch larger than area.

Remove both the patch and the original flooring material and thoroughly clean surface where the damaged flooring lay.

Check the fit of the patch in the opening. Trim as necessary with sharp knife and sandpaper, checking fit frequently.

Apply floor tile adhesive to the bottom of the patch and install the patch. Wipe up excess adhesive with a cloth.

Fit the replacement patch into position. Weight it down and leave the weights in place until the adhesive has dried.

Double-hung windows

Components and operation

A double-hung window is so-called because it has an upper, or outside, sash that slides down and a lower, or inside, sash that slides up. These movements may be controlled by pulleys equipped with cords and weights or by springs concealed in the side jamb sections of the unit. Some double-hung sashes are aluminum, but most are wood. This type of window is adaptable to many architectural styles and has been used in houses for centuries.

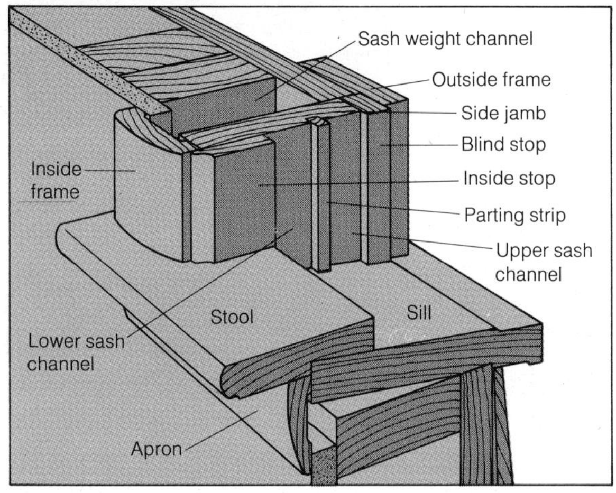

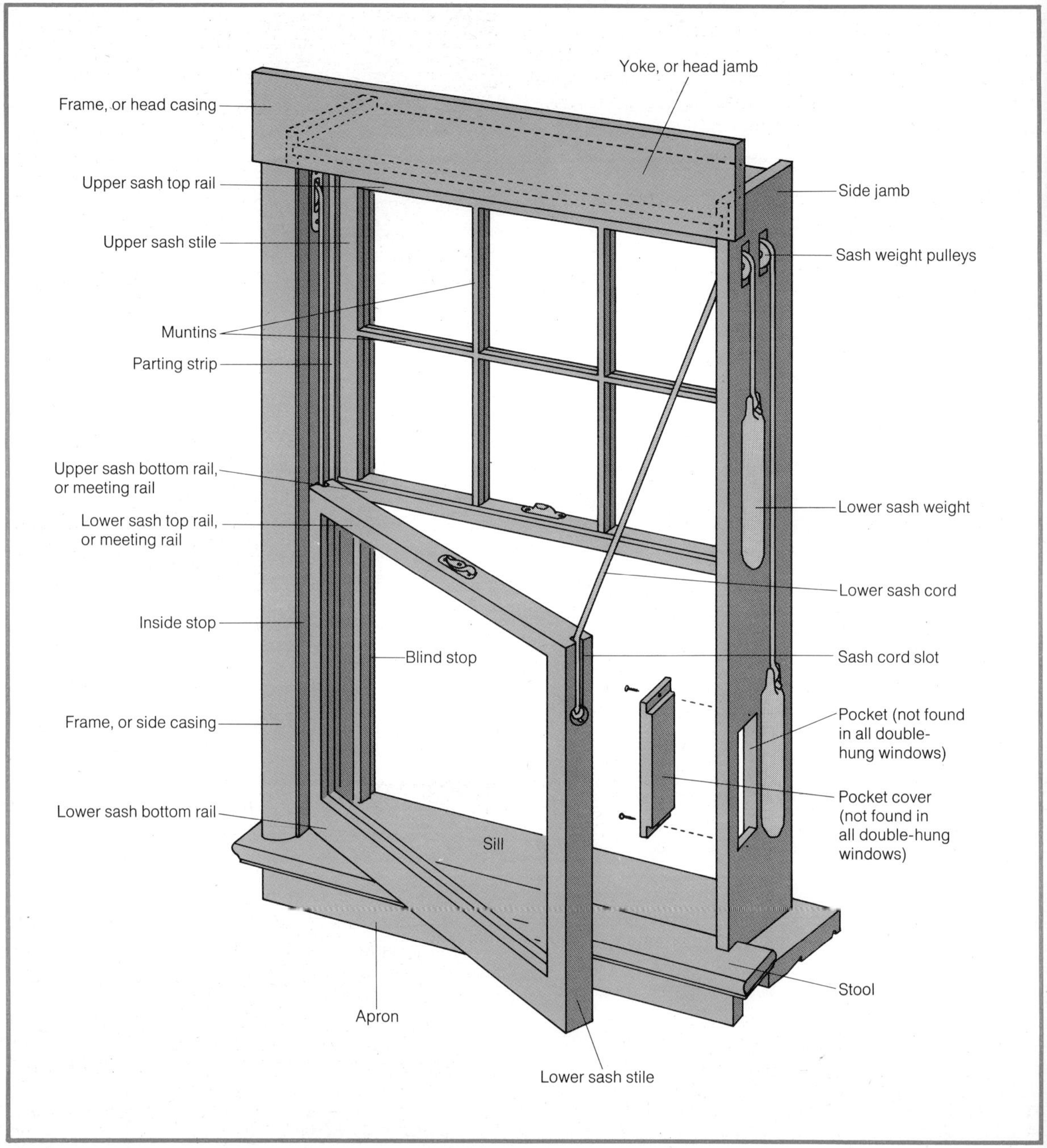

Sash weight channel
Outside frame
Side jamb
Blind stop
Inside stop
Parting strip
Upper sash channel
Inside frame
Stool
Sill
Lower sash channel
Apron

Frame, or head casing
Yoke, or head jamb
Upper sash top rail
Side jamb
Upper sash stile
Sash weight pulleys
Muntins
Parting strip
Upper sash bottom rail, or meeting rail
Lower sash weight
Lower sash top rail, or meeting rail
Lower sash cord
Inside stop
Blind stop
Sash cord slot
Frame, or side casing
Pocket (not found in all double-hung windows)
Pocket cover (not found in all double-hung windows)
Lower sash bottom rail
Sill
Stool
Apron
Lower sash stile

Attaching sash cord or chain

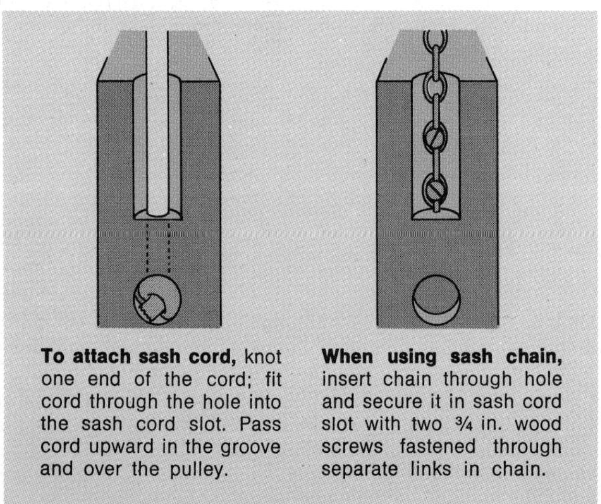

To attach sash cord, knot one end of the cord; fit cord through the hole into the sash cord slot. Pass cord upward in the groove and over the pulley.

When using sash chain, insert chain through hole and secure it in sash cord slot with two ¾ in. wood screws fastened through separate links in chain.

How to correct sticking

Windows of this type usually stick for one of three reasons: (1) Paint or dirt has accumulated in the grooves or on the edges of the various stop moldings; (2) humidity has caused expansion or swelling of wood parts; or (3) weatherstripping fits too snugly.

The first of these problems can be eliminated by sanding and cleaning, usually without completely dismantling the window unit. The other two can generally be overcome by lubrication or by gently tapping a block of wood, the width of the sash groove, along the groove to expand the frame.

If none of these remedies works, you will have to remove the sash from its frame and lightly plane down one or both of its sides just enough to permit free movement when it is replaced.

Break a paint seal by running a wide putty knife between the parting strip and the window sash as shown above.

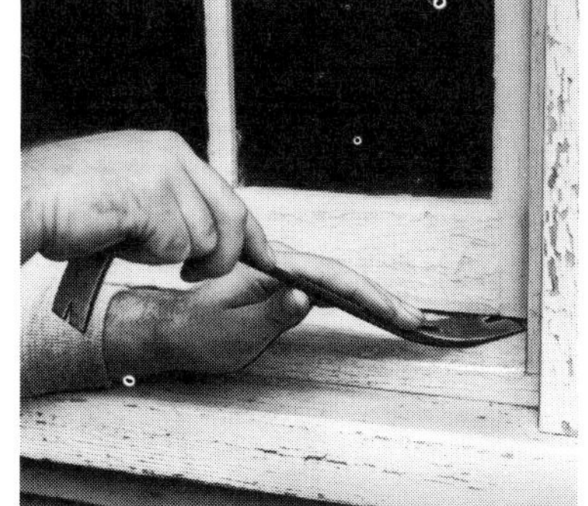

Use a pry bar alternately under outer extremes of bottom rail of lower sash and over top rail of upper sash.

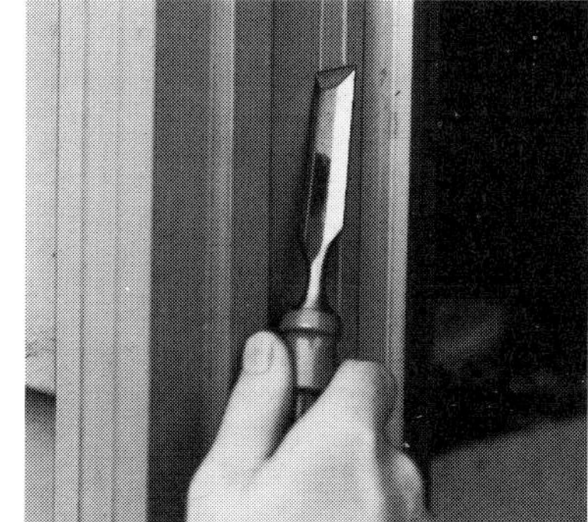

Cut all globs of dried paint from the edges of the parting strip and both stops, using an old 1-in. chisel.

Sand the edges of the parting strip, the inside stop, and the blind stop from which the paint was chiseled away.

If the sash still binds, gently tap on a block of wood along the sash grooves to force the frame outward.

If all else fails, pry out inside stop on one side to remove lower sash and parting strip on same side for upper sash.

While inside stop and parting strip are removed, restore them to original size by planing, then sanding them smooth.

Pull on one side to release sash from frame, remove cord on both sides of sash, then lift out entire sash for repair.

After lightly planing the sides of the sash, test it in the frame for fit, then reassemble as originally installed.

Lubricating sash

If a double-hung window will move but will not slide smoothly, rub hard soap or paraffin as a lubricant along the edges of the blind stop, the inside stop, and the parting strip. Wipe off any excess.

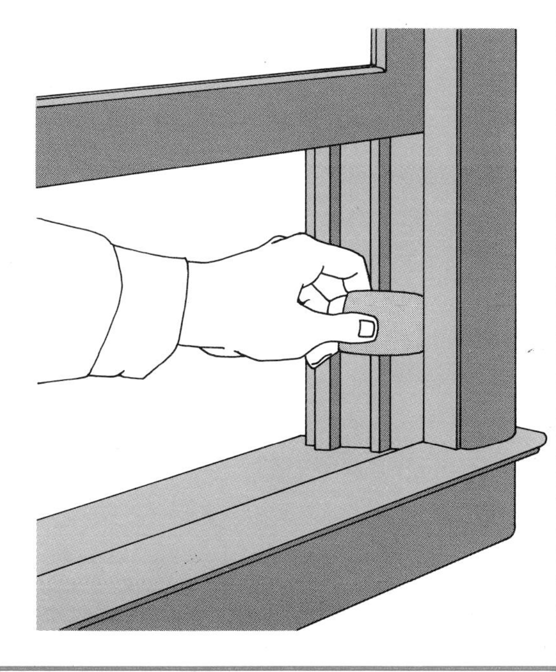

Replacing sash cord with chain

Use wide chisel or stiff putty knife to remove the inside stop on the side of the window frame where the broken cord is to be replaced.

Turn lower sash partly sideways, raise to clear window ledge, then swing out from frame far enough to expose knot in sash cord.

Remove knotted end of cord from sash cord slot in edge of sash. Ease cord upward until knot holds at the pulley. Lift sash from frame.

To replace cords in some windows, it is necessary to remove the window frame in order to gain access to the sash weights.

Other windows are equipped with sash weight pockets. Remove screws from pocket cover; then remove cover to expose weight inside.

Lift weight from pocket and unknot end of cord tied to weight. Have new sash chain of same length as old cord ready as replacement.

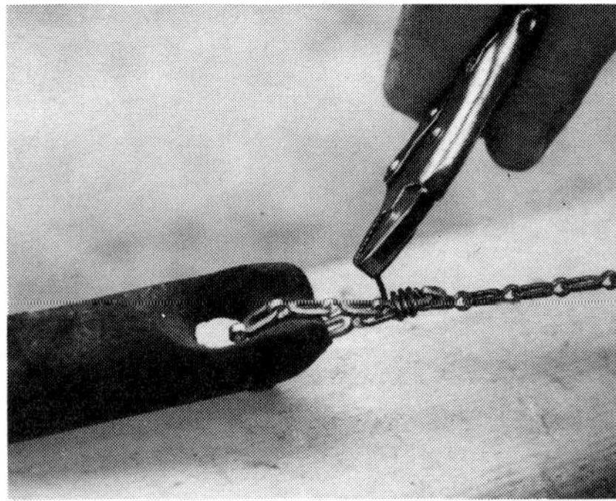
Secure one end of chain to window. Thread other end through pulley to sash weight; fasten to hole in weight; bind tightly with wire.

Proceed similarly when substituting chain for cord in a window without pockets. After attaching chain, put weight back in opening.

Take hold of chain on outside and pull weight up. When it touches pulley, secure chain on outside with a nail passed through a link.

With weight secured, attach chain in sash cord slot on side of sash; use wood screws or nails. Replace cord on opposite side in same way.

When replacing upper sash cord, it is necessary to remove lower window and parting strip before upper sash can be removed.

Replacement technique for upper cord and sash is the same as for lower sash. Change to chain is always advisable when replacing old cord.

Spring lift sashes

Spring lift sash windows are recognizable by a tube that runs from the top of the window casing channel. A spring mechanism in the tube permits the window to be either raised or lowered with a minimum of effort. This type of sash is inexpensive and is virtually maintenance-free.

There are two types of spring sash balances. The tube type is the most common. Inside the tube is a spring attached to a twisted rod. The rod keeps the spring taut so that the window sash will stay in any desired position. There is just enough tension, however, to enable the window sash to be moved up or down with very slight pressure. Occasionally it is necessary to adjust the spring tension to allow the windows to move more easily. The photographs below show how to do this, or how to replace the entire spring assembly should it break.

The second spring type is a steel strap design in which one looped end fastens to the window sash and the other fastens to the window casing. This type is not adjustable and should be replaced if the window action is unsatisfactory.

To adjust spring tension, hold the tube firmly with thumb and remove the screw that holds the tube in place.

If window tends to creep up, the spring is too tight. Keep finger firmly on screw and let spring unwind 2 or 3 turns.

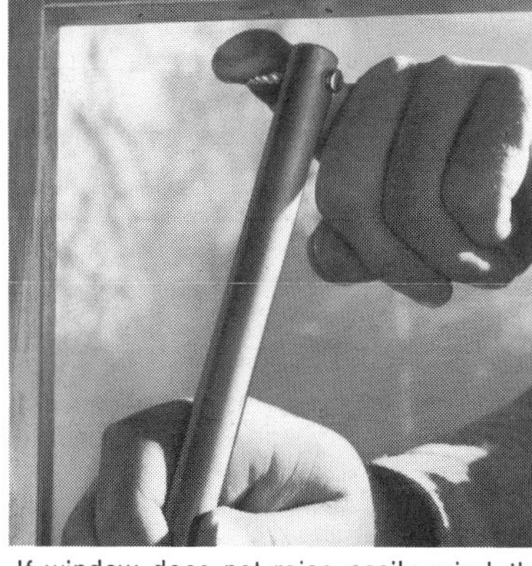

If window does not raise easily, wind the spring tighter by 2 or 3 turns. Hold tube firmly at all times.

Broken spring assembly calls for removal of sash. Flatten aluminum sash channel with light hammering.

With tube screw removed, insert pry bar between sash and frame to hold sash channel flat. Pull sash from frame.

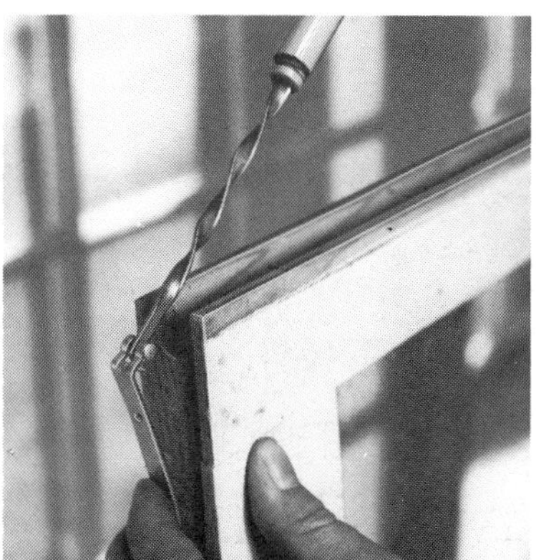

Remove twist rod from sash frame. Install replacement unit the same way. Refit sash and adjust spring tension.

Sash balance

This device is bought as a kit and eliminates sash weights and the problem of broken cords or chains. It consists of a spring inside a revolving drum. The unit is inserted in the pulley hole after the old sash pulley has been removed. A tape attached to the spring is secured to the window sash by means of an adapter hook. This metal strip is installed on the side of the sash in the space between the old cord and the window jamb. The precise spring needed to operate different-size windows is specified in a chart which accompanies each kit.

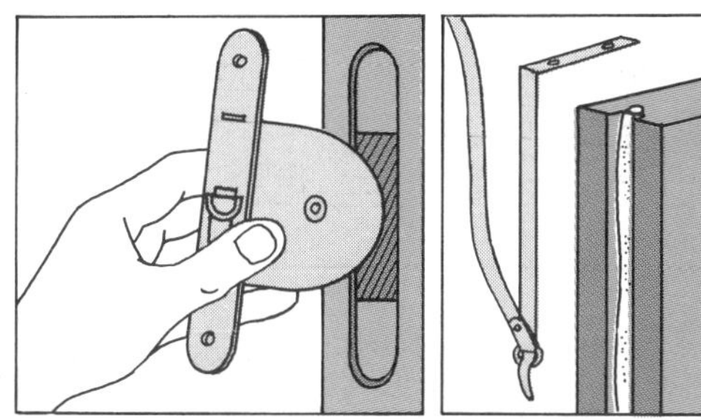

Insert sash balance unit in pulley hole and secure with screws. Attach loop on end of tape to bottom prong of adapter.

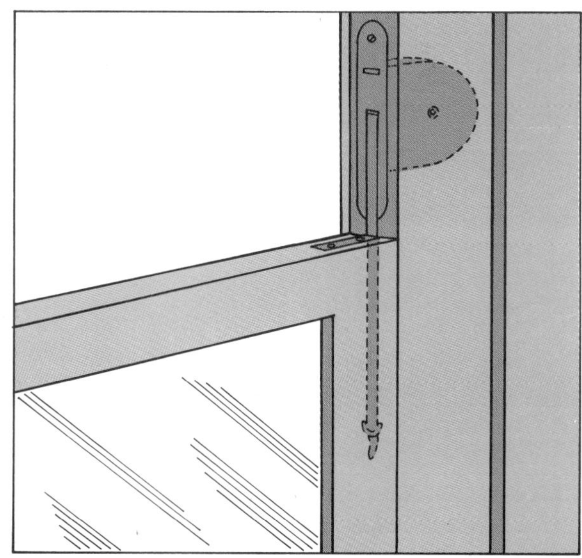

With adapter positioned snugly against side of window sash, attach L-shaped arm to top of sash with screws. Use flathead screws; make sure they are flush with the arm.

Weatherstripping windows

Basic types

Most windows, especially in older houses, should be weatherstripped to seal cracks and openings that permit heat loss and cold air penetration. You can buy weatherstripping by the foot or yard, or in kits complete with rustproof tacks for installation.

For double-hung windows, there are several basic types of weatherstripping that can be applied without special tools: (1) Thin spring-metal strips; (2) vinyl, available in tubular form and as a covering over a sponge core; and (3) adhesive-backed foam. All attach to molding and fit snugly against sash.

Metal-framed windows of the casement, awning, or jalousie type can be weatherstripped with a transparent vinyl tape that goes over their edges, or an adhesive-backed foam that is installed at the joints. There is also an aluminum strip made especially for casements. All let windows open freely, then close tightly against all parts of their frames.

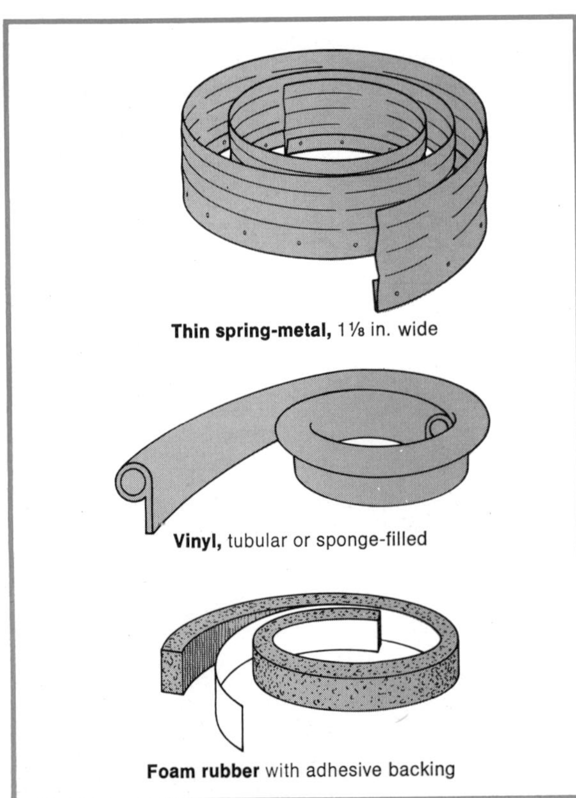

Thin spring-metal, 1⅛ in. wide

Vinyl, tubular or sponge-filled

Foam rubber with adhesive backing

Installation

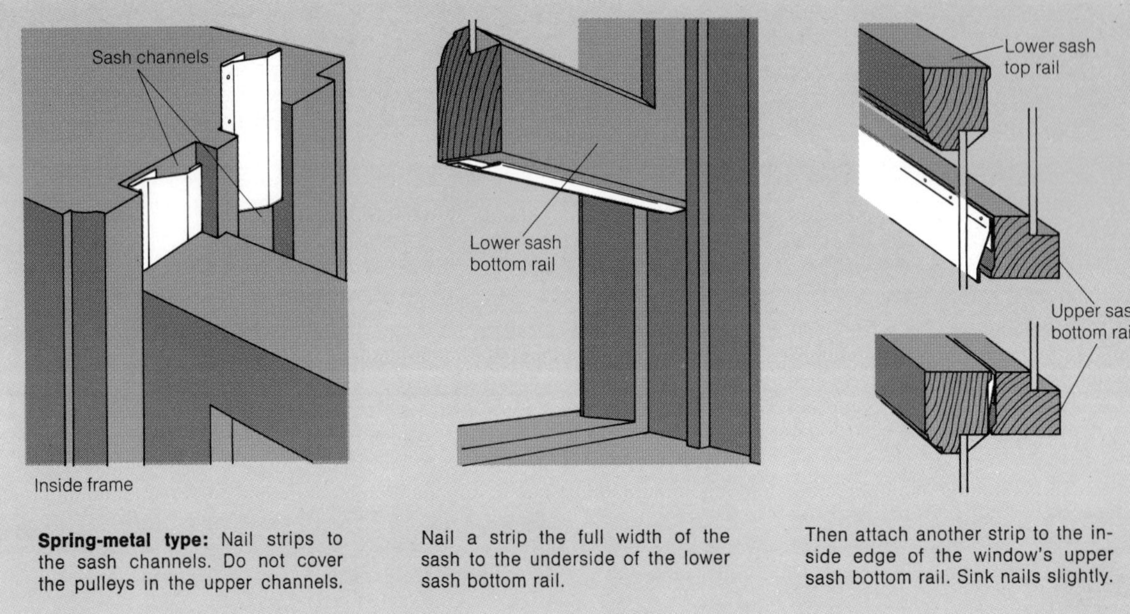

Spring-metal type: Nail strips to the sash channels. Do not cover the pulleys in the upper channels.

Nail a strip the full width of the sash to the underside of the lower sash bottom rail.

Then attach another strip to the inside edge of the window's upper sash bottom rail. Sink nails slightly.

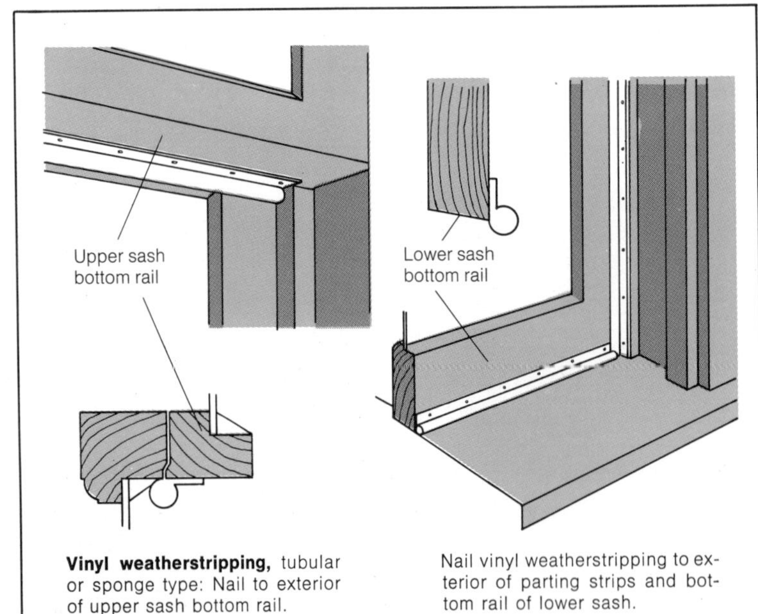

Vinyl weatherstripping, tubular or sponge type: Nail to exterior of upper sash bottom rail.

Nail vinyl weatherstripping to exterior of parting strips and bottom rail of lower sash.

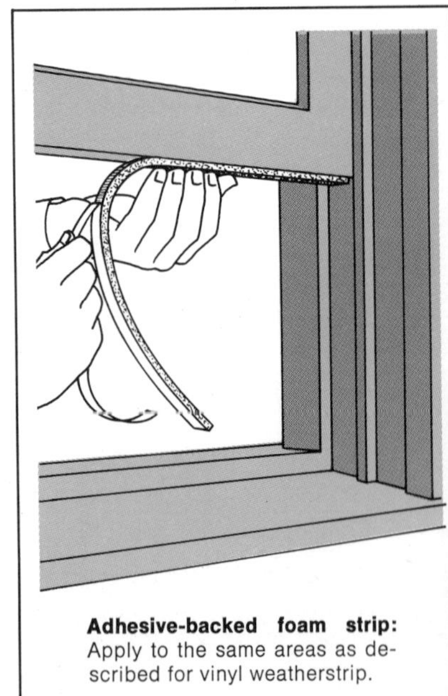

Adhesive-backed foam strip: Apply to the same areas as described for vinyl weatherstrip.

Replacing panes

Wear heavy gloves to remove broken glass. Take out old putty, softening it, if necessary, with a soldering iron or a torch with a soldering head. Extract glazier's points. Remove bedding putty carefully to avoid gouging groove; sand groove and coat with linseed oil or thinned exterior paint to prevent absorption of oils from fresh putty or glazing compound.

Cut new pane, preferably of double-strength glass, about ⅛ inch smaller than opening in length and width to allow for irregularities. Apply a thin bed of glazing compound to the groove and press replacement pane in place. Secure it on all four sides with glazier's points spaced about 4 to 6 inches apart. Drive them into the sash about halfway, using the side of a chisel, putty knife, or screwdriver.

Roll glazing compound into a rope about ⅜ inch in diameter and press it along the edges of the pane; draw a putty knife over it at an angle to form a neat triangular bead. Let compound dry for a week or so, then paint to protect it against the weather.

Making a glass-cutting jig

Lay a sheet of ¾-in. plywood, larger than glass to be cut, on workbench. Place a hardwood strip near bottom edge of plywood; nail strip to bench through plywood. Position glass on plywood against hardwood strip so cutter will clear strip. Use kerosene or turpentine to wipe line to be cut, then score with glass cutter in a single stroke along rafter square. Move glass so scored line is just beyond plywood's edge; tap glass lightly to break at score mark.

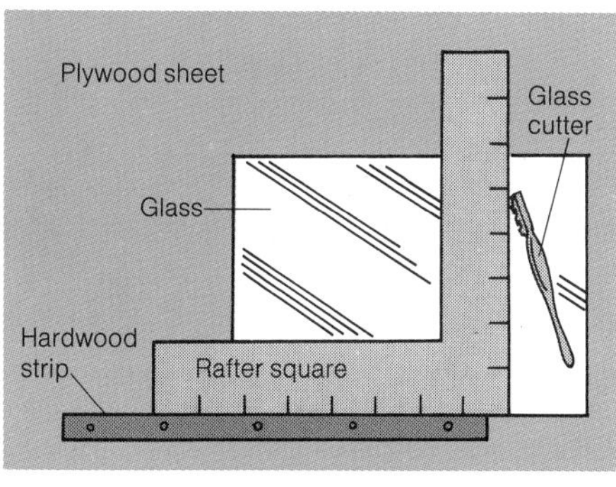

Take broken glass from frame. Remove old putty, softening it with soldering iron or torch with soldering head, if necessary.

Clean out the old bedding putty, remove the glazier's points, and then sand the groove smooth on all four sides.

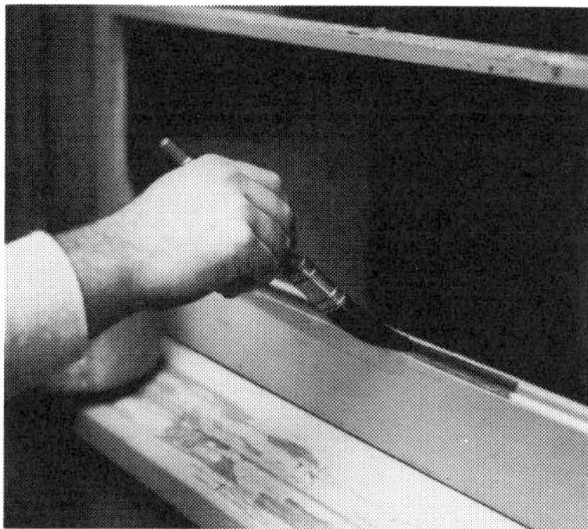

Coat groove with linseed oil or thinned exterior paint to prevent absorption of oil from fresh glazing compound.

Cut new pane of glass ⅛ in. smaller than the opening in length and width to allow for any irregularities and expansion.

Apply a thin bed of glazing compound along all four sides to cushion the glass against stress and leakage.

Press glass against glazing compound and tap in glazier's points 4 to 6 in. apart. Drive them halfway into sash.

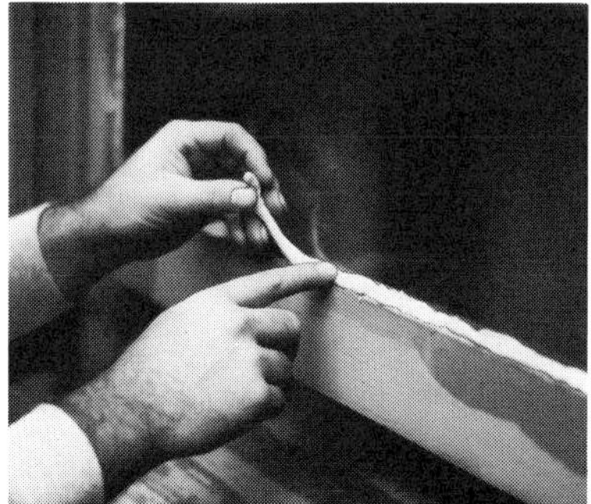

Form the glazing compound into a rope ⅜ in. in diameter. Press compound into groove along edges of the glass.

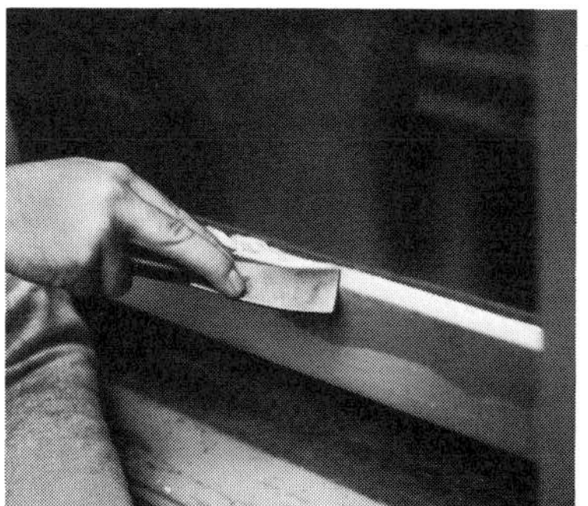

Hold the putty knife at an angle and draw it over the glazing compound rope to form a neat triangular bead.

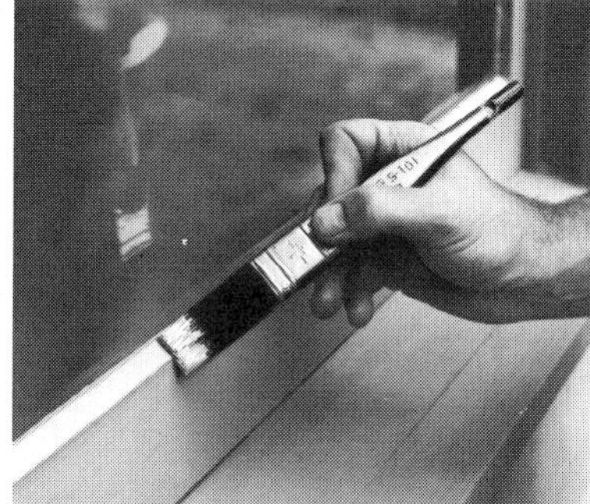

Allow compound to dry for a week or so, then paint, overlapping glass about 1/16 in. as a seal against moisture.

Casement windows

Operation and maintenance

A casement window is attached to its frame by means of hinges and is operated by the turning of a crank. Except for broken panes of glass, this type of window seldom needs repair beyond occasional tightening of a loose hinge and cleaning and lubrication of the operator crank and arm.

If opening or closing becomes increasingly difficult, however, inspect the concealed gear mechanism. (To get at it, remove the screws from the crank assembly.) If you find the gears are badly worn, the entire assembly must be replaced. Should old, hardened grease be causing the problem, wash it out with a solvent and relubricate.

Make sure that the operator arm slides smoothly in its tracks as the window is opened and closed. Difficulty in operation may be caused by accumulations of rust or hardened grease, or by a bent arm. Remove the operator to straighten the arm or to clean out accumulated debris. Usually a generous application of fresh grease is sufficient to restore proper operation upon reassembly.

If you feel a draft even with the window closed tightly, adjust or tighten the locking handle; if that does not seal out the air satisfactorily, install a thin layer of adhesive-backed foam weatherstripping between the sash and the frame.

To remove casement window operator, open window part way and unscrew bolts that hold operator to frame.

Slide the arm to left or right (depending on window) until arm leaves window track, then draw arm straight out.

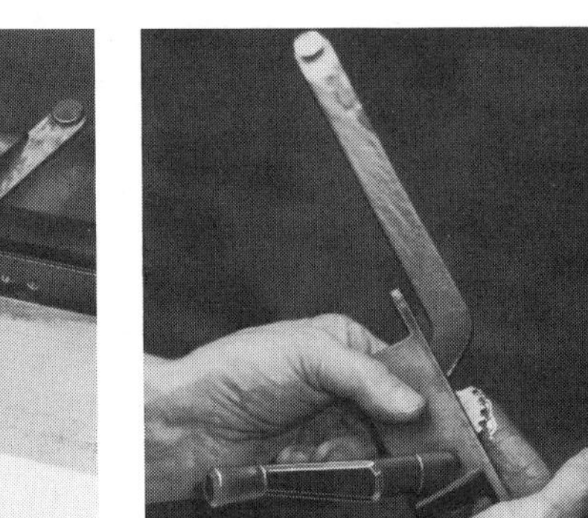

Inspect all parts of the crank handle mechanism and arm for broken parts. Make sure that the gears mesh properly.

Use wire brush to clean out accumulated rust, hardened grease, or other debris from under sash, frame, and window track.

Thoroughly lubricate track underneath sash. Use automobile grease or petroleum jelly. Apply with fingers; wipe off excess.

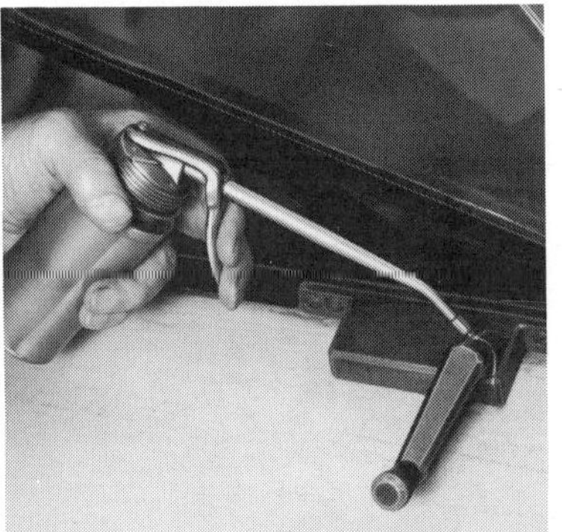

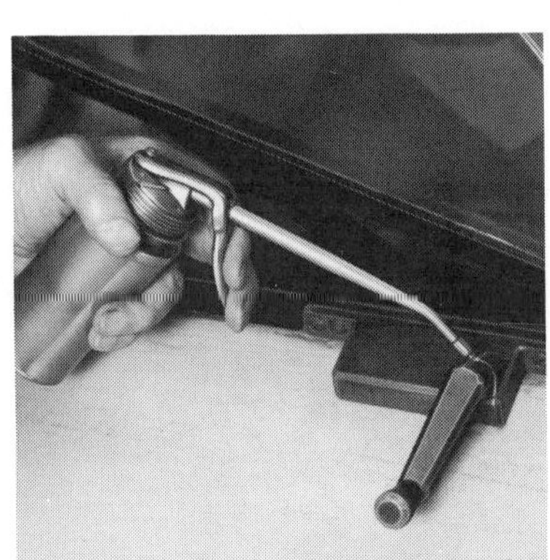

Oil crank handle and hinges so that they operate smoothly and evenly. Lubrication is needed at least once a year.

Replacing panes

Pane replacement in casement windows is much the same as the procedure for double-hung windows. The panes in casement windows, however, are held in place by spring clips instead of glazier's points.

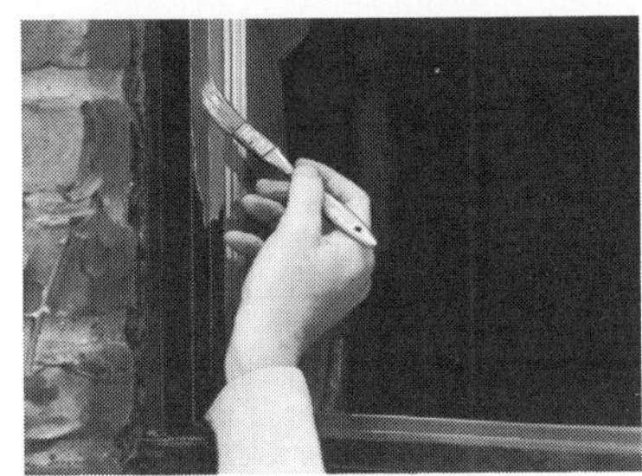

The first step is to remove broken glass, spring clips, and old putty. Then paint to stop rusting.

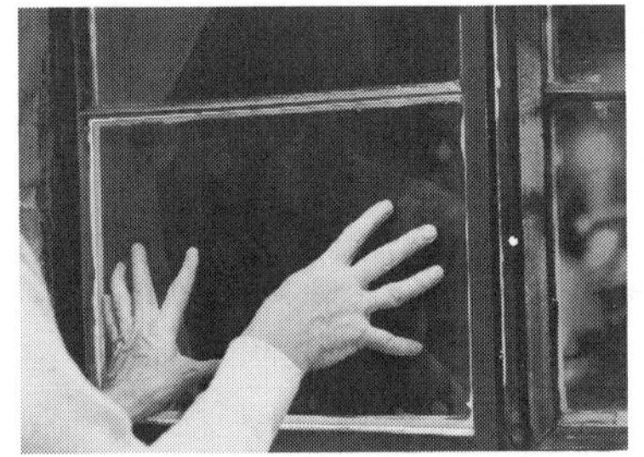

Apply a thin bed of glazing compound to the frame and press the glass gently against it.

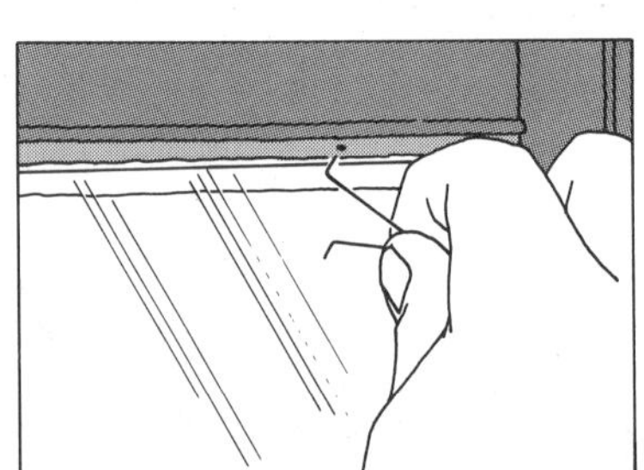

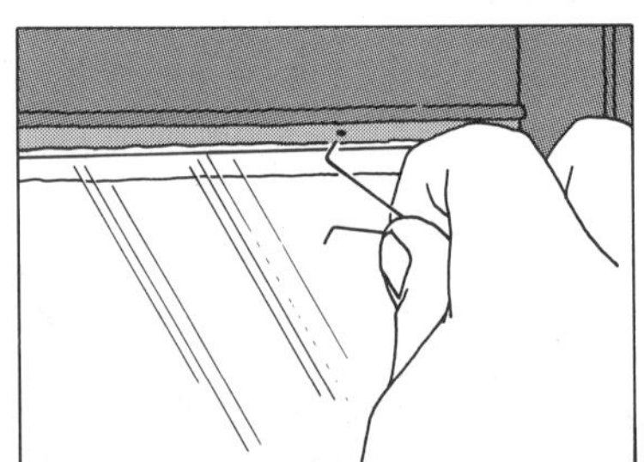

Insert the spring clips in the holes provided for them in sash and press them into position.

Apply moro compound to edges of glass and frame; draw putty knife over it at an angle to form a triangular bead.

Operation and maintenance

Though some are made of wood, most sliding windows are aluminum and they move along a closely fitted track at top and bottom. To facilitate ease and smoothness of window operation, the bottom track contains nylon glides.

The sash itself is removable and can be dismantled for replacement of broken panes by taking out the screws or pins that hold the upper and bottom rails to the side stiles. The glass is fitted tightly in the frame with either a plastic glazing channel around its perimeter or a flange (glazing bead) mounted to hold it against a glazing tape.

Screens for sliding windows are usually located on the outdoor side of the window with the storm windows between the screen and the window. Screens and storm windows are self-storing; they are not removed except for repair. Screens are one piece, covering the entire window area, storm windows consist of two halves, pushed to one side in summer.

Maintenance consists primarily of removing the sash and cleaning and applying wax to the surface of the metal weatherstripping and in its groove at the sash edges. The wax used may be either stick paraffin or paste wax.

Oxidation deposits can be removed from aluminum windows with a light household abrasive cleaner, mild detergent, or fine steel wool. When the aluminum is clean, an application of automobile paste wax will protect it for at least a year.

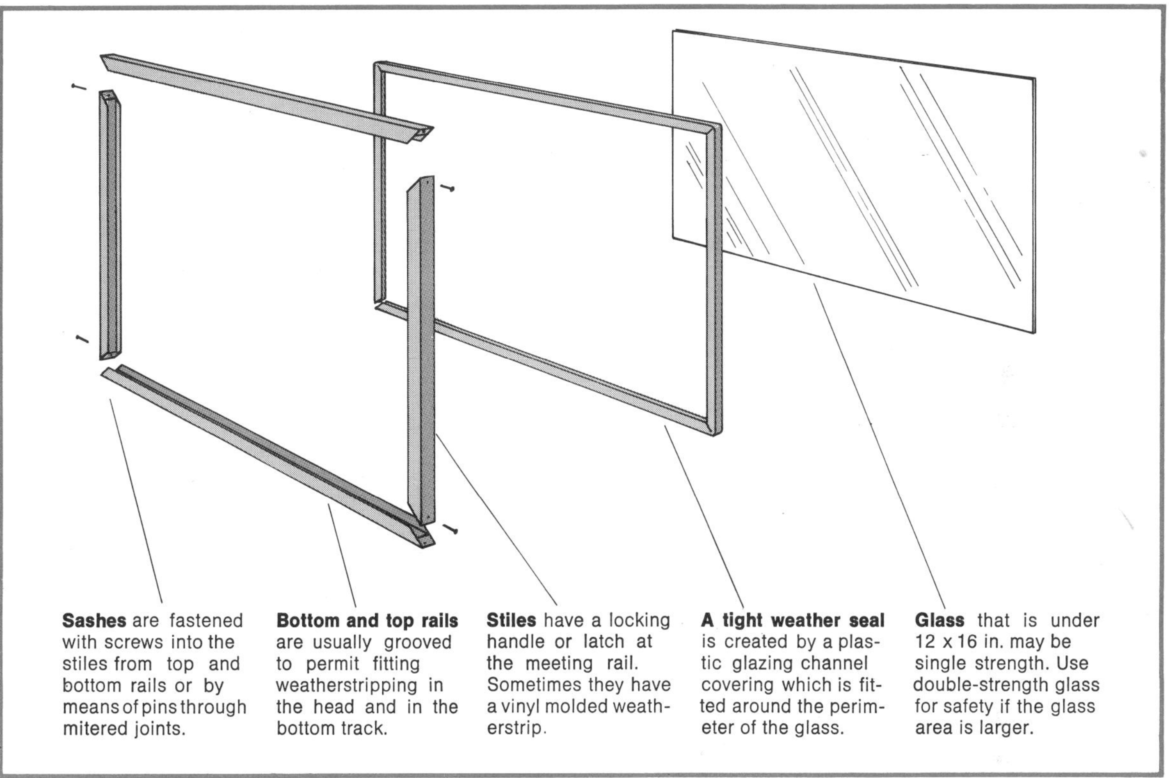

Sashes are fastened with screws into the stiles from top and bottom rails or by means of pins through mitered joints.

Bottom and top rails are usually grooved to permit fitting weatherstripping in the head and in the bottom track.

Stiles have a locking handle or latch at the meeting rail. Sometimes they have a vinyl molded weatherstrip.

A tight weather seal is created by a plastic glazing channel covering which is fitted around the perimeter of the glass.

Glass that is under 12 x 16 in. may be single strength. Use double-strength glass for safety if the glass area is larger.

Replacing storm window panes

The glass in some vertical sash aluminum windows is held in place by a gasket which must be pulled from under the retaining lip.

Wear gloves when lifting the damaged glass from the frame. Run a screwdriver around the frame to clear away small bits of glass.

Have new glass cut approximately 1/32 in. smaller than the frame. Lay the new pane in the frame carefully. Wear gloves.

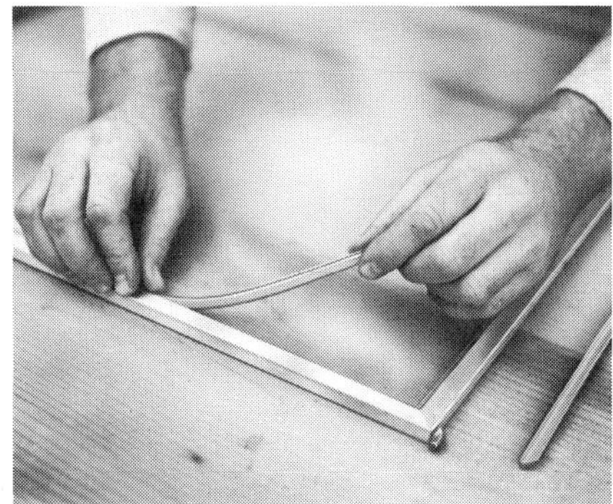

Replace the plastic gasket by pressing it under the frame lip with your thumb. Start at the corner and work along the frame.

Awning and jalousie windows

Awning windows: Use, operation, maintenance

Awning windows are hinged at the top and swing out at the bottom; they may have one or more sashes. This type of window provides maximum ventilation plus protection against rain damage while the window is open. Screens or storm sash can be readily attached and removed from inside the house.

Usually awning windows are operated by means of a crank (like casement windows) or by a scissors-type linkage that permits rapid adjustment. Most awning windows may be tilted flat for washing from the inside. Detachable hinges permit removal of the sash for maintenance or repair.

To remove sash for such maintenance as replacement of panes, release sash from operator mechanism and tilt flat.

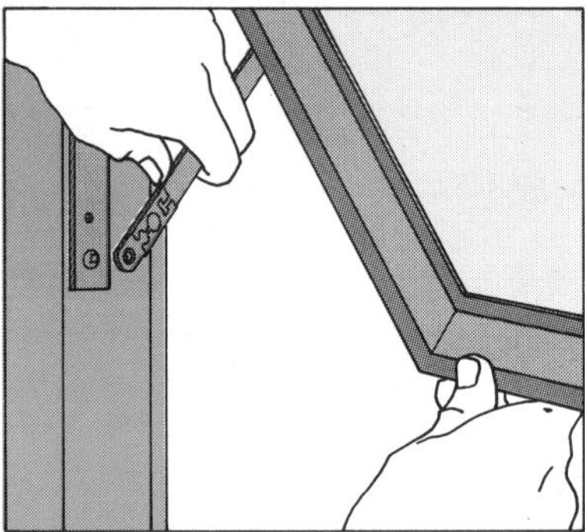

The hinges are now exposed. Detach them from the sides of the sash so that the window can be removed.

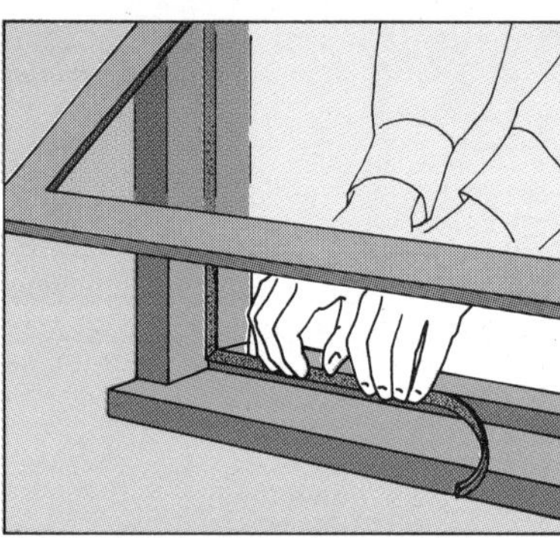

Older types of awning windows may need adhesive-backed foam weatherstripping around exterior of frame.

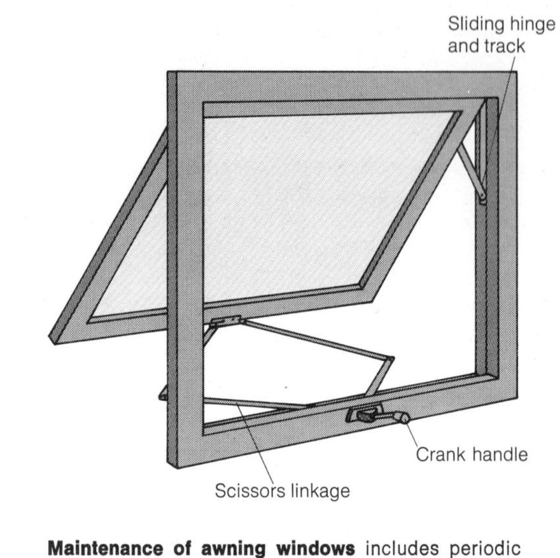

Maintenance of awning windows includes periodic lubrication of parts pointed out above.

Jalousie windows: Use, operation, maintenance

Jalousie windows are made of horizontal glass slats held by a metal frame at each end. The metal frames are connected by levers. Jalousies operate like awning windows but they do not protrude as far and so can be used in more limited space. Because of their relatively large numbers of panes, jalousie windows cannot be made completely weather-tight. Transparent vinyl weatherstripping remedies this to some extent, but these windows are still better suited to warm than to cold climates. Jalousies are also acceptable for rooms that you do not keep heated in the winter or air-conditioned during the summer.

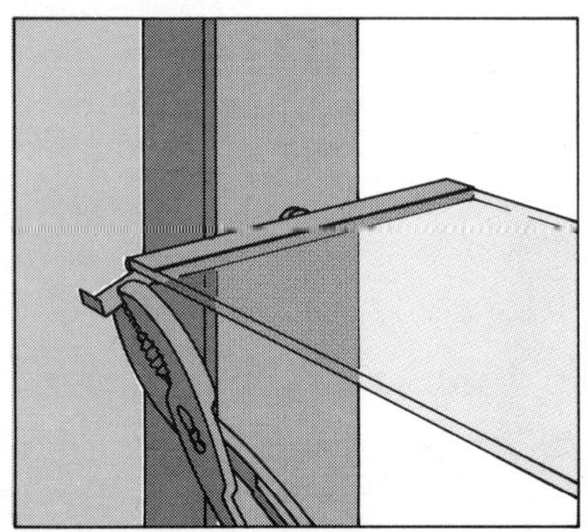

To replace a jalousie glass slat, first bend the clip holders just enough to clear the thickness of the glass.

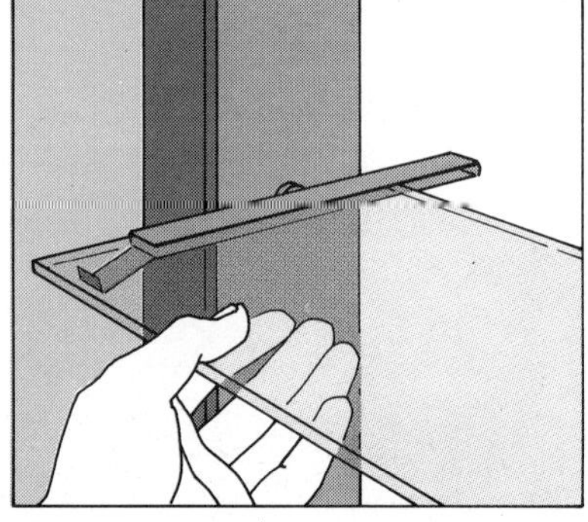

Set the metal frame in a horizontal position and then slide the replacement glass slats into position.

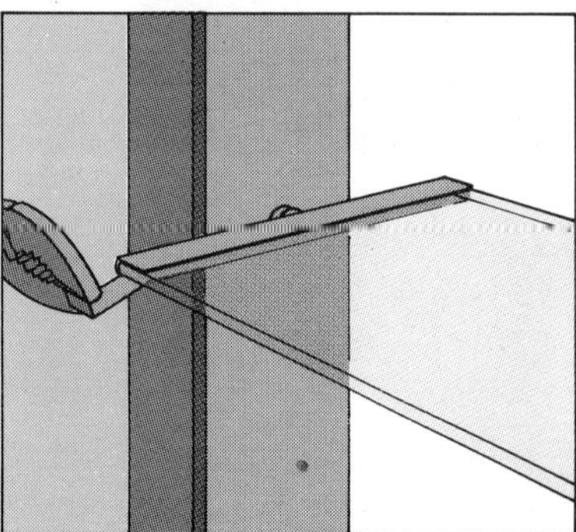

Bend over the ends of the clip holders into their original shape. This holds the glass slats firmly in place.

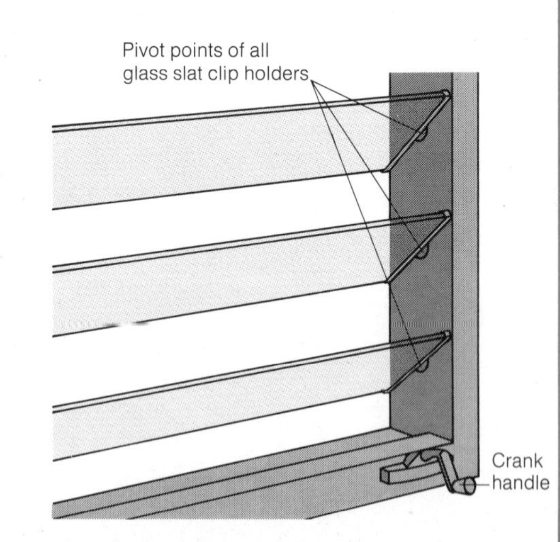

For smooth operation of jalousie windows, lubricate pivot points and all moving parts regularly.

Preparation and procedure

Installing a new window frame is comparatively easy if the replacement frame is an exact duplicate of the old one. You simply buy a new frame to match the original (possibly salvaging the old sash), remove the old frame, and put in the new.

In older dwellings, which often lack natural light, the installation may not be straight substitution, but supplementary—putting in a larger window or adding one or more new windows to the room you want to brighten. In either case, choose a standard-size ready-made window unit, being sure that it will blend architecturally with the existing windows.

Be careful not to cut a new opening in a part of a wall that contains electrical, plumbing, or heating lines unless they can be relocated. In some cases, you can determine their presence by inspecting the wall from the basement.

The framing must be square and true and should be installed according to standard practices as closely as possible. It must be sturdy enough to bear the weight above the opening without sagging or distortion and also to support the weight of the window unit. To assure that it will do this, use double 2 x 4s in both headers and sides.

When an opening is more than 4 feet wide, the header size is increased and the header also trussed if possible in order to divert some of the weight from above to the side so that it will be carried down to the sill. A span of 5½ feet requires two 2 x 6s; a 7-foot span, two 2 x 8s; more than 7 feet, two 2 x 10s.

Cross section of window frame

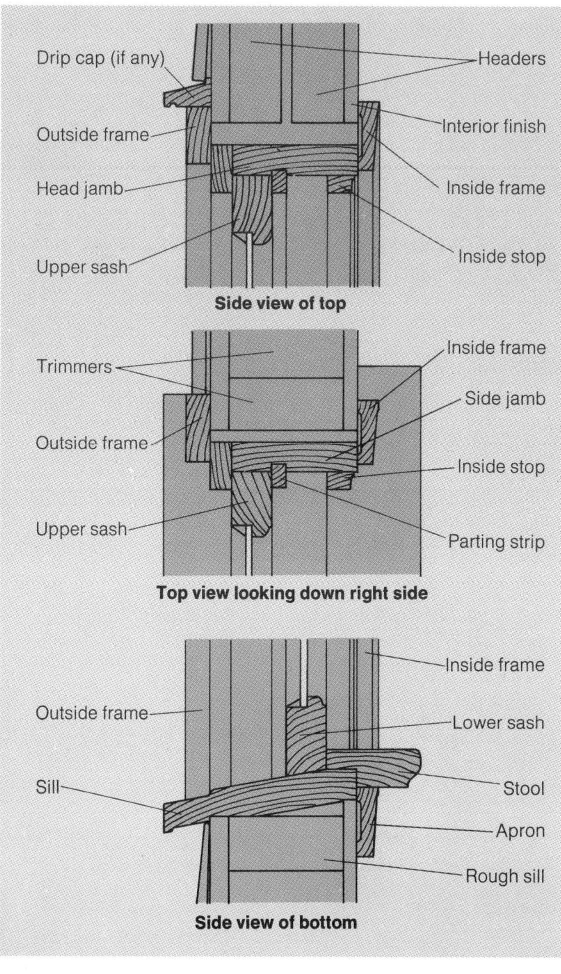

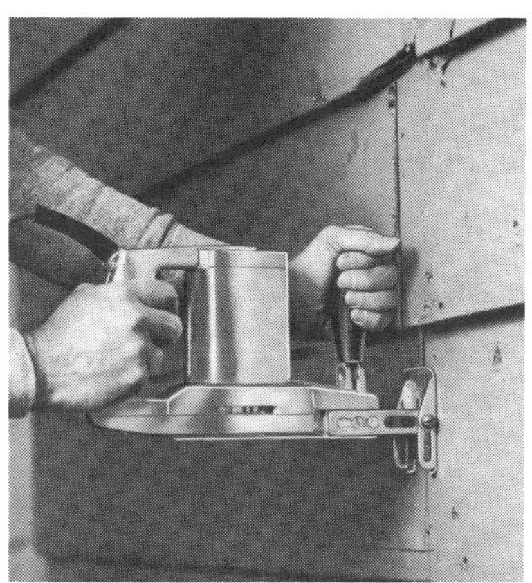

To cut opening in exterior wall: Drill holes at corners. Start cut with keyhole saw, then switch to reciprocating power saw.

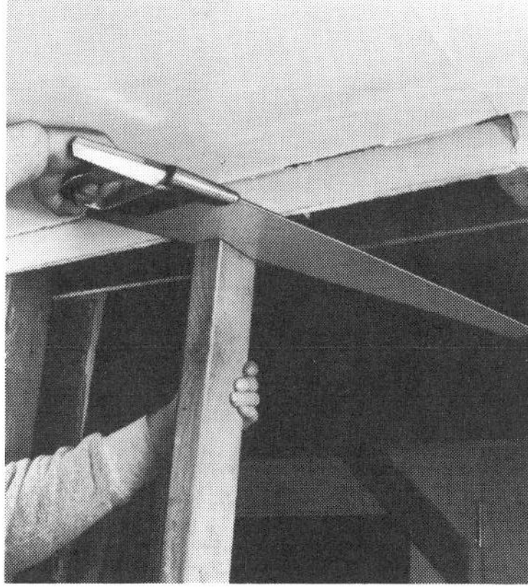

With the window cut, saw off the studs in the opening, first at the bottom, then at the top. Be sure to make the cuts square.

Install 2 x 4 double headers set on edge. Toenail them into the side of the opening to give the frame extra strength.

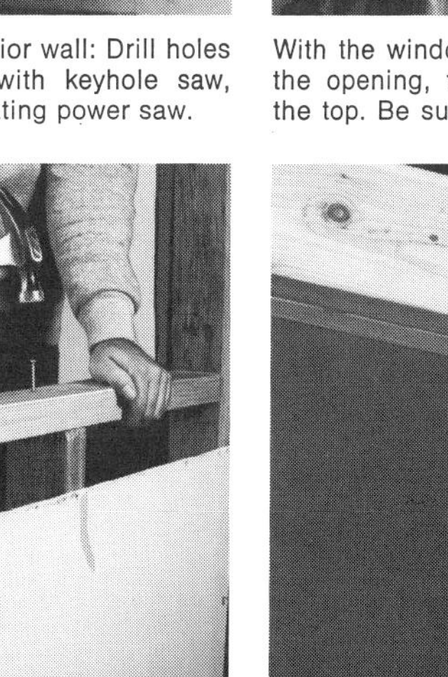

The lower support is constructed of double 2 x 4s set in position and nailed to the vertical studs.

Place supporting 2 x 4 studs at sides of window opening. Nail the side jambs securely into the wall.

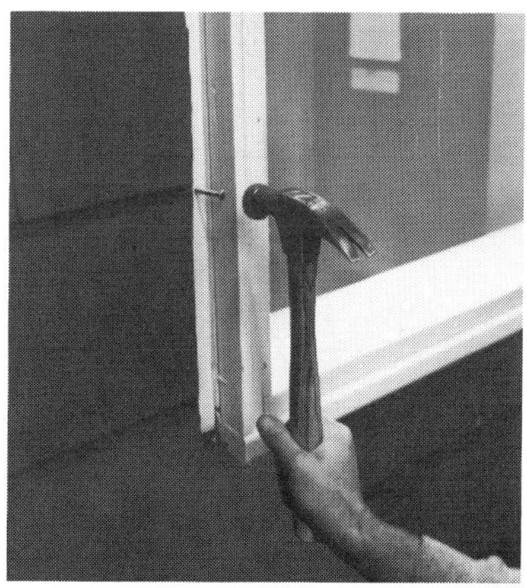

With the frame set in the window opening, check for level and plumb. Shim whereever necessary, then nail in place.

How to make aluminum storm windows

Measuring

Aluminum storm windows can be built at home at a fraction of the cost of ready-mades. Aluminum sash is sold in most hardware stores and comes fitted with glazing channels that protect and seal the glass.

If the area to be covered is 9 square feet or less, the storm sash will carry a single piece of double-strength glass; if the area is larger, it is necessary to divide the window into two or more parts.

Make all measurements on double-hung windows just outside the blind stop so that the storm sash will fit against it when put in place. Measurements given below allow space for hanging brackets, meeting rail channels, and slight errors in cutting.

A single full-length storm sash requires four pieces of aluminum sash section. The top and bottom rails should be ⅛ inch smaller than the width of the opening, and the two vertical side rails should be ⅛ inch smaller than the height of the opening.

A two-piece storm sash has eight aluminum sections. Make the four horizontal pieces ¼ inch smaller than the width of the opening, and the four vertical pieces ¼ inch smaller than the height of the opening divided by two.

A three-piece storm sash for extra-tall windows is made up of 12 sections. The horizontal pieces are ¼ inch smaller than the width of the opening, and the vertical pieces ⅜ inch smaller than the height of the opening divided by three.

Casement window frames usually have holes along the sides and middle for screws and clips to hold screens or storm sash on the inside of the window. Measure width just inside these holes; measure length from the top of the operator to the inside of the frame at the top and add ¼ inch for overlap.

Awning window storm sash is also attached on the inside with screws in the sash and into the blind stop. You will probably have to attach a wood filler strip with a hole for the crank at the bottom of the window opening. Take measurements just inside the blind stop. Width is ⅛ inch less than the opening; height is ¼ inch less than the distance from the top of the filler strip to the top of the opening.

Basement windows can be fitted with storm sash on the inside or the outside. Dimensions are ¾ inch more than the width and height of the opening to provide a ⅜-inch overlap on wood frames; secure the storm sash with wood screws. If the frames are metal, fit the storm sash the same as for a casement window.

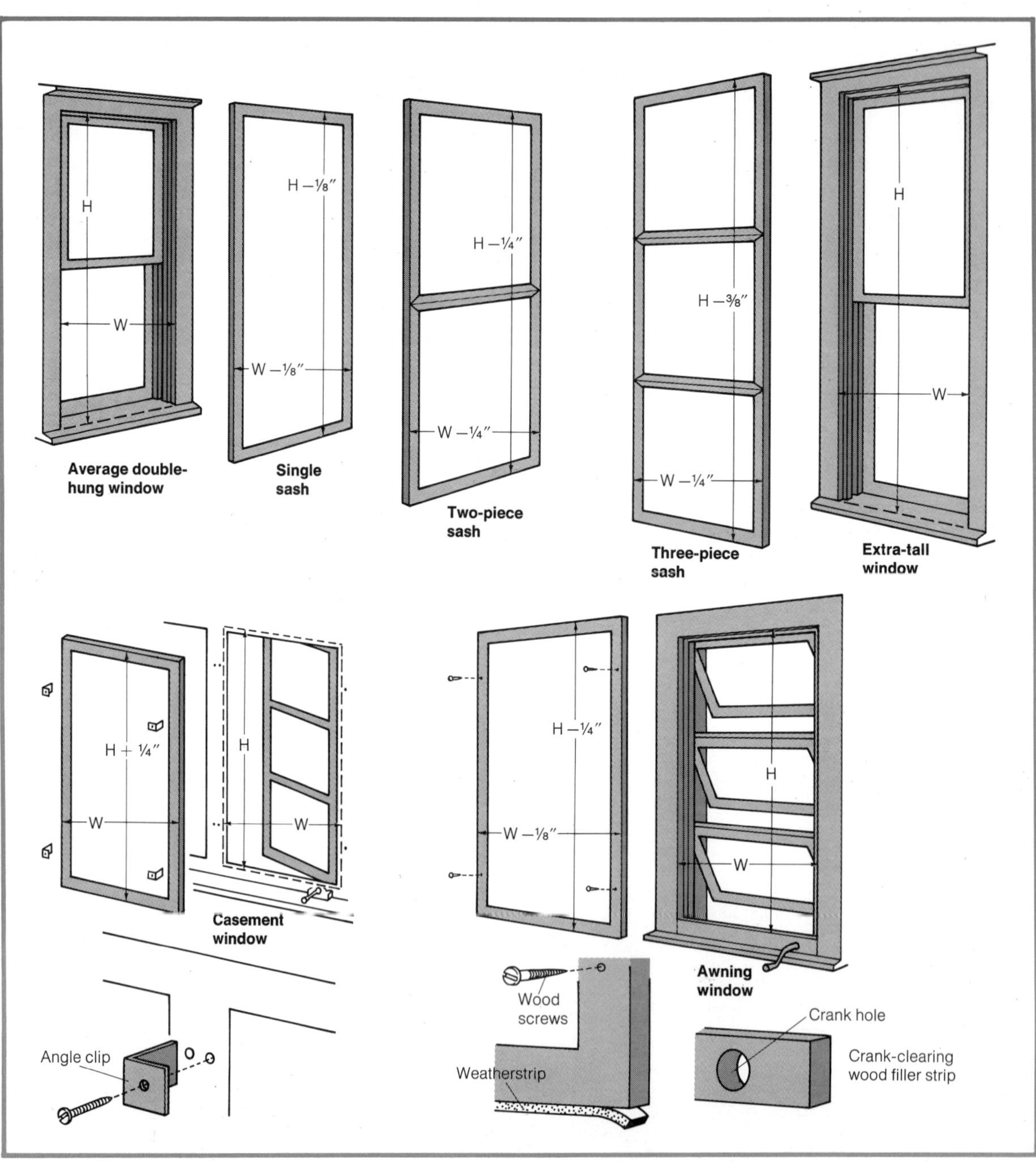

Assembly

Before marking or cutting, check the measurements of the original aluminum storm sash if available. If you have several windows to assemble, consider buying a small miter box for use with a hacksaw.

Although single-strength glass is acceptable for panes up to 9 square feet, double-strength is recommended even for these smaller sizes; it costs very little more. Glass must be cut accurately and with square corners so that the sash can be assembled properly. You can order glass cut to your measurements or cut it yourself (p. 438).

When cutting the glazing channel for the mitered corners, cut only the edges so that the channel will not separate at this point.

Friction-fit corner locks are used to secure the mitered corners. Push them into place or tap gently with a wood mallet. Do not use a hammer—it might damage the sash. Stake the corner locks into the sash side members with a 3½-inch nail. Be careful not to damage the lock; drive the nail just hard enough to dimple the aluminum of the sash.

All aluminum storm windows should have adhesive-backed foam weatherstripping around the perimeter to make a tight seal against frame or blind stop. No matter how accurate the construction, storm sash will not function right without a complete seal.

Maintenance: Besides cleaning the glass, you should remove oxidation or stain from the metal parts. Use a special aluminum oxide remover combined with a polish, or very fine steel wool; follow with paste wax.

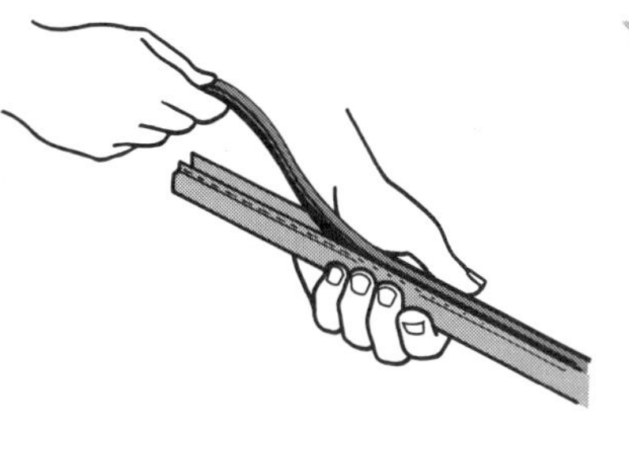
Before marking or cutting sash section, remove and save glazing channel.

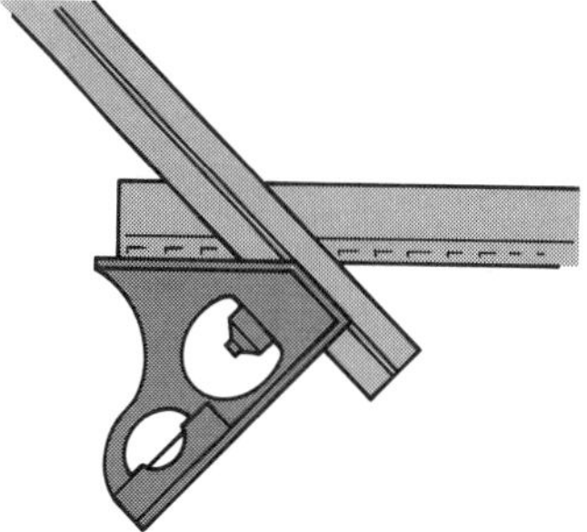
Miter sash at corners. Use combination square to scribe 45° angles.

Cut on scribed lines with fine (32-tooth) hacksaw blade; file off burrs.

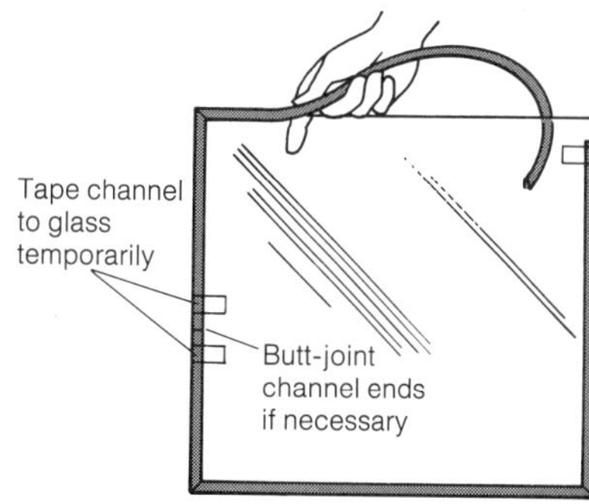

Use glass 1¹⁄₁₆ in. smaller than the outside measurements of the frame.

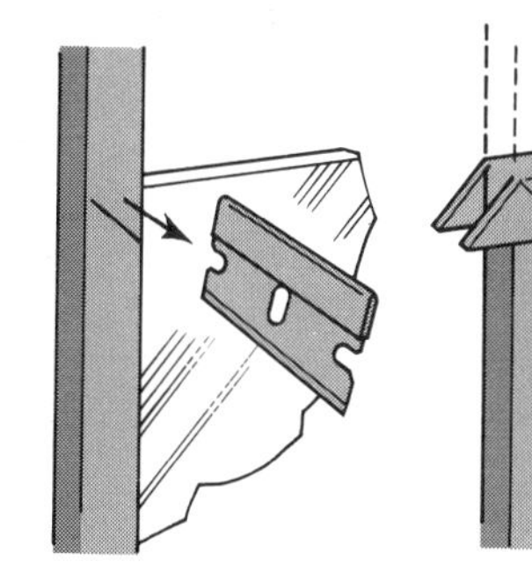
Apply glazing channel. Make 45° cut from corner with a sharp razor blade.

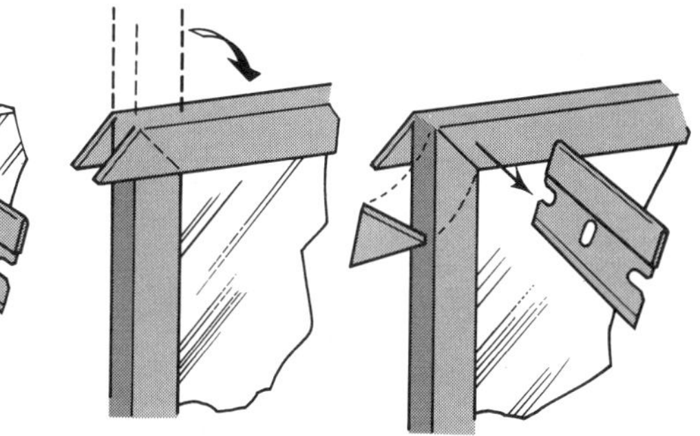
Fit channel over top of glass, then cut the mitered corner joint.

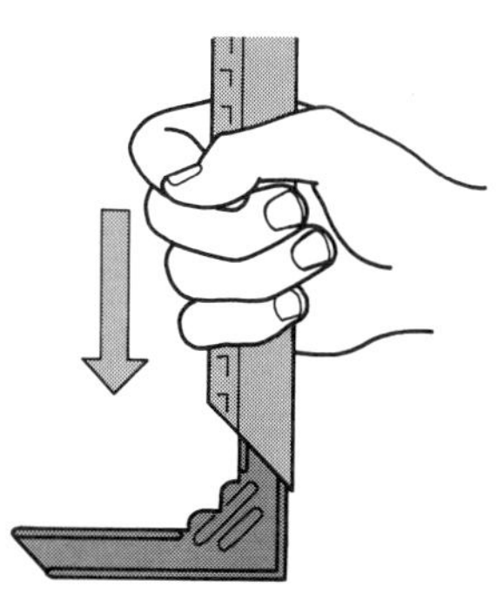
Push corner lock on each mitered end of the sash side members.

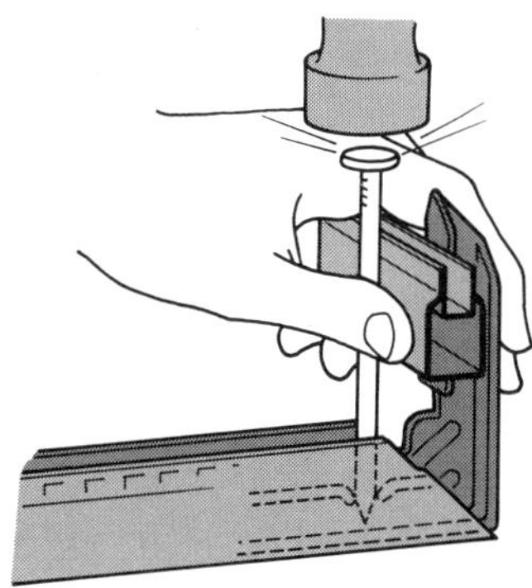
Stake each corner lock in place by dimpling with 3½-inch nail.

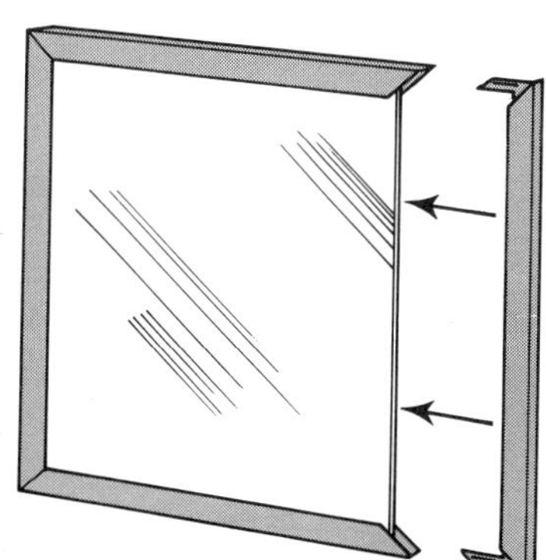
Center top and bottom sash members over glass; add sides to complete.

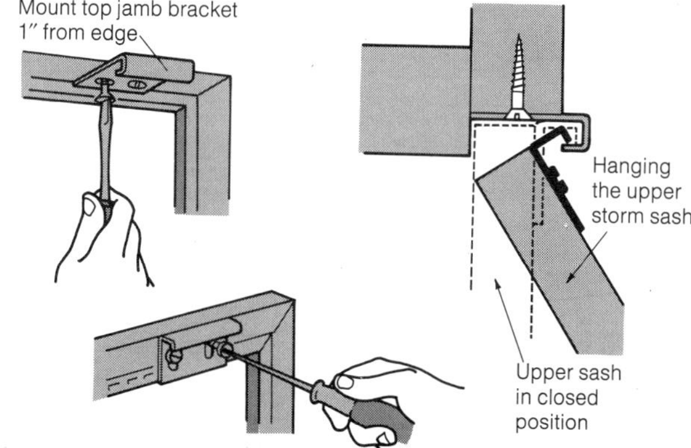

Use brackets to mount storm sash to top of window for easy hanging, removal, and screen substitution.

Wood sash storm windows

Maintenance and repair

Storm windows reduce drafts, help hold down fuel bills, and make heating and air-conditioning systems function more efficiently.

Install a storm window so that it fits snugly into the window frame; weatherstrip the window to make the seal even tighter. If both inner and outer windows are completely sealed, neither will sweat. An insulating dead-air space between the windows reduces heat loss to the outside and keeps out cold air during the cold-weather months; in air-conditioned houses, this dead-air space helps to retain the cool air and keeps heat out when the weather is hot.

Good maintenance of wood sash storm windows requires periodic removal for repainting, needed to prevent swelling and distortion from absorption of moisture. While the window is down, inspect it for bent hangers and hooks; loose screws, joints, and adjusters; crumbling or missing putty; broken glass.

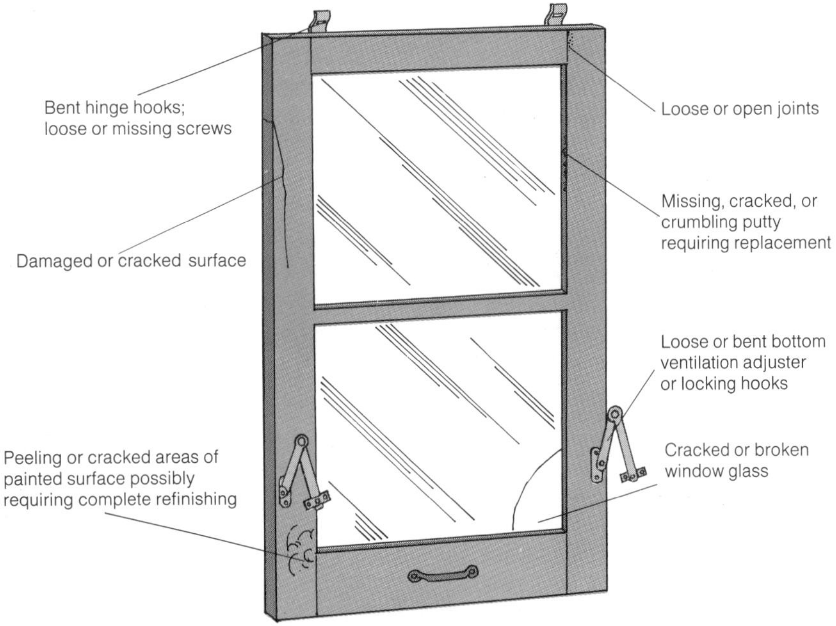

Bent hinge hooks; loose or missing screws

Damaged or cracked surface

Peeling or cracked areas of painted surface possibly requiring complete refinishing

Loose or open joints

Missing, cracked, or crumbling putty requiring replacement

Loose or bent bottom ventilation adjuster or locking hooks

Cracked or broken window glass

Periodic check of points indicated, with repairs made as needed, will keep storm windows in good condition.

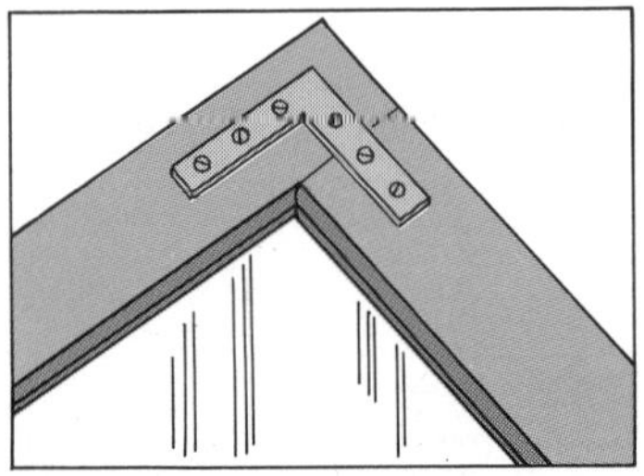

Open a loose butt or miter joint; reglue and reinforce with a fastener.

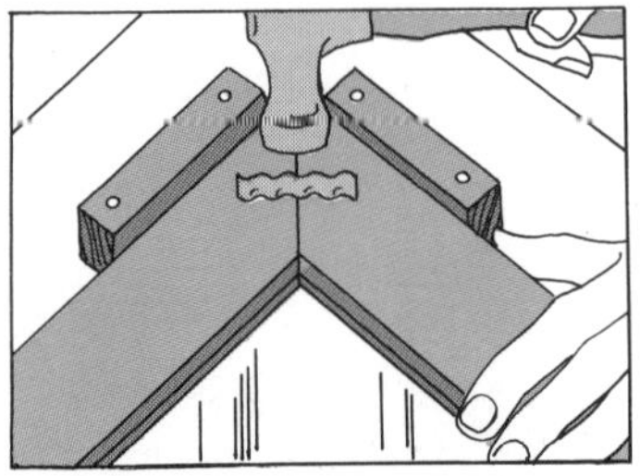

Nail two wood strips to workbench to hold corner square while reinforcing.

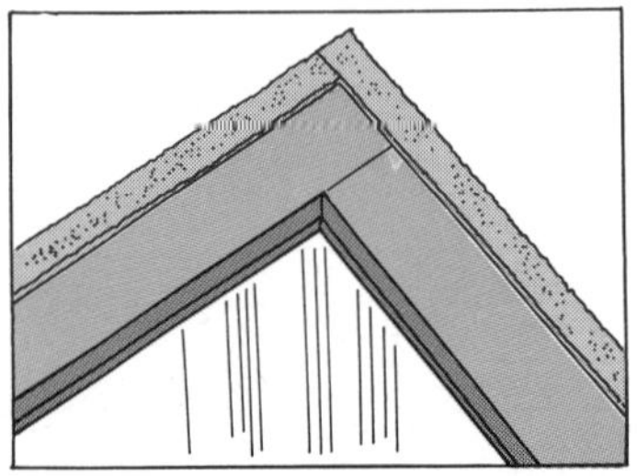

Put adhesive-backed foam weatherstripping on inner edge of sash.

Sweating windows

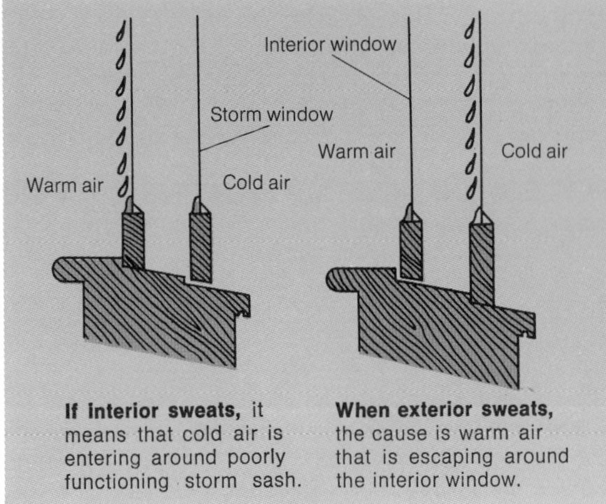

If interior sweats, it means that cold air is entering around poorly functioning storm sash.

When exterior sweats, the cause is warm air that is escaping around the interior window.

Painting storm sash

To paint all sides in one operation, install storm window hangers in ceiling joist and suspend storm sash from it; steady sash with a weight.

Maintenance and repair

Black-enameled steel wire is no longer used as screening, and galvanized steel wire has practically disappeared from the market. These have been replaced by screening of such rustproof materials as bronze, copper, plastic, and aluminum, and a louver type of either brass or aluminum. Other popular new types are a fiber-glass screen and one of anodized aluminum available with a baked enamel finish.

Any screen will do a good job of keeping even the smaller insects out of the house, if it is made of fine enough mesh (18 x 16 is a practical choice). With reasonable care, modern screens will last many years. Accidental holes, however, are just about unavoidable. It is important to repair them before they get so large that replacement is required. Plastic or wire screening will become dirty; wire, in addition, will corrode. Clean both types periodically; use the round brush attachment on a vacuum.

Keep wood frames painted, not just for looks but to prevent absorption of moisture that may cause swelling, distortion, or even rotting. Aluminum frames will probably need occasional cleaning and a coat of wax to deter oxidation.

If joints loosen, reglue them and add reinforcements—corner plates, T plates, mending plates, corrugated or chevron-shaped fasteners, wood screws, or glued-in dowels—to make the repair permanent.

Inspect the hangers for damage to the bracket on the house or the hook on the screen, and also to see if any screws are loose or missing. Also check the interior fasteners to be certain that they are all functioning properly.

Close a small hole in metal screen with quick-drying waterproof glue. Use acetone-type glue for plastic screen.

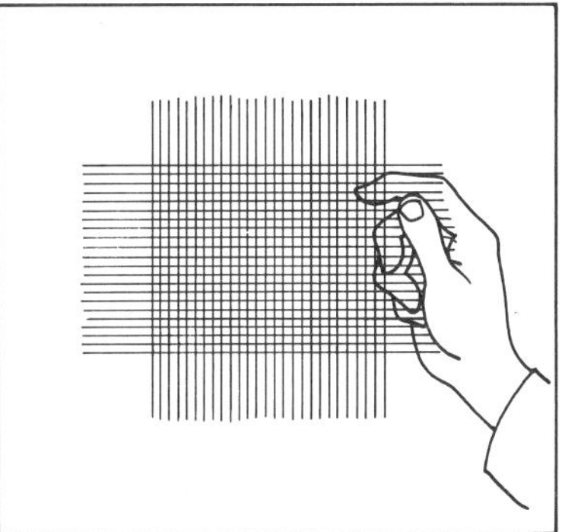

To repair a large hole, first make a patch by cutting a piece from scrap screening larger than the hole in the screen.

Bend the free end wires of patch and push them through mesh around hole. Bend ends back to hold. Cement plastic ends.

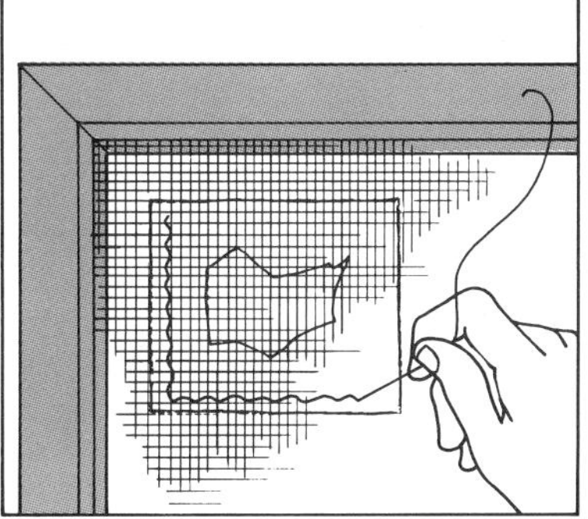

You can mend small holes by weaving or darning strands from scrap screening, or wire from a lamp cord.

To clean off rust and dirt, brush both sides with a soft wire brush, then use vacuum-cleaner round brush attachment.

After cleaning, apply thinned screen enamel, paint, or varnish to both sides of screen. Use brush or piece of carpet.

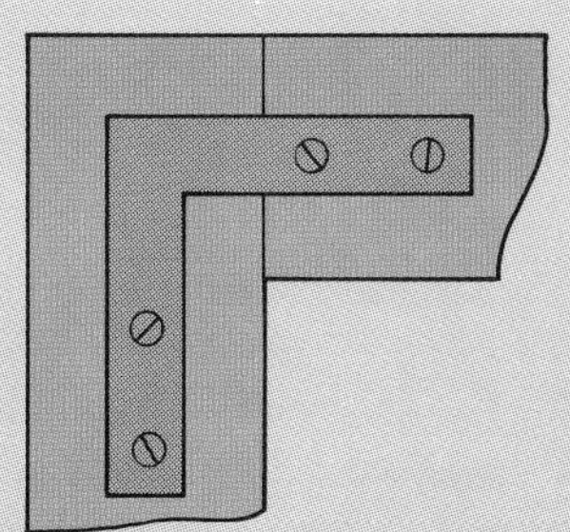

When loosened joint has been reglued, reinforce with metal mending plate of corner-iron type.

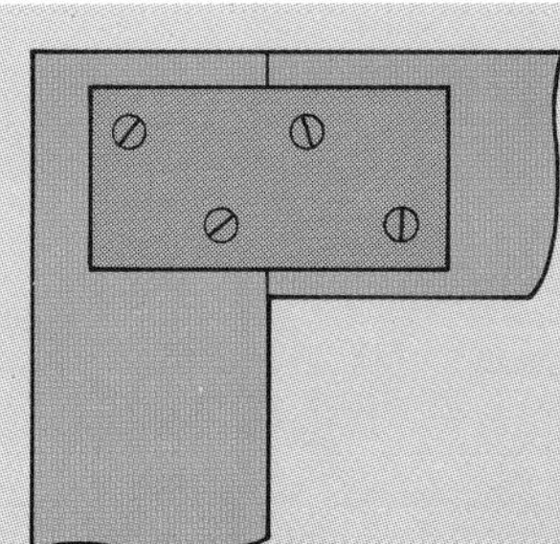

Other types of mending plates, such as T's or rectangular shapes, are also suitable.

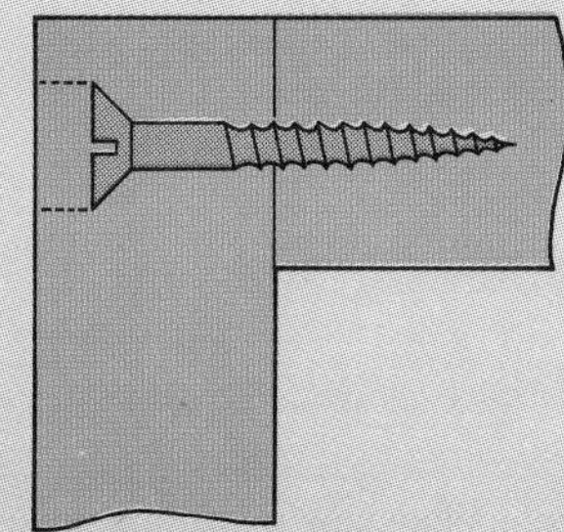

To strengthen joint, sink long wood screw as shown; fill hole with dowel or wood dough.

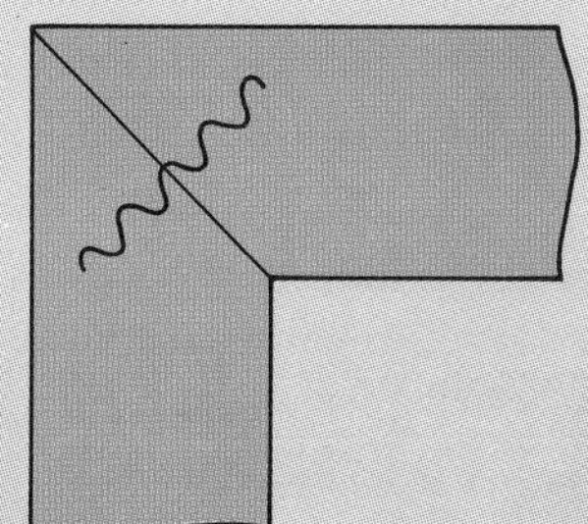

Mitered joints can be reinforced with corrugated or chevron-shaped miter joint fasteners.

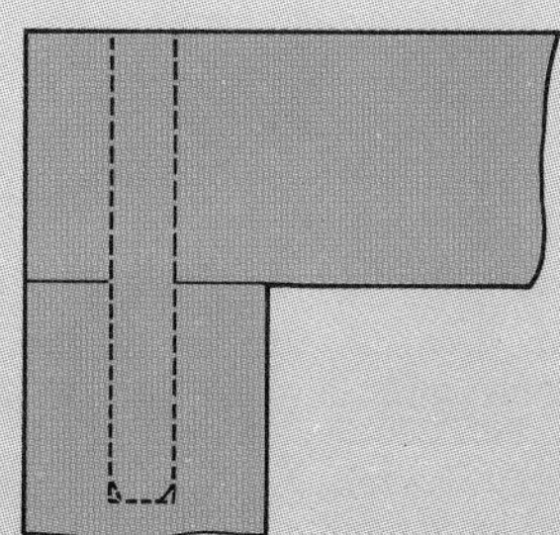

Strengthen a corner by gluing a hardwood dowel into hole bored through both pieces of joint.

Replacing a wood-frame screen

Even so-called lifetime screening cannot take such a severe blow as would be inflicted by, say, a hard-hit baseball, so any type of screen might sometime need replacement. When a galvanized metal screen begins to rust, it is advisable to replace it right away, not just because rust is unsightly, but to keep it from staining adjoining areas.

When replacing a wood-frame screen, remove the molding carefully so it can be used around the new screening. Choose one of the newer rustproof types of screening (p.131) for the replacement. Buy a piece of screening larger than the area to be covered; excess at the edge gives you something to hold on to when pulling the screen taut to fit it to the frame.

Place screen on sawhorses; use a putty knife or wide chisel to lift off old molding. Work outward from center.

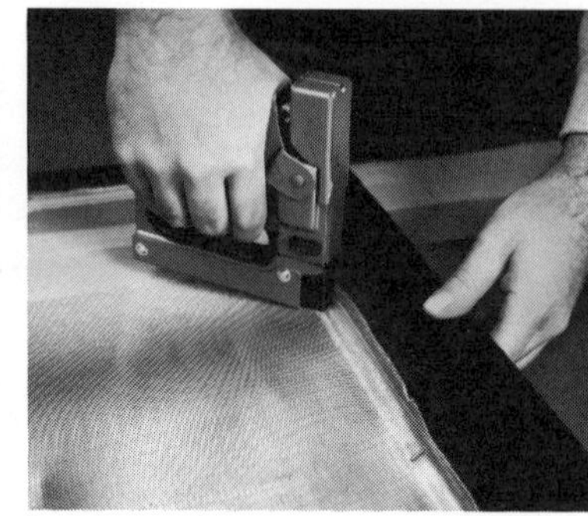

Cut screen to correct size; staple or tack it to one end of frame only. If plastic, fold all edges for 1½ in. hem.

Bow frame (see drawing at left) and draw screening taut. Tack down second end. Then remove clamps and blocks.

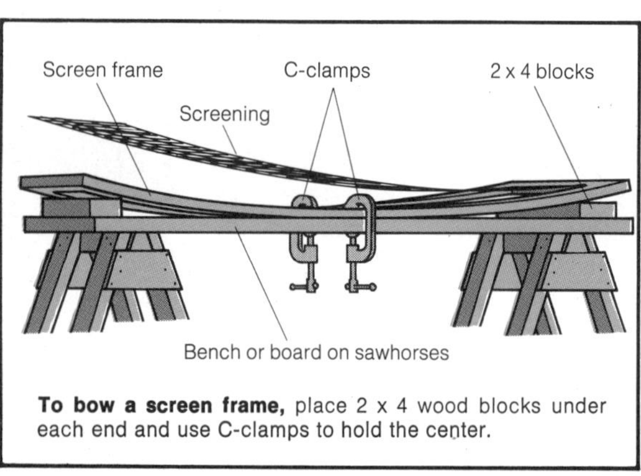

To bow a screen frame, place 2 x 4 wood blocks under each end and use C-clamps to hold the center.

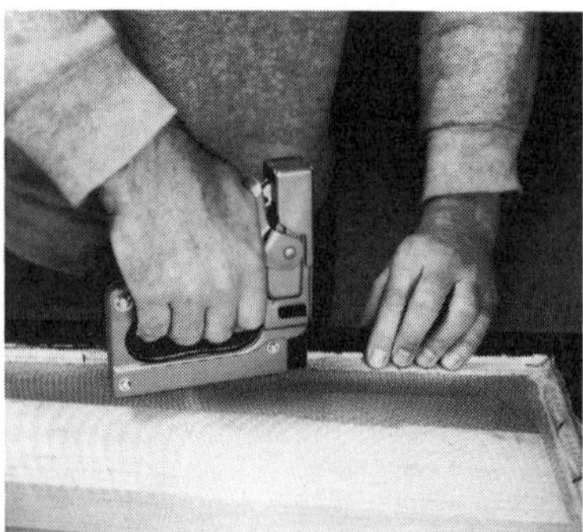

Fasten the sides, pulling screen tight. Work from center of each side toward the ends. Fasten center rail last.

Trim off excess screening with a heavy-duty knife, household shears, tin snips, or razor blades (for plastic).

Attach molding (use old molding if it is sound). Sink brad heads, fill the holes, prime, and repaint the entire frame.

Replacing half a screen

If only half of a screen containing a center rail is damaged, you can replace just this section rather than the entire screen. Use a matching screening material, if you can, for appearance' sake.

Since the bow method that is shown above will not work for this partial repair, follow this alternate method: First, secure the new screening to the center rail. Then make a clamp of two boards and nail it to the bench top to secure the screening. A pair of wedges driven between this clamp and the end of the screen frame will supply the required tension in the new screening.

All other steps in the replacement process are the same as given above for a full-length screen.

Remove trim molding; use shears or snips to cut away damaged section from center rail; leave good half intact.

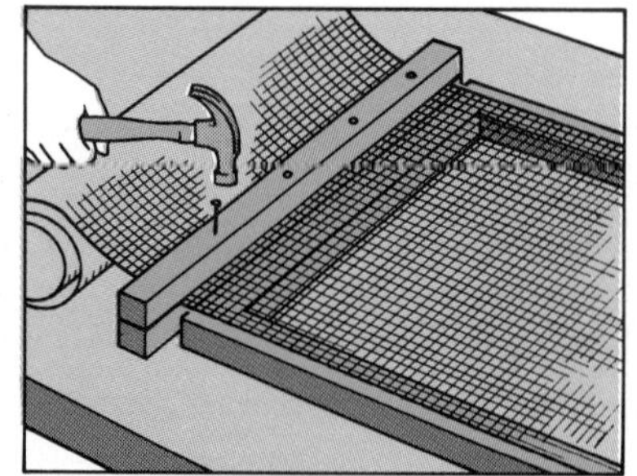

Fasten new screening to center rail; unroll it along frame and put it in clamp just beyond frame; nail clamp to bench.

Drive wedge at each end between clamp and frame for tension; finish rescreening as for full-length screen, above.

Assembling aluminum screens

The various parts that make up an aluminum screen frame can be purchased from stores that carry do-it-yourself aluminum products. The screen frame parts, which are the same size as those used for storm windows, also take the same corner locks and other fittings, and are therefore interchangeable with storm window parts. The difference between the two is that the opening in a screen frame is in the face and is fitted with a thin aluminum tongue called a spline rather than with a glazing channel.

Window measurements for aluminum screen frames are made in the same way and from the same points as described for storm sash (p.128).

Since only half of a double-hung window can be opened at a time, you can save money, labor, and time by making only half-screens. These can then be used to replace the lower half of the matching storm window, with the upper half left in place. Window types other than double-hung will need full-length screens and will be fitted following the same procedures as specified for their storm sash.

Though the metal spline that comes with the aluminum screen frame section will work perfectly for the initial installation, it may not work so well if you have to later replace the screening. For replacement purposes, the screening can be secured by using a plastic spline that compresses slightly when installed. You can use a special tool, an inexpensive roller made for the purpose, to force the plastic spline into the frame channel.

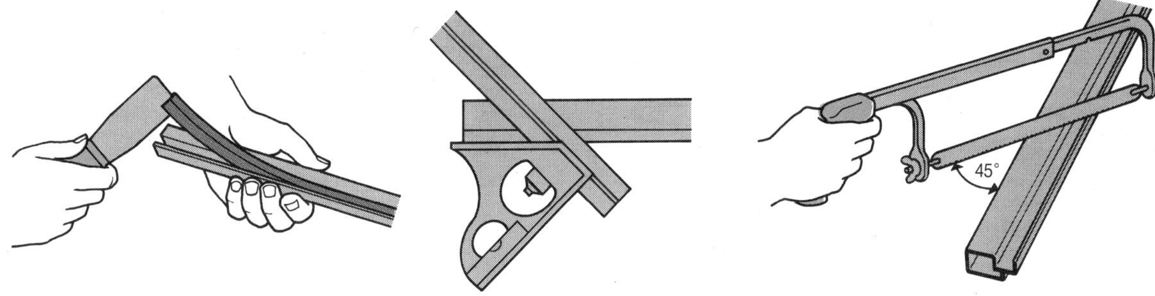

Remove spline from frame member with putty knife; do not bend spine.

Measure as for storm windows (p.128); scribe 45° angles on frame members.

Miter corners with a fine-tooth hacksaw blade; remove burrs with a file.

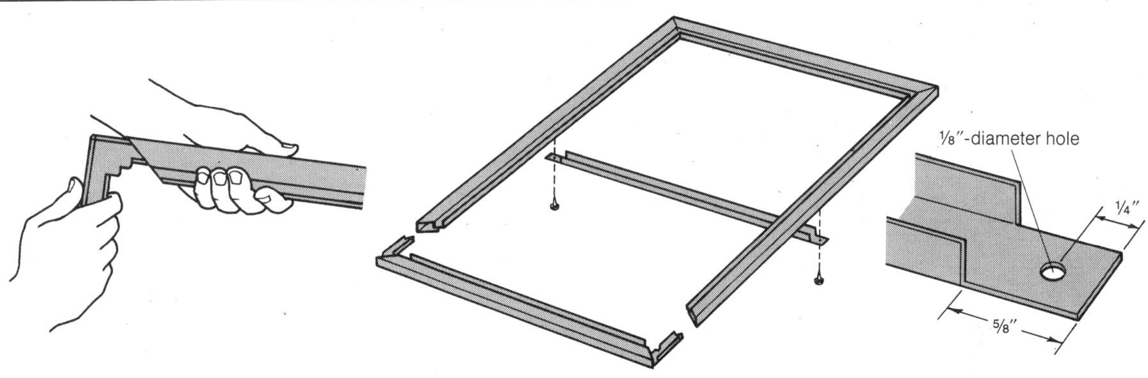

Insert a corner lock into both ends of the end frame sections.

Insert exposed ends of corner locks into side pieces to complete frame.

Add a section of channel as a cross brace for screens over 6 sq. ft.

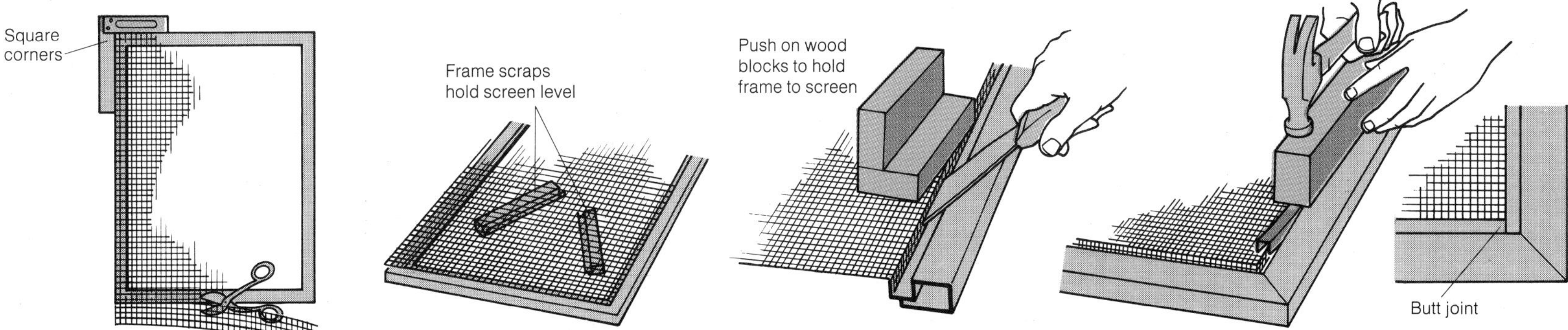

Cut the screening to the outside dimensions of the assembled frame.

Align screening with outside edge of groove on one side and one end.

With a putty knife, bend the screen edges down into the groove. Trim excess.

Drive the spline into the groove with a wood block and hammer; butt-joint the spline at corners.

Window shades

Solving shade problems

Improper winding: If a shade will not wind up satisfactorily even when it is correctly installed, remove it from its brackets and increase the spring tension by rolling the shade up by hand, then return it to the brackets. Repeat if the tension is still too slack.

If a shade winds up with a bang, take it down and partially unroll it, then put it back and check its operation. If tension is still too great, repeat.

Broken spring: If you cannot correct a lack of tension in the spring, replace the entire roller.

Binding: When a shade binds, the roller fits too tightly between brackets. Tap brackets lightly with a hammer to flatten them a bit. If that doesn't work, move the brackets farther apart. If this is impossible because the brackets are mounted inside the window casing, remove the round fixed pin and its barrel from the roller and cut the pin down slightly.

Falling: When a shade repeatedly falls out of its brackets, the brackets are too far apart. If they are mounted outside the window casing, move one of them in a little closer. If they are mounted inside the casing, put a cardboard shim under either bracket to decrease the spacing.

Wobbling: A bent roller pin will make the shade wobble when operated; straighten the pin with pliers. If pin is rusty or dirty, clean it with sandpaper.

Failure to catch: A shade will not catch when pulled down if the pawls, or catches, do not engage the notches in the ratchet. Clean the area and lubricate with graphite. An accumulation of threads from a cloth shade will also prevent pawls from catching.

Worn shade cloth: A shade can be salvaged if it is worn only at the bottom edge. Trim off the damaged part; remove cloth from roller and remount by tacking or stapling cut bottom end to roller. Be sure it is straight so the shade will not pull to one side.

Cutting a shade: If the spring cavity in the roller is not disturbed, a shade can be cut down to fit a narrower window. Remove the cloth from the roller and the slat from the hem. Saw the roller to the predetermined length on the round pin side. Put the barrel on the newly cut end and hammer its pin straight in. Make sure the pin is in the exact center of the roller. Stretch the cloth out and mark its new width at several points; join the points with a straight line and carefully cut with scissors or razor blade. Shorten bottom slat to fit the new hem. If shade has a pull cord, drill a new hole for the cord.

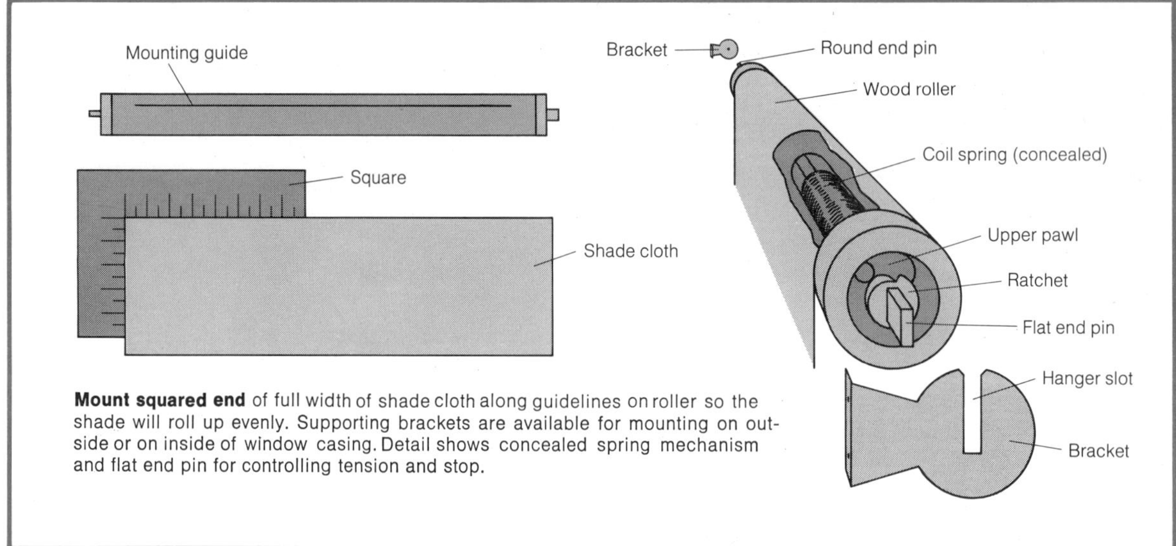

Mount squared end of full width of shade cloth along guidelines on roller so the shade will roll up evenly. Supporting brackets are available for mounting on outside or on inside of window casing. Detail shows concealed spring mechanism and flat end pin for controlling tension and stop.

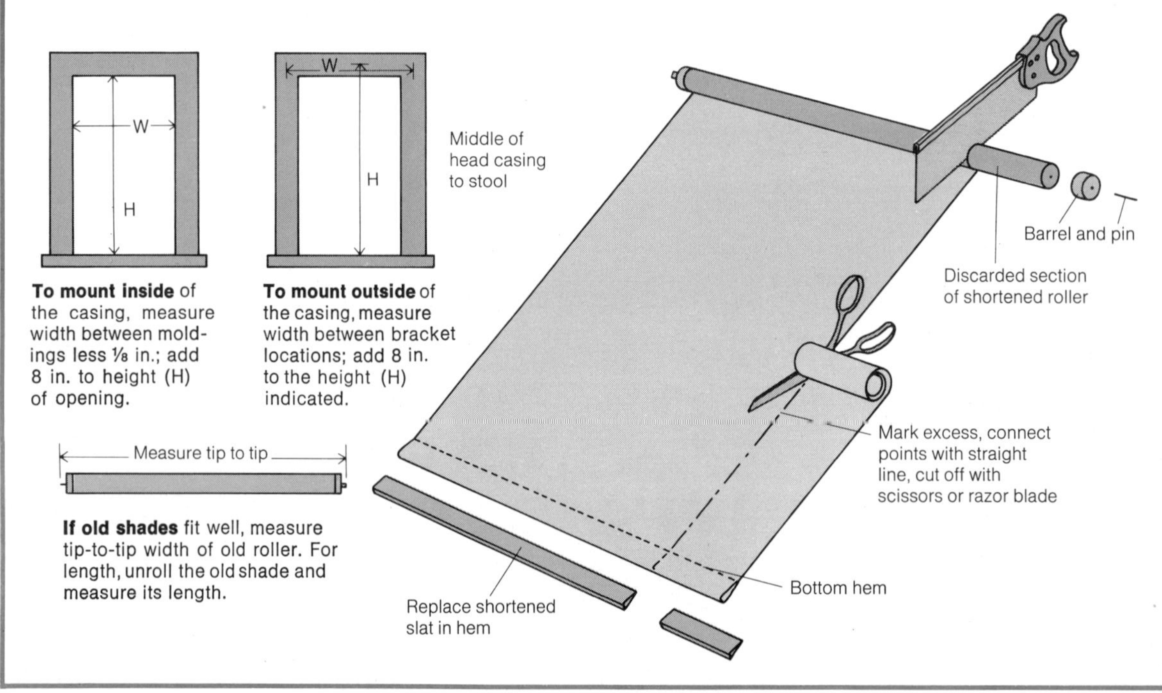

To mount inside of the casing, measure width between moldings less ⅛ in.; add 8 in. to height (H) of opening.

To mount outside of the casing, measure width between bracket locations; add 8 in. to the height (H) indicated.

If old shades fit well, measure tip-to-tip width of old roller. For length, unroll the old shade and measure its length.

Replacing cords and tapes

To replace a worn lift cord on a Venetian blind, first remove the end caps and the metal cover from the bottom slat. (A wooden blind has an extra-thick bottom slat through which the cord passes.)

Untie the knot on the tilt cord side and butt-join the old cord to the new cord with transparent tape. Now it is just a matter of gently threading the new cord up through the holes in the slats and continuing over the entire route of the old cord until the knot on the opposite side is reached. The tilt cord should be changed at the same time; this is done by simply pushing it through the opening and placing it over the pulley.

When it becomes necessary to replace soiled or worn tapes, take off the bracket clips, lift out the head box (if any) and remove the blind from the window. Stretch it out on a table or the floor and remove the metal cover from the bottom slat. Both ends of the cord should be untied and pulled free. This will release the slats so that they may be pulled out and washed or painted. The old tapes may be discarded after they have been unfastened from the clamping arrangement at top and bottom.

When you buy new tapes, make certain that they have the same number of ladders as the old tapes and that they are for the same width slats. Install the new tapes by fastening them to the top and bottom, then thread the lift cord through the tapes.
Important: Make certain that you thread the cord through alternate sides of the woven ladder in the tapes. When replacing tapes, it is always advisable to replace lift and tilt cords at the same time.

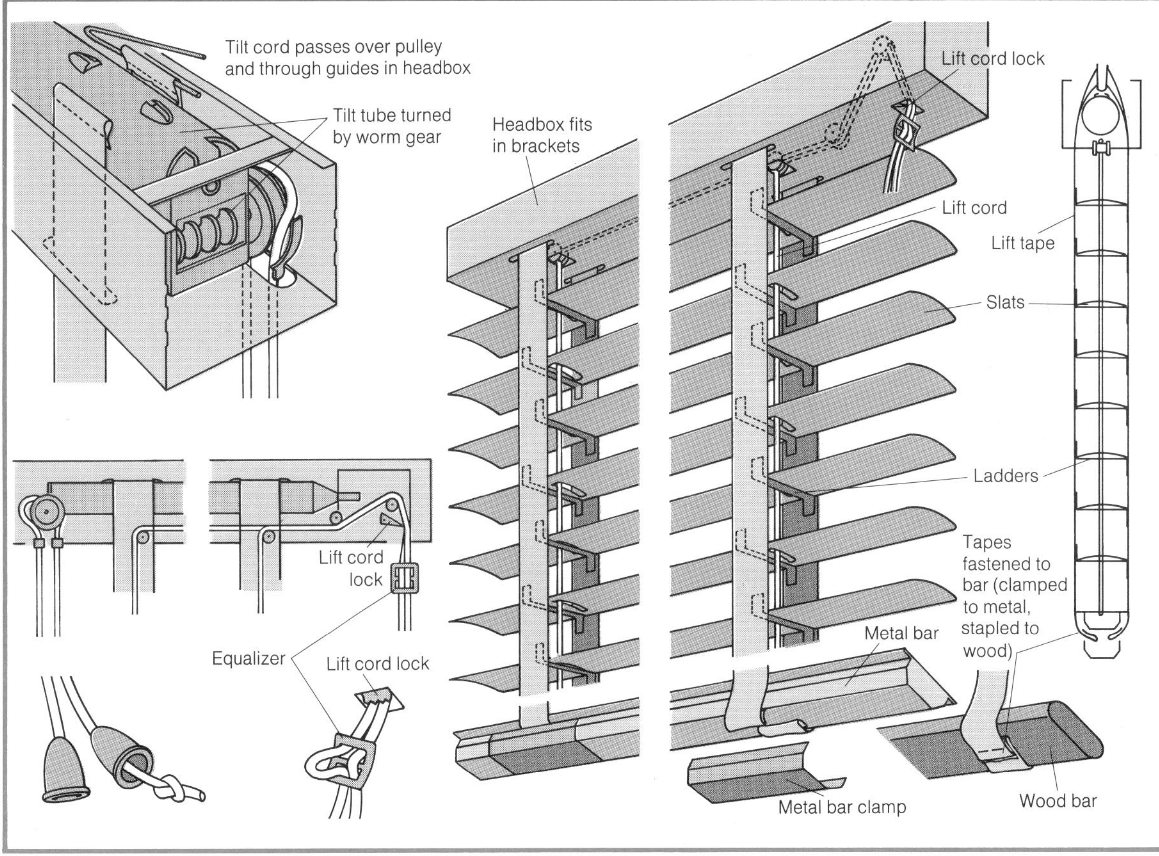

To remove metal blind from holder, pull out lock lever and lift up. On wood blinds, remove face board.

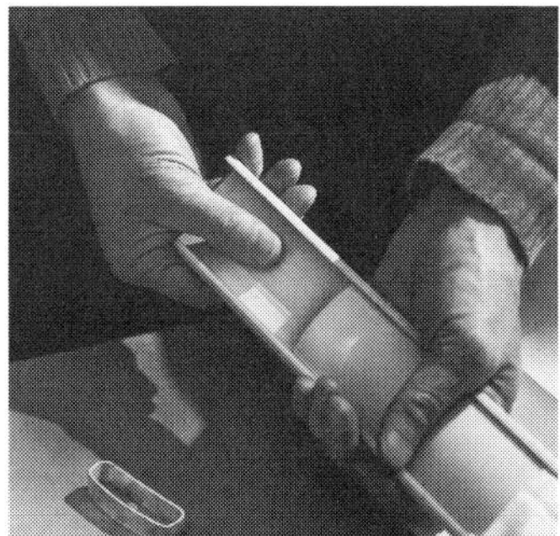
Remove the end caps and the metal cover from the bottom bar to expose the knotted ends of the lift cord.

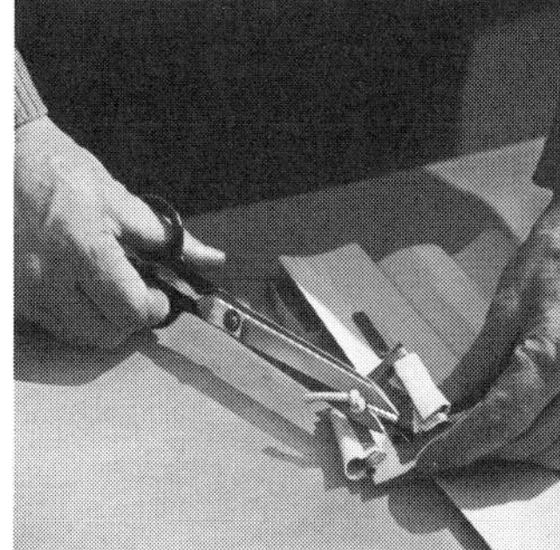
Snip off or untie both knots. Draw released cord up to headbox. Slats are now free to be pulled out.

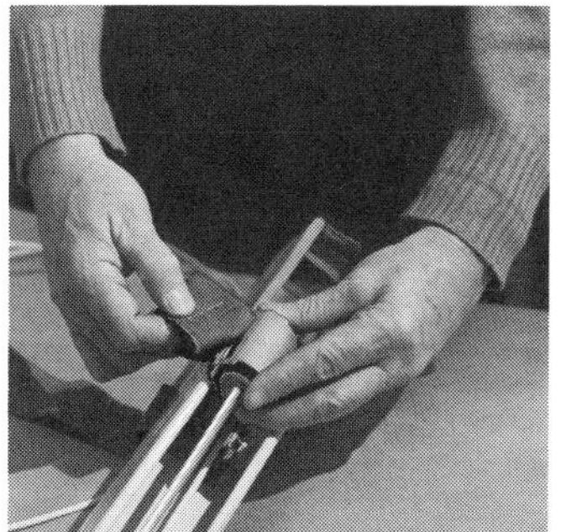
Remove old tape. Fold over and insert ends of new tape in clamps at top and in bottom bar.

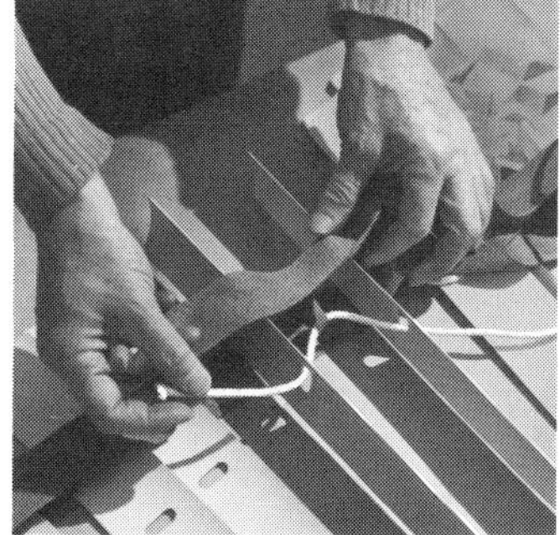
When rethreading the new lift cord through the slats, be sure it passes on alternate sides of ladders.

Drapery hardware

Stationary and traverse installations

Window draperies designed to remain more or less stationary can be hung on fixed curtain rods or poles. But when frequent adjustment is necessary or desirable for the sake of privacy, to control light, or to obtain a decorative effect, a traverse rod is recommended. A traverse rod can be operated manually or by a remotely controlled electric motor. When draperies are traverse-hung, no matter how wide an area they cover, you can open both sides with one motion, and close them just as easily, all or part of the way.

The traverse rod can be mounted on the window casing, the walls, or the ceiling, regardless of the type of hardware used to hold the draperies. If any curtain rod is more than 48 inches in length, make certain that it has adequate intermediate support—one or more brackets spaced equidistantly or, in traverse rod installations, whatever is specified in the instructions for the span the rod will cover.

Draperies can offer the additional advantage of changing a window's apparent size—giving the impression of increased height or width. You might want, for example, to hang draperies beyond the frame to take full advantage of window width and let in maximum natural light. This can be achieved by using extender plates, which are mounted directly on the window casing so no wall mounting is needed. They can also be used to make windows seem taller.

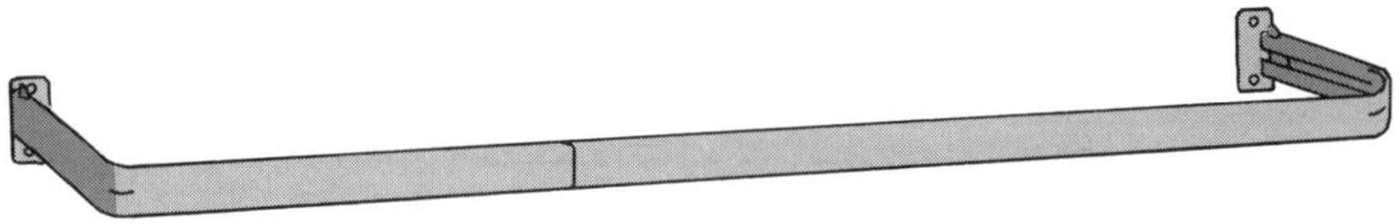

Adjustable stationary curtain rod

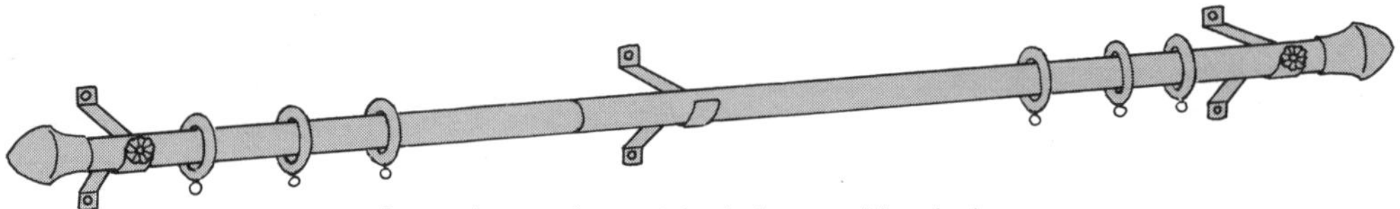

Decorative wood or metal pole for use with cafe rings

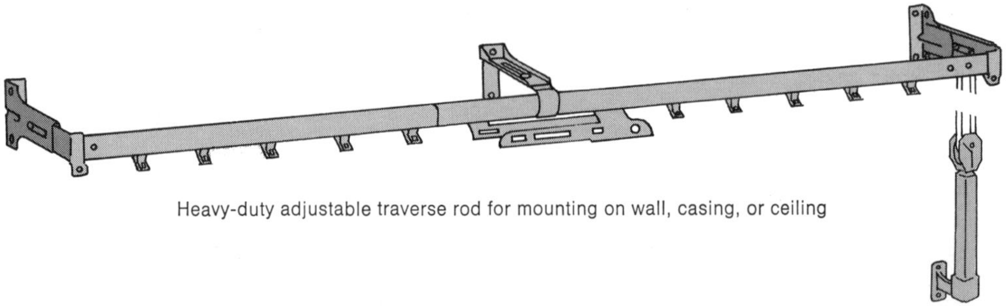

Heavy-duty adjustable traverse rod for mounting on wall, casing, or ceiling

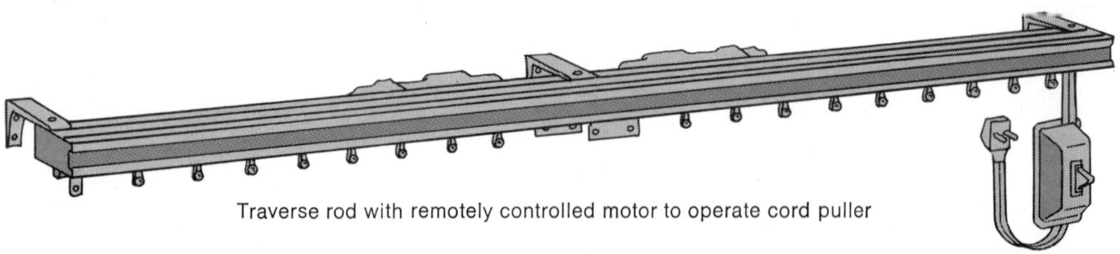

Traverse rod with remotely controlled motor to operate cord puller

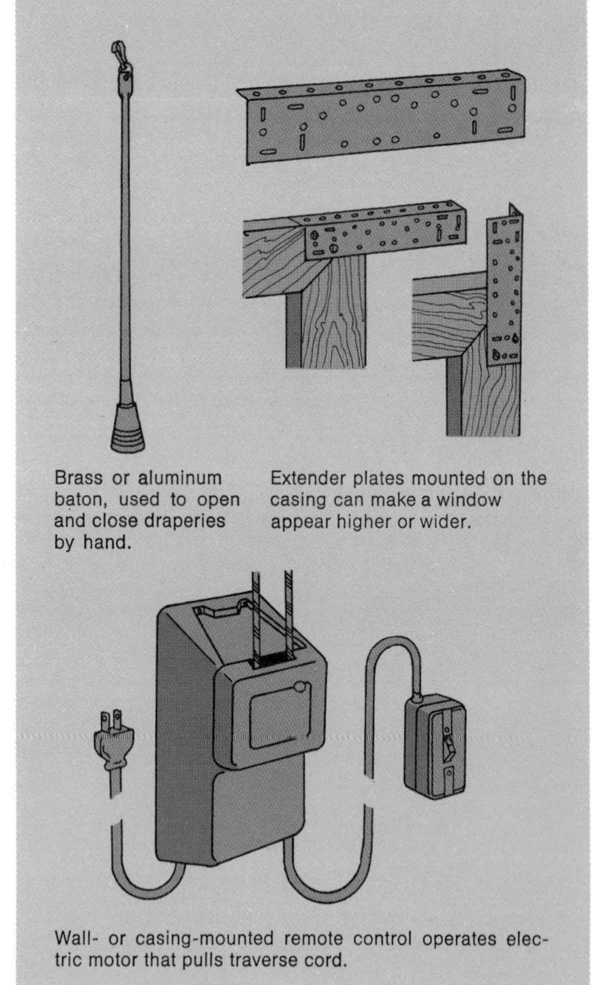

Brass or aluminum baton, used to open and close draperies by hand.

Extender plates mounted on the casing can make a window appear higher or wider.

Wall- or casing-mounted remote control operates electric motor that pulls traverse cord.

Mounting

When either a traverse or a stationary curtain rod is to be attached directly to the window casing, position the brackets at the upper corners of the casing. Add one or more intermediate supports for rods more than 48 inches long.

For windows that do not have casings, drapery mountings are usually placed 4 inches above the window and from 6 to 18 inches out from each side so that when draperies are pulled back, the room gets all the available natural light. If the rod is near the ceiling, make sure that you mount it parallel with the ceiling. Use toggle bolts or screw anchors to mount a rod on a hollow wall (p. 76).

Brackets and supports for ceiling installations are the same as for wall installations and are mounted substantially the same way; where ends of rod fit flush to walls, brackets are not necessary.

With the brackets in place, you can adjust the rod for length and for simultaneous closing and opening. Put the rod face down on the floor and adjust to the correct length to fit between and into the brackets. Pull the outer cord to draw the left master slide as far as it will go. Then, with the cord held taut, move the right master slide as far to the right as it will go. Attach the cord securely under the lug on the front of the right master slide.

When the rod is placed in its brackets, the cord can be properly tensioned. You can mount the base of the spring-loaded pulley on the baseboard, wall, or floor. Pull the yoke up and insert a nail in hole in pulley stem. Open the yoke and place cord loop under pulley wheel; close the pulley yoke. Pull out right-hand knot behind master slide until cord is slack-free; tie new knot, cut off the surplus, and remove the nail from the pulley stem.

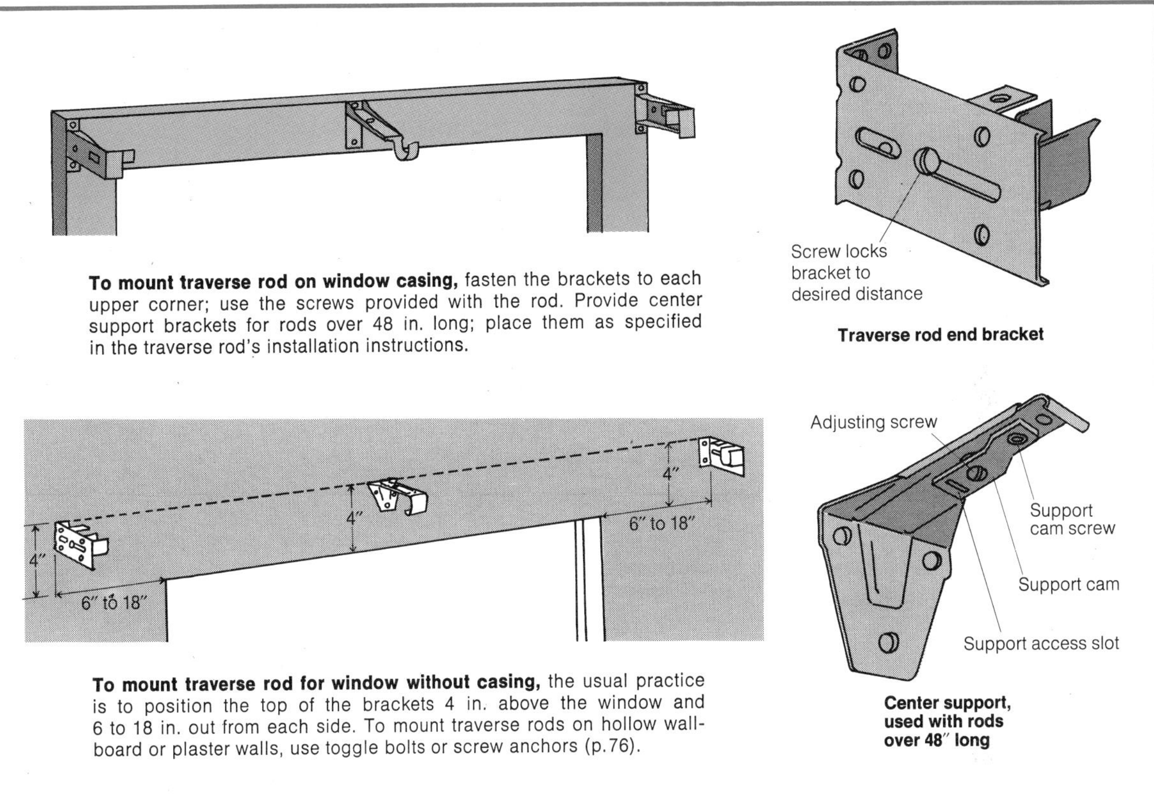

To mount traverse rod on window casing, fasten the brackets to each upper corner; use the screws provided with the rod. Provide center support brackets for rods over 48 in. long; place them as specified in the traverse rod's installation instructions.

Traverse rod end bracket

To mount traverse rod for window without casing, the usual practice is to position the top of the brackets 4 in. above the window and 6 to 18 in. out from each side. To mount traverse rods on hollow wallboard or plaster walls, use toggle bolts or screw anchors (p.76).

Center support, used with rods over 48″ long

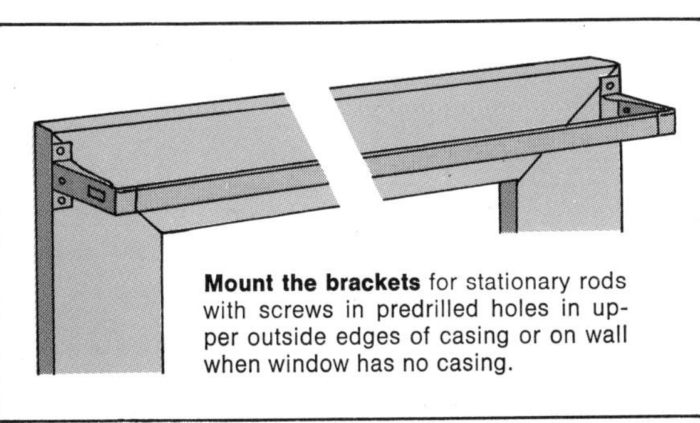

Mount the brackets for stationary rods with screws in predrilled holes in upper outside edges of casing or on wall when window has no casing.

Adjusting a traverse rod

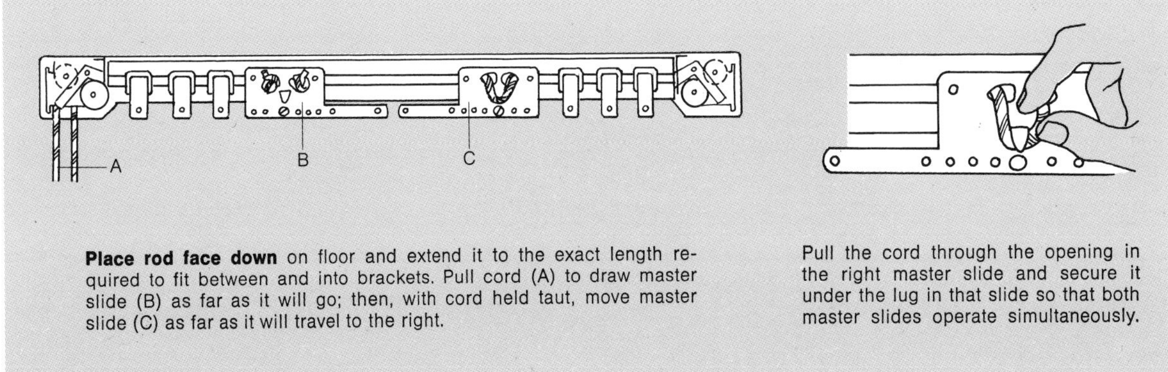

Place rod face down on floor and extend it to the exact length required to fit between and into brackets. Pull cord (A) to draw master slide (B) as far as it will go; then, with cord held taut, move master slide (C) as far as it will travel to the right.

Pull the cord through the opening in the right master slide and secure it under the lug in that slide so that both master slides operate simultaneously.

Drapery hardware

Mounting

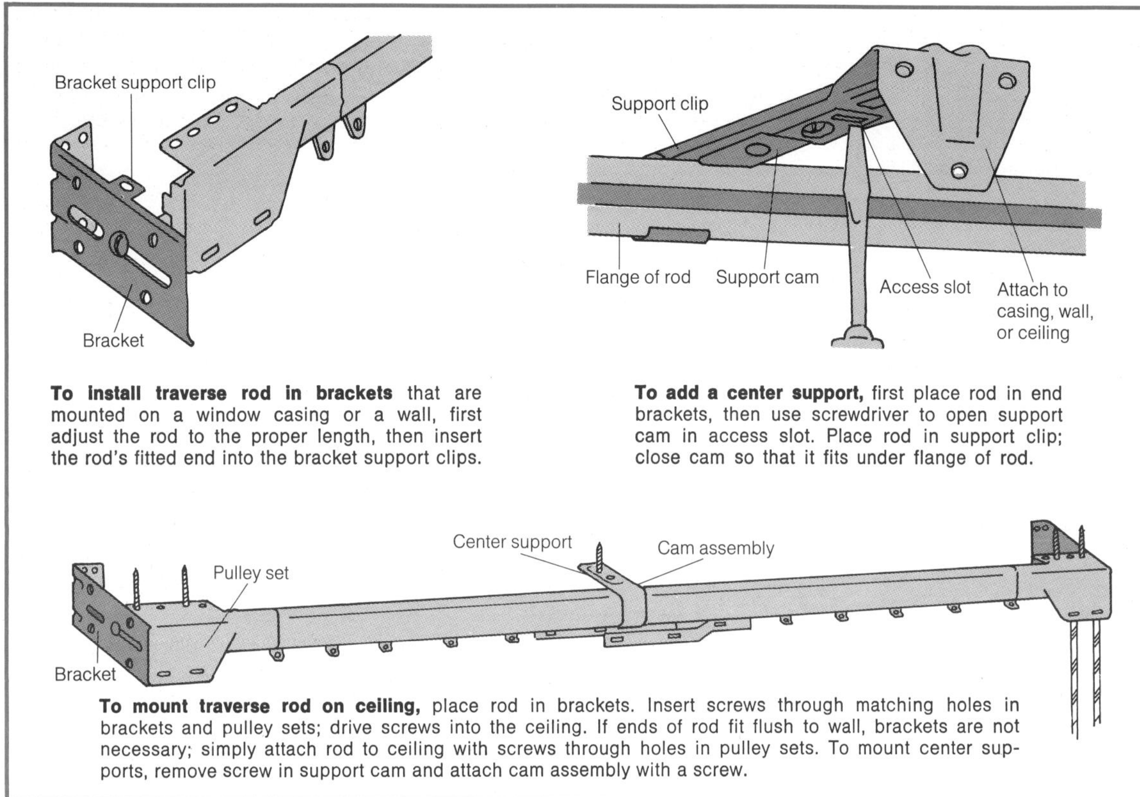

To install traverse rod in brackets that are mounted on a window casing or a wall, first adjust the rod to the proper length, then insert the rod's fitted end into the bracket support clips.

To add a center support, first place rod in end brackets, then use screwdriver to open support cam in access slot. Place rod in support clip; close cam so that it fits under flange of rod.

To mount traverse rod on ceiling, place rod in brackets. Insert screws through matching holes in brackets and pulley sets; drive screws into the ceiling. If ends of rod fit flush to wall, brackets are not necessary; simply attach rod to ceiling with screws through holes in pulley sets. To mount center supports, remove screw in support cam and attach cam assembly with a screw.

Adjustments

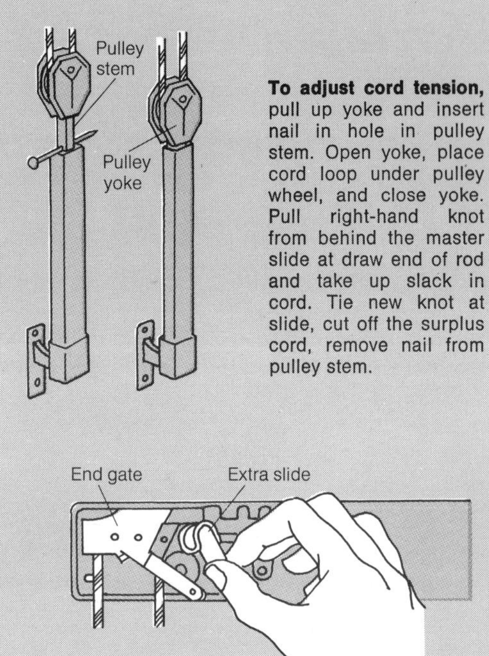

To adjust cord tension, pull up yoke and insert nail in hole in pulley stem. Open yoke, place cord loop under pulley wheel, and close yoke. Pull right-hand knot from behind the master slide at draw end of rod and take up slack in cord. Tie new knot at slide, cut off the surplus cord, remove nail from pulley stem.

To remove unneeded slides, push down on end gate, slip out the extra slides (save them for possible later use), and push gate back to original position.

Installing a traverse rod cord

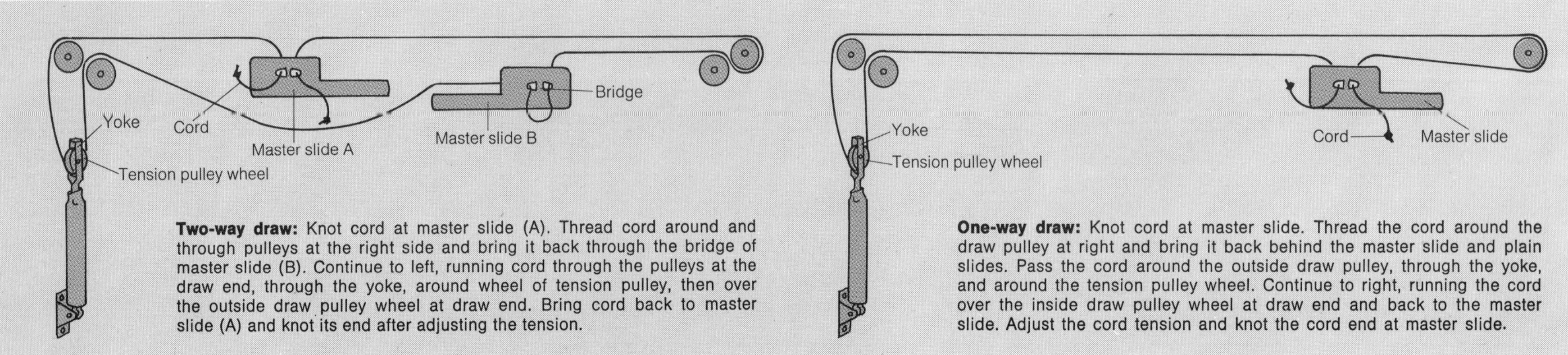

Two-way draw: Knot cord at master slide (A). Thread cord around and through pulleys at the right side and bring it back through the bridge of master slide (B). Continue to left, running cord through the pulleys at the draw end, through the yoke, around wheel of tension pulley, then over the outside draw pulley wheel at draw end. Bring cord back to master slide (A) and knot its end after adjusting the tension.

One-way draw: Knot cord at master slide. Thread the cord around the draw pulley at right and bring it back behind the master slide and plain slides. Pass the cord around the outside draw pulley, through the yoke, and around the tension pulley wheel. Continue to right, running the cord over the inside draw pulley wheel at draw end and back to the master slide. Adjust the cord tension and knot the cord end at master slide.

Binding and looseness

A door may stick because of loose or improperly mounted hinges, swelling of the wood, or even settling of the house. Correct the first difficulty by readjusting the hinges; correct the others by sanding or planing some wood from the door. When wood is removed, finish the raw wood to match the door and prevent moisture absorption, which causes swelling.

Open the door to inspect hinges and strike plate for loose screws. If any are loose because holes are enlarged, try longer screws or fill the holes with plastic wood or glue-coated wood plugs and reset the screws. If the door still binds, locate the points where it rubs by sliding thin stiff cardboard between the edges of closed door and jamb.

If the door is free near the bottom but binds near the top on the latch side, the bottom hinge may have been mortised too deeply. Open the door and secure it with a wedge. Remove the screws from the bottom hinge leaf in the jamb, insert a cardboard shim under the hinge leaf, and reset the screws. This will push the lower part of the door out from the jamb and tilt it back square in its frame.

If the door binds near the bottom on the latch side, insert a shim under the upper hinge leaf in the jamb. If the door still binds slightly near the top or bottom edge after either hinge has been shimmed, sand or plane off a small amount of wood at the rubbing point (can be done without removing the door).

If the door is now clear along the latch side but binds on top, wedge it open and sand or plane down the wood. If the binding is at the bottom, you must first remove the door (p.140). If the door binds along the entire latch side, remove it and sand or plane down the hinge side. It is easier to plane this side than the latch side because the lock need not be removed. Also, since the hinge side is less conspicuous, it may be easier to refinish.

When the door moves freely and the latch is lined up but will not reach the strike plate, a shim under it may move it out near enough to the door to hold. If the door resists closing or tends to open by itself when not latched, insert a narrow cardboard shim under half the hinge leaf on the pin side only of each hinge on the jamb. These can be inserted if the hinge leaf is removed from the jamb.

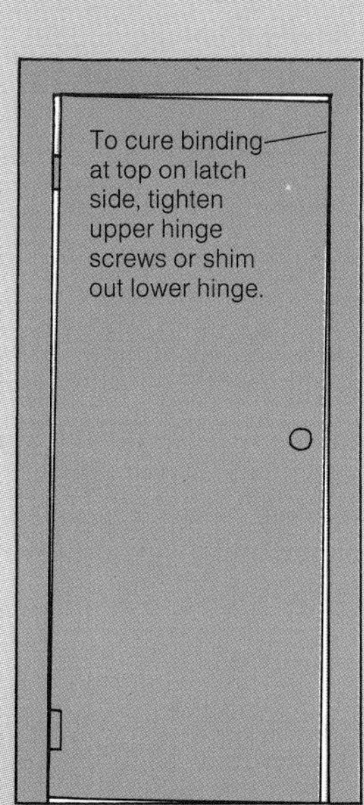

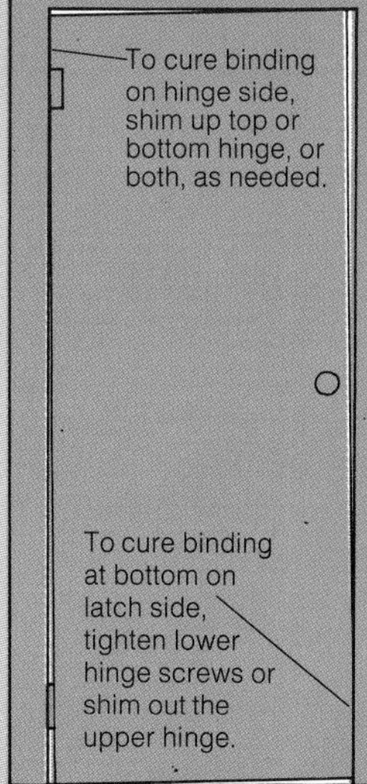

First check the hinges and strike plate to make certain that they are not loose. Slide a sheet of thin stiff cardboard between the door and the jamb while the door is closed. The door is binding at those points where the cardboard does not move freely.

Put cardboard shim under bottom hinge leaf in jamb if door binds at top on latch side; shim up top hinge if bottom binds.

To tighten hinges, use longer screws or fill holes with plastic wood or glue-coated wood plugs and reset old screws.

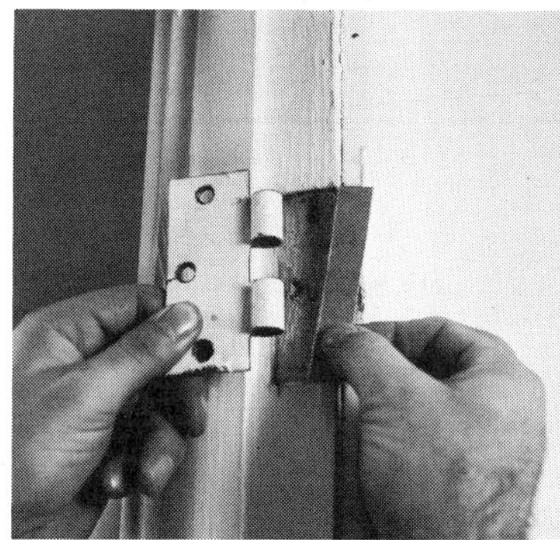

If a door resists closing, insert a narrow cardboard shim between the jamb and leaf of each hinge.

Insert a wedge under the outer edge of the door to hold it steady for sanding or planing or when working on one hinge.

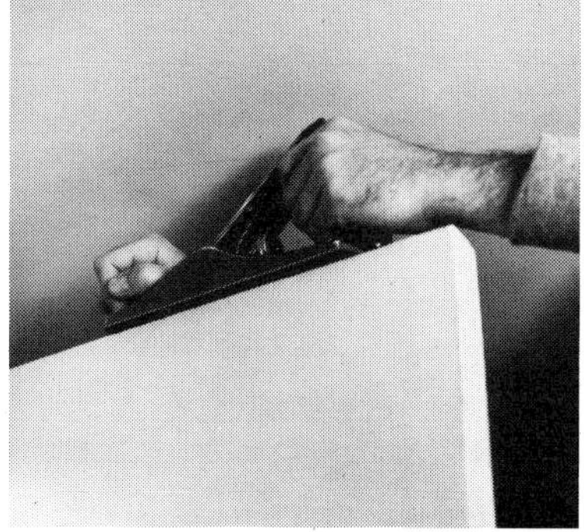

Use a sanding block or a plane to remove small amount of wood from top of door; no need to remove door from hinges.

If latch bolt fails to reach the strike plate opening, insert cardboard shim under strike plate to move it nearer door.

Doors

Binding and looseness

A door must be removed when its bottom edge or hinge side needs planing. If the door is hung with loose-pin hinges, drive them up and out with a hammer and a screwdriver. Remove the pin from the bottom hinge first and the top hinge last so that the door will not fall while still held by one hinge. If the door is hung with hinges that do not have loose pins, remove the screws from one leaf of each hinge on the door's jamb side. Do this with the door wide open and a supporting wedge under its outer corner.

Planing the hinge side: Before removing the door, mark the spot or spots where it binds. Then plane to these marks. Plane with great care; it is easy to remove too much wood. In some cases it may be necessary to deepen the hinge mortises so the position of the door in the frame will not be changed.

Planing the bottom: Prop the door so that it stands on one long edge with the bottom perpendicular to the floor. Plane from the top corner of the bottom edge toward the center; then turn the door over so that it stands on the other long edge and plane from the other corner to the center.

Relocating the strike plate: A door will not stay closed if the latch tongue does not enter the strike plate opening. Correct this condition by filing the strike plate to make the opening slightly larger. The strike plate should be moved if it is too much out of line. To do this, remove the strike plate, extend the mortise, and fill the exposed part with plastic wood. Plug up the old screw holes.

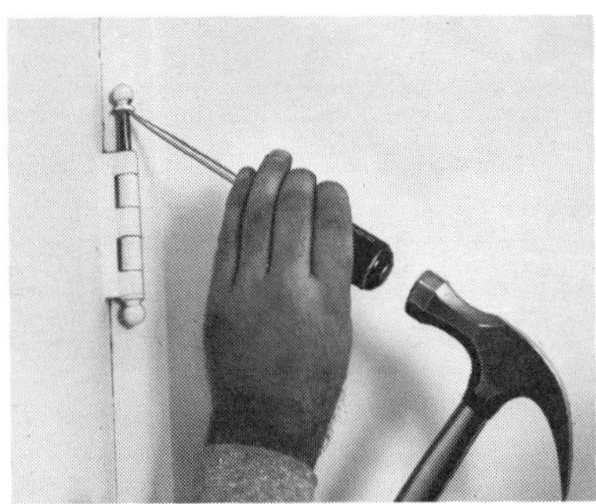

To remove loose-pin hinges, drive pins up and out with a hammer and screwdriver. Remove bottom hinge first and top last.

Plane to a reference mark on the door to make sure just the right amount of wood is removed from all the high spots.

To move a door away from the jamb on the latch side, use a hammer and chisel to deepen the hinge mortises in the jamb.

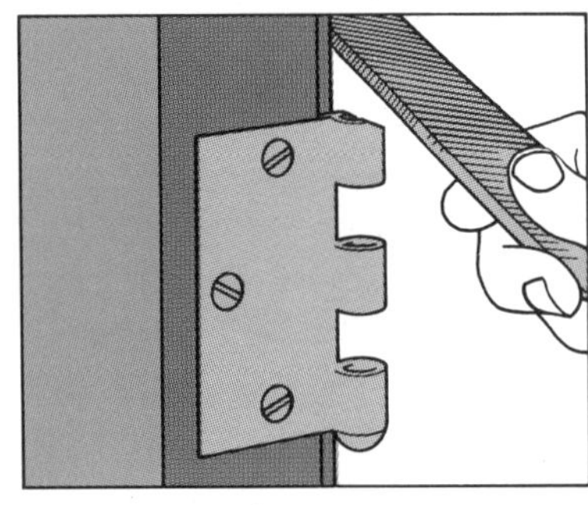

Before reinstalling a door, file a slight notch on the top of its hinge leaf barrel to expedite future pin removal.

Correct minor misalignment of the latch bolt and the strike plate opening by enlarging the opening with a file.

If strike plate and latch bolt are too much out of line, or if door rattles, relocate strike plate in new mortise.

Correcting warps

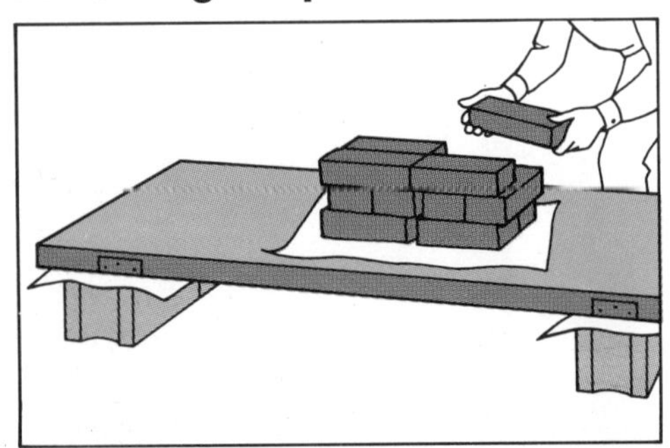

Straighten a bowed door by applying heavy weights over the bulged part for about 24 hours. Rest door on supports under both ends, bulged side up.

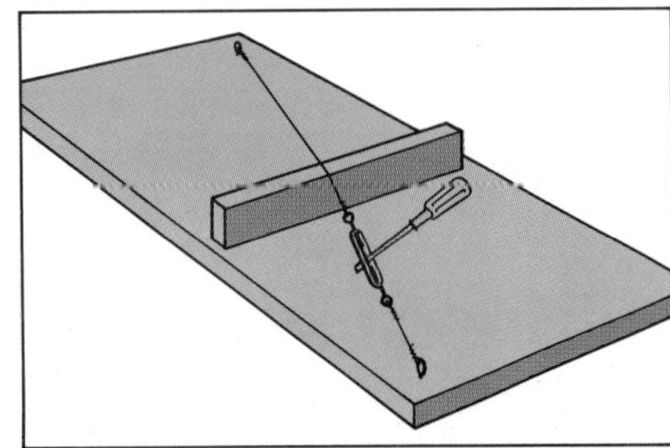

Pull a warped or twisted door back into shape by tightening a turnbuckle in a wire connecting screw eyes at both ends and over a bridge in the center.

If a door is warped on hinge side, difficulty may be corrected by installing a third hinge between present hinges.

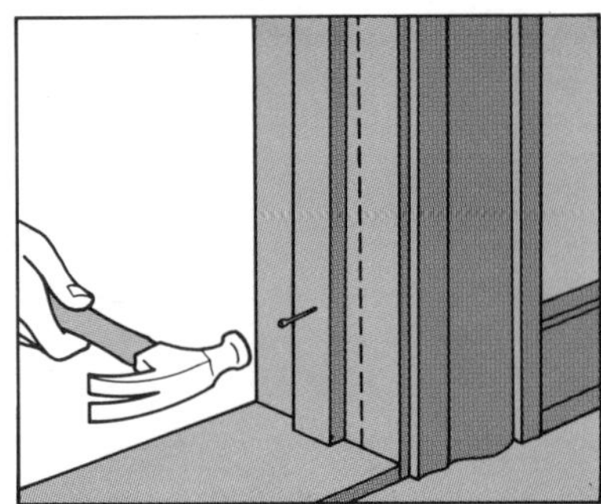

For door warped on latch side, remove stop, close door, draw line on jamb along edge of door, renail stop to line.

Hanging a new door

To hang a new door, first saw off the protective ends that project from the stiles. Measure and mark the door for width and height, then cut it to size; use a plane to trim the edges of hinge and latch stiles and the bottom rail.

Place door in opening and put wedges under bottom rail to raise it ¼ inch for clearance; if door will open out over a rug, increase this to ⅞ inch. Allow ⅛-inch clearance at top and on each side.

Locate hinges 6 or 7 inches from the top and 10 or 11 inches from the bottom. Mark their position on door and jamb with a chisel. Cut mortises for hinges.

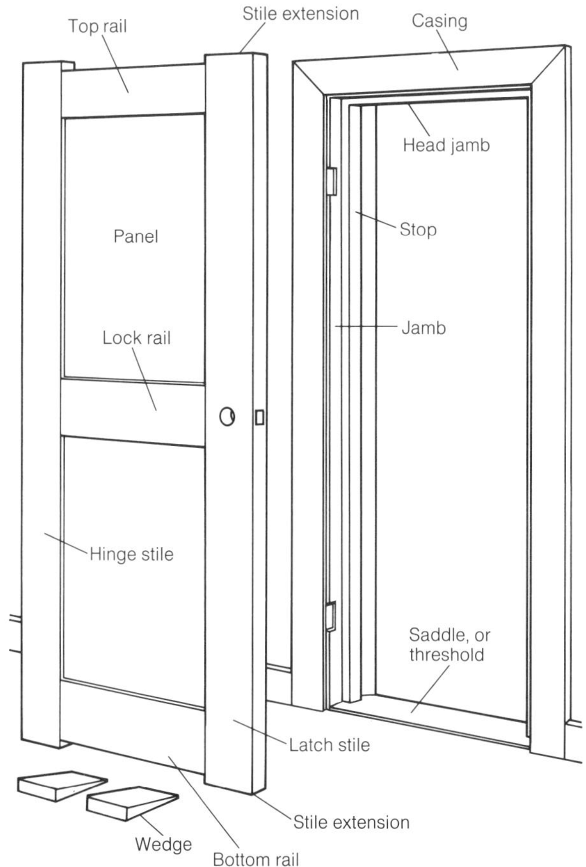

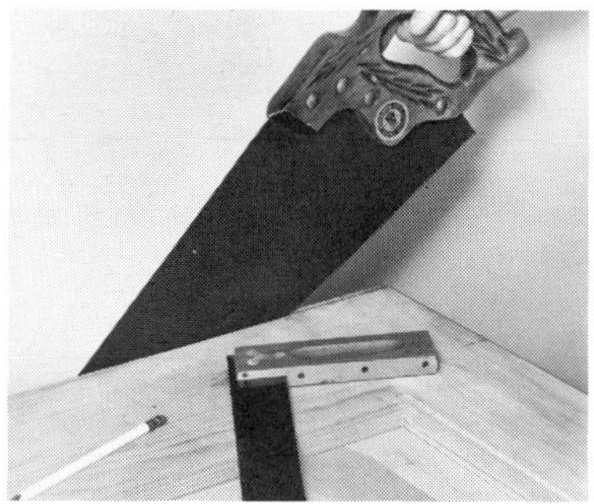

Place new door on sawhorses and cut off the ends that project from the stiles.

Plane bottom rail and both stiles; bevel latch side slightly toward stop.

Prop door in opening and insert wedges to provide proper clearance all around.

Hammer in the wedges on all four sides of the new door to hold it in position.

Mark position of hinges on door and jamb simultaneously with a chisel.

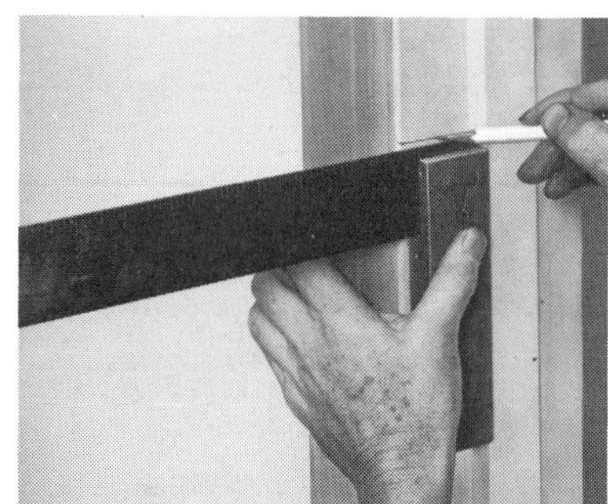

Remove door and use a try square to extend the hinge marks onto the jamb.

Fitting hinges

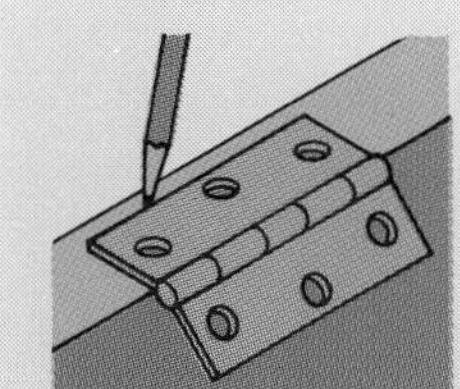

Outline the mortise with a pencil, using the hinge leaf as a guide. Barrel of hinge should extend beyond inner face of door. Mark hinge thickness on inside door face.

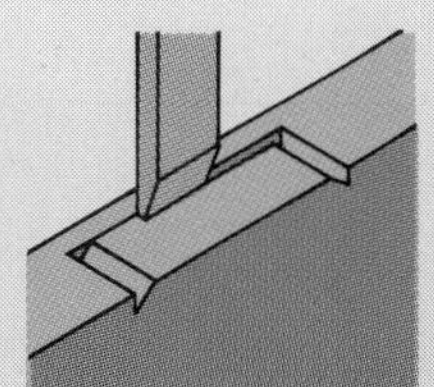

Score hinge outline with chisel inside pencil mark. Hold chisel vertically and drive it to approximate hinge depth. Keep beveled face of chisel toward the opening.

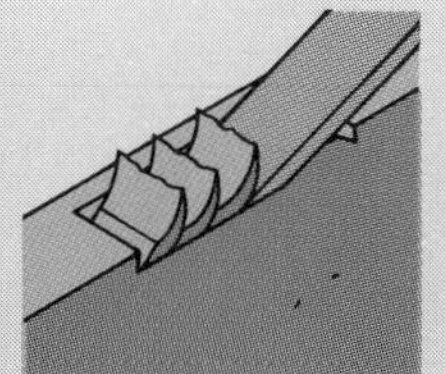

Make shallow feather cuts to clean mortise to depth line. Hold the chisel's beveled edge downward. Several smaller cuts make a cleaner mortise than a few large ones.

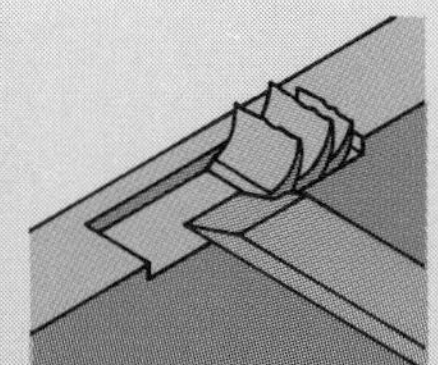

Hold chisel along depth line and tap lightly across grain of mortise to shave off feather cuts. Hold the chisel with the beveled side of the blade facing up.

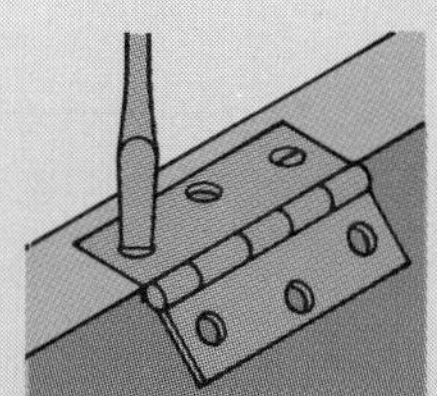

Drill or punch holes for the screws, then drive screws home. Check that hinge leaf is flush with door edge. If mortise is too deep, shim hinge with cardboard until it is flush.

Weatherstripping doors

Weatherstripping outside the jamb

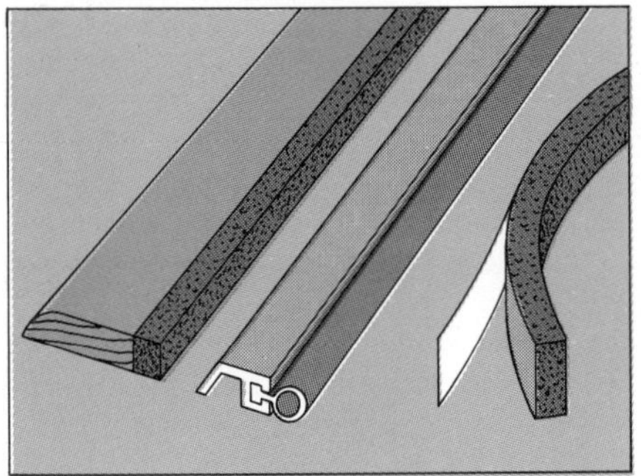

Three basic outer jamb weatherstrips: Wood strip with foam backing; aluminum channel with vinyl backing; adhesive-backed foam strip.

To apply the wood strip, nail it snugly against the closed door. Cut strips to size with a back saw. Space nails 8 to 12 in. apart.

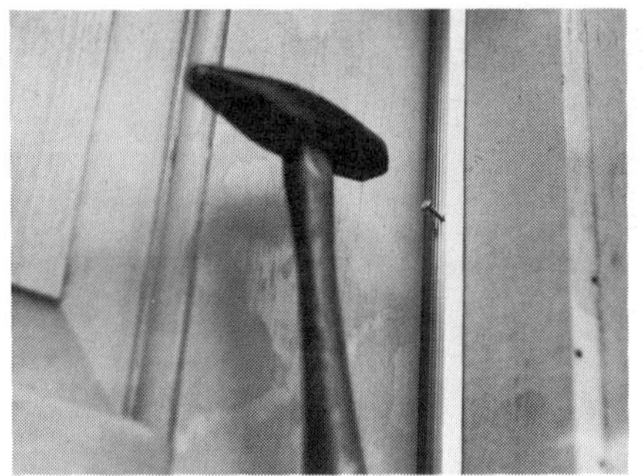

Aluminum/vinyl stripping must be cut with a hacksaw. Nail cut channel to the jamb snugly against the closed door.

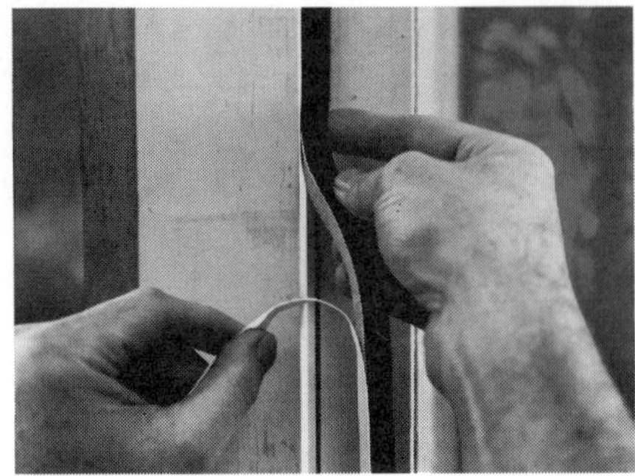

Adhesive-backed foam is applied to the inside face of the jamb; when the door is closed, the foam is compressed, making a tight seal.

Sealing gaps at the bottom of a door

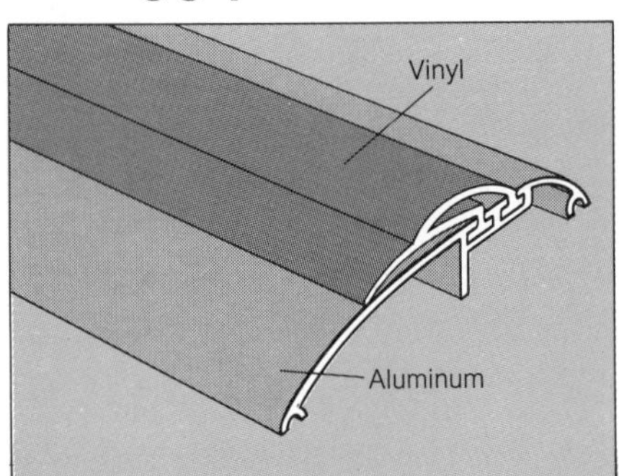

Aluminum channel with a heavy-duty vinyl flap may be used to seal the gaps between door bottoms and thresholds.

Cut the aluminum with a hacksaw to fit snugly against both sides of the door jamb. Install with flap toward outside. Fasten with screws.

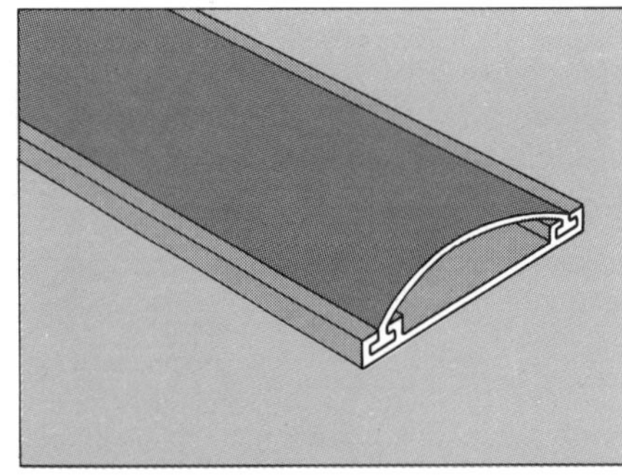

An alternative for sealing the threshold is an aluminum/vinyl channel that is fitted to the bottom of the door.

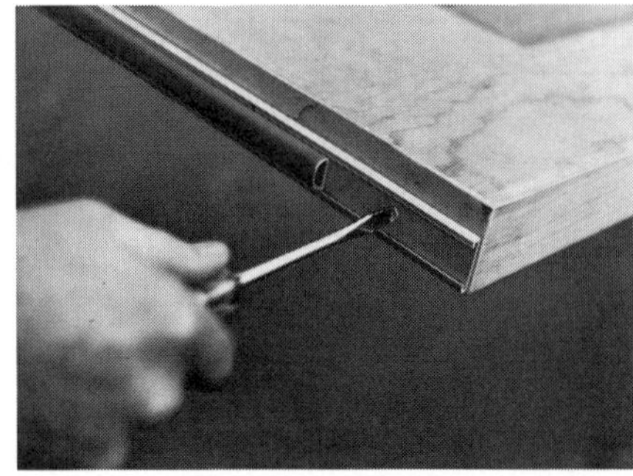

To install, first remove the door. Cut channel to door width with a hacksaw. Slide vinyl out of channel to fasten screws.

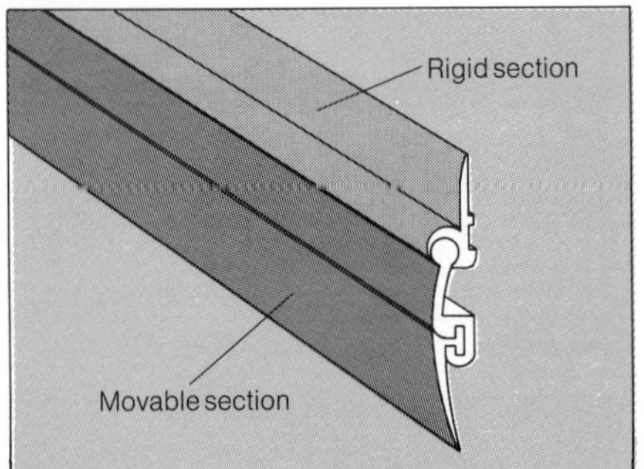

Flap-type seal fitted to the outside of the door flips down when door is closed, springs up out of the way when door is opened.

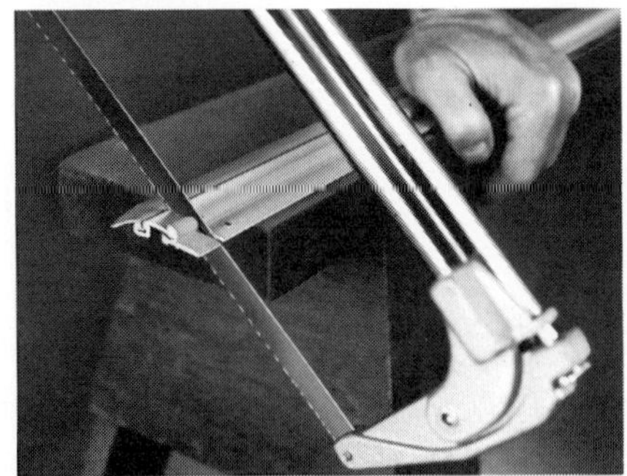

Cut strip with hacksaw so it is 1/16 in. in from sides of door jamb. Apply light saw pressure so as not to damage hinge joint.

Position the strip on the outside of the door 1 13/16 in. above the threshold. Measure this distance while the door is closed.

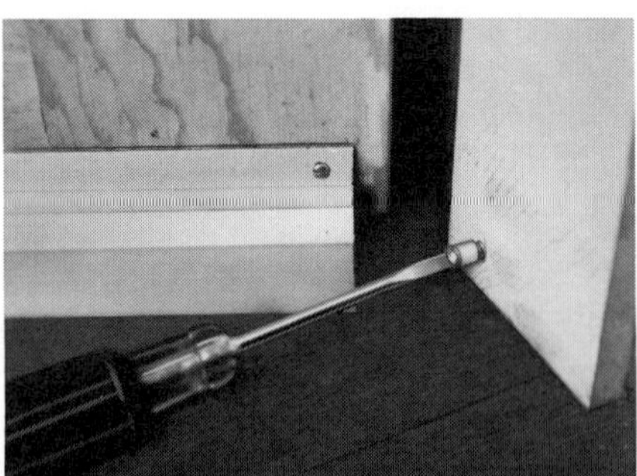

Install the top roller 11/16 in. above the threshold on the door jamb. The roller fits on the hinge side of the door.

Inside the jamb (new doors)

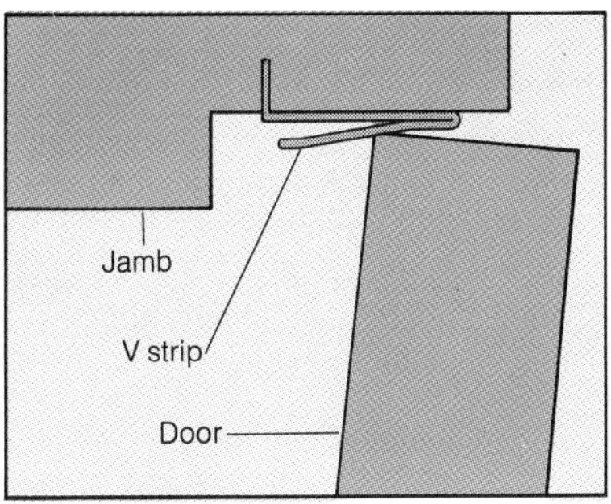

V strip metal channel seals door gaps as the closed door compresses the metal up against the jamb.

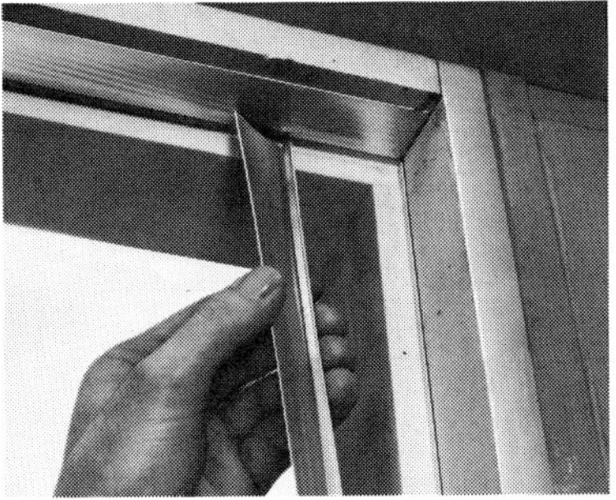

The installation calls for a groove to be cut in the jamb. The metal lip of the V strip slips into the groove.

On hinge side of door, install hinges before V strip. Tack along the edge of the strip so only tack heads rest on strip.

Inside the jamb (old doors)

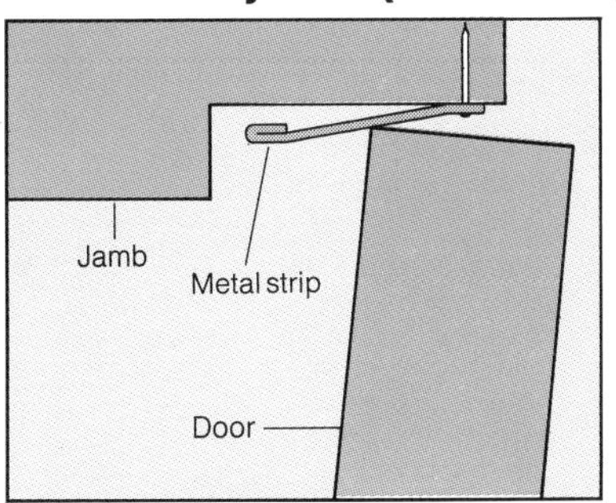

Metal strip for old or new doors seals similarly to V strip when door is closed.

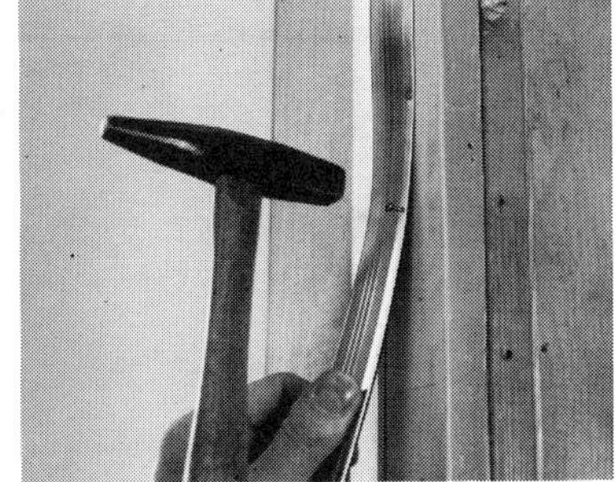

Installation does not require groove to be cut in jamb. Simply tack in place.

For better seal, lift outer edge of strip with screwdriver after tacking.

Interlocking weatherstripping

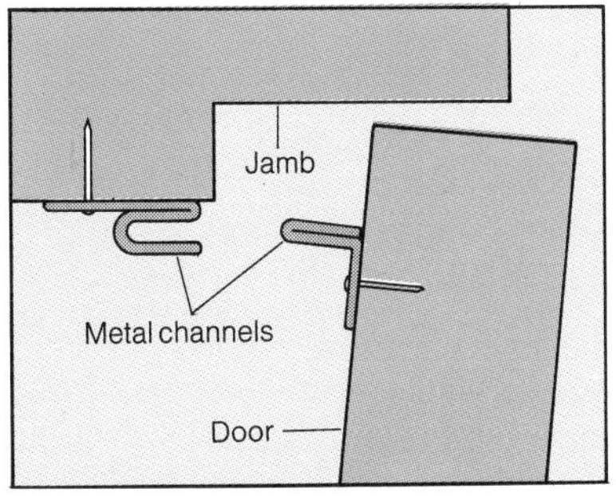

Interlocking metal channels provide excellent seal. Male channels are fitted to door surface; female channels to jamb.

Cut and fit strip to head of door first. On in-swinging doors, install on the outside; on out-swinging doors, the inside.

Installation sequence, hinge side of door: Male strip on jamb; female strip on door. On lock side, reverse the sequence.

J strips

The most efficient door weatherstripping system is a set of interlocking aluminum channels that are fitted around a door's edge.

One J strip is applied in a rabbet that is made in the top and latch side of a door to interlock with a matching strip fitted in a rabbet cut in the frame. A rubber-backed flat strip is attached in a rabbet in the bottom of the door. This fits a groove of a metal threshold. Another flat strip is installed in a rabbet on the surface of the hinge side of the door and positioned so that ¼ inch projects into a groove cut in the frame.

This method cannot be used on a badly warped door. Because some specialized tools are required, it is best to have this installation done professionally.

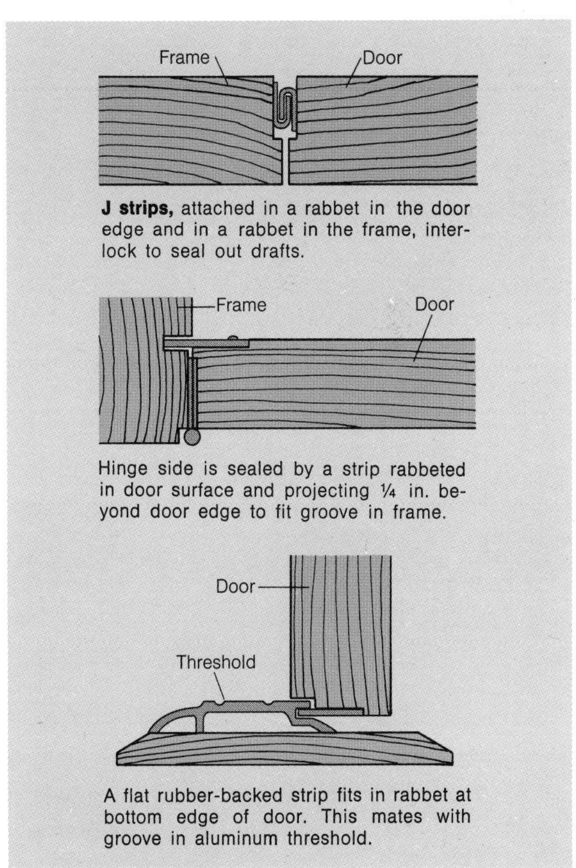

J strips, attached in a rabbet in the door edge and in a rabbet in the frame, interlock to seal out drafts.

Hinge side is sealed by a strip rabbeted in door surface and projecting ¼ in. beyond door edge to fit groove in frame.

A flat rubber-backed strip fits in rabbet at bottom edge of door. This mates with groove in aluminum threshold.

Replacing a threshold

The part of a doorway that receives the most wear is the saddle, or threshold. To remove a worn saddle, swing the door wide open; if more clearance is needed, take the door off. If necessary, remove the door stops from the jamb. Lift up the old saddle with a pry bar or the claws of a hammer. If the saddle is badly worn, it may be easier to split the wood with a chisel and remove it in pieces. If the saddle extends under the jambs, try to remove it intact; if you can't, cut the saddle in three sections with a back saw, remove the middle section, then work out the end pieces. Where possible, use the old saddle as a pattern for the new one. If this cannot be done, take measurements carefully and cut the new piece accordingly. Cut so that protruding ends fit snugly against the door casing. Drill holes and sink nails (or countersink screws) to secure the new saddle to the floor. Fill holes with wood putty.

If saddle extends under door jamb, it may be necessary to remove the door stop. Check for nails or screws in middle of saddle.

Another method of removing the saddle is to split it with a chisel and hammer and remove it piece by piece.

If you can't remove the old saddle intact for use as a pattern, cut it in three parts with back saw; remove middle, then work out ends.

If the old saddle cannot be used as a pattern for the new one, transfer the measurements to new saddle and trim to fit.

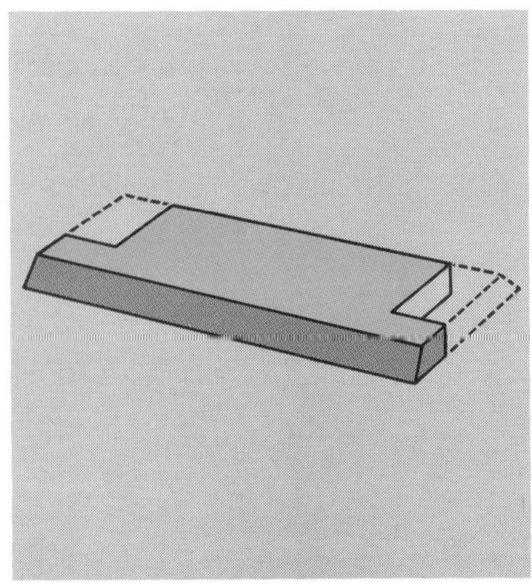

Saddle, ready for insertion, should look somewhat like this. Countersink holes if screws are to be used for fastening.

After vacuuming area where new saddle is to go, tap it in lightly. Do not force. If fit is too tight, pull saddle out and trim.

Since saddles are generally made of hardwood, chiefly oak, it is advisable to drill pilot holes for the nails to avoid splitting.

Drive 2½-in. finishing nails into predrilled holes. Sink nailheads with a nail set; fill holes with wood putty; sand when dry.

Installing a handle

A door can often be made better looking and easier to close by the addition of a decorative handle. Such handles are available in a number of finishes; some can be installed over the existing knob without removing knob or the rose.

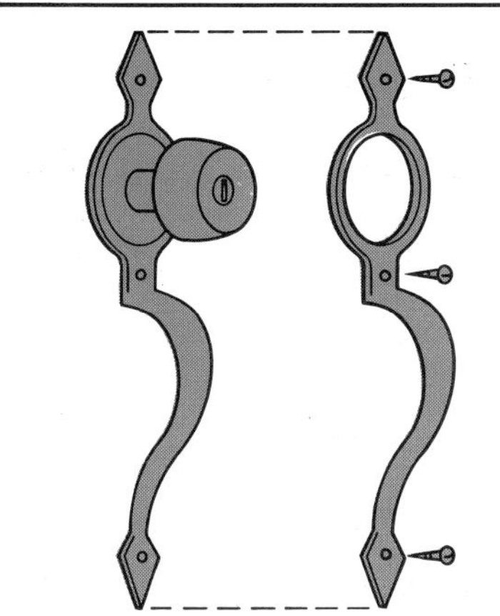

Slide the handle over knob and rose and attach it securely to the door, using the screws provided. If the circumference of the knob is greater than the handle opening, remove the knob.

Adding decorative molding

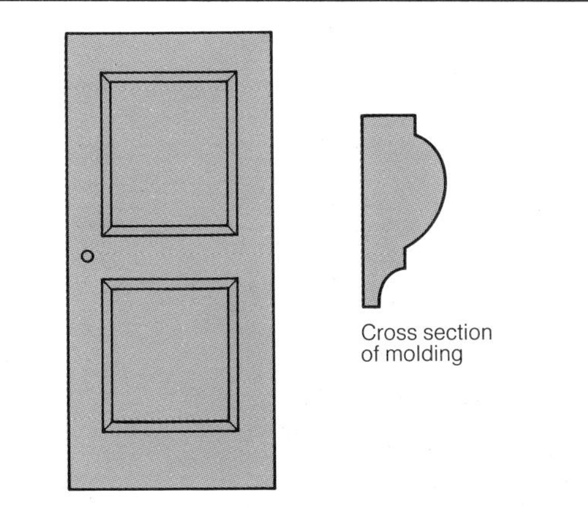

Cross section of molding

A flush door can be converted to a traditional type by means of picture-frame molding. Miter-cut the joints to form the panels. Use glue at all corner joints. Fasten the molding to the door with brads; sink the brads with a nail set and fill holes with wood putty; sand when putty is dry and finish to suit.

Installing a peephole

A peephole, or viewer, allows the householder to see a caller before opening the door. Some peepholes are simply a swinging cover over a hole in the door. A better type is equipped with lenses that give you a wide-angle view of the exterior.

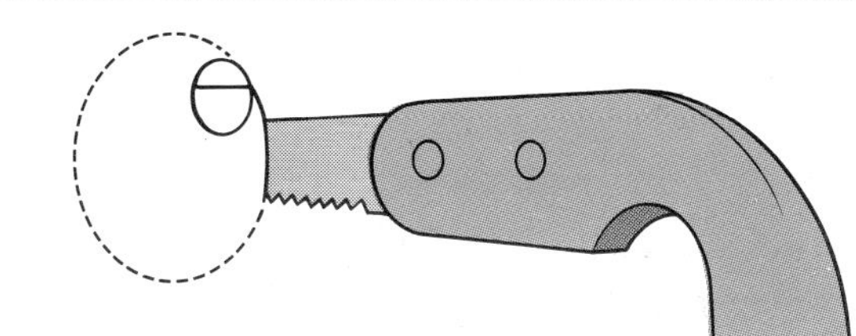

Mark on the door the eye level of the household's shortest adult. Cut a hole to accommodate the peephole in the center of the door. Use keyhole saw or a hole cutter mounted in an electric drill.

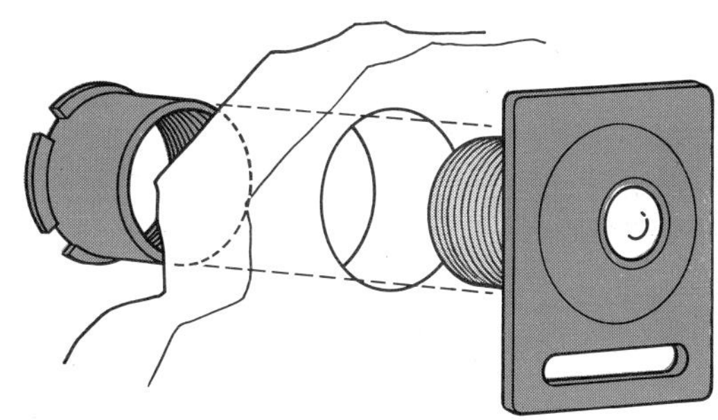

To install on a door more than 1⅛ in. thick, insert the viewer in the hole; thread on the large flanged ring and tighten it securely by running it through the hole in the door; then screw on the cover.

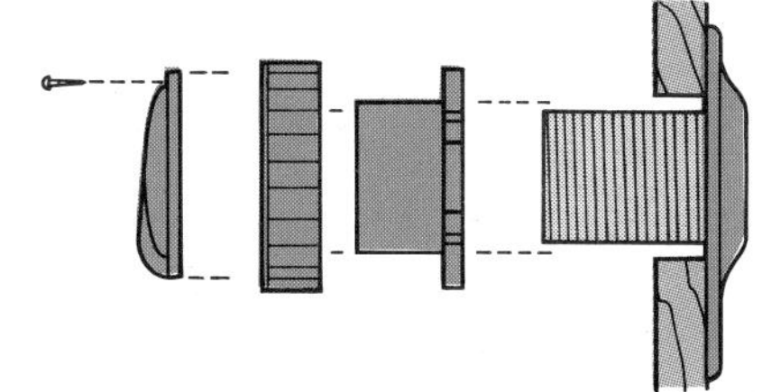

To install on a door less than 1⅛ in. thick, reverse the large flanged ring to fill the space between viewer tube and door surface, then secure the unit with the smaller fluted ring enclosed in kit; screw on the cover.

Installing a mail slot

A mail slot should be at least 1½ inches wide and 7 inches long, and be set at least 30 inches above the floor in the thicker part of the door—never the panel part if the door is that type. Hollow-core doors need a metal chute between inside and outside plates.

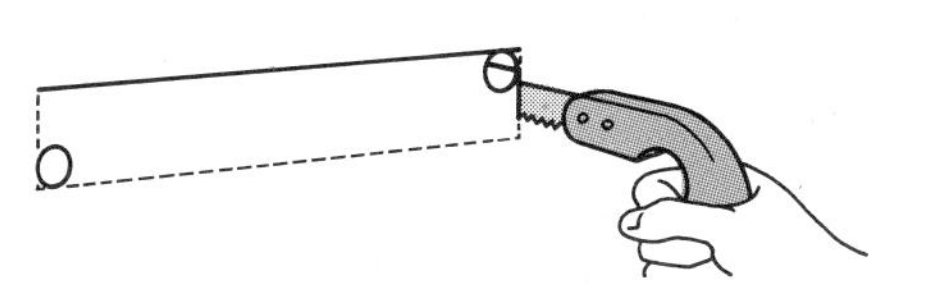

Mark on the door the size of the opening for the unit you have chosen. Drill holes at the four corners and cut out the opening with a keyhole saw.

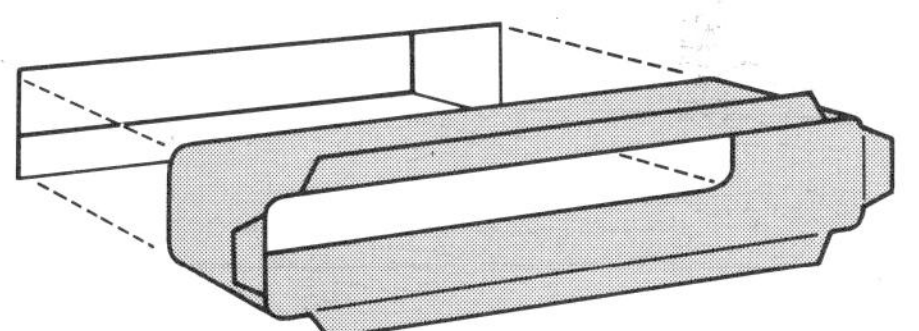

Insert and secure the metal chute between the inside and outside plates. Use a heavy-gauge aluminum or brass unit when installing slot in a hollow-core door.

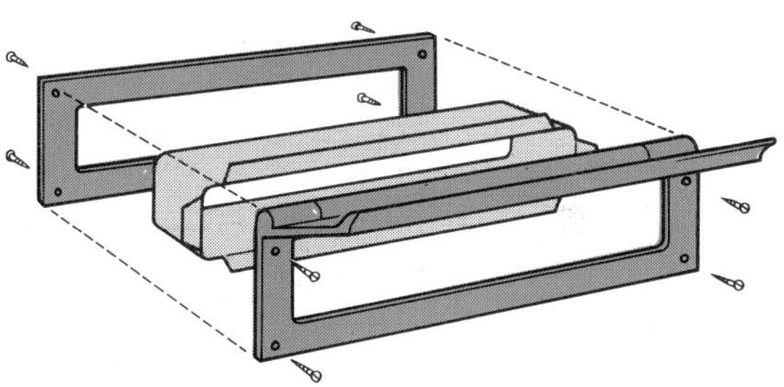

Fasten inside and outside plates with screws provided in the mail slot kit. Before doing so, make sure that the spring or gravity cover is on the outside.

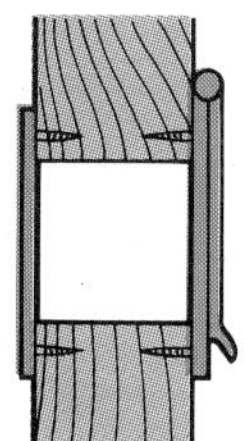

Cross section view of a door mail slot to which a hood has been added on the inside. Such hoods give privacy and protect against theft.

Installing glass

When glass is to be substituted for one or more panels of a door in order to admit light, the first step is to take the door down and place it across padded sawhorses or on a bench top. Remove the molding carefully so that it can be used again, then pry out the panel and clean its bed of glue and dirt. Apply exterior paint to the bed where the glass will be placed, then lay a thin layer of glazing compound in the bottom before installing the glass.

When you have the glass positioned, press it down slightly to force some compound up around the edges. Run another layer of compound around the perimeter of the glass. Use the old molding, or a new one if necessary, to hold the glass in place; drive brads through the molding into the stiles and rails. Rehang the door. Molding or glazing compound on the outside of the door should be protected against weather by at least two coats of exterior paint.

Use a wide, stiff putty knife to pry out molding from around panel. Do this carefully so molding can be used again.

Remove the panel and clean out the bed. Sand down any wood splinters until the bed is perfectly smooth.

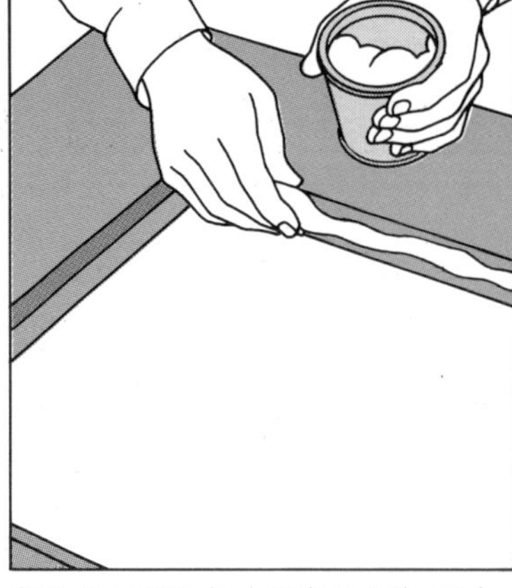

Coat the entire bed surface with outdoor paint. Then lay a thin strip of glazing compound in the bottom of the bed.

Glass should be a double-strength pane cut ⅛ in. smaller than opening. Press it down to force compound up around edges.

Place another layer of compound around perimeter of glass. Replace the molding; drive in and sink brads; fill holes.

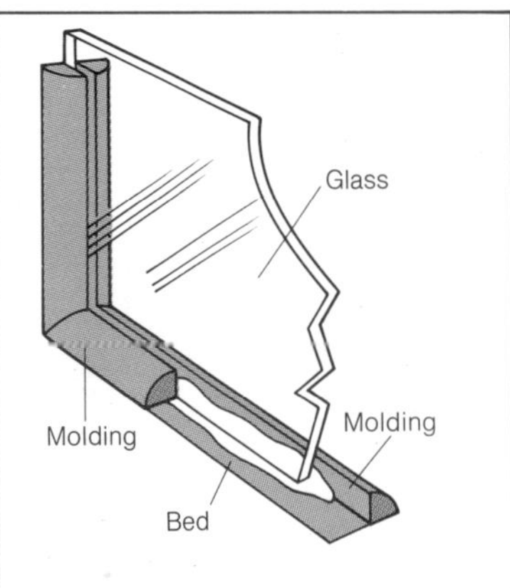

Cross section of glass installed in exterior door. Make sure that outside molding is sealed against the weather.

Installing a drip cap

A drip cap of wood or metal is installed on the outside of a door over the threshold to keep rain from draining or blowing under the door. One metal type, shown above, is mounted just on the face of the door.

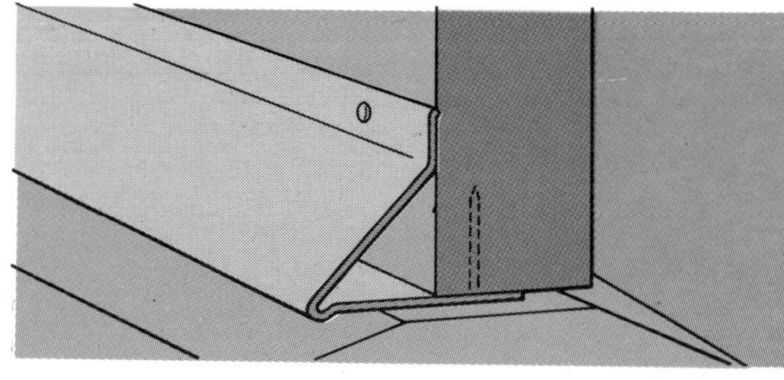

Another type of metal drip cap extends under the bottom of the door, as shown above.

Installing a kick plate

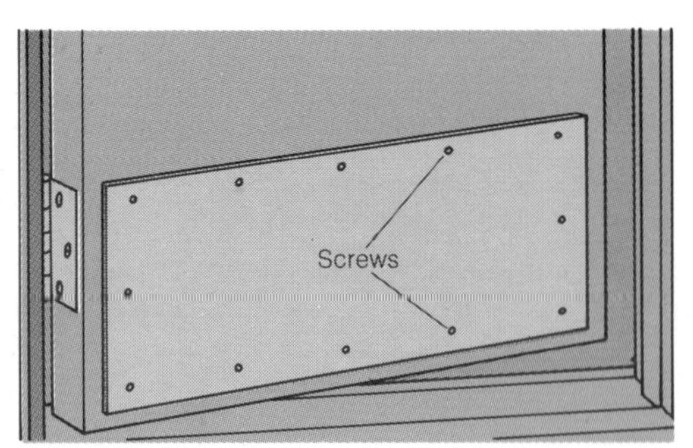

A kick plate of plastic or metal can be attached to the base of a much-used door to protect its lower surface. The plate is beveled on three sides and measures 2 in. narrower than door width to allow for door stops.

Adding flush paneling

You can turn an old-fashioned paneled door into a modern flush door by covering it on both sides with a sheathing of thin plywood, veneer, hardboard, or plastic laminate.

All of the old hardware can be used, but a longer doorknob spindle may be needed because of the door's added thickness. First remove the knobs from the door and then the lock or latch. Next, remove the door from the jamb by driving out the hinge pins. Take each hinge leaf off the door so that you will have unobstructed access to the surface of the door when you place it on a bench or sawhorses.

All nails and screws and any decorative trim must be removed. Use a scraper or a sander fitted with coarse sandpaper to remove old paint or varnish that is in poor condition; sand the door down to a solid surface to which glue can adhere properly.

Plane down any molding that cannot be removed, watching out for nails. Build up hollow sections with plywood or paneling, and secure the filler with glue and brads. This will provide a suitably even gluing surface for the new sheathing; on large panels it will also prevent buckling.

Instead of glue and clamps, you can use contact cement, which does not require clamping. Apply the cement to the door surface and to the panel. Wait until both surfaces are dry to the touch, then cover the cemented door surface with a large sheet of wrapping paper. Next, position the panel over the paper. Make sure it is exactly where you want it to be. Have someone hold down one end while you lift the other end and tear away part of the paper. Lower the panel so that that end "grabs." Then lift the opposite end, tear away the rest of the paper, and lower the remainder of the panel into place.

If the sheathing selected is to cover the entire surface of the door, cut it slightly larger initially and plane it down later for a precise fit. If the sheathing is to be a raised panel with a small strip of the old door showing around its perimeter, square it off and carefully finish its edges.

White glue can be used for an interior door. For an exterior door, use a waterproof glue such as resorcinol-resin or powdered plastic resin.

As soon as the glue has been applied and the sheathing positioned, place over it a sheet of ¾-inch plywood large enough to cover the sheathing or panel and apply clamps or weights at about 6-inch intervals. Leave them in place overnight or longer.

Work on one side of a door at a time. When you have removed the clamps or weights from the first side, bore the holes for the lock and knobs before gluing and clamping the second side.

When the gluing has been completed, the lock and latch holes have been bored in the second face, and all hardware has been replaced, the newly paneled door is ready to be rehung. If the new sheathing is the raised-panel type, there will be no need to adjust hinges and stops. It is usually necessary to compensate, however, for the extra thickness added by completely flush sheathing by relocating both hinges and stops. If you use a comparatively thin covering material, such as plastic laminate or veneer, you may not have to reset hinges or stops.

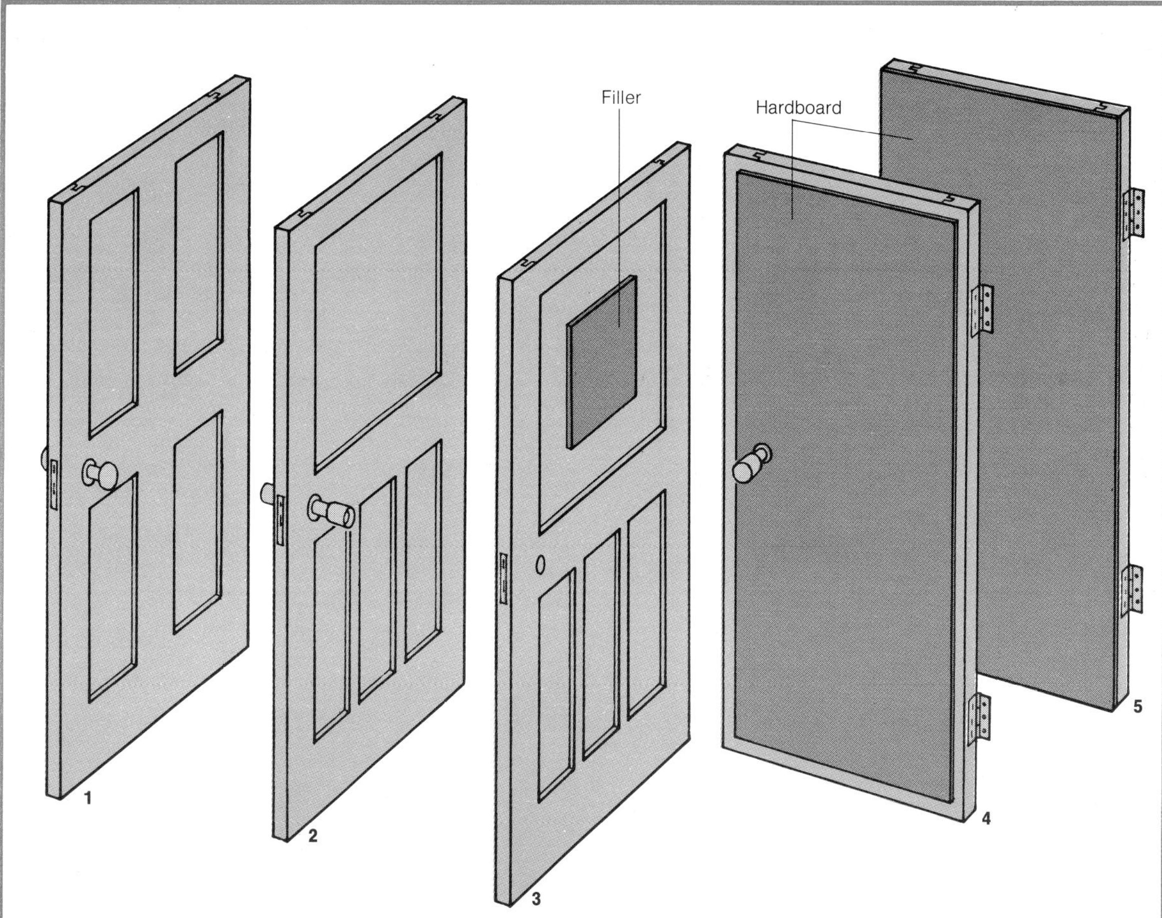

Doors 1 and 2 are suitable types for modernizing by the addition of full or partial flush paneling. No. 3 has filler added. No. 4 has been modernized by partial paneling; the margin around the door permits it to be rehung without resetting hinges or stops. No. 5 has been completely sheathed, which requires resetting hinges and stops and possibly a new lock if the old one cannot accommodate the extra thickness the paneling adds to the door.

Cutting a new doorway

Determine the general position of the proposed opening, then tap the wall or drill ⅛-inch pilot holes to locate studs. (Also check from the basement to be sure that the opening contains no heating ducts or pipes. Electrical wires can be easily relocated.) Try to have one side of the new doorway close to a stud. Location of other stud depends on the size of the door; the opening should be 5 inches wider and 5½ inches higher than the dimensions of the new door.

Cut plaster or gypsum board with a chisel and hammer. Wood laths can be cut with a coarse compass saw, metal laths with tinsnips or a hacksaw. Remove center studs, then sole plate at bottom. Studs may be reused to make the double header.

The opening constructed for the frame should allow enough extra space for adjustments as well as for the hinge and lock blocks (if these are needed).

When the frame has been properly secured by means of wedges, it should be permanently nailed to the studs and header with nails placed ¾ inch in from the edges and spaced 16 inches apart.

The final step is to apply the trim molding. You can then hang the door (p.141), fit in the strike plate, and attach the stop molding.

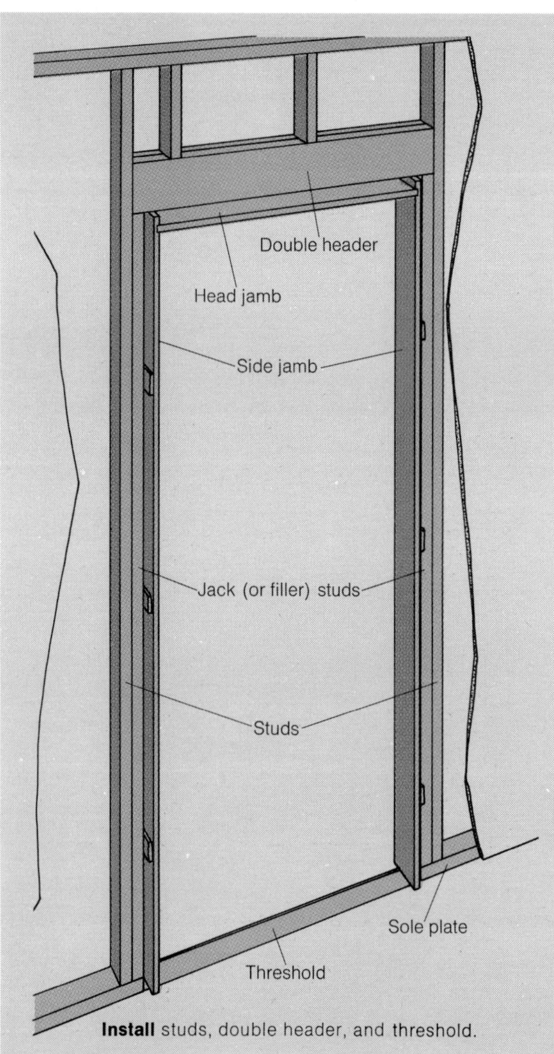

Install studs, double header, and threshold.

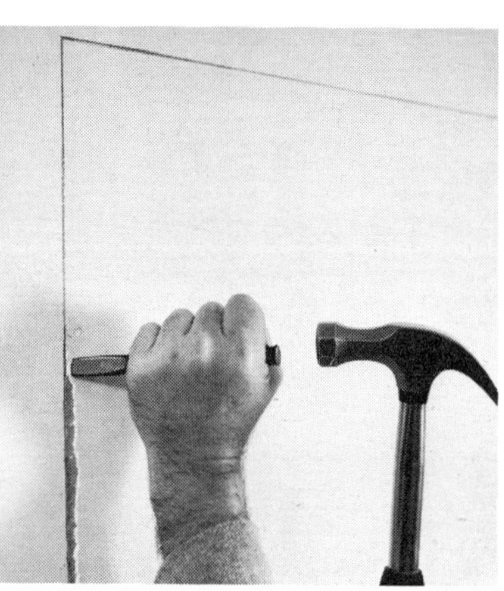

Have one side of door near stud. Outline opening 5 in. wider and 5½ in. higher than door. To expose studs, chip out plaster (and remove lath) or wallboard.

Saw off studs at bottom, then top. Mark studs at top with a square and saw accurately. Cut the lower ends 2 in. above the sole plate to avoid nails.

A header, consisting of two 2 x 4s, is always installed at the top of a doorway. Nail it to the studs, with additional toenailing for extra strength.

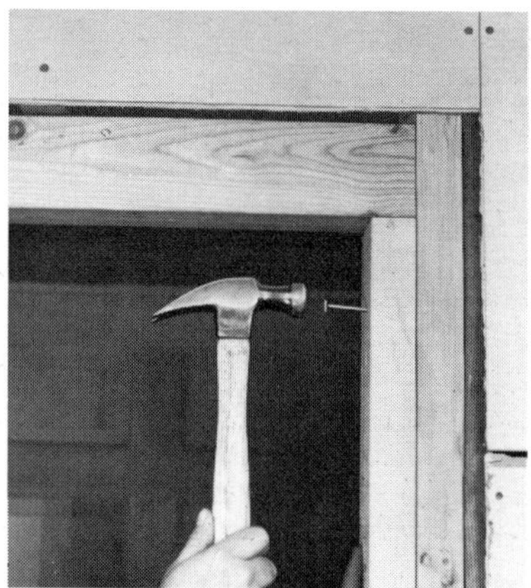

Install an extra stud on each side of the opening. These extra jack, or filler, studs under the header provide additional support and a nailing base.

After installing head and side jambs or preassembled frame, saw off the sole plate and install saddle (threshold). Use wedges to insure proper fit of frame.

Fit blocks (if needed) between jamb and studs for hinges and lock. Use level and adjust frame as needed. Apply casing, hang door, install stops and strike plate.

Closing a doorway

To close up a doorway, it is necessary, first, to remove the door and its hardware. Then pry off the casing, taking care to avoid damaging the adjacent wall. Pry the side jambs loose, starting at the bottom; use a wrecking bar if necessary. Pull the side jambs out at the bottom; this will loosen the head jamb and permit the entire frame to be removed as a unit. Pull out any nails that remain in the studs; if a nail puller won't get them out, cut them off flush. Remove the threshold (p.144). Nail a 2 x 4 at the top of the opening, another at the bottom, one at each side, and one upright in the center. Install wall materials to match existing walls. Use wallboard (p. 93) to close an opening in a plaster wall. Add baseboard and molding. Staple insulation to studs in cavity when closing an exterior doorway.

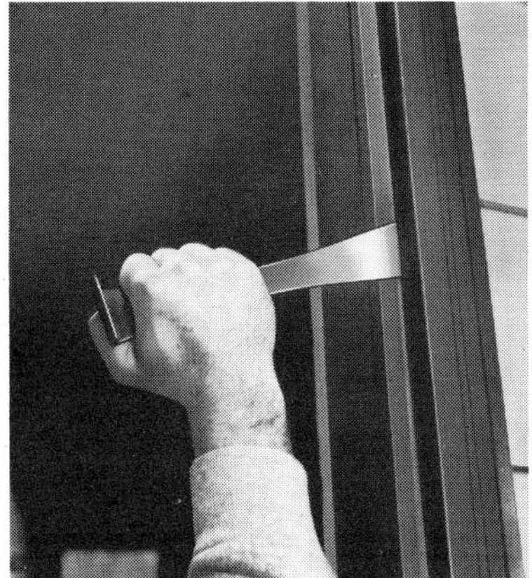

After removing door and its hardware, pry off the casing with a pry bar or a wide flat chisel. Work carefully; try not to damage the casing or the wall.

Pry out side jambs, starting at bottom; use a wrecking bar if necessary. Many nails will remain in the studs; remove with a nail puller or cut them off flush.

After removing nails from side jambs, pull the jambs out from bottom. This will provide enough leverage to free head jamb so that entire frame can be removed.

Remove threshold or saddle. If this is difficult because jambs rest on it, cut it in three parts and remove in sections. Take care to avoid damaging floor.

Nail a 2 x 4 at bottom of opening, at top, at both sides, and upright in the center. Make sure that all 2 x 4s are flush with the existing wall studs.

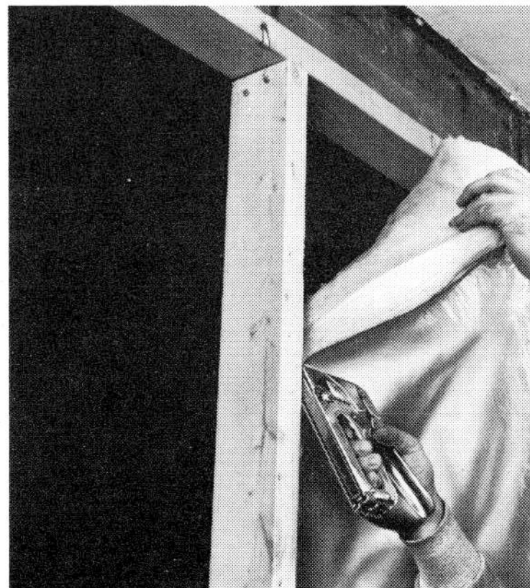

When closing an outside doorway, pack insulation into the cavity and fasten it with staples. Add baseboard and molding and refinish to match existing walls.

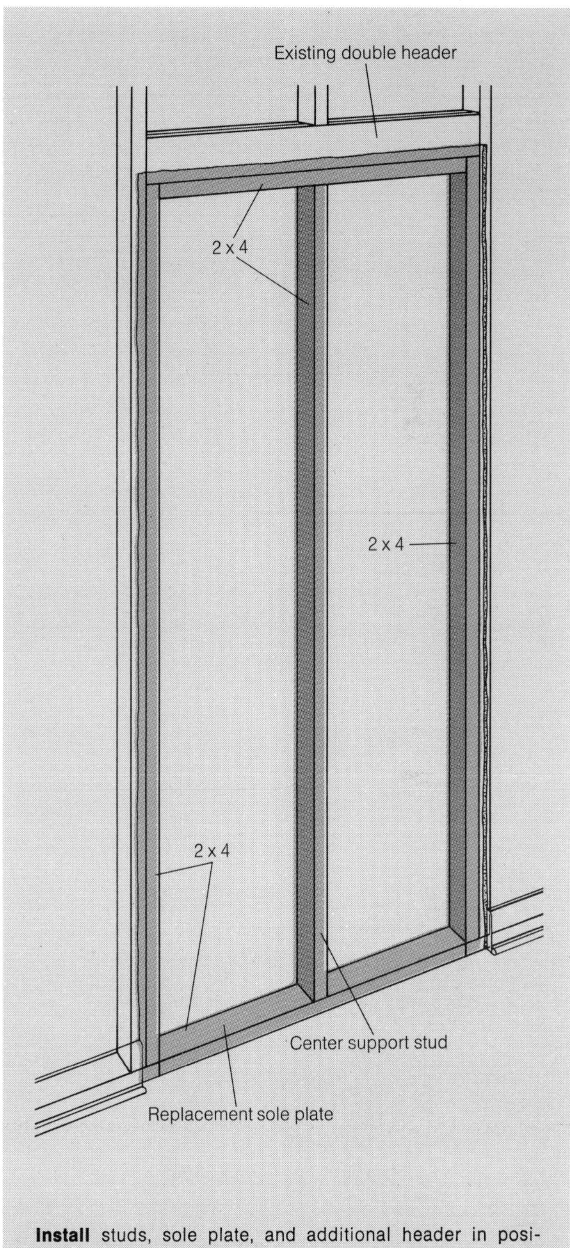

Install studs, sole plate, and additional header in positions shown to close up a doorway.

Basic types

Three basic lock types are in common residential use: Rim locks, mortise locks, and cylindrical locks. Although all three types of locks have key cylinders, the term "cylindrical lock" is used only for the type with the keyway in the knob. Some cylindrical locks, known as tubular locks, do not actually contain key cylinders; they are used on interior doors and are installed the same way as other cylindrical locks.

Mortise locks

Mortise locks are installed in a recess that is cut into the edge of the door; they cannot be installed in a door that is less than 1⅜ inches thick. The "hand" of a door should be specified when ordering a mortise lock (p. 78) even though the latch can be reversed in the lock if necessary.

In addition to the spring-loaded latch, the mortise lock has a dead bolt. When the key is inserted and fully turned, the dead bolt is extended to "double lock" the door. The dead bolt can be retracted and extended from inside the house by turning a knob—the use of a key is not necessary. Mortise locks are also available with a dead bolt that can only be operated with a key from either side.

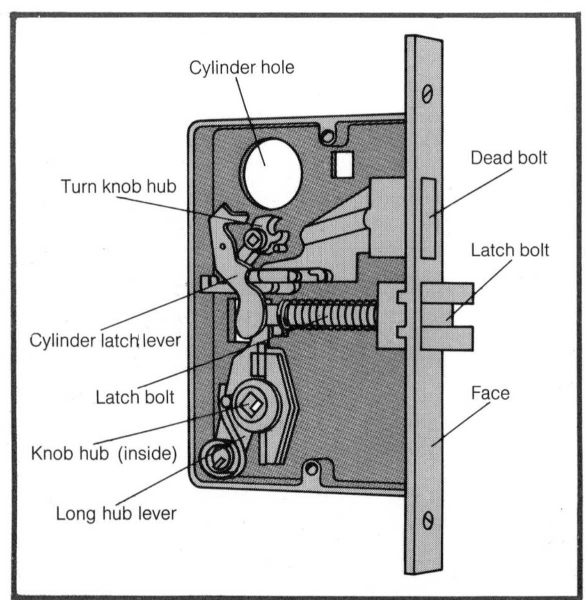

Replacing a mortise lock

An old-style mortise lock can be replaced with a modern cylindrical lock using a lock replacement kit. These replacement locks are available in a wide range of styles and finishes. They can be installed in most residential doors. The kits include templates to aid in installation, and decorative escutcheons, or trim plates, large enough to cover holes and scars left by removal of the old lock.

After removing the knobs and hardware, slide the old lock out of the mortise in edge of door. Use template to find position for cylinder hole. Drill hole with expansive bit or hole saw.

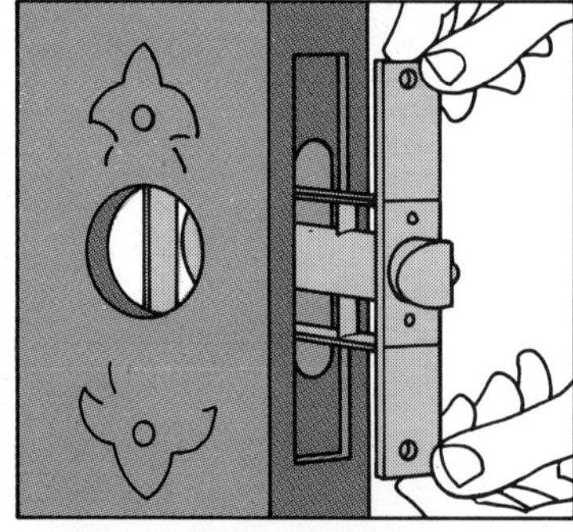

Insert new latch assembly. To ensure a good fit, it may be necessary to enlarge mortise with a chisel or to build up low spots with wood dough. Mount new strike plate in the jamb.

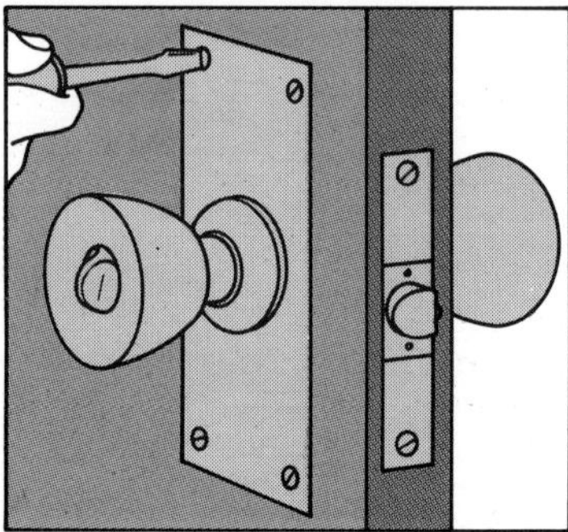

Install decorative escutcheon on door face to cover up any old scars and holes. Slide the cylinder into place. Make certain that the latch mechanism meshes and operates smoothly.

Mortise lock maintenance

To clean a mortise lock, wash it thoroughly in paint thinner or a grease solvent; then lubricate it with powdered graphite, silicone spray, light oil, or light grease. Lubricate the tumbler pins and the keyway in the cylinder by blowing in graphite. Apply graphite to the key. Never use oil in the cylinder; it will gum the tumblers. Lubricate the latch with light oil; wipe off the excess.

Correcting lock faults

PROBLEM	REMEDY
Frozen lock: Key will not enter cylinder	Chip ice from cylinder opening, then partially insert warmed key in cylinder. Remove key and repeat until full penetration is possible. Applying alcohol to key may help. Turn key gradually and carefully to free tumblers if they are also frozen.
Stuck bolt: Key partially turns in cylinder but bolt does not move	Check alignment of door to see if bolt lines up with strike plate. If it does not, realign door if possible. It may be necessary to change location of strike plate or enlarge its opening. If bolt is paint-bound, scrape off all dried paint and lubricate the bolt.
Binding key: Key fits in cylinder but will not turn	Cylinder may have turned slightly in lock face plate so that cam will not throw bolt. Loosen setscrew and turn cylinder back to correct position. If duplicate key is being used, it may be a poor duplication; check against the original. If an attempt has been made to pick the lock, or if a wrong key has been used, the tumblers may be damaged; in either case a replacement cylinder will be needed.
Broken key: Key has broken and part remains in keyway	Loosen setscrew and unscrew cylinder from lock face plate. Hold face down and gently tap to dislodge broken part. If this fails, insert thin, stiff wire through cam to push out broken part or run a thin crochet hook along top of keyway to pull the part out.

Rim locks

Rim locks, also called night locks or night latches, are mounted on the inside face of the door, often as supplements to mortise locks. Some have a spring-loaded latch that locks automatically when door is closed; others have dead bolts.

To install the lock illustrated, mark the location for the key cylinder and drill a hole for it. Secure the mounting plate on the face of the door. Next, fasten the cylinder to the mounting plate with connecting screws cut to match door thickness. Fit the lock case to the mounting plate, making sure the connecting bar enters the locking mechanism. Shorten connecting bar if necessary. Some locks have no mounting plate and are mounted directly on the door surface.

Position the strike plate on the jamb so that the latch bolt will match the strike plate opening. Finish by cutting a mortise for the strike plate and mount the plate on the jamb.

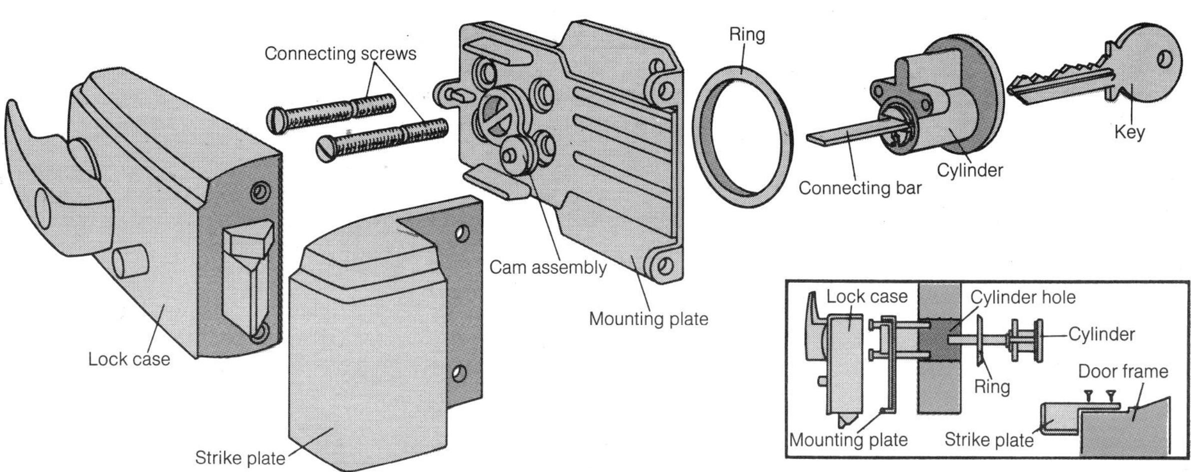

Tubular locks

Tubular locks are used on interior doors. Installation requires only two holes: A large one cut all the way through the door for the spindle and stems; a smaller one in the door edge for the latch bolt.

Some models have a push button in the knob or a small lever or button on the rose on the interior side. This locks the latch bolt so the door cannot be opened from the outside; it can be released by turning the inside knob or by pushing a rod or nail into a hole in the outside knob.

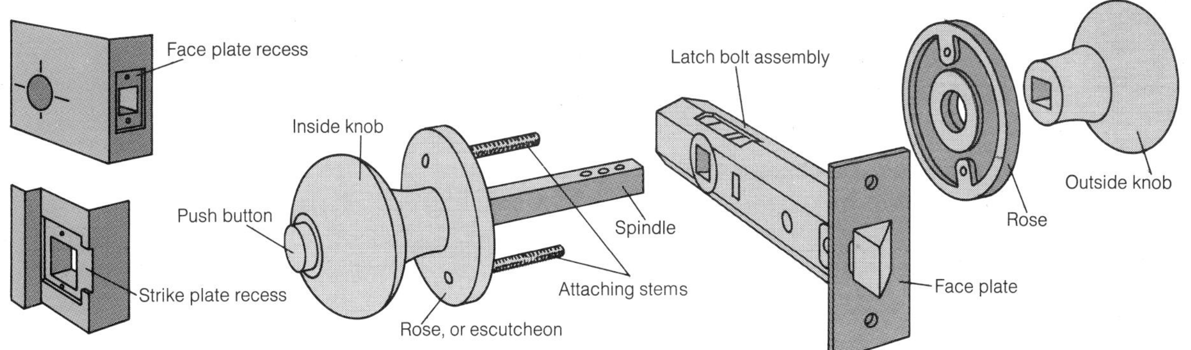

Cylindrical locks

Cylindrical locks are larger and stronger than tubular locks and provide the more substantial security required for exterior doors. These units are locked by means of a key in the outer knob and with a turn knob or push button in the inner knob. When the key is inserted in the keyway in the knob handle, it activates pin tumblers, permitting the cylinder to rotate and the lock to open. The knobs on cylindrical locks have a hollow spindle and are attached by a spring catch; the outside roses are screwed in or attached with screws from the inside to prevent tampering with the lock from the outside.

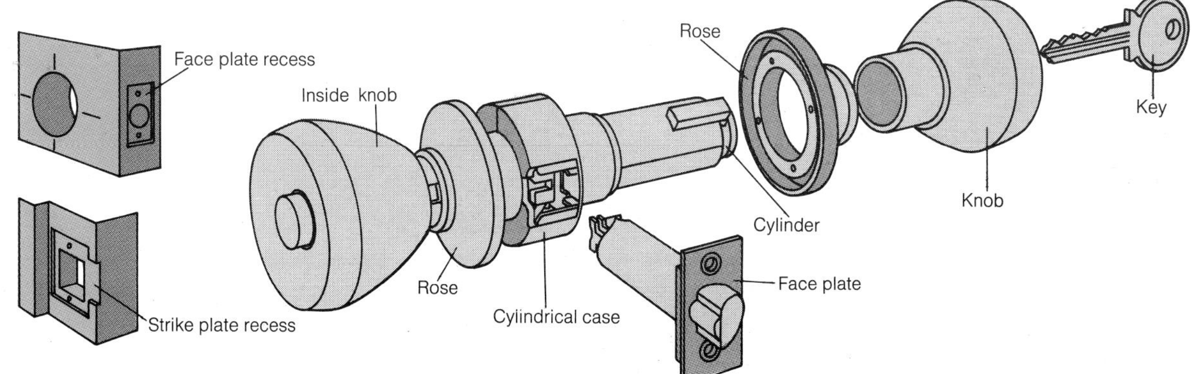

Door locks

Installing a cylindrical lock

Installing a cylindrical or tubular lock is not a complicated job. It does, however, demand close attention to detail and the precise following of the manufacturer's step-by-step instructions that come with each lock set.

Installation requires the drilling of two holes: A large hole through the faces of the door for the cylindrical case or the spindle and stems, and a smaller hole in the edge of the door for the latch bolt. Mortising is necessary only for the latch plate in the door and the strike plate in the jamb.

Cylindrical and tubular locks are usually mounted about 36 inches above floor level.

1. Use template packed with kit to mark center of hole for lock on door face and center of latch bolt hole in edge.

2. Drill 2⅛-in. hole in face with expansive bit or hole saw; stop when tip of bit breaks surface and drill from other side.

3. Drill 15⁄16-in. hole for latch bolt in edge until you reach large hole. Be sure bit is at right angle to door edge.

4. Insert latch bolt; mark latch plate position on door. Remove bolt and chisel out wood until plate is flush with edge.

5. Reinsert latch bolt in small hole in door edge and fasten the latch plate securely to edge with screws provided.

6. Push in latch bolt and insert exterior knob, making sure stems are correctly positioned through the latch holes.

7. Insert interior knob and rose, aligning screw guides and stems. Push flush against door; fasten securely with screws.

8. Locate strike plate with template on jamb. Open door and drill 15⁄16-in. hole ½-in. deep in jamb to take latch bolt.

9. Mark position of strike plate on jamb. Chisel out jamb so that plate fits flush. Insert plate and fasten with screws.

Installing a deadlock

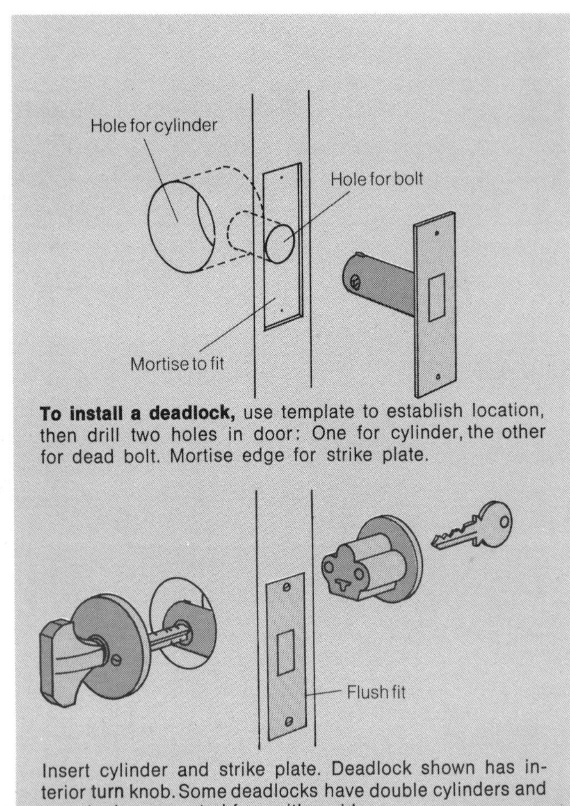

To install a deadlock, use template to establish location, then drill two holes in door: One for cylinder, the other for dead bolt. Mortise edge for strike plate.

Insert cylinder and strike plate. Deadlock shown has interior turn knob. Some deadlocks have double cylinders and must be key-operated from either side.

Installing a replacement mortise lock

Mortise locks, either standard or heavy-duty, offer a wider variety of lock functions than cylindrical locks. For this reason and because they often produce a desired decorative effect, mortise locks are often used to replace cylindrical locks. They come with one or two cylinders that contain up to six tumbler pins. Some have a deadlock of hardened steel for greater security.

When a modern mortise lock is being installed in place of a cylindrical lock, it is often necessary to fill the holes used for the old lock. When these are neatly patched, sanded, and painted, the repair will not be noticeable. For a major repair, covering a cylinder hole, for example, cut a diamond-shaped patch for each door face. Bevel the patch sides and the sides of the cutout areas in the door faces to make sure the patches will fit snugly. Glue the patches into position; clamp until dry. Fill any spaces; when filler is dry, sand smooth. Finally, give the entire door a coat of paint before installing the lock.

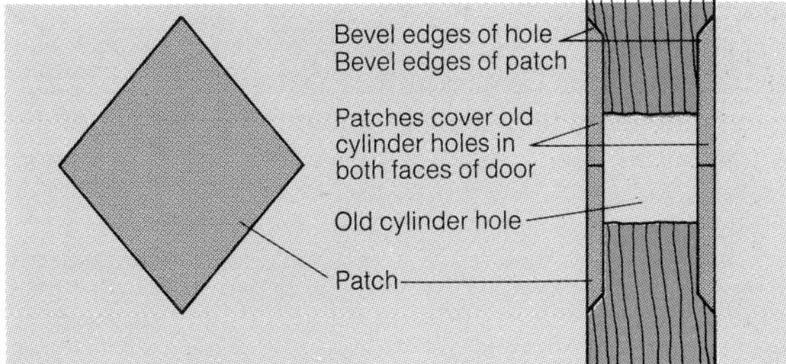

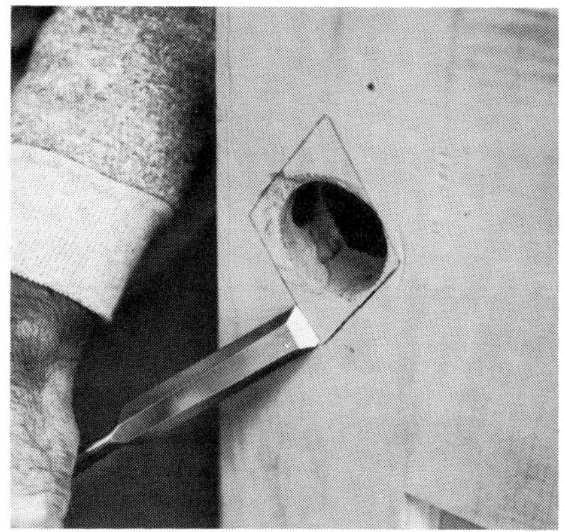

1. Cut two diamond-shaped patches from scrap wood. Bevel edges as shown in diagram above. Pencil an outline of the patches on the door. Chisel recesses.

2. Fit patches so they do not protrude more than 1/32 in. above the door surface. Coat patch edges and the recesses with glue. Fit and clamp for 24 hours.

3. Fill any spaces with wood putty. When it is dry, plane and sand the patched surfaces thoroughly until the juncture of patches and door surfaces is level and absolutely smooth.

4. Use template or the lock body to mark the location of (1) the spindle, 36 in. above floor, and (2) the center of the cylinder hole. Drill both holes as manufacturer specifies.

5. When holes for spindle and cylinder are completed, drill a series of holes 1/16 in. wider than the lock body into the edge of the door to the full depth of the lock.

6. Remove wood between holes in door edge with chisel and insert lock body into recess. Mark outline of face plate on door edge. Remove the lock; cut mortise so lock will fit flush.

7. Replace the lock in its recess and fasten the face plate securely to the door edge. Mount the knob on the interior face of the door and the handle on the exterior face.

8. Mark location of strike plate on door jamb. Make certain it matches position of lock, then mortise for a flush fit. Chisel out holes to receive both latch bolt and dead bolt.

Replacing floor or wall tiles

Ceramic floor tile is so hard that it rarely gets damaged but it does come loose on occasion. Repair is simply a matter of resetting the loosened tile with a waterproof adhesive for tiles that is available at most paint and hardware stores. All of the old cement must always be completely removed before any new adhesive is applied. Brush or vacuum thoroughly.

Loose wall tiles can be reset with the cement that is used for floor tiles. Wall tile failure may be due to a movement of the wall support, to warping of the studs, to shifting of the foundation, or to improper preparation and installation.

Wall tile may sometimes have to be removed and replaced because of crazing (a pattern of hairline cracks over the glazed surface of the tile). Unless the contractor left a few extra tiles behind from the original job, it may take some shopping around to find a replacement that is a perfect match.

1. Remove the defective tile by scoring out the old cement along the joints. Then use a chisel and hammer to break it out.

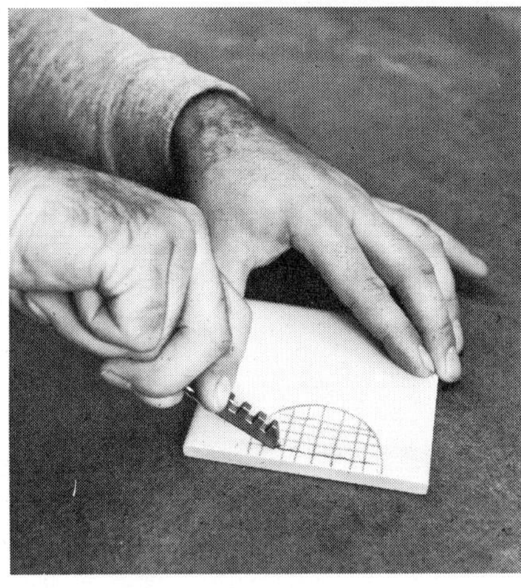

2. If new tile needs special shaping, use glass cutter to score outline of part to be removed, then score crisscross lines over that part.

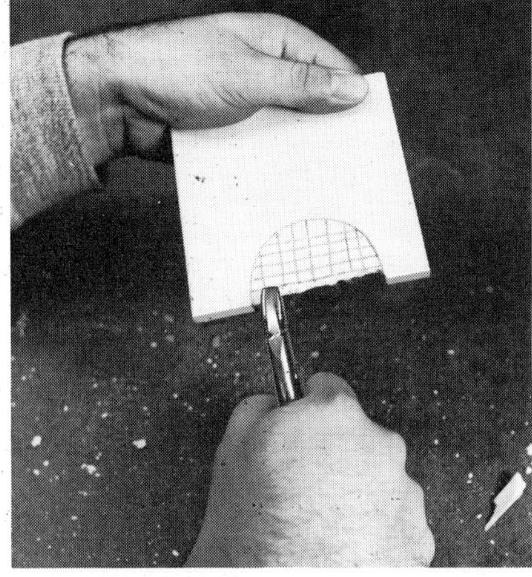

3. Use pliers or end cutting nippers to nibble out scored part of tile, one small piece at a time. Smooth the unglazed edges with a file.

4. Apply the adhesive to the back of the new tile with a putty knife. Keep adhesive ½ in. away from the edges of the tile.

5. Holding the tile by the edges, force it gently into cleaned-out space. Check to see that it fits flush with adjacent tiles.

6. Use grouting cement to fill the spaces between the adjacent tiles. Force the grout into the joints with your fingers.

7. Let the grout set for 15 minutes before removing the excess. If any gaps appear, apply more grout to fill the space.

8. Use a damp cloth or sponge to remove any remaining grout. Paint thinner will remove adhesive that may be left on the tiles.

Recaulking

The inevitable crack that appears between the bathtub and the wall tiles is caused by the tub being filled and emptied several times a week. This constant weight change eventually splits the plaster or grout along the joint. The remedy is to caulk the joint around the entire rim of the tub with a waterproof flexible caulking compound.

Cut the spout of the caulking tube and squeeze out the compound, working as shown.

With a smaller opening, the tube can be used to caulk openings between the tiles above the tub.

Replacing a ceramic soap dish

Soap dishes, and sometimes toothbrush holders, are the ceramic fixtures most frequently in need of repair or replacement. If the fixture is broken, remove it with a chisel and hammer; be very careful not to damage any of the adjoining tiles. Select a replacement dish or holder that will take up the same number of tile spaces as the old one. It may have edges that fit flush with the adjoining tiles, or its edges may overlap them while its base occupies the same tile space as the old fixture. If you cannot get an exact color match, a dish in a contrasting color will do, provided it is harmonious.

Use a chisel and a hammer to break up and remove the damaged soap dish from the bathroom wall. Take extreme care to avoid chipping any of the adjoining tiles. Be sure to remove all the old grout or adhesive from the cavity.

Apply a liberal coating of grout made of white Portland cement and water to the back of the replacement soap dish. Use a putty knife to spread it and be sure to keep the grout ½ in. away from the edges of the soap dish.

Press the dish firmly into the wall cavity. Center a flush-type fixture to make all joints equal. If the fixture is the overlapping type, seat it so that the projecting lips will be plumb and butted flat against the adjoining tiles.

Use masking tape to hold the new fixture immovably in position until the grout has set. If it is an extra-heavy dish, give it additional support by propping it up during the drying period. Fill spaces between joints with grout.

Eliminating dampness

The exterior foundation walls of a basement should be waterproofed when they are built, but this is not always done. Drain tile, at the level of the basement floor, should run parallel to any wall that has the ground sloping toward it. The drain should terminate at a dry well or, better yet, a storm sewer. A poured concrete wall, and especially block-type walls, should be covered with black mastic waterproofing compound, plastic sheeting, and a final coat of the compound. Backfill should be gravel, to obtain rapid and complete drainage, and should fill to within a foot of the surface.

If seepage is caused by porous walls, the best repair is waterproofing from the outside. Try first, however, to correct the fault by applying one of the many waterproofing materials made for masonry walls. They are troweled or brushed on according to label directions. When they enter the pores of the concrete or cinder block, they expand and harden to form a waterproof coating.

If, despite your best efforts to waterproof the wall from the inside, water still leaks through, you have no recourse but to waterproof the offending wall from the outside. There are three possible methods. One is to grade the ground so that it slopes away from the wall (or walls). Or you can dig away the earth from around the wall and install a drain tile system. Third, get an estimate from a commercial waterproofing company. This last approach may prove the least expensive. The professional technique is to seal up all cracks from the inside with a thick epoxy and then pump a special sealing compound into the earth a few inches from the problem walls. This compound flows toward the wall, following the same path that the water took to penetrate the wall. When it meets the wall surface, it solidifies and seals the wall against water penetration.

During warm, humid weather, an entire house may become so saturated with moisture-laden air that enough condensation appears on toilet tanks and cold-water pipes to make them "sweat" and drip water. This is the result of the warm, moist air coming in contact with a cold object in the same way that warm air causes drops of water to appear on the outside of a glass filled with an ice-chilled drink.

Condensation forms in a basement that is cool or cold more readily than in the rest of the house because the temperature difference is greatest between the cool basement air and the warm outside air.

Condensation in a basement can be reduced by sealing the basement with storm windows and keeping doors closed to prevent the warm outside air entering; or, alternatively, by opening all windows and doors to equalize outside and inside temperatures.

Condensation problems may also be solved by covering cold-water pipes with insulation and by the use of a dehumidifier. A dehumidifier in a basement will remove much of the moisture in that area. A good one will collect more than a gallon of water from the air in 24 hours.

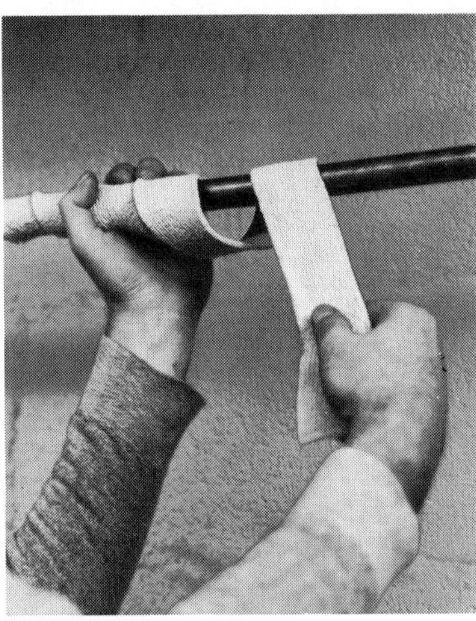

Wrap a layer of fiber-glass insulation around cold-water pipes to stop dripping during humid weather.

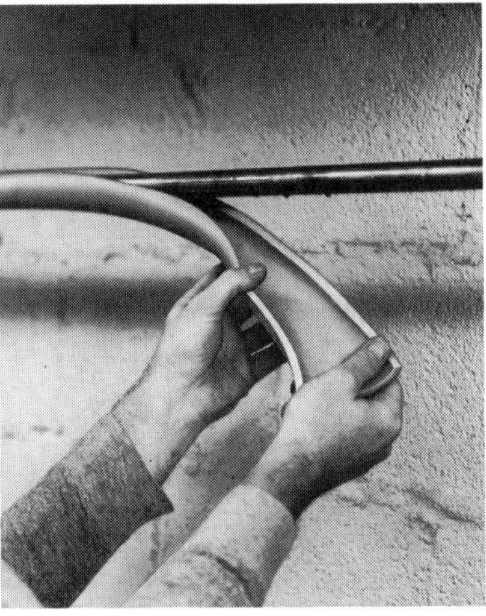

Foam plastic sleeves can also be used; slit them (if they are not already cut) and seal the slits with adhesive tape.

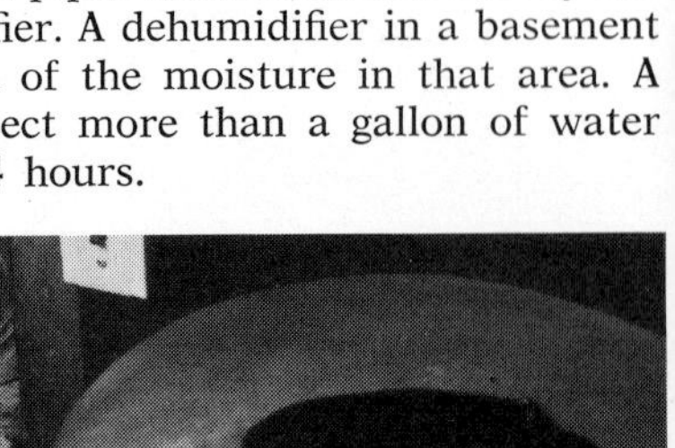

A thick coating of mastic can be used to insulate a tank to stop condensation; apply with a trowel, ¼-inch-thick coat.

Spray basement walls with water before applying cement-base waterproofing material; apply while walls are still damp.

Mix compound according to directions and apply with a stiff brush. Rub well into all crevices and holes in the wall.

A second coat of the compound should be applied within 24 hours. Dampen the wall again before applying the second coat.

How to fix a wall leak

Water may enter a basement through cracks in the wall, in the mortar joints, or in the floor. If a crack continues to enlarge, it should be examined by an expert; major repairs may be needed. A stable crack should be repaired as soon as possible, preferably in a dry season, and before frost can enlarge it.

Any crack over ⅛ inch should be chiseled to a wedge shape, wider at the rear to keep patching material from falling out. Dust and concrete particles should be brushed out and vacuumed.

If the crack can't possibly leak during repair, it may be patched with a stiff mixture of 1 part mortar cement to 3 parts fine, sharp sand. The crack should be wet, but not glistening, and the mortar forced in until it completely fills the cavity. The patch should be kept damp for curing for several days.

A two-part epoxy mix can also be used to repair wall cracks. It costs more than mortar, but works better. Trowel it into place after mixing. Can be smoothed with a moistened finger after half an hour.

Enlarge the crack with a chisel and a light sledge hammer. The crack should be wider at the rear than the front. Clean out debris with a brush and vacuum thoroughly.

Mix the two parts of the epoxy, half and half, until the color is uniform throughout the batch. The mixed epoxy should be applied within a half-hour or less after mixing.

Apply the epoxy with a trowel, forcing it well into the rear of the crack. Epoxy is especially suitable for small areas, but is more expensive than mortar.

After the epoxy has set for at least a half-hour, it can be smoothed out level with the adjacent surface. Wet the trowel with water to prevent sticking.

Plugging a leaking hole

During a wet season or indeed at any other time because of a flooding condition, water may enter a basement through a crack or a hole. The solution is to undercut the hole and then fill it with a quick-setting hydraulic cement. Mix the cement according to the manufacturer's instructions and form it into a carrot-shaped plug. Just as the material starts to stiffen, it should be inserted as you would a cork to stop the flow of water. Hold it in place for several minutes until it hardens.

Use a chisel to undercut the opening of the hole through which water is entering, either as a trickle or under pressure. Clean out cut with a stiff brush.

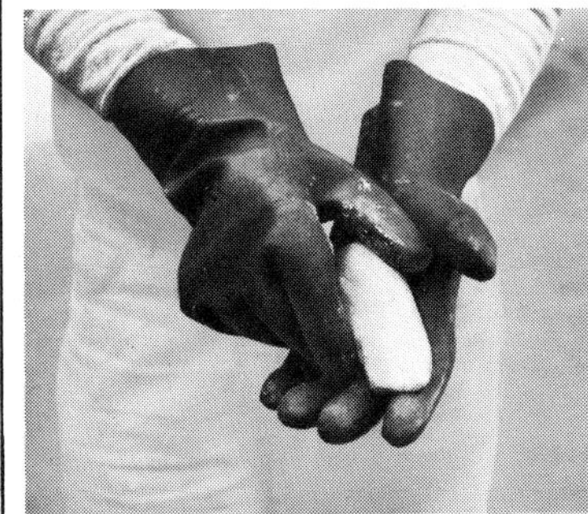

Wearing soft rubber gloves, shape a plug in the form of a carrot and large enough to fill the hole. Prepare the plug according to the directions given for the particular plugging cement used.

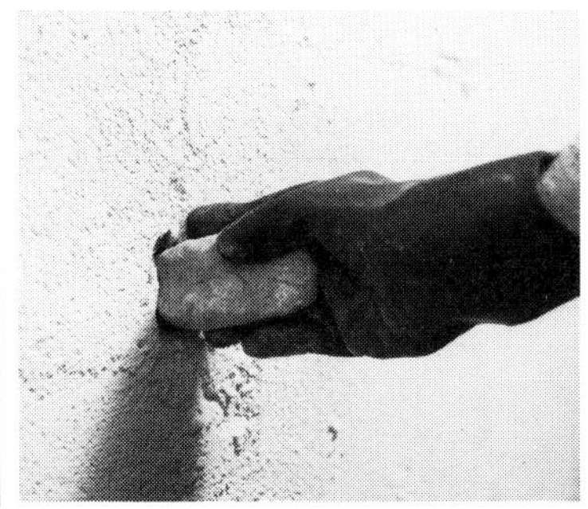

Just as the plug begins to stiffen, press it into the hole; hold it in place with your hand or a trowel until it has set. Smooth the surface with a trowel before it has had time to harden completely.

Watertight seam at wall and floor

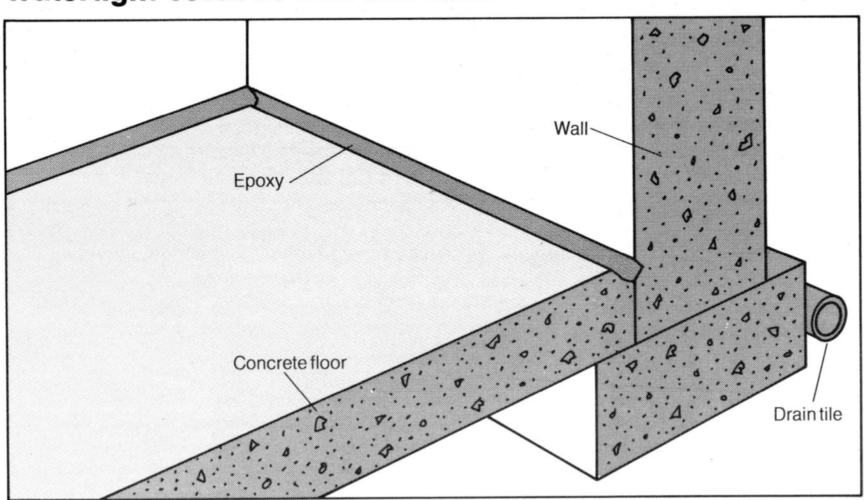

Unless a foundation has been made absolutely watertight, there are times when some water may be forced up through the joint where the floor meets the wall. You can remedy this condition by undercutting the joint surface with a cold chisel, then filling the cavity with a two-part epoxy patching mix to seal the joint. This job should be done during a dry spell.

First, use a chisel to cut out the joint where floor meets wall, making the cavity wider on the inside than the outside. Remove loose material with a stiff brush, then vacuum.

Prepare the epoxy according to directions. Trowel the mixture into the cavity. Smooth with the bowl of a water-moistened spoon to produce a neat seam. Epoxy cures in 24 hours.

Leveling a basement floor

To level a depression in a concrete floor, first roughen the surface with a hammer and a cold chisel. Clean up chips; remove all dust and cement particles with a vacuum cleaner.

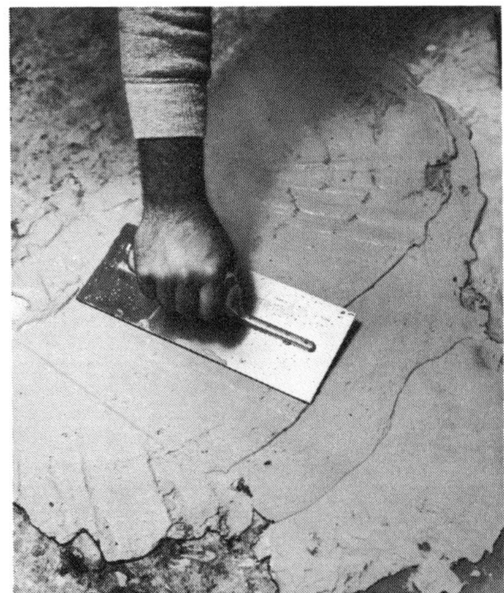

Next, dampen roughened area and fill depression with 1 part mortar cement to 3 parts fine, clean sand and enough water to make a thick paste. (Or use an epoxy if area is small.)

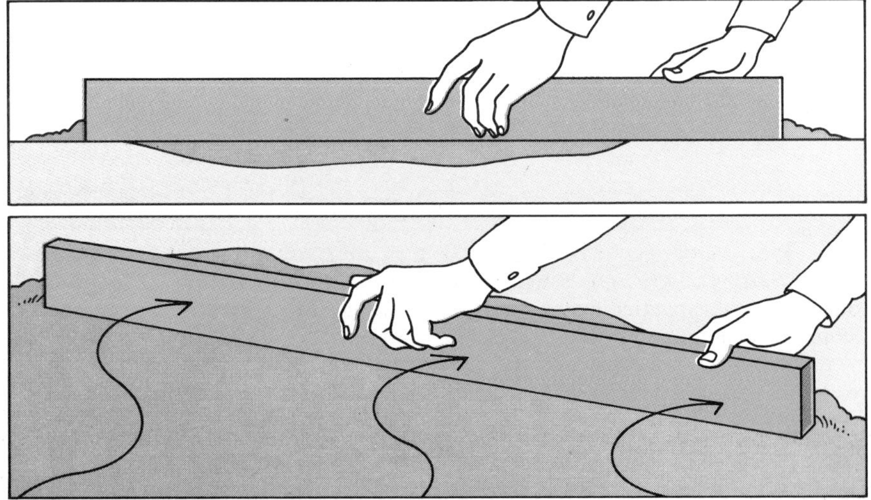

Level the surface with a wooden strip, called a strike-off board or screed. Fill in any low spots and go over area again with screed, using a sawing motion. Do this until the surface is level. Check from two directions. After cement has partially set, finish surface with wood float or steel trowel to the desired smoothness. Keep the patch damp for a week to cure.

Insects

Preventive measures: Be sure screens fit tightly and are undamaged. Do a thorough cleaning job, especially in corners, in cabinets and closets, around water pipes and bathroom fixtures, and under sinks. Store food in tightly sealed containers. Seal garbage and trash in sanitary containers and store them outside to await disposal. Use caulking compound to seal openings, such as where pipes enter the house. Since pests often hide in packages, get rid of cartons as soon as they are emptied. Always wash clothing or have it cleaned before storing.

Elimination: Destroy insects in the house with insecticides, which are available as surface sprays, space sprays, powders, and chemically treated strips. **Surface, or residual, sprays** are applied by spray gun, aerosol bomb, or by brush to surfaces where the insects breed or travel. The liquid in surface sprays leaves a fine film that will kill insects on contact even weeks after application. **Space sprays** dispensed from a spray can or aerosol bomb kill flying insects but have no residual effect. Insecticide **powders** are dusted in breeding or feeding areas.

Safety: Before using any insecticide, carefully read the instructions and precautions on the container's label. Use the insecticide only as directed; failure to do so could cause serious injury. Do not let an insecticide spray get on food or on eating or cooking utensils or surfaces. Be careful not to inhale it or get it on your skin or in your eyes. Wash hands and face thoroughly with soap and water after handling any insecticide. Never use a spray near an open flame, such as a pilot light, or near a furnace; do not smoke when handling a spray. Leave the room as soon as you have used a space spray; keep the room closed and stay out of it for at least half an hour, then ventilate it. Do not hang a chemically treated strip in rooms where people will be present for prolonged periods, particularly infants or sick or old people; do not use it where food is prepared or served. Do not let children touch surfaces where residual sprays have been used. Store insecticides in a cool, dry place out of reach of children and pets—and never near food. Dispose of insecticides in such a way that they cannot contaminate water or wildlife; do not flush them down toilets, sinks, or sewers. If any insecticide should get in your mouth or be swallowed, call a doctor immediately. Follow the antidote instructions on the insecticide label.

INSECT	HABITAT	CONTROL MEASURES
Ant	Lives in colonies; can usually be found by following a single path from food supply to nest.	Form chemical barrier across path to nest; use oil-based residual spray with minimum of 2% chlordane. Baygon, diazinon, and malathion are also effective. Apply around sinks, window sills, baseboards, table legs. If nest is indoors, use residual spray; if outdoors, dust with powder containing 5% chlordane.
Bedbug	Infests mattresses and box springs. Also lays eggs in cracks in floor, furniture, and wallpaper. Sucks human blood. Flat and brown when empty; round, bright red when full.	Use residual spray containing .2% pyrethrum or 1% malathion. Spray in all possible hiding places, especially around tufts and in crevices in mattresses, then leave bed unmade for 2 hours. For badly infested house, call in professional exterminator.
Carpet beetle Clothes moth	Both moth and beetle lay eggs and hatch larvae in rugs, furs, and wool clothing, which they eat. Carpet beetle is the more active.	Apply nonstaining residual spray along edges of carpets, behind radiators, and in clothes closets; remove clothing from closets so that interiors can be thoroughly sprayed. Store moth-free clothing in sealed containers with paradichlorobenzene moth crystals. Clean rugs, upholstery, and slipcovers frequently. Dispose immediately of vacuum cleaner sweepings from infested rugs, bedding, and upholstered furniture.
Cockroach	Hides in any dark place. Brown in color, ½ to 1 in. long. Nocturnal, hides by day. Eats glue, starch, food, garbage.	Use residual spray wherever roaches might hide. Most will develop resistance to chlordane. If insecticide used is not effective, switch to .5% oil solution or water emulsion of diazinon.
Housefly	Breeds in food, decaying organic matter, garbage, and filth. Spreads germs of many diseases harmful to man and beast.	Use screens on all windows and doors. Kill flies in house with space spray or fumes from chemically treated strip. Seal garbage in sanitary containers outdoors; spray interior of containers with residual spray. Keep yard free of garbage and manure.
Mosquito	Grows from larvae found in stagnant water. Feeds on animal and human blood. Some types transmit disease, notably malaria.	Indoors, use space spray in closed room; keep room free of people and animals for half an hour. Outdoors, drain all stagnant water or cover with thin layer of oil. To avoid bites, use insect repellent on skin.
Silverfish	Lives in cool places. Eats starch, protein, sugar, and materials that have been sized. Active after dark.	Use residual spray containing chlordane or malathion. After spraying, dust or blow pyrethrum powder into infested places.
Spider	Not a true insect. Except for black widow, most found in U.S.A. are harmless, even beneficial. Spins webs in crevices and corners.	Use a space spray on those you can see. Then destroy all webs and use a residual spray in protected crevices and corners. Cleanliness and order deny them hiding places; do not store junk indoors or outdoors.

Termites

More than 40 species of termites can be found in the United States and Canada; the most destructive is the subterranean termite. These voracious insects are often called white ants—erroneously, because their appearance is actually very different from that of the ant. The body of the termite is comparatively straight and of approximately equal thickness throughout its length, while the ant has a narrow-waisted body that is shaped like an hourglass. The winged termite has wings of the same length; the hind wings of an ant are shorter than its forewings.

Termites live off of cellulose, which they get from dead trees, rotting plant material in the soil, and wooden objects such as fence posts, house timbers, and furniture. In colder climates the subterranean termite will stay below the frost line and can live for as long as 10 months without a taste of the cellulose found in wood; in areas where there is no frost it can eat the year round. Although this species is especially fond of softwoods such as pine, it will just as eagerly attack any type of wood.

The destruction wrought by termites is hidden from view and may take place slowly over a long period of time, but it can be devastatingly thorough and a wise homeowner takes precautions against it. Termites do their destructive work in large numbers; as many as 4000 have been found in a single cubic foot of wood. They eat only the interior sections of a timber or piece of furniture, leaving just a hollow shell. And no opening ever shows on the surface.

The subterranean termite requires moisture to survive. It lives in social colonies wherever it finds a source of wood in the soil. The colonies are composed of three groups: Reproductive termites, soldier termites, and worker termites.

The reproductive termites are dark in color and have wings, which they shed after they leave the nest to mate and form a new colony.

The soldiers are wingless and blind and have especially strong jaws. Their function is to defend the colony, principally against ants.

The workers are the ones that do the damage. They are wingless, blind, and white. Their job is to provide food for the colony. Since workers cannot endure exposure to light and open air, they will build tunnels from the ground up to wood, if this is necessary to reach a new source of food.

Where to look for termites

Houses in areas that are subject to termite infestation should be inspected twice a year. Use the checklist below as a guide when examining your premises for termites, or hire a competent, reliable exterminator to conduct the inspection for you.

1. During the termite mating season in spring or early summer, be alert for large numbers of flying insects. These could be reproductive termites as they emerge from their nest to form a new colony.

2. Also watch, during the spring and early summer, for the discarded wings of reproductive termites. These wings are whitish and opaque, and their presence in significant numbers probably indicates that a new termite colony has been established somewhere nearby. Look for the wings in basements and crawl spaces, and near the house foundation.

3. Be especially on the lookout for the earthen shelter tubes, or tunnels, that connect the termite colony in the moist soil with the wood that the worker termites convert into food for themselves and the colony. These tunnels are ¼ to ½ inch wide and are half-round in shape. They may be found on masonry foundation walls, basement walls, piers, even on the surface of metal pipes. Indeed, there have been some instances of tunnels having been built straight up from the ground without support to reach the wood over a crawl space.

Check for tunnels around the openings where pipes enter a foundation wall or the wall of a house; while you're checking, examine the pipes as well. Use caulking compound to seal the openings.

4. Check foundation walls on the inside of the house as well as on the outside. Be alert for cracks or loose mortar and pay particular attention to the joint where the floor meets the wall. Take a close look at the joint where any slab, such as a garage, patio, or porch floor, touches the wall.

5. Inspect wood trellises and fences that touch the house or are near it. Do not overlook boxes or piles of stored lumber or firewood. Check any lumber or wood structure that is near the ground.

6. Check basement or cellar window sills.

7. Inspect window sills, thresholds, wood stairs and their stringers. Be on the lookout for paint that has blistered or peeled on any wood structure that is close to the ground.

8. Look into crawl spaces and any interior area that has a dirt floor. Remove any scrap lumber that you find in crawl spaces.

9. Use a sharp-pointed instrument, such as an ice pick, penknife, or awl, to probe any wood you suspect of being infested. When the instrument, with just hand pressure, penetrates to a depth of ½ inch or more, this is a strong indication of deterioration caused by termites or dry rot.

10. During any new construction, make certain that no scrap lumber or other debris is buried anywhere near the house.

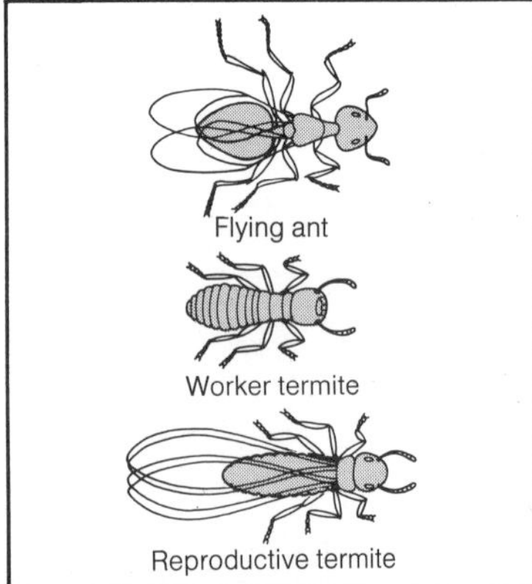

Reproductive termite has straight body, equal-length wings. Ant is narrow-waisted, has hind wings shorter than forewings.

Worker termites build half-round tunnels from moist earth to wood supply. Width is ¼ to ½ in.; length may be several feet.

If a sharp-pointed tool penetrates to a depth of ½ in. under hand pressure, wood has probably suffered termite damage.

How to control termites

The most effective total extermination method is poisoning the soil under the infested building and the entire wall surface of the masonry foundation as well. The chemical commonly used for this purpose is chlordane. It must be used with extreme caution because it can be poisonous to humans and to animals. The chlordane comes in concentrated form and the concentrate is diluted with water to produce a solution of the correct strength as specified by the directions that accompany the concentrated product.

The diluted chlordane can be poured from a watering can, with the sprinkler head removed, into a shallow trench dug close to the foundation and all the way around the building. Chlordane should also be applied indoors, near the foundation wall of all crawl spaces and other areas having a soil floor, and into any visible cracks at the point where a concrete floor joins a foundation wall. Since the chlordane is toxic, it is advisable to ventilate the room when using it indoors. Then vacate the room and do not use it or allow pets into it for several days after the chemical treatment.

Chlordane can be relied on to be effective. Some of the termites that cross the chemical barrier will die; those that do not will carry the poison back to the colony, where it will kill the insects.

Note: Dry wood termites occur in the southwestern U.S. One way to exterminate them is with a nonpoisonous chemical, fluoridated silica aerogel. This chemical is a very fine white dust that absorbs the wax coating on the dry wood termite's shell. This causes the body fluids to evaporate, and the insect dies. The dust is blown into the attic, between the walls, and on the underside of the house.

Siding
Joist
Sill
Termite shield
Foundation

The best method of control is to deny termites access to the wood parts of a structure by installing copper termite shields during construction. Shields should extend 3 or 4 in. beyond each side of the masonry and be anchored to the top of the foundation every 3 ft.

To treat the soil chemically to eliminate termites, first dig a trench 6 in. wide and 2 ft. deep all the way around foundation.

Pour part of the diluted chlordane solution into the trench; mix the rest with the soil as you refill the trench.

Wet rot and dry rot

Wet rot is fungus that attacks timbers subject to saturation—the bottoms of posts set in soil, for example, or timbers in wet cellars. It can spread rapidly to wet timbers nearby. The affected timber looks charred, with splits along the grain or dark, veinlike strands. It is spongy when wet; painted timbers show splits and flaking of paint in the early stages. The cure is to eliminate the moisture source and improve ventilation; for minor outbreaks, thoroughly dry the area. Replace timbers with wood treated with pentachlorophenol or zinc napthenate.

Wet rot splits wood along and across the grain.

Dry rot is a microscopic fungus spread by spores that are airborne or carried on shoes or clothing. They settle on timber and, in suitable conditions of dampness, warmth, and poor ventilation, germinate rapidly, causing deterioration of the timber. Dry rot appears as thin white strands that develop into woollike sheets; from these, tendrils spread, seeking more timber to provide moisture and nourishment for the fungus.

Inspect regularly for dry rot. Check roof timbers, under staircases, in cellars, and under suspended ground floors. The test for dry rot is the same as that for termites. Wood that is spongy and shows a multitude of tiny open cells should be removed and replaced. Use timbers treated with a preservative containing pentachlorophenol or zinc naphthenate.

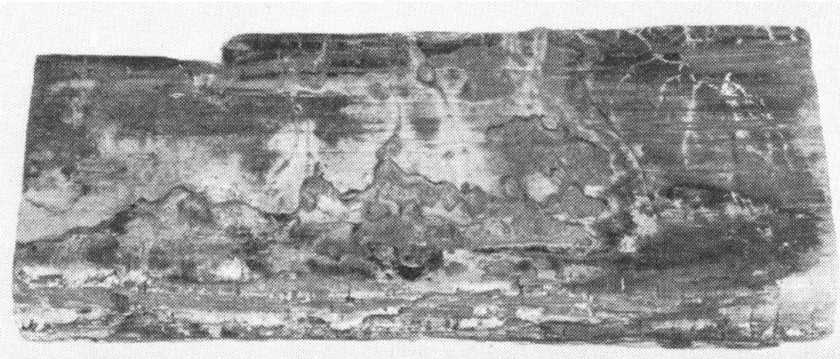

Dry rot, spread by spores, turns wood to powder.

Household pests

Animals

Though not all the animals described below are rodents, most of them damage property as rodents do —by gnawing. Many are capable of causing considerable damage to the inside of a house or to outbuildings.

Of the four chief methods of control, three are appropriate to all the pests mentioned; the fourth applies only to those that enter the home:

1. Destruction of the animal itself. In most cases, poison is the most efficient means. Traps can be effective, but results are unpredictable.

2. Elimination of the shelter or nesting place. In addition, you should remove materials that could be used to construct a new shelter.

3. Cutting off food supplies. Eventually the pests will be forced to leave in search of food.

4. Seal up or screen all possible places of entry. Do not overlook the chimney, drains, and kitchen vents.

ANIMAL	CHARACTERISTICS	CONTROL MEASURES
Bat	Bats are destroyers of insects and therefore beneficial to man. However, if they find a means of entry and exit in a house, they are capable of creating extreme disorder. Bats may be rabid, and a bite from one should never be ignored. Though active at night, they may be seen indoors during the daytime, generally at rest.	Use naphthalene flakes as a repellent to keep bats from entering or to force them out. A bat that is indoors may be drawn outside by turning on a porch light or automobile headlights while keeping the house in darkness and a door, window, or other suitable exit wide open. If the bat was in the attic, the point of entry should be sealed or screened.
Chipmunk	A small reddish-brown animal with dark and light stripes on face and sides, the chipmunk prefers to live underground and hibernates during cold winters. Each pair of chipmunks produces from three to five offspring annually. A chipmunk is a rodent of the squirrel family.	Use a live animal trap baited with rolled oats, corn, or dry peanuts to catch chipmunks (sometimes called ground squirrels); release chipmunk in woods. Be sure that points of entry are closed. Chipmunks are repelled by moth balls or crystals.
Mole	The mole is a blind animal about the size of a rat; it has an excellent sense of smell. Though moles never enter a house, they can ruin a lawn or garden. They live underground and dig tunnels several inches below the surface in search of food.	Although difficult to trap, moles can be caught by the use of a special trap. A better method is to drive them away by killing off the worms they live on. This is done by poisoning the soil with a dilute solution of chlordane. Apply every two years.
Mouse	Mice are found wherever man makes his home. They usually build their nests between walls or in holes. Mice breed at any time of year, mating when the female is only 40 days old. There are from four to seven or more mice in a litter.	Mice can be controlled to some extent by the use of traps. Bait traps with oatmeal, peanut butter, bacon, or cheese. Use poison only out of reach of children or pets and use the type that kills after forcing mouse to leave premises to seek water.
Rabbit	Rabbits will seldom if ever enter a house, but they can cause a considerable amount of damage outside by eating vegetables and flowers. Rabbits damage and kill trees by eating the bark.	A rabbit can be driven off, shot, trapped, or poisoned. It may be discouraged by spraying an animal repellent near where the damage occurred, or caught in a live animal trap baited with carrots or apples; release rabbit in woods. Protect tree trunks on your property with a fence of hardware cloth about 1 ft. high.
Rat	Rats enter dwellings in search of food and water and will gnaw through wood to reach food. They also bite people. Never place poisoned bait, or dead rodents that have been poisoned, in garbage that might become food for other animals.	Large traps are useful, but bait them only after hands have been thoroughly washed; rats are very wary of human scents. Poisons work better. Use warfarin, ANTU (alpha-naphthylthiourea), or red squill, all relatively harmless to humans. Close all entry points.
Squirrel	Squirrels usually live in holes in trees or in bulky leaf nests, but they will enter an attic or an unoccupied house in search of food. They are destructive, and will tear draperies and furniture in an effort to escape. A chimney is usually the point of entry, but check other openings that could allow access into the house.	Bait a live animal trap with shelled walnuts, dry peanuts, or similar food; release trapped squirrel in woods. To drive squirrels out of a building, scatter moth balls or crystals in areas they occupy. Close all points of entry after making sure no squirrels are still in the house.

section 5:

Major and minor exterior repairs

Though a house means many things to a family, its basic purpose is shelter. If your house is to be the haven you expect, you must remember that it is vulnerable—to weather, to wear, to the passage of time. And you must pay constructive attention to its weak points. This section helps in two ways: It points out potential trouble spots and explains how to solve any problems you find. After covering the house from roof to basement, it deals step by step with other outside repairs—to fences and gates, to garages and driveways.

contents

Exterior maintenance

Inspection checklist

Exterior maintenance can best be described as preventive care with the primary purpose of keeping a house weatherproof. The sensible way to assure adequate weatherproofing is not to attend haphazardly to each bit of trouble as it develops, but to conduct a regular campaign of maintenance as outlined below. If you follow the checklist faithfully, making necessary repairs at vulnerable points, you can rest assured that your house is snug in any kind of weather.

1. Roof: Apply roof tar cement to loose shingles; replace missing or damaged shingles (p.166).

2. Flashing: Examine for looseness between chimney, roof, and flashing. Seal with caulking compound or roof cement (p.175).

3. Gutters: Remove accumulated debris; check for proper pitch and renail if necessary; check for leaks at seams (p.170).

4. Downspouts: Clean leaf strainer, if one is used; check for loose joints (p.170).

5. Louvers: Should be open for ventilation but screened to keep out insects. Remove leaves; check caulking (p.182).

6. Roof line: Check for separation and loose flashing (p.175).

7. Siding: Renail loose siding; replace rotted areas; paint siding if required; check for carpenter ants and wasps' nests (p.181).

8. Rain diverter: Make sure that it is set in the proper position. It is best to drain the downspout into a dry well (p.173).

9. Garage door: Lubricate hinges and hardware; check for loose putty in windows; paint the door if necessary (p.189).

10. Driveway: Chip out and fill cracks, or seal if blacktop; add gravel if needed; align curbing (p.194).

11. Foundations: Check flashing and termite shield. Look for termite tunnels (p.160).

12. Windows: Remove loose putty, apply new putty and paint; lubricate casement operators (p.123).

13. Doors: Tighten loose hinges; rehang doors if necessary; check condition of weatherstripping; apply graphite to the lock (p.139).

14. Caulking: Remove crumbling caulking; clean, and apply new caulking where doors and windows meet siding or brick (p.182).

15. Chimney: Replace loose mortar; check for birds' nests; check condition of draft deflector; cover the chimney if it is not used (p.174).

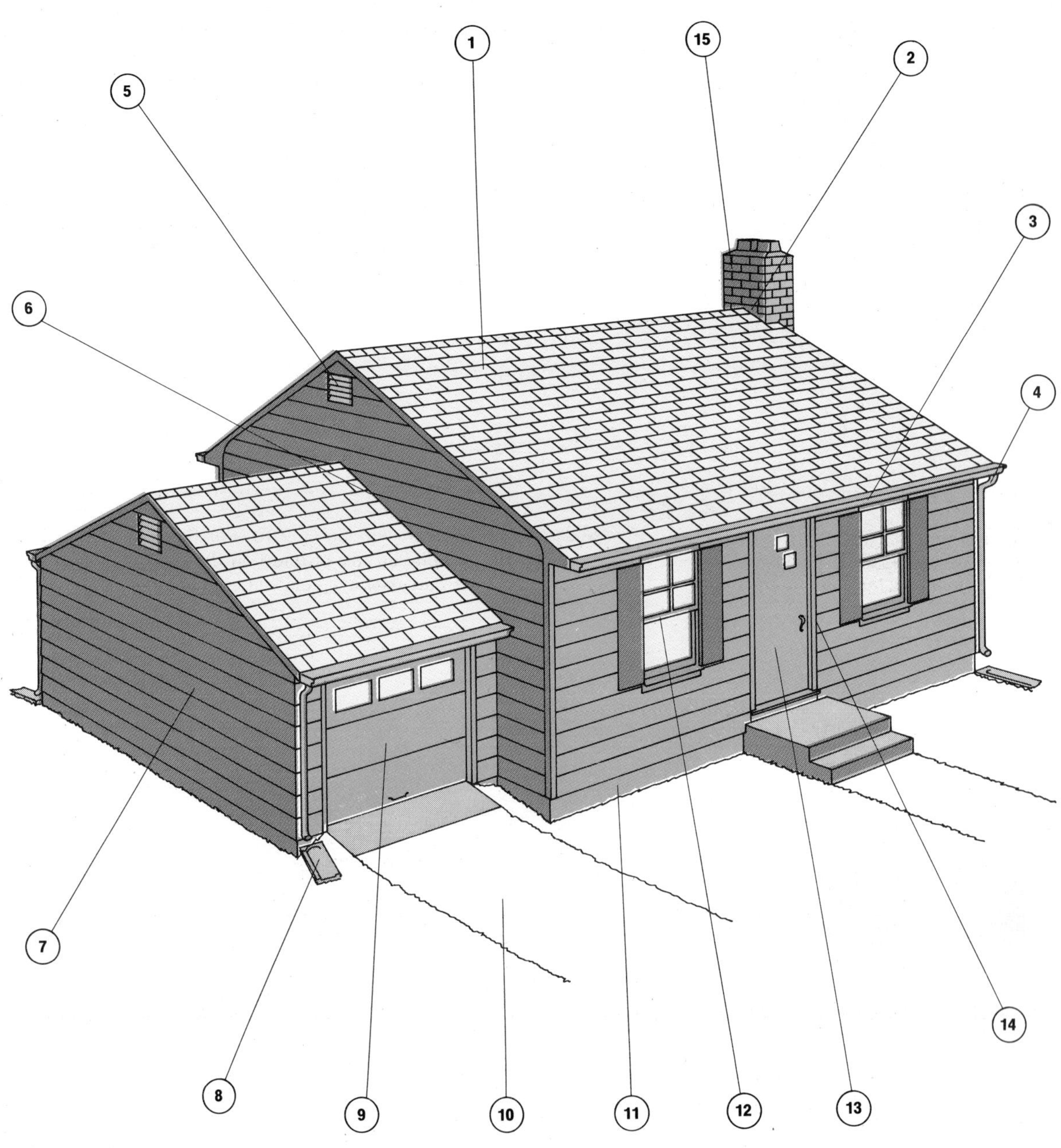

Using an extension ladder

Before using ladder, check it for loose rungs and cracked side rails. Place it in area where it is to be used, then pull the rope to raise it to desired height.

Set the bottom one-quarter of ladder's length from base of house. Make sure it is resting on a firm support.

Keep hips between rails when reaching out. Keep one hand on the ladder, the other free for work. Ladder should be at least 2 feet longer than the highest point you are working on.

Locating leaks

Locating a leak in a roof can be a frustrating experience because quite often the leak in the roof is not directly over the wet spot on the ceiling. If the cause of the leak is defective flashing around a chimney or along a roof extension, the leak will show up close to where the chimney passes near the wall or near the roof line.

If the house has an open attic that allows you easy access to the underside of the roof, the task of locating the leak is much easier. During a storm, just climb into the attic and look at the underside of the roof directly above the wet spot on the ceiling. You may find that the roof is dry at that point. If it is, keep looking (use a strong light) toward the high side of the roof. Chances are that it will be possible to see water leaking through the roof, following a path along the rafters or roof boards and then dropping to the attic floor boards.

After you have located the leak from the inside, circle the hole with a crayon. The purpose of the circle is to lead you to the leak when the storm subsides. Drive nails or push wire through this spot so that you will be able to tell the leak's exact location when you are outside on the roof.

You can make a very temporary repair by applying a sealer of caulking compound to the hole, working it well into and around the area. This will keep water from leaking into the house until the storm stops, and you can make a more permanent repair.

If the inside of the roof has insulation between the rafters, remove batt after batt until you find the leak. Examine the insulation carefully as you pull the batts out. If it is damp or discolored, you know the leak is nearby.

Of course, if the attic is finished with a ceiling, it will be impossible to make a visual inspection of the underside of the roof. In such cases it is necessary to do some careful measuring and transpose the measurements to the outside of the roof. For example, count the number of joists or rafters from the wet spot to the chimney, the end of the house, or some such well-defined area. Multiply this number by 16 inches, divide by 12, and this will give you the number of feet that must be measured off to get to the leak area. Quite likely the problem will turn out to be a cracked or missing shingle. Other possible sources of leaks are a poorly fitting skylight and the area around the sewer vent pipe or chimney. Complete information about solving roof problems is given on the next few pages.

When climbing on a roof, wear soft-soled shoes to prevent slipping. Besides being slippery, hard soles can damage shingles. Make sure your ladder is well secured. A roof ladder arrangement of the kind shown below is a good safety device. The safest arrangement of all is to have a friend hold the ladder while you climb. A safety precaution you should always observe: Stay off the roof in bad weather.

On steep roof, ladder should be anchored in place with framework as shown.

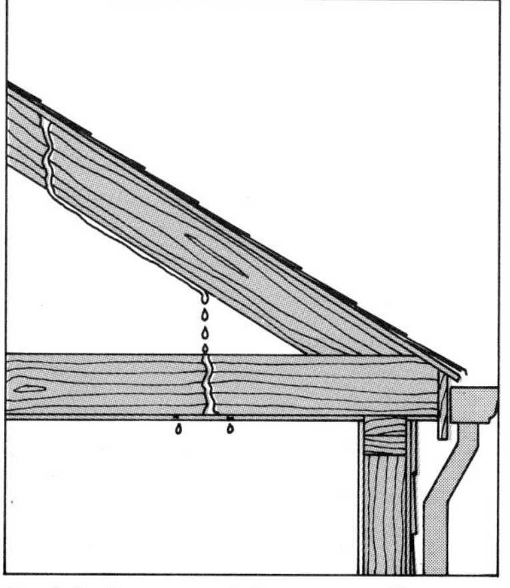

Roof leak may not be over ceiling wet spot. Examine rafters for water path.

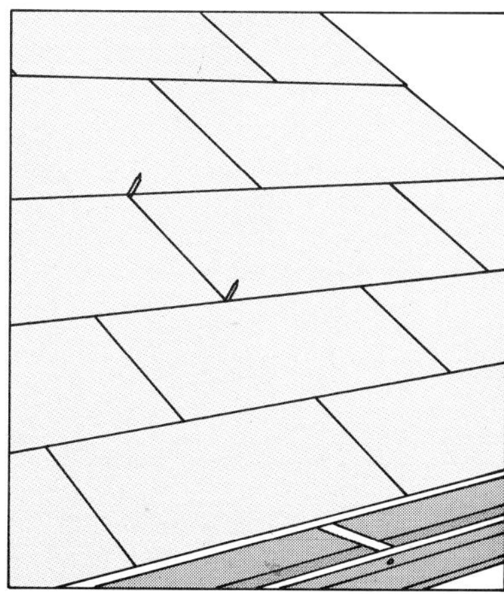

After finding roof leak, drive nails from inside of roof to show location.

Asphalt shingles

Repair and replacement

With a little care, damaged and missing shingles can be replaced without reroofing. Shingles are applied from the lower edge of the roof surface to the top in an overlapping pattern; you will have to lift the good shingles above the damaged ones to slip the new shingles underneath and maintain the pattern.

Safety: Never work on the roof in wet or windy weather. Wear soft-soled shoes. Make sure the ladder is secure. On a steep roof, use the auxiliary ladder arrangement shown on page 165. While on the roof, walk in a crouch and have supplies close at hand.

Repair: Shingles lifted by a storm can usually be repaired. Try to do this on a warm day when shingles are pliable. Stiff shingles tend to crack. To repair minor splits and lifted shingles you need roof cement, a trowel, roofing nails, and a hammer.

Replacement: The first step is to raise the shingles above the damaged one. Take care not to crack the good shingles. Remove the nails with a pry bar or chisel.

Slip the new shingle in place under the raised shingles. If the shingle sticks, cutting off the corners may help. Be careful not to tear the roofing paper.

Holding up the shingles above, nail down the new shingle. Use special roofing nails with broad heads. Apply a dab of roof cement to the nailheads.

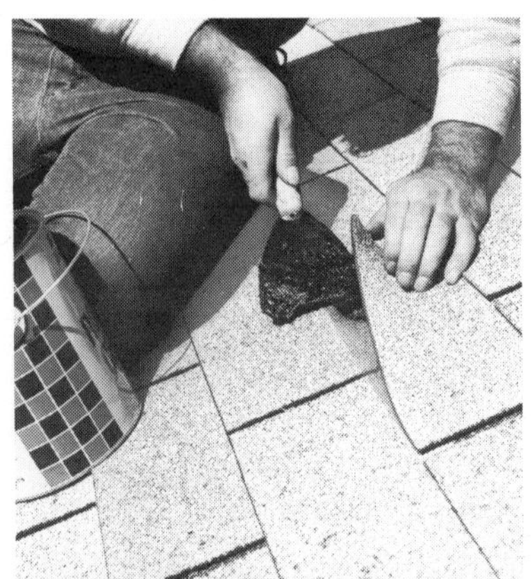

Repairs: Partially lifted or curled shingles can be repaired with a dab of roof cement under the lifted area. Best done in warm weather to prevent cracking.

To salvage badly torn or damaged shingles, apply roof cement liberally to the underside. Press cemented shingle down; nail edges; cover nailheads with cement.

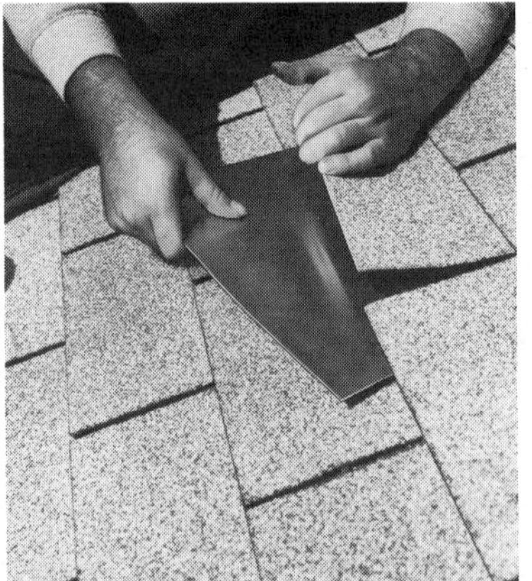

Use sheet aluminum or copper to make a repair if you haven't a spare shingle on hand. Coat bottom with roof cement; push as far as you can under damaged shingle.

Hip shingles

Hip joint shingles that show cracks can be repaired with black asphalt roof paint. Use roof cement if cracks are wide or shingles are badly damaged.

Replacement hip or ridge shingles should have at least a 3-in. overlap. Nail down bottom shingle at all four corners under the overlap. Apply roof cement to the nailheads.

Next apply a coating of roof cement or asphalt paint to the bottom of the new ridge shingle before laying it down. Again nail and apply cement to nailheads.

Replacing slate roof shingles

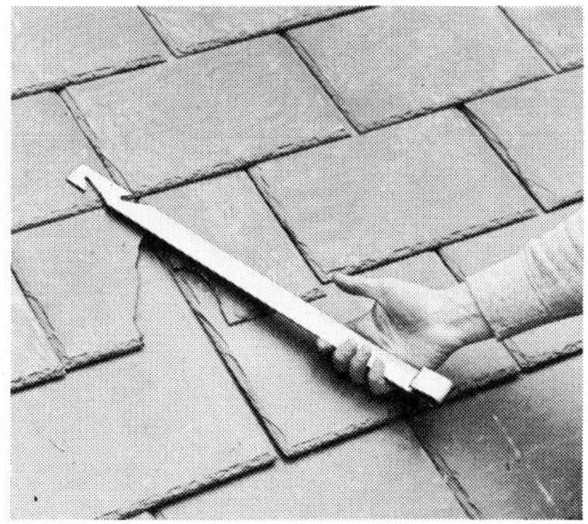

Make a nail puller out of strap iron. File two notches in it as shown and bend the end over for a hammering surface.

Hook the tool over the nail; drive it out with a hammer. Driving the nail from inside the house for a start will help.

Slates can be cut to fit by scoring each side with a chisel or screwdriver. Make certain lines match up.

Tap the slate along the scored lines to deepen score marks. Then break it off by snapping it over a straight edge.

Any ragged edges can be smoothed out by light hammer blows. It is best to practice first—slate is quite brittle.

Next step is to put slate in position and mark the locations of the required nail holes. Two holes are needed.

Nail holes can be punched through the slate with a nail set, or to be on the safe side use an electric drill.

Apply roof cement to the missing slate area and to the back of the new slate. Push up new slate under upper slates.

Drive in two roofing nails through the previously drilled holes. Cover the nail heads with roof cement.

Alternate method

Alternate method of replacing a slate shingle is by means of two copper strips. Nail them in place as shown, leaving 2 in. for overlap. A sharp blow will penetrate shingle without splitting it.

Cover each nailhead with roof cement. It is best to use galvanized or copper roofing nails for this step. Do not remove excess cement; it will help hold new shingle in place.

Next, slide the new slate shingle up as far as it will go and bend over each strip to hold the slate in place. Strips should be flush to surface of the new slate.

Repairing slate shingles

A cracked slate shingle that is in position should be protected with a liberal application of roof cement. Use a putty knife to apply the cement.

Repairing a flat roof

Repairing a flat roof is comparatively simple compared to the work required on a steep-sloped roof. When a flat roof develops a leak, it will generally be right over the damaged section in the ceiling below. Most flat roof leaks develop around chimney areas and at low spots where water can collect. If the roof is covered with gravel or pebbles (sometimes used to protect flat roofs from sun), you must first sweep these away with a stiff broom. Keep sweeping until the roof surface is clean and visible. Do not use a shovel; the edge might tear the roof.

If the entire roof is in bad shape, it is best to cover it with black asphalt roof paint—not roof cement. The paint comes in 5-gallon buckets, is inexpensive, and covers about 100 square feet to the U.S. gallon and 125 square feet to the imperial gallon. Apply it with a long-handled brush especially made for roof paint. Work a 5-x-5-foot section at a time, making sure the surface is free of dirt and pebbles. Don't worry about replacing the pebbles—most new flat roofs have no gravel cover. All flat roofs have a slight pitch, to drain water to a gutter or downspout. Determine which way the roof is pitched and start applying the roof paint to the highest area, working down to the low part. Leave yourself a path for getting down, and cover it when the rest of the roof is dry enough to walk on, usually two days later.

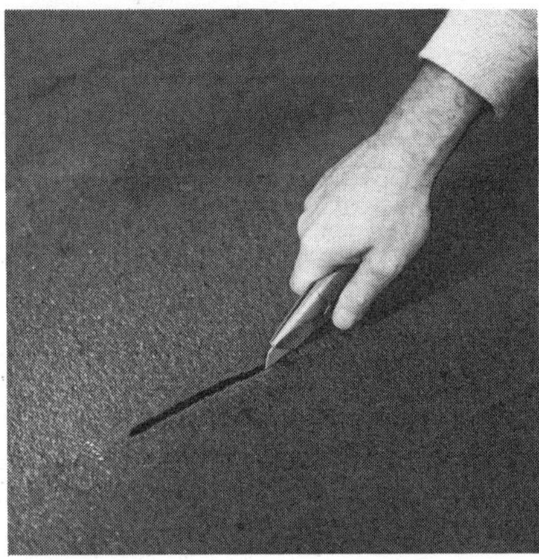

Blister on roof should be cut through the middle with a sharp knife. Be careful not to cut through the lower layer.

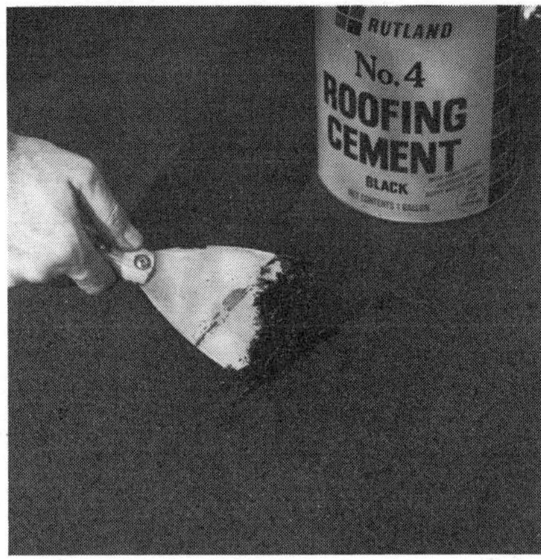

Force some roof cement under both sides of the cut with a putty knife. (It is best to do this on a fairly warm day.)

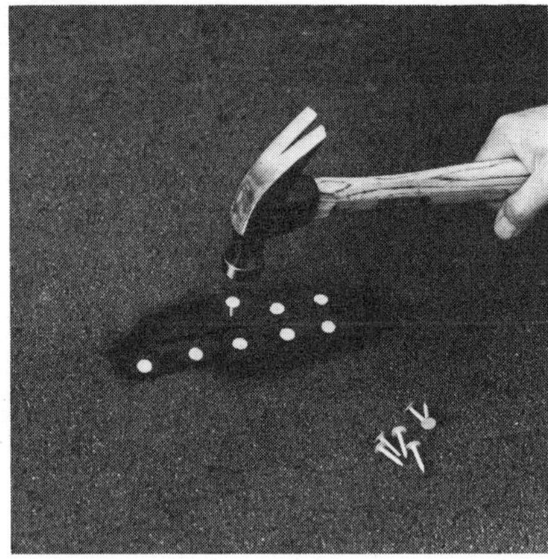

Nail down both sides of the cut with wide-headed roofing nails. Use galvanized or copper nails to prevent rusting.

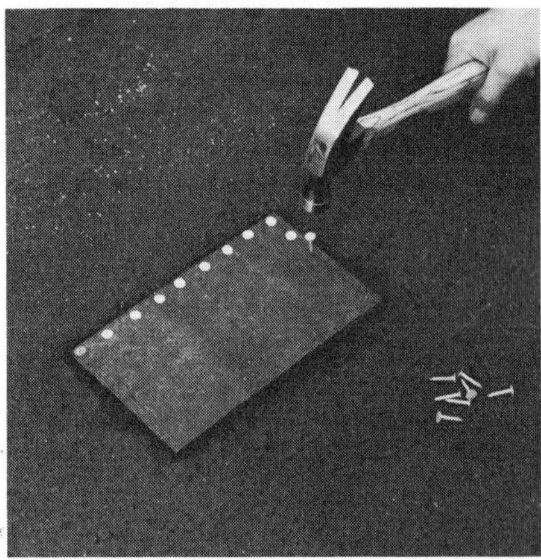

Cover cut and nails with roof cement and apply a patch (tarpaper or shingle) over area. Nail and cover with cement.

A large area is best repaired by cutting out the damaged section. Make the cut in a square or rectangular pattern.

Apply roof cement to the exposed area and to the underside of all four edges. Lift gently to avoid unnecessary tearing.

Nail down a patch of roofing felt over the cemented area. There should be at least a 2-in. overlap all around.

Make a second oversize patch to go over the first; nail it down and apply roof cement to nailheads and edges of patch.

Cleaning and maintenance

Roof gutters need cleaning at least twice a year, once before the start of winter and again right after spring. If your house is located in a heavily wooded area, more frequent cleaning may be required—leaves, twigs, and seed pods are the worst culprits when it comes to clogging. When they are allowed to accumulate and clog gutters and downspouts, back-up water during a heavy rain has no place to go, and will cascade over the gutters, washing away topsoil and damaging the plants below. Furthermore, the constant wetting and drying, in time, will rot the fascia boards under the gutters.

To clean gutters, you need a ladder long enough to reach the highest gutter. Clean out as far as possible on either side of the ladder; about 2 feet in each direction is average. Caution: Do not be tempted to stretch beyond a normal reach to avoid moving the ladder. Move it—and avoid a fall.

Sagging gutters: A gutter that sags will also be a dripping gutter. Gutters should be slanted or pitched to the downspout about ⅛ inch for each foot of their length. Important: Quite often a long gutter will slant toward two downspouts, one at each end with the high spot in the middle.

Removal of debris from the gutters is best done by hand; use gloves. A garden hose will flush away remaining material.

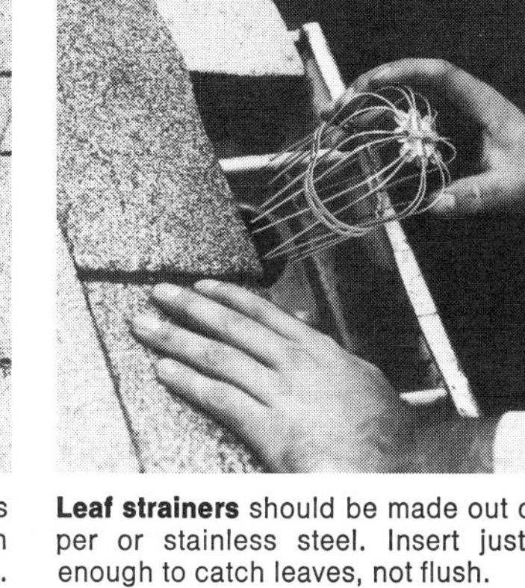

Leaf strainers should be made out of copper or stainless steel. Insert just deep enough to catch leaves, not flush.

Leaf guards fit between shingle ends and lip of gutter. They shed large leaves and allow water to flow into the gutter.

Check the gutter hangers. Renail if necessary with nonferrous or galvanized nails. Cover nailheads with roof cement.

Many gutters are supported with a long copper spike passing through a metal sleeve and driven into the roof board.

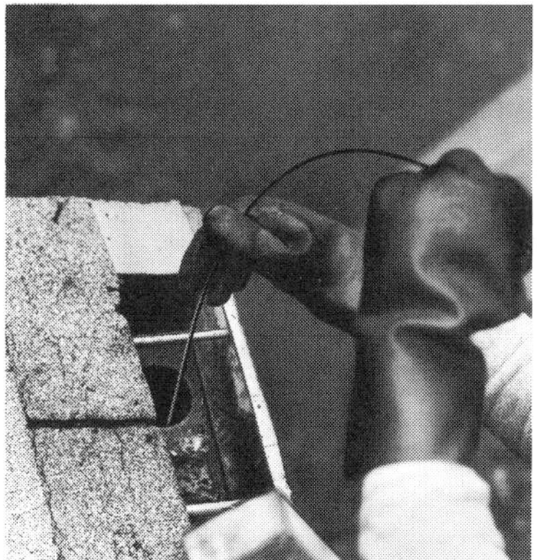

Stoppage often occurs at elbow between downspout and gutter. An electrician's snake can be used to clear out debris.

Adjusting gutter hangers

The three styles of gutter hangers shown below should be adjusted so that each one bears its share of the load supporting the gutters. Use a support every 30 in. and a support at each end of a corner installation.

Sleeve and spike hanger: Sleeve fits within the gutter and spike is driven into roof board.

Bracket hanger: Bracket is nailed or screwed to fascia board right below the roof.

Strap hanger: Strap is nailed to roof under shingle. Cover nailheads with roof cement.

Gutters and downspouts

How to repair them

Gutters and downspouts are made of steel, copper, plastic, aluminum, or wood. Wood gutters are seldom installed nowadays, but if your house has them, they should be preserved with a paint job every three years. The best paint to use for the inside of the gutters is asphalt roof paint, thinned to brushing consistency with 1 part paint thinner to 4 parts paint. Do the job after several days of sunshine so the gutters will be reasonably dry. Two thin coats are better than one heavy coat. The asphalt paint will flow into the tiny cracks in the wood, effectively sealing them against further deterioration. Be careful not to get this paint on the outside of the gutter; it will bleed through any conventional paint that may later be applied to the outside.

The best way to repair small—and not so small—leaks in metal gutters is with asphalt roof cement, as shown below. Such repairs can also be made by a method that involves fiber glass used in combination with a two-solution epoxy mix. If the gutters—and downspouts—need considerable repair, it may be better to replace them than to keep patching them.

Gutter and downspout leaks often develop at seams. However, the water may travel from a leaky seam along the bottom of the gutter, and then drop off some distance from the actual leak. Tracing it is somewhat like finding a roof leak. Check the underside of the gutter. Chances are you will be able to see the water travel along the gutter, then drop off when it can no longer support its own weight.

Sweep away all dirt from damaged area. Use coarse sandpaper or a wire brush to clean the section to be repaired.

Wipe away any grit with a solvent-soaked rag (paint thinner) and apply a liberal coating of black asphalt roof cement.

A crack more than ¼ in. wide should be covered with light sheet metal or canvas before applying cement.

For a very large hole, you will have to cut a piece of sheet metal for a patch. First cut a pattern out of paper.

Press the patch over the hole, making sure that it overlaps the damaged area by at least ½ in. all around.

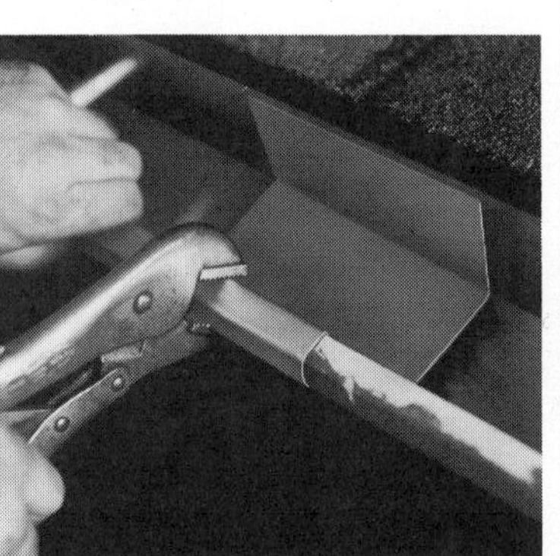

Crimp outer edges of patch over edge of gutter with pliers. Apply thick layer of roof cement under and over the patch.

Wood gutter repair

Wood gutters should be painted every three years. After a dry spell of several days, clean out any debris and thoroughly sand the interior surfaces.

Wipe the interior with paint thinner. Next, apply a thinned coat of asphalt roof paint. Apply second coat after the first has dried, two days later.

Sand the exterior to remove scaling and blistered paint, wipe with paint thinner, and apply appropriate exterior house paint. Two coats are best.

Selecting gutters and estimating needs

Your choice of gutters and downspouts for partial replacement is often governed by the type on the house at present, especially when you must match a new gutter to an old one. (Never connect aluminum to steel to copper in any combination because of the corrosive electrolytic action between them.) When you are planning to replace all gutters, however, or to install them on a new house, you can use whatever you wish.

Steel gutters are available galvanized and with a white enamel finish. Enameled gutters and downspouts are slightly more expensive. Steel guttering is about the lowest-priced drainage system you can buy. Its chief drawback is its short life compared to other materials. Painting helps to make steel last longer. Do not paint galvanized gutters and downspouts, however, until they have weathered for at least a year. Also paint will flake off galvanized steel unless it is preceded by a special primer.

Copper gutters and downspouts are usually installed by a professional roofer because joints must be soldered instead of just clipped together. Copper gutters are virtually corrosion-resistant, though leaks may develop at the soldered joints. As the gutters age, they will take on copper's typical green patina, so it is best to leave them unpainted.

Aluminum gutters and downspouts come white-enameled as well as unfinished. They can be cut to size with a fine tooth hacksaw. Being lighter in weight than steel or copper gutters, they are much easier to handle. Also they offer better corrosion resistance than steel. Remember, however, that they do not have the strength of steel; they can be dented by mere pressure from a ladder.

Plastic gutters are practically maintenance-free. When installing them, make allowance for expansion; they will buckle if installed too tightly. A special mastic is used at all joints to make connections. Metal is used only for the hangers.

Wood gutters are specified by some architects for aesthetic reasons (compatibility with the character of the house), or sometimes because they can be put up by the builder's carpenter instead of a roofer. See opposite page for care of wood gutters.

How to calculate your needs. Generally, it is best to replace an entire gutter run rather than just a section of it. When you do replace only a section, measure the old piece or pieces carefully from seam to seam and determine the number of lengths needed. Most gutters are available in 10-foot lengths, though a few manufacturers make longer sections. Also measure the size of each fitting and count the number of hangers or spike and ferrule sets needed. Take a small section of the old gutter to your building supply dealer to be sure you get a good match.

When installing a completely new run, make a sketch of the roof area involved. From this, determine the number of 10-foot lengths needed, as well as the number of other fittings required. Keep in mind that you need one slip connector at each point where gutter sections meet or where outlet and corners are installed, and that one hanger or ferrule set should be installed for every 3 feet of gutter run.

Regardless of the arrangement on the old gutter, plan to have one downspout for each 35 running feet of gutter. Offset elbows are needed to permit the downspout to be mounted flush against the house, and one is required at the bottom of the leader to keep the water away from the house (unless, of course, the downspout leads to a dry well). A little paperwork at the planning stage will cut down on material waste and trips to the dealer.

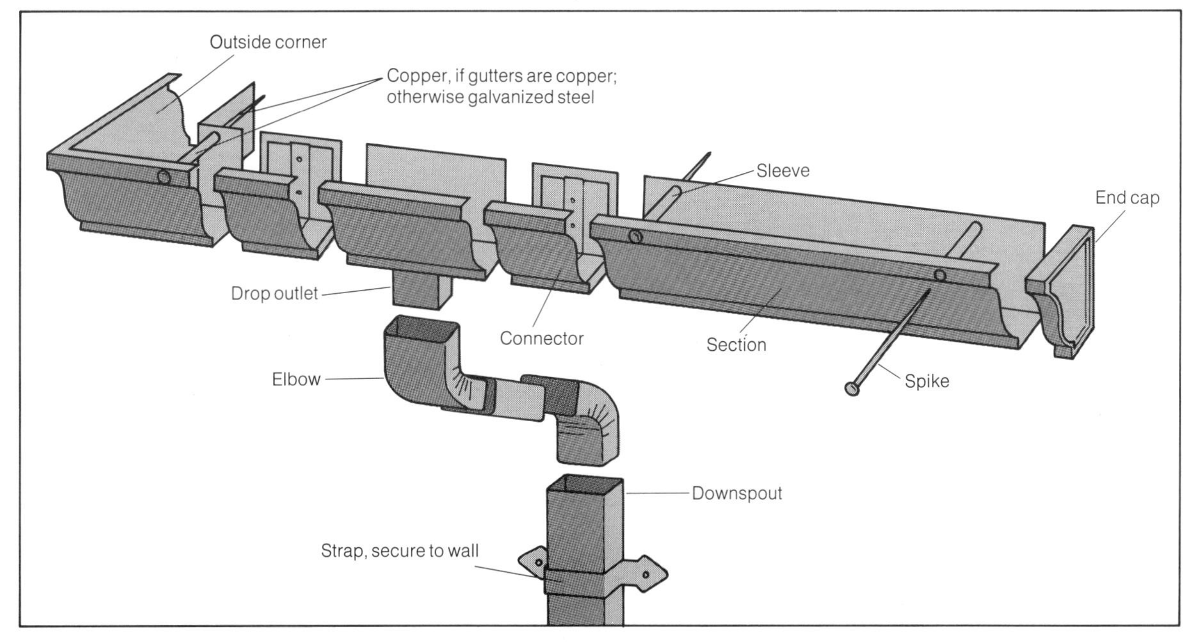

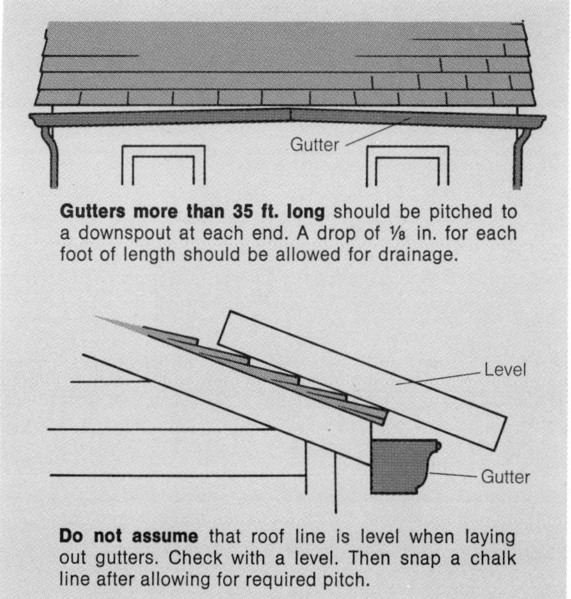

Gutters more than 35 ft. long should be pitched to a downspout at each end. A drop of ⅛ in. for each foot of length should be allowed for drainage.

Do not assume that roof line is level when laying out gutters. Check with a level. Then snap a chalk line after allowing for required pitch.

Installing new gutters

How to cut and fit gutters

Support the inside of the gutter with a 2 x 4 and use a hacksaw to cut it to length.

File away all burrs. This will make it easier to install the slip connectors.

If using spike supports, drill holes through front and back of the gutter near top edge.

Fit the cap to the end of the gutter after first applying caulking compound as a seal.

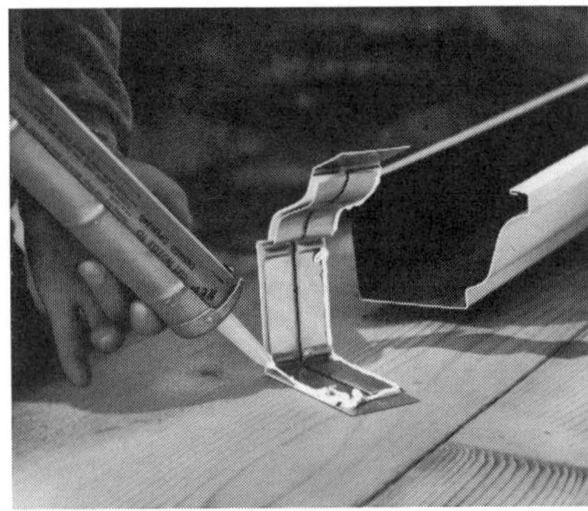

Apply caulking to connectors before joining with gutters to make a waterproof joint.

Slip-joint connectors are used to join all sections. Make certain they fit tightly.

After parts have been inserted, bend edge of connectors down against gutter with pliers.

Drive the spike through the front lip of gutter, sleeve, and fascia board into rafter.

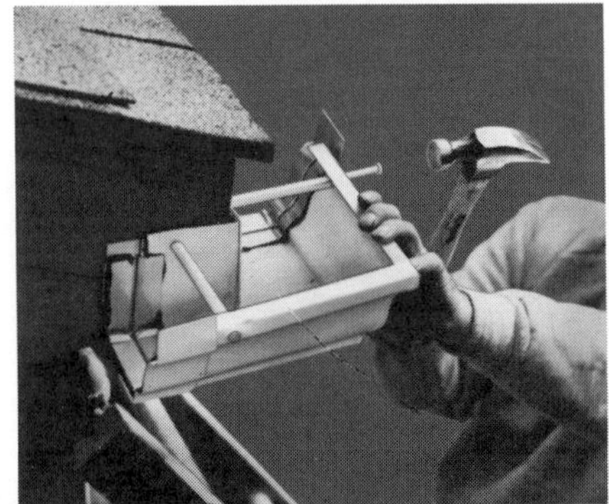

Corner joints should be reinforced by nailing a spike on each side of the corner.

If strap hangers are used to support the gutter, lift shingles and nail as shown.

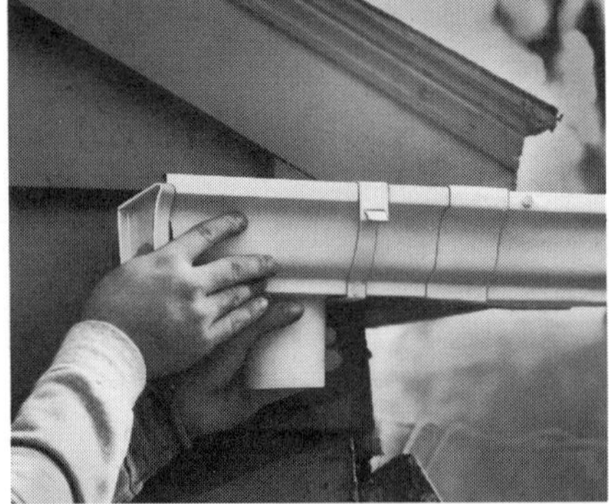

Install cap at end of gutter adjacent to downspout. Seal with caulking compound.

Downspout is connected by slipping it over the stub-length downspout connector.

Splash blocks

Water that is allowed to pour directly from downspout to ground may ultimately find its way through the foundation wall and into the basement. One way to prevent this: Let the water fall on splash blocks. These prevent soil erosion under the downspout and also tend to lead water away from the foundation.

There are several other devices more effective than masonry splash blocks. Among them are fabric sleeves which fasten directly to the downspout. Perforations along the extended sleeve cause the water to flow gently rather than pour out. One sleeve type even has a spring that coils it up between rains; the weight of the descending water unrolls it.

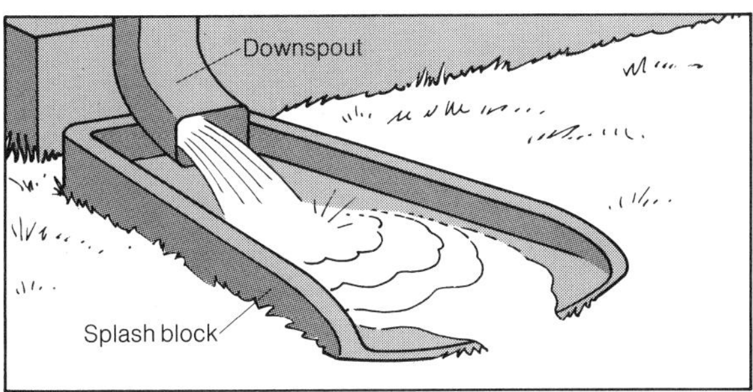

Ready-made concrete splash blocks are available from building supply dealers; use them to divert rainwater.

Dry wells

The best solution to roof water drainage problems is to connect all downspouts to a storm sewer or dry well. Such an arrangement calls for the installation of drainage pipes or tiles in an underground trench about a foot below the surface near the downspout and sloping about ½ inch per foot as it runs away from the house to the storm sewer or dry well.

A dry well, used where storm sewers are not available, is just a large hole in the ground filled with rocks and covered with wood planks or a concrete slab to keep out topsoil. One way to build a dry well is to remove both ends from a 55-gallon oil drum, cut a hole in one side to accept the drainpipe, and punch a few dozen random holes in the metal to permit water seepage. Then bury the drum in the ground (at least 18 inches deep) and fill it with rocks and rubble. Cover it with wood planks to keep spaces between the rocks from filling up with dirt.

A dry well may also be built using concrete blocks laid on their sides and separated a few inches at the joints to form a hollow square in the center. A hole 3 feet square is minimum; a 3-x-6- to 3-x-8-foot hole is best. All dry wells should be located at least 10 feet from foundation walls.

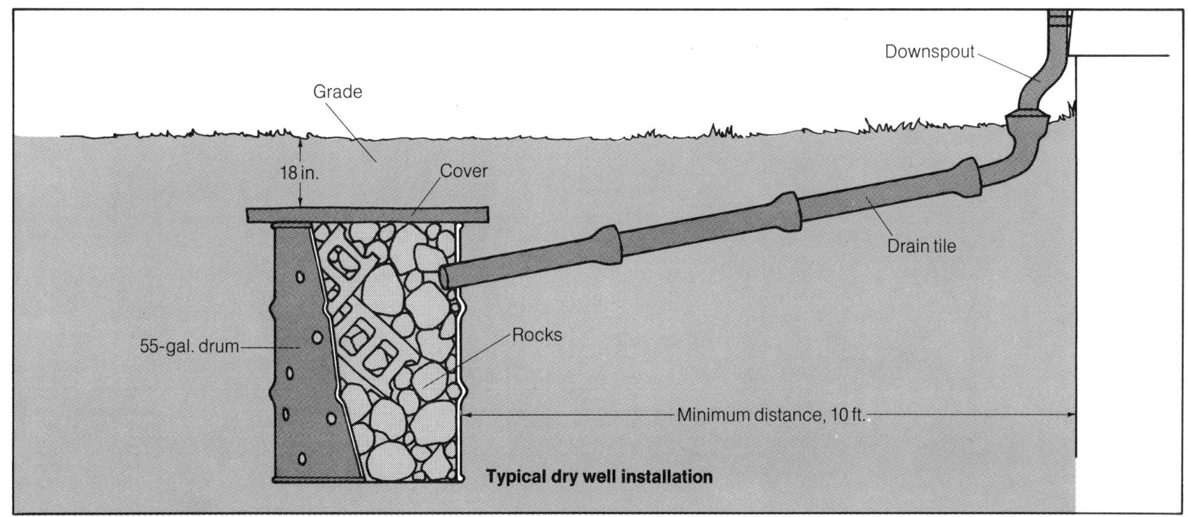

Typical dry well installation

Preventing an ice dam

Use electric heating tapes along the roof edges to prevent snow and ice formations. The tape is laid along the roof in a zigzag pattern and held in place with special clips. Then during stormy weather the tape can be plugged into the closest available outdoor outlet. The front entrance light could serve this purpose, or the tape might be drawn through a window and plugged into an indoor outlet.

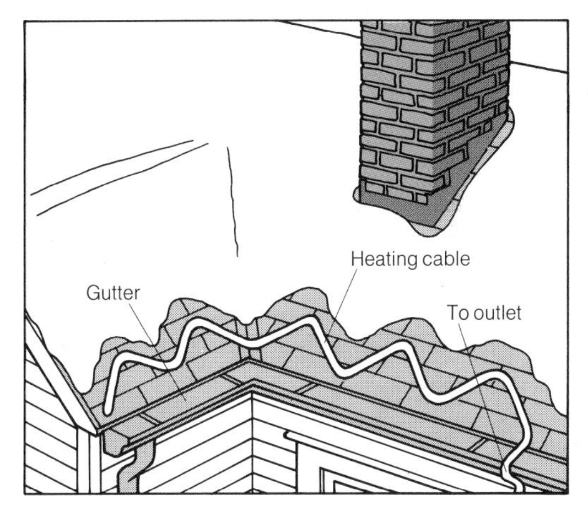

Snow guards

Install snow guards to stop "avalanches" of snow and ice from sliding off the roof. These guards are available at hardware dealers; the precise type of guard and method of installation will depend on the style of your roof. As a rule, the steeper the roof, the more guards you will need to use. Space the guards out evenly over roof near eaves.

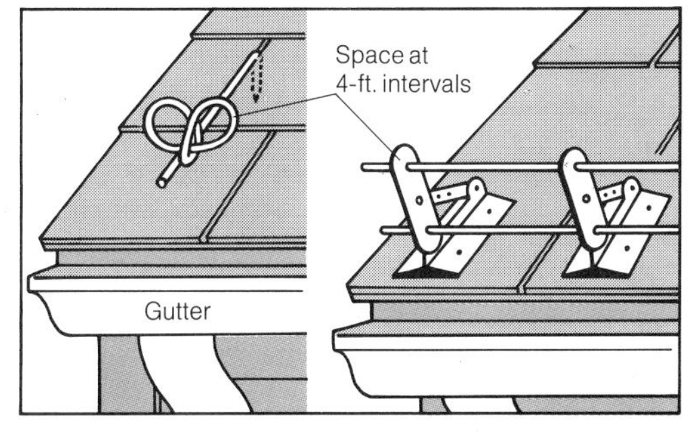

Upkeep and improvements

A chimney should be inspected yearly and cleaned when necessary. Dirt and soot will not only reduce the effective flue area, but they can cause a fire in the chimney. If the top is accessible, look down the chimney with the aid of a flashlight or reflect sunlight down into it with a mirror. If the chimney is not accessible from the top, you can inspect it with a mirror and flashlight from the fireplace or from the clean-out at the chimney's base.

If you see thick deposits of soot, the chimney needs cleaning. To clean a flue, tie a weighted bag stuffed with straw, paper, or cloth to a stout nylon rope. Lower the bag, moving it up and down as you do. This will force the dirt and soot down the chimney flue. First make sure, however, that the fireplace damper is closed and the opening sealed to keep soot from entering the room. Professionals now use vacuum cleaners for this soot-removal job.

Once the chimney is clean, inspect it carefully for cracks in the flue linings and leaks around the furnace connection. If you find any cracks, seal them with a mixture of 1 part masonry cement and 3 parts sand. Any cracks in the chimney's masonry surfaces should be repaired (p. 462).

Installing spark arresters and rain guards: The tops of some chimney flues are covered with a galvanized wire mesh basket to prevent sparks and embers from blowing out and possibly setting nearby areas afire. To make such a basket for your chimney, cut a piece of wire mesh (hardware cloth) to the proper size and fold it to fit over the flue (see illustration, top left). The mesh basket should be cleaned or replaced every so often so that accumulations of soot do not hamper the draft of the flue.

Chimney caps also are often used to prevent sparks from flying out, and to keep water from entering the chimney as well. A chimney cap may be either a reinforced concrete slab or a large flat stone and should be supported so that it is 6 to 12 inches above the top of the chimney (top right).

If rain continues to come in the chimney, change to a cone-shape chimney cap. These come in several styles, among them the shanty type with a plain metal hood, and the weathervane type, which contains a turbine activated by the wind. All of them serve to prevent downdrafts and keep out water. These caps can be purchased to fit almost any size flue, or you can make one as illustrated at the right.

Spark arresters and rain guards

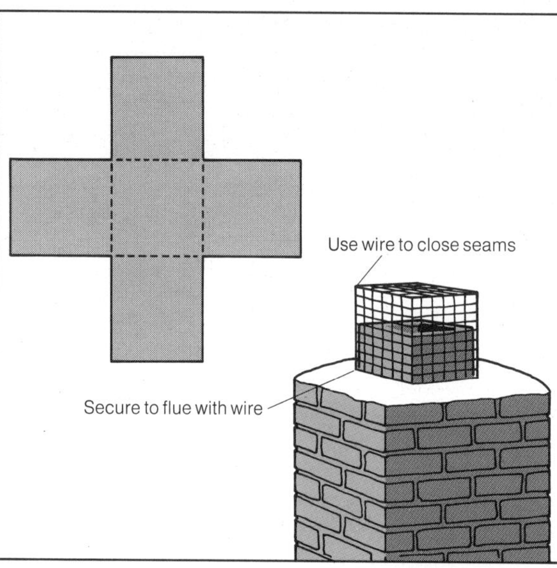

Spark arrester can be easily made of wire mesh. Measure chimney opening and cut cloth with tin snips to required size in the shape shown. Fold into basket form; wire edges together.

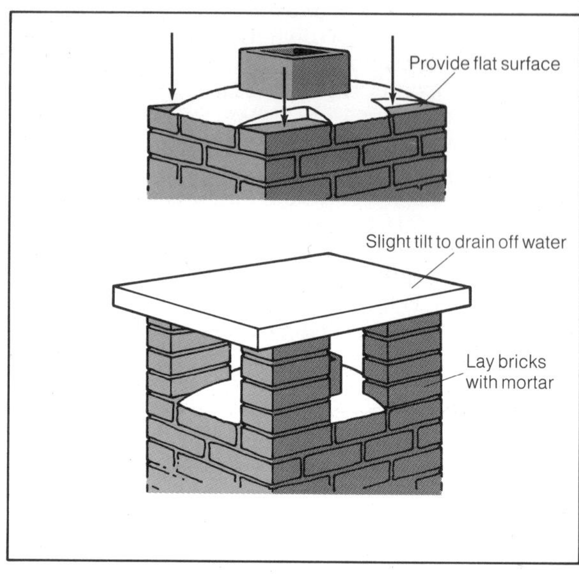

Rain and draft deflector consists of concrete slab or flat stone supported 6 to 12 in. above chimney top by bricks. Chip away mortar with chisel to make flat surface for bricks.

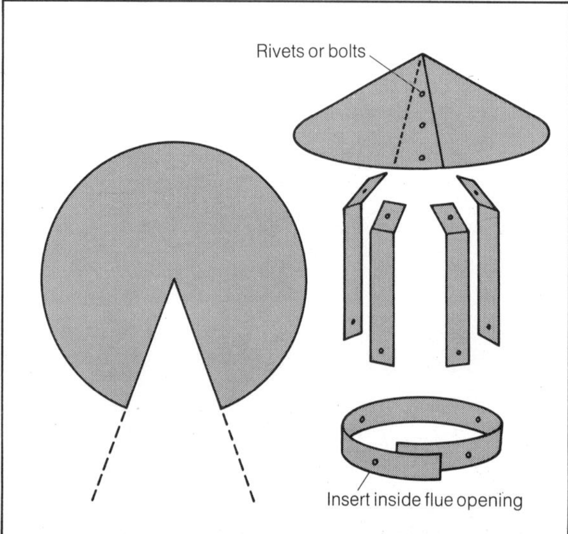

Make the coolie-hat draft and rain guard of a round piece of metal, preferably copper, notched and seamed as shown. Actual diameter will depend on size of opening to be covered.

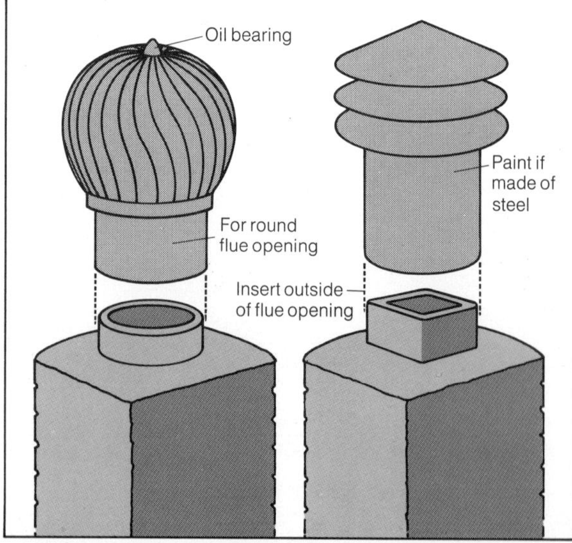

These two types of rain and draft deflectors are sold commercially. Turbine at left rotates in a slight breeze; one at right is used if chimney is in a particularly gusty area.

Care and repair of flashing

Flashing is used wherever roof surfaces, walls, and chimney meet. Thus you will find flashing around chimneys, around vent pipes, in roof valleys, and around dormers. Many materials are used for flashing, including galvanized steel, copper, lead, aluminum, plastic, felt, and rubber.

Flashing joints are usually sealed with roofing cement; after many years of weathering, there may be small breaks at these joints. An actual gap is obvious, but pinholes are not. You should therefore inspect flashing carefully at least once a year. If you have doubts as to its condition, apply asphalt roof paint or roofing cement. You may have to fill larger gaps with roof felt and cover it with cement.

Sometimes chimney flashing separates from the mortar in which it is embedded. This requires immediate action, because the separated flashing acts as a scoop for water running down the protrusion's sides, sending all of it under roof shingles, through sheathing, and into rooms below. In such a situation, the old mortar along the defective line must be cleared away, the channel cleaned, and the flashing repositioned in the line. The line is then filled with a fresh mix of patching mortar.

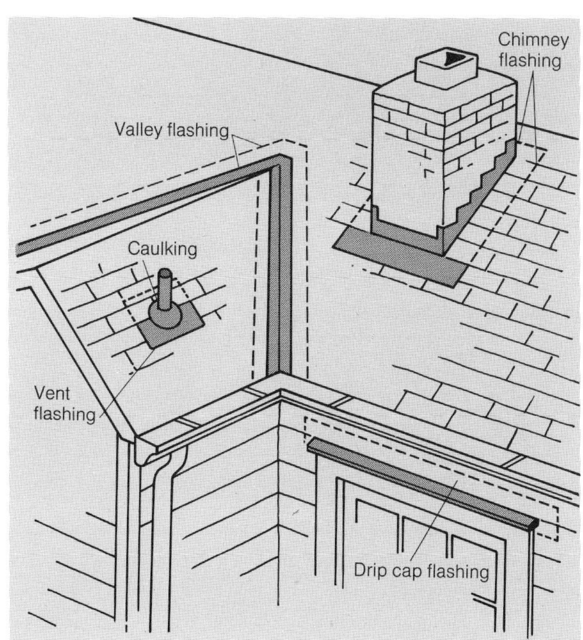

Chimney flashing may leak at the corner joints or at the mortar line. Seal with liberal application of black roof cement.

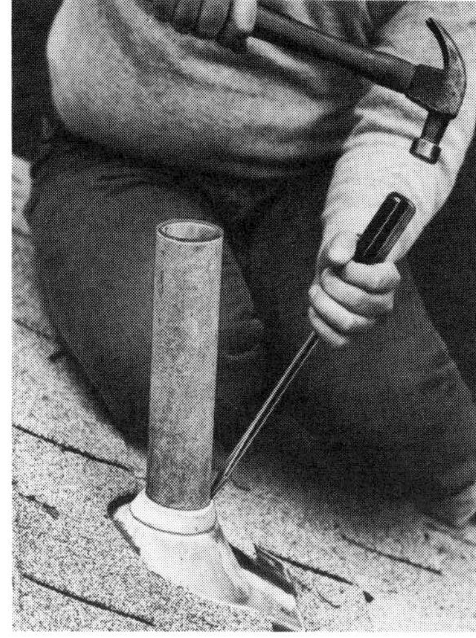

Vent pipes sometimes leak around the lead caulking at the neck. Use a screwdriver to tap the lead against the pipe.

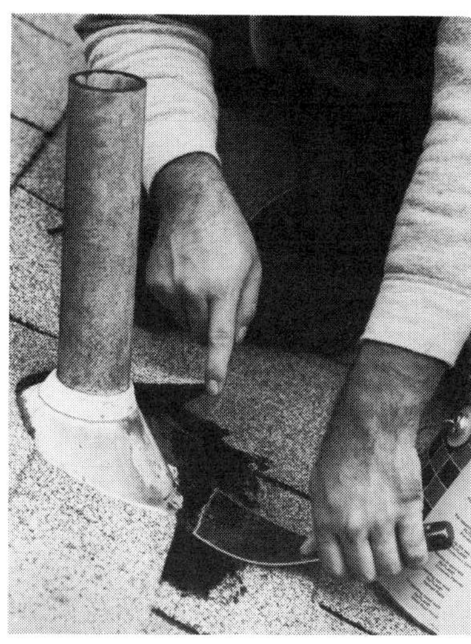

Apply a liberal coating of asphalt roof cement all around the flashing area and partway up the vent pipe.

Reflashing a vent pipe

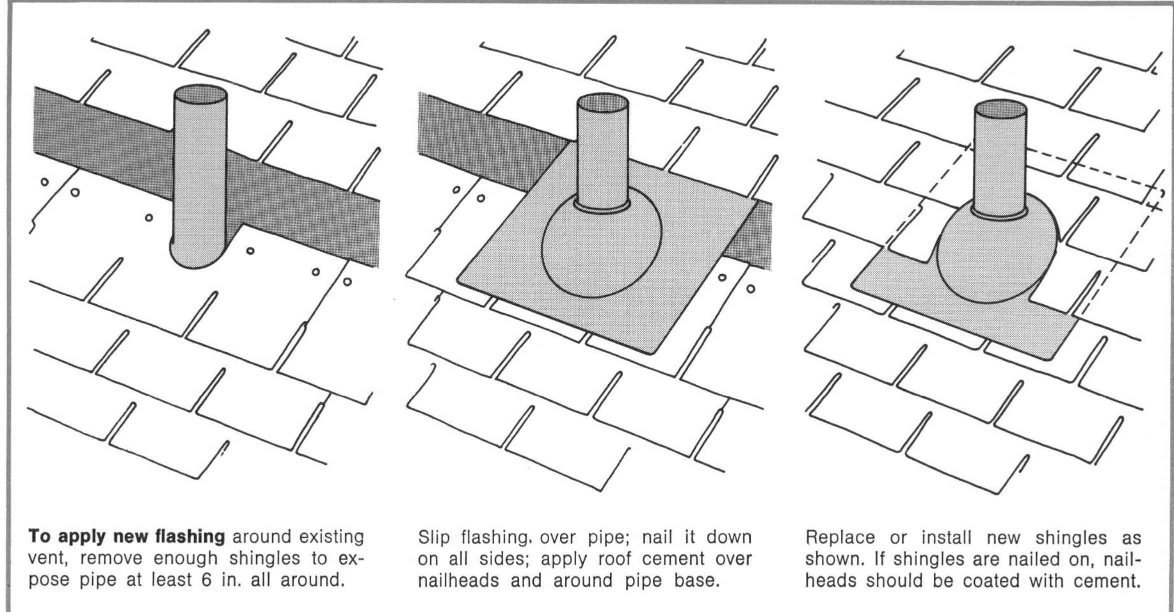

To apply new flashing around existing vent, remove enough shingles to expose pipe at least 6 in. all around.

Slip flashing over pipe; nail it down on all sides; apply roof cement over nailheads and around pipe base.

Replace or install new shingles as shown. If shingles are nailed on, nailheads should be coated with cement.

Method of flashing

It is impossible to lay any type of shingle tightly enough against a chimney to keep water from entering the joint where the chimney passes through the roof. This is because chimneys are masonry construction, and the roof is of wood, asbestos, slate, or other material that is almost impossible to fasten to masonry. The solution is flashing, which is used to seal the roof-chimney joints.

A good chimney flashing system consists of two sections of sheet metal, generally copper. The two sections cover all four sides of the base—including wrap-around lips for the corners. One section is the step, or base, flashing. It is bent to conform to the slope of the roof and positioned flush against the chimney, going partly up the side and also onto the roof, where it is covered with shingles.

The second part of the system is called the cap, or counter, flashing. It is placed over the base flashing, but only a small portion of it extends onto the roof. The portion against the chimney's side extends beyond the step flashing, and its top edge is bent 90 degrees and inserted directly into the chimney mortar. This system puts flashing at every joint where the chimney meets the roof.

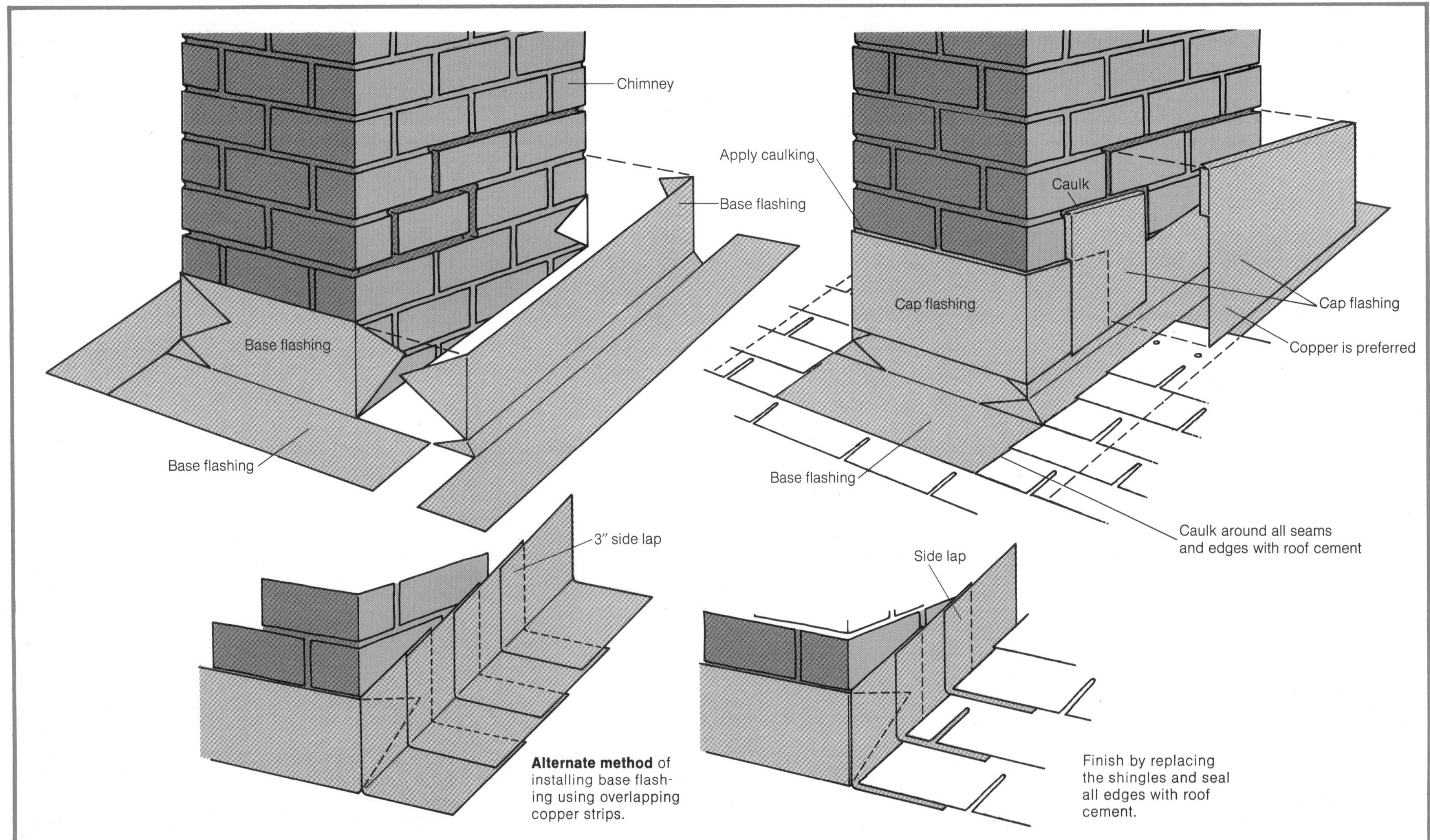

Alternate method of installing base flashing using overlapping copper strips.

Finish by replacing the shingles and seal all edges with roof cement.

How to replace chimney flashing

Even with the two-part counter-flashing system, leaks can develop where the cap flashing is inserted and at corners. When leaks occur at these points, patching is usually a temporary measure. It is better to rip out the old flashing and install new.

Examine the mortar line closely. If the cap flashing has pulled away from the joint or is for any reason suspect, rake out the old mortar and remove and discard the flashing. To do a complete job, you may have to remove the shingles around the chimney.

Use the old flashing as a pattern or make a new one as shown below. Cut all the pieces from sheet copper and make all necessary bends. Then, using asphalt roof cement, fasten the front base, or step, flashing in place and apply the side pieces. The base flashing at the back of the chimney is applied last. When these steps are taken, the shingles can be replaced.

Cut the cap flashing pieces to size. Then bend the edges up and around in the shape of a J. Push the flashing all the way into the brick joints and fill with mortar or black roof cement. The cap flashing on the front of the chimney can be one continuous piece, but the sides must be stepped up in sections to align with the roof slope.

Chisel out old mortar and caulking holding the cap flashing in place. Then remove flashing from around chimney.

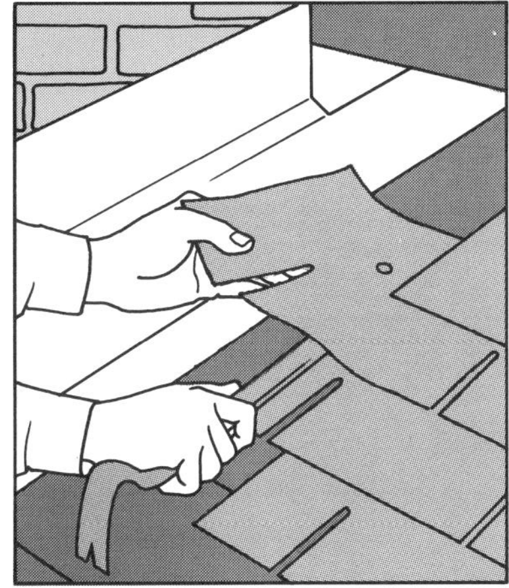

Carefully remove shingles from around chimney. Use pry bar or nail puller and make sure you don't crack shingles.

Next remove the old base flashing, using pry bar. Be careful not to tear the roofing paper underneath the flashing.

Fit new base flashing, cut to size, around the chimney. Cement all sections together as they are applied.

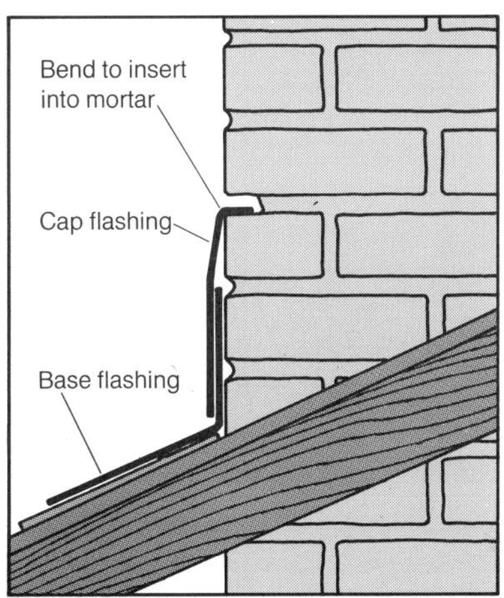

Bend the cap flashing down over the base flashing and set it into the mortar joints to a depth of 1½ to 3 in.

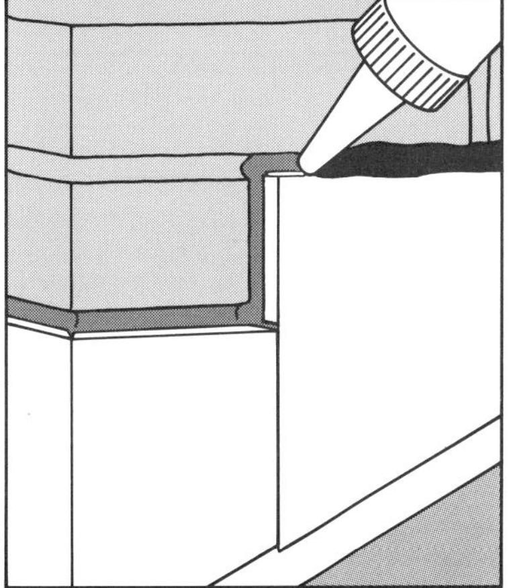

To complete the job, use mortar or black roof cement to waterproof and fasten the cap flashing in place.

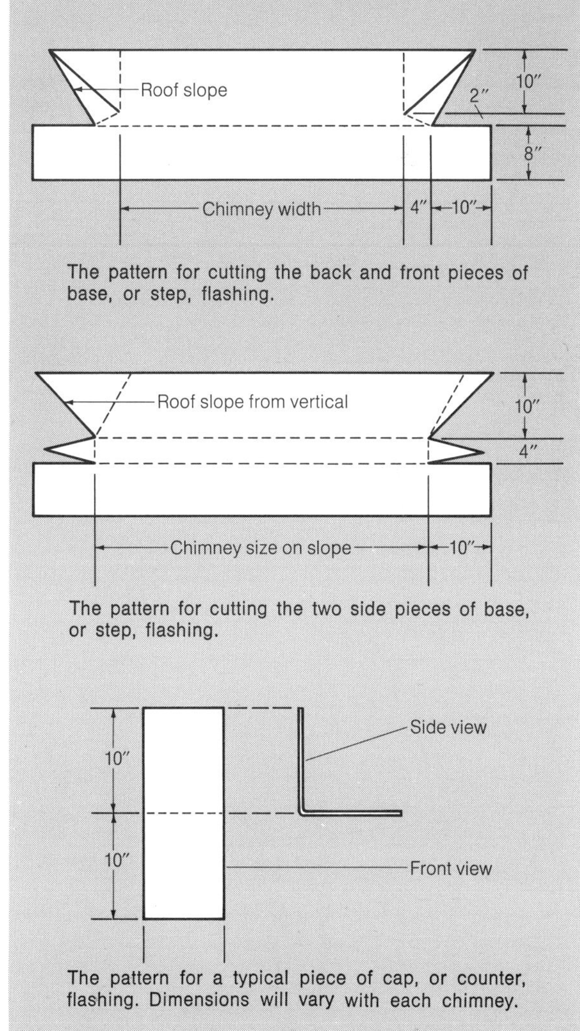

The pattern for cutting the back and front pieces of base, or step, flashing.

The pattern for cutting the two side pieces of base, or step, flashing.

The pattern for a typical piece of cap, or counter, flashing. Dimensions will vary with each chimney.

Flashing valley and dormers

Roof and window flashing

Valley flashing is done by two methods, known as **open** valley and **closed** valley. Shingles on an open valley stop right before the valley, leaving an open space. Those on a closed valley are butted together in the valley center. Open valleys are easier to install and usually preferable to closed. Also water seepage is less likely with open valleys. Actually, the only reason for using closed valleys is their appearance; by covering up flashing material, they present an unbroken shingle surface.

Small holes and gashes in open valley flashings can be repaired without replacing the flashing. Cut a piece of metal flashing material to lap the hole 1 inch on all sides. Apply roof cement to the hole and surrounding surfaces. Press the piece of flashing into the cement and hold it firmly a few minutes.

Leaks that develop in closed valley flashing frequently require the removal of shingles in the leak area and the replacement of the valley flashing. Often, however, leaks in closed valley can be patched with squares of copper or aluminum, bent to fit the valley angle. Bending makes it easier to push the metal pieces past obstacles such as nails. If nails interfere too much, they can be cut off under the shingle, or pulled out with the tool shown on page 181 and later replaced with new nails. The exact size of the squares depends upon the pitch of roof and the exposure of the shingles to the weather, but they should be large enough to fit up under the second shingle at least 2 inches.

The bent squares are pushed up under the shingles and over the top of old flashing. Start at the bottom of the valley and work until you reach the top or until all damaged flashings have been covered.

Dormer flashing: The flashing around dormers, between the roof and the siding, or between any wall and the roof should extend up under the siding and out over the shingles. It is generally best applied as a series of overlapping sheets. If the siding is already in place, it can be bent and shoved up under the siding. Shingles are laid as flashing is installed, with the flashing overlapping so as to provide a watertight joint between meeting surfaces.

The roof is not the only part of the house that requires flashing. For example, window and door jambs usually need this protection from the weather. Remember that the wall joints most vulnerable to the entrance of water are around windows and doors.

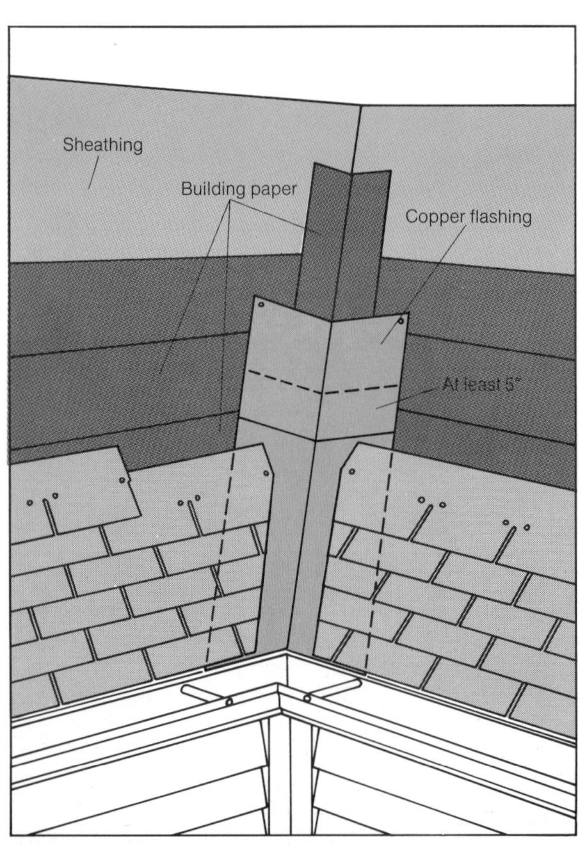

Open valley flashing, usually of copper

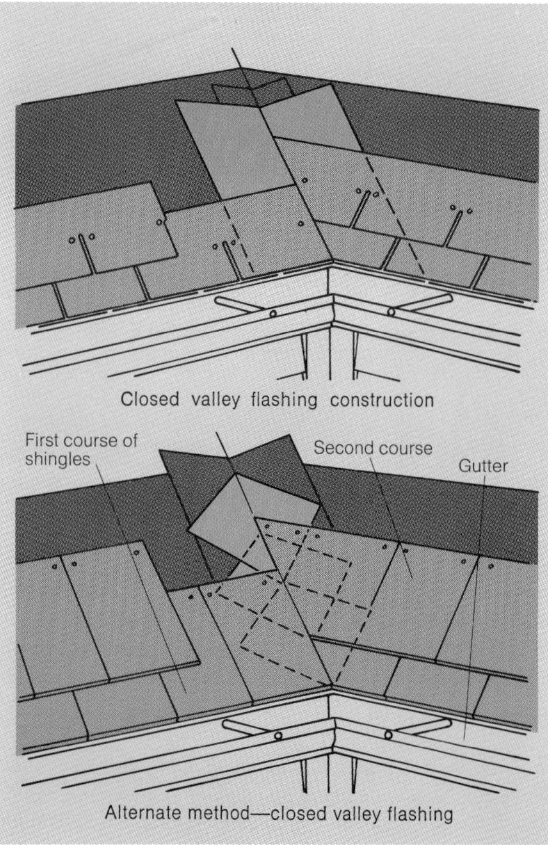

Closed valley flashing construction

Alternate method—closed valley flashing

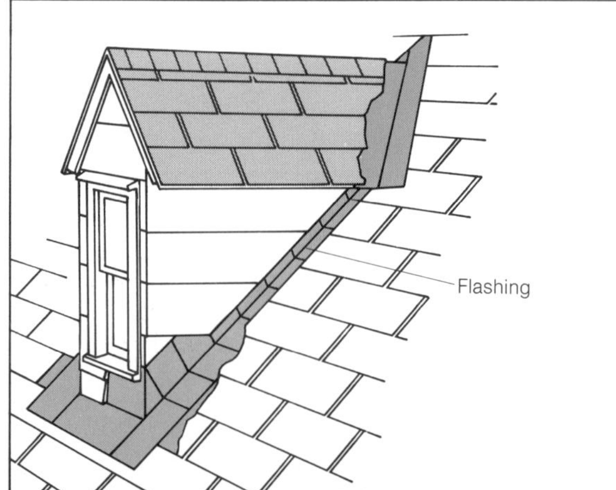

How flashing is used around a dormer

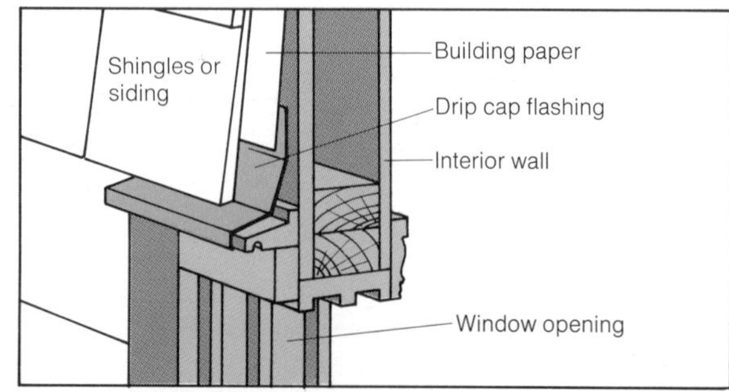

Application of flashing around a window

Materials and construction

The roof, on the basis of square footage, is one of the most expensive parts of a house, so it makes good sense to transform any flat roof space into a usable living area, such as a sun deck or roof patio. Before any roof can be used for such a purpose, however, it must be properly protected. The average residential flat roof is covered only with rolled roofing, which cannot take much traffic or abuse.

As previously noted on page 168, all "flat" roofs have a degree of pitch; how you construct a roof deck will depend on this slope. For instance, where the pitch exceeds the minimum drainage requirement of ¼ inch per foot, the deck can be leveled with "sleepers"—simply floor joists placed on the existing roof. Depending on the slope, sleepers can be anything from 1 x 2s blocked up at intervals to 2 x 10s cut on a diagonal to form long wedges. They are usually placed at the same distance as floor joists—16 inches on centers. In planning the location of sleepers, however, be sure that the original roof drainage will not be blocked. The deck surfacing material is fastened over the sleepers.

Several materials are suitable for deck surfacing: Exterior-grade plywood, hardwood, lumber planking, and materials made especially for the purpose. When planking is used, duckboard construction is most popular. Actually duckboards are square platforms (3 x 3 feet is a good size) laid side by side over the entire deck. If sleepers are wedge-cut, duckboards can be accommodated to slight changes in roof pitch.

Finish off the roof deck with a protective railing on open sides. To provide access to this new living space, you can usually convert a window to a door.

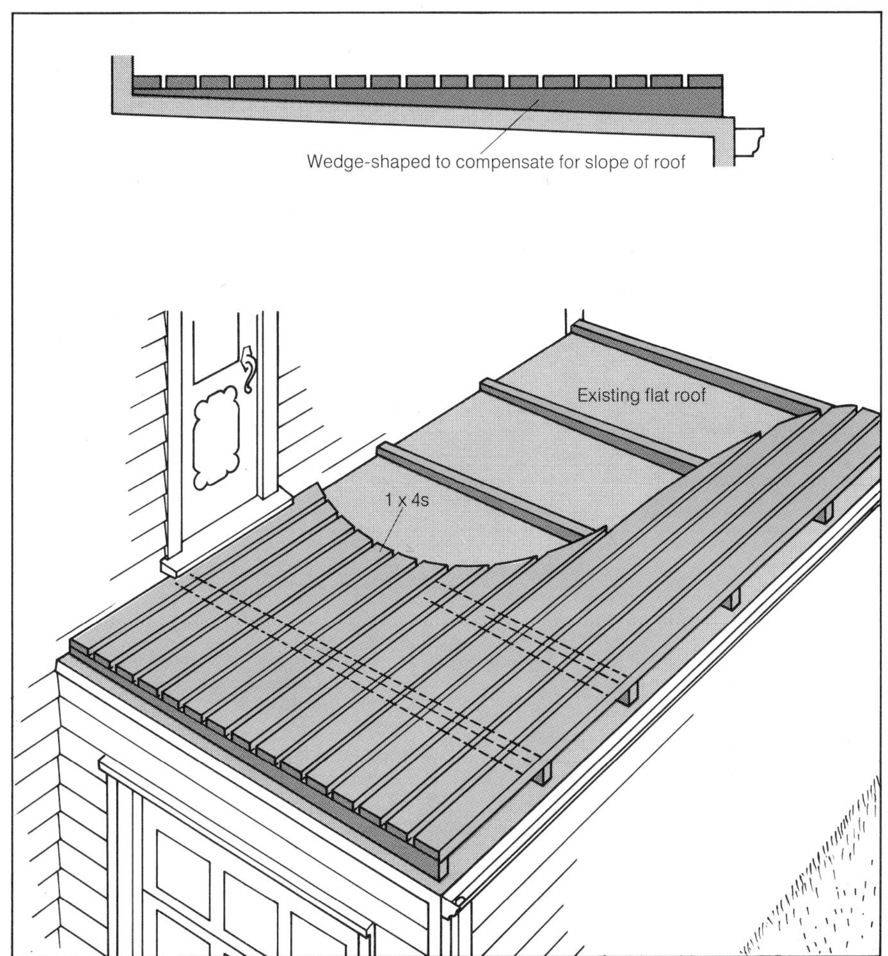

In single-unit installation, sleepers run across the surface at same distance as floor joists.

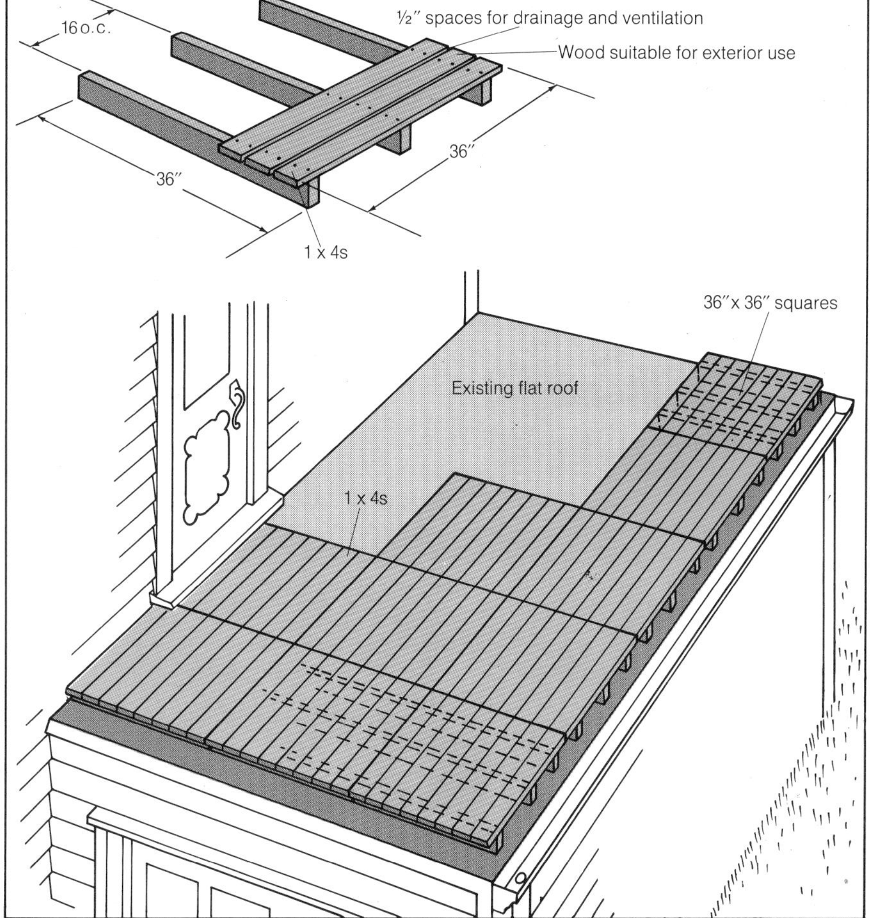

Duckboard construction is advisable when deck is of planking. Modules permit lifting for cleaning.

Repairing damaged clapboard

How to repair clapboard

Whenever you find a piece of warped or split clapboard, repair it immediately. Moisture entering the wall beneath the warp or through the crack will, in time, rot out a section of the wall from the inside before there are any external signs of damage. The first indication of this: When the paint starts to peel in the room adjacent to the damaged section.

Because clapboards are overlapped and nailed together, it might seem that disturbing one board would require removing the next one above, and so on up the wall to the top. This is not so. One board or even a part of a board can be pulled up or out and repairs made without tearing down the wall.

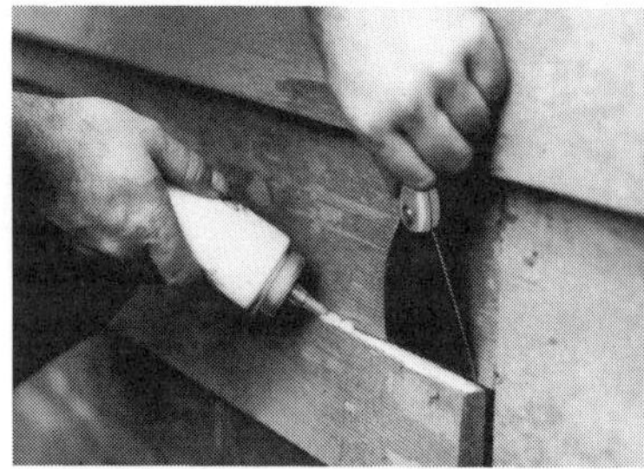

To repair split clapboard, pry out loose portion and coat both edges of the split with waterproof glue.

Clamp split together by driving nails below lower edge and bending them up to close crack. Remove nails when glue sets.

When renailing warped clapboard, drill pilot holes to prevent splitting. Drive nails so heads are slightly countersunk.

How to replace clapboard

Cut out damaged section with backsaw. Avoid damaging the good board below by using point of saw for final cut.

Use sharp chisel and hammer to remove chunks of the cut board. Be careful not to cut the building paper or felt paper below.

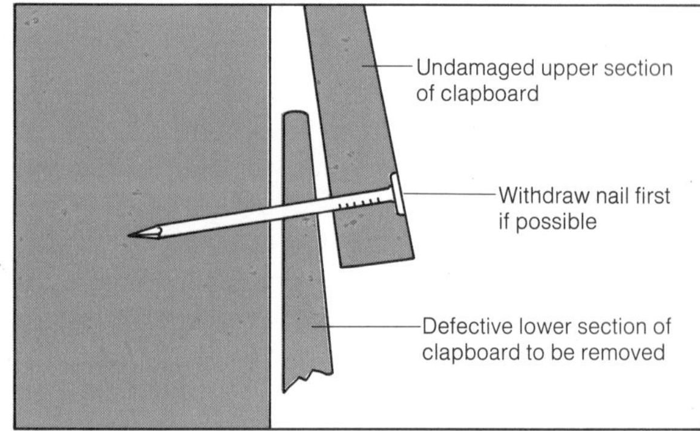

Cross section of clapboard shows the rotted lower board which is to be removed and the nails that are holding it.

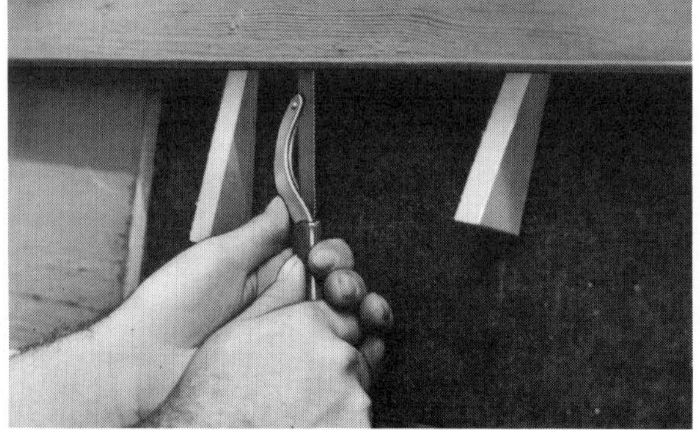

Insert wedges or screwdriver gently under the upper board; cut the nails holding the overlapping board with hacksaw.

With upper board wedged in place, chisel out ends of cut board flush to saw cuts. Replace rotted building paper.

Drive in new board; nail in place with aluminum or galvanized nails. Countersink nails, fill holes with putty, and paint.

Wood and asbestos shingles

Wood shingles, as a rule, are easier to repair than clapboard. You can usually fix those that have split or warped by simply nailing them down with aluminum or galvanized nails. If the shingle is on the exposed side of the house, however, where strong wind-driven rains could penetrate the cracks, cut a piece of roofing paper approximately the size of the shingle and slip it underneath the shingle before nailing it down. This will help to waterproof the patch.

Ordinarily, asbestos shingles, because they are not vulnerable to rot or weather, need little maintenance. Since they are relatively brittle, however, some shingles, especially in the lower courses, may become damaged and require replacement.

If you find that more than 10 percent of the shingles on a wall require replacement, it is best to replace the entire wall. If you are replacing an entire wall of asbestos shingles, save the old undamaged shingles—they can be used again. In wood shingle replacement, the old ones are left in place and used as the undercourse for the new wall.

Replacing wood shingles

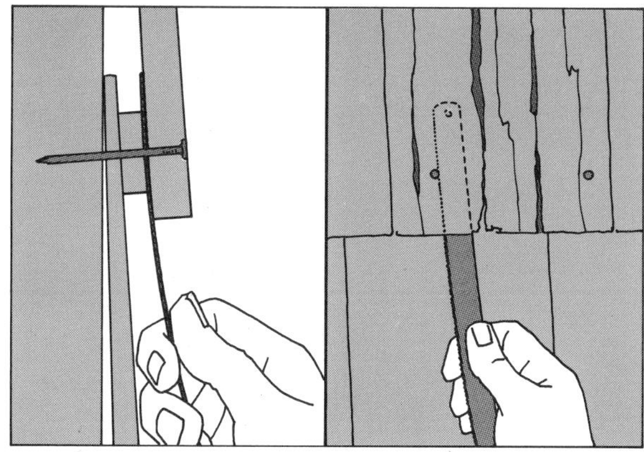

Slip a hacksaw blade under the bottom of the good shingle and cut the nails that hold the top of the damaged shingle. In the same way, cut nails at bottom of the damaged shingle.

To remove the damaged shingle, it is necessary, first, to splinter it. Then remove stubs of previously cut nails with a claw hammer or with pincers.

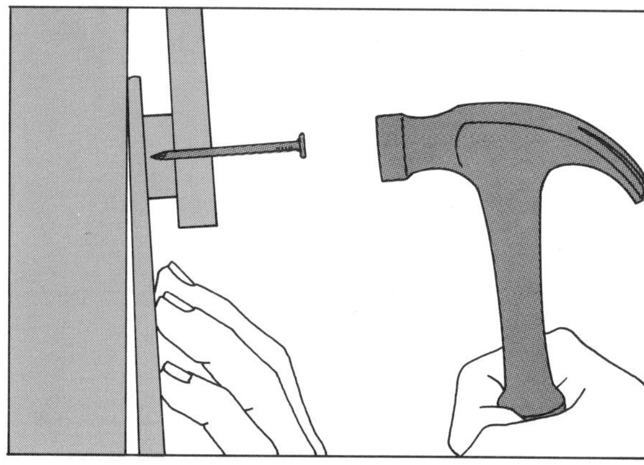

Slip a new shingle, the same size and thickness as the old one, into the open cavity. Top of new shingle is overlapped by upper shingle course; bottom overlaps lower shingle course.

Replacing asbestos shingles

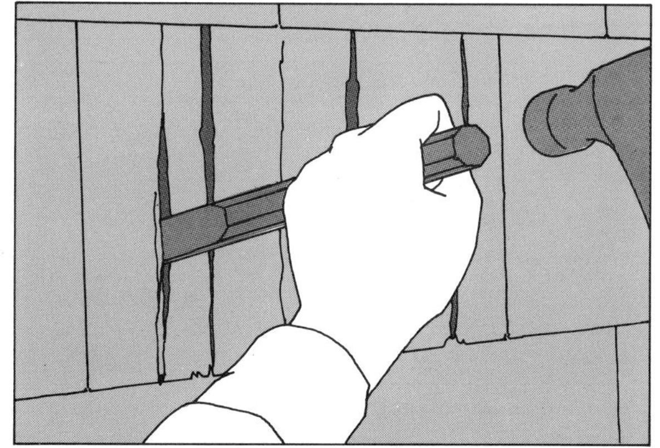

To remove an asbestos shingle, break it into pieces with a chisel and hammer. Do this carefully to avoid damaging nearby shingles. Remove nails with claw hammer or pincers.

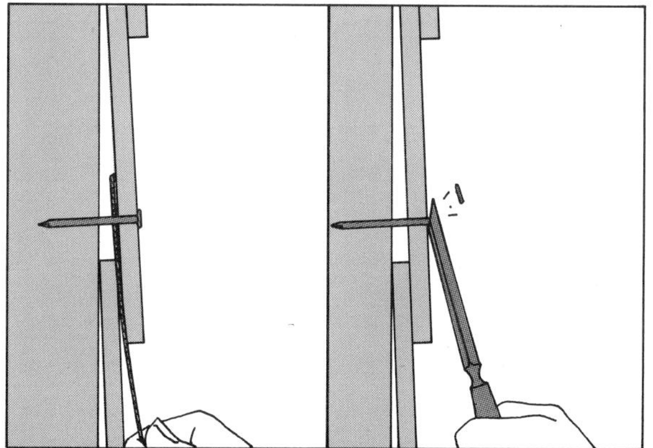

Shingles can also be removed by sawing through nails with a hacksaw or prying them out with a screwdriver, or by drilling through the nailheads or cutting them with chisel.

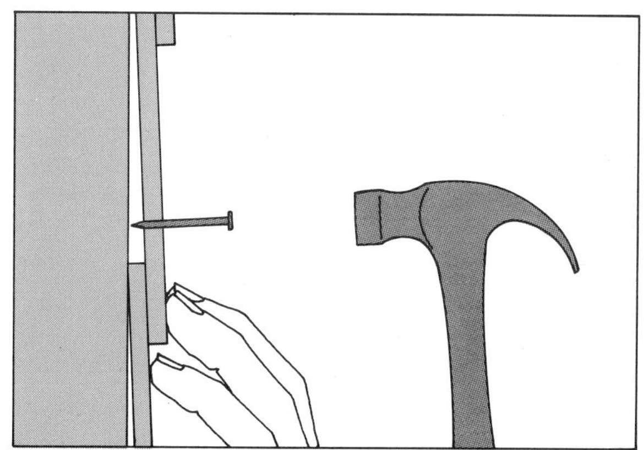

Asbestos shingles are not nailed at the top edge, so the new shingle is slid up from below, placed in position, then nailed in place through predrilled holes along bottom edge.

Caulking

How to buy and use caulking

Caulking is very important to the soundness of any house, helping to keep it air- and watertight where the windows and doors meet the walls.

Caulking compound is composed of a semisolid substance combined with a binder of natural and synthetic oils added to keep the caulk elastic and resilient. Caulking is available in bulk in gallon and 5-gallon cans and in disposable cartridges made for use with a caulking gun. Caulking guns are made in two types: The **full-barrel** type, which is designed for bulk filling, and the half-barrel or drop-in type, intended for use with the disposable cartridges. In addition, some types of caulking compound are available in squeeze tubes that are similar in look and function to giant toothpaste tubes.

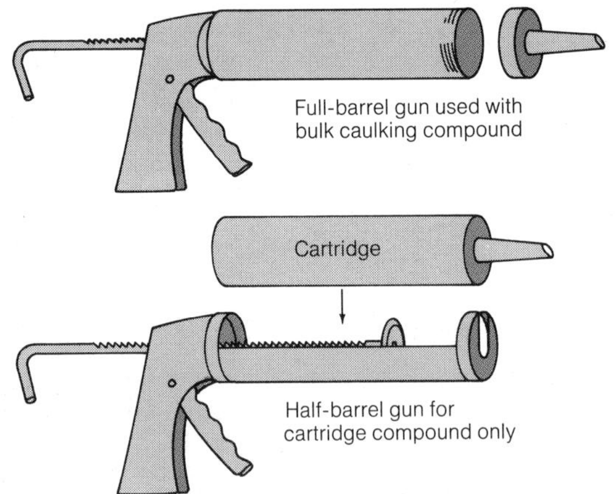

Two types of caulking guns; the more common uses cartridge

Caulking compound is available in five basic types:

1. Oil-base caulking is the most common and will bond to most surfaces—wood, masonry, and metal.

2. Latex-based, water-thinned caulking is fast-drying and will take paint very well.

3. Butyl rubber caulking is long-lasting and best suited for making metal-to-masonry joints.

4. Polyvinyl acetate caulking is a durable material that adheres to all surfaces, including paint.

5. Silicone caulking is the longest-lasting of all of the compounds and takes well to all surfaces, with the exception of paint.

All caulking compounds, regardless of form or composition, are available in white, gray, and black.

Where to use caulking

Caulking should be used wherever two different materials or parts of a house are joined. For specific places, check the following list:

1. Where the chimney meets roof shingles.
2. Between dormer cheeks and roof shingles.
3. All roof flashing.
4. Between underside of eaves and gable molding.
5. Beneath window sills at siding.
6. Between masonry steps, porches, patios, and the main body of the house.
7. At all corners formed by siding.
8. Between siding and window and door drip caps.
9. At joints between siding and window and door frames.
10. Between siding and vestibule or entrance roofs, or any protrusions from main body of house.

Getting a good bead

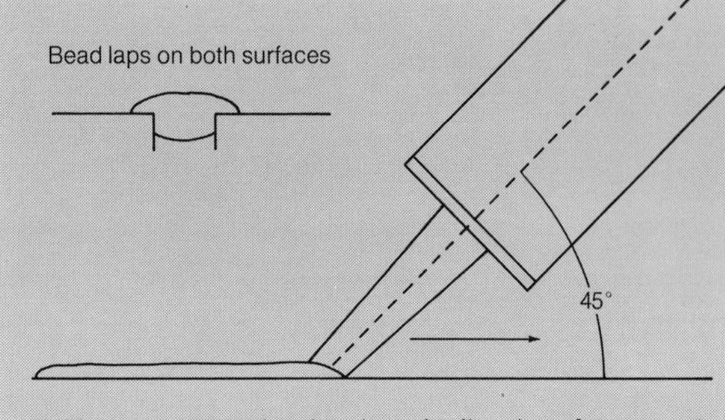

Hold gun at 45° angle; slant base in direction of movement

How to load the half-barrel caulking gun: Cut the tip off the nozzle; break inner seal; insert rear of cartridge first.

Before starting, remove all the old caulking. Wipe the area with a solvent-soaked rag. Work in warm weather.

The caulking compound should adhere to both sides of the joint to be sealed; a wide bead may be necessary.

Fill extra wide cracks with oakum, then apply the compound in one or more beads as needed to span the area.

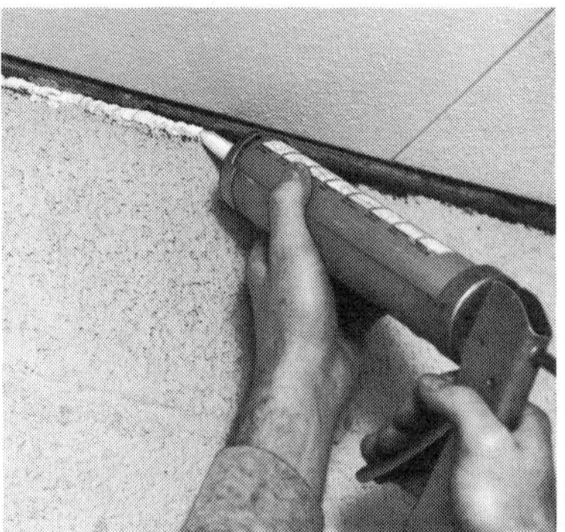

Hold the gun at a 45° angle to the work and slant the base of the gun in the direction of movement.

Caulking compound can also be bought in rope form. Unwind as shown and force it into cracks with your fingers.

How to replace a window sill

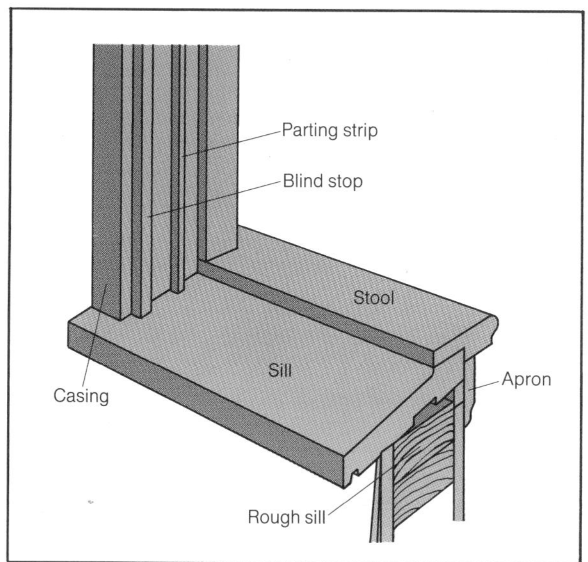

Cutaway drawing shows construction of a typical window sill. The exterior part of the sill should always slope toward the front of the house to drain water away from the sill.

First step is removing the old sill. Raise the window and cut the rotted sill in one or more places as shown. Be careful that you do not cut into the stool on the inside of the room.

If the cut parts cannot be pulled out, use a chisel to split the sill into smaller pieces for removal. Check for nails that may be holding the sill in place.

Use the old sill as a guide for trimming the new sill. Beveling the ends slightly will make it easier to install the new sill. Sand the new sill before installing it.

Use brads to anchor the new sill to the window casing. Sink the heads slightly below the surface of the wood, fill depressions with putty or wood dough, and seal with shellac.

Seal the edges of the window sill where they meet the window frame with a caulking compound. Finally, paint the exterior part of the sill with outdoor paint.

Waterproofing basement walls

Repairing from the outside

A wet basement can be caused by either surface or ground water leakage. **Surface water** usually shows up as stains on the wall starting at a level with the outside ground surface and diminishing as the wall approaches the floor. Surface water originates in overflow from puddles, streams, or roof gutters, or from rain or thawing snow. If water seepage occurs after rainy periods, suspect surface water.

A common cause of surface water problems is improper roof drainage. A dry well arrangement (p. 173) usually corrects this. If a house is in a natural drainage path, the only cure is to use ditches or retaining walls, or have the surrounding ground regraded (this usually calls for professional help).

Ground water in the basement is often identifiable by water stains low on the wall. It will ooze through the floor or enter at junctures of floor and wall. Persistent flooding generally comes from ground rather than surface water. You can prevent ground water penetration by: (1) Laying a tile drain around the cellar; (2) waterproofing the outside wall surface; or (3) treating the inside wall surface (p. 158).

Outside waterproofing, though it is more work, is generally considered more effective than treating inner walls, for it deflects water pressure instead of letting it push through to the inner surface. Where there is considerable water pressure—as in moist clay soil—exterior treatment may be necessary.

If only a small crack is involved, you can use a liquid sealer or patching compound; for a major problem, the best waterproofing solution is a coat of asphalt roofing cement or a plastic sealer. For added protection, asphalt or vinyl sheeting is often applied to the outer side of the foundation. This method requires digging away the soil from around the outside of the walls.

The professional technique involves forcing a special sealing compound along the base of the wall under pressure; it tends to flow to the wall and seal fissures and cracks. The job can be done professionally without digging. The cost depends upon the severity of the problem; ask for an estimate.

First step in exterior waterproofing is to dig away the earth from the problem wall. To lay drainage tile, you will have to dig down to the base of the footing.

Scrape away all loose earth. Place a tarp on the adjacent ground to protect the grass. Cracks in the wall should become apparent at this stage.

Next, use a stiff brush and warm water to clean the foundation. Chisel and rake out all cracks or faulty joints. Fill all cracks with a mortar mix (p.447).

Using a liquid sealer

To use a liquid sealer as a waterproofer, you must first dig a shallow trench next to the foundation and above the leak, then pour the sealer into the trench. Usually, two applications will do the job.

After the wall is dry, trowel on a heavy coat of asphalt roof cement, asphalt roof paint, or any of the many available sealers. Problem walls take two coats.

Ground water can be led away from the wall with special drainpipes and tiles. Drainpipes, sloped ½ in. per foot, should lead to a sewer or a dry well.

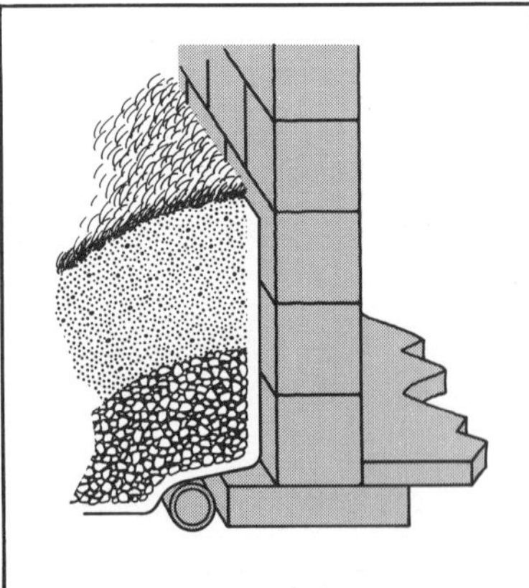

Cross section showing relationship of drain tiles to footing and foundation. Note use of asphalt paper to protect wall, and gravel to facilitate drainage.

Loose hinges

If screws cannot be tightened or do not hold, remove them, fill the holes with wood slivers and waterproof glue, and drive the screws back. Using longer screws or moving hinges to solid wood will sometimes work. If not, drill through the hinge holes to the other side of the post and secure hinge with nuts and bolts.

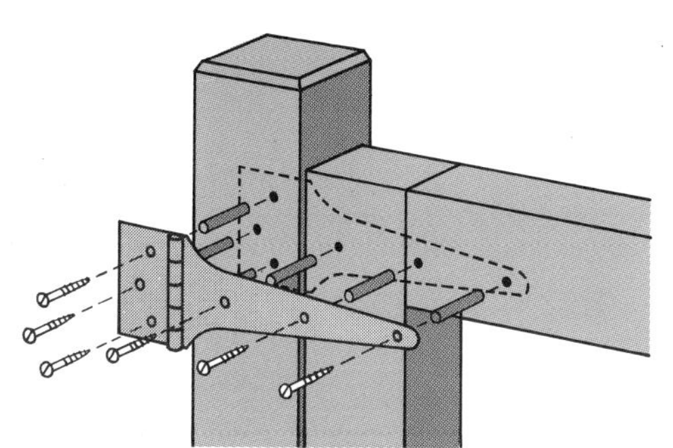

Remove loose screws, plug oversize holes with wood dipped in waterproof glue, and drive screws back.

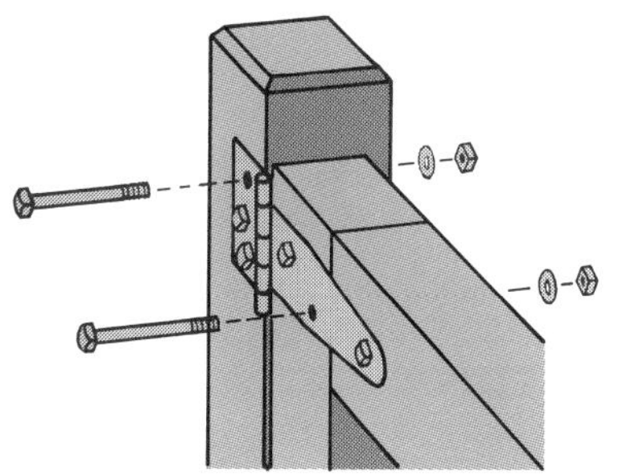

If hinges cannot be moved to a new position or holes successfully plugged, try bolting the hinges.

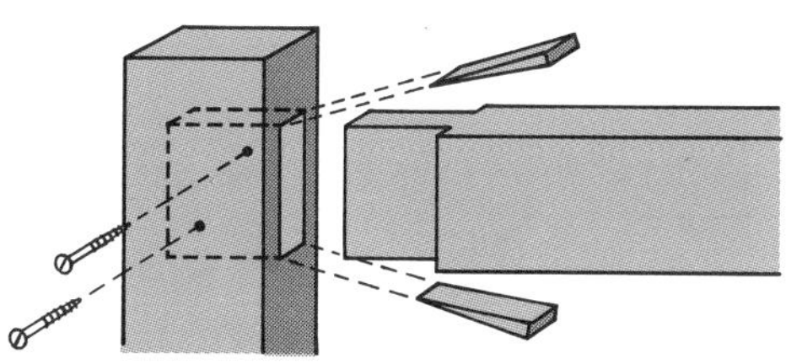

Wedges and waterproof glue can also be used to tighten loose gate joints. Make wedges of hardwood.

Loose frame

If the gate's frame isn't square, but it is not broken, use a wire and a turnbuckle to bring it back to its proper shape. Or you can install a brace, made out of a 1 x 4, from the bottom rail to the top rail. On wider gates, make it an X brace with a half-lap joint in the middle (p. 394).

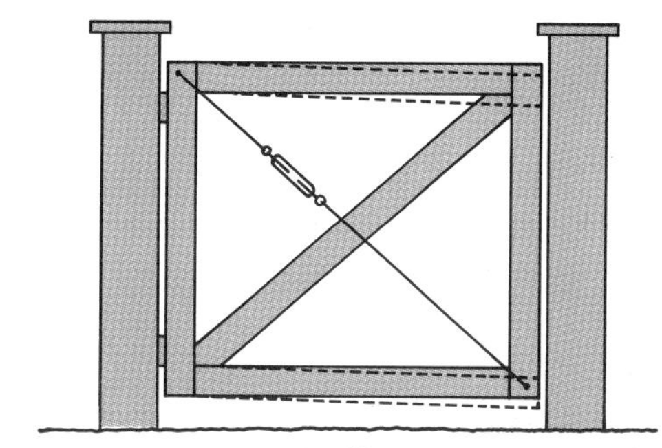

Use a wire and a turnbuckle to square up a sagging gate. Connect the wire to a screw eye at each end.

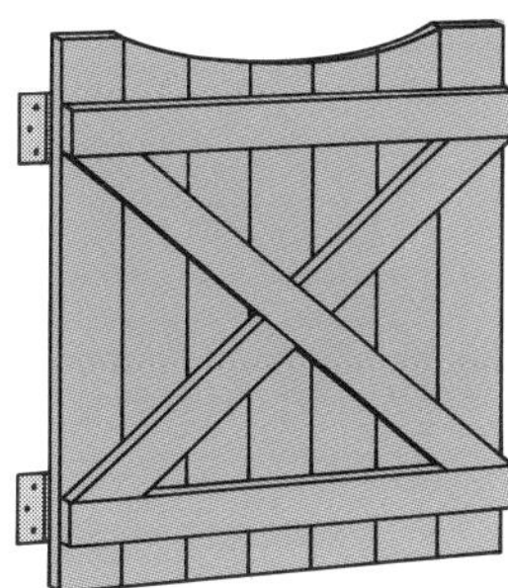

An X frame gives strong support to a wider frame. Use 1 x 4 lumber; miter ends to fit the corners.

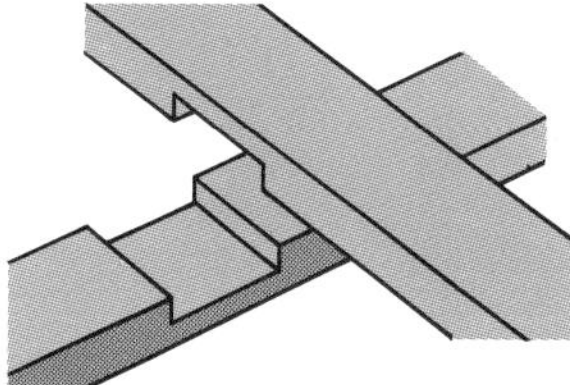

Make a half-lap joint where the two parts of the X frame cross. Add a screw for greater strength.

Sagging post

A sagging post can cause a gate to operate poorly. If a post set in concrete has shrunk, try driving a hardwood wedge between post and concrete; seal with asphalt paint or roof cement. If a post has loosened from a masonry wall, fasten it with lead anchors. For more about sagging posts, see next two pages.

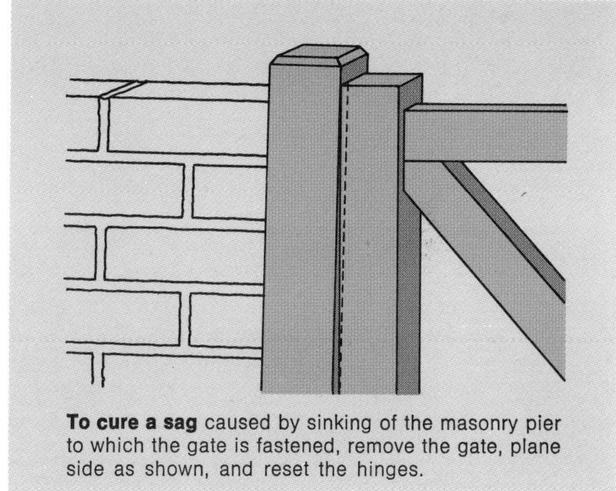

To cure a sag caused by sinking of the masonry pier to which the gate is fastened, remove the gate, plane side as shown, and reset the hinges.

Installing a gate stop

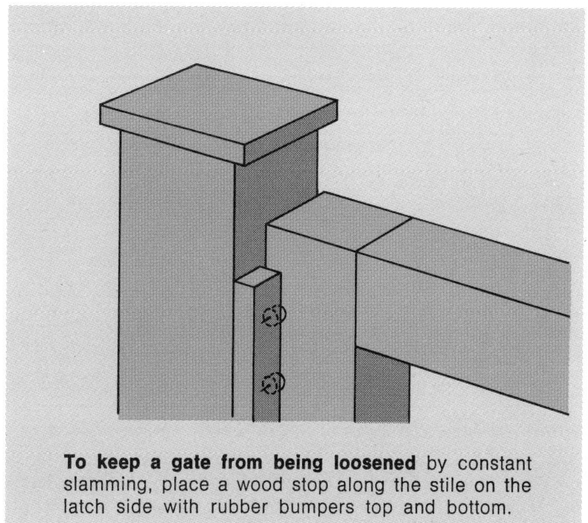

To keep a gate from being loosened by constant slamming, place a wood stop along the stile on the latch side with rubber bumpers top and bottom.

Repairing fence posts

How to set a post

You can avoid unnecessary fence repairs by setting posts correctly and protecting them against decay. Wood posts should be set with one-third of their length in the ground. They should be treated before setting with a preservative, the most popular being creosote and pentachlorophenol (penta). The best application method is to let the posts stand overnight in a can containing the preservative. This gives the end grain time to absorb the chemical.

When setting a post, place a flat rock or layer of gravel in the bottom of the hole and rest the post on it. Concrete fill is not necessary in firm, well drained soil, providing the earth is compacted around the base, and the post is properly treated before setting. In loose soil, prepare a mixture of concrete (p.469) and pour it into the hole, tamping it tightly in place. Make the post hole slightly larger at the base than at the top. Set the post and fill the area around it to ground level. Top off with a cement cap troweled at a 45-degree angle from the post to the ground. Apply roof paint or asphalt cement to any cracks between the post and the concrete after the concrete has hardened. Steel posts should be set the same way, except the lower end should be liberally coated with asphalt paint to prevent rusting. Provide posts with a flange at the base, or a crossbar passing through drilled holes, to keep the post from turning in the concrete.

Use a post-hole digger to make holes. Try not to disturb the surrounding earth.

Paint or dip posts in preservative for protection against insects and decay.

Place a couple of shovelfuls of gravel in the bottom of the hole for drainage.

Set posts vertically and check with level. Hold in place with braces.

Make up a batch of concrete (p.469) and shovel it into the hole around post.

Tamp concrete to eliminate air bubbles. Slope at top so water will drain off.

Wobbly and heaved posts

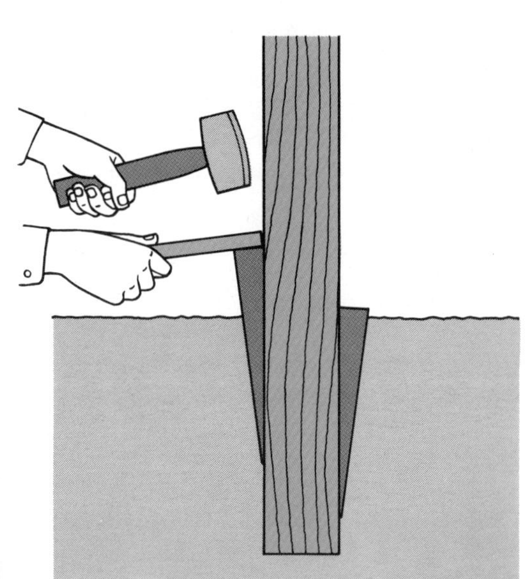

To give temporary support to a wobbly wooden post, drive 2 x 2 wedges in on opposite sides. Bind the wedges to the post with wire.

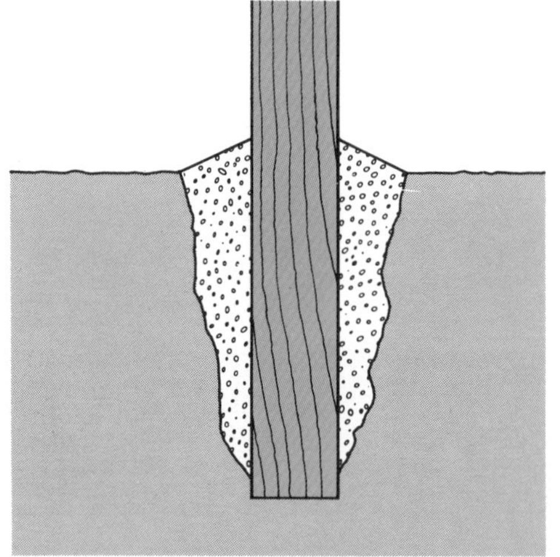

Heaved post caused by frost action should be set as described at left, except that concrete should be set below frost line to prevent future heaving.

Repairing wood and metal posts

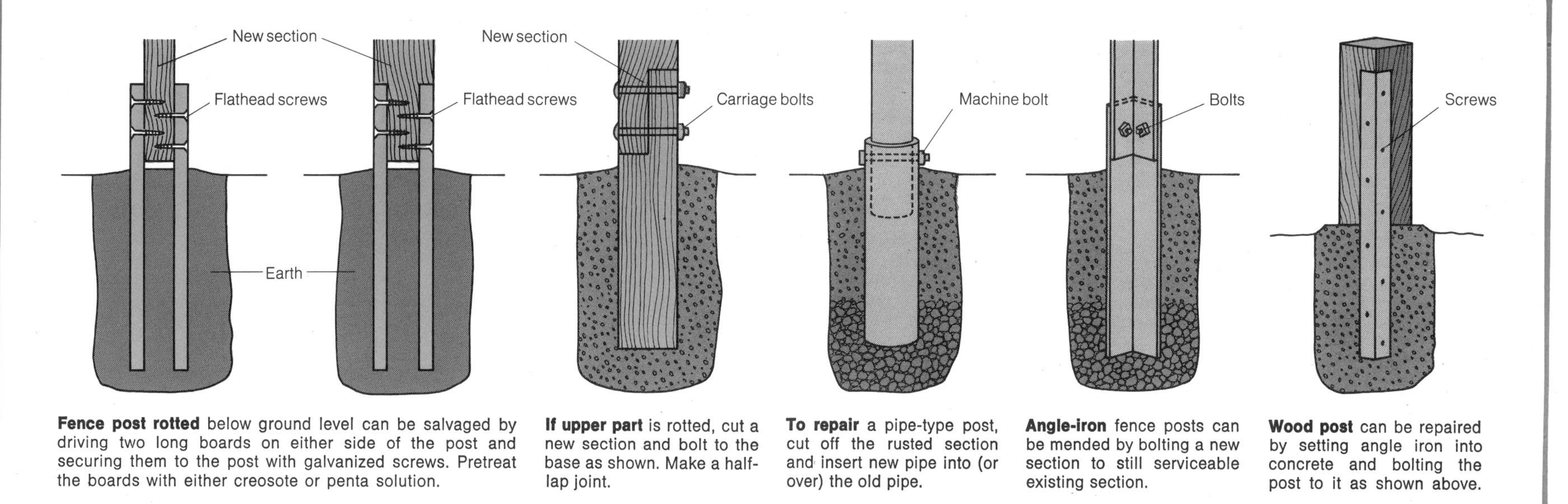

Fence post rotted below ground level can be salvaged by driving two long boards on either side of the post and securing them to the post with galvanized screws. Pretreat the boards with either creosote or penta solution.

If upper part is rotted, cut a new section and bolt to the base as shown. Make a half-lap joint.

To repair a pipe-type post, cut off the rusted section and insert new pipe into (or over) the old pipe.

Angle-iron fence posts can be mended by bolting a new section to still serviceable existing section.

Wood post can be repaired by setting angle iron into concrete and bolting the post to it as shown above.

Posts in concrete

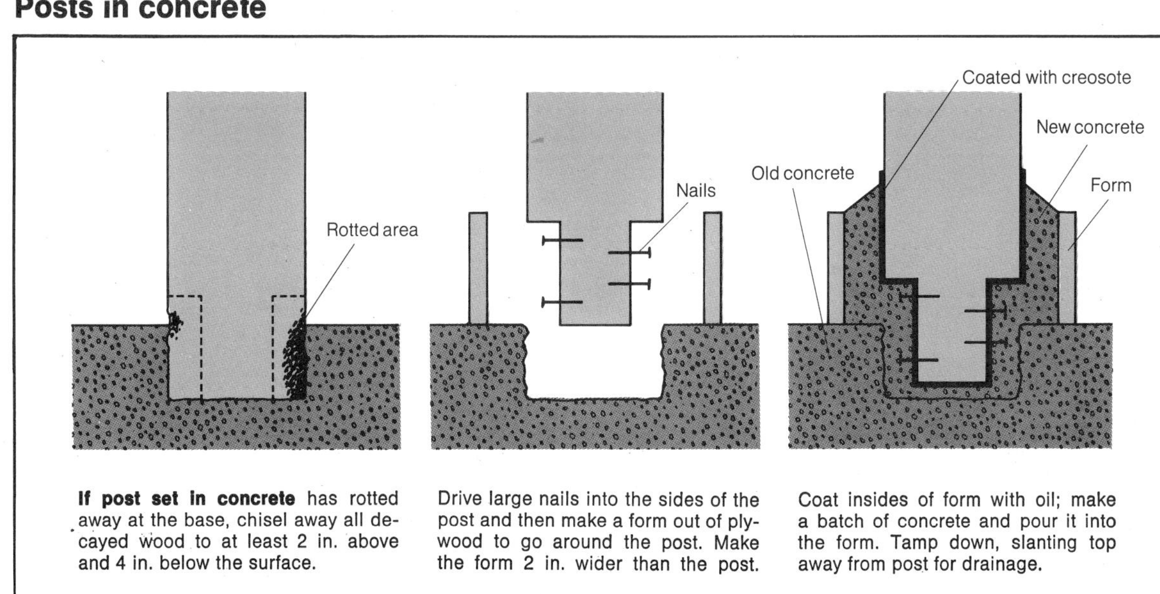

If post set in concrete has rotted away at the base, chisel away all decayed wood to at least 2 in. above and 4 in. below the surface.

Drive large nails into the sides of the post and then make a form out of plywood to go around the post. Make the form 2 in. wider than the post.

Coat insides of form with oil; make a batch of concrete and pour it into the form. Tamp down, slanting top away from post for drainage.

Removable post

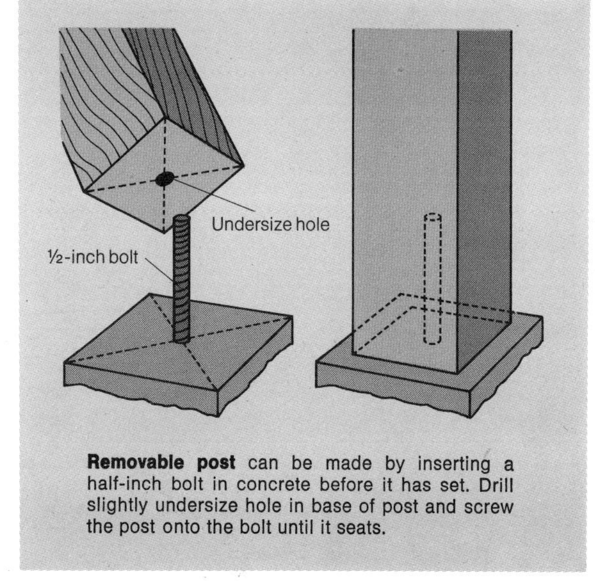

Removable post can be made by inserting a half-inch bolt in concrete before it has set. Drill slightly undersize hole in base of post and screw the post onto the bolt until it seats.

Repairing a wood fence

Replacing a damaged rail or picket

The best solution for a badly rotted fence post is a new one, set in concrete (p.186). Fence rails, however, can usually be repaired or replaced without disturbing the posts. Usually the end of the rail rots first. Nails rust out and the resulting openings let rain into the end grain. If no more than an inch or two is damaged, the rail may be salvaged by cutting away the rotted section and nailing a 2 x 4 extension to the remainder of the rail and then to the post. Other replacement methods are shown below.

Broken or rotted pickets are best replaced individually, using a discarded one as a model for new ones. They can be quickly cut from standard stock obtainable in lumberyards. Nail the pickets to the top and bottom rails with rust-resistant nails, sinking them slightly, and fill the holes with a wood putty or sawdust mixed with waterproof glue. Steel nailheads, being prone to rusting even when covered with paint, should first be shellacked and then the entire picket replacement (or the whole fence, for appearance' sake) given a coat of outdoor paint.

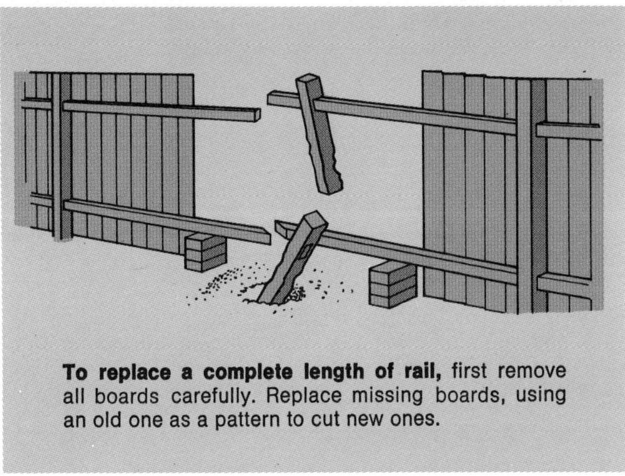

To replace a complete length of rail, first remove all boards carefully. Replace missing boards, using an old one as a pattern to cut new ones.

How to space pickets

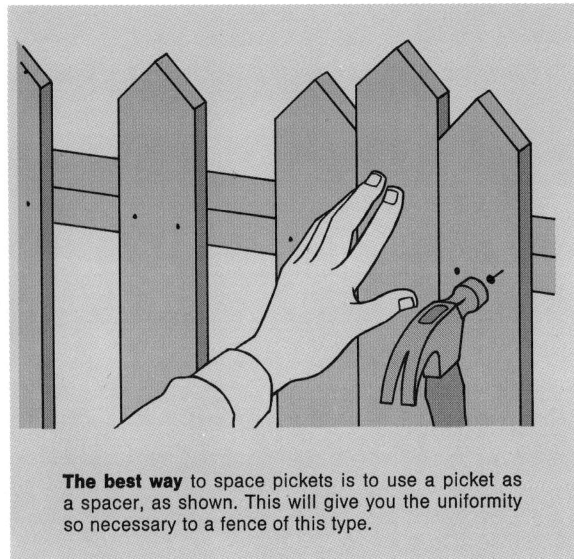

The best way to space pickets is to use a picket as a spacer, as shown. This will give you the uniformity so necessary to a fence of this type.

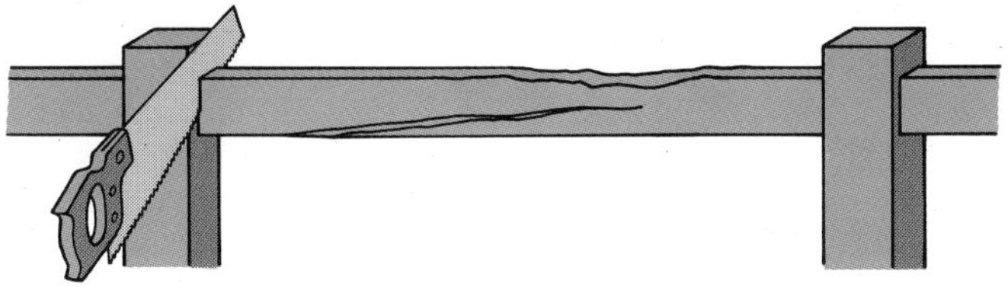

To replace a rotted rail, saw it off as close to the post as possible. Do the same at the other end.

Force each post inward so you can saw off a part of the remaining rail at each end equal to half the post width.

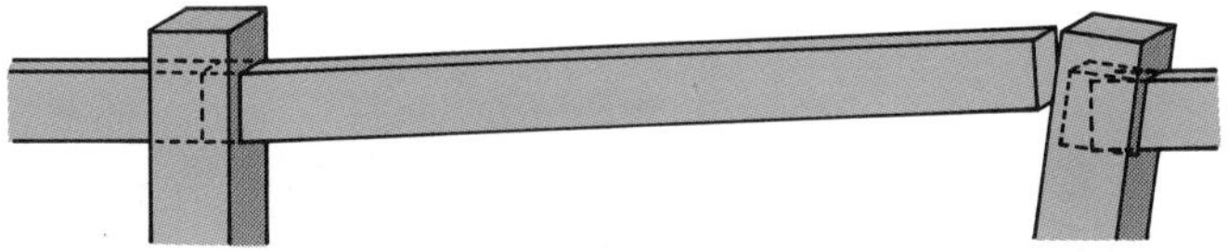

Now force one of the posts outward far enough that the new rail can be slipped into the post sockets.

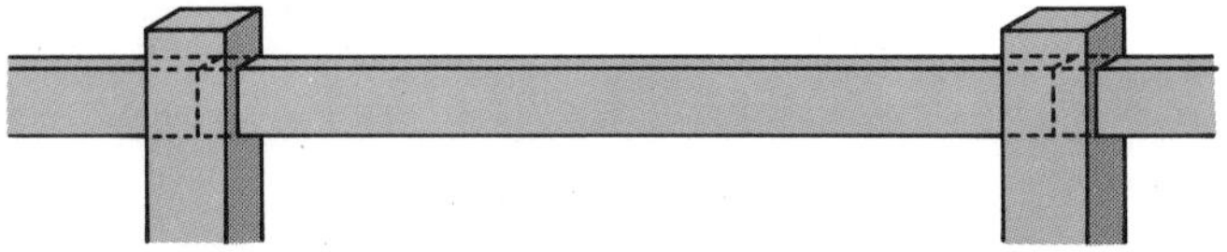

Straighten tilted post. Tamp down earth so that it will support the post properly. Paint the new rail.

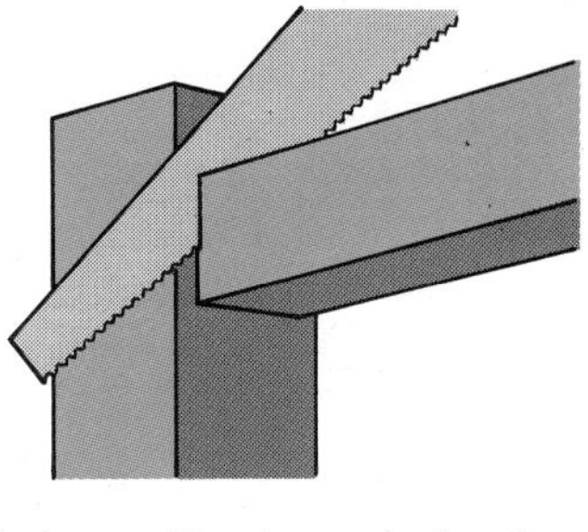

If post is immovable, draw out all nails and saw off the rotted rail as close to the post as possible.

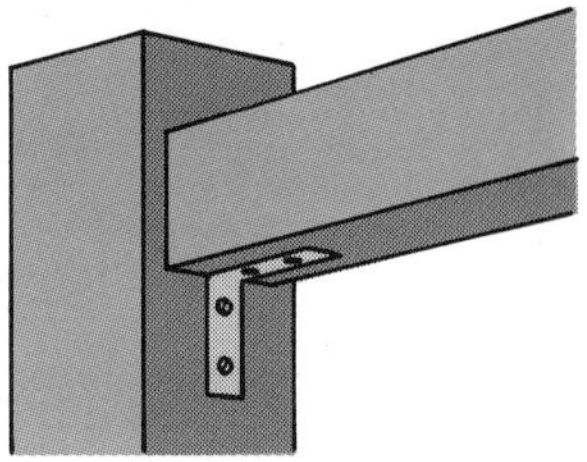

Cut a new rail to the exact length required. Attach one angle iron at each end to support the new rail.

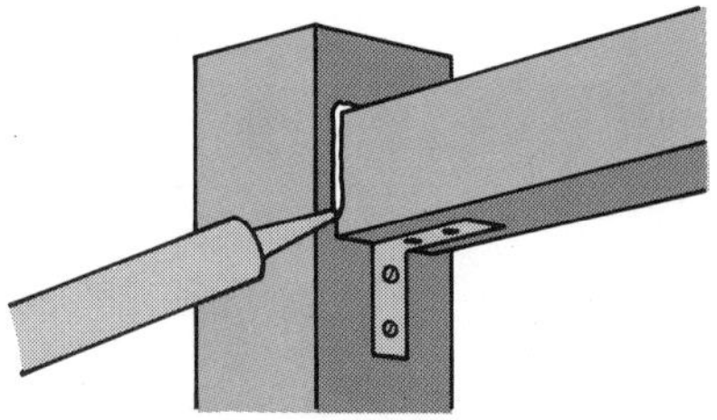

Prevent future rot at the joint by caulking the juncture with sealing compound. Paint the angle irons to prevent rusting.

Sagging door

Hinge-mounted garage doors have a tendency to sag and often can be opened and closed only with difficulty. You can correct this sagging by driving wood wedges under the dropped corner of the door until it hangs straight. When it is hanging properly, tighten all the hinge screws. If the existing screws cannot be tightened, replace them with longer screws or reposition the hinges so that the screws can be driven into solid wood.

If the screws cannot be tightened because the wood has rotted, remove the screws. Then drill all the way through the hinge holes and secure the hinges with rust-resistant bolts and nuts. Replace the hinges if they are damaged or twisted.

Sagging frame

If a swinging garage door sags, and its hinges are tight, the chances are that the door is not square. To make the door square and plumb, drive wedges under the door until it hangs straight. Strengthen the corners with right-angle steel mending plates. Then install a metal door brace with a turnbuckle.

When making this installation, be sure to extend the brace to its full length. Screw one end of the brace to the bottom rail at the sagging corner and the other end as far up as possible on the hinge side of the stile. Then tighten the turnbuckle until the corner is raised. You can also use a wood brace made out of 1 x 4 lumber installed between the lower outside corner and the upper inside corner as shown.

Maintenance

The hinges of these garage doors should be kept oiled. Also the doors, especially the bottom part, should be kept painted for protection against the weather. If rot along the bottom has not progressed to the point where you need a new door, cut away the decay only and patch with new wood. Then saturate the entire area with a wood preservative. Next, cut a strip of aluminum wide enough to fold over both sides of the bottom of the door. Attach it with rust-resistant nails and seal the edges so that rain cannot penetrate between metal and door.

If a panel has rotted, remove it carefully, cut a new panel from ¼-inch exterior plywood and secure with ½-inch quarter-round molding and brads.

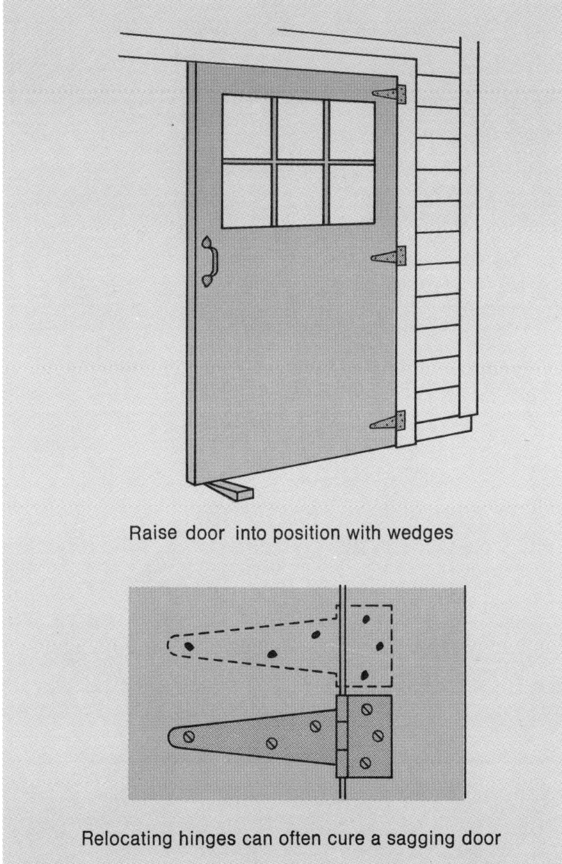

Raise door into position with wedges

Relocating hinges can often cure a sagging door

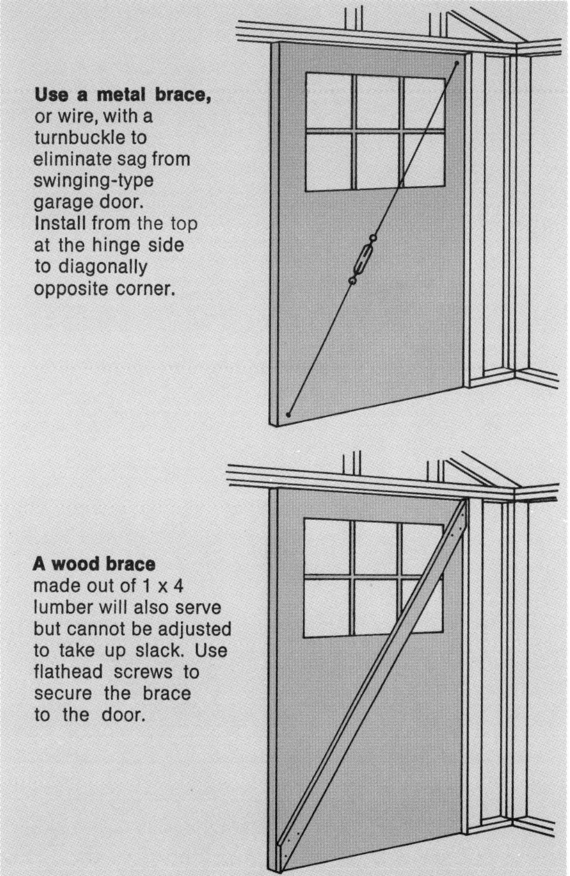

Use a metal brace, or wire, with a turnbuckle to eliminate sag from swinging-type garage door. Install from the top at the hinge side to diagonally opposite corner.

A wood brace made out of 1 x 4 lumber will also serve but cannot be adjusted to take up slack. Use flathead screws to secure the brace to the door.

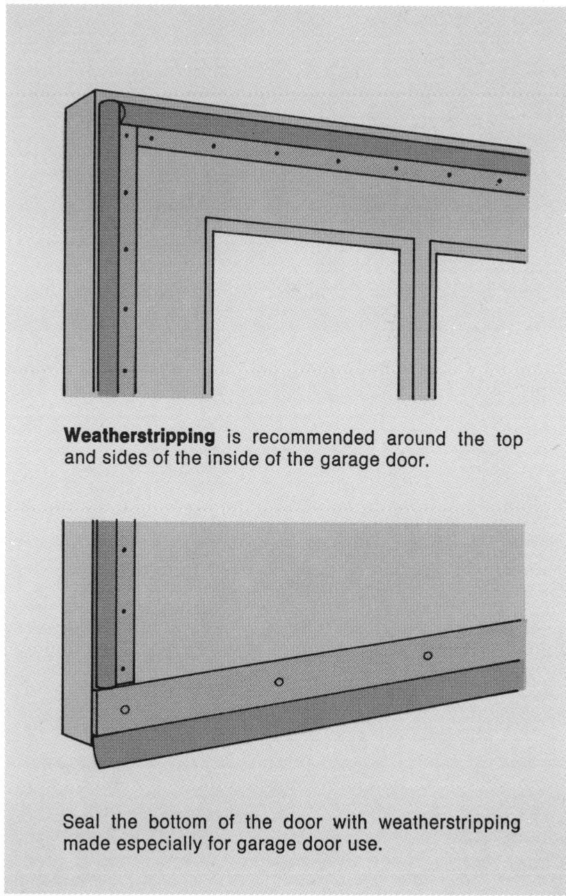

Weatherstripping is recommended around the top and sides of the inside of the garage door.

Seal the bottom of the door with weatherstripping made especially for garage door use.

Overhead garage doors

Roll-up doors

Most dragging or binding of overhead garage doors can be traced to improper track alignment or lack of lubrication. The vertical tracks must be plumb and the two curved sections at the same height. Track mounting brackets have slots for adjustment, made by loosening the screws or lag bolts. Also, when checking the track, make sure the overhead track is set to slant slightly downward toward the rear of the garage so the raised door will stay in the "up" position. Replace any bent or distorted track.

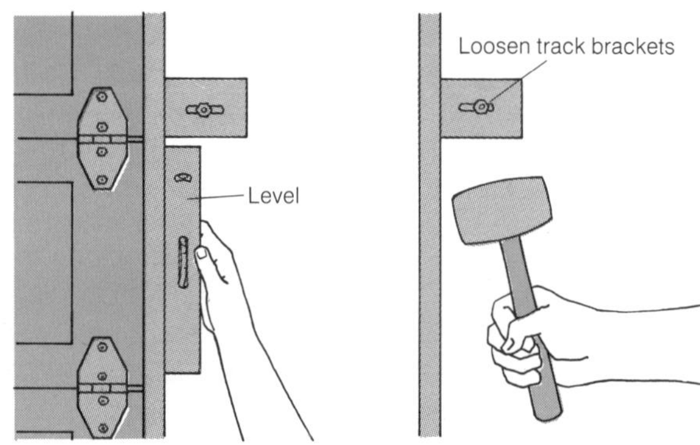

Check if door is plumb with a level. Make adjustment, if necessary, by loosening the brackets and tapping track with a mallet or a block of wood.

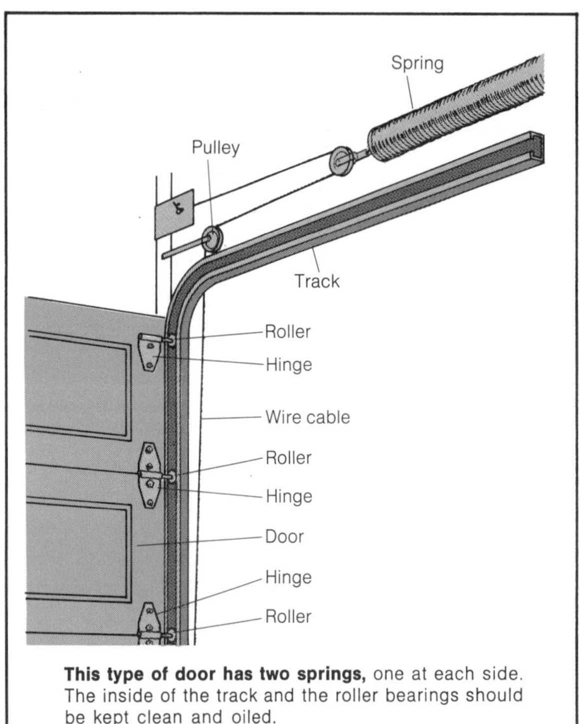

This type of door has two springs, one at each side. The inside of the track and the roller bearings should be kept clean and oiled.

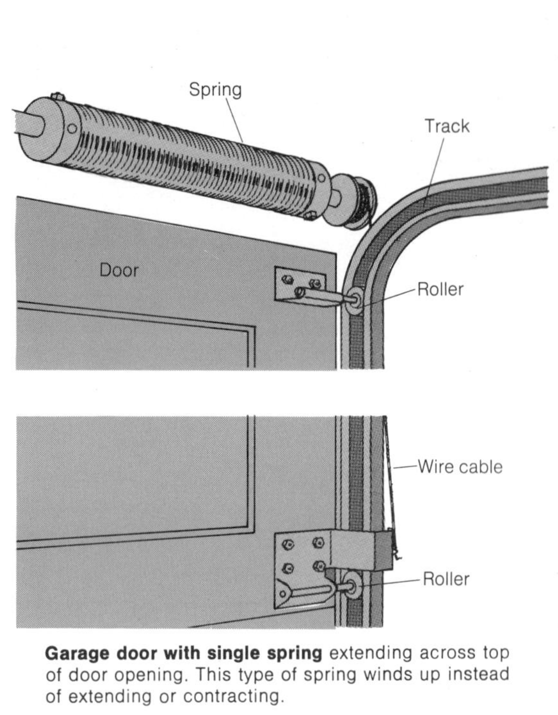

Garage door with single spring extending across top of door opening. This type of spring winds up instead of extending or contracting.

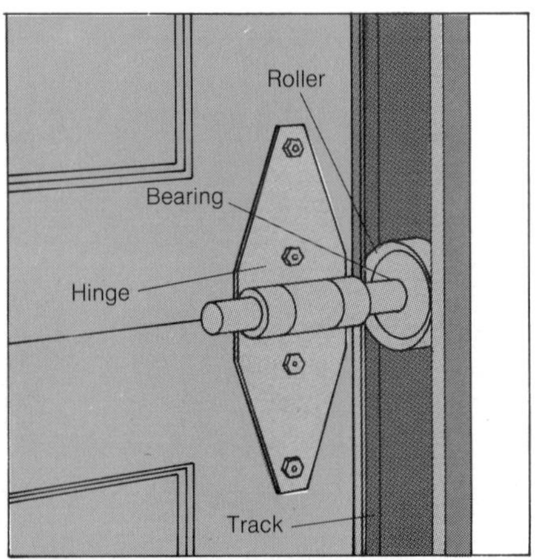

Loose or bent hinges will cause rollers to bind in their tracks. Binding can also be caused by a broken roller shaft. Keep rollers oiled.

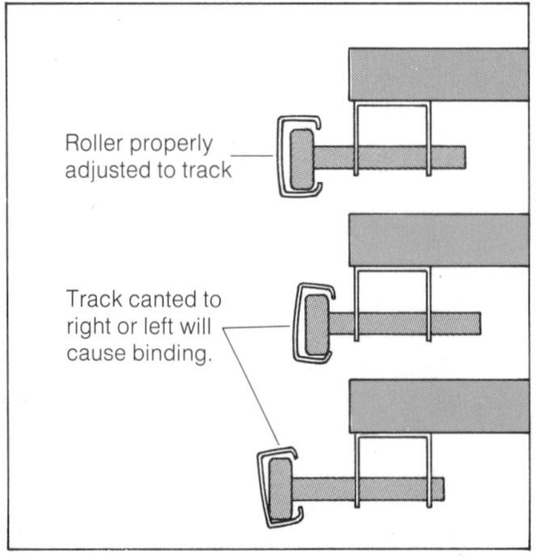

Rollers should be properly adjusted to track. Too tight a fit will cause binding, may even stall the motor if door is power-operated.

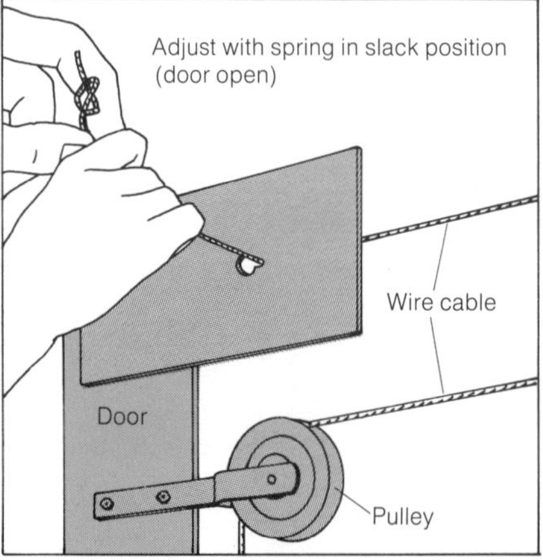

Spring tension in this type of door is adjusted by shortening the cable or by taking up the slack. Make sure the cable end is secured.

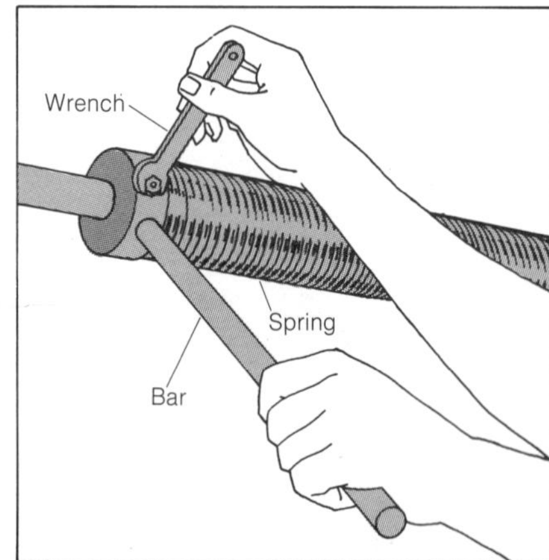

Adjust tension in the spring of this type of garage door by loosening locknut and winding spring tighter with bar inserted in collar.

Swing-up doors

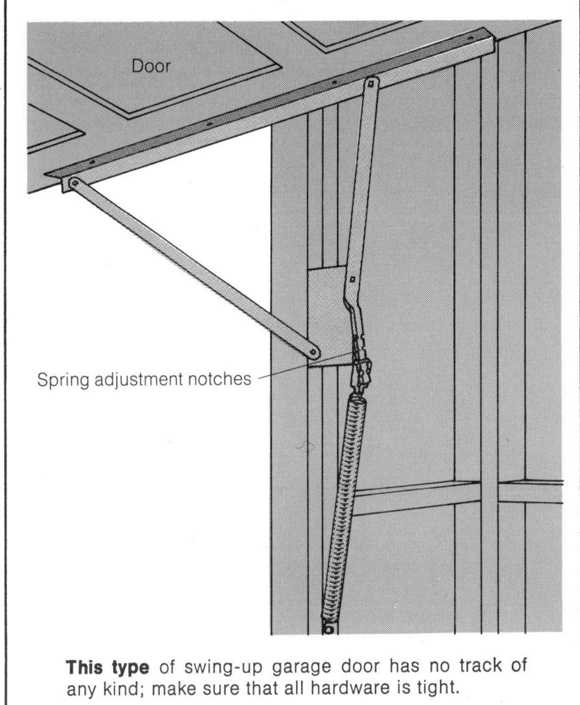

This type of swing-up garage door has no track of any kind; make sure that all hardware is tight.

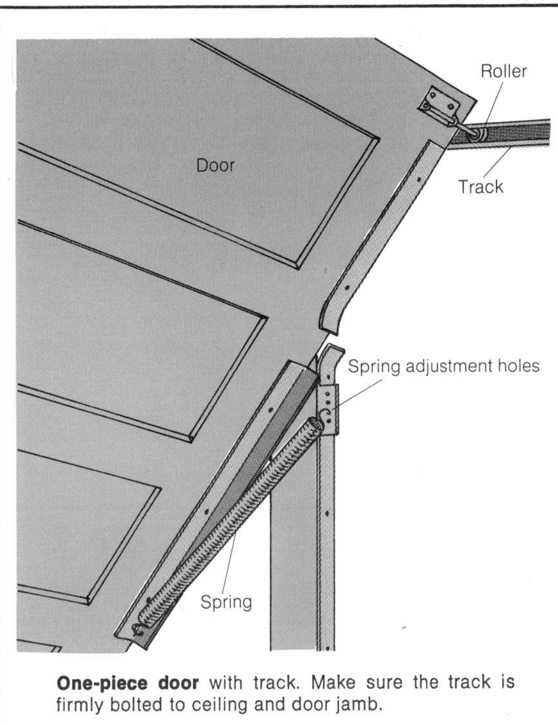

One-piece door with track. Make sure the track is firmly bolted to ceiling and door jamb.

Garage door locks and latches

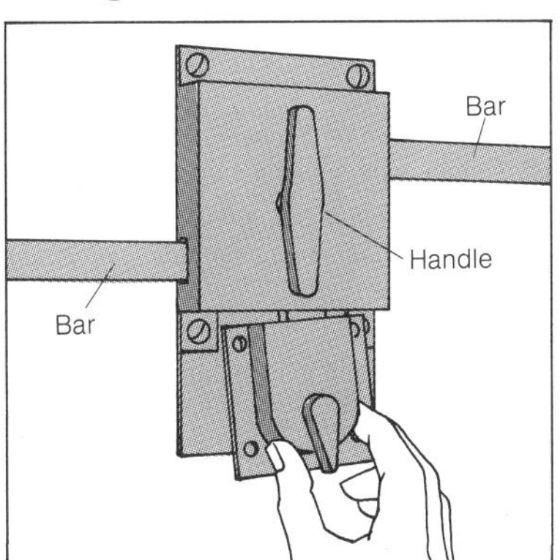

Typical garage door lock consists of two spring-loaded bars controlled by a key on the outside. You remove the screws to get at and lubricate the latch mechanism.

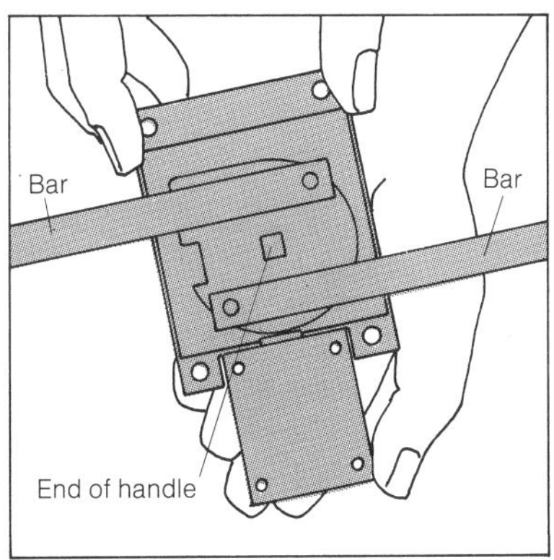

The crank handle lock mechanism creates locking bars that latch in door rail tracks. Once a year lubricate all moving parts. Use powdered graphite rather than oil.

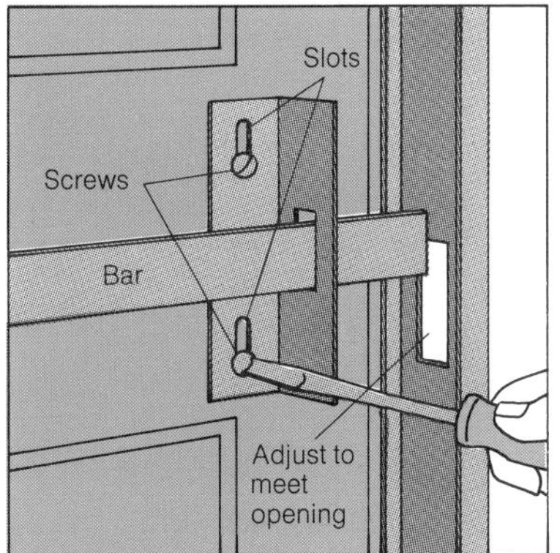

Guides at the edge of each side of the door can be adjusted so the locking bars glide freely through their openings. Tighten bracket screws after adjusting.

Maintenance of doors

Swing-up garage doors do not generally require much maintenance, except for the moving hardware, which should be kept lubricated with oil or powdered graphite. Lubricate the hinges and rollers with the door in the "down" position. Since oiled tracks collect dirt, it will be necessary to clean the tracks occasionally with a rag dampened with paint thinner. Straighten out any nicks you notice in the tracks. Be sure to keep overhead garage doors well painted, especially the bottom edge, to protect them from rain, snow, and sun.

Weatherstripping

Like the other exterior doors of the house, garage doors should be weatherstripped. The type of stripping shown gives an especially good fit because the weight of the door compresses it against the concrete floor, creating a tight seal.

Raise the door. Sand and paint the bottom with wood preservative before installing any weatherstripping.

Install the weatherstripping with galvanized nails. Stagger the nails. Roofing nails with large heads are best to use.

Electric garage-door opener

Preparation for installation

Electric garage-door operators are for installation on overhead doors that slide up and down on tracks. Most units are suitable for either sectional doors that glide in curved tracks, or one-piece doors that glide on straight tracks. Make certain which type of door you have before ordering an opening unit.

Also measure the door's height and width, since these measurements can affect the size of the control unit you need. Check the distance between the highest arc of door travel and the garage ceiling. Most opening units require at least 2 inches clearance.

Prior to installation, prepare the door by checking that all hardware is working properly. Oil the rollers and apply a liberal coat of grease to the tracks. Be sure the door is balanced.

Make the existing door locks inoperable by jamming them in the open position, or hacksawing off the locking bar ends. The door operator unit could become seriously damaged if it strains to open a locked door. It is not necessary to be able to lock the door, since a door equipped with the automatic opener cannot be opened manually from outside the garage. In the event of electrical failure, however, the connecting arm can easily be disconnected from the carrier to permit manual operation.

One safety feature you should not fail to look for in the control unit you buy is an automatic return switch. This device causes the automatic reversal of the door when it encounters an obstruction during its downward slide.

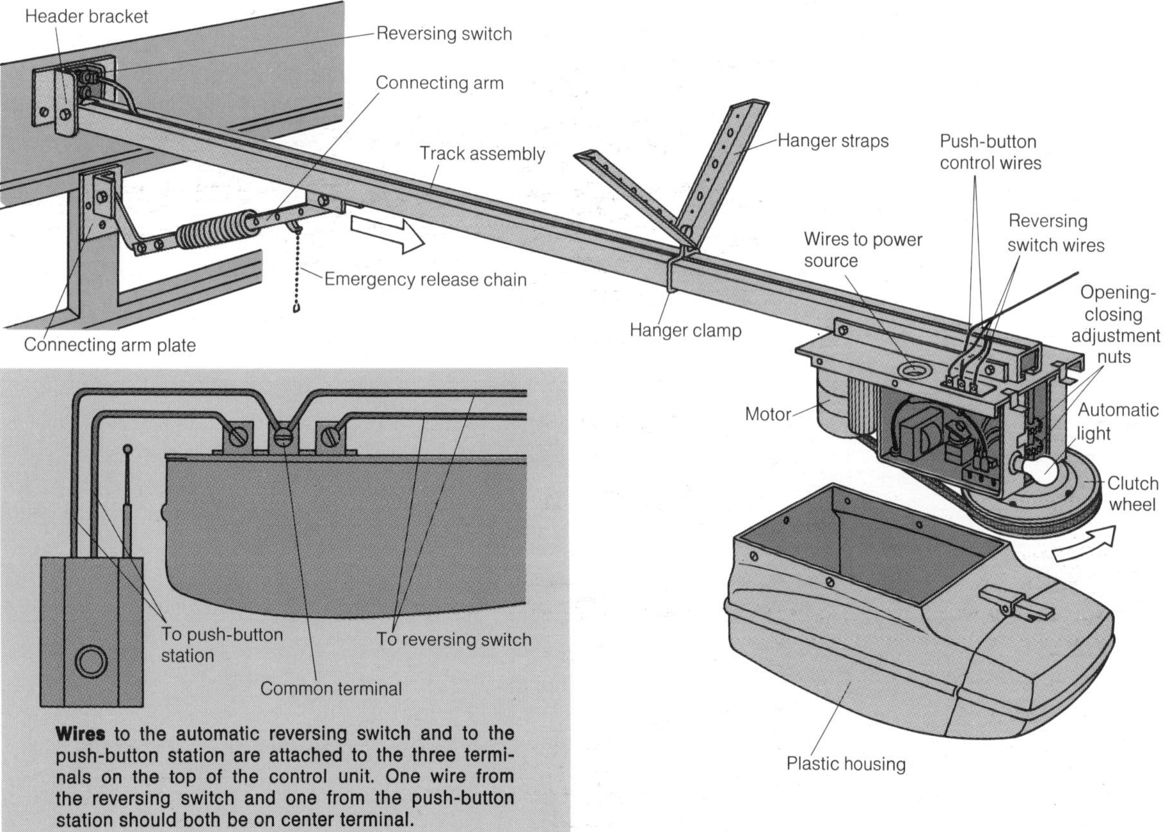

Wires to the automatic reversing switch and to the push-button station are attached to the three terminals on the top of the control unit. One wire from the reversing switch and one from the push-button station should both be on center terminal.

Adjustments

Your door opener will require adjustment right after installation, to make it close more snugly or open wider. A clutch adjustment for the drive belt permits it to slip if the door's downward travel is obstructed. This slippage is an extra safety factor which occurs before the automatic reversal control takes over.

Opening adjustment (with door closed): Turn bottom nut to left if door opens too wide; to right if not wide enough. **Closing adjustment** (with door open): Turn upper nut left to close tighter; to right to close less.

Automatic reverse adjustment (so doors reverse with minimum pressure): Tighten nut nearest switch until spring has about ⅛ in. between coils. Test door. Loosening bottom spring nut will decrease required pressure.

Adjust clutch by using large wrench to tighten wheel nut so clutch is just tight enough to move door through its cycle but will slip if movement is obstructed. Then adjust wheel nut a quarter turn tighter.

Installation

Screw reversing switch and header bracket to exact center of door header beam. Leave at least 2 in. clearance to ceiling.

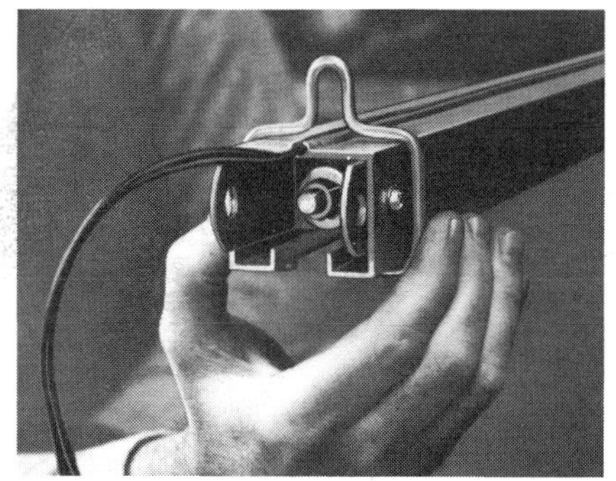

Slip wire hanger clamp over the track assembly with the loop side up. This hanger clamp will later fasten to the supporting straps.

Raise the end of the track assembly to mate with the header bracket. Fit the retaining bolt; do not tighten.

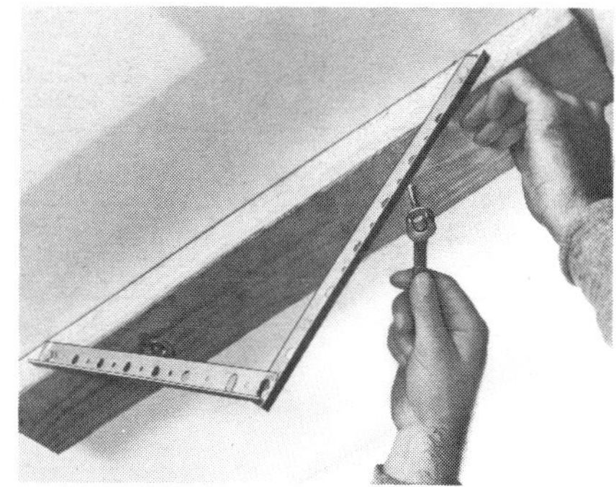

Fasten the hanger straps to the ceiling 2 ft. ahead of the operator unit. If ceiling is closed in, fasten a 2 x 4 to joist.

With an open ceiling, screw the hanger straps to the face of the beam. In either fastening application, use 1½ in. lag screws.

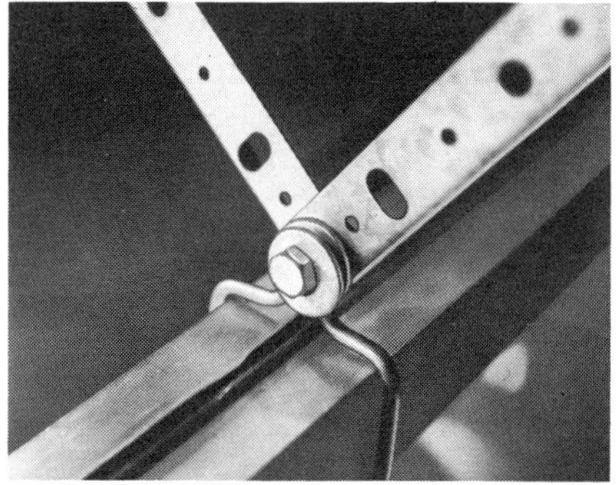

Lift operator unit to meet hanger straps and bolt hanger clamp to straps. This is an awkward step, so do it with a helper.

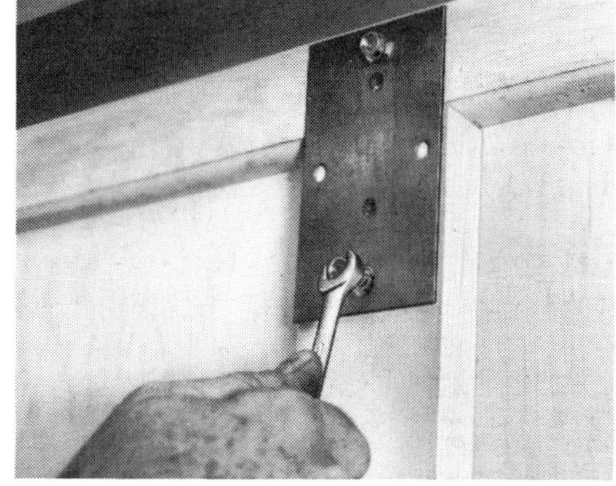

Center the door bracket plate on the door; bolt it in place. At this stage, tighten the track assembly bolt in the header bracket.

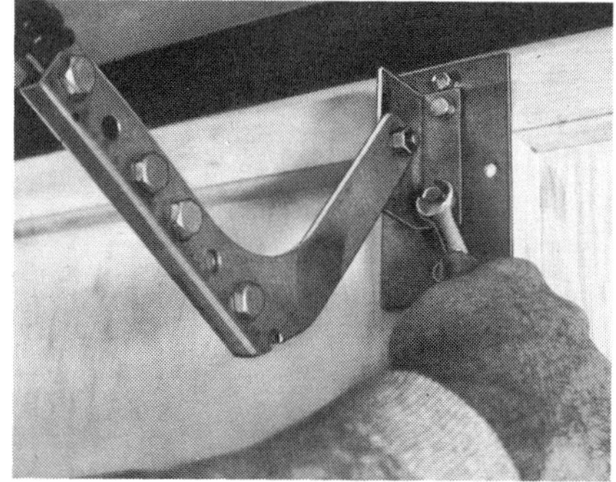

Fit the connecting arm unit to the door plate. Turn the operator unit by hand until the connecting arm can latch onto the carrier.

Connect automatic reversing switch wires and push-button control wires to appropriate terminals as shown in the diagram (opposite page).

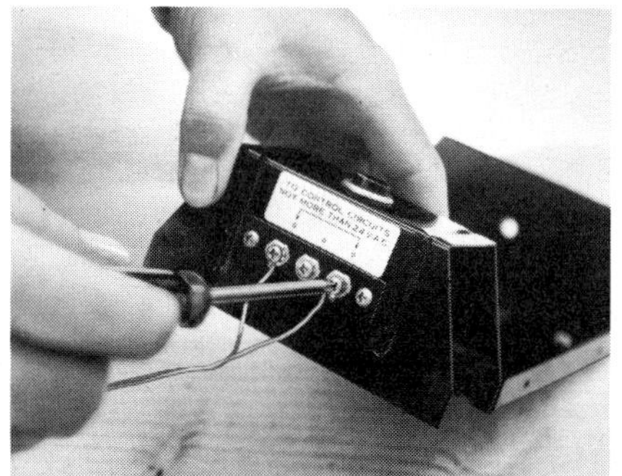

Dismantle the push-button control unit to expose the terminals. Run the wires from the operator unit to the push-button control.

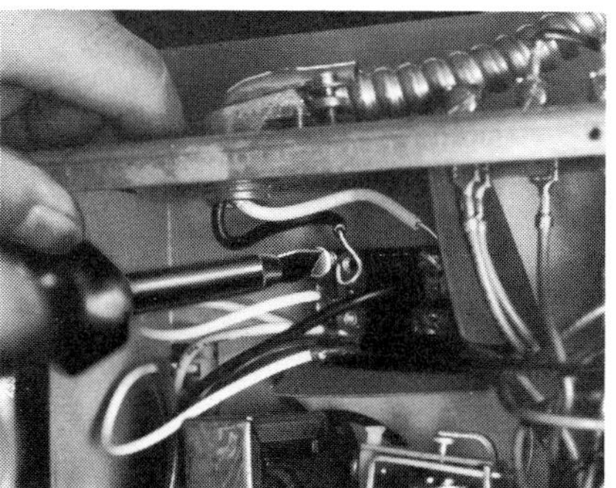

Make permanent electrical hookup by running BX cable from a junction box. Some control units are equipped with a cord and plug.

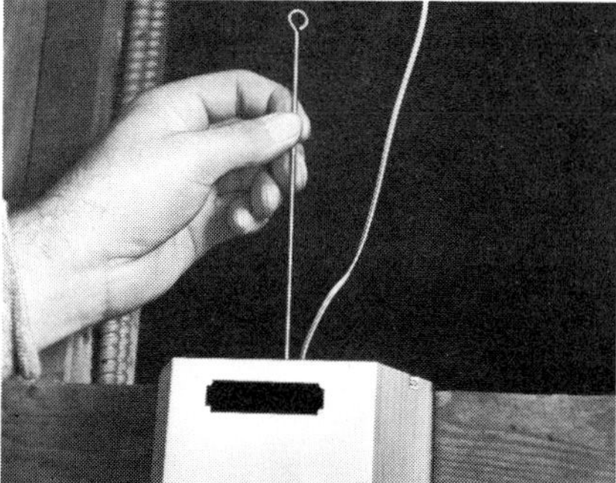

Be sure to install antenna in control box. Install batteries in hand transmitter units and test door for proper opening and closing.

Patching a blacktop driveway

Repairing a hole in blacktop

To patch a blacktop driveway, thoroughly clean the hole or the depressed area of all debris—chunks of old asphalt, dirt, and pebbles. A deep hole should be partially filled with coarse gravel.

In patching, use a cold-mix asphalt material which is available in 66-pound paper bags. The material should be loose in the bag for proper application. If it is hard, warm it for several hours indoors, perhaps overnight. When the material is workable, it can be brought to the site.

Fill the cavity to within an inch of the top with the patching material. To eliminate any air pockets, slice the fill with the shovel and then tamp it with the end of a 4 x 4. Finish filling the hole by shaping the asphalt into a mound. Then level this mound flush to the adjacent surface with the flat part of the shovel or with a roller.

To keep the fresh asphalt from sticking to your shoes, spread a thin layer of sand over the surface of the patched area.

Dig out all the loose blacktop paving and crumbling edges; clean out all dirt and loose fill. Edges of hole should be firm.

If it is a deep hole, fill it to within 3 or 4 in. of the top with coarse gravel. Tamp gravel down firmly.

Next, fill the hole to within an inch of the top with the blacktop mix. Slice with spade to eliminate any air pockets.

Use a 4 x 4 to tamp down the mix. Make certain that the mix is pressed firmly against all sides of the hole.

Complete the patch by adding enough of the mix to bring the patch about a half-inch above the level of the driveway.

Now tamp the patch down to make it flush with the surrounding area. Drive your car over the patch to compact it.

Blacktop sealer

Waterproof blacktop sealers are available at building supply dealers. Their purpose is to protect driveway surfaces against sun, snow, and water.

Most sealers come ready-mixed in 5-gallon cans; that quantity will coat from 200 to 300 square feet, depending on the porosity of the surface. Sealers are applied with a long-handled push broom. Before application, see to it that the driveway is swept clean of all dirt and debris. It is best to apply two coats, the second within 48 hours.

To fill breaks and cracks, use special blacktop sealer. Fill cracks partially with sand, then pour sealer into crack. Best to do this job during warm weather.

Large cracks can be patched by making a mix of sand and sealer, then troweling the mixture into the crack as shown. If mix settles, add more to bring it up to driveway level.

If entire driveway is to be treated, pour enough sealer from the can to cover a section at a time, spreading it around with a push broom. Be careful not to track the sealer into the house.

section 6:

Furniture: How to repair and restore it

Many families give up unnecessarily on damaged furniture because they fear they can't manage the kind of repair it needs. A wasteful and costly practice, and one this section is designed to put an end to. No matter what's wrong with your furniture—scrapes, scratches, or stains; sticking drawers or doors; weak joints; broken legs; sagging springs—chances are there's a remedy. Some renovations, such as new upholstery or cushions for chairs, are surprisingly simple too.

contents

Cleaning and care of fabrics

Fabrics

When upholstery fabrics need a thorough cleaning, the method depends on the fabric. Synthetics and cottons are often washable; most other fabrics require dry cleaning. In between, however, most fabrics can be sponge-cleaned safely and satisfactorily with the foam from a suds made of mild detergent or a commercial cleaning product and water. **Use only the foam** and wipe it off quickly—fabric should not be soaked. Test for colorfastness on a concealed area.

Leather and vinyl

Cleaning of either natural or artificial leather means more than mere removal of dirt and fingermarks; their sheen and suppleness must also be preserved. Saddle soap is excellent in all these respects, as is commercial wax made for use on appliances. Both are applied with a damp cloth or sponge, then buffed with a soft, dry cloth. Leather cream (made for shoes) is good for occasional polishing; a mild detergent suds, well rinsed and buffed, for spot-cleanings.

Removing stains from fabrics

Cause of stain	Washable fabrics	"Dry-clean only" fabrics
Alcoholic beverages	Blot immediately, rinse in cold water, and launder.	Blot immediately. Sponge with a solution of 1 teaspoon white vinegar to 1 pt. water.
Beverages: Cocoa, coffee, tea, milk, soft drinks	Blot, then launder in a solution of 1 oz. borax to 1 pt. warm water. Rinse and launder.	Blot, then apply commercial stain remover with a towel.
Blood, egg	Rinse immediately in cold water and launder. For white fabrics, add a few drops of ammonia to the wash water.	Dab with a solution of cold water and ammonia, 1 or 2 drops of ammonia per cup. If stain persists, make a paste of cold water and laundry starch; let it dry on the stain and brush off.
Burns and scorches	Soak in glycerine or sponge with a solution of 1 oz. borax to 1 pt. water. Launder.	Make a paste of borax and glycerine; let dry on stain; brush off. Sponge with a damp cloth.
Fat	Rub lightly with methylene chloride or commercial stain remover.	Same as for washable fabrics.
Fruit	Blot immediately; launder. If stain persists, try solution for Beverages.	Wipe with alcohol. Apply commercial cleaner.
Glue	Soak in water as hot as the fabric can endure without damage. If stain persists, soak in warmed white vinegar for 1 minute; rinse and launder. Use nail polish remover on resin glues, but not on synthetic fibers.	Sponge with suds and rub liquid detergent into the stain. Sponge with cold water.
Ink	Fresh ink: Sponge with detergent suds immediately. Sprinkle white cotton and linen fabrics with lemon juice and salt; leave for an hour, then launder. Ballpoint pen ink: Hold a cloth dampened with alcohol against the stain to absorb ink. Launder.	All inks: Same as recommended for washable fabrics. Then dry-clean.
Mildew	Apply lemon juice and leave to dry.	Moisten with lemon juice, sprinkle with salt, and leave to dry, in sun if possible. Sponge lightly.
Oil, grease, tar	Sponge with a little turpentine. Rinse and launder.	Same as for washable fabrics, but sponge instead of launder.
Paint	Oil-based: Dab with turpentine and launder. Latex paint: Soak in cold water. Lacquer-based: Dab with nail polish remover or acetone (do not use this on synthetic fibers) and launder.	Same as for washable fabrics, but sponge instead of launder.

Caution: Many commercial cleaners contain carbon tetrachloride or ammonia. The fumes from these chemicals are dangerous and products containing them should be used in well-ventilated areas. Carbon tetrachloride is an effective cleaning agent, but safety experts advise methylene chloride (from a pharmacist) as a safer substitute.

Marks and stains on wood

Heat marks on wood generally show up as white rings or patches; water marks are dark. In most instances, commercial furniture cleaners, used as directed on labels, will correct the condition. If these do not work, try rubbing lighter fluid or benzine into the marks with a clean, dry cloth.

Water spots that resist these treatments can often be removed by brushing on a solution of oxalic acid (½ cup of acid crystals to a quart of hot water). For heat marks that resist conventional methods, make a thick paste of cigar ash and water and rub it into the spot. Heat marks may also respond to a light scrubbing with undiluted ammonia.

Treat minor cigarette burns with commercial cleaner, lighter fluid, benzine, or the oxalic acid solution described above. Deeper burns must be scraped away and the area refinished to match its surroundings. A simple method of spot refinishing is with artist's oil paints. Mix a color match; then, with your fingertip, apply as thin a coat as possible to the discolored area. (A thin coat will dry more quickly and to a harder finish than a thick one.) Keep the coat thin by applying paint sparingly—do not thin the paint with turpentine. When the paint dries, spray the repair with clear lacquer, let it dry, and spray a second time to get an even sheen. Rub the surface with 000 grade steel wool, then wax it.

To remove a superficial ink or acid stain, rub the discolored area lightly with 000 grade steel wool, abrasive paper, pumice, or rottenstone. A deep stain of either of these types must be bleached. Brush on the oxalic acid solution recommended above. When the surface is almost dry, brush on a second solution, called a stop, made from a cup of borax (not boric acid) dissolved in a quart of hot water. Let the surface dry overnight and then sand it smooth. Use oil paints as specified above for cigarette burns to refinish the bleached area.

Removing stains from marble

Most marble stains can be bleached out with a thick homemade paste made of hydrogen peroxide and powdered whiting. Spread the paste over the stained area, add a few drops of household ammonia, and keep the paste damp by covering it with plastic wrap. Allow the paste to stand on the surface for a few minutes, then wash it off (see p. 459).

Correcting minor defects

Small abrasions on wood surfaces can often be repaired without major refinishing. On a varnished surface, for example, merely brush turpentine around the damaged area. The turpentine liquefies the varnish, which then flows into the scratch or crack and hardens. Use the same technique on a lacquered surface, but with lacquer thinner rather than turpentine.

A common imperfection on varnished wood is checking—a crazed pattern of tiny surface cracks. To correct this condition, first scrub with a stiff brush and mild detergent suds. Let dry and then apply a solution of 2 parts turpentine, 3 parts varnish, and 4 parts boiled linseed oil. Rub this mixture into the checked surface; if all of the cracks have not disappeared when the area is dry, repeat the process.

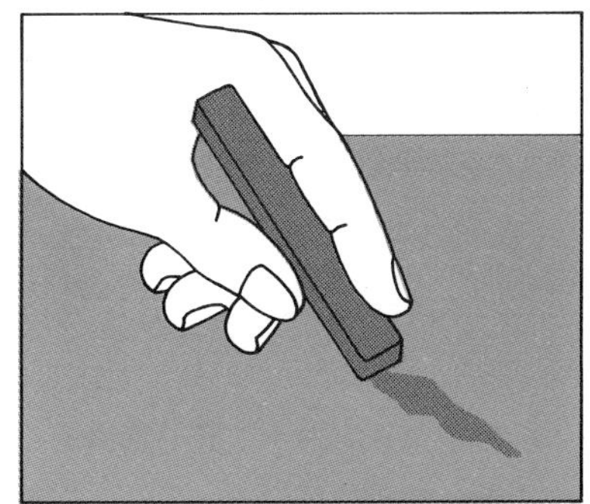

Hairline scratches on hardwood finishes can be easily and successfully camouflaged with a wax-like tinted touchup stick.

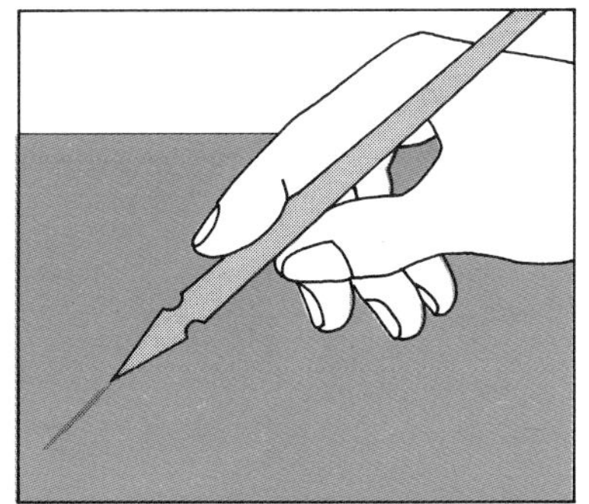

Apply iodine with an India ink pen to conceal scratches or other minor imperfections on a dark-colored surface.

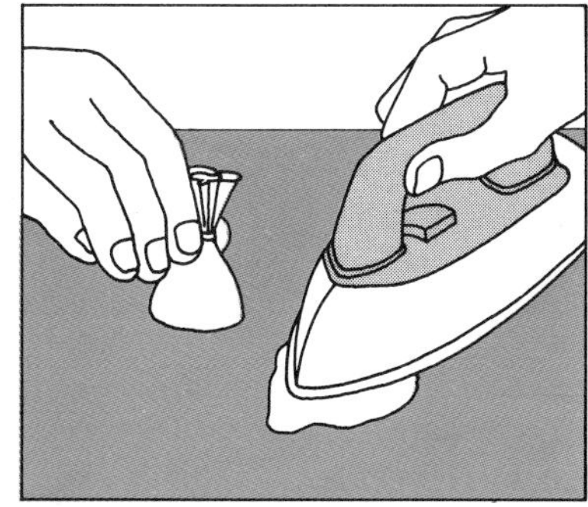

Moisture (sprinkled water, or steam from an iron on a damp cloth) can cause wood fibers to expand and fill a dent.

Deep scrapes and scratches

As a rule, even fairly deep scrapes and scratches on finished wood can be repaired quickly and easily with stick shellac, available in a variety of colors and at most hardware stores. If you cannot find exactly the color you need, it is possible to blend several sticks together into the desired hue. Simply heat the sticks over a gas or alcohol flame until the shellac flows and can be mixed.

After you have selected or mixed a color, heat the hard shellac with a soldering iron until it is soft enough to flow into the crack. To smooth the shellac, use a spatula that has been heated over an alcohol flame. Carefully scrape off any excess and then rub the repair with a felt pad dipped in rottenstone to make it level with the surrounding surface.

To fix a deep gouge, clean out the damaged area and fill cavity with wood putty, tinted with dry pigment to proper hue.

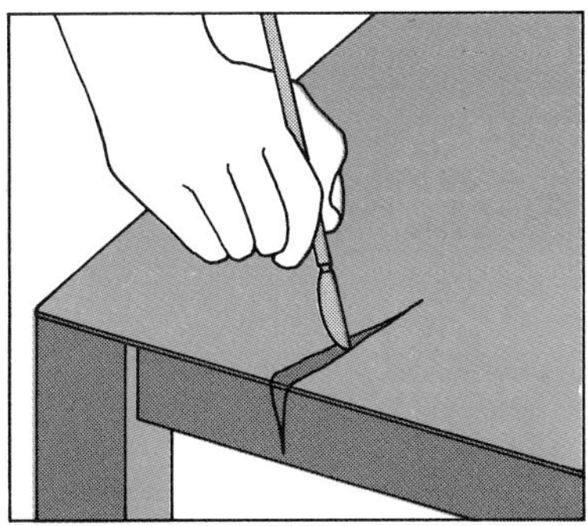

Let the putty dry and then apply a layer of stick shellac that is the same color as the surrounding area.

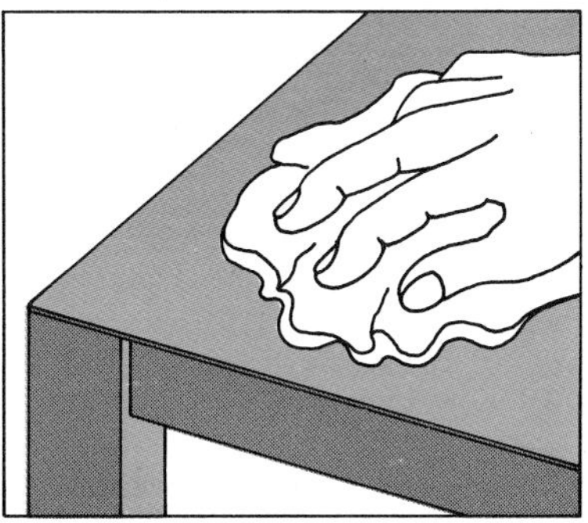

Rub down the repair with a felt pad or extra-fine steel wool until the patch is level with the surrounding surface.

Patching solid wood

A solid wood patch can most conveniently be made from some hidden element, such as bracing. Make a cardboard template of the patch and scratch its outline on the surface to be repaired. With a chisel, gouge out a cavity to the shape and thickness of the patch. Outline the patch with the template, then cut it out with a fine-toothed coping saw. White-glue patch into the cavity; apply pressure until dry.

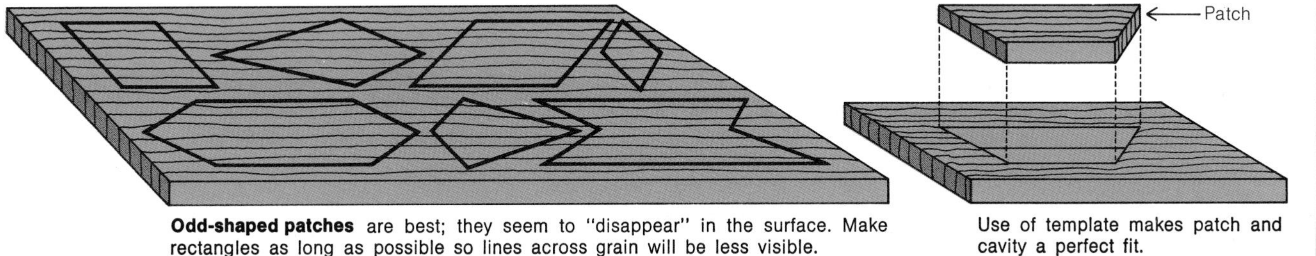

Odd-shaped patches are best; they seem to "disappear" in the surface. Make rectangles as long as possible so lines across grain will be less visible.

Use of template makes patch and cavity a perfect fit.

Scratched, loose, and blistered veneer

Furniture finished with veneer is subject to several types of damage. As with any wood surface, scratches and abrasions are common occurrences. In addition, however, veneer often pulls away from its base wood. Blistering—small bubbles on the surface—is another problem that afflicts veneer. All these defects are usually simple to fix provided the repairs are made as soon as possible and not allowed to get worse. Veneer is brittle and delicate, and minor damage, left unattended, can quickly become a serious, perhaps irreparable, condition. Loose veneer, for example, is much more likely to split or chip than veneer that is tightly glued to its base wood.

To repair a simple scratch or abrasion, use the techniques recommended on page 197 for surface faults on solid wood. When working with loose veneer, or a blister, however, remember that this material is thin and easily broken and requires special precautions. Put a damp cloth over the problem area and a hot iron on top of the cloth. This will force moisture into the veneer, making it more flexible and less likely to split as you work with it.

To repair loose veneer, scrape out the old glue from the base wood with a small, sharp knife, working it in as far as possible. If all the glue does not come up, squeeze hot water from a sponge under the loose veneer. The water will eventually melt the glue, which can then be scraped up with the knife. Re-attach the veneer to the base wood with white glue, then lay plastic sheeting over the repaired area to keep excess glue from sticking to whatever clamping device you use to hold the repair while the bond sets. After the bond has set, wash away any excess glue with hot water. If it is not possible to use a clamp to hold the bond, wind masking tape tightly around the repaired area. Secure repairs that can neither be clamped nor taped with a weight, such as a sandbag. Allow the bond to set for at least 12 hours before removing the clamps, tape, or sandbag.

A hot iron on damp cloth moistens loose veneer, making it more pliable so that it can be lifted without cracking.

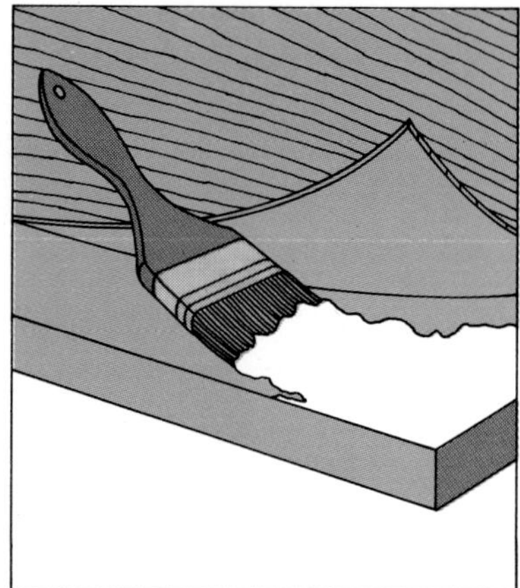

After scraping out old glue, apply a new coat of glue to the base wood and then to the underside of the loose veneer.

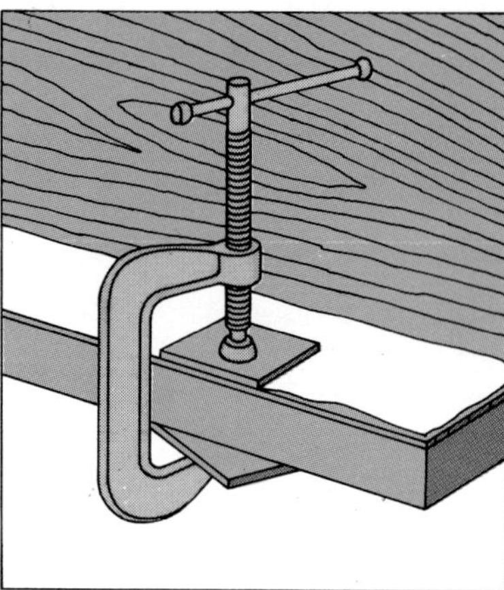

When clamping repair to secure bond, insert hardwood blocks between clamp jaws and surfaces to prevent marring.

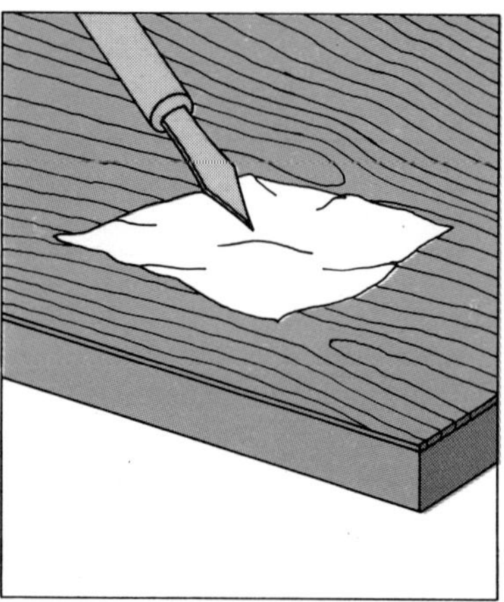

To flatten a bubble in veneer, place a damp cloth over the affected area. Next, slit the bubble open with a sharp knife.

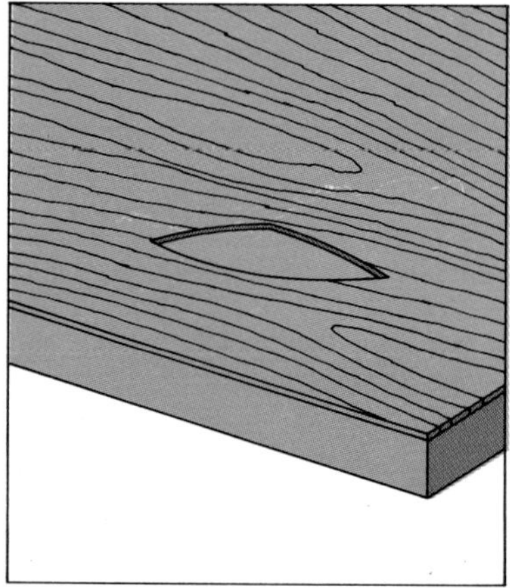

Put white glue into the slit and onto the underside of the loosened veneer. Press the veneer back in place.

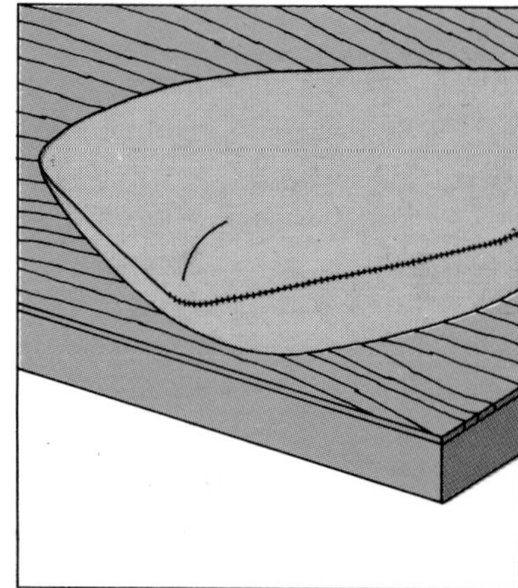

If you cannot use a clamp or masking tape to secure the bond, weight the repair with a heavy sandbag for about 12 hours.

Plastic laminate repair

Minor scorches, rust rings, or black marks from cooking utensils left on plastic laminates sometimes respond to scouring powder. More serious damage will probably require patching; if the laminate is a standard pattern or color, a match should be no trouble. An edge-to-edge patch is easier to make and less noticeable. To patch or recement an area, first dissolve the old cement (use lacquer thinner or other appropriate solvent) so it can be scraped up. Pry up the laminate with a small, sharp knife so you can get solvent underneath. Make a patch by scoring its outline, then cutting it out with a fine-toothed hacksaw blade. Cut slightly beyond the scored mark, then file down to the line. Score the patch pattern onto the surface being repaired, scrape out excess glue, and, using a sharp knife, cut the hole for the patch. Recement both surfaces. Clamp the bond, putting wax paper between so excess glue won't stick.

Sticking drawers

A drawer can stick because it is too full, or the problem may be rough runners. To remedy roughness, remove the drawer, then use a hard wax or soap to lubricate the runners and the drawer edges that glide along them. Dampness can also cause wood drawers to expand; if you suspect this, remove the drawer, check for signs of where it is binding, then use a plane to shave some wood from the affected area. Loose joints or runners can be another cause. Reach inside and push the loose member back in place; then remove the drawer and glue the loose member in position. If a drawer bottom is coming loose from its frame, take out the drawer below and push up on the loose bottom to remove the drawer. Refasten bottom to drawer as shown.

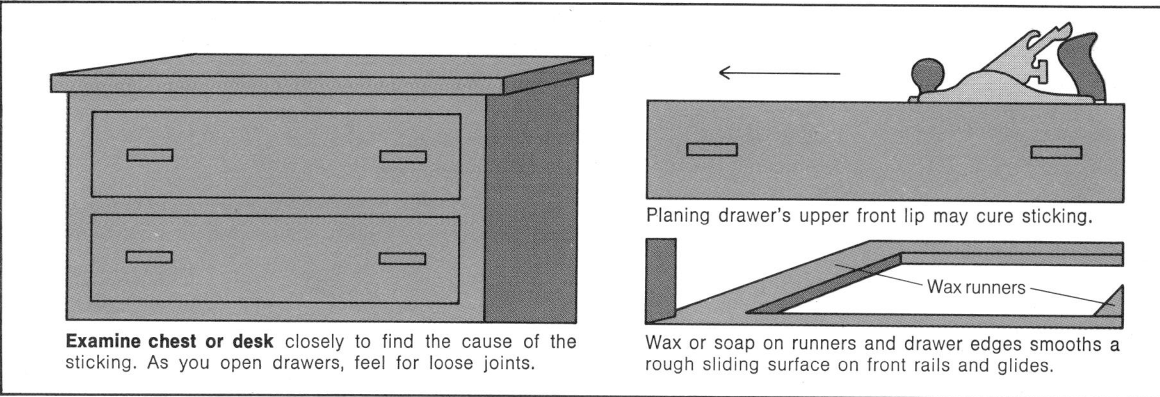

Examine chest or desk closely to find the cause of the sticking. As you open drawers, feel for loose joints.

Planing drawer's upper front lip may cure sticking.

Wax or soap on runners and drawer edges smooths a rough sliding surface on front rails and glides.

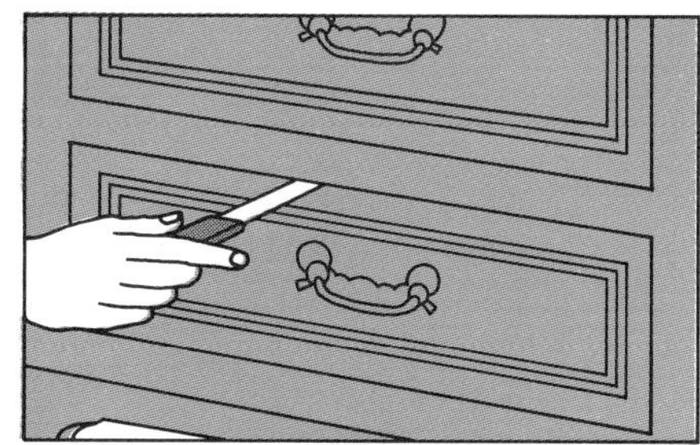

If an overfilled drawer will open a crack before it sticks, try working a thin metal rule or knife blade inside, then move it around to rearrange the drawer's contents.

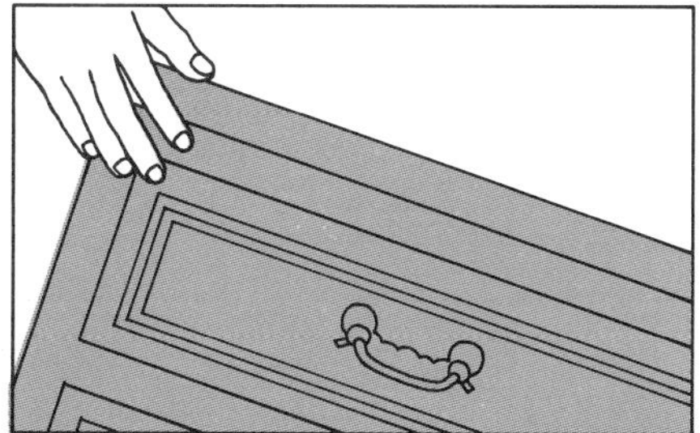

Remove drawers above and below stubborn one; feel sides and bottom runners for loose joints. These can usually be pushed back in place. Remove drawer; reglue damaged joint.

Some chests have no dividers between drawers. If a drawer sticks because it is too full, remove the one below and pound the bottom of the stuck drawer to shake down its contents.

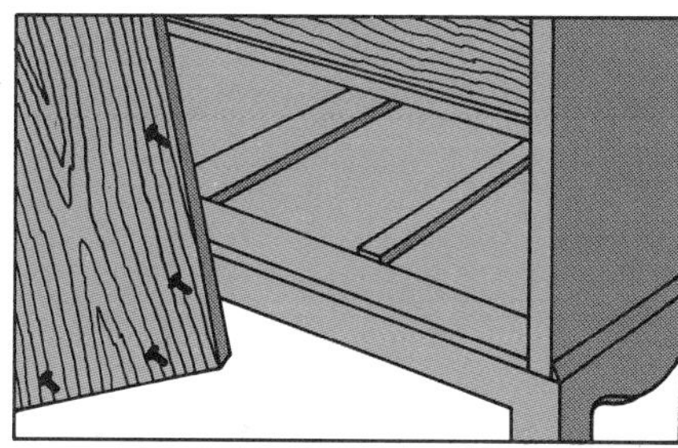

As a last resort, pry off the back of the cabinet with a putty knife to expose the backs of the drawers. Tap sides of the problem drawer alternately to force it out to the front.

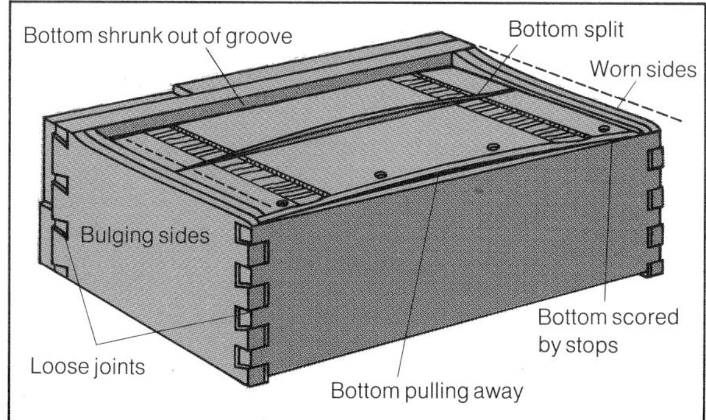

This typically worn drawer illustrates a variety of troubles. The bottom is pulling away from the frame, the facing around the front joints is broken, and the joints are loose. Such a drawer must be completely taken apart and reglued.

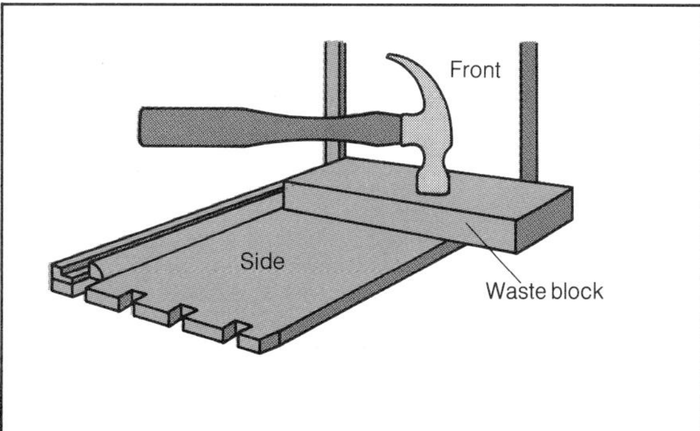

When separating the elements of a drawer, beware of chipping or breaking the wood. If possible, gently pull joints apart by hand. If you must use a hammer, do not strike directly but on a wood block placed between hammer and drawer.

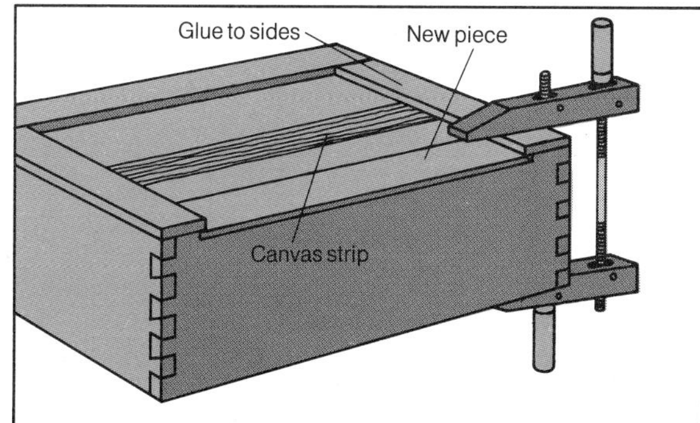

A split drawer bottom is a common fault. Fix it by gluing a canvas strip across the split to reinforce the bottom. On the frame around the bottom use white glue, not nails, for joining, and clamp the assembly to obtain a good bond.

Structural and functional problems

Tightening joints

To fix loose joints in chairs, you must first pull structural elements—legs, rungs, rails, etc.—from their sockets.

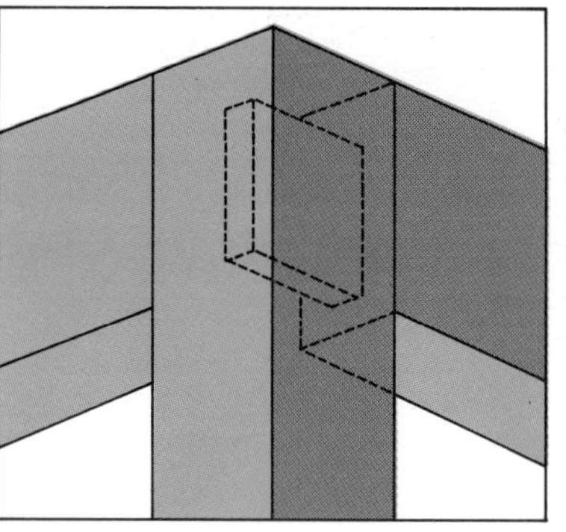

Clean off all old glue or cement from sockets and tenons and apply a fresh coat of white glue to both.

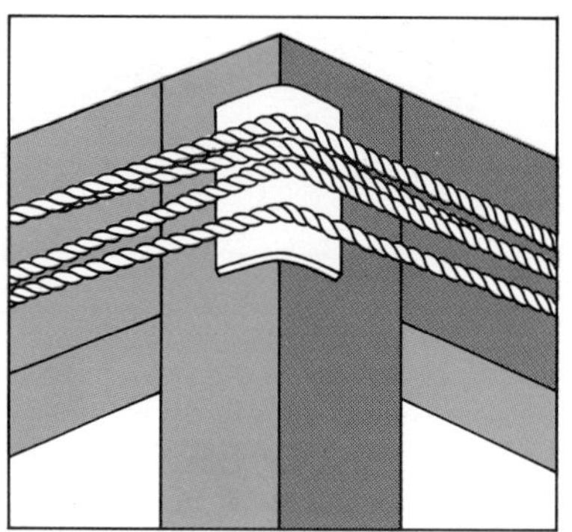

After refitting element in socket, clamp to secure the bond. Cord twisted tight around the joint makes a good clamp.

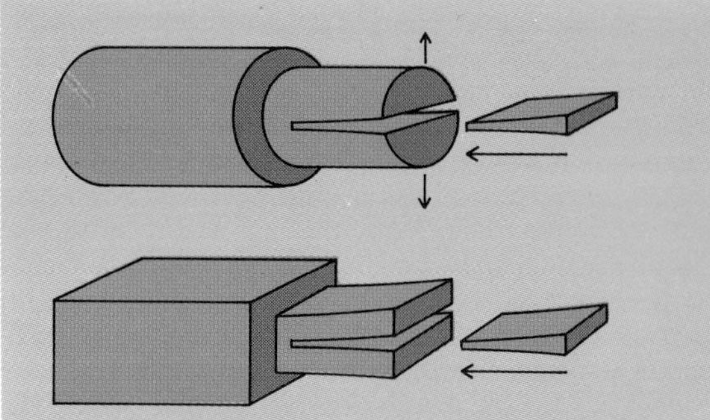

To insure tight fit, cut a slot in each tenon and insert a thin wedge projecting just beyond its end. When tenon is driven into socket, wedge will expand it.

Repairing cracks and breaks

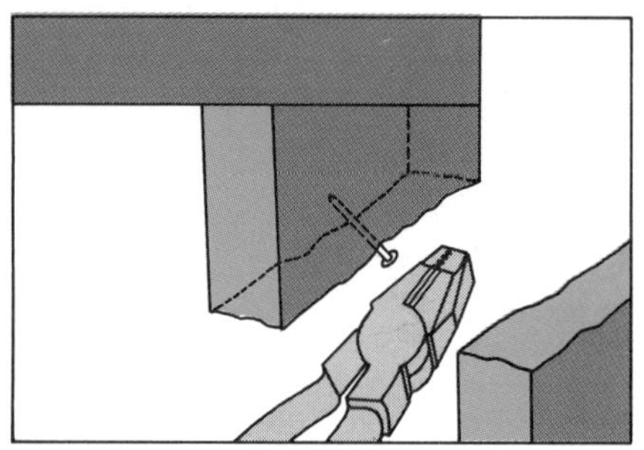

To fix a broken chair leg, drive brad into the center of the break on one piece. Clip brad so only 1/16 in. protrudes.

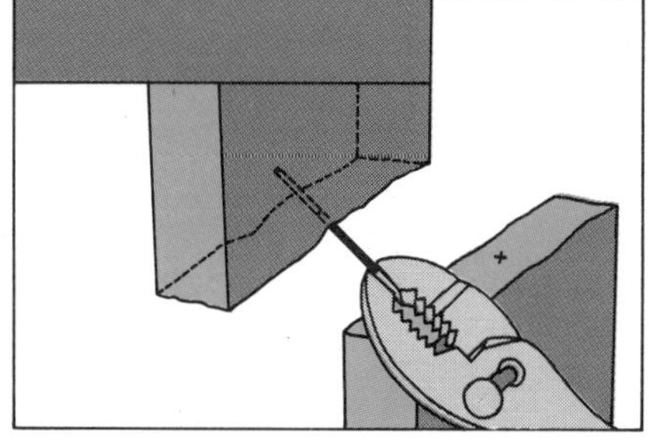

Fit the two pieces together carefully and press firmly. Then pull the pieces apart and remove the brad.

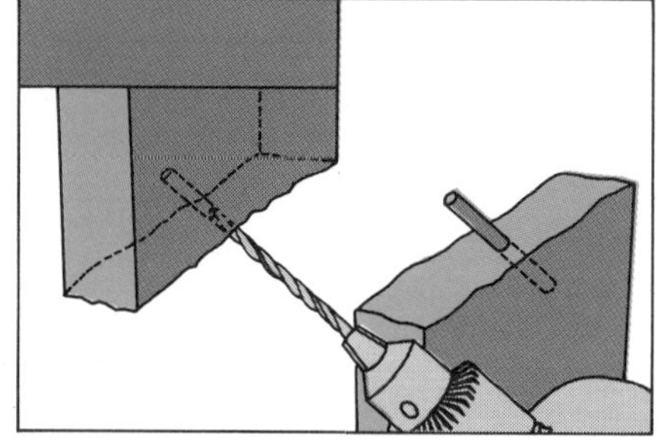

The mark left on each piece by the brad will show you where to place the drill point. Drill holes to accept a round peg (dowel).

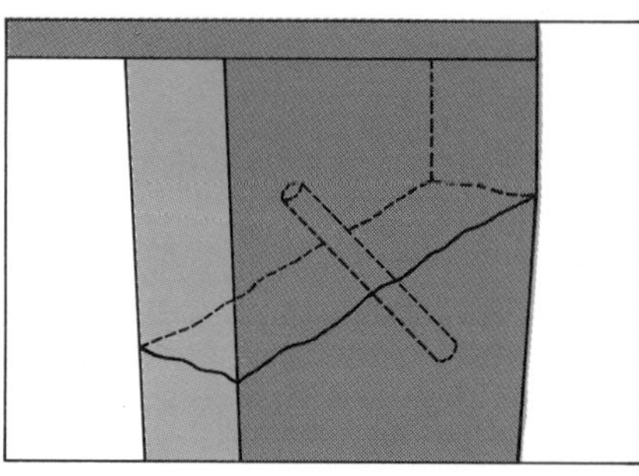

Coat one dowel socket with white glue and insert dowel. Coat other socket and push piece over protruding part of dowel.

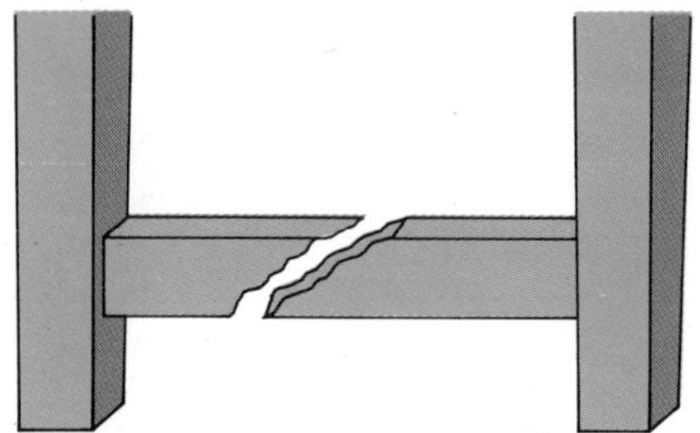

A break in a nonsupporting element can often be fixed without doweling. Separate the broken pieces, making certain that no bits of the original wood are missing from them.

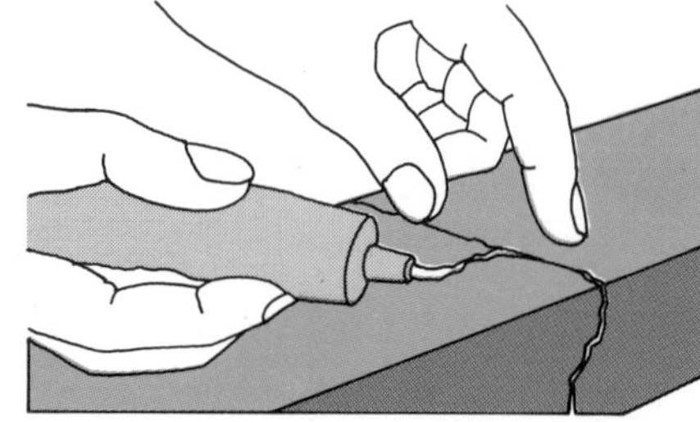

Apply white glue to both surfaces of the break and press the two pieces together. Scrape off excess glue, taking care to keep pieces pressed together as you work.

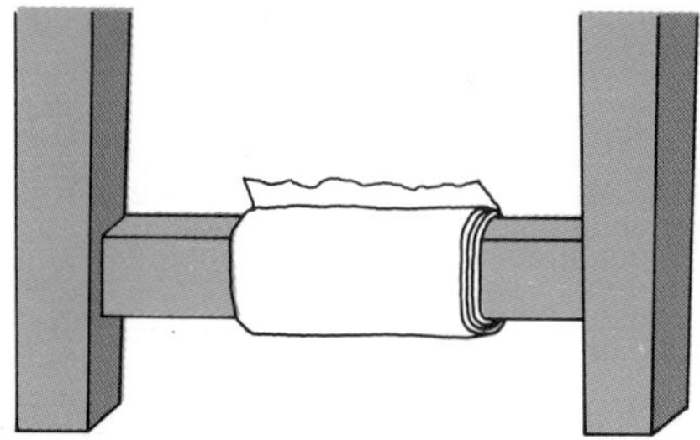

Wrap wax paper or plastic wrap around the repaired area. This will prevent any glue that may remain on the surface of the wood from sticking to the clamp.

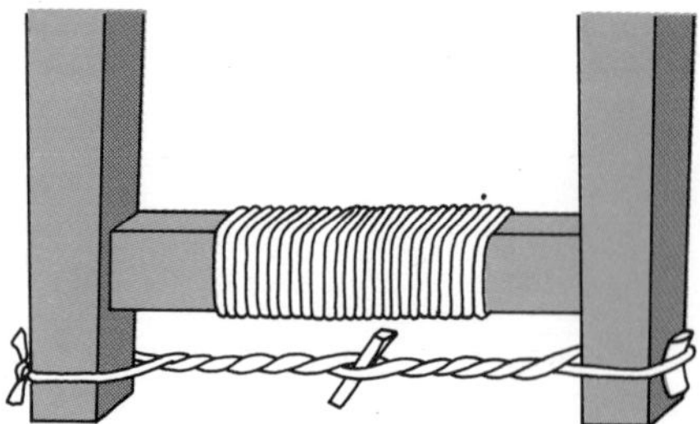

Wind heavy rope or cord around the repair to clamp it. Using wood and additional rope, make and apply a tourniquet as shown. Padding on legs prevents marring.

Reinforcing weak shelves

How you reinforce weak or sagging bookcase or cabinet shelves depends primarily on the type of piece being fixed. If it is a tool-storage shelf, for example, where appearance doesn't matter, or a kitchen cabinet shelf, in which the joint between shelf and upright is not usually visible, reinforcement may involve nothing more than attaching an angle iron, with no attempt made to conceal the repair. Shelves in a living room, bedroom, or dining room, however, generally should be strengthened in such a way that the repair is invisible or, in any case, will not detract from the appearance of the piece.

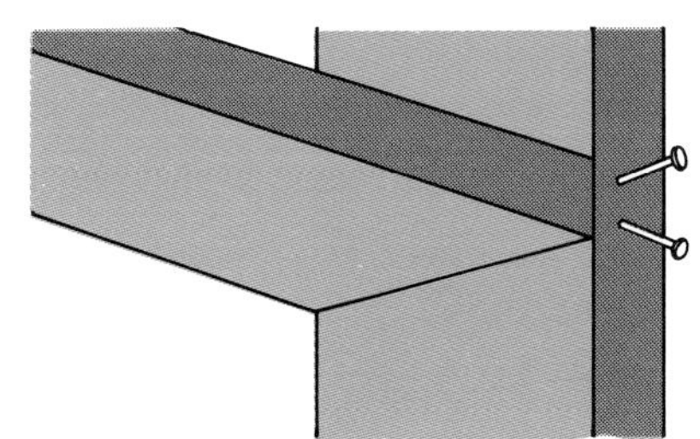

The simplest strengthening technique involves two nails driven to form a V through the upright into the shelf.

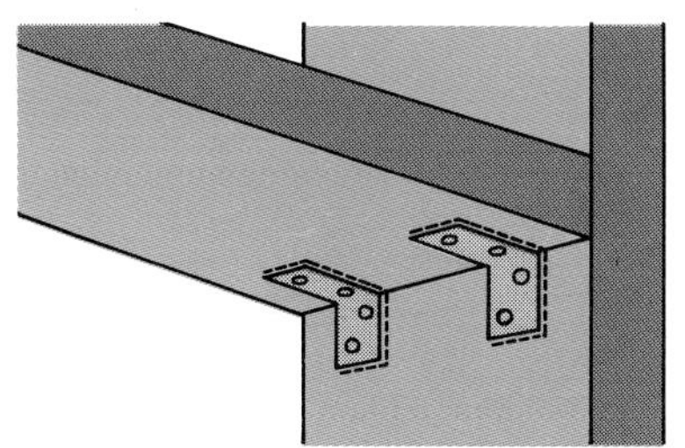

A stronger repair is made with angle irons, fitted into grooves routed out with a chisel, then covered with wood filler.

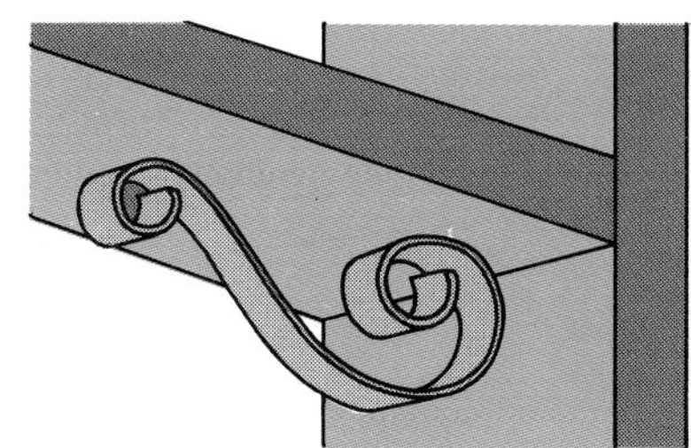

Wrought iron supports screwed to shelves and uprights are a good and attractive choice for some bookcases.

Casters, glides, and levelers

For small pieces of furniture, such as dining room chairs or occasional tables, rubber cushion glides are sufficient. Installation is simple—just drive the nail that forms the shaft into the chair leg.

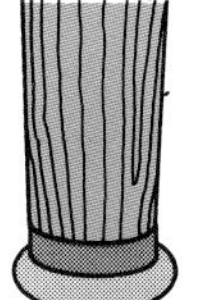

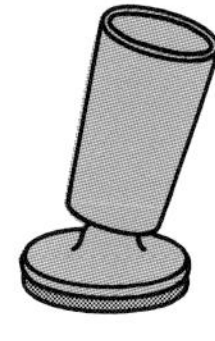

Hollow-shafted glides are designed for modern furniture with tapered legs. These glides come in sizes to fit the various diameters of most contemporary chair and table legs. To install, tap the shaft over the leg.

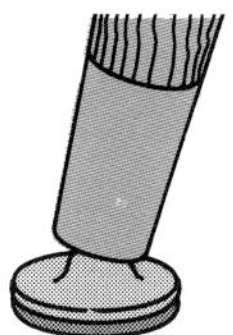

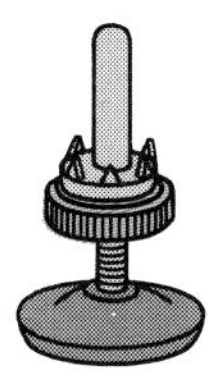

Adjustable furniture levelers offer a quick and effective solution to the problem of tables and chairs that wobble on an uneven floor or uneven legs. To adjust height, simply turn the ring above the base.

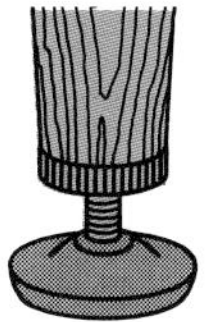

Wide-base furniture glides swivel at base to compensate for legs that are not absolutely perpendicular to the floor, and can also be adjusted to uneven floors or legs. Wide base distributes weight without marring rug.

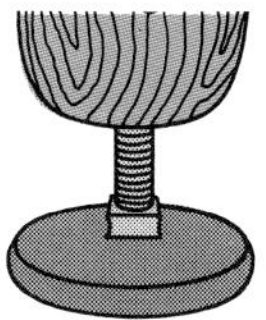

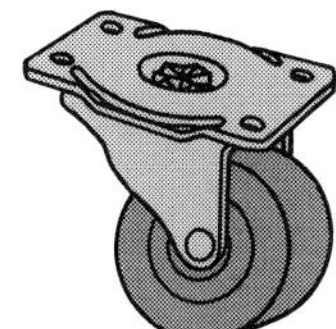

The flat-plate swivel caster is intended mainly for hand trucks and dollies. Plate is screwed to the underside of the truck. Wheels are made either of powder iron or soft rubber and can support heavy weights.

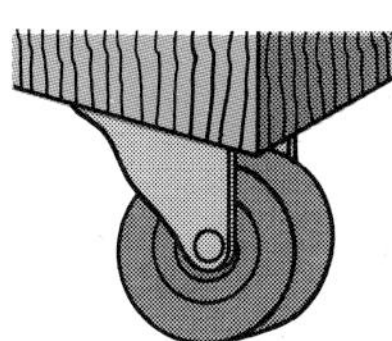

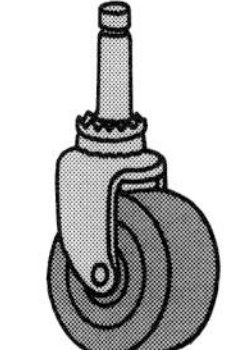

This general-purpose caster is usable on both light- and medium-weight furniture, from cribs to double beds. Caster has a grip-neck yoke that is tapped into the wood base of the leg to insure a tight fit.

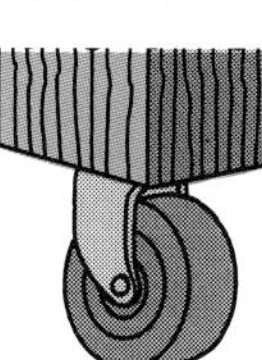

Adjustable casters are designed for use with furniture having tubular metal legs. Can be adjusted, after furniture is in place, to compensate for uneven floors or legs. Also made for wooden-legged furniture.

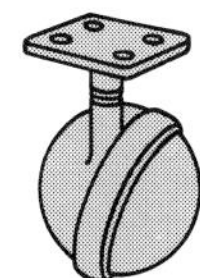

Ball-type casters are made primarily for furniture that is frequently moved across carpets and rugs, such as coffee tables. Available with a plate-type mount, as shown, or a socket-type, grip-neck mount.

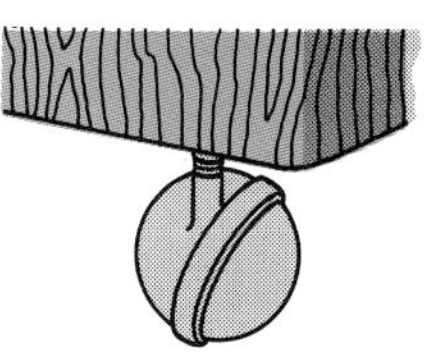

Structural and functional problems

Sticking (hinged doors)

Dampness may have expanded the wood fibers so the door cannot close properly. To remedy this, remove the door and its hinges. From the hinge side, plane the wood back to the desired level, planing a stroke or two at a time and checking fit frequently. Deepen hinge recesses to compensate for shaved-off wood.

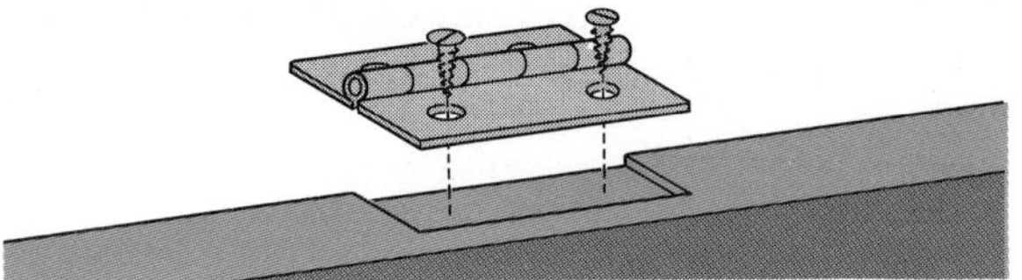

1. To repair a door that sticks because of wood expansion, you must first remove the door and its hinges.

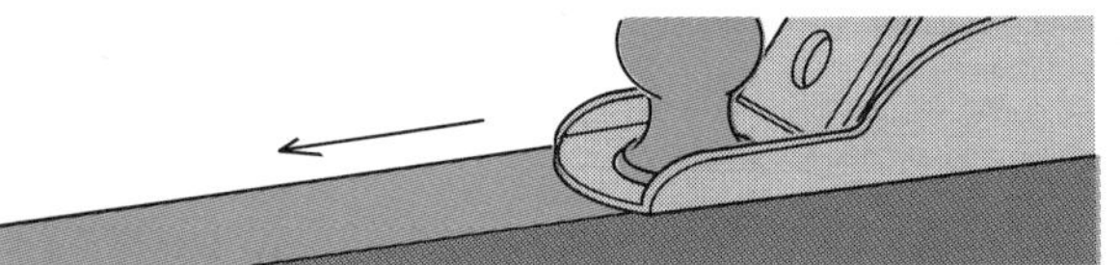

2. Planing of excess wood is done on the hinge edge of the door. Plane with the grain, checking often for fit.

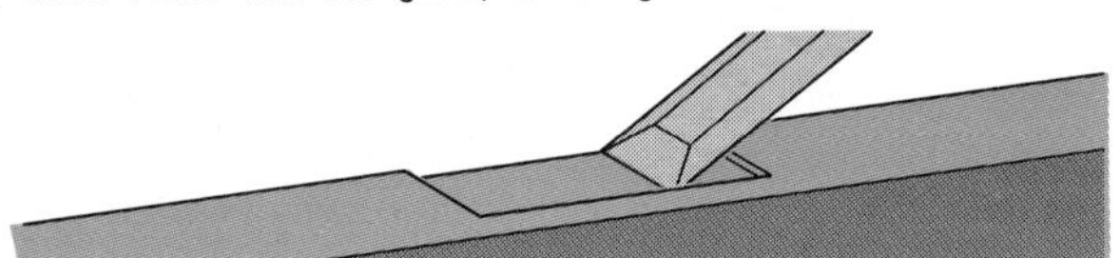

3. Chisel the recesses to proper depth before replacing hinges.

Sticking at corners

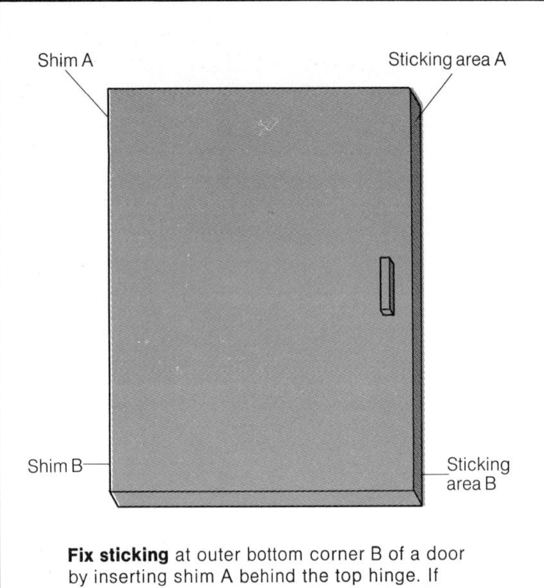

Fix sticking at outer bottom corner B of a door by inserting shim A behind the top hinge. If door sticks at upper corner A, put a shim B behind lower hinge. Check for loose hinges that may cause binding. Reset hinges with longer screws or plug up screw holes with slivers of wood dipped in glue. After glue dries, insert hinge screws.

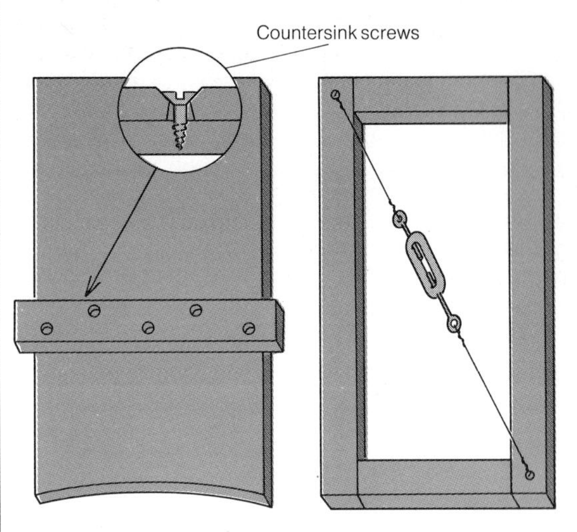

To repair a warped cabinet door, screw a wood brace across the warp on the inside of the door. Another method is to attach a cable and turnbuckle from one corner to the diagonally opposite corner; tighten until the warp straightens. Wet the wood to make it more pliable. Leave the cable assembly attached to the inside of the door.

Sticking (sliding doors)

Sticking in a cabinet door that runs on tracks may also be caused by wood expansion. To correct it, remove the door and plane down the edges that slide in the track. If the problem is looseness, shim the top and bottom slides with wood strips.

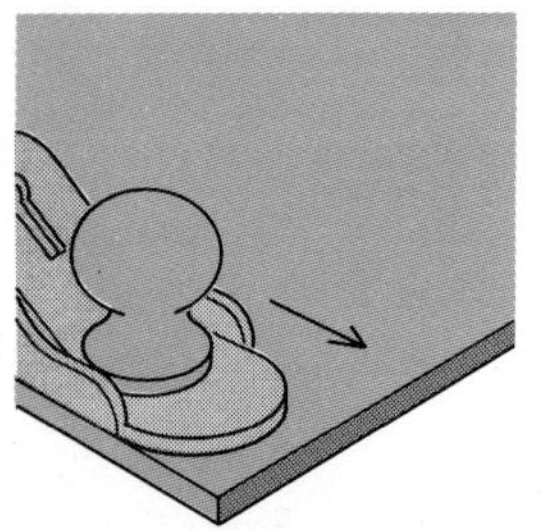

Plane edges that stick

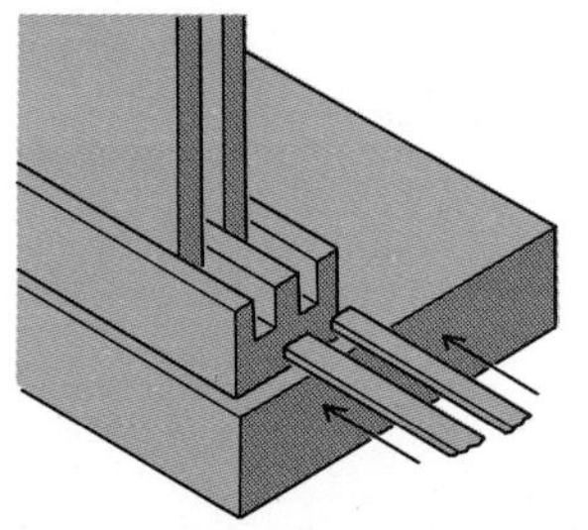

Shim edges that are loose

Loose door joints

Corner plates

The simplest method of repairing loose joints on a cabinet door is to screw in L-shaped mending plates on the inside surface of the door at the corners as shown.

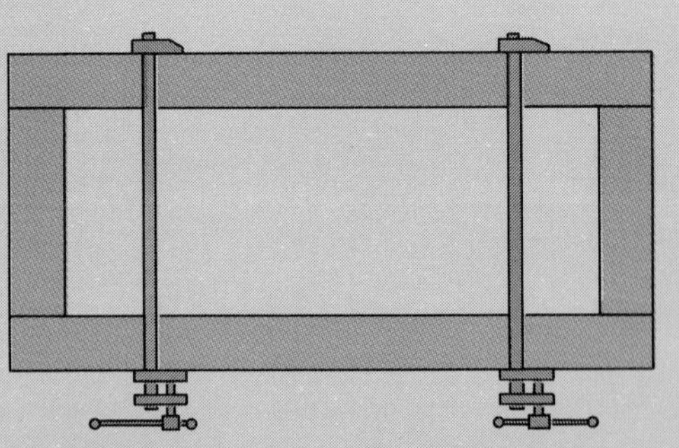

The neatest way to tighten loose door joints is to dismantle the door, clean off the old glue, and reglue. Clamp the repair as shown during drying to get a stable, durable bond.

How to correct warping

Warping is a natural tendency in wood that usually affects an unbraced element, such as a table top or leaf. It is the result of uneven expansion and shrinkage caused by moisture and heat. Heat and moisture can be put to work, however, to help reverse the curl and straighten the surface. In a table top that is to be completely refinished, first remove all the old finish, then soak the bare wood, by covering it with rags, sawdust, or other material that can be kept wet, for 4 or 5 days. You may be able to cut this time by a day or so if you apply steam from a household iron through the dampened material several times each day. After a thorough soaking, the wood will be pliable enough to benefit from clamping to reverse the curl. If you do not intend to do a complete refinishing job and the concave surface is on the underside, you will only need to strip and soak the top surface.

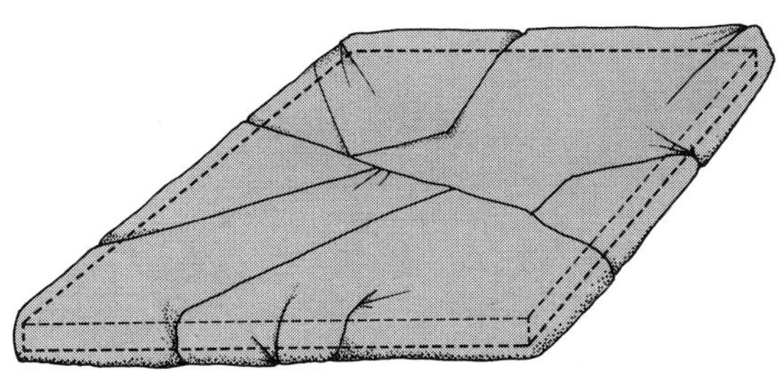

Soak a warped table top under a covering of wet sawdust, rags, or newspaper for 4 or 5 days. Moisture causes fibers of wood to expand, making the wood pliable enough that a clamp can be applied without danger of splitting.

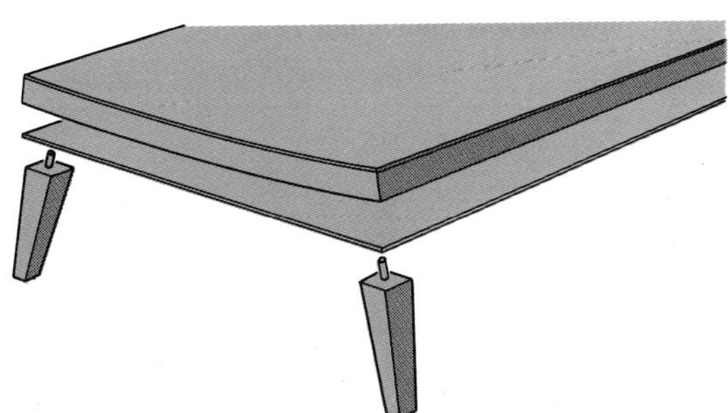

A laminated coffee table top will often warp if only the top is laminated. The cure is to glue another piece of laminate to the bottom. It need not be a matching piece.

Homemade clamp to cure warping

A warped surface requires a clamp for roughly every 10 inches of length, so you will probably need several to straighten a table top or leaf. A single clamp consists of two rough-cut 2 x 4s, each piece the same length (and several inches longer than the width of the surface to be repaired). Hold the 2 x 4s together in a vise and drill a hole at both ends through both pieces large enough to accept a ¼-inch bolt.

When the clamps are in position, insert the bolts and hand-tighten the nuts, using washers under nuts and bolt heads. Finish the tightening with a wrench. Equalize the pressure while tightening by turning a bolt only two or three times, then doing the same to the next, and the next, until all bolts are tight. When the clamps are secure, place the assembly in a warm, dry room for several days. During this period, loosen and then quickly retighten the bolts several times each day. This will prevent shrinkage cracks. Refinish the repaired surface as soon as possible to seal it against moisture.

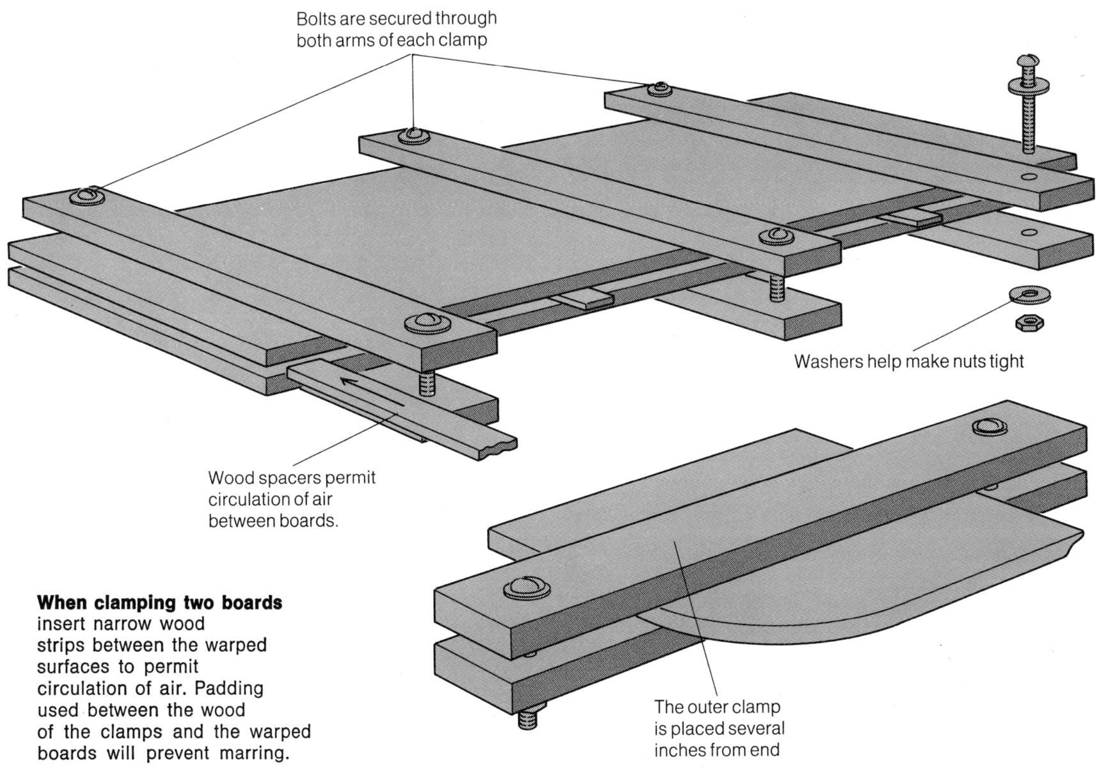

When clamping two boards insert narrow wood strips between the warped surfaces to permit circulation of air. Padding used between the wood of the clamps and the warped boards will prevent marring.

Retying springs and rewebbing

Retying coil springs is an easy repair and a worthwhile one. The condition of the springs determines not just a chair's shape, but how comfortable it is to sit on. To retie a spring, turn the chair upside down, remove the dust cover, and use a flashlight to look under the webbing for the loose or broken tie. With scissors or a sharp knife, cut away the hanging twine, and retie the spring with upholsterer's twine. Professionals use a clove hitch knot, but almost any well-tied knot—even a square knot—will do.

Rewebbing is a simple job, too. Webbing is inexpensive, so it pays to buy the best (recognizable by a woven-in red stripe). Upholsterer's twine and needle do the best and easiest stitching job.

In typical coil pattern, each twine length is tied to tacks on frame and at two points to each spring in its row.

To reweb a chair, first untack the old webbing. Then cut new strips, long enough so that the ends can be folded under.

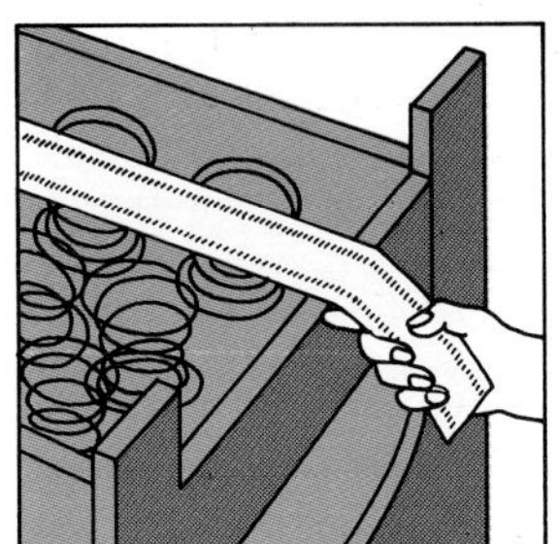

Tack one folded-under end of a strip to the frame; pull strip taut with web stretcher; tack to opposite rail to hold.

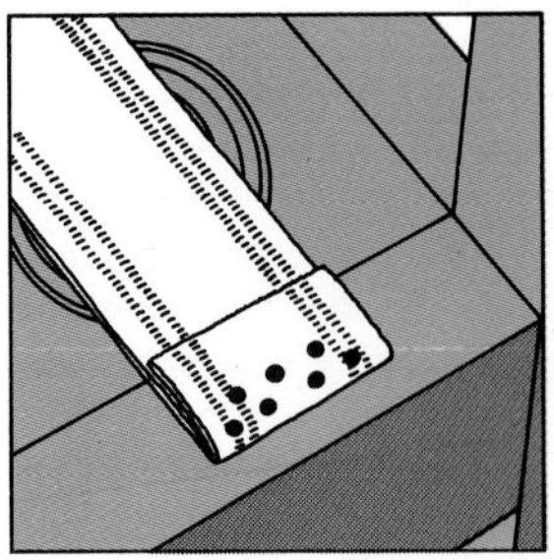

Fold down second end of strip and tack securely. When all strips are in place, stitch webbing to springs with twine.

Reinforcing loose webbing

An easy way to give sagging springs a new lease on life is by means of plywood supports. First strip away all the worn webbing. Then cut 2-inch-wide slats of ½-inch-thick plywood, slightly shorter than the width of the chair or sofa bottom. You will need one slat for each row of springs. Screw each slat across the bottom of the chair so that a row of springs is centered on it. Tie the springs to their respective slats with twine so that they will not shift under pressure. The ends of each slat should be beveled slightly so they will not be visible. Of course, if your furniture has a skirt, this bevel is not necessary—the ends will be concealed.

Screw slats to chair frame with two flathead screws at each end. Drill clearance holes in the slats and pilot holes in the frame to avoid splitting.

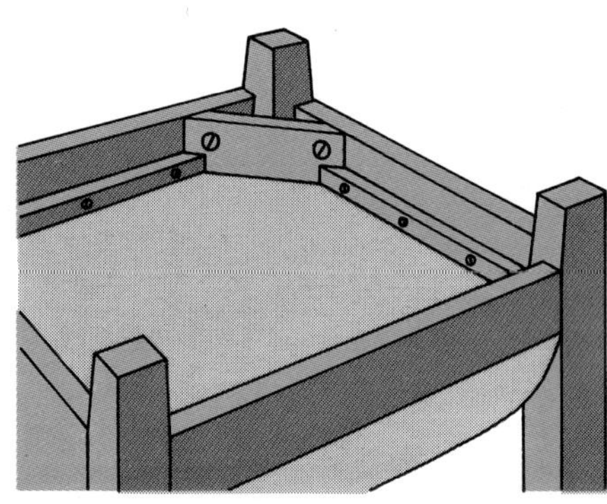

Padded-seat chair is given support by a plywood panel cut to fit inside frame and held tight against the webbing by thin hardwood strips screwed to the rails.

Installing helical springs and straps

In the ideal installation, the helicals hold the straps flat, with no spreading of coils. Under pressure, the coils open; when it is released, they spring back. Careful measuring is the key to a successful installation. If, for example, a frame opening is 24 inches, each helical is 3 inches, and each hook eye will protrude ¼ inch from the frame, straps should be 17½ inches long. On a flat frame, install screw eyes midway between top and bottom of rails. Those with slots or lips are installed differently (see sketches). Install springs and attached straps 4 to 5 inches apart, front to back first, then side to side, interweaving side-to-side straps. When straps are in place, tack a sturdy cloth over them to prevent contact between cushion and springs.

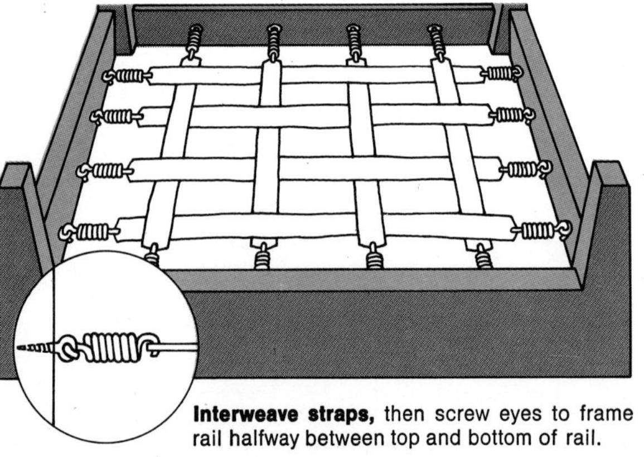

Interweave straps, then screw eyes to frame rail halfway between top and bottom of rail.

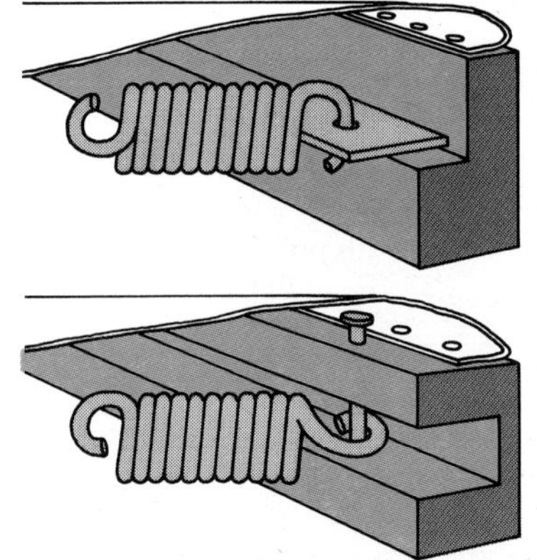

Where a flat lip protrudes from frame, use mounting plates rather than round eyes for a spring-and-strap installation. Plates extend beyond lip to allow clearance for fitting in hook.

On a slotted frame, drive a nail through the top lip, through hook of spring, then into bottom lip. When measuring for a slot-and-pin mount, remember no allowance need be made for eyes.

How to use different fillings

Cushions have traditionally been filled with such materials as goose and duck down or feathers. Today, a variety of fibers is used, foam fillings—molded foam rubber and polyfoam—being the most popular. Though comfortably soft, they quickly regain their shape after distortion. Foam is available in sheeting or crumb form; both are relatively inexpensive.

Sheet foam: Cut a cardboard pattern the desired shape, ¾ inch larger all around than actual size. With a ballpoint pen, trace the pattern on two pieces of 2-inch-thick soft-cavity foam rubber or sheet polyfoam. Reverse pattern to cut second piece so pieces will match exactly when put together, cavity side to cavity side (if foam rubber is used). Cut foam all around to taper sides. Cement (p. 86) tapered edges and press together. For a plumper cushion, cut a

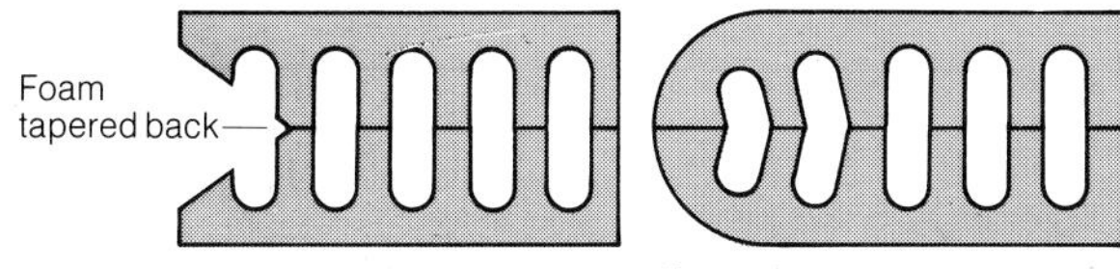

Foam pieces pressed together

piece of ½-inch sheet foam or polyfoam about 2½ inches smaller all around than the core foam, and cement it between the two layers. If outer cover will be thick fabric, a muslin inner cover is advisable.

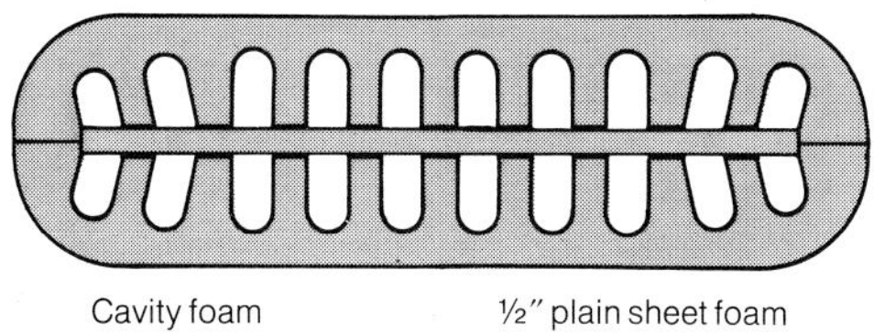

Loose fillings: The shape of cushions filled with loose materials, such as down or crumb polyfoam, is determined by the inner cover. Make a cambric inner cover for down or feathers; they will penetrate other fabrics. To make inner cover, cut two pieces of fabric to the desired size, plus ½ inch all around for seams. With right sides together, machine-stitch the pieces together, using double or French seams, and leaving a small opening for inserting fill. (Outer cover is made the same, except one entire side is left open.)

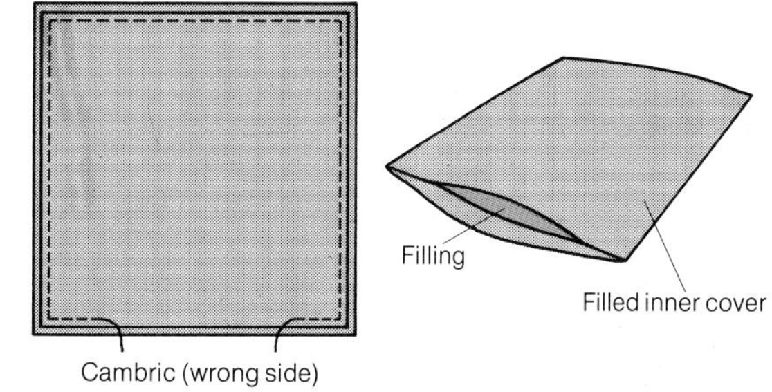

Make a small hole in the corner of the bag of filling material; push this into the opening in the inner cover and gently work filling from bag to cover.

Waterproof cushions

For this type of cushion, you will need polyurethane foam, leather-like vinyl (1 linear yard covers a 21-inch square cushion), waterproof cement, and masking tape. Cut a piece of vinyl 5 inches larger all around than the foam. Place vinyl face down with foam centered on top. Fold the excess up and over, making corners as you fold. Cement the edges and both surfaces of corner folds; after about 15 seconds, press surfaces together. Tape to hold. When dry, cement (p.86) a square of vinyl over the exposed foam.

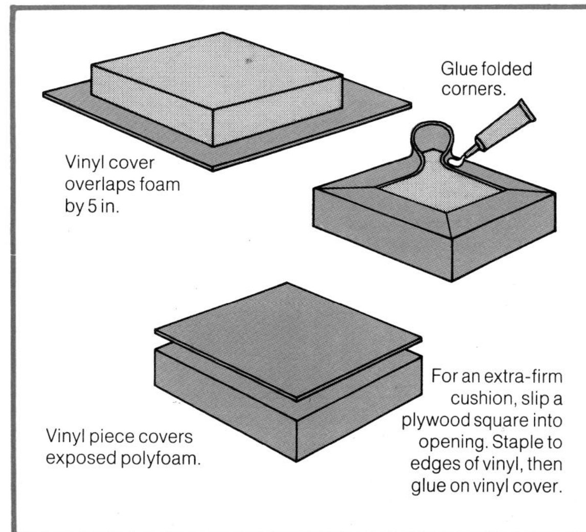

Piping seams

To make piping (fabric-covered cotton cord), cut (1) and join (2) bias strips of fabric; fold joined strips over cord and stitch (3), using cording foot. Cut front and back cover panels. Lay the piped cord along an outside edge of one panel, with end in center. Starting 1 inch from end of piping, stitch almost to corner. Notch corners as shown. Raise the cording foot and pivot the cover so the piping falls into place on the next side. Near end of stitching, cut piping, leaving ¾ inch extra at ends. Open ends and cut excess cord from each. Turn in ends of casings, tuck them into

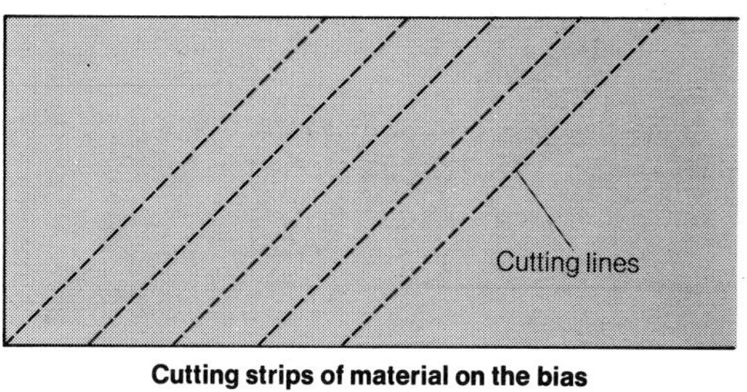

Cutting strips of material on the bias

Joining bias strips by machine

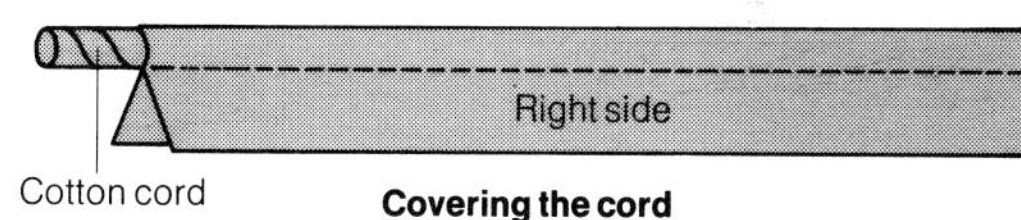

Covering the cord

one another, and finish stitching. With right sides together, join front and back panels, leaving one side open. Turn cover right side out; insert cushion; slipstitch the open edge.

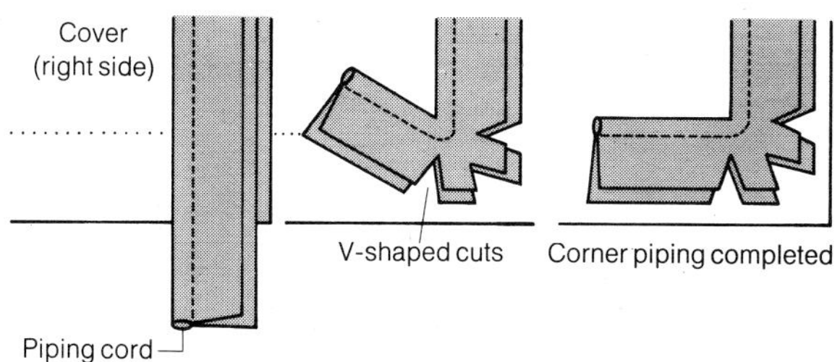

Cane seating

Maintaining, cleaning, restoring

Cane—the thin bark of the rattan palm cut into narrow strips—is a remarkably resilient seating material when properly maintained. Although it is exceptionally light in weight—the caning for an average seat weighs only about 2½ ounces—the average household will get years of use from a cane seat before replacement becomes necessary.

The characteristic color and mellow glow of cane can be preserved by frequent cleaning, using the simple technique that is shown at the immediate right. To keep cane in shape to give the resilient and comfortable support for which it is famous, follow the shrinking technique shown at the far right at the first sign of stretching.

For all its resilience, however, cane is a relatively delicate material in certain respects and is more susceptible to damage from just minor abuse than most other furniture materials. Take special care to keep children from using caned chairs in their play or as ladders for reaching distant objects.

Clean cane by scrubbing vigorously with a solution of about a tablespoon of common salt in a quart of hot water. Use a cloth or soft brush to avoid damage.

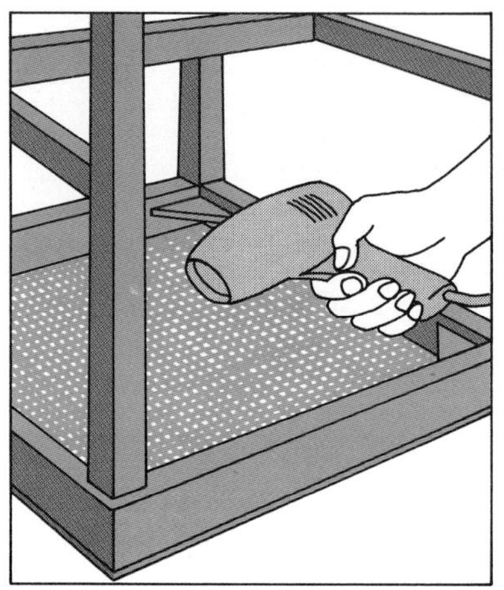

After scrubbing, wipe off excess moisture with a clean cloth, then dry the cane completely with warm air from a hair dryer or vacuum cleaner.

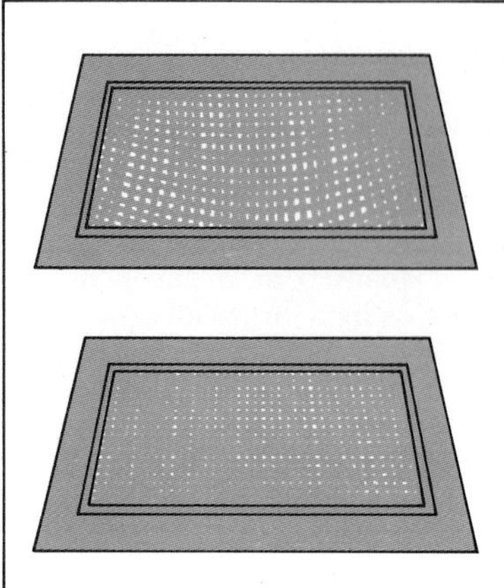

Shrinking will restore stretched cane to its original tautness. To accomplish this, place the cane seat in warm water for several minutes; let dry naturally.

Replacing a damaged seat

Cane seats are usually constructed with factory prewoven cane, which can be replaced by the procedure illustrated at the right. Pre-woven cane for replacement purposes is available in both an open basket weave and an open octagonal weave. Many upholstery repair shops stock this material; for other sources, look in your classified telephone directory under the listing "Chair caning."

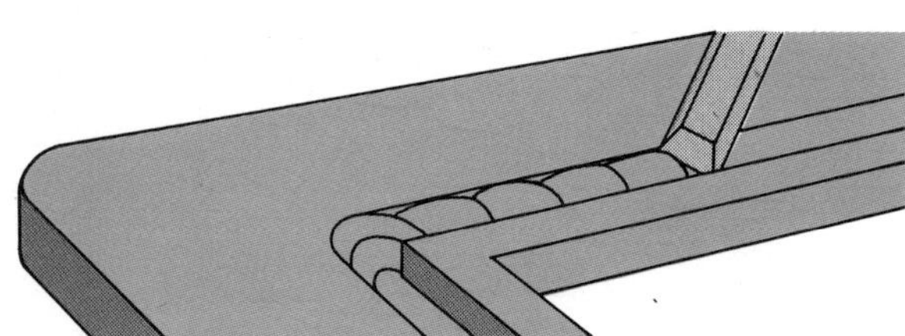

Clean old spline from groove with a chisel

Cane is most commonly sold in an 18-inch width, but other widths, from 8 to 36 inches, are available if the conventional width doesn't suit your purpose. You buy cane as you do fabric, by the yard. Before attempting to install pre-woven cane, soak it for several minutes in hot water to make it pliable enough to work without cracking.

Center the cane on the seat. Make certain that it extends at least 2½ in. over the spline groove near the seat edge. Use a hardwood wedge and mallet to drive the cane into the groove, working from front to back first, then doing sides.

With the cutting edge of a chisel set along the bottom outer edge of the spline groove, cut away excess cane by hitting the butt end of the chisel with a mallet. Set cane into groove by squeezing white glue into the cavity.

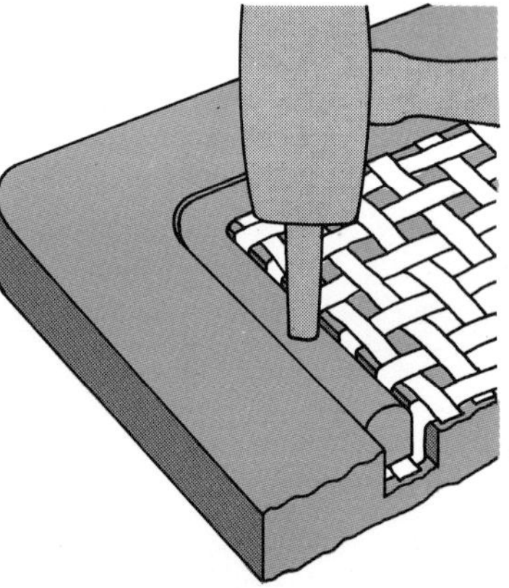

After soaking spline in hot water until it is flexible, set it into the groove on top of the cane. Again using wedge and mallet, drive spline into place, then wipe away excess glue. Let cane and spline dry out before sitting on seat.

Tools and materials

Cane strips for making chair seats, and sometimes backs, come in several widths, ranging from very fine (about .065 inch wide) to common (.130 inch wide). If you are undertaking a recaning job for the first time, you will probably find the medium width (.115 inch wide) easiest to work with. Enough cane for the replacement of a single average-size seat costs about a dollar. If your local upholstery shop does not carry cane strips, ask the owner where you can buy or order some.

You will also need, for either a recaning job or for caning a new seat, an awl for reaming out the holes on an old seat, or a drill and 3/16-inch bit for making holes around the perimeter of a new one; thick binding cane for covering the holes when the job is completed; and two wire bodkins—one for separating the strands that are already in place, the other for drawing the cane strips through them.

Installing the cane

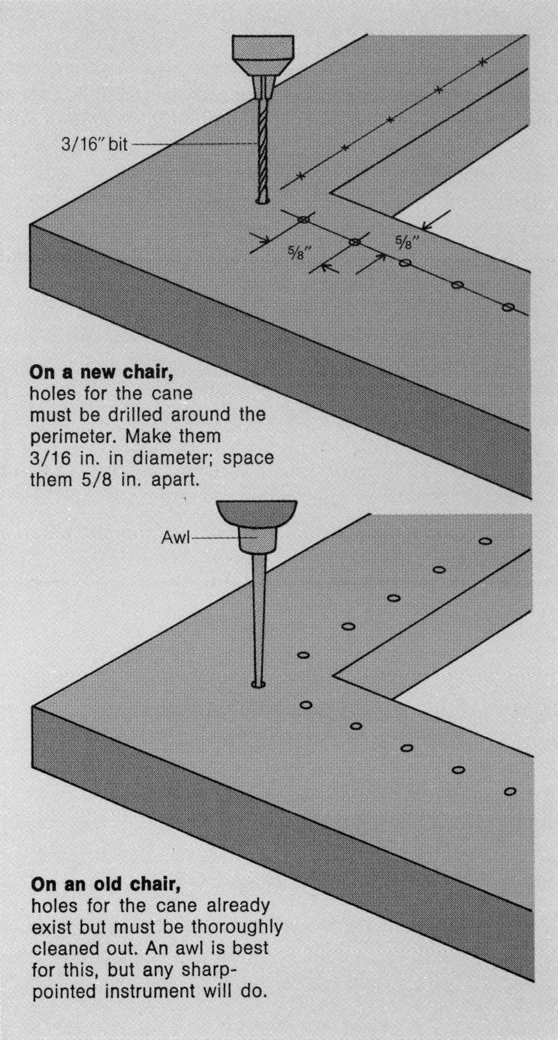

On a new chair, holes for the cane must be drilled around the perimeter. Make them 3/16 in. in diameter; space them 5/8 in. apart.

On an old chair, holes for the cane already exist but must be thoroughly cleaned out. An awl is best for this, but any sharp-pointed instrument will do.

Soak the cane in warm water until pliable. Find the center holes at front and back of seat. Draw a strand of cane down through the front center hole for half its length, then up through the next hole to the left. Take both ends of the strand through the corresponding back holes.

Wedge the cane in the front center hole with a peg and continue threading the other end—along the underside, up through the next hole, and across to the other end of the seat. Keep the strands parallel, with the shiny side showing. Leave some slack at this stage; the cane will tighten as work progresses.

Secure the end of a completed or new strand by winding it twice around the cane running between the holes on the underside and pulling it tight. When the left half of the seat is covered, unpeg the end of the first strand and complete the right half. Then thread the cane from side to side, on top of and at right angles to the front-to-back strands. Thread another set of front-to-back strands on top of the first two, then another side-to-side set, this time weaving the cane over and under the intersecting strands. Beginning at one corner, weave diagonally, under the sideways pairs and over the front-to-back pairs. Take two diagonal strands from the corner hole to get correct spacing, only one from the other holes. Weave diagonally in the other direction, that is, over the sideways pairs and under the front-to-back pairs.

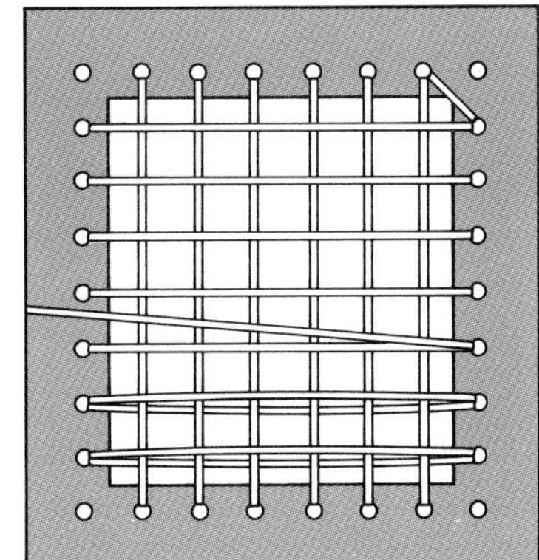

The first sets of strands run from front to back and from side to side, forming squares. A front-to-back set goes in place first and a side-to-side set goes over that. Then a second front-to-back set is added over the first side-to-side set.

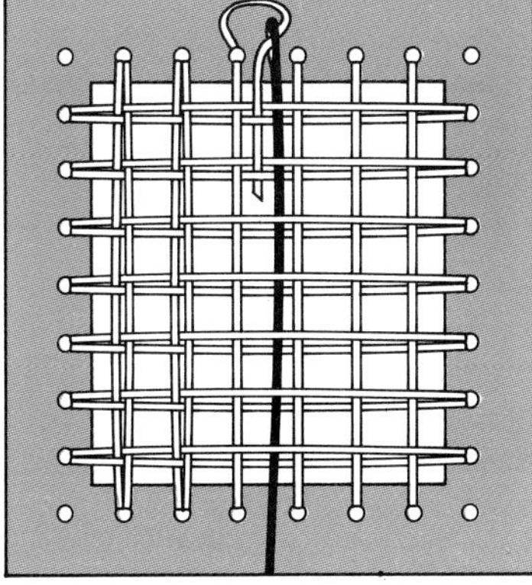

Next you weave the second set of side-to-side strands over and under the front-to-back strands as shown. Use a wire bodkin to separate the strands so that there is enough space for the new ribbon of cane to be woven through.

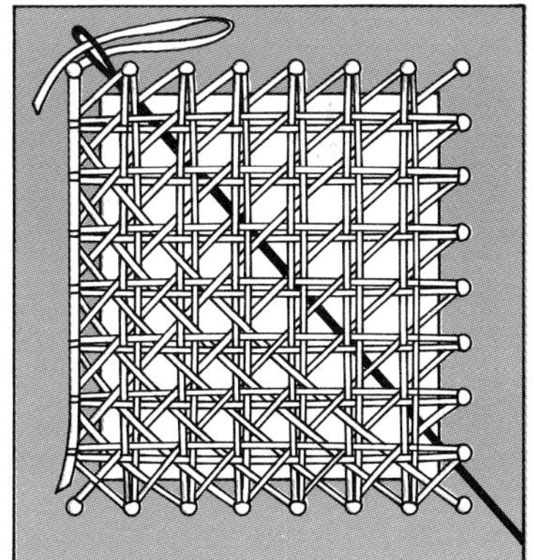

Starting from a corner hole, begin to weave the diagonal strands. Weave under the sideways pairs and over the front-to-back pairs. Then weave in the other direction—that is, over the side-to-side pairs and under those that go from front to back.

Reupholstering attached seats

Kitchen and dining room chairs on which webbing and covering material are attached directly to the rails, are called overstuffed seats. Repairing a chair of this type involves stripping off and replacing all of the upholstery.

To do the job, you need upholsterer's webbing or rubber webbing; burlap (for upholsterer's webbing); sheet foam rubber or polyfoam, 1½ or 2 inches thick; 3-inch-wide calico strips; tacks as specified; adhesive; and covering material.

Strip off all the old upholstery, including the webbing, and remove old tacks, leaving the chair frame bare. Fix new webbing to the seat frame, interweaving it and spacing it evenly so that the gaps do not exceed the width of the webbing.

If you use upholsterer's webbing, pull it taut with a web stretcher (1) and fix each end with three tacks. Cut off the ends, leaving an inch or so to be folded back and secured with two more tacks.

Rubber webbing is not turned back as upholsterer's webbing must be, but is stretched by hand 5 to 10 percent beyond its normal length.

If upholsterer's webbing is used, tack a piece of burlap over it.

Cut a pattern of the seat out of stiff paper, allowing an extra ½ inch all around. Lay the pattern on the foam (if you are using cavity latex foam, lay the pattern on the smooth surface) and mark around it with a ballpoint pen (2). If slight doming is required, glue a piece of ½-inch sheet latex foam or polyfoam, 2½ inches smaller all around, to the bottom side of the foam base.

Cut out the foam with a sharp knife or with kitchen scissors dipped in water. Make sure the cut is vertical and not jagged.

Form a firm "cushioned" edge by gluing the calico strips to the outside edges of the top surface of the foam (3), leaving just over an inch of each strip free to tack to the seat rails.

Lay the foam on the chair seat, allowing an overlap of ½ inch around all four sides. Pull the calico strips down and fix them with ⅜-inch tacks to the seat rails (4). When you have a smooth, even contour, drive the tacks home.

Put on the covering material, using ⅜- or ½-inch tacks. Cut the cover fabric at least 1½ inches larger all around than the seat size, to allow for turning in and tacking.

Lay the cover over the seat and tack it temporarily to the center of the undersides of the front and back rails, using one tack per rail. Repeat for the side rails. The cover should now be correctly positioned and under slight tension.

Starting at center front and working outward, drive in the final tacks to within 2 inches of the front legs. Do the same on back and sides.

Turn out the corners at the back legs and cut a V from each (5). Turn in the raw edges and tuck fabric down around the back legs, turning the folded end under the seat and tacking it down. Finish off the front corners by folding the material, cutting away excess inside the fold to give a smooth finish (6).

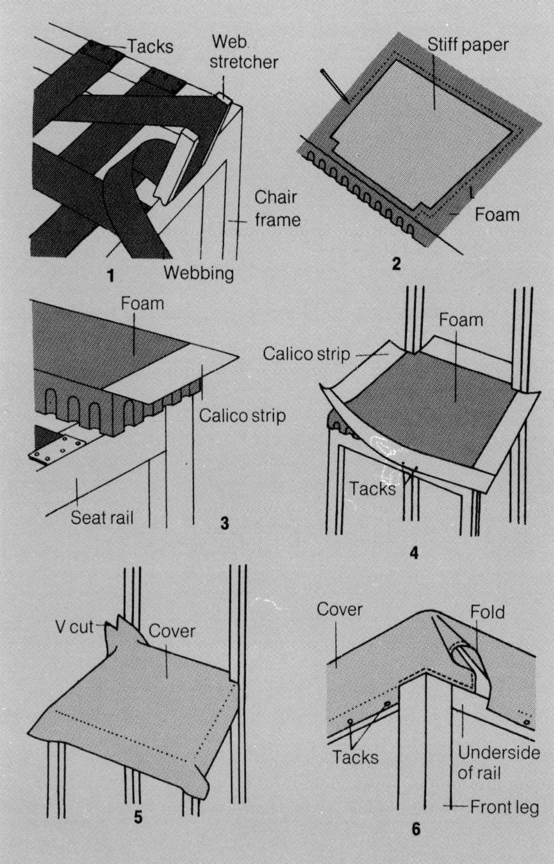

Reupholstering removable seats

A removable seat can be repaired with sheet foam. Use covering material no bulkier than the original, or the seat may not drop back into place. If you want to use a heavier material, you may have to plane down the edges of the seat so that it will fit, with its new heavier covering, into the chair's frame.

For this repair job, you will require upholsterer's webbing or rubber webbing; burlap (for upholsterer's webbing); sheet foam rubber or polyfoam 1 or 1½ inches thick; 3-inch-wide calico strips; tacks as specified; adhesive; and covering material.

Strip off all the old upholstery and webbing and fit the new webbing as specified at the left for an overstuffed seat.

Tack down a layer of burlap over upholsterer's webbing if this is the type you have used.

Using the seat as a pattern but allowing an extra ½ inch all around, cut out the foam for the seat. Tape the edges of the foam with calico as described, left, for an overstuffed seat.

Lay the foam on the seat frame so that the ½ inch overlap is even all around. Starting from the center of the front edge, pull the calico down and tack it temporarily to the frame's underside, keeping tension even all around. Drive the tacks home.

Put on the final cover, allowing an extra 1½ inches all around for turning and tacking. Lay the cover on the seat, then hold the two together and turn them over. The seat is now upside down.

Tack the cover temporarily, making it tight enough to compress the foam slightly but not so tight that its resilience is restricted. Drive tacks home in the same way as for an overstuffed seat.

Finally, tack the overlapping cover fabric at the corners. Tack the corner of the fabric first, then fold in the sides and tack down. If the fabric is bulky, trim some of the excess before tacking down.

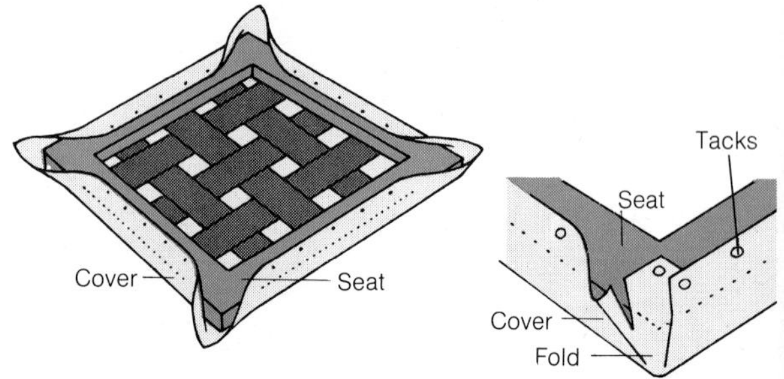

Invisible repairs

Because dining room furniture is usually expensive, and bought as much for looks as for service, it cannot be mended with the kind of simple and visible repair that will do for kitchen or utility furniture. Good furniture calls for repairs that are both strong and nearly invisible—a more difficult task but well worth the effort when you consider the cost of replacing the parts of a valuable set, providing it is possible for them to be replaced.

Loose rails, broken legs and chair arms, separating earpieces on cabriole legs—these are among the most common difficulties that develop in dining room furniture. You will find suggestions below for making several such repairs in ways that will restore the strength of furniture—and preserve its good looks.

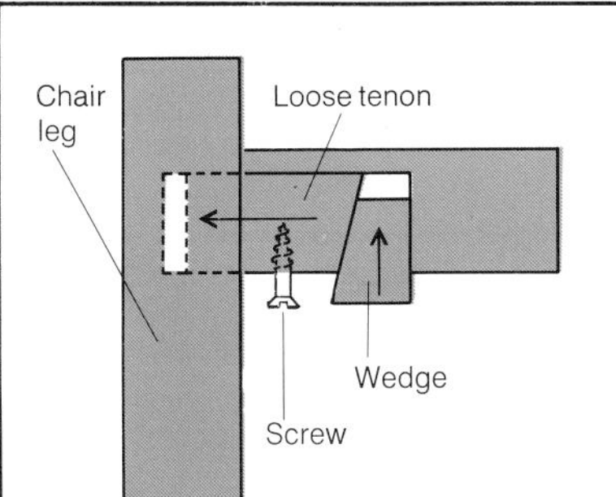

Loose center rail on a chair: To fix, cut a deep slot along the rail's end and base. Slip a tenon in from the base and insert a small screw in the bottom of the tenon. Position the rail by the mortise and, holding the screw head, move the tenon forward. Lock the tenon in place with a wedge behind it and remove the screw.

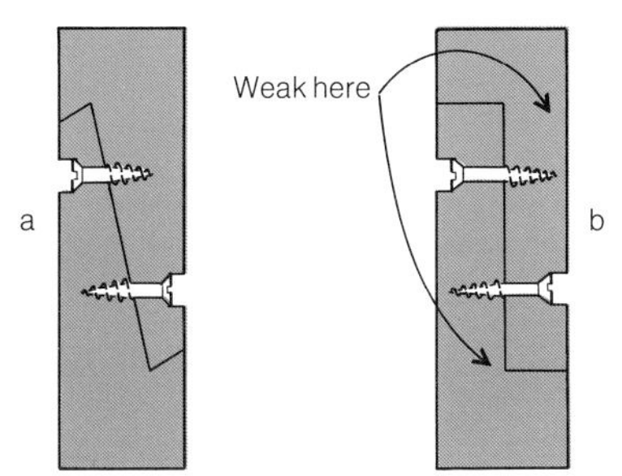

A tapered joint (a) is the best way of dealing with a broken square front leg. Ordinary pressure on straight joints (b) can cause them to fail. In method (a), the new piece is glued to the old, the joinings reinforced with screws. Counterbore the screw holes and countersink the screw heads. Cover the heads with wood putty, then stain.

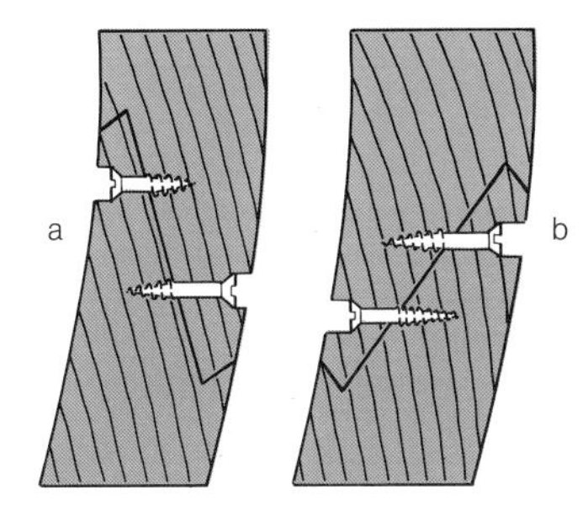

In splicing curved back legs, keep the joint running in the direction of the grain (a) as much as possible. If the joint runs opposite to the grain, as in illustration (b), the splice will be weak. Just as with front legs, add screws in counterbored holes for strength; countersink screw heads, fill the depression with wood putty, and then stain.

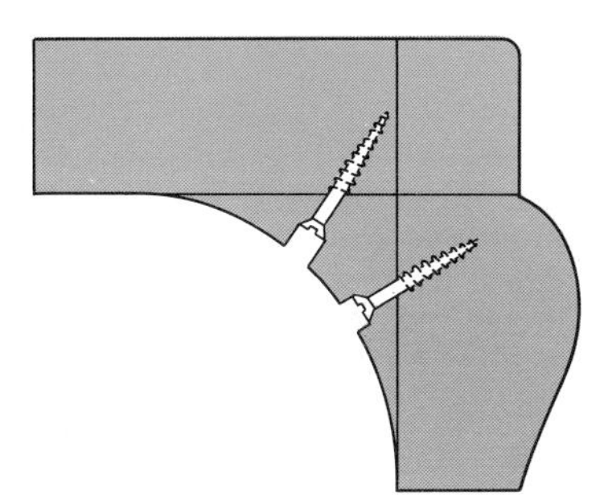

If an earpiece adjoining a cabriole table or chair leg comes loose from its frame, chip away the old glue and reglue the piece in place. Use a rope or web clamp around the repair to hold it and, when the glue has set, counterbore (and countersink) holes for screws. Set the screws in place and fill depressions with wood putty.

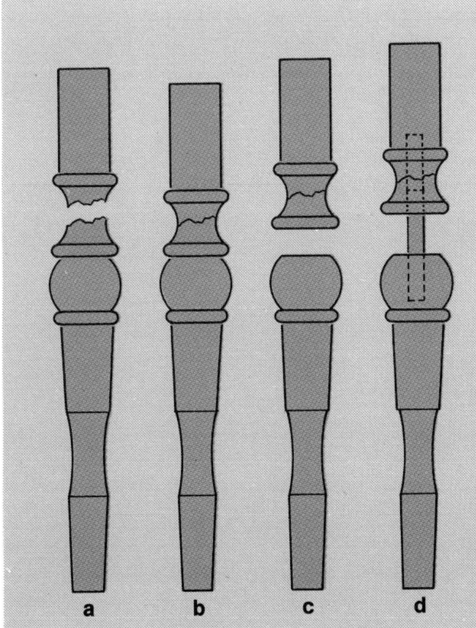

To repair a turned leg broken near the top, use a dowel joint. Illustration (a) shows the broken leg. Glue the break together (b), clamping the repair while the bond sets. Then saw the leg apart below the original break (c). Tap a brad into the center of the top of the lower section. Clip the top of the brad so that less than an inch is exposed. Fit the two sections together, then pull them apart; the brad will leave a mark on the top section to guide you in placing the bit. Drill holes in both pieces to accept a dowel. Spread glue in the holes; insert the dowel to join the pieces (d). Let the glue set overnight before putting weight on the leg.

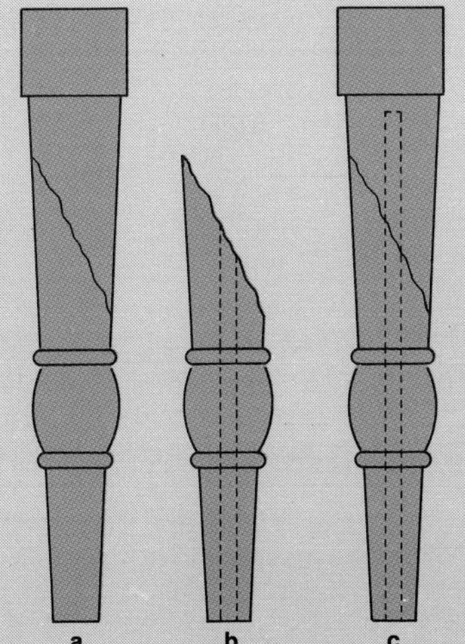

A split on a turned leg can be repaired with a dowel. The split leg is shown in illustration (a). Separate the pieces, apply cement to both ragged edges (b), and fit the two pieces together. Clamp the assembly with tightly wound rope and allow the bond to set for several hours. Then drill a hole for the dowel through the center of the leg at the base, drilling all the way through the bottom part and well into the upper part of the leg. Squeeze cement inside the hole and also cement the dowel well to be sure cementing is ample. Insert the dowel (c). Let the cement set thoroughly (at least overnight), then cut away the excess doweling at the base of the leg.

Patio, lawn, and den chairs

Renovating a director's chair

To renovate a director's chair, all you need is a paintbrush and paint for the wood portions and a few yards of canvas for new seat and back slings. First you must remove the screws that connect the chair arms and back to the legs and lift the upper elements off. Carefully remove the tacks that connect the seat sling to the legs and lift off the back sling. Rip out all stitches from the back sling and use both slings as patterns for cutting new ones.

Because the seat sling is merely a flat piece of canvas, you need only hem the edges to prevent unraveling. The back sling is almost as simple. You first hem the edges, and then sew two cylinders, one on each end. These fit over the two back uprights. (You can measure the stitching on the old sling to see how much space to allow.) Repaint the chair and let it dry; then install the slings. Slip the back sling down over the uprights and tack the seat sling along the base of the sling supports. Put frame back together, tightening screws well.

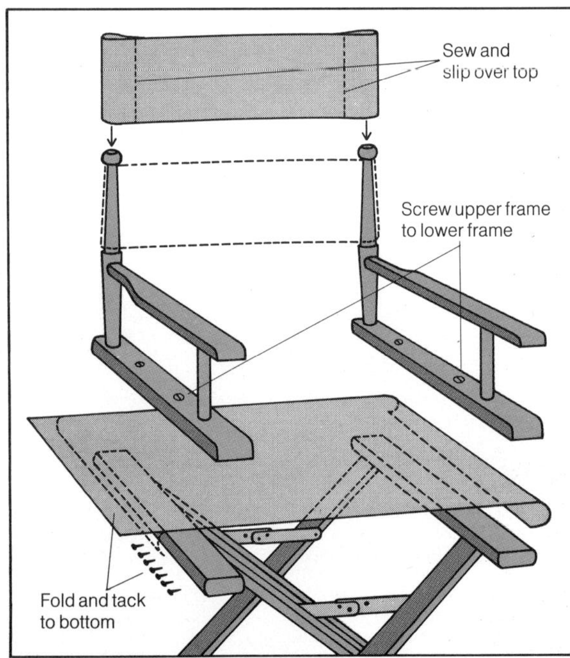

Using old slings as patterns, you can make a new set fast. Canvas for the job is inexpensive and sturdy, comes in many colors and patterns. Wood parts can be painted.

Renovating porch and patio chairs

Cushions: You can make any porch or patio chair, sofa, chaise longue, or glider more comfortable by putting cushions over the webbing. Lightweight canvas and sailcloth both make suitable coverings, although waterproof vinyl over a filling of polyfoam (p.205) is the most durable choice, particularly if the cushions will be exposed to the elements. Scatter cushions (p.205) filled with foam or kapok probably offer the easiest solution to the problem of cushioning porch furniture. To cushions that will go on larger pieces, such as chaise longues, you can add buttons if you would like a tufting effect. You will need two buttons for each tufting point, one at the cushion's top and the other on its underside. Pull the attaching thread between the two tight enough to achieve the desired depth. Finish by tying the thread to the button on the underside.

Plastic tape webbing for porch and patio furniture can be found in most hardware stores. Although you should not expect this material to last for more than a year or so, look for brands that carry guarantees concerning their durability to be sure you get the maximum possible wear. Attach this webbing as you would webbing on indoor furniture (p.204). Do not, however, use a spiked stretcher—plastic webbing tears easily. Other types of stretchers might be useful in pulling the web tape taut, but you may find it easier just to stretch the material by hand.

Plastic-covered cord is a relatively new form of upholstery for porch and patio furniture and very easy to use. You simply wind it back and forth across the chair frame. On most chairs that are built to take this material, the line is looped to rivets on the underside of the frame and stretched across the frame, then looped and stretched again and again. When you are winding, do not cut the line, but keep it continuous. When you begin to install new cord, leave some of the old cord in place as a pattern to follow.

Cord and canvas is another fairly new upholstering possibility for patio furniture. The canvas is stretched across the frame, tying the canvas to the rails with a strong cord. To renovate a chair with cord and canvas, cut the canvas somewhat smaller than the frame opening and hem the edges. Then install grommets (or reinforced buttonholes) near the edges, spacing the holes about 2 inches apart. You are then ready to lace the cord through the holes, winding the cord tightly around the rails as you go.

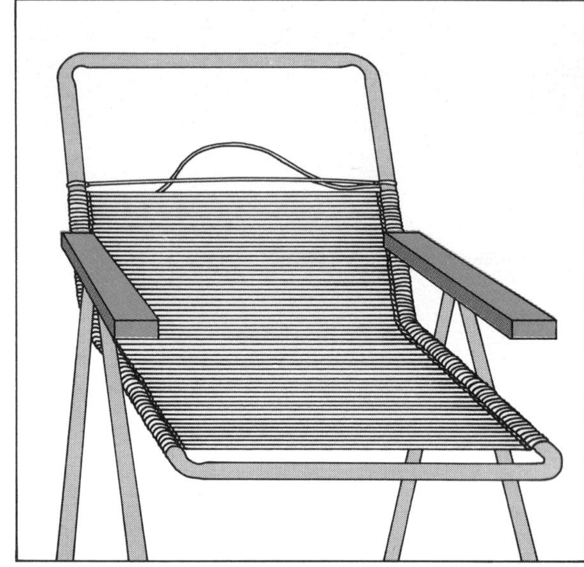

Stretch plastic-covered cord back and forth across the frame of the chair. It makes a resilient, comfortable seat that stands up well in both the sun and the rain.

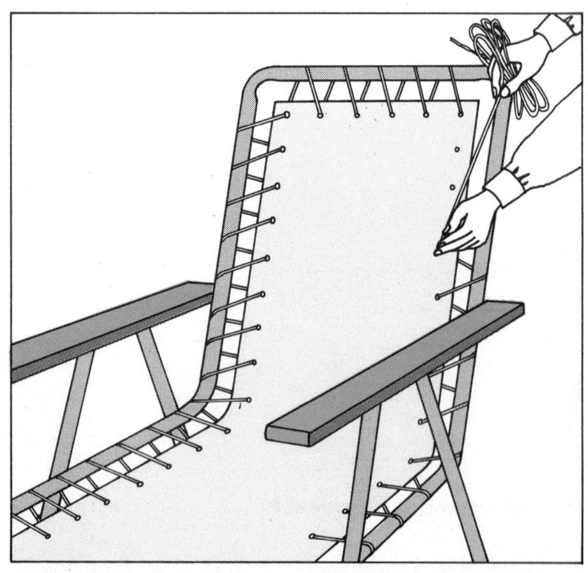

Cord-and-canvas installation: Lace cord through grommets (or holes) near the edges of the canvas and wind the cord around the chair frame. Knot each end of cord to secure it.

section 7:

Plumbing: How to keep it in working order

A trouble-free plumbing system is one of the real comforts of home, and you can do more than you may realize to keep yours that way. This section tells exactly how. Of course it goes fully into plumbing fundamentals. And it also takes you step by step through repairs and replacements, making clear which you can do yourself and which call for outside help. Either way, you benefit: In savings and satisfaction when you do the work; in the best possible job when you hire it done.

contents

Plumbing emergencies

General recommendations

A correctly designed and installed home plumbing system is practically trouble-free. Should problems occur, there are standard methods for dealing with them. And there are good reasons as well—a neglected leak inside a wall, on the floor, or in the ceiling can cause serious damage.

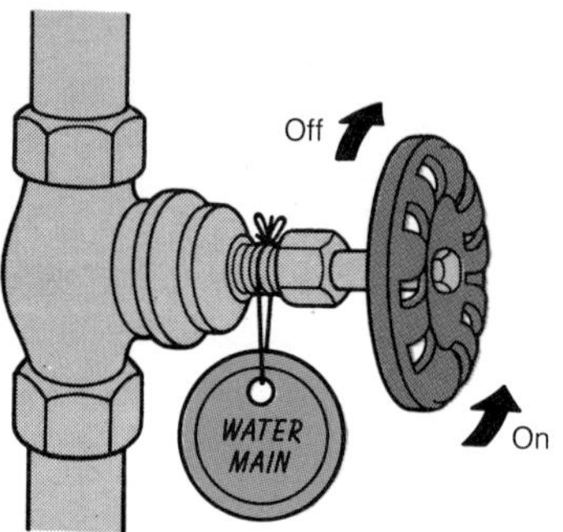

Label main water shutoff valve

Most plumbing systems provide numerous shutoff valves for controlling water flow in the supply system. Sinks and lavatories have individual shutoffs for hot and cold water; toilets have just one. The first thing to do in an emergency at a fixture is to close its shutoff valve. Most shutoffs are located just underneath the fixtures they control; some are in the basement, utility room, or crawl space below.

Generally you can shut off the hot-water supply for the whole house at the hot-water heater.

Whether or not a house has individual fixture controls for the water supply, you will always find a main shutoff near the water meter or at the wall where the main enters the house. Leaks or overflowing that cannot be stopped at a fixture can always be stopped by closing this shutoff valve.

Close all shutoff valves by turning their handles clockwise. You should become familiar with shutoffs in your house—especially the main shutoff—so you can get to them without delay in case of trouble. Houses served by water mains have additional shutoffs located underground near the sidewalk or lawn. Sometimes a special wrench is needed to operate the valve, which is reached through a lined hole in the ground.

What to do in an emergency

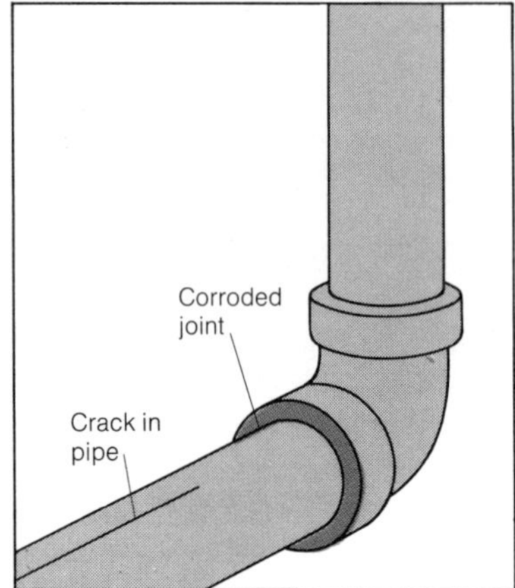

Pipe leaks: Joints that have corroded and pipes that have frozen (and burst) will leak. Tightening a threaded joint or re-soldering a soldered joint may cure it. Burst pipes can sometimes be mended with a clamp-on pipe patch. If not, they must be replaced. Emergency clamp can be made of piece of rubber and C-clamp.

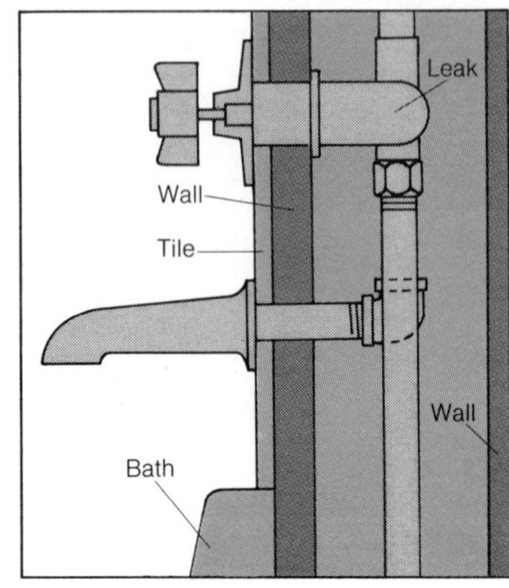

Leak in wall: Most often caused by faulty riser pipe to a shower or to fixtures on the next floor. Best to get professional help. Plumber will tell you whether he can make the repair—installing new pipe—with or without cutting hole in the covering wall. Some communities insist upon access panels to pipes located behind walls.

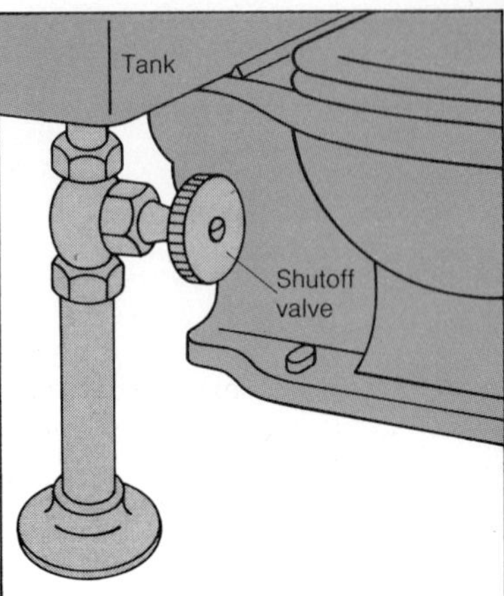

Overflowing toilet tank: A toilet tank overflowing into the bowl will be heard running long after flushing. Close the tank shutoff valve between tank and floor. See p. 222 for information on correcting this trouble. Take care when removing porcelain top—it is easily damaged. Place on heavy towel or pile of newspaper.

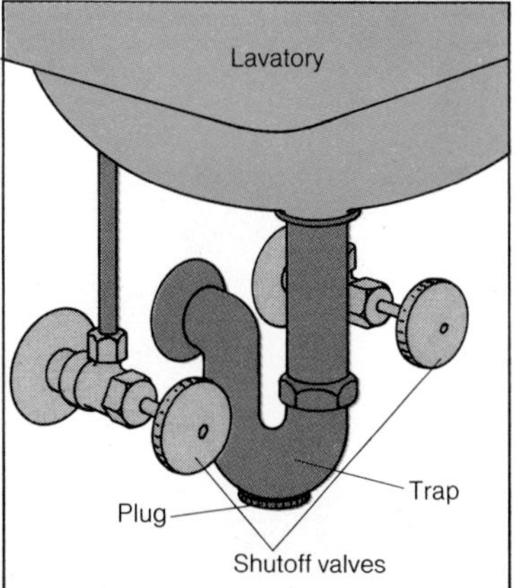

Sluggish or stopped sink drain: First try a rubber force cup. If this doesn't work, try a chemical drain-opener, following directions on container. If this doesn't work either, put a pail under the trap and remove the plug. Use a wire to remove the debris, usually hair and grease. Replace plug and run water scalding hot to clean the drain and keep it clean.

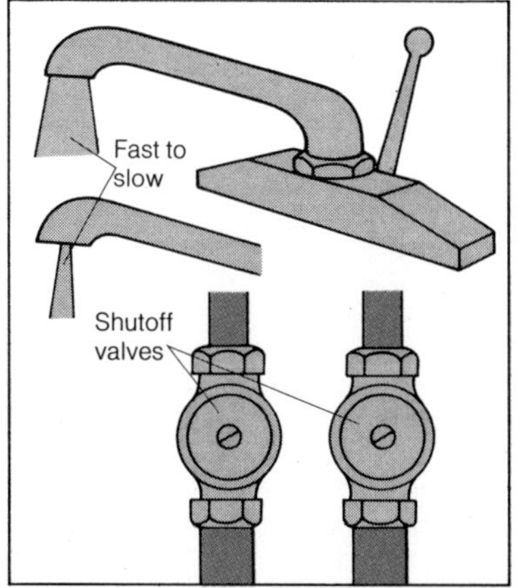

Scale-restricted supply pipes are a problem in old houses and hard-water areas. Turn water on full force, first making sure all valves are fully open. If the water comes out fast and then slows, there is a restriction in the pipe. The cure? Replace all affected pipes. Avoid galvanized pipes; they are prone to scaling. Use brass pipe or copper tubing instead.

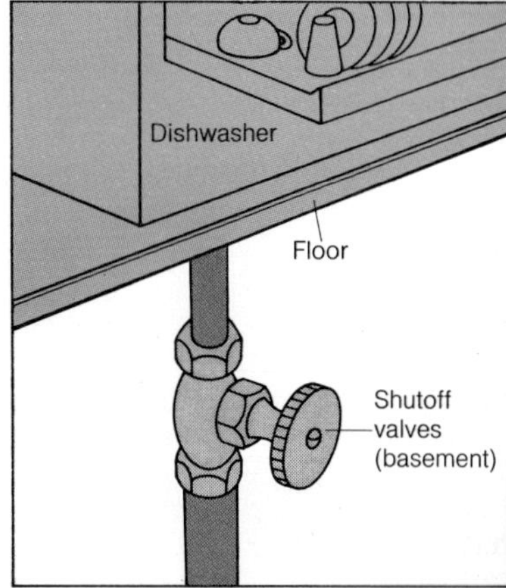

Overflowing dishwasher: The first thing to do: Turn off the valve controlling the water supply to the dishwasher. Then check the screen around the drain. It may be clogged with grease or a rag. If water keeps flowing in before shutoff valve has been turned off, electrical controls may be at fault. Turn off current, or pull the plug if it is a portable model.

How they work

Your home's plumbing system is basically simple. It is made up of an incoming water supply, outgoing drainage pipes, fixtures, and appliances. Toilets, lavatories, bathtubs, showers, kitchen sinks, and laundry tubs are fixtures. Clothes washers, dishwashers, garbage disposers, hot-water heaters, and the like are appliances. Some water-supply pipes end in outdoor faucets for garden hoses.

Fresh water is carried under pressure from the house water-service entrance (or from the well pump in a private system) to each fixture and appliance. Water-supply pipes are relatively small, with inside diameters from 3/8 to 1 inch.

The incoming water pipe is divided at the hot-water heater into hot- and cold-water systems. Pipes for the two usually run parallel throughout the house.

The drainage system is completely separate. Drainpipes are larger than incoming water-supply pipes, varying from 1¼ to 4 inches, inside diameter.

At each fixture the drain passages contain a U- or S-shaped bend, called a **trap.** The trap retains water that acts as a seal to prevent gases, bacteria, and vermin from entering the house.

The drainage system handles drain water removal, waste removal, and venting, and so is called the drain-waste-vent or DWV system.

Waste pipes carry wastes by gravity away from each fixture into larger drainpipes, which carry the flow downward into the house sewer line.

Vent pipes carry off sewer gases and keep the whole DWV system at atmospheric pressure, necessary to maintain the water seal in each trap. Without venting, pressure from collected gases in any portion of the DWV system could force and break the trap's water seal. If atmospheric pressure were not maintained, trap water would siphon away.

Main vents serving toilets, and secondary vents serving other fixtures, extend through the roof where they are open to the air. Some systems have revents that connect their fixtures to a main or secondary vent instead of directly through the roof. DWV pipes that serve toilet waste are called **soil pipes** and are 3 inches or larger in diameter. A toilet vent is termed a **soil stack.**

Every DWV system contains plugged openings called **cleanouts.** There is one in each horizontal run of drainage line. Cleanouts provide access to the inside of the DWV system for removal of any blockage.

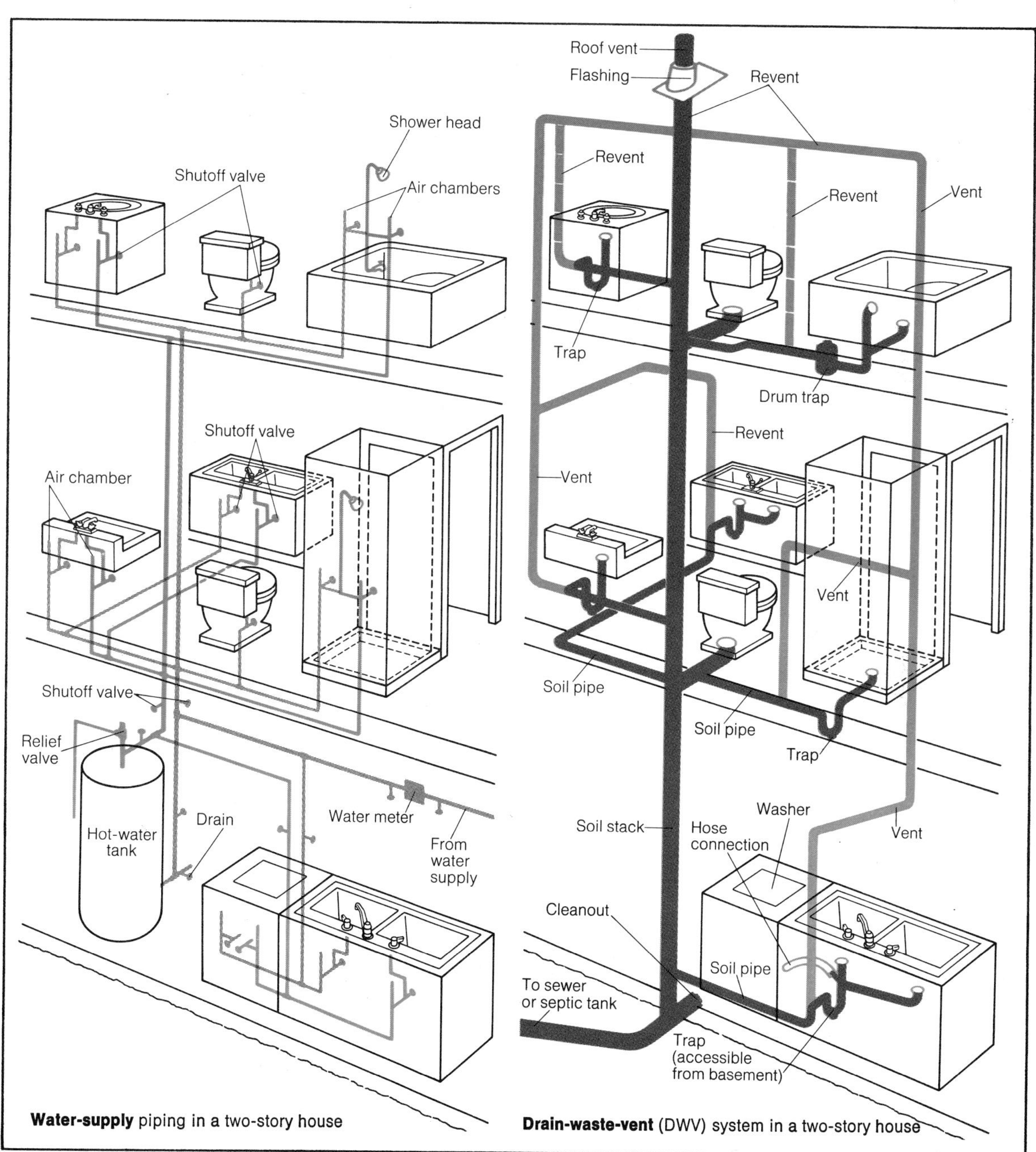

Water-supply piping in a two-story house

Drain-waste-vent (DWV) system in a two-story house

Water supply and disposal

Water-supply system

Where your water comes from. Water is supplied to most homes by private, public, or municipal water systems; some homes have their own systems. All water originates as rainfall. Rainwater may be collected directly in reservoirs or cisterns; it may be found as surface water, as in lakes and rivers; or it may be obtained from springs or from shallow or deep wells. After collection by whatever method, pipes carry the water to your house.

Both rainwater and surface water almost always contain pollutants. Such water must be treated to make it pure enough to drink. The usual method is by the addition of chlorine.

Ground water generally is pure enough to drink unless it is taken from a shallow well that has been contaminated by polluted surface water. However, ground water often contains large amounts of dissolved or suspended solids—minerals—that make it "hard." To make it more suitable for home use, hard water can be softened by running it through demineralizing agents that change the composition of the minerals or remove them. This is usually done in homes with commercial softeners (p.247).

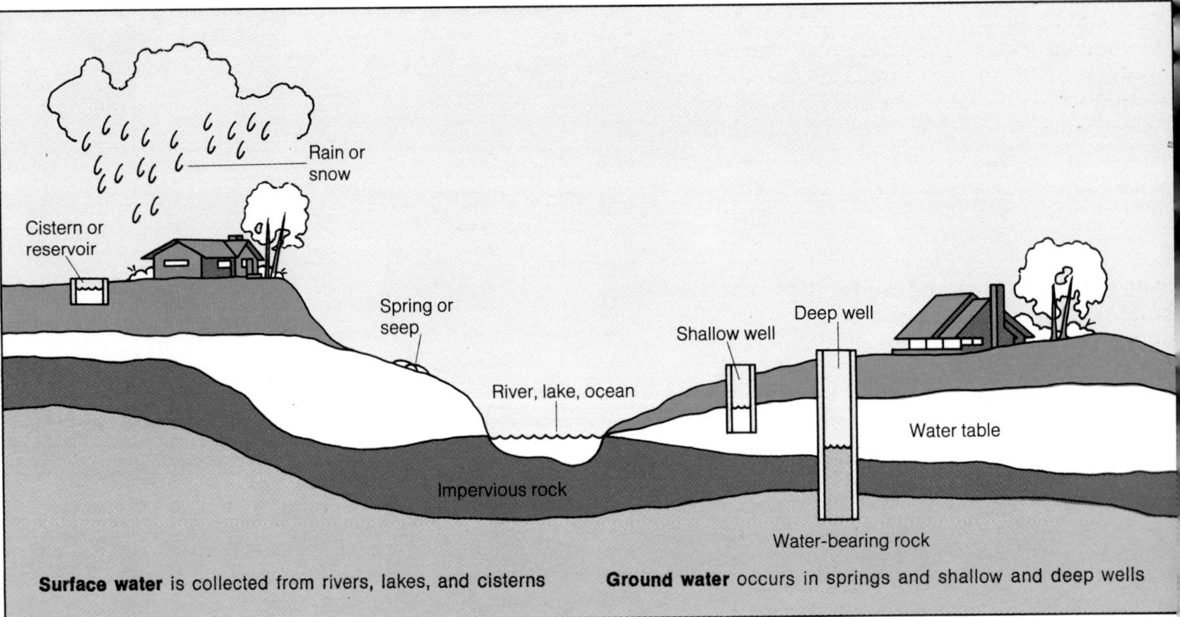

Surface water is collected from rivers, lakes, and cisterns

Ground water occurs in springs and shallow and deep wells

Drainage

Outgoing "used" water may be handled either collectively or privately. Collective sewage treatment is much more efficient than private disposal. In a collective sewer system, drain water and wastes enter a network of pipes from each house, and flow, most often by gravity, to a sewage-treatment plant.

Modern sewage-treatment plants then aerate the sewage to hasten bacteriological action and breakdown, to settle out the remaining solids, and to dry them, selling the residue for fertilizer. The effluent is further aerated, filtered, and chlorinated to kill any remaining bacteria. When the process is complete, the water is pure enough to drink and it is discharged into a nearby stream.

Most private sewage-disposal systems consist of a septic tank and disposal field, and serve one family. The septic tank breaks down the sewage into liquids and solids by bacteriological action. Solids settle to the bottom of the tank and must be cleaned out every few years. Effluent runs out of the tank and is distributed throughout a system of underground trenches or pits where it seeps into the soil. In time, all septic disposal fields become clogged by suspended solids in the effluent and they have to be enlarged. Better, but more expensive, are one-family disposal systems that work much like collective sewage-treatment plants, but on a smaller scale.

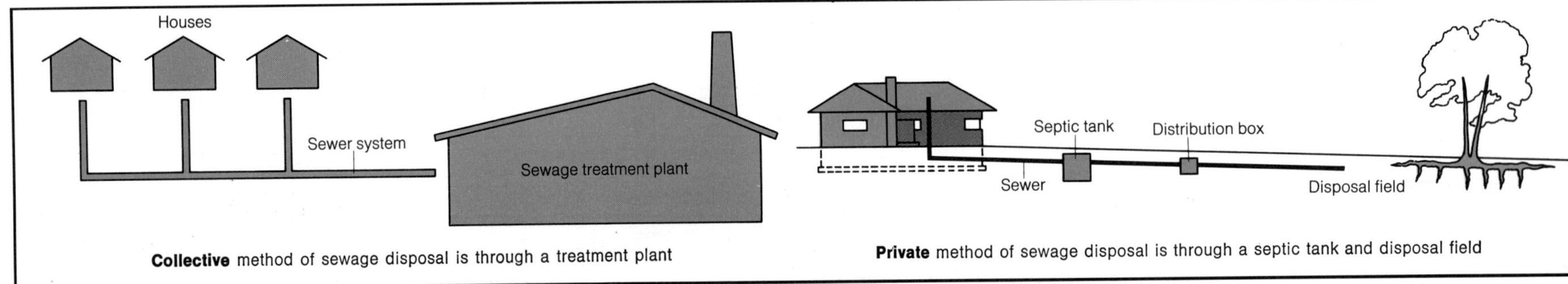

Collective method of sewage disposal is through a treatment plant

Private method of sewage disposal is through a septic tank and disposal field

Piping

The diameters of most pipe and tubing are expressed in nominal sizes which sometimes bear little relation to the actual inside or outside diameter. For example, 1/8-inch steel pipe has an inside diameter of more than 1/4 inch and an outside diameter of a little less than 1/2 inch; 3/4-inch pipe has an outside diameter of more than an inch. You need not worry about these discrepancies so long as you order and use pipe by its nominal size. Actual outside diameters are only important when you want to cut exact-size clearance holes through joist and studs.

Pipe fittings (p.227) are made to fit all pipe and tubing made in the United States and Canada. If you can't figure out how to make a particular connection and no fitting seems to be available or made, try a combination of two or more. The chances are the problem can be solved. One of the most important plumbing fittings is a "union." It enables you to remove and install a section of pipe in the middle of a run without having to start at the very beginning or end. When a pipe is unscrewed from a fitting, the other end will screw further into the fitting at the other end—this is why unions are so important.

Water-supply piping can be steel, copper, plastic—and, in problem-water areas, sometimes brass. Drain-waste-vent piping can be cast iron, copper, plastic—and sometimes steel. Most older houses have steel water-supply and cast-iron DWV pipes; modern ones may have any combination. All piping consists of pipes plus fittings to join them in line, at angles, and branching off in various ways. Copper water-supply tubing can be bent to make turns without fittings.

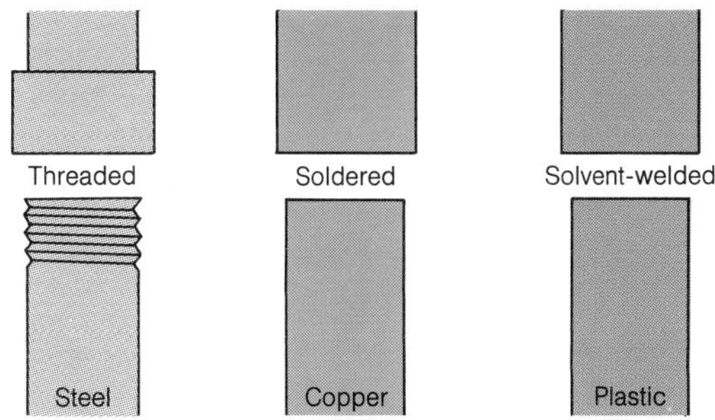

Water-supply pipe types

Drainpipe types

Another kind of pipe—polyethylene—is used for certain cold-water applications, but not normally inside the house. It, too, has fittings for joining.

Joining: Steel water-supply and DWV pipes are connected to their fittings with threaded joints. Outside threads on the pipe screw into inside threads on the fittings. The pipe threads are tapered to form a tight seal. Pipe-joint compound or Teflon is used on the threads to make a leakproof joint.

Copper water-supply tube and DWV pipe are joined by sweat-soldering. The joint absorbs molten solder, which hardens into a tight seal. Some copper water-supply installations use flare joints (p.231).

Plastic water-supply and DWV piping are joined to their fittings by fusing with a solvent cement.

Cast-iron DWV pipes are joined with neoprene rubber sleeves or lead joints (p.227).

Codes: Plumbing codes govern the type of materials that may be used and how the system must be designed and installed. Before you tackle any plumbing, check your local plumbing code.

A cross-connection is any connection between water that you might drink (in the water-supply system) and water that is unfit to drink. Almost every home has some cross-connections. Yours probably does too.

A faucet in a bathtub, sink, or lavatory that would be submerged if the basin should overflow is a cross-connection. Should the bowl become filled with backed-up drain water, the contaminated water could be drawn into the water supply used for drinking. Siphonage could occur even through a closed faucet if there were a vacuum in the water supply. A vacuum could be caused by a heavy water draw elsewhere in the house or a pressure drop from a nearby hydrant.

A garden hose with its end left in a swimming pool is a cross-connection. So is a hair-rinse hose that is left attached to the faucet and lying in the bowl.

Some older toilet tanks have cross-connected water inlets. Look under the tank lid. If the inlet valve in the tank does not extend above the high-water line, replace the valve with a vacuum-breaker inlet.

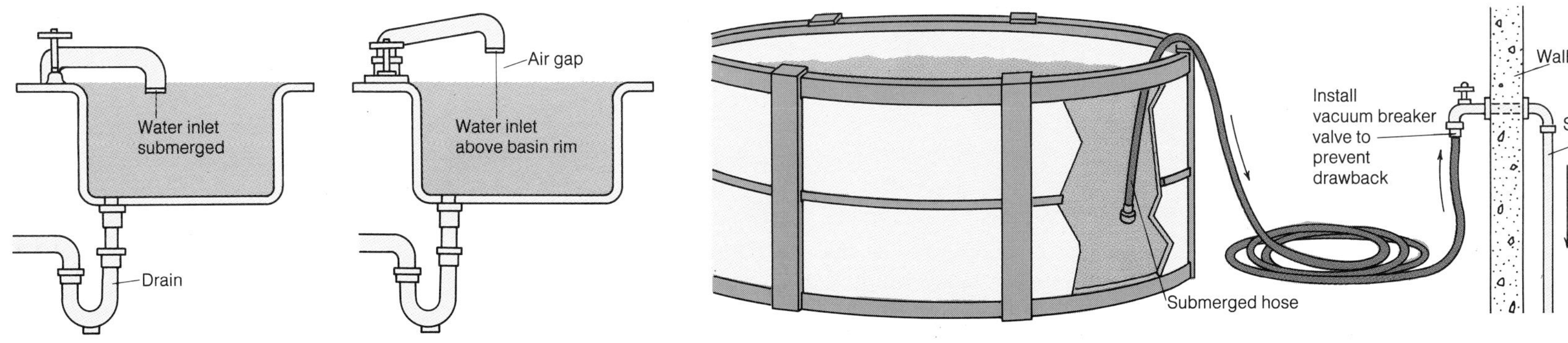

Cross-connection in an old fixture

Air gap in modern fixture

Cross-connection formed by hose and faucet can be prevented by the installation of a vacuum breaker

Clogged fixture drains

Unclogging a sink drain

How to unclog a fixture drain: When a sink, lavatory, shower, or bathtub drains slowly or not at all, the usual cause is an accumulation of hair, grease, or other debris lodged somewhere near the drain.

First try cleaning it with a rubber force cup, sometimes called a plumber's friend or plunger. The best type of plunger for this job is one with a wide, flat face that enables it to make good contact with the near-flat fixture bottom.

Run an inch or two of water into the basin. Remove the stopper if there is one. Plug up the overflow opening with a wet cloth or have someone hold his hand tightly over it. This will keep the plunger pressure from by-passing the clogged area and blowing out of the overflow outlet. Tip the force cup up to expel its air and place it directly over the drain. Plunge it down and pull it up firmly and rhythmically to build up force. Then pull the plunger off the drain opening to draw up the stoppage.

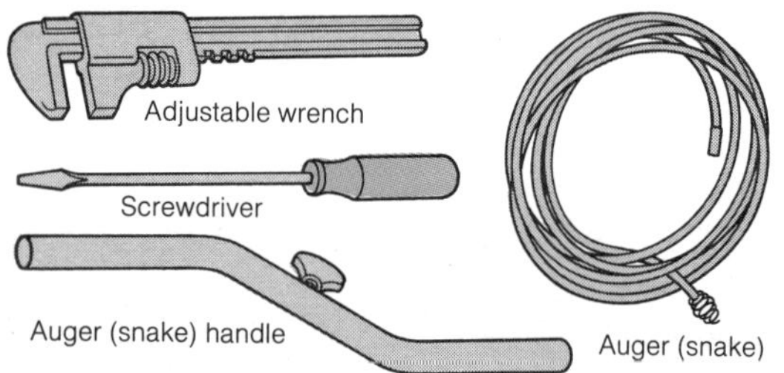

Drain cleanout tools (crank fits over end of auger)

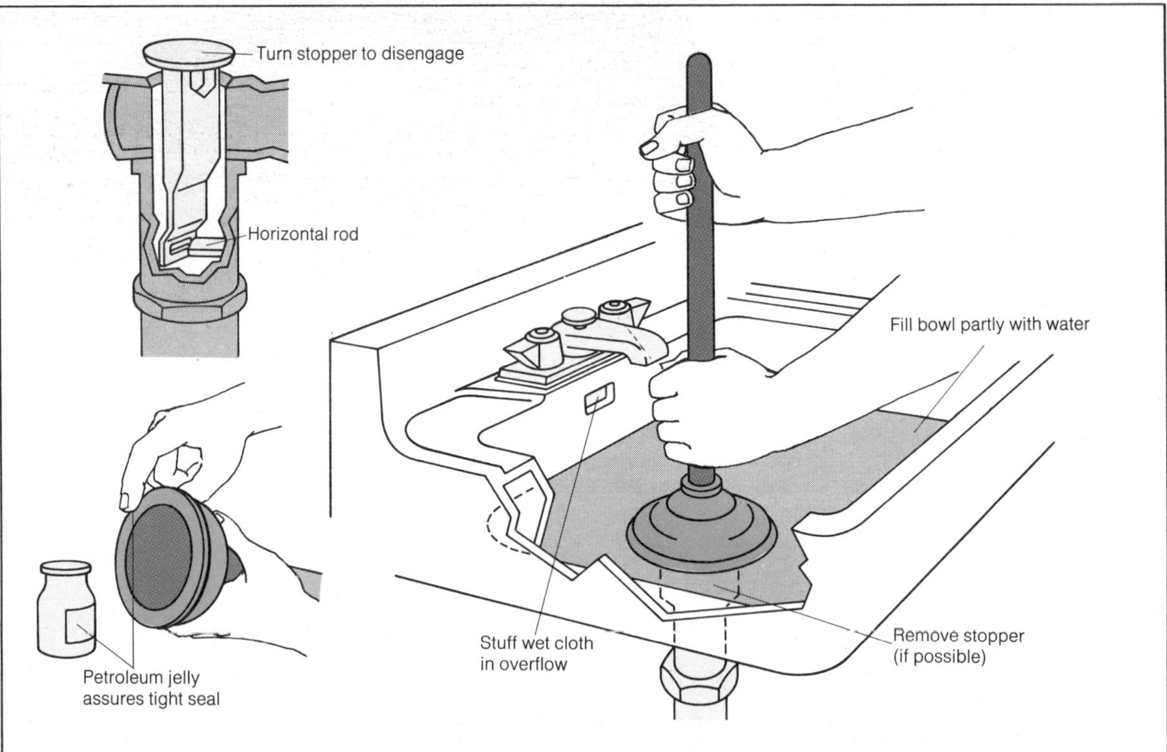

You can also try doing this with a special compressed-air plunger that acts like a pump (p. 217).

If plunging has not worked after several minutes, try a liquid chemical drain cleaner. If the stoppage is still there, use a sink auger, also called a plumber's snake. The auger is rotated into the drainpipe and will generally cut its way through the obstruction. Also a garden hose will sometimes do the job. Try it with and without water pressure.

If none of these work, remove the cleanout plug at the bottom of the trap. Some traps have no cleanout plugs and may themselves have to be removed. Others, called drum traps, used chiefly on tubs and showers, have screw-off covers accessible below the floor near the fixture. Insert the snake at the trap to remove debris. As a last resort, you may have to remove the trap to locate and clear out the clog.

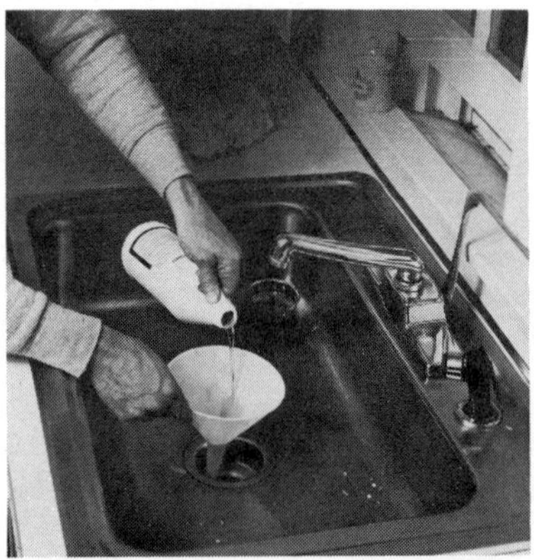
Liquid chemical cleaner is heavier than water and will settle to stoppage through standing water. Use it only according to directions on the container. Be careful not to splash, the chemical is caustic.

Drain auger is rotated into the drain until it contacts the stoppage. Turn the crank to work auger around the bends in the trap. In one type of auger, the cable is housed in a self-container.

Cleanout plug can be unscrewed to remove the stoppage, by hand or with an auger. Place a pan under the trap to catch the drain water. If trap has no plug, you may have to remove entire trap.

Unclogging a toilet

Toilets have built-in trap passages that can become clogged. Chemical cleaners cannot penetrate the trap area enough to be effective. Instead, try using a force cup—the kind with the fold-out or extra brim that will fit the toilet bowl passage snugly.

If several minutes of plunging doesn't work, switch to a toilet auger. This has a housing with a sharp bend that gets the snake started in the toilet trap. Aim the auger into the trap area, turn the crank handle, and keep moving the auger up the trap to the obstruction. Try to hook the blockage and pull it down or break it up rather than push it in deeper. When broken up, the debris can be flushed away.

If you do not have a closet auger, a sink auger may work. It is difficult, however, to get started into the trap. With your arm in a plastic garbage-pail liner, reach down under the water to get the auger started. Work the snake up and around the first sharp bend, then beyond to the blockage. Try to hook it and pull it out if you can.

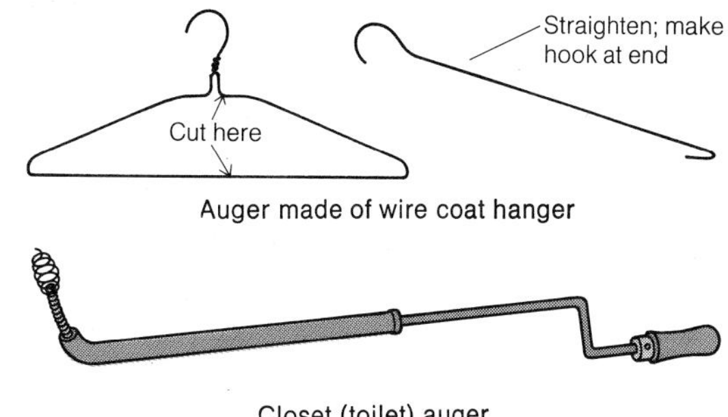

Auger made of wire coat hanger

Closet (toilet) auger

You can make an effective cleanout tool from a wire coat hanger. Probe the toilet trap area with it, trying to snag whatever is causing the stoppage. A child's toy, or a toothbrush, lodged in a toilet trap often resists easy removal. If you cannot get out an obstruction any other way, you will have to remove the toilet from the floor, invert it, and work at the blockage from the lower end (p. 237).

A toilet bowl that clogs every so often may have a partial blockage. Try running the auger through the passage once the toilet is flushing normally. If the problem is not partial blockage, and the bowl is a washdown or a reverse-trap type, replace the toilet with a siphon jet model, distinguishable from less expensive toilets by the jet, a ⅝-inch hole at the back of the bowl well below water level.

Compressed air cleaner

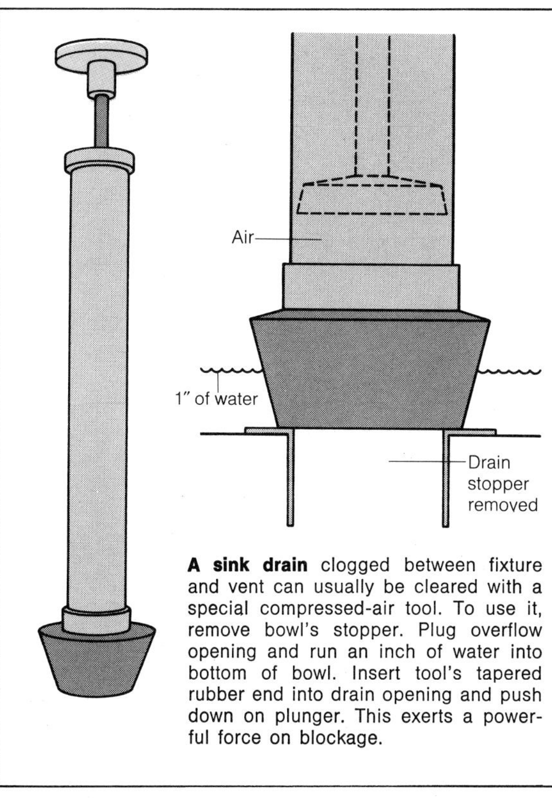

A sink drain clogged between fixture and vent can usually be cleared with a special compressed-air tool. To use it, remove bowl's stopper. Plug overflow opening and run an inch of water into bottom of bowl. Insert tool's tapered rubber end into drain opening and push down on plunger. This exerts a powerful force on blockage.

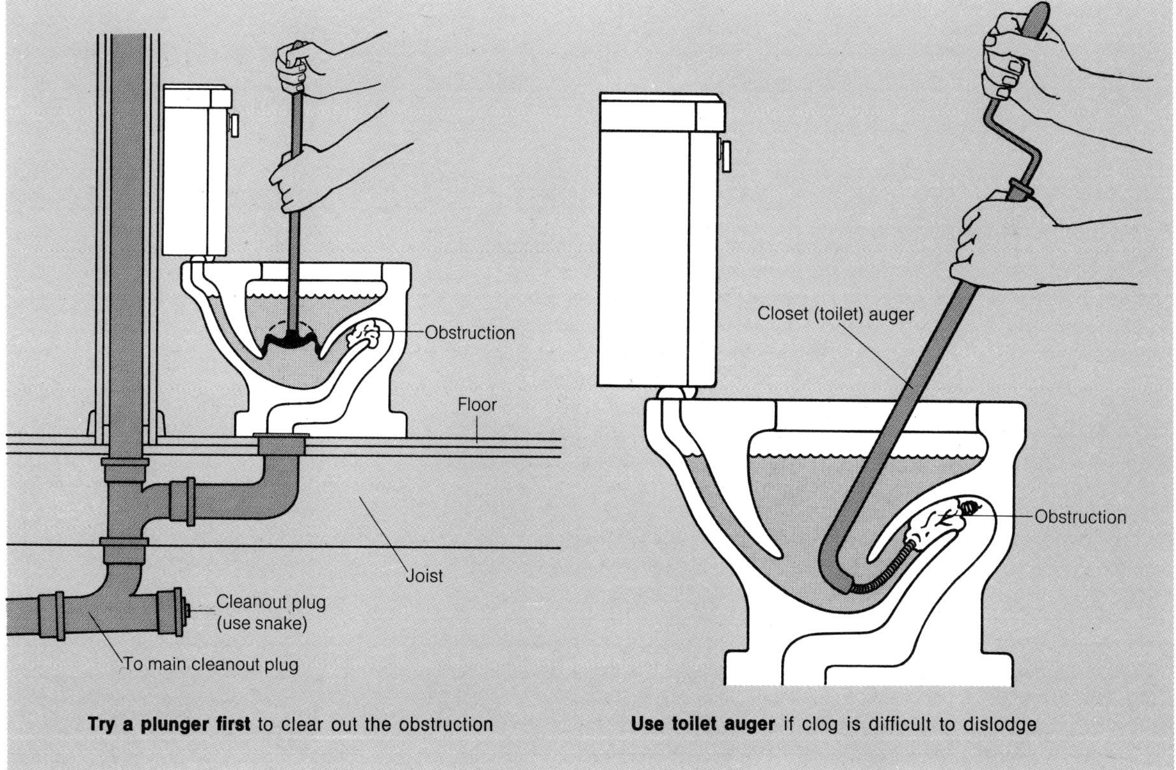

Try a plunger first to clear out the obstruction

Use toilet auger if clog is difficult to dislodge

Clogged main drainpipe

Unclogging the main drainpipe

Sometimes fixture drains back up because of a blockage in one of the drainpipes rather than in the fixture. You can quickly find out if this is so by loosening a cleanout plug in the drain beneath and close to the fixture. If water runs out around the loosened plug, the blockage is beyond that point.

Drain all water from the blocked-up DWV system at the cleanout plug nearest the clogged fixture. Just loosen the plug, and let the water drip into a pail.

If the clog is close to the cleanout, you may be able to clear it out with a wire. Sometimes, jamming a garden hose down the pipe will remove the blockage. Turn on the water gradually. (No one should drink from that hose until it is thoroughly flushed.)

If you have a drain auger or a plumber's snake, run that into the pipe until it meets soft resistance. Then crank or push and pull to remove the obstruction. Hard resistance usually indicates a bend or joint in the pipe that must be passed.

If the blockage turns out to be further from the cleanout than your drain auger or snake will reach, you can rent heavy-duty augers that will extend to 25, 50, or 100 feet. For clearing house-to-sewer lines, you will need a power rooter.

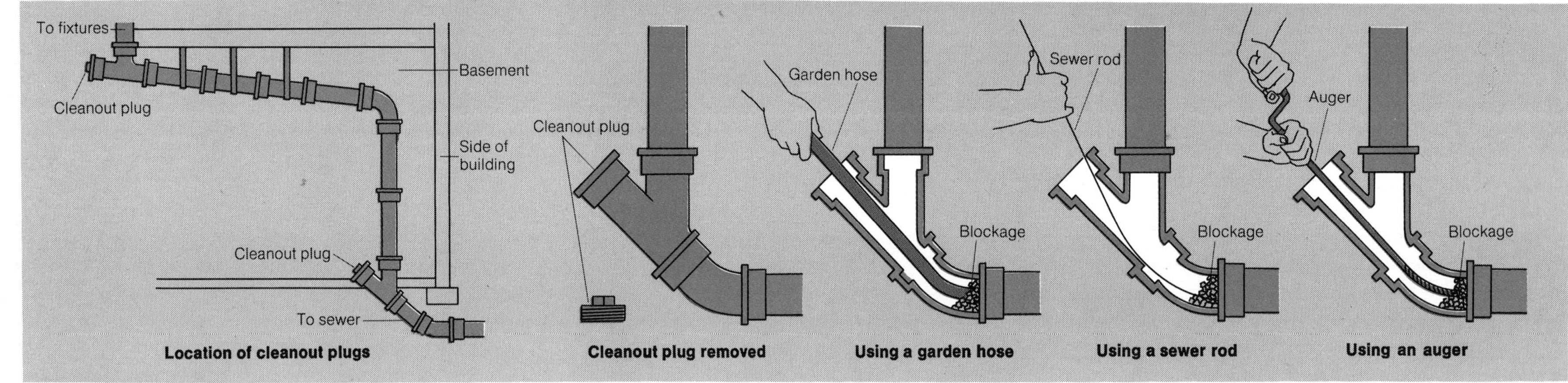

Removing roots from sewer pipe

Tree roots that grow through joints in underground pipes and sewer lines can be removed by a power auger. This machine, which has a special root-cutting head, can be rented from most tool-rental firms.

Before getting the machine, determine where the blockage is and remove the closest cleanout plug—usually located in the basement or crawl space, sometimes outside the house. Feed the auger cable slowly into the pipe until you feel the cable strain as its cutting head meets root resistance. Then feed more slowly so the head will cut steadily.

Once you've made a breakthrough, run water from a garden hose into the cleanout to help wash away cuttings; at the same time, work the auger over the area again. When the cutter hits a hard, impassable object, you have probably reached the main sewer. Back out slowly. Before you clean the cable and return the machine, test the drain by replacing the cleanout plug and flushing a toilet several times.

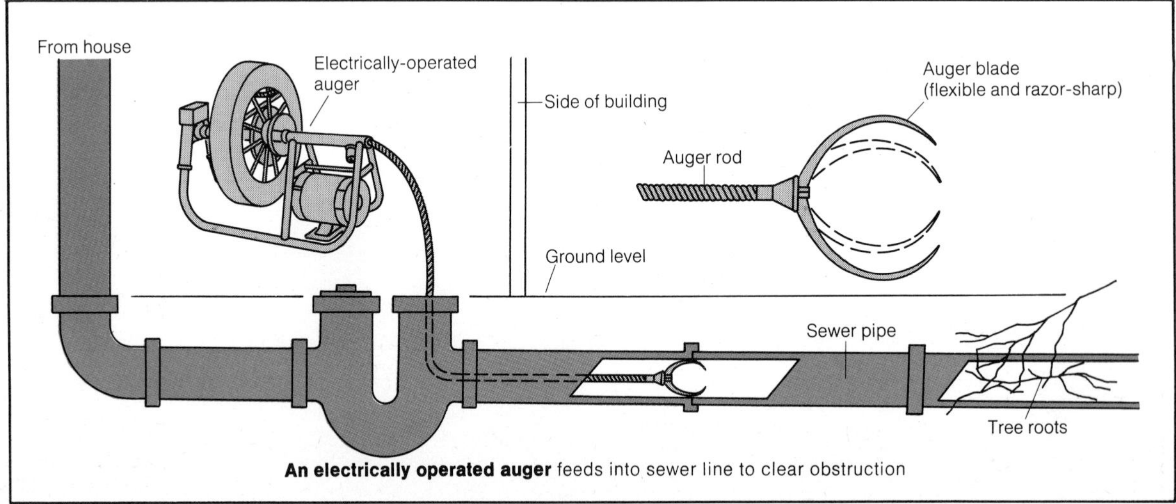

An electrically operated auger feeds into sewer line to clear obstruction

Repairing a washer-type faucet

Ordinary faucets leak for one of two reasons: The washer at the valve seat no longer fits the seat, or the packing around the faucet spindle is worn. Dripping indicates a worn washer, or seat, or both. Leaking around the handle indicates worn packing.

Some modern faucets use rubber O-ring seals instead of packing. Keep an assortment of faucet washers, O-rings, small brass bolts, and packing material on hand to make repairs as needed.

The first step is to remove the faucet handle. Some handle screws are hidden under threaded or snap-in caps that must be removed. Follow the steps illustrated to complete the repair. Your faucet's construction may vary somewhat from the one shown, but the repair steps will be similar. They apply to sink, lavatory, tub, and shower faucets with washers. To repair washerless faucets, see the next page.

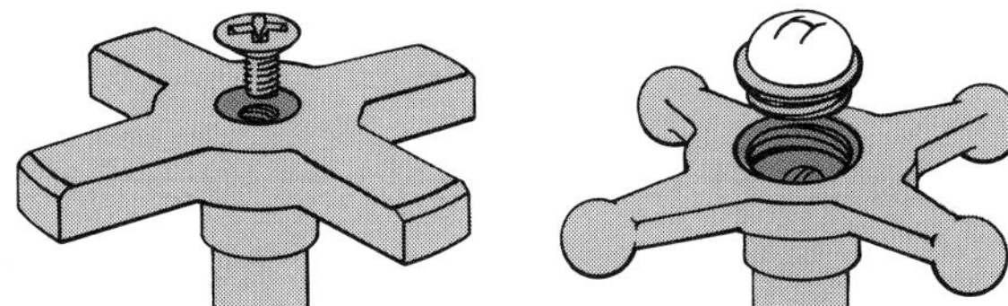

Handle screws may be hidden beneath threaded or snap-in caps

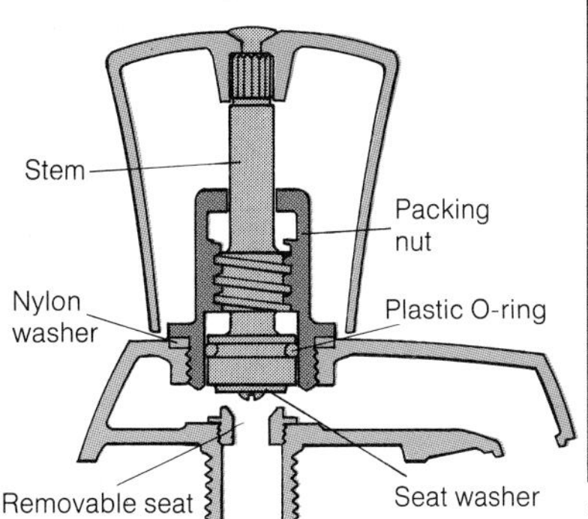

Valve seat grinding tool

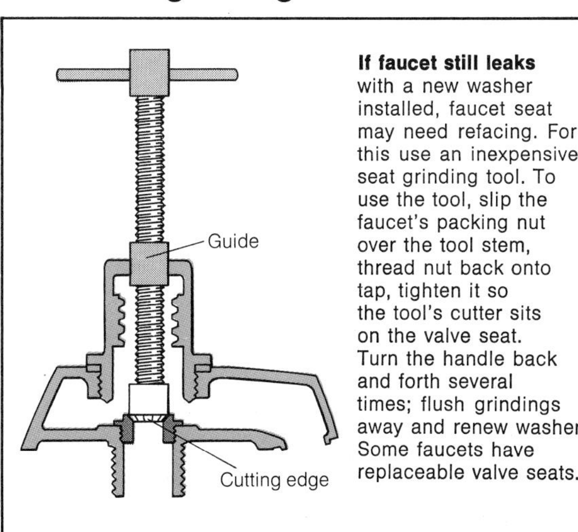

If faucet still leaks with a new washer installed, faucet seat may need refacing. For this use an inexpensive seat grinding tool. To use the tool, slip the faucet's packing nut over the tool stem, thread nut back onto tap, tighten it so the tool's cutter sits on the valve seat. Turn the handle back and forth several times; flush grindings away and renew washer. Some faucets have replaceable valve seats.

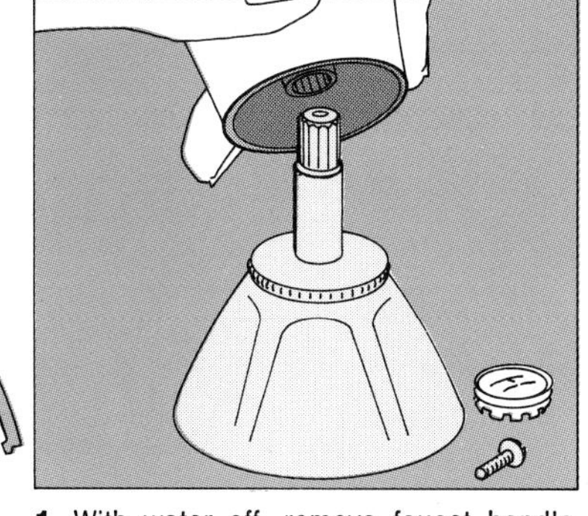

1. With water off, remove faucet handle. The handle can stay on if it does not cover the packing nut.

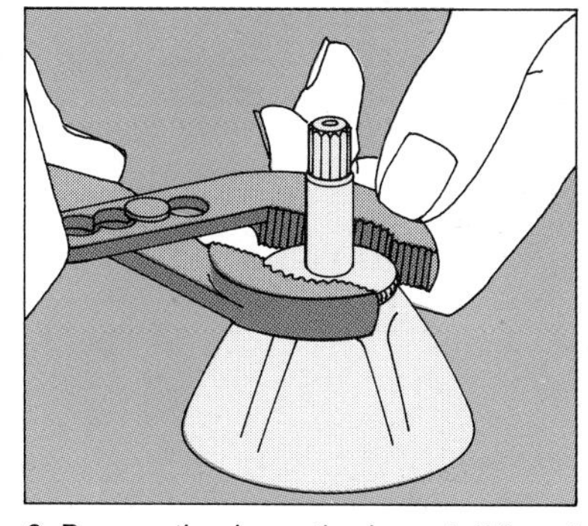

2. Remove the decorative bonnet, if faucet has one, to get at packing nut beneath. Use tape to avoid scratches.

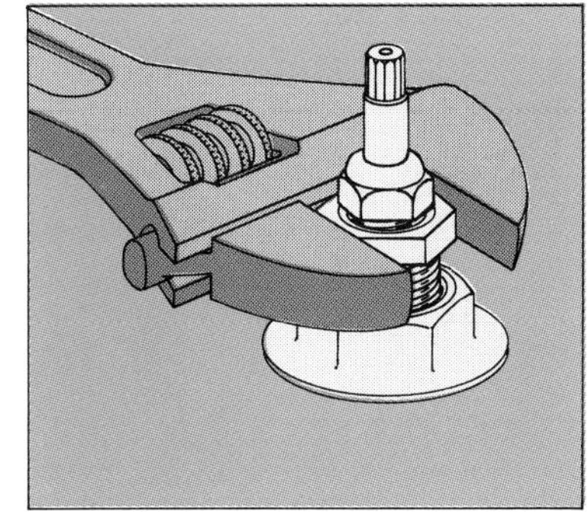

3. Remove packing nut (turn it counterclockwise with wrench), then spindle and washer assembly.

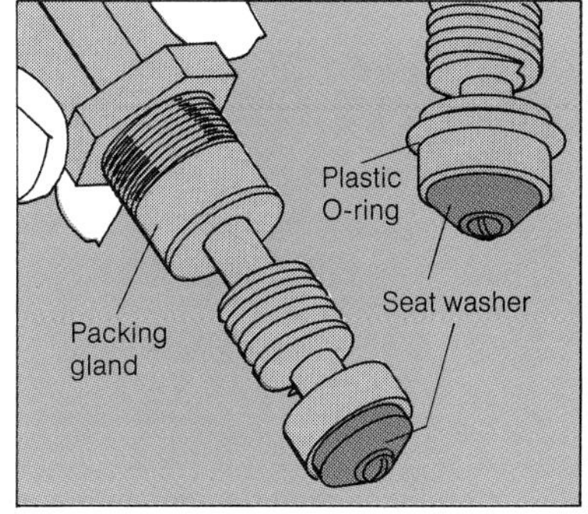

4. The renewable parts of the spindle assembly vary with the manufacturer. All have washers, some packing, others O-rings.

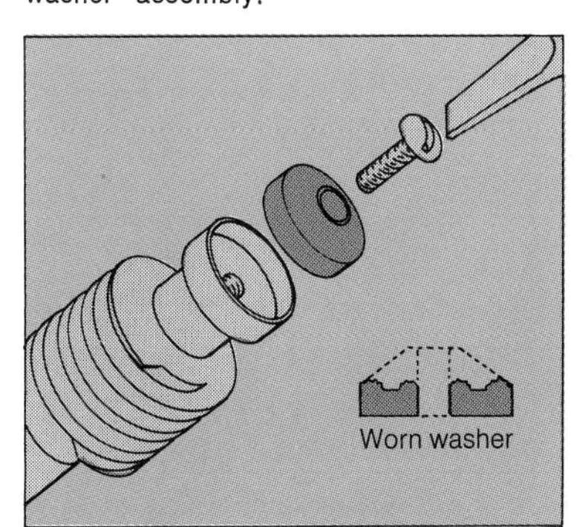

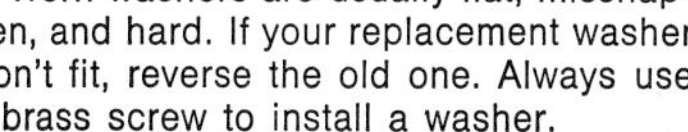

5. Worn washers are usually flat, misshappen, and hard. If your replacement washer won't fit, reverse the old one. Always use a brass screw to install a washer.

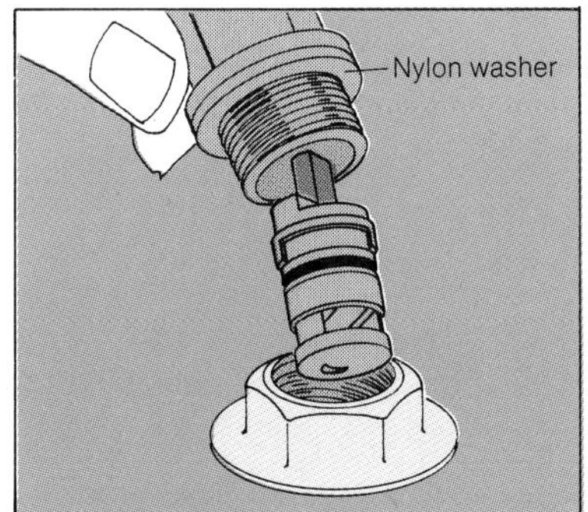

6. Some spindle assemblies lift from the base in a removable sleeve. The sleeve contains the valve seat, and can easily be replaced if seat is badly worn.

Faucets

Repairing washerless faucets

Modern washerless faucets look and work differently from those with washers. They are less apt to give trouble, and when they do, are easier to repair. Most are designed for easy replacement of wearing parts.

If working parts are hidden by the handle, remove the Phillips screw and lift the handle off. If the screw isn't exposed, look for an insert in the center of the knob that you can pry out or unscrew.

There is rarely a packing nut—merely a stem nut holding the parts together. Instead of the washer, a rubber diaphragm or a metal-to-metal contact stops the flow of water.

Unscrew the stem nut with a wrench and lift out the assembly. If the diaphragm stays in, pick it out with a small screwdriver. Take the unit to a plumbing supply dealer and get a kit of all the parts needed to renew the faucet. Insert them, replace assembly and handle, and the faucet is as good as new.

Metal-to-metal valve assemblies sometimes need a strong pull to get them out past the O-ring seals. If necessary, put the handle back on temporarily to get a good grip without using a wrench or pliers. When one of these faucets gives trouble, the entire valve assembly is replaced.

Because the stem action in washerless faucets generally stays dry, you should lubricate it whenever you take it out. Use white lube, petroleum jelly, or grease. Do not get lubricant on rubber parts.

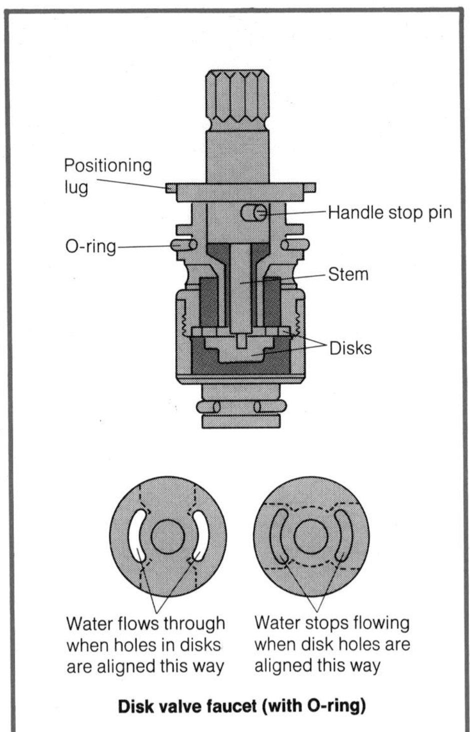

Disk valve faucet (with O-ring)

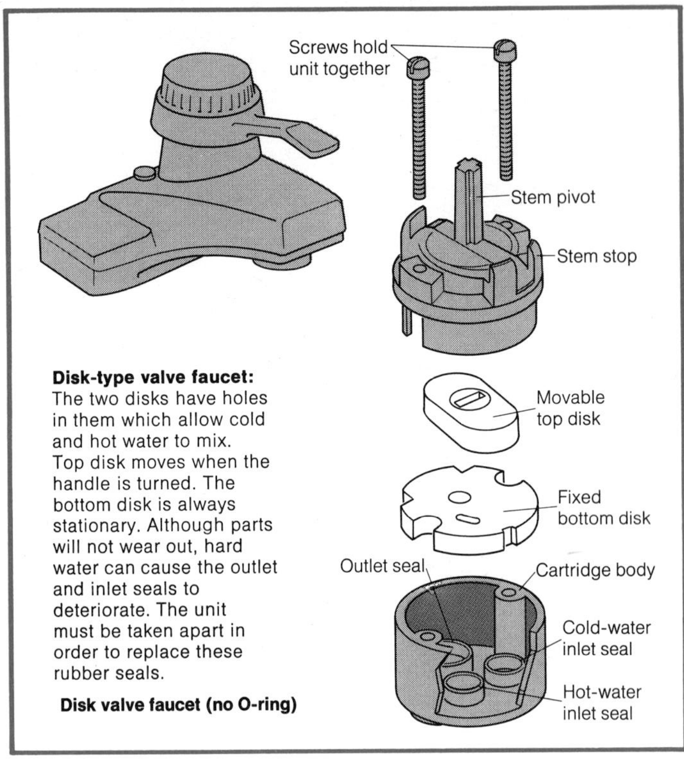

Disk-type valve faucet: The two disks have holes in them which allow cold and hot water to mix. Top disk moves when the handle is turned. The bottom disk is always stationary. Although parts will not wear out, hard water can cause the outlet and inlet seals to deteriorate. The unit must be taken apart in order to replace these rubber seals.

Disk valve faucet (no O-ring)

Single-handle tub or shower control

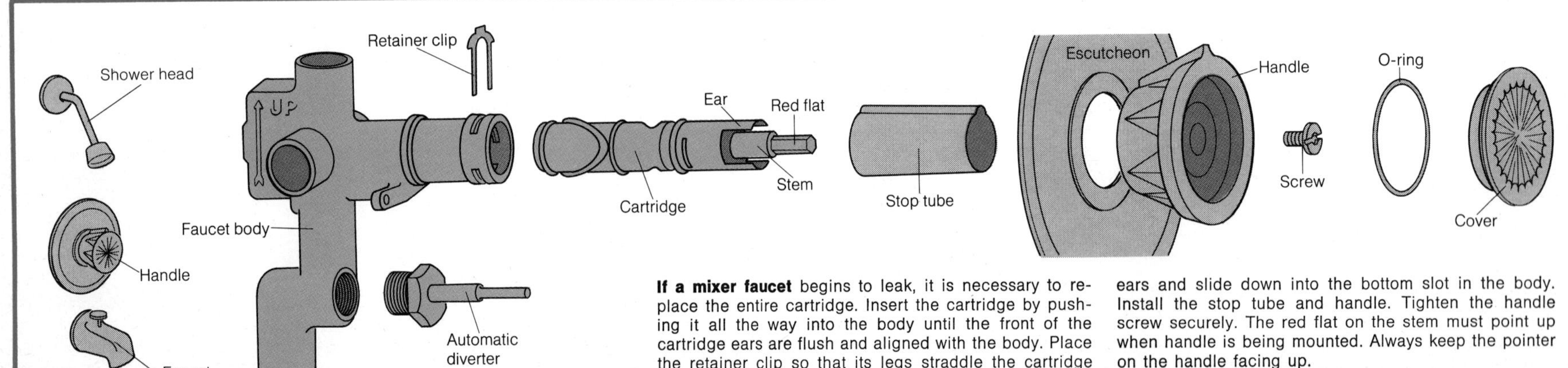

If a mixer faucet begins to leak, it is necessary to replace the entire cartridge. Insert the cartridge by pushing it all the way into the body until the front of the cartridge ears are flush and aligned with the body. Place the retainer clip so that its legs straddle the cartridge ears and slide down into the bottom slot in the body. Install the stop tube and handle. Tighten the handle screw securely. The red flat on the stem must point up when handle is being mounted. Always keep the pointer on the handle facing up.

Single-handle faucets and sink spray hoses

Sink spray hose repairs: You can repair automatic spray-hose valves that no longer divert water from the faucet through the hose when the button is pressed. However, a slight flow from the faucet while spraying is normal in some.

If yours is malfunctioning, first make sure that faucet and spray-head aerators are clean. You can buy replacements if the old ones are beyond cleaning.

If this does not cure the problem, look beneath the sink to see if the hose is kinked. If you suspect a restriction in the hose, turn off the faucet and remove the hose (loosen the hex nut connection below the faucet) and replace it with the identical type.

The last place to look for trouble is the diverter valve. It can be taken out by removing the faucet spout. Valve parts can then be lifted or screwed out from above and the diverter valve replaced.

Single-handle faucet installation and repair: Older sinks, lavatories, tubs, and showers are easily modernized by installing new single-handle faucets. One lever controls both hot and cold water, mixing them to the desired temperature in one motion.

First turn off all water to the fixture. Remove the old faucets, disconnecting them from the supply pipes beneath the sink. Measure the distance between centers of fixture holes—generally, 4, 6, or 8 inches—and buy a single-lever faucet to match this measurement. Also tell your supplier the type and size of water-supply pipes you will be connecting to; he will sell you the proper adapters if your supply lines do not match the parts that come with the new faucet.

Slide the new faucet through the fixture holes, arranging parts as the manufacturer specifies. Stuff plumber's putty under the escutcheon to prevent leaking. Clamp faucet down firmly to fixture ledge by tightening jambnuts below.

About the only service a single-handle faucet needs is cleaning the strainers. When water flow gets sluggish, they have probably begun to fill with sediment. The manufacturer's instruction sheet will explain how to get at them; if you do not have one, ask your plumbing supply dealer. You can usually reach the strainers by removing the faucet spout and escutcheon and unscrewing the plugs on each side of the faucet body (see drawing). If the spout's O-ring shows signs of leaking, put in a new one during reassembly. Keep the handle-adjusting screw tight to prevent possible drift of the temperature setting.

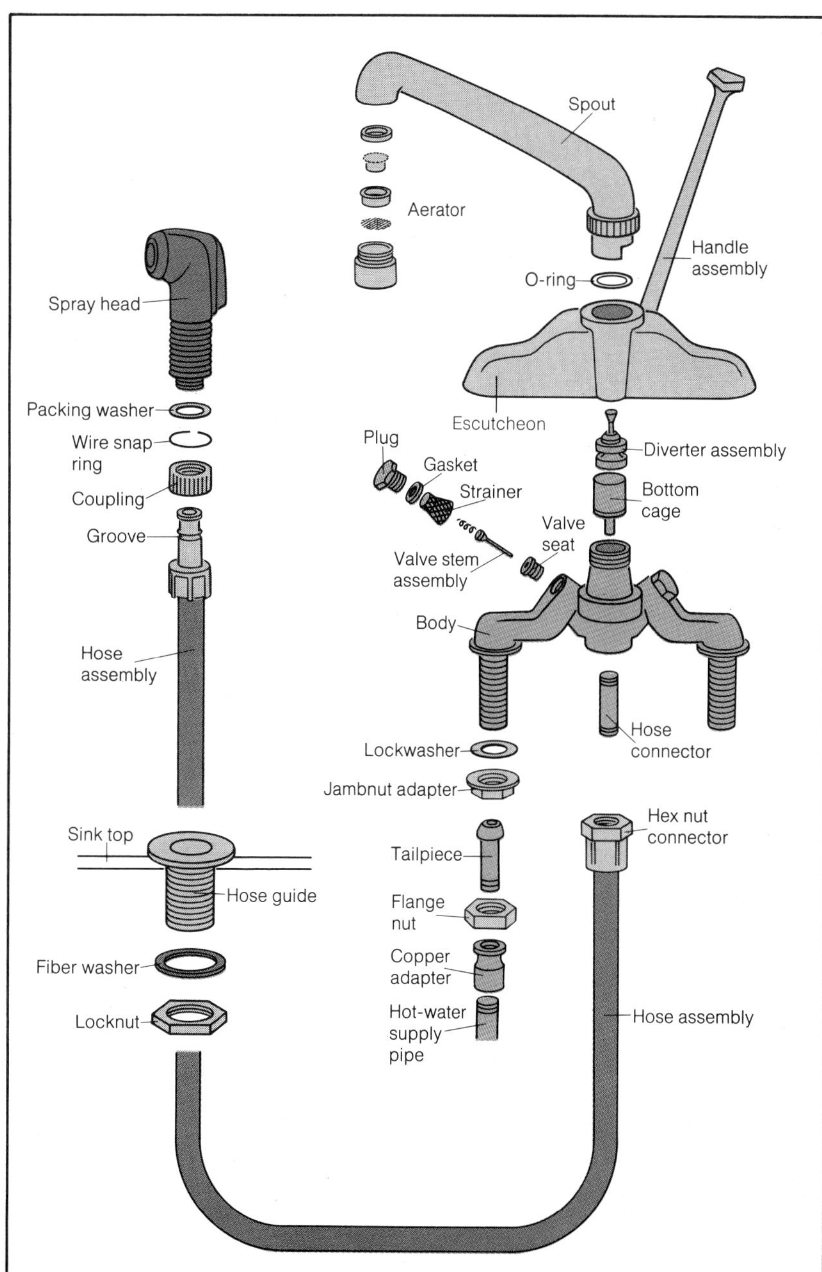

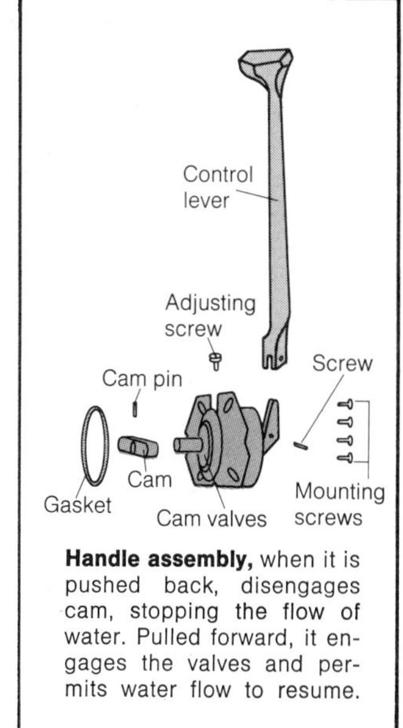

Handle assembly, when it is pushed back, disengages cam, stopping the flow of water. Pulled forward, it engages the valves and permits water flow to resume.

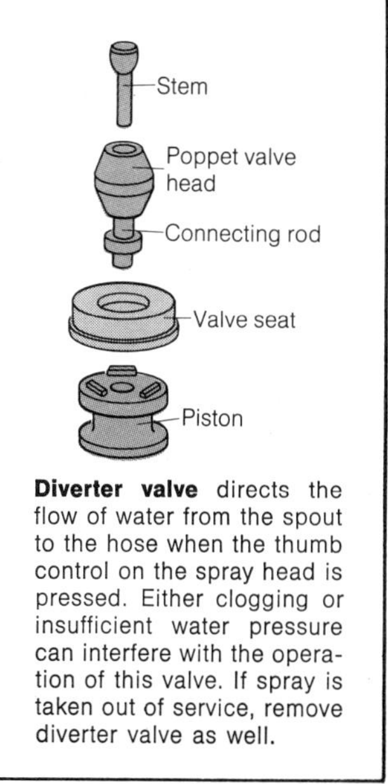

Diverter valve directs the flow of water from the spout to the hose when the thumb control on the spray head is pressed. Either clogging or insufficient water pressure can interfere with the operation of this valve. If spray is taken out of service, remove diverter valve as well.

How a flush tank works

All toilet flush tanks work about the same. When the toilet is flushed, the trip handle lifts the tank ball (or rubber flapper or tilting bucket), opening the outlet and letting water flow into the bowl. When the tank is nearly empty, the ball falls back in place over the outlet. The float falls with the water level, opening the water-supply inlet valve just as the outlet is being closed, and the tank is refilled through the filler tube. Water also flows through the bowl refill tube into the overflow pipe to replenish trap-sealing water. As the water level in the tank nears the top of the overflow pipe, the float closes the inlet valve, completing the cycle.

Most toilet tank trouble centers around the tank ball and its lift wires. The best cure is to replace lift wires, guide arm, and tank ball with a rubber flapper which is slipped down on the overflow pipe and raised for flushing by a stainless steel chain fastened to the trip lever.

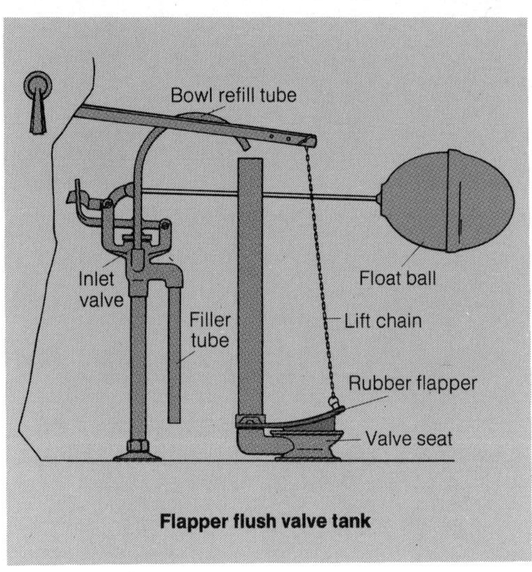

Flapper flush valve tank

Troubleshooting checklist

PROBLEM	SOLUTION
Water keeps flowing; tank does not refill after a flush	Check for binding of the trip handle, trip lever, lift wires, or tank ball. Bend parts to reshape, or install new ones. See if tank ball is centered in its valve seat. If not, rotate the guide arm on the overflow tube to reposition ball.
Tank fills, but water keeps flowing	Lift float ball. If flow stops, bend float arm to lower the ball a bit. If this fails, remove screws from inlet valve levers, disassemble and pull out valve assembly. Replace inlet valve washer. If inlet valve seat is badly corroded, replace it; if seat is not replaceable, then replace entire inlet valve unit. Be sure bowl refill tube does not go into overflow tube below the tank water level. Remove mineral scale on flush valve seat with fine wet-or-dry sandpaper. Replace deteriorated tank ball.
Water level is too high or too low	Level should be ¾ inch below top of overflow tube. Bend float arm down to lower water level, up to raise it. If level is too high, water will run over. If too low, water may be inadequate for a complete flush.
Tank flushes partially	Tank ball may not rise enough; shorten upper lift wire slightly and rehook it through hole in trip lever. Follow manufacturer's instructions for pivoted tip-type flush valve.
Splashing sound inside tank during refill	Be sure bowl refill tube ejects into overflow tube. Flush and look for leak at inlet valve. If more than a trace leaks, remove valve and replace split O-ring seal or washer.
Tank sweats (humid air condenses on cold porcelain surface)	1. Simplest method is to put a terry cloth cover on tank; it soaks up condensation, which then evaporates. 2. More effective cure is to line tank with foam sheets. Buy in kit from plumbing-supply or mail-order house. Flush toilet, dry inside of tank, apply foam sheets as directed by kit's instructions. 3. Most permanent method is to use a device called a tempering valve, available from plumbing-supply house. This valve admits a little warm water to the tank, raising temperature of water in tank sufficiently to prevent condensation; it also stops toilet bowl from sweating. Insert valve in cold-water line that leads into toilet tank inlet. Then attach hot-water line to tempering valve.

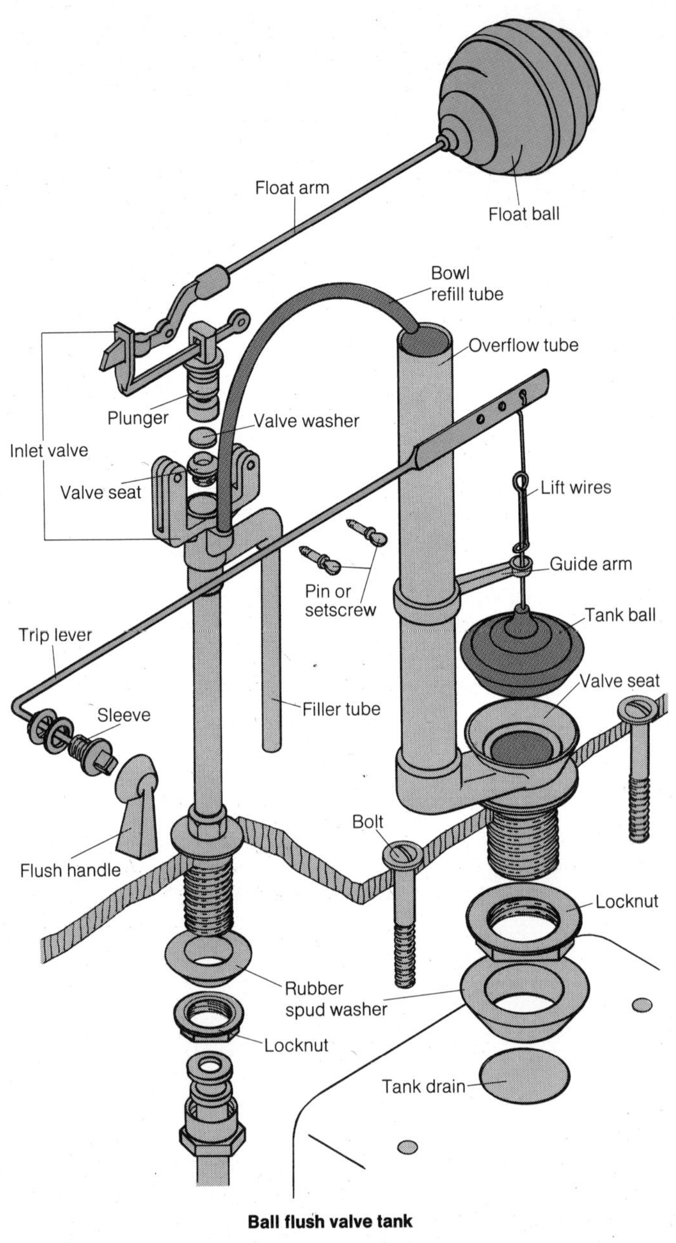

Ball flush valve tank

Repairing a flush-valve toilet

A flush valve is an automatic metering valve that, once actuated, will complete its cycle and shut off by itself. Valves may be the diaphragm or piston type. Both kinds will last for years without attention, and the operation and service needs of each are similar. All should be adjusted for the minimum water discharge that will flush the toilet effectively. Flow is regulated by turning the regulating screw right (for less) or left (for more) water per flush.

If the valve will not shut off completely, take it apart by removing the cover, top plate, and relief valve or piston. Wash the working parts thoroughly, especially the relief valve, piston, and seat. Make sure the screen is clean, then reassemble.

Short-flushing (insufficient water for a complete flush) may be caused by an improperly set adjustment screw or by some problem inside the valve. First be sure the control valve is all the way open. If the valve turns out to be the trouble, disassemble it and make sure the diaphragm or piston is hand-tight in its guide and that its bypass openings have not been enlarged.

Diaphragm, piston, and valve replacements come in kit form so you can rebuild a worn-out flush valve.

New toilet tank equipment

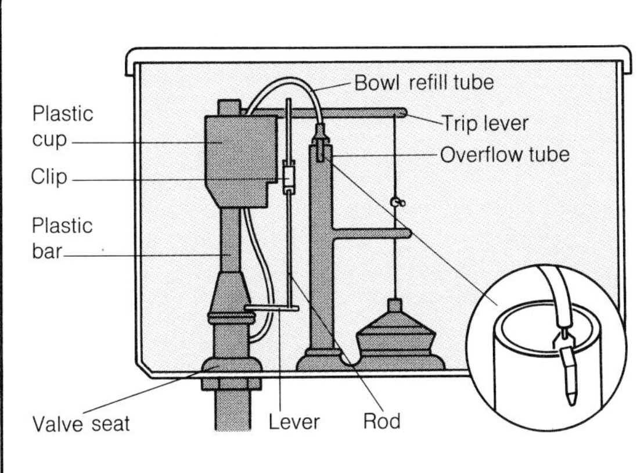

A faulty tank valve can be replaced by a new type of flush control. Called Fluidmaster ballcock, the plastic device has no float ball assembly. Water pressure controls the inlet valve, thereby providing more accurate water level control. The device also eliminates hissing and gurgling noises.

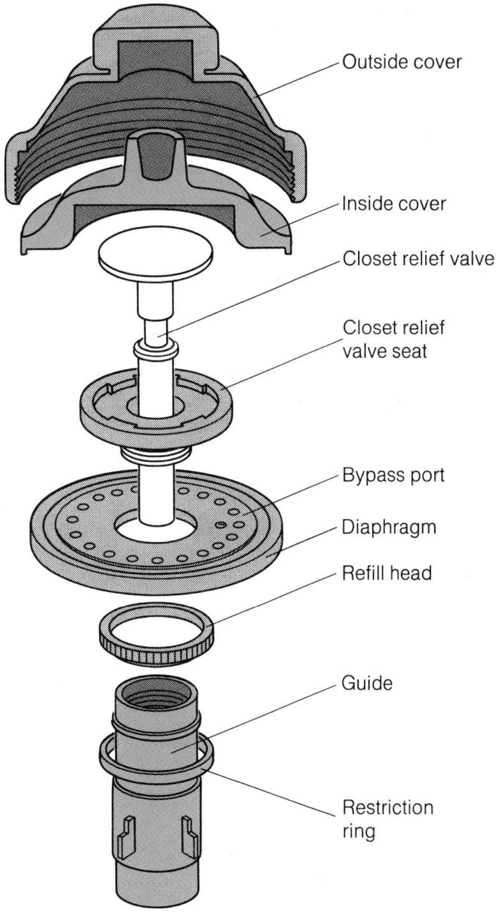

Diaphragm-type flush valve

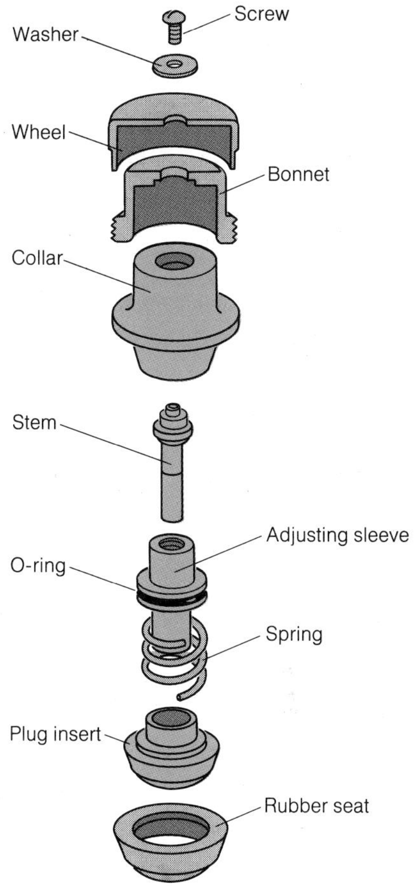

Stop valve assembly

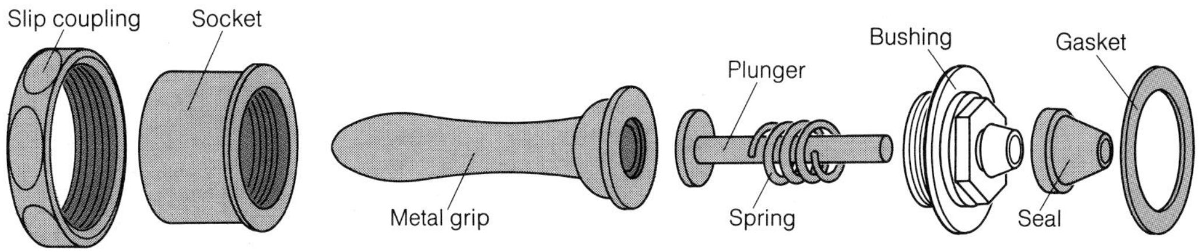

Handle assembly

Plumbing noises

Causes and cures

Ticking in pipes: When hot water flows into a cold hot-water supply pipe, the pipe expands, producing a ticking sound. Be sure the expanding pipe has room to slide on its hangers.

Gurgling drain: Improper venting and wrong drain-pipe size are the usual causes. Try installing an anti-siphon trap as a remedy.

Whistling sound: Water under high pressure that must flow past a restriction can produce a high-pitched whistle. The most common instance is a whistling toilet inlet valve. Some toilets have an adjusting screw that permits you to reduce the flow below the whistling level. If yours does not have this feature, you can turn the tank's shutoff valve until the flow is reduced and the whistle stops.

Check all valves in the water-supply system to be sure that none of them are partially closed.

Running water: Check into the sound of water running through pipes when nothing is turned on. Many dollars in water costs can go needlessly down the drain from an undetected water leak. Try to locate the source of the sound. A leaking toilet tank may be the cause (p. 222). Sometimes it's just a partially open faucet somewhere in the house. Sound caused by a vibrating pipe can be silenced by wrapping the pipe with felt or installing extra pipe hangers.

Some furnace humidifiers are connected into the cold-water line and make a mild running-water sound while they are operating. An automatic water softener that is back-flushing will produce a loud running-water noise. If its timer fails to switch from "Regenerate" to "Soften," it can waste a lot of water. Find out which is faulty, timer or valve.

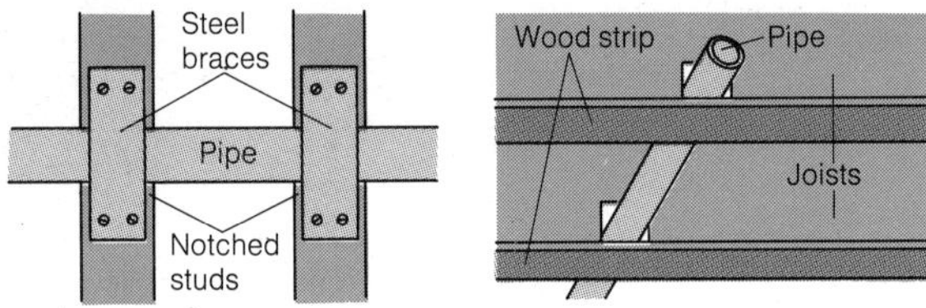

Pipe secured to stud and joints

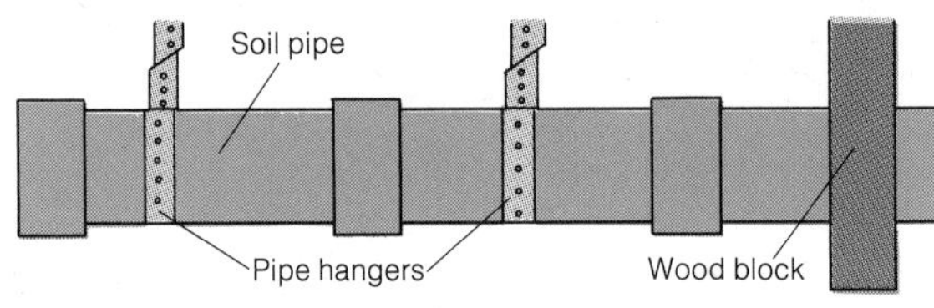

Pipe secured with hangers and blocks

Correcting water hammer

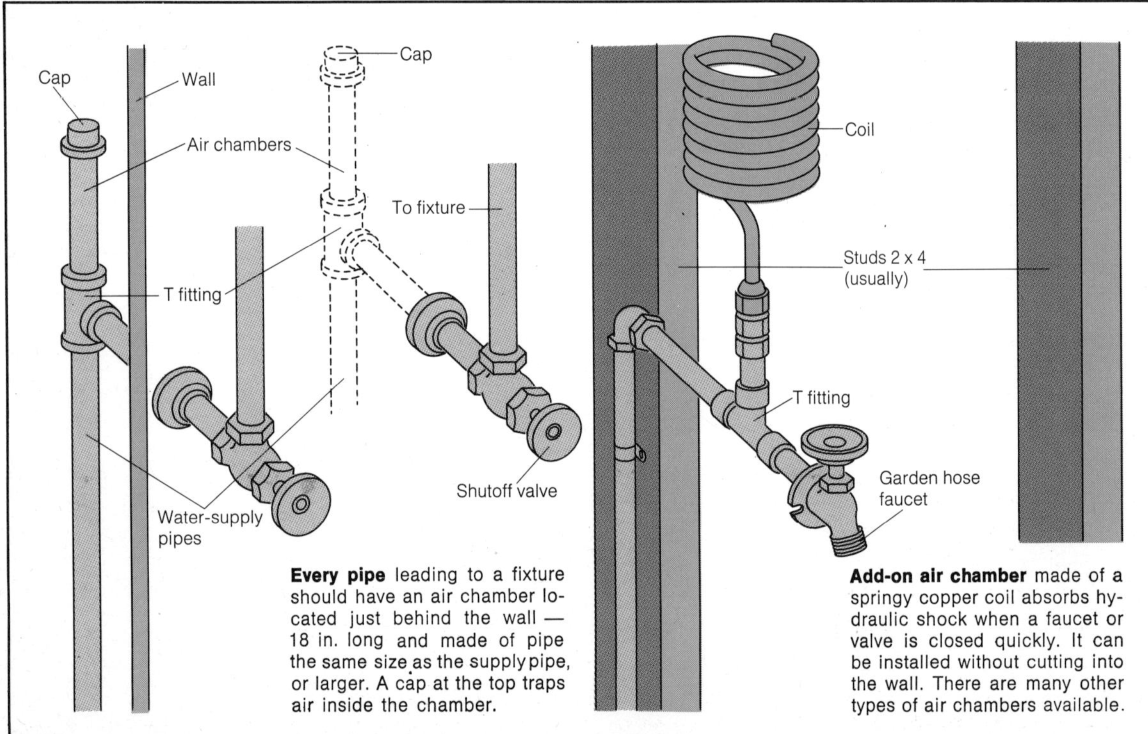

Every pipe leading to a fixture should have an air chamber located just behind the wall — 18 in. long and made of pipe the same size as the supply pipe, or larger. A cap at the top traps air inside the chamber.

Add-on air chamber made of a springy copper coil absorbs hydraulic shock when a faucet or valve is closed quickly. It can be installed without cutting into the wall. There are many other types of air chambers available.

Water hammer is a harsh, hammering sound in the piping when a faucet or an automatic washer solenoid valve turns off rapidly. Water moving swiftly through the pipes while the valve is open comes to an abrupt halt as the valve is closed, and heavy pressures are put on the entire water-supply system. Eventually the pipe or one of its fittings could burst —which makes this more than just a nuisance.

The problem is lack of, or improperly operating, air chambers. The air chamber lets rushing water bounce gently against a cushion of air when a valve closes, taking the strain off the pipes.

Commercial air chambers (also called water-hammer arresters or air cushions) are made in several types. The most common is a flexible copper tube, wound in a spiral, with one end sealed and the other connected by means of a fitting to the cold- or hot-water line. Another consists of a rubber bag in a metal sleeve; a third looks like a giant doorknob. All work on the same cushion-of-air principle.

An air cushion can fill with water. To restore the air to all air chambers, turn off the main shutoff valve and completely drain the water-supply system. Open all faucets to let air in. Then close the faucets and turn the water on again.

If, after all this, water hammer is still present, install separate air chambers at each problem location or a large air chamber at the service entrance.

Thawing frozen pipes

Water can freeze in pipes that pass through a cold location, such as an open crawl space or unheated cellar. Water expands when it freezes; unless the pipe through which it runs also expands, it will rupture. Insulating gives pipe some protection at low temperatures but may not prevent freezing. To keep a pipe from freezing, wrap electrical heating cable around it—one turn every 2 feet—then cover the pipe with insulation to conserve the heat. Plug in the cable when the temperature drops below freezing. The same cable device can be used to thaw a pipe.

There are other effective thawing methods. One of the best is pouring boiling water over rags wrapped around the frozen pipe. Heating with a propane torch works quickly, but take care that steam pressure does not burst the pipe. Do not heat a pipe to a higher temperature than your hand can stand.

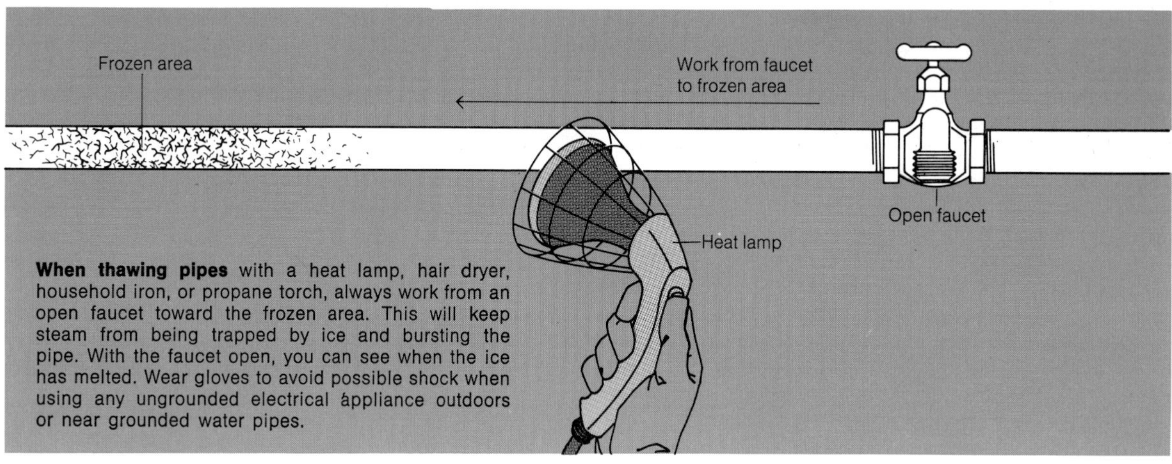

When thawing pipes with a heat lamp, hair dryer, household iron, or propane torch, always work from an open faucet toward the frozen area. This will keep steam from being trapped by ice and bursting the pipe. With the faucet open, you can see when the ice has melted. Wear gloves to avoid possible shock when using any ungrounded electrical appliance outdoors or near grounded water pipes.

Insulating pipes

Pipe insulation gives two kinds of protection. It will keep cold-water pipes from sweating in warm weather and will reduce heat losses from hot-water piping as well. It comes in a number of forms. The type easiest to use and effective for cold-water pipes is a liquid material containing finely ground cork. This is brushed on in one or more applications to build up the necessary thickness.

More effective is a self-sticking tape that has special insulating qualities. Several versions are available. The putty-like tape is wound spirally around the pipes (see illustration). It is easily formed around fittings and makes a neat installation.

Another kind that works well: Asbestos tape wrapped over paste applied to the pipes. At fittings, the tape is soaked in the paste and molded in place.

Excellent insulation is obtained with 3-foot-long plastic foam, air-cell asbestos, wool felt, or fiber glass pipe jackets. The thick insulating sections are split so they can be slipped over straight pipe runs. Sections can be cut to length with a fine-toothed saw, such as a hacksaw.

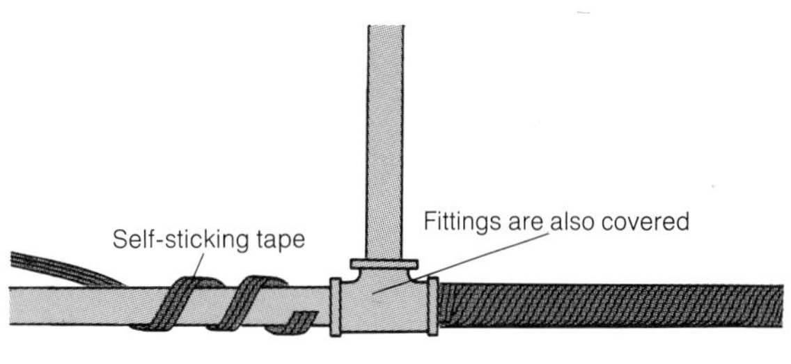

Pipe wrapped with self-sticking tape

Burst pipes

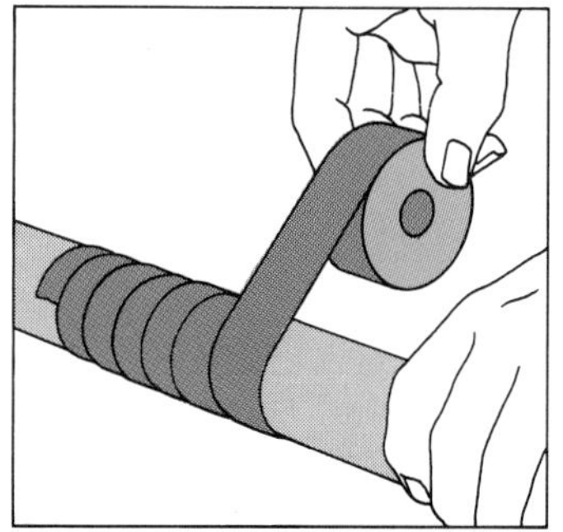

Tape wrapped tightly around a small leak will serve as a temporary repair.

Epoxy paste seals breaks around joints. Water must be off; pipes dry.

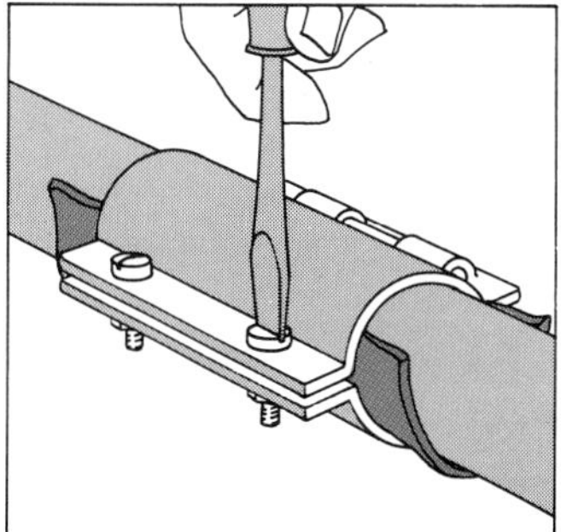

Pipe clamp bolted over a rubber pad seals larger cracks permanently.

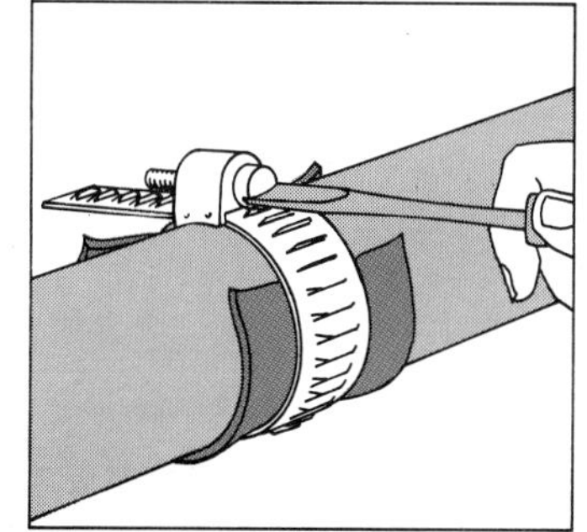

Hose clamp compressing a rubber pad can cure pinpoint leaks or cracks.

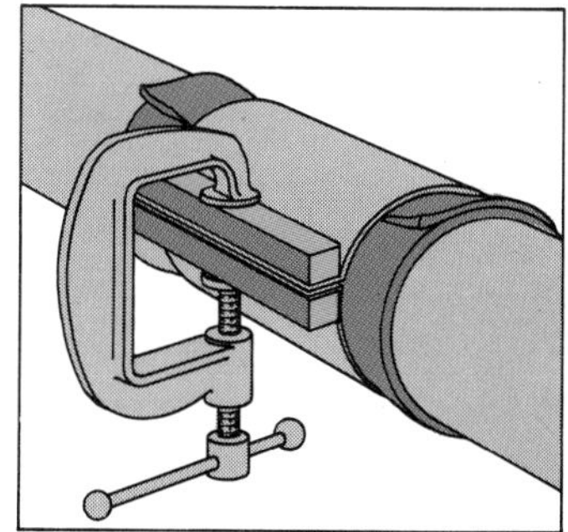

Tin can cut along the seam and clamped between two blocks of wood.

Planning your work

Most plumbing jobs involve more drudgery than skill. Knowing what equipment you need and understanding basic plumbing principles will enable you to perform numerous repairs and improvements without calling in professional help.

Seemingly big jobs, such as installing a new sink or toilet bowl, adding a new water-supply line, or replacing a length of damaged pipe, can often be accomplished without the use of specialized tools, and do not require extensive skill. The diagrams on the following pages will guide you in making basic repairs and understanding requirements for bigger jobs.

Always check local building ordinances to make certain that the work you intend to do will not violate any regulations. Before beginning a project, carefully read any instructions that come with a fixture or appliance. Assemble all the tools and materials needed for the job. For jobs you do not feel competent to handle, call in a professional plumber.

If you do much work around the house, you should already have many of the tools necessary for the average plumbing job: Tape measure, screwdriver, pliers, hammer, hacksaw, electric drill, and chisels. Specialized plumbing tools may have to be purchased or rented. Major mail-order houses will often lend or rent you a set of plumbing tools if you purchase the materials for the job from them.

Wrench sizes and uses: Wrench sizes are designated according to overall size, from the bottom of the handle to the top of the upper jaw. A 10-inch wrench should be used for pipes up to 1 inch in diameter and an 18-inch wrench for pipes up to 2 inches in diameter. Really large pipes—2½ inches and more in diameter—require a 24-inch wrench. Never extend the turning power of a wrench by inserting a length of pipe over the handle to gain extra leverage. You will only break the wrench or damage the pipe. Never use a pipe wrench or Stillson wrench on plated or polished pipe—they will mar the surface.

It is a mistake to tighten the jaws of a pipe wrench to a too-snug fit. The wrench gets tighter as you turn it and will tend to crush the pipe. When using a pipe wrench, always fit and turn it so the turning force is directed to its open end—this tightens the wrench on the pipe. And never turn a wrench sideways. When using two wrenches to hold fitting and pipe, position the left-hand wrench in front to loosen the joint, right-hand wrench in front to tighten it.

Basic plumbing tools

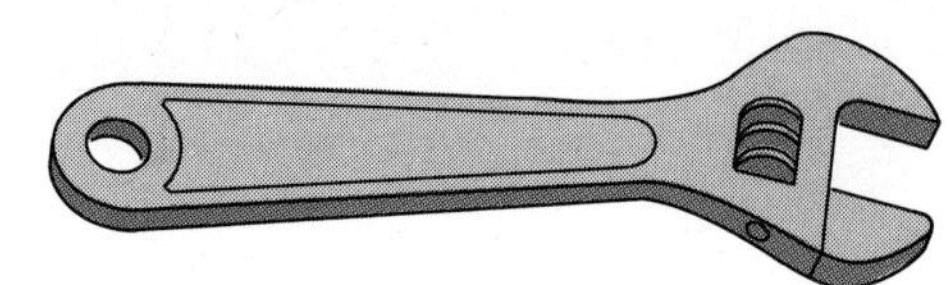

Adjustable open-end wrench is useful for removing nuts, fittings, etc., from faucets and other fixtures.

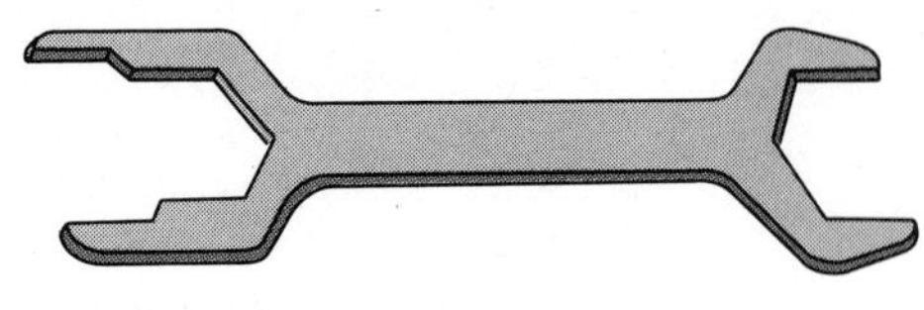

Fixed spud wrench is used for large spud nuts on toilet tanks and sinks. Adjustable type is also available.

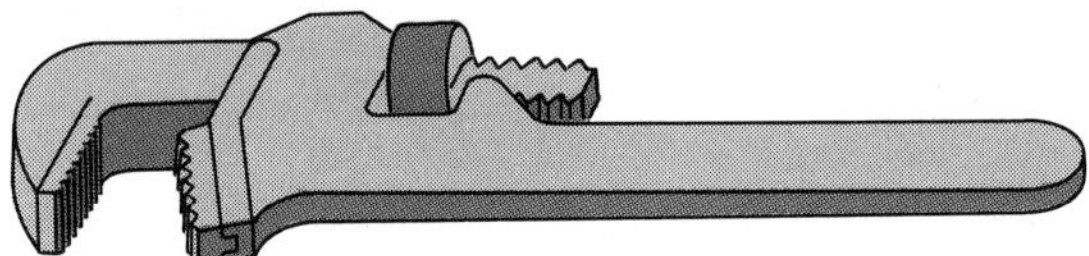

Pipe wrenches are used in pairs, one on the threaded pipe and the other on the fitting attached to the pipe.

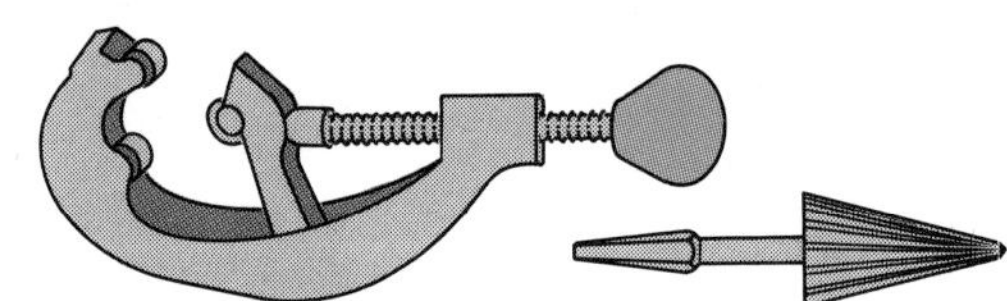

Pipe and tubing cutter is turned around pipes or tubes to cut them.

Pipe reamer removes burrs from cut pipe.

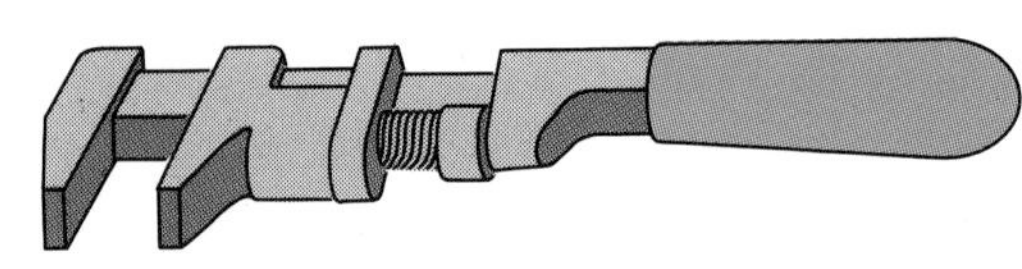

Monkey wrench has smooth jaws that adjust to fit nuts of various sizes such as those on fixture traps.

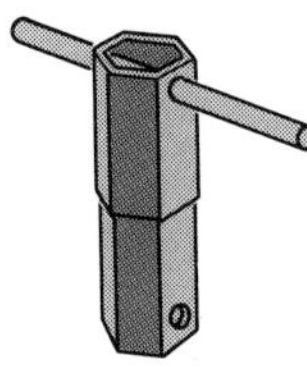

Socket wrench is used to remove some faucet parts.

Flaring tool makes flare joints in copper tubing.

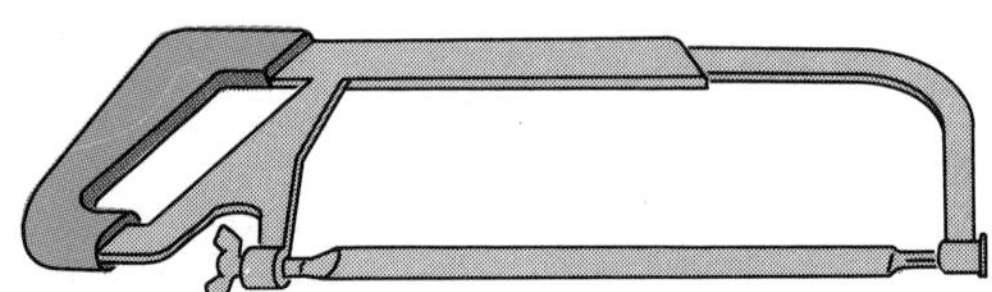

Hacksaw equipped with a blade that has 24 or 32 teeth per inch will cut metal or plastic pipe to needed sizes.

Strap wrench is used instead of a pipe wrench to prevent damage to the finish of chromed pipes and tubes.

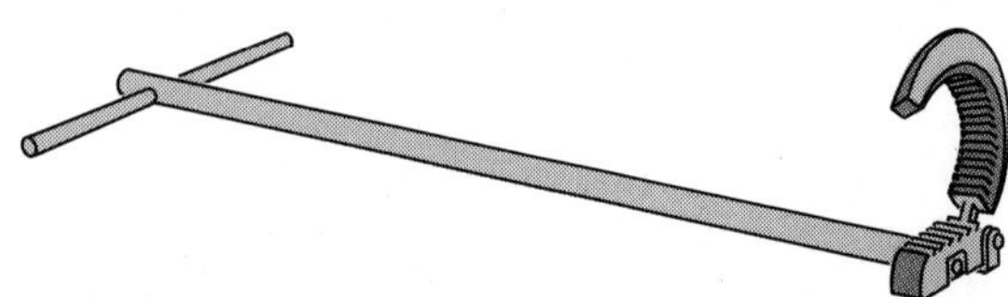

Basin wrench is used to work on hard-to-reach water-supply pipes and faucets behind sinks and lavatories.

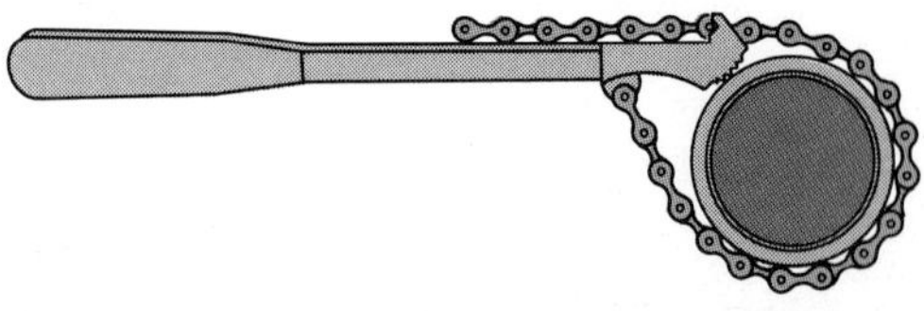

Chain wrench can be used on pipe, tubing, and fittings in places that are too small for a pipe wrench to fit.

The right fitting for the purpose

While some kinds of pipe will serve for both water supply and drainage, the fittings will not. Drainage fittings have smooth inner contours so nothing will hamper movement of solids through them. In a drain-waste-vent system, regular fittings can only be used in the vent system, where no liquids flow.

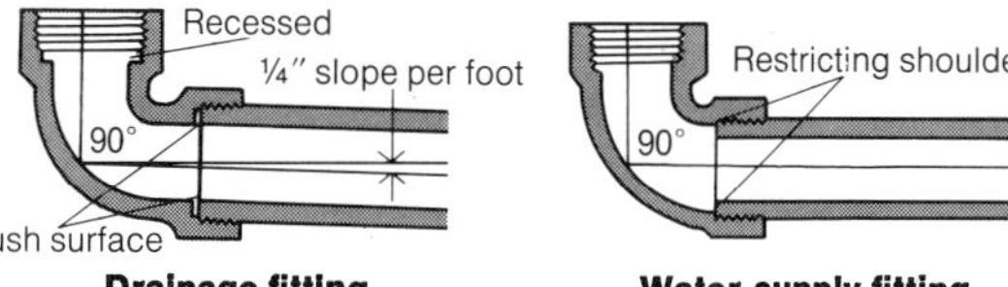

Recessed
¼″ slope per foot
90°
Flush surface

Drainage fitting

Restricting shoulders
90°

Water-supply fitting

Cast-iron fittings are made for drainage only; galvanized steel, copper sweat-type, and solvent-welded plastic fittings come in regular and drainage types.

Black iron fittings and pipe are used for gas lines only; flare-type copper fittings, brass, bronze, and slip-on plastic pipe fittings, just for water supply.

For cast-iron pipe (hub)

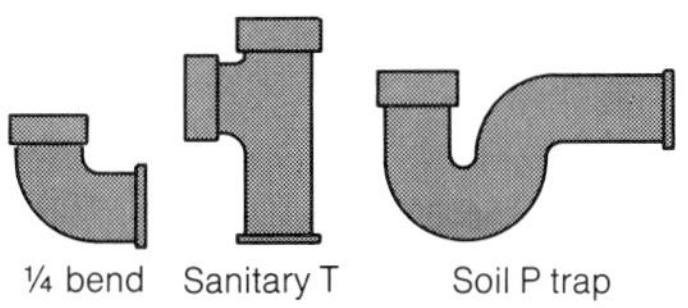

¼ bend
Sanitary T
Soil P trap

For cast-iron pipe (hubless)

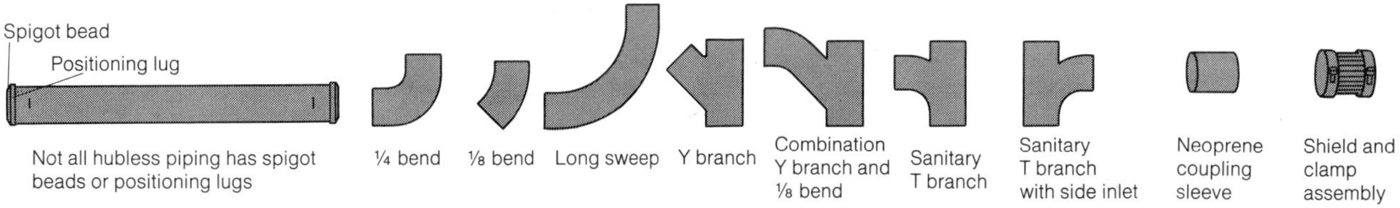

Spigot bead
Positioning lug
Not all hubless piping has spigot beads or positioning lugs
¼ bend
⅛ bend
Long sweep
Y branch
Combination Y branch and ⅛ bend
Sanitary T branch
Sanitary T branch with side inlet
Neoprene coupling sleeve
Shield and clamp assembly

For galvanized and black steel, brass, and bronze pipe

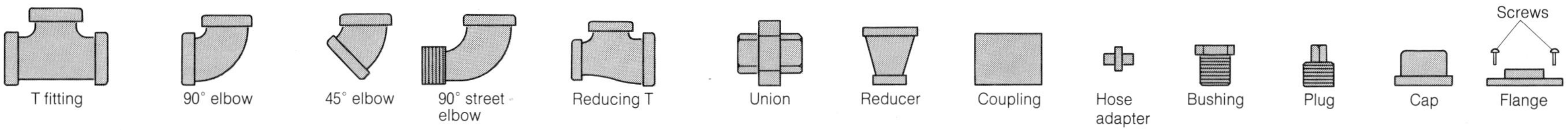

T fitting
90° elbow
45° elbow
90° street elbow
Reducing T
Union
Reducer
Coupling
Hose adapter
Bushing
Plug
Cap
Screws
Flange

For copper pipe

Sanitary T
Closet flange
Drum trap with cover
45° Y branch
¼ bend
⅛ bend
Sanitary T with side inlet
Cast-iron pipe adapter
Closet bend
Coupling
Copper-to-steel pipe adapter
Cleanout with plug
Slip coupling
90° street elbow

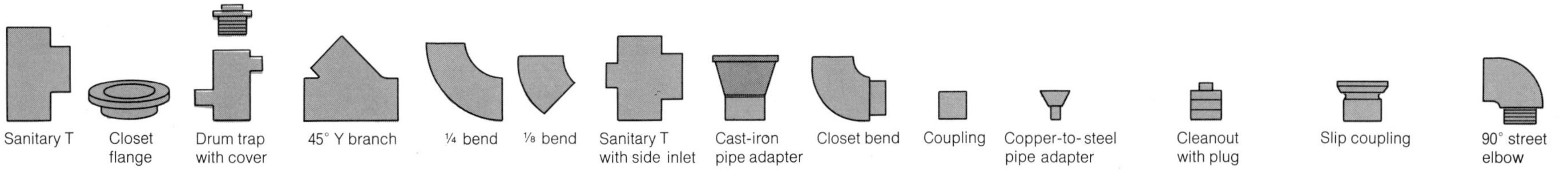

For copper tube (sweat-solder)

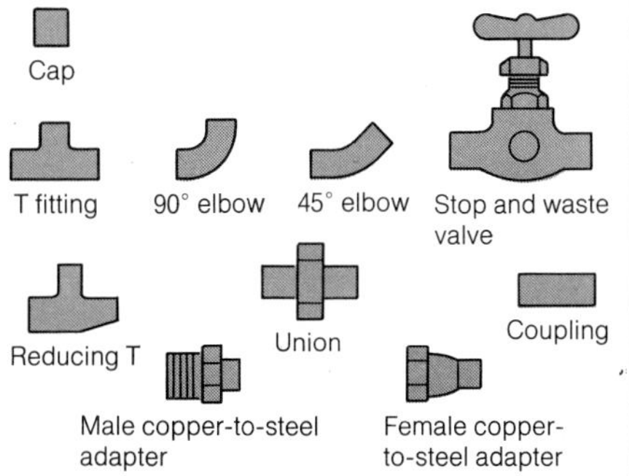

Cap
T fitting
90° elbow
45° elbow
Stop and waste valve
Reducing T
Union
Coupling
Male copper-to-steel adapter
Female copper-to-steel adapter

For copper tube (flare)

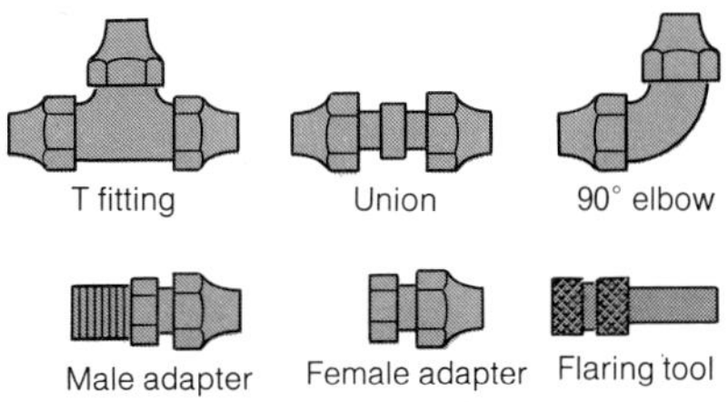

T fitting
Union
90° elbow
Male adapter
Female adapter
Flaring tool

For plastic pipe (rigid)

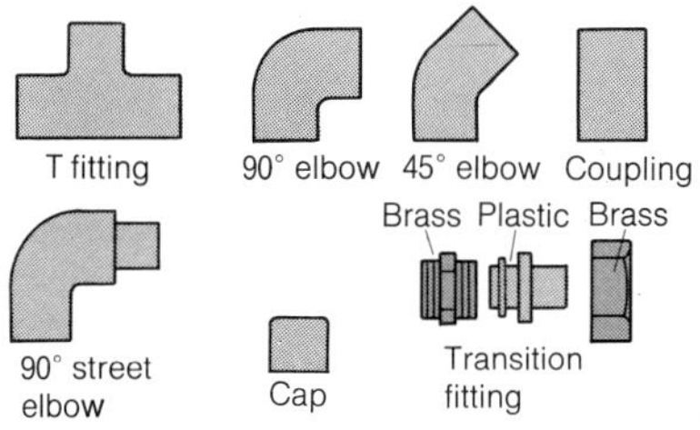

T fitting
90° elbow
45° elbow
Coupling
Brass
Plastic
Brass
90° street elbow
Cap
Transition fitting

For plastic pipe (flexible)

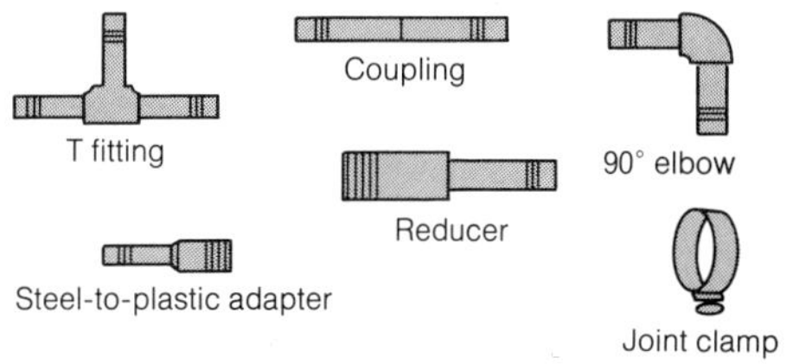

T fitting
Coupling
90° elbow
Reducer
Steel-to-plastic adapter
Joint clamp

Cast-iron pipe

Working with cast-iron pipe

Cast-iron pipe is the most popular pipe for soil and waste stacks. It is available in service weight as well as extra-heavy grade. Service, or standard weight pipe can be cut with a hacksaw. Make a 1/16-inch deep cut around the pipe, rest the pipe on a 2 x 4, and tap the overhang with a hammer close to the cut until the section breaks off. You can, if you prefer, cut the pipe all the way through with the hacksaw. Extra-heavy cast-iron pipe is cut with a cold chisel and hammer. Apply the chisel all around the required cut, striking the chisel until the pipe breaks off. If you plan carefully, very few cuts will be needed, as this pipe comes in 5-foot lengths.

Cast-iron soil pipe has a bell-shaped hub at one end and a ridge around the other called a spigot, which fits into the hub of the same size pipe. Because the fit is loose, the joint must be caulked. The space is first filled with oakum, a stringy fiber, which is wrapped around the inner pipe and packed down to within an inch of the top of the hub. Then molten lead is poured into the hub over the oakum. An important rule when working with hub-type pipe: Install it so the hub faces up, never down. This is so solid matter won't become lodged at the joint.

Installation is simpler with new no-hub pipes and fittings. Instead of caulked joints, neoprene gaskets are used that permit slight misalignment of pipes and fittings without leaking. Also there are no wasted pieces with hubless pipe. All cutoffs are usable. Any accessible no-hub joint can be taken apart for repairs or additions just by loosening the clamp screws. To take hub-type pipe apart, the lead must be melted with a torch, or the pipe cut on both sides of the fitting. After a hub-type system has been opened up, no-hub fittings and pipes are compatible with it (provided local plumbing code approves). If your code permits, no-hub can be used below grade. Hubless pipe comes in 2-, 3-, and 4-inch diameters and 5- and 10-foot lengths. There is no required direction of flow through the pipe as there is with hub-type pipe. The fittings must be arranged, however, so the flow follows the smooth inner curves.

Joining cast-iron pipe

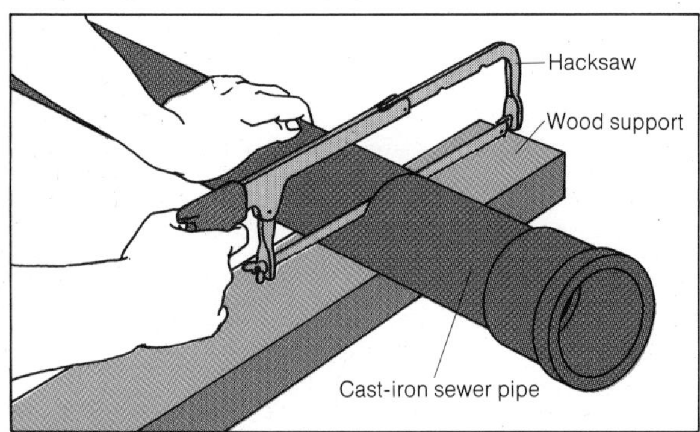

1. Measure pipe. Mark it all around with chalk or crayon, then score it at mark with a hacksaw to a depth of 1/16 inch.

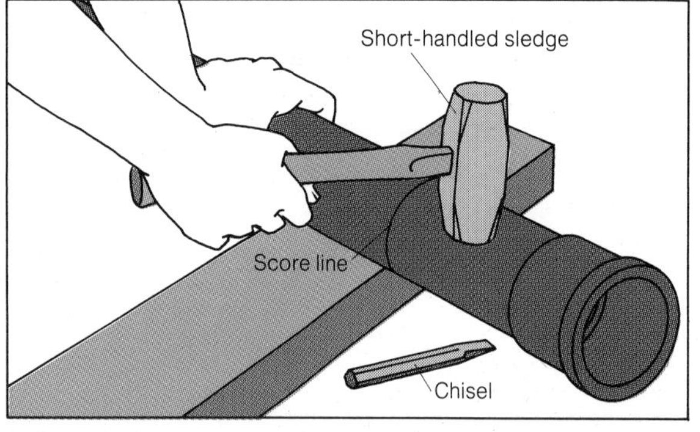

2. Support pipe on a board and tap all around at score mark until end falls off. Heavy pipe may have to be chiseled off.

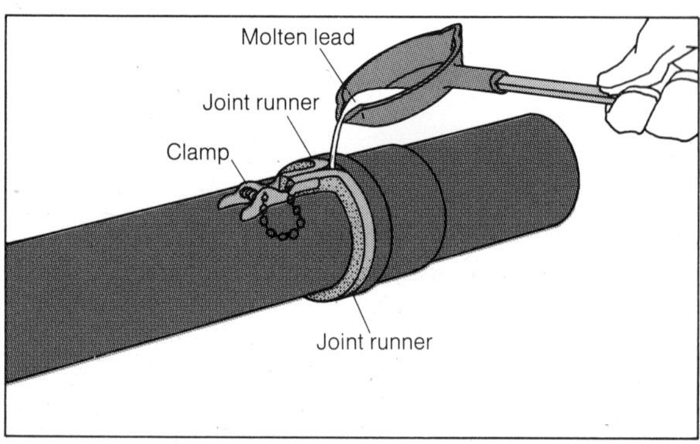

3. After joint is packed with oakum, molten lead is poured into asbestos joint runner that confines lead to joint area.

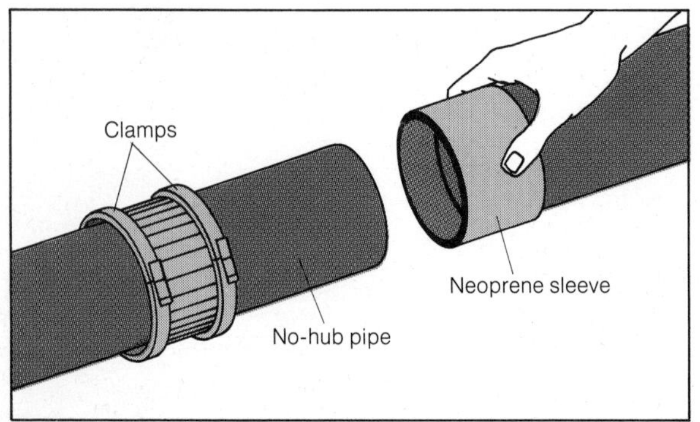

1. No-hub pipe is joined with a neoprene sleeve and clamps. No allowance need be made for joints with this type of pipe.

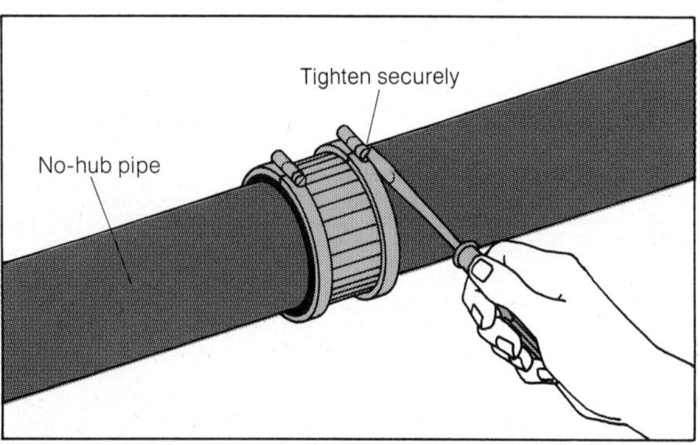

2. After pipes have been aligned, sleeve and clamps are centered over the joint. Sleeve permits slight pipe misalignment.

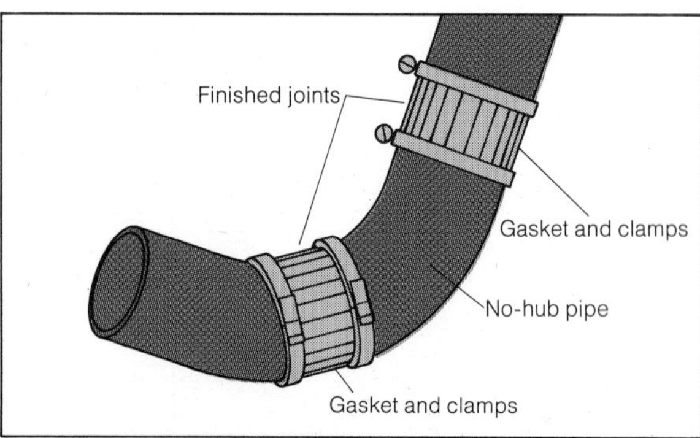

3. Finished no-hub joint. Adapters are available to connect this pipe to other types and sizes of sewer pipe. Consult code.

Working with brass and steel pipe

You can expedite small steel and brass piping projects by ordering pipes from your dealer already cut to length and threaded. Standard pipe nipples—short lengths of pipe threaded on both ends—are stock items, available in lengths from 1 to 12 inches. Chart and diagram below show how to calculate the length needed to complete a connection.

Because a run of threaded pipe needs a starting point for disassembly, fittings known as **unions** must be installed wherever you cut through a pipe to add a branch or to replace a pipe. A thoughtful plumber also installs unions wherever frequent access may be needed, such as at a water heater or water softener, or at the start of an outdoor run of pipe.

Calculating pipe length

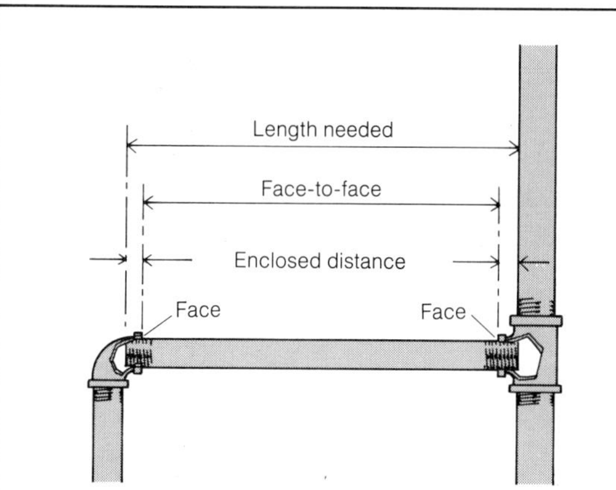

To determine the length of pipe needed to complete a connection, measure the distance from the face of one fitting to the face of the other. Add to this face-to-face measurement the length of the pipe that will enter the fittings at both ends.

Pipe size (inches)	**Enclosed length** (inches)	
	Standard fittings	Drainage fittings
½	½	(none)
¾	½	(none)
1	⅝	⅝
1¼	⅝	⅝
1½	⅝	⅝
2	¾	⅞
3	(none)	1
4	(none)	(none)

Cutting and threading brass and steel pipe

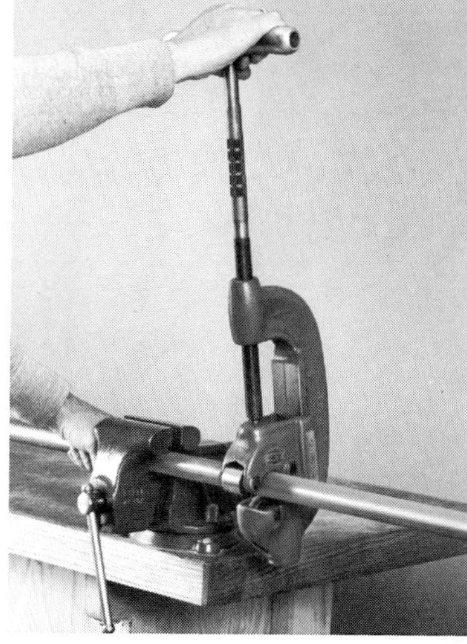

1. To use a pipe cutter, secure the pipe in a vise and clamp cutter on the pipe with the wheel on the cutting mark. Rotate the cutter around once. Tighten and rotate. Repeat until the pipe is cut.

2. To thread pipe, install the right size die in the die stock, push and rotate clockwise until die bites into pipe. Use oil, back off to remove chips, and stop when pipe end is flush with die.

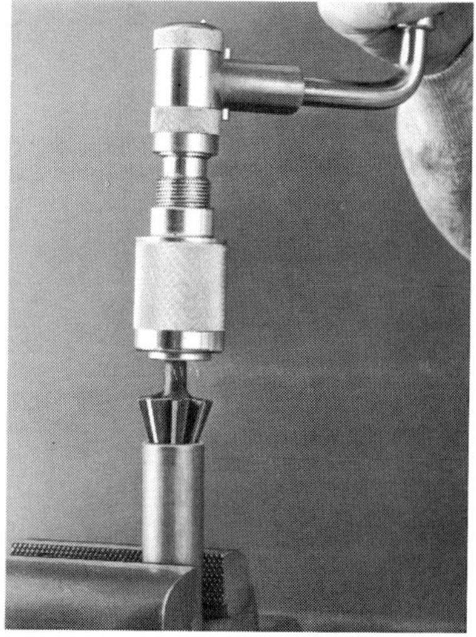

3. With pipe still in vise, place point of reamer squarely into the end of the pipe and turn clockwise. Use moderate pressure. Stop when burr around inside of pipe has been cleared away.

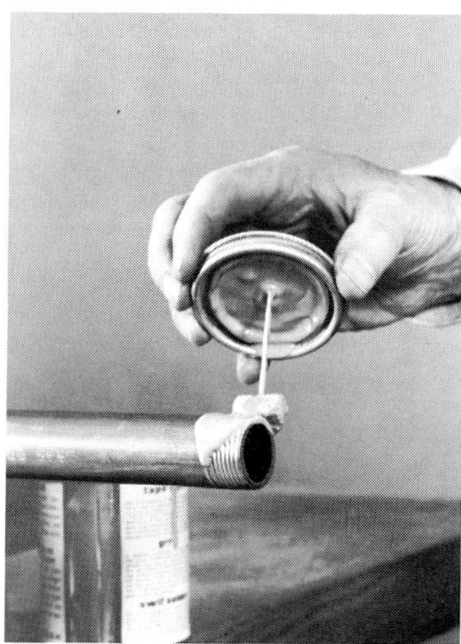

4. Pipes should have pipe joint compound applied to their threads. Compound helps seal the joint and makes it easier to take apart if necessary later. Teflon tape may be used instead of compound.

5. Screw fitting onto pipe (or pipe onto fitting) as far as you can by hand. This should be several turns. Finish by tightening with pipe wrench. Two or three threads are usually left showing.

6. To prevent strain on a pipe assembly, use two wrenches, facing in opposite directions, to hold and tighten a pipe or loosen it from its fitting. Turn wrenches toward their openings.

Working with copper pipe

Though comparatively expensive, rigid copper pipe is unusually easy to work with, add to, and repair; involves little or no waste; and resists corrosion and scaling. Small sizes are used for water supply, larger sizes for DWV systems. Sweat-soldered joints are made the same in either case.

Copper pipe comes in 10- and 20-foot lengths in three weights: Thin-walled Type M, medium-walled Type L, and thick-walled Type K. Code permitting, Type M is adequate for house plumbing with soldered joints. For a line to be buried below ground or that may be subject to mechanical damage, use Type K.

Outside diameter of copper pipe is ⅛ inch more than its nominal size. Sizes suitable for home plumbing are ⅜, ½, ¾, 1, 1¼, 2, and 3 inches.

As with steel pipe, allowance must be made for the distance this pipe slips into fittings. To measure for copper pipe, determine the distance from face to face of fittings, then add twice the depth from the face to the inner shoulder of each fitting.

A good way of building a copper pipe run is to assemble everything dry, make adjustments, then disassemble and go through the sweat-soldering procedure. On long pipe runs, prepare and solder four or five joints, if this is possible, at the same time.

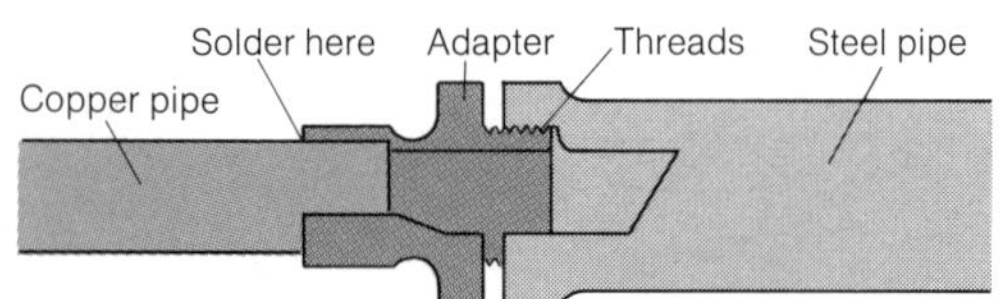

Copper-to-steel adapter (Dielectric types available.)

If you have to solder a joint after another one at the same fitting has cooled, wrap the cooled joint in damp cloths. Heating very large DWV pipes may call for an extra-large tip on your propane torch.

Soldered joints can be removed by heating and tapping them apart when the solder has melted. All water must first be drained from the pipe. DWV piping is always sloped to a drain. Similarly, all water-supply piping should slope back to a drain point so it can be emptied to prevent freezing in an unheated house. The drain point is usually a basement laundry tub or a low hose outlet, sometimes a shutoff valve incorporating a drain plug. Once removed, soldered joints in copper pipe can be cleaned and resoldered.

Making a solder (sweat) joint

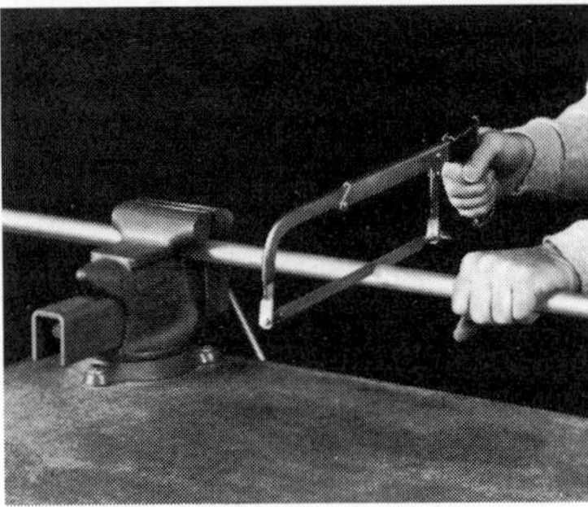

1. The best way to cut copper pipe is with a hacksaw. A miter box helps to make a square cut. Use the saw dry—no oil. A tubing cutter may also be used.

2. Use a half-round file to remove burrs left by the cutting operation. Burr removal takes longer on pipe that is cut with a tubing cutter.

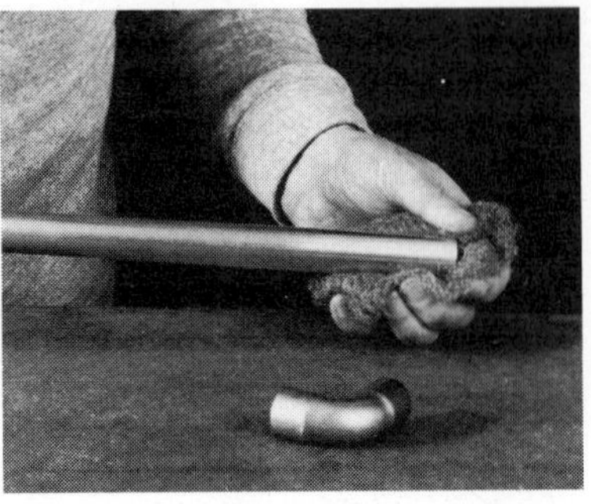

3. Polish the end of the pipe with steel wool or fine, cloth-backed sandpaper until it is bright all around. The tube end must be round—not dented or flattened.

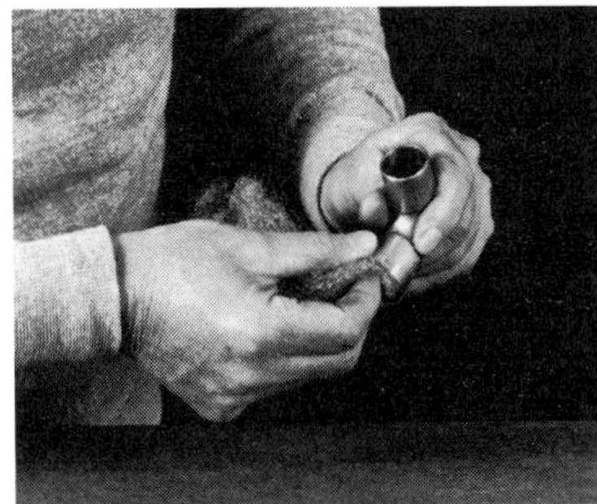

4. Clean the inside of the fitting all around and down to the shoulder with the steel wool or abrasive paper. Fitting must also be round and free from dents.

5. Apply a light coat of soldering flux (soldering paste) to the cleaned outside of the tube. Use fingers or an old toothbrush to apply the flux.

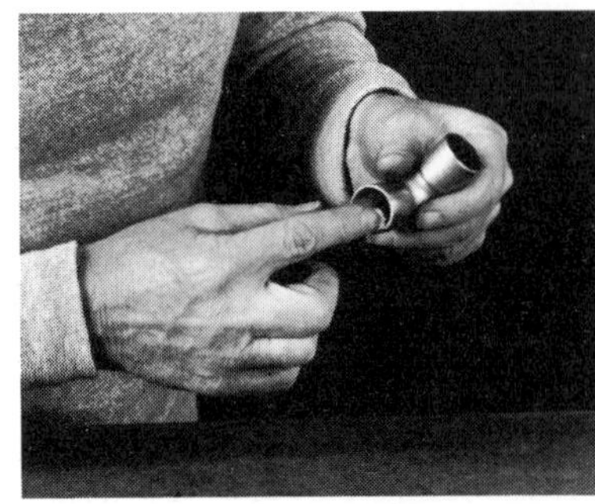

6. Apply the flux around the inside of the cleaned fitting. Flux will keep the copper from oxidizing when heated. Don't use acid as a pipe-soldering flux.

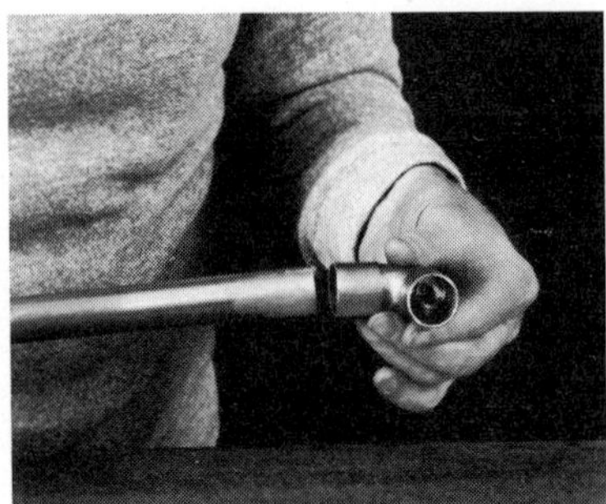

7. Assemble the fluxed joint, pushing the pipe into the fitting until it contacts the shoulder inside. Remember to adjust direction of fitting before soldering.

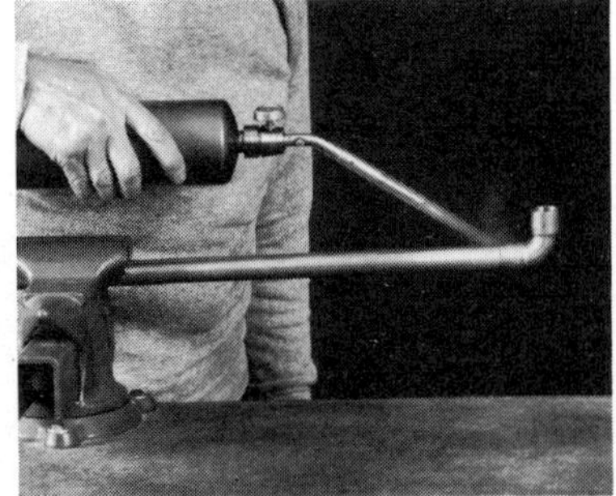

8. Heat the fitting to soldering temperature with a torch. Large fittings should be heated front and back. Do not overheat. Test by touching with solder.

9. When joint is hot enough, solder will flow into it by capillary action. Flow solder in until fillet appears all around fitting. Use solid-core wire solder.

Working with copper tubing

The chief advantage of soft-temper copper tubing is its flexibility. Often an entire run of pipe can be made with fittings only at the ends. Bends are taken in stride. Because of the long, gentle curves that are possible, resistance to water flow is reduced and more water delivered at the tap. If flexible copper tubing is used with solder-type fittings, it is handled, measured, and cut the same as rigid tubing.

Flexible copper tubing is sold in 15-, 30-, and 60-foot lengths. It is made in Type L (for most uses) and Type K (for hard service). It is excellent for plumbing remodeling jobs, since it can be snaked in behind walls and through small openings. Flexible tubing does not, however, produce as neat a job as rigid pipe with its straight lines and precise right angles. For this reason, flexible tubing is usually installed where it will not show.

Flexible copper tubing may be joined with soldered fittings or with convenient flare and compression fittings. Compression fittings are similar to flare fittings, but without the flaring. Both are self-sealing. The advantage of flare and compression fittings is that any accessible joint can be taken apart at any time with a pair of open-end wrenches. The disadvantage is their relatively high cost compared to soldered fittings. If cost need not be considered, flare and compression fittings could be used much more widely in house plumbing systems for ultimate flexibility in repair and remodeling.

The making of a flared joint is shown on this page. Unless flare joints are carefully made, they can leak. Be sure that you test flare joints under pressure.

If the tubing end is slightly dented, the flaring tool will bring it back into shape. And always remember to remove the flange nut from the fitting and slide it over the tubing before flaring the tube. Use two wrenches when making up the connection—one to hold the fitting, the other to turn the flange nut. If a joint does leak, cut off end of tube and reflare it.

Flexible copper tubing can be bent across your knee or straightened out by unrolling the coil. The larger the tube diameter, the gentler the bend must be to avoid kinking. To make sharper bends in short lengths, fill the tube with sand before bending it. This prevents kinking. Or use a spring, as shown.

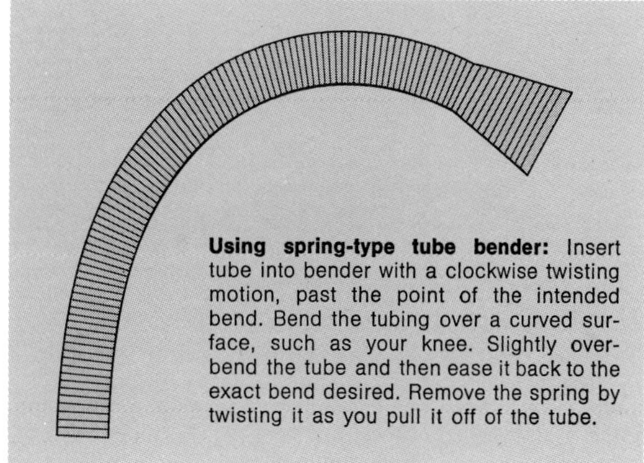

Using spring-type tube bender: Insert tube into bender with a clockwise twisting motion, past the point of the intended bend. Bend the tubing over a curved surface, such as your knee. Slightly overbend the tube and then ease it back to the exact bend desired. Remove the spring by twisting it as you pull it off of the tube.

Making a flare fitting mechanically

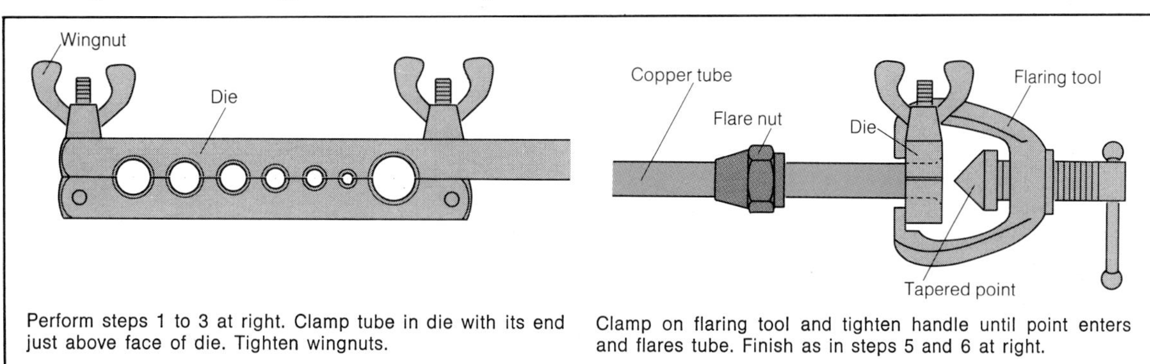

Perform steps 1 to 3 at right. Clamp tube in die with its end just above face of die. Tighten wingnuts.

Clamp on flaring tool and tighten handle until point enters and flares tube. Finish as in steps 5 and 6 at right.

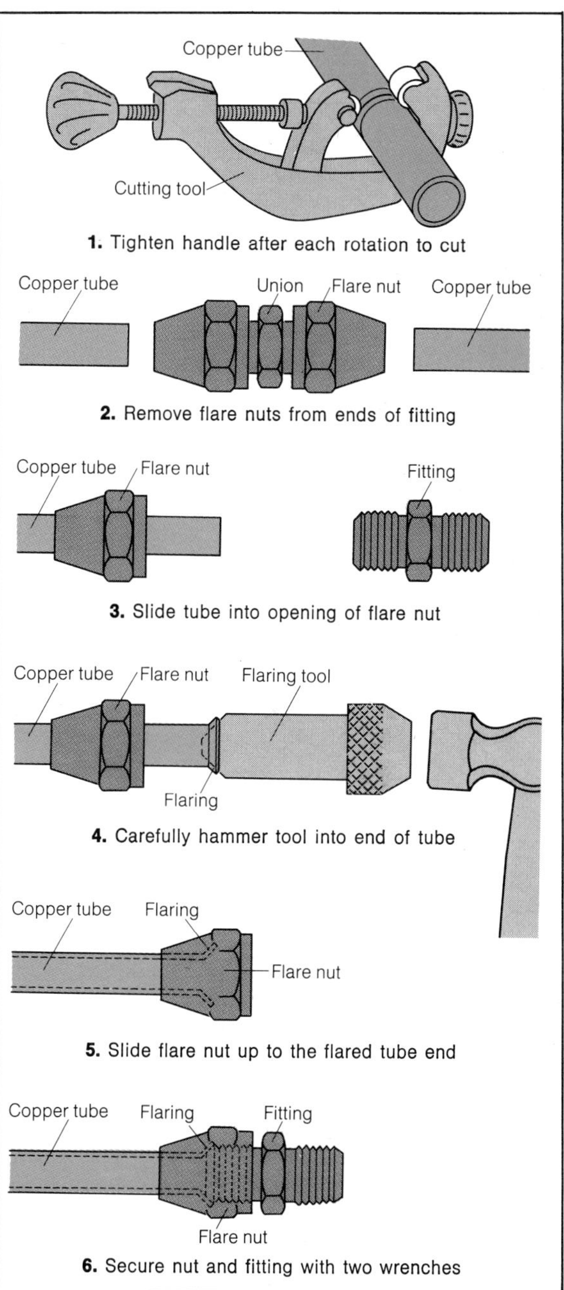

1. Tighten handle after each rotation to cut

2. Remove flare nuts from ends of fitting

3. Slide tube into opening of flare nut

4. Carefully hammer tool into end of tube

5. Slide flare nut up to the flared tube end

6. Secure nut and fitting with two wrenches

Working with rigid pipe

The three types of rigid plastic pipe produced for use in home plumbing are designated PVC (polyvinyl chloride), ABS (acrylo-mitrile butadiene-styrene), and CPVC (chlorinated polyvinyl chloride). Local codes generally forbid their use behind or within walls, though most of them permit the use of plastic pipe for lawn sprinkler systems.

All three types of piping can be used for cold-water supply as well as for drainage systems. Only CPVC, rated to take 100 pounds water pressure per square inch (psi) at a temperature of 180°, can be used for both hot- and cold-water piping—provided that local building codes permit. Some hot-water heaters are fitted with temperature-pressure relief valves (p. 241) with relief settings as high as 125 pounds pressure per square inch at 210°. To use CPVC pipe with such a system, it is necessary to replace the relief valve with one rated at 100 psi, 180° (the rating appears on the valve).

In addition to the need for a new pressure relief valve, the CPVC pipe must be connected to the water heater with a transition fitting (see p. 227) that will absorb heat from the tank wall. Since plastic piping expands and contracts more than other types of piping, hangers made especially for plastic pipe should be used to permit movement without damage to pipe walls. Install the pipe hangers every 32 inches or on alternate overhead joists.

Joining pipe: All types of plastic pipe can be joined to plastic fittings by means of a special **solvent cement** (solvent-welded). But before using this, try sliding the pipe into its fitting. The pipe should slide all the way into the fitting before it touches the shoulder inside the fitting. This preliminary test is advisable because the solvent sets too fast to permit major repositioning.

Do not attempt to solvent-weld at temperatures below 40°. If the solvent in the can has discolored or thickened, discard it. Solvent weld for CPVC pipe comes in two cans (one can contains a cleaning agent); solvents for ABS and PVC, in a single can. To apply solvents of any type, use only brushes with non-synthetic bristles (use a separate one for each of the two CPVC cans). Wait three minutes before attempting to move solvent-welded joints. Do not attempt to pressure-test plastic pipe for at least 16 hours after it has been welded.

Rigid plastic pipe can be joined to copper tubing by means of flare fittings (p. 227). Warm the pipe end with a torch before flaring. Plastic-to-steel joints can be made with a special adapter. This adapter is threaded on one end to accept steel or brass pipe. The other end has a plastic bushing that cements to a plastic pipe. Copper-to-plastic adapters are also available. Do not mix different plastics in the same system, as ABS pipe and PVC fittings or vice versa. This can cause leaks. But one type may be used for water supply, another for drains.

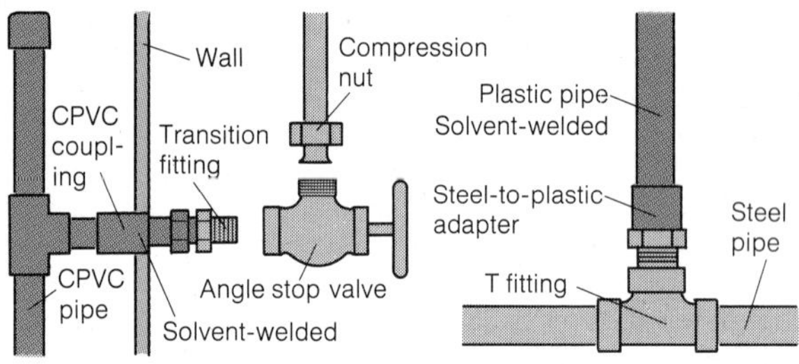

Joining pipe to fixture **Joining plastic to steel**

Solvent-welding a joint

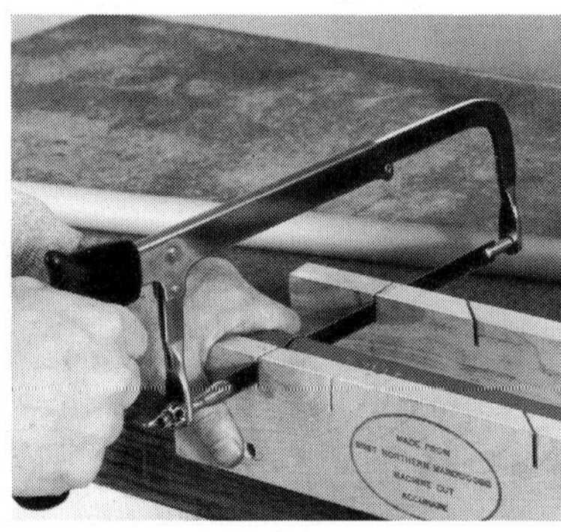

1. Cut plastic pipe in a miter box with a hacksaw to get smooth, square cuts. A 24-tooth blade works best. Ordinary hand saws can be used, but their cuts are rougher.

2. Remove the burr inside the pipe with a knife, a file, or sandpaper. Any burr around the outer edge should also be removed. Use fine sandpaper for this.

3. CPVC pipe is joined with two solvents. No. 1 is a cleaner to remove wax, oil, and dirt. Brush No. 1 solvent on the outside of the pipe and on inside of fitting.

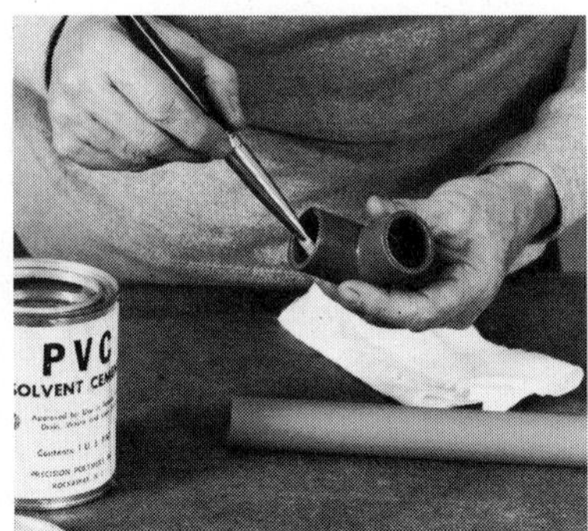

4. Next brush No. 2 liberally on outside of pipe and lightly inside the fitting. On PVC and ABS pipe, use the recommended single solvent. Coat all mating surfaces.

5. Without waiting, push the fitting and pipe together with no more than a quarter twist until the pipe bottoms. Next, quickly adjust fitting to desired direction.

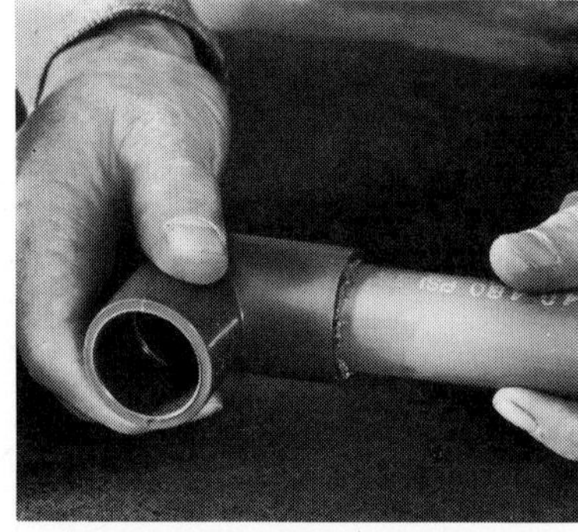

6. A properly solvent-welded joint will show a bead of fused solvent. If joint leaks, it must be cut out and replaced with a new coupling or fitting.

Working with flexible tubing

Flexible plastic polyethylene tubing is black and comes in 100-foot coils. It is an "outdoor" pipe suitable for use in wells, underground sprinkler systems, and water-service entrance lines. Polyethylene tubing should never be used, however, for hot water.

Three qualities are available. The best is rated to take pressure up to 125 pounds pressure per square inch (psi). Use it for deep wells to 200 feet. Medium quality, the one most commonly used, will withstand pressures up to 100 psi and can be used in wells to 80 feet deep, but not with a submersible pump. The third, utility-grade, should not be used for high pressure at all, nor for drinking water. It is suitable, however, for underground sprinkling systems.

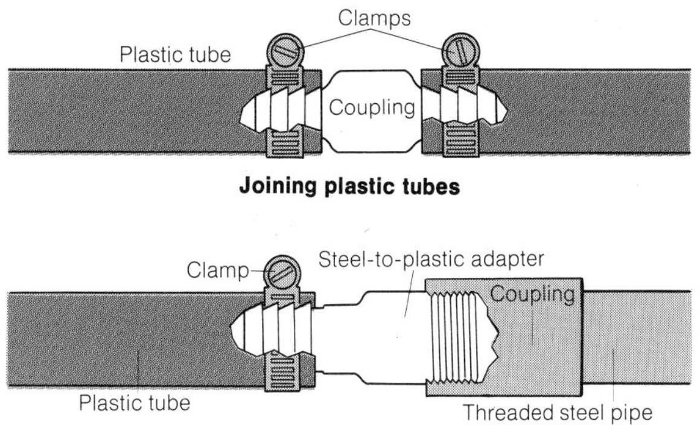

Joining plastic tubes

Joining plastic to steel

Polyethylene tubing is lightweight and easy to use. Since few joints are required in an installation because of its length, the tubing presents minimum resistance to water flowing through it.

Tubing can be connected to threaded steel pipe and to itself with polystyrene fittings and couplings. Do not tighten plastic adapters into a threaded fitting more than one turn beyond hand-tight. Use an open-end wrench—not a pipe wrench.

Stainless steel worm-drive clamps are used to secure tubing to non-threaded fittings. Joints can be loosened, pulled apart, and put back together as often as needed. Hot water poured on a joint will soften the tubing and help it come off more readily.

Underground lawn sprinkler systems

You can install a lawn sprinkler system as simple or as complex as you need for the area you want to cover and the operational convenience you would like. The simplest of the various available systems attaches to a T fitting in an outdoor faucet line. It has half a dozen pop-up sprinkler heads and will water up to 900 square feet of lawn.

More complex systems (such as the one illustrated) even have built-in pumps to pressure-feed water to dozens of sprinkler heads. A clock-operated programmer will turn separate zones of the system on and off according to a preset plan.

Sprinkler systems of this more complex kind must be fitted with an antisiphon valve to prevent the submerged sprinkler heads from feeding contaminated water into the house water-supply system if a vacuum should occur in the house plumbing. Most sprinkler systems nowadays use flexible plastic pipe buried in trenches below the lawn.

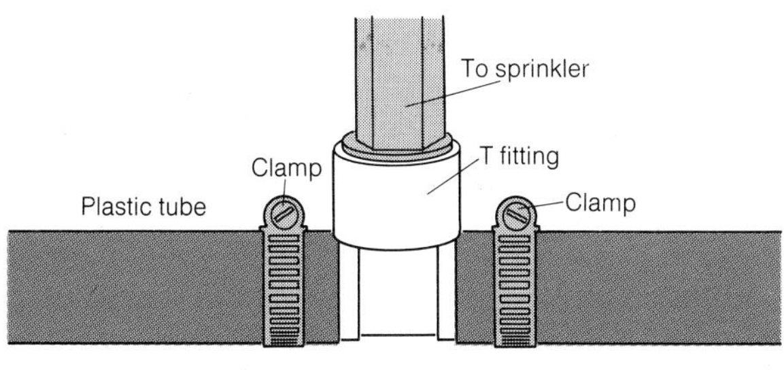

Basic sprinkler connection

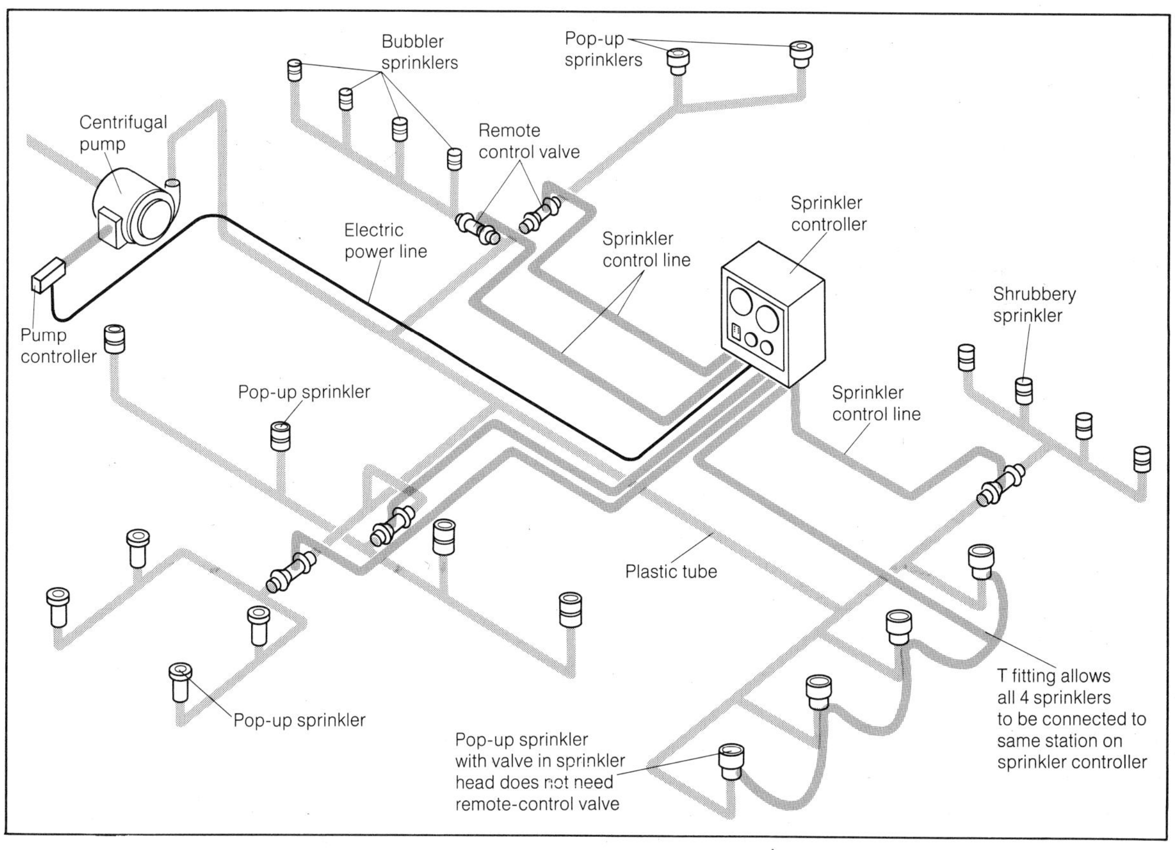

Planning your installation

Installing plumbing for a house addition or converting a room to an extra bathroom involves installation of water-supply and drain-waste-vent piping in walls, floors, and ceiling. These preliminary provisions are called **rough plumbing.**

The water-supply system generally has a ¾- or 1-inch service entrance; ¾-inch hot and cold main lines to rooms; ½-inch branch lines to sinks, tubs, showers, washer, laundry tub, and dishwasher; ⅜-inch lines to toilets (except flush-valve-operated toilets) and lavatories. The drain-waste-vent system uses 4-inch sewer lines; 3- or 4-inch main drains and vents, serving toilets and groups of fixtures; 3- or 4-inch toilet drains; 2-inch shower drains; 1½-inch drains for sinks, tubs, laundry tubs, washers, and dishwashers; 1¼-inch lavatory drains.

Always plan piping layouts to take the most direct route, avoiding obstacles wherever possible. DWV piping takes precedence over water-supply piping because it is bulkier and costlier. The smaller water pipes usually can be routed along with DWV.

Pipes in the floor should parallel the joists where possible. Pipes in the attic can easily run across the tops of attic floor joists. Pipes below the first floor can be run under first-floor joists. Joists between floors must be notched or have holes cut in them for pipes running across them.

When making additions to existing plumbing, you will not have the choice of pipe location that is available in new construction. New pipe runs can be made by cutting into an existing line and using a T and a union to make the connection. Vents for new toilets, sinks, and tubs can be hooked up to the existing vent pipe by means of revents (p. 235). Check your local code, as most codes specify just how far a fixture can be from the main vent.

You must be a bit of a carpenter to do plumbing work; it requires considerable cutting through walls, joists, studs, and floors. In addition to the usual hand tools, an electric drill capable of driving a hole saw will not only make the job easier, but neater as well. A hole drilled through a floor to pass a pipe makes a neater job than an irregular hole cut with a keyhole saw. If pipes have to cross a steel I beam, it will pay you to have a hole cut in the beam with a torch instead of dropping the pipes under the beam. Get professional help for this, under Welding in the classified telephone directory.

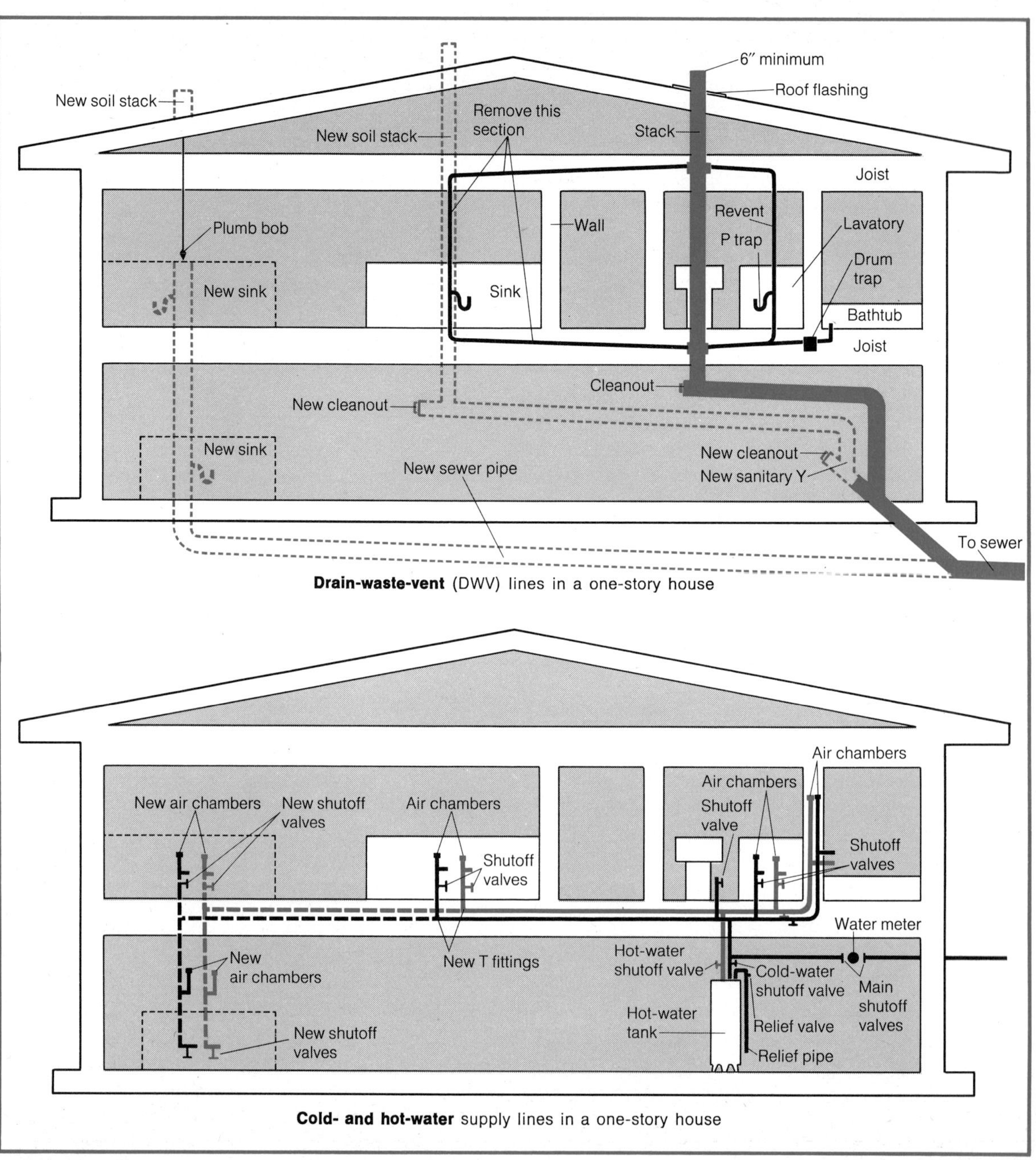

Drain-waste-vent (DWV) lines in a one-story house

Cold- and hot-water supply lines in a one-story house

Notching joists and studs

Notch joists according to these rules: Notch only in the end quarter of each joist. Never notch near the center. Never notch out more than one-quarter of the joist depth (in a 2-x-8-inch joist, a 2-inch notch, maximum). Nail a steel brace or a 2 x 2 piece of wood across each notch, front and back.

Holes can be cut in the joist anywhere along its length if these rules are followed: Center the holes between the top and bottom no closer than 2 inches to the edge. Hole diameter should be less than one-quarter of the joist depth.

Pipes across notched studs should conform to these rules: Never notch deeper than two-thirds of stud depth (2½ inches on a 2 x 4 stud). In the lower half of the stud, do not notch deeper than one-third without reinforcing with a steel strap or wood brace across the notch. In a nonbearing wall, which excludes most outside walls and center partitions, you can notch the upper half of the stud to half its depth if there are at least two unnotched studs left. Of course, to notch any stud, the existing wall covering must be removed and the wall later recovered.

To notch a joist or stud, saw in on both sides and cut out the plug with a sharp chisel.

Pipes crossing under joists can be hung from perforated metal pipe strapping that is cut to length and nailed to the joist; pipes running between two joists can be supported on wood braces nailed across the joists. A vertical run of pipe, such as a soil stack, for example, is supported by resting the bottom fitting on a wood brace that is nailed into position. Other horizontal drain and vent lines entering the soil stack will also help to support it.

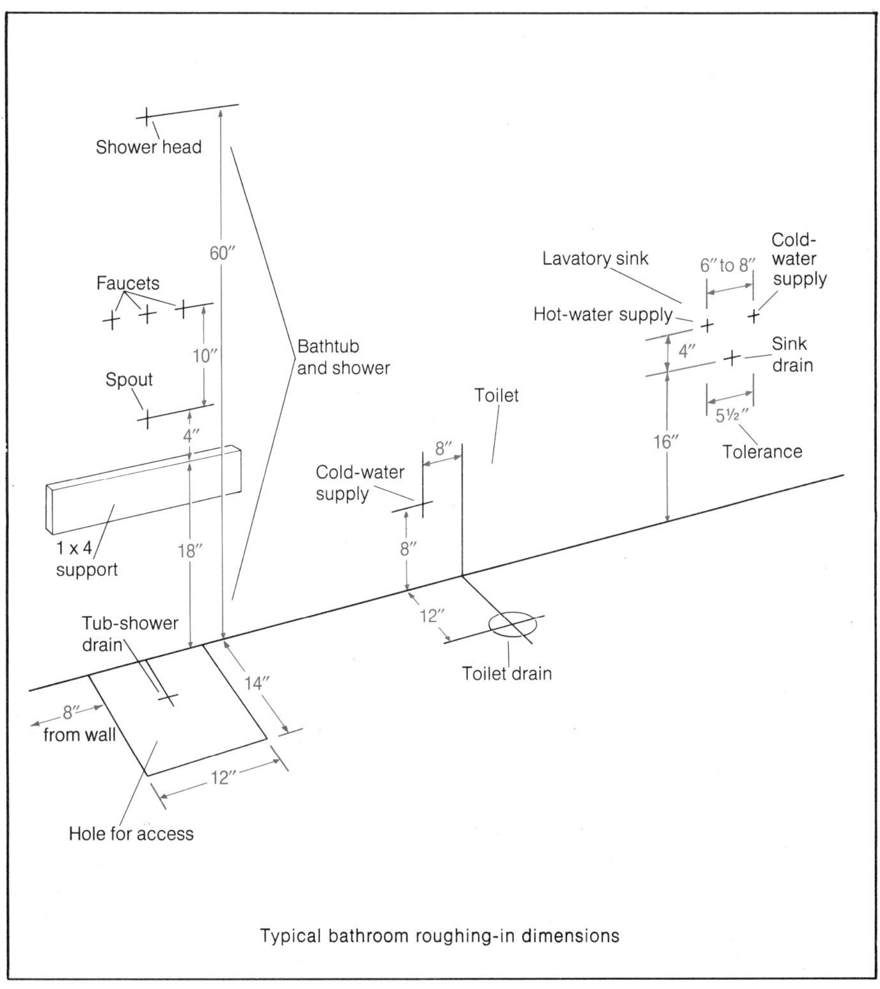

Typical bathroom roughing-in dimensions

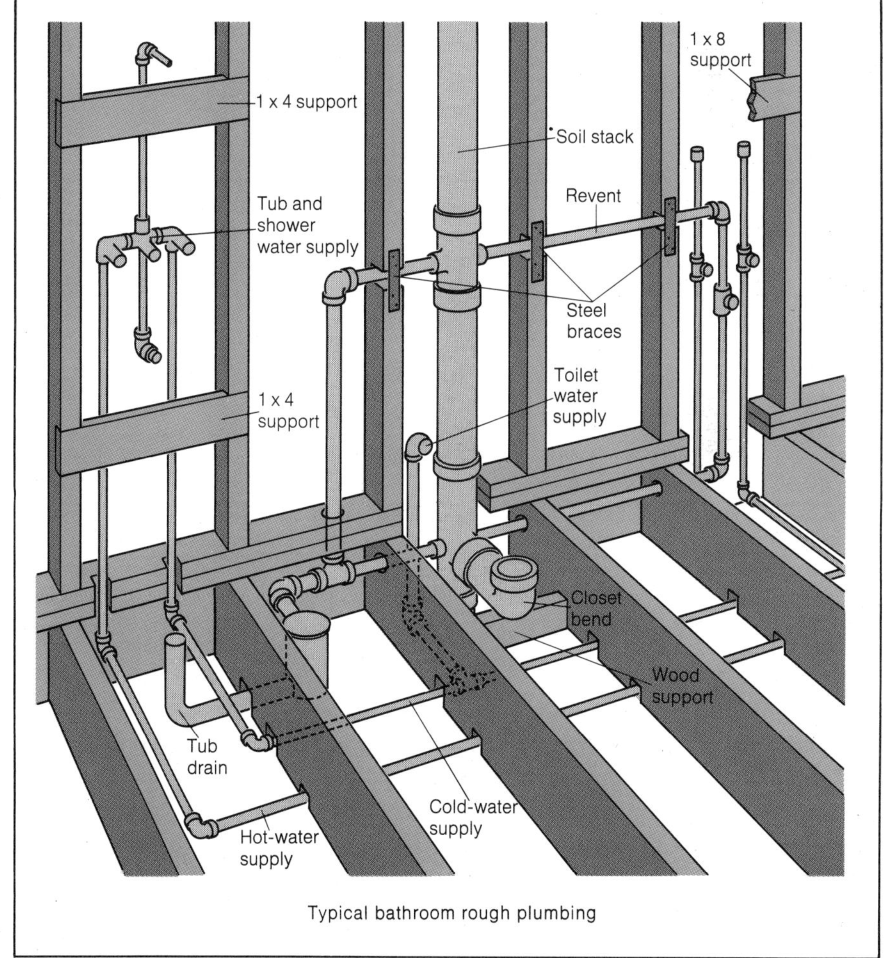

Typical bathroom rough plumbing

Installing pipes

The closet bend, which connects the toilet floor flange to the soil stack, presents a special problem. Try to run it between two joists. If a joist must be cut to accommodate, cut it only as deep as necessary. Then nail 2-inch-thick wood braces on both sides of the notch. Instead of making a deep notch, cut a section of the joist out and install two **headers** (short boards the same thickness and depth as the joists).

Pipes through walls need ample clearance. DWV sizes up to 3 inches in steel, plastic, or cast iron will fit into a standard 2 x 4 framed wall. All threaded pipes must be given sufficient additional clearance to allow for tightening.

DWV assembly is done first, starting at the toilet drain. Cut and suspend the closet bend and sanitary T. Then work from the sewer or building drain back to the closet. Be sure to install accessible cleanouts in every horizontal drain run.

If the drainage portion of the soil stack must be offset to clear framing, use two ⅛ bends; if the vent portion must be offset, use two ¼ bends.

Because of the cramped space involved when installing a closet bend, many plumbers use a lead pipe for the connection between the toilet and the drain. The lead pipe permits fitting into awkward areas with slight bending—and straightening—after the closet bend is in place. Lead-pipe closet bends are often used when two toilets are mounted back to back in adjacent bathrooms. The joint between the lead pipe and the cast-iron drain is made by a process that is called "wiping"—using molten lead to make the connection.

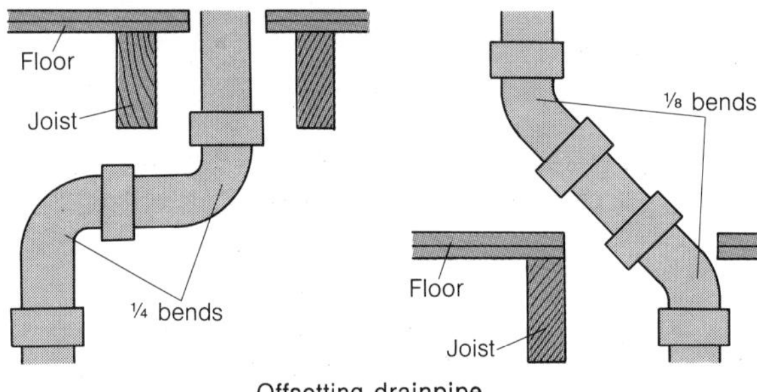

Offsetting drainpipe

Build the soil stack up from the toilet and out through the roof. Code may require that vent size be increased to 6 inches just below the roof with a vent increaser. Install flashing below the roofing and around the vent; caulk well with roofing cement.

Work out from the stack, building the branch waste and revent lines. Build up a secondary stack, if needed. Bring out all fixture drains, positioning them according to dimensions shown in the drawings on page 238. Bring the waste lines out of the wall and cap them temporarily. These can be cut off or threaded out later and proper fittings installed.

When assembling pipes for the water-supply system, extend the existing cold- and hot-water mains. Install reducing T's for the branches as you go. Then install the branch and fixture runs. If it is practical to do so, bring out all water-supply pipes through the wall. Otherwise, bring them up through the floor. Use the rough-in dimensions on page 235 as a guide.

A fixture run should be brought to the point of entry into the room. Install a T with the branch of the T facing into the room. The branch takes a short capped pipe reaching at least an inch into the room. For the top of the T, use an 18-inch capped air chamber pipe, the same size as the supply line.

When installing pipe branches, bear in mind that the hot-water pipes go on the left and the cold-water pipes go on the right of the fixture's center line. Remember to install cutoff valves below each sink and lavatory.

Secure bathtub faucets with a 2 x 4 wood brace to hold the faucet body in place. Do the same with a shower outlet. For quiet plumbing, all pipes should be well supported. A support block is also needed behind a wall-hung lavatory. Locate it according to the requirements of the fixture you are using.

Both DWV and water-supply systems should be tested before redecorating the room. Do it this way: Rent a set of rubber plugs for the closet bend and sewer line and install them. Turn on the water and look for leaks in the water-supply lines. Look again several hours later. Run water from a garden hose into the main soil stack until full. Wait 20 minutes, then look for leaks in the DWV lines. If there are none, you can remove the plugs and close in the walls confident that your plumbing system is leak-free.

Supporting the closet bend

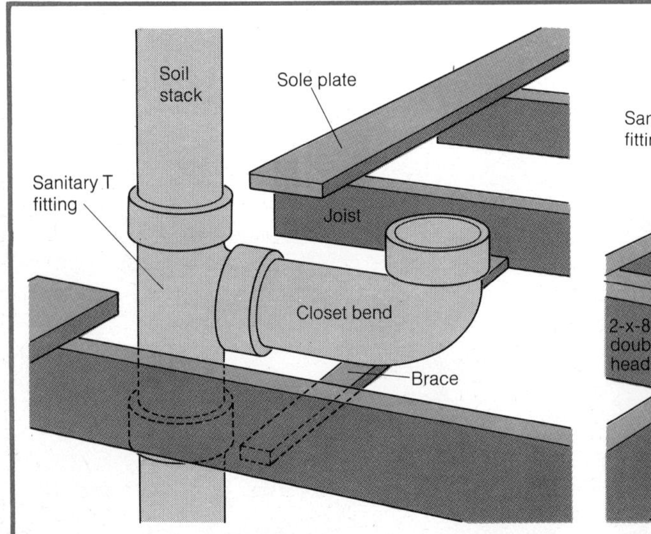

If the closet bend is parallel to the joists, install a brace as shown between the two joists to support the closet bend. Shim up if a space remains.

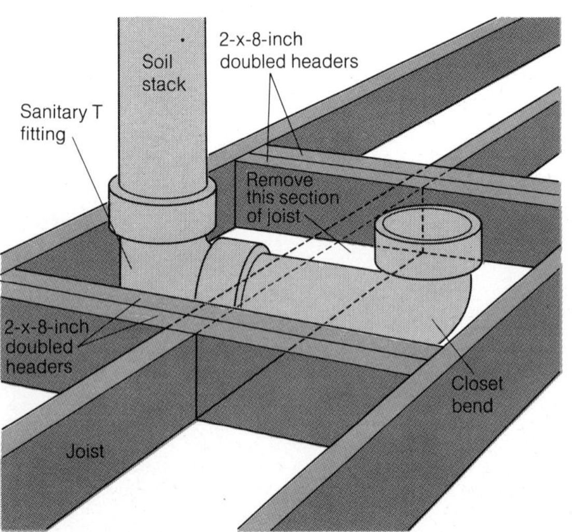

If you have to cut away a joist in order to make room for the closet bend, reinforce the cut joist at each end, as shown, with double headers.

Removing and installing a toilet

When buying a new toilet, select one that matches the **rough-in** of the old toilet. Rough-in is the distance from the finished wall behind the toilet to the center of the floor flange to which the bowl is attached (see drawing). Fortunately, most old and new toilet rough-ins are 12 inches.

The first step is to turn off the water supply. Flush the toilet and bail out all the water from both tank and bowl with a can and sponge. Remove the old water-supply line leading from the floor or wall to the tank. If it does not contain a shutoff valve, leave only the coupling or short pipe for attaching the new supply parts.

Remove the tank-to-bowl pipe couplings. If these are corroded, saw them off. Remove the two screws that are holding the tank to the wall. Support the tank as it comes off.

Pry off the caps on the bolts holding the bowl to the floor and unscrew the bolts. Rock the bowl from side to side, then lift, and twist from side to side.

Place the new toilet bowl upside down on newspaper padding to keep it from being scratched. Clean off all old gasket material from around the toilet bowl's floor flange. Position a new toilet bowl gasket around the bowl outlet horn, with flat surface down on the bottom of the bowl. Put plumber's putty in a 1-inch-thick ring around the bowl's bottom rim.

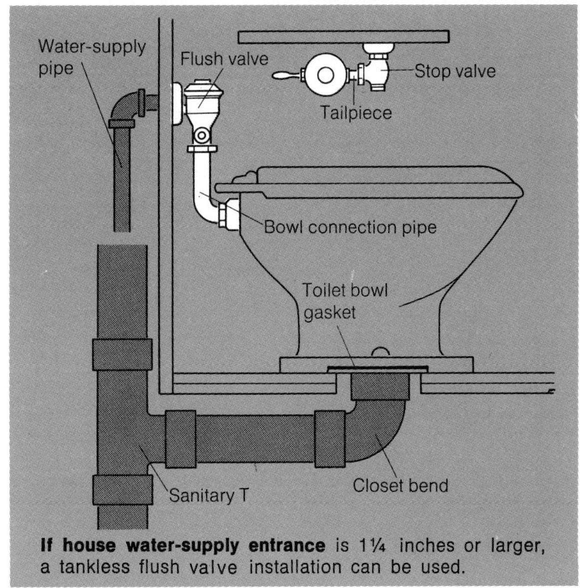

If house water-supply entrance is 1¼ inches or larger, a tankless flush valve installation can be used.

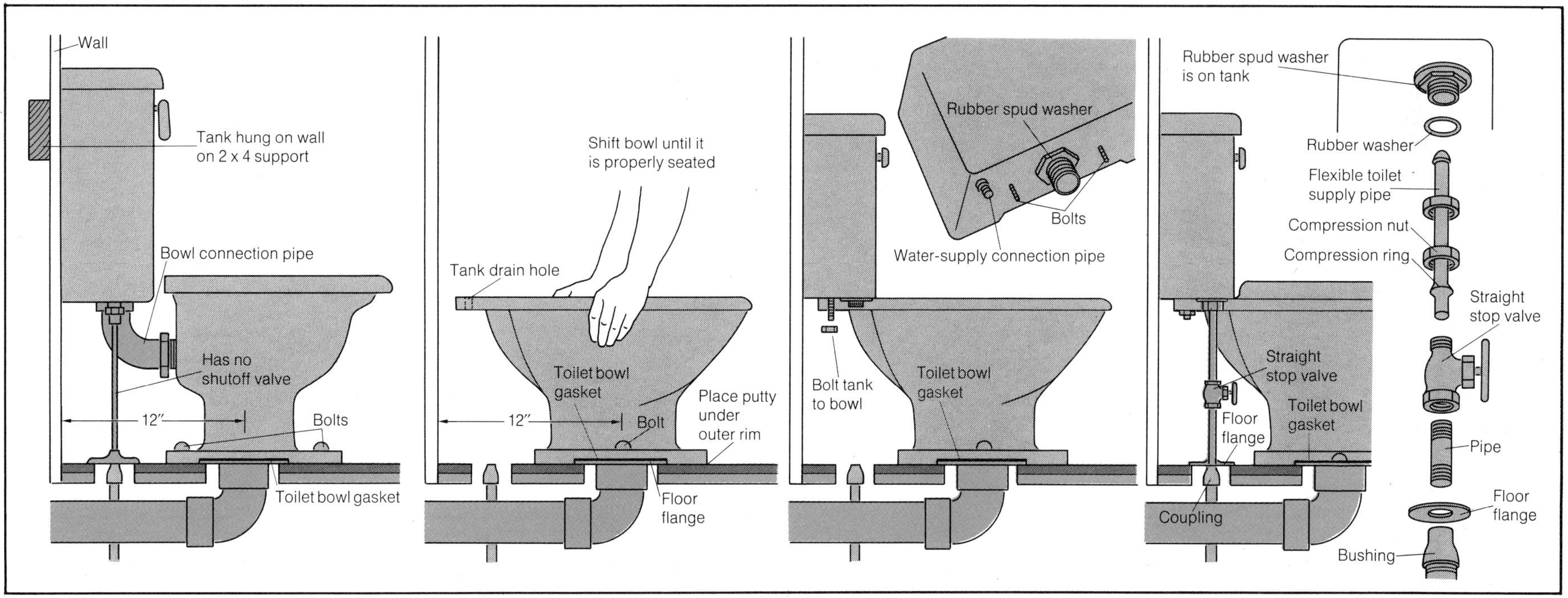

Install new floor flange bolts in the slots in the floor flange. Most modern toilets have just two bolts. If your old one had four, remove the extra ones. Turn the bowl right side up and lower it with the outlet horn centered over the floor flange. Press down and twist slightly, left to right, to compress the gasket as you bring the toilet down onto the floor. Avoid raising any part of the bowl once it is down. Check across the top of the bowl with a level. Shim the bowl if the floor is not level.

Mount the tank to the bowl, if it is separate, using the gasket and bolts furnished. Align the tank with the wall by twisting the bowl without raising it. Now gently tighten the floor flange bolts.

Make the water-supply connection with compression fittings to the flexible supply tube. Turn on the water, flush the toilet, and check for leaks.

Wall
Tank hung on wall on 2 x 4 support
Bowl connection pipe
Has no shutoff valve
12″
Bolts
Toilet bowl gasket
Shift bowl until it is properly seated
Tank drain hole
Toilet bowl gasket
Place putty under outer rim
12″
Bolt
Floor flange
Rubber spud washer
Bolts
Water-supply connection pipe
Bolt tank to bowl
Toilet bowl gasket
Rubber spud washer is on tank
Rubber washer
Flexible toilet supply pipe
Compression nut
Compression ring
Straight stop valve
Straight stop valve
Toilet bowl gasket
Floor flange
Pipe
Coupling
Floor flange
Bushing

Extending existing piping

When you are adding a sink, laundry tub, or lavatory to your house, the new installation should be located as close as possible to a soil stack so it can be drained and vented through the same pipe. This arrangement is called **wet-venting.**

As specified by the National Plumbing Code, the maximum wet-vented distances between trap outlet and soil stack are: With 2-inch pipe, 5 feet; 1½-inch pipe, 3½ feet; 1¼-pipe, 3½ feet; and 1¼-inch pipe, 2½ feet. If you exceed these maximums, your local code may require the reventing of the fixture or the installation of a new soil stack. Either procedure could be costly and difficult. Wet-venting below a toilet is not permitted.

Position the new fixture with its outlet pipes and trap loosely in place. Then plan the routing of the waste pipe, sloping it 1 inch for every 4 feet of run to assure good drainage.

If the existing soil stack is made of cast iron, cut it as shown in the drawing to make room for the new parts. A copper soil stack is handled similarly, with the new T installed with special slip couplings (local

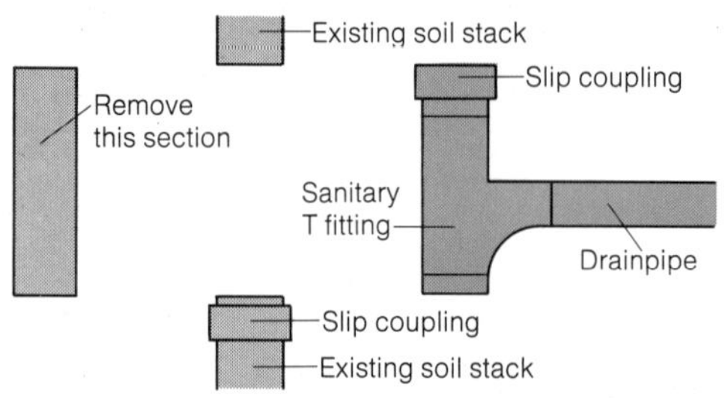

Installing branch in copper or plastic soil stack

code permitting). A plastic soil stack is not cut apart. Instead, an opening is cut and a solvent-welded saddle installed.

The water-supply lines to the new fixture (½-inch for a sink or laundry tub and ⅜-inch for a lavatory) call for tapping into nearby hot- and cold-water supply lines. You can do this with T's, nipples, and unions, as illustrated here; or you can install tapping T's on the existing water lines. Tapping T's are made with rubber gaskets that are clamped around holes drilled in the pipe. They are threaded to accept new ½-inch piping.

To make water-supply, trap, and waste hookups at the sink, see the next page.

Pipe connections to existing lines

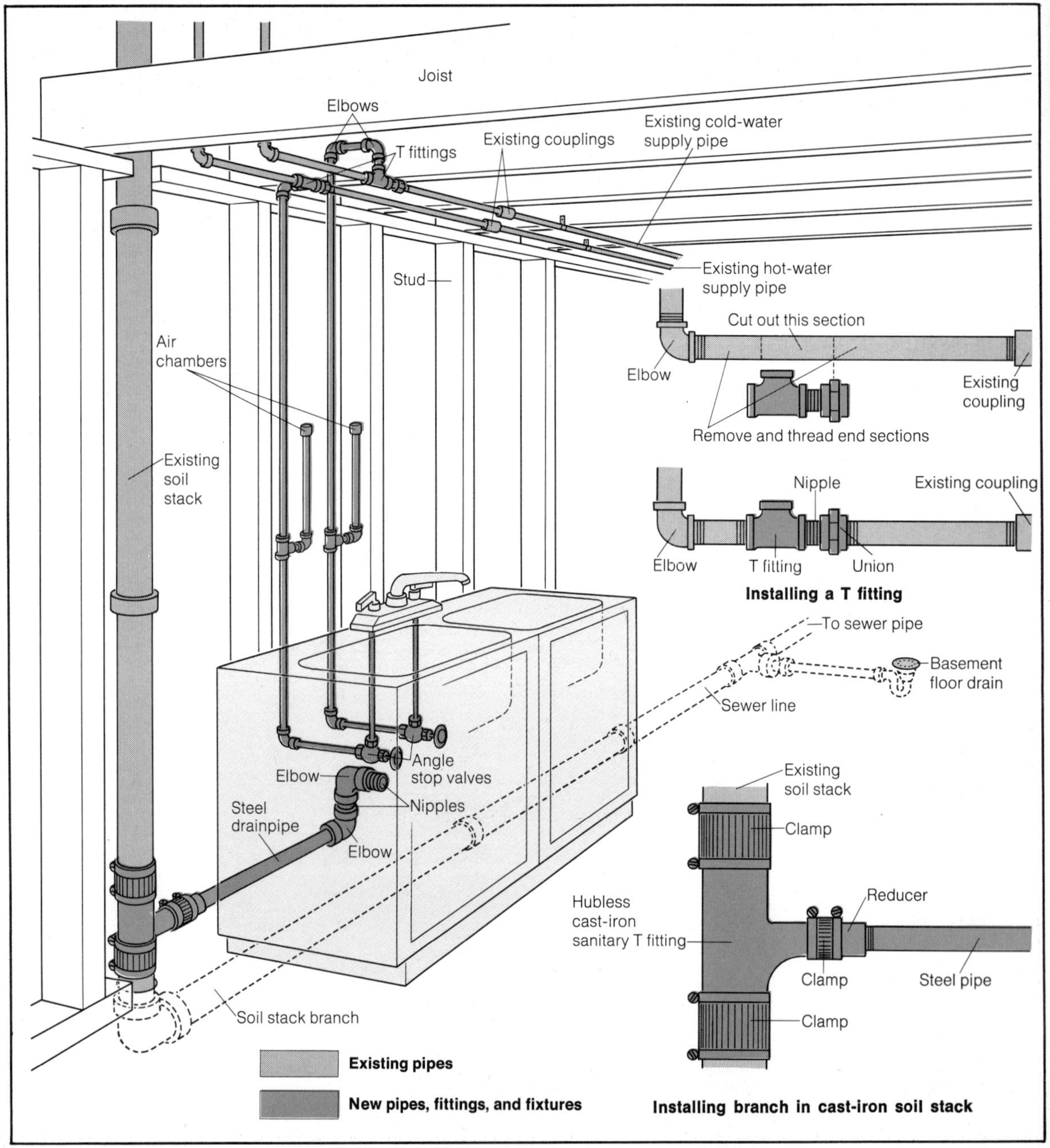

Joist
Elbows
T fittings
Existing couplings
Existing cold-water supply pipe
Existing hot-water supply pipe
Stud
Air chambers
Existing soil stack
Angle stop valves
Elbow
Nipples
Steel drainpipe
Elbow
Soil stack branch
Sewer line
To sewer pipe
Basement floor drain

Cut out this section
Elbow
Existing coupling
Remove and thread end sections
Nipple
Existing coupling
Elbow
T fitting
Union

Installing a T fitting

Existing soil stack
Clamp
Reducer
Hubless cast-iron sanitary T fitting
Clamp
Steel pipe
Clamp

Installing branch in cast-iron soil stack

Existing pipes

New pipes, fittings, and fixtures

Connecting a new sink

Whether you are making a new installation or replacing an old sink, water-supply and waste connections are similar. Sinks and lavatories may be wall-hung, supported by legs or a pedestal, mounted in a cabinet, or a combination of legs and a wall support with the legs adjustable to carry some of the weight and to compensate for unevenness in the floor. A wall-hung sink should have a horizontal 1-x-8-inch board screwed to at least two studs in the wall and flush with wall. Bracket supplied with sink is screwed to the board and the sink hung on the bracket.

Once the fixture is in place, you can install the drains. Note the exact arrangement of parts in the manufacturer's instruction sheet. Tighten the large sink basket-drain flange nuts with a spud wrench (p. 226). Plumber's putty is often required on the inside between the new drain and the fixture bottom.

If the fixture has a short chromed-brass tailpiece with fine threads at one end, use pipe-joint compound on the threads and screw the tailpiece into the bottom of the drain from below. A slipnut and rubber washer go onto this, then the trap is attached. Put a slipnut on the tailpiece of the trap, then a rubber washer, and slide the trap into the end of the waste pipe coming through the wall. If it is a 1½-inch pipe and the trap is 1¼ inches (lavatory size), use a reducing slipnut with an extra-large rubber washer to make the connection. Assemble the trap halves loosely with a rubber washer between, holding them with a slipnut. Trap design makes it possible to accommodate variation in waste-pipe position. Adjust all the trap parts so they do not bind. Tighten the slipnuts with a monkey wrench or spud wrench.

If yours is a new installation, be sure to install a pair of shutoff valves for the hot- and cold-water lines. Without them, you would have to turn off the main valve in the basement just to replace washers.

Mount the faucet on the fixture (as described on p. 221) with a ring of plumber's putty around the faucet escutcheon. Consult the drawings below for details on how the water-supply pipes are connected to the sink or lavatory. Use pipe-joint compound on all pipe threads. Turn on the water and check your installation for leaks. Also check and adjust the operation of the pop-up lavatory stopper.

Pipe connections

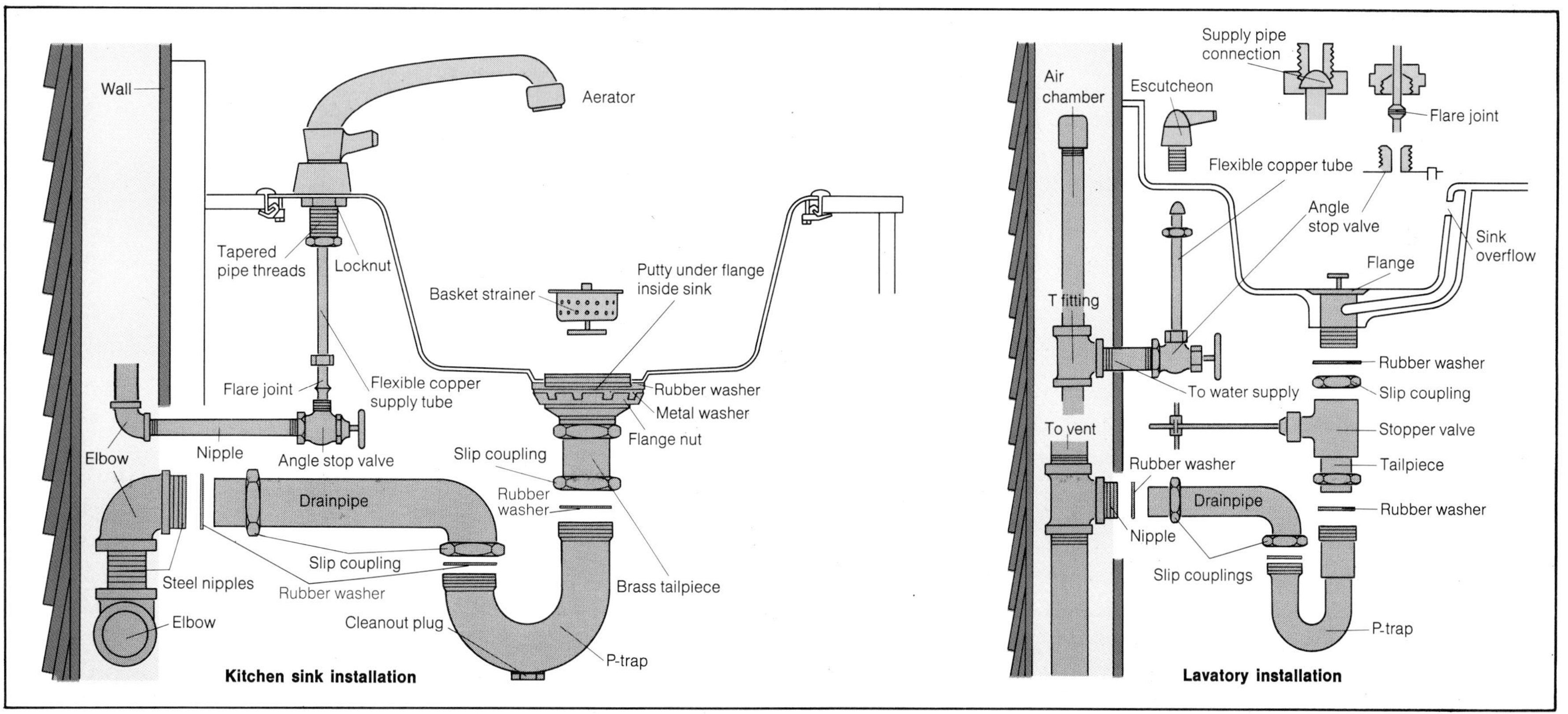

Tubs and showers

Installing a combination tub/shower

You can modernize a bathroom by installing a built-in bathtub and shower. Use existing water-supply and waste pipes to simplify the job.

First make sure you have room for a new tub. Most new bathtubs are 5 feet long (though you can get shorter models), designed to be closed in on three sides. If the available space is too small, you may have to move a wall (p. 404). Do this, however, only if it is a non-load-bearing wall. Excess space can be filled in by adding a ledge flush with the tub.

If the original tub was not closed in at all (see the small drawing, upper right), build a new wall at the head end of the tub, using 2 x 4 plates with studs on 16-inch centers. Notch all framing members for the pipes. Nail 1 x 4 tub supports to the three walls, having their tops level at the required height for the tub flanges to rest on. (Cast-iron tubs do not require any supports.)

Extend all piping as necessary. The water-supply lines are extended upward and attached 32 inches above the floor. The tub spout is centered 22 inches off the floor. The shower pipe is run up and elbowed out, usually 5 feet above the floor and centered on the tub width. Use a 2 x 4 support board to hold the faucet and shower outlets.

Next, lower the tub onto the supports and secure it with screws. The walls around the tub can be finished and tiled as desired.

Either build an access panel in the wall behind the head of the tub or use permanent connections for the tub drain. Faucets with large escutcheon plates should be used to permit faucet repairs from the tub wall. In a no-access installation, the trap installed should be of a kind that will permit auger-cleaning through the tub drain.

With an access panel, ordinary waste fittings and the existing tub trap may be used. The 1½-inch tub drainpipe slips into the similar-sized threaded pipe with a slipnut connection.

The last step in the installation is to put in the tub compartment parts of the drain, faucet, tub spigot, and shower head.

A flow-control shower head is recommended as a water-saving measure. When your installation work is finished, turn on the water and look for leaks. Caulk around the tub with silicone sealant; this will keep water from getting behind the wall. Finally, install the shower rod and the job is complete.

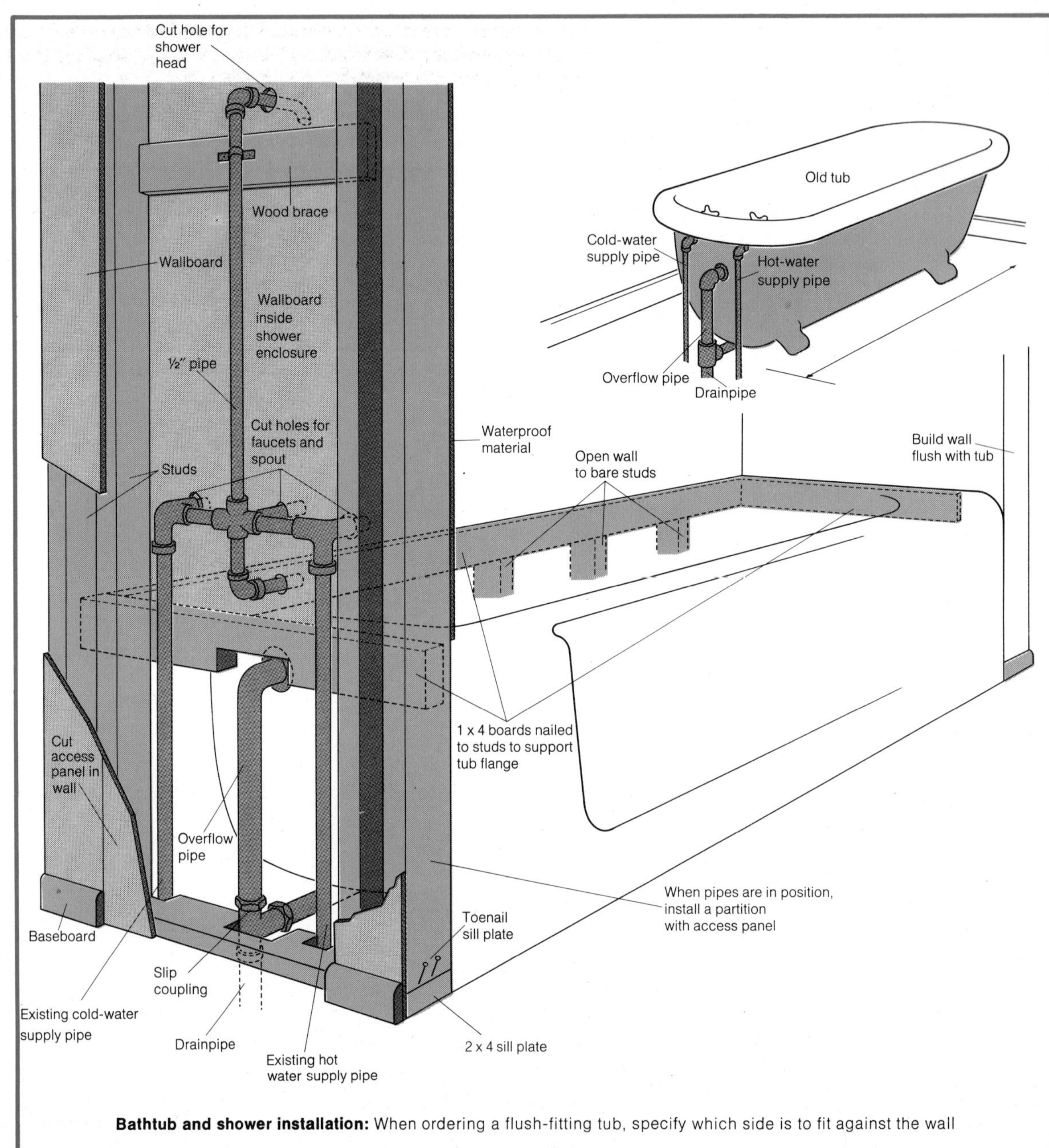

Bathtub and shower installation: When ordering a flush-fitting tub, specify which side is to fit against the wall

Installing a hot-water heater

When a hot-water heater fails, the usual cause is tank corrosion. The tank develops a pinhole and leaks water, which calls for a new water heater. It is simplest to replace the old heater with one of the same size using the same fuel. A change of fuel or increased tank size is possible, however. Some water heaters are connected to the house hot-water heating system and are merely storage tanks for water heated in coils as it flows through the boiler.

A hot-water heater is always full of water. Its temperature is controlled by thermostat, usually set at from 120 to 180 degrees F. As hot water is drawn off, cold water enters through a dip tube and flows to the bottom of the tank.

To remove the old water heater, turn off both water and fuel supply. Remove heater's fuel line (or electric wires) and flue pipe. Take apart the unions in the hot- and cold-water pipes. If there are none, saw through the pipes, remove the stubs, and replace with unions. Empty the tank, using a garden hose led to a drain. Turn the emptied tank on its side and roll it away. If it has a suitable temperature and pressure relief valve, remove that and reuse it. Set the new heater in place. If it is a different height, make the necessary adjustments in the water-supply pipes to connect it to the unions. Install the draft diverter (gas) or draft regulator (oil), normally supplied with the heater. Connect flue pipe, fuel line, or electric wires.

Fill heater with water before lighting burner or switching on electric heater, by turning on the water supply and opening a hot-water tap. When water begins flowing steadily, the tap may be closed and the heater fired up. Set the thermostat to normal (about 140 degrees). If hot water runs low or you have a dishwasher, you may have to increase the setting.

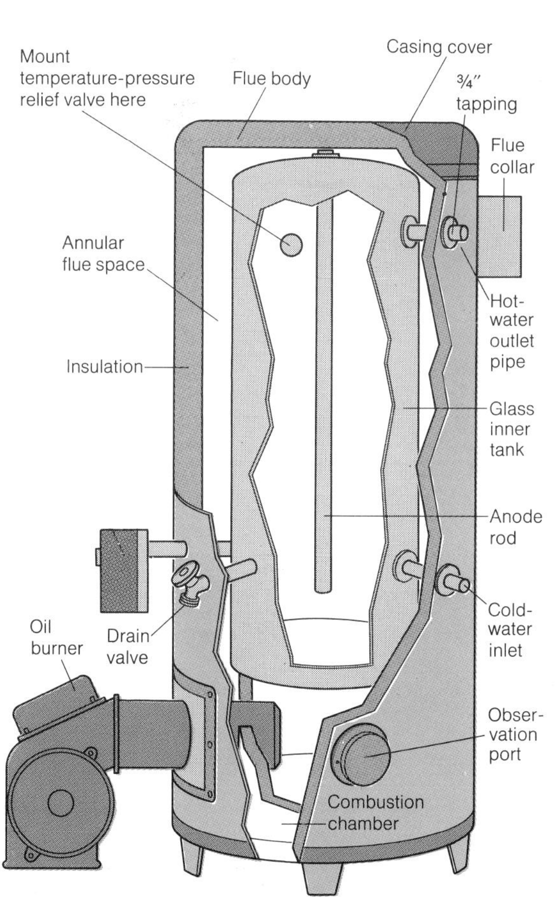

Oil-fired

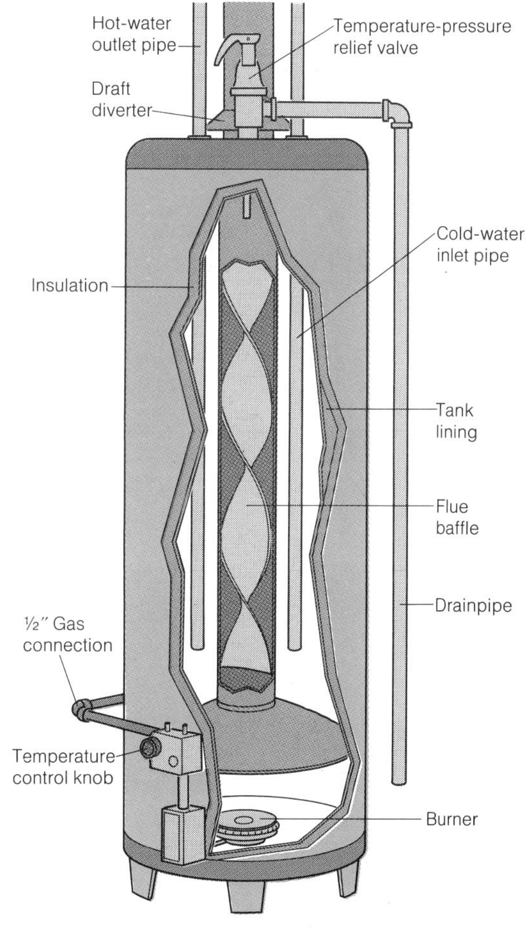

Gas-fired

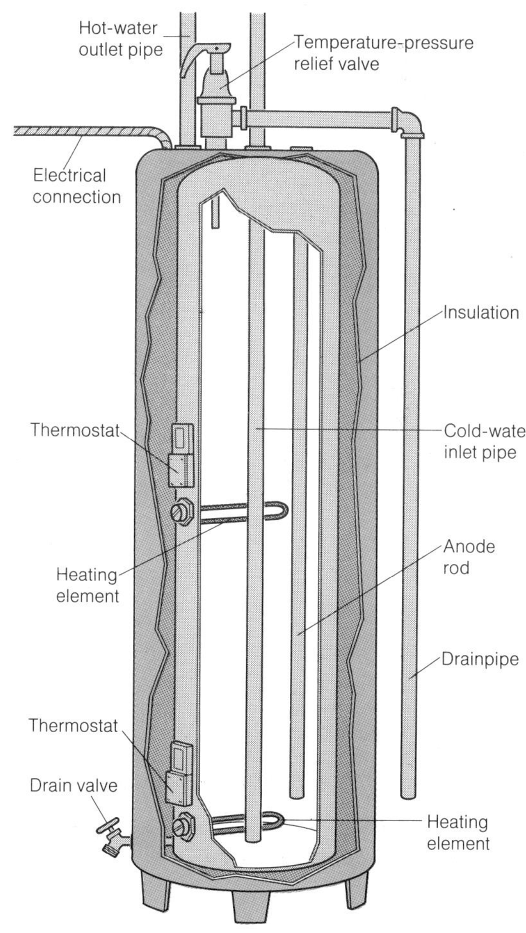

Electric-powered

Installing a clothes washer

An automatic clothes washer needs ½-inch hot- and cold-water supply pipes. Such a washer also requires a 1½-inch standpipe connection to the drainage system or basement floor drain for the disposal of waste water. If a floor drain is used, it must lead into a sewer or septic tank system. Also needed is a 117-volt outlet protected with a 15-ampere time-delay fuse or circuit breaker (p. 252).

Water-supply pipes should be equipped with air chambers to prevent water hammer when the electrically operated washer inlet valves snap shut after a fill or rinse cycle. Air chambers for clothes washers are usually one pipe size larger than the water-supply pipes and 24 inches long to enable them to cushion abrupt shutoffs.

Shutoff valves for the water-supply pipes are also necessary. Closing them when the washer is not in use takes the water pressure off the washer's valves. Shutoff valves also permit servicing without having to turn off the water supply for the entire house.

The washer must be electrically grounded. Most washers are grounded through a third prong on the plug of the electric cord. If the receptacle is not a three-wire grounding type, you can install a grounding adapter, but be sure to connect the adapter's green pigtail lead to a good ground, such as the center screw of the receptacle cover—provided that it is grounded (p. 257).

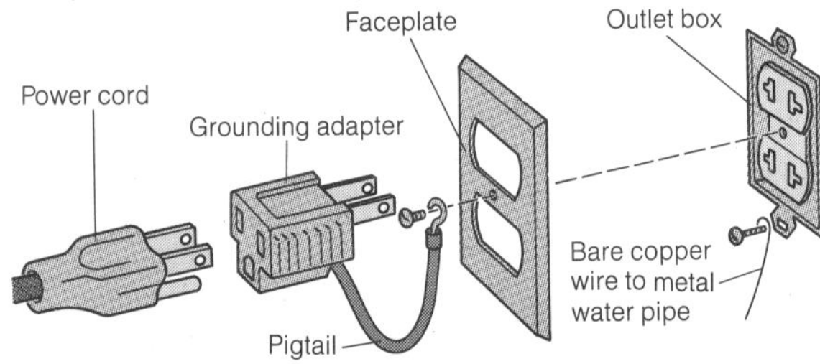

Pigtail adapter is used to ground 3-wire plug

After all the pipe and drain connections have been made, adjust the locknuts on the four bolts at the corners of the washer to level it. Use rubber pads between the bolts and the floor. Some manufacturers supply retractable casters with their washers at extra cost. If these are available, get them. Casters will enable you to roll the washer away from the wall for servicing and cleaning.

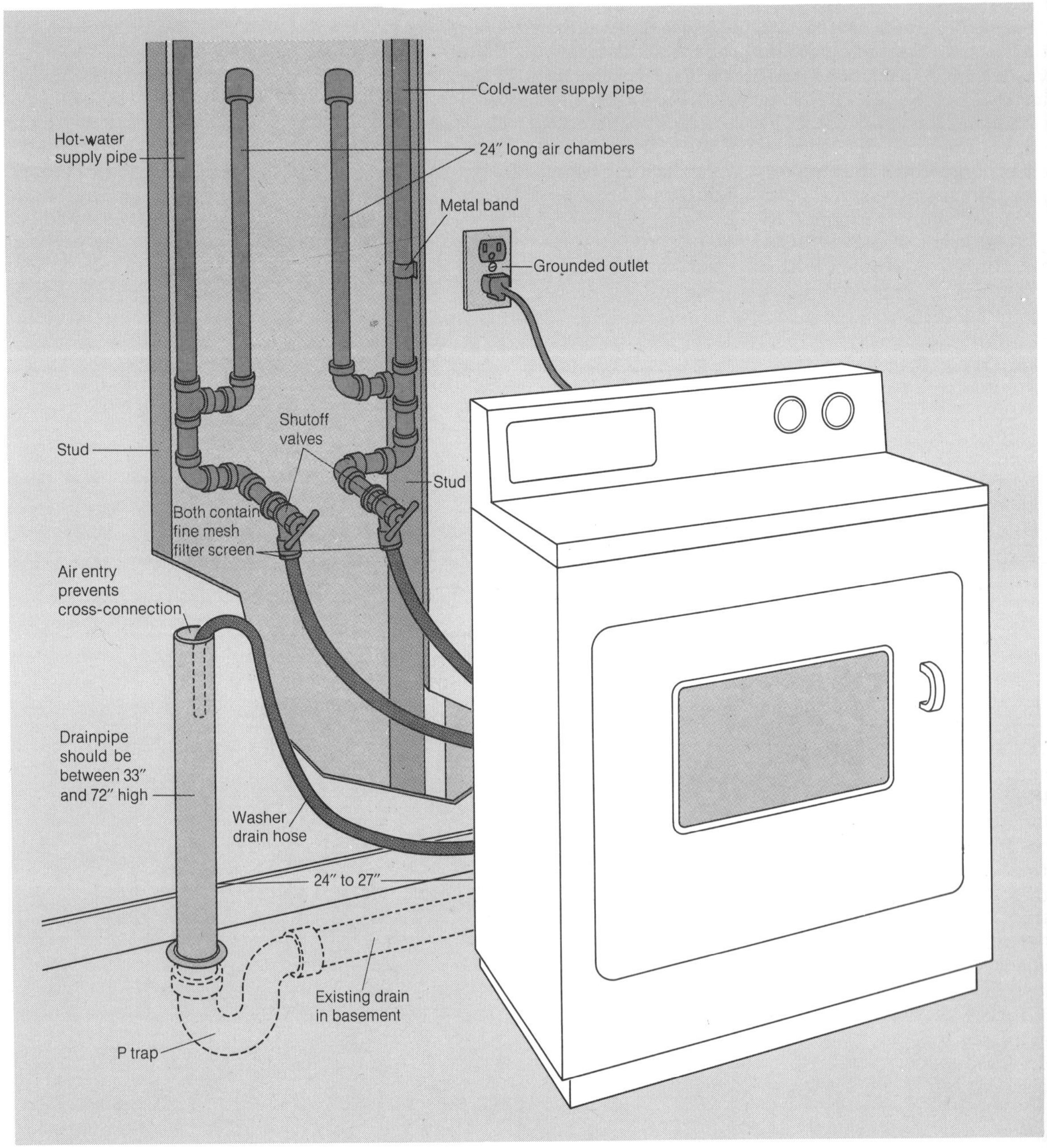

Repairs and maintenance

The most common complaint with dishwashers is that they are not washing properly. Before calling a serviceman to remedy this, study the machine's operating instructions to be sure you are following the precleaning, loading, and detergent specifications recommended by the manufacturer. If you are doing everything properly, the next most probable cause for poor washing is too low a water temperature.

Water flowing into a dishwasher should be between 140 and 160 degrees. Check the gauge on the hot-water tank or heater to see if it is set properly.

Dishwashers occasionally require some simple maintenance such as cleaning out the drain strainer. If a residue of coarse food particles is left on dishes following a wash cycle, a clogged strainer is the most likely cause. Rinse it under a tap.

Another common dishwasher complaint is about leaks around the door during the wash cycle. This is a minor problem usually found in older machines. The rubber seal, or gasket, around the door deteriorates with age and loses its sealing qualities. On most machines, this is a simple replacement task. Buy a new gasket through a dealer in the appropriate brand and install it by reversing the steps you took in removing the old one.

If the machine will not start at all, check the fuse or circuit breaker before calling a serviceman. If a newly replaced fuse blows immediately, you can be sure that servicing is required.

Faulty timer switches are often the cause of dishwasher breakdown. This switch controls the machine's various wash cycles and automatically regulates the length of time for each cycle. The following symptoms indicate a faulty timer switch: Machine will not turn on (fuses or circuit breakers okay); machine runs through one or more cycles, then stops; machine continues to operate on one cycle and will not switch to the next one.

Timer switch replacement is fairly simple. First check the machine's make and model number. Obtain a replacement switch from a local dealer.

The timer switch has numerous wires running to and from it. Reconnecting them will be easier if you draw a diagram showing the position of each before disconnecting them from the old switch.

For problems that do not seem to be related to the timer switch or cannot be solved by the simpler repairs mentioned, it is best to call in a repairman.

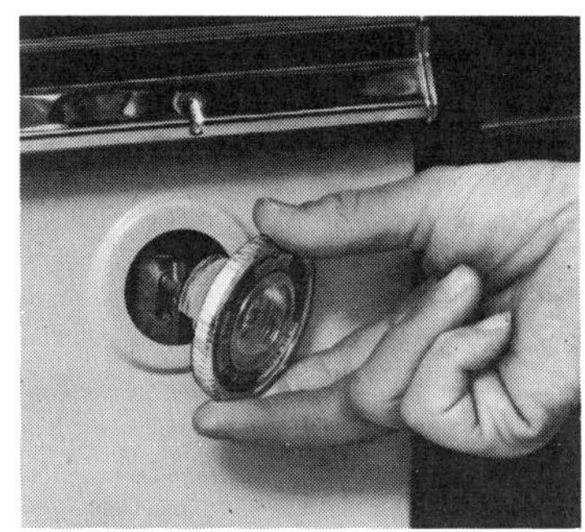

To expose the timer switch on most models, first remove the cycle control knob, then remove all screws holding the front panel in place.

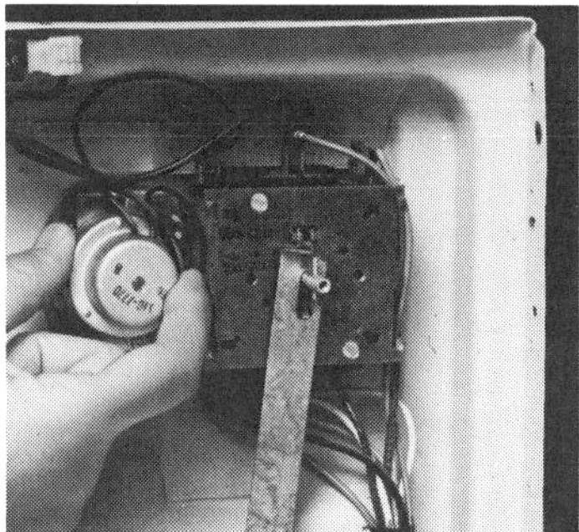

Unplug the machine before touching the timer. Place the wires one by one from the old switch onto the new one to avoid wrong connections.

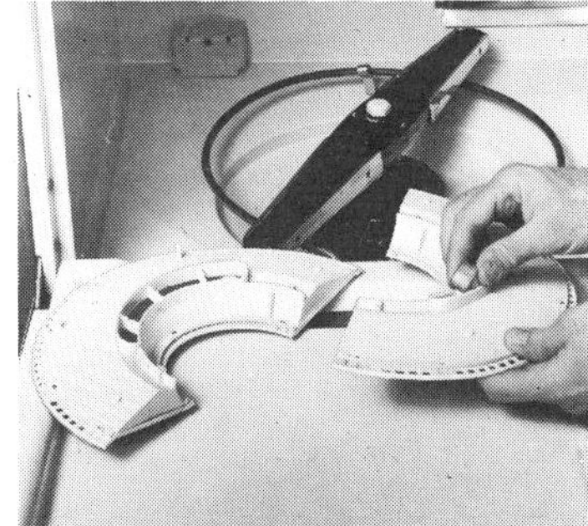

Clogged strainers are easily remedied by removing the unit for cleaning. Most units are plastic or metal and can be cleaned with a tap rinse.

Dishwasher service chart

TROUBLE	POSSIBLE CAUSE	REMEDY
Machine fails to start	Door partly open	Close door securely
	Defective switch or timer	Replace
	Check switch linkage	Adjust, if necessary
	Open circuit	Check fuse or circuit breaker
Dishes do not come clean	Wrong soap used	Use only recommended detergent
	Improper loading	Load dishes as per instructions
	Not properly pre-cleaned	Pre-clean dishes
	Low water temperature	Adjust water-heater thermostat
	Not enough water	Unclog water inlets
	Strainer clogged	Remove strainer and clean
	Timer faulty	Replace timer unit
	Solenoid coil inoperative	Replace solenoid coil (call serviceman)
	Measuring coil inoperative or out of adjustment	Replace or repair as required (call serviceman)
Water does not stay in tank	Leaking drain valve	Tighten flange on drain valve
	Inlet valve not opening	Adjust linkage, have solenoid repaired or replaced as required
Machine noisy	Solenoid core not centered in coil	Realign core to assure perpendicular and centered action
	Motor out of alignment	Realign motor (call serviceman)
	Vibration	Machine not on solid footing
	Impeller scraping against impeller screen	Check and adjust as necessary
Door or cover will not close	Door or cover seal binding inside of tank	Loosen screws on seal retainer and reset to retain seal
Insufficient fill	Low water pressure	Check water pressure at faucets. Check inlet at machine
Slow draining	Drain solenoid inoperative	Check and replace drain solenoid (call serviceman)
Dishes do not dry	Incorrect water temperature	Adjust water thermostat to 150°F
	Leaking inlet valve	Replace valve-seat washer
	Inoperative heating element	Turn timer to heating cycle; check if heating element is working. If not, timer may be faulty. If timer okay, problem is with element
Tarnishing silverware	Chemicals in water	Try reducing amount of detergent. A water softener or mineral filter may be required in areas having hard water

Installing a sump pump

Sump pumps suck out rain or waste water—from around a foundation, from under the basement floor, and from basement floor drains—that has collected in a sump pit. A pump is needed when the sewer-line level is above the basement floor. Often, a pit and pump are used to cure basement flooding. A pit is usually made of 24-inch-diameter sewer tile set vertically on a gravel base below the basement floor.

When the float is forced up by rising water, it reaches a stop that turns on the pump motor. As the water level drops, the float moves down to another stop which turns the motor off. Stops are adjustable and can be set for the desired control level. All sump pumps have built-in float-operated switches. Strainer screens remove solids that might clog the pump.

To connect a sump pump, lead 1¼-inch flexible plastic pipe from pump's discharge outlet to cellar drain. The pump sometimes discharges into a slop sink instead of directly into sewer; pumps that drain only basement floors and foundations usually can discharge into a storm drain, seepage pit, or outside to the ground. Install 1¼-inch brass check valve in discharge line, with its arrow pointing away from pump, to prevent backflow of water into pump.

Set the float level as described in instructions that come with pump. Make a cover of ¾-inch exterior plywood. Plug the pump into a 117-volt 3-wire grounding outlet and test the pump's action.

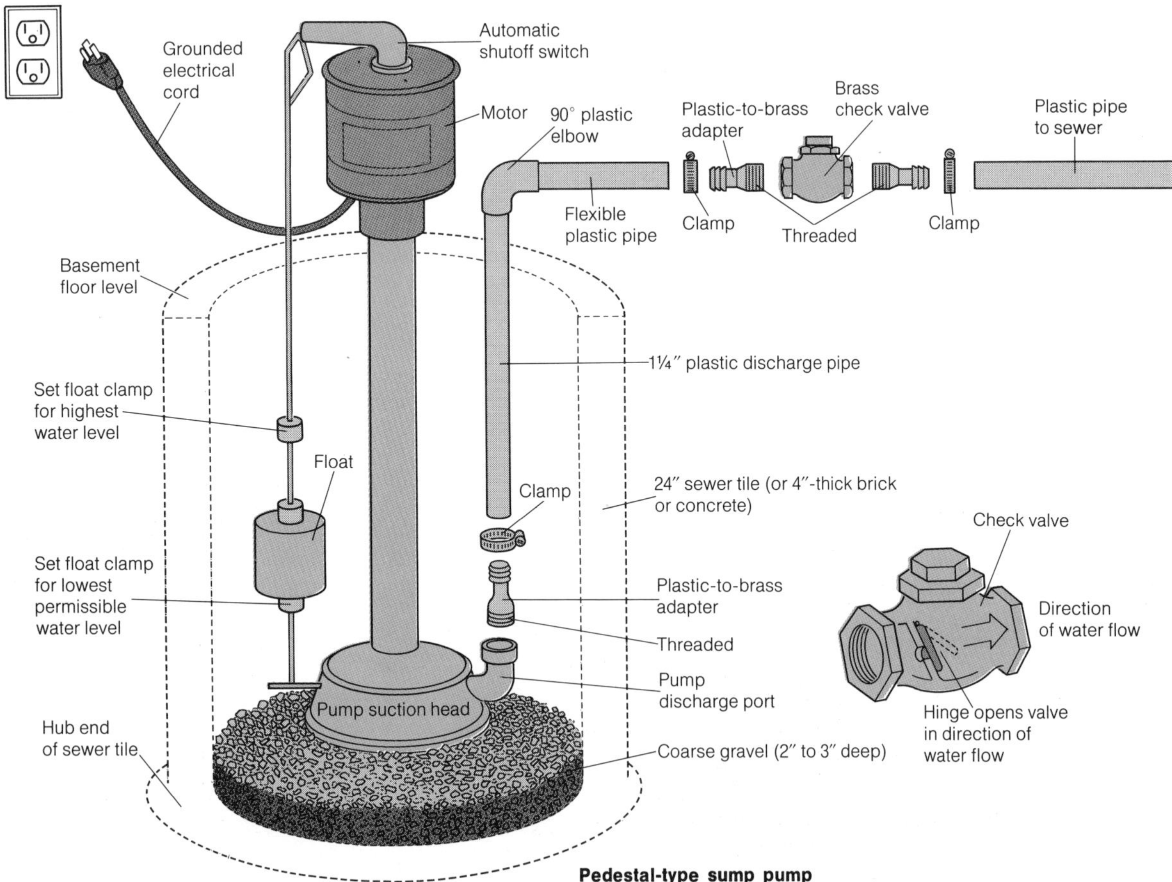

Pedestal-type sump pump

Portable sump pump

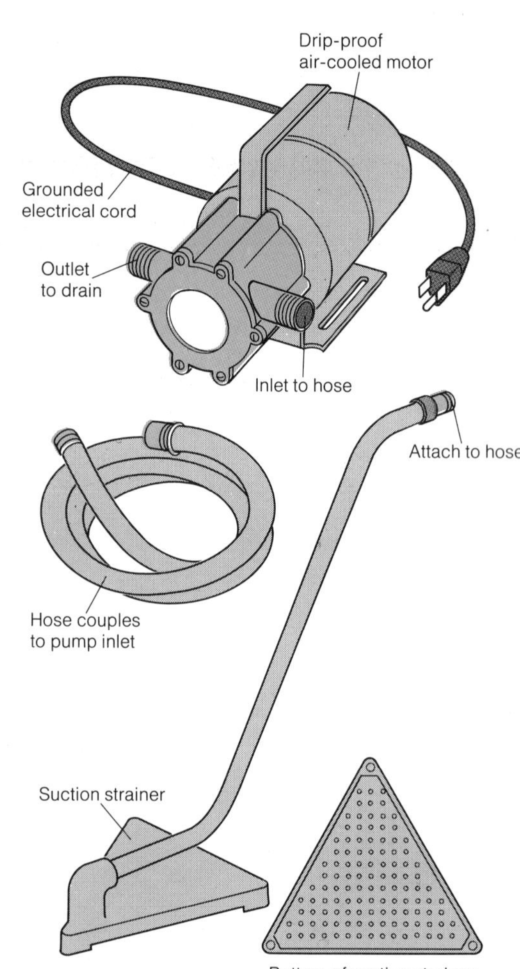

Pumping water into or out of basements, cisterns, ponds, pits, septic systems, and boats is easy with an integral water pump-power unit. The handiest ones are self-priming and will pump even trash-laden water. Pumps are designed to accept standard garden-hose fittings. Two hoses are needed, one for suction, another for discharge. Suction lifts from water to pump should not be more than 20 feet in elevation. Discharge lifts can usually be 30 feet or more above the pump. Suction hose should be fitted with a strainer to screen out large debris. You can get an attachment that sucks up puddles like a vacuum cleaner.

Pressure-reducing valve

When house water pressure is more than 60 pounds per square inch (psi), a pressure-reducing valve is often introduced to improve plumbing performance. Too much pressure encourages faucets to leak, increases plumbing system noises, and wastes water at fixtures. Also, the chances of damage from water hammer (p.224) are much greater when water pressure is high.

First test the water pressure by connecting a pressure gauge to a hose faucet. (It costs less to buy the gauge than to hire a plumber to do this.)

If the pressure tests at more than 60 psi, you should install a pressure-reducer. This valve is smaller than a water meter and is installed in the entrance line beyond the main shutoff valve. It contains a union for easy hookup. You can then adjust the pressure for 50 psi, or whatever level you wish.

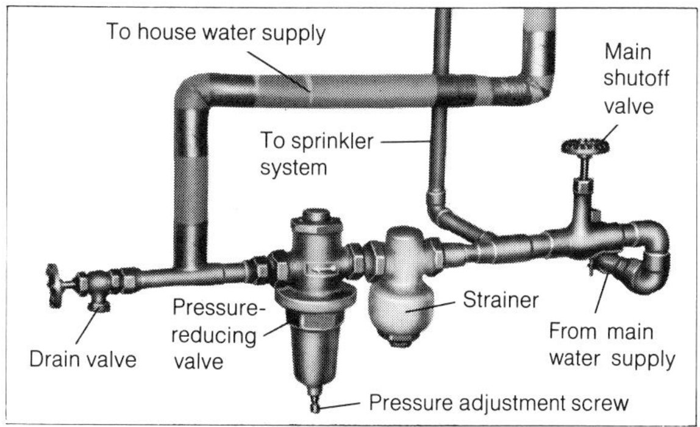

Pressure regulator lowers and steadies pressure that is high and varying. Most are factory-adjusted to 50 psi but can be reset lower. Install beyond main shutoff valve. Branch to lawn sprinkler system should be taken off before regulator.

Up-flush sink

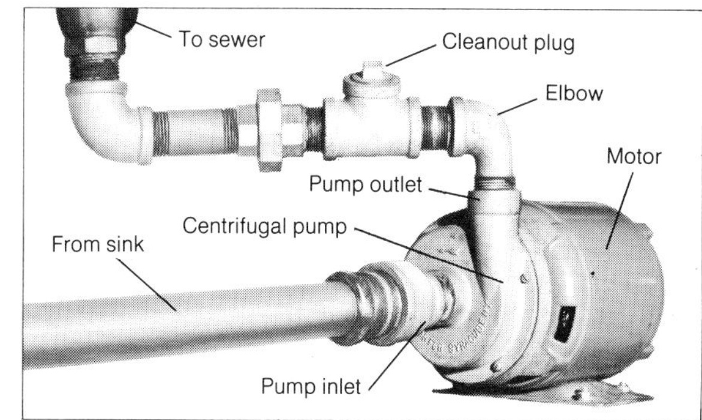

Sink below house sewer-line level will require a pump in order to discharge waste water into the sewer line. A pump, combined with a motor, is available for this purpose. Motor is switched on only when the sink is in use.

Up-flush toilet

The up-flush toilet lets you put a toilet in the basement, even if the sewer is above basement-floor level. The unit needs no pipes below the basement floor. Instead, water enters the toilet's patented flushing system through a double-acting flush valve supplied by a ½-inch or larger cold-water pipe. A vacuum breaker on the flush valve prevents any backflow of contaminated water. When the flush lever is pushed, the flush valve sends water through a small flexible pipe to a disintegrating jet located on the T fitting behind the white porcelain bowl. This breaks up solids. Next the valve switches to its flush mode and sends water to the flushing jet. This carries the liquefied waste out of the bowl and up through the sewer riser to a gravity drain. Required water pressure is 40 psi for a maximum 10-foot lift.

Everything from the water-supply pipe to the sewage riser pipe is furnished with the fixture. Plumbing for it is not difficult to provide. Full instructions come with every toilet and should be carefully followed. In general, this is the procedure:

Set the bowl in wood putty at its base to make it rock-free. Mount the flush valve solidly 6 inches or more above the bowl and connect it with a union to the water-supply pipe. Run the riser to full height, then into a gravity drain. Turn on the water and flush several times to clear air from the system.

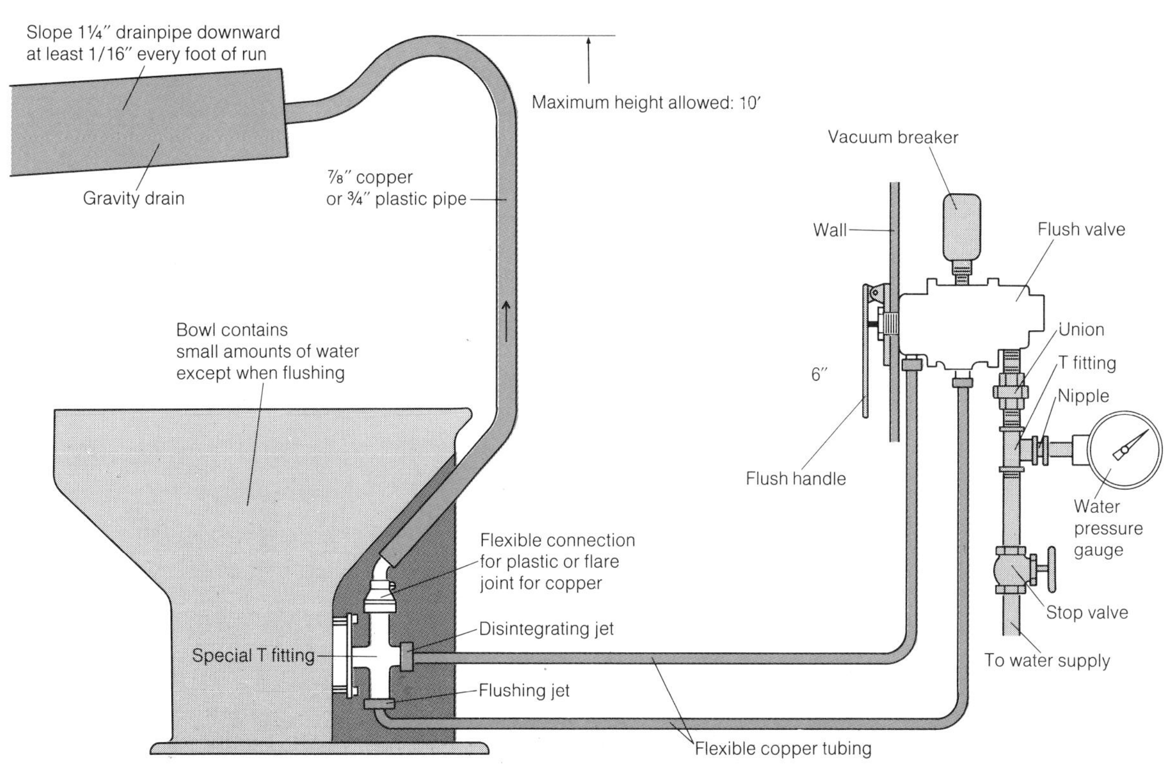

Up-flush toilet uses only 2½ gallons of water per flush. It needs no pipes beneath the basement floor.

Home water treatment

Softening water

Rain is natural water in its purest form. As the water filters through the earth, however, it absorbs calcium, magnesium, and other minerals. When such materials are not dissolved in the water but suspended in it, the water is called "hard."

Hardness is often measured in grains per gallon of calcium carbonate as follows:

Less than 1	soft
1 to 3.5	moderately hard
3.5 to 7.0	hard
7.0 to 10.5	very hard
More than 10.5	extremely hard

Most American and Canadian water supplies are in the 3-to-30-grains-per-gallon range. Hard water takes more soaps and detergents, causes bathtub rings, streaks on dishes, dingy laundry, tough cooked vegetables, and clogged pipes.

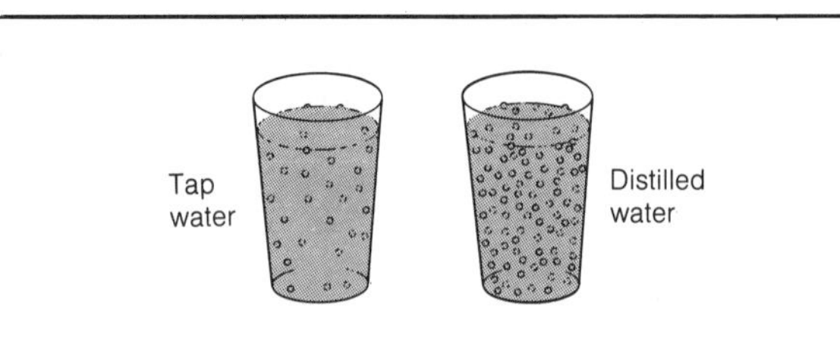

You can test water for hardness by comparing it with bottled distilled water. Put distilled water and tap water into two separate glasses. Add 10 drops of liquid dishwashing detergent to each glass and shake to make suds. Compare the suds level in each glass. The tap water is hard if it makes less suds than the distilled water. Add 10 more drops of detergent to the tap water and shake the samples again. If the suds level is now the same in both glasses, your water is twice as hard as pure water. If it takes 40 drops of detergent in the tap water to equalize the suds, your water is four times as hard, and so on.

Other water problems are red iron (visible), colloidal iron (invisible), manganese (black deposits), hydrogen sulfide (rotten egg odor), corrosive water (containing acid, oxygen), turbidity, fluorides (some may be desirable), and nitrates (poisonous).

Most water problems can be solved with the proper equipment. The first step is to find out what treatment, if any, is needed. Any equipment supplier can have a test made for you, often at no cost.

The most common water-treatment process is softening, accomplished by running the water through a mineral or synthetic resin compound that exchanges troublesome magnesium and calcium ions —electrically charged particles—for trouble-free sodium ions. The compound is regenerated by passing salt water through it. High sodium concentration in the salt water forces out the calcium and magnesium ions, they are flushed away, and the softener is ready for another cycle.

Water softeners can be purchased, or rented on a service basis. A rented unit is picked up regularly and taken to a plant for regeneration. The owner of a unit must regenerate it himself by adding salt.

Some softeners have sensors to indicate when regeneration is needed, and do it automatically. In semi-automatic softeners, it is handled by a timer.

Only some of the water in a house requires softening. Hose water, and sometimes water to toilets, need not be soft. Sometimes only hot water is softened; in such cases, people on sodium-free diets, who should not drink softened water, can drink the system's unsoftened cold water. If all water is softened, they may need a separate drinking water tap.

Installing a water softener is easy, using flexible pipe. Cut through the water service pipe beyond the water meter, main shutoff valve, and branches to outdoor faucets. If all household water is to be softened, make the cut before the pipe reaches the water heater. If only hot water is to be softened, make the opening in the cold-water line to the water heater. Install elbows on both ends of the cut pipe, and suitable adapters. Run one pipe from the water entrance pipe to the softener inlet and another pipe from the water-supply side to the softener outlet. Turn on the water and you have softened water.

Waste water from the regenerator may be run out on the ground or into the house sewer through a trap. It will not affect a septic tank system.

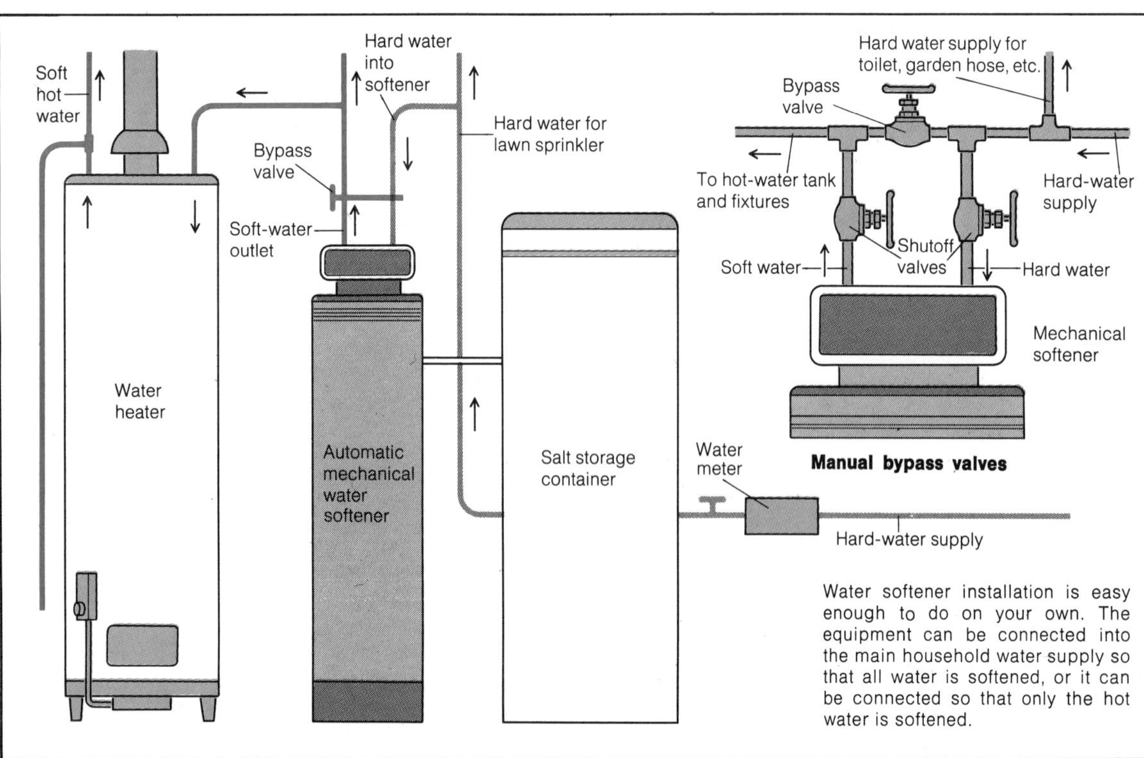

Water softener installation is easy enough to do on your own. The equipment can be connected into the main household water supply so that all water is softened, or it can be connected so that only the hot water is softened.

Removing impurities from water

Water softeners will remove some iron, but large amounts of iron in water call for a special iron filter, which removes both dissolved and suspended iron. The iron filter contains a mineral that traps iron and must be regenerated periodically by backwashing to rinse out the collected oxidized iron. Most iron filters work automatically. When used with water that has a low oxygen content, an iron filter may require flushing with potassium permanganate. This is poisonous and should be flushed out thoroughly before the iron filter is put back into service.

Well water containing sulfides can be cleared of them with an iron filter used in combination with an activated-carbon filter. As a general rule, an activated-carbon filter attaches to the under-sink piping or to the kitchen faucet.

Water that is only slightly contaminated can be treated with an automatic chlorine feeder. The feeder injects chlorine into the water main line to kill bacteria and precipitate some undesirable solid particles. A chlorine feeder used in conjunction with a sediment filter makes a good iron remover. A sediment filter uses sand and gravel or a replaceable cartridge to remove suspended particles. A chlorine feeder, combined with an activated-carbon filter, does a good job of improving sulphur-water.

Corrosive water can be corrected with a neutralizing filter and a polyphosphate feeder, in the main water line. A neutralizing filter injects agents into the water to reduce corrosiveness. The filter needs occasional replenishment and cleaning. A phosphate feeder dispenses phosphate crystals, which are slowly dissolved into the water. These form a protective coating on pipes and water heaters, slowing the process of corrosion. Of course, the phosphate crystals need periodic replenishing.

Cloudy water can sometimes be cleared with a water softener. A better solution is a sediment filter used in combination with an activated-carbon filter. A serious clouding problem requires a chemical feeder, plus a sediment filter.

Bad-tasting water can be improved by filtration through an activated-carbon filter. Brackish, salty water presents special treatment problems, as does water that must be delivered sodium-free or free of other minerals. Two high-quality water-treatment methods will deal with problems of this kind: Reverse osmosis and deionization.

Reverse osmosis makes use of a cellulose acetate membrane to separate water from the impurities it contains. The impurities end up on one side of the membrane and are flushed away. The water that leaves the opposite side of the membrane is pure. A reverse-osmosis unit costs about $200, and will treat enough water for the average family's drinking and cooking needs, steam-iron-filling, and auto battery replenishment. There are no moving parts and there is nothing to regenerate. Normal household water pressure supplies all the energy necessary to operate the unit. About every two years the membrane needs replacing, at a cost of about $40. A reverse-osmosis unit is usually connected into the kitchen cold-water line under the sink.

A water deionizer can remove practically all dissolved solids, rendering water pure enough for most routine uses. The process is accomplished in two steps by means of two different ion-exchange resins. These may be in two containers or just one. The first mineral is the same as the one used in water softening, except that it is charged with hydrogen ions rather than sodium ions. As water passes through it, the positively charged hydrogen ions are released into the water, and the positive mineral ions—iron, carbonates, etc.—are held. The water then passes immediately through another bed of resin that has been charged with negative hydroxide ions. These ions are released into the water, and the negative mineral ions—chlorides, bicarbonates, etc.—are picked up and held. Hydrogen and hydroxide ions released into the water unite to form additional pure water.

These resins, like those used in softening, become exhausted and their ions must be regenerated by what is essentially a plant process: A strong acid is used to regenerate the first mineral, a strong alkali to regenerate the second.

Though it is invaluable in certain situations, deionization of water is costly. Deionization units, also called demineralizers, come ready for connection to plumbing or for faucet attachment. The latter are generally discarded when they are used up.

Once you have identified the impurity problem in your water, one or more of the aforementioned water-conditioning units can be counted on to correct it. You can install a water softener and any of the filters yourself. The feeder units should be installed and serviced by professionals.

Activated carbon filter

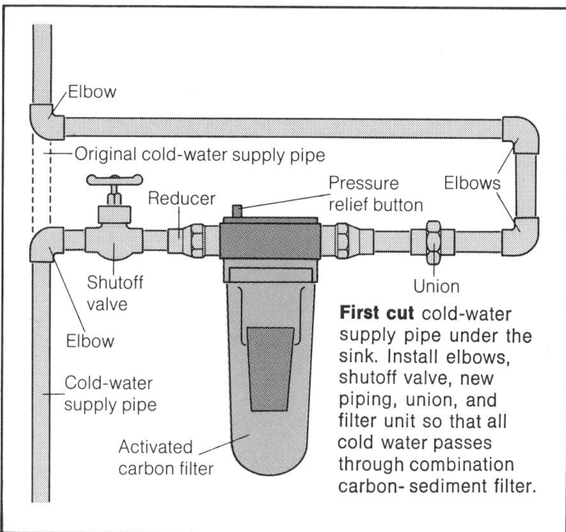

First cut cold-water supply pipe under the sink. Install elbows, shutoff valve, new piping, union, and filter unit so that all cold water passes through combination carbon- sediment filter.

Reverse-osmosis unit

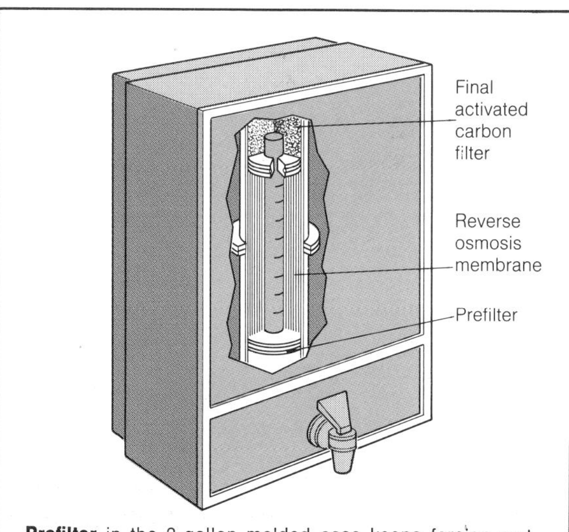

Prefilter in the 3-gallon molded case keeps foreign matter away from reverse-osmosis membrane. Membrane is wound spirally around a central core and allows only purified water to pass through. Final activated-carbon filter removes any odor or taste that might be left in water. Unit requires little plumbing.

Sewage disposal

Private disposal systems

Because of the amount of digging involved, it is not likely that you will want to attempt to build your own sewage disposal system. The job involves a sewer line, septic tank, and absorption field. Enough information is given here that you can plan an installation and discuss it knowledgeably with local health authorities who must approve the system.

Unless the water-absorption characteristics of your soil are known, you will be required to conduct what is called a percolation test. To do it, dig about six holes where the proposed absorption field is to be located. Use a post-hole digger and dig down to the depth of the drainage trenches, usually 18 to 36 inches. Fill the holes with water. After 24 hours, adjust the water level in each hole to about 6 inches deep. Then insert a yardstick and clock how many minutes it takes for the water level to fall 1 inch. The table gives the minimum square feet of absorption area you will need for each bedroom in your house.

In laying out the septic tank and absorption field, observe the code-specified distances to houses, wells, property lines, and trees. A watertight sewer line leads from the house to the septic tank. This can be cast-iron pipe, solvent-welded plastic pipe, self-sealing vitrified clay tile, tapered-joint fiber pipe, or self-sealing cement-asbestos pipe. The size is usually 4 inches; the slope is ¼ inch per foot. Codes often call for the use of cast-iron pipe within about 5 feet of house.

Minutes for water to fall 1 inch	Absorption area required in square feet for each bedroom
2 (or less)	85
3	100
4	115
5	125
10	165
15	190
30	250
60	330
More than 60	**Not suitable for trenches**

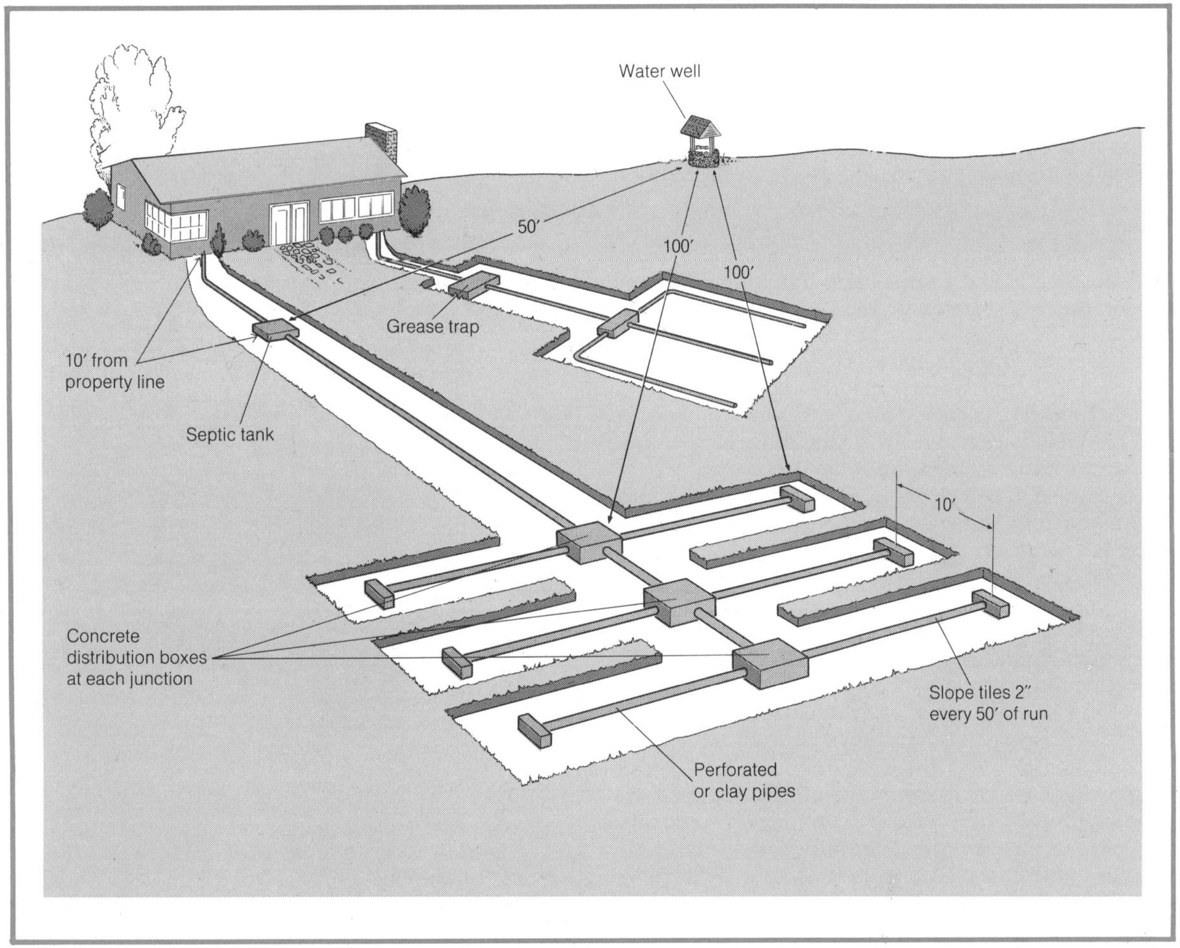

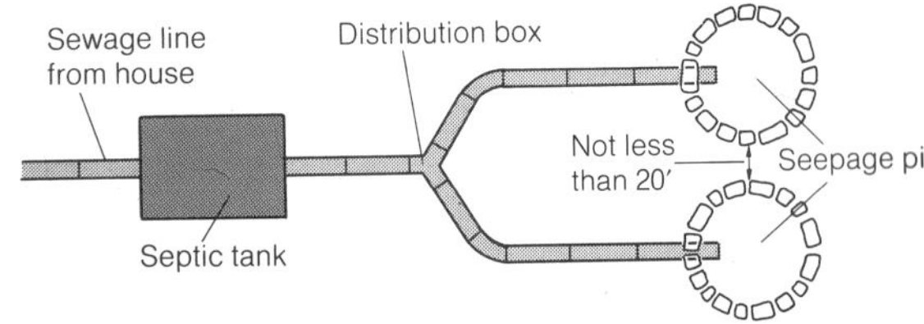

Seepage pits for areas too small for a drain field

The septic tank can be precast concrete, asphalt-coated steel, concrete block, redwood, clay tile, or brick. In it sewage settles and decomposes. The tank's outlet is lower than its inlet to keep sewage from backing up into the sewer line. The entire tank is below ground. When it becomes necessary to clean the tank, a hole is dug at the access cover and the cover removed. Locate the tank where a truck can get to it for the purpose of cleaning it out.

A septic tank must be sized to suit the house, as indicated in the table. The sizes given take into account use of such waste-producing appliances as garbage disposers, clothes washers, and dishwashers.

Codes vary on what wastes can go into a septic tank. Some codes require separate grease traps for kitchen wastes. Some will allow you to run toilet wastes into the septic tank and conduct other wastes directly to the drainage field. Most require that all wastes be handled through the septic tank.

Installing a septic tank

Let a contractor install the septic system. He will probably use a tractor-mounted machine, called a **backhoe,** to dig the pit for the septic tank and drainage trenches leading away from the tank. A layer of gravel or crushed stone will then be spread in the trenches. A watertight line will be laid from the septic tank to a small buried concrete vault called a **distribution box.** Its purpose is to regulate the flow of septic tank effluent among two or more drainage lines. These lines will be laid on gravel, either level or sloped away from the distribution box no more than 6 inches every 100 feet.

The drainage line may be of 4-inch concrete or clay tiles or perforated plastic or fiber pipe. The 1-foot-long tiles are laid with slight spaces between them to permit seepage. Perforated pipes come in 10-foot lengths. Their holes permit seepage. Drainage lines are not meant to be watertight.

Once set, the drainage tiles will be covered with gravel. A layer of building paper may be laid over the top of the stones to prevent infiltration of the soil backfill. After the system has been inspected, it will be covered with soil and graded. When this is done,

Number of bedrooms	Minimum tank capactiy
2 or less	750 gallons
3	900 gallons
4	1000 gallons
5	1250 gallons

you can plant it with grass and moisture-loving trees.

On hilly or sloping land, a different type of drainage field, called a **serial distribution field,** must be built. To make it, level trenches are dug along contours of land, each lower than the next. Connections between trenches are arranged to transfer effluent to a lower trench only when effluent depth in the trench above reaches the top of the gravel fill. Thus, the first trench in the system must work to full capacity before the second trench receives any effluent. No distribution box is needed with the serial distribution system.

No attempt need be made to lay the septic tank and its drainage lines below frost depth. Warm house water entering the system and the heat of bacterial action keep the whole system warm.

A new septic tank needs no special treatment to start the bacterial action. Each year a sludge depth should be checked by removing the access cover and inserting a stick into the tank. The stick should be

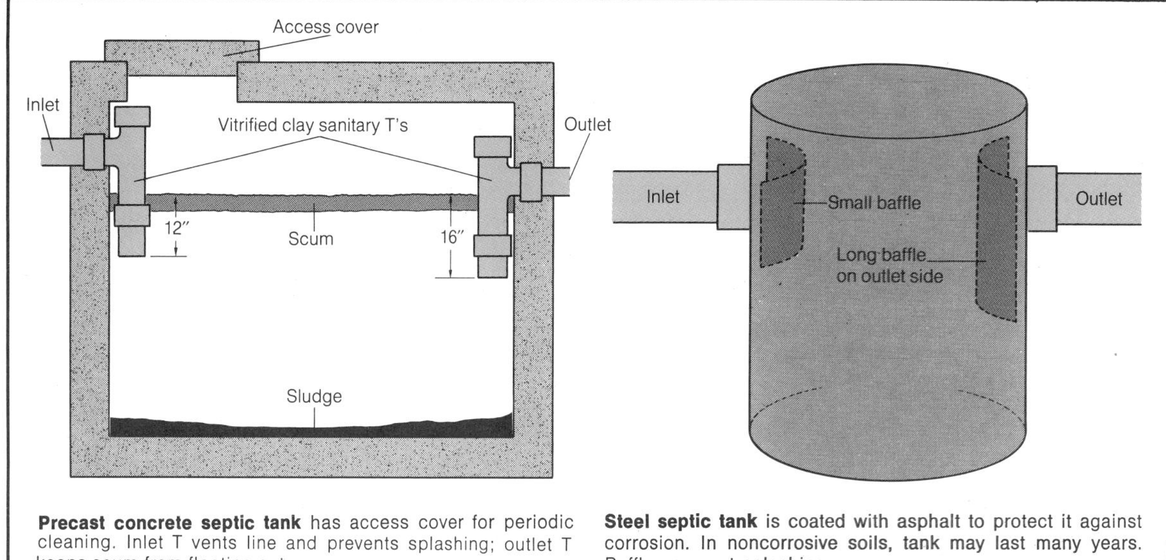

Precast concrete septic tank has access cover for periodic cleaning. Inlet T vents line and prevents splashing; outlet T keeps scum from floating out.

Steel septic tank is coated with asphalt to protect it against corrosion. In noncorrosive soils, tank may last many years. Baffles prevent splashing.

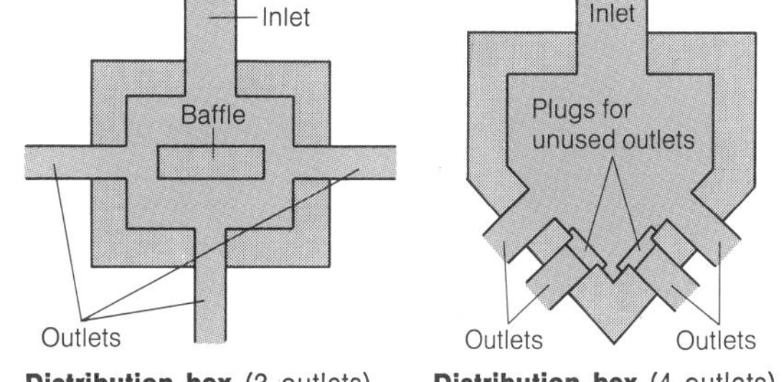

Distribution box (3 outlets) **Distribution box** (4 outlets)

pushed to the bottom of the tank and pulled up. If the end is first wrapped with a light-colored rag, the sludge depth will show on it. The allowable sludge accumulation in inches is shown in table at right.

When the sludge reaches these levels, the tank should be pumped out. For this operation, it is best to call in a septic tank cleaning company.

Chemicals are sometimes added to sewage to speed up precipitation. The choice of chemicals depends upon the sewage and local conditions. Frequently used chemicals are lime and sulphate of alumina. Yeast is sometimes added to speed up the bacteriological action. Mix the yeast with warm water in a pail and empty it into the toilet bowl. A half-pound of brewer's yeast is sufficient.

Cesspools: The chief difference between a cesspool and a septic tank is that a cesspool does not make any provision for the breakdown and treatment of the sewage. It is simply a collecting tank that permits raw sewage to be leached into the ground. Cesspools are highly unsanitary and can be a menace to health. If a cesspool is located near an underground source of water, it will gradually pollute the water and make it unfit and dangerous to drink. Also, polluted matter will ultimately find its way up to the

DISTANCE FROM BOTTOM OF TANK OUTLET TO TOP OF SLUDGE

Tank capacity (gallons)	Liquid depth (feet) 3	4	5
500	11"	16"	21"
750	6"	10"	13"
900	4"	7"	10"
1000	4"	6"	8"

Note: Sludge depth increases slower in tanks with large bottom areas.

surface, where it will decompose and emit foul odors. For these reasons, codes often ban cesspools.

Sewage disposal

Installing a seepage pit

Steeply sloped, hilly land or a small lot may not be suitable for trench-type absorption of septic tank and treatment-plant effluent. In such cases, a seepage pit may be advisable. The arrangement may consist of one or more holes in the ground lined with stone, bricks, or concrete blocks. There the effluent is absorbed into the ground. Seepage pits are characterized by earth bottoms where some of the seepage takes place and porous sides where more of it occurs. Pits without strong walls are filled with stones. Removable covers permit inspection and cleaning, if necessary. Inlet T's in the pits vent the tile lines and cut down on splashing.

Seepage pits are fed through open-joint tile lines coming from a distribution box, just like those in a trench-type absorption field. Seepage pits may be any size. They need not be round. A huge one could be scooped out with a bulldozer, filled with stones, and then have a thin covering of backfill pushed over it. Much of the seepage in a smaller pit takes place through its walls, which makes larger pits less efficient per square foot of area. Therefore, to do its job, a large pit must cover a much greater area than the total of several smaller seepage pits.

A seepage pit can be built even on a steep slope. As soon as tree roots find the pit and grow into it, they will help absorb effluent. Unwalled, stone-filled pits are sometimes put near trees to encourage root infiltration. Absorption field tile runs sometimes end in seepage pits that handle overflow.

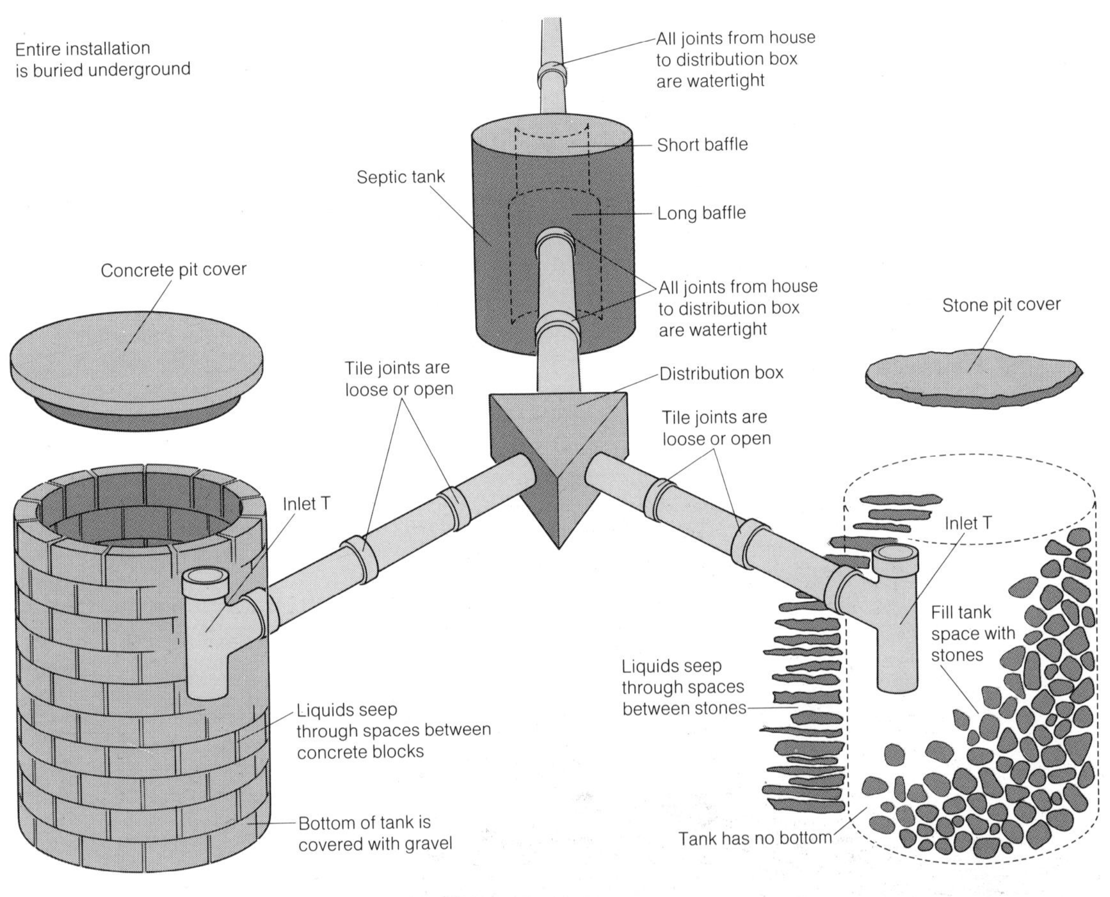

Concrete pit is made of concrete block with uncemented joints

Stone pit has mortarless stone walls and is filled with gravel

Sloping drain fields

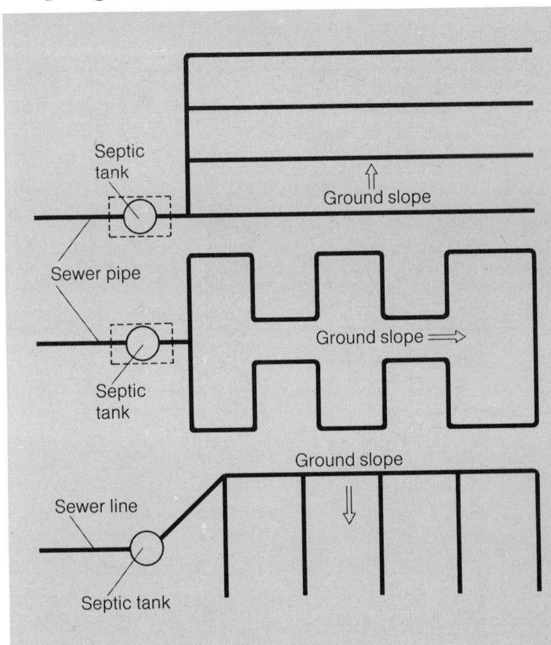

Relatively level drain fields can be built on land that slopes no more than 6 inches every 100 feet. Hilly or steeply sloping land requires a **series drain field** constructed by digging level trenches along contours of land, each trench lower than the one preceding it. Connections between trenches are arranged to transfer liquids to a lower trench only when the liquid depth in the trench above reaches the top of the gravel fill. Thus each trench overflows into the next lower one. No distribution box is needed with a series drain field. In this type of drain field, the outlet of the septic tank must be at least 4 inches lower than the inlet.

section 8: Electricity: Solving power problems safely

The intent of the section on electricity is simple: To save you from feeling helpless when the power goes off or a vital appliance stops working. It succeeds by putting a complex subject in understandable terms and easy-to-follow order, with detailed drawings every step of the way. The section tells you everything you'll ever need or want to know: How the system works; how to improve it, add to it, make emergency repairs; and — perhaps most useful of all — how to deal knowledgeably with an electrician.

contents

Fuses and circuit breakers

The job they do

Fuses and circuit breakers might be called the watchmen of your electrical system. When a fuse blows or a circuit breaker trips, it is telling you that something is wrong. What is wrong may be two bare electric wires touching because of worn insulation; too many appliances on the same circuit; or an overloaded motor. It makes no sense to replace a blown fuse or reset a circuit breaker unless you have found and corrected the cause of the trouble. If the condition exists when you make the replacement, you will blow another fuse or trip a circuit breaker again.

The most common cause of fuse-blowing is too many appliances on the same circuit. If a fuse blows when you push down the toaster handle, there is a good chance that you may be operating, say, a broiler or an electric iron on the same circuit. If you are, unplug the iron or broiler, and then replace the fuse or reset the circuit breaker.

A fuse that has been blown by a short circuit will usually have a blackened or discolored mica window. A fuse that has blown because of an overload will usually show a clear window, but there will be a break in the flat metal strip. The circuit breaker just flips to the "tripped" (off) position when there is an overload or short circuit.

It is practical to keep spare fuses handy near the fuse box. When you replace a fuse, be sure that the new one is of the same capacity. In other words, if you blow a 15-ampere fuse, replace it with a 15-ampere fuse, never a 20 or 25.

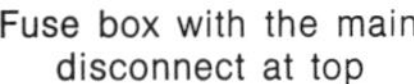

Fuse box with the main disconnect at top

Circuit breaker panel with main disconnect

Types of fuses and circuit breakers

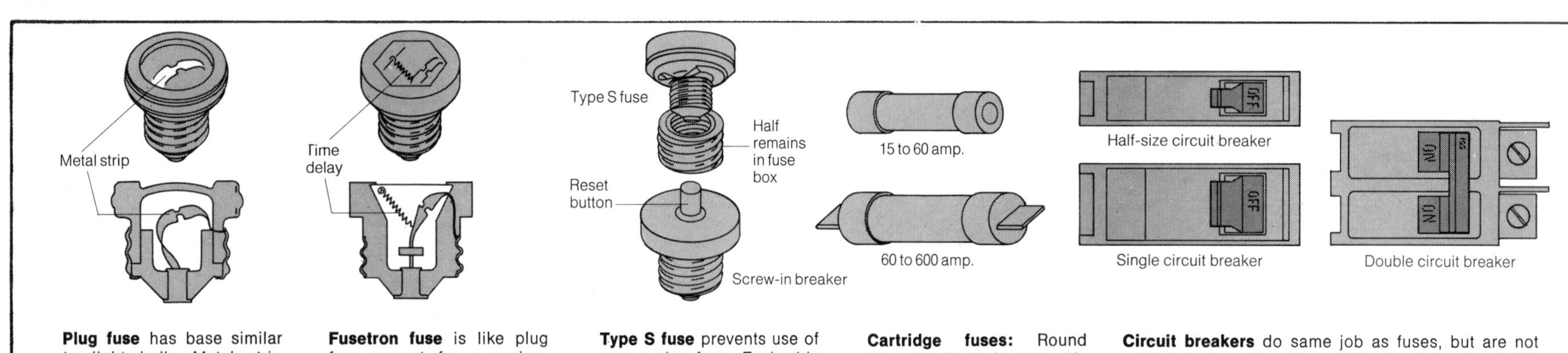

Plug fuse has base similar to light bulb. Metal strip shows through mica window if fuse is good. Blackened window or break in strip means blown fuse.

Fusetron fuse is like plug fuse except for a spring-loaded metal strip that allows a temporary overload. Used mainly on circuits for washers, large power tools.

Type S fuse prevents use of wrong size fuse. Each side has a different thread. **Screw-in breaker** replaces fuse. When blown, button pops out. Push to reset.

Cartridge fuses: Round type, top, is made up to 60-amp. capacity; bottom type, with knife-edge contacts, from 60 amp. up. Use fuse puller to remove safely.

Circuit breakers do same job as fuses, but are not replaced when they "blow." Instead, toggle switch is pushed to "reset" or "on." Made in same capacities as fuses. Double circuit breaker with connecting bar is used to protect 240-volt circuits; two-in-one circuit breaker has two breakers in the space of one.

How to replace a blown fuse

Remove the fuse by turning it counterclockwise (first shut off the main switch). If it is a 15-ampere fuse, make sure the replacement is the same. Pull a cartridge-type fuse straight out. Large ones are best handled with a fuse puller. To "replace" a tripped circuit breaker, push the toggle handle to "reset" or "on." Always be sure your feet are on a dry surface and keep one hand at your side or in your pocket.

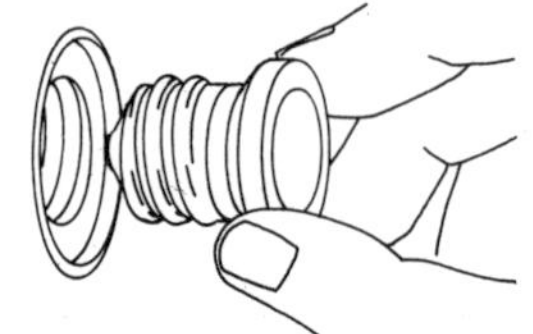

Remove blown fuse by turning counterclockwise. Be sure new one has same capacity.

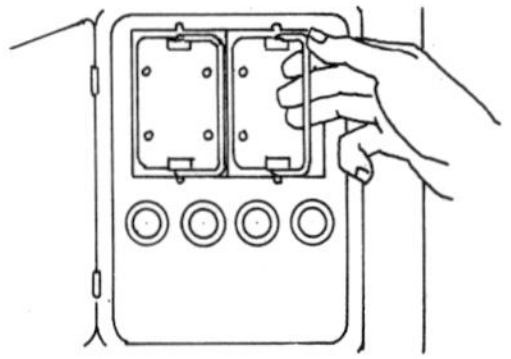

If fuse box has main disconnect of type above, pull it out to get at main fuses. This will

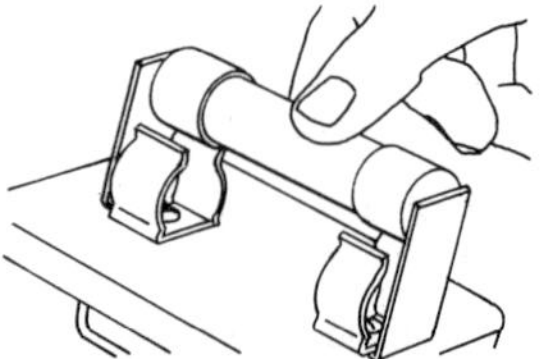

expose cartridge-type fuses. Pull straight out; put in new fuse of same capacity, type.

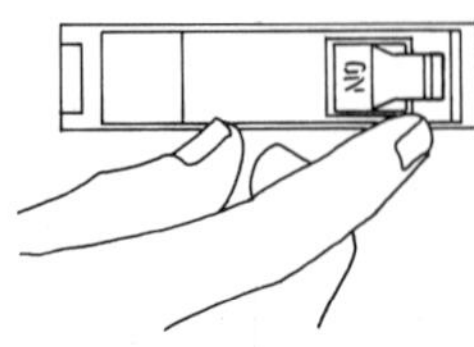

Tripped circuit breaker: Easy to "replace." Just push switch to "reset" or "on."

Electrical terms and their meaning

In order for electricity to travel through wiring, it has to be under pressure–much the same way water is under pressure in your plumbing system. This electrical pressure is measured in **volts** or **voltage.** Modern homes receive 240 volts of electrical power. This power enters the home through an electrical service entrance and passes through a meter where the amount that the household uses is measured and distributed throughout the house. Most appliances operate on 120-volt current; heavy-duty appliances such as an electric range or oven, clothes washer or dryer require 240 volts.

Current, or rate at which electricity is delivered to an appliance, is measured in **amperes.** It is limited by the diameter of the wire it must flow through. Just as a larger diameter pipe can deliver more gallons per minute, a larger diameter wire can conduct more amperes. Since excess current causes a wire to overheat, fuse size must be matched to wire size so that if necessary the fuse will blow before the wire becomes a fire hazard.

The wiring that travels through the walls and ceilings of a house is divided into **circuits.** Each circuit connects with a series of wall outlets and switches. Each heavy-duty appliance has its own separate circuit. Every household circuit is protected by a **fuse** or a **circuit breaker.** These devices break (or interrupt) the circuit when it is overloaded.

The number of electrical circuits in a house determines how many electrical appliances you can use conveniently and safely. If your home is over 20 years old and has never been rewired, it undoubtedly needs improvements in its wiring system.

What to look for

Buying a new home: Check the size of the electric service wires and the electric service panel. An ideal service is 3-wire 150- to 200-ampere (wire of suitable size). A home equipped with an electric range, hot-water heater, dryer, and central air conditioning, along with the usual lighting and appliances, needs a 150-ampere service as a minimum. With electric heating, the need increases to 200 amperes.

Buying an old home: Check the capacity of the electric service panel. A home with a 3-wire service is more valuable than one with two wires. The information on the following pages will help you to calculate your needs and make a more informed decision.

Appraising the wiring in an existing home: The great majority—an estimated 90 percent—of the nation's homes need some rewiring. If your electrical system displays any of the symptoms described on the following page, use this section as the basis for a review of your requirements with an electrical contractor.

How to read a meter

When the needle is between two numbers, always read the lower number. The dials in this illustration, for example, read 8187. The needle for each dial must have reached a number before you read that number. Note that the needle for the second dial from the left has passed the 1 mark but has not reached the 2.

Hookup from power lines

Never attempt to work on the electric power hookup entering the house. These wires carry high voltage and are dangerous. Should they become damaged or worn, call your power company to make repairs.

The local utility, in many communities, supplies only the wiring and the actual hookup as far as the electric meter. Beyond that point, it becomes the responsibility of the homeowner or electrical contractor. In most new homes in the United States and Canada, the meter is located on an exterior wall, generally quite close to the service head. Fuses and circuit breakers are always inside the house. Three-wire 150-ampere service is best, though many homes are still equipped with 2-wire 30-ampere service.

How to shut off main power

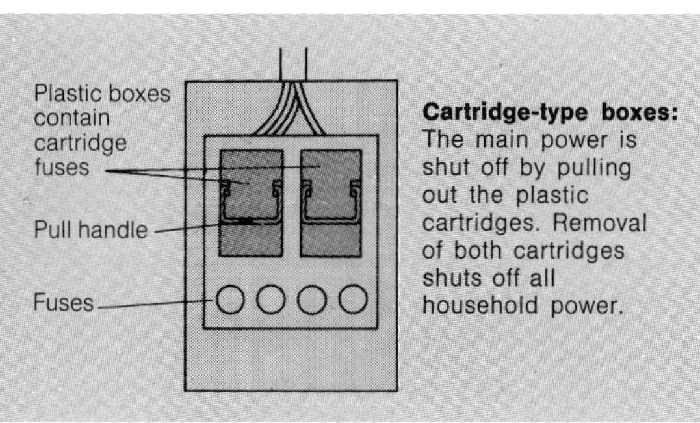

Cartridge-type boxes: The main power is shut off by pulling out the plastic cartridges. Removal of both cartridges shuts off all household power.

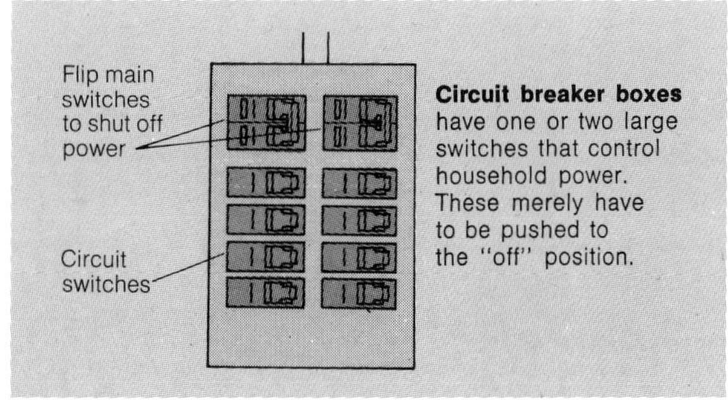

Circuit breaker boxes have one or two large switches that control household power. These merely have to be pushed to the "off" position.

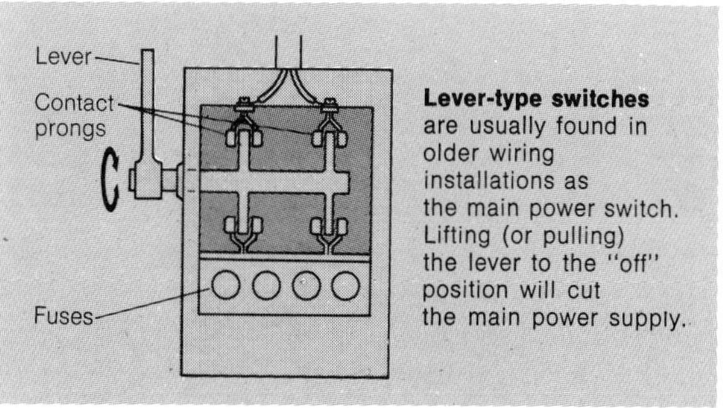

Lever-type switches are usually found in older wiring installations as the main power switch. Lifting (or pulling) the lever to the "off" position will cut the main power supply.

Defining electrical needs

Is your wiring adequate?

Your home needs more wiring if it exhibits any of the following symptoms: **Fuses** or circuit breakers blow or trip often; **lights** flicker when appliances are turned on; **appliances** do not operate at full power; **TV image** shrinks when a heavy appliance is on; you use too many **extension cords.** Most people can manage with their present wiring only because not all circuits are in use at the same time.

List the watts used by all appliances that would normally be operated simultaneously. Be sure to include light bulbs and fluorescent tubes. Appliance wattage usually appears on the nameplate. If any of your nameplates are missing or illegible, check the appliance's needs in the chart below. Add up the wattage of all lights and appliances on each 110-volt circuit and divide by 110. If the result is more than 1,650 on a circuit with a 15-ampere fuse, or 2,200 for 20-ampere fuse, you may blow the fuse when all appliances are on. To avoid trouble, plug one or more of the items into another circuit. Circuits carrying 240 volts are almost always used for a single appliance; check its amperage against fuses.

REPRESENTATIVE WATTAGE RATINGS

Item	Watts	Item	Watts
Air conditioner (room)	1350	Lamp (floor)	300
Air conditioning (central)	5000	Lamp (outdoor)	100
Blender	250	Lamps	60–150
Can opener	150	Lathe	300
Coffeemaker	600	Mixer	150
Dishwasher	1800	Radio	50
Drill press	300	Range (electric)	8000 to 16000
Dryer	6000	Refrigerator	250
Fan	75	Roaster	1380
Food warmer	500	Rotisserie	1400
Freezer	350	Saw	570
Fryer	1320	Shaver	10
Furnace	250	Stereo hi-fi	300
Garbage disposer	900	Sump pump	300
Grill	1300	Sun lamp	275
Heater (hot water)	2500	Television	300
Heater (room)	1600	Toaster	1100
Hot plate (2-burner)	1650	Vacuum cleaner	400
Iron (hand)	1000	Ventilator	100
Ironer	1650	Washer	350

To obtain amperes, divide watts by volts. Use 110 for the latter—it is close enough for practical purposes. Line voltage runs generally between 110 and 120.

Balanced circuits are important

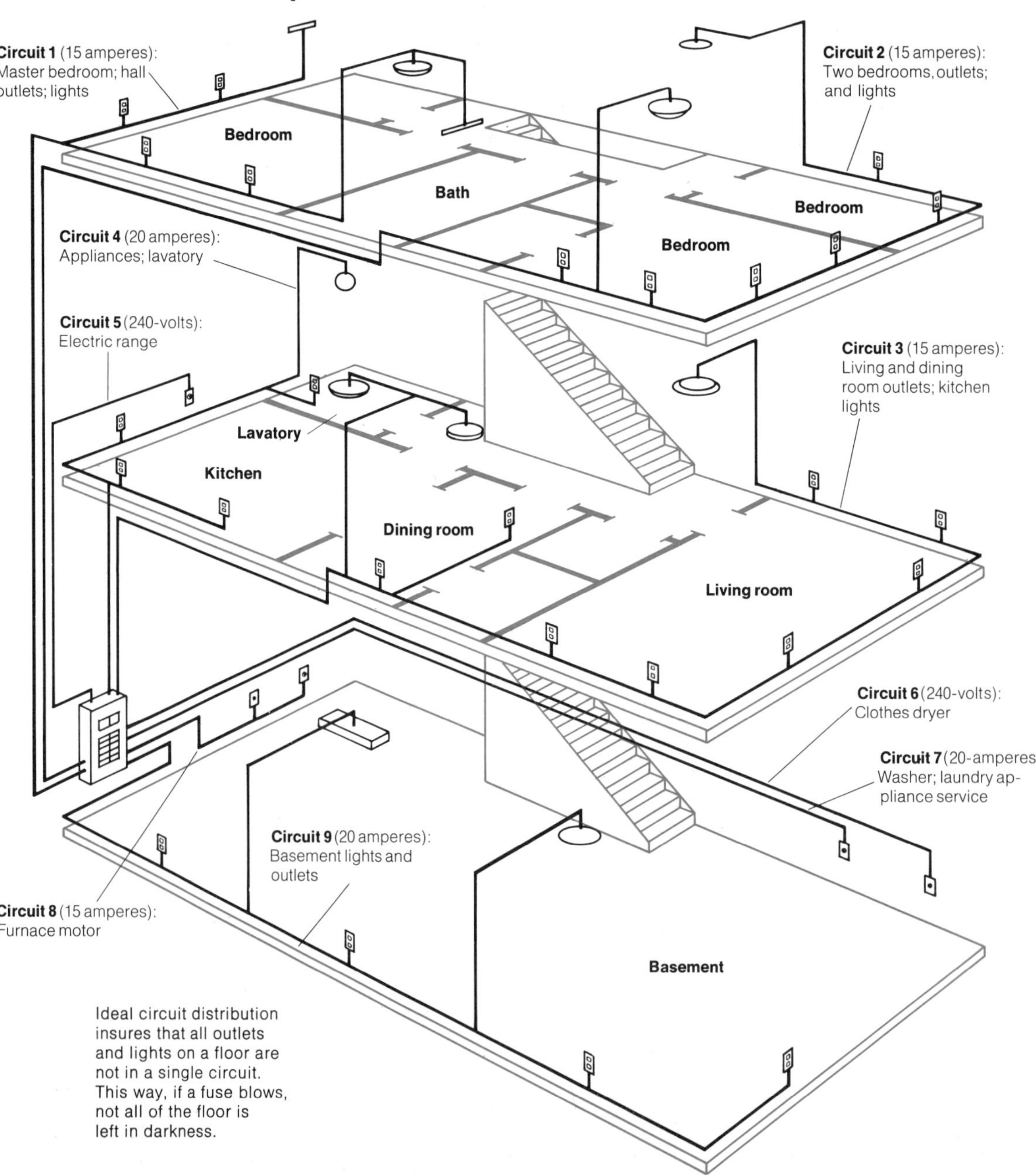

Ideal circuit distribution insures that all outlets and lights on a floor are not in a single circuit. This way, if a fuse blows, not all of the floor is left in darkness.

Tips to get you started

Inadequate power in the home does not mean that you must completely renew all wiring plus the service panel. Wiring can often be updated by the installation of additional circuits to your existing system. Completely renewed wiring should be left to the licensed electrician, but by following the recommendations in this section, you can put more "horsepower" in your home's electrical supply.

The first step is to learn something about local codes from your city or town building inspector. In some areas you are not permitted to do your own wiring. Many communities will permit you to install new circuits up to the service entrance panel, but insist that a licensed electrician complete the final hookup. This is a wise practice, since the high cost of additional circuits is in the routing of the wire. Most electricians will be happy to inspect your work before making final connections for only a fraction of what they would charge for the entire job.

The code determines what type of wire you must use. Some areas use "Romex" (wire with nonmetallic sheathing); others use "BX" (armored cable). Wire size is important. Wires are rated by numbers, the lowest numbers indicating larger diameter wire (p. 261). Number 12 wire is generally recommended throughout the home. Number 14 wire can be used, however, for 15-ampere circuits.

Part of your planning includes checking the existing electrical service panel to see if there is room for new circuits. Be sure to check also with the local utility company to be certain that the lines leading into your home have the capacity to deliver the extra power the new circuits would require.

Refer to the electrical service panel illustrated here for help in determining what circuits should feed various appliances and lighting needs in an efficient circuitry plan. Try to plan circuits so that lighting is kept separate from heavy-duty circuits such as those in the kitchen and laundry areas. A kitchen circuit should allow for several outlets, at least one for every 4 feet of counter space.

Circuits for lighting and convenience outlets, except for the kitchen and laundry, should be planned on the basis of a single 20-ampere 120-volt circuit for every 500 square feet of floor space, or one 15-ampere 120-volt circuit for every 375 square feet of floor space. Outlets should be spaced every 12 feet around the walls of each room.

Efficient light and appliance circuits

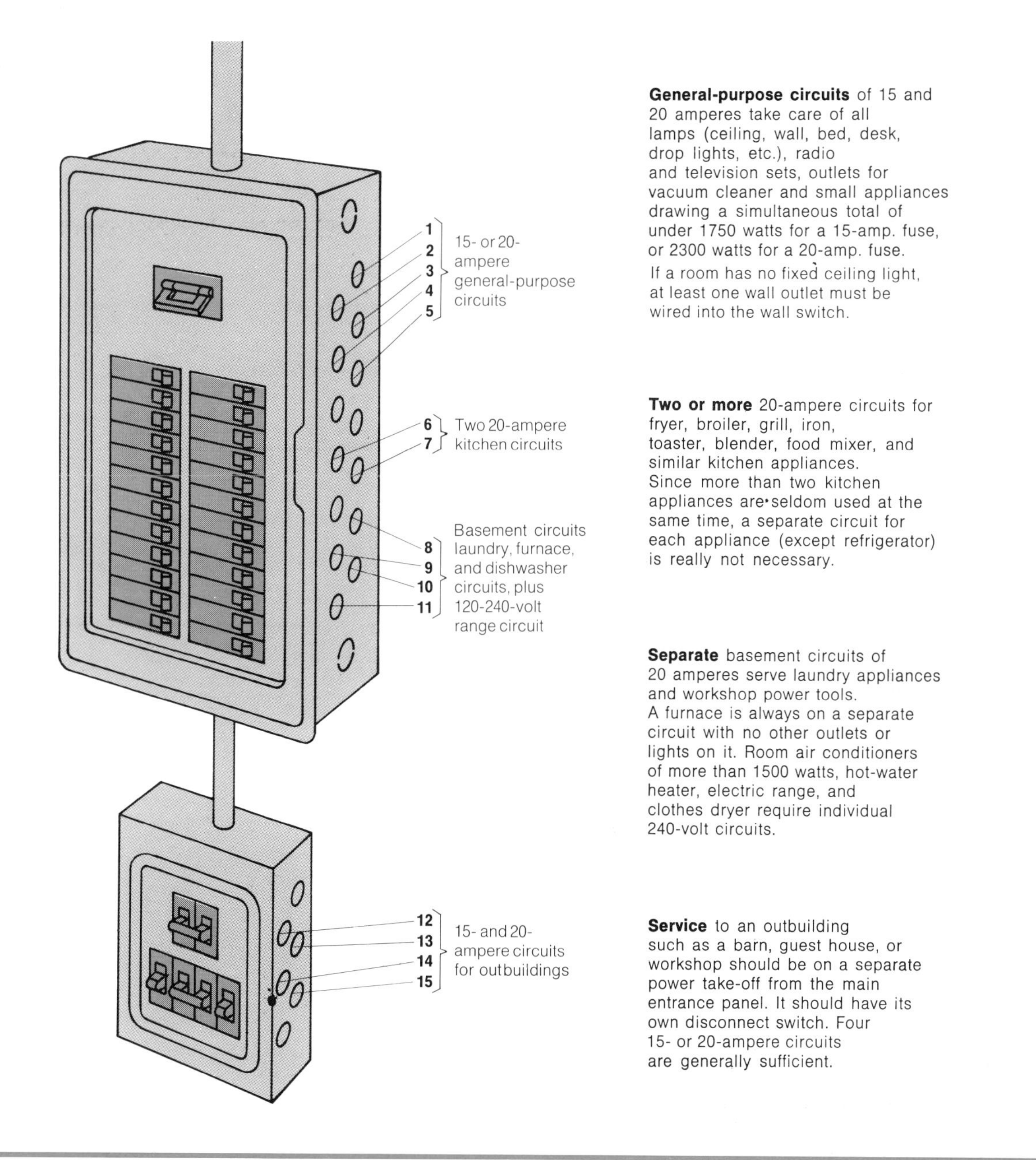

General-purpose circuits of 15 and 20 amperes take care of all lamps (ceiling, wall, bed, desk, drop lights, etc.), radio and television sets, outlets for vacuum cleaner and small appliances drawing a simultaneous total of under 1750 watts for a 15-amp. fuse, or 2300 watts for a 20-amp. fuse.
If a room has no fixed ceiling light, at least one wall outlet must be wired into the wall switch.

Two or more 20-ampere circuits for fryer, broiler, grill, iron, toaster, blender, food mixer, and similar kitchen appliances. Since more than two kitchen appliances are seldom used at the same time, a separate circuit for each appliance (except refrigerator) is really not necessary.

Separate basement circuits of 20 amperes serve laundry appliances and workshop power tools.
A furnace is always on a separate circuit with no other outlets or lights on it. Room air conditioners of more than 1500 watts, hot-water heater, electric range, and clothes dryer require individual 240-volt circuits.

Service to an outbuilding such as a barn, guest house, or workshop should be on a separate power take-off from the main entrance panel. It should have its own disconnect switch. Four 15- or 20-ampere circuits are generally sufficient.

Improving electrical service

Relieving overloaded circuits

Overloaded circuits are caused by the use of too many appliances at the same time. For example, if the kitchen electrical outlets share the same circuit with the lights, a refrigerator, a radio, or some other appliance, the chances are that your fuses blow whenever all of these are operating simultaneously and you switch on a fry pan or toaster.

You can eliminate this kind of overloading by connecting a 4-outlet appliance plug box directly to the electrical service panel. Top sketch shows a 120-volt split circuit connecting appliance outlets to two spare fuse locations in the entrance panel. This hookup allows you to use four appliances simultaneously at up to a 4400-watt capacity.

Before planning this installation, see if your fuse box has two unused power takeoffs. These can be recognized by two empty spaces that would accept a fuse (or a circuit breaker, in homes so equipped). If all power terminals are in use, you will have to install an "add-on" electrical panel.

Once two power takeoff terminals are established, follow the wiring configuration of the upper diagram to run a No. 12, 3-wire cable from the appliance plug to the service panel.

Installing an "add-on" panel: These units do the job of a small electrical service panel. The power from the main service entrance flows into the add-on panel and is distributed to the supplementary circuits.

Most service entrance panels have two power takeoff screws located between the two left and the two right plug fuses. Wires leading to the add-on panel are connected to these terminals as shown. The two black wires go to the terminals and the white wire goes to the neutral bar.

At the add-on panel, both black wires are joined to the fuses' screw terminals and the white to the neutral bar. New circuits are then connected.

How to avoid danger

Working with electricity is not hazardous as long as you obey strict safety rules. Always shut off or disconnect power before handling wires. If you are working on the electrical service entrance, do not stand on a damp floor. Protect yourself by wearing rubber gloves and rubbers, and stand on a rubber mat or a piece of dry wood. Above all, if you are in any doubt about how to do any particular job, call in a licensed electrician.

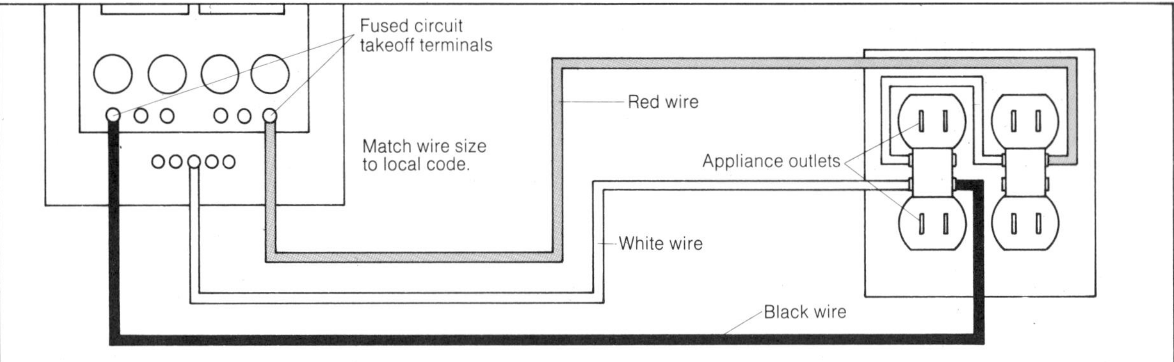

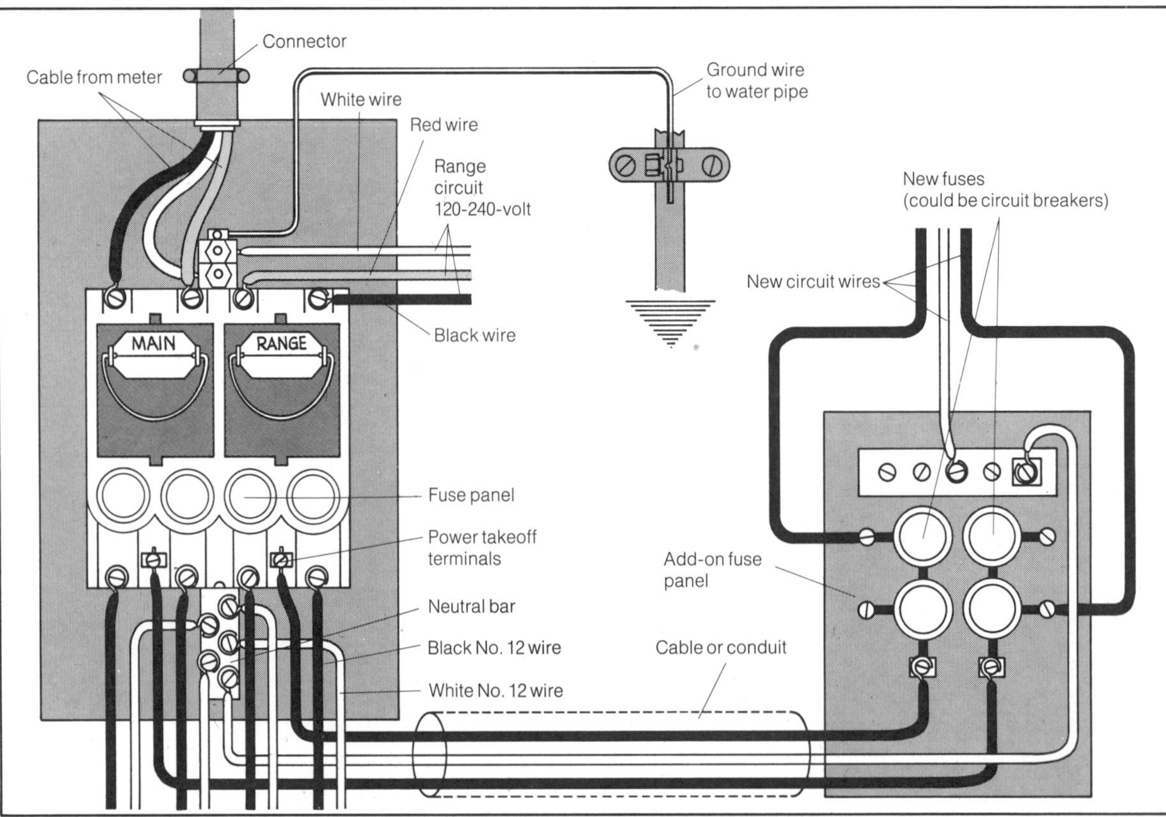

Three-wire electrical cable in older homes will have two black wires and one white one. In more recent construction, this has changed to one black, one red, and one white. Present electrical codes call for a fourth wire, which is a ground. This ground wire is bare metal. To avoid confusion, ground wires have been left out of these illustrations.

Grounded wiring

Household wiring is color coded. In 120-volt circuits one wire, called the *neutral* wire, is white; the other, the *hot* wire, is black or another color but never white. Both are live wires. In circuits carrying 240 volts only, one wire is usually black and the other another color, but neither should be white. In 3-wire circuits carrying both voltages one wire is white, the other two black or colored. You get 120 volts by connecting the white wire and a colored wire to an outlet, 240 volts by connecting the two colored wires to an outlet.

The fuse or circuit breaker panel of your home is **grounded,** that is, there is a wire connecting the service panel to a rod which is driven into the earth. In residential areas, this ground wire is usually attached to the water-supply pipe which leads into the ground. The white neutral wires of the various branch circuits throughout the house are also connected to grounded terminals in the service panel. This is necessary for a number of reasons, such as reduction of the possible effects of lightning.

Grounded wiring systems are those in which all metal outlet and switch boxes, cable armor, and exposed metal parts of the wiring system are connected back to grounding terminals in the fuse or circuit breaker. Grounding terminals of grounded receptacles are connected to the box by a jumper wire or other means. A 3-prong appliance cord continues the grounding to an appliance or power tool. If a loose wire touches the frame of such an appliance or tool, the grounding wire will protect the user from shock and may cause a fuse to blow or a circuit breaker to trip. Appliances or tools that do not have such protection can be dangerous—you could get a shock if something should go wrong with the internal wiring.

Check your system for grounding by seeing what type of wiring is installed in your home. If the wiring is of nonmetallic cable, that cable should have a third wire (which has no plastic sheathing) that is connected directly to the electrical outlet boxes. If your wiring is of BX cable, you know the system is grounded, because the metallic sheathing of BX cable acts as a grounding conductor. Metal conduit also serves as a grounding conductor.

Once you have determined how your electrical wiring is grounded, you can carry grounding safety one step further by installing 3-prong electrical outlets throughout the house. Be sure that the third wire of the three wires (the bare one) is attached to the ground terminal on the outlet receptacle.

A less expensive and easier method would be to equip all 3-prong appliance cords with a grounded adapter plug. Be sure to connect the small wire of the plug to the screw on the electrical box plate. If you neglect to do this, the grounded circuit will be ineffective.

In double-insulated tools, all wiring is protected by an extra layer of insulation. With this extra layer, even if the primary insulation fails, no part of the tool can become electrically "live." The casings of these tools are usually plastic, which further reduces shock hazard. Such tools do not require a 3-prong plug nor a grounded 3-wire extension cord. All tools that are equipped with 3-prong plugs, however, must be connected to grounded receptacles and used in conjunction with 3-wire extension cords.

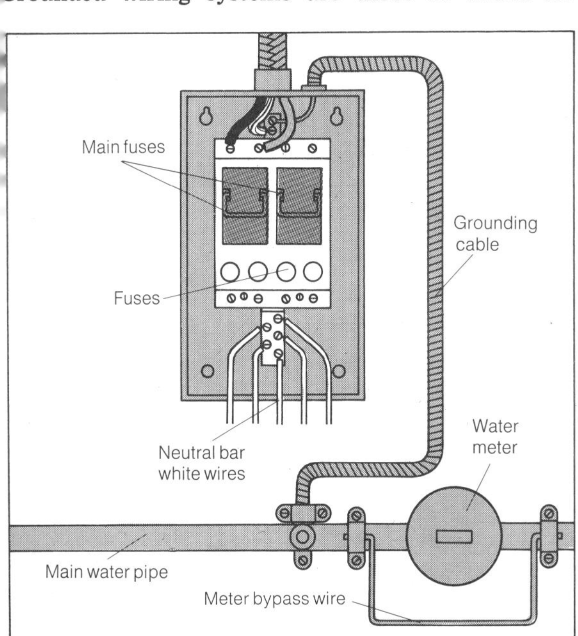

Electric service entrance is grounded to metal water-supply pipe or to a special metal rod driven into the earth.

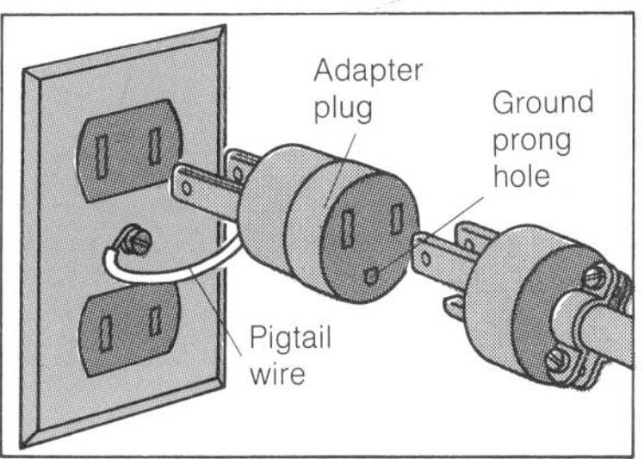

Fit 3-wire adapter plugs with pigtail attached to receptacle plate.

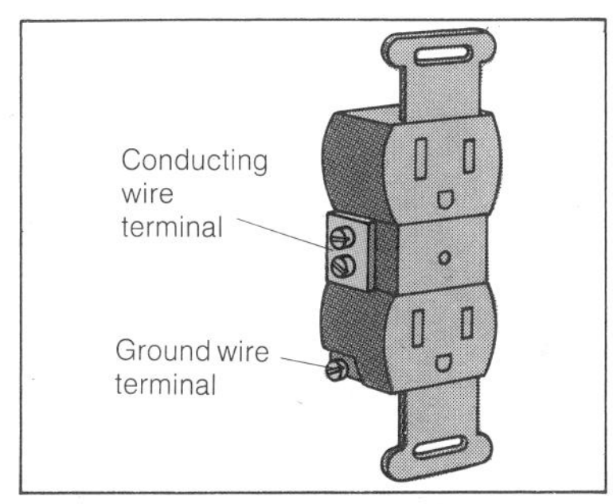

Three-hole receptacle has a green terminal screw for the grounding wire.

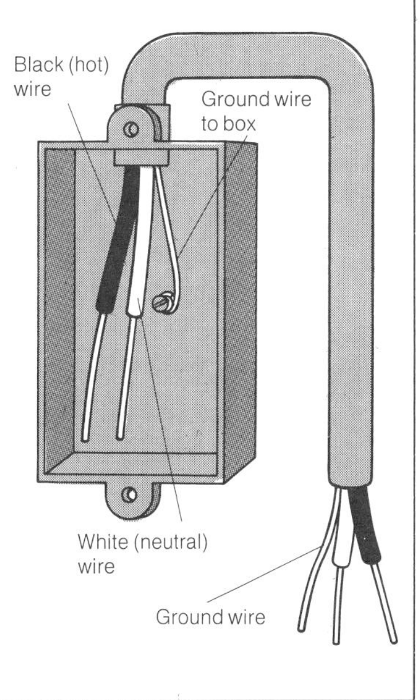

Copper ground wire of nonmetallic cable connects directly to outlet box.

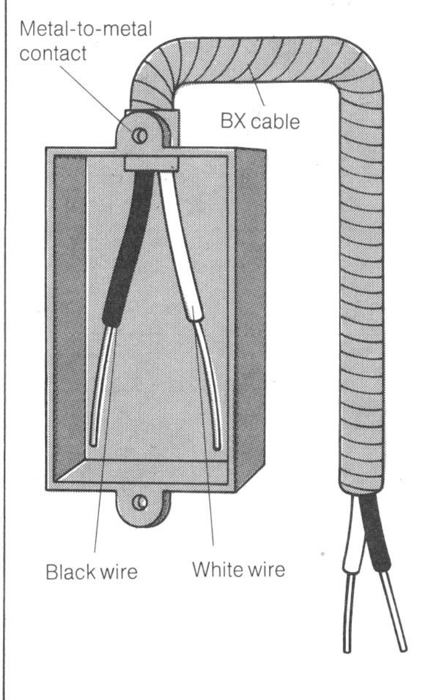

Metallic sheathing of BX cable acts as ground conductor in older homes.

Aids to easy repair

If you can follow the operating instructions for a dishwasher, dryer, or modern electric range, you can learn the necessary technical facts and techniques to handle dozens of minor electrical repairs. Replacing an old wall switch with a new silent type, installing a dimmer switch, replacing broken lamp switches, hanging a new ceiling fixture—these are all tasks that can be easily accomplished with a minimum of skills and tools.

Even the seemingly more complex jobs, such as installing an additional electrical outlet or wiring a new circuit, are a simple matter of following the step-by-step instructions in this section.

Important: Unplug appliances you are working on. If changing switches or electrical wiring, remove the fuses or shut off the circuit breakers that supply power to the circuits you are working on.

You probably already have most of the tools that are required for minor electrical repairs or wiring. These include screwdrivers, knife, ruler, hammer, saw, chisel, brace and bit, electrician's pliers, metal snips, and locking pliers.

More complicated jobs can be simplified with inexpensive specialized tools, such as **screwdrivers** with a device on the end that holds small screws for insertion in inaccessible areas, such as electrical boxes; **Phillips-type screwdrivers** for the cross-slotted screws often used in appliances; **nut drivers** that have a socket on their end to drive or remove nuts in areas in which a wrench would not fit.

Another necessity is a **neon lamp tester,** a small light with two wires that are inserted into an electrical outlet to see whether power is present.

Long-nose pliers are used to hold screws, nuts, and similar small hardware so that you can insert or remove them in hard-to-reach places inside walls or appliances. They are equipped with side cutters which can be used for cutting wires.

Wire strippers slice neatly through the insulation covering a wire and remove it without disturbing the wire itself. This is a necessary step prior to making connections with new wire. There is also a **multipurpose tool** that cuts and strips wire and can crimp terminals (fasteners) to the ends of a wire, joining them without the use of solder.

In electrical work, a **soldering gun** is a better choice than a soldering iron because it heats faster and has an easily held pistol grip.

Tools and their uses

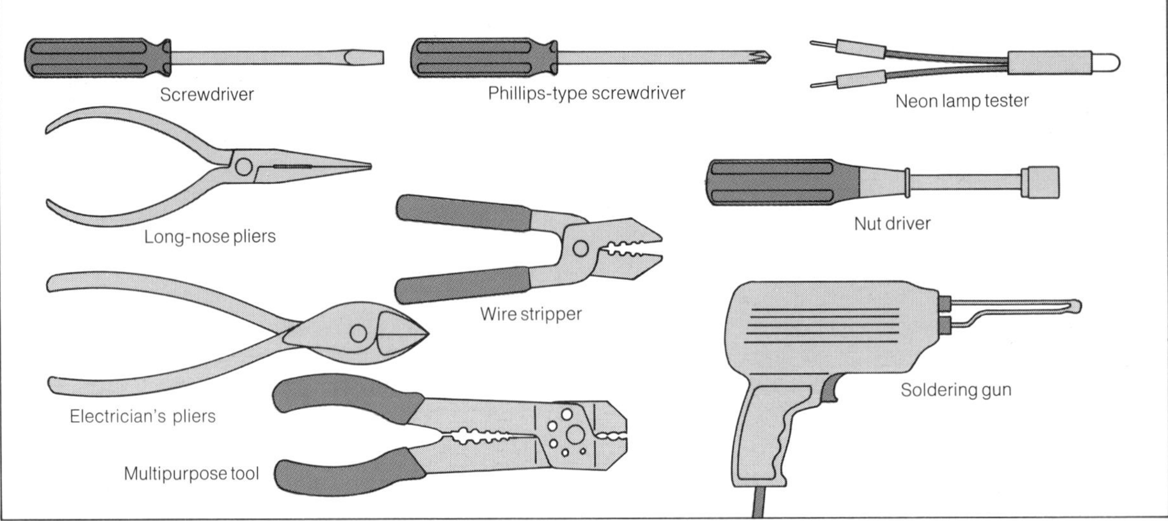

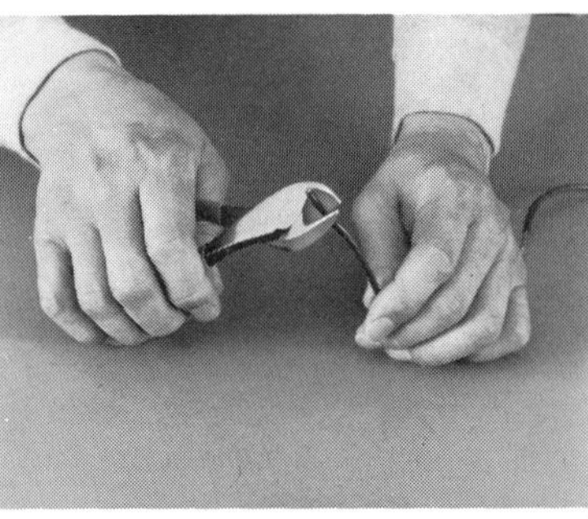

Side cutters of electrician's pliers cut through wire. Can be used as strippers.

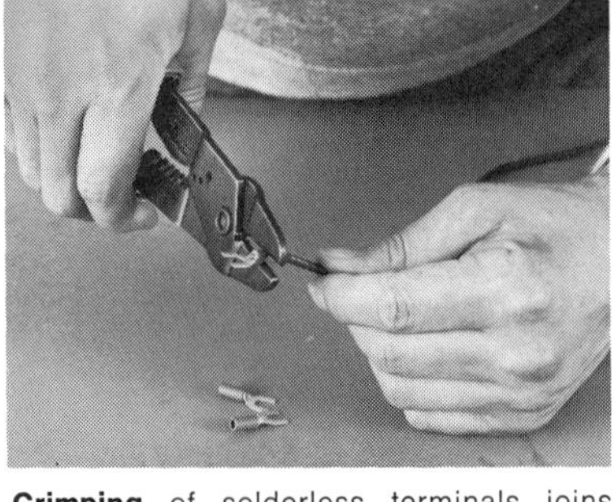

Crimping of solderless terminals joins wires without the use of solder.

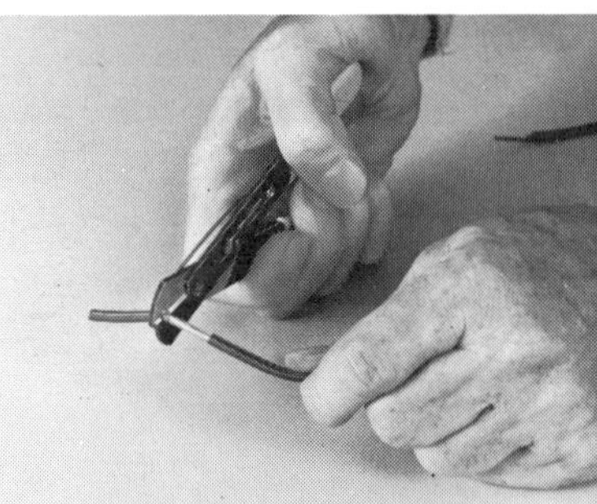

Stripper removes outer covering of wire, leaving the wire itself untouched.

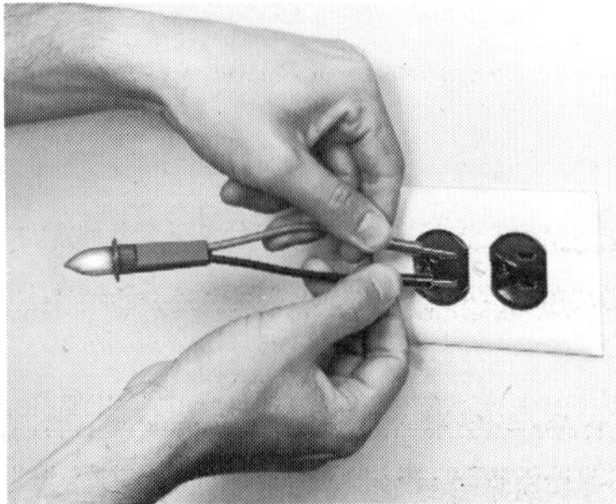

Test lamp inserted in outlet lights up, signaling presence of electricity.

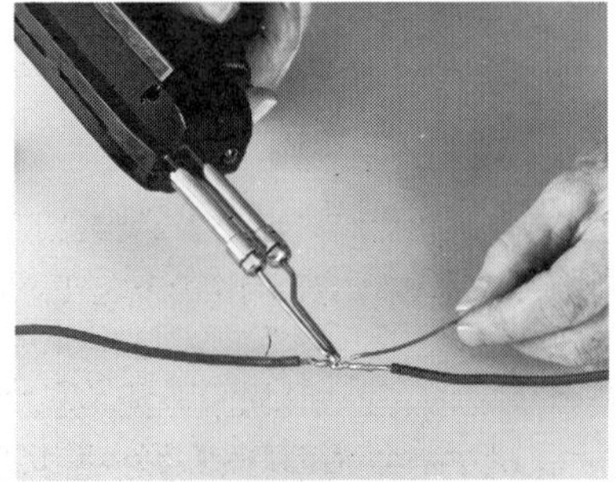

Soldering gun melts solder to form permanent electrical connections.

Nut driver reaches nuts in cramped areas where wrenches do not fit.

Extension cords

Household extension cords usually have only two wires inside and are adequate only for the operation of one or two small appliances. The thinner the cord, the lower its capacity for conducting electricity. Too many appliances or lamps plugged into the same cord will cause it to overheat, creating a possible fire hazard.

Length is also important. A longer cord wastes current. If it is too long, the drop in current can reduce an appliance's efficiency. The table below recommends suitable extension cord wire lengths and diameters for various electrical loads.

Remove extension cords from an outlet by grasping the plug body. Otherwise, the wires may tear loose, resulting in a shock or short circuit.

Three-wire extension cords are used for electric power tools and outdoor appliances. The third wire is a grounding wire; plug this type of cord into a grounded outlet or ground it with a suitable adapter plug (p. 48). Use only 3-wire extensions for tools and appliances that have 3-wire cords.

Most cords are sheathed in plastic that can take rugged use. Rubber-sheathed cords are more flexible and easier to store.

Selecting the proper length

Length	To 7 amp.	7-10 amp.	10-15 amp.
To 25 ft.	No. 18	No. 16	No. 14
To 50 ft.	No. 16	No. 14	No. 12
To 100 ft.	No. 14	No. 12	No. 10

Wire diameter to use (p. 261)

Splicing cord wires

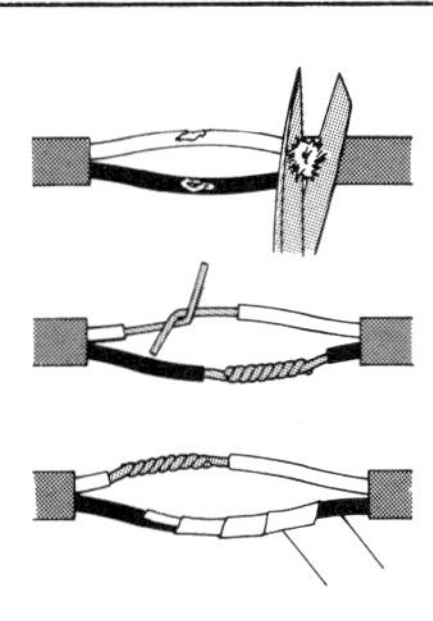

1. Cut away damaged insulation with scissors. Cut both wires in half with wire cutters. Strip 1 in. of insulation from wires with wire stripper or sharp knife. **2.** Twist ends of both wires. **3.** Wrap each wire with tape, then wrap wires together. Overlap tape onto cord. Splicing is an emergency repair not approved by electrical code. **Do not splice house wiring.**

Replacing damaged plugs

Types of plugs

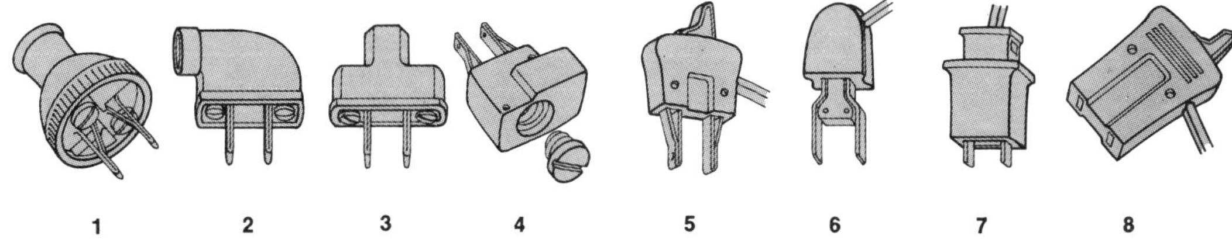

Plug replacement is easy with these readily available plugs. In addition to the new plug, you'll need wire cutters, a screwdriver with a small tip, and a sharp paring knife. Replacement of round-wire plugs (Nos. **1–3**) and flat-wire plugs (Nos. **5–8**) is illustrated below. For plug No. **4**, loosen screw, slip wire into casing, and tighten screw.

Flat-wire plugs

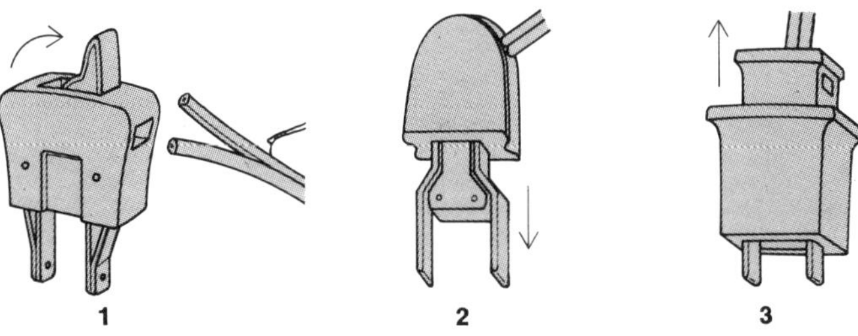

1. Lift top clamp. Slit cord ¼ in. between wires. Push cord into plug; close clamp. **2.** Grasp prongs and pull firmly to remove from casing. Spread prongs. Insert wires through plug and into terminal. Close prongs and place securely in casing. **3.** Remove casing. Insert wire and push through plug. Replace casing. **Flat-wire plugs are easiest to replace because no wire stripping is involved.**

Round-wire plugs

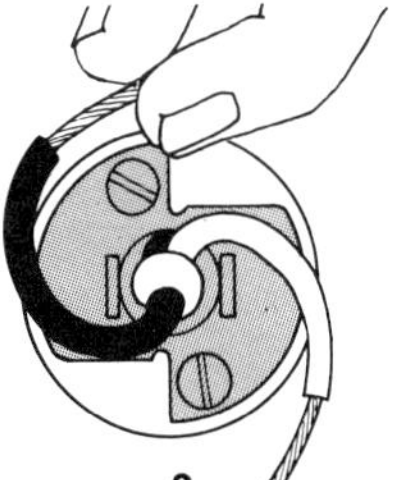

1. Loop both wires exactly as shown to tie an "Underwriters" knot. Pull the knot down into the plug casing between the prongs. This knot is important because it protects the wires from strain should the plug be pulled from a socket by the cord. **2.** Strip ½ in. of sheathing from each wire. Twist wires in clockwise direction. **3.** Loop wires around screws in clockwise direction. Tighten screws and clip off any excess wire. Be sure that no strands from the black wire are in contact with those of the white wire.

3-prong plugs

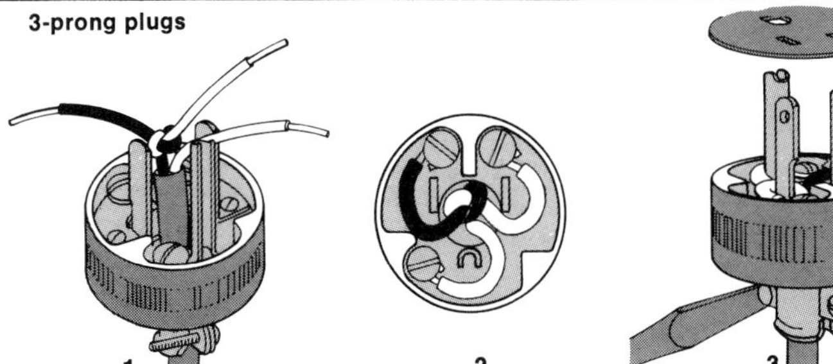

1. Loop all three wires together if plug space permits. If space does not permit, tie black and white wires in "Underwriters" knot (as above) and leave third wire free. **2.** Strip plastic sheathing from all three wires. Twist wire strands clockwise. Loop wires clockwise around screws. (Wires must not be allowed to touch each other.) **3.** Tighten both outside screws to secure cord to plug. Slip protective cover over prongs and push down to cover exposed wires; this is an important safety precaution.

Electrical boxes and accessories

Wall boxes

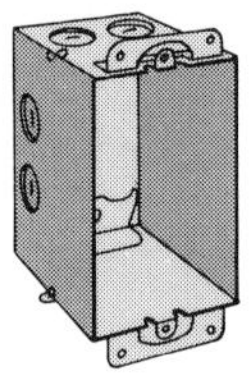

1. Metal box is flush-mounted in lath wall. Surface-mounted also available

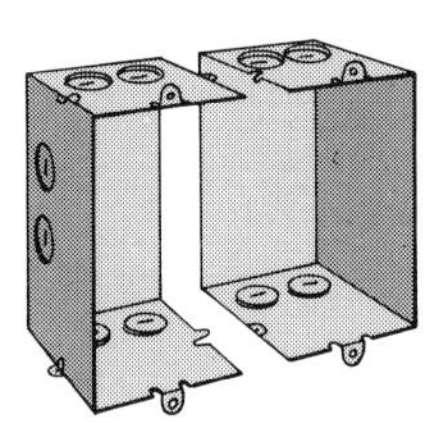

2. Several metal boxes are joined together by removing their side plates.

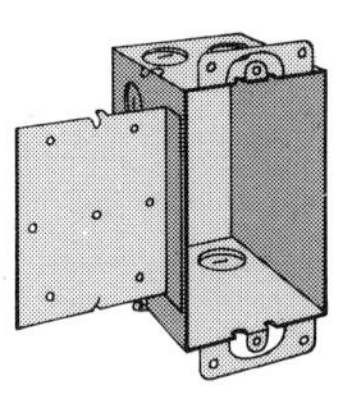

3. Metal box with a flange is nailed to the front or rear of stud in drywall.

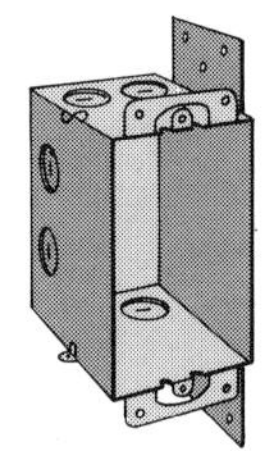

4. The flange on this box can be screwed to the side of stud in drywall

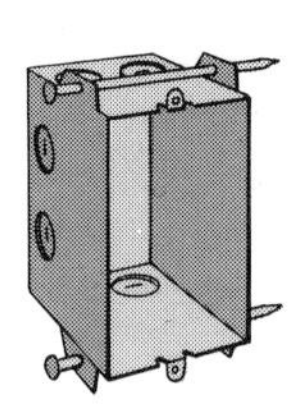

5. Small side flanges of this box can be nailed to side of stud in drywall.

Wall box accessories

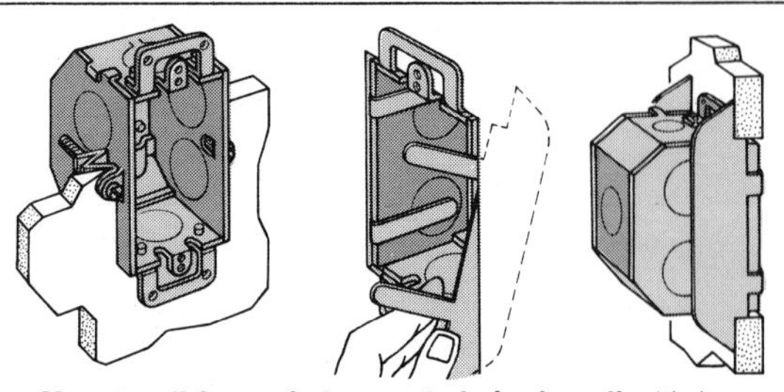

Mount wall boxes between studs in drywall with box clamps, left, which grip rear side of wall as side screws are tightened. Or use metal supports, right, that slip in hole; projecting tabs are bent into box.

Boxes for damp locations

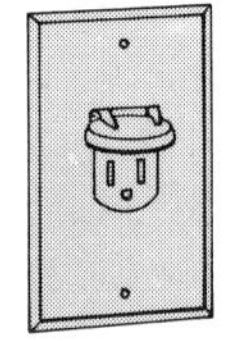

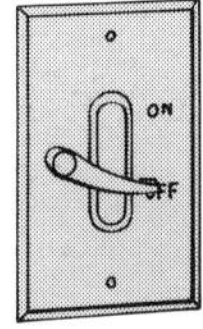

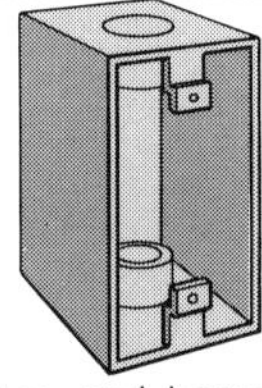

Weatherproof outlets, switches, and boxes for outdoor installation. Single or multiple outlets have snap covers. Both single and three-way switches are available.

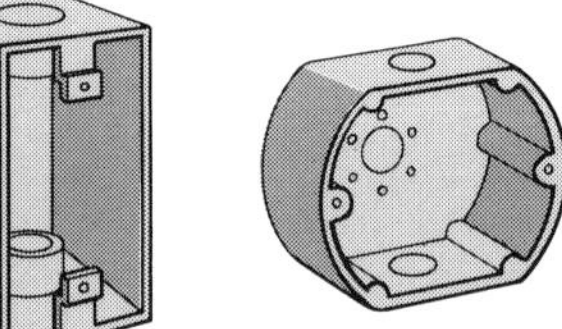

Bakelite wall and ceiling boxes used in damp areas cannot be ganged together.

Ceiling boxes and accessories

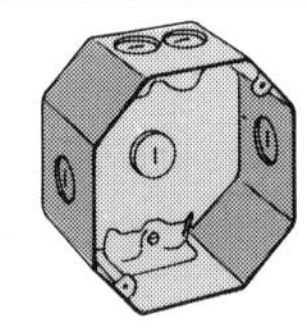

Metal boxes for ceiling mounting are made square, octagonal, and round.

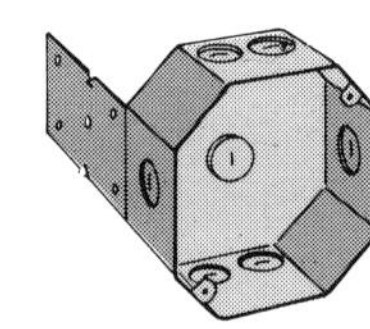

Flange on this metal box permits it to be nailed or screwed to joists in a ceiling.

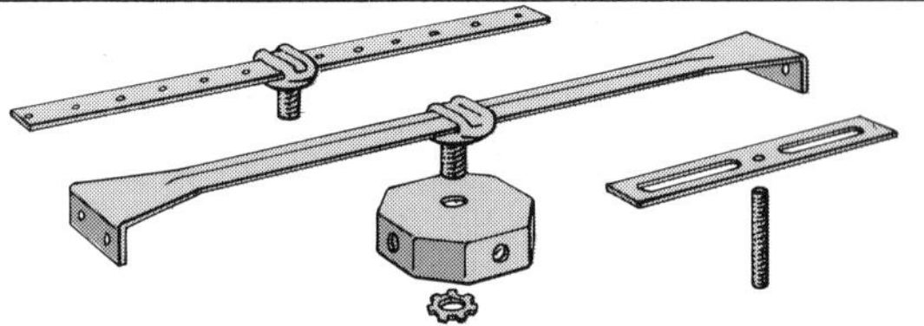

Adjustable hangers, left, permit ceiling boxes to be fastened between ceiling beams. Shallow box hangers, right, rest on ceiling laths.

Thin-walled conduit and accessories

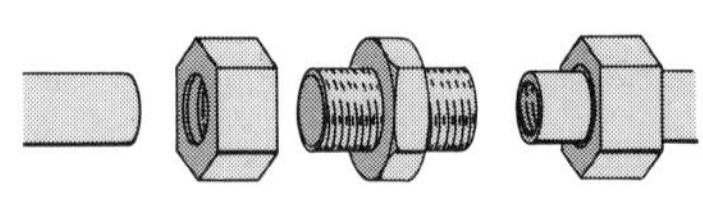

Fiber ring inside nut clamps conduit pushed into it. Tightening coupling joint secures both pieces.

Adapter on end of unthreaded conduit attaches conduit to threaded box.

Various types of metal clamps and screws attach the conduit to a wall.

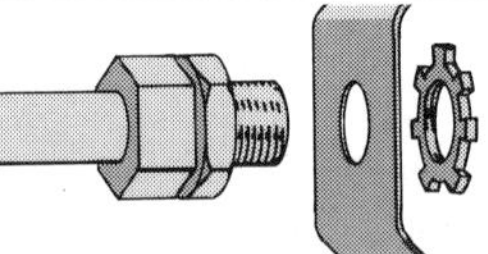

Fiber ring inside this nut clamps conduit and coupling joint. Coupling joint is secured to box with locknut.

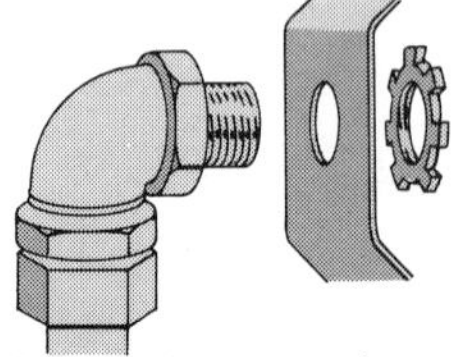

Fiber ring inside nut attaches conduit to right-angle adapter. Adapter is held to the box with a locknut.

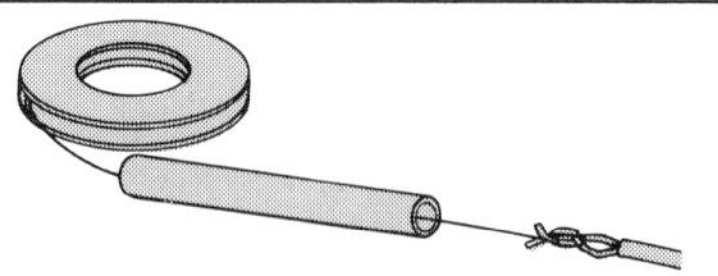

A 50-ft. fish tape (p. 264) attached to the wire is used to pull the wire through a conduit or through a wall.

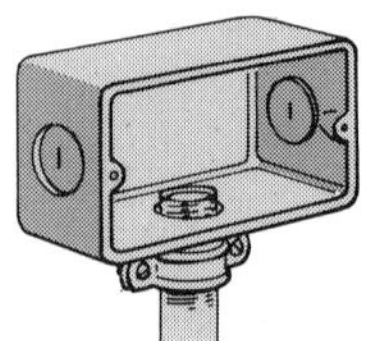

Rigid threaded conduit inserted into neck of threaded box is securely attached to the box with metal clamps.

Bending conduit with a hickey

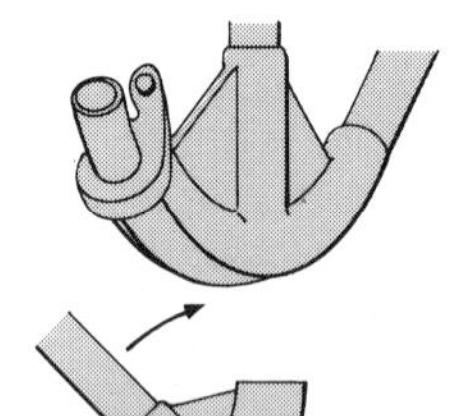

Make bends in conduit with an electrician's hickey. The total bend angles in a length of conduit between two boxes must not exceed 360°.

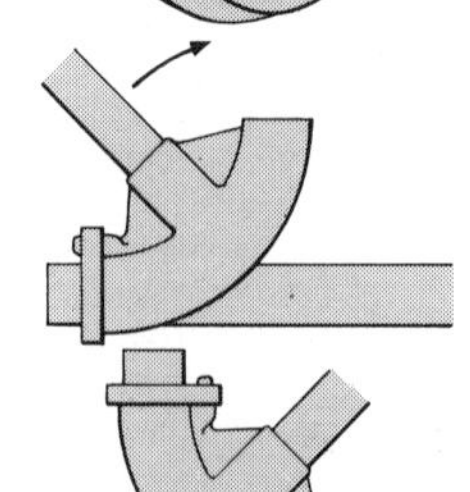

Hook bender over conduit with the inside of the grip hook at mark. Bend the conduit by pulling the handle back in the direction of the bend.

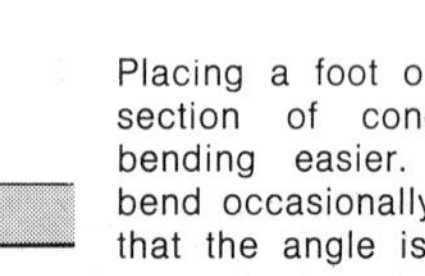

Placing a foot on a straight section of conduit makes bending easier. Check the bend occasionally to be sure that the angle is correct.

Types and uses

Nonmetallic and metallic cable

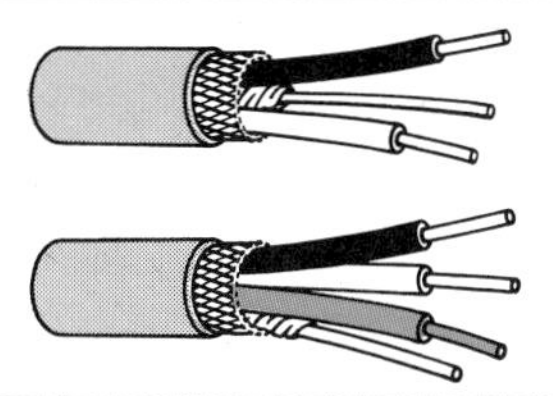

Buying cable: Cable is classified according to the number of wires it contains and their size or gauge. Two-wire cable actually contains three wires: The black (hot) wire, the white (neutral) wire, and a third which is the ground wire. Similarly, 3-wire cable contains four wires: Black, white, and red (which is also a hot wire) and a ground wire.

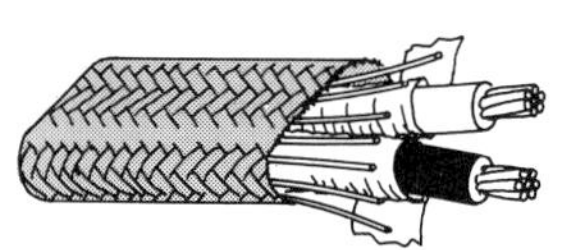

Service entrance cable: Used to transmit power to main entrance switch. Can be used indoors or outdoors. Also used to wire large appliances such as ranges and water heaters. Usually a 3-wire cable.

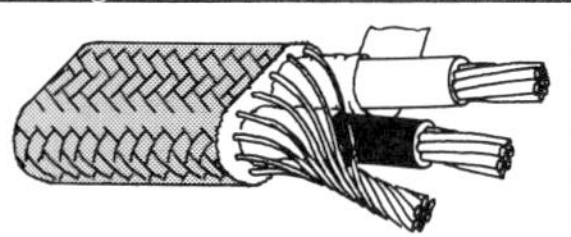

Nonmetallic sheathed cable: For indoor use. Has a moisture-resistant, flame-resistant covering. It is made with and without a ground wire. The wires are copper or aluminum. No. 6 and larger are stranded.

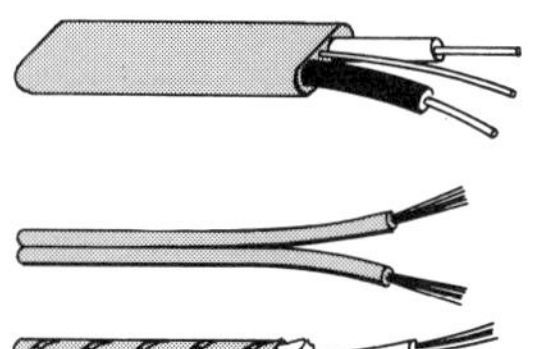

Underground feeder and branch circuit cable: Can be used underground, indoors or out. Does not require a conduit when buried. Resists water and corrosion.

Extension and appliance cords: Come in light- and heavy-duty types. Lamps usually use plastic-covered types. Appliances and motors take heavier forms with wire size to suit the load. Extension cords are sold with connectors at each end.

Armored and special-purpose cable

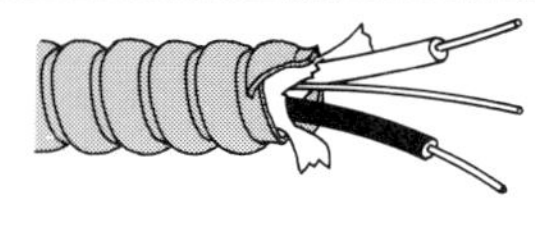

Armored BX cable: Used only in dry, indoor locations. Wires are copper; bare ground may be aluminum. Must be used with steel junction and switch boxes. Made in 2- and 3-wire types.

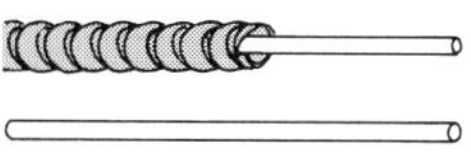

Ground wire: Used to ground an electrical system to a cold-water line or to a copper rod buried in the ground. Generally single-wire armored cable. Wire size depends on service wire size. Check local code.

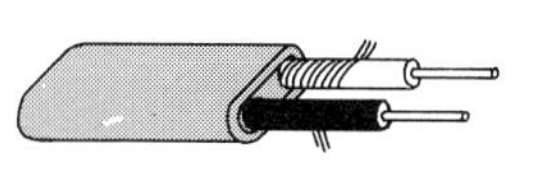

Lead-encased underground cable: Generally used to transmit power to outbuildings from main power source. Must be substituted for plastic-covered wire if local electrical code requires it.

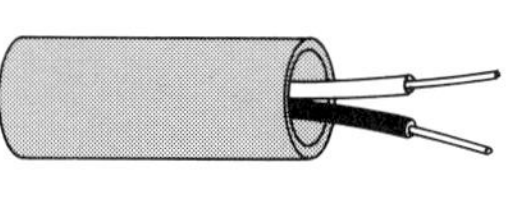

Thin-wall steel conduit: Required by some towns. Installed same way as piping; wires are pulled through afterward. Acts as its own grounding conductor. Made in 10-ft. lengths; joined by special connectors.

Wire sizes

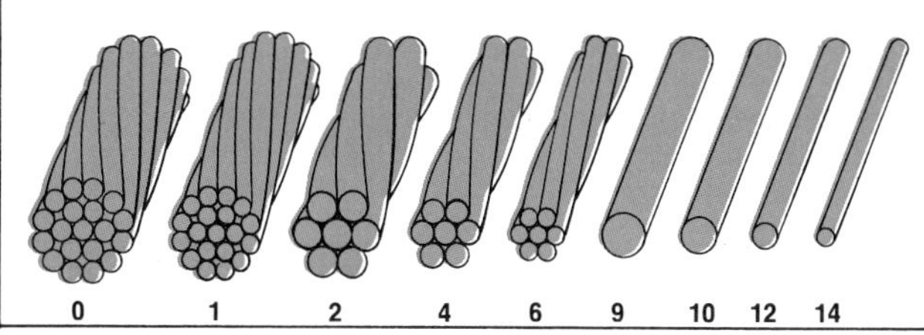

Wire sizes for residential wiring vary from No. 14, the smallest permitted, to No. 0. (Sizes to 0000 available for special work.) The smaller the number, the larger the size. The wires shown are actual sizes. No. 6 and larger wires are stranded.

Installing nonmetallic cable

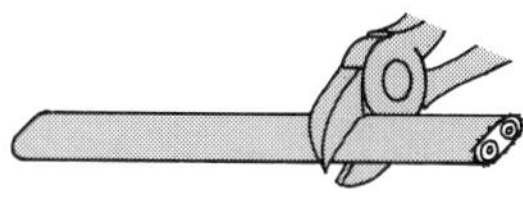

1. Strip off about 6 in. of the cable covering. Be careful not to cut insulation.

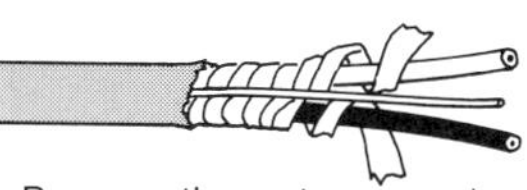

2. Remove the outer wrapping from each of the wires. Insulation is inside wrapping.

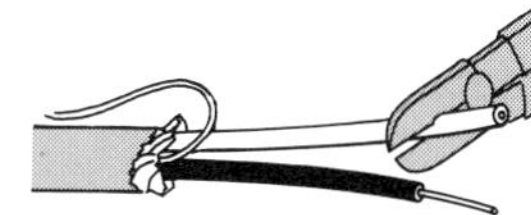

3. The next step is to strip off insulation to expose about 1 in. of the solid copper wire.

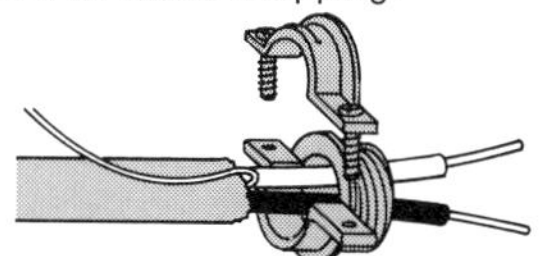

4. Install the connector. Use the kind made for nonmetallic cable with two locking bolts.

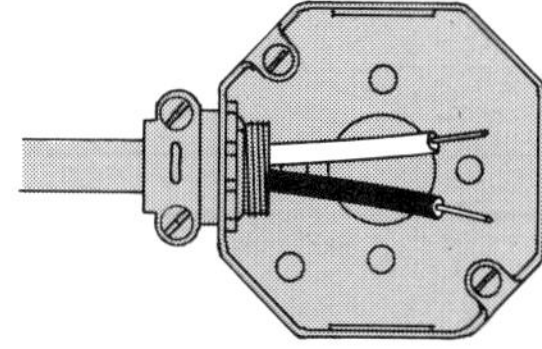

5. Tighten the bolts so connector is secured to cable. Insert into box, install locknut.

Installing BX cable

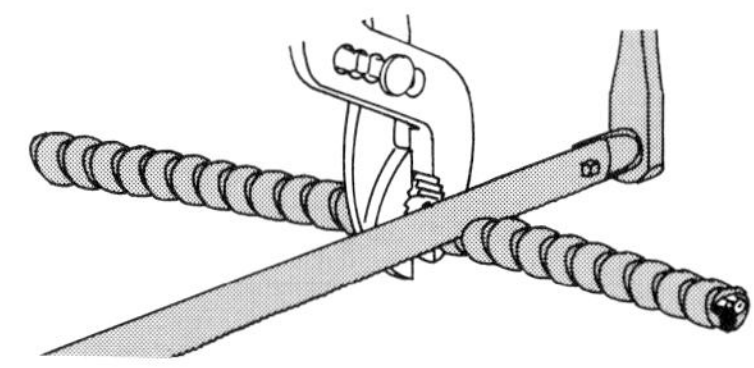

1. Use a hacksaw to cut off about 6 in. of the armor. Be careful not to cut into the wires.

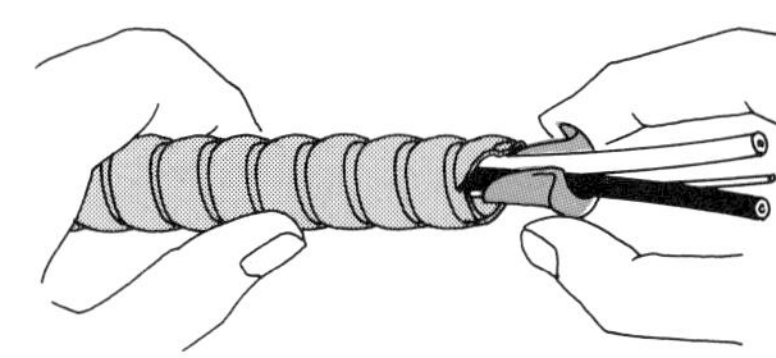

2. Remove 1 in. of insulation from each of the two wires; insert insulating fiber bushing.

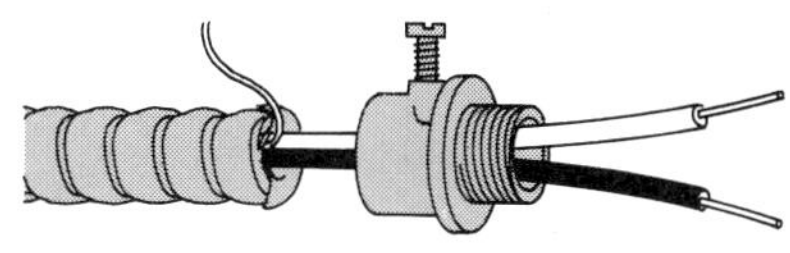

3. Install special BX cable connector. Make sure cable fits snugly in it; tighten screw.

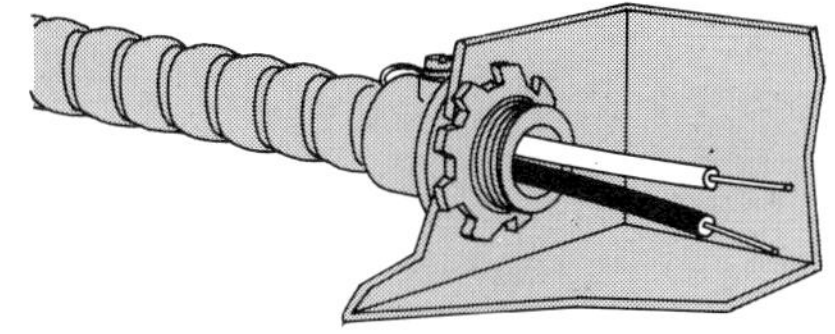

4. Push cable into junction or switch box and install locknut. Allow 6 in. for connection.

Switches and outlets

Replacing a switch

Switches are always in the hot (black wire) side of the circuit, never in the neutral (white wire) side. So they connect to black wires only, except in switch loops (at right and p. 270) or multiwire switching.

To remove old switches, you must first remove the fuse (or turn off the circuit breaker) that controls the switch (p. 252). Then remove the switch plate and the screws holding the switch in the switch box. Tug the switch out of the box so that the wires are accessible. Release the wires from their respective terminals and replace them in the same position on the new switch. Tighten all connections and tuck the wires and the switch back into the box. Fasten the screws and replace the switch plate.

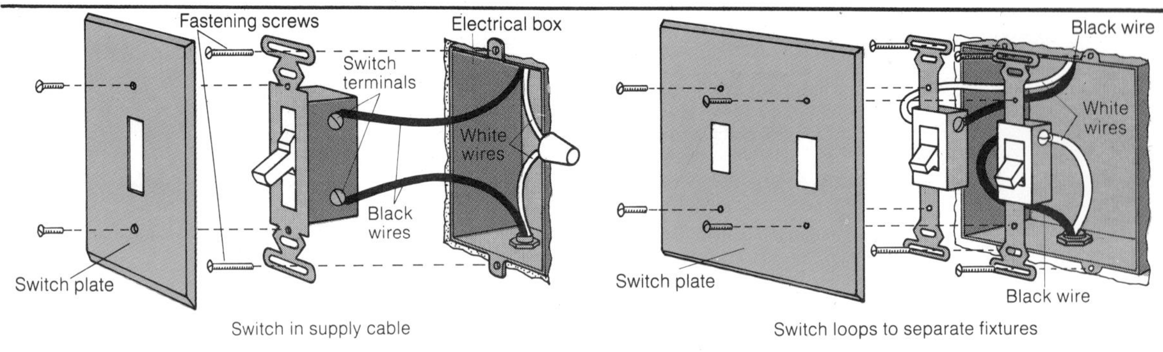

Switch in supply cable

Switch loops to separate fixtures

Replacing an outlet

If an electrical outlet is faulty, it will short circuit and blow a fuse (or trip a circuit breaker) whenever an appliance or lamp is plugged into it. To test whether or not an outlet is defective, plug in a lamp you know is working. If the lamp doesn't go on, and the circuit is all right, then the outlet is faulty.

To remove a damaged outlet, turn off the power to the affected circuit (p. 253). Remove the outlet plate, remove the two screws holding the receptacle, and pull the unit out of the box. Remove the wires from their respective terminals and replace them in the same arrangement on the new receptacle. Many new receptacles are the 3-wire grounded type, in which case you can either ignore the ground terminal, or join a short length of wire from the ground terminal directly to the outlet box; follow local code.

Multiple switches and outlets: Usually you would only have to replace one switch or outlet from a faulty multiple hookup. These multiple units should be tested in the same way as the single units.

Position of terminals of multiple switches or outlets may vary slightly on some brands. The important thing is to place all the wires removed from the old switch or outlet on the same screw terminals of the new unit.

Combination units: Combination switch/receptacle units are wired similarly to the single and double switches and outlets. Each switch, outlet, or pilot light requires one common wire obtained by using jumpers to connect all three terminals.

Grounding wires not shown on this page.

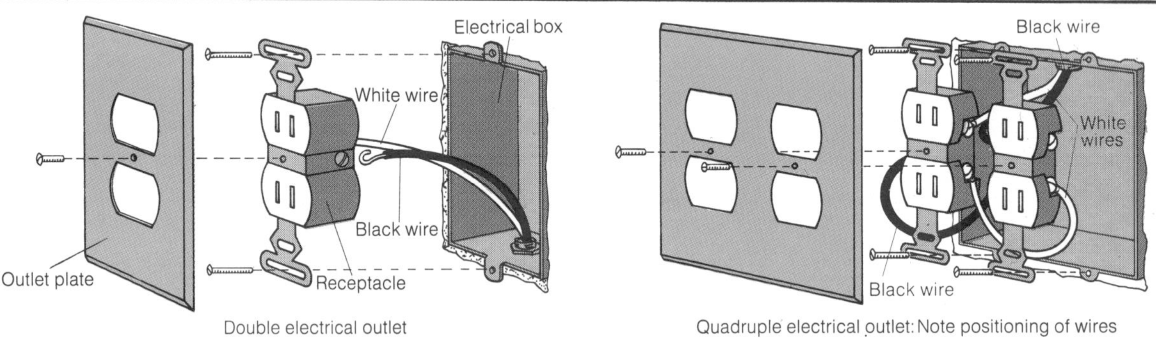

Double electrical outlet

Quadruple electrical outlet: Note positioning of wires

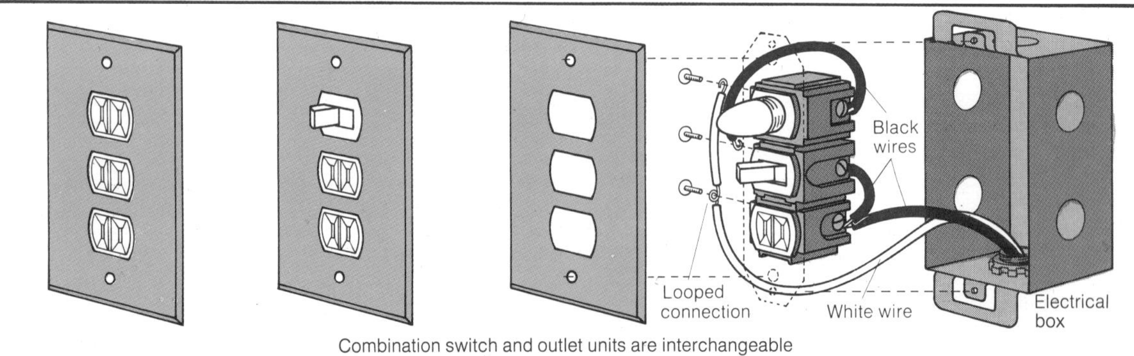

Combination switch and outlet units are interchangeable

Receptacles and dimmer switches

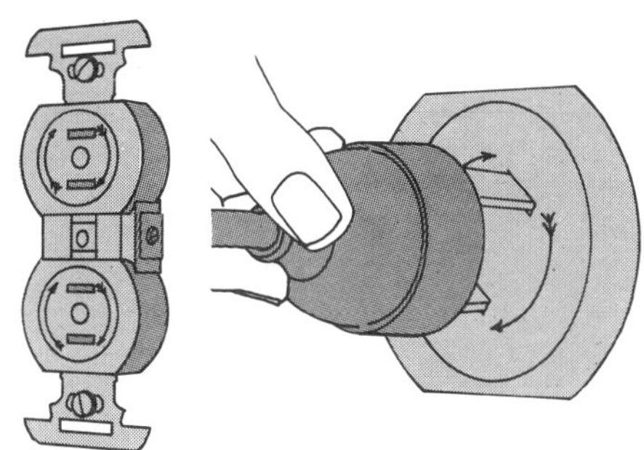

Safety outlet has plastic disks which are turned to open slots in the receptacle before the plug is inserted. Outlet is virtually childproof since it takes adult finger strength to twist the disks.

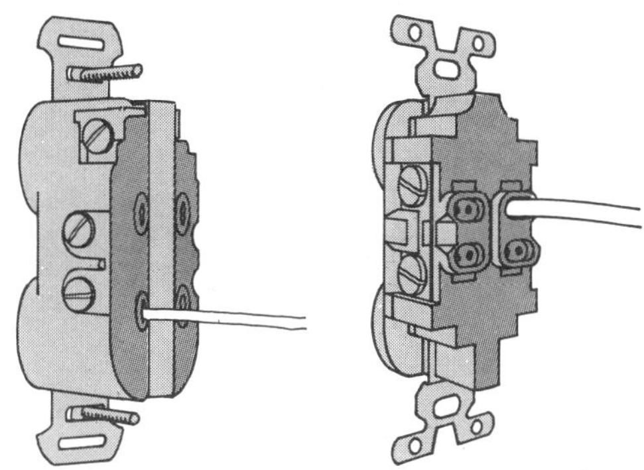

Backwired receptacles make wiring jobs easier. Instead of being looped, wires are pushed into holes. Some switches and receptacles have push-in connectors that eliminate screw terminals.

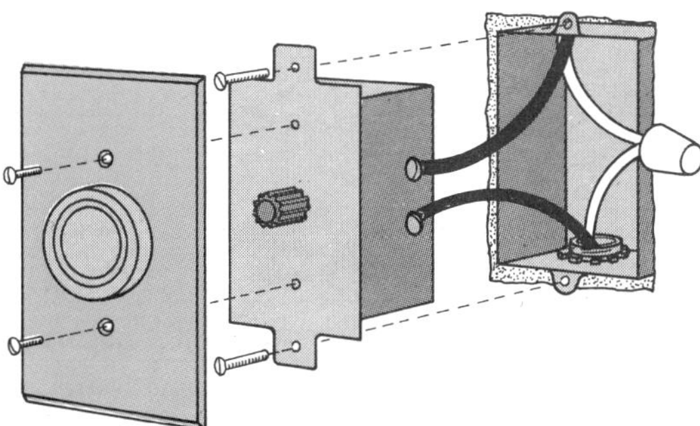

Dimmer switch controls replace ordinary switches. They are wired in the same way as single switches. Wattage capacity of switch must be higher than total wattage of lighting being controlled.

Wiring on wall surfaces

If you have to add electrical service to a room, the easiest and least expensive way is with surface wiring. This wiring method eliminates the need to cut into walls to install electrical boxes, to drill through studs, and to fish wires (p. 264). Several forms of surface wiring are available:

1. Plug-in strips: These are rigid plastic strips which are fastened to the wall or baseboard. The starting end plugs into an existing wall outlet. Wherever you need a receptacle, a molded plastic outlet is inserted into the strip.

2. Multioutlet strip: This is a flexible plastic ribbon that has wires running along each side under a plastic lip. The starting end of the strip is connected directly into the house wiring inside an electrical box. Once the strip has been fastened to the wall, outlets can be clipped into the cable wherever they are needed.

3. Metal raceways: These are metal channels through which wires are run. The raceways are fastened to the wall; some types even take the place of baseboards. Outlets, switches, and light fixtures can be mounted right in the metal channels. This type of unit is most appropriate for major electrical expansions, such as would be involved, for example, in adding a new section to a home.

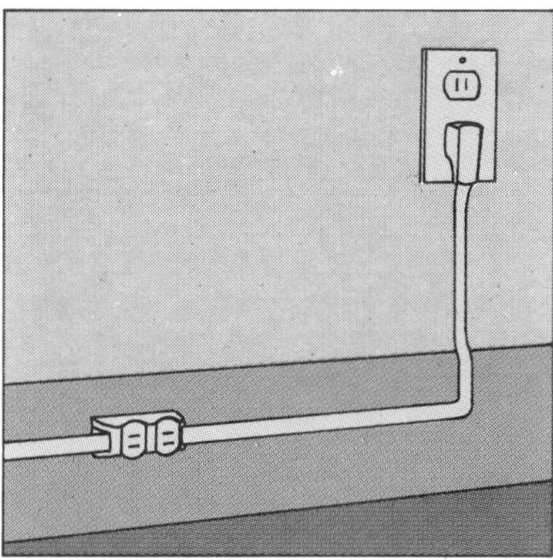

Plug-in surface wiring is fastened to wall or baseboard and receptacles are located where needed during assembly.

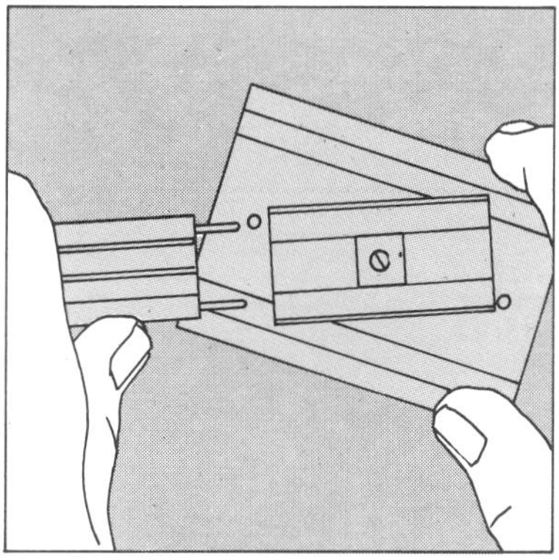

Multioutlet strip is connected directly into existing wall box and the strip is screwed to the wall or baseboard.

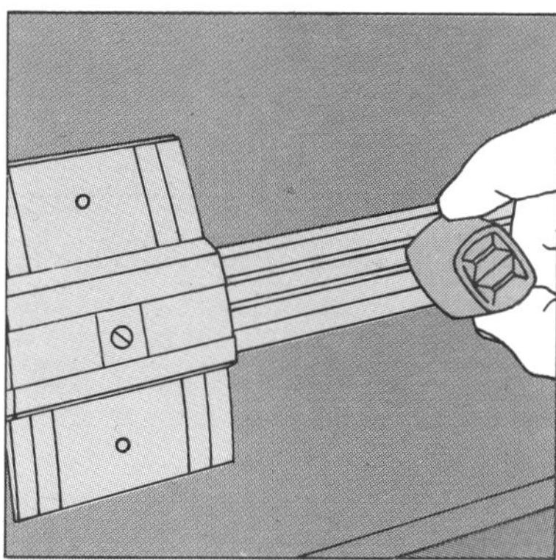

Outlets can be inserted anywhere along the strip. They twist into plastic channels and lock in place.

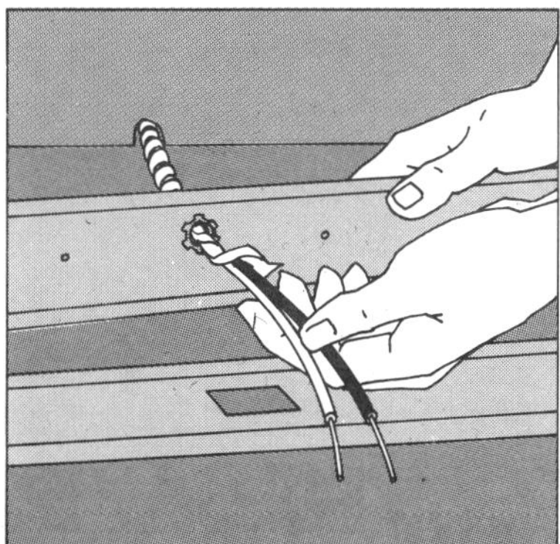

Metal raceway is fed by BX cable from household wiring. Base of raceway is fastened to the wall or baseboard.

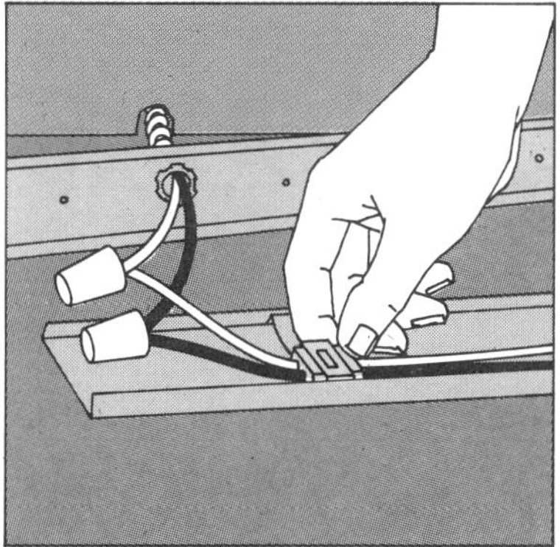

Wires from BX cable are connected to raceway wiring with wire nuts. Outlets are held in cover openings by spring clips.

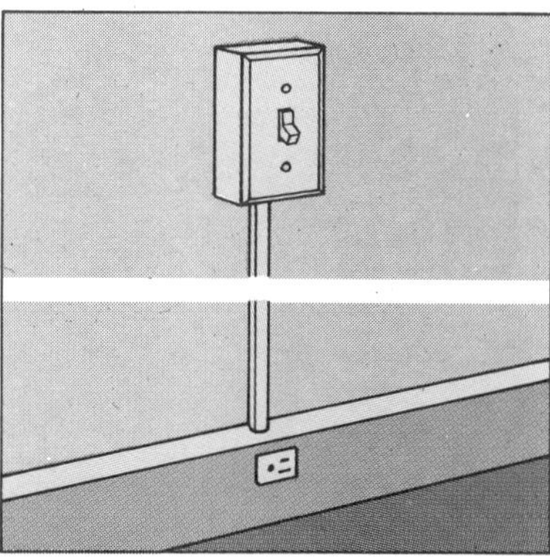

Metal raceways can be fitted with adapter plates that permit 2-wire channels to be connected with wall switches.

Wiring new circuits

Wiring in old construction

Wiring in new construction is seldom a problem since all studs and ceiling joists are exposed and accessible. Running wires in an existing structure, however, poses the problem of working inside walls. In the case of plaster walls or ceilings, channels must be gouged out for the wires and later replastered. In such instances, surface wiring (p. 263) is easier.

For drywall construction, it is necessary to wire through the spaces between walls and ceilings. The method of doing this is known as "fishing." This is done with a fish tape, a springy length of wire that is hooked at one end. It is fed through pre-drilled access holes in ceilings, floors, or walls. The electrical cable is attached to the hook, then pulled through the construction.

Wherever possible, plan to run wires across an attic floor or across the open ceiling of a basement. This will minimize the amount of fishing.

Fishing a wire

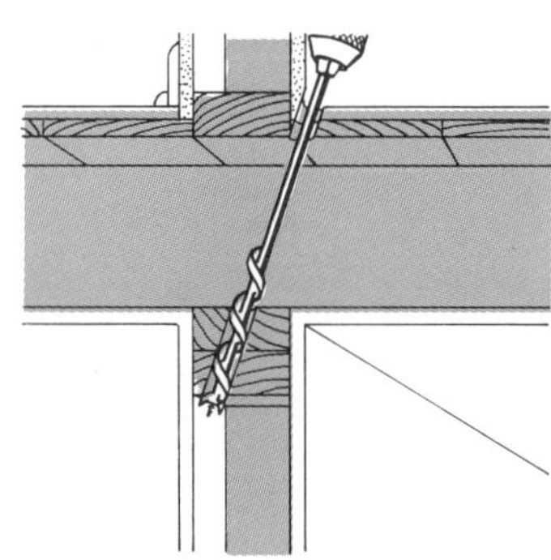

If there is a room or attic above, remove baseboard and drill diagonally through supporting beams into wall cavity. Use a brace and 18-in. bit.

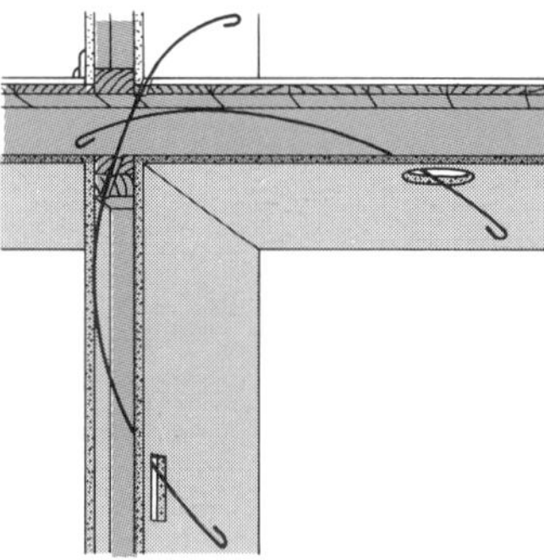

Feed a 12-ft. fish tape down from upper room and out the electrical box hole in the wall. Feed a second tape through ceiling hole. Hook the tapes.

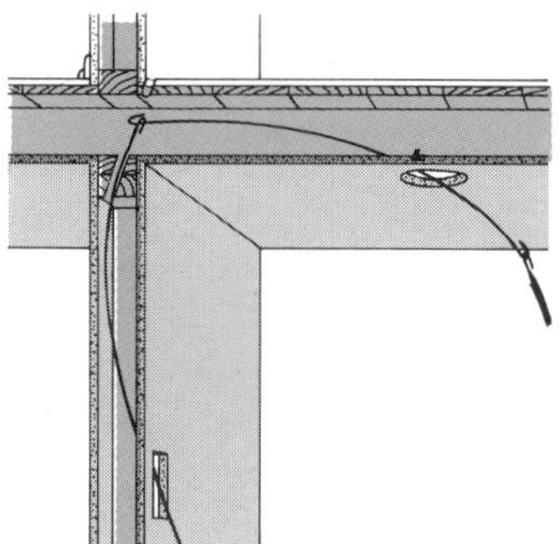

Withdraw both tapes through ceiling hole. Bind wire cable around hook, making sure no part of the binding is larger than the bored hole.

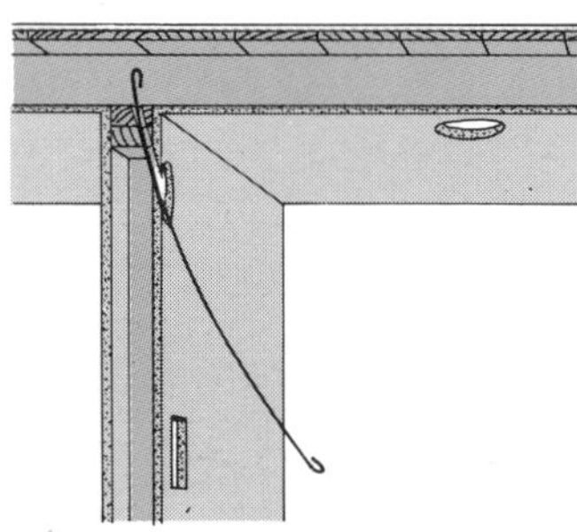

If there is no access above, cut large hole in wall 5 in. from ceiling. Bore diagonally up through support beams into ceiling cavity. Insert fish tape.

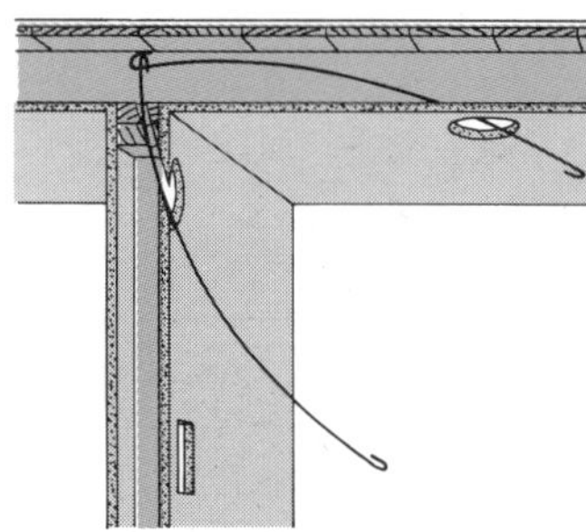

Insert second fish tape through ceiling hole. Fish until tapes interlock. Withdraw tapes through ceiling hole until hook of wall tape can be grasped.

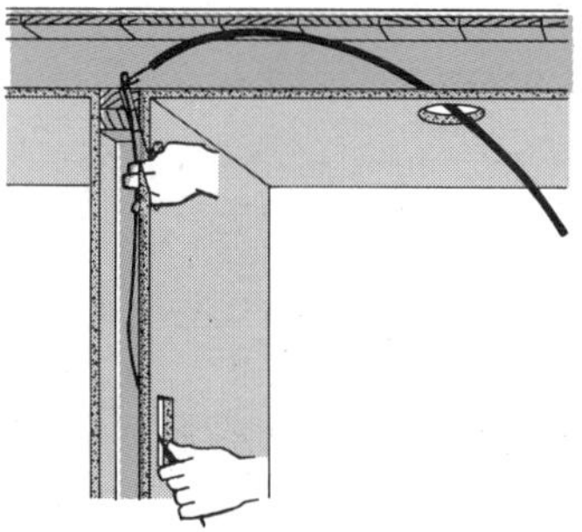

Attach cable to tape hook, then withdraw tape and cable by pulling down through large hole in the wall. Feed free end of tape out box holes.

How to run a wire

Wiring around door frame: Remove baseboard and door trim. Notch wall and spacers between frame and jamb. Use an 18-in. bit in a brace to drill through headers and uprights.

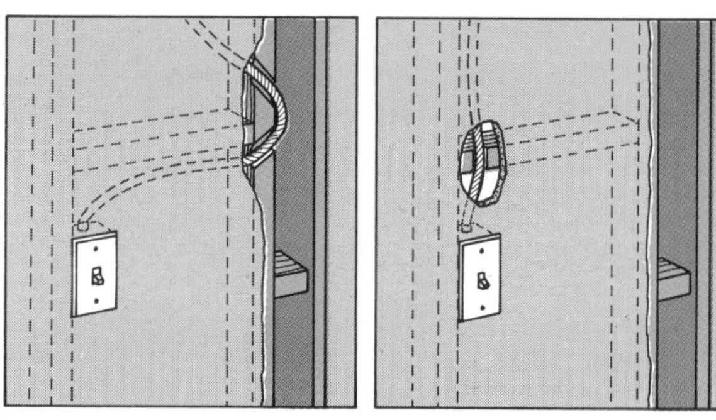

Wiring around door-frame headers: Notch upright twice and wire through both notches. Or make hole in wall, notch header, pass wiring through notch in header. Replaster hole (p. 92).

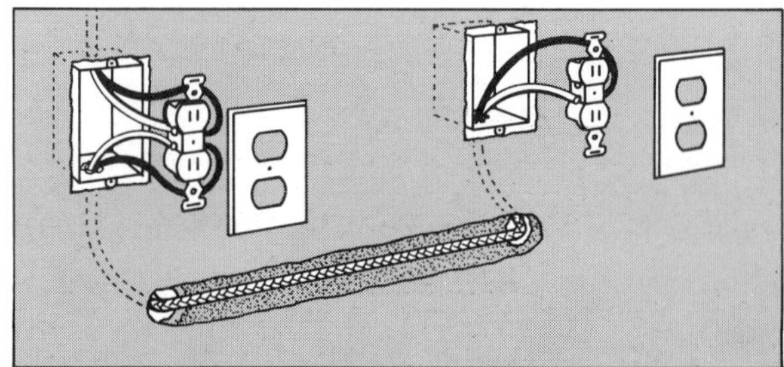

Wiring from one outlet to another in plaster walls: Notch plaster so the wire can run in a channel inside the wall. Notch hole for box. Connect wires and replaster.

Lath and plaster walls

Ideal positioning for switch boxes is about 4 feet from the floor; for outlet boxes, roughly 12 to 18 inches off the floor. Outlets for wall-mounted light fixtures should be 60 to 70 inches above the floor. Be sure to mount switches on the opening side of a door rather than on the hinged side. Always use 2½-inch-deep electrical boxes rather than the shallow ones, unless some structural problem will not permit the deeper box. With lath and plaster construction, you can locate an electrical box almost anywhere along the wall, since the wooden lathwork is strong enough to hold the box securely.

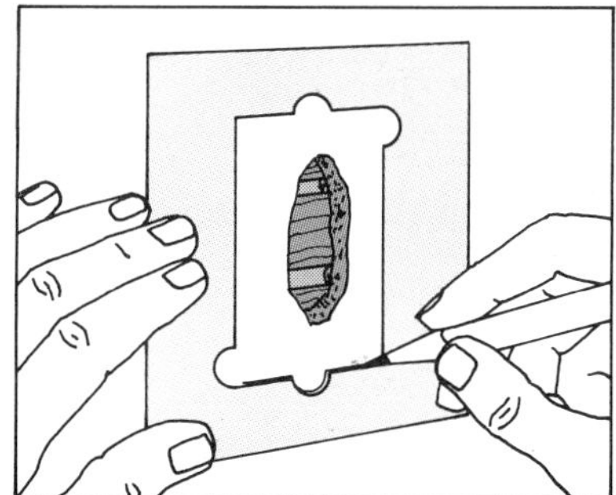

Locate stud. Cut an opening in the plaster 5 in. out from stud, large enough to expose laths. Use template at right to outline hole to be made in the wall.

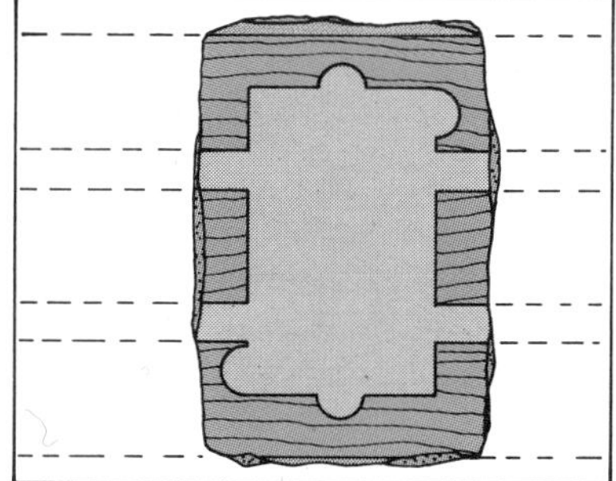

Remove plaster. Drill saw holes. Hold your hand against wall to prevent cracks. Cut away center lath completely. Cut sections from laths above and below.

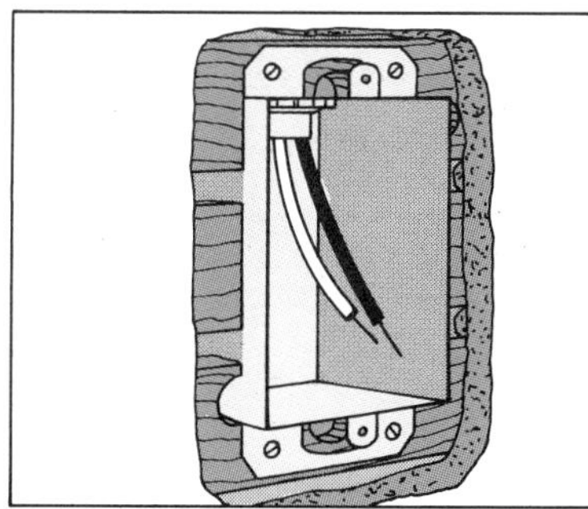

Punch knockout disks from box. Pull wiring through hole. Attach connector. Install locknut. Push box into hole. Anchor box to lath with wood screws.

Drywall installations

In drywall or wood paneling, boxes can be mounted between studs by means of special clamping devices (p. 260) that grip the inside of the hollow wall. The strongest point in this type of construction, however, is at the studs. You can get boxes equipped with brackets that can be nailed or screwed directly to the face of the studwork. To fit boxes directly onto the studs, you must first locate the stud, then chip a notch out of the drywall large enough to accept the fastening bracket. Connect the wires to the box before placing it in the hole. When installation is complete, patch the hole (p. 99).

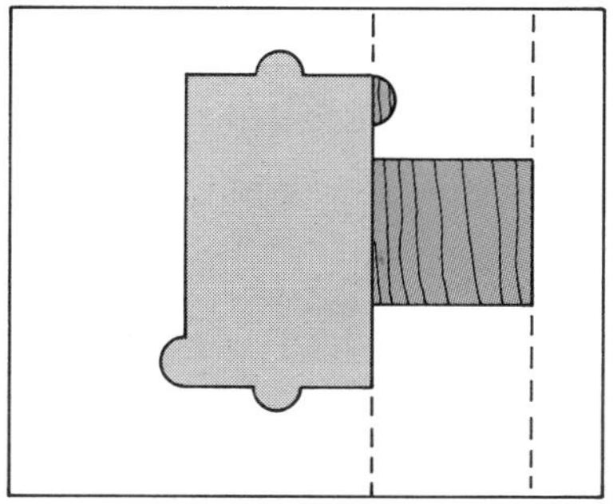

Locate stud. Notch drywall to expose stud. Outline area next to stud with template. Drill saw holes. Hold hand against wall to prevent cracks. Saw out section.

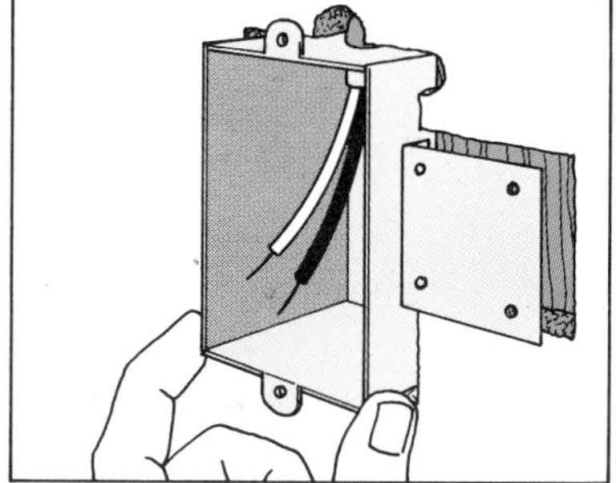

Punch knockout disks from box. Pull wiring through hole. Attach connectors. Install locknut. Line up bracket with stud and push box into hole.

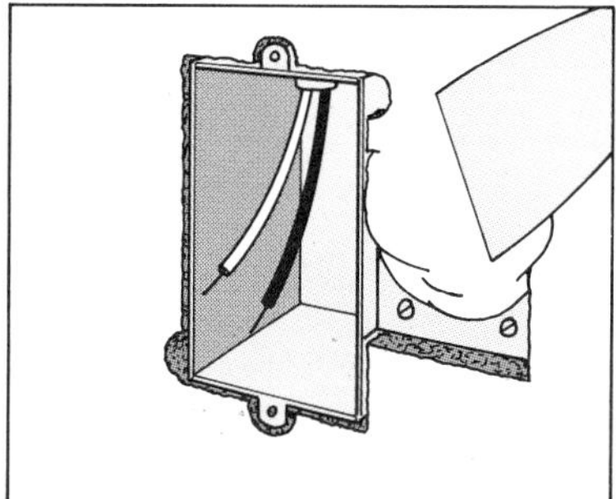

Anchor box bracket to stud with screws. Fill area around box and bracket with either plaster or spackle so that it is flush with the wall surface.

Locating studs

There are several methods for locating studs. One of the following should work for you:

1. Tap the wall lightly at points above the nails in the baseboard. A hollow sound means there is no stud. A solid sound indicates the presence of a stud. To be sure that you have found the stud, use a small drill (⅛ inch) to bore holes in the wall slightly above the baseboard. Drill several holes side by side until you bore into the stud.

2. Baseboard removal: With the baseboard off, check to see where two panels of drywall meet. This point will indicate the center of a stud. This method also works with paneled walls.

3. Measuring from the corner: Studs are generally located either 16 or 24 inches apart. Which it is depends on local building codes. Try measuring out from the corner of a room to find the approximate location of a stud, then use the drilling technique described above to find the exact stud location.

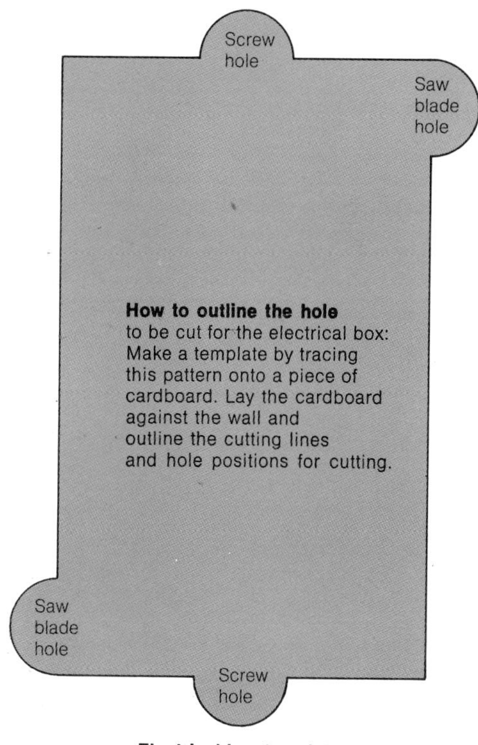

Electrical box template

Mounting a ceiling box

If you plan to install a ceiling light and the space above the ceiling is not accessible, you will have to work from below. Cut away plaster or other ceiling material to fit a shallow box, then any backing that is in the way. Fish the BX cable through the opening. Next install a hanger bar across the opening. Thread the cable through one of the holes in the box; secure with a locknut. The stud on the hanger passes through the center hole of the box. Tighten the nut until box is secure against backing. A shallow box is recommended; few chandelier canopies are large enough to cover a full-size box.

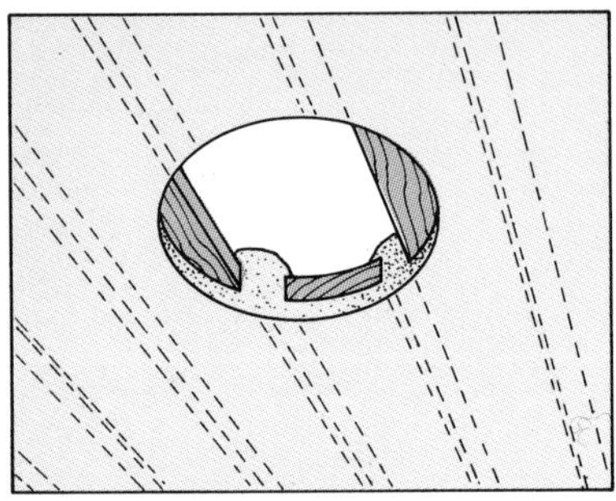

Draw box outline on ceiling and remove plaster or other ceiling material up to backing. Carefully cut away any backing that is visible through the hole.

Fish the BX cable through the hole. Insert hanger bar so it will rest across the backing material. Stud on hanger bar should be long enough to pass through box.

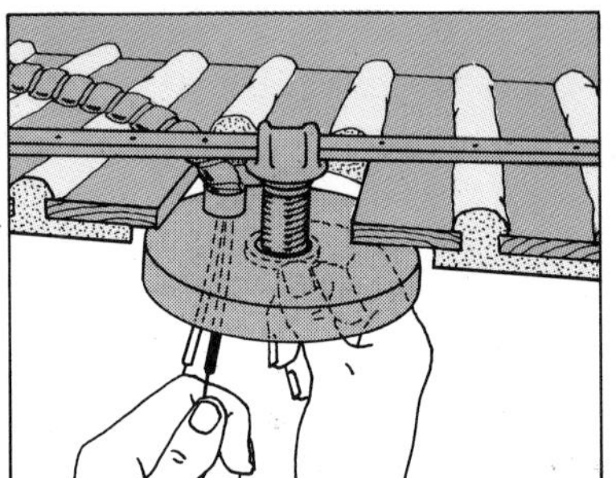

Pass the cable through one of the holes in the box and secure it with a locknut. Raise the box so that stud will pass through the center hole; secure with nut.

Recessed ceiling fixture

To install a recessed ceiling fixture, first locate the ceiling joists, by touch and sound or, if necessary, by drilling a few holes with a small drill. Outline the space between the joists for the box. (Joists are usually 16 inches apart.)

Saw out the required section with a keyhole saw. Next screw wood strips between joists to support the box. Some manufacturers supply metal support strips as well as junction boxes as part of the fixture.

Bring the cable to the junction box and secure it with a locknut. Allow 4 inches of wire beyond the locknut for connecting. Make sure that the cable end is protected with an insulating sleeve. Connect the white wire to the nickel-plated binding post and the black wire to the brass-plated post. Push the fixture into the opening; secure it with roundhead screws.

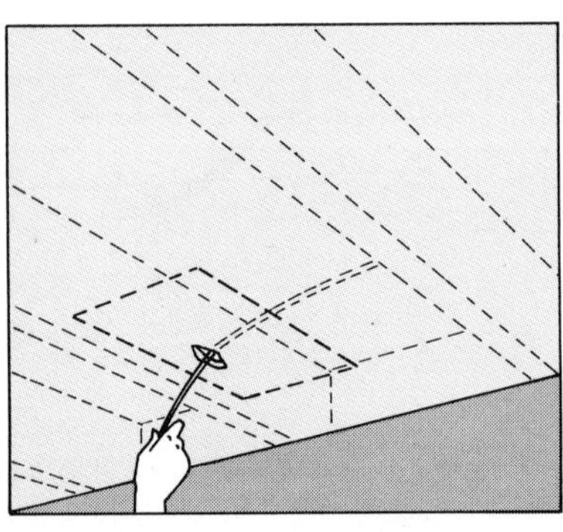

Locate joists by tapping or drilling pilot holes and probing with a wire.

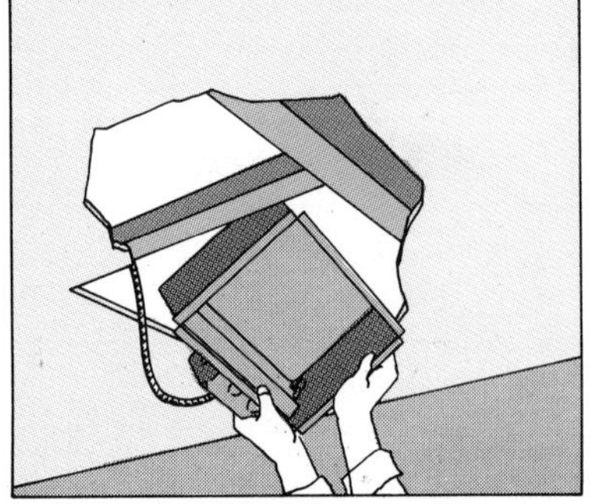

Cut opening between joists to accept the fixture. Secure cable to junction box.

Insert the ceiling fixture box and secure it to the wood strips with screws.

Installing a floor outlet

A floor outlet is convenient because you need not fish wires. Installation is easiest above a basement; the required power for takeoff is usually available from a cable running along or between basement joists. First locate—and avoid—the joist at the installation point by drilling a hole, through basement ceiling and floor above, at each side of joist. The holes mark joist width, so make opening at either side.

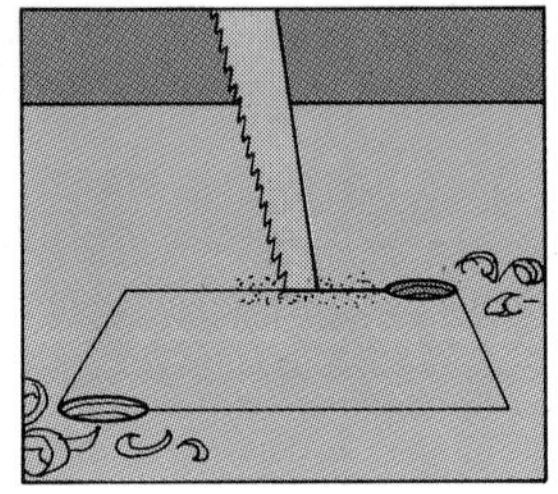

Draw an outline of the box between the floor joists. Drill a clearance hole in each corner and saw out opening.

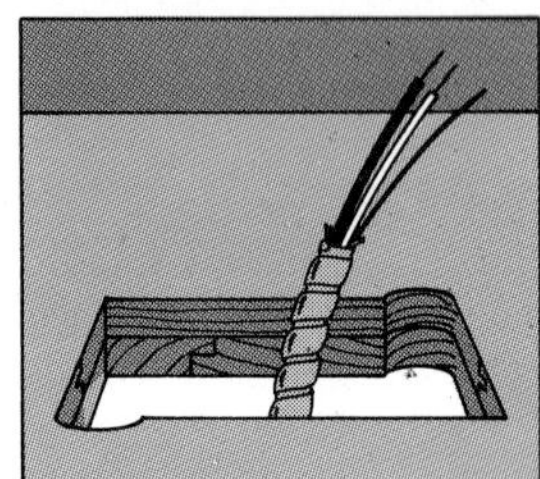

Pull the BX cable through the opening and anchor it to the ceiling below. Strip off armor to expose 4 in. of wire.

Pass the cable through one of the knockouts in the box and secure with a locknut. Use insulating bushing at cable end.

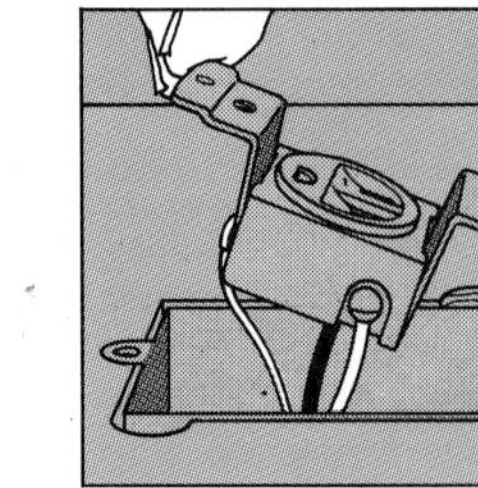

Screw the box to the floor with flathead screws. Connect black wire to brass screw and white wire to nickel-plated screw.

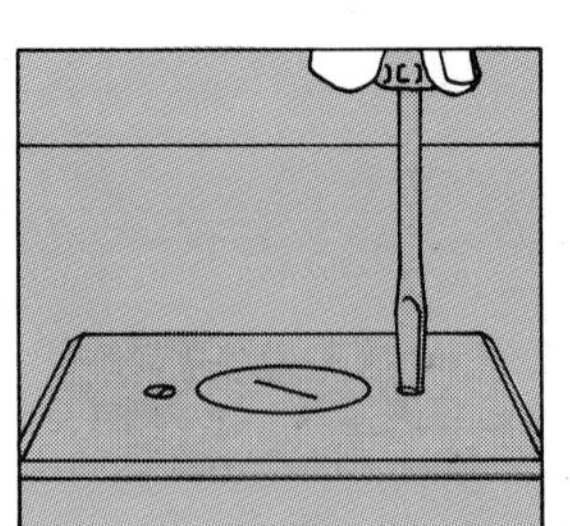

Install the outlet plate after the receptacle has been bolted to the outlet box. Note dust cover over the plug opening.

Connect other end of cable to power source. Remove cover and insert appliance plug which can take dust protector.

How to install a chandelier

Use a sturdy ladder to work on ceiling fixtures. Check whether you can do the job or if it must be done by a licensed electrician (or approved by one).

Before beginning any work, turn off the main power source or the circuit controlling the light (p. 253). Use a test light to find out if the wiring is still "hot." If the old fixture hanger or bracket is the same as the one that comes with the new fixture, use the old one.

You will need to support the fixture as you work. You can do this by bending a coat hanger to size and hooking it to the new fixture and ceiling box, or you can tie the fixture to the box with strong cord.

Connect the black wire in the ceiling box to the black wire of the fixture, and the white wire to the white wire. Make sure the wiring doesn't rub against any surface that might wear through the insulation. Apply tape to any such possible areas. If you use wiring nuts, tape them so that they won't loosen. If you prefer soldered connections, tin wires first, solder them together, then apply enough tape to equal the thickness of the scraped-away insulation.

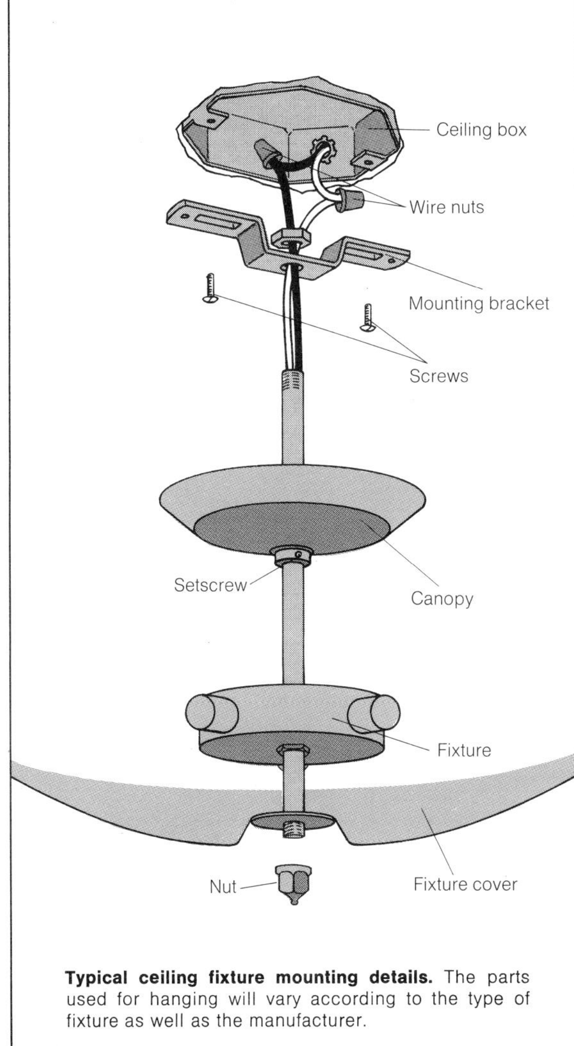

Typical ceiling fixture mounting details. The parts used for hanging will vary according to the type of fixture as well as the manufacturer.

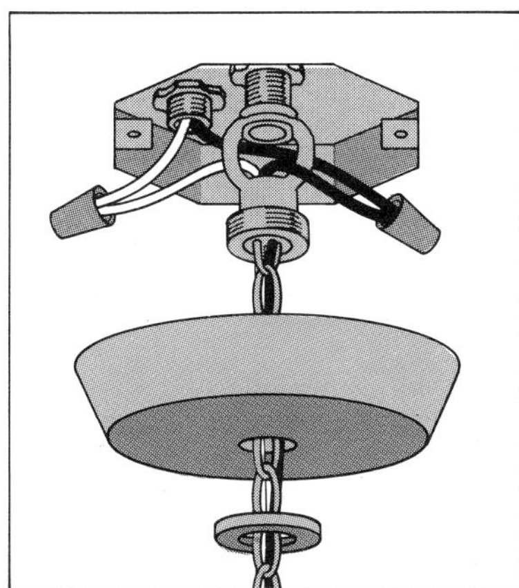

1. Turn off power. Loosen and remove the chains. Holding canopy in one hand, loosen setscrew or locknut at bottom of canopy. Lower canopy.

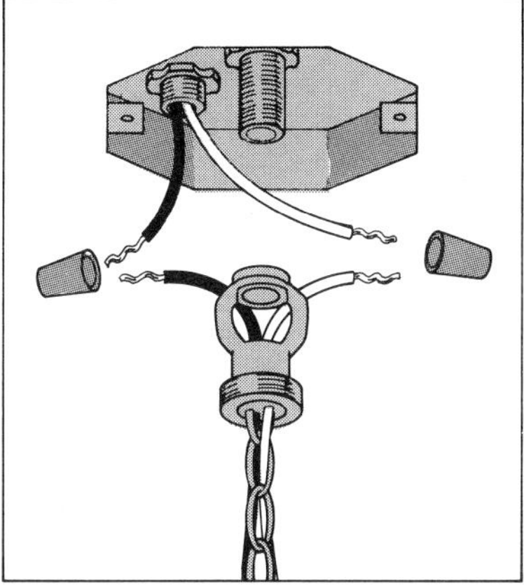

2. Support the fixture; pull out wires. Remove nuts holding wires together or cut the connections. Unscrew the nipple from the stud in ceiling box.

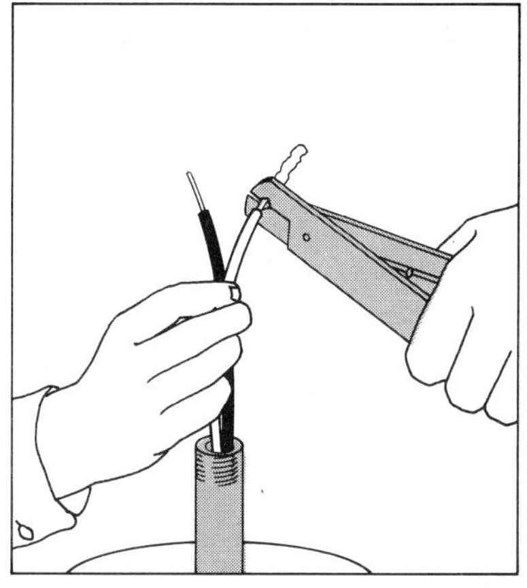

3. Strip a 2-in. length of insulation from the wires of the new fixture. Use wire nuts to make connections between fixture wires and the wires from ceiling box.

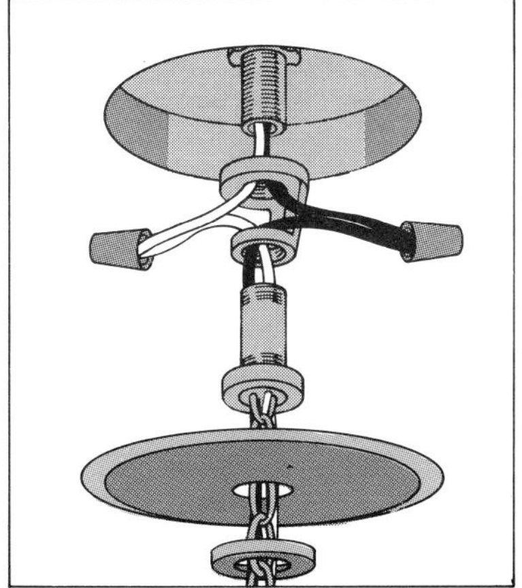

4. Screw nipple back to ceiling box stud. Connect fixture and ceiling wires, black to black, white to white. Push up canopy and secure with locknut or setscrew.

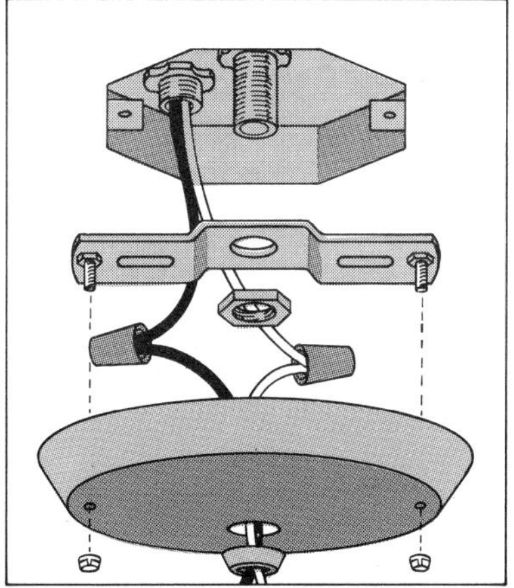

You may encounter this type of installation, where a steel bracket is connected to a stud in the center of the box and fixture is bolted to the bracket.

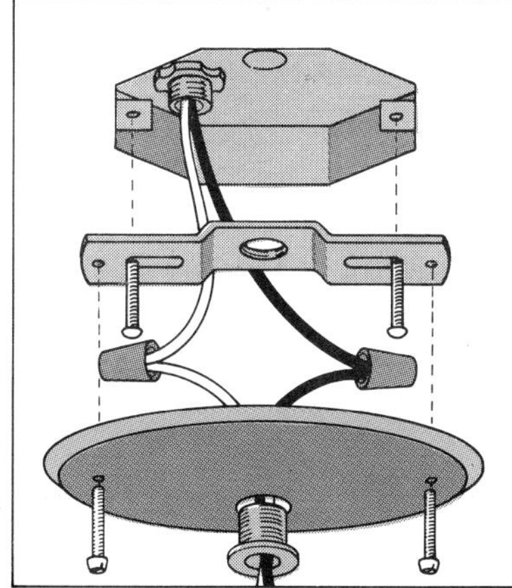

Another possibility: The bracket is bolted to the ears on the sides of the box, and the fixture is also bolted to the bracket as shown in drawing above.

Wiring switches, outlets, and fixtures

Wiring 2-, 3-, and 4-way switches

How a switch, outlet, or fixture is wired depends upon its location in relation to the wires that lead from the main service entrance. The diagrams on the following three pages show a variety of common switch, outlet, and fixture wiring installations. To use these, find the diagram that most closely resembles your wiring arrangement. Then follow the pattern of joining white wires to white wires and black to black.

The white wires are always neutral, the black ones always hot; however, in certain switch installations both black and white wires are hot. In such cases, you should dab black paint on the white wires at the switch and fixture to indicate a hot wire. **Drawings on pages 268 and 269 are diagrammatic, without grounding wires.**

Two-wire joining methods

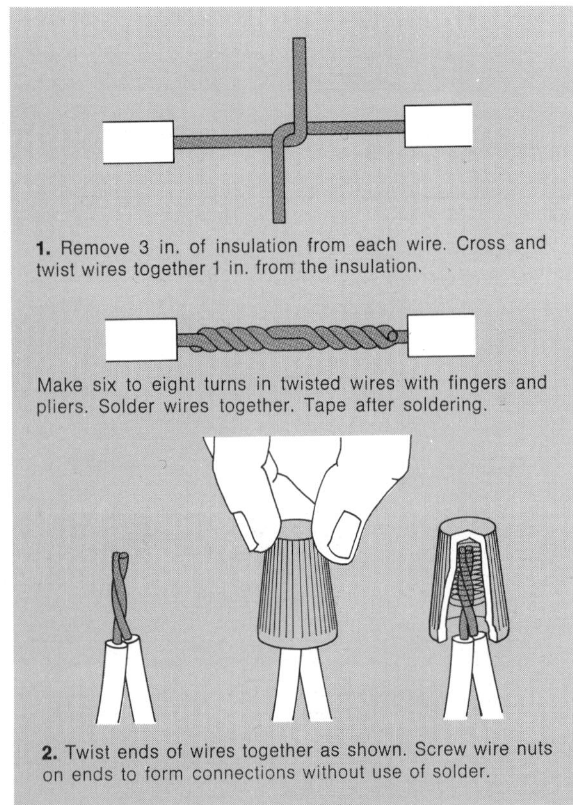

1. Remove 3 in. of insulation from each wire. Cross and twist wires together 1 in. from the insulation.

Make six to eight turns in twisted wires with fingers and pliers. Solder wires together. Tape after soldering.

2. Twist ends of wires together as shown. Screw wire nuts on ends to form connections without use of solder.

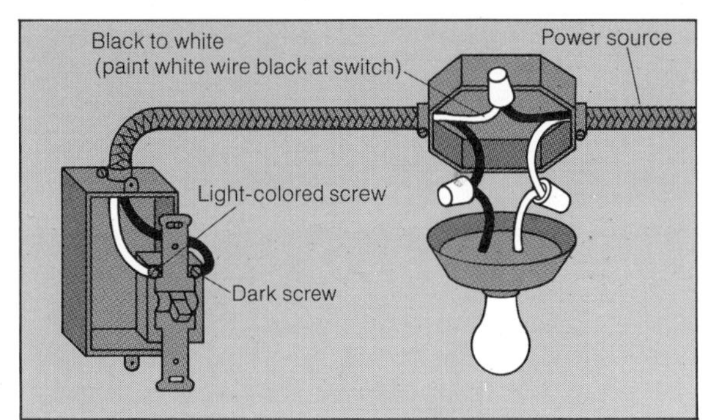

Wall switch to control ceiling fixture at the end of its run: Note that black feed wire is connected to white wire from the switch. Paint white wires at fixture and switch black.

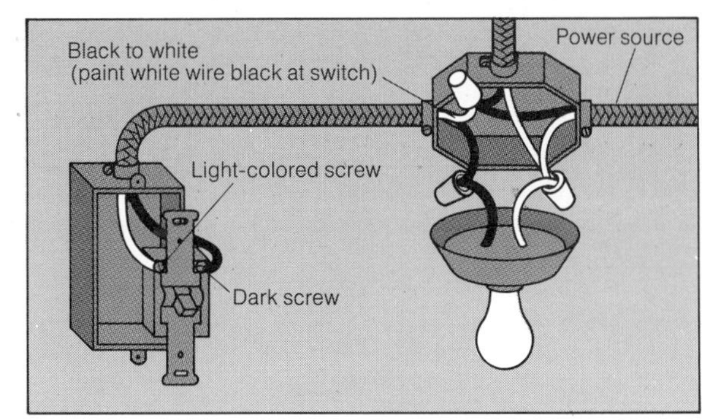

Wall switch to control ceiling fixture in the middle of run: This wiring hookup is similar to wiring at left. Paint white wires at switch and fixture black to indicate they are hot.

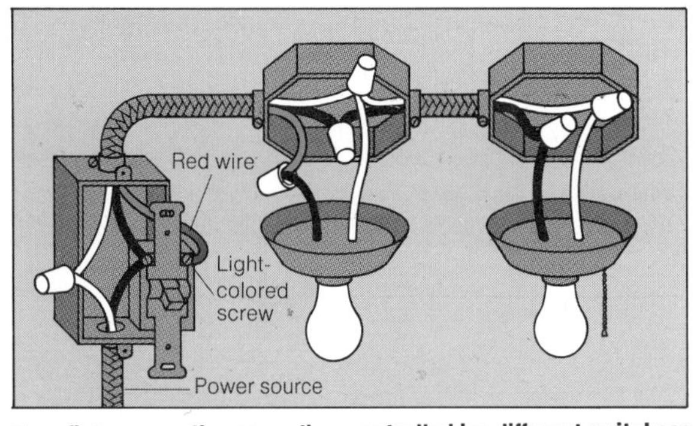

Two fixtures on the same line controlled by different switches: Fixture on left is controlled by switch to the left. Fixture on right is controlled by pull chain on fixture.

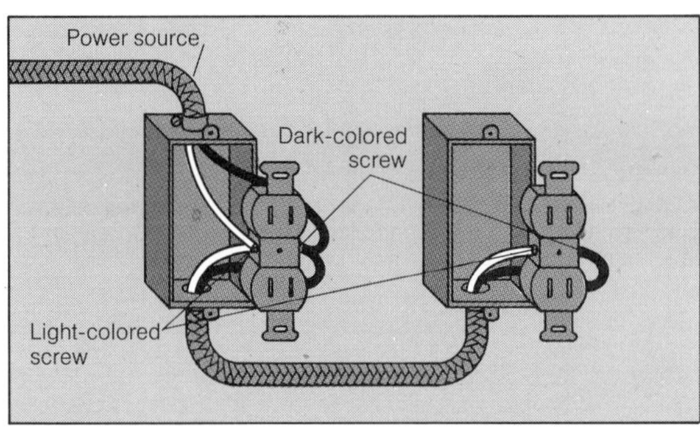

Adding a supplementary outlet to an existing outlet: Connect feed wire to top terminals on existing outlet (left). New outlet is connected to lower terminals.

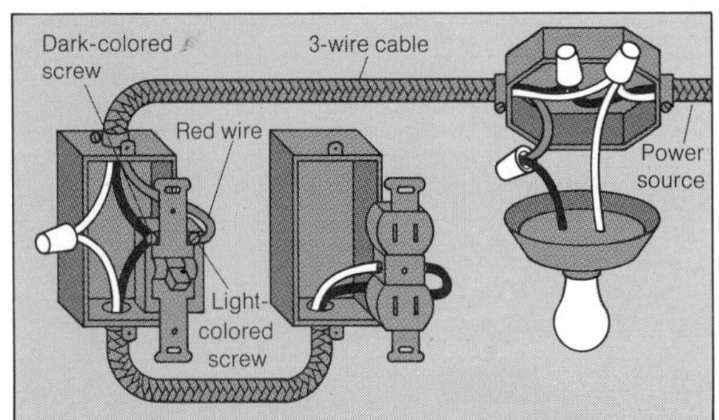

Adding a new switch and outlet to an existing ceiling fixture: Fixture is controlled by wall switch. Operation of new outlet is unaffected by operation of wall switch.

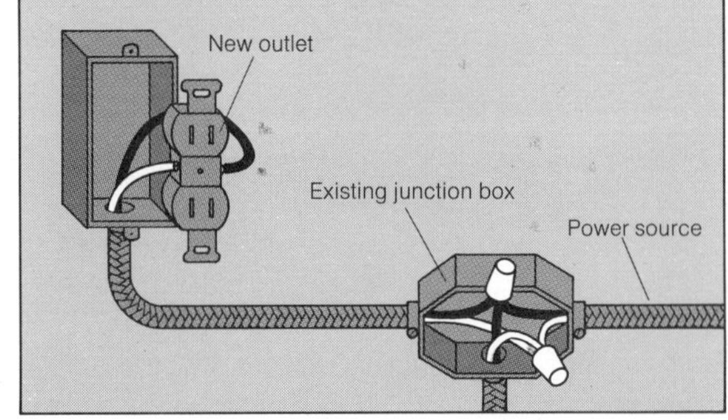

Adding a new outlet or fixture to an existing junction box: Same wiring arrangement as for outlet could be used to connect a new ceiling fixture instead of an outlet.

Wiring 2-, 3-, and 4-way switches

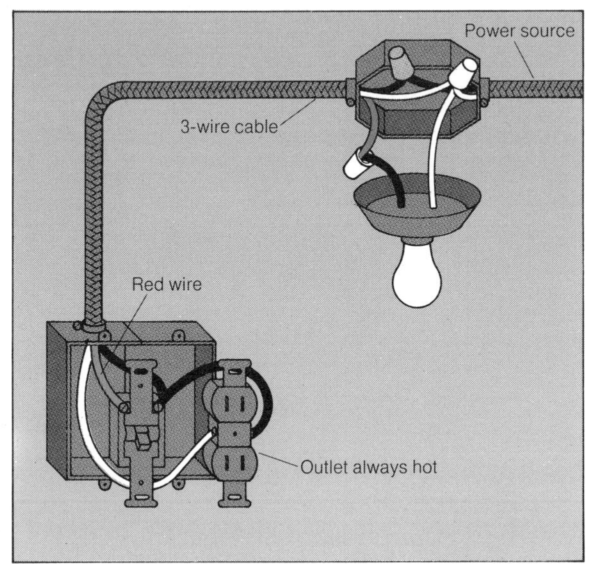

Adding switch and outlet in the same box to ceiling fixture: Existing ceiling fixture is controlled by new switch. Operation of new outlet is unaffected by new switch.

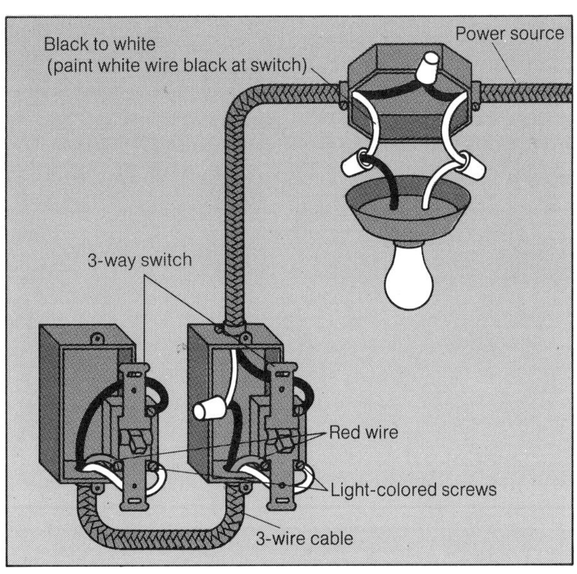

Same ceiling fixture controlled by two different switches: Three-wire cable must be used between switches. Either switch, each located at a different spot, can control fixture.

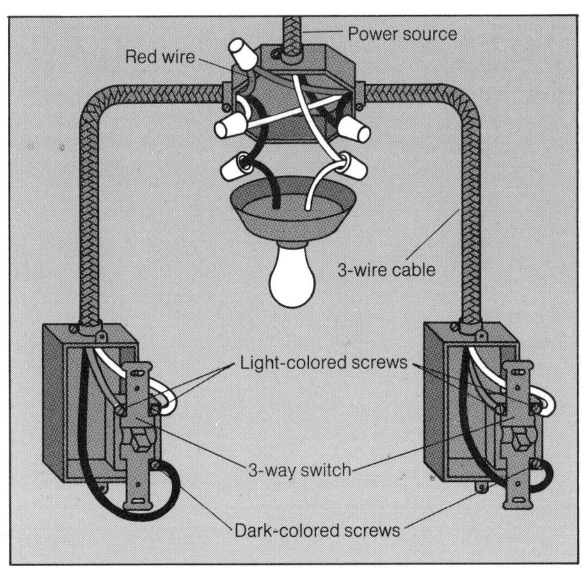

Ceiling fixture between two switches, controlled by either: Three-wire cable connects each switch to the fixture. Feed wire to fixture is a 2-wire cable.

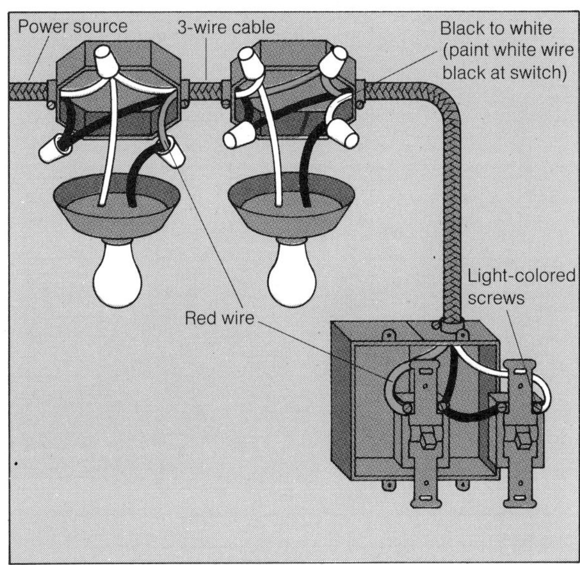

Two separate fixtures controlled by two switches: Left fixture controlled by left switch. Feed wire is 2-wire cable. Fixture and switch connections are 3-wire.

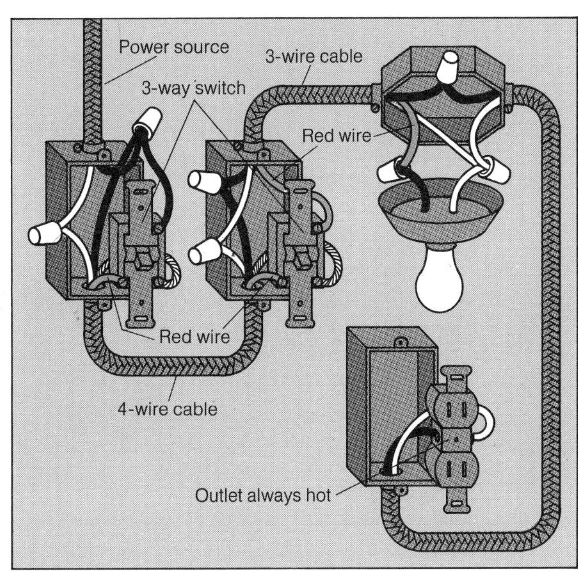

Fixture controlled by separate switches; outlet always hot: Feed wire and outlet connections are 2-wire cable; connections between switches and outlet, 4-wire cable or two 2-wire cables.

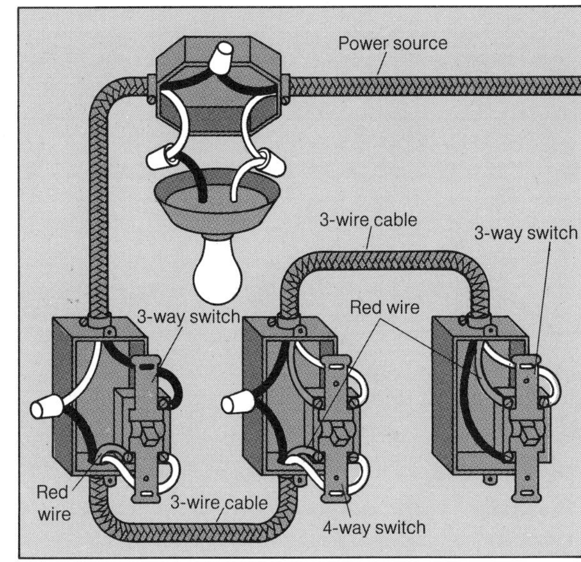

Ceiling fixture controlled from three separate locations: Two 3-way switches and one 4-way switch are required. Each extra control point requires an additional 4-way switch.

New grounding requirements

The National Electrical Code now requires that new residential outlets be grounded by a grounding wire, or "jumper," connected between a grounded outlet box and the grounding terminal of the receptacle. A grounding screw is provided for this purpose in many new boxes; if it is lacking, buy a special grounding connector. The reason for the jumper is to provide a secure grounding path. Grounding may be established by contact between the outlet box and the receptacle's metal yoke where this type of contact is adequate, as on surface-type boxes. Flush-type outlet boxes, however, are frequently installed too deeply in the wall to permit sound metal-to-metal contact between yoke and box. Grounding, in these cases, depends upon the uncertain electrical path provided by the mounting screws; so the jumper is used. If the yoke is specially designed to provide a reliable grounding circuit between box and receptacle, it will suffice. Check your local code.

Not all switches have grounding terminals, which are often used with nonmetallic boxes.

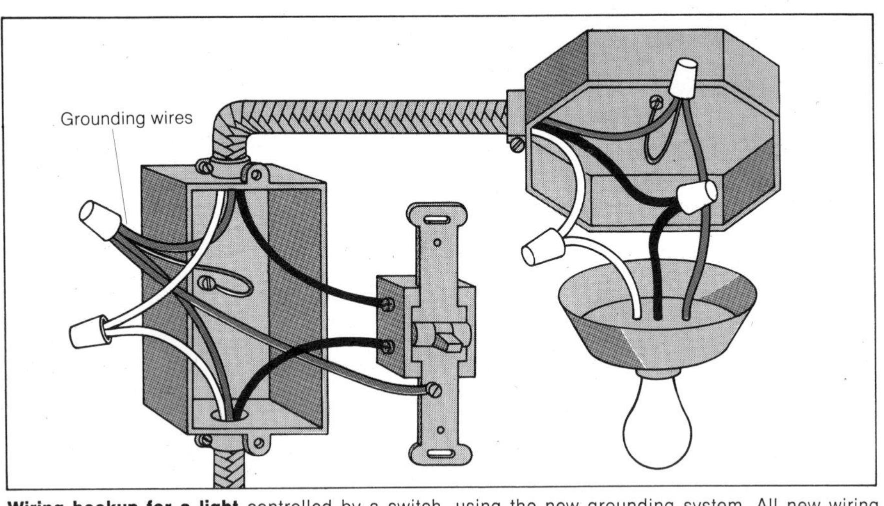

Wiring hookup for a light controlled by a switch, using the new grounding system. All new wiring must have an extra wire as a ground; with Romex, use the bare middle wire.

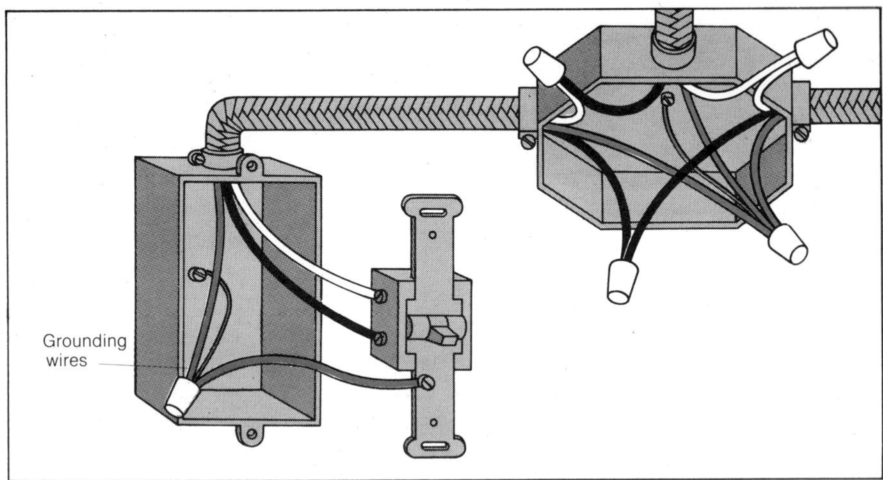

Switch wired through junction box controls light at far end of cable. This type of wiring is called a switch loop. White wire leads to switch; black wire leads from switch to fixture.

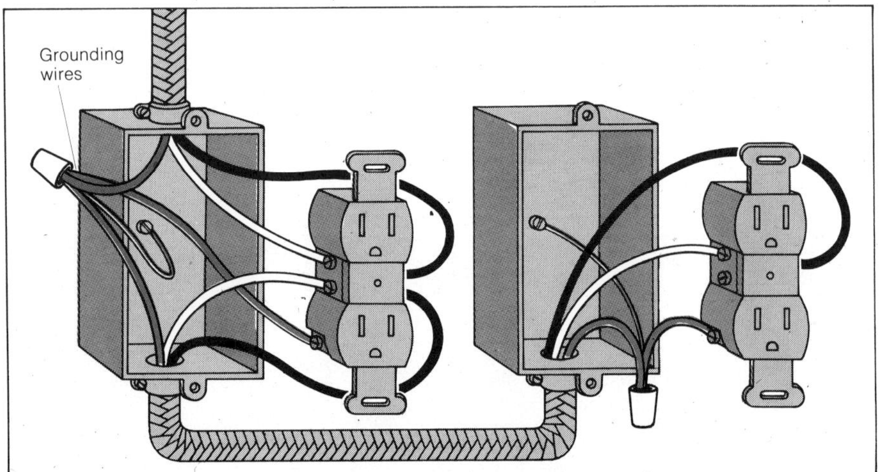

Extending power to a new outlet. Both outlets have a self-grounding strap and binding post that is connected by means of the jumper wire to the grounding post in each box.

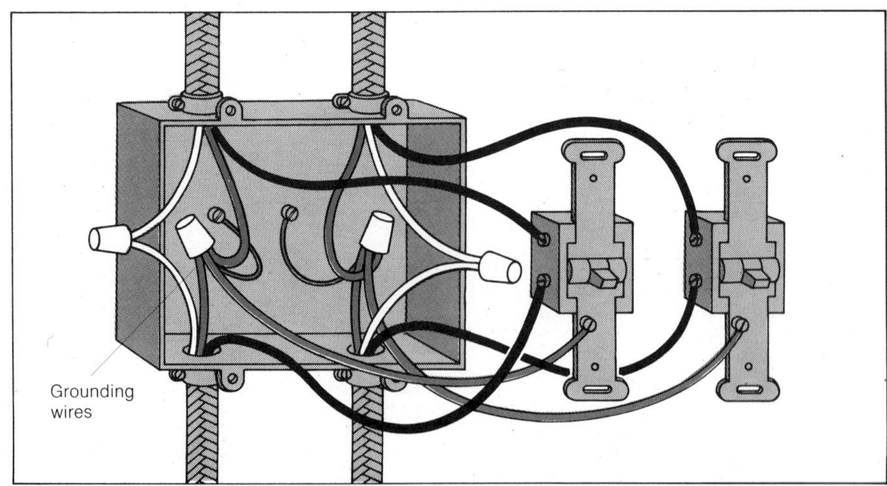

Two switches independently controlling two ceiling fixtures and wired according to the revised code. Grounding terminal is lacking on many switches but must be used if required by local code.

Installation requirements

Outdoor receptacles must be the weatherproof type. They usually have a spring-loaded cover to seal them when they are not in use. The juncture between the cover plate and the wall surface must also be made water-tight with a caulking compound.

Surface-mounted receptacles also have a weatherproof outlet box mounted on the outside face of the wall rather than flush with the wall. Wiring for either type is led to the box through a length of threaded conduit (p. 272). All wiring to outside outlets must now be protected by a ground fault interrupter (GFI). Grounding and wiring connections are the same as for an indoor receptacle.

Only fixtures and wire approved for outdoor use should be used for outdoor lighting. If the bulb will be exposed to the weather, it should be a weatherproof type to prevent its shattering from contact with rain or snow while in operation.

One type of outdoor lighting fixture is designed to fit a small box in which the connections between fixture wires and supply wires can be made. The box is equipped with a cover and a gasket for protection against rain after the connections have been made.

One way to make the wiring passage through the house wall is with conduit (the rigid, threaded type) screwed to the back of the box. If the conduit leads to a grounded junction box inside the house, and is properly connected, it serves to ground the outside fixture. If the conduit merely passes through the wall and serves only as a channel for the cable, the cable must be grounded.

Any tools or appliances that are plugged into an outdoor outlet should be of the grounding or double-insulated type; make certain that their cords are not frayed. Extension cords should be of sufficient capacity that they will convey current to the tool without a drop in the voltage (p. 259).

An outdoor soffit light, such as is shown at the right, can be hooked up with a photoelectric eye to turn the light on at dusk and off at dawn. The bulb is screwed into the photoelectric eye adapter and the adapter is then screwed into the socket. No further wiring is required.

Caution: Before doing any wiring, always make certain that you have turned off the current and that you will be complying with your local electrical code.

Outdoor outlet

Wire an outdoor receptacle to the nearest junction box in the house. Switch can be used to control outlet.

Cut hole in wall of house to exact size of outlet box. Secure cable; leave 4 in. of wire for connections.

Install the receptacle with weatherproof faceplate. Caulk opening around box to prevent water getting into outlet.

Eave light

Connect cable to power inside house and pass it through a 1-in. hole drilled in the soffit. Work with current off.

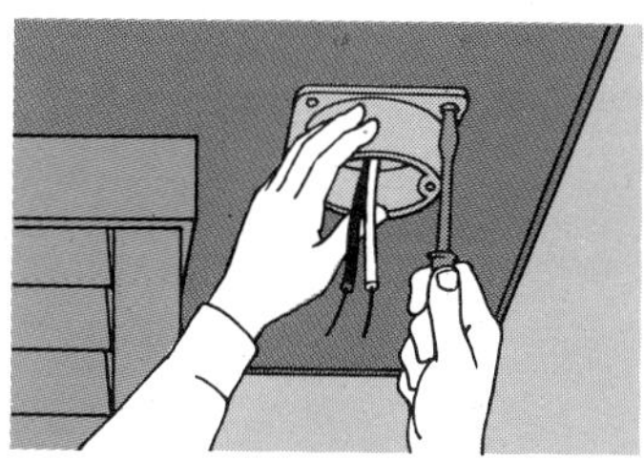

Secure the cable end to special outdoor box with locknut. Allow 4 in. of wire for connections.

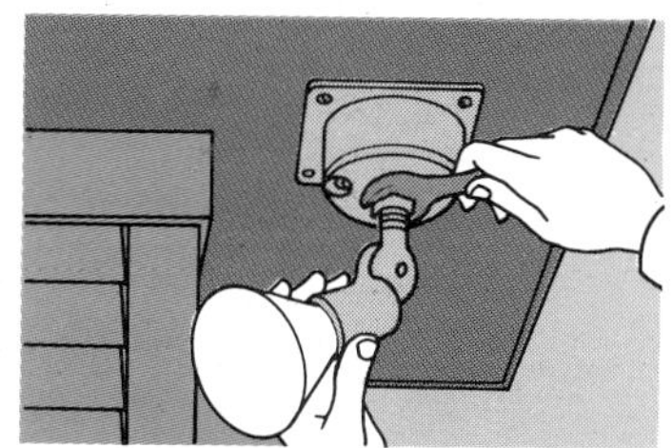

Connect white wire to white wire and black to black. Secure socket assembly with the bolts provided.

Accessories

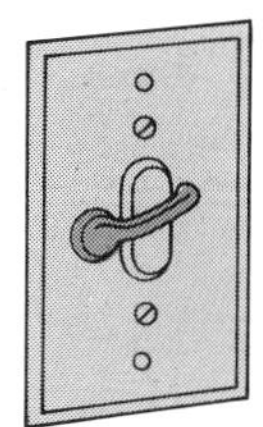

Switch for outdoor use is especially designed to be weatherproof.

Weatherproof outlets have screw-on caps or spring-loaded lids to protect the openings from the elements.

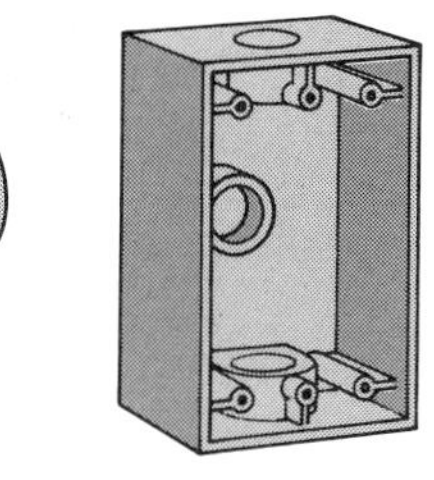

Special outdoor boxes must be used with outdoor switches, outlets.

Portable outdoor outlet is grounded by third wire in the cord.

Outdoor wiring

Installation

Plan your outdoor wiring so that each circuit is protected by its own fuse or circuit breaker. Wire directly to the main service entrance, or to an add-on panel (p. 256). Wiring through conduit (p. 260) is preferred, but grounded underground-type cable can also be used. Check local building and electrical codes before doing any actual wiring.

Plan the number of outlets and permanent lights carefully to avoid having to use extension cords. Add 10 to 20 feet to whatever the distance is between your house and the projected outlets and fixtures to get the number of feet of wiring you will need to buy. This will provide plenty of slack for buried wiring. Use No. 14 or heavier wire.

Cut or drill holes in the side of the house close to the fuse or circuit breaker box. If your house is wood, make certain that holes are located between studs. Holes in concrete or stone can be made with a star drill (p. 77). Areas around the holes and each end of conduit should be plugged with caulking compound after the wiring or cable is installed.

To prevent damage to the lawn when you dig a trench between house and fixtures, cut sod into blocks with a long-handled spade and lay them aside on burlap. Locate electrical boxes and fixtures at least 18 inches above ground and anchor them in concrete. Bury cable at least 18 inches below the ground to protect it from gardening tools. You can bury cable as little as 6 inches below the ground if it is covered to protect it against damage or, safer still, routed through galvanized conduit.

Make sure all outdoor wiring is complete and all terminals connected before connecting the wiring to the fuse or circuit breaker box.

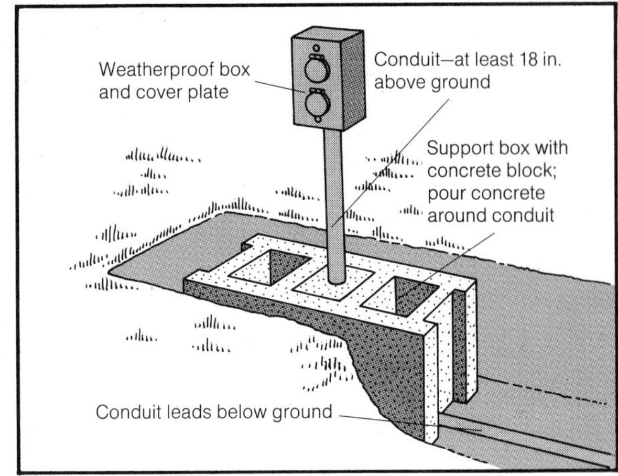

Freestanding electrical boxes should be at least 18 in. above ground level. Set them atop a length of galvanized conduit that is embedded in a concrete support block.

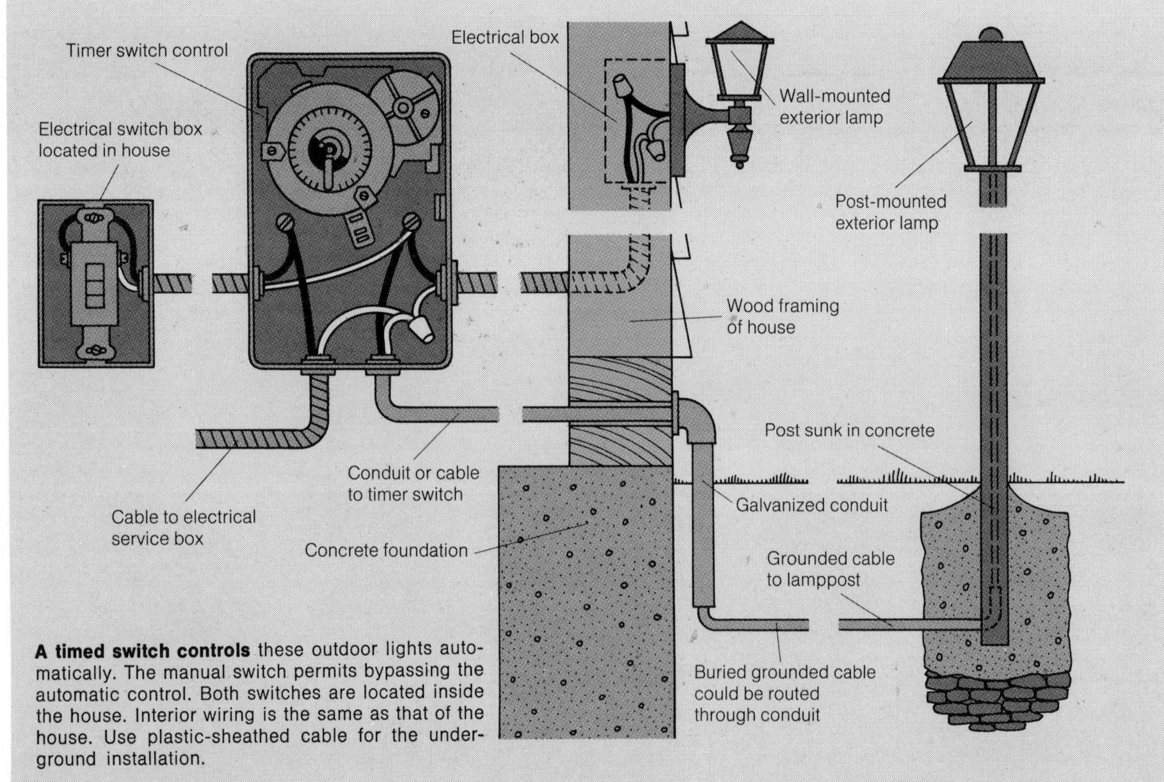

A timed switch controls these outdoor lights automatically. The manual switch permits bypassing the automatic control. Both switches are located inside the house. Interior wiring is the same as that of the house. Use plastic-sheathed cable for the underground installation.

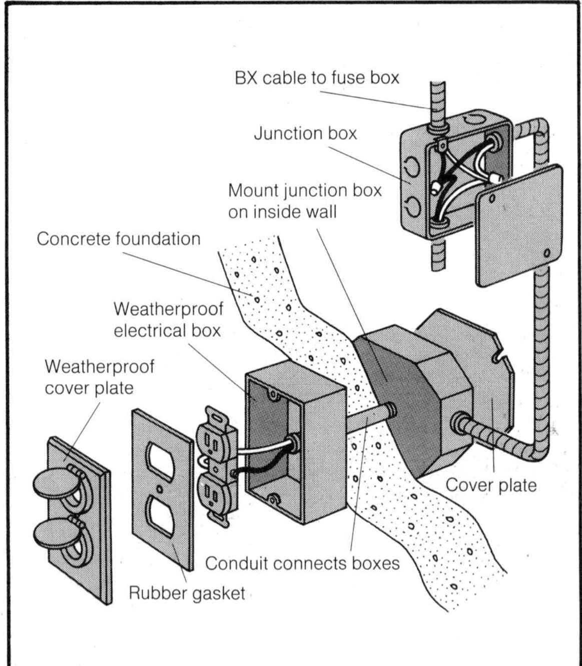

Use this electrical box arrangement when running wires from inside the house to a weatherproof box mounted on the exterior wall. Run connecting cable through conduit.

Probable sources of trouble

If a lamp flickers or will not go on, check to be sure that the bulb is still sound and tightly seated, and that the plug is firmly in its outlet and the socket is functioning. If none of the above is causing the problem, unplug the lamp and check the cord for fraying, cracks, bare wires, or loose connections at the plug. If the cord is damaged, follow the instructions below to replace it. If the cord is not the problem, the difficulty may be in the switch. If it is necessary to install a new switch, examine the old one closely before disconnecting the wires, then connect the new switch in the same way.

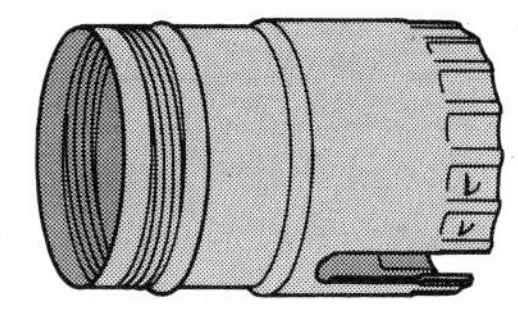

Outer shell is made out of brass or aluminum.

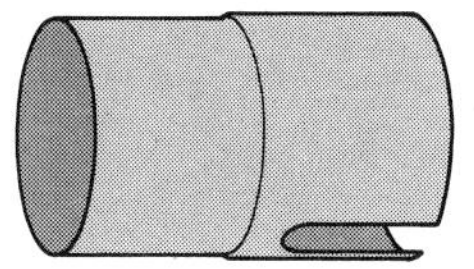

Insulating sleeve fits between shell and socket.

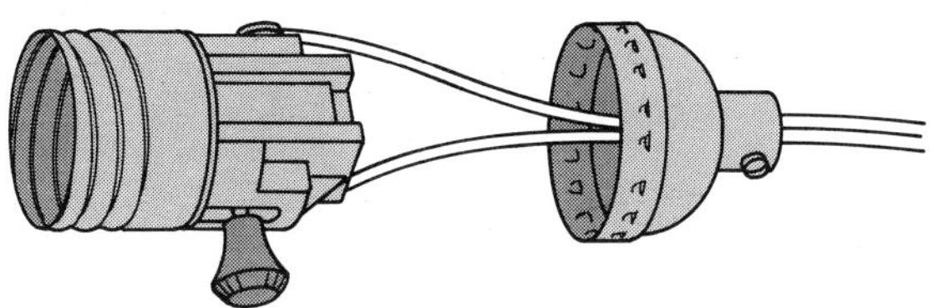

Socket has two terminals for connecting wires.

Cap has insulating liner; clips to shell.

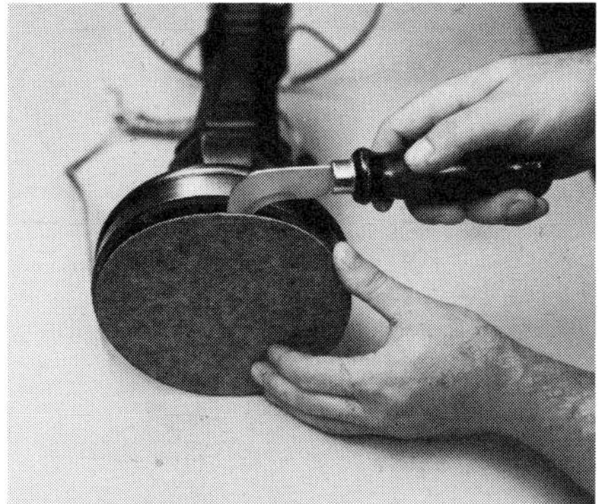

Repair procedure. First disconnect the lamp from the wall outlet. Use a knife to pry off the protective felt cover to give access to the wiring in the base of the lamp.

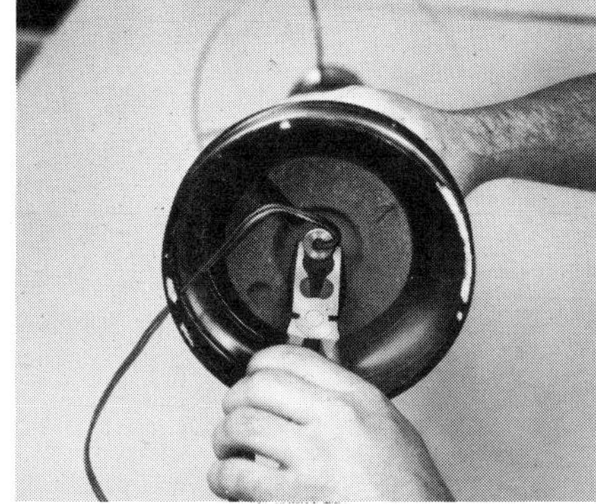

Use a wrench, or pliers, to remove the nut that secures the long, threaded tube to the base of the lamp. Most lamps will contain a lead weight; remove this from the base as well.

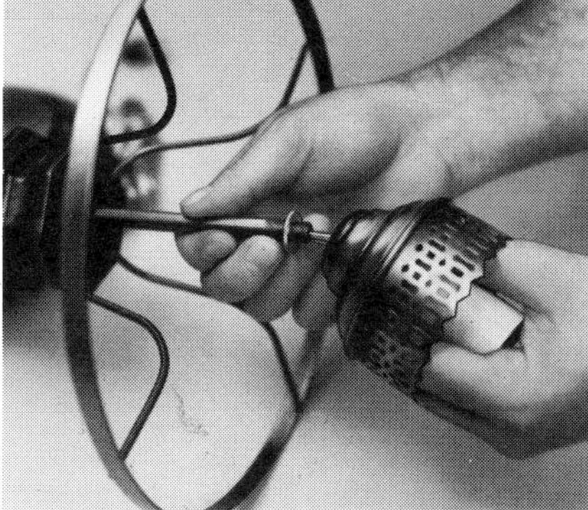

Pull the tube partway out from the top of the lamp. Unscrew the socket from the tube by turning it counterclockwise. If you are renewing a cord, cut the old one to make dismantling easier.

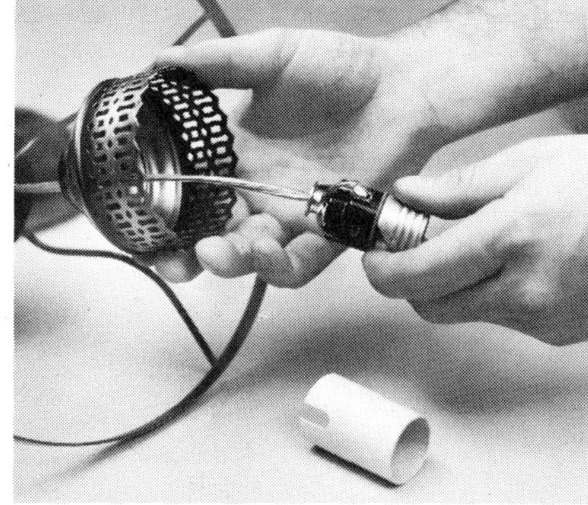

Remove the outer shell of the switch socket by pressing at the base and pulling it straight up. Slide off the cardboard insulating sleeve to expose the socket's screw terminals.

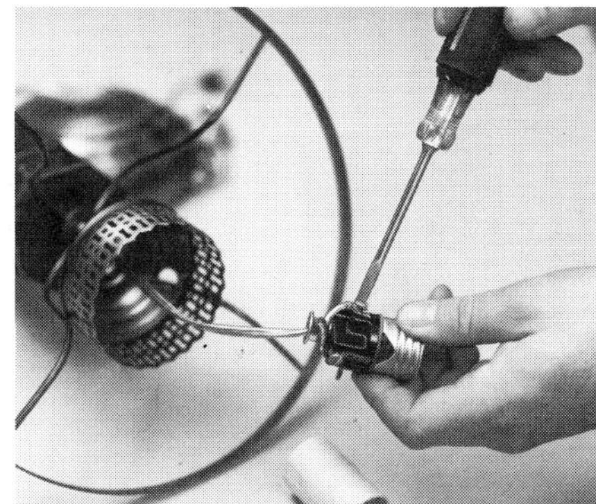

Unscrew the two wires on the terminals. If you are replacing the switch or socket, fit the wires onto the new unit in the same way as they were attached to the old one.

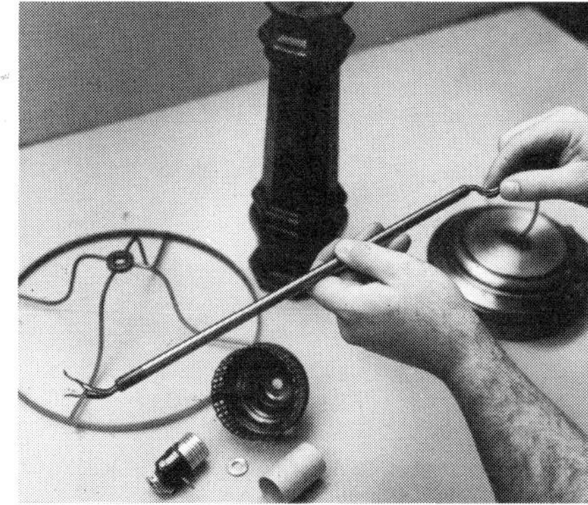

If fitting a new wire and plug, feed the wire through the lamp base and threaded tube. Connect wires to switch or socket. Reassemble lamp in same order that it was dismantled.

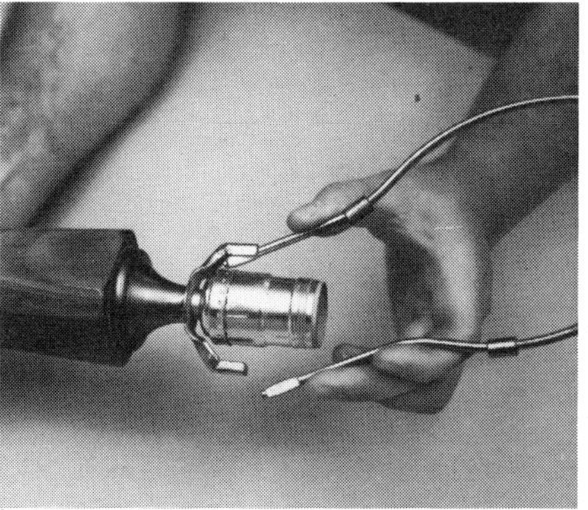

Some lamp models have a harp which must be removed before further dismantling. Remove by pressing the two bottom arms together. Some types are held by finger nuts.

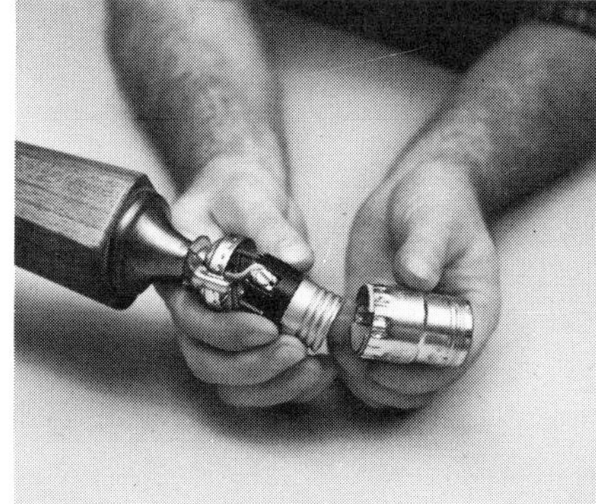

Some sockets and switches have metal shells which are removed by pressing at their base. Use same procedure as above for switch or socket replacement in this type of fixture.

Fluorescent fixtures

Starter-type and rapid-start

Fluorescent tubes need special fixtures to operate properly. Straight-tube fixtures contain a **socket** at either end into which their pins fit. The pins of a circular tube plug into a socket and are held in place by spring clips. All fluorescent fixtures contain a ballast for each tube the fixture accommodates. Fixtures for most tube types contain **starters.** Rapid-start tubes, however, do not use them.

The ground wire on rapid-start fluorescent fixtures, whether the straight or circular type, should be connected either to a ground wire in the fixture or to a grounded ceiling mounting assembly.

To install a starter, push it into the socket, press it down, then give it a half turn to secure it. Install a straight tube by aligning the pins with the socket slots on either end of the fixture, then push the tube in and secure it with a quarter turn.

Replacement tubes, starters, and ballasts must be of exactly the same type and rating as those being replaced. Adapters are needed to operate fluorescent tubes with direct current. Fluorescents are designed to operate in areas with a temperature of 50 degrees or higher. To operate a tube in a colder area, you need a special fixture. Turn off all power to a fixture before working on it.

Fluorescent tubes will last much longer if they are kept burning than if they are constantly turned on and off. In fact, manufacturers rate the life of these tubes by the number of starts they are subject to. The life of a 40-watt fluorescent tube, turned on for 3 hours at a time, is about 12,000 hours.

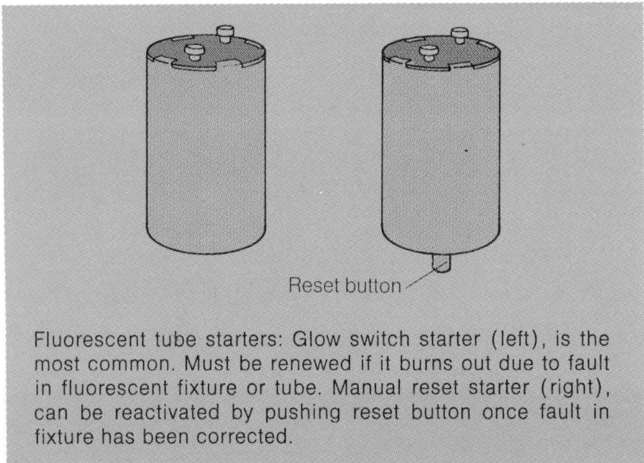

Fluorescent tube starters: Glow switch starter (left), is the most common. Must be renewed if it burns out due to fault in fluorescent fixture or tube. Manual reset starter (right), can be reactivated by pushing reset button once fault in fixture has been corrected.

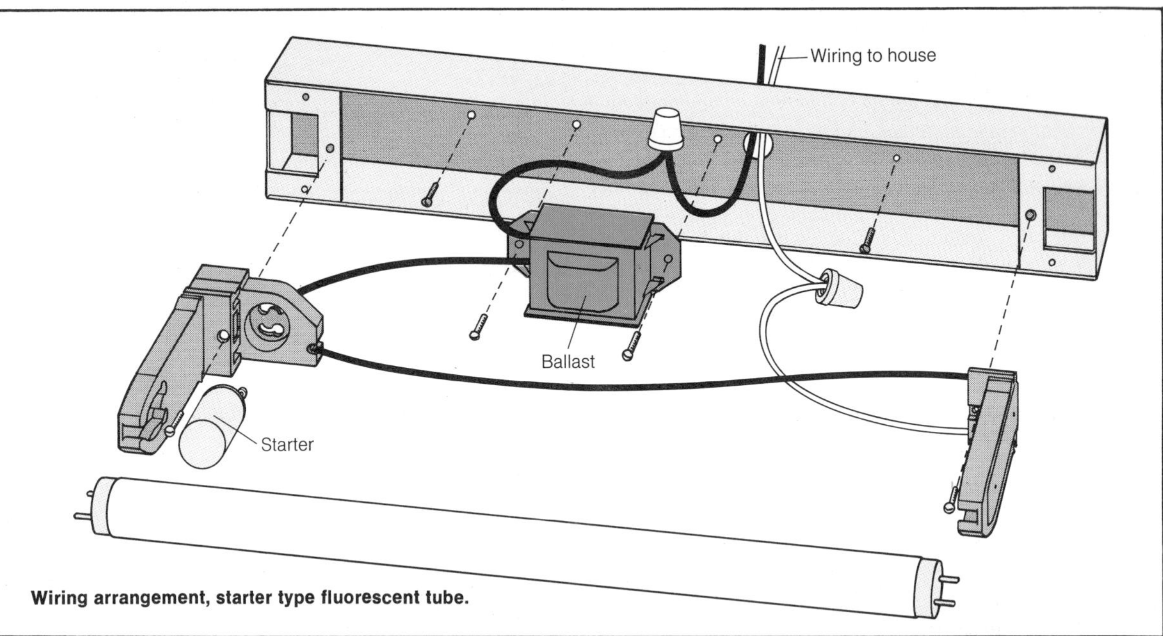

Wiring arrangement, starter type fluorescent tube.

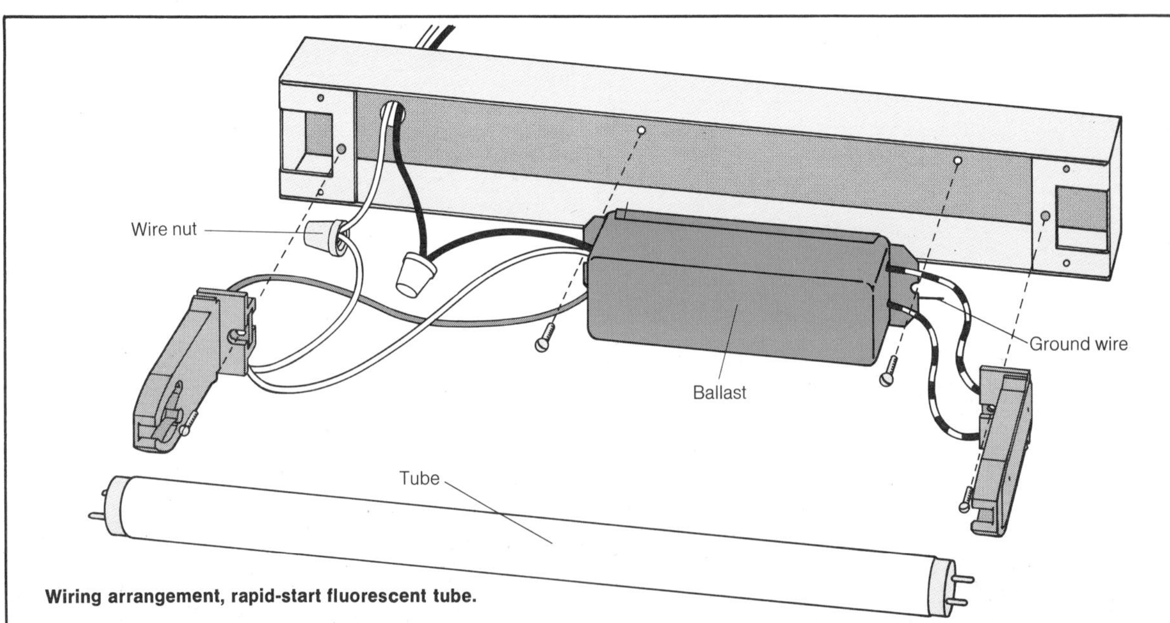

Wiring arrangement, rapid-start fluorescent tube.

Troubleshooting checklist

Before making repairs, be sure power is off.

Problem	Solution
Tube will not light	**(1)** Make sure that **fuse or circuit breaker** is not blown or tripped (p. 252). **(2)** If fuse or circuit breaker is intact, try replacing the **starter.** **(3)** If this does not work, renew the tube. **(4)** As a last resort, replace the **ballast.**
Light flickers and swirls around inside tube	**(1)** If tube is new, this condition will disappear with use. **(2)** If tube has been in operation for some time, replace the **starter.** **(3)** If replacing the starter does not correct the condition, replace the **ballast.**
Light blinks on and off	**(1)** Tube is probably not properly seated in its socket. **(2)** Remove the tube and examine the pins on the end. If pins are bent, straighten them with long-nose pliers. Reinstall the tube in its socket. **(3)** If it still blinks, remove it again and lightly sand the **pins.** **(4)** Turn off power to fixture. Straighten socket contacts with long-nose pliers. Sand socket **contacts.** Brush out residue with a toothbrush. **(5)** Remove tube and fixture cover. Tighten any **loose connections.** Reinstall tube. **(6)** Replace **starter** **(7)** Replace **ballast** **(8)** If fixture is in area of low temperature, replace **tube** with jacketed all-weather tube. **(9)** Replace **starter** with low-temperature starter. **(10)** Replace **ballast** with low-temperature ballast. **(11)** Replace entire **fixture** with low-temperature type.
Fixture hums but otherwise works properly	**(1)** Make sure ballast **connections** are not loose. **(2)** Replace present ballast with special low-noise ballast.
Ends of tube are discolored	**(1)** A brown color is normal. **(2)** If color is black and tube is new, replace the **starter.** **(3)** If tube is old, replace it. **(4)** Make sure **ballast** is correct and that its connections are secure. **(5)** If **tube** is discolored on only one side, remove tube, turn it over, and reinstall it. **(6)** If tube is new and one end darkens before the other, reverse the tube in its socket, end for end. **(7)** Check **power** (see "Tube will not light" above). Replace tube.
Tube burns out too fast	**(1)** Tube has probably been turned on and off too often. Replace **tube.** Leave new tube on for longer periods of time. **(2)** Replace **starter.** **(3)** Replace **ballast.** **(4)** Make sure connections are secure.

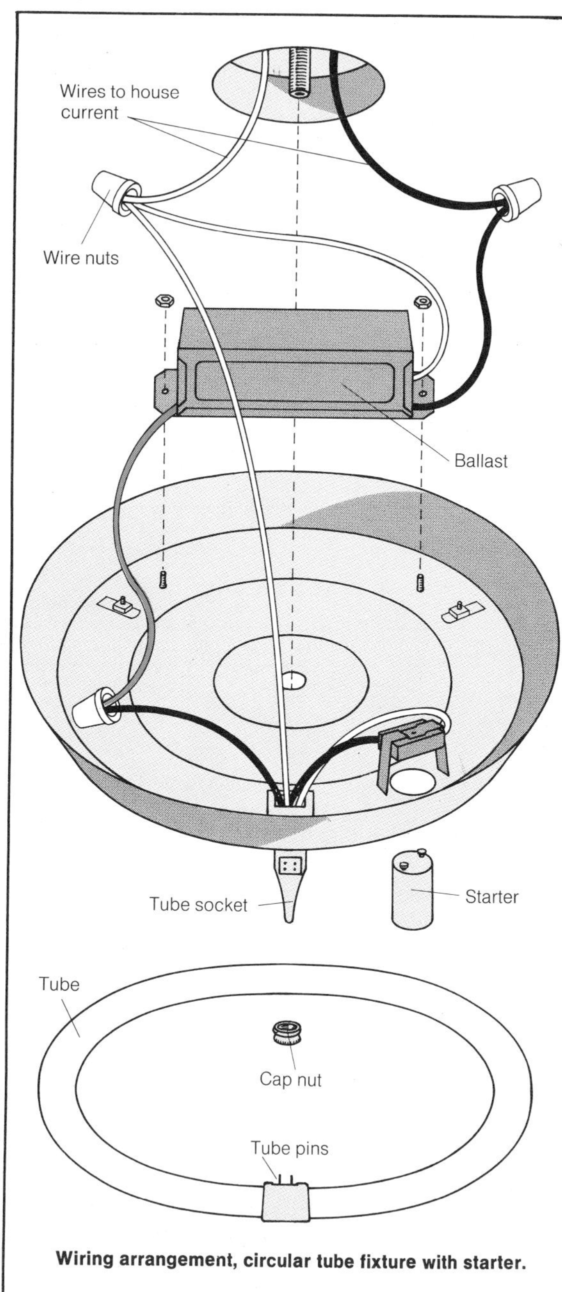

Wiring arrangement, circular tube fixture with starter.

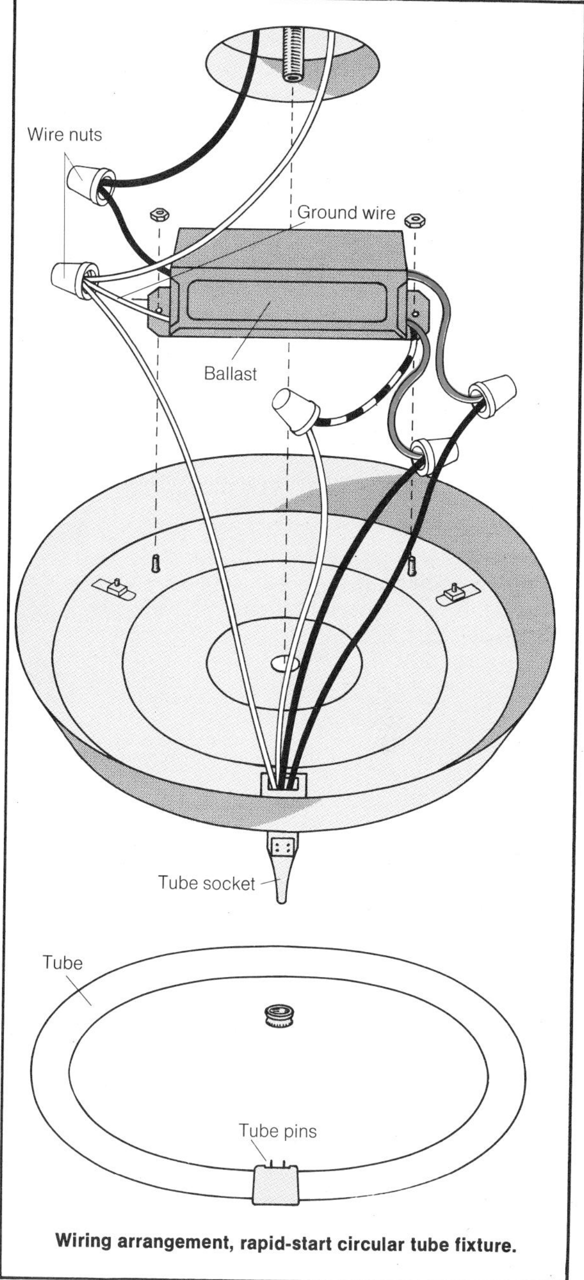

Wiring arrangement, rapid-start circular tube fixture.

Door chimes, bells, and buzzers

Troubleshooting and repair

Door chimes and bells operate on low-voltage current reduced by a transformer from 120-volt household current. The reduced voltage will not give you a shock, so it is safe to work on a chime or bell system without shutting off the power.

Chime or bell failure: The first thing to check is the wiring between button and transformer. The thin wire might be broken or shorting out at some point. If so, simply rejoin or tape the wire.

If the wiring is intact, the probable cause is the entrance button. These tend to become corroded from the weather. If the contact points are accessible, clean them with sandpaper. If they are hard to get at, try replacing the button. If the button is not the problem, check connections at the chimes or bell. Vibration sometimes loosens them. The problem is not likely to be in the chime or the bell mechanism. If investigation leads you to believe it is, replacement is probably easier than repair.

Installing new chimes: Locate the transformer unit, then run wires to the chime unit and, subsequently, to the entrance button. Check whether chimes and transformer operate on the same voltage. Labels will tell you. Many transformers provide a variety of voltage levels with separate terminals marked for each. Be sure to use only those suited to your chime or bell.

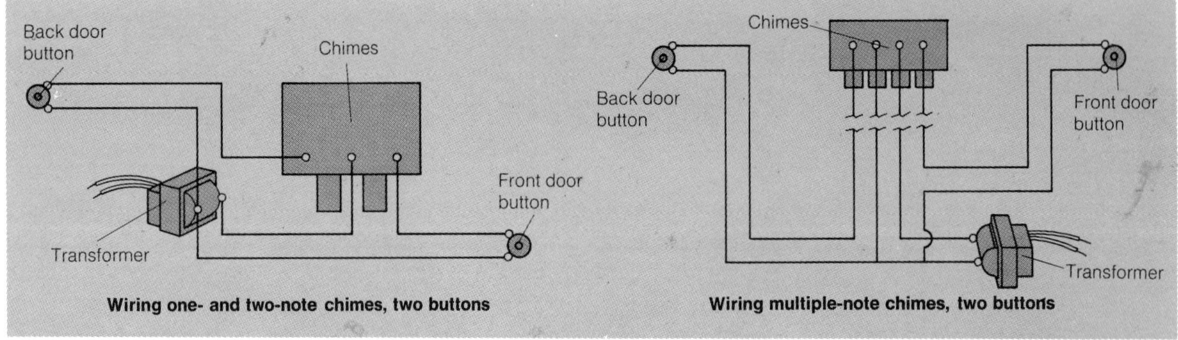

Wiring one- and two-note chimes, two buttons

Wiring multiple-note chimes, two buttons

Transformer
Bell
Button

Wiring a one-door system

Rear entrance button
Bell
Front entrance button
Transformer

Wiring one bell operated by two buttons

Bells
Transformer
Button

Wiring three bells to work off one button

Installing chimes

Install the transformer in a convenient junction box. With power off, punch out disk and insert transformer wires.

Transformer is fastened with a nut. Some transformers must be mounted outside the junction box; only the wires go in box.

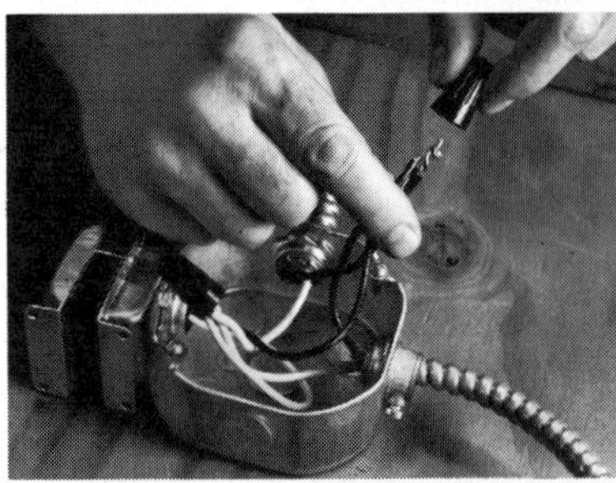

Using wire nuts, fasten wires from transformer to house wiring. Black is joined to black and white to white.

Connect low-voltage bell wiring to transformer terminals. Run the wire through the house to location of chime unit.

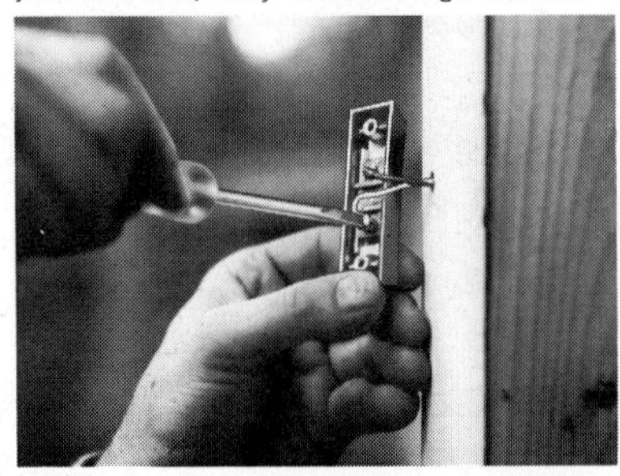

Push-button wires may be run on outside or inside of door molding. Bore hole in molding and connect wires to button.

Connect all wires to correct terminals on chime unit. The terminals are usually marked by the manufacturer.

section 9:

Climate control: Heating and air conditioning your home

Heating and air conditioning don't just keep a home warm or cool. Modern systems, at their most efficient, also control moisture and keep air fresh and clean. One that isn't working properly can be a hazard to health, not to mention a drain on the budget. Whatever you're considering—a new installation, a conversion, or just improvements in the system you have—read this section before you proceed. You'll be amply repaid in results.

contents

Heating and air conditioning

Basic facts

All heating and air conditioning systems have a common purpose: Treating air to maintain comfortable levels of temperature and humidity (moisture content). In the past, houses were heated by an open fireplace or stove, and ventilation was accomplished by opening doors and windows. Today, more attention is being given to maintaining the proper temperature in a house and the correct moisture content in the air as well, as it is increasingly recognized that both have a bearing on health and comfort.

It is important to know a few facts about heat—that, for example, it is constantly on the move in one of the following three ways:

Conduction. Heat will always leave an object that is warm for one that is less warm, and it will always flow in the direction of the cooler object. When heat passes through the walls and roof of a house, it travels by "conduction."

Convection. Air tends to rise when it is heated, so warm air always rises to the ceiling of a room while the cold air drifts down. The current formed by warm air's tendency to rise is called "convection."

Radiation. The traveling, or transference, of heat from one object directly out into the air is known as "radiation."

These three characteristics of heat are the basis, in varying degrees, of all our present home heating and cooling systems.

Central heating systems: These general systems create the heating for an entire building at one central point. The heat is then delivered to the places where it is required.

There are two main kinds of central systems. The first is **indirect** or **warm-air** heating. In the second, **steam** or **hot water** is carried by pipes to radiators where the heat is given off.

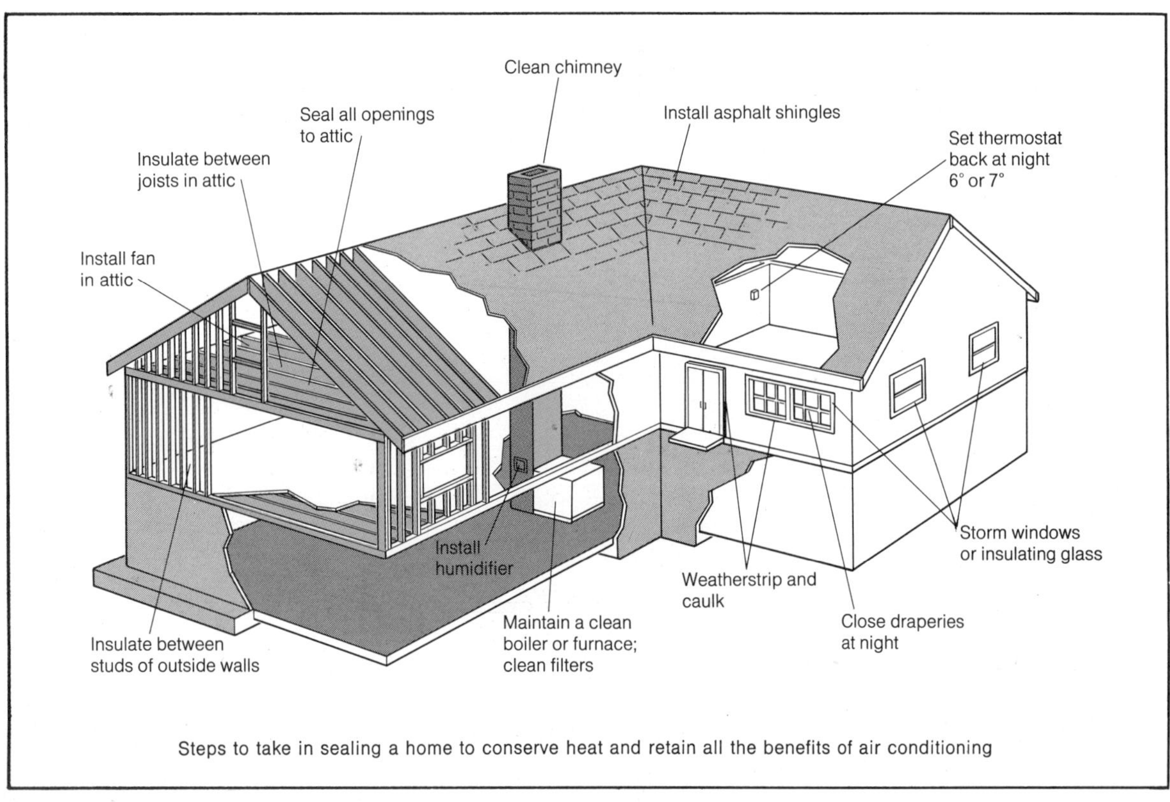

Steps to take in sealing a home to conserve heat and retain all the benefits of air conditioning

Kinds of fuel: Most central heating systems burn coal, oil, or gas, or are powered by electricity. Coal, gas, and electricity are burned or consumed directly. Oil is changed into a fine mist which burns when it is mixed with air. Most central heating systems today are automatically controlled by a thermostat. When the temperature drops below a certain point, the thermostat makes an electrical contact which turns the burner or heater on. When the temperature reaches a higher point, the thermostat turns the heat source off or down.

Air conditioning controls the temperature, moisture, cleanliness, and movement of indoor air. It cools the air when the weather is hot, and can warm it when the weather is cold. Air conditioning removes or adds moisture as needed, which affects comfort; it removes dirt or dust; it controls air movement, replacing stale air with fresh.

Economy tips: If you are to get maximum comfort from such systems, your house must be insulated. Insulation is a thermal barrier that keeps heat in during cold weather and out during hot. Besides insulation to reduce heating and cooling loss, you can save money in other ways: (1) Develop good **heat conservation habits.** Lock windows to pull sash tightly together. Close fireplace dampers except when a fire is burning. Close draperies at night, open them on sunny days. (2) Use **storm windows** or **insulating glass.** Double-thickness glass resists heat loss almost twice as much as single-thickness. (3) Use **storm doors.** Keep them tightly latched. (4) **Weatherstrip** windows and doors to keep warm air in, cold air out. (5) **Caulk cracks** around the outside of window and door frames. (6) Have a **serviceman** clean and adjust the furnace and check balancing of the heat distribution system to make sure no room gets more heat than it needs. (7) Clean or replace **furnace filters.** Dirty filters can severely hinder movement of warm air. (8) Set the **thermostat** back at night, but only 6 or 7 degrees. A greater setback will require extra fuel for morning pick-up. Always set the thermostat back if you are going away for a weekend or longer. (9) **Turn off heat** in rooms that are not used. If you have zone thermostats to control your heating, consider keeping bedrooms at a lower temperature during the day. (10) Install a **humidifier.** When relative humidity is high, you will be comfortable at a lower temperature.

Types and operation

Gravity warm-air: The furnace in this type of system utilizes the fact that warm air is lighter than cold, so that hot air rises and cold air settles. In operation, the air in the furnace's air jacket becomes heated from its close contact with the outer wall of the combustion chamber or fire box. It then rises through ducts and passes through registers into various rooms. As it does, it replaces colder air, which drifts downward through the cold air ducts and into the lower part of the air jacket, where it is heated and again begins the same cycle.

Besides central heating furnaces, the gravity warm-air principle is used in floor furnaces and space-heating systems. In these, several smaller furnaces are used, located either under the floor or at the wall of the room to be heated, each furnace serving only its immediate vicinity. Heated air from the furnace rises and circulates into the room space; cool air at the floor is drawn back to the furnace for reheating. Many space heaters have fans to increase air circulation and automatic controls to regulate the amount of heat produced.

The major difficulty with any gravity system is that there must be a considerable difference in temperature between rising hot air and descending cold air to obtain good air movement and equal heat distribution in all parts of the home.

Forced warm-air: The furnace in this system is an improvement over the gravity type in that it employs a blower to force air to circulate between furnace and registers and need not depend on natural convection. Besides making warm air distribution more equitable, this system minimizes the difference between warm air entering and cold air leaving rooms.

With a forced warm-air system it is possible to send heat just to rooms that require it. To accomplish this, the house is divided into zones, each with its own thermostat to call for heat, and individual blower arrangements or louver devices that direct the heat where it is needed.

There are four basic designs of forced warm-air furnaces, the choice depending on the planned location. (1) The **upflow highboy,** which discharges warm air from the top and takes return air in the back, is best for full basement areas. (2) The **downflow model,** designed to take return air in through the top and discharge warm air from the bottom, is generally a main floor installation. (3) The **upflow lowboy,** with both duct systems coming through the top, is fine for small or partial basement areas. (4) The **horizontal furnace,** which takes return air in one end and discharges warm air through the other, is good for crawl space or attic installations.

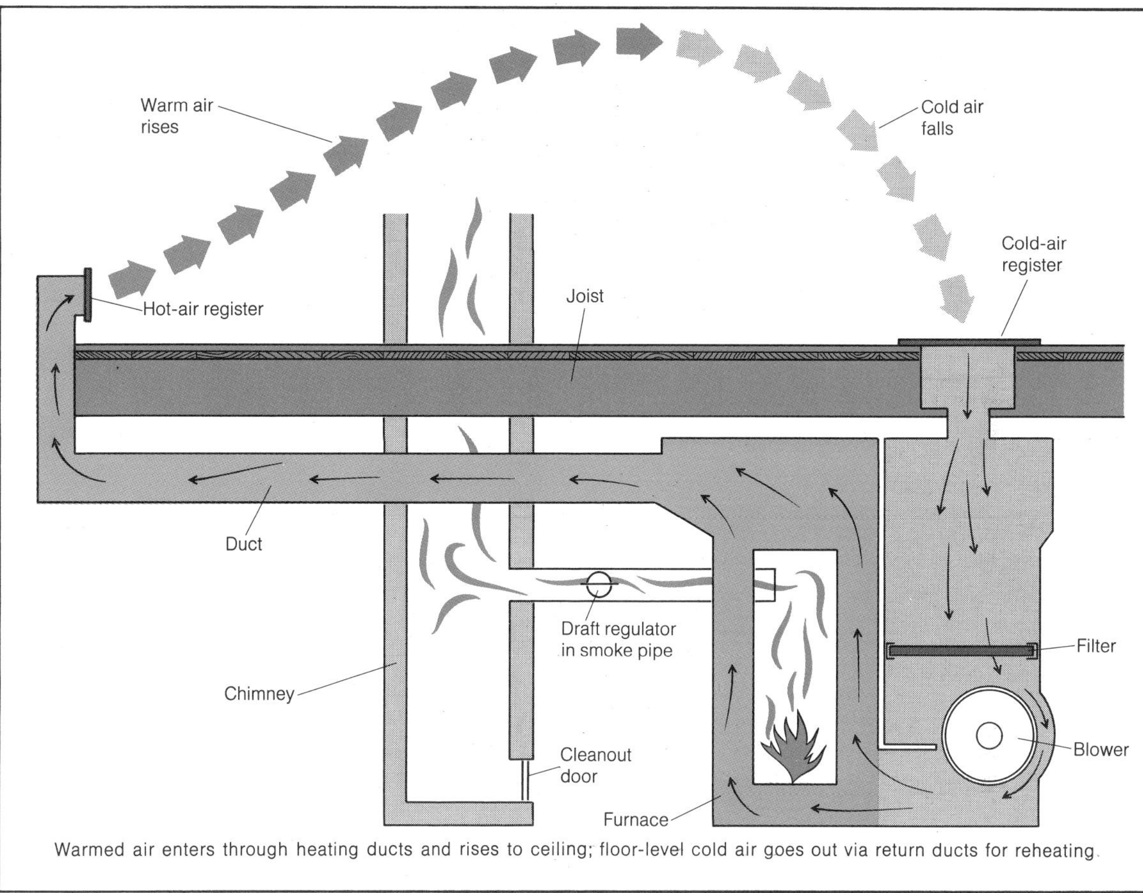

Warmed air enters through heating ducts and rises to ceiling; floor-level cold air goes out via return ducts for reheating.

The blower of a forced warm-air furnace may be used to cool the home in summer. Usually a manual blower switch can be turned on to circulate air. A furnace of this type can often be adapted to work with modern central air conditioning systems.

Most forced warm-air furnaces have an air filter to clean the circulating air, usually a loosely packed pad of fiber glass or other nonflammable substance which traps the dust and keeps it from returning to the rooms. Permanent filters are washable; the throwaway type must be replaced.

Some furnaces have evaporative-plate humidifiers which add some moisture to the air. Complete humidification requires the powered-type humidifier.

Furnace controls: Both gravity and forced warm-air systems are usually thermostat-controlled. In addition, most furnaces have a high-limit control engineered to shut down the burner if the air in the plenum (warm-air supply duct) gets hotter than the manufacturer's design limit. When the temperature returns to normal, the limit switch closes and the burner restarts. In a forced warm-air system, this control often works in conjunction with the blower.

Hot-water systems

Types and operation

In this method of heating, water is employed as the medium for transmitting heat, principally by means of two systems: (1) the gravity system and (2) the hydronic, or forced system.

The **gravity system** works on the principle that when water is heated it expands; it then occupies more space for its weight and so becomes lighter and rises. The water, when heated in the boiler, rises through pipes to the radiators, its place being taken by the cooler and heavier water in the return pipes. Giving up some of its heat to the radiators—and to the room—the cooler water returns to the boiler through a separate return pipeline. All of the water is thus put into circulation when the heat is applied. The speed of its circulation will depend on the difference between the temperature in the boiler and that of the returning water. The greater the difference, the faster the water will move. The temperature as the water leaves the boiler is usually about 180 degrees, the return temperature about 140.

Piping arrangements in gravity systems may be open or closed. In the open arrangement, the increase in volume that occurs when the heated water expands is taken up by an expansion tank located above the highest point in the system, usually the attic. This tank is open, with an overflow pipe near the top; if the tank gets too full, the water will flow through the pipe and not over the side.

The closed gravity system has an expansion tank installed near the boiler. The tank has no overflow pipe but is completely airtight. When the water expands, it compresses the air in the tank and puts the water in the entire system under pressure, making it possible to maintain a higher water temperature. There is a limit to how much pressure the system can sustain; a relief valve in the supply line will relieve excess pressure should the need arise.

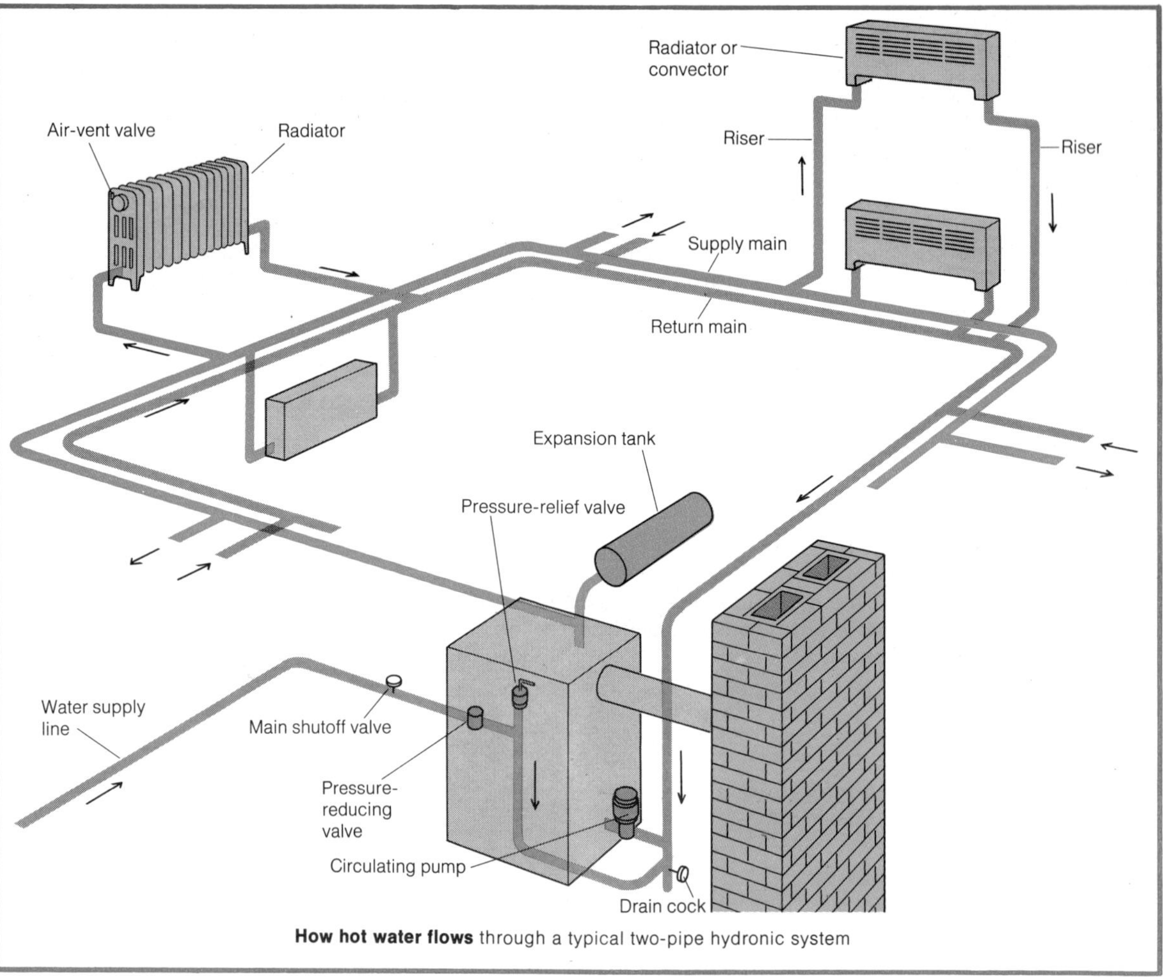

How hot water flows through a typical two-pipe hydronic system

The **hydronic,** or **forced hot-water system** is a closed gravity hot-water system with a circulating pump driving the water through the pipes and radiators. This pump, usually in the return line, controls the flow of water through the system and operates whenever the room thermostat calls for heat. Its function is similar to that of the fan in forced warm-air heating—helping to get the heat quickly to where it is needed. A flow-control valve in the main supply line prevents any flow of water when the pump is not operating. If that valve were not functioning properly, the water would continue to rise as in the gravity-flow system, and overheat the rooms.

The hydronic system supplies hot water not only to the radiators, but also to the hot-water faucets in the house, whether or not the heating system is in operation. Hot water for the faucets does not come directly from the boiler but from a coil inside it. Whatever the fuel, the burner operates whenever the hot water in the boiler must be brought to the desired temperature. By conduction, the heat of the boiler water is transferred to the inside of the built-in coil, which then becomes the hot water supplier for the sinks, tubs, and showers.

Most hot-water system boilers have a high-limit control, or Aquastat. It is often combined with the pump controls and will keep the system inoperative if the water in the hydronic system exceeds the design pressure or temperature.

The two-pipe forced hot-water heating system has two water-supply pipes. One pipe supplies the hot water to the radiator; the other returns the cooled water to the boiler for reheating (see drawing).

Series-loop system

The first of the hydronic heating systems installed in homes made use of the two-pipe arrangement that is employed in the hot-water gravity systems. The two-pipe system is still considered the best choice for use in heating large, rambling-type homes. In today's houses, however, two other piping arrangements also are used.

The series-loop system is the simplest of all hydronic piping systems. In its operation, the hot water leaves the boiler at the top through the main supply line and continues on a straight line through each radiator in the loop, finally returning at the bottom of the boiler.

Related as they are to the system, the radiators, for all practical purposes, are sections or integral parts of the supply pipeline. While this type of installation has the advantage of requiring a minimum of fittings and materials, it has a limitation that should be kept in mind: No one radiator in the loop can be turned off. Because each is an integral part of the main supply, shutting off one radiator would stop the flow throughout the entire circuit. This limitation confines the use of the series-loop system, as a rule, to small homes where room-by-room heating adjustments will not be required.

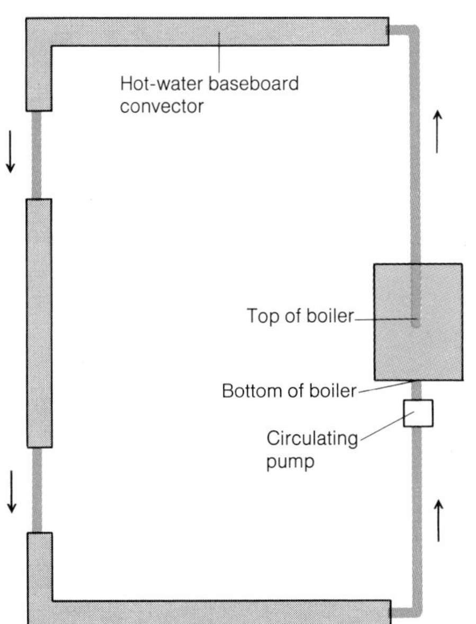

One-pipe system

In the one-pipe system, as in the series-loop system, the main supply line comes from the top of the boiler and completes its circuit by returning at the bottom of the boiler. There is, however, the significant difference that in the one-pipe arrangement the radiators are not an integral part of the supply pipelines. In this system, branch pipes run from the supply pipeline to both ends of each radiator in the circuit, with a heat-control valve at the inlet side of each radiator. If an individual radiator is shut off, the hot water does not stop but simply flows past this radiator and continues its journey around the circuit. To divert the water from the main line through the radiator when the valve is open, a special forced-flow T fitting is used at the point where the return pipe from the radiator connects back into the supply pipeline.

Both cost and convenience are considerations here. While the one-pipe system does give individual room-by-room heat control, it is more expensive to install than the series-loop—less, however, than the two-pipe. One further point of comparison: The temperature difference between the first and last radiators along the one-pipe supply line is considerably greater than in a two-pipe system (see opposite page).

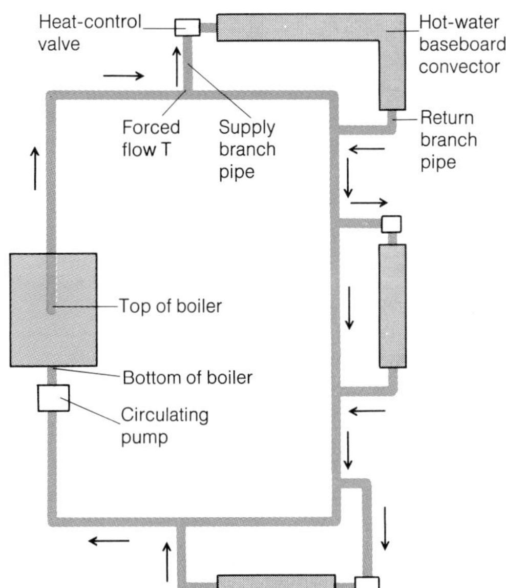

Zone heating

A hot-water heating system can be installed with independent temperature controls for any area, or even for each room, but, as emphasized earlier, zone heating is a more practical and economical way to achieve area control. The hydronic zone system consists of two or more separate circuits of pipelines which feed the radiators. It will work with most piping systems. The house may be divided into the desired zones, each with its own thermostat. In addition, each zone has its electrically operated valve on the radiator supply line, controlled by its own thermostat, so that the valve opens only when its thermostat calls for heat.

In a hydronic zone system, only one boiler is needed, and generally one circulator, except in larger systems where each zone has its own circulating pump. This is insurance against the possibility that water might cool off before it reaches the rooms furthest from the boiler and thus not give off enough heat at these points. It is also much easier to circulate the water through a few radiators than it would be to move it in one continuous passage through an entire house. Generally, bedrooms and living areas are controlled by separate thermostats to achieve zone-area heating, with bedrooms at a lower setting.

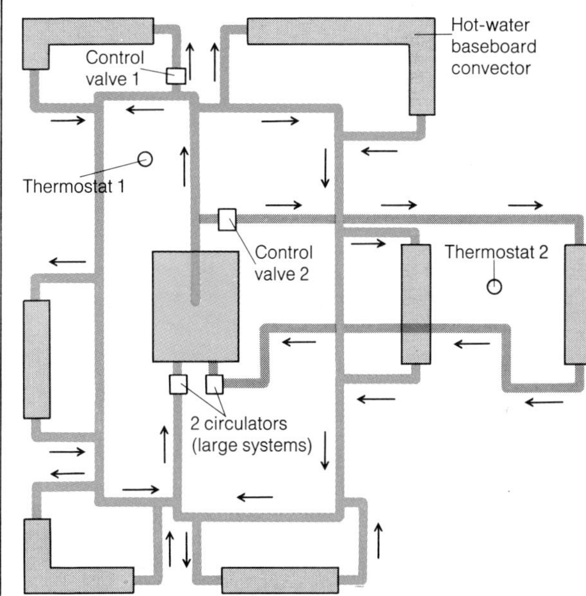

Radiant systems

Operation and advantages

Radiant heating is a method of supplying heat, in the form of radiant energy (radiation), in automatically controlled amounts. The heat is generated, just as in any hot-water heating system, by a boiler, and then conveyed by hot water pipes to surfaces, called panels, in the rooms.

In most cases, parallel rows of pipes or tubes, connected by return bends or headers, are embedded in a concrete floor slab or in a plastered ceiling or wall. A circulating pump near the boiler forces the water through the piping system. The heat from the water is transmitted to the room through the embedding material; thus the radiant heat does not actually come from the embedded piping, but from the surface of the panel.

Two advantages of such a system: Heat sources are invisible—no radiators, convector cabinets, registers, or grilles—and no floor space need be sacrificed for heating devices. When the system is operating, air is heated only as it comes in contact with the warm surfaces. Room-air temperatures, therefore, are somewhat lower than with conventional systems.

Radiant heating is most valuable in basementless houses where other types of heat cannot produce completely warm floors. The heat given off by the panels is absorbed by all other room surfaces that are at lower temperatures than the panels and in direct line with the heat rays, so the floors can be warm even if the panels are in the ceiling.

Although the location of panels is of little importance from the standpoint of comfort, other factors that can affect panel location should be kept in mind. Large pieces of furniture will intercept the heat from a floor panel and thereby reduce the effective panel area. Rugs and carpets will also reduce the heat output from floor panels.

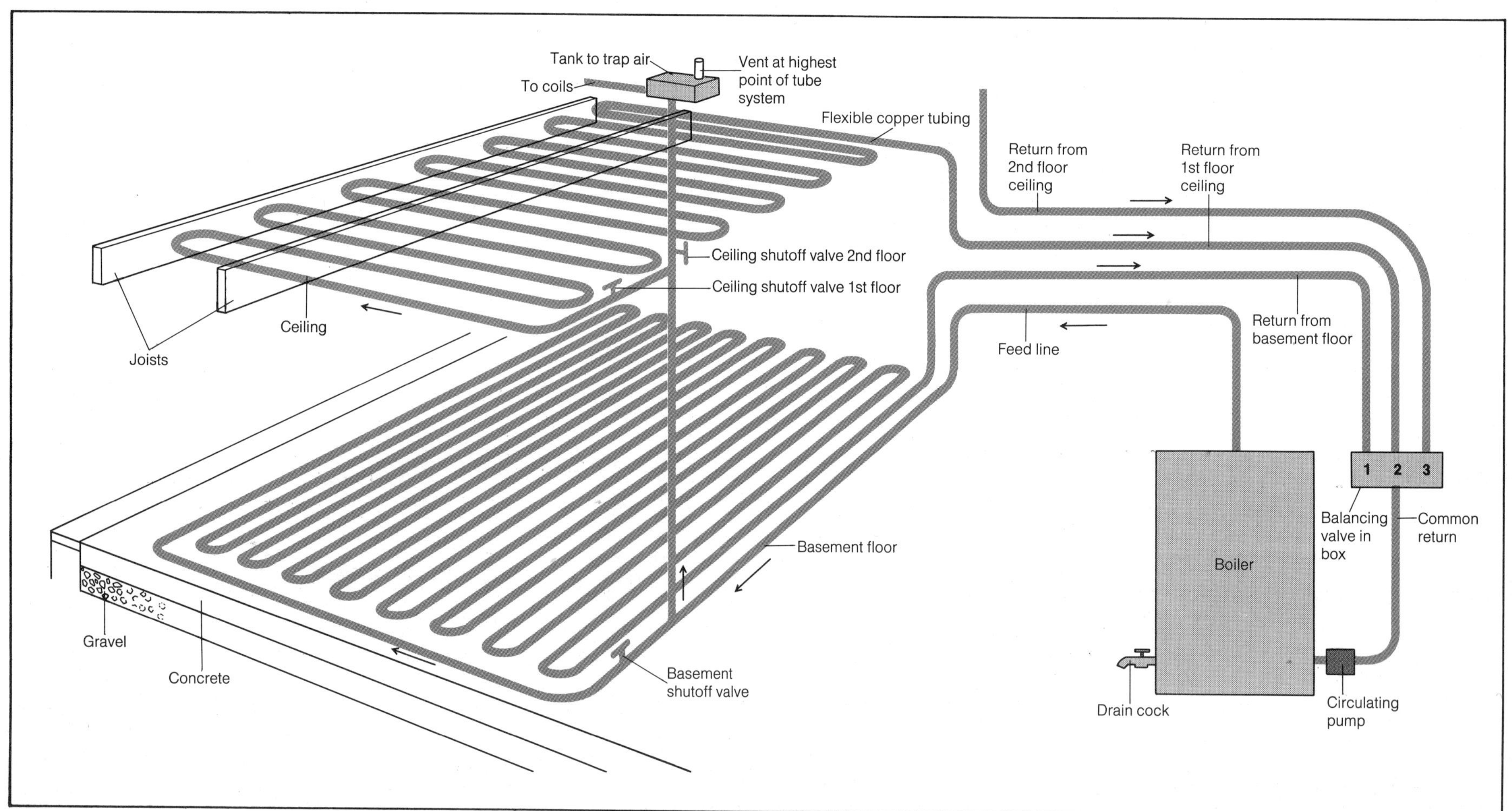

Types of installations

Wall installations: Heat panels are rarely installed in exterior walls because the heat loss would be too great. Extra-heavy insulation would reduce this loss, but it would greatly increase installation costs. For interior wall installations, the heating coils are embedded in the plaster facing the room. Though it sounds good in theory, it is not possible to heat the rooms on both sides of a wall efficiently with the same coils. This would necessitate putting the coils in the exact center of the wall structure instead of in their normal location, which would make labor costs very high, and require the design and heating needs of the two adjoining rooms to be identical.
Ceiling installations: This type of installation is ideal for two-story homes. Its greater per-square-foot capacity to transfer heat brings it the nearest of all to a true radiant-heat application. That is, the radiant waves can angle off in all directions, warming walls, occupants, objects, and floors. Temperature control is also maximized because ceiling panels can react comparatively fast to temperature changes.

As with adjoining rooms in a wall installation, it is not practical to heat two adjoining levels with the same heating coils. With the installation shown in the drawing, only about 25 percent of the warmth in the coils will heat the upper room, most of the heat being directed downward to the room below. It is best to embed heating coils in the ceiling plaster of the room to be heated and not depend upon any heat from the coils heating the room below. Ceiling panels should be well insulated to direct their heat to the room for which it is intended.
Floor installation: The most common method of radiant heating is floor or slab installation. Usually the coils are embedded in a concrete slab, with at least 1 inch of concrete above and never less than ½ inch below. Usually, a gravel base is put down first, then a waterproof insulation at least ¾-inch thick, before the concrete slab, in which the coils are to be embedded, is poured. Because contact between slab and footings permits heat to escape to the ground by conduction, it is usually recommended that this contact be broken by a 1- to 1½-inch thick separating strip of insulation around the perimeter of the slab. Also before pouring, a ground analysis for moisture content should be made; if water is present and in contact with the concrete, it will literally drain off heat from the panel.

Because concrete heats up slowly, the best thermostat to use with a concrete-slab radiant floor installation is an outdoor type. It senses a drop in temperature long before a room thermostat would call for heat, and "tells" the furnace in advance.

Wall panels

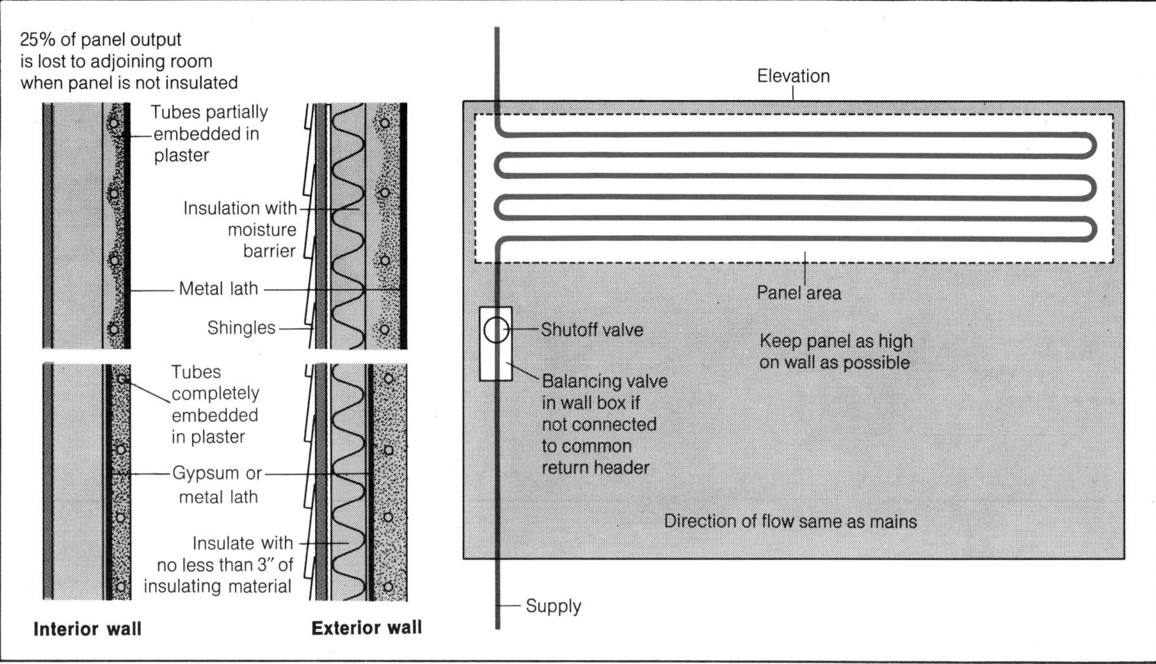

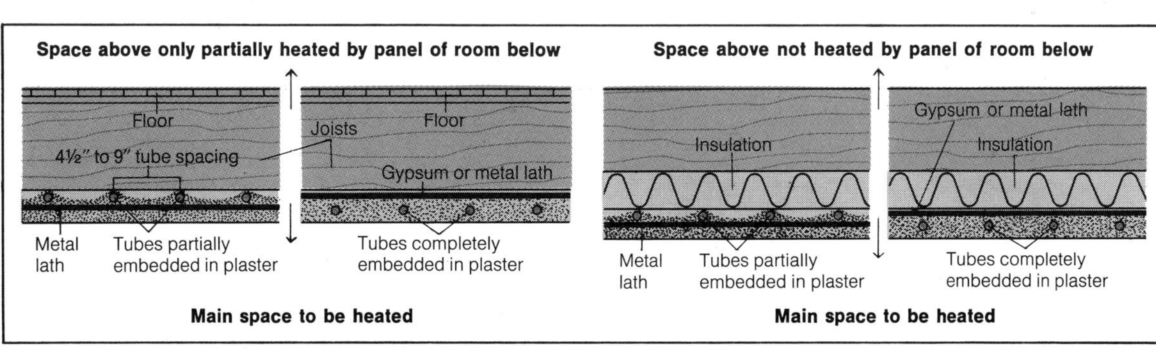

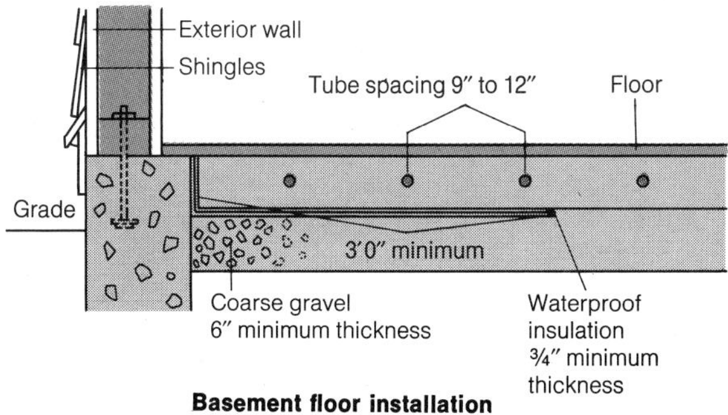

Basement floor installation

Steam system

Basic operation

In this system water is heated in the boiler until it boils, or turns to steam, and rises through pipes to radiators. As it contacts the cooler metal of the radiators, the steam condenses; the resulting water returns to the boiler for reheating. The two-pipe system is like the hot-water system in that steam flows to the radiator through one pipe and the water flows back to the boiler through another. In the one-pipe system, a single pipe carries both the steam to each radiator and the condensed water back to the boiler.

There are several major differences between the two systems. Whereas the maximum water temperature in a hot-water system is rarely over 180 degrees, steam leaves a boiler at about 212 degrees, the boiling point of water. Thus, steam radiators can be smaller and still give the same heat. Also, steam moves through pipes more rapidly than hot water, so steam radiators heat up faster.

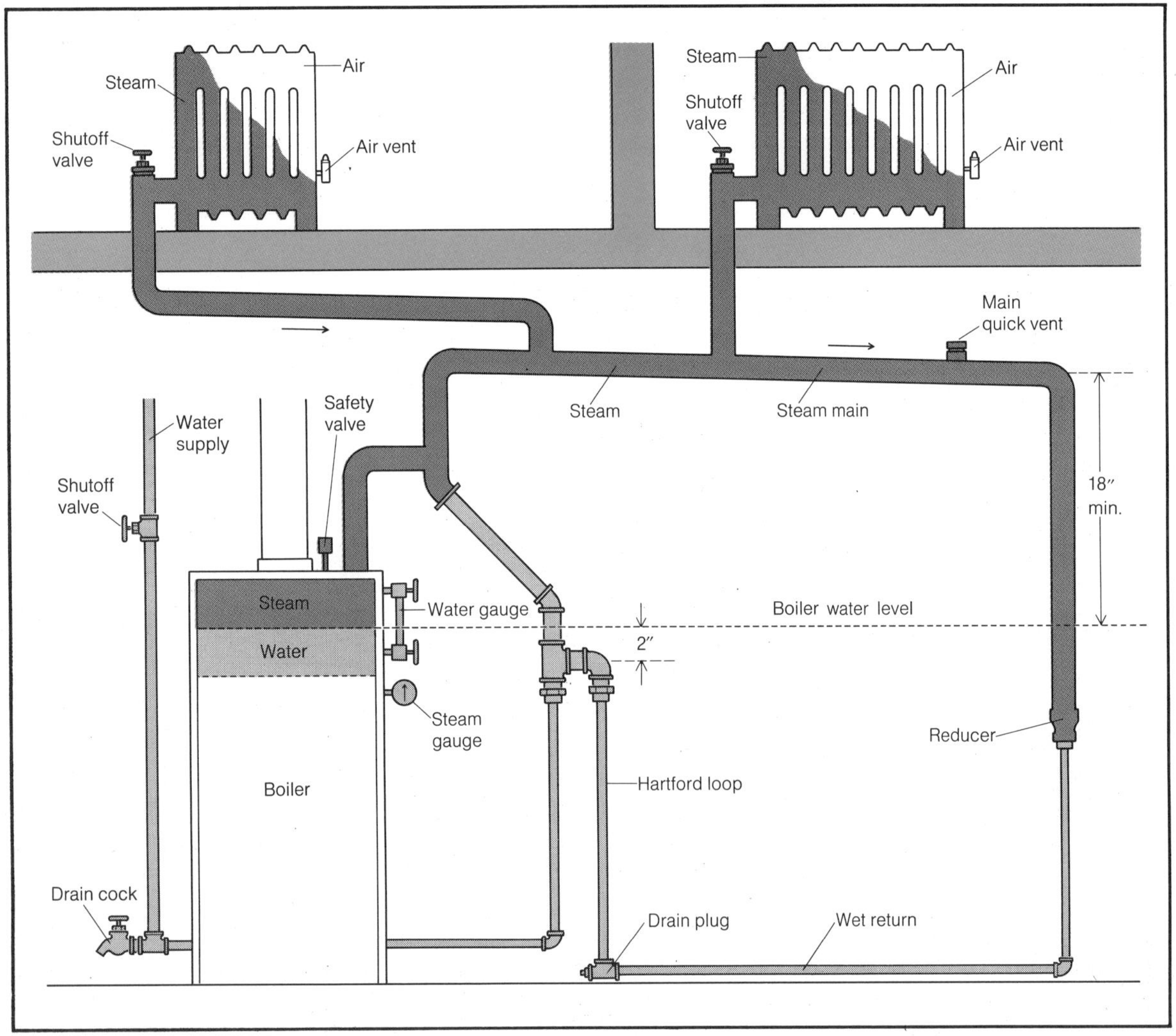

Valves and gauges

Safety valve: When water is heated into steam, a severe pressure is created in the boiler. To insure that this pressure never exceeds the capability of the system to contain it, every steam boiler has a safety valve which is set to open and release excess steam before this safety limit is reached.

On most residential systems the safety valve is usually set to open, or blow off, at 15 pounds pressure. The valve will remain completely open until a predetermined lower pressure is reached, at which time the valve will close again.

Water gauge: The glass water gauge provides a convenient means of checking the water level in the boiler. The proper water level is midway between the upper and the lower cocks. If no water is visible, turn off the furnace immediately, wait half an hour to let the boiler cool, and then add water.

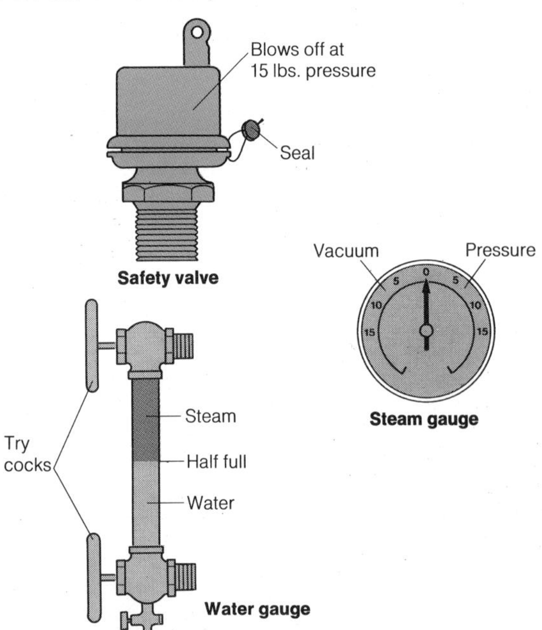

Steam gauge: This device measures—in pounds per square inch (psi)—the steam pressure at the top of the boiler. In typical installations, this reading ranges from 2 to 10 psi—the larger the system, the higher the reading. About 12 psi is usually marked as a danger zone. Some gauges also have a negative-reading scale which indicates a vacuum at top of boiler.

Types, structural requirements, maintenance

Central heating systems that work by combustion require a chimney to provide the necessary draft to keep furnace or boiler in operation, and to let combustion gases escape. Chimneys expand and contract with heat, so they must be built solidly on a base.

Chimneys may rise outside or inside a house. Interior chimneys are generally preferable; the heat they conduct is transmitted to the house from four sides, whereas with an outside chimney most of the heat is lost. Outside brick chimneys are usually built to a thickness of at least 8 inches, inside chimneys to 4 inches. Masonry chimneys require 4 to 6 inches more. The draft must be free; chimney top should not be less than 4 feet above a flat roof, at least 2 feet above the highest point of a gable roof.

Chimneys for most modern homes contain a furnace flue and a fireplace flue. For the average small home, the flue area should not be less than 8 by 12 inches, or 100 square inches in another shape. The flue should be tight for its entire length, and preferably lined with a fire-clay flue lining.

The flues should be kept clean and the chimney in top repair. Before cleaning a chimney, disconnect the flue at the furnace and seal the duct end with paper and tape so soot won't get into the basement. Similarly close all fireplace openings and any other connections to the chimney. Soot and dirt will collect against the paper and can easily be removed after cleaning. When you are sealing off the duct, check it for holes and rust spots. These should be repaired or you may have to replace the duct later.

Then, from the roof, clean out all dirt and soot from inside the chimney for efficient operation and maximum warmth, and to keep smoke from backing up into the house. Fill a burlap or canvas bag with excelsior or rags for bulk and bricks for weight until it fits snugly into the flue. Tie it with a strong rope, spray water into the chimney, and then raise and lower the bag in the flue.

Holes and cracks in the chimney diminish its efficiency and permit the entry of water that could freeze and crack the masonry. If you cannot spot a leak that you know exists, start a fire at the chimney base and add a material to it that will cause a lot of smoke, such as damp rags. When you see the leak, repair it with a mixture of 1 part masonry cement and 3 parts sand. Clean out any loose mortar and moisten the joints before applying the new mortar.

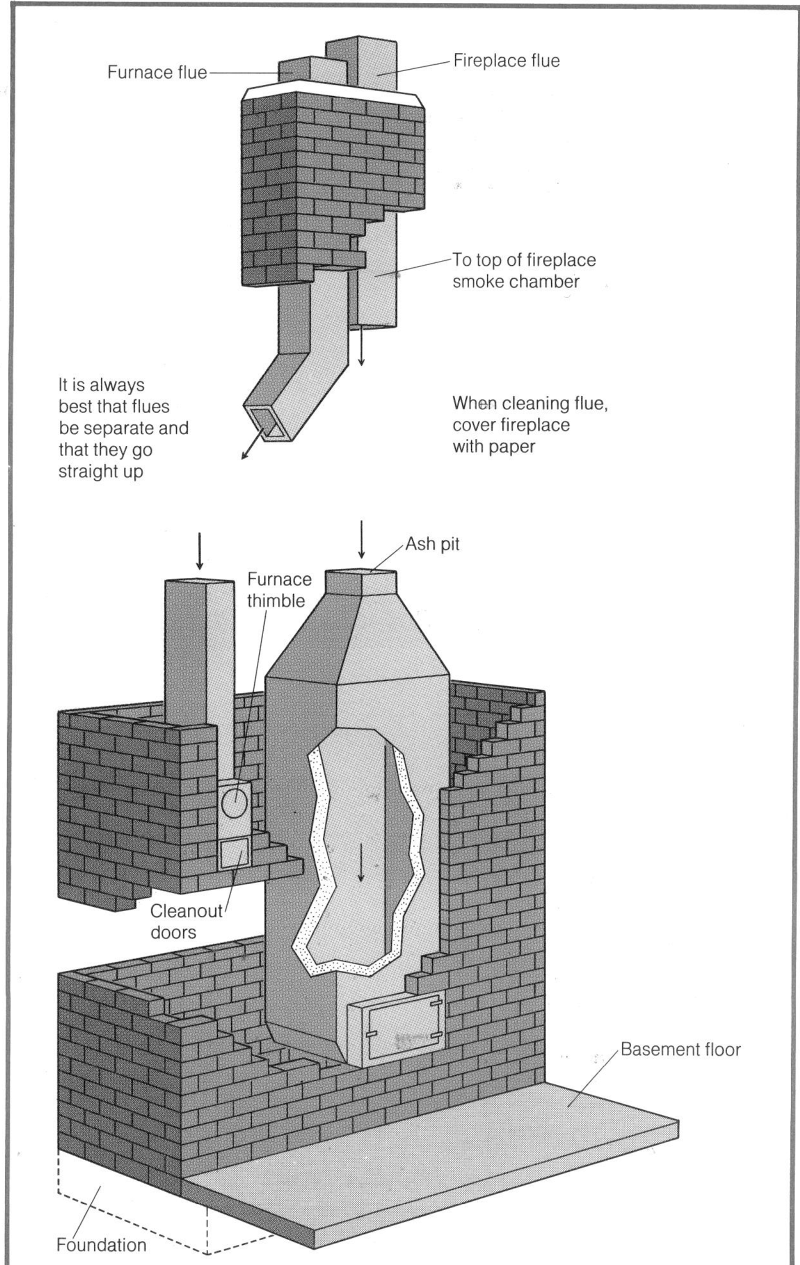

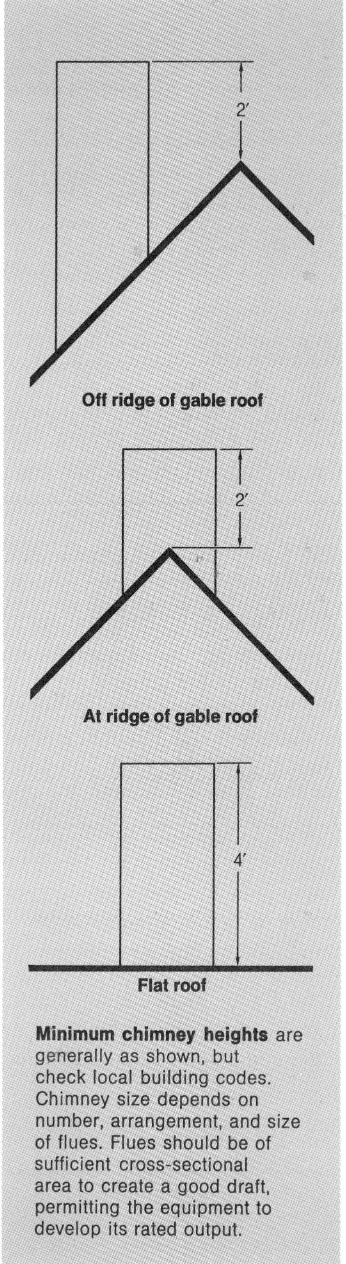

Minimum chimney heights are generally as shown, but check local building codes. Chimney size depends on number, arrangement, and size of flues. Flues should be of sufficient cross-sectional area to create a good draft, permitting the equipment to develop its rated output.

Heat distribution

Warm-air systems

Usually the only parts of a heating system visible in the room are the registers or radiators which distribute the heat—registers in homes with warm-air heating; radiators with steam or hot-water heating.

Registers: Registers are designed for two types of warm-air heating—gravity and forced. In a gravity system, registers are usually located in or next to the baseboard on inside walls. Be sure the joint between the register face and the wall is completely airtight, or you will get dirt streaks on the adjoining woodwork or wall. Most better-made registers come with a flexible gasket for making a tight seal. Floor grilles, located near the outside walls, are generally used for the cold-air return.

In forced warm-air heating, diffusion-type registers are recommended. They distribute the air evenly and without drafts. These are best located so that the room's occupants are not in the direct path of the warm-air supply. The supply registers of a modern forced warm-air system may be in any of a room's walls; if not in the baseboard, they should be low on the wall or near the ceiling. Because a high location doesn't interfere with furniture arrangement, this method is popular. The cold-air return intakes are best located at or near the baseboard, or in the floor, but not too close to the supply grilles.

Duct systems: The ductwork is, of course, crucial to a warm-air distribution system. While furnace location and the layout of the house determine its exact routes, two basic systems, the **radial** and the **extended-plenum,** are now in use.

In the radial system, warm-air outlets are located around the perimeter of the house, along the rooms' outside walls. Each run of ductwork extends, as directly as possible, outward from the furnace plenum to the room register. The return is usually led back through inside wall registers.

With the extended-plenum system, a very large rectangular duct extends in a straight line from the plenum. From it, smaller ducts lead to individual registers. This system, while more costly to install, permits better register placement, and the large duct means less resistance to the flow of air.

Either rectangular or round metal ducts may be employed. Round ducts (like stovepipe) are easiest to install but their use is limited. Rectangular ducts are the most popular for larger installations and those where air conditioning is planned.

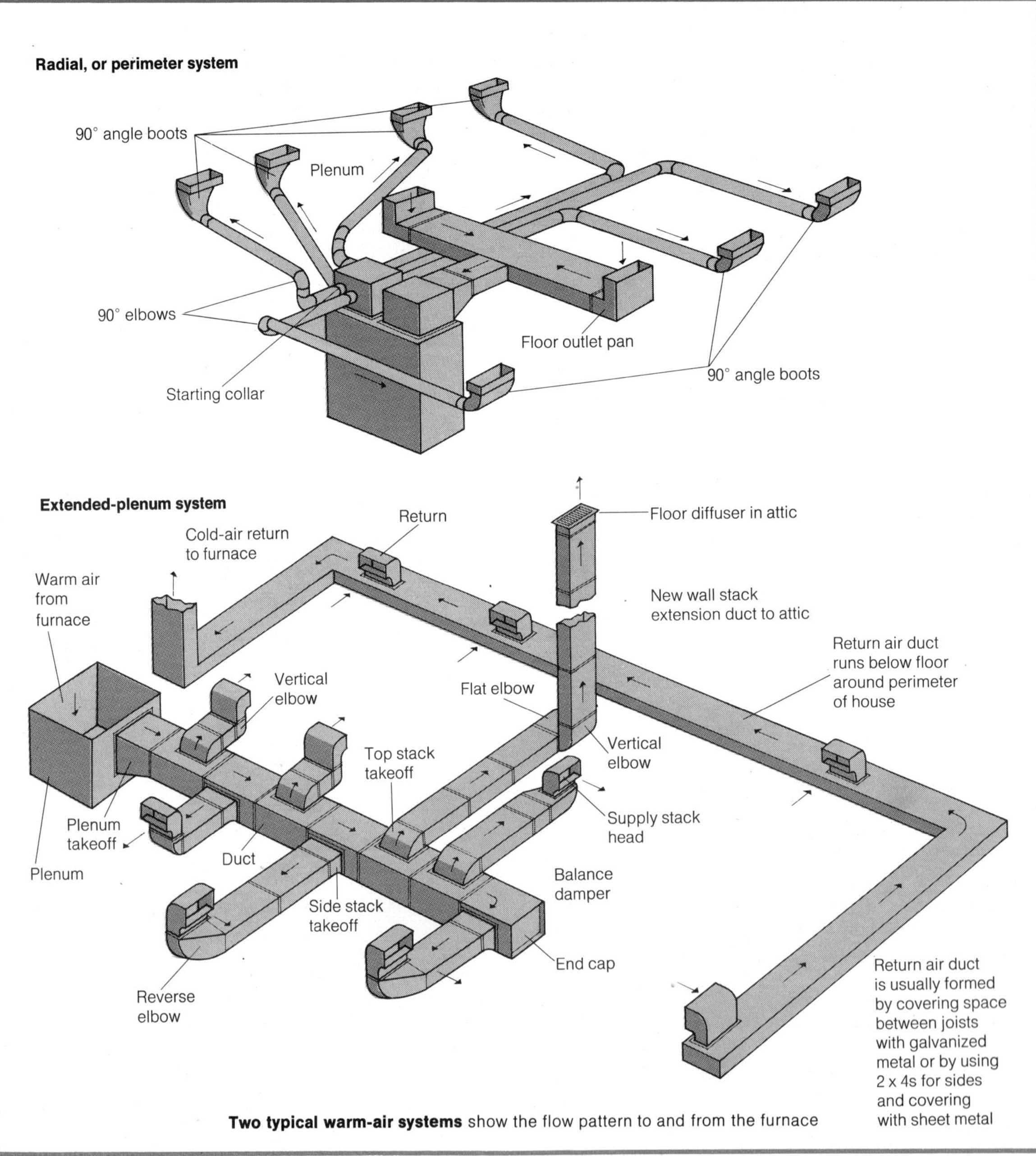

Two typical warm-air systems show the flow pattern to and from the furnace

Radiators

All three kinds of radiators—cast-iron, convector, and baseboard—work the same with either hot water or steam.

Cast-iron radiators deliver heat (1) by **convection**—air in contact with the hot metal is heated and rises, mixing with cooler air, and its place is taken by air drawn up from the floor; (2) by **radiation**—nearby objects are warmed by heat waves from the hot metal. Of the total heat thrown off by a cast-iron radiator, from 10 to 30 percent will be radiated. Since the amount of heat thrown off is directly proportionate to the amount of exposed metal, the newer thin tube-and-fin types are much more efficient than earlier ones. Also they take up 40 percent less space, so a much more efficient radiator can be put in the same area. A long, low radiator will heat a room better than one that is shorter and higher, because of the greater volume of warm air rising from it.

A good location for a radiator is near an outside wall, under a window. This permits better circulation of air and prevents drafts across the floor.

Covered and built-in radiators may be less conspicuous than the freestanding type, but they are not quite as effective. To function properly, they need a continuous passage of air from bottom to top, also some sort of reflective material at the back of the enclosure to direct the heat back into the room.

Convectors: In the convector, or "built-in" radiator, the hot water or steam is circulated through a finned metal tube in a cabinet. Cool air enters the bottom of the convector and rises through the fins, which warm it. The warmed air expands, mounts through the convector's top and is circulated by already moving air currents. Cabinet may be recessed in a wall.

Baseboard radiators are very efficient, delivering heat at the floor, where natural convection will cause the air to rise and warm the outside walls. Also they can be painted for partial concealment. They may be the radiant cast-iron or finned-tube type. The latter are generally used with hydronic systems.

As a rule, only outside walls are equipped with baseboard radiators. In the series-loop system, the main supply pipe may run around the outside walls of rooms where radiators are not needed and covered with matching metal baseboard, eliminating a great deal of basement piping.

All radiators have air valves to vent trapped air. Steam systems also have safety valves at the boiler.

Cast-iron radiators for water or steam

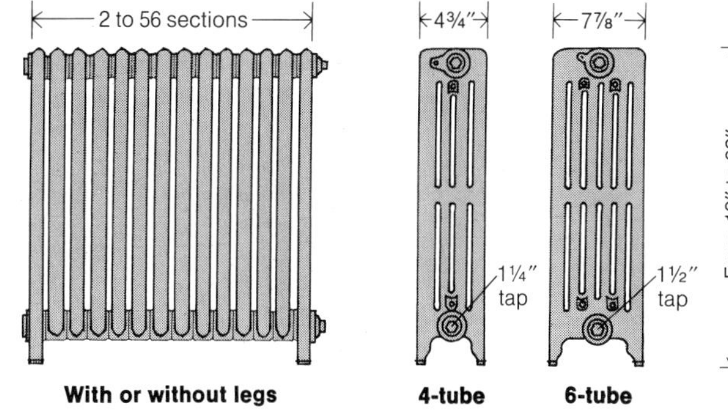

With or without legs **4-tube** **6-tube**

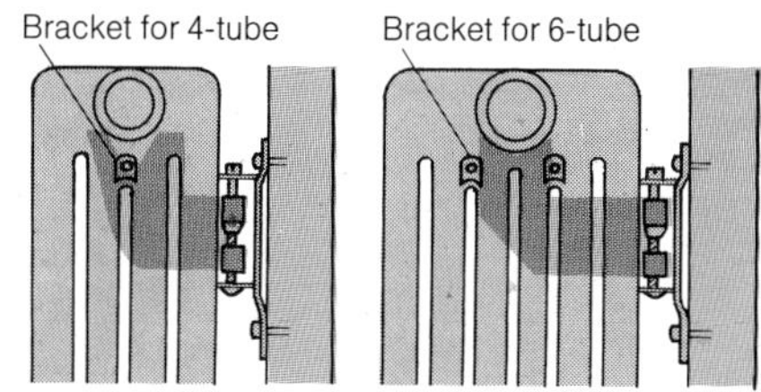

To suspend wall-hung radiators, use bracket-wall plate combination. Two are sufficient for radiators of up to 28 sections; from 30 to 45 sections, three are needed. Spacing between brackets should not exceed 42 in.

Nonferrous convectors for hot water or steam

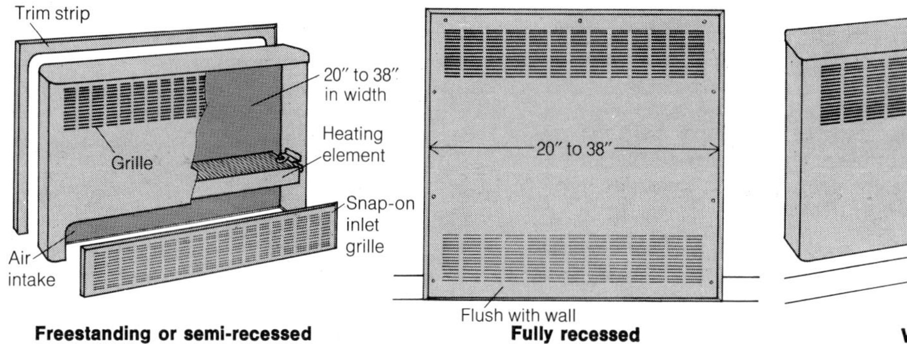

Freestanding or semi-recessed **Fully recessed** **Wall-hung**

Cast-iron baseboard for hot water or steam

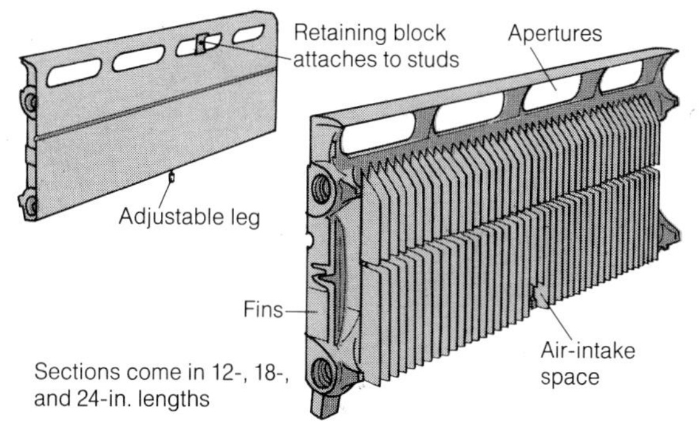

Installed against wall or recessed to depth of plaster

Nonferrous baseboard for hot water

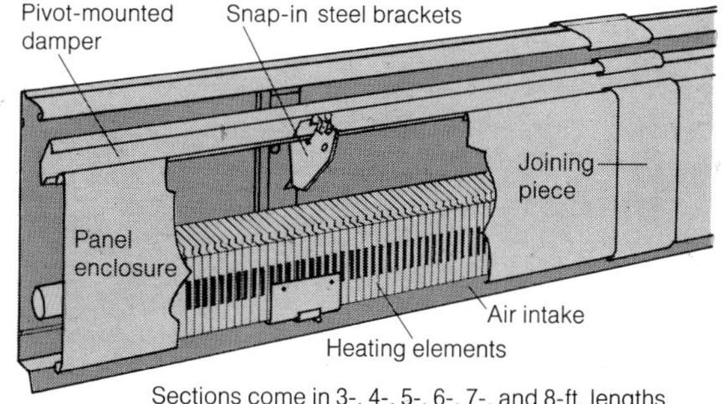

Installed against wall or recessed to depth of plaster

Warm-air system

Filters are generally employed in forced warm-air heating systems to keep air cleaner. Permanent-type filters require occasional washing; filters of the throwaway type need replacement from time to time. If the filters are permitted to become clogged with dust and dirt, the circulation of air will be diminished and the efficiency of the heating plant reduced.

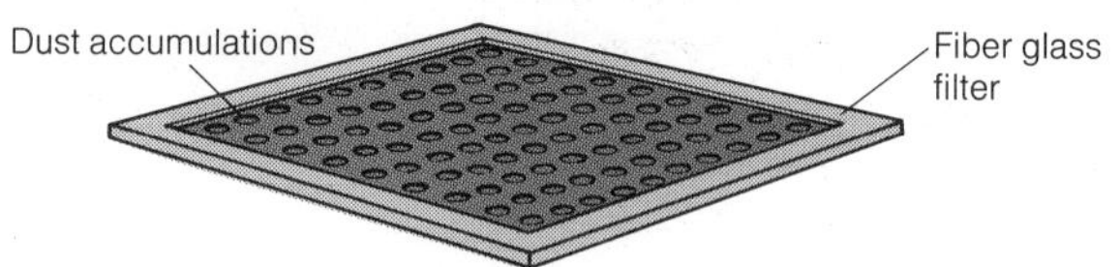

Replace or clean filter

Grilles: Floor grilles or registers also require frequent cleaning, since dust and small objects can easily fall into them. This kind of cleaning can usually be done with a vacuum cleaner. If large objects become lodged in the warm-air supply pipe, however, it may be necessary to dismantle the pipe to remove them. Wall grilles or registers are not directly subjected to dust or other accumulations in the way that floor grilles are but may require dismantling for cleaning if they become clogged.

Blower cleanliness: Keep the fan blades clean. When they become loaded with lint, as often happens, their ability to move air, and thus their efficiency, is cut down. Many blowers have blades that are easily accessible for cleaning. You can get at them with a small brush. If the blades are not accessible, a serviceman should disassemble, clean, and adjust the blower every second year. The belt that powers the blades should not be stiff or too loose. Properly adjusted, it has ½ to ¾ inch of slack. If worn, replace.

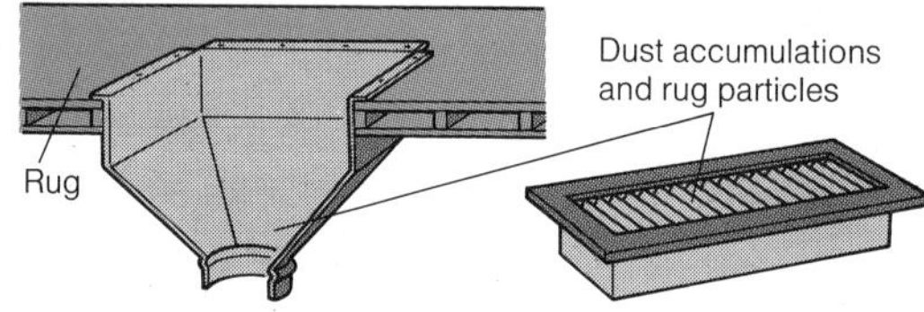

Cleaning ducts and inlet and outlet registers

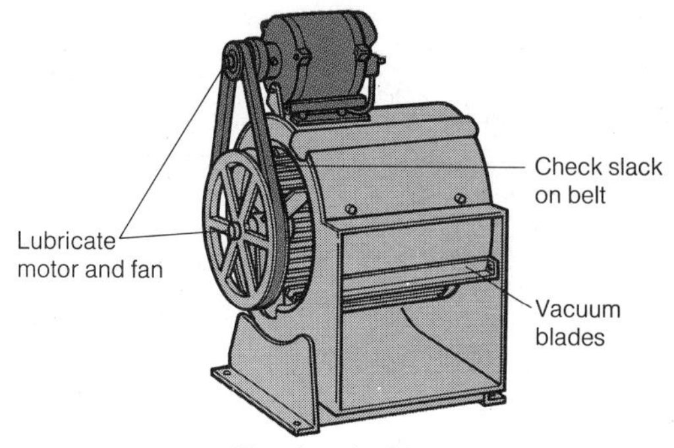

Cleaning the blower

Hot-water system

The expansion tank usually requires periodic draining. Do this by shutting off the valve that lets water into the tank from the boiler, then opening the valve at the bottom of the tank. To make the job easier, attach a hose to the tank and run it to a pail or drain.

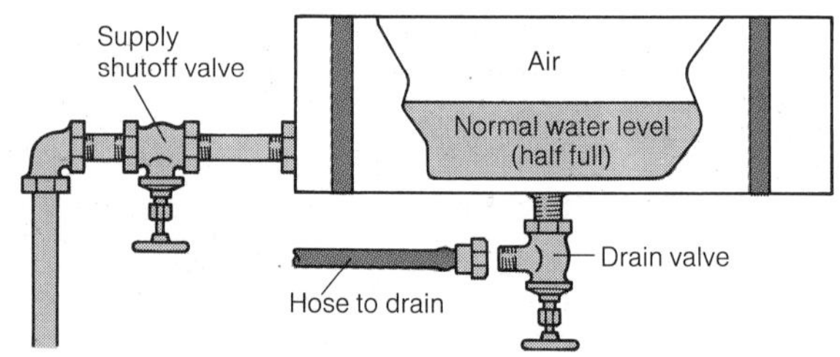

Flushing out boiler: How much dirt gets into the boiler depends on the water supply. To drain your boiler: (1) Turn off the burner. (2) Shut off the water-supply inlet to the boiler. Attach a hose to the drain outlet at the lowest level in the system (generally at the base of the boiler) and lead it to the cellar drain —or use several pails. Open the drain outlet. (3) When water begins to flow through the hose, open the venting valves on the highest radiators. (4) After the sediment has drained out, open the water-supply inlet to the boiler and flush the boiler with clean water. (5) To refill, leave the water-supply inlet open but shut off the drain outlet at the base of the boiler. Turn the burner back on. Keep the venting valves open on the highest radiators until you hear water filling the pipes, then close them. Later in the day, vent all valves of trapped air.

Bleeding a radiator: Air, freed from freshly added water as it is heated for the first time, will rise and trap itself in the radiators. This blocks circulation of water, causing the radiators to stay cold. Bleeding is necessary to get rid of the trapped air. To bleed a radiator, open the vent screw in the valve at one end, and keep it open until water spurts out. The water will be hot—catch it in a cup. This must be done to each radiator. An automatic valve is worth considering here—it is low-priced, easy to install, and does away with the necessity for hand venting.

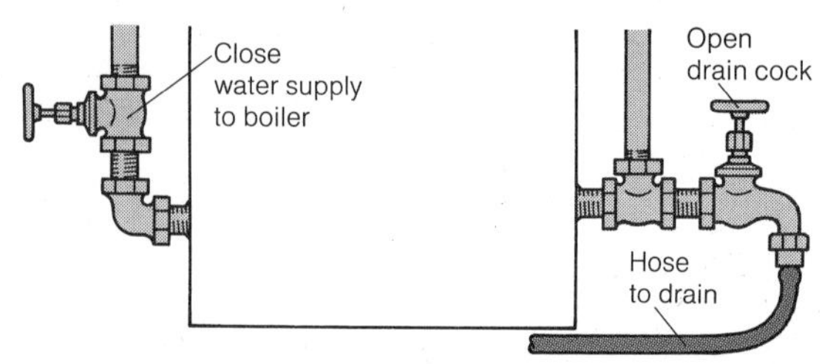

Flushing out boiler

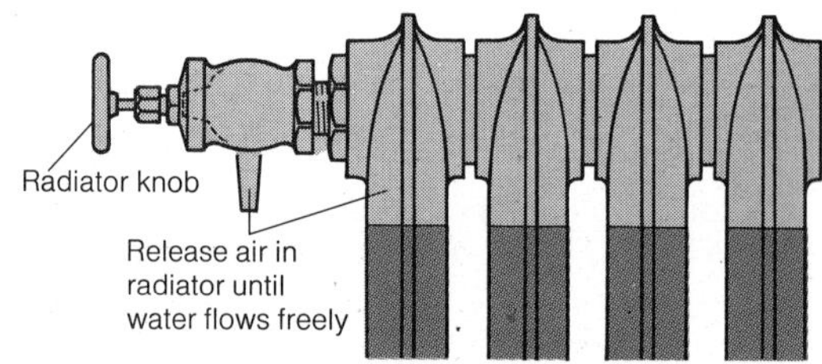

Bleeding the radiator

Insulating pipelines: Insulate mains and risers in the cellar, to avoid heat loss at that point, with asbestos. The asbestos, available at heating-supply outlets, comes in two sections that are wrapped around the pipe and held by metal bands (p.225).

Hot-water shutoff valves may be set partly open or closed and used as throttling valves to regulate the heat to each radiator, permitting you to balance the system by favoring radiators that are not hot enough and cutting down on those that are too hot.

Steam system

In operation, steam boilers should be kept filled with water at least to the center of the water gauge or to the level recommended by the manufacturer.
Noise in a system: Several conditions can make a steam system noisy. A knocking sound is often traceable to the improper pitch of the pipes. All pipes must have a downward slope, so water will flow easily from the radiator to the boiler. If for some reason a section of pipe has sagged, water will collect in this low spot and become an obstacle to the oncoming steam. The meeting of steam and trapped water results in pounding. When this occurs close to a radiator, it can usually be corrected by placing small blocks of wood under the radiator's legs. This will increase the pitch of the radiator, and the pipe connected to it, giving the water an easy path back to the boiler. When hammering occurs in some other part of the system, check whether a section of pipe has sagged, causing the same kind of depression.

Another reason for pounding may be the position of the steam valve between radiator and steam pipe. This valve should be fully opened or fully closed.
Dirty water gauge: The glass water gauge on the boiler can get so dirty inside that an accurate reading is impossible. To remove it for cleaning, close valves at top and bottom, take off top and bottom nuts and washers, pull glass up and out the bottom.
Leaking steam valve: If steam escapes around a steam valve stem, it is a sign that the packing is loose. It can be tightened by turning down the packing nut on the stem. If this does not correct the leaking, the stem should be repacked. This can be done by turning off the valve, unscrewing the packing nut, and replacing the washers or the packing cord, depending on the type of packing.

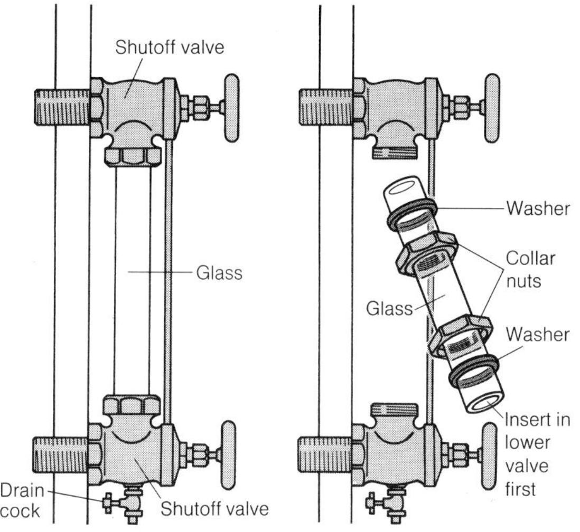

Replacing glass on water gauge

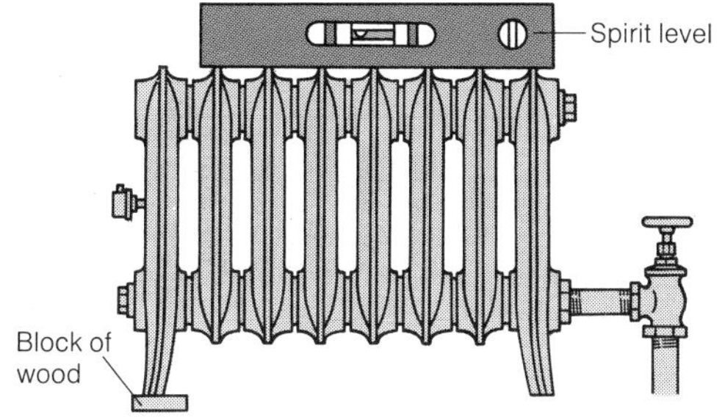

Radiator should slant to outflow

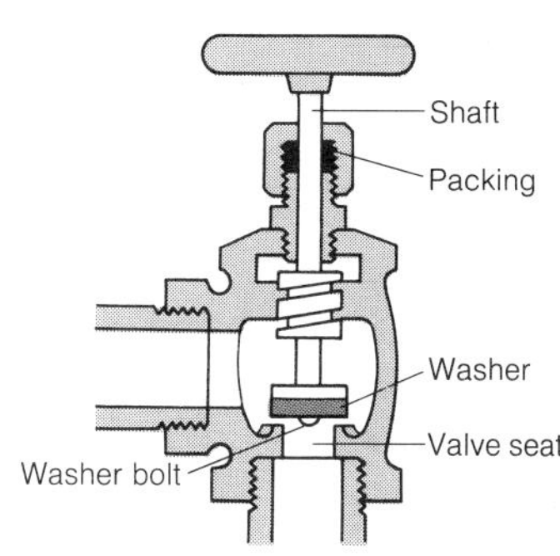

Cross section of radiator valve

Setting a surface Aquastat controller

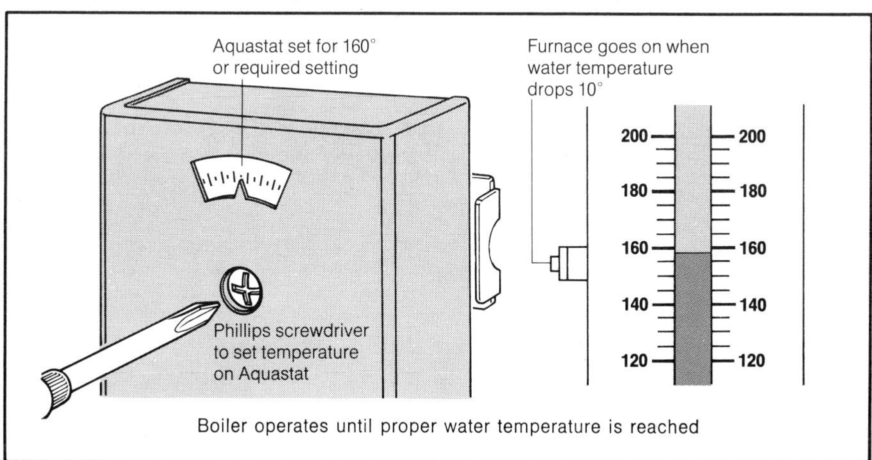

Boiler operates until proper water temperature is reached

How an altitude gauge works

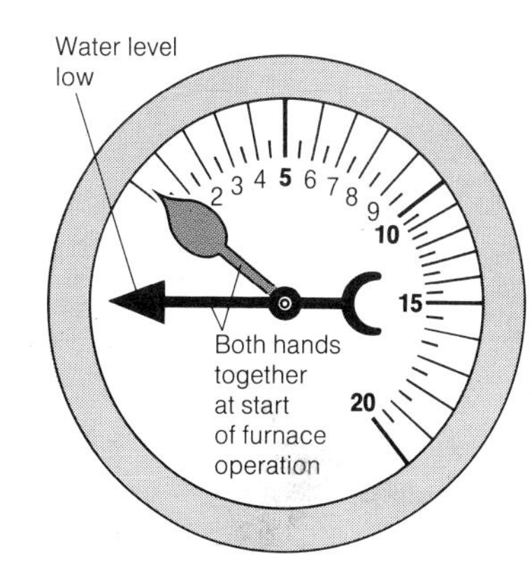

The purpose of the gauge on a hot-water boiler is to show the level of water proper for and actually present in the system. This gauge has two needles, one black and the other usually red. The red needle is set for the water level that is required for the highest radiator in the house. The black needle indicates the actual level of water in the system and varies with changes in water content. When the red needle is over the black one, the system is properly filled. In pressure systems, the amount of water is automatically controlled by a valve. By reading the altitude gauge, you can tell whether the valve is operating correctly. If for some reason the gauge reads higher than it should, have the valve examined and the malfunction corrected before turning on the furnace.

Oil burners

Types and operation

Oil burners use fuel oil, spraying it into a combustion chamber where it burns to create heat. While many designs exist, there are only two basic types on the market: The pressure, or gun type; and the vaporizing, or pot type. The once popular rotary burner is now used only in big commercial installations.

Pressure burners. The high-pressure oil burner is by far the dominant type in home use today. In operation, the oil is pumped into the burner unit under high pressure, sprayed through a nozzle into a fine mist, and then mixed with air by a fan. The resulting combination is ignited by an electric spark. The ignition system, much like that of an automobile, contains a transformer which changes the house electrical system into a high voltage that jumps a spark gap directly in the path of the oil spray.

The low-pressure burner looks much like the high-pressure type, but employs a low-pressure pump and mixes air and oil within the nozzle. The mixture is sprayed as a vapor through an opening many times larger than the opening in a high-pressure nozzle. Ignition takes place within the combustion chamber in the same way as in the high-pressure type.

Pressure burners do not operate continuously but on demand of the thermostat. They usually project beyond the firebox and so are readily serviced.

Pot-type, or **vaporizing burners** are frequently used in small central and space-heater furnaces. Principal features are a pot containing a pool of oil and a control for regulating its flow. The fire is started by hand or by an electric spark, and the resulting heat vaporizes the oil. Air necessary for burning is admitted by natural draft or by a small fan. A low pilot flame keeps the fire alive once it starts. Oil is fed into the pool as needed. Because the burner has few moving parts, it is very quiet. Both fuel and air must be carefully adjusted by a competent serviceman familiar with the particular burner, to avoid a smoky, sooty flame. All burners, regardless of type, should be given a yearly CO_2 indicator test to make sure combustion is proper.

All oil burner installations require a small but steady draft, best provided by an automatic draft regulator placed in the vent pipe.

Oil supply: The label of the Underwriters' Laboratories on the burner will specify the recommended grade of oil. This will be the heaviest and least expensive grade the burner can consume safely. Tanks for storage of this oil should be installed as stipulated by the National Board of Fire Underwriters. Small tanks generally go in the basement; they should be at least 7 feet from the furnace. Individual tanks should not exceed 275-gallon capacity, and two are the maximum allowed in a basement; if greater capacity is needed, the tanks must be buried in the ground. Each tank must be vented to the outside and equipped with an outside pipe for filling.

Oil burner control: Beside the room thermostat, most oil burners have a stack-control relay which shuts off the oil pump motor if the spray does not ignite within a short time. Without this relay, located either on the smoke pipe (which runs to the chimney) or on the furnace, the oil pump could continue to pump oil into the combustion chamber, causing it to overflow. The stack-control is designed to operate as the hot gases from the combustion chamber pass through the smoke pipe. If no hot gases pass through, indicating no combustion, the stack-control relay shuts off the pump motor. If it shuts off the burner, reset it once only, by pressing the button or pushing the tab. If the unit starts, fine. If it starts but shuts down again, the trouble is within the burner and calls for professional service.

Conversions: Coal-burning furnaces can be converted to oil by installation of a specially designed gun-type oil burner. If the conversion is properly planned and made, good heating efficiency can be obtained, though some authorities claim that any converted unit will be less efficient than a furnace especially designed and built to burn oil.

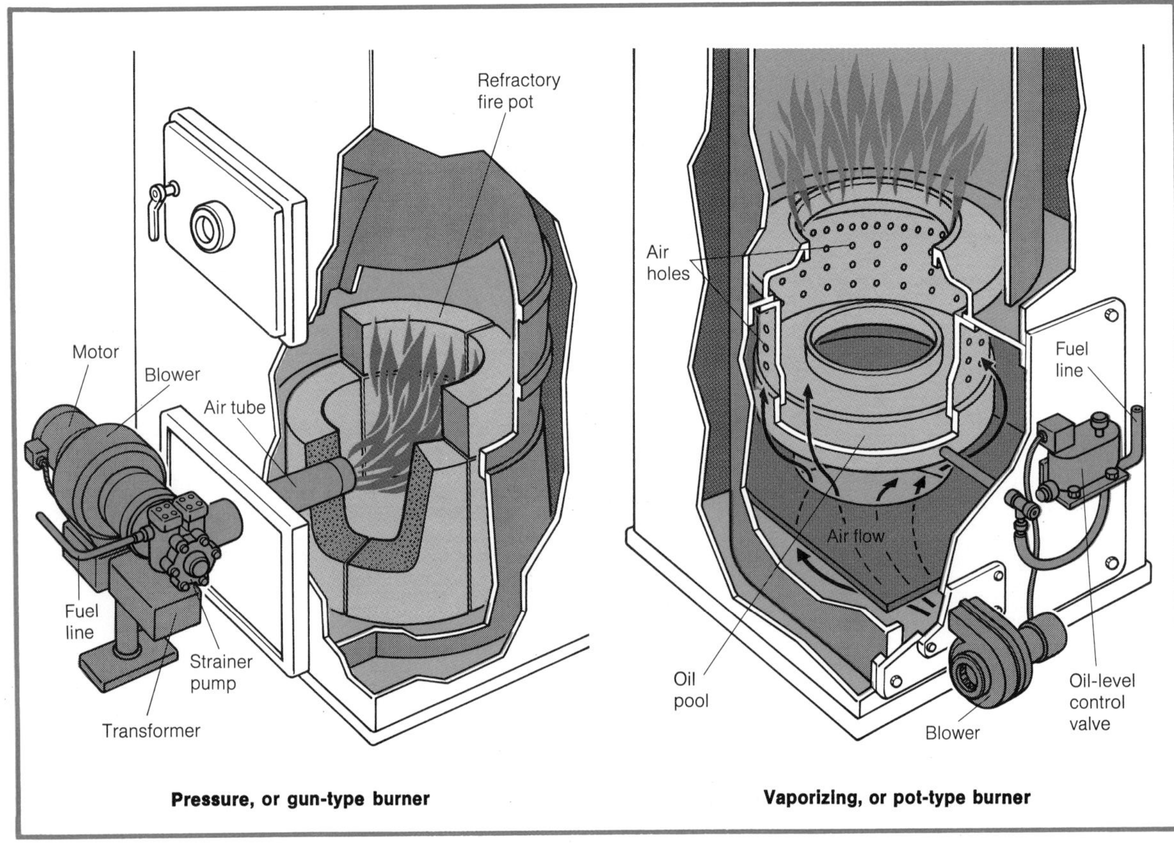

Pressure, or gun-type burner **Vaporizing, or pot-type burner**

Basic operating principles

Gas burners are much like oil burners except that they are considerably simpler and require only a burner arrangement and automatic valve instead of the oil pump and oil reservoir tank. The gas burner may have either a single jet which shoots a flame against a deflecting surface that spreads it over the surface to be heated, or a multi-jet arrangement similar to the burners on a gas range. Another kind is a ribbon-type burner, used on furnaces designed exclusively for gas. All three can use natural, artificial, or LP (liquefied petroleum) gas.

With all gas systems, a pilot is used to light the jet or burners. Its flame heats a device called a thermocouple which converts its heat into a tiny electric current. This current holds an electrical valve open in the main gas-supply line to the burner. If the pilot light goes out, the thermocouple cools off. Because it does not then supply any current, the gas supply valve closes, and will stay closed until the pilot is relighted (p.293).

For any gas-fired heater to function properly, the gas must be supplied at low pressure into the burner head where it is mixed with the air required for burning. Hot gases caused by the resulting combustion pass through the furnace or heater into the vent pipe and then out through the chimney. A gas-control valve regulates the amount of gas supplied to the burner; pressure is controlled by an automatic pressure regulator. A draft diverter hood, located on the vent pipe, maintains a small draft, at the same time preventing air currents from backing down the chimney and blowing out the pilot light flame. The pilot keeps moisture from condensing in the chimney and retaining the acid by-products of gas combustion which, though weak, can cause damage to the mortar joints. Such conditions are especially dangerous in older homes where flue linings have been omitted in the chimney. In gas heating systems, the chimney is usually referred to as a vent.

Though furnaces and boilers designed specifically for gas are the most efficient, existing systems which use other types of fuel can be made to burn gas satisfactorily by the installation of a conversion gas burner. This transformation should be done only by a competent technician employed by the gas company. All gas-burning equipment should bear the American Gas Association seal, which guarantees that a prototype has been tested for safety.

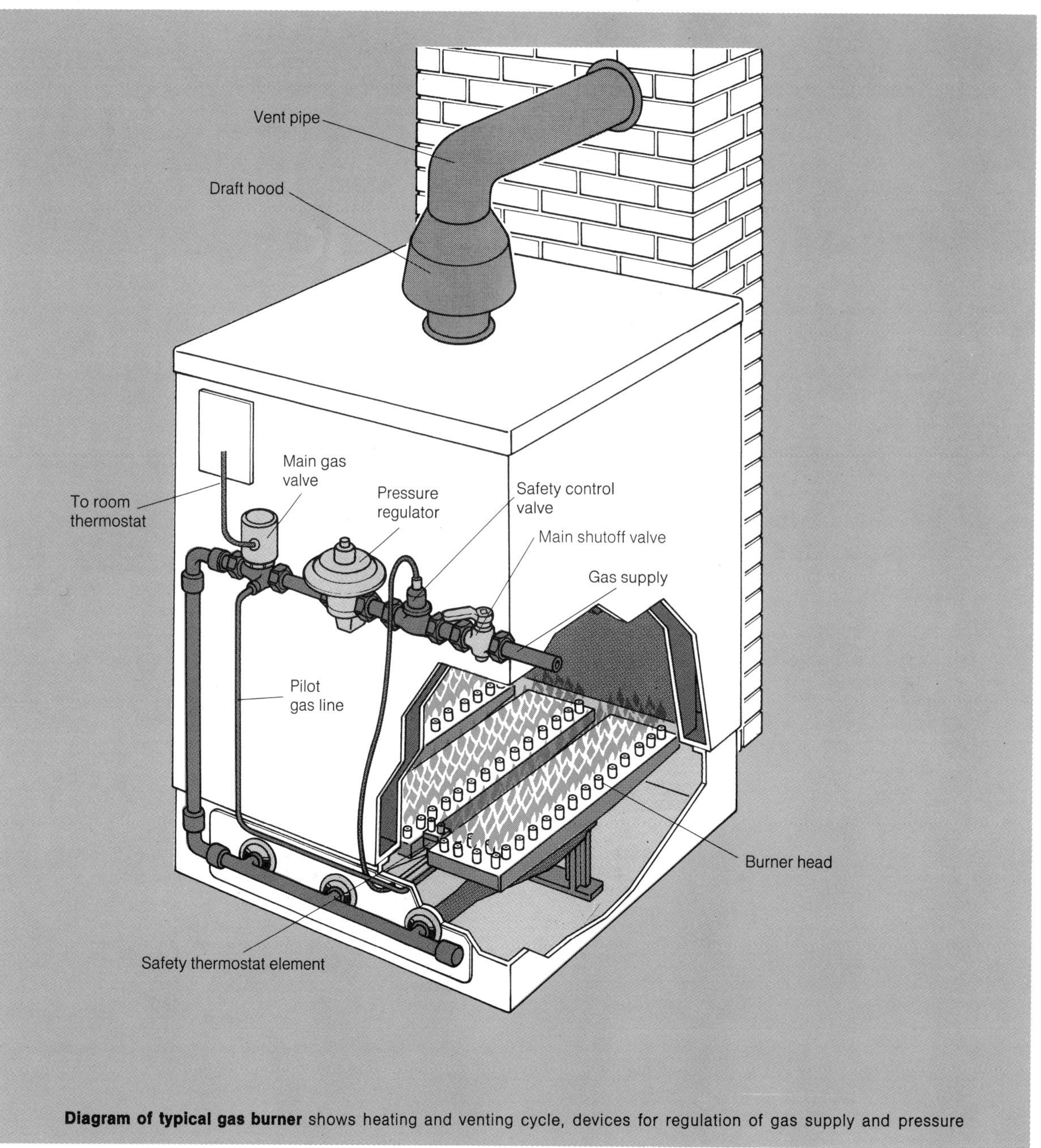

Diagram of typical gas burner shows heating and venting cycle, devices for regulation of gas supply and pressure

Oil burners and controls

Furnace does not operate. There are a number of points that you can check before calling the serviceman:

1. See that the emergency switch has not been accidentally turned off. This switch, usually found close to the furnace or in the basement stairwell, resembles a regular light switch usually painted red.
2. Examine the fuse that controls the furnace. If it is blown, replace it. If your home is equipped with circuit breakers and one is tripped, reset it. If a new fuse blows, or if the circuit breaker trips again, call for servicing.
3. If fuses and switches are in order, check the oil tank. Often the gauge can stick, indicating that the tank is full when it is actually empty.
4. Try moving the thermostat up a few degrees. If it is the type that has a night and day setting, remove the thermostat cover and check the dial to see if a recent power failure may have caused the timer to operate out of cycle.

While the cover is removed, check the thermostat contact points. Dirt or corrosion on the points could keep the furnace from turning on.

5. Try resetting the furnace relay switch, which is usually located on the furnace or on the smoke pipe leading to the chimney. This safety switch shuts down the furnace in case of ignition failure.

Press the reset button once only. If the furnace starts and then stops, call for service.

Furnace operates but heat is low. This usually indicates trouble in the heat-distribution system rather than the oil burner. Study page 288 for maintenance details on various heat-distribution systems.

If you have a **hot-water system,** check the circulator pump. This pump circulates the heated water from the furnace to the radiators. If the pump is not operating while the furnace is running, push the reset button found on some pump motors.

Lack of heat in a **forced-air heating** system usually means that the circulator fan is not working. Often this will require only replacement of the fan belt that connects the fan and the electric motor. If the belt is intact, push the reset button located on the side of fan motor. If this fails, call for service.

If your furnace is linked to a **steam heat** distribution system, check the water level in the boiler. When the water level drops too low, the furnace will shut off if it has a low-water cut-off switch. Allow the boiler time to cool before refilling. At about the halfway point the furnace should start. If it does not, call for servicing.

Spasmodic operation. If the furnace is sputtering, or going on briefly then shutting down, there may be dirt in the oil filters. This condition can also keep the furnace from running at all. Normally you might call a serviceman to clean the filters. But you can follow the instructions in the drawing below to clean the filters yourself.

Unusual noise and rumble. This is usually an indication of air trapped in the radiators or pipes. Bleed the air by opening or unscrewing the valves in a hot-water system until water starts to escape. If the circulator pump is running but making a loud noise, the coupling shaft joining the motor to the pump may be broken. Call for servicing. Both chimney and furnace should be cleaned of soot at least once a year.

Cleaning thermostat contacts

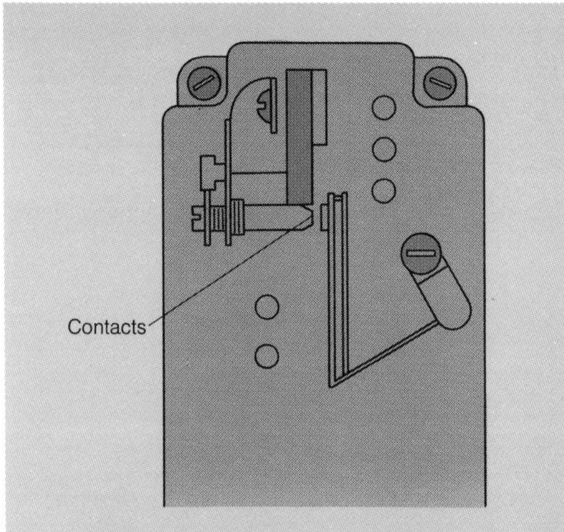

If thermostat contact points have gotten dirty in use, this could hinder the entire heating operation. To correct, remove the control cover and clean the points by passing a crisp, new dollar bill or business card between them. Be sure never to use an abrasive—this would scratch and damage the contacts. When the thermostat is a mercury vial-type, cleaning is not necessary. Such a thermostat is sealed by the manufacturer.

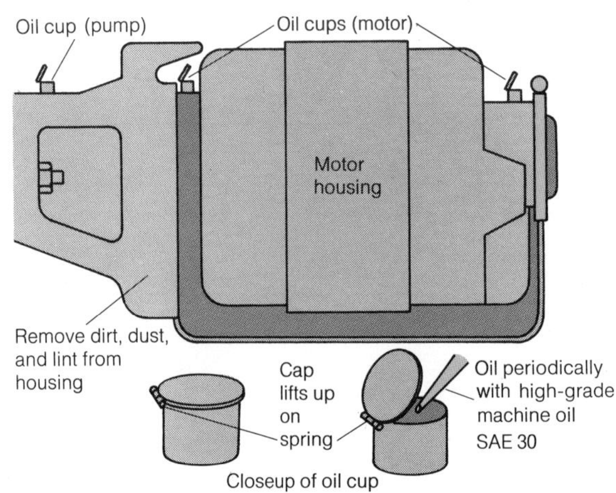

Pump motors need periodic attention—a few drops of high-grade machine oil to cups and removal of dust and dirt

Cleaning the filters

Filters are located at the end of the furnace motor in a cast iron pump housing. The housing lid is held in place by six or eight bolts. With the furnace switch off, remove the bolts and the housing lid. Take care not to damage the gasket underneath. Lift out the filters and clean them in kerosene.

Gas-fired burners

A gas-fired system requires no regular annual maintenance by a serviceman. Most gas companies inspect gas heaters every three years, primarily to make sure that the heater fuel passages and the vent pipe to the chimney are clean and clear. Also their servicemen will respond quickly to customer calls regarding any problems they encounter with their heating systems. Major utility companies do not usually charge for service.

Although gas-fired heating systems do not need much periodic maintenance, certain malfunctions can occur. Actually, the most frequent difficulties encountered with gas burners are the sticking of the plunger of the main valve, the accumulation of gum or other foreign matter in the pressure regulator, and the loss of the pilot light. Repairs to the gas valve and regulator should be made only by utility company representatives.

A pilot light may be relighted by the homeowner after ample opportunity has been given for the combustion chamber to be aired out and after making certain that the main gas valve of the appliance has been closed. Follow the directions printed on the tag or plate attached to the unit. But never try this unless you know what must be done. To avoid inconvenience, call the local utility company in advance and have someone show you the proper way to do the job. If the pilot light goes out for an unknown reason, the furnace's operation should be watched carefully for a time after relighting to determine whether further repair is needed.

Another source of trouble is improper adjustment of the primary air nozzle. To adjust the air setting, allow 5 minutes for the burners to heat up; open the air shutter until the flame lifts off the burner (a sign that it's getting too much air), then close it until the flame returns to the burner. There should be no yellow in the flame.

Manual operation: Some gas furnaces can be operated manually during power failures by: (1) Turning the switch on the limit-relay control to the "manual" position and (2) opening all water-flow control valves in the system. It is important to remember that this is an abnormal operating condition, and the boiler should therefore be supervised throughout the manual operation period. (3) When power resumes, return the switch to the "automatic" position and flow-control valves to original adjustments.

Flames

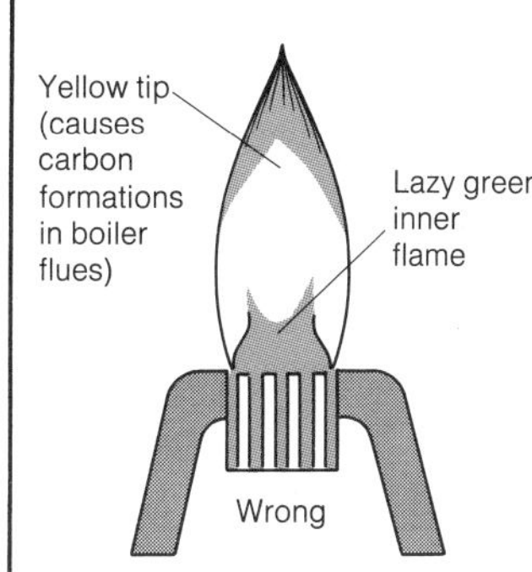

Not enough primary air

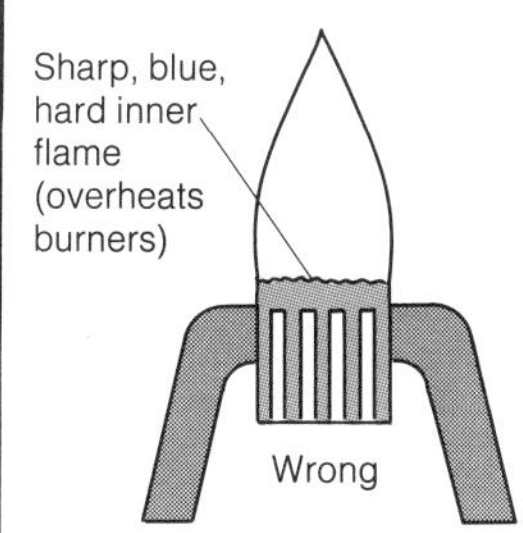

Too much primary air

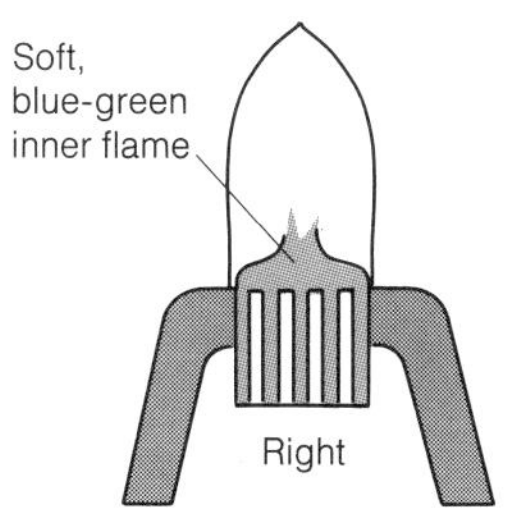

Ribbon burners: LP (liquefied petroleum) gas burner flames must be adjusted properly to prevent excessive burner temperatures. Adjust the air shutter to a blue-green inner flame with no yellow in the flame.

Relighting the pilot

1. Set the room thermostat to the lowest temperature on the scale.

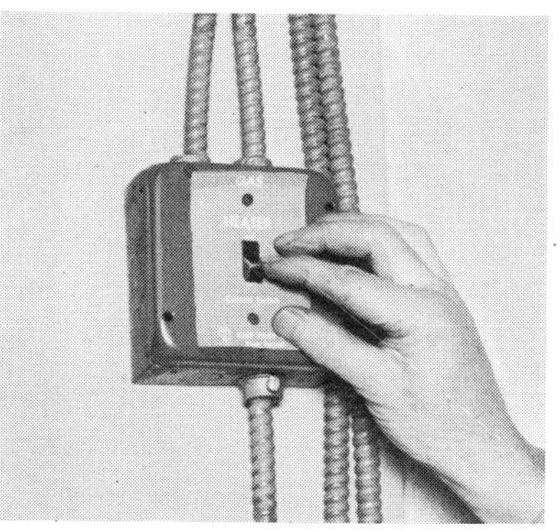

2. Flip to "off" the switch that controls current to the gas furnace.

3. Shut off the gas supply to the furnace but leave on the gas to the pilot light.

4. Light pilot; turn on current, open main gas valve, and adjust thermostat.

For manual operation, turn switch on limit-relay control to "manual."

Open the water control valve, usually located right above the furnace.

Stoker-fired burners

Types, functions, maintenance

Stokers are intended primarily to feed coal automatically into a furnace or boiler. In addition, many units provide for automatic removal of ashes from the firebox directly into covered ash cans. This makes for cleanliness in the heater room and avoids a messy job for the homeowner.

Though there are several design variations available, stokers are of two basic types, the hopper and the bin. Both employ a screw, or auger, to transport the nut-size stoker coal from the supply bin to the firebox. The hopper-type stoker pushes the coal from the bottom of the hopper; the bin-type pulls the coal from the coal bin. With the former, it is necesary to fill the hopper at least once a day. In the latter system, coal handling is eliminated.

Through openings in the retort, a fan draws in the necessary air for proper burning of the fuel. After the fire has been started—this may be done with kindling—it is maintained by a "hold-fire" control which runs the automatic stoker a few minutes each day. A room thermostat keeps the stoker in operation when a demand for increased heat arises. Sometimes the hold-fire control will feed in too little coal, allowing the fire to go out. Or it may feed in too much, causing the house to be overheated in mild weather. Adjustments to correct such conditions should be made by a mechanic familiar with the equipment and trained by its manufacturer.

Maintenance: The coal used for a stoker-equipped heater should be treated for the elimination of dust and should be uniformly 1 inch or smaller in diameter. A shear pin is usually located in the shaft of the coal screw to protect the other parts of the mechanism in the event that the feed screw gets jammed with large pieces of coal or other solid material which may be present in the coal supply. If this should occur, it is necessary to remove the obstruction and replace the shear pin. Some stokers are not equipped with a shear pin, but are designed to jump out of gear if the screw gets jammed.

At the end of each heating season, the burner should be completely cleaned of all coal, ash, and clinkers. This cleaning necessity applies to the stoker as well. At the time of cleaning, oil the insides of both coal screw and hopper to prevent rust. Before the system is put back in operation, the stoker should be inspected, repaired if necessary, and adjusted by a competent serviceman.

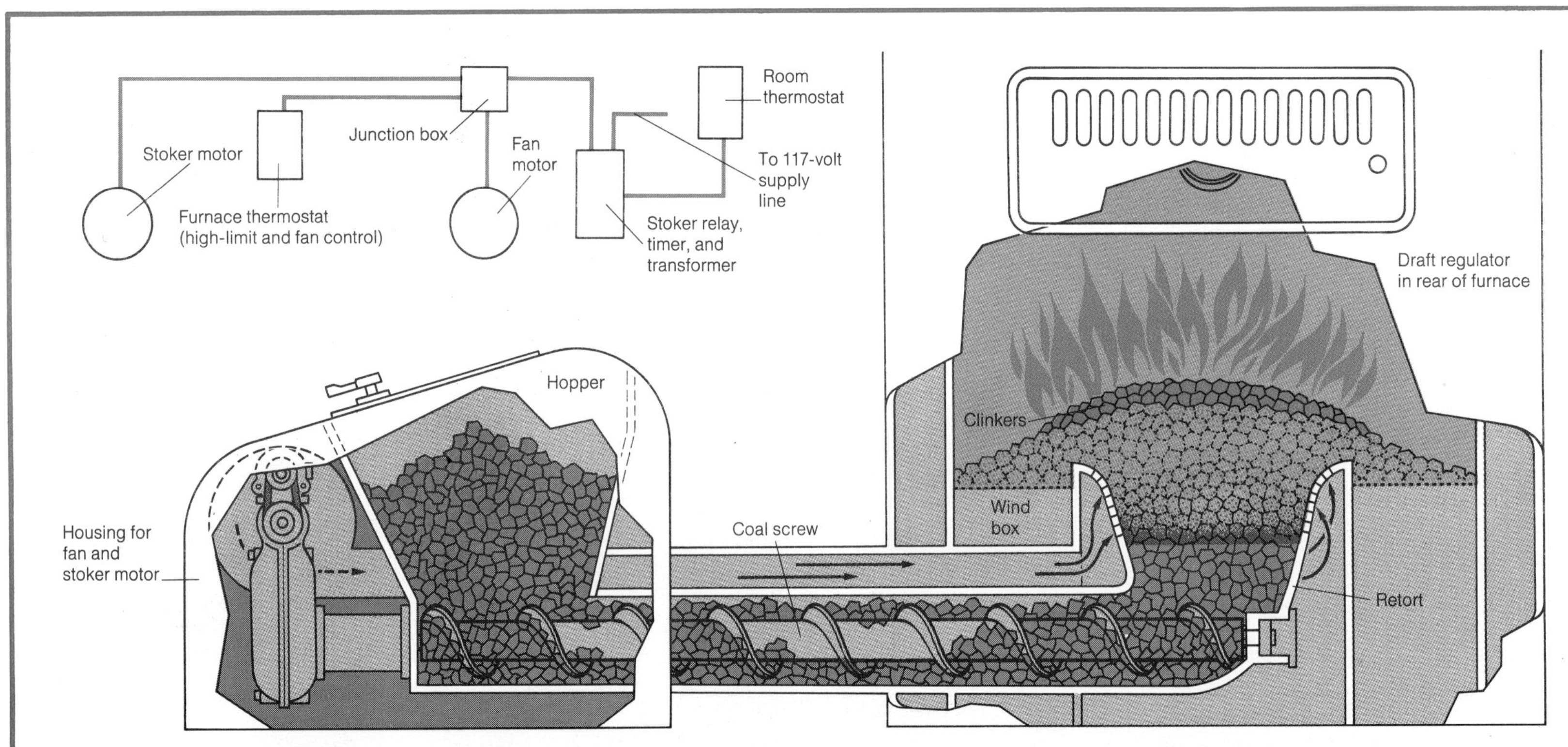

The stoker fire burner system, found in areas where coal is easily obtainable, feeds fuel to the furnace automatically. In some systems the hopper must be filled once a day. Others are equipped with automatic feeders leading from the coal supply into the hopper. There are also screw systems for automatic removal of the ashes.

Basic design and operation

The fireplace, once a major source of heat for the home, is used today only as a source of supplementary heat and for decorative purposes.

The usual fireplace is a recessed niche in the wall, lined with firebrick, usually on three sides and the floor, open at the front, with a chimney above it. The fireplace throat is normally equipped with a damper that will close off the chimney when the fireplace is not in use. This prevents heat loss in the winter and the entrance of small animals in the summer. The smoke shelf just above the fireplace prevents downdrafts from entering the fireplace and blowing smoke out into the room. The ash pit has a small hinged door that tilts to permit the ashes to fall into a pit below the fireplace. The hearth, whether brick or tile, should be well supported to prevent it sagging and breaking away from the fireplace floor.

All fireplaces should be built in accordance with a few simple design principles for satisfactory performance. The size should suit the room in which they are to be used, for the sake of both operation and looks. For example, the opening should be approximately 10 to 12 times the flue area. For an 8- by 12-inch flue, that would mean about a 960-square inch opening. The width of the opening should always be greater than its height. The depth, on this basis, can be 2 feet or more.

Because fireplace construction is exacting, preformed metal fireboxes are popular today. Their sides and upper parts have double walls so that air can be drawn in at the bottom and discharged through vents at the top. Air passing through this space will be heated by the fire and projected into the room, much the same way as it is with a warm-air gravity system.

Maintenance: Before starting a fire, check the damper to make sure it is open. You should be able to look up the chimney and see daylight even if the chimney has a slight offset. No daylight may mean an obstruction, such as a bird's nest, and a need to clean the chimney (p. 174). If your fireplace has a trap door for ashes, remove ashes regularly.

Removing stains and soot: Stains on brick and stone can be removed with detergent and water. For stubborn stains, use a half-and-half solution of muriatic acid and water. Wear gloves and eye protection. Commercial products from hardware stores can be thrown on a fire to burn excess soot from the chimney.

Masonry

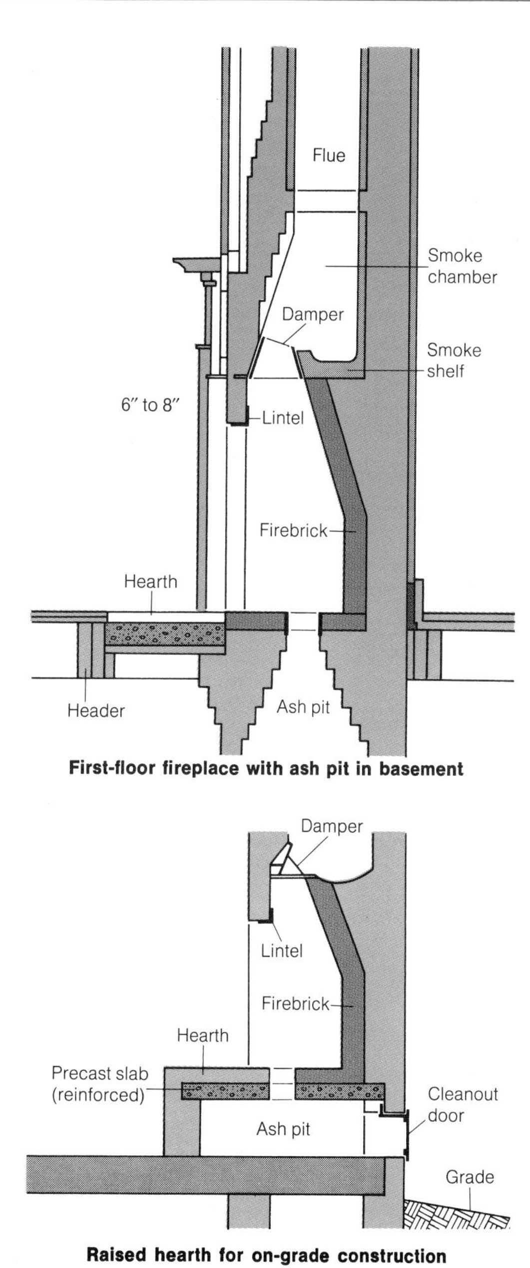

First-floor fireplace with ash pit in basement

Raised hearth for on-grade construction

Metal

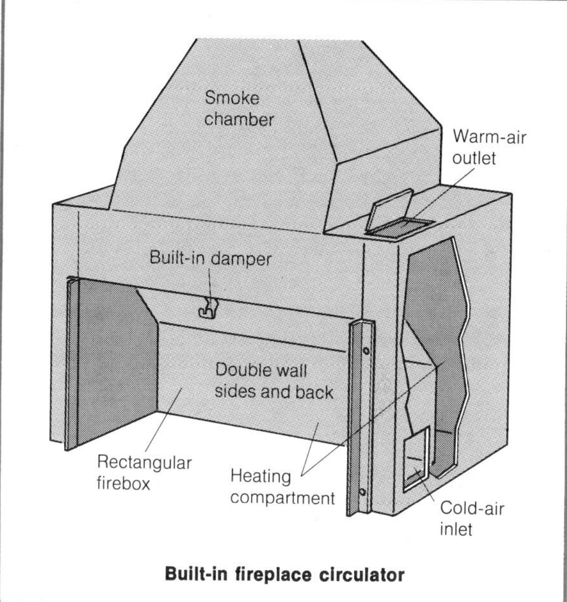

Built-in fireplace circulator

Freestanding

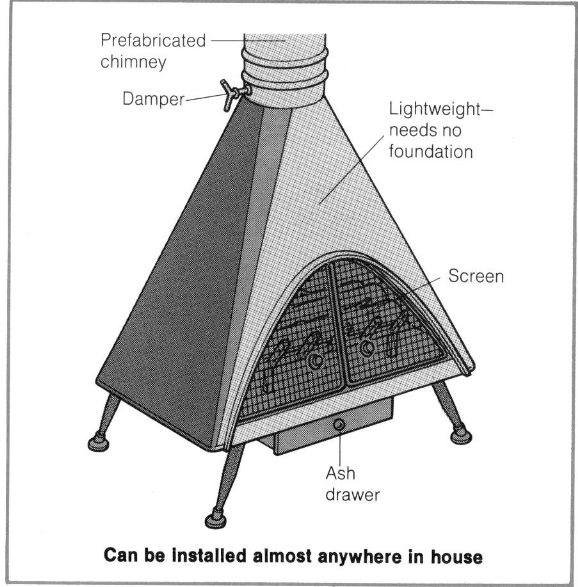

Can be installed almost anywhere in house

Electric heat systems

Types of installations

Any electrical conductor with resistance to electricity will get hot when current passes through it. This is the basis of all electric-resistance heating systems. Operating on this simple principle, most electric heating systems have no moving parts to wear out or cause service problems. Maintenance is unusually low and fuel supply constant. There is no fuel combustion, so there is no need for a chimney, which helps to make electric heat the least expensive type to install (not, however, to operate).

For successful electric-heat operation, the house must be properly insulated. Also, in certain regions, the high cost of electric power may make this type of heating too expensive to be practical.

Radiant ceilings: Electric radiant ceilings, which operate similarly to a radiant hot-water system, may involve either heating cables or panel units. The radiant cable installations utilize a woven grid of slim electric heating cables which may be embedded in the plaster or sandwiched between plasterboard layers. Radiant panels are nothing more than wallboard sections with heating elements that are built in at the factory. Both types of radiant ceilings can be painted as you would any ceiling to blend with the room's decor. Panel installations are usually the choice for remodeling work because they mount easily on existing ceilings. Heating cables are preferable for use in new construction.

Wall heater: These electric resistance units are generally used to supply supplementary heat to problem or special-function areas, such as baths, utility rooms, basements, and entries. They are actually small panel units and most are equipped with fans to circulate room air over the electric heating elements and into the room.

Baseboard heat: Perimeter baseboard heating is currently the most popular form of electric heating. Basically, the heating units need only be wired into the outer walls of your home. They consist of an electric heating element concealed in a slim metal casing which is mounted along the walls in place of the usual wooden baseboard. Each room or living area, as a rule, is separately wired to its own thermostat, enabling you to regulate the temperature of any room independently of other areas. Common quarters, such as kitchen and living room, can be kept at a moderate temperature, and family members can heat individual rooms as they prefer.

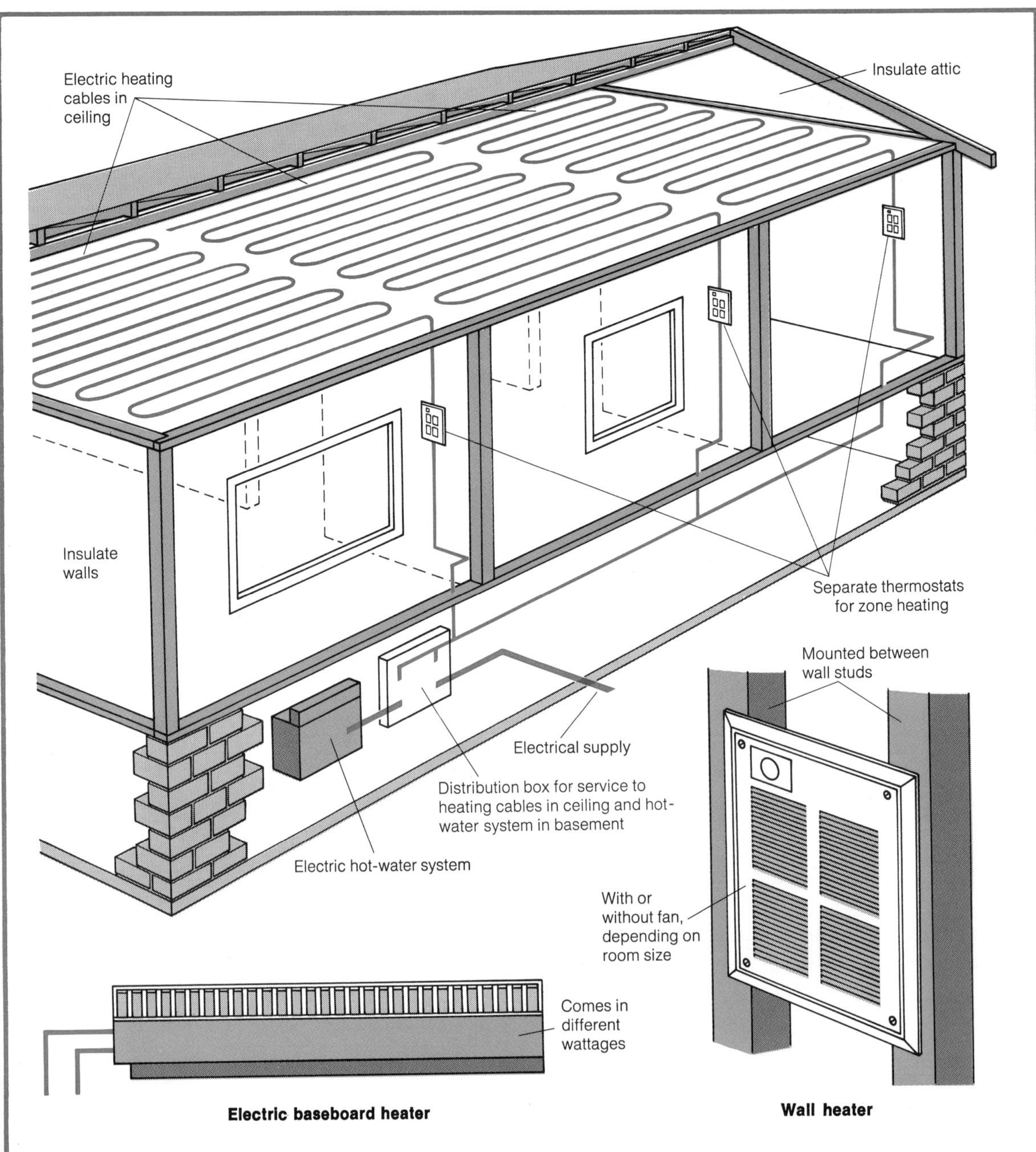

Electric baseboard heater

Wall heater

How hydronic heating systems work

A less common but equally effective type of electric baseboard heating is the hydronic system. Normally this means that a central electric boiler heats a liquid, usually water, which is then pumped throughout the home and circulated through the baseboard unit. In another type of electric-hydronic system, there are special immersion heaters in each baseboard unit. This type of hydronic heat requires no plumbing, only wiring similar to that of the resistance heat baseboard.

The central electric hot water boiler is very compact—the average home-size unit takes up only about 3 cubic feet of space—because the heating elements are immersed directly in the water that is being heated. All of the heat produced by the elements is transferred directly to the boiler water. The heated water is then piped directly to the room baseboard radiators or convectors.

The control system for an electric boiler is similar to that of any other furnace, its components being a room thermostat, relay, and circulator control. The boiler uses a fast-acting immersion-type high-limit control and a mechanical pressure-temperature relief valve to keep the unit from overheating or building up a head of steam. An adaptation of the electric boiler involves the connection of a large storage vessel which permits "off-peak" water heating, that is, heating and storage of water when the lower off-hour electrical rates apply. When the thermostat calls for heat, a pump circulates the heated water from this reservoir to the room units.

The central hydronic boiler is especially suited to converting a conventionally fueled boiler system in an older home to electric heat. No changes are required in the heat distribution apparatus—the circulating pump, piping, and radiators. In other words, the old coal- or oil-fueled boiler is simply replaced with an electric boiler the size of a portable television set which is usually mounted on a wall, freeing valuable floor space. Such adaptability makes electric baseboard heat suitable for remodeling as well as for new construction. The units can be painted to blend into any decor, and they require little maintenance beyond an occasional dusting or vacuuming. However, you must keep in mind that the addition of central air conditioning to your home would require ductwork. Incidentally, electric-hydronic installations are readily adaptable to zone control.

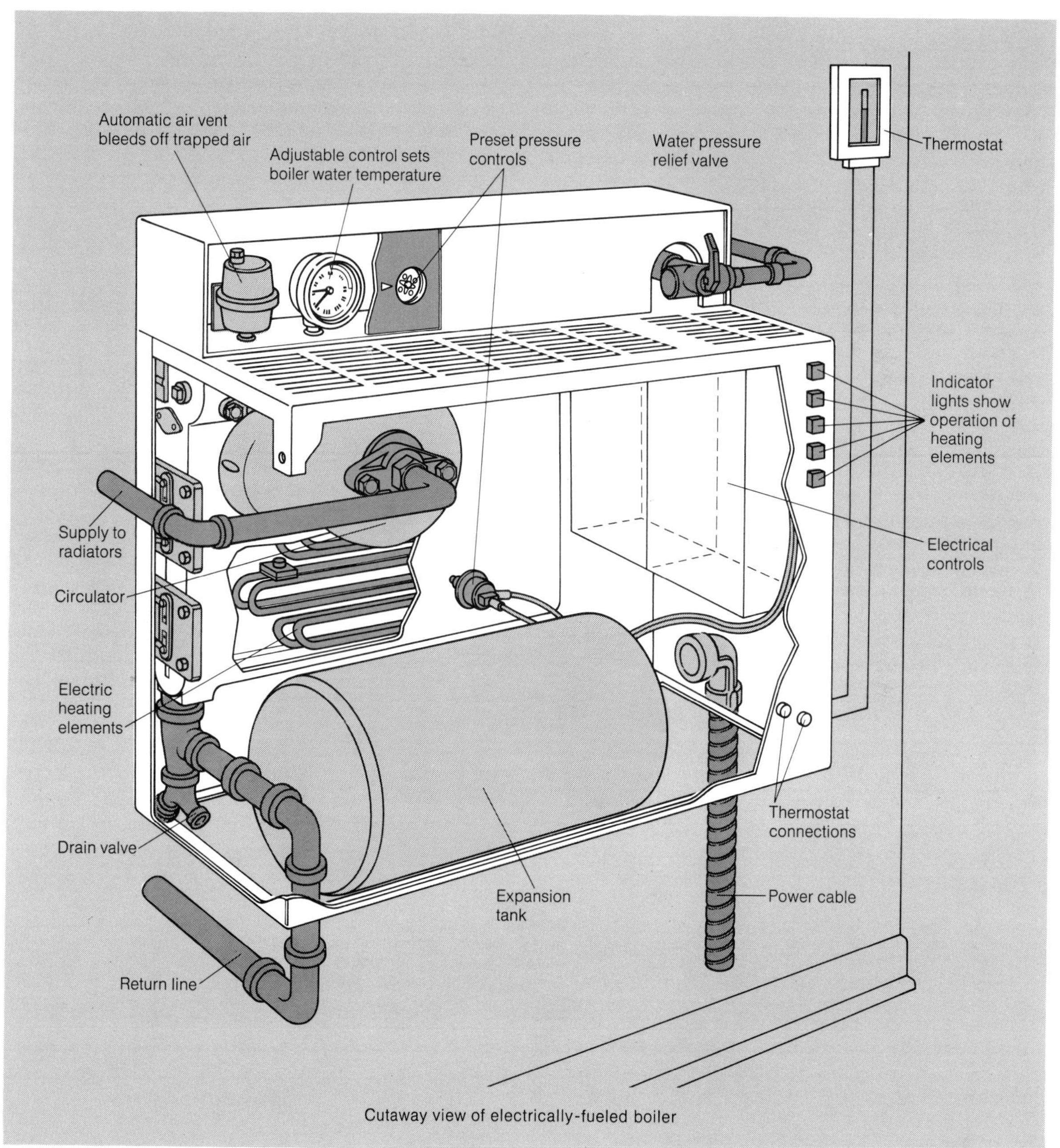

Cutaway view of electrically-fueled boiler

Electric furnaces

Installing and operating an electric system

Electric warm-air furnaces operate basically the same as conventionally fueled furnaces do, except that a series of two to five electric-resistance heating elements takes the place of the burner unit. The electric system works in a very simple way. When an electric current is fed into these heating elements, they give off a concentrated flow of heat in a manner similar to an electric iron. The heat is then circulated throughout the entire home with the aid of a blower fan located in the furnace housing. This fan is actually the only moving part in the whole unit. The heating elements themselves operate in sequence, the steps depending upon the temperature increase that is desired. Temperature-limit control of the overall system is provided by a low-voltage thermostat, relay, and fan control.

Unlike other forced-air systems, the electric furnace needs no chimney since there are no combustible fuels and thus no gases to be vented. This means that you can install an electric furnace almost anywhere inside a house. Most units are small enough that they can be tucked into space as limited as a main floor closet. They can also be suspended from overhead joists in basements, or mounted on basement floors without greatly affecting the floor plan.

The duct system of an electric furnace can be used to cool the house as well as heat it. A central air conditioning unit can easily be connected to the existing duct system when the electric furnace is installed, or later if you wish. It is advisable to include in the original furnace installation an electric air cleaner in the cold-air return ducts.

When you are planning the duct system for the electric furnace, it is recommended that you locate your heat-supply register on the outside walls of the home, preferably below window level. This insures that your home will be heated along the perimeter, where about 75 percent of heat loss occurs.

It is best to have your return-air registers located on an inside wall, up near the ceiling. This facilitates air circulation and promotes even temperature at all levels. This positioning is especially important if you plan to add central air conditioning at some later time. When return air registers are high up on the walls, the fresh, cooled air enters near the floor and quickly displaces the stale, warm air. Without the high return registers, a pocket of hot air would be trapped in the room.

Duct heaters: If individual room-temperature controls are desired with a warm-air system, electric duct heaters should be used. These are small resistance heaters that can easily be mounted anywhere in a forced-air duct system. There is no need to rebuild existing ductwork to accommodate these units. They can be used to heat an entire house or in conjunction with an electric furnace. In any case, each duct heater can be fitted with its own thermostat, so that temperatures can be individually adjusted.

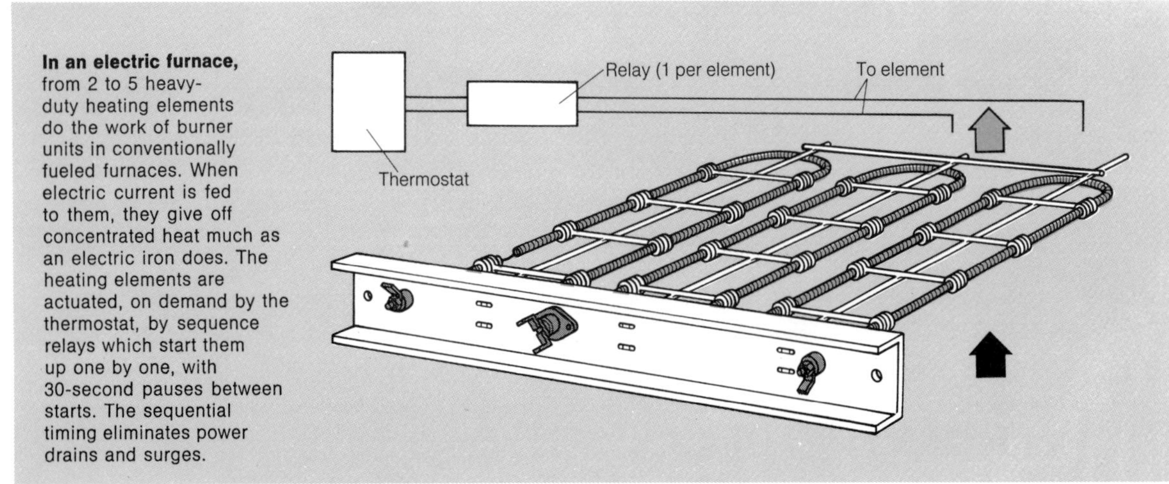

In an electric furnace, from 2 to 5 heavy-duty heating elements do the work of burner units in conventionally fueled furnaces. When electric current is fed to them, they give off concentrated heat much as an electric iron does. The heating elements are actuated, on demand by the thermostat, by sequence relays which start them up one by one, with 30-second pauses between starts. The sequential timing eliminates power drains and surges.

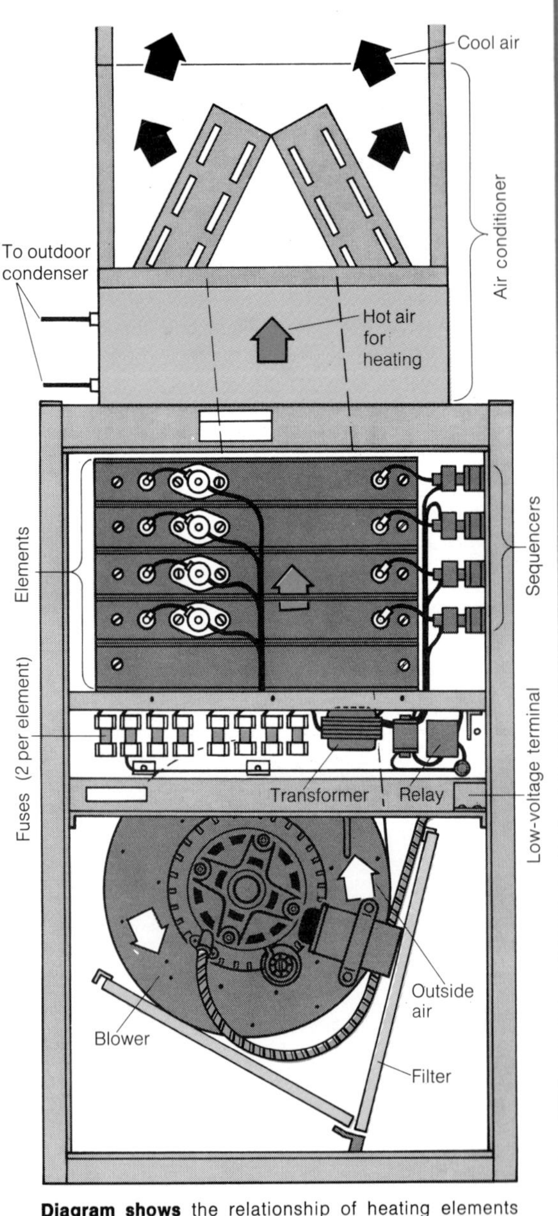

Diagram shows the relationship of heating elements to the relay system and to the blower.

Basic facts about heat-pump operation

The heat pump is a very special type of electric heating system. It extracts heat from outdoor air (or water) and transfers it indoors in winter; in summer it reverses the cycle, absorbing heat indoors and disposing of it to the outdoor air (or to water). In other words, the same unit heats a house in winter and cools it in summer. To make it work, you need only set the themostat for the desired temperature and it will be maintained the year round. The heat pump will automatically reverse itself to cool or heat, depending upon outside weather changes.

Basically, a heat pump consists of an outdoor coil, indoor coil, and compressor. In warm weather, the indoor coil picks up heat from the indoor air and transfers it by means of a circulating refrigerant to a compressor from which it is dispersed outdoors. In cold weather, the opposite takes place. A reversing valve automatically changes the direction of refrigerant flow, and heat from the outside air is transferred indoors. Indoor air is circulated throughout the house by means of a blower and a duct system, similar to the way circulation is accomplished in a standard forced-air heating system.

In exceptionally cold climates, where below-zero winter readings are not uncommon, it is necessary to have supplemental resistance-heating coils installed. The heat pump is fully capable of providing adequate heat approximately 85 percent of the time during the heating season. When the outside temperature drops to near zero and below, however, the supplementary coils automatically add enough heat to keep the home warm. Though supplemental heat may be required on these few extra-cold days, the system makes up for this cost with savings in late fall and early spring. On days when most homeowners will have to change their thermostat settings several times, a heat pump owner will be able to keep his home comfortable without any special adjustments. If the morning temperature is 40 degrees, he will have heat; if the temperature rises into the high 70s by mid-afternoon, his home will be cooled—all without his realizing that the outside temperature has fluctuated greatly.

The addition of a power humidifier to compensate for winter dryness and an electronic air cleaner to keep indoor air consistently clean will make the heat-pump system one of the most effective of all available interior climate controls.

As in all electric-powered heating systems, insulation is very important to satisfactory heat-pump operation. At least 6 inches of insulation should be installed (or enough added to make a total of 6 inches) over the ceiling under the attic. Exterior walls should contain 4 inches of insulating material and all floors at least 2 inches. Storm windows and doors are necessities. Double insulating glass—the Thermopane type—should be specified in new installations, as should vapor barrier linings in all sidings.

Independent unit for heating and cooling

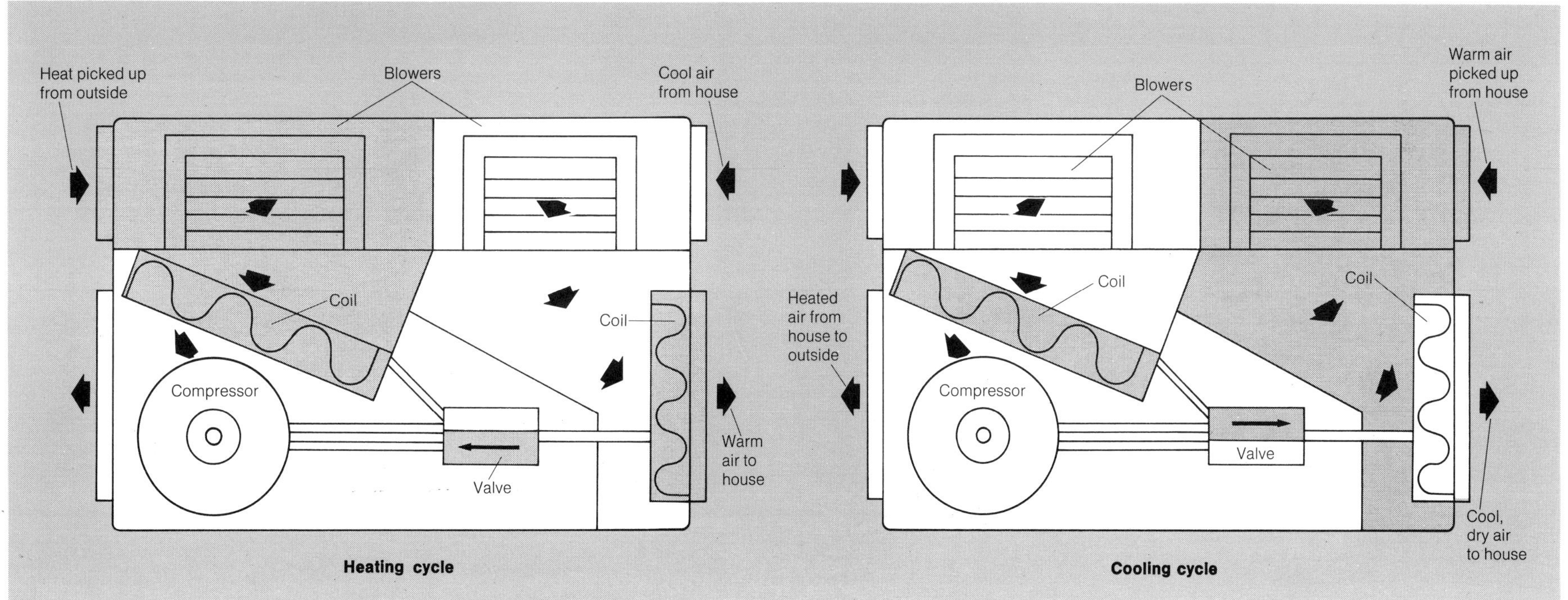

Insulation

Purpose and methods

Total insulation can cut down as much as 75 percent on a home's heat loss. If the house is already built, total insulation is not always possible or practical, but even partial insulation can effect a saving of up to 30 percent. Thus in a very short time insulation pays for itself in reduced fuel bills.

If a home is air conditioned, full insulation will save on power—from electricity, oil, or gas—in summer, too. Adequate insulation alone can often make smaller-capacity air conditioning equipment, requiring less power, equal to the cooling job. And if the home does not have air conditioning, insulation still will shut out heat.

Types of insulation: Though there are several different varieties, most home insulating materials fall into one of four general categories: Rigid boards, flexible batts or blankets, loose fill, and reflective. All except the reflective type work on the same basic principle: They trap air in thousands of tiny pockets within the material, preventing heat passage in either direction. The reflective types have foil surfaces that reflect heat. Some insulating materials combine both the reflective and entrapment principles; for example, foil-covered batts.

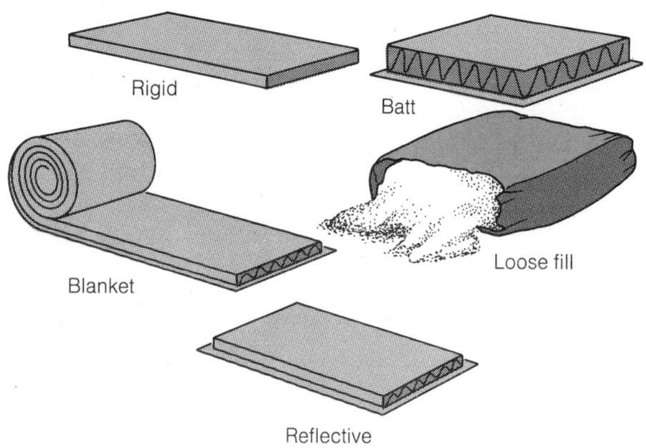

The type of insulation used in new construction is a matter of preference. If a house is old or is improperly insulated, the fill type is easiest to install. It is blown in by machine by workmen especially trained for such jobs. This can be done without any outward signs of disturbance.

Using blankets or batts for walls and ceiling

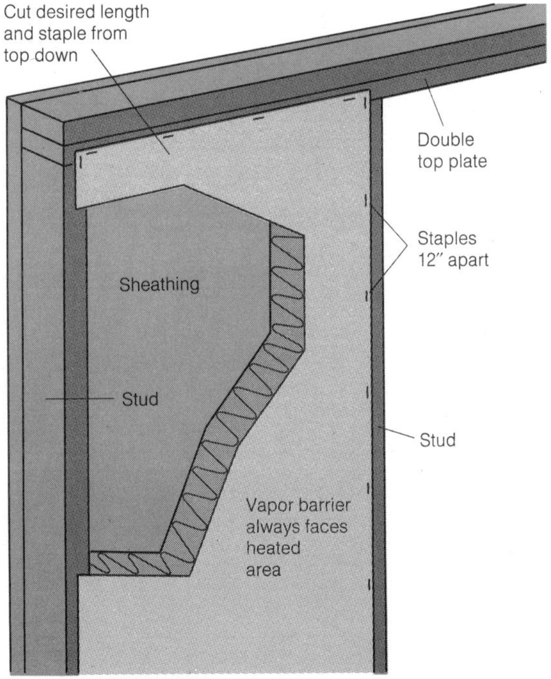

Cut desired length and staple from top down
Double top plate
Staples 12″ apart
Sheathing
Stud
Stud
Vapor barrier always faces heated area

Blanket wall insulation

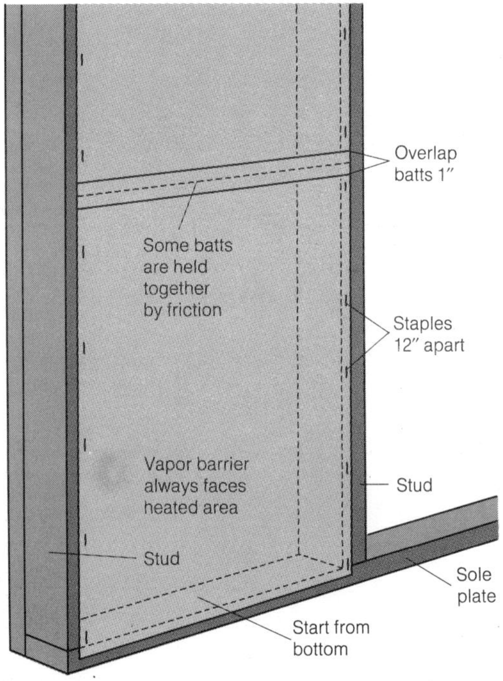

Overlap batts 1″
Some batts are held together by friction
Staples 12″ apart
Vapor barrier always faces heated area
Stud
Stud
Sole plate
Start from bottom

Batt wall insulation

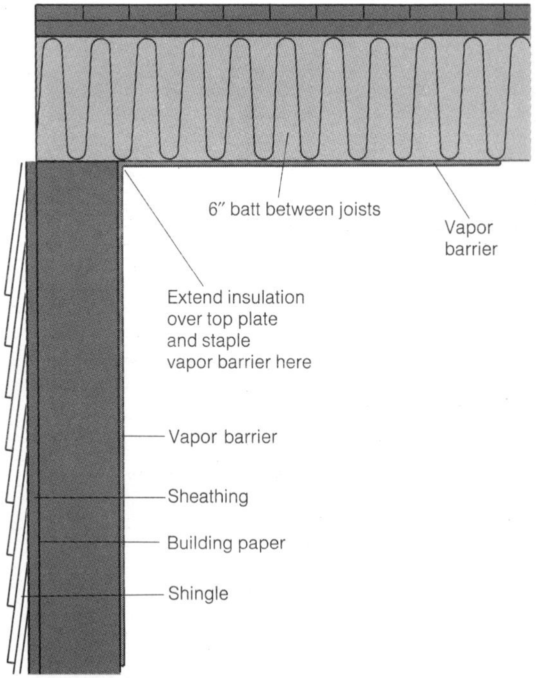

6″ batt between joists
Vapor barrier
Extend insulation over top plate and staple vapor barrier here
Vapor barrier
Sheathing
Building paper
Shingle

Batt ceiling installation (heated area)

Vapor barriers

Soon after insulation came into use as a means of reducing heat loss, it became obvious that without a vapor barrier, the insulation would get wet and lose much of its insulating value. A vapor barrier is a material that will not absorb moisture or let moisture pass through it. Commonly used materials are plastic film, metal foil, or asphalt between layers of brown paper. Though installed primarily to keep the insulation from getting wet, a vapor barrier is also a means of retaining room moisture.

The vapor barrier may completely enclose the insulation, as in so-called blanket insulation. It may be

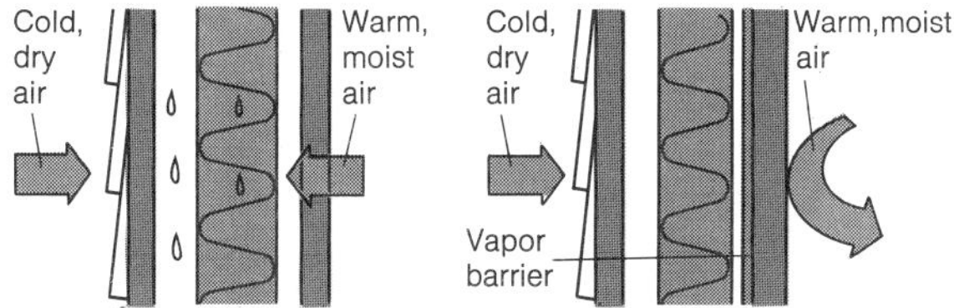

How a vapor barrier protects a wall from condensation

applied to only one side of the batts and installed with the vapor barrier on the indoor side even if air conditioning is planned. Another method is to install the insulation blanket or similar material between the framing members, then cover the inside surfaces with the vapor barrier before applying the wall finish. It is important that care be taken not to damage this moisture barrier during or after installation; if it should become torn or punctured, the openings should be effectively closed (patched).

Finished attic insulation: To insulate just the living space in an attic, staple insulation across collar beams, down rafters and knee-wall studs, and along ceiling joists to the wall plate. It is also good to insulate walls and undersides of stairways to unheated attics. Do not try to run a continuous blanket across collar beam and down rafters and knee wall—use separate sections to avoid buckling and gaps. Lap vapor barriers at junctures. In either case, ventilation above collar beams is necessary. Be sure, also, that there is space for ventilation between insulation and roof sheathing when attaching insulation to rafters, and that recessed lighting fixtures and exhaust fan motors protruding into the ceiling are not covered. Staple at 8-inch intervals. Check for gaps along the stapling flange.

Finished and unfinished attics

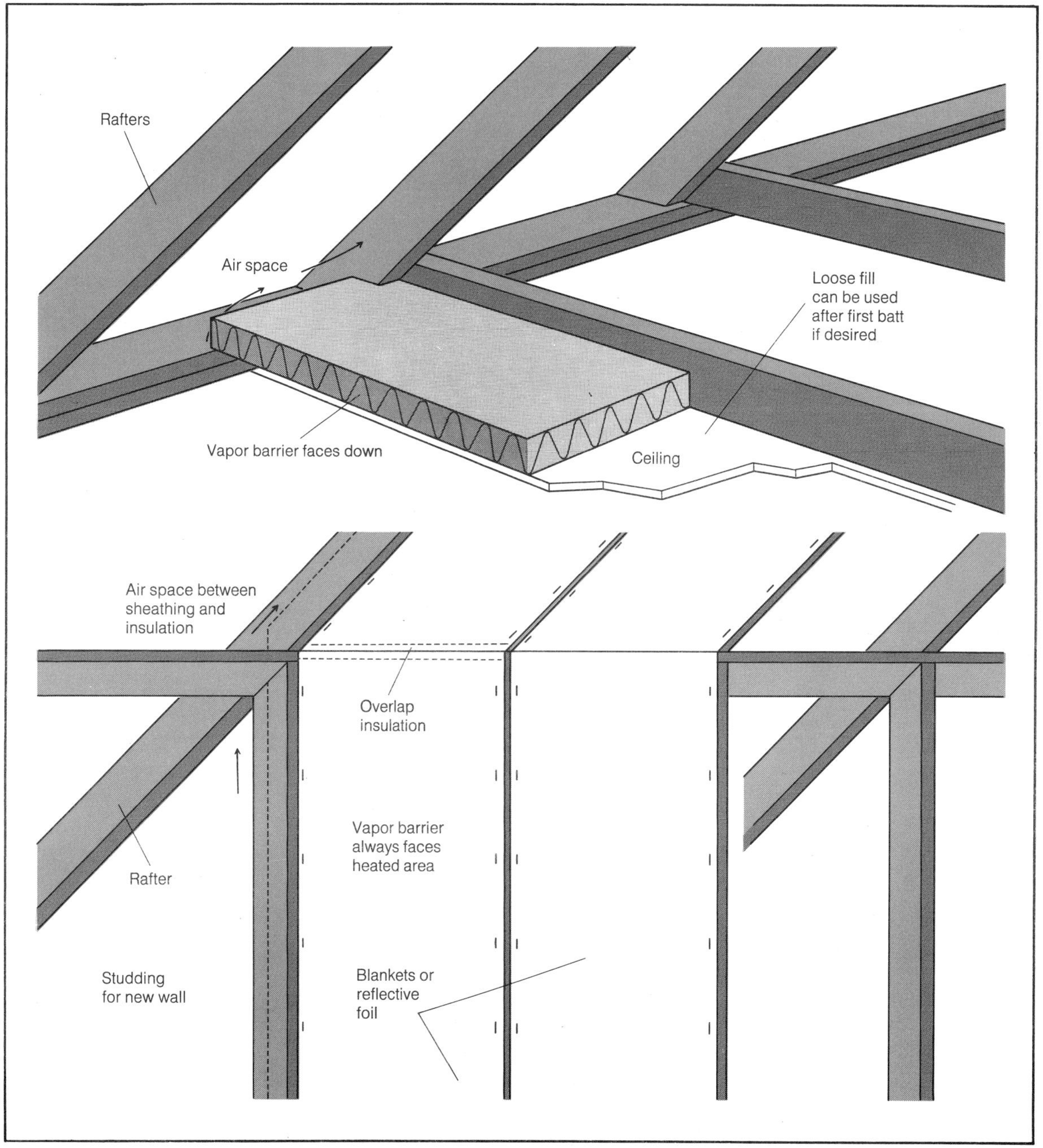

Rafters
Air space
Loose fill can be used after first batt if desired
Vapor barrier faces down
Ceiling
Air space between sheathing and insulation
Overlap insulation
Vapor barrier always faces heated area
Rafter
Studding for new wall
Blankets or reflective foil

Ceilings, walls, floors

Ceiling insulation: Starting at the outside wall plate, peel back an inch or two of the vapor barrier at the end of the insulation and, using this as a stapling flange, staple the vapor barrier to the plate. Be sure insulation lays firmly on top of plate to prevent infiltration of air. With the end of the insulation attached to the plate, staple the insulation inset along the sides of the joists. Reflective insulation must have at least a ¾-inch air space for full insulating value.

If the ceiling is in place, insulation may be laid in from above, vapor barrier side down. Lay insulation over outside plate, being sure not to block the eave vents.

If there is clearance, compress the insulation under the bridging. Or cut away the material, carry vapor barrier under bridging and staple it in place, then stuff the material in and around bridging. Or add a separate piece of vapor barrier under bridging, overlapping barriers of adjoining batts, then fill space in and around bridging with insulation.

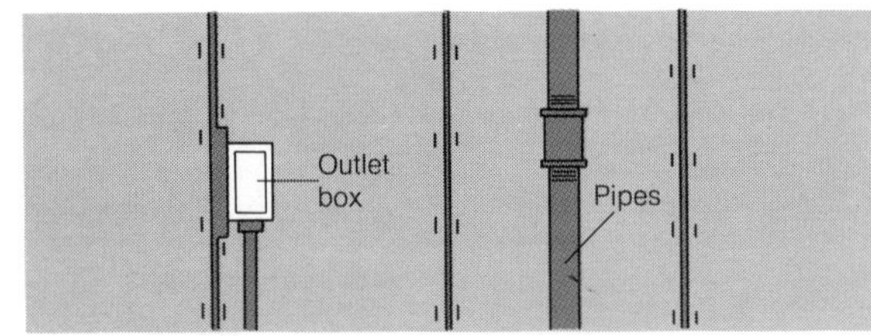

Fit insulation around outlet boxes and plumbing

Wall insulation: Staple the insulation from the top, installing it so it touches the exterior sheathing. Blanket ends should be snug against the top and bottom plates. When stapling to horizontal framing members, pull away the material to allow an extra inch of vapor barrier as a stapling flange.

Where it is possible, batts and blankets should be compressed and tucked behind piping and ducts. Where it is not, split the insulation (it is easy to do) and place as much as possible behind the obstruction. (Omit insulation in front, on the warm side.) Where you encounter outlet boxes, electrical receptacles, and wall projections, place the insulation behind the obstruction, carefully cutting and fitting the vapor barrier to insure full protection.

Where they are accessible, stuff the small spaces between rough framing and the heads, jambs, and sills of windows and doors with insulation. Cover these with a small, separate vapor barrier.

Floor insulation: Place the insulation with the vapor barrier up except where vapor-barrier paper is used in place of the building paper over the subfloor, in which case it may face down.

Floors over a crawl space should be protected with as much insulation as the walls, as well as a vapor barrier on top of the joists, between the joists and the subflooring. Put at least 2 inches of insulation around the walls of crawl spaces to help keep the cold air from seeping up through the floors and walls at points of contact.

Installing batts under bridging

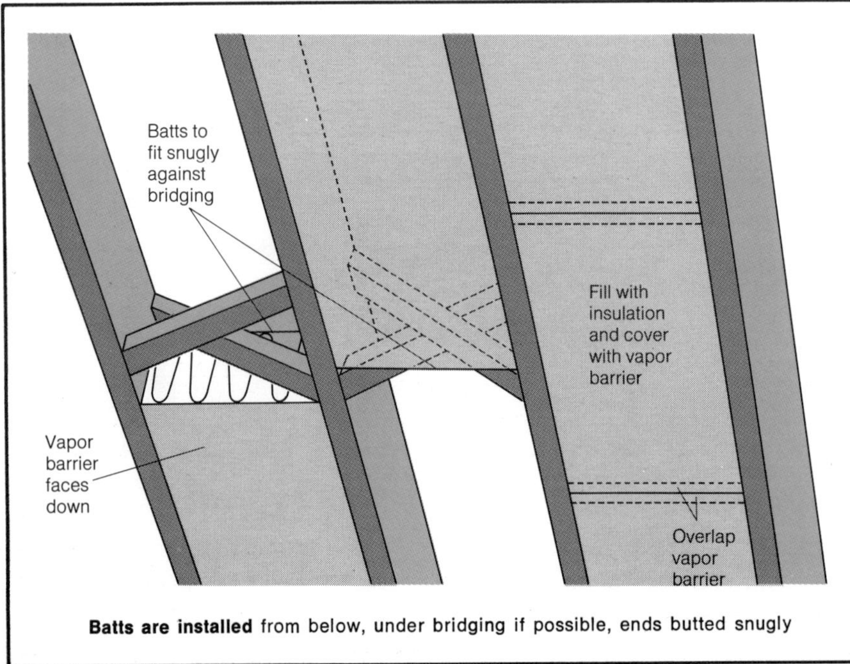

Batts are installed from below, under bridging if possible, ends butted snugly

Insulating windows and doors

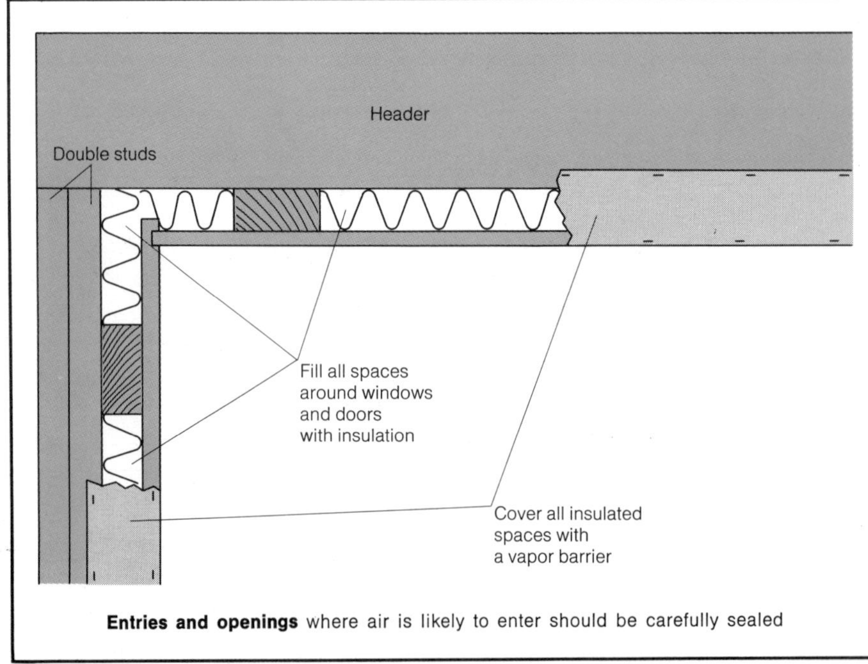

Entries and openings where air is likely to enter should be carefully sealed

Condensation

Condensation, as the word is used here, means the change of water from a vapor to a liquid or solid state. This familiar phenomenon can be a problem to the owner of even a well-insulated home, especially in attic and basement crawl spaces.

Attic condensation: Most homes with unused attics have a layer of insulation spread over or beneath the attic floor. This keeps heat in the rooms below, but it also lowers the temperature of the attic. Adding to the chill are roof boards, usually much colder in winter than at any other time. When warm, humid air from the house rises and enters the attic through cracks or other apertures or up stairways, it contacts the cold roof boards and loses its moisture, which condenses into water. This condensed water works its way down through the ceiling or walls, staining them and, if the condition is allowed to continue, causing rot in other parts of the home.

The cure for this is louvers. Louvers placed at gable ends or under the eaves in a ratio equal to 1/300 of the attic floor area will suffice to ventilate the attic, letting humid air escape with its moisture, yet without undue loss of heat. In an attic 20 by 30 feet, or 600 square feet, for example, the total louver area should be at least 2 square feet. Where louvers are protected by screens, the area should be increased at least 1½ times.

If the attic is used, insulation with a vapor barrier should be inserted between all rafters, with air space allowed between the vapor barrier and roof boards and vented to the ridge or eaves.

Crawl space condensation: The ventilation ratios for crawl spaces are: 1) With moisture seal, 1 square foot of vent area for each 1500 square feet; 2) with no moisture seal, 1 square foot of vent area for each 150 square feet. The addition of a ground moisture seal over the bare earth will help to keep crawl space humidity at a safe level. Roll roofing (55-lb.) or polyethylene sheeting (4-mil or thicker), lapped at least 3 inches, will make a satisfactory seal.

Attic and crawl space ventilation are both just as necessary in winter as in summer. Leave the louvers open in winter. Always provide at least two vent openings as well. If possible, place them so that air can flow in through one, over the insulated area or ground surface, and out the other. In areas that are difficult to ventilate naturally, an exhaust fan should be installed.

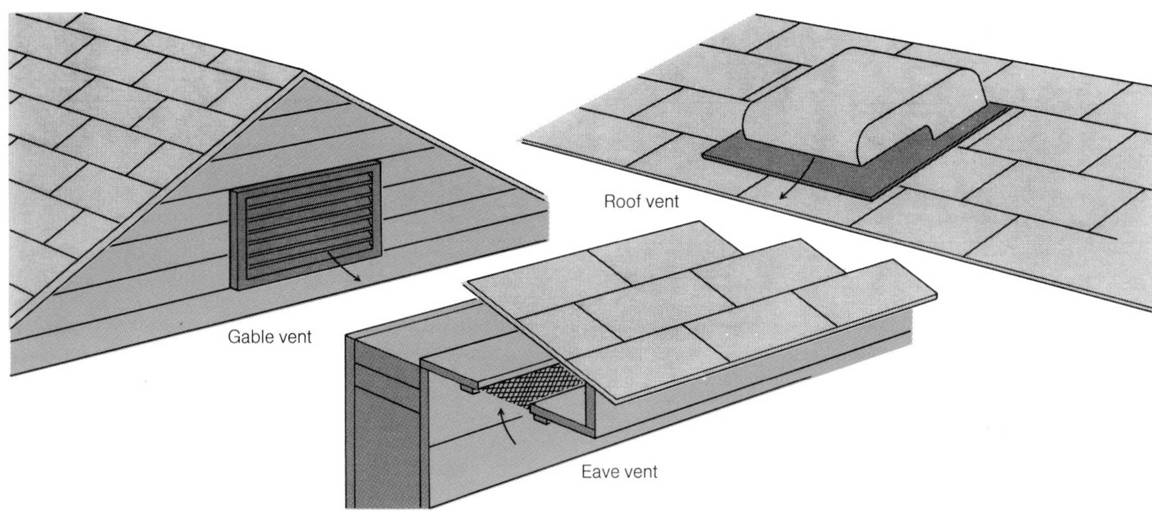

Insulating and venting crawl spaces

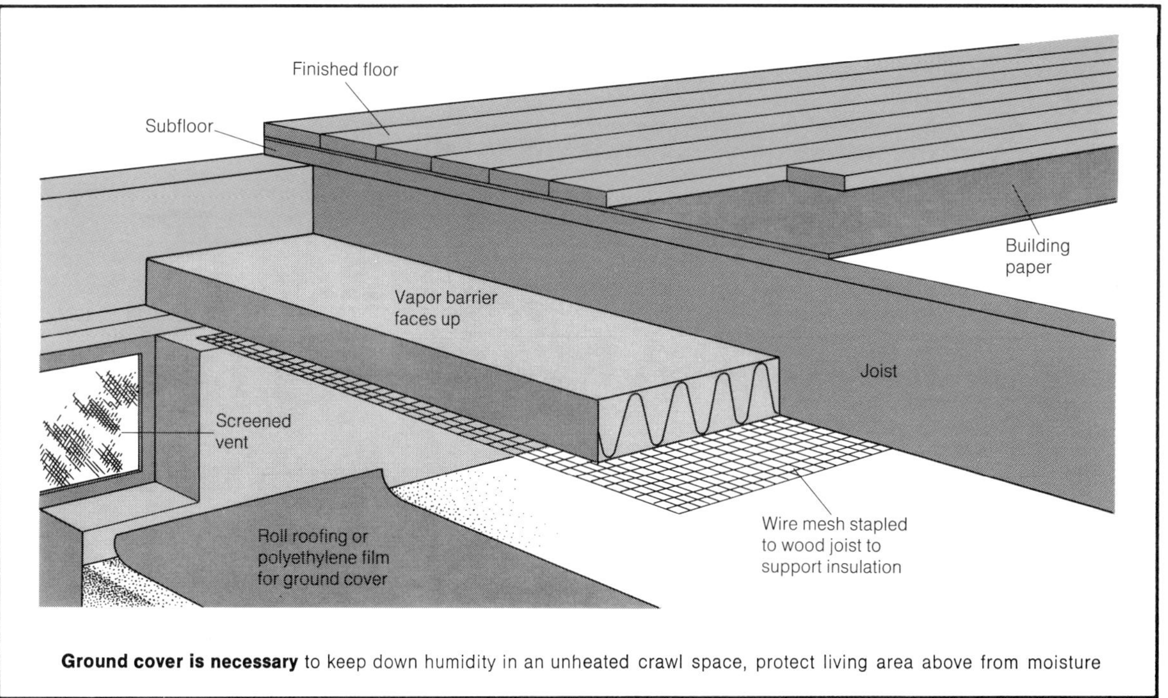

Ground cover is necessary to keep down humidity in an unheated crawl space, protect living area above from moisture

Determining unit size

Air conditioning systems are of two general types: **Central** conditioning, which cools an entire house; and individual **room** units, which cool only the room in which they are placed. The two systems have different attributes and limitations, so the choice you make depends on your needs.

Air conditioning terms: Three terms are basic to making a selection: (1) **BTU,** or British Thermal Unit; (2) **tonnage;** and (3) **horsepower.**

One BTU is the amount of heat required to raise the temperature of 1 pound of water 1 degree F. An air conditioner's BTU measurement indicates the amount of heat it will remove.

Tonnage is another means of rating performance, used especially in connection with room units. It relates to a conditioner's cooling capacity, 1 ton of cooling being comparable to the cooling effect achieved by melting a ton of ice in an hour. A useful rule of thumb in relating BTUs and tonnage: An air conditioner will provide 12,000 BTUs of cooling in an hour for every ton at which it is rated.

Though horsepower ratings are still applied to a few models, it is not considered an accurate method, and it is best to avoid units that are rated this way. The horsepower referred to is that of the compressor motor. Many other components, however, have a bearing on the cooling effect of a unit. A 1 HP air conditioner, for example, may vary from fewer than 8000 BTUs to well over 10,000.

Determining cooling capacity: Before you consider installing any air conditioning system or model, you must determine the cooling capacity required by the area that is to be cooled.

One way is to have a competent and reputable dealer come to your home and estimate its needs. He can then compute the size and type of unit he believes is necessary to do the job properly.

If you are considering a central system, get bids from several air conditioning contractors. Be sure each bidder stipulates the number of BTUs he recommends, then compare all bids and BTU requirements carefully. Be wary of a bidder whose cost and BTU estimates are too high or too low—reliable bids won't differ greatly from one another.

You can make a fairly accurate estimate yourself, using the guide given here. But be sure you understand the variables—there are pitfalls for the untrained estimator. Use your estimate only as a guide.

FLOOR AREA IN SQUARE FEET

Width \ Length	10	12	14	16	18	20	22	24	26	28	30	32	34	36	38	40	42	44	46	48	50
10	100	120	140	160	180	200	220	240	260	280	300	320	340	360	380	400	420	440	460	480	500
14	140	168	196	224	252	**280**	308	336	364	392	420	448	476	504	532	560	588	616	644	672	700
18	180	216	252	288	324	360	396	432	468	504	540	576	612	648	684	720	756	792	828	864	900
22	220	264	308	352	396	440	484	528	572	616	660	704	748	792	836	880	924	968	1012	1056	1100
26	260	312	364	416	468	520	572	624	676	728	780	832	884	936	988	1040	1092	1144	1196	1248	1300
30	300	360	420	480	540	600	660	720	780	840	900	960	1020	1080	1140	1200	1260	1320	1380	1440	1500
34	340	408	476	544	612	680	748	816	884	952	1020	1088	1156	1224	1292	1360	1428	1496	1564	1632	1700
38	380	456	532	608	684	760	836	912	988	1064	1140	1216	1292	1368	1444	1520	1596	1672	1748	1824	1900

In estimating the BTUs required to cool a particular space, you must bear several things in mind. (Including the fact that your estimate is only that—a rough and very broad guide.) As a rule of thumb, figure 1 ton of cooling capacity (12,000 BTUs) for every 500 square feet. The example below shows how to determine the square feet in a given space; the chart above may make this unnecessary if your room is within its range. Find the room's length and width, then follow the horizontal and vertical columns to the point where they meet. The number there is the size in square feet. The table at the right relates BTU requirements to size in square feet. Note that up to about 400 square feet a small unit is usually sufficient; beyond that, you need a large one, requiring a 230/240-volt circuit—which may mean expensive rewiring, a possibility that points up the importance of buying no more capacity than you need. Factors other than floor area affect cooling needs—construction, insulation, outside wall expanse, windows, exposure, roof style, even the activity in a room. If your installation will be large and complex, it's wise to use the industry form that provides for all these elements and weighs their relative importance.

Example:

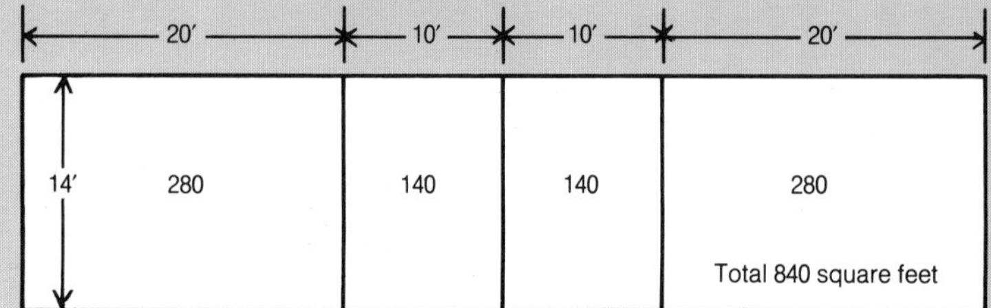

Unit approximately 20,000 BTUs

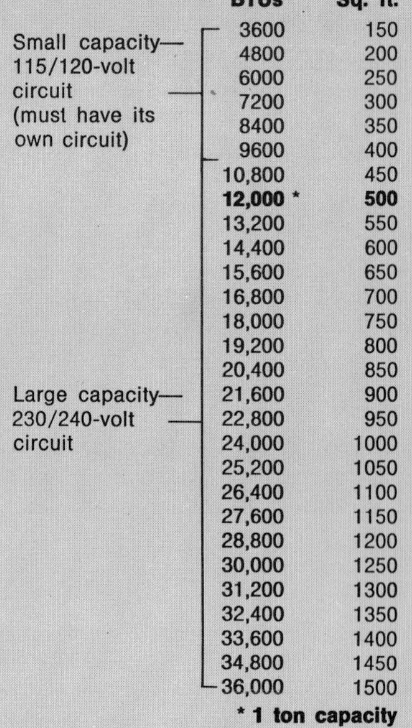

	BTUs	Sq. ft.
Small capacity—115/120-volt circuit (must have its own circuit)	3600	150
	4800	200
	6000	250
	7200	300
	8400	350
	9600	400
Large capacity—230/240-volt circuit	10,800	450
	12,000 *	**500**
	13,200	550
	14,400	600
	15,600	650
	16,800	700
	18,000	750
	19,200	800
	20,400	850
	21,600	900
	22,800	950
	24,000	1000
	25,200	1050
	26,400	1100
	27,600	1150
	28,800	1200
	30,000	1250
	31,200	1300
	32,400	1350
	33,600	1400
	34,800	1450
	36,000	1500

*** 1 ton capacity**

Function and features of individual units

A room air conditioner's basic function is to provide comfort by cooling, dehumidifying, filtering or cleaning, and circulating air. The units can be placed on a window sill or in a wall. The latter type fits into a built-in through-the-wall sleeve. Both vent heated air from the motor and condenser to the outside. Most models also draw outside air in through the coils (while filtering and cooling) to the room. Console-type units are also designed to provide heating, by reverse cycle operation (heat pump, p.299), steam or hot water coils, or electric-resistance elements.

In the operation of a typical room air conditioner, warm room air passes over the cooling coil, giving up its actual and latent heat. The conditioned air is then circulated by a fan or blower. The heat from the warm room air causes the cold (low-pressure) liquid refrigerant flowing through the evaporator to vaporize. The vaporized refrigerant then carries the heat to the compressor, which compresses the vapor and increases its temperature to a point higher than that of the outdoor air. In the condenser the hot (high-pressure) refrigerant vapor liquefies and gives up the heat from the room air to the outdoor air. The high-pressure liquid refrigerant then passes through a restrictor which reduces its pressure and temperature. The cold (low-pressure) liquid refrigerant then re-enters the evaporator, and the entire refrigeration cycle is repeated again.

Operation: Room air conditioners are simple to operate. Usually one control operates the unit while a second regulates temperature. Additional operating knobs or levers are provided for louvers, deflectors, ventilation, exhaust dampers, or other special features. These are usually on the front of the unit, or concealed behind an accessible panel; they may also, however, be on the top or sides.

Types of room air conditioners: One type is the integral chassis design, with the outer cabinet fastened permanently to the chassis, and provision made for servicing most components by partially dismantling the control area without displacing the unit. Another type is the slide-out chassis design, which permits the outer cabinet to remain in place while the chassis is removed for service.

Features to look for: A thermostat, which prevents wide temperature fluctuations. **Multiple fan speeds,** to blow the cool air into the room and to circulate it. Most air conditioners have two fan speeds. Economy models may have only one; deluxe models may have more than two. An **automatic control,** which regulates the fan speed to disperse the right amount of cool air to maintain a preset degree of comfort. **Condensation disposal,** which disposes of water removed from the air. **Air direction control,** which regulates the direction of the cool air. There are many versions of this. Most let you direct the air up, to the right and left, and straight ahead, or in combinations. Other air conditioners actually change the air direction automatically by means of moving louvers or an oscillating device in the unit. **Protection against overload,** a built-in device that shuts off the compressor to avoid overheating of the motor windings. **Dehumidification,** the removal of excess moisture from the room air. **Filters,** which remove airborne dust so clean air is supplied to the room. They may be metal mesh or plastic (which can be cleaned and reused), or glass fiber (which must be replaced from time to time). **Fresh air intake,** a feature that exhausts stale air, or brings in fresh air, or both. This feature makes your air conditioner valuable the year round. It is important to check exactly what type of ventilation any given model provides in terms of stale-air exhaust and fresh-air inlet.

There are other features to look for, such as the sound level of the unit, which is particularly important when an air conditioner is to be installed in a bedroom. A certain amount of sound is to be expected because of the movement of the air through the unit and the operation of the compressor. The sound level of well-designed room air conditioners, however, is relatively low and free from excessive vibration and noise.

Room air conditioners require a durable finish, especially on all parts exposed to the weather. Good design calls for baked finishes over rustproof or zinc-coated steels, and the use of such corrosion-resistant materials as plastic, aluminum, and stainless steel. Remember that quality sometimes costs a little more. A price cut can be a poor exchange for a reputable brand name and dealer.

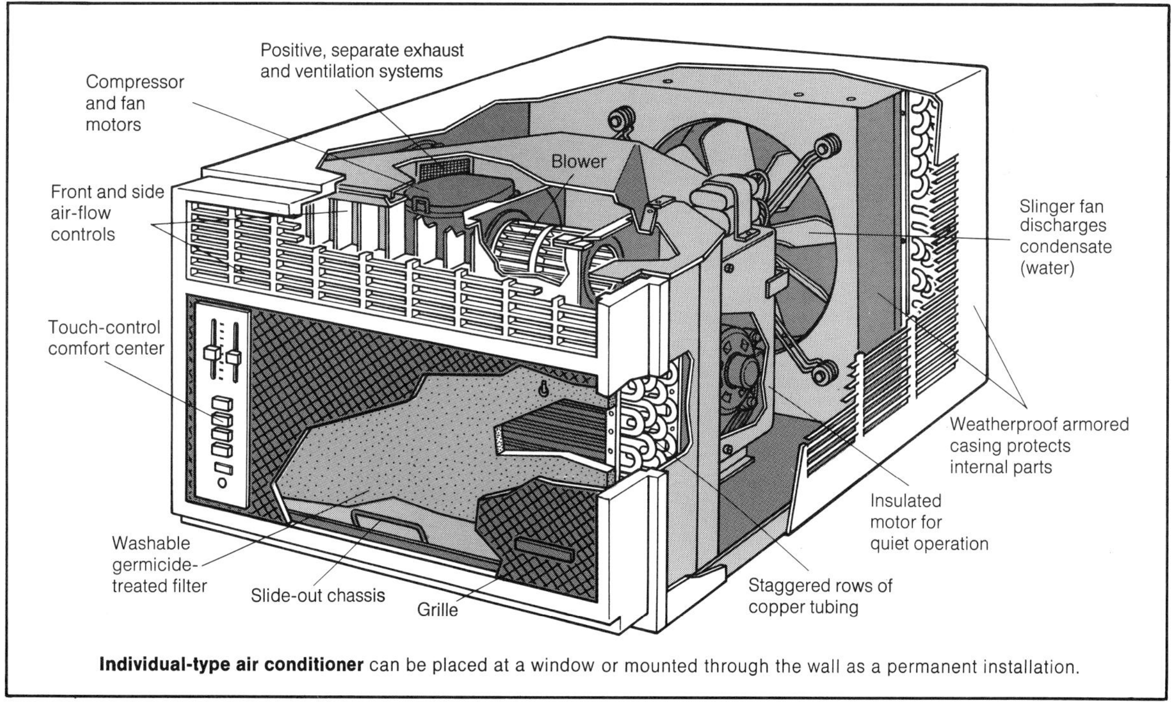

Individual-type air conditioner can be placed at a window or mounted through the wall as a permanent installation.

Mounting methods

Many lightweight, smaller-capacity, through-the-window air conditioners come with a do-it-yourself installation kit, which provides all the parts for proper mounting: Gaskets, panels, and weather-tight seals. Instructions and procedures make installation easy for you and a helper, but should be followed carefully to ensure satisfactory results.

Installation of larger-capacity models generally calls for an expert. Let your dealer handle the job to be sure it is done properly and the unit is working efficiently. Through-the-wall and some large window units have a permanent sleeve. Small air conditioners can be removed and stored over the winter.

Installation procedures differ considerably because room units can be mounted several ways. It is therefore important to consider what mounting is most suitable to existing conditions and local building codes. Common mounting methods are:

1. Outside flush mounting: Outer face of unit is flush or slightly beyond outside wall.

2. Inside flush mounting: Interior face of conditioner is approximately flush with inside wall.

3. Balance mounting: Unit is installed approximately half inside and half outside the window.

4. Interior mounting: Unit is completely inside the room, permitting the window to be closed.

5. Upper sash mounting: Unit is mounted in the top of the window.

6. Special mounting: Unit designed for casement windows and horizontal sliding windows.

Through-the-wall mounts, or sleeves, are used to install window-type chassis, complete units, or consoles in walls. Units with hot-water or steam coils are usually permanently wired with armored cable or conduit. Generally a plug-in wiring arrangement is provided to facilitate working on the cooling portion without disturbing the heating system.

Location of unit: Install a room conditioner as far as possible from exterior doors to prevent drafts and cross-ventilation from interfering with the cooled air. Make sure there are no obstructions in front of the unit, such as chairs or draperies. Direct the vents upward so you get cool air at the upper levels (it will drift naturally down to the floor).

Exterior doors and windows in the room should be completely weatherstripped. If too much outside air comes in through cracks, the unit will have to work harder to remove heat and humidity.

Typical double-hung window mounting

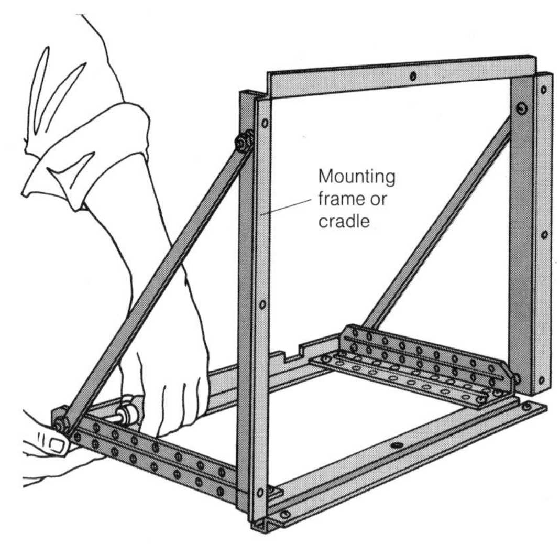

1. To install a room air conditioner, first assemble the mounting frame or cradle that comes with the unit. Frame is designed to bear the weight of the unit.

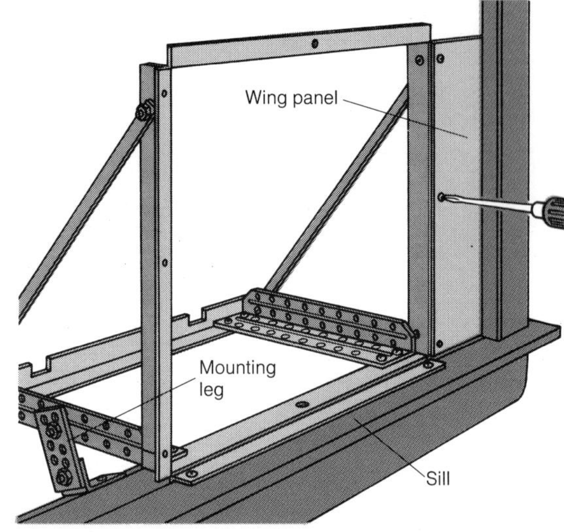

2. The mounting frame is centered in the window. Small mounting legs screw to sill near outer edge. A slight pitch to outdoors lets water drain outward.

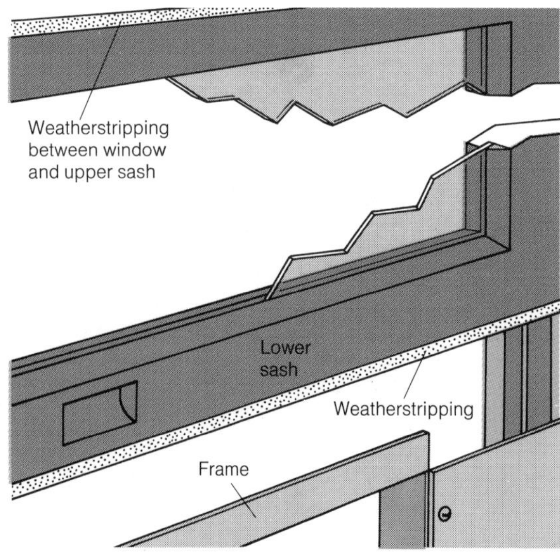

3. Sash is weatherstripped full width and lowered to top of frame. Additional weatherstripping is installed against upper sash of lower window to shut out all drafts.

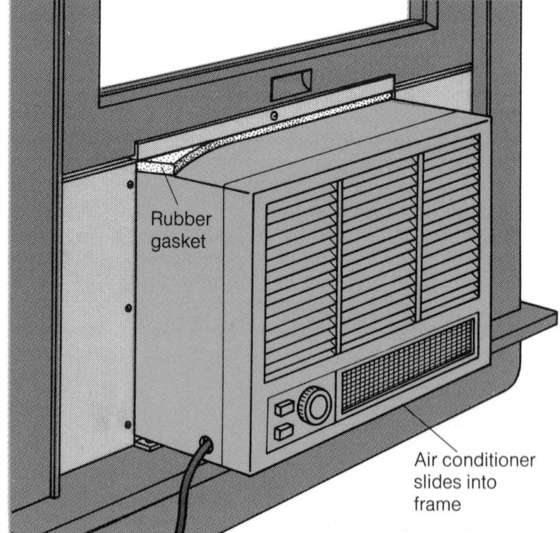

4. Air conditioner slides into frame until flush with window. A heavy rubber gasket tucks into place all around it, sealing the space between frame and unit.

Power supply

Voltage supply: When the unit is running, the voltage must always remain within plus or minus 10 percent of the rated voltage. Check when compressor is operating.

Grounding: All units come equipped with grounding-type plugs on the service cord. Receptacles used where units are installed should have the correct grounding contact to fit that plug.

Fuses: Use a special time-delay fuse in the circuit of the size recommended by the manufacturer. These fuses allow an overload during the starting period.

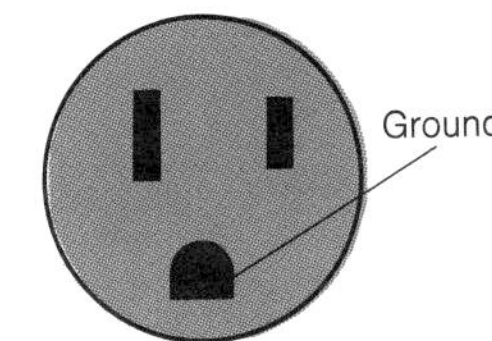

15-amp. 120-volt receptacle

Time-delay fuse

Service: Be sure the unit is plugged in and fuses are sound before contacting the dealer. Have the unit cleaned and checked once a year.

Care and maintenance

Grille: Clean with soft cloth, mild soap, and warm water—no waxes or cleaners. Keep insect sprays away; some contain solvents that may corrode the grille.

Filter: Clean often. Remove as service booklet directs. Vacuum and wash in warm water; shake off excess water; dry and replace filter and grille.

Condensation on grille: Moisture may collect on the grille when the unit is first turned on because of high humidity in the room. If doors and windows in the room are closed, the humidity will be lowered sufficiently to evaporate this moisture.

Typical through-the-wall mounting

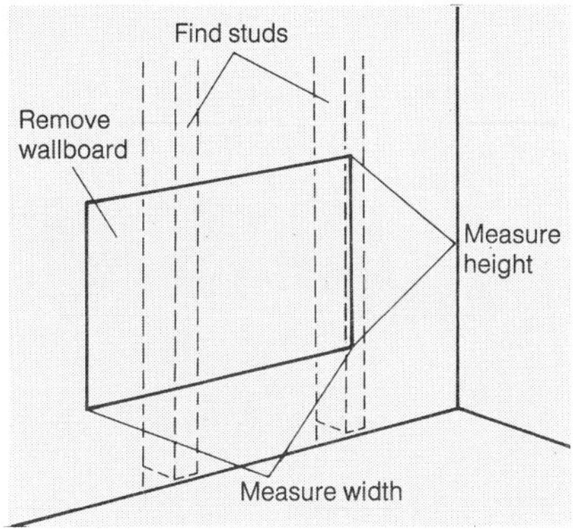

1. Cut out premarked area with keyhole saw

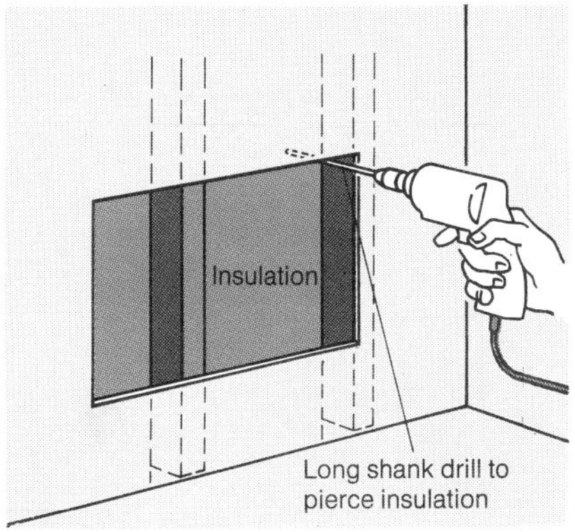

2. Mark outside from inside

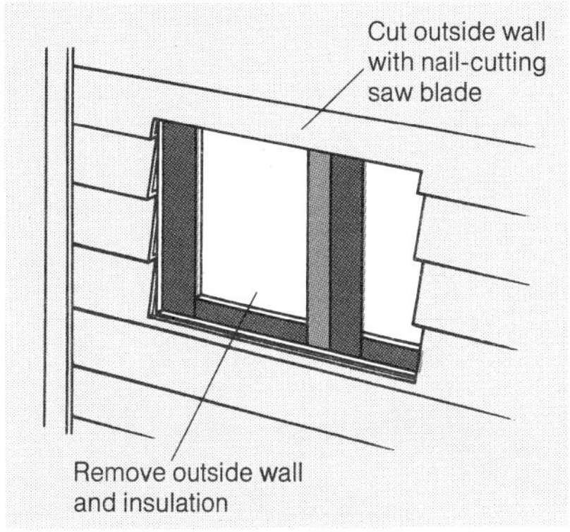

3. Cut through outside shingle and insulation

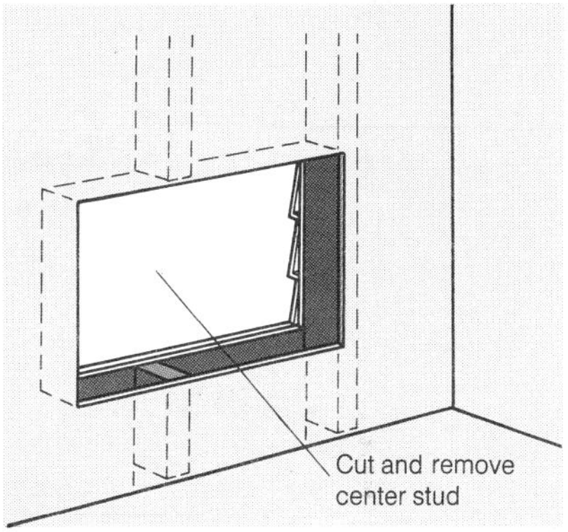

4. Saw off center stud and remove

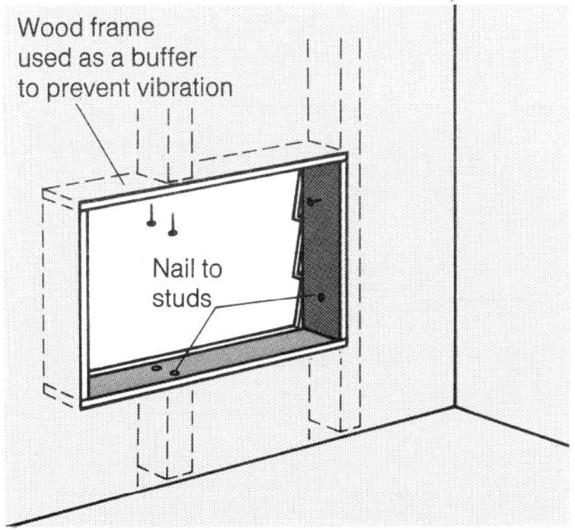

5. Insert preassembled frame

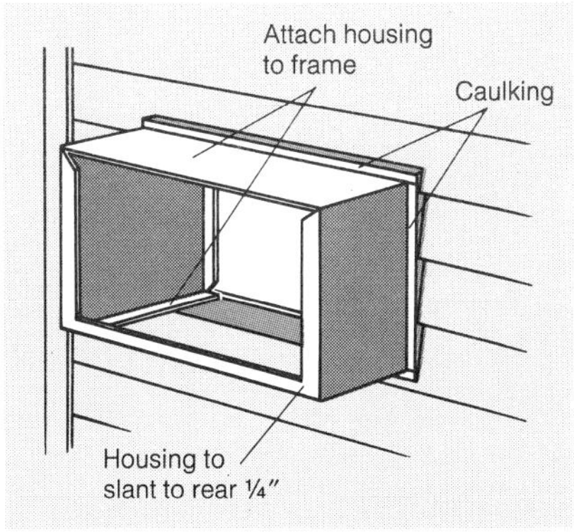

6. Insert metal sleeve

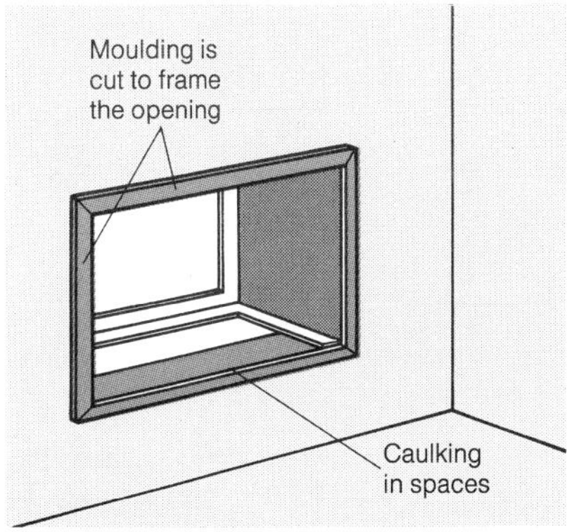

7. Finish inside assembly

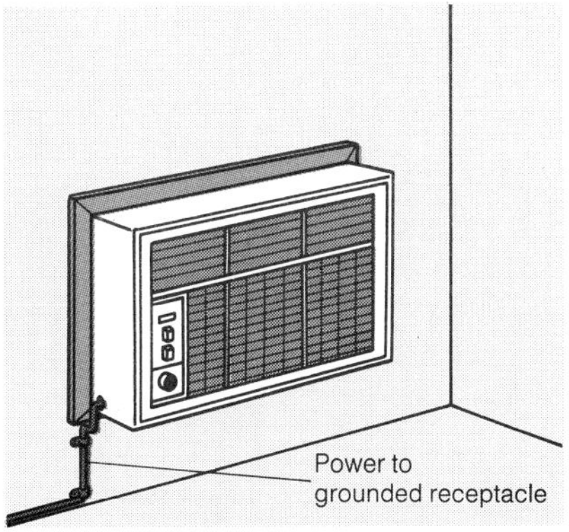

8. Insert unit in frame

Central air conditioning

Installation

Central air conditioning, as explained previously, means whole-house conditioning 24 hours a day the year round. It is designed to distribute conditioned air through a series of ducts already in existence or installed for the purpose.

Lower operating cost, better overall cooling efficiency, and quieter operation are the major advantages of central systems. In most installations, it is proportionately less expensive to centrally air condition an entire home than to get the same amount of cooling from individual units. Central systems can, however, be more expensive to purchase and install than room units if no usable ductwork is available. Ripping open walls and ceilings, when this is necessary, can be quite costly. On the other hand, in a one-story house with open attic or basement, ductwork can be easily and economically installed.

The heating for a year-round central comfort system that is to work in conjunction with an air conditioning system may be oil- or gas-fired, or all electric. Complete central units, which are quite small compared to earlier models, can be installed virtually anywhere in the home—in basement, crawl space, or attic, in a central hallway, closet, garage, etc.

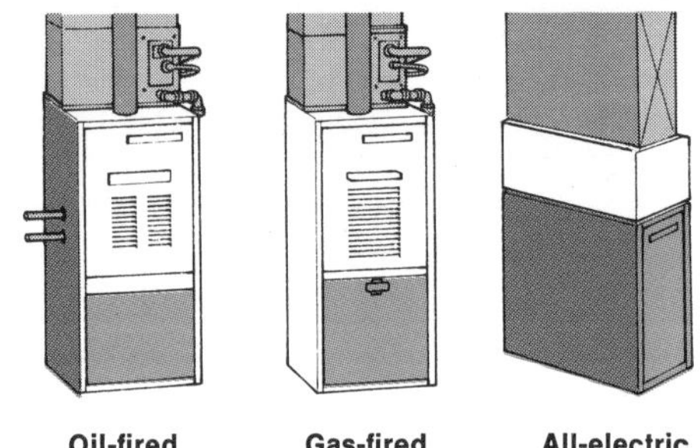

Single-package unit

There are two types of central air conditioning, the single-package unit and the split system. The single-package unit is self-contained; that is, all the necessary components are together in the package. This is the least expensive system, but the noise of the compressor makes an outside location preferable. In the split system, the components are separated—the cooling coil inside the house and the condenser and compressor outside—so that all the noise and vibration are kept out of the house.

When the single-package unit is used in conjunction with a heating system, it is coupled to the furnace and uses the furnace's ductwork; when it is used independently, as a cooling-only unit, arrangements must be made for a distribution system (ductwork and blower). For an outdoor installation of this type of unit, it is necessary to run a connecting duct from air conditioner to ductwork.

Independent unit for cooling only

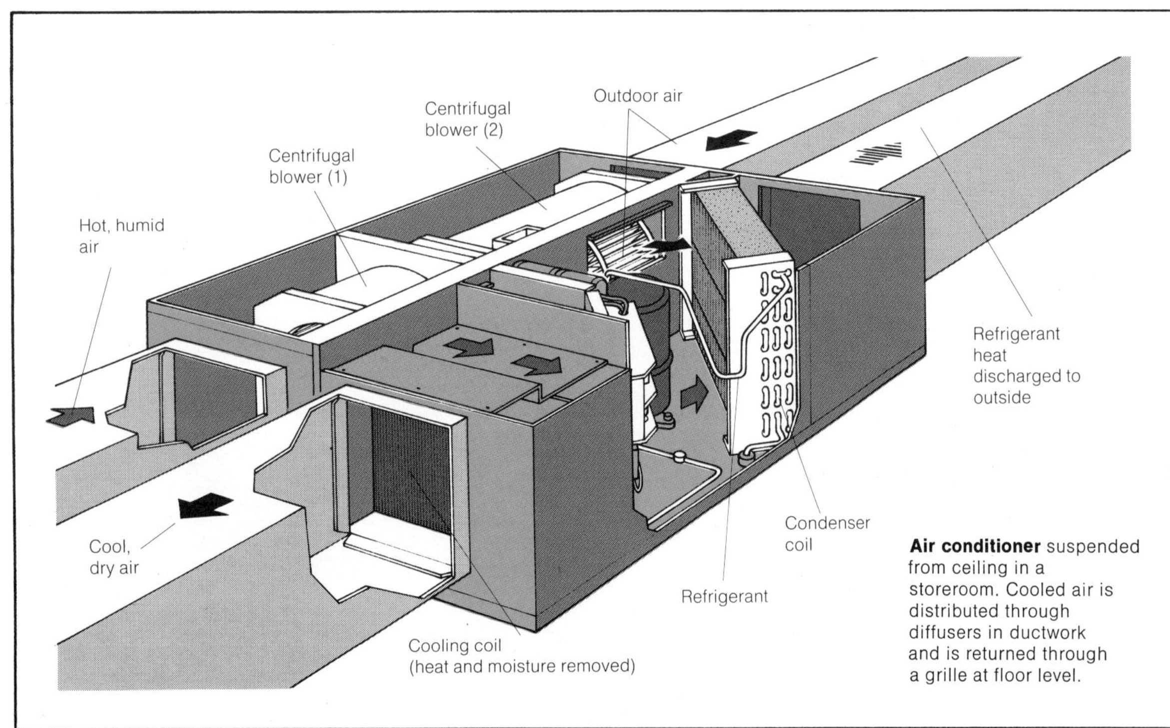

Air conditioner suspended from ceiling in a storeroom. Cooled air is distributed through diffusers in ductwork and is returned through a grille at floor level.

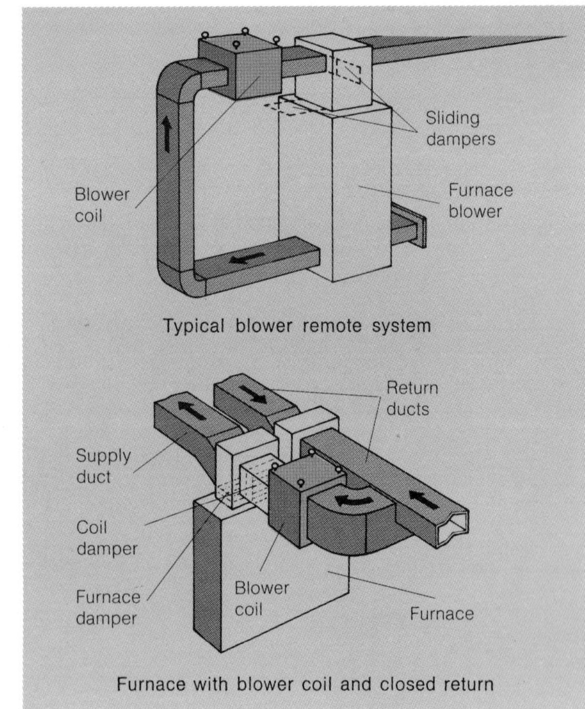

Split system

This second type of central unit is suitable for every kind of home and heating system. The condensing unit is located outdoors at the most convenient place and connected by small-diameter copper tubing to the evaporator cooling coil located at the furnace, using the furnace blower and ducts for summer cool-air distribution. The vertical air-flow evaporator, or cooling coil, is installed on top of the air discharge outlet of an upflow-type forced air furnace. The evaporator can be the horizontal type. A horizontal evaporator can also be installed at the air-discharge outlet of a horizontal furnace. This is ideal for attic or crawl space installation. The downflow evaporator is placed underneath a downflow furnace and is commonly used in slab construction and basementless houses or in houses which are built above a crawl space.

For homes with non-ducted heating systems, a special blower is used; it may have its own duct system or discharge cool air directly into the room through a directional air-flow grille. These independent units are ideal for installation in central hallways, attics, or closets. They often offer an optional electric-heat module for winter-summer operation.

Although slightly more expensive than a single-package unit, the split system's specifications automatically eliminate interior noise and the need for large holes through an exterior wall (necessary to accommodate the connecting duct in a single-package, outside installation). Split systems are the dominant choice for installation in new and existing homes.

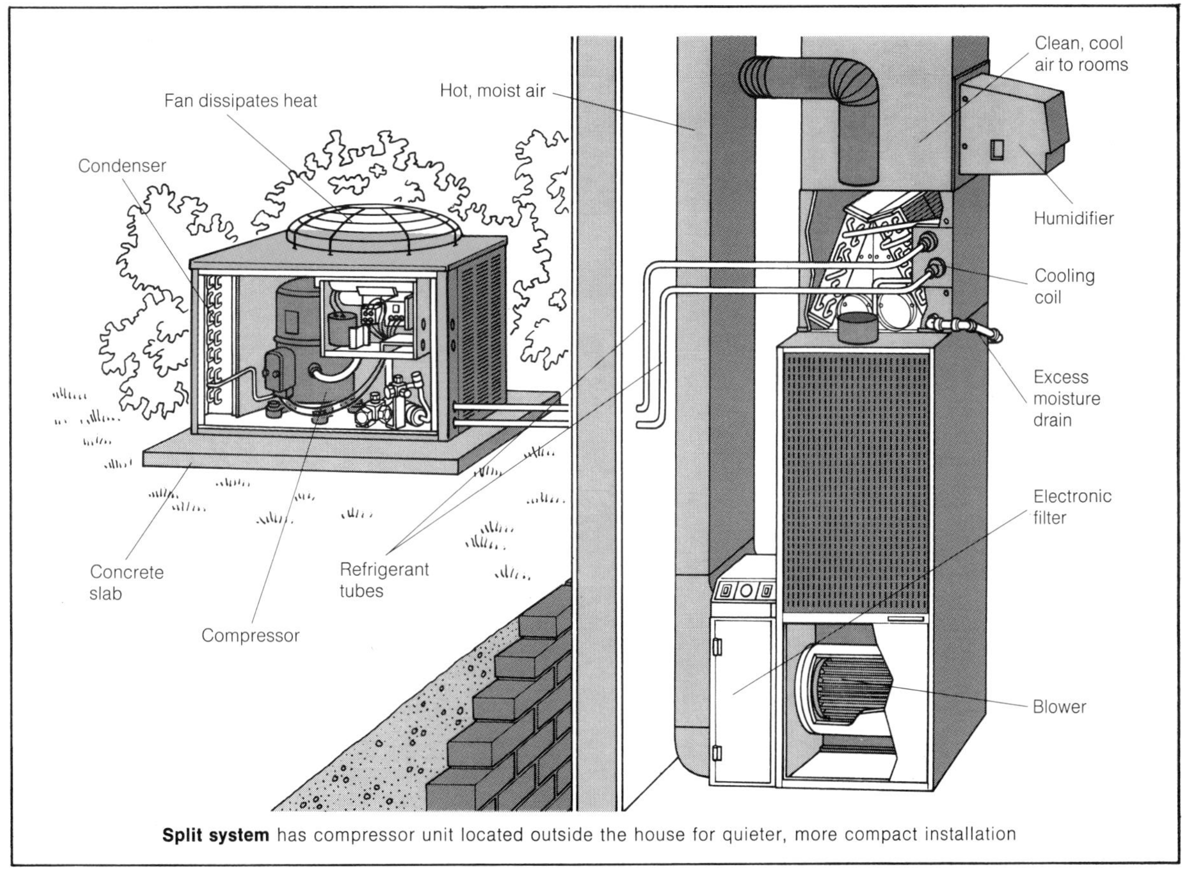

Split system has compressor unit located outside the house for quieter, more compact installation

INSTALLATION CHECKLIST

1. In most units, heat is dissipated from the condenser by a stream of air directed over the coils by a fan. Other models require special cold water connections and a drain or water evaporator "tower" outside. In these devices, cold water in a jacket around the coils removes heat created by compressed refrigerating gases. Check local ordinances. They may prohibit this arrangement because of the excessive water use and loss involved.

2. Ductwork passing through areas that are not air conditioned should be insulated to prevent condensate problems and heat gain. Also if furnace ductwork is to be used for cold air, check the size. Warm and hot air can travel in ducts smaller than those usually required for cold air. Ducts should be insulated.

3. Some air conditioners require 230 volts to operate the motor. This generally necessitates a special line to the fuse box. A separate line should always be run from the fuse box to the air conditioner regardless of the unit's voltage requirements. This prevents the overloading of other household circuits.

4. The condensing unit should be located, if possible, where it will receive a minimum of direct sunlight. There should be at least 10 feet between the condenser air discharge and any wall or obstruction which might return heated discharge air to the air intake. The air intake should be at least 12 inches from any obstruction.

5. Electrical wiring and refrigerant tubing should be installed so they are protected against being walked on or accidentally damaged in any way.

6. The blower coil can be used when it is not practical to use the furnace blower for air conditioning as well as heating. The blower coil is mounted in its own duct along with its own blower and connected to the main duct of the heating system. A damper (usually it will be a sliding type) shuts off the distribution system during the winter, when the heating system is in operation.

7. Be sure that your proposed installation satisfies local building codes and FHA requirements.

8. Check whether draining of evaporator condensate could present any problems.

9. Care should be taken in locating and mounting the condensing unit so that the operating vibrations (even though slight) are not exaggerated by the building construction or by the mounting mechanism.

10. If the unit is to be installed in the furnace, the cooling coil should be placed downstream. If it is placed otherwise, cold air will collide with warm air flowing into the furnace from the flue before the cold air reaches the ductwork. This collision will cause condensation to form inside the furnace, which can lead to rust and corrosion in the unit. When the flow of cold air is downstream, the cooling coil section is usually butted against the furnace's heat exchanger. With this arrangement, the cold air passes directly into the exchanger and ductwork, bypassing any warm air that is in the furnace.

Electronic air cleaners

Types, operation, maintenance

Electronic air cleaners electrically remove not only dust particles from the air but smoke and pollen as well. They are available in **self-contained** units for room use and in **central** systems which are attached to a warm-air heating plant. Since most air cleaners are guaranteed to remove up to 95 percent of the particulates in the air (the standard warm-air furnace filter is capable of removing only up to about 10 percent), they make house cleaning easier and less frequent, keep air more healthful to breathe, and give relief to sufferers from hay fever and other allergies.

How they work: "Electrostatic precipitation" is the scientific name for the process by which the air cleaner traps airborne particles. When these particles are carried into the cleaner unit, they pass through a powerful electrical field and receive an intense positive electrical charge. When they reach the collecting section, the particles enter a second electrical field set up between a series of metal plates or screens. In a way similar to a magnet's attraction of iron filings, the positively charged particles are hurled against the negative collecting plates, where they stay until they are washed off. The process is continuous. As the air is recirculated through living areas and back into the air cleaner, it is recleaned to remove new dirt particles that enter from outside or are stirred up indoors.

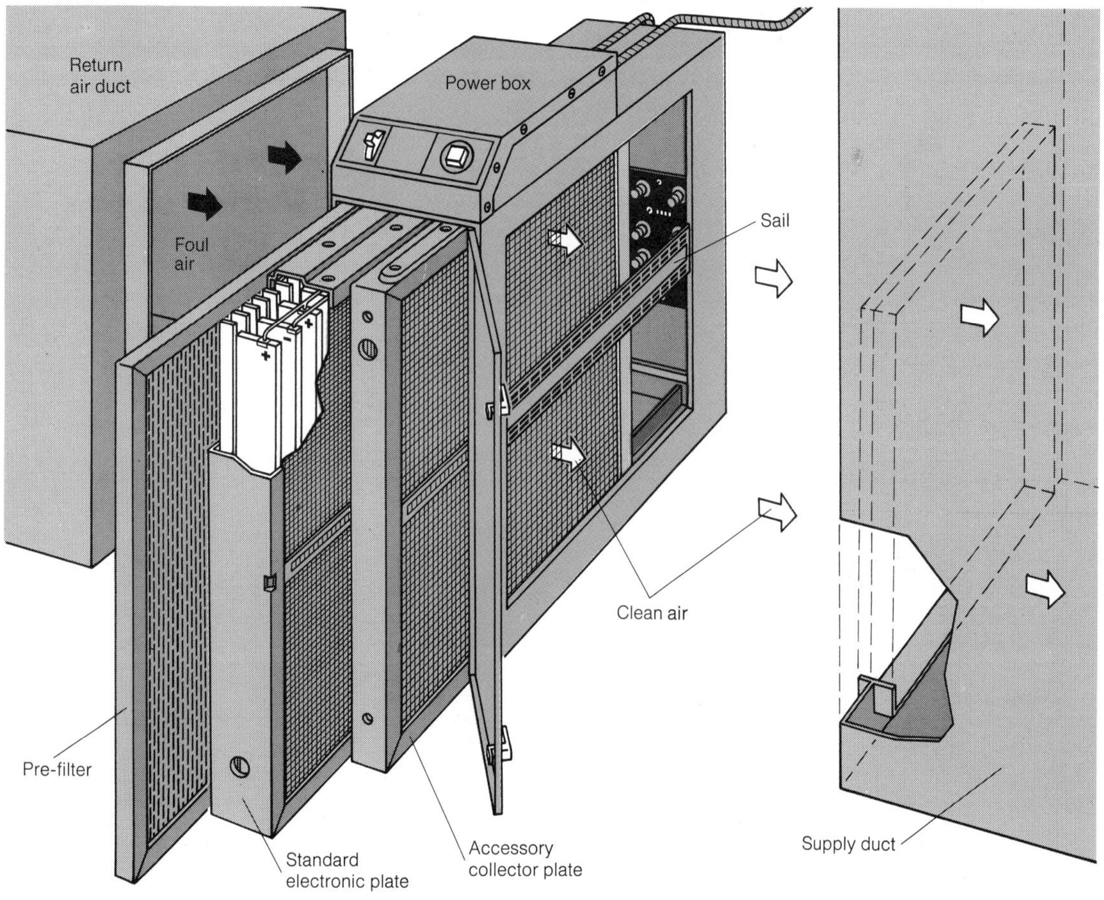

Self-contained models. These are easily movable, and are designed for use wherever you wish air to be cleaned. All of them employ a built-in motor-driven fan to circulate air through the unit. The self-contained types are ideally suited for selective air cleaning, or for applications where installation of a central system unit is impractical.

Electronic air cleaner can be mounted vertically or horizontally; cells reverse for right or left air flow

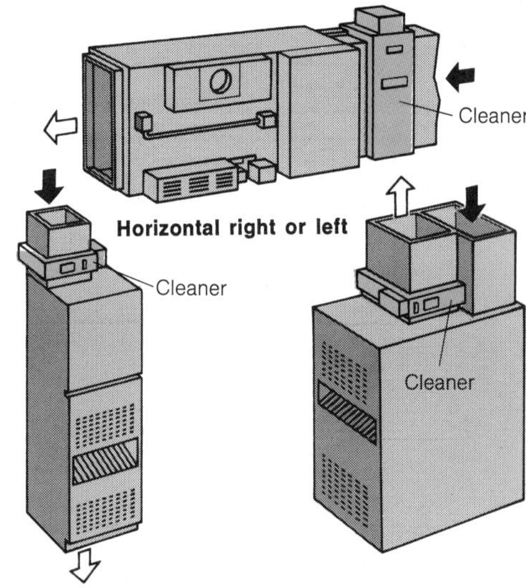

Central system models. These units are designed for permanent mounting in the ductwork of a central system—forced warm-air, air conditioning, or heat-pump. Air flow through the electronic cleaner is provided by the system's circulating fan.

Maintenance: About the only maintenance required is occasional cleaning of the collector plates. You simply remove the slide-out plates and wash them. Some models feature a wash-in-place unit which permits plates to be washed without removal. A few units even have a light bulb arrangement to indicate when plate cleaning is necessary.

Solving the problem of too little moisture

Physicists define relative humidity as the ratio of the amount of water vapor that air contains to the total amount of water it could contain at a given temperature. This is always stated as a percentage.

When the air around us is chilled, it becomes drier, because the capacity of air to hold moisture decreases as the temperature drops. We feel cooler or warmer in proportion to the rate of evaporation of moisture from our bodies. The temperature and moisture content of the air, and the moisture evaporation rate, are important and related factors in comfort control. In winter, heating makes air extremely dry, producing rapid evaporation of body moisture. To keep comfortably warm, we must maintain an air temperature between 75 and 80 degrees. If we add moisture to the air, we can be comfortable at lower temperatures, as low as 70 degrees. For comfort and health in wintertime, relative humidity should be between 30 and 50 percent. You can buy a humidity guide which will indicate, by means of a pointer, the percentage of moisture in the air.

The best way to maintain a proper home humidity level is with a power humidifier. Such a unit helps to correct the condition of extreme dryness that can cause not only personal discomfort, but damage to furniture and other household furnishings as well. An automatic humidistat permits selection of the desired humidity level, after which the humidifier takes over, automatically maintaining that level.

Types of humidifiers: Power humidifiers work on two basic principles. **Evaporator** types capitalize on the fact that warm air moving over water can pick up moisture by simple evaporation. **Atomizer** types mechanically break up water into fine particles which the surrounding air can readily absorb.

There are several powered evaporative types on the market. One is the **stationary pad** type in which a motor and fan assembly draws the warm air from the supply duct, passes it through the evaporator pad, and returns humidified air back into the supply duct. This provides a constant, positive stream of humidified air into the supply duct and the living area any time the warm air furnace is in operation.

Another type might be called a **dip-and-dry** design. It relies on motor power to dip evaporative media into the water; then exposes the wetted surface to the moving warm air.

While primarily designed for homes with forced warm air, powered evaporative units can also be designed with a blower and used in homes equipped with other heating systems. Evaporation is accomplished by means of hot water, rather than heated air. The humidified air is circulated through a duct to a centrally located grille.

Operating on a completely different principle—mechanical break-up of water into particles which the surrounding air absorbs—the **atomizer** type is independent of the movement of warm air, and when installed in ductwork, is located in the cold-air return. Some models can also be installed in a closet, over a cabinet, almost anywhere that water and electrical connections are available. All that need show is a small opening with free access to the house air. If you provide reasonably good air movement between rooms, it is possible to humidify all of them from this one point, since water vapor tends to spread evenly. Both atomizer and evaporative types are also available in portable form.

It should be pointed out that many warm-air furnaces are equipped with an evaporative-plate humidifier. These units, however, rarely have adequate capacity, and because they work on capillary action, they are subject to clogging from mineral deposits. A powered unit is the only sure way to supply a home with a proper and consistent humidification level.

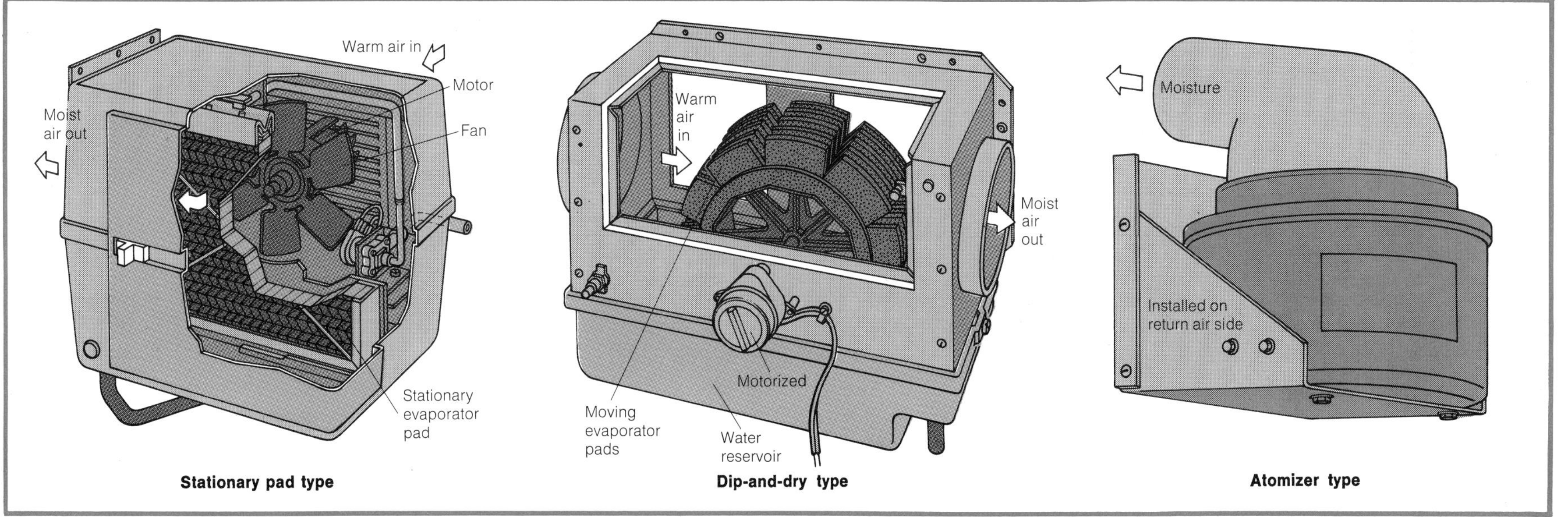

Stationary pad type

Dip-and-dry type

Atomizer type

How dehumidifiers lower the humidity level

At some seasons, even a tightly constructed home can have problems of undesirably high humidity. These may be attributable to a combination of factors, such as frequent showers, wet towels, drying clothes, cooking, floor washing, or ground moisture. Two common methods of reducing the humidity are: 1) mechanical dehumidifiers; 2) attic fans to replace warm, moist air with cool, dry outside air.

Mechanical dehumidifiers consist of a refrigerated surface (often called the air-drying coil), a condenser, an air-circulating fan, a humidistat, and a cabinet to house these components.

How a dehumidifier works: Moisture-laden air is drawn over the refrigerated coils by the fan. As the damp air hits the cold surface, the moisture condenses and drips off into the collection bucket, or is carried off to a drain by a hose connected to a drip tray. Most dehumidifiers have a hose connection designed to fit a standard garden hose. Get one long enough to reach the nearest basement drain. Or set the dehumidifier over a sink or washtub.

Continuous recirculation of room air in this way gradually reduces the relative humidity. The addition of a humidistat control to the system will automatically help maintain a preselected relative humidity. Controls are normally supplied in an adjustable range of 30 to 80 percent relative humidity and can hold the circulating air to within plus or minus 3 percent of the selected humidity.

Capacity and performance ratings: A powered dehumidifier is rated according to the pints of water it will remove in a 24-hour period from air that is at 60 percent relative humidity and 80 degrees temperature. Most home power dehumidifiers have from 10- to 30-pint capacity. Performance is generally evaluated in terms of pints of condensate per kilowatt hours. In a one-room basement, one unit should suffice. Or, depending upon air movement in your home, you may need one for each main living area.

The refrigerated, or air-drying, surface may take the form of bare-tube or finned-tube coils in vertical or horizontal tube arrangements. Exposed vertical tubes tend to collect smaller drops of water, encourage quicker run-off and less re-evaporation than horizontal tubes. Because header connections of closely spaced multiple-vertical tubes involve high construction costs, spiral evaporator tubes can be a good compromise. These coils are often staggered for maximum exposure to the flow of damp air. In any unit, be sure that the coils are held firmly in position to provide good drainage and to eliminate the possibility of rattles or vibration.

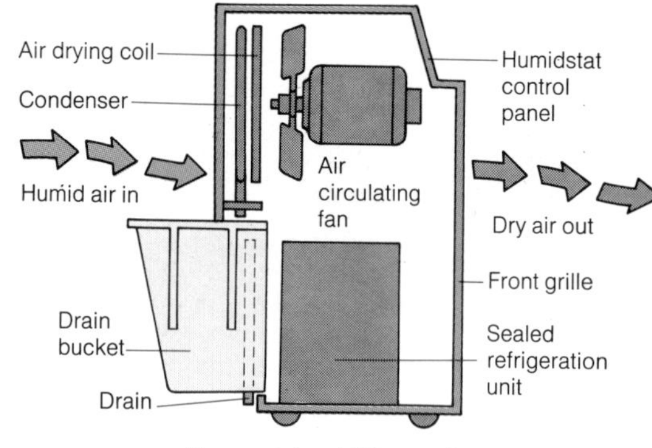

How a dehumidifier works

Operation of dehumidifier: Dehumidifiers are used winter and summer in some parts of the country. Regardless of season, they work best with doors and windows closed. Remember that the rate of moisture discharge will vary with the weather. Generally, the hotter the day, the faster the flow of water.

The only maintenance a unit usually requires is removal of dust and dirt from the refrigeration coils, the condenser, and the fan units. Most other problems should be left to an experienced serviceman.

Features to look for

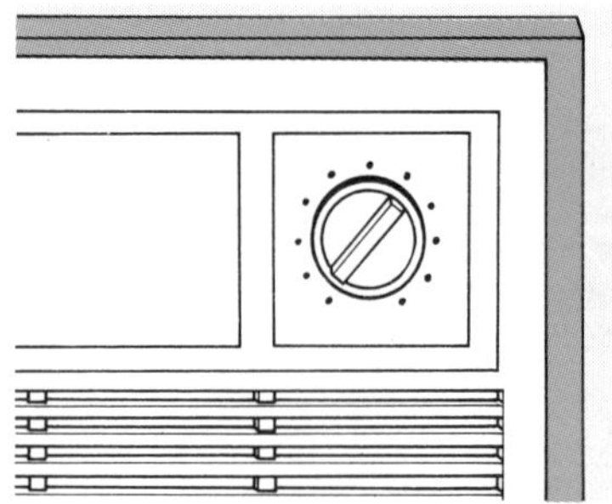
Adjustable humidistat: Humidity control starts the dehumidifier and automatically cycles on and off as required to maintain selected humidity conditions.

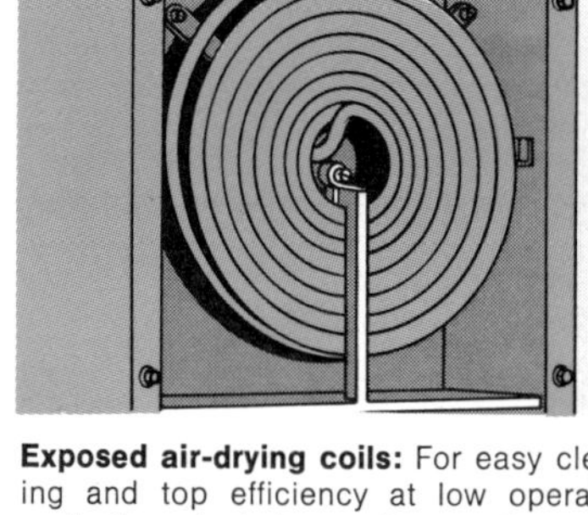
Exposed air-drying coils: For easy cleaning and top efficiency at low operating cost, the air-drying coils are frequently staggered and left exposed.

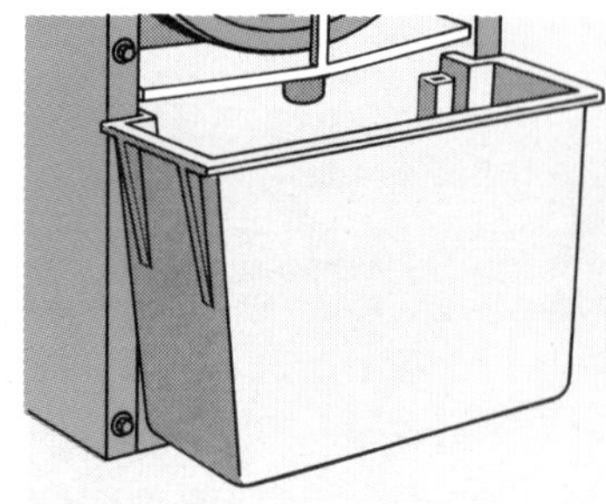
Catch bucket: When used, the water catch bucket should hold at least 10 qts. and should be so arranged that it can be easily removed and emptied without spilling.

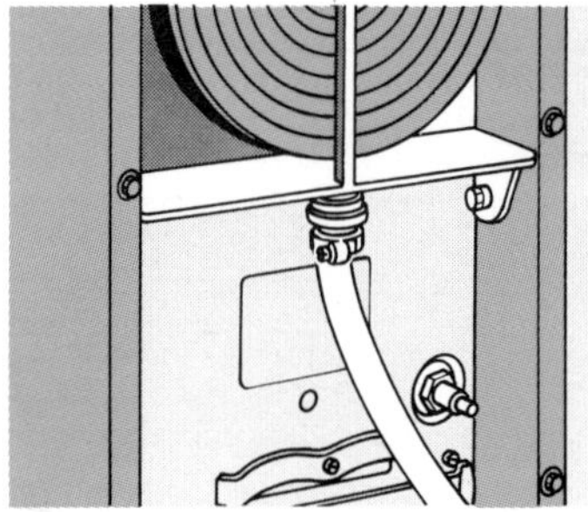
Threaded hose connection: A connector for a standard garden hose should be available for direct and continuous removal into the nearest floor drain.

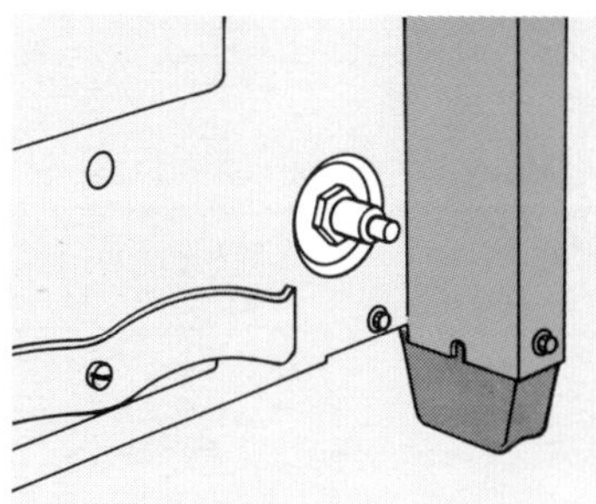
Automatic water overflow control: To prevent overflow of bucket, many models have an automatic shutoff switch. A signal lamp lights up when the bucket is full.

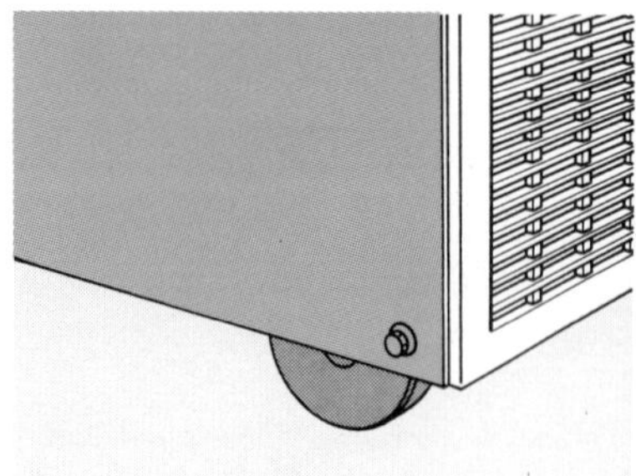
Recessed wheels: For complete mobility and greater stability, recessed wheels plus easy-roll casters should be provided. Usually two recessed wheels are sufficient.

Attic fans

Though an attic fan does not reduce temperature, the air movement it causes helps to cool the body by evaporating perspiration, creating more than just an illusion of comfort. Furthermore, the fan will ultimately reduce temperature and humidity as it replaces hot indoor air with cooler night air drawn in from outdoors. By adjusting doors and windows according to needs and conditions, the fresh, moving air can be routed through any part of the house.

Types: Attic fans are of two basic types. One is placed in an opening cut in the gable end; the rest of the attic is then sealed except for a louver through the ceiling to the area below. Indoor air moves into the attic as the fan pulls the attic air out. The other type of fan is placed in the ceiling beneath the attic and pulls air directly from the living area into the unused space above. The attic air then moves outdoors through ventilating louvers, usually in the gable ends. Louvers must always be large enough for the volume of air the fan can move to pass freely.

Size: Fans are made in a variety of sizes. Blade size and speed determine how many cubic feet of air the fan can move per minute. To determine the appropriate size (take all of the dimensions in feet), multiply house length by house width by room height by the number of floors of living space. (Do not consider the basement as a floor in making your calculations.) From the result, deduct 10 percent (for closet space and other areas the fan will not have to ventilate). The final figure is the number of cubic feet of air that the fan must move.

In the South, the fan should be able to handle the total volume once a minute; in the North, two-thirds of that amount. For example, take an average two-story-plus-basement house in Georgia 35 feet long, 22 feet wide, and with 8-foot ceilings. Multiply 35 by 22 by 8 by 2 (stories) and you get 12,320 cubic feet; deduct 10 percent and the figure is 11,088—the cubic feet of air per minute the fan should be able to move. If the house was in New Hampshire, the fan would need only two-thirds of that capacity, or 7392 cubic feet.

Mounting the fan: The type, size, and method of operation govern construction details. A fan mounted directly over the grille should be on vibration absorbers, usually rubber, or on felt padding, to deaden noise and vibration. A fan mounted directly before the louver is best suspended on springs.

Typical truss construction installation

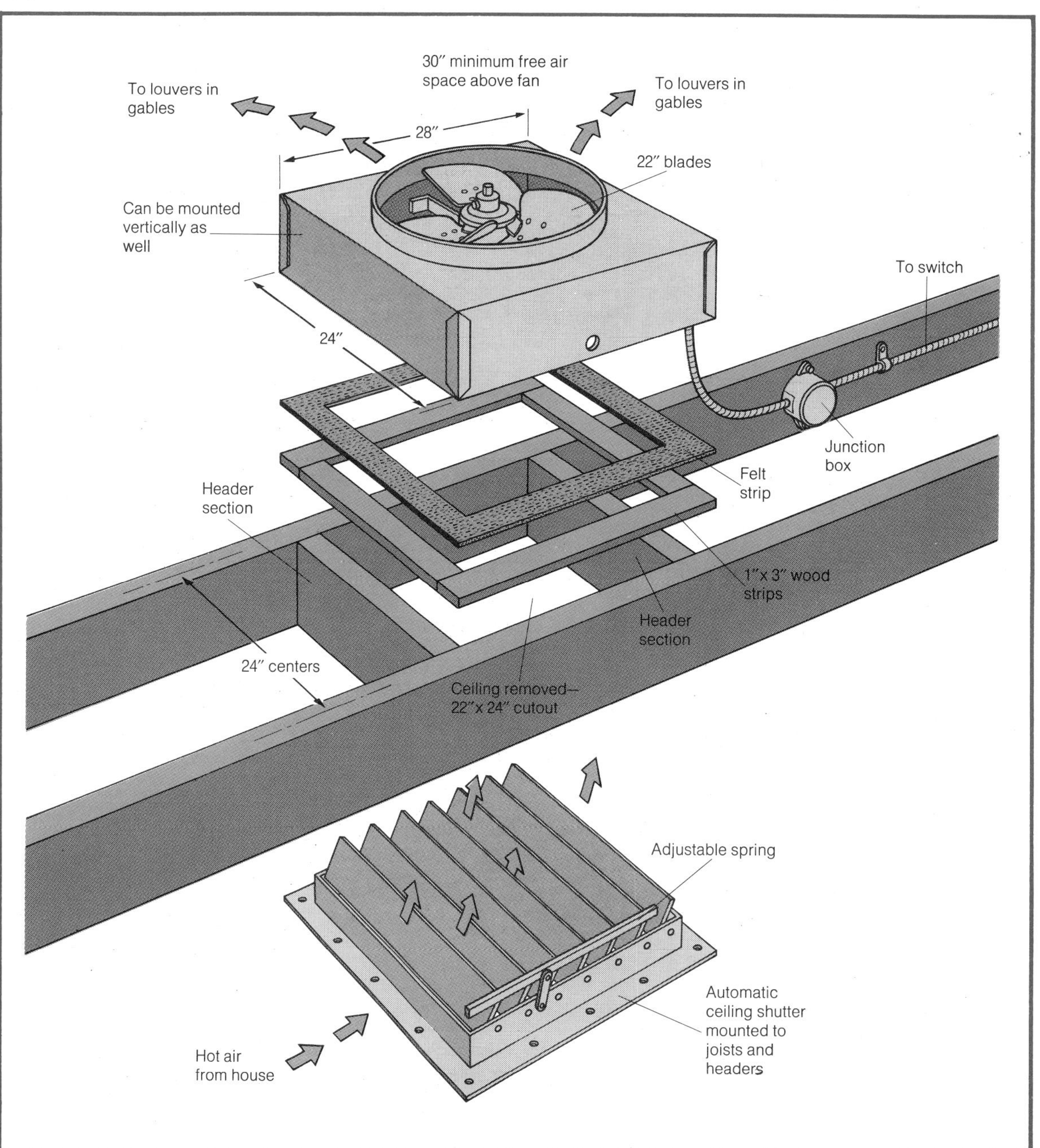

Controls for heating and cooling systems

Thermostats and humidistats

If the heart of any heating or cooling system is the heating unit, air conditioner, or heat pump, the controls of these units might appropriately be called the brain and nerves.

Room thermostats: The primary control in any heating and cooling system, to the homeowner, is the room thermostat. While there are several types, most are based on the principle of unequal expansion or contraction of metals when subjected to temperature changes. Different metals, when heated or cooled, expand and contract at different rates. Hence, if two different metals are joined into a bimetal strip, this strip, or arm, will bend with temperature changes; this movement is utilized to open or close an electric circuit which turns on the appropriate unit.

The correct placement of a thermostat is most important. This will vary, of course, according to the house plan, but a thermostat should never be placed in the path of a draft. Since it must regulate heat or coolness for the entire house, it should be located where the surrounding air will be average for the whole house. Never place a thermostat near a fireplace or other source of heat, since this will tend to shut off the conditioning source before the rest of the rooms have reached their desired temperature. Conversely, a hallway that receives gusts of wind every time the front door is opened, is also an unsatisfactory spot for the thermostat.

Multi-stage thermostats: A single-location temperature control for a house is often insufficient, since variations of exposure are certain to cool some parts of a house more rapidly at some times and less rapidly at others. Such control is bound to lead to constant complaints of "too hot" or "too cold." You can overcome this problem by laying out a zone control of the home's heating and/or cooling system in such a way that a separate thermostat can be provided to control the heat to each area, and the desired temperature maintained in each zone at all times.

Manual timer thermostats: This model of thermostat is made for people who are away from home much of the day or who have irregular sleeping schedules. A spring-wound timer on the thermostat lets the homeowner lower the temperature to cut down on fuel while he is away or asleep. At the end of the lowered-need time period, it automatically returns to the higher comfort setting.

Electric clock thermostat: Designed to provide complete care-free control, this thermostat requires no attention from the homeowner. On a preselected schedule, it automatically lowers the temperature each night and raises it each morning. Should the homeowner wish some evening to stay up later than usual, he need only shift the night setting to the daylight level. The clock is a working timepiece that is an asset on the wall.

Heating-cooling thermostats: Various models are available; among them you can obtain such features as manual or automatic changeover from heating to cooling or the reverse, manual or automatic fan control, two-stage control, and system "off." Automatic day-and-night control is also available in some heating-cooling thermostats.

Thermostats/humidistats: Some control units combine thermostat and humidistat. Such an arrangement permits the control of both the humidity and the temperature. A few home comfort panels even include electronic air-cleaner status signal lights and an odor control. The latter is a device which is installed in the ductwork of a forced-air furnace or central air conditioning system and neutralizes any unpleasant household odors.

To add for total home comfort

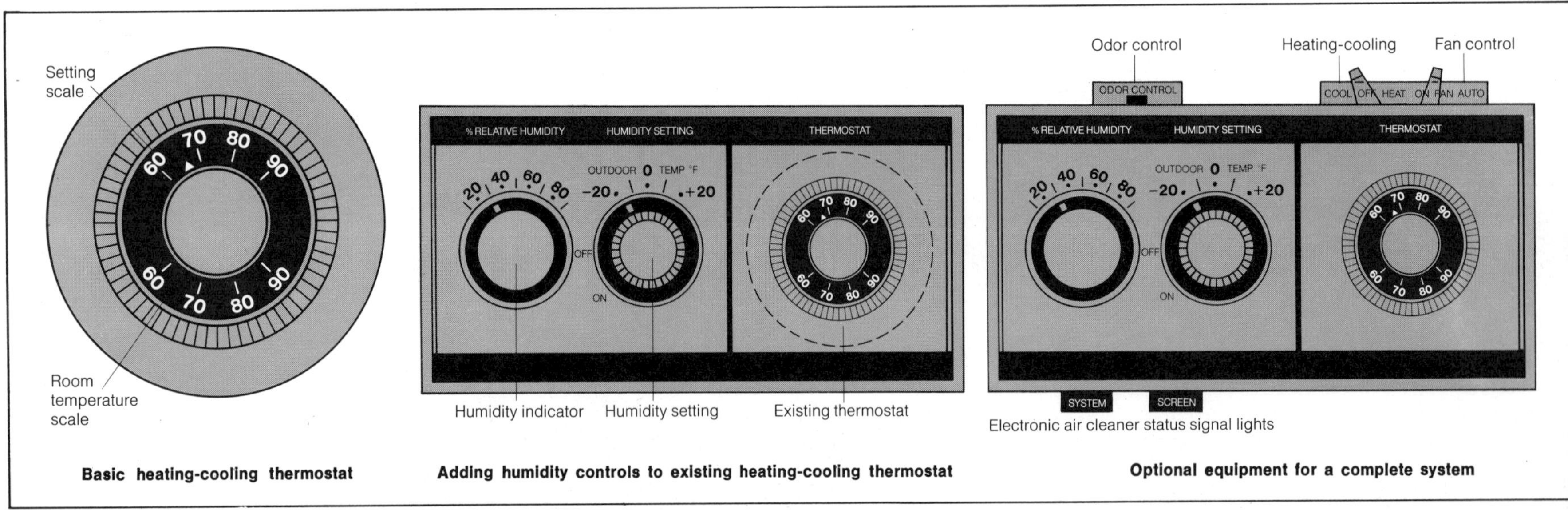

Basic heating-cooling thermostat

Adding humidity controls to existing heating-cooling thermostat

Optional equipment for a complete system

section 10:

Painting and decorating walls, ceilings, and floors

If you like a lot of results for your efforts, consider resurfacing walls, ceilings, or floors. There's no job so rewarding. The change is total and striking, and below the surface satisfactions lie such practical ones as easier maintenance and greater durability. Techniques are not difficult, but success depends on proper preparation and procedures. This section details these for every resurfacing medium: Paint, wall coverings, tiles and panels for every purpose, wood flooring, and carpeting.

contents

Brushes

Selecting the right paintbrush

Quality is a very important consideration in brush selection regardless of size or style. A good brush will hold more paint and make it possible for you to paint more smoothly with less effort.

Bristles on all good brushes are "flagged," a term that signifies splits on the bristle end. The more flags the better—they help retain paint. Hog bristle is naturally flagged, synthetic bristle artificially flagged. About 75 percent of the brushes sold today have synthetic bristles.

Test for "bounce" by brushing bristles against the back of your hand; they should feel springy and elastic. When the brush is gently pressed on any surface, good bristles will not fan out excessively. Check the setting, too. Bristles should be solidly set to prevent fallout while painting. Jar the brush and fan the bristles—any loose bristles will be apparent. The metal band on a brush, the ferrule, is generally stainless steel or aluminum on better brushes.

Both the area to be painted and the type of paint have a bearing on the size and style of brush. Calcimine brushes with very long, tough, and elastic bristles are best for applying water-thinned paints to large areas. Enamel and varnish brushes, both flat and chisel-shaped, are best for alkyd paints and lacquers. The shape and lengths of the latter help achieve a smoother flow and prevent lap marks. A special brush with very tough fiber or nylon bristles, ranging in width from 4 to 6 inches, is recommended for rough stucco or masonry surfaces.

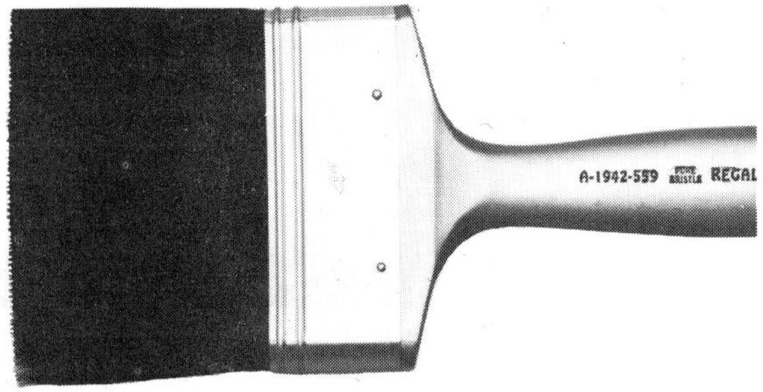

4″ wall brush for outside or inside work

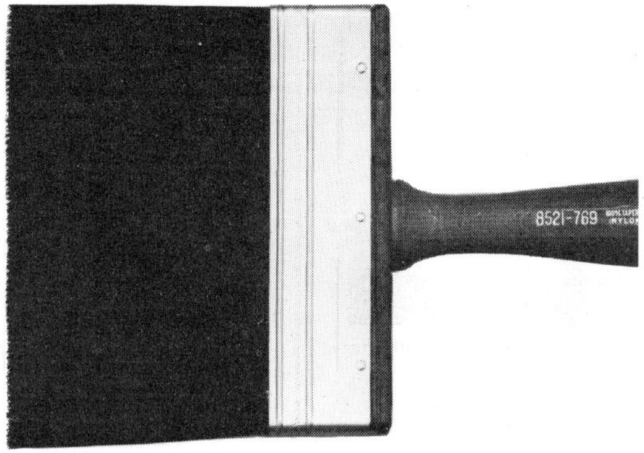

6″ outside wall brush for masonry surfaces

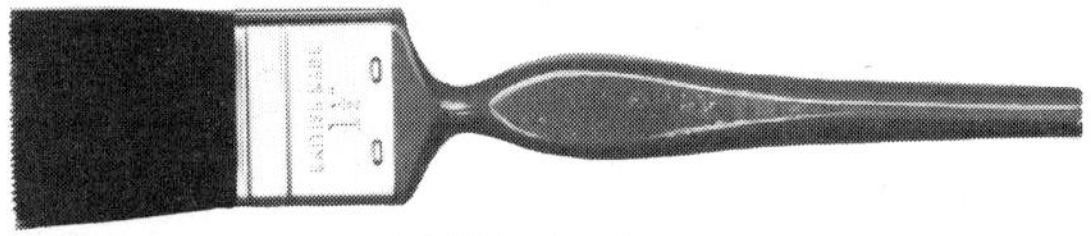

1½″ trim brush

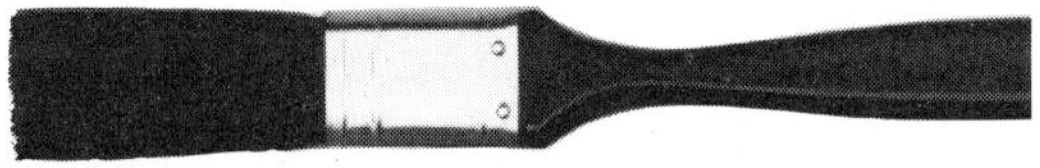

1″ high-quality trim brush

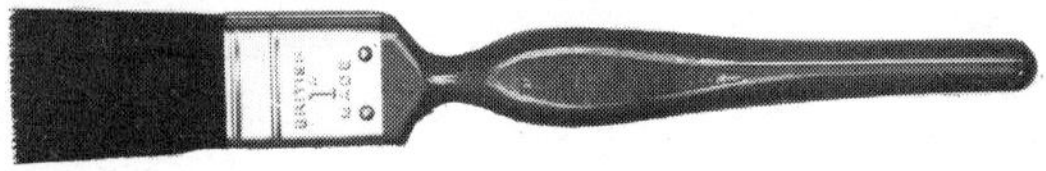

1″ varnish or enamel brush

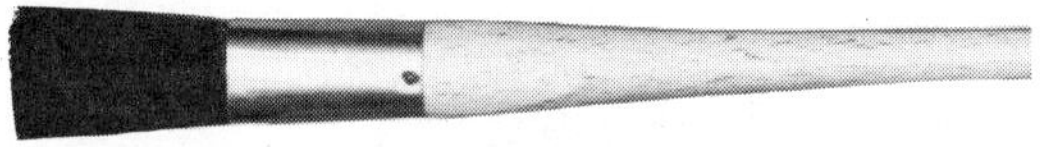

Round sash brush

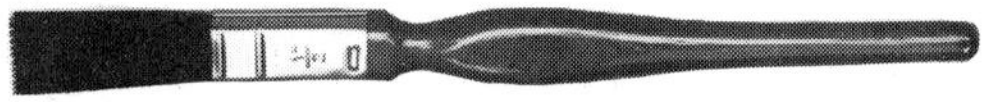

Varnish touchup brush

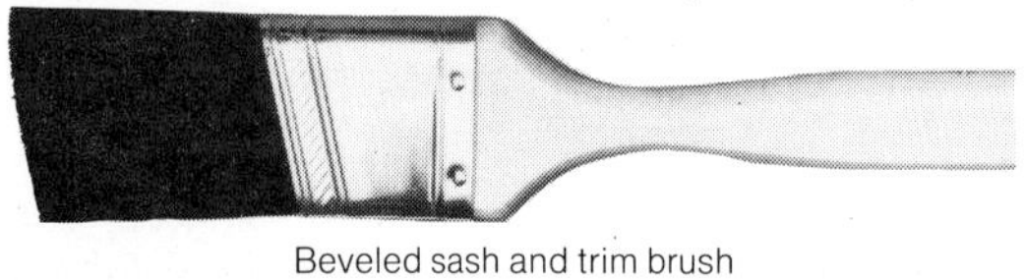

Beveled sash and trim brush

New painting devices can often simplify the job:

1. **Tilting tray** that hooks on ladder rung or step holds 1/2 gal. Tilting the entire unit allows tray to fill with paint from container below.

2. **Exterior brush pad** applies paint twice as fast as a 4-in. brush. Use with exterior latex paint on siding, shingles. Refill pads are available.

3. **Small brush pad** made of foamed urethane. Use to paint interior or exterior trim.

4. **Disposable brush** made of foamed urethane is available in widths to 3 in. Cheap enough to use once and discard. Eliminates cleanup.

Proper care of brushes

Always clean a brush right after painting. Use the thinner or solvent for the paint with which the brush has been used. For example, to remove oil-base or alkyd paints, use turpentine followed by benzine or paint thinner; for brushes used to apply shellac or alcohol-base stains, alcohol or lacquer thinner. Follow cleaning with a thorough washing with soap and warm water. Brushes used with latex or water-base paints are very easy to clean; just use warm water.

Proper storage is important to the condition of a brush. A good procedure is to drill a hole in the base of the brush handle. You can then, for overnight storage, insert a wire rod through the hole and rest it on top of a paint or coffee can with the brush suspended in the solvent. Be sure the can is taller than the bristles—they should not rest on the bottom. For longer storage, brushes should be wrapped in foil or heavy paper after cleaning.

To clean a paintbrush, saturate the bristles in appropriate solvent right after use. Latex or water-base paints require only warm water.

Work the bristles between your fingers all the way to the heel of the handle. Gloves are advisable with some types of solvent.

Rinse in solvent several times, shake out excess, then comb the bristles thoroughly. This will straighten the inner bristles.

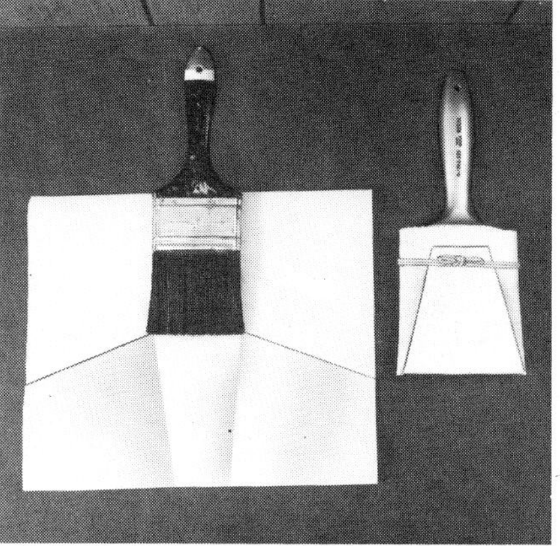
For prolonged storage, wrap brushes in foil or heavy paper as shown. Bristles should be dry before brush is wrapped for storage.

How to salvage old brushes

Brushes that have hardened because they weren't properly cleaned or protected can often be made usable by soaking in a paint-remover type of brush softener sold in paint stores. Success depends upon the amount of paint left in the brush and how long it has dried. If needed, comb bristles and resoak.

Storing brush without wrapping causes bristles to fan out

Dried-out paint on lower half of sash brush

Dried-out paint extends up to handle on this brush

To soften dried paint, soak bristles of neglected brush in a commercial brush softener. In method shown, brush is suspended by means of a wire rod inserted in hole drilled in handle. Length of soaking time depends on brush condition.

Scrape off caked surface paint with putty knife, taking care not to cut bristles. To remove scale from inner bristles, use the back edge of a knife. Comb out remaining paint with a metal comb and soak bristles overnight in brush softener.

If some paint still remains, wash it out with soap and water, adding some turpentine to the suds—about a cup to a quart of water. Rinse in clear water, use the metal comb to straighten the bristles, and let dry thoroughly before storing.

Paint rollers

Selecting the right roller

Always choose a paint roller to suit the job. They come in various sizes and with handles of different lengths. Many are designed to take extensions, making it possible to paint ceilings or stairways as high as 12 feet while standing on the floor, or to paint a floor without stooping or bending.

Roller covers are made in many widths for use on different size areas. For amateur use on walls and ceilings, good choices are the 7- or 9-inch models; for finishing woodwork, doors, and trim, the 3-inch is best. You can also get smaller sizes for cutting in corners and for use on window frames and moldings.

Special-purpose rollers include a doughnut-shaped type that will coat both sides of a corner at once. To enable you to paint a wall without getting the paint on the ceiling, there are special edging rollers. Flat painting "pads" (some with guide wheels) are available for use on fencing, siding, shakes, and other hard-to-get-at surfaces.

The fabric on the roller cover should conform to type of paint that is to be applied. Lamb's wool, for example, is excellent with latex or alkyd paints but should not be used with enamels. Enamel will cause the wool to mat.

Mohair rollers work with any type of interior flat paint but are especially suitable for applying enamel and producing a smooth finish. Rollers made from synthetic fibers can also be used with all types of flat paint, inside and out. Where a stippled finish is desired, use a roller made of carpeting.

Another factor to consider when choosing a roller is the length of the nap or pile, which can range from 1/16 to 1½ inches. In general, the rule is: The smoother the surface, the shorter the nap; the rougher the surface, the longer the nap. Use short-napped rollers for painting walls, ceilings, woodwork, and smooth concrete. The longer naps are for use on rough masonry, brick, stucco, wire fences, and other irregular or uneven surfaces.

In buying a roller, be sure the roll is easy to remove and change. If both oil and water paints are to be applied, get separate rolls for each. Make sure that neither water nor oil will soften the tube (frequently it is made of treated cardboard) that supports the pile. It is best to get a roll on which the material is stretched over a plastic tube. Always keep a small brush on hand to cut in where it is impossible for a roller to fit.

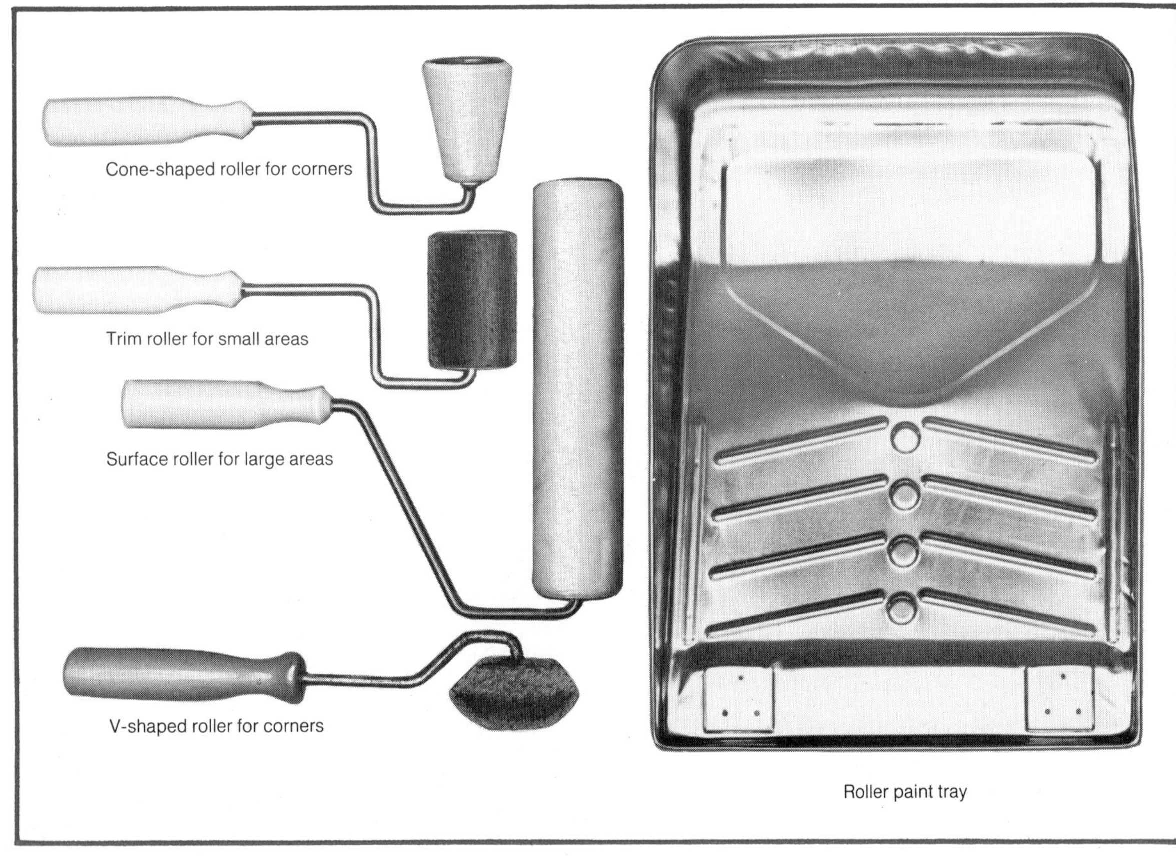

Cone-shaped roller for corners

Trim roller for small areas

Surface roller for large areas

V-shaped roller for corners

Roller paint tray

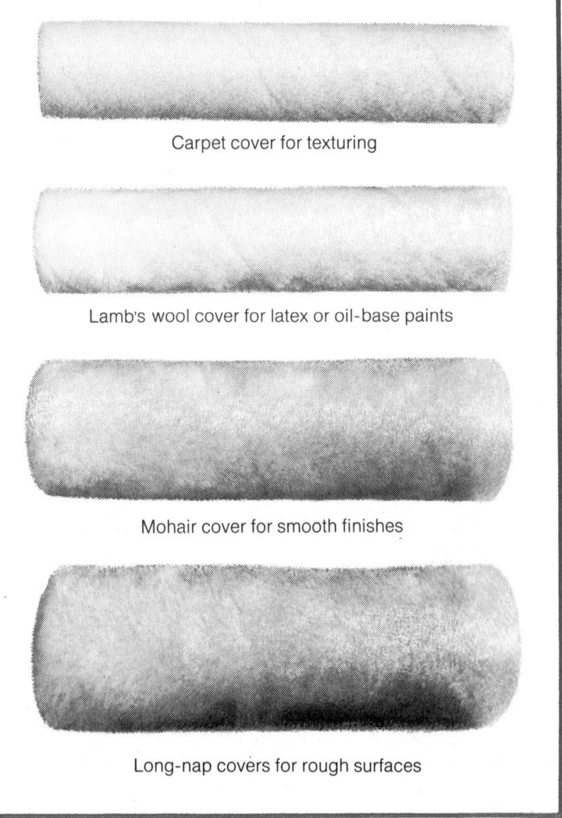

Carpet cover for texturing

Lamb's wool cover for latex or oil-base paints

Mohair cover for smooth finishes

Long-nap covers for rough surfaces

Care of rollers

A roller, like a paintbrush, should be cleaned as soon as possible after use. To clean roller, first roll out excess paint on newspaper until no more comes off. Then slide the roller cover from its support.

Wash the roller cover in the appropriate thinner or solvent for the type of paint being used. For latex paints, it will be water. Work the nap of the cover between your fingers to get out any embedded paint.

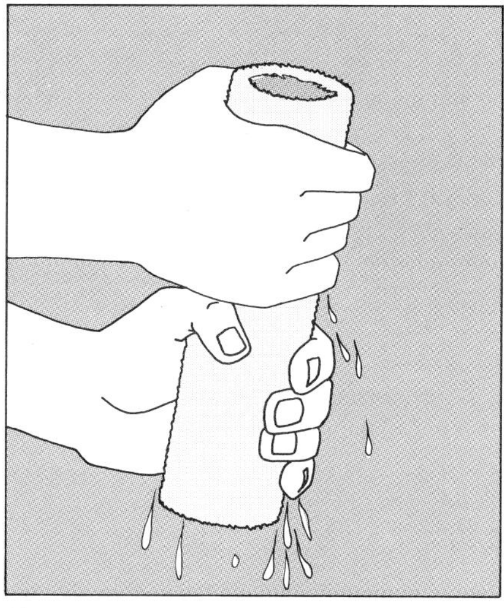

When the cover has been thoroughly washed, wring out the excess liquid, then dry the cover by rubbing it vigorously with a clean, absorbent cloth. Wrap the dried cover in aluminum foil to keep it clean.

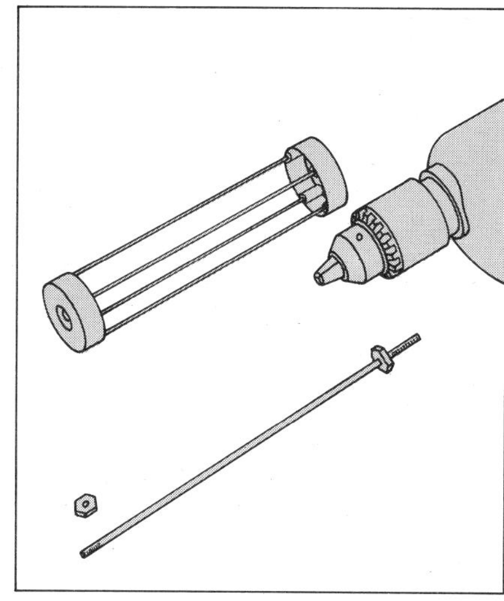

You can make a dryer for roller covers with a length of threaded rod, the core from an old roller, and two nuts. Place the assembled unit, including damp cover, in chuck of drill and spin the cover dry inside a paper bag.

Care of brush pads

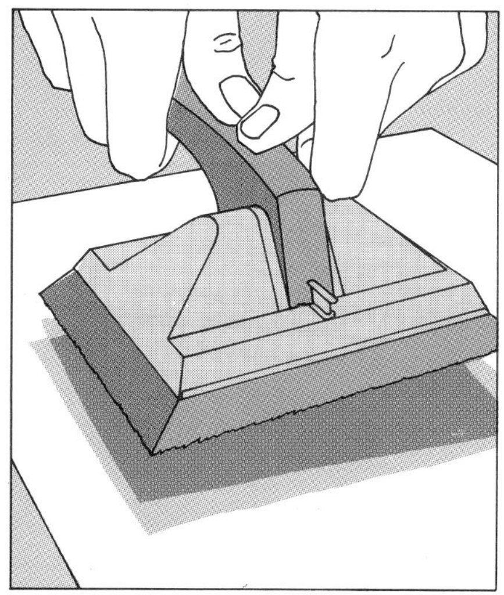

To clean a brush pad, first squeeze as much paint as possible on several layers of newspaper. Then carefully remove the pad portion from the handle unit.

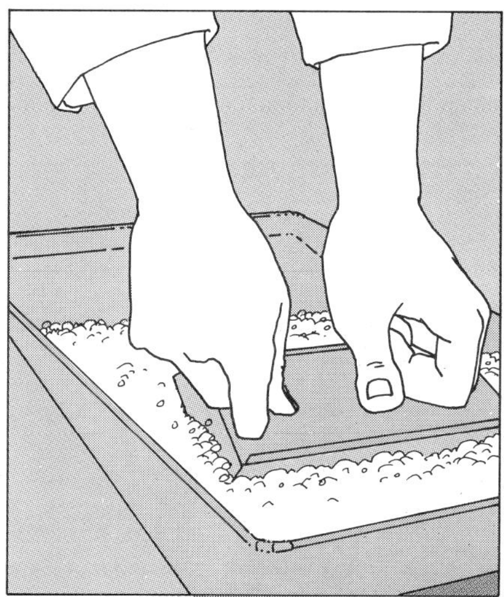

Wash out the pad in the appropriate thinner or solvent for the type of paint used—water for latex paint; turpentine or paint thinner for oil-base and alkyd paints.

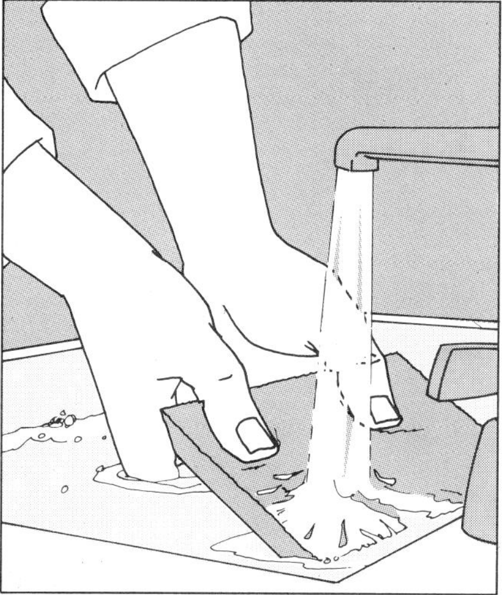

When most of the paint has been removed, wash the pad a second time in a solution of detergent or soap and water. Rinse it well in clear water to remove the last traces of paint.

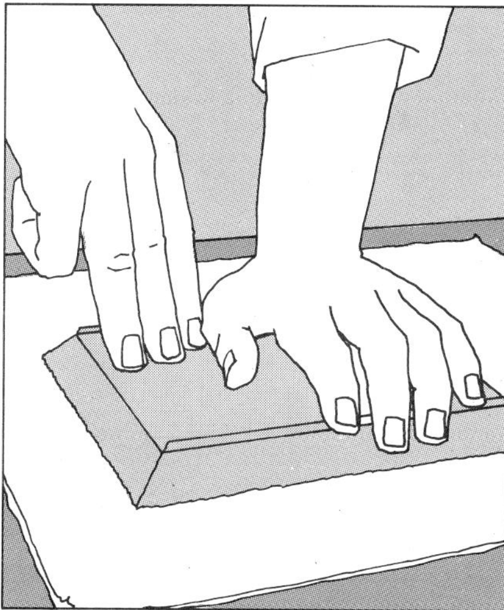

When you are satisfied that the pad is clean, squeeze out all excess water and leave pad to dry. Wrap the dried pad in aluminum foil or heavy brown paper to protect it from dirt.

Spray-painting

Selecting the right spray equipment

Spray equipment ranges from painting attachments for use with vacuum cleaners to large air compressor sprayers which can be rented for a low fee.

The vacuum cleaner sprayer is satisfactory for most household painting projects. Before deciding to spray-paint, however, consider whether the time gained will be lost in the extra work of masking windows and hardware. While practically any paint product that can be brushed or rolled on can also be sprayed, spray-painting is best suited for large wall areas, fences, or furniture that can be placed in an open space while it is being painted.

The width of the spray should be adjusted to the size of the article that is to be coated. A narrow fan is best for spraying small or narrow articles; a full-width fan should be used to spray broader areas such as table tops or walls.

It is important to experiment beforehand. Test for the thickness of the paint, the size of the spray area, and the motion of the gun before actually painting any surface. Excessive paint thickness can cause rippling of the wet film by the sprayed air or lead to blistering later. On vertical and inclined surfaces, it can cause runs.

The spray fan should be perpendicular—at right angles—to the surface being coated. The stroke, or motion of the hand holding the spray gun, should start with the spray pointed beyond the surface to be painted. This assures a smooth, uninterrupted flow when you reach the surface to be coated.

As you spray, move the gun parallel to the surface, and keep moving with an even stroke back and forth across the area being coated. Corners and edges should always be sprayed first.

Regardless of the type of equipment used, there are certain precautions you should take. The room in which you are spraying should be well ventilated. Keep a fire extinguisher within reach. Make sure all flammable liquids are stored in safety cans. If you are spraying in a confined area, wear a mask to avoid breathing in vapors and paint.

Spray equipment should be thoroughly cleaned immediately after use. The simplest method is to spray a suitable solvent through the equipment. A broom straw can be used to unclog the fluid tip. Never use wire or a nail to clear the holes in the spray tip. They are precision-machined openings and can easily be damaged by such sharp objects.

Thin the paint with the appropriate solvent or thinner to obtain the correct consistency for spraying. Remove lumps by straining the paint through a nylon stocking.

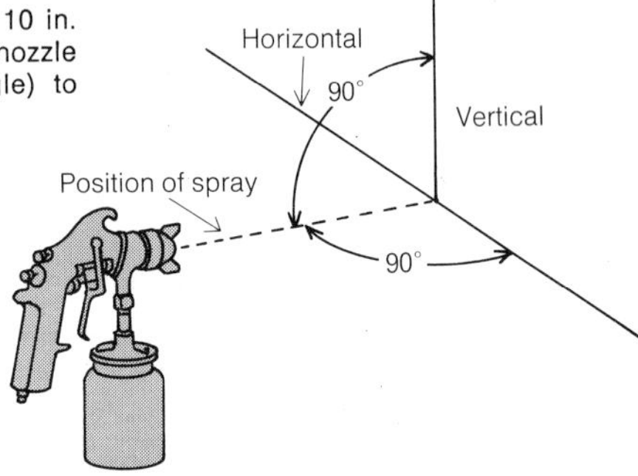

Hold the gun between 6 and 10 in. from the work and keep the nozzle perpendicular (at a 90° angle) to the surface at all times.

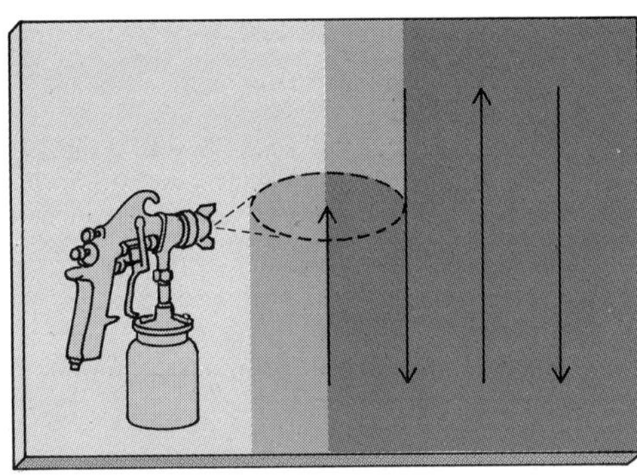

Overlap strokes by one-half and do not concentrate the spray on one area; this will cause runs.

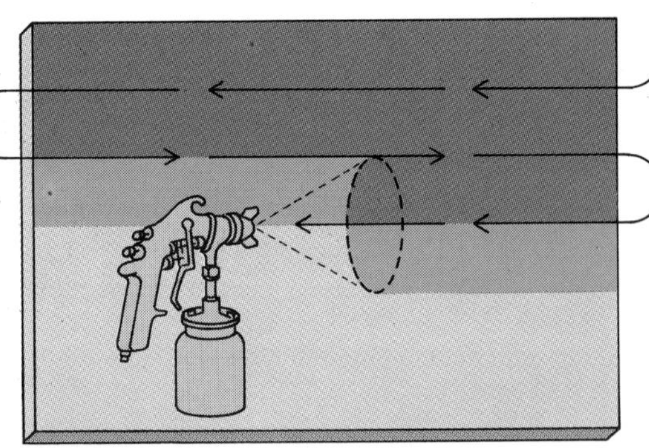

Always spray slightly beyond area to be painted to avoid a double thickness of paint on return stroke.

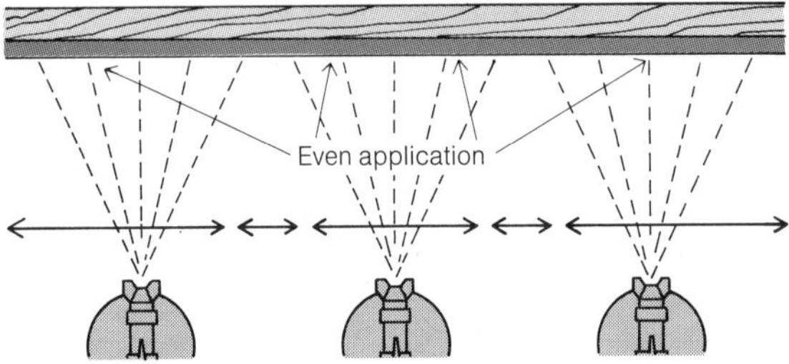

Right way: Move the spray gun parallel to the work surface, keeping the wrist flexible at all times.

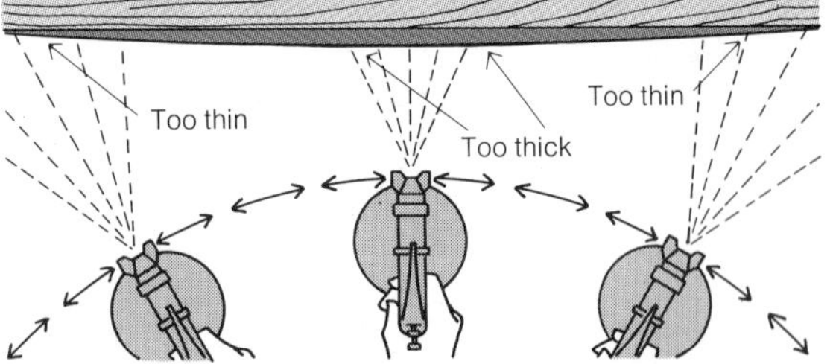

Wrong way: Never swing the gun in an arc; this motion will produce an uneven paint coat.

How to use a spray can

There are four basic components in aerosol-packed paints: Container, valve, propellants that produce the pressure, and paint. The operating principle is simple. With the injection of the propellant, the pressure within the container becomes greater than that in the atmosphere; when the valve is opened, the pressure produces a fine spray of paint.

Most aerosol paints are mixed by the movement of a small ball within the container, accomplished by shaking the can. This shaking is a very important step. If you don't take it, the paint may come out too thin, or the can may run out of pressure before all the paint is used up.

Hold the container 10 to 12 inches from the surface being painted. Keep the nozzle parallel with the piece. Press the valve button all the way down and move the can evenly over the surface; release the pressure before you end each stroke. The trick is to work across the surface, starting beyond the left edge and continuing beyond the right. Overlap the first stroke with at least one-third of the next.

Be sure to use rapid, smooth strokes. If the can is moved too slowly, or stopped, you will get streaking. Never spray too long in one area; this causes drips and runs. Results are best when the paint is sprayed in very thin coats (two or three for maximum coverage) with ample drying time allowed in between. When a particularly smooth finish is desired, sand between the coats, using a fine grade of sandpaper.

Aerosol paints are flammable, so keep them away from open flames, particularly during use. Store the cans in a cool place. Keep them away from hot-water and heating pipes. If the spray tip gets clogged, clean it with a fine copper wire (a strand from a lamp cord works well). Before discarding a used-up spray can, remove the tip; in a pinch it can be used to replace the clogged tip on another can. Two final precautions: Aerosol cans should never be punctured, and you should never discard them in an incinerator—they could explode.

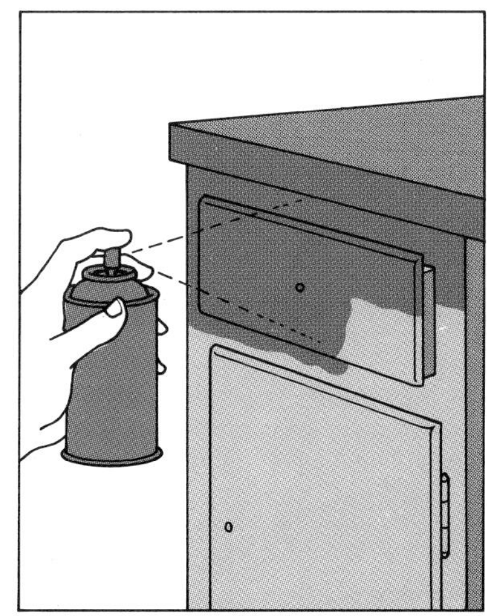

When painting drawers, open them about ¼ in. so that the spray will be sure to cover their edges.

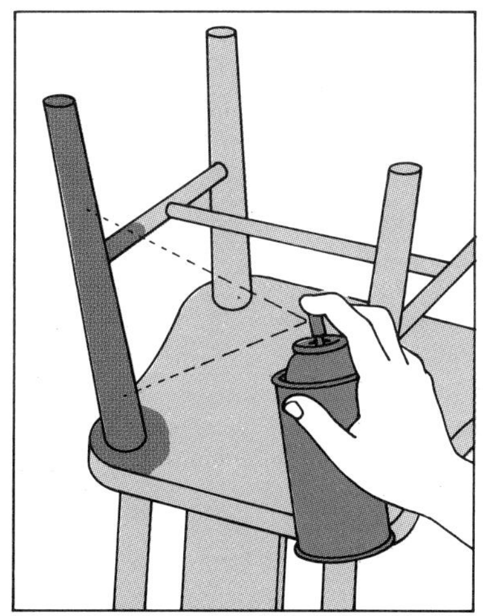

When spraying a chair, turn it upside-down and work along legs and rungs first. Reverse it to paint top surfaces.

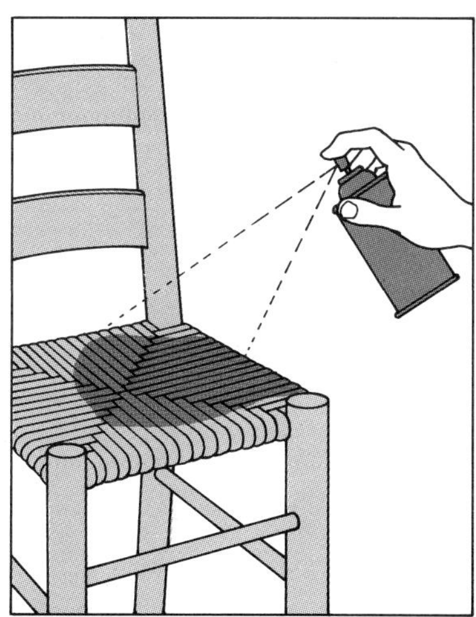

When spraying openwork, tilt the can 45°. This will ensure that too much paint does not pass through the openings.

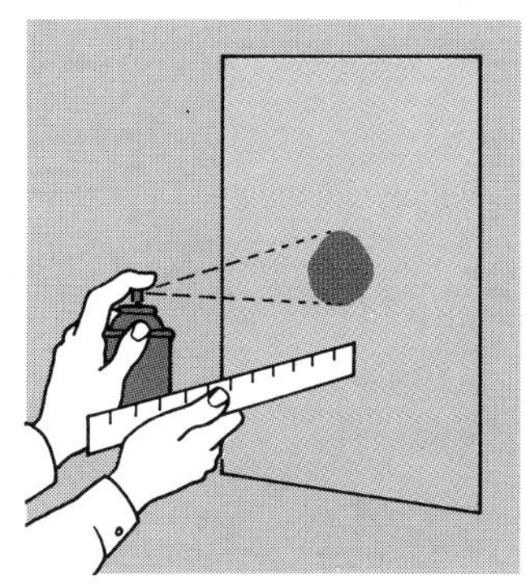

Before starting actual painting, experiment to find the proper holding distance for the best spray pattern. Use a piece of cardboard as target.

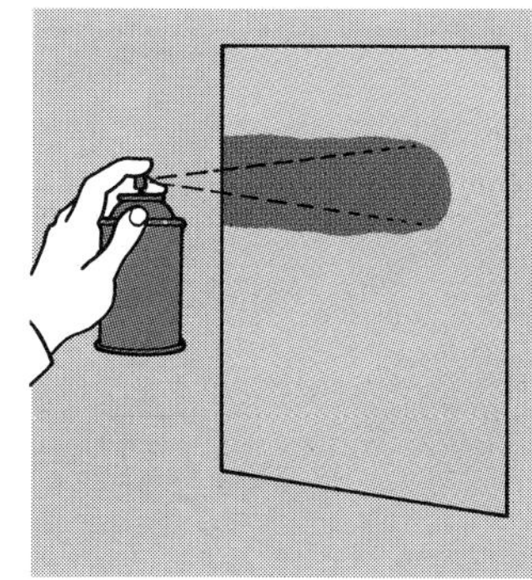

Apply coverage from left to right, carrying spray slightly past both edges. Maintain an equal distance from the work at all times.

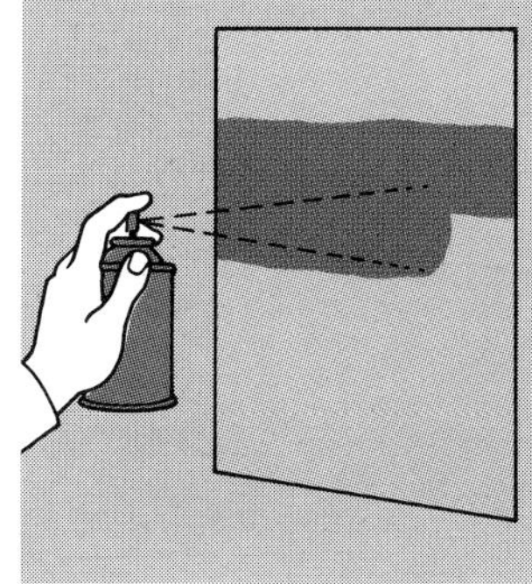

Overlap the first stroke with about one-third of the next. Take care to use a rapid, smooth stroke to prevent streaks when spraying.

Hold can as nearly perpendicular as possible. Tilting puts top and bottom of spray at different distances from work and makes spray uneven.

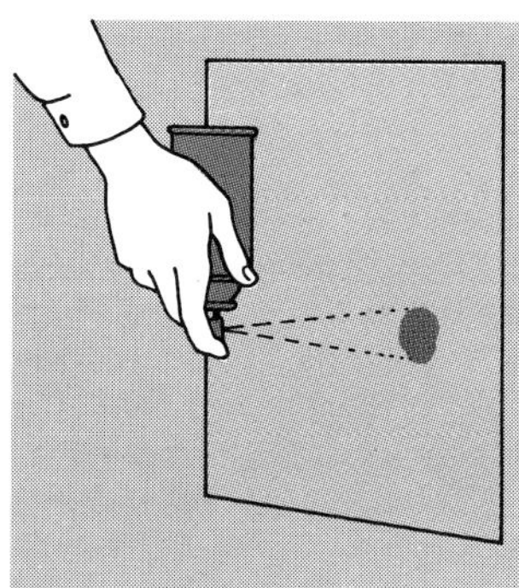

When you finish painting, turn the can upside-down and spray until the paint stops coming out. This will clear out the nozzle.

Preparation

Before painting interiors

Prepainting preparations should include a thorough cleanup of the walls and ceiling. Remove all nails and picture hangers from the walls. Check the walls and ceiling for cracks and blemishes. Carefully fill hairline cracks with spackling material, using a putty knife, kitchen knife, or even your fingers. Larger cracks should be filled with special patching plaster which has been mixed according to the directions on the container.

To insure proper adhesion of the plaster filler, chisel out a triangular channel in the wall, narrow on the surface and wider inside. Then feed the plaster into the channel through the narrow opening. When the patching material has thoroughly dried, sand the surface smooth, and apply undercoating or primer to the patched areas.

Check for joint separation on moldings around walls, doors, and windows and correct by resetting the strips or filling in the cracks with spackle.

Next remove all hardware from doors and windows and loosen the lighting fixtures, or cover these areas with masking tape, paper, or cloth. This will make after-painting cleanup much easier.

Dust the walls thoroughly with a dry mop, except in the kitchen or bathroom, where grease or steamed-on dirt tends to accumulate on walls. These walls should be washed with household cleaner or detergent before repainting. Woodwork should be given a final wiping with a rag dampened with paint thinner if you are going to use an oil-base or alkyd paint. Except for kitchen and bathroom walls, where a gloss is sometimes desirable, flat paint is generally used on walls. On woodwork and doors, gloss or semi-gloss paint is usually the choice.

Before painting, remove switch covers and other hardware. This makes painting easier and avoids the risk of spattering.

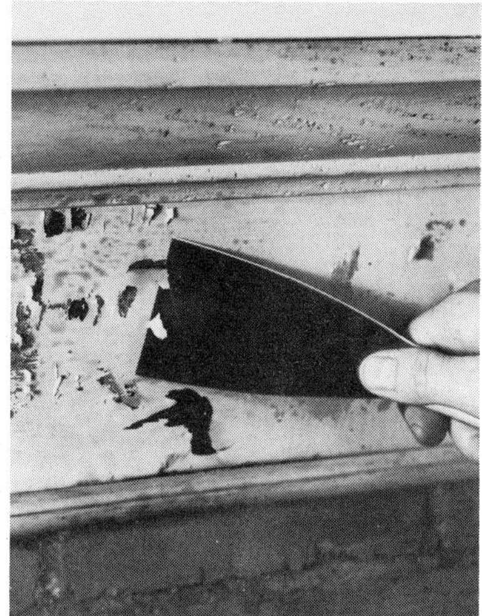

Scrape off any flaking, peeling, or blistered paint with a putty knife. Sand to blend edges and smooth the surface.

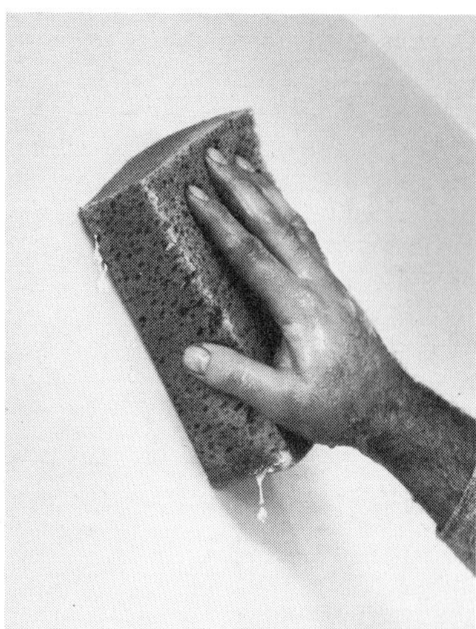

The final prepainting step: A thorough cleaning with detergent and water. Let walls dry completely before painting.

Scrapers and knives

Four basic types of scrapers and knives should be part of a homeowner's painting equipment.

1. Hook scraper. This is useful for scraping down a rough surface and can be used with paint remover or a blowtorch. Hook scrapers usually consist of a steel blade, with a hook at one end. Some hook scrapers have removable and reversible blades.

2. Razor blade scraper. Especially handy for scraping paint from glass. Made in a variety of styles.

3. Wall scraper. Knife-type wall scrapers, for removing paint and other general scraping and cleaning. Available in sizes from 1¼ to 5 inches wide with both flexible and stiff blades. Usually a 2- to 4-inch width with a stiff blade works best.

4. Putty knife. Knife with a flexible steel blade used for applying and smoothing putty. Also handy for filling, scraping, and cleaning.

In addition you should have a supply of coarse, medium, and fine grades of sandpaper.

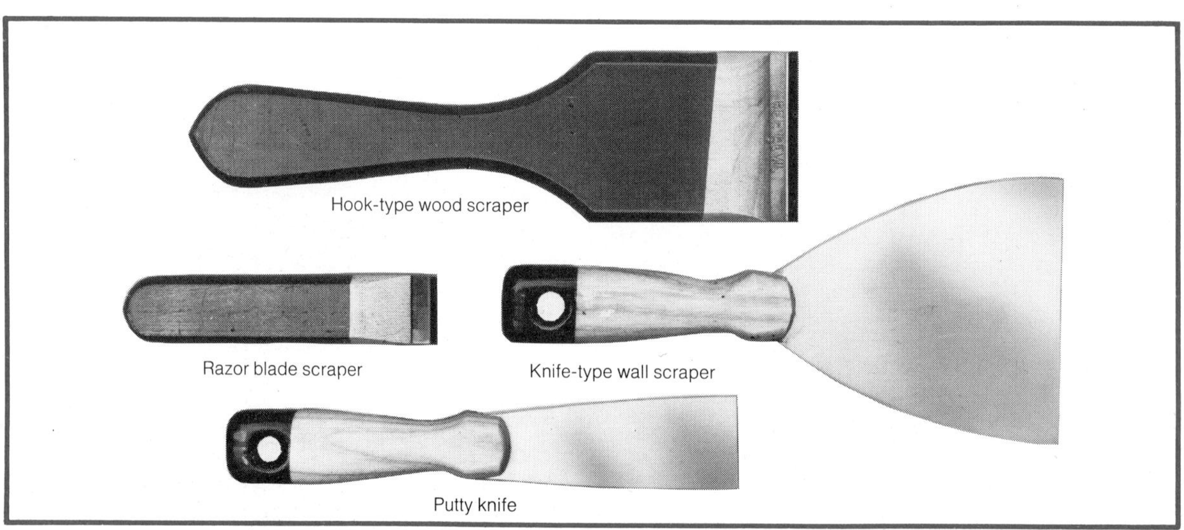

Stripping old paint

Proper surface preparation sometimes requires stripping away all the old finish. The easiest way to do this is with a paint remover.

Apply the remover with a broad, thick brush that will hold an ample supply. Lay on a good full coat. Brush in one direction only. Cover and work on an area no more than 2 feet square at a time. Give it some time to soften, then go back to where you started and, with your scraping knife, test to see if the film has softened all the way down to the wood. If it has, scrape it off. If not, recoat the area. This will give you an idea of the work and time involved in removal. Unless the original finish is very old, two coats and an hour of time should be sufficient to soften the paint.

After you have scraped all of the old paint from the surface, remove the remaining sludge and thoroughly clean the surface with coarse steel wool. Let the surface dry for at least 4 hours before doing any refinishing.

On broad, flat, accessible surfaces, such as doors, a power sander can be useful for final finishing to achieve the smoothness that is desired for painting.

Removing interior woodwork finish may require more time, because of the extra care required to protect surrounding areas—covering or moving of furniture, etc.—and of the intricacy of the woodwork itself. Do not coat too large a surface at a time, particularly if there is a good deal of detail work involved. As soon as the finish has softened, scrape it off. Allow the surface to dry for 4 hours before applying a new finish. Wipe it down with a rag dampened with paint thinner before painting.

Apply a generous coat of paint remover to an area at a time. Use short strokes and work in one direction—do not brush out or back.

After about 20 minutes, test to see if film has softened. If it has, scrape off with putty knife or scraper. If not, recoat area.

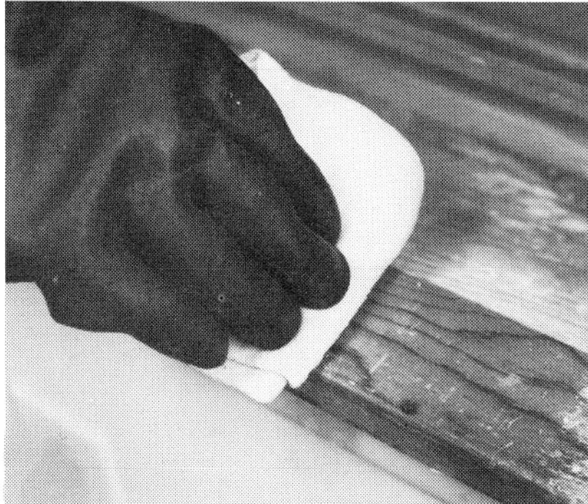

When remover has been used on entire surface and old paint scraped off, remove sludge and clean with coarse cloth or steel wool.

A finishing sander, used after a belt sander on large, flat surfaces such as doors and sills, speeds up the final prepainting preparation.

Removing paint with heat

A comparatively easy way to remove all the paint from the outside of a house, or other large surface, is to burn it off. You will need a propane or blowtorch for this. Remember, in using a blowtorch, that you do not want to burn the wood, so don't keep the flame on the surface too long. After heat has been applied, the paint may be scraped off with a putty knife just as with paint remover. Do not worry if wood is slightly scorched; this is almost inevitable and does no harm—just take care not to char it.

For those who do not like working with a blowtorch, there are electric paint softeners with a built-in scraper that lifts off the heat-softened paint as you move the tool forward. The higher their wattage, the faster these electric paint removers work. When all of the paint has been burned off, the surface should be sanded before painting.

Propane torch is useful for softening on very broad areas. Scrape off paint immediately after application of heat.

If a torch seems too risky, an alternative is an electric paint softener which uses no flame and scrapes as it softens.

Preparation

Preparing existing paintwork

Plaster surfaces must be clean and smooth before paint is applied. Fill all cracks with patching plaster. Paint that is loose or badly cracked or chipped should be completely removed. Sand off any pimples, ridges, and paint runs.

Fresh plaster can be painted with latex paint as soon as the trim is nailed; use two coats. With oil-base paint use three coats and let the plaster cure for 90 days before painting. If you choose not to wait 90 days and you still want to use oil-base paint, the plaster can be prepared for painting by treating the surface with a solution of 2 pounds of zinc sulfate dissolved in 1 gallon of water.

It is not advisable to paint over wallpaper, though it can be done if the paper does not have a texture that will show through the paint. Be sure there are no colors in the paper that will bleed through the paint and make certain the paper is sound and tight over the entire wall; use latex paint.

Walls of plywood and most composition wallboards are painted in the same way as plaster walls. Some wallboards, however, are extremely porous and will require a sealer coat. Your paint dealer can suggest a suitable sealer for the purpose.

Whether you should apply one or two coats depends on the condition of the surface, the color change involved, and the type of paint. Modern paints cover better and wear longer than earlier ones, so if you are repainting in approximately the same color, one coat will usually be enough. If there has been much peeling and chipping, or if you are changing color radically, two coats will probably be required, regardless of manufacturers' claims. You can apply a suitable undercoat or primer as the first coat, or use two coats of the same paint.

To estimate how much paint you need for any interior decorating job, you need to know the square feet of wall surface to be painted and the number of square feet a gallon of the paint you are planning to use will cover. The label on the paint can usually specifies how many square feet a gallon will cover. Remember, an imperial gallon covers 25 percent more than an American gallon.

Walls and ceilings are usually rectangles. To determine ceiling area, multiply length by width. To calculate the square footage of walls, measure the perimeter of the room and multiply this figure by its height. The result is the square footage of wall space to be covered. Do not deduct for windows unless they measure together more than 100 square feet.

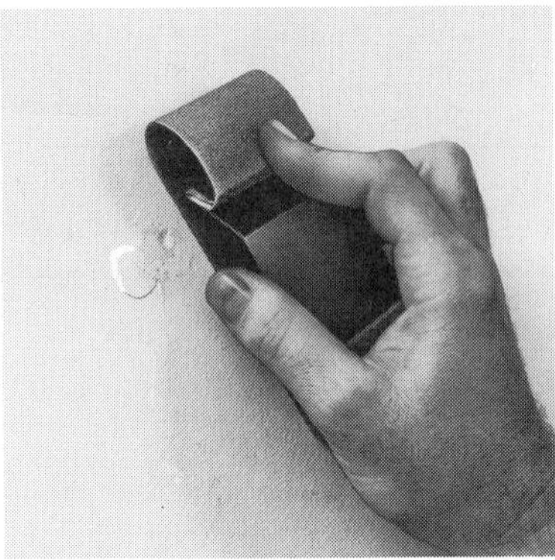

When sanding on flat surfaces, make the task easier by using a sanding block.

Sandpaper is sometimes easier to handle when folded into four thicknesses.

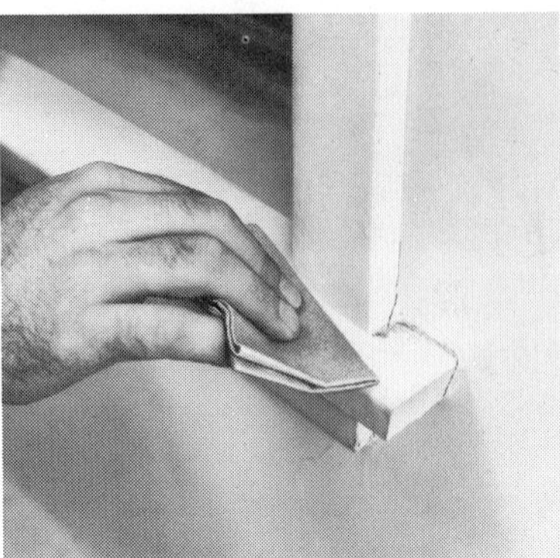

Try the V fold shown above to sand trim, molding, and hard-to-get-at areas.

If moldings need to be removed or relocated, do this before repainting.

Fill in screw holes and slight separations at mitered joints with wood putty or spackle.

Sand rust from metal surfaces; use powered wire brush if rusting is severe.

Divide the number of square feet to be painted by the number of square feet a gallon will cover. The result is the number of gallons or fractions of a gallon you will need to complete the job. The same formula applies, of course, to determining how much paint you will need for the ceiling.

When you buy paint, have the dealer put it in a shaker; this minimizes the amount of stirring you will have to do at home. Stir the paint with a flat board until you are positive that no pigment is left at the bottom of the can.

Some manufacturers recommend no stirring. Check the label. Certain paints should never be stirred. These are the jelly-like thixotropic paints.

Every paint job will go faster if you follow the right sequence. Do ceilings first, walls second, then woodwork (doors, windows, and other trim). Where you put floors in the sequence depends upon what is being done to them. If the floors are simply being painted, they should be done last; if they are to be completely refinished, including sanding or scraping, do them first, and cover them with paper or drop cloths while you paint the room.

Important: When you paint the lower portion of the woodwork and especially the baseboards around the room, keep the family out until the paint has a chance to dry. Walking in a room raises dust particles which adhere to a freshly painted surface.

Safe working platforms

A ladder with three or four steps is a good choice for painting walls or ceilings. When you are painting high ceilings, a stepladder, with a folding platform, is essential. Be sure that your ladder is sturdy. Don't use a makeshift arrangement of whatever you can unearth or borrow—invest in a new ladder if necessary; it will amply repay you in safety and in efficiency.

Do not go higher than the second step from the top. Also remember that a stepladder is firmly footed only when the spreader is fully opened and locked. Do not try to climb a stepladder that is in any other position; it is likely to slip or topple. When painting near a door, be sure it is either fully opened, or closed and locked. Otherwise, if someone opens the door, down you go.

You can make wall and ceiling painting considerably easier by rigging a raised platform to work from. Such an arrangement will eliminate the necessity to

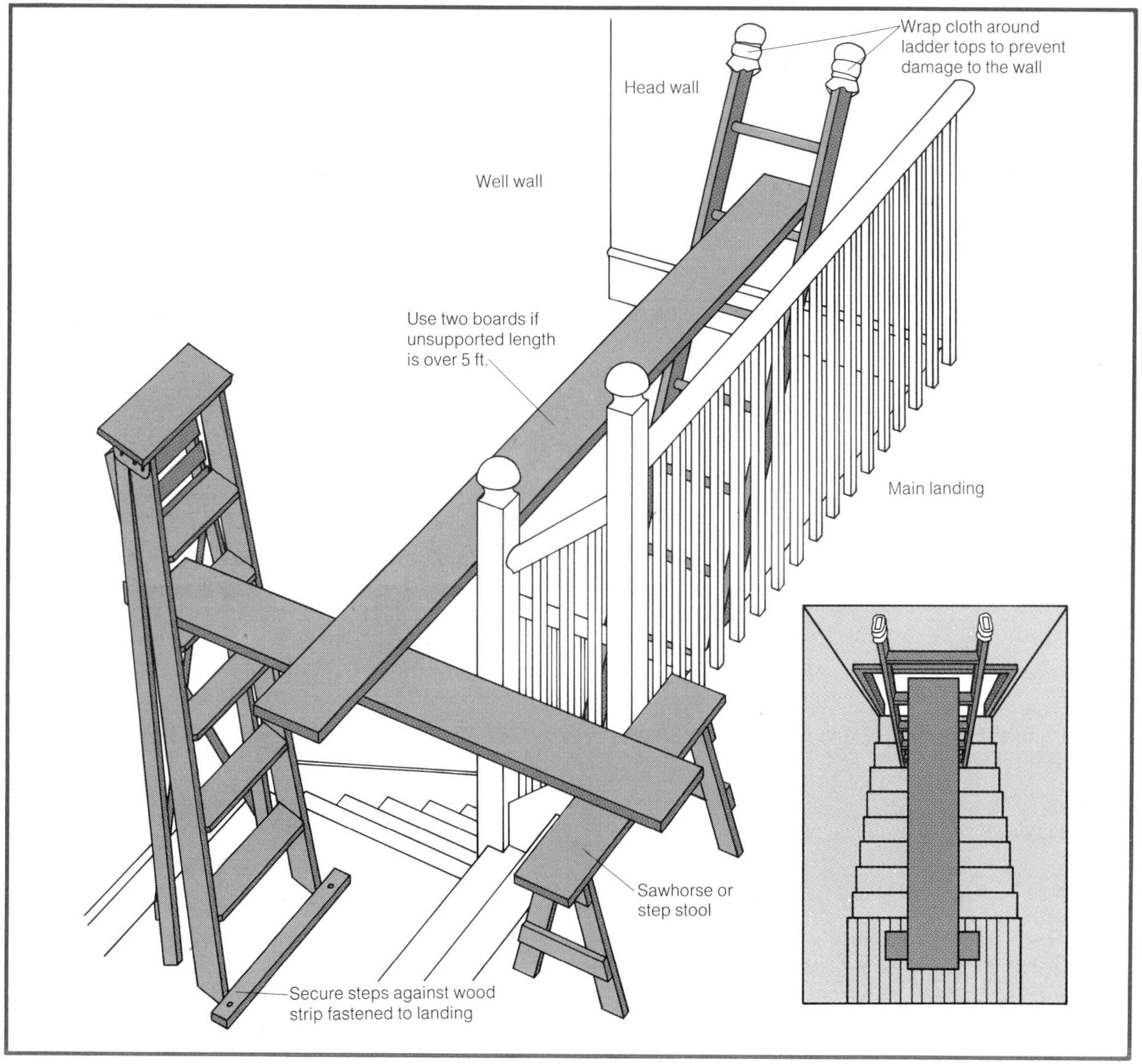

A simple step stool-to-stepladder platform

get up and down constantly to move the stepladder.

For high work—above 8 feet—you will need a platform made of two sturdy stepladders or high sawhorses and a wide scaffold plank; for jobs below 8 feet but above head level, you can work on a scaffold plank laid across two low sawhorses or step stools. In either situation, always place the scaffold plank so that it extends at least a foot beyond the step of the ladder or sawhorse on which it rests.

Scaffold planks (2 x 8 and up to 18 feet long) are sold at lumberyards, and are often available on a rental basis from paint stores. A 10-foot length is generally the most useful. Boards longer than this need support in the center as well as at the ends.

When decorating a stairwell, arrange a scaffolding system with ladders and planks, so that there is easy access to both head wall and well wall (see illustration at left). Make sure that the ladders are perfectly secure. If boards are longer than 5 feet from support to support, place one board on top of another for added strength. Use drop cloths to protect stairs, carpeting, and floors from paint spatters.

When decoration of the well is finished, remove the scaffold board and complete the head wall, working from a ladder placed on the main landing.

Wrap cloth around ladder tops to prevent damage to the wall

Head wall

Well wall

Use two boards if unsupported length is over 5 ft.

Main landing

Sawhorse or step stool

Secure steps against wood strip fastened to landing

Interior painting

Types of paint

So many new paints have been introduced in recent years that it is difficult for nonprofessionals to be sure when and where particular types should be used. For the home decorator, the most significant innovation is water-thinned latex paints.

The common belief that latex means rubber-based is wrong, for latex paint contains no rubber. Latex means here what the dictionary calls it—a whitish, milky emulsion. All latex paints (1) thin with water; (2) dry quickly, usually in about an hour; (3) spread easily; and (4) have little or no "paint" odor. Also the brushes used with them can be cleaned with warm water and soap.

Most manufacturers state on their labels the uses to which their products should be put, and what preparations each requires. Remember, multipurpose paints represent a compromise. A flat finish, even if labeled "washable," cannot be scrubbed the way a high-gloss or semi-gloss enamel can be. Though many paints are labeled flat enamels, this is really a misnomer. They may be washable compared to old-style flats, but you still cannot scrub them repeatedly as you can a semi-gloss or glossy enamel.

Paints are divided into interior and exterior types. The exterior paints are discussed on page 336; interior types and their uses are described here.

For interior work there are three types of paint: Flat for walls and ceilings; semi- or high-gloss enamel for woodwork, furniture, and bathroom or kitchen walls; and deck enamel for floors.

Flat paints come in alkyd and latex types. The once-popular oil-base flats are seldom seen any more. Both latex and alkyd types are quick-drying and free of odor; the latter has more hiding power than you would get from a latex flat. Alkyd paints are thinned with a paint thinner or turpentine.

Flat paints can be used both on walls and ceilings. Enamel finishes are usually used on doors, windows, and other woodwork. In addition to high-gloss types, enamels are also available in a semi-gloss or satin finish, and a duller luster, usually referred to as eggshell (meaning degree of gloss, not color). Enamels will take more scrubbing and abuse than flats. They are available in both alkyd and oil-base types, but latex enamels are available only in semi-gloss.

Deck paints are enamel-type finishes sometimes used on interior floors and steps. The most widely used are varnish-based, which dry to a high gloss.

The most suitable protective coatings for the items listed in the left-hand column are shown in this chart. A solid block means that the product listed directly above it is recommended. For example, for kitchen and bathroom walls, follow the line to the solid blocks, look above them, and you will find the recommended products.

	Semi-gloss—latex	Flat paint—latex	Flat paint—alkyd-type	Semi-gloss—alkyd	Gloss enamel—alkyd	Rubber-base paint (not latex)	Interior varnish	Shellac	Wax (liquid or paste)	Wax (emulsion)	Stain	Wood sealer	Floor varnish	Floor paint or enamel	Aluminum paint	Sealer or undercoat	Metal primer	Cement-base paint	Clear polyurethane	Catalyzed enamel
Dry walls	■ •	■ •	■ •	■ •	■ •			■				■				■				■ •
Plaster walls and ceilings	■ •	■ •	■ •	■ •	■ •	■										■				■ •
Wallboard	■ •	■ •	■ •	■ •	■	■										■				■ •
Wood paneling	■ •		■ •	■ •	■	■	■	■	■		■	■							■	■
Kitchen and bathroom walls	■ •			■ •	■ •	■										■				■
Wood floors						■		■	■	■ •	■ •	■	■ •	■ •					■	■
Concrete floors						■			■ •	■ •	■			■				■	■	■
Vinyl and rubber tile floors									■	■										
Asphalt tile floors										■										
Linoleum								■	■	■			■	■						
Stair treads						■		■			■	■	■	■					■	■
Stair risers			■ •	■ •	■ •	■	■	■			■	■							■	■
Wood trim	■ •		■ •	■ •	■ •	■	■	■	■		■					■			■	■
Steel windows	■ •		■ •	■ •	■ •	■									■		■			■
Aluminum windows	■ •		■ •	■ •	■ •	■									■		■			■
Window sills	■ •				■ •	■	■													■
Steel cabinets			■ •	■ •	■ •	■											■			■
Heating ducts	■ •		■ •	■ •	■ •	■									■		■			■
Radiators and heating pipes	■		■ •	■ •	■ •	■									■		■			■
Old masonry	■	■	■	■	■	■									■	■		■		■
New masonry	■ •	■ •	■ •	■ •	■ •	■										■		■		■ •

■ • Black dot indicates that a primer or sealer may be necessary before the finish coat (unless surface has been previously finished).

How to use color

Color is the least expensive way to beautify your rooms, and of all the means of providing it, paint is by far the most economical.

The more you know about color, the more effective use you can make of it. Get to know colors, and the color wheel, at the right, which is a color spectrum arranged in a circle. Fill in the circles with crayons or water colors in the indicated colors, and you will have a practical working tool.

You will recognize the three **primary** colors, yellow, blue, and red, and the **secondary** hues (formed by pairing the primaries), orange, purple, and green. The others are mixtures of primaries and secondaries, called **tertiaries.** Using tints, tones, and shades of these twelve basic hues, you can work color magic.

By combining the colors on the wheel as shown by the arrows, you will get various harmonious effects. Whether you wish to stay with this conventional harmony or change color "keys" depends on your personal taste. The use of the color wheel to obtain a limited range of predictable harmonious effects assures you of a non-clashing color scheme.

As a general rule, the ceiling has the lightest color in a room, followed by the walls, with the woodwork (especially the baseboards) the darkest color. Kitchens should always be painted in a light, cheerful color. Avoid a "hot" color scheme; the kitchen gets warm enough without outside help. Stick to colors that keep things cool, such as white, light blue, pale yellow, light green, and beige.

Paint styling is the technique of using color to emphasize the good features of a room, a house, or a piece of furniture, and to minimize the unattractive ones. An important facet of paint styling is the creation of optical illusions. Suppose two identical houses are built side by side on adjoining plots. If one is painted in light colors and the other in dark, the light house will seem larger.

The same principle also works indoors. If you paint the walls and ceiling in a light tint, the room will seem more expansive than it would in a dark tone. The "largest" of the colors is yellow, followed by red, then green, blue, and finally black.

This "fool the eye" principle can be applied in other ways to problems inside and outside a home. Just as light colors make a room appear larger, a dark, warm color on the walls will reduce the apparent size of an overly large room.

To widen a very narrow room, put a dark, warm color on each end wall and lighter, receding colors on the side walls. Similarly, you can "bring down" a ceiling that looks too high by painting it a darker color than the walls, or raise a low ceiling by painting it white or a lighter tint than the walls. If a room is perfectly square and uninteresting in shape, you can give it variety and dimension by making a focal point of one wall with bright or warm colors.

What works on ceilings will have the same modifying effect on roofs. A light-colored roof that seems too high for its width can be lowered to scale by the use of dark-colored shingles.

Finally, color can give unity to a house. If too great a variety of building materials has been used in its construction, for example, the use of a single paint color can do much to unite all the materials into a harmonious whole.

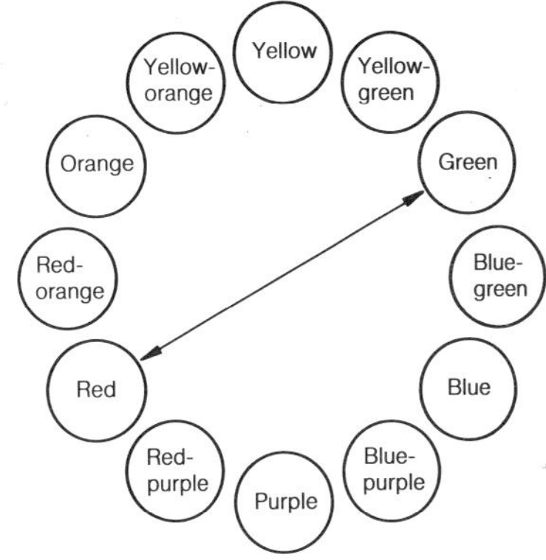

Complementary colors are any two opposite each other on the color wheel. These are familiar contrasts, generally considered harmonious.

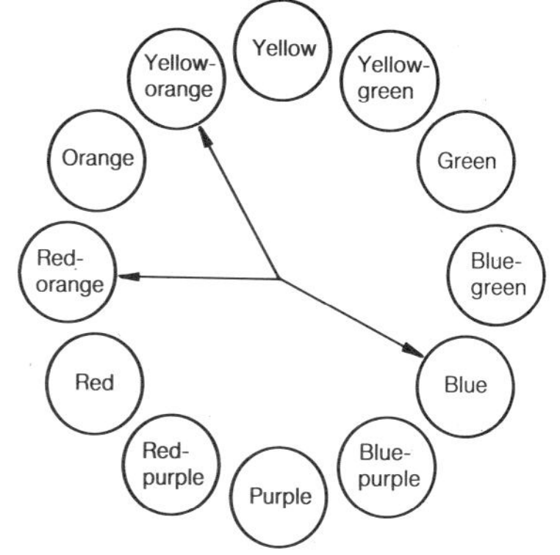

Split complementaries are a foolproof way to choose tri-color schemes. Turn the Y pointer 180° for opposite split complementary colors.

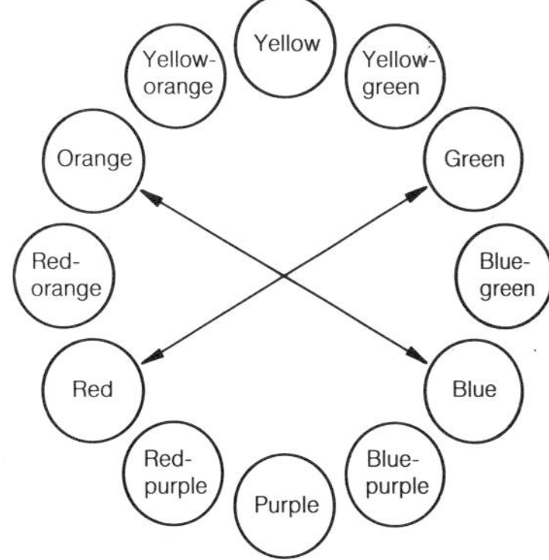

Double complementaries combine two pairs of opposite colors and are a sound basis for selecting harmonious four-way combinations.

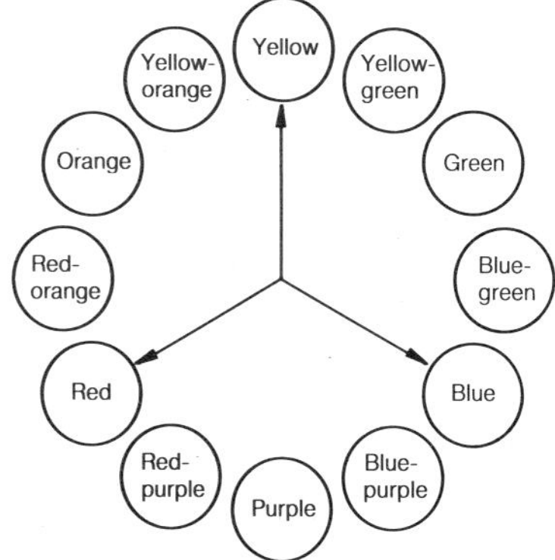

Triad harmony utilizes three equidistant colors on the color wheel, achieves variety by using different tints of principal colors.

Painting ceilings

Using a brush: When applying alkyd paint to a ceiling, work across the width, rather than the length, of the room. This permits beginning the second lap before the first has dried completely. Never try to paint a strip more than 2 feet wide for the same reason. This means moving ladders frequently, but that is better than having the dried edges of the laps mar the job. Latex paints are less apt to show lap marks and are nearly always used on ceilings.

Using a roller: A roller can be used on a ceiling. It is possible to paint a ceiling with a long-handled extension roller while standing on the floor, if the walls will be painted later, as they usually are.

When using latex paint, brush a narrow strip around the entire perimeter of the ceiling. Fill in the center area later with the roller. When using an alkyd paint, work across the narrow dimension of the ceiling. Start in a corner and brush a narrow strip 2 or 3 feet wide against the wall. Then load your roller and roll on a strip of the same width, working from the unpainted area into the still-wet wall-side strip. At the far side of the room, paint the area near the wall with brush or roller. Work backward into the wet edge of the previous strip. Crisscross the strokes to cover the area completely. For a really large ceiling, you can buy or rent a pressure-fed roller which eliminates the need to constantly replenish the roller with paint.

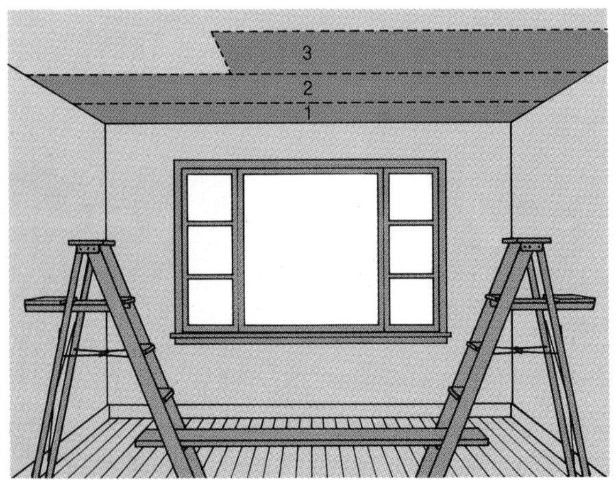

Stepladder platform: Do not work from a single ladder when painting a ceiling. Best to make an arrangement as shown.

When painting a ceiling, use the brush edge-on to cut in with a straight line where the ceiling meets the wall.

To minimize spattering, begin work with a dry brush. Dip bristles into paint—never more than one-third their length.

Lay off—that is, smooth over while the paint is still wet—every 4 ft. or so, working from a wet edge back to the paint.

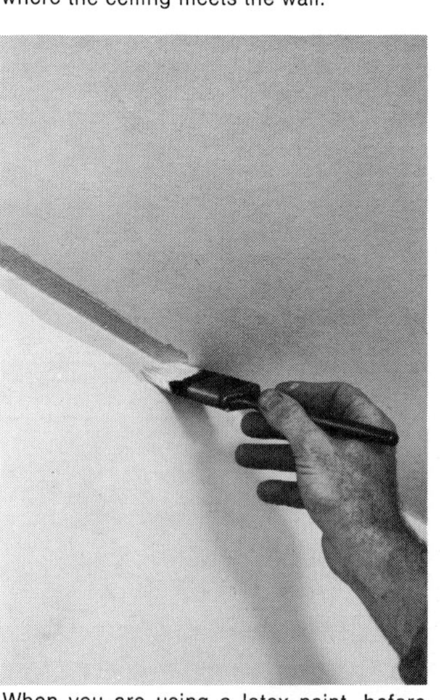

When you are using a latex paint, before starting work with roller, brush a strip of paint around entire perimeter of room.

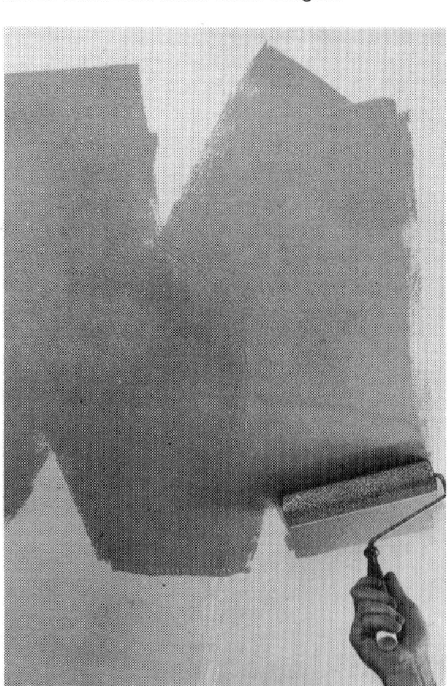

Then cover the ceiling surface with alternating diagonal strokes. To prevent spattering, never let roller spin freely.

Then cross-roll to assure even coverage. It is best to start in a dry area and roll toward one that was just painted.

Painting walls

Using a brush: To eliminate lap marks when applying alkyd-type paints, begin at the top of the wall and paint a panel about 3 feet wide down to the baseboard or floor. Then start at the top and paint another 3-foot panel. This way, you will be starting the second panel before the top part of the first one has had time to dry.

For best results, apply the paint rather liberally to the surface and then spread it, without additional dipping into the paint can, brushing it out thoroughly. Brush marks can be minimized if you avoid painting with a "dry" brush. Keep a rag dampened with water for latex paints, or with turpentine for alkyd paints, to clean up paint spatters.

Using a roller: Before applying paint with a roller, first cut in the edges of the wall with a brush or an edging roller, taking care not to get paint on the ceiling or the adjacent wall.

Make your first stroke upward even if the general direction of the painting will be downward. Follow with a down stroke over the same area and then roll crosswise to assure even coverage. As you progress, always start in a dry area and roll toward one that was just painted, blending in the laps.

Avoid rolling too fast; this causes spatters, as does spinning the roller at the end of the stroke. Always stop the roller before you lift it from the wall. Feather out the final stroke by using lighter pressure.

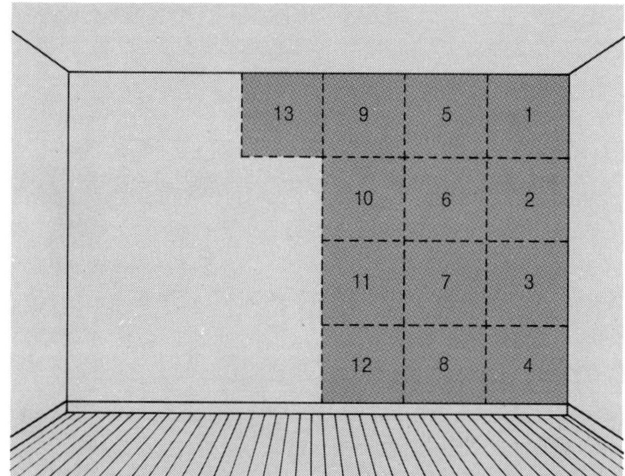

When using gloss or semi-gloss paints, apply with vertical strokes in 2 x 3 ft. sections following the sequence shown.

Apply paint with short strokes, lifting brush at end of each stroke. Do not use uniform, same-direction brush strokes.

Level paint after application with back-and-forth motion. Never put just-dipped brush on bare wall—start at wet area.

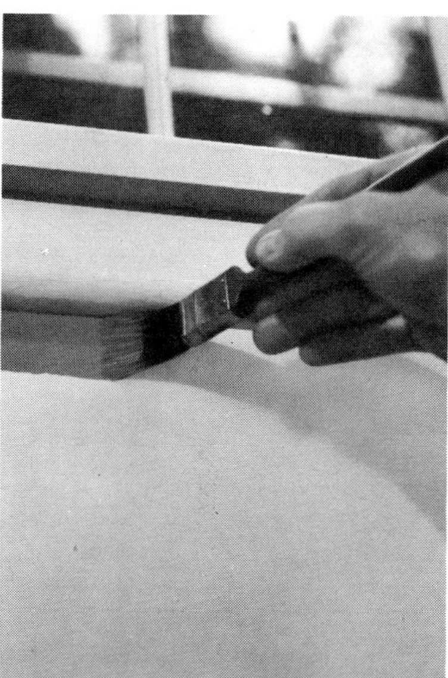

Work from confined area to broad expanses around windows. Work part way across top of window, then part way across bottom.

Making the first stroke in an upward direction, increase the pressure on the roller until all paint is deposited.

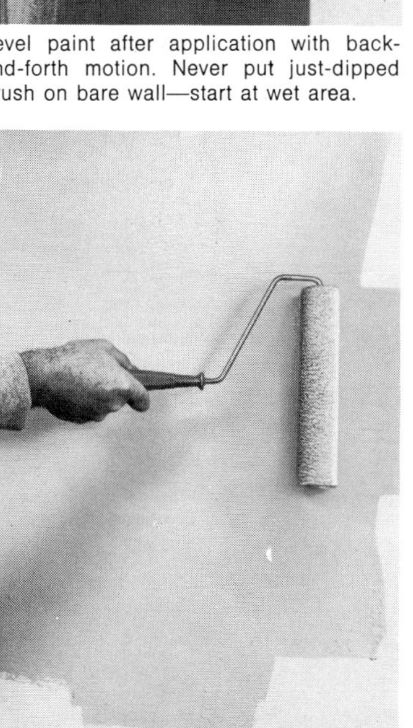

Then smooth out zigzag pattern with horizontal strokes in both directions. Do not follow uniform pattern. Check for skips.

Corners are hard to do with an ordinary roller. Special doughnut-shape edging roller coats both sides of corner at once.

Painting woodwork

Walls are usually given a flat finish, and woodwork and trim finished with a gloss or semi-gloss enamel, which will not show dirt as much as flat paint tends to do. Many people, however, prefer to use flat paint on woodwork as well as walls; others prefer gloss or semi-gloss enamel throughout. This decision is largely a matter of taste. Some enamels require a prime coat before application.

Woodwork and trim should be prepared as previously described (p. 324) and paint applied very much the same as specified for ceiling and walls (p. 328). There is only one problem that sometimes occurs with wood—certain types of wood stains bleed through the paint and cause a discoloration. Before you paint over wood that has been stained, apply the paint to be used to a small area and let it dry for several days to be sure the stain does not bleed through. If there is any bleeding, it means that a component in the paint has dissolved the coloring material in the stain. The solution is to apply two coats of thinned white shellac to the wood before applying the paint.

When applying paint to woodwork, dip the brush into the paint at least one-third of the length of the bristles. When the brush is well filled, remove it and tap the tip lightly against the inside of the can. Hold the brush comfortably near the base of the handle, exerting light pressure with your fingertips. Do not bear down but exert enough pressure to make the bristles flex slightly toward the tip as you begin a brush stroke. Be sure to brush out runs and sags as they occur.

When enameling, be sure to use a cross-brush technique—that is, brush the enamel on in one direction, and then brush across to level it. Use slow brush strokes when you are painting on wood. If you brush too fast, you will get little skips where the enamel literally did not have time to reach into tiny depressions. Slow brushing permits the bristles to force the paint into contact with the surface and insures better coverage with less brushing.

As a rule, the baseboard is painted after the ceiling and walls, window trim next, then doors and door frames. Shelves, built-in cabinet trim, and other trim work are done last.

If a semi-gloss enamel is too glossy it can be mixed half-and-half with a flat enamel of the same brand. Make a test with the flat, the semi-gloss, and the half-and-half to see which finish looks best.

An important part of trim work is painting the radiators. If your radiators have never been painted, be sure that they are thoroughly cleaned of grease and rust. Rust must be removed if you expect the paint to stick. The best prime coat for radiators is a red-lead paint. After this prime coat, the radiators can be painted with any interior paint you choose. Paint only the visible portions, leaving the rest bare metal for greater heating efficiency. Never use aluminum or any metallic paint on a radiator; they reduce heat.

If the radiators were previously painted, and the paint is cracked or peeling, it will be necessary to remove all of it with paint remover or a wire brush before repainting. After using paint remover, wipe off surfaces with turpentine or paint thinner before you apply new paint.

If you have some paint left over, keep it for later touchups. A thin film of paint thinner carefully poured over the surface will prevent skinning for a few weeks. Ultimately the air trapped inside the covered can will cause a skin to form on the top of the paint, but this is easily removed. To provide a seal and minimize skinning, place a sheet of plastic wrap under the lid before replacing it and pound the lid down securely.

Use masking tape or a shield to keep paint from getting on the glass.

A sash and trim brush is the best choice for painting in confined areas.

Paint can lid makes good "palette" for painting trim. Holds ample paint, is easy to carry.

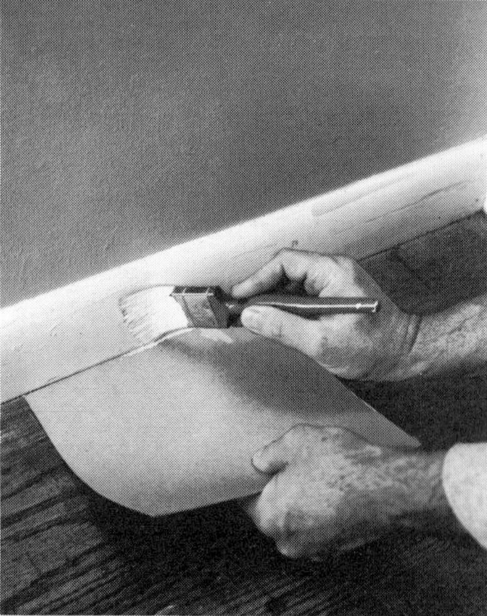

Paint top edge of baseboard first, then floor edge. Protect floor with cardboard shield.

Procedure

Doors: Panel doors must be painted in a strict sequence. Do the whole job in one session; pauses will result in hard-to-remove edges. Paint the panels from each end, toward the middle. When painting flush doors, start at the top and work down in sections. Work quickly so the paint does not harden before the adjoining section is painted.

Windows, like doors, must also be painted in order, governed by their construction. For casements this is the sequence: (1) Muntins (where the glass joins the wood); (2) crossbars; (3) cross rails; (4) meeting sill; (5) frame.

To paint a double-hung window, push the lower sash up and upper sash down so you can get at the meeting rail, then paint in this order: (1) Meeting rail, including the bottom edge; (2) the two uprights as far as you can go on the top sash; (3) bottom edge of the lower sash; (4) soffit; (5) the inside of the outer channels. Then lower both windows and paint (6) the inside channels as far as you can go. When painting the outside of the window, following the same procedure as for the inside, paint (7) the bottom of the inside channels, and (8) a short way up the inside channels. A nail, lightly driven into the bottom of the upper and lower sash, will enable you to move the windows without marring the paint. After drying overnight, move windows to prevent sticking.

7 1 2 8 3 4 11 12 13 9 5 6 10

Paneled door painting sequence

1. Laying on
2. Cross-brushing
3. Laying on
4. Cross-brushing
5. Brushing in
6. Smoothing out
7. Laying on
8. New section

Flush door painting sequence

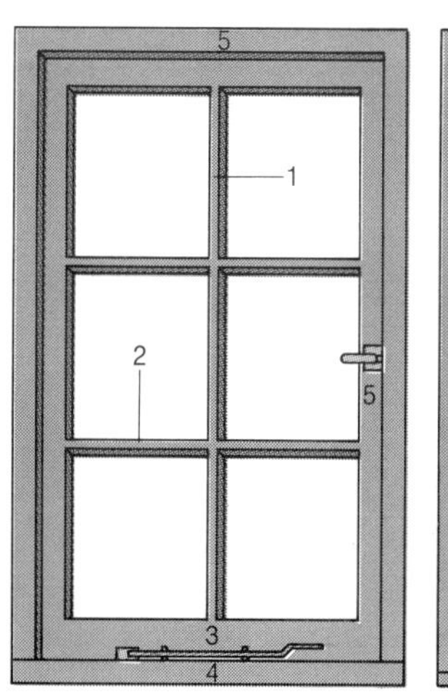

Casement sequence

Double-hung sequence

Interior painting summary

1. Select your color scheme, then determine the type of finishes and the amounts of materials required.
2. Remove all lightweight furniture.
3. Move all heavy furniture to the center of the room.
4. Cover the floor and remaining pieces of furniture with drop cloths.
5. Collect all necessary tools.
6. Set all nails; remove hardware from doors, curtain rods, and any other removable obstructions that are not to be painted.
7. Remove all switch plates and outlet plates from the walls. Cover openings with masking tape.
8. Clean the ceiling of calcimine; or wash flat paint; or remove paper.
9. Sand walls; or wash paint; or remove paper.
10. Use coarse sandpaper to remove hardened paint runs on woodwork, doors, and walls. Finish with fine sandpaper.
11. If the wallpaper is to be painted over, make an advance test to see if any color in the paper bleeds.
12. Remove damaged paint from woodwork and trim; or wash undamaged painted surface with ammonia solution or household cleaner to remove grease.
13. Nail down any squeaking floorboards (p. 109) and sink all nails before next step.
14. Sand the floors, if necessary, or remove the old finish (p.408).
15. Patch plaster walls and ceilings.
16. Fill holes in woodwork and trim.
17. Fill floor cracks as needed.
18. Paint the ceiling.
19. Paint the walls.
20. Paint woodwork and trim.
21. Paint windows.
22. Refinish or clean the floors (p.115).
23. Wash brushes with soap and warm water if used with latex paints; use paint thinner for cleaning paintbrushes used with oil-base or alkyd paints.

Painting concrete

Floors and walls

Several paint types are suitable for concrete walls. Latex paints are the easiest to use because they can be applied to damp walls and cleaned up with water. Also highly regarded are Portland cement paints, swimming pool paints, and reinforced masonry paints. For optimum resistance to moisture, frequent cleaning, or chemical attack, use epoxy paints.

After selecting paint color and type, prepare the surface. In most instances, you will only have to remove dirt and loose or crumbling material with a wire brush. Grease or oil should be scrubbed off with detergent. Be sure to patch all cracks and holes. Before using latex paints, prime any bare metal in the walls with an anticorrosive metal primer.

Portland cement paints are frequent choices because they are long-lasting and keep moisture under low pressure from penetrating the walls. No paint, however, will be a complete moisture barrier. Find and correct moisture problems before painting to avoid dampness from the outside of the wall (p. 184).

Portland cement paints cannot be used over surfaces to which any other type of paint has been applied. Walls must be kept damp while cement paint is curing. Once it has dried, it provides a tough and durable coating that bonds strongly with the walls.

Durability and excellent adhesion are the best features of epoxy paints. These paints are based on resins to which a catalyst is added immediately before application. They harden chemically to a smooth, tile-like surface. Epoxy, polyurethane, and polyester types are all good for walls that are washed often and for floors that take heavy traffic. Application of epoxy paints takes a little extra care. The surface preparations must be made carefully in order for the coating to bond properly to the wall or floor. A filler should be applied before painting if a smooth surface is desired. Before painting, read the manufacturer's directions, and follow them carefully.

For concrete floors you can also use a chlorinated rubber paint. It is made in a wide range of colors and adheres well to a fairly new concrete floor. You can use latex floor paints, which are easier to apply but do not wear as well as epoxy paints or alkyd-type enamels. Regardless of the paint you use, preparation is most important. Floors should always be vacuumed after normal preparations before applying paint. The best way to paint a large basement floor is by sections. Mentally divide the floor into 3-x-3-foot squares. Prepare one section, paint it, and then go on to the next square.

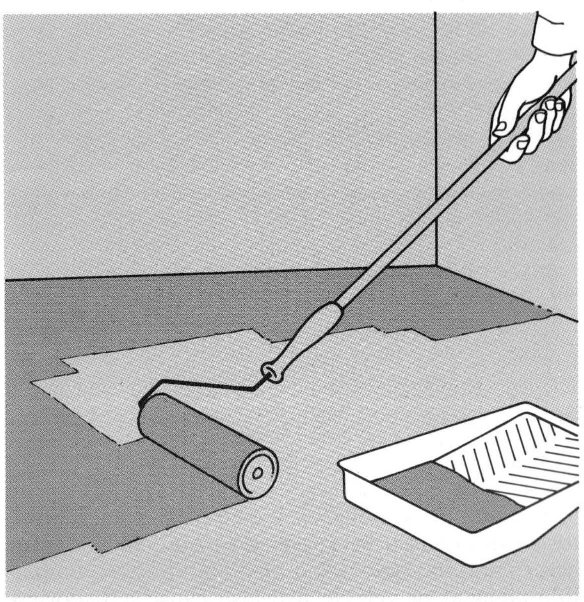

A roller speeds application on flat masonry surfaces such as walls and floors. Paint should be rolled on with light, even strokes in different directions. Do not roll too fast.

Concrete steps and walls

Remove grease and oil from surface by washing with trisodium phosphate (TSP) and hot water. Rinse with clear water; vacuum when dry.

Apply the paint generously and work it well into all cracks and crevices; add a second coat after 24 hours' drying time.

A long-nap roller is necessary when painting a rough-textured masonry surface. It is used in the same way as a standard roller.

Use a stiff-bristled brush to apply paint to rough walls such as cinder block, concrete block, and poured concrete.

Types, causes, cures

An unsatisfactory paint job can be caused by any of the following faults:

1. Improper painting techniques, or failure to follow mixing, priming, and application instructions.
2. Inadequate protection of the exterior walls against moisture.
3. Use of the wrong type of paint for the existing surface conditions.
4. Use of inferior paints.
5. Excessive intervals between repaintings.
6. Too frequent repainting.
7. Wrong paint thinner used.
8. Mixing incompatible paints.
9. Excessive thinning.
10. Painting over grease and rust.

Listed below are the paint defects you are most likely to encounter and the causes of each.

Alligatoring is the term for a pattern of coarse, interlacing lines that look very much like an alligator's skin. Caused by applying second coat of paint before first has dried. Too much oil or an incompatible pigment or vehicle will also cause alligatoring.

Checking is like alligatoring except that cracks are smaller and less noticeable. Causes are the same.

Cracking and scaling: These two conditions are closely related, scaling being actually a later stage of cracking. While checking and alligatoring affect only the surface coat, a crack in the paint film goes right down to the wood and lets moisture get behind the paint, causing it to scale off.

Paint that behaves this way lacks elasticity and will not move with the wood when it expands and contracts. The only way to correct a badly scaling paint finish is to remove all the paint and start over again with a paint that is not so brittle.

Blistering and peeling: This is the result of paint applied to a wood surface that is damp or wet. The presence of water prevents the paint from gripping the surface properly. The solution is to make sure any surface is thoroughly dry before you apply paint. Then after the prime coat has been applied, allow an extra-long drying period to permit the surface behind the paint to dry even more thoroughly.

Wrinkling: This is a problem that comes from putting paint on too thick. When the top surface of a thick coat dries before the paint underneath has dried properly, wrinkles will appear on the surface. The remedy is to use a thinner paint and to brush it out thoroughly when applying. Before applying another coat, sand the surface if you want a smooth finish. In extreme cases, it may be necessary to remove the old paint before proceeding with further painting.

Tackiness and slow drying: These could be traceable to any of a number of factors. There may not have been enough drier in the paint; the solvent may have been of poor quality; a somewhat slow-drying oil may have been used in the paint's manufacture. Or improper application may be to blame—application during damp weather, over paint that had never really dried, or, as in the case of wrinkling, of too thick a coat. Good paints will eventually dry no matter how carelessly they have been applied. A poorly formulated paint, however, may never dry. The only cure, if this is the problem, is to remove all of it.

Running and sagging: These are nearly always caused by too heavy an application of paint. The problem could be your brushing technique. Make a point of brushing the paint out, and you will have less trouble with runs and sags. As for those you already have, they can be removed with sandpaper.

Chalking: This is a defect only when it is excessive. Good outdoor paint is designed to chalk so rain will wash away the dirt, leaving a clean surface. **Important:** Never apply lacquer to a painted surface. The lacquer will act as a sort of paint remover, lifting and wrinkling the paint below. Paint, however, can be safely applied to a lacquered surface. Also, floor enamel applied to a concrete floor will very often lift and flake off because of alkaline salts in the concrete. These can be neutralized by scrubbing the concrete with a solution of muriatic acid and water—1 part acid to 2 parts water. Rinse with clear water, and allow to dry before painting.

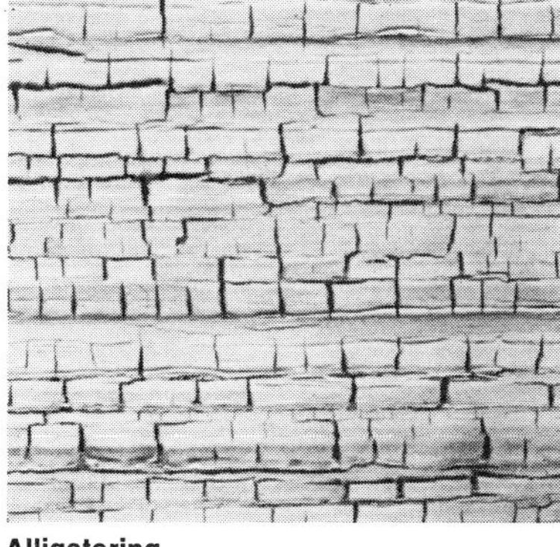
Alligatoring

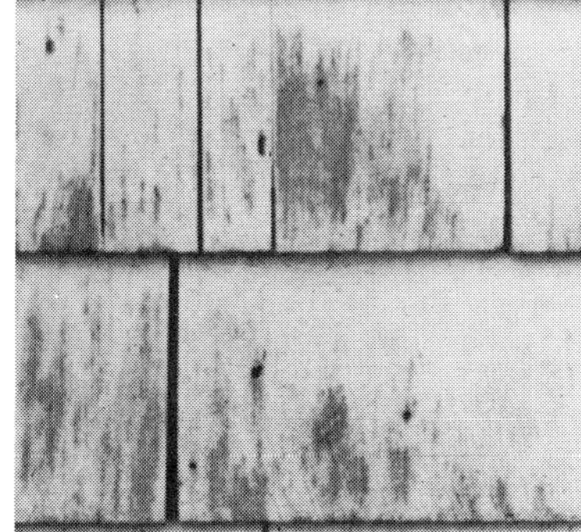
Bleeding

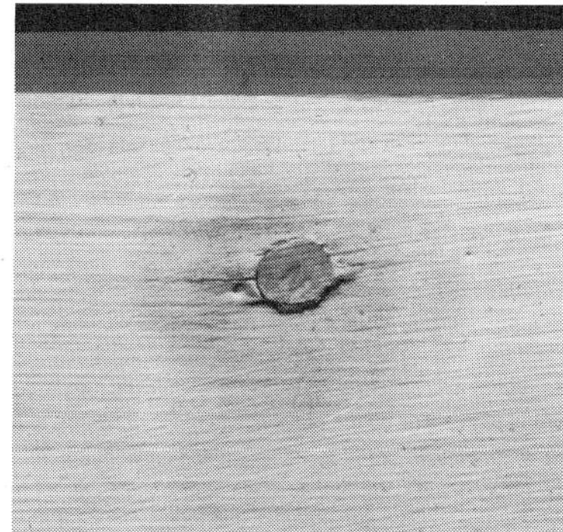
Nail staining

Blistering and peeling

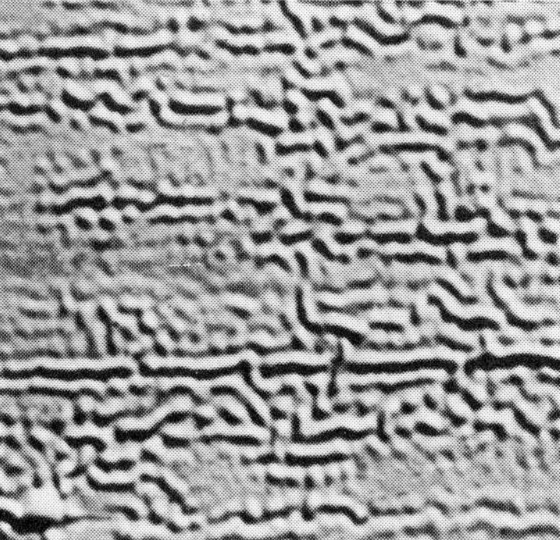
Wrinkling

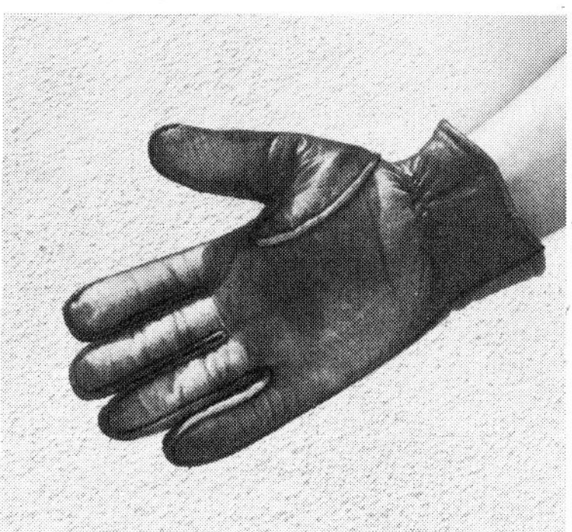
Chalking

Exterior painting

Preparing clapboard siding

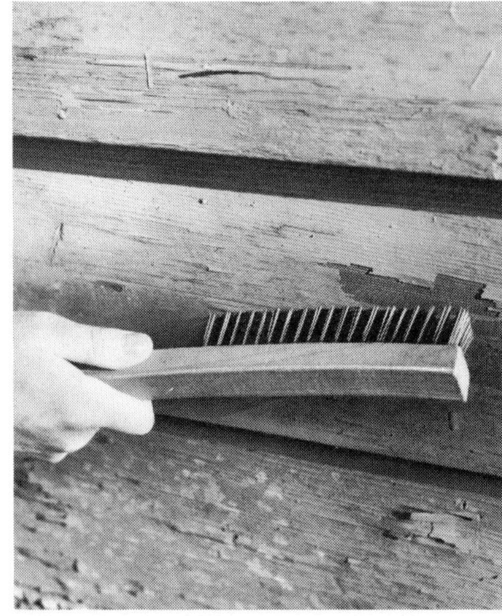

Brushing: Use a stiff wire brush to clean off dirt and scaling paint. A putty knife will come in handy to lift off loose paint. Pay special attention to bottoms of clapboards. Clean exposed cracks and fill with putty.

Scraping: Blistered or peeling paint should be removed down to the bare wood with a paint scraper. Then use sandpaper or steel wool to feather down the edges of the sound paint. Follow with a fine-grade sandpaper.

Removing paint: Where there are very large areas of scaling, it may be necessary to use a blowtorch or chemical paint remover. On vertical surfaces, use a semi-paste paint remover. Apply to a small section at a time.

Priming: Apply a primer coat to all bare wood spots before painting, making certain that the primer used is compatible with the final coat. If you are using a latex paint, do the painting when the wall is in shadow.

Nailing: Loose boards should be nailed in place. Countersink all exposed nailheads, then fill holes with putty to prevent rust stains from discoloring newly painted surfaces.

Sanding: Roughen with coarse sandpaper any areas where the surface looks too glossy. Remember, paint does not adhere well to slick, shiny surfaces. Finish with fine sandpaper.

Puttying: Remove all cracked or loose putty or caulking compound. Then, after priming the surfaces, replace with new putty or caulking, following the technique on page 182

Caulking: Apply caulking compound (p. 182) in joints at doors and windows and around chimney. Lay down a wide bead of caulking. Smooth it with a putty knife before it sets.

Preparation

The condition of the surface to which paint is applied is of great importance to the durability of the painted surface. Wood siding and trim, provided they are properly dried, offer an excellent surface for painting. Structural defects that permit water to penetrate the wood behind the paint will cause blistering and peeling; prevent this by eliminating the source of the moisture before applying paint.

A paint job will be more durable if the surface is free of dust and dirt. New wood should be brushed to remove all dust immediately before applying the primer. All open joints should then be sealed with a caulking compound. Wood siding which contains knots should be shellacked to prevent discoloration of the paint by the resin in the knots.

Nailheads should be checked to make sure that they have been set below the surface and the holes puttied. Nonrusting siding nails are often set flush with the surface of the wood, in which case puttying is unnecessary. All iron or steel must be primed with a rust-inhibitive primer.

If the old paint is merely faded, dirty, and chalking, the only preparation necessary is dusting the surface before painting. If the surface is extremely dry, or very dirty, wash it with a mild detergent or household cleaner solution and rinse thoroughly with clear water. Let the surface dry before painting. Remove rust marks around nailheads with sandpaper or steel wool, then set, prime, and putty.

Remove all loose, flaking, or blistering paint with a wire brush, putty knife, and scraper. Where blistering, cracking, or alligatoring of old paint is extensive, the old film should be removed down to the bare wood, and the edges of the sound paint feathered with sandpaper or steel wool before priming and repainting. Paint new wood with a paint primer before applying the finish coats.

For best results, paint should be applied in clear, dry weather with temperatures above 40 degrees. Wait until the morning dew has evaporated. If siding has been wet by a recent rain, let it dry for several days before painting. With latex paint, you can leave some moisture on the wood. Paint new, dry woodwork as soon as possible after installation.

A three-coat job is the best for new work—one coat of primer and two finish coats. Do not, however, make the serious error of assuming that if three coats are desirable, more coats are bound to be even better. One coat is often sufficient when repainting a surface in good condition. When the old paint is very thin or a long time has elapsed since the last painting, two coats are recommended.

House paint normally covers about 500 square feet of surface per American gallon, 625 square feet per imperial gallon. With these estimates and the dimensions of the house, it is easy to determine the approximate number of gallons of paint required by the following procedure:

1. Average height of house = distance from foundation to eaves for flat-roof types; add 2 feet to this for pitched roofs.

2. Average height x distance around foundation = surface area in square feet.

3. $\frac{\text{Surface area}}{500}$ = number of gallons of paint (or primer) required for each coat.

There is no need to calculate trim paint. The average house—six to eight rooms—requires a gallon.

Preparation also means having on hand all other paraphernalia required for painting (p. 316)—brushes, thinners, scrapers, sandpaper, ladders, and drop cloths—and some old clothes. It is best to wear hard-soled shoes with heels, rather than sneakers. You won't feel the ladder's rungs through hard soles.

Now that you are all set, where do you start? Set up the ladder and start at the highest point of the house. Don't lean out from the ladder—reach out a comfortable, normal distance, keeping your hips between the rails. Keep one hand on the ladder and with the other hold the brush. Make an S hook out of a wire coat hanger from which to suspend the can of paint. Suspend the can so that it hangs on the outside of the ladder—on the right if you are right-handed. This way you will avoid having to reach the brush between the rungs when the time comes to refill. If the top of the house has trim that requires painting, you may want to paint the trim at the same time to avoid setting up the ladder twice in the same spot. The choice is yours. If you do want to follow this technique, you will need a separate, smaller brush for the trim paint. Keep a rag dampened with paint thinner on hand to wipe off paint spatters as soon as they happen. Make sure you have a drop cloth below the area in which you are painting so paint will not drop on shrubbery or plants.

When painting the trim, take care to use trim paint or outdoor enamel. The paint used for the main part of the house should never be used to paint the trim.

If part of your paint job includes porch steps, try this technique: Paint alternate steps, and when these are dry, paint the skipped steps. This way you will not be deprived of the use of the stairs while the paint is drying. Another technique is to paint just the right half of the treads and risers, using the left side for traffic while the right side dries.

Outdoor railings around steps should be painted last of all. Generally a black enamel is used. Chip away all loose paint, sand the surface, apply a metal primer, and then paint. Pay special attention to the underside of railings. This is the place professional painters too often overlook, and it is the place where rusting starts. A wire brush will remove the old rust. You can check the thoroughness of your work by holding a hand mirror under the railing.

Points to check before starting

1. Downspouts and gutters should be checked and necessary repairs made (p. 170). If they have defects that are not corrected, overflowing water will cause rapid deterioration of the paint job.
2. Caulking and flashing should be in good repair at windows, door frames, and other structural joints (pp. 178 and 182).
3. Window sash should be reputtied (p.123) if the old putty is crumbling or missing. First remove the old putty and paint the muntins, then apply new putty and paint over it.
4. Loose boards should be nailed in place.
5. Cracks or nail holes in the wood should be filled with wood putty. Rough surfaces should be sanded.
6. Check for loose, flaking, or blistering paint and use a wire brush, putty knife, and scraper to remove it. If such conditions are extensive, the old paint in the affected areas should be taken off down to the bare wood, and the edges of the sound paint sanded smooth before finishing.
7. Protect iron or steel with a coat of rust-inhibitive primer.
8. Be sure that all surfaces to be painted are clean and thoroughly dry.

Exterior painting

Choosing the right paint

Different surfaces require different paints, so the type you choose depends on the surface to be painted. For wood siding, use a conventional oil-base paint, an alkyd-base paint, or latex paint. Shingle stain is recommended for shingles and shakes. Use an exterior latex paint for asphalt siding; asphalt will not bleed through latex. Paints for masonry houses must be resistant to the alkali present in concrete and mortar; exterior latex paints, solvent-thinned masonry paints, colorless silicone-base water repellents, and Portland cement paints (over unpainted concrete only) are recommended.

Trim paints are glossy, enamel-like finishes for windows, doors, and other exterior trim. They have a varnish or alkyd resin base, and dry to a hard, dense finish. Deck paints are enamel-type finishes used on porch floors, steps, patios, and terraces. The most widely sold varieties are varnish-based, which dry to a hard gloss. For concrete surfaces, latex and chlorinated rubber-base paints are suitable.

Latex paints are easy to apply, and the surface to which they are to be applied need not be absolutely dry. Their quick-drying qualities keep down dirt and bug collection during drying and make it possible to apply a second coat within an hour or two. They give a good-looking, long-lasting finish and, since latex paints are generally permeable to moisture, are less likely than oil-base paints to blister.

Many of the new house paints are designed to be self-cleaning; they chalk gradually and rain washes away the outer layer to which dirt adheres, keeping the paint fresh and bright. If there is masonry or a darker color below upper portions of your home, chalking paints will stain the lower areas. In this case, use non-chalking paint for the upper surfaces.

Location is another factor you must consider in choosing the proper paint. If your home is in an area that is subject to fumes from nearby industrial plants, a paint with a fume-resisting formula is advisable and available. These paints will hold to a minimum the discoloration caused by smoke and fumes. In an area where atmospheric conditions might cause mildew, a paint with a mildew-resistant additive should be used; this will constitute an effective barrier against mildew. Additives must, of course, be compatible with the ingredients of a particular paint. Your paint dealer can assist you in matching additives to particular brands.

Use this chart to determine the best protective coating for any of the outdoor, around-the-house items listed in the left-hand column. For example, for shutters and other trim, follow the line to the solid blocks, and look above them, for recommended products.

	Exterior masonry paint—latex	House paint—latex	House paint—oil-base	Transparent sealer	Cement-base paint	Exterior clear finish	Aluminum paint—exterior	Wood stain	Roof coating	Roof cement	Asphalt emulsion	Trim paint	Awning paint	Spar varnish	Porch-and-deck enamel	Primer or undercoat	Metal primer	Latex types	Water-repellent preservatives
Wood siding		■	■ •				■									■		■ •	
Brick	■	■	■ •	■	■		■									■		■	
Concrete block	■ •	■	■ •	■	■		■									■		■	
Asbestos cement	■	■	■ •													■		■	
Stucco	■	■	■ •	■	■		■									■		■	
Natural wood siding and trim						■		■						■					
Metal siding		■	■ •				■ •					■ •					■	■ •	
Wood frame windows		■ •	■ •				■					■ •				■		■ •	
Steel windows		■ •	■ •				■ •					■ •					■	■ •	
Aluminum windows		■ •	■				■					■ •					■	■ •	
Shutters and other trim		■ •	■ •									■ •				■		■ •	
Canvas awnings													■						
Wood shingle roof								■											■
Metal roof		■ •	■ •														■	■ •	
Coal tar-felt roof									■	■	■								
Wood porch floor															■				
Concrete porch floor															■			■	
Copper surfaces														■					
Galvanized surfaces		■ •	■ •				■ •					■ •		■			■	■ •	
Iron surfaces		■ •	■ •				■ •					■ •					■	■ •	

■ • Black dot indicates that a primer or sealer may be necessary before the finish coat (unless surface has been previously finished).

Order of working

When painting exteriors, start with the main part of the house—shingles, siding, and other large surfaces. The trim (windows, doors, cornices, etc.) comes next. Then paint decks, porches, and patios. Do storm windows, screens, and shutters last, or save them for a rainy day's work inside the garage.

Start at the top of the house, working all the way across in horizontal stretches to the bottom. That is, start with the gables and work down to the eave lines. Paint all dormers before painting the lower sections. Use a clean drop cloth to protect the roofing beneath you from spatters and drips. Check carefully for skips—missed areas—before coming down the ladder; you will save a lot of steps.

Remember that exterior painting is a fair-weather job; plan to do it in the spring or fall when the weather is fairly settled. Another reason for choosing these seasons is that nearby leaf-bearing shrubbery will be bare. Many painting failures, as previously noted, can be traced to a surface that was either damp or exposed to strong sunlight while being painted. If you must paint in hot weather, paint "behind the sun"; that is, start working in the morning on a portion of the house that the sun has just left and follow the sun around as the day progresses. Then the oils in the paint won't be drawn to the surface by the sun's heat.

Priming: New wood always requires a coat of the primer recommended by the manufacturer of the finish paint coat. This is also a prerequisite where the old paint is badly weathered or where an oil-base paint is to be used. Otherwise it is only necessary to prime any bare spots and follow with a single coat of quality house paint.

After priming and before applying the finish coat, replace window sash putty that was removed during the preparatory stage and fill all cracks and nail holes with putty. Where necessary, caulk joints around chimney, doors, and window frames. Do this after the wood surfaces have been primed; caulking adheres better to a primed surface. Most caulking compounds will take paint without bleeding.

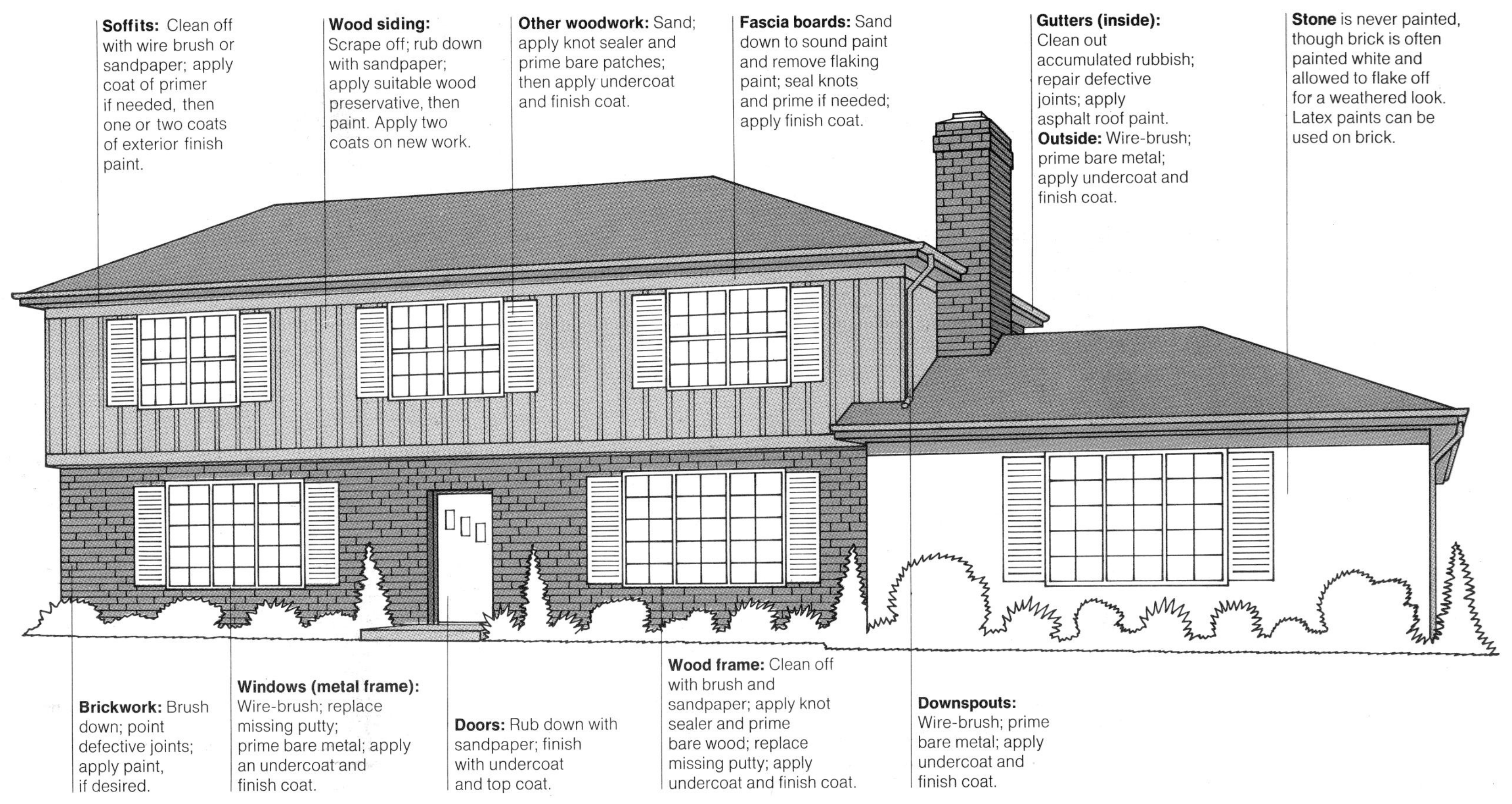

Application techniques

Make sure the paint is thoroughly mixed, even if your dealer has mixed it mechanically. Pour some into a separate can. Stir the paint that is left with a wooden stick or paddle until all pigment is mixed. Pour the paint in the separate can back into the original container and stir until the mixture is uniform. As final "insurance," pour the paint back and forth a few times from one can to the other.

Work out of one can, which should be about half full. To apply the paint, immerse the paint brush about one-third to one-half its bristle length into the paint. Tap the brush gently on both sides of the paint can before lifting it out. This eliminates excess paint that would run down the handle.

On lap siding, paint underneath the projections first, making sure they are completely covered (skips can be easily seen from the ground). Run the brush tip along these projections, about five boards at a time. Check for runs that may have leaked down the surface of the siding directly under the projections.

Next paint the surface of the siding, spreading the paint out and working it into the wood with long, back-and-forth strokes. If the wood is rough, shorter, more forceful, diagonal strokes may be necessary. Finish strokes, however, must always be horizontal on a horizontal surface. To cover nail holes, you may have to slap the brush smartly against the hole, wiping away excess paint with the next stroke.

Once a course across the siding is started, it should be finished. A prolonged interruption will result in a lap mark when painting is resumed. The exception is when using latex paint, which is much less apt to show a lap mark. It is still the best policy, however, to continue on the course till the end has been reached, if for no other reason than to develop good professional habits.

When painting the exterior of doors and windows, follow the same sequence as that given on page 331. The only exception is casement windows; on these you paint the top, side, and bottom edges first, finishing with the mullions, rails, frames, casing, and sills. A metal shield can be used to keep paint off the glass. If you should get paint on the glass, remove it at once with a cloth dampened in the proper paint solvent. Should you miss a few spots, no harm is done—they can easily be scraped off with a razor blade after the paint has dried. Incidentally, if the door swings out, paint the lock edge with exterior paint; if it swings in, paint the hinged edge.

A roller may be used to apply paint to brick, concrete, cinder block, or stucco. It may also be used to paint porches, steps, and patios. When using a roller, paint an edge first with a brush, then use the roller. Be sure to keep the overlap with the edge as narrow as possible; roller texture is noticeably different from brush marks. Roll the paint on with light, even strokes in different directions.

If your front door has a natural wood look, then it has been protected with spar varnish. This is a special high-grade varnish made for outdoor use. To refinish such a door, sand it lightly with fine sandpaper, wipe off the dust with a cloth slightly dampened with paint thinner, and apply the varnish with long, flowing brush strokes.

When painting siding, paint the underside of the board first.

Apply paint in short strokes, across siding, or up and down if it is vertical.

Then spread the paint out with smooth, even strokes to complete section.

Remember to paint unseen surfaces such as door tops and window frames.

Paint alternate steps so that you can use the steps while the paint dries.

Finish inside of gutters with asphalt, outside with house paint.

Refinishing shingles and shakes

If your shingles are already painted, you have no choice but to paint them again. If they are only stained, you can refinish them with a stain or a preservative. A stain differs from paint in amount of pigment. Paint is opaque and hides the wood beneath it; stain has enough pigment to color the wood but not to hide its grain. A preservative is clear.

Refinishing of shingles and shakes follows the same procedure as for any wood surface. Remove all loose material. If mildew is present, treat it with a commercial mildew remover.

Most cedar shingle and handsplit shake roofs are left untreated and give long and satisfactory service. If you want to undertake color treatment of a cedar roof, use a light-bodied stain. When special circumstances make a preservative treatment advisable, use a 5 or 10 percent pentachlorophenol solution, or a solution of phenyl-mercuroleate. These chemicals are highly toxic to wood-attacking bacteria. In applying them, avoid contact with the solutions, and protect nearby lawns and shrubs.

Shingled sidings can also be painted. However, it is best to check for bleeding. Some stains, in time, will penetrate the paint and cause discoloration. Paint a few shingles in an inconspicuous place and wait a few weeks. If bleeding occurs, stick to staining; if it doesn't, it's safe to paint.

Shingle stains are easily applied with a roller or brush. To assure uniform color, stir stain periodically during application.

Foam-and-pile brush pads make shingle staining considerably easier. When using a pad, move it in the direction of the grain.

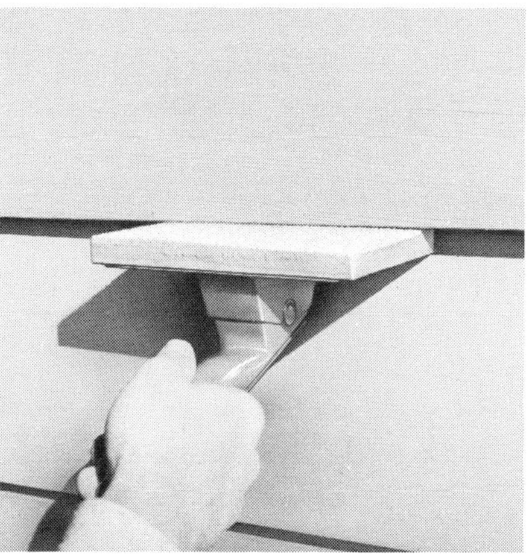

Brush pads are also handy for painting clapboard. Load the pad with paint, then apply it first to the underedges of the boards.

To apply the paint on a horizontal surface, push the applicator slowly over the board. Overlap as needed if pad is narrower than board.

Ladder safety

To paint in high places, you need an extension ladder, but use it with care. Before climbing, make sure the ladder is firmly footed. Stand on the bottom rung to press feet well into ground. On a smooth surface, use safety treads. If the ground is muddy, it is best to rest the ladder feet on a wide plank. Always climb facing the ladder and never go higher than the third rung from the top. Do not lean out; reach a comfortable distance to the right or left, keeping both feet solidly on the ladder. If you need both hands free, "lock" yourself to the ladder by slipping one leg over the rung and holding the rung below with the heel of your shoe. At high levels, it is more convenient to paint above the ladder; you can then reach both ways. Never place a ladder against a window sash, or in front of an unlocked door.

To raise a ladder without help, brace one end against the house and "walk" it —hand over hand—into position.

The bottom of a ladder can be secured firmly by tying it to a stake driven well into the ground.

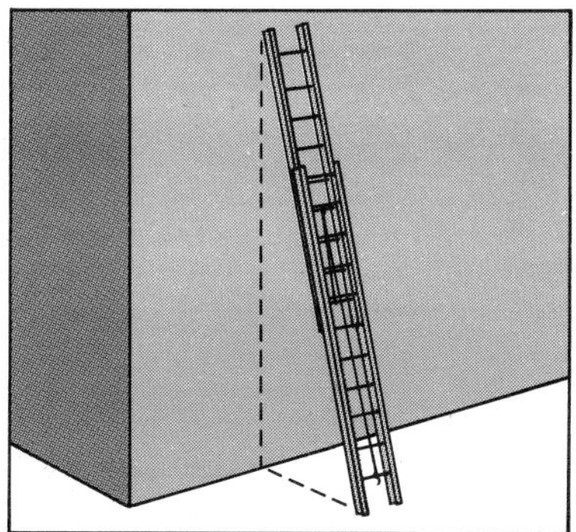

Position the ladder so that it is about one-fourth of its height from the wall. Make sure the rope is not frayed.

Wallpapering

What you need for the job

To hang wallpaper, you need the following items:
Smoothing brush for smoothing the paper on the wall. Good brushes have firm yet soft bristles which will not scratch the paper.
Plumb line and chalk. A length of string with some kind of weight on one end is fine. Use colored chalk to coat the string.
Shears for cutting and trimming the paper.
Seam roller for pressing seams.
Sponge and bowl for wiping down strips.
Wheel knife or trimming knife for trimming at baseboards and around windows.
Wallpaper paste for attaching paper to walls.
Wall size for preparing walls before papering.
Paste bucket and brush for applying wall size and wallpaper paste. Tie a string across the top of the bucket to rest the brush on when it is not in use.
Yardstick for measuring strips.
Patching plaster and wall scraper for repairing cracks in walls and ceiling.
Sandpaper for sanding patched wall areas.
Straightedge as guide for trimming the selvage.
Stepladder to reach ceiling and other high areas.
Soft rags for cleaning and removing excess paste.
Paste table. If you do not buy or rent a professional folding paste table, a kitchen table or two card tables side by side will work. You can also use a piece of plywood set on a pair of sawhorses. Cover the surface with brown paper. Do not use newspapers—the ink will rub off and soil your work.

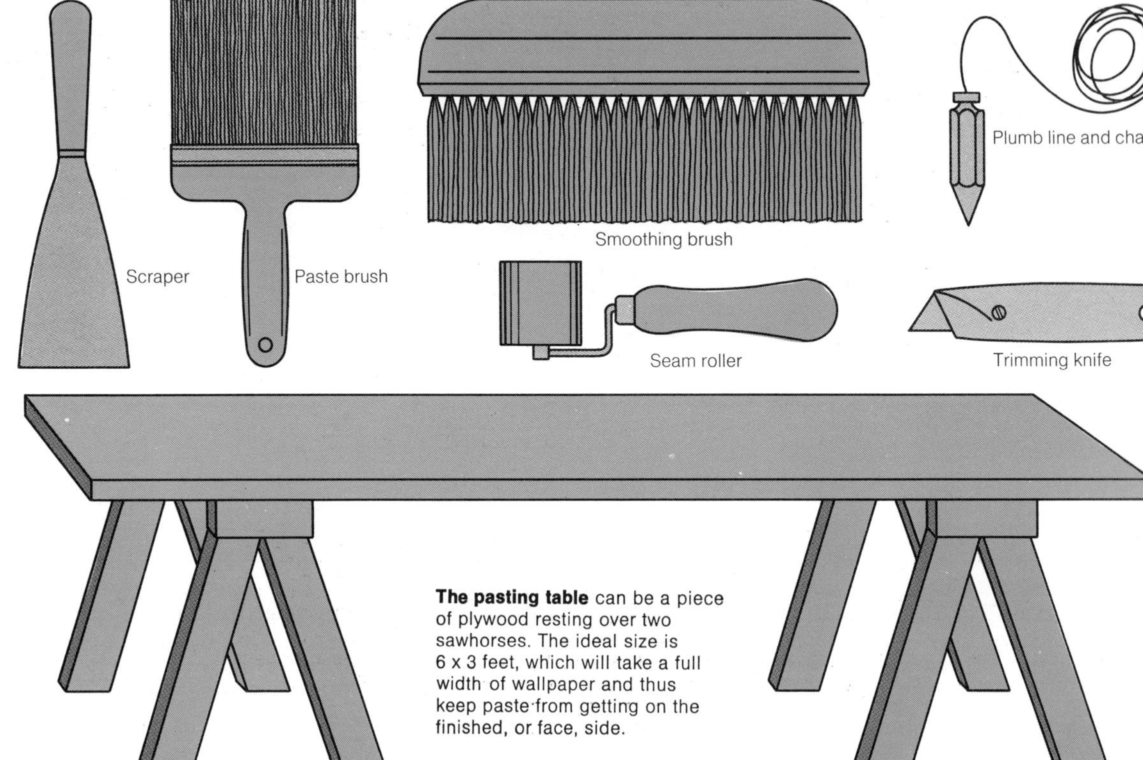

The pasting table can be a piece of plywood resting over two sawhorses. The ideal size is 6 x 3 feet, which will take a full width of wallpaper and thus keep paste from getting on the finished, or face, side.

Pre-pasted wallpaper

Several types of wallpaper and wall coverings come pre-pasted. Most of these also come pre-trimmed so you don't have to cut the selvages as each strip is hung. If the paper is not pre-trimmed, it must be cut and matched the same as unpasted paper (p. 343).

To ready the wall covering for hanging, immerse it in a tray of water for the time specified by the manufacturer, then lift it out onto the wall. Most trays sold with pre-pasted wallpapers are folded to shape from pre-scored, heavily waxed cardboard. A bathtub or kitchen sink will also work. Hanging techniques for pre-pasted coverings are the same as for regular unpasted papers. Smooth the paper on the wall with a brush. Pay particular attention to seams to be sure they adhere firmly.

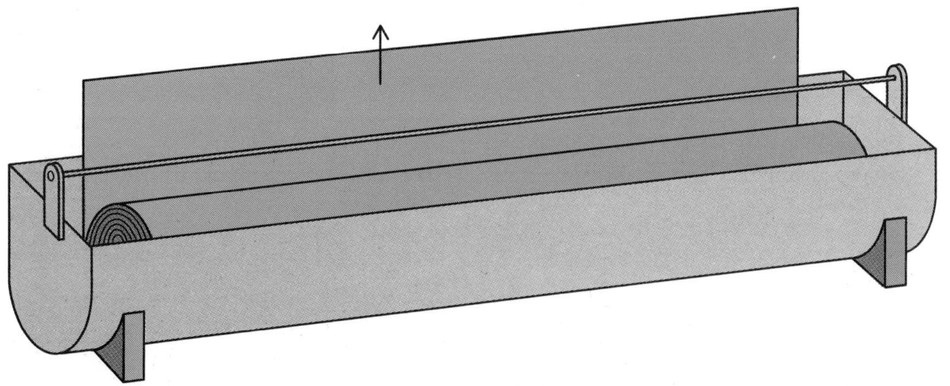

Water tray for immersing pre-pasted wallpaper

Types of modern wallpapers

You can buy wallpapers today that are washable, pre-pasted, scuff-resistant, pre-trimmed, and even strippable—a feature that allows easy removal of the paper should you decide to change it at a later date.

Many new "wallpapers" are not made of paper. They are made of vinyl, metallic foil, burlap, fabric, cork, and even wood. In fact, so many modern wall products are paperless that most manufacturers now refer to their products as wall covering rather than wallpaper. Vinyl-faced wall coverings (*Wall-tex, Fashon, Satinesque*) are the most popular. Their surface of vinyl and printing with vinyl inks make them washable, resistant to fading, and virtually impervious to household stains. Their backing may be of cloth or paper. Although cloth backing is stronger, it is somewhat more expensive.

Some vinyl wall coverings are colored and textured to resemble wood paneling, handwoven grass cloth, burlap, and other high-style decorator materials. For bathroom or powder room you can get wall coverings with a metallic or velour face that will withstand moist conditions.

Most vinyl wall coverings, like wallpaper, come in rolls that are 27 inches wide. However, heavier and better grade vinyl wall coverings are available in 54-inch widths. These are more difficult to handle and generally require an assistant to help with application. Their chief advantage is that fewer seams are needed—and visible. Another advantage with vinyl wall coverings is that they are much easier to remove than paper at redecorating time. They can be pulled off the wall without soaking, scraping, or steaming. Each sheet will come off in a single piece—just grasp a corner and pull. A second important advantage of the vinyls, especially the heavy-duty 54-inch-wide materials, is the way they hide cracks in the walls and render invisible any crack that may develop later.

When selecting wall coverings, remember that the pattern of a wallpaper or other wall covering can be used to alter the appearance of a room. For example, a room with a low ceiling can be made to appear higher by using a wallpaper with strong vertical pattern. A paper that has a horizontal pattern can be used to make a narrow room appear wider. Light colors make rooms appear larger; dark colors make walls appear closer or a room seem smaller.

Selecting adhesives: Many vinyl wall coverings (as well as conventional wallpapers) are available in pre-pasted form.

Lightweight vinyl wall coverings can be hung with ordinary wallpaper paste, but it is best to use adhesives designed especially for vinyl—essential when hanging the heavier grade vinyl wall coverings. These special adhesives are stronger and more resistant to mildew.

How many rolls? In calculating how much wallpaper or wall covering will be required, remember that a roll is a standard unit of measure in the wall covering industry. Whether the material comes in single, double, or triple rolls, each "roll" contains approximately 36 square feet; a double roll has 72 square feet, a triple roll 108. In hanging the material, there will always be some waste because of trimming, matching, and cutting strips to size; so figure on getting only about 30 square feet of material out of each roll.

To determine the number of rolls needed for a given room, measure the room's perimeter—its overall length and width (ignore windows and doors at this time). For example, a 10 x 12-foot room would have a perimeter of 44 feet. To get the square feet of wall space, multiply perimeter by height. If the walls are 8 feet high, the room in the example has 352 square feet of wall space—ignoring windows and doors. Dividing this by 30—the approximate number of usable square feet in a roll—it would take roughly 12 rolls to cover this room.

From this, deduct one roll for every two average-size openings (windows, doors, fireplaces, etc.). Supposing the room in the example had a total of four such openings, you would deduct two rolls and end up with a total of 10 rolls needed for the job. The table at the right will help you calculate the number of rolls needed for most average-size rooms.

Borders: When papering a room, you may want to add a border along the top of the wall for decoration. Borders are sold by the linear yard, not by the roll. They come in various widths for application between the ceiling and the wall. To determine how much border material you need, add the distance around the room in feet and divide by three to get the number of yards required .

Ceilings: To estimate the amount of paper needed to cover a ceiling, multiply its width by length (in feet) and divide by 30 to get the number of single rolls required.

ROOM ESTIMATING CHART

Distance around room in feet	Single rolls for wall areas Height of ceiling 8 feet	9 feet	10 feet	Number yards for borders	Single rolls for ceilings
28	8	8	10	11	2
30	8	8	10	11	2
32	8	10	10	12	2
34	10	10	12	13	4
36	10	10	12	13	4
38	10	12	12	14	4
40	10	12	12	15	4
42	12	12	14	15	4
44	12	12	14	16	4
46	12	14	14	17	6
48	14	14	16	17	6
50	14	14	16	18	6
52	14	14	16	19	6
54	14	16	18	19	6
56	14	16	18	20	8
58	16	16	18	21	8
60	16	18	20	21	8
62	16	18	20	22	8
64	16	18	20	23	8
66	18	20	20	23	10
68	18	20	22	24	10
70	18	20	22	25	10
72	18	20	22	25	12
74	20	22	22	26	12
76	20	22	24	27	12
78	20	22	24	27	14
80	20	22	26	28	14
82	22	24	26	29	14
84	22	24	26	30	16
86	22	24	26	30	16
88	24	26	28	31	16
90	24	26	28	32	18

This table is based on a single roll covering 30 square feet of wall area. Deduct 1 single roll for every 2 doors or windows of average size.

Preparing walls for papering

You can paper over old wallpaper, provided it still adheres tightly. If it is loose in spots, remove the loose parts and sand torn edges. If a large area is loose or there are more than two layers, it should all be removed. Never hang a vinyl wall covering over old paper; it will pull the paper off when it dries.

Old wallpaper can most easily be removed with steaming equipment, which you can usually rent locally. Soaking with a sponged-on solution of water and removal concentrate also works, but it takes longer. Remove loosened covering with a scraper.

Before new plaster walls are papered, they must be thoroughly cured, then coated with a commercial wall sizing available at wallpaper stores. Treat "hot spots" (recognizable by their dull appearance) as the package instructions specify. Other unpapered walls should be treated as described on page 322, then prepared with a single coat of sizing.

You can strip off old paper with a wallpaper steamer, or soak it off with a mixture of water and special wallpaper remover.

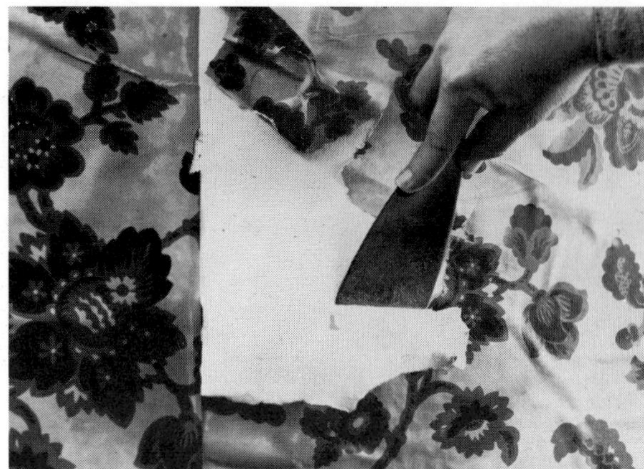

When the paper has soaked long enough to soften and shred, scrape it off with a putty knife. Take care not to gouge wall.

Planning the work

The usual place to put the first strip of wallpaper is to the left or right of a doorway, next to a window, or at the end of a wall, working toward the longest unbroken wall area. With a large or very definite design, however, it is usually desirable to create a center of interest over a fireplace or directly above a sofa. In such cases, make the center of this area the starting point.

When cutting the strips of wall covering, make the first piece from 4 to 6 inches longer than the height of the room; hold the cut piece up to the wall to assure that it is the proper length and will give you a pleasing pattern placement. Then lay the cut piece, pattern side up, on the pasting table. Cut a second piece to match the pattern and length of the first, and then hold it up to the wall to check the length and effect again. Continue until you have cut enough pieces to cover the entire wall.

There are two ways of joining the seams in hanging wallpaper, butt and overlap. The butt method, in which the edges fit tightly up against each other with no overlap, is the one preferred by professionals. If the paper you buy is not pretrimmed, the selvage—the undecorated border—must be cut off both edges of the roll. Most of the wallpaper sold today is pretrimmed by the manufacturer.

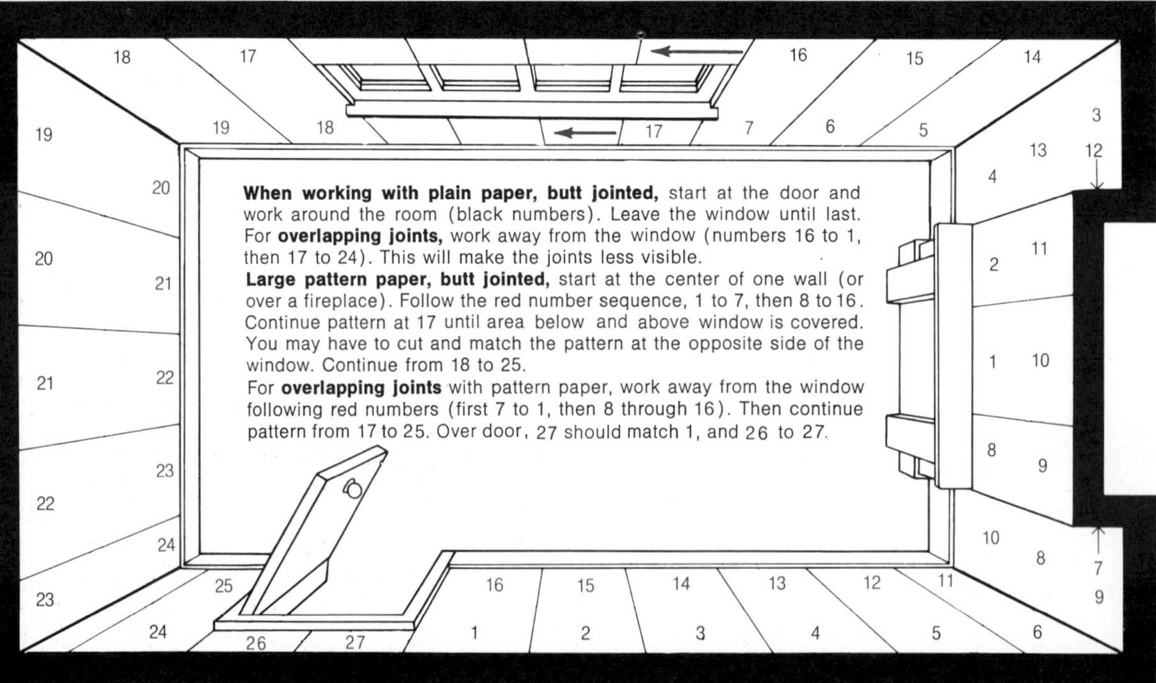

Matching, aligning, and pasting

Walls and ceilings are often not exactly square; to be sure paper hangs straight, you must establish a true vertical with a plumb line. To do this, hang a weight at the end of a string; tack the string at the top of the wall so it is closer to the starting door or window than the width of the wall covering roll, and the weight hangs just above the floor. Chalk the string, hold it taut near the weight, and snap it against the wall. Do this as each new wall is begun.

Stack cut sections of unpasted wallpaper face down on the pasting table. Apply paste with a clean pasting brush to each piece just before hanging. Spread paste evenly and completely (unpasted spots will blister. Start working from the top of the strip at the center. Leave an inch or two unpasted at the top edge. Apply heavy coating of paste to both edges. Fold the top half over itself paste side in and paste the bottom half, working from the center.

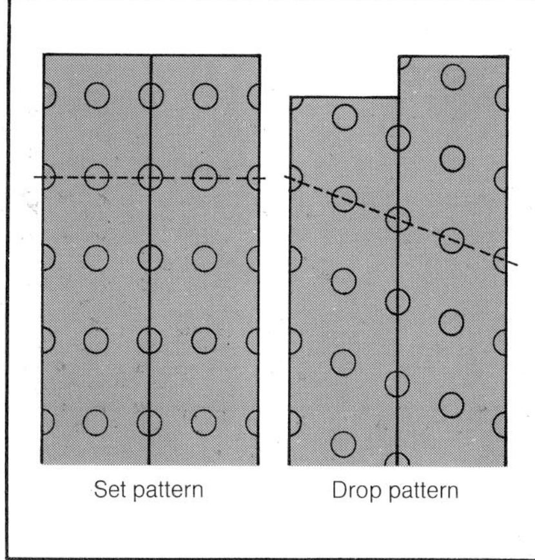

Match the pattern carefully when cutting wallpaper to length. As shown above, there are two types of pattern match—the set and the drop. The latter is more difficult to hang.

To "plumb" the wall, suspend a chalked line from a tack driven in just below the ceiling. Draw the line tight against the wall at the bottom and snap it. This mark is the true vertical.

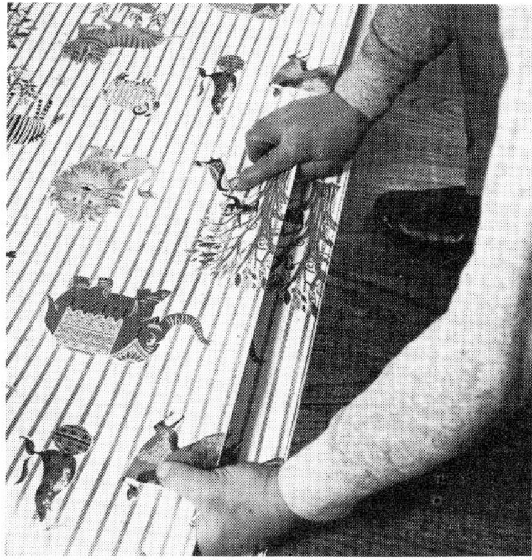

Place the trimmed lengths of unpasted wallpaper on the pasting table. Make sure the patterns will match. Cut enough paper for at least one wall. Then flop them over.

Start brushing on the paste from the top of the strip (imprint on selvage or back of the paper will indicate which end is "up"), leaving an unpasted inch or two at the top.

Continue brushing on the far side of the paper, paying particular attention to the edge. The paper should be adequately supported along both edges to prevent its creasing.

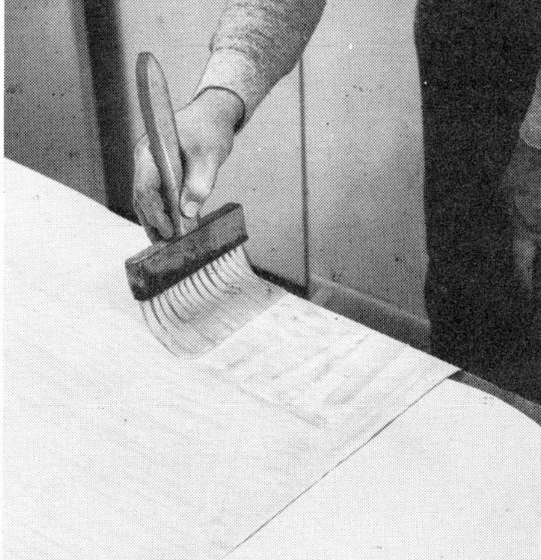

Next apply paste to the near edge. Use a full stroke and make certain that all parts of the strip are pasted. An unpasted spot will show up as a blister after paste has dried.

Paste half a length. Then fold up this half over itself as shown and paste up the other half. Be sure not to crease the paper along the fold line; this would show as a crack in the paper.

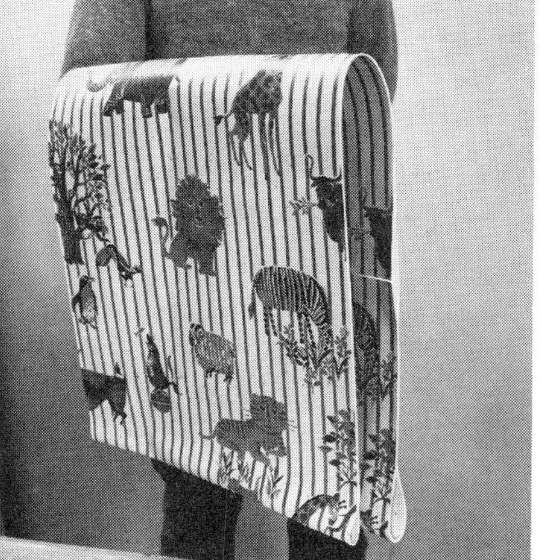

To carry the pasted paper to the wall, loop the folded section over your arm. The top of the fold should be in position to be installed next to the ceiling line.

Hanging, trimming, turning corners

Place each strip high on wall, with about a 2-inch overlap at ceiling, and line up with plumb line or previous piece. Stroke top several times with smoothing brush to hold strip in place. Then open and line up lower folded portion and smooth onto wall from top to bottom. When entire piece is in place and aligned, smooth again from top to bottom, brushing from center toward edge to remove any air pockets.

Brush paper firmly into casing joint and trim as at baseboard and ceiling. When hanging paper from a corner, brush overlap into corner and onto adjoining wall; it will be covered by the final strip.

Corners are seldom "true." When approaching one, measure distance from the last strip hung to the corner at ceiling and baseboard; add ½ inch to wider measurement; cut a full-length strip to this width and hang as usual, brushing tightly into corner. Strip should now overlap about ½ inch on adjoining wall.

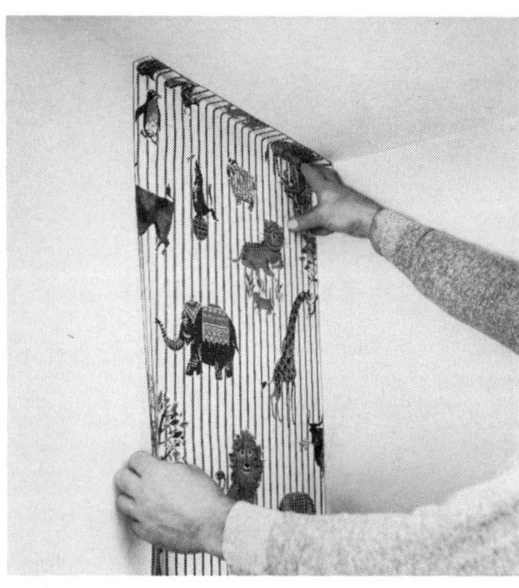

Take first strip and open up longer folded section by grasping unpasted area at end. Position strip at ceiling and align right-hand edge with chalked guideline.

Run the smoothing brush down center of paper and work it toward the edges to force out any air bubbles, wrinkles, or excess paste. Make certain paper is adhering to wall.

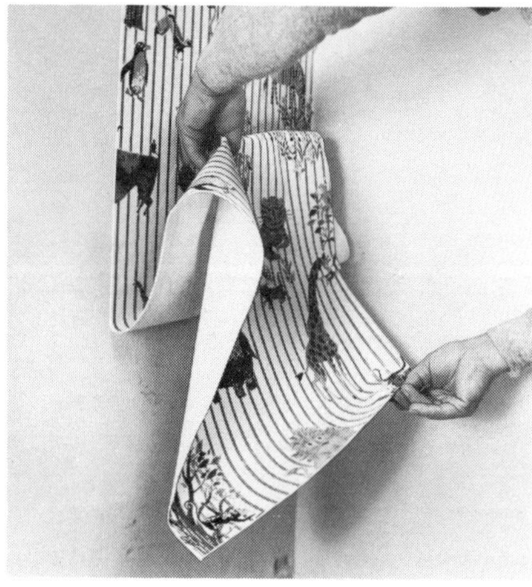

Reach behind the strip, unfold the shorter folded section, and guide gently into place. When lower section is in proper position, go over entire strip with smoothing brush.

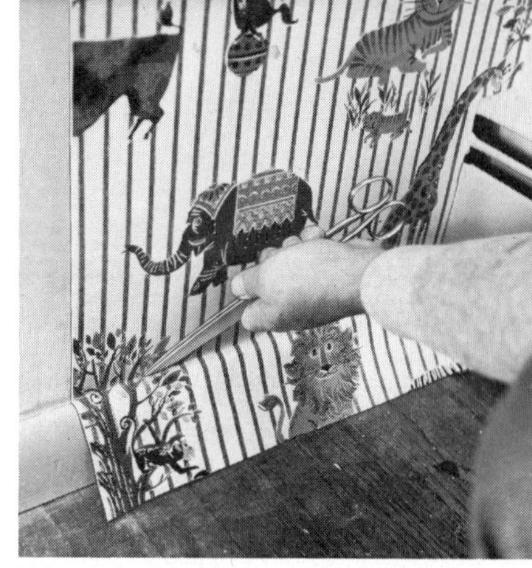

Using a putty knife as a guide and a razor blade cutter, trim off the excess paper at baseboard and ceiling. To make paper hold, it may be necessary to add more paste.

Paper can also be trimmed by first scoring it with back of a knife or scissors. Then pull it away slightly from wall, cut with scissors on scored line, and brush back in place.

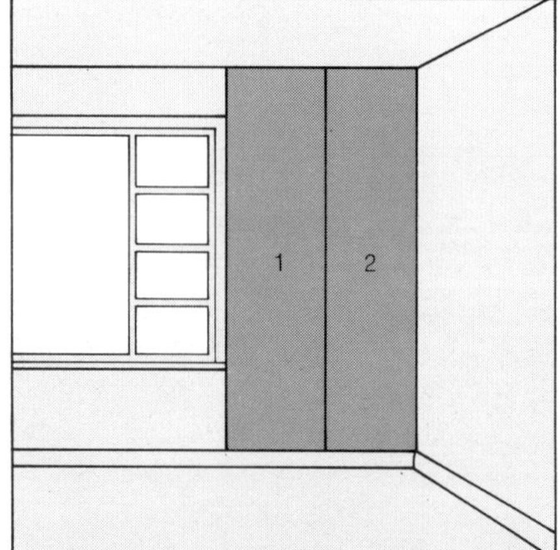

Follow the same procedure with succeeding strips, hanging them in the order in which they were cut. To butt seams, slide edge of one strip against edge of another.

After strips have been hung for 10 to 15 minutes, press the seams lightly with a seam roller—except in the case of embossed paper, where seams are not rolled.

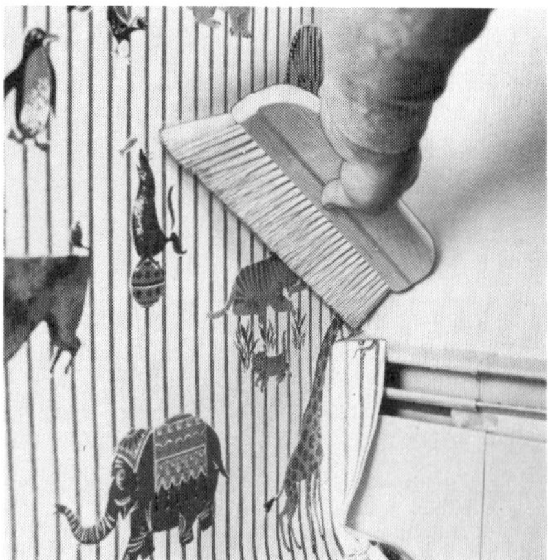

Unless a corner is perfectly straight, which they seldom are, it is impossible to get a perfect butt match. The slight overlap, however, will not be noticeable.

Fireplaces, windows and doors

Some mismatching is inevitable, particularly in corners and around fireplaces, windows, and doors. With the last two, the problem is to keep the pattern continuous, with the edge pattern of the wall covering extending beyond the vertical line established by the window or door frame. Whether the last strip falls short by a few inches or almost its full width, cut the full-length strip to extend at least an inch beyond the frame, then hang it from ceiling to baseboard. Snip it at the top of the door, or the top and bottom of a window, and it will lay flat against the wall. Trim off any surplus at the casing.

If you pick, say, a door for the mismatch point, select a part of the pattern for the over door join which blends with but does not match the strips that end there. Actual matching would have to be continued above doors and above and below windows, using parts from full-width strips—very wasteful.

If your room has a fireplace, and you are using a wallpaper with a large, definite pattern, hang the first strip centrally over the fireplace as the focal point of the room.

Take special care when trimming paper along edges of fireplace. The weight of the paper could cause it to tear at its narrowest point, where it turns around end of mantelpiece.

Trim the paper along the mantelpiece and remove as much waste as possible before smoothing it into place and cutting it to fit around the molding beneath the mantelpiece.

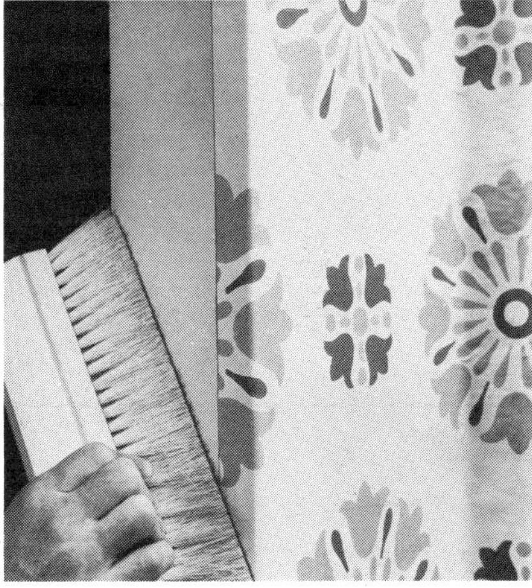

Use smoothing brush to bring the paper around the bend. Any paste forced out and deposited on brush should be cleaned off. Use sponge to wipe away paste from front of paper.

Cover plates on outlet boxes and on switches should be removed before start of papering, and wall-mounted fixtures removed or loosened. Paper over opening, then trim paper away.

After trimming, replace the outlet or switch plate. Follow the same procedure when doing a paint job. It makes for a much neater and more professional result.

At large obstructions, such as door frames, crease a trimming line with a putty knife. Then cut along this line, pressing the paper into the angle before trimming it off.

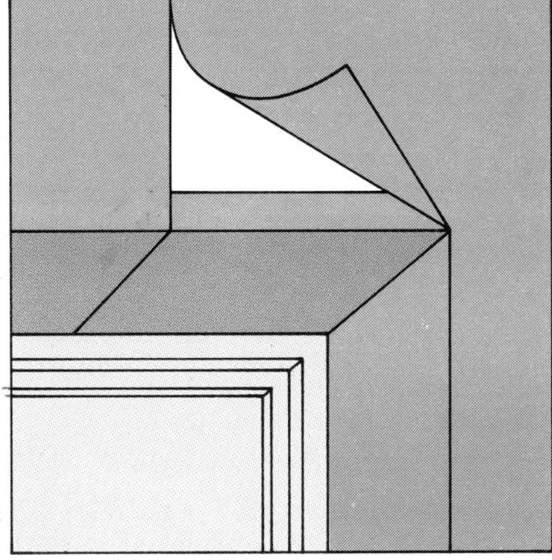

When you come to a recessed window, paper the inside first, then overlap, as shown, to conceal the join. Paper the areas above the recess as you would an unbroken wall.

Papering ceilings

Because shorter strips are easier to handle, ceiling strips are always hung across the room rather than lengthwise. It is best to do ceiling before walls. Mark a guideline along ceiling to assure that the first strip parallels the starting wall. Cut, paste, and fold as for walls, adding about 2 inches to ceiling measurement. Unfold top end of pasted strip and lift to ceiling, supporting still-folded other end with roll of paper. Allow 1 inch overlap at end. Trim surplus according to whether pattern will go all the way down, or only part way to a molding. Use of same pattern on walls and ceiling is an advantage when main entrance is opposite a room's narrow side. Pattern can then be hung so it seems to continue up and across ceiling, adding to the room's apparent height.

Some papers can go up a wall and across a ceiling, but not down the opposite wall because of a definite right-side-up design, such as flowers on stems.

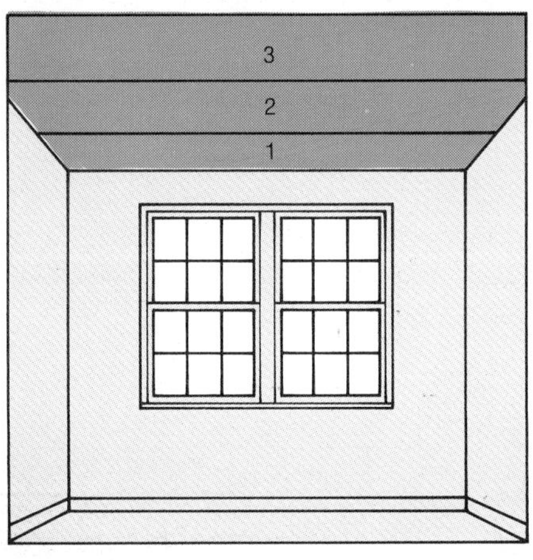

Hang wallpaper across a ceiling rather than lengthwise. Start working at a window and continue hanging toward back of room. Chalk a line on the ceiling to use as a guide.

Cut paper into ceiling-width lengths, allowing a slight overlap for trimming at each end. Apply paste as specified for walls and fold the paper accordion-fashion as shown.

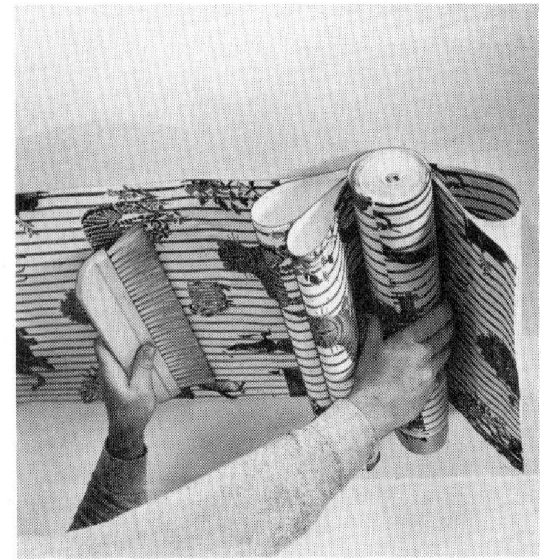

Using a spare roll to support the folded paper from underneath, start putting the strip up. Unfurl it one fold at a time, smoothing it onto the ceiling with a brush.

Slit paper, as shown, around light fixtures. Fit the paper into place around the fixture. When that entire length of paper is in place, trim off the waste with a razor blade.

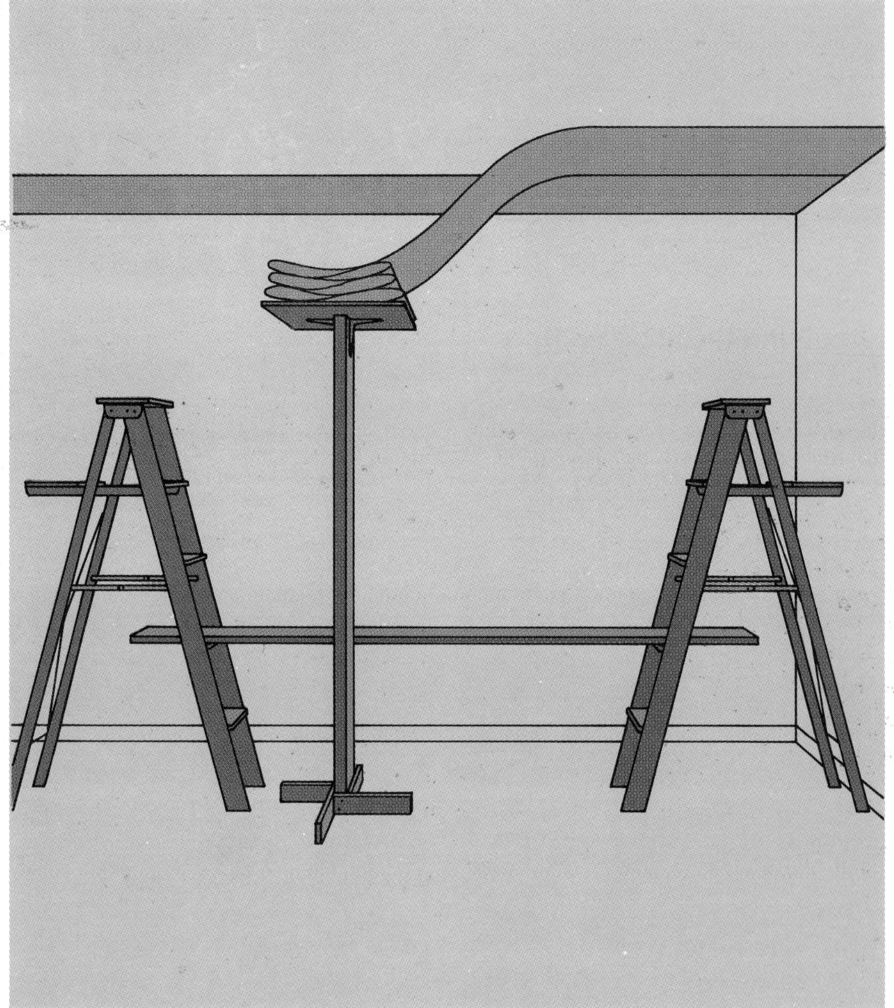

When papering a ceiling, set up a platform, using two stepladders and a plank, so that you can cover the full width of the ceiling without having to get down. Your head should be 6 in. below the ceiling. A holder for the paper can be made of 1 × 3s as shown and used instead of an assistant, to support the paper while you are working on the platform.

Renovating a ceiling with tiles

Tiling is a fast, easy, and attractive way to transform an unsightly ceiling. Standard tile sizes are 12 x 12, 12 x 24, 24 x 24, and 24 x 48 inches. The larger sizes are made for commercial use; these are called panels rather than tiles. Most tiles are made of wood fibers, some treated for fire resistance. There are also tiles and panels of completely fireproof materials.

Ceiling tiles may be installed either of two ways:

1. Direct application, in which the ceiling material is fastened to furring strips on the existing ceiling with staples or special ceiling tile cement.

2. Grid system, in which a metal grid is suspended from the ceiling. The panels slip into place without special fastening and can be lifted out for cleaning or replacement, and for access to pipes and wiring. This is ideal where there are exposed pipes, wires, ducts, joists, or seriously damaged ceilings.

Before doing any work, lay out the design to scale on paper. Mark openings, light fixtures, and other obstructions; then relate the unit size of the material to the layout. Borders should be the same size all around; if a fraction of a course is needed to complete the ceiling, apportion half to each side.

Pattern or design must be considered in buying and installing tiles. Some permit a checkerboard installation, or one with the pattern running the same way from end to end. Such tiles must be installed to contrast with, or match, the adjacent pattern. Random-pattern tiles can be installed any way you wish.

The required tools are few and simple, regardless of the tile application method—such everyday items as a hammer, nails, chalk line, sharp knife, stapling gun. If you plan to mount the tiles directly on the ceiling, you will need 1 x 3 furring strips. When you buy the suspended grid-type tiles, the grids come with the tile order.

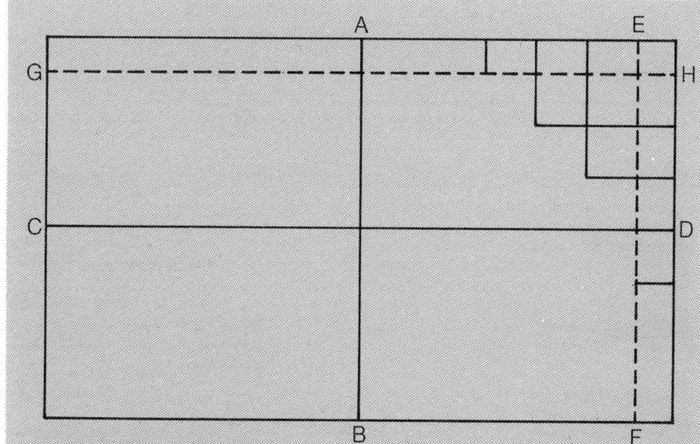

Guidelines on ceiling assure even placement. Start application at corner. Be sure lines E-F and G-H between border tiles and first course of full tiles are always parallel to lines A-B and C-D which meet at center of room.

Applying tiles to a ceiling

If there is no existing ceiling, as in an unfinished basement, or if a ceiling is badly cracked and damaged, 1 x 3 furring strips are installed at right angles to the joists or rafters. Install the first strip flush where wall and ceiling meet; the location of the second depends on the width of your border tile. Space this second strip so that the stapling edge of the border tile will be centered on it. Work across the ceiling from the second strip, installing parallel furring strips on 12-inch centers for 12 x 24-inch tiles. A spacer strip will expedite the work. The next to the last strip should be the same distance from the wall as the second strip; the last is nailed flush against the wall.

Start the installation at a corner. Cut border tiles to previously determined size. Make sure the stapling edges of the tiles face into the center of the room. Apply the first tile, staple in place, and face-nail at wall. Leave a small space between first tile and wall for possible movement (molding will cover it). Be sure tongue-and-groove edges fit together snugly, but do not force them. Work across the room, installing two border tiles at a time and filling in with full-size tiles, keeping stapling edges out. Make sure all joints are continuous and straight.

On sound ceilings, tiles may be cemented directly to the existing surface.

1. When nailing up furring strips, use spacer strip to assure parallel spacing.

2. Nail furring strips on 12-in. centers. Spacer strip eliminates measuring.

3. Staple tiles to furring, using a staple at each corner of exposed tongue.

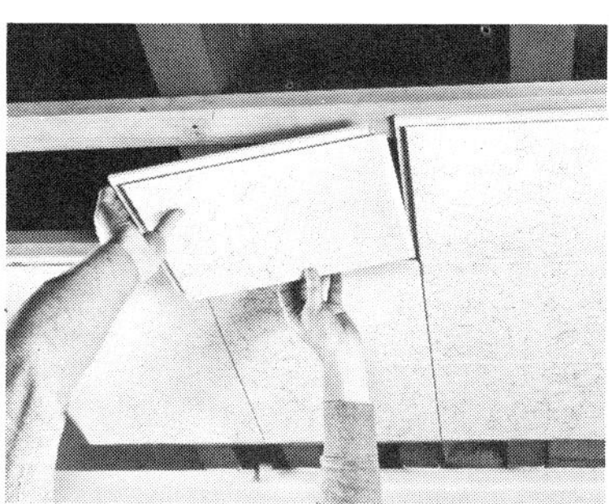

4. Grooved side of tile is slid into the projecting tongue of preceding tile.

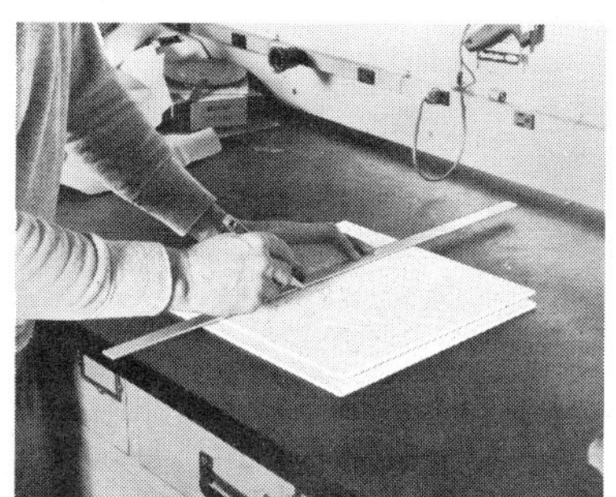

5. Use straightedge and sharp knife when tiles must be cut down to fit.

6. Final step: Installation of crown molding at joint between ceiling and wall.

Installing a suspended ceiling

Suspended ceilings, also known as dropped ceilings, are often used to lower and modernize an existing ceiling, to cover a damaged ceiling, or to hide exposed plumbing, wiring, and joists.

Before starting any installation work, sketch a diagram of the ceiling, indicating each panel and lighting fixture. Use graph paper, letting one square equal one square foot.

Suspended ceiling panels for home use come in two sizes—2 x 2 and 2 x 4 feet—and in several patterns. Keep in mind the decorative effects that are possible with this kind of installation. For example, you can make long, narrow rooms seem wider and more expansive by installing rectangular panels perpendicular to the length of the room.

Lighting fixtures should be planned at this time and indicated in the sketch. This is also the time to balance the borders. For instance, if your room is 15 feet wide, use three 2 x 4-foot panels with two 1½-foot border panels. The border panels at the sides of the room should always be equal. The grids in which the ceiling panels rest are white but there is no reason why you cannot paint them.

One important advantage with a suspended ceiling is that you can always have access to pipes and wiring without having to tear down the tiles. You can just slide them out of their grids.

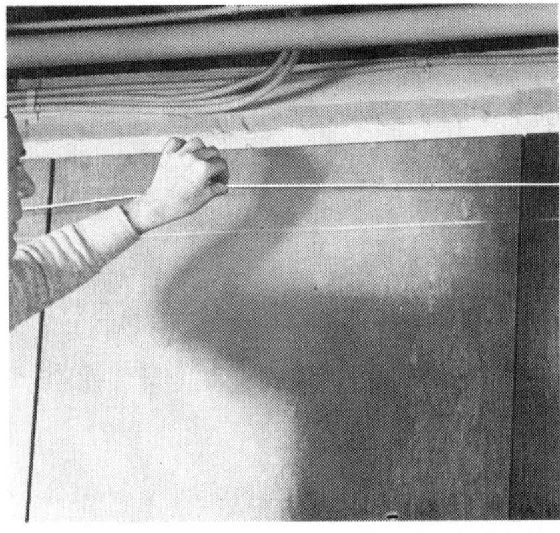

1. Snap a chalk line at the desired ceiling height. Bear in mind that you must allow 4 in. of head room to permit the panels to be maneuvered into place

2. Fasten the L-shaped wall angles (supplied with the panels) at the chalk-line height. Use nails for preliminary fastening and follow with screws every 2 ft.

3. Stretch strings across the room from wall angle to wall angle as guides for mounting the main runners and the crosspieces which will ultimately form the grid system.

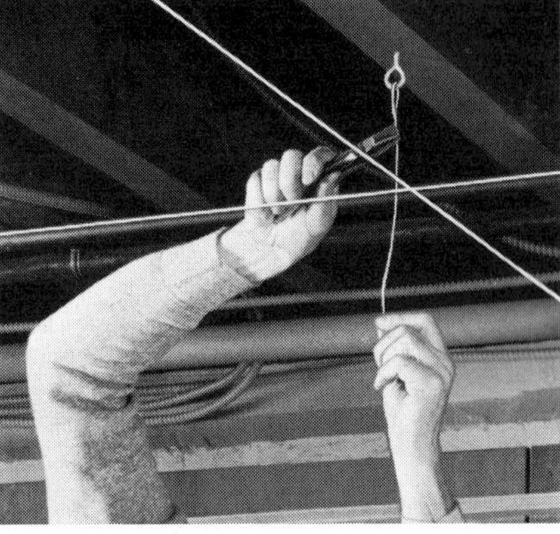

4. The next step is to insert a screw eye at each intersection where the strings cross. Insert a length of wire through each screw eye and twist it to lock it in place.

5. The main runners are suspended from the wires. You can adjust the height of the runners by means of the wires. A fine adjustment can be made by means of the screw eyes.

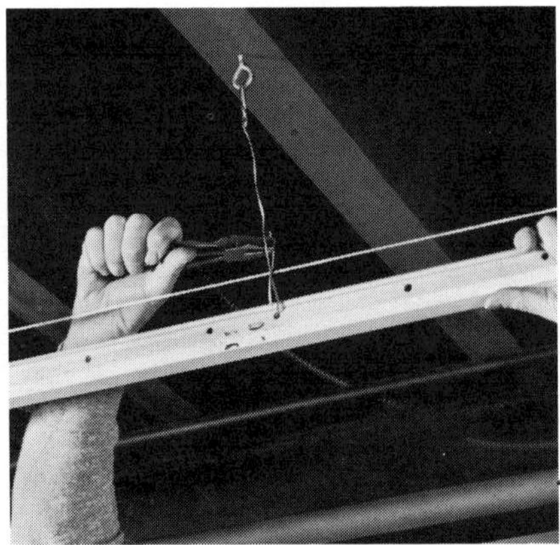

6. A screw eye and wire installed below every other ceiling beam serves to support the long main runners. Runners can be spliced, end to end, for an extra-long ceiling.

7. Next insert the crosspieces every 2 ft. into the main runners. The crosspieces have tabs at each end which fit into slots on the main runners. Check for alignment.

8. The final step consists of installing the panels. This is a simple matter of tilting them slightly to fit between the grids and then lowering them into place.

Installing recessed fixtures

Another advantage of a suspended ceiling is the ease of installing lighting fixtures. If you insert translucent panels in some of the openings, light from the fixtures above will show through, softly lighting the room. These panels—which range from louvered or "eggcrate" styles to plain white frosted panels—can be placed wherever you please. Lighting can be located above every work center in a room, or where you plan a seating arrangement. In a smaller room, such as a bathroom, you can even illuminate the entire ceiling, flooding the room with light.

Fluorescent lighting is generally employed with a suspended ceiling unit and recessed incandescent lamp fixtures with a ceiling tile system. The recessed units are the same size as standard tiles and are set in the ceiling in place of a single tile. They may be located wherever light is needed. Never use a bulb of higher wattage than is recommended by the fixture manufacturer. To avoid the chilly outdoor-light effect of ordinary fluorescent tubes, the kind most frequently sold, use the warm-white type, which produces a light much like that of incandescent lamps.

New lighting fixtures for grid-type ceilings are attached directly to the grids, not to the ceiling, thus avoiding interference problems with pipes and ducts. The fixtures can be mounted flush with the ceiling panels or below them.

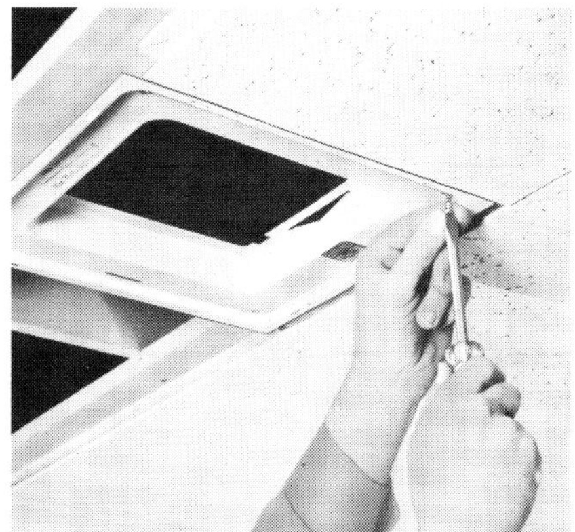

An incandescent ceiling fixture is the same size as a ceiling tile, 12 x 12 in. Screw the special adapter plate to the furring strips that hold the tiles.

Next install the junction box on the adapter plate and connect the wires from the socket to a power line (p. 266). Be sure to make provision for an on-off switch.

Snap the reflector dome in place. The reflector's highly polished surface serves to amplify the light from the bulb. Polish with a dry cloth to remove any fingerprints.

The final step is to insert a 100-watt (or smaller) bulb and slip the holder-springs of the framed diffuser into the slots provided. Fixture will project about 3 in. below ceiling.

To install a fluorescent light fixture in a suspended ceiling system, first attach the mounting brackets to the flanges of the runners. Tighten with screws provided.

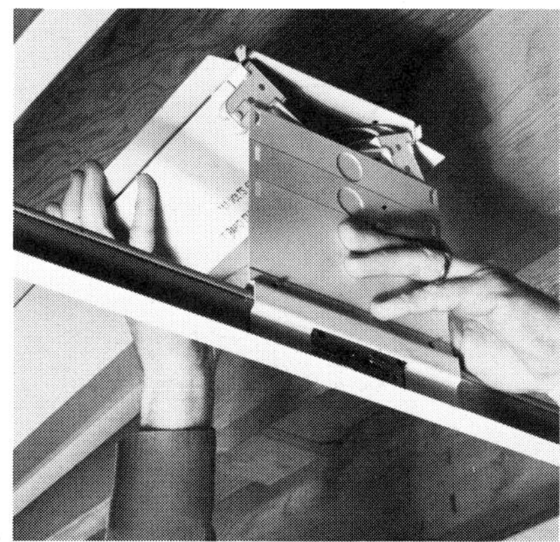

Next attach the fixture to the mounting brackets by sliding the two tabs at each end of the fixture through the matching slots of each opposing bracket.

Install the reflector panels over the top of the fixture. Make connection to a suitable source of power, plus provision for a switch, and insert the fluorescent tubes.

The final step consists of sliding the diffusing panel into place below the fixture. These panels come in many styles, including plain translucent, eggcrate, and louvered.

Wall paneling materials

Today's homeowner has many different interior wall surfacing materials to choose from. They vary in thickness from a minute fraction of an inch for wallpaper to almost an inch for solid wood boards. Actually, the material possibilities are limited only by the imagination of the decorator. In addition to conventional wall materials—solid wood, plywood, hardboard, gypsum board, ceramic tile, plaster—you will find plastic laminates, fiber glass panels, corrugated plastic panels, stone and brick veneers, polystyrene panels, metal sheets, and three-dimensional vinyl reproductions, to list just a partial selection. Page 341 fully describes wallpapers and other roll wall coverings; what follows are descriptions of so-called rigid types.

Solid wood paneling: This material offers an infinite variety of grain patterns, from plain pine to elegant polished hardwoods. Among wood's many natural assets is the fact that age increases its beauty; also it is an effective insulator against heat and noise. Besides the interior types of tongue-and-groove boards, some exterior forms can be used as well. Even beveled siding is finding a place in the home, often on a single wall as a contrast to paint or wallpaper on the other walls. Interior planking varies in thickness from ⅜ to ¾ inch, and in widths from 3 to 12 inches; it comes in lengths up to 8 feet.

Solid paneling's major disadvantage is cost. Most hardwoods—walnut, oak, cherry, mahogany—are rather expensive, especially when purchased prefinished. Solid softwood panels of redwood, knotty pine, and western red cedar cost less.

Plywood: Besides offering a variety of veneers and textures, plywood wall panels have the advantages of being nonsplitting, resistant to warping, and easy to install. Plywood also has fair insulating and sound-absorbing qualities and imparts structural rigidity when properly installed.

Plywood comes faced with many fine hardwoods and several textured softwoods. Many of the hardwood panel surfaces are factory-finished. Panel widths range from 16 inches to 4 feet. The ¼-inch thickness is the most popular for wall work, and is usually installed by one of the following methods:

1. Contact-type cement can be used to secure the plywood panels in place—no nails needed. This method is recommended with prefinished panels.
2. The clip method makes it possible to nail panels and yet conceal the nailheads behind the panels.
3. It is, of course, possible to nail directly through the panel into studs or furring strips. This is suitable with textured woods, but nailing will mar the finish of prefinished panels.
4. Another variation is V-plank panels. Here, the random-width V grooves are arranged so there is a groove every 16 inches on center. Driving nails through the V groove does not mar the panel's finish, and it is easy to conceal the nailheads.

Prefinished hardboard: These fabricated sheets are tough and moisture-resistant, and won't crack or split. The baked-on finish and the vinyl-faced types are available in many colors and in a variety of patterns, some of them simulating polished hardwoods and veined marble.

Nearly all factory-finished hardboard panels come in standard 4 x 8-foot sheets and are ¼ inch thick. Many brands can be ordered from 6 to 10 feet in length; a few come in 16-inch-wide "planks" for paneling walls. Sheet hardboard is applied by cementing, cementing and nailing, or nailing (or screwing) over solid backings, studs, or furring strips.

The perforated hardboards so popular for display backgrounds and tool and utensil racks make handsome wall coverings. When using this type of hardboard, space framing members 16 inches apart. Where holes fall over solid supports, the studs can be painted black to simulate a hollow space, or the support may be grooved where a line of holes falls for the insertion of brackets.

Insulating wallboards: Insulation-type wallboards are inexpensive, and their light weight makes them easy to handle. Their surfaces are textured and come in many prefinished colors. Also, their application possibilities are almost unlimited. Because of their insulating properties, they are often substituted for other types of insulation. Though insulating wallboards are easily marred, walls are rarely subject to puncturing shocks, and where this possibility does exist, the boards can be applied over a hard surface. Insulating wallboard is installed over furring strips, or directly over rough framing; boards are secured with nails or staples through the tongues.

Gypsum wallboard: Still one of the most widely used wall materials, this product consists of a gypsum core sandwiched between layers of specially treated paper which provides an ideal surface for paint or for wallpaper and other roll wall coverings. It is also available with colorful vinyl surfaces and in simulated wood grain as well as textured patterns; these do not require additional decoration.

Plastic laminates: These will give your walls the same rugged surface that you get with a plastic-laminated counter top. Laminates are available in a wide range of surfaces including textures and wood grains, in solid colors and many distinctive patterns. Being resistant to almost everything, this paneling is especially practical in high abuse areas. It comes 24 to 60 inches in width and 6 to 12 feet in length. The 1/32-inch thickness is generally tough enough for walls, but it must be applied, of course, to a backing of some kind (plywood, hardboard, or gypsum wallboard) with contact cement.

Fiber glass panels: These panels come in several colors, offering varying degrees of light transmission. They are made in thin sheets corrugated like sheet metal and in plain flat sheets. Popular for outdoor walls, they have indoor uses as well. While they can be applied as coverings, a better use for them is as actual walls, serving as dividers or partitions. The panels are rigid enough that they require support only at the top and bottom.

Polystyrene panels are similar in many respects to fiber-glass except that they are intended primarily for interior installations. They come in several designs that create a stained-glass effect.

Cork: Cork for wall use is generally available in tiles 6 x 12, 12 x 24, and 24 x 48 inches, and in three thicknesses from ⅛ to 5/16 inch. They come in light and dark browns (which may be intermixed) and in a range of tones that are factory finished. Cork is fixed to a wall with adhesive.

Other materials: There are other rigid materials that can be employed as wall coverings. For example, it is possible to cover a wall from floor to ceiling with mirrors, either panels or tiles. Metal sheets, available in various designs and several finishes, can be used to achieve special effects on walls. There are also new types of paneling, such as particle boards. These are compressed panels, made of wood flakes and chips bonded together with a special synthetic resin, usually in 4 x 8-foot sheets and in thicknesses from ⅜ to ¾ inch. They take paint and most other wood finishes very well and are installed the same as other rigid paneling types.

Brick veneer

Real brick veneer and vinyl brick are installed much the same way. Starting from the top, apply mastic to the wall with a trowel. Let it set several minutes to assure that the brick will stay where it is placed. Slightly dampen the back of the brick with water and press it firmly into the mastic with a side-to-side motion, using both hands. This motion sets the brick into the mastic and forces the mastic from behind to make a mortar joint. Allow ⅜ to ½ inch between bricks. Wet the stick which comes in each carton and smooth the mortar area between bricks. The stick also acts as a ⅜-inch spacer. To cut real brick veneer, score the back with a hacksaw. Place face down on counter, score line at edge, and snap.

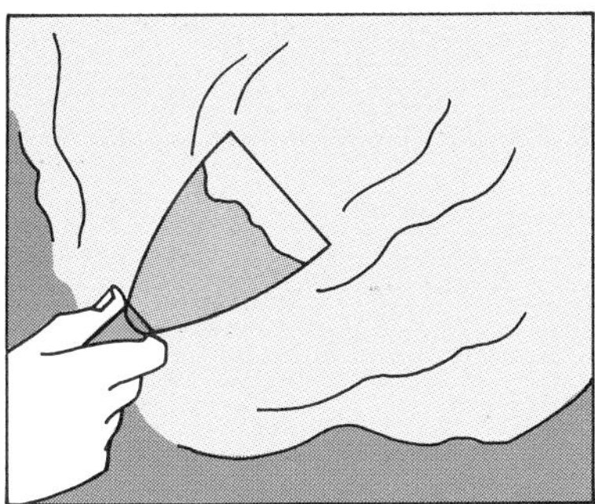

Apply recommended mastic over 3-foot square area with a wide putty knife.

Use a damp cloth to moisten back of brick. This delays "setting" of bricks.

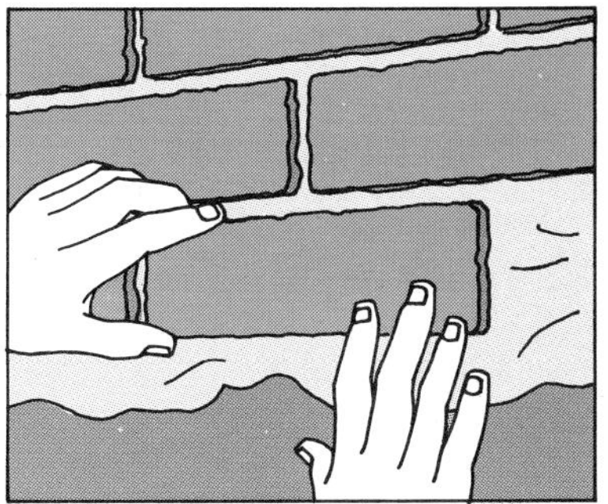

Press brick onto mastic with side-to-side motion, keeping a ⅜-in. mortar space.

Stone veneer

Stone, a much-neglected interior building material, can add richness and beauty to a home—and easily. Packaged stone veneer, ¾-inch thick, can be applied right over old walls with metal clips and screws. These clips fit in grooves on the top and bottom edges of each stone, securing it to the wall and providing proper spacing between stones.

The joints between the stones are filled with a mortar mix of 1 part cement and 2 parts sharp sand, with just enough water so that mortar is fairly stiff. Use an old paintbrush to wet edges of stone before filling joints. When the mortar starts to set, tool the joints with a round stick or dowel and remove excess mortar from stones with a soft brush.

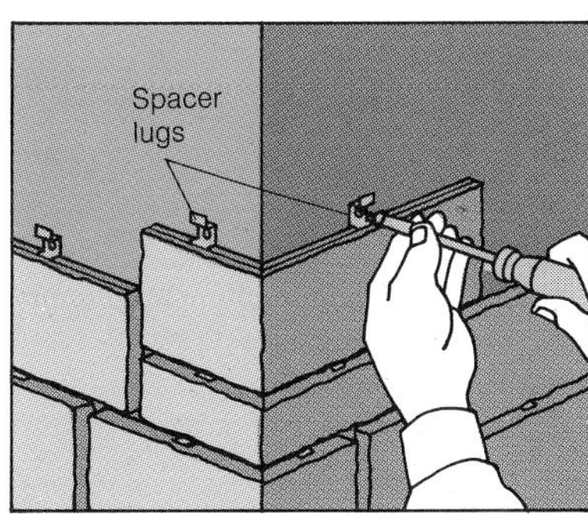

Small metal clips secure stone to wall, provide proper spacing between stones.

Some systems employ a caulking gun to fill the joints with special mortar.

Set and clean mortar joints with a dowel as soon as the mortar starts to harden.

Plastic wall covering

Another popular type of wall covering (though not a rigid type) is a heavy plastic that comes in 54-inch rolls. This material should not be confused with vinyl-coated "wallpaper" as it is much thicker and requires a special technique in application as shown at right. It is a heavy-grade material similar to vinyl upholstering material. Formerly it was used only in stores and offices but now it is available for residential use. It is especially suitable for covering cracked plaster walls and for application over painted walls, but old wallpaper should be removed first. This material may be scrubbed repeatedly without affecting its texture or color. However, it does require a special adhesive for application.

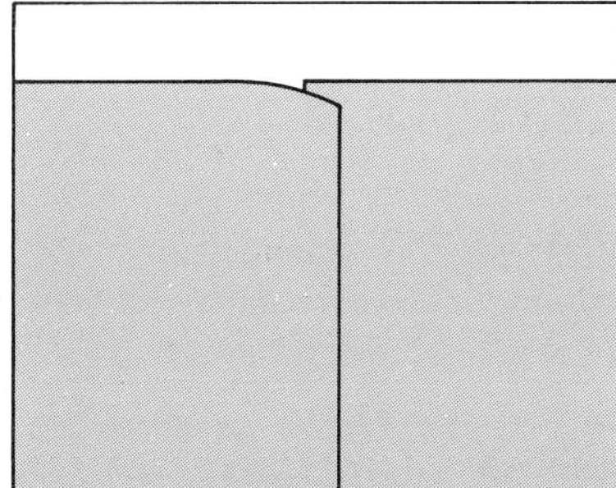

Smooth-fitting butt joint can be made with plastic wall covering by first overlapping adjacent panels 1 inch.

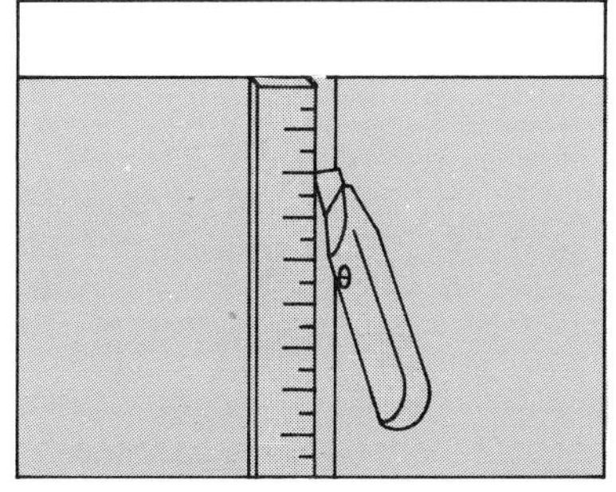

Cut through both panels with a sharp knife. Use a metal straightedge as a guide. Do not go over the cut.

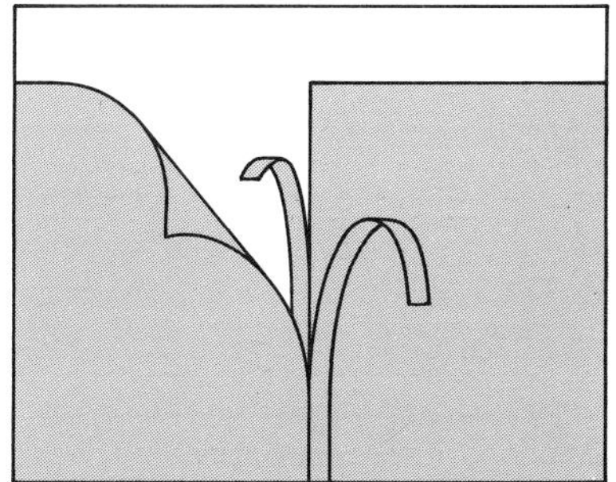

Peel away the outside strip and the inside strip. Then press down for a smooth fit. Wipe away excess paste.

Ceramic wall tiles

Surface preparation

Before planning a retiling job, determine whether existing tiles are mounted on a solid wall surface such as wallboard or plywood, or if the tiles are encased in plaster. This latter installation is known as a "mud job." Retiling this type of wall is a complex task that should be left to a professional. If the mud job tile surface is sound, however, you could tile directly over it.

When tile is to be applied over a solid surface such as wallboard, hardboard, or plywood, be sure that the surface material is exterior grade. The following pretiling treatments are recommended:

Plaster: A newly plastered surface must be allowed to cure for at least a month before tiling. When a wall is made of old plaster, make certain that it is perfectly sound. Patch any crumbling areas and seal the new patches with shellac.

Paint: Either remove the old paint or scratch at least 50 percent of the painted surface to expose a suitably clean base for the tile.

Wallboards (plaster board, Sheetrock, rock lath, and gypsum boards): All of these materials provide an ideal surface for tiling, but they must be properly supported so that no movement or warping can take place. Fasten these boards at 12-inch intervals for ⅜-inch-thick boards and at 16-inch intervals for boards that are ½ inch thick.

Plywood: Ceramic tiles can be installed over plywood, but it must be the waterproof exterior grade; do not use the interior grade.

Tools for tiling

You should have the following tools available when doing tile installation work:

Trowel. Buy one that has notches along one edge and is smooth on the other.

Tile cutter. Scriber with a tungsten carbide tip is the most efficient tool for cutting tiles. A glass cutter can be used, but it will dull quickly.

Tile nippers. It is possible to buy carbide-tipped nippers made especially for this purpose, but you can use a pair of ordinary pliers in a pinch.

Rubber-surfaced trowel. Use this tool for grouting.

In addition, have on hand a Carborundum stone, sponge, hammer, plumb line, carpenter's level, joint-striking tool (use a toothbrush handle), a small trowel for mixing grout, and a long straightedge.

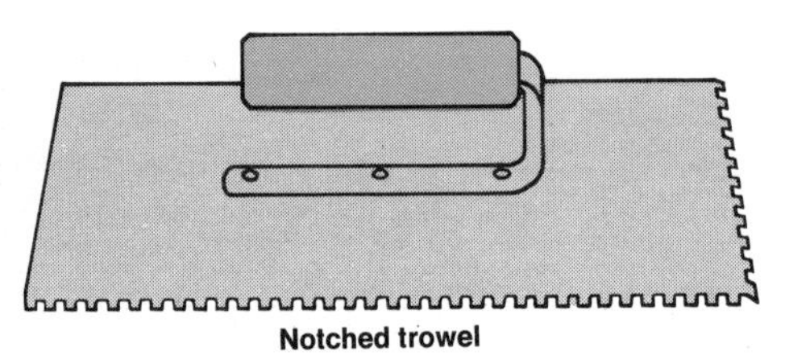
Notched trowel

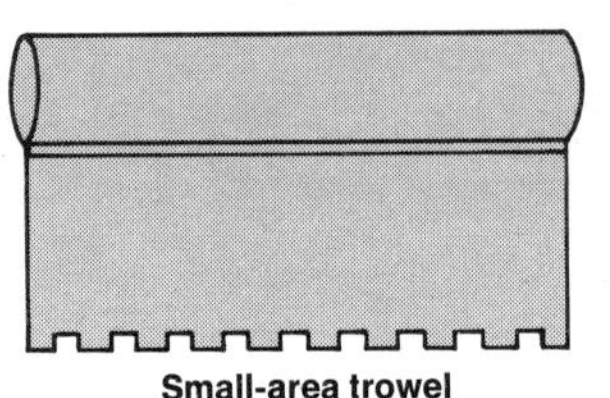
Small-area trowel

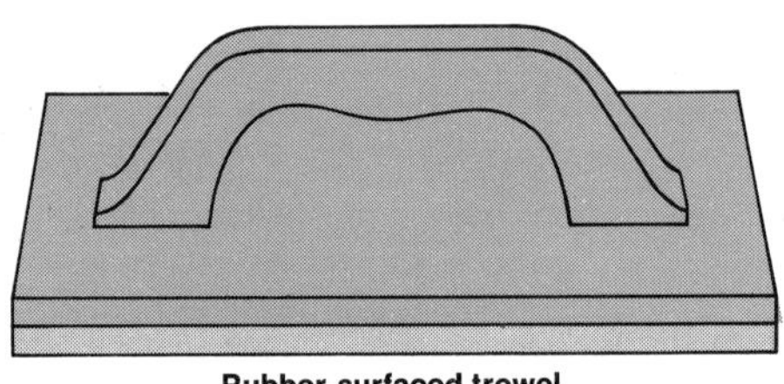
Rubber-surfaced trowel

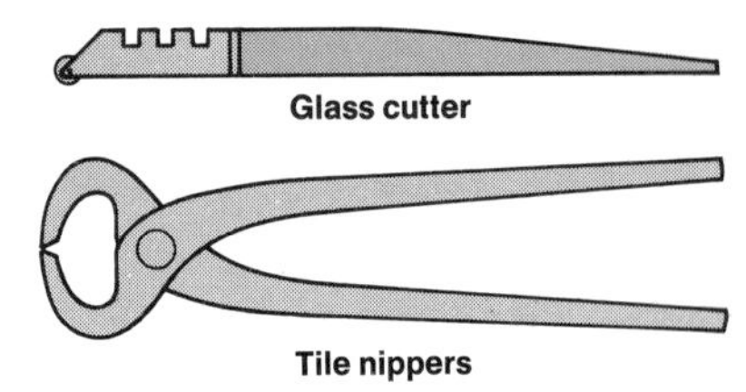
Glass cutter

Tile nippers

Estimating

Tile: Find, in the adjoining table, the number of tiles required for the length and height of the area to be covered, and multiply the two. Example: A length of 10½ feet takes 30 tiles; height of 9 feet, 26 tiles; 30 x 26 equals 780, the total needed. Subtract the number of tiles that would cover doors and windows. Add a dozen tiles for possible breakage.

In addition to 4¼-inch tiles, you will need trim tiles for inside and outside corners, and cap and base tiles. You can get base tiles with a special cutout for use where two walls meet. Measure for these separately; most of them come in 6-inch lengths.

Mastic: One gallon of waterproof wall-tile mastic adhesive will cover about 50 square feet.

Grout: One pound, after mixing, will cover approximately 18 square feet.

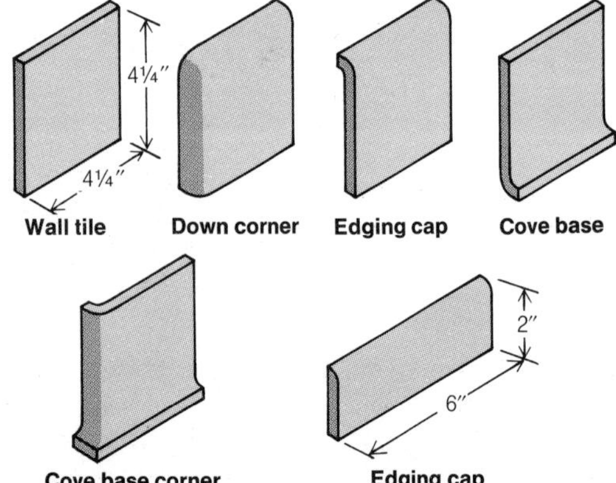

Ft.	No. of tiles	Ft.	No. of tiles
5	15	10½	30
5½	16	11	32
6	17	11½	33
6½	18	12	34
7	20	12½	36
7½	22	13	37
8	23	13½	39
8½	24	14	40
9	26	14½	41
9½	27	15	43
10	29		

Estimating table. This is for 4¼ x 4¼ in. tiles. If one of your wall measurements falls between two dimensions given on the table, use larger dimension for estimating number of tiles.

Installation procedure

The key to a professional-looking ceramic tile job is to start working with a squared-off area. Most rooms do not have perfectly square corners, as indicated by the exaggerated diagram below. The first step is to mark off a square area in such a way that fractional tiles at the corners (edges) are approximately the same size.

To mark off the squared area, first find the lowest point of the wall you are tiling; in this example, it is the low point of a bathtub line. From this corner draw a horizontal line a full tile height above the tub line.

Use a piece of scrap wood about 36 inches to 48 inches in length to mark up a tile-measuring stick (see photo). Lay this stick on the wall and shift it back and forth to determine the starting point for laying the tile so that equal widths of fractional tiles are left at the end of each row.

At both ends of the horizontal line draw vertical lines to form the squared-off area. To make tile application easier, you can fasten battens to the wall on the outside of the drawn lines.

Use a trowel to spread the mastic over approximately a 3 x 3-foot area of the wall. Use the notched side to form ridges in the mastic, pressing hard against the surface so that the ridges are the same height as the notches on the tool.

Start tiling at either of the vertical lines and tile half the wall at a time, working in horizontal rows. Press each tile into the mastic, but do not slide them or else mastic will be forced up the edges onto the tile surface. After each course of tile is applied, check with the level before spreading more mastic. If a line is crooked, remove all the tiles in that line and apply fresh ones. Do not use the removed tiles until the mastic has been cleaned off. Finish tiling the main area before fitting edge tiles.

Grouting: Allow the mastic to set for 24 hours before applying grout. Follow the manufacturer's mixing instructions closely and use a rubber-surfaced trowel to spread the grout over the tile surface. Work the trowel in an arc, holding it at a slight angle so that grout is forced into the spaces between the tiles.

When grout begins to dry, wipe the excess from the tiles with a damp rag. After the grout is thoroughly dry, rinse the wall and wipe it with a clean towel.

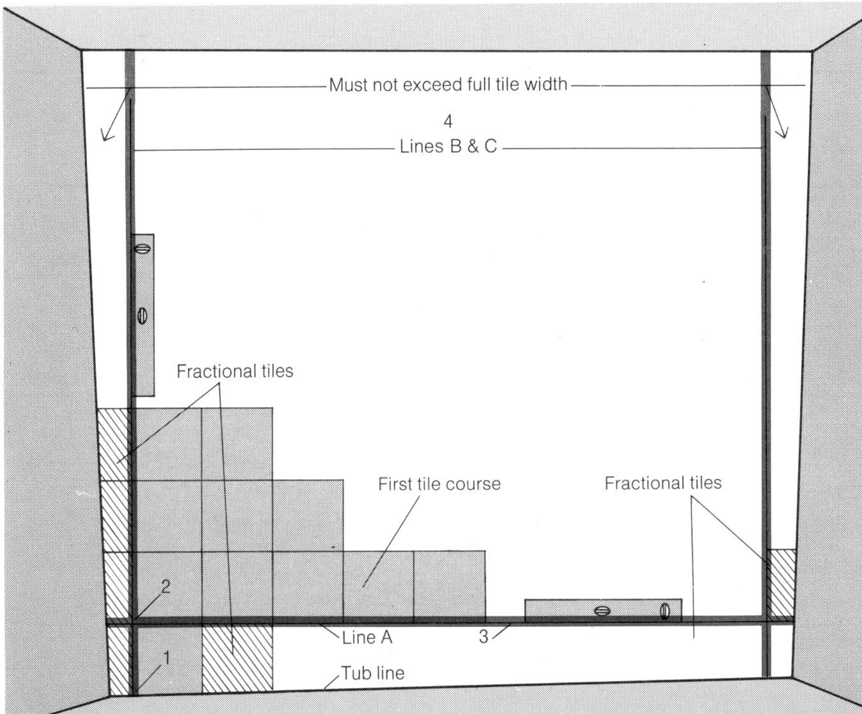

To square off wall for tiling: 1. Find low point of tub. **2.** Measure up height of one full tile at low point. Draw horizontal line A. It must be level. **3.** Use tile-measuring stick to determine position of full-width tiles in such a way that fractional tiles at each corner (edge) are equal. **4.** Draw vertical lines B and C perpendicular to line A. Apply tiles to squared-off area first. Then cut and apply fractional tiles.

Mark off a long length of wood with a series of lines equal to the width of a tile.

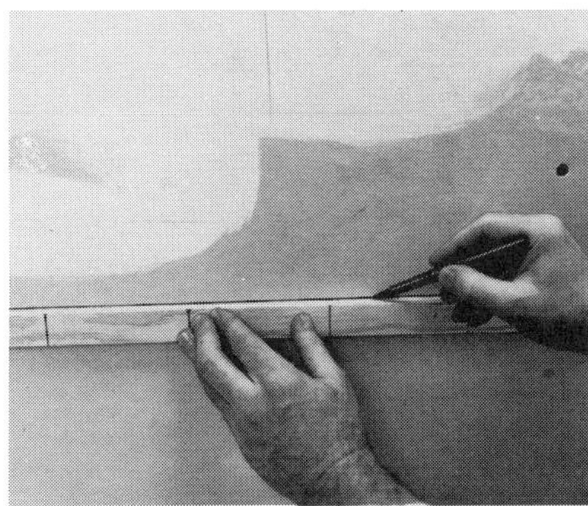

Extend the horizontal level line across the entire width of one wall.

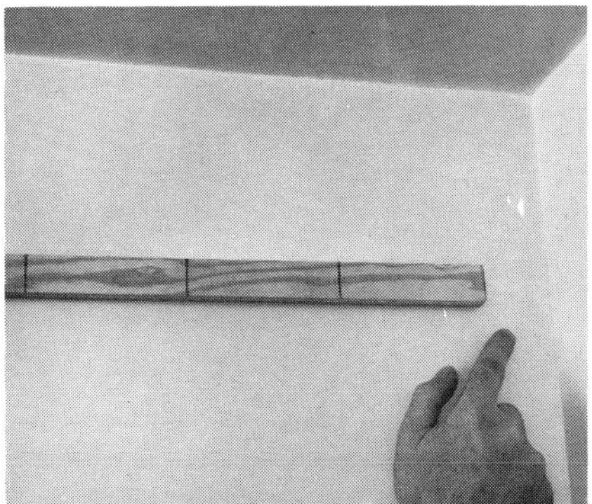

Shift the marked stick so you will have an even margin at both left and right sides.

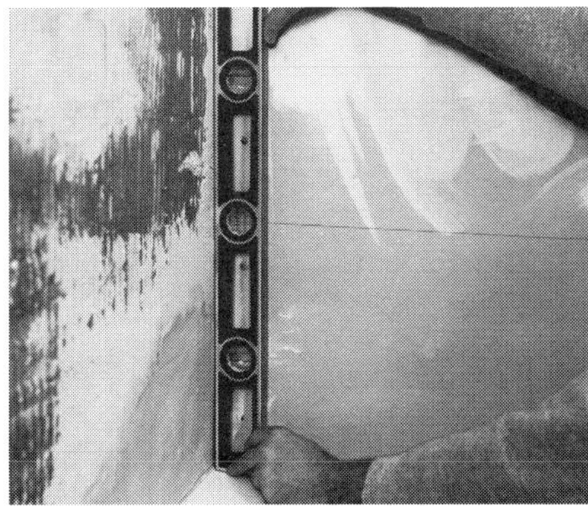

Use a level to establish a line perpendicular to the horizontal starting line.

Ceramic wall tiles

Applying the tiles

1. Apply tile cement after the wall surface has been prepared and cleaned.

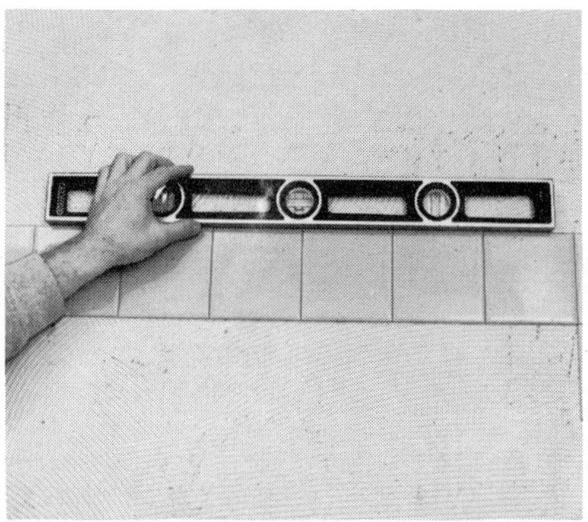

2. Lay out first row of tiles along the horizontal line above the tub.

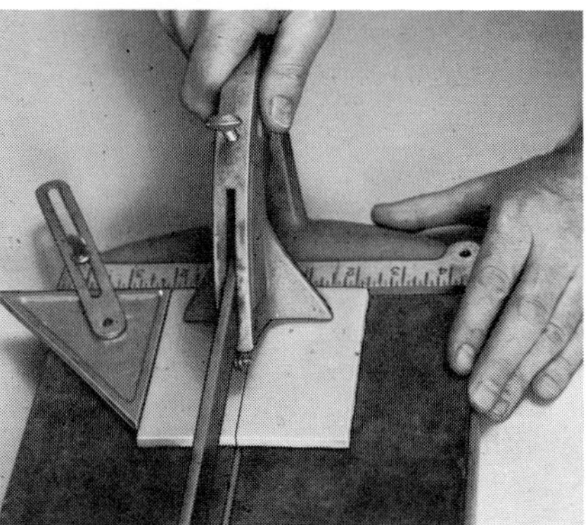

3. A commercial tile cutter can be rented to cut tiles to size.

4. Another method is to score the glazed surface with a glass cutter.

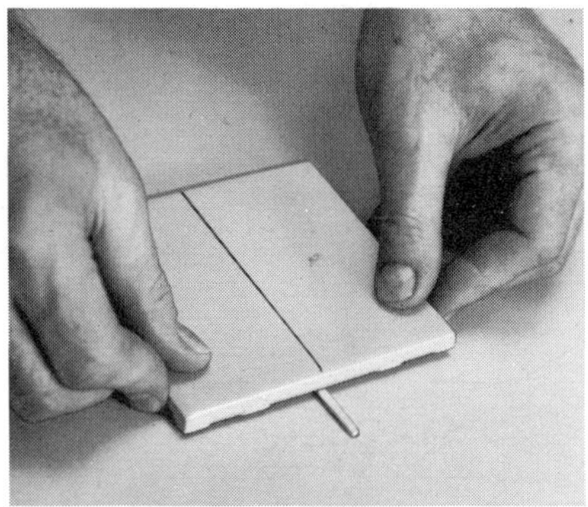

5. Then break the tile by pressing, as shown, over a nail or dowel.

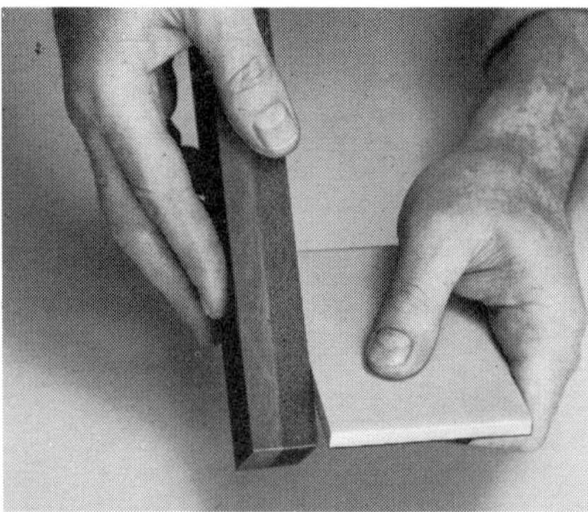

6. If the break leaves a rough edge, smooth it with a whetstone and water.

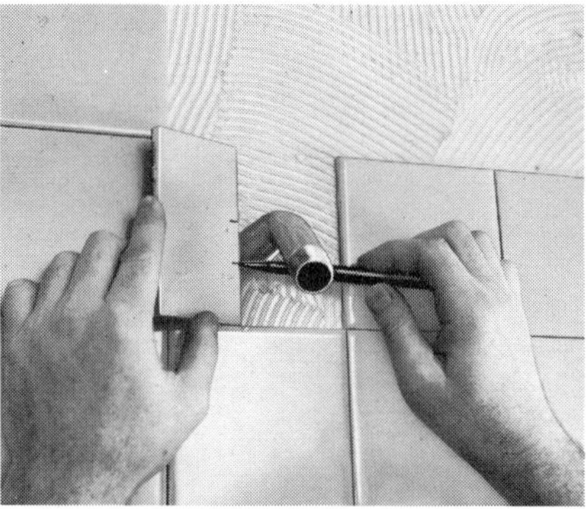

7. To fit tiles around fixtures, mark cut-out lines on half-tiles.

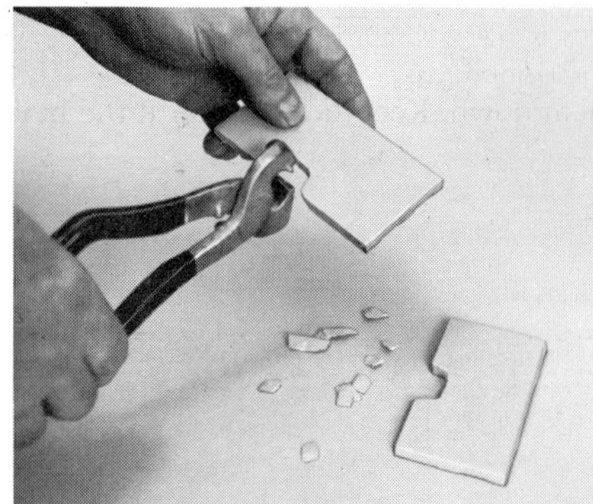

8. Then cut out tile with tile nippers to fit around the fixtures.

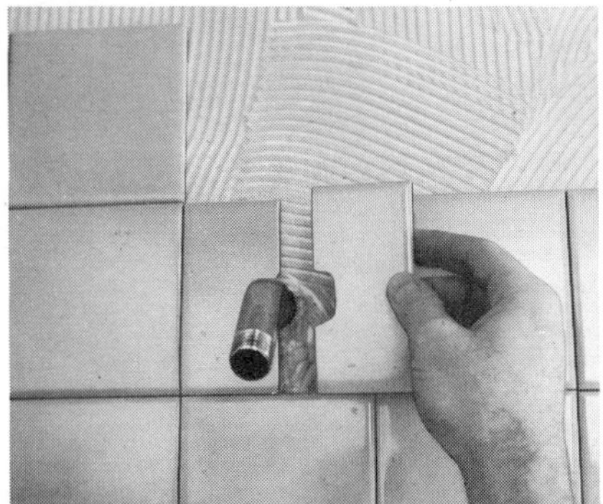

9. Fit both halves of the tile around the fixture after applying mastic.

10. Apply grout with rubber-surfaced trowel after mastic has set for 24 hours.

11. Clean out intersections with the handle of an old toothbrush.

12. Finally, wipe off excess grout with a dampened sponge.

Mosaic floor tiles

Mosaic floor tiles are sold in 1- x 1- or 1- x 2-foot sheets. Some come with a paper backing which holds the sheet together. Others have a protective paper covering on the top surface which must be peeled off after installation.

Before mosaic tiles are laid, the floor surface must be leveled, all cracks filled, and in the case of rough hardwood floors, they should be sanded. In the case of badly warped floors, a plywood or hardboard underlayment is the easiest way of preparing a good tile base.

The floor area should be squared-off as described for standard tiles (p. 356). Apply mastic with a notched trowel over a 3-foot square at a time. Lay the sheets of tile lightly on the mastic. Slide into proper position, then press firmly in place.

Be sure that the spaces between the sheets of tile equal the size of the spaces between the individual tiles. After every three or four sheets of tile have been positioned, use a rubber-surfaced trowel to tamp them down. Keep tamping until the mastic begins to ooze up between the individual tiles.

When the main area of the floor is completed, you will have to cut and fit narrow pieces of tile around the edges. If the tile has a pattern, be sure to follow it when fitting smaller pieces in place. Very small gaps, such as along the edge of the bathtub and around fixtures and pipes, will have to be filled with individual tiles. You may have to cut and shape some of the tiles. Do this with a pair of tile nippers.

If the tile is covered with protective paper, soak the paper with warm water and a sponge. Peel off the paper, wipe off excess water and let the tile set 24 hours prior to grouting.

Grouting: To fill the spaces between the tiles, mix 3 parts Portland cement with 1 part water. Continue adding water until the mixture is creamy. Use a rubber-surfaced trowel to spread the grout over the tile, forcing it between the cracks. Let the grout dry at least 12 hours before walking on the floor.

Wipe the excess grout from the floor immediately with a damp sponge. After the floor has thoroughly dried, the cement will leave a hazy film. Remove this with a mixture of muriatic acid and water (1 part acid to 10 parts water). Apply the solution with a rag, wipe thoroughly, and dry with a clean rag. Wear rubber gloves when working with the acid solution. Two applications may be necessary.

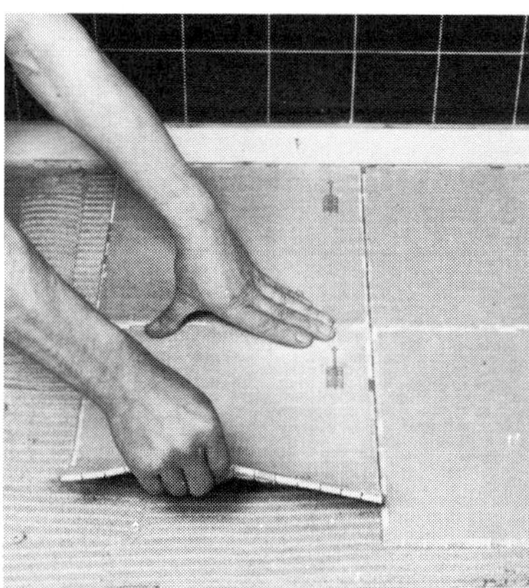

1. The space between the sheets should be the same as between the tiles.

2. Tamp the sheets down so that they are firmly embedded in the adhesive.

3. Mark the edge to be cut after laying sheet, down side up, over the vacant area.

4. Apply mastic to bottom of cut sheet before setting it in place.

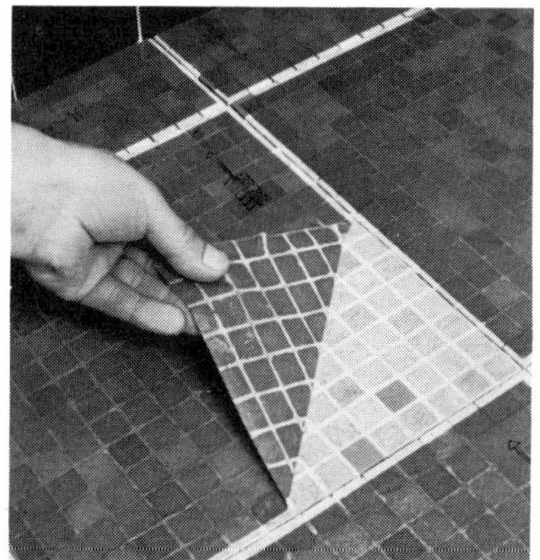

5. Soak tiles covered with protective paper with warm water. Peel the paper off.

6. Use squeegee or rubber-surfaced trowel to fill gaps with grout.

Covering old floors

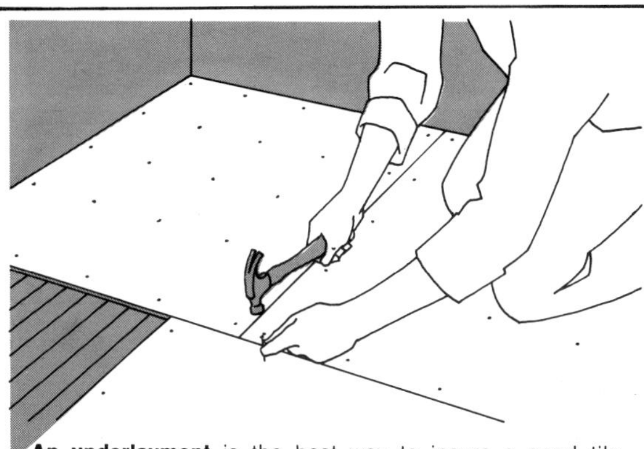

An underlayment is the best way to insure a good tile floor installation. When nailing hardboard underlayment, observe the following precautions: (1) Never butt sheets of underlayment together. Leave about 1/32-inch expansion space between them. (2) Always stagger seams to avoid the possibility of four corners meeting at a single point. (3) Use cement-coated nails or annular-ring nails to fasten the underlayment to the floor.

Preparations for ceramic tile

Lay ceramic tiles so they are square in relation to the doorway—that is, so the line of tiles runs squarely from the entry toward the back of the room. This is especially important with odd-shaped rooms.

Mark a line on the floor at right angles to the doorway, running from the center of the door to the back of the room. Take a square length of wood and divide it into lengths as described for wall tiling (p. 353). Floor tiles do not have spacer lugs, so you must allow a 1/16-inch gap between the tiles. Use the piece of wood as a measuring stick.

Starting from the door jamb with your first full tile, use your measuring stick to divide the center line into tile widths. (You may have to cut tiles at the far wall—full tiles rarely fit room length exactly.) Mark the point where the last full tile will finish. Nail a wooden batten across the width of the room at this point. The batten must be at precise right angles to the center line, no matter what angle the back wall makes. Nail another batten at the left-hand end of the first to give you a perfectly square corner. This is where tiling will start.

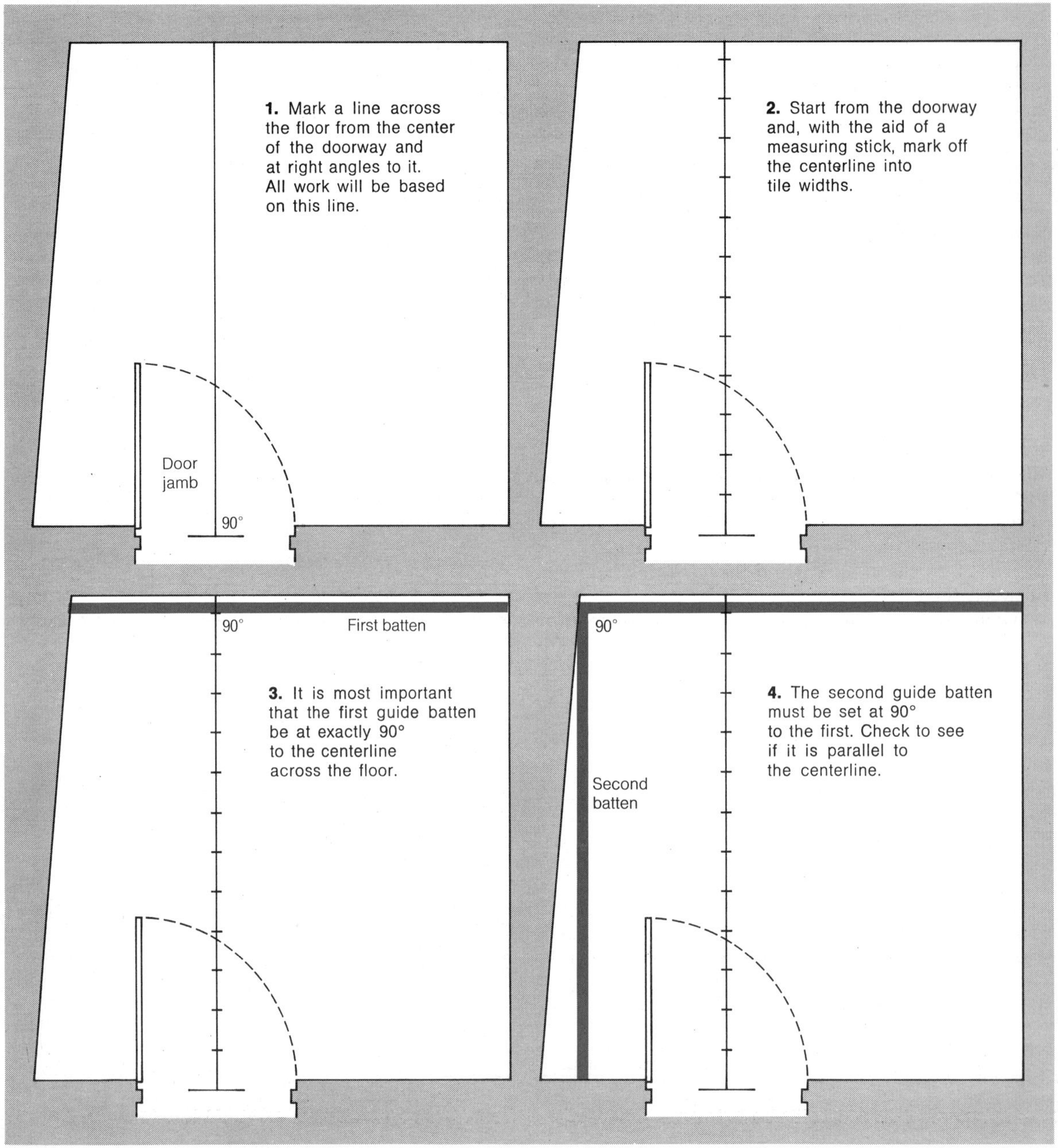

1. Mark a line across the floor from the center of the doorway and at right angles to it. All work will be based on this line.

Door jamb

90°

2. Start from the doorway and, with the aid of a measuring stick, mark off the centerline into tile widths.

90°

First batten

3. It is most important that the first guide batten be at exactly 90° to the centerline across the floor.

90°

Second batten

4. The second guide batten must be set at 90° to the first. Check to see if it is parallel to the centerline.

Cutting tiles

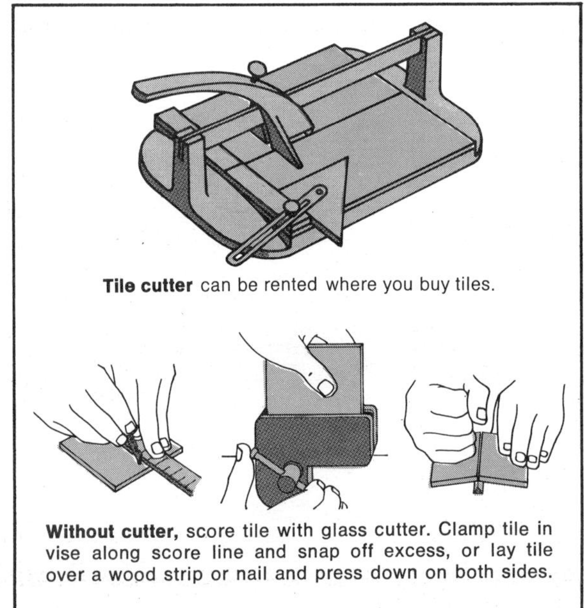

Tile cutter can be rented where you buy tiles.

Without cutter, score tile with glass cutter. Clamp tile in vise along score line and snap off excess, or lay tile over a wood strip or nail and press down on both sides.

Laying a ceramic tile floor

Ceramic floor tiles are made either 4 inches square by ⅜ inch thick or 6 inches square by ½ inch thick. They may have a mat or a glazed surface. Unlike wall tiles, they do not have spacer lugs. Wood floors are the best surfaces for them. Concrete or brick floors are generally unsuitable for ceramic tiling because they are rarely flat and must be accurately leveled—a job that is best left to a professional—before the tiles can be laid.

Make sure that the floor to be tiled is perfectly flat and firm—nail down any loose boards, and sand the surface if necessary. Very uneven or rough floors should be covered with an underlayment of hardboard. Another preliminary requirement: Some adjustment will have to be made to the doors to compensate for the thickness of the tiles.

Be sure to use a floor-tile mastic to lay ceramic tile; these mastics are usually rubber-based and have the needed flexibility to allow for movement while tiles are being set. Apply the mastic according to the directions on the container. Use a notched trowel to spread it over a 3-foot-square area of the floor in the corner where you have laid out the battens. Press the tiles into the adhesive and insert 1/16-inch spacers between them.

When you have finished tiling the first section, scrape off any excess adhesive from around the tiles and coat the next area, continuing in this way until the main floor area is complete.

If you find as you work that the tiles are getting closer together, or farther apart, this could mean that your battens were not at an exact 90-degree angle. Try manipulating the tiles so that they are even (the flexible mastic permits some adjustment). If you cannot, you will have to take them all up and start over, carefully repositioning the battens at the correct 90-degree angle.

When the main area of the floor is complete, remove the battens and cut the tiles to fit the spaces around the edges of the room. Place a tile upside-down over the space to be filled and mark it at least at two points to indicate where it must be cut (allow 1/16 inch for spacing). Carry these marks around to the face of the tile and carefully score a line into the surface with a tile cutter.

To break the tile at the score mark, kneel on the floor and grip a spare tile between your knees. Hold the tile to be cut on each side of the score line and strike the scored area on the edge of the tile you are holding between your knees. The tile should break cleanly. Smooth the cut edge with a whetstone, rubbing along, not across, the edge. Butter the entire back of the tile with adhesive and place it in position with spacers and with the cut edge against the wall.

Allow at least 24 hours for the adhesive to set before removing the spacers and rubbing grout into the joints. Grout the floor as described for wall tiling (p. 354) but use a rubber squeegee instead of a sponge to make sure that the grout penetrates well into the gaps. To complete the job, wipe up any excess grout and smooth the joints. Apply a second coating of grout to fill in any small gaps. Wait at least 24 hours.

Apply special mastic to about a 3-foot-square area. Use a notched trowel for the job; cover surface thoroughly.

Press the tiles into place. Do not slide them or you may displace the adhesive and push it up between the tile joints.

Use pieces of 1/16-in.-thick cardboard or wood as spacers to keep the joints between the tiles to a uniform size.

When marking tiles for cutting to fit around the edges of the room, make an allowance of 1/16 in. for the spacers.

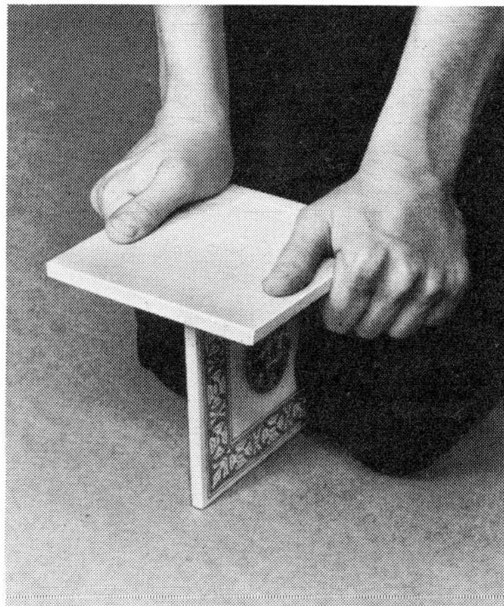
To get a clean break, use both hands to strike the glazed surface along its scored line against edge of another tile.

The cut edge of the tile should be set against the wall to make a perfect fit after the spacers have been inserted.

Floor coverings

Resilient flooring

Resilient floors come in **sheet** form, such as linoleum and vinyl, and **tiles**—asphalt, vinyl, vinyl-asbestos, and cork. Except for linoleum and cork tile, most of today's resilient flooring materials can be installed anywhere in the house, including the basement.

Asphalt tile is the least expensive. However, for a few cents more per tile you can get vinyl-asbestos, which has all of asphalt tile's advantages, plus better color, easier care, and grease resistance.

More **vinyl-asbestos tile** is sold than any other kind. It can be installed anywhere, above, on, or below grade. It does not require waxing—buffing gives it a low sheen. Vinyl-asbestos tiles are made of a mixture of vinyl resins and asbestos fiber. Colors and gloss are less brilliant than in pure vinyl, but this has an advantage—scratches and soil do not show up as readily. Other maintenance characteristics are about the same as those of vinyl. Many vinyl-asbestos tiles have a vinyl-formula wearing surface fused to a vinyl-asbestos base.

Vinyl is unquestionably the most popular above-grade flooring material, and deservedly so. A good vinyl in the right pattern and color is easy to maintain. The original shiny vinyl showed scuffs and smudges, but this "plate finish," as it was called, is rarely seen today. Embossing has helped vinyl, and other tile materials, to conceal wear marks. Carved, pitted, fissured, or grained effects are more than just good-looking—they are easier to maintain. Dirt lies loosely in the recesses instead of being walked on and ground in. Texture makes even white floors almost practical, and also hides seams, floor irregularities, and dents left by furniture.

Cork tile is the only natural material among the resilient floorings. Its richness and beauty are an asset to a room, it is soft and warm underfoot, and tends to deaden the sound of footsteps. When coated with vinyl, it is easy to maintain.

Worth a final mention are so-called **"wood tiles"**—a 5/16-inch layer of fine wood, usually oak, on a ⅛-inch foam base, protected by a top coat of factory-applied finish. These tiles, usually 12-inch squares, are laid like vinyl tiles but with a special adhesive available at the same stores that sell the tiles. Leave ½-inch expansion space between wall and tiles.

Estimating and planning for tiling

Vinyl and vinyl-asbestos tiles are 9 or 12 inches square and come in a wide variety of colors. Thickness is ⅛ or 1/16 inch. Avoid solid colors if you want easy maintenance. White and black are especially difficult. The more textures and variations in a tile, the better it will hide seams, floor irregularities, scratches, and soil. Remember, too, that some colors bleach when continuously exposed to sunlight, especially light shades, such as pinks and yellows.

To estimate the number of resilient tiles you need of one color only, first measure the length and width of the room in feet. For 12-inch tiles, you need only multiply length times width to get the number of tiles. For 9-inch tiles, find your length and width measurements on the chart and follow them across and down to the point where they intersect. The number there is the number of tiles required. For instance, you will need 252 9-inch tiles for a room 13 feet long by 10 feet wide. If a fireplace or other structure protrudes into a room, measure this obstruction separately and subtract the appropriate number of tiles. Divide irregularly shaped rooms into two or more rectangles, calculate the number of tiles needed for each, then combine the totals.

If tiles of two colors are to be laid in a checkerboard pattern or in alternate rows, halve the total amount and buy equal quantities of each color. For more complex patterns, shade in the pattern on graph paper—letting each square equal one tile—and count up the number needed of each color.

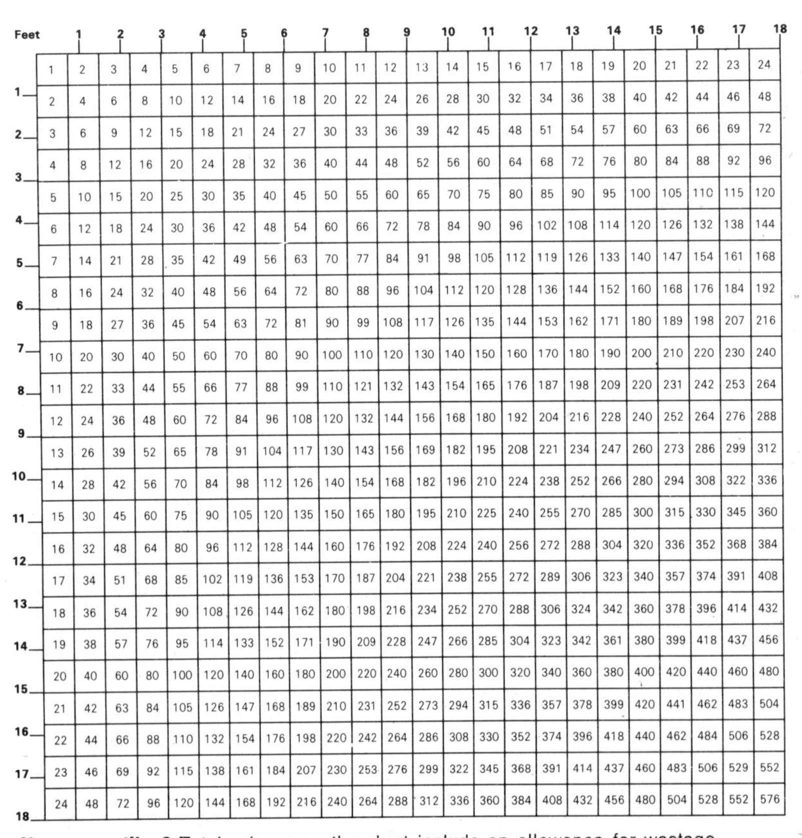

1	2	3	4	5	6	7	8	9	10	11	12	13	14	15	16	17	18	19	20	21	22	23	24
2	4	6	8	10	12	14	16	18	20	22	24	26	28	30	32	34	36	38	40	42	44	46	48
3	6	9	12	15	18	21	24	27	30	33	36	39	42	45	48	51	54	57	60	63	66	69	72
4	8	12	16	20	24	28	32	36	40	44	48	52	56	60	64	68	72	76	80	84	88	92	96
5	10	15	20	25	30	35	40	45	50	55	60	65	70	75	80	85	90	95	100	105	110	115	120
6	12	18	24	30	36	42	48	54	60	66	72	78	84	90	96	102	108	114	120	126	132	138	144
7	14	21	28	35	42	49	56	63	70	77	84	91	98	105	112	119	126	133	140	147	154	161	168
8	16	24	32	40	48	56	64	72	80	88	96	104	112	120	128	136	144	152	160	168	176	184	192
9	18	27	36	45	54	63	72	81	90	99	108	117	126	135	144	153	162	171	180	189	198	207	216
10	20	30	40	50	60	70	80	90	100	110	120	130	140	150	160	170	180	190	200	210	220	230	240
11	22	33	44	55	66	77	88	99	110	121	132	143	154	165	176	187	198	209	220	231	242	253	264
12	24	36	48	60	72	84	96	108	120	132	144	156	168	180	192	204	216	228	240	252	264	276	288
13	26	39	52	65	78	91	104	117	130	143	156	169	182	195	208	221	234	247	260	273	286	299	312
14	28	42	56	70	84	98	112	126	140	154	168	182	196	210	224	238	252	266	280	294	308	322	336
15	30	45	60	75	90	105	120	135	150	165	180	195	210	225	240	255	270	285	300	315	330	345	360
16	32	48	64	80	96	112	128	144	160	176	192	208	224	240	256	272	288	304	320	336	352	368	384
17	34	51	68	85	102	119	136	153	170	187	204	221	238	255	272	289	306	323	340	357	374	391	408
18	36	54	72	90	108	126	144	162	180	198	216	234	252	270	288	306	324	342	360	378	396	414	432
19	38	57	76	95	114	133	152	171	190	209	228	247	266	285	304	323	342	361	380	399	418	437	456
20	40	60	80	100	120	140	160	180	200	220	240	260	280	300	320	340	360	380	400	420	440	460	480
21	42	63	84	105	126	147	168	189	210	231	252	273	294	315	336	357	378	399	420	441	462	483	504
22	44	66	88	110	132	154	176	198	220	242	264	286	308	330	352	374	396	418	440	462	484	506	528
23	46	69	92	115	138	161	184	207	230	253	276	299	322	345	368	391	414	437	460	483	506	529	552
24	48	72	96	120	144	168	192	216	240	264	288	312	336	360	384	408	432	456	480	504	528	552	576

How many tiles? Totals shown on the chart include an allowance for wastage.

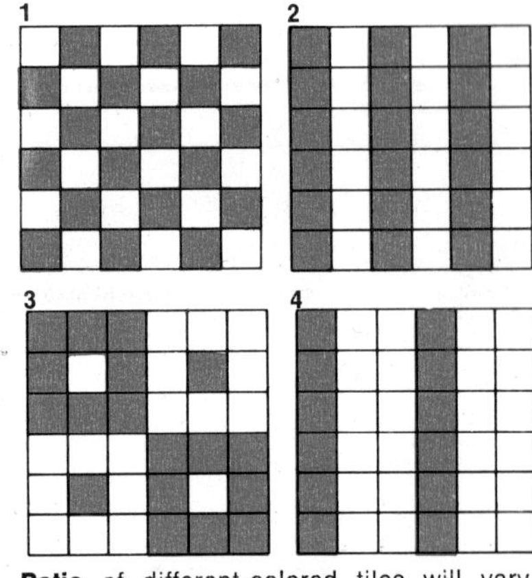

Ratio of different-colored tiles will vary with pattern—½ of each in Nos. 1, 2, 3; ⅓ of one and ⅔ of the other in No. 4.

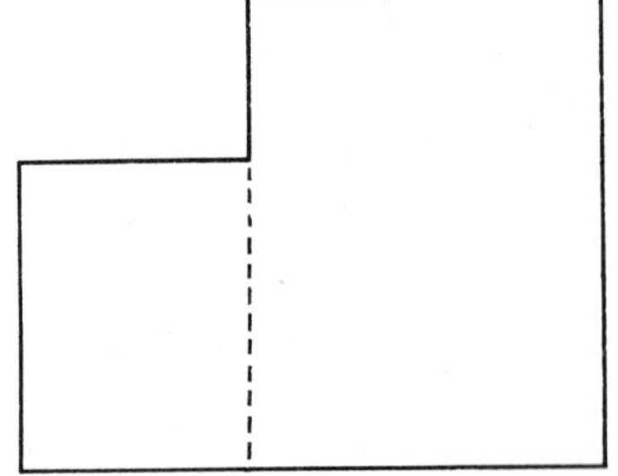

Divide odd shapes into rectangles.

Preparations for resilient floor tiling

For best results, the subfloor should be smooth and dry, free of dust, grease, and wax or other finishing material. On painted floors, paint must adhere tightly, with no cracking or peeling. Old floor coverings, too, must be firmly and evenly attached. Remove any covering except asphalt and vinyl-type tile on subfloors that are on or below grade. On wood floors, replace any badly worn boards and renail loose ones. Cover single-layer or wide board (over 3¼-inch) double flooring with underlayment of plywood or hardboard. Drive all nails flush.

Both brush-on and trowel-type adhesives are good. Professionals prefer the troweled material because they are used to it. The brush-on type is better for the handyman because it avoids the risk of applying too much or too little cement. The tendency of the amateur is to use too much—a real problem with some adhesives, which squeeze up between the tiles. Apply trowel-type adhesive with a notched trowel.

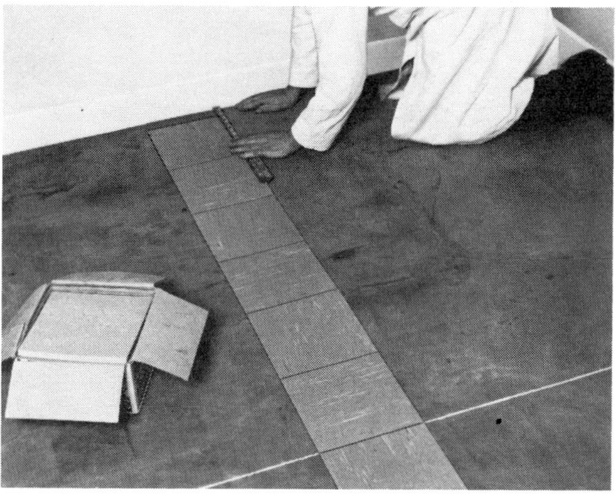

Measure the distance between the last of a row of "dry" tiles and the wall to get border width.

For a wider border, move the row of tiles 4½ in. toward the center of room, away from the wall (6 in. for 12-in. tiles).

Snapping a chalk line: On long lengths, press the center of the string on the floor and snap each of the sides in turn.

Lining up the tiles

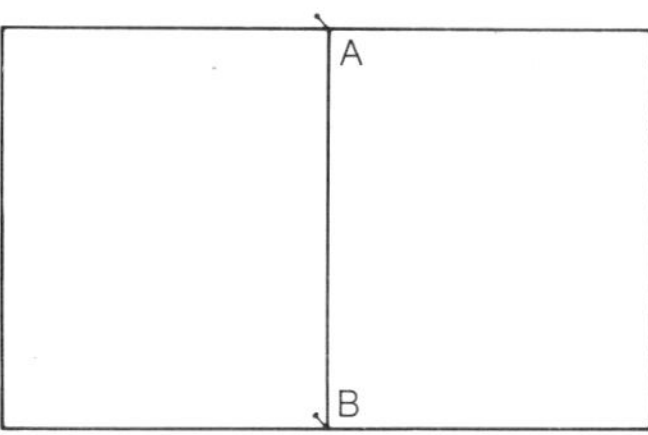

1. Chalk a string slightly longer than room width and tie it between two nails positioned at opposite sides of the room. Nails should extend about an inch above the floor.

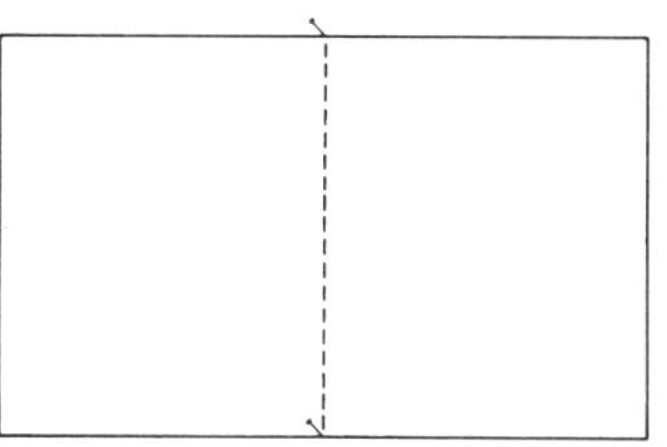

2. Make certain that the string is tight so it will snap properly. Raise it a few inches and then let it snap free to mark a chalk line on the floor.

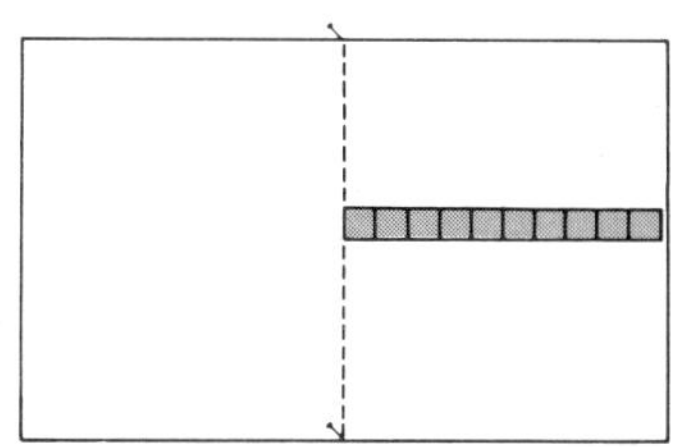

3. Determine center of chalk line; place a line of "dry" tiles from the chalk line to the side wall, lining up the first tile with the chalk line and the center mark.

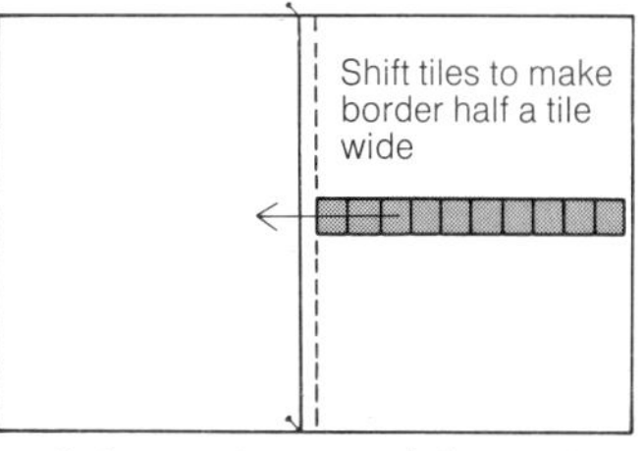

4. If the gap between wall and closest tile is 3 in. or less (for 9-in. tiles), move row 4½ in. from wall. Set new nails and snap second line.

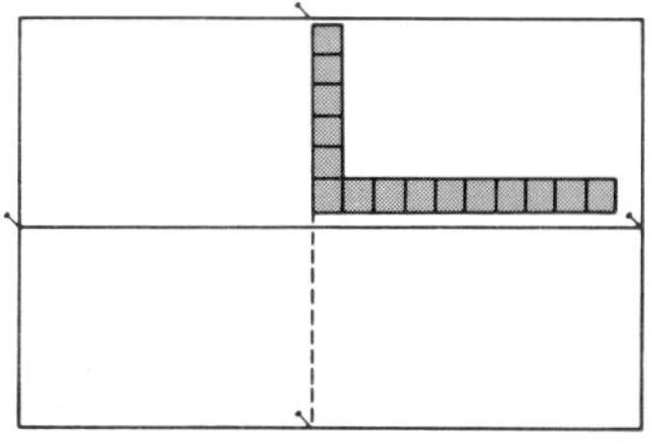

5. If gap is more than 3 in., leave tiles alone and lay out second row at right angles to first. If gap at end is 3 in. or less, follow step 4.

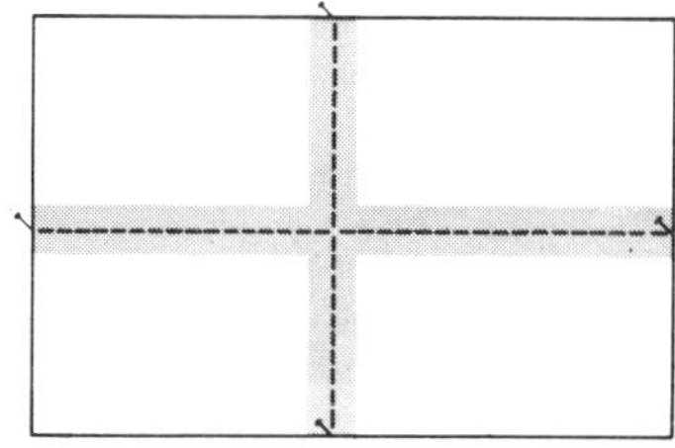

6. This establishes lines against which to lay the tiles. Leave the nails and string in place temporarily as a guide for laying the tiles.

Laying the tiles

Tile half the room at a time, first spreading adhesive over about a square yard of floor on each side of the center line. Place the first two tiles in the right angles made by the chalk lines and work outward from each side to form a pyramid pattern. Lower the tiles into the adhesive—do not slide them into place; this forces the adhesive up. Lay marbleized or grained tile so that the pattern in adjacent tiles runs in opposite directions. Continue spreading adhesive and laying tiles up to the borders.

To cut the border tiles, place a "dry" tile exactly over an adjacent fixed tile; hold another on top, flush with the wall, and score along the inner edge. The trimmed part of this tile will fit the border.

Do the same when cutting a tile to fit against a door frame. First place and mark a tile as though you were cutting it for a straight border. Then move the tile, without turning it, to the other side of the door frame, again place it over a fixed tile, and draw a line at right angles to intersect the first. Cut along the lines up to the intersection with a sharp knife.

Treat more complicated shapes, such as thresholds, the same way, but take separate measurements from each surface in both tile positions. In the bottom example at the right, the tile is in its first position, and lines are drawn a tile-width away from surfaces A, B, C, and D. If the outline is curved, draw a freehand line between the marks after marking intersections from the second tile position. Wire solder, bent to fit, can be used to transfer curves.

1. Lay the tiles outward to make a pyramid shape, starting with tiles 1 and 2 in the angles made by the lines. Where you can, kneel on the tiles as you work.

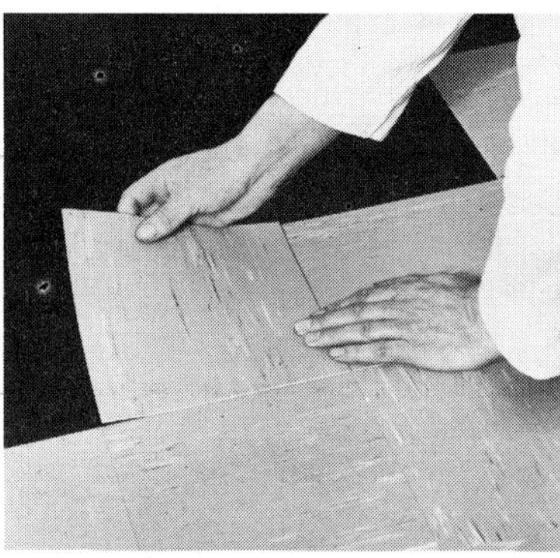

2. Butt each tile against the adjacent ones and lower it into place.

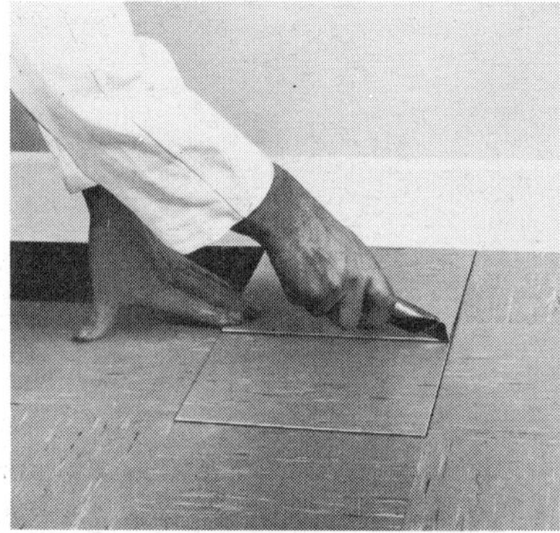

3. Use a knife to scribe border tiles, then bend tile to complete the break.

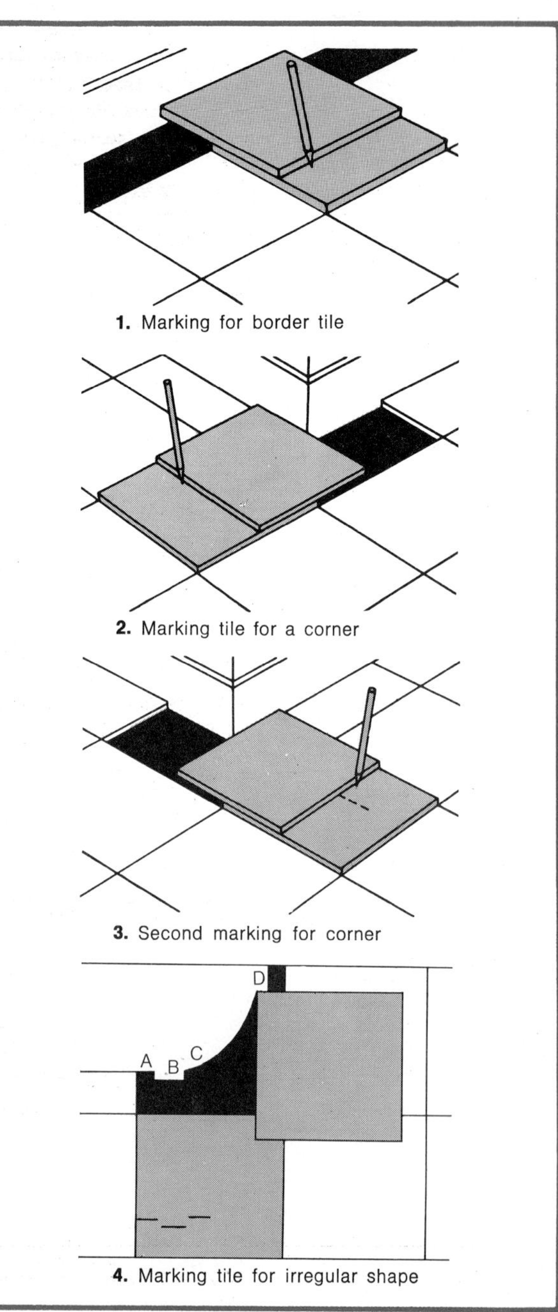

1. Marking for border tile

2. Marking tile for a corner

3. Second marking for corner

4. Marking tile for irregular shape

How to lay sheet vinyl

Standard sheet flooring that is installed permanently with adhesive is not generally recommended as a do-it-yourself material. Loosely laid vinyl flooring, however, is well within a handyman's skills.

Most cushioned vinyls are available in 6-, 9-, and 12-foot widths. Seaming is needed only for rooms that are more than 12 feet wide and is accomplished as follows: To match the pattern across the seam, the second piece of material must be overlapped along the seam edge. Be sure to allow enough material in both width and length to match the pattern. After the pattern is matched, weight or tape the matched pieces so that they will not shift. Cut to fit at the walls, allowing for ⅛-¼ inch clearance at the edges.

Using a metal straightedge as a guide, cut through both pieces of material in the overlapped area with a sharp knife. As you cut, keep the knife vertical, not leaning to the right or left. Remove the cut-off pieces, both top and bottom.

Next lay back one piece of flooring at the seam. Draw a pencil line on the floor along the edge of the second piece. Lay back the second piece and spread a 6-inch band of adhesive under the seam area, centering it on the pencil line. If the back of the vinyl has been waxed, sand the area lightly. Use a vinyl cement recommended by the flooring manufacturer and spread it with a notched trowel. Lay the vinyl sheeting onto the wet adhesive and wipe down with a damp cloth to ensure good contact with the adhesive.

In trimming the vinyl sheeting, allow a minimum clearance gap of ⅛ inch between the edge of the material and each wall to provide for expansion and contraction of the underfloor. If molding is used, it will conceal the gap.

Clearance must also be allowed between the vinyl and the floor molding to permit the walls and subfloor to move without affecting the flooring. Removed moldings should be renailed to the baseboard (not the floor), with a piece of cardboard inserted between the molding and the floor. When the cardboard is removed, you will have the proper clearance. If a rubber or vinyl cove base is used, it can be cemented to the wall. Install a metal threshold at doorways, fastening it to the floor but not through the vinyl.

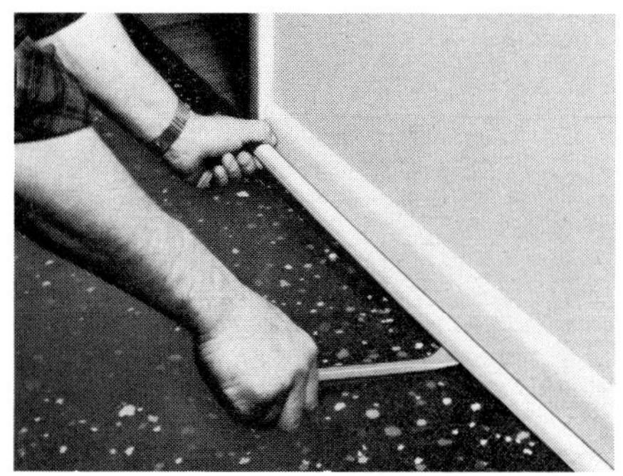

1. To loose-lay sheet vinyl, first remove the wood molding between the baseboard and the floor by prying up gently from the floor and away from the wall.

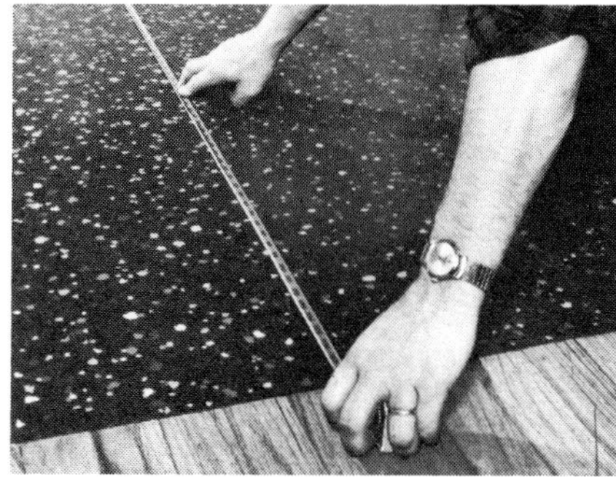

2. Measure the room where the vinyl is to be installed. Roll the vinyl out in another room and let it reach room temperature. Transfer the measurements to it.

3. Snap a chalk line across the rolled-out vinyl to establish a true edge for one side of the room. Mark as many cutouts as possible—for pipes, radiators, etc.—on the vinyl.

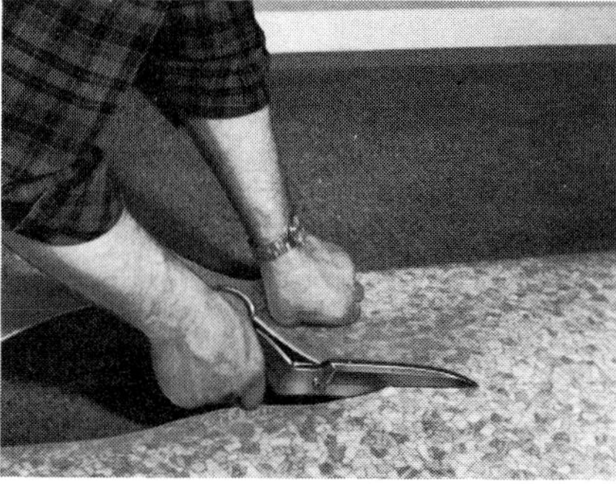

4. Using heavy shears, cut the vinyl on the marked lines. Roll up the material, with the pattern side showing, and carry it to the room where it is to be laid.

5. Start at the longest and most regular wall of the room and butt the sheeting against it. Unroll it across the room, allowing excess material to curve up at other walls.

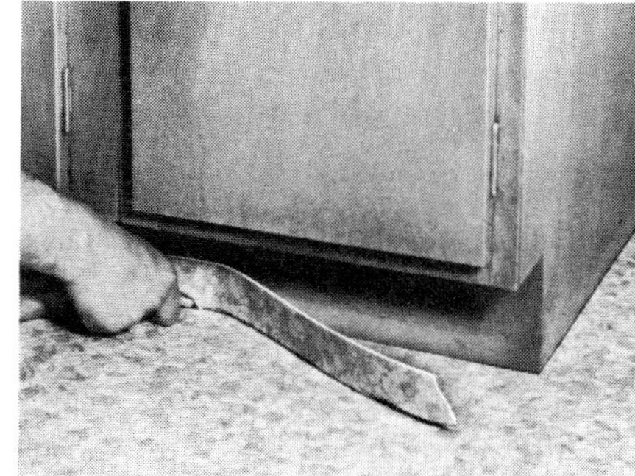

6. Press the flooring material gently into place and trim excess with a knife or scissors. Allow ⅛ in. for clearance at all walls and other vertical surfaces.

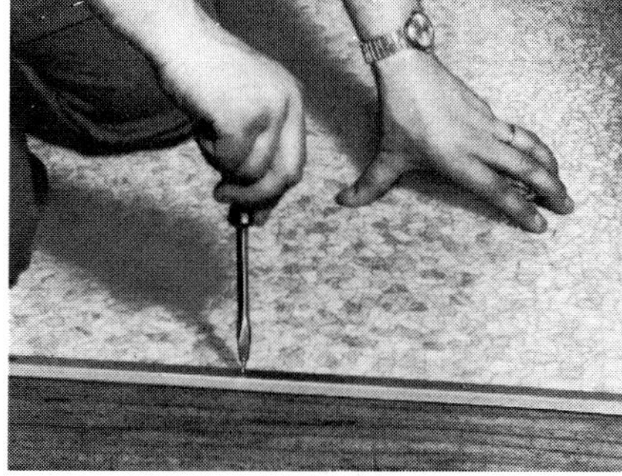

7. At a doorway, it is best to protect the edge of the vinyl with a metal threshold. Screw the threshold to the floor and not through the vinyl. Use roundhead or oval screws.

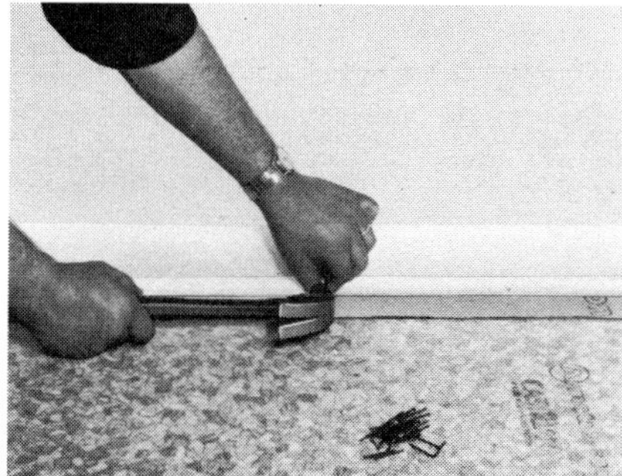

8. The final step is replacing the floor moldings. Slip a piece of cardboard between the molding and the vinyl to provide clearance. After nailing, remove the cardboard.

How to lay a wood floor

Wood floors can be secured directly over joists or even concrete. A subfloor is usually used, however, for added strength; many today are of plywood which is nailed across the joists. This is generally covered with a layer of 15-pound asphalt-saturated building felt, lapped 3 inches at seams and held in place by the finish floor.

Tongue-and-groove strip or board flooring—the kind most commonly used—comes prefinished as well as unfinished, and is usually laid the long way of the room. Take care, in laying a wood floor, not to mar the wood with the head of the hammer. Nail into the tongue at a 45-degree angle and into the subfloor. Use 2-2½ inch steel-cut flooring nails, the choice depending upon the thickness of the finish floor. Start the nails on the tongue side approximately where the shoulder of the tongue comes out. To avoid splitting the tongue, use a nail set to drive the last ¼ inch or so. If there is a subfloor, the nails need not go into the joists. Leave a gap of at least ¼ inch at each side of the room.

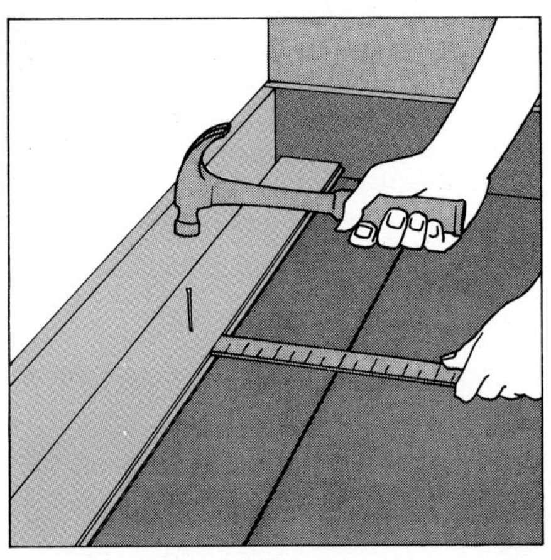

1. Stretch a string across the room as a guide for laying the first course of flooring. Leave a gap of ¼ in. between first course and wall; this will be covered by molding.

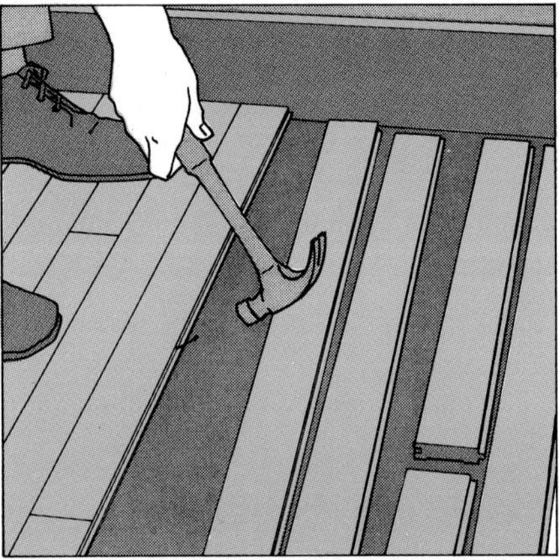

2. For appearance's sake, avoid laying out the floorboards so that too many joints appear in one area. It is best to lay the boards out in a dry run before doing actual nailing.

3. Hammer on a piece of scrap to keep the flooring tight. Each tongue-and-groove board is secured to the next one by blind-nailing diagonally through the tongue.

4. Measuring a piece of flooring in order to fill out a course. If the flooring you are using has a tongue on its width, make sure you cut off this end as the waste.

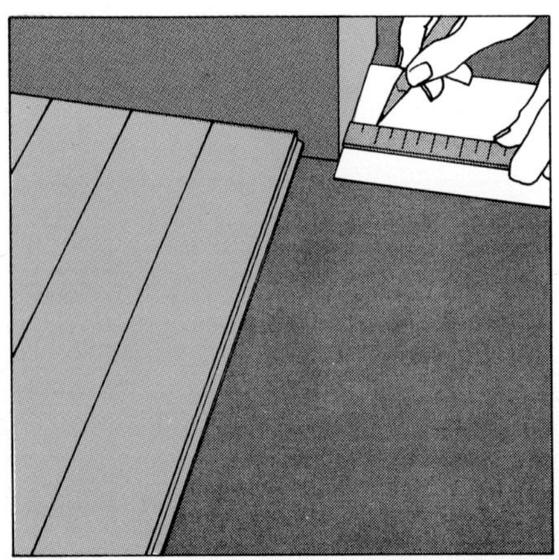

5. To fit flooring around a door frame, make a cardboard pattern to fit around the frame. Then use the cardboard as a template and cut the flooring to fit.

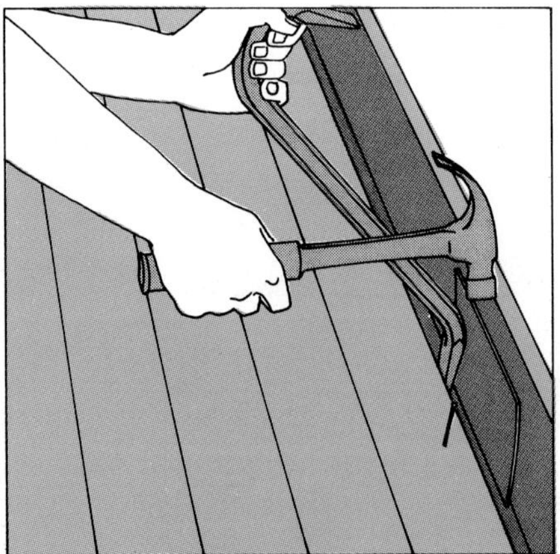

6. Since the last course, and sometimes the one next to it, cannot be blind-nailed, face-nail them in place. Pull them up tight with a crowbar and sink the nailheads.

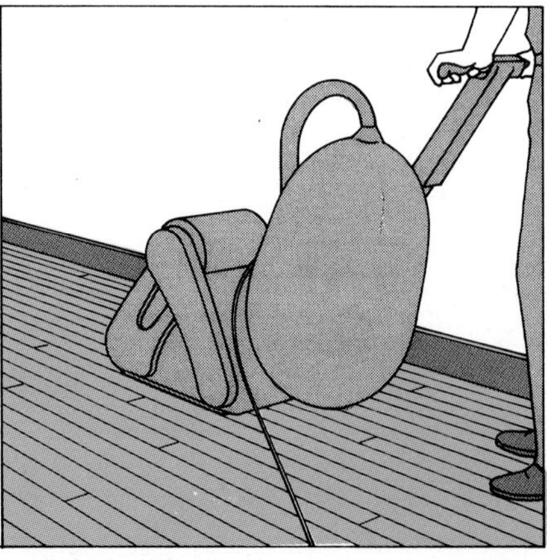

7. The finished floor should be given at least two sandings, first with coarse sandpaper and then with medium or fine. Turn to page 114 to see how to use a sanding machine.

8. The final step consists of applying the baseboard and the shoe molding. Then give the floor two coats of varnish, polyurethane, or shellac. Polish with steel wool and wax.

How to lay a wood floor over concrete

A wood floor can be laid over concrete, using 2 x 4 screeds (short lengths to which flooring can be nailed). Use random lengths 18 to 48 inches long and 2 x 6 or 2 x 8 pieces along the walls. Screeds are set in mastic about ⅛ inch thick, which is spread over the whole floor. If adhesive is applied only under the screeds, it is spread ¼ inch thick; compression by the screeds will spread it further.

With this base, only tongue-and-groove flooring should be used. It is best to stack flooring indoors for at least a week before laying; damp flooring can shrink considerably and leave cracks to be filled. Short lengths are usable, but be sure each piece rests on at least two screeds, preferably more. Nail at every point where a screed is crossed by a piece of flooring. Pieces must be nailed into screeds at laps; this ties the substructure together.

Cover entire floor with ⅛-in.-thick coating of mastic. Use a notched trowel.

Lay random length 2 x 4 screeds so that the ends are overlapping.

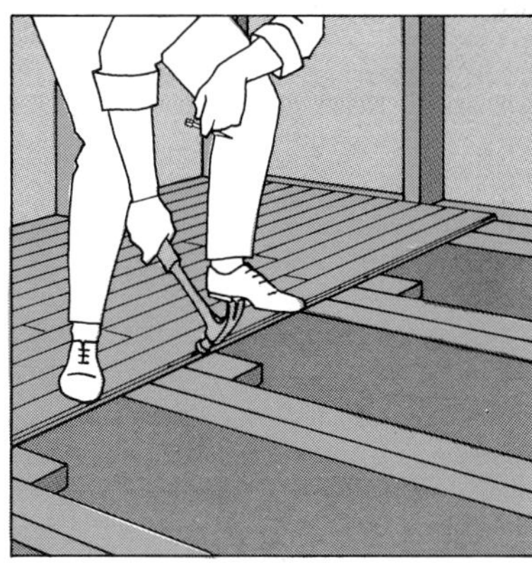

Lay flooring across the screeds. Nail into the screeds through the tongue.

How to lay a wood block floor

Block, or parquet, flooring may be purchased finished in many sizes and thicknesses. Most parquet is made of oak, but other woods are available. The blocks are usually composed of wood strips glued together into a unit; one type is laminated of layers of wood much the same way as plywood. To give wood flooring time to adjust to atmospheric conditions, it should be unpacked and left in the room where it will be used for at least 72 hours beforehand.

You can install block flooring over most types of subfloor, but for on-grade or below-grade concrete, put down polyethylene film before installing the blocks. Do not lay a wood floor over a subfloor that is damp or subject to moisture.

Blocks may be laid either square (parallel to the wall) or diagonally. It is best to have full blocks in the doorway where traffic is concentrated. To accomplish this, start from the center of the wall where the door is located and lay loose blocks to a point about 4 feet into the room. Measure the exact distance from there to the opposite wall. Chalk a line and snap it to mark the center of your starting boundary. Spread the mastic over the part of the marked-off area that is opposite the entranceway.

The first block is located in the right angle at the center point and blocks then laid in a pyramid sequence the same as vinyl tiles (p. 359). When the main area is completed, lay the rest of the blocks.

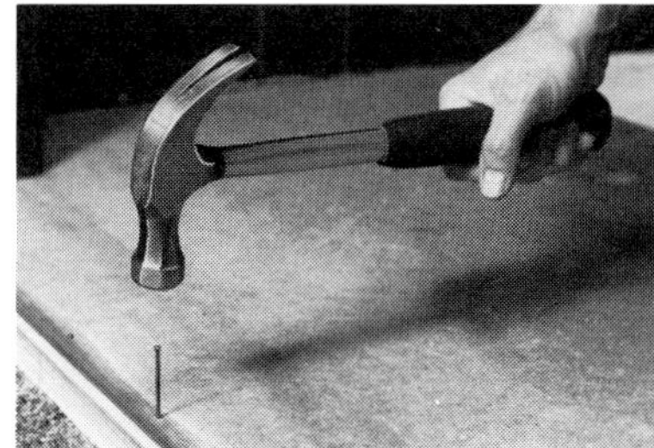

1. If a floor is badly warped or uneven, apply a hardboard underlayment. For tiled floors, remove loose tiles and level spaces with patching cement.

2. For concrete floors, a plastic vapor barrier must be laid first. Dampness from the concrete could cause the floor to warp. Apply adhesive, then roll plastic onto it.

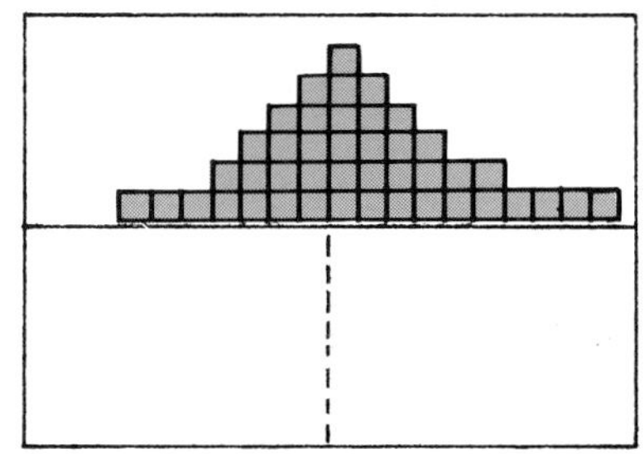

3. Plan to lay the flooring squares in this order, working on half the room at a time. Use a chalk line to mark the room off into square segments.

4. Spread the adhesive with a notched trowel. Hold the trowel at a slight angle so that ridges are left in the adhesive. Coating should be about ⅛ in. thick.

5. Drop the parquet blocks into place with a minimum of sliding. Press the blocks together so that they interlock. Tap the edges to assure a snug fit.

6. Leave at least ¼ in. between the wall and the flooring to allow for expansion. The gap will be covered by the molding. Do not nail molding to the floor.

Laying slate tiles

Slate tiles make particularly good vestibule floors because they are unaffected by water or dirt. They seldom need polishing; an occasional damp wiping is usually sufficient. Slate tiles also make fine garden paths and walks leading to front entrances.

Slate can be laid over any sound wood, concrete, or composition flooring. Loose boards should be nailed down tight. Clean up the area to be tiled, remove all wax, grease, and loose paint. Lay tiles for outdoor use over a concrete base at least 4 inches thick.

A dry run is advisable before laying the tiles. In an area adjacent to and the same size as the proposed floor or walk, arrange the tiles in a pleasing pattern. Place them ground (smooth) side down; the fissured side is the "walking" surface. Number the tiles; this makes them easy to replace in proper order.

If any tiles arrive broken from the dealer, do not despair. They can be fitted together and the natural fissure, or cleft, will hide the break.

Slate tiles are sold by masonry supply dealers loose or packaged—usually enough in a carton to cover 10 square feet. Tiles can be random colors or you can specify one color. Thicknesses are ¼ to ½ inch. Tiles come in an irregular flagstone pattern or in rectangles to lay in a square ashlar pattern.

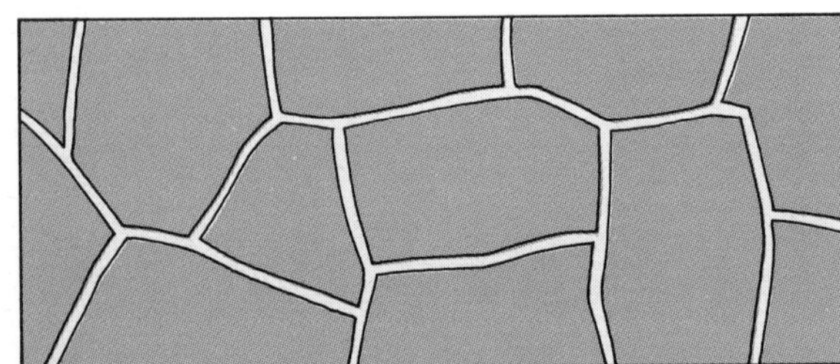

Random pattern tile installation

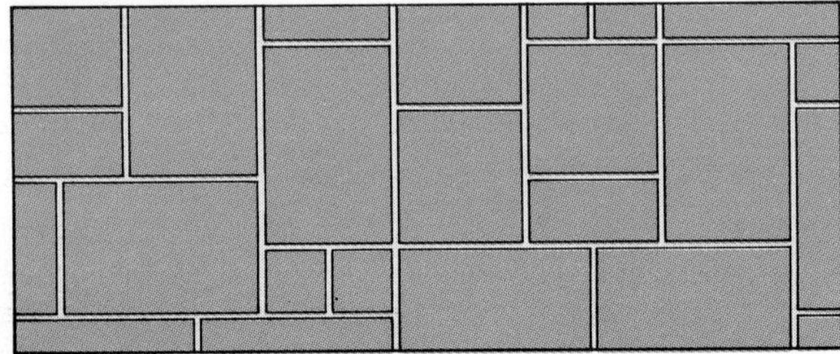

Tiles installed in an ashlar pattern

Snap a chalk line down the center of the longest dimension of the floor.

Make a dry run, allowing a ⅜-in. space between tiles for later grouting.

Use a notched trowel to spread the adhesive over a 2-ft.-square area.

A slate cutter, which you can rent, is used to cut down tiles to fit odd spaces.

Slate cutter can also be used to nibble tiles to fit irregular openings.

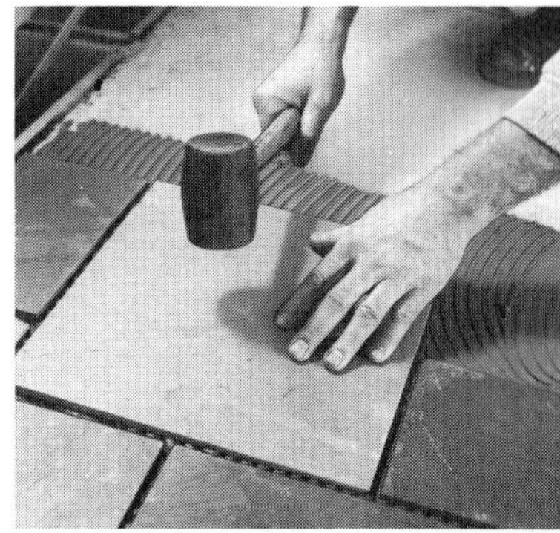

Place a flat board on top of the tiles and lightly tap them into place as shown.

To assure uniform spacing, place a ⅜-in. strip of wood between adjacent tiles.

Let tiles set overnight, then apply grout to joints; fill spaces flush to surface.

Wipe off surplus grout with a damp sponge. Finally, polish with a dry cloth.

Wall-to-wall carpeting

Wall-to-wall carpeting can make a small room look larger, insulate any room against drafty floors, and do a certain amount of soundproofing. Fortunately for the home decorator, carpeting of this type is not too difficult to install.

All carpets consist of surface pile and backing. The surface pile may be nylon, polyester, polypropylene, acrylic, wool, or cotton. Each has its advantanges and disadvantages; which you select depends on your needs and pocketbook. Carpeting can be purchased in 15-, 12-, and 9-foot widths.

Measuring and estimating: Measure the room in the direction in which the carpet will be laid. To broaden long, narrow rooms, lay patterned or striped carpeting across the width. For conventionally rectangular rooms, measure the room lengthwise. Include the full width of door frames so the carpet will extend slightly into the adjoining room.

Most wall-to-wall carpeting is priced by the square yard. To determine how many square yards you need, multiply the length by the width of the room in feet and divide the result by 9.

Choosing a padding: Except for so-called "one-piece" and cushion-backed carpeting, underlay or padding

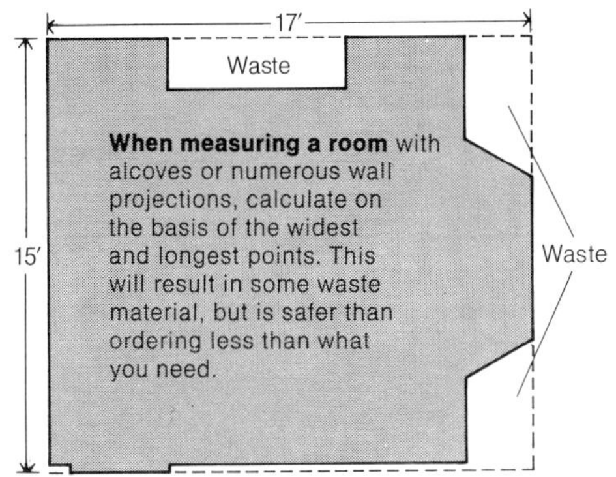

Maximum carpet width is 15 feet.

is essential to a good carpet installation. It prolongs the life of the carpeting, increases its soundproofing capacity, and adds to underfoot comfort.

The most common types of carpet padding are latex (rubber), sponge-rubber foams, soft- and hard-back vinyl foams, and felted cushions made either entirely of animal hair or of a combination of hair and jute. Of all types, the latex and vinyl foams are generally considered the most practical. Their waffled surface tends to hold the carpet in place. Most carpet padding comes in a standard 4½-foot width.

Cushion-backed carpeting is increasing in popularity, especially with do-it-yourself homeowners. The high-density latex backing is permanently fastened to the carpet, which eliminates the need for a separate underpadding. It is non-skid and heavy enough to hold the carpet in place without the use of tacks. In addition, the foam rubber backing keeps the edges of the carpet from unraveling so that it need not be bound. Foam rubber is mildew-proof and unaffected by water, so the carpet can be used in basements and other below-grade installations. It can even be laid directly over unfinished concrete.

The really key feature of this backing, however, is the "dimensional stability" it imparts to the carpet. This added characteristic means that the carpet will not stretch, nor will it expand and contract from temperature or humidity changes. Thus these carpets can be loose-laid, with no need for adhesives or tacks to give them stability.

Preparing the floor: To lay carpets successfully on wood floors, they must be warp-free, with all nails hammered flush and old tacks removed. Nail down any loose floorboards and plane down the high ridges of warped boards. Fill wide cracks between floorboards with strips of wood or wood putty. Cover floors that are warped and cracked beyond reasonable repair with hardboard or plywood.

Stone or concrete floors that have surface ridges or cracks should be treated beforehand with a floor-leveling compound in order to reduce carpet wear. These liquid compounds are also useful for sealing the surface of dusty or powdery floors. A thin layer of the compound, which is floated over the floor, will keep dust from working its way up through the underlay and into the carpet pile.

The best carpeting for concrete and hard floor-tile surfaces is the so-called indoor-outdoor carpet. The backing of this carpet is made of a closed-pore type of either latex or vinyl foam which keeps out most moisture. It is not wise to lay any of the standard paddings on top of floor tiles unless the room is well ventilated and free of condensation. Vinyl and asbestos floor tiles accumulate moisture when carpeting is laid over them; this condensation soaks through into the carpet and will eventually cause a musty odor and will also produce ugly mildew stains.

Methods of fastening carpets: The standard fastening methods are with tacks or by means of tackless fittings. Carpets can also be loose-laid with only a few tacks at entrances. Carpet tack lengths are ¾ and 1 inch. The first is long enough to go through a folded carpet hem and anchor it firmly to the floor. The 1-inch tacks are used in corners where the folds of the hem make three thicknesses.

Tackless fittings are a convenient fastening method. They consist of a 4-foot wooden batten with a number of spikes projecting at a 60-degree angle. The battens are nailed to the floor around the entire room, end to end and ¼ inch out from the baseboard,

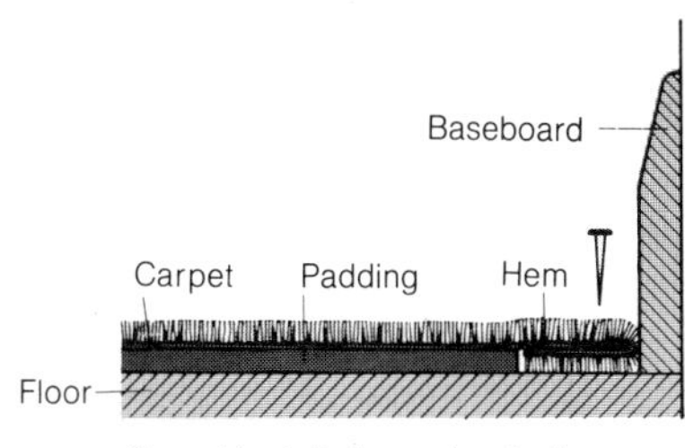

Carpet installation using tacks.

with the spikes facing toward the wall. The spikes grip the backing of the carpet to hold it in place. On stone or concrete floors, the battens are glued in place with special adhesives.

Though cushion-backed carpeting will stay in place without fastening, it is best to hold it down with double-face tape. Carpets can also be held down with

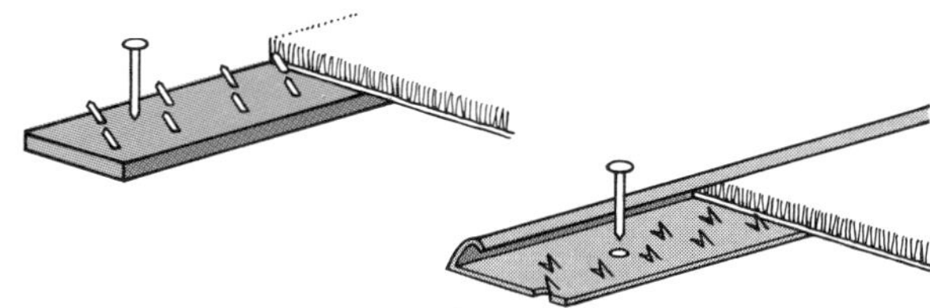

Tackless fitting for wall and doorway (right).

Velcro tape where the frequent removability of the carpet for cleaning and maintenance is a factor. Velcro consists of two tapes, one having thousands of tiny nylon loops and the other tiny hooks which mesh when they are pressed together.

Standard carpet installation method

To install a carpet you will need a hammer large scissors, a sharp knife, a 3-foot rule, needle and carpet thread, chalk and a chalk line, latex adhesive, and carpet tape. The only special tool is a carpet stretcher, called a kicker, which can usually be rented from the carpet dealer.

Cutting and seaming of a new carpet is often done prior to delivery, and final fitting and adjustments made when the carpet is in the room. Before starting the job, remove all furniture and any doors that swing into the room. If you are cutting the carpet yourself, spread it out on a suitable floor space and chalk the exact pattern of the room on the pile surface. Then cut along the chalk line with the scissors or sharp knife.

Join unseamed carpet by placing the two pieces so the pile surfaces meet edge to edge. Match patterned carpets carefully; with plain carpets, lay each piece so the piles run the same way. Join the pieces with carpet thread, taking stitches at 18-inch intervals along the seam. Pull the carpet tight after each stitch to take up slack. Sew along the seam between stitches, tucking any protruding fibers back into the pile. Carpet can also be seamed by cementing carpet tape to the backing threads with latex adhesive. Open carpet to room length and position it before starting to put down the padding. The pile should fall away from windows to avoid uneven shading in daylight. Fold one end of carpet back halfway and put the padding down on the exposed part of the floor. Do the same at the other end. This avoids wrinkles caused by movement of the padding.

Using tacks: Start at the corner of the room that is formed by the two walls with the fewest obstructions; butt the carpet up against the wall, leaving about 1½ inches up the baseboard for hemming. Attach carpet temporarily with tacks about 6 inches from the baseboard along these two walls. Use the kicker to stretch the carpet, first along the length, then the width. Start from the middle of the wall, stretching alternately toward opposite corners. When it is smooth, tack down the stretched area temporarily.

Cut slots for pipes, fireplace protrusions, and radiators. Trim back the padding to about 2 inches from the wall to leave a channel for the carpet hem. Fold the hem under and tack the carpet in place with a tack every 5 inches through the fold.

Using tackless fastenings: Position the carpet in the room and put down the padding. Trim the padding so that it meets the strip at the wall. Nail the carpet along two walls with temporary tacking, then use the kicker to stretch it over the spikes of the tackless fastenings. Remove the temporary tacking and restretch the carpet, allowing a 3/8-inch overlap. Turn down the overlap and press it firmly into the channel between the wall baseboard and the tackless fittings. Protect the exposed edge of the carpet at doorways with a special metal binder strip, or bar. The strip is nailed to the floor at the doorway and the carpet slipped under a metal lip which is then hammered down to grip the carpet edge.

Tacks can be used as an alternative to a binder strip. Before tacking, tape the exposed edge of woven carpet to prevent fraying if the selvage has been trimmed off. Cement carpet tape to the backing threads with latex adhesive. Nonwoven or latex-backed carpet will not fray, but tape is still advisable to protect exposed edges. If the door drags, remove it from its hinges and trim accordingly.

Tackless fittings are nailed all around the room, ¼ in. away from the wall. Remove shoe molding before installing; move out all furniture.

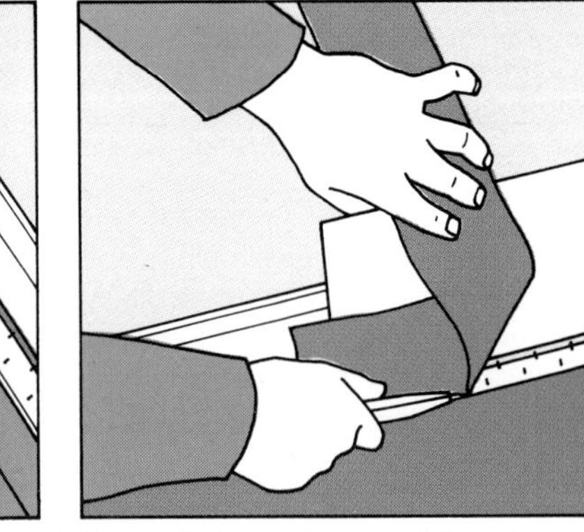

The underlayment, or padding, is next nailed down and trimmed so that it is flush with the tackless strip. Then tack it down so that it will not move.

A special tool called a kicker is used to stretch the carpeting over the nails projecting out of the tackless strip. Bend kicker down to hook carpet over nails.

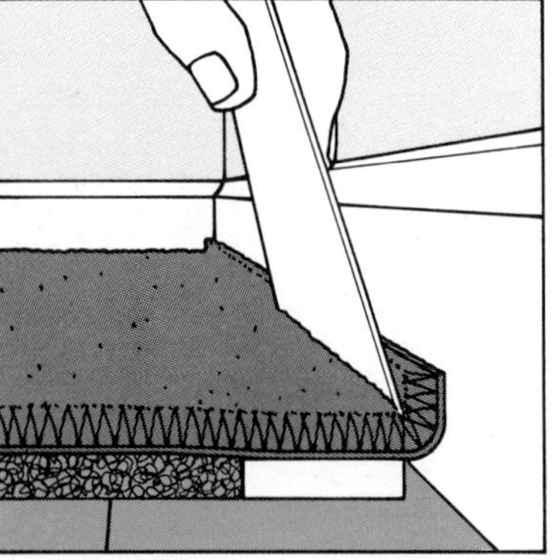

Next step is to trim the carpet, leaving a 3/8-in. overlap, which is tucked into space between the wall and the tackless strip with help of a putty knife.

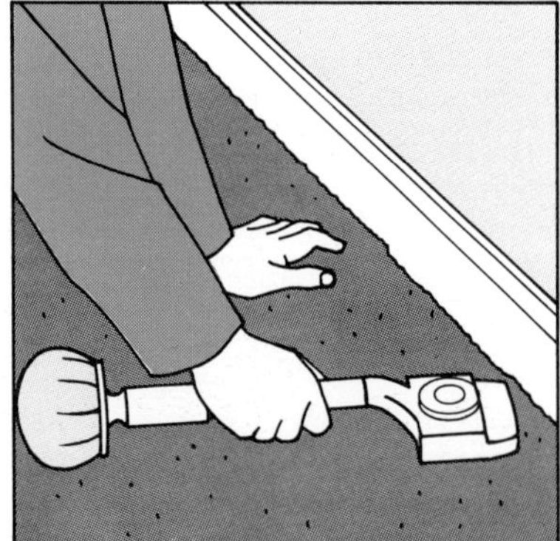

If too much of carpeting has been trimmed, lift the carpeting off the spikes of the tackless fitting and use knee-kicker to fit carpeting to wall.

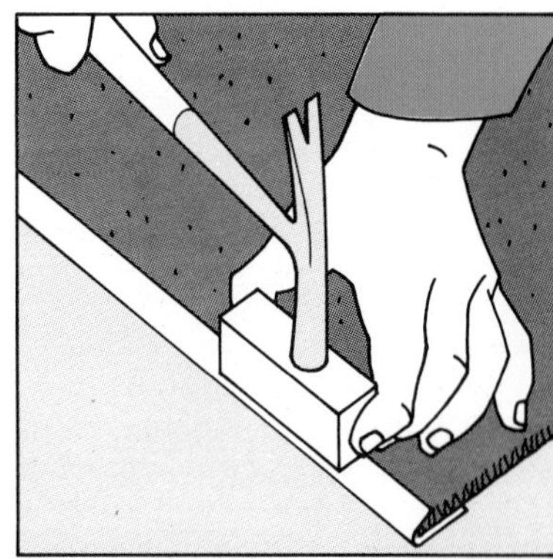

At doorways, the end of the carpet is inserted under the lip of a metal binder bar. The lip is then flattened down over it with a block of wood and mallet.

Carpeting stairs

Stairways can be covered either with fitted carpets, best laid by a professional, or strip carpets, called runners, which are easier to lay and less costly.

Measuring and estimating: Stairway runners come in standard widths of 27 and 36 inches and are usually sold by the running yard.

Straight staircases: To find the length needed, measure in inches the depth of one tread and the height of one riser; add the two measurements together and multiply by the number of stairs; divide the result by 36 to determine the number of linear yards needed.

Staircases with bends: First estimate the total required length for straight stairs and landings. Measure each winding tread separately at the widest point that will be covered by the carpet. Add these figures to the first total and divide the grand total by 36 to get number of yards required. Be sure to allow for some excess to fold under at top and bottom landings so that carpet can be shifted.

Padding: Choose a good-quality rubber or felt underlay to run continuously or to function as individual pads on each tread. Runner underlays need be tacked only at the top landing; individual pads must be tacked separately and are advisable when tackless fittings are used. Be sure that the stair pads are deep enough to butt against the riser and extend about 2 inches over the stair nosing.

Fastening: Stair carpeting may be installed with tacks, tackless fittings, double-face tape, or stair rods—metal rods that slide through eyelets screwed to the bottom of each stair riser. Tape is placed on both sides of the intersection between riser and tread, and over the tread nosing. Tackless fittings are metal strips nailed at the point where treads and risers meet; their metal teeth bite into the carpet, holding it firm. Stair carpets can be tacked down, but tacks, besides being unattractive, must be removed if you ever want to shift the carpet.

Laying: Lay stair carpeting with pile facing down the stairs for maximum wear resistance. To check the sweep of the pile, stroke it back and forth lengthwise. The smoother stroke is the lay of the pile.

When using stair rods, start with the upper landing. Drape the carpet against the riser of the step below and temporarily tack it in place. Let the carpet drop over the next step. Screw an eyelet at each side of the stair riser, near the tread and about ½ inch beyond the edges of the runner. Next slide a stair rod through the eyelets, remove the temporary tacking and continue doing the same with each stair and riser until you reach the bottom. A few inches of extra length, folded under at either the top or bottom landing, will provide the necessary excess for tread-shifting when the carpeting runner becomes worn, which most often happens at the nose of the steps. To shift the runner, slide out the stair rods, move the carpeting up or down, and you will have a fresh wearing surface all the way along.

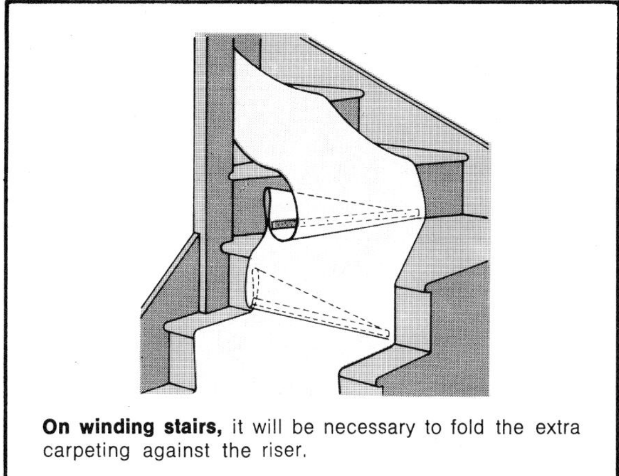

On winding stairs, it will be necessary to fold the extra carpeting against the riser.

When using double-face tape, install it first on the riser-tread joints and nosing. Keep the protective paper on, removing it as you progress down the staircase. Remove it from the first two stairs, lift the carpet over the nosing of these first two treads, and tuck it into the point on the first stair where tread and riser meet. After making sure the carpet is secure, press it firmly against the nosings. Continue this way until you reach the bottom landing.

When using tackless fittings, nail a right-angle strip to the treads and risers of each step. Install a pad for each step. Attach the end of the carpet to the tackless strip on the first riser and tread and stretch the carpet over the tread nosings. Keep it taut and continue to the next tread.

Winding stairs require folds in the carpet to take up slack at the narrow point of the stairs. With stair rods, fold the slack down toward the lower stair rod and drive three tacks through the doubled carpet across the width of the fold, working from the broadest to the narrowest part. Pull the carpet taut. Position it on the next tread and repeat.

With tackless fittings, nail a flat metal grip to the tread of the first step to hold the carpet. Stretch the carpet over the tread, swinging it around to follow the turn of the stairway. Fold the resulting slack downward to meet the flat strip just installed. Mark the back of the carpet at the base of the fold on both sides. Turn the carpet back down the stairs, holding the two marks well into the angle where tread and riser meet. Secure the fold with a second flat strip nailed into the riser through a double thickness.

Hammer down the tackless fittings so they hold down the underlayment pads at the same time. Fold pads over nosing.

Instead of pads, you can use strip underlayment. Nail tackless fittings to riser, over the underlayment.

Drape the carpeting over the nosing, stretching and fitting it to each strip of tackless fitting; continue to next step.

Cushion-backed carpeting

With cushion-backed carpeting, many steps can be eliminated. No tack strips are used, and separate padding is not needed. Although these instructions suit most such carpeting, read the manufacturer's instructions for any deviation in technique.

To install cushioned carpet, 2-inch-wide double-face tape is applied flush with the wall around the entire room; then the carpet is rolled out. Protective paper is removed from the tape, and the carpet pressed down firmly over the tape. A metal binder strip is generally used in doorways. Most cushion-backed carpeting comes in 12- and 15-foot widths; if your room is wider, an extra strip must be added. To seam a carpet, you will need 5-inch-wide tape, tape activator, seam adhesive, and a long metal straightedge. All of these items can be purchased from your carpet dealer or he can tell you where to buy them.

On wood floors, make the seam perpendicular to the direction of the floorboards. To prevent shading, position the second piece so the nap runs in the same direction as the first. Edges, if not straight, must be trimmed before seaming; use metal straightedge as a guide. Using the seam edge as a guide, mark the floor with a soft pencil. Fold back both lengths and center the 5-inch tape along the pencil line. Pull the tape out in 3-foot strips (do not cut); do not remove protective paper. Let the first length of carpet down over the tape. Then lower the second. Adjust second length until it forms a slight peak with the first. Fold back both lengths about 18 inches, and peel the paper from the tape. Apply the tape activator to the tape and spread with carpet scrap until tape is slippery. Smooth the first length on the tape. Next apply a bead of the seam adhesive at the pile level all along the edge of first piece of carpet. Take care not to get the adhesive on the carpet face. Then let the second length down. Form the seam by gently easing the second width away from the first until it drops onto the tape, then slide it forward until seam is closed.

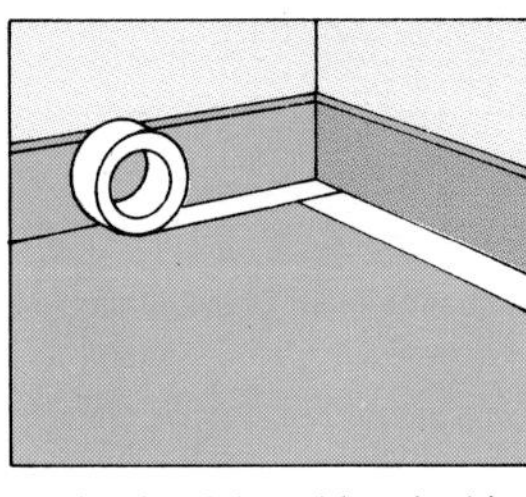

1. Apply 2-in.-wide double-face tape flush to wall around entire perimeter of room. Do not remove protective paper.

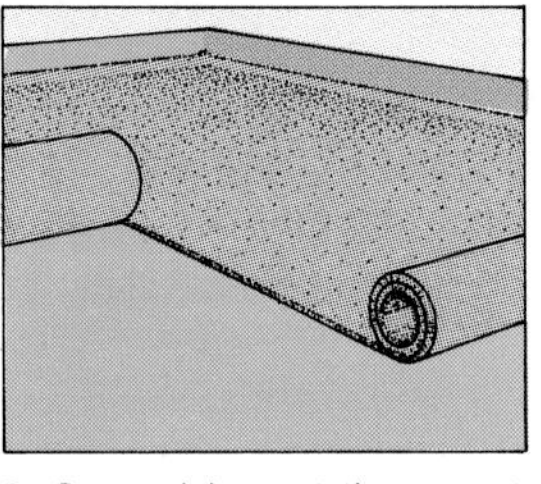

2. Cut and lay out the carpet in the room. Pay attention to the lay of the pile. This is a dry run to check placement.

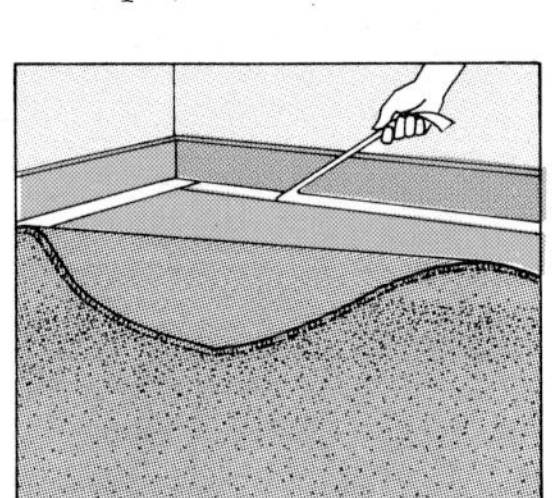

3. Fold back the carpet from around the sides of the room and peel off the protective paper from the tape.

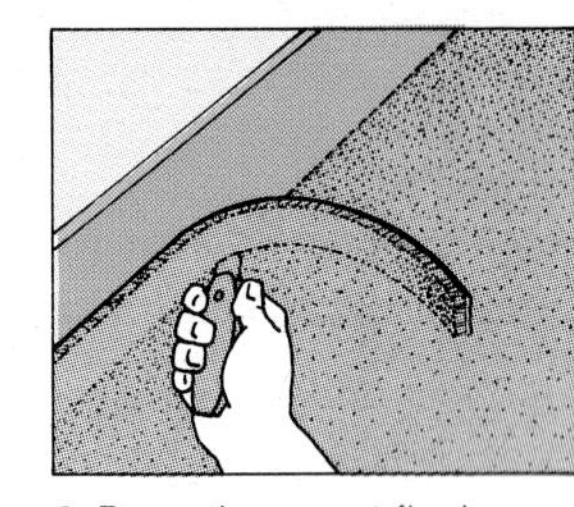

4. Press the carpet firmly over the exposed tape and trim away the excess with a sharp knife or a trimming tool.

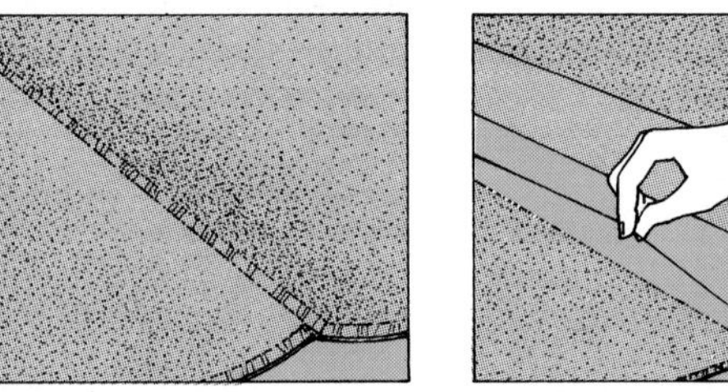

5. To make a seam, adjust edges to form a slight peak. Seaming is needed with narrow-width carpet.

6. Fold back one piece of carpet and snap a chalk line (or draw a pencil line) along the edge of the second piece.

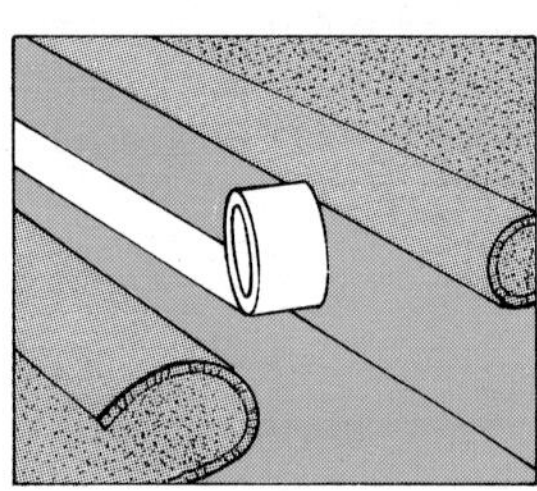

7. Apply the 5-in.-wide tape, exactly centering it over the pencil line. Press the tape down as you unroll it.

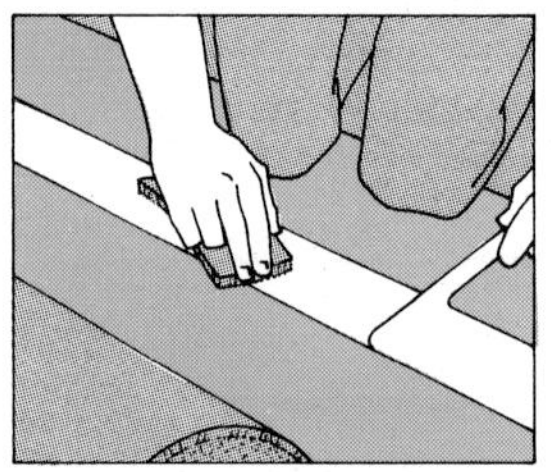

8. Peel off the protective paper and activate the tape, using a piece of scrap carpet soaked with the activator.

9. Let down one length of the carpet on the tape. Next apply the seam adhesive along edge of first piece of carpet.

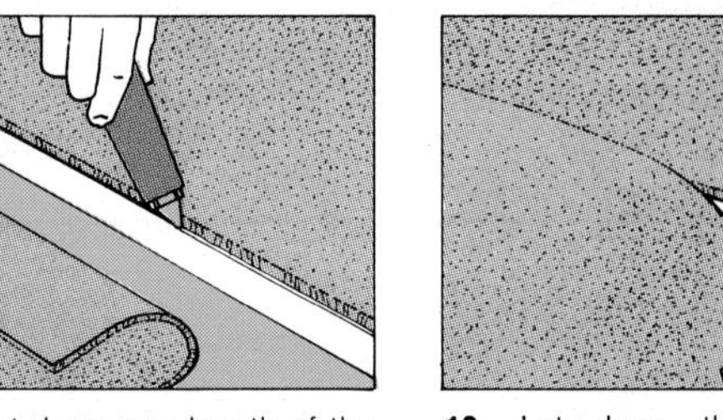

10. Let down the second length (take care not to shift the carpet). Second length will overlap first as shown.

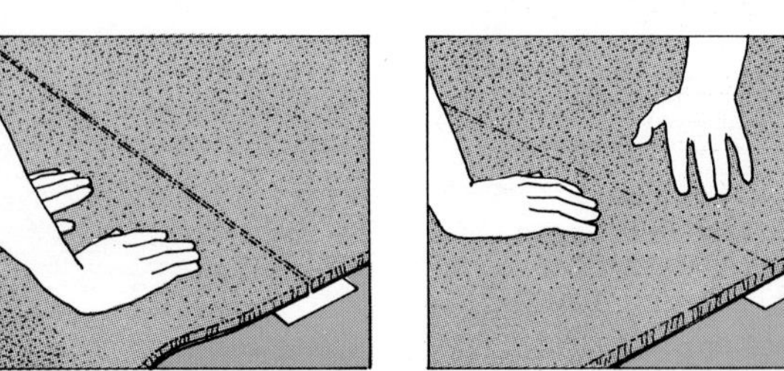

11. Ease away the second length slightly until the edge drops into line and the peak is no longer visible.

12. Smooth down both edges with a roller or by patting. Check entire seam for fit. Push from side to close gap.

13. Remove excess adhesive with solvent. Solvent, tape, and adhesive can be purchased from carpet dealer.

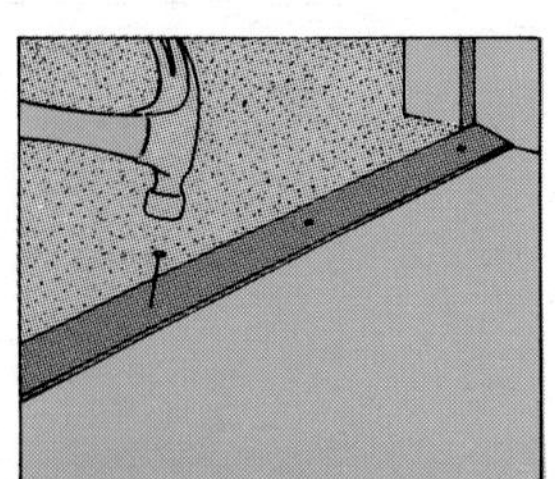

14. Edges of carpeting at doorways should be protected with either a metal binder strip or an aluminum saddle.

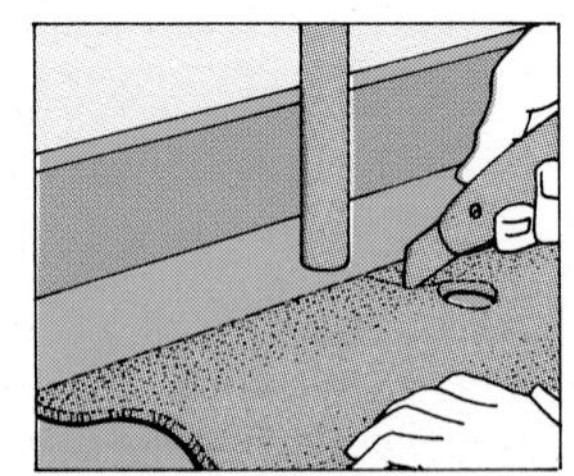

15. Cut a slit in carpeting for protruding pipes, etc. Then trim to fit the outline of the protrusion for a snug fit.

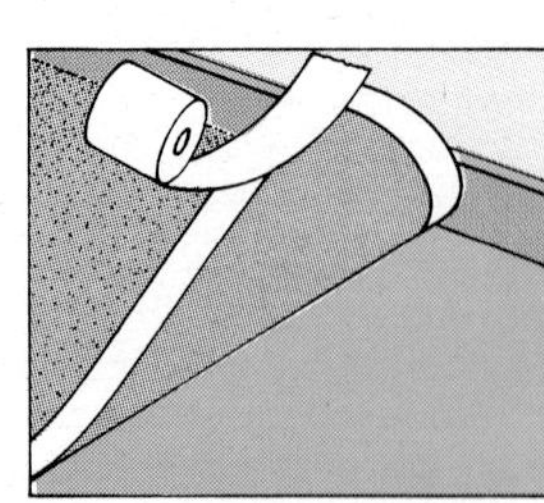

16. To take up taped-down carpet, remove it with tape attached; put toilet tissue on tape to prevent sticking.

section 11:

Working with wood

The best tools and techniques won't count for much unless you understand the materials they are to be used on. In making home repairs, wood is the material you will encounter most frequently. It will give you uniformly satisfying results provided you use the right wood in the right way. To supply the necessary knowledge, this section covers wood from start to finish, with detailed how-to instructions for major uses in and around the house.

contents

Understanding wood

The origins of lumber

All woods are composed of approximately 60 percent cellulose and 28 percent lignin. These substances make up the woody and fibrous cell walls of plants and trees and the cementing material between them. The remaining 12 percent consists of the elements that give each species individual qualities, like the rich color of the mahogany used in cabinetwork, the unmistakable aroma of cedar in blanket chests, and the rot-resistance that makes redwood so ideal for lawn furniture. The other characteristics that match lumber to specific uses are the result of the way it is sawed from the log and seasoned. After that, it is up to you and your tools to cut it, shape it, join it, and finish it into the object you have in mind. The following pages are designed to help you accomplish this.

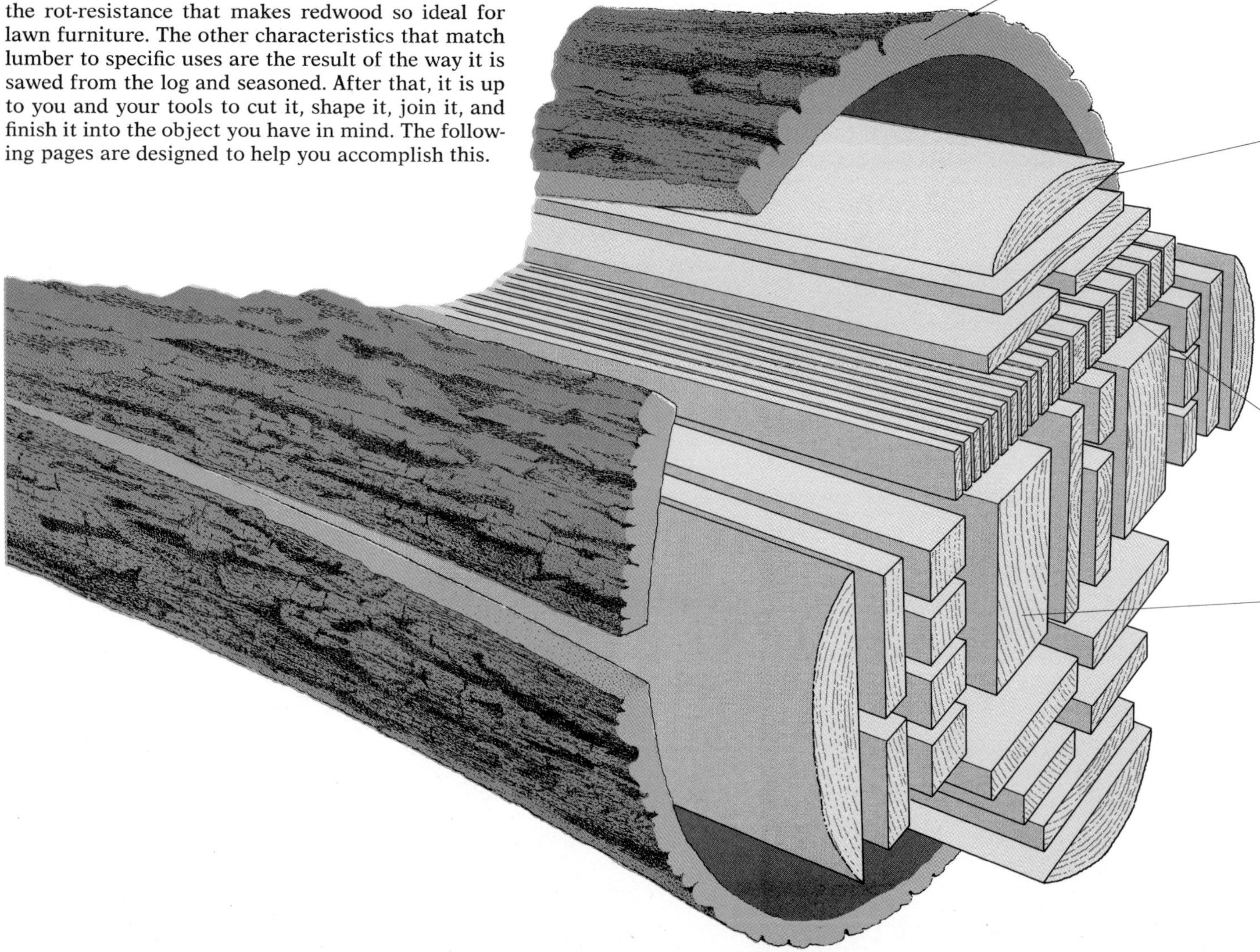

The bark, or outside covering of a tree, has little commercial value except as fuel and, with some types, as a garden mulch. Just below the bark is the only living part of the tree—the cambium layer, which extends from the tips of the roots to the tips of each branch. The cells on the outside layer of the cambium form the bark, those on the inside the wood, of the tree.

The rounded sides of the log are called "slabs." In the drawing, the entire log is being used for lumber with the exception of the slabs, which are going to a chipping machine. The machine grinds them into chips and flakes for use in making chipboard, a kind of coarse-grained hardboard. As cutting continues, other pieces not suitable for lumber (edges and trim) are also fed to the chipper.

The outer portions of a log usually have the fewest knots. This so-called clear lumber is made into boards or planks from one to three inches thick.

Toward the center of the log, the oldest part of the tree, the number of knots increases. Knots mark the joints of branches that were cut or broken off, as well as damage to the bark caused by disease or animals. Wood in this center portion is not well suited for boards and is generally cut into heavy planks and square or rectangular beams used mainly for construction work. The reason is the weakening effect of knots, which does not affect large, thick lumber as much as it would smaller cuts such as 4 x 4s or 3 x 10s.

Hardwoods

Hardwoods come from broad-leafed, deciduous trees, such as the oak, walnut, maple, birch, and mahogany. Woods in this group cost more than softwoods, but as a general rule the hardwoods are stronger and longer lasting.

Don't be afraid to use hardwoods. As long as your tools are sharp, these woods can be cut, turned, and jointed as successfully as softwoods.

The decorative effect of most hardwoods is superior because of better surface finishing properties.

The quality of hardwood depends on how it has been seasoned and stored. Modern kiln-drying or air-drying is satisfactory but wood should still be given time to adjust its moisture content to the conditions under which it will be used.

When lumber is improperly air-dried, or neglected during storage, water can collect around the stacking boards (sticks), causing permanent stick marks ingrained deep into the boards.

Because the ends of boards dry out faster than the centers, apply paint or pitch to the ends to protect them during air-drying.

SPECIES	CHARACTERISTICS	USES
Mahogany:	Fine-grained; reddish brown; durable; resists swelling, shrinking, and warping; easy to work	Choice cabinet wood; boat construction; plywood facings; veneers; high-grade furniture
Walnut:	Strong; fine-textured; free from warping and shrinking; easy to work; finishes well	Solid and veneered furniture; gunstocks; wall paneling; turnings; novelties; cabinetry
Oak:	Strong; durable; good bending qualities; finishes well; resists moisture absorption	Furniture; interior trim; boat frames; desks; barrels; floors; piles; handles; crossties
Maple:	Strong; hard; machines well; resists shock; fine-textured; moderate shrinkage	Flooring; fine furniture construction; woodenware; bowling alleys; agricultural implements
Cherry:	Close-grained; resists warping and shrinking; ages well; reddens when exposed to sunlight	Cabinetmaking; boat trim; novelties; solid furniture; handles; turned projects
Rosewood:	Very hard; dark reddish brown; close-grained; fragrant; hard to work; takes high polish	Musical instruments; piano cases; tool handles; art objects; furniture; levels; veneers
Teak:	Hard; durable; resistant to moisture and rot; resists warping, cracking, and decay	Fine furniture; paneling; shipbuilding; doors; window frames; flooring; general construction

Softwoods

Softwood is lumber from coniferous (cone-bearing or evergreen) trees, such as pine, cedar, fir, hemlock, redwood, spruce, cypress, and basswood. It is usually sold sawed and, since timber from the saw is rough, planed to finished dimensions. Because of shrinkage and planing, lumber is actually smaller than the nominal size by which it is sold. As an example, mill machining and drying reduce the dimensions of a piece sold as 1 x 6 inches to approximately ¾ x 5½ inches. If the exact size is vital, order your lumber to that full size. It will be milled from the next larger standard size. Since you will be paying for that size, the cost will be somewhat greater.

Softwoods vary in their resistance to weather. Common structural species, like pine, must be protected with preservatives or paints. Others, like redwood, have natural weather resistance.

For posts that are to be imbedded in the ground, order lumber chemically impregnated against rot and insect damage. Softwoods for floors, walls, and ceilings need protection against dirt. There are finishes made specifically for this purpose.

Many softwoods have hard, brown pockets (knots) that give off a sticky liquid. These should be cleaned with turpentine, then shellac-sealed (loose knots white-glued first, then shellacked) before finishing. Softwoods are susceptible, too, to very rough or split ends; allow for this by ordering 5 to 10 percent more boards than you need.

SPECIES	CHARACTERISTICS	USES
Pine:	Uniform texture; works easily; finishes well; resists shrinking, swelling, and warping	House construction; paneling; trim; furniture; crates; boxes; millwork; patterns; moldings
Hemlock:	Light in weight; uniformly textured; machines well; low resistance to decay; nonresinous	Construction lumber; sheathing; doors; planks; boards; paneling; subflooring; crates
Fir:	Easily worked; finishes well; uniform texture; nonresinous; low resistance to decay	Furniture; doors; frames; windows; plywood; veneer; general millwork; interior trim
Redwood:	Light in weight; durable; easy to work; naturally resistant to decay	Outdoor furniture; fencing; house siding; interior finish; veneer; paneling
Spruce:	Strong; hard; low resistance to decay; finishes well; moderate shrinkage; light in weight	Masts and spars for ships; aircraft; crates; boxes; general millwork; ladders
Cedar:	Fresh sweet odor; reddish color; easy to work; uniform texture; resistant to decay	Chests; closet lining; shingles; posts; dock planks; novelties; Venetian blinds

Deciding what to buy

Shopping for wood

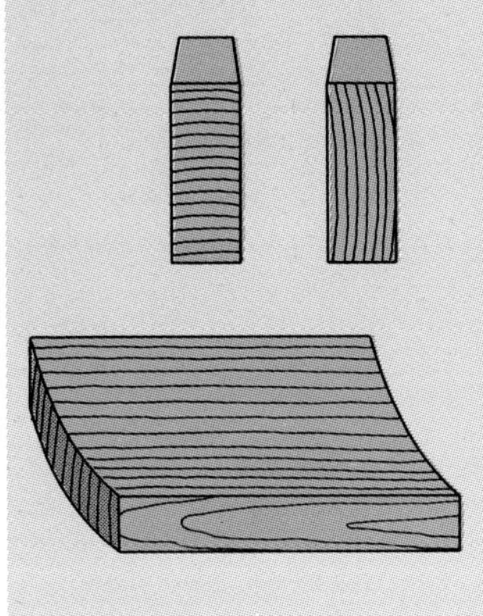

Quarter-sawed lumber, cut at right angles to growth rings, has vertical end-grain (far left). Plain- or flat-sawed lumber is cut straight through log (near left). Most often used, usually cheaper.

Warping, often from faulty seasoning, can distort boards several ways. Sight along board to spot twist. Prolonged wetting of concave side may help but warped lumber is generally best avoided.

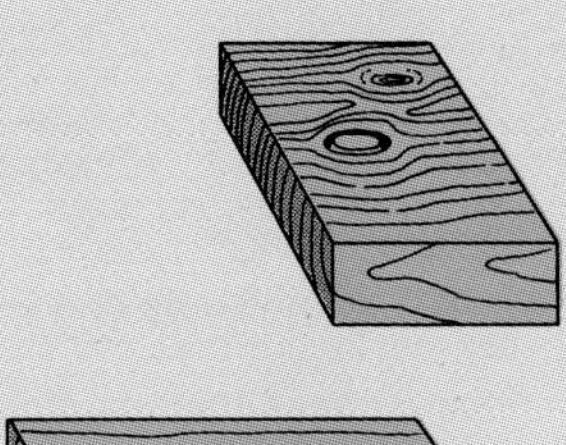

Sound knots: Acceptable in such uses as framing lumber if they occur within grade's size limits and not at points where they would impair strength. For furniture, buy clear grades.

Wane edge: Bark and sapwood, sometimes left on hardwoods to make maximum use of lumber width (wider board end is not trimmed to make edges parallel). Most sapwood shows as a paler band.

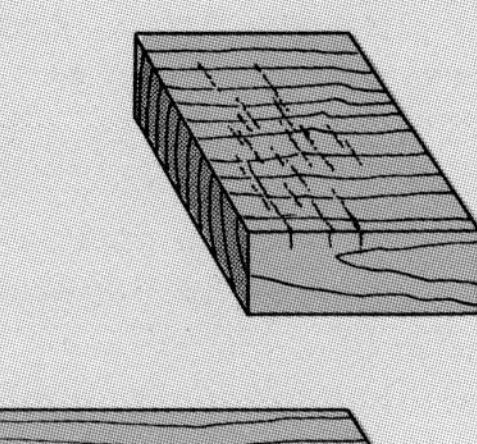

Felling or compression failures are areas distorted by a blow to the log. Recognizable by irregular lines crossing the grain of a board. Use for hidden, low-stress cabinet parts.

End shakes, from faster drying at board ends, occasionally occur in most lengths but are limited in size by grade. If feasible, affected end may be cut. Appear along grain, between rings.

Shrinkage and warping

All lumber, when first cut, contains considerable moisture. Much of this is removed by a seasoning process before the wood is shipped to a dealer. As the lumber dries out, it shrinks and tends to warp.

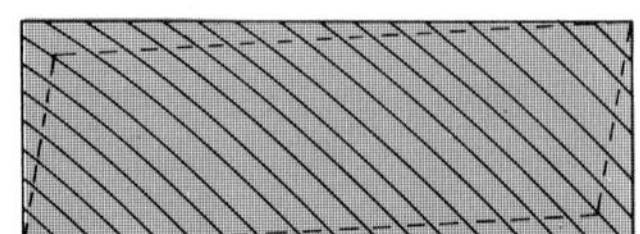

Dotted line indicates shrinkage

Greatest shrinkage takes place in the circumference of the annual rings. Length along the grain shrinks only about ⅛ inch in 12 feet.

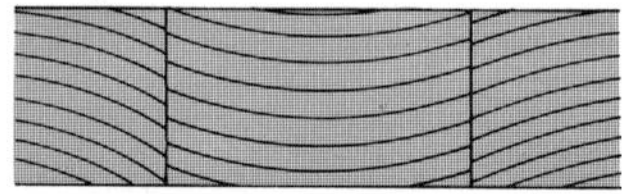

Alternate grains equalize movement

When joining a series of boards edge to edge, place the boards so that the end grains alternate. This changes the direction of the annual rings from board to board, the technique most likely to balance stresses or movement so the work will stay flat.

Solid lumber behaves in a different way from hardboard, chipboard, and other composition boards. You should not, for instance, join a drawer side made of hardboard to a drawer front of solid wood if it will be exposed to high humidity. Joint distortion or splitting may result.

There is no harm, however, in fixing a plywood bottom to a drawer made of solid lumber, since almost no change takes place in the length of the sides or in the plywood. Nor is there a problem in joining a solid long-grained piece of molding to one of the nonmoving types of board such as plywood. Here too, change in length is negligible.

If you are uncertain about how to cope with the problem of solid-lumber movement, take a look at some pieces of old furniture and see how they are put together. (This also applies to joint details when designing furniture.)

Methods to correct or alleviate warping during air-drying have limited success, but they are worth trying. Stacking the lumber with one layer in one direction and the next at right angles is a common practice. This alternate-stacking method is also a good way to store lumber if you buy it in quantity.

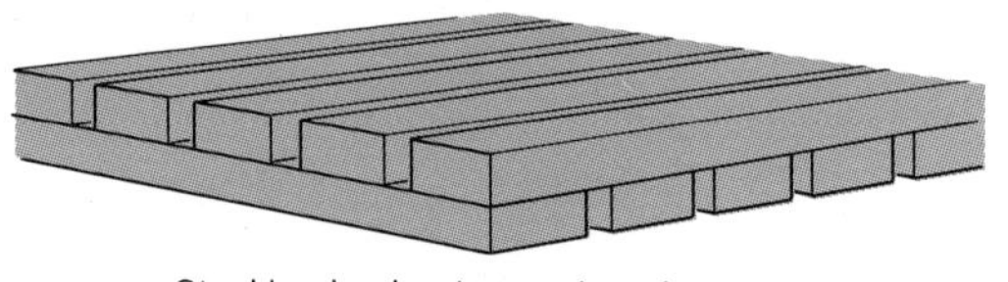

Stacking lumber to counteract warpage

To straighten a bent board, first wet it thoroughly, then rest the board ends on bricks and place a heavy weight on the center. After a few days, the pressure from the weight will force the board to flatten out.

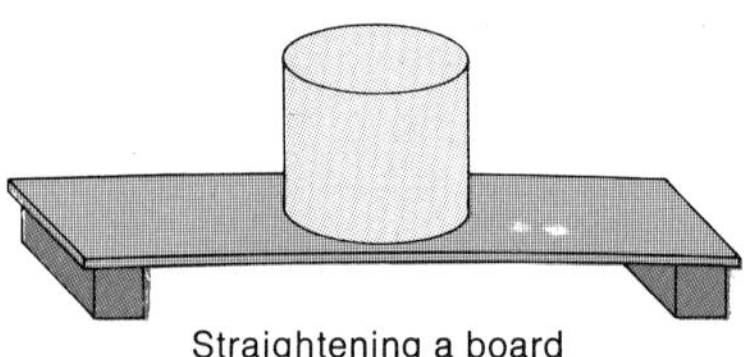

Straightening a board

Warping of two boards may be corrected by placing them together, convex sides outside, and clamping the centers together. (Place scrap softwood between clamp jaws and boards to prevent denting.) Wetting the wood thoroughly before clamping will hasten the straightening process.

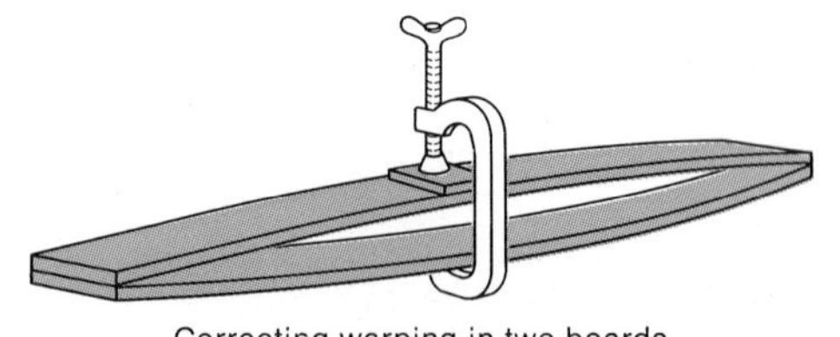

Correcting warping in two boards

Wood grades

There are two basic classifications of lumber: (1) **Select lumber**—excellent quality; for use when appearance and finishing are important; and (2) **common lumber**—has defects; used for construction and general-purpose projects.

The grades of select lumber are: **B and Better grade** (or **1 and 2 clear**)—devoid of any but minute blemishes; **C select grade**—has some minor defects, such as small knots; **D select grade**—has larger imperfections which can be concealed by paint.

The corresponding select grades of Idaho White Pine are designated Supreme, Choice, and Quality.

The grades of common lumber are: **No. 1 grade**—contains tight knots, few blemishes; suitable for natural knotty finish or paint; **No. 2 grade**—has more and larger knots and blemishes; used for flooring and paneling; still suitable for knotty finish or paint; **No. 3 grade**—has loose knots and knotholes and other pronounced flaws; used for shelving, sheathing, fencing, nonvisible purposes; **No. 4 grade**—low quality; used for sheathing, subflooring, crating, and concrete forms; **No. 5 grade**—lowest board grade, for limited use where strength and appearance are not essential to the finished result.

The corresponding grades of Idaho White Pine are Colonial, Sterling, Standard, Utility, and Industrial.

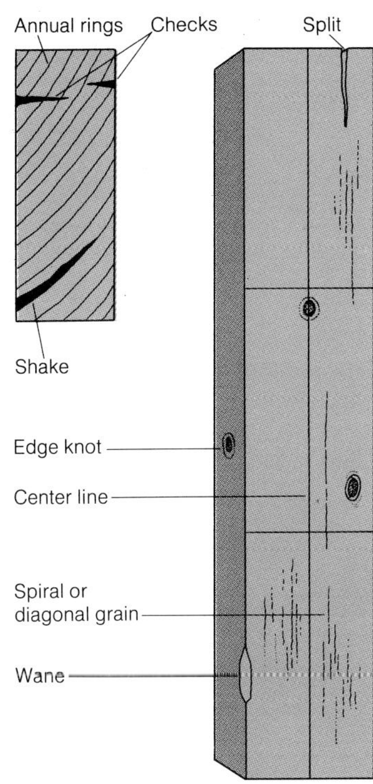

Ordering wood

Board foot, the unit used in buying lumber, equals the amount of wood in a piece of lumber measuring 1 foot long, 1 inch thick, and 12 inches wide. To calculate the number of board feet, multiply length in feet by **nominal** thickness and width in inches and divide by 12. Thus, the number of board feet in a piece of lumber 6 feet long, 2 inches thick, and 6 inches wide would be:

$$\frac{6 \text{ ft.} \times 2 \text{ in.} \times 6 \text{ in.}}{12} = \frac{72}{12} = 6 \text{ board ft.}$$

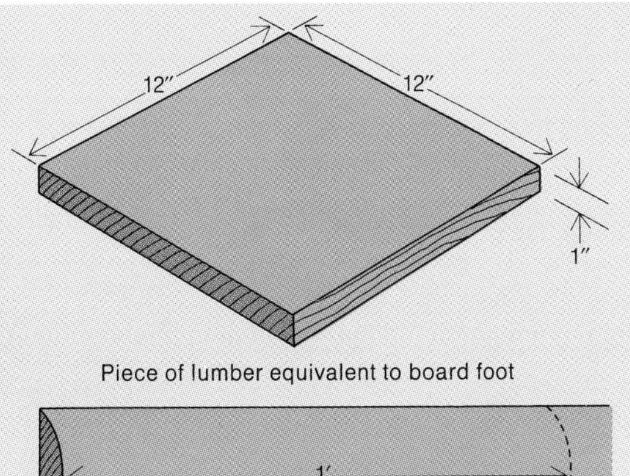

Piece of lumber equivalent to board foot

Linear or running foot is the buying unit for such products as moldings, dowels, furring strips, railings, poles, sometimes 2 x 4s. Length, not thickness or width, is the only consideration. Shingles and laths are usually sold by the bundle, plywood and wallboard by the panel.

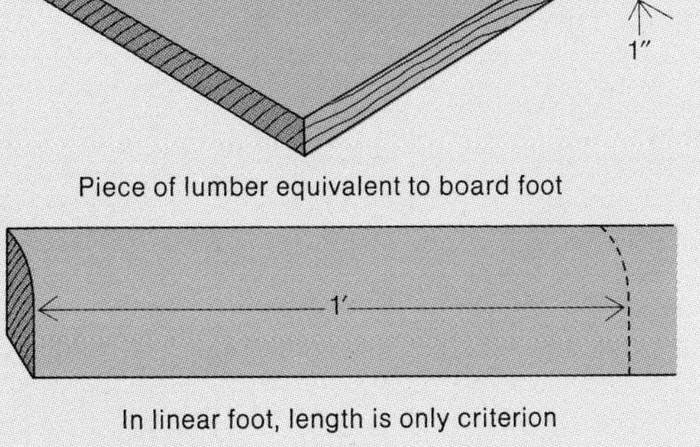

In linear foot, length is only criterion

Standard sizes

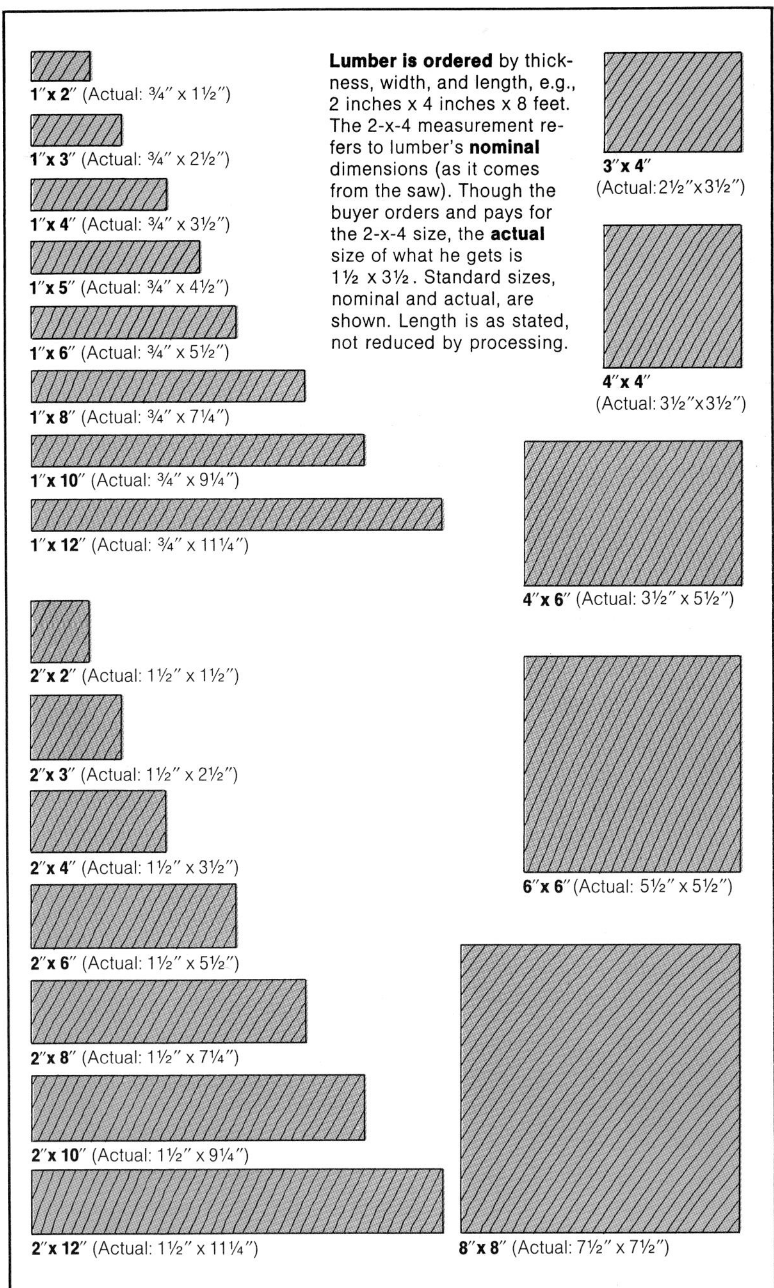

Working with plywood

How plywood is made

Plywood is made from an odd number of thin sheets of wood, or veneers, glued face to face, with grains running in alternate directions. Lumber core plywood has a solid center ply with thin crisscrossed veneers glued to both its surfaces. Use of an odd number of veneers stabilizes plywood in this way:

If two veneers are bonded together, tensions created by the glue lines, and inherent in the opposite grain directions, will cause warping. But two veneers, each bonded to the opposite sides of a middle panel, will equalize the tension.

New veneers are added in pairs, one on each side, building up to as many as required. Whatever the thickness, the total is always an odd number.

Plywood can still twist, because no two veneers are completely identical and the tensions are never perfectly balanced. Another factor that can cause warping is the wetting or heating of one face of the plywood. This will cause the veneer to expand or contract and may pull the board out of true.

Plywood for specific uses is factory-processed accordingly. For example, plywood for concrete forms is available with oiled surfaces. Where appearance matters, one or both sides are sanded.

The most widely used plywoods are softwood types made from fir, pine, or spruce, and graded according to the quality of the outer plies. Hardwood types include those with all-hardwood veneers and combination types with softwood interiors and hardwood exteriors. Hardwood plywoods (oak, walnut, mahogany, etc.) are generally used where appearance is a factor, as in the construction of furniture.

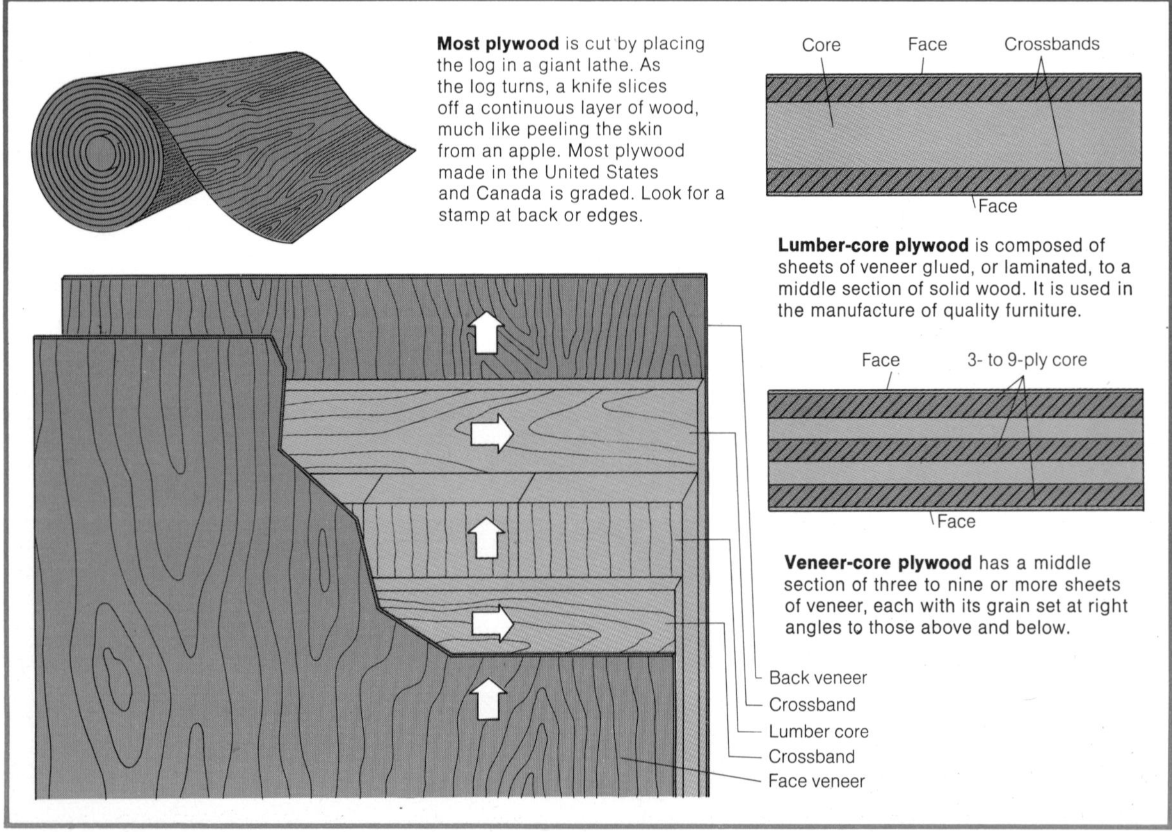

Most plywood is cut by placing the log in a giant lathe. As the log turns, a knife slices off a continuous layer of wood, much like peeling the skin from an apple. Most plywood made in the United States and Canada is graded. Look for a stamp at back or edges.

Lumber-core plywood is composed of sheets of veneer glued, or laminated, to a middle section of solid wood. It is used in the manufacture of quality furniture.

Veneer-core plywood has a middle section of three to nine or more sheets of veneer, each with its grain set at right angles to those above and below.

Plywood grades

Most plywood made today is graded by the American Plywood Association. Look for a rubber stamp at the back or along the edges with the letters DFPA, which stand for Department For Product Approval.

The large capital letters on the grade stamp indicate the quality of the face and back: N (natural finish grade, free of defects); A (smooth and paintable, also usable for less exacting natural finish); B (allows circular repair plugs and tight knots); C (allows knotholes and splits of limited size); D (permits similar flaws, somewhat larger).

The group number indicates the species group used and relative strength ranging from Group 1, the strongest, down to Group 5. Group 1 includes, for example, plywood made from birch, Western larch, sugar maple, loblolly pine, long and short leaf pine,

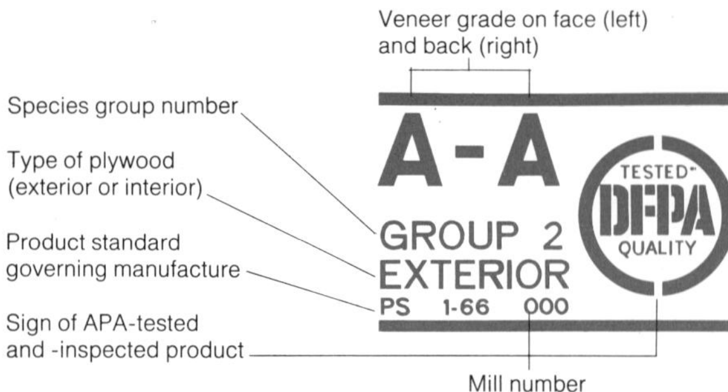

and Douglas fir from Washington, Oregon, California, Idaho, British Columbia, and Alberta. Group 2 plywood is made from cedar, Western hemlock, black maple, red pine, Sitka spruce, and Douglas fir from Nevada, Utah, and New Mexico. Group 3 comprises plywood made from Alaska cedar, red alder, jack pine, lodgepole pine, Ponderosa pine, and red, white, and black spruce. Woods used in Group 4 are aspen, paper birch, Western red cedar, Eastern hemlock, sugar pine, and Engelmann spruce. Plywoods in the fifth group are made from balsam fir and poplar.

The term **Exterior** describing plywood means waterproof glue between plies; **Interior,** moisture-resistant glue, not suited to outdoor or marine use. If there are two additional numbers, such as 48/24, the first indicates maximum spacing between rafters for roof decking, the second between joists for subflooring. When the second number is zero, as 24/0, the plywood is not suitable for subflooring.

Choosing and using plywood

Plywood is generally sold in 4-x-8-foot sheets and in thicknesses ranging from ¼ inch to ¾ inch. However, large lumberyards frequently stock, or can order for you, nonstandard sizes and thicknesses. The corners of plywood sheets are often chipped or splintered, so always make allowances for such waste when measuring and ordering.

Douglas fir plywood is one of the most commonly used plywoods—and also the least expensive. Because the grain darkens when it is exposed, this plywood is best suited to work where appearance is not a factor, or which will be ultimately covered by some other material. Examples are concrete forms, backs of furniture, temporary structures, shelving, and work of a similar nature.

Plywood can be mortised, dovetailed, mitered, and otherwise worked in the same ways as solid wood, provided it is thick enough. Avoid using plywood for drawer sides—it has a tendency to cut the runners rather than slide on them.

Sawing: A fine-toothed saw should be used for cutting plywood. Score the cut line with a knife when cutting across the grain and score both sides of the sheet in order to prevent splintering.

If you are cutting plywood with a circular saw or a radial arm saw, always have the good side facing up. However, when cutting with a portable power saw, have the good side facing down. If the plywood has two good faces and you want to avoid splintering either face, score the plywood or apply masking tape along the line of cut.

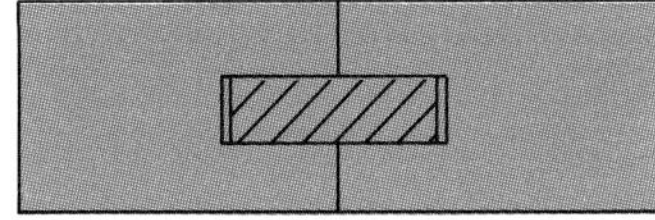
Leave slight gaps when using splines

Screwing: Always drill pilot holes before using screws. And remember screws do not hold as securely in the edges of the plywood as they do in the face.

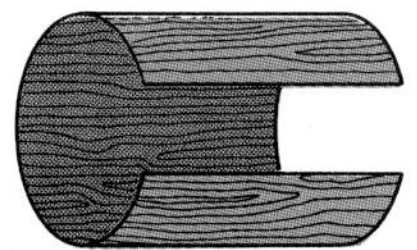
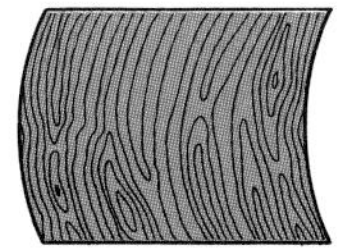
Plywood bends tighter when grain runs across curve

When soft plywood is being attached with screws, there is a danger that the screw heads may sink too far into the wood. Use screw cups to reduce this risk —if the job permits.

Gluing: Roughen surfaces so the glue has something to grip; use coarse sandpaper. Apply as much even pressure as possible with clamps or weights while the glue is setting. For marine or outside work, use a waterproof adhesive.

Jointing: Plywood that is more than ¼ inch thick can be jointed the same as ordinary wood. Joint edge to edge by the loose-spline method (p.395) but do not bend the sheets after joining.

Repairing: If small pieces of veneer lift up during work, glue and clamp them in place again, using a wood block, paper, and a clamp.

Protection: Wherever possible, use plywood so that its edges are supported. Protect edges with molding if there is a possibility of damage. Alternatively, remove all sharp edges with a small chamfer.

Bending: The thinner the sheet, the more it will bend. Birch plywood is one of the best for bending.

Fairly simple, even curves will hold their shape if you bend two or more sheets and glue them together, using a temporary jig. Slight dampening of what will be the outer curve of each sheet will help it to bend, but do not glue the sheets together while they are still wet. Let them dry out thoroughly—overnight should be ample—in the new shape. Plywood will bend to a tighter curve when the grain is running across the curve than when it is running with it. For further instruction, see drawings below.

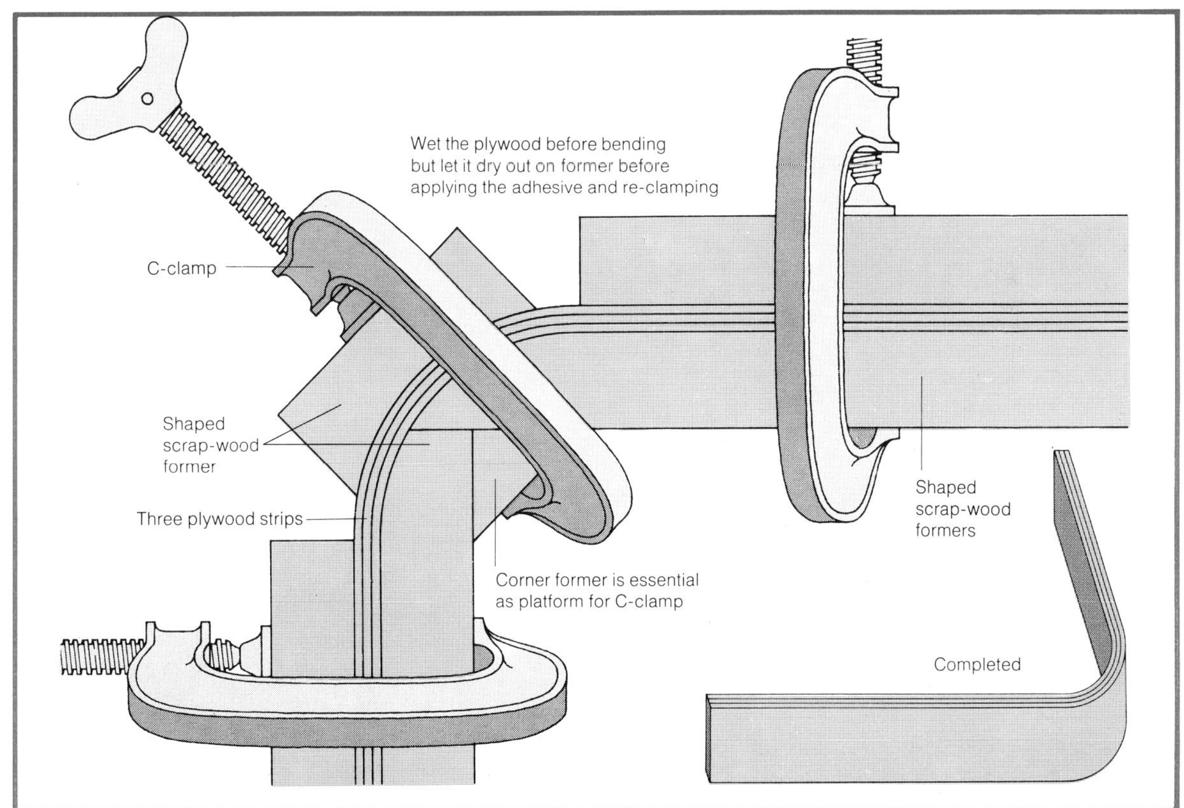

Making curved forms: Simple curved shapes can be made by gluing pieces of plywood together between scrap-wood formers

Manufactured wood

Types and uses of hardboard

This versatile material is made from softwood pulp which is forced into sheets under heat and pressure. It is available in a variety of forms.

Hardboard may be tempered or untempered. The tempered kind has been treated with oils and resins, which make it harder and more moisture-resistant. It is darker in color than the untempered kind.

Hardboard is made smooth on one side (S1S) or smooth on two sides (S2S). It can be bought in a variety of perforated patterns, the best known being pegboard. Hardboard panels are usually 4 feet wide and come in standard lengths of 8, 10, and 12 feet. Various thicknesses are available, ⅛ and ¼ inch being the most common. Like plywood, hardboard is sold by the square foot.

Some dealers will cut to the size you need, using a panel saw to assure an accurate and square cut. For a number of long cuts on large panels, allow for the thickness of the saw blade. Uncut factory sheets are true and square-cornered for easy modular construction.

Standard: Usually finished on one side, textured on other. Used in cabinet work, drawer bottoms, concealed panels.

Enameled: Prepainted surface, often with tile or plank patterns embossed. Used for wall or bath paneling. Very hard-wearing.

Plastic-laminated: Often used for sliding doors. Decorative; easy to clean. Not suitable for surfaces subject to abuse.

Perforated: Single or double thickness. Perforations range from spaced round holes to intricate grillwork.

Particle board: Exterior and interior. Durable, quite light. Strongest and best is 3-layer, single next, extruded last.

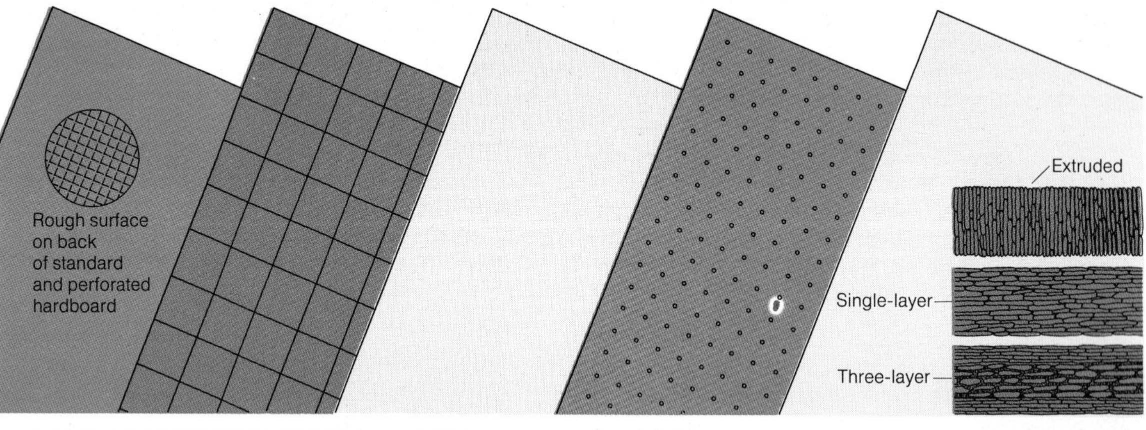

Working with hardboard

Store panels flat, taking care to protect corners and edges from damage. Standard woodworking tools can be used for cutting, shaping, and cleaning up edges. Avoid damaging the surface; once the smooth top crust is broken, sandpapering will not restore the original smoothness.

Cutting: Use a fine-toothed saw and always cut on the face side. On prepainted and plastic-covered boards, score the cutting line with a knife before sawing. This minimizes chipping. To prevent tear-away, support both ends of the sheet on the underside. Battens clamped along the cutting line can prevent the saw veering from the cutting line and avoid saw jump-out and damage to the surface.

Gluing: All woodworking adhesives work well on untempered hardboard. When gluing to the face of the board, roughen the surface with sandpaper to give adhesive the texture needed for a good grip.

Fitting: Always drive screws through hardboard, not into it. When nailing, use special hardboard nails. They have very small heads that are barely visible after they have been driven into the hardboard.

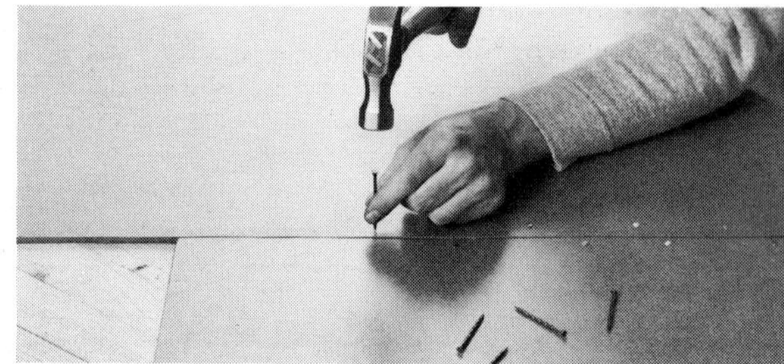

Hardboard is used as an underlayment before putting down tile

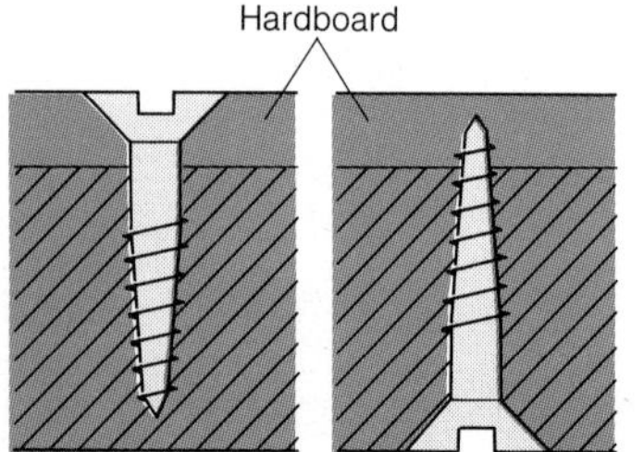

Drive screws into hardboard as shown at left, not as at right.

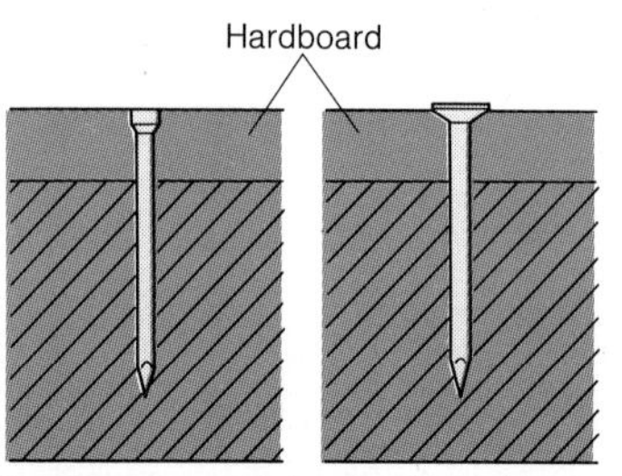

Brads can be sunk into hardboard (left); heads of nails will show.

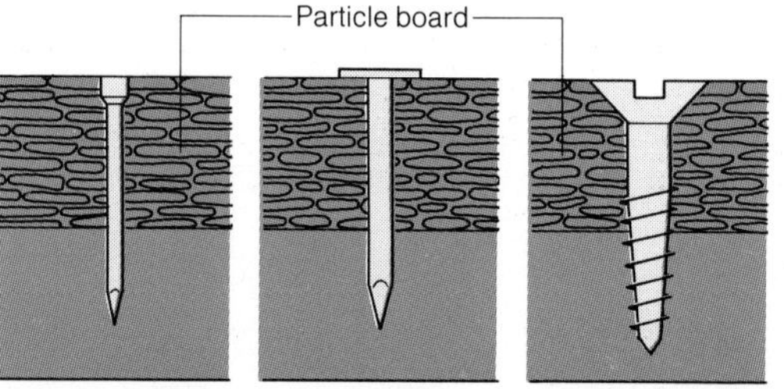

Brads, nails, and screws should be driven through particle board for maximum holding power.

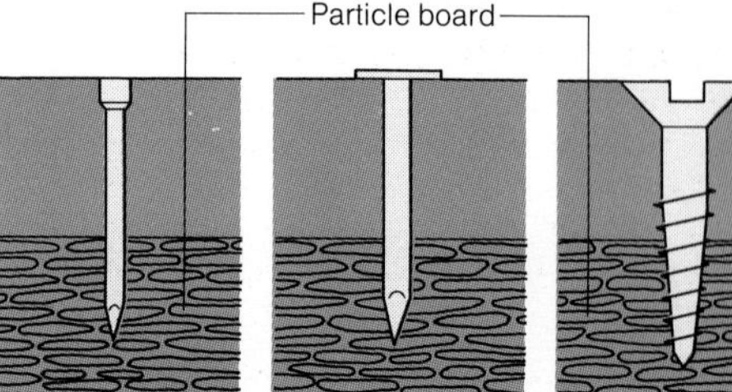

Driving brads, nails, or screws into particle board is not as strong a method of fastening.

House framing

Composition sheathing: These panels, as a general rule, come ½ inch thick, and are made in four sizes: 4 x 8 feet, 4 x 9 feet, 4 x 10 feet, and 4 x 12 feet. Composition sheathing has many uses in the building of a house, insulation being a significant one.
Joists: Parallel beams placed horizontally from wall to wall of a structure to support floor and ceiling loads.
Roof rafters: A series of sloping parallel beams which give support to a roof. The size of rafters required for different spans is generally specified by local building codes.
Studs: Usually made of 2 x 4s, and used vertically in a building's framework for the various walls and partitions to which laths, wallboard, and sheathing are attached.
Furring: Material, such as strips of wood or metal, that is attached to walls or ceilings to be used as a base for paneling, tiles, and other comparable finishing materials.
Subflooring: The first, or rough, floor of a building. This is nailed to floor joists and acts as support for the finish flooring, which is nailed directly onto it.
Construction plywood: Plywood grade intended for use where appearance doesn't count, such as sheathing, subflooring, and roof decking. Usually unsanded. Use-graded by the industry.
Insulation board: Material that is made from plant fibers or wood pulp and formed into light, stiff panels suitable for use as walls or partitions, and in similar applications.
Building paper: Inexpensive, heavy paper that is used as a draft seal in the construction of walls, also "sandwiched" between the first or subfloor of a building and the finish flooring.
Clapboard: A type of siding, made up of boards with one edge thinner than the other. Clapboard siding is nailed in overlapping fashion to form the outside covering of a house.
Gypsum board: Wallboard panels composed of a core of gypsum with outside surfaces of tough, durable paper. Can be bought in standard 4-foot-wide panels in lengths from 6 to 12 feet. The paneling is easily nailed to both joists and studs; is inexpensive and fireproof; takes paint or wallpaper well (seams must be taped over). These boards are available with a paper finish made to resemble various wood patterns, which eliminates the need for further finishing.

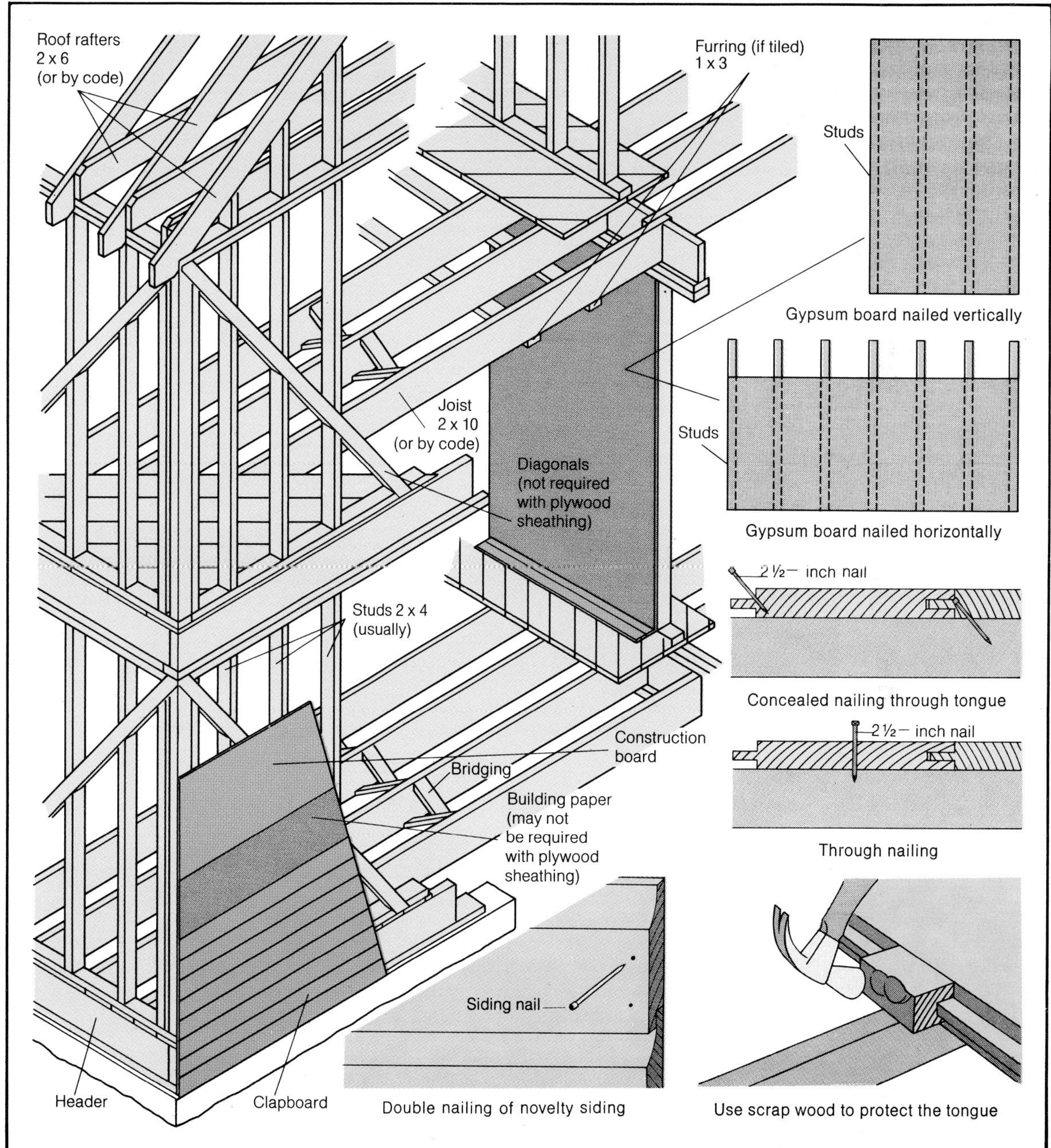

Wall paneling

Planning the work

You may experience one difficulty in paneling a room—choosing from among the many finishes, styles, and effects that are available. You will find, for example, some fifty or more wood grains veneered, lithographed, or printed on wall panels. All of these facsimiles are done so expertly that it takes a trained eye to tell them from real wood. Philippine mahogany, knotty pine, cherry, oak, and walnut are some of the possibilities. Some are stained deep red, blue, or an exotic green.

If you would like something other than wood effects, panels can be bought that resemble delicately veined marble or rough-hewn stone. Others are wall-sized murals or reproductions of old engravings. (See the decorating section, p.350, for more about paneling possibilities.)

Once you have made your choice, your next move is to estimate how much paneling you will need. Details of how to arrive at an estimate are given elsewhere on this page.

Have the panels delivered to your home several days before you plan to install them. Put them in the room that is to be paneled so they will be exposed to the room's normal humidity and will have a chance to adjust to it.

When stacking the panels, be sure to separate them by inserting thin sticks between layers to permit air to circulate.

Calculating panel needs

An easy way to estimate: Draw your room to scale on graph paper. Suppose the floor is 16 x 20 feet. Pencil in a rectangle to represent it. Using the suggested scale (1 square = 2 square feet), it will be eight squares wide by ten long.

Next measure ceiling height and sketch in walls (treat them like the dropped-down sides of a box). Then determine size and location of doors, etc.

Wall panels are generally 4 x 8 feet. If it weren't for door and window allowances, you could just add up the room's perimeter—here it would be 72 feet—and divide by four (the width of a panel). The result, 18, would be the number of panels needed to cover your walls.

Subtract, on the average, ½ panel for each fireplace or window, ⅔ for a door. The example shows three windows (1½ panels) and the equivalent of three doors (2 panels). Subtract the allowance for these—3½—from 18, and you get the panels you need: 14½. Panels must be bought whole; when the result is a fraction, round out to the next whole number, in this case 15. Window and door cutouts can be used on adjoining wall areas. Not all calculations come out even, but the difference will be fractional, and might come in handy.

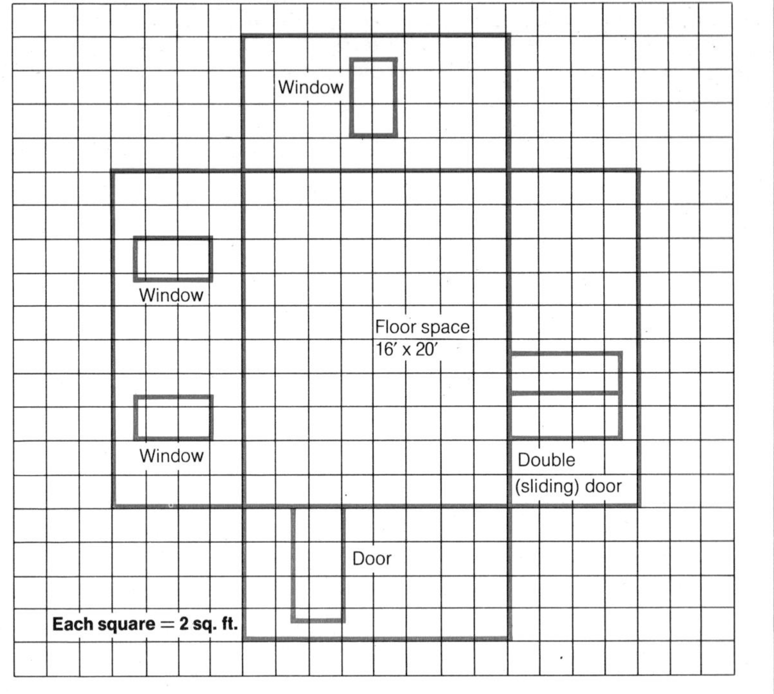

Solid wood paneling

If the idea of imitations just doesn't appeal to you, you can get paneling that is wood all the way through. Solid wood paneling is available in an attractive range of hardwoods and softwoods, and can also be bought tinted, if your decorating preferences lean toward color.

In any of the available forms, the paneling is easy to install and maintain. Interesting effects can be obtained by installing the panels horizontally or vertically, or in combination. Vertical paneling in random widths can also be striking. Some paneling materials are made with simulated board-and-batten joints and others are constructed with tongue-and-groove joints.

If your room is inclined to be damp, or if you are paneling over masonry, coat the walls before you begin with a waterproofing material.

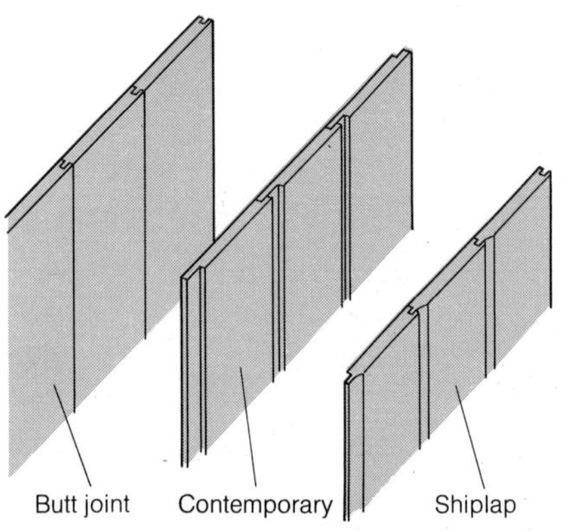

Types of boards available

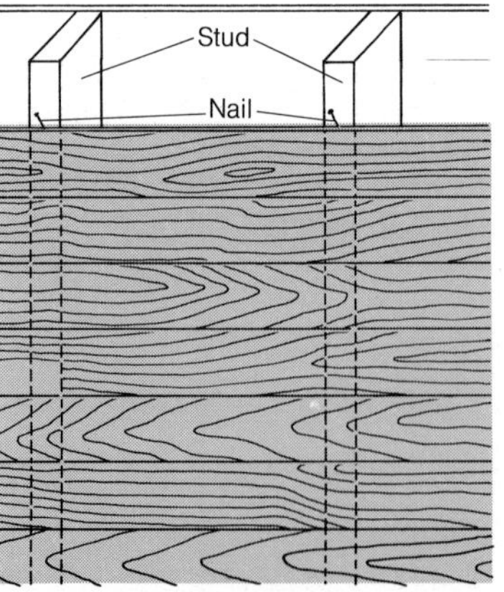

Horizontal application

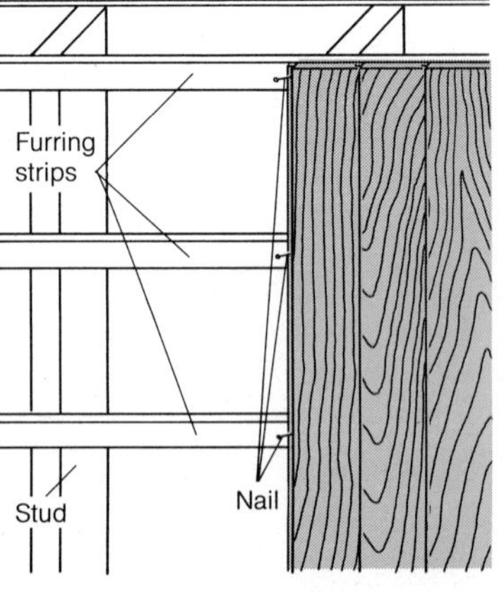

Vertical application

Trims and moldings

Many makers of prefinished paneling manufacture a coordinated line of hardwood moldings and trims made to match the panels in finish and in contour. These accessory products allow the home craftsman to handle the intricate finishing that is necessary around doors, windows, and corners with complete confidence in the end result.

Another molding now available to simplify the installation of paneling is made of aluminum, with an unfinished face veneer of matching hardwood bonded to the metal base. The molding strips are attached to studs or furring and the panels slide into place along the molding lip.

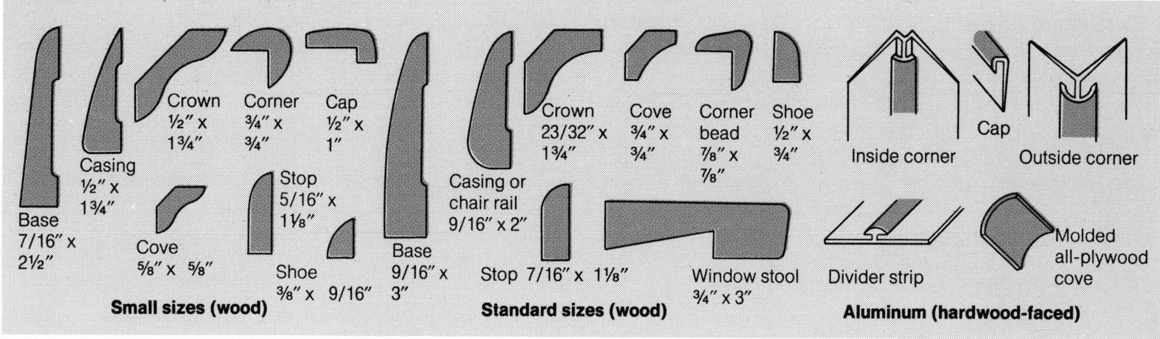

Installing panel sheets

1. Apply furring strips (1 x 2s or 1 x 3s) vertically at 16-in. intervals for full size panels and horizontally at 16-in. intervals over the existing 2 x 4s for random-width paneling.

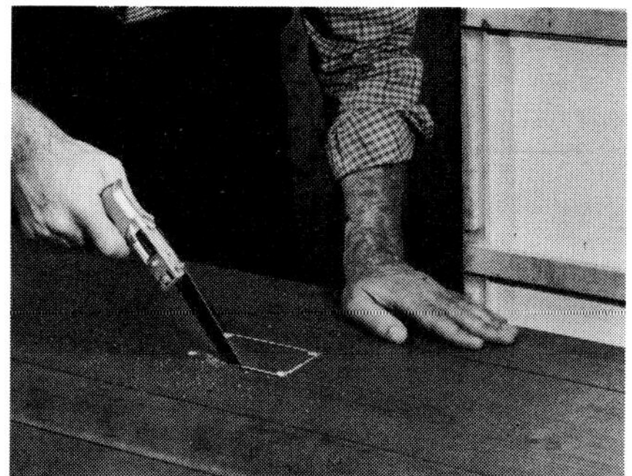

2. Measure carefully and mark on paneling where openings for wall switches, etc., are to go. Drill pilot holes in corners of each area to be cut, then use keyhole or saber saw.

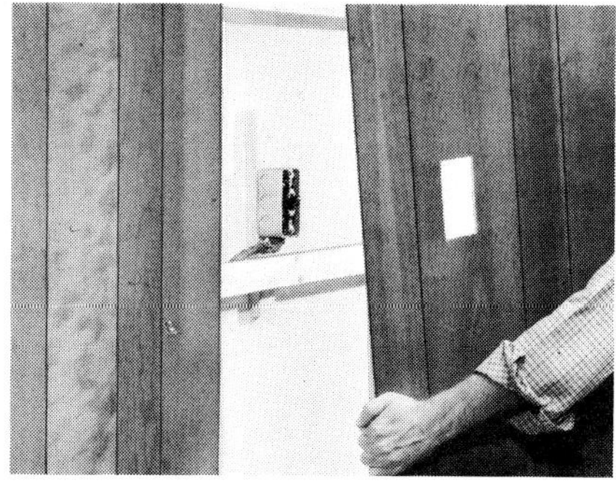

3. Try the panel for fit before applying the adhesive. If panel is to be mounted directly to the wall, apply the adhesive at 16-in. intervals, horizontally and vertically.

4. Apply beads of cement to all furring strips that will contact the panel. If necessary, use cleats between strips so that butt joints on large panels will have support.

5. Position panel against furring; drive small nails partway into top of panel to create hinge action. Press panel against framework to transfer some adhesive to back of panel.

6. Pull bottom of panel about 10 in. away from furring strips and prop out with wood block. This will separate the two until the adhesive has time to develop needed tackiness.

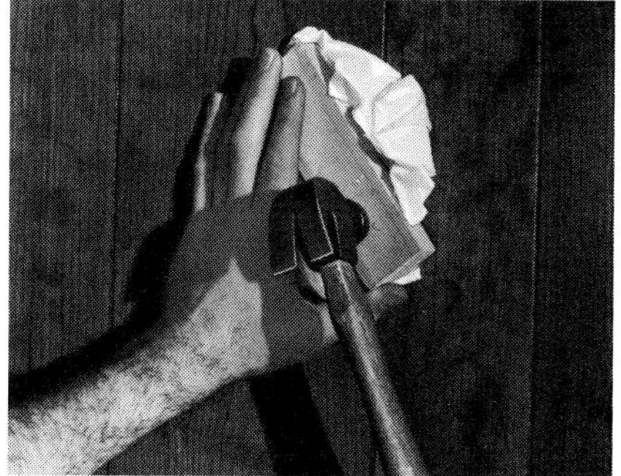

7. After eight to ten minutes, remove block and push panel in position, checking alignment carefully. Using a hammer on a cloth-covered block, tap sheet to spread adhesive evenly.

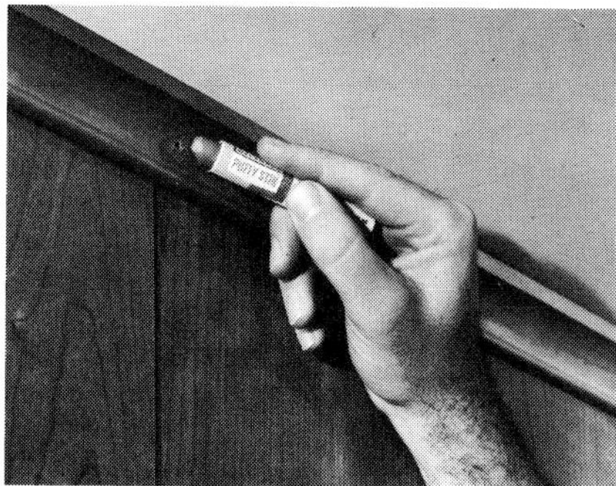

8. Leave nails at top until adhesive is set hard; then sink or pull them. Fill nail holes with putty stick to match panel. Sometimes it is advisable to face-nail panel at bottom as well.

Working with laminates

Laminate uses

Plastic laminates are made from layers of resin-impregnated paper bonded under high temperature and pressure into rigid sheets.

Decorative laminates for home use are sold in standard-size sheets measuring from 2 x 5 feet up to 5 x 12 feet. Thickness is generally 1/16 inch for durability on horizontal surfaces and 1/32 inch for use on vertical surfaces.

The range of decorative effects includes plain colors, patterns, wood grains, and abstract designs, with a choice, in most instances, of mat or gloss finish.

Laminates can be used on most flat and dry surfaces. Chipboard and plywood make ideal bases. Take painted and varnished surfaces down to the bare wood before cementing laminates in position.

Boards covered with laminate should be backed with an inexpensive backing laminate to prevent absorption of moisture, which might warp the board. It is advisable to back all laminate-covered surfaces, but it is not so necessary when the board is to be firmly attached to a frame, such as the top of a counter.

The best adhesives for normal household use are contact cements (p.86).

Laminates can be damaged by extremes of heat. Never place dishes and pans straight from the oven on a laminate, as they can scorch or blister it. Some chemicals, such as hydrogen peroxide, and certain cleansers and bleaches containing chlorine, may stain the surface. The best policy is to wipe up any spillage immediately, regardless of chemical content.

Covering with laminates

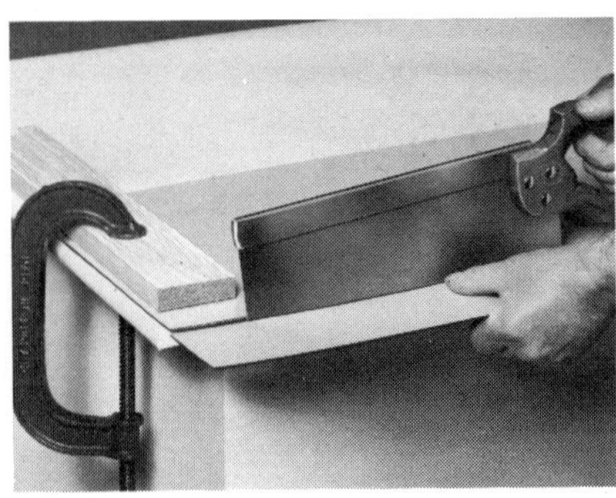

For counter and table tops, laminates can be bought cut to size or you can cut them to size yourself. Use a fine-toothed saw at a low angle on the decorated side of the laminate. Cut pieces slightly oversize to allow for trimming.

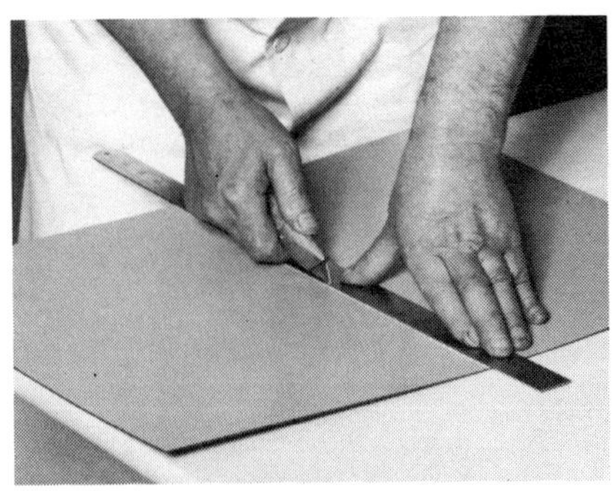

An alternate tool is a knife with a special laminate-cutting blade. Using a straightedge as a guide, score a line through the decorated surface. Hold a piece of wood along the cut and lift and break off free side of laminate.

Roughen surface to be covered (here, a table top) with sandpaper. Brush contact adhesive on the back of clean laminate, spreading it evenly over entire surface. Do the same on the table top. Let dry for about 15 minutes.

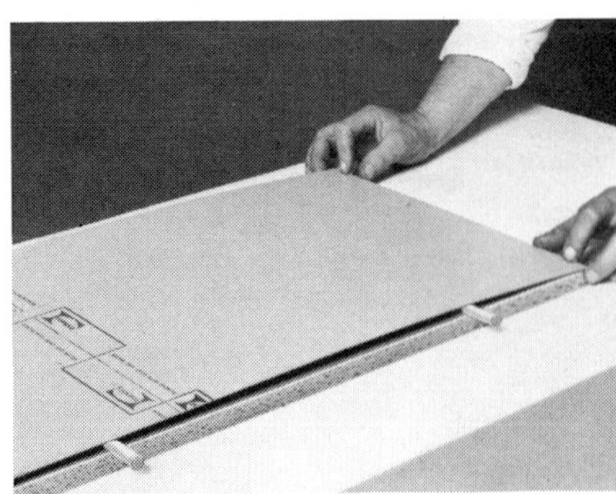

Cemented surfaces cannot be moved, so work carefully. Lay several strips of wood on table top; position laminate on them. Press one end of laminate down; move strips back toward other end, pressing laminate down as you go.

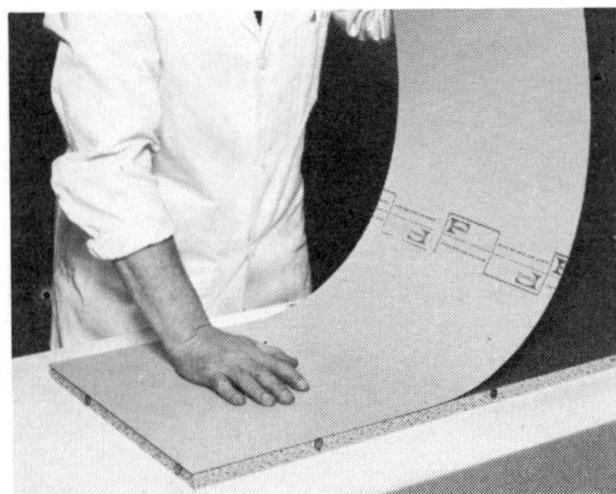

Another way: Push thumbtacks into table top edges as guide. Lay brown paper on dried, cement-coated table top. Align dried, cement-coated laminate on top. Withdraw paper, pressing down on laminate as it contacts table top.

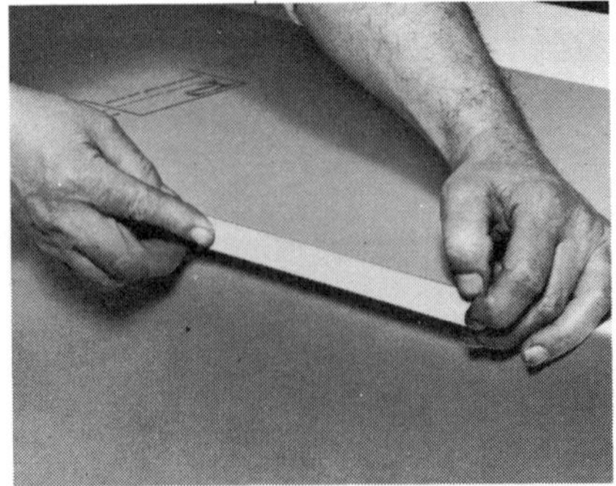

Use thin edging strips, or molding made especially for this purpose, to finish the table edges. Cement the edge strips to the table edges in the same way as the laminate, with adhesive on both surfaces to be joined.

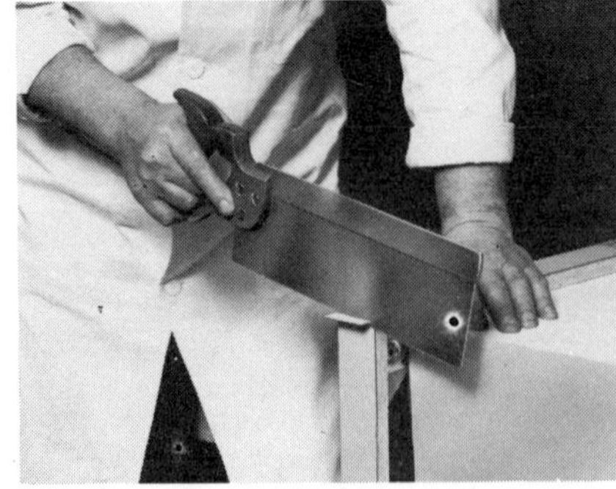

Use a backsaw to trim the edging strips so they are not quite flush with adjoining surface. Keep the saw at a shallow angle as shown. After 30 minutes' drying time, complete final trimming with a fine-tooth file.

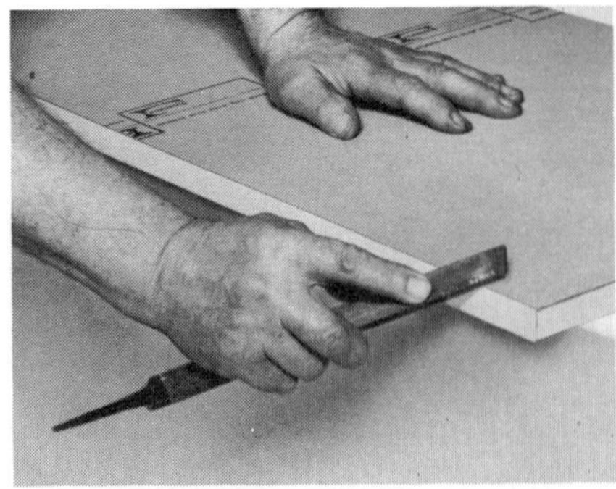

When filing down the edges, keep the file at a 45° angle to the work to avoid possible chipping of the laminate. Use light strokes. A plane or a router with a special bit can also be used for trimming (p.55).

Veneer types

Veneers are thin slices of wood cut from round logs or log segments called flitches. Their primary advantage to the woodworker is their ability to give an attractive face to the most ordinary and inexpensive piece of wood.

There are two basic veneer types: **Construction veneers,** which are often thick and are used in some plywood and factory-produced laminated shapes; and **face veneers,** usually 1/28 inch thick and intended for decorative applications.

Various methods are employed to produce veneers, such as sawing, slicing, and rotary cutting. In rotary cutting, the log is mounted on a lathe, and a knife peels off a continuous ribbon of veneer. Sliced veneer is cut crosswise by a tool operating like a giant plane. The veneer is the shaving that is produced by this slicing process.

In each case the grain of the veneers varies, producing distinctive effects and patterns.

A single sheet of veneer is called a leaf and several are a parcel. Veneer is priced by the square foot.

Much sharper bends than possible with plywood or lumber can be made by gluing thin veneers together over a form to produce a laminated shape. The grain of the layers is laid parallel, not crisscrossed as it is in plywood.

For decorative cabinet veneering, a wide variety of ready-made inlays, including fraternal emblems and checkerboard faces, is available from cabinetmakers' supply houses.

Applying veneer

For general veneering work, you need a veneer hammer (or roller), marking knife, straightedge, toothing plane (for scratching wood to get a good bonding surface) or coarse abrasive paper and block, gummed paper, glue and brush.

Cut veneers larger than the surfaces to be covered (½-inch overlap on all edges). Moisten veneers (if they are wavy) on both sides; stack them flat between boards. After several hours they will be pliable and ready for use with water-mixed-type glue. (For contact cement, they must be completely dry.) Brush a thin coat of glue on the surface to be veneered; let the glue dry.

Arrange the sheets as they will be laid. Place the surface to be veneered flat and spread glue on it, the width of the first sheet to be attached. Spread glue on the underside of this first sheet and move it into position, overlapping edges about ½ inch. Rub the sheet with the veneer hammer or roller until firmly bonded. Use the hammer or roller to work out bubbles to the nearest edge.

Each new sheet should overlap the previous one by about ¾ inch. Using a trimming knife and a straightedge, cut along the center line of each overlap, through both layers of veneer. Remove waste and close the joint by rubbing hard with the veneer hammer or roller, pressing in a herringbone pattern from both sides toward the joint, until the meeting edges are flat.

If a veneering glue is used, the veneered work should be held in a veneer press until the glue sets. (You can make such a press with stock lumber and special clamps.) For a contact-cement-type adhesive, the procedure is the same as with plastic laminates; no clamping arrangement is required.

Begin by rubbing down the first piece of veneer. Work air bubbles out toward the edge. Pencil lines help alignment.

Press the second piece of veneer in place, with its edge overlapping the first by approximately ¾ in.

Cut completely through both thicknesses of veneer at the joint and carefully pull away the waste strips.

Rub the joint down firmly, working the hammer toward the joint from alternate sides to close any gap.

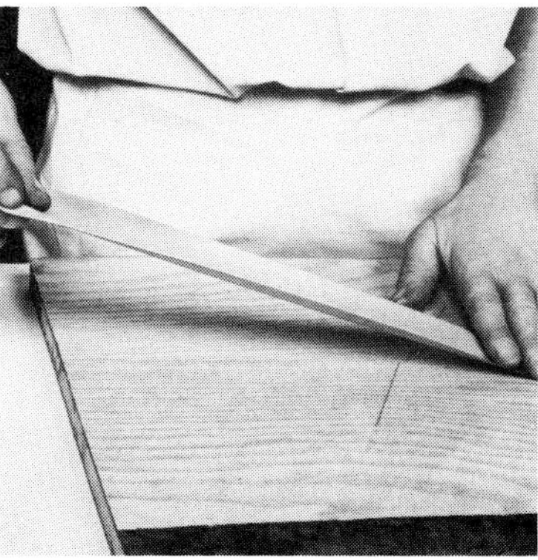

Apply gummed paper along joint to hold it in place until dry—also along any splits there may be at edges.

Patching veneer: Press a boat-shaped patch in position and clamp it until the cement is thoroughly dry.

Measuring and marking

Some basic definitions

Almost all woodworking procedures require some knowledge of simple mathematics, so that tools can be properly set and correct measurements made for the work at hand. The following are a few basic terms necessary for calculating various sizes and shapes, and indispensable to the "working vocabulary" of the home handyman.

Circumference: The distance around a circle; the length of the diameter times 3.1416 (pi).

Diameter: The distance across a circle through its center; equal to the length of the circumference times .3183.

Radius: A straight line from the center of a circle to a point on the circumference or surface.

Arc: Part of a curved line, especially a circle.

Drawing circles

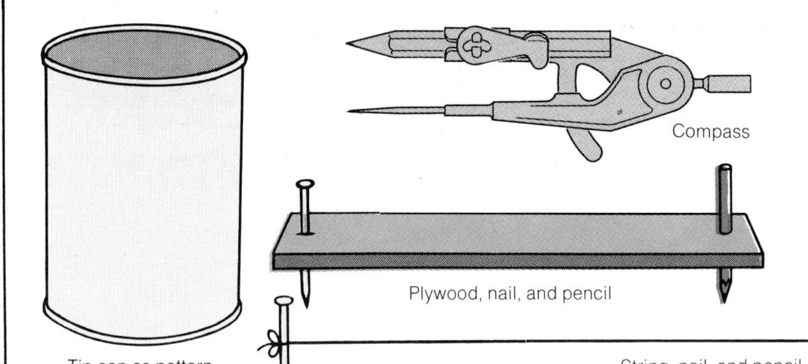

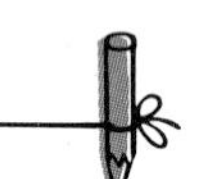

You can draw a circle: Using a compass; with a strip of wood and a nail (as the point) at one end and a pencil, at a distance equal to the radius required, at the other (or use ready-made "trammel points" on the wood strip); with a nail, string, and pencil; by tracing a coin, tin can, or plate.

Calculating sizes and shapes

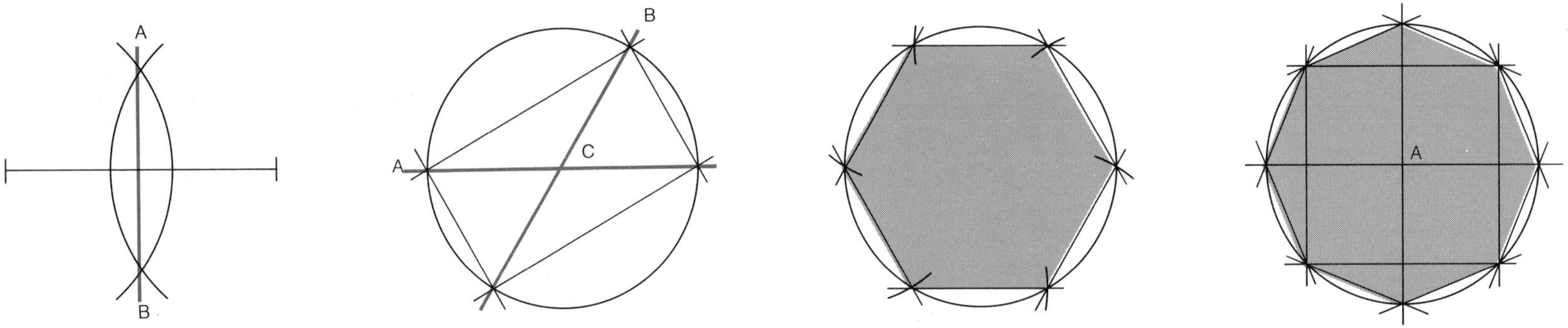

Halving line at 90°: Draw intersecting arcs, with same compass setting, from each end of line. Line drawn between two intersections (AB) will divide first line in half at 90°.

Finding center of circle: Draw a chord (AB). With this as base, use a square to draw a rectangle in circle. Where diagonals of rectangle cross (C) is center of circle.

Hexagon: Draw a circle with radius equal to required side length. Using same compass setting, step out radius on circumference six times. Connect stepped-out points.

Octagon: Mark out a square and bisect each side. Draw circle with compass point at intersection of bisecting lines (A) to enclose square exactly. Join points where bisecting lines cut circle to original corners of the square.

Ellipse: Draw on center line (AB) bisecting line (CD) at 90° so they halve each other. Make line AB equal to length of ellipse, CD to width. Set two thumbtacks along center line at distances from D equal to half length of AB (AE). Tie loop of string around tacks so it will reach D. With pencil in loop and string taut, draw ellipse.

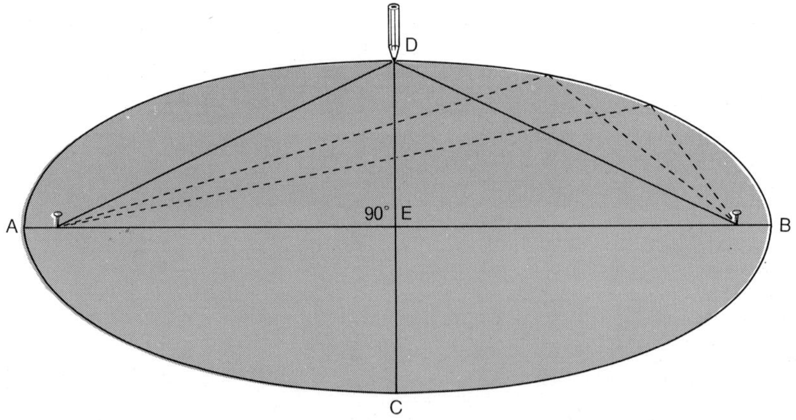

Methods of marking angles

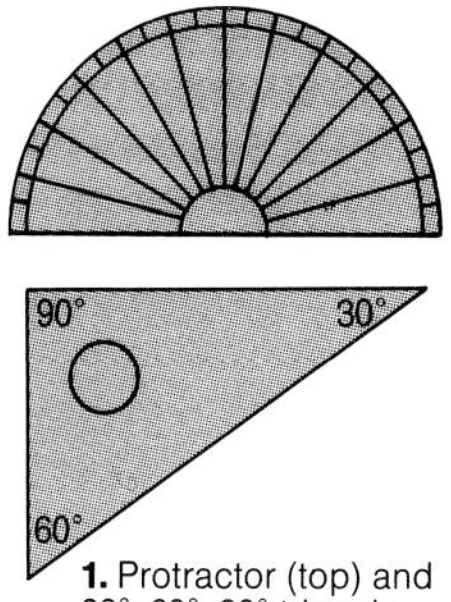

1. Protractor (top) and 30°, 60°, 90° triangle

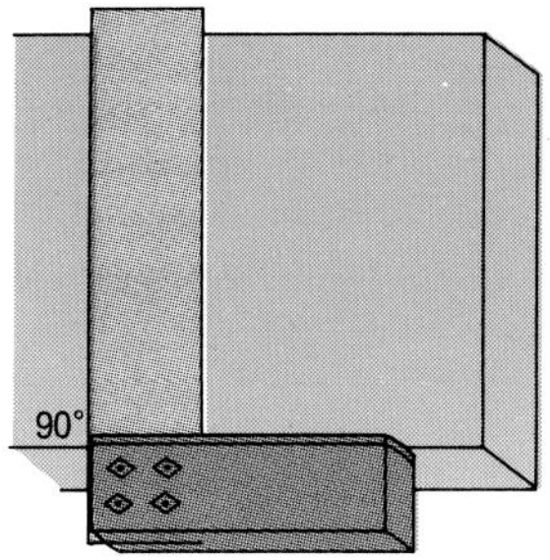

2. Using a try square

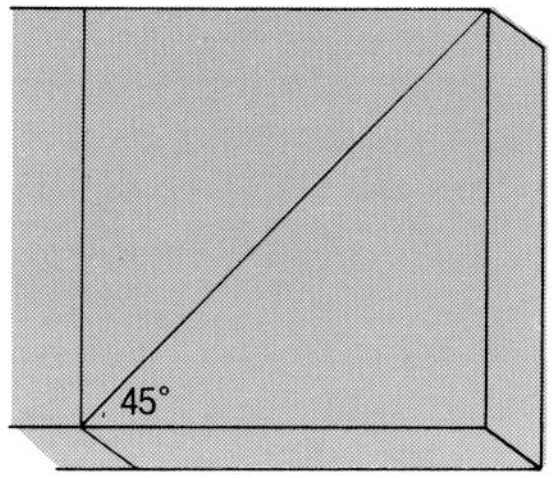

3. Finding 45°

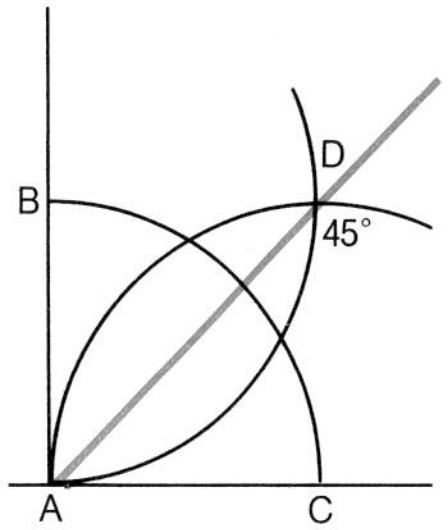

4. Finding 45° with compass

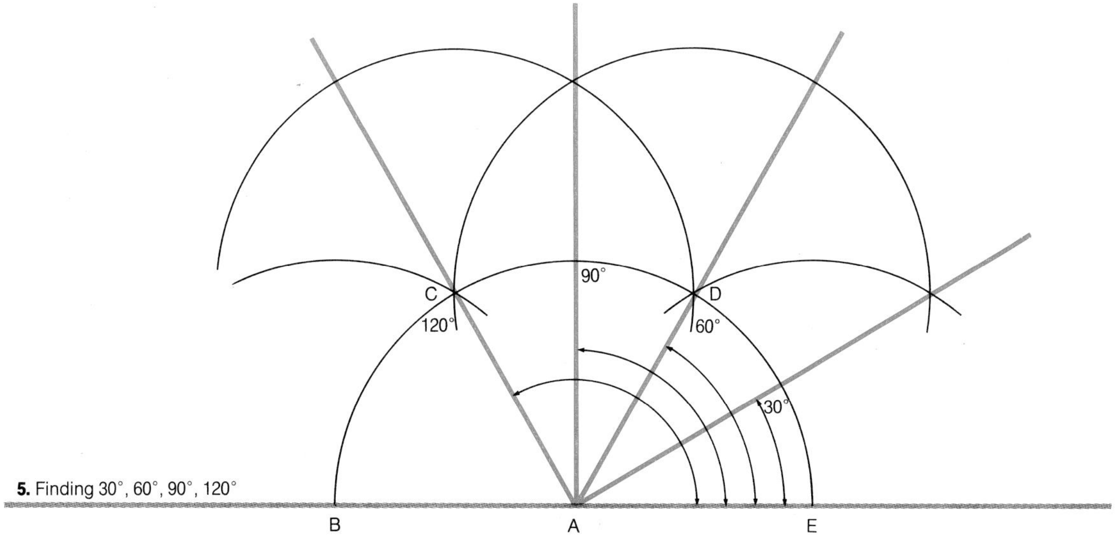

5. Finding 30°, 60°, 90°, 120°

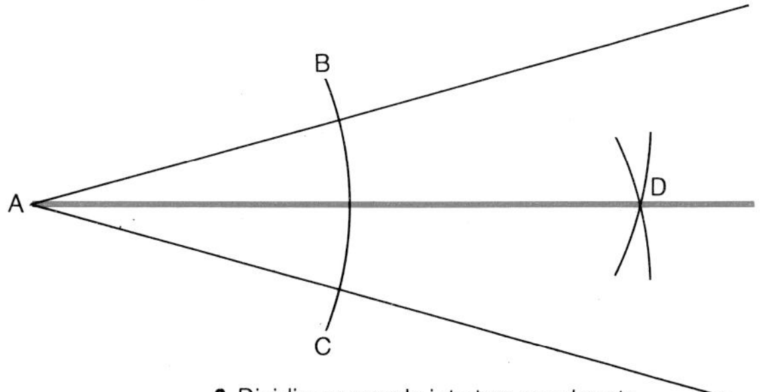

6. Dividing an angle into two equal parts

1. Using protractor, angle once found can be copied by transferring setting to sliding T bevel.
2. Using try square for 90° angle.
3. Marking a square with sides equal to width of wood and drawing a diagonal to get 45°.
4. Finding 45°, having marked 90° with try square. Divide that angle with three compass swings on same setting from A, B, C. Join A with intersection D.
5. Finding 30°, 60°, 90°, 120° angles, using compass with single setting. Draw arcs from points A, B, C, D, E. Join intersections with point A.
6. Dividing unknown angle into two equal parts with single compass setting. Draw arcs from points A, B, C. Join intersection at point D with point A.

Marking corner curves

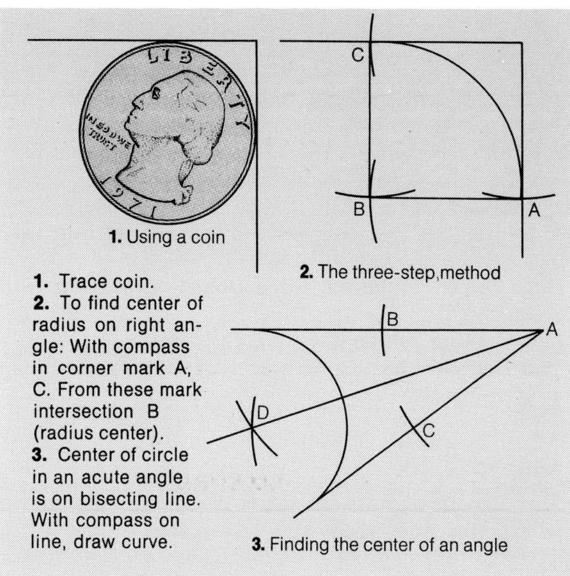

1. Using a coin

2. The three-step method

3. Finding the center of an angle

1. Trace coin.
2. To find center of radius on right angle: With compass in corner mark A, C. From these mark intersection B (radius center).
3. Center of circle in an acute angle is on bisecting line. With compass on line, draw curve.

Drawing a triangle

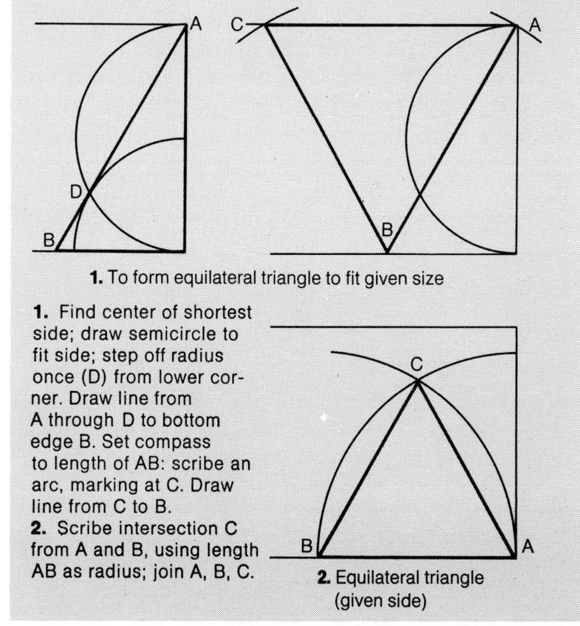

1. To form equilateral triangle to fit given size

1. Find center of shortest side; draw semicircle to fit side; step off radius once (D) from lower corner. Draw line from A through D to bottom edge B. Set compass to length of AB: scribe an arc, marking at C. Draw line from C to B.
2. Scribe intersection C from A and B, using length AB as radius; join A, B, C.

2. Equilateral triangle (given side)

Which joint for the job?

This section deals with the variations on basic joints, from the simplest through the more difficult. T joints, for example, start with basic nailed joints and finish with mortise, tenon, and dovetail joints. Joints can be divided into six groups:

T joints: One piece joined at right angles to the face or edge of another, forming a T shape.
L joints: Two pieces joined to form a corner.
X joints: The pieces crossed over or fixed into each other to form a cross.
Edge (-to-edge) joints: Edges that are joined to produce wider surfaces.
Lengthening joints: Two pieces joined end to end.
Three-way joints: Three pieces of wood joined; e.g., a chair leg and rails.

Nailed T joints

Simple nailed joints are satisfactory for light frames where the sides meet the crosspieces squarely. Be sure the butt ends of the crosspieces are square and the sidepieces are smooth. Otherwise the joint cannot form a true right angle.

Use three nails: Hammer the middle one in first to hold the wood firm, then drive in the other two on either side of it, sloping them inward at angles of 20 to 30 degrees. These nails form a dovetail.

Toe nailing from the inside of a frame requires care. Hammer from both sides alternately and realign the work as the nail points bite into the sidepiece. Drive nails in line with the grain, but stagger them to avoid splitting.

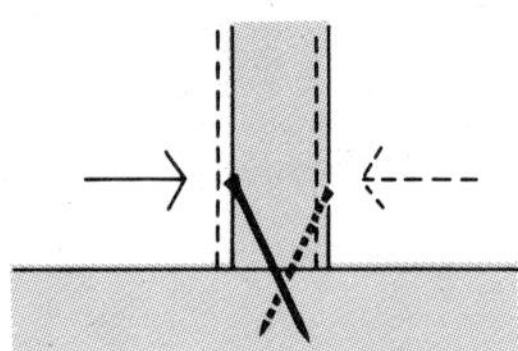

Take care that wood does not move as you hammer

Set the nailheads below the surface of the wood for extra tightness. Fill holes with filler or putty.

Use finishing nails on trim and exposed work, common nails on structural framing. The nail length should be at least three times the thickness of the wood through which it is driven.

Using braces and fasteners

Metal braces and mending plates are helpful in making flat T joints. There are four types: One, known as an **inside corner brace,** is a strip of drilled metal bent into a simple L shape for fitting into corners; another, called a **T plate,** is a flat T shape, and screws flat onto the work. The **flat corner plate** is similar, but L shaped, for corner use. The **mending plate** is straight, for straight line reinforcement.

Use these whenever the appearance and thickness of the brace do not matter, as in light framing, which needs a little more strength than nailed joints would provide, also for repairs. Obviously, the stronger the brace the stronger the joint, but, in some applications, the braces will bend unless you use one on each side of the joint.

The screws should fit the drilled holes snugly. Drill pilot holes in the wood to prevent splitting. Drive the screws home flush with the top.

A far quicker way to make T joints (where high strength isn't required) is with corrugated metal fasteners which are hammered straight into the work. These fasteners are sharpened on one edge. They are best used on light indoor work, such as screen frames and box-making.

Make sure that the joint is as tight as possible before you drive the fasteners home.

Position the fasteners well in from the edges of the crosspiece to prevent splits. Tap gently until they are going in evenly, then hammer them along the top until they are flush with the surface.

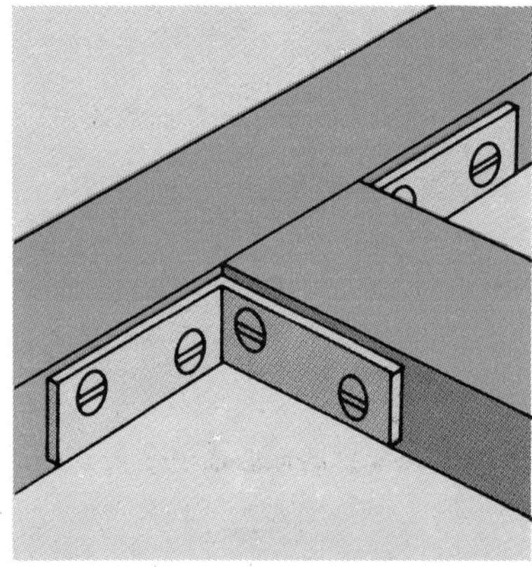

Two corner braces prevent bending

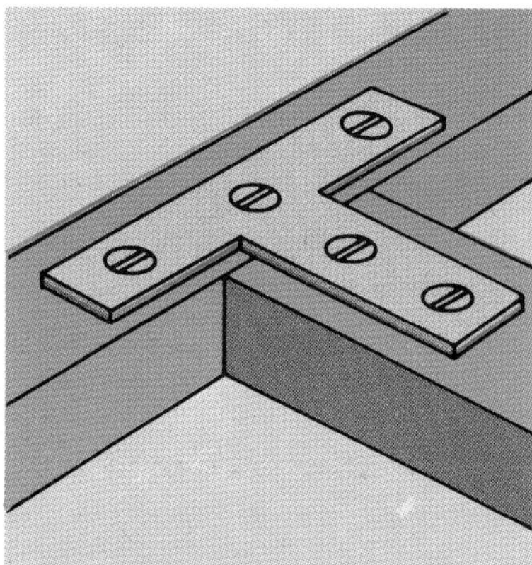

Screw T plates flat on the surface

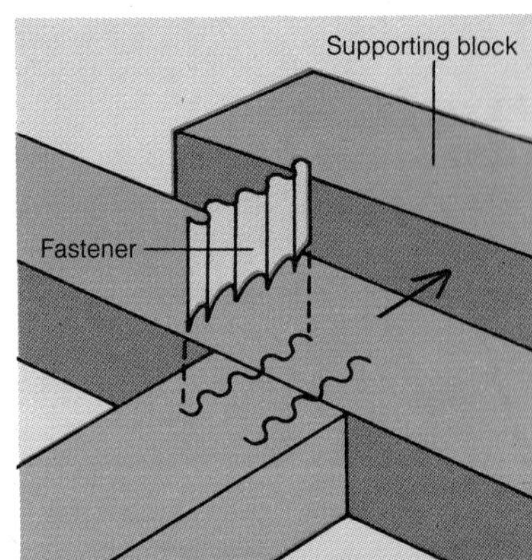

Hammer in corrugated fasteners

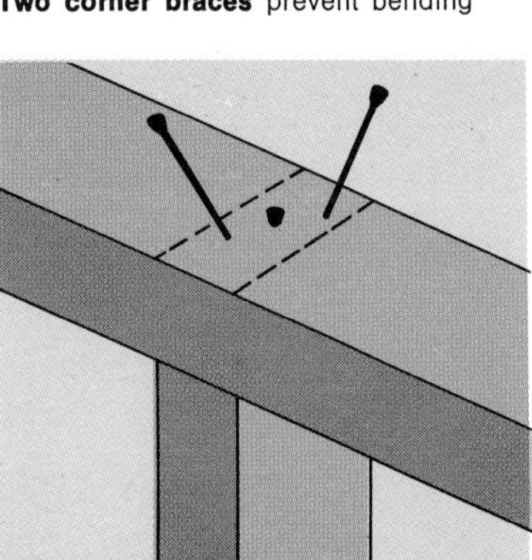

Direct nailing: Two-thirds of the nail length should be in the crosspiece.

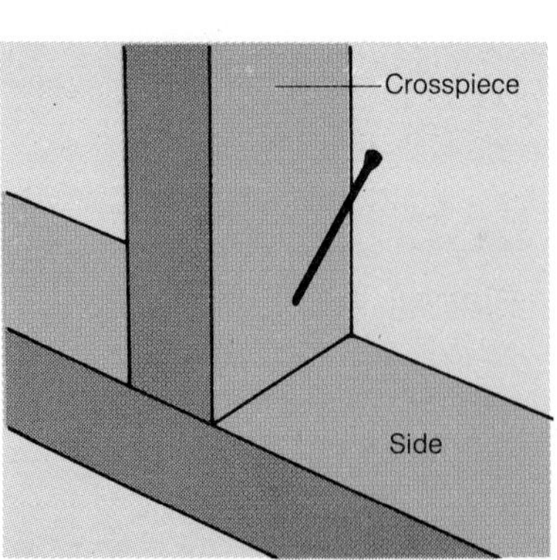

Toe nailing: Drive nails from opposite sides at about a 30° angle.

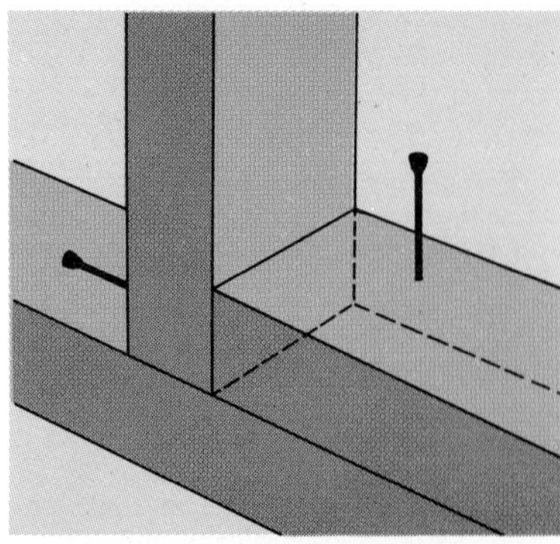

A block may be nailed to one member to receive nails driven through the other.

Overlap joints

The overlap T joint is used for general-purpose jobs. It can be secured by screws, nails, or bolts, and, for strongest results, may also be glued.

To make a strong screwed-overlap joint, clamp both pieces of wood together with a C-clamp (p. 36). Drill a clearance hole through the top piece and a pilot hole in the lower piece, using a bit small enough for the screw thread to bite firmly. Countersink holes in top piece, coat inner surfaces with glue, fit pieces together, then drive screw home.

A simple glued-and-screwed T joint, combined with supporting blocks, produces sturdy shelving units. Glue and screw blocks to each side of the casing, then glue and screw the shelving to the blocks.

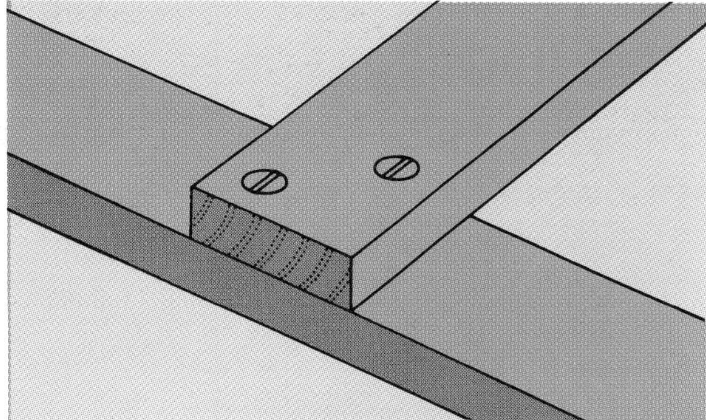

Overlap T joint: Screw diagonally to avoid splitting wood

Shelf support: Screw block to upright; screw in shelves

Full and half lap joints

Use these strong, neat joints for fitting crossrails flush into frames to be paneled.

In a **full lap joint** the side rail is cut out to accommodate the whole of the crossrail. To make it, mark the exact shape of the cutout on both faces of the side rail and across its top edge.

Cut out the waste gradually from each side with a backsaw and chisel until the base of the cutout is level. Check the fit, glue all mating surfaces, and complete the joint by nailing or screwing.

In a **half lap joint,** the crossrail and the side rail are both cut away to give a flush fit when they are mated.

Mark the width of the crossrail across the face of the side rail and halfway down both edges.

On the back of the crossrail, mark a shoulder line across at a distance from the end a little greater than the width of the side rail.

Continue the line halfway across the edges. Set a marking gauge to half the thickness of the wood and gauge lines from the face of both pieces.

Saw a center slot in the crossrail, skimming the gauge line on the waste side. Remove the waste block by cutting across the shoulder line.

Saw just inside the lines marking the side rail cutout. Saw an extra cut in the center to make waste removal easier. Using a chisel, remove the waste from both sides to complete the cutout, check for fit, fix, and trim. If you have difficulty assembling the pieces, sand the leading edges lightly. If the joint is to be glued, use the glue sparingly.

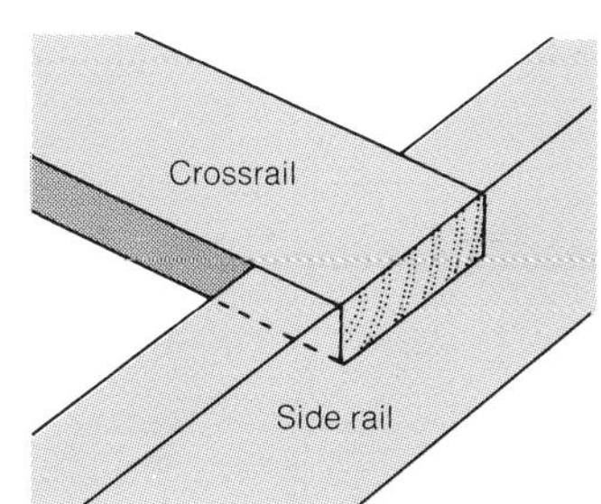

Full lap joint: Set in flush with the face of a frame, joint provides strength as well as a neat look.

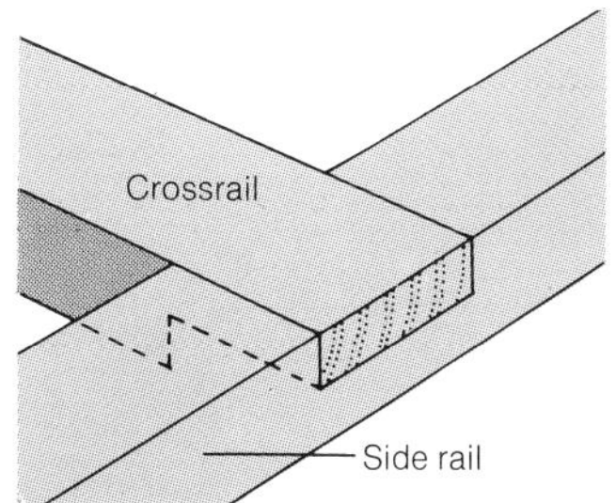

Half lap joint: Quick and simple method of joining wood of equal thickness. Glue and nail the pieces together for greater strength.

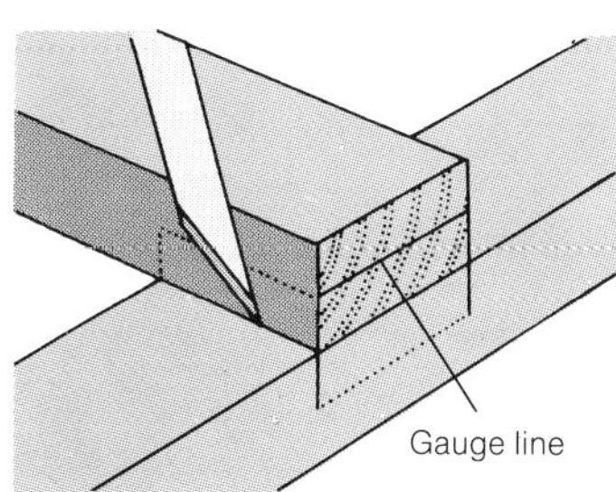

1. To make the half lap joint, mark off the width of the crossrail. Keep the pieces perpendicular to each other.

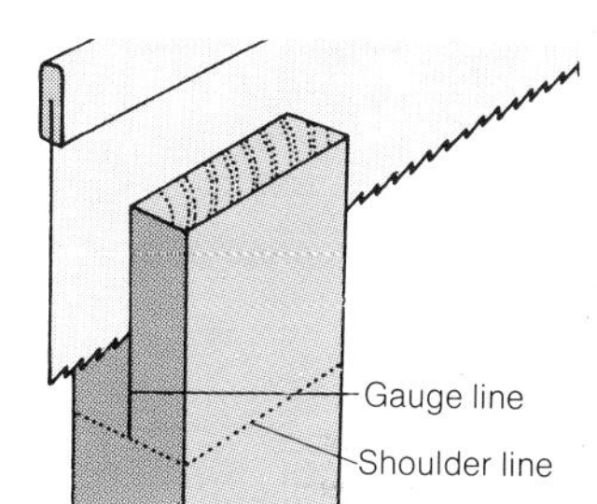

2. Next saw down the center of the crossrail, skimming the gauge line on the waste side.

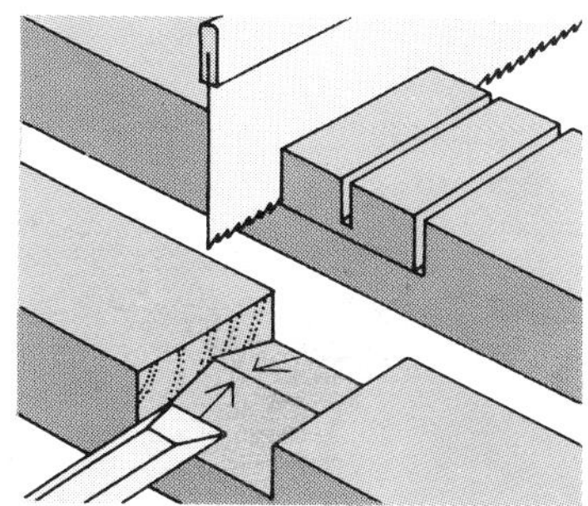

3. Make three backsaw cuts—one on each side of the cutout and one in the middle. Chisel the waste away from both sides down to the gauge lines.

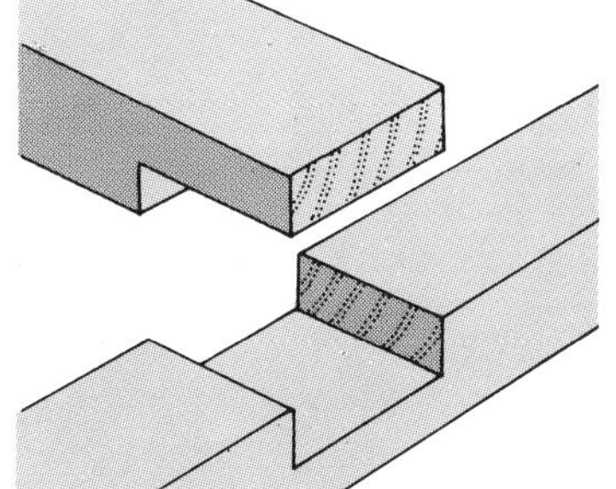

4. The finished joint should tap together easily. Make sure the shoulders are secure. Glue and nail. Allow the glue to set, then trim.

Plain and stopped dadoes

The dado joint is the classic way of joining the end or edge of one board into the cut surface of another. There are two principal types: The **plain dado,** in which the cutout continues all the way across the joining member, and the **stopped dado,** in which the dado extends only part way.

Both types can be dovetailed by cutting one side of the housing and the matching edge of the cross member at an inward sloping angle (p 389).

The stopped dado is the type that is used for display and cabinet work.

Making the joint: First, mark a line at right angles across the inner face of the piece to be dadoed. Hold the cross member against the line and draw a line along its other side to give the exact width of the dado.

Continue these lines across both edges of the upright. Mark the depth of the dado—usually it is one-third of the wood thickness from the face side of both edges.

Cut down carefully to depth on both sides of the housing with a backsaw.

Chisel away the waste from each edge. Start with a sloping cut and gradually reduce the paring angle until the center is chiseled away. Finish the cut with a hand router.

If you do not have a hand router available, take extra care with the paring and check frequently with a straightedge for depth and flatness. The dado can also be cut on a table or radial arm saw, using a dado set in place of the blade and setting it for the width and depth of the cut (this is the easiest way).

The stopped dado joint: Construction is similar to that of the regular joint except that the cutout ends a short distance from the front edge (or edges) of the dadoed member. The corner of the inserted member is cut away to overlap this distance.

Mark as usual for the joint but also mark the stopped end (or ends) of the dado from the edge.

To make space for a saw, chisel out a recess from the stopped end to near the correct depth. Saw to depth from the unstopped edge on both sides. Chisel away the waste and clean out to depth with a router. If both ends are stopped, cut the dado with a chisel, or with a router.

On the inserted member, mark the cutout to depth and length and cut away the corners for the overlap. Saw away the waste with a backsaw.

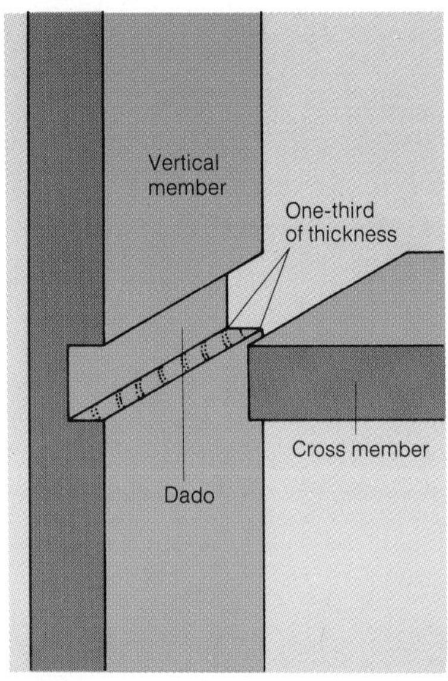

Dado joint: A clean, strong joint. The cross member takes considerable weight and is ideal for bookshelves.

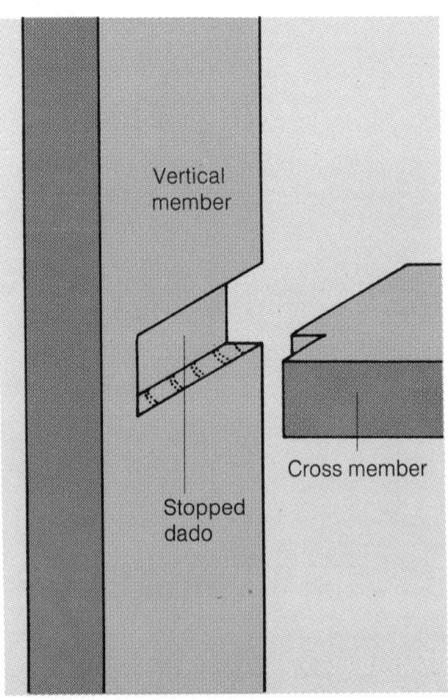

Stopped dado joint: Use this joint where appearance matters. Overlap neatly conceals its construction on the front.

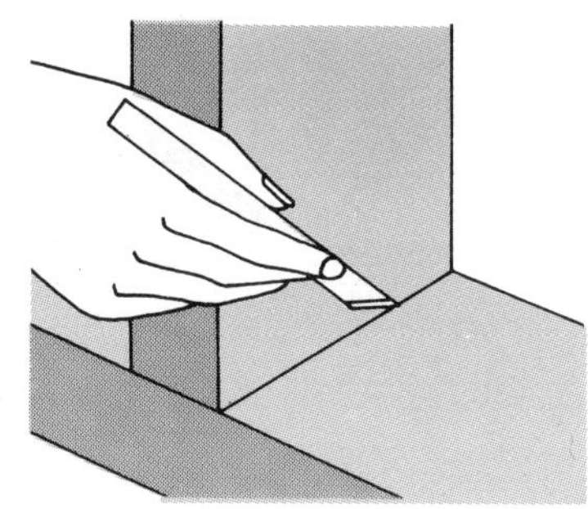

To make a dado joint: Place cross member against a squared line on the inner face of the upright and mark on other side for the exact cut.

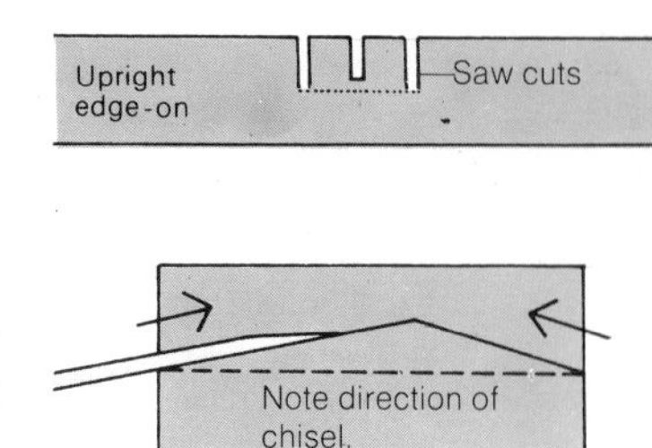

After sawing to depth, gradually chisel out the waste from each edge until the center is completely removed. Then trim to depth.

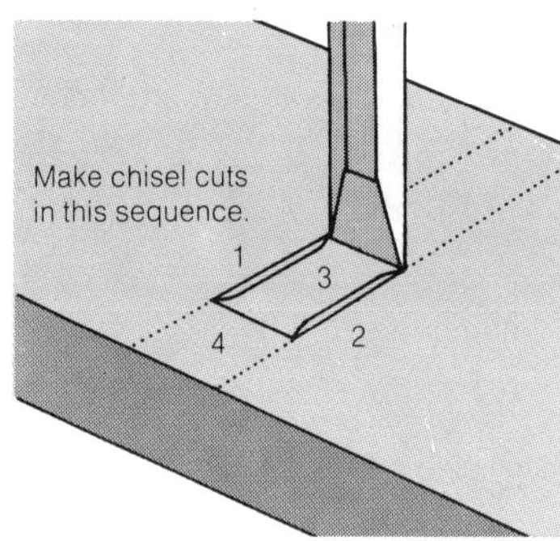

To make a stopped dado joint: Make room for saw movement by chiseling a recess at stopped end of joint.

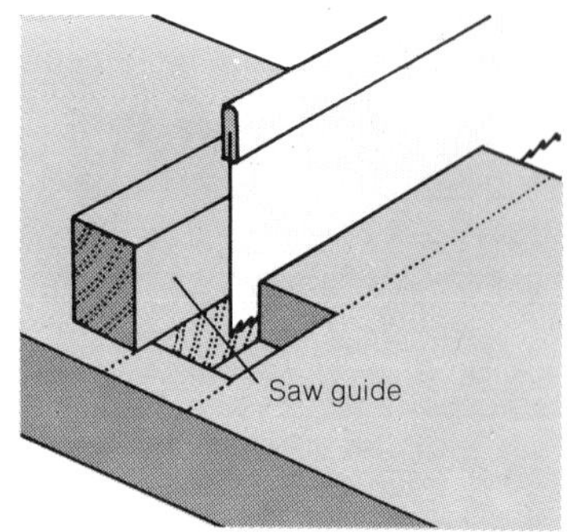

On long cuts, run the saw against a guide batten that is temporarily clamped to the work.

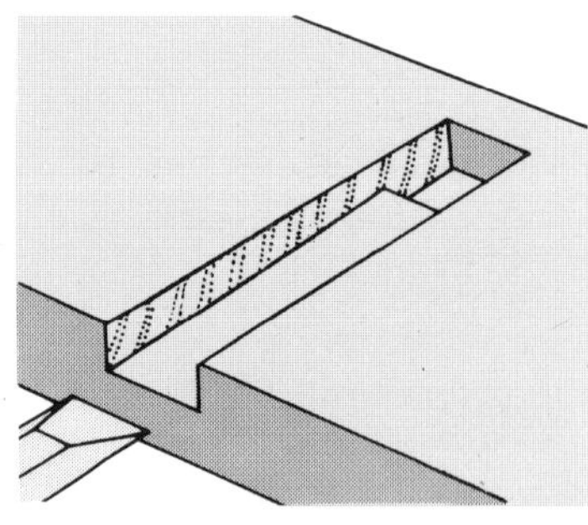

Chisel out waste, then finish cut with hand router or paring chisel.

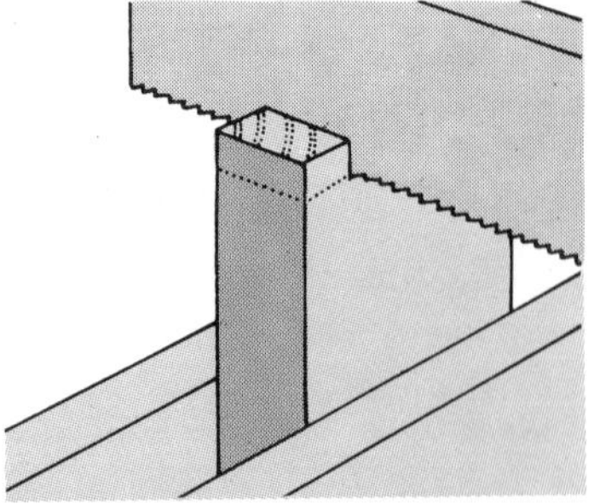

Saw off cut-away corner on cross member to the depth of the housing.

Making the basic joint

The strongest of the T joints, used for heavy framing and in general furniture work. The thickness of the tenon should not exceed one-third the thickness of the mortised member.

To make the joint, mark the width of the member to be tenoned **(rail)** on the member to be mortised **(stile)** and continue the lines as a guide. On the ends of the mortise outline, mark lines for wedges—about ⅛ inch outside existing lines—if joint is to be wedged. Square a shoulder line right around the member to be tenoned, to give a tenon length just greater than the mortise depth.

Select your chisel and set mortise limit points to its width. (You may use a regular marking gauge by resetting it after first marking.) Center the mortise

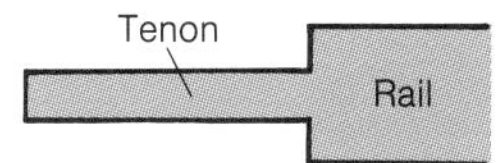

Tenon thickness: One-third of stock

(for methods, see p 382), then cut back to edge lines on outer edge. You can speed the mortise by boring through at each end with an auger bit, then chiseling between holes. Saw down tenon line faces and cut carefully across at shoulder lines.

Apply glue, assemble, clamp, and hammer in glued wedges. Sand off protrusions when glue has set.

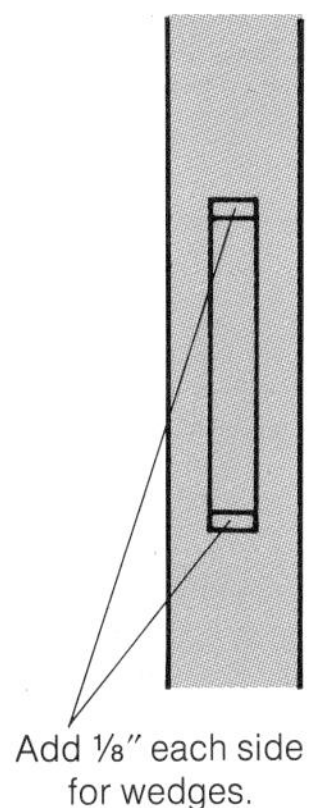

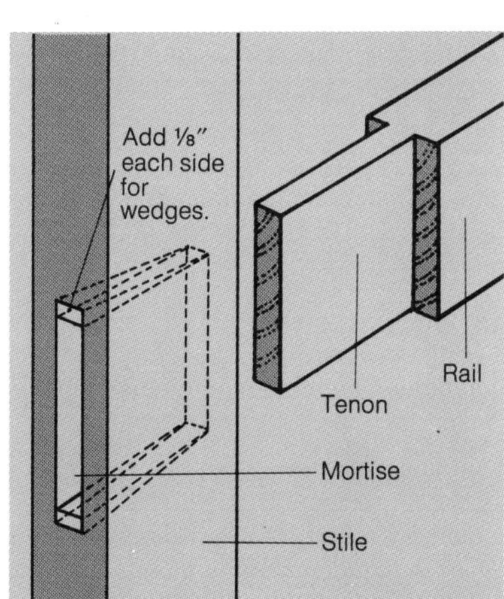

Marking out: Make tenon long enough to project slightly beyond mortise.

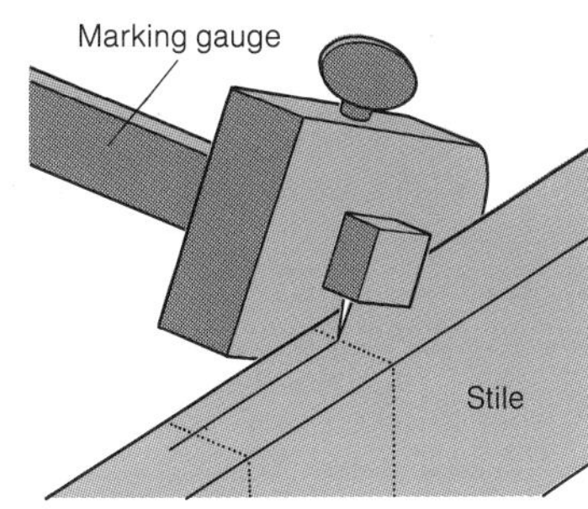

1. Set the point of the marking gauge for the outside limit of the mortise to be cut in the rail.

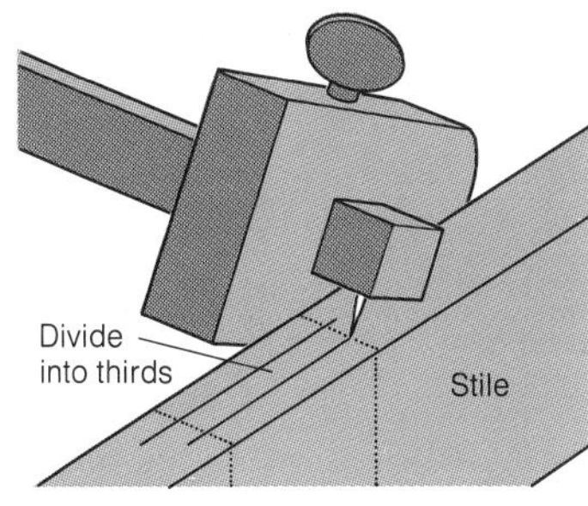

2. Extend the point and mark the width of the mortise. Make it equal to one-third the total thickness of the wood.

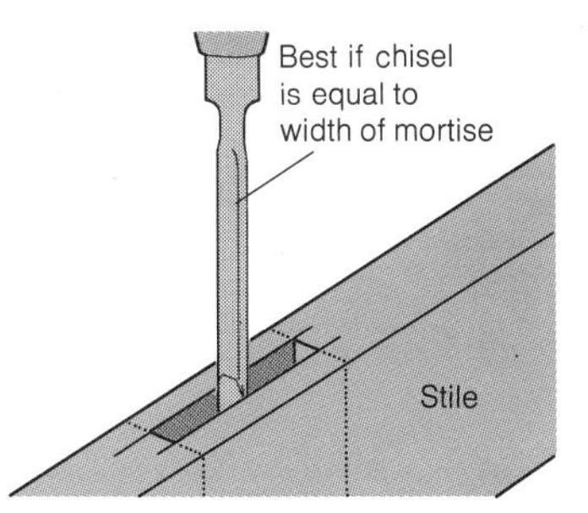

3. Cut out the mortise, working from both sides until recesses meet. Trim out, then cut back for wedges.

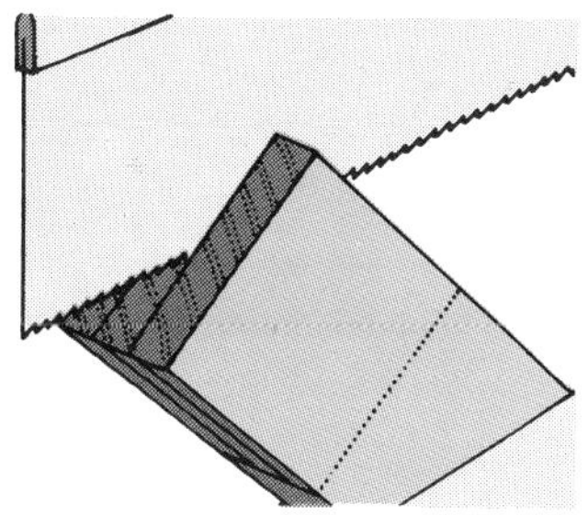

4. Make sloping cuts down both tenon lines alternately from each edge. Skim the lines on the waste side.

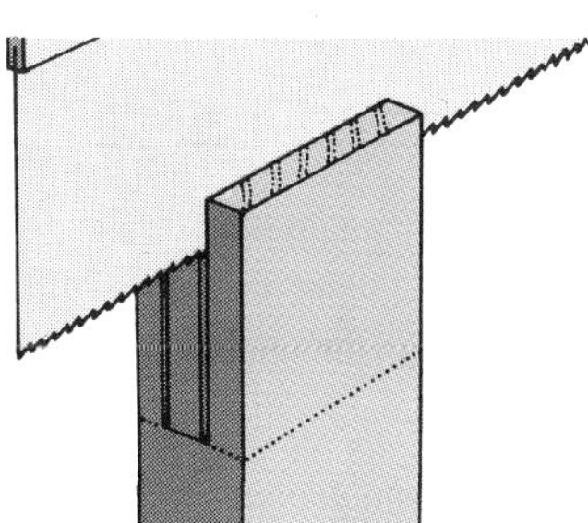

5. Clamp the work upright in vise, then saw the waste down squarely to the shoulder lines.

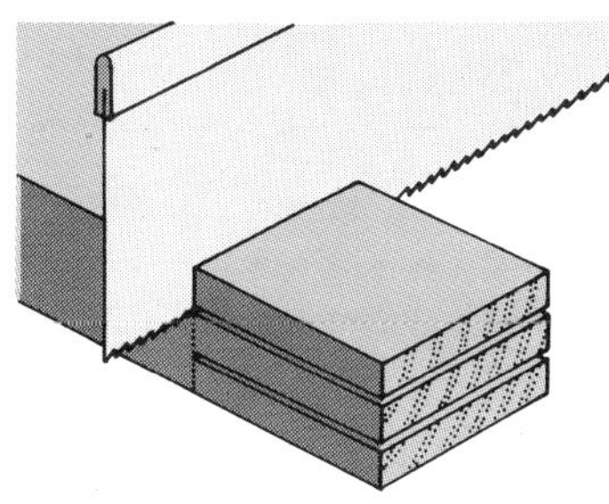

6. Cut across shoulder lines to complete tenon, making sure the saw is straight. Fit tenon into mortise.

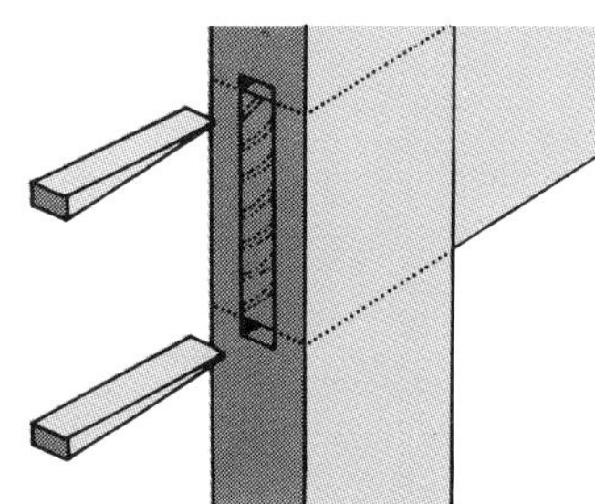

7. Apply glue to the tenon and inside the mortise. Fit the parts together. Cut finely tapered wedges to fit part way into the ⅛-in. slots at the ends of the mortise.

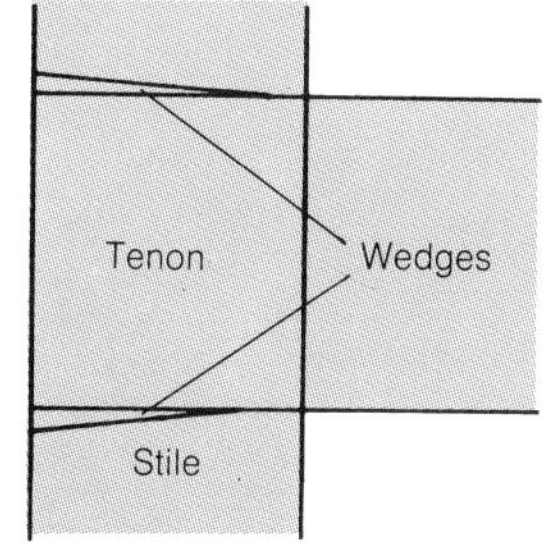

8. Apply glue to the wedges and drive them into the slots. Hammer both in at the same time, striking them alternately to keep tenon straight in mortise. Clamp the assembly.

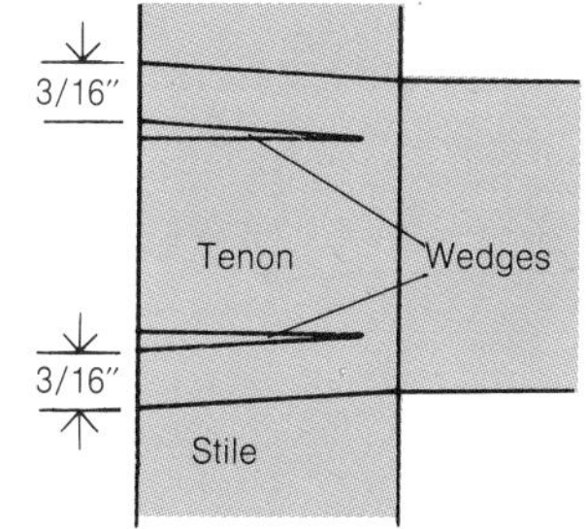

9. Another wedging method is to saw wedge slots about two-thirds down the length of the tenon, 3/16 in. in from the edges. The wedges jam the tenon into the shape of the mortise.

Mortise and tenon joints

Variations on the basic joint

The mortise and tenon joint strengthens furniture construction and provides a pleasing appearance. Extra shoulders may be cut, reducing the width of the tenon by ⅛ to ½ inch top and bottom to completely hide the ends of the mortise slot.

Rabbeted or haunched tenon: A very strong joint for window frames, doors, and furniture. It can be used as an L joint—on corners—as well as a T joint. The haunch can be sloping, instead of square as shown. The haunch resists twisting, but does not weaken the stile, as a full width tenon would.

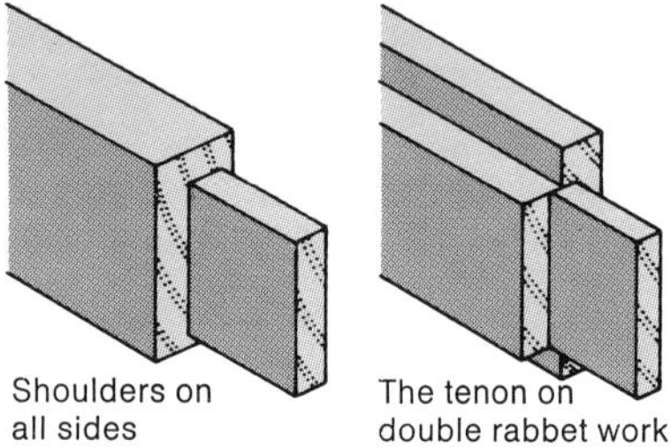

Proportions are important. Make the mortise and tenon about one-third the thickness of the wood—if too wide, the joint will be weakened.

Make the length of the haunch not more than one-third the length of the tenon. Its depth should be no more than a quarter of the width of the mortised member, or ½ inch—whichever measurement is the smaller. Often the depth is determined by a groove in the frame.

Leave at least ½ inch of waste on the end of the mortised member to prevent splitting while making and fitting the joint. Trim when the glue sets.

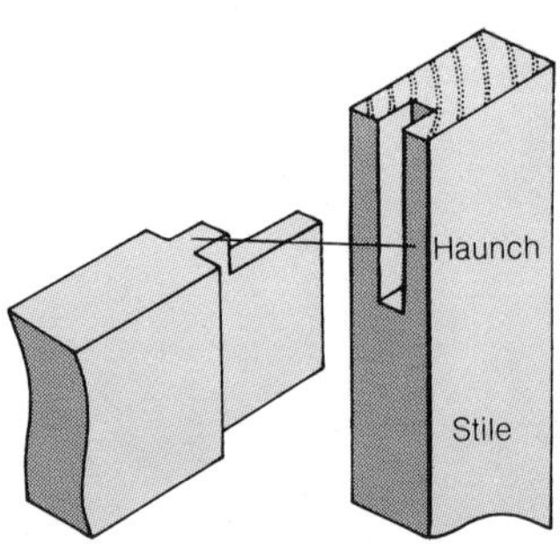

Make the haunch one-third the length of the tenon

Double tenon: Use a double tenon where a single tenon would be so wide as to weaken the upright.

The joint has great resistance to twisting where extra-wide rails have to be fitted to uprights. Set it out and cut the same as for a single tenon.

Stub tenon: This joint serves much the same purpose as the plain mortise and tenon, but the tenon in this type is stopped short so that it does not appear on the outside.

The depth of the mortise should be about two-thirds the width of the wood. Cut the tenon about ⅛ inch short of this depth measurement. This will keep it from touching the bottom of the mortise.

Scribed tenon: The scribed tenon is used on work in which one or both edges have molding, such as window frames.

Cut the tenoned piece oversize by the depth of the molding. Then, with a chisel, cut away the shoulders of the tenon to match the molding on the other member. Trim to fit.

Twin mortise and tenon: This joint is mainly used on the center rail, or lock rail, of door frames. The divided tenons span the lock, which is mortised from the outside.

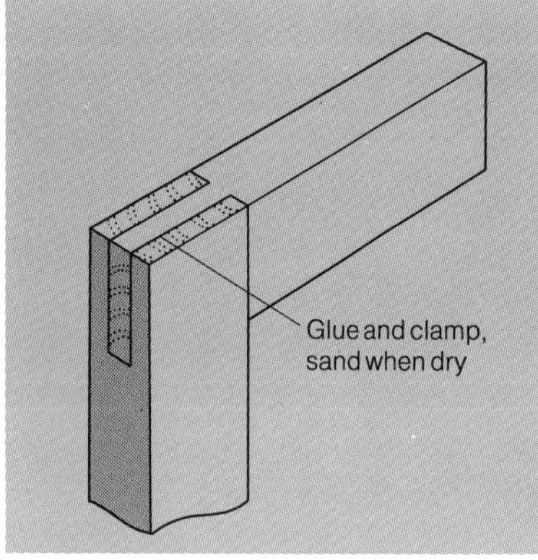

Open mortise and tenon: Easy to make, and strong using modern resin glues.

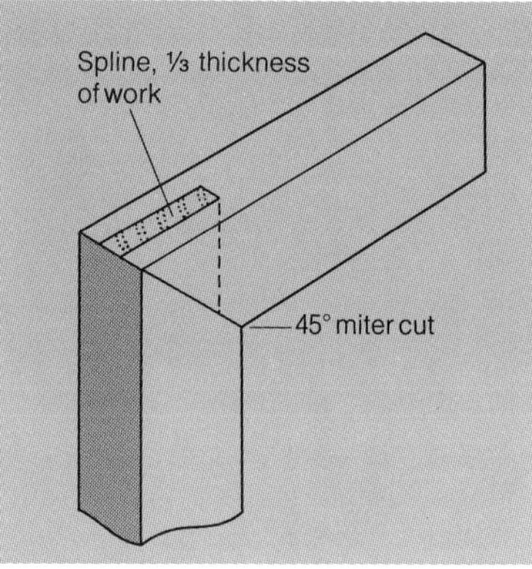

Miter with feather joint locked by square spline fitted into outer corner of joint.

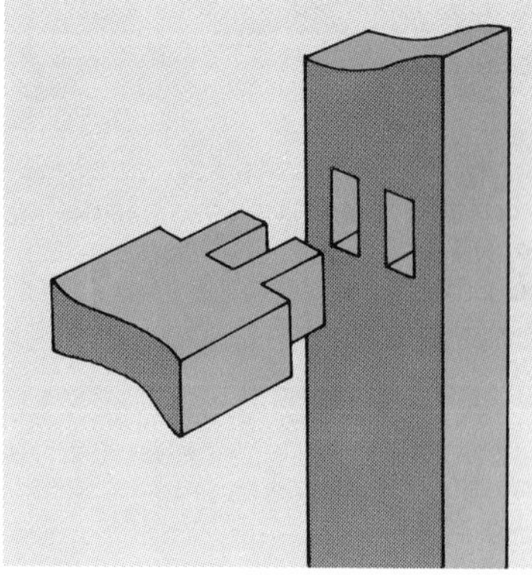

Double tenon should have tenon widths the same as the gaps between them.

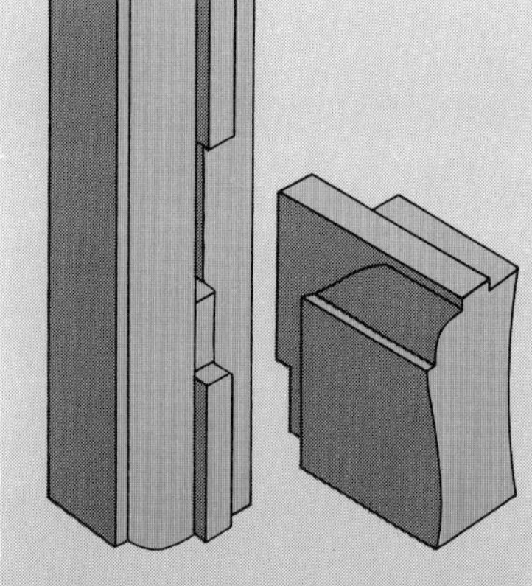

Scribed tenon, used where moldings meet; tenon shoulders match joining part.

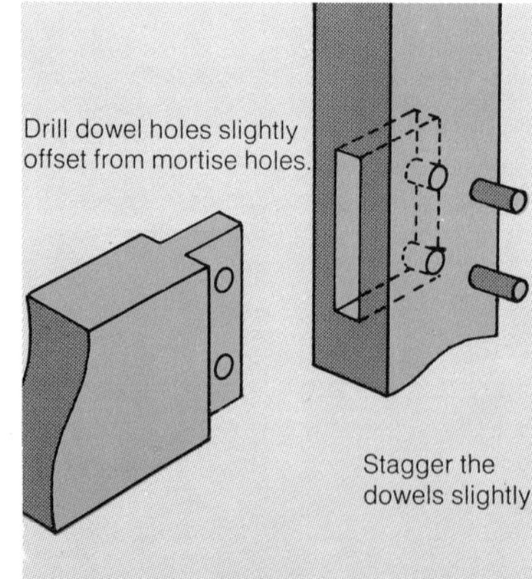

Stub tenon runs part way through; may be locked with staggered dowels plus glue.

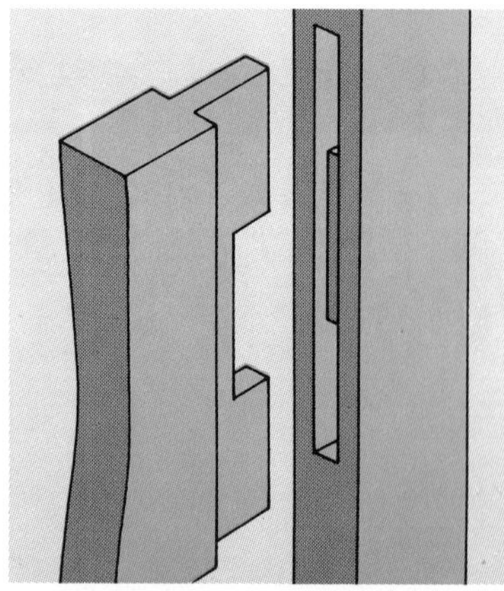

Twin mortise and tenon is often used for wide rail of door at lock location.

Single dovetail

The single dovetail is a mechanically strong joint for furniture rails that have to bear weight.

To construct it, first mark out and cut the pin (this is the flared projection at the end of the rail or board) with either a backsaw or a dovetail saw (2). Make the angle of the pin 1:6 for softwood (1) and 1:8 for hardwood.

Transfer the pin shape to the other frame piece (3) by marking with a pencil or knife.

Saw down the shoulders of the dovetail cutout and make an extra cut in the center of the waste to facilitate chiseling work (4). Put joint together dry (before gluing) to check for fit (5). Then glue and clamp (6), wiping off excess glue to reduce required sanding later.

The same type of single dovetail can also be cut very quickly with a jigsaw that has a tilt adjustment. Use the saw with the blade in vertical position to cut the pin. Then mark the shape of the pin on the second piece. Cut this part of the joint by adjusting the table tilt to the marked joint angle and cutting inward from the edge. Use a chisel to separate the waste piece between cuts.

Small dovetails and multiple types, as in drawer corners, can be cut rapidly with a router, using a dovetail bit. If a dovetail attachment is available for the router, as is the case with many models, a complete drawer-corner dovetail can be cut in about one minute, as both parts are cut simultaneously by the dovetail-shaped bit.

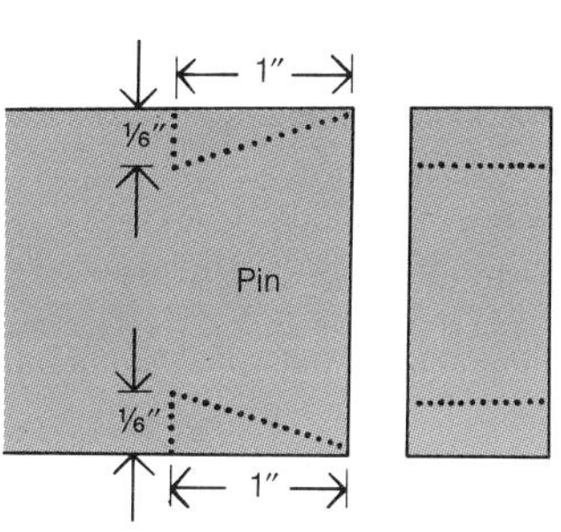

1. Mark both of the dovetail parts for cutting. Cut on the waste side, then trim.

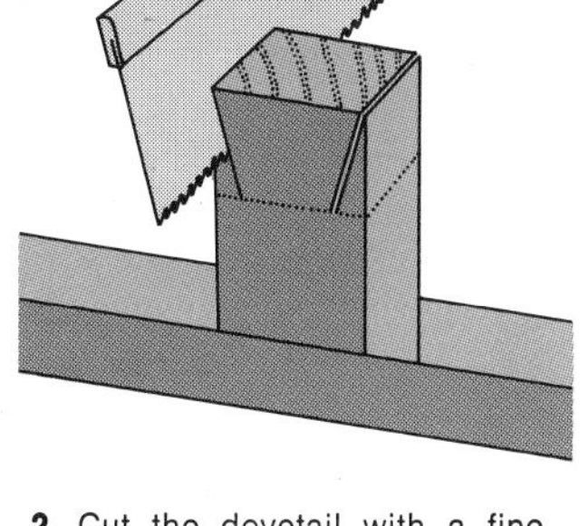

2. Cut the dovetail with a fine-toothed backsaw or saber saw for smoothness.

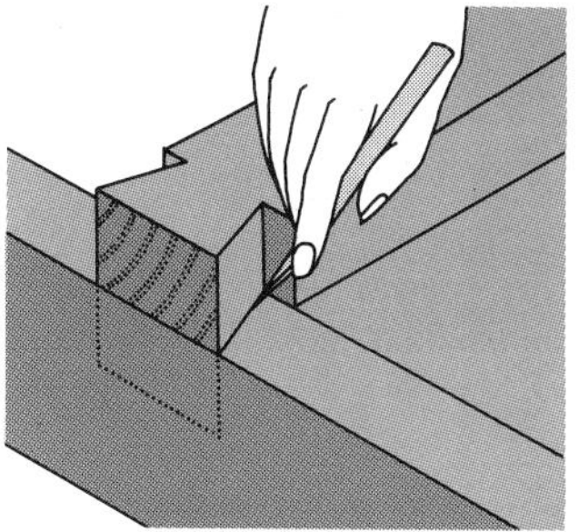

3. Mark the cut dovetail on the mating part of the joint for precise cutting.

4. Cut the second part with a backsaw or saber saw. Chisel out the waste wood.

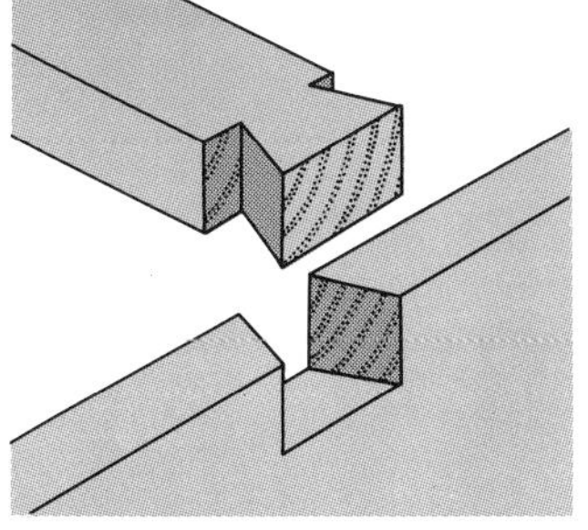

5. Fit the joint parts together dry to check fit. Trim them before applying the glue.

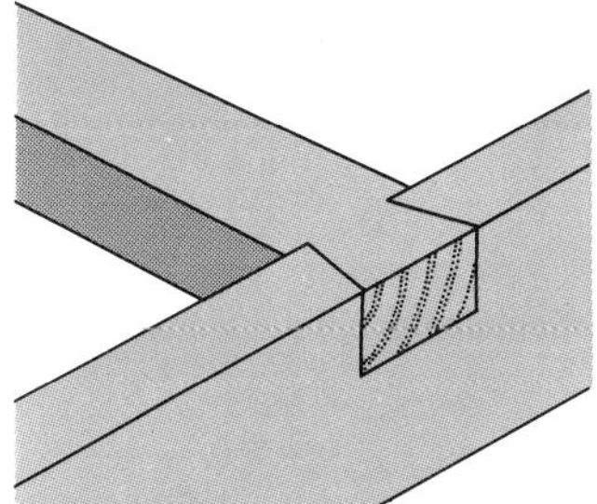

6. Glue and clamp the joint, wiping off any excess glue to reduce amount of sanding.

L joints: Six ways to make corners

Six corner joining methods are shown on the right. Wooden blocks can be square or triangular in cross section. Triangular ones (1) are neater.

The strength of glued joints depends mainly on the glue, though screws or dowels can reinforce them. Hammer the nails home dovetail-fashion (p. 70). Stagger dowels or screws to avoid splitting. Make sure the dowels or screws do not meet in the middle. Metal reinforcements can either be screwed to the top and bottom of the corner (4) or screwed only on the inside of the joints (5). The first method is the stronger.

Triangular plywood gussets (6), or glue blocks, at top and bottom, are glued and bradded to the corner. Trim outside edges when glue is dry.

1

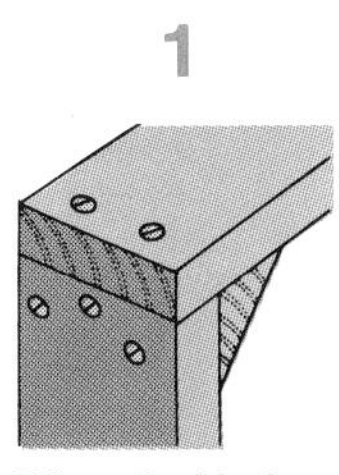

Triangular block makes smooth inside corner in cabinetwork. Has same glue grip as square block.

2

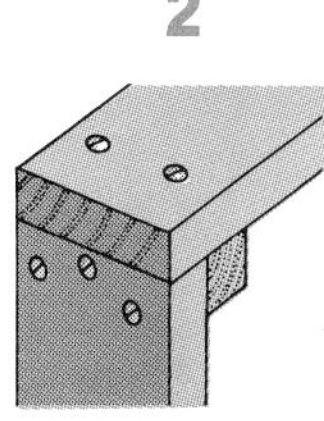

Square block allows greater depth for screws. Often used where appearance is not essential.

3

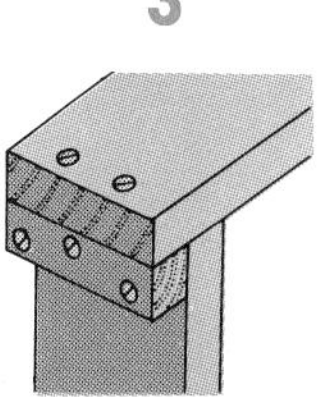

Outside glue block permits screw fastening where unobstructed inner corners are needed.

4

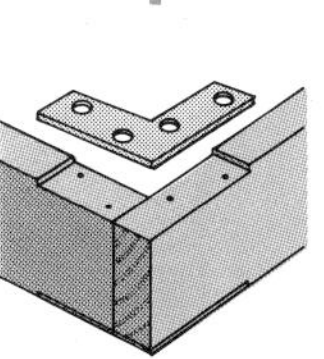

Flat corner plates recessed into edges at corners produce a strong joint with minimum effort.

5

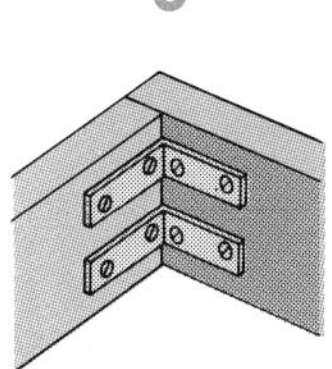

Inside corner braces do job when edges must be smooth, as when plywood will be attached.

6

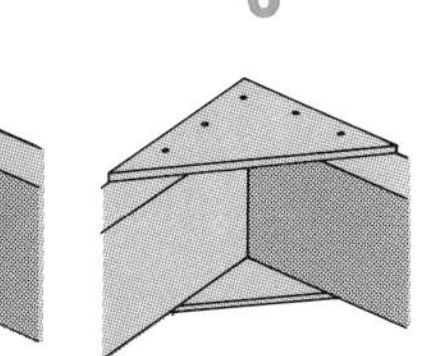

Plywood gussets and triangular pieces make a very rigid joint when nailed and glued.

Dovetail variations

Through dovetail

The through dovetail is the strongest and most decorative of the corner joints. It is used extensively for backs of drawers and in general cabinetwork.

Assemble the wood to be joined, marking the matching pieces forming the corners. Plane the end true and square, allowing $\frac{1}{16}$ inch for overall waste. Set the marking gauge to the wood thickness plus $\frac{1}{32}$ inch (the allowance for waste on each corner). Mark gauge line (a) on all sides and edges.

Use a dovetail template (angles 1:6 for softwoods; 1:8 for hardwoods) to mark the dovetails. Square the lines across the ends.

Cut down the dovetails with a backsaw (1); remove the waste with a coping saw (2); trim out with a chisel (3).

Use the dovetails as patterns to mark out the pins on the ends of the side pieces (4). Saw along the marked lines (5); remove the waste with a coping saw; then trim with a chisel.

Save time when making several joints by cutting all the dovetails at once with the dovetail pieces clamped together in the vise.

Test the joints for fit (6). Do this with the parts dry in case further trimming is needed; if all is well, glue and clamp.

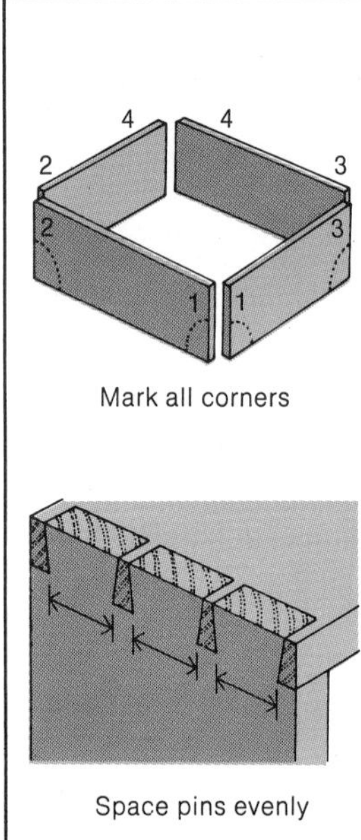

Mark all corners

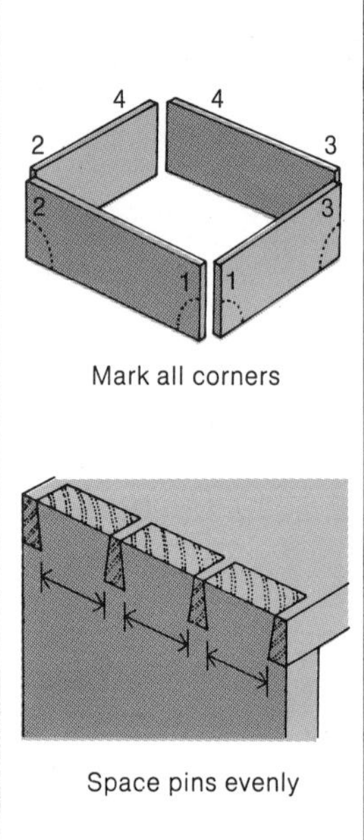

Space pins evenly

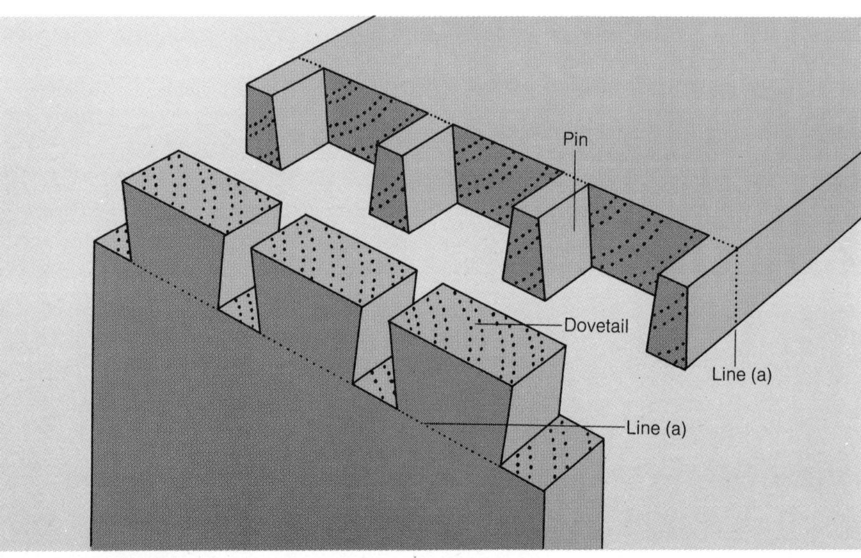

Marking out dovetails: The dovetails give the greatest strength when positioned at both sides of drawers, packing boxes, and upright frames.

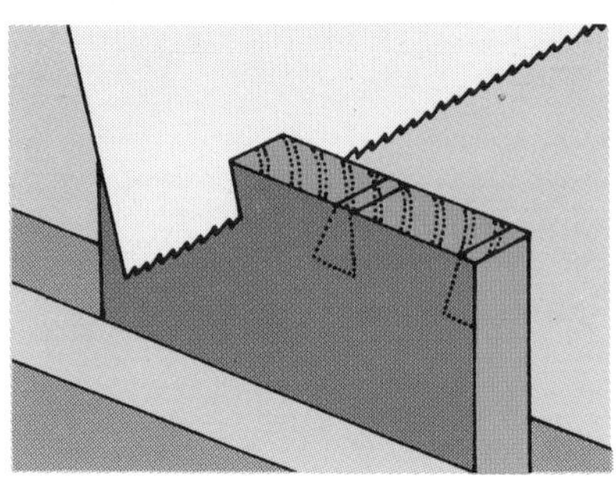

1. Cut the dovetails in the vise with a backsaw. Saw within the waste.

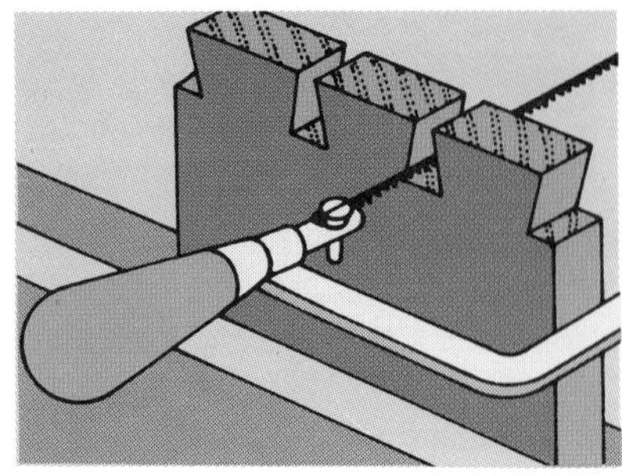

2. Remove the bulk of the waste with a coping saw. Take care not to saw into the dovetails. Hold the saw level.

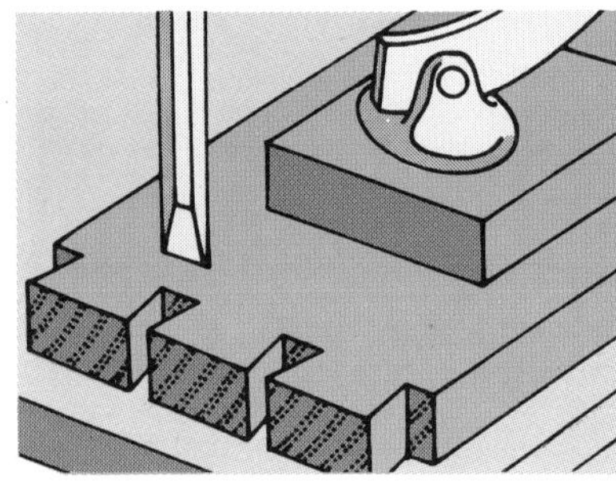

3. Trim out the socket, using a narrow chisel. Keep the work steady by securing it with a clamp.

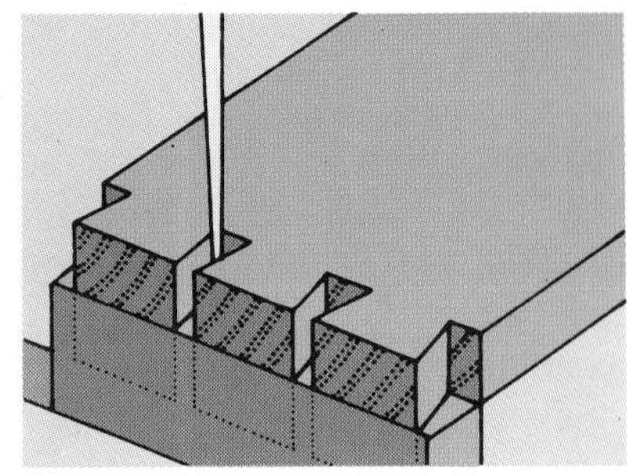

4. Mark out the pins, using a sharp pencil or the front tooth of the saw.

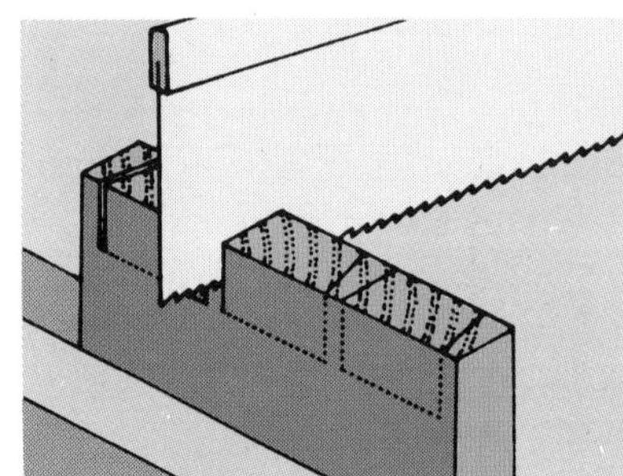

5. Saw down the pin lines, then remove the waste with a coping saw. Trim out with the largest possible chisel.

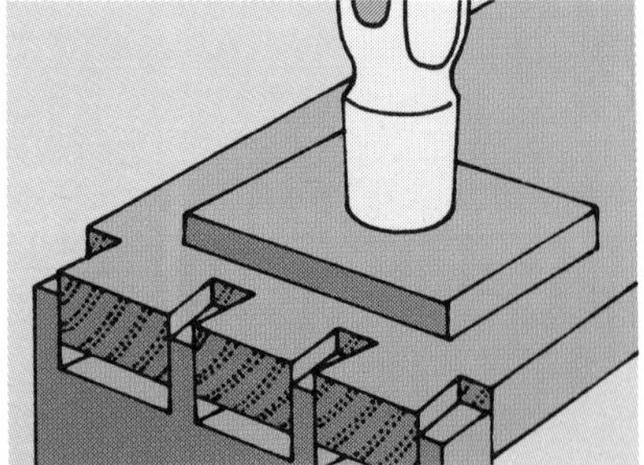

6. The completed joint should fit firmly when tapped in place. Use a spare block so the hammer won't damage the surface. Position the pins at the top and bottom on frames, at the back for drawers.

Lap, double-lap, and secret dovetails

The lap dovetail is used where the ends of the dovetails would spoil the appearance of the work.

Cut and plane the side to the length of the drawers, less the thickness of the lap (⅛ inch on ¾-inch wood, a proportion of 1:6). Cut and plane the front to the size of the opening it must fit.

Set the cutting gauge to the thickness of the front, less ⅛ inch for the lap. Gauge line (a) on the end of the front and on the inside and line (b) all around the end of the side, with the cutting gauge at the same setting. Mark the dovetails as for the common dovetail and cut the same way.

Butt the tails against line (a) on the front and mark off the shape of the pins.

Mark the depth of the pins on the inside of the front. Saw the pins at 45 degrees, with wood held upright in the vise. Chop out the waste, keeping the chisel short of line (a) until the bulk is removed.

The overhang of the pins prevents cutting straight into their corners. Ease out the waste at these points with a narrow chisel.

Trim the inner faces of the pins by paring them with a chisel. Finally, run a groove for the drawer bottom through a dovetail so that it will be covered by the lap.

Variations on the joint are the **double-lap dovetail,** and the **secret,** or **miter dovetail.**

In both the double-lap and the miter dovetail joints, cut the pins first.

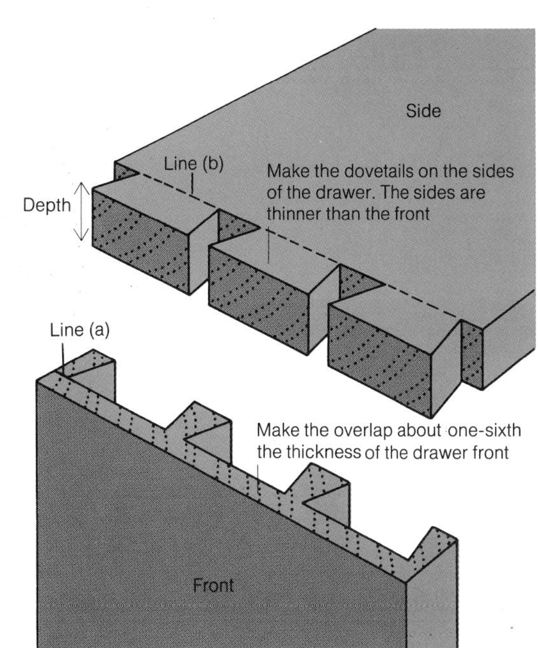

Lap dovetail is the ideal joint for the fronts of drawers and the corners of bookcases. Cut the dovetails in the sides and the pins in the overlapping pieces.

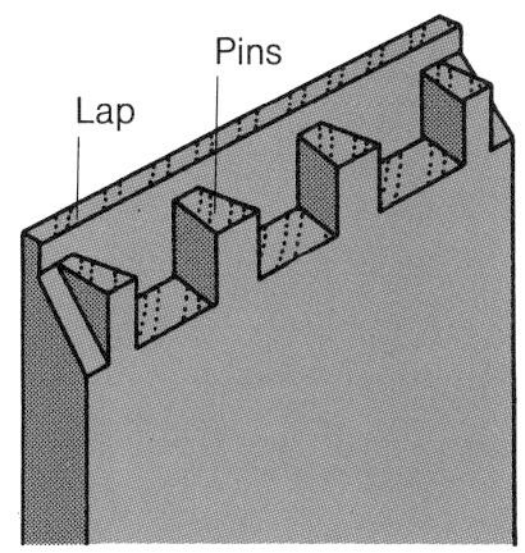

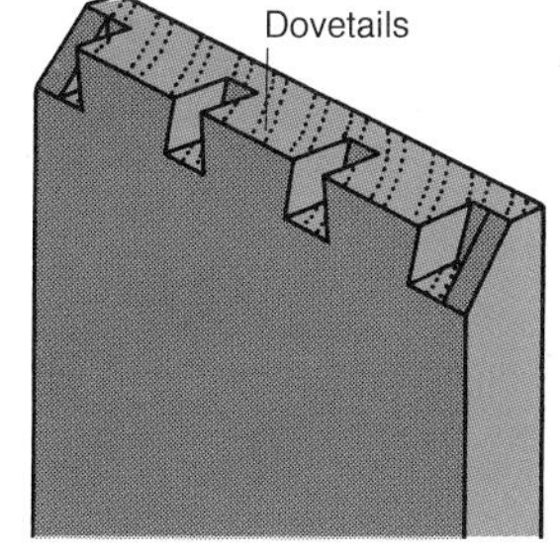

Double-lap dovetail shows only a small amount of end grain. It is neat, but demands care in construction. It incorporates miters at corners and provides a strong joint.

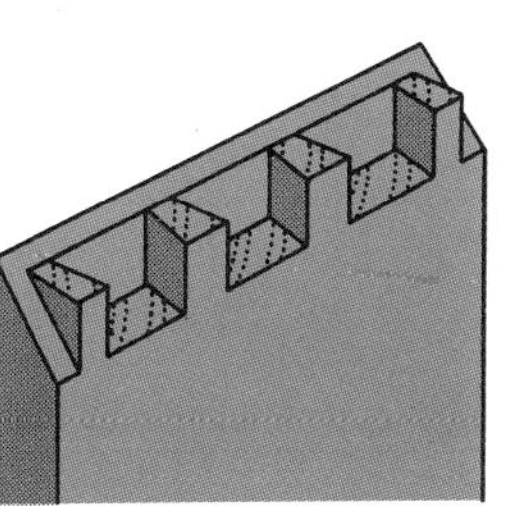

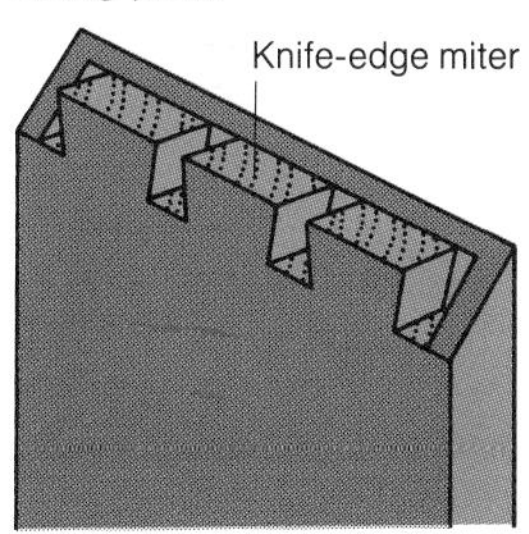

Secret, or miter, dovetail is an uncommon joint used chiefly for quality work. It takes practice to achieve the undamaged knife-edge that gives the miter a perfect fit.

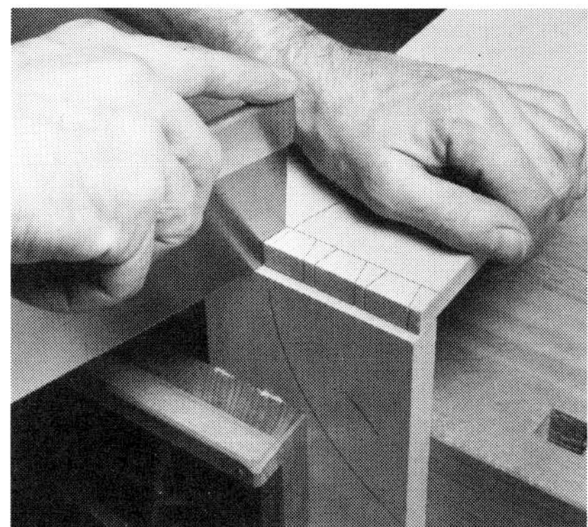

Cutting the lap on a lap dovetail joint requires, first, that you place the dovetail side piece on top of the front piece, then use the saw cuts, as shown, to mark the pins.

Hold the front piece upright in the vise and saw down the pins at 45° as far as possible. Be careful not to saw into the lap. The waste area should be clearly marked.

The next step is cutting out the waste. Be very careful as you work to keep the chisel always well back from the gauge line until most of the waste has been removed.

Use a very narrow chisel to trim the corners covered by the overhang of the pins. It is recommended that you secure the wood with a clamp during this part of the operation.

Right-angle joints

Rabbeted and grooved joints

You can simplify drawer construction and other projects normally requiring dovetailed corners by substituting rabbeted or grooved joints. They are quick to make and strong enough for most jobs.

Allow a little extra length on the front so that you can make the rabbet slightly wider than the thickness of the wood it joins. This allows for final cleaning up. The depth of the rabbet should be not more than three-quarters the thickness of the wood it joins.

Cut the rabbet with a backsaw or on a power saw with a dado attachment. Glue and nail the joint. Nail the brads in opposite directions.

Use this joint on the front corners of drawers with the rabbet overlapping the sides.

For drawer fronts that extend beyond the sides, use a groove and rabbet joint. Cut the groove in the inner face of the drawer front and the rabbet on the inner face of the side. Both groove and rabbet can be dovetail-shaped for extra strength.

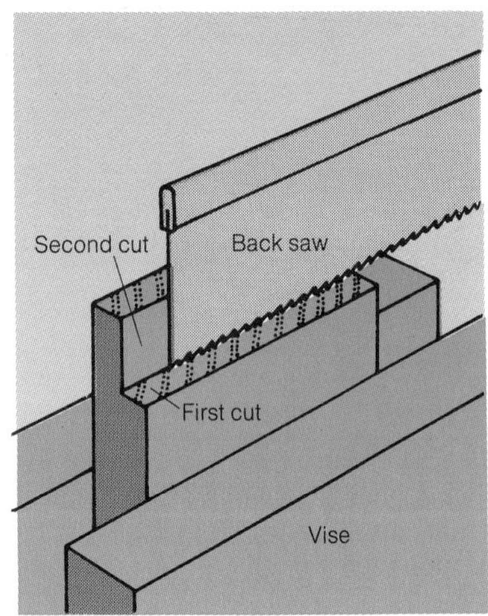

Rabbet joint: First make the horizontal cut, then the vertical; use a back saw.

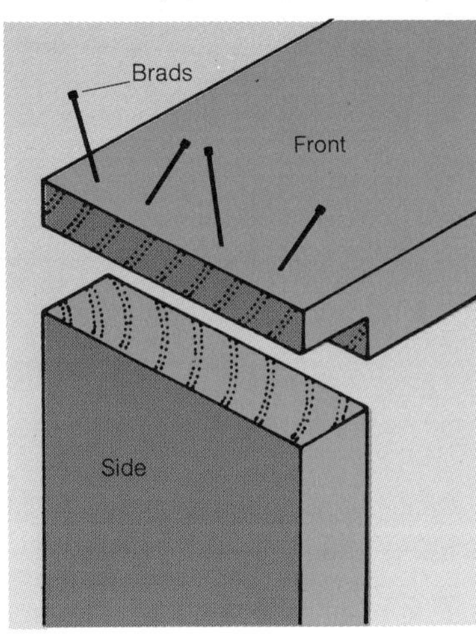

Check fit, apply glue; nail brads in opposing directions for added strength.

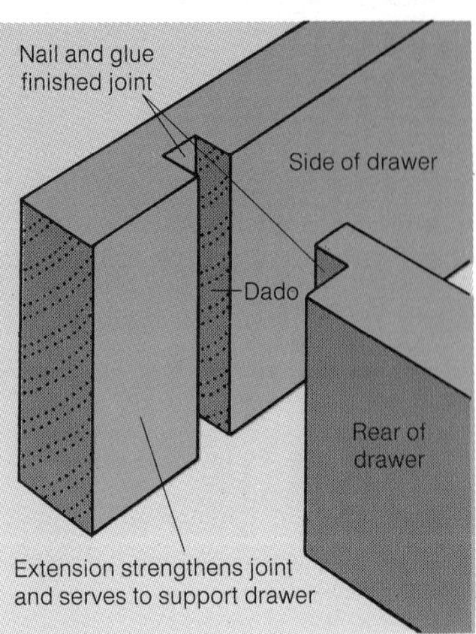

Dado-rabbet joint: Overhang strengthens joint, gives support to extended drawer.

Bridle and box joints

A bridle or a finger (box) joint is strong but needs to be well made for a pleasing effect. Both are ideal for such jobs as joining legs to chair arms.

Use the bridle joint at a corner—where it becomes an open mortise and tenon—or at a T joining, where it is more decorative than a plain half lap joint. For both types, divide the edge of the work into thirds. Square off the shoulder lines on both pieces and mark the finger and cutout lines from the face sides.

Mark the waste wood clearly with Xs so that there will be no mistakes. Saw down the cutout section, skimming the gauge lines in the waste. Remove most of the waste by cutting across near the bottom with a coping saw. Next, square off at the shoulder line with a narrow chisel.

Cut the finger of a corner joint as you would a tenon. On the through joint, cut out from both sides. Saw down to the gauge marks and chisel out the waste from both sides.

Both joints can be strengthened with dowels. To get extra tightness, offset the dowel holes slightly so that the dowel, when driven home, forces the finger against the bottom of the cutout.

The box, comb, or finger joint is machine-made as a general rule, but it can be made by hand as an alternate to dovetailing on light furniture and in box construction.

One of the pieces must contain two end fingers, so the total number of fingers will be uneven.

Score each shoulder with a knife. Darken to make the lines clearer and mark off the waste. Check one piece against the other before you cut the joint.

In the construction of these joints, follow the axiom of measuring twice and cutting once. It's easy to correct an error on paper; wood is another story.

All of the joints described should be reinforced with brads and white glue. When making a drawer, be sure it will fit the opening it is designed for with adequate clearance all around.

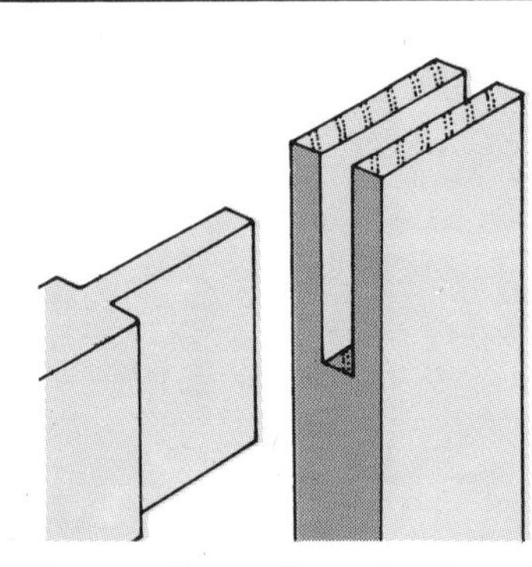

Open mortise and tenon: Use for such jobs as joining legs to chair arms.

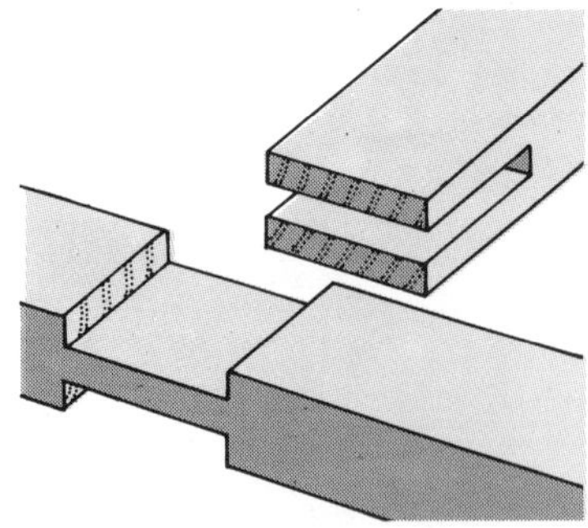

T joining or through bridle: Better appearance than plain half lap joint.

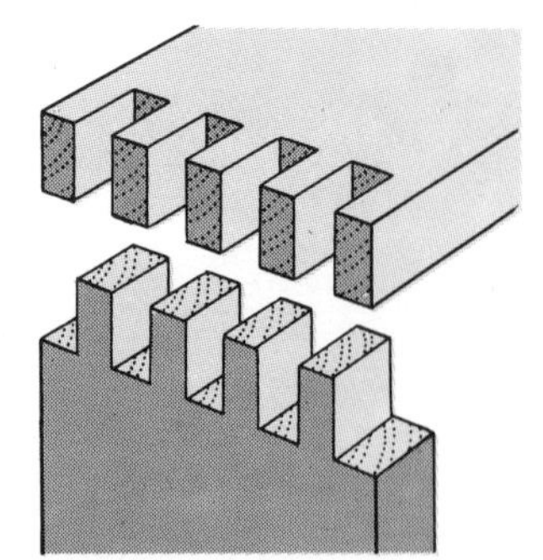

Box joint: Has many uses in construction of light furniture and drawers.

Four ways to make miter joints

Miter joints are used for picture frames and larger jobs such as bookcases. The miter angle of 45 degrees must be cut and trimmed accurately. It must also be strengthened in one of several ways.

The simplest method is to glue both surfaces, then clamp the corner in a vise (use padding). This prevents the hammer from knocking the joint out of shape. Nail the brads home in opposite directions and fill the holes.

A stronger method is to saw slots dovetail-fashion across the outer edge of the corner, with both pieces held together in a vise. Insert "keys" of veneer and trim when the glue dries.

Splined or tongued miters are even stronger. Avoid damaging the edge of the miter by making a 45-degree block the same width as the work. Clamp the block and the work together in a vise and cut the groove, using the block as a guide. Cut the tongue from stiff plywood.

Doweling is effective, but the holes need careful drilling. Locate them exactly by tapping brads at the dowel positions in one miter face. Cut the brads and drill both sets of holes at right angles to the miter. Set the holes nearer the inner work face to allow for a reasonable length of dowel.

A necessity for making accurate miter joints is a well-constructed miter box and backsaw.

Nailing a miter joint

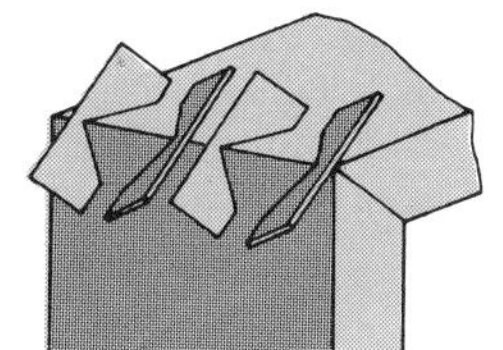

Using veneer in slots

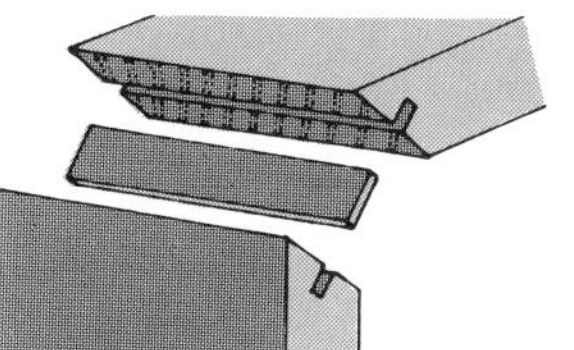

Spline reinforces miter

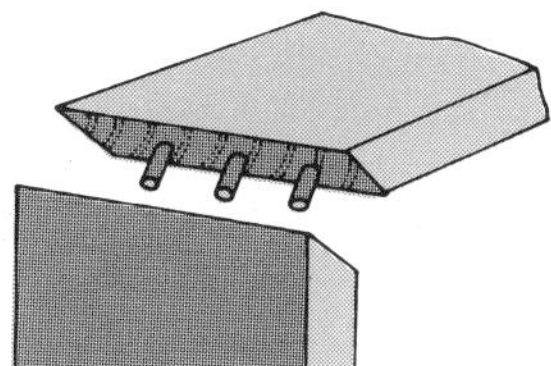

Doweled miter joints

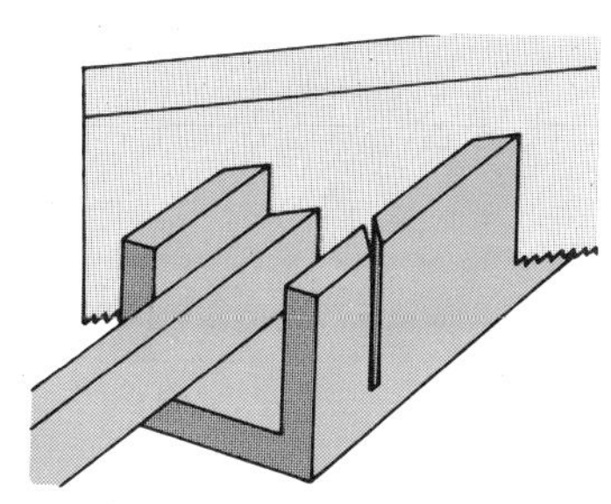

1. Cut the miter carefully in a miter box using a backsaw. Make sure molding faces the right way before cutting.

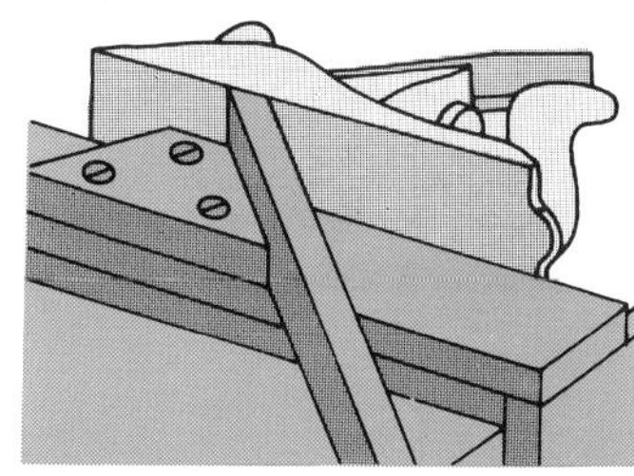

2. Trimming with a plane shortens the work, so allow about 1/32 in. for this when sawing the miter. Trim to exact length with plane on miter board. Make sure plane is sharp; give it a fine setting.

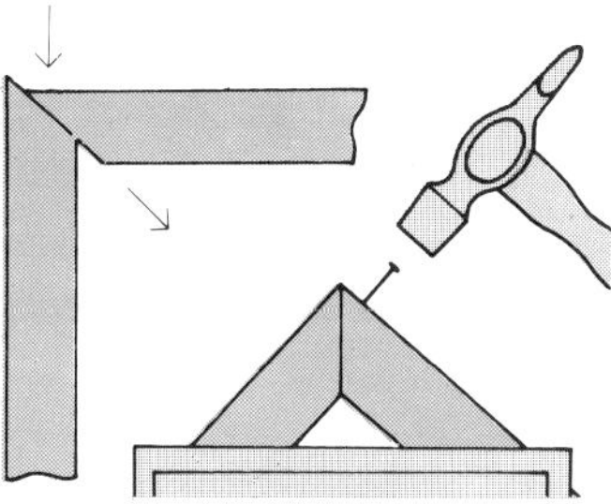

3. If possible, nail a mitered corner with the joint held firmly in a vise to prevent the hammer knocking it out of line.

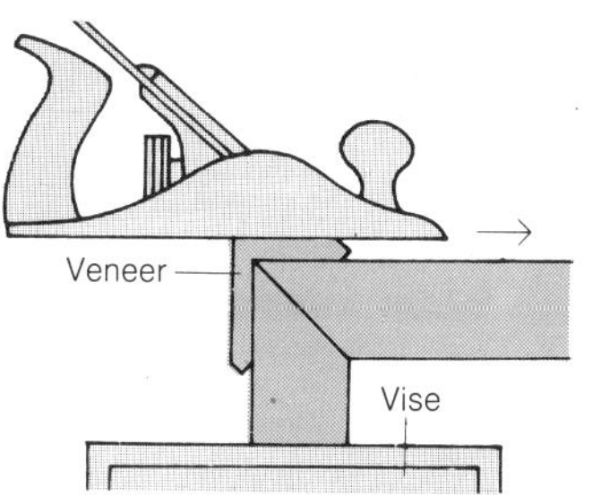

4. Plane toward the center of the work when trimming veneer that is set into the corners.

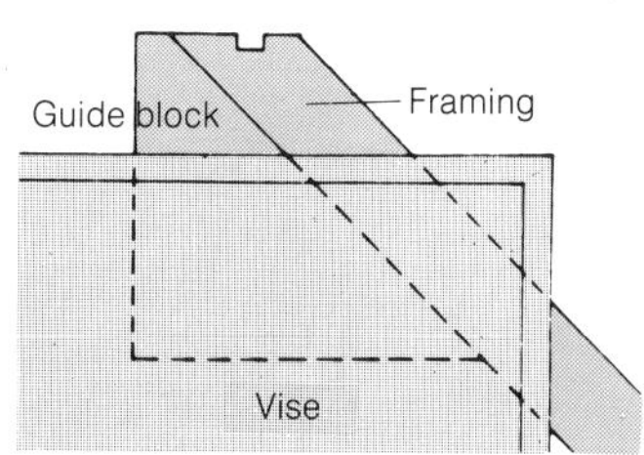

5. Use a 45° block the same width as the work as a guide for cutting a groove for a spline across a miter.

6. Locate dowel positions by temporarily nailing brads into one face. Cut them off short and make their impressions on the other face. Remove the brads and exact positions for all dowels are marked. Use depth gauge when drilling.

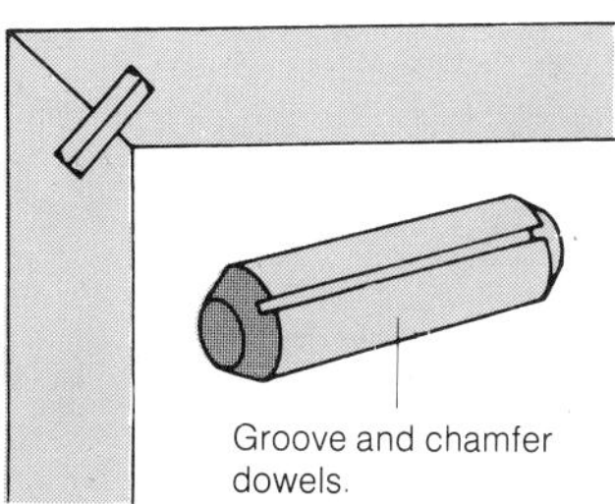

7. Dowels should have a groove cut the long way to let glue escape. Chamfer the ends so they will fit into the holes easily. Coat the dowels with white glue.

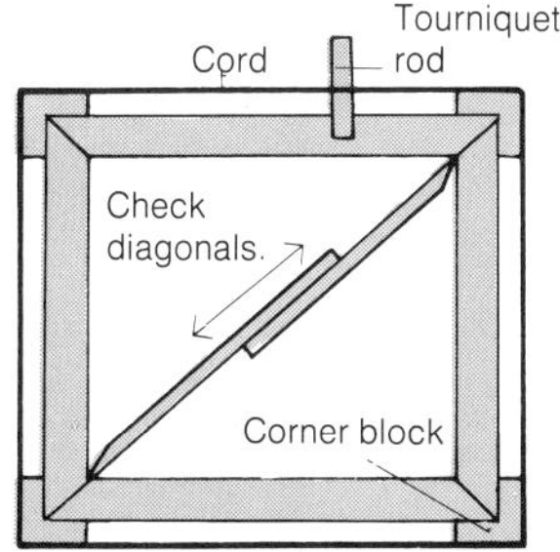

8. Pull a mitered frame tight with a cord running around corner brackets and tightened with a turnbuckle. Check the diagonals—they should be equal.

X or crisscross joints

Five ways to make them

The simplest of the X joints is the plain overlap. Held together with glue and screws for greatest strength, it can also be bolted, clinch-nailed, glued and doweled, or glued and nailed.

The cross-lap—one of the easiest and most useful of the various joints—is cut in the same way as the half lap joint. Whether it is made flat or on edge, the eggcrate construction is the same. Glue and clamp the pieces together firmly. Trim the joint when the glue is thoroughly dry.

By reducing the depth of the cutout, one rail can be made to project over the other.

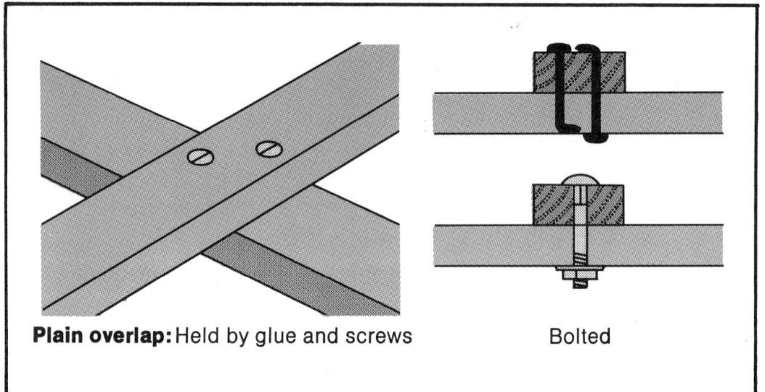

Plain overlap: Held by glue and screws

Bolted

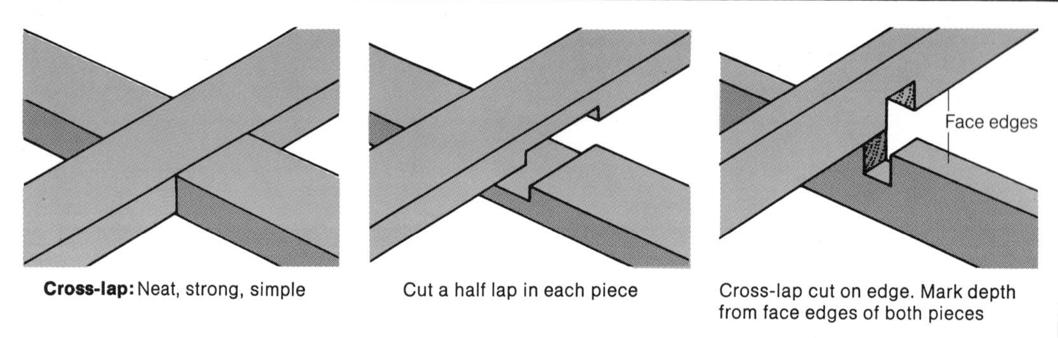

Cross-lap: Neat, strong, simple

Cut a half lap in each piece

Cross-lap cut on edge. Mark depth from face edges of both pieces

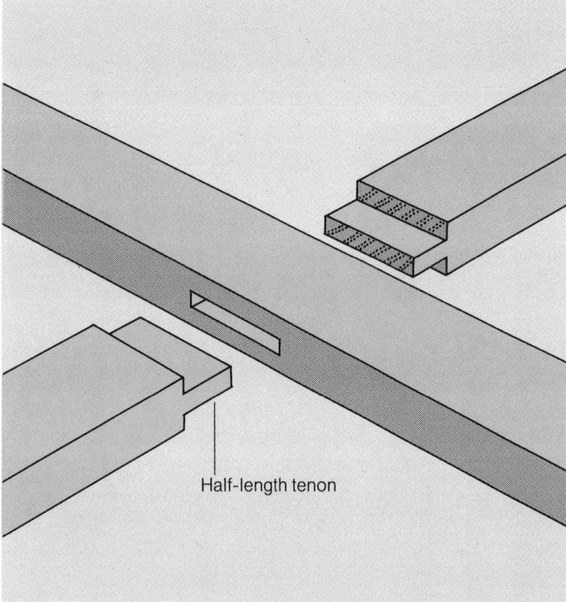

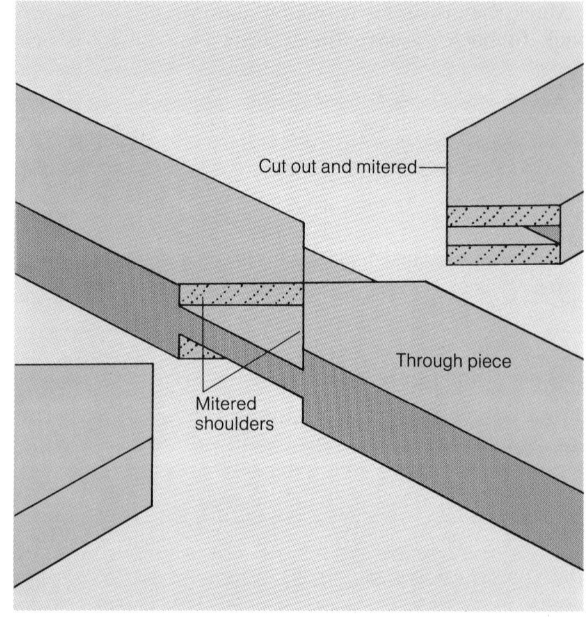

Doweled joint: Make an X joint on a heavy frame by using dowels and drilling out with a doweling jig. This joint has many advantages. It has more strength than a nailed joint, is neater, and is relatively easy to construct.

Mortise-tenon joint: An alternate method of making a strong and attractive X joint is to cut a mortise on the through piece and half-length tenons on the joining rails. Then glue and clamp the pieces together.

Mitered bridle joint: Mark the edges as for the bridle joint and scribe miter lines across all faces. Work to a fine point in the center of the through piece by cutting each of the mitered shoulders individually.

Edge-to-edge joint

Edge-to-edge joints are used when it is necessary to increase the width of lumber for table tops or for wide shelving. There are three methods of making them: Gluing, doweling, and loose-tongue (or spline) joining.

Before joining, the boards must be planed to a perfect edge-to-edge match. Preparatory to planing, clamp both boards together with the edges to be joined uppermost. Then, using a jointer plane (p. 28), plane both edges at once until they seem to the eye to be flat and even.

Check the result for accuracy by holding the planed edges together. No daylight should show through at any point if they are evenly planed.

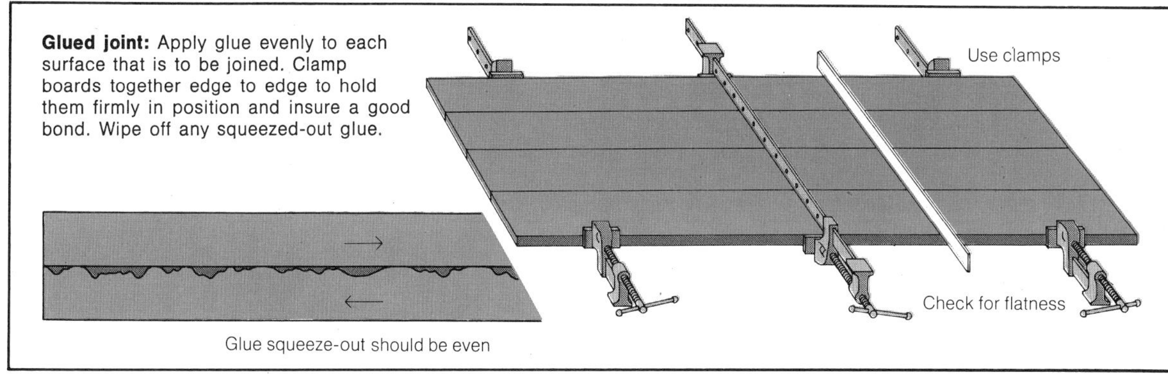

Glued joint: Apply glue evenly to each surface that is to be joined. Clamp boards together edge to edge to hold them firmly in position and insure a good bond. Wipe off any squeezed-out glue.

Dowel joint

A dowel jig insures the needed accuracy for this joint. Plane the edges straight and square.

Mark the dowel locations by clamping both boards back to back; square lines across to allow for one dowel every six or nine inches. Intersect marks with a central gauge line from each face side (1).

Drill holes, checking often for squareness. Use a depth gauge on the bit to give a hole slightly deeper than half the dowel length (2).

Chamfer the dowels at each end to aid location in assembly. Saw a groove along each dowel to allow trapped glue to escape. Glue and insert the dowels in one board; fit the other board over the protruding dowels and clamp the two together.

1. Clamp both boards together back to back when marking. Mark lines across and along each board—centers for dowels are where lines intersect.
2. Drill the dowel holes centrally and square, making sure they are deep enough. Chamfer the dowels at each end; groove them to let excess glue run out.

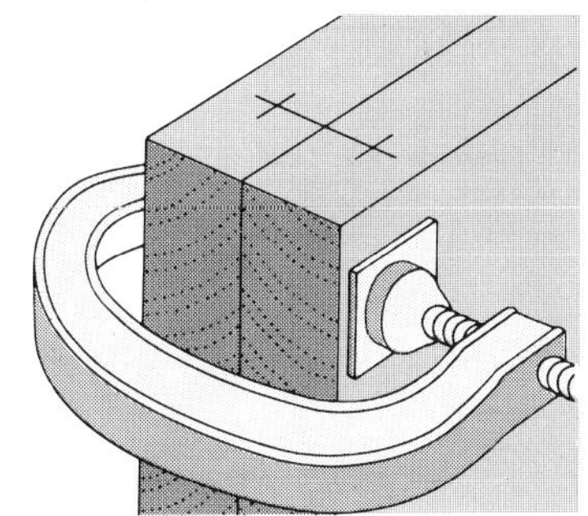

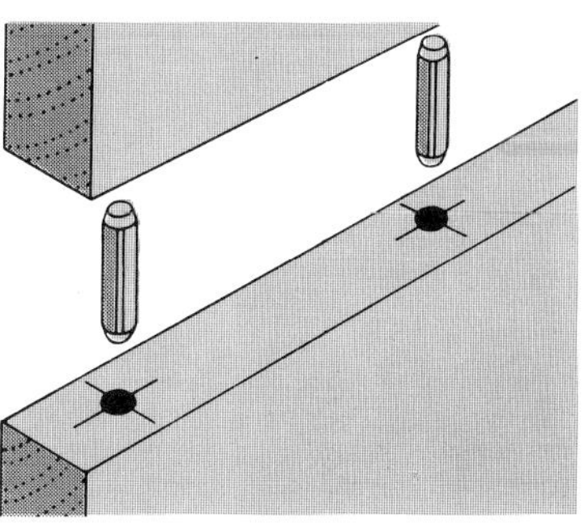

Splined joint

These joints are more suitable for longer work and are easier to make accurately than doweled joints.

Cut the tongue (spline) from cross-grained plywood and select a plow-plane blade of exactly the same thickness, or groove the edges on a table saw.

Cut a groove along both prepared edges, running the plow fence along the face side. The combined depth of both grooves is just slightly greater than the width of the spline (1).

Glue and assemble the joint (2) and clamp the assembly together.

Make a final check for flatness, then wipe off any excess glue. Cut and trim for overall size only after the glue has set.

1. Cut the grooves to the exact width of the tongue. Make the combined depths of the grooves about 1/16 in. greater than the width of the spline.
2. Glue both edges and grooves. Fit the plywood spline into one board and set the other board on it. Clamp and check for flatness. Wipe off surplus glue.

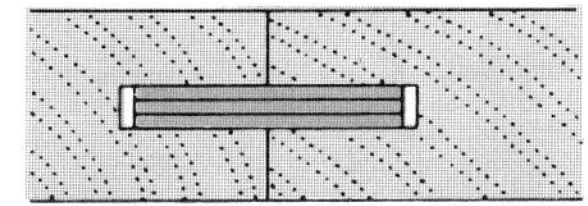

Make grooves deeper than spline width

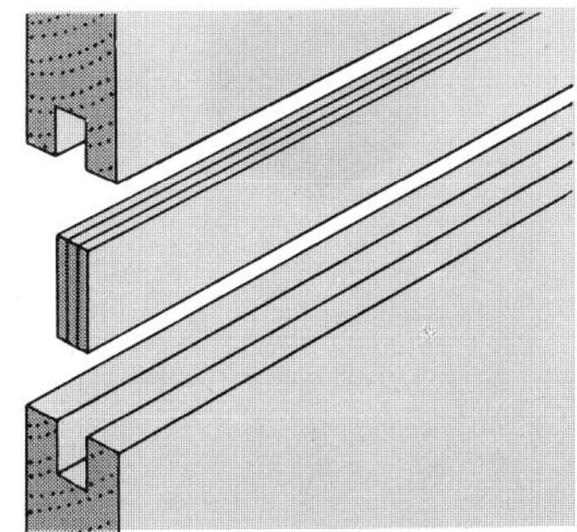

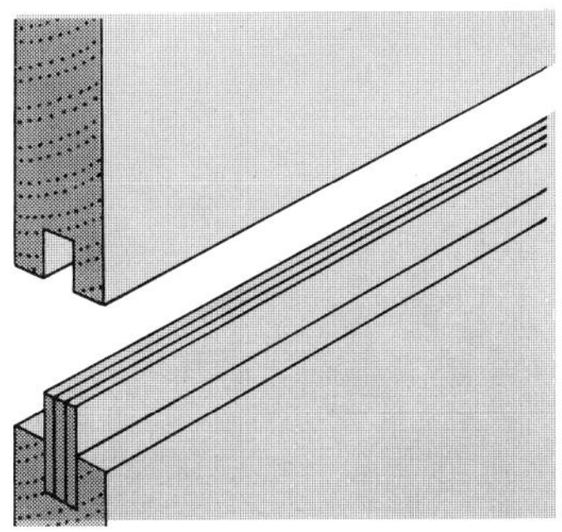

Lengthening joints

Choosing the correct joint

Lumber often has to be lengthened for big projects, such as garages, carports, or floor renovation. Smaller jobs, too, such as furniture repairing, occasionally require greater length than is available. What follows will give you a basis for selecting the proper joint, in terms of comparative strength and complexity of construction.

Lapped joint: The simplest of all the lengthening joints and suitable for use in lightweight structures. Cut the laps to half the thickness of the lumber; be sure that both shoulders butt exactly against the end of the joining pieces or the joint will be weakened.

Secure the joint with glue and screws. The screws should be staggered—this is in order to avoid splits along the grain.

Splayed lap: A variant of the half lap, with the lap cut in the thickness instead of the width. Can be used where the joint itself is supported by a joist or wall. Its chief use is to keep decorative, nonsupporting ceiling beams in line where center nailing has to be straight for fastening sheet materials such as wallboard.

Cut a splay along the grain to resist any tendency of the joint to pull apart. Make the length of the joint equal to the width of the lumber.

Drive a cut nail diagonally through the lower lap into the joist or supporting wall plate (lumber running along the top of the wall). Butt on the joining length and secure with another nail driven diagonally through from the top.

Bolted joint: Carriage bolts used with lumber connectors make strong face-to-face joints in beams and trusses.

Insert the connectors—metal washers with toothed edges—on the bolts between the joining faces. Tighten the nuts and the connectors will bite into the wood, increasing the shear strength of the joint. Use washers under the nuts.

Using joining plates: A sandwich construction using joining plates gives great strength to end-to-end joints. Cut the joining plates (sometimes called fish plates) four times longer than the width of the timber. They should be the same width as the lumber but only half its thickness.

Glue all surfaces, and stagger the screws or carriage bolts. Carriage bolts pass through the wood; screws should be just short of passing through.

Scarf joint: This is cut on a long slant and is used where great strength is required.

A scarf joint is usually just glued, but the angle-cut faces need to be cut and planed with great accuracy. Properly made, it is as strong as the lumber that it joins.

Ideally, the slant of the scarf should be eight to one or greater in order to achieve full wood strength. Screws need not be used for extra strength with modern resin glues. Clamp the joint while the glue is setting.

V-spliced joint: This is used mainly in furniture repairs or in applications where appearance is an important consideration.

Cut the V with a fine-tooth saw. Then cut and plane the joining piece to an exact fit. Glue the pieces, join, and clamp in position.

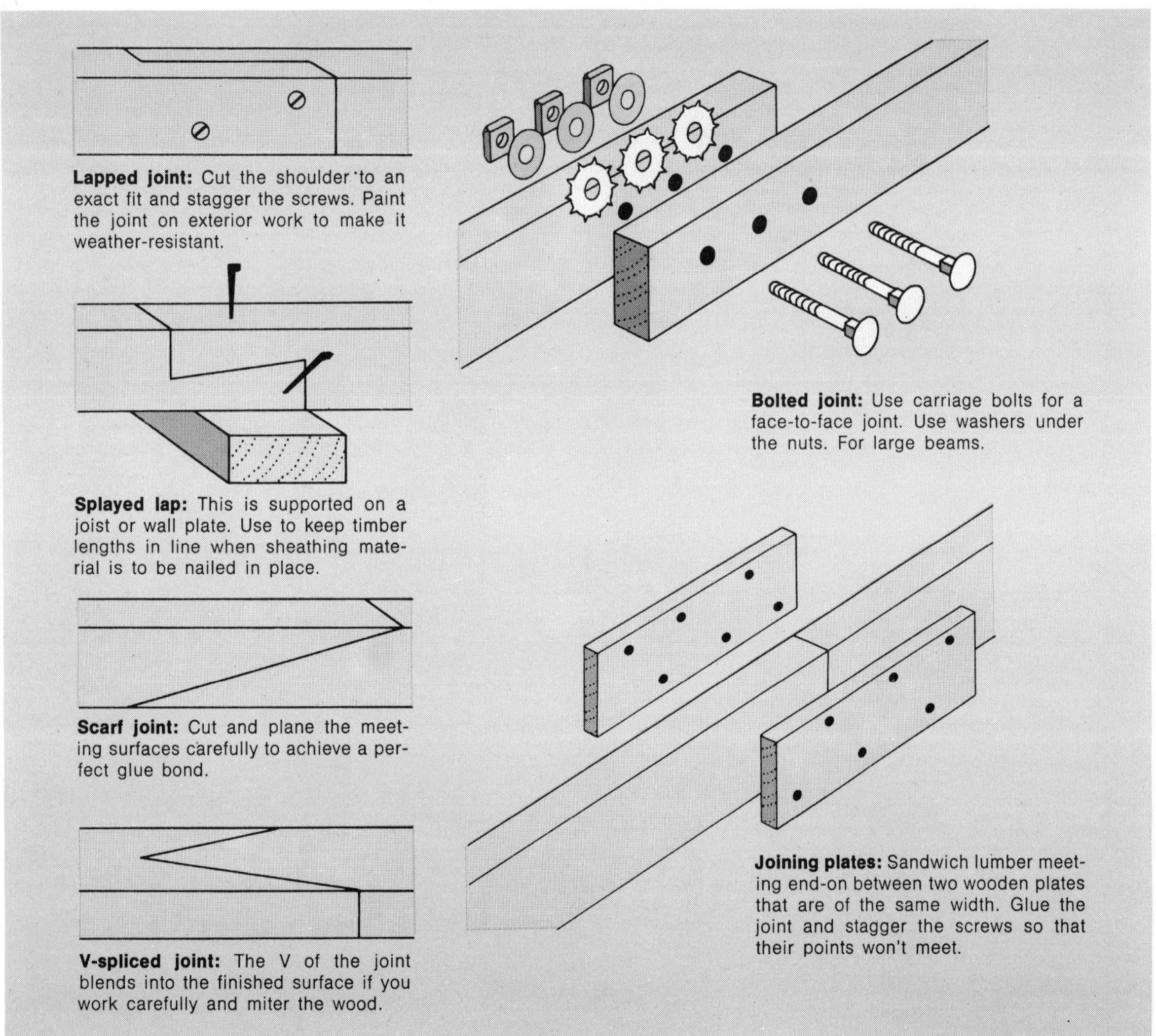

Lapped joint: Cut the shoulder to an exact fit and stagger the screws. Paint the joint on exterior work to make it weather-resistant.

Splayed lap: This is supported on a joist or wall plate. Use to keep timber lengths in line when sheathing material is to be nailed in place.

Scarf joint: Cut and plane the meeting surfaces carefully to achieve a perfect glue bond.

V-spliced joint: The V of the joint blends into the finished surface if you work carefully and miter the wood.

Bolted joint: Use carriage bolts for a face-to-face joint. Use washers under the nuts. For large beams.

Joining plates: Sandwich lumber meeting end-on between two wooden plates that are of the same width. Glue the joint and stagger the screws so that their points won't meet.

Six ways to attach legs at corners

Three-way joints are essential for making tables and chairs and certain types of framing. Construction methods range from the use of glue and screws to doweling and tenoning.

A simple way of joining a leg to two rails is with a commercially produced chair and table corner brace that fits into slots in the rails (1). These braces come in a number of sizes. The joint is held together by a screw which is passed through the brace into the leg.

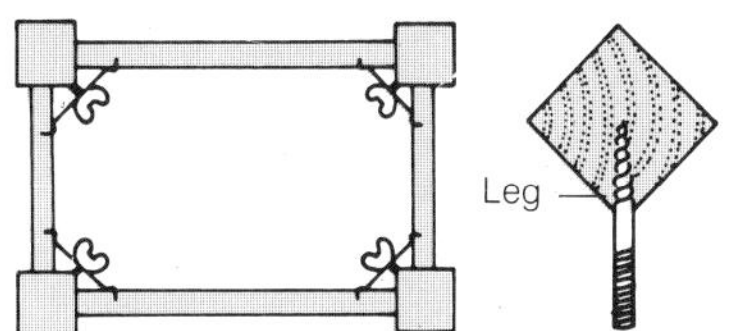

Frame fixed with chair corner braces

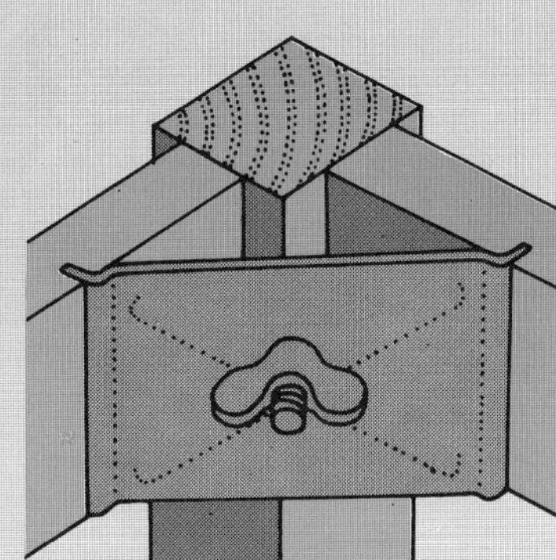

1. The chair corner brace, available in several sizes, holds corner together with a hanger bolt. The plate fits into slots in the rails.

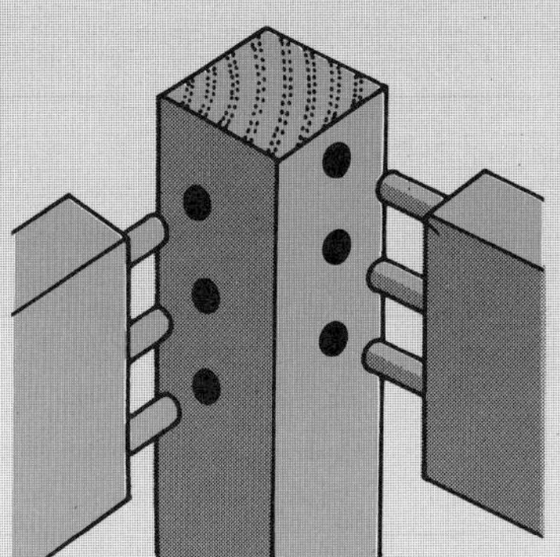

2. Dowels must be staggered to prevent their meeting in the middle of the leg. Space them as evenly as possible; use at least three to a rail.

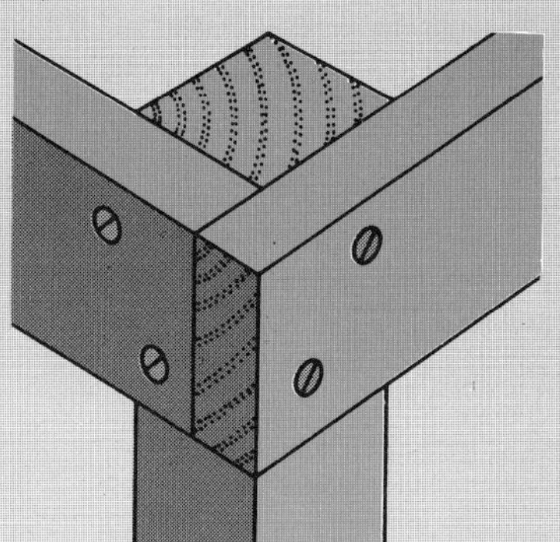

3. Glue and screw the rail to the legs for a quick and strong corner joint. Stagger the screws to prevent splits; countersink their heads.

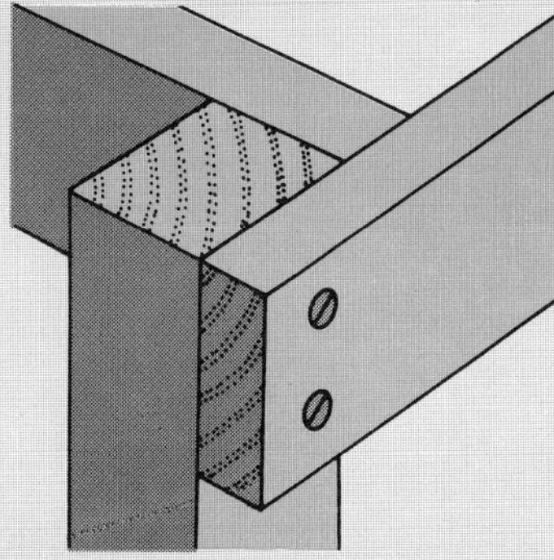

4. A similar joint can be made with the leg on the outside. Both joints rely solely on the strength of the glue and screws. Wood plugs can cover recessed screw heads.

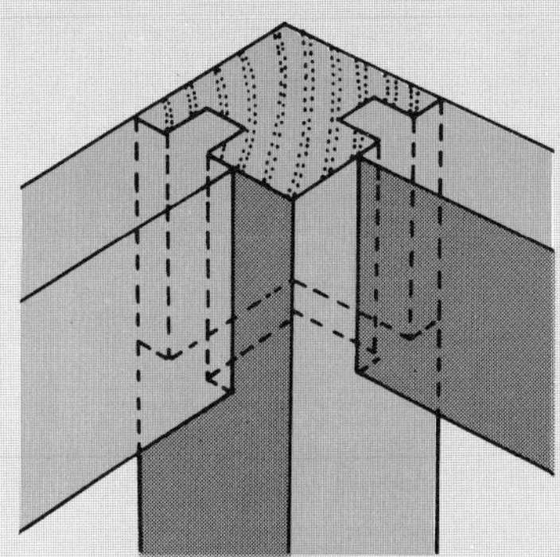

5. The haunched and mitered mortise and tenon is the strongest of the leg joints. Leave about ½ in. of waste at the top of the leg; trim it off when the joint is complete.

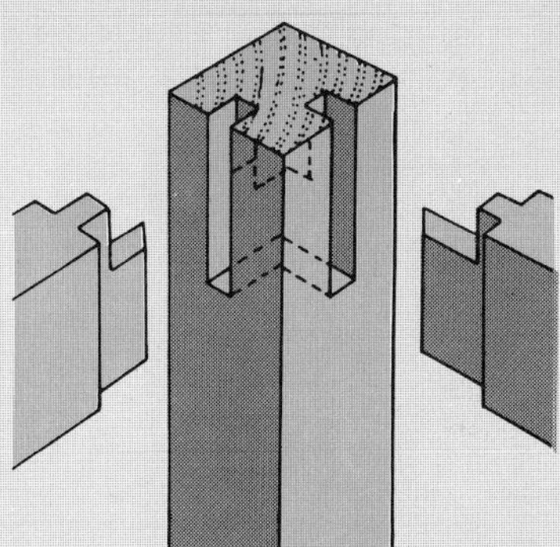

6. An exploded view of the joint, showing the miters on the ends of the tenons. Trim the miters so there is a small gap between them on assembly to allow for excess glue.

Some types of braces also provide holes for screws.

Mark the positions of the legs and rails on the underside of the chair or table top. Cut the rails to exact size. Position the braces at 45 degrees in the corners on the penciled outline and mark the location of the slots that will house the brace ends in the rails. Transfer these positions to the wood and cut the slots to fit.

Mark on the inner corner of each leg the place where the plate screw is to go and drill a hole deep enough for the wood screw to get a start.

Attach the rails to the table top with glue or small metal inside corner braces, then drive a hanger bolt into the pre-drilled hole in each leg. Insert the other end of the bolt in the corner plate and tighten the wing nut.

Dowels on corner joints (2) need to be staggered to prevent their meeting in the middle of the leg. Use at least three on each rail (if space permits) and space them evenly. The dowels should be one-third the thickness of the rails.

Glued and screwed corners are strong and can be made quickly. They can be arranged so that the leg is inside (3) or outside (4) the rails.

The strongest corner joint of all is the mitered mortise and tenon (5 and 6). Basically, the joint is just two rabbeted stub tenons meeting at right angles in the center of the leg.

Mark out and tenon the rails and mortise the inner faces of the leg. Fit rails separately, then miter the tenon ends so there is a small gap between them when the joint is assembled.

Leave about ½ inch of waste at the top of the leg; trim it off when the joint is completed. This prevents splitting.

Cabinet corner joints: In cabinet construction, tongue and groove the panels into solid corner pieces. The tongue should be one-third the thickness of the panel.

Solid tongues can be cut at either surface of the panel, or the grooves can be cut into the panel ends and the tongues on the corner pieces. These joints are chiefly used with solid wood, not plywood.

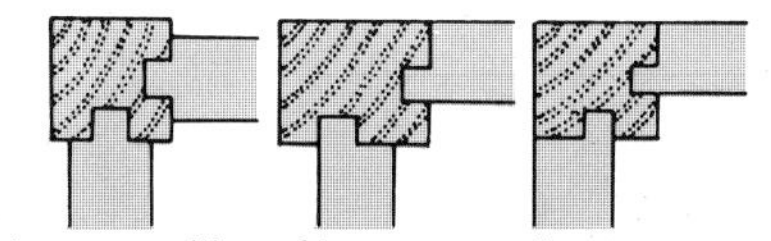

Joints vary position of tenon according to construction

How to use moldings

Window and baseboard trim

Moldings are decorative strips of wood that serve as trim for woodwork and as a covering for seams and joints. They are made in many types, each according to its purpose.

Shown below are moldings for interior window trim. The first type to be applied is called the **stool.** It is placed horizontally atop, and overlapping, the sill. **Side casing** comes next, to the left and right of the window. For paired windows, a piece of **middle** or **mullion casing** is placed on the vertical member between the two windows.

Head-casing molding, mitered at the ends, is then mounted across the top and fitted into the mitered upper ends of the side casing. (For mitered corners, head and side casing should be of identical molding.) To complete the trim, the **apron** is nailed in place under the stool, closing any gap between sill and inner wall.

Also shown, at lower right, are **baseboard** and **shoe** moldings. These are used to cover the joint between wall and flooring. The shoe molding covers the joint between baseboard and floor. Nail it to the floor rather than the baseboard to minimize shrinkage gaps where floor and baseboard meet.

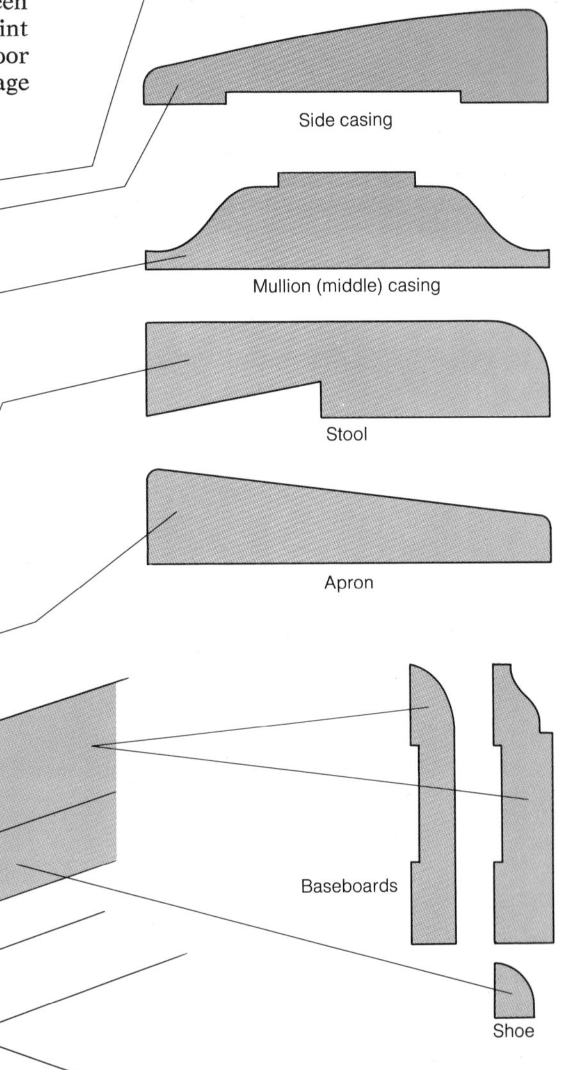

Trim for a window or for the baseboard of a room calls for a particular kind of molding. Each section of molding must be carefully measured, cut, and fitted.

Two ways to make a coped joint

The coped joint is used where moldings meet at inside corners. Its advantage over a mitered joint: It conceals irregularities better.

To make the coped joint, you first cut molding to fit the two longest and opposite sides of the room, with ends square so they butt against the walls. The lengths for the shorter sides are coped to fit. If the molding is flat on the back, you can do this by using scrap molding as a pattern. Trace the contour on the flat side, tape the front—to avoid splintering—and cut through the molding along the outline with a coping saw. If the molding back is irregular (crown molding), get the desired result with this method: Cut a 45 degree miter, then cut away the excess wood along the miter outline.

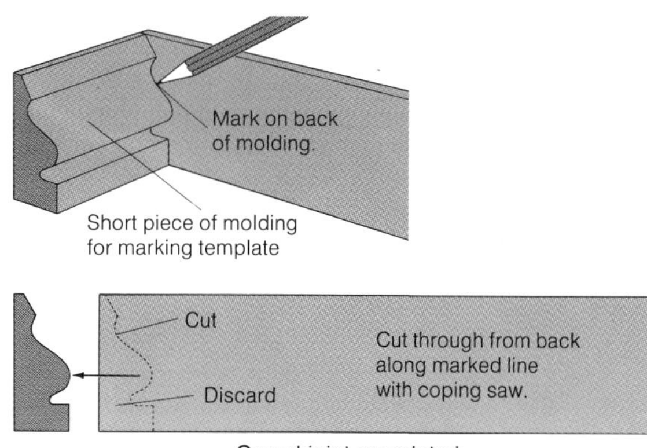

Coped joint completed

Top view 45° miter
Face of molding
90° cut
Cut back to contour of molding.
Fit to wall

Back view of completed coped joint

Measuring for miter; cutting return miter

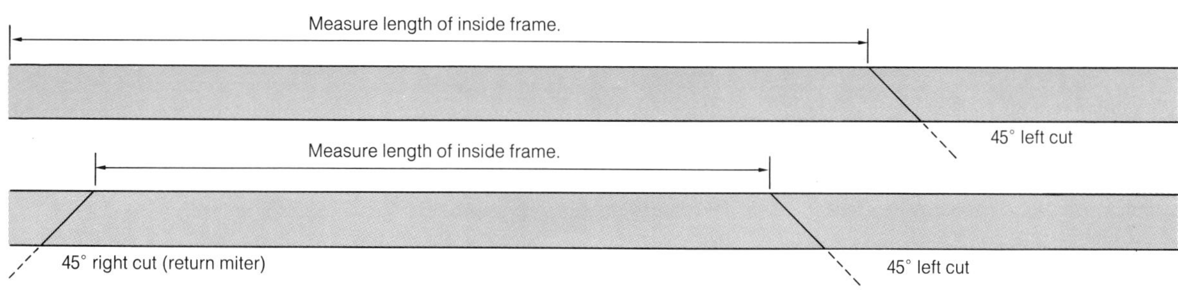

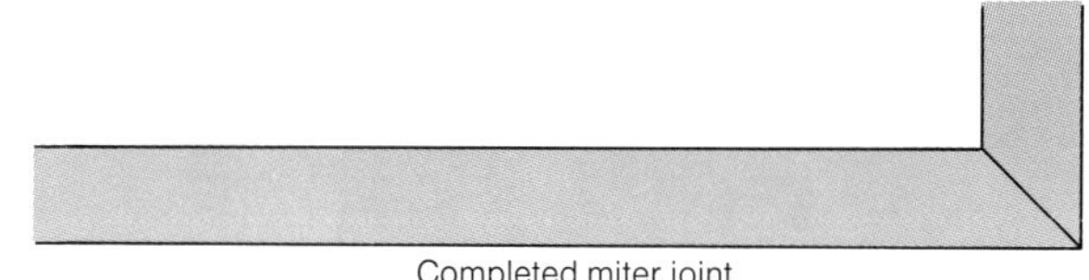

Completed miter joint

Window casing's inner edge is flush with inside of window unit frame. For top mitering, measure as shown (see drawing, above left). Cut head casing (drawing, below left) to fit between side piece miters. Cutting head slighly oversize permits sanding miters to fit.

Other types of molding

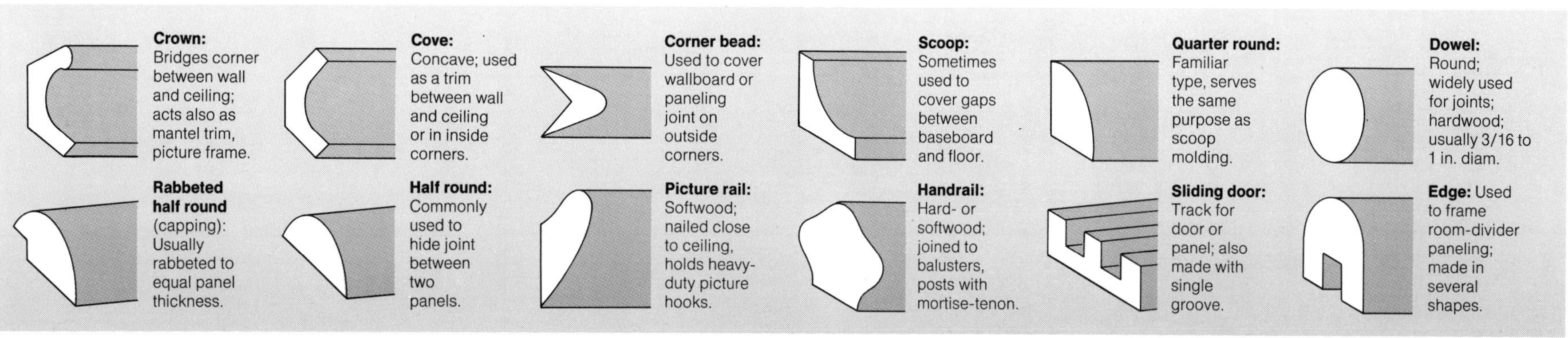

Accurate verticals and horizontals

Finding a vertical line

A spirit level, used to check surfaces for precise horizontals or verticals, has a bubble in a glass vial with either **one** center mark, or a **pair** of marks separated by a distance equal to the bubble's length. A surface is level (or plumb) in the single-mark type when the bubble is centered; in the two-mark type, when the bubble is between the two. The tubes running crosswise of the level's length are "plumb" vials, used, as

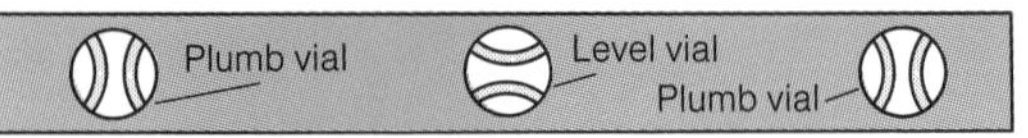

This level type is good for eye-height use

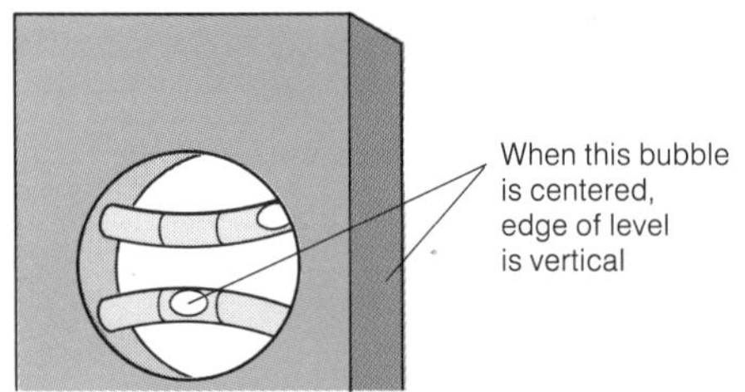

shown in the drawing, to check the accuracy of vertical surfaces.

By attaching a plumb bob and line to a board, you can take a vertical line from the board's edge with a pencil. In a 4-x-4-inch board five or six feet long, cut a hole (1) a half-inch longer and two inches wider than the bob (2) and mark a center line on the board (3). Fix a nail into the center line near the board's top (4). Draw a pencil line along board edge to get a true vertical.

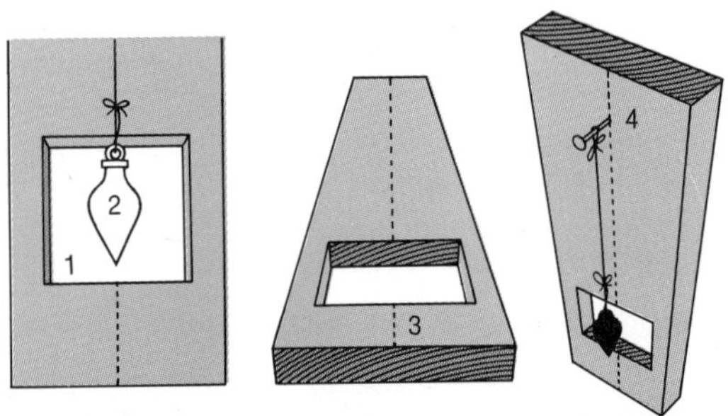

When using a plumb bob and board to find a true vertical, make sure that the line swings free of the board.

Finding a horizontal line

In using a spirit level to check a horizontal surface, read the "level" vials—those that run parallel to the level's length. Spirit levels come with extra vials set at 45 degrees for checking certain angular braces. Others include an adjustable protractor dial on one set of vials to give angle readings from 0 to 90 degrees. A line level hangs on a taut string to provide a level line for masonry and other structural work.

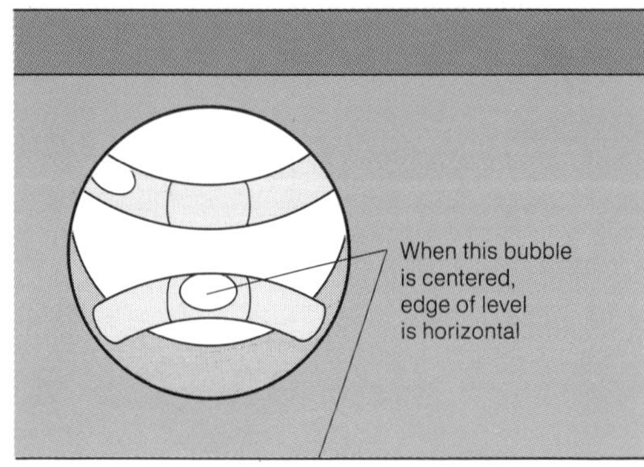

Combination squares, another option, are described at the right.

To establish a horizontal without the use of a level, make a plywood pointer with nail hole at top and point at bottom, both centered. Fix an upright, wider than pointer, to a straightedge and draw a center line through the board at a 90-degree angle to straightedge. Loosely nail pointer to board through center line. Rest straightedge on object to be leveled; move object until pointer aligns with center line.

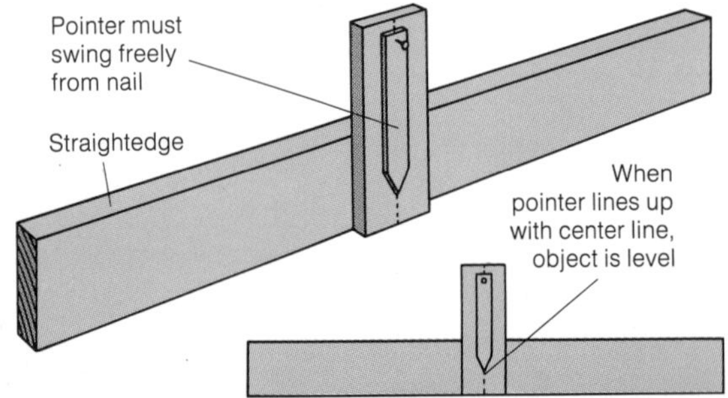

Easy-to-make alternative for a spirit level consists of free-hanging plywood pointer and a board attached to a straightedge.

Making a straightedge

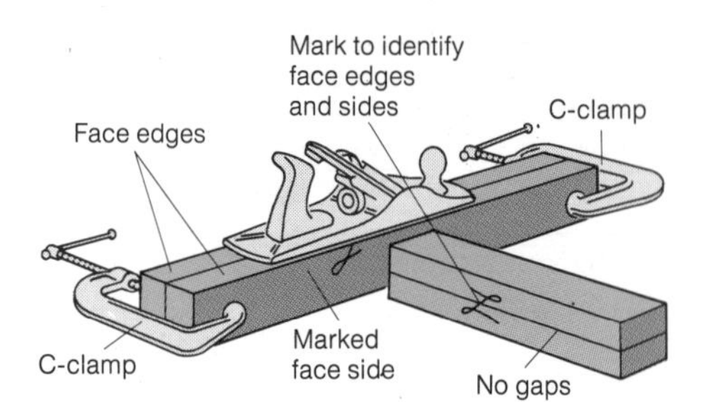

To make a straightedge you need two pieces of 1-x-3-inch long-planed, straight, even-grained lumber, each four feet long. Hold pieces together, face sides out and face edges together, with a pair of C-clamps. Run a long plane over the butted edges until continual, even, fine shavings appear. Unclamp pieces, place face edges together, and hold up to a strong light. If light shows through the joint, the edges are not true and must be replaned. Mark the gaps and plane as before until edges are true.

Combination square

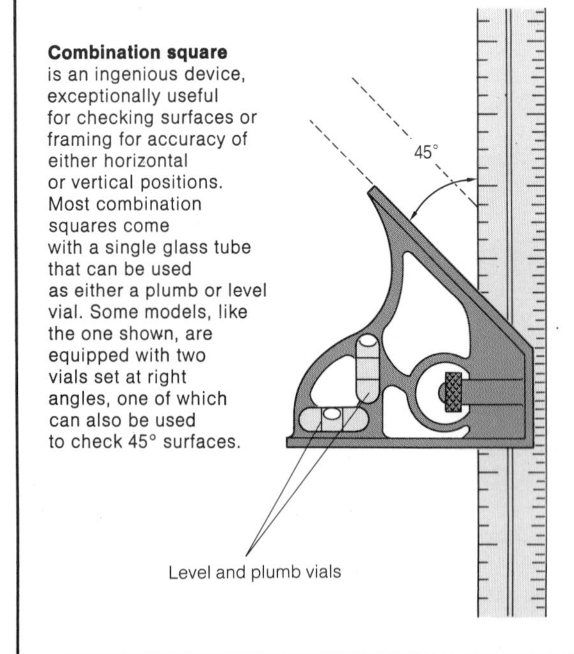

Combination square is an ingenious device, exceptionally useful for checking surfaces or framing for accuracy of either horizontal or vertical positions. Most combination squares come with a single glass tube that can be used as either a plumb or level vial. Some models, like the one shown, are equipped with two vials set at right angles, one of which can also be used to check 45° surfaces.

Making a simple box

Learn to build this basic unit and you will be on your way to many more complex structures. The steps are easy to follow:
1. Fasten together the four sides of the box, each cut on the square.
2. Before attaching the back section (or bottom, as the case may be), nail two strips of wood diagonally across the front of the box to stiffen the structure and hold it square.
3. Nail or glue the back to the box; remove the strips. Should you wish to make your box into a bookcase, simply turn it on end and add shelves.
4. You can do this by attaching plastic tracks or molding to the sides and sliding the shelves into position. (Shelves may be nailed to molding.)
5. Tracks may also be produced by attaching two strips of molding on either side as shown.

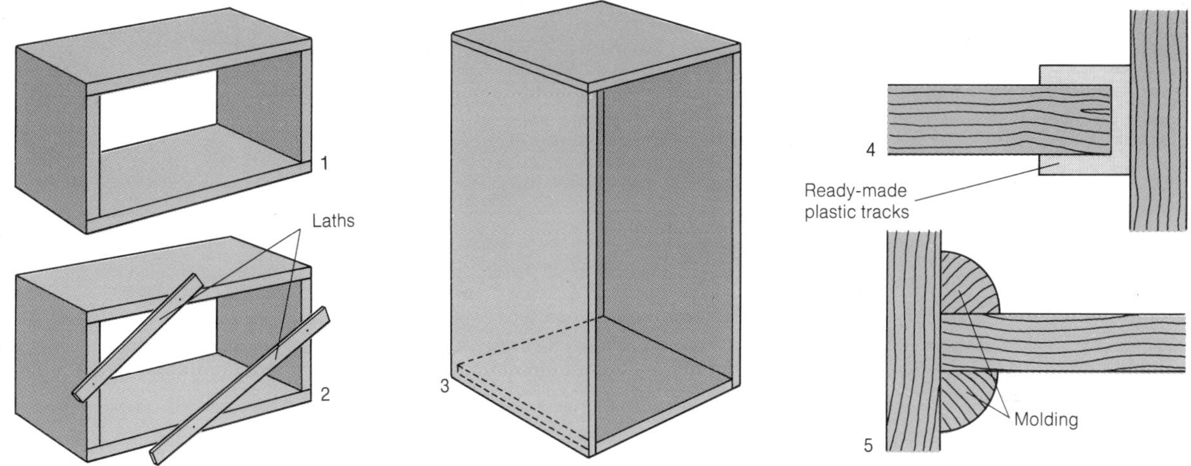

Making a simple drawer

A drawer is simply a box, four sides and a bottom (1), but it can be constructed several ways. Drawing 2 shows the side pieces fitted into slots in the front, permitting nails to be driven from two directions (3) for extra stability.

By placing the bottom of the drawer in grooves cut in the side pieces (4), you provide a narrow bearing area between side and runner. The back slides into grooves in the sides; the bottom is grooved to the front. It is then possible to nail the bottom to the back and front from beneath.

In another variation (5), grooves are cut in the sides to act as tracks for runners, which are fastened to the walls of the basic unit (6).

In drawing 7, drawer fronts are slightly deeper than the drawers themselves, giving the unit, when they meet, a neat, finished look.

Instead of grooves, two strips of wood may be added, the slot between them acting as a track (8). Or single strips may be nailed to the sides as runners (9), which travel along grooves in the unit's side (10). Tracks may also be made by attaching twin strips to the unit's sides (11). Simplest of all: Ready-made plastic tracks (12).

A drawer may be suspended under a desk or table on L-shaped molding (13) or plastic tracks on wood strips (14), fastened in either case to the underside.

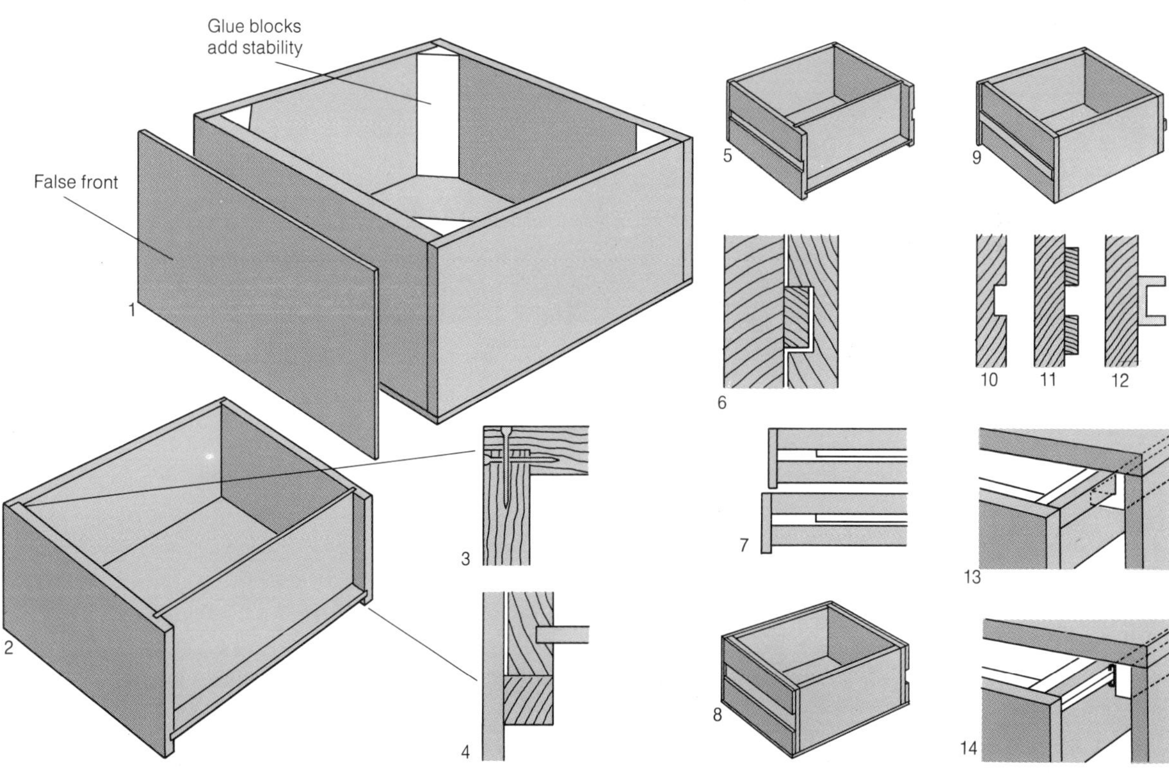

Drawer construction

Rabbeted-front drawers

The rabbet and dado joint shown on the drawer at the right can be made easily on a table saw or radial arm saw with a dado head or by repeated passes over (or under) the saw blade, with the cutting depth adjusted to suit. The back of the drawer front, like the drawer back and sides, is dadoed to take the edge of the plywood bottom. If the drawer is to have side runners, the sides should be dadoed before assembly, as shown in the detail sketch.

To assemble the individual parts, you first join the sides to the back, using glue and nails. Next, slide the bottom panel in place after coating its edges, and the grooves into which they fit, with glue. Then coat the bottom dado and end rabbets of the drawer front with glue, along with the front edge of the bottom panel and the front ends of the sides, and fit the parts together. The angle nailing of the sides and front (as indicated) locks the assembly while the glue sets. If the stopped dadoes are made on a power saw, stop the saw cut well short of the dado end and finish to the stopping point with a chisel. Attach drawer hardware after glue has set.

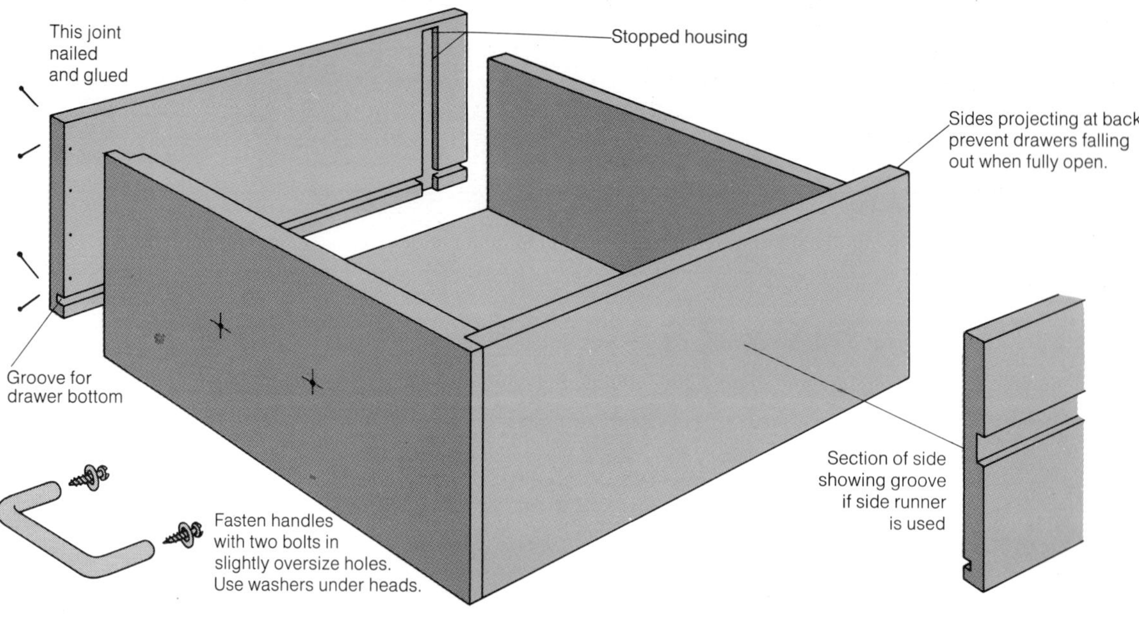

Overlapping-front drawers

If the drawer front overlaps the sides, as in the unit at right, to conceal all framing behind it, the joint between the sides and front may be "dovetail dadoed" for added strength, as shown in the sketch at the lower right. The same type of joint (or a plain dado joint) may be used where the sides join the back. In either case the dado is stopped below the top, and, if it was cut on a power saw, finished with a chisel. The plywood bottom of the drawer is fitted in dadoes all around, as in the drawer above.

If you decide you want to make a dovetail dado, it can be easily cut by setting the saw for the desired depth of cut and adjusting the blade tilt to the dovetail angle. Use the same tilt in cutting the mating piece. If you have not previously made this type of joint on the saw, make a few trial joints in scrap wood to practice the technique. The plain dadoes to take the drawer bottom are made by simply setting the blade for the depth of cut and the fence for the correct distance from the edge. Reset the fence to shave the cuts to the groove width and remove intervening material with in-between passes.

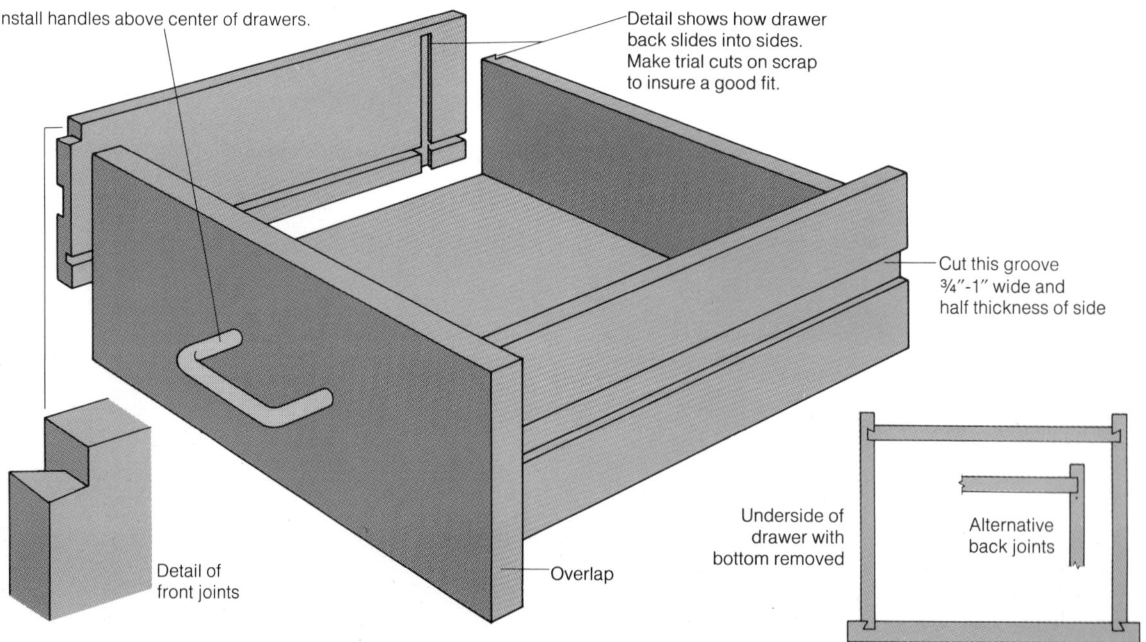

Drawer guides

To assure that drawers move straight in and out without jamming at an angle, they can be equipped with tracklike guides. **Corner guides** fit around the lower outside corners of the drawer sides. The bottom of each guide serves as a supporting track, the raised portion as a curb to prevent turning. A "kicker" strip of wood is often mounted above the drawer to prevent the back from tipping upward (and the front downward) as the drawer nears full extension. **Side guides** consist of grooves in the outer surface of the drawer sides which fit stationary runners mounted in the frame of the furniture. As no additional support is necessary, the cross members between the drawers can be reduced in thickness or even eliminated, adding to overall drawer volume. **Center guides** consist of a grooved or twin rail unit

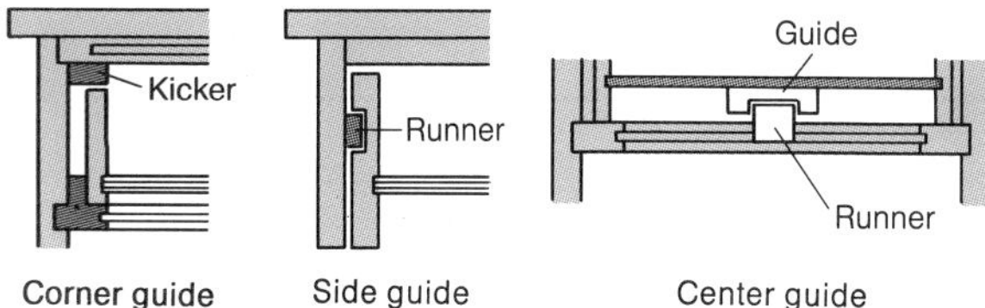

on the underside of the drawer with a stationary rail (attached to the framing) in the middle. This assures that the drawer moves straight in and out, while allowing clearance at the sides. The weight of the drawer may be supported by the lower edges of the sides riding on flat rails without the curb strips of corner guides.

All wood-to-wood guides operate more smoothly and easily if lubricated, either by waxing or applying a spray lubricant made for the purpose. In either case, the wood surface should first be given a coat of sealer and allowed to dry.

Manufactured drawer slides are available in many forms, usually comparable to the center guide and side guide, but with special advantages, including low-friction rollers. Full extension types with telescoping rails permit the drawer to be pulled out to its full length without disengaging or tipping. In planning for the use of ready-made slides, however, clearance at drawer sides or bottom must be allowed for the make and model of slide to be used. Typical clearances: Allow one inch for track between drawers with center slides and a half-inch clearance at sides for side slides.

Hardware installation

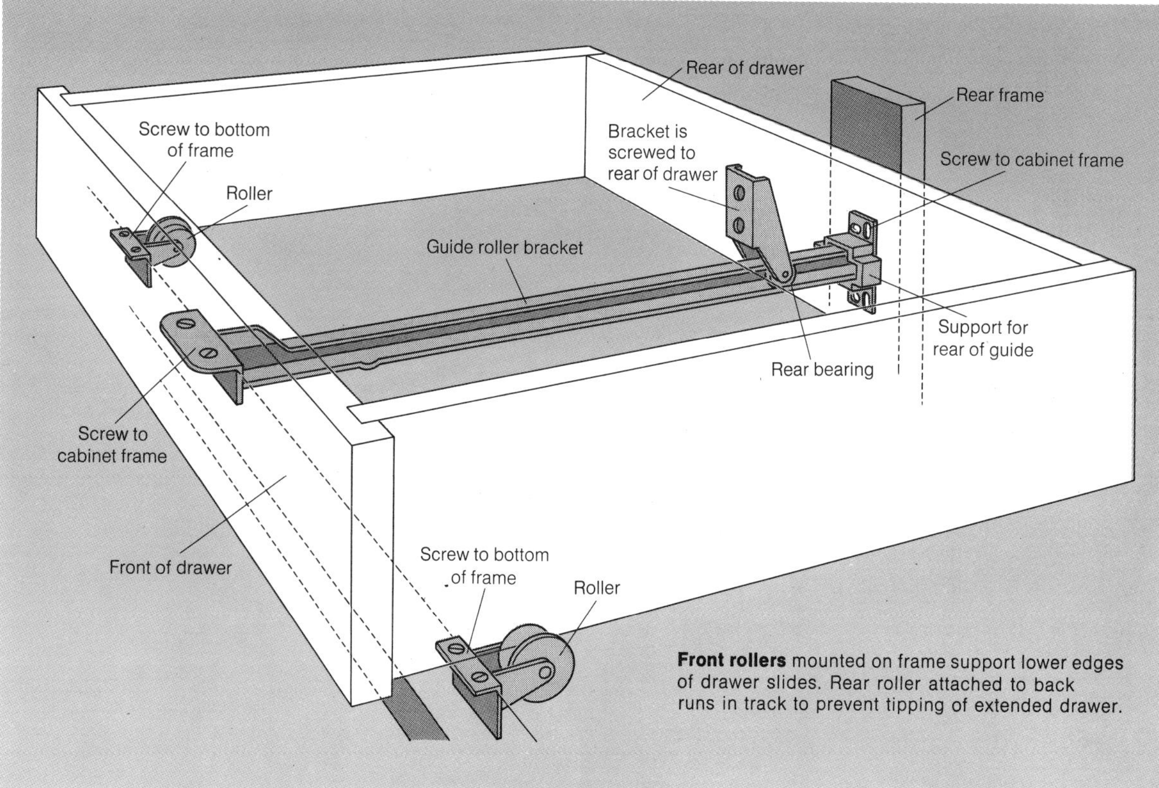

Front rollers mounted on frame support lower edges of drawer slides. Rear roller attached to back runs in track to prevent tipping of extended drawer.

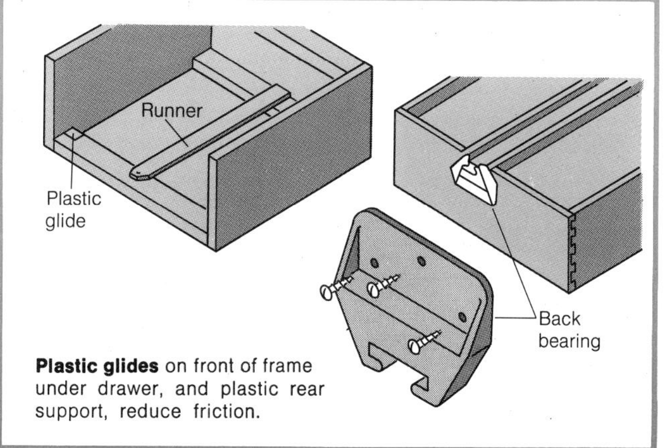

Plastic glides on front of frame under drawer, and plastic rear support, reduce friction.

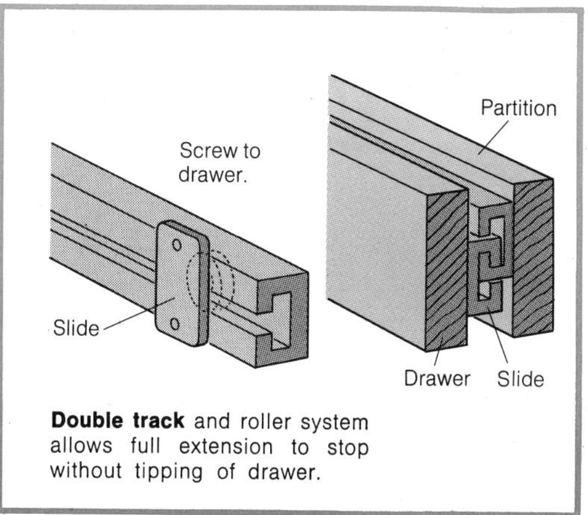

Double track and roller system allows full extension to stop without tipping of drawer.

Building a partition

The simplest way to build a room-divider partition is flat on the floor. Lay out the framework with studs (uprights) 16 inches apart, center to center. The length of the partition depends on the room, so the final stud at one end will usually be spaced differently from the others. The entire frame, including studs, sole, and plate, is of 2-x-4 stock. Make the overall height of the framing 1½ inches shorter than ceiling height, using a single 2 x 4 for sole and plate. You can then stand the completed framing up without a corner of the plate jamming against the ceiling. Fasten the studs by driving two 3½-inch common nails through the sole and plate directly into the ends of each stud. No toe nailing is required. Stand the fully assembled framework up and, with someone holding it, slip an extra length of 2 x 4 under the sole of the framing to raise it snug against the ceiling. Mark the floor position of the extra 2 x 4, then, with the framework temporarily removed, nail the 2 x 4 to the floor. Replace the framing, holding it vertical during the process, and nail its sole to the extra 2 x 4.

Use a level to square up the partition, and mark the ceiling (or joists) above it at that point. Then nail upward through the plate into each joist, if the partition runs crosswise. (If the partition runs parallel, it is most practical to locate it under a joist. You will seldom have to shift a planned location more than a few inches to accomplish this, since joists are on 16-inch centers in standard construction. See detail drawing below.)

Apply the covering of paneling or wallboard after the framing is in place. (The ends of the framing can be nailed through the end studs into the existing walls before the covering is applied, as studs in those walls are usually located directly under the joists.) Start the paneling from the end of the framing where the studs are spaced evenly on 16-inch centers, trimming the final panel as required. Molding and trim may then be added. Molding should, of course, be stained and finished to coordinate with the paneling before this step is taken.

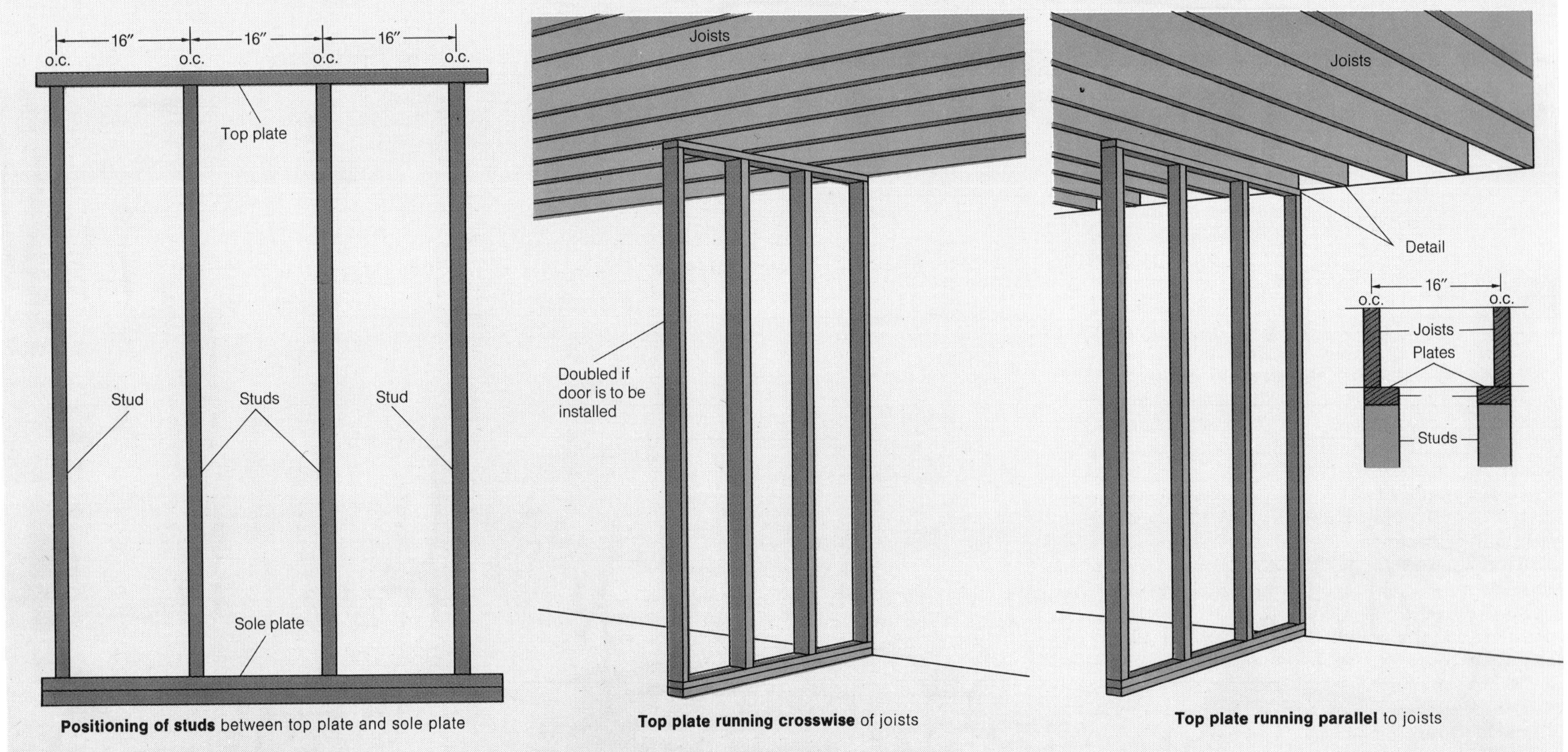

Positioning of studs between top plate and sole plate

Top plate running crosswise of joists

Top plate running parallel to joists

Framing a door

The kind of framing required for a door depends on the nature and function of the wall. If it is not a load-bearing partition wall, a pair of 2-x-4 pieces, edge-up, will act as an adequate "header" across the top. However, if the wall is a part of an addition to the house and must support part of the load of the floor or roof above, a much heavier header (usually paired 2-x-8 pieces) must be used above the door opening, with the framing fitted as is shown at the right.

Your local building code will specify the size of the header to use in most cases. The purpose of the doubled studs at the header ends is to assure positive support for the header, which, in turn, supports the floor or roof above, by means of the short intervening studs resting on it. Doubled studs are also used on each side of the door opening to prevent vibration from door closing. The sole of the framing does not extend across the bottom of the door opening. Base the overall door-opening dimensions on the size of the actual door and trim that are to be used, allowing for the clearances that are recommended by the manufacturer.

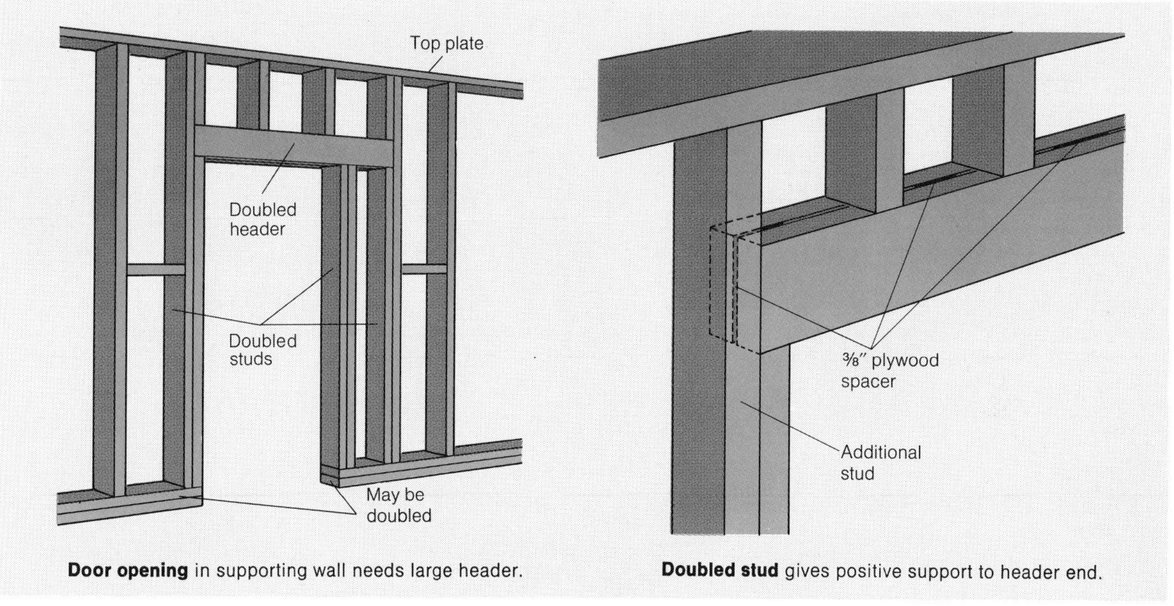

Door opening in supporting wall needs large header.

Doubled stud gives positive support to header end.

Framing a window

Framing methods for window openings follow the same rules as those for framing a door. As most windows (except for kitchen pass-through openings) are in outside walls, they are more often involved with structural support.

In general, walls that run parallel to the ridge of the roof are supporting walls. Those that run across gable ends usually are not. If the window opening is of more than average width, however, a fairly large header should be used even when you are dealing with non-load-bearing walls, to provide the stiffness required to prevent cracks in plaster or wallboard, especially at corners.

The dimensions of the window opening should be based on the actual size of the window to be installed, as there is wide variation among the newer types made by different manufacturers. If the window affords an attractive view, it should be set low enough not to block the vision of the room's occupants when they are seated. A sill height of about 30 inches usually assures this. (Higher sills tend to obstruct your view of lawn or garden.)

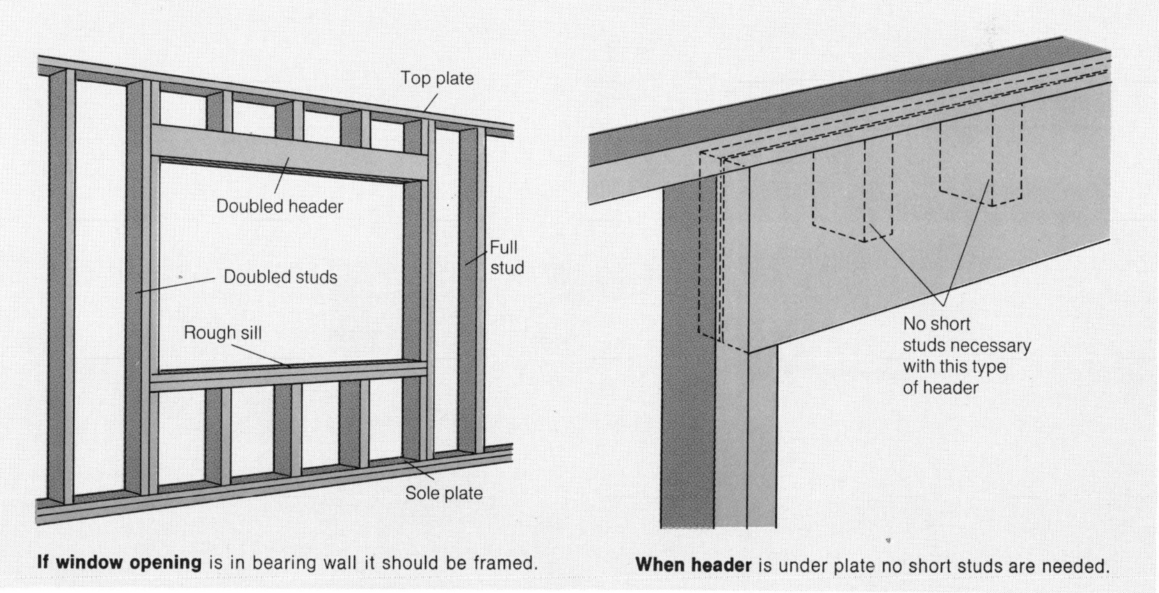

If window opening is in bearing wall it should be framed.

When header is under plate no short studs are needed.

Laying a basic floor

Before installing strip flooring, sweep or vacuum the subfloor and cover it with building paper from wall to wall.

Finish strip flooring is laid at right angles to subfloor boards, if the subfloor is laid at right angles to the joists. If the subflooring is diagonally laid, or is made of plywood, the finish flooring may be laid in any direction except parallel to the subfloor. Begin by putting down the first strip, parallel to a wall, with grooved side toward the wall. Leave a half-inch expansion space between strip and wall (will be covered later by the baseboard and molding).

Face-nail the first strip into place every 10 inches. Drive the nails close to the grooved edge so that they will be concealed by the molding. The nails should be driven through the flooring strip into the subfloor. On the tongue edge, blind-nail at a 50-degree angle. You can rent a floor-nailing machine to handle this part of the job.

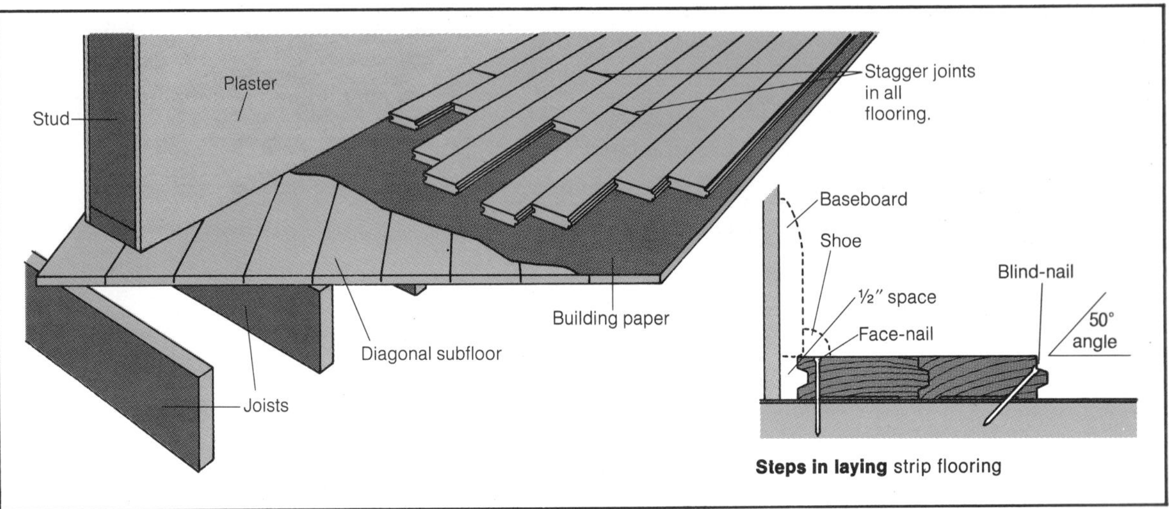

Steps in laying strip flooring

Installing ceiling furring strips

Furring is the name for the inch-thick strips of wood that are fixed to ceiling or wall to provide a level base for a surface material such as ceiling tiles or wall panels.

The furring strips shown are nailed at right angles across the joists. (The strips can also be mounted directly on the surface of an old ceiling.) Space the strips according to tile size so that tile edges will meet at centers of strips. (If 16-inch-wide tiles are used, position the furring strips 16 inches apart, measuring center to center.) Use 2½-inch nails to secure the strips to the joists, two nails to each of the joist crossings.

There are two basic methods for installing furring strips. In one, you start from the center of the ceiling and work out toward each side, so that side tiles, trimmed if necessary, will match on both sides. In the other, you start flush with one wall and trim, as necessary, at the other.

Use a level to check strip alignment every two strips. Use small pieces of wood to shim between strips and joists when adjustments are needed.

Tiles can be fastened to the furring strips with nails or cement, though as a general rule they are stapled in place. The tongue-and-groove edges keep the seams smooth.

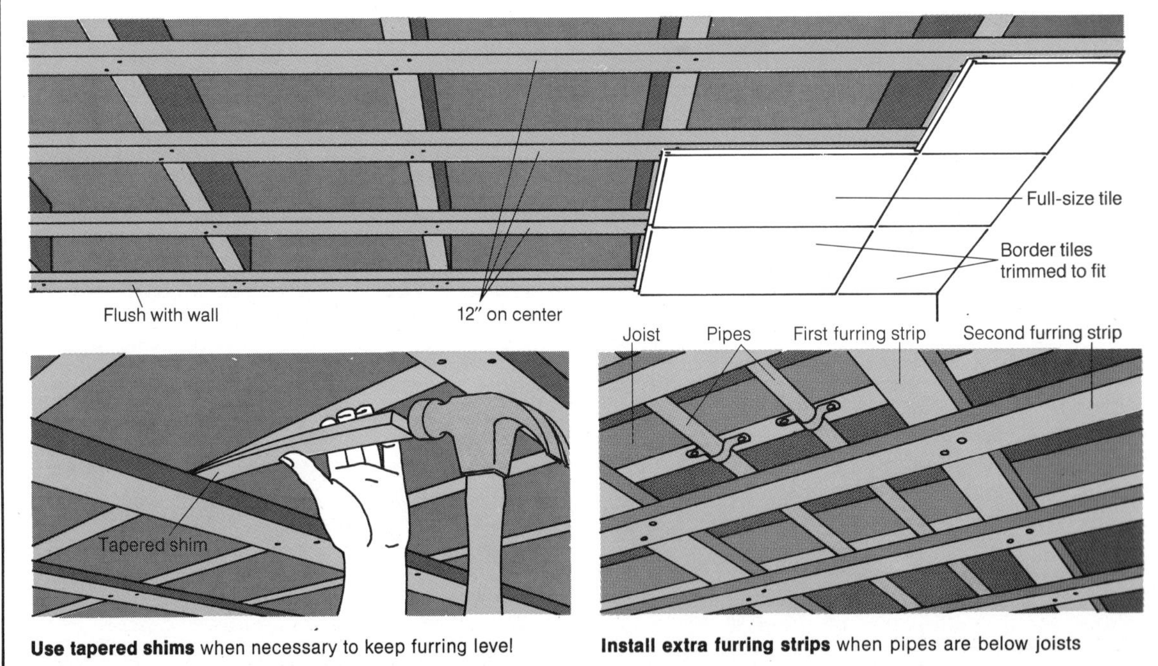

Use tapered shims when necessary to keep furring level

Install extra furring strips when pipes are below joists

Preparation

No matter what you want a wood finish to do—enhance grain patterns, color the wood, provide a durable surface—correct and patient preparation is critical. The first step is to determine whether the wood is an open- or closed-pore type. (Pores are the tiny natural holes that run along the grain.) This will dictate whether or not you have to use a wood filler before applying the final finish. Common open-pore woods are mahogany, walnut, oak, rosewood, teak, korina, and avodire. Closed-pore or tight-grained woods are pine, maple, birch, cherry, and gumwood. Woods in the latter group usually do not require the use of fillers.

Absorbency is also important. Softwoods, such as pine, are generally more absorbent than hardwoods. An absorbent wood tends to soak up the finish coat so sealers must be used after initial staining.

Sanding is crucial to the success of any furniture finish. Although power tools can do much of the rough sanding, only careful hand sanding will guarantee a smooth, professional final result.

Sand in stages, using finer-grained paper at each stage (p. 42). Start with 80 grit for rough work, followed by 120 grit for smoothing. Use 220 grit, working along the grain, only when you want to produce a super-smooth surface. Grits up to 280 may be used on hardwoods. After sanding, vacuum the surface to remove all traces of dust and grit, then wipe with a rag dampened with turps or paint thinner.

Fill blemishes, such as nail holes or splits in the wood, with stick shellac or wood dough. Both come in colors to match most woods. Stick shellac is melted into the hole or crack. Wood dough is applied with a putty knife. When the filling material has dried thoroughly (follow the manufacturer's instructions on this), sand the filled area smooth with 120 grit sandpaper.

Before beginning final finishing, take temperature and humidity into account. Finishing is not recommended under conditions of extreme cold or dampness, such as in a basement. (Polyurethane finishes are not adversely affected by dampness.)

If you are staining or coloring a piece of furniture, this work should be done in the same light as the piece will receive in use. This is particularly important if you are only partially refinishing an item of furniture and want to match the previous finish as closely as possible.

Sanding

Properly used, power sanders can nearly complete most sanding jobs. Some hand sanding is usually then required, the amount depending on the work and the final finish you plan for it. Best and easiest method: Wrap sandpaper around a smooth, flat block and sand with consistent, moderate pressure.

Large rough surfaces: Sand these with a belt sander (p. 57) or a disk sander (p. 46). Use a belt sander diagonally across the wood grain, first one way, then on the opposite diagonal. It is important to start with coarse sandpaper (p. 42) and work down to medium, never skipping more than one grit size. When the surface is smooth and level from diagonal sanding, work along the grain, starting with medium grit paper and proceeding down to fine. Don't use a belt sander for veneered work (p.381). It cuts too deep and is liable to damage the work. Hand sanding is best for these surfaces.

Disk sanders: Follow the same sandpaper progression as for the belt sander. Move back and forth along the grain with fine paper until the surface is smoothed. Finish by hand, working along the wood grain to eliminate any marks left by the disk.

Semi-smooth surfaces: The orbital or vibrating sander (p. 57) works well on previously painted pieces and on work that is fairly smooth. It is useful for sanding on inside corners. For paint removal and rough work, start with a coarse or open grit sandpaper and finish with fine. Hand sanding is not always necessary, especially if you plan to finish with paint. If the finish is to be stained and varnished, hand sanding is recommended.

Belt sander is used for initial sanding. Use it at a slight diagonal to the grain. Do not apply pressure; let the weight of the machine do the work.

Disk sander should be applied with a slight pressure and tipped so that only the nearest half of the disk contacts the work. Always keep it moving.

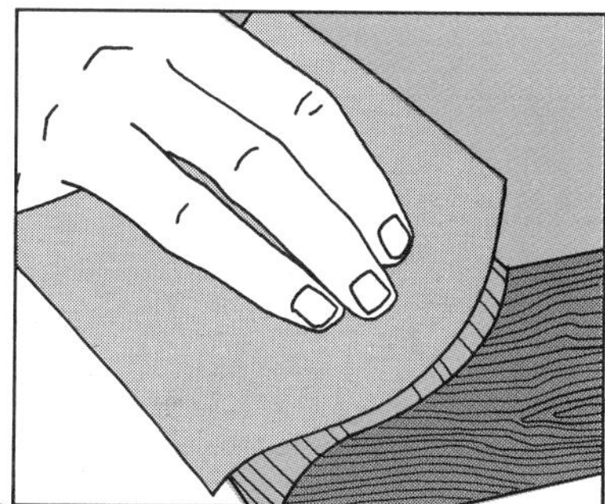

Concave surfaces are best sanded by hand. Always sand with the grain. Use successively finer grades of sandpaper until desired smoothness is obtained.

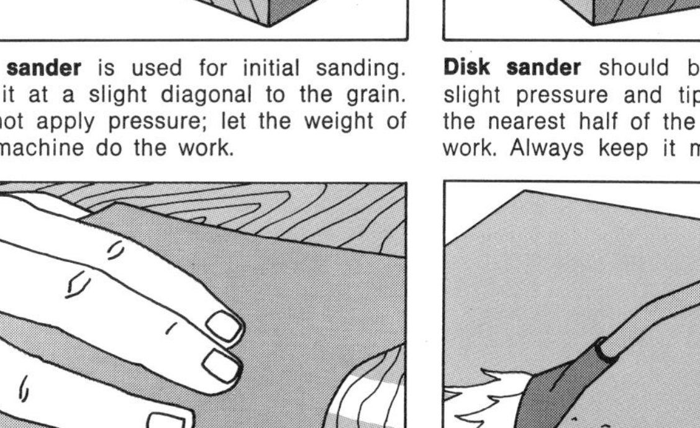

When sanding an edge by hand (or with power), sand toward the middle to avoid splintering edges. A good idea is to bevel ends slightly before starting sanding.

Propane torch with a flame spreader can be used to take off hard-to-remove finishes. Follow flame with a putty knife. Work rapidly, don't allow finish to cool.

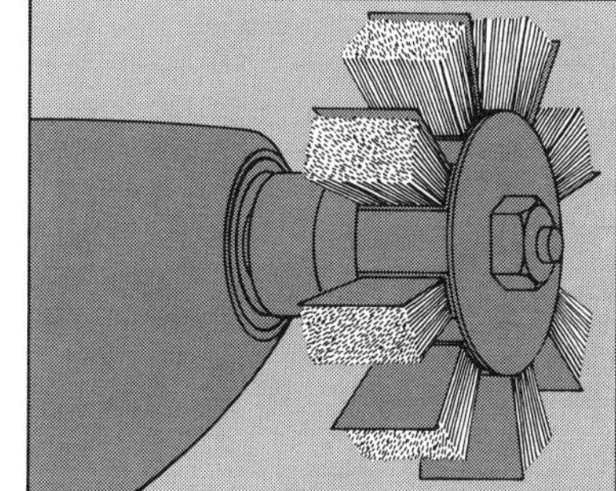

Contour sander, which attaches to an electric drill, is useful for sanding intricately shaped sections that are hard to sand by conventional means.

Finishing wood

Removing old finishes

Old finishes can be sanded and scraped until all previous coats of varnish or lacquer are gone, but the simplest and quickest method is to use a remover. These liquids or creams soften almost any finish and won't damage the wood. (Sanding can leave scratches, especially on veneers.)

The best way to apply a remover is to spread a generous amount on the work surface. Try to work on a horizontal plane. Use a natural bristle brush to cover about two square feet at a time. In about 5 minutes the surface will start to peel and blister. Some old surfaces simply become gummy. Lift the old finish off with a putty knife, pressing down firmly and moving with the grain when possible. If the old finish is several coats thick and extremely old and hard, you may have to repeat the process.

For vertical surfaces, cream remover is the best choice. It forms a jelly-like cover that clings long enough to lift the old finish. Use it also for intricate chair and table legs. When the old finish begins to lift, use a stiff brush and coarse steel wool to scrub away the residue.

Work the cream into cracks and crevices until all the original finish is gone. Wipe off excess with old towels or newspaper.

With open-pore woods (p.371), it is necessary to get as much of the finish out of the pores as possible. To do this, use a medium-grade steel wool dipped in remover and rub the surface with hard, continuous pressure.

Once the old finish is gone, neutralize the remover that has been absorbed by the wood. Use turps or lacquer thinner and steel wool to wash down the entire surface. Rub along the grain when you can.

If at this point the remaining color or stain on the wood is satisfactory, you can begin to carry out the finishing techniques described on the pages that follow. If the remaining color is not to your liking, you will have to stain over the existing color to darken or deepen it, or remove the old stain completely by sanding or bleaching.

If you notice, while sanding, that the surface looks blotchy and the blemishes do not seem to be coming out, this probably means that the original stain was a penetrating oil stain. This can be difficult, even impossible, to remove. You might try bleaching (p.409). If this fails, the surface must either be painted or a darker stain applied.

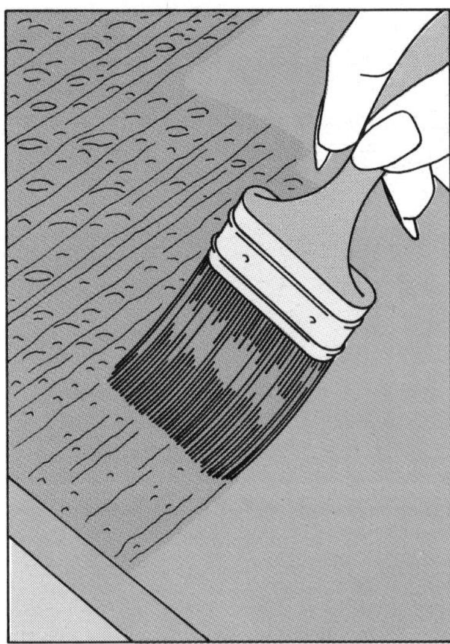

Flow a heavy coat of remover on the item or area to be stripped, working it well into the grain of the wood. Do not brush out, as this will tend to thin the coat. Don't let the remover dry.

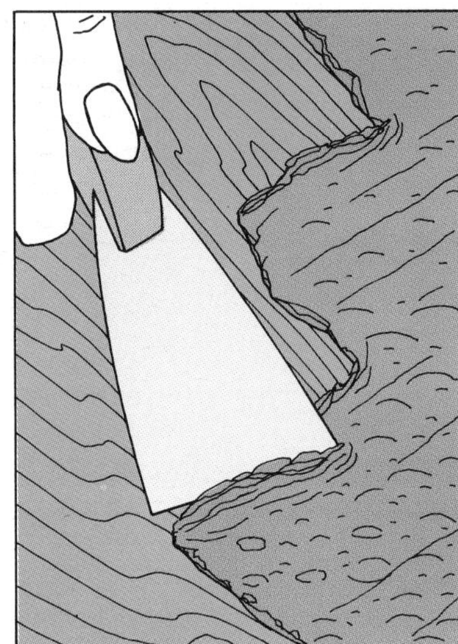

When the surface softens, use a putty knife to remove and lift off the old finish. Be careful that the knife does not gouge the surface. On large, flat surfaces it is best to use a scraper.

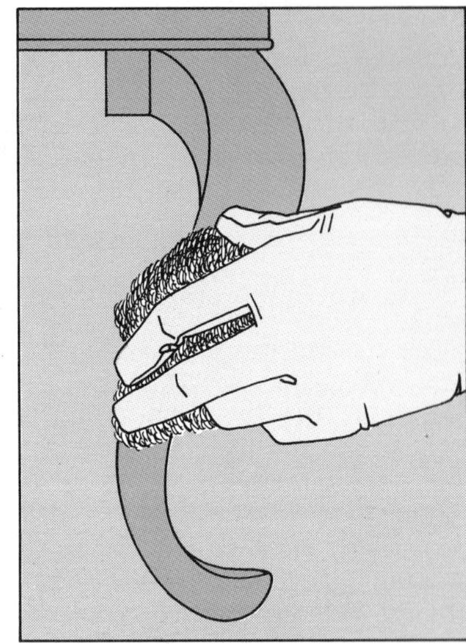

Burlap or steel wool is extremely useful for removing finish from rounded areas where a putty knife or scraper cannot be successfully used. Spread newspapers to catch drippings.

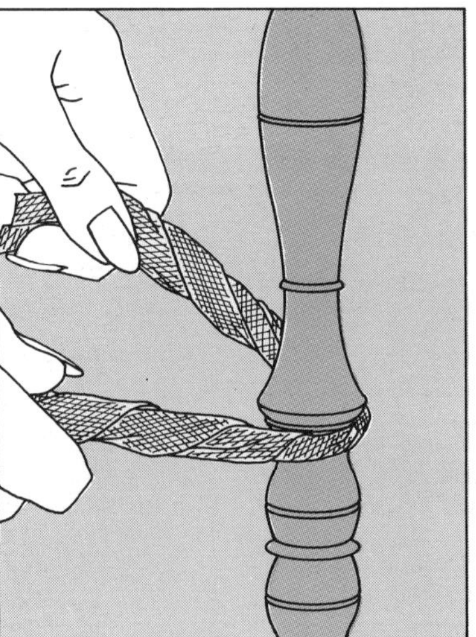

Another use for burlap: Twisted and applied as shown, it can be used to remove the finish from turned legs and posts. Use twine or coarse string to get into narrow openings.

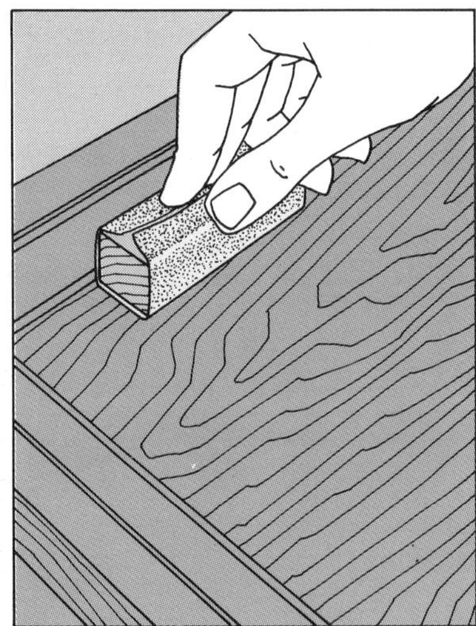

Use a block of wood and sandpaper as shown when you have to remove stubborn finish from corners. Work with the grain. Keep your pressure light to avoid any possibility of scratching.

Before applying new stain or any new finish, go over the entire area as shown with turps or lacquer thinner. This step is necessary to neutralize the effects of the remover.

Colors and bleaching

The color of the final finish on furniture is best determined by experimentation. If you are attempting to achieve a finish that matches other furnishings, prepare test pieces for color comparison.

Stain kits are available which contain test-size amounts of several basic stain colors. If you have some stains left over from other jobs, experiment with those. Make your comparison test on a scrap piece of the wood used to make the furniture. (If you are refinishing, select an area on the side or back of the furniture.) Sand the surface carefully, and apply the stain mixtures 2 square inches at a time. Make the mixtures with an eyedropper or by the teaspoon. Keep a record of them and their concentrations. When your sample board or area has dried, coat the entire surface with a sealer to bring out the color. The shades you see will be slightly darker than the actual final finish. Test for final color by applying three coats of lacquer or varnish (whichever will be the final coat) to a piece of clear glass. Hold this glass over the sample finishes to see the true colors.

Bleaching: Each application of a finishing material further darkens the wood surfaces. If you desire a light blond or pastel finish, it is necessary to bleach the raw wood to a lighter shade.

Professional wood bleaches are classified by numbers 1, 2, and 3. Bleach surfaces by applying bleach No. 1 to the entire area. Use only a clean white rag. Let dry 10 minutes, then apply bleach No. 2 over No. 1. Allow to dry at least 12 hours before taking the next step. The bleach is water-soluble and will cause the wood grain to lift, so follow the drying with a light sanding, using 220 or 280 sandpaper. (If at this stage a still lighter color is desired, apply a second coat of No. 2 bleach.) Bleached wood must be neutralized before finishing. Do this with a 50/50 solution of white vinegar and water. Rub the solution into the surface with fine steel wool. Wait 24 hours, then sand the lifted grain.

A less efficient but simpler bleaching method is to use a combination of bleaches Nos. 1 and 3 in a single application. Make the mixing ratio 4 parts No. 1 to 1 part No. 3. Apply two or three coats of this mixture, followed by vinegar neutralization.

Caution: When using bleach, wear gloves of the type recommended by the bleach manufacturer, and work only in a well-ventilated area.

Fillers and sealers

Wood fillers are important because finishing magnifies every hole and crevice in unfilled wood. Fillers come in paste or liquid form. The paste type must be thinned with benzine or turpentine. Turpentine is best for the beginner since it dries more slowly and thus allows more working time. Fillers come in a wide range of colors or can be colored lighter or darker with japan colors (p.410).

Apply filler over the surface about two square feet at a time. Brush first across, then along the grain. When the filler turns gray or dull (10 to 15 minutes), wipe the surface across the grain with a rough towel or burlap. This will force the filler into the wood pores. When most of it has been wiped off, wipe lightly along the grain with a rag. Timing is important so follow the manufacturer's instructions. If wiped too soon, the filler pulls out; wait too long, and it won't come off at all.

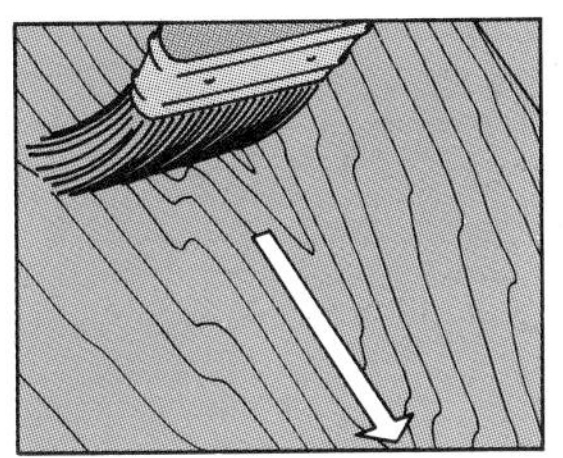

Apply stains and fillers with and across grain.

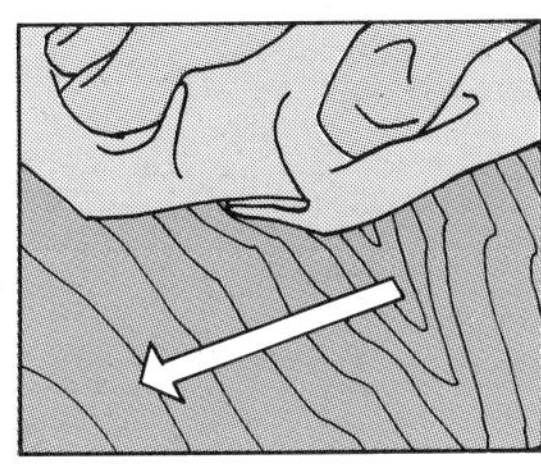

Wipe off either one with a clean cloth before it dries.

Wait overnight before applying a finish coat. Most fillers look dry after only a few hours but this is deceptive, and premature application of a final finish can seal filler liquids in crevices. These show up later as gray blotches in the finish.

Sealers act as a buffer between colors, stains, and fillers, and final finish coats. A sealer fills wood pores and reduces absorbency to keep the number of finish coats to a minimum. If an oil stain has been used, the sealer keeps it from bleeding into the finish coats. The best sealer to prevent bleeding is shellac. For sealing, shellac can be mixed with 5 to 10 percent of denatured alcohol. Most shellacs are yellow or orange; used as a sealer, they alter the color of the final finish. Test for color change by shellacking a piece of glass and placing it over the finish to view the change.

Shellac has some disadvantages. It deteriorates on the shelf, usually in four to six months. Old shellac will not dry. Another problem is that shellac is very hard and brittle. It will develop "alligator" cracks if exposed to damp conditions.

Professional sealers are available which have no shelf-life limitations. They can be thinned with lacquer thinner and can be painted or sprayed right from the can. Some ready-mixed stains on the market combine a sealer with the stain. This of course eliminates the extra step of sealing—provided available stains include the color you want.

Hardware protection

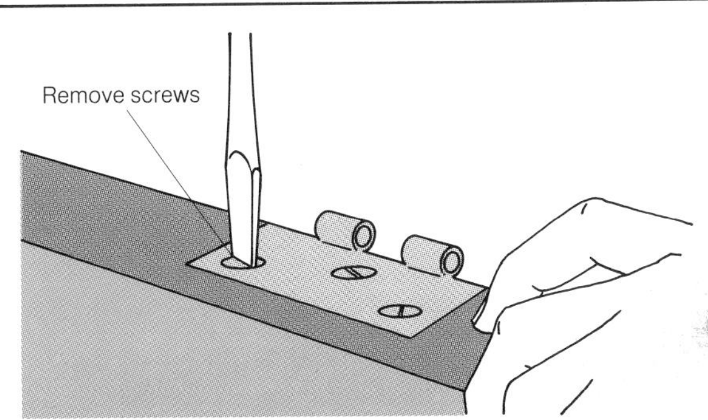

Before starting a refinishing job, remove as much hardware as possible. This will make the job much easier.

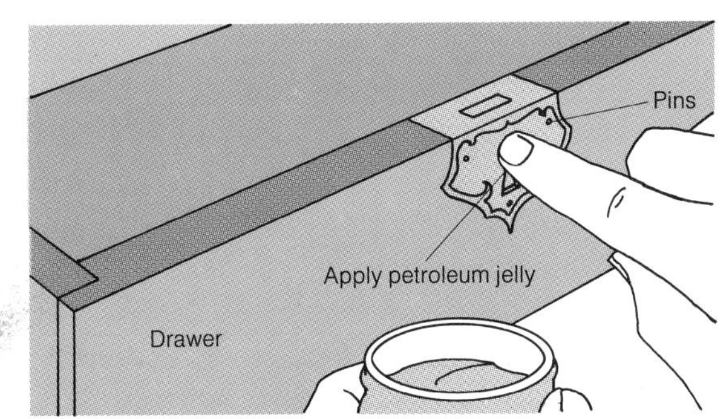

If hardware cannot be removed, it should be protected against bleaches and stains with petroleum jelly.

Staining

Stain has two functions: It brings the wood to the desired color and it emphasizes the beauty of the grain. If you prefer a natural wood finish, use a light stain that will not alter the wood's color, but will emphasize the grain lines. Or you can simply not stain the work at all.

In refinishing, it is staining that matches the color of your new work to other finished sections or perhaps to different pieces. When selecting a stain, bear in mind that the final finish coats usually make the actual result a little darker.

There are several types of stains, oil stains and water- or alcohol-soluble stains being most common.

Pigmented, or oil stains are finely ground powders which are used in paste form—mixed with turpentine or benzine so they can be brushed or wiped onto the work surface. Pigmented stains are fairly thick when mixed with turpentine and they tend to cover the grain when applied. An oil stain can be applied with a rag or a brush. Rub the stain across as well as with the grain. Let it dry for 10 to 15 minutes and then wipe it off with a clean rag. If the staining is too light, don't make the mistake of applying a thick coat and letting it dry. Instead, wipe off the first coat after a longer wait, of not more than 20 minutes, and then apply a second coat the next day. An oil stain should be wiped off—never allow it to dry, as it will discolor and conceal the grain of the wood, like a sort of paint. But if you should happen to let the stain dry, all is not lost: Dampen a rag with turps or benzine and wipe off the stain. You may have to apply considerable pressure, as dried stain is difficult to remove.

Dye stains generally are both water- and alcohol-soluble. They are applied as very thin liquids that soak into the wood quickly. Use a dye stain to bring out and sharpen grain lines. These stains come in powdered form and are mixed in water slightly below boiling temperature. They are best applied by spraying, although a rag or sponge will do. For best results, work at room temperature. When mixing, a light color can be darkened by adding more powder; dark colors can be made lighter by adding more water, either cold or hot. Apply the stain slightly lighter than you want it to finally look, using a second application to bring it to the desired intensity. Be sure to mix enough stain to complete the entire job. Getting a second batch to match could be difficult. After opening, these stains should only be stored in glass containers.

If you should put too much stain on the work and find that it looks blotchy and uneven, try reducing the concentration by wiping the surface immediately with a rag soaked in cold water.

Water stains, however, will raise the grain of the wood. After an overnight drying, sand the surface lightly with fine sandpaper. Another disadvantage is that they tend to cause swelling and warping.

Applying alcohol-soluble stains: These stains are often called N.G.R., N.B. (non-grain-raising, non-bleeding) stains. They have all the advantages of other stains, except that they are not as colorfast as water stains. They are sold already mixed in eight basic colors and can be intermixed to make your own custom color. Their intensity can be reduced by adding an alcohol solvent.

You can apply these stains by spraying, brushing, or wiping on with a rag. Beginners should use the brushing method for best results. Brushing is easier if the stain is thinned 1 part stain to 3 or 4 parts alcohol. Clean brushes after use by rinsing them thoroughly in warm, soapy water.

If too dark an application has been made, try making it lighter by wiping immediately with a solvent-soaked rag. If this does not work, you will have to sand the work and begin again.

Wear gloves when using these stains. If any should get on your skin, wash with warm water and soap. As a safety precaution, do not smoke while using alcohol stains.

Japan colors are pigment-type stains popular with professional finishers because of their versatility. They can be used for staining, glazing, toning, painting, blending, graining, and shading.

Japan-color pigments are normally ground six to twelve times, the finer the grind, the better—and also the costlier—the results.

The colors are available in standard wood shades plus white, black, blues, and greens. Used on raw wood, they will hide the grain rather than enhance it; in a strong enough concentration they behave like paint. Mixed with lacquer, they give it color to form a toner. Mixed with sealers, they become a colored glaze.

Japan-color mixture applied on the end grain of plywood makes the end match the rest of the wood. The colors can also be used for antiquing effects; wiped on the work after it has been dye-stained, they give the surface an undercolor of stain and an overlayer of color.

Because they are pigmented stains, follow-up coats of japan colors should be sprayed. Brushing will tend to pull the pigments off and mix them with the lacquers. If brushing is unavoidable, let the first coat dry at least 24 hours and apply the second with very light brush strokes.

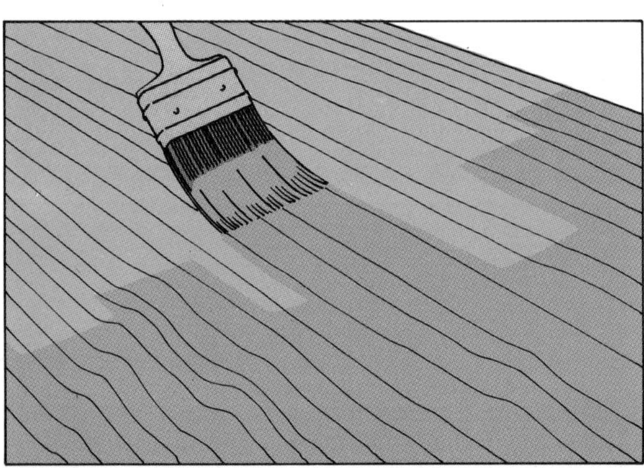

Stain can be applied either by brush or with a rag. Whichever method you use, rub the stain in thoroughly both with the grain and across the grain.

After about a 10- to 15-minute wait, wipe away the excess stain with a clean rag. Don't permit the stain to dry. Dried stain will cake and affect the finish.

Varnish and shellac

The object of final finishing is to protect the surface, and to reflect as much light from the surface as is necessary for the desired effect, such as a high gloss, a satin finish, or a flat finish.

Varnish is available in many grades and colors. Quality grades will expand and contract with the furniture without cracking and will dry hard enough to be rubbed down for the final finish. Colors range from nearly clear to dark brown.

Some varnishes are available with additives to give them resistance to salt water. These are called spar varnishes. Generally speaking, the more resistant they are, the softer they are and thus the more difficult to rub to a final finish. Varnish can be thinned with turpentine; suitable cleaning agents are benzine and turpentine.

Before varnish is applied, it is essential that the work be completely dust-free. Particles left from sanding will appear as small bumps in the finish, as will dust that settles on the unfinished work. Have the working area as dust-free as possible, with a minimum of air currents.

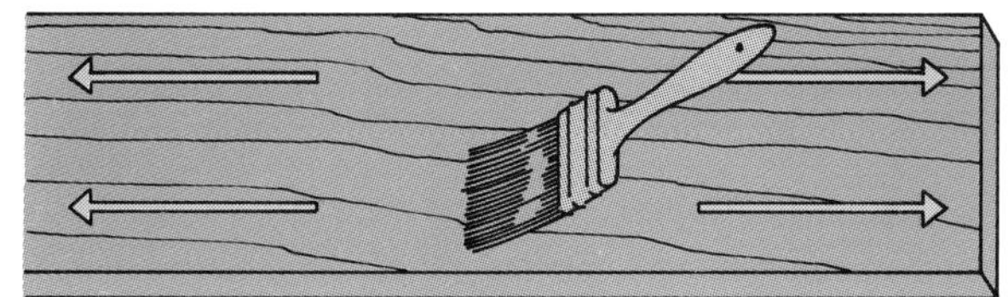

Flow varnish along grain, working from wet to dry area. Use slow brush strokes; brush out air bubbles.

When varnish is used on bare wood, it is best to thin it (1 part turpentine to 4 parts varnish) for the first coat. Brush this mixture in as a sealer (p. 409). Let it dry thoroughly and, after light sanding, apply flow coats with light hand sanding between them. As you sand, you can feel the finish smooth as dust particles and bubbles flatten. Be generous about drying time. It is better to allow a little extra than to try to rush the job. The harder the coat, the smoother it will sand. Clean the surface with a tack rag after sanding.

For most satisfactory application of successive coats, use the varnish just as it comes from the can, but watch the quantity. A full-flowing coat will level itself, but too much will increase the drying time and the danger of dust accumulation. Too little will leave bare spots that will demand sanding to blend between coats. It pays to practice on scrap wood to see just how heavily to load the brush for best results. If possible, turn the work as finishing progresses, so you are always working on a horizontal surface. This eliminates sags and runs, which are difficult to remove.

Shellac used as a finish is very easy to work with. It dries dust-free in half an hour or less, and is ready for between-coat sanding in an hour, except in humid conditions. Shellac has a limited shelf-life of four to six months. When stored longer, it deteriorates. First indication of this is excessive drying time. When making your purchase, try to find out how old the stock is. Shellac is thinned with denatured alcohol to the desired "cut." (Cut means the number of pounds of shellac dissolved in a U.S. gallon of alcohol or four-fifths of an imperial gallon.) Knowing the right cut for a job comes from experience. There are some basic rules, however, for determining how thick or thin shellac should be for different uses. Floors usually need a three-pound cut; fine finishing on furniture or a hand-rubbed effect on paneling requires a thinner mix. The thinner the coat, the smoother the job. A built-up finish of many thin coats is better than a few thick ones.

Shellac comes in white and orange, the orange type giving a deeper grain tone than the white, with a tendency toward amber in coloration. If a special wood hue is desired, white shellac can be tinted with shellac colors (alcohol-soluble aniline dyes). These can produce modern effects and are also used for blending or matching, which are crucial in refinishing old work. When restoring furniture, some experimenting on scrap wood will make it possible to duplicate color and tone so that replacement parts closely match the original finish.

Apply shellac freely so that the surface is good and wet. Work toward the wet edge and do not worry too much about visible laps. You will find that shellac softens and blends with previous brush coverage. The first coat tends to raise any fine fibers left from original sanding; these will disappear with the first sanding. (A light wash coat of thin shellac can be used under other finishes just to eliminate these fibers before application of slow-drying finishes. This wash coat also balances absorption between the hard and soft grains of some plywoods.) Keep the brush soft between coats by immersing it in denatured alcohol. Shellac can also be applied with a lint-free cloth pad.

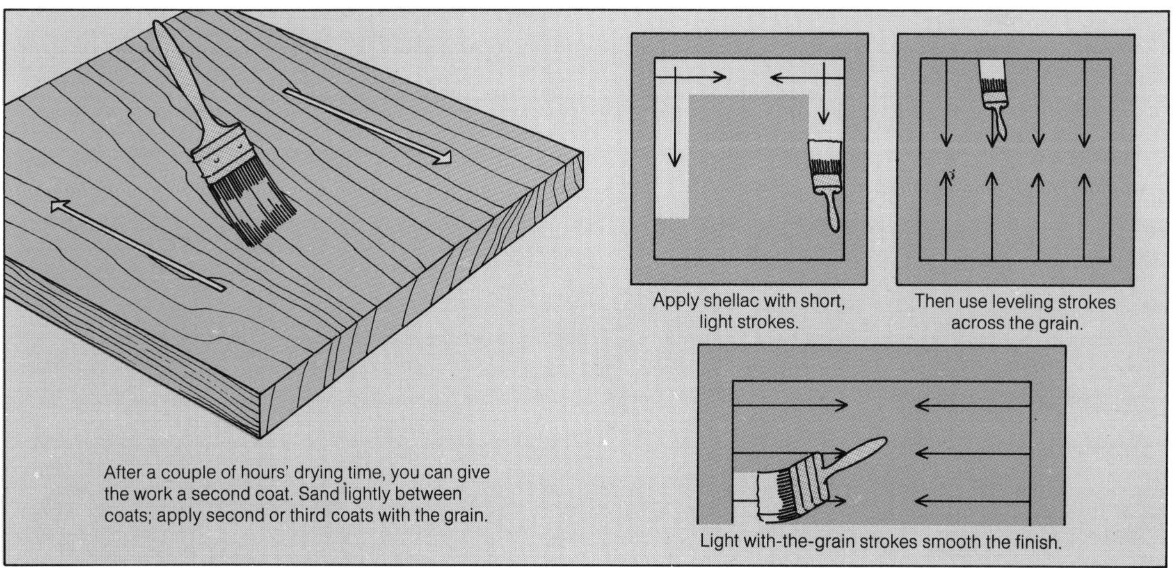

After a couple of hours' drying time, you can give the work a second coat. Sand lightly between coats; apply second or third coats with the grain.

Apply shellac with short, light strokes.

Then use leveling strokes across the grain.

Light with-the-grain strokes smooth the finish.

Final finishes

Applying lacquers

Lacquer—readily identifiable by its banana-like odor—is popular among many woodworkers because it dries rapidly and does not conceal the grain of the wood. This latter quality is due to the fact that it is always applied in thin coats (because of its light body), whether this is done by spraying or by brushing. One important precaution: Never apply lacquer over a painted surface. It will lift the paint, acting as a kind of paint remover. Lacquer is made for spraying or for brushing. The brushing type takes longer to dry than the spray type. Never use the spray type for brushing; it will dry too fast to brush out. Both types of lacquer are made in flat and glossy finishes. When the lacquer is dry and rubbed down, it is impossible to tell if it has been sprayed or brushed. The advantage of spraying, of course, is that it is time-saving.

After the work has been sanded (and stained, if this is required), brush or spray on the first coat of lacquer. For spraying use an external mix gun. A spray job should always consist of three or more light coats. Heavy spraying will give you trouble—generally in the form of runs which cannot be picked up the way you can pick up a paint run with a brush. If a brushing lacquer is to be used for spraying, thin it with lacquer thinner—do not use any other solvent for this purpose.

To apply lacquer, use a clean brush that has never been used for paint. Flow on the first coat as evenly as possible, following the grain of the wood. After 24 hours' drying time, you can apply the second coat. Sanding is not necessary between coats as each succeeding coat of lacquer tends to dissolve into the preceding one. Keep the lacquer brush in the can while you are working with this finish, as lacquer dries very quickly and may cause the brush to take a set within a very short time.

After a surface has been sprayed or brushed with lacquer you may feel or see tiny pits, dust particles, and possibly uneven layers of lacquer. Such imperfections can be eliminated and the finish vastly improved by rubbing the surface with fine steel wool and wax. But wait to do this until the lacquer has dried for at least 48 hours. Make a steel wool pad about 3 inches square and rub it over the paste wax until it is thoroughly charged. Next, rub the waxed pad over the wood with long strokes parallel to the grain. Do a small section at a time, no more than a 10 x 20-inch area. Wipe off the wax with vigorous strokes, using terry cloth or a coarse towel as a polisher. Do this polishing before the wax has a chance to dry and set. Rub the tips of your fingers over the polished surface to detect any areas you might have missed.

Clear polyurethane finishes are termed varnishes by some manufacturers, lacquers by others. They are durable, highly water-resistant, and moderately quick-drying. Though two-part types are made for certain industrial uses, the one-part type (in a single can) is common for home use. Because of variations among brands, follow the instructions on the can you have selected after preparing the work. (Polyurethanes can be applied over an existing finish, if it is sound.) Any staining or filling must be thoroughly dried before applying polyurethane to new wood. This finish may be brushed, sprayed, or rolled, and in most types need not be sanded between coats if each is applied within the manufacturer's specified time after the preceding one. (Proper timing enables the coats to fuse chemically.) If you wait beyond the set time, sanding is necessary to provide a "bite" for proper adhesion of the next coat. The first coat serves as a primer sealer. Unlike traditional varnishes, which should not be applied in humid weather, the polyurethanes harden more readily when the atmosphere is humid. Select the type—gloss or mat—for the desired results.

Colored transparent polyurethane finishes have the same general characteristics as the clear varnish versions, but offer a wider range of decorative possibilities. To determine the hue a given color will produce on a particular wood, make a test on scrap. Remember that each successive coat will deepen the tone, somewhat like layers of colored glass laid one on top of the other. If the desired depth of color is reached before sufficient coats are applied to produce the required surface luster, use clear polyurethane varnish for the remaining coats. This has a minimal effect on the color tone. Commonly available in several colors, in gloss and mat finish, colored polyurethane can be used to develop a wide variety of combinations—using one color for a panel area, another for trim and regulating depth of tone by the number of coats. Like the clear types, the colored polyurethanes are highly water-resistant, well suited to table and bar tops.

Preparing the surface

The first step in the preparation of any wood for finishing is a thorough sanding. For ease of handling and greater efficiency, wrap the sandpaper around a block of wood.

After sanding, carefully wipe the entire surface with a piece of clean cheesecloth. Run your hand over the surface to detect any areas you might have left unsanded.

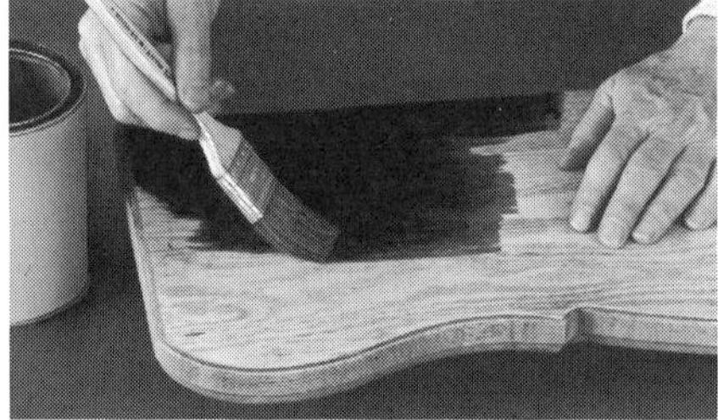

Staining is the next step. Stir the stain in the can and then apply it generously both with and across the grain. Wipe the excess off after about 20 minutes.

Apply lacquer, or any of the polyurethane finishes, in long, flowing strokes, always with the grain. A second coat can be applied after a drying period of 24 hours.

Linseed oil

The so-called classic oil finish is inexpensive, and it is simple to apply, maintain, and repair, but it does require elbow grease. Use boiled linseed oil, thinned with turpentine in proportions ranging from half-and-half to 2 parts oil to 1 part turpentine. Adjust the formula to your liking. This finish is excellent on walnut, and many fine antiques owe their luster to this time-honored method.

On old work, the original finish must be removed down to the bare wood; the pores must be exposed to permit the oil to be absorbed. New work merely needs sanding and thorough dust removal to make sure that the pores are clean. Oil darkens wood considerably, so test on a scrap of the wood or the underside of the piece to see whether a stain will be required under the oil. Brush the oil on freely, and allow time for thorough penetration. If dull spots show, add more oil to be sure you get an even finish. When it is apparent that the wood will accept no more oil, wipe off the surplus with a clean, dry, lint-free cloth. After wiping, rubbing down with a cloth pad, such as old linen, produces a satiny sheen. The secret is rubbing hard enough to generate heat. Pressure exerted with the heel of the hand is a good method, as is a felt bonnet on an orbital sander. Let the work dry for at least two days in a warm, dry atmosphere, then repeat all of the steps—five times to achieve a true classic finish.

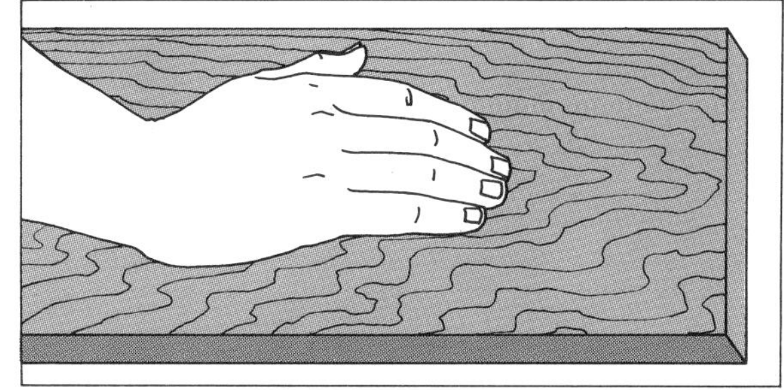

A crucial step in the boiled linseed oil finish is a firm, vigorous rubdown. Pressure from the heel of your hand helps to generate the heat that is needed to set the finish.

French polish

French polishing methods vary in detail, but all of them are based on the wipe-on application of shellac. The traditional applicator is a "rubber" that consists of cotton wool wrapped in linen to make a pad of a size convenient for hand rubbing. Shellac, thinned to a one-pound cut, is poured on the cotton wool, with the linen wrapper open. Then, with the linen closed, the rubber is moved gently, with the grain, over the surface to be finished, applying the shellac as it soaks through the linen. After letting the shellac dry briefly, the process is repeated to build up the desired depth of finish. To prevent the rubber from sticking and dragging the finish during the final coats (these should be rubbed with a figure-8 polishing motion), a few drops of linseed oil may be added as a lubricant. This, however, must not be overdone, as too much oil can adversely affect the polish.

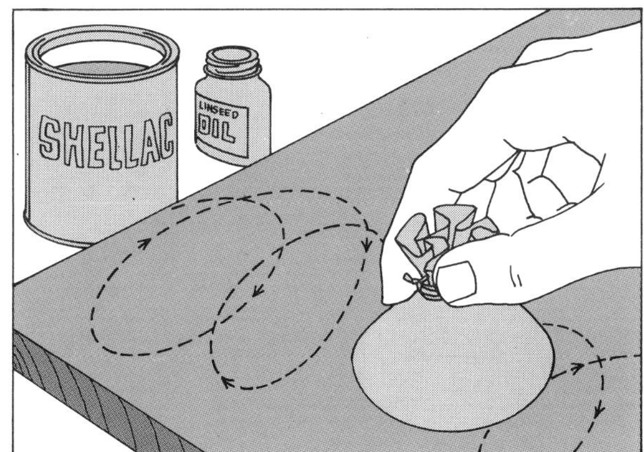

Rubbing pad for French polishing is shellac-soaked, lubricated during final stages with just a few drops of linseed oil. Do not overdo lubrication—excess oil can gum up the finish. Recommended rubbing motion: In the shape of a figure 8.

For those who would like to closely approximate the effect of this type of polish with a simpler method, a wad of soft, lintless cloth can be used to apply the shellac. Allow each application to dry thoroughly, sand lightly with fine sandpaper, and repeat the process until the required degree of finish is attained. By allowing the shellac to dry thoroughly, and by using very light pressure in the wiping-on process, the need for lubrication can be avoided. The finish can be built up to a high luster, if this is desired, or rubbed down with rottenstone (p.196) and oil after final drying. The wiping method of application, of course, eliminates the possibility of brush marks.

Either white or orange shellac may be used, depending on the finish tone you want. Any filling or staining of the wood should be done before the shellac application begins, and should be allowed to dry thoroughly. An alcohol-type stain or a non-grain-raising type may be used with this process.

Wax

A good paste wax adds life to the oil finish, minimizes care, and adds a protective layer to vulnerable surfaces. Follow manufacturer's directions for application; some require that the cloth applicator be wet, then wrung out before using. The wax should be applied to an area about two or three feet square at a time. Then, if a damp cloth was used, any remaining moisture should be wiped away and the paste evened out before the area is polished.

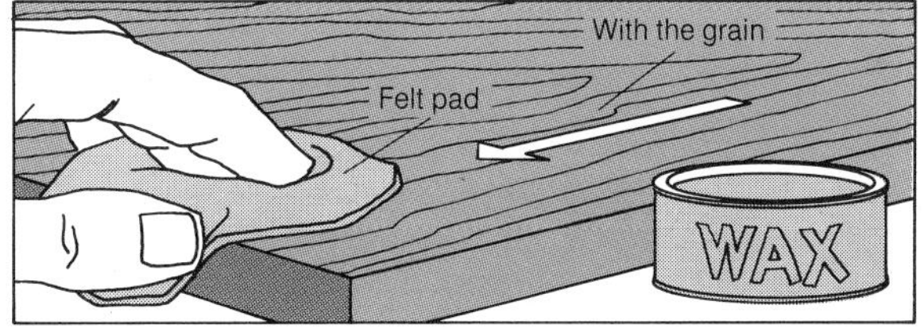

Paste wax, applied with a damp cloth, protects the final finish

For a really good buffing job, the polishing bonnet on the rubber disc of a power sander is ideal. After the first area reaches the desired sheen, polish an adjacent area, being careful to blend the entire finish so there are no laps or bare spots.

Some paste waxes are made with a built-in color for use on dark finishes. The colored wax adds a slight darkening effect, desirable where staining is uneven or too light.

Aerosol spray

A professional-looking finish with no brush marks can be applied quickly and easily with an aerosol spray on natural or stained wood. Use a lacquer for water resistance, aerosol shellac for a warmer tone. Have the work thoroughly prepared and dust-free. To avoid spraying nearby objects, work in an open area, well away from walls. Use newspapers and masking tape to protect parts not to be finished.

Any filling or staining should be finished and dry before spraying begins. Follow the instructions on the aerosol can, which usually require a temperature between 70 and 90 degrees. Maintain a distance of 10 to 12 inches from work while spraying. Keep the can moving and avoid runs by applying several light coats rather than a single heavy one. Sand lightly between coats, allowing ample drying time.

Ebonizing

With the use of an ebony (black) stain, available from large paint dealers, many inexpensive woods can be made to resemble ebony, and still retain a grain pattern. (The relatively simple straight and parallel pattern of real ebony exists in many woods.) However, to produce the desired tone (ebony finishes differ), base your staining and finishing on an example you like. The darkest tones may require several applications of stain, especially on naturally light-colored species. If the piece is to be purely ornamental, soft as well as hardwoods may be included in a test group. Wipe off the stain after different drying periods to control the depth of the color. Finish with clear lacquer or varnish (polyurethane is suitable). Finish may be mat, or rubbed to a low luster with fine steel wool and paste wax.

Fuming

The fumed oak finish is named for the method once used to produce it—exposing the wood to strong ammonia fumes in a sealed chamber. The final color varied, of course, with the species of oak and the portion of the log from which it was cut. The heartwood of both red and white oak, for example, is brown (reddish brown in red oak), while the sapwood is close to white. As the graying effect of fuming produces an effect considered drab by some, fumed oak stains are also available with warmer tints. As with most wood finishes, the best procedure is to base your choice on an example that you find attractive. Control the tone by the length of time the stain is allowed to remain on the wood before it is wiped off and by the number of applications. A mat finish is preferable.

Liming

The term "limed oak" describes several finishes applicable to the open grain of oak. In one popular version, white filler is applied and wiped thoroughly across the grain. After it has dried completely, thinned white paint is brushed over the wood and wiped off while still wet, leaving a faint white overtone with the grain showing through. When this is dry, several coats of a compatible clear finish are applied. Another method calls for a brushed-on "wash coat" of thinned shellac (about one pound cut, p.411). After this dries, white filler is applied and wiped off. The wash keeps the filler out of the pores, leaving the white only in the open grain fissures. Clear finish completes it. For a grain-textured surface, thinned white paint is applied, worked well into the open grain, and wiped off to leave a faint white overtone. The textured finish may also be varied with a shellac wash, retaining the wood tone except in the open grain. A clear finish goes over either one. In some variations, the wood is stained before whitening so a mellower or deeper tone shows through. Novelty finishes using the same methods can be made with pigmented fillers and thinned paint in colors other than white.

Test any method beforehand on scrap. Even after a piece is completed, its overall tone can be varied in a single step by applying a coat of colored transparent polyurethane over the clear finish. A mat finish softens the color, a gloss emphasizes it.

Ribboning

The striped "ribbon" tops used on many modern tables are easily made from plywood, preferably with a face veneer of a light, close-grained wood such as birch. Conceal the plywood edges with molding or with strip veneer made for this purpose.

Width of the stripes should be planned to produce an odd number of stripes, so that the same tone (light or dark) will appear at both edges and the center stripe will be of the opposite tone. For maximum concealment of edge-trim seams, have the end stripes dark. As the table top must be cut from a 4-foot width in most cases, cut it to a width divisible by 5 or 7. Thus, a typical dinner table could be 35 inches wide (not including edge molding) and have seven stripes each 5 inches wide, or five stripes each 7 inches wide.

Narrow grooves (the width of a saw blade) must be cut between the stripes to prevent the stain migrating from the dark stripes to the light ones. This can be done easily on a table saw with table extensions. Simply set the blade to cut about ⅛ inch deep, or at least through the surface veneer, and clamp a wooden fence to the table extensions, repositioning it for successive cuts. If you don't have a table saw, you can cut the grooves with a handsaw drawn back and forth between 1 x 2-inch guides clamped to the plywood, as shown. A crosscut saw or backsaw is best for this job.

Stain alternate stripes; allow ample drying time for the stain, and then apply a thin wash coat of shellac over both the stained and unstained stripes to seal the wood pores. Then fill the grooves with spackling compound, level with a putty knife, and wipe any excess or smears of the compound from the adjacent surfaces. When the spackling compound is hard, apply several coats of compatible varnish or lacquer over the entire table top, allowing ample drying time between them.

Narrow grooves between the stripes keep stain from migrating.

Step-by-step method

Antiquing is a term applied to several aspects of woodworking. When used with regard to paint finishing, it refers to a two-tone effect produced by laying a glaze over a contrasting undercoat, and then wiping the glaze to suit. On molding-trimmed panels and similar areas, the glaze is most often applied over the entire area after the base coat is dry. The central area is then wiped to remove the glaze (a thin film always remains), the wiping cloth lifted gradually as it nears the edges, to blend out the tone. Another wipe-off technique utilizes crumpled paper, a cellulose sponge, or steel wool, turned against the fresh glaze to form swirl patterns closely spaced over the antiqued area.

On molding and other contoured areas, a fairly stiff cloth pad is used in wiping, to remove the glaze from the "high" portions while permitting some to remain in the channels and grooves for emphasis. The same general procedure is followed on carvings. As most glazes are not fast-drying, they allow ample time for reworking if the first wiping does not give the desired effect.

Other forms of antiquing (called "distressing") are designed to simulate, by mechanical means, the effects of age and wear on furniture. On pieces such as cobbler's benches and dry sinks, originally designed for hard use, a short length of chain (such as a tire chain) is often laid on the surface and struck with a hammer to dent the wood without breaking its fibers. The dents give the impression of long use and hard wear, yet do not materially impair finishing qualities. Sharp corners (as on unfinished furniture) are frequently sanded to simulate natural rounding from years of wear. Machine-planed surfaces, too, are given slight hollows, to simulate both wear and the unevenness of early lumber processing methods, by local sanding with a disk sander. Medium-grit abrasive is used first across the grain and then with the grain. The hollow is then smoothed with fine abrasive, the contact area of the disk traveling with the grain. Abrasive shaping methods should not be used, however, where they would remove the actual patina of age.

Before using any method intended to approximate authenticity, it is advisable, if possible, to examine a genuine antique of the same type. The surface can then be treated to resemble actual texture and wear patterns as exactly as possible.

Fir panel was antiqued by first scorching with a propane torch, then scoring with a stiff wire brush along the grain. Next came a deep brown stain and sealer. Finish is clear lacquer.

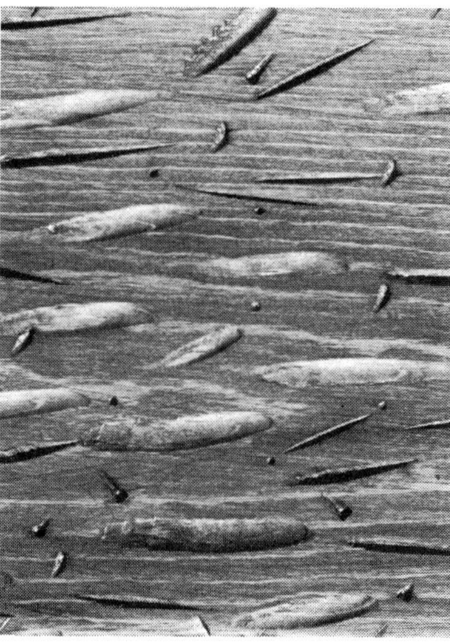

Pine was distressed with a dog chain and the edge of a hammer. Additional marks were made with chisel and gouge. Next step was staining and sealing. Finish is good for ceiling beams.

Fir plywood was given a sealer, then a heavy coat of white lacquer. After three minutes of drying, a wire brush was used to make striations. Gray paint was brushed into grooves the next day.

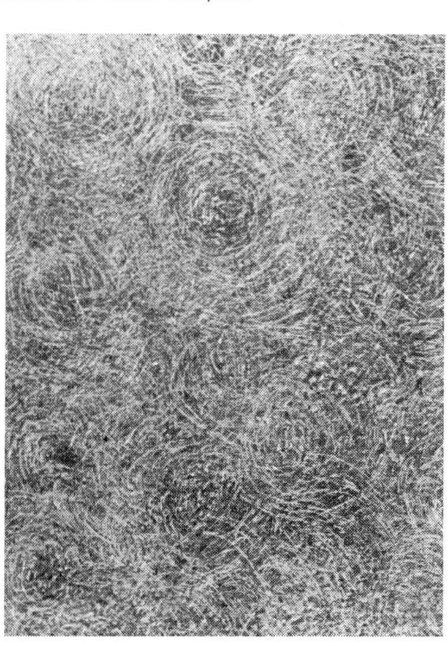

Birch panel was distressed with a group of nails held with a rubber band and applied in a random pattern. After distressing, wood was hand sanded, stained, sealed, and then varnished.

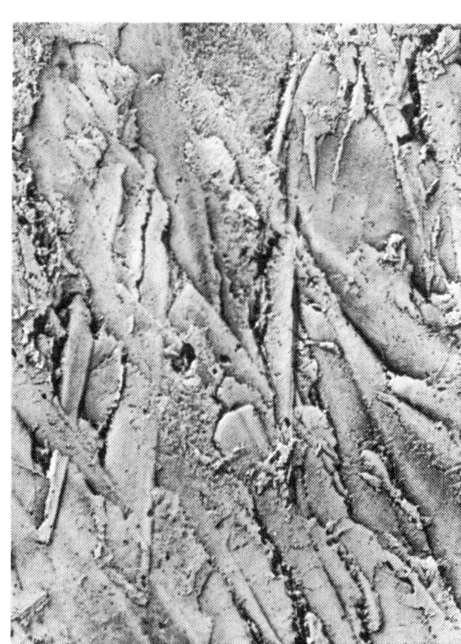

Plaster, water, and white glue, ¼-in. thick; marks made with sponge and knife. After setting, walnut stain was applied and wiped off, a green stain brushed on high spots. Finish is lacquer.

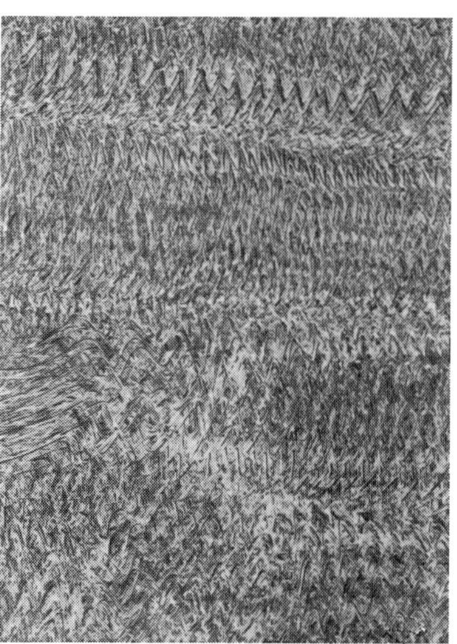

"Frostiquing" is done by first applying a base coat of light paint. Then a contrasting coat is applied. A sponge, steel wool, or a brush is used to make designs before paint sets.

Achieving surface effects

Flake patterns

A wide variety of color combinations is available in flake-pattern finishing systems. Originally introduced for floors, these epoxy-based formulas are also widely used to produce colorful and extremely durable table and counter tops. Typically, the application begins with spreading by roller the mixed two-part epoxy base coat on the prepared surface. In water-base types, the base coat is first sprayed with a water mist, as from a garden or insecticide spray. The system's color chips are then scattered like confetti and again mist-sprayed. After overnight drying, loose chips are brushed off and the fixed chips given a sealer coat. After this dries, final glaze coats are applied. The result: Sparkling color patterns embedded in glass-like plastic.

Marbleizing

An attractive marble-like look can be produced on appropriate cabinet work areas with "marbleizer" paints. One of the easiest to use is applied with a vacuum-cleaner attachment that sprays the contrasting marble streaks in realistic patterns over a base coat. (The attachment comes with the marbleizing kit.) Made in seven different color combinations, this type of finish has been in use for many years, originally on walls. A clear coating is also available for added protection of the marbleized surface where this is required. Take the usual care not to spray over nearby objects.

Tiger-striped fir

Accentuated, the natural grain of fir plywood can be a decorative feature. First saturate the surface with an aniline dye of any desired brilliant color that contrasts with the deeper-toned veins of the plywood grain. The dye will soak into the more porous lighter areas (the summer growth). Wipe the plywood surface after a few minutes to remove as much dye as possible from the surface of the less porous areas. When the plywood is dry, sand it with fine sandpaper. Object: To remove any surface dye from the hard-grain surfaces. This increases the contrast greatly, as the porous areas are then deep-dyed. Remove the resulting dust with a cloth, then a tack rag. Follow with a clear wood finish. Use two or more coats to produce a smooth luster.

Fabric dyes

By using ordinary aniline fabric dyes as wood stains, you can coordinate colors of modern cabinet woodwork with upholstery and draperies. As the final color varies with the type of wood, and some types of fabric, experimental applications (including the final finish) are essential. Intensity of the color on wood can be controlled by the concentration of dye in the water-mix and by the number of applications. Follow the manufacturer's instructions regarding fabric dyeing. Mix the dye with very hot water and apply with brush or pad to the wood, using rubber gloves (with pad application) to keep color off the hands. After the dye has dried, smooth any raised grain by very light sanding with a fine sandpaper, and apply a clear wood finish.

Multicolor paints

Multicolor paints that create the effect of a solid color speckled with a contrasting color, are available in about a dozen combinations. They can be applied in one step by spray or special roller, depending on brand. One special advantage they offer: Avoiding color-match problems, as in coordinating new units with an existing room finish that can no longer be obtained. Their camouflage effect also conceals minor surface flaws. Prepare the surface for them in the usual manner. Vacuum-cleaner spray attachments are available from manufacturers; some others call for a conventional spray gun.

Textured surfacing

Where a textured surface is desired for decorative effect or concealment of surface flaws, a "sand" paint is commonly used, containing fine mineral particles. It is applied like conventional paint, but stirred often to keep the particles in suspension. Many latex-type paints can be given a similar texture by mixing in cornmeal thoroughly before application. Because of variations in paint chemistry, a small sample should be mixed first, applied to scrap, and allowed to dry as a test. For bold patterns and maximum concealment of surface flaws, a cellulose sponge is often worked against the texture-painted surface with a rotary motion to create closely spaced swirl patterns. The size of the sponge determines the pattern size.

Metallic tones

Painted furniture may be decorated with metallic-tone designs by several methods. The simplest uses metallic paints, available in gold, bronze, silver, and even chrome. Pencil the designs on the surface to be decorated, using stencils, and apply the metallic paint with an artist's brush. For certain traditional effects, use dry powdered metal and a sand-filled velvet "pouncing" bag. In this method, you apply varnish to the area to be decorated, let it become tacky, and press a waxed-paper stencil on it. Pat the bag first in the powder, then on the tacky varnish in the stencil's open area to deposit the powder. Wipe excess powder from stencil, then lift it off. When the original varnish hardens, coat the entire design area with varnish.

Glitter

Called "glitter" by many paint dealers, the sparkling particles often seen on holiday decorations and musical instrument stands may also be used on game room accessories such as dart boards, and on children's furniture and toys. An easy way to apply the material is by sprinkling it on the tacky surface of a freshly applied finish, usually a contrasting color. For even distribution, use a salt shaker as a dispenser (with holes suited to particle size) held a few feet above the tacky surface, if it is horizontal. Glitter can be blown by a vacuum cleaner's outlet air stream on vertical surfaces.

Wood-grain simulations

A natural-looking wood grain can be simulated artificially on wood or metal surfaces by means of a simple two-step procedure. The materials, often sold in kit form, consist of a base coating, graining "glaze," and brushes, and sometimes a special "graining pad." Colors as well as natural wood tones are available. Apply the base coat to the surface (which may be painted or varnished) and let it dry. Then apply the graining glaze. A fairly stiff brush or a graining pad (depending on the kit) may be used to form the streaks that are characteristic of wood grain. Either allows the base coat to show through. Straight or wavy grain patterns are easily imitated. Experiment with the procedure on scrap for different effects before beginning the actual job.

section 12:

Metals: How to use them in home repair

Metals are second only to wood in their incidence in home repair. Certain procedures—filing, sawing, drilling, for example—work with either. But metals have very different physical characteristics and must be handled accordingly. To work with them successfully, you must know the significance of brittleness, ductility, malleability; when and how to anneal, temper, solder, weld. The section that follows is a short course in metals in general and as they relate to home repair.

contents

Working with metals

Metalwork terms

Alloy: Combination of two or more metals, usually a fine and a baser metal. Chromium steel, nickel steel, and tungsten steel are examples of ferrous alloys; brass, bronze, and pewter, of nonferrous alloys.
Annealing: Gradual heating and cooling of metal in order to reduce brittleness.
Brittleness: The quality of being fragile or breakable; for example, glass, some cast iron, hardened steel.
Brazing (hard soldering): Joining of two or more pieces of metal by means of an alloy, or "spelter," and heat.
Case hardening (carburizing): Hardening the surface of low carbon steel.
Chasing: Ornamenting metal by indenting the outline of a design. (See **Repoussé.**)
Coloring: Using heat and/or chemicals to change the surface color of metals.
Conductivity: Ability to carry heat or electrical current.
Corrosion resistance: Ability to withstand the oxidation and other chemical action of metals that is caused by contact and chemical union with oxygen and dampness.
Ductility: Ability of a metal to be drawn out into a wire.
Elasticity: Ability of a metal to return to original form after being bent or twisted.
Etching: The cutting action of an acid through lines scratched with a needle on a wax-coated surface.
Ferrous metals: Composed mainly of iron with small amounts of other metals or substances added. Examples are cast iron, wrought iron, mild steel, carbon steel. Nonferrous metals contain little if any iron. Examples are aluminum, brass, bronze, copper, gold, lead, nickel, pewter, tin, zinc.
Fusibility: Ability to join with other metals after being melted by heat.
Galvanizing: Depositing a zinc coating on iron or steel.
Hardness: Resistance to being dented or penetrated.
Heat treatment: Heating or cooling ferrous metals, such as steel, to bring them to their highest efficiency.
Lapping: The fine finishing of external or internal surfaces by hand or machine.
Magnetic: Containing forces of attraction and repulsion.
Malleability: Capable of being hammered, rolled, or bent without breaking or cracking.
Planishing: Hammering or rolling metal in order to make its surface smooth.
Repoussé: Working up a design from the reverse side of thin metal. (See **Chasing.**)
Saw piercing: Cutting out a design in the interior of a sheet of metal with a jeweler's saw.
Soldering: Joining two pieces of metal by means of another metal or alloy, generally a combination of lead and tin. Heat, applied with a soldering iron or flame, is required.
Spinning: Pressure applied to thin sheet metal, while it is rotating in a lathe, to form bowl-shaped articles.
Sweating: The process of heating and joining two tinned metal parts without the use of a soldering iron.
Tensile strength: The resistance of a particular material to longitudinal pull.
Toughness: Resistance to forces that tend to break, bend, stretch, or crack.
Welding: Metals united by heat and pressure to make them melt and blend.

Types of metals

IRON

Pure iron: Silvery white metal, one of the chemical elements; high in malleability, ductility, and tenacity; too soft for most industrial work.
Pig iron: After impurities are burned out of iron ore in a blast furnace, the melted iron is poured into iron or sand molds to form pigs, or bars, each weighing approximately 100 pounds.
Cast iron: Pig iron remelted and poured into molds of various shapes for machine parts or such other objects as heating radiators or hydrants; contains 3.0 to 5.0 percent carbon; is very brittle and breaks easily.
Malleable iron: Cast iron that has had some of its carbon burned out so that its structure is changed from granular to fibrous; not only malleable but also strong, tough, and soft; used to advantage in parts that are subject to shock, such as farm tools and railroad equipment.
Wrought iron: Pig iron purified by the removal of most of its carbon and foreign elements. (Today's wrought iron furniture is usually made of mild steel.)

CARBON STEEL

Low carbon steel: Contains .05 to .30 percent carbon; also known as mild, machine, or machinery steel; its rather soft, tough, malleable, and ductile characteristics make it suitable for rivets, chains, screws, nails, and low strength machine parts, and as a replacement for wrought iron; may be welded.
Medium carbon steel: Contains .30 to .70 percent carbon; somewhat stronger than low carbon steel; is used to make bolts, crankshafts, axles, hammers, screwdrivers, and similar items.
High carbon steel: Contains .70 to 1.55 percent carbon; known also as tool steel or carbon tool steel; can be hardened to a brittle state when made red-hot, then suddenly quenched in water or oil (the higher the carbon content and the faster the cooling, the harder the resulting metal); used for such tools as drills, taps, dies, files, and cold chisels, as well as for springs, needles, ball bearings, and razors.
Drill rod: High grade of carbon steel produced in short lengths that are accurately ground to standard sizes for use in making small cutting tools, punches, and other articles that require strength and hardness. These may also be obtained in high-speed steel.

ALLOY STEEL

(The classification "alloy steel" comprises steels to which one or more metals have been added to give them, when they are properly heat-treated, characteristics that are desirable in certain applications.)
Manganese steel: Extremely hard, usually cast into other form for wearing parts on such equipment as rock or ore crushers.
Nickel steel: Has great strength plus a high degree of elasticity and ductility; used for armor plate, marine shafting, axles, and wire cables.
Vanadium steel: Ability to resist shocks makes it desirable for springs, car axles, and gears.
Chrome-vanadium steel: Used for parts which must be strong and tough but not brittle.
Nickel-chromium steel: Has great strength, hardness, and ductility; used for armor plate and automobile parts.
Tungsten steel: Self-hardening; used in tools made for cutting metals at high speeds.
Tungsten carbide: Nearly as hard as diamond; will cut up to four times faster than high-speed steel.
Molybdenum ("Molly") steel: Stands heat and blows; used to make roller and ball bearings and very fine wire.
Chromium steel: Used for safes; also the basis for noncorrosive stainless steel.

NONFERROUS METALS

Aluminum: Metal made from bauxite ore; too soft in its pure state for most commercial uses but ideal for a wide variety of applications when combined with other metals to produce an alloy.
Copper: One of the most useful of all metals; long-lasting; good conductor of heat and electricity; malleable and ductile; when hardened by hammering may be annealed by heating, then suddenly quenched in water (the opposite of annealing steel).
Gold: Heavy, lustrous, yellow, precious metal; harder than lead but softer than silver or copper; generally mixed with copper, silver, or other metal to make costume jewelry and other articles in which the use of pure gold is not practical.
Lead: Found in the form of lead ore; a soft metal used primarily for white lead (in paints), also for batteries, pipes, and sheet roofing.
Magnesium: In pure form burns easily and must be handled with care; this difficulty overcome when properly combined with aluminum, copper, or other metals.
Nickel: Noncorrosive, highly magnetic metal (next to cobalt and iron); used for plating iron and brass; also used under chromium plating.
Silver: Best conductor of electricity and heat; very soft, malleable, white metal; made from silver ore.
Tin: Primarily used to make tin plate (hot sheet steel coated with melted tin); also used in many alloys.
Zinc: Used in paint manufacture and many alloys; also as rust-resistant coating on iron and steel (galvanizing).

ALLOYS

An aluminum alloy may contain one or more other metals to improve its physical properties. The first digit of its coded number indicates the main alloying element as follows: 1, pure aluminum; 2, copper; 3, manganese; 4, silicon; 5, magnesium; 6, magnesium and silicon; 7, zinc; 8, other elements; 9, special.
Babbitt: Noted for its anti-friction qualities; contains tin, antimony, and copper, occasionally some lead.
Brass: Contains copper and zinc; may be made harder by addition of some tin.
Bronze: Harder than brass, made of copper and tin; may also contain some zinc.
German (or nickel) silver: Contains copper, zinc, nickel.
Green gold: Made of gold, silver, copper.
Monel metal: Composed mainly of nickel and copper.
Pewter (Britannia metal): Contains tin, antimony, copper.
Sterling: Silver with a small amount of copper added to make it harder.
White gold: Has from 15 to 20 percent nickel combined with the gold.

Layout tools and their uses

Laying out is the preliminary marking of lines, circles, arcs, and centers on the surface of metal as a guide for a metalwork project. The surface is often coated with a marking solution so that the lines of the layout can be seen more clearly.

Steel rules, available in various lengths, are used for linear measuring, for testing plane surfaces, and for marking straight lines. These guidelines are drawn, or scratched, with a **scriber** (sometimes referred to as a metalworker's pencil), a steel instrument that has a sharp point at one end and frequently a point bent at a right angle at the other. The bent point is used to mark lines that are out of reach of the straight end.

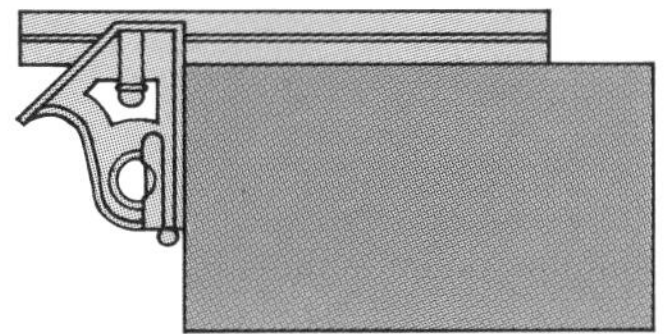

Using a square to check the squareness of a plate

When the lines are to be drawn at an angle of 90 degrees, a **square** (also used for testing) should be used. If it is a **combination set,** it may also be used to lay out and measure angles (same as a **protractor**) and find the center of a circle. These lines may also be scribed accurately with a **combination bevel** after the angle has been located.

The spring-type **divider,** the kind most commonly used, is a two-legged instrument with hardened points that is used for measuring or marking off short spaces, and for scribing small circles and parts of circles. In order to secure the leg of the divider, a very light center mark is made with a **prick punch** tapped lightly with a machinist's hammer. When the holes are to be drilled, the prick punch marks are enlarged with a **center punch.**

A more advanced layout might require the use of other tools such as an angle plate, hermaphrodite calipers, parallel clamps, parallels, spirit level, surface gauge, bench or surface plate, trammels, or V blocks. Trammels are used to lay out and measure circles that are too large to be managed with more limited dividers or compass. They can be used with beams of unlimited length.

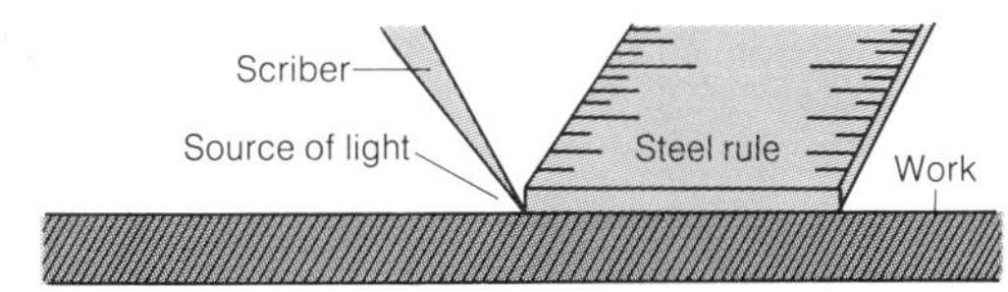

Scribe accurately by holding the scriber so its point draws a line along the lower edge of the steel rule.

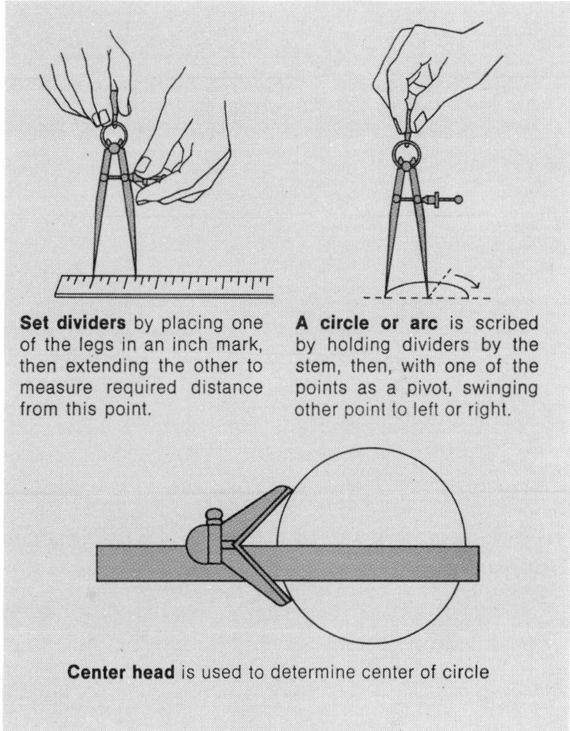

Set dividers by placing one of the legs in an inch mark, then extending the other to measure required distance from this point.

A circle or arc is scribed by holding dividers by the stem, then, with one of the points as a pivot, swinging other point to left or right.

Center head is used to determine center of circle

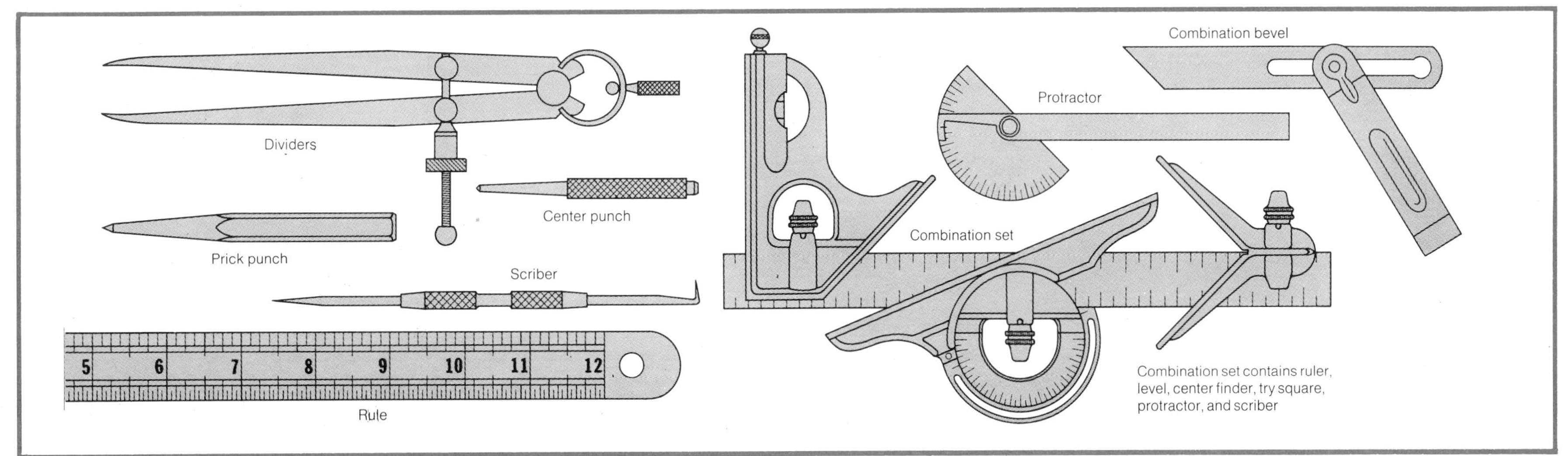

Combination set contains ruler, level, center finder, try square, protractor, and scriber

Filing techniques

Most files have cut teeth running in diagonal rows. Single-cut files with teeth in single diagonal rows are best for hard metals, and rasp-cut files, with individually formed teeth, for soft metals. The more teeth to the inch, the smoother the cut.

A file should have a handle to help prevent injury. Exceptions are such small files as needle or jeweler's, auger bit, and ignition files.

The work piece should be clamped tightly in a vise so it will not vibrate. If the piece has finished surfaces, protect them with soft vise-jaw caps. If possible, the work piece should be held at elbow level and should project slightly above the vise jaws.

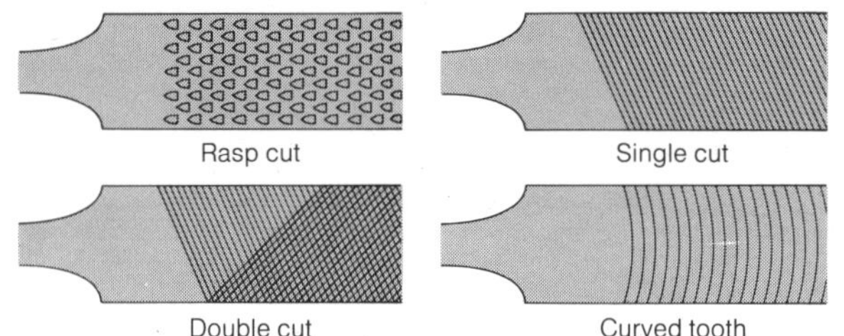

To begin operations, grasp the file handle in the right hand with palm down and thumb lengthwise along the handle. In normal work, hold the point or tip end with thumb on top and first two fingers of left hand below; for heavy work, place your entire palm on top of the file.

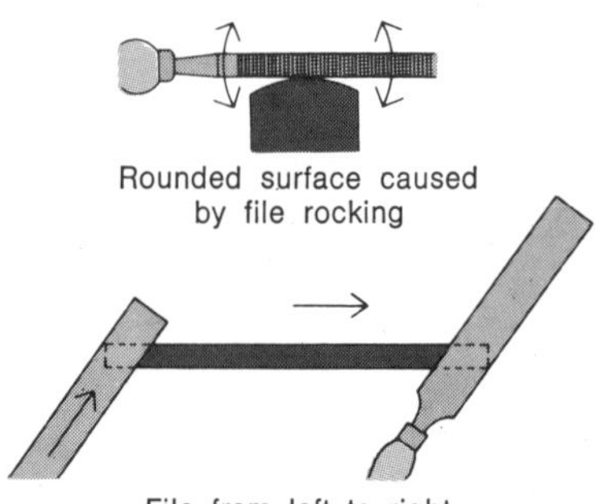

Rounded surface caused by file rocking

File from left to right

The file should be guided only by the hands and arms, with the body assuming the same stance as for sawing. Exert pressure on the full forward cutting stroke. Release the pressure, or lift the file free, on the return stroke. Do not move your body when making the stroke. This can rock the file, resulting in rounded edges instead of a completely flat surface.

Larger and coarser files should be used for rough cutting, finer files for finishing. When filing a wide, flat surface, it is advisable to start the stroke on the left side with the file held at about a 30-degree angle. Move it across the entire width of the work to finish the stroke, then reverse the angle and cross the stroke by filing from right to left. Test the results for accuracy with a straightedge and a square.

A very smooth surface is produced by **draw filing** with a single-cut (mill) file. A shearing cut is made by holding the file flat, at a slight angle, and with one hand on each side and quite near the work. As it is drawn back and forth, all cross-filing marks will be removed. A flat file may be used for draw filing all flat surfaces and outside curves but a round or half-round file must be used on inside curves.

Keep the file free from the chips and filings called "picks" or "pins"—they will scratch the work. Go over a file frequently with a wire brush (file card) and remove picks with a pointed wire or small, thin piece of sheet metal. Rubbing chalk in the file's teeth before use will help keep it clean. Avoid tapping files on a metal or masonry surface to clean them.

Hold the file with both hands. Bear down on the forward stroke, relieve pressure on the return stroke.

Aluminum and other soft metals are best filed with a coarse, single-cut file. Use light pressure.

Test the accuracy of filing at frequent intervals, using a straightedge and a square against the work surface.

Draw filing gives a smooth surface after the metal has been cross-filed. Pull the file along the length of the work.

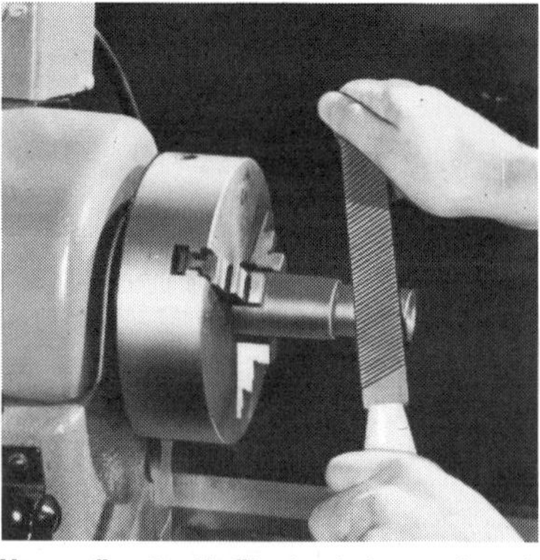

Use a fine-tooth file for lathe work; adjust lathe to moderately high speed. Hold file firmly in position shown.

Clean files regularly with a file card. Brush in the direction teeth are set to get rid of "pins" and "picks."

Filing techniques

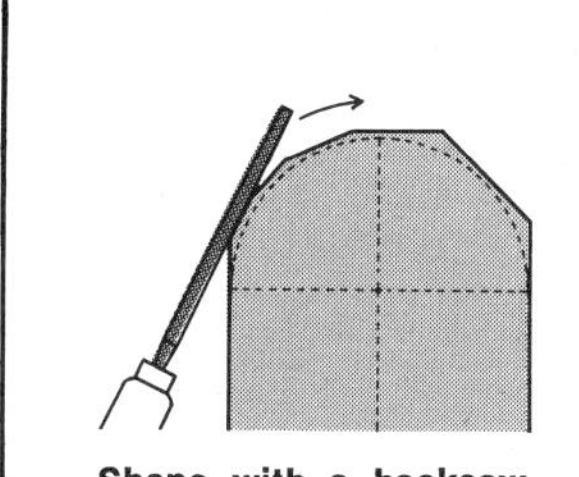

Shape with a hacksaw to outside layout lines, smooth with rough file.

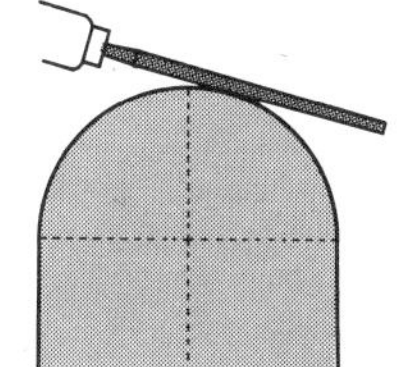

Use smooth file to obtain final finish, rocking it along curved edge.

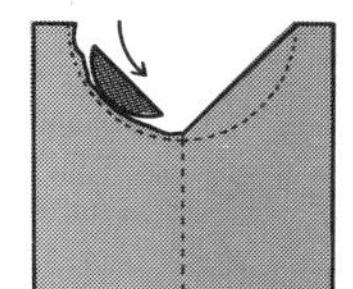

Cut V notch with hacksaw, then shape curve with half-round file.

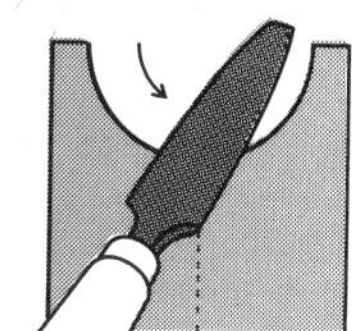

Finish with smooth file, following the curve on the forward stroke.

Finishing metals

It is desirable to polish metalwork to a high finish to remove all traces of surface irregularities. The work should first be filed smooth, then finished with an abrasive cloth or a light emery paper (p. 42). Use a power buffing wheel, or do it by hand.

The abrasive may be natural emery or an artificial one such as silicon carbide or aluminum oxide. For the initial polishing, select a grade that is coarse enough to have an effect on the metal surface. Then use progressively finer grades to remove the marks made by each preceding abrasive. Continue changing abrasives and rubbing until you reach the finest grade of cloth or the desired degree of polish.

To finish by hand, tear a strip from the sheet of abrasive wide enough to cover a solid backing, such as a file. Fold one end over the end of the file, then move the file back and forth across the work. With each change to a finer abrasive, shift the direction of polishing so it is at right angles to the direction of the polishing that preceded it.

To polish large, flat surfaces, cover a sanding block with the abrasive cloth.

Chisels

Cold chisels are forged from tool steel and used to cut or chip metal. Principal types are: **Flat cold chisel,** for cutting and shearing metal and cutting bars and rivets; **cape chisel,** for chipping narrow grooves such as for keyways in pulleys and shafts; **diamond point,** for cleaning out sharp corners and cutting V-shaped grooves; **round nose,** for cutting grooves and moving improperly started drill holes.

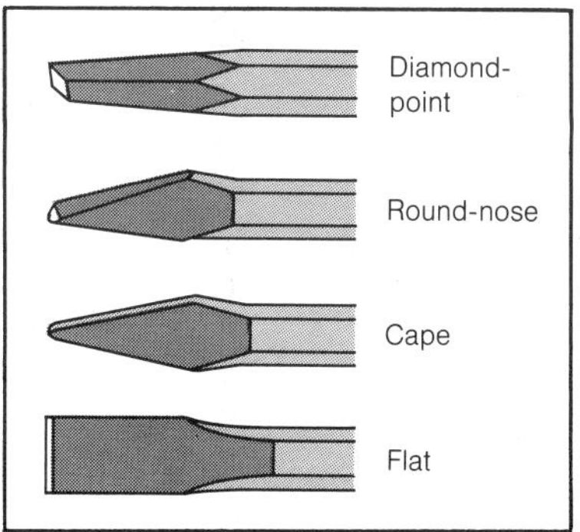

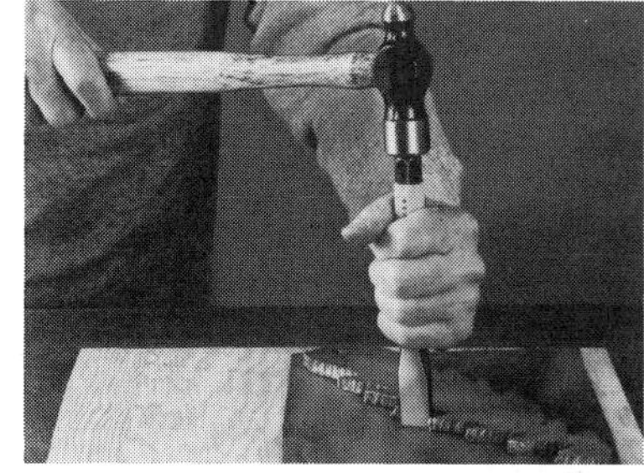

An inside design is cut by applying cutting edge of chisel to the metal inside layout lines, then smoothing with file.

Sheet metal too heavy for snips may be sheared off at the layout line with a chisel, while being held in a vise.

How to harden and temper tools

When a tool's cutting edge has lost its hardness because of excessive sharpening or overheating, it must be rehardened and retempered. Steel is rehardened by heating it to between 1350 and 1500 degrees F. At this temperature, chemical and structural changes take place. If the hot steel is cooled quickly in oil or water, these changes are trapped in its internal structure, making the steel fine-grained and very hard. In this state steel is too brittle for most purposes and must be tempered, that is, reheated to a moderate temperature and again quenched.

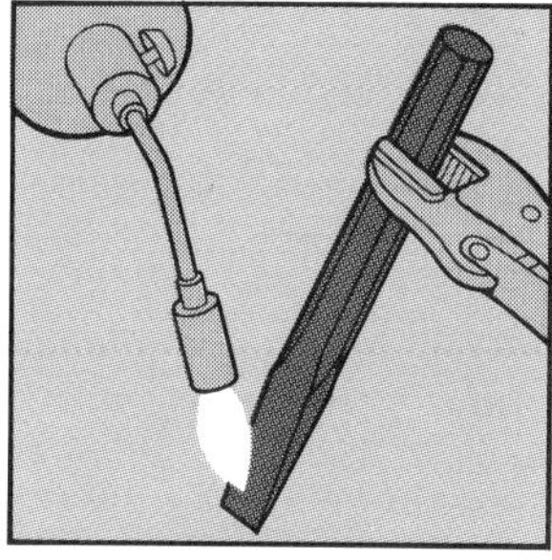

To harden such tools as cold chisels, wood chisels, or screwdrivers, heat 1″ of cutting end with a blowtorch until it turns bright red. Then immerse 2″ in cold water just long enough for the metal to cool to the touch. Remove, polish the end with an emery cloth, and wipe with an oily rag.

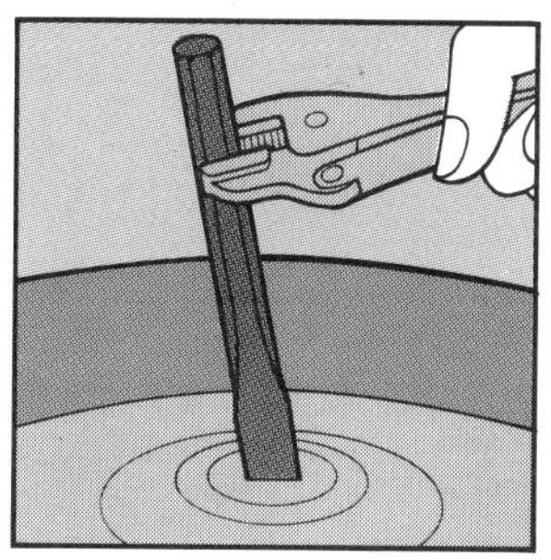

Tools become brittle when they are hardened; to correct this, they must be tempered. Heat the tool until it reaches the proper temperature, recognizable by a change in the color of the metal. The chart below tells you what color to watch for in various tools. When the color reaches the tip, quench the entire tool in water.

TEMPERING GUIDE

Color	Temp.	Tools
Faint yellow	420	Knives, hammers
Light yellow	440	Lathe tools, scrapers
Straw	460	Dies, punches, bits, reamers
Light brown	480	Twist drills, large taps
Dark brown	500	Axes, wood chisels, drifts
Purple	540	Cold chisels, center punches
Blue	560	Screwdrivers, springs, gears
Dark blue	600	Scrapers, spokeshaves

Locate the tool to be tempered in the chart above. After hardening, reheat the cutting end to the color shown; then quench to obtain the proper temper. If tool is not listed, follow instructions for one that does similar work.

Cutting metal

Tools and methods

The **hacksaw** is the tool most often used for cutting metals. It may have either a fixed or adjustable (8 to 12 inches) frame with a pistol grip or a straight handle. Blades are available in 8-, 10-, or 12-inch lengths, with standard or wavy set teeth 18, 24, or 32 to the inch. Blades on which only the teeth are hardened are sometimes called "unbreakable" or flexible. The hacksaw makes it possible to cut in any of four directions, down, up, right, or left, depending on how the blade is mounted in the frame. Regardless of how the blade is mounted, the teeth should point away from the handle so as to cut on the forward stroke.

Keyhole hacksaws (they come with a replaceable blade) are useful for making inside cuts in blind holes. Other hard-to-reach places can be handled by using a loose blade that has tape wrapped around one end for protection.

A rule for blade selection is that two or more teeth must always be in contact with the surface being sawed. This means that thin metal or tubing requires a fine blade. If it is not possible to apply this rule, for example, when cutting very thin metal, place the metal between two clamped boards. Both wood and metal will be sawed at the same time, and the metal kept from bending and tearing.

Pierced work in thin metals may be cut out by hand with metal-cutting blades in a jeweler's saw or in a scroll or jigsaw. Blades are also made for cutting metal with a portable saber saw.

Round holes may be cut in thin sheet metal with either a hole saw or a circle or fly cutter. Use these carefully—they can be dangerous. The circle or fly cutter is similar to the hole saw except that the hole is cut with a tool similar to a lathe bit, secured in a rod that can be adjusted to cut holes up to 8 inches in diameter.

Sheet metal of 20 gauge and lighter may also be cut with tinsnips. Tinsnips should never be used to cut wire, nails, or hardened steel.

The commonly used straight-pattern snips range in overall length from 8 to 15 inches, with cutting edges from 2 to 5 inches long. Snips of this type will follow a straight or curved line and will cut with maximum efficiency if opened as far as possible. More accurate work can be done on curves when scrap metal is removed to within ¼ inch of the layout line before the final cut is made.

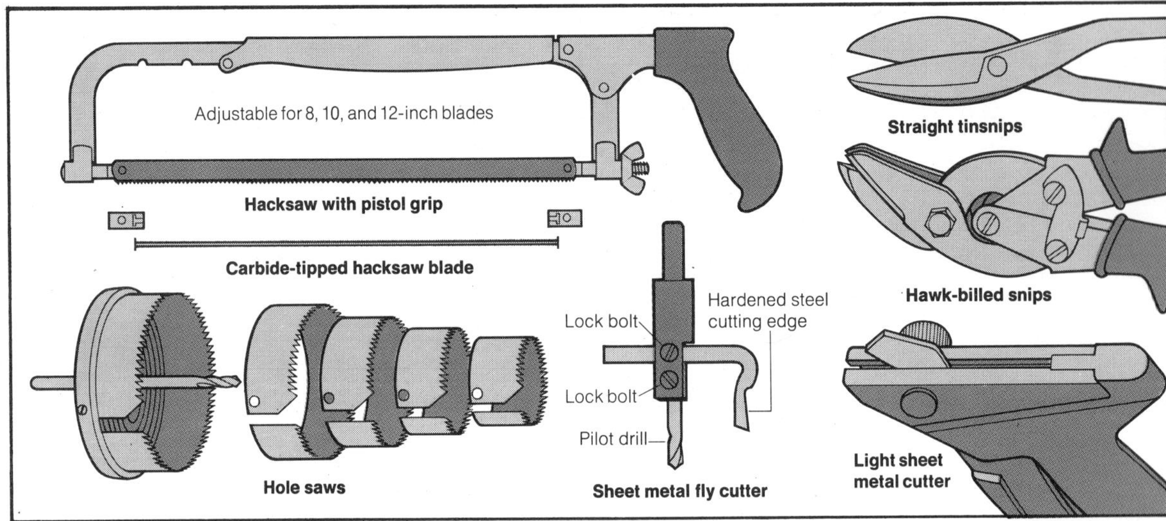

Tungsten carbide-tipped blade for use with hacksaw will cut glass, hardened steel, and ceramic tile.

The fly cutter makes holes in light gauge metal, is adjustable for holes up to 8 in. in diameter.

Hole saws vary in diameter from ¾ to 2½ in. They can be used on a drill press and electric drills.

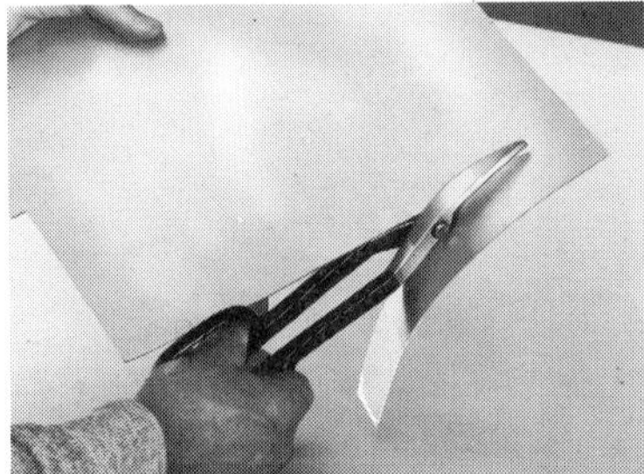

Upper blade of straight snips is kept over layout line; opening the jaws as wide as possible makes cutting easier.

Compound-action snips make it easy to cut such materials as sheet metal, vinyl tile, and air conditioning ducts.

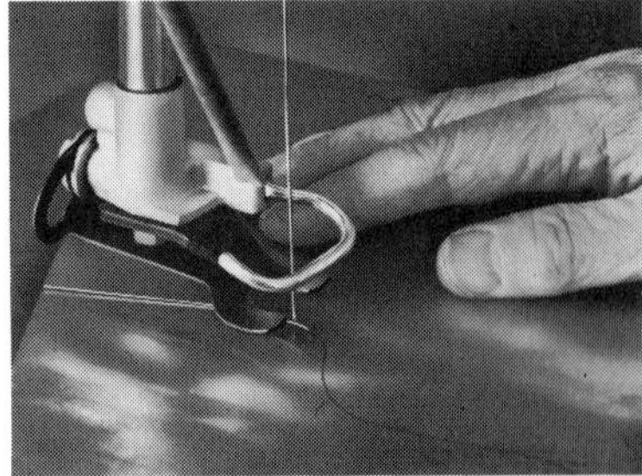

Scroll or jigsaw fitted with a metal-cutting blade permits accurate cuts to be made in thin sheet metals.

Types of drills

The **twist drill,** used for cutting holes in metal, may be made of either carbon or high-speed steel. It has three principal parts, a **shank,** a **body** with two spiral-like grooves called flutes, and a cone-shaped cutting end called the **point.**

The **flutes** act as channels for the escape of metal chips from the hole that is being drilled and permit the lubricant to travel down to the cutting edges at the point.

The **cutting lips** of most drills are ground to equal length at an angle of 59 degrees. The trailing lip must have clearance so the leading lip can cut into the metal. When sharpening is necessary, it is advisable to use a drill grinding attachment (p. 41) rather than attempt to do the sharpening freehand.

A **countersink** is a tool used to enlarge and bevel the end of a drilled hole so that when a flathead rivet, bolt, or screw is inserted, the head will be flush with the surface of the work.

Though not strictly drills, a **burring reamer,** to remove burrs from cut pipe, and a **taper reamer,** to increase the size of holes, are handy to have.

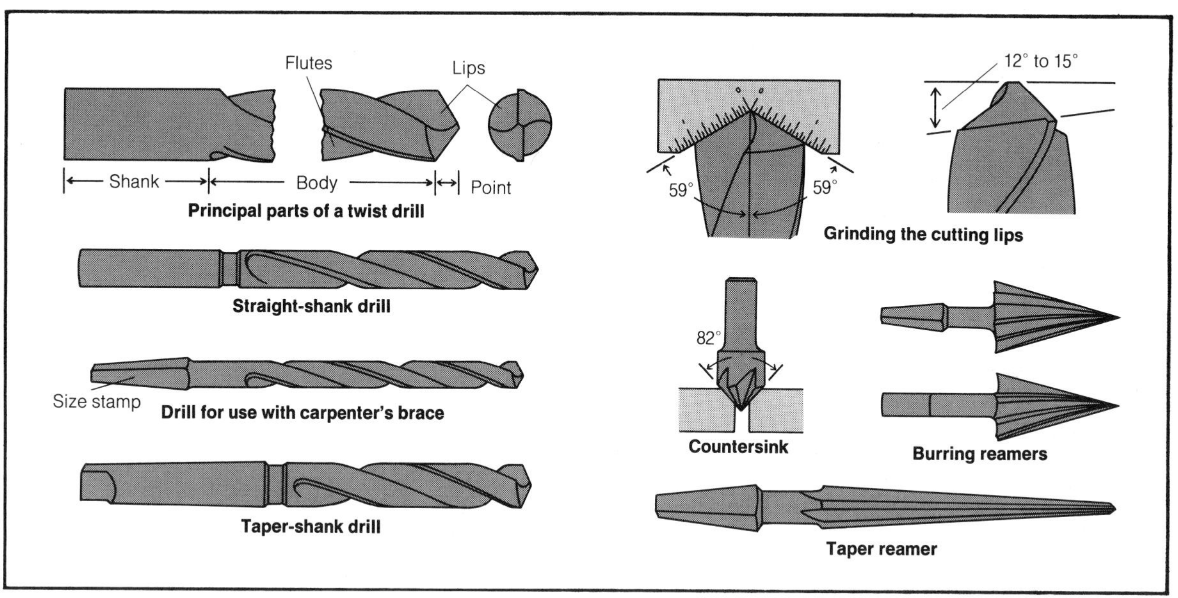

Principal parts of a twist drill

Straight-shank drill

Drill for use with carpenter's brace

Taper-shank drill

Grinding the cutting lips

Countersink

Burring reamers

Taper reamer

How to drill accurately

A small indentation to guide the drill should be made with a center punch at the exact location for a hole. If this mark proves not to be correctly located, it can be moved by slanting the punch, that is, relocating it in the exact spot, then straightening the punch and enlarging the mark.

The work should be secured in a vise or clamp, the rotating drill placed over the center punch mark, and a slight cone-shaped cut made to see if the hole is on center. If it is, the drilling can be completed. Ease up on drilling pressure just before the drill breaks through the work. This will keep the bit from grabbing and jamming.

Use a light oil to lubricate the drill bit when drilling wrought iron or steel. On aluminum, use kerosene or turpentine. Cast iron, copper, brass, bronze, and babbit may be drilled dry.

Feed and speed are essential when drilling metal. Feed should be constant and as fast as the drill will cut the metal. Speed must be varied with the material and the size of the drill. As a general rule, the larger the drill, the slower the speed; the smaller the drill, the faster the speed.

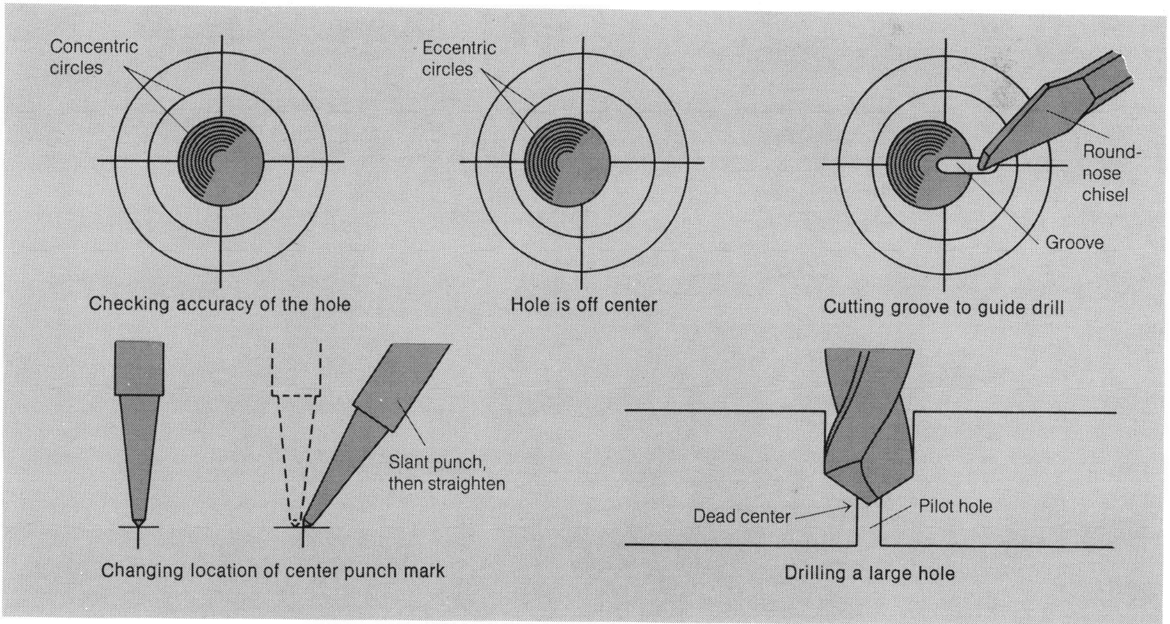

Checking accuracy of the hole

Hole is off center

Cutting groove to guide drill

Changing location of center punch mark

Drilling a large hole

Cutting internal threads

The tool for cutting a thread inside a hole is called a tap. Taps are made from a round bar of hardened steel, ground square on one end and threaded for part of its length on the other. On the threaded portion are several parallel grooves called **flutes,** one edge of each forming a cutting edge.

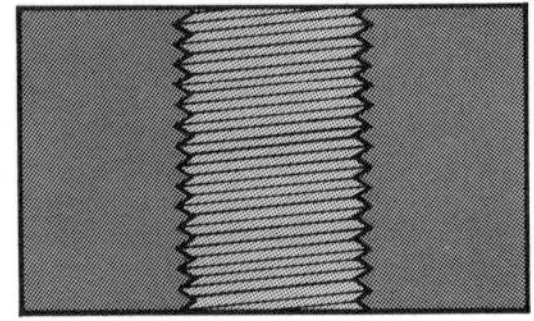
Fully tapped hole

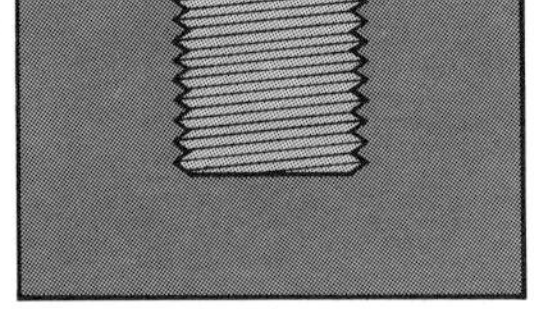
Closed, or blind, hole

Taps are usually one of three types: **Taper, plug,** or **bottoming.** Approximately the first six threads of the taper tap are tapered for easy starting. In the plug tap, the one most commonly used, the first three or four are tapered. The untapered bottoming tap is used to cut full threads to the bottom of a hole. Tap size (outside diameter and number of threads per inch) is stamped on the shank.

To cut internal threads, drill a hole slightly smaller than the tap's outside diameter. For drill size, see table below. Secure the work with hole vertical or horizontal, whichever is most convenient.

When the hole is drilled completely through, or partially through, as in a closed or blind hole, insert the tap and check that it is square with the work surface. If the tap is large, use a wrench to turn it. Small taps are turned with a special tap wrench.

The slight downward pressure needed at the start should be released once the tap threads begin to bite. Lubricate the work with lightweight oil; reverse the tap every two or three turns to clear metal shavings. Continue threading in and out of the hole until the tap turns smoothly with little pressure.

When threading a blind hole, use a taper tap until it touches the bottom, then change to a plug. Complete the thread with a bottoming tap.

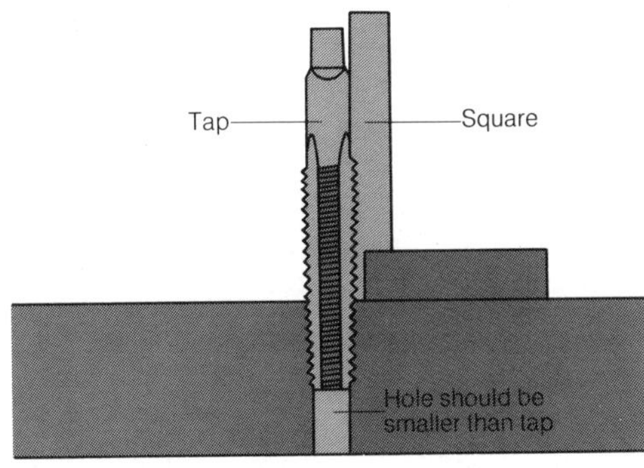

Tap must be square with work

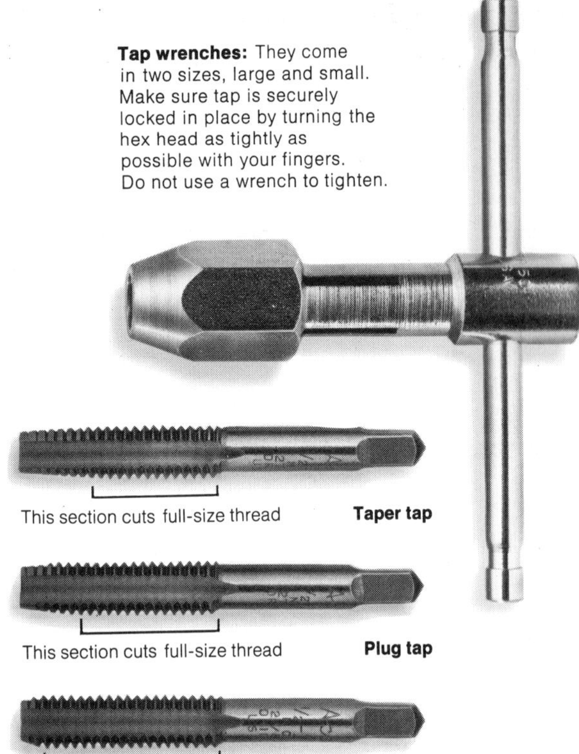

Tap wrenches: They come in two sizes, large and small. Make sure tap is securely locked in place by turning the hex head as tightly as possible with your fingers. Do not use a wrench to tighten.

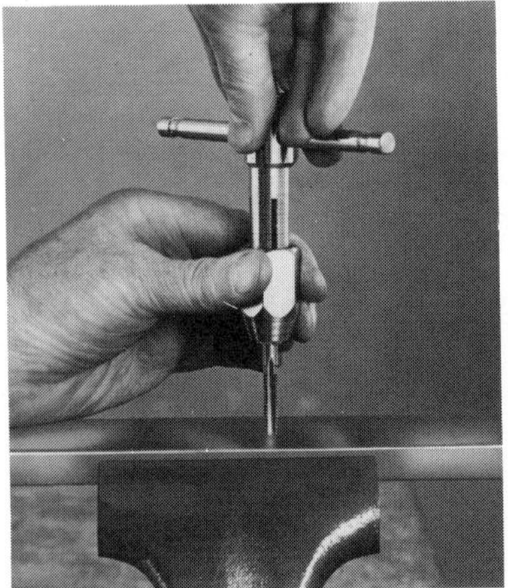
A small tap wrench is used to turn a small tap when cutting a thread on the inside of a hole in metal.

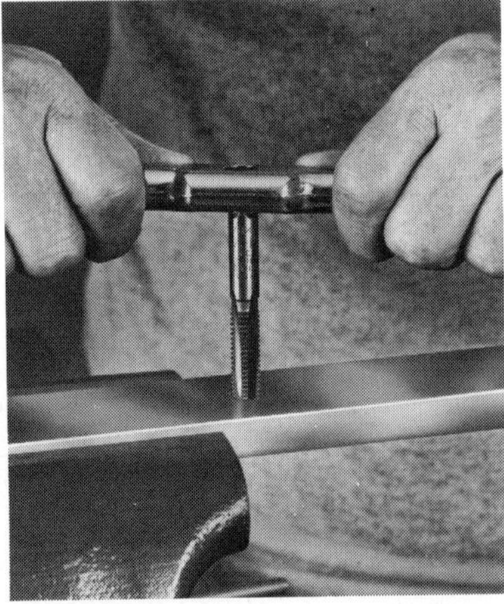
If the tap is large, a two-handled tap wrench is used for turning. Be sure the tap is at right angles to the work.

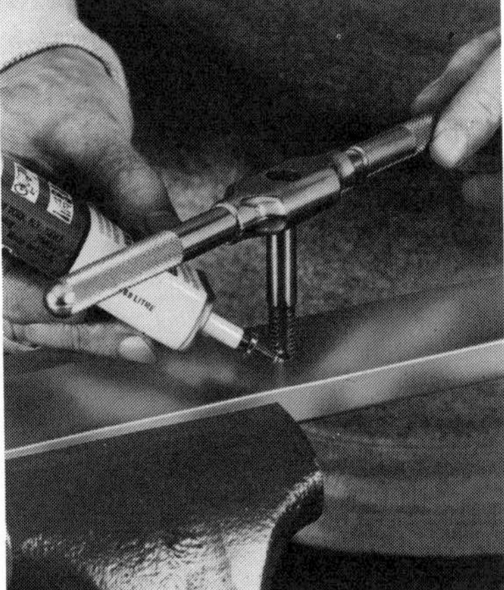
Light oil applied to the tap will help in cutting the thread. Reverse every two or three turns to remove chips.

TAP DRILL CHART

Bolt size		Drill size	Bit size
6–32	NC	35	7/64
8–32	NC	29	9/64
10–24	NC	25	5/32
12–24	NC	16	3/16
1/4–20	NC	7	13/64
1/4–28	NF	3	7/32
5/16–24	NC	F	17/64
3/8–16	NC	5/16	
3/8–24	NF	21/64	
1/2–13	NC	27/64	
1/2–20	NF	29/64	

To check threads per inch, lay the bolt along a rule and count the grooves in one inch. The most common thread standard is the American National—NC standing for **coarse** and NF for **fine.** Most home workshop tap and die sets produce both types to that standard.

Cutting external threads

Die cutting is the term that describes the method of cutting a thread around the outside of a piece of metal such as a long bolt, pipe, or rod. This is done by hand in a manner similar to the procedure followed when cutting an internal thread with a tap but using, in this case, a die.

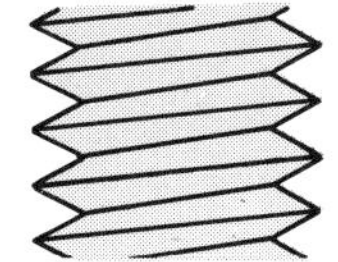
Dies cut external threads

A threading die is a block of very hard steel, round, square, or hexagonal in shape, with internal threads provided with flutes which form cutting edges. These threads are ground away slightly on one side to make starting easier.

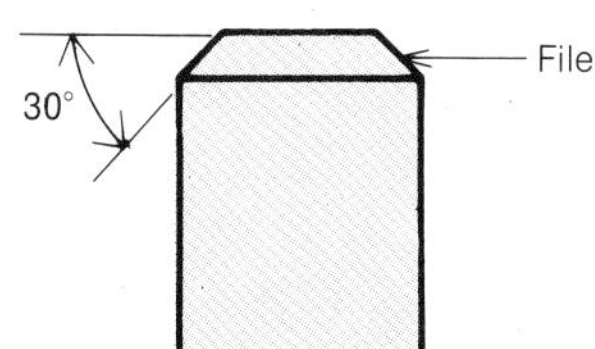

Bevel before threading

The most useful dies for the homeowner are those that cut threads on stock measuring 3/16, 1/4, 5/16, 3/8, and 1/2 inch. The die you select depends on the thread to be cut, the number and kind (fine or coarse) of threads per inch, and the diameter to be threaded.

To use a die, first grind a slight bevel on the edge of the pipe or rod to be threaded, then clamp the work in a vise, vertically or horizontally, beveled end up. Fasten the die in a diestock or holder and place it squarely over the end of the work. Applying downward pressure, turn the stock slowly to the right until the threads catch. After three or four threads have been cut, remove the diestock and check to be sure the threads are perfectly formed and the die is cutting square.

Keep the threads moist with oil and continue with the threading. Once the thread has been started, the downward pressure is no longer needed; the die will continue cutting on its own. Back off after each half turn to release the metal chips.

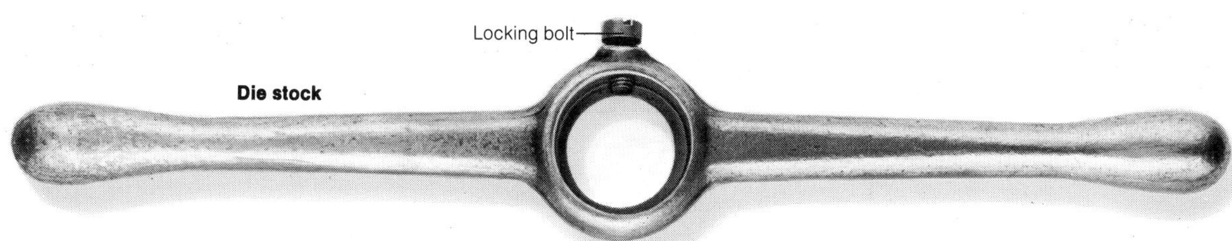

Adjustable die: These dies have a recessed adjusting bolt so threads can be cut slightly undersize or oversize

Solid die: Inexpensive solid dies, called button dies, are 1-in. wide. They will thread rods up to ½-in. diameter

Hexagonal die: These are also used for restoring damaged threads. Hex shape allows them to be driven in cramped quarters with a wrench

Use a file to make a bevel on round bar stock before starting the threading operation to help get die started.

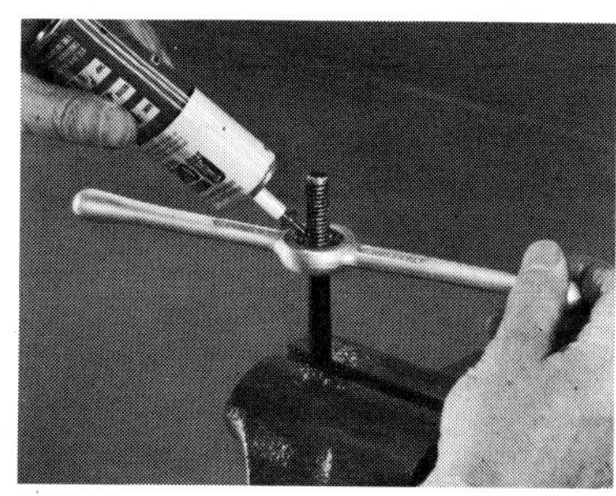
Apply a light oil to the die during the cutting operation. Back off die every half turn to remove chips.

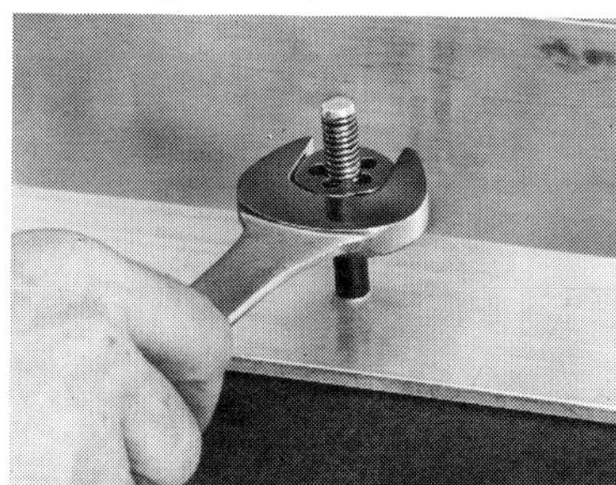
Open-end wrench can be used to turn a hex-shaped die. Wrench is handy to use when working in close quarters.

Bolt extractors

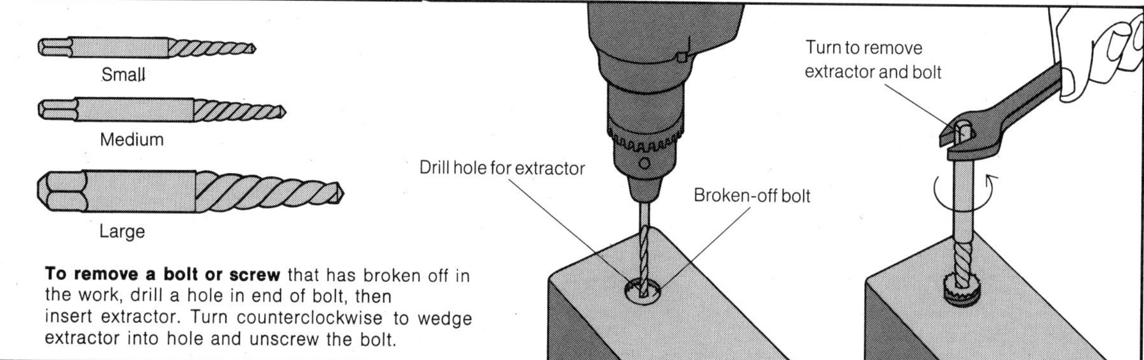

To remove a bolt or screw that has broken off in the work, drill a hole in end of bolt, then insert extractor. Turn counterclockwise to wedge extractor into hole and unscrew the bolt.

Riveting

Types of rivets

One of the most useful if often overlooked items for the home workshop is the rivet, a bolt-like fastener that joins pieces firmly and simply, quickly and inexpensively—primarily pieces of metal, but plastics, wood, canvas, and leather as well.

In form, a rivet is a soft metal pin with a head and shank—a sort of short bolt without threads. It may be made of any of a number of metals, such as iron, brass, copper, or aluminum.

The majority of rivets are solid but some, made for special purposes, may be hollow or tubular. Those of thin metals or soft materials are reinforced with a washer-type device called a burr that is placed over the rivet before the head is formed.

Large rivets of the kind used on boiler, structural, or other heavy work must be heated and the point or new head formed while the metal is hot. Such rivets shrink as they cool, forming an even tighter joint.

Rivet size classification includes both diameter and length. On rivets designed to be set in a countersunk hole, the length measurement includes the head.

Whatever the size or kind of rivet to be used, it should extend 1½ times the rivet diameter beyond the pieces to be riveted for the formation of the head. If it is too long, it should be cut shorter.

Roundhead

Flathead

Countersunk

Bifurcated

Stem allowance needed to form a countersunk head is equal to diameter of rivet.

Allowance needed to form a round head is 1½ times the diameter of the rivet.

Spacing between two rows of adjacent rivets should always be staggered.

Pop rivets

A device known as a **pop,** or **blind riveter** will install and set rivets without the use of a tool to support the work. Rivets made of aluminum, copper, monel, or steel are available for the device. Each rivet has a pin, or mandrel, which is automatically broken off, removed, and discarded after the rivet has been set.

The stem of the rivet is inserted in the tool and placed through the hole. As the tool is squeezed, the mandrel draws the concealed end of the rivet back, expands it to completely fill the hole, then breaks off as soon as the head is formed.

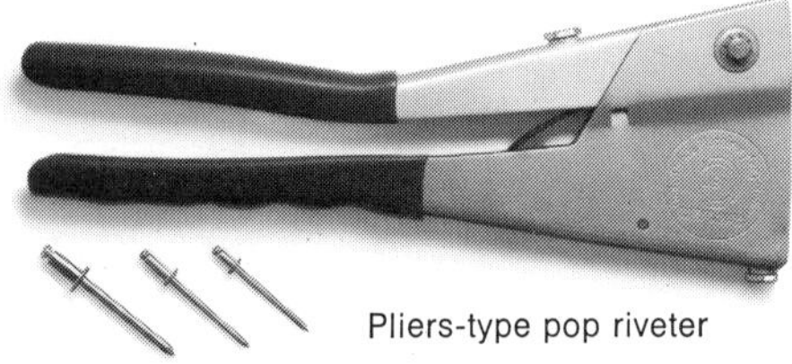

Pliers-type pop riveter

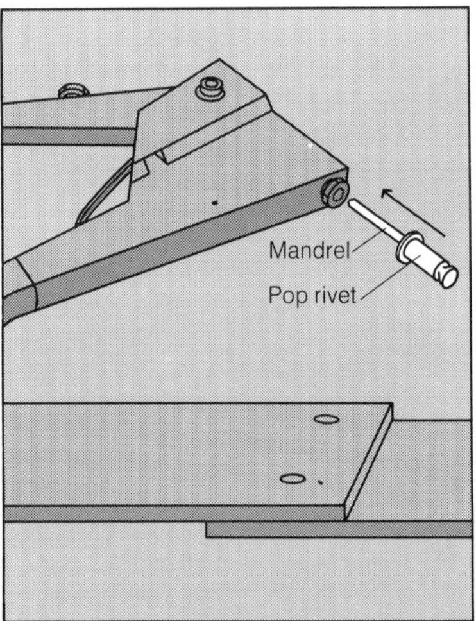

Select proper size rivet and drill holes. Insert mandrel into setting tool.

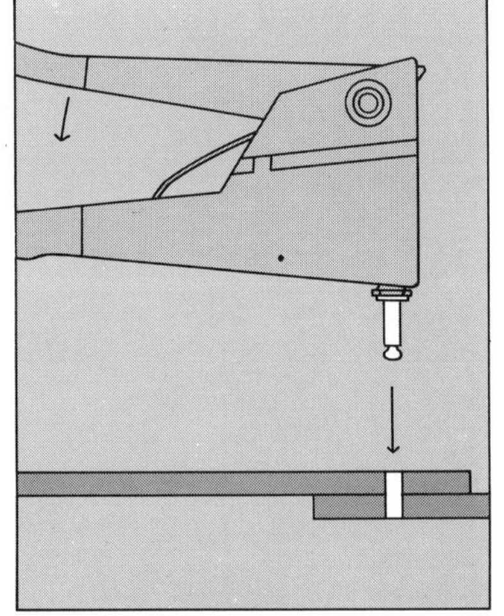

Apply enough pressure on tool handle to hold pop rivet. Insert rivet in hole.

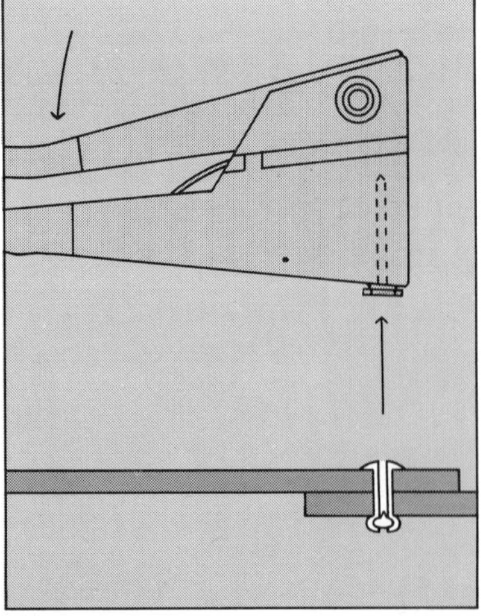

Squeeze handle. Mandrel breaks and rivet is set when handle is released.

Using a rivet set

A rivet set is a short length of hardened tool steel. One end, which is called the face, contains a hollow, or cupped depression, that is used to form a head, or point, on a rivet. Also in the face, at the bottom, is a deep hole. The hole is placed over the rivet shank and the rivet set struck with a hammer. This serves to flatten the metal around the rivet and draw the work together. Rivet sets come in many sizes to fit rivets of different diameters. In a pinch, you can cut off the end of a rivet that is too long, in order to match it to the job in hand.

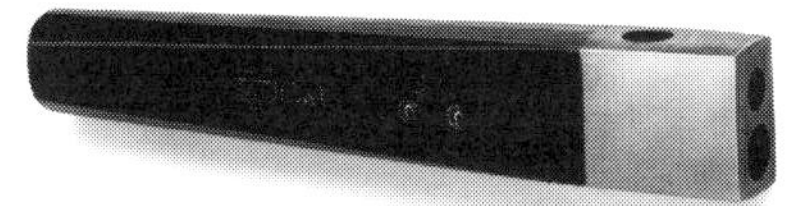

Rivet set, a steel punch used to set and head rivets

Sheet metal rivets, actual size. Rivet size is derived from a rivet's weight per thousand. For example, 1,000 12 oz. rivets weighs 12 ozs.

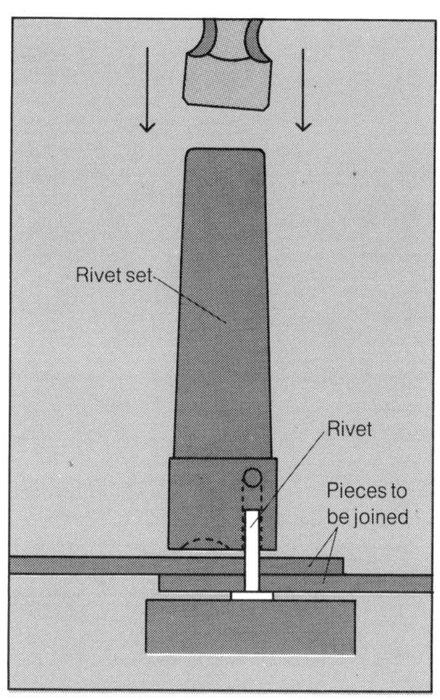

Sheet metal pieces to be riveted are positioned with the rivet inserted in the deep hole of the rivet set.

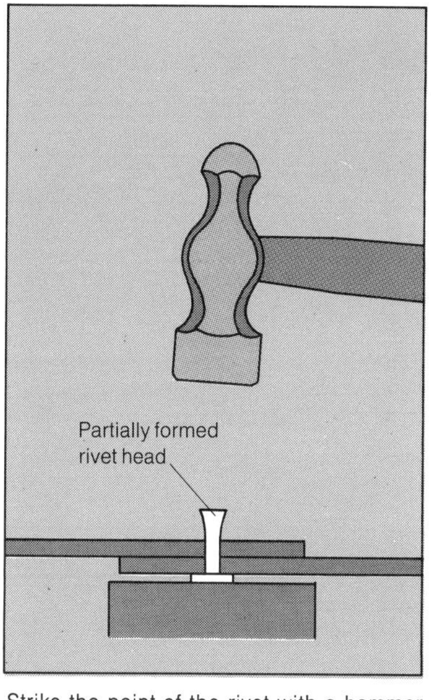

Strike the point of the rivet with a hammer to fill the hole and to flatten the rivet slightly at the head.

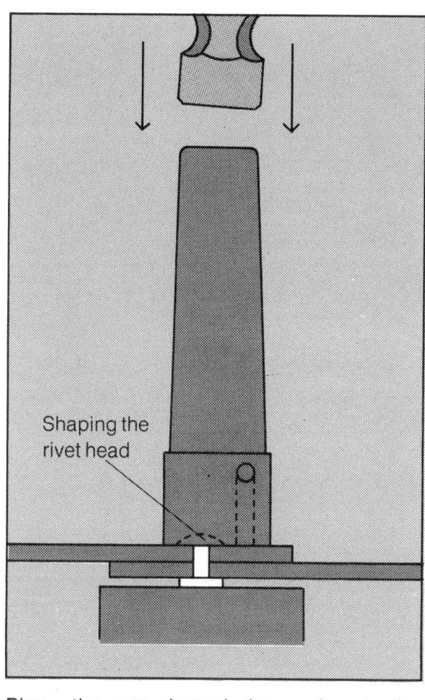

Place the cup-shaped depression in the set over the shank of the rivet. Strike with the hammer to round the head.

How to install a rivet

Mark the position for the rivet with a center punch, then drill a hole slightly larger than the selected rivet through both of the metal pieces to be joined. Place the rivet in the hole. Fit the rivet set over the projecting end of the rivet and strike it with a hammer. The metal pieces will then be tight against each other. Remove the rivet set and strike the protruding part of the rivet, spreading the rivet inside the hole and thereby securing the joint.

Using slanting blows of the hammer, roughly shape the rivet head to a dome-like configuration. The rounded end of a ball peen hammer (p.14) does this shaping job best. Finally, use the rivet set's cupped face to give the rivet a round, smooth surface.

Keep the original head on other than flathead or countersunk rivets from being flattened by using either a riveting block or a second rivet set as a backing tool. A piece of steel with a small hollow drilled in it can be used satisfactorily as a substitute for the riveting block.

Riveting mistakes and corrections

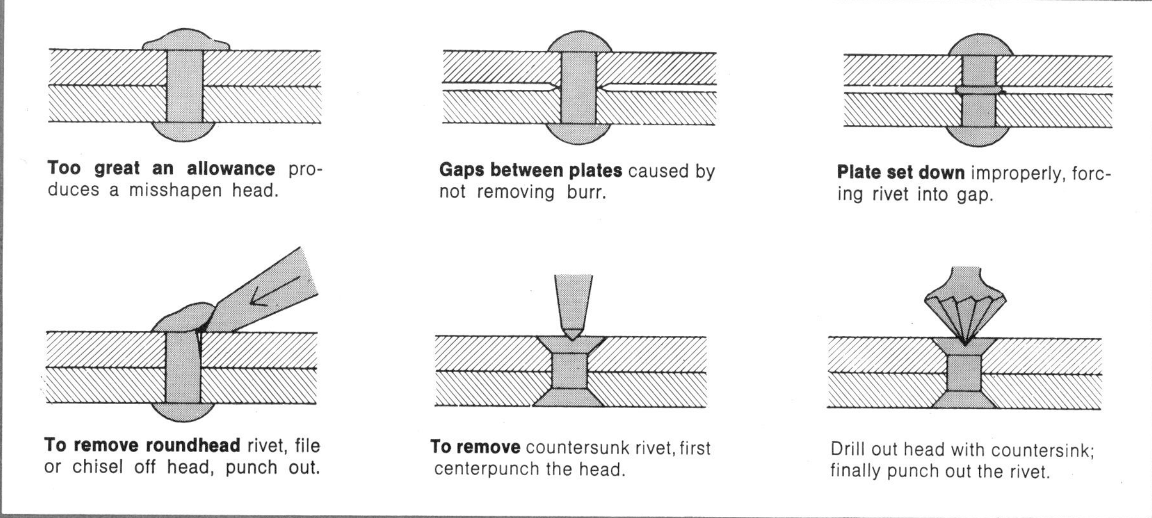

Too great an allowance produces a misshapen head.

Gaps between plates caused by not removing burr.

Plate set down improperly, forcing rivet into gap.

To remove roundhead rivet, file or chisel off head, punch out.

To remove countersunk rivet, first centerpunch the head.

Drill out head with countersink; finally punch out the rivet.

Other ways to attach metals

Bolts

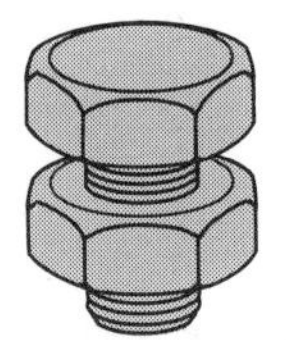

Hex-head machine bolt

Bolts are used to join pieces that may have to be taken apart later. A bolt requires two wrenches for tightening, a machine screw requires a wrench and a screwdriver.

Square-head Carriage Flathead Roundhead

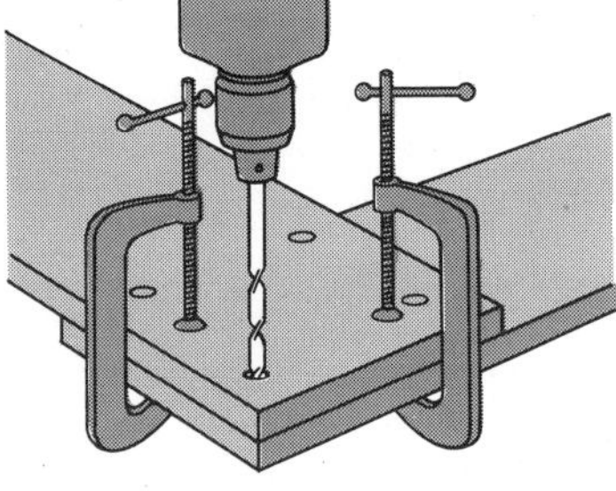

Lay out all holes accurately. Clamp pieces to be joined, drill corner hole only.

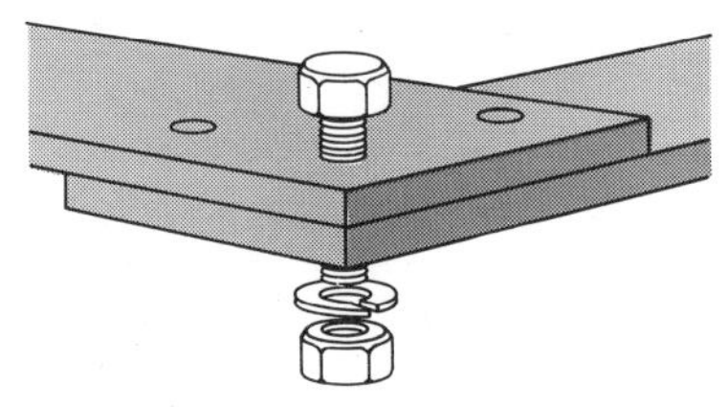

Secure the corner with a bolt, drill a second hole and pass a bolt through it.

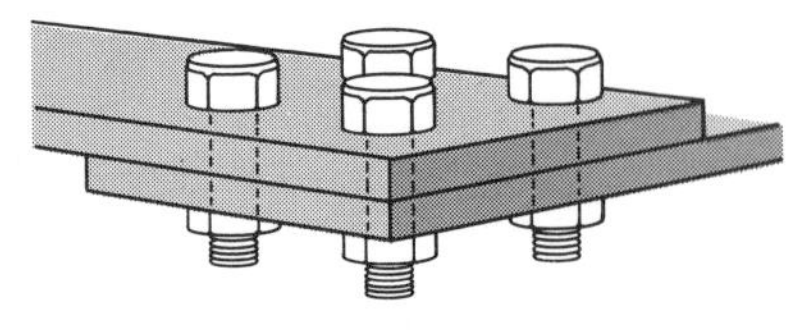

Drill all remaining holes. Remove clamps and fasten the pieces together.

Self-tapping screws

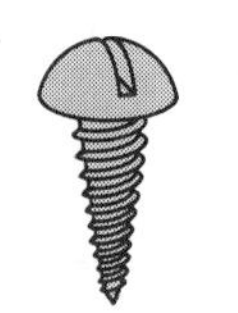

Self-tapping screw

Self-tapping screws, also called sheet-metal screws, are made of hardened steel and cut their own threads as they are turned. Lengths and diameters are similar to wood screws.

Pan-head Roundhead Flathead Oval-head

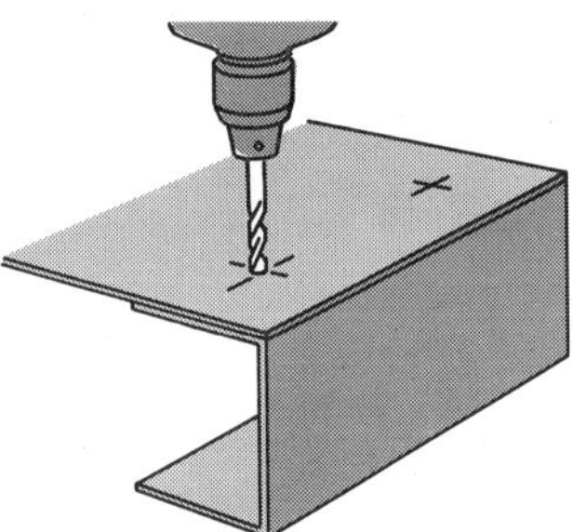

Make punch marks; drill the pilot holes through both sheets to be joined.

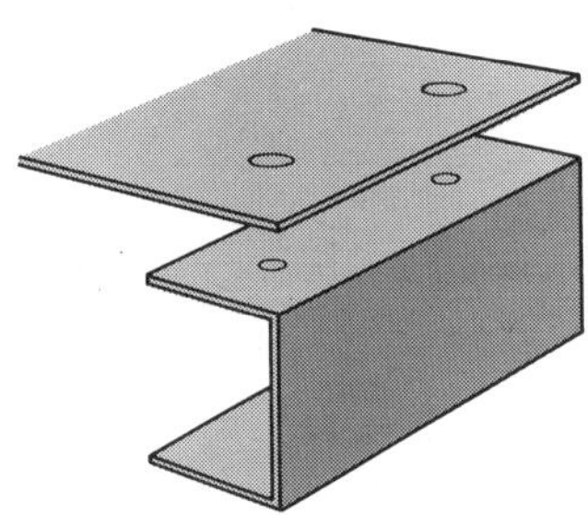

Enlarge the holes on top so they will pass the screws without binding.

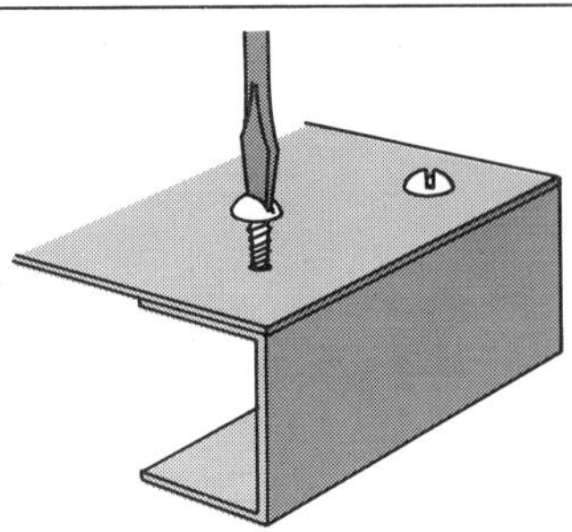

Screw will bite into smaller hole at bottom drawing metal up to top sheet.

Epoxy adhesive

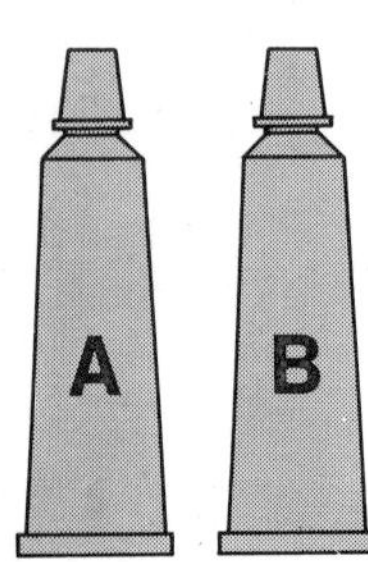

Epoxy adhesive makes strong metal-to-metal bonds. It comes in separate tubes of (A) hardener and (B) resin that must be mixed in equal amounts. Most epoxies take several hours to cure to full strength, but 5-minute curing types are available.

Place equal parts of resin and hardener on one surface; mix them together.

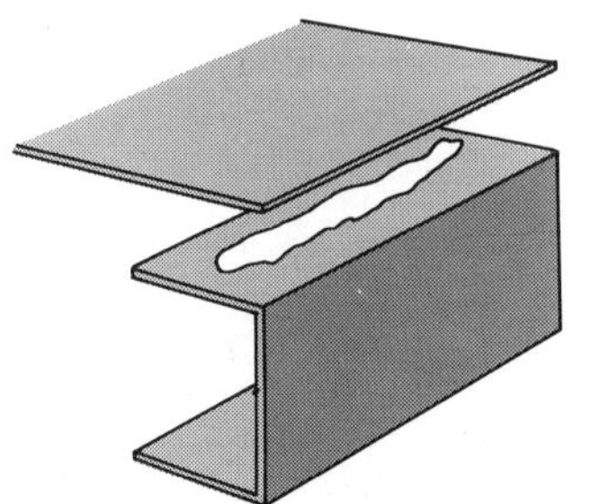

Spread mixture thinly over both surfaces to be joined, then fit them together.

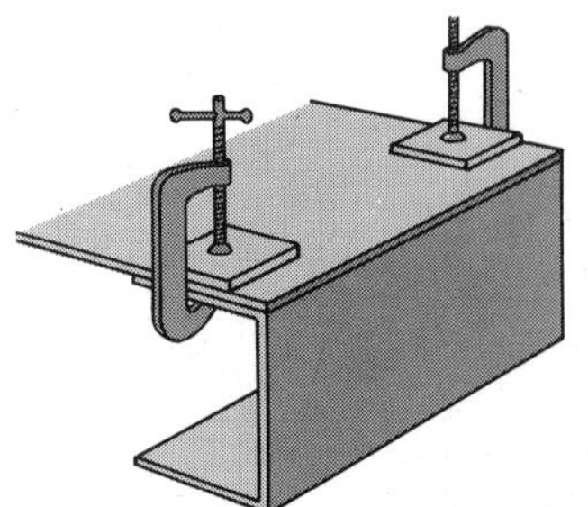

Secure with clamps for drying time recommended on tubes or containers.

Soldering technique

Soldering is an easy way to join metals and wires if you know and use the correct procedures. The first step in soldering is to "tin" the soldering iron or gun. First clean the copper tip with steel wool until it is bright. Next, plug in the iron and wait until it gets hot, then melt some solder onto the tip. The tip will turn silver; this is called "tinning." An iron that has not been properly cleaned and tinned will produce a poorly soldered joint.

The work surfaces you are going to solder must also be cleaned. For this, use coarse steel wool, being sure not to touch the cleaned surface with your bare fingertips. The oil from your fingers can keep the solder from sticking.

Next, apply flux to the metal surfaces to be joined. The flux prevents oxidation on the metal surface, which would keep the metals from fusing. You can apply flux with your fingers or a brush.

A properly soldered joint can only be achieved when the iron is at its hottest. Apply the tip of the iron to the surface of the work to be soldered. It is important to understand that you apply the solder when the **work surface,** not the iron, is hot enough to melt the solder. When this temperature has been reached, the solder will flow around and over the cleaned and fluxed surfaces. If the solder does not adhere to the surfaces, the work has not been properly cleaned and fluxed.

If you are soldering small joints, such as two wires together, or wires to electrical terminals, you can save time and effort by using rosin-core (flux-core) solder. This soldering wire has a core of rosin which acts as a flux during soldering.

Solder comes in both wire and bar form. You would most likely use the bar type when doing large soldering jobs such as sheet metal work.

METAL	RECOMMENDED FLUX
Aluminum	Aluminum solder and special flux or flux combined with aluminum solder
Brass, bronze	Clean to bare metal and use rosin as flux
Cadmium plate	Rosin or flux used for galvanized iron
Copper	Clean to bare metal and use rosin as flux
Galvanized iron, iron	Zinc chloride flux containing hydrochloric acid. Made by dissolving zinc in hydrochloric acid, diluting with equal amounts of water
Lead	Tallow
Monel, nickel	Same as for galvanized iron
Pewter	Flux made of 1 oz. glycerine and 5 drops hydrochloric acid
Silver	Use rosin-core solder
Stainless steel	Special stainless-steel flux
Steel	Same as for galvanized iron
Tin	Same as for galvanized iron
White metal	Same as for galvanized iron
Zinc	Same as for galvanized iron

If the soldering iron is badly corroded and pitted, clamp it in a vise and clean the tip with a file. File all surfaces until bright copper is exposed. Finish cleaning with steel wool.

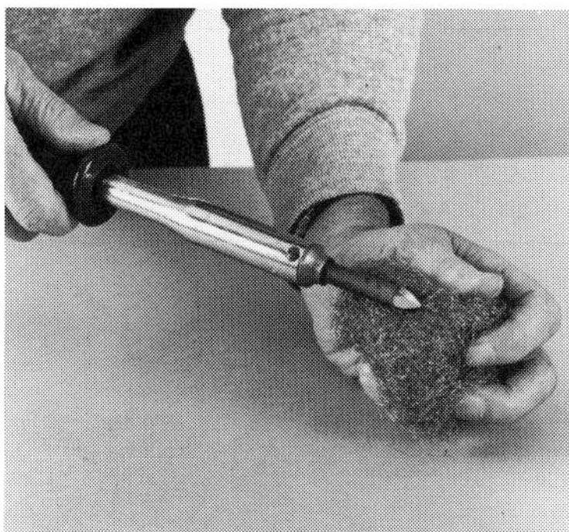

If the iron tip is dirty but not corroded, clean all sides with coarse steel wool. Avoid touching the cleaned tip with your fingers; this leaves an oil film which keeps solder from adhering.

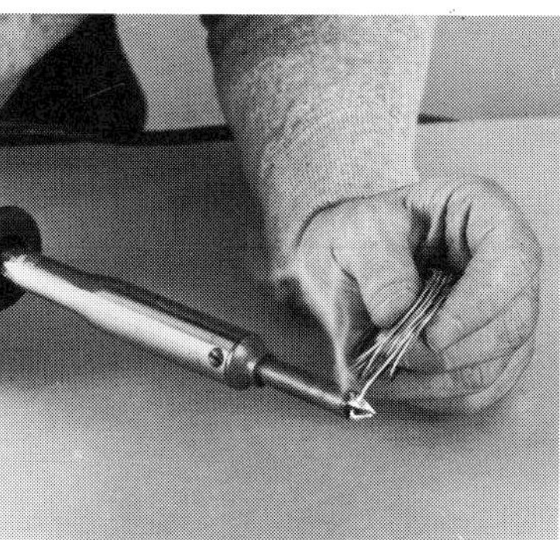

The iron must be at maximum heat for tinning. Plug it in and let it heat for at least 5 minutes. Then apply the flux-core solder so that it flows evenly over all sides of the tip.

Making a soldering pot

A soldering pot is handy when making many similar connections, such as joining wires. You can make one of a brass block, hacksawed as shown. Drill series of ¼ in. overlapping holes for well. Recess should fit snugly over tip of iron. Solder melts in about 4 minutes.

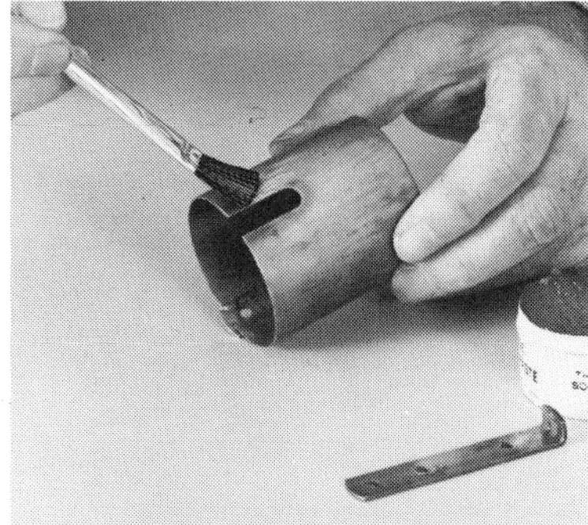

Clean the surfaces of the pieces to be soldered with steel wool and apply paste flux to the cleaned areas. If you are using rosin core (flux-core) solder, there is no need to use flux.

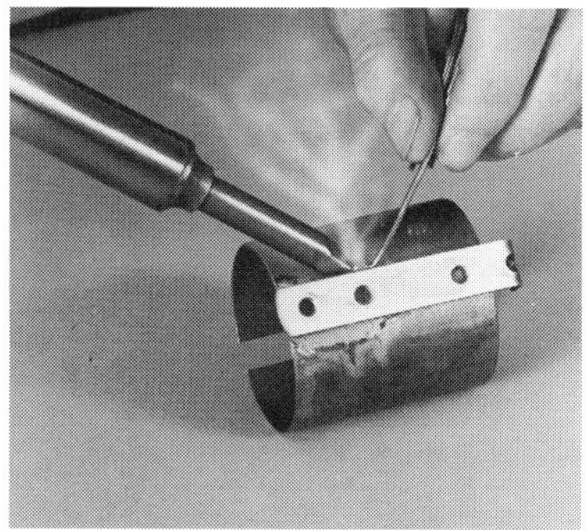

Apply the iron to the work until the work gets hot enough to melt the solder. Feed the solder along the work and slightly behind the iron. Use a large iron for heavy work.

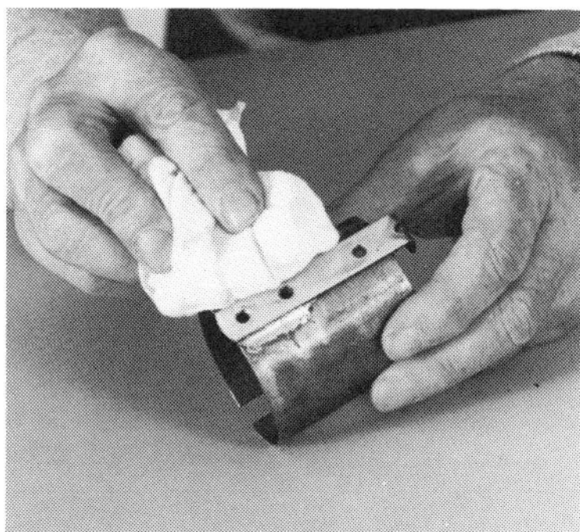

Wipe off excess flux from the soldered joint with a clean rag. Do this while the soldered joint is still warm. Flux stains can be removed from a cold joint with paint thinner.

Hard soldering and welding

Hard soldering (used on steel, silver, gold, and bronze) makes a neater, stronger, and more permanent joint than soft soldering. A torch is needed to supply the high heat required for hard soldering. A propane torch is most convenient but a Bunsen burner with a blowpipe can also be used.

The first step in hard soldering is to clean the area where the pieces are to be joined. For this use a file, emery cloth, or wire brush. Clamp the pieces in position, apply flux to the joint, and then the recommended solder. Heat the metal until flux and solder melt. Insert thin sheets of solder into the joint. Keep the joint hot and continue to apply solder until all crevices are filled.

Use solder that is colored to match the metals being joined. For example, when joining silver, use silver solder, an alloy of 8 parts silver, 3 parts copper, and 1 part zinc; for gold, the proper solder is an alloy of silver, copper, and gold.

If you are doing a large job and do not have sufficient flux, a substitute can be made of powdered borax mixed with water to the consistency of cream.

Melted flux leaves a brownish residue that can be removed from the soldered joint by submersion in a solution of 1 part sulphuric acid to 2 parts water. Let the work soak in this for about 30 minutes. Always add acid to water, never water to acid, when diluting sulphuric acid, and wear rubber gloves as well as protective goggles when you do it. Flux residue can sometimes be removed with boiling water alone if the joint is soaked before it cools.

Welding is a method of joining metals by melting them together. The extreme heat required may be attained by electricity (arc welding) or gases (oxy-acetylene welding). Welding is an economical way to join metals where it is impossible or impractical to use conventional fasteners such as bolts or rivets—for example, to repair a cracked furnace door, a broken railing, or garden and farm equipment.

Inasmuch as welding equipment is comparatively expensive, and the technique beyond the skill of the average homeowner, it is much more practical—and cheaper—to take the work to a local commercial welder. Home welding outfits that sell for about $20 are not recommended, are even in many cases unsafe. The least expensive welding outfit that will do a fairly satisfactory job will cost at least $125—quite an investment for a tool you will not use frequently.

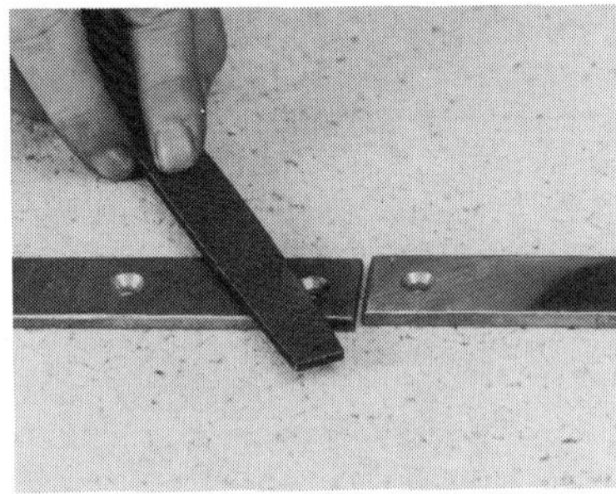

Sections to be joined by hard soldering must be cleaned with a file or emery cloth and placed on a fireproof surface such as firebrick or asbestos board.

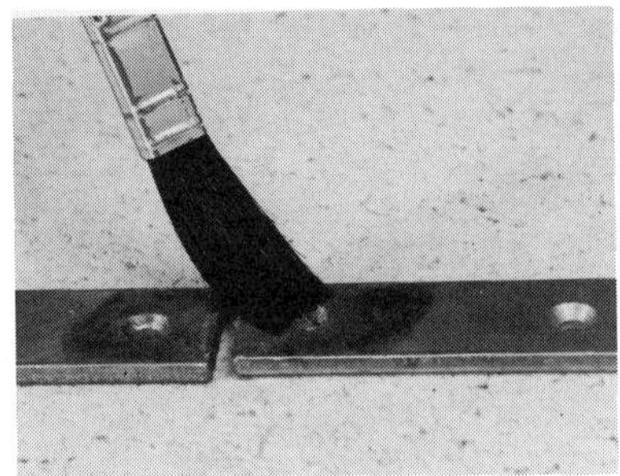

A flux, such as borax and water paste, is then liberally applied to the cleaned surface with a small brush. Too much flux is better than too little.

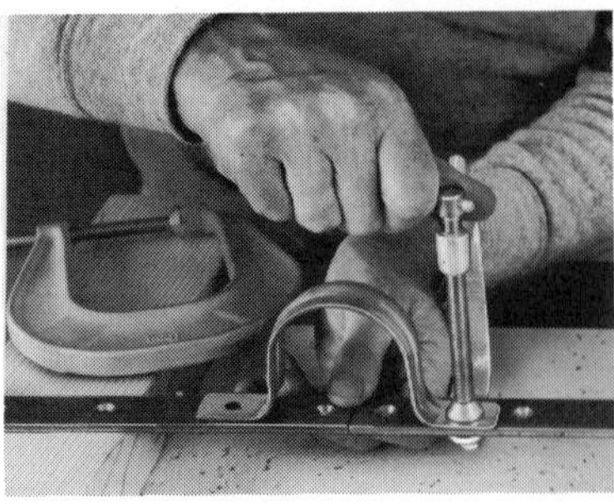

A bridge should be made from a piece of scrap metal bent in the middle to keep it away from the joint. A pair of clamps will also be needed.

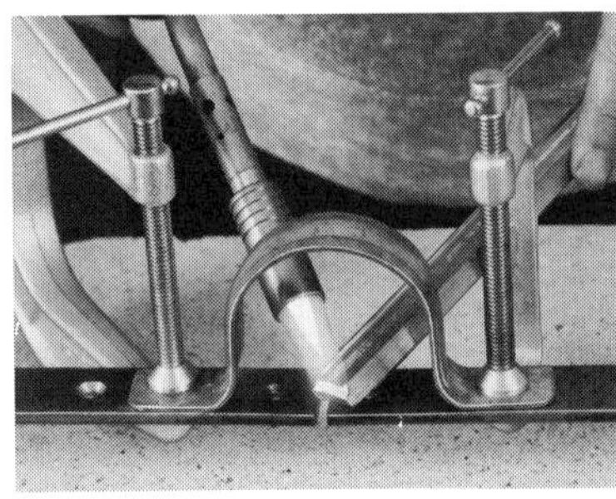

The metal is heated to melt the hard solder as it is fed into the joint. Use the tip of the inner core of the flame, which is the hottest part.

The finished hard-soldered joint. Note that the clamps have been placed as far as possible from the joint in order to avoid heat loss at joint area.

After the solder has cooled, remove the flux by submerging the joint in a solution of 1 part sulphuric acid to 2 parts water, then file it smooth.

Soft soldering sheet metal

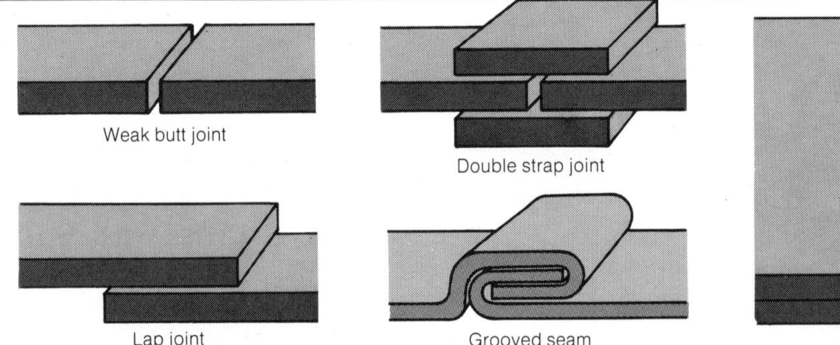

If a butt joint is unavoidable, it should be strengthened with metal sweat-soldered to both surfaces. A lap joint is better, a locked grooved seam stronger still. Large sheets should be tack-soldered before the joint is soldered.

Sweating

Sweating is a form of soldering in which the solder alone holds the pieces of metal together. The areas to be joined are cleaned and the surfaces made as smooth as possible so they can be brought into close contact. They are fluxed, coated with solder (tinned), assembled, clamped if possible, and heated until the solder re-melts and unites. The joints must be held in position until the solder cools. Additional solder in the form of a fillet may be run along the joint edges for greater strength, waterproofing, and improved appearance.

A solder fillet adds to the strength of a right-angle joint.

A fillet on an unlocked (folded) grooved seam.

Tin both surfaces to be joined before sweating.

Solder united on a sweated joint.

Securing the joint

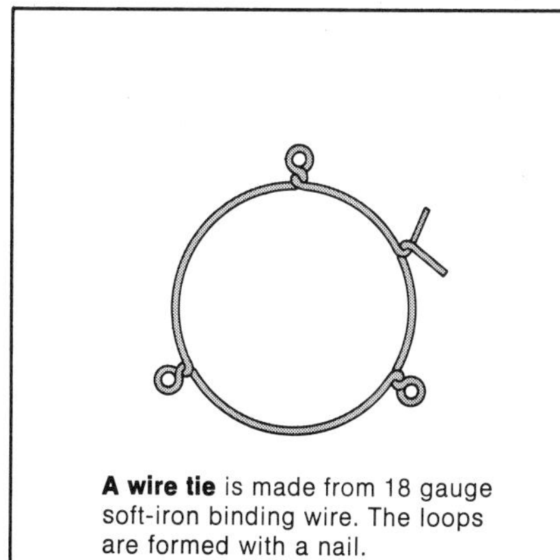

A wire tie is made from 18 gauge soft-iron binding wire. The loops are formed with a nail.

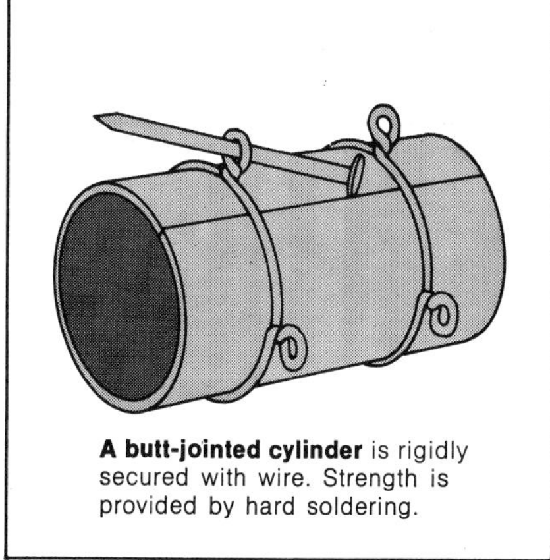

A butt-jointed cylinder is rigidly secured with wire. Strength is provided by hard soldering.

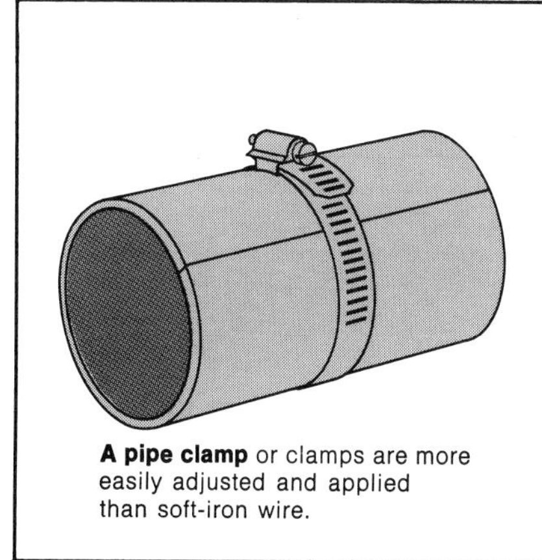

A pipe clamp or clamps are more easily adjusted and applied than soft-iron wire.

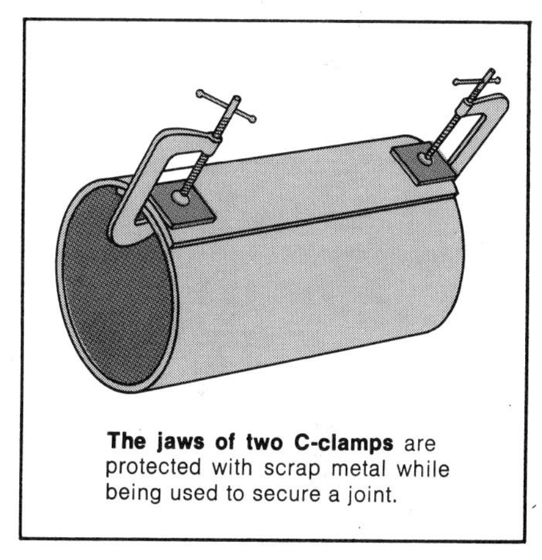

The jaws of two C-clamps are protected with scrap metal while being used to secure a joint.

Permanent rivets or temporary screws may be used to hold the joint in place before soldering.

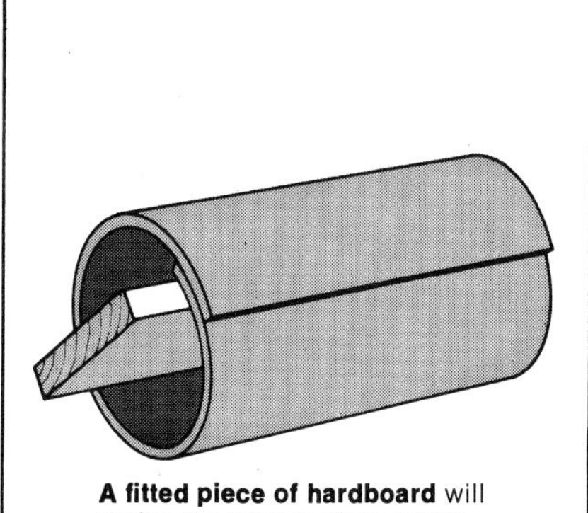

A fitted piece of hardboard will spring the joint in place and is easily removed later.

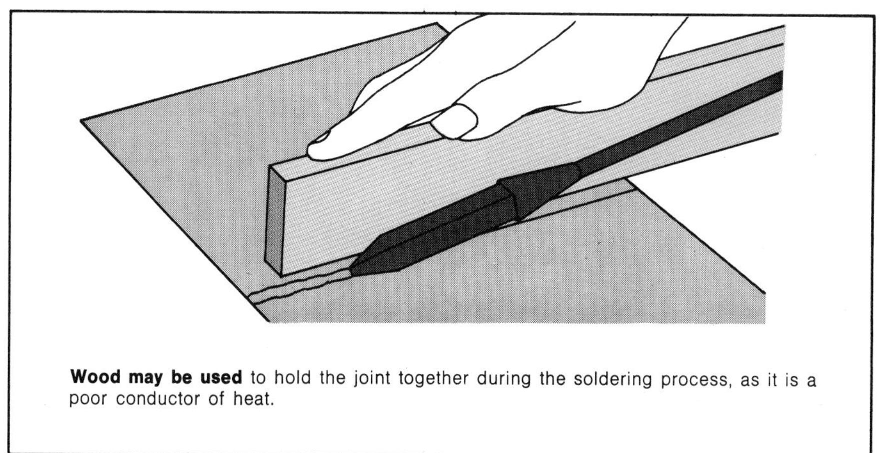

Wood may be used to hold the joint together during the soldering process, as it is a poor conductor of heat.

Sheet metal

Introduction

A sheet of aluminum, brass, copper, galvanized iron, iron, tinplate, or zinc that is up to $\frac{3}{16}$ inch in thickness, is referred to as sheet metal. (Thicker sheets are called plate.) Also included in this group are perforated steel sheets and welded wire mesh, of the type used for decorative effects, window guards, pet cages and similar structures. Few of the tools needed to work sheet metal are specialized, and you can use homemade forms and jigs to lay out, cut, bend, hammer, and assemble sheet metal projects.

Annealing

Bending and hammering can harden and stiffen metal to a point where it must be resoftened to its former flexibility. This is accomplished by annealing, a process of heating the metal to its critical point (recognizable by color change), then cooling it. Copper and brass, for example, should be heated to a dull red or until you see "rainbow" colors.

Plunge the heated metal into water or set it aside to cool. After cooling it will again have its original softness and pliability.

To soften and reduce the brittleness of hardened steel, heat it to its critical point (when it will no longer attract a magnet). Then let it cool slowly. Annealing is accomplished in soft metals during the heating; in hard metals, during cooling.

You will probably never have to anneal hardened steel, but all soft metals should be annealed after frequent bending.

Annealing is important when the work is to be machined, as it gives the metal a finer grain.

Bending

Sheet metal can be bent by hand in the home shop using anything that will give it solid support on both sides for its entire length. Supports for a long bend, used either singly or in combination, may be a bench top, a pair of angle irons or thick hardwood boards, clamps or a vise. A hand screw or vise may be sufficient to support a short bend.

There will be less surface damage if a rubber or rawhide mallet is used to strike the metal. You can make a satisfactory substitute by covering the face of a regular hammer with a piece of rubber.

Forming curves: Malleable metals such as soft aluminum, brass, copper, lead, or zinc can be formed with a mallet over hardwood forms made to exactly the size and shape needed. The forms should be made slightly undersize for harder metals such as aluminum, galvanized iron, or tinplate, as these tend to spring back when the pressure is removed.

Bending jig made by clamping sheet metal between boards

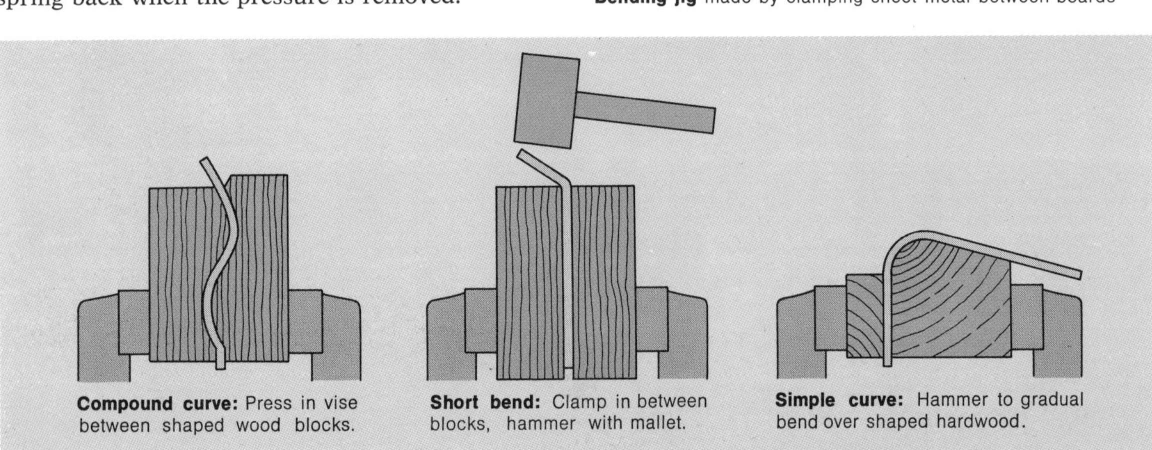

Compound curve: Press in vise between shaped wood blocks.

Short bend: Clamp in between blocks, hammer with mallet.

Simple curve: Hammer to gradual bend over shaped hardwood.

Making a safe edge

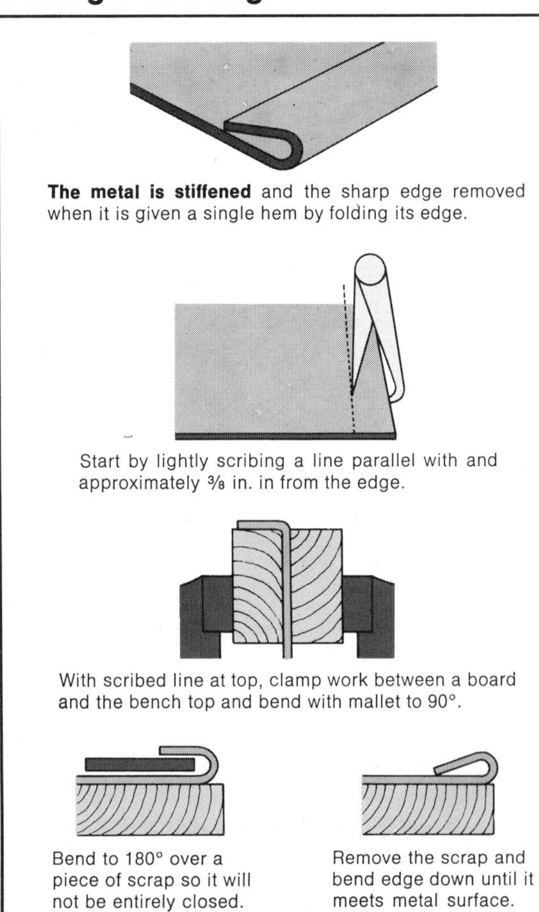

The metal is stiffened and the sharp edge removed when it is given a single hem by folding its edge.

Start by lightly scribing a line parallel with and approximately $\frac{3}{8}$ in. in from the edge.

With scribed line at top, clamp work between a board and the bench top and bend with mallet to 90°.

Bend to 180° over a piece of scrap so it will not be entirely closed.

Remove the scrap and bend edge down until it meets metal surface.

Reinforcing lip

Sheet metal can be easily reinforced by adding a lip, a seam, or a rolled edge to the end of the sheet. Not only does this technique serve to reinforce the metal, but it also acts as a sort of safeguard, as the raw edge of sheet metal is quite sharp and can inflict a nasty cut. Follow the drawings at the right for the proper technique for making a reinforcing lip on sheet metal. Small sheets can be reinforced in the home workshop. Large sheets are best farmed out to a commercial sheet-metal shop where they have machines for making special bends, seams and lips. Incidentally, if you are planning any sheet metal work, bear in mind that sheet metal comes in standard widths of two feet and lengths up to eight feet long. Sheet metal is available commercially in galvanized steel, tin plate, black annealed iron, aluminum, copper, brass and nickel silver. When handling sheet metal, particularly large sheets, wear gloves to protect your hands from being cut.

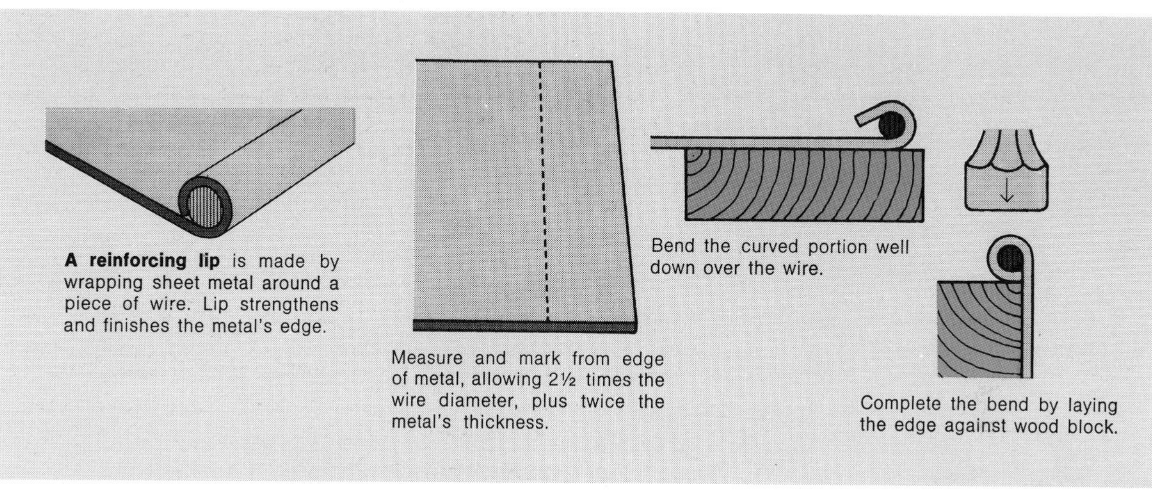

A reinforcing lip is made by wrapping sheet metal around a piece of wire. Lip strengthens and finishes the metal's edge.

Measure and mark from edge of metal, allowing 2½ times the wire diameter, plus twice the metal's thickness.

Bend the curved portion well down over the wire.

Complete the bend by laying the edge against wood block.

Folded and grooved seams

A **folded seam** is made by simply hooking two single hems together. Because the edges are only bent, the seam is not flush, though it does come apart easily.

A **grooved seam** is made by forming and hooking two single hems as with a folded seam, then hammering them flat. An alternative way is to use a "hand groover." It is placed over the seam and struck with a hammer. This first locks each of the ends, then the entire seam, making it flush. Soldering will make the seams waterproof.

To make a box out of sheet metal, make a wood form and bend the sheet metal around it.

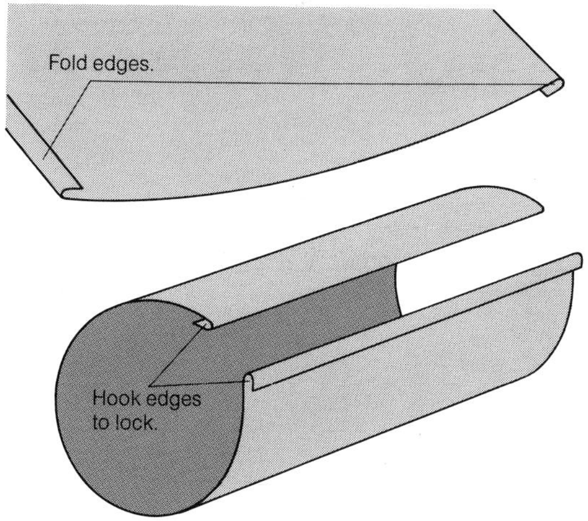

Fold edges.

Hook edges to lock.

Fold back edges of opposite sides of metal sheet, then hook folded edges together to form a cylinder.

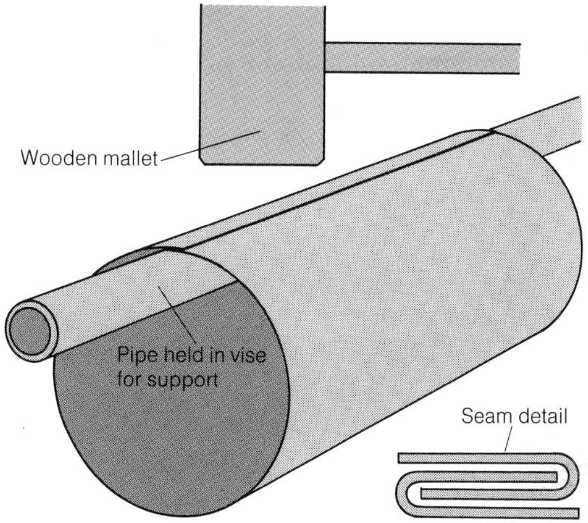

Wooden mallet

Pipe held in vise for support

Seam detail

A folded seam is made by striking along hooked edges with a wooden mallet. Use a pipe held in a vise for support.

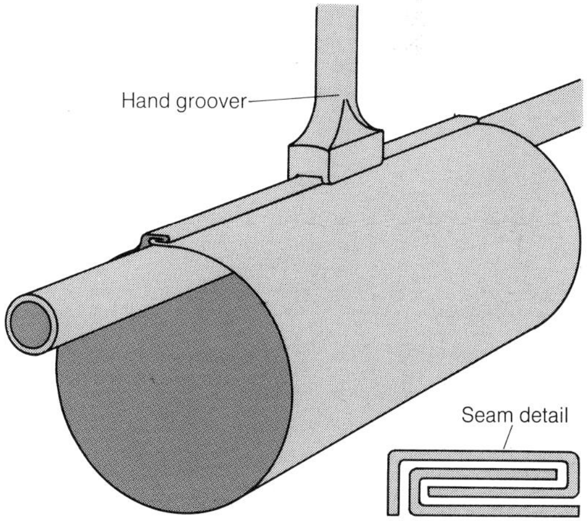

Hand groover

Seam detail

To make a grooved seam, place hand groover over hooked edges, strike with hammer to close ends and seam.

Repairing minor dents

A **slight dent in thick metal** is fairly easy to repair. Build up a bit above the surface with filler, then grind or file level. A **bad dent stretches thin metal** and it must be "shrunk" back before filling and smoothing. If the **domed part** of a dent in thin metal is accessible, and you can't push it back by hand, hammer the metal back to shape against a sandbag. A wooden or hide mallet minimizes surface damage. If a **narrow neck** prevents your reaching the domed part, try inserting a wooden stake and pressing it against the dent. Sometimes hammer-tapping causes a stake to vibrate and act as an internal hammer.

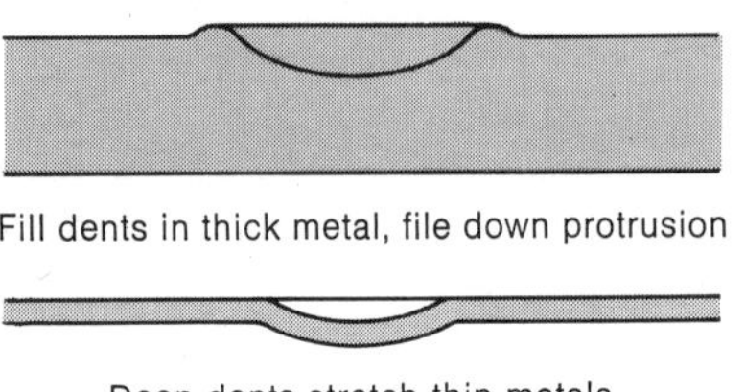

Fill dents in thick metal, file down protrusion

Deep dents stretch thin metals

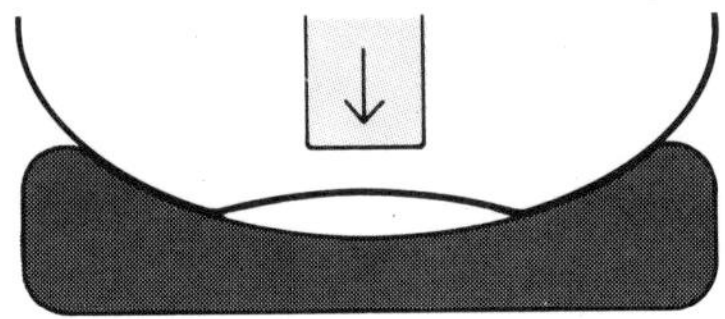

Hammer out dent against sandbag backing

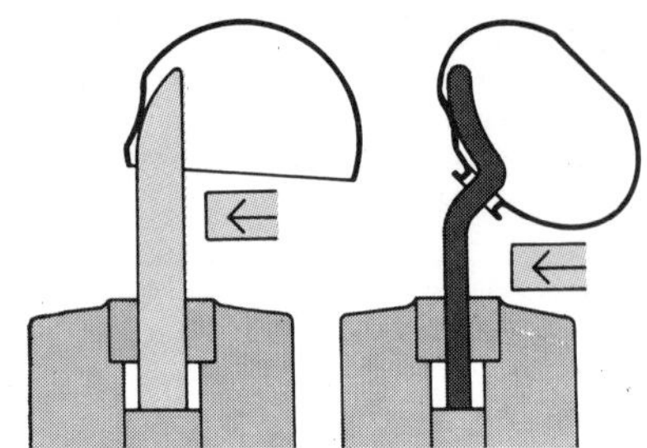

Use wood stake or metal bar to force out dents

Repairing holes with epoxy

Use a metal repair kit to fill such holes as a rusted-out area on a car. Kits consist of fiber glass screening and a two-part epoxy mix. Make the repair by first sanding down to the bare metal. Fit a piece of the screening over the hole. Use the epoxy mix to build up the rusted-out area or hole.

Let the patching dry for about 30 minutes, then sand it flush with the metal surface. Finish up the smoothing process with a final hand sanding. Make sure the filler is completely cured before starting the finishing process.

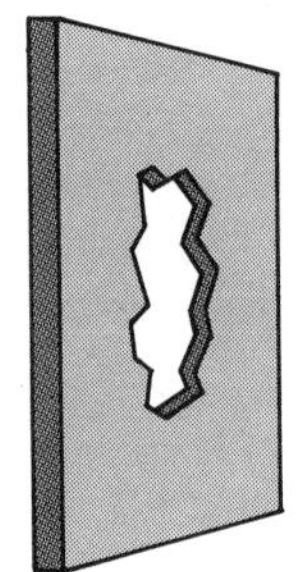

Sand surrounding area down to bare metal.

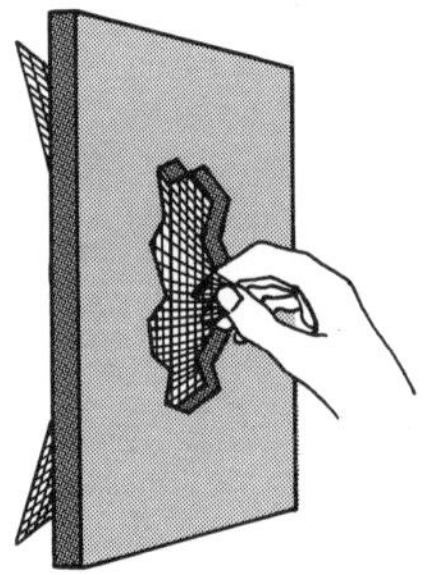

Attach screening, using epoxy, with ½ in. overlap.

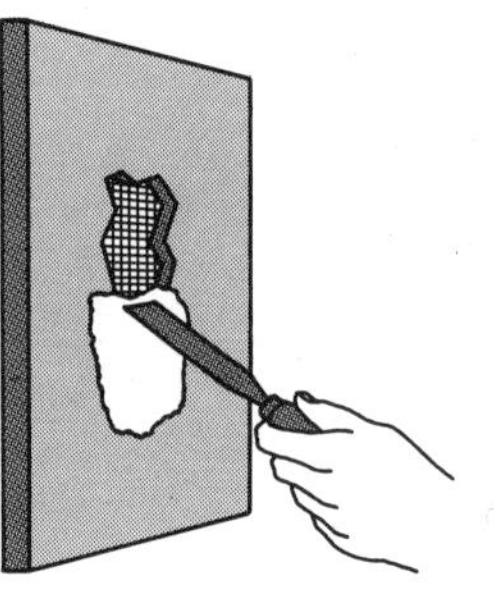

Apply the epoxy mix over the screening.

When the epoxy mix is dry, sand it smooth.

Repairing large dents

To repair dents in thick metal, it is necessary to fill in the entire cavity with the epoxy mix from the metal repair kit. First drill a series of small anchor holes in the metal. Fill in the depression slightly above the surface with the compound. Apply pressure when you are filling in the dent so that the mix will penetrate the drilled holes. When the application has dried thoroughly, the mix will be anchored in the holes. A deep dent in metal can sometimes be pulled out, or at least made shallower, by inserting sheet metal screws, spanning the opening with a block of hardwood, and pulling on the screws, slowly and steadily, with a claw hammer.

Drill a series of holes to anchor the epoxy mix.

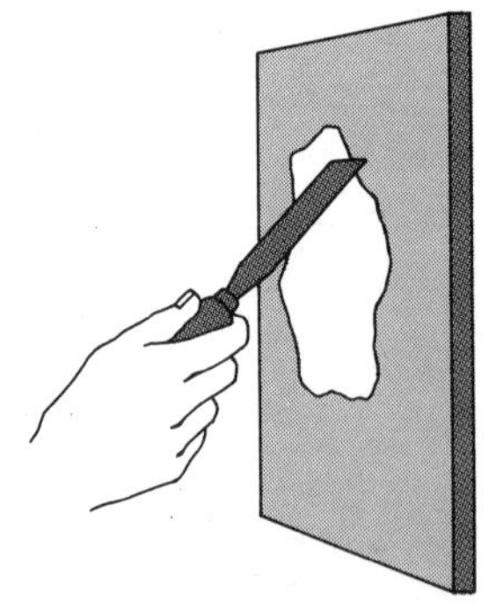

Fill the dent to slightly above the surface with the mix.

Sand flush and let curing time elapse before finishing.

Introduction

Light, soft strap metals such as aluminum, Duralumin, brass, copper, mild steel, and wrought iron (up to ¼ inch thick) may be bent cold without risking a fracture or seriously impairing their strength. Mild steel and Duralumin will offer greater resistance than the other metals mentioned.

When metal is bent cold, it will stretch on the outside and, at the same time, be compressed on the inside, causing distortion in the area of the bend. This is a greater problem in thick metal than in thin.

When metal is bent hot, or forged, the distortion will not be as great and is easily corrected. This is

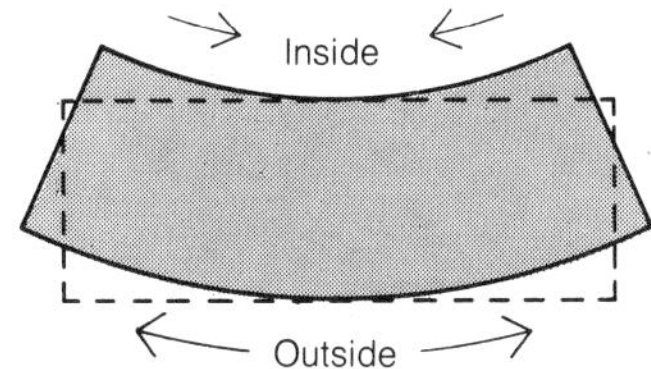

done by letting the corner of the bend equal one-half the thickness of the metal and adding this to the length. As the inside is compressed, the metal must go somewhere, and so it becomes wider at this point. Often the outside half becomes concave as well.

Since all of the metal is still there, the distortion can be corrected by laying the bend on its side on an

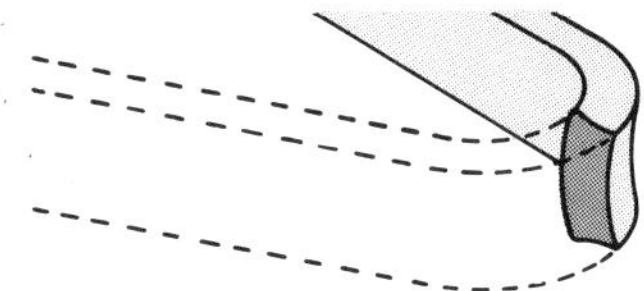

Bending distortion in metal

anvil and hammering it back to its original shape, reheating it white-hot if necessary.

The average home handyman isn't likely to have access to a forge to heat the metal to this point. The gas ring of an ordinary kitchen range will serve the purpose, especially for small pieces, or you can use a blowtorch.

To obtain a completely sharp angle in the heavier mild steel, wrought iron, or some of the harder aluminum alloys, you will need to heat the area of the bend with a torch. For this kind of sharp bending, wrought iron should be brought to a white heat if possible. If it is struck when it is yellow, it is liable to split rather than bend.

Some of the nonferrous metals may have to be annealed (p.432) if they are hard initially or have been hardened while being worked. If any difficulty is encountered, bending should be done in stages, with the heating and cooling of the annealing process performed between stages.

Strap metal can be twisted to shape for making light fixtures, sconces, and decorative brackets. Clamp one end in a vise and use a monkey wrench at the other end to do the twisting. The twist can be a left-hand or a right-hand twist depending on which way you turn the wrench. Twisting "shrinks" the metal considerably so make adequate allowance for this before starting.

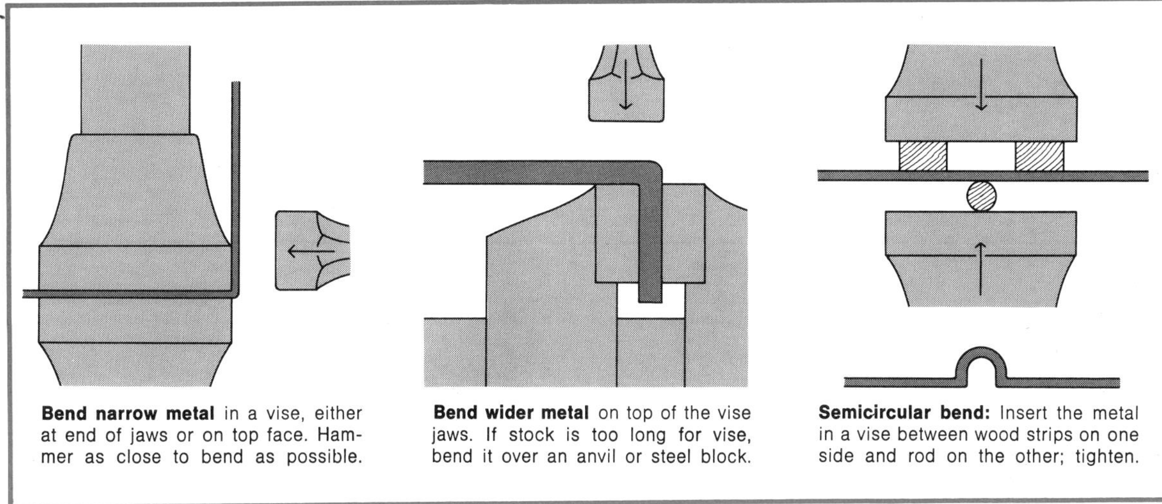

Bend narrow metal in a vise, either at end of jaws or on top face. Hammer as close to bend as possible.

Bend wider metal on top of the vise jaws. If stock is too long for vise, bend it over an anvil or steel block.

Semicircular bend: Insert the metal in a vise between wood strips on one side and rod on the other; tighten.

Curved bending

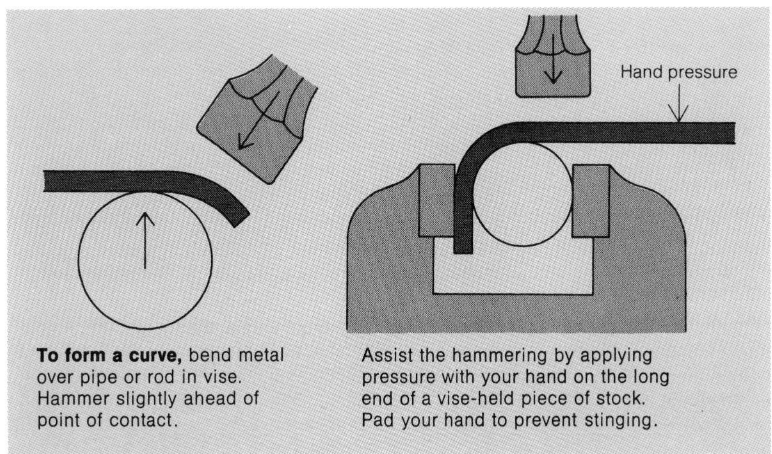

To form a curve, bend metal over pipe or rod in vise. Hammer slightly ahead of point of contact.

Assist the hammering by applying pressure with your hand on the long end of a vise-held piece of stock. Pad your hand to prevent stinging.

Bending jigs

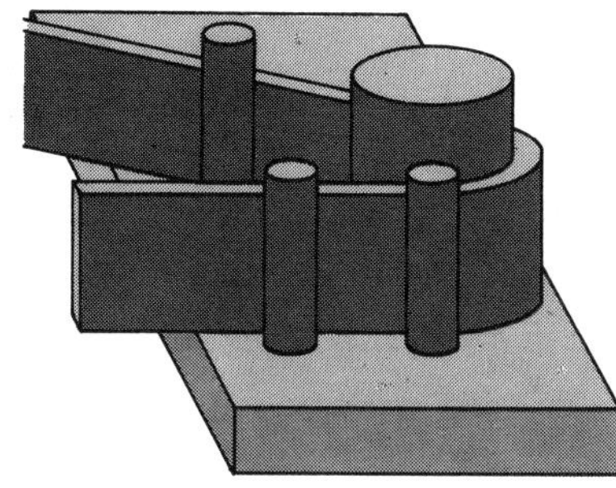

Curves, including scrolls, may be formed in light materials by bending the metal cold. If the jig used is made entirely of metal, this type of bending may be done with red-hot metal.

Tube and bar metal

Working with tubing

In working with plumbing, heating, oil feed lines, conduit, chair frames, etc., a homeowner often needs tubing—generally of aluminum, brass, copper, or steel. To order tubing, you usually need to know outside diameter and thickness of wall. When tubing is bent, the outside stretches and the inside contracts; unless handled properly, it can break or flatten. To prevent this, pack the tube with sand, seal the ends, then bend gradually. The easiest and safest way is to use an electrician's hickey (p.260) with a bending jig, or a coil spring. Before bending thick-walled tubing, heat the bend area to soften it.

Plug	T-butt connector	Coupling
Floor flange	Elbow connector	Swivel connector

Connectors shown above are used to join aluminum tubing in various combinations to make furniture, workbenches, and garden equipment. Made to fit ¾ and 1 in. tubing.

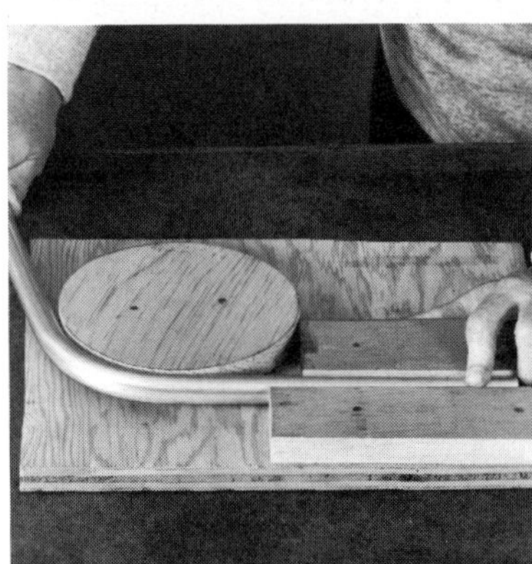

Make bends by packing tubing with sand, then bending it around a wooden form. An electrician's hickey (p.260) can also be used to bend most tubing.

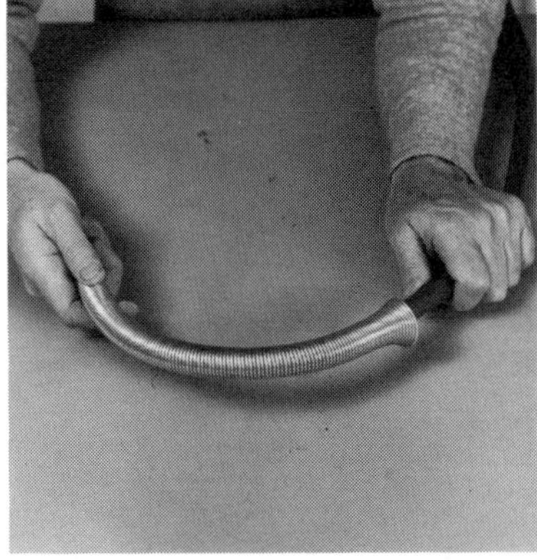

When you bend small diameter tubing, slip a heavy spring around it. The spring coils will hold the tubing in shape while it is bent to the desired radius.

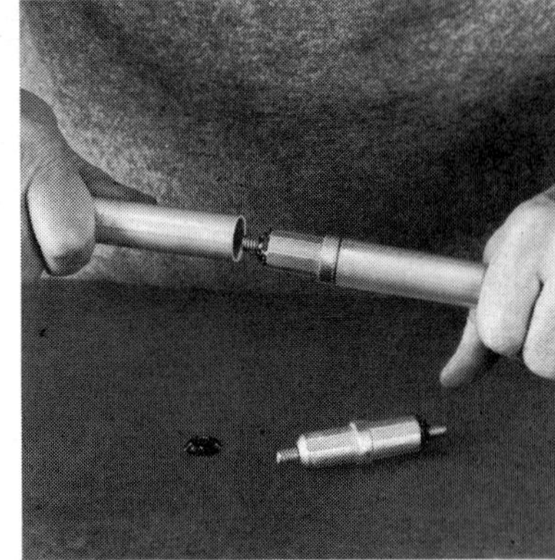

To join tubing, use a coupling, shown in drawing at far left; a tight fitting dowel; or a piece of scrap tubing with lengthwise slit cut down the middle.

Working with bar metal

Metals such as aluminum, brass, bronze, copper, and various steel bar metals come in a wide variety of sizes and shapes—round, square, flat, hexagonal, octagonal—and in lengths to 20 feet.

The techniques of drilling, cutting, threading, joining, and finishing described in the preceding pages apply to bar metal. Bar metal is too large to be bent cold; it must be heated and forged to the desired size and shape.

Bar metal with a ½-inch square section can easily be cut into short lengths for burglarproofing basement windows. Drill holes at each end for one-way screws (p. 72) and fasten the bars to the framework of the window at 5-inch intervals. Instead of one-way screws, you can use ordinary screws and grind down the screw slot so the screw cannot be removed.

Strap iron, ⅛-inch thick and 1 inch wide, is a handy metal to have around to reinforce garage doors and shelving. Because of strap iron's light weight, short sections of it can be bent in a vise without heat. This can be done by hand when the radius is fairly large.

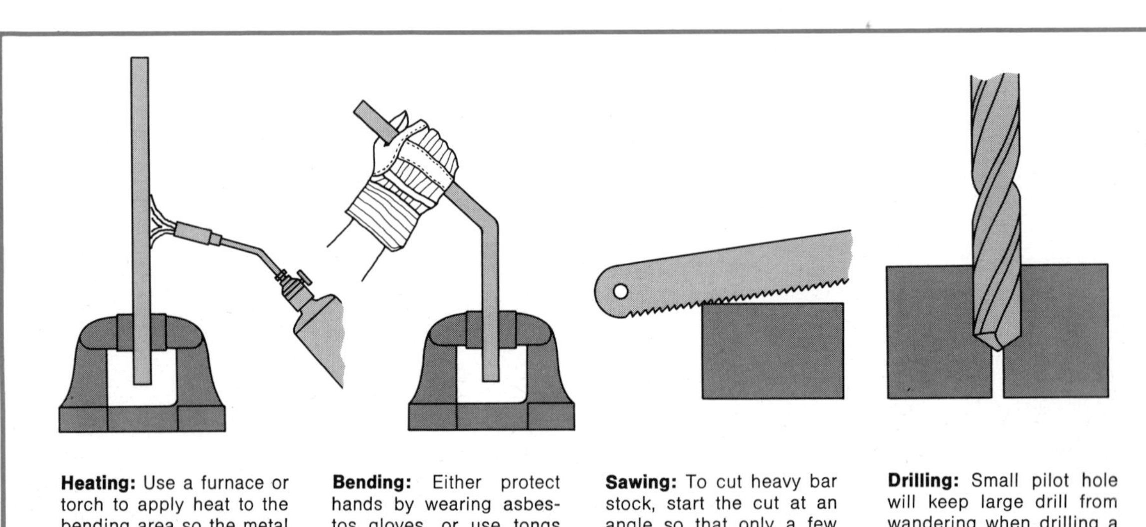

Heating: Use a furnace or torch to apply heat to the bending area so the metal may be worked easily.

Bending: Either protect hands by wearing asbestos gloves, or use tongs when handling hot metal.

Sawing: To cut heavy bar stock, start the cut at an angle so that only a few teeth contact the metal.

Drilling: Small pilot hole will keep large drill from wandering when drilling a large hole through metal.

section 13:

Glass, ceramics, and plastics

The susceptibility of glass to breaking (and of china and pottery as well, which this section also covers) makes it a material the home repairman should be knowledgeable about. The breakage problem partly explains why plastics are replacing glass in some applications; however, plastics have functions and characteristics well worth knowing on their own merits. In addition to repair, this section describes special uses and installations sure to be of interest to the improvement-minded homeowner.

contents

Cutting

Cutting glass is a matter of confidence—and experience. You can gain both by practicing on scrap glass before trying to cut window glass to size. You will need a glass cutter; a good one costs under a dollar.

To cut a piece of glass, lay a straightedge along the proposed cut. Hold it down firmly with one hand and, with the glass cutter in the other, make one continuous smooth stroke along the surface of the glass with side of cutter pressed against the straightedge. The object is to score the glass, not cut through it. You should be able to hear the cutter bite into the glass as it moves along. Make sure the cut is continuous and that you have not skipped any section. Going over a cut is a poor practice as the glass is sure to break awry at that point. Snap the glass immediately after cutting it by placing a pencil under the score line and pressing with your hands on each side of the cut. Frosted or patterned glass should be cut on the smooth side. Wire-reinforced glass can be cut the same as ordinary glass except that you will have to separate the wires by working the two pieces up and down until the wire breaks or by cutting the wires with side-cutting pliers.

To cut a narrow strip from a large piece of glass, score a line and then tap gently underneath the score line with the cutter to open up an inch or so of the score line. Next, grasp the glass on each side of the line and gently snap the waste piece off. Press downward, away from the score mark. If the strip does not break off cleanly, nibble it off with pliers or the notches in the cutter. Slivers less than ½ inch wide are cut off by scoring the line and then nibbling off the waste. Do not nibble without scoring a line first. You can smooth off the edges of glass intended for shelving or table tops with an oilstone dipped in water. Rub the stone back and forth from end to end with the stone at a 45-degree angle to the glass. Rub the stone side to side only, not up and down.

Measuring: Always measure the length and width of the opening in which the glass is to fit at more than one place, as windows are often not absolutely square. If there is a difference between two measurements, use the smaller—and then deduct ⅛ inch from the final result to allow for expansion and contraction. Otherwise the glass may crack with changes of weather. This is especially true with steel casement windows. See pages 123 and 124 on how to install glass in wood sash and steel casement windows.

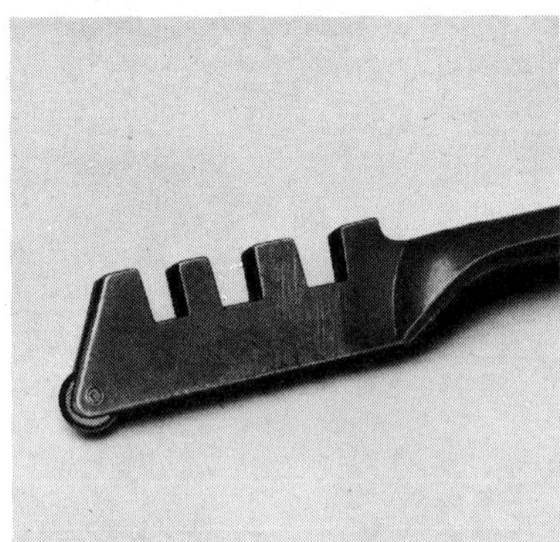

Lightly oil the cutting wheel with a thin machine oil or use kerosene.

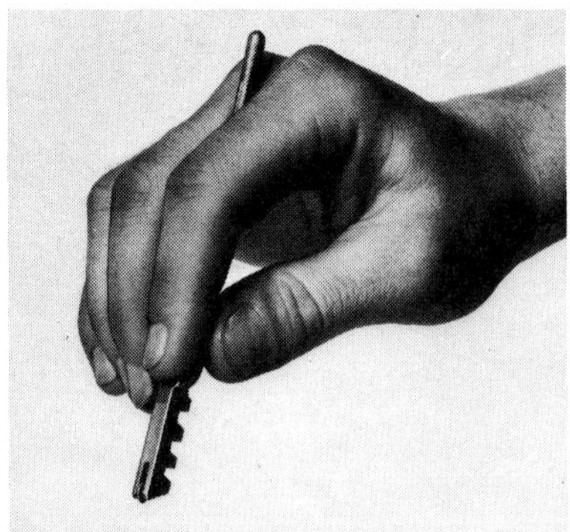

Hold the cutter by resting your index finger on the flat part of the handle.

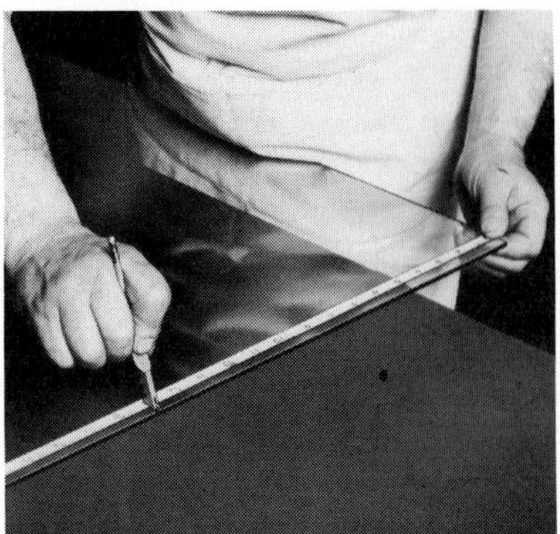

Mark start of cutting line by lightly nicking the edge of glass with cutter.

Score the glass along the straightedge in one continuous smooth stroke.

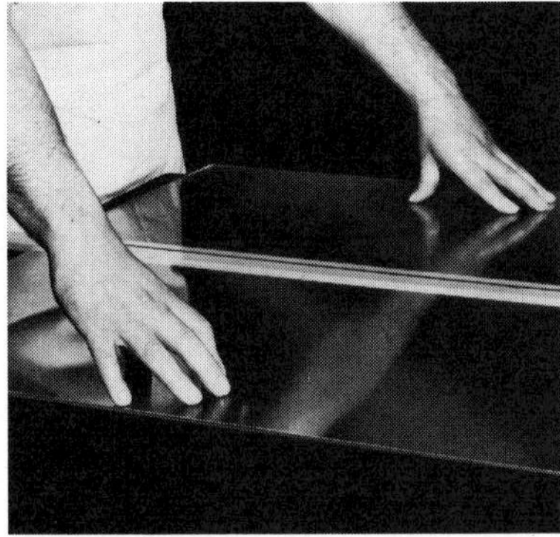

Place the glass over a pencil or long dowel. Press on each side to snap it.

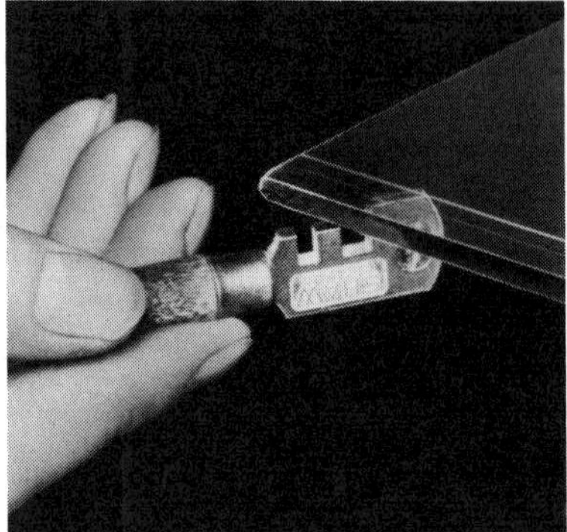

Open out narrow strips by tapping the underside of the glass with the cutter.

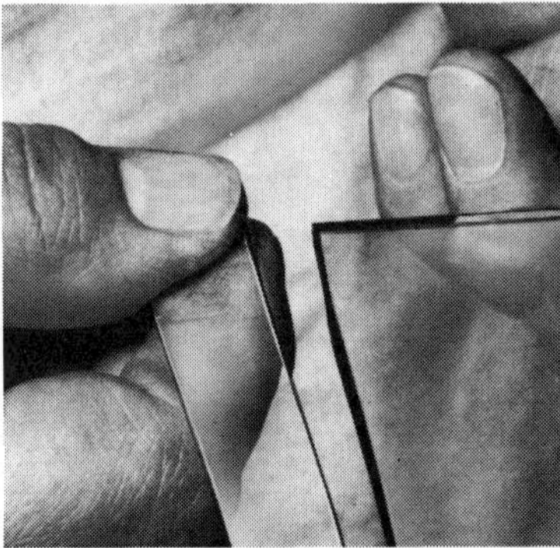

Grasp the glass on each side of the cut and snap off by bending glass back.

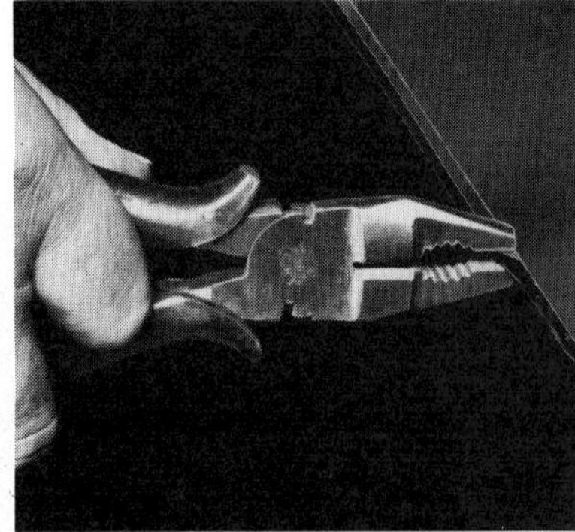

Slivers can be removed by scoring a line and nibbling with pliers as shown.

Raw edges can be smoothed with an oilstone dipped in water. Rub the long way.

Bending glass tubing

Glass tubing can be bent easily with the application of heat from a torch. Excessive heat will actually melt glass. The trick in bending the tubing is to apply the heat slowly and gradually so that the glass has a chance to expand evenly. Too much heat at once will inevitably crack the glass, just as too-hot water poured into a glass cracks it. Wipe the outside of the glass and make certain that there is no moisture on the inside, or it will crack. Wear goggles and gloves when bending short lengths of tubing. Rotate the glass so that the heat is evenly distributed over its surfaces and keep moving it from side to side. Adjust the flame so that it has a lazy blue center.

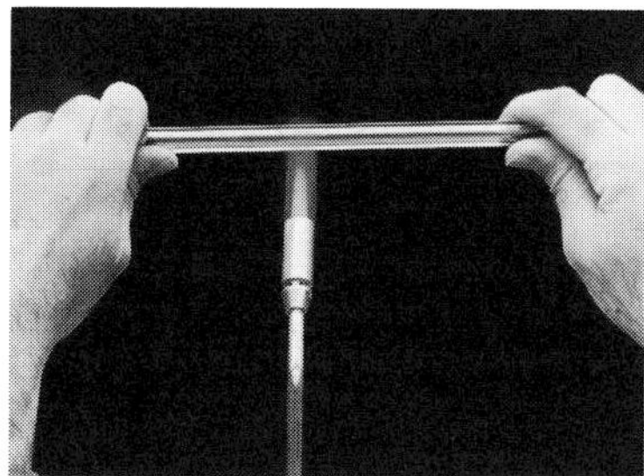

Propane torch is used to heat the glass tube. Move tube from side to side so the flame heats the glass evenly.

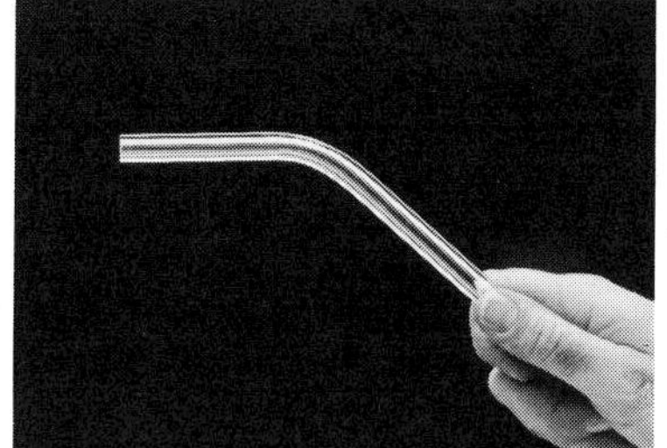

As soon as the glass turns red, apply pressure gently to bend the glass. Pictures show a glass drinking "straw."

Cutting a bottle

Set the glass cutter (part of a kit) to the desired height; rotate bottle to make cut.

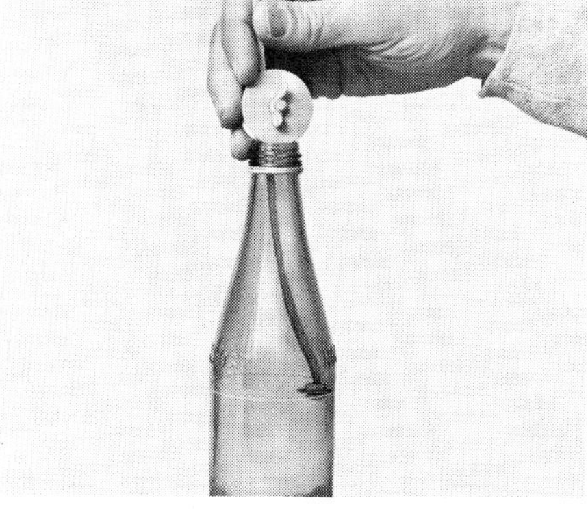

Tap the bottle from the inside along the scored line; keep tapping slightly ahead of crack.

When the crack on the inside is continuous, bottle will separate along scored line.

The separated parts of the bottle. The upper part can be made into a candle holder.

Edge of the cut glass should be smoothed by rubbing on wet-or-dry abrasive paper.

The finished product makes an inexpensive drinking glass. Select bottle free of bubbles.

Repairing crystal

A chip on the lip of a glass you value can be repaired by pre-heating the glass in an oven to about 350°. Then heat the chipped area with a propane torch until the glass starts to melt. The finished job will leave only a slight indentation where the chip was originally—far safer than drinking from a chipped glass.

Drilling glass and ceramics

Glass and pottery

Cutting holes in glass and ceramic ware sounds risky, but it is actually quite easy, provided you have a drill press, or access to one in a school or shop. For this job, you will need an abrasive powder—silicon carbide (Carborundum, or Cristolon)—putty, a piece of pipe, and some water. Support the bottom of the work with a block of wood. Next build a dam of putty around the area to be cut. Place a teaspoonful of the abrasive powder and some water within the dam area, notch the pipe and insert it in the drill press chuck, turn on the switch, and gently lower the tubing. Don't be concerned by the harsh, rasping noise; it means all is as it should be. Keep raising and lowering the pipe to let the mixture of abrasive and water flow into the ring being cut.

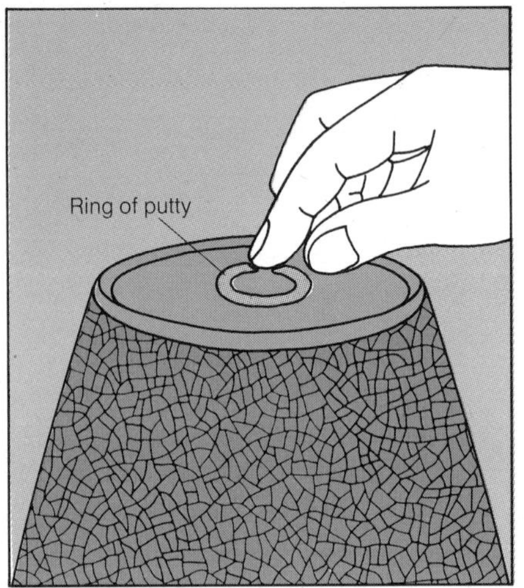

Make a dam with putty. Vase bottom is supported with block of wood to prevent splintering.

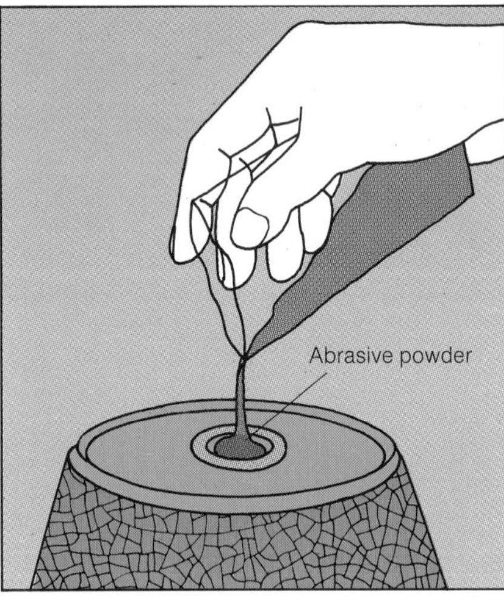

Next, pour a teaspoonful of the powder into the dammed-up area on top of the vase bottom.

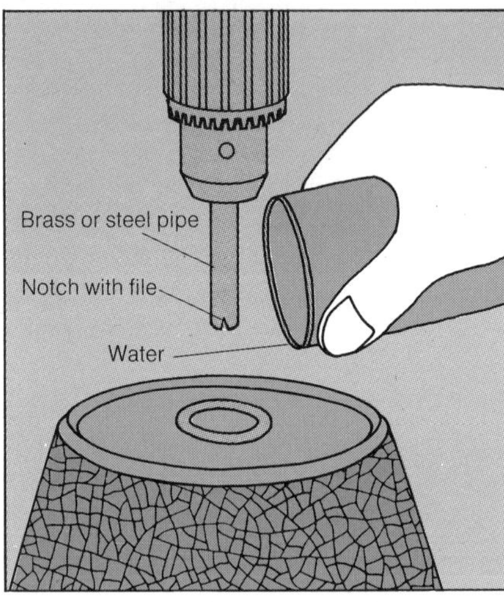

Add a little water. Outside diameter of the pipe or tubing should be equal to hole size.

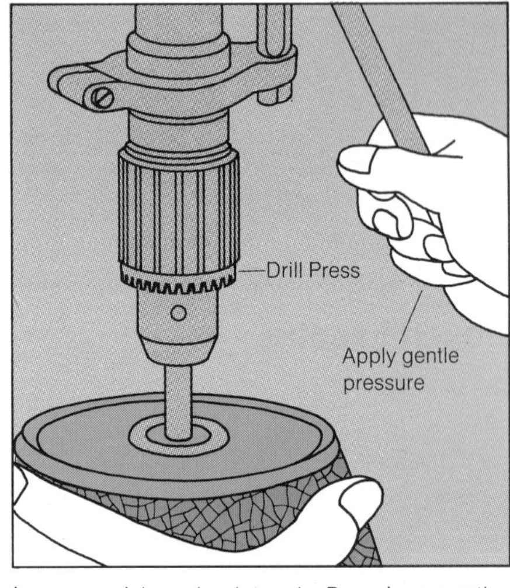

Lower revolving pipe into mix. Bear down gently, adding more powder, until hole is cut.

Ceramic tile

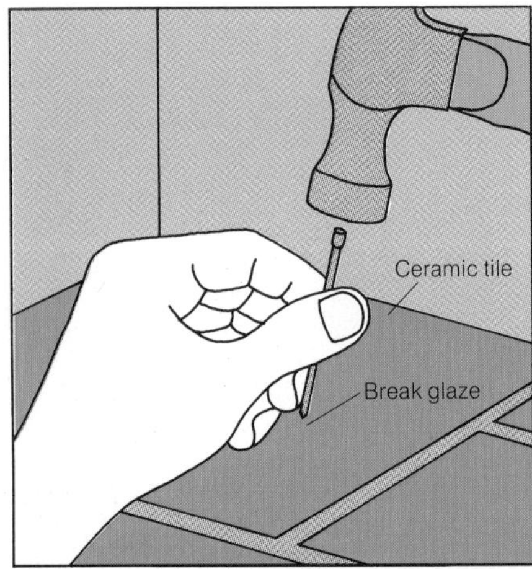

To drill a hole in a ceramic floor tile, lightly punch or score a starting mark.

Make sure the starting mark has penetrated the glaze of the tile; apply oil.

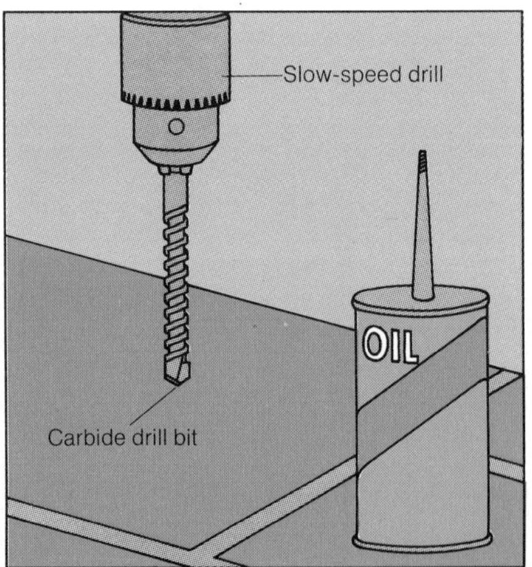

Use a carbide-tipped bit mounted in a slow-speed electric drill. Drill gently.

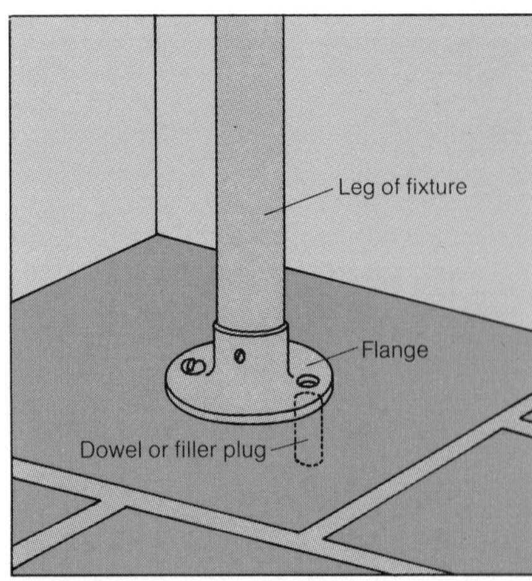

Before securing the fixture, drive dowels into holes; fasten with roundhead screws.

Preparation and procedure

Before mending china, glass, earthenware, or stoneware, clean pieces thoroughly. Adhesives will not stick to greasy or damp surfaces. Select an adhesive (p. 86) which will withstand conditions under which the repaired item will be used. Epoxies provide the strongest bonds and can be washed repeatedly in hot water. Cellulose-base adhesives can take limited washing and they harden faster, but they are not as strong as epoxies. Gap-filling cements are useful for filling chips and can also be used as adhesives.

Before gluing the item, rebuild it without adhesive to see how parts fit together. Always glue small pieces to large ones, allowing the adhesive holding one part to harden before fixing another in place.

Repairing glass

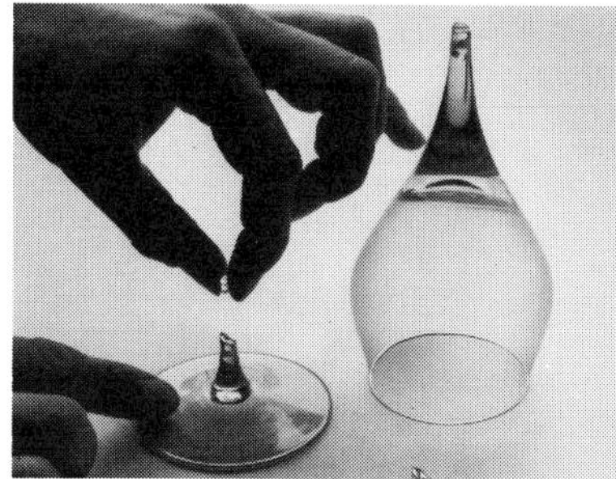

Glass usually breaks into small fragments. Gather up the pieces and arrange in order of rebuilding. Use a clear epoxy cement.

Score each piece with silicon carbide paper; cement small pieces to larger ones. Speed up curing with hair dryer.

Make up a jig from scrap wood to hold upper part of glass against base while epoxy cures; rubber band applies pressure.

Broken handles

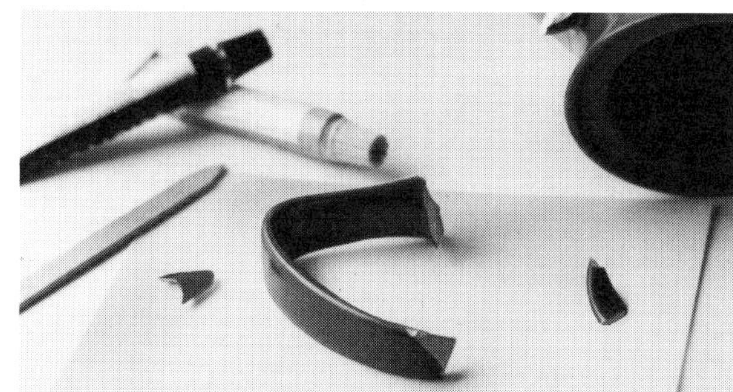

Repair broken handles with epoxy adhesive, since bond strength is important. Clean the parts. Allow them to dry and arrange them in order of replacement. Join small pieces to large ones, allowing the epoxy to harden between each step.

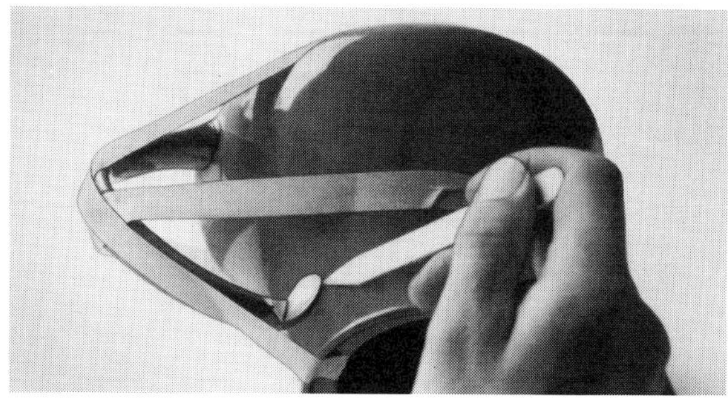

When all parts are joined and the epoxy has hardened, attach the handle to the main body of the vessel and tape it in place. If damage has left a small hole through the vessel, use enough epoxy to fill the hole through to the inside.

Fill large cavities left by missing chips with a thick epoxide filler such as Devcon 2-Ton or Duro E•Pox•E Cement & Filler. For a stronger bond, coat cavity with regular epoxy before using epoxide filler.

Build the filler up slowly, smoothing it with fingers moistened in soapy water. When the shape is right, clean the epoxide filler off surrounding surface. Scrape the filler until it is slightly below the glazed surface.

When set (in about 15 hours), a colored adhesive can be mixed to match the vessel. Do this by mixing a small amount of epoxy with paint pigments. Epoxy adhesives dry to a shiny smooth surface which resembles the original glazed finish.

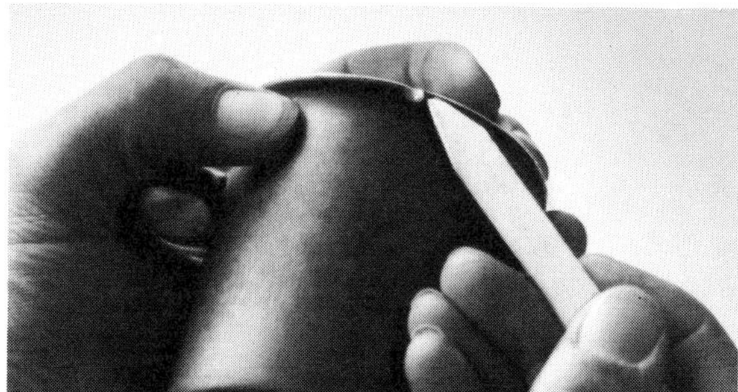

For smaller chips, such as on the rim of this mug, mix a little epoxy adhesive with paint pigment to match the color. Smooth the mixture into the cavity. Speed-up hardening with slight heat—excess heat will discolor the pigments.

Cutting and fabricating

Rigid plastics can be cut and drilled using woodworking tools. When sawing plastics, use fine-tooth blades; drill plastics at low speeds and support the work on a wood base to keep the drill from deforming the plastic when it penetrates. To bend plastics, heat lightly with a propane torch. Move the torch back and forth across the area which you wish to bend, then make the bend by gently forming it over a wood block for a 90 degree bend, or over a dowel if you wish to make a rounded corner.

Plastics can be joined by gluing. Use adhesives recommended by the manufacturer. An alternative joining method is to use a right angle aluminum channel to form corner joints.

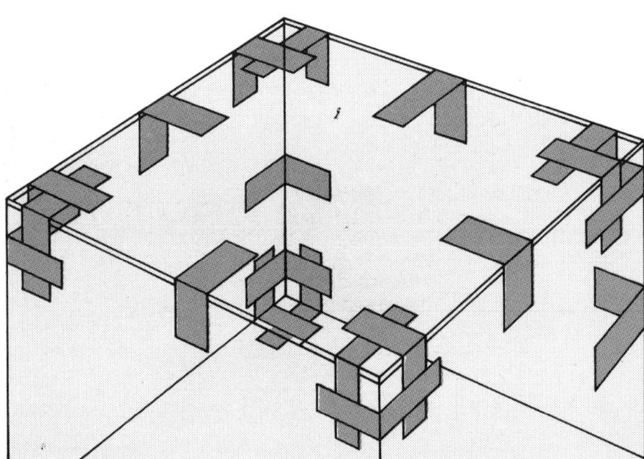

An easy method of joining plastics is with cement. Edges should be lightly sanded, not polished. Use the special cements recommended; tape the edges until the cement sets.

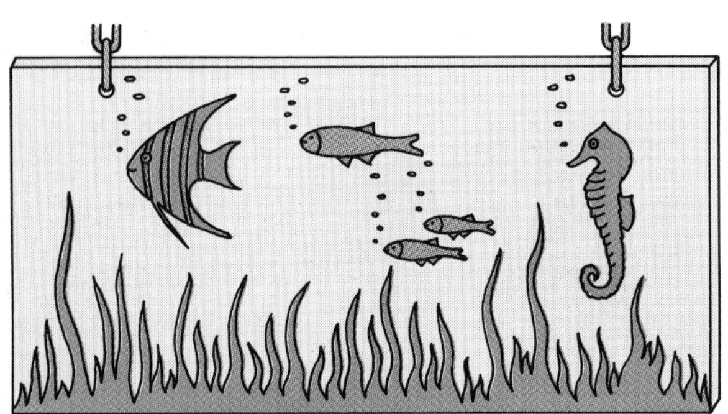

Plastic can be decorated with enamel, lacquers, and oil-base paints, but not with latex-type paints. Spray paint can also be used. For outdoor use, protect paint with clear spray.

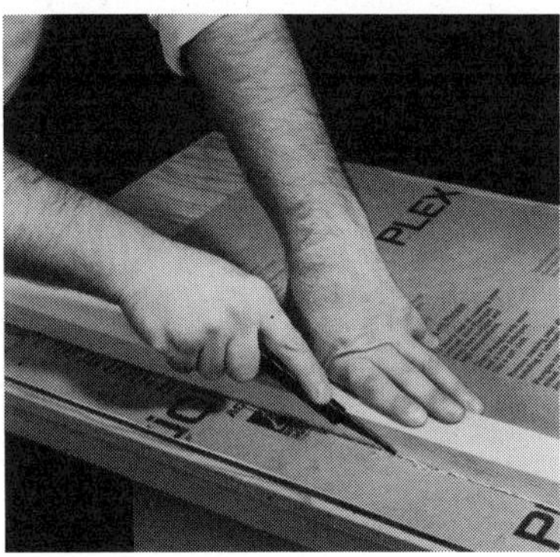

Plexiglas can be cut to size by scribing several lines along a straightedge.

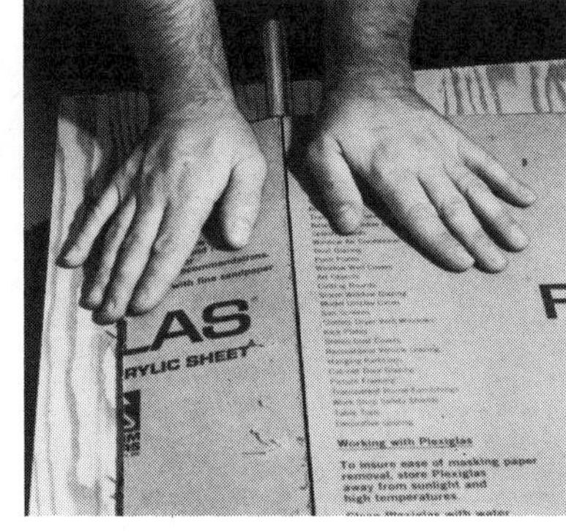

Make the break by pressing down on each side of the scribed line as shown.

Curved cuts can be made with jigsaw, following line marked on cover paper.

Jigsaw and a batten clamped at each end can also be used to cut the plastic.

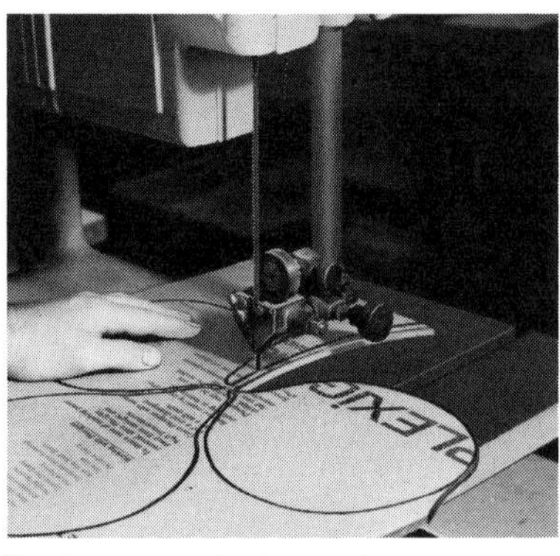

Band saw can also be used to cut curves. Use a fine-tooth blade and feed slowly.

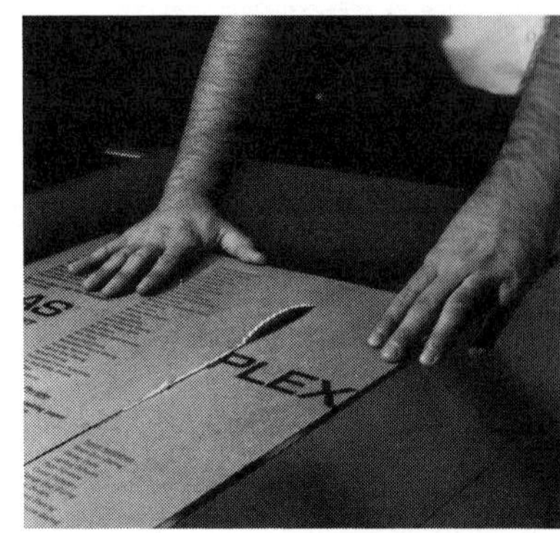

Use a hollow-ground or plywood-type blade to cut the plastic on a circular saw.

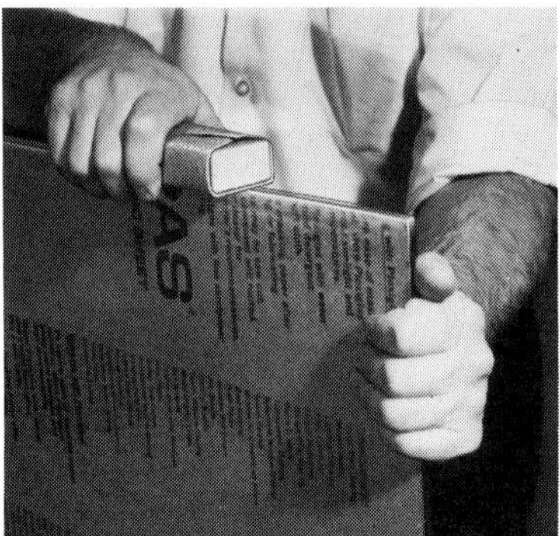

Raw edge should be smoothed with a medium-grade wet-or-dry sandpaper.

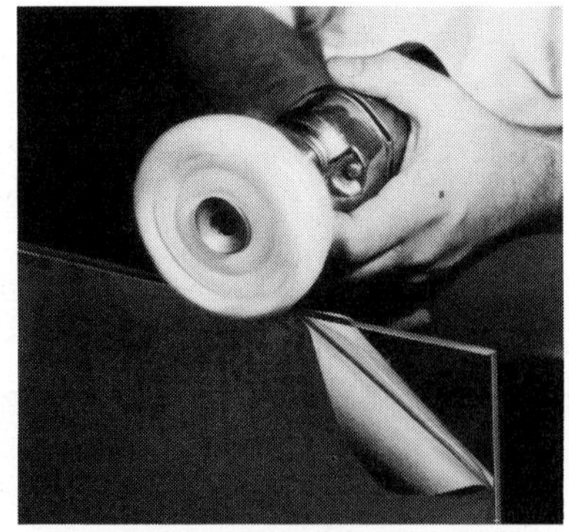

For transparent edge, use buffing wheel, after sanding with extra-fine paper.

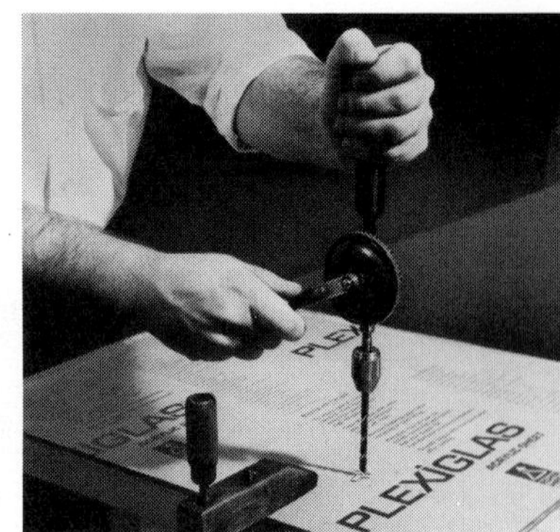

Plexiglas can be drilled the same as wood. Back plastic up with block of wood.

Fixing a storm door

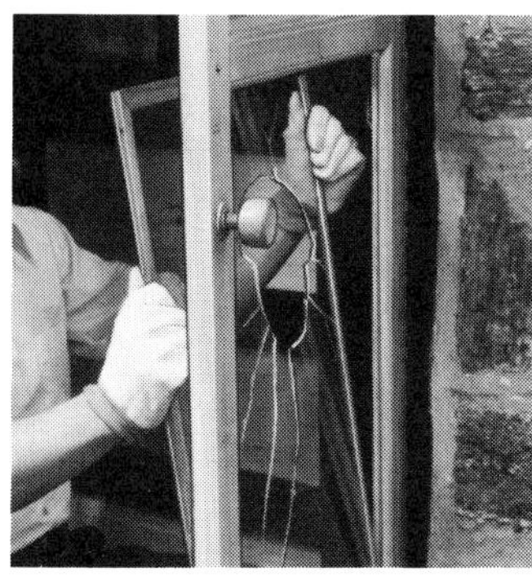
Remove the broken storm door glass as well as the surrounding frame.

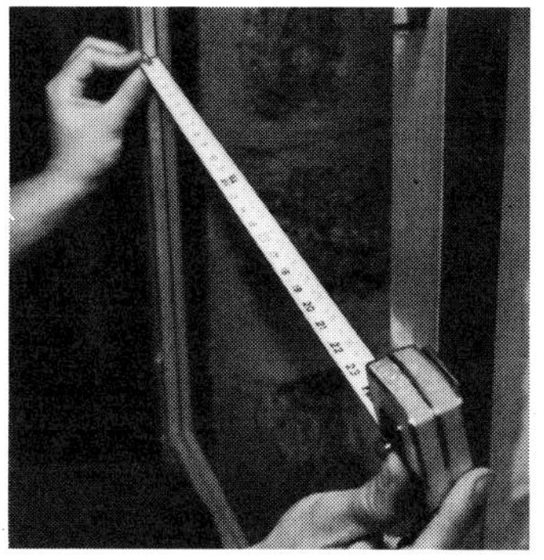
Measure the opening; allow 1/32 in. per foot for thermal expansion.

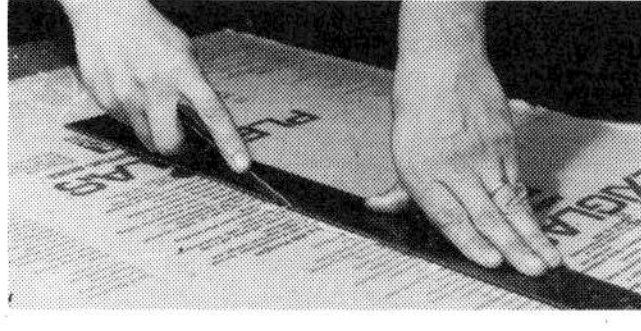

Plastic can be cut with a circular saw or by scribing and breaking.

Remove the protective paper and install the plastic into opening.

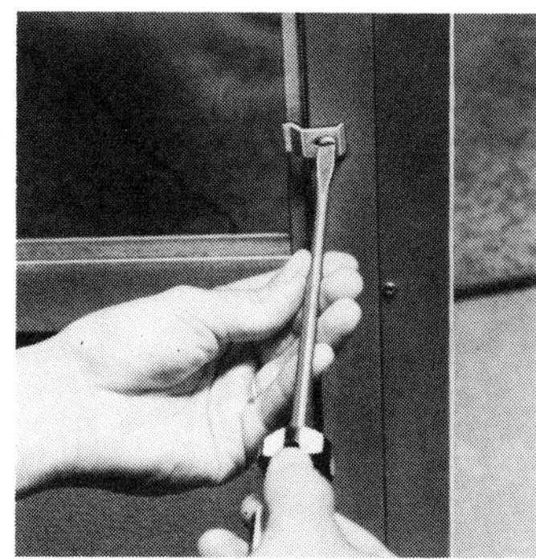
No frame is required; tighten clips just as though frame were present.

Fixing a shower door

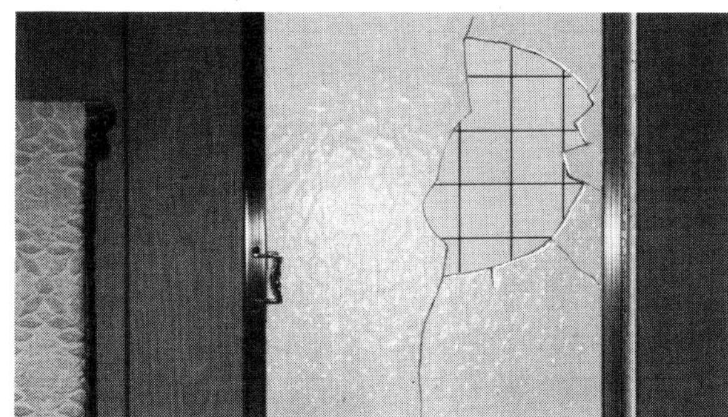
Broken glass shower door can be replaced with a plastic one, thus eliminating the hazards of breakage in the future.

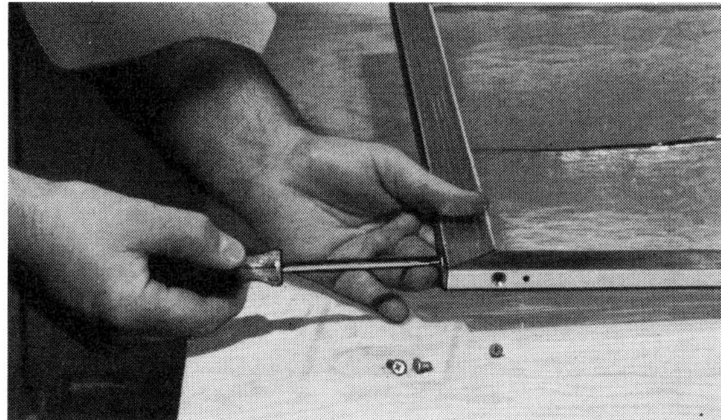
First remove the door from its hinge. Then remove the screws at all four corners of the shower door. Save the screws.

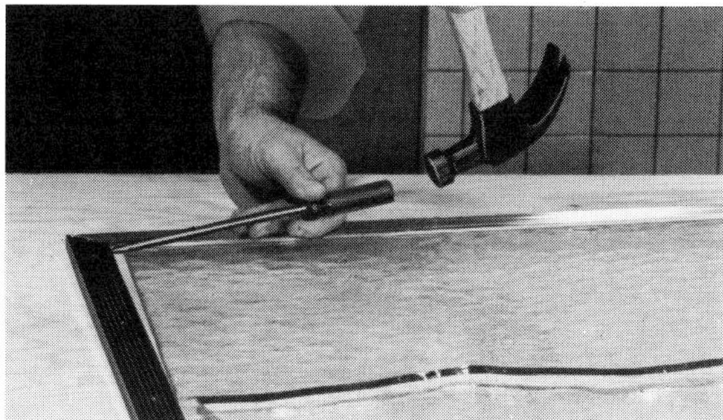
Remove the top and bottom of the door frame and disassemble the entire frame. Work carefully to avoid making burrs.

Carefully remove the broken glass. Clean the gasket and frame. Measure the opening and cut the plastic slightly undersize.

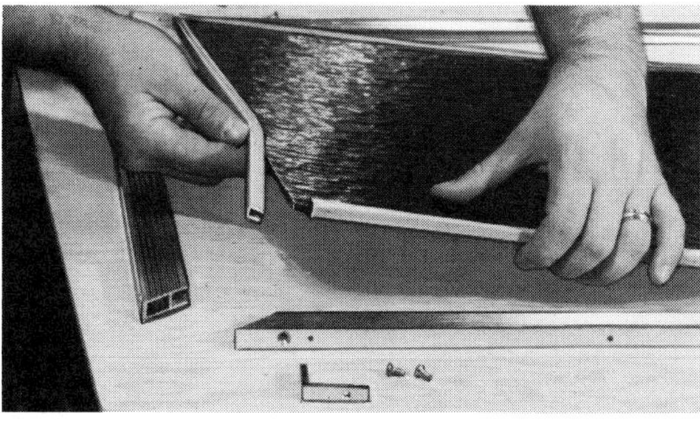
Lightly sand the edges of the plastic. Fit the rubber gasket around the 1/8-in.-thick plastic sheet.

Press the frame over the rubber gasket on all four sides. Replace all screws at each corner and rehang the door.

Special-purpose glass

Making ground glass

Ground glass is useful for glazing windows when privacy is desired. Also, ground glass windows in a basement or attic, disperse light so that a greater area is softly illuminated. All you need to make your own ground glass is a few ounces of silicon carbide (Carborundum or Cristolon). These abrasive powders come in grades from coarse to extra-fine. The finer the grit, the more translucent the glass will appear when the job is done. For the grinding process, you will need a "glass trowel." Make this by gluing a wood handle to a piece of scrap glass. Use epoxy adhesive.

Start grinding by mixing a paste of silicon carbide and water. Rub the paste into the glass with a circular motion. As you grind, the grit will lose its cutting action. When it does, add more grit and water. Frequently wash away the sludge to see where you have missed spots. Once the desired ground glass surface is achieved, wash the glass and stand it on edge to drain dry. When you are installing ground glass windows, make sure the ground surface is on the inside so that they will be less apt to collect dirt.

Ground glass finish is achieved by rubbing two sheets of glass together with a silicon carbide abrasive slurry between them.

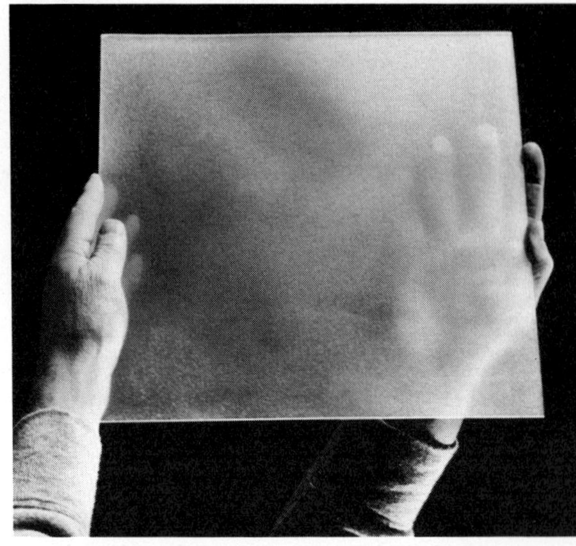

This is the result. The coarseness or fineness of the finish will depend upon the grade of grit used for grinding.

Glass blocks

Glass blocks are often used to seal on-grade cellar or basement windows against water or for privacy, as well as for burglar-proofing. They are also used extensively for partitions and room dividers. Glass blocks, (glass bricks) are installed similarly to brickwork. The blocks are made in three sizes— 8 x 8, 12 x 4 and 8 x 4 inches—all 4 inches thick. Some are especially designed to diffuse light and some are made so as to direct light. They are also available in transparent or translucent designs.

When measuring a window for glass blocks, allow for the thickness of the mortar, about ⅜ inch per block. For example, if you plan to use 8 x 8 blocks, consider the measurements on the basis of 8⅜ x 8⅜. If the width of the window sill does not accept an exact number of whole blocks, install a frame around the top and bottom or sides so that whole blocks will fit. Cutting glass blocks is not possible for the home handyman.

Install glass blocks using white mortar. Allow about a quarter pound of mortar per block. Glass blocks may be laid up to any height without any special support. However, if the blocks are to extend only part way, such as building a half wall, the tops of the blocks should be covered with a wooden shelf. For external installations, such as filling in a window area, first cover the sill area on which the glass blocks are to rest with a thick coat of asphalt roof paint. Next, lay an expansion strip of heavy felt on each side of the frame. When the asphalt has dried, lay a ⅜ inch mortar bed on the sill (p. 447) for the first course of blocks. After the first course has been laid you may want to install steel reinforcement bars for extra-strength burglar protection. Lay the reinforcing bars in the grooves of the lower course. Then lay down the mortar bed for the second course of blocks. Continue this way until the entire area to be covered with the glass blocks has been filled. A caulking compound should be applied all around the periphery of the new glass block window. Apply it to all surfaces where the glass blocks meet the frame or original wall. Areas which are filled with caulking compound should be raked out to a depth of at least ⅜ inch. If a jamb is part of an installation, pack oakum tightly between the glass blocks and the jamb leaving some space for the caulking compound.

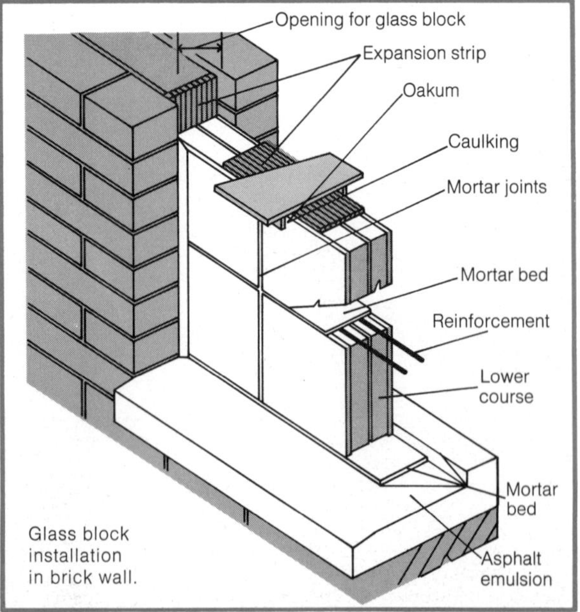

Glass block installation in brick wall.

section 14:

Brickwork and stonework

One of the charms of brickwork or stonework is its rough, apparently artless look. Appearances were never so deceiving. Every element—choice of components, order of work, pattern of laying—is part of a careful plan. Looks are almost a by-product; the point of the meticulous construction is strength. Before undertaking any masonry project, study this section carefully. It can guide you to a finished product that will stand up to whatever it's exposed to, including the elements.

contents

Ordering bricks

The right brick for the job

Before planning any brickwork, consider the conditions the finished structure will be subjected to in use. Bricks for interior applications, for example, have different characteristics than those used outdoors. Similarly, outdoor bricks differ; those used in moderate climates are not suitable for jobs involving exposure to sub-zero temperatures. Bricks also vary in size, texture, and color.

There are three grades of building, or common, brick: SW (severe weathering), MW (medium weathering), and NW (no weathering). SW bricks have a high degree of resistance to frost action. Retaining walls, foundations, patios, or other structures where bricks come in contact with the ground call for SW grade. MW bricks are for use where temperatures are likely to drop below freezing. They have a moderate degree of resistance to frost action and can be used in the exposed faces of walls above the ground. NW bricks are intended for interior walls that are not exposed to the weather.

When buying bricks, check to be sure that all are of uniform size, straight, and hard. Poorly burned bricks are subject to crumbling. Two bricks when struck together should produce a ringing sound, indicating that they are of good quality.

Facing bricks, also called face bricks, are made especially for use in finished wall surfaces that are exposed to the weather. These bricks should have good weathering qualities. Available in a variety of colors, shapes, sizes, and textures, facing bricks usually have sharp edges and square corners. Colors include many shades of red, plus yellows, browns, and even purple and black. You can obtain facing bricks with either rough or smoothed surfaces. Some types are even enameled. There are two grades of facing bricks, SW and MW.

Firebricks are made of a clay that is capable of withstanding extremely high temperatures. Domestically they are used in fireplaces and in the fireboxes of barbecue pits. The mortar used in laying firebricks must also contain fire clay.

Reclaimed bricks can often provide an antique decorative effect. They may also be used to match the bricks in an existing structure. Often they can be purchased through a brickyard, although the most reliable source would be a demolition contractor. When working with reclaimed bricks, examine each one before laying for cracks and other defects.

How many do you need?

Before planning a job, it is essential to know what size brick you will use. This can depend on the sizes your local brickyard stocks. Building bricks, however, are usually 2¼ inches high, 3¾ inches wide, and 8 inches long.

Estimating: To estimate the number of bricks for a wall, first determine the wall's total square footage, next calculate the square footage of doors and windows, then deduct door and window area from total area; the result is the area you have to cover with brick. Figure 6.16 bricks per square foot. Be sure to allow extra bricks for breakage and waste.

To allow for the ½-inch mortar joint between bricks, use the nominal, or working, brick dimensions of 2¾, 4¼, and 8½ inches. For example, if a wall is to be 17 feet tall and 11 feet long, divide the length, in inches, by the nominal brick length of 8½ inches and divide the height by the nominal brick height of 2¾ inches. You would need 24 bricks laid end to end for each course, or layer; the wall would be 48 courses high and would require a total of 1,152 bricks to build.

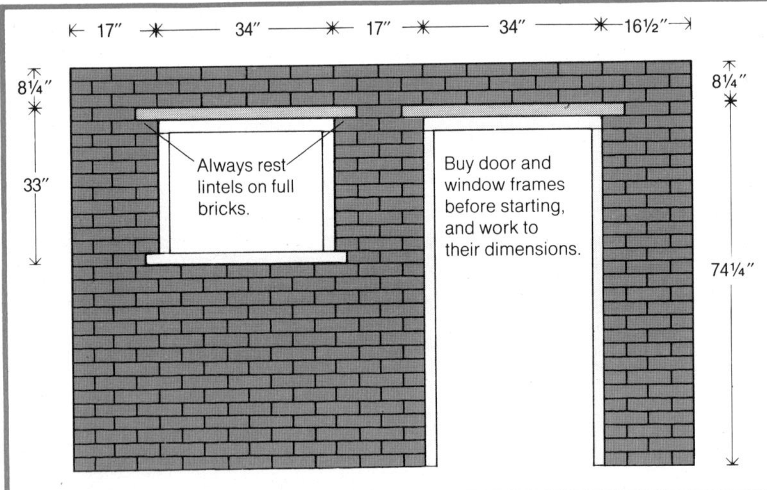

Planning a brick structure: Sketch the project to scale. Keep all height measurements to multiples of 2¾ in., the nominal brick height. Try to keep the length of brick structures to multiples of 8½ and 4¼ in. By working to these brick and half-brick sizes, you eliminate unnecessary brick cutting and give the job a neater appearance. To determine the number of square feet to be covered by bricks, subtract from the total wall area the square footage to be occupied by windows and doors.

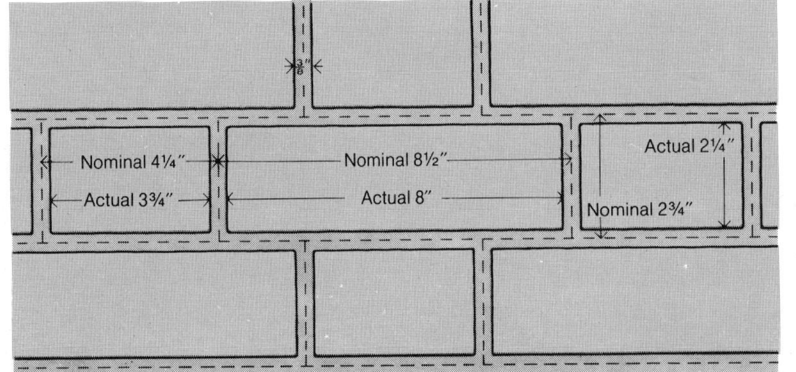

To estimate the number of bricks for any structure, use nominal brick sizes. Mortar joint between bricks makes nominal sizes ½ in. larger than actual sizes.

To stack bricks safely, allow the end walls to slope inward toward the top.

Composition of mortar

Mortar consists of a binder (cement, lime, or both), an aggregate of sand, and water; proportions by volume are usually 1 part binder to 3 parts sand.

You can be assured of the quality of Portland cement if the approval of the ASTM (American Society for Testing and Materials) is printed on the bag.

The sand must be clean and free of clay, shale, and vegetable matter. To test it, squeeze a handful; it should fall apart when the fingers are opened and it should not stain or soil the hand. Do not use sea sand; it contains salts that cause the mortar to remain damp and to discolor.

The water used for mixing mortar should be clean. Floating dust and foreign matter in the water will produce inferior mortar. Never use salt water.

Selection and mixing of mortar

The amateur bricklayer will usually use a dry-mix mortar or masonry cement mortar, depending on the size of the job.

Use a garden hoe to mix mortar in small batches in a mortar box or a clean metal wheelbarrow, adding enough water to make it smooth and plastic. Mix only enough to use within an hour or an hour and a half. Mortar that is of the proper consistency will slide readily from the trowel and will be stiff enough to keep its shape and not sag when piled on the trowel.

Always use fresh cement products. Cement deteriorates with age, so there is no point in saving it from one year to the next.

For a small project that requires no more than 1 cubic foot of mortar, buy dry-mix brick mortar. This contains all the necessary ingredients except water and is the easiest mortar to mix. It is, however, the most expensive.

For a larger job, it is less expensive to use masonry cement mortar. To make it, mix three units of sand and one unit of masonry cement (mortar cement, which already contains the correct amount of lime). Mix until every grain of sand is completely covered. Add a little water at a time and mix until mortar is a uniform color and has a smooth texture.

Cement-lime mortar requires the user to mix Portland cement, lime, sand, and water. It is a little cheaper than masonry cement mortar and is used for large projects and special jobs, such as laying sills. Hydrated lime is easier to use than quicklime; add it dry to the mixture, but slake (mix with water) quicklime first. To make cement-lime mortar, mix sand and cement thoroughly; add lime and mix completely again; then add water little by little and mix until you get smooth mortar of uniform color.

Mortar coloring, sold as powder or paste, may be used to conceal or emphasize joints. Up to 10 percent by weight may be added to the cement. With quicklime, add coloring only after lime has been slaked at least 24 hours; then mix thoroughly and strain through a coarse sieve before adding to sand. With masonry cement, blend coloring powder thoroughly with dry masonry cement and sand. Make a sample batch and let it set before doing a job.

Grout is a thin mixture of Portland cement, lime, sand, and water. It is poured into places where regular mortar would be difficult or impossible to apply. Use grout sparingly; water weakens cement.

Freezing weather: Laying bricks in sub-zero temperature is a professional's job. Severe cold freezes the mortar, causing severe cracking. For emergency repair jobs, keep bricks, sand, and cement warm under a tent-like tarpaulin. Use an oil heater under the tarp to keep the temperature up. Use warm water when mixing mortar. Cover the finished job with a tarp; if possible, keep it warm until mortar sets.

EQUIVALENT MORTAR MIXES

Type of brickwork	Cement-lime mortar	Masonry cement mortar
Retaining walls; sills and copings	1 part cement ½ part lime 4½ parts sand	1 part masonry cement 3 parts sand
Freestanding walls; work below moisture line; uncoated parapets	1 part cement 1 part lime 6 parts sand	1 part masonry cement 4½ parts sand
Severely exposed walls above moisture line; mortar-coated parapets; inner leaf of cavity wall	1 part cement 1 part lime 6 parts sand	1 part masonry cement 4½ parts sand
Internal non-load-bearing walls	1 part cement 2 parts lime 9 parts sand	1 part masonry cement 6 parts sand

The general purpose mix (1 part masonry cement, 3 parts sand) is recommended for almost all home repair jobs. Judging when other mixes are suitable is beyond the experience of most amateurs.

HOW MUCH MORTAR?

For 100 square feet of brick wall surface

Wall thickness	Number of bricks	Cubic feet of mortar	Mix by volume 1:3	
			Masonry cement bags	Cubic feet of sand
4″	616	9	3	9
8″	1,232	21	7	21

The mortar quantities in this table are approximations. They allow for roughly 20% waste for a 4 in. wall, 12% waste for an 8 in. wall. These allowances are conservative since waste can be higher than 50%, depending on the care and skill of the bricklayer. Table is based on standard building bricks—2½ x 3¾ x 8 in. All mortar joints are assumed to be ½ in. thick. A 70-lb. bag of masonry cement holds 1 cu. ft.

The basic kit

In addition to the tools pictured here, you'll need a 4-foot spirit level, a metal wheelbarrow, a mason's line, either line pins or blocks to hold line, a 50-foot measuring tape, a garden hoe, and a flat shovel. Safety glasses are a wise precaution against flying chips when you are cutting bricks or cleaning out old mortar joints.

If your project requires the use of a scaffold, you can rent one or improvise by using ladders and planking. With any scaffolding, be sure that planks are free of large knots and other defects. Pretest planking by suspending it a foot or so above ground level, then have two adults stand in the center. Always have the same side of a plank facing up; mark the top side so you'll know.

Specialty tools: You will probably have to buy some of the tools shown here. Bear in mind that it is better to purchase quality tools than so-called bargains that won't stand up to rough use. **1.** Brick trowel. To lay mortar, form brickwork joints, tap bricks into place, and trim cut bricks. **2.** Bricklayer's hammer. To cut bricks. **3.** Heavy-duty 2½-pound hammer. To remove damaged bricks, chip mortar, cut bricks. **4.** Bricklayer's 4-inch chisel. To cut bricks, split stone, chip mortar, remove damaged bricks. **5.** Cape chisel with ⅜-inch blade. To clean out mortar joints for repointing. **6.** Square brick jointer. To shape and smooth mortar joints.

Tools you can make: 1. Story pole, or gauge rod. To ensure that brick courses are rising evenly. Make from a length of 1 x 2 equal to the height of the wall being built. Use a saw to make a cut marking the height of each course (2¾ inches—the height of a brick plus the mortar bed). **2.** Slope, or "batter," gauge. To check the "batter," or slope, of walls or chimneys. Make from 1 x 2s to size dictated by the job. **3.** Hawk. To hold a small amount of mortar for pointing and small mortar-patching jobs. Make this tool 1 foot square, using ⅜-inch marine plywood (for strength and lightness). The handle is screwed on; use a piece of old broom handle or 1½-inch dowel 6 inches long. **4.** Spot board. To hold a reserve of mortar. Make from ⅜-inch marine plywood or ¼-inch tempered hardboard 3 feet square. Cleats that support it can be 1 x 3s, 2 x 2s, or 2 x 4s. **5.** Large builder's square. For checking corners. Keep the measurements in the ratio 3:4:5. Using 1 x 2s, make it 18 x 24 x 30 inches.

Tools to buy

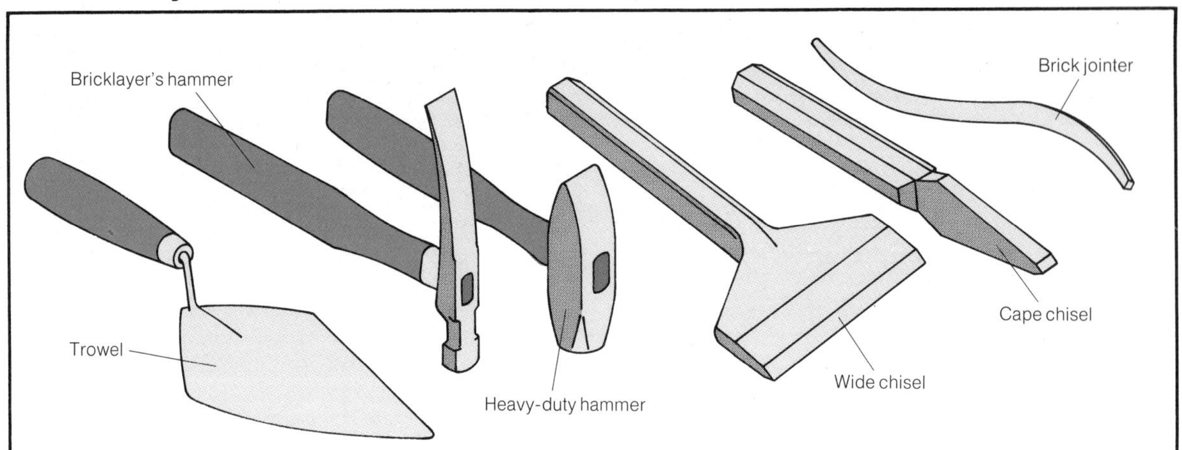

Tools to make

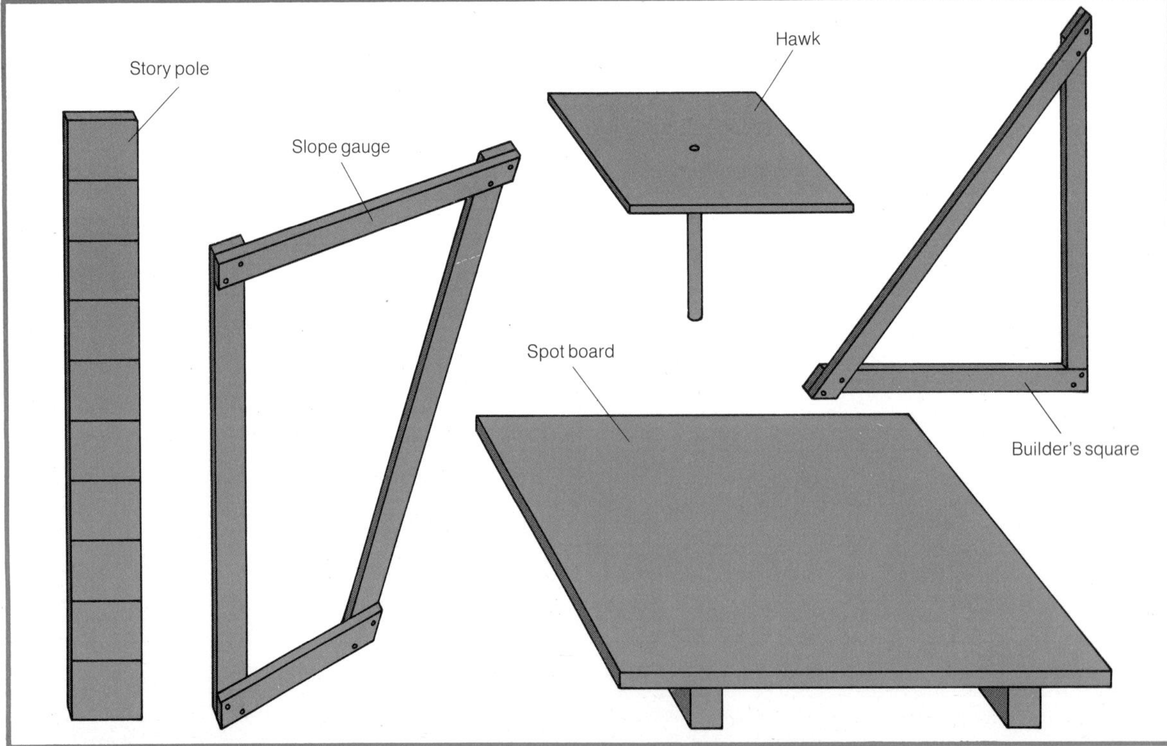

Using a trowel

Handling a trowel properly is the key to laying bricks correctly and quickly. A strong, even bond requires that mortar be properly placed before the bricks are laid, and only careful attention to trowel techniques will make this possible.

If you are laying bricks for the first time, take the trouble to build a small practice wall before actually undertaking your major project. This will help develop the knack of handling the trowel properly. This preliminary step is not expensive, since the practice bricks can be used again if the mortar is cleaned off of them within two hours.

Study the techniques shown in the accompanying photographs. With practice, the sequences of scooping up and laying mortar should become one smooth operation that will be done almost automatically.

Some beginners will find that they are able to work more comfortably and efficiently if they use the smaller and lighter pointing trowel instead of the standard-size brick trowel for placing and trimming the mortar (p.455).

Although the edge of the trowel can be used to cut bricks, a beginner is likely to find this difficult to manage. It is safer to use the trowel only for placing and trimming the mortar and for cleaning up the cut after the bricks have been severed with a bricklayer's chisel.

Use the trowel handle to tap a brick gently into place in the mortar bed (p.455). Use the edge of the trowel to form brickwork joints (p.456).

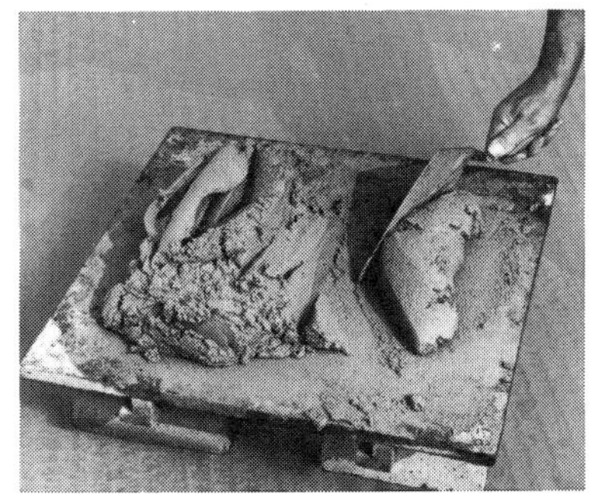

To pick up mortar, saw off a slice with trowel; draw it toward you. With sawing action, form back of slice into curve.

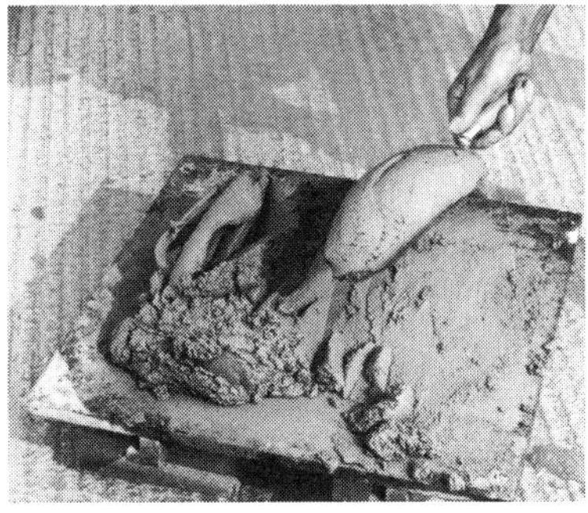

Lift mortar by sweeping trowel under it from behind, thus loading trowel fully with an easy-to-lay mortar "sausage."

To place sausage accurately, hold trowel above brick, pull trowel back and roll mortar off of it in one smooth motion.

Use point of trowel to smooth mortar into bed about ½ in. thick, ready to receive bricks. Note proper length of bed.

To form vertical joints, "butter" one end of each brick before laying; doing so after laying may push it out of line.

Trim off excess mortar around edges. Lay brick with buttered end against adjoining brick. Make joint ½ in. thick.

Using a bricklayer's chisel

Before cutting bricks, try to determine how many half-bricks you will need so that they can be cut in batches. This will also give you practice.

Test each brick to be cut by tapping it with a hammer or striking it against another brick. You should hear a clear ringing note, indicating that the brick is good. If the resulting sound is dull, the brick is likely to crumble when it is cut.

You can use the chisel with any standard hammer, but a heavy-duty hammer with a 2½-pound head works best. Place the chisel blade on the cutting point of the brick. Tilt the handle slightly toward the waste end of the brick and strike sharply. Generally, the sharper the blow, the cleaner the cut. Wear safety glasses when doing this work.

To cut a brick with a heavy-duty hammer and chisel, use a sharp pencil and rule to mark face side where it is to be cut.

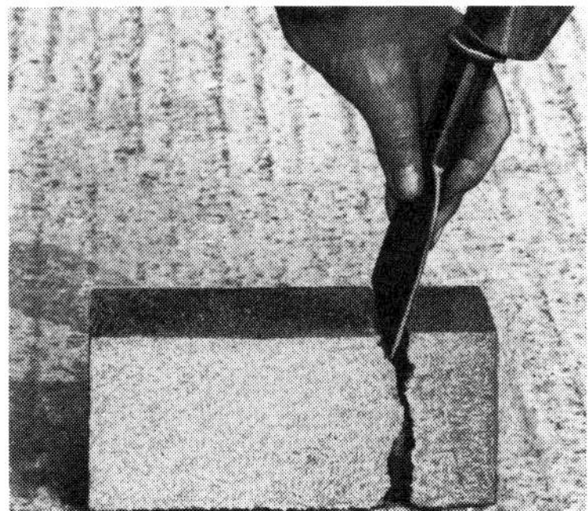

Place chisel on mark. Tilt handle toward waste end. Strike sharply once. Some bricks must also be cut from the back.

Clean the cut by chopping it with curved edge of trowel. Brick is usable if the face side is the right length.

Using a line

To lay a course of bricks level, plumb, and aligned, use a line with blocks or use pins or nails. After the first course is completed, build up leads (several courses laid at a corner, each course successively shorter) square and level and with the exact amount of mortar between the joints.

The easy way to use a line is with plastic line blocks. Fit line into groove and draw it taut; the tension of the line will hold the plastic blocks in place.

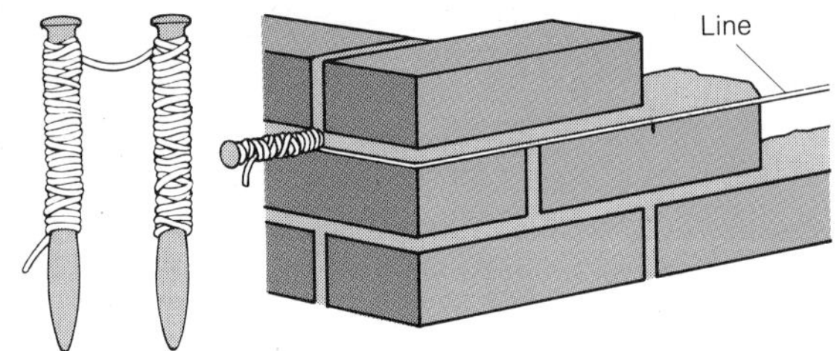

Pins stuck in mortar hold line taut.

To use a line without blocks, stick flat-bladed pins (or drive nails) into mortar joints around the corners from the course to be laid. Attach line to pins so it will be flush with upper outside edge of the corner bricks and the course you will lay between them. Keep the line taut. For a long wall, lay up leads at intermediate points to support the line.

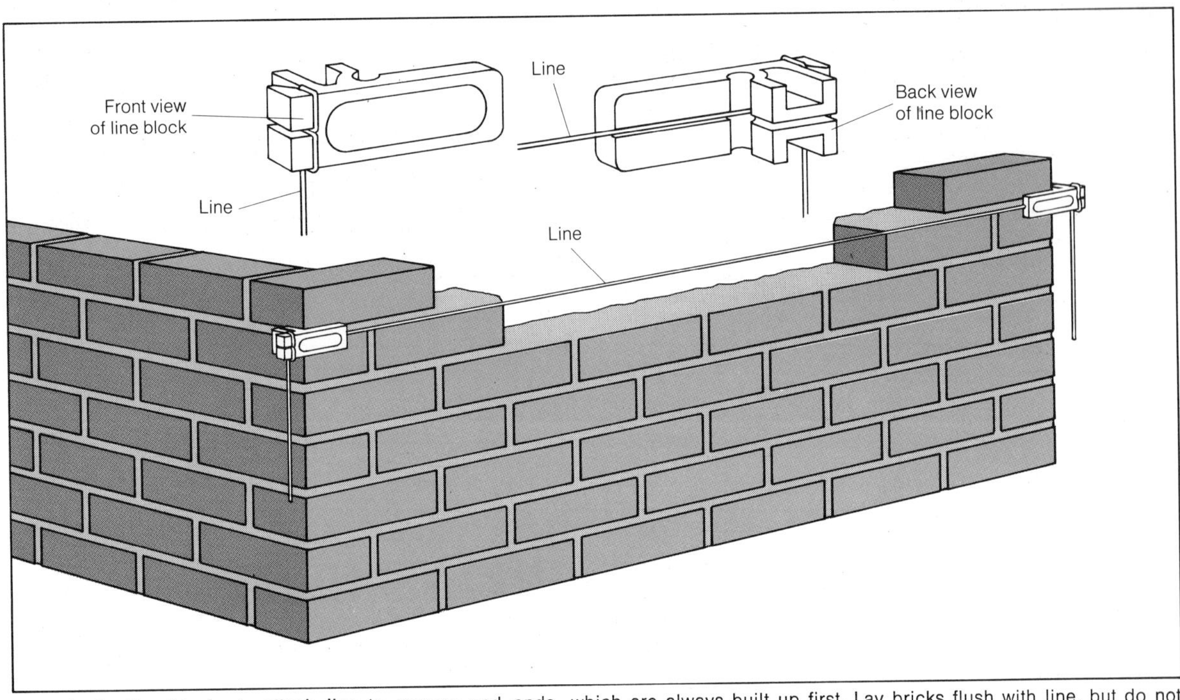

Use plastic line blocks to attach line to corners and ends, which are always built up first. Lay bricks flush with line, but do not push it out. Line blocks, unlike pins and nails, leave no holes in mortar to be filled in later.

Checking with a spirit level

Use a 4-foot level to check brickwork four ways before the mortar sets. The level's vertical and horizontal bubbles will tell you whether or not your work is level in those directions. You can use the level as a straightedge to check both diagonals; in this use the position of the bubbles has no significance. Hold the level diagonally across the face of the wall and see if there are any gaps between level and wall. If gaps occur, the wall is out of true; correct this by gently tapping the bricks back into line against the level. Vertical and horizontal irregularities may also be corrected by gently tapping the level with your trowel handle.

Keep the bottom of the level clean; even a small dab of mortar on the surface will make it inaccurate.

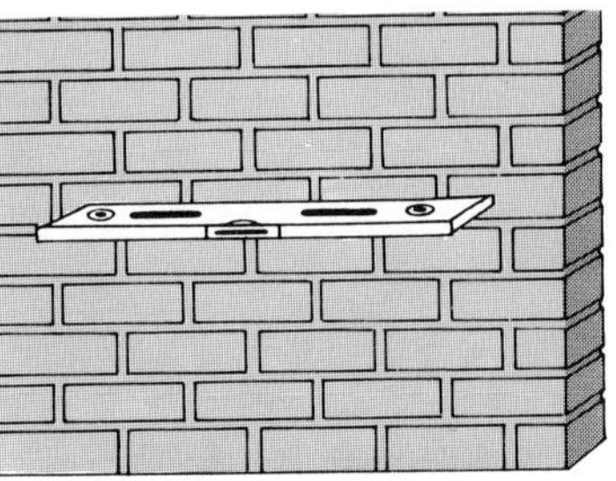

Bubble readings are used to check wall face vertically and horizontally.

Ignore vertical and horizontal bubbles when using level as a straightedge.

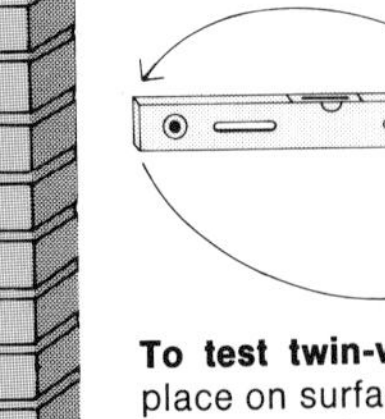

To test twin-vial level place on surface that gives a level reading; turn it around; if it doesn't read the same, have level adjusted.

Types of bond

The bond is the pattern formed by the courses in a brick wall. Courses are laid on top of each other so that the vertical joints in one course never fall directly above the vertical joints in the course below. In most bonds, however, the vertical joints of alternate courses should coincide exactly.

In all bonds, the bricks laid end to end in the wall are called stretchers, and those laid crosswise are called headers.

Although the interlocking pattern creates an interesting decorative effect, the main reason for bonding is that it produces a stronger wall. The staggered vertical joints cause the downward dead-load pressure of the bricks themselves and of such components as the roof and floor joists to be spread over the entire wall. The stronger wall also gives better support to these components.

To see how well a particular bond will match its surroundings, build a small test wall without mortar. Such a test structure will also show you the need for bats and closers in every bond to achieve staggered vertical joints. A bat is a partial brick. A closer is the last brick laid in a course; it can be either a whole or a partial brick.

Running bond is the simplest type. All bricks except corners and ends are laid as stretchers. Corners are headers; ends are half-bats. This bond is very strong longitudinally, very weak transversely.

American bond, also called common bond, is a modification of the running bond. Every sixth or seventh course is a header course. The result is a great increase in the wall's transverse strength.

English bond, for walls 8 in. thick, is made by running alternating courses of all headers, then all stretchers. The staggered vertical joints are achieved by the use of half-header bricks (a).

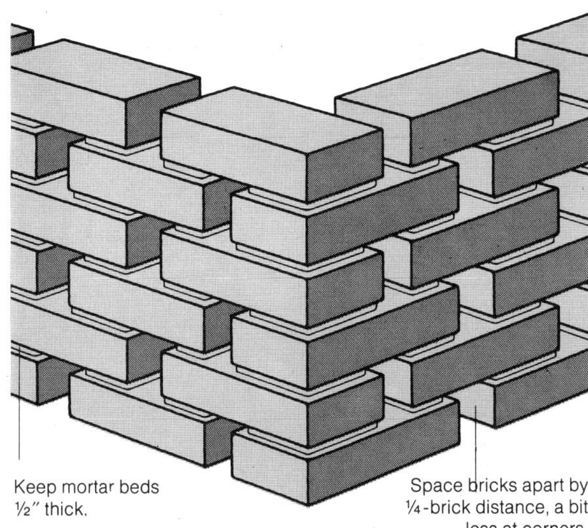

Open bonding makes a fine decorative wall for garden or patio. Lay each course as stretchers with a quarter-brick space between bricks. To maintain the bond, reduce slightly the space on each side of the corner bricks. If tied to the bank and kept low, open bonding can be used for retaining walls.

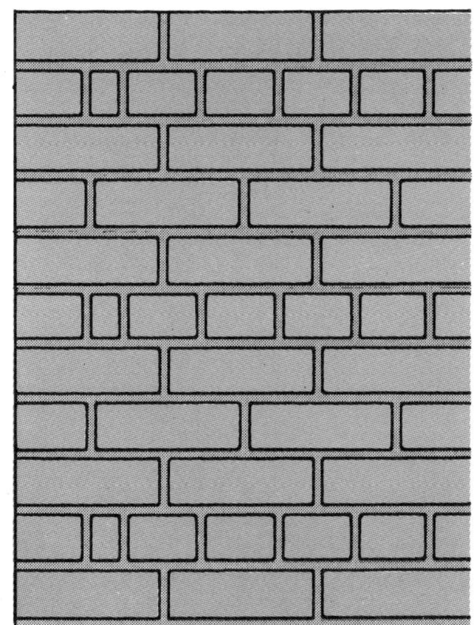

English garden wall bond, for walls 8 in. or more thick, is laid with three courses of stretchers for every course of headers. It is less strong than English bond, almost as strong as Flemish bond.

Flemish bond, also for 8-in.-thick walls, has identical courses, each consisting of pairs of stretchers laid side by side alternating with headers. Joints are staggered by using half-header bricks (a).

Dutch, or English cross, bond has alternating stretcher and header courses. Coinciding vertical joints of stretcher courses are separated by two header courses and one stretcher course.

Corners, ends, junctions

Running bond

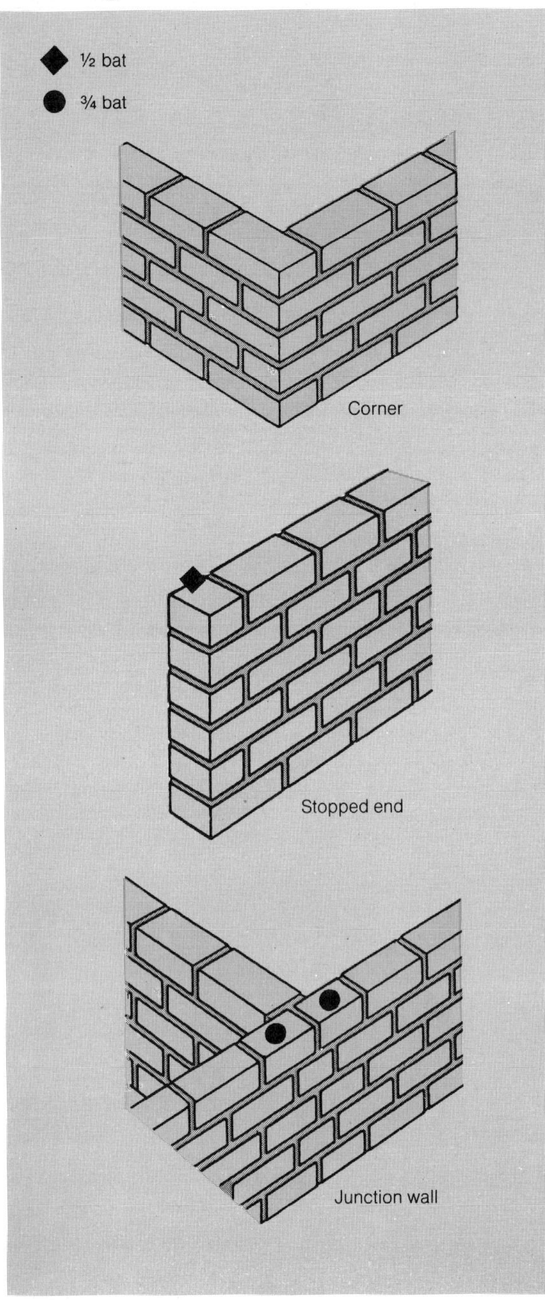

English bond

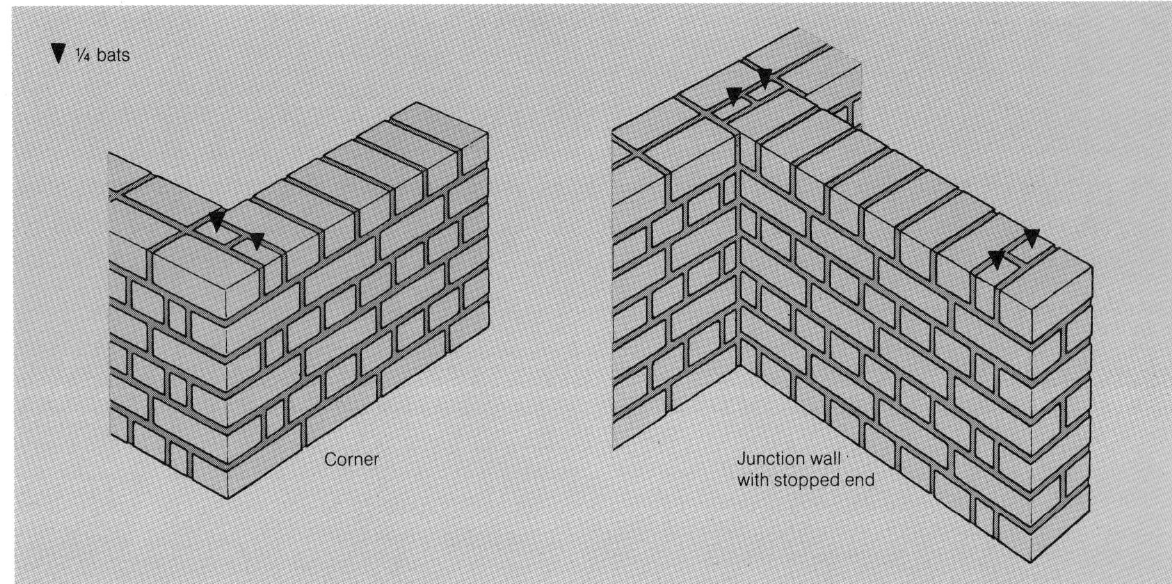

Flemish bond

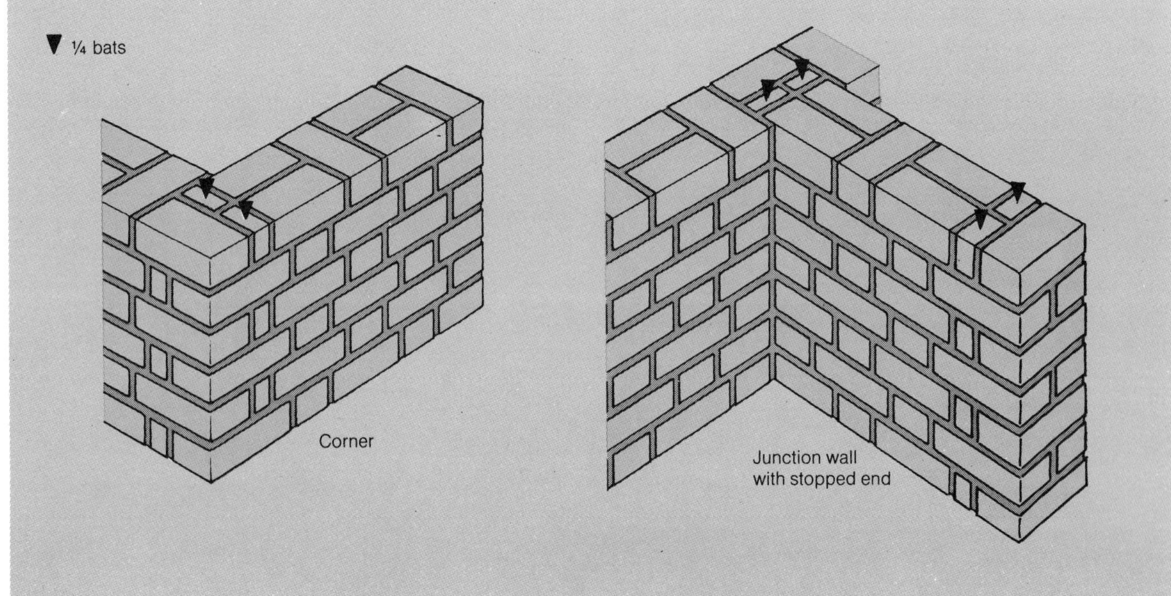

Moisture from the air

A **brick cavity wall** consists of two parallel tiers of brick separated by a 2-inch air space and joined by metal wall ties. Use facing brick for the outer wall, NW brick (p.446), hollow tile, or concrete block for the inner wall. Cavity wall ties are corrosion-resistant metal, usually steel, about $\frac{3}{16}$ inch in diameter and rectangular or Z-shaped. Build up the inner and outer tiers of a cavity wall simultaneously so that the ties can be placed in parallel horizontal mortar joints; for a tile or concrete block inner wall, adjust vertical spacing of ties to match joints in outer brick wall.

A **brick veneer wall** is made by laying a single-tier brick outer wall over a frame wall. A 1-inch air space separates the two walls, and metal ties connect them. Cover the frame wall with heavyweight waterproof building paper. Veneer wall ties are 6-inch-long corrugated metal strips; copper is the best metal for the purpose. Nail the ties to the frame wall so that about 3 inches of each tie can be embedded in the horizontal mortar joints as the bricks are laid. Use nails of the same metal as the ties. After a brick veneer wall is laid, seal the air space by nailing and caulking brick veneer moldings around all openings. A brick veneer wall added to an existing frame structure requires a full foundation; this is a job to be done by a professional.

The still air between the two wall surfaces in brick veneer and cavity walls keeps a house cooler in summer, warmer in winter. Moisture that penetrates the outer wall runs down between the walls, leaving the inner wall dry. To expedite drainage, make "weep holes" in the outer wall. Place metal or plastic tubes ⅜ inch in outside diameter 2 to 3 feet apart in the first bed of mortar, under the first course of bricks and on top of the termite shield. In termite-infested areas place copper flashing over foundation flush with inside and about 1 inch beyond outside; bend extension slightly downward. Tubes must extend from air space to flush with the face of the wall; slope their outside edges downward.

Mortar or other debris that falls into the air space when a brick veneer or cavity wall is being built will cover weep holes and will form "bridges" between the walls, allowing moisture to reach and penetrate the inner wall. To trap debris, lay a batten with wire loops at both ends over the wall ties. Use a batten almost as wide as the air space and as long as you can conveniently handle. When you reach the next course that contains ties, raise the batten by means of wire loops, clean it, install the ties, and place the batten over them.

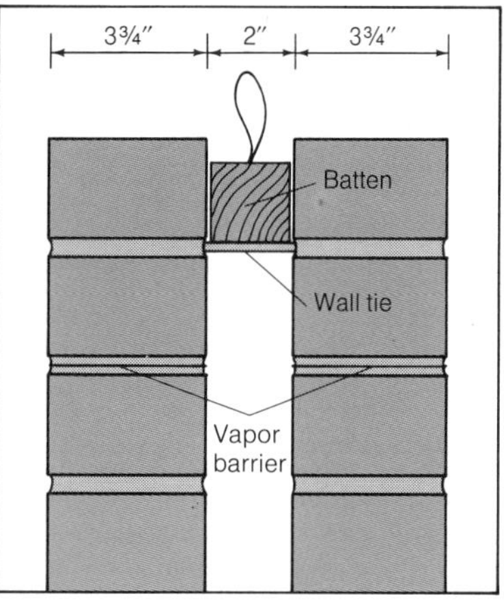

Batten rests on ties between tiers of cavity wall, catches mortar droppings.

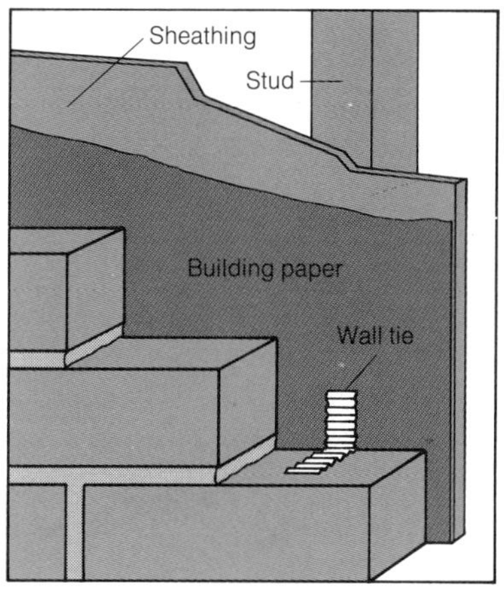

A brick veneer wall is separated from the frame wall by a 1-in. air space.

Stagger wall ties every 2 ft. in every fourth or fifth course.

Moisture from the soil

Bricks in direct contact with a wet surface draw moisture like a blotter. If the condition persists, the entire brick structure becomes damp and sweats. To prevent this, any brick structure must have a vapor barrier. This is provided by a layer of waterproof building paper or polyethylene. Lay a thin bed of mortar, about ¼ inch thick; put down the vapor barrier, covering the width of the course; complete the bed with the other ¼ inch of mortar. Where one end of the vapor barrier stops and another starts, overlap generously.

Building codes demand vapor barriers at breaks in external house walls and where gaps in cavity or brick veneer walls are sealed. It is advisable to use them for any brick structure.

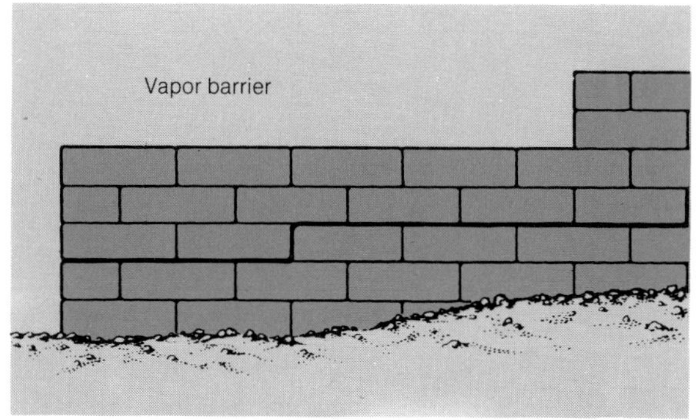

Embed vapor barrier in horizontal mortar joint two courses, or 5½ in., above the normal soil level. Follow slope of land.

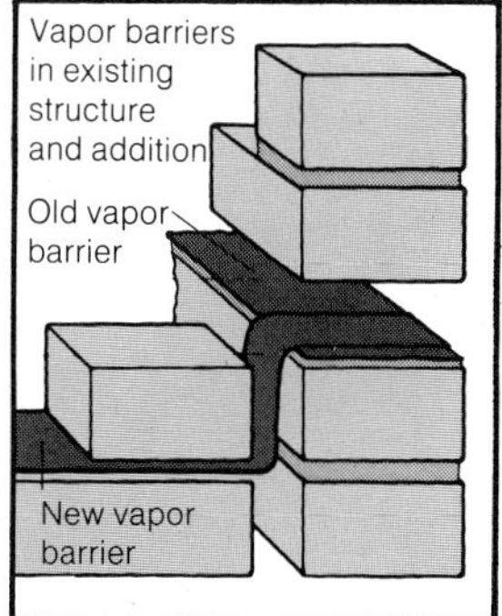

Where two vapor barriers meet, they must overlap.

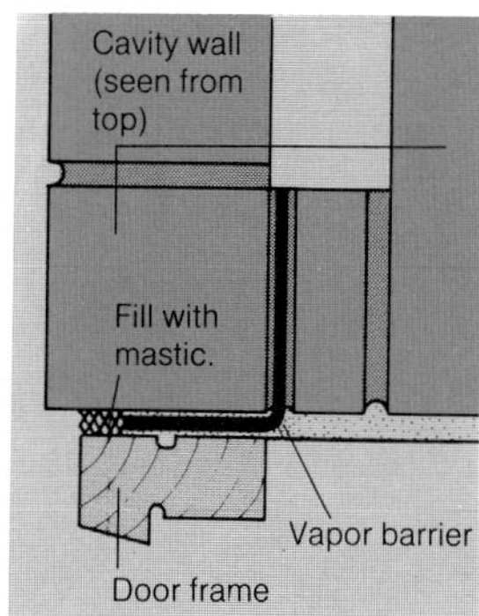

Sandwich vapor barriers between cavity-closing bricks.

Laying the bricks

Preparation and procedure

Order all materials and mark out and build footings and foundations (p.472) well before you plan to begin laying the bricks. Have enough plastic sheeting or canvas on hand to cover the materials and to protect the work overnight or in bad weather.

Place piles of bricks at convenient intervals around the job. Keep a bucket of water nearby to clean off tools as you use them. Mortar dries out the skin; so try not to handle it too much. Rubber gloves are a good idea.

Bricks should be damp when laid. Wet them thoroughly with spray from a garden hose, especially in hot, dry weather. Dampen spot boards (p.448) also.

To verify how many bricks to cut, set out the first course without mortar on the foundation wall or slab on which it will be laid. Allow for the ½-inch mortar joint between bricks and mark the position of each brick on the outer edge of the foundation. Mix the first batch of mortar, making up no more than can be used in an hour or two.

Follow the sequence in the photographs. A foundation wall should extend above ground level, but for the sake of clarity the work is shown here beginning at the surface.

Build up corners or stopped ends first. Make sure they are vertical and level. Use a builder's square to check the corners.

Lay ample mortar beds. You cannot squeeze mortar into a joint after bricks are laid. So butter ends generously with mortar; butter headers on the side. Shove the brick into the mortar bed and tap it gently with the trowel handle to level and bed it properly. With trowel, scrape off mortar that oozes out of joints. To lay the closer (last brick in course), butter both ends and put mortar on the ends of the bricks it will lie between. For a 2-brick-wide 8-inch wall, butter one end and one side of each brick in inner wall; build up both tiers simultaneously.

Do not move a brick that has been laid. If bricks are not level or plumb or aligned, tap them gently before the mortar sets. Avoid heavy tapping; it might dislodge brick or cause a hollow space in a joint. If a brick is improperly laid and the mortar has set, remove that brick and all bricks above it; remove the mortar too. Put down new mortar and lay a clean brick or bricks in it.

Brush off loose mortar before it hardens; you may have to use a wire brush for stubborn spots.

1. To mark the front face of the wall (the building line), set out two stakes at each corner as shown in photograph. Stretch strings between the corners, forming a right angle at each corner.

2. Lay a thin layer of mortar beneath the strings. This mortar is used for marking out the guidelines for the first course of brick. Hold the spirit level against the string, taking care not to deflect it. Keep the level upright; steady it with a batten. Where the foot of the spirit level touches the newly laid mortar, scratch a mark with the point of the trowel, directly under the string.

3. Make another mark for the same line about 2 ft. from the first. Join the two marks with a straightedge to form line A. Mark line B at a right angle to line A. Repeat at all corners or stopped ends. The building line is now transferred from the strings to the mortar. Take plenty of time with this; if it is wrong, all your later work will be out of line. When finished, remove the strings.

4. Lay a ½-in. mortar bed at one corner; take care not to cover the lines. Very carefully lay the corner brick against the lines. Level it lengthwise and crosswise. Measure its height.

5. Lay six or so bricks along both arms of corner; keep to lines. Check against corner brick with level. Lay it on bricks and tap it gently with trowel handle to make row level with corner brick. Make cross joints ½ in. thick. Build up the corner to the second course above ground level, the base for the vapor barrier. Inaccuracies in the foundation must be taken up by the time you reach it.

6. Make frequent use of the spirit level as you build up the courses. Use it for checking the bricks crosswise as well as lengthwise. Use it also as a straightedge to keep bricks in alignment.

7. Lay ¼-in. mortar bed and place vapor barrier (p.453) on it. Start at corner; overlap ends. Smooth barrier flat with trowel (do not puncture). Cover barrier with ¼ in. of mortar; lay bricks on it.

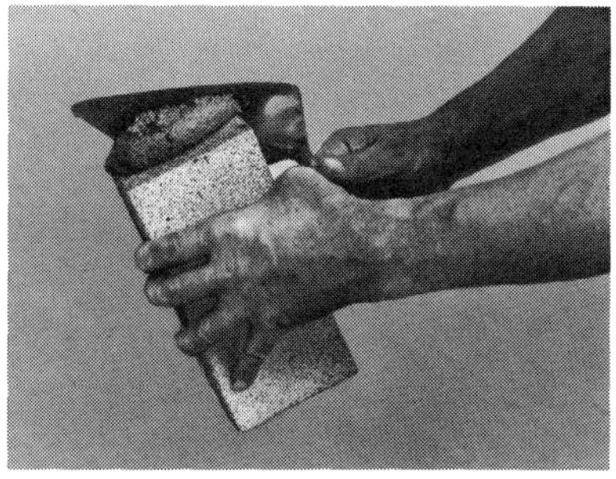

8. Form cross joints by wiping a dab of mortar on one end of the brick, spreading it all over the end and trimming it to size. You need butter only one end of each brick in this fashion.

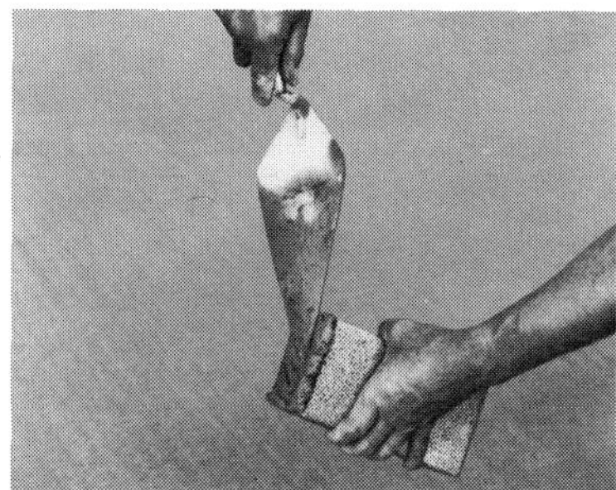

9. Use point of trowel to make sure that the mortar is spread evenly all over the end of the brick. By buttering a brick before it is laid, you avoid the risk of moving it out of line.

10. With vapor barrier placed, lay up corner for several courses, each half a stretcher length shorter. Use story pole to ensure that the courses rise evenly; each line marks the top of a brick.

11. At this stage, use spirit level also to check accuracy vertically, horizontally, and diagonally. For a diagonal check, hold the level against the wall from the corner brick. With trowel handle, tap level gently over any bricks out of line. Build up the other corners to the same height. String a line between two corners and fill in the courses. Repeat this procedure until you reach the top of the wall.

12. The inner side of a wall can be left rough if it will not show or if it is to be stuccoed over. But keep the face side clean and free of mortar droppings; wipe them off before they harden.

13. Before the mortar hardens, it must be pointed (p.456). To form a tooled joint, use a jointer or a metal rod. Rub it up and down the vertical joints first, forming a slight hollow.

14. Next rub the horizontal joints in the same manner, again forming a slight hollow. Then brush off the excess mortar. For details on how to form other brickwork joints, see the next page.

Garden and retaining walls

A garden wall, to have sufficient strength, should be at least 8 inches wide. Choice of bond (p.451) is a matter of preference. The foundation should be below the frost line. If the wall is to be on a slope, the foundation will have to be stepped in multiples of 2¾ inches, the height of a brick.

The procedure for building a garden wall is the same as for any other wall (p.454). Either SW or MW bricks (p.446) may be used. Set out the first course of bricks without mortar, allowing for the mortar joints, to verify the number of bricks to cut. Use a dry-mix mortar or mix 1 part masonry cement with 3 parts sand. Work from both ends toward the middle; build up all tiers simultaneously. If the wall is exceptionally long, build up leads (p.450) at 8- to 10-foot intervals.

Cover the top of the wall with a coping (a weather-resisting course). The coping should be sloped to shed water. It may be made of bricks laid on end and sloped to form an inverted V, or of a rich mortar, cast concrete, or coping or cornice tile.

A retaining wall is built basically like a garden wall, but it must be built to withstand the pressure of the earth behind it, and it must be properly drained. Use SW brick (p.446). Mix mortar of 1 part masonry cement and 3 parts sand. The face of a retaining wall is vertical or nearly so. The foundation should be below the frost line unless the wall is on well-drained soil. The wall's thickness is greatest at the base and is gradually decreased with height. Strengthen a retaining wall by inserting metal rods in the holes of cored brick or by inserting flat metal bars vertically in the mortar between tiers. Or tie the bricks to the earth with metal rods or bars 3 to 4 feet long; place them in a staggered pattern 4 to 5 feet apart in the horizontal mortar bed every 2 feet of the wall's height.

To drain off moisture that builds up behind the wall, install drainpipes at least 2 inches in outside diameter 4 to 6 feet apart at the bottom of the wall. It is wise to add several additional pipes about 2 feet above the first row. Drainpipes must extend from the earth behind the wall to flush with face of wall. A fill of coarse gravel (1 foot thick to within about 1 foot of the top) behind the wall aids drainage. Strength is increased if retaining wall is made of poured concrete and faced with brick; the same provision should be made for drainage.

Pointing

The process of finishing off brickwork joints is known as pointing (sometimes also called jointing). Various shapes can be given to the joints between bricks to provide interesting and attractive decorative effects. But the principal purpose of pointing is to compress the mortar and seal the joint against moisture.

If you are putting joints in new brickwork or are completely repointing a wall, you can choose any of the joints shown below. Weathered joints give maximum protection from moisture and are not particularly difficult to form.

Regardless of which type of joint you select, pointing must be begun before the mortar gets too hard. It should be undertaken while the mortar is still workable and sufficiently plastic to "give" when you press your thumb into it. Be especially watchful when the weather is hot and dry, because the mortar will harden faster.

Start finishing the joints after you have laid two or three courses, before the mortar has begun to set. This will seal the joints and prevent the penetration of moisture. Point the vertical joints first and then the horizontal ones.

Vertical weathered joints are sloped with a pointing trowel to match the horizontal ones.

Raked joints, with mortar scraped out and smoothed, can be made with a brick jointer.

An improvised tool can be used to scrape out the mortar to ¼-in. depth for raked joints.

Complete a raked joint by rubbing with stick or jointer to smooth and compact the mortar.

To make flush, weathered, or struck joints, cut off excess mortar with edge of trowel. For most other types, run a jointing tool along the joint to scrape out and compress the mortar. Some joints require the use of a brick jointer. For some joints, you can improvise by using a metal rod or a piece of pipe. You can use a rod with a curved, pointed end to scrape out the mortar for a raked joint. You can form a concave joint with a metal rod. To make the straightedge needed to form a rodded joint, cut ¼-in. tempered hardboard to a convenient length and attach a square of the same material at each end so that the straightedge will stand slightly away when it is held against the wall.

A flush joint is formed by cutting off the excess mortar with the edge of the trowel.

A weathered joint. Make the sloped surface with edge of trowel. Bottom of horizontal joint is flush with lower brick; top is recessed.

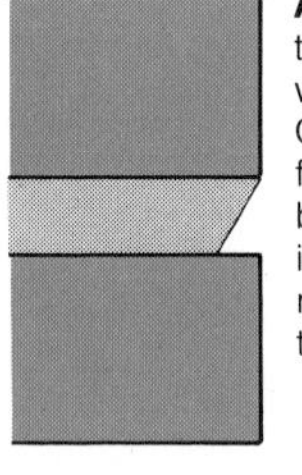

A struck joint, the reverse of the weathered joint. Outer edge is flush with upper brick and is slightly recessed from the lower.

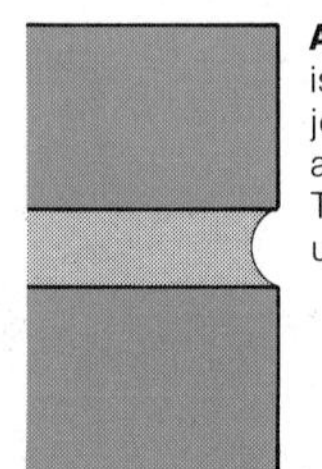

A concave joint is a tooled joint made with a brick jointer. To improvise, use a metal rod.

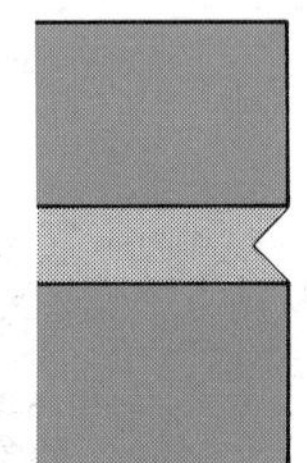

The V joint, like the concave joint, is a form of tooled joint. Use a brick jointer to make it.

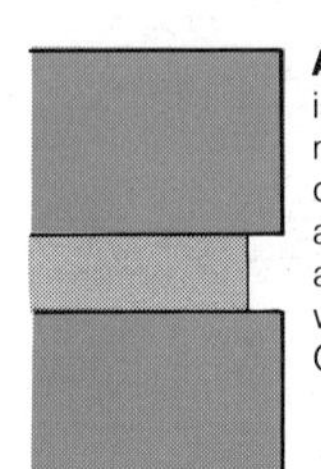

A raked joint is made by removing mortar to a depth of ¼″ with a pointed rod and smoothing with a stick. Or use jointer.

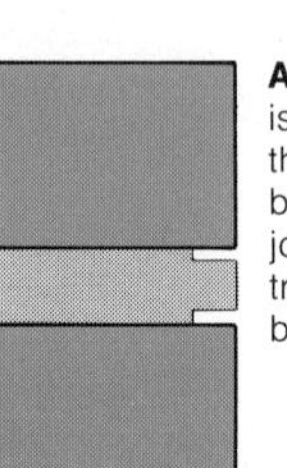

A rodded joint is made by scoring the top and bottom of the joint with edge of trowel guided by straightedge.

A grapevine, or colonial, joint. To make it, you need a jointer designed for the purpose.

Procedure

Crumbling mortar joints in old brickwork allow moisture to penetrate the wall. The remedy is repointing, or tuck pointing—removing the old mortar to a depth of at least ½ inch and replacing it with new waterproof mortar. If you are repointing an entire wall, you can do it in stages—about 1 square yard at a time. Use scaffolding if the wall is high; do not work on a ladder. Wear goggles or safety glasses while raking or chipping out mortar. Remove mortar in "bites" about 1 inch long. Hold chisel at a sharp angle; avoid wedging it in the joint; do not hit it hard enough to chip the bricks.

If you are repointing only part of a wall, you will need to match the joints with the existing ones. The new mortar should match the composition of the old. If you do not know the mix for the old mortar, you can use a dry mix that contains all the ingredients except water; or you can mix 1 part masonry cement and 3 parts sand; or use 1 part Portland cement, 1 part hydrated lime, and 6 parts sand. Mortar coloring can help you to match color of old mortar. Make new mortar slightly darker than the shade of the old when the old mortar is wet; the new mortar will get lighter as it dries.

Deteriorated jointing lets rain penetrate. Use ⅜-in. cape chisel and 2½-lb. hammer to remove old mortar from about 1 sq. yd. of wall. Clear vertical joints, then horizontals, to a depth of at least ½ in.

Brush joints clean; dampen them and surrounding bricks with fine spray from garden hose to prevent absorption of moisture from new mortar.

Mix enough mortar for about an hour's work. Practice picking up mortar from hawk with a smooth upward sweep of the back of the pointing trowel.

Force mortar into joints—first the verticals, then the horizontals above and below. For weathered or struck joints, form slope as you go; leave mortar flush for other joints. After mortar hardens, brush off waste.

Classes and types of stone

Six kinds of natural stone are generally used for do-it-yourself work: Granite, marble, slate, limestone, sandstone, and bluestone.

There are three classes of stonework construction: Rubble, ashlar, and trimmings.

Rubble masonry consists of uncut stones or stones that are not cut to a specific shape. This style of stonework is used for rough masonry such as retaining walls or foundations. When stones of this type are assembled with mortar joints, a liberal amount of mortar must be used because of the stones' irregularities. This type of construction is weak compared to other stone structures. Rubble stonework is well suited for dry walls where no mortar is used.

Ashlar is stone cut on four sides to roughly resemble brick. The surfaces can be smooth (dressed) or rough. Laid in regular courses, it is referred to as **coursed** ashlar. Laid in broken courses without regard to the continuity of the joints, it is called **broken,** or **ranged,** ashlar.

Trimmings are cut on all sides. They are used for sills, lintels, moldings, and ornamental purposes. Trimmings used for sills have beveled tops so they will shed water.

Granite is a hard, sparkling stone that polishes well and is nonporous. It is durable and expensive. It varies in texture from very coarse to very fine and comes in red, pink, white, gray, and green. When buying granite, avoid stones with knots that look much like knots in wood, stones with surface stains, and stones with cracks or seams.

Marble is a fairly hard stone that polishes well. It is available at a considerable range of prices and in a variety of colors. It is suitable for keystones and window sills on the exterior and for such interior uses as fireplace facings, floor tiles, table tops, and hearthstones.

Slate is dense, brittle, and nonporous and is easily split into thin laminations. Available in black, gray, and green, it is used outdoors primarily as roofing; indoor uses include decorative facings, hearthstones, and sills. Bear in mind that slate should always be set flat, not on edge.

Limestone is a chalky stone that varies in hardness, durability, and price. Colors range from buff, cream, and ivory to brown and green. It is used chiefly for paving, walls, steps, and rock gardens.

Sandstone is strong and durable. Its color varies from buff, cream, and ivory to brown. It is used for sills and copings. Soft seams or soft spots that can be picked out with a nail indicate poor quality.

Bluestone is a fine-grained fossilized clay stone used for paving and veneer. Its nonskid surface makes it suitable for stair treads.

Buying stone

Natural stone can be purchased in three finishes:

1. Dressed describes fully dressed stone, supplied cut to your requirements and the most expensive of the three finishes.

2. Semidressed stones are cut to approximate sizes.

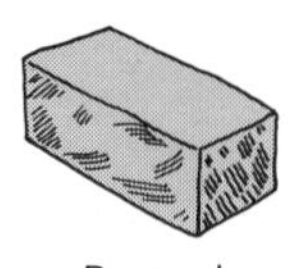
Dressed

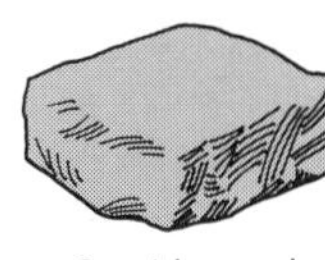
Semidressed

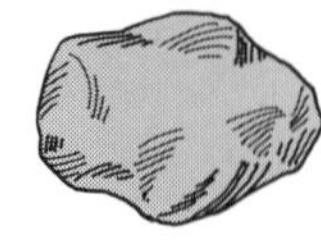
Undressed

Trimming and cropping with a cold chisel and a heavy hammer (p.459) will be necessary.

3. Undressed stone, the cheapest finish, is simply chunks of raw stone direct from the quarry.

Artificial stone blocks and slabs closely resemble natural stone but are much cheaper. They require no dressing. Artificial stone is available in a variety of colors, sizes, and finishes; it is used for walls and exterior paving. Some types are made by applying a facing of crushed stone and colored cement to plain concrete blocks. In others, the same crushed stone aggregate is used throughout. Artificial stone is known by various names, such as cast, precast, imitation, and reconstructed.

Masonry styles

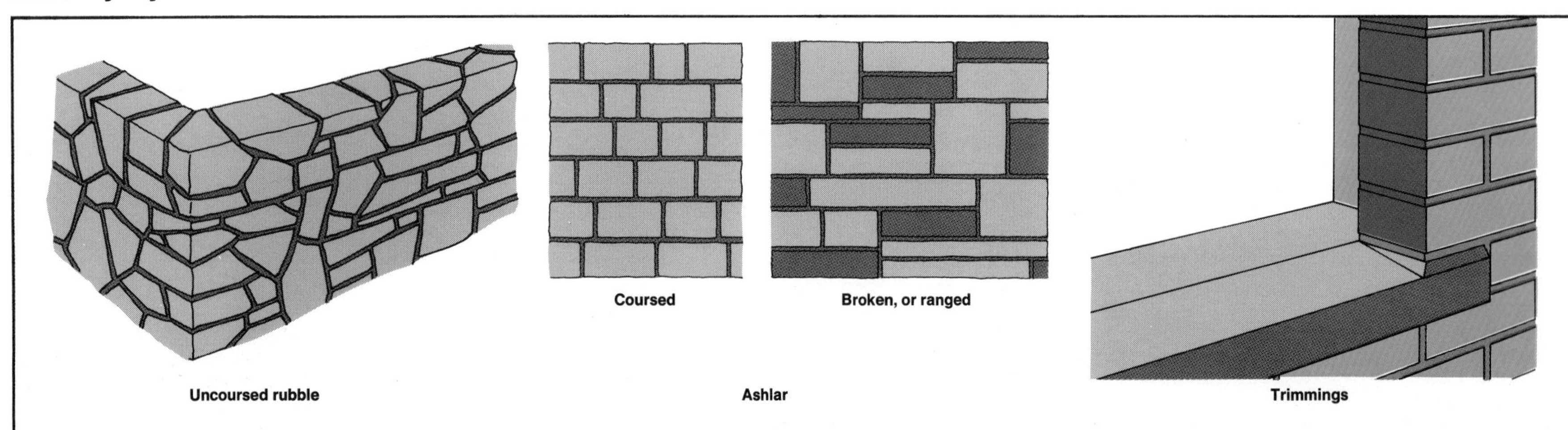

Uncoursed rubble

Ashlar

Trimmings

Drilling and splitting

Wear goggles or safety glasses when cutting, splitting, or drilling stone.

Drilling: Use carbide-tipped masonry bit with power drill; use slower speed with two-speed drill, or use a speed reducer with single-speed drill. Apply moderate pressure and drill in short, sharp bursts; withdraw drill frequently to prevent overheating the bit. For hand drilling, use a star drill and a small sledge hammer; twist the drill between blows and withdraw it frequently to clean out hole (p.77).

Splitting: Bore a hole several inches deep at the grain line and into it drive a three-piece stone-splitting tool, called a set of plug and feathers, with the plug between the feathers. Some stones will require boring more than one hole; others can be split with hammer and chisel.

Cutting a slab

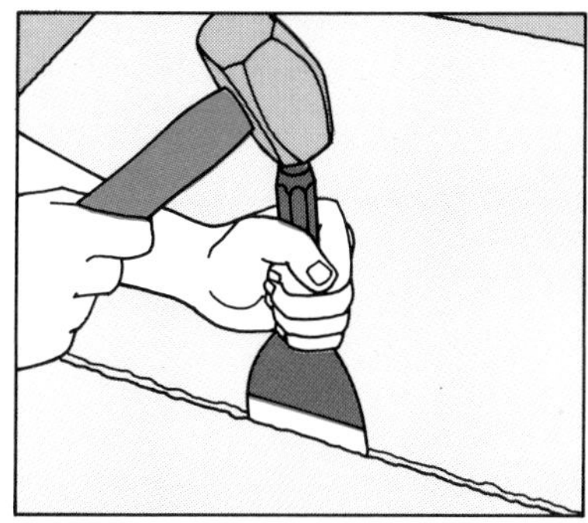

With slab evenly supported from below, scribe a line for cut; use masonry nail or corner of chisel. Cut V-shaped groove about ½ in. thick along the line.

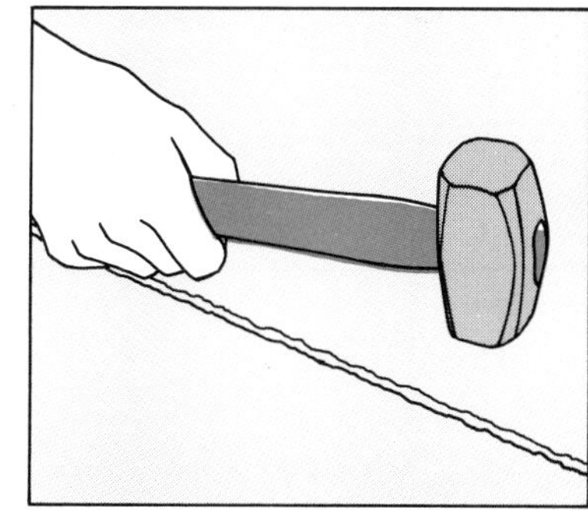

Lift up one end of slab; strike along cut line with small hand sledge until slab snaps. Or lay slab in sand bed; with chisel in groove, strike sharply along line.

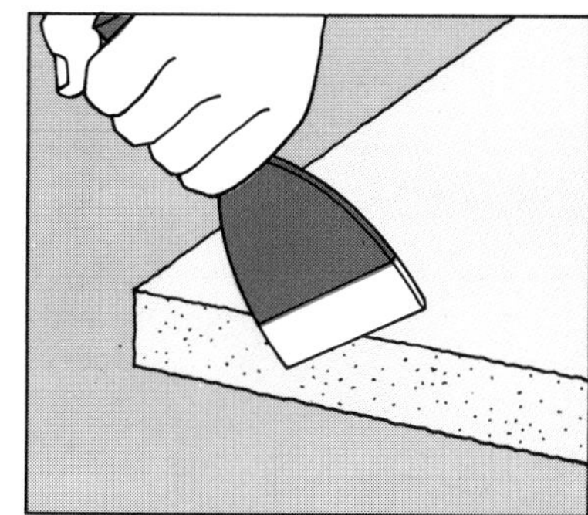

Trim off any ragged edges from the cut slab with a bricklayer's chisel. If you want a smoother finish, you can use a sharp, coarse rasp (p.34).

Polishing, cleaning, removing stains

If you want polished stone for decorative purposes, such as a marble table top or a slate hearth, or if you need to clean or remove stains from stone, follow the appropriate procedure described below.

Polishing slate and marble: Use an abrasive wet-or-dry paper on a finishing sander. Lubricate the surface to be polished with water; then buff with wet-or-dry paper in small circular movements. Continue sanding until dust particles mix with the water to form a cream-like slurry. After a few minutes, clean off the slurry; the surface will be developing a sheen. When the surface is polished to your satisfaction, wash off the slurry and dry with a lint-free cloth. The surface can be protected with a colorless wax polish.

Slate can be given a coat of polyurethane varnish. Do not varnish marble; the varnish will turn yellow with age and discolor the marble.

Generally, polishing is a difficult job that is best left to a professional mason who has the special equipment required.

Polishing granite: For the initial surfacing, use a finishing sander with a cloth pad and abrasive powder in progressively finer grades to buff the stone. Follow this with a finer polishing agent, such as rouge powder, to form the slurry. Wash, dry with a lint-free cloth. Finish with a colorless wax polish.

Cleaning marble, granite, and bluestone: Nonabrasive acid-free detergents can be used to remove grease, provided all traces are rinsed away. Wipe the surface clean; then polish with a piece of chamois. Never use a liquid detergent on marble flooring; it invariably leaves slippery patches on the surface. Clean the surface frequently with a soft brush to remove abrasive dust.

Cleaning limestone and sandstone: Use a fiber scrubbing brush, plenty of water, and lots of energy. Avoid detergents, especially those that contain alkalis such as caustic soda, because they break down the surface of the stone. The appearance of internal stonework can usually be improved by brushing the surface with a soft-bristled brush to remove the dust.

Cleaning slate: Wash with hot water and a mild detergent. Rinse, then polish with pumice powder or rottenstone on a dampened felt pad.

Cleaning artificial stone: If the use of a moderate detergent fails to clean up the stone and the surface is reasonably flat, use a medium-fine pumice powder and a bristled scrubbing brush. Be sure to use plenty of water.

Stain removal: The procedures for removing stains vary for the different types of stone.

Marble: The usual cause of stains is spilled liquids that are not wiped up before they eat into the stone's surface. Simple washing will seldom remove such ingrained stains. The longer a stain is permitted to set, the more difficult it becomes to remove.

Most marble stains can be bleached out with a thick homemade paste made of hydrogen peroxide (from a drugstore) and powdered whiting (from a paint store). Spread the paste over the stained area, add a few drops of ordinary household ammonia, and keep the paste damp by covering it with a sheet of plastic wrap. Allow the paste to stand on the surface for a few minutes, then wash it off. Rinse with hot water, repeat the process if necessary, then wipe dry with a lint-free cloth.

Rust or stains can sometimes be washed off with ammonia or a paste made from equal parts of amyl acetate and acetone mixed with whiting. Surface scratches can be removed by using very fine wet-or-dry abrasive paper and water.

Smoke stains can be removed by gentle scrubbing with powdered pumice and water. If the stains are persistent, try rubbing with a cut lemon. **Do not use carbon tetrachloride** in any form under any trade name; its fumes are extremely dangerous.

Limestone and sandstone: A stone hearth that has been slightly burned can be cleaned by a light rubbing with a medium-grade abrasive paper. Deep burns generally cannot be removed.

Moss-colored stains on garden ornaments can be removed by using a wet scrubbing brush dipped in a little hydrated lime. Be sure to wear heavy rubber gloves while doing this kind of work. Also be sure to store the lime beyond the reach of children—it can be extremely hazardous for them.

Settlement and shrinkage

Settlement, or movement cracks in bricks as well as in the mortar are caused by movement of the ground beneath the building. The ground may be "made land" where voids were filled without enough time being allowed for complete compacting. Clay under the foundation may have dried out and shrunk or it may have moved as the result of flooding. Drainage and waterproofing of the foundation may have been deficient, or it may have been built above the frost line. Soil under hillside homes sometimes moves down the slope. Rotting or drying timbers may on occasion cause movement. Roots of large trees may move or bulge a foundation. Whatever the cause, settlement cracks left unattended usually erode and become worse.

Running cracks on outside walls are an indication of settlement trouble. They are most apparent where an extension has been built on or where a garage or garden wall meets the house wall. Cracks also develop around door tops, sills, and window frames.

The first thing to do is to determine whether or not the movement has stopped. Movement in a new house may be a one-time occurrence that will not happen again once the house has thoroughly settled. Test outside walls to find out whether the movement has stopped by one of the following methods:

Bridge the crack with a piece of flat glass, fastening the glass tightly over the crack with epoxy cement. The slightest movement or shift in the house will cause the glass to break.

The second test is to bridge the crack with plaster of Paris; the hardened plaster will crack if there is any movement in the building.

You may have to wait several months before you see results from either test. If the crack continues to open and close, even slightly, this indicates a serious settlement crack. To cure this problem, the soil under the footings of the foundation will probably have to be shored up, or the footings replaced. These are big jobs, best handled by experts, although you could save money by doing your own digging.

Shrinkage: Open cracks should be filled to prevent further damage. Minor cracks in the mortar are caused by shrinkage, the result of the bricks having absorbed water too rapidly from freshly laid mortar. This is a one-time occurrence that happens only during construction. Chip out the defective mortar and repoint the joints (p.457).

If the crack is long and deep, and if it occurs in the bricks as well as in the mortar joint, it may be difficult to point with a trowel. In such situations it is necessary to feed grout (p.447) into the fissure. Do this by first wetting the crack. Then use wide adhesive tape or a board to temporarily seal the lower portion of the crack. This will keep the fresh grout in place. Pour the grout into the top of the crack, using a funnel attached to a tube. Get the tube well into the wall; it should reach to the center of the crack. After the grout has set about a day, remove the temporary covering and point (p.456) the surface of the crack. Move up the wall, repeating the process as often as necessary to fill the crack completely. Use mortar coloring to match brick color when fixing cracks in brick; or make a powder of a similarly colored brick and incorporate it in the mortar. If you use such a powder, be sure to reduce the amount of sand used in the mortar mix by an amount equivalent to the added powder.

Shrinkage cracks around window and door frames may be caused by the shrinkage and expansion of timber and not by movement of the brickwork. Point these cracks with a caulking compound that will avoid such problems by flexing with any slight movement between the bricks.

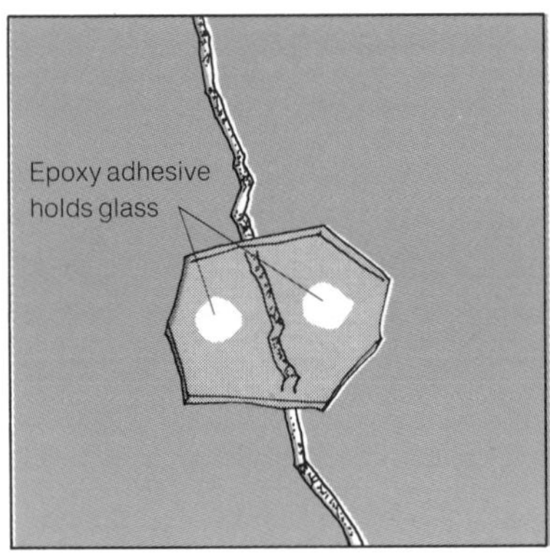

Test structures for movement by using epoxy adhesive to glue glass onto the wall. Movement will crack the glass.

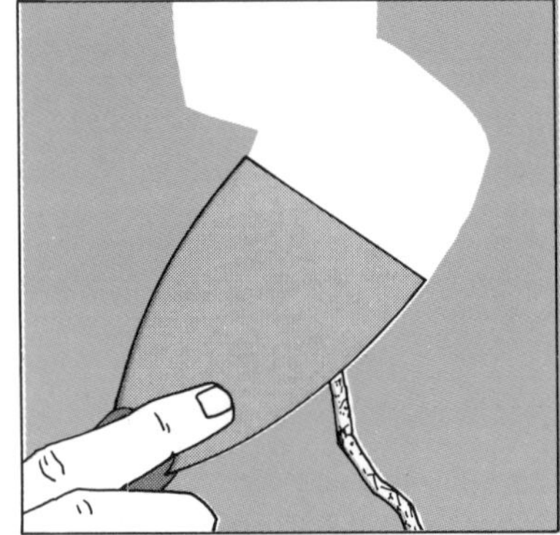

Another way to test for movement is to bridge crack with plaster of Paris; it, too, will crack with movement.

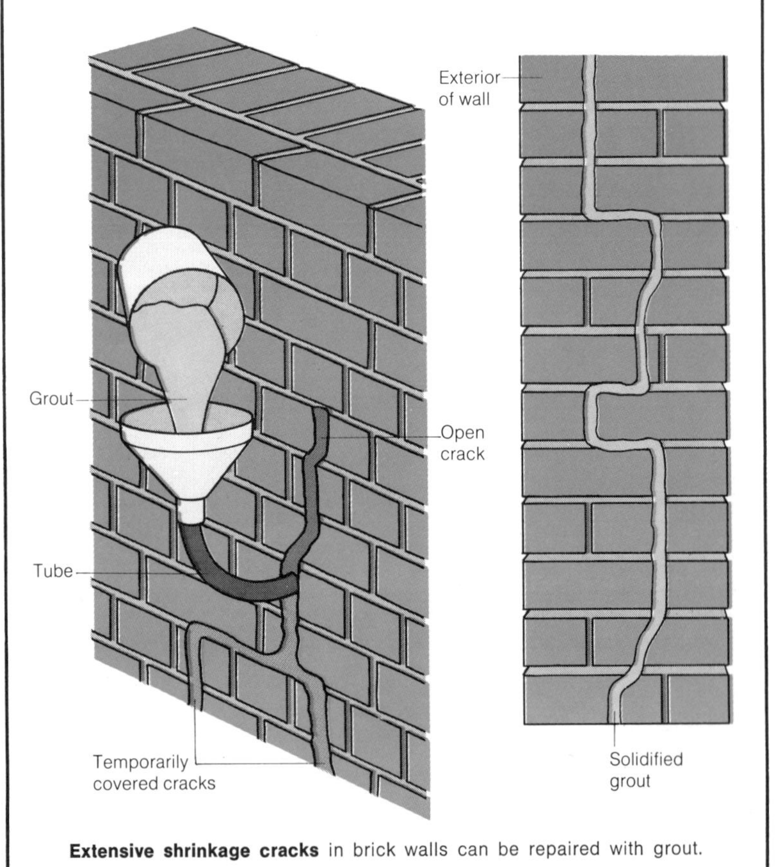

Extensive shrinkage cracks in brick walls can be repaired with grout.

Damaged brickwork

Brick absorbs large quantities of moisture when it is rained upon and then permits it to evaporate in dry weather. In cold weather, moisture absorbed by the bricks can freeze. The expansion caused by freezing often causes bricks to "spall," or crumble at the edges. Such bricks should be replaced.

Remove mortar around the damaged brick, using a ⅜-inch cape chisel. Chip the brick with a 4-inch bricklayer's chisel until it can be removed. Remove any remaining mortar; clean the cavity with a wire brush and hose out the cavity. Protect your eyes with goggles or safety glasses during all of these operations.

Replace the brick by laying mortar on the horizontal surface of the cavity; press the new brick firmly into place. Then, use a pointing trowel to force mortar around brick, fill in cavity completely at the top and both ends. After replacing damaged bricks, apply a coat of clear brick or masonry sealer to prevent further frost damage to brickwork; this is a good idea even if no bricks are broken. If the wall does not look attractive after patching, apply a coat of waterproof masonry paint.

Water penetration: If water penetrates the joints or cracks in a brick veneer or cavity wall, and if it cannot be kept out by repointing, it will collect at the bottom. There it will either seep through to the inner wall and cause damage, or it will freeze, in which case it could break the wall. The remedy: Using a carbide-tipped bit in a ½-inch power drill, bore drain holes (known as weep holes) through the bottom mortar joint. Space the holes approximately 2 feet apart; make them at least ½ inch in diameter and slope their outside edges downward.

Decayed stonework

Natural stones do not as a rule flake as much as brickwork does, except for the softer sandstones and limestones. Chemical impurities in the air can cause some stones to decay. This type of decay shows up as flaking and pitting on the stone's surface. It can be treated with chemical preservatives available from brick and stone dealers.

Where such decay has destroyed a stone, chop out the damaged stone, using a bricklayer's 4-inch chisel. Remove all loose debris. Prepare a mortar mix of 1 part masonry cement and 3 parts sand. Dampen both replacement stone and cavity thoroughly. Lay mortar in cavity, insert new stone, and repoint.

If a matching stone is not available, you can make a facsimile using 1 part masonry cement, 2 parts sand, and 5 parts small crushed stone. Add mortar coloring to match the old stone. Mix a small batch first, let it dry, then test the color match.

To make a large imitation stone, embed pieces of scrap clay tile in the mortar to build up the hole. Then fill to the surface with mix. Whether large or small, the surface area must be made to match the surrounding stones. If they are smooth, cover the surface with a stucco coat of mortar; if they are irregular, match the surface with a pointing trowel and jointing tools.

Small damaged areas can be repaired with epoxy-based fillers made for concrete. These give a very strong bond and are ideal for repairs to steps, especially treads. They are expensive, however.

Stone can be protected from impurities in the air by regular scrubbing with cold water. Do not add acids, detergents, or chemicals to the water. For very grimy walls, call in professional cleaners.

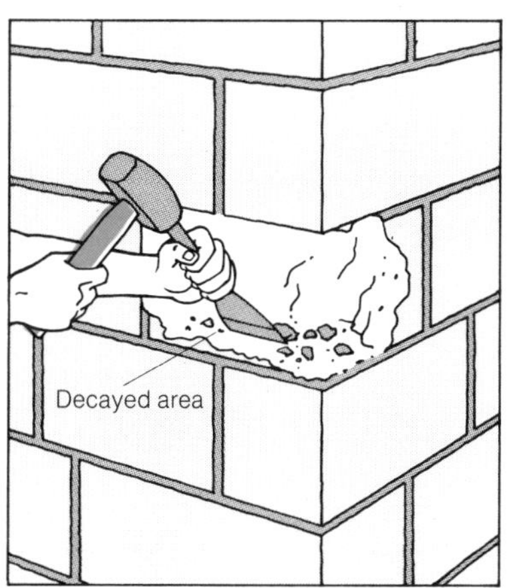

Chop out decayed stone with hammer and chisel. Remove all loose debris.

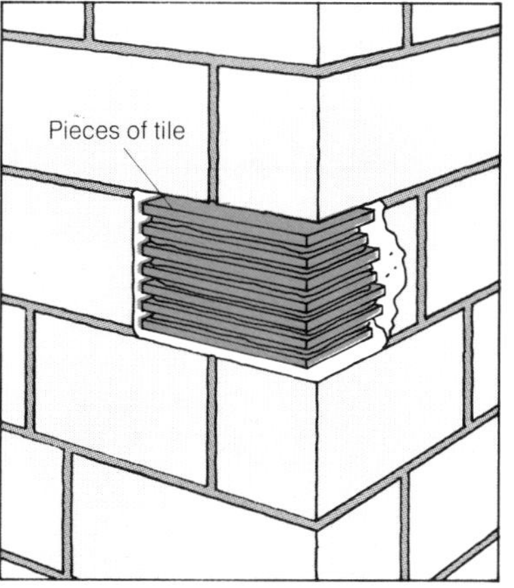

To make large imitation stone, build up hole with clay tile bedded in mortar.

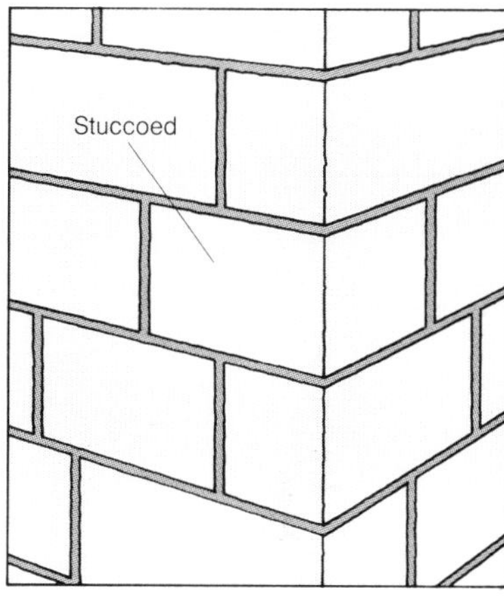

Make the surface of the imitation stone match that of the surrounding stones.

Efflorescence

Efflorescence is a whitish powdery stain formed on masonry walls when water-soluble salts in the brick, stone, or mortar are washed to the surface, where they crystallize. New structures, in which a lot of water must evaporate from the freshly laid mortar, are most prone to this condition. In an old wall efflorescence indicates a leak that must be located and fixed. After the leak has been corrected, you can probably remove the deposits with a wire brush. If wire brushing does not remove the efflorescence, buy (from your building supplies dealer or a brickyard) a solution that will penetrate the brick and neutralize the salts.

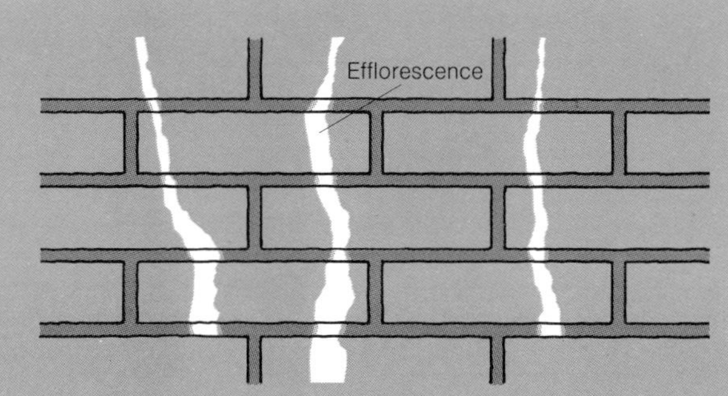

Repairs

Defects in chimneys are often neglected because they cannot easily be seen. Such neglect can be dangerous. Binoculars or the long lens of a reflex camera enable you to do a preliminary check. Look for leaning brickwork, serious cracks, damaged cap, loose or deteriorated flashing.

Anything questionable should be given a close inspection as soon as possible. But be careful: Use a sturdy ladder to reach the roof. To scale the roof, you'll need some safe means, such as a roof ladder that hooks over the ridge.

Chimney stack: If your close inspection reveals that the chimney stack is leaning, call in professional help. Curing this serious fault is probably beyond the scope of the average home handyman.

The minor defect of crumbling pointing can be easily fixed and should not be neglected; it can lead to water penetration, which will damage the chimney stack. Clean out the crumbling mortar to a depth of at least ½ inch. Use a ⅜-inch cape chisel and a 2½-pound hammer, wearing goggles to protect your eyes. Brush away loose mortar and dust. Dampen the joints and repoint with new mortar (p.457). It is simplest to use a dry-mix mortar, but if you prefer you can mix your own of 1 part masonry cement and 3 parts sand.

Close off the damper in the fireplace to confine any soot that may be loosened when you are working on any part of the chimney. Many chimneys have more than one flue, and the dampers for all of them should be closed.

You may sometimes see smoke leaking out of a chimney stack through chinks in the mortar. This probably indicates a cracked or broken flue lining and is a fire hazard. This is a job for a professional, and the chimney should not be used until the trouble has been remedied.

To test a chimney for leaks, build a fire in the fireplace and when it is burning briskly, add to the wood or coal some material that will smoke profusely, such as damp straw; then cover the chimney with a heavy wet cloth to force the smoke to seek some exit other than the normal one. Be sure the windows and doors are open to let smoke escape from the house.

Ordinarily the smoke would be drawn harmlessly past the joints in the flue lining, but this test will force it through these joints if there are cracks in them. And if there are cracks in the joints of the chimney stack, the smoke will leak through these. If there are only a few small leaks, repoint the offending brickwork joints.

If there are many leaks in the chimney stack, or if they are large, consult a chimney expert. He can tell you whether the chimney can be repaired or whether it must be rebuilt. Regardless of the number and size of the leaks, do not use the chimney until all existing defects are corrected.

If the main part of the stack is sound, and if you find loose bricks, you can remove and replace them.

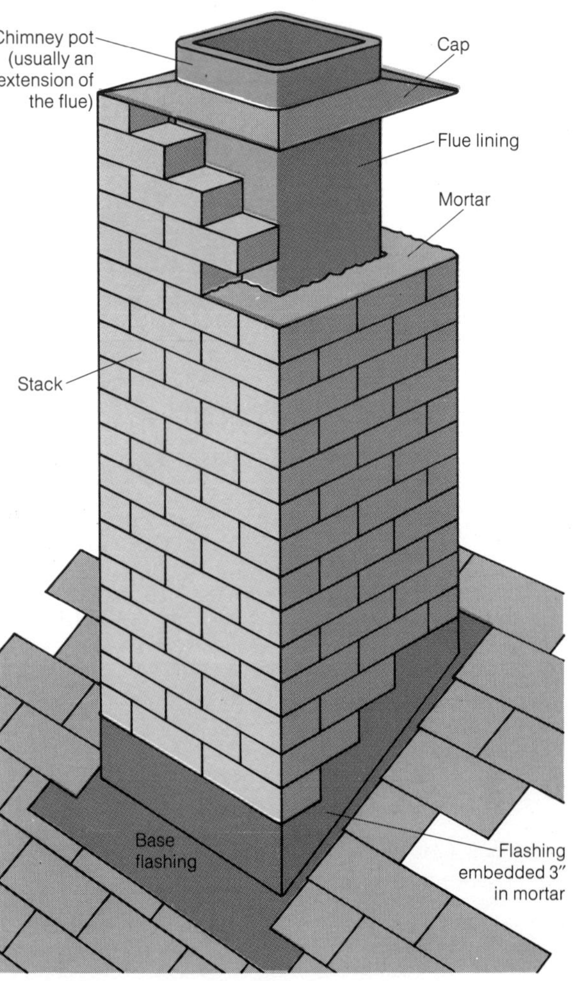

To remove mortar from around a loose brick, use a ⅜-inch cape chisel and a 2½-pound hammer; wear goggles. Ease the brick out and take it to the ground to clean it. Scrape all loose and crumbling mortar from the hole (goggles are important here). Dampen the brick and those surrounding it and the cavity as well. Add new mortar (p.447) and press the brick back into place, being sure to fill the joints completely with mortar. Then repoint the joints, finishing them off to match the type of joint originally used in the chimney.

Flashing, if it is defective at any point, can be the cause of interior water stains that appear anywhere near the chimney. If the flashing has merely come loose, the joints it was embedded in should be raked out, the flashing edge reinserted, and the joint remortared. But if the flashing was made of metal that has in any way deteriorated, it should be completely replaced with a metal that will not corrode, such as copper or aluminum.

This replacement should be embedded 3 inches into the brick or stone mortar at a point 6 inches above the roof line, and the seam and the portion that extends over the roofing should be liberally coated with roofing cement (p.177).

Whether you are reinserting loose flashing or installing new, use a dry-mix mortar or mix 1 part masonry cement and 3 parts sand.

Cap: The top of the chimney, or cap, is made of mortar sloped so that rain can run off. It is a common trouble spot.

Fill any cracks or holes in the cap with mortar. You can use a dry-mix mortar to which you need add only water, or mix a mortar made of 1 part masonry cement and 3 parts sand.

If the cap is badly cracked or the mortar is loose and pulling away from the bricks, it should be replaced. To remove it, use a bricklayer's chisel and a 2½-pound hammer; be sure to wear goggles. It is a good idea to put the broken pieces in a bucket and lower them to the ground with a rope; do not let them bounce down off the roof. Clear away all loose material, then clean and dampen the top course of bricks and you are ready to form the new cap. Build it up with dry-mix mortar or a mortar that you make yourself using 1 part masonry cement to 3 parts sand. Trowel on several thick layers of mortar, sloping them so that the water will run off.

Repair and removal

Crumbling mortar and cracked or loose bricks in a fireplace are fire hazards and should be repaired as soon as they are discovered.

Remove mortar from crumbling or cracked joints with a ⅜-inch cape chisel and a 2½-pound hammer. Dampen the joints and repoint (p.457). To lay firebricks or repair firebrick joints, buy masonry cement that contains fire clay; mix 1 part of this with 3 parts of sand.

Remove cracked bricks (p.461) and loose bricks (p.462). Dampen the cavity and the surrounding bricks and put in the replacement firebricks; use a fire-clay mortar mix.

If the fireplace opening is too large, the flue will not draw properly. You may be able to correct this by laying additional firebricks on the floor of the fire chamber, at the sides, or at the back. You should have the trouble diagnosed by a fireplace expert before laying the bricks. You can experiment, however, by putting a layer of firebrick on the floor without mortar. If this cures the trouble, lay the bricks permanently with fire-clay mortar.

If the expert you consult finds the fireplace too wide, the disproportion can be corrected by laying additional firebrick at the sides; if the fireplace is too deep, lay a course against the back.

Removal: An old fireplace may not fit the decorative scheme in a modern home, or it may be beyond repair. In either case removal is a simple job.

If the screws or nails that hold a wooden mantel to the wall are hidden under a molding, remove the molding and pry outward on the mantel shelf. This will show you where the mantel is fixed to the wall, and you can then remove the screws or nails. Use a crowbar to pry the mantel from the wall. To keep the mantel from falling, have someone support it while you remove the screws or nails and when you pry it loose from the wall.

To remove brick or stone mantel trim, clean out the mortar between the joints with a ⅜-inch cape chisel and a 2½-pound hammer. Then use a crowbar to remove the brick or stone.

The fireplace opening should be bricked up or sealed off with asbestos board. Be very careful not to inhale dust when sawing or breaking asbestos. The flue at the chimney top should be completely capped to keep out water (p.462). Provide a small vent at both ends of the flue to prevent condensation.

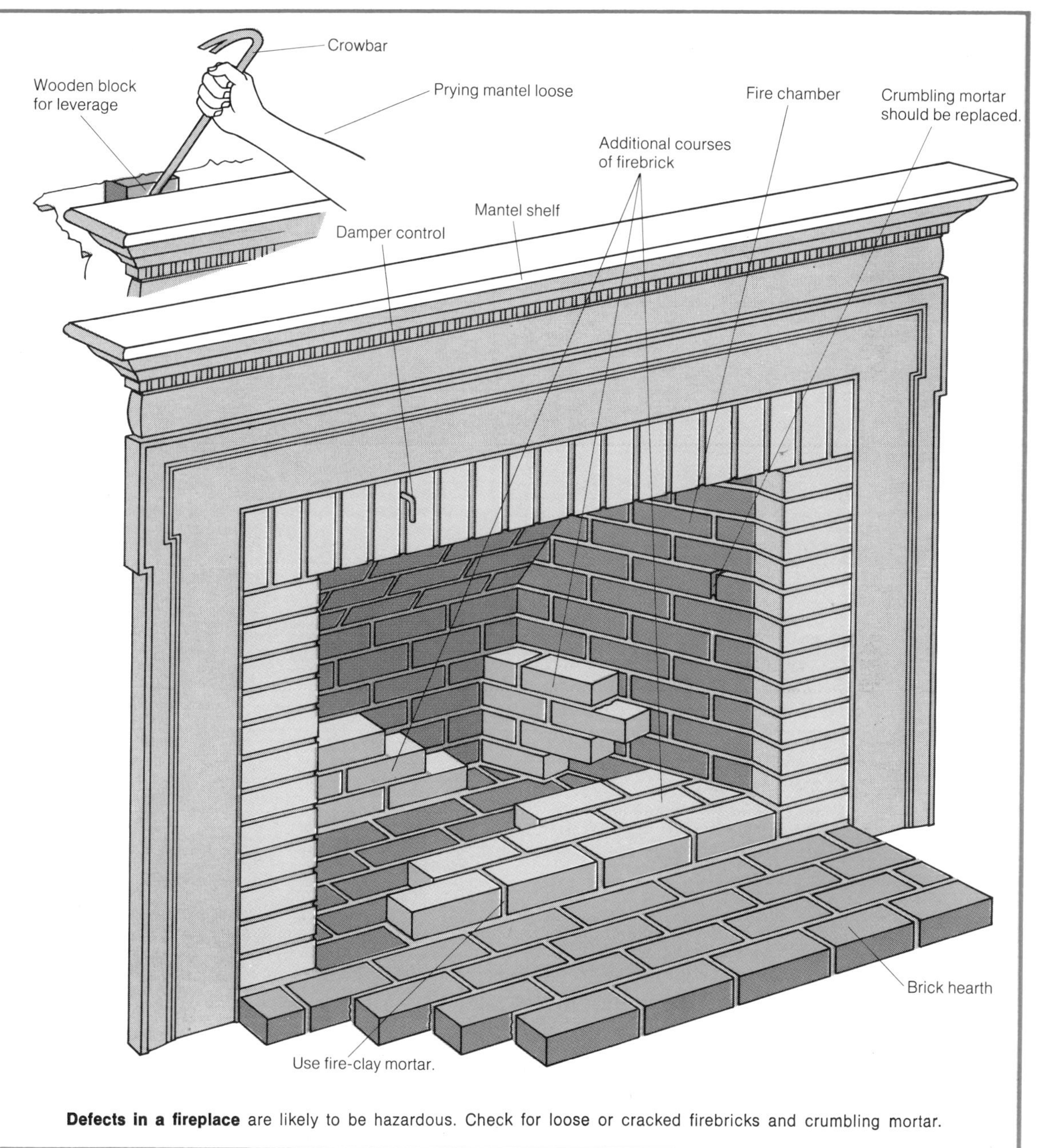

Defects in a fireplace are likely to be hazardous. Check for loose or cracked firebricks and crumbling mortar.

Walks, patios, drives

Use SW brick (p.446) for walks, patios, and driveways. Dig out the area for a brick walk or patio to a depth of approximately 4¼ inches. This allowance accommodates the thickness of the brick as well as a 2-inch bed of sand. Slope a patio away from the house about ⅛ to ¼ inch per foot; if the area does not adjoin a building, make the highest point in the center. On level ground, slope paths and walks slightly to one side.

To form the border, set bricks on edge in a trench 5¾ inches deep (2 inches for the sand bed, 3¾ inches for the brick). For a patio, set out only two adjoining edges of the border at this stage. Spread 2 inches of sand and roll or tamp it smooth. Put down a layer of heavy impregnated building paper to discourage weeds. Lay the bricks in the desired pattern for a walk. For a patio, lay them for the entire paved area, starting where the border is in place; finish by completing the border for the remaining sides. Spread sand over the paved area and sweep it over the bricks until cracks are filled.

Driveways: To make a brick driveway, lay bricks on edge in 2 inches of crushed stone or compacted sand. Begin by excavating the driveway area to a depth of 5¾ inches (2 inches for the bed, 3¾ inches for bricks on edge). Stand bricks on end for driveway border. If you do not want a curb, dig a trench 10 inches deep to accommodate the 2-inch bedding material and the bricks on end. To make a 4-inch curb, dig the trench 6 inches deep, then put down the 2-inch bed and lay bricks on end. Do not slope a driveway more than 1¾ inches per foot. Form the cross slope by making the drive higher in the middle or sloping it to one side. Sweep sand over the finished surface until cracks are filled. Flagstones set in the same kind of bed may be used for driveways. Patios, walks, and driveways can be set in mortar on a concrete foundation (p.475).

Flagstones: Lay flagstones in sand at least 2 inches deep to make a walk or patio. Keep the stones at least ½ inch apart. Wet them down; also wet the sand between them. Mix 1 part Portland cement with 3 parts sand; use no water. Spread the dry mixture on the flagstones and fill the gaps between stones by sweeping. Wet the walk or patio with the fine spray from a garden hose until the cement-sand mixture is saturated. Repeat the process two or three times at 15-minute intervals to wet the mortar to its full depth.

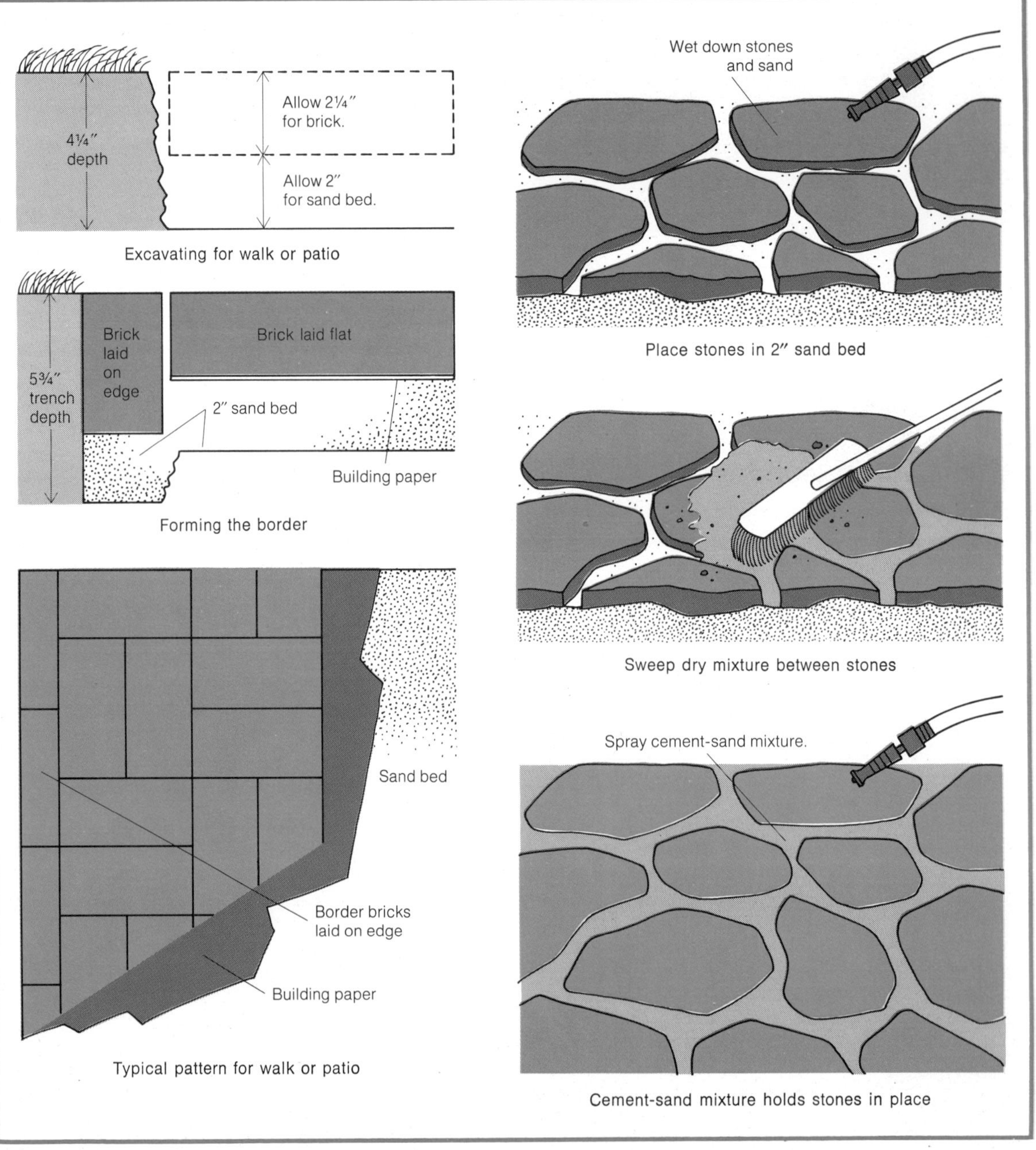

Excavating for walk or patio

Forming the border

Typical pattern for walk or patio

Place stones in 2″ sand bed

Sweep dry mixture between stones

Cement-sand mixture holds stones in place

section 15:

Working with concrete

Although most homeowners realize how much they could save by doing their own concrete work, many hesitate because of the degree of expertise supposedly involved. Professional know-how is needed, but this can be acquired—with the help of this section. It goes thoroughly into such fundamentals as matching the concrete mix to the job, the timing and conditions of curing, putting in foundations. With this preparation, you are ready for the building and repair jobs that are spelled out here as well.

contents

Composition of concrete

The proper ingredients

Concrete is one of the least expensive of all building materials. It is suitable for a wide range of uses in and about the home and, when concrete work is properly done, very durable.

Concrete is a mixture of Portland cement, fine aggregate (sand), coarse aggregate (gravel or crushed stone), and water. These ingredients are carefully proportioned, and the proportions of the resulting mix expressed in three numbers. For example, a 1:3:4 mix means that the concrete is made of 1 part Portland cement, 3 parts sand, and 4 parts gravel.

Portland cement is a manufactured product, made finer than flour. You can be assured of its quality if the approval of the ASTM (American Society for Testing and Materials) is printed on the bag. Cement must be free-flowing when it is used; keep it dry or lumps will form. If lumps will not pulverize easily when squeezed between your thumb and finger, do not use the cement.

When Portland cement combines with water, it forms **cement paste,** which binds the aggregates into concrete. The paste makes up 25 to 40 percent of the total volume of the concrete.

Standard Portland cement is gray, but you can buy white Portland cement for such uses as lawn ornaments, flower pots, or other decorative applications.

Air-entraining Portland cement contains an agent that forms billions of microscopic air bubbles in concrete. After air-entrained concrete hardens, there is virtually no scaling of the kind caused by freezing and thawing, and by salts used for de-icing. Air-entrained concrete should be used for all applications that will be exposed to any of these conditions.

Aggregates make up about 60 to 75 percent of the finished concrete. It is important to the strength of the concrete that you use the correct ratio of fine to coarse aggregates.

Fine aggregate is sand that will pass through a ¼-inch screen. It should be clean and free of foreign matter. Clay or vegetable matter in the sand will prevent the cement paste from bonding with it. If you are using noncommercial sand, test it for silt content. Put 2 inches of sand in a quart jar and add water until the jar is about three-quarters full. Shake it vigorously for one minute, let stand for one hour, then inspect for a layer of silt on top of the sand. If the silt layer is more than 3/16 inch thick, the sand is too dirty to use unless it is washed first. Do not use seashore sand; it contains substances that will cause the concrete to disintegrate. And do not use mortar sand; its particles are too small for concrete.

Damp sand, which falls apart when you try to squeeze it into a ball, requires more water in the mix.

Wet sand, the most usual kind, forms a ball when squeezed but leaves no noticeable moisture on your palm.

Very wet sand, such as that exposed to a recent rain, forms a ball when squeezed and leaves moisture on your palm.

Good coarse aggregate separated into three sizes—¼ to ⅜ in., ⅜ to ¾ in., ¾ to 1½ in.—looks like this.

When combined, the smaller pieces fill the spaces between the larger ones in a well-graded coarse aggregate.

The dampness of the sand must be considered, too. The moisture in the sand combines with the cement, affecting the amount of water to be used in mixing concrete. If your sand is very wet, add less water (p.470). To test sand for moisture content, squeeze a handful. Damp sand will feel only damp and leave very little moisture on the hand; wet sand, the most usual kind, feels wet and leaves some moisture on the hand; very wet sand is dripping wet and leaves a lot of moisture on the hand when it is squeezed.

Coarse aggregate may be either gravel or stone ranging from ¼ inch to 1½ inches in breadth. It should be hard, clean, and free of earth and vegetable or organic matter such as manure. You can order gravel by size or bank run. This is gravel with several sizes mixed together, plus some sand.

Water for mixing concrete should be clean and free of oil, acid, or vegetable matter. Sea water should never be used; it contains salts that are harmful to concrete. As a general rule, water fit to drink is all right for making concrete.

Tools for concreting

The usual household collection includes some of the tools needed for concrete work: Wheelbarrow, for mixing small batches and for hauling; bucket, for measuring cement and aggregate; watering can, for measuring water and adding it to mix; 50-foot steel tape. Handling wet concrete cracks the skin, so wear waterproof gloves and boots.

There are other concrete specialty tools that you will have to buy or make:

Wood float, to level the concrete and give it a rough surface finish.

Steel finishing trowel, to give the concrete a smooth, hard surface finish.

Groover, or jointer, to cut joints between slabs.

Edger, to round off the edges of concrete slabs.

Trowel, to place mortar on blocks.

Square-pointed shovel, to mix and place concrete.

Strikeoff board, or straightedge, to remove excess concrete and bring surface to grade. Use an unwarped 2 x 4 long enough to extend about 6 inches beyond each side of the slab.

Bull-float, to smooth and level the surface. Make one from a 4 foot x 8 inch piece of 1-inch board; use broom handle or 1-inch dowel for handle.

Mason's line and blocks or pins, to lay concrete blocks level, plumb, and aligned.

Four-foot spirit level, to obtain true horizontal and vertical lines on paths, foundations, and walls.

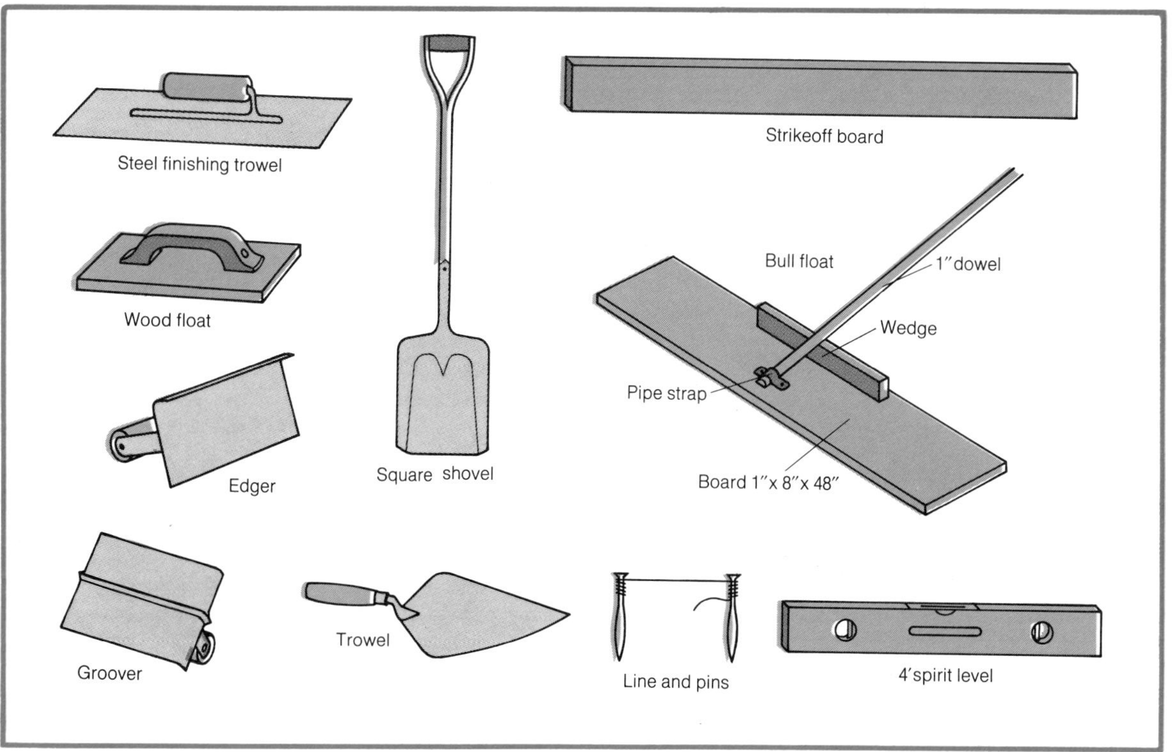

How to store raw materials

Always store cement in a dry place. It is advisable to store the bags on a platform with at least 4 inches of air space below. Stack the bags close together. Give them additional protection by covering or, better still, completely enclosing the bags in a large sheet of plastic. Keep the cement away from other materials, such as lime or plaster, that might contaminate it. If you must store an opened bag, even for a short time, close the bag securely and put it in a sealed plastic bag.

Store fine and coarse aggregates separately on a clean, hard surface. If you must store them next to each other, place a wooden barrier between the piles. Outdoors, cover with plastic sheeting.

If piles of aggregate must be left in a roadway, post red warning flags around them in the daytime and red warning lights at night.

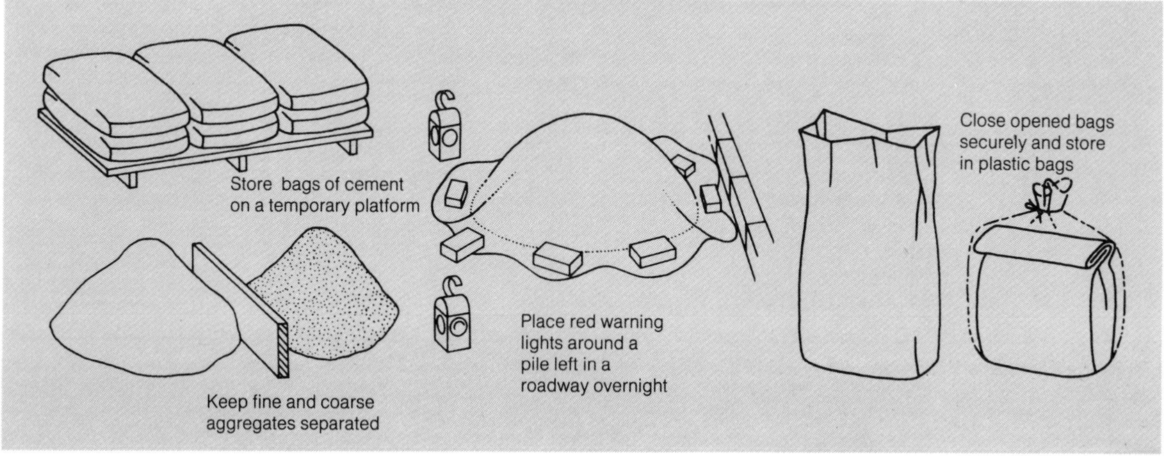

Estimating

Area and volume

The first step in estimating how much concrete you will need is to calculate the area in square feet that the structure will cover. Measure the dimensions of the space and determine its square footage as explained at the right. Multiply the square footage you get by the thickness in feet of the planned structure. The result will be the total volume of concrete required, which is expressed in cubic feet. To convert this number into cubic yards—the unit by which concrete is calculated and sold—divide it by 27, the number of cubic feet in a cubic yard. For example, a 4-inch-thick concrete floor 25 x 15 feet would require 4.63 cubic yards of concrete: 25 times 15 times ⅓ (4 inches is ⅓ foot) equals 125 cubic feet; this, divided by 27, equals 4.63 cubic yards.

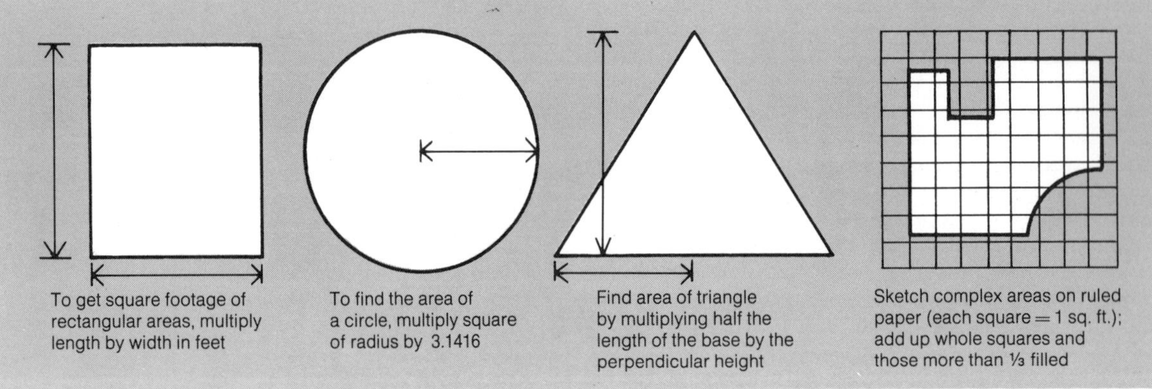

To get square footage of rectangular areas, multiply length by width in feet

To find the area of a circle, multiply square of radius by 3.1416

Find area of triangle by multiplying half the length of the base by the perpendicular height

Sketch complex areas on ruled paper (each square = 1 sq. ft.); add up whole squares and those more than ⅓ filled

How much concrete?

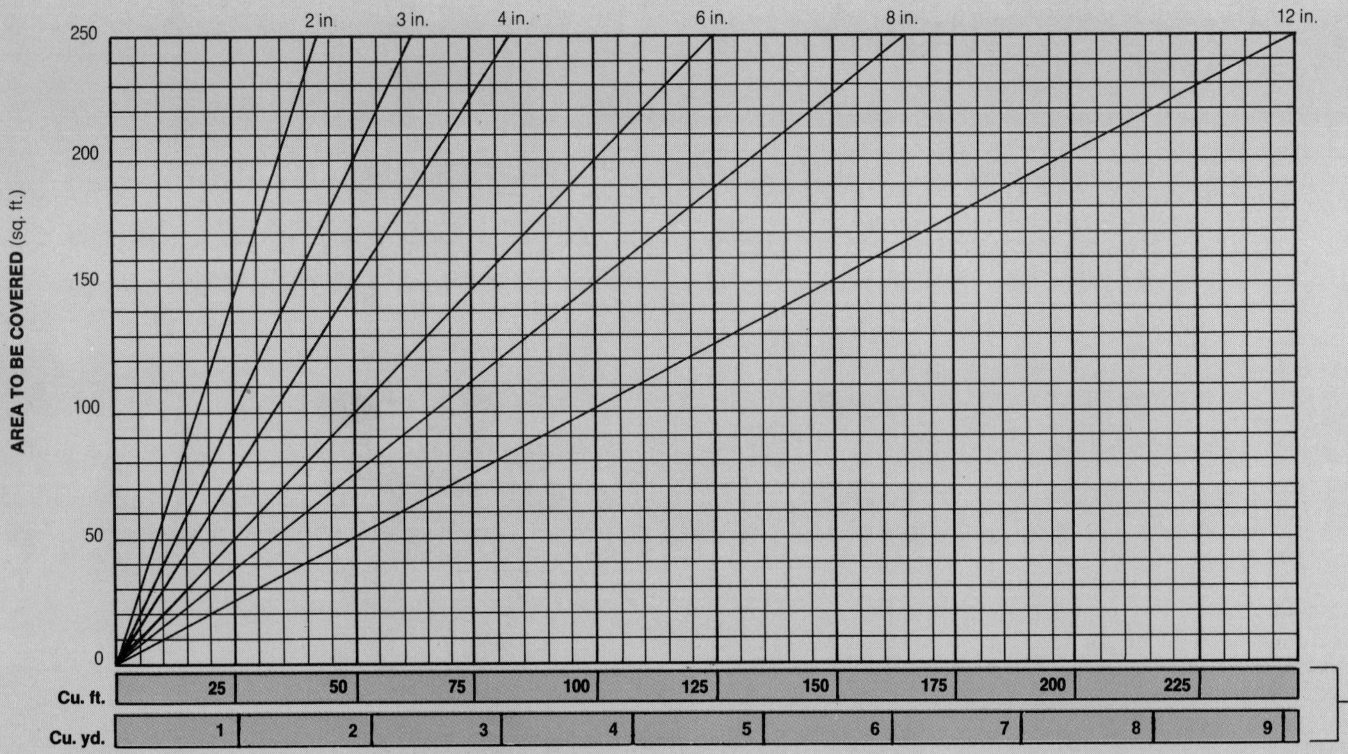

AREA TO BE COVERED (sq. ft.)

250 200 150 100 50 0

2 in. 3 in. 4 in. 6 in. 8 in. 12 in.

Cu. ft. 25 50 75 100 125 150 175 200 225

Cu. yd. 1 2 3 4 5 6 7 8 9

TOTAL MIX REQUIRED

Use this chart to calculate the amount of concrete needed. Read across from the area scale on the left to the line for the thickness of concrete, and then down to the total quantity scale to get the number of cubic feet or yards required. For example, to cover an area of 240 sq. ft. with a 4-in. slab takes about 80 cu. ft., or 3 cu. yds. Thicknesses and square footages not given can be calculated by addition. For instance, for a 5-in. slab, add the amounts needed for 2-in. and 3-in. slabs; for 375 sq. ft., add the amounts required for 200 and 175 sq. ft. at the thickness desired.

The right mix for the job

Before ordering materials for any concreting project, you must determine what mix is proper for the job. The table at right lists mixes suitable for most amateur concrete work. Note that the precise amount of water is specified for each mix. Be sure to follow this exactly; it is the water-to-cement ratio that determines the strength of the cement paste that binds the aggregates together. Too much water will make the paste thin and the concrete weak and porous; too little will make the concrete too stiff to be worked and placed in position.

Ready-mixed concrete: If your project calls for a cubic yard or more of concrete, you can prepare it in a mixer or buy it ready-mixed, as you prefer. Ready-mixed is usually more convenient and also more economical. When ordering ready-mixed concrete, be sure to specify the following:

1. Maximum-size aggregate. The coarse aggregate should not exceed one-third the slab thickness.
2. Minimum cement content. This will usually be six bags per cubic yard. For some jobs, however, such as footings and foundation walls, it can be five bags per cubic yard.
3. Maximum slump. The slump is a rough measure of the concrete's consistency and workability. Order a slump that does not exceed 4 inches.
4. Load-bearing capacity at 28 days should be no less than 3500 pounds per square inch.
5. Entrained air content of 6 percent. Air entrainment is required for good durability in concrete that will be exposed to freezing and thawing conditions, or to de-icing salts.

Mix-it-yourself: For jobs that require less than a cubic yard, mix the concrete yourself. If you need more than a few cubic feet, you'll find it more convenient and efficient to use a mixer; they can be rented in most areas.

For very small jobs that require only a few cubic feet, mix the concrete by hand. Buy the ingredients separately and mix them, or use a pre-packaged dry-mix concrete that contains all the ingredients except water. Quality dry-mix meets standards specified by the American Society for Testing and Materials; it comes in a bag bearing the printed statement that the product complies with ASTM C387. Since hand-mixing is not vigorous enough to make air-entrained concrete, do not hand-mix concrete that will be exposed to freezing and thawing, or to de-icing salts.

How to choose proper mix — Recommended proportions of water to cement and suggested trial mixes*

Kinds of work	Add U.S. gallons of water to each sack batch if sand is:			Suggested mixture for trial batch**			Materials per cu. yd. of concrete**		
					Aggregates			Aggregates	
	Very wet	Wet (aver. sand)	Damp	Cement sacks	Fine (cu. ft.)	Coarse† (cu. ft.)	Cement sacks	Fine (cu. ft.)	Coarse† (cu. ft.)
Concrete subjected to wear and weather: Watertight floors, such as basements, barns, and foundations. Driveways, walks, swimming and wading pools.	4¼	5	5½	1	2½	3½	6	15	21
Concrete not subjected to wear and weather: Foundation walls, footings. Uses where watertightness and abrasion resistance are not important.	4¾	5½	6¼	1	3	4	5	15	20

* Use air-entrained concrete where concrete will be subjected to freezing, thawing, or de-icing salts, or where it is exposed to weather.

† Maximum-size aggregate 1½ in.

** Large aggregates are more economical than smaller aggregates but not essential. Most commonly used aggregate is ¾-in. gravel.

Guide for ordering ready-mixed concrete for driveways, walks, and patios

Maximum-size aggregate (inches)	Minimum cement content (lb. per cu. yd.)	Maximum slump (inches)	Compressive strength at 28 days (lb. per sq. in.)	Air content (percent by volume)
⅜	610	4	3,500	7½ ±1
½	590	4	3,500	7½ ±1
¾	540	4	3,500	6 ±1
1	520	4	3,500	6 ±1
1½	470	4	3,500	5 ±1

Quantities of materials required for 100 sq. ft. of concrete of various thicknesses *

Thickness of concrete (inches)	Amount of concrete (cu. yd.)	Proportions					
		1:2½:3½ mix			1:3:4 mix		
		Cement sacks	Aggregate Fine (cu. ft.)	Aggregate Coarse (cu. ft.)	Cement sacks	Aggregate Fine (cu. ft.)	Aggregate Coarse (cu. ft.)
3	0.92	5.5	13.8	19.3	4.6	13.8	18.4
4	1.24	7.4	18.6	26.0	6.2	18.6	24.8
5	1.56	9.4	23.4	32.8	7.8	23.4	31.2
6	1.85	11.1	27.8	38.9	9.3	27.8	37.0

* Add 5 to 10% to compensate for loss caused by such factors as spillage and uneven subgrade.

Handling concrete

Mixing

Whether you are mixing by hand or with a mixer, the amount of water you add to the mix will depend a good deal upon the "wetness" of the sand. After you have decided what concrete mix you are going to use (p.469), never change the ratio of cement, sand, and gravel. The mix should be mushy, but not soupy, and stick together without crumbling. If it is too dry, add a little water; if too wet, add cement, sand, and aggregate in the proportion you started with.

To use a mixer: After measuring all ingredients to the correct proportions, follow this procedure:

1. With the mixer stopped, load in all the coarse aggregate and half the water. If you are using an air-entraining agent, mix it with this part of the water. Since the amount of the agent depends on the brand, follow the manufacturer's directions. An easier and more dependable way to make air-entrained concrete is to use Portland cement that contains the air-entraining agent.
2. Start the mixer. With the mixer running, add the sand, the cement, and the rest of the water.
3. Continue mixing for three minutes, or until all the materials are thoroughly mixed and the concrete is a uniform color.

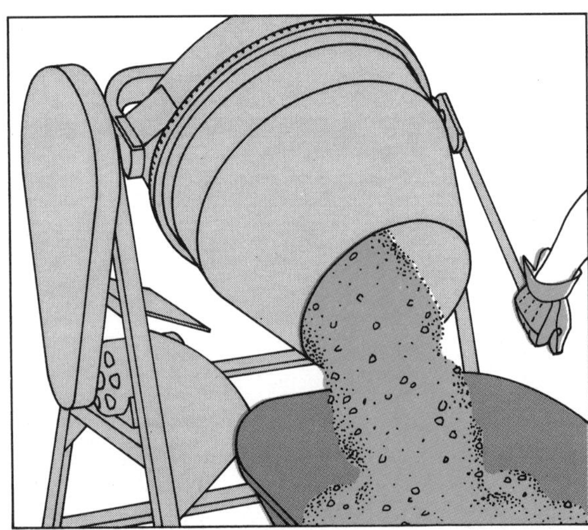

A mixer's batch size, or mixing capacity, is usually 60 percent of its total volume; never exceed the batch size. Wash out the drum after each batch. To scour the drum at the end of the day, add water and a few shovelfuls of coarse aggregate while drum is turning; then hose it out and dry it.

How to mix by hand

1. Tools and materials needed for hand mixing. To measure aggregates, fill bucket and level off with shovel. Measure cement the same way, shaking it well down in bucket and scraping it off level.

2. Spread the sand in a ring on the mixing area, add the cement, mix until you get a uniform color without brown or gray streaks. Add coarse aggregate and turn the mix over at least three times.

3. Form a depression in the middle of the heap, add some of the measured water, and work it into the center of the mixture. Add more of the water as needed and mix until entire pile is damp.

4. Shovel the dry part of the mix into the depression until the water has been absorbed (take care not to let the walls collapse). Then turn the whole heap over until it is evenly moist.

5. Form a new depression, as here, if more water is to be added. If only a little water remains to be added, sprinkle it on the surface of the heap. Never change the ratio of cement and aggregate.

6. To test the mix, draw the shovel backward over the heap in a series of jabs; try to leave clearcut ridges. If mix is too dry, they will be indistinct; if too wet, they will level out.

Placing, finishing, curing

The dry materials in concrete settle to the bottom and force the water to "bleed" to the surface. Any work done to the surface of the concrete while this water is present will cause scaling or dusting (p.466). Placing, striking off, and bull-floating must be done before the water bleeds to the surface; edging, jointing, floating, and troweling must be done after all such water has evaporated from the surface.

Placing: Planning is the secret of successful concrete work. Before you mix concrete or take delivery of ready-mixed, prepare the surface you are going to cover, have the forms in place, have tools at hand —and a helper or two. Try to have ready-mix unloaded directly into the forms. Always place concrete as near its final position as possible. Do not dump concrete in widely separated piles and rake them together; dump each succeeding load against the previous one. Never place concrete on frozen ground, on mud, or on ground covered with standing water. If the ground is extremely dry, dampen it so it won't absorb water from the mix. Start the placing in a corner. Use a shovel with a square end to spread concrete. Do not use a garden rake or hoe; they separate coarse aggregate from the rest of the concrete mix.

Striking off, or screeding, brings the surface to the correct elevation. Place strikeoff board (p.467) across edge forms, or screeds, and move it back and forth in a sawing motion to remove excess concrete and fill in low spots.

Bull-floating: Immediately after striking off, use a bull float (p.467) to level ridges and fill voids left by the strikeoff board and to embed coarse aggregate slightly below the surface.

Finishing cannot begin until the water sheen leaves the surface and the concrete stiffens slightly. This waiting period is absolutely essential if you are to get durable surfaces. On cool, dry days the waiting time can be several hours; on hot, dry, windy days the period is short; there may be no waiting with air-entrained concrete.

Edging: Immediately after bull-floating, run a trowel between the concrete and the side forms to a depth of 1 inch. Wait until the concrete has set enough to hold the shape of the edger (p.467); then run it back and forth between concrete and side forms.

Jointing: After edging, use a groover (p.467) to cut control joints 4 to 5 feet apart in sidewalks, 10 to 15 feet apart in floors, drives, and patios; cut a joint down the center of 10-foot and longer slabs. These joints control the location of possible cracks. Using a 1 x 10 as a guide, run the groover across the slab; turn it around and run it back the opposite way.

Floating embeds large aggregate just below the surface, levels off humps and voids, and brings the fine aggregate to the surface for further finishing. Hold the float flat on the surface and swing it in a sweeping arc. Wood floats produce a rougher finish than metal floats do. Use an aluminum or magnesium float for air-entrained concrete.

Troweling produces a smooth, hard surface and is done immediately after floating. For the first troweling, hold the steel trowel (p.467) flat against the surface. Additional trowelings will make the surface smoother and harder. Begin the second troweling when your hand pressed against the surface leaves only a slight impression; tilt leading edge of trowel upward this time.

Brooming. Pull a damp stiff-bristled broom over a floated surface to produce a nonskid finish.

Curing keeps concrete moist and warm while it is hardening and greatly increases its strength and durability. Curing time of 6 days is sufficient on the average, with slight variations for warm weather (5 days) and cooler weather (7 days). You can cure concrete by any of the following methods:

1. Seal the surface with plastic sheeting or waterproof paper; seal these coverings at the joints, lay them flat, and anchor them at the edges.
2. Cover the concrete with burlap or canvas and keep this covering continuously wet during the curing period.
3. Keep the concrete moderately moist with a lawn sprinkler or soaking hose.
4. Spray a pigmented curing compound on the damp concrete. It is essential that coverage be complete. Curing compounds should not be used in the late fall in the northern United States or in Canada because they may prevent proper air-drying, which is needed to resist de-icing salts.

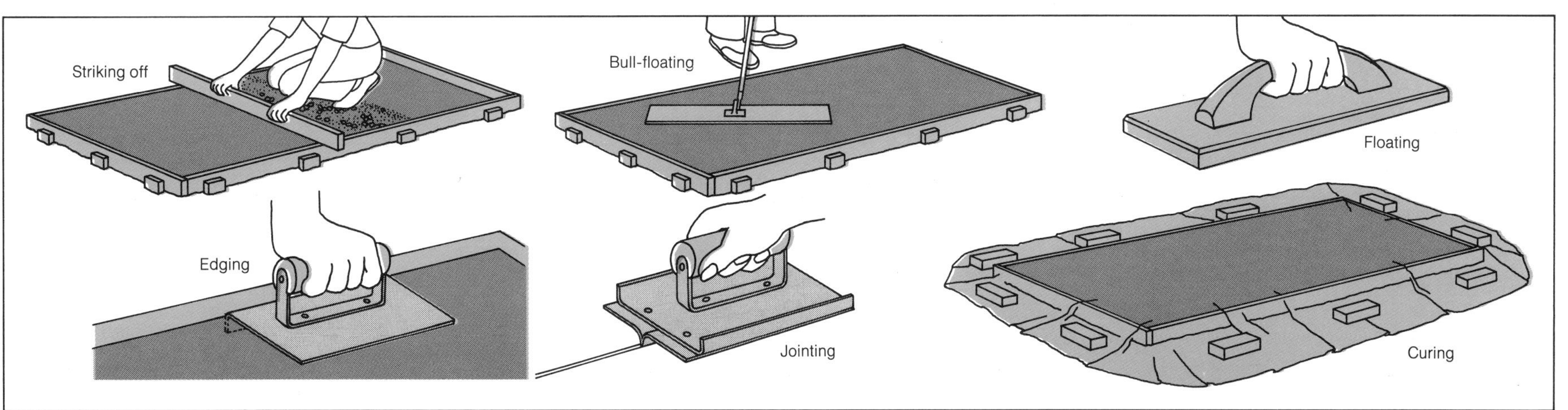

Placement of footings

Footings must rest on undisturbed soil below the frost line. Place footings on slightly dampened soil, but be sure that the soil is not wet. The depth that footings must extend below grade is specified by agencies of the federal government and varies widely, depending upon such divergent factors as depth of frost penetration, soil conditions, local building custom and experience, and whether or not the area is in an earthquake zone. In certain parts of Florida, for example, footings need be only 6 inches below grade, but in some parts of Maine they must be 4½ feet under the surface. Local building regulations sometimes differ from national requirements; check your local building code.

In cold climates, a crowned bed slab without footings is used for outbuildings. The slab is laid over a thick bed of gravel as shown. Heaving caused by frost raises the entire structure as a unit.

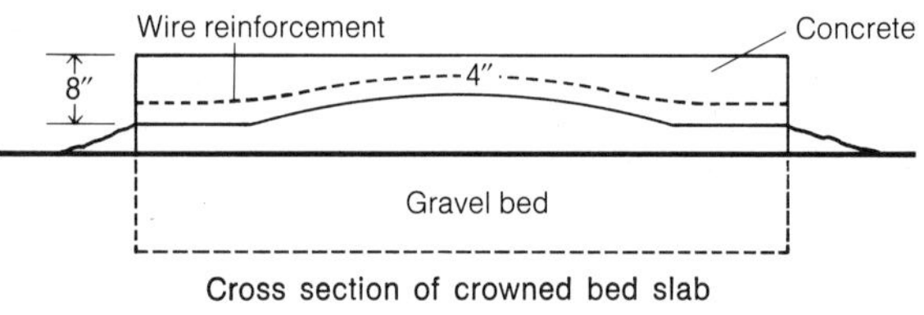

Cross section of crowned bed slab

GOVERNMENT REQUIREMENTS FOR DEPTH OF FOOTINGS

Area	**Depth of footings** (inches)
Albany, New York	42
Albuquerque, New Mexico	18
Anchorage, Alaska	42
Bangor, Maine	48
Camden, New Jersey	30
Charleston, West Virginia	24
Columbus, Ohio	32
Fort Worth, Texas	6
Greensboro, North Carolina	12
Helena, Montana	36
Knoxville, Tennessee	18
Los Angeles, California	12
Minneapolis, Minnesota	42
Omaha, Nebraska	42
Seattle, Washington	16
Shreveport, Louisiana	18
Tampa, Florida	6

Local regulations may vary; check building code

Types of footings

Among the most commonly used concrete footings are (1) the flat top, which looks like a small slab, and (2) circular piers, or columns. The flat-top footing can be perfectly flat across the top or it can have a keyed joint into which concrete for the foundation wall is placed. The first of these types of flat top is used when the foundation wall is made of concrete blocks, and frequently with a poured concrete wall as well. Make a keyed footing by laying a 2 x 4 on edge in the top of the footing concrete; remove it as soon as the concrete has set.

Concrete piers of sufficient diameter, usually 12 inches, can serve as both foundation and footing with no additional footing beneath them. They are spaced around the perimeter of the structure and under the interior construction as local building codes specify. Dig postholes to hold laminated fiber forms and fill the forms with concrete.

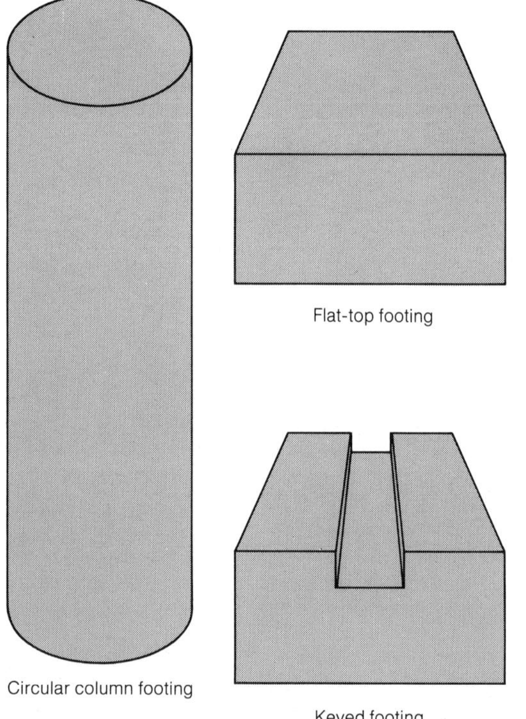

Flat-top footing

Circular column footing

Keyed footing

Establishing building lines

First determine the front line, which is the outer face of the foundation wall for the front of the structure. Locate this line by measuring carefully from the property line or from an existing structure. Stretch a line between two temporary stakes driven into the ground to mark the front line. Then check your plan and locate one of the outside corners of the front foundation wall. Drive a stake to mark this point, and then drive a nail into the exact center of the top of the stake.

Next, measure along the temporary front line to the spot where the other outside corner of the front foundation wall should be. Drive a stake at that point and drive a nail into the center of this stake. The exact front line of the foundation is the line between the two nails.

Stretch a line between the two front corner stakes and set up the other three sides in the same way.

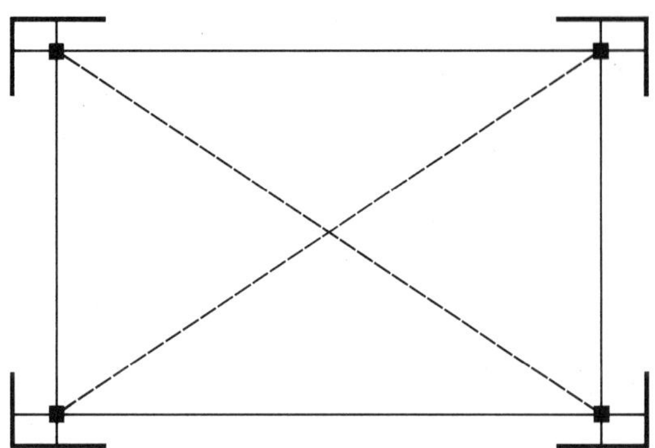

Test building lines of a rectangle or square by measuring diagonally; lengths must be equal.

After the building lines are laid out, check the measurements against your plan. For a square or rectangle, the distance between the rear stakes will be the same as between the front stakes, and the diagonals will be equal. Corners will be located where lines for outside surfaces intersect.

To check your corners to be sure they are exactly 90 degrees, measure 3 feet in one direction from a corner and then 4 feet at a right angle to the first direction; if the corner is square, the diagonal must measure 5 feet. Or you can check the angles with a large builder's square (p.448).

Batter boards

Before you can excavate for footings and formwork, and in order to provide working space, you will have to remove the building layout stakes driven to mark the building lines. To preserve the building lines, set up batter boards about 4 feet beyond the building layout stakes, far enough from the stakes that the excavation will not disturb the batter boards. Where an existing wall adjoins the new site and prevents batter boards being set into the ground, fix flat boards to the wall. To make batter boards, use 2 x 4s for the stakes and 1 x 6s for the crosspieces along the top.

Set up a right-angle batter board with the crosspiece slightly above the top of the foundation at each corner; make the boards approximately level with each other. Stretch a line from each batter board and use a plumb bob to determine where the lines intersect directly over the nail in each layout stake. Drive a nail into the top of each crosspiece to mark the correct location of the building lines. With these nails in place, you can locate the exact corners of the structure even when the layout stakes have been dug up. All you have to do is run lines from each nail; the corners will fall directly under the spots where the lines intersect.

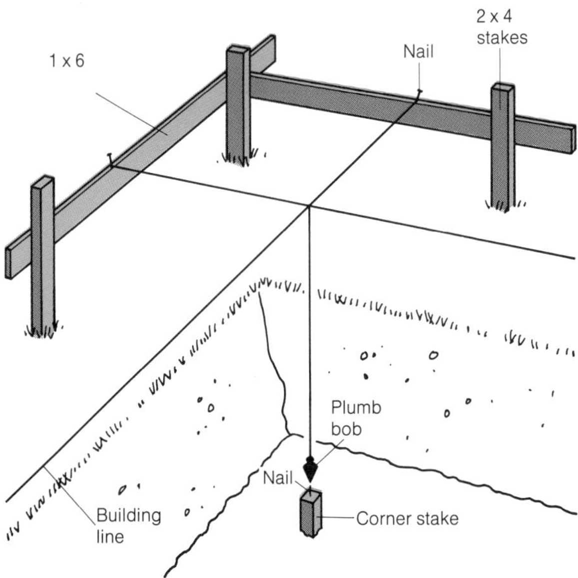

Right-angle batter boards preserve building lines

Excavation and formwork

Excavation: Set out stakes to mark the boundaries of the footings. Remove lines from batter boards. Remove loose dirt and debris from the ground that the footings will rest on.

Building the forms: Double-headed nails are easier to remove than regular nails would be. Always nail through the stakes and into the form boards. Use old crankcase oil to oil the form surfaces that will touch the concrete.

Footing forms: After excavating, replace lines on batter boards and locate corners again. Mark their position with stakes at the bottom of the excavation. Then drive a number of grade stakes along the footing line level with the corner stakes.

Set up the outside forms first. Make their tops level with the grade stakes. Use ¾-inch plywood or 1-inch boards for the forms; hold them in place with 2 x 4s driven into the ground every 2 to 3 feet. Space 1 x 2s as long as the footing width every few feet along its length. These spacers will keep the forms apart and will locate the correct position for the inside forms.

Remove the corner stakes and grade stakes before placing the concrete. Remove the spacers as you place the concrete.

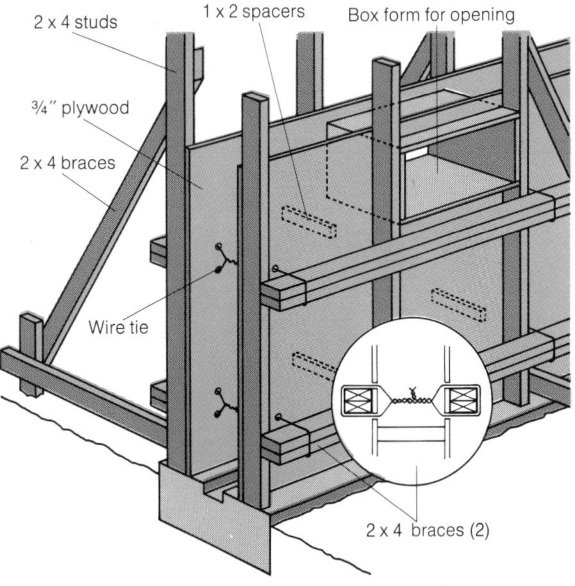

Formwork for concrete foundation wall

Wall forms: Use ¾-inch plywood or 1-inch boards for the side forms. Support them with 2 x 4 studs every 2 feet; use 2 x 4 braces at each stud as shown. For a wall higher than 4 feet, attach 2 x 4 braces horizontally to the studs. Tie the forms together with soft iron wire. Drill holes in the forms and insert a couple of lengths of twisted wire, or use two wires twisted to form an X across the wall's width at 2-foot intervals. Before removing forms, cut off the wire ends on the outside.

Keep inside and outside form boards the proper distance apart with 1 x 2 spacers cut to the wall's exact width; space them about 2 feet apart. Remove spacers as you place the concrete. Walls 4 feet or higher need ties and spacers about every 2 feet between the top and bottom of the forms. Build a wood box into the form to allow for openings such as basement windows in the foundation wall.

Fasten sills to foundation wall with ½-inch anchor bolts 8 inches long. Space and insert the bolts 4 feet apart before the concrete has set. If the foundation wall is concrete block, install bolts 18 inches long in cores filled with concrete (p.483).

Foundation without forms

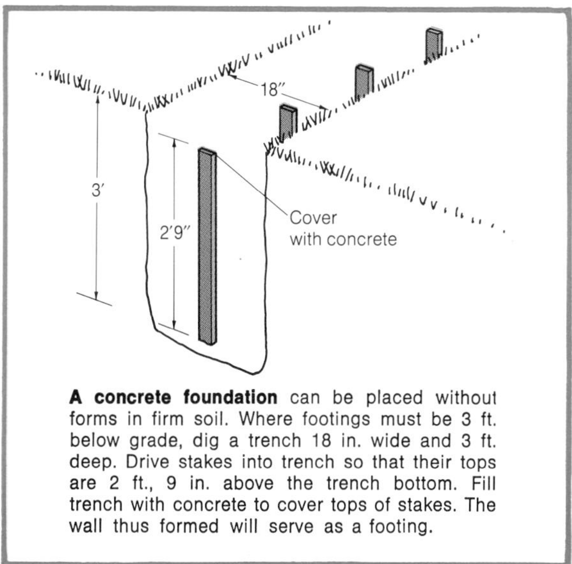

A concrete foundation can be placed without forms in firm soil. Where footings must be 3 ft. below grade, dig a trench 18 in. wide and 3 ft. deep. Drive stakes into trench so that their tops are 2 ft., 9 in. above the trench bottom. Fill trench with concrete to cover tops of stakes. The wall thus formed will serve as a footing.

Laying walks and drives

Preparation

If the soil where you plan to lay a walk or drive is firm and compacted, lay the concrete directly on the ground. Disturb the soil as little as possible. Dig out grass and weeds and level off bumps, then roll to provide a smooth, hard base. If the soil is poorly drained and water-soaked most of the time, lay a 4- to 6-inch subbase of gravel or crushed stone. Compact it thoroughly. If the base has a few soft spots, fill them with crushed stone or gravel and tamp well.

If you are laying concrete on an existing concrete base that is cracked, break up the cracked base and compact the rubble with a roller; otherwise the new slab will almost certainly crack or scale.

Make forms of 2 x 4s for walks and of 2 x 6s for drives. Support the forms every 3 feet with 2 x 4s from 12 to 18 inches long. Oil the form surfaces that will touch the concrete in order to prevent sticking.

Provide a slope of at least ⅛ inch per foot of width to carry off surface water. You can make one edge lower than the other, or make a crown in the center by using a concave strikeoff board. The slope must always be away from any buildings.

A concrete driveway should be 6 inches thick if it will be used by heavy trucks; 4 inches for cars and light trucks. Most sidewalks are 4 inches thick, but check your local building code. Where heavy trucks cross a walk, make it 6 inches thick.

To control cracking, cut control joints every 10 feet in a drive, every 4 to 5 feet in a walk. Or install wood joints as shown on the next page.

Use a 1:2½:3½ mix for walks and drives; use air-entrained concrete in cold climates.

Setting out the forms

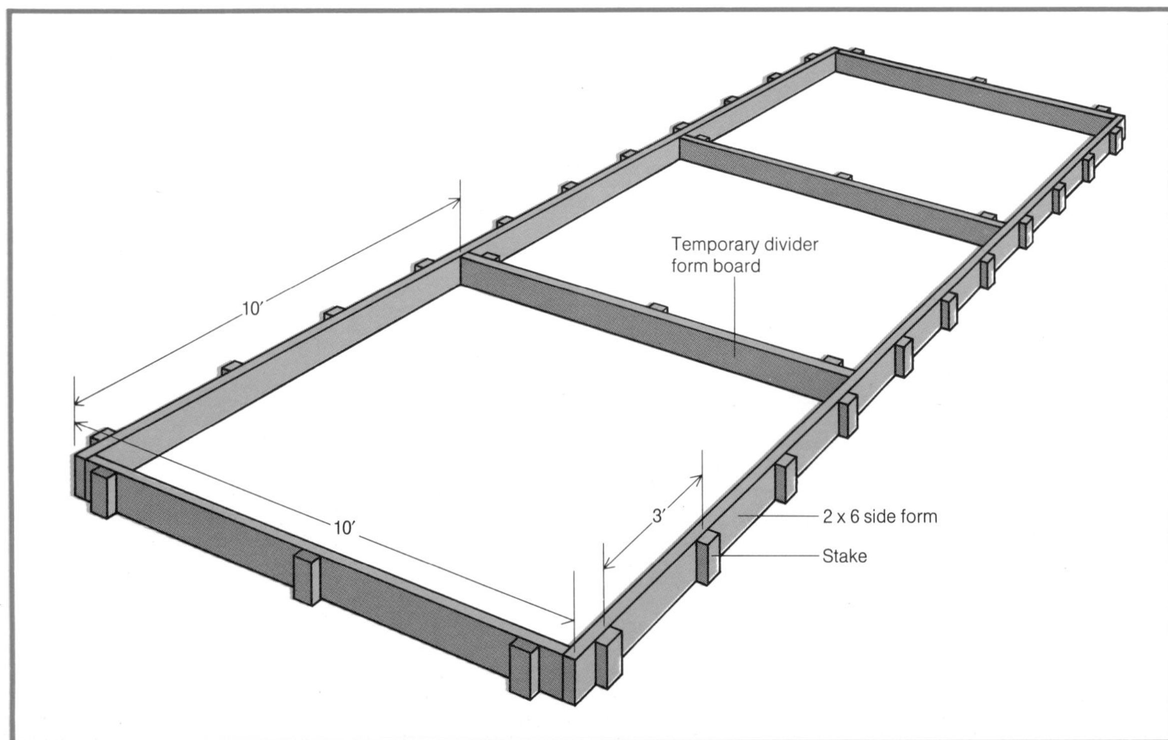

Driveway forms: Prepare a base 3 in. larger all around than the finished slab will be, so that the forms can be placed on firm ground. Stakes must resist sideways pressure of concrete. Place joints on the side where the concrete pour will start.

Stoop and steps

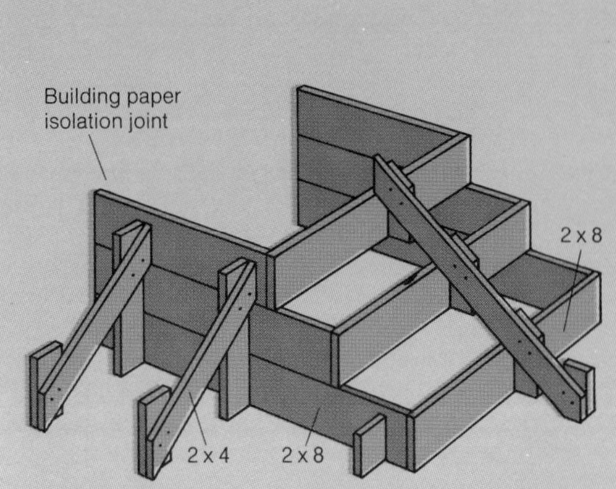

Put footings 6 in. below frost line or 2 ft. deep in a no-frost area. Tie steps to the wall with metal anchors. Make forms rigid and tight; oil them. Make steps at least as wide as the walk, treads 11 in., risers 7½ in. Pitch treads ¼ in. to front for drainage.

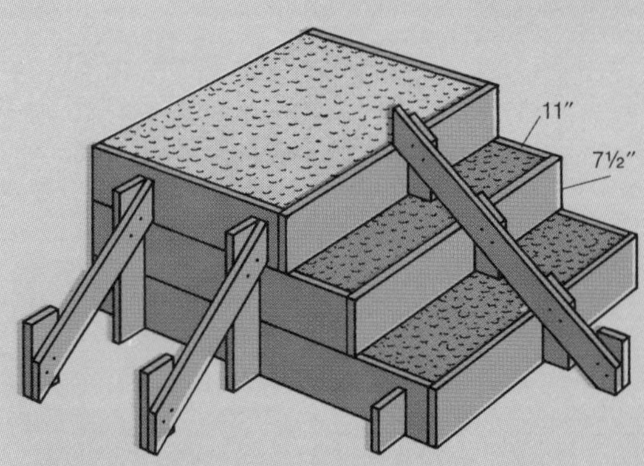

You can reduce amount of concrete needed by using fill, such as stone, covered with well-tamped sand; keep fill 4 in. below top of forms. Use a 1:2½: 3½ mix, air-entrained in cold climates. Spade concrete well next to forms. Tap forms lightly to release air bubbles. Broom surface to make it nonskid. Cure for 6 days with forms in place.

Laying step by step

1. Drive 2 x 4s along the outside of the forms at 3-ft. intervals, with extra stakes where form boards are butted together. Drive nails through the forms into the stakes. Leave no gaps between boards. Forms must withstand the pressure of compacted concrete.

2. Use a spirit level to check the forms. One side of the form of a 10-ft.-wide slab should be raised 1¼ in. to ensure minimum pitch (⅛ in. per foot) for drainage. Place a 1¼-in. wood strip over the lower side and check across both sides with a level.

3. Pour concrete straight into the forms. Place it as accurately as possible to reduce subsequent handling. This is especially important with ready-mixed concrete. Use a shovel to spread mix evenly to about 1 in. above the forms to allow for compacting.

4. Run a spade down the inside edge of the form; then tamp the concrete, using a strikeoff board to which you have attached handles. Lift a few inches and drop it; move it forward about half its thickness each time. Use the same board to strike off excess concrete.

5. Insert control joints every 10 ft., using ⅜-in. softwood boards of the same length and width as the temporary divider board. Place one for each joint, positioned so that a knot-free edge is up, between the divider board and the untamped concrete.

6. Spread the concrete up to the joint; strike it off and bull-float it (p.467). Remove the temporary divider and its supporting stakes. The joint must remain vertical and level with the side forms and the compacted concrete. Continue concrete work on far side of joint.

7. When water sheen has disappeared, run an edger along the sides. Then float the concrete (p.471). Use a stiff brush to give it a rough, skid-resistant surface; pull the brush across the slab toward you. For a smoother surface, make the final finish with a wood float.

8. Cover newly laid concrete with plastic sheeting or waterproof paper, or use straw or burlap kept continuously wet. Leave forms in place for several days. Cure for at least 6 days; concrete can then take light loads, but keep heavy loads off for 6 days more.

Concreting alongside a wall

If you lay a walk alongside a wall or building, you cannot use the strikeoff board, with or without handles, across its width. The solution is to lay the concrete in alternate bays, compacting and leveling it by using the strikeoff board lengthwise between the end stops.

When placing formwork, insert a strip of ½-inch-thick asphalt-impregnated fiber material to form an expansion joint between the wall and the slab. Use one wherever the slab abuts curbs, foundations, or steps. Slope the walk away from the wall ¼-inch per foot to carry off surface water.

When laying the first bays, make sure the divider forms are firmly in place so that they cannot be displaced by the pressure of the concrete.

Leave the divider forms in place while the concrete hardens; then remove them and fill in the empty bays. When all of the concrete has thoroughly hardened, the side form can be removed.

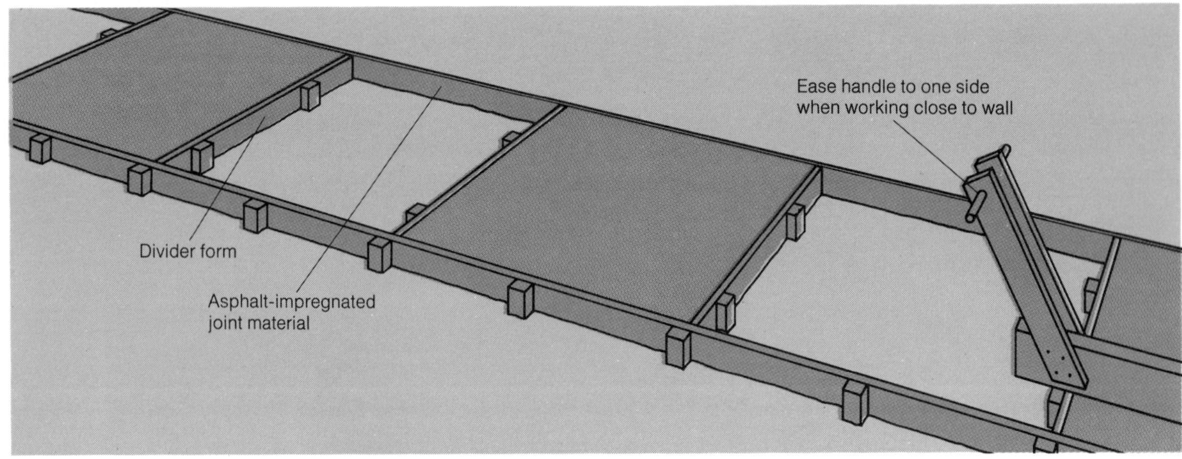

A keyed control joint is required when a concrete pour is stopped before completion. To make one between bays, nail a double-beveled 1- x 2-in. strip along the inside length of the divider form. This will keep all slabs level.

Sloped and curved sites

On a steep slope, allow shorter spaces between the divider forms.

For a curved walk or drive, make the forms of ¼- or ½-inch plywood or hardboard, or use 1 x 4s. Soak 1 x 4s to make them easier to bend. Set the supporting stakes closer together than the usual 3-foot spacing used for straight forms.

A reverse slope may be so steep that there may be danger of water entering the building after the gutter has been made, as in the illustration below. In such a situation, build a small curb or dam at the sill. A long slope may require more than one such diversion point; space them about 30 feet apart. If the slope is long and curved, pitch it about ¼ inch per foot toward the shorter side.

For reverse slope, lay slab to a point below floor, then run it upward. Make gutter a gradual slope as shown.

How to cast slabs

Home-cast slabs are suitable for patios and walks. They are usually 2 inches thick. Make the formwork ½-inch deeper than the slab thickness to allow for a ½-inch sand bed to pour the concrete on; this sand base will make it easier to lift the slabs after they have hardened. Dampen the sand bed before placing the concrete.

Use a 1:2½:3½ mix of air-entrained concrete. Place concrete in forms, strike it off, and bull-float it (p.467). Run an edger along the forms to round off the sides of the slabs. Use a wood float to produce a textured surface. A rougher, skid-resistant surface can be made by dragging a stiff-bristled brush over the concrete after troweling.

Cut slabs with trowel 1 to 2 hours after pouring; slice through the concrete. For rough edges, cut only one-third through and break at trowel marks when lifting.

Cure the slabs for 6 days, then lift them carefully and stack on edge.

Laying paving slabs

1. Remove 3 to 4 in. of soil. (Dig deeper in poorly drained soil and put in 4 in. of gravel.) Lay a 2-in. sand bed. String line to mark edges and height of path.

2. Make a mortar mix of 1 part masonry cement and 3 parts sand. Place baseball-sized dabs of mortar in center of bed for each slab and just inside corners.

3. Lay slabs either touching one another or ½ in. apart. If they are spaced, obtain uniformity by inserting a ½-in. wood spacer. Spacing will improve appearance of walk.

4. Press slabs firmly into mortar bed. Tap gently on a wood block placed over the surface until slab has no tendency to rock and is level with adjacent slabs and with line.

5. Fill open joints with wet mortar or a dry mixture of masonry cement and sand. Pack wet mortar (as here) into dampened joints and trowel it to just below slab level.

6. When using a dry mixture of masonry cement and sand, pour it into joint from edge of trowel. Brush away surplus. Moisten joints with fine spray from a garden hose.

Making steps with paving slabs

Paving slabs make excellent treads for garden steps, with the risers made of bricks or smaller slabs. If homemade slabs are used, they can be cast to exactly the required size. If you buy slabs, get them textured to prevent slipping in wet weather.

Plan your steps so that each tread (the part that is walked upon) is at least 11 inches from front to back; make the risers (the vertical parts) no more than 7½ inches high. Allow a ¼-inch pitch for drainage on each tread.

Cut out the rough outline for the steps, taking care not to disturb the rest of the soil; finish the cutting as the work progresses. To support the riser of the first step, dig a trench 4 inches deep and the same width as the steps; fill the trench with concrete to provide a secure footing. Use a 1:3:4 mix; in cold climates, use air-entrained concrete.

When the concrete has hardened, lay small slabs or bricks to form the bottom riser; bed them in mortar made of 1 part masonry cement and 3 parts sand. Firm and level the soil behind the riser. Using the same mortar mix, lay a slab to form the bottom tread so that the front protrudes 1 inch beyond the riser. Use the back of the tread as a base for the next riser.

If the steps go up the face of a bank, build side walls to prevent soil from being washed onto the steps whenever it rains.

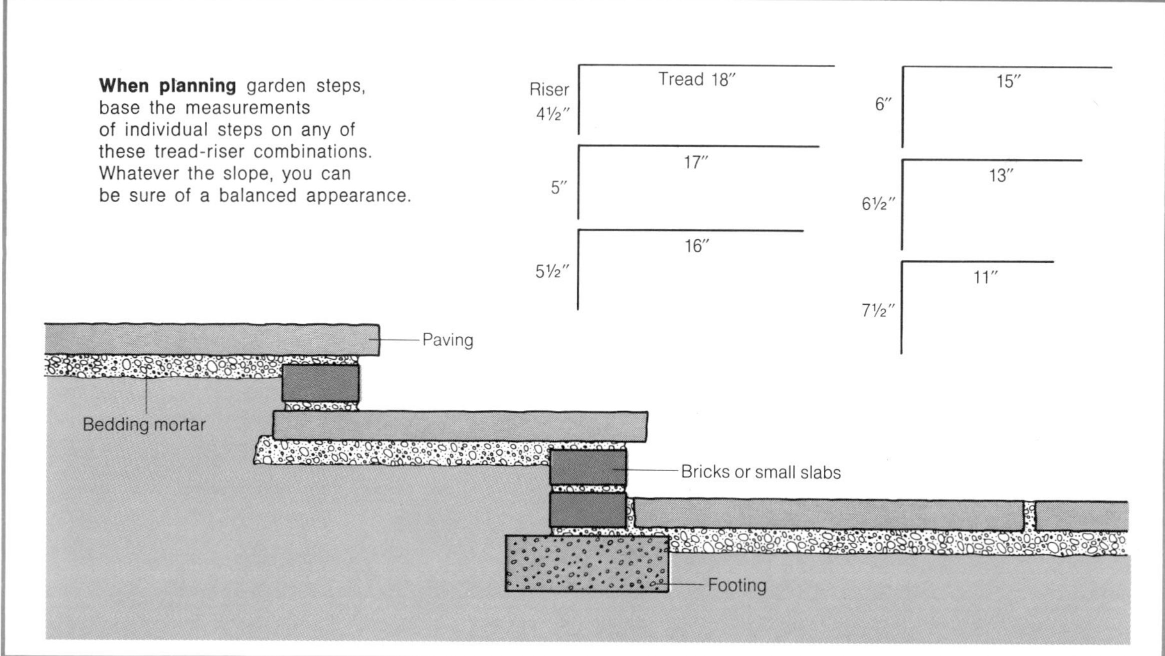

To build steps into a bank or a raised lawn, first cut out the rough outline of the steps; do not loosen the rest of the soil. Complete the cutting as building proceeds. Side walls may be needed to prevent mud from washing onto steps.

Concrete floors

Planning and preparation

Check your town's building code for requirements regarding floor design and construction.

If the base soil is well drained, compact it and lay the floor directly on it. If the soil is soft or loose, you will need to dig it out and lay a subbase of 4 inches of crushed stone and 1 inch of sand; compact the subbase thoroughly.

Slope concrete floors for drainage; basement floors should slope toward drains, garage floors toward the garage door. Obtain uniform floor thickness by sloping the subgrade under the floor. To keep a basement or garage floor from bonding with the footing, spread 1 inch of sand over the top of the footing before placing the concrete.

Provide ducting for pipes and cables below the slab. To hold the side forms, drive 2 x 2s into the ground about 8 inches, making their tops flush with the surface.

Install a vapor barrier of heavy polyethylene sheeting over the base after you have driven in the stakes; overlap the joints of the sheeting about 4 inches. Run the vapor barrier up the wall to the full height of the floor; run it to the first course above grade in a masonry wall.

Use 6-foot lengths of 2 x 4 for the side forms. After laying the vapor barrier, attach the side forms, driving the nails only ½ inch into the stakes. Side forms in this instance are used only as supporting surfaces for the strikeoff board and are therefore merely tacked to the stakes so that they can be removed without difficulty.

Separate floor from walls with a ½-inch-thick isolation joint made of asphalt-impregnated material. Isolation joints of the same thickness should also be put around steel drains and Lally columns.

Make a garage or basement floor 4 inches thick, using a 1:2½:3½ concrete mix. Use a 2 x 4 slightly shorter than the width of the room for your strikeoff board.

Prevent cracks by spacing the control joints (p. 471) about 10 feet apart. Make them with a groover, cutting the joints one-fifth to one-fourth as deep as the floor and all the way across the slab.

Finish the surface (p.471), then cover it with polyethylene sheeting and let it cure for 6 days. For a smooth surface that can be painted or to which tiles are to be applied, finish the concrete with a steel trowel.

Laying procedure

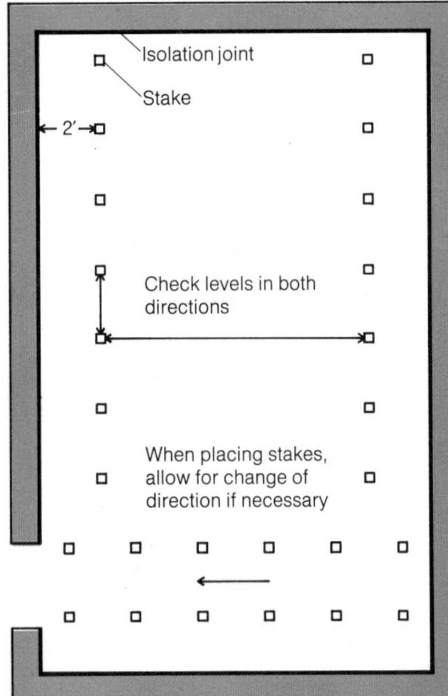

1. While preparing the base, drive stakes to support the formwork; do this before laying the vapor barrier. Place the stakes so that the forms can be drawn back to the exit.

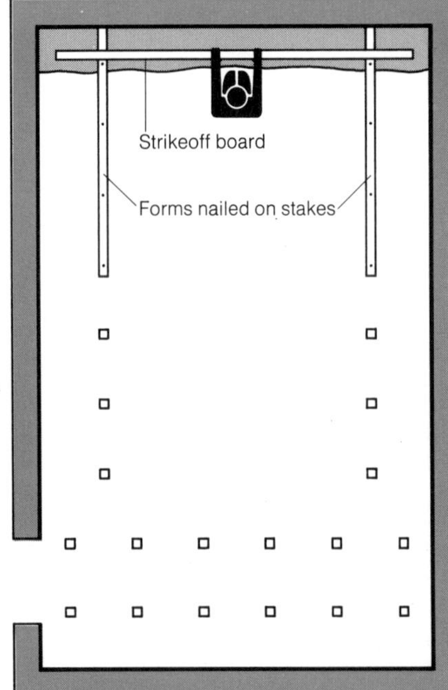

2. Stand the forms on edge on the stakes; drive nails through forms to penetrate ½ in. into stakes. Check levels; then lay a 3-ft. strip of concrete as for a walk.

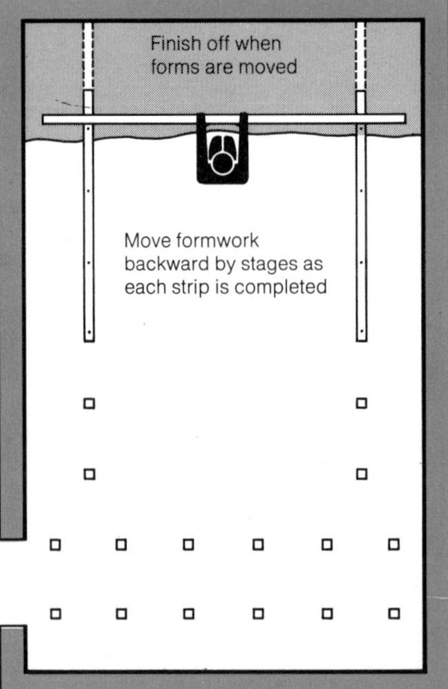

3. Lift the forms; draw them back and attach them to the next set of stakes. Fill and compact the spaces left by removal of the forms. Finish the surface with a float.

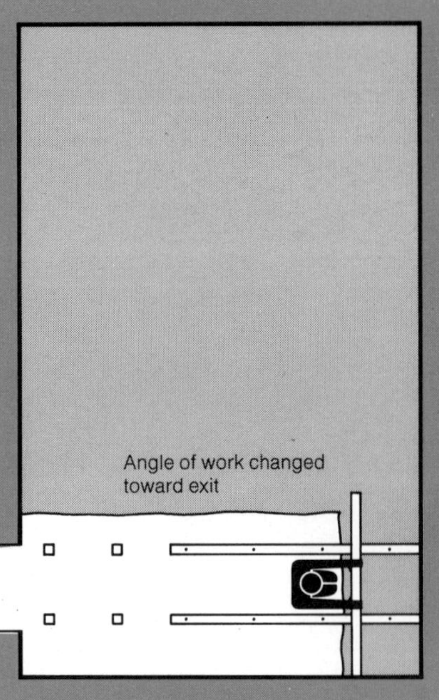

4. Continue working backward, checking levels often, so that you finish at the exit. Make sure at each stage that you have sufficient reach for compacting and finishing.

Damaged walks and drives

If the damage is not extensive, you can use any of the patching compounds—latex, vinyl, or epoxy—following instructions that come with them.

For bigger jobs, however, these are too expensive and fast-drying. Repair more extensive damage with a dry-mix (gravel mix) concrete or make your own stiff mix of 1 part Portland cement, 2 parts sand, and 2 parts fine gravel.

Surface repairs: Chisel out loose or broken fragments of concrete to a depth of 1 inch, then use the chisel to thoroughly roughen the base of the cavity (wear goggles). Undercut the edges of the damaged area. Wire-brush the surface and wash out all loose particles.

The surface to be patched should be damp, not wet, so sponge out any water that remains. Coat the surface with a thick, creamy mixture of Portland cement and water and fill the cavity with the patching mix before the creamy mixture dries. Tamp the patching mix in firmly, overfilling the cavity slightly to allow for shrinkage. Smooth the patch lightly with a wood float. When the concrete begins to stiffen, finish with a wood float or steel trowel. Let the patch cure for 6 days and keep traffic away from it during that time.

Cracks must be similarly cleaned out, undercut, dampened, and filled as for a surface repair. If a large section of a walk or drive has been cracked or damaged, it must be removed and replaced with new concrete. If a crack is too narrow to take gravel, you can use mortar made of 1 part Portland cement and 3 parts sand.

Undercut the edges of a damaged surface to lock in the patch. Patching mix will not adhere to edges such as those shown below.

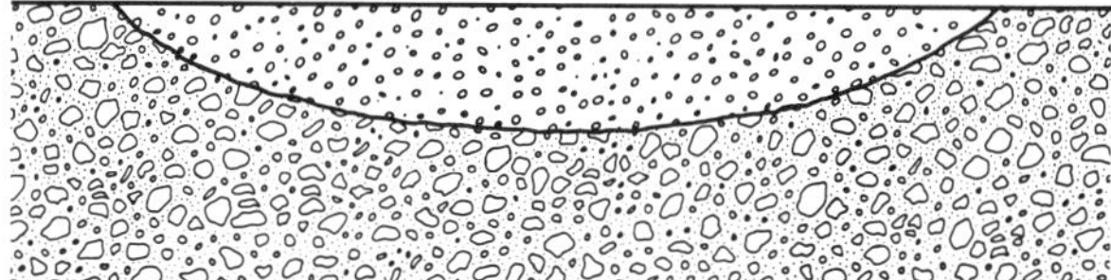

Uneven flagstones

Use a crowbar or sturdy spade to pry up one end of the slab. To avoid having to lift a heavy slab, slip a broomstick or length of pipe under the raised end and roll the slab clear. If the slab was laid on sand, level the surface and add sand as needed; if it was laid on dabs of mortar, replace with fresh mortar. Always tamp the foundation and fill low spots with sand or gravel. Remove the roots or other obstructions that caused the flags to tilt; fill the area they occupied with gravel and tamp solidly.

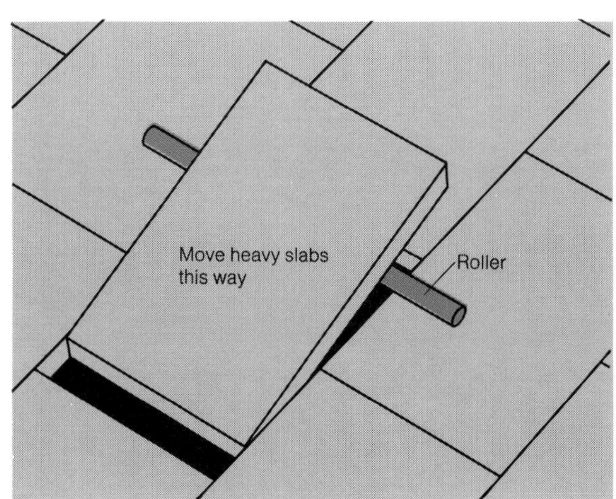

Cracked walls

Use a cold chisel to remove all loose material to a depth of 1 inch, undercut the area just beneath the surface, brush out all dust, and thoroughly dampen the area to be patched. Make a thick paste of 1 part masonry cement and 3 parts sand and fill the crack completely with it. Smooth the surface and cure for 6 days. Repair cracks in joints by removing mortar ½ inch deep and repointing (p.457). If cracks are severe or continue to enlarge despite repair efforts, seek professional advice.

Cracked floors

Prepare the patch area as you would for a wall crack. Use mortar made of 1 part Portland cement and 3 parts sand. When the crack is filled, the surface should be slightly higher than the surrounding floor. After it has set for 48 hours, grind the patch area flush with the floor, using an abrasive stone or a sheet of coarse emery paper over a block of wood.

Dusting

Dusting appears as fine powder on concrete slabs. To correct it, apply a commercial concrete sealer or scrub on two or three coats of a solution of 1 part sodium silicate and 3 parts water. Apply either remedy to a clean, dry slab. Paint adheres well to concrete treated with sodium silicate.

Damaged steps

To repair a crumbling stair edge, chisel out a V-shaped section until you reach solid concrete. Then brush away loose material and dampen the exposed area. If the tread nosing was flush with the riser, place a form board against the riser as shown. If the tread nosing extended beyond the riser, make a form and reinforce the patch with coat-hanger wire. Paint the V-shaped area with cement paste and fill with a mortar made of 1 part Portland cement and 3 parts sand. Finish and cure for 6 days.

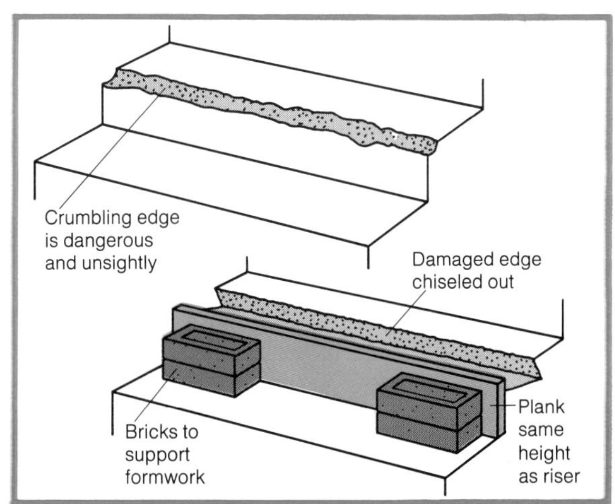

Stucco

Stucco mixes: To fill cracks or to patch a larger area, use a dry-mix mortar to which you only add water; or make a mix of 1 part masonry cement and 3 parts sand. Stucco should be pliable but firm enough to stand in a pile. You can make colored stucco by adding mineral pigments to the mortar for the final coat and mixing sufficiently to produce a uniform color. Use white cement if it is available. The pigment added should never total more than 5 percent of the weight of the masonry cement.Pigments are added to stucco ir pastel shades, such as pink, yellow, and green.
Mending cracks: Use a knife or spatula to open the crack to sound stucco; then use a hammer and cold chisel to make the edges of the crack wider on the inside than they are at the surface, forming a key to "lock in" the new stucco. Brush away loose material. Dampen the crack and use a putty knife or trowel to fill it, packing the stucco in tightly. If a crack extends through the stucco to the base, overfill the crack slightly. Let the stucco dry for about 15 minutes, then work it down with a trowel to the approximate level of its surroundings. Moist-cure a deep crack by dampening it with fine spray from a garden hose once in the morning and once at night for three days.

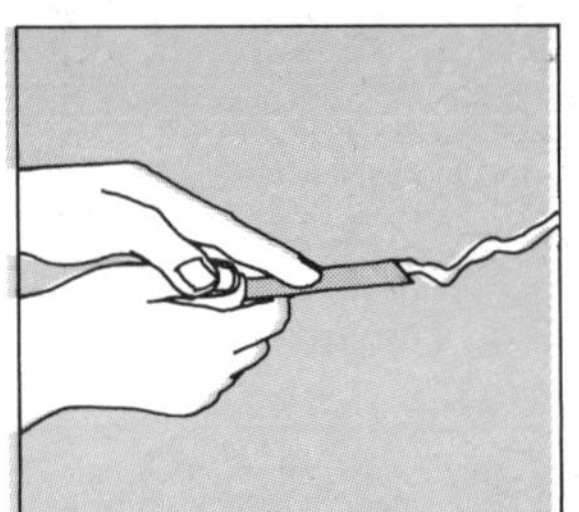

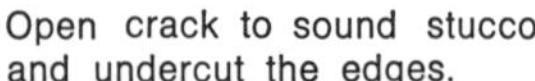

Open crack to sound stucco and undercut the edges.

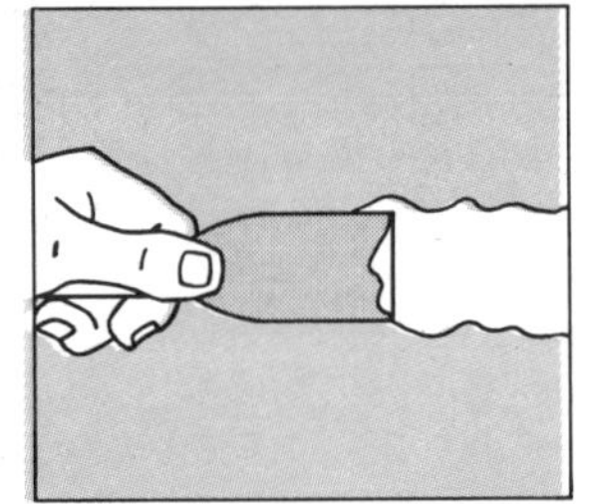

Fill crack with stucco, packing it in tightly.

Patching stucco: If a large section of a stucco wall is damaged, remove the stucco down to the bare wall surface. Clean a concrete or clay masonry surface thoroughly before stuccoing. With clay tile or brick surfaces, rake out about ¼ inch of mortar from the joints to help key the first coat, wire-brush the surface, and then wash it thoroughly. A smooth concrete wall should be wire-brushed or chipped to roughen it. Wear safety goggles to protect your eyes during all these operations.

In open-frame wood construction, stretch wires across the face of the studs horizontally about 6 inches apart. Then nail waterproof building paper to the studs over the wires; use galvanized nails. Overlap the paper by at least 3 inches. Place wire mesh stucco netting over the building paper; nail it to studs with nails that will keep a ¼ inch space between the reinforcement and its support. Use galvanized or rust-resistant nails or staples. Do not use aluminum nails; they react chemically with cement.

If the wood frame is sheathed, cover the sheathing with waterproof building paper and apply the metal reinforcement, keeping it furred out ¼-inch from the building paper.

Never apply stucco to a surface that contains frost or at a time when the temperature is likely to fall below freezing.

Stucco is usually applied in three coats. If the base is masonry or concrete, two coats may be sufficient, especially in hot, dry climates; in these cases, the base coat is approximately ⅜ inch thick and the finish coat about ¼ inch.

The first, or scratch, coat should be about ½ inch thick and should be pushed through the mesh to ensure that the metal reinforcement is completely embedded in stucco. Dampen a masonry or concrete wall with the fine spray from a garden hose before applying the scratch coat.

Place a liberal amount of stucco on a hawk (p.448) and tilt the hawk's outer edge downward. Use a steel trowel (p.467) to scrape stucco off hawk onto wall; trowel will be almost upside-down as mix is scraped off. Use a 2 x 4 as a strikeoff board (p.467).

As soon as the first coat is firm but not hard, scratch it to form horizontal ridges; these provide a key for the second coat. Drive a row of nails through a board to make a scratcher, or use a piece of the reinforcing mesh.

The second, or brown, coat is applied as soon as the first coat has set enough to carry the weight of both coats. This usually takes about four or five hours. In hot, dry, or windy weather it will be sooner; in cool weather, later. But with open-frame wood construction, the scratch coat must set at least 48 hours before the brown coat is applied.

Keep the scratch coat moist with occasional fine sprays of water until you are ready to apply the brown coat. Dampen the scratch coat just before you start to apply the brown coat.

Make the brown coat about ⅜ inch thick. Use a straightedge to smooth it. Float the brown coat (p. 471) to provide a good bond for the finish coat. Moist-cure the brown coat for at least 48 hours, then let it dry for at least 5 days, preferably longer, before applying the finish coat. Make the finish coat at least ⅛ inch thick. Do not begin moist-curing the finish coat until the day after application. Then fog-spray it very lightly with a garden hose; do not saturate it. Continue the moist-curing for a full day.

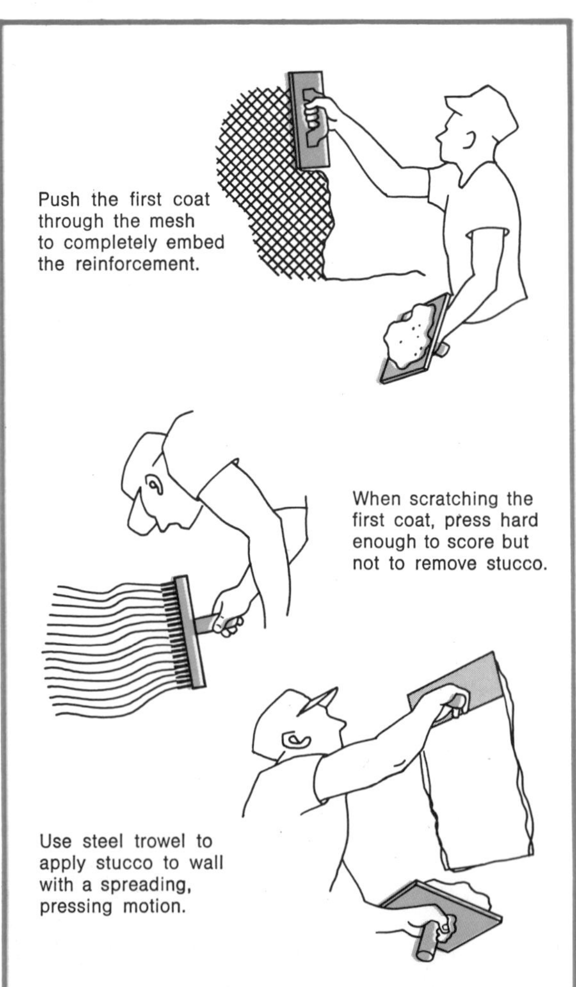

Push the first coat through the mesh to completely embed the reinforcement.

When scratching the first coat, press hard enough to score but not to remove stucco.

Use steel trowel to apply stucco to wall with a spreading, pressing motion.

What you can buy

A wide variety of ready-made precast concrete units is available from concrete products manufacturers. They are made to standards that are difficult or impossible to match using do-it-yourself methods.

Precast paving slabs for patios and walks, for example, save the amateur a great deal of work and are less liable to chip and crack than slabs made at home. Other precast units include septic tanks, lintels, sills, splash blocks, benches, bird baths, steps, and roof tiles.

The most widely used of the precast concrete units, however, are blocks. Hollow-core concrete blocks of 6-, 8-, 10-, and 12-inch thicknesses are in standard use for load-bearing walls. In addition, special-purpose blocks are made in various sizes, shapes, and colors. Split block has a rough face that resembles stone. Slump block looks much like adobe. Screen, or grille, blocks are among the most popular precast concrete units. They provide privacy and still admit sunshine and air. Screen blocks are widely used for garden walls and indoors as room dividers. In warmer climates screen blocks serve as windows in garages and other outbuildings. The most common size for screen blocks is 4 x 12 x 12 inches.

HOW MANY BLOCKS? HOW MUCH MORTAR?

Blocks: To estimate the number of blocks (8 x 8 x 16) needed for a wall, use this formula:
Height of wall in ft. x 1½ = number of courses (A). Length of wall in ft. x ¾ = number of blocks in each course (B). Then A x B = total number of blocks.
Mortar: Buy 1 70-lb. bag of masonry cement and 3 cu. ft. of sand for each 100 blocks.

Screen blocks of precast concrete can make decorative privacy screens when laid to form a wall. The blocks should be based on a poured concrete footing. Mortar joints are the same as for regular building blocks.

Types of building blocks

Concrete blocks are available in widths of 2, 3, 4, 6, 8, 10, and 12 inches and in heights of 4 and 8 inches; they are all 16 inches long. Blocks are made with either heavyweight or lightweight aggregates and may be solid or hollow.

The most commonly used block is the lightweight hollow-core **stretcher** block. It is 8 x 8 x 16 inches, weighs about 30 pounds, has a half-core at each end and two or three internal cores. A matching **corner** block is the same except one end is smooth; the manufacturer usually includes a proportionate number of corner blocks with an order of regular blocks.

Partition blocks are smooth on both ends and are half as thick as stretcher blocks. They are used to form half a wall to permit installation of heating or air-conditioning ducts, to form a dado in a wall to lock in another internal wall at right angles, and to form non-load-bearing partition walls.

Solid-top blocks (their top 4 inches are solid concrete) are used to support floors and joists.

Jamb, or wood joint, blocks are used at the sides of door and window openings to permit installation of wood frame members.

Bullnose blocks provide rounded corners; a double bullnose has two rounded corners.

Half units, with both ends smooth, are made for openings and ends of walls.

The most common special size is the **half-height,** made for almost all units and needed where a wall's height is not a multiple of 8 inches.

When planning a block structure, check a manufacturer's catalog for other available types.

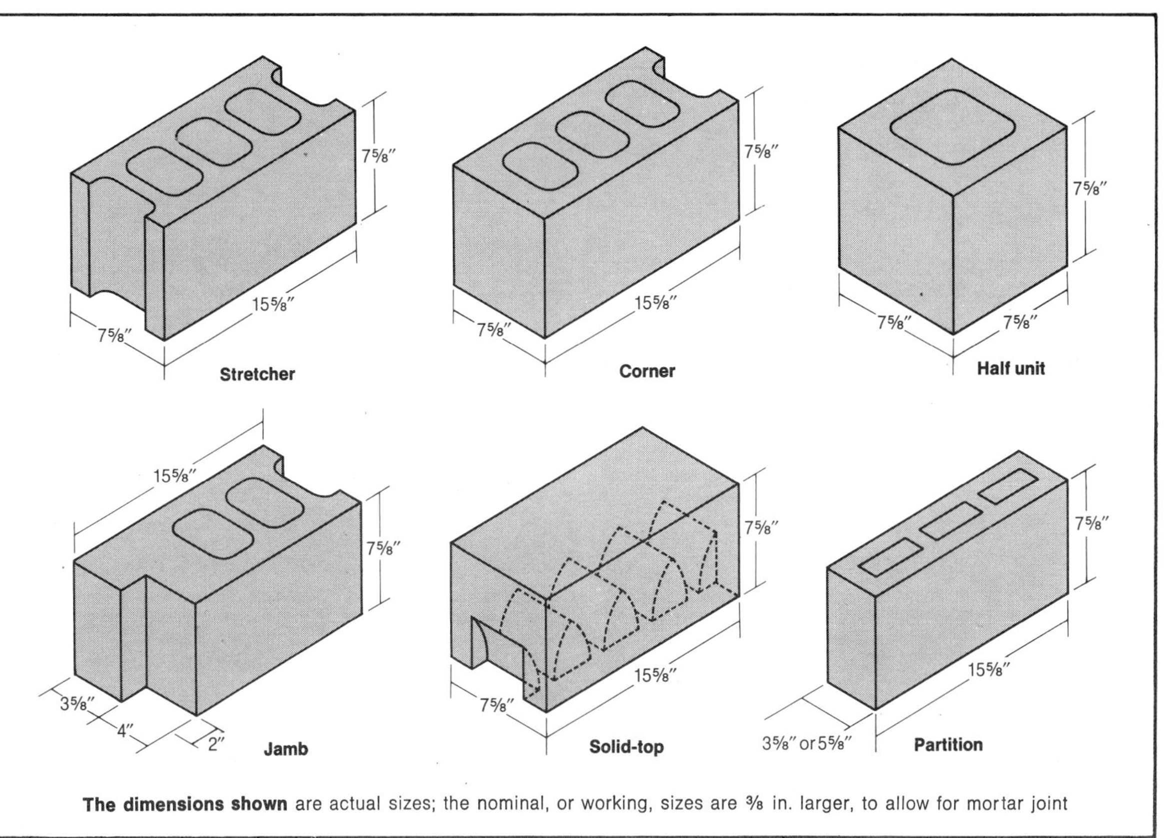

The dimensions shown are actual sizes; the nominal, or working, sizes are ⅜ in. larger, to allow for mortar joint

Building with blocks

Planning

Design your project so that all dimensions will be multiples of nominal full-size and half-size blocks—this reduces the necessity for block cutting. Choose window and door frames in sizes that will take advantage of the modular sizes of concrete blocks. With the standard 8 x 8 x 16 block, both horizontal and vertical dimensions should be in multiples of 8 inches. Be sure your design and construction conform to local building codes.

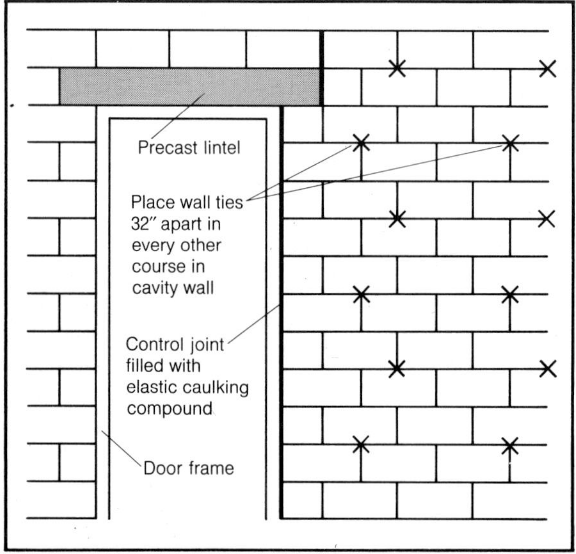

Maximum dimensions for concrete block walls

	Thickness of block (inches)	Maximum spacing (feet) of horizontal and vertical supports
Load-bearing walls		
Solid block	8 10 12	13 16 20
Hollow block or cavity wall (cavity wall thickness is sum of two tiers)	8 10 12	12 15 18
Non-load-bearing walls		
Solid or hollow block	8 10 12	24 30 36

Walls must be reinforced horizontally by pilasters or intersecting walls, vertically by floors. Rules here are general; local codes govern.

Block walls

Concrete blocks are laid in much the same way as bricks (p.454), with three important differences:

1. Concrete blocks must be dry when they are laid. Store them on planks so they won't be in contact with the ground; protect them from the rain. If you have to stop work before finishing a wall, cover its top to keep the rain off.

2. Mortar joints between blocks are ⅜ inch.

3. Unlike brick walls, long concrete block walls are not bonded continuously; they must have control joints at intervals of about 20 feet to prevent cracking. Control joints are also required at openings for doors and windows, at junctions of two walls, and at junctions of walls and columns. These joints run the full height of the wall and must have lateral support (p. 483). After mortar stiffens, rake out the joint to a depth of ¾ inch. This joint is later filled with an elastic caulking compound; prime the joint as the caulking manufacturer recommends.

Set out the first course, or horizontal layer, of blocks without mortar all around the footing; make any adjustments necessary to obtain proper spacing between the blocks and to minimize cutting. Use a ⅜-inch-thick strip of wood between blocks to ensure that they are correctly spaced. Mark with chalk the location of each joint on the footing.

Make your mortar of 1 part masonry cement and 3 parts sand (p.447). Because blocks are heavy, the mortar should be stiffer than it would be for bricklaying. Avoid making your mortar too wet. Use only enough water to make it workable.

The first course is laid in a full bed of mortar on the footing; that is, the webs of the blocks, as well as the face shells, or outer edges, are bedded in mortar.

Lay the first corner block carefully, with the thinner part of the web down. Place about ½ inch of mortar on the footing and push the block into it firmly so that you get a ⅜-inch mortar bed. Check the block crosswise and lengthwise with a spirit level. Use your trowel handle to tap the block into position and to level it. Lay the block for the other section of the corner in the same way.

To lay the second block for each section, stand a block on end and butter the two projecting ends with mortar; then put the block firmly in place and level it. Trim off excess mortar with the edge of the trowel. Lay the corner block for the second course; then set up the opposite corner in the same way. Fill in the first course, working from the corners toward the center.

Use line blocks or pins (p.450) to stretch a line between corners; if the distance is so great that the line sags, position a block at an intermediate point to support it.

As the work progresses and the mortar begins to stiffen, compress it with a jointer. A ⅝-inch metal rod or pipe will serve as a jointer for concave joints; a ½-inch square bar can be used to make V joints. Bend the jointing tool at the leading end to avoid gouging the mortar.

Where bearing walls intersect, you will need a control joint. You must also tie the walls together with a ¼-x-1¼-x-28-inch metal tie bar with a 2-inch right-angle bend at each end. Embed the ends of the bar in cores filled with mortar or concrete supported by metal lath. Space tie bars not more than 4 feet apart vertically.

Courses that support floor beams or slabs must be solid masonry. Use solid-top blocks or fill hollow-core blocks with concrete or mortar; embed metal lath in the bed joint of the course below to support the concrete or mortar filling the cores. Check your local building code to see if mortar may be used for filling cores. Garden walls need to be capped this way to keep out water.

For a wall that will support a frame roof, embed ½-inch anchor bolts 18 inches long in concrete or mortar in the cores of the top two courses; space bolts no more than 4 feet apart. Metal lath two courses down supports the bolts.

Cavity walls (p.453) require wall ties of 4-x-6-inch noncorroding metal; place them 32 inches apart in every other course.

The insulating properties of concrete block walls can be increased by filling the cores with a granular insulation such as vermiculite.

To make concrete block walls weathertight, apply either two coats of Portland cement base paint or a ½-inch coat of the mortar that was used for laying the blocks.

For garden walls 4 to 6 feet high, use ½-inch-diameter reinforcing bars every 4 feet of the wall length. Bars must be long enough to extend 2 feet above ground level and halfway down the thickness of the footing. Embed the bars in the footing and fill the cores with concrete around the bars.

Block walls

Stand blocks on end and butter the two projecting ends with mortar. Set a block firmly into place and level it.

Above the first course, apply mortar only to face shells, or outer edges. Some codes require full mortar bedding; check yours.

To lay last block in row, butter all ends of block and the opening. Place block carefully. Start over if you go wrong.

Tie nonbearing walls to other walls with metal lath or ¼-in. galvanized hardware cloth in every other course.

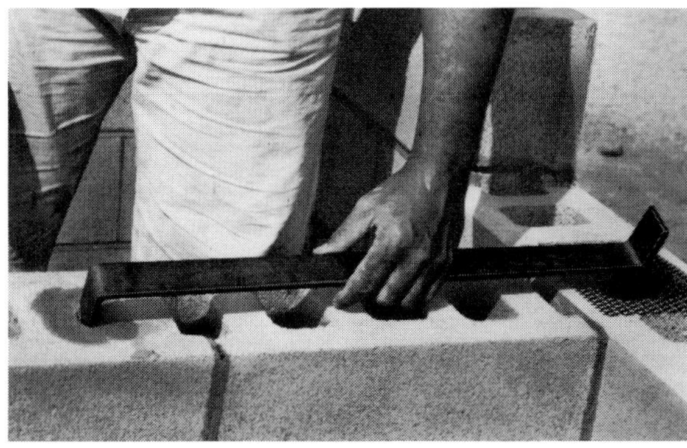

Tie bearing walls together with a ¼-x-1¼-x-28-in. metal tie bar with 2-in. right-angle bend at each end.

Use ½-in. anchor bolts 18 in. long to fasten wood plates to wall. Space bolts not over 4 ft. apart in filled cores.

A solid masonry course is required to support floor beams. Use solid-top block or fill cores. Cap garden walls also.

Fill cores of beam-supporting courses with concrete (1:3:4) supported by metal lath in course below. Check your code.

To give lateral support to a control joint, line one side of joint with building paper and fill the core with mortar.

Building with blocks

Putting up a screen wall

1. Dig a trench 12 in. wide and below frost line; in no-frost areas footing goes at least 18 in. below grade. Put ¾-in. layer of gravel on bottom. In loose soil use forms.

2. Fill trench with 1:3:4 concrete mix. Run a spade down the edges and tamp the surface with a 4 x 4 to compact concrete and eliminate air pockets. Be sure surface is level.

3. Place mortar, made of 1 part masonry cement and 3 parts sand, for the first block. The mortar bed should be ⅜ in. thick and wider than the thickness of the block.

4. Place first end block on mortar bed. Line it up with the foundation; check its top surface in both directions with spirit level. Tap block into position with trowel handle.

5. Mortar an edge of the second block; lay it in mortar bed and push it against the first block. Lay a third block on top of the first one, checking level and alignment.

6. Lay the rest of the first course dry to position each block; allow ⅜ in. for mortar joints. Build up the far end as you did the first. Stretch a line between ends.

7. With both ends in place, fill in the first course; build other courses the same way. If coping pieces are to be used, set them in a mortar bed on the top course.

8. To finish the joints, use a piece of hardwood with one end cut to a 45° angle. Run it along the vertical joints first, then the horizontal, to make a recessed joint.

section 16:

Guide to better planning

Planning is the first step in any job. If you are like most homeowners, you are perhaps unconciously planning home improvements regularly. For example, if you think that the kitchen needs more counter space, you have begun planning a kitchen improvement. If you are dissatisfied with a room arrangement, available closet space, the number of bathrooms in your home, you have started a major improvement plan. The fact is, once you establish in your mind that you are unhappy with some aspect of your home, you are on the way to planning improvements. The purpose of this section is to help you turn thoughts into reality. The next 19 pages offer suggestions and advice as to what elements should be considered when you want to solve problems related to making your home more convenient. You will learn how to deal with contractors and suppliers and how to assure yourself of satisfactory results, how to arrange financing, and how much you can do yourself.

contents

How to make plans and estimate costs

What does your home really need?

If you are like most homeowners, you probably have many improvements in mind that you would like to make—if you only knew how and where to start, and how much they would cost.

Perhaps you wish you could get rid of the morning traffic jam by adding another bathroom or simply another lavatory in the present bathroom. Maybe you would like to modernize the kitchen with new cabinets and appliances or update the house wiring for more voltage to accommodate additional appliances, such as an air conditioner, some workshop tools, or other electrical equipment. Whatever you have in mind, major or minor, your first move—and perhaps the hardest—is deciding to begin and finding out how.

A good way to start is to get to know your house as you have never known it before. With a notebook in hand, go over the house room by room. As you move through the house, act like a prospective buyer sizing it up. Jot down everything that must be done to put the house in excellent repair. Also, itemize all those things that you feel are wrong. For instance, see if your home suffers from any of these common problems:

1. An inconvenient traffic pattern. Does everyone seem to walk through your kitchen on his way in and out of the house? Do you have to walk through a bedroom to get to the extra bathroom?

2. Unused and wasted space. Is there some way to make new rooms in the attic? Could more useful space be created by conversion of the basement or closing in a porch or perhaps even turning a garage into a family room or guest house?

3. Minor annoyances. Do doors open the wrong way? Are there electrical outlets where you need them? Is there insufficient storage space? Are there closets with too few shelves? Do you have difficulty heating some rooms in winter?

4. Bland decoration. Does every room live up to its full appearance potential? Which rooms need painting, papering, or perhaps some kind of new floor covering? Would more lighting improve some rooms?

5. In need of repairs. Do all doors close properly? Are all floors and stairs free of squeaks and warping? Do plumbing fixtures need replacement? Are walls and ceilings cracked?

By the time your house tour is complete, you will have the beginning of a master improvement plan in your notebook. Very likely it will be too extensive—and expensive—to accomplish all at once; but with all your desires spelled out, you should be able to decide what projects take priority over others.

The first steps in any project are to establish in your own mind exactly what you expect the finished job to achieve and how you want it to look. Knowing these objectives will help you to determine what kind of work is involved and the types of materials that are needed. Armed with this information, you can then intelligently approach a contractor to discuss the project, or start initial planning to do the job yourself.

Photo credit: American Brick & Stone Co.

Careful planning and materials selection turned a dull room into this interesting family area. A variety of do-it-yourself materials held the cost to only a fraction of what it might appear to be. The brick wall, for example, is actually veneer brick glued to the existing wallboard underneath. The mantel is a hollow box of cedar bolted to the wall studs. The solid-looking beams are actually styrofoam imitations glued to the wall and ceiling. Paneling on the far wall is 3-inch rough-sawn cedar glued to the wallboard at ½-inch intervals.

How much will it cost?
To estimate the cost of your project, make a rough sketch of the structure and fill in the measurements. Then make a materials list, allowing about 10 percent extra for wastage on each item.

One of the most convenient shopping guides for hardware and decorator materials is a mail-order house catalog. Usually, catalog prices are slightly lower than those you would pay local dealers. If you feel confident enough about planning the job, you can save money by ordering as many materials and fixtures through the catalog as possible. Basic building materials, such as lumber, plywood, and wallboard, are generally more easily obtained from a local building supplier.

There is no simple formula for calculating labor expenses on a project. In most instances they will vary from 60 to 75 percent of the total materials cost. That is, if the materials cost for a project amounts to $2,000, a rough labor estimate would be $1,200, bringing the total project cost to $3,200. This is not a firm rule however; a reputable local contractor will give you a more precise estimate based on your materials list.

Understanding materials

Many products on the home improvement market are specifically designed for installation by the homeowner. These products help to achieve desired effects quickly and inexpensively. Prefinished wall panels, for example, are far easier and cheaper to install than a wall of individual planks that have to be hand finished. Veneered surfaces of brick or stone, imitation wood beams of plastic, embossed wall coverings—all offer short cuts and savings that could make the difference between doing a job and not being able to afford it. Familiarize yourself with home improvement materials so that when planning your project, you will have the knowledge to deal intelligently with suppliers or contractors.

Among the best sources of information on materials are the various shelter magazines. By writing to specific advertisers, you can obtain hundreds of brochures and pamphlets that will help you evaluate the newest building products.

If you are thinking about improving your home substantially, it is a good idea to organize a home improvement file system. One way to do it is to use a large envelope or folder for each room. When you see a magazine illustration of something you may be able to use, file it for later reference. Or you might keep separate folders for wall coverings, flooring materials, building materials, hardware, and even furnishings. Also include sales brochures and, wherever possible, prices. In this way, when planning an improvement project, you will have an up-to-date guide for fresh ideas as well as information that will help contractors understand your plans.

If you are modernizing a kitchen or bathroom, plan to visit showrooms of suppliers who sell complete cabinets, countertops, and sink units that are delivered ready for installation. Since such units are mass-produced, they are often less expensive than those installed for a custom-built job.

Custom-made built-ins are often the only answer to home improvement problems. These book shelves and cabinets accentuate the windows and make full use of the surrounding space for storage. Professional quotes for constructing these units ranged from $900 to $1,200, but they were home built for less than $200 in materials and took roughly 60 hours to complete. Redwood was used throughout. Uprights are construction-grade 2 x 8s. Shelving and cabinets are 1 x 12s. Each cabinet is a separate box attached to the uprights with screws.

How to finance home improvements

Where will you get the money?

If the improvements you plan are relatively minor, you may be able to manage them by digging into your savings or stretching the family budget. If they are major, however, you may have to arrange a loan.

It is not hard to borrow money for home improvements, provided of course that your credit is good. Most banks are willing, even eager, to advance funds for such enterprises.

There are several types of loans available, however, and you should investigate them all to determine which ones you are eligible for and which fit your needs best. Also, terms and interest rates vary from one locality to another and sometimes from bank to bank in the same community; so do some shopping around. See the table below for details about different types of loans.

Practices with regard to interest rates, however, should not vary. Since July 1, 1969, they have been regulated by law—the Truth in Lending Law, as it is called. Under this law, a borrower must be told the total interest he will be paying and exactly what annual rate that represents. This outlaws such dubious earlier practices as, for example, the add-on loan, in which the borrower ostensibly paid $6 for every $100 he borrowed. The amount was added to the principal, and the $106 was paid off in 12 monthly installments. The borrower's payments steadily reduced the principal; yet he continued to pay interest on the original amount—not at the 6 percent claimed but at about 11.1 percent. Another dodge was the discount loan, in which the $6—again called 6 percent—was deducted at the outset from each $100. The borrower thus paid $6, not on $100, but on

TYPE OF LOAN	AMOUNT	SECURITY	INTEREST	TERM	WHERE OBTAINABLE
FHA (Federal Housing Administration) **TITLE I LOAN** One of the lowest cost loans available, and a popular one. Application must be made before work project is completed. Loan can be used only for improvement and livability of the property—not for nonessentials such as a swimming pool, tennis court, etc. Lender is insured by FHA against loss, but FHA does not guarantee workmanship or materials.	Up to $5,000	No security required	9.4 percent per year simple interest	Up to 5 years	Apply directly to banks, savings and loan associations, and mutual savings institutions
FHA 203 (K) LOAN Loan is used for extensive structural improvements on a house at least 10 years old. Loans may be preceded by a first mortgage. If improvement work has already begun, FHA will not insure a loan. Though the cost is extremely low, the loan is not popular because of restrictions and paperwork involved.	Up to $10,000	Second mortgage	7.5 percent per year	Five to 20 years	FHA-approved bank or savings and loan association
BANK HOME IMPROVEMENT LOAN Readily available type of loan, advanced by many banks and savings and loan associations. Extremely flexible, with no restrictions on use of borrowed funds such as in FHA Title I loan. Money may be used for any kind of improvement, including such luxuries or nonessentials as construction of a greenhouse, patio, or swimming pool, or landscaping.	Up to $5,000, sometimes higher	If credit has not been established satisfactorily, collateral may be required	From 10 to 14 percent straight interest. Lower rate if borrower is an A-1 credit risk	Up to 7 years	Loan departments of most banks, savings and loan associations, and mutual savings institutions
CONTRACTOR'S LOAN Often arranged by a home improvement contractor to take care of homeowner's financial involvement. Usually costlier than loan taken out by property owner himself.	The estimated cost of the job	Usually none from the homeowner	Often higher than other forms of similar loans	One to 5 years	Contractor handles loan with lending institution
OPEN-END MORTGAGE LOAN Highly recommended way to finance home improvement project if original mortgage has an open-end clause permitting the homeowner to borrow as much money as he has paid out to date. Such a provision is not carried by all mortgages.	Equal to payment made on mortgage to date	Original mortgage acts as security	Often at same rate as original mortgage. Some lenders insist on increase to current interest rates	Usually the term of the mortgage is extended, with the same payments.	The bank or other financial institution that handled the original mortgage
SECURED LOAN Favored by homeowners who hold stocks, bonds, or other securities sufficient to cover the cost of the home improvement. Bank holds enough securities to insure repayment of loan; borrower pays only interest.	From 50 to 75 percent of market value of securities	Good-quality securities or cash deposit in a savings account	0.5 to 1 percent over the current interest rate	Arrangement with bank	Usually at the bank where homeowner has an account

Note: This chart is only a general guide to sources of home improvement loans. Interest rates, amount and type of security, and terms vary from community to community and from one financial institution to another. These factors also vary from month to month and from year to year. Be sure to check with local sources of home improvement loans for details prevailing at the time you wish to obtain the loan.

the $94 he actually got—a rate of more than 13 percent. Further, many loan companies "loaded" contracts with unexpected service charges, insurance premiums, and processing and investigation fees. The 1969 law eliminates such surprises by stipulating that a lender clearly specify "all borrowing costs" on loans.

It should be understood, however, that the law does not fix or regulate interest rates; so you should look around for the best "buy" in money just as you would with any major purchase.

Do you need life insurance on a loan?

With many types of loans you automatically acquire life insurance—for which you may or may not pay directly, depending on the source of your loan. The life insurance buys protection for the lender—not for your family—against your death and the possibility that your estate may not be able to pay off the debt. It may sometimes appear that you are getting a particularly good deal—a competitive rate of interest plus insurance. A closer look at the terms of the contract, however, may prove otherwise. You and your family would derive no personal benefit from the insurance—except for the coverage of the debt in case of death; when you take the full cost into consideration, you may find that the overall contract is no bargain.

You may be offered "free insurance" as part of the agreement. It may be called "free," but the cost is probably built into the interest charge you pay. Sometimes, in addition, you will be offered the benefits of accident and health insurance for "pennies a day." In either case, the insurance may turn out to be overpriced in comparison to life and medical insurance that is not part of a loan package. Before signing up for loan insurance, check the coverage you already have in case of accident or disability and try to estimate what the general state of your finances would be in such an eventuality.

Spend your money wisely

All the thought you've put into getting money at the best rates from the most appropriate source can be wasted if you don't spend it with equal care. Beyond finding a reliable contractor and suppliers, there are more and less advantageous payment methods. Ask your dealers about the possibility of payments being extended—over a 30-, 60-, or 90-day period—without a carrying charge. Also request that suppliers bill you; some expenses may be deductible from income taxes, and detailed bills are the best possible verification. Get written verification, too, from any outside help you hire. If billing is too formal for, say, a part-time worker, date and fill out your own receipt and ask the man to sign it.

Beware of home improvement frauds

The home improvement business has become a source of easy picking for fast-talking operators who dupe American homeowners out of an estimated billion dollars a year. A little knowledge of how they operate is your best defense against such swindlers. These seem to be the most flagrant deceptions:

1. The "model home." Here the victim is led to believe that if he allows improvements to be made on his property, he will receive commissions from similar sales made to persons impressed by the work done at his home, and thus recoup his investment.

A salesman convinced one suburban housewife, whose husband was unemployed, that an aluminum re-siding job could be done without cost. All she had to do was sign a contract for a $1,600 job; they would receive a $100 check for every sale made to a neighbor impressed with the work. To date there have been no $100 checks, the husband is still out of work, and the finance company is pressing for payment.

2. "Bait and switch" advertising. A typical "bait" ad featured an "aluminum patio" for $79.50 and showed a happy couple relaxing on a flagstone terrace under a gleaming metal awning.

Most people who responded to the ad were switched to awnings costing from $300 to $1,900. Of 67 cases investigated, only one person held out for the $79.50 "patio" as advertised; he got a plain sheet of metal suspended on 2 x 4s.

3. The "easy contest." This attracts many gullible people. A couple is notified that the wife's entry in a "Match the Stars" contest has won first prize. Because she could tell two film stars apart, they get free siding for their home. The sponsoring "contractor" said he would not only make a gift of the siding but would install it at a giveaway price of $300. When the winner's husband said he would install it himself, the entry was ruled ineligible.

4. The "left over from another job" scheme. This is the bait of itinerant repairmen who claim they can give you a good price "because we have material left over from another job." "Sealing" driveways is a favorite use of "leftovers." The operators spray on a thin coat of asphalt, collect up to $125 for 10 minutes' work, and the coating weathers away in a few weeks.

Says the president of a legitimate company specializing in such work: "It should take two men several hours to seal the average driveway, using a coal-tar pitch emulsion with silica sand added. The surface should last from 5 to 10 years."

5. Fake chimney, roof, and furnace "inspectors." These operators prey largely on widows and elderly couples, using fear as their chief weapon. A big-city homeowner tells of his experience: "The chimney was working fine, but these 'free inspectors' insisted on checking it for me; so I finally agreed. They smashed at it with crowbars, and bricks came tumbling down, sealing the chimney. When I asked the crew boss what he was doing, he handed me a contract for $230, and said I would have to sign or they wouldn't fix the chimney. It was winter, and I had to have heat; so I signed."

6. The signed completion certificate. This enables the crooked contractor to collect his money from the bank or loan agency financing the work and leave the homeowner with uncompleted repairs or a half-finished job. One contractor pleaded: "Just sign so I can pay the boys before Christmas." The "boys" never returned to finish the work.

7. Debt consolidation. Under this agreement, a homeowner who owes, say, $7,000 and wants $5,000 worth of work done on his house may sign a new mortgage to pay the builder $12,000. The builder supposedly pays off the $7,000. The catch is that the builder doesn't pay off. Instead, he sells the mortgage to a finance company and skips town with a pocketful of cash. The homeowner ends up with no repairs and a higher mortgage.

To protect yourself against these and similar practices, check out all firms and any questionable or unusual offers with the Better Business Bureau, Chamber of Commerce, or Board of Trade.

As the president of the Association of Better Business Bureaus has eloquently put it: "If an offer or claim sounds too good to be true, it usually is."

Should you be your own contractor?

How to determine when to get help

If you are already a handyman or have ambitions to become one, you may elect to do most, perhaps all, of the work yourself on your home improvement project. However, if it is a large-scale or somewhat involved project—a major plumbing or electrical installation, for example—some outside help may be needed or even required by local building codes. In determining whether or not you will need or want at least some professional assistance, these are some of the deciding factors:

1. When your improvement plans include plumbing, heating, air conditioning, or electrical work, check relevant local ordinances before going ahead. They may require that certain portions of the work be done by licensed professionals.
2. Some jobs require special tools. Though these usually can be rented at a reasonable rate, such specialized tools are part of the professional's equipment. If you're short of time, this could be a convenience.
3. Another suggestion in the interests of time: It can take much study, and sometimes a bit of legwork, to develop the knowledge of materials—lumber, roofing, tiling, plumbing and heating components—that a professional already has. If your project is a rush job, you may have to call in an expert, at least the first time. If you have sufficient "lead time," spend it reading the appropriate sections in this manual; they will teach you what you need to know.
4. Once the project is under way, you may find it is taking longer than you had planned because you can't give it the time you had hoped. Such delays, on a big project, can be a serious inconvenience to you and your family. When this happens, professional help may be the only sensible solution.

It should be clear, from the tone of the above suggestions, that the question of professional assistance is rarely either/or—either you do the work yourself or you hire someone to do it. Oftener it is a matter of deciding at what points professional assistance will be most practical and least costly to you.

Money-saving jobs you can do

You can always do a lot of the work yourself, no matter how much professional help is required. You can usually handle all of the preliminary preparation. For instance, if a job calls for pulling down partitions or ripping up worn floor coverings, you can be your own wrecking crew—at a considerable saving in labor costs. You can help dig trenches for water pipes, level the foundation for a new carport, prepare holes for casings. You can scrape off old paint and put on new when the time comes. You can put up wallpaper, replace broken window panes, staple insulation in place. You can lay floor tiles, build shelving, put on shingles, install wall paneling. If you examine beforehand what particular projects actually entail—this manual will be a great help in doing that—you will find you can do more than you would have believed, regardless of the kind of home improvement you are making.

Could you handle the total job?

As contractor, you would have to deal with professionals in many trades—plumbers, electricians, carpenters, masons, and so on—and synchronize all of their skills into a smooth work flow. You would also need to become knowledgeable about building codes and local ordinances. You will be better able to decide this finally when you have read the fuller discussion below of the qualifications of professional contractors. In the meantime, you should first consider an intermediate step—hiring an architect if your project requires one.

When do you need an architect?

Many homeowners think of architects only in connection with big, complicated projects, not with modest home improvement jobs. However, if you are contemplating any remodeling that calls for structural change, such as adding a new wing or revamping interior space, an architect can be a tremendous help. Their fees vary but usually they run about 10 percent to 15 percent of the project's total cost. The guidance of a competent man, brought in at the beginning, will more than repay that investment. If you are hazy about what should be done or where to begin, he will discuss the basic problems with you and make rough sketches of practical solutions.

When you have reached agreement on precisely what the work will entail, he will prepare detailed drawings and specifications. Copies of these papers will then be submitted by the architect to a number of contractors—at least three or four—as a basis for bids. When the bids are in, he will go over them carefully and advise you which to accept. It may not be the lowest, but it will be the one that in his judgment is the best.

When work is about to begin, the architect will attend to such matters as obtaining a building permit and will also make sure you do nothing contrary to local codes and ordinances. He will supervise the contractor's work as it progresses, seeing that the requisite grades of materials and workmanship go into the job and that time schedules are adhered to. He will keep close watch on the budget and inform you of any increased construction costs so that you will know how much money is being spent and for what.

The architect will make a final inspection of the completed work and sign a certificate of approval only when both you and he are completely satisfied.

It is well to remember that an architect is a highly trained specialist in the blending of esthetics and practicality in construction. He would, for instance, design a new wing to be a harmonious part of the existing structure, not a makeshift eyesore.

If your home improvement project is relatively uncomplicated and calls for no structural change, an architect probably won't be necessary. You may, however, need the help of an experienced contractor.

Selecting a contractor

If you live in or near a fairly large community, look in the classified directory under the heading "Contractors—General," and you will see scores of names and advertisements. (A general contractor is one who can take over and do your entire job; a subcontractor usually specializes in just one type of work—heating, wiring, carpentry, etc.)

Contractors are so numerous these days that the problem is not to find one but to narrow down an extremely wide choice to a suitable single one. Consult friends or neighbors who have had remodeling work done by contractors. Get their recommendations and, if possible, inspect the finished work.

Don't stop, however, with just one recommendation. Get several names. If a particular individual is suggested by more than one person, he certainly merits further investigation. Speak to your local banker and to building supply people, hardware merchants, appliance wholesalers, and the like.

Other excellent sources of information are the subcontractors in the area—electricians, plumbers, masons, carpenters—who have dealt with local contractors and should know, if anyone does, which ones do the best work.

Your next job, after you have compiled a list of recommended contractors, is eliminating names. This brings you to the all-important question: How do you recognize a good contractor?

Any contractor you seriously consider should be a reputable businessman who is known for competent work at reasonable prices. Above all, he should be reliable—the kind of man who will do the job he said he would do, with the specified materials, at the quoted price, and within the agreed-upon period of time. And since many decisions must be made during the course of the work, you must know he'll be there when you need him.

You would do well to check the following before deciding finally on a contractor:

1. How long has the contractor been in business? This will give a good indication of his reliability. The contracting trade has an extraordinarily high mortality rate. It is estimated that about 70 percent of new contractors go out of business within three years.

2. Does he have a business office and a regular staff? He need not be a big operator to do a good job; but a business office, no matter how small, and a staff of permanent employees are signs that he is not a fly-by-night.

3. Is he a member in good standing of a trade organization? Building trade associations have codes of ethics that their members must honor. Any complaints lodged against a contractor's work or conduct would be registered with the association to which that contractor belongs.

4. Does he carry adequate insurance of the necessary types? A contractor should have sufficient workmen's compensation, property damage, and personal liability coverage that you won't be sued for an injury to a workman or a visitor on the site of your home improvement project.

5. Is he familiar with State, county, and local regulations pertaining to remodeling and rebuilding? Be sure he is, or you could find yourself with a finished job that doesn't conform to local laws or rules.

6. Will he provide all the permits required by local building regulations? To the experienced contractor, this is a routine matter, but it is still a question worth raising.

After you have eliminated the contractors you feel do not measure up, you may be left with three or four who seem like good possibilities. Set up meetings (including your architect if you are using one) with each of the contractors to discuss the prospective work so that they can submit bids for the job. Be sure to give each man exactly the same requirements—what you want done, the quality of materials to be used, the time you think the job should take.

Ask for bids in writing by a date set by you. There is a point in informing each man that he is competing with others—it might cause him to trim his figures a bit. Never reveal or suggest, however, what another man has bid. This could cause another contractor to make his bid lower than his competitor's but still higher than he had first intended.

Before you make a firm commitment to any contractor, take one last look at the financial obligation you will be undertaking. The figures on the submitted bids are your only guide to the probable cost of the job. If they are higher than is really feasible, perhaps you need to cut down somewhere.

The written contract

When you have decided which contractor to hire, the next step is the written contract. It should be prepared by a lawyer and signed before witnesses by both you and the contractor. The contract should clearly state:

1. The work the contractor agrees to do. This includes dimensions, specifications, and type and quality of materials to be used.

2. The date the work is to commence and a time schedule of how the project is to proceed step by step until its termination.

3. A schedule of payments. A common arrangement is an agreed-upon payment of money when the work begins, another predetermined amount at the halfway mark, and the balance upon completion.

4. A precise statement of the appliances or fixtures to be bought, if any. This section should specify the size, model, price, and make of each unit. This protects you against, say, ending up with a type of dishwasher that you did not order but that was picked up at a bargain.

5. Cleanup and removal of debris from the premises. An agreement that your house or site will be left "broom clean" daily or at stated intervals may sound trivial, but it can be important, especially if you plan to live in the house during remodeling.

6. Release for you from all liability should the contractor go bankrupt before he has completed your work. This is a vital clause. Under the mechanic's lien law, an owner can be held accountable for any money owed by the contractor for labor or materials used on the owner's project. You can be liable even if you have lived up completely to your financial agreement with the contractor. If you wish, this clause may be handled as a separate agreement.

Finally, before you sign your name to the contract, check—or have your lawyer check—that the following items have not been overlooked:

1. Make certain that the changes you are planning will not void any of your insurance coverage. This could happen, for example, if you were to put in a swimming pool. Check beforehand with your insurance agent. If the improvement is important enough to you, you can get additional coverage.

2. See whether your mortgage papers contain a clause that states that you must have the agreement of the mortgage holder to do any remodeling or improvement of your property. This permission is usually just a formality, but it is a necessary one.

You need a building permit when—

- The improvement you contemplate will change your home's use or "occupancy" from, say, a single-family to a multi-family dwelling.
- You build a carport or garage, or convert the garage you have to another use.
- You plan to wall in, roof, or attach a patio to your existing house.
- The pool you're building is deeper than 24 inches.
- You build a retaining wall more than 4 feet high.
- You plan to install plumbing or electricity inside or outside the house.
- You build a barbecue with a chimney that is more than 6 feet high.
- You drill a well or install an underground lawn-sprinkler system.
- Your radio or TV antenna, tower, or flagpole will exceed 45 feet in height.

Note: Specifications will vary according to the code in use in your locality.

How to plan kitchen improvements / 1

Planning an efficient layout

The first step in planning an improved kitchen is to list the shortcomings of your present kitchen. A typical list would include such items as insufficient counter space, inefficient appliances, awkward layout, inadequate storage space, dreary decoration, poor lighting, deficient ventilation. These are just a few of the many complaints people have about their kitchens, but they are the primary areas of concern when you are contemplating kitchen remodeling.

Once you have your list, select the one item that is the most disturbing. Usually this will be the problem that involves the most work. For example, a kitchen with a poor traffic pattern will call for extensive alterations that will affect every other item on your list. If you can solve the major problem, the smaller ones will generally fall into place.

Shop for ideas by visiting appliance centers, kitchen equipment showrooms, and model homes, and by clipping designs that interest you from magazines. Then use the information below as a guide in planning a rough design on paper. Use this design as a basis for discussion with a contractor or as a guide for buying the materials and equipment you will need to do the job yourself.

Storage and mixing center

This center should be designed for sorting of groceries and the preparation of dishes in which ingredients are combined, such as baked foods, salads, and desserts. The refrigerator is the major appliance and is best located near the kitchen entrance to save steps when carrying in groceries. The refrigerator may be freestanding, built-in, or suspended from a wall. But even in the most modern kitchen this center should include a working counter at least 15 inches wide. This counter should be located so that access to it will not be blocked by the refrigerator door.

The storage and mixing center should include cabinets with ample space for storing mixing bowls and spoons, measuring cups, sifter, beater, grinder, rolling pin, baking pans and casseroles, and ingredients used in mixing (sugar, flour, shortening, spices).

Cleaning and preparation center

The sink is the heart of this center, and there should be a minimum of 30 inches of working counter at each side of the sink, plus sufficient storage near the sink for unrefrigerated foods, such as potatoes, that need to be washed and peeled. Small pans, coffee pot, everyday dishes, brushes, utensils, and cleaning supplies should also be stored near the sink. Garbage cans can be a problem if you do not have a garbage disposal unit. Try to place the garbage can where it is readily accessible but easy to store out of sight when not in use. Incidentally, if a dishwasher is not in the budget now, it is wise to plan for one by installing a storage cabinet adjacent to the sink; the interior width of the cabinet should be at least 24 inches. The shelves and partitions in the cabinet can be replaced later with an automatic dishwasher.

Cooking and serving center

The range and oven are the major appliances in this center. There should be storage space nearby for items used at the range: Skillets, saucepans, and lids; stirring spoons, testing implements, ladles, and spatulas; canned vegetables and foods that require boiling water for preparation (tea, coffee, raw cereals, macaroni). Serving dishes for hot food may be stored here too. This area is also the serving center and will have storage space for electrical equipment (such as toaster and waffle iron), trays, ready-to-eat foods (cookies, crackers, cake, bread). This center should be located near the dining area.

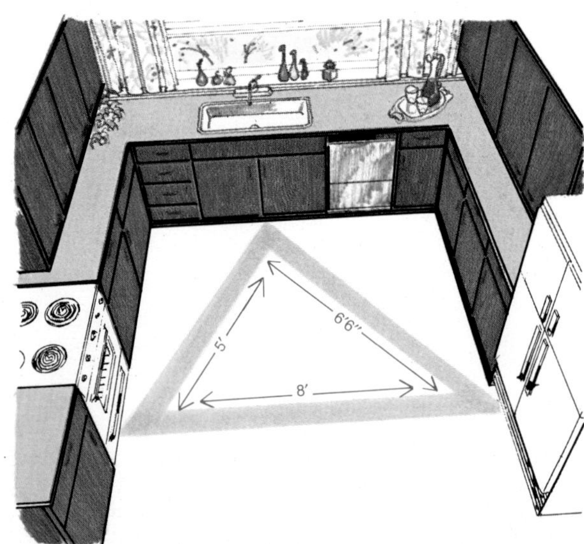

Most efficient is work triangle of no more than 22 ft.

The work triangle

The distances between the three centers usually form a "work triangle" that serves as a measure of a kitchen's efficiency. The sum of the sides of this triangle should be no more than 22 feet. The recommended limits, measured from the front of the three appliances, are: refrigerator to sink—4 to 7 feet; sink to range—4 to 6 feet; and range to refrigerator—4 to 9 feet. In planning a kitchen around the triangle, try to prevent the normal traffic lanes of the home from crossing it. If they do cross it, the work triangle's efficiency is reduced.

Height of countertops and cabinets

In most kitchens 36 inches is the standard height for the countertops. Stock base cabinets are 36 inches high, 24 to 25 inches deep, and from 12 to 48 inches wide. Wall cabinets are generally 12 to 14 inches high, 13 inches deep, and from 12 to 48 inches wide.

Ventilation

Proper ventilation is essential to a modern kitchen. Home management experts estimate that approximately 200 pounds of moisture, smoke, and greasy vapor are released during a year's cooking. These lodge in furnishings and eventually cause discolor-

6'4" Seldom-used storage
5'4" Easy-access storage
4'4" Comfortable height for use when standing
3' Frequently used storage
18" Seldom-used storage

Plan storage at these levels for greatest convenience.

ing and musty odors. They can leave your kitchen walls greasy and cause paint to peel.

The solution is to vent the vapors to the outside or to remove the moisture and grease by filtering the kitchen air. Venting can be done with a kitchen fan built into a wall near the range; filtering, by a ventilating hood directly above the range.

Exhaust fans come in a variety of shapes and sizes. All models require cutting through the kitchen wall for installation. There are two types of ventilating hoods: ducted and unducted. Ducted hoods require venting to the outside. This type of vent is best

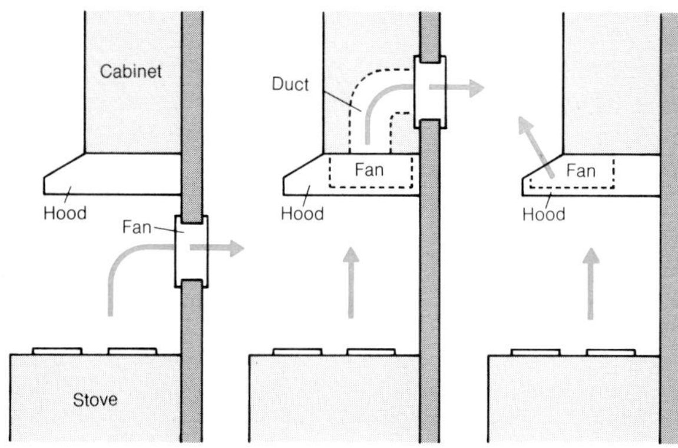

Air flow of exhaust fan, ducted and ductless hoods.

installed as part of a major kitchen remodeling wherein walls, ceilings, and cabinets are all being renewed. Ductless vents have a fan that draws cooking vapors through a charcoal filter that eliminates odors and grease, before releasing cleaned air back into the kitchen.

When installing a ducted system, ducting should be planned so that it follows a direct route to the outdoors with a minimum of angles, or "elbows." It is also important to avoid changes in the size of the duct pipe leading from fan to outside vent, since grease accumulates wherever the duct size changes.

Ductless ventilators fit in a hood over the range and can be hung on a wall or suspended below a cabinet. They are generally used where it is impossible or too expensive to have a duct to an outside wall. While nonducted ventilation does an effective job of reducing grease, odors, and smoke, it cannot remove heat and moisture from the kitchen air like a ducted system. In addition, the filters, which are made of strong aluminum mesh and fiberglass, granulated charcoal, or activated carbon, must be cleaned or replaced every few weeks. It is also a good idea to clean a ducted system at least twice a year.

In either the ducted or ductless ventilating systems the proper fan capacity, rated in cubic feet per minute (c.f.m.) of air delivery, should be a major consideration. Fan capacity must relate directly to the size of the room or area in which it is to function. Ventilating experts offer this guide for fan size in relation to square footage of floor space in a kitchen with an 8-foot ceiling: 60 sq. ft.–120 c.f.m. 110 sq. ft.–225 c.f.m.; 160 sq. ft.–325 c.f.m.; 200 sq. ft.–400 c.f.m.

Lighting

Light in the kitchen should be of sufficient intensity that you can easily read the small print on food packages. It should be evenly distributed so that you can see into cabinet corners and so that you do not have to work in your own shadow. Light should help to make the room a cheerful, pleasant place to work. In some kitchens it may be possible to satisfy all these requirements by using carefully placed ceiling fixtures that do the job with virtually no additional local lighting fixtures. In most cases, however, ceiling fixtures will have to be supplemented by specific lighting of particular work centers.

As a general rule, every 50 square feet of kitchen takes a combination of ceiling and local fixtures that will supply 150 to 175 watts of incandescent or 60 to 80 watts of fluorescent lighting. Plan on a 30-watt fluorescent fixture mounted 22 inches above the range; two 30- or 40-watt fluorescents above the sink; two 20-watt fluorescents set just under the cabinets over each 30-inch length of counter. A minimum of 150 watts incandescent is recommended for a dining area. The use of light colors for the walls and ceiling of the kitchen will further brighten the room and decrease the amount of artificial lighting required.

It is most important to plan the wiring in the kitchen so that it is adequate to handle all the appliances and lights in use at any one time. Provide wiring that permits countertop appliances, such as coffee maker, toaster, and blender, to be plugged in to an electrical circuit that is separate from the major appliance circuits (p. 256).

Some planning do's and don'ts

1. **Do** include adjacent to your range a heat-resistant work counter on which hot baking dishes, saucepans, etc., can be placed for serving. A minimum width of 9 inches is recommended.

2. **Don't** install a built-in oven too high. Place it so that the oven door opens out to about the same level as the countertops–36 inches from the floor. Or mount the oven to position the open door 2 inches below the elbow of the homemaker.

3. **Do** make your kitchen aisle wide enough to permit all appliance doors and cabinet doors and drawers to open fully without interfering with each other. Minimum recommended aisle is 42 inches; 48 inches is better.

4. **Don't** install your dishwasher next to the refrigerator if you can avoid it. Both refrigerator and dishwasher emit heat; thus they will work more efficiently and last longer if separated. If they must be placed side by side, insert a panel of insulation between them.

5. **Do** allow ample space between range and sink. This is the busiest area in the kitchen. Too little space between range and sink increases the risk of brushing against a hot pan or knocking it off the stove.

6. **Don't** place a dishwasher at right angles to the sink. In such a position the dishwasher door, when open, blocks access to the sink and makes movement awkward.

7. **Do** eliminate kitchen doors that open against the face of an appliance. Hang doors on the other side of the door jamb, hinge them to swing out rather than in, or use a sliding door.

8. **Don't** place oven and burners side by side if installing a countertop range with separate oven. Leave at least 9 inches of counter space between them to manipulate hot pots, pans, and dishes. This counter space should be covered with a heat-resistant material.

9. **Do** plan corners so that these awkward spaces are put to good use. Cabinets with revolving shelves work well in corners. Major appliances do not; their doors interfere with other doors and drawers.

10. **Don't** overlook ventilation. Try to place the range where it will be convenient to vent cooking odors and moisture to the outside. Consider installation of a through-the-wall air conditioner to ensure maximum comfort.

U-shaped kitchen

Of the four basic floor plans shown on these pages, the U-shaped kitchen has the greatest potential for giving you the best possible working arrangement. Since the U is closed on three sides, there is no through traffic from one room to another to interfere with kitchen work. This design is also a saver of wasted steps because the highly efficient triangular pattern between range, refrigerator, and sink is easiest to arrange in a U-shape. Storage space is plentiful; even the corner areas can be utilized with a revolving shelf arrangement.

One popular and attractive variation of the U-shaped kitchen is the use of one arm of the U as a pass-through serving counter into the dining room or into a family room.

The only disadvantages to the U-shape are economic. U-shapes usually require more expensive countertops and special cabinets to fit the corners. U-shaped kitchens should be 10 feet wide or wider at the base of the U. Anything narrower results in a cramped work area around the sink, decreasing the efficiency of the work triangle.

U-shaped arrangement produces an uncluttered working space.

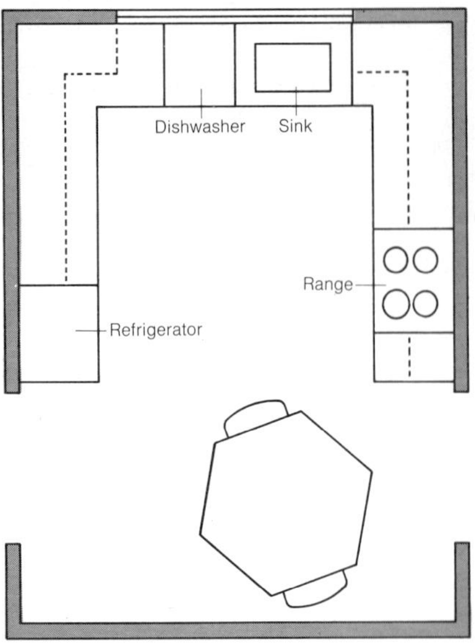

L-shaped kitchen

The L-shaped kitchen features continuous counters and appliances located on two adjoining walls. This design generally permits more space for eating in the kitchen. The corner of the room opposite the kitchen equipment is often the best place to locate your table and chairs. These may be freestanding or built in. The L-shape is also adaptable to almost any space and has a very efficient work triangle. Through traffic is kept to one side, away from the work triangle, but it may interfere with the serving path between work area and dining area.

There can be problems with this plan. In many L-shaped kitchens, for example, the wall space is broken by two doors, one at each end of the L. This is not bad planning, but traffic through these doors does interfere with movement between the kitchen counter and the dining table. Another problem is wasted storage space. Given the same square footage, the U-kitchen provides considerably more space for storage than the L. Also, the compact efficiency of the kitchen can be destroyed if the walls of an L-shaped kitchen are too long.

Open side of L-shaped kitchen provides room for dining area.

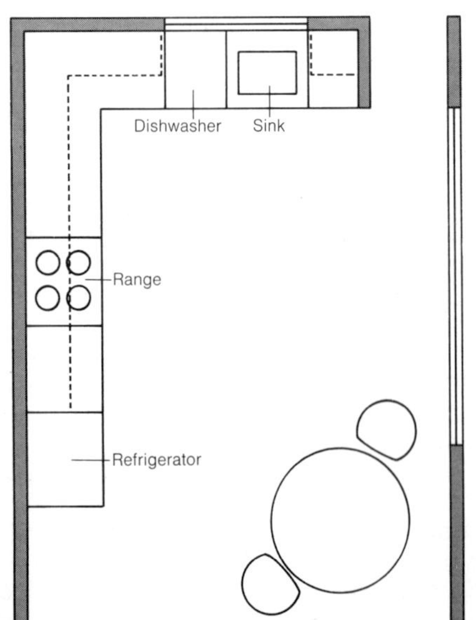

Corridor kitchen

The corridor, or galley, kitchen arranged along two walls is very efficient for apartments or long narrow rooms. It takes up very little floor space, is the best step-saver of all, generally permits extra counter space, and provides more than adequate room for storage if you use your ingenuity in planning countertops and cabinets.

The major drawback of a corridor kitchen is that it is often built along a busy thoroughfare from one section of the house to another or to outdoors, thus greatly cutting down the efficiency of the work triangle. This flaw can be overcome to some extent by closing off one end of the corridor. Traffic jams also can be eased by widening the floor space between the two walls of kitchen equipment. A width of 4 feet is good; 5 feet excellent; more than that and this design's floor-space-saving quality is lost.

If one end of the corridor kitchen is closed off, the "dead end" can be put to a variety of uses. A breakfast bar can be fitted easily into this space or, if there is plenty of room, the end can accommodate a pantry or utility closet.

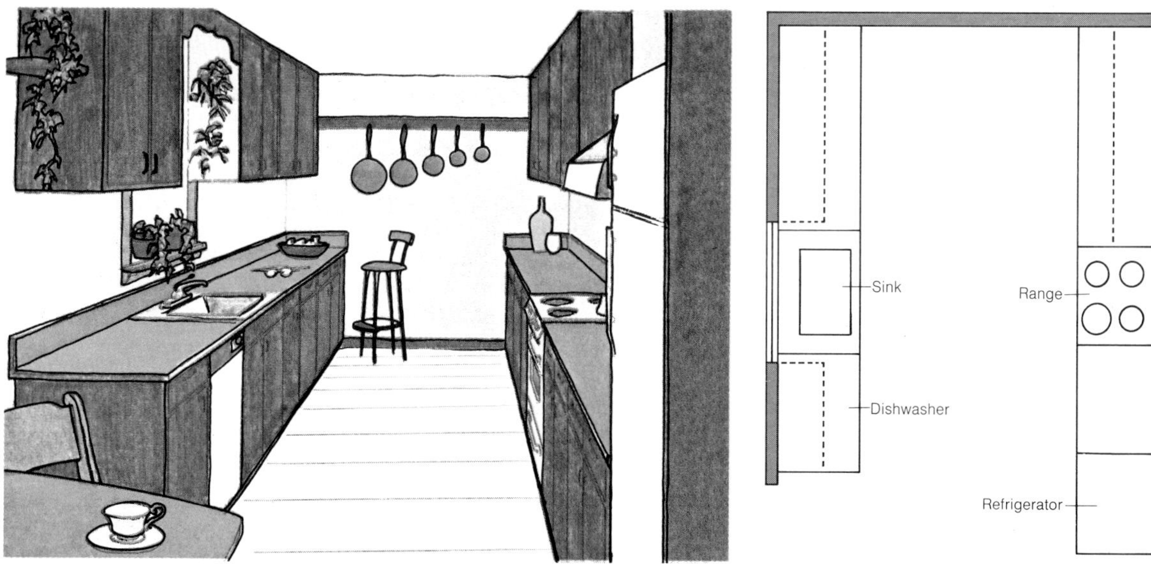

Compact corridor kitchen makes best use of limited floor space.

One-wall kitchen

The one-wall kitchen is an excellent plan for small apartments and cabins or houses in which little space is available. The work centers are located in one line and produce a compact, efficient arrangement. However, care must be taken to avoid stretching out the space between appliances, for this would destroy the efficiency of the one-wall plan. If space is extremely limited, compact appliances may serve your needs better than standard sizes.

A disadvantage of the one-wall kitchen is that counter and storage space are sacrificed in order to fit in the necessary major appliances. To solve the storage problem, a nearby closet can be converted to a pantry for canned goods or space for brooms, mops, and other cleaning supplies.

Since one-wall kitchens are often built into rooms that serve other purposes, many attractive variations are possible. In the illustration at right, a low room divider serves as both a counter and storage space for table linen and silverware. If the kitchen is part of an informal game room, a similar low room divider can serve as a bar.

Versatile one-wall kitchen blends easily into larger room.

How to make laundering more convenient

Layouts to suit your needs

The first thing to consider when planning a laundry center is the volume of work your family requires. If you do six or seven loads of wash a week, plus ironing and occasional mending, you may need a central clothes-care center. A central installation brings washer, dryer, ironing board, and sewing machine into the same room. An elaborate arrangement could include storage for linens and blankets as well as storage for out-of-season clothing.

Basements, with their ample—and often unused—floor space usually provide the best locations for laundry centers, although one room of the house can be used if you have no other need for it. However, there are some disadvantages in taking the laundry center out of a basement. First, the plumbing will generally require extensive alterations in order to accommodate the water supply and drainage needed by the washer. Second, the 240-volt electrical hookup for the dryer also has to be routed to the new location. These alterations can be expensive.

Planning the space

For greatest efficiency, locate the appliances and work areas of the laundry in the order in which they will be used. There are four steps in the laundry process: Receiving and sorting laundry, washing, drying, ironing and storage. The equipment needed for each of these steps should be grouped so that you can move from one step to the next with a minimum of time and effort.

A washer and dryer together require approximately 5 feet of wall space. The depth of most appliances, including washer-dryer combinations, is about 28 inches. To this should be added 36 to 42 inches of floor space for adequate work room.

If you are planning to build the washer and dryer into a countertop and cabinet arrangement, be sure to allow space behind each unit for the plumbing hookup and ventilating ducts. Also, allow space along the sides for both units to be pulled away from the wall when servicing is required.

Where space is a problem, a high-rise laundry arrangement can be employed. It is possible to cut the amount of floor space needed for laundry appliances by one third to one half by mounting a portable dryer above the washer. Even though the portable dryer holds only half a wash load, this compromise may be practical for an apartment-dwelling family whose weekly washing consists of small, rather than large, loads.

Ideal clothes-care center is a laundry room with sewing and mending facilities and ample storage space.

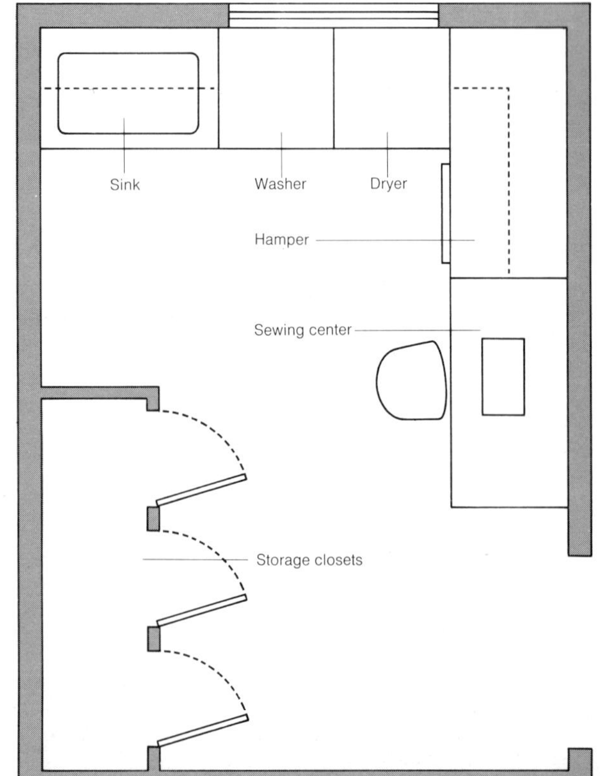

Lighting and ventilation

If you are arranging a room as a complete clothes-care center, make it as comfortable as possible. A large weekly volume of ironing and mending requires the homemaker to spend a substantial amount of time in the room. For this reason, plan to light the area as you would a kitchen, and be sure there are plenty of electrical outlets for the various appliances. If the laundry is in a basement, you should consider installing a telephone extension.

With the dryer and washer operating, room temperature can be uncomfortably warm; so plan to install an exhaust fan. This will also serve to carry away any unpleasant odors from detergents, bleaches, and dry-cleaning fluids.

Appliances, plumbing, and electricity

The washer will, of course, require hot- and cold-water taps and an outlet for the drain. If you launder frequently, consider installing a supplementary hot-water tank to serve the laundry center.

In addition, many dryers require an outside venting arrangement. About 30 feet is the maximum amount of venting ductwork that can be used without elbows if the dryer is to operate efficiently. Each elbow reduces this figure by 4 feet (i.e., maximum efficiency with one elbow is 26 feet, with 2 elbows 22 feet, etc.). Gas dryers are slightly less expensive to operate than electric dryers, but gas is not always available in every community. If you move frequently, you'd better stick with an electric dryer. Gas dryers must always be vented to the outside.

All electric washers require a standard 120-volt circuit. In addition, electric dryers should have a 240-volt circuit. Many electric dryers can operate on less, but drying time increases substantially. Gas dryers require a 115-volt circuit.

Sinks

Although many home laundry facilities do not have sinks, your plans should include one if you are thinking in terms of a fully equipped facility. An extra sink is the perfect place for soaking out stains, pretreating heavily soiled laundry, mixing starch solutions, spot treating clothing before washing, and dyeing garments. A tall gooseneck faucet will make filling pails easier.

The minimum laundry facility

A clothes-care center need not be so elaborate as an entire room set aside solely for laundering and mending. For example, many people arrange a washer and dryer in an extra-large closet near the second-floor bath. This eliminates the need to carry clothes downstairs for washing and drying and then back upstairs for storing. New, small-load washers and dryers designed for apartment living can easily fit into a standard-size closet.

Two basic laundry center plans

The size of your clothes-care center will depend on the size of your family and the amount of wash you do every week. The floor plans shown here contain many ideas that can help you decide what you need:

Optimum laundry center

- Separate, large-capacity washer and dryer
- Built-in hampers to store soiled clothes sorted by type of washing load
- Cabinets for storing laundry aids and other household supplies
- Counters for sorting and folding clothes
- Ample floor space for ironing board
- Sewing center
- Closets for storing linens, vacuum cleaner, mops, etc.
- Large sink

Minimum laundry center

- Washer and dryer or combination
- Appliance tops for sorting and folding
- Cabinet for storing laundry aids
- Small sink

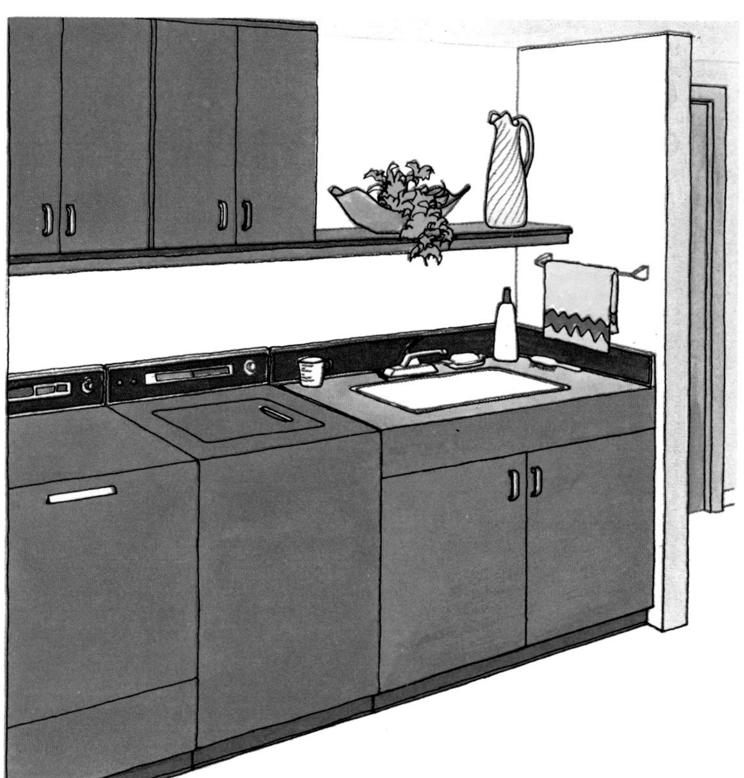

Compact, efficient laundry centers often can be installed in an upstairs closet.

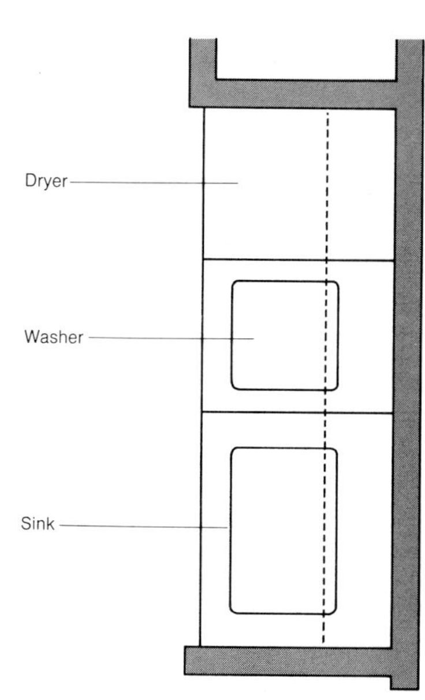

New ways to brighten your bathroom

Planning renovations

Second only to kitchens, bathrooms are the most remodeled and redecorated rooms in North American homes. This is true in large part because of the many new materials that are available for bathroom renovation. Also, updating an old bathroom is a job that an amateur with limited skills can tackle successfully.

In response to the new interest in bathrooms, manufacturers of fixtures and accessories are producing coordinated colors and designs often geared to do-it-yourself installation. If you are tired of your bathroom or feel that you need additional facilities, start your planning by collecting information about these new materials, fixtures, and accessories. Then work up a budget based on the parts of the job you think you can handle, the going local rate for professional help, and estimated material costs.

Bathroom rejuvenation can start with something as small as a new moisture-resistant wallpaper. Other wall treatments (apart from paint) include wood paneling treated to resist moisture, plastic laminates that can be applied in sheet form, and moisture-resistant hardboard. The commonest and most durable of bathroom wall materials, of course, is ceramic tile.

Bathroom floors can be improved in many ways by the do-it-yourselfer. The use of carpets in bathrooms has become more practical with the advent of indoor-outdoor carpeting. Vinyl and asbestos floor tiles come in many colors and designs and can easily be installed by the amateur (p. 355). A floor that is currently tiled could even be resurfaced with mosaic tiles if carpeting or vinyl tiles do not appeal to you.

Apart from the decorative additions you can bring to your bathroom, think seriously about new fixtures. Color-matched toilet bowls and lavatory units are not prohibitively expensive and can transform your bath. Most installations that involve an exchange with the old units do not require much in the way of plumbing skills (p. 237). Even if done professionally, this job won't take a costly length of time.

Mirrors and cabinet fixtures are favorites with most handymen since they add instant convenience with minimal installation effort. Ready-made lavatory units built into finished cabinets are an exceptionally efficient and attractive replacement choice. Removing the old lavatory takes less than an hour in most instances. If you can sweat copper pipes (p. 225), you are all set to handle the trickiest part of the new installation. The cabinet/lavatory combinations come in standard sizes to fit almost any bathroom.

An excellent addition to the tub area is the sliding glass door enclosure. Such a unit takes less than an hour to install and will cut down considerably on the mopping up that shower curtains so often cause. Glass shower enclosures also come equipped with full-length mirrors. These help to make a small bathroom look larger.

A case history

The small bathroom (5 by 8 feet) shown on these pages was transformed with a series of do-it-yourself projects at a total cost of less than $600. (The transformation involved no major plumbing installation.) The 15-year-old bathroom was of drywall construction, painted, with the tub area surrounded by ceramic tiles. The walls had cracked badly; the linoleum floor had heaved; and the ceramic tiles were chipped, cracked, and falling out.

The owner selected ceramic tile for the wall surface and mosaic tile for the floor, with a random pattern of decorative wall tiles to break up the

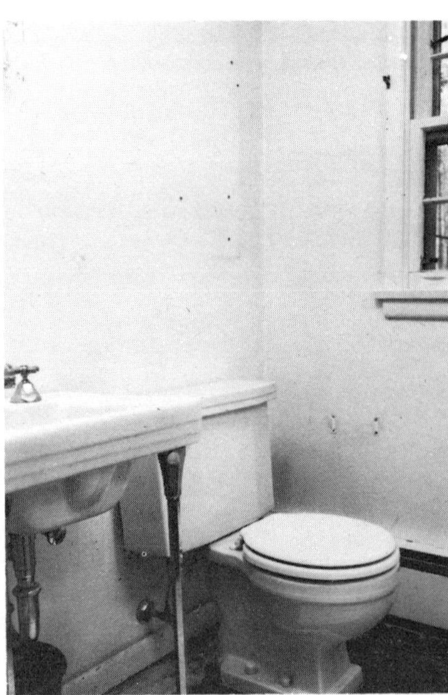

The facelift given this tired bathroom took fewer than six days and cost less than $600. The old toilet with its high tank was replaced by a contemporary unit that flushes silently. An oval lavatory set in a marble top replaces the old sink. The ready-made cabinet hides the lavatory pipes and adds welcome storage space to the room's limited facilities. Tile is lavishly used for its looks and easy maintenance—mosaic on the floor and ceramic on the wall. Moisture-resistant paneling covers the upper part of the wall; a floating mirror runs the entire length of the room.

Photo credit: Montgomery Ward & Co.

large tile areas. The tile job also included matching accessories. Tiles surrounding the tub area were taken full height to the ceiling and continued around the lower half of the room to make cleaning easier around toilet and lavatory areas. To further break up the large expanses of tile, the untiled portion of the wall was covered with moisture-resistant plywood. (This would also have been a good place to use a patterned washable wallpaper.)

An exterior-grade plywood subfloor was laid over the linoleum, and patterned mosaic tiles then put on over that. New fixtures and accessories include a toilet, lavatory, and prefinished cabinet, as well as a floating mirror and matched cabinet. The mirror runs the full length of the wall to give the illusion of the room's being larger.

The existing tub was sound; so it was left in place and enclosed with sliding glass panels, one of which is mirrored. Not shown in the photographs is a combination ceiling fan and heat lamp, which was installed to improve ventilation. This required only the cutting of a hole through the ceiling from the attic and a simple electrical hookup. The unit keeps the room free of moisture during baths and showers.

Prior to installing new tile, all the old tiles were chipped and scraped off, and the wall beneath was examined for deterioration caused by dampness. Damaged sections were cut out and replaced with exterior-grade wallboard. Before tiling, the wallboard around tub and shower faucets was cut away, and the plumbing was modified for more modern fixtures.

The whole installation took fewer than six days; full facilities were unavailable for only two.

In the tub area ceramic tiles accomplish the major transformation; a pattern of decorative tiles breaks up larger areas. The new tiles were taken to the ceiling, then continued around the entire room to make cleaning easier. The existing tub was in satisfactory condition; so it was kept. Sliding glass doors now enclose the tub-shower area; one of the panels is a full-length mirror. When the old tiles were off, the wallboard covering the tub and shower faucets was removed so that the plumbing could be inspected; new fixtures were then installed.

Photo credit: U.S. Ceramic Tile Co.

Finding space for a new bathroom

Most homes with only one bathroom could probably use another, and even families with one and a half or two full baths often wish they had an extra one for guests or just for added convenience.

If you are converting your basement to a family room or den, set aside some space for an additional bathroom. Even if you do not build the room immediately, you will have the space when you are ready to start work on it. The best location for basement bathrooms is as close as possible to existing plumbing for the main drainage system and the hot- and cold-water supply pipes.

Finding additional bathroom space in the living areas of the house can be difficult. For a toilet and lavatory, you need, at the very least, an area no smaller than 4 by 5 feet. Many people convert a small bedroom into a large bathroom. If it's positioned right, such an installation can have more than one entrance, thereby serving another bedroom.

When considering a new bathroom location in the house, determine where the main drainpipes and water-supply pipes run in relation to the spot you've selected. The most expensive part of adding a new bathroom is roughing in the new plumbing (p. 234) —complicated work that should be left to a plumber.

Prefabricated bathrooms

Entire bathrooms made of fiber glass come in easy-to-handle sections—good to know if you plan to do a major home improvement job on your own. You simply build the framing for the bathroom area, then insert the prefabricated unit a section at a time. In such units all the fixtures—electrical, lavatory, toilet, tub, and shower—are built in and ready for connection to the appropriate systems. Considering the cost of building a full bathroom and installing new fixtures, you will probably come out ahead with prefabricated units.

How to make a small house bigger

Which way to grow

It's amazing how many families go on living uncomfortably in cramped quarters without ever considering either the very real possibility of enlarging their house or of making more efficient use of the space that it contains. The usual response to seriously inadequate space is to look for a larger house, but this solution, particularly in today's market, can be prohibitive. Before you contemplate making such a move, take some time to examine the expansion possibilities that exist in your present home.

In the average house the areas likeliest to offer room for expansion are the basement and attic (p. 502). There are practical limits, however, to the kind of supplementary facilities that these areas can provide. If you need a larger living room, dining area, or kitchen, you will probably have to add on to your existing structure. Almost any house built on an average-size lot can accommodate at least one additional room.

The first step in planning such an addition is to check local building codes and zoning laws. In many communities such laws or regulations prohibit the addition of rooms to the front or side of a house. The possible restrictions are of course too numerous to list here, but a talk with local housing authorities or a local contractor will clarify what types of expansion are and are not permissible in your area. Bear in mind that for an exterior addition, detailed plans and drawings must be submitted to local authorities for approval.

When planning an exterior addition, it is always wise to seek the help of an architect. His fee will not be exorbitant, and his expertise can save you time and money in the long run. Furthermore, he will know enough about local codes and zoning regulations to draw up plans to the specifications that are necessary to obtain a building permit. Finally, by creating a design appropriate to the existing structure, he will avoid another worry this kind of addition entails—the esthetic effect on your home.

On smaller jobs, such as enclosing a porch or breezeway, a general contractor can function for you as an architect would on a larger one, from the planning and permit stage through the finished job. In most communities drawings and specifications for these simpler additions need not be prepared professionally; usually rough sketches indicating the dimensions are sufficient for the issuance of a building permit. If this is the first time you've tackled such a job yourself, it will pay to talk to a builder before you start any planning.

Extending out
This method of adding a room is feasible with almost any house regardless of its structural strength. Unlike rooms built above a house or garage, as shown on next page, it adds no weight on the structure. For exterior additions, an architect's help is indispensable. His knowledge of local codes ensures conformity to pertinent regulations; his technical and design expertise assures you of getting a sound addition that harmonizes with the rest of your house.

Going up
When you want to build a room on top of an existing structure, the need for an architect or contractor is imperative. It takes a professional to judge the capacity of the structure to withstand the additional weight and to determine where and how it needs to be strengthened. In the long run, it is probably most economical to let a contractor build the shell for any exterior addition, and to confine your efforts to whatever interior work you feel equipped to handle.

Building a new wing
An addition of this kind will involve construction of a new foundation (p. 472), or a concrete slab with footings may suffice if the building code permits. You can usually build without disturbing the interior of the house up to the point where the framing is completed and you are ready to knock through the wall. The two most difficult construction steps with this type of addition will be cutting the new roof into the existing one, and blending the new walls with the old. Again looking toward the long run, it is probably best to have a contractor build the shell, and do your economizing by completing the interior on your own.

Building on top of an existing structure
If you decide to build upward onto an attached garage or some lower portion of the house, it is vital that you call in an architect or contractor. The existing structure must be examined to determine whether or not it can support the weight of an added floor, and only an experienced professional is equipped to make this judgment. And if it should turn out that existing walls and footings need to be strengthened, only plans prepared by a professional can tell you precisely what has to be done.

Unless you have had considerable previous experience with such work, it is advisable to let a contractor handle the job of building the floor, walls, and roof of the addition. Once this part of the job has been accomplished, you can take over as much of the light construction and interior finishing as you feel that your skills will permit.

Garage conversions
Rather than build on top of an attached garage, consider the possibility of using the garage itself for supplementary living space. The enclosed structure is essentially complete, having the requisite floor, walls, and roof. The necessary heating, plumbing, and electrical connections are usually close by.

You will need to make some basic modifications in the existing structure. The garage door opening or openings can be closed in with glass or a structural wall. The floor can be raised to house level by the use of sleeper beams, and the heating system and electrical leads run under the new floor. Plywood is an excellent material for this purpose; it can be covered with carpet or vinyl flooring, whichever is more practical for the room's intended use. The walls, after they have been insulated, can be covered with any paneling material you desire; the ceiling can be closed in with wallboard or, if you prefer, a suspended ceiling can be installed (p. 348).

If yours is a double garage, you could partition it to serve two purposes. One part, with a single overhead door, could continue to function as a one-car garage, leaving the rest for living space.

Basements and attics can be livable

Planning a basement conversion

Creating a room in a basement can be one of the most rewarding of home improvement projects. There are few places in the home that look less appealing than an unfinished basement. But in a timespan of a few weekends you can transform a little-used, unattractive area into a family room, a workshop, a laundry center, or a combination of these.

Plan to finish the basement by phases. This procedure will enable you to purchase materials as you need them—by phase—thereby spreading the cost of the work over a period of weeks or months. Also, it will leave you plenty of working space to install the materials without having to shift around lumber that you aren't using.

Phase 1—Planning the area

Draw a rough diagram of the basement area you plan to close in. If you are doing the entire basement, you will probably want to try to complete a section at a time. For example, plan to do the family room first, laundry second, furnace room and workshop last. Consider any special construction that may be needed, such as a soundproof wall between the living area and the workshop or furnace room, or wall areas where a brick or stone veneer would look better than wall paneling.

If a wet bar is part of your plan, be sure to place it close to existing plumbing. Indicate where you will need electrical outlets and switches. Also, plan how the room will be heated. If you have a forced-air heating system, a simple branch line heating duct into the living area can often be enough for a small room. For larger rooms (20 x 15 feet and bigger), plan at least two heating ducts. These ducts can be directed down from the ceiling; but generally the lower they are placed in a room, the more efficient heating you will have.

If your home is heated by hot water or steam, it will probably mean calling in a plumber to install a separate heating circuit for the basement. There are, however, several self-contained hot-water heating systems that work off electricity and do not depend on the main furnace. These systems are called hydronic heating units (p. 297) and can generally be installed by an amateur.

Once you have a general plan drawn up, make up a list of the materials you would like to use during each phase of construction.

Phase 2—Preparing floors, walls, and ceilings

A damp basement will have to be dried out as thoroughly as possible before any work begins. Any cracks in the floor or walls should be filled with a sealing compound (p. 156). Coat basement walls with asphalt paint. If the basement tends to be extremely damp, cover the walls with a sheathing of clear plastic. This can be applied directly on the asphalt paint.

Construct partition walls (p. 404) and fasten them to the floor joists over the basement. Use masonry nails or stronger concrete anchor bolts to fasten partitioning to the floor.

The concrete walls of the basement must be lined with furring strips. Space the strips 16 inches apart from center to center. Strips can be fastened to the wall with masonry nails or by using a construction adhesive. If a plastic vapor barrier has been applied to the wall, use nails to fasten furring strips.

Phase 3—Applying wall covering

The most convenient covering for basement walls is prefinished wood paneling. Wallboard can be used, but it involves a series of subsequent operations, such as taping the joints, sanding, and painting. Prefinished paneling can be applied with either finishing nails or with special adhesive (p. 379). Prior to installing walls on partition framing, install electrical cable and outlet boxes (p. 265).

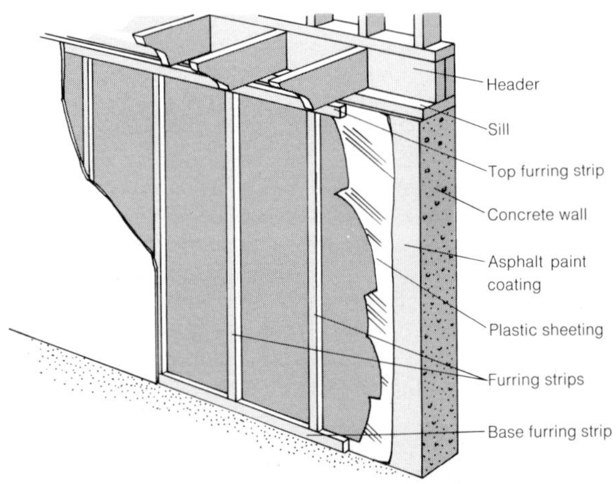

Dampness can be minimized if walls are coated with asphalt paint, then covered with a vapor barrier consisting of a polyethylene sheet. Apply furring strips at 16-in. intervals.

Phase 4—Ceiling installation

All plumbing, heating, and electrical work should be complete before putting up the ceiling. There are basically three types of ceilings: Wallboard, tile, or suspended. Wallboard ceilings are the least expensive of the three, but installation is somewhat awkward (p. 95). Tile ceilings require furring strips laid across the joists, but these are simple to install (p. 406).

If the room area has numerous heating ducts and plumbing pipes hanging from the floor joists, a suspended ceiling is probably the best type (p. 348). This will eliminate the need for boxing in pipes and ducts, since the framing structure that holds the ceiling panels hangs 4 inches or more below the joists. With this type of installation the distance from joists to floor must be at least 8 feet to allow headroom.

Phase 5—Floor installation

Flooring can be of hardwood, vinyl or asphalt tile, wood parquet, or carpeting. The prime consideration is how damp the basement tends to become in wet weather. If moisture and condensation tend to accumulate on the concrete floor, consider installing a plastic vapor barrier and a wood subfloor. Apply the plastic, then lay 2 x 4 sleeper beams on top of the plastic. First, coat the sleepers with a wood preservative. Install a layer of ¾-inch exterior-grade plywood on top of the sleepers.

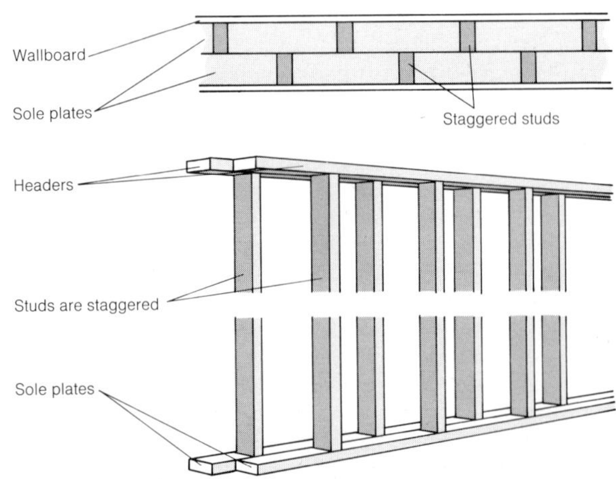

Construct a soundproof partition by laying two sole plates side by side. Erect studs on both sole plates in a staggered pattern. Insulation will provide further soundproofing.

Creating a room in your attic

It is usually practical to convert an attic only when the upstairs space (1) is of sufficient size to make a reasonable room, (2) has ample head clearance of at least 7 feet 6 inches over a large area, (3) has a regular stairway leading up to the attic, and (4) has floor joists that are large enough to support the added load of materials and furnishings. Generally, homes of Cape Cod and some bungalow designs have high peaked roofs that make them easily adaptable to attic conversion.

Unused attic space converts easily into extra room.

What rooms are correct for the attic?
Bedrooms, for certain. Extra sleeping quarters rate as the number one project among all converted attics; and if the bedrooms go in, a bath is a handy convenience. To save money, try to locate a new bath above an existing bath to use the same vent stack and plumbing lines. Hobby rooms and workshops make as good sense in the attic as in the basement. And a playroom is a natural addition, especially if children are going to have their bedrooms in the area. Many people plan an "adult" family room in the attic. An attic can often be converted into an attractive separate apartment for an older relative.

While the pitch of the roof limits the living area, it can provide excellent storage space. The space behind the knee walls, where the overhead is low, is ideal for storage purposes, particularly for out-of-season garments, sports gear, luggage, etc. Be sure to complete the floor and walls under the eaves so that the storage area is dust-free.

What work is involved?
Most of the jobs involved in attic conversion are within the capabilities of the average handyman. These include installing insulation, flooring, framing partitions, putting up studding and ceiling joists, installing wiring and electrical fixtures and outlets, and finishing the walls and ceilings.

If the attic needs more floor space, dormers will have to be added. This means cutting into the existing roof and building an extension. Unless you have had considerable construction experience, this task should be left to a carpenter. Plumbing needs should also be left to a contractor.

To heat the attic, you can either hook onto the central heating system or install an electrical baseboard heating system complete with its own thermostat. Hooking onto the existing heating system is easiest if your home is equipped with forced-air heating. Generally, all you need to do is add lengths of hot- and cold-air ducting and join them to an existing system. Before doing this, however, check with a heating contractor to ensure that your existing furnace blower has sufficient capacity to heat the attic. Similar advice should be sought regarding capacity of hot-water heating systems.

Good ventilation can sometimes be a problem in attic rooms, especially in the summer. The simplest solution is to install a large-capacity attic fan that will draw hot air from the rooms below and exhaust it through the openings used to vent the roof.

Attics are ideally suited for spare bedrooms, separate apartments, or upstairs family and hobby rooms.

Basements and attics can be livable

How to brighten an attic

The two basic problems with attics are insufficient natural light and limited floor space. There are numerous ways to solve these problems. Getting more light into the attic is a task that most do-it-yourselfers can tackle using some of the suggestions on this page. Creating more floor space, however, calls for major structural alterations in the roof. To save time and frustration, leave this job to a professional contractor.

Dormers

One of the most conventional ways of getting light into an attic, as well as adding extra headroom, is to use dormers. The two types of dormers most commonly used are the gable and the shed. A gable dormer usually provides only one window; a shed dormer, which raises the entire roof line of a house except at the ridge, may contain a series of windows. It is possible to give so-called Cape Cod gable dormers a contemporary look by opening the front area to the peak.

Lightscoops

These are smaller forms of the shed-type dormer. While they do not produce the extra headroom of a shed dormer, they are easier to construct. When installing either dormers or lightscoops, make certain that flashing is installed alongside the walls and the junction of the dormer or lightscoop and the existing roof (p.178).

End Windows

The easy way to increase the daylight in a dark attic is to increase the size of the end windows already present; that is, use a bigger window or two windows, or install a complete glass wall.

Bubble Skylights

Ready-made plastic bubbles add variety and versatility to attic lighting. They may be set into the roof wherever a source of daylight is needed—over desks, work or game tables, or in the bathroom. The bubbles come in frames in a variety of sizes and shapes.

Strip Skylights

These give the attic the most daylight and will create a cheery studio effect. For the most satisfactory light, put skylights on north or east slope of the roof. Construction of strip skylights is a fairly easy task. Shingles and sheathing are removed from the skylight area and a 2- x 4-inch curb is nailed to existing rafters. The tempered glass or ¼-inch plastic panes are set in place and caulked with glazing compound; then stop molding is nailed over the caulked lines.

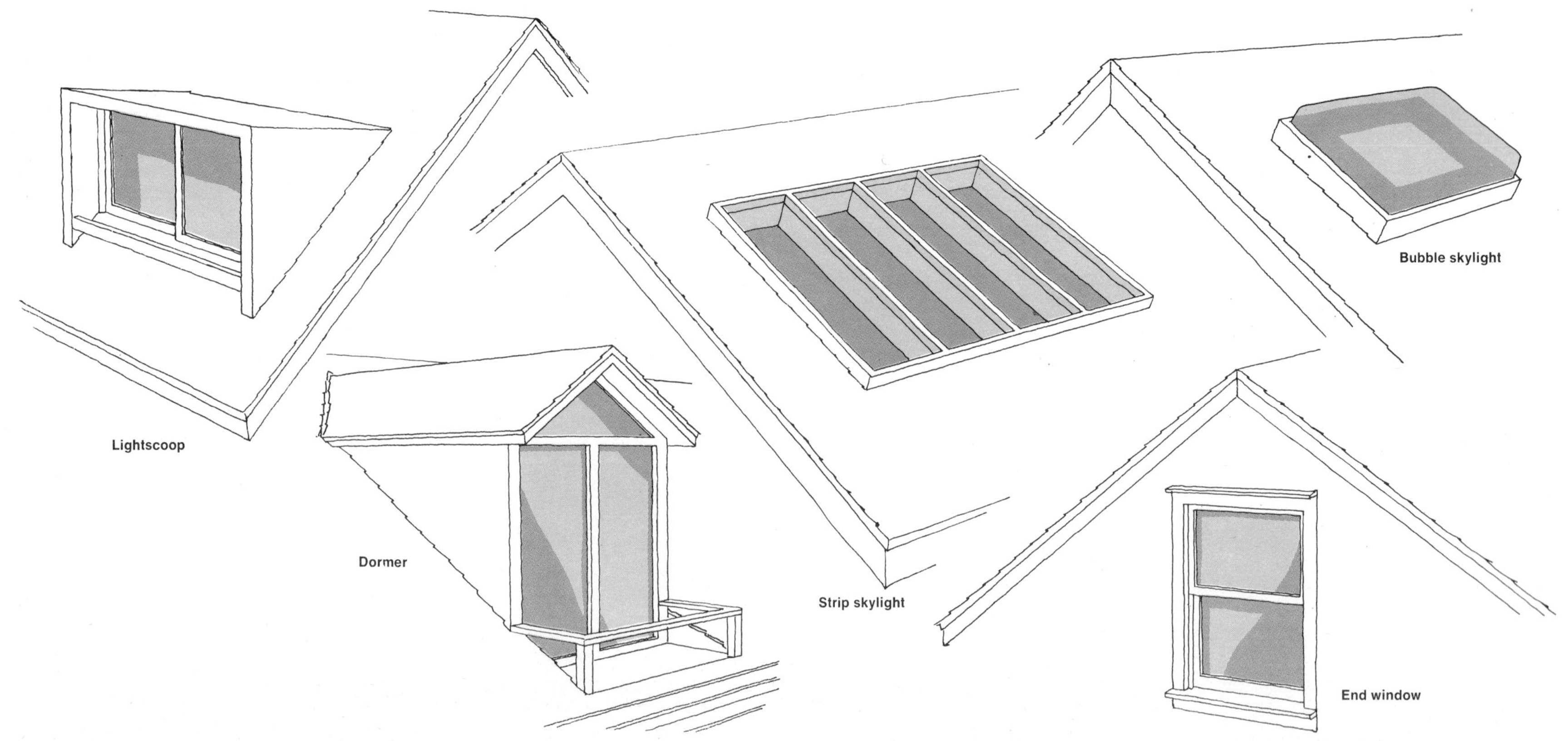

section 17: Fifty projects you can build

How to use this section

This section describes more than 50 projects that you can build for your home and garden. Color photographs show how each finished project will appear, a parts list gives dimensions of the components, exploded-view drawings show how they fit together, and construction notes give the order of work.

In building any of these projects, use the techniques sections of the book to assist in developing unfamiliar skills. Follow this procedure:

1 Select the project you want to build. Study the photograph, diagram, and parts list. Read the instructions to see what special tools or skills will be needed to do the job.

2 The parts list will tell you what wood to buy, what hardware is needed, what amounts of other materials are necessary to produce the project in the photograph. Dimensions given in the parts list are based on nominal-size lumber. This will enable you to order materials using the parts list as a shopping guide.

3 The cross-references at the top of the page lead you to other sections of the book. There, step-by-step photographs and drawings show you how to do unfamiliar jobs. You will often find several different ways of doing the same job; so you can select the method best suited to your skills and equipment.

4 Use the exploded-view drawing as a visual guide while your work progresses. The drawings show how the various parts fit together, and they serve as a valuable tool in the overall construction. Parts numbers on the drawings correspond to the numbers on the parts list.

5 Step-by-step instructions explain how the work should be put together and in what order parts are to be assembled. When building these projects, do not cut all the pieces to size and then try to assemble them. Instead, cut parts as they are needed, checking them for fit as work advances. This way, you can alter dimensions slightly to make up for unavoidable discrepancies.

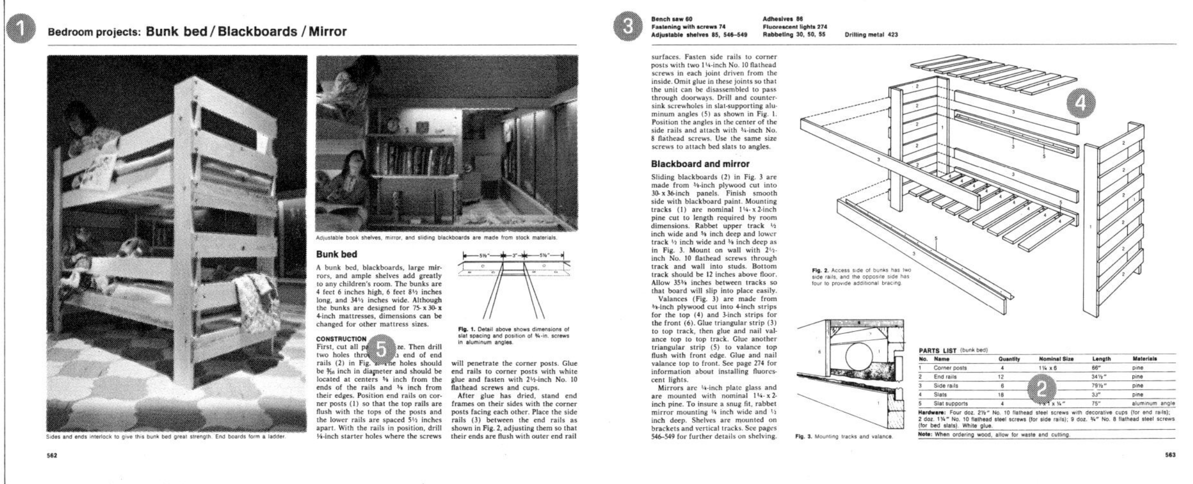

contents

Cabinet system can be adapted to any kitchen. Request lumberyard to cut door plywood to size to minimize work.

Built entirely of standard lumberyard materials, these kitchen cabinets require no complex woodwork. They can be adapted for any size of kitchen, and the three types of cabinets can be built independently of each other. A dishwasher can be installed between bottom cabinets. Drawers can be used instead of shelves and a door. The dimensions given in the Parts List are based on the units shown. Two possible cabinet depths are given, 18 and 24 inches, the latter for the wider counter top required by a standard-size sink. To assure ample width for the sink, get the measurements of the sink you plan to use before you start building the cabinet. Fasten front rails to cleats (18), nailed to the floor with 3-inch nails spaced 1 foot apart.

CONSTRUCTION

Bottom cabinets

Cut the upper rails (1) and the bottom rails (2) to the length required by your kitchen dimensions. Fasten the rear rails to the wall, with their tops 17½ and 35 inches above the floor; drive 3-inch nails through the rails and wall into the studs.

Fix the uprights (3) to the outer side of the bottom rail and both top rails at 20-inch intervals as shown in Fig. 2. Make right-angle junction between two cabinets as shown in Fig. 1. Use white glue and one 1½-inch No. 8 flathead steel screw at each joint; place outer upper rails at same heights as rear upper rails.

Notch the divider panels (4) for all rails and fasten them to the uprights with brackets of aluminum angle, as in Figs. 3 and 4, drilled for ¾-inch No. 8 flathead screws. Fasten the bottom rail to the floor with 3-inch nails. Nail the bottom rail to the cleats with 2-inch finishing nails, driven from the front. Cut sink panel (7) and fix it to back of uprights with two No. 8 flathead steel screws in each upright. Cut the shelves (5) to fit between panels; fix them to the tops of the middle rails with white glue and 2-inch finishing nails. Install the countertop (6) and cover it with plastic laminate (p. 380).

Hang the doors (8) (p. 78) and mount door pulls 2¼ inches from top edge and latch edge. Install magnetic catches (p. 81).

Drawer cabinet

Build the drawer cabinet in the same way as the shelf cabinet except that drawer runners take the place of divider panels and shelves. Make three to five drawers (p. 402) to suit your needs. Drawer fronts project above and below drawer sides to cover drawer runners. Allow about ⅛-inch clearance between drawer fronts. Fasten the runners (10) to the end panels with white glue and finishing nails. Brace each runner with two triangular blocks (11) glued and nailed as in Fig. 5; be sure drawer sides clear the blocks. Drawers are of simple box construction. Sides are held to front by glue and 1½-inch finishing nails driven through the front into their ends. Back is fastened between sides in the same manner. Corner angles (1½-inch) halfway up each inside corner reinforce the joints. The front is set ⅜ inch below sides to conceal the ⅜-inch plywood bottom. The bottom is glued and secured with 1-inch brads to the sides and back, and butted against the rear of the drawer front. A 1½-inch corner angle reinforces the bottom-to-front joint at the center of the drawer.

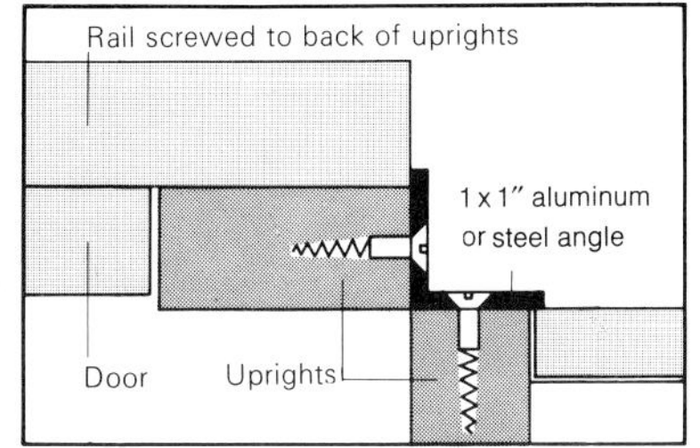

Fig. 1. Right-angle junction between cabinets is fastened with metal angle.

Upper cabinets

All rails are 1 x 2s, and uprights (12) extend ¾ inch above top rail. Use only two divider panels (13), one on each side of central door. Otherwise, follow same procedure as for bottom cabinets. Construct the unit so the end upright (if against a wall) will be at a stud location so it can be fastened through the wallboard to the stud with corner angles or aluminum angle brackets (9) and 2-inch No. 8 flathead screws. The center divider panels should also be located at studs and fastened the same way to provide firm cabinet suspension.

Nail rear top rails to studs. Set upper rail 85½ inches above floor, middle rail 64 inches, lower rail 55½ inches. Fasten shelf that serves as cabinet top to rails and divider panels before fastening other shelves to rails; mount cabinet top like countertop. Mount doors (14).

Tall cabinets

Build these in the same way as bottom cabinets, and make uprights (15) overlap the upper top rail by ¾-inch. Fix all three top rails at the same height as the top cabinets. If 18-inch-deep upper or bottom cabinets are next to 24-inch-deep tall cabinets, screw end panel (16) of the tall cabinet to the frame of upright of the bottom cabinets. Any floor-mounted cabinets can have a false floor mounted

Rustproof wire kitchen trays make vegetable drawers in sink cabinet.

Brooms, mops, vacuum cleaner store in tall cabinet, with additional storage space above.

Natural wood paneling can be used on wall between base and upper cabinets to match furniture.

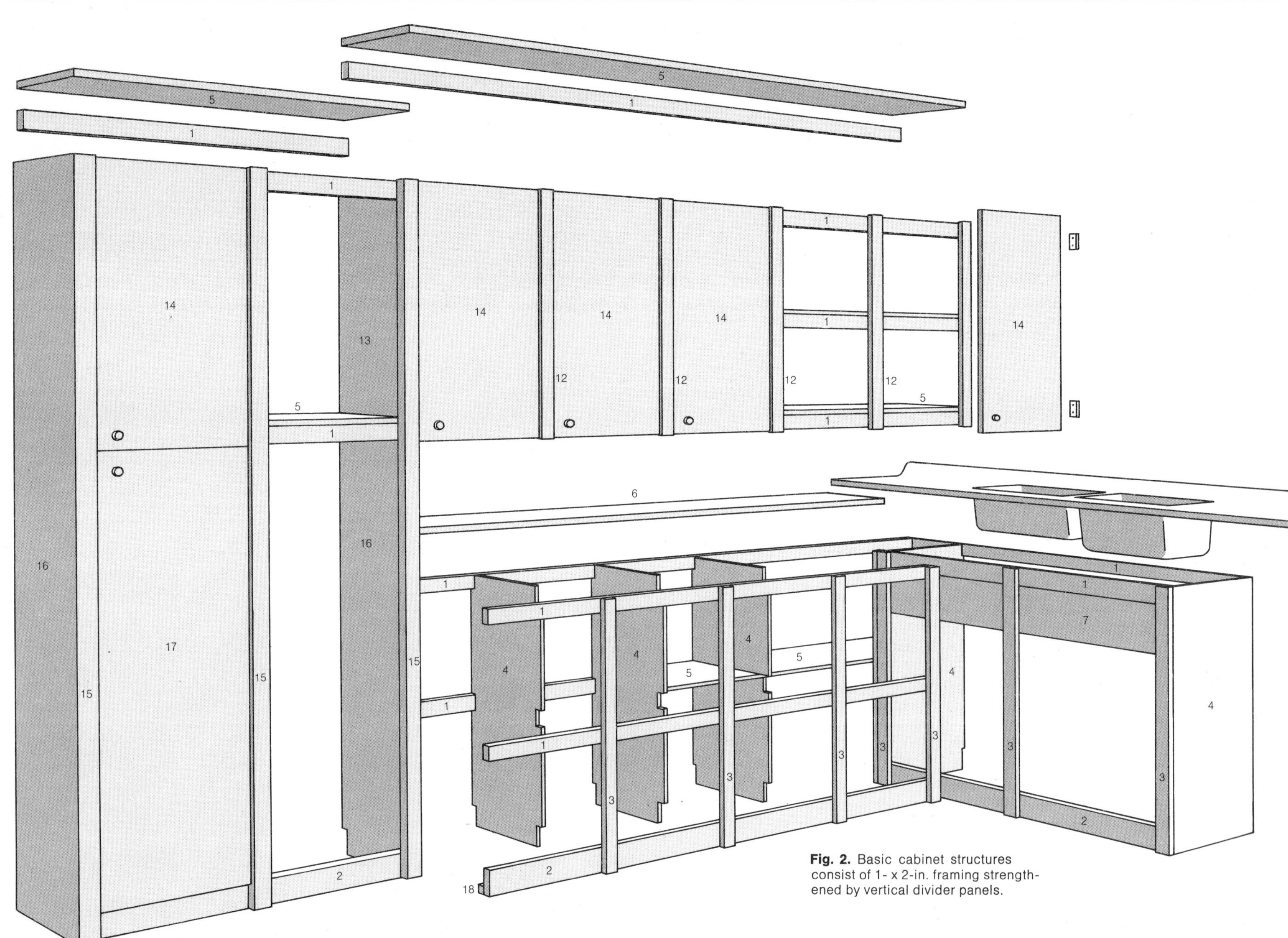

Fig. 2. Basic cabinet structures consist of 1- x 2-in. framing strengthened by vertical divider panels.

on top of the bottom rails so that stored items need not be lifted over the bottom rail. Mount doors (17).

Finish all cabinet doors in semi-gloss enamel, uprights with a clear polyurethane varnish. Rough in (p. 234) any necessary plumbing before fastening the countertop for the sink in place. Be sure under-sink doors provide easy access to the sink trap in case a sink drain stoppage requires disassembly of the trap to clear the drain pipe.

Countertop

Cut the countertop (6) from ¾-inch plywood or 1-inch particle board. Width will be 18 inches or 24 inches, depending on cabinet's depth. Make a countertop splash board (not illustrated) to fit along the back edge. Make splash board from the same stock as the countertop. Width should be 4 inches to 6 inches. Rabbet the lower edge to half the thickness of the stock. Glue and screw it to the countertop. Use 1½ inch No. 6 flathead screws.

An alternative to making a countertop is to buy a readymade unit that has a preformed splash panel. Such units come already covered with laminate. If you also plan a readymade sink unit, make sure the units match.

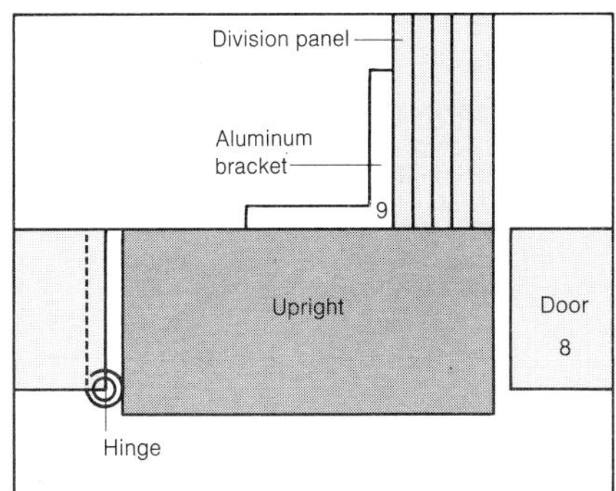

Fig. 3. Aluminum angle bracket drilled for ½-in. flathead screws holds dividers to uprights. Doors are attached with 2½ in. butt hinges. Use three hinges on tall cabinet doors, two hinges on all other doors.

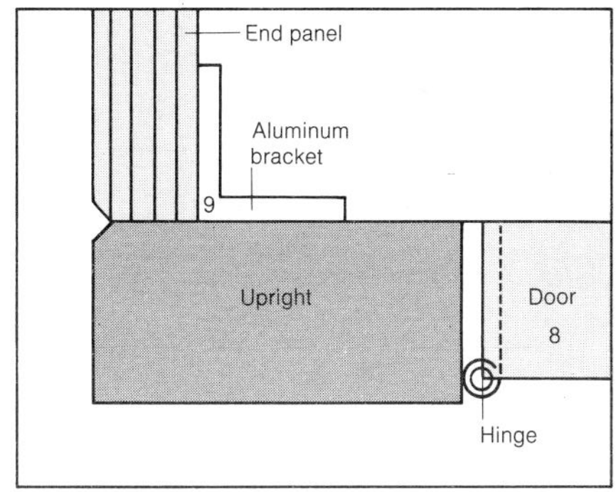

Fig. 4. For a neater joint, use a plane to chamfer edges of end panels and uprights where they meet. This is not necessary if a kitchen appliance will be placed so that it hides the end panel.

Countertop can be made from plywood and covered with laminate. Or purchase a readymade unit that contains standard-size sink openings.

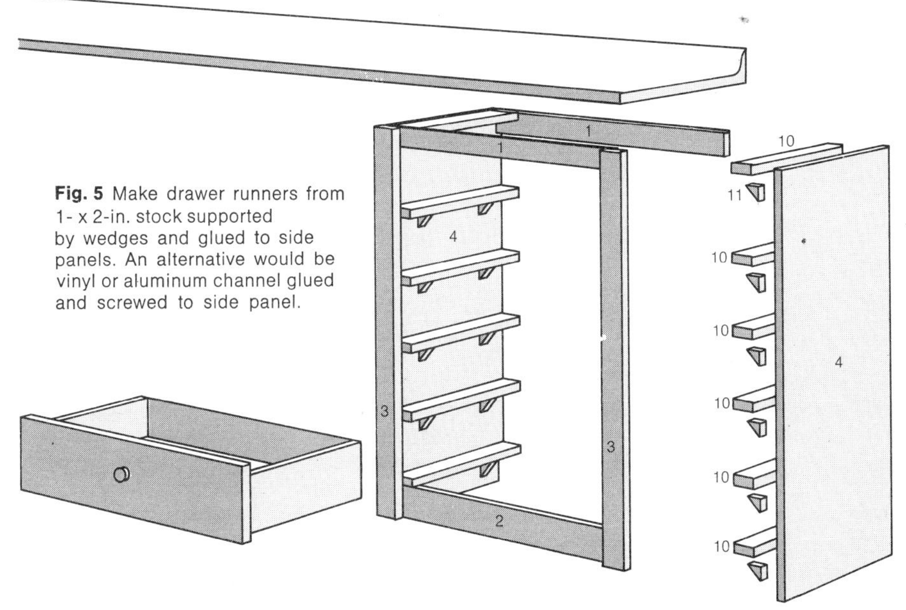

Fig. 5 Make drawer runners from 1- x 2-in. stock supported by wedges and glued to side panels. An alternative would be vinyl or aluminum channel glued and screwed to side panel.

PARTS LIST

No.	Name	Quantity	Nominal Size	Length	Width	Material
1	Upper rails	as needed	1 x 2	as needed		pine
2	Bottom rails	as needed	1 x 4	as needed		pine
3	Frame uprights	as needed	1 x 2	35″		pine
4	End/divider panels	as needed		35″	17¼ or 23¼″	½″ fir plywood
5	Shelves	as needed		as needed	17¼ or 23¼″	¾″ particle board
6	Countertop	as needed		as needed	19″ or 25″	1″ particle board
7	Sink panel	as needed		as needed	as needed	½″ fir plywood
8	Doors	as needed		33″	19¹¹⁄₁₆″	¾″ fir plywood
9	Brackets	as needed	1 x 1	6″		⅛″ aluminum angle
10	Drawer runners	as needed	1 x 2	17¼ or 23¼″		pine
11	Triangular blocks	as needed	2 x 2		1″	pine
Upper cabinets						
12	Frame uprights	as needed	1 x 2	as needed		pine
13	End/divider panels	as needed		30″	17¼″	½″ fir plywood
14	Doors	as needed		30″	19¹¹⁄₁₆″	¾″ fir plywood
Tall cabinets						
15	Frame uprights	as needed	1 x 2	as needed		pine
16	End/divider panels	as needed		as needed	17¼″	½″ fir plywood
17	Doors	as needed		as needed	19¹¹⁄₁₆″	½″ fir plywood
18	Floor cleats	as needed	2 x 2	as needed		fir

Hardware: Two 2½″ hinges per door for base and upper cabinet doors, three per door for high doors of tall cabinet, with screws to match. One magnetic catch per door. Door and drawer pulls as required. Nails: 3″; 2″ finishing; 1″ brads. Flathead screws No. 6—½″, 1½″; No. 8—¾″, 1½″, 2″. Corner angles, 1½″. White Glue.

Note: Door widths are based on 20″ door opening. Drawer fronts, sides, and backs are of nominal 1″ pine.

Stain-resistant fabric is ideal for chairs.

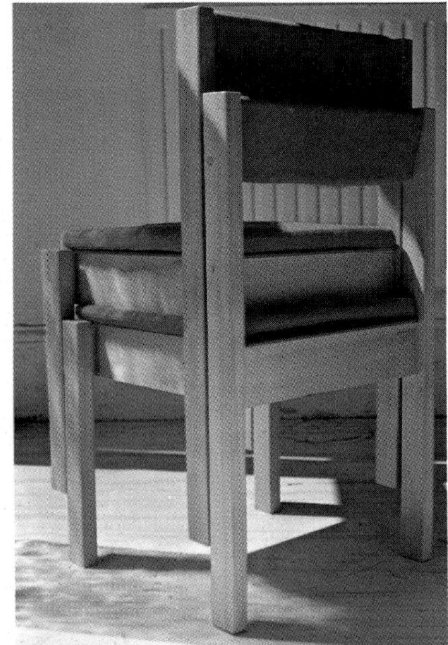
Extra chairs lock into storage stack.

This table and chair set requires minimum space; chairs slide snugly under the table and extra chairs stack neatly, even in a closet.

CONSTRUCTION

Table

Each table leg is made of a narrow piece (1), cut to length from nominal 1 x 3 stock, joined at a right angle to a wide piece (2), ripsawed from a nominal 1 x 4, to form a squared V-channel leg measuring 3¼ inches across both outside faces. Cut mortises ¼ inch wide and 1½ inches deep in outer edges of all leg pieces, starting ½ inch from the top and extending 3 inches down the side. Haunched tenons on end (3) and side (4) rails, with upper edges ½ inch below rail tops, fit into the mortises. Cut tenons slightly oversize and use rasp and sandpaper to bring them to a snug fit for gluing.

Assemble leg and rail frame in two halves, each including one complete two-piece leg consisting of one narrow leg piece and one wide leg piece at each

Easy-to-clean plastic laminate comes in colors to match most kitchen decors.

Cushions 205
Dowel joints 394
Haunched tenon 388
Laminates 380
Protractor 383
Mortise and tenon joints 387
Rasp 35

end (Fig. 1). To complete assembly, locate end leg pieces so that a wide one and narrow one meet. Join leg pieces with glue and 2-inch No. 6 flathead screws at 5-inch intervals. Screws pass through wide pieces into edges of narrow pieces; 2-inch finishing nails can be used instead of screws.

Glue and nail ledger strips (5, 6) inside rails ¾ inch below rail tops; use 1½ inch finishing nails. Side ledger strips fit between end strips. Table top (7) fits inside rails and is glued to ledger strips. Plane top edges to achieve snug fit. Apply plastic laminate top with contact cement.

Chair

Mortise and tenon joints and dowel joints provide rigidity for chair frames. Front and back rails (8) and side rails (9) of seat frame are joined by three ¼ inch dowels from side rail ends into front and back rails. Cut tenons on front and back rail ends ⅜ inch thick and ⅞ inch long, with their tops and bottoms ½ inch from rail edges. Side rails are set in ½ inch from tenon shoulders so that legs will be held out from side rails. Drill ¼-inch-diameter dowel holes through front and back rails into side rails or use a doweling jig to align the holes. Cut 2 x 2 stock into diagonal corner blocks (10) and fasten with glue and 1½-inch finishing nails to reinforce corners.

Cut mortises matching front/back rail end tenons starting ½ inch from top of front legs (11) and 14 inches from top of rear legs (12). Cut tenons slightly oversize and rasp and sand down to a snug fit before gluing. Fasten seat panel (13), extending ¼ inch onto seat rails all around, with glue and 1-inch brads.

Glue and nail corner blocks (14) to back rest (15). Polyurethane foam back pad (16) is held in place by upholstery fabric stapled to back rest edges and corner blocks. Staples are concealed by a gimp. Set back rest top flush with leg tops and slanted back at about 78 degrees (mark angle with protractor) for comfortable fit. Drive two 1¾-inch No. 8 flathead screws from the outside through each back leg into back rest corner blocks.

Seat pad (17) is slipped into the unsewn rear edge of a fabric cover, which is then stitched. Pad is held to seat panel by tapes sewn to underside of cover and tied through two holes in seat panel. Finish all exposed wood on table and chairs with polyurethane varnish.

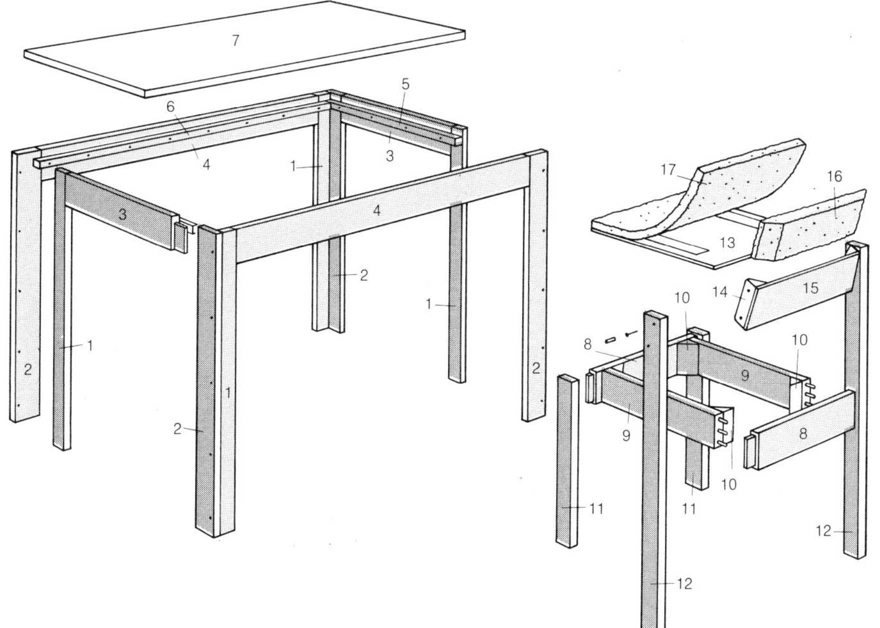

Fig. 1. Chair and table assembly. Join wide and narrow leg pieces as shown.

PARTS LIST

No.	Name	Quantity	Nominal Size	Length	Width	Material
Table						
1	Narrow leg pieces	4		28″	2½″	¾″ pine
2	Wide leg pieces	4		28″	3¼″	¾″ pine
3	End rails	2	1 x 4	22″		pine
4	Side rails	2	1 x 4	46″		pine
5	End ledger strips	2	1 x 1	24″		pine
6	Side ledger strips	2	1 x 1	46½″		pine
7	Table top	1		48″	24″	¾″ particle board
Chair						
8	Front/back rails	2	1 x 4	18¼″		pine
9	Side rails	2	1 x 4	14¼″		pine
10	Corner blocks	4	2 x 2	3½″ diagonal		fir
11	Front legs	2	1¼ x 2	16½″		pine
12	Rear legs	2	1¼ x 2	30″		pine
13	Seat panel	1		14¾″	14½″	¼″ plywood
14	Back corner blocks	2	1¼ x 1¼	4½″ diagonal		fir
15	Back rest	1		16½″	4½″	⅜″ plywood
16	Back rest pad	1		17½″	5½″	1″ polyfoam
17	Seat pad	1		15¾″	15½″	1″ polyfoam

Hardware: Table: Twenty 2″ No. 6 flathead screws or ¼ lb. 2″ finishing nails. Quarter-pound 1½″ finishing nails. One pt. plastic resin glue. **Chair:** Box 1″ brads. Box 5/16″ staples for staple gun. Four 1¾″ No. 8 flathead screws. One ¼″-dia. dowel 36″ long. One pt. contact cement. Minimum 2 sq. ft. fabric to cover pads. Fabric tape.

This 18- x 17-inch table and matching wall-hung shelf unit can be varied in size to suit available space in any small room. If table is to be used with stools, the top should be 3½ feet above the floor. For use with chairs, table height should be 2½ feet. If the table is to serve as additional counter space, make it the same height as existing counters.

CONSTRUCTION

Wall-hung shelves

Cut shelves (1) and partitions (2) to size. Clamp partitions in a vise with the grain running vertically. Drill two ¼-inch holes 1 inch in from each edge and ¾ inch deep. Do this to both ends of the partitions.

From a length of ¼-inch doweling, cut 20 pieces 1½ inches long. Coat half of each dowel with glue and fit them into the holes in the partitions.

Rest the partitions on edge across the bottom shelf, one at each end and the others at the desired intervals. Draw lines to mark the locations. Within the lines drawn to mark the locations of the partitions on the bottom shelf (1), mark the spots for the dowel holes. Drill ¼-inch holes. Mark and drill the top shelf (1) in the same way.

Fit all parts together and check that the assembly is square. Take it apart. Glue all mating surfaces and clamp.

Cut the back (3) to fit the box assembly. You may prefer not to use a back, as in the photograph. If a back is used, fasten it to the box with 1½-inch No. 6 screws.

Mount the unit 20 inches above the table surface. Use 2½-inch No. 8 flathead screws through the back (3) into the studs. If no back is used, fasten the unit to the wall with 2 corner brackets screwed to the inside of the end partitions with ½-inch flathead screws. Fasten angle brackets to the wall with 2-inch screws if going into studs. If stud locations do not match bracket positions, use a Molly bolt or other hollow-wall fastener (p. 76).

Flexible living space: This drop-top table serves as a snack bar, desk top, or hobbies center.

With its top against the wall, the table makes a decorative backdrop. Instructions recommend a particle board table top covered with plastic laminate, but you can plan your own alternative. This design, for example, has 1- x 4-in. pine slats cleated to the support brackets. Stools here are purchased, but you can make your own rustic units from the instructions on the right.

Drop-top table

Cut the parts to sizes in Parts List or as required by available space. Mount the uprights (8) spaced so that they can be screwed through wall into studs with 2½-inch No. 8 flathead screws. Mount cross rail (7) above the uprights with 2½-inch No. 8 screws driven into the studs. Mount top rail (6) on the upper edge of cross rail (7) with its edge against the wall; screw in place with 2-inch No. 6 flathead screws. Mount the folding shelf brackets with their tops in open position snug against the underside of the top rail (6). Use 1-inch No. 6 screws.

Cut the table top (4) to size. If laminate is to be used, apply it (p. 380) before mounting top. Apply finishing trim to rear edge and ends of the top.

Mount the top (4) on shelf brackets. Use ½-inch No. 6 flathead screws to fasten it. Attach front trim (5) to top. Glue it and fasten it with 2-inch finishing nails.

Adhesives 86
Corner braces 384
Doweled joints 395, 397
Fasteners 74, 76
Mortise and tenon joints 387
Particle board 376
Working with laminates 380

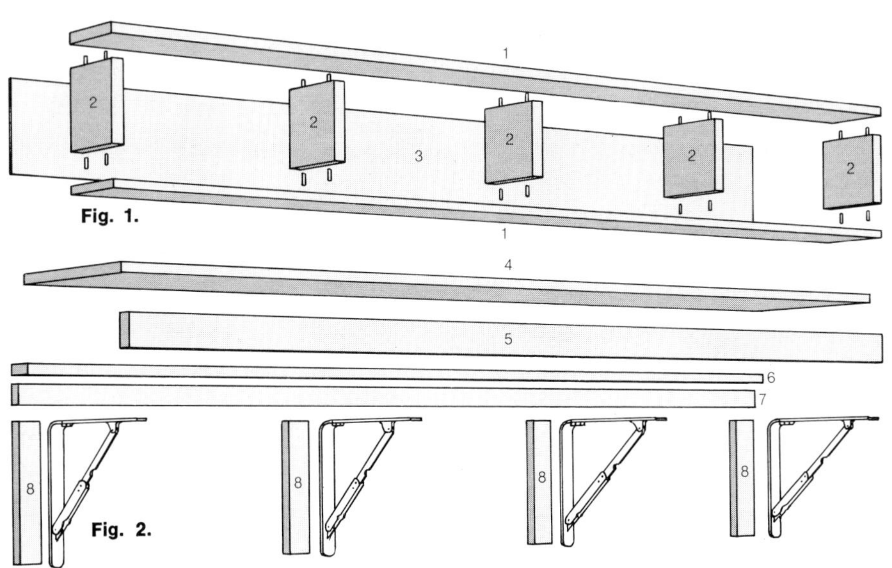

Fig. 1.

Fig. 2.

PARTS LIST

Wall-hung shelves

No.	Name	Quantity	Nominal Size	Length	Width	Material
1	Top/bottom	2	1 x 6	72″		pine
2	Partitions	5	1 x 6	6″		pine
3	Back	1		72″	7½″	⅜″ fir plywood

Hardware: Three dozen 1½″ No. 6 flathead screws. Two 2½″ No. 8 flathead screws per stud location, as required for mounting. One ¼″ diameter dowel, 38″ long, to be cut for doweling. Resorcinol adhesive.

Drop-top table

No.	Name	Quantity	Nominal Size	Length	Width	Material
4	Table top	1		71⅞″	15″	¾″ particle board
5	Front trim piece	1	1 x 3	72″		pine
6	Top rail	1	1 x 3	72″		pine
7	Cross rail	1	1 x 2	72″		pine
8	Uprights	4	1 x 2	12½″		pine

Hardware: Four 12″ x 12″ folding shelf brackets. Plastic laminate as required, if used. No.6 flathead screws: twelve ½″, twelve 1″, six 1½″, twelve 2″. Eight 2½″ No.8 flathead screws for wall mounting. Vinyl or aluminum trim for back edge and ends of table top.

Stool features oak frame and pine slats.

Kitchen stool

Cut top, bottom, and foot rails (2, 3, 5) to size. Use a plane to round a ¼-inch radius on each. Cut curve in seat rail (4) (p. 30) top edges so that center is 1 inch below ends. Cut seat slats (6) and plane edges.

Foot and seat rail length allows for 1¾-inch-long tenons (p. 387). These pass through legs, and overlap is trimmed and sanded after glue sets. Cut 1-inch-long tenons on top and bottom side rails. Cut tenons ¼ inch from top and bottom of lower rails. Top of upper side rail tenon (2) is ¾ inch from top of rail. Start the mortise ¾ inch down the edge of the leg (1) so that top edge of leg and side rail are flush. Seat rail tenons (4) are cut flush with the rail's top edge. They fit mortises ½ inch below leg tops (1). Glue side frames (1, 2, 3) and join them by gluing in seat rails (4) and foot rails (5). Screw slats (6) to seat rails with centered 1¼-inch No. 6 screws.

PARTS LIST

No.	Name	Quantity	Nominal Size	Length	Width	Material
1	Legs	4	1¼ x 3	30″		oak
2	Top side rails	2	1¼ x 3	12¼″		oak
3	Bottom side rails	2	1¼ x 3	12¼″		oak
4	Seat rails	2	1¼ x 3	17″		oak
5	Foot rails	2	1¼ x 3	17″		oak
6	Seat slats	9	1 x 2	16″	1½″	pine

Hardware: Eighteen 1¼″ No. 6 flathead screws.

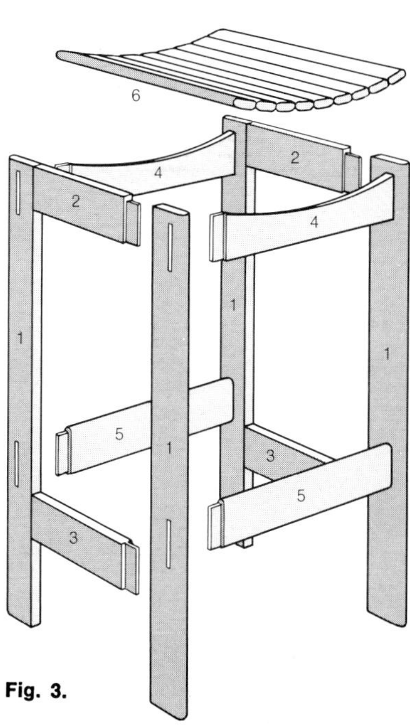

Fig. 3.

This table seats four with drop leaf raised. With leaf down, it seats three. Either way, no one need straddle a leg.

Adhesives 86
Doweled joints 395, 397
Drilling wood 27, 44
Working with laminates 380

Lowered leaf rests against table legs.

To expand this table, simply raise the drop leaf and slide it up on the table frame. When the top is pushed beyond the legs, wooden tracks on its underside lock it in place.

CONSTRUCTION

Table frame is nominal 3 x 3 fir with dowel fasteners to provide the strength of fitted joints without having to cut them. To join leg (1) and top end rail (2), drill two ⅜-inch holes through leg and 1½ inches into rail. Space the holes ⅝ inch and 1⅞ inches from leg top and center both on width of leg. Set top end rails ⅛ inch lower than leg tops to allow hinges to clear. For each side long rail (3), drill two ⅜-inch holes through leg and 1½ inches into rail, both 1¼ inches from leg top, centered ⅝ inch from the side. To join leg and bottom end rail, drill same size holes through leg and rail, one ⅝ inch from leg bottom, one 1⅞ inches, both centered on width of leg. To join bottom long rail to bottom end rails, drill ⅜-inch holes through end rails 1½ inches into long rail; center holes in end rails 10⅜ inches from each end.

Assemble end frames first, with ⅜-inch dowels at least 4 inches long and resorcinol glue. After inserting dowels, saw outer edges off flush and sand smooth.

Wooden slides (7, 8), and runners (4), keep the table top from moving sideways, tipping down, or sliding too far when extended. Glue and nail runners (4) inside top long rails, flush with rail tops; use 2-inch finishing nails. Fasten drop leaf (5) to top (6) with three 1½-inch butt hinges, one centered, the others 6 inches to each side. Clamp slide (7) and slide batten

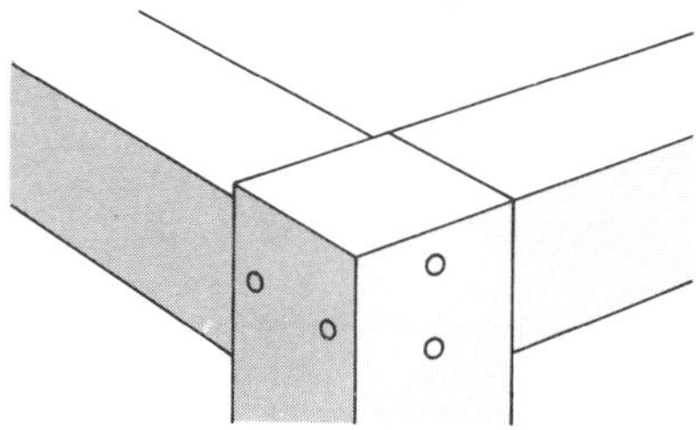

Fig. 1. Staggered dowels bypass each other.

(8) with C-clamps and drill four evenly spaced ⅛-inch holes through both. With top in place, flap down against legs, nail slides temporarily under top, flush against runners and end rail at leaf end. Slide top to check that hinged seam stops near frame midpoint. If slide positions are correct, glue them in place, then glue slide battens to them and fix battens with 2-inch No. 8 screws.

Paint top and leaf or cover them with laminate. Paint or varnish frame. Wax slides and runners.

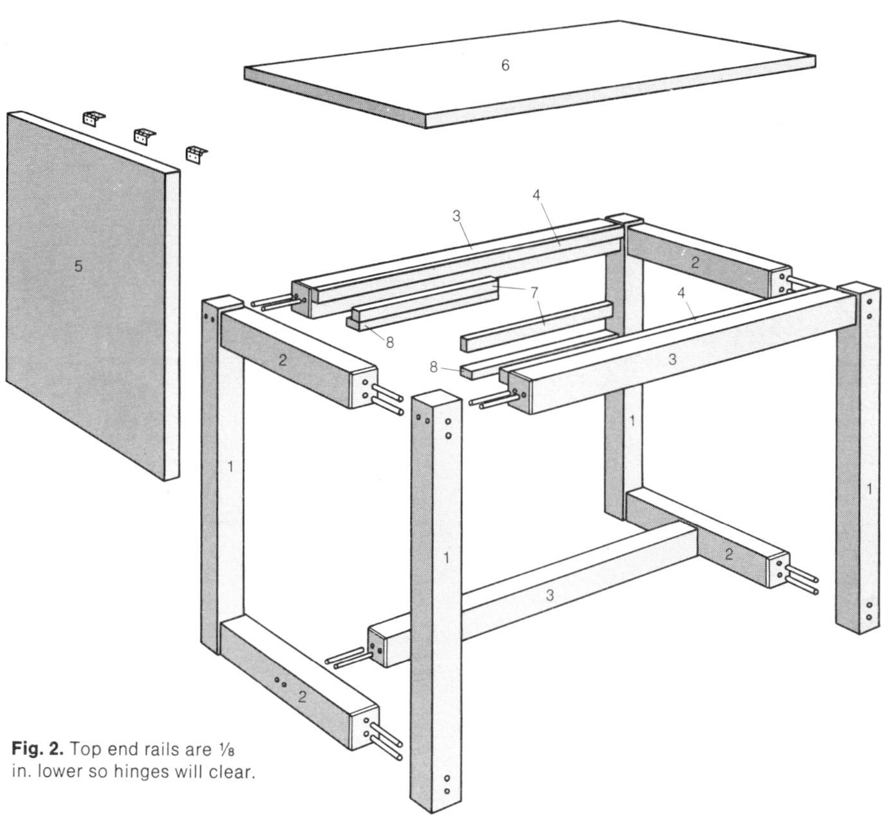

Fig. 2. Top end rails are ⅛ in. lower so hinges will clear.

PARTS LIST

No.	Name	Quantity	Nominal Size	Length	Width	Material
1	Legs	4	3 x 3	27″		fir or pine
2	End rails	4	3 x 3	22″		fir or pine
3	Long rails	3	3 x 3	35″		fir or pine
4	Runners	2		35″		¾″ x ¾″ hardwood
5	Drop leaf	1		20″	27″	¾″ plywood
6	Top	1		40″	27″	¾″ plywood
7	Slides	2		14″		¾″ x ¾″ hardwood
8	Slide battens	2	1 x 2	14″		hardwood

Hardware: Twenty-eight 4″x ⅜″ dowels. Resorcinol glue. Three 1½″ butt hinges with ½″ flathead screws to match. Eight 2″ No. 8 screws (for slides). Finishing nails, 2″. Paint, plastic laminate, and glue, and/or varnish for finishing.

Note: If frame is to have natural finish, select the 3 x 3 stock to minimize knots and surface checks.

Making drawers for cabinet is simplified by fitting plastic containers to drawer fronts.

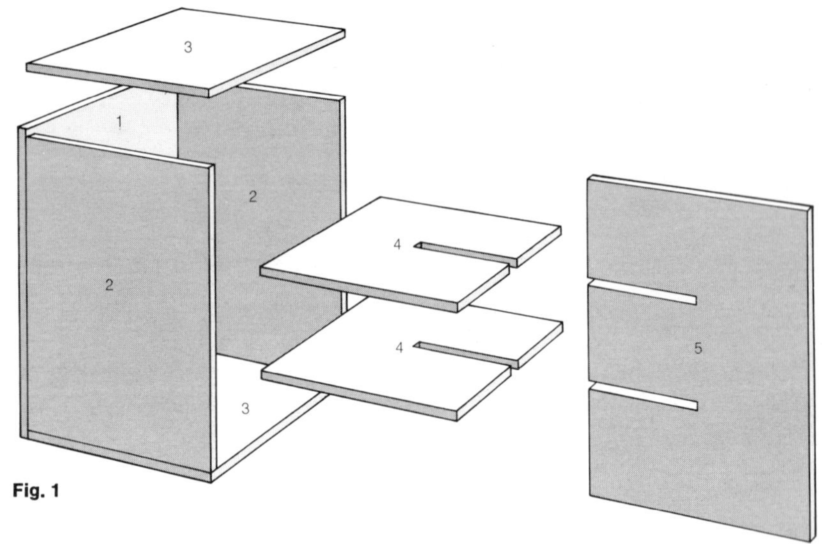

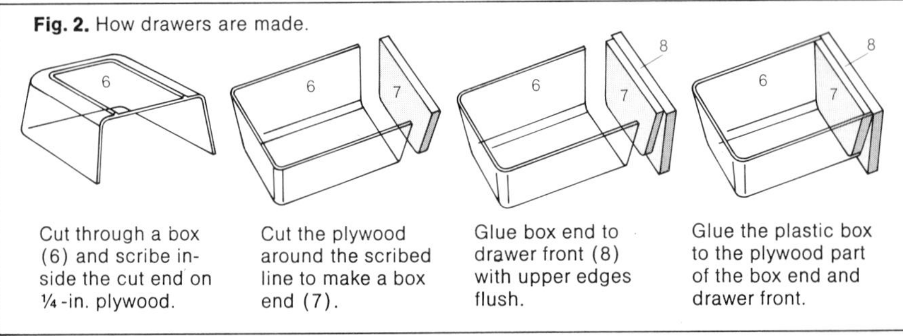

Rack and six drawers

The two racks on these pages are suitable for storing dried fruits, beans, garlic, or similar items.

The plastic boxes used for the drawers can be bought in various shapes and sizes. If you cannot find a set that suits the dimensions of this box unit, the rack dimensions can easily be adjusted to suit any available box sizes.

CONSTRUCTION

Cut and plane to size back (1), sides (2), and top and bottom (3) of rack.

If rack is to be hung on wall, drill clearance holes in back (1).

Glue and brad back, sides, top, and bottom together. To cut slots in shelves (4), clamp the two shelf pieces in a vise. Outline ¼-inch-wide slot at the center 2¾ inches deep. Cut out slots with a coping saw. Mark and cut ¼-inch-wide slots 2¾ inches deep in panel (5). Space slots 2¼ inches apart on center. Join two shelves (4) and division panel (5) together. Glue and brad shelf unit assembly into rack. Cut and plane drawer fronts (8) to size. Construct drawers (Fig. 2).

PARTS LIST

No.	Name	Quantity	Length	Width	Material
1	Back	1	7¼″	8″	¼″ plywood
2	Sides	2	6¾″	5½″	¼″ plywood
3	Top/bottom	2	8″	5½″	¼″ plywood
4	Shelves	2	7½″	5½″	¼″ plywood
5	Division panel	1	6¾″	5½″	¼″ plywood
6	Plastic boxes	6	5″ maximum	3⅝″ maximum	clear plastic
7	Box ends	6	See Fig. 2	—	½″ plywood
8	Drawer fronts	6	3⅝″	2″	pine*

Hardware: Six ⅝″ diam. brass knobs. White glue. Epoxy adhesive.
Note: *Cut from nominal 1 x 3 pine.

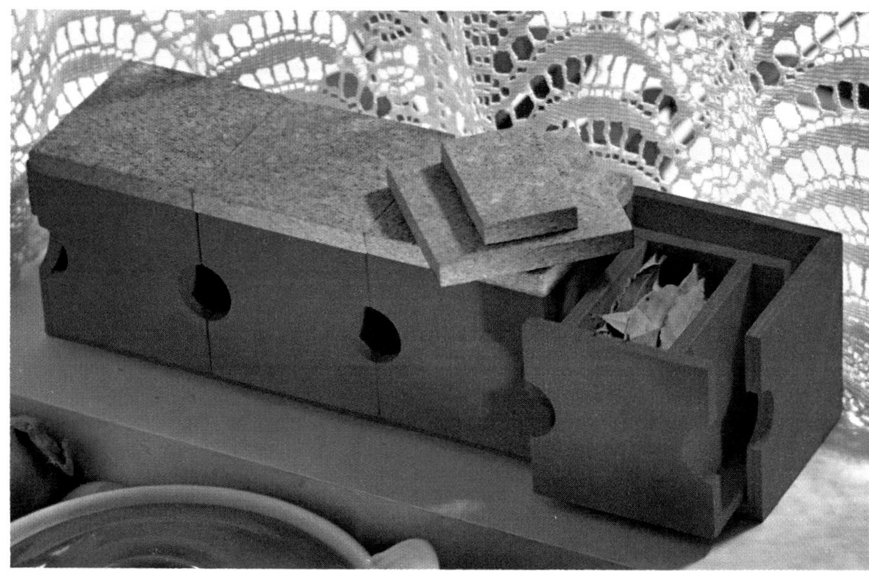

Plywood storage boxes have cork tops. Units can be wall or shelf mounted.

Rack and four storage boxes

CONSTRUCTION

Mark out on one length of plywood eight box fronts (1) allowing 1/16 inch for sawcut between them (Fig. 2).

Bore 1-inch-diameter holes at the center of each line.

Cut and plane box fronts, sides (2), and bottoms (3). Assemble boxes by fitting sides ½ inch from edges of box fronts. Glue and brad front and bottom to sides.

Lids can be cut out from cork sheeting as pictured or from plywood. Cut lid bottoms (4) so that they fit within the boxes. Cut lid tops (5) and glue to lid bottoms. When dry, put lids in position and sandpaper lid-top edges flush with box.

Mark out two rack sides (6) on one length of plywood. Allow 1/16 inch for saw-cut between them. Bore 1-inch-diameter hole at the center of each line.

Cut and plane sides, bottom (7), and back (8) of rack to size, then glue and brad them together.

If rack is to be hung on wall, drill screw clearance holes through the back (8).

Finish the box with a lead-free paint. If cork lids are used, they can be coated with a clear lacquer.

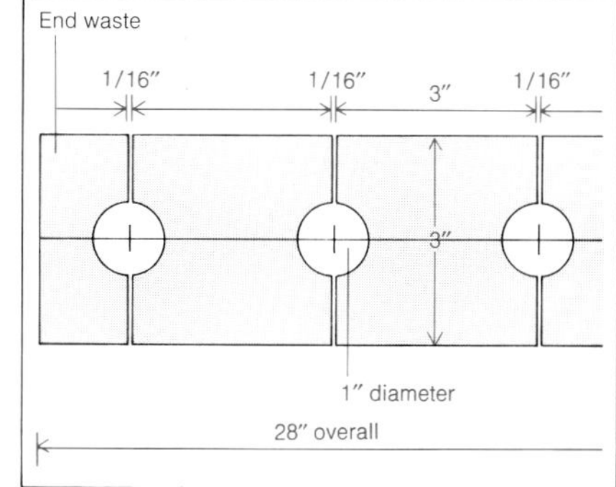

Fig. 2 Mark out box fronts on a single strip of plywood.

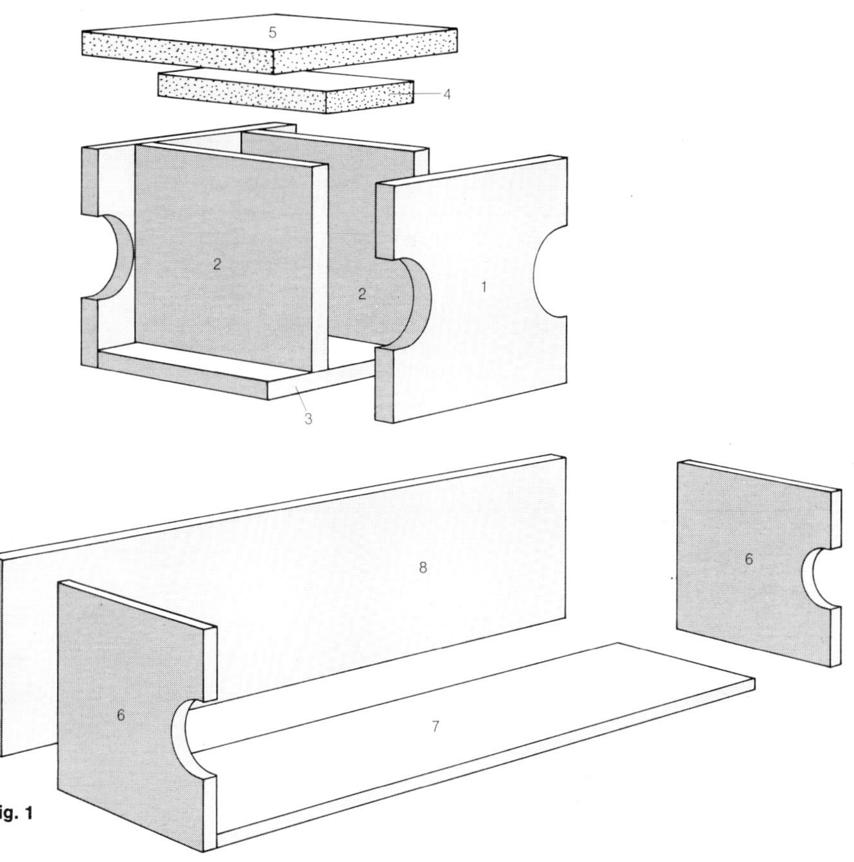

Fig. 1

PARTS LIST

No.	Name	Quantity	Length	Width	Material
1	Box fronts	8	3″	3″	¼″ plywood
2	Box sides	8	2½″	2¾″	¼″ plywood
3	Box bottoms	4	2½″	3″	¼″ plywood
4	Lid bottoms	4	2½″	1½″	⅜″ cork
5	Lid tops	4	3″	3″	⅜″ cork
6	Rack sides	2	3¼″	3″	¼″ plywood
7	Rack bottom	1	12 1/16″	2¾″	¼″ plywood
8	Rack back	1	12 1/16″	3¼″	¼″ plywood

Hardware: Screws—1¼″ No. 8 brass roundhead. White glue.
Note: Cut rack sides from one length of plywood at least 6½″ long.

Compact nine-bottle rack is a space-saver that looks well anywhere.

Wine rack

A rack for nine bottles of wine can be made from 16 lengths of $\frac{3}{8}$-inch dowel and 16 lengths of $1\frac{3}{8}$-inch closet pole dowel. The dimensions provided in this text are suitable for most wine bottles but can be modified to take other sizes.

A drill press or drill press stand for a portable power drill should be used to make certain that the holes bored in the closet pole dowel are perpendicular. Mark the location of the holes with a pencil and make an indentation with an awl so that the drill won't slip off the mark. Hold the work while drilling by resting it in a V-notch cut in scrap wood.

CONSTRUCTION

Cut 16 pieces of $1\frac{3}{8}$-inch closet pole, each 9 inches long. Cut 16 pieces of $\frac{3}{8}$-inch dowel, each 12 inches long.

For the simplest job, drill $\frac{3}{8}$-inch holes parallel to each other through all the closet pole sections on centers $1\frac{1}{16}$ inches from each end. Then drill a second set of holes at right angles to the first set. Locate the second set of holes on centers $\frac{9}{16}$ inch from each end. To assemble the rack, push the dowels through the holes to form the framework. Drive 1-inch finishing nails to pin the assembly as shown in Fig. 1. If you wish to conceal the dowel ends, drill holes only halfway through the outer posts.

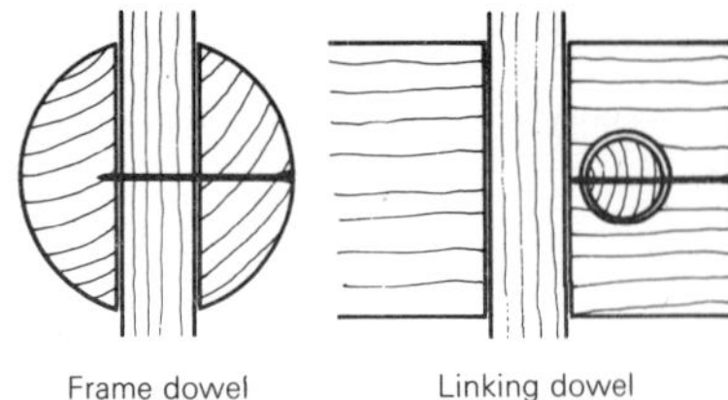

Fig. 1. Secure dowels with finishing nails.

Meat mallet

Mallet-head teeth are cut with triangular file, then smoothed by sanding.

The mallet head is a 4-inch length of 3 x 3 fir with all surfaces sanded to bring out the natural wood tone. On each end of the mallet use a triangular file to cut four parallel grooves $\frac{1}{4}$ inch deep at centers $\frac{1}{2}$ inch apart. File a second set of four grooves perpendicular to the first. Bore a 1-inch hole $1\frac{1}{2}$ inches deep on one side for the handle. The handle is a 1-inch dowel epoxy-glued to the head to withstand washing. A $\frac{3}{16}$-inch hole in the handle accommodates a rawhide thong for hanging the mallet.

Knife rack 1. Not all blades will stick to magnets. Test before building rack.

Knife rack 2. Hidden weatherstripping holds knives firm in simple five-piece rack.

Knife rack 3. Tilted mounting keeps knives from falling when placed between blocks.

Knife racks

Simple hand tools and a few pieces of scrap material make it easy to unclutter your kitchen with a choice from one of the simple, convenient designs on this page.

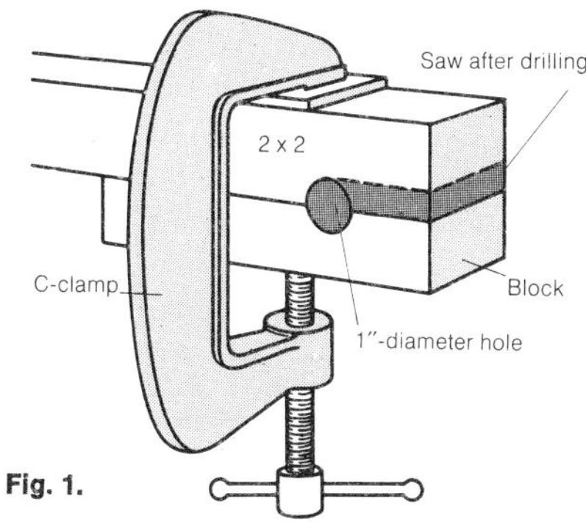

Fig. 1.

Knife rack 1

This is made from nominal 2 x 2 fir of a length suited to the number of knives. Ends are cut back for screws to hold the rack to the wall. To make the cutbacks, clamp a block to the 2 x 2 and bore a 1-inch hole through both the block and the 2 x 2 at their juncture; then saw the 2 x 2 back to the bored hole as shown in Fig. 1.

The knives are held in place by magnetic door catches. Choose the most suitable type available at your hardware store and attach them to the rack, leaving 2 inches between centers and 1⅜ inches at each end. Drill and countersink a screw hole at each end of the 2 x 2 and attach it to wall with two 2½-inch No. 10 screws.

Knife rack 2

As shown in Fig. 2, this rack consists of two 1½-inch-wide strips of ¼-inch plywood (1) long enough to hold the desired number of knives. Spacer blocks of ¼-inch plywood (2) at the ends of the strips provide the gap into which the knife blades fit. A strip of plastic weatherstripping (3), tacked to

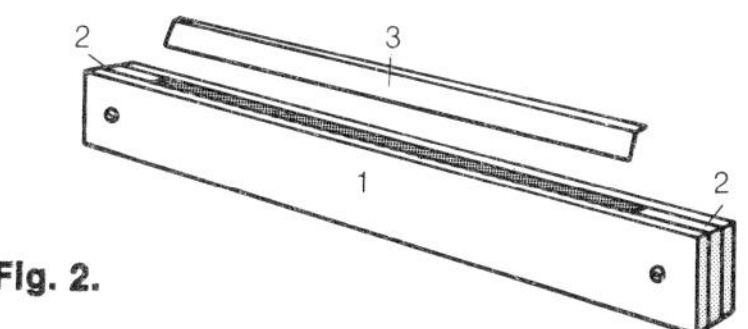

Fig. 2.

the inside of one of the strips, helps grip the blades. Attach to wall with either chromium-plated 2½-inch No. 10 roundhead screws or same size flathead screws with cups as shown.

Knife rack 3

This rack is made by gluing triangular wood blocks to a backboard of pine or spruce so that the knives hang between the blocks. The backboard may be ¾- x 4-inch plywood or solid stock. The blocks are cut from nominal 2 x 2 stock. Cut the 2 x 2 into 1½-inch lengths, then cut these in half diagonally. Plan the length of the rack by laying the blocks on the backboard in the positions they will occupy on the finished piece. Allow ⅛ inch between corners for blade thickness and leave 1½ inches at the ends for the mounting screws.

Cut the backboard to the desired length, clean up blocks and backboard with sandpaper and mount the blocks with a high-strength, water-resistant adhesive such as plastic resin glue (urea type) or resorcinol. Glue or tack a strip of felt weatherstripping to the bottom of the backboard so that the rack tips slighly inward to hold the knives. Spray-paint with a gloss enamel. Mount the rack with two roundhead chromium-plated 2½-inch No. 10 screws or same size flathead screws with cups.

These shakers are rosewood; walnut, mahogany, or other hardwoods could be used.

Salt and pepper shakers

Make handsome salt and pepper shakers of straight and clear wood that is free of knots and all other blemishes.

Cut wood for each shaker 2 inches long by $1\frac{5}{8}$ inches square. Mark top and bottom centers. With a drill press or a portable drill in a stand, drill a $1\frac{3}{8}$-inch hole $\frac{5}{16}$ inch deep in each bottom. Remark centers and drill a $\frac{7}{8}$-inch hole $1\frac{3}{4}$ inch deep (Fig. 1). Drill slowly to prevent overheating and possibly splitting wood.

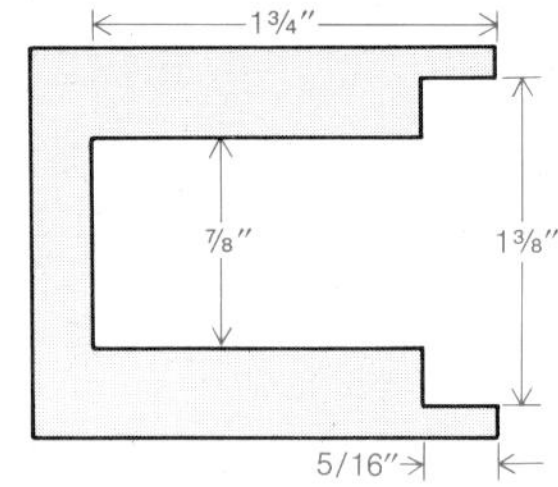

Fig. 1. Drilling out shaker insides.

Trace Fig. 2 design and transfer to a card or draw design on a card with compass at $\frac{3}{4}$-inch radius. Drill (and later countersink) seven $\frac{1}{16}$-inch holes through marks on card into salt shaker top, and a single $\frac{3}{64}$-inch hole in pepper shaker. Sand lightly to remove sharp edges. Plug bottoms with $1\frac{3}{8}$-inch corks.

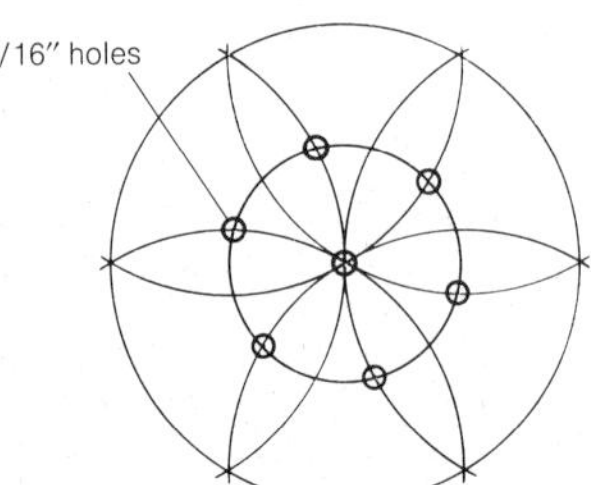

Fig. 2. Intersecting arcs produce this symmetrical pattern for the salt shaker's top holes.

Copper squares keep pots warmer longer.

Casserole stand/1

Cut $8\frac{1}{2}$-inch-square base from $\frac{1}{4}$-inch plywood. Cut four $8\frac{3}{4}$-inch lengths of $\frac{3}{8}$- x $\frac{1}{8}$-inch hardwood strip; miter ends.

Use white glue and brads to fasten the molding flush with the bottom of the base. Sink brad heads and fill the holes with wood putty; then wax molding and enamel the base bottom. Glue four $4\frac{1}{4}$-inch squares of copper flashing to the base.

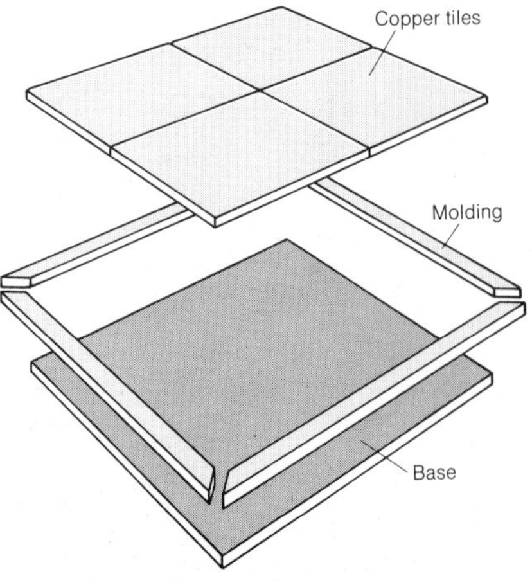

Fig. 3. Squares are glued to top of the base.

Joints for this stand's interlocking hardwood strips are all cut in one operation.

Casserole stand /2

Rich, dark woods such as rosewood, walnut, or mahogany are ideal for this attractive stand, as they will not show stains. Or use a light-colored wood and stain it dark.

The hardwood strips that form the stand are clamped together so that the half-lap joints can be cut in one operation. Each joint is cut with a circular saw as a series of grooves or with one pass of a router. Cut test grooves in spare strips first to make sure that finished strips will lock together.

Cut and plane ten hardwood pieces to 6¾- x 1- x ¼-inch size. Clamp together with C-clamps into a block; check with a try-square to make sure they all line up and are exactly square with the first piece.

Set a circular-saw blade to cut ½ inch deep; adjust fence to make first cut ¾ inch from the edge. Cut across the grain of the clamped strips. Adjust fence so that second cut widens the first. Continue adjusting fence and widening cut until a ¼-inch-wide groove is made or use a router to make the groove in a single pass. Continue until all grooves are cut. Solid areas between grooves should measure 1 inch, as shown in Fig. 5.

Make a trial fit. If strips fit well, disassemble, apply a dab of plastic resin glue to joints, reassemble, and

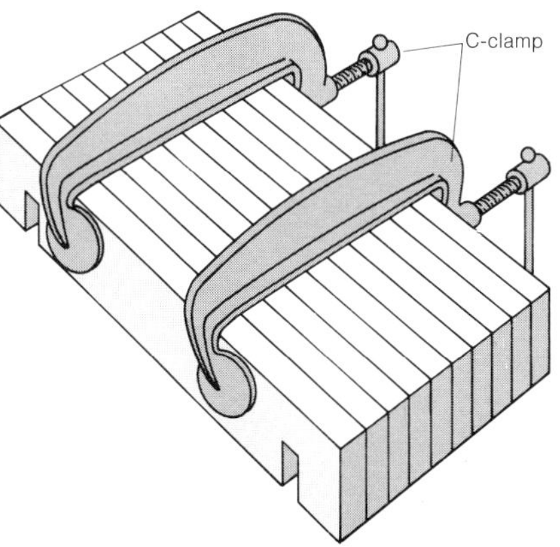

Fig. 4. Two C-clamps hold the ten strips together so all grooves can be cut at once.

leave overnight to dry. If strips are too loose, reassemble as before, with a drop of glue on each joint and drive a small brad into the underside of any loose joint. Sink brad head so that it won't scratch the tabletop. If the finished stand is wobbly, sand or plane the offending area until the stand rests securely on the table.

Sand corners of all projecting strips to a slight bevel to prevent splintering. Finish with two coats of varnish, clear lacquer, or a polyurethane finish.

With projects such as these casserole stands, it is almost as easy to

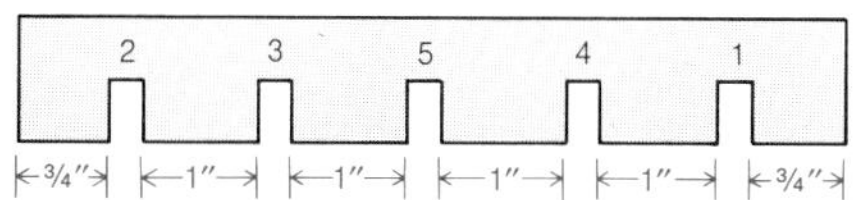

Fig. 5. Cutting order and spacing of grooves.

make several as it is to make one. No gift is nicer than something you have made; so while you're at it, think about making additional stands for your friends.

Unfinished maple is ideal for this stand.

Teapot stand

Make this rugged stand of hardwood. If you use hard maple, there will be no need to finish it, because maple can take considerable wear without a protective coat.

Plane a 5⅝- x 5⅝- x ¾-inch block square and flat. Set a circular-saw blade to cut 3/16 inch deep and lock the

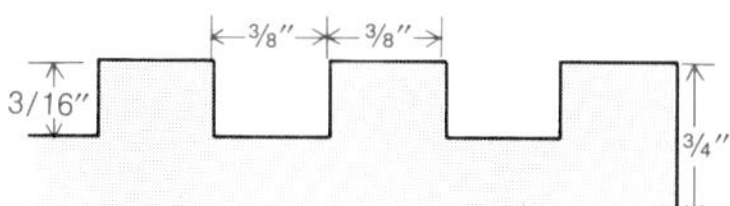

Fig. 6. Dimensions of stand grooves.

fence so that first cut—made across the grain—is ⅜ inch from edge, as shown in Fig. 6. Adjust fence to make the second groove ⅜ inch from the first. Continue adjusting fence and cutting until the block is covered with seven ⅜-inch-wide grooves ⅜ inch apart. Repeat along the grain to make a pattern of squares.

Finish with varnish, clear lacquer, or a polyurethane finish.

The unusual double candlestick shown at the left below is made from an ordinary 1½-inch-diameter plastic sink trap. The triple candlestick to its right consists of three wooden balls, each 2 inches in diameter (sold in toy stores), which are joined together with dowels and glue. U-shaped unit needs no finishing; triple unit is painted.

Double candlestick is cut from plastic sink trap.

Triple candlestick is made from three wooden balls.

Double candlestick

Use a hacksaw to cut the pipe into a U-shape, making sure that the cuts are straight and the tops level with each other. To flatten the base, cut away the base of the U as shown in Fig. 1—straight across from axis to axis of the vertical sections. Smooth cut edges with a file; remove burrs.

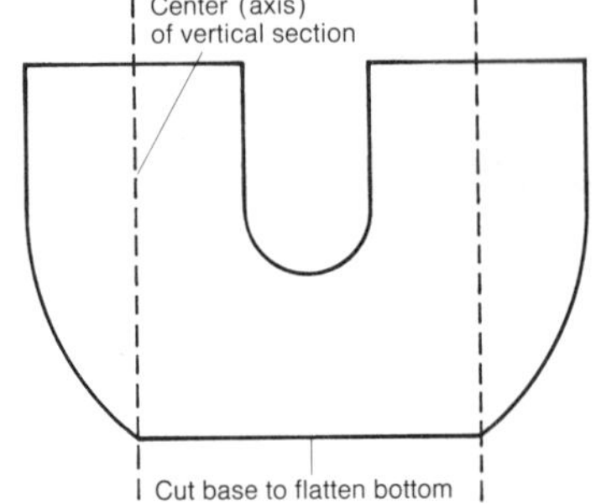

Fig. 1. Establishing cutting line for base.

Triple candlestick

Arrange the balls on a flat surface so that they touch. Mark the points of contact (use carbon paper or chalk); at each of these points drill a ¼-inch hole, 1 inch deep, along the radius. Cut three 2-inch lengths of ¼-inch dowel. Coat

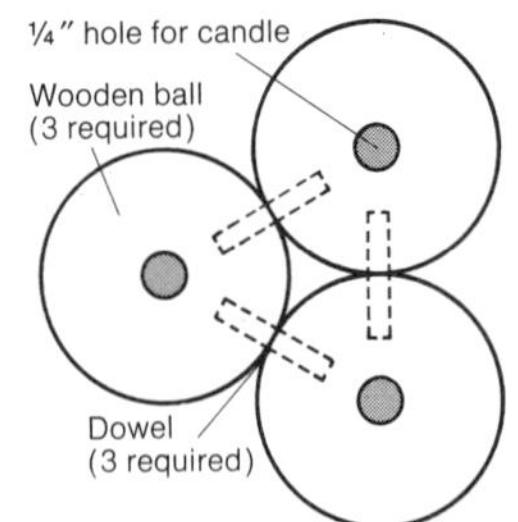

Fig. 2. Dowels hold balls together.

ends lightly with white glue, insert into holes, and push all three balls together at once. Drill a hole in the top of each to accept the candles you will use. To hold candlestick for painting, wedge a piece of dowel into one of the holes.

Adhesives 86
Cutting metal 422
Joints 393

Breakfast tray

Start by gluing and nailing the side strips (2) to the underside of the panel (1). Center strips so that they are ⅝ inch shorter than the panels at each end. Miter-cut end strips (3) at inner end, then glue and nail them to underside of the panel (Fig. 2). Next, miter the ends of the tray sides (4) and the tray ends (5). Cut a finger grip at each end (Fig. 1). Glue sides and ends so that they project ¾ inch above the upper surface. Fill the nail holes and paint the tray a color that harmonizes with your china. Finish tray by gluing sheet vinyl to bottom.

Leftover vinyl flooring is used for bottom of tray.

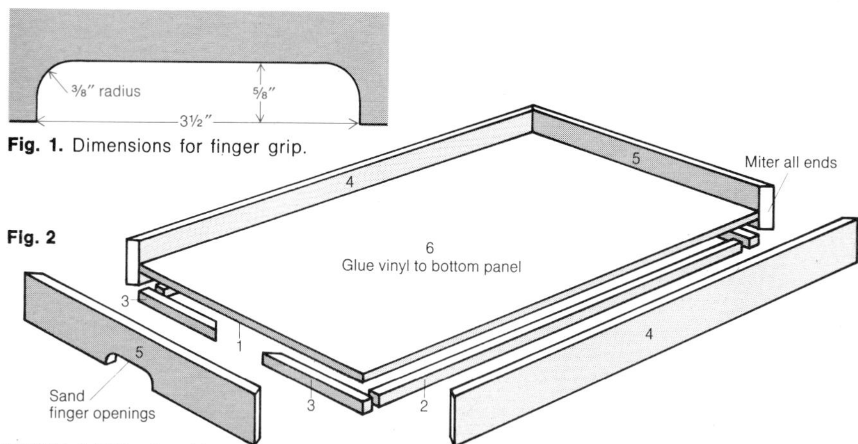

Fig. 1. Dimensions for finger grip.

Fig. 2

PARTS LIST Breakfast tray

No.	Name	Quantity	Nominal Size	Length	Width	Material
1	Panel	1		23	13	¼" plywood
2	Side strips	2	½" x ½" (cut)	22"		pine
3	End strips	4	½" x ½" (cut)	4¾"		pine
4	Tray sides	2	½ x 2	24"		pine
5	Tray ends	2	½ x 2	14"		pine
6	Panel lining	1		23¼"	13¼"	sheet vinyl floor covering

Note: When ordering materials, allow for waste and cutting.

Cork tiles line bottom of the tray.

Teatime tray

Cut tiles (2) slightly longer than 9 inches and glue to panel (1) at center line. With a razor blade, trim flush to panel edges. Miter moldings (3, 4) and screw to underside of panel with countersunk screws. Finish tiles and panel with clear polyurethane varnish. Glue felt pads to bottom.

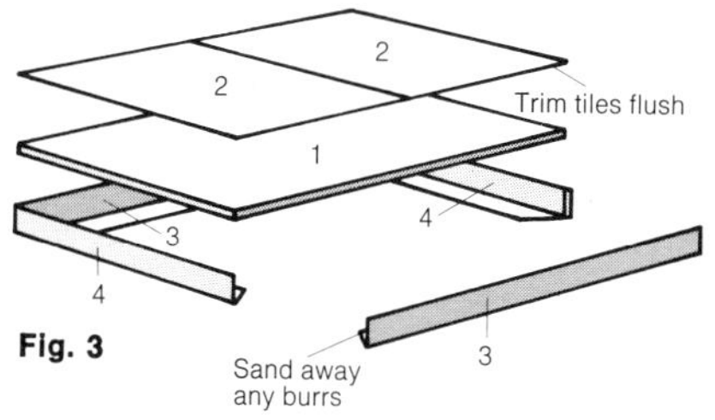

Fig. 3

PARTS LIST Teatime tray

No.	Name	Quantity	Length	Width	Material
1	Panel	1	18"	12"	¼" plywood
2	Tiles*	2	9"	12"	⅛"cork
3	Side molding	2	18¼"	1" (both lips)	⅛" aluminum angle
4	End molding	2	12¼"	1" (both lips)	⅛" aluminum angle

Note: *Buy two 12" x 12" cork tiles as specified and cut to 9" lengths.

Back panel ends part way down. Handy screw-in hooks in shelf and sides hold items.

Open Cupboard

Sides (1) of this handy kitchen shelf unit are dadoed to width of shelves (2, 3) and rabbeted for back (4). Shelves have 3/8- x 3/8-inch rabbets at ends to fit dadoes. Unit is attached to wall with 2½-inch No. 8 flathead screws driven into studs. Secure joints with white glue and 1½-inch finishing nails.

PARTS LIST

No.	Name	Quantity	Nominal Size	Length	Width	Material
1	Sides	2	1¼ x 8	24″		pine
2	Top/bottom shelves	2	1 x 6	20½″		pine
3	Middle shelves	2	1 x 4	20½″		pine
4	Back	1		20½″	10″	3/8″ plywood

Hardware: Six 2½″ No. 8 steel flathead screws. White glue. Finishing nails (1½″).
Note: Back runs only from top to bottom of lower narrow shelf, but it can run full length of unit.

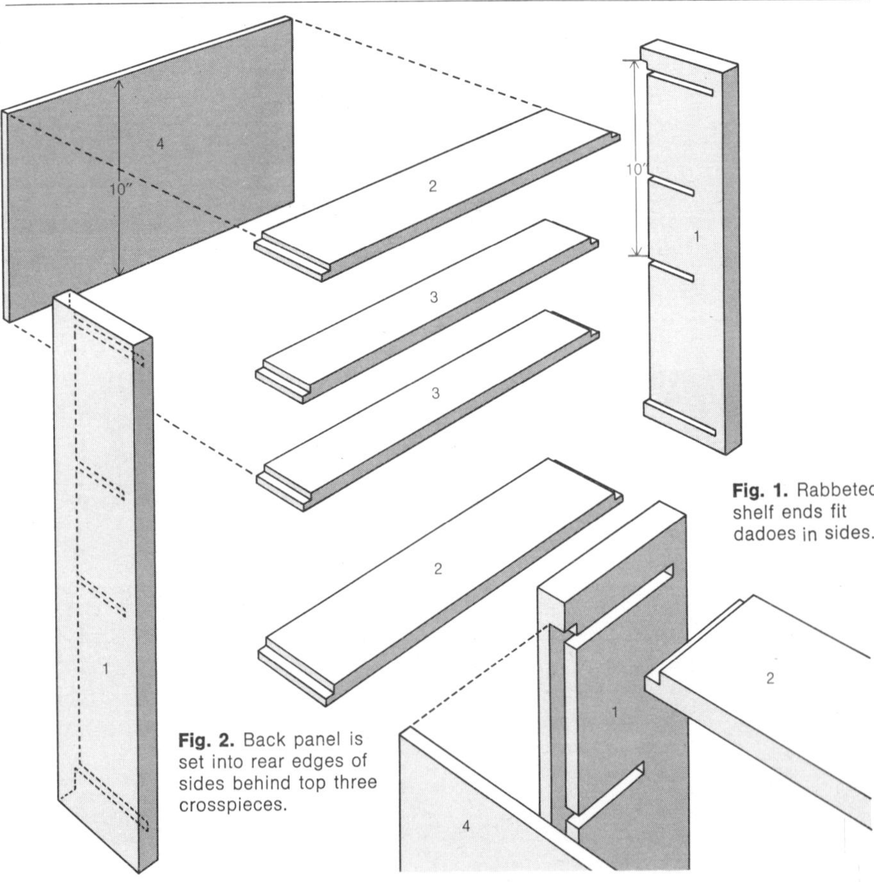

Fig. 1. Rabbeted shelf ends fit dadoes in sides.

Fig. 2. Back panel is set into rear edges of sides behind top three crosspieces.

Adhesives 86
Dado joints 386
Door catches 81
Door hinges 79
Junction box 260
Plastic panels 442
Shelving 548–549

Vanity Cabinet

Ideal for a powder room off a kitchen area, this cabinet has adjustable glass shelves and diffused lighting.

Cut ¼- x ¼-inch rabbets across ends of top shelf (1) to fit dadoes cut 5 inches from top edges of sides (2). Similar rabbets on bottom shelf and base (3) fit dadoes in sides located as desired. Drill holes in sides ½ inch in front of base for toothbrush rail. Assemble with glue and 1½-inch finishing nails; glue and nail back panel (5) and divider (6) in place. Attach door, mirror, light fixtures and diffuser as shown.

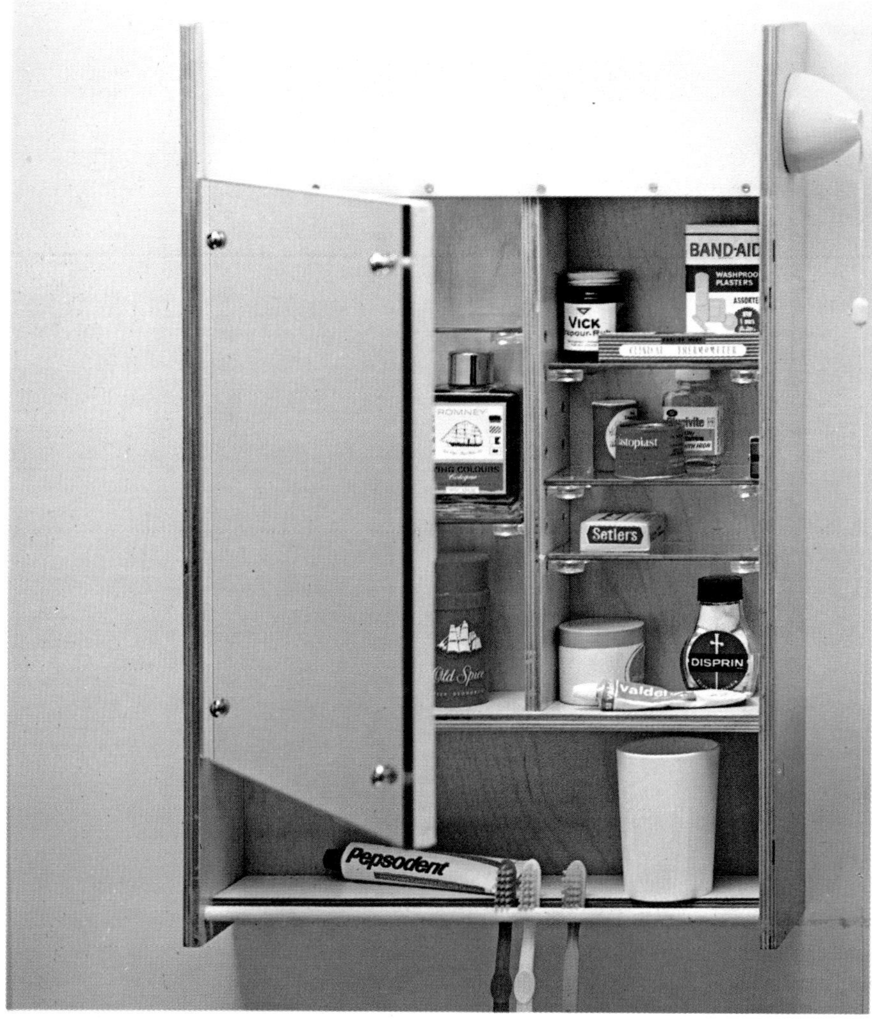

Door overhangs bottom shelf by several inches to provide grip for pulling it open.

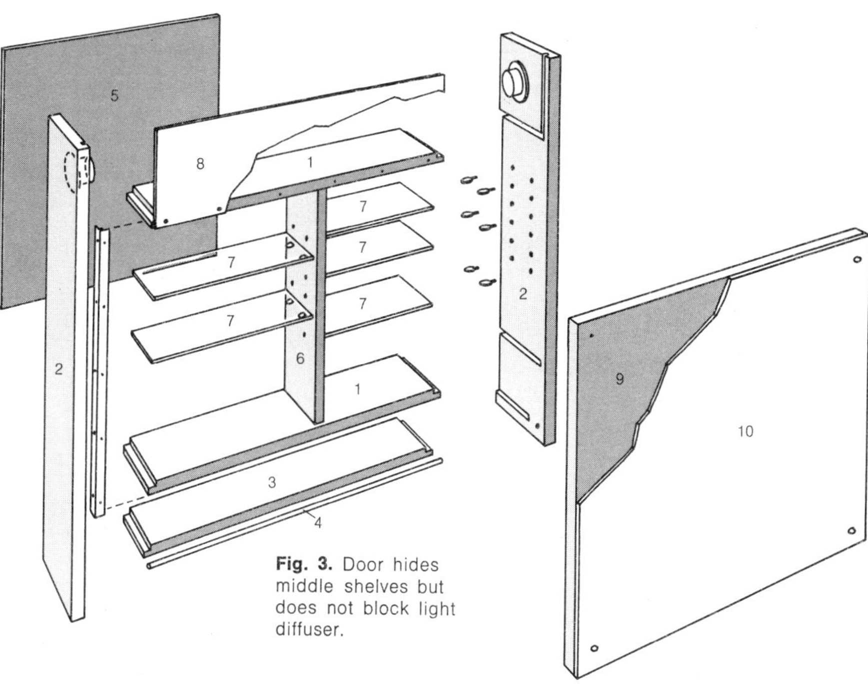

Fig. 3. Door hides middle shelves but does not block light diffuser.

PARTS LIST

No.	Name	Quantity	Length	Width	Material
1	Top/bottom shelves	2	15½″	3¼″	½″ plywood
2	Sides	2	24″	4″	½″ plywood
3	Base shelf	1	15½″	2¾″	½″ plywood
4	Toothbrush rail	1	16″		⅜″ dowel
5	Back panel	1	19½″	15½″	¼″ plywood
6	Divider	1	to suit	3″	½″ plywood
7	Intermediate shelves	to suit	7″	2¾″	¼″ glass
8	Light diffuser	1	15½″	5″	⅛″ frosted plastic
9	Door	1	15″	15″	½″ plywood
10	Mirror	1	15″	15″	¼″ glass

Hardware: Light: Two 3¼″ metal junction boxes, two 3½″ porcelain lamp receptacles to fit boxes, wire as needed, two 25-watt bulbs. **Door:** 15″ chrome piano hinge, screws to match, one magnetic catch, mirror glue from glass supplier or four mounting rosettes if mirror is drilled for screw mounting. **Cabinet:** White glue, ¼ lb. 1½″ finishing nails, four bracket clips for each glass shelf, six 2½″ No. 8 flathead screws (for mounting to wall through back).
Note: Have supplier cut, bevel, and polish edges of glass shelves and mirror, and drill mirror holes if you wish to screw-mount.

Furnishings for living areas: **Wall-fitted shelves/Mobile filing unit /1**

Roll filing cabinet out for access to files on top. The unit provides drawers on one side and storage space on the other.

Adhesives 86
Bench saw 60
Doweling 395, 397
Hacksaw 19
Half-lap joints 385
Linoleum 117
Locating studs 76
Making grooves 54
Rabbeting 392
Rabbet plane 30

Wall-fitted shelves

This built-in desk unit, designed to fit into an alcove, can be adapted to a straight wall.

Nail desk support cleats (1–4) through wall into studs. Drill blocks (5) for 2-inch No. 8 flathead screws to be driven up into desk. Fasten blocks to cleats, spaced a foot apart, with 2½-inch roundhead screws. Glue desk top (6) and extension (7) on cleats and drive screws in from below. Cover with linoleum, trim carefully, and fasten reinforcing strip (8) to edge flush with linoleum, with glued tongue and groove (Fig. 2.) or with glue and nails 4 inches apart.

Drill uprights (9) for No. 6 flathead screws 6 inches apart and mount on alcove walls from desk top to ceiling. Hacksaw shelf standards to upright length and screw on. Be sure bracket holes in standards are level. Notch shelf (10) corners to fit between uprights. Cover shelves with linoleum, rest on brackets in standards, and glue and nail reinforcing strips (11) to front edges. Before finishing, lightly sand all edges.

PARTS LIST

No.	Name	Quantity	Nominal Size	Length	Width	Material
1	Cleat	1	1 × 2	alcove length		pine
2	Cleat	1	1 × 2		alcove width	pine
3	Cleat	1	1 × 2		projection-side width	pine
4	Cleat	1	1 × 2	projection-front length		pine
5	Blocks	as needed	2 × 2	3″		fir
6	Desk top	1		alcove length	projection-side width	¾″ particle board
7	Desk extension	1		projection-front length	10″	¾″ particle board
8	Desk edge strip	1	1¼ × 3	desk length		pine
9	Uprights	4	¾ × ¾	desk-ceiling ht.		pine
10	Shelves	3		alcove length	9″	¾″ particle board
11	Shelf edge strips	3	1¼ × 2	shelf length		pine
12	Light diffuser	1		shelf length	4½″	⅛″ opal glass
13	Sliding doors	2		½ shelf length + 1″	12″	⅛″ hardboard
14	Door stiffener	1	1 × ½	12″		pine

Hardware: Four metal shelf standards, 12 matching clips or brackets. Two alcove-long lengths of sliding-door track for ⅛″ hardboard. For three 12″ door handles: 36″ length of ¾″ x ¾″ x ⅛″ aluminum angle; or 36″ length of ¾″ x ¾″ pine. Linoleum or plastic laminate. Finishing nails (2½″) for edging strips. Common nails (2½″). Flathead screws—2″ No. 8, 1½″ No. 6.

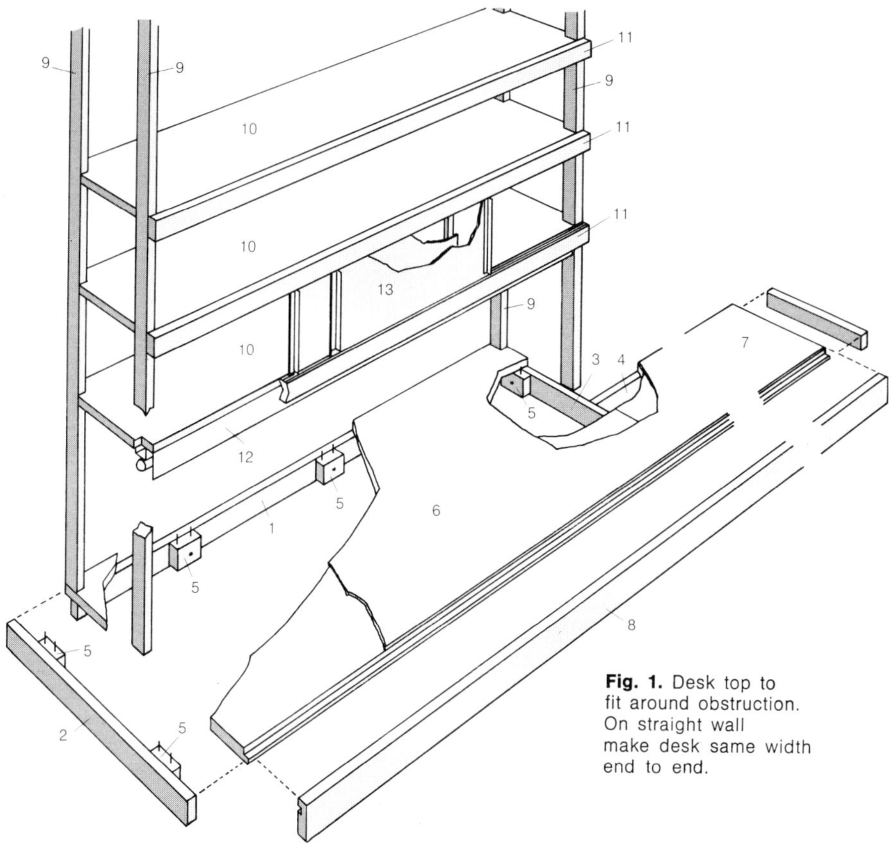

Fig. 1. Desk top to fit around obstruction. On straight wall make desk same width end to end.

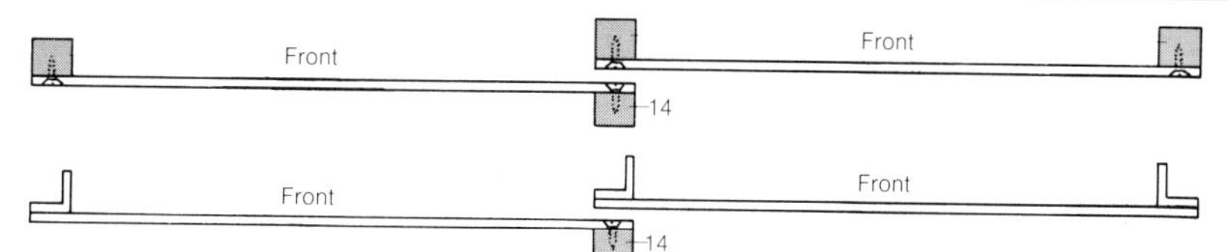

Fig. 2. Wood (top) or aluminum (bottom) door handles can be used on cabinet doors (13). Stiffener (14) supports door.

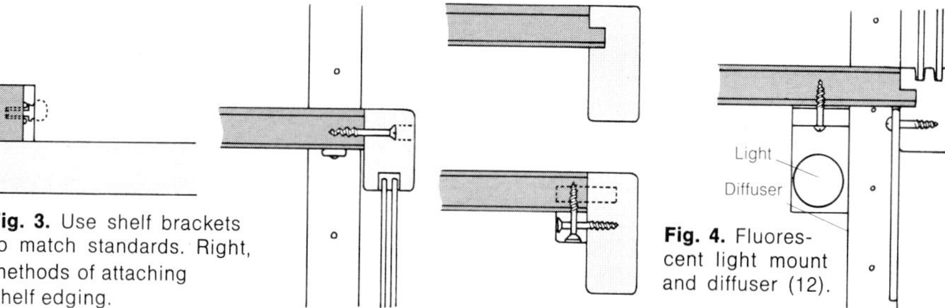

Fig. 3. Use shelf brackets to match standards. Right, methods of attaching shelf edging.

Fig. 4. Fluorescent light mount and diffuser (12).

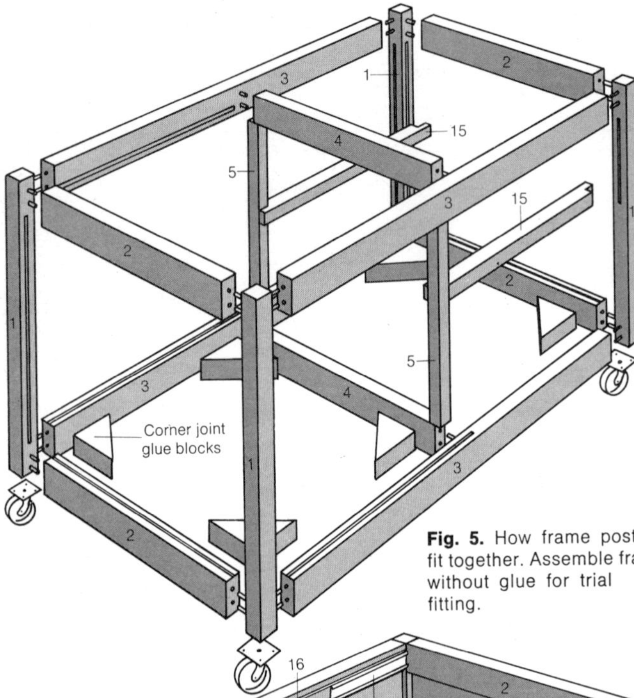

Fig. 5. How frame posts and rails fit together. Assemble frame without glue for trial fitting.

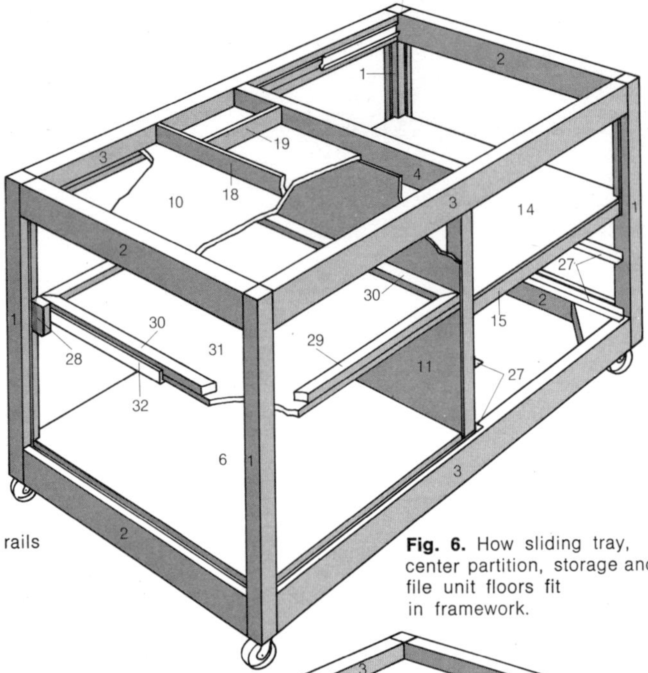

Fig. 6. How sliding tray, center partition, storage and file unit floors fit in framework.

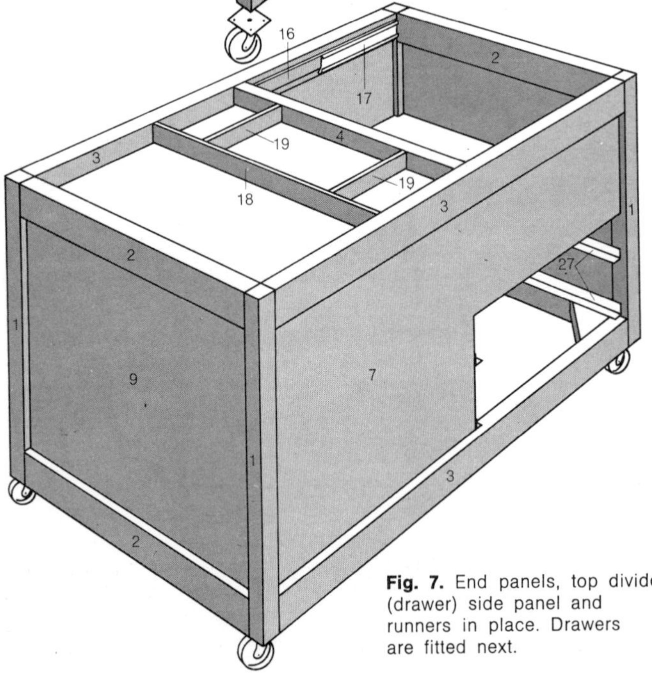

Fig. 7. End panels, top dividers, (drawer) side panel and runners in place. Drawers are fitted next.

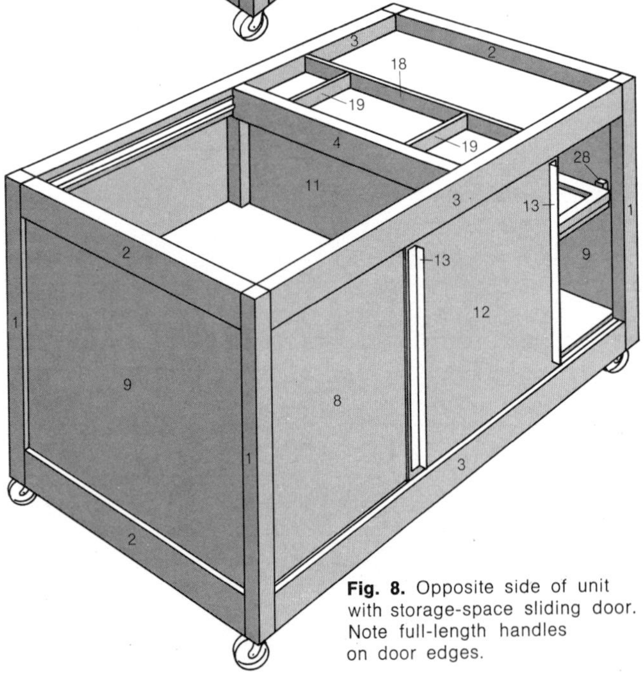

Fig. 8. Opposite side of unit with storage-space sliding door. Note full-length handles on door edges.

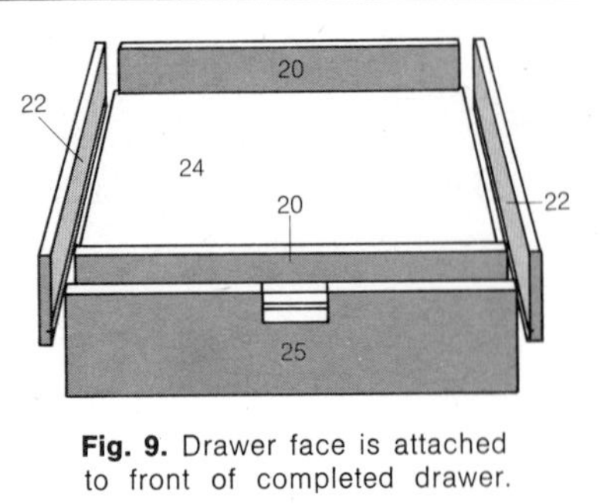

Fig. 9. Drawer face is attached to front of completed drawer.

Shelf light and cabinet

For typing clearance and space for the optional fluorescent light and diffuser shown in Fig. 4, the bottom shelf should be about 20 inches above the desk. This shelf is the sliding-door cabinet bottom; the next shelf, placed 1 foot higher, is the top. Cut sliding-door tracks to length with a hacksaw. Surface-mount with brads or recess atop bottom shelf edging strip and beneath second shelf strip. Trim doors for easy sliding, attach three handles, Fig. 2, and screw wood stiffener to back of handleless door edge.

Mobile filing unit

This handy rolling unit is vertically divided in two. One side has an open-top file and two drawers underneath. The other side is general storage space, with an optional sliding tray. Drawers open on one long side; storage-space door slides open on opposite side. Top dividers hold paper clips and pencils.

Framework and panels

Cut corner posts (1) and other frame parts and drill holes for the ⅜-inch-diameter dowels that will join them; use a doweling jig or dowel points to align the holes. If you don't mind visible dowel ends, drill through corner

Adhesives 86
Bench saw 60
Doweling 395, 397
Hacksaw 19
Half-lap joints 385
Linoleum 117
Locating studs 76
Making grooves 54
Rabbeting 392
Rabbet plane 30

PARTS LIST

No.	Name	Quantity	Nominal size	Length	Width	Material
Framework and panels						
1	Corner posts	4	2 × 2	1′ 11″		fir
2	End rails	4	2 × 3	1′ 4″		fir
3	Side rails	4	2 × 3	3′ 7½″		fir
4	Cross rails	2	2 × 3	1′ 4″		fir
5	Center posts	2	2 × 2	1′ 6″		fir
6	Storage-space floor	1		1′ 9″	1′ 4″	½″ plywood
7	Side panel (drawer)	1		3′ 8″	1′ 6½″	⅛″ hardboard
8	Side panel (storage)	1		1′ 11½″	1′ 6½″	⅛″ hardboard
9	End panels	2		1′ 6½″	1′ 4½″	⅛″ hardboard
10	Storage-space top	1		1′ 9½″	1′ 4½″	¼″ plywood
11	Partition panel	1		1′ 7½″	1′ 5″	¼″ plywood
Fittings						
12	Sliding-door panel	1		1′ 10″	1′ 6½″	⅛″ hardboard
13	Door handles	2	¾ × ¾	1′ 5″		⅛″ aluminum angle
14	File compartment floor	1		1′ 11″	1′ 5″	¼″ plywood
15	File compartment rails	2	2 × 2	1′ 9½″		fir
16	File folder rails	2		1′ 8¾″	¾″	⅛″ aluminum strip
17	File rail spacers	2	½ × ¼	1′ 8¾″		pine
18	Storage-top divider	1		1′ 4″	2″	½″ plywood
19	Storage-top dividers	2		9½″	2″	½″ plywood
Drawers						
20	Upper drawer ends	2		1′ 7½″	3¾″	½″ pine
21	Lower drawer ends	2 (not shown)		1′ 7½″	4¼″	½″ pine
22	Upper drawer sides	2		1′ 4¼″	3¾″	½″ pine
23	Lower drawer sides	2 (not shown)		1′ 4¼″	4¼″	½″ pine
24	Drawer bottoms	2		1′ 8″	1′ 3¾″	¼″ plywood
25	Upper drawer face	1		1′ 8⅝″	4½″	½″ pine
26	Lower drawer face	1 (not shown)		1′ 8⅝″	4⅜″	½″ pine
27	Drawer runners	4	¾ × ¾	1′ 5″		⅛″ aluminum angle
28	Spacer glue blocks	as needed	¾ × ¾			pine
29	Tray rim sides	2	½ × ½	1′ 4½″		pine
30	Tray rim ends	2	½ × ½	1′ 8½″		pine
31	Tray bottom	1		1′ 8½″	1′ 4½″	½″ plywood
32	Tray supports	2	¾ × ¾	1′ 4½″		⅛″ aluminum angle

Hardware: Four ball-type plate-top casters and ¾″ roundhead screws to match. Screws—1½″ No. 6 flathead, 1½″ No. 8 roundhead, 1″ No. 8 flathead, ½″ No. 6 flathead. One box ¾″ brads. Approx. 6′ of ⅜″-dia. maple dowel. Two by six fir for glue blocks. Plastic resin glue.

posts into end (2) and side (3) rails to align holes automatically. Dowels will simply be pushed in from outside, trimmed off flush, and sanded smooth to resemble decorative pegs. Drill through side rails into cross rails (4) the same way. At corners with two sets of dowels, stagger crossing holes so that they don't intersect. Center posts (5) sit inside side rails, fitting between (and doweled to) top and bottom cross rails.

With a bench saw or rabbet plane, make centered grooves ⅛ inch wide by ¼ inch deep for the frame panels on the tops of all bottom rails, bottoms of all top rails, and inner edges of corner posts. For storage-space top and center partition, make grooves ¼ inch wide. Do not make groove on half of bottom side rail on drawer opening side where there will be no panel. On storage-space opening side make grooves for panel only halfway across (covering file-drawers side), but cut parallel outer grooves for sliding door full length of rails. Cut top door groove 1 inch deep so that door can be inserted after frame is complete.

Reinforce corner joints of frame bottom with wedge-shaped glue blocks cut from 2 x 6 fir, set ½ inch below tops of bottom rails. Drill holes through blocks into rails, toward block centers so that 1½-inch No. 8 roundhead screws used in final assembly will hold blocks securely.

Storage-space floor (6) is screwed on glue blocks with 1-inch No. 8 flathead screws. Side panels (7, 8), end panels (9), storage-space top (10), and partition panel (11) fit in frame grooves. Assemble the frame and panels without glue to check the fit, then glue together.

Sliding door (12) for storage space has handle (13) at each side.

Interior fittings and finishing

Filing compartment floor (14) rests on rails (15) from corner posts to center posts. Dowel rails to center posts and rabbet other ends ½ inch deep to half-lap corner posts but stop short of the end-panel grooves. Glue rails and attach floor with glue and 1½-inch No. 6 flathead screws. Files slide on aluminum rails (16) glued to spacers (17) attached to the side rails.

Drawer ends (20, 21) and sides (22, 23) are grooved ¼ inch deep ¼ inch above the bottom edges to take drawer bottoms (24). Glue on drawer faces (25, 26), slightly larger than front ends, and also screw on fronts from within drawers. Drawer pulls can be leather, as shown, or as desired. Drawers slide on aluminum angle runners (27) glued to corner post (1). Use epoxy adhesive. If drawers are to contain heavy items, reinforce the glue joint with ¾ inch No. 4 screws countersunk into the aluminum angle.

Sides (29) and ends (30) of optional sliding tray are simply glued and nailed flush to bottom (31). Set support (32) at desired height in storage space, attached at back to corner and center posts and at front to glue blocks (28) glued and screwed to side and partition panels to be clear of the sliding door.

Glue and nail storage-top dividers (18, 19) to top. Screw four ball-type plate-top casters to bottom glue blocks with ¾-inch roundhead screws sized to match plate holes. Paint panels to match linoleum color on desks and shelves; coat wooden frame with clear polyurethane varnish.

Staining of the frame is optional. However, if you use a stain, sand after 24 hours to remove raised wood fibers. Then finish with two coats of polyurethane varnish; apply the second coat after 24 hours.

This matched set of furniture, with sleek modern lines, is easily constructed. One basic unit serves as table, plant container, or chair underframe and, with modifications, as underframe for the four-seat sofa. Pine frames can be given a clear finish or stained dark, and the choice of upholstery fabric is almost limitless. The tabletop can be thick glass, marble, or plywood or particle board painted or surfaced with a plastic laminate such as Formica or Micarta. (Use contact cement to apply the laminate.)

Table underframe

This table can be varied in size to suit available space by cutting its frame rails shorter or longer. Using longer rails and legs, you could even build a dining table.

Bevel one edge of each leg (1) so that leg halves can be miter-joined. The miter can be tongued and glued, as shown in Fig. 1 detail, or simply glued with plastic resin glue. Finishing nails hold leg halves together while the glue dries.

To cut lap joints in frame, set leg against side rail (2) and mark for ¾-inch-deep lap cut, leaving a ⅜-inch-thick lap at back of rail. Hold leg in side rail lap, butt front rail (3) up against inside surface of side rail, and mark front rail for lap cut. The resulting joint structure is shown in two views in Fig. 1. Legs are attached to rails with mortise and tenon joints or with three evenly spaced 2- x ¼-inch dowels (drill ¼-inch holes). Drill and countersink ⅛-inch-diameter pilot holes through laps into legs.

Assemble legs and side rails, then slip front and back rails in place, gluing all meeting surfaces and dowels. Fasten laps to legs with ¾-inch No. 8 flathead screws.

Plant container

Cut ¼-inch exterior plywood to exact size of table frame top. Place plywood on floor, stand frame on it, and trace legs; cut away traced areas. Bevel plywood edges, attach to bottom of frame rails with plastic resin glue, and 1-inch galvanized nails. For extra waterproofing, line plant box with fiberglass or soldered copper flashing. The best way to make a copper tray for the plant container is to line the inside with light cardboard, cut to fit the bottom and sides. Place the cardboard over a sheet of copper and use it as a pattern for cutting and bending. Use lightweight plastic flower troughs no higher than 3 inches. If pots are heavier, substitute ¾-inch plywood for bottom and additionally secure to frame with four or eight 1-inch angle irons and ½-inch flathead screws to match.

Chair underframe

Adding a base for the back unit converts the table underframe into a chair underframe, as shown in Fig. 2. The central rail (4) and mounting plates (5) must be installed before the final side rail.

Cut a ½-inch-long tenon ½ inch thick across the bottom of each mounting plate end. Cut matching mortises in central and back rails so that mounting plate tops will be flush with rail tops, and the gap between rails 5⅝ inches. To join central rail to sides, cut two tenons ¾ inch long and ½ inch thick at each end of central rail, centered on width. Cut mortises to match in side rails. Assemble like table underframe with plastic resin glue.

Sloping seats and backs make this sofa and chair especially comfortable.

Bending metal, soldering, 431–432
Dowels 394, 397
Lap joints 385, 392
Miter joints 393
Mortise and tenon joints 387
Upholstery 204–205

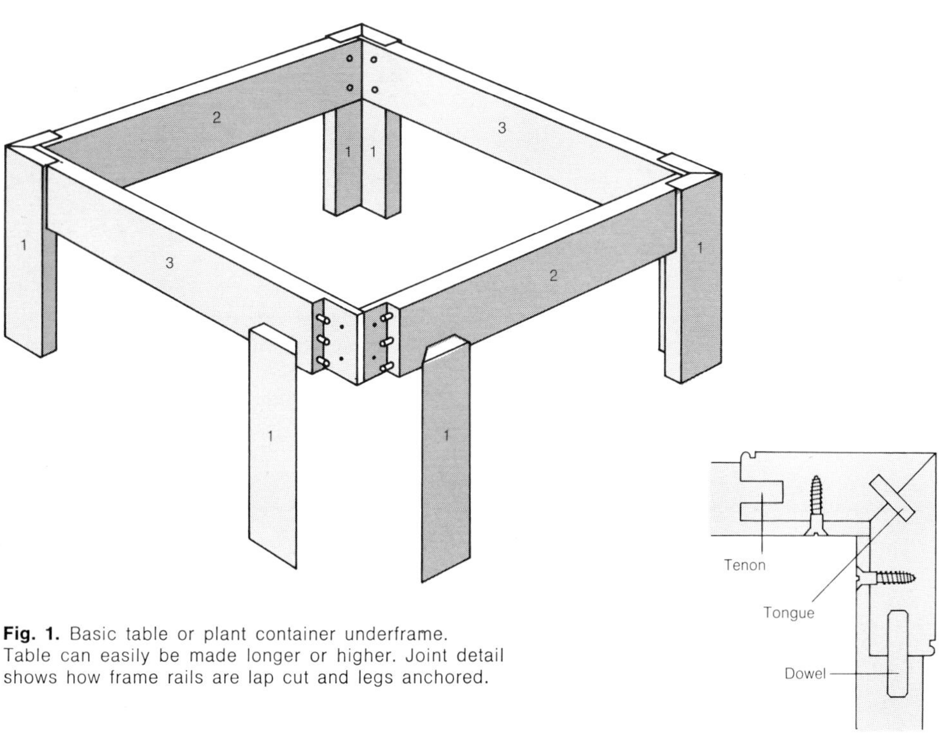

Fig. 1. Basic table or plant container underframe. Table can easily be made longer or higher. Joint detail shows how frame rails are lap cut and legs anchored.

Chair has generous proportions and resilient foam padding over webbing.

PARTS LIST

No.	Name	Quantity	Nominal Size	Length	Width	Material
Table underframe						
1	Legs	8	1¼ × 4	10″		pine
2	Side rails	2	1¼ × 4	27⅛″		pine
3	Front/back rails	2	1¼ × 4	25⅝″		pine
Chair underframe						
1	Legs	8	1¼ × 4	10″		pine
2	Side rails	2	1¼ × 4	27⅛″		pine
3	Front/back rails	2	1¼ × 4	25⅝″		pine
4	Central rail	1	1¼ × 4	27⅛″		pine
5	Mounting plates	2	1¼ × 4	6⅝″		pine

Hardware: For each underframe, eight ¾-inch No. 8 flathead screws and plastic resin glue.
Note: For optional plant container, ¼″ exterior plywood 27⅛″ × 25⅝″; 1″ galvanized nails; fiberglass or copper flashing for lining if desired. For stronger bottom, ¾″ exterior plywood 27⅛″ × 25⅝″; four or eight 1″ angle irons; ½-inch flathead screws to match.

No.	Name	Quantity	Nominal Size	Length	Width	Material
Low arm unit						
6	Ends	2 (not shown)	1 × 4	8¼″		pine
7	Tops/bottoms	2	1 × 4	30¼″		pine
8	Corner blocks	4	2 × 2	3½″		fir
9	Inner panel	1 (not shown)		30¾″	11¾″	⅛″ hardboard
10	Outer panel	1 (not shown)		30¾	8¼″	⅛″ hardboard
Back unit						
11	Side panels	2		14″	7⅞″	¾″ pine
12	Top rail	1	2 × 2	21″		fir
13	Bottom panel	1		20¼″	7⅞″	¾″ pine
14	Corner blocks	2	2 × 2	7″		fir
15	Back panel	1		21″	15″	⅛″ hardboard

Hardware: Arm: 3″ angle iron; two ¾″ No. 8 flathead screws; plastic resin glue; 1½″ finishing nails; four 2½″ No. 8 flathead screws (to attach to frame). **Back:** Plastic resin glue; 1½″ finishing nails; 1″ common nails; four 2½″ No. 8 flathead screws (to attach to frame).

Low arm unit

Low arms can be used for chair or sofa. Prepare a base by screwing 3-inch angle iron to front corner of frame flush with top (Fig. 2).

Make ½-inch-deep lap cut ¾ inch long at each end of arm end (6). Set top and bottom (7) between laps, assemble with plastic resin glue and 1½-inch finishing nails, adding corner blocks (8). Notch inner hardboard panel (9) to fit between underframe rails, then attach it and outer panel (10) with glue and 1-inch common nails.

After upholstering, lock arms to underframe. Drive four 2½-inch No. 8 flathead screws through corner angles at front and mounting plates at rear (drill and countersink ⅛-inch pilot holes) into arm bottoms. Use corner angles with countersunk openings.

Back unit

Taper side panels (11) from 7⅞ to 1½ inches wide. Make lap cuts ¾ inch deep by ¾ inch wide in top rail (12) ends and ¾ inch deep by ⅜ inch wide at bottoms of side panels. Set bottom panel (13) between sides; set sides up against top rail laps. Plane front edges of top rail and bottom panel to angle of sides. Assemble with plastic resin glue and 1½-inch finishing nails, adding corner blocks (14). Glue and nail on back panel (15) with 1-inch common nails.

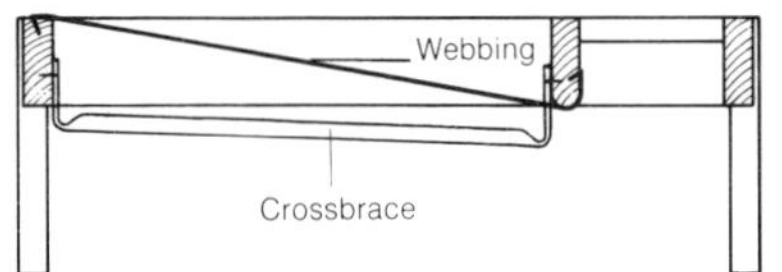

Fig. 3. Side view of webbing, brace.

After webbing and upholstering, lock back unit to underframe, overhanging back rail by ¾ inch. Drive four 2½-inch No. 8 flathead screws up through mounting plates (drill and countersink ⅛-inch pilot holes) into bottom panel.

Sofa underframe

The sofa is simply an elongation of the chair. Front and back (3A) and central (4A) rails are longer and five mounting plates are used, but joints and assembly are identical.

Cut a ¼-inch outer lap and ⅜-inch centered tenon in center legs (16), as shown in Fig. 6, and matching mortises in front and back rails. Glue center legs to rails.

Make three evenly spaced cross braces between front and central rails from ½-inch thin-walled metal electrical conduit. Hammer 2 inches flat at ends, bend up and drill a clearance hole in each end for ¾-inch No. 8 roundhead screws. Hang braces so that tubular part is 1 inch below front rail, 1½ inches below central rail.

High arm unit

High arm construction and fastening to underframe are the same as for low arm. For extra strength, keyhole and screw assembly locks high arm to back. In upper back corner of arm substitute joining block (17) for corner block. Be sure to make left- and right-hand units. A 1¼-inch No. 10 roundhead screw in joining block locks into a keyhole plate on back unit side (Fig. 4). Try keyhole plate in position to ensure that screw head can be inserted through large hole and moved into narrow slot. Then screw keyhole plate to back side and drill hole for arm-unit screw. Hole in keyhole plate can be enlarged with a rattail file if necessary.

Sofa back units

Sofa backs, each identical to chair back, are screwed to underframe mounting plates, locked to high arms by keyhole/screw, and joined together by 1½ x ¾-inch-diameter dowels glued into matching holes drilled into the sides of adjacent back units.

Upholstery—webbing

On chair or sofa underframe stretch jute or rubber webbing strips, spaced ¼ inch apart, from front rail top to central rail bottom, and tack. On back unit stretch webbing over top rail and tack under bottom panel front. Crossweave added webbing and tack strips to side panels.

Upholstery—back and arm units

Cut 4- or 5-inch-thick polyurethane foam for top and front of back unit and ½-inch foam for back panel. Tack down upholstery fabric under back bottom, draw up taut over top rail and down to tack under bottom front. Overlap about ¾ inch onto side panels and tack as in Fig. 4. Fold fabric into short overlaps to lie flat at corners. Practice such tricky jobs first with muslin.

Next to a low arm a back unit needs a side pad. Cut ½-inch foam to fit, cover with fabric, and sew to tacked-down back unit cover.

Cover arm unit with ½-inch foam pulled over top, sides, and ends and tacked on bottom. Sew fabric into pullover case, continuous over top and sides with sewn-in end panels. Pull case over arm unit and tack under bottom. For high arm, cut out hole for keyhole-screw head.

Make sure that arm and back units are same height, adjusting with extra-thin foam layers if necessary. Polyurethane foam slabs are available in most large department stores.

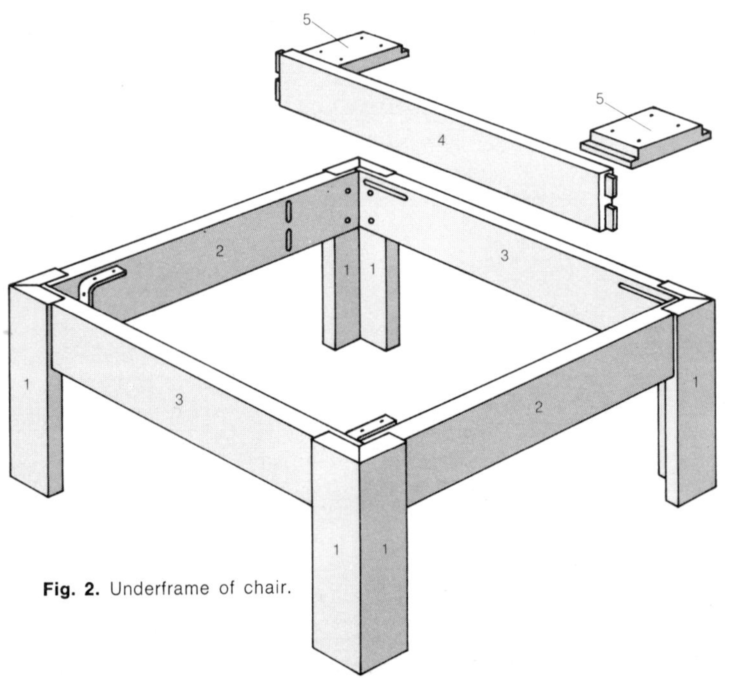

Fig. 2. Underframe of chair.

Bending metal, soldering, 431–432
Dowels 394
Lap joints 385, 392
Miter joints 397
Mortise and tenon joints 387
Upholstery 204–205

Upholstery—seat cushions
Each seat cushion matches back unit in width. Cut 5-inch foam slightly oversize so that cushion will fit snugly at sides and overlap front rail about 2 inches. Wrap fabric around top and sides, fold underneath, and pin. Remove foam to machine-sew front and side seams. Reinsert foam through open rear seam and sew seam closed by hand. For extra strength, use transparent nylon thread. Knot thread at finish to prevent unraveling.

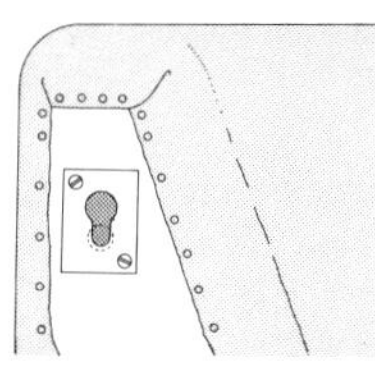

Fig. 4. Keyhole plate in back unit locks arm in place. Tacks secure folded-in fabric edge.

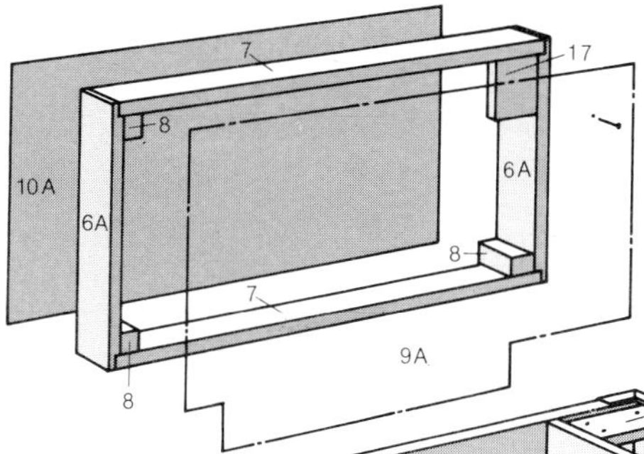

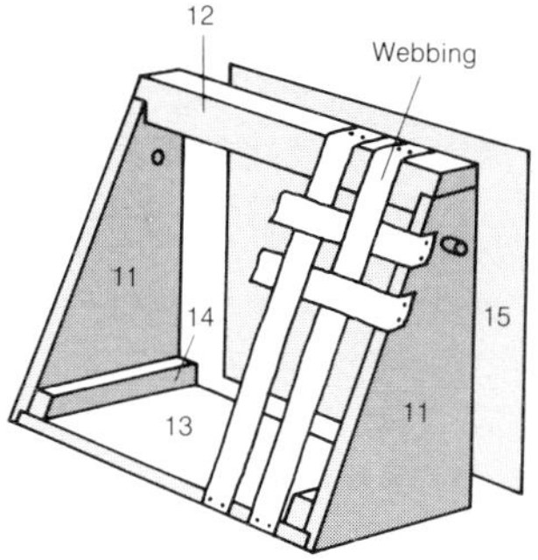

Fig. 5. Back units are linked by dowels. Interlaced webbing provides firm, flexible support.

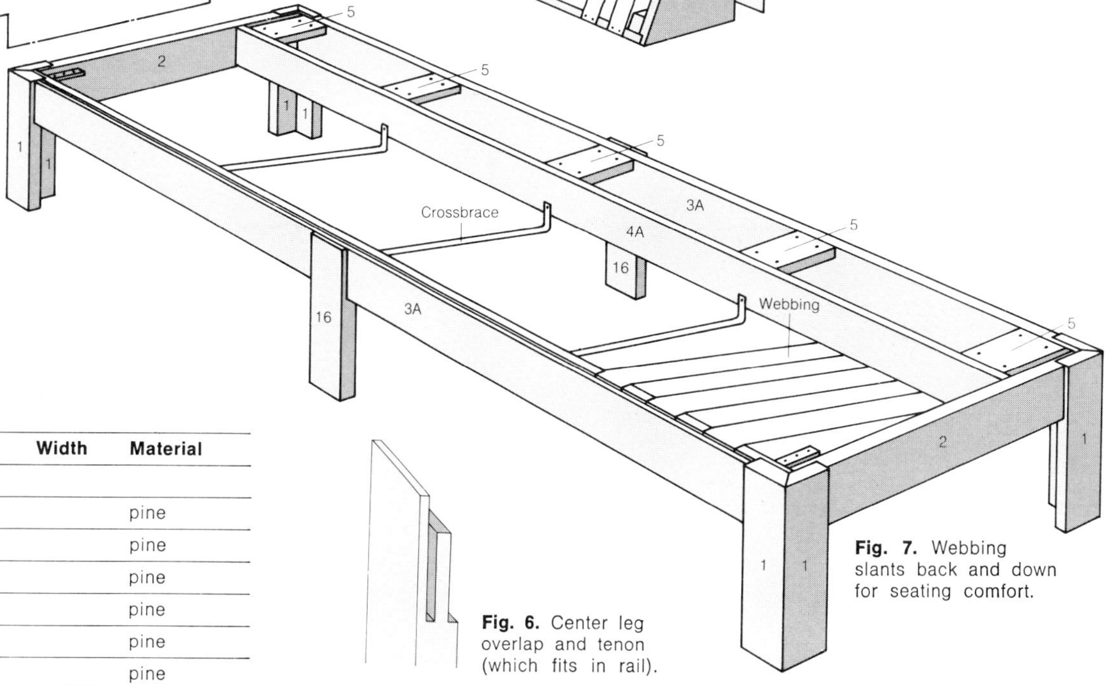

Fig. 6. Center leg overlap and tenon (which fits in rail).

Fig. 7. Webbing slants back and down for seating comfort.

PARTS LIST

No.	Name	Quantity	Nominal Size	Length	Width	Material
Sofa underframe						
1	Legs	8	1¼ × 4	10″		pine
2	Side rails	2	1¼ × 4	27⅛″		pine
3A	Front/back rails	2	1¼ × 4	89⅛″		pine
4A	Central rail	1	1¼ × 4	90⅝″		pine
5	Mounting plates	5	1¼ × 4	6⅝″		pine
16	Center legs	2	1¼ × 4	10″		pine
High arm unit						
6A	Ends	2	1 × 4	15″		pine
7	Tops/bottoms	2	1 × 4	30¼″		pine
8	Corner blocks	3	2 × 2	3½″		fir
9A	Inner panel	1		30¾″	18½″	⅛″ hardboard
10A	Outer panel	1		30¾	15″	⅛″ hardboard
17	Joining block	1	1 × 4	4″		pine

Hardware: Sofa: Eight ¾-inch No. 8 flathead screws; plastic resin glue; 10′ length ¼″ thinwall metal electrical conduit; six ¾″ No. 8 roundhead screws. **Arm:** 3″ angle iron; two ¾″ No. 8 flathead screws; plastic resin glue; 1½″ finishing nails; four 2½″ No. 8 flathead screws (to attach to frame).

Note: 3A, 4A, etc., are same size as in chair underframe and low arm unit, except for length. Chair and sofa back units are identical. To fasten high arm to back, use keyhole plate (back), 1¼″ No. 10 roundhead screws (arm). To lock back units together, use 1½″-× ¾″-diameter dowels.
Polyurethane Foam: Seat cushion: 5″ foam approx. 22″ square. Back unit: 4″ or 5″ foam approx. 18″ × 22″; ½″ foam 15″ × 21″; (side pad) ½″ foam 14″ long tapering from 7⅞″ to 1½″. High arm unit: ½″ foam approx. 36″ square. Low arm unit: ½″ foam approx. 24″ × 36″.
Webbing: Chair underframe approx. 12′; sofa underframe approx. 36′; back unit approx. 8′.
Fabric: Quantities given are for plain fabric. Allow ample extra fabric for match if using striped or patterned fabric. Seat cushion: approx. 36″ square. Back unit: approx. 2′ × 3′ plus extra for side pads. High arm unit: approx. 36″ square. Low arm unit: approx. 2′ × 3′.

Compact trio of tables stacks neatly when not in use. Each table is 17 in. high; each additional table increases the height of the stack by 2¾ in.

Adhesives 86
Finishing wood 407
Screws 72
Screwing applications 74

These versatile, lightweight tables are made from stock materials and have alkyd-enameled tops to resist stains.

CONSTRUCTION

First, make the clamping jig. Set three rails (1) in a triangle, inner corners touching, as in Fig. 1. Lay the triangle on scrap plywood and nail 2- x 2- x 16-inch cleats to the plywood around it.

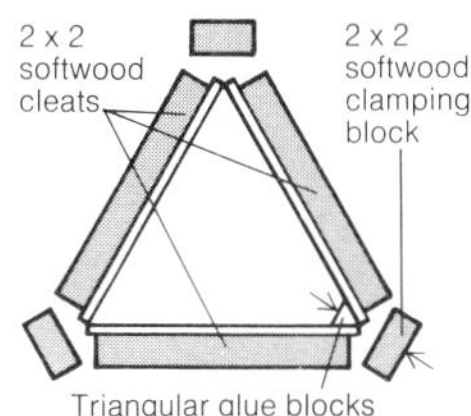

Fig. 1. Jig for clamping frame.

Use this same jig for each table.

Cut three equilaterally triangular gluing blocks (2) from 2- x 2-inch stock, making them 1½ inches on each side.

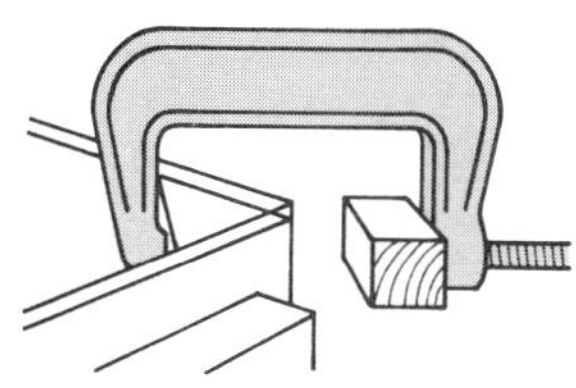

Fig. 2. How blocks are glued to rails.

Glue blocks to rails as in Fig. 2, preferably with waterproof glue. (Place paper under blocks so that they won't stick to the jig.) Let glue harden overnight, then trim rail ends as in Fig. 3.

Glue and screw legs (3) to frame, as in Fig. 4, so that tops of legs project ¼ inch above frame. Use two 2-inch No. 8 roundhead screws, through ⅛-inch

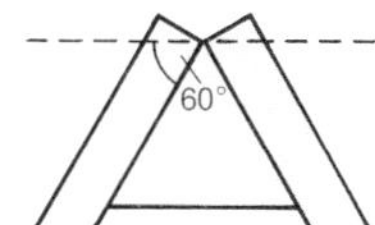

Fig. 3. Cut off rails to line shown.

holes predrilled through each block. Stagger holes to avoid splitting.

Make top from a 20¾-inch triangle of ¼-inch plywood, with corners cut to fit snugly against leg tops. Paint top (4) with high-gloss alkyd enamel. Glue top to rails with resorcinol adhesive or white glue; edges overlap rails a bit.

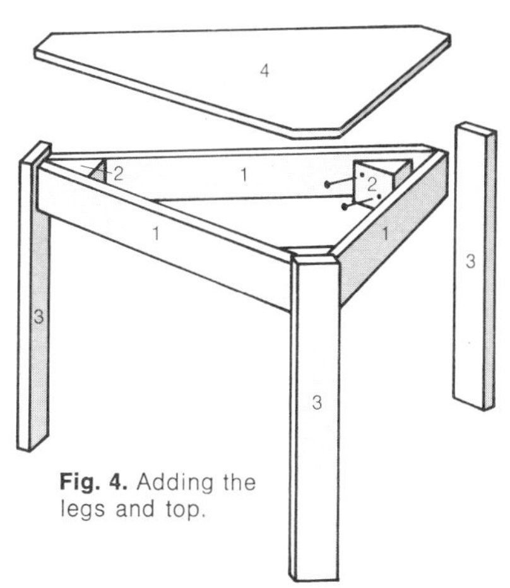

Fig. 4. Adding the legs and top.

PARTS LIST (for one table)

No.	Name	Quantity	Nominal Size	Length	Material
1	Rails	3	1 x 3	17″	pine
2	Blocks	3	2 x 2 triangular		fir
3	Legs	3	1 x 3	17″	pine
4	Top	1		20¾″ equilateral triangle	¼″ plywood

Hardware: Six 2″ No. 8 roundhead screws and washers. High-gloss alkyd enamel. Resorcinol adhesive or white glue.

The stack forms a spiral as the tables are added.

Although its chief purpose is to house stero equipment, this cabinet also provides storage space for liquor and miscellaneous items. It can easily be varied in size to fit available space. The units are versatile and have the same depth from front to back, simplifying construction and cutting costs. End sections are topped with white plastic laminate, center section with teak veneer. The right-hand top, shown in the photograph as a single piece, can also be divided, as shown in the drawing.

CONSTRUCTION

After cutting the parts as indicated in the Parts List, assemble the left-hand cabinet first, because its simplicity makes it a good starting project. All panel joints in the three cabinets are made with white glue, and 2-inch finishing nails if the material is plywood. With particle board, use 2-inch No. 6 flathead screws. Clamp or weight glued joints until the glue has dried.

Begin by fastening the sides (1) to the ends of the base (4) and to the upper wall bearer (27). Use shelf (5) to mark the base for the location of divider (2). Notch the divider at top corner around the upper bearer. Install the divider and mount the shelf at a height that suits your purpose. Attach the top (3), then the lower bearers (28 and 29). Fasten the rear lower bearer (28) with glue and nails driven through the base. Attach the side wall bearer (29) with glue and 2½-inch finishing nails driven through predrilled holes in the bearer into left side (1). Set the legs 3 inches from the side and 2 inches from the front as in the photo. Attach them with glue and 2-inch finishing nails driven down through the base. Mount the hinge and hang the door last.

Cover all exposed panel edges with veneer strips affixed with contact cement. Apply the cement to edges and to the back of the strips. When the cement is no longer tacky, align the strips, and press them down firmly.

Plastic laminate panels are also applied to the top with contact cement. Coat the cabinet top and the undersurface of the plastic laminate with cement and allow it to dry. Then place a wrapping paper slip sheet over the cabinet top. Align the laminate exactly on top of this. Then carefully slip the paper out and press the cemented surfaces together. Finish all the wood parts with two coats of clear polyurethane varnish before unit is mounted.

Drill pilot holes in the bearers for 2½-inch No. 8 flathead screws, spaced to match wall studs. Use scrap wood blocks under the lower bearers to hold the cabinet level while the screws are driven with a long screwdriver.

Basic procedure is the same for all cabinets. Note that the right cabinet top (20) can be fitted in three pieces as shown in Fig. 3 to provide access to the space behind false front (24). Use ready-made metal track for the sliding glass doors, which should have edges polished after cutting. The track used for the sliding glass doors should be of the type that has small bearings in the bottom track to ease movement of the doors. Drop-in bases (13 and 14) of the center unit rest on ¾- x ¾-inch aluminum angles.

Cabinet extends from wall to wall and is supported at ends by wall-mounted bearers. If not mounted to walls at ends, add an extra leg at each end.

Adhesives 86
Attaching to hollow surfaces 76
Finishing wood 407
Screws 72
Working with laminates 380

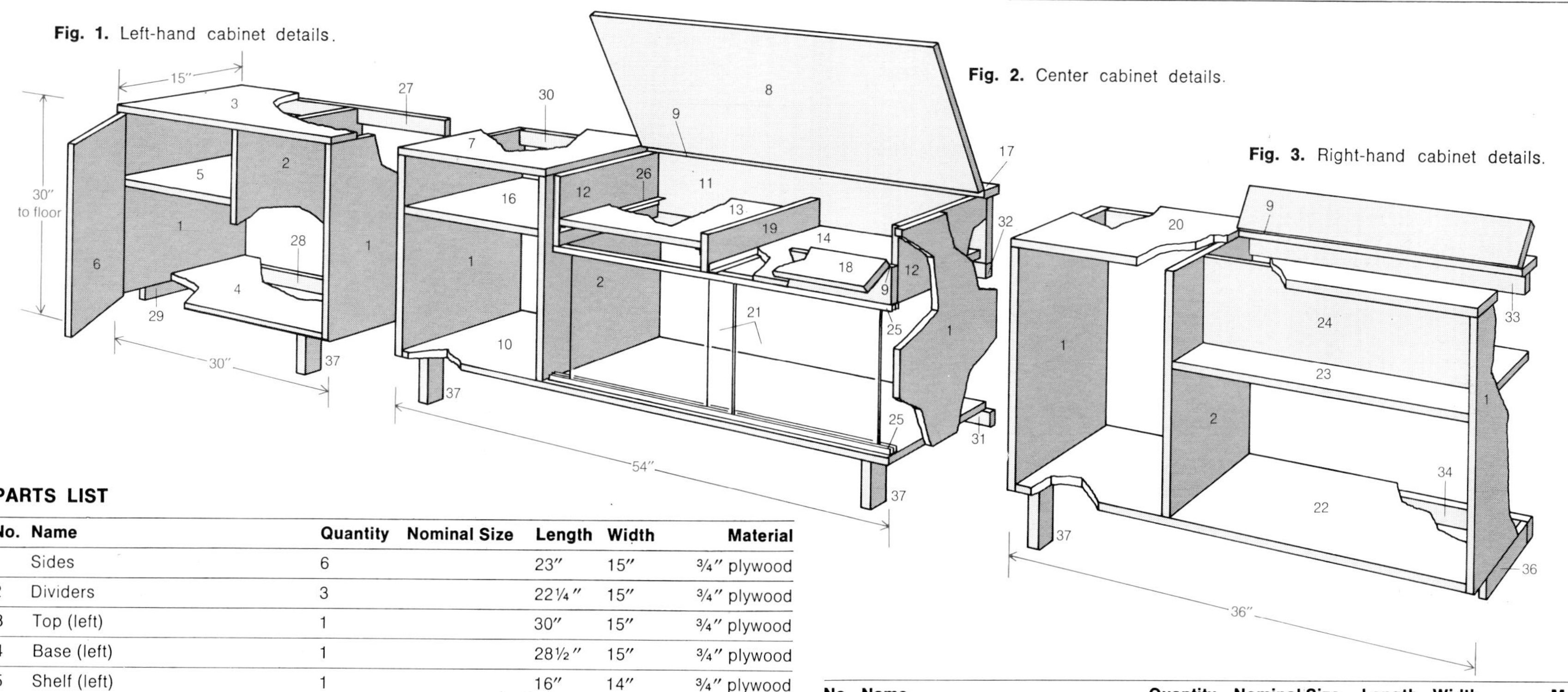

Fig. 1. Left-hand cabinet details.

Fig. 2. Center cabinet details.

Fig. 3. Right-hand cabinet details.

PARTS LIST

No.	Name	Quantity	Nominal Size	Length	Width	Material
1	Sides	6		23"	15"	¾" plywood
2	Dividers	3		22¼"	15"	¾" plywood
3	Top (left)	1		30"	15"	¾" plywood
4	Base (left)	1		28½"	15"	¾" plywood
5	Shelf (left)	1		16"	14"	¾" plywood
6	Door (left)	1		22⅛"	16"	¾" plywood
7	Fixed top (center)	1		18"	15"	¾" plywood
8	Lift-up lid (center)	1		36"	13½"	¾" plywood
9	Piano hinges	4		to suit		
10	Base (center)	1		52½"	15"	¾" plywood
11	Back panel (center)	1		35¼"	8½"	¾" plywood
12	Lid supports (center)	2		13¼"	8½"	¾" plywood
13	Left drop-in base (center)	1		13¼"	15½"	¾" plywood
14	Right drop-in base (center)	1		13¼"	17½"	¾" plywood
15	Veneer strip (not shown)			to suit	¾"	teak
16	Hi-fi shelf (center)	1		16½"	15"	¾" plywood
17	Rail for hinged lid (center)	1		36"	1½"	¾" plywood
18	Hinged front and support (center)	1		35¼"	4¼"	¾" plywood
19	Shallow divider (center)	1		13½"	4½"	¾" plywood
20	Top, overall (right)	1		36"	15"	¾" plywood
21	Glass doors	2		18½"	13½"	¼" plate glass
22	Base (right)	1		34½"	15"	¾" plywood
23	Shelf (right)	1		22"	15"	¾" plywood
24	Compartment, false front (right)	1		22"	8"	¾" plywood
25	Sliding door channels (center)	2		35¼"		metal
26	Aluminum angles	4		13¼"	¾"	
27	Upper wall bearer (left)	1	1 × 2	28½"		pine
28	Lower wall bearer (left)	1	1 × 2	30"		pine
29	Side wall bearer (left)	1	1 × 2	12"		pine
30	Upper wall bearer (center)	1	1 × 2	16½"		pine
31	Lower wall bearer (center)	1	1 × 2	54"		pine
32	Mid wall bearer (center)	1	1 × 2	35¼"		pine
33	Upper wall bearer (right)	1	1 × 2	34½"		pine
34	Lower wall bearer (right)	1	1 × 2	36"		pine
35	Handle (optional)	1				hardwood
36	Side wall bearer (right)	1	1 × 2	12"		pine
37	Legs (all units)	4	1 × 2	6¼"		hardwood

Hardware: Twelve 3" No. 10 roundhead screws. Box of 1¼" No. 8 flathead screws. Nails. Glue. Three-quarter-inch veneer strip. Sliding door tracks (cut to suit). Length of Aluminum angle.

Bar-server door hinges at bottom, is held steady by drop-lid stays.

Cabinets are held to the wall by means of interlocking wall and back rails.

The expensive appearance of these two side-by-side cabinets was achieved by using plywood with a teak veneer. Apply veneer to all surfaces before cutting. Or buy a face-veneered plywood. Available in thicknesses from ¼ to ¾ inch, these are not stocked by many lumberyards but they can be special ordered.

CONSTRUCTION

Dimensions of the two units vary slightly because of the sliding glass doors; so cut parts to size and build units one at a time. The glass-door cabinet is simpler to build; make it first.

In this unit, inch-wide grooved door strips (3) are glued and fastened with 2 inch finishing nails to the front edges of the top and bottom panels (1); thus these panels are 1 inch narrower than those of the plywood-door cabinet. The grooves in the top track are deeper than those in the bottom track (Fig. 1) so that the glass doors (7) can be installed by lifting them into the upper grooves, then lowering into bottom ones.

Corner pieces (4) are cut from full 1 x 1 inch stock milled and planed from nominal 1¼ x 1¼, and cut on the bench saw to produce centered ¼ x ¼ inch tongues (Fig. 2). The top and bottom edges of the end panels (2) and the ends of the top and bottom panels are grooved to take these tongues. A router is a good tool for this. Similar ¼ x ¼ inch grooves are also cut lengthwise in bottom surface of top panel, upper surface of bottom panel, and vertically in inner surfaces of end panels. For all panels, the rear edge of these grooves is ¾ inch from the rear edge of the panel. The back panel (5) will be glued in the grooves. The corner pieces (4) must be notched to take the back panel's corners.

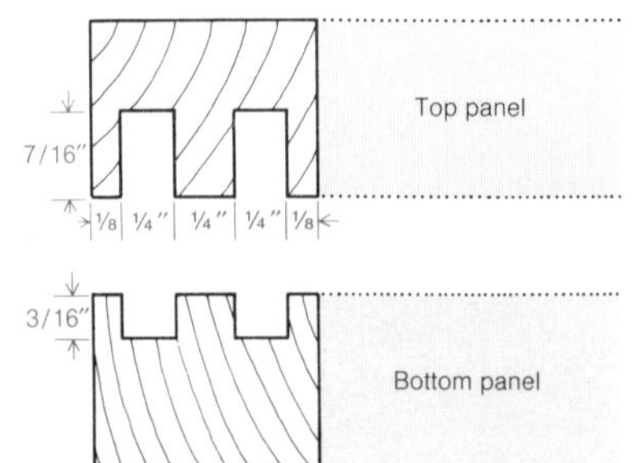

Fig. 1. Track strips are grooved on bench saw, fastened to panel edge with finishing nails and glue. Grooves are deeper in top track.

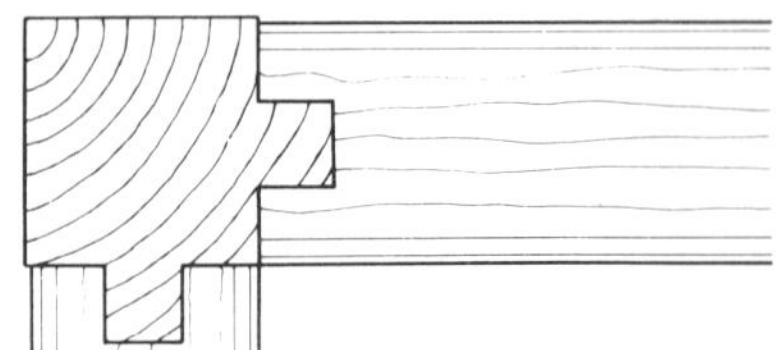

Fig. 2. Corner tongues match panel end grooves.

The bottom edge of back rail (6A) is beveled downward toward the wall at 45 degrees. It is glued and screwed to the back panel directly under the top panel, using ¾ inch No. 8 flathead screws driven from inside the panel. The bevel on back rail (6A) mates with the bevel on the top edge of the wall rail (6B), which slants upward at 45 degrees. Cabinets are mounted by lifting them above the wall rail (6B), then lowering them so that 6A and 6B will mate.

The front edges of the top, bottom, and end panels (track strips in glass-door cabinet) are covered with ¼-inch-thick edge strips (9), mitered at the corners. The wooden pulls are bonded to the glass doors with epoxy adhesive.

In final assembly fasten lower corner pieces (4) to bottom panel (1) and one end panel (after attaching track strips with glue and finishing nails), then glue back panel (5) into bottom

Adhesives 86
Bench saw 60
Clamping 38
Corner joints 389, 392
Cutting grooves 386
Dovetailing 390–391
Drawer making 402
Router 54
Veneering 381

and end grooves. Next, join top (1) and other end panel to both upper corner pieces and lower them onto back panel and other end panel. Clamp with a long band clamp (p. 38) around all four corner pieces until glue sets.

Mount back rail and shelf, and glue and brad the edge strips after main assembly glue joints have set.

The plywood door and drawer cabinet is made the same way, except that no track strips are required. Grooves for partitions must be cut ¼ inch deep and ¾ inch wide across the underside of the top panel and the upper side of the bottom panel centered 17 inches from the inside of each end panel. Drawer fronts are lap-dovetailed (p. 391) to sides; back is through-dovetailed (p. 390), with bottom set in ¼ x ¼ inch grooves all around, ¼ inch from bottom. Use simple corner joints (pp. 389, 392) if you lack tools for dovetailing. Magnetic catches serve as stops and hold the doors shut. Wood door and drawer handles are glued and screwed in notched door and drawer edges with 1 inch No. 6 flathead screws. Mount wall rail (6B) with 2½ inch No. 8 flathead screws driven into wall studs.

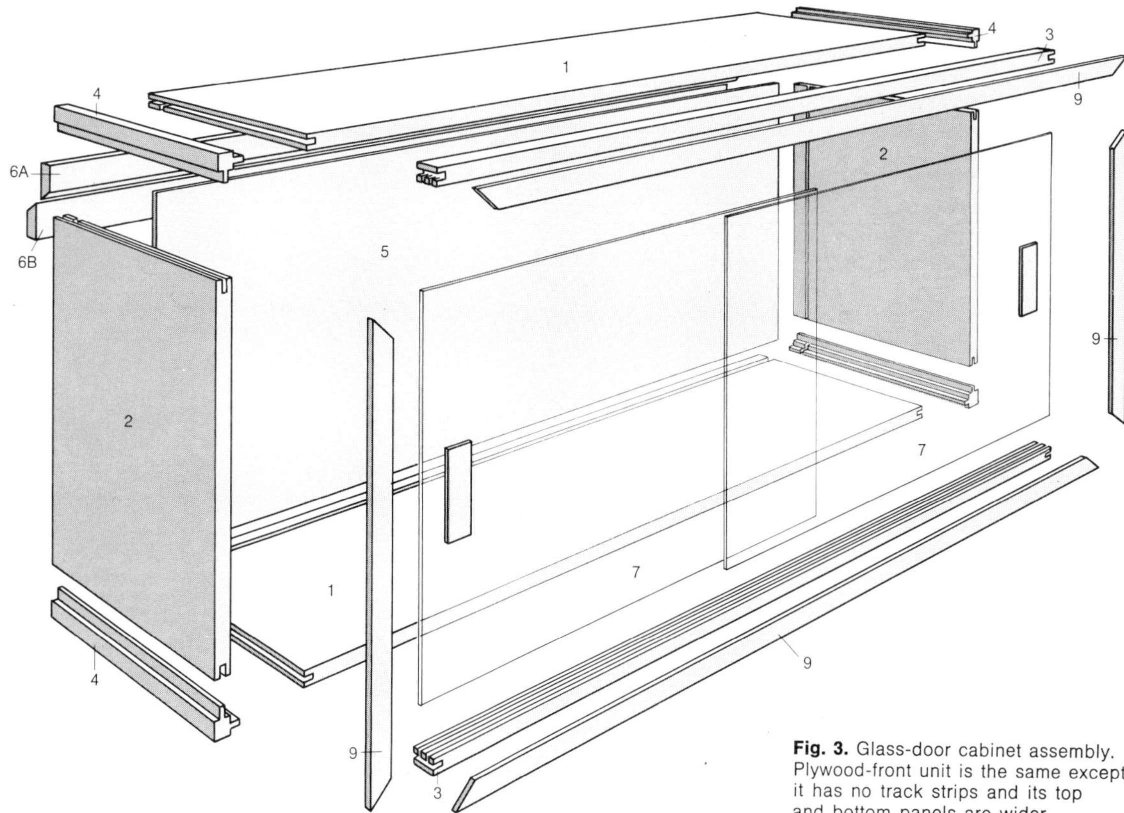

Fig. 3. Glass-door cabinet assembly. Plywood-front unit is the same except it has no track strips and its top and bottom panels are wider.

PARTS LIST (Glass-door cabinet)

No.	Name	Quantity	Nominal Size	Length	Width	Material
1	Top/bottom panels	2		52½″	12¾″	¾″ plywood
2	End panels	2		16½″	13¾″	¾″ plywood
3	Door track strips	2	1 x 1¼ (cut)	52½″		pine or to suit
4	Corner pieces	4	1¼ x 1¼	13¾″		pine or to suit
5	Back panel	1		53″	17″	¼″ plywood
6A	Back rail	1	1 x 4	52¼″		pine
6B	Wall rail	1	1 x 2	52½″		pine
7	Doors	2		28¼″	16⅞″	¼″ plate glass
8	Shelf	1	(not shown)	52½″	10½″	¾″ plywood
9	Edge strips	8		30′ cut as required	¾″	¼″ pine

Note: Have glass doors smooth-polished on all edges by glass supplier.

PARTS LIST (Door and drawer cabinet, not shown)

No.	Name	Quantity	Length	Width	Materials
10	Top/bottom panels	2	52½″	13¾″	¾″ plywood
11	Partitions	2	17″	12¾″	¾″ plywood
12	Doors	2	16⅝″	16⅛″	¾″ plywood
13	Shelves	2	17″	10½″	½″ plywood
14	Drawer fronts	4	16¾″	4¹⁄₁₆″	¾″ plywood
15	Drawer sides	8	12¼″	4¹⁄₁₆″	½″ plywood
16	Drawer backs	4	16¾″	4¹⁄₁₆″	½″ plywood
17	Drawer bottoms	4	16¼″	16¼″	¼″ plywood
18	Drawer runners	8	11¾″	¾″	³⁄₁₆″ hardwood

Hardware: One doz. ¾″ No. 8 flathead screws, 1 doz. 1″ No. 6 flathead screws, 1 doz. 2½″ No. 8 flathead screws. Two brass cabinet hinges; one 16½″ piano hinge. Two friction stays.
Note: Additional parts needed are shown as parts 2, 4, 5, and 6A and B for glass-door cabinet.

Furnishings for living areas: **Dining room alcove unit**

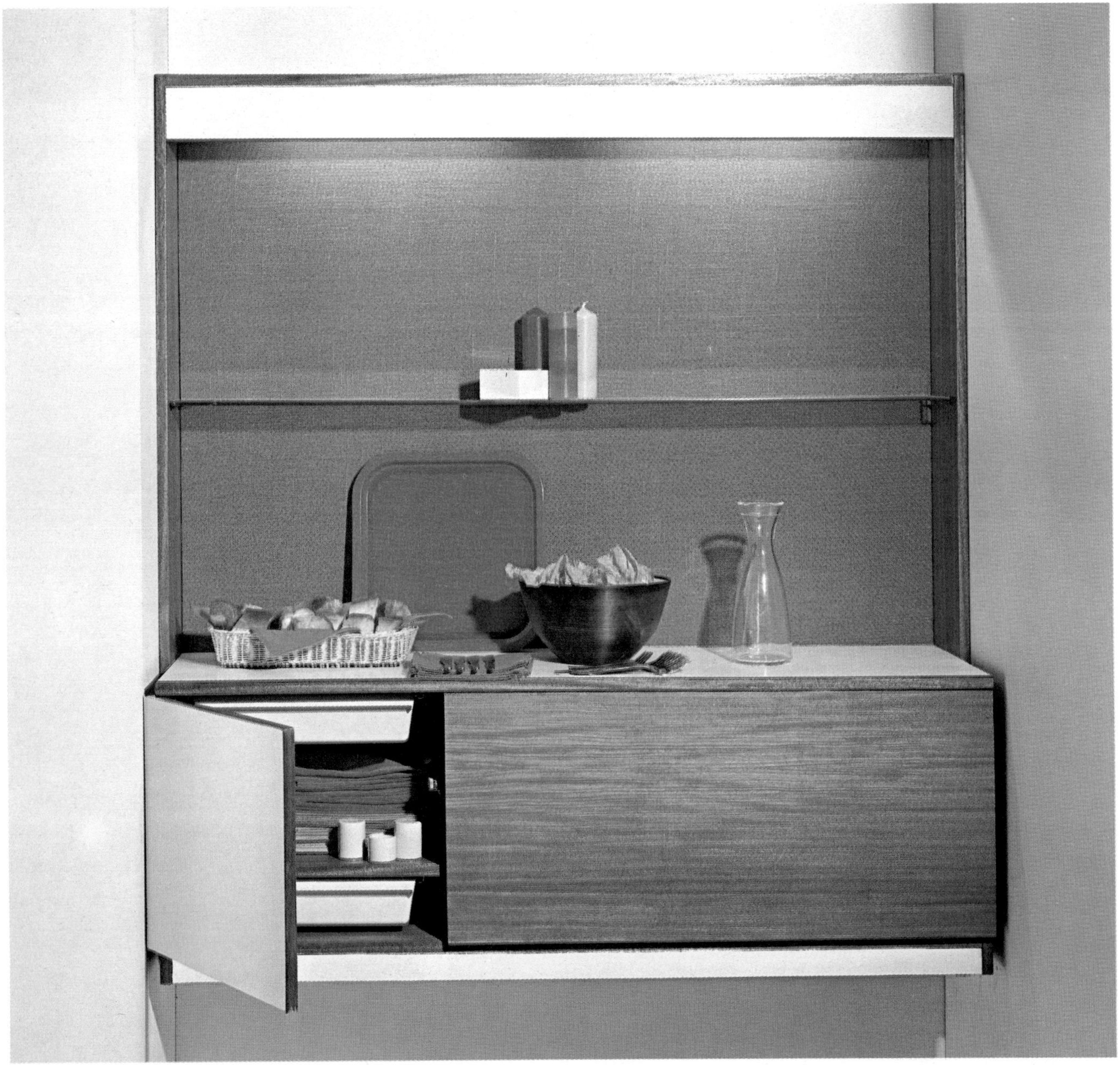

Backboard is covered with washable vinyl in a color suited to the room's decor. Cabinet top and door are faced with plastic laminate.

CONSTRUCTION

Assemble the main frame first. Mark and drill holes in sides (2) for metal spade pins (p. 548); provide four or five, 1 inch apart, so that shelf height can be adjusted. Top (1) is rabbet joined to sides with white glue and 2-inch finishing nails. Glue and nail fascia (3) to top. Insert frame into alcove and fasten back support strips (4) to wall with toggle bolts, Molly bolts, or screws into studs. Locate top and bottom support strips so that they will be 4 inches inward from top and bottom edges of main frame backboard (5). Mount remaining strip midway between the other two. Nail sides to support strip ends.

Build the cabinet next, modifying dimensions as necessary to fit frame when in place in alcove. Cut dado grooves in sides (6) 3/8 inch deep and 3/4 inch wide for cabinet base (8). Locate bottom edge of groove 2 inches above bottom edge of sides. Divider (9) fits into 3/4- x 3/8-inch dado grooves in base and top (7). Before assembling cabinet shell with glue and nails, try the unit (with nails only partly driven) to be sure it fits easily between main frame sides. Note that top should overlap front edge of sides by 3/4 inch.

Position divider when glue is dry in assembled cabinet; mark and drill holes for metal spade pins for left and right shelves (10, 11). Glue and nail

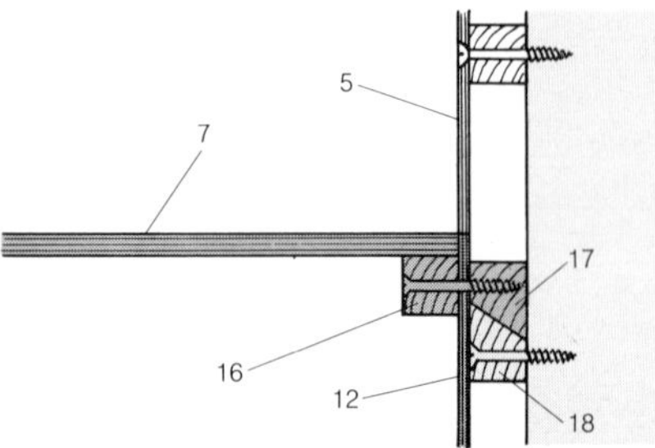

Fig. 1. How cabinet is mounted.

Adhesives 86
Fluorescent lights 274
Hinges 78
Locating studs 265
Shelving 85
Fasteners 76
Wood joints 384
Working with laminates 380

divider, back (12), and cabinet crossrail (13) in place. Glue cabinet support strips (16) in position and secure them with countersunk 1½-inch No. 8 flathead screws driven down through top and base and into support strips. Bevel lower edge of hanger strip (17) and upper edge of wall strip (18) at matching 45-degree angles as shown in Fig. 1. Attach hanger strip to cabinet back with glue and countersunk 2½-inch No. 8 flathead screws driven through support rail into hanger strip.

Apply plastic laminate to fascia (3), cabinet top (7), crossrail (13), and door (14). Attach hinges and lid supports (see Fig. 2) and hang door and drop flap (15).

Temporarily place main frame backboard (5) and cabinet in position and mark off locations for wall strip and spacer strip (19). Attach wall strip and spacer strip to wall with screws into studs. Lift cabinet into place.

Install wiring and fixtures for fluorescent light tube. After wiring is installed, attach frame backboard to support strips with three countersunk 1½-inch No. 8 flathead screws per rail. Cover backboard with fabric-backed vinyl (or other material of your choice) after backboard is in place.

PARTS LIST

No.	Name	Quantity	Nominal Size	Length	Width	Material
1	Main frame top	1		55½″	9″	¾″ veneered plywood
2	Main frame sides	2		57″	9″	¾″ veneered plywood
3	Main frame fascia	1		54″	4″	¾″ pine
4	Back support strips	3	2 x 2	54″		fir
5	Main frame backboard	1		54″	36″	½″ plywood
6	Cabinet sides	2		17¼″	17¼″	¾″ veneered plywood
7	Cabinet top	1		54″	18″	¾″ veneered plywood
8	Cabinet base	1		53¼″	17¼″	¾″ veneered plywood
9	Cabinet divider	1		17¼″	15¼″	¾″ veneered plywood
10	Cabinet shelf, left	1		16½″	17¼″	¾″ veneered plywood
11	Cabinet self, right	1		35¼″	12″	¾″ veneered plywood
12	Cabinet back	1		54″	18″	¼″ plywood
13	Cabinet front crossrail	1		52½″	2″	¾″ pine
14	Cabinet door	1		17⅝″	14½″	¾″ veneered plywood
15	Cabinet drop flap	1		36⅜″	14½″	¾″ veneered plywood
16	Cabinet support strips	2	2 x 2	52½″		pine
17	Hanger strip	1	2 x 4	53½″		pine
18	Wall strip	1	2 x 4	53½″		pine
19	Spacer strip	1	2 x 2	53½″		pine
20	Glass shelf	1		54″	6″	¼″ plate glass

Hardware: Two drop-leaf supports with screws to match. One 36″ chrome piano hinge with screws to match. One pair ¾″ x 2″ chrome butt hinges with screws to match. Magnetic catches for door and drop leaf. One dozen metal spade pins. No. 8 steel flathead screws—2 doz. 1½″, 1 doz. 2½″. Molly bolts, toggle bolts, or lag screws (for fastening to wall). Box 2″ finishing nails. One 40-watt fluorescent strip fixture with wiring as required. Plastic laminate and contact cement. Fabric-backed vinyl 54″ x 36″.

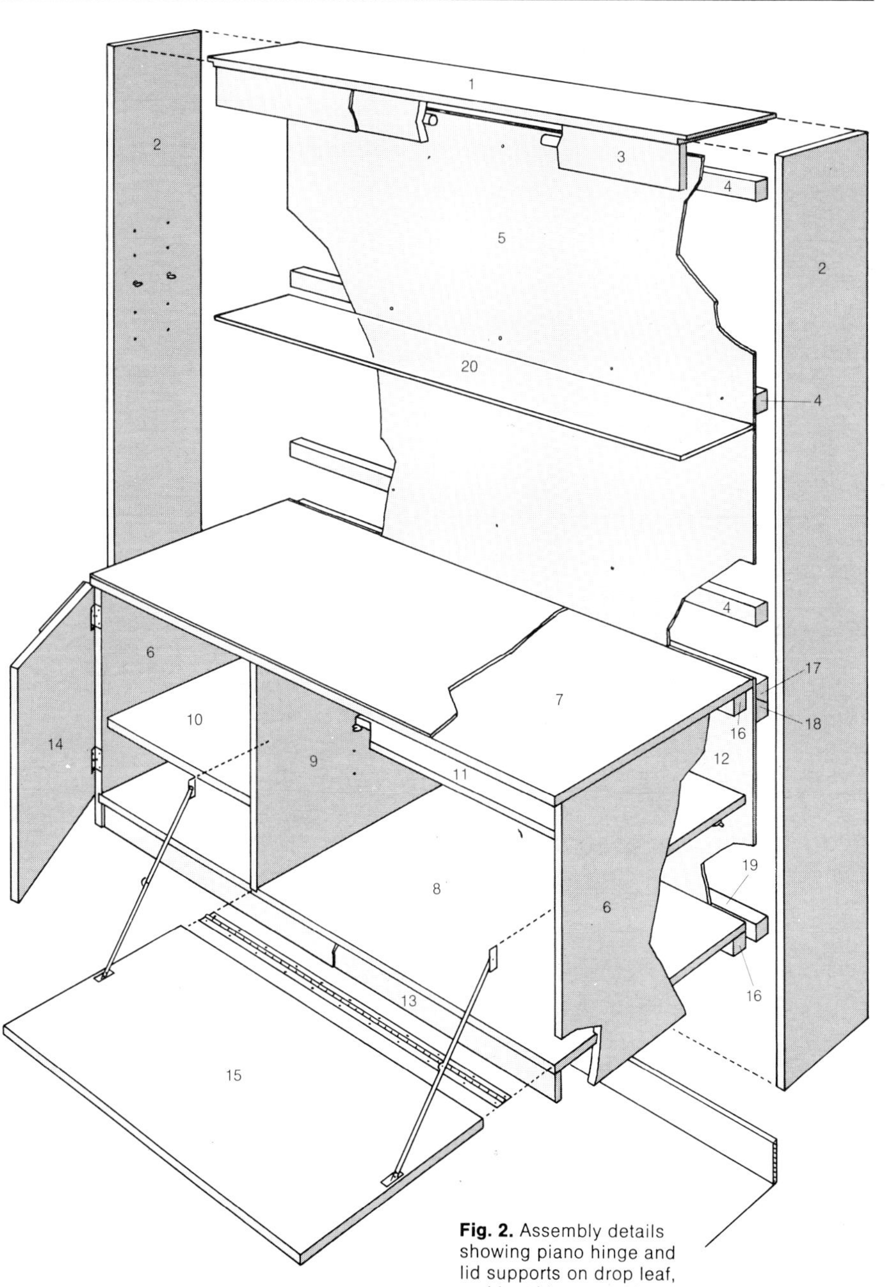

Fig. 2. Assembly details showing piano hinge and lid supports on drop leaf, and butt hinges on door.

For a child's desk, a worktop is placed across two floor-standing boxes.

Adhesives 86
Drawer making 402
Finishing wood 407
Joints 384
Magnetic catches 81
Piano hinge 79
Rabbeting 392
Shelving 85

The simplest possible boxes—plain plywood panels screwed to stock-size pine frames—are the basis of every unit in this versatile system. The secret of the boxes' adaptability lies in their ingenious fittings—shelves, racks, doors, partitions, and drawers. With these you can turn the basic boxes into attractive arrangements that will brighten any room in your house.

The boxes are 19½ inches high and 18 inches wide and deep. They can stand on the floor or be hung from a wall at any convenient height. For instance, if your plans call for a dressing table or a desk for adults, hang the boxes so that their tops are 30 inches from the floor and place a worktop between them. Floor-standing boxes fit into a base that produces an overall height of 21 inches—just about right for a child. Or the boxes can be placed on the floor without bases to give a worktop height of 19½ inches. Boxes stacked more than two high are held together with cleats.

Shelves rest on dowels. If you plan to use them with a door, fit the shelves before hanging the door. They must be ¾ inch shallower than in an open box.

Floor-standing and wall-hung units with a variety of fittings serve many storage purposes.

CONSTRUCTION

Basic box

Cut a rabbet ¾ inch wide and ⅜ inch deep at each end of front and back frames (1). Fasten side frames (2) with glue and 1½-inch finishing nails. Glue and nail top and bottom panels (3) to frames with 1-inch finishing nails.

Set side panels (4) so that they overlap back edges of frames by ¼ inch and are flush with top panel and bottom of frame. Fasten side panels to frames with glue and four 1-inch No. 6 screws.

Vertical cleats (5) are glued and

Box system is adapted here to fit an odd-shaped corner.

nailed to side panels flush with back edges of frames. Set back panel (6) flush with bottom edge of box and fasten to cleats and back frames with glue and ¾-inch brads.

Drill 3/16-inch holes through upper back frame, ¼ inch from bottom edges, for two 2-inch No. 10 screws to attach box to wall. Locate holes so that screws will penetrate studs when box is in position. Finish by filling screw and nail holes and painting all surfaces.

Shelves

Before attaching side panels to frames of basic box, drill two rows of ¼-inch holes ⅜ inch deep in side panels at centers 4 inches from front and back edges. Centers are 3⅞ inches apart, starting 5½ inches from the bottom edge. Glue the shelf support dowels (7) in their respective holes. Cut shelves (8) to size, paint, and insert after box is assembled.

Bottle rack

Mark off the shorter side of the vertical panels (9) and the longer side of the horizontal panels (10) into three equal parts (Fig. 4). Cut ⅜-inch slots halfway across each panel at the marks.

Mask off the joints where the glue is to be applied and paint the panels. When the paint is dry, remove the tape and glue panels together.

Fig. 1. How the basic box is constructed.

PARTS LIST

No.	Name	Quantity	Nominal Size	Length	Width	Material
Basic box						
1	Front and back frames	4	1 x 2	17″		pine
2	Side frames	4	1 x 2	16¼″		pine
3	Top and bottom panels	2		17″	17″	⅛″ hardboard
4	Side panels	2		19½″	18″	½″ plywood
5	Vertical cleats	2		15½″	½″	½″ pine
6	Back panel	1		19½″	17″	¼″ plywood

Door

Glue and nail frame rails (11) to frame uprights (12). Nail panels (13) to each side of the frame (Fig. 5). Plane the door to fit the box, allowing for the thickness of the piano hinge.

Drill holes for attaching the handle 1¼ inches from edge of door and midway between the top and bottom edges. Fill nailheads, then paint the door. Attach handle and magnetic catches.

Record or magazine rack

Before side panels of basic box are attached, cut ½-inch deep notches ¾ inch wide in side pieces of upper frame to take upper cleats (14). The front cleat is 5½ inches from front edge of frame, and the back edge of the rear cleat is 1½ inches from back edge of frame (Fig. 5).

Mark off the upper cleats into three equal parts and cut 3/16-inch-wide notches ¼ inch deep at the marks. Glue and nail the upper cleats to upper frames.

Cut a 3/16-inch groove ¼ inch deep along center line of lower cleats (15). Round off top edges of cleats.

Next, cut away top corner of partitions (16) as in Fig. 2 and round off all corners.

Glue lower cleats to box with partitions in position. Line up grooves in lower cleats with those in the upper cleats, using a try square to make sure partitions are at exact right angles to base. Let glue set before removing partitions from cleats.

Drawers

Cut groove ⅜ inch deep and ¾ inch wide along outside center line of sides (18) to accommodate runners (21). Grooves are wider than runners to prevent binding. Cut groove on inside of fronts, backs, and sides ⅛ inch wide and ¼ inch deep for bottom (20). Locate these grooves ¼ inch from bottom edge. Fronts (17) and backs (19) are rabbeted to sides. Cut rabbets ¾ inch wide and ⅜ inch deep on ends of fronts and backs.

Assemble sides, front, back, and bottom temporarily with finishing nails. Check for fit and trim as necessary. Cut notches in backs to unblock runner grooves, then cut a ¼- x ⅛-inch rabbet along lower front edge of drawer fronts. Assemble permanently with white glue and 1-inch finishing nails.

Position drawer runners (21) along inside of box so that they correspond to grooves on drawer sides. Fasten runners with glue and ½-inch brads.

Paint edges and face of drawer fronts and attach handles when paint is dry.

Worktop

Rabbet long rails (22) to end rails (23). Cut rabbets ¾ inch wide and ⅜ inch deep. Glue and nail all joints. Glue and

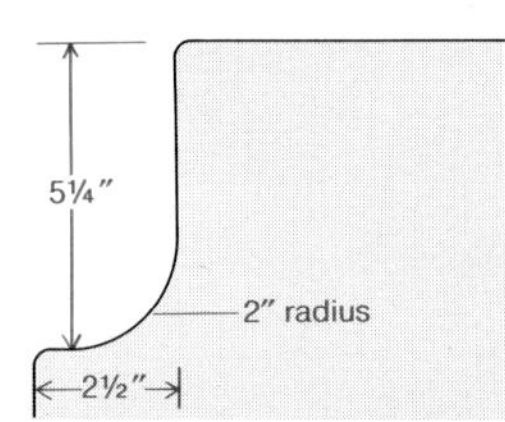

Fig. 2. Cut record cabinet partitions as shown.

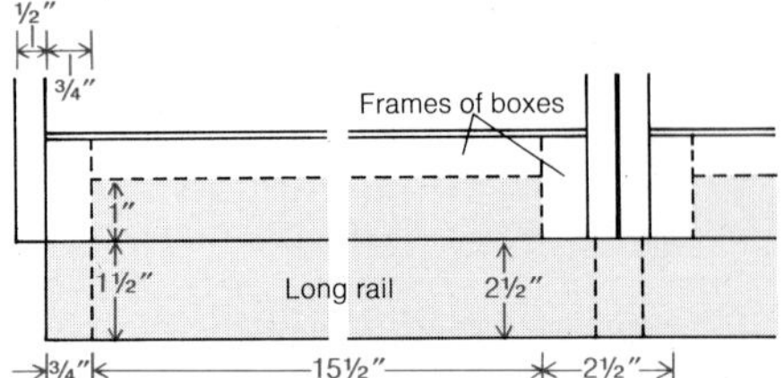

Fig. 3. Detail of box base.

Adhesives 86
Drawer making 402
Finishing wood 407
Joints 384
Magnetic catches 81
Piano hinge 79
Rabbeting 392
Shelving 85

nail cross rails (24) squarely between long rails, 10¾-inches from inside face of each end rail (Fig. 7). Install triangular glue blocks (25) in all corners of the frame. Glue and nail top panel (26) to top of frame. Install worktop between boxes with 1½-inch No. 10 screws passing through end rails into box sides and top frames. Fix worktop flush with tops of boxes.

Base

Cut long rails (27) to required length (long rail for one box is 17 inches; add 18 inches for each additional box). Cut grooves in long rails to take boxes (Fig. 3). Join the long rails to the end rails (28) with simple butt joints as in Fig. 8. Glue and nail all joints. Next, glue and nail crossrails (29) between long rails. Glue triangular blocks (30) in corners.

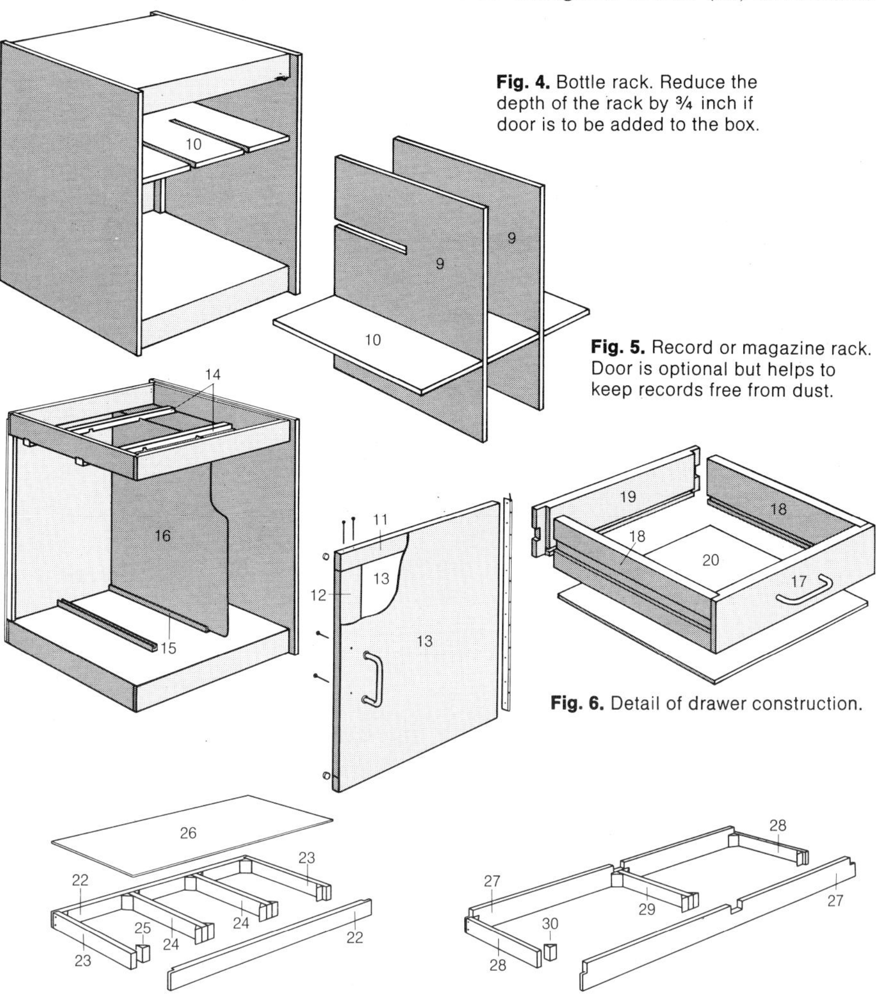

Fig. 4. Bottle rack. Reduce the depth of the rack by ¾ inch if door is to be added to the box.

Fig. 5. Record or magazine rack. Door is optional but helps to keep records free from dust.

Fig. 6. Detail of drawer construction.

Fig. 7. How worktop is made.

Fig. 8. Details of base construction.

PARTS LIST

No.	Name	Quantity	Nominal Size	Length	Width	Material
Shelves						
7	Shelf supports	12		⅞″		¼″ dowel
8	Shelves	3		17″	16½″	½″ plywood
Bottle rack						
9	Vertical panels	2		16½″	16½″	⅜″ plywood
10	Horizontal panels	2		17″	16½″	⅜″ plywood
Door						
11	Frame rails	2		17″	1″	½″ pine
12	Frame uprights	2		14¼″	1⅞″	½″ pine
13	Panels	2		17″	16¼″	⅛″ hardboard
Hardware: One piano hinge 16½″ x ¾″; one 3″ handle; two magnetic catches.						
Record or magazine rack						
14	Upper cleats	2		17″	¾″	¾″ pine
15	Lower cleats	2		12½″	¾″	¾″ pine
16	Partitions	2		15¾″	15″	⅛″ double-faced hardboard
Drawers						
17	Drawer fronts	4		16⅞″	4″	¾″ pine or plywood
18	Drawer sides	8		15¾″	4″	¾″ pine or plywood
19	Drawer backs	4		16⅞″	4″	¾″ pine or plywood
20	Drawer bottoms	4		15½″	15⅞″	⅛″ hardboard
21	Drawer runners	8		16″	⅝″	¼″ pine
Hardware: Four 3″ D-handles.						
Worktop						
22	Long rails	2	1 x 3	36″		pine
23	End rails	2	1 x 3	16¼″		pine
24	Cross rails	2	1 x 3	15½″		pine
25	Glue blocks	12	1¼ x 1¼	1½″		pine
26	Top panel	1		36″	17″	⅛″ hardboard
Base						
27	Long rails	2	1 x 3	as needed		pine
28	End rails	2	1 x 2	13¾″		pine
29	Cross rails	as needed	1 x 2	13¾″		pine
30	Glue blocks	as needed	1¼ x 1¼	1⅞″		1⅛″ pine

Hardware: Flathead screws—1″ No. 6, 1½″ No. 10, 2″ No. 10. Finishing nails—1½″. Brads—½″, ¾″, 1″. Plastic resin adhesive. Door and drawer handles. Magnetic catches.

Adjustable light-duty shelves feature built-in book ends.

Planning and design

Nearly every home project involves the use of shelves. A new kitchen cabinet, a workbench, or a built-in for the family-room stereo—all these require shelves. In addition, most homes have an ever-increasing need for shelf space, a need easily met by erecting open shelves.

Consider future use before starting work. If shelves are to carry heavy loads, such as books, the type of shelving material used is important, as is the structural arrangement to support the shelves. Try to design bookshelves that are the same width as the books or even a bit wider. This reduces the amount of open shelving to be dusted and prevents a book's being accidentally pushed behind others and misplaced. For these reasons, book shelving is generally 8 or 10 inches wides. Spacing shelves 9 inches apart will suit most books, and a shelf or two with an 11- or 12-inch vertical clearance will accommodate larger volumes.

When planning shelving, remember that shelf loads most likely will continue to increase. Shelves built to hold a few magazines may have to bear the weight of growing stacks. Vertically adjustable shelves are much more useful than fixed ones because they can be adapted to specific storage needs.

Shelving materials

Solid lumber, plywood, and particle board are best for utility shelves. The length of the shelf and the load it must carry will determine the material, its thickness, and its supports. Lumber and plywood are stronger than particle board, which tends to bend under fairly light loads (a cleat or support glued under the shelf will increase its strength).

Plate glass ¼ inch thick is suitable for shelves up to 42 inches long if they

Coping saw 18
Dowels 395
Fasteners 76–77
Saber saw 52

carry only light loads, such as bric-a-brac. Glass shelves can be purchased in standard sizes with the edges beveled and polished. A local glass dealer can cut and polish glass to any other size and shape.

A light load for a 9-inch-wide solid wood shelf is about 10 pounds per linear foot, a medium load about 20 pounds per foot, and a heavy load 30 to 40 pounds. Large books and stacks of phonograph records constitute heavy loads.

Fastening shelves to walls

Before erecting shelving, consider the wall and the type of fastening best suited to it. Remember that methods suitable for alcove (or inside cabinet) installation are not necessarily best for an open wall. An alcove shelf can be supported by cleats—narrow horizontal wood strips attached to vertical studs or solid walls—fastened to each side wall.

Shelf brackets can be fixed almost anywhere on a brick, concrete block, or concrete wall, but the position of the studs in a plaster or wallboard partition will govern placement of shelf brackets and also the shelves. If a particular shelf arrangement is important, brackets can be screwed to cross supports or cleats fastened to the studs.

A shelf can bear more weight without bending if supports are not set right at its ends. Reducing the unsupported span of the middle of the shelf prevents sagging, so common in long shelves (Figs. 1, 2).

Before installing shelves, check the wall for bulges, as they can throw the shelves out of square. Shim supports if necessary so that shelves will be level (Fig. 3).

Shelving that fits inside a furniture unit, such as a cabinet, can generally be supported by wood cleats. Cut the cleats to match the width of the shelf, then glue and screw them to the cabinet frame. If you want adjustable shelving inside a cabinet, use clip-type supports (p. 85). These comprise perforated metal tracks into which metal clips can be hooked at various levels. Another method is to drill a series of ¼-inch-diameter holes in the cabinet side walls. Drill the holes 1½ inches apart in two sets of vertical lines spaced slightly narrower than the width of the shelf. These holes will accept metal spade pins.

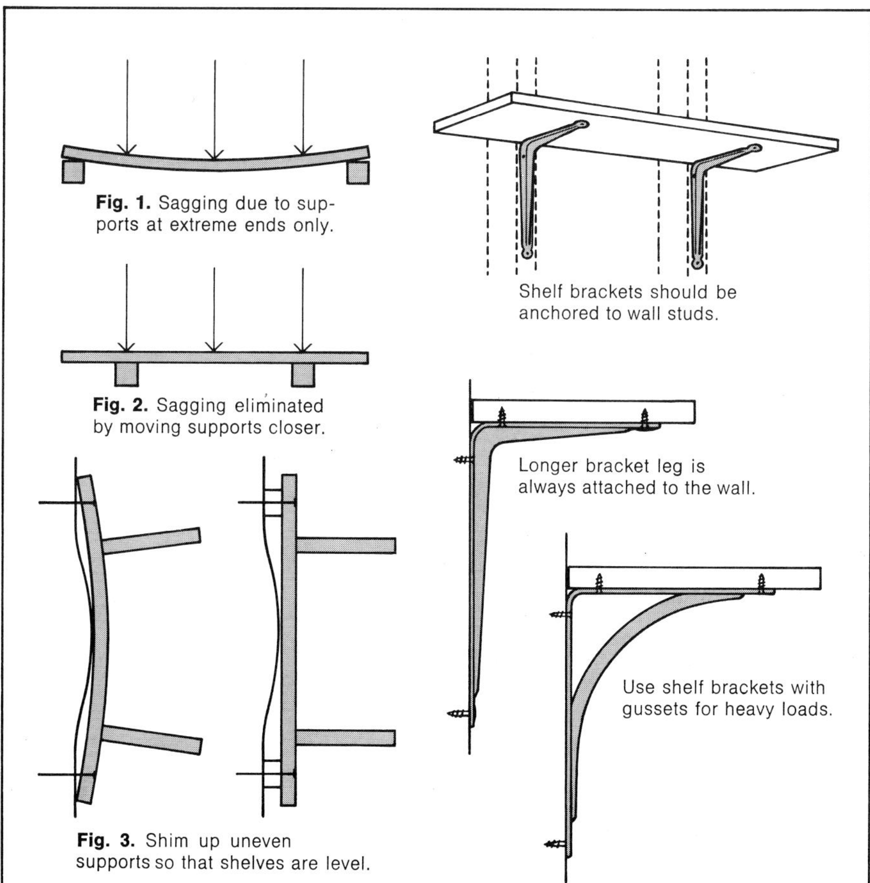

Fig. 1. Sagging due to supports at extreme ends only.

Fig. 2. Sagging eliminated by moving supports closer.

Fig. 3. Shim up uneven supports so that shelves are level.

Shelf brackets should be anchored to wall studs.

Longer bracket leg is always attached to the wall.

Use shelf brackets with gussets for heavy loads.

Adjustable shelving

Each adjustable shelf in the light-load unit shown on the facing page is held in place at each end by two dowels pushed through the upright. One passes through the end panel; the other engages a cleat fixed under the shelf.

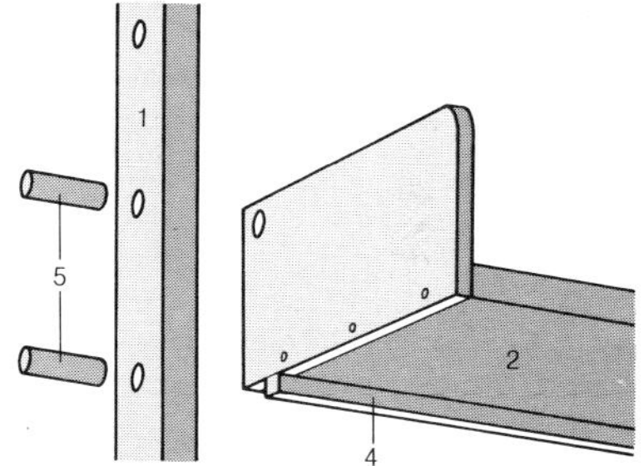

Cut upright (1) bottoms flush to baseboard. Drill ½-inch holes 4 inches apart through upright, and clearance holes for screws into wall 14 inches apart. Countersink screw holes. Screw uprights to wall studs at 32-inch intervals, or anchor the uprights with collapsible anchor bolts (p.76).

Round off top front corner of shelf end (2) to ½-inch radius with saber saw or coping saw. Drill ½-inch hole in end centered 1⅜ inches from top, ¾ inch back. Screw end to shelf (3). Glue and nail cleat (4) under shelf 1 inch from back edge.

PARTS LIST

No.	Name	Quantity	Nominal Size	Length	Width	Material
1	Uprights	2 per shelf	1¼ x 2	72″		pine
2	Shelf ends	2 per shelf		9¼″	5″	½″ plywood
3	Shelves	as needed	1 x 10	29⅞″		pine
4	Shelf cleats	1 per shelf	½″ x ½″ (cut)	30″		pine
5	Dowels	4 per shelf	½″ dia.	1⅝″		maple

Hardware: Six 1½″ No. 6 flathead screws per shelf (for shelf ends). Five 3½″ No. 10 flathead screws per upright. Plastic resin glue. Finishing nails (1″).
Note: Two shelves side by side can share a vertical support; use longer dowels.

Shelf supports

The simplest method of supporting shelves is to hold up the shelf at each end with cleats fastened to side walls or panels. This is suitable only for shelves less than 36 inches long.

Shelves of any length can be cantilevered from the wall on brackets, as long as enough supports are used. A wide variety of metal braces, brackets, and angle irons can be used for supports. If a heavy load will be placed on the shelving, or if extra bracing is required at several points on a long span, use metal brackets. If stock brackets will detract from the appearance of the shelving, choose ornamental brackets available in a variety of styles.

The easiest (and weakest) way to fasten shelves permanently is the butt joint (Fig. 1), but cleats are most frequently used (Fig. 2). The professional way to construct shelves is with dadoes (Figs. 3, 4). A dado is cut into each side, and the shelf is slipped into place and held with nails, screws, adhesive, or simply a friction fit.

Dowels provide adjustable supports. Drill two vertical series of holes in each side of a cabinet and insert two short dowels below the shelf at each side. Metal and plastic pins or studs can be used instead.

Shelves that might sag under a heavy load can be stiffened by nailing or screwing a facing lip across the front of the shelf (Fig. 2). This lip should be at least twice as wide as the shelf is thick. The lip will also hide the cleats at each end—if that support is used for the shelf. If a shelf is backing against a wall, sagging can be corrected by fastening a cleat to the wall to support the back edge of the shelf. Remove the shelf when installing the cleat. Replace the shelf with its bottom side up to straighten the bend.

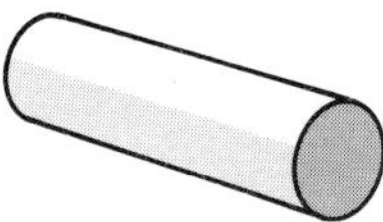

Hardwood dowels provide one of the simplest means of supporting adjustable shelves.

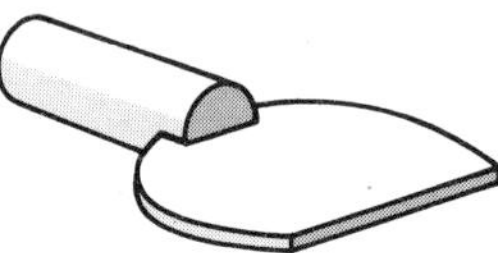

Metal spade pins that fit into predrilled holes can be used instead of dowels.

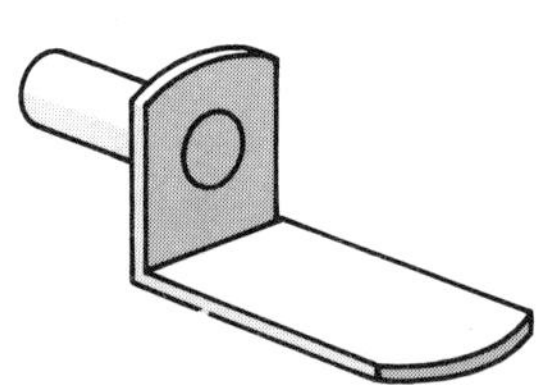

Bracket clips also fit in predrilled holes.

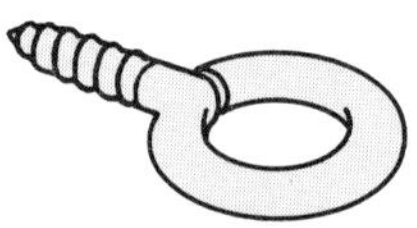

Screw eyes can be used for light loads.

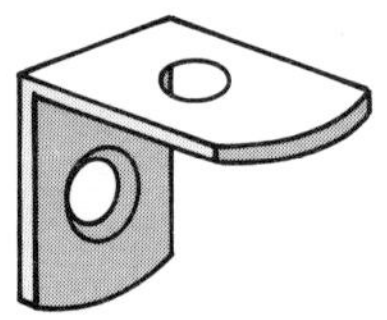

L-brackets are suitable for medium loads.

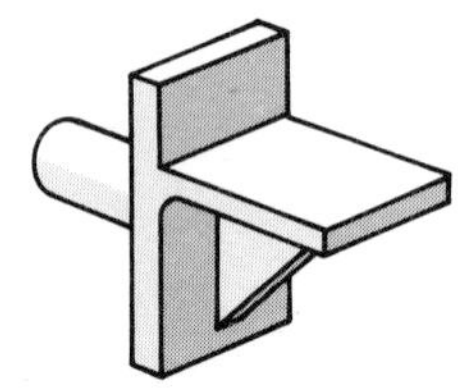

Reinforced brackets are for heavier loads.

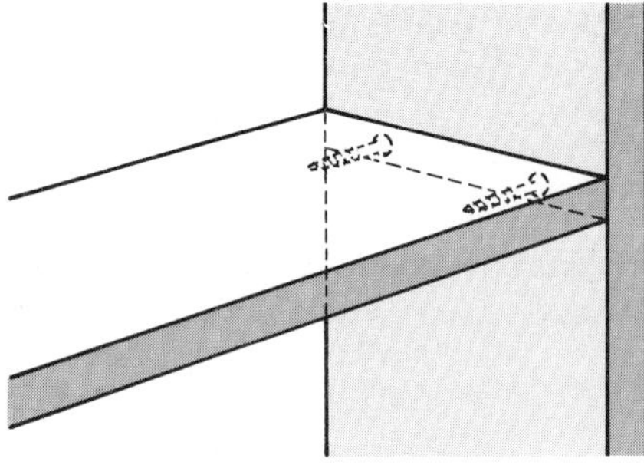

Fig. 1. With the butt joint, end of shelf is set against the side and permanently secured with nails or screws through side.

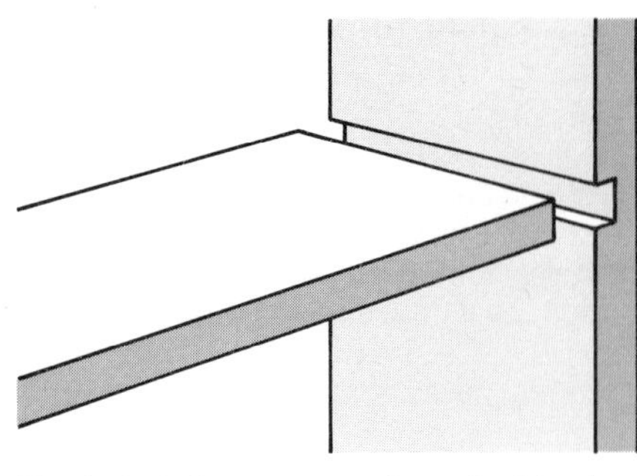

Fig. 3. A dado groove cut in each side of a cabinet with backsaw and chisel or a router is the method professionals use.

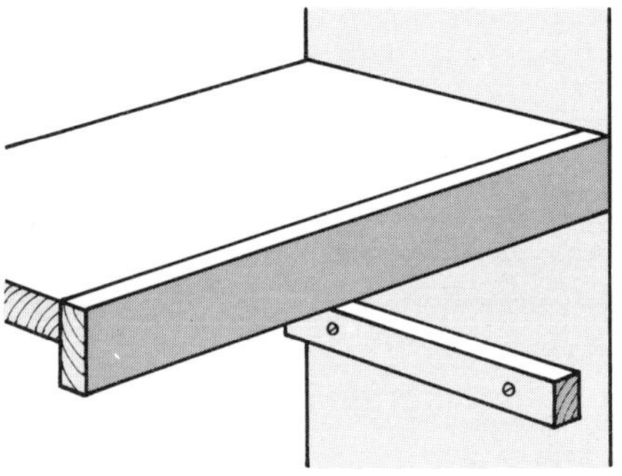

Fig. 2. A cleat of quarter-round or square stock should be used if the butt-joint shelf is to support any substantial weight.

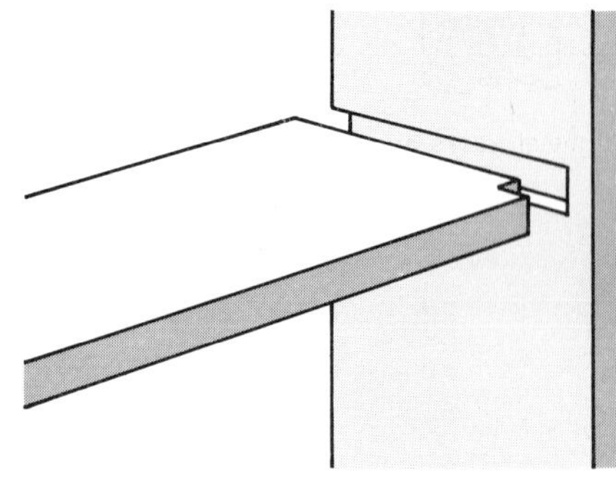

Fig. 4. A partial groove (a stopped dado) gives a more finished look. From the front, groove opening does not show.

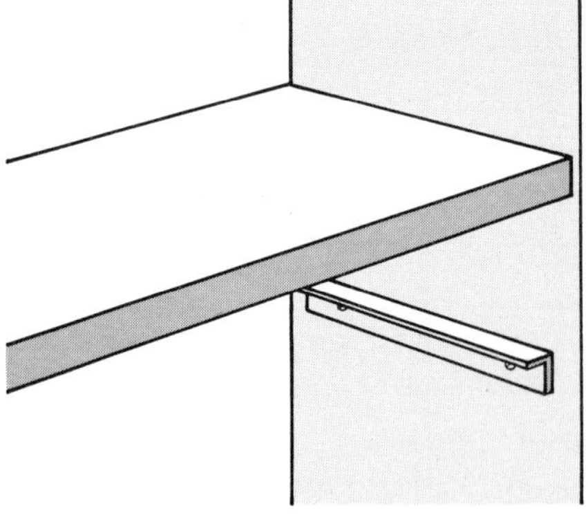

Metal angle irons, screwed to the side pieces, are sometimes substituted for wood cleats, especially in the case of glass shelves.

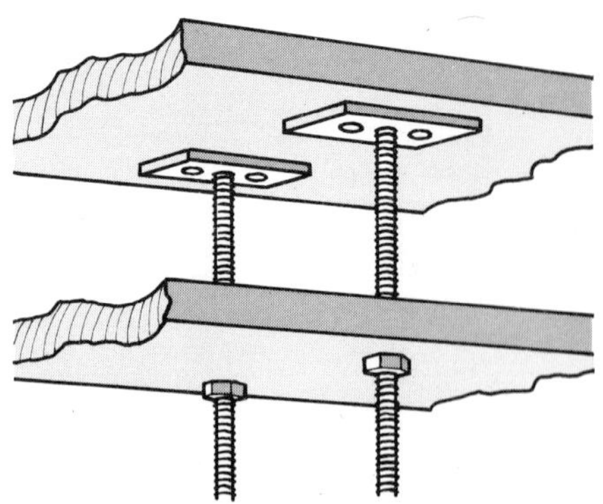

Threaded metal rods fitting into a threaded plate, plus nuts and washers, are suitable to prop up home workshop shelves.

Dado joints 386
Fasteners 76–77

Adjustable standards and brackets

Two metal tracks are screwed to each side of a cabinet. Matching clips can be inserted at 1-in. intervals. Tracks and clips are made in many finishes with tracks up to 12 ft. long.

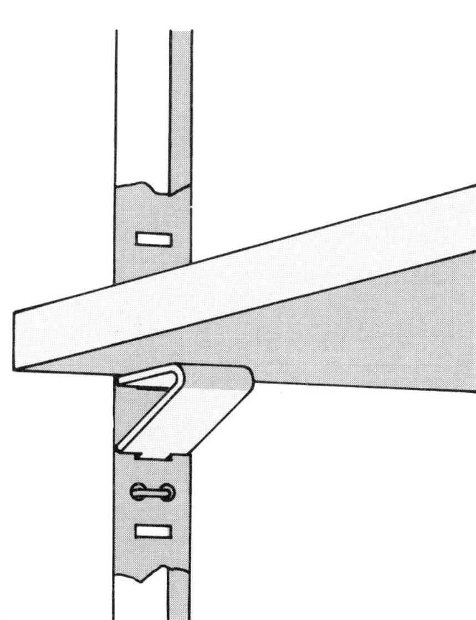

Metal tracks can also be flush mounted. Cut grooves in cabinet sides equal to the depth of the track. Clips with gussets, shown here, are stronger than flat clips but take up slightly more room.

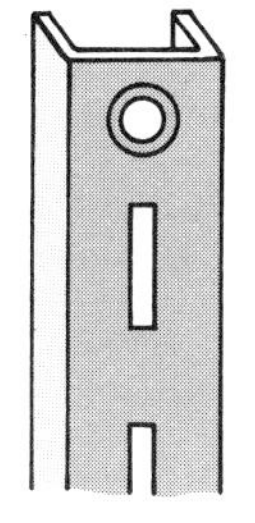

Two or more tracks can support shelves from rear. Slots permit flexibility in shelf arrangement. Bracket below locks in slots.

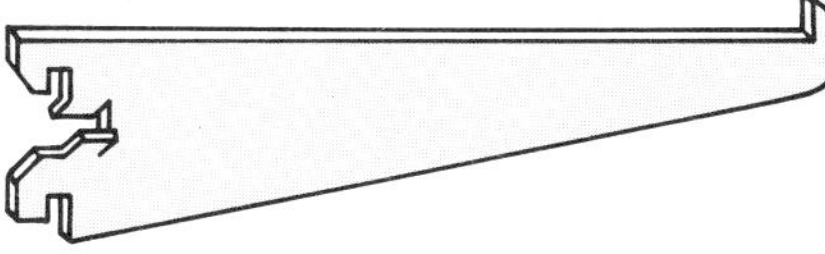

Support bracket, available in various sizes to suit shelf width, fits into track slots.

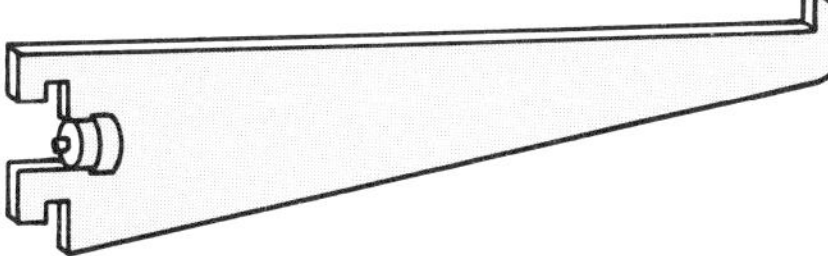

Some brackets, after snapping into place, are secured with a locknut.

Wider tracks with double rows of slots are perfect for shelves that bear heavy loads.

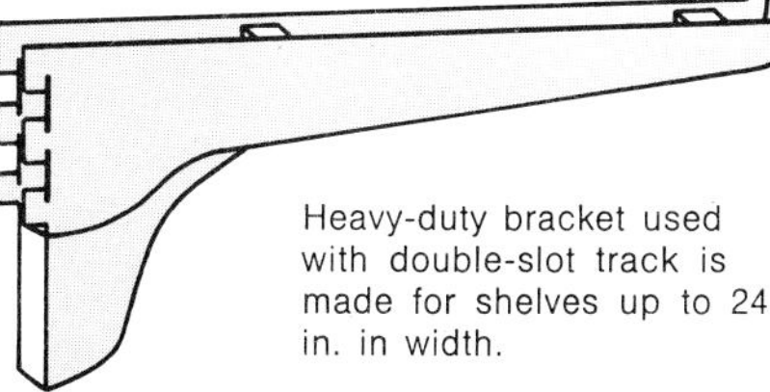

Heavy-duty bracket used with double-slot track is made for shelves up to 24 in. in width.

Another heavy-duty track has keyhole openings for the shelf brackets.

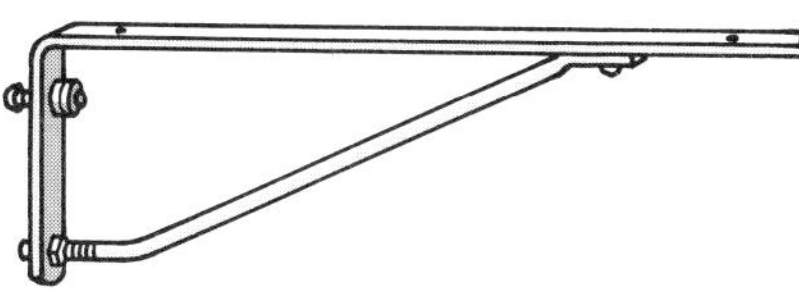

Bracket for keyhole-slot track has a reinforcing gusset and threaded knob to secure the bracket to the track.

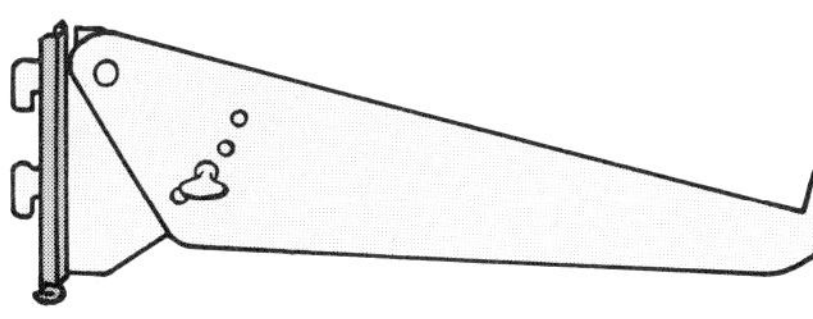

This bracket can be adjusted to slant at 15, 30, or 45 degrees to hold a magazine shelf.

Stationary brackets

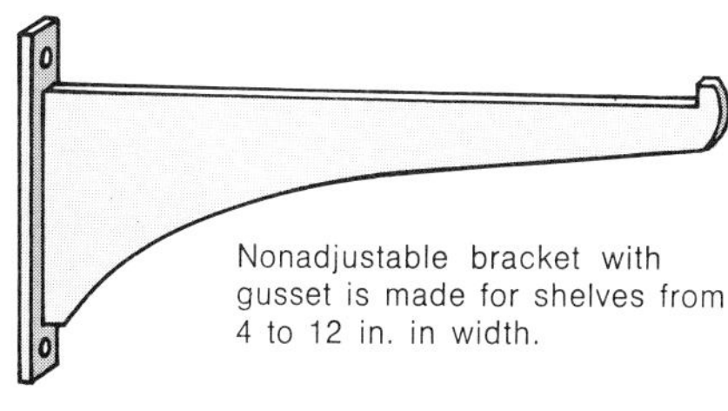

Nonadjustable bracket with gusset is made for shelves from 4 to 12 in. in width.

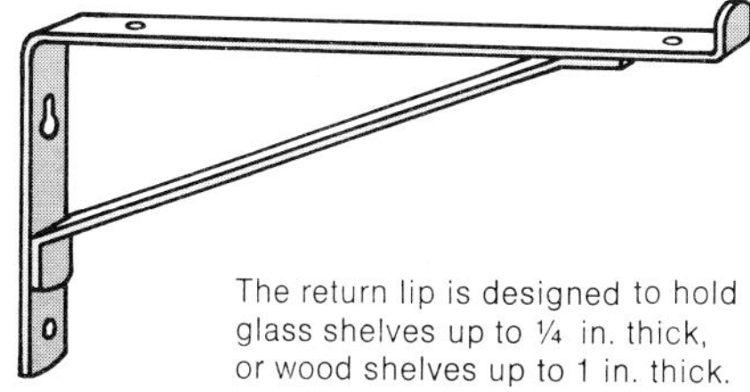

The return lip is designed to hold glass shelves up to ¼ in. thick, or wood shelves up to 1 in. thick.

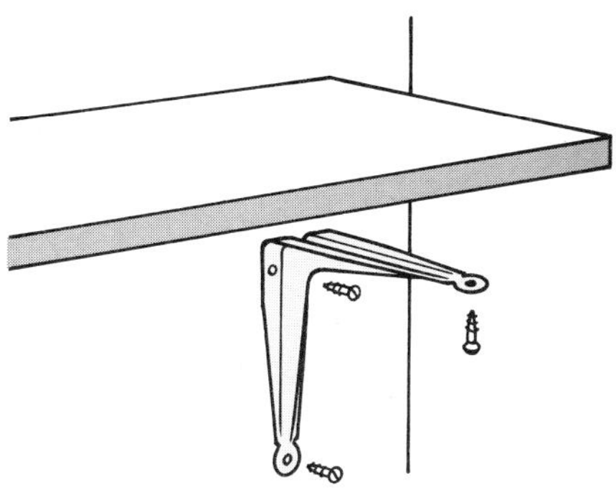

For storage shelves where appearance is not important, pressed-steel brackets screwed to the back wall will support medium loads.

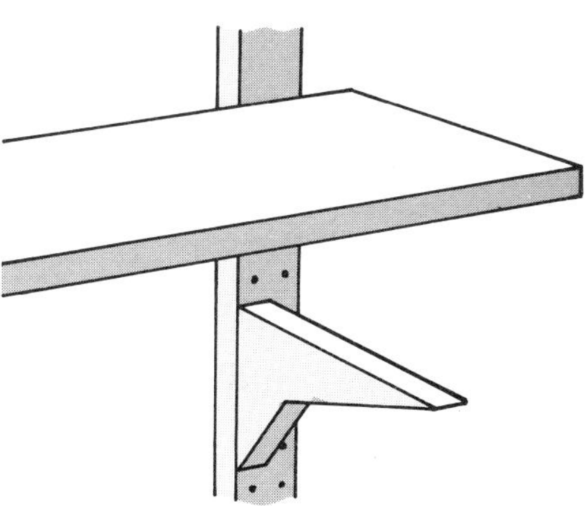

Triangular wooden blocks "toe-screwed" into uprights make sturdy shelf supports. Best material is hardwood, stained, finished, and waxed to match other furniture in room.

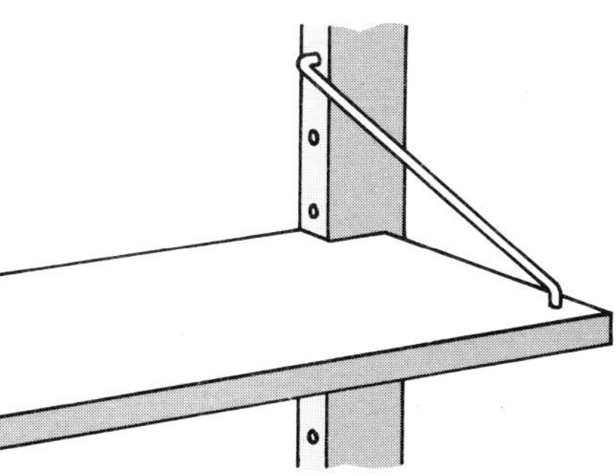

While most brackets support shelves from below, the suspended type is used where styling is a factor.

Bed frame and headboard-night table assembly; mattress base omitted to show framing details.

A 75- x 54- x 5½-in. foam mattress completes bed.

Double bed frame

Inconspicuous leg panels make this elegant double bed appear to float. An optional night table unit with convenient sliding tops can be attached to the headboard. The unit is described on page 552.

The bed described here was designed specifically to accommodate the night tables. If you wish to include them in the project, read instructions on page 552 before proceeding with construction of bed unit.

CONSTRUCTION

Starting 8 inches from each end, curve foot rail (1) down from full width to 5 inches with spokeshave or saber saw. Cut simple box joints in ends of foot, head (2), and side (3) rails with backsaw or saber saw. After trial assembly, round corners with belt or disk sander and coarse abrasive, then smooth with fine abrasive. Screw ledger strips (4, 5) inside rails so that all bottom edges are flush. For extra stability, glue and screw glue blocks (6) inside ledger strips at corners.

Cut leg panel (7) ends to 2-inch depth to match ledger-strip width. These cuts extend in 5 inches, slanting to about 3-inch depth, then curve down steeply to leg panel bottom edge. Straight part of bottom edge should be 38 inches long.

With a saber saw, cut 1½-inch-wide notches 4 inches deep in top edges of leg panels, inner edge of each notch 9 inches from center of panel. Cut 1½-inch-wide notches 3¼ inches deep in the bottom edges of the stringers (8), outer edge of each notch 12 inches from stringer end. When leg panels and stringers fit together, top edges should be flush. Cut central portion of stringers down to 2½-inch depth so that cross beam (9) can rest on stringers. Join beam to stringers with ¼-inch carriage bolts 7½-inches long, heads sunk flush in beam.

Assemble legs, stringers, and beam without glue and fit inside ledger strips, supporting outer frame on blocks or boxes so that leg and stringer tops are flush with ledger strip tops. Where inner and outer frames meet, drill two ⅜-inch-diameter holes through rails 1½ inches into leg and stringer ends. Before gluing, insert dowels (¼ inch overlong for easy removal) dry. At this stage trim inner frame and mattress base (11) to fit.

Take frame apart, then reassemble with glue on both faces of joints,

Backsaw 17
Box joints 392
Countersinking 74
Dowels 395
Saber saw 52
Sanders 57, 59
Spokeshave 30

on dowels, and in dowel holes. Trim dowels to exact length before gluing. Fasten mattress base with glue and 1-inch finishing nails. Wipe off excess glue with damp cloth; after glue hardens, sand smooth any remaining glue with fine sandpaper.

Paint legs and stringers flat black and finish frame with clear polyurethane varnish. For extra stability, center a 47½-inch-long 2 x 3 fir rail between legs 6 inches off floor (for cleaning ease). Attach with ⅜-inch dowels and glue.

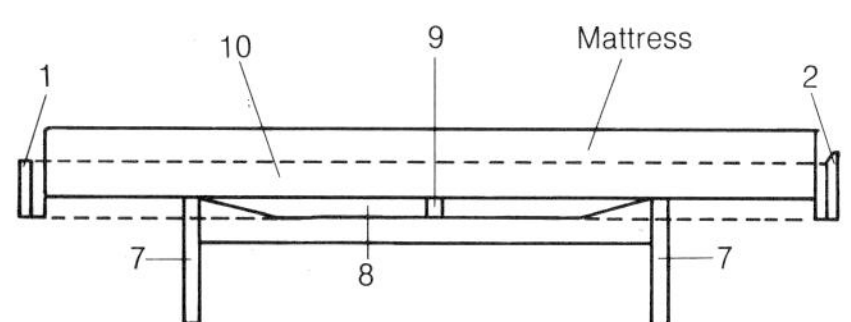

Side view with mattress in place.

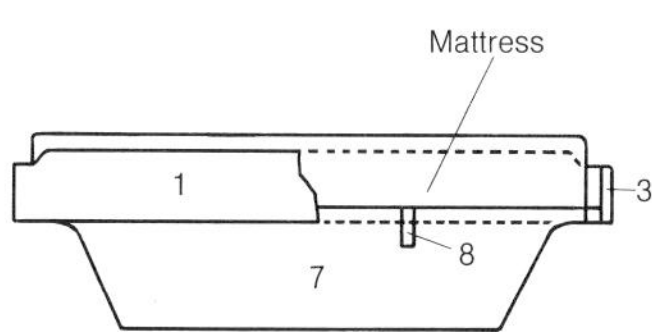

Cutaway end view of construction.

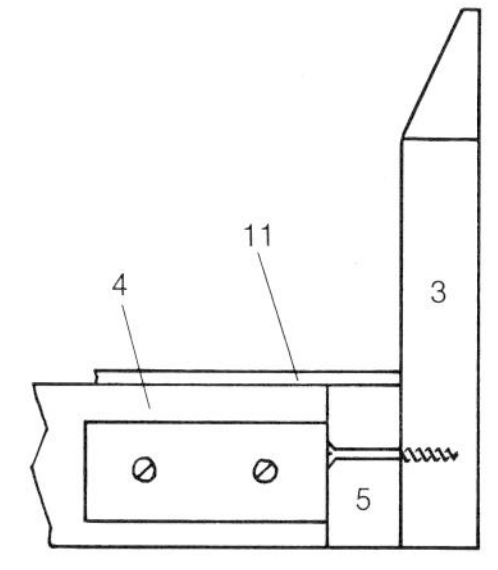

Frame joints are cut square, then rounded.

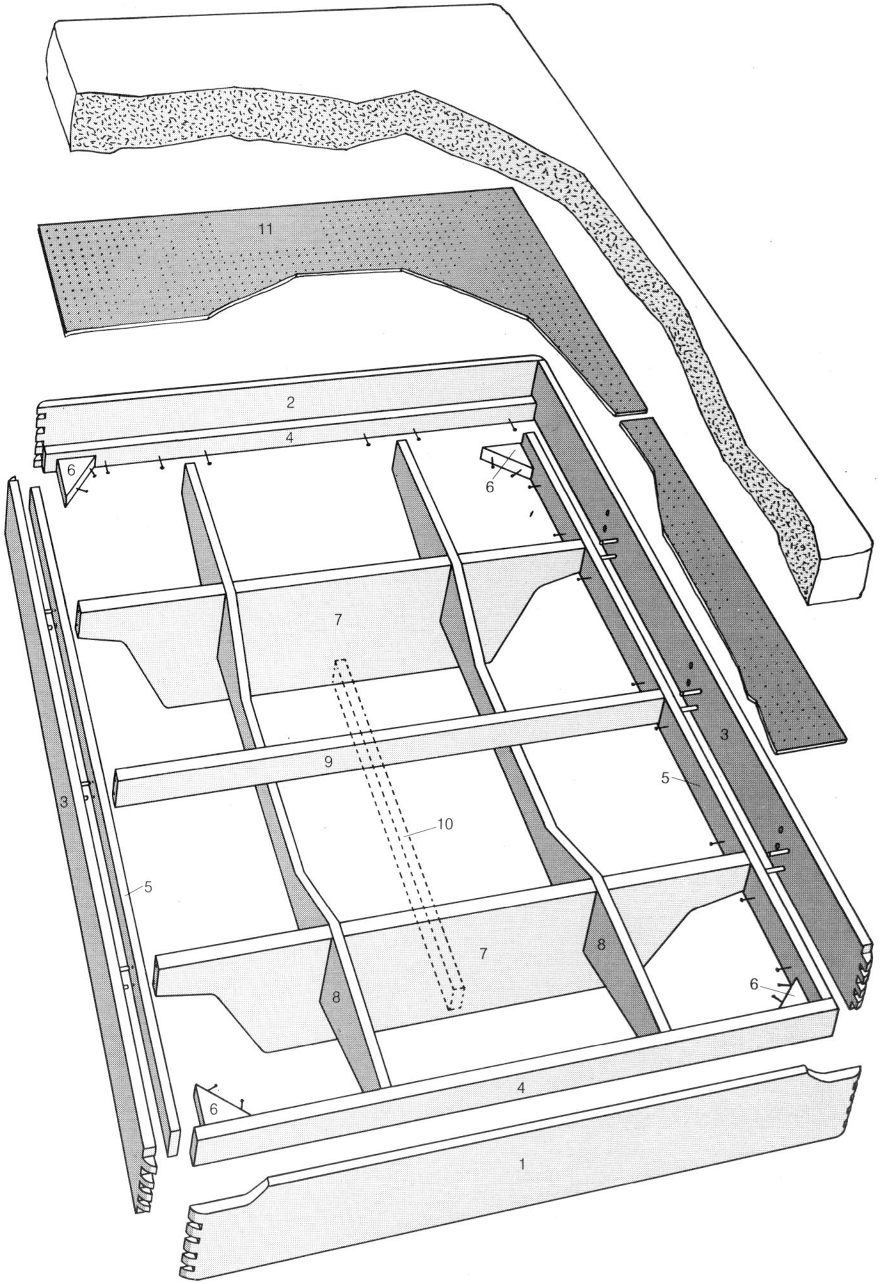

PARTS LIST

No.	Name	Quantity	Nominal size	Length	Width	Material
1	Foot rail	1		58″	6½″	1¼″ pine
2	Head rail	1		58″	5″	1¼″ pine
3	Side rails	2		79″	5″	1¼″ pine
4	End ledgers	2		55¾″	2″	1¼″ pine
5	Side ledgers	2		74½″	2″	1¼″ pine
6	Glue blocks	4	1¼ × 4	triangles		pine
7	Leg panels	2	2 × 12	53½″		fir
8	Stringers	2	2 × 8	74½″		fir
9	Cross beam	1	2 × 3	53½″		fir
10	Support rail	1 (optional)	2 × 3	47½″		fir
11	Mattress base	2 (halves)		38⅜″	55¾″	⅛″ perforated hardboard

Hardware: No. 8 flathead steel screws—twenty eight 1¾″ (to attach ledger strips), eight 2¼″ (to attach corner blocks). Dowel ⅜″-dia., 36″ long. Quarter lb. 1″ finishing nails for mattress base. One qt. plastic resin glue. Two ¼″-dia. carriage bolts 7½″ long.
Note: If head and side rails are ripsawed at lumberyard from nominal 1¼ × 8 lumber, strips left after cutting the rails to size can be used for head and side ledger strips. Sawed edges should be planed smooth. Foot rail (and its ledger strip) must be bought separately because of the width required.

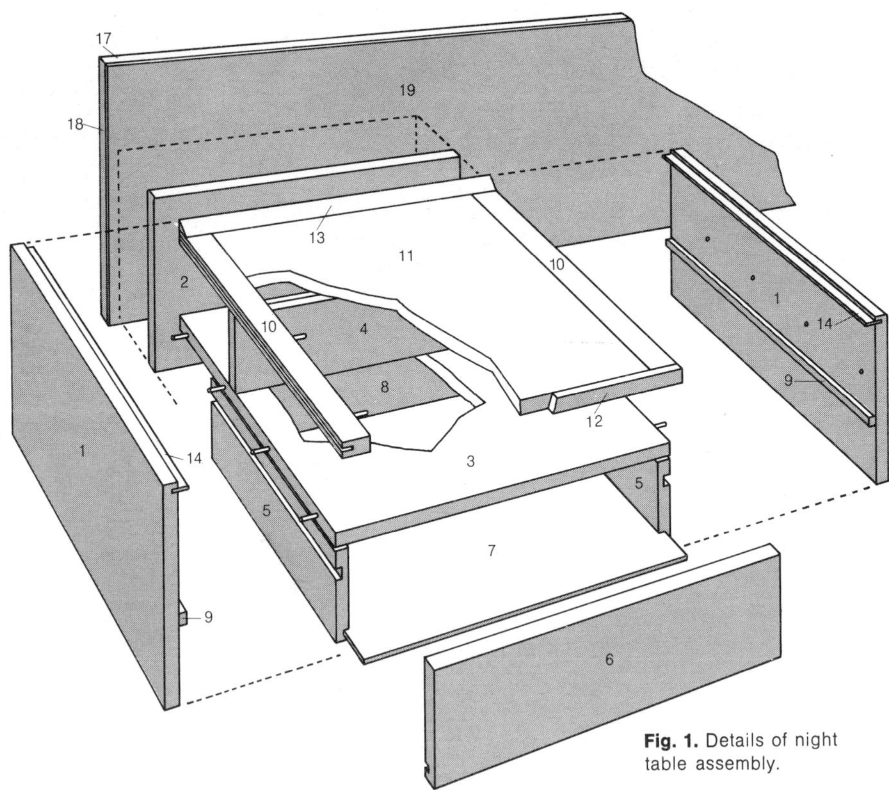

Fig. 1. Details of night table assembly.

PARTS LIST

No.	Name	Quantity	Nominal Size	Length	Width	Material
Each night table						
1	Sides	2		18″	7½″	¾″ plywood
2	Back	1		16¾″	8″	¾″ plywood
3	Shelf	1		17″	16¾″	¾″ plywood
4	Partition	1		16¾″	3¼″	¾″ plywood
5	Drawer sides	2		16″	2¾″	½″ plywood
6	Drawer front	1		16½″	3¾″	½″ plywood
7	Drawer bottom	1		16″	15½″	¼″ plywood
8	Drawer back	1		16½″	3″	½″ plywood
9	Drawer runners	2	½ × ¼ (cut)	16″		pine
10	Top side strips	2	1 × ¾ (cut)	17″		pine
11	Sliding top	1		17″	14⅜″	¾″ plywood
12	Top front trim	1	1 × ½ (cut)	16⅜″		pine
13	Top finger pull	1	1 × ½ (cut)	16⅜″		pine
14	Top tongues	2	½ × ⅛ (cut)	17″		oak
15	Side top/ bottom trim	4 (not shown)	¾ × ¼ (cut)	18¼″		pine
16	Side front trim	2 (not shown)	¾ × ¼ (cut)	8″		pine
Headboard						
17	Top trim	1	¾ × ¼ (cut)	96″		pine
18	Side trim	2	¾ × ¼ (cut)	11¼″		pine
19	Headboard	1		95½″	11″	¾″ plywood
20	Spacers	2	½ × 4 (cut)	18″		pine

Hardware: Box of 1″ brads; ¼ lb. 1½″ finishing nails to hold parts together while glue sets. One pt. plastic resin glue. No. 8 flathead screws; eight 1¾″ (headboard-bed); eight 1½″ (headboard-tables); four 2¼″ (side rails-tables). Dowels (side strips-top), ¼″ dia.
Note: Plywood used for headboard and tables can be birch or pine face veneered. It can be given a natural polyurethane finish or stained to contrast with pine bed frame.

Night table unit

The headboard and matching night tables described here are illustrated in the photographs on page 550. They were designed to harmonize with the double bed shown on that page. Dimensions can be modified, however, to fit any bed of similar size.

Saw ⅛-inch grooves on inner side of table side pieces (1) ⅜ inch from top. Glue and nail sides and back (2) to edges of shelf (3) so that shelf bottom is 3½ inches above bottom edges of sides. Glue and nail partition (4) 5 inches from back, to form a compartment accessible when top is forward.

For drawer, cut ⅝-inch-wide grooves slightly more than ¼ inch deep, 1 inch from outside top edges of drawer sides (5), for the runners. Cut ¼- x ¼-inch grooves ¼ inch from bottom inside drawer sides and front (6), for drawer bottom (7). Assemble with glue and brads. Fit back (8) between sides with bottom edge glued and nailed to drawer bottom. Mount runners (9) with glue and brads so that drawer top edges will clear underside of shelf by 1/16 inch.

Cut centered grooves ⅛ inch wide in sliding top side strips (10). Glue and dowel (with ¼-inch dowels) side strips to top (11). Glue front trim (12) flush with top surface of top; chamfer finger pull (13) with router, or saw off front edge at angle, then glue on back edge of top. Glue tongues (14) into side strip grooves and slide top into table.

Fig. 2. Front view of table construction.

Glue and nail trim strips (15, 16) to table sides; glue and nail trim strips (17, 18) on headboard (19).

Center headboard against bed head rail, bottom edges flush, and screw on. Use no glue, to permit disassembly. Drive screws through headboard into tables, tables positioned so that spacers (20) fit between them and side rails, and bottoms of tables and side rails are flush. Drive screws from inside each side rail through spacer into table side.

Dowels 395
Drawer construction 402
Grooves 386
Rabbet plane 30

Wall-mounted headboard

This headboard-night table unit was designed to fit a double bed with an overall frame width of 56½ inches, but it can be modified to suit queen- or king-sized beds. The entire unit, mounted on the wall, can be removed easily.

CONSTRUCTION

Drill four evenly spaced ¼-inch holes through each end panel (1) into headboard ends (2) and attach with dowels, or make blind-dowel joints. Rear edges of end panels project ¾ inch behind headboard to allow space for wall rail (3) and top rail (4). Bevel upper edge of wall rail 45 degrees downward toward wall and attach to studs with 2½-inch No. 8 flathead screws. Bevel lower edge of top rail to match so that it will lock on when headboard is lowered onto wall rail. Glue and screw top rail to back of headboard with 1¼-inch No. 8 flathead screws. Glue and dowel shelf (5) and drawer guide (6) to headboard with four ¼-inch dowels in shelf, one in guide. Glue and nail end panel and guide to shelf.

For drawer runners, cut ⅝-inch-wide grooves slightly more than ¼ inch deep 1 inch from top edges of sides (7). Glue and nail front (8) and back (9) to ends of sides; glue and nail bottom (10) to bottom edges of drawer assembly. Nail and glue runners (11) on end panel and drawer guide (6) so that top of drawer clears shelf by 1⁄16 inch.

No drawer pulls are needed; the open bottoms of the tables provide an easy grip. Paint or varnish the completed unit as desired. Veneer plywood edges.

Space tables to clear bed side by comfortable margin.

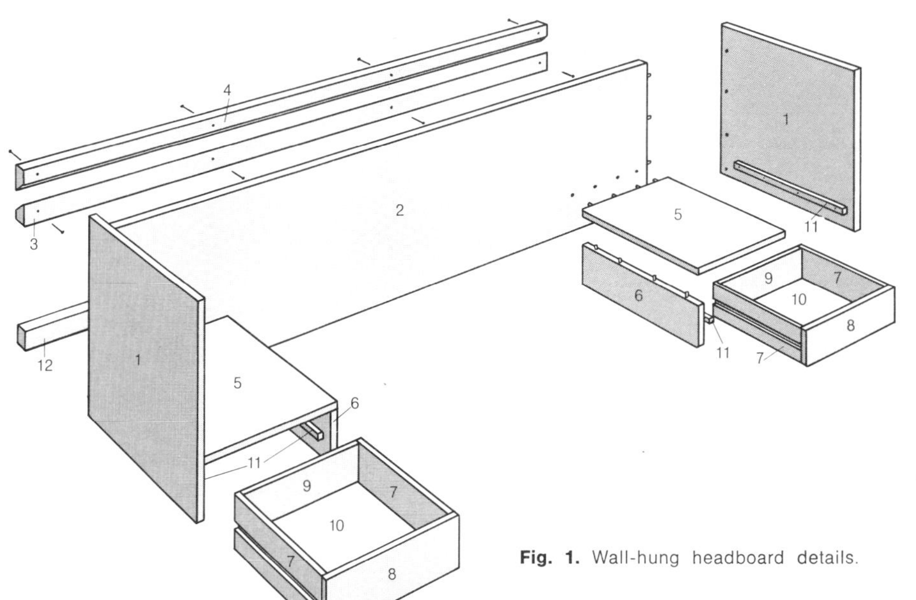

Fig. 1. Wall-hung headboard details.

PARTS LIST

No.	Name	Quantity	Nominal Size	Length	Width	Material
1	End panels	2		14¾″	14¼″	¾″ plywood
2	Headboard	1		83½″	14¾″	¾″ plywood
3	Wall rail	1	1 × 2	82″		pine
4	Top rail	1	1 × 2	83½″		pine
5	Shelves	2		12¾″	12¾″	¾″ plywood
6	Drawer guides	2		12¾″	3″	¾″ plywood
7	Drawer sides	4		11¼″	2⅝″	¾″ plywood
8	Drawer fronts	2		12½″	2⅝″	¾″ plywood
9	Drawer backs	2		12½″	2⅝″	¾″ plywood
10	Drawer bottoms	2		12½″	12½″	¼″ plywood
11	Drawer runners	4	½ × ¼ (cut)	11″		pine
12	Spacer	1	1 × 2	82″		pine

Hardware: Small box 1½″ finishing nails for drawer corners; box ¾″ brads for drawer bottoms. Dowels, ¼″ dia. Veneer plywood edging as needed (approx. 18′). One pt. plastic resin glue. No. 8 flathead screws—eight 1¼″, eight (or as needed for wall studs) 2½″.

 Comprehensive wall-to-wall closet /1

This closet storage plan can be arranged in an existing closet, or you can build a wall to wall unit comprising two of these cabinets.

Coping saw 18
Dado joints 386
Fasteners 76
Hanging doors 141
Wall paneling 379

This closet storage unit is a two-part project. Part 1 is a closet storage cabinet that can be built into an existing closet. Part 2 is a comprehensive storage wall that can be built across an entire room. The wall-to-wall framework would contain two of the storage units described in Part 1.

Part 1: Closet storage cabinet

Before starting construction, shop for plastic tray storage drawers and storage basket units. If the units available in your area are of different measurements from those shown here, (trays 15 inches wide, 16 inches deep; baskets 12 inches wide, 18 inches deep), alter the measurements of the tray and basket compartments (3, 4, and 8) in the project to suit the components available. An alternative to the trays would be to build eight storage drawers (p. 402).

CONSTRUCTION

Mount end panel (5) to the closet wall. If fastening to hollow walls, use collapsible anchors (p. 76), inserting one at each corner of the panel. Use two 3-inch angle irons to attach second end panel (5) to the floor. Space it 36 inches from wall-mounted end panel as in Fig. 1. Mount cabinet top (1) to end panels (5). Glue and fasten with 1½-inch No. 6 flathead screws.

Cut tray compartment shelf (3) and use it as a spacer to position divider panel (6). Fasten divider panel to the floor with two 3-inch angle irons. Use two 1½-inch No. 6 flathead screws to fasten panel through cabinet top (1).

Cut shelves (4) and drill ¼-inch shelf-mounting holes in wall-mounted end panel (5) and in divider panel (6).

Mount bridge shelf support (11) to rear wall of closet so that its top edge is flush with top edge of end panel (5). Fasten to wall with collapsible anchors or screw into studs. Install closet pole supports (12) and closet pole (13). Install bridge shelf (2). If building the cabinet unit into an existing closet, one closet pole support is mounted on the end divider panel (5), and the other is wall mounted and fastened with collapsible anchors. When building the cabinet into the wall-to-wall closet, both closet pole supports are screwed to the end panels (5) of both storage cabinets. Fig. 1.

Mount basket compartment sides (8). One side is screwed to end divider panel (5) with 1½-inch No. 6 flathead screws. The other is fastened to the floor with two 3-inch angle irons. Mount basket compartment top (7) to sides. Glue and fasten it with 1½-inch No. 6 flathead screws.

Cut shoe rack panels (9). The panels are slotted at about 35 degrees to the top and back edges, 45 degrees near the base of the front edge, as in Fig. 2. Make the slots oversize to accept ¾-inch dowels. To determine the spacing of the slots, lay a shoe, toe down on its side, against the panel surface. Mark the notch for the dowel between heel and sole and at a point about halfway along the sole. Use a coping saw to cut the down-slanted notches to these marks. The spacing will differ for men's and women's shoes. Glue the shoe rack sides to the end panel and divider panel. Install the dowel shoe supports (10). To store other items in the shoe rack space, simply lift out the dowels.

Install tray and basket racks as per manufacturer's instructions.

Part 2: Wall-to-wall closet

Before planning construction for this unit, determine what size and style louver door you will use. This will enable you to build the door openings of the closet to suit standard door sizes rather than trying to fit doors to odd-sized openings. Standard louvered

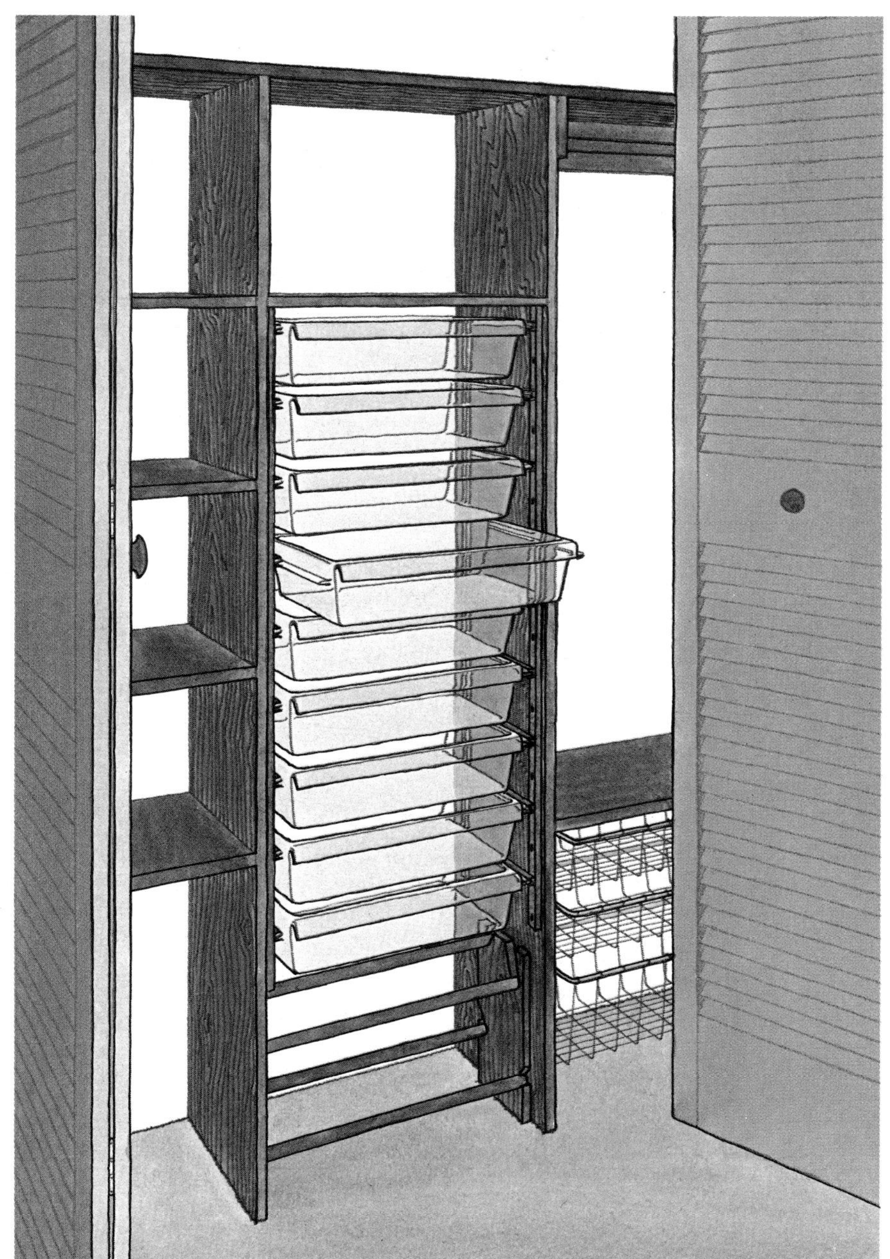

Clear plastic trays are mounted on runners to serve as drawers. Baskets are installed in same manner.

door heights are 48, 60, and 72 inches. The average room will require either a 60-inch or 72-inch door, depending on the height of the ceiling. Doors are also made to fit door openings of 24, 32, 36 inches. Double doors, such as those pictured, will fit openings of 48, 64, or 72 inches.

Doors are often sold in complete kits that include hinges, tracks and knobs. If your dealer does not carry the doors in kit form, be sure to order hanging tracks and related hardware when you buy the doors.

If the unit is to be built into a room with wall-to-wall carpeting over carpet padding, it should be built on its own base floor of three 2 x 8s plus a 2 x 3 laid side by side. This will assure that the door bottoms clear the carpeting.

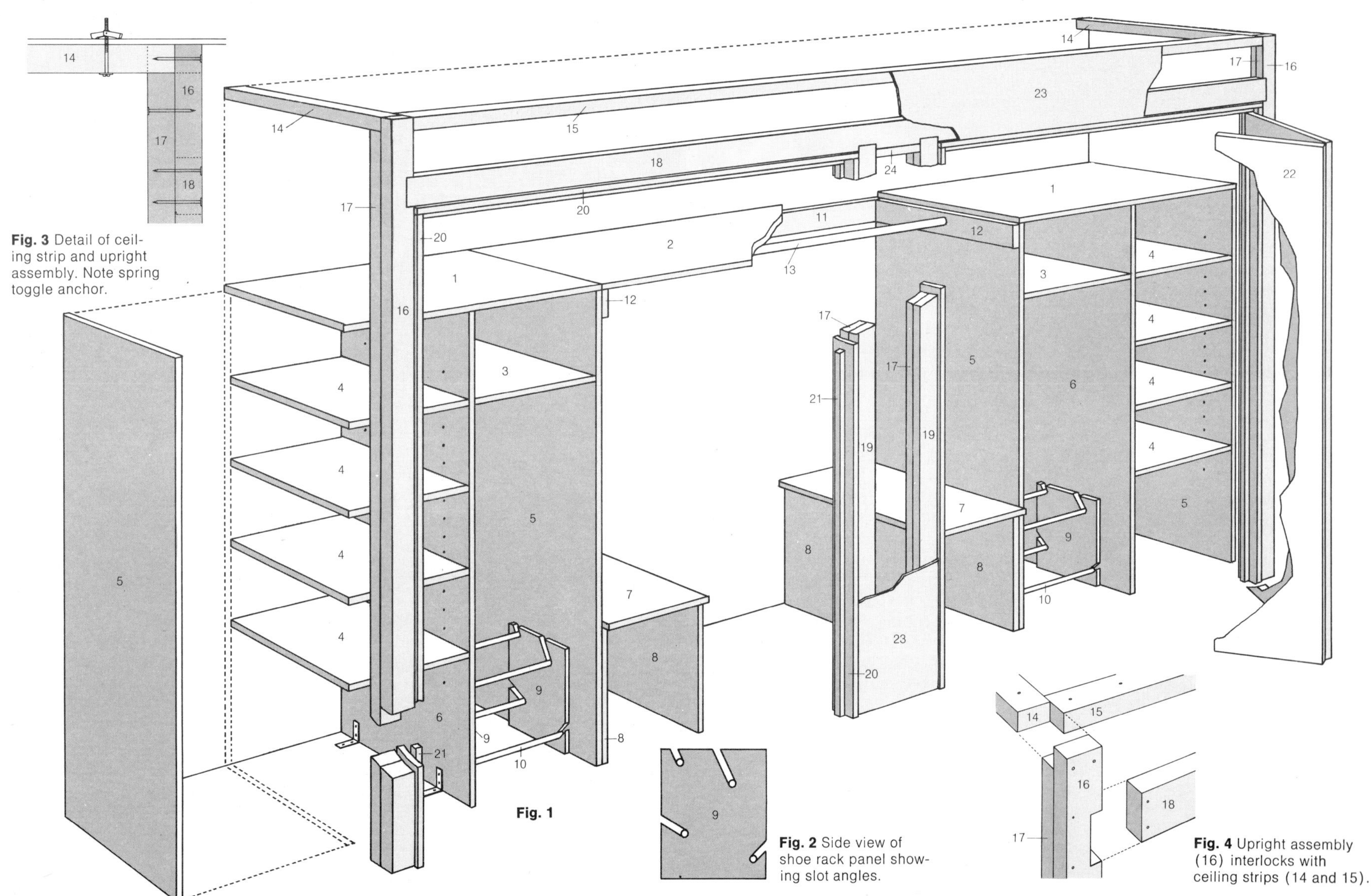

Fig. 3 Detail of ceiling strip and upright assembly. Note spring toggle anchor.

Fig. 1

Fig. 2 Side view of shoe rack panel showing slot angles.

Fig. 4 Upright assembly (16) interlocks with ceiling strips (14 and 15).

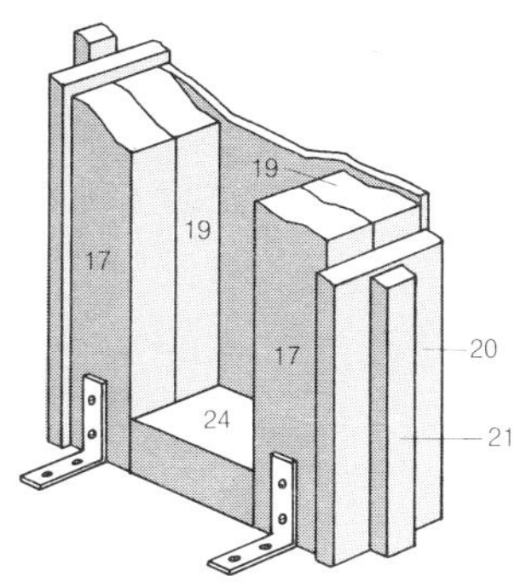

Fig. 5 Floor fastening detail for center uprights.

CONSTRUCTION

Cut end ceiling strips (14). Fasten both strips to the ceiling. Nail them in place if a ceiling beam is present. If not, anchor them with 3-inch split-wing toggles (p. 76) as in Fig. 3. Mount front ceiling strip (15) so that the front edge protrudes 1½ inches beyond the end of the ceiling strips (14) as in Fig. 4. Fasten by screwing into beams with 3-inch lag screws (p. 72).

Cut corner uprights (16) so that they fit snugly from floor to ceiling. From bottom end of upright, measure the height of the louvered door. To this measurement, add ¾ inch to allow for the thickness of the door jamb, plus additional clearance between the door bottom and the floor. At this point, mark a line for a dado cut.

For example, if door height is 72 inches, the bottom of the dado mark would be 73¼ (72″ + ¾″ + ½″) inches from the floor end of the upright. Make a 3½-inch-long dado 1 inch deep (p. 386). This dado holds door header (18).

Complete upright assembly by cutting upright support strip (17) 1½-inches shorter than the upright (16). Nail upright support strip to corner uprights (16) so that bottom ends are flush. Install upright assembly. Nail the top end to the end ceiling strips (14) as in Fig. 4. Use 3-inch angle irons to fasten the bottom ends to the floor.

Cut door header (18) to fit snugly between upright assemblies (16). Make dado cuts for center upright assemblies (19). Space dadoes so that door openings are the same size as louvered doors. Allow 1½ inch additional space for thickness of door jambs. Install door header (18) by nailing it into upright support strips (17).

Cut center uprights (19) to fit snugly between the door header (18) and the floor. Cut upright support strips (17) 2½ inches longer and nail them to the uprights. Fit the upright assemblies into the door header dadoes. Fasten the top end by nailing through support strips (17) into the header. Use two 3-inch angle irons to fasten the bottom to the floor as in Fig. 5. Nail one spacer cleat (24) to the floor between the center uprights. Nail another to the door header to provide a nailing base for wall covering. Cut and fit door jambs (20). If doors have sliding-track hardware, install it on the upper jamb.

Close in framework with wallboard or prefinished wood panel (23).

Build storage cabinet units as described in Part 1 of this project. Complete both cabinets prior to installing bridge shelf support (11), bridge shelf (2), and closet pole (13). For spans 6 feet or longer, use a 1-inch-diameter galvanized steel pipe rather than a wooden pole. Most plumbing suppliers will cut the pipe to length. No threading is required. Be sure the pole is mounted far enough below the shelf to allow easy withdrawal of coat hangers.

Mount doors (22). Follow the manufacturer's instructions in using the folding door hardware, and try the doors before mounting the stop strips (21). Install the strips so that they close any gap between the door and surrounding trim. The strips should also conceal the folding-door track.

PARTS LIST Shelf cabinet (for building one cabinet only)

No.	Name	Quantity	Nominal Size	Length	Width	Material
1	Cabinet top	1		36″	18″	¾″ particle board
2	Bridge shelf	1		to suit	18″	¾″ particle board
3	Tray compartment shelf	1		18″	16¼″	¾″ particle board
4	Adjustable shelves	4		18″	17½″	¾″ particle board
5	End panels	2		60″	18″	¾″ particle board
6	Divider panel	1		60″	18″	¾″ particle board
7	Basket compartment top	1		20″	15″	¾″ particle board
8	Basket compartment sides	2		19″	18″	¾″ particle board
9	Shoe rack panels	2		10″	10″	⅜″ plywood
10	Shoe supports	4		16¼″		¾″-dia. dowel
11	Bridge shelf support	1	1 x 4	to suit		pine
12	Closet pole supports	2	1 x 4	17¼″		pine
13	Closet pole	1		to suit		1⅜″-dia. fir

Hardware: Six 3″ angle irons to attach divider panels to floor. Seven collapsible anchors to fasten to hollow wall. Twenty-four 1½″ No. 6 flathead screws. Adjustable shelf hardware; 16 shelf supports to fit holes in dividers.

Note: Dimensions are for cabinet shown in picture. Depth of cabinet can be adjusted to suit deeper or shallower closets.

PARTS LIST Wall to wall closet

No.	Name	Quantity	Nominal Size	Length	Material
14	End ceiling strips	2	2 x 3	22½″	fir
15	Front ceiling strip	1	2 x 3	to suit	fir
16	Corner upright assemblies	2	2 x 3	to suit	fir
17	Upright support strips	4	2 x 3	to suit	fir
18	Door header	1	2 x 4	to suit	pine
19	Center upright assemblies	2	2 x 3	to suit	fir
20	Door jambs	6	1 x 4	to suit door width and height	pine
21	Door stops	6	¾ x ¾	to suit door width and height	pine
22	Louvered doors	4 pair	standard sizes available		
23	Wall covering	1 sheet	4 x 8		wallboard or wood panel
24	Spacer cleats	2	2 x 3	to suit	fir

Hardware: Four 3″ angle irons to fasten uprights to floor. Collapsible anchors as needed to fasten end ceiling strips. Six 4-inch lag screws for fastening front ceiling strip. Quarter-lb. 3½″ common nails. Construction adhesive, if applying wood panel; wallboard nails, tape, and joint compound if installing wallboard. Louvered door track hardware. Twelve 1″ x 3″ butt hinges. Four door pulls.

Note: Uprights (19) and door header (18) can be positioned to suit standard louvered door sizes.

Bedroom projects: **Fitted closet**

Frame of the closet is built along one side wall and rear wall of a room.

By varying length, width, and height to fit available space, you can adapt both the natural-finish and the painted versions of this space-saving double closet to fill a recess or a corner of a room of different dimensions from those illustrated here. The use of sliding doors eliminates the problem of door swing clearance.

CONSTRUCTION

Start by measuring the space to be occupied by the closet. Cut grooves in top and bottom rails (1) and middle rail (2) equal to the width of the door track (Fig. 2). Stop the grooves 3 inches from the ends of the rails. A mortise and tenon joint is used at each end (see drawing).

Cut a ¾- x ¾-inch rabbet along the outer face of the free end upright (3) to take end panel (5) and along top face of middle rail (2) to take the long shelf (6). Cut a ¾-inch rabbet ⅜ inch deep for the partition (7) in the center of the middle rail. Cut mortises in uprights so that top of middle rail will be 76¾ inches above the floor.

Painted version with extra shelves.

Glue uprights (3,4) and rails (1,2) squarely together to form the front frame; then fasten them with 1½-inch No. 8 flathead screws.

Cut a filler strip (8) to fit the contour of the side wall with its front face 26 inches from the back wall. The filler strip must be straight and vertical on its outer edge and no thicker than the baseboard. Screw the filler strip to the wall. Next, fasten the long cleat (9) to the wall.

Screw the front frame to the filler strip and floor, with the front edges 26 inches from back wall. If floor is uneven, use shims to level the front frame.

Cut ¾-inch-wide slots for the short shelves (10) in partition (7) 9 inches and 18 inches from top. Cut ¾- x ⅜-inch rabbets in end panel (5) also 9 inches and 18 inches from the top. Cut identical rabbets for the long shelf, level with rabbet in middle rail (2).

Cut the back of the partition (7) to fit the baseboard and fit the partition behind the bottom rail (1) and middle rail (2). Cut the long shelf to length. Cut a ¼-inch-deep rabbet in it to take the partition. Nail ¾- x ¾-inch cleats to back of middle rail (2), ¾ inch from rail top to support shelf edge. Next, screw short cleats (11) to the wall. Cut the short shelves to length.

Lift short shelf outer ends and slip inner ends into partition slots. Then rest outer ends on cleats. Toenail partition to the floor.

Cut the back of the end panel (5) to fit the baseboard. Screw the end panel to the upright (3).

Screw closet pole brackets (13) in place 3 inches below long shelf and 11

Adhesives 86
Finishing Wood 407
Measuring and marking 382
Rabbeting 392
Wood joints 384

inches from wall. Install closet poles (14).

Doors should have ⅛-inch clearance on all sides. Insert the plastic tracks in the top and bottom rails (1). Install the rear door first. Raise it into the upper track so that it clears the lower track and then lower the door into the lower track. Repeat for the outer door. The short upper doors (15) are installed the same way.

Install recessed pulls on the doors at same height as handles on other doors of the room.

The smaller photograph shows a painted version of the closet with the addition of four shelves at the left for storing sheets, blankets, and towels.

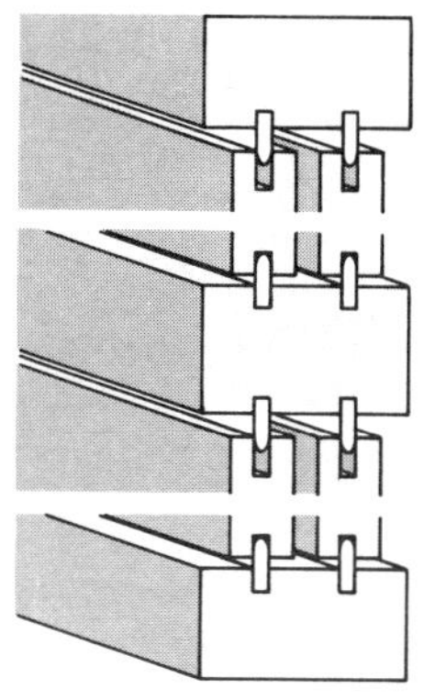

Fig. 2. Upper and lower doors ride on thin plastic splines that fit into groves cut in top, middle, and bottom rails as well as door tops and bottoms.

If you want to make either version of the closet into a freestanding unit, you will have to add a back, back frame, and base. Make the back of ¼-inch plywood. Inasmuch as this material comes only in 4-foot widths, you will use two pieces for the back. Cut them so that the "seam" meets the center partition. Nail the back to the back frame with 1½-inch finishing nails.

The base should be sturdy enough to withstand occasional moving of the closet. Use ¼-, ½-, or ¾-inch plywood.

Regardless of which version you decide to build, paint the interior a light color. The unpainted closet is finished by lightly staining the trim and doors.

Before finishing, carefully sand the inside as well as the outside. Round all sharp corners with coarse sandpaper, followed by fine sandpaper. Finishing consists of two coats of lacquer (with light sanding between coats) and a coat of paste wax buffed to a soft luster with a buffing bonnet on a power drill.

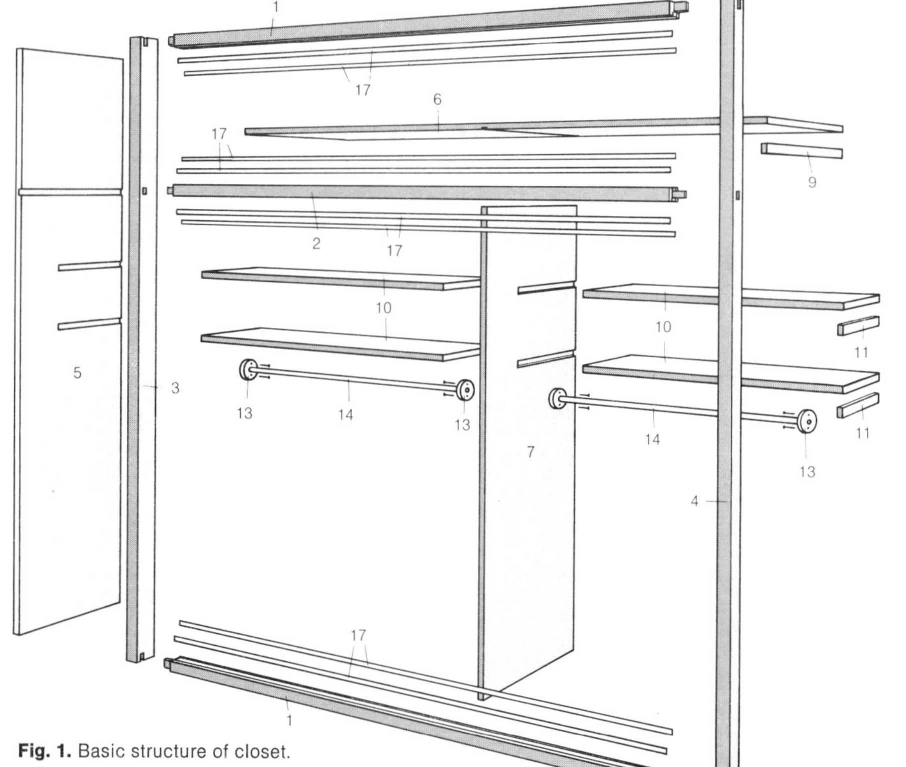

Fig. 1. Basic structure of closet.

PARTS LIST

No.	Name	Quantity	Nominal size	Length	Width	Material
1	Top/bottom rails	2	2 X 3	as needed		pine
2	Middle rail	1	2 X 2	as needed		pine
3	Free end upright	1	2 X 2	as needed		pine
4	Wall end upright	1	2 X 3	as needed		pine
5	End panel	1		as needed	26″	¾″ plywood
6	Long shelf	1		as needed	23½″	¾″ plywood
7	Partition	1		76¼″	23½″	¾″ plywood
8	Filler strip	1	1 X 3 (not shown)	as needed		pine
9	Long cleat	1	1 X 2	23½″		pine
10	Short shelves	4		as needed	16″	¾″ plywood
11	Short cleats	2	1 X 2	16″		pine
12	Vertical molding	1	¾″ quarter round	as needed		pine
13	Closet pole brackets	4				wood or metal
14	Closet poles	2		as needed		1⅜″—dia. fir
15	Upper doors	2		to fit		½″ plywood
16	Lower doors	2		to fit		½″ plywood
17	Door tracks	4		as needed		plastic (see Fig. 2)

Hardware: One doz. 1½″ No. 8 flathead screws. Nails, 1½″ finishing. Four recessed door pulls. One half pt. stain. One pt. polyurethane varnish.

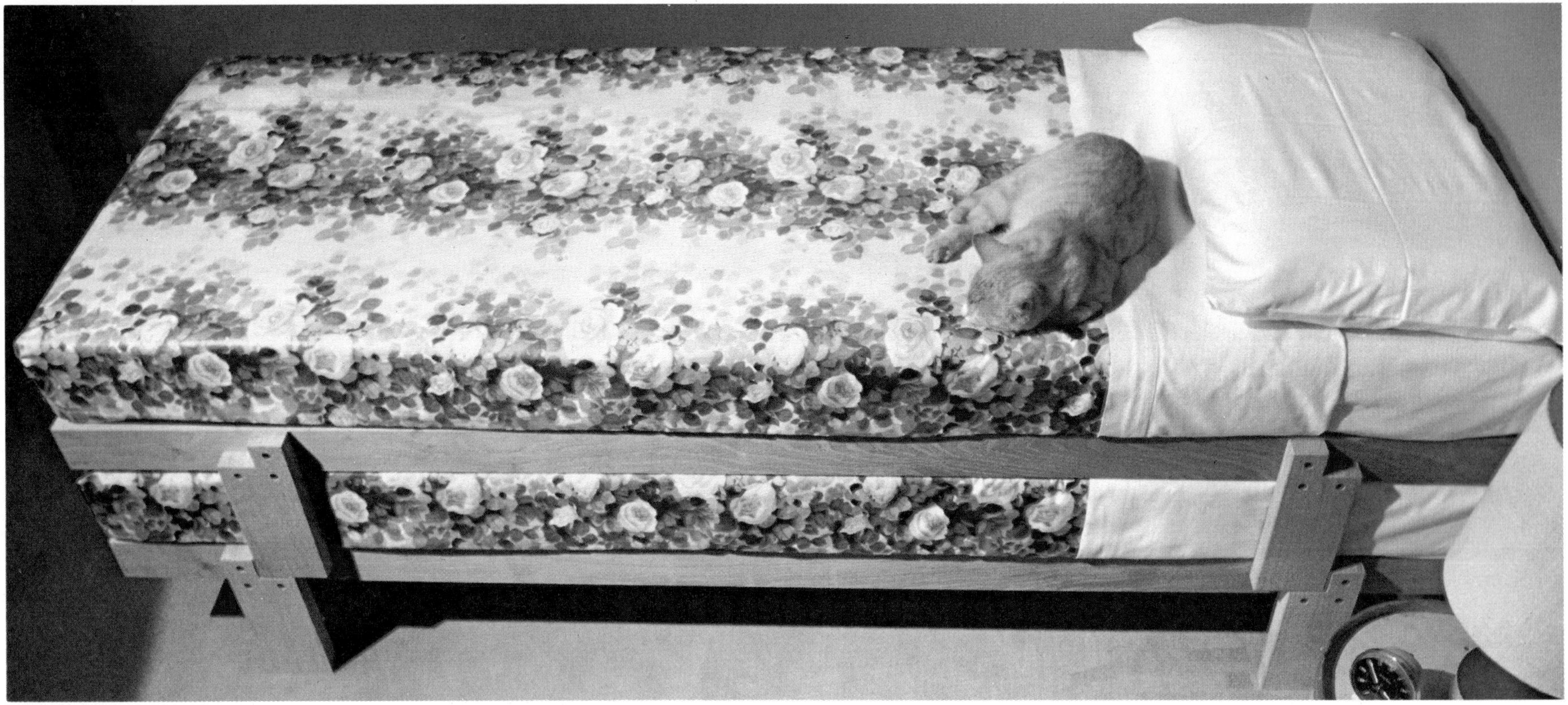

When stacked, these two beds occupy the space of one. The notching of the leg tops allows either bed to rest on top of the other.

When separated, the unit becomes a set of twin beds.

The lightweight construction of these two sturdy beds makes them easy to rearrange for extra guests. Stack one atop the other and the unit can be used as a single bed. In the "piggyback" position the legs interlock so that the top bed will not become dislodged. When a second bed is needed, the upper unit is simply lifted to allow a twin-bed arrangement. The beds are the same height, and either can be stacked on top of the other.

CONSTRUCTION

The dimensions given here are based on the use of 75- x 30-inch mattresses 4 inches thick. If 5-inch mattresses are used, increase the leg length 1 inch. Outside dimensions of mattresses may vary slightly; so it is a good idea to measure them before buying the lumber.

The nominal size of the side rails and end rails is the same as that of a standard 2 x 4; so ordinary fir 2 x 4s can be used if costs are to be kept to a minimum. Otherwise, use hardwood, available in the same size at larger lumberyards. With either material, the box joints at the corners can be cut with a saber saw or by hand with a backsaw. Coat all meeting surfaces with

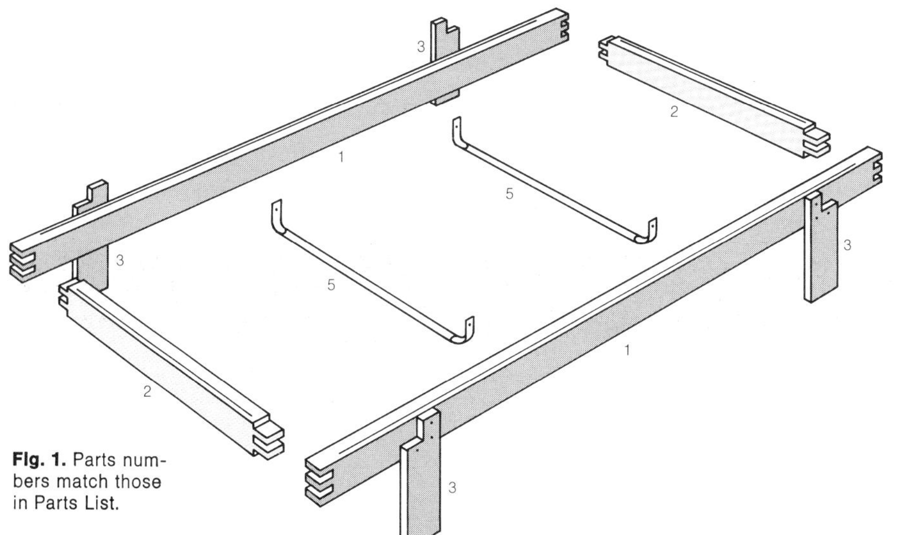

Fig. 1. Parts numbers match those in Parts List.

PARTS LIST

No.	Name	Quantity	Nominal Size	Length	Material
1	Side rails	4	2 × 4	78″	fir or hardwood
2	End rails	4	2 × 4	30″	fir or hardwood
3	Legs	8	1¼ x 4	10″	hardwood
4	Webbing	approx.	2″	120′	rubber, jute or canvas
5	Spacer bars	4	¾″	34″	thin-wall electrical conduit

Hardware: Twenty-four 2½″ No.10 brass flathead screws. Eight 1½″ No.10 steel roundhead screws. Two boxes of No. 12 tacks. Pint of white glue.

Note: If beds are for continuous rather than occasional use, add one lengthwise webbing strip and two crosswise webbing strips for additional strength. Buy added webbing accordingly.

white glue before assembling the joints. If the fit isn't snug, fill in the gaps with glue-coated shavings or wood shims. Be sure the corners are square and allow the glue to harden overnight.

The spacer bars are made by flattening the ends of 34-inch lengths of electrical conduit in a vise or by hammering on a hard surface. The flattened ends are then bent so that there are 30 inches between the bends. Drill the flattened ends for screwing to the inner faces of the side rails. Mount them so the tubular portion extends about 1 inch below the bottom of the side rails. Set each one 24 inches from the end of the frame and fasten with one No. 10 roundhead screw at each end of the two bars.

Notch the legs as shown in Fig. 2. Clamp the legs to the side rails with C-clamps, positioning them for a fit when the beds are stacked as in Fig. 4. Drill and countersink 3 holes in each leg while the assembly is still clamped together. Remove the clamps, coat the meeting surfaces with white glue, and screw the legs in place with 2½-inch No. 10 flathead screws.

Webbing can be applied by either of the methods shown in Fig. 5. If the webbing is rubber, it can be pulled taut by hand. If jute or canvas, it can be tightened with a web stretcher, available from an upholstery supply dealer.

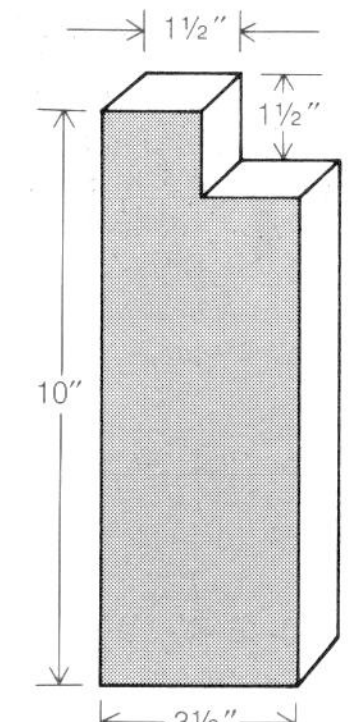

Fig. 2. Notches in legs permit easy stacking.

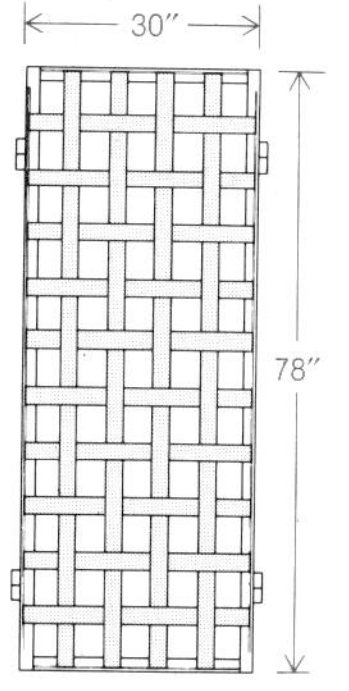

Fig. 3. Use number of webbing strips shown, spaced evenly.

Fig. 4. Space legs as indicated above but double-check position by clamping them temporarily and making trial fittings in both stacked positions.

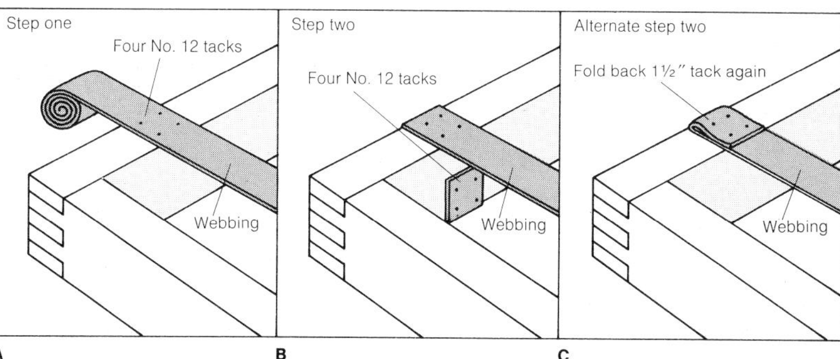

Fig. 5. If wraparound fastening is used to add extra strength as in A and B above, select webbing color to go with side rail wood tone. If webbing is to be concealed, fasten it as in C above.

Sides and ends interlock to give this bunk bed great strength. End boards form a ladder.

Adjustable book shelves, mirror, and sliding blackboards are made from stock materials.

Bunk bed

A bunk bed, blackboards, large mirrors, and ample shelves add greatly to any children's room. The bunks are 5 feet 6 inches high, 6 feet 7½ inches long, and 34½ inches wide. Although the bunks are designed for 75- x 30- x 4-inch mattresses, dimensions can be changed for other mattress sizes.

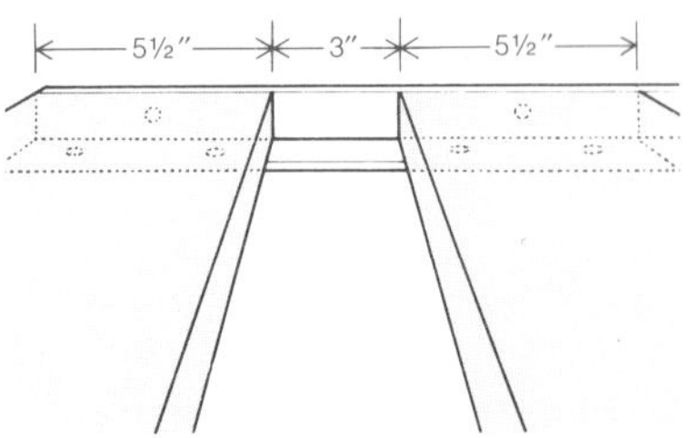

Fig. 1. Detail above shows dimensions of slat spacing and position of ¾-in. screws in aluminum angles.

CONSTRUCTION

First, cut all parts to size. Then drill two holes through each end of end rails (2) in Fig. 2. The holes should be $\frac{3}{16}$ inch in diameter and should be located at centers ⅝ inch from the ends of the rails and ⅜ inch from their edges. Position end rails on corner posts (1) so that the top rails are flush with the tops of the posts and the lower rails are spaced 5½ inches apart. With the rails in position, drill ⅛-inch starter holes where the screws will penetrate the corner posts. Glue end rails to corner posts with white glue and fasten with 2½-inch No. 10 flathead screws and cups.

After glue has dried, stand end frames on their sides with the corner posts facing each other. Place the side rails (3) between the end rails as shown in Fig. 2, adjusting them so that their ends are flush with outer end rail surfaces. Fasten side rails to corner posts with two 1¾-inch No. 10 flathead screws in each joint driven from the inside. Omit glue in these joints so that the unit can be disassembled to pass through doorways. Drill and countersink screwholes in slat-supporting aluminum angles (5) as shown in Fig. 1. Position the angles in the center of the side rails and attach with ¾-inch No. 8 flathead screws. Use the same size screws to attach bed slats to angles.

Blackboard and mirror

Sliding blackboards (2) in Fig. 3 are made from ⅜-inch plywood cut into 30- x 36-inch panels. Finish smooth side with blackboard paint. Mounting tracks (1) are nominal 1¼- x 2-inch pine cut to length required by room dimensions. Rabbet upper track ½ inch wide and ⅝ inch deep and lower track ½ inch wide and ⅜ inch deep as in Fig. 3. Mount on wall with 2½-inch No. 10 flathead screws through track and wall into studs. Bottom track should be 12 inches above floor. Allow 35⅜ inches between tracks so that board will slip into place easily.

Valances (Fig. 3) are made from ⅜-inch plywood cut into 4-inch strips for the top (4) and 3-inch strips for the front (6). Glue triangular strip (3) to top track, then glue and nail valance top to top track. Glue another triangular strip (5) to valance top flush with front edge. Glue and nail valance top to front. See page 274 for information about installing fluorescent lights.

Mirrors are ¼-inch plate glass and are mounted with nominal 1¼- x 2-inch pine. To insure a snug fit, rabbet mirror mounting ¼ inch wide and ½ inch deep. Shelves are mounted on brackets and vertical tracks. See pages 546–549 for further details on shelving.

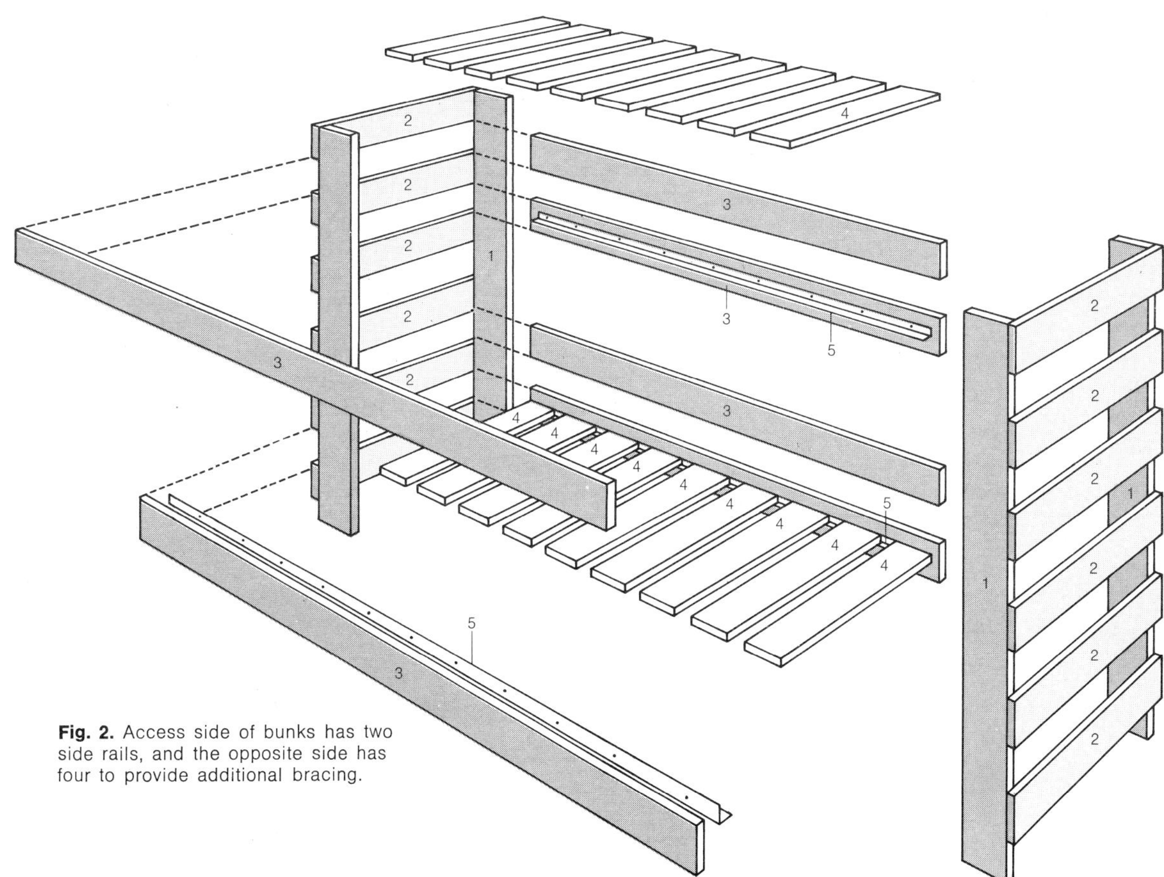

Fig. 2. Access side of bunks has two side rails, and the opposite side has four to provide additional bracing.

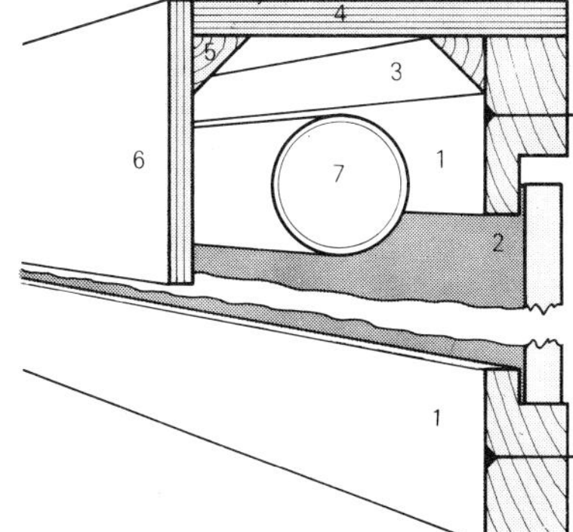

Fig. 3. Mounting tracks and valance.

PARTS LIST (bunk bed)

No.	Name	Quantity	Nominal Size	Length	Materials
1	Corner posts	4	1¼ x 6	66″	pine
2	End rails	12	1 x 6	34½″	pine
3	Side rails	6	1 x 6	79½″	pine
4	Slats	18	1 x 6	30 3/16″	pine
5	Slat supports	4	* 1 x 1 x ¼″	75″	aluminum angle

Hardware: Four doz. 2½″ No. 10 flathead steel screws with decorative cups (for end rails); 2 doz. 1¾″ No. 10 flathead steel screws (for side rails); 9 doz. ¾″ No. 8 flathead steel screws (for bed slats). White glue. *Or use nearest size aluminum or steel angle for Part No. 5.

Note: Mattresses fit snugly. For additional clearance, add 1″ to length of parts 2 and 4.

Tidying up a room is easy with toy boxes on movable bases (foreground) that also store along a wall.

Roomy toy boxes give children an incentive to keep their playthings off the floor when not in use. Two special design elements add to the usefulness of the boxes illustrated here: They can be hung out of the way on a wall at a height convenient for small children, and the cart feature of the base makes them easily movable. The base becomes a cart, a toy in its own right, when the boxes are hanging on the wall. Each box is a 1-foot 3-inch cube.

CONSTRUCTION

Toy box

Cut side, front, back, and bottom panels and lid from ¼-inch plywood according to the sizes given in the Parts List. Use the smoother side of the plywood for the outer side of the box. To make the hand holes in the lid and side panels, bore two 1-inch holes with centers 2½ inches apart and 1½ inches from the edge. Use a keyhole saw to complete the cutout.

Cut ¾- x ¾-inch corner posts and front, back, and side strips to lengths given in Parts List. Fix corner posts (3) to front and back panels (2) with white glue (the front and back panels are the ones without hand holes). Set bottom of posts 1¼ inches above bottom edge of panel and flush with vertical edge. Nail through panels to posts with ¾-inch brads at 3-inch intervals. Then glue and nail side panels (1) to corner posts, setting side panel edges flush with vertical edges of front and back panels.

Next, turn assembly upside down and set bottom panel (4) on ends of corner posts. Glue side strips (5) and front and back strips (6) in position and nail them to panels all the way around. Turn the box right side up and drop lid (7) into place, planing or sanding as necessary to make it lift out easily.

Drilling wood 26, 45 **Plywood 374–375**
Casters 201 **Planing 28**
Adhesives 86 **Keyhole saw 18** **Power saw 49–50**

Cut hanger strip (8) from nominal 1 x 2 and make a 30-degree bevel by planing or by using a power saw with a tilted blade (p. 49). Glue hanger strip to back panel 2½ inches from the panel's top edge and secure it with ¾-inch No. 8 flathead screws driven from the inside.

Cut the wall strip (9) from nominal 1 x 2 long enough to accommodate the number of boxes planned, allowing 2 inches between boxes to permit access to the hand holes. Bevel the upper edge of the wall strip to match the beveled lower edge of the hanger strip as shown in Fig. 2. Mount the wall strip 23 inches from the floor, using 2-inch common nails through strip and wall into studs. Mount the spacer strip (10) the same way, setting it 10 inches below the wall strip to prevent the boxes from tilting.

Cart

Cut all parts to sizes given in Parts List. Round off front corners of base (11) to ½-inch radius. Drill two ¼-inch-diameter rope holes and two ½-inch-diameter clearance holes in the base at centers 6½ inches from the sides and ¾ inch from the front edge as shown in Fig. 3. The rope passes through the small hole, and a knot lodges in the larger hole on the underside. Glue side strips (12) and front and back strips (13) to base in positions shown in Fig. 1, making sure that the toy box fits in the square formed by the strips. Nail strips to base with 1-inch brads driven from the underside at 3-inch intervals.

After painting with lead-free paint, attach flat-plate swivel casters to underside of base; set them at the corners 2 inches from each edge.

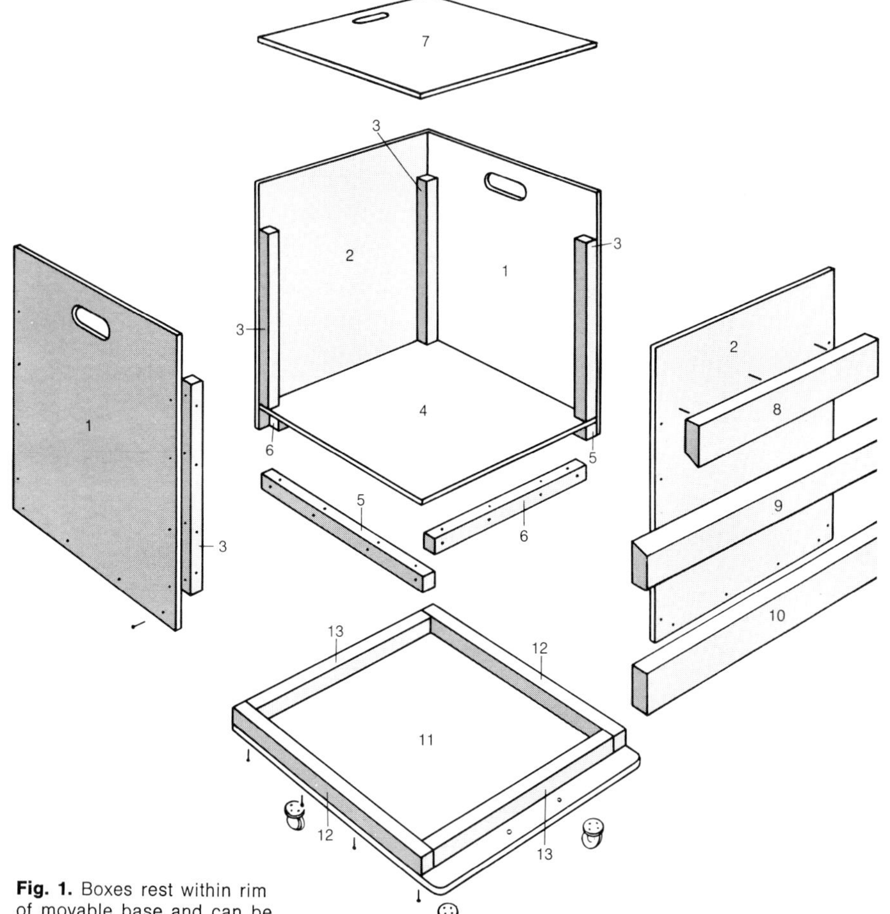

Fig. 1. Boxes rest within rim of movable base and can be lifted out and hung on wall.

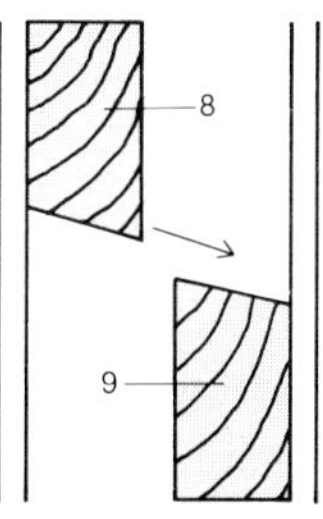

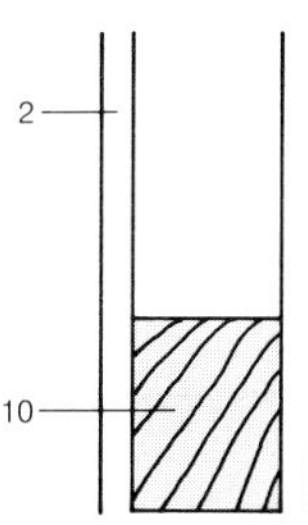

Fig. 2. Detail of beveled strips (8) and (9) at left and spacer (10), right.

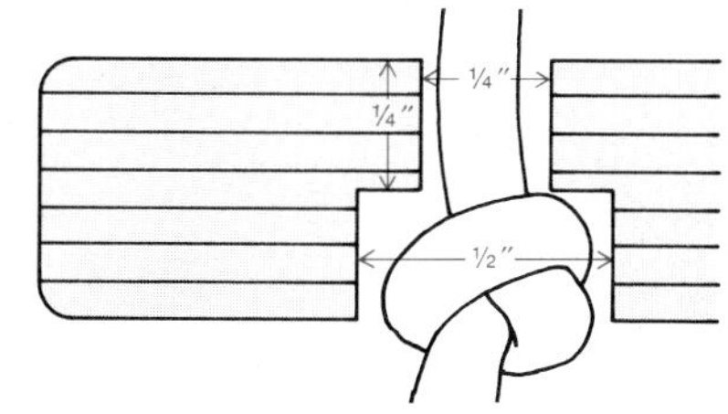

Fig. 3. Knotted end of rope is anchored within larger hole of the movable base.

PARTS LIST (for one toy box and one cart)

No.	Name	Quantity	Nominal Size	Length	Width	Material
Toy box						
1	Side panels	2		15″	15″	¼″ plywood
2	Front and back panels	2		15″	14½″	¼″ plywood
3	Corner posts	4	¾ x ¾	11″		pine
4	Bottom panel	1		14½″	14½″	¼″ plywood
5	Side strips	2	¾ x ¾	14½″		pine
6	Front and back strips	2	¾ x ¾	13″		pine
7	Lid	1		14½″	14½″	¼″ plywood
8	Hanger strip	1	1 x 2	14½″		pine
9	Wall strip	1	1 x 2	as needed		pine
10	Spacer	1	1 x 2	as needed		pine
Cart						
11	Base	1		18½″	17″	½″ plywood
12	Side strips	2	¾ x ¾	17″		pine
13	Front and back strips	2	¾ x ¾	15½″		pine

Hardware: One-inch and ¾″ brads. Common nails (2″) as needed. Four ¾″ No. 8 flathead screws. Four flat-plate swivel casters and mounting screws. Rope for pull handles. White glue.

Toys tag along in this wagon and toy box combination. Sturdy and easy to build, it will delight any two to five year old.

Wagon and toy box

CONSTRUCTION

Bore ¾-inch-diameter holes through side rails (1) 1½ inches from front ends. Round off front end corners of rails. Drill ¼-inch axle holes ½ inch above bottom edge, 3¾ inches from front end 2½ inches from back end.

Dowel end rails (2) to sides with ¼-inch dowels but do not glue yet. Make rear end rail flush with ends of side rails. Set front end rail with its rear surface 12¼ inches from front surface of rear end rail.

Bore ¾-inch-diameter holes ½ inch deep in tops of handlebar uprights (3) centered ¾ inch from ends. Bore similar holes all the way through lower ends. Glue handlebar (4) and pivot bar (5) into handle uprights, pivot bar projecting 1 inch on each side.

Varnish handlebar uprights and pivot bar; enamel handlebar white.

With pivot bar inserted in side rails, glue dowel joints in wagon frame. Glue and brad stop strip (6) to front end rail, top edges flush. Glue and nail side and end ledger strips (7, 8) to wagon frame flush with bottom.

Round all sharp corners of wagon by sanding. Varnish wagon except for ledger strips. Enamel top surface only of bottom panel (9) white. When dry, glue it to unpainted ledger strips.

Cut plywood panels for box. Cut ¾- x 3-inch hand holes in box sides (10) centered 1 inch from top edges. Glue and brad sides to box ends (11). Glue and nail box bottom (12) to edges of assembled sides and ends.

Cut axles from ¼-inch steel rod so that they project far enough beyond wheel hubs to allow for drilling 1⁄16-inch cotter pin holes. Use a washer on both sides of each wheel.

Blocks shown in wagon were cut from 2 x 2, sanded and varnished.

Dowel joints 395
Fastening with screws 74
Hand drills 26–27
Resorcinol adhesive 86
Power drill 45
Table saw 60

PARTS LIST

No.	Name	Quantity	Nominal Size	Length	Width	Material
1	Side rails	2	1 x 3	16½″		pine
2	End rails	2	1 x 3	9¼″		pine
3	Handlebar uprights	2	1 x 2	13½″		pine
4	Handlebar	1		8½″		¾″ dowel
5	Pivot bar	1		11¼″		¾″ dowel
6	Stop strip	1	½″ x ½″ (cut)	9¼″		pine
7	Side ledger strips	2	½″ x 1″ (cut)	12¼″		pine
8	End ledger strips	2	½″ x 1″ (cut)	8¼″		pine
9	Bottom panel	1		12″	9″	⅜″ plywood
10	Box sides	2		12″	7″	⅜″ plywood
11	Box ends	2		8¼″	7″	⅜″ plywood
12	Box bottom	1		12″	9″	¼″ plywood

Hardware: Box of 1″ brads. Four 3″-diameter wheels (or nearest available size), axles to match hub diameter. Eight flat washers; 4 cotter pins. Resorcinol glue.

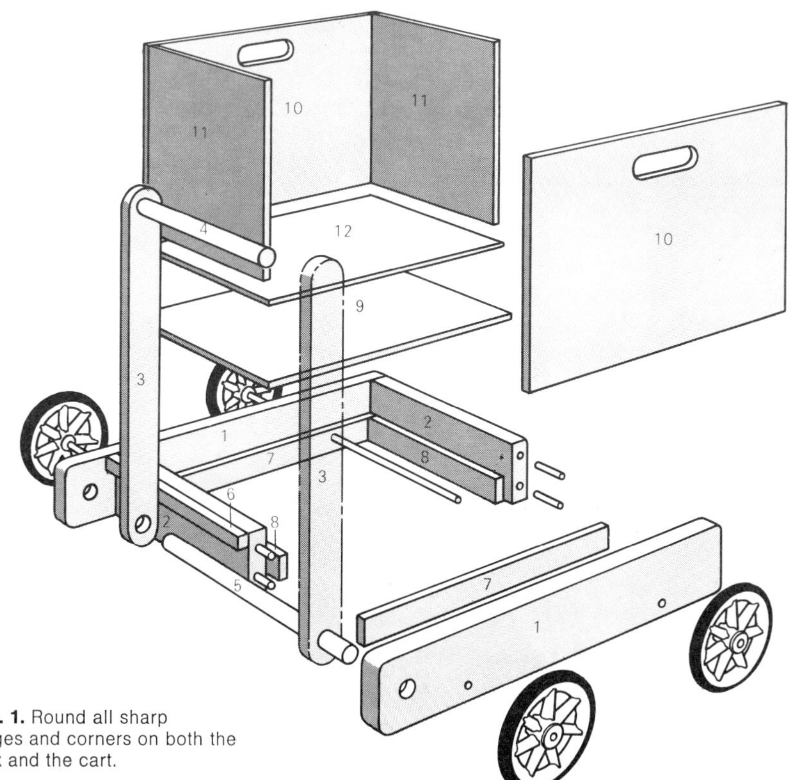

Fig. 1. Round all sharp edges and corners on both the box and the cart.

Blackboard

This double-sided blackboard can keep two children happy at the same time. Blocks under the hinges minimize the chance of legs closing and pinching small fingers, and carpet tape stops the legs from opening too far.

CONSTRUCTION

If you have a table saw, set it for ½-inch depth to cut the grooves in inside edges of legs (2) to accept hardboard panels (1). Glue panels in grooves, flush at top. If you have no table saw, cut the panels 26 inches wide with a rip saw and screw them to the wide surfaces of the legs. Glue hinge blocks (3) to tops of legs and hinge the two assembled panels together. Use medium-grade sandpaper to round off tops of the tape blocks (4) to protect tapes. Position tape blocks on inside of panels, centered ½ inch above bottom edges. Fasten each tape (5) between panel and tape block with two ¾-inch No. 8 flathead screws. Countersink screws and fill holes with wood putty so that panels will be smooth. Tape should limit angle between legs to about 30 degrees.

Use blackboard paint on the panels or a colored flat latex paint for use with contrasting chalk. Allow either type to harden thoroughly before use. Varnish the legs with clear varnish.

A fold-away blackboard made from hardboard and 1 x 2s.

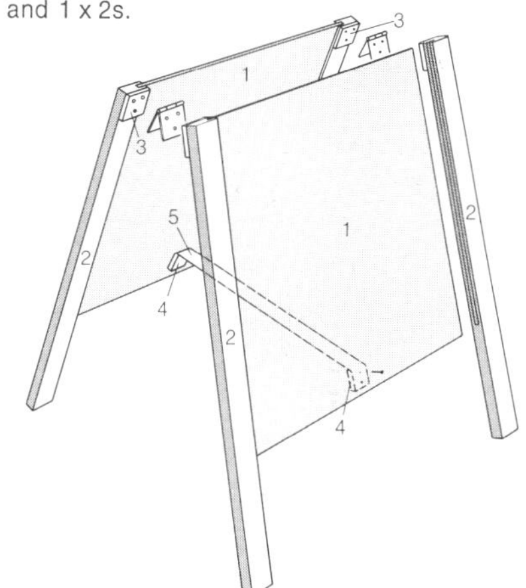

Fig. 2. The hinged boards are kept from opening too far by carpet tape.

PARTS LIST

No.	Name	Quantity	Nominal Size	Length	Width	Material
1	Panels	2		25″	24″	⅛″ hardboard
2	Legs	4	1 x 2	36″		pine
3	Hinge blocks	4	2″ x ½″	2″		pine
4	Tape blocks	2	2″ x ½″	2″		pine
5	Tape	1		18″	1½″	carpet binding tape

Hardware: Two 1½″ galvanized butt hinges with screws. Four ¾″ No. 8 flathead steel screws; 16 screws if panels are screwed to legs.

CONSTRUCTION

House

Start by cutting all parts to size. Next, mark outlines of windows and door in facade (13) and side walls (7). Cut out windows and door. Mark and cut stairwell and doorways in partitions (4), which enclose the landing (8).

Front door and window openings in facade are centered in each room. The lower window's upper edges are level with the door top. Bottom edges of upper windows are 10⅝ inches above base. All front windows are 4½ inches high. Left ones are 9 inches wide. Center one is 3 inches wide, right ones 3¾ inches wide. Front doorway is 6¾ inches high, 3 inches wide. Partition doorways, 6⅝ inches high, 2¾ inches wide, 1¼ inches from front edge. Stairwell is 5¾ inches square, 7 inches from right end of floor. Kitchen window in right wall is 3½ inches high, 4 inches wide, starting 2 inches from back.

Attractive six-room dollhouse with furnishings in place before the facade is installed.

Cut ¼- x ¼-inch groove along back and side skirting (2) and (3). Miter ends of back skirting (2) and glue and nail to base (1). Miter back ends of side skirting (3) and cut front ends square so that side grooves are 11¾ inches long. Fasten side skirting to base.

Start assembly by gluing side walls (7) into side skirting (3). Glue right-hand first-floor partition (4) 7 inches from right wall, with bottom rear corner notched over back skirting. Mount left partition similarly, 5¾ inches to the left. Glue second floor (5) between walls (7) and brad through walls into its edges. Also glue partition tops to its underside and nail into partition edges. Edges of stairwell should be flush with inner partition surfaces. Install the stairs at this stage. They're made by gluing and nailing together 2⅞-inch lengths of ½- x 1-inch pine, overlapped in steps. They run up the left partition to a half-height rear landing (8) of ¼-inch plywood, then from the landing forward, up the right partition to the stairwell opening above.

Mount second-floor partitions same as the first. Glue ceiling (6) to upstairs partitions (4) and to inside of side walls (7). Cut roof pitch in back wall (9) so that wall edges are level with the side wall edges (7), and the peak is 4⅞ inches higher. Cut the same angle on gable (10). Glue soffit strips (11) to gable and back wall. Glue back wall (9) into back skirting (2) and fasten it to rear edges of side walls (7). Glue lap strip (14) to gable front so as to overlap facade ¼ inch. Facade can be tipped out at bottom for removal. Glue gable to side walls (7), to the celing (6), and to upper partitions (4). Rest roof panels (12) on soffit strips. Mark and cut angle where roof panels meet at peak. Glue roof panels to soffit strips.

Adhesives 86
Joints 384
Miters 393
Mortise and tenon joints 387
Splines 395

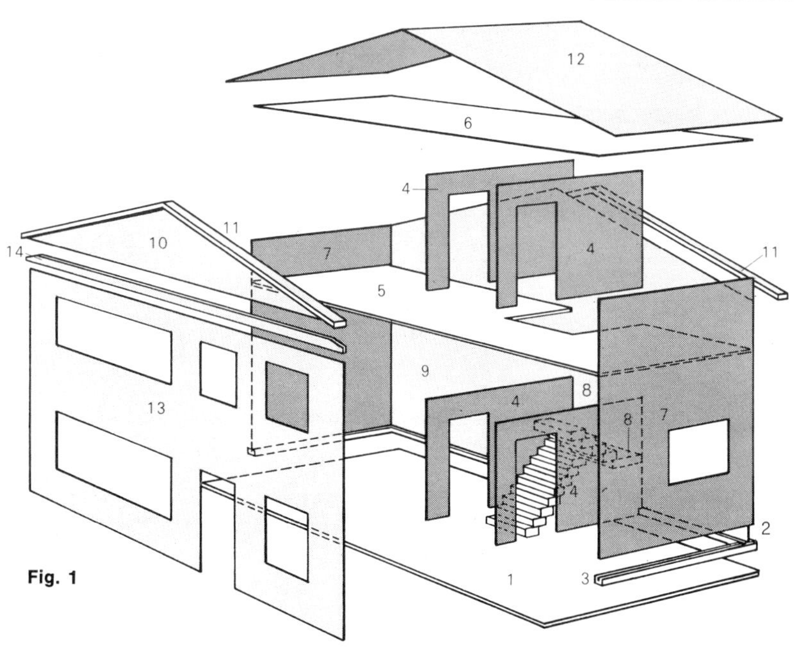

PARTS LIST

No.	Name	Quantity	Nominal Size	Length	Width	Material
1	Base	1		25⅜″	15″	⅜″ plywood
2	Back skirting	1	¾ x ¾	25⅜″		pine
3	Side skirting	2	¾ x ¾	to fit		pine
4	Partitions	4		11½″	7¾″	¼″ plywood
5	Second floor	1		24⅝″	11½″	⅜″ plywood
6	Ceiling	1		24⅝″	11½″	⅜″ plywood
7	Side walls	2		16″	11½″	¼″ plywood
8	Landing	1		5¾″	2¾″	¼″ plywood
9	Back wall	1		25⅛″	20⅞″	¼″ plywood
10	Gable front	1		25⅛″	5¼″	¼″ plywood
11	Soffits	4		14″	¾″	½″ pine
12	Roof panels	2		15¼″	15″	¼″ plywood
13	Facade	1		25⅛″	15¾″	⅜″ plywood
14	Lap strip	1		25⅛″	¾″	½″ pine
15	Front door	1	(not shown)	6 9/16″	2⅞″	¼″ plywood

Note: List does not include material for stairs or window trim. The 16 stairs required can be cut from 2′ of ½″ x 1″ pine. This can be ripped (cut lengthwise) from ½″ x 2″ pine, usually the nearest stock size. Window trim can be made from ¼″ x ¼″ or similar balsa strip. It should be stained or painted before gluing.

This doll's bed can easily be made from scrap wood in less than an afternoon.

CONSTRUCTION

Bed

Cut the 8- x 18-inch base (1) from 1- x 10-inch pine and saw ⅝- x ⅝-inch notches in the corners for the ¾- x ¾-inch bedposts. Cut headposts (4) 9 inches long from nominal 1 x 1 pine, footposts (5) 8 inches, all mitered at top to take 8¼-inch-long top rails (2). Nail and cement posts in notches so that they project 3½ inches below the base. Cut four ⅜- x ⅜-inch bars (3) to fit between top rails and base at head and foot. Mortise them 3/16 inch into rails and base or cement them in place. Miters may be reinforced with veneer splines (6) or glued and nailed with brads.

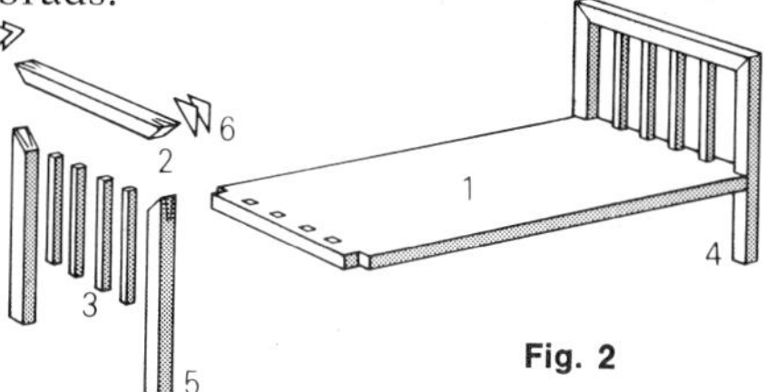

Outside leg frame, with wide bottom rails for stability, leaves plenty of clearance for children's legs.

Use weather-resistant exterior plywood to make these chairs and table so that they can be left outdoors without danger of damage from summer showers. The chairs have spacers between the side rails and legs so that they can be stacked for storage. The frames are glue and screw fastened, or they can be doweled and glued.

CONSTRUCTION

Table

Round off lower corners of top rails (1) and upper corners of bottom rails (2) to a ¼-inch radius. Round off all other exposed edges and corners.

Join uprights (3) to top and bottom rails with lapped T-joints as shown in Fig. 1. Dowel-joint cross rail (4) to uprights so that cross rail center is 8 inches from each end of upright.

Glue and screw top panel (5) to top rails so that edges are flush to sides. Fill screw holes and paint all surfaces. If the top panel is to be a different color from the underframe, paint underframe after top has dried. Sand edges smooth and round off all corners of top before painting.

Chair

Round off all exposed edges. Screw side rails (6) to legs (7 and 8) with spacer (9) glued between each leg and side rail. Ends of side rails are flush with legs. Top edges of side rails are ½ inch below top of front leg and at corresponding height on back leg, 11⅞ inches from floor. Dowel-joint cross rails (10) to side rails 1⅞ inches from each end. Screw seat (11) to side rails and cross rails, front and side edges flush with rails.

If seat is to be different color from the frame, paint the frame after the seat has dried. Cover cushions with sailcloth and use it for back too. Wrap it around back leg tops and tack it.

Counterboring 74
Cushions 205
Dowel joints 395
Lapped T-joints 385

PARTS LIST

No.	Name	Quantity	Nominal size	Length	Width	Material
Table						
1	Top rails	2	1¼ × 2	22″		pine
2	Bottom rails	2	1¼ × 2	17″		pine
3	Uprights	2	1¼ × 3	16″		pine
4	Cross rail	1	1¼ × 2½	32″		pine
5	Top panel	1		36″	22″	¾″ exterior plywood
Chair						
6	Side rails	2	1¼ × 2½	13″		pine
7	Front legs	2	1¼ × 2	12⅜″		pine
8	Back legs	2	1¼ × 2	22″		pine
9	Spacers	4		2¼″	1⅞″	⅛″ exterior plywood
10	Cross rails	2	1¼ × 2½	10¾″		pine
11	Seat	1		13″	13″	½″ exterior plywood
12	Cushion	1		13″	13″	1″ polyurethane

Hardware: No. 8 brass flathead screws (1½″). Waterproof glue.
Note: When ordering wood, allow for waste and cutting.

Chairs can be stacked without removing cushions.

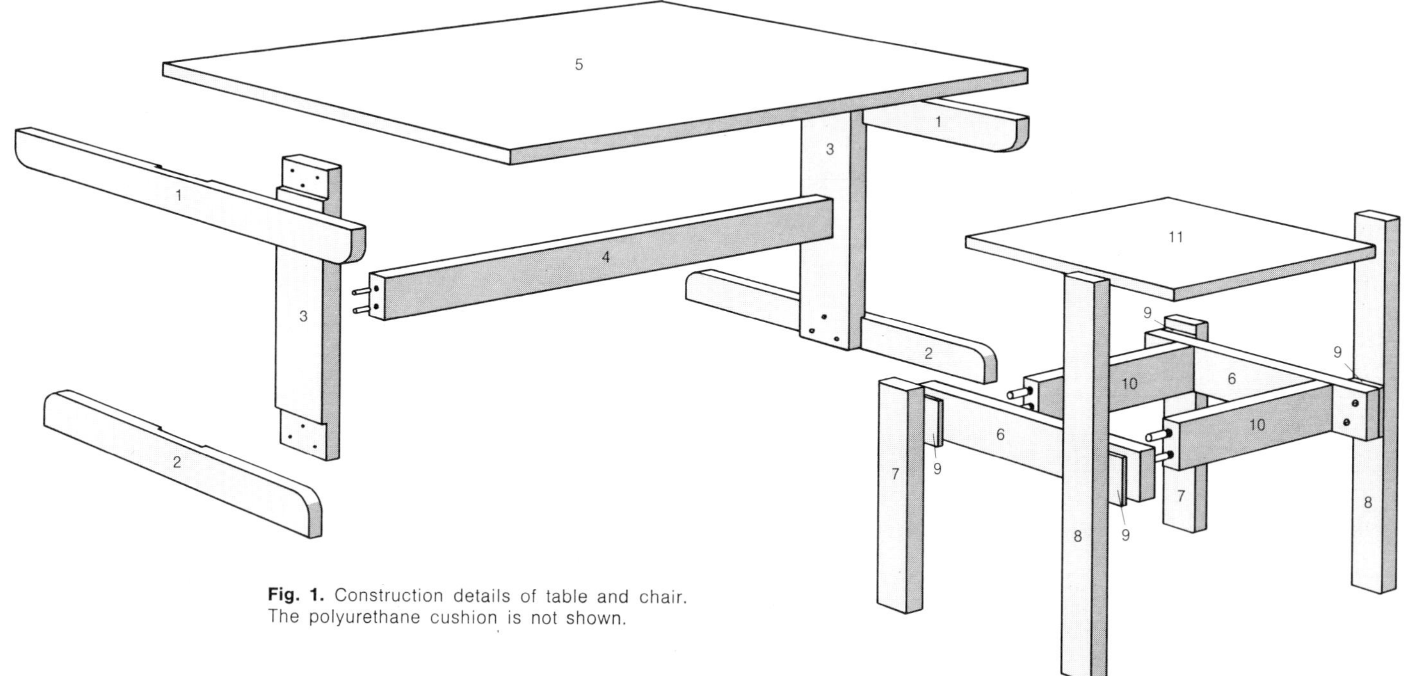

Fig. 1. Construction details of table and chair. The polyurethane cushion is not shown.

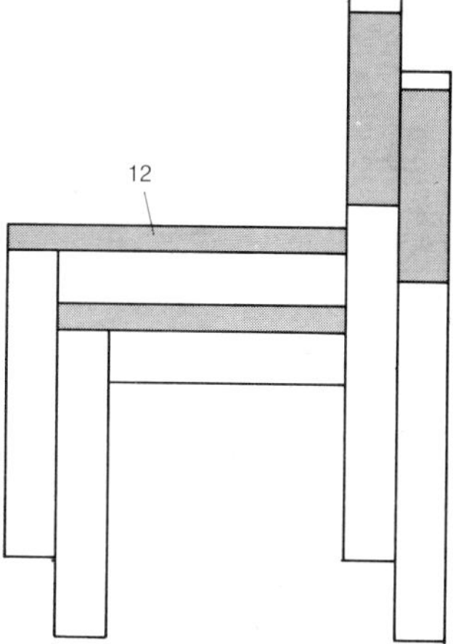

Fig. 2. Make 10-in.-high canvas-sling back to slip over back legs. Use selvage for bottom edge and turn seam over for top edge.

Mouse cage

This two-story indoor mouse cage is suitable for a maximum of three mice.

After parts are cut, as per Parts List, cut a ⅜ inch-wide groove across the upper surface of the bottom panel (2) and the under surface of the upper floor (4) 5⅝ inches from the right-hand end of each. The first-floor ramp wall (5) will fit in these. Cut similar grooves ¼ inch wide across the top surface of the upper floor and the under surface of the top panel (3) 5¾ inches from the left-hand end of each. The partition wall (10) of the nesting box will fit in these. Also cut ⅛ inch grooves a little more than ⅛ inch wide $\frac{3}{16}$ inch from the long edges of the side panels (1). The removable front and rear glass walls (11) of the cage will fit in these.

Fasten the ramps (6, 7, and 8) to the ramp wall with glue and ¾ inch brads driven through the wall into their edges. All ramps are inclined about 30 degrees. Top and bottom ramps are on the right side of the wall, the middle ramp on the left. Bore 2 inch-diameter holes (p. 46) just above the base of the lower ramp and at the two crossing points between left and right ramps so that the mice can go through the wall from one ramp to another.

Cut a 2 x 4 inch hole in the upper floor flush to the upper end of the top ramp. Round the other end of the hole. The mice can climb through this hole to the upper floor after ascending ramps. Bore 1 inch ventilation holes in the centers of the end panels and glue screening to the inside.

Fasten the side panels (1) to the bottom panel (2) with glue and 1 inch brads driven through the bottom into the lower panel ends. Fit the ramp wall in its grooves, with upper floor above it, and fasten all joints with glue and 1 inch brads. Edges of the upper floor should be same distance from front and rear edges of the side panels. Fasten nesting box walls (9) the same way. Do not nail or glue the front of the box (10); it must be removable for cleaning. Glue and nail the top panel equidistant from front and rear edges of the side panels. Then, while the glue is still fresh in all the joints, slip the glass in the grooves of the side panels so that it rests on the bottom. This will hold the cage square while the glue sets. Be sure no glue sticks to the glass in the grooves. The gap between the glass and the top panel provides ventilation, as do the holes in the side panels. For safe handling, dull the edges of the glass by rubbing with aluminum oxide cloth and water. Paint the cage inside and out with lead-free enamel and sprinkle sand on the freshly painted ramps to provide traction.

Mouse cage should be kept out of sun to avoid excess heat. Buy water and food receptacles and exercise wheels at a pet shop.

Adhesives 86
Bench saw 60
Circular power saws 50
Electric drills 46
Hand drills and braces 26
Hand router 30
Mitering 393
Router 54
Working with glass 438

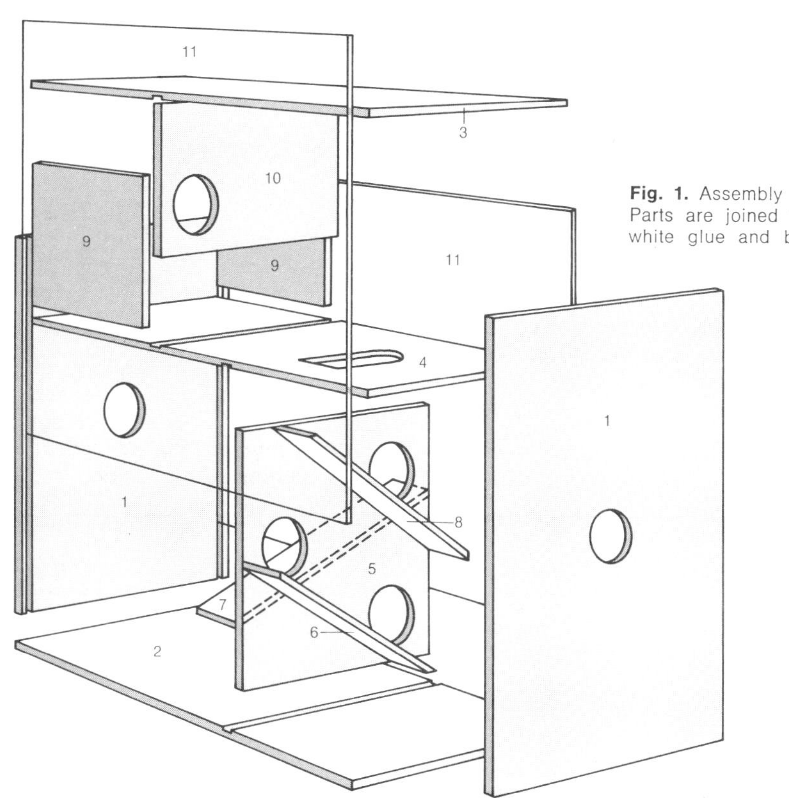

Fig. 1. Assembly details. Parts are joined with white glue and brads.

PARTS LIST

No.	Name	Quantity	Length	Width	Materials
1	Side panels	2	15⅝″	9½″	⅜″ plywood
2	Bottom panel	1	16″	9½″	⅜″ plywood
3	Top panel	1	15¼″	8⅝″	⅜″ plywood
4	Upper floor	1	15¼″	8⅝″	⅜″ plywood
5	Ramp wall	1	9½″	8⅝″	⅜″ plywood
6	Bottom ramp	1	8⅜″	2″	⅜″ plywood
7	Middle ramp	1	10⅛″	2″	¼″ plywood
8	Top ramp	1	7⅛″	2″	¼″ plywood
9	Nesting box walls	2	5¾″	5⅝″	¼″ plywood
10	Nesting box front	1	8⅝″	5⅞″	¼″ plywood
11	Front/back	2	15⅝″	15½″	⅛″ glass

Hardware: Scrap screening for two 1″-dia. screens.
Note: If glass for front and back walls is purchased to order, get it with edges polished. If you cut your own, use aluminum oxide cloth and water to dull the edges.

Birdhouse

The size of the entrance hole determines the species of bird likely to use this birdhouse. Make a 1 inch hole for wrens, 1⅛ inch for chickadees, and 1⅜ for tufted titmice or nuthatches.

Parts are ⅜ inch exterior plywood. Cut two 8 inch equilateral triangles for front and back (1). Bore entrance hole in one triangle, centered 2½ inches below apex. Drill a ⅜ inch hole 4 inches below apex for a 1¾ inch-long dowel perch. Cut an inverted keyhole in the other triangle, as shown, so that house can be mounted on a nail. Bottom (3) is a rectangle 8¼ x 5 inches, with ends beveled 60 degrees. Roof panels (2) are 8¾ x 6 inch rectangles mitered to meet at the top. Assemble front, back, bottom, and one roof panel with glue and 1½ inch finishing nails. Mount the other roof half with 1¼ inch No. 6 brass screws so it can be removed for cleaning.

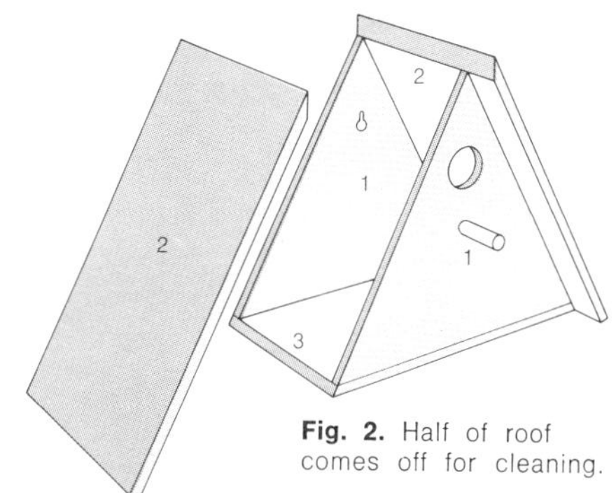

Fig. 2. Half of roof comes off for cleaning.

Set house on solid branches about 6 ft. above a lawn rather than sidewalk or patio.

Tree house size can be tailored to suit the tree and arrangement of branches.

A tree house can bring the world of fantasy right into your own backyard. You can build this one with a minimum of materials and anchor it securely with 2 x 4 braces and nylon ropes. Sturdy trees with spreading branches about 6 feet above the ground make the best tree house sites.

CONSTRUCTION

Make the platform frame of five 2 x 4s (fir, spruce, or pine), four for the ends and sides and one across the center. Set the center 2 x 4 parallel with the shorter sides if the frame is rectangular. Dovetail-nail the frame with two 3½-inch galvanized nails in each joint. The floor is ½-inch exterior plywood, nailed with 1½-inch galvanized nails about 6 inches apart. Platform size depends on the layout of the tree and branches (the one shown is approximately 4 x 5 feet). Finish the platform with clear polyurethane varnish. Lash it to the tree with ¼-inch nylon rope run through ⅜-inch holes drilled in the frame, and nail supporting blocks to the frame wherever necessary to make the platform level.

Access to the tree house is by ladder. The rungs are foot-long 1-inch dowels; the sides are ¼-inch nylon rope. Tie the rungs into the ropes at 12-inch intervals, using the type of knot shown in Fig. 1. Drill ⅜-inch holes horizontally through platform frame and knot the rope ends through the holes to secure them. Extend the side ropes below the lowest rung; stake them to the ground to prevent excessive ladder swing.

To add a canopy roof, cut two vertical canopy supports 4 to 5 feet long from 1-inch dowels or old broomsticks. Bore 1-inch holes for the supports on opposite sides of the platform, ¾ inch from the edge and 2 inches deep, through the floor and into the framing 2 x 4s. To secure the canopy supports solidly, drill ⅛-inch pilot holes through frame and dowel and fasten with 1½-inch No. 8 roundhead screws. Finish with clear polyurethane varnish.

For the ridgepole, use another 1-inch dowel, cut about 2 inches shorter than the space between the supports. Insert a screw eye into each end of the ridgepole and a screw hook about 1 inch from the top of each support. Two canopy-end rods, the same length as the ridgepole, can be ½-inch dowels with screw eyes inserted in each end, or old extendible drapery rods.

The tree house canopy can be awning canvas or a tarpaulin. Make the canopy as wide as the ridgepole is long. Length is determined by the size of the tree house, but allow extra inches for sleeves (like curtain rod pockets) for the ridgepole and canopy-end rods. Insert ridgepole and end rods into sleeves and hook the ridgepole to the vertical supports. Tie ⅛-inch nylon rope to the canopy-end rods and secure to branches to support the canopy at the desired height.

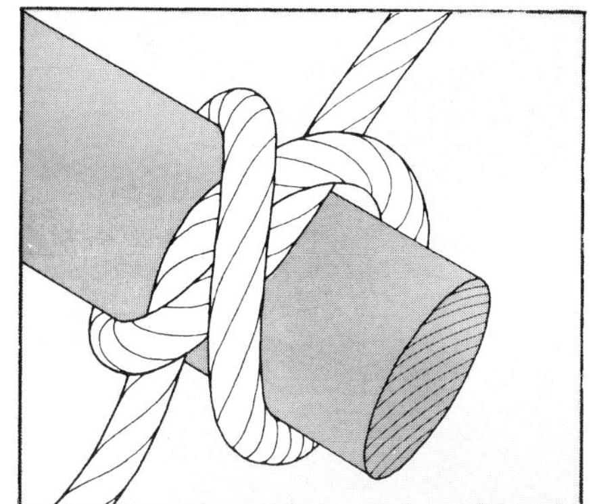

Fig. 1. How to tie rope ladder knots.

Nail 2 x 4 braces to tree to make platform level.

Ladder rungs are 12 in. wide and 12 in. apart.

Hooks and eyes link ridgepole and uprights.

Nylon ropes bind frame to branches and keep platform firmly in place.

The ladder is made of tough nylon rope to withstand any amount of hard usage.

Periscope

Make this periscope for your children out of 1/16-inch-thick cardboard. Mark the cutting and folding lines (Fig. 1) and then paint the inside with a flat black paint.

Rubber-cement tab A to inside face of flap W, tab B to inside face of flap X, tab C to inside face of flap Y, and tab D to inside face flap Z. Repeat at other end. Cover the periscope with adhesive-backed paper.

Secure a handbag mirror to inside face of flap Y with double-faced tape. Secure another mirror on flap at other end.

Double-faced tape can be used instead of glue to hold the tabs to the flaps, or staple surfaces together.

Ideal for around-the-corner viewing, this periscope is made of cardboard.

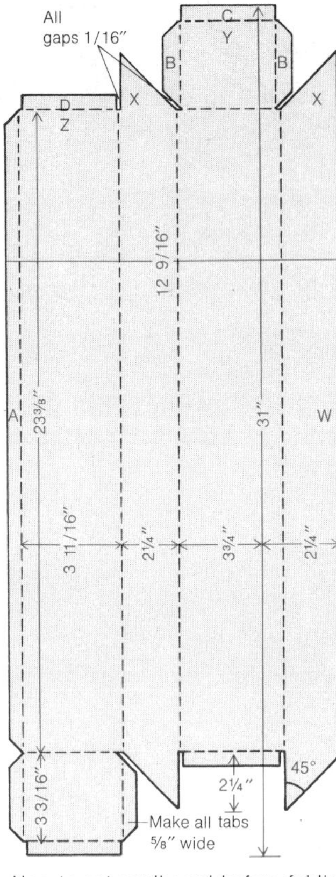

Fig. 1. How to cut cardboard before folding.

Use periscope to look over a hedge.

Tent

This play tent can be made from 54-inch-wide cotton cloth. Cut two pieces of the cloth to shape shown (Fig. 2). Join them with a center seam. Hem edges and sew sleeve seams. Pattern has ¾-inch allowances for hems and seams. Cut ridgepole (1) and edge poles (2) from 1-inch-thick closet pole, all 65 inches long. Cut 36-inch-long support poles (3), also from a closet pole. Attach screw eyes in the ends of ridge and edge poles and roundhead screws in support poles. Hold poles to ground with skewers or wire coat hangers.

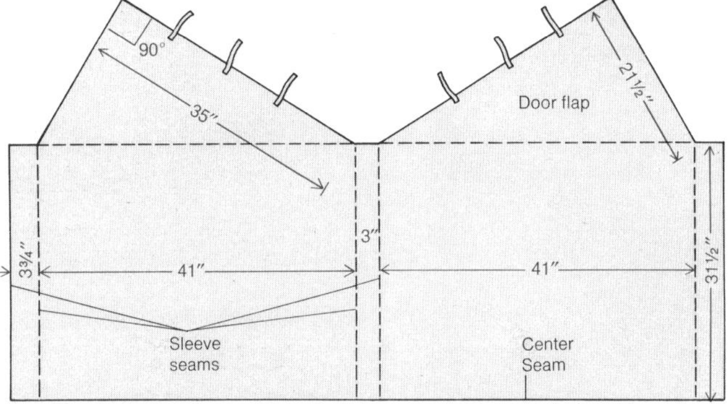

Fig. 2. Cutting pattern for the tent.

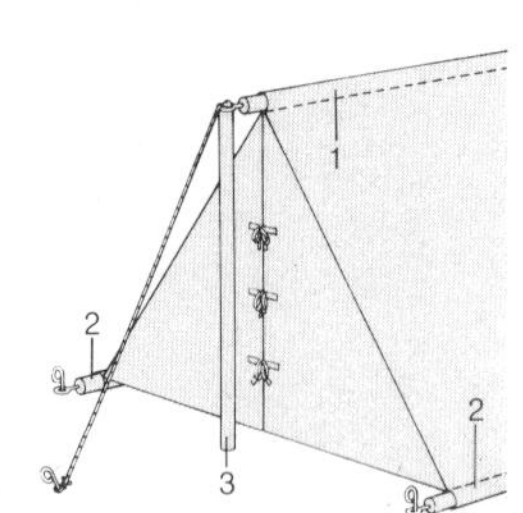

Fig. 3. Arrangement of poles.

Ridgepole can be suspended from branch.

Stilts

Cut these 54-inch-long stilts from straight-grained, knot-free nominal 1¼- x 2-inch wood. Shape the handles as shown in Fig. 5.

Drill eight ⅜-inch holes on center line 2 inches apart, starting 6 inches from the bottom. Make footrests from nominal 1¼-inch-thick wood (Fig. 4). Next, drill ⅜-inch hole ½ inch deep in edge of footrest. Insert and glue a 1- x ⅜-inch dowel in the hole. Drill ⅜-inch hole through edge of footrest centered 2 inches above dowel center. Glue and nail ¼-inch-thick rubber pads to bottoms of stilts.

Locate footrest dowel in hole in stilt and pass a 4½- x ⅜-inch carriage bolt through hole above. Secure with wing nut against stilt.

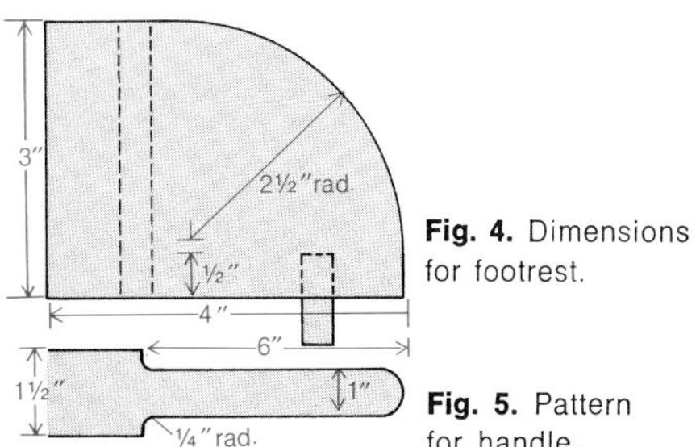

Fig. 4. Dimensions for footrest.

Fig. 5. Pattern for handle.

Bolt and wing nut hold footrest.

Stilts can turn any kid into a backyard star. Footrests adjust from 9 in. to 21 in. off the ground.

Paint front axle board and rest of racer before assembly. Racing stripe is stick-on tape.

CONSTRUCTION

Cut frame board (1) to length and plane edges. Drill a 7/16-inch hole through frame board, centered 4 inches from one end. Center back edge of rear axle board (2) 4½ inches from the other end of frame board. Drill four 5/16-inch holes at least ¾ inch from all edges; countersink for flathead bolts. Bolt boards with ¼-inch flathead steel bolts 2½ inches long.

Round off front and back edges of seat (3). Clamp seat over frame board with back edges flush. Drill four 5/16-inch holes through seat into frame board at least ¾ inch from all edges; countersink for flathead bolts in seat. Bolt boards with ¼-inch flathead steel bolts 2½ inches long.

Cut seat sides (4) so that front ends slant back about 15 degrees at the top; round off front corners. Cut half-circle arcs with a saber saw or coping saw.

Align sides so that their bottoms are flush with bottom of rear axle board and front edges are flush with seat front edge.

Drill and countersink four evenly spaced 1/16-inch pilot holes through each side into seat board. Attach sides with resorcinol adhesive and 1½-inch No. 6 flathead steel screws. Glue four small triangular bracing blocks at seat-side joints as shown in Fig. 2.

Taper back edge of front axle board from full width at center to 3¾ inches at ends. Round off front and back edges. Drill 7/16-inch holes through board at center and 1 inch from each end, 2⅞ inches from front edge.

Cut front and rear axles to size and drill ⅛-inch holes ¼ inch from the ends for cotter pins. Anchor each axle to its board with four evenly spaced electrical cable straps attached with ¾-inch screws. If straps don't fit, build up axle diameter at strap locations by wrapping with tape.

Four wheel stops (6) prevent wheels from jamming against axle boards. Hacksaw and file axle-width slots into one face of an angle iron, as shown in Fig. 1. Set each stop with outside edge just past axle board end and trace the stop on the board. Chisel a recess ⅛ inch deep so that stop lies flush with board. Mount each stop with two ¾-inch No. 8 roundhead screws.

Cut a spacer disk (7) with a saber saw or coping saw; drill a 7/16-inch hole through its center. Bolt frame board, disk, and front axle board together with a 3- x ⅜-inch carriage bolt. Place 2-inch washers on each side of disk to reduce friction.

Hold front axle board at a 45-degree angle to frame board and mark for a stop block (8) beneath frame board to limit turning angle of wheels. Attach stop block with glue and two 1½-inch No. 10 roundhead screws.

Drill 5/16-inch holes through centers of brake blocks (9) and cut off rounds 1 inch below the holes; cut up at an angle of 120 degrees 2¾ inches from curved edge of block, as shown in Fig. 3. Round off brake lever (10) ends and drill a centered 5/16-inch hole 3¼ inches from one end of each. Finish brake blocks and levers with two coats of clear polyurethane varnish.

Place rear wheels on axles temporarily and set brake blocks on seat sides, bottom edges flush, just in front of wheels. Drill and countersink two ⅛-inch pilot holes through each block into side. Attach blocks with glue and 1¼-inch No. 8 flathead screws.

Drill 5/16-inch holes through sides where brake block holes are. Bolt brake assembly with 2½- x ¼-inch carriage bolts from the inside out. Use washers between brake parts and wing nuts outside brakes to tighten bolts.

Drive a 1½-inch No. 12 roundhead

Coping saw 18
Drawing circles 382
Drilling metal 423
Hacksaw 19
Planing 28
Saber saw 52
Sawing metal 422
Fastening with screws 74

screw into each brake block to make stops. Position each so that when brake lever lies against it, bottom of lever clears wheel by ¼ inch. To keep lever from dropping forward, staple a 1¼-inch-long tension spring to each brake lever and block.

Mount wheels on axles with washers on inside and out. Cut clothesline or ¼-inch rope to desired length, push ends through 7/16-inch holes in front axle board, and knot underneath.

Fig. 3. Easy-to-reach brakes control speed.

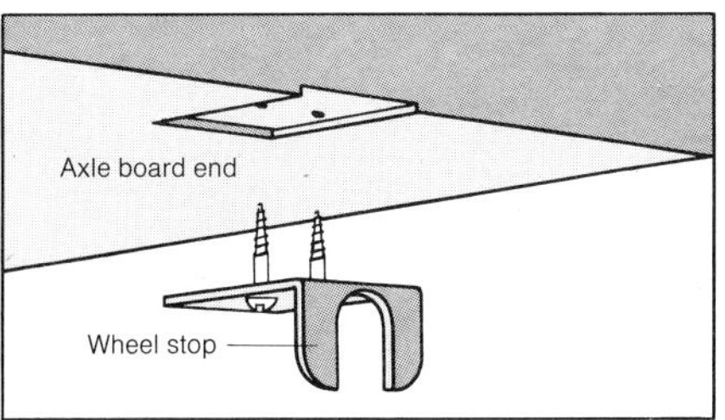

Fig. 1. Stops reduce wheel friction.

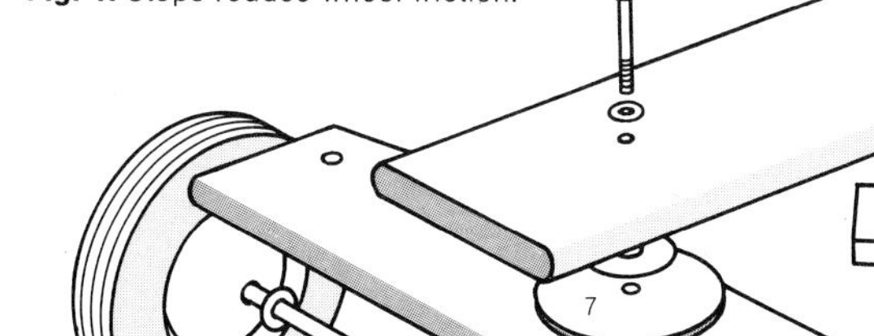

Fig. 2. All exposed edges are rounded with plane.

PARTS LIST

No.	Name	Quantity	Nominal Size	Length	Width	Material
1	Frame board	1	1¼ x 6	38″		pine
2	Rear axle board	1	1 x 4	16¾″		pine
3	Seat	1		16¾″	16½″	⅝″ plywood
4	Seat sides	2	1 x 6	18″		pine
5	Front axle board	1	1 x 6	21″		pine
6	Wheel stops	4		1″	1¼″ x 1¼″	⅛″ angle iron
7	Spacer disk	1			4″ dia.	¼″ plywood
8	Stop block	1		3″	3″	1″ pine
9	Brake blocks	2			4½″ dia.	⅝″ plywood
10	Brake levers	2	1 x 2	12″		pine

Hardware: Wheels shown are 7″ diameter, held to axles by spring clips. New or used wheels of other diameters can be used with axles to match. Rod for axles is sold in various diameters, usually 18″ and 36″ lengths. Screws: eight 1½″ No. 6 flathead steel; twenty-four ¾″ No. 8 roundhead; four 1¼″ No. 8 flathead; two 1½″ No. 10 roundhead; two 1½″ No. 12 roundhead. Bolts: eight ¼″ flat-head steel 2½″ long, plus washers and nuts; one 3″ x ⅜″ carriage, plus two 2″ washers, nuts; two 2½″ x ¼″ carriage, plus washers and cap nuts. Brads. Four cotter pins (if rod is used for axles). Four-foot stick-on tape (for racing stripe). Resorcinol adhesive. One pint lead-free high-gloss enamel. Approx. five feet clothesline or ¼″ rope. Two 1¼″-long tension springs.

Children between the ages of two and six will have loads of fun with this slide and seesaw.

The sliding surface is 8 feet long and 3 feet from the ground at its highest point. The slide is best set up on grass, but it can be used on paving or indoors if some cushioning material is placed under the lower end.

The seesaw supports are set in concrete. The seat, which can be lifted off the supports for storing indoors during the wintertime, is 8 feet long, and it raises a child to a height of 2 feet 7 inches.

Both the slide and the seesaw can be made from readily available standard-size materials.

The gentle slope of the slide makes it safe for small children.

CONSTRUCTION

Ladder

Cut ladder sides (1) and rungs (2, 3, 4, 5, and 6) to length. Mark positions of rungs on outer face of ladder sides, upper edge of top rung 25¾ inches from top of ladder sides and remaining four rungs spaced 6¼ inches apart. Lay ladder sides on edge, with outer faces 27 inches apart at the top and 36 inches apart at bottom. Place rungs in position on ladder sides. Mark off exact lengths of rungs between inner faces of ladder sides. Cut ½-inch-thick tenons on rungs and matching mortises in the sides. Clamp ladder sides to the rungs. Cut the strut sides (7) to length and the strut rails (8 and 9) to approximate lengths indicated in Parts List.

Slide can be dismantled for storage.

Mark positions of strut rails on strut sides, upper edge of top rail 9⅝ inches from top of strut sides, and lower rail 14 inches from bottom.

Lay strut sides on edge, with outer faces 29¾ inches apart at top end and 36 inches apart at bottom end.

Lay the strut rails in position on clamped-up ladder so that both sides are at same angle. Mark the lengths of the strut rails. Cut ½-inch-thick tenons on strut rails and matching mortises in strut sides.

Temporarily clamp the strut rails to the strut sides. Cut top ends of strut sides to a 44-degree angle and cut bottom ends of strut and ladder sides to a 68-degree angle. Cut slots in all tenons to take wedges and glue the joints with waterproof glue. Check ladder frame against strut frame for matching angles, and drive home wedges. When glue is dry, plane down tenons and wedges. Install the hinges to hold strut (7) to ladder sides (1).

Slide

Cut slide panel (10) and slide sides (11) to length indicated in Parts List. Clamp sides to panel and drill pilot holes for screws through panel about 12 inches apart.

Cut crosspiece (12) to length and clamp to underside of slide panel 4 inches from top end.

Screw slide panel to the crosspiece with one countersunk screw through center of panel and another 8 inches on each side. Round off the top edges of the sides. Glue and screw the slide panel to the slide sides.

Screw brackets between the crosspiece and the slide panel. Fill screw heads and finish slide and ladder with three coats of polyurethane varnish. The additional varnish coats will safeguard against any surface splinters.

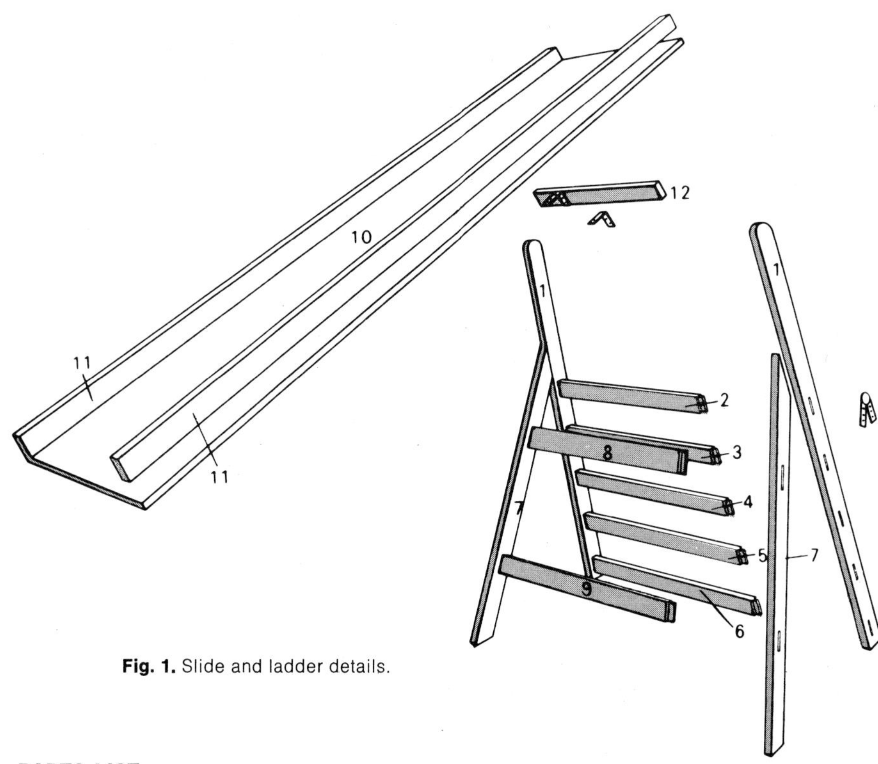

Fig. 1. Slide and ladder details.

PARTS LIST

No.	Name	Quantity	Nominal Size	Length	Width	Material
1	Ladder sides	2	1 X 3	66¾″		hardwood
2	Rung	1	1 X 3	31″		hardwood
3	Rung	1	1 X 3	32″		hardwood
4	Rung	1	1 X 3	33½″		hardwood
5	Rung	1	1 X 3	34½″		hardwood
6	Rung	1	1 X 3	36″		hardwood
7	Strut sides	2	1 X 3	47″		hardwood
8	Strut rail	1	1 X 3	32″		hardwood
9	Strut rail	1	1 X 3	34½″		hardwood
10	Slide panel	1		96″	24″	½″ plywood
11	Slide sides	2	1 X 3	96″		hardwood
12	Crosspiece	1	1 X 3	23¾″		hardwood

Hardware: Two 5″ X 1¼″ flat-mounted hinges; strap hinges can be used. Two 2½″X ¾″ steel angle brackets. Flathead screws—thirty-six ¾″ No.6, four 1½″ No.8 Plastic resin glue. Polyurethane varnish.

Seesaw

Cut a U-shaped notch 1¼ inches deep and 1¼ inches wide in center of spine board (2). Glue and screw spine board to underside of seat board (1) along center line. Counterbore the screw holes 1 inch deep.

Push pivot bar (3) through notch so that it projects 1¼ inches on each side of the seat board. Attach the pivot bar to the seat board with two pipe clamps on each side of the spine.

Cut a 1¼-inch-wide U-shaped notch 2½ inches deep in top of supporting uprights (4). Next, drill a ¼-inch hole 5½ inches deep in edge of supporting uprights centered 1⅜ inches from top and ¾ inch from outside faces. Hammer locking pins (5) into holes after pivot is in notches. Set uprights in concrete.

Round off all corners of seat and spine boards and all edges. Apply three coats of polyurethane varnish to prevent splintering.

Seat board can be removed from its supports.

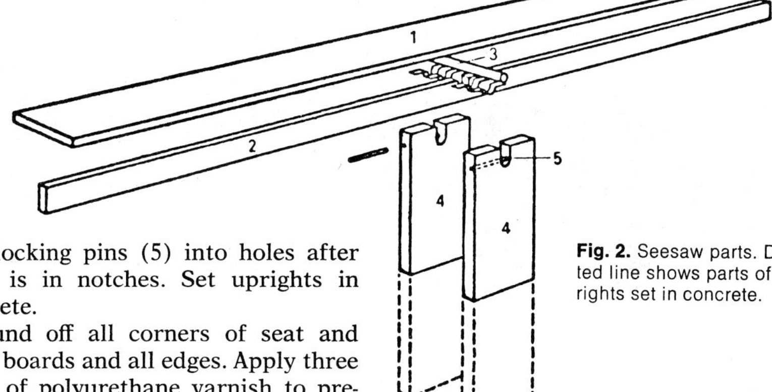

Fig. 2. Seesaw parts. Dotted line shows parts of uprights set in concrete.

PARTS LIST

No.	Name	Quantity	Nominal Size	Length	Width	Material
1	Seat board	1	1 X 8	96″		pine
2	Spine board	1	1 X 3	96″		pine
3	Pivot bar	1		10¼″		1″ int. dia. galvanized pipe
4	Supporting uprights	2	2 X 8	36″		fir
5	Locking pins	2		5½″		¼″-dia. steel rod

Hardware: Four 1¼″ pipe clamps. Eight 1½″ No.8 flathead screws. Plastic resin glue. Polyurethane varnish.

As box is bottomless, it is self-draining and assures quick drying of sand if a sudden shower catches it with the lid off.

Laying concrete slabs 477
Fastening with screws 74
Clinch-nailing 70

A simple base of patio blocks permits this sandbox to be built without a bottom so that rainwater drains freely instead of collecting in puddles. A convenient lid keeps pets from using the sandbox as a bathroom.

The box and lid are built entirely of nominal 1 x 4 stock (Fig. 1), and only a hammer, saw, and screwdriver are required. If redwood is used, no wood preservative is needed because the wood has high natural rot resistance. If white pine is used to cut costs or to provide a wider range of staining possibilities, use a nontoxic wood preservative or paint the box.

To minimize waste, buy lumber in standard lengths of 1 x 4. You will need seven 8-foot lengths, one 10-foot length, and two 12-foot lengths. Use 8-foot pieces for side boards, lid crosspieces, end boards, and the uprights. Cut side boards and lid crosspieces first, then cut end boards and use the leftover 3-foot lengths for the uprights. Use the 10- and 12-foot lengths for lid boards.

Nail the uprights to the boards on sides and ends with 2-inch nails driven from the outside. Use two nails through each upright into each board and stagger them to prevent splitting. As nominal 1 x 4 stock is actually ¾-inch thick, nail points will project ½ inch from the inside surface. Clinch-nailing (p.70) will bend these points over so that they can't scratch and will make a stronger bond. Assemble side and end boards and fasten corner joints with 2½-inch nails.

Position lid crosspieces 10 inches apart on lid boards, adjust their ends so that they will fit inside ends of box, and clinch-nail with 2-inch galvanized nails driven from the outside. Set mending plates outside crosspieces to reinforce end strips and attach with ½-inch screws.

Set box on patio blocks and anchor by driving two rods into the ground on each side and one at each end in spaces between blocks. Fill box with about ⅓ cubic yard of sand.

The sandbox lid can also serve as a low play table.

PARTS LIST

No.	Name	Quantity	Nominal Size	Length	Material
1	Side boards	6	1 x 4	48″	redwood or white pine
2	End boards	6	1 x 4	26″	redwood or white pine
3	Uprights	10	1 x 4	12″	redwood or white pine
4	Lid boards	14	1 x 4	28½″	redwood or white pine
5	Lid crosspieces	2	1 x 4	46″	redwood or white pine

Hardware: Four mending plates with ½″ screws as required. Galvanized nails: 2″ and 2½″. Two 36″ lengths of ⅜″ steel curtain rod cut into six 12″ pieces. Twenty 8 x 16 x 2 patio blocks.

Mending plate

Fig. 1. Parts numbers match those in Parts List.

Outdoor living ideas: Brick barbecue

Large grill area allows the preparation of an outdoor party meal of many courses. Storage bin keeps charcoal dry.

If your patio has a sound base, you can use it as the foundation for this brick barbecue. But if you wish to locate the barbecue in an open area in your yard or along the edge of an existing brick or stone patio, a new slab is required.

To make the slab, first remove sod and soil to a depth of 4 inches and rake the area level. If the soil is well drained, lay the base directly on the ground; if it is not, you'll need a sub-base of gravel or crushed stone (p. 474). Use 2 x 4s set on edge to build a form 61 x 22 x 4 inches for base slab. Use a 1:2½:3½ concrete mix or a dry-mix (p. 469) to which you add only water.

Make the top for the storage bin at the same time that you make the base slab, using the same concrete mix. Make a form 20¾ x 20¾ x 2¾ inches. Cut a piece of scrap the same size as the door frame top (1) and set it in the front edge of the form to make the door frame indentation. Place the form on a flat surface, fill it and finish and cure the concrete.

Cut door frame sides (2) and drive 2-inch nails through them, spacing nails to penetrate mortar, not brick.

Use a triangular file or a hacksaw to cut 11 V-shaped notches ½ inch deep and 1½ inches apart in narrower

Brick design blends well in garden setting.

Bending sheet metal 432 · Bricklaying 454 · Casting slabs 476 · Clinch nailing 70 · Concrete mixes 469 · Cutting metal 422 · Grades of bricks 446 · Handling concrete 471 · Mixing mortar 447 · Mixing concrete 470 · Ripping 17

face of grill rod supports (7).

When the base slab has cured, begin bricklaying (p. 454). Use SW grade bricks (p. 446). Buy dry-mix brick mortar, which contains all the necessary ingredients except water, or mix your own mortar according to the instructions on p. 447. After the first course of bricks is laid, fill the floor of the storage bin with the same concrete mix used for slab. Set tray supports (9) into mortar on fourth, fifth, and sixth courses—2 in. at sides, 1 in. at back. Set door frame sides (2) in place, pushing nails into wet mortar.

Nail door frame top (1) to sides. Lay storage bin top in mortar bed on sixth course. Spread mortar on storage bin top, set the grill rod supports (7) 2 inches into it, and lay the final course of bricks.

Door cross strips (3) and hinge strip (4) are clinch-nailed to panels (5) from the outside with 2-inch galvanized nails. Attach hinges, pull, and catch mentioned in Parts List.

The brazier tray (8) is made by bending up four sides of sheet metal 2 inches after cutting out corners. Fasten corners with 2-inch angle irons.

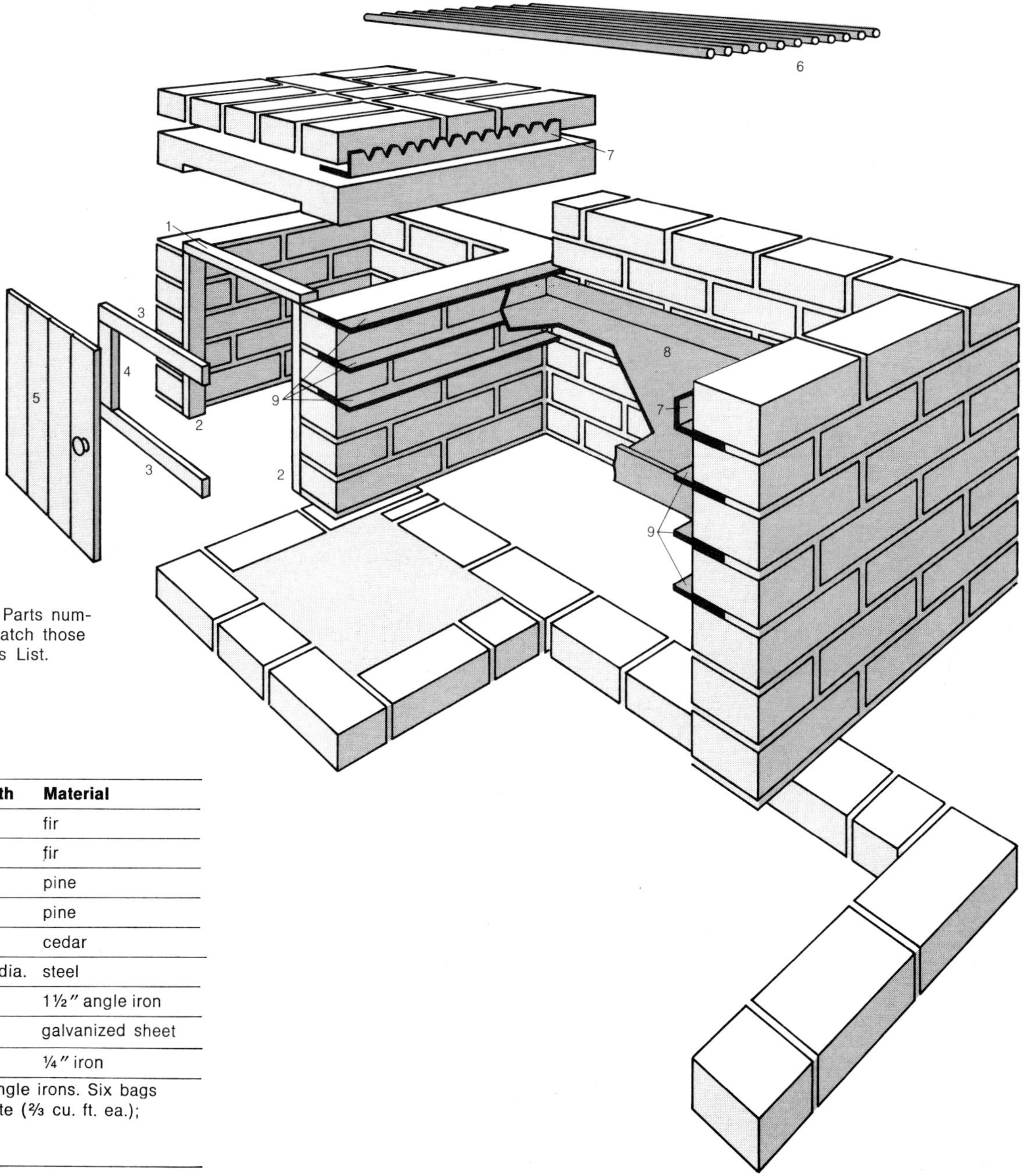

Fig. 1. Parts numbers match those in Parts List.

PARTS LIST

No.	Name	Quantity	Nominal Size	Length	Width	Material
1	Door frame top	1	1 × 2	13¼″		fir
2	Door frame sides	2	1 × 2	to fit		fir
3	Cross strips	2	1 × 2	11¼″		pine
4	Hinge strip	1	1 × 2	9″		pine
5	Door panels	4	1 × 4 (ripped)	to fit		cedar
6	Grill rods	11		33¾″	½″ dia.	steel
7	Grill rod supports	2		17″	3″	1½″ angle iron
8	Brazier tray (sheet)	1		37¼″	20″	galvanized sheet
9	Tray supports	6		18″	3″	¼″ iron

Hardware: Two 2″ brass butt hinges. Door pull. Spring catch. Four 2″ angle irons. Six bags dry-mix mortar (½ cu. ft. ea.); 120 SW bricks. Eight bags dry-mix concrete (⅔ cu. ft. ea.); or 1 bag Portland cement, 2 cu. ft. sand, 3 cu. ft. gravel.
Note: Fire cavity shown is 17″ deep, 34″ wide.

The table and chairs shown are variations of the same design. With it, you can make fixed-top tables, or chairs that convert into tables when the backrests are lowered. For a table, you need only the first four items in the Parts List; for chairs, you need all. Protect all the wood parts of the table and chairs with two coats of clear spar varnish or polyurethane varnish. Sand lightly between coats after 24 hours' drying time. Paint all the metal parts with a good grade of exterior enamel. Finish the base with walnut, redwood, or cedar stain.

Four units are shown above: Two fixed-top tables placed side by side and two convertible chairs.

CONSTRUCTION

To make the base for either table or chair, use ⅜-inch dowels and glue to hold sides (1) to front and back (2), three dowels (3) for each joint. Cut slats (4) and lightly bevel all edges.

Fixed-top table

Leaving a 1½-inch overhang all around and a ¼-inch gap between slats, screw all seven slats to base. Drill two ⅛-inch clearance holes 2¼ inches from the ends and 1 inch from the sides of the slats, 2¼ inches from outer edges of end slats. Counterbore a ½-inch hole ½ inch deep around clearance holes. Fasten slats with 2-inch No. 8 flathead screws. Fill holes with plugs cut from waste (p. 33).

Convertible chair

Screw only four slats to the base. Cut a 45-degree bevel at one end of each upright (5). Drill a ⅜-inch hole for back support (6) through the center line of each upright, 3½ inches from the end. Glue and screw the remaining three slats to the uprights 2¾ inches from the ends, with the upright ends flush with the inner edge of the first slat. Hinge the back to the seat slats. Heat and bend the back support (6) to fit into holes drilled in the uprights. Prime and paint the metal. When the paint is dry, spring the ends into the holes. Screw the support cleat (7) into the back of the base 1½ inches from top edge.

Cushions

Either awning canvas or vinyl is suitable for covering outdoor cushions. Insert ventilation eyelets to allow air to escape when cushion is compressed. Double-sew covers with nylon thread for strength. Use 2-inch-thick polyurethane foam for padding.

Adhesives 86
Cushions 205
Dowels 394
Fastening with screws 74
Joints 384
Plug cutting 33
Wood finishes 407

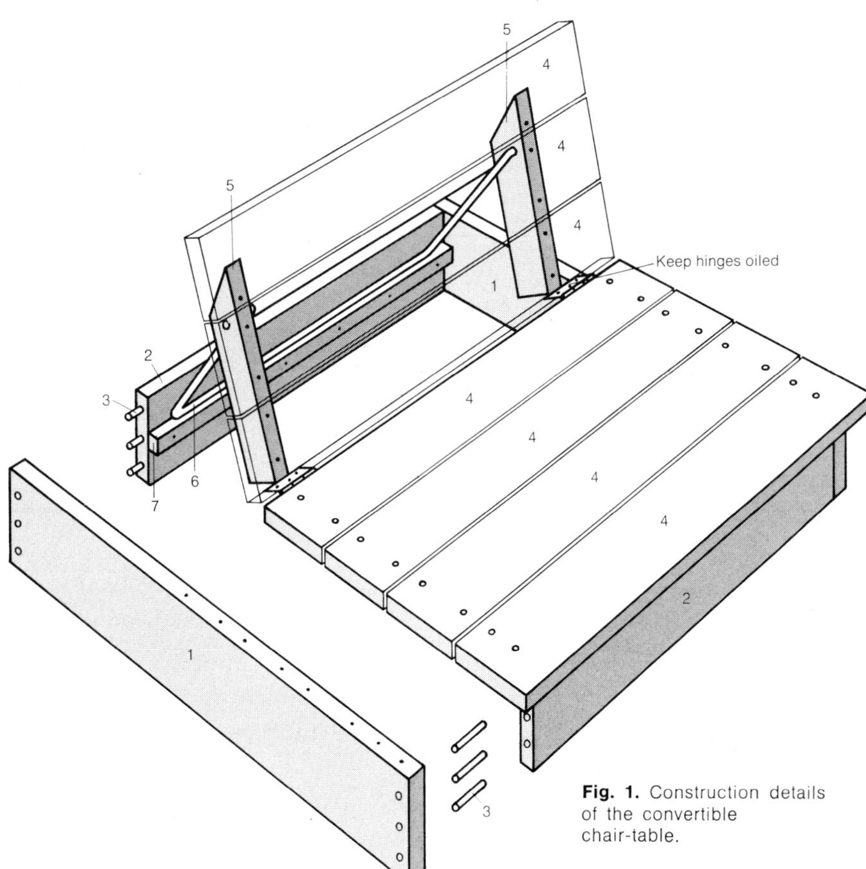

Fig. 1. Construction details of the convertible chair-table.

Chaise longue consists of two chairs, one with the backrest down.

PARTS LIST

No.	Name	Quantity	Nominal size	Length	Material
1	Base sides	2	2 × 6	32″	fir
2	Base front/back	2	2 × 6	25″	fir
3	Dowels	12		2	⅜″-dia. hardwood
4	Slats	7	2 × 4¾ (cut)	31″	fir
5	Uprights	2	2 × 3	12½″	fir
6	Back support	1		50″ (approx.)	⅜″-dia. mild steel rod
7	Support cleat	1	1 × 1	25″	pine

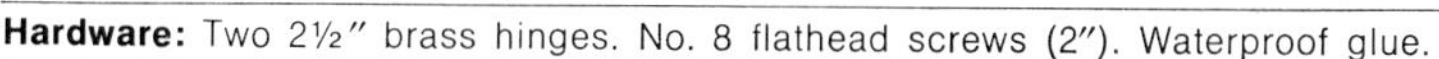

Hardware: Two 2½″ brass hinges. No. 8 flathead screws (2″). Waterproof glue.

The metal support rod holds the back at a comfortable angle.

A finish of clear polyurethane varnish protects the boards of the garden seat.

Garden seat

This simple garden seat consists of two boards bolted to steel frames. The boards are set at a slight angle and have a gap between them to shed water.

For frames (1) and connecting strips (2), you will need two 6-foot lengths of ¼- x 2-inch strap iron. Boards for seats (3) are 48- x 8- x 1⅜-inch pine. The two connecting strips are 6 inches long. Cut one from each length of steel. Bend strips to an angle of 170 degrees across the center and drill four $^3/_{16}$-inch holes in each strip as shown in Fig. 1.

To form the two frames, mark off and bend each length of steel at intervals of 6¾, 14¼, 14½, 14¼, and 6¾ inches. Top angles are 85 degrees; bottom angles are 90 degrees. Use a vise and heat the bend area with a propane torch before bending. Drill $^5/_{16}$-inch holes in top of frame 1¼ and 6 inches from the ends.

Drill $^5/_{16}$-inch clearance holes through the seat boards 3½ inches from ends and 1½ inches from sides. Then bolt seat boards to frames with 2- x ¼-inch carriage bolts. Attach the connecting strips beneath seats 4 inches from insides of frames with 1½-inch No. 8 roundhead screws.

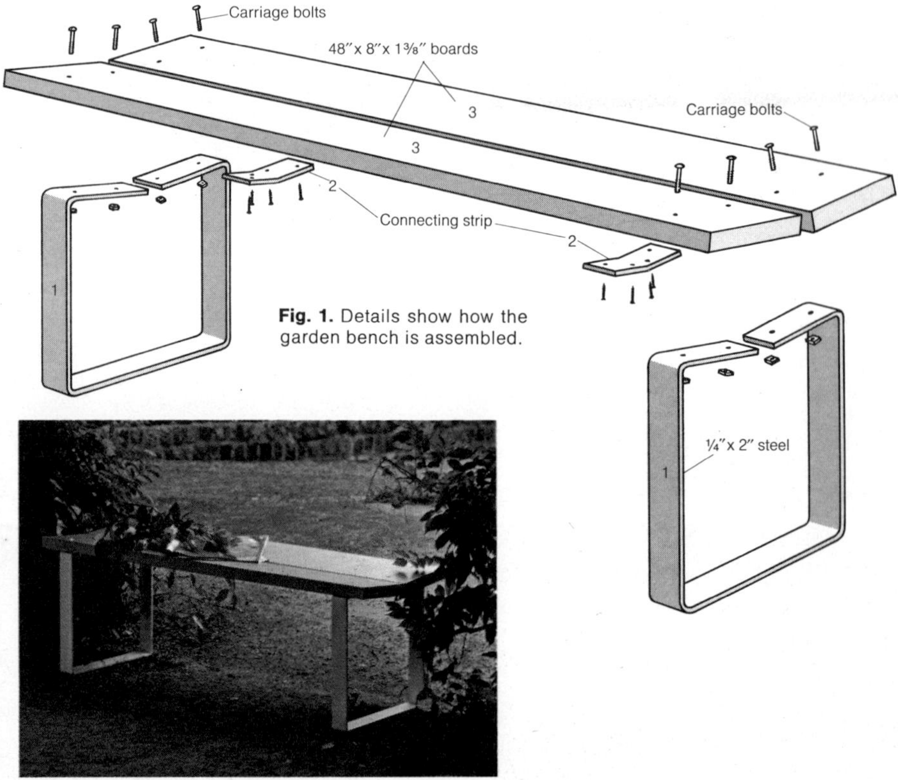

Fig. 1. Details show how the garden bench is assembled.

Broad metal frame will not harm lawn.

Bending metal 435
Drilling wood 44
Exterior finishes 336

Diagonals brace the potting bench.

How diagonals meet crossrails.

Potting bench

A single unit (Fig. 3) of this simple design can be made up to 6 feet long. For more work space, separate sections (Fig. 4) can be bolted together.

Cut crossrails (1) from nominal 2 x 4s. Make them 8 inches shorter than the desired width of the bench. Cut legs (2) from nominal 4 x 4s. Make them 31 inches long for a convenient working height. Bolt crossrails to legs with 3¾- x ¼-inch carriage bolts and serrated washers in ⁵⁄₁₆-inch holes (Fig. 1). Set upper crossrails flush with tops of legs. Bottom edges of lower rails should be 2 inches above the floor.

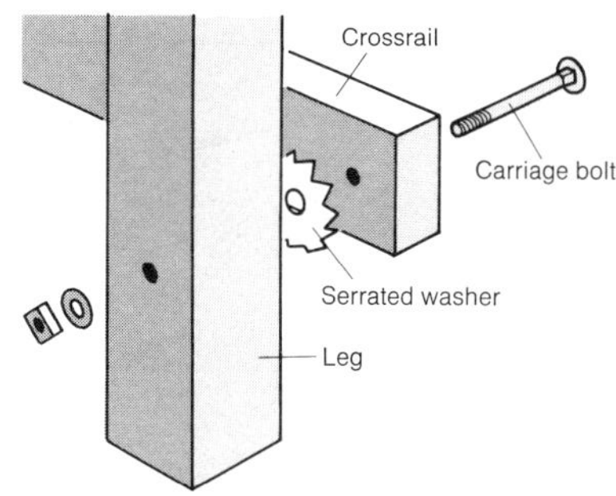

Fig. 1. Bolting crossrails to legs.

Long rails (3) are nominal 2 x 4s. cut to desired length and screwed to the outside of the legs with 2½-inch No. 12 flathead screws. Diagonal braces are 2 x 4s. with bird's-mouth joints (Fig. 2). Screw braces to rails with 2½-inch No. 12 flathead screws.

Cut ¾- x 2-inch strips (5) so that they overhang the framing by 1½ inches in front and 4 inches in back. Space strips 1 inch apart and nail in place with 2-inch nails. Nail ¾-inch molding (6) to front ends of the strips.

If you make the bench in sections, use 2 x 4s. for legs at joining areas; when bolted together, they form 4 x 4-inch legs. Screw crossrails to each pair of half-thickness legs. To avoid splitting legs when fastening long rails, screw 4 x 4 corner blocks to crossrails as in Fig. 4 and screw rails to the blocks instead of legs.

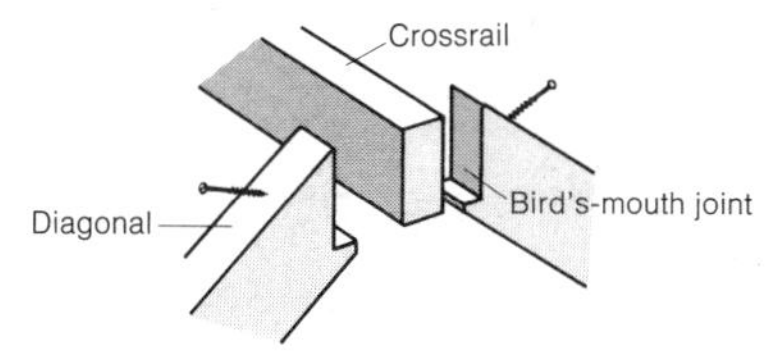

Fig. 2. Detail of bird's-mouth joints.

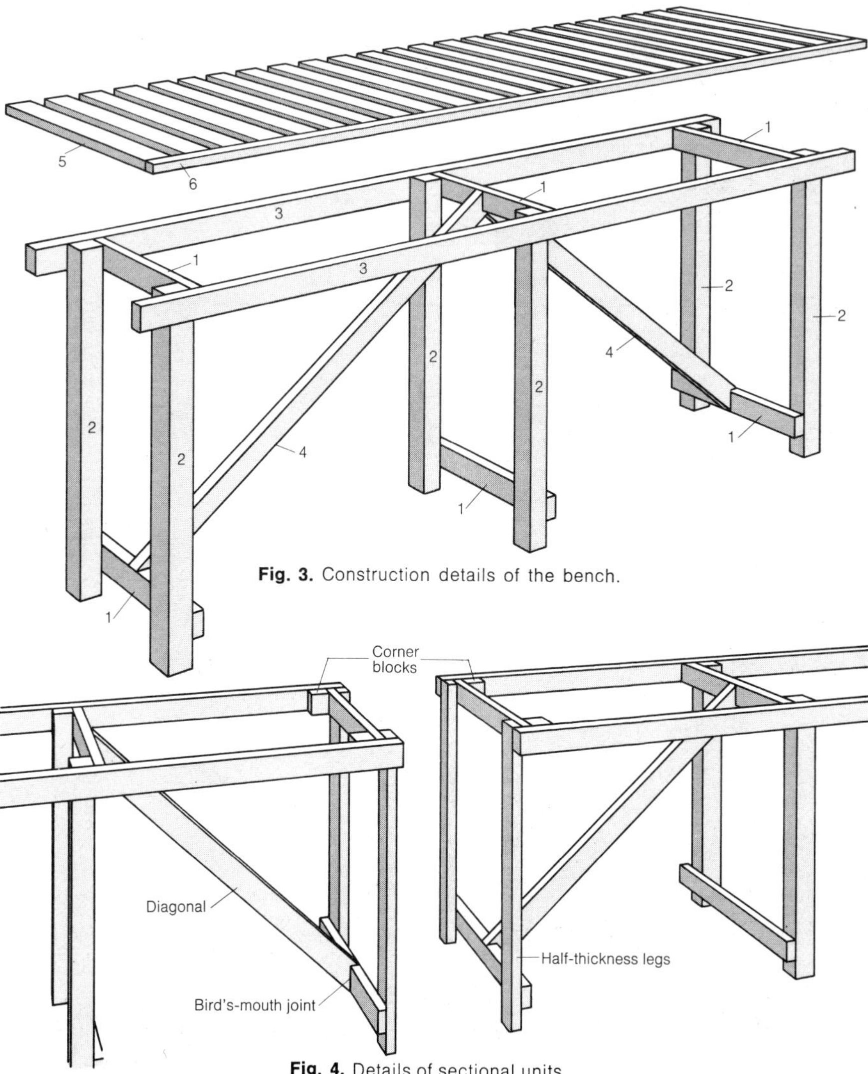

Fig. 3. Construction details of the bench.

Fig. 4. Details of sectional units.

Outdoor living ideas: Garden frame

A single course of bricks laid without mortar provides a level base for the frame.

Set tallest plants at rear of frame.

Front should face south in sunny, not too windy area.

CONSTRUCTION

To make two sloping sides (1) with one cut, mark a straight line on a 28 x 48 inch piece of plywood (surface grain lengthwise), between a point 12 inches from a long edge at one end to a point 16 inches from the same long edge at the other end; then cut along this line. Nail through sides into front (2) and back (3) at corners. Nail on side rails (4) 1 inch from tops of sides. Make notches 2½ inches wide and 2⅛ inches deep for gutter (5) in center of front (2) and back (3). Nail on gutter sides (6) before nailing gutter in notches.

For the glass tops, cut ⅜ x ⅜ inch rabbets—to hold panes—on both sides of dividers (7) and one side of sides (8) with table saw or rabbet plane. Cut half-lap joints 2½ inches long in divider ends and matching notches 1½ inches wide in ends (9), as shown in Fig. 1. Fasten with 1-inch galvanized nails. Join ends to sides with two ¼ inch dowels in each joint. Overlap panes (10) shingle fashion with 2-inch S-shaped strips of aluminum flashing gripping edges to keep upper panes from sliding down. Drive two ¾ inch No. 8 roundhead galvanized screws close to bottom edge of each lower

Half-lap joints 385
Rabbet plane 30
Table saw 60
Bricks 446
Dowels 397
Electrical wiring 271–272

pane to keep it from slipping. Drive glazier's points into sides and dividers to keep wind from lifting glass.

Place the frame on a single course of bricks to keep plywood edges off the ground. Paint frame inside and out with exterior latex; paint top frames or finish with spar varnish or wood preservative, as shown.

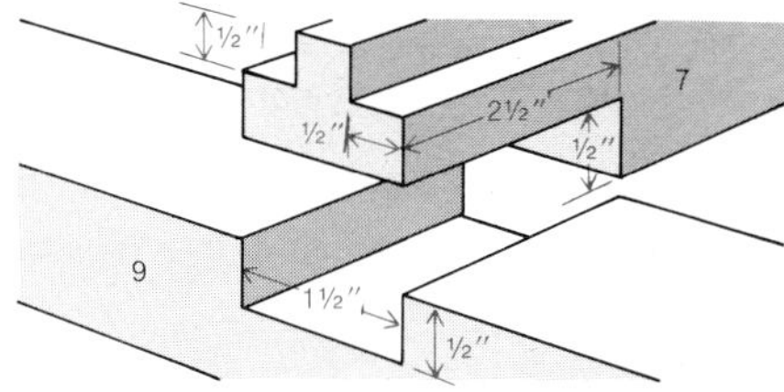

Fig. 1. Rabbeted dividers half-lap ends of glass-topped frames.

PARTS LIST

No.	Name	Quantity	Nominal Size	Length	Width	Material
1	Sides	2		48"	16"	¾" exterior plywood
2	Front	1		70¼"	12"	¾" exterior plywood
3	Back	1		70¼"	16"	¾" exterior plywood
4	Side rails	2	¾ x ¾	48"		pine
5	• Gutter	1	1¼ x 3	49"		pine
6	Gutter sides	2	1 x 3	46½"		pine
7	Glass-top dividers	2	2 x 2	49"		fir
8	Glass-top sides	4	1¼ x 2⅛ (cut)	49"		pine
9	Glass-top ends	4	1¼ x 3	34¾"		pine
10	Glass-top panes	8		25"	17⅜"	⅛" glass

Hardware: Quarter-pound 2" galvanized nails. Eight ¾" No. 8 roundhead galvanized screws. One ¼"-dia. dowel 36" long. Small twin tubes epoxy glue for dowels. Aluminum flashing ½" wide. Glazier's points.
Note: If you have old windows or storm windows available, alter frame dimensions to suit them.

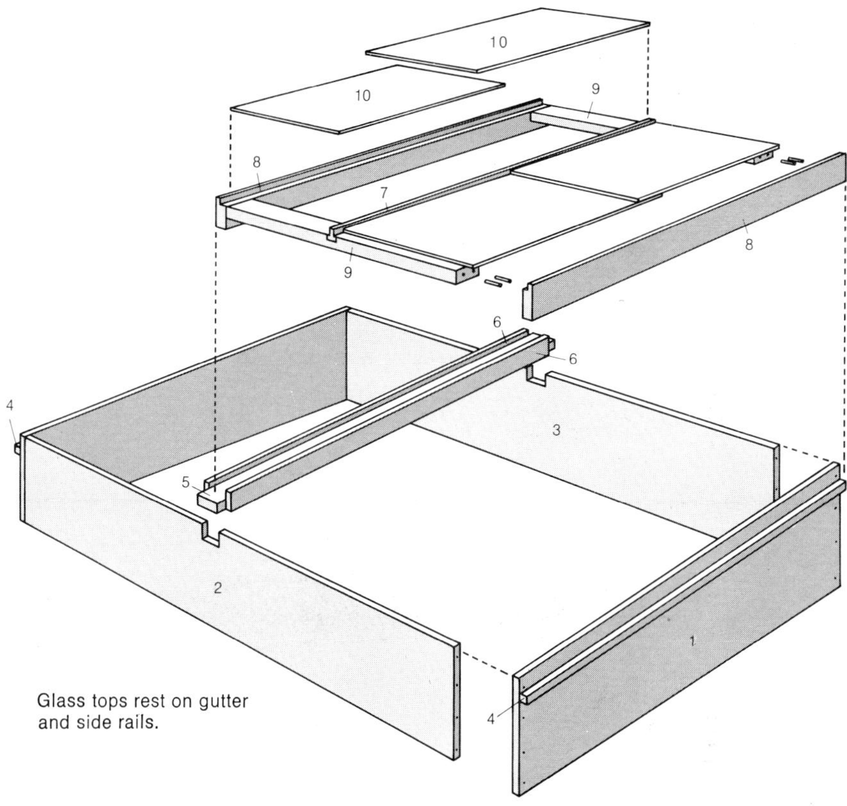

Glass tops rest on gutter and side rails.

Heating a frame

Electric heating cable on a bed of sand under frame or on inner walls extends the growing season to practically year round. In typical cold-winter areas, for example, lettuce can be planted in October for use at Christmas. To assure adequate warmth, temperature is controlled by a thermostat. Purchase heating cable specifically for hotbed use and follow manufacturer's installation instructions. Check local electrical code for the type of supply wiring required from house to frame.

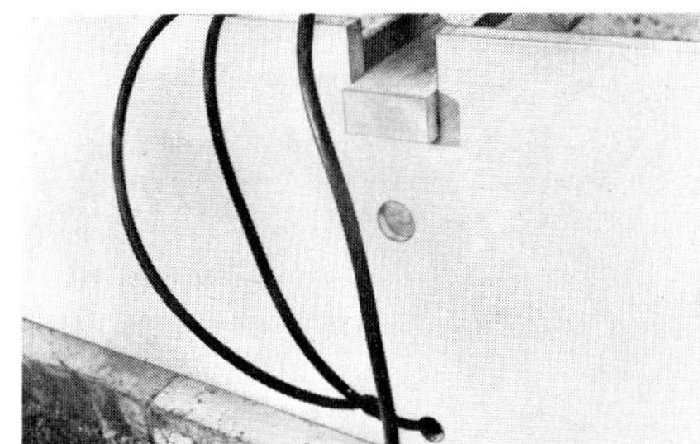

If control box is outside frame, wire the soil and wall heating cables through separate holes and mount box to cover holes. If control is inside frame, run supply cable to control and wire heating cables from there. Wiring details vary with heating kit used.

Ready-made clips can be used to mount wall heating cable. Large screw eyes can be substituted to keep cable away from the wall to avoid heat loss. Cable shown here terminates in thermostat (needed to keep heat constant); some types start from thermostat.

The cable used to heat the soil should lie on a 2-in. bed of moist coarse sand. When laying the cable, work from left to right and avoid making any sharp bends in it; space the lengths of wire about 5" apart. Cover the cable with a 2-in. layer of moist coarse sand.

Index

The page numbers in **bold type** indicate a principal reference to a subject; in many cases there is more than one principal reference to the same subject. Page numbers in ordinary type refer to pages in which some other aspect of the subject is covered, or where the subject is mentioned briefly.

A

B

C

Index

D

E

F

Index

Index

Q

R

S

T

Index

U

V

W

Y

Z